HOLT BIOLOGY
Visualizing Life

Texas
Annotated
Teacher's
Edition

George B. Johnson

HOLT, RINEHART AND WINSTON
Harcourt Brace & Company

Austin • New York • Orlando • Atlanta • San Francisco • Boston • Dallas • Toronto • London

HOLT BIOLOGY
Visualizing Life

From the Leader in Biology!

TEACHING
RESOURCES

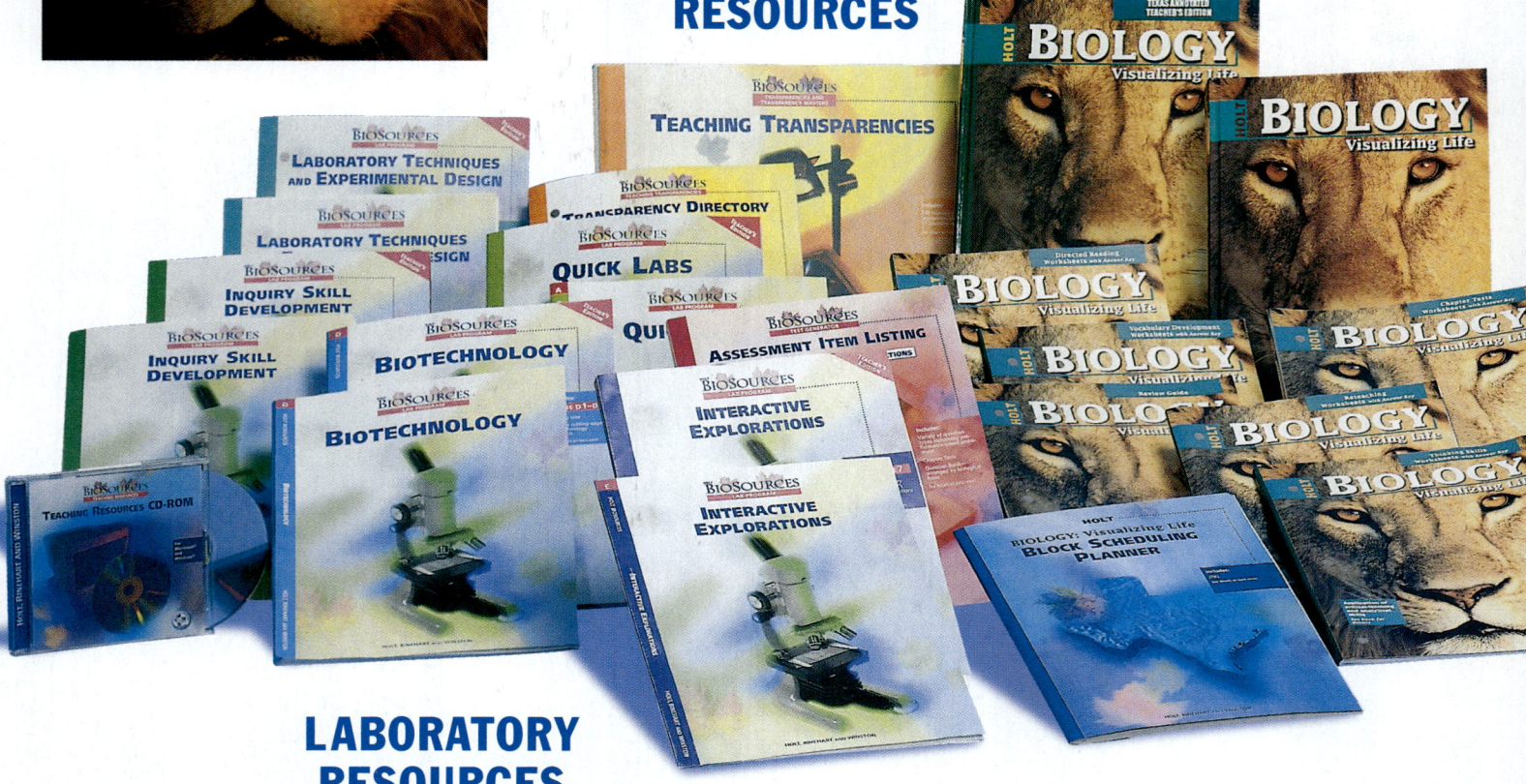

LABORATORY
RESOURCES

Focusing on fundamental biological concepts, Holt Biology: Visualizing Life presents students with more concise coverage, fewer details, and an engaging narrative. Spanning coverage from genetic engineering to environmental awareness, Holt Biology: Visualizing Life presents real-life issues that affect students today.

The Texas Annotated Teacher's Edition includes effective teaching strategies, expansive assessment options, creative reinforcements, thought-provoking extensions, and correlations to the Texas Essential Knowledge and Skills (TEKS).

TECHNOLOGY RESOURCES

TEXAS RESOURCES

HOLT

BioSources

LABORATORY PROGRAM

All labs

bench-tested

by WARD'S™ for

effectiveness

and safety.

5 different lab manuals to meet every need

- 34 Quick Labs provide concise demonstrations or focus activities to introduce biological concepts (see page T30).

- Inquiry Skills Development labs improve students' practical skills and laboratory techniques (see page T31).

- The Laboratory Techniques and Experimental Design manual contains two types of labs. The first provides guided procedures to develop specific laboratory skills. The second simulates real-world laboratory applications (see page T32).

- BioTechnology labs incorporate cutting-edge research techniques and challenge students to use precise skills (see page T33).

- The Interactive Explorations in Biology Laboratory Manual allows students to record data and answer questions from the activities on the interactive CD-ROMs (see page T33).

FREE Software to order your lab materials—making your life easier

WARD'S™ Materials Ordering Software saves you time and lists all supplies and materials—per lab group or class size—needed for every lab investigation (see page T 745-12 to T 745-16).

The Biggest and the Best!

3 distinct types to meet every need

TEACHER MATERIALS

The **Holt BioSources Teaching Resources CD-ROM** provides customizable scoring rubrics and hundreds of pages of additional worksheets such as science research paper worksheets, portfolio projects, and occupational-applications worksheets (see pages T35).

CLASSROOM PRESENTATIONS

- **Holt BioSources Teaching Transparencies** with 238 color transparencies and 71 transparency masters will help make your points crystal clear. Teacher's Notes in the unique **Transparency Directory** make planning more convenient than ever (see page T35).

- Sophisticated—yet easy to use—the **Holt BioSources Test Generator with TestBuilder Software** facilitates selecting test items from a bank containing thousands of questions (see page T39).

- **Holt Biology Videodiscs** enliven instruction with vivid images, videos, and photos tied directly to the text lessons (see page T37).

- With **Concepts of Biology,** customize your presentations and engage your students with this award-winning multimedia system (see page T37).

STUDENT INTERACTIVE EXPERIENCES

- The **Interactive Explorations in Biology** CD-ROMs allow students to manipulate variables and to study phenomena that they otherwise could not observe in the classroom (see page T36).

- Using **Concepts of Biology,** students working in small groups can develop and present their own multimedia reports (see page T37).

RESOURCES—

The Texas Block Scheduling Planner includes:

- **Lecture Concepts**
- **Lecture Resources**
- **Classwork Options**
- **Assignment Options**
- **Review**
- **Assessment**
- **TEKS**

The Texas Block Scheduling Planner—Manage Your Resources with Flexible Options

A four-page planner for each chapter provides you an organized and easy-to-use system with a variety of options to complement your teaching style and block-scheduling needs.

Each chapter planner includes:

- **Lecture Concepts,** which focuses on instructional objectives

- **Lecture Resources,** which suggests materials to make your lecture powerful and effective

- **Classwork Options,** which recommends in-class work for students, including laboratories

- **Assignment Options,** which proposes optional homework assignments

Applicable TEKS are listed under **Lecture Resources, Classwork Options,** and **Assignment Options,** so you know which TEKS are covered.

The **Texas Block Scheduling Planner** also includes **Chapter Review** and **Assessment** sections, which focus on the mastery of content through a variety of options, including materials to prepare your students for the new Texas Biology End-Of-Course Exam.

just for Texas!

The Texas Environmental Guide—Presenting Issues Close to Home

The Texas Environmental Guide consists of 34 student activity worksheets. Each worksheet is divided into four sections: **Introduction, Materials, Procedure,** and **Analyses and Conclusions**. An Answer Key is included.

With the **Texas Environmental Guide,** students explore the Texas environment in a variety of ways including:

- **Interspersed maps that highlight the different regions of Texas**

- **Detailed illustrations that show Texas flora and fauna**

- **Insightful chronologies that present students with a historical perspective of the Texas environment**

- **End-of-section discussion questions that challenge students to use critical thinking**

- **Thought-provoking Going Further sections that encourage students to extend their understanding with further investigation and research**

The Texas Environmental Guide

includes awareness

activities, providing

complete coverage

of the climatic,

geographic, and

biological diversity

of Texas.

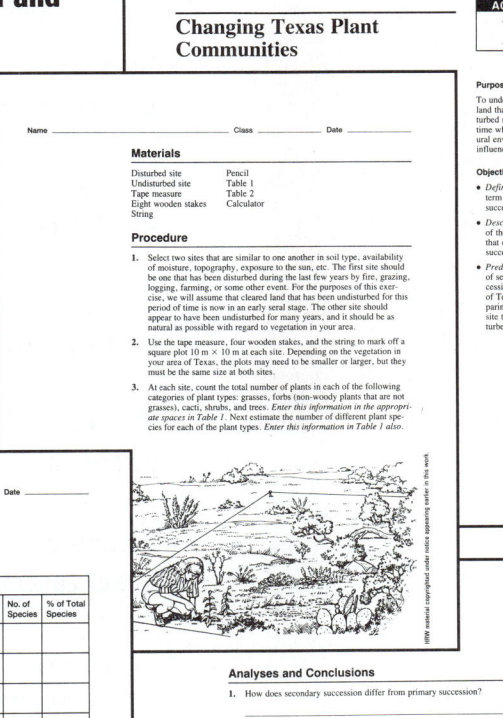

RESOURCES

The Texas End-of-Course Exam Preparation Guide

includes:

- **weekly activities**

- **test-taking tips**

- **practice exams**

- **performance test**

- **and much more!**

The Texas End-Of-Course Exam Preparation Guide—Prepare Your Students for Success

The best preparation does not take place the night before or even the week before an exam. The best preparation comes from continuous review and practice over time. Our Texas End-Of-Course Exam Preparation Guide will give your students the opportunity to succeed.

The Texas End-Of-Course Exam Preparation Guide delivers a wide range of hands-on and written assessment activities including:

- 30 Weekly Activities engaging students in 15-minute experiments/assignments

- Practice Exams (2 sets) containing 40 multiple-choice items for thorough review

- Practice Performance Test (1 set) containing 3 open-ended items with a scoring rubric provided for each question

- Tips on taking tests, including general test-taking guidelines and strategies for students, parents, and teachers

- A general introduction and exam overview listing objectives and instructional targets from the Texas Education Agency

- Data from the Texas Education Agency conveying general results from state-wide administration

- Answer Keys providing answers to Weekly Activities, Practice Exams, and the Practice Performance Test

—*just for* Texas!

Students Will

- **Learn effective test-taking strategies**

- **Simulate actual testing conditions**

- **Practice frequently to keep test-taking skills sharp**

- **Apply decision-making and problem-solving skills**

Teacher Benefits

- **30 Weekly Activities to reinforce instructional objectives**

- **Timely and periodic assessment options**

- **Additional assessment options: hands-on and written**

- **Multiple approaches to prepare students for the exam**

- **Practice exams to prepare students for actual testing conditions**

- **Complete Answer Keys including scoring rubrics to most effectively assess student responses**

- **Biology performance levels for the state of Texas, provided by the Texas Education Agency**

Holt Biology: Visualizing Life has 2 types of correlations to the Texas Essential Knowledge and Skills for Biology (TEKS)

We have the TEKS covered!

TEKS to HOLT BIOLOGY: VISUALIZING LIFE

1 Use this correlation to assure that all TEKS are being met and to quickly reference pages which focus on specific TEKS.

HOLT BIOLOGY: VISUALIZING LIFE to the TEKS

2 Use this correlation to track TEKS coverage in each section of every chapter, to organize lesson delivery, and to easily reference which TEKS are understood and which need reteaching.

1 TEKS Correlation to Holt Biology: Visualizing Life

1a The student develops a study using appropriate procedures applied to a real-world situation, such as an evaluation of the impact of commercial chemicals and the destruction of habitats

PE 8, 9, 198, 289, 290, 291, 292, 339, 377, 498, 499

ATE 9, 289, 367, 759

1b The student uses safe practices during laboratory investigations and fieldwork

PE 45, 157, 341, 342, 486, 496, 752, 753, 754, 755, 757, 758, 759, 761, 762, 763, 764, 765, 766, 767, 774, 775, 776, 777, 780, 782, 783, 784, 785, 788, 789, 790, 792, 793, 794, 795, 798, 799, 800, 801, 802, 804, 805, 806, 808, 812, 813, 816, 818, 820, 821, 822, 823

ATE 41, 45, 341, 368, 480, 585, 587, 737, 757, 761, 762, 763, 764, 765, 767, 771, 774, 775, 776, 777, 781, 782, 784, 785, 787, 788, 789, 791, 792, 793, 794, 795, 796, 798, 799, 800, 801, 802, 803, 804, 805, 806, 807, 809, 812, 813, 817, 818, 819, 820, 821, 822, 823

1c The student practices conservation in using biological materials and resources

PE 261, 295, 296, 302, 303, 304, 305, 306, 307, 308

ATE 8, 259, 296, 297, 299, 302, 303, 304, 417, 421

2a The student plans and implements appropriate investigative procedures including formulation of testable hypotheses and selection of appropriate equipment and technology

PE 11, 12, 13, 14, 15, 19, 20, 21, 56, 57, 58, 59, 60, 192, 233, 234, 239, 247, 248, 307, 476, 520, 536, 538, 571, 756, 757, 758, 760, 761, 762, 763, 764, 767, 768, 770, 776, 777, 786, 787, 790, 791, 792, 793, 794, 798, 799, 803, 809, 812, 813, 816, 817, 818, 819, 820, 821

ATE 12, 13, 14, 15, 19, 25, 33, 41, 45, 49, 62, 83, 87, 91, 109, 110, 118, 129, 194, 197, 199, 203, 208, 226, 234, 237, 244, 245, 253, 257, 279, 283, 290, 291, 293, 344, 358, 363, 469, 554, 556, 568, 586, 625, 638, 669, 687, 721, 756, 758, 776, 790, 792, 816

2b The student, working independently and in teams, makes observations and measurements to collect data in a variety of ways

PE 24, 37, 43, 271, 433, 497, 571, 649, 677, 715, 759, 760, 761, 762, 763, 764, 765, 766, 767, 769, 770, 775, 777, 783, 784, 785, 786, 787, 788, 791, 795, 798, 801, 803, 805, 809, 813, 816, 817, 818, 819, 820, 823

ATE 8, 9, 15, 18, 23, 24, 27, 28, 40, 41, 42, 43, 45, 46, 48, 51, 53, 54, 55, 56, 62, 65, 67, 69, 70, 73, 79, 83, 84, 87, 92, 94, 107, 109, 112, 118, 121, 125, 131, 132, 133, 141, 143, 156, 165, 166, 167, 171, 173, 174, 176, 180, 181, 184, 190, 191, 203, 213, 214, 215, 219, 221, 228, 237, 238, 239, 242, 246, 254, 257, 260, 264, 276, 281, 282, 294, 295, 301, 305, 308, 313, 315, 316, 320, 323, 324, 326, 327, 331, 332, 336, 337, 338, 339, 345, 347, 356, 360, 365, 366, 368, 372, 374, 375, 378, 379, 382, 383, 392, 394, 395, 398, 400, 403, 405, 414, 418, 419, 423, 424, 426, 427, 428, 429, 442, 444, 449, 450, 453, 460, 468, 471, 472, 479, 480, 481, 483, 488, 492, 493, 494, 495, 498, 503, 507, 509, 515, 516, 525, 527, 529, 530, 534, 541, 542, 543, 546, 549, 553, 556, 557, 560, 562, 564, 565, 575, 578, 583, 596, 597, 601, 605, 610, 614, 615, 620, 622, 626, 631, 635, 645, 646, 652, 658, 666, 669, 670, 672, 674, 675, 678, 682, 684, 687, 688, 691, 692, 693, 694, 701, 706, 709, 711, 725, 729, 741, 758, 759, 760, 761, 762, 764, 765, 766, 767, 768, 769, 770, 771, 772, 774, 776, 778, 780, 782, 783, 785, 787, 788, 790, 791, 792, 793, 794, 798, 802, 804, 806, 807, 808, 812, 814, 816, 817, 818, 819, 820, 821, 822, 825

2c The student organizes, analyzes, makes inferences from, and evaluates data

PE 4, 5, 6, 10, 20, 21, 22, 23, 24, 25, 36, 37, 56, 57, 58, 60, 61, 74, 75, 96, 97, 115, 134, 135, 150, 151, 168, 169, 188, 189, 210, 211, 230, 231, 233, 234, 235, 236, 237, 239, 240, 241, 244, 245, 246, 247, 248, 249, 258, 270, 271, 282, 286, 287, 293, 298, 299, 301, 306, 307, 329, 338, 344, 350, 352, 353, 355, 357, 358, 359, 370, 371, 388, 389, 406, 408, 409, 413, 418, 421, 422, 423, 424, 426, 427, 429, 430, 431, 432, 433, 438, 456, 457, 476, 477, 496, 497, 520, 521, 531, 538, 539, 554, 570, 571, 582, 596, 598, 599, 609, 610, 615, 621, 628, 629, 635, 637, 643, 644, 645, 646, 648, 649, 656, 664, 669, 675, 676, 677, 681, 682, 684, 685, 686, 687, 689, 692, 693, 694, 696, 697, 699, 700, 701, 702, 703, 704, 712, 714, 715, 717, 726, 727, 730, 739, 740, 741, 742, 743, 756, 757, 759, 760, 761, 762, 763, 764, 765, 767, 768, 769, 770, 771, 772, 773, 774, 775, 776, 777, 778, 779, 780, 781, 782, 785, 786, 787, 788, 789, 791, 792, 793, 794, 795, 796, 797, 798, 799, 800, 801, 803, 804, 805, 806, 807, 809, 810, 811, 812, 813, 814, 815, 816, 817, 818, 819, 820, 821, 822, 823, 824, 825

ATE 4, 5, 6, 7, 9, 10, 11, 15, 16, 17, 22, 23, 24, 25, 27, 28, 29, 30, 31, 34, 41, 42, 44, 45, 48, 50, 51, 52, 57, 58, 59, 63, 64, 65, 66, 68, 69, 71, 72, 76, 77, 78, 79, 80, 81, 82, 83, 85, 87, 89, 90, 93, 94, 95, 100, 102, 103, 104, 105, 110, 112, 113, 116, 117, 118, 119, 121, 122, 124, 126, 128, 129, 131, 133, 137, 138, 139, 143, 146, 148, 149, 153, 154, 157, 159, 161, 163, 173, 174, 175, 176, 177, 178, 179, 182, 183, 184, 190, 192, 193, 194, 196, 197, 198, 199, 200, 201, 202, 203, 204, 205, 206, 207, 208, 209, 212, 215, 216, 217, 218, 219, 222, 223, 226, 227, 228, 232, 233, 234, 235, 236, 237, 238, 239, 240, 241, 243, 244, 245, 246, 247, 258, 259, 260, 261, 262, 265, 268, 274, 275, 277, 279, 280, 282, 284, 288, 291, 292, 293, 294, 296, 297, 298, 301, 303, 304, 308, 315, 319, 321, 322, 325, 330, 331, 332, 333, 334, 336, 338, 339, 340, 343, 344, 346, 347, 350, 351, 355, 357, 359, 361, 363, 364, 365, 366, 367, 368, 369, 372, 373, 374, 376, 379, 380, 381, 382, 385, 387, 391, 393, 395, 398, 399, 401, 406, 407, 410, 411, 412, 413, 416, 417, 420, 422, 423, 426, 427, 428, 430, 431, 438, 439, 440, 447, 448, 451, 452, 453, 458, 461, 464, 465, 467, 472, 474, 475, 479, 481, 482, 483, 484, 485, 487, 489, 490, 491, 494, 498, 502, 505, 508, 510, 515, 516, 518, 522, 528, 532, 533, 534, 535, 537, 540, 542, 543, 544, 547, 548, 549, 551, 552, 553, 554, 555, 557, 558, 561, 563, 567, 569, 574, 577, 580, 581, 582, 584, 586, 587, 589, 590, 592, 593, 596, 603, 609, 613, 615, 616, 618, 620, 621, 623, 626, 627, 632, 634, 635, 640, 641, 644, 645, 647, 651, 652, 654, 655, 657, 658, 659, 661, 664, 666, 667, 668, 671, 673, 674, 678, 680, 681, 682, 685, 686, 687, 690, 692, 694, 695, 699, 700, 701, 702, 704, 706, 709, 712, 713, 716, 717, 723, 725, 726, 727, 731, 732, 734, 735, 736, 737, 738, 739, 740, 741, 756, 758, 759, 764, 766, 767, 768, 772, 773, 774, 776, 778, 779, 786, 787, 788, 790, 792, 793, 794, 796, 798, 800, 802, 804, 806, 807, 808, 809, 810, 812, 813, 816, 818, 820, 822, 824, 825

2d The student states valid conclusions and predicts trends based on scientific data and information, and communicates conclusions and trends effectively

PE 74, 134, 188, 234, 235, 248, 328, 687, 757, 765, 767, 769, 771, 775, 781, 785, 787, 791, 793, 795, 799, 803, 804, 805, 809, 813, 817, 818, 819, 821

ATE 17, 46, 83, 112, 118, 129, 140, 174, 175, 182, 246, 255, 299, 301

3a The student evaluates promotional claims that use biological data, such as product labeling and advertisements

PE 169, 171, 354, 355
ATE 38, 120, 147, 170, 241, 354, 355, 512

3b The student examines scientific evidence and information to test, modify, or challenge biological theories

PE 14, 15, 19, 192, 193, 194, 498
ATE 14, 227, 545

3c The student evaluates the relationship between scientific research findings and their impact on society and the environment

PE 5, 6, 7, 8, 9, 10, 13, 19, 20, 39, 115, 157, 166, 167, 168, 169, 170, 171, 287, 293, 294, 296, 299, 301, 302, 304, 305, 306, 307, 308, 309, 343, 344, 349, 351, 353, 379, 498, 499, 513, 692, 693, 694, 697, 716, 717

ATE 4, 6, 8, 10, 13, 39, 128, 160, 166, 171, 265, 280, 300, 302, 308, 348, 349, 499, 692, 693, 717

3d The student uses a variety of sources to gather information about possible careers

PE 21, 55, 61, 115, 131, 151, 165, 238, 249, 267, 353, 425, 511, 629, 665, 677, 705, 715, 757, 761, 763, 765, 771, 775, 785, 787, 789, 795, 797, 799, 801, 805, 813, 821, 823

ATE 55, 109, 125, 131, 165, 216, 238, 267, 315, 339, 355, 363, 402, 416, 425, 511, 594, 665, 705

4a The student microscopically examines different cell types and identifies their parts and functions, such as the prokaryotic and eukaryotic cells of plants and animals

PE 40, 41, 42, 43, 45, 50, 51, 52, 53, 54, 59, 60, 61, 64, 65, 66, 73, 74, 144, 147, 332, 333, 351, 352, 476, 605, 606, 608, 636, 637 , 638, 649, 676, 681, 695, 760

ATE 40, 50, 51, 52, 53, 54, 58, 62, 64, 72, 92, 104, 144, 325, 332, 333, 334, 335, 606, 637, 638, 760

4b The student designs and performs an experiment or produces a model to explain cellular processes including, but not limited to, permeability, energy production, transportation of molecules, disposal of wastes, and synthesis of new molecules

PE 16, 18, 25, 35, 36, 47, 48, 59, 60, 62, 67, 68, 69, 70, 71, 72, 73, 74, 75, 78, 79, 80, 82, 83, 88, 88, 91, 92, 93, 94, 95, 96, 97, 334, 335, 464, 602, 603, 605, 606, 607, 628, 670, 673, 675, 762, 778, 779

ATE 54, 67, 68, 70, 72, 361, 396, 602, 671, 699, 730, 762, 778

4c The student describes the role of the environment in maintaining homeostasis in cells

PE 52, 63, 64, 65, 74, 81, 543, 711, 713, 714, 824, 825

ATE 63, 711, 824

5a The student compares and contrast the structure and functions of viruses to various cells, including, but not limited to, their roles in causing diseases, in the environment, and as sources of food

PE 330, 345, 346, 347, 348, 349, 350, 351, 352, 353, 683, 687, 691, 692, 693, 695, 696, 697, 737, 738, 742, 743

ATE 25, 345, 346, 347, 350, 740

6a The student compares and contrast cells from different parts of plants and animals, such as roots, stems, leaves, epithlium, muscle, and bone, to show specialization of structure and function

PE 356, 357, 358, 359, 360, 362, 363, 364, 365, 372, 373, 374, 375, 376, 377, 391, 392, 393, 394, 395, 396, 397, 402, 403, 407, 412, 439, 440, 464, 465, 466, 467, 468, 469, 471, 472, 473, 474, 475, 479, 480, 526, 528, 529, 530, 542, 553, 575, 576, 578, 580, 583, 585, 587, 591, 593, 597, 601, 602, 604, 618, 619, 622, 623, 624, 627, 652, 653, 655, 657, 667, 668, 671, 673, 679, 680, 682, 683, 684, 685, 689, 690, 691, 695, 696, 697, 708, 709, 710, 711, 719, 721, 725, 728, 729, 794, 795

ATE 7, 31, 358, 360, 362, 374, 391, 393, 395, 397, 413, 415, 439, 441, 473, 474, 564, 575, 576, 577, 578, 580, 581, 585, 589, 590, 595, 601, 683, 728

6b The student examines stages in the development of organisms to analyze changes that occur during cell differentiation and result in multicellular organism to other organizational systems

PE 436, 437, 440, 441, 442, 443, 444, 445, 446, 447, 449, 450, 451, 452, 455, 456, 457, 481, 482, 509, 519, 734, 735

ATE 440, 441, 443, 446, 509, 734

6c The student sequences the levels of organization in a multicellular organism in order to relate the parts to each other and to the whole, and to compare the organism to other organizational systems

PE 307, 436, 438, 441, 442, 443, 444, 445, 446, 447, 448, 449, 450, 451, 452, 453, 454, 455, 456, 457, 460, 461, 462, 463, 464, 466, 467, 468, 469, 470, 471, 472, 473, 474, 475, 476, 477, 490, 494, 495, 509, 515, 519, 524, 527, 528, 529, 533, 538, 561, 575, 577, 597, 598, 616, 617, 629, 662, 663, 676

ATE 436, 437, 443, 446, 447, 448, 453, 454, 469, 516, 576, 616, 617, 650, 662, 663

7a The student develops a pedigree to determine the advantages and disadvantages of selective breeding

PE 130, 131, 133

ATE 130, 226, 235

7b The student compares and contrasts genetic variations observed in plants and animals

PE 116, 117, 118, 119, 120, 121, 122, 123, 124, 125, 126, 133, 134, 135, 730

ATE 116, 117, 119, 121, 122

7c The student makes predictions and solves real-world problems relating to genetic combinations, including as examples plant, animal, and human characteristics

PE 39, 118, 119, 120, 121, 122, 123, 124, 125, 126, 129, 130, 133, 134, 135, 773, 774, 776, 777

ATE 16, 39, 111, 118, 119, 120, 121, 122, 123, 124, 125, 126, 129, 130, 133, 164, 183, 226, 405, 656, 774

7d The student identifies and analyzes karyotypes for genetic anomalies

PE 128, 129

ATE 103

7e The student compares and contrasts the processes of mitosis and meiosis and their significance to sexual and asexual reproduction

PE 100, 103, 104, 105, 106, 107, 108, 110, 111, 112, 113, 114, 115, 334, 375, 376, 483, 719, 770, 771, 772, 773

ATE 100, 101, 105, 106, 108, 116, 148, 690, 721, 770, 771, 772

8a The student interprets how genetic materials are affected by changing environmental conditions such as radiation, chemicals, or viruses

PE 109, 115, 140, 292, 582, 583, 598, 731, 732, 742

ATE 309, 731

8b The student illustrates how instructions for specifying characteristics of an organism are carried in the DNA

PE 17, 101, 106, 107, 112, 113, 114, 135, 136, 137, 138, 148, 149, 150, 193

ATE 136, 138, 322

8c The student uses models of DNA and RNA to explain replication, transcription, and translation

PE 140, 141, 142, 143, 144, 145, 146, 147, 149, 150, 151, 780, 781

ATE 139, 140, 142, 144, 145, 215

8d The student evaluates the appropriate use of genetically engineered organisms as well as the use of genetic engineering in the production of biochemical products, including insulin, growth-stimulating hormone, oil-consuming bacteria, tissue growth, and interferon

PE 7, 8, 19, 20, 38, 39, 61, 117, 132, 151, 152, 153, 154, 155, 156, 157, 158, 159, 160, 161, 162, 163, 164, 166, 167, 168, 169, 170, 171, 333, 334, 337, 342, 344, 379, 430, 433, 782, 783

ATE 152, 153, 156, 157, 158, 159, 160, 161, 162, 167, 170, 171, 337, 342, 410, 429, 782

8e The student illustrates how changes in DNA (mutations) occur spontaneously at low rates, and evaluates the significance of these changes

PE 61, 108, 109, 113, 114, 115, 127, 132, 133, 134, 135, 181, 690, 695, 780

ATE 108, 127

9a The student compares and contrast evidences of change in organisms using fossils, DNA sequences, or anatomical similarities with existing species of plant and animals

PE 50, 151, 155, 174, 176, 178, 179, 187, 188, 189, 190, 191, 195, 196, 199, 200, 201, 202, 203, 204, 205, 207, 209, 210, 213, 214, 215, 216, 217, 218, 219, 220, 221, 222, 224, 226, 227, 228, 229, 230, 231, 322, 325, 329, 331, 333, 460, 461, 466, 468, 477, 505, 523, 525, 531, 532, 539, 552, 555, 556, 558

ATE 17, 172, 174, 177, 178, 179, 195, 201, 202, 212, 217, 220, 221, 222, 224, 225, 460, 488, 523, 531, 552

9b The student formulates and defends a hypothesis to explain speciation and extinction of organisms

PE 177, 197, 323, 547, 548, 569, 570

ATE 524, 545, 559

9c The student develops a model to illustrate the results of natural selection including, but not limited to, speciation, diversity, adaptation, or extinction

PE 17, 19, 172, 173, 174, 175, 180, 181, 182, 183, 184, 185, 186, 187, 188, 189, 206, 208, 212, 213, 214, 225, 226, 227, 228, 229, 230, 232, 235, 240, 241, 242, 243, 244, 245, 246, 247, 248, 249, 279, 438, 458, 459, 460, 461, 462, 463, 464, 465, 467, 472, 473, 475, 476, 490, 502, 503, 504, 506, 510, 520, 521, 525, 528, 533, 541, 542, 545, 546, 554, 559, 561, 562, 564, 566, 568, 569, 625

ATE 180, 181, 185, 186, 187, 204, 212, 232, 243, 335, 458, 459, 462, 463, 471, 473, 506, 525, 526, 530, 537, 546, 555, 558

10a The student uses taxonomic nomenclature to understand the relationships among organisms and develops a hierarchical classification system based on similarities and differences

PE 197, 204, 205, 206, 207, 208, 209, 210, 220, 221, 222, 223, 224, 225, 226, 228, 229, 230, 231, 313, 314, 315, 316, 317, 318, 319, 320, 321, 323, 327, 328, 329, 331, 332, 358, 359, 360, 361, 363, 364, 365, 366, 367, 368, 369, 370, 371, 374, 376, 377, 378, 379, 380, 381, 382, 388, 401, 437, 439, 440, 443, 445, 447, 448, 449, 451, 453, 454, 456, 459, 478, 479, 481, 482, 483, 484, 485, 486, 487, 488, 489, 490, 491, 492, 493, 494, 495, 496, 497, 500, 501, 503, 504, 505, 507, 508, 514, 515, 516, 517, 518, 519, 520, 521, 522, 523, 525, 526, 527, 528, 530, 531, 532, 533, 535, 536, 537, 538, 539, 540, 541, 544, 545, 546, 547, 548, 549, 550, 551, 552, 555, 556, 557, 558, 559, 560, 562, 563, 564, 565, 567, 568, 569, 570, 571, 796, 797, 806, 807, 808

ATE 207, 208, 222, 224, 312, 313, 314, 316, 318, 319, 320, 321, 323, 324, 332, 373, 395, 404, 450, 455, 478, 486, 492, 500, 501, 505, 507, 514, 517, 519, 526, 527, 531, 533, 535, 536, 544, 550, 551, 560, 562, 563, 796, 806, 807, 808, 809

10b The student classifies organisms using a dichotomous key of a classification system that includes several kingdoms

PE 196, 312, 324, 325, 326, 327, 328, 329, 332, 333, 351, 357, 360, 361, 369, 370, 373

ATE 196, 326, 327, 356

10c The student applies the principles of classification to everyday objects such as books in a library, products in a store, and the organization of types of music or computer files

PE 328, 329

ATE 312, 317, 323

11a The student uses three-dimensional models to demonstrate parts, interactions, changes, and relationships within a complex biological system such as DNA, chemical interactions, cell division, and body organs

PE 26, 27, 28, 30, 31, 32, 33, 34, 35, 37, 44, 45, 46, 47, 49, 53, 61, 64, 65, 70, 71, 72, 73, 75, 80, 83, 87, 88, 89, 88, 89, 91, 92, 93, 94, 95, 102, 139, 140, 141, 142, 149, 198, 477

ATE 26, 193

11b The student explains how a physical model is similar to and different from the real-world object or event

PE 119, 120, 121, 192, 193, 194, 209, 210, 211, 770, 771, 788, 789, 790, 791, 804, 809

ATE 32, 33, 44, 47, 48, 80, 93, 106, 107, 111, 144, 146, 147, 154, 155, 190, 191, 194, 229, 255, 441, 462, 468, 480, 608, 612, 624, 659, 674, 698, 718, 770, 780, 790, 791, 804

11c The student develops analogies to explain parts, interactions, and relationships within a complex biological system, such as comparing the heart to a pump, the kidney to a filter, and a cell to a factory

PE 60, 96, 114, 134, 150, 210, 248, 270, 306, 328, 352, 388, 408, 432, 456, 496, 520, 598, 628, 648, 714, 742

ATE 47, 49, 51, 66

11d The student evaluates analogies according to their adequacy in representing a specific real-world biological object or event

PE 24, 41, 42, 46, 47, 48, 51, 53, 64, 66, 77, 80, 88, 88, 94, 142, 144, 145, 146, 148, 164, 255, 297, 317, 328, 347, 352, 368, 448, 471, 681, 684, 780

ATE 66, 278, 445, 620

12a The student examines and compares the structure and functions of different types of biomolecules such as carbohydrates, lipids, proteins, and nucleic acids

PE 22, 29, 30, 31, 32, 33, 34, 35, 36, 46, 47, 49, 60, 77, 78, 79, 80, 81, 89, 89, 136, 192, 193, 699, 700, 701, 702, 713, 714, 800, 801, 802, 803

ATE 22, 30, 31, 32, 34, 35, 45, 49, 78, 136, 636, 699, 700, 800, 802

12b The student compares and contrasts energy flow in photosynthesis and respiration

PE 76, 84, 85, 86, 87, 88, 89, 88, 89, 90, 95, 96, 97, 768
ATE 84, 85, 86, 88, 89, 94, 334, 768

12c The student experimentally demonstrates the effects of enzymes on food molecules

PE 77, 703, 706, 707, 708, 709, 713, 714, 820, 821
ATE 77, 703, 707, 708, 820

12d The student experimentally calculates the amount of energy released from food molecules in order to assess his or her own nutritional requirements

PE 701, 715, 742, 761, 763, 777, 810, 811

ATE 701, 811

13a The student compares and contrasts the circulation, digestion, nutritional requirements, and release of energy and wastes of organisms

PE 18, 77, 466, 470, 471, 475, 476, 477, 487, 497, 527, 533, 534, 542, 553, 559, 560, 566, 579, 650, 651, 652, 653, 654, 655, 656, 657, 658, 659, 660, 661, 662, 663, 664, 666, 667, 668, 669, 675, 676, 677, 698, 706, 707, 708, 709, 710, 711, 712, 713, 714, 715, 804

ATE 466, 467, 470, 566, 607, 653, 654, 655, 657, 658, 660, 661, 662, 663, 664, 698, 706, 707, 708, 709, 710, 804

13b The student describes the functions of body systems including nervous, endocrine, reproductive, integumentary, skeletal, respiratory, muscular, and immune

PE 462, 463, 464, 465, 466, 467, 468, 469, 472, 473, 474, 475, 476, 477, 480, 481, 484, 485, 493, 496, 529, 534, 537, 538, 553, 560, 574, 575, 576, 577, 578, 579, 580, 581, 584, 585, 586, 587, 588, 589, 590, 591, 592, 593, 594, 595, 597, 598, 599, 600, 601, 602, 603, 604, 605, 606, 607, 608, 609, 611, 612, 613, 614, 616, 617, 618, 619, 620, 621, 622, 623, 624, 625, 626, 627, 628, 629, 630, 631, 632, 633, 634, 635, 636, 637, 638, 639, 640, 641, 642, 643, 644, 645, 646, 647, 648, 650, 670, 671, 672, 673, 674, 675, 676, 677, 678, 679, 680, 681, 682, 683, 684, 685, 686, 687, 688, 689, 690, 691, 695, 696, 697, 718, 719, 720, 721, 722, 723, 724, 725, 726, 727, 728, 729, 731, 732, 733, 734, 735, 736, 740, 741, 742, 743, 814, 815

ATE 463, 469, 472, 486, 536, 583, 584, 585, 588, 589, 591, 593, 596, 600, 604, 605, 611, 612, 617, 618, 619, 630, 631, 633, 637, 638, 639, 642, 643, 644, 646, 664, 673, 679, 680, 681, 682, 684, 689, 719, 720, 722, 723, 724, 726, 729, 730, 733, 736, 812, 814

13c The student describes the interrelationships of the human body systems to each other and to the body as a whole

PE 189, 646, 648, 668, 671, 673, 674, 675, 676, 711, 713, 725, 726, 727

ATE 576, 632, 650, 710, 711, 713, 724, 727

14a The student identifies and describes the relationships between internal feedback mechanisms to maintain homeostasis

PE 16, 19, 20, 21, 25, 37, 543, 564, 579, 620, 621, 622, 627, 628, 629, 632, 634, 635, 642, 643, 644, 647, 648, 649, 722

ATE 18, 43, 579, 623, 634, 635, 722

14b The student designs experiments to demonstrate how plants and animals, including humans, respond to external stimuli

PE 639, 818

ATE 619, 622, 818, 819

15a The student describes the flow of energy through various cycles including, but not limited to, carbon, oxygen, nitrogen, and water cycles

PE 84, 252, 259, 260, 261, 262, 269, 270

ATE 84, 252, 262, 422

15b The student describes interactions between organisms exhibiting predation, parasitism, commensalism, or mutualism, and evaluates how each example affects the organisms' ecosystems

PE 199, 203, 209, 210, 211, 276, 277, 285, 286, 287, 335, 338, 340, 341, 366, 367, 368, 369, 370, 371, 377, 378, 387, 408, 483, 484, 485, 486, 491, 495, 496, 497, 502, 503, 504, 505, 513, 518, 519, 520, 521, 524, 537, 538, 570

ATE 276, 277, 365, 377, 378, 444, 485, 504

15c The student designs food chains, food webs, and food pyramids and explains the interactions between the organisms within each system

PE 256, 257, 258, 263, 269, 270, 271, 335, 336, 337, 353, 362, 375, 388, 513, 518

ATE 252, 254, 256, 257, 258, 266, 362, 517, 518

15d The student compares and contrasts variations and tolerances in plants and animals in different biomes

PE 264, 265, 266, 268, 269, 270, 271, 273, 274, 275, 281, 282, 283, 285, 286, 289

ATE 265, 266, 268, 272, 273

15e The student describes the effects of natural or human disturbances on a biome

PE 21, 214, 216, 231, 253, 254, 255, 262, 264, 265, 269, 270, 271, 272, 273, 274, 275, 278, 279, 280, 281, 282, 283, 284, 285, 287, 288, 290, 291, 292, 293, 294, 295, 296, 297, 298, 299, 300, 305, 306, 307, 308, 309, 432, 497, 498, 499, 512, 561, 571

ATE 253, 254, 256, 263, 264, 265, 269, 272, 275, 280, 284, 288, 367, 421, 513

15f The student designs an investigation to illustrate interactions in an ecosystem

PE 255, 788, 789

ATE 254, 285, 788

16a The student surveys and describes methods of reproduction, growth, and development of various types of plants in order to understand their roles in the environment

PE 380, 381, 382, 383, 385, 386, 387, 388, 389, 390, 398, 399, 400, 401, 402, 403, 406, 407, 408, 409, 420, 428, 429, 431, 432, 798, 799

ATE 381, 382, 390, 392, 398, 399, 400, 403, 406, 420, 428, 798

16b The student identifies structural and physiological adaptations to predict the probability of survival in a particular habitat or habitats

PE 380, 381, 382, 383, 384, 385, 386, 387, 388, 389, 390, 391, 392, 393, 394, 395, 396, 397, 401, 402, 404, 405, 407, 408, 409

ATE 381, 383, 384, 385, 386, 390, 394, 401, 404, 406, 410

16c The student recognizes and justifies the significance of plants in all environments

PE 295, 297, 305, 382, 386, 388, 389, 410, 411, 412, 413, 414, 415, 416, 417, 418, 419, 420, 431, 432, 433

ATE 417, 431

CHAPTER CORRELATION TO TEKS

Chapter Section	Page Number	TEKS

1.1 PE 4 — 2C
 5 — 2C, 3C
 6 — 2C, 3C
 7 — 3C, 8D
 8 — 1A, 3C, 8D
 9 — 1A, 3C
 10 — 2C, 3C

 ATE 4 — 2C, 3C,
 5 — 2C
 6 — 2C
 7 — 2C, 3C, 6A
 8 — 1C, 2B, 3C
 9 — 1A, 2B, 2C
 10 — 2B, 2C, 3D

1.2 PE 11 — 2A
 12 — 2A
 13 — 2A, 3C
 14 — 2A, 3B
 15 — 2A 3B

 ATE 11 — 2C
 12 — 2A, 2C
 13 — 2A, 3C
 14 — 2C, 2D
 15 — 2A, 2B, 2C,

1.3 PE 16 — 4B, 14A
 17 — 8B, 9C
 18 — 4B, 13A

 ATE 16 — 2C, 7C
 17 — 2C, 2D, 9A
 18 — 2B, 14A

HIGHLIGHTS
 PE 19 — 2A 3B, 3C, 8D, 9C, 14A

 ATE 19 — 2A

REVIEW
 PE 20 — 2A, 2C, 3C, 8D 14A
 21 — 2A, 2C, 3D, 14A, 15E

2.1 PE 22 — 2C, 12A
 23 — 2C
 24 — 2B, 2C, 11D
 25 — 2C, 4B, 14A

 ATE 22 — 2C, 12A
 23 — 2B, 2C
 24 — 2B, 2C
 25 — 2A, 2C, 5A

2.2 PE 26 — 11A
 27 — 11A
 28 — 11A

 ATE 26 — 11A
 27 — 2B, 2C
 28 — 2B, 2C

2.3 PE 29 — 12A
 30 — 11A, 12A
 31 — 11A, 12A
 32 — 11A, 12A
 33 — 11A, 12A
 34 — 11A, 12A

 ATE 29 — 2C
 30 — 2C, 12A

 31 — 2C 6A, 12A
 32 — 11B, 12A
 33 — 2A, 11B
 34 — 2C, 12A

HIGHLIGHTS
 PE 35 — 4B, 11A, 12A

 ATE 35 — 12A

REVIEW
 36 — 2C, 4B, 12A
 37 — 2B, 2C, 11A, 14A

SCIENCE TECHNOLOGY AND SOCIETY
 PE 38 — 8D
 39 — 3C, 7C, 8D

 ATE 38 — 3A
 39 — 3C, 7C

3.1 PE 40 — 4A
 41 — 4A, 11D
 42 — 4A, 11D
 43 — 2B, 4A
 44 — 11A
 45 — 4A, 4B, 11A

 ATE 40 — 2B, 4A
 41 — 1B, 2A, 2B, 2C
 42 — 2B, 2C
 43 — 2B, 14A
 44 — 2C, 11B
 45 — 1B, 2B, 2C

3.2 PE 46 — 11A, 11D, 12A
 47 — 4B, 11A, 11D, 12A
 48 — 4B, 11D
 49 — 11A, 12A

 ATE 46 — 2B, 2C
 47 — 11B, 11C
 48 — 2B, 2C, 11B
 49 — 2A, 11C, 12A

3.3 PE 50 — 4A, 9A
 51 — 4A, 11D
 52 — 4A, 4C
 53 — 4A, 11A, 11D
 54 — 4A
 55 — 3D
 56 — 2A, 2C
 57 — 2A, 2C
 58 — 2A, 2C

 ATE 50 — 2C, 4A,
 51 — 2B, 2C, 4A, 11C
 52 — 2C, 4A
 53 — 2B, 4A
 54 — 2B, 4A, 4B
 55 — 2B, 3D
 56 — 2A, 2B
 57 — 2C
 58 — 2C, 4A

HIGHLIGHTS
 PE 59 — 2A, 4A, 4B

 ATE 59 — 2C

REVIEW
 PE 60 — 2A, 2C, 4A, 4B, 12A
 61 — 2C, 3D, 4A, 8D, 8E, 11A

4.1 PE 62 — 4B
 63 — 4C

 64 — 4A, 4C, 11A, 11D
 65 — 4A, 4C, 11A
 66 — 4A, 11D

 ATE 62 — 2A, 2B, 4A
 63 — 2C, 4C
 64 — 2C, 4A
 65 — 2B, 2C
 66 — 2C, 11C, 11D

4.2 PE 67 — 4B
 68 — 4B
 69 — 4B
 70 — 4B, 11A
 71 — 4B, 11A
 72 — 4B, 11A

 ATE 67 — 2B, 4B
 68 — 2C, 4B
 69 — 2B, 2C
 70 — 2B, 4B
 71 — 2C
 72 — 2C, 4A, 4B

HIGHLIGHTS
 PE 73 — 4A, 4B, 11A

 ATE 73 — 2B

REVIEW
 PE 74 — 2C, 2D, 4A, 4B, 4C
 75 — 2C, 4B, 11A

5.1 PE 76 — 12B
 77 — 12A, 12C, 11D, 13A
 78 — 4B, 12A
 79 — 4B, 12A
 80 — 4B, 11A, 11D, 12A
 81 — 4C, 12A

 ATE 76 — 2C
 77 — 2C, 12C
 78 — 2C, 12A
 79 — 2B, 2C
 80 — 2C, 11B
 81 — 2C

5.2 PE 82 — 4B
 83 — 4B, 11A
 84 — 12B, 15A

 ATE 82 — 2C
 83 — 2A, 2B,
 84 — 2B, 12B, 15A 2C, 2D

5.3 PE 85 — 12B
 86 — 12B
 87 — 11A, 12B
 88 — 4B, 11A, 11D, 12B
 89 — 11A, 12A, 12B

 ATE 85 — 2C, 12B
 86 — 2C
 87 — 2A, 2B, 2C
 88 — 12B
 89 — 2C, 12B

5.4 PE 90 — 4A, 4B, 12B
 91 — 4B, 11A,
 92 — 4B, 11A
 93 — 4B, 11A
 94 — 4B, 11A, 11D

 ATE 90 — 2C
 91 — 2A
 92 — 2B, 4A
 93 — 2C, 11B
 94 — 2B, 2C, 12B

HIGHLIGHTS

PE	95	4B, 11A, 12B

ATE	95	2C

REVIEW

PE	96	2C, 4B, 12B
	97	2C,4B, 12B

6.1

PE	100	7E
	101	8B
	102	11A
	103	7E

ATE	100	2C, 7E
	101	7E
	102	2C
	103	2C, 7D

6.2

PE	104	7E
	105	7E
	106	7E, 8B
	107	7E, 8B
	108	7E, 8E
	109	8A, 8E

ATE	104	2B, 4A
	105	2C, 7E
	106	7E, 11B
	107	2B, 11B
	108	2C
	109	2A, 2B, 3D

6.3

PE	110	7E
	111	7E
	112	7E, 8B

ATE		
	110	2A, 2C
	111	7C, 11B
	112	2B, 2C, 2D

HIGHLIGHTS

PE	113	7E, 8B, 8E

ATE	113	2C

REVIEW

PE	114	7E, 8B, 8E
	115	2C, 3C, 3D, 7E, 8A, 8E

7.1

PE	116	7B
	117	7B, 8D
	118	7B, 7C
	119	7B, 7C, 11B
	120	7B, 7C, 11B
	120	7B, 7C, 11B
	122	7B, 7C

ATE	116	2C, 7B, 7E
	117	2C, 7B
	118	2A, 2B, 2C, 2D, 7C
	119	2C, 7B, 7C
	120	3A, 7C
	121	2B, 2C, 7B, 7C
	122	2C,7B, 7C

7.2

PE	123	7B, 7C
	124	7B,7C
	125	7B, 7C
	126	7B7C

ATE	123	7C
	124	2C, 7C
	125	2B, 3D, 7C
	126	2C,7C

7.3

PE	127	8E
	128	7D
	129	7C, 7D
	130	7A, 7C
	131	3D
	132	8D, 8E

ATE	127	8E
	128	2C, 3C
	129	2B, 2C, 2D, 7C
	130	7A, 7C
	131	2B, 2C, 3D
	132	2B

HIGHLIGHTS

PE	133	7A, 7B, 7C, 8E

ATE	133	2B, 2C, 7C

REVIEW

PE	134	2C, 2D, 7B, 7C, 8E
	135	2C, 7B, 7C, 8B, 8E

8.1

PE	136	8B, 12A
	137	8B
	138	8B
	139	11A
	140	8A, 8C, 11A

ATE	136	8B, 12A
	137	2C
	138	2C, 8B
	139	2C, 8C
	140	2D, 8C

8.2

PE	141	8C, 11A
	142	8C, 11A, 11D
	143	8C
	144	4A, 8C, 11D
	145	8C, 11D

ATE	141	2B
	142	8C
	143	2B, 2C
	144	4A, 8C, 11D
	145	8C

8.3

PE	146	8C, 11D
	147	4A, 8C
	148	8B, 11D

ATE	146	2C, 11B
	147	3A, 11B
	148	8B, 11D

HIGHLIGHTS

PE	149	8B, 8C, 11A

ATE	149	2C

REVIEW

PE	150	2C, 8B, 8C
	151	2C, 3D, 8C,8D, 9A

9.1

PE	152	8D
	153	8D
	154	8D
	155	8D, 9A
	156	8D
	157	1B, 3C, 8D

ATE	152	8D
	153	2C, 8D
	154	2C, 11B
	155	11B
	156	2B, 8D
	157	2C, 8D

9.2

PE	158	8D
	159	8D
	160	8D
	161	8D

ATE	158	8D
	159	2C, 8D
	160	3C, 8D
	161	2C, 8D

9.3

PE	162	8D
	163	8D
	164	8D, 11D
	165	3D
	166	3C, 8D

ATE	162	8D
	163	2C
	164	7C
	165	2B, 3D
	166	2B, 3C

HIGHLIGHTS

PE	167	3C, 8D

ATE	167	2B, 8D

REVIEW

PE	168	2C, 3C, 8D
	169	2C, 3A, 3C, 8D

SCIENCE TECHNOLOGY AND SOCIETY

PE	170	3C, 8D
	171	3A, 3C, 8D

ATE	170	3A, 8D
	171	2B, 3C, 8D

10.1

PE	172	9C
	173	9C
	174	9A, 9C
	175	9C

ATE	172	9A
	173	2B, 2C
	174	2B, 2C, 2D, 9A
	175	2C, 2D

10.2

PE	176	9A
	177	9B
	178	9A
	179	9A

ATE	176	2B, 2C
	177	2C, 9A
	178	2C, 9A
	179	2C, 9A

10.3

PE	180	9C
	181	8E, 9C
	182	9C
	183	9C
	184	9C
	185	9C
	186	9C

ATE	180	2B, 9C
	181	2B, 9C
	182	2C, 2D
	183	2C, 7C
	184	2B, 2C
	185	9C
	186	2A, 9C

HIGHLIGHTS

PE	187	9A, 9C
ATE	187	9C

REVIEW

PE	188	2C, 2D, 9A, 9C
	189	2C, 3C, 9A, 9C

11.1 PE 190 — 9A

PE	190	9A
	191	9A
	192	2A, 3B, 11B, 12A
	193	3B, 8B, 11B, 12A
	194	3B, 11B
ATE	190	2B, 2C, 11B
	191	2B, 11B
	192	2C
	193	2C, 11B
	194	2A, 2C, 11B

11.2 PE

PE	195	9A
	196	9A, 10B
	197	9B, 10A
ATE	195	9A
	196	2C, 10B
	197	2A, 2C

11.3 PE

PE	198	1A, 11A
	199	9A, 15B
	200	9A
	201	9A
	202	9A
	203	9A, 15B
ATE	198	2C
	199	2A, 2C
	200	2C
	201	2C, 9A
	202	2C, 9A
	203	2A, 2B, 2C

11.4 PE

PE	204	9A, 10A
	205	9A, 10A
	206	9C, 10A
	207	9A, 10A
	208	9C, 10A
ATE	204	2C, 9C
	205	2C
	206	2C
	207	2C, 10A
	208	2A, 2C, 10A

HIGHLIGHTS

PE	209	9A, 10A, 11B, 15B
ATE	209	2C

REVIEW

PE	210	2C, 9A, 10A, 11B, 15B
	211	2C, 11B, 15B

12.1 PE

PE	212	9C
	213	9A, 9C
	214	9A, 9C, 15E
	215	9A
	216	9A, 15E
	217	9A

ATE	212	2C, 9A, 9C
	213	2B
	214	2B
	215	2B, 2C, 8C
	216	2C, 3D
	217	2C, 9A

12.2 PE

PE	218	9A
	219	9A
	220	9A, 10A
	221	9A, 10A
	222	9A, 10A
ATE	218	2C
	219	2B, 2C
	220	9A
	221	2B, 9A
	222	2C, 9A, 10A

12.3 PE

PE	223	10A
	224	9A, 10A
	225	9C, 10A
	226	9A, 9C, 10A
	227	9A, 10A
	228	9A, 9C, 10A
ATE	223	2C
	224	9A, 10A
	225	9A
	226	2A, 2C, 7A, 7C
	227	2C, 3B
	228	2B, 2C

HIGHLIGHTS

PE	229	9A, 9C, 10A
ATE	229	11B

REVIEW

PE	230	2C, 9A, 9C, 10A
	231	2C, 9A, 10A, 15E

13.1 PE

PE	232	9C
	233	2A, 2C
	234	2A, 2C, 2D
	235	1D, 2C, 9C
	236	2C
	237	2C
	238	3D
	239	2A, 2C
ATE	232	2C, 9C
	233	2C
	234	2A, 2C
	235	2C, 7A
	236	2C
	237	2A, 2B, 2C
	238	2B, 2C, 3D
	239	2B, 2C

13.2 PE

PE	240	2C, 9C
	241	2C, 9C
	242	9C
	243	9C
	244	2C, 9C
	245	2C, 9C
	246	2C, 9C
ATE	240	2C
	241	2A, 3A
	242	2B
	243	2C, 9C
	244	2A, 2C
	245	2A, 2C
	246	2B, 2C, 2D

HIGHLIGHTS

PE	247	2A, 2C, 9C
ATE	247	2C

REVIEW

PE	248	2A, 2C, 2D, 9C
	249	2C, 3D, 9C

14.1 PE

PE	252	15A
	253	15E
	254	15E
	255	11D, 15E, 15F
	256	15C
	257	15C
	258	2C, 15C
ATE	252	15A, 15C
	253	2B, 15E
	254	2B, 15C, 15E, 15F
	255	2D, 11B
	256	15C, 15E
	257	2A, 2B, 15C
	258	2C, 15C

14.2 PE

PE	259	15A
	260	15A
	261	15A
	262	15A, 15E
ATE	259	1C, 2C
	260	15A
	261	1C, 15A
	262	2C, 15A

14.3 PE

PE	263	15C, 15E
	264	15D, 15E
	265	15D, 15E
	266	15D
	267	3D
	268	2C, 15D
ATE	263	15E
	264	2B, 15E
	265	2C, 3C, 15D, 15E
	266	15C, 15D
	267	3D
	268	2C, 15D

HIGHLIGHTS

PE	269	15A, 15C, 15D, 15E
ATE	269	15E

REVIEW

PE	270	2C, 15A, 15C, 15D, 15E
	271	2B, 2C, 15C, 15D, 15E

15.1 PE

PE	272	15E
	273	15D, 15E
	274	15D, 15E
	275	15D, 15E
	276	15B
	277	15B
ATE	272	15D, 15E
	273	15D
	274	2C
	275	2C, 15E
	276	2B, 15B
	277	2C, 15B

15.2 PE 278 15E
279 9C, 15E
280 15E
281 15D, 15E
282 2C, 15D, 15E
283 15D, 15E
284 15E

ATE 278 11D
279 2A, 2C
280 2C, 3C, 15E
281 2B
282 2B, 2C
283 2A
284 2C, 15E

HIGHLIGHTS
PE 285 15B, 15D, 15E

ATE 285 15F

REVIEW
PE 286 2C, 15B, 15D
287 2C, 3C, 15B, 15E

16.1 PE 288 15E
289 1A, 15E
290 1A, 15E
291 1A, 15E
292 1A, 8A, 15E
293 2C, 3C, 15E

ATE 288 2C, 15E
289 1A
290 2A
291 2B, 2C
292 2C
293 2A, 2C

16.2 PE 294 3C, 15E
295 1C, 15E, 16C
296 1C, 3C, 15E
297 1C, 11D, 15E, 16C
298 2C, 15E
299 2C, 3C, 15E

ATE 294 2B, 2C
295 2B
296 1C, 2C
297 1C, 2C
298 2C
299 1C, 2D

16.3 PE 300 1C, 15E
301 2C, 3C
302 1C, 3C
303 1C
304 1C, 3C

ATE 300 3C
301 2B, 2C, 2D
302 1C, 3C
303 1C, 2C
304 1C, 2C

HIGHLIGHTS
PE 305 1C, 3C, 15E, 16C

ATE 305 2B

REVIEW
PE 306 1C, 2C, 3C, 11C, 15E
307 1C, 2B, 2C, 3C, 15E, 16C

SCIENCE, TECHNOLOGY AND SOCIETY
PE 308 1C, 3C, 15E
309 3C, 15E

ATE 308 2B, 2C, 3C
309 8A

17.1 PE 312 10B
313 10A
314 10A
315 10A
316 10A

ATE 312 10A, 10C
313 2B, 10A
314 10A
315 2B, 2C, 3D
316 2B, 10A

17.2 PE 317 10A, 11D
318 10A
319 10A
320 10A
321 10A
322 9A
323 9B, 10A

ATE 317 10C
318 10A
319 2C, 10A
320 2B, 10A
321 2C, 10A
322 2C, 8B
323 2B, 10A, 10C

17.3 PE 324 10B
325 9A, 10B
326 10B

ATE 324 2B, 10A
325 2C, 4A
326 2B, 10B

HIGHLIGHTS
PE 327 10A, 10B

ATE 327 2B, 10B

REVIEW
PE 328 2D, 10A, 10B, 10C, 11D
329 2C, 9A, 10A, 10B, 10C

18.1 PE 330 5A
331 9A, 10A
332 4A, 10A, 10B
333 4A, 8D, 9A, 10B
334 4B, 7E, 8D
335 4B 15B, 15C

ATE 330 2C
331 2B, 2C
332 2B, 2C, 4A, 10A
333 2C, 4A
334 2C, 4A, 12B
335 4A, 9C

18.2 PE 336 15C
337 8D, 15C
338 2C, 15B
339 1B
340 15B
341 1B, 15B
342 1B, 8D
343 3C
344 2C, 3C, 8D

ATE 336 2B, 2C
337 2B, 8D
338 2B, 2C
339 2B, 2C, 3D
340 2C
341 1B
342 8D
343 2C
344 2A, 2C

18.3 PE 345 5A
346 5A
347 5A, 11D
348 5A
349 3C, 5A
350 2C, 5A

ATE 345 2B, 5A
346 2C, 5A
347 2B, 2C, 5A
348 3C
349 3C
350 2C, 5A

HIGHLIGHTS
PE 351 3C, 4A, 5A, 10B

ATE 351 2C

REVIEW
PE 352 2C, 4A, 5A, 11D
353 2C, 3C, 3D, 5A, 15C

SCIENCE, TECHNOLOGY AND SOCIETY
PE 354 3A
355 2C, 3A

ATE 354 3A
355 2C, 3A, 3D

19.1 PE 356 6A
357 2C, 6A, 10B
358 2C, 6A, 10A
359 2C, 6A, 10A

ATE 356 2B, 10B
357 2C
358 2A, 6A
359 2C

19.2 PE 360 6A, 10A, 10B
361 10A, 10B
362 6A, 15C
363 6A, 10A
364 6A, 10A
365 6A, 10A
ATE 360 2B, 6A
361 2C, 4B
362 6A, 15C
363 2A, 2C, 3D
364 2C
365 2B, 2C, 15B

19.3 PE 366 10A, 15B
367 10A, 15B
368 10A, 11D, 15B

ATE 366 2B, 2C
367 1A, 2C, 15E
368 1B, 2B, 2C

HIGHLIGHTS
PE 369 10A, 10B, 15B

ATE 369 2C

REVIEW

PE	370	2C, 10A, 10B, 15B
	371	2C, 10A, 15B

20.1

PE	372	6A
	373	6A, 10B
	374	6A, 10A
	375	6A, 7E, 15C
	376	6A, 7E, 10A
	377	1A, 6A, 10A, 15B
	378	10A, 15B
	379	3C, 8D, 10A
ATE	372	2B, 2C
	373	2C, 10A
	374	2B, 2C, 6A
	375	2B
	376	2C
	377	15B
	378	2B, 15B
	379	2B, 2C

20.2

PE	380	10A, 16A, 16B
	381	10A, 16A, 16B
	382	10A, 16A, 16B, 16C
	383	16A, 16B
ATE	380	2C
	381	2C, 16A, 16B
	382	2B, 2D, 16A
	383	2B, 16B

20.3

PE	384	16B
	385	16A, 16B
	386	16A, 16B, 16C
ATE	384	16B
	385	2C, 16B
	386	16B

HIGHLIGHTS

PE	387	15B, 16A, 16B
ATE	387	2C

REVIEW

PE	388	2C, 10A, 15C, 16A, 16B, 16C
	389	2C, 16A, 16B, 16C

21.1

PE	390	16A, 16B
	391	6A, 16B
	392	6A, 16B
	393	6A, 16B
	394	6A, 16B
	395	6A, 16B
ATE	390	16A, 16B
	391	2C, 6A
	392	2B, 16A
	393	2C, 6A
	394	2B, 16B
	395	2B, 2C, 6A, 10A

21.2

PE	396	6A, 16B
	397	6A, 16B
	398	16A
	399	16A
ATE	396	4B
	397	6A
	398	2B, 2D, 16A
	399	2C, 16A

21.3

PE	400	16A
	401	10A, 16A, 16B
	402	6A, 16A, 16B
	403	6A, 16A
	404	16B
	405	16B
	406	2C, 16A
ATE	400	2B, 16A
	401	2C, 16B
	402	3D
	403	2B, 16A
	404	10A, 16B
	405	2B, 7C
	406	2C, 16A, 16B

HIGHLIGHTS

PE	407	6A, 16A, 16B
ATE	407	2C

REVIEW

PE	408	2C, 15B, 16A, 16B
	409	2C, 16A, 16B

22.1

PE	410	16C
	411	16C
	412	6A, 16C
	413	2C, 16C
	414	16C
	415	16C
	416	16C
	417	16C
	418	2C, 16C
	419	16C
ATE	410	2C, 8D, 16B
	411	2C
	412	2C
	413	2C, 6A
	414	2B
	415	6A
	416	2C, 3D
	417	1C, 2C, 16C
	418	2B
	419	2B, 16C

22.2

PE	420	16A, 16C
	421	2C
	422	2C
	423	2C
	424	2C
	425	3D
	426	2C
	427	2C
	428	16A
	429	2C, 16A
	430	2C, 8D
ATE	420	2C, 16A
	421	1C, 15E
	422	2C, 15A
	423	2B, 2C
	424	2B
	425	3D
	426	2B, 2C
	427	2B, 2C
	428	2B, 2C, 16A
	429	2B, 8D
	430	2C

HIGHLIGHTS

PE	431	2C, 16A, 16C
ATE	431	2C, 16C

REVIEW

PE	432	2C, 15E, 16A, 16C
	433	2B, 2C, 8D, 16C

23.1

PE	436	6B, 6C
	437	6B, 10A
	438	2C, 6C, 9C
	439	6A, 10A
	440	6A, 6B, 10A
	441	6B, 6C
ATE	436	6C
	437	6C
	438	2C
	439	2C, 6A
	440	2C, 6B
	441	6A, 6B, 11B

23.2

PE	442	6B, 6C
	443	6B, 6C, 10A
	444	6B, 6C
	445	6B, 6C, 10A
	446	6B, 6C
	447	6B, 6C, 10A
ATE	442	2B
	443	6B, 6C
	444	2B, 15B
	445	11D
	446	6B, 6C
	447	2B, 6C

23.3

PE	448	6C, 10A, 11D
	449	6B, 6C, 10A
	450	6B, 6C
	451	6B, 6C, 10A
	452	6B, 6C
	453	6C, 10A
	454	6C, 10A
ATE	448	2C, 6C
	449	2B
	450	2B, 10A
	451	2C
	452	2C
	453	2B, 2C, 6C
	454	6C

HIGHLIGHTS

PE	455	6B, 6C
AT	455	10A

REVIEW

PE	456	2C, 6B, 6C, 10A
	457	2C, 6B, 6C

24.1

PE	458	9C
	459	9C, 10A
	460	6C, 9A, 9C
	461	6C, 9A, 9C
	462	6C, 9C, 13B
ATE	458	2C, 9C
	459	9C
	460	2B, 9A
	461	2C
	462	9C, 11B

24.2

PE	463	6C, 9C, 13B
	464	4B, 6A, 6C, 9C, 13B
	465	6A, 9C, 13B
	466	6A, 6C, 9A, 13A, 13B
	467	6A, 6C, 9C, 13B
	468	6A, 6C, 9A, 13B
	469	6A, 6C, 13B
	470	6C, 13A
	471	6A, 6C, 11D, 13A,

ATE	558	2C, 9C
	559	9B
	560	2B, 10A
	561	2C
	562	2B, 10A
	563	2C, 10A

28.4 PE	564	9C, 10A, 14A
	565	10A
	566	9C, 13A
	567	10A
	568	9C, 10A

ATE	564	2B, 6A
	565	2B
	566	13A
	567	2C
	568	2A

HIGHLIGHTS

PE	569	9B, 9B, 10A
ATE	569	2C

REVIEW

PE	570	2C, 9B, 10A, 15B
	571	2A, 2B, 2C, 10A, 15E

29.1 PE	574	13B
	575	6A, 6C, 13B
	576	6A, 13B
	577	6C, 13B

ATE	574	2C
	575	2B, 6A
	576	6A, 6C, 13C
	577	2C, 6A

29.2 PE	578	6A, 13B
	579	13A, 13B, 14A
	580	6A, 13B
	581	13B
	582	2C, 8A
	583	6A, 8A

ATE	578	2B, 6A
	579	14A
	580	2C, 6A
	581	2C, 6A
	582	2C
	583	2B, 13B

29.3 PE	584	13B
	585	6A, 13B
	586	13B
	587	6A, 13B
	588	13B
	589	13B

ATE	584	2C, 13B
	585	1B, 6A, 13B
	586	2A, 2C
	587	1B, 2C
	588	13B
	589	2C, 6A, 13B

29.4 PE	590	13B
	591	6A, 13B
	592	13B
	593	6A, 13B
	594	13B
	595	13B
	596	2C

ATE	590	2C, 6A
	591	13B
	592	2C

	593	2C, 13B
	594	3D
	595	6A
	596	2B, 2C, 13B

HIGHLIGHTS

PE	597	6A, 6C, 13B
ATE	597	2B

REVIEW

PE	598	2C, 6C, 8A, 13B
	599	2C, 13B

30.1 PE	600	13B
	601	6A, 13B
	602	4B, 6A, 13B
	603	4B, 13B
	604	6A, 13B
	605	4A, 4B, 13B
	606	4A, 4B, 13B
	607	4B, 13B
	608	4A, 13B
	609	2C, 13B
	610	2C

ATE	600	13B
	601	2B, 6A
	602	4B
	603	2C
	604	13B
	605	2B, 13B
	606	4A
	607	13B
	608	11B
	609	2C
	610	2B

30.2 PE	611	13B
	612	13B
	613	13B
	614	13B
	615	2C
	616	6C, 13B
	617	6C, 13B
	618	6A, 13B
	619	6A, 13B
	620	13B, 14A

ATE	611	13B
	612	11B, 13B
	613	2C
	614	2B
	615	2B, 2C
	616	2C
	617	6C, 13B
	618	2C, 13B
	619	13B, 14B
	620	2B, 2C, 11D

30.3 PE	621	13B, 14A
	622	6A, 13B, 14A
	623	6A, 13B
	624	6A, 13B
	625	9C, 13B
	626	13B

ATE	621	2C
	622	2B, 14B
	623	2C, 14A
	624	11B
	625	2A
	626	2B, 2C

HIGHLIGHTS

PE	627	6A, 13B, 14A
ATE	627	2C

REVIEW

PE	628	2C, 4B, 13B, 14A
	629	2C, 3D, 6C, 13B, 14A

31.1 PE	630	13B
	631	13B
	632	13B, 14A
	633	13B
	634	13B, 14A
	635	2C, 13B, 14A

ATE	630	13B
	631	2B, 13B
	632	2C, 13C
	633	13B
	634	2C, 14A
	635	2B, 2C, 14A

31.2 PE	636	4A, 13B
	637	2C, 4A, 13B
	638	4A, 13B

ATE	636	12A
	637	4A, 13B
	638	2A, 4A, 13B

31.3 PE	639	13B, 14B
	640	13B
	641	13B
	642	13B, 14A
	643	2C, 13B, 14A
	644	2C, 13B, 14A
	645	2C, 13B
	646	2C, 13B, 13C

ATE	639	13B
	640	2C
	641	2C
	642	13B
	643	13B
	644	2C, 13B
	645	2B, 2C
	646	2B, 13B

HIGHLIGHTS

PE	647	13B, 14A
ATE	647	2C

REVIEW

PE	648	2C, 13B, 13C, 14A
	649	2B, 2C, 4A, 14A

32.1 PE	650	13A, 13B
	651	13A
	652	6A, 13A
	653	6A, 13A
	654	13A
	655	6A, 13A
	656	2C, 13A
	657	6A, 13A

ATE	650	6C, 13C
	651	2C
	652	2B, 2C
	653	6A, 13A
	654	2C, 13A
	655	2C, 13A
	656	7C
	657	2C, 13A

32.2 PE 658 13A
659 13A
660
661 13A
662 6C, 13A
663 6C, 13A
664 13A
665 3D
666 13A
667 6A, 13A
668 6A, 13A, 13C
669 2C, 13A

ATE 658 2B, 2C , 13A
659 2C, 11B
660 2C, 13A
661 2C, 13A
662 6C, 13A
663 6C, 13A
664 2C, 13A , 13B
665 3D
666 2B, 2C
667 2C
668 2C
669 2A, 2C

32.3 PE 670 4B, 13B
671 6A, 13B, 13C
672 13B
673 4B, 6A, 13B, 13C
674 13B, 13C

ATE 670 2B
671 2C, 4B
672 2B
673 2C, 13B
674 2B, 2C, 11B

HIGHLIGHTS

PE 675 2C, 4B, 13A, 13B, 13C

ATE 675 2B

REVIEW

PE 676 2C, 4A, 6C, 13A, 13B, 13C
677 2B, 2C, 3D, 13A, 13B

33.1 PE 678 13B
679 6A, 13B
680 6A, 13B
681 2C, 4A, 11D, 13B
682 2C, 6A, 13B

ATE 678 2B,2C
679 13B
680 2C, 13B
681 2C, 13B
682 2B, 2C, 13B

33.2 PE 683 5A, 6A, 13B
684 2C, 6A, 11D, 13B
685 2C, 6A, 13B
686 2C, 13B
687 2C, 2D, 5A, 13B

ATE 683 6A
684 2B, 13B
685 2C
686 2C
687 2A, 2B, 2C

33.3 PE 689 2C, 6A, 13B
690 6A, 8E, 13B
691 5A, 6A, 13B
692 2C, 3C, 5A
693 2C, 3C, 5A
694 2C, 3C

ATE 689 13B
690 2C, 7E
691 2B
692 2B, 2C, 3C
693 2B, 3C
694 2B, 2C

HIGHLIGHTS

PE 695 4A, 5A, 6A, 8E, 13B

ATE 695 2C

REVIEW

PE 696 2C, 5A, 6A, 13B
697 2C, 3C, 5A, 6A, 13B

34.1 PE 698 13A
699 2C, 12A
700 2C, 12A
701 2C, 12A, 12D
702 2C, 12A
703 2C, 12C
704 2C
705 3D

ATE 698 11B, 13A
699 2C, 4B, 12A
700 2C, 12A
701 2B, 2C, 12D
702 2C
703 12C
704 2C
705 3D

34.2 PE 706 12C, 13A
707 12C, 13A
708 6A, 12C, 13A
709 6A, 12C, 13A

ATE 706 2B, 2C, 13A
707 12C, 13A
708 12C, 13A
709 2B, 2C, 13A

34.3 PE 710 6A, 13A
711 4C, 6A, 13A, 13C
712 2C, 13A

ATE 710 13A, 13C
711 2B, 4C, 13C
712 2C

HIGHLIGHTS

PE 713 4C, 12A, 12C, 13A, 13C

ATE 713 2C, 13C

REVIEW

PE 714 2C, 4C, 12A, 12C, 13A
715 2B, 2C, 3D, 12D, 13A

SCIENCE , TECHNOLOGY AND SOCIETY

PE 716 3C
717 2C, 3C

ATE 716 2C
717 2C, 3C

35.1 PE 718 13B
719 6A, 7E, 13B
720 13B
721 6A, 13B
722 13B, 14A

ATE 718 11B
719 13B

720 13B
721 2A, 7E
722 13B, 14A

35.2 PE 723 13B
724 13B
725 6A, 13B, 13C
726 2C, 13B, 13C
727 2C, 13B, 13C

ATE 723 2C, 13B
724 13B, 13C
725 2B, 2C
726 2C, 13B
727 2C, 13C

35.3 PE 728 6A, 13B
729 6A, 13B
730 2C, 4B
731 8A, 13B
732 8A, 13B
733 13B
734 6B, 13B
735 6B, 13B
736 13B

ATE 728 6A
729 2B, 13B
730 4B, 13B
731 2C, 8A
732 2C, 3C
733 13B
734 2C, 6B
735 2C
736 2C, 13B

35.4 PE 737 5A
738 5A
739 2C
740 2C, 13B

ATE 737 1B, 2C
738 2C
739 2C
740 2C, 5A

HIGHLIGHTS

PE 741 2C, 13B

ATE 741 2B, 2C

REVIEW

PE 742 2C, 2D, 5A, 8A, 13B
743 2C, 5A, 13B

LAB SAFETY

PE 752 1B
753 1B
754 1B
755 1B

ATE T745-9 1B
T745-10 1B
T745-11 1B

EXPLORATION

1.A PE 756 2A, 2C
757 1B, 2A, 2C, 2D, 3D

ATE 756 2A, 2C
757 1B

1.B PE 758 1B, 2A
759 1B, 2B, 2C

758 2A, 2B, 2C
759 1B, 2B, 2C

EXPLORATION

3.A PE 760 2A, 2B, 2C, 4A
761 1B, 2A, 2B, 2C, 2D, 3D

ATE 760 2B, 4A
761 2A, 1B, 2B, 2C, 2D, 3D

EXLORATION

4.A PE 762 1B, 2B, 2C, 4B
763 1B, 2A, 2B, 2C, 2D, 3D

ATE 762 1B, 2B, 4B
763 1B

EXPLORATION

5.A PE 764 1B, 2A, 2B, 2C
765 1B, 2B, 2C, 2D, 3D

ATE 764 1B, 2B, 2C
765 1B, 2B

5.B PE 766 1B, 2B
767 1B, 2A, 2B, 2C, 2D

ATE 766 2B, 2C
767 1B. 2B, 2C

EXPLORATION

5.C PE 768 2A, 2C, 12B
769 2B, 2C, 2D

ATE 768 2B, 2C, 12B
769 2B

EXPLORATION

6.A PE 770 2A, 2B, 2C, 7E, 11B
771 2C, 2D, 3D, 7E, 11B

ATE 770 2B, 7E, 11B
771 1B, 2B, 7E

EXPLORATION

6.B PE 772 2C, 7E
773 2C, 7C, 7E

ATE 772 2B, 2C, 7E
773 2C

EXPLORATION

7.A PE 774 1B, 2C, 7C
775 1B, 2B, 2C, 2D, 3D

ATE 774 1B, 2B, 2C, 7C
775 1B, 2B, 2C, 2D, 3D

7.B PE 776 1B, 2A, 2C, 7C
777 1B, 2A, 2B, 2C, 2D

ATE 776 1B, 2A, 2B, 2C
777 1B

EXPLORATION

7.C PE 778 2C, 4B
779 2C, 4B

ATE 778 2B, 2C, 4B
779 2C

EXPLORATION

8.A PE 780 1B, 2C, 8C, 8E, 11D
781 2C, 2D, 8C

ATE 780 2B, 11B
781 1B

EXPLORATION

9.A PE 782 1B, 2C, 8D
783 1B, 2B, 8D
784 1B, 2B
785 1B, 2B, 2C, 2D, 3D

ATE 782 1B, 2B, 8D
783 2B
784 1B
785 1B

EXPLORATION

10.A PE 786 2A, 2B, 2C
787 2A, 2B, 2C, 2D, 3D

ATE 786 2B, 2C
787 1B, 2B, 2C

EXPLORATION

14.A PE 788 1B, 2B, 2C, 11B, 15F
789 1B, 2C, 3D, 11B, 15F

ATE 788 1B, 2B, 2C, 15F
789 1B

15.A PE 790 1B, 2A, 11B
791 2A, 2B, 2C, 2D, 11B

ATE 790 2A, 2B, 2C, 11B
791 1B, 2B, 11B

18.A PE 792 1B, 2A, 2C
793 1B, 2A, 2B, 2C, 2D

ATE 792 1B, 2A, 2B, 2C
793 1B, 2B, 2C

EXPLORATION

19.A PE 794 1B, 2B, 2C, 6A
795 1B, 2B, 2C, 2D, 3D, 6A

ATE 794 1B, 2B, 2C
795 1B

EXPLORATION

20.A PE 796 2C, 10A
797 2C, 3D, 10A

ATE 796 1B, 2C, 10A
797

EXPLORATION

21.A PE 798 1B, 2A, 2B, 2C, 16A
799 1B, 2B, 2C, 3D, 16A

ATE 798 1B, 2B, 2C, 16A
799 1B

EXPLORATION

22.A PE 800 1B, 2C, 12A
801 1B, 2B, 2C, 3D, 12A

ATE 800 1B, 2C, 12A
801 1B

22.B PE 802 1B, 12A
803 2A, 2B, 2C, 2D 12A

ATE 802 1B, 2B, 2C, 12A
803 1B

EXPLORATION

24.A PE 804 1B, 2C, 2D, 11B, 13A
805 2B, 2C, 2D, 3D

ATE 804 1B, 2B, 2C, 3A, 11B, 13A

805 1B
26.A PE 806 1B, 2C, 10A
807 2C, 10A

ATE 806 1B, 2B, 2C, 10A
807 1B, 2B, 2C, 10A

28.A PE 808 1B, 10A
809 2A, 2B, 2C, 2D, 11B

ATE 808 2B, 2C, 10A
809 1B, 2C, 10A

EXPLORATION

29.A PE 810 2C, 12D
811 2C, 12D

ATE 810 2C
811 12D

EXPLORATION

30.A PE 812 1B, 2A, 2C
813 1B, 2A, 2B, 2C, 2D, 3D

ATE 812 1B, 2B, 2C, 13B
813 1B, 2C

EXPLORATION

30.B PE 814 2C, 13B
815 2C, 13B

ATE 814 2B, 13B
815

31.A PE 816 1B, 2A, 2B, 2C
817 2A, 2B, 2C, 2D

ATE 816 2A, 2B, 2C
817 1B, 2B

32.A PE 818 1B, 2A, 2B, 2C, 2D
819 2A, 2B, 2C, 2D

ATE 818 1B, 2B, 2C, 14B
819 1B, 2B, 14B

EXPLORATION

34.A PE 820 1B, 2A, 2B, 2C, 12C
821 1B, 2B, 2C, 2D, 3D, 12C

ATE 820 1B, 2B, 2C, 12C
821 1B, 2B

EXPLORATION

34.B PE 822 1B, 2C
823 1B, 2B, 2C, 3D

ATE 822 1B, 2B, 2C
823 1B

EXPLORATION

34.C PE 824 2C, 4C
825 2C, 4C

ATE 824 2C, 4C
825 2B, 2C

BIOLOGY

Visualizing Life

Your Evaluation Checklist

Fulfilling the Promise: Biology Education in the Nation's Schools, a report by the National Research Council, tells you what to look for when choosing a biology text.

✳ Factual accuracy

Read George Johnson's statements on accuracy, pages T20–T21.

✳ Appropriateness of students' level and interest

See the many high-interest lessons and features throughout the text.

- Biology and You, page 10
- DNA Profiling: Promise or Peril? page 38
- The Puzzle of Sickle Cell Anemia, page 183
- Career Opportunities: Veterinary Technician, page 238
- Environmental Problems Can Be Solved, page 300
- Exploration of an Arthropod, page 450
- Tour of a Frog, page 535
- Nutrition and Health, page 699

✳ Clarity in explanation and effectiveness of illustrations

Look at the careful integration of all illustrations throughout the text. Note the extended captions (such as on pages 92, 140, 184, 217, 543, 548, and 576) that aid in the visual presentation of concepts.

✳ Incorporation of current conceptual understanding and new subject matter

See the Table of Contents, pages T6–T19, for important highlights.

✳ Adequate but not encyclopedic coverage

See the *Biology: Visualizing Life* Table of Contents on pages T6–T19 and "What Students Need to Know" on pages T24–T25.

✳ Logical coherence

Read George Johnson's philosophy on pages T20–T25, and see the Author's Rationale section on the first page of every chapter.

✳ Representation of biology as an experimental subject

See pages T28–T29 and pages T745-1 through T745-8 to learn how *Biology: Visualizing Life* labs provide opportunities for students to act as independent, self-directed investigators.

Author

George B. Johnson

**Professor of Biology
Washington University
St. Louis, MO**

Staff Credits

Executive Editor
Ellen Standafer

Managing Editor
William Wahlgren

Senior Editor
Susan Feldkamp

Project Editors
**Carolyn Biegert
Mitchell Leslie
Jennifer Linn
Encarnacion Perez, Jr.
Annette Ratliff
Tracy Schagen
George F. Spiegel, Jr.**

Copyediting
**Amy Daniewicz
Denise Haney
Steve Oelenberger**

Prepress
**Beth Prevelige
Simira Davis
Rose Degollado**

Media
Susan Mussey

Manufacturing
Michael Roche

Design
Foca, Inc.

Cover Design and Electronic File Production
Morgan-Cain & Associates

To learn how a lizard changes its body temperature, see page 543.

Acknowledgments

Contributing Writers

Mary Pitt Davis
Science Teacher
Long Reach High School
Columbia, MD

David Jaeger
Will C. Wood High School
Vacaville, CA

Jacqueline Jarzem, Ph.D.
Instructor
Austin Community College
Austin, TX

Lynne Krenicky
Biology Teacher
Clifton High School
Clifton, NJ

Judy A. Leavell, Ph.D.
Assistant Professor
Curriculum and Instruction
 Department
Southwest Texas State
 University
San Marcos, TX

Nancy Morvillo, Ph.D.
Howard Hughes Medical
 Institute
Undergraduate Biology
 Educational Program
State University of New
 York at Stony Brook
Stony Brook, NY

Karen M. Nein
Science Consultant
Denver, CO

William H. Peltz
Greenwich Academy
Greenwich, CT

Barbara A. Scroggie
Dripping Springs High
 School
Dripping Springs, TX

Salvatore Tocci
Science Department
East Hampton High School
East Hampton, NY

Suzanne Weisker
Science Teacher and
 Department Chair
Will C. Wood High School
Vacaville, CA

Lab Reviewers

George Nassis
Ken Rainis
Geoffrey Smith
WARD'S Natural Science
 Establishment
Rochester, NY

Ted Parker
Forest Grove, OR

Mark Stallings, Ph.D.
Chair, Science Department
Gilmer High School
Ellijay, GA

Jay A. Young, Ph.D.
Chemical Safety
 Consultant
Silver Spring, MD

Reviewers

Lois Bergquist, Ph.D.
Professor of Microbiology
Los Angeles Valley College
Van Nuys, CA

Margaret Bradley-Schwartz
Biology Teacher
Lexington High School
Lexington, MA

G. Lynn Carlson, Ph.D.
Senior Lecturer/Lab
 Manager
University of Wisconsin–
 Parkside
Kenosha, WI

Pat Carter
Biology/Physics Teacher
Central High School
Evansville, IN

Phillip Creighton, Ph.D.
Dean, School of Science
 and Technology
Salisbury State University
Salisbury, MD

Mary Pitt Davis
Science Teacher
Long Reach High School
Columbia, MD

Michael Dole
Science Teacher/Dept.
 Chairperson
Covina High School
Covina, CA

William J. Ehmann, Ph.D
Chair
Department of Environ-
 mental Science
Trinity College of
 Washington, DC
Washington, DC

David G. Futch, Ph.D.
Associate Professor
Department of Biology
San Diego State
 University
San Diego, CA

Jim Gardner
Science Department Chair
Central High School
Evansville, IN

Herbert Grossman, Ph.D.
Associate Professor
 of Botany
Pennsylvania State
 University
State College, PA

How does this flower attract pollinators? See page 386.

Do these dogs have the same name? See page 313.

Acknowledgments, continued

Frank Harrold, Ph.D.
Professor of
  Anthropology
Department of Sociology
  and Anthropology
The University of
  Texas–Arlington, TX

Arthur Hulse, Ph.D.
Department of Biology
Indiana University of PA
Indiana, PA

Clifford Keller, Ph.D.
Institute of Neuroscience
University of Oregon
Eugene, OR

Hillar Klandorf, Ph.D.
Associate Professor
Division of Animal and
  Veterinary Science
West Virginia University
Morgantown, WV

Patty Korn
McLean High School
McLean, VA

Lynne Krenicky
Biology Teacher
Clifton High School
Clifton, NJ

Jo Ann D. Lane
Science Department Chair
St. Ignatius High School
Cleveland, OH

Sheila Logiudice
Biology Instructor
Science/Technology
Lowell High School
Lowell, MA

Dan Millin
Biology Instructor
West Bend East High School
West Bend, WI

Martin Nickels, Ph.D.
Professor of
  Anthropology
Anthropology Program
Illinois State University
Normal, IL

David O. Norris, Ph.D.
Professor of Biology
E.P.O. Biology
University of Colorado
Boulder, CO

William H. Peltz
Greenwich Academy
Greenwich, CT

Sharon Perlman
Biology Teacher, Environ-
  mental Specialist
Dade County Public
  Schools
Center for Environmental
  Education
Miami, FL

**Terence M. Phillips,
Ph.D., D.Sc.**
Professor of Medicine/
  Immunochemistry
George Washington
  University Medical Center
Washington, DC

Joseph B. Schiel, Jr., Ph.D.
Biology Teacher
Artesia High School
Artesia, NM

Betty H. Smith
Assistant Principal/
  Curriculum Coordinator
Pineville High School
Pineville, LA

Richard Storey, Ph.D.
Professor and Chair of
  Biology
Department of Biology
Colorado College
Colorado Springs, CO

Peter Swanson
Biology Teacher
Quincy High School
Quincy, MA

Mary Kay Thomas
Bowling Green High
  School
Bowling Green, MO

Donald W. Tuff, Ph.D.
Department of Biology
Southwest Texas State
  University
San Marcos, TX

E. Peter Volpe, Ph.D.
Professor of Basic Medical
  Sciences
Division of Basic Medical
  Sciences
Mercer University School
  of Medicine
Macon, GA

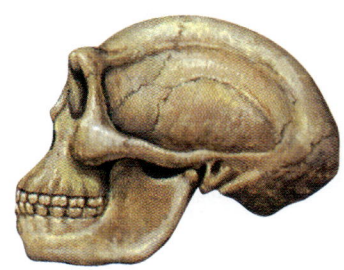

What does this skull reveal about
human origins? See page 225.

Contents in Brief

Table of Contents

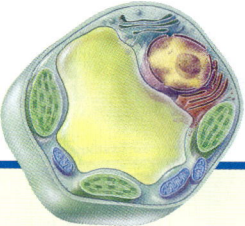

What's inside this plant cell?
To find out, see page 54.

Unit One | Study of Life

Section 1-1
Science literacy is tied to personal decision making.

Section 1-3
Six essential themes provide a framework for learning biology.

Unit Two   Continuity of Life

How does this structure turn light energy into chemical energy? See page 88.

How do bacteria divide? Find the answer on page 104.

What makes the
Gulf seaside sparrow
unique? See page 184.

Chapter 10
highlights the story
of evolution and natural
selection.

Chapter 11
Students take an
evolutionary journey.

Take a tour of a dinosaur
on page 207.

> **Chapter 13 covers the principles of animal behavior.**

Unit Three   The Environment

> **Unit 3 Environmental issues are presented early in the course.**

> **Chapter 14 gives practical strategies for solving environmental problems.**

How can community action transform this vacant lot? See page 304.

Unit Four Diversity of Life

Section 18-3
HIV is covered here and in Chapter 33.

How does a *Paramecium* move? See page 361.

Chapter 20
covers the evolutionary changes that took place during the transition to life on land.

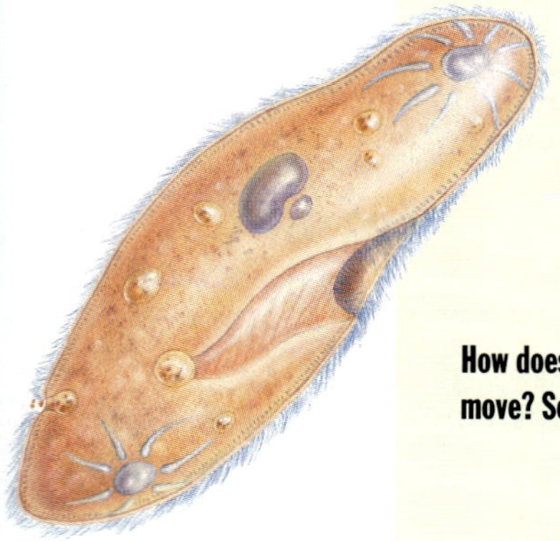

What is "double-loop" circulation? To find out, see page 466.

Unit Five continued

How is this beetle beneficial to humans? See page 508.

Chapter 25 summarizes key features of the animal phyla.

To learn about the biology of this turtle, see page 548.

Unit Six   Human Life

Sections 33-2 and 33-3 include descriptions of AIDS transmission and prevention.

A taco tastes great, but now what happens? Learn about digestion starting on page 706.

What key events occur during fetal development? See page 733.

Lab Program 744

Lab Program: Teacher's Overview

Pages 746–755 introduce students to the lab program.

Reference and Skills Appendix 826

Reference and Skills Appendix provides opportunities to learn and practice skills needed for success.

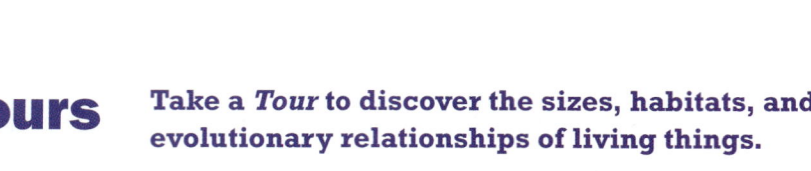

Features

Tours

Take a *Tour* to discover the sizes, habitats, and evolutionary relationships of living things.

A Closer Look

Discover key structures and learn how they function by taking *A Closer Look*.

Evolutionary Journeys

Travel on an *Evolutionary Journey* through time as you trace the development of each of these major organs.

FEATURES

Career Opportunities

How can your knowledge of biology lead to an exciting job? Find out in *Career Opportunities.*

Science, Technology, and Society

Science, Technology, and Society explores the conflicts that can arise between new technologies and the needs of society.

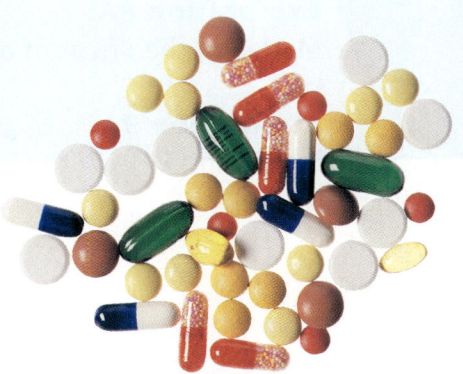

Lab Program

- *Explorations* teach you laboratory skills and techniques. You'll apply these skills in *Investigations* as you design experiments to solve real-world problems.

- Using CD-ROM technology, *Interactive Explorations* allow you to see and control biological phenomena in ways never before possible.

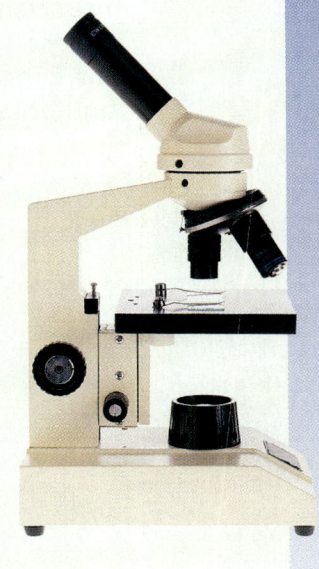

Breaking new ground in curriculum and instruction

"In designing a course, we must identify the central concepts and principles that every high school student should know and pare from the curriculum everything that does not explicate and illuminate these relatively few concepts."

Fulfilling the Promise: Biology Education in the Nation's Schools

Why I Wrote This Book

No one who teaches biology today can fail to be aware of the current clamor for better ways to teach science in our classrooms. As science becomes more important to our everyday lives, we see national studies repeatedly indicating that today's students are not learning the science they will need to know to live in the twenty-first century. This concern of educators has led to a flurry of proposals for improving how science is taught, including the recommendation of the National Science Education Standards that we get away from encyclopedic detail and focus more on teaching a few fundamental science concepts. It is in response to these concerns that this book was written. In writing Biology: Visualizing Life, I set out to accomplish five things.

1 Get the Science Right

Working as a research scientist for some 27 years with over 50 research papers to my credit has given me the background and experience needed to get the science right. The experience of writing three successful college biology textbooks has given me the experience to write a high school text that is authoritative, accurate, and up-to-date.

2 Focus on Concepts

The most common complaint about high school texts is that they are too long and are filled to the brim with detail that is too much for any student. What you don't hear as often but can easily demonstrate to yourself by opening any of the texts is that these texts are hard to learn from. Just turn, for example, to the chapter on photosynthesis. It's not just that they present too much detail, but that the basic concepts that the details are intended to explain are not themselves presented clearly.

In writing *Biology: Visualizing Life*, I have stressed at every stage a clear presentation of ideas and concepts, rather than a listing of detailed information. In every chapter, I try to present how things work and why things happen the way they do, rather than naming parts and stressing definitions.

Focus on Concepts

Themes serve as unifying concepts in a conceptual approach to biology. The table below shows how the six themes, introduced in Chapter 1, become focal points for students as they review their knowledge.

Theme	Chapter																																		
	1	2	3	4	5	6	7	8	9	10	11	12	13	14	15	16	17	18	19	20	21	22	23	24	25	26	27	28	29	30	31	32	33	34	35
Cell Structure and Function			X	X	X	X	X	X			X							X	X	X	X	X	X	X	X	X	X	X	X	X	X	X	X	X	X
Stability and Homeostasis			X	X	X		X		X	X				X	X						X							X	X	X	X	X	X	X	X
Heredity						X	X	X	X	X						X					X	X		X					X						X
Evolution				X				X	X	X	X	X	X	X	X		X		X	X	X	X	X	X	X	X	X	X	X	X	X	X			
Interdependence		X			X				X	X	X	X	X	X	X				X	X	X				X	X									
Matter, Energy, and Organization	X	X	X	X										X	X	X	X	X	X	X	X			X						X	X	X		X	

3 Write Well

In teaching biology for more than 25 years, I have come to the unpleasant but unavoidable conclusion that today's students can't read as well as those in the past. Whether this is the result of substituting television for reading as entertainment during childhood, or for some other reason, the fact is that students today neither read nor write with facility. It is the job of the text to bridge this gap. What I have done is to teach with analogies rather than detail whenever possible. When the student confronts the complex problem of how a repressor protein prevents RNA polymerase from reading a gene, the text points out that the locations of the DNA overlap where these two proteins attach, and that "two people can't sit in the same chair at the same time." Simple analogies are effective teaching tools.

4 Relate to the Student

Biology: Visualizing Life was written in the firm belief that you cannot teach a student who is not paying attention. Students will not learn if they see no relationship between their lives and what is going on in the classroom. This simple fact has colored every aspect of *Biology: Visualizing Life*. There is no concept or idea presented without emphasizing why it is important to students.

Relate to the Student
Students are shown throughout the text actively engaged in everyday biology.

5 Teach Visually

Today's students, raised on video screens and computers, learn most easily through visual presentations, and that is how we must teach them. In *Biology: Visualizing Life*, illustrations do not supplement the text, but rather are active partners with it. This lively presentation captivates students and makes the task of learning seem less intimidating, and it is actually a better way to teach. Exploratory learning, both effective and fun, is fostered in *Biology: Visualizing Life* with interactive CD-ROM exercises that are coupled to the teaching of many key concepts.

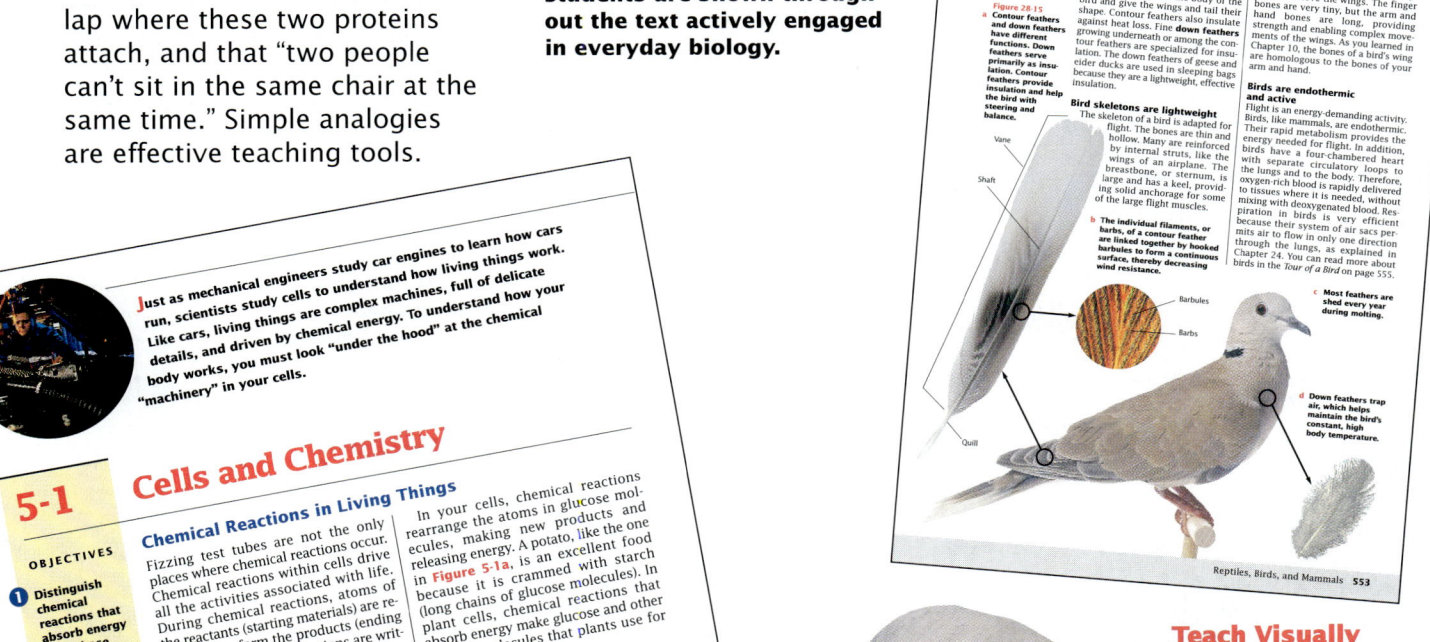

Teach Visually
Illustrations and photographs are an integral part of the delivery of scientific information, not simply decorative elements. Visual learning is enhanced, and students become eager to master the content.

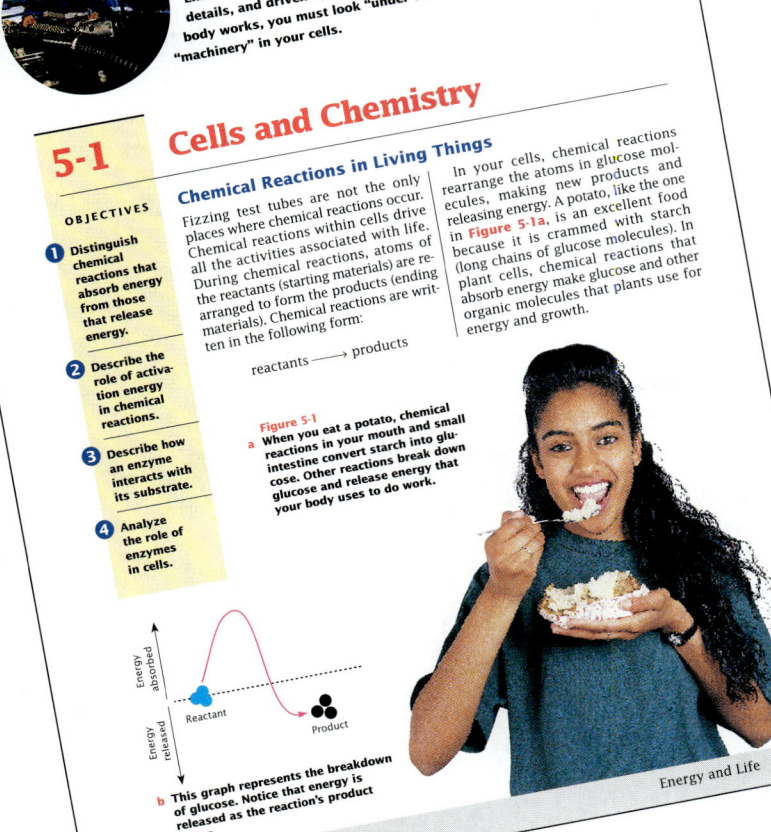

Just as mechanical engineers study car engines to learn how cars run, scientists study cells to understand how living things work. Like cars, living things are complex machines, full of delicate details, and driven by chemical energy. To understand how your body works, you must look "under the hood" at the chemical "machinery" in your cells.

Cells and Chemistry

5-1 Chemical Reactions in Living Things

OBJECTIVES

1 Distinguish chemical reactions that absorb energy from those that release energy.

2 Describe the role of activation energy in chemical reactions.

3 Describe how an enzyme interacts with its substrate.

4 Analyze the role of enzymes in cells.

Fizzing test tubes are not the only places where chemical reactions occur. Chemical reactions within cells drive all the activities associated with life. During chemical reactions, atoms of the reactants (starting materials) are rearranged to form the products (ending materials). Chemical reactions are written in the following form:

reactants ⟶ products

In your cells, chemical reactions rearrange the atoms in glucose molecules, making new products and releasing energy. A potato, like the one in Figure 5-1a, is an excellent food because it is crammed with starch (long chains of glucose molecules). In plant cells, chemical reactions that absorb energy make glucose and organic molecules that plants use for energy and growth.

Figure 5-1
a When you eat a potato, chemical reactions in your mouth and small intestine convert starch into glucose. Other reactions break down glucose and release energy that your body uses to do work.

b This graph represents the breakdown of glucose. Notice that energy is released as the reaction's product forms.

Energy and Life **77**

What This Text Is Like

These five goals, taken together, describe not so much what I did in writing Biology: Visualizing Life, *but rather how I set out to do it, the tools I used as I sat down to write. What sort of book is* Biology: Visualizing Life?

Table of Contents

My first act was to attack the traditional table of contents, a straitjacket that forces the teaching of biology in overwhelming detail and away from the core concepts that we should be teaching students. Traditionally, biology is taught from a phylogenetic point of view, starting with the little stuff. After learning a little about cells, students are taken on a long tour of the biological kingdoms, passing through detailed chapters on the different kinds of animals and other organisms. It is not by accident that these books are overloaded with detail—detail is the very essence of what a biology course has become.

A Conceptual Approach

In *Biology: Visualizing Life*, I abandon traditional approaches and focus instead on key concepts—on those ideas that explain biology—that tell us why and how rather than what. You can see the result of this conceptual approach in the early chapters of the text. Instead of starting the text with a student-terrifying chapter on chemistry, *Biology: Visualizing Life* integrates the chemistry into the flow of the text, teaching only as much as students need to know in order to understand what they are reading.

Coverage of the Animal Kingdom

The focus on concepts can be clearly seen in Unit 5, which is devoted to the animal kingdom. Instead of a progression of chapters devoted to "systems" of each phylum, the unit opens with Chapter 23, which describes the evolutionary journey that produced animals in terms of a series of key adaptations. This organization serves to highlight both the progressive nature of animal evolution and the important role of certain key elements of body architecture. Each advance is coupled to a pedagogical overview of the phylum, called an **Exploration**, that represents this advance—Exploration of a Mollusk, for example—so that the student can put the information into perspective. The intent is to minimize the presentation of detail, focusing instead on the process of evolution and recounting how it has produced the diversity we see today. If we are to succeed in substituting concepts and principles for encyclopedic

Coverage of the Animal Kingdom
The overview of animals includes significant milestones in the evolution of the animal body.

A Conceptual Approach
In covering the phyla, representative organisms are used in illustrating adaptive characteristics.

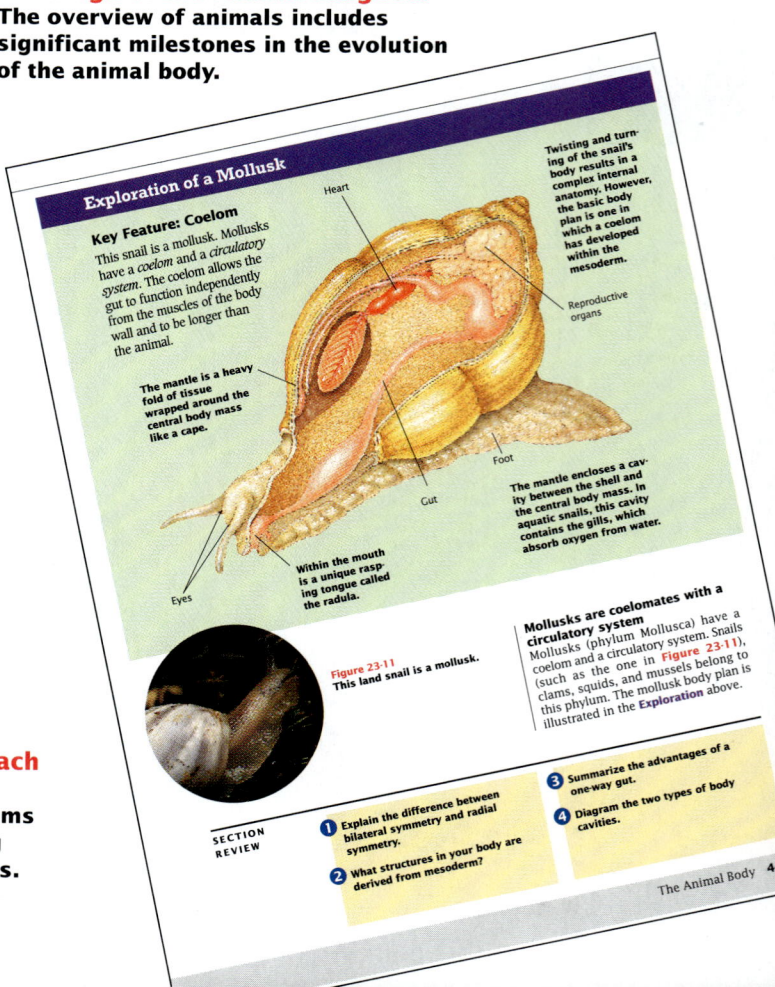

detail, then this principle—how evolution explains the animals we see—is surely one of the most important to convey.

Chapter 24 continues the evolutionary journey, considering key adaptations involved in the invasion of the land from the sea. In each case, the solution says a great deal about the relation between structure and function, and the possibility of different successful solutions to the same adaptive problem. The focus here is on how adaptation has driven progressive evolutionary change, a lesson that permits students to see themselves as part of a larger evolutionary picture. If students can come to view themselves as the product of a long evolutionary history, they will gain a sense of themselves as being part of life's tapestry, not separate from it. This lesson is far more important than memorizing the structural details of animals.

Coverage of Environmental Issues

Another clear example of the focus on concepts is seen in the organization of Unit 3, which is devoted to ecology. First, note where it is—up front, and not at the tail end of the book! Ecology is often skipped in high school courses for the simple reason that it comes at the end of the course. In today's world, with the need to understand environmental issues, that omission is a tragedy. Besides, it is difficult to properly teach animal and plant diversity without ecology. What is diversity but the product of evolution and ecology? In *Biology: Visualizing Life*, ecology is presented early in the sequence, where it makes the most sense.

Now take a look at the three chapters of Unit 3. They are not the traditional "levels of organization"

chapters (populations, ecosystems, biomes). Instead, Chapter 14 focuses immediately on ecosystems, the basic unit of the environment. Students learn how ecosystems work—how they cycle nutrients and process energy, and how climate shapes who and what lives where. Chapter 15 focuses on the key issue in environmental science today—how ecosystems respond to disruption. The biodiversity and complex relationships built over centuries of coevolution tend to make ecosystems more stable, while humans today are disrupting natural ecosystems. The principles students learn here will guide their thinking for years to come. Chapter 16 provides a careful and honest evaluation of where we are now and what is being done to save our environment. The approach is positive and pragmatic. There are few issues that students will encounter in biology that deserve more careful treatment.

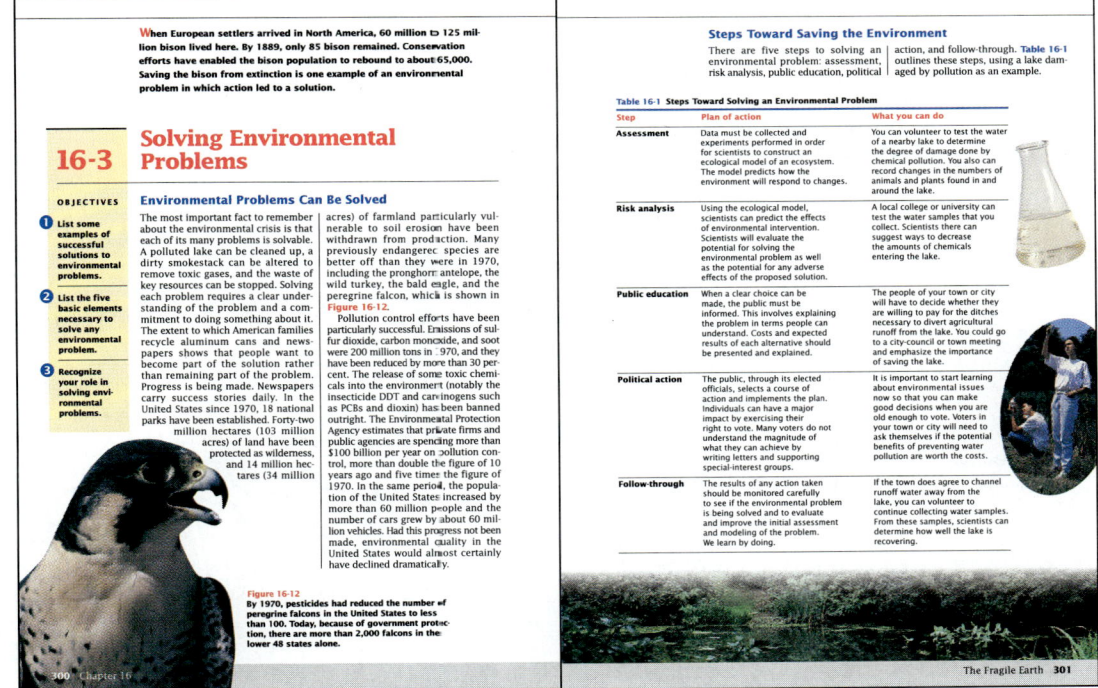

Coverage of Environmental Issues
Students develop practical solutions to today's world environmental problems using a systematic method of analysis.

What Students Need to Know

At some point, anyone who writes a text needs to sit down and ask a simple question: What things do students really need to know? When I went through this exercise, I came up with a short but powerful list—things that impact students in ways that change their lives. The list included teaching students how to avoid contracting AIDS, why smoking cigarettes will kill them, why drugs are dangerous, and how their bodies work. You will find all these topics in Biology: Visualizing Life and will find many others that directly affect the lives of students. This approach isn't taken for entertainment, but because I regard it as my responsibility to tell students about the science behind these issues, for this knowledge will affect their futures.

Coverage of Adolescent Issues

To get some sense of what I mean, look at Chapter 30, which includes a pointed discussion of drugs. Almost every high school text discusses drugs, but this one is different in that it does not devote the bulk of its space to a boring litany of drug types or preaching about the evils of drug abuse. Instead, it focuses on explaining just how drugs work to create addicts. In my teaching I have found that if I explain the mechanism of addiction to students so that they see it is a simple cause-and-effect process, then I don't need to preach to them, because the danger is so obvious. The basic idea of lowering the numbers of drug receptors within nerve synapses as a compensation for increased levels of neurotransmitters is not difficult to teach or understand. Few students can read this chapter and contemplate taking drugs, and that decision is based on their own reasoning process—not on the acceptance of my opinions on the subject. The same approach is taken in discussing cigarette smoking and cancer. Students read a clear description of how chemicals in cigarette smoke cause mutations at random in DNA. They learn that when key growth-regulating genes are hit by these mutations, cancer results. Smoking is like going into a dark room and letting someone shoot a gun at you—you might not be hit at first, but how many times would you let them shoot? Every cigarette is one more bullet. Because the presentation of how cancer works is very concrete, grounded in basic concepts that students can grasp, no one fails to get the point.

Teen Focus
Students see the importance of biology by studying topics that will directly affect them now and in the future.

Smoking
The hazards of smoking are covered in relation to mutations of DNA.

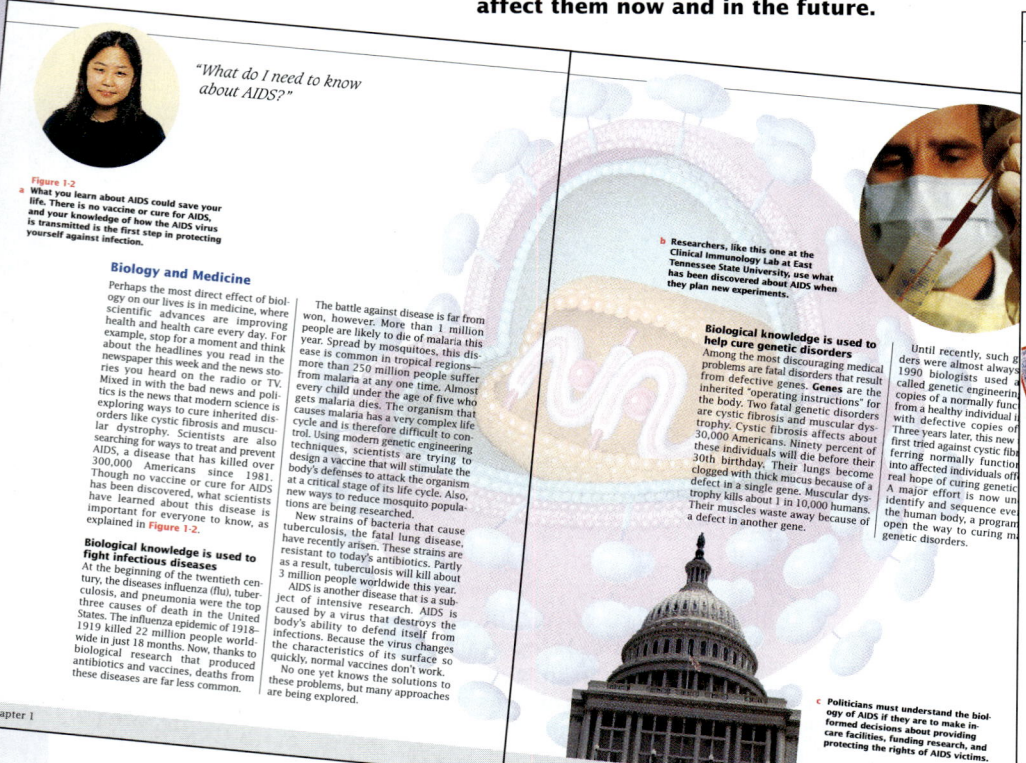

"What do I need to know about AIDS?"

Figure 1-2
a What you learn about AIDS could save your life. There is no vaccine or cure for AIDS, and your knowledge of how the AIDS virus is transmitted is the first step in protecting yourself against infection.

Biology and Medicine

Perhaps the most direct effect of biology on our lives is in medicine, where scientific advances are improving health and health care every day. For example, stop for a moment and think about the headlines you read in the newspaper this week and the news stories you heard on the radio or TV. Mixed in with the bad news and politics is the news that modern science is exploring ways to cure inherited disorders like cystic fibrosis and muscular dystrophy. Scientists are also searching for ways to treat and prevent AIDS, a disease that has killed over 300,000 Americans since 1981. Though no vaccine or cure for AIDS has been discovered, what scientists have learned about this disease is important for everyone to know, as explained in **Figure 1-2.**

Biological knowledge is used to fight infectious diseases

At the beginning of the twentieth century, the diseases influenza (flu), tuberculosis, and pneumonia were the top three causes of death in the United States. The influenza epidemic of 1918–1919 killed 22 million people worldwide in just 18 months. Now, thanks to biological research that produced antibiotics and vaccines, deaths from these diseases are far less common.

The battle against disease is far from won, however. More than 1 million people are likely to die of malaria this year. Spread by mosquitoes, this disease is common in tropical regions—more than 250 million people suffer from malaria at any one time. Almost every child under the age of five who gets malaria dies. The organism that causes malaria has a very complex life cycle and is therefore difficult to control. Using modern genetic engineering techniques, scientists are trying to design a vaccine that will stimulate the body's defenses to attack the organism at a critical stage of its life cycle. Also, new ways to reduce mosquito populations are being researched.

New strains of bacteria that cause tuberculosis, the fatal lung disease, have recently arisen. These strains are resistant to today's antibiotics. Partly as a result, tuberculosis will kill about 3 million people worldwide this year.

AIDS is another disease that is a subject of intensive research. AIDS is caused by a virus that destroys the body's ability to defend itself from infections. Because the virus changes the characteristics of its surface so quickly, normal vaccines don't work. No one yet knows the solutions to these problems, but many approaches are being explored.

b Researchers, like this one at the Clinical Immunology Lab at East Tennessee State University, use what has been discovered about AIDS when they plan new experiments.

Biological knowledge is used to help cure genetic disorders

Among the most discouraging medical problems are fatal disorders that result from defective genes. **Genes** are the inherited "operating instructions" for the body. Two fatal genetic disorders are cystic fibrosis and muscular dystrophy. Cystic fibrosis affects about 30,000 Americans. Ninety percent of these individuals will die before their 30th birthday. Their lungs become clogged with thick mucus because of a defect in a single gene. Muscular dystrophy kills about 1 in 10,000 humans. Their muscles waste away because of a defect in another gene.

Until recently, such g ders were almost always 1990 biologists used called genetic engineeri copies of a normally func from a healthy individual l with defective copies of Three years later, this new first tried against cystic fibr ferring normally function into affected individuals off real hope of curing genetic A major effort is now un identify and sequence eve the human body, a program open the way to curing m genetic disorders.

c Politicians must understand the biology of AIDS if they are to make informed decisions about providing care facilities, funding research, and protecting the rights of AIDS victims.

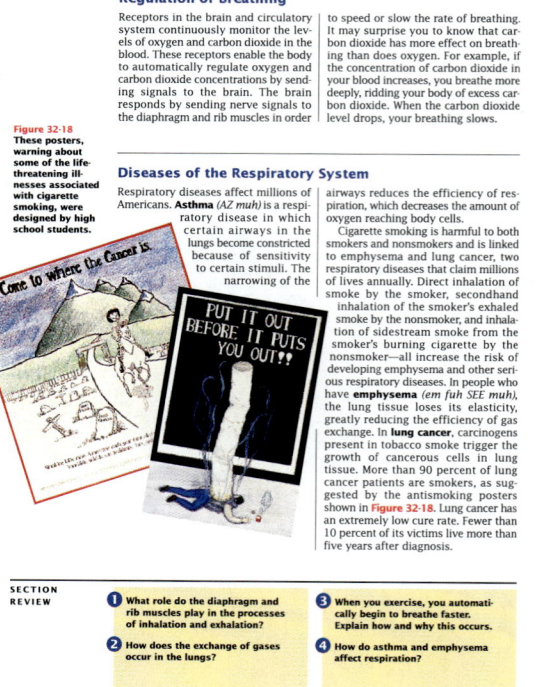

Regulation of Breathing

Receptors in the brain and circulatory system continuously monitor the levels of oxygen and carbon dioxide in the blood. These receptors enable the body to automatically regulate oxygen and carbon dioxide concentrations by sending signals to the brain. The brain responds by sending nerve signals to the diaphragm and rib muscles in order to speed or slow the rate of breathing. It may surprise you to know that carbon dioxide has more effect on breathing than does oxygen. For example, if the concentration of carbon dioxide in your blood increases, you breathe more deeply, ridding your body of excess carbon dioxide. When the carbon dioxide level drops, your breathing slows.

Figure 32-18
These posters, warning about some of the life-threatening illnesses associated with cigarette smoking, were designed by high school students.

Diseases of the Respiratory System

Respiratory diseases affect millions of Americans. **Asthma** (AZ muh) is a respiratory disease in which certain airways in the lungs become constricted because of sensitivity to certain stimuli. The narrowing of the airways reduces the efficiency of respiration, which decreases the amount of oxygen reaching body cells.

Cigarette smoking is harmful to both smokers and nonsmokers and is linked to emphysema and lung cancer, two respiratory diseases that claim millions of lives annually. Direct inhalation of smoke by the smoker, secondhand inhalation of the smoker's exhaled smoke by the nonsmoker, and inhalation of sidestream smoke from the smoker's burning cigarette by the nonsmoker—all increase the risk of developing emphysema and other serious respiratory diseases. In people who have **emphysema** (em fuh SEE muh), the lung tissue loses its elasticity, greatly reducing the efficiency of gas exchange. In **lung cancer**, carcinogens present in tobacco smoke trigger the growth of cancerous cells in lung tissue. More than 90 percent of lung cancer patients are smokers, as suggested by the antismoking posters shown in **Figure 32-18.** Lung cancer has an extremely low cure rate. Fewer than 10 percent of its victims live more than five years after diagnosis.

Come to where the cancer is.

PUT IT OUT BEFORE IT PUTS YOU OUT!!

SECTION REVIEW

① What role do the diaphragm and rib muscles play in the processes of inhalation and exhalation?

② How does the exchange of gases occur in the lungs?

③ When you exercise, you automatically begin to breathe faster. Explain how and why this occurs.

④ How do asthma and emphysema affect respiration?

Using Technology

As every classroom teacher knows, hands-on exploration is far and away the most effective way to learn anything. To best learn the science of biology, students should do experiments, freely exploring the concepts and ideas they are attempting to master.

Unfortunately, there is a limit to how much science can be taught "hands on" in a classroom or in a laboratory. Thus it is with genuine excitement that teachers and students greet the new interactive CD-ROM technologies now beginning to appear in today's classrooms.

Biology: Visualizing Life contains six interactive CD-ROM labs for use with Macintosh® or Windows®. The *Interactive Explorations in Biology Laboratory Manual* contains an additional seven interactive CD-ROM labs. What does a CD-ROM lab offer that slide collections and laser discs cannot? In a word—*interactivity*. Each of these labs provides back-and-forth interaction, an environment in which true inquiry and analysis can take place. This is why the CD-ROM explorations in *Biology: Visualizing Life* play such an important part in the learning experience provided by this text.

New Beginning

I took time from a busy teaching schedule to write this book because I felt it was important to make a start at improving how we teach biology. Anyone who looks at this book will think of things I could have done differently. I hope you will tell me about them by writing to me in care of Holt, Rinehart and Winston. No single person can get the job done alone, and I certainly appreciate any help that experience and interest can provide. Thank you in advance.

Drugs

The biological basis of addiction is the core of the coverage of drugs.

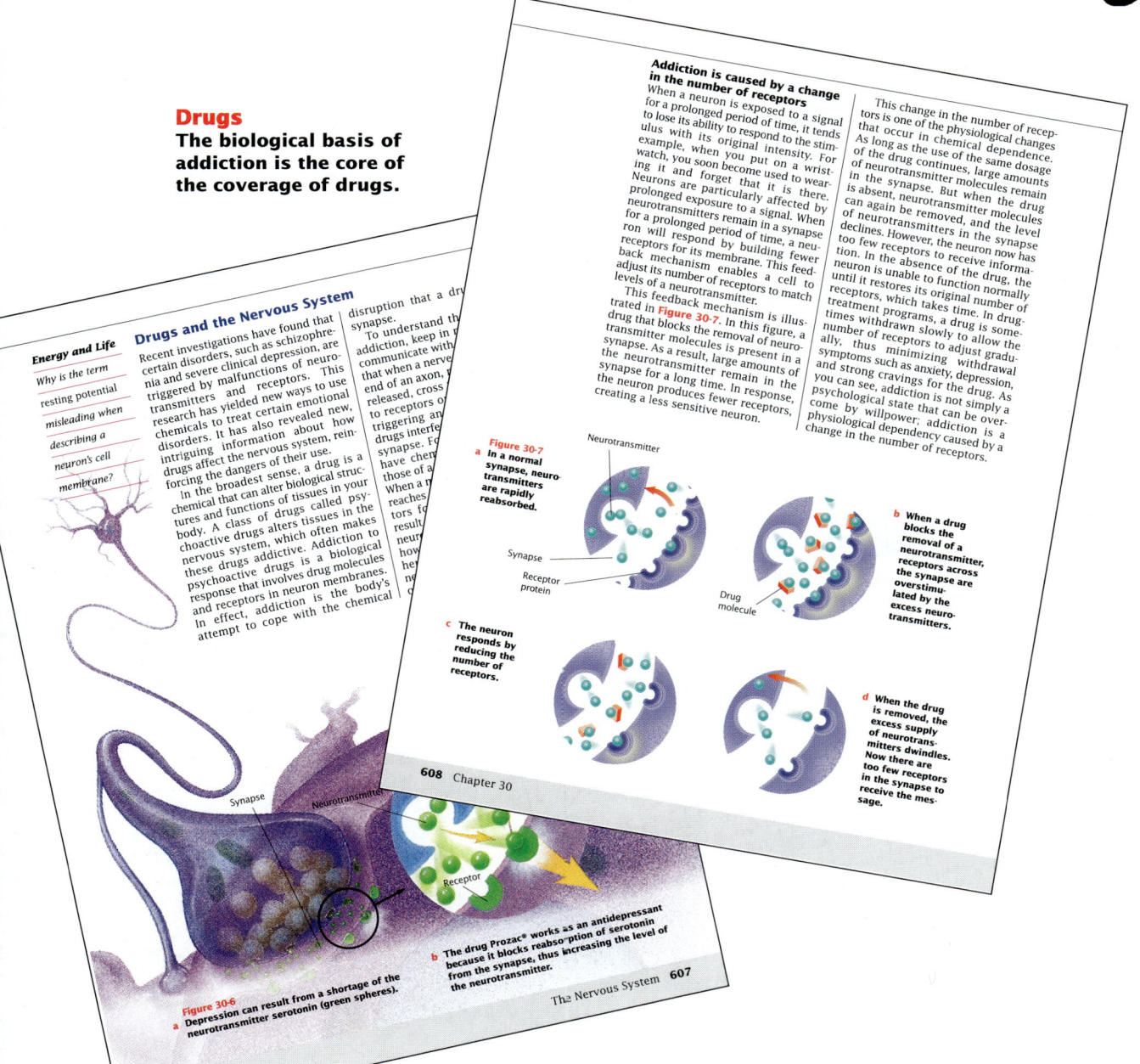

Energy and Life

Why is the term resting potential misleading when describing a neuron's cell membrane?

Drugs and the Nervous System

Recent investigations have found that certain disorders, such as schizophrenia and severe clinical depression, are triggered by malfunctions of neurotransmitters and receptors. This research has yielded new ways to use chemicals to treat certain emotional disorders. It has also revealed new, intriguing information about how drugs affect the nervous system, reinforcing the dangers of their use.

In the broadest sense, a drug is a chemical that can alter biological structures and functions of tissues in your body. A class of drugs called psychoactive drugs alters tissues in the nervous system, which often makes these drugs addictive. Addiction to psychoactive drugs is a biological response that involves drug molecules and receptors in neuron membranes. In effect, addiction is the body's attempt to cope with the chemical disruption that a dru[...] synapse.

To understand th[...] addiction, keep in [...] communicate with [...] that when a nerve [...] end of an axon, [...] released, cross [...] to receptors o[...] triggering an [...] drugs interfe[...] synapse. Fo[...] have chem[...] those of a[...] When a n[...] reaches [...] tors fo[...] result[...] neur[...] how[...] he[...] ne[...] o[...]

Figure 30-6
a Depression can result from a shortage of the neurotransmitter serotonin (green spheres).

b The drug Prozac® works as an antidepressant because it blocks reabsorption of serotonin from the synapse, thus increasing the level of the neurotransmitter.

Synapse

Neurotransmitter

Receptor

Addiction is caused by a change in the number of receptors

When a neuron is exposed to a signal for a prolonged period of time, it tends to lose its ability to respond to the stimulus with its original intensity. For example, when you put on a wristwatch, you soon become used to wearing it and forget that it is there. Neurons are particularly affected by prolonged exposure to a signal. When neurotransmitters remain in a synapse for a prolonged period of time, a neuron will respond by building fewer receptors for its membrane. This feedback mechanism enables a cell to adjust its number of receptors to match levels of a neurotransmitter.

This feedback mechanism is illustrated in **Figure 30-7**. In this figure, a drug that blocks the removal of neurotransmitter molecules is present in a synapse. As a result, large amounts of the neurotransmitter remain in the synapse for a long time. In response, the neuron produces fewer receptors, creating a less sensitive neuron.

This change in the number of receptors is one of the physiological changes that occur in chemical dependence. As long as the use of the same dosage of the drug continues, large amounts of neurotransmitter molecules remain in the synapse. But when the drug is absent, neurotransmitter molecules can again be removed, and the level of neurotransmitters in the synapse declines. However, the neuron now has too few receptors to receive information. In the absence of the drug, the neuron is unable to function normally until it restores its original number of receptors, which takes time. In drug-treatment programs, a drug is sometimes withdrawn slowly to allow the number of receptors to adjust gradually, thus minimizing withdrawal symptoms such as anxiety, depression, and strong cravings for the drug. As you can see, addiction is not simply a psychological state that can be overcome by willpower; addiction is a physiological dependency caused by a change in the number of receptors.

Figure 30-7
a In a normal synapse, neurotransmitters are rapidly reabsorbed.

Neurotransmitter

Synapse

Receptor protein

Drug molecule

b When a drug blocks the removal of a neurotransmitter, receptors across the synapse are overstimulated by the excess neurotransmitters.

c The neuron responds by reducing the number of receptors.

d When the drug is removed, the excess supply of neurotransmitters dwindles. Now there are too few receptors in the synapse to receive the message.

Breaking new ground

to deliver instruction with a comprehensive resource package as diverse as your student body

Biology: Visualizing Life

gives you the coordinated support you need to address various learning styles.

- **Student Review Guide** (0-03-050613-1)
  - **Directed Reading Worksheets**
  - **Vocabulary Development Worksheets**

- **Directed Reading Worksheets with Answer Key** (0-03-051398-7)

- **Vocabulary Development Worksheets with Answer Key** (0-03-051397-9)

- **Thinking Skills Worksheets with Answer Key** (0-03-051393-6)

- **Reteaching Worksheets with Answer Key** (0-03-051394-4)

- **Language Development and Reading CD Audio Program for *Biology: Visualizing Life* and *Essentials of Biology*** (0-03-050618-2)

- **Chapter Tests with Answer Key** (0-03-050614-X)

- **Holt BioSources Assessment Item Listing for *Biology: Visualizing Life*** (0-03-050707-3)

- **Spanish Resources** (0-03-050617-4)

- **Holt Biology Videodiscs Teacher's Correlation Guide to *Holt Biology: Visualizing Life*** (0-03-050612-3)

See page T34 to discover how these resources help students build and check content comprehension.

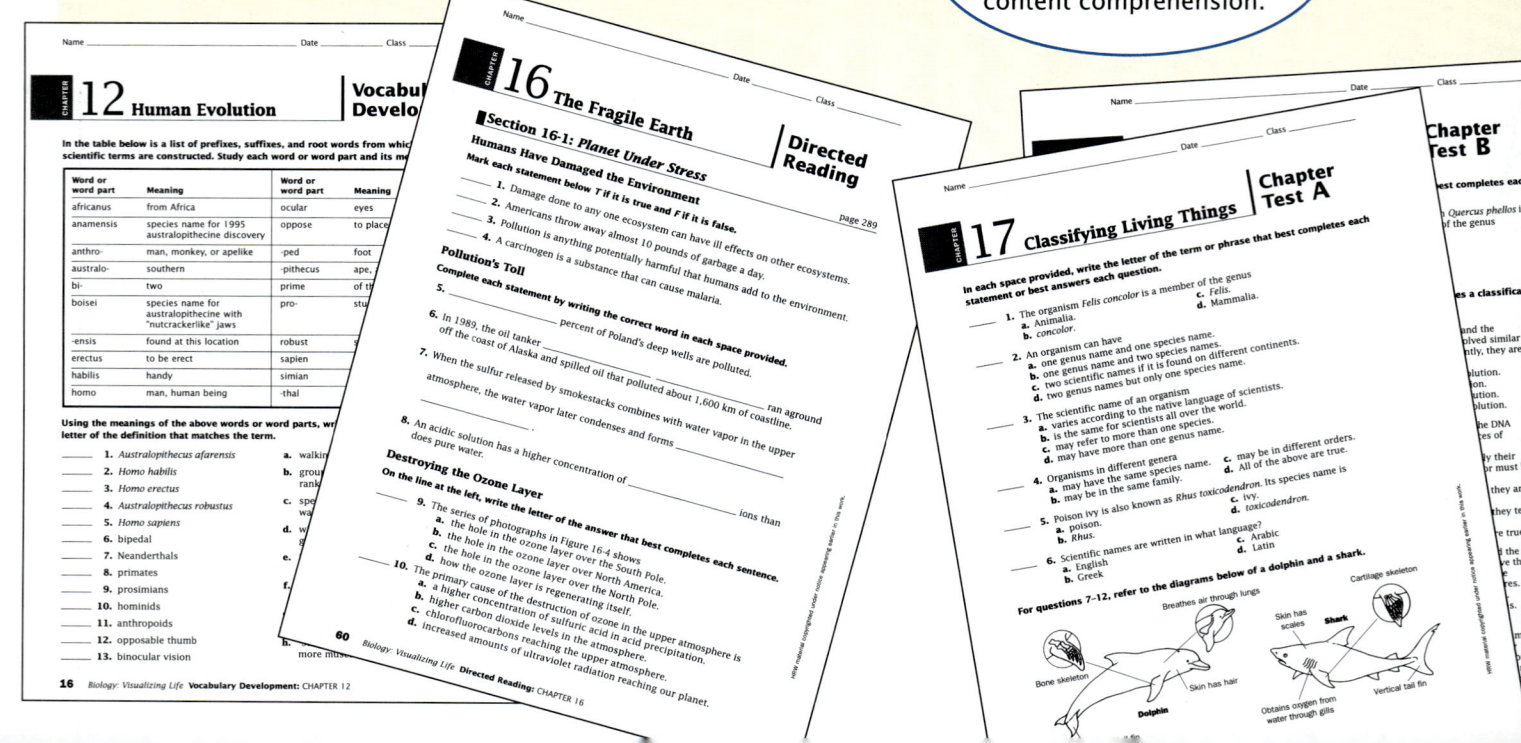

HOLT
BIOSOURCES™

allows you to customize your course to meet your needs.

Holt BioSources Lab Program

- **Quick Labs** (0-03-050693-X)
- **Quick Labs, Teacher's Edition** (0-03-050694-8)
- **Inquiry Skills Development** (0-03-051399-5)
- **Inquiry Skills Development, Teacher's Edition** (0-03-051402-9)
- **Laboratory Techniques and Experimental Design** (0-03-051403-7)
- **Laboratory Techniques and Experimental Design, Teacher's Edition** (0-03-051404-5)
- **Biotechnology** (0-03-051407-X)
- **Biotechnology, Teacher's Edition** (0-03-051408-8)
- **Interactive Explorations in Biology Laboratory Manual** (0-03-050483-X)
- **Interactive Explorations in Biology Laboratory Manual, Teacher's Guide** (0-03-050484-8)

Additional Holt BioSources components

- **Holt BioSources Teaching Transparencies** (0-03-050702-2)
- **Holt BioSources Transparency Directory with Teacher's Notes** (0-03-050703-0)
- **Holt BioSources Teaching Resources CD-ROM For Macintosh® and Windows®** (0-03-050697-2)
- **Holt BioSources Test Generator with TestBuilder Software** (0-03-050704-9)

> **Laboratory exercises for a wide range of styles and abilities**
> See pages T30–T33 for a complete listing of all laboratory titles.

Holt Biology Technology

is your passport to the exciting world of curriculum-based multimedia instruction.

- *Interactive Explorations in Biology: Human Biology for Macintosh® and Windows®* (0-03-050473-2)
- *Interactive Explorations in Biology: Cell Biology and Genetics for Macintosh® and Windows®* (0-03-050478-3)
- *Holt Biology Videodiscs*
- *Concepts of Biology*

> Turn to pages T40–T41 to see how each chapter's Lesson Planning Guide integrates the components of Holt BioSources and Holt Biology Technology into each lesson of *Biology: Visualizing Life*.

TO ORDER, CALL TOLL FREE
800-225-5425   FAX 800-874-6418

Breaking new ground

to bring a renewed emphasis on inquiry into your science labs

What's the best design for a wildlife zoo?

How can a pet store most effectively raise brine shrimp?

Which soap kills the most bacteria?

Which foods have the most nutrients?

Labs have changed. For today's students, success in the laboratory must be measured by more than just demonstrating and verifying content. ***Biology: Visualizing Life*** offers you three kinds of labs—all within the pupil's edition. These labs provide your students with step-by-step opportunities to attain goals emphasized in the new National Science Education Standards:

- **Working in groups to analyze data and defend conclusions**
- **Acquiring new skills, practical techniques, and scientific habits of mind—not just content**
- **Relating newly acquired skills to past and present activities**
- **Recognizing science as argumentation and explanation**

Your students will do more than just "get the answer." They'll learn:

- **biological techniques and their applications**
- **practical skills needed for success in the real world**
  - **Working as a team member**
  - **Selecting appropriate technology**
  - **Managing and allocating resources**
  - **Communicating effectively**
  - **Finding information**

1 Explorations

teach your students laboratory skills and procedures in the context of solving a real-world problem.

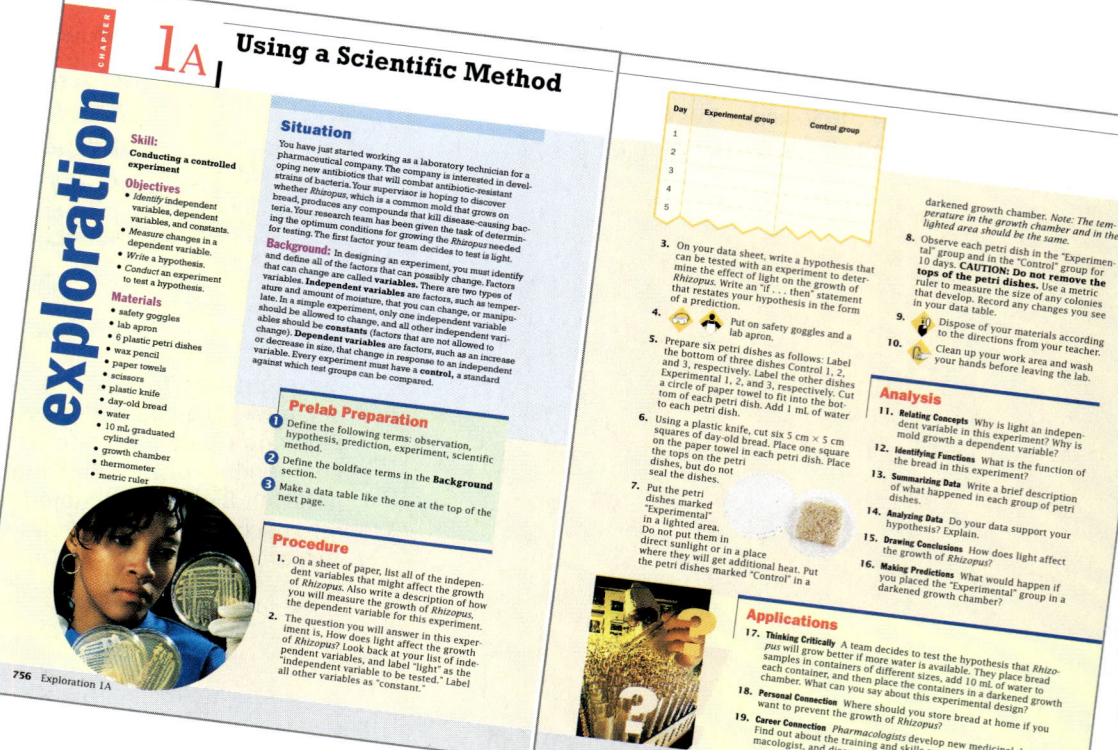

2 **Investigations** require your students to apply these skills to design their own experiments as they take the role of an employee of a scientific consulting firm.

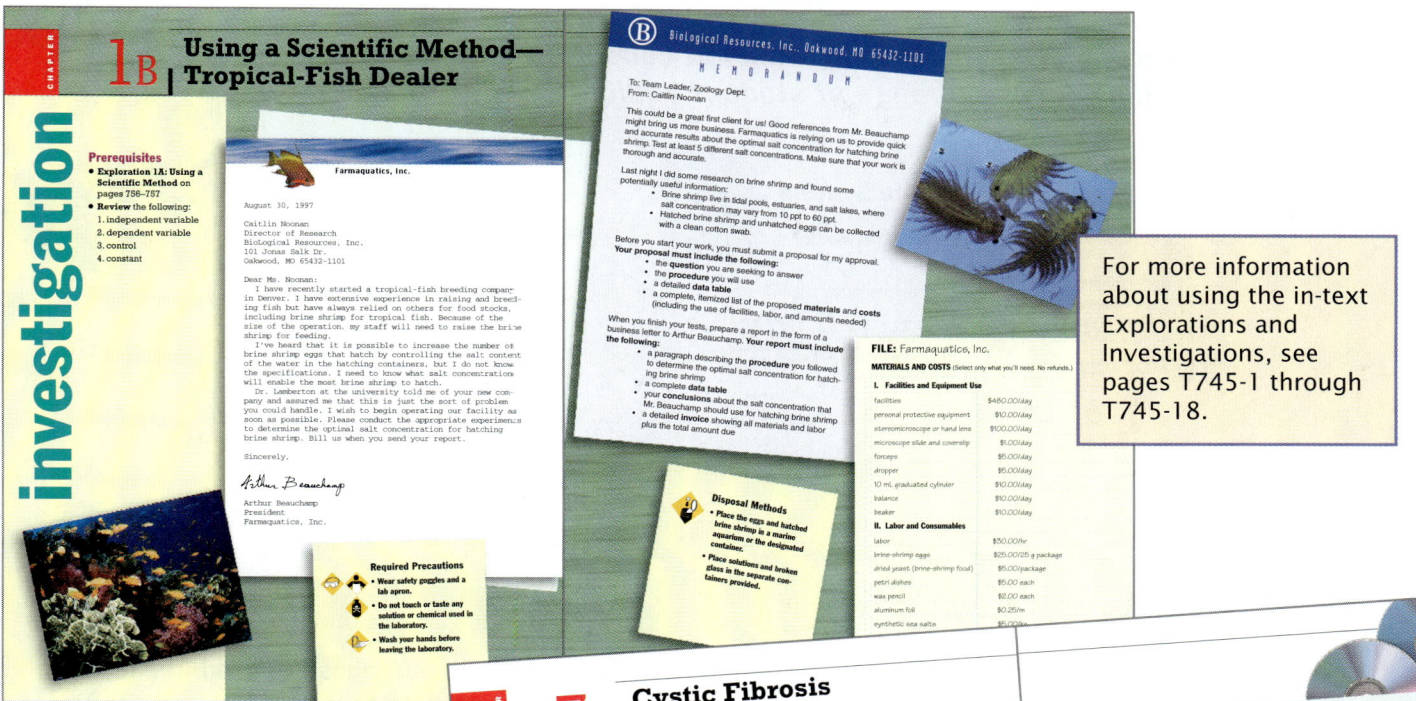

For more information about using the in-text Explorations and Investigations, see pages T745-1 through T745-18.

3 **Interactive Explorations**

use CD-ROM technology to allow students to see biological phenomena and manipulate variables in ways never before possible.

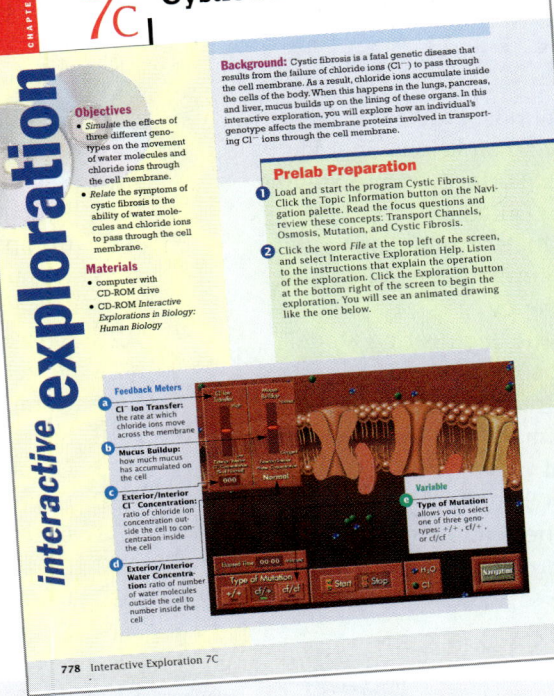

Holt, Rinehart and Winston/**WARD'S**™
Together We Make Teaching Biology Easier for You!

WARD'S Natural Science Establishment, Inc. is the "Official Materials and Equipment Supplier" for *Biology: Visualizing Life* and *Holt BioSources Lab Program*. Holt, Rinehart and Winston's unique partnership with WARD'S guarantees that:

• WARD'S lab materials and supplies are selected to specifically satisfy the needs of the lab activities in *Biology: Visualizing Life* and *Holt BioSources Lab Program*.

• All lab activities in *Biology: Visualizing Life* and *Holt BioSources Lab Program* are bench tested by WARD'S technical staff to guarantee successful lab results and experiences.

See the titles of 135 additional labs found in the *Holt BioSources Lab Program* on pages T30–T33.

Five Lab Manuals Bring You Unprecedented Variety

Holt BioSources gives you an unparalleled collection of labs, extending across a range of student ability levels.

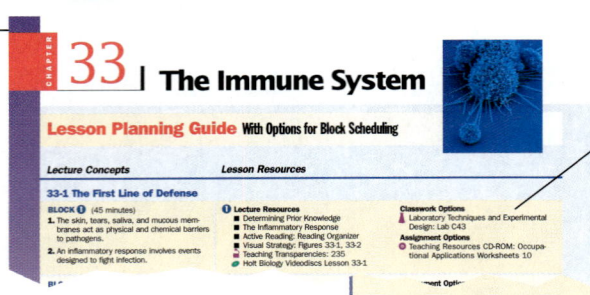

CHAPTER 33 | **The Immune System**

Lesson Planning Guide With Options for Block Scheduling

> Selecting labs is easy! Each chapter's Lesson Planning Guide identifies the appropriate lab or labs to use with each lesson. See pages T38–39.

A Quick Labs

Quick Labs are just that. Inexpensive, easy-to-obtain supplies are used in each of these short lab activities. Use them as brief labs or even to introduce a new topic.

A1 Imagining Solutions: Problem Solving	A18 Comparing Plant Adaptations
A2 Comparing Living and Nonliving Things	A19 Inferring Function From Structure
A3 Modeling Cells: Surface Area to Volume	A20 Relating Root Structure to Function
A4 Demonstrating Diffusion	A21 Recognizing Patterns of Symmetry
A5 Interpreting Labels: Stored Food Energy	A22 Comparing Animal Eggs
A6 Interpreting Information in a Pedigree	A23 Observing Some Major Animal Groups
A7 Making Models	A24 Observing Insect Behavior
A8 Making a Genetic Engineering Model	A25 Observing a Frog
A9 Comparing Observations of Body Parts	A26 Vertebrate Skeletons
A10 Analyzing Adaptations: Living on Land	A27 Comparing Skeletal Joints
A11 Comparing Primate Features	A28 Bias and Experimentation
A12 Making a Food Web	A29 Graphing Growth Rate Data
A13 Using Random Sampling	A30 Collecting Data Through a Survey
A14 Determining the Amount of Refuse	A31 Determining Lung Capacity
A15 Grouping Things You Use Daily	A32 Relating Cell Structure to Function
A16 Using Bacteria to Make Food	A33 Reading Labels: Nutritional Information
A17 Observing Protists	A34 Culturing Frog Embryos

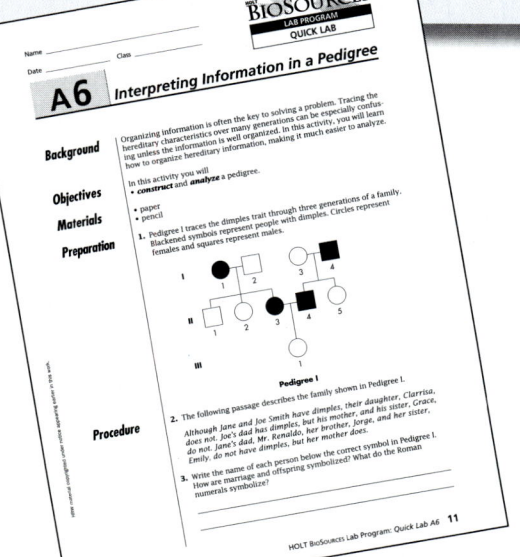

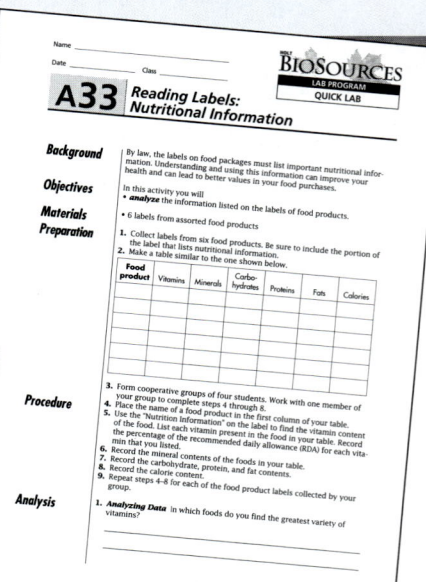

B *Inquiry Skills Development*

Inquiry Skills Development labs teach students practical skills and techniques they'll need throughout their classroom lab experience—and beyond.

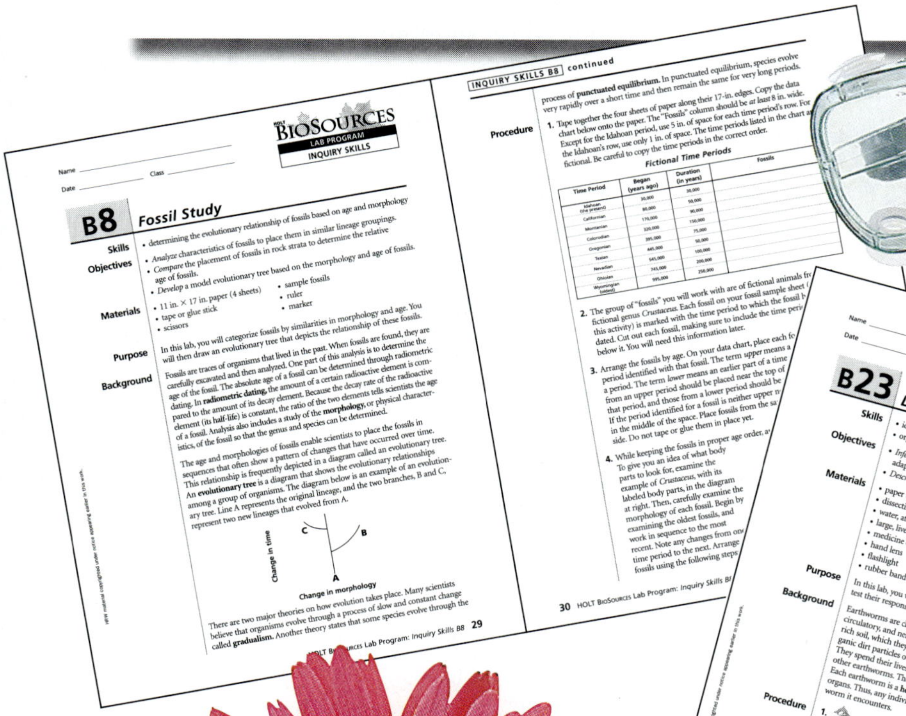

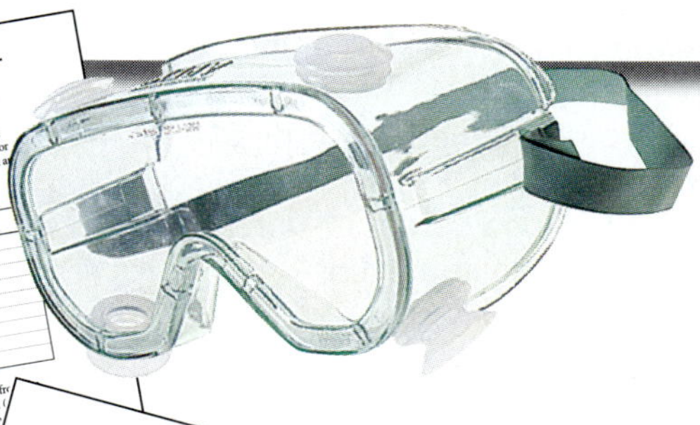

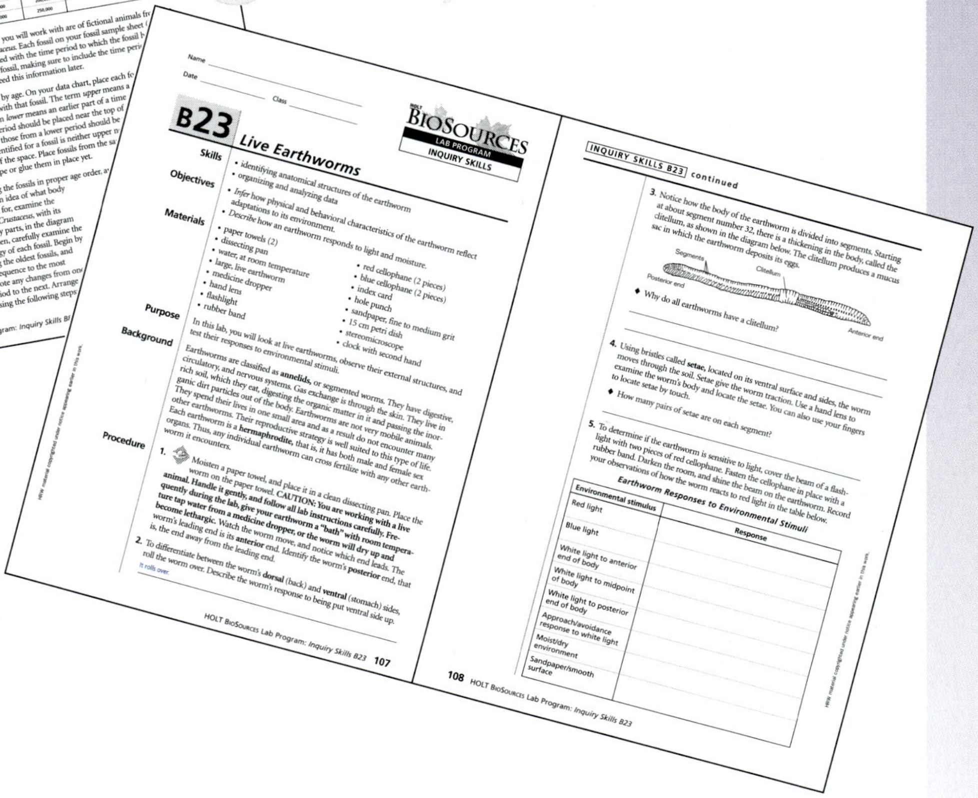

FOR MORE LABS, TURN THE PAGE.

C Laboratory Techniques and Experimental Design

Laboratory Techniques and Experimental Design labs follow the formats used in the in-text *Explorations* and *Investigations*, requiring students to apply skills and techniques they've mastered earlier to design their own experiments.

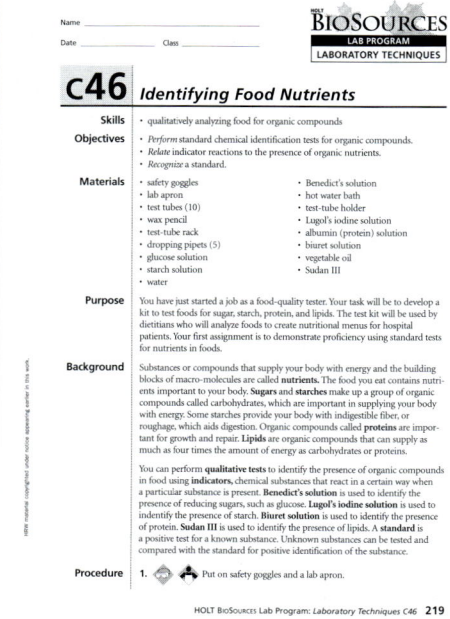

Name _____

Date _____ Class _____

BioSources
LAB PROGRAM
LABORATORY TECHNIQUES

C46 Identifying Food Nutrients

Skills · qualitatively analyzing food for organic compounds

Objectives · *Perform* standard chemical identification tests for organic compounds.
· *Relate* indicator reactions to the presence of organic nutrients.
· *Recognize* a standard.

Materials
· safety goggles
· lab apron
· test tubes (10)
· wax pencil
· test-tube rack
· dropping pipets (5)
· glucose solution
· starch solution
· water
· Benedict's solution
· hot water bath
· test-tube holder
· Lugol's iodine solution
· albumin (protein) solution
· biuret solution
· vegetable oil
· Sudan III

Purpose You have just started a job as a food-quality tester. Your task will be to develop a kit to test foods for sugar, starch, protein, and lipids. The test kit will be used by dietitians who will analyze foods to create nutritional menus for hospital patients. Your first assignment is to demonstrate proficiency using standard tests for nutrients in foods.

Background Substances or compounds that supply your body with energy and the building blocks of macro-molecules are called **nutrients**. The food you eat contains nutrients important to your body. **Sugars** and **starches** make up a group of organic compounds called carbohydrates, which are important in supplying your body with energy. Some starches provide your body with indigestible fiber, or roughage, which aids digestion. Organic compounds called **proteins** are important for growth and repair. **Lipids** are organic compounds that can supply as much as four times the amount of energy as carbohydrates or proteins.

You can perform **qualitative tests** to identify the presence of organic compounds in food using **indicators**, chemical substances that react in a certain way when a particular substance is present. **Benedict's solution** is used to identify the presence of reducing sugars, such as glucose. **Lugol's iodine solution** is used to indentify the presence of starch. **Biuret solution** is used to identify the presence of protein. **Sudan III** is used to identify the presence of lipids. A **standard** is a positive test for a known substance. Unknown substances can be tested and compared with the standard for positive identification of the substance.

Procedure 1. ⚠ Put on safety goggles and a lab apron.

HOLT BioSources Lab Program: *Laboratory Techniques* C46 **219**

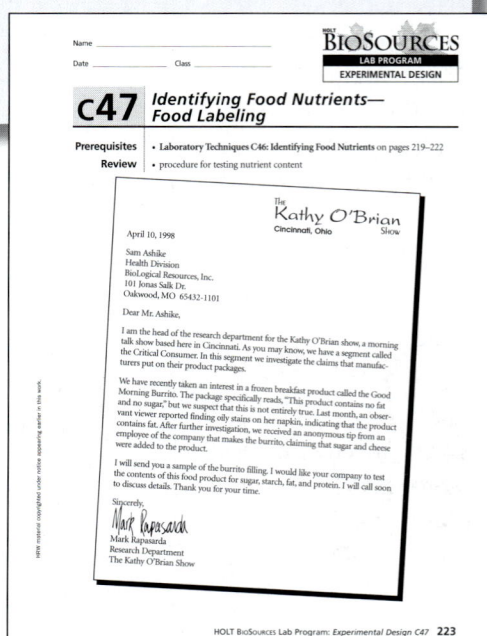

Name _____

Date _____ Class _____

BioSources
LAB PROGRAM
EXPERIMENTAL DESIGN

C47 Identifying Food Nutrients—Food Labeling

Prerequisites · Laboratory Techniques C46: Identifying Food Nutrients on pages 219–222
Review · procedure for testing nutrient content

The Kathy O'Brian Show
Cincinnati, Ohio

April 10, 1998

Sam Ashike
Health Division
BioLogical Resources, Inc.
101 Jonas Salk Dr.
Oakwood, MO 65432-1101

Dear Mr. Ashike,

I am the head of the research department for the Kathy O'Brian show, a morning talk show based here in Cincinnati. As you may know, we have a segment called the Critical Consumer. In this segment we investigate the claims that manufacturers put on their product packages.

We have recently taken an interest in a frozen breakfast product called the Good Morning Burrito. The package specifically reads, "This product contains no fat and no sugar," but we suspect that this is not entirely true. Last month, an observant viewer reported finding oily stains on her napkin, indicating that the product contains fat. After further investigation, we received an anonymous tip from an employee of the company that makes the burrito, claiming that sugar and cheese were added to the product.

I will send you a sample of the burrito filling. I would like your company to test the contents of this food product for sugar, starch, fat, and protein. I will call soon to discuss details. Thank you for your time.

Sincerely,

Mark Rapasarda
Research Department
The Kathy O'Brian Show

HOLT BioSources Lab Program: *Experimental Design* C47 **223**

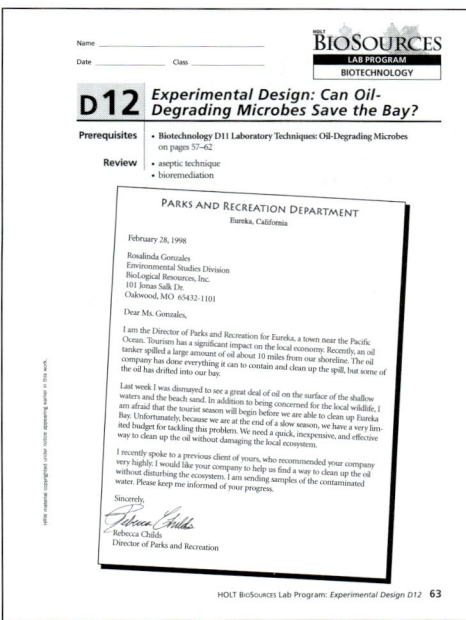

D Biotechnology

Biotechnology labs apply the formats used in the in-text *Explorations* and *Investigations* to bring the latest in cutting-edge biotechnology research techniques into your classroom.

D1 Staining DNA and RNA
D2 Extracting DNA
D3 Genetic Transformation of Bacteria
D4 Genetic Transformation—Antibiotic Resistance
D5 Introduction to Agarose Gel Electrophoresis
D6 DNA Fragment Analysis
D7 DNA Ligation
D8 Comparing DNA Samples
D9 Introduction to Fermentation
D10 Ice-Nucleating Bacteria
D11 Oil-Degrading Microbes
D12 Can Oil-Degrading Microbes Save the Bay?

E Interactive Explorations in Biology

Interactive Explorations in Biology enable your students to study phenomena that otherwise could not be observed in the classroom. Using CD-ROM technology, students will manipulate variables, predict consequences, and study outcomes in ways never before possible.

E1 Cell Size
E2 Oxidative Respiration
E3 Thermodynamics
E4 Gene Regulation
E5 Heredity in Families
E6 Hemoglobin
E7 Diet and Weight Loss

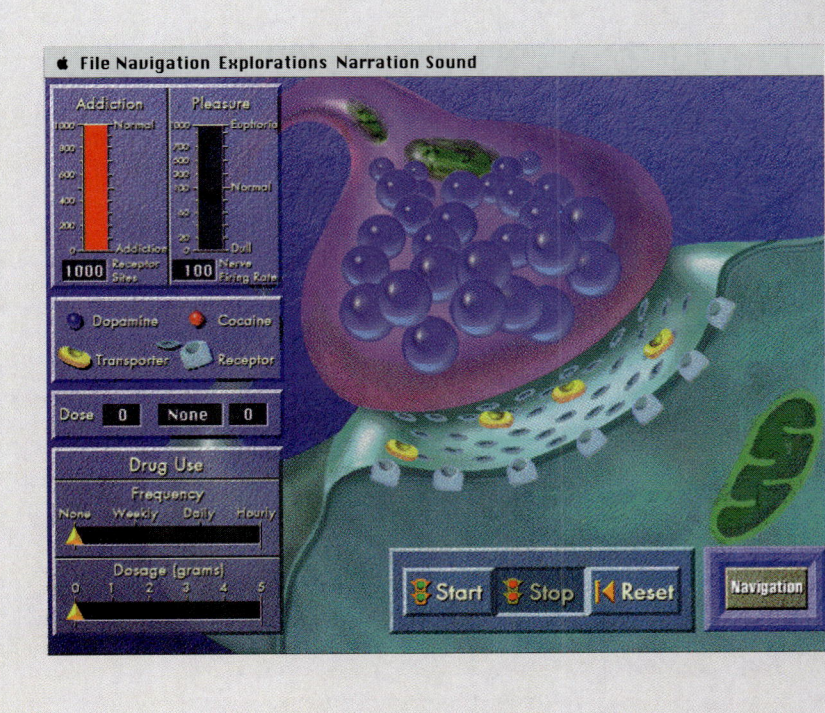

Extensive Resources Support Various Teaching Styles and Learning Modalities

Biology: Visualizing Life **resources help students build and check content comprehension.**

Vocabulary Development Worksheets provide practice in understanding and using essential terms in biology.

Directed Reading Worksheets help students to remain focused while they read, enabling them to understand key concepts on a lesson-by-lesson basis.

Thinking Skills Worksheets challenge students to use analytical and critical thinking as they apply their understanding of chapter content to new settings and situations.

Reteaching Worksheets offer additional practice for learners having difficulty.

Language Development and Reading CD Audio Program provides auditory lessons that guide the listener through each lesson of the text.

Spanish Resources includes Spanish translations of the *Glossary*, end-of-chapter *Highlights*, 160 Teaching Transparencies with accompanying worksheets, and audio compact discs.

Name _____ Date _____ Class _____

CHAPTER 12 Human Evolution

Vocabulary Development

In the table below is a list of prefixes, suffixes, and root words from which a number of scientific terms are constructed. Study each word or word part and its meaning.

Word or word part	Meaning
	Word or word part	Meaning
ocular	eyes
oppose	to place opposite
africanus	from Africa
anamensis	species name for 1995 australopithecine discovery
-ped	foot
-pithecus	ape, apelike
anthro-	man, monkey, or apelike
australo-	southern
prime	of the highest rank
pro-	sturdy, muscular; before
bi-	two
boisei	species name for australopithecine with "nutcrackerlike" jaws
robust	strong, healthy
sapien	wise
-ensis	found at this location
simian	monkey
erectus	to be erect
-thal	valley
habilis	handy
homo	man, human being

Using the meanings of the above words or word parts, write in the space at the left the letter of the definition that matches the term.

___ 1. *Australopithecus afarensis*
___ 2. *Homo habilis*
___ 3. *Homo erectus*
___ 4. *Australopithecus robustus*
___ 5. *Homo sapiens*
___ 6. bipedal
___ 7. Neanderthals
___ 8. primates
___ 9. prosimians
___ 10. hominids
___ 11. anthropoids
___ 12. opposable thumb
___ 13. binocular vision

a. walking on two feet
b. group of animals that is the highest rank in its class
c. species once thought to be the first to walk erect
d. wise individuals who are the latest group of the human family
e. individual that made simple tools, used hands well
f. means "southern ape" from Afar, a region in Africa
g. like modern humans; found near the valley of the Neander river in Germany
h. "southern ape" that was sturdier and more muscular than its close relatives

16 *Biology: Visualizing Life* **Vocabulary Development;** CHAPTER 12

Name _____ Date _____ Class _____

CHAPTER 16 The Fragile Earth

Directed Reading

■ Section 16-1: *Planet Under Stress*

Humans Have Damaged the Environment

Mark each statement below *T* if it is true and *F* if it is false.

___ 1. Damage done to any one ecosystem can have ill effects on other ecosystems.
___ 2. Americans throw away almost 10 pounds of garbage a day.
___ 3. Pollution is anything potentially harmful that humans add to the environment.
___ 4. A carcinogen is a substance that can cause malaria.

Pollution's Toll

Complete each statement by writing the correct word in each space provided.

5. _____ percent of Poland's deep wells are polluted.

6. In 1989, the oil tanker _____ ran aground off the coast of Alaska and spilled oil that polluted about 1,600 km of coastline.

7. When the sulfur released by smokestacks combines with water vapor in the atmosphere, the water vapor later condenses and forms _____ .

8. An acidic solution has a higher concentration of _____ ions than does pure water.

Destroying the Ozone Layer

On the line at the left, write the letter of the answer that best completes each sentence.

___ 9. The series of photographs in Figure 16-4 shows
  a. the hole in the ozone layer
  b. the hole in the ozone layer over the South Pole
  c. the hole in the ozone layer over North
  d. how the ozone l...

___ 10. The prim...

page 289

60 *Biology: V...*

Name _____ Date _____ Class _____

CHAPTER 3 Cells

Thinking Skills

A scientist designed the following experiment to test the limits of cell population growth. Cells were grown in six flasks under different temperature conditions. Each flask contained a nutrient broth of the same concentration. The table below shows the data obtained from the experiment. Study the table and answer the questions that follow. NOTE: Read all the questions before beginning to write your answers. If you need more space for your answers, use a separate sheet of paper.

DATA TABLE

Flask	Temp. (°C)	Vol. of Nutrient (mL)	No. of Cells (millions) Day 1	No. of Cells (millions) Day 2	No. of Cells (millions) Day 3
1	0 (32°F)	500	1.0	1.0	1.0
2	20 (68°F)	500	1.0	1.2	1.2
3	30 (86°F)	1000	1.0	2.6	3.2
4	40 (104°F)	500	1.0	2.2	2.2
5	50 (122°F)	500	1.0	2.0	2.0
6	60 (140°F)	500	1.0	1.4	1.4

Critical Thinking

1. What was the experiment devised to test? _____

2. A mistake was made in setting up the experiment. In which flask was the mistake made, and what were its consequences? _____

3. Based on the data, what was the optimal temperature for cell growth? Exclude results obtained from the flask with the faulty data. _____

Holt BioSources **components enable you to customize your course, while offering you unprecedented variety.**

Teaching Transparencies with Transparency Directory With Teacher's Notes contains 238 full-color images of key illustrations accompanied by 71 blackline masters.

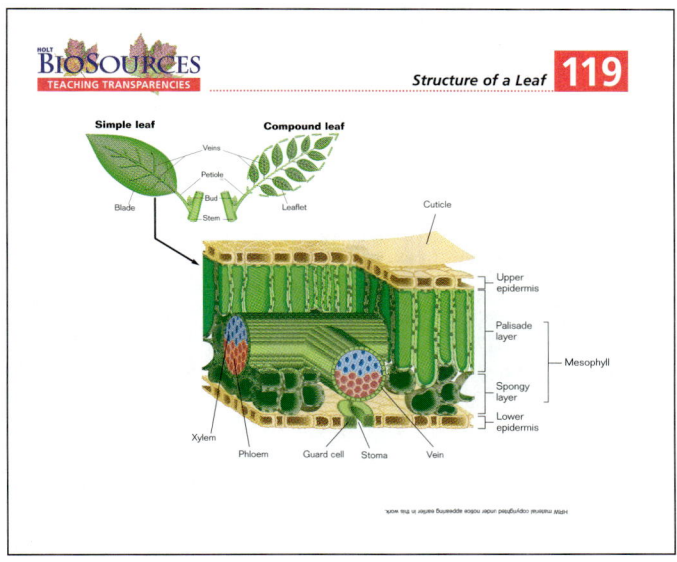

Teaching Resources Disk is a CD-ROM collection of more than 70 worksheets, rubrics, reading guidelines, portfolio projects, professional readings, and checklists. All electronic files can be copied from the CD-ROM to a diskette or hard drive. All rubrics are fully editable. Click on any of the titles below to see a list of the files contained within.

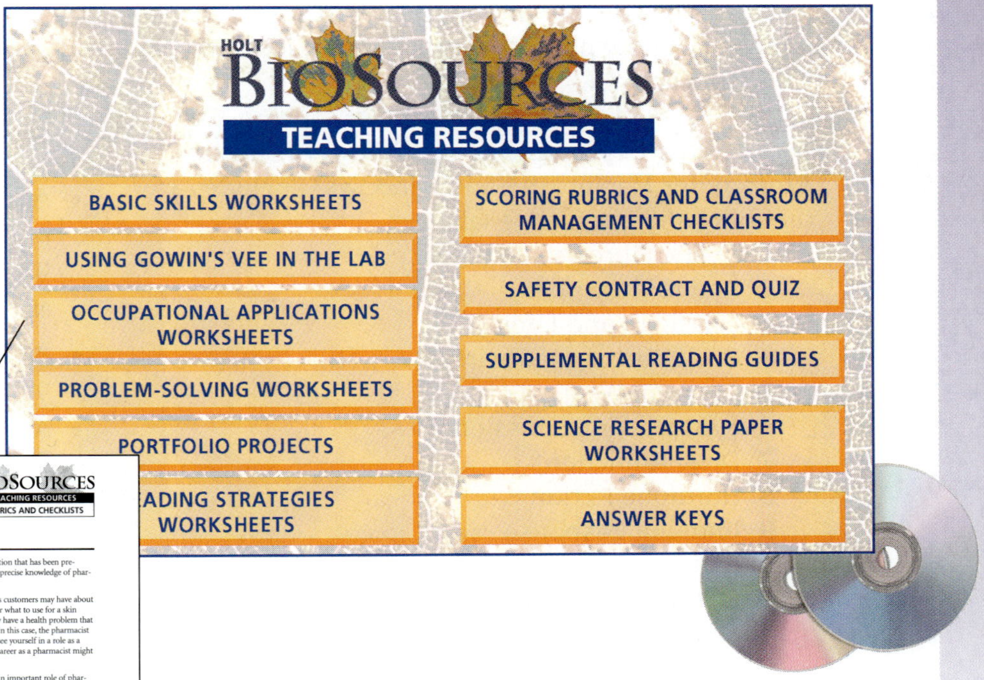

HOLT BIOSOURCES
TEACHING RESOURCES

BASIC SKILLS WORKSHEETS	SCORING RUBRICS AND CLASSROOM MANAGEMENT CHECKLISTS
USING GOWIN'S VEE IN THE LAB	SAFETY CONTRACT AND QUIZ
OCCUPATIONAL APPLICATIONS WORKSHEETS	SUPPLEMENTAL READING GUIDES
PROBLEM-SOLVING WORKSHEETS	SCIENCE RESEARCH PAPER WORKSHEETS
PORTFOLIO PROJECTS	
READING STRATEGIES WORKSHEETS	ANSWER KEYS

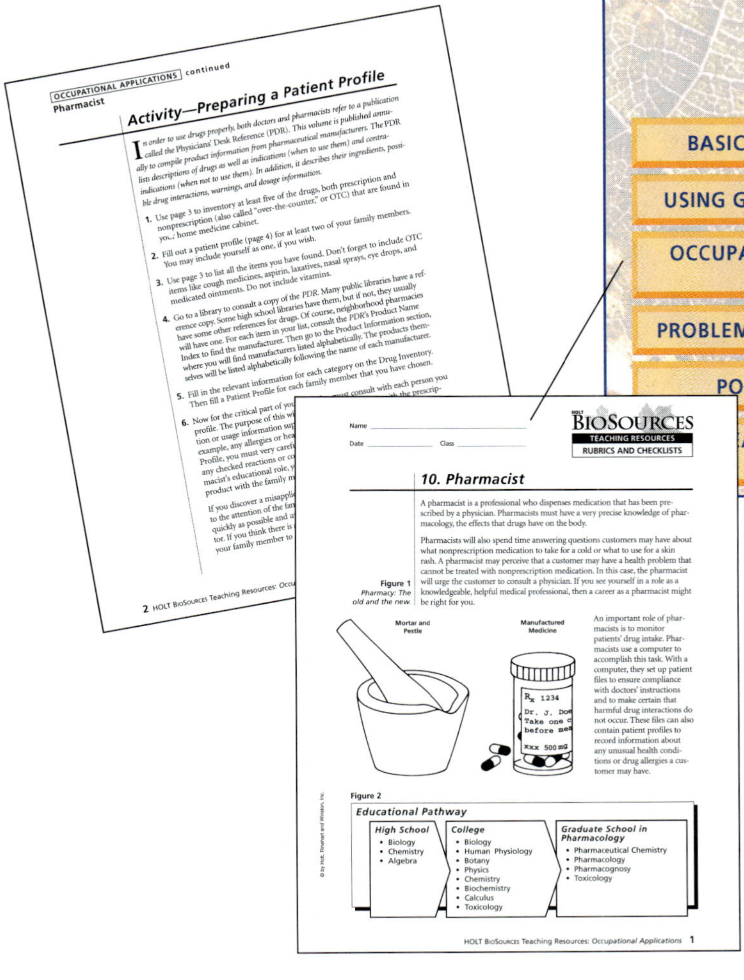

HOLT BIOSOURCES ALSO INCLUDES OPTIONS FOR ASSESSMENT. SEE PAGES T38–39.

Curriculum-Based Multimedia Instruction is Fully Integrated With Each Lesson of *Biology: Visualizing Life*

 ***Interactive Explorations in Biology* brings interactive CD-ROM technology into the lab.**

Imagine students learning about photosynthesis. Until now, their learning experience consisted of viewing a text diagram illustrating a chloroplast and listening to you describe how chlorophyll in the chloroplast captures light energy. Using the Interactive Exploration *Photosynthesis*, found on page 768, students can witness the electrons energized by light traveling through the chloroplast membrane and driving the synthesis of ATP. Then—and this is the key to the hands-on learning experience—your students can manipulate variables and see the effect on the animation! By exploring the influences of variables such as wavelength and light intensity, students learn for themselves how photosynthesis works, instead of simply being told.

Interactive Explorations in Biology: Human Biology for Macintosh® and Windows® includes the following interactive labs:

1 Cystic Fibrosis
2 Active Transport
3 Life Span and Lifestyle
4 Evolution of the Heart
5 Diet and Weight Loss
6 Synaptic Transmission
7 Drug Addiction
8 Hormone Action
9 Immune Response
10 Heredity in Families
11 Pollution of a Freshwater Lake

Each **Interactive Exploration** provides a simulation of a key biological concept. Each Interactive Exploration includes:

- A narrative overview of the biological concepts presented, followed by auditory instructions for using the meters and sliders in each simulation
- Narration in both English and Spanish
- A navigation bar that makes it easy to access other parts of the program
- A User's Guide containing questions and answers for each Interactive Exploration
- A list of additional videos and recommended readings

Interactive Explorations in Biology: Cell Biology and Genetics for Macintosh® and Windows® includes the following interactive labs:

1 Hemoglobin
2 Cell Size
3 Active Transport
4 Thermodynamics
5 Oxidative Respiration
6 Photosynthesis
7 Meiosis: Down Syndrome
8 Gene Regulation

Holt Biology Videodiscs offers you a comprehensive array of visuals tied directly to the lessons in *Biology: Visualizing Life.*

- Four double-sided videodiscs provide thousands of images:

  - More than 30 video segments offer visual examples of the ways in which complex processes work.

  - More than 40 original animations allow students to explore sophisticated biological phenomena.

  - More than 350 photographs reinforce material covered in the text.

  - More than 650 step-frame illustrations enable you to demonstrate and explain biological structures, processes, and conceptual relationships.

  - More than 650 glossary terms—all of which are available on each videodisc—can be accessed as needed.

  - Also included are concept maps, graphic organizers, Gowin's Vees, and suggestions for student portfolios.

- **Teacher's Correlation Guide to *Holt Biology: Visualizing Life*** contains barcodes and descriptors correlated specifically to each lesson in *Biology: Visualizing Life.*

- **Image Directory** contains a topic index, a subject matter index, and a glossary index, enabling you to locate the images you want quickly and easily.

Also available: **Management Software System**, a Macintosh® software program that enables you to create, save, and even print your own customized media play lists or to select preset media play lists included with the program.

Concepts of Biology adds interactive lesson plans and extensive tools for customization.

Concepts of Biology includes:

- **Holt Biology Videodiscs**

  - Four double-sided videodiscs provide thousands of images, including live-action and animated videos.

- **Four CD-ROM discs** with:

  - All media from **Holt Biology Videodiscs**
  - Complete on-line lesson plans
  - Media search and sort features
  - Interactive glossary
  - Customization features for multimedia presentations
  - Fully functional word processor
  - Digital labs

- Teacher's Guide
- Image Directory
- User's Guide
- Interactive Investigations and Laboratories, Teacher's Edition
- Interactive Investigations and Laboratories, Pupil's Edition

Both *Holt Biology Videodiscs* and *Concepts of Biology* feature a comprehensive table of contents consisting of 26 topics divided into four units.

Unit 1 Cells, Energy, and Genetics

- Cell Structure and Function
- Cell Division
- The Chemistry of Life
- Energy and Enzymes
- Photosynthesis and Cellular Respiration
- Fundamentals of Genetics
- How Genes Work

Unit 2 Evolution and Ecology

- Evolution and Natural Selection
- Evolution of Life on Earth
- Ecosystem Structure and Function
- Global Ecology
- Classification of Life
- Bacteria and Viruses
- Protists and Fungi

Unit 3 Plants and Animals

- Plant Evolution
- Plant Structure and Function
- Animal Evolution
- Invertebrate Diversity
- Evolutionary Trends in Vertebrates
- Vertebrate Diversity

Unit 4 Human Biology

- Body Systems
- Circulation and Respiration
- Digestion and Excretion
- Nervous and Endocrine Systems
- Drugs and the Human Body
- Reproduction and Development

Flexible Assessment Options Touch on All of Your Broad Instructional Goals

Chapter Tests assess content mastery

- Two *Chapter Tests* are provided for each of the 35 chapters in *Biology: Visualizing Life*. Each of these printed tests exists in two formats. Test A is all multiple choice. Test B includes short-answer and essay formats.

Holt BioSources Teaching Resources CD-ROM includes additional assessment support

- Scoring rubrics help you evaluate student-designed experiments, performance tasks, and concept maps.

- An *Informal Assessment Direct Observations Checklist* facilitates informal assessment.

- A *Portfolio Assignment Student Evaluation Form* and an *Assessment Rubric for Portfolio Items* help students and teachers evaluate portfolio assignments.

- Specialized rubrics for Holt BioSources *Quick Labs, Inquiry Skills Development* labs, and *Laboratory Techniques and Experimental Design* labs help you assess laboratory performance.

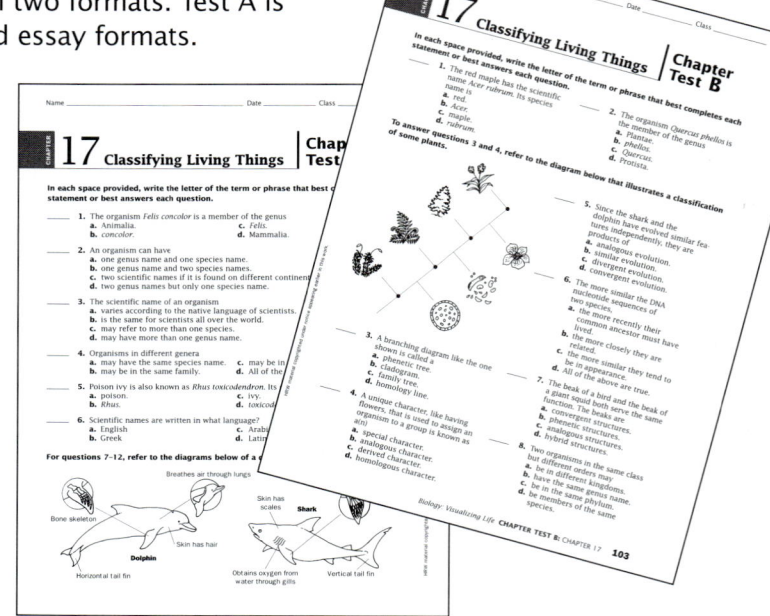

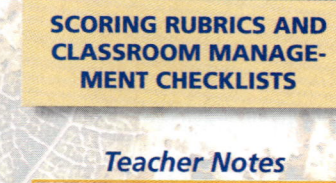

SCORING RUBRICS AND CLASSROOM MANAGEMENT CHECKLISTS

Teacher Notes

1 Introduction to Scoring Rubrics

2 Student Designed Experiments Rubric

3 Informal Assessment Direct Observations Checklist

4 Evaluating Concept Maps

5 Performance Tasks Scoring Rubric

6 Assessing Portfolios

7 Portfolio Assignment Student Evaluation Form

8 Assessment Rubric for Portfolio Items

9 Assessment Rubric for Exploration, Quick Labs, Inquiry Skills, and Laboratory Techniques

10 Assessment Rubric for Experimental Design and Investigation Labs

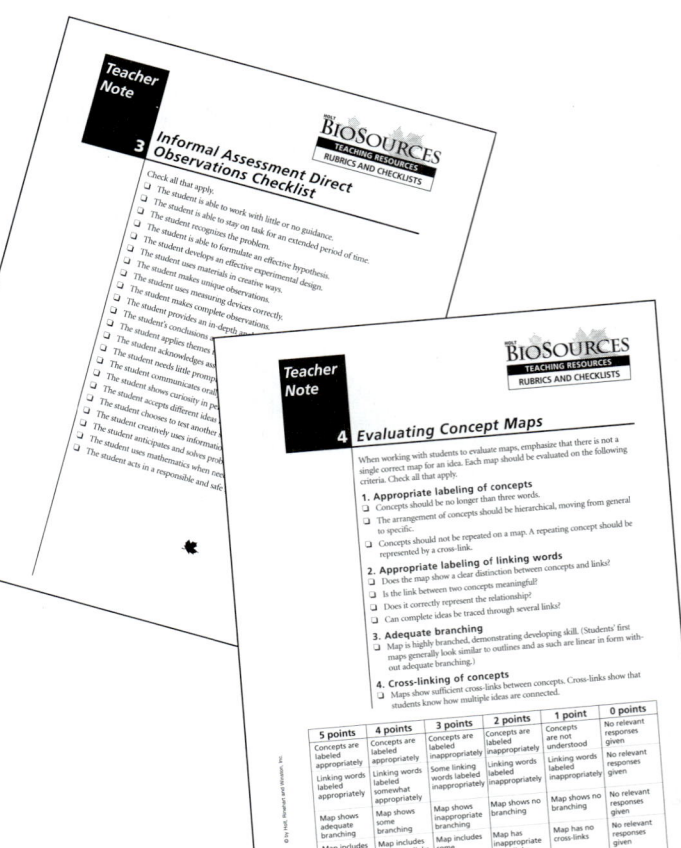

Create customized tests using *Holt BioSources Test Generator with TestBuilder Software*

- Hybrid CD-ROM disc for use with either Windows® or Macintosh®

- Contains more than 3000 multiple choice, analogy, short answer, and essay items. Includes *Holt BioSources Assessment Item Listing for Biology: Visualizing Life,* a printout showing all items.

- Sort items by lesson objective or difficulty level to construct your own customized tests to assess mastery of the lesson objectives.

- *Critical Thinking* and *Analytical Thinking* items challenge students to go beyond rote recall to analyze and apply chapter content.

- Includes 10 *Performance-Based Assessment Activities,* laboratory-based activities that challenge students to design, perform, and analyze their own experiments to solve an assigned problem.

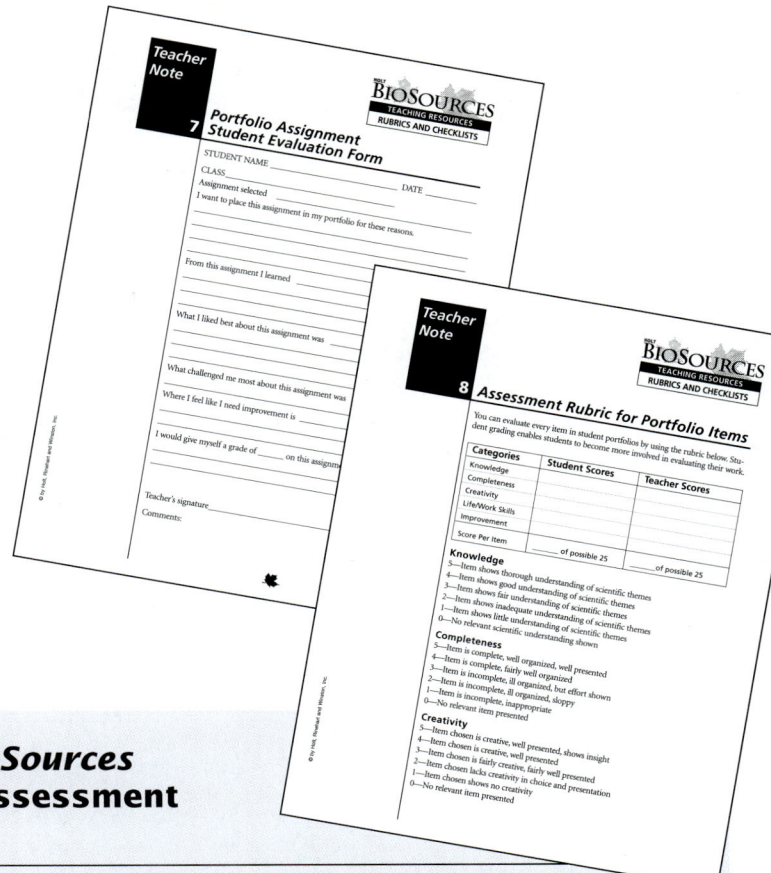

Biology: Visualizing Life and *Holt BioSources* help you make performance-based assessment a reality in your classroom.

Portfolio Assessment

 The portfolio icon denotes items that may be appropriate for inclusion in a student portfolio. Students should select their best work and provide a self-reflective rationale (see *Portfolio Assignment Student Evaluation Form**) for each selection. Use the *Assessment Rubric for Portfolio Items** to evaluate portfolios.

Students can make selections in the following areas:

1 **Content**   One concept map from the chapter. See the rubric *Evaluating Concept Maps** for evaluation criteria.

2 **Reading Comprehension**   One *Directed Reading* worksheet. Use the Answer Key to evaluate for accuracy.
   Or: One *Reading Strategies Worksheet**
   Or: One *Active Reading* assignment from the lesson wrap

3 **Writing**   *Vee Form**, concept map, or report summarizing one of the following:
   - An activity or a reading in the *Chapter Review*
   - A newspaper or magazine article relating to the chapter topic
   Or: A research paper on a subject related to the chapter topic. See *Science Research Paper Worksheets.**

4 **Performance Assessment**   One lab report or *Vee Form** for an in-text lab or a **Holt BioSources Lab Program** lab. See assessment rubrics for *Explorations, Investigations, Quick Labs, Inquiry Skills,* and *Laboratory Techniques and Experimental Design* labs.* For Vee forms, see *Assessing Student-Constructed Vee Reports** for evaluation criteria.
   Or: A student-designed experiment. See *Student-Designed Experiments Rubric** for evaluation criteria.

Teachers can make selections in the following areas:

1 **Formal Assessment**   *Chapter Test* (from **Chapter Tests** or **Holt BioSources Test Generator with TestBuilder Software**). The teacher-scored test should be reviewed by the student. Incorrect responses should be corrected by the student before the test becomes part of the portfolio.

2 **Informal Assessment**   Use *Informal Assessment Direct Observations Checklist** during a laboratory or other cooperative learning experience.

3 **Performance Assessment**   Assign the appropriate *Performance-Based Assessment Activity* from **Holt BioSources Test Generator with TestBuilder Software.**

* found in **Holt BioSources Teaching Resources CD-ROM**

Biology: Visualizing Life Presents Effective Teaching Strategies That Will Help You Meet the Demands of Block Scheduling

Lesson Planning Guide With Options for Block Scheduling Coordinates Weekly and Daily Planning

The *Biology: Visualizing Life* Annotated Teacher's Edition consists of two parts. Teacher's interleaf pages preceding each chapter assist you with *weekly planning*, while teacher's lesson wrap surrounding the reduced pupil's pages offers strategies for *daily planning*.

The **Lesson Planning Guide With Options for Block Scheduling** gives you the flexible options you need to make block scheduling a success!

Lesson Resources lists resources available for each lesson, including options for group learning, student presentations, and project-oriented instruction.

Lecture Concepts summarizes the key points of each lesson.

Use the Lesson Planning Guide to help you with the following:

❶ *Plan lessons* **Lesson Resources** makes it easy for you to "switch gears" and keep your class engaged throughout the longer class periods required by block scheduling.

Each lesson includes options for lecture and classwork that will support various learning modalities for the longer periods required by block scheduling. Select from **Lecture Resources**, **Classwork Options**, and **Assignment Options** to create the lesson plan that works for you.

CHAPTER 28 | Reptiles, Birds, and Mammals

Lesson Planning Guide With Options for Block Scheduling

Lecture Concepts	Lesson Resources	
28-1 Reptiles		
BLOCK ❶ (45 minutes) 1. Reptiles are well adapted to life on land. 2. Reptiles are ectotherms. Their body temperature changes with their surroundings.	**❶ Lecture Resources** ■ Determining Prior Knowledge ■ Active Reading: Discussion ■ Visual Strategy: Videodisc ■ Demonstration: Identifying Structures ■ Teaching Transparencies: 171, 173, 174 ● Holt Biology Videodiscs Lesson 28-1	**Classwork Options** ■ Life/Work Skills: Finding Information ▲ Quick Labs: Lab A22 **Assignment Options** ■ Warmblooded Dinosaurs? ■ Island Speciation
BLOCK ❷ (45 minutes) 3. Extinct reptiles include dinosaurs, ichthyosaurs, plesiosaurs, and pterosaurs. 4. Virtually all large animals became extinct about 65 million years ago.	**❷ Lecture Resources** ■ Tied to Land ■ Reptile Lands ■ Active Reading: Reading Organizer ■ Teaching Transparencies: 141A, 142A ● Holt Biology Videodiscs Lesson 28-1 **Classwork Options** ■ Lizards and Snakes	■ Closure: Determining the Validity of a Claim **Assignment Options** ■ Reteaching ■ Section Review ■ Chapter Review, questions 1a, 2a, 4, 5, 6, 7, 24, 25, 27, 29 ■ Directed Reading Worksheet
28-2 Birds		
BLOCK ❸ (45 minutes) 1. Birds evolved from reptiles, and they still share many characteristics. 2. Birds are the only animals that have feathers.	**❸ Lecture Resources** ■ Are Birds Reptiles? ■ Demonstration: Comparing Structures ■ Teaching Transparencies: 175, 176 ● Holt Biology Videodiscs Lesson 28-2	**Classwork Options** ▲ Laboratory Techniques and Experimental Design: Lab C40 **Assignment Options** ■ Life/Work Skills: Finding Information
BLOCK ❹ (45 minutes) 3. Feathers, a lightweight skeleton, and endothermy enable a bird to fly. 4. The feet and beaks of birds are important in determining how birds are classified.	**❹ Lecture Resources** ■ Teaching Transparencies: 143A, 182 ● Holt Biology Videodiscs Lesson 28-2 **Classwork Options** ■ Life/Work Skills: Being a Team Member ■ Closure: Relating Concepts	**Assignment Options** ■ Small Group Reteaching ■ Section Review ■ Chapter Review, questions 1b, 2b, 8, 9, 10, 21, 22, 26, 28 ■ Directed Reading Worksheet
28-3 Introduction to Mammals		
BLOCK ❺ (45 minutes) 1. True mammals evolved from therapsids, have fur, and are able to produce milk. 2. Mammals took over ecological roles previously occupied by dinosaurs.	**❺ Lecture Resources** ■ How Long Ago? ■ Best Adapted? ■ Visual Strategy: Figure 28-17 ■ Teaching Transparencies: 177, 178 ● Holt Biology Videodiscs Lesson 28-3	**Classwork Options** ● Teaching Resources CD-ROM: Occupational Applications Worksheets 1 ■ Investigation 28A **Assignment Options** ■ Life/Work Skills: Being a Team Member
BLOCK ❻ (45 minutes) 3. Mammals are endotherms and can regulate their body temperature. 4. Monotremes lay eggs. Marsupials give birth to young that then develop in their mother's pouch. Placental mammals develop inside their mothers before birth.	**❻ Lecture Resources** ■ The Evolution of Mammals ■ Active Reading: Reading Organizer ■ Teaching Transparencies: 181 ● Holt Biology Videodiscs Lesson 28-3 **Classwork Options** ■ Closure: Organizing Information	**Assignment Options** ■ Reteaching ■ Section Review ■ Chapter Review, questions 3, 11, 12, 13, 20, 23 ■ Directed Reading Worksheet

539A   Chapter 28   Teacher's Interleaf

The **Teacher's Interleaf** is your master plan for integrating all the materials available for the program into your teaching plan for each chapter. Whether you teach on a traditional schedule or follow a block schedule, the use of varied teaching strategies, classwork options, and assignment options is essential to sustaining student interest.

A variety of lecture and classwork options will keep your students on task—and your lesson on target.

The Teacher's Interleaf presents all of the options available from *Biology: Visualizing Life* and *Holt BioSources* for use with each section.

The **Key** lists the components of your comprehensive resource package.

1 *Biology: Visualizing Life* resources help students master the content of each lesson of the text.

2 **Holt BioSources** enables you to extend and customize your course to meet your needs.

3 **Holt Biology Technology** gives you options for curriculum-based multimedia instruction.

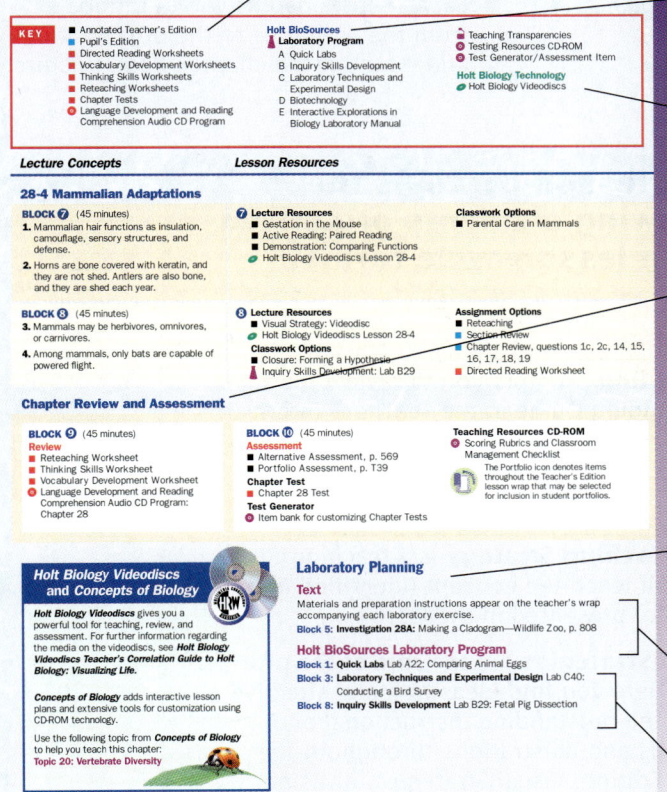

KEY
- Annotated Teacher's Edition
- Pupil's Edition
- Directed Reading Worksheets
- Vocabulary Development Worksheets
- Thinking Skills Worksheets
- Reteaching Worksheets
- Chapter Tests
- Language Development and Reading Comprehension Audio CD Program

Holt BioSources
Laboratory Program
- A Quick Labs
- B Inquiry Skills Development
- C Laboratory Techniques and Experimental Design
- D Biotechnology
- E Interactive Explorations in Biology Laboratory Manual

- Teaching Transparencies
- Testing Resources CD-ROM
- Test Generator/Assessment Item

Holt Biology Technology
- Holt Biology Videodiscs

Lecture Concepts

Lesson Resources

28-4 Mammalian Adaptations

BLOCK 7 (45 minutes)
1. Mammalian hair functions as insulation, camouflage, sensory structures, and defense.
2. Horns are bone covered with keratin, and they are not shed. Antlers are also bone, and they are shed each year.

7 Lecture Resources
- Gestation in the Mouse
- Active Reading: Paired Reading
- Demonstration: Comparing Functions
- Holt Biology Videodiscs Lesson 28-4

Classwork Options
- Parental Care in Mammals

BLOCK 8 (45 minutes)
3. Mammals may be herbivores, omnivores, or carnivores.
4. Among mammals, only bats are capable of powered flight.

8 Lecture Resources
- Visual Strategy: Videodisc
- Holt Biology Videodiscs Lesson 28-4

Classwork Options
- Closure: Forming a Hypothesis
- Inquiry Skills Development: Lab B29

Assignment Options
- Reteaching
- Section Review
- Chapter Review, questions 1c, 2c, 14, 15, 16, 17, 18, 19
- Directed Reading Worksheet

Chapter Review and Assessment

BLOCK 9 (45 minutes)
Review
- Reteaching Worksheet
- Thinking Skills Worksheet
- Vocabulary Development Worksheet
- Language Development and Reading Comprehension Audio CD Program: Chapter 28

BLOCK 10 (45 minutes)
Assessment
- Alternative Assessment, p. 569
- Portfolio Assessment, p. T39

Chapter Test
- Chapter 28 Test

Test Generator
- Item bank for customizing Chapter Tests

Teaching Resources CD-ROM
- Scoring Rubrics and Classroom Management Checklist

The Portfolio icon denotes items throughout the Teacher's Edition lesson wrap that may be selected for inclusion in student portfolios.

Holt Biology Videodiscs and Concepts of Biology

Holt Biology Videodiscs gives you a powerful tool for teaching, review, and assessment. For further information regarding the media on the videodiscs, see *Holt Biology Videodiscs Teacher's Correlation Guide to Holt Biology: Visualizing Life.*

Concepts of Biology adds interactive lesson plans and extensive tools for customization using CD-ROM technology.

Use the following topic from *Concepts of Biology* to help you teach this chapter:
Topic 20: Vertebrate Diversity

Laboratory Planning

Text
Materials and preparation instructions appear on the teacher's wrap accompanying each laboratory exercise.
Block 5: **Investigation 28A:** Making a Cladogram—Wildlife Zoo, p. 808

Holt BioSources Laboratory Program
Block 1: **Quick Labs** Lab A22: Comparing Animal Eggs
Block 3: **Laboratory Techniques and Experimental Design** Lab C40: Conducting a Bird Survey
Block 8: **Inquiry Skills Development** Lab B29: Fetal Pig Dissection

Teacher's Interleaf   Chapter 28   539B

2 *Review and assess* Review the chapter using any or all of the options shown here. Select from the assessment options to evaluate content mastery.

3 *Choose one or more labs* **Laboratory Planning** recommends labs to incorporate into your lesson curriculum.

These labs are found in the *Biology: Visualizing Life* Pupil's Edition.

These labs are found in the Holt BioSources Laboratory Program.

4 *Select media to support and extend your lesson* **Holt Biology Videodiscs** contains thousands of images correlated lesson-by-lesson to *Biology: Visualizing Life.* Use the topic from *Concepts of Biology* listed here to enrich your lesson curriculum.

The Teacher's Wrap Gives You the Teaching Strategies You Need for Daily Planning Using the Lesson Cycle

Each chapter opens with the following items:

Determining Prior Knowledge helps you assess how much your students know—and what misconceptions they may have—before you begin teaching.

Active Reading provides a variety of strategies to help your students become truly *active* readers, responsible for their own learning. Many Active Reading strategies are supported by *Reading Strategies Worksheets* from Holt BioSources Teaching Resources CD-ROM.

CD-ROM Resources identifies the appropriate lesson in *Concepts of Biology*.

Author's Rationale
Each chapter begins with a rationale from the author as to the organization and intent of the chapter. Read this first.

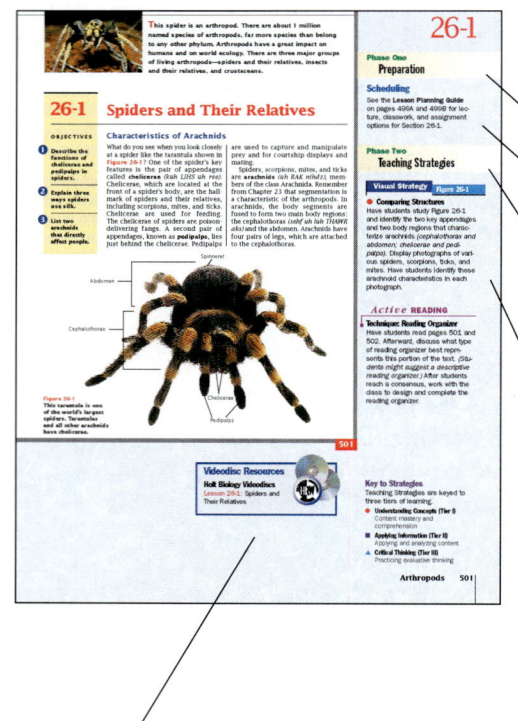

Each lesson contains the following elements organized into a lesson-cycle format:

Phase 1
Preparation

Scheduling prompts you to review the Lesson Planning Guide in the Teacher's Interleaf.

Phase 2
Teaching Strategies

Each **Teaching Strategy** is a teaching tip to help you teach the concept (identified in the tip's title) presented in the lesson.

Visual Strategies are the core of the program. Here you find ideas to make effective use of the outstanding instructional photographs and illustrations throughout the Pupil's Edition. Visual Strategies for using specific images found in *Holt Biology Videodiscs* are also included.

Teaching Strategies are coded according to three tiers of learning:

● Understanding Concepts (Tier I)
■ Applying Information (Tier II)
▲ Critical Thinking (Tier III)

Videodisc Resources identifies the corresponding lesson in *Holt Biology Videodiscs*.

Demonstrations provide concrete modeling for abstract ideas.

Connections highlight interrelationships. You'll find *Connections* for other subjects like mathematics and social studies and *Connections* to previous chapters.

Life/Work Skills require students to apply five skills needed for success:

- Communicating
- Allocating Resources
- Finding Information
- Being a Team Member
- Selecting Technology

Problem-Solving or **Decision-Making** asks students to practice problem-solving or decision-making skills.

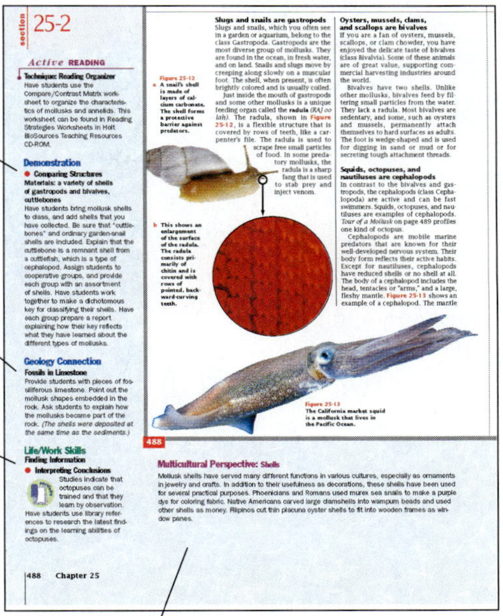

Informational items along the bottom of the lesson wrap help you support and extend the lesson content.

Community Connections suggest ways you can bring creative contributions from your community into your classroom.

Historical Perspectives are historical backgrounds related to the text.

Multicultural Perspectives provide information about people of various cultures who have been associated with ideas presented in the text, or about the influence of culture on a biological issue.

Matter of Fact provides a useful bit of information related to the ideas in the text.

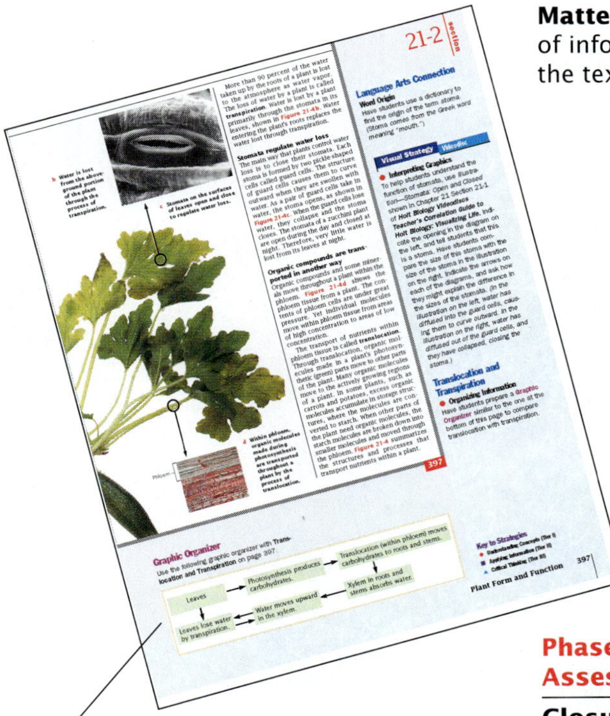

Graphic Organizers are visual tools that help you describe particularly complex information. A nearby teaching strategy offers suggestions for using the graphic organizer.

Phase 3 Assessment Options

Closure is a strategy for helping students summarize key concepts from the lesson.

Section Review assesses mastery of the section objectives.

Reteaching provides a strategy for additional instruction in a major concept of the section.

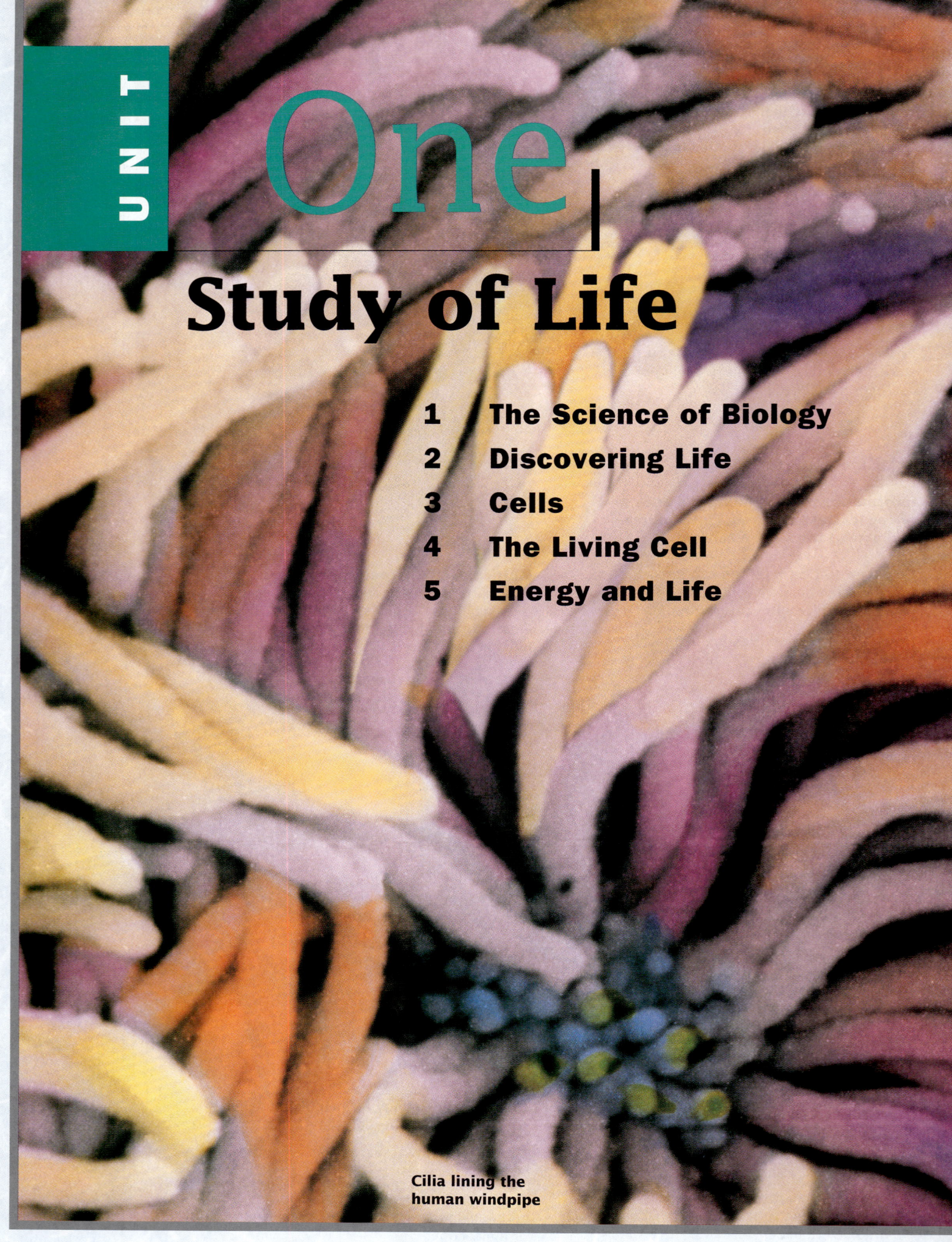

One

Study of Life

Cilia lining the
human windpipe

GENES AND INHERITANCE

You are a unique combination of traits—hair color, eye color, body shape, and others—controlled by genes inherited from your parents and your ancestors. But some genes passed from parent to child are defective and cause diseases like cystic fibrosis (CF), a lung condition that causes death in nine out of ten patients before age 30.

Making a Diagnosis

Doctors discovered that people with CF have very salty sweat. They also learned that high levels of salt collect in the cells of the lungs, pancreas, and liver of people with this disease. The salt pulls water out of normal mucus, leaving the mucus thick and sticky.

Finding the Cause

The CF gene, like all genes, carries instructions for making proteins. In CF patients, certain protein structures that pump water and salt into and out of cells are built incorrectly. A defective gene carries the wrong instructions for making these proteins and is the cause of this inherited disease.

LOOKING AHEAD

- How could you find out if you are a carrier of a defective gene? See **Science, Technology, and Society: DNA Profiling: Promise or Peril?** pages 38–39.
- Where in a cell are instructions for making proteins? See **A Closer Look: Eukaryotic Cell,** page 53.
- Who helps scientists find answers to the mysteries of cell structure? See **Career Opportunities: Science Technology,** page 55.
- How do protein channels restrict the kind of particles that enter and exit a cell? See pages 69–71.

1 | The Science of Biology

Lesson Planning Guide With Options for Block Scheduling

Lecture Concepts	Lesson Resources

1-1 Biology Today

Block ❶ (45 minutes)

1. Biology is the study of living things.
2. Biology involves a search for solutions to medical problems.

❶ Lecture Resources
- Determining Prior Knowledge
- Active Reading: Brainstorming
- Visual Strategy: Figure 1-2b
- Teaching Transparencies: 238, 203A
- Holt Biology Videodiscs Lesson 1-1

Classwork Options
- Laboratory Techniques and Experimental Design: Lab C1

Assignment Options
- World of Work: Biological Research
- Teaching Resources CD-ROM: Basic Skills Worksheets 9

Block ❷ (45 minutes)

3. Biology involves a search for answers to environmental concerns.
4. A knowledge of biology will provide information that is useful in making critical personal decisions.

❷ Lecture Resources
- Active Reading: Reading Organizer
- Demonstration: Comparing Structures
- Teaching Transparencies: 65
- Holt Biology Videodiscs Lesson 1-1

Classwork Options
- Life/Work Skills: Finding Information
- Closure: Recognizing Relationships

Assignment Options
- Reteaching
- Section Review
- Chapter Review, questions 2a, 4, 5, 6, 16, 20
- Directed Reading Worksheet

1-2 Science Is a Search for Knowledge

Block ❸ (45 minutes)

1. Biologists begin their search for a solution to a particular problem or question by forming a hypothesis.
2. Biologists make predictions based on hypotheses.
3. Biologists may test their prediction in a controlled experiment.

❸ Lecture Resources
- Testing a Claim
- Active Reading: Reading Organizer
- Visual Strategy: Figure 1-6
- Holt Biology Videodiscs Lesson 1-2

Classwork Options
- Life/Work Skills: Finding Information
- Exploration 1A

Assignment Options
- Scientific Experiments

Block ❹ (45 minutes)

4. Biologists reject any hypotheses not supported by the results of their experiments.
5. Biologists may formulate a theory if their hypothesis is tested in many ways and supported by the results of experiments.

❹ Lecture Resources
- Theories
- Science Publications
- Visual Strategy: Figure 1-7
- Holt Biology Videodiscs Lesson 1-2

Classwork Options
- Reteaching
- Closure: Recognizing Verifiable Facts
- Investigation 1B

Assignment Options
- Pasteur's Words
- Section Review
- Chapter Review, questions 1a, 3, 7, 8, 9, 10, 12, 15, 17
- Directed Reading Worksheet

1-3 Studying Biology

Block ❺ (45 minutes)

1. All organisms are composed of cells.
2. All organisms must maintain homeostasis.
3. Instructions for development are passed from parent to offspring.
4. Evolution is inherited change over time.

❺ Lecture Resources
- Active Reading: K-W-L
- Demonstration: Relating Concepts
- Teaching Transparencies: 7
- Holt Biology Videodiscs Lesson 1-3

Classwork Options
- Life/Work Skills: Communicating
- Inquiry Skills Development: Lab B1

Assignment Options
- World of Work: Paleontology

Lecture Concepts

Lesson Resources

1-3 Studying Biology, *continued*

BLOCK ⑥ (45 minutes)

5. Living things interact with their environment in complex ways.

6. The physical principles that apply to stars or computers apply to all living things; they differ only in degree.

⑥ Lecture Resources
- ■ Interdependence
- ■ Demonstration: Interpreting Data
- 💿 Holt Biology Videodiscs Lesson 1-3

Classwork Options
- ■ Reteaching
- ■ Closure: Relating Concepts

Assignment Options
- ■ Section Review
- ■ Chapter Review, questions 1b, 1c, 2b, 2c, 11, 13, 14, 18, 19
- ■ Directed Reading Worksheet

Chapter Review and Assessment

Block ❼ (45 minutes)
Review
- ■ Reteaching Worksheet
- ■ Thinking Skills Worksheet
- ■ Vocabulary Development Worksheet
- ◉ Language Development and Reading Comprehension Audio CD Program: Chapter 1

Block ❽ (45 minutes)
Assessment
- ■ Alternative Assessment, p. 19
- ■ Portfolio Assessment, p. T39

Chapter Test
- ■ Chapter 1 Test

Test Generator
- ◉ Item bank for customizing Chapter Tests

Teaching Resources CD-ROM
- ◉ Scoring Rubrics and Classroom Management Checklist

The Portfolio icon denotes items throughout the Teacher's Edition lesson wrap that may be selected for inclusion in student portfolios.

Holt Biology Videodiscs and *Concepts of Biology*

Holt Biology Videodiscs gives you a powerful tool for teaching, review, and assessment. For further information regarding the media on the videodiscs, see *Holt Biology Videodiscs Teacher's Correlation Guide to Holt Biology: Visualizing Life.*

Concepts of Biology adds interactive lesson plans and extensive tools for customization using CD-ROM technology.

Use the following topic from *Concepts of Biology* to help you teach this chapter:
Topic 1: Cell Structure and Function

Laboratory Planning

Text
Materials and preparation instructions appear on the teacher's wrap accompanying each laboratory exercise.

Block 3 **Exploration 1A:** Using a Scientific Method, p. 756

Block 4 **Investigation 1B:** Using a Scientific Method—Tropical Fish Dealer, p. 758

Holt BioSources Laboratory Program

Block 1 **Laboratory Techniques and Experimental Design** Lab C1: Using a Microscope

Block 5 **Inquiry Skills Development** Lab B1: Introduction to Experimental Design and Data Presentation

Determining Prior Knowledge

- Have students search current periodicals to find photographs of people engaged in various activities that require some knowledge of biology. Have students suggest examples of how biology is a necessary part of life.
- Have students provide examples of how biology has had an impact on their lives.
- Have students discuss the meaning of the following terms: hypothesis, control experiment, and theory.
- Ask students to list some biological concepts or theories and discuss what they know about them.

Active READING

Technique: Brainstorming

Before students begin Chapter 1, write the word *Biology* on the chalkboard. Ask students to think of other words that include the prefix *bio (biology, biodegradable, biosphere, biography, bionic)*. Then have students generate a list of words that include the suffix *logy (psychology, sociology, ecology, geology)*. Using the student-generated lists of words as a guide, have students use dictionaries to find the meanings of the prefixes and suffixes. Students should discover that the Greek roots *bio* and *logy* mean "life" and "science" or "theory," respectively. Explain to students that the study of life is what biology is all about. For fun, have students brainstorm a list of their favorite silly "ologies" *(sleepology, sportsology)*. Some of the silly words might have real-world equivalents. For example, a person who studies sleep is probably an *electrophysiologist*.

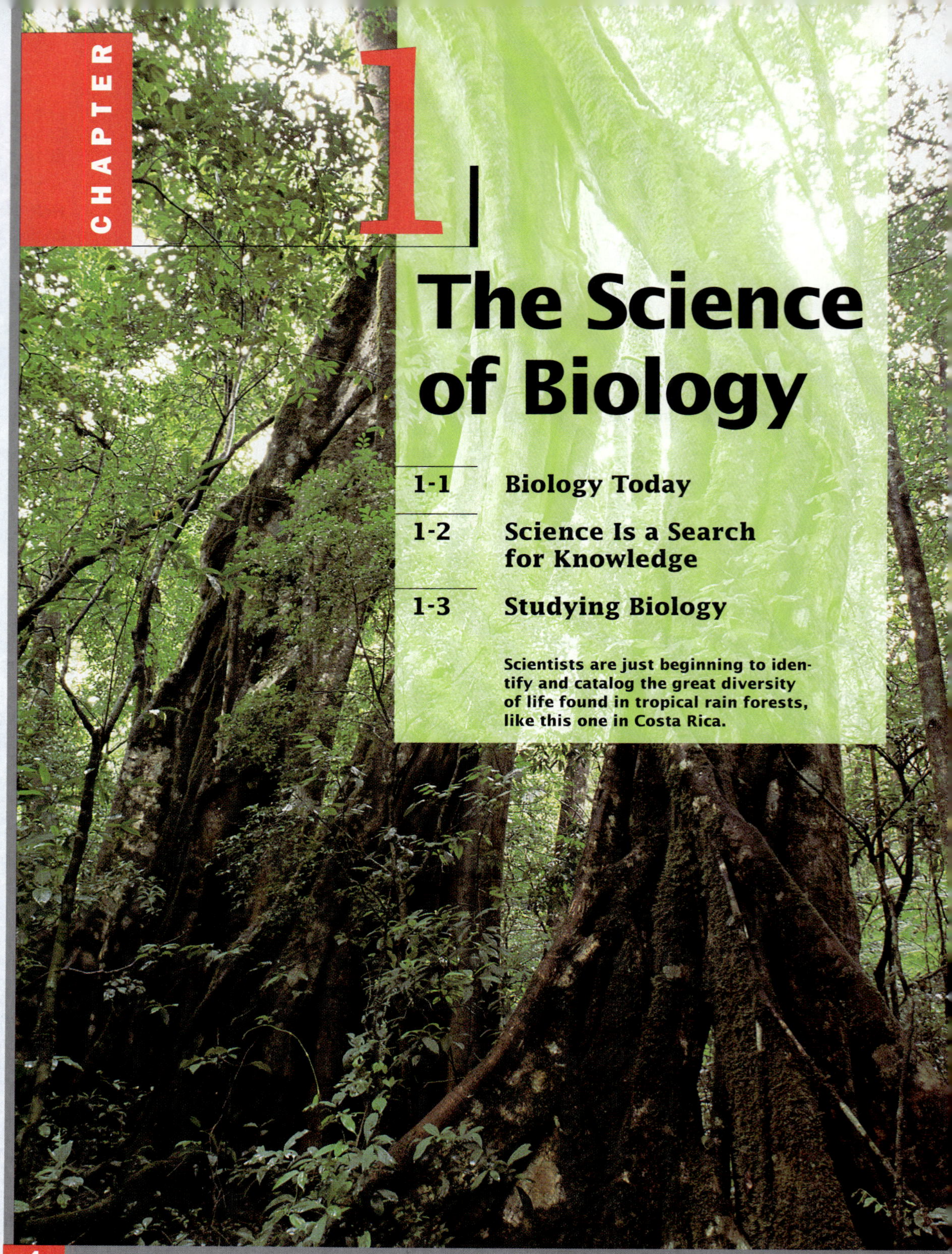

The Science of Biology

1-1	**Biology Today**
1-2	**Science Is a Search for Knowledge**
1-3	**Studying Biology**

Scientists are just beginning to identify and catalog the great diversity of life found in tropical rain forests, like this one in Costa Rica.

4

Author's Rationale This chapter introduces the importance of biology to students who may not have much interest in science and who probably don't plan to study the subject further in college. The chapter starts with the importance of biological knowledge in making personal decisions. It then focuses on how biology is studied—the nature of scientific inquiry. Students will apply the knowledge they acquire from this section as they study various topics throughout the year. At the core of the chapter is a description of major themes that will be encountered repeatedly throughout the course.

Biology is the study of the living world. Biologist Terry Erwin, at left, collects and studies tropical insects. Biologists also study how a child grows, what dinosaurs were like, and many other topics. People have puzzled about life for thousands of years, but only in the last 150 years have we really begun to understand how the world came to be the way it is.

1-1 Biology Today

OBJECTIVES

1 List three diseases for which scientists are seeking cures.

2 Describe two environmental problems and the ways scientists are trying to solve them.

3 Explain three ways you can use biological knowledge to improve your health.

Studying Life

Science is a way of investigating the world in order to form general rules about what causes things to happen. A scientist is an observer who searches for knowledge to find solutions to problems. Science has changed the world rapidly in modern times, and new and important scientific discoveries, like the one shown in **Figure 1-1**, continue to be made. What scientists have learned about life and how they learned it are the subjects of this text.

You are about to embark on the study of biology, the science of life.

Biology is the study of living things, including ourselves. While biological scientists, called biologists, continue to learn new things all the time, they now have a pretty clear picture of what living things are like and how they function. Biologists have learned enough, in fact, to begin to make genetic tools that can change the living world in new and important ways—an exciting and sobering prospect. Biology's impact on our daily lives has become so great that every person needs to know about biology in order to make many personal decisions.

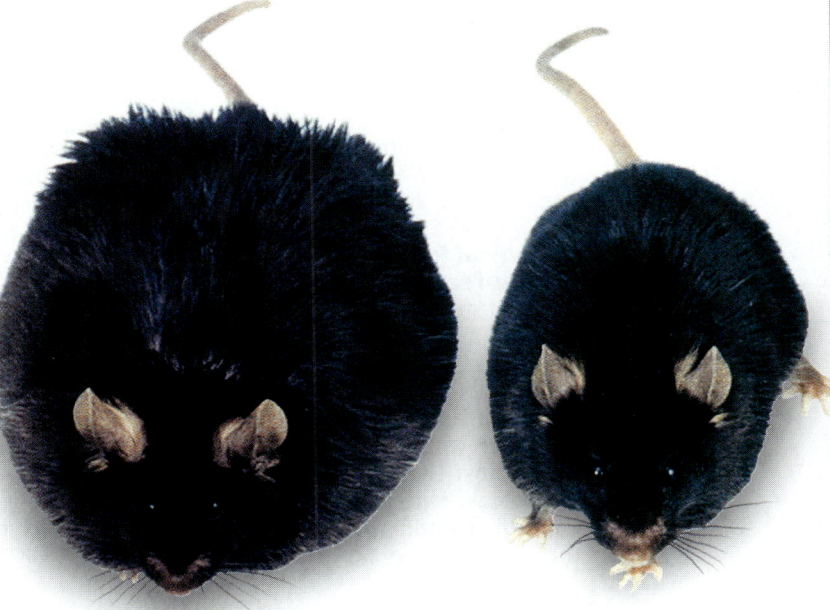

Figure 1-1
Biologist Jeffrey Friedman and his colleagues have discovered a protein that helps the body regulate weight. Mice that produce too little of this protein, like the one on the left, become grossly overweight. Friedman and other scientists are investigating how this protein functions in humans.

5

Videodisc Resources

Holt Biology Videodiscs
Lesson 1-1: Biology Today

Phase One
Preparation

Scheduling
See the **Lesson Planning Guide** on pages 3A and 3B for lecture, classwork, and assignment options for Section 1-1.

Phase Two
Teaching Strategies

Active READING

Technique: Reading Organizer
Have students read Section 1-1, then design a spider map reading organizer to show the main ideas and supporting details of the section. Maps will vary, but students should begin by writing the main idea in the center of the diagram and the details of the section arranged around the center. For more information about reading organizers, see Reading Strategies Worksheets in Holt BioSources Teaching Resources CD-ROM.

Key to Strategies
Teaching Strategies are keyed to three tiers of learning.

● **Understanding Concepts (Tier I)**
Content mastery and comprehension

■ **Applying Information (Tier II)**
Applying and analyzing content

▲ **Critical Thinking (Tier III)**
Practicing evaluative thinking

"What do I need to know about AIDS?"

Health Connection

Top Three Diseases

Ask students what they think are the top three leading causes of death in the United States today *(heart disease, cancer, and stroke).*

World of Work

Biological Research

Have students use the library or on-line references to obtain information about current biological research. Assign topics so that several areas of research are covered. Areas of research could include genetics, ecology, agriculture, behavioral science, veterinary medicine, anthropology, or nutrition. Ask students to prepare reports summarizing their findings. Provide students with the following questions to get them started: (1) What educational preparation is needed to become this type of scientist? (2) Where would this research scientist work? (3) What problems are the scientists in this area presently trying to solve? (4) How might their findings affect people's lives? (5) What would you like and dislike about this particular career?

Figure 1-2

a What you learn about AIDS could save your life. There is no vaccine or cure for AIDS, and your knowledge of how the AIDS virus is transmitted is the first step in protecting yourself against infection.

Biology and Medicine

Perhaps the most direct effect of biology on our lives is in medicine, where scientific advances are improving health and health care every day. For example, stop for a moment and think about the headlines you read in the newspaper this week and the news stories you heard on the radio or TV. Mixed in with the bad news and politics is the news that modern science is exploring ways to cure inherited disorders like cystic fibrosis and muscular dystrophy. Scientists are also searching for ways to treat and prevent AIDS, a disease that has killed over 300,000 Americans since 1981. Though no vaccine or cure for AIDS has been discovered, what scientists have learned about this disease is important for everyone to know, as explained in **Figure 1-2**.

Biological knowledge is used to fight infectious diseases

At the beginning of the twentieth century, the diseases influenza (flu), tuberculosis, and pneumonia were the top three causes of death in the United States. The influenza epidemic of 1918–1919 killed 22 million people worldwide in just 18 months. Now, thanks to biological research that produced antibiotics and vaccines, deaths from these diseases are far less common.

The battle against disease is far from won, however. More than 1 million people are likely to die of malaria this year. Spread by mosquitoes, this disease is common in tropical regions—more than 250 million people suffer from malaria at any one time. Almost every child under the age of five who gets malaria dies. The organism that causes malaria has a very complex life cycle and is therefore difficult to control. Using modern genetic engineering techniques, scientists are trying to design a vaccine that will stimulate the body's defenses to attack the organism at a critical stage of its life cycle. Also, new ways to reduce mosquito populations are being researched.

New strains of bacteria that cause tuberculosis, the fatal lung disease, have recently arisen. These strains are resistant to today's antibiotics. Partly as a result, tuberculosis will kill about 3 million people worldwide this year.

AIDS is another disease that is a subject of intensive research. AIDS is caused by a virus that destroys the body's ability to defend itself from infections. Because the virus changes the characteristics of its surface so quickly, normal vaccines don't work.

No one yet knows the solutions to these problems, but many approaches are being explored.

6

Matter of Fact: HIV Cases

The World Health Organization estimates that by the year 2000 there will be 30–40 million people with HIV and 10 million cases of AIDS. For free information about HIV, referrals, and pamphlets, call the Centers for Disease Control National AIDS Information Hotline: 800-342-AIDS.

You can also contact the CDC at the following Internet address: **http://www.cdc.gov/**

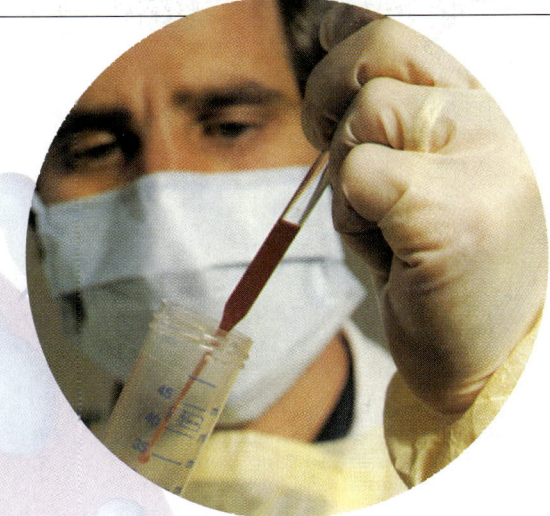

b Researchers, like this one at the Clinical Immunology Lab at East Tennessee State University, use what has been discovered about AIDS when they plan new experiments.

Biological knowledge is used to help cure genetic disorders

Among the most discouraging medical problems are fatal disorders that result from defective genes. **Genes** are the inherited "operating instructions" for the body. Two fatal genetic disorders are cystic fibrosis and muscular cystrophy. Cystic fibrosis affects about 30,000 Americans. Ninety percent of these individuals will die before their 30th birthday. Their lungs become clogged with thick mucus because of a defect in a single gene. Muscular cystrophy kills about 1 in 10,000 humans. Their muscles waste away because of a defect in another gene.

Until recently, such genetic disorders were almost always fatal. But in 1990 biologists used an approach called genetic engineering to transfer copies of a normally functioning gene from a healthy individual into a patient with defective copies of that gene. Three years later, this new therapy was first tried against cystic fibrosis. Transferring normally functioning genes into affected individuals offers the first real hope of curing genetic disorders. A major effort is now underway to identify and sequence every gene in the human body, a program that may open the way to curing many other genetic disorders.

c Politicians must understand the biology of AIDS if they are to make informed decisions about providing care facilities, funding research, and protecting the rights of AIDS victims.

Demonstration

● **Comparing Structures**

Use electron micrographs to point out the differences between bacteria and viruses. *(Viruses have only the genetic material surrounded by a protective protein and sometimes lipid coat. A cell is more complex, having many structures inside the cell membrane.)* Emphasize that bacteria are considered life-forms but that viruses are not, for reasons that will be discussed in Chapter 2. Students may be surprised to learn that although effective against bacteria, antibiotics do not kill viruses. Ask students what they know about AZT and Acyclovir. *(AZT is a drug that inhibits HIV reproduction inside the infected cell, but the drug produces serious toxic side effects and does not cure the disease. Acyclovir is used to reduce the rate of growth of the herpes virus and its relatives, but it does not cure the disease.)*

Visual Strategy **Figure 1-2b**

● **Identifying Functions**

Ask students to suggest what role politicians play in biological research. Emphasize that most research is supported through grants given by government agencies such as the National Institutes of Health, the National Science Foundation, and the Department of Energy.

Historical Perspective: Ernest Everett Just

Ernest Everett Just, an American biologist, was one of the first individuals to challenge the generally accepted theory that the nucleus controls cell activity. He contended that the cytoplasm was important in directing the activities of the cell. Cell activity is now believed to be a result of chemical information being exchanged between the nucleus and the cytoplasm. Just held a teaching job at Howard University, earned his Ph.D. in 1916 from the University of Chicago, and carried out research at the Marine Biological Laboratories at Woods Hole, Massachusetts.

Key to Strategies

● Understanding Concepts (Tier I)
■ Applying Information (Tier II)
▲ Critical Thinking (Tier III)

The Science of Biology 7

"What can I do to help preserve the environment?"

Mathematics Connection

Population Growth

Assume that the planet's population is 6 billion and increasing annually at 1.6 percent. Have students use a calculator to estimate population for several consecutive years. Ask students how long it would take for the population to double. *(6 billion multiplied by 0.016 equals 96 million. Add 96 million to 6 billion to get the new population. This can also be done by multiplying the population by 1.016 each time. Do this calculation until students see that in 44 years the population would double.)* Ask students to imagine having twice as many people, cars, etc., in their community. Ask students what factors could affect the population growth rate *(family planning, disease, food shortage, wars, economic conditions)*.

Figure 1-3
Humans are changing the planet faster and on a greater scale than ever before in history. Scientists are seeking solutions to the environmental problems created by this rapid change.

a In 1989, the *Exxon Valdez* spilled its load of oil on the coast of Alaska. This cleanup crew is using high-pressure sprayers to help remove the oil from the beach.

Biology and the Environment

When you were born, the world contained just over 4 billion people. By the year 2000, the world's population will exceed 6 billion. The exploding human population is placing great stress on the planet by using more energy, consuming more resources, and producing more waste than ever before. One of the greatest challenges we face is finding ways to support so many people without harming the Earth. **Figure 1-3** shows examples of some of the environmental problems we face and describes some of the ways these problems are being addressed.

Biological knowledge is used to help feed a hungry world

One of the most immediate challenges facing today's world is producing enough food to feed its expanding population. Only three kinds of plants (rice, wheat, and corn) provide half of all human energy requirements worldwide. Researchers are presently working to increase the amount of food that can be obtained from a farm without requiring large amounts of fertilizers, pesticides, and expensive, energy-consuming equipment. New varieties of plants are being developed that are more resistant to disease and more tolerant of poor growing conditions. Also, scientists have used genetic engineering to add genes to existing crop plants. These genes increase the productivity of the crop plants by increasing resistance to pests, increasing growth rates, or improving nutritional quality.

Our effect on the environment is often negative

Think for a moment about the materials you use and discard in a day—plastic, paper, glass, and metal. We are beginning to exceed the Earth's capacity to absorb the waste we generate. Releasing pollutants into the atmosphere, for example, can produce acid rain that kills forests and poisons lakes. Industrial chemicals once considered harmless are destroying the ozone in the atmosphere that shields us from the sun's harmful rays. And the burning of gasoline, oil, natural

Community Connection: Managing Our Waste

Sort and bag the contents of a trash can into three categories: recyclable, compostable, and garbage. Have students compare the weight and size of each bag and estimate the amount of landfill space that could be saved if certain items were recycled or composted. Use the *Yellow Pages* to locate companies that pay cash for certain items. Contact the environmental protection agency in your state for information about waste-reduction programs, motor-oil recycling, chemical disposal, and other programs designed to help protect the environment. This information will also be helpful for Chapter 16.

c The productivity of agricultural land is threatened by the loss of topsoil. Scientists are developing crops that can be grown without tilling the soil to remove weeds, thus reducing soil erosion.

b More kinds of animals and plants live in tropical rain forests than anywhere else on Earth. Scientists like E. O. Wilson of Harvard University are trying to slow the rapid destruction of tropical rain forests.

gas, and coal releases large amounts of carbon dioxide into the atmosphere, causing the Earth's average temperature to rise because carbon dioxide traps the sun's heat.

Preserving a healthy world for your children

An old saying that is attributed to many different sources, from Native Americans to Amish farmers, states that "we do not inherit the world from our parents; we borrow it from our children." To ensure that our children have the resources they need tomorrow, we must stop wasting precious resources, such as topsoil and ground water, that are in limited supply.

Most important, we must not destroy the world's biological diversity. Unfortunately, we are doing just that, and on a very large scale. For example, the world's tropical rain forests are being destroyed at a breathtaking rate, along with much of the world's biological richness. Every second, about 3 hectares (1.3 acres) of tropical rain forest are destroyed—cut for lumber, burned to create fields for growing crops, or cleared to make pastures for grazing cattle. If this practice continues at such an alarming rate, only small patches of rain forest will remain by the middle of the twenty-first century. About half of the world's species live in tropical rain forests, and many of them will disappear as the rain forests are destroyed. Within the next 100 years, more than two-thirds of the species of organisms on Earth may become extinct—about the same percentage of species as disappeared 65 million years ago at the end of the age of the dinosaurs. Biologists and others are working to save as much as possible by creating preserves and by educating the public about the need to save some of the world's biological richness for future generations. However, if we wish to save biological diversity around the world, we all will have to take an active role.

9

Matter of Fact: Greenhouse Gases

Carbon dioxide is called a "greenhouse gas" because the molecules act like the glass of a greenhouse, trapping the radiant energy from the sun. The energy's wavelength is changed when it bounces off the surface of the Earth. The new, longer wavelength prevents the energy from passing a second time through the carbon dioxide layer. If students are not familiar with greenhouses, have them consider what happens when a car is parked in the sun with the windows closed. Take this opportunity to discuss child and pet safety in cars. There may be local news stories about children or pets who have died in cars due to the trapped heat.

Demonstration
■ **Recognizing Relationships**
Materials: photographs and products of rain forests
Display pictures and products of tropical rain forests. Some products you may be able to find are Brazil nuts; cashews; and teak, balsa, and mahogany woods. Discuss plants that yield raw materials for pharmaceuticals. Cinchonas provide the drug quinine; and curare, a muscle relaxer, comes from various woody vines that grow in tropical rain forests. Encourage students to find out why saving the rain forest is considered such a top priority by environmental groups. Have students write or call The Rainforest Action Network, 450 Sansom Street, Suite 700, San Francisco, CA 94111, 800-989-7246.

Life/Work Skills
Finding Information
▲ **Evaluating Viewpoints**

Have students obtain information about recent oil spills. *(The 1989 Exxon Valdez disaster resulted in about 11 million gallons of oil being released into Prince William Sound in Alaska, and the 1993 spill near the Shetland Islands resulted in just over twice that amount being spilled into the North Sea.)* Ask each student to arrive at some decisions concerning restrictions, guidelines, or requirements that should be imposed on the shipping industry. Discuss the viewpoints of environmentalists and shipping companies. *(Environmentalists might propose laws prohibiting supertankers from coming within a certain distance of environmentally sensitive coastal regions, while shipping companies might propose a law that would require oil companies to establish funds to clean up oil spills.)*

Key to Strategies
● **Understanding Concepts (Tier I)**
■ **Applying Information (Tier II)**
▲ **Critical Thinking (Tier III)**

The Science of Biology 9

"My uncle died of a heart attack three years ago, at age 45. Will I have heart problems too?"

Figure 1-4
Asking questions is the first step toward finding answers. A knowledge of biology will help answer many of the questions these young adults have.

"My mother had to have a skin cancer removed. Will I get cancer too?"

Biology and You

Much of the information provided in this course will help you answer important personal questions like the ones asked by the students shown in **Figure 1-4**.

Should I smoke? Biologists now know how cigarette smoking causes lung cancer. Chemicals in the smoke enter the cells of your lungs and damage them, and cancer results. Most people who die of lung cancer today are smokers. Smoking is also associated with other lung diseases and with heart disease. One out of three teenagers who take up smoking will die prematurely as a result. You will learn more about the dangers of smoking in Chapters 30 and 32.

How can I avoid developing heart disease? Biologists have learned that diet and exercise have a major influence on whether you are likely to have a heart attack or stroke. You will learn some things you can do to prevent heart disease in Chapter 32.

What are the risks in taking drugs? Most mind-altering drugs are addictive and thus very harmful. This includes the nicotine in cigarettes and the alcohol in wine, beer, and spirits. Biologists have learned much about the physical basis of drug dependency and about the far-reaching effects drugs can have. You will learn about the harmful effects of drugs in Chapter 30.

Will I get cancer? Cancer is the second leading cause of death in the United States. The good news is that scientists have learned that many cancers, including skin cancer, are related to lifestyle and diet and can thus be prevented. You will learn more about cancer in Chapters 6 and 33.

"Many of my friends smoke, and they say smoking is all right as long as you quit when you're older. Is that true?"

"I see other kids using drugs. They say they can stop whenever they want. I wonder if that's true."

SECTION REVIEW

1 Why is research in the field of genetic engineering considered so important to medicine?

2 What environmental problems are being created by the rapidly growing human population?

3 List two personal decisions that a knowledge of biology can help you make.

10

Science is a way of investigating the world. A scientist is an observer who is driven by the search for new knowledge and who uses methods that differ from those of writers or public officials. Public officials may make conclusions after thinking through a problem. However, scientists make hypotheses after observing a number of specific cases.

1-2 Science Is a Search for Knowledge

OBJECTIVES

1 **Describe the role of testing in verifying hypotheses.**

2 **Describe the importance of controls in testing hypotheses.**

3 **Compare the scientific definition of *theory* with the use of the word in everyday language.**

A Case Study in Science

Perhaps the best way to see how science works is to look at a real case in which science has been used to solve a problem and improve human health. One good example is the deadly disease malaria. **Figure 1-5** shows the global distribution of malaria. In 1941, more than 4,000 Americans died of malaria. In the year 2000, by contrast, fewer than five people are likely to die of malaria in the United States. This disease has been virtually eliminated from the United States and many other countries as a result of work begun by one man. His story is a very real example of how science works. His investigations were simple. They involved careful observation and the formulation of clear questions. Finding the cause of malaria was one of the greatest medical advances of all time.

Observations suggest questions to investigate

In the summer of 1897 an English physician, Ronald Ross, was working in a remote field hospital in Secunderabad, India. Ross set out to discover how malaria was transmitted. Of all tropical diseases, malaria was the greatest killer, taking more than a million lives a year in India alone. Doctors knew that the disease was caused by a microscopic parasite called *Plasmodium*, which could be found in the blood of malaria victims. However, no one was sure how the parasite was transmitted from one person to another. Working alone, Ross discovered how malaria is spread.

Ross observed that patients in the field hospital who did not have malaria were more likely to develop the deadly

Figure 1-5
Malaria kills more than 1 million people per year. The disease is found mainly in tropical regions in Africa, Latin America, and Asia (areas shown in red on the map).

11

Videodisc Resources

Holt Biology Videodiscs
Lesson 1-2: Science Is a Search for Knowledge

Scheduling

See the **Lesson Planning Guide** on pages 3A and 3B for lecture, classwork, and assignment options for Section 1-2.

Phase One
Preparation

Active READING

Technique: Reading Organizer
Display a series-of-events chain on the overhead projector or chalkboard. Have students read the section and fill in the graphic as they review the steps taken by Dr. Ronald Ross. Answers will vary but should include the steps taken by Dr. Ross. For more information about reading organizers, see Reading Strategies Worksheets in Holt BioSources Teaching Resources CD-ROM.

Phase Two
Teaching Strategies

Language Arts Connection
Malaria
The word *malaria* comes from the Italian words meaning "bad air." It derives from the once commonly held idea that evil spirits and the night air caused diseases. Ask students to identify other words with the prefix *mal*, meaning "bad" or "wrong" (*maladjusted*, *malice*, *malpractice*).

Key to Strategies
● Understanding Concepts (Tier I)
■ Applying Information (Tier II)
▲ Critical Thinking (Tier III)

The Science of Biology 11

Visual Strategy   Figure 1-6

● **Identifying Processes**

Use this figure to guide students through the various processes scientists use. Emphasize that a hypothesis does not have to be tested by conducting an experiment in a laboratory. To verify a hypothesis, a scientist might simply make careful observations in the field.

Testing a Claim

■ **Designing an Experiment**

Hold up a breath mint or vitamin tablet and tell students that it is a "magic pill" that will prevent the common cold. Have them describe how they would design a control experiment to test the pill's effectiveness. *(Student answers will vary but should demonstrate an understanding of scientific methods.)* Use the **Graphic Organizer** at the bottom of page 12 to help students design their experiment.

Scientific Experiments

▲ **Justifying Conclusions**

A scientist testing the effectiveness of a drug or therapeutic treatment on humans will most likely conduct an experiment in which two groups of subjects (experimental and control) do not know whether they are receiving the drug or a placebo. The scientist may even conduct a "double blind" experiment, in which the scientist is also unaware of what treatment each group is getting. Ask students to explain how such experiments enable scientists to justify their conclusions. *(If the test subjects and the scientists knew what treatment or placebo was being administered, psychological factors, such as expectations, could affect the results.)*

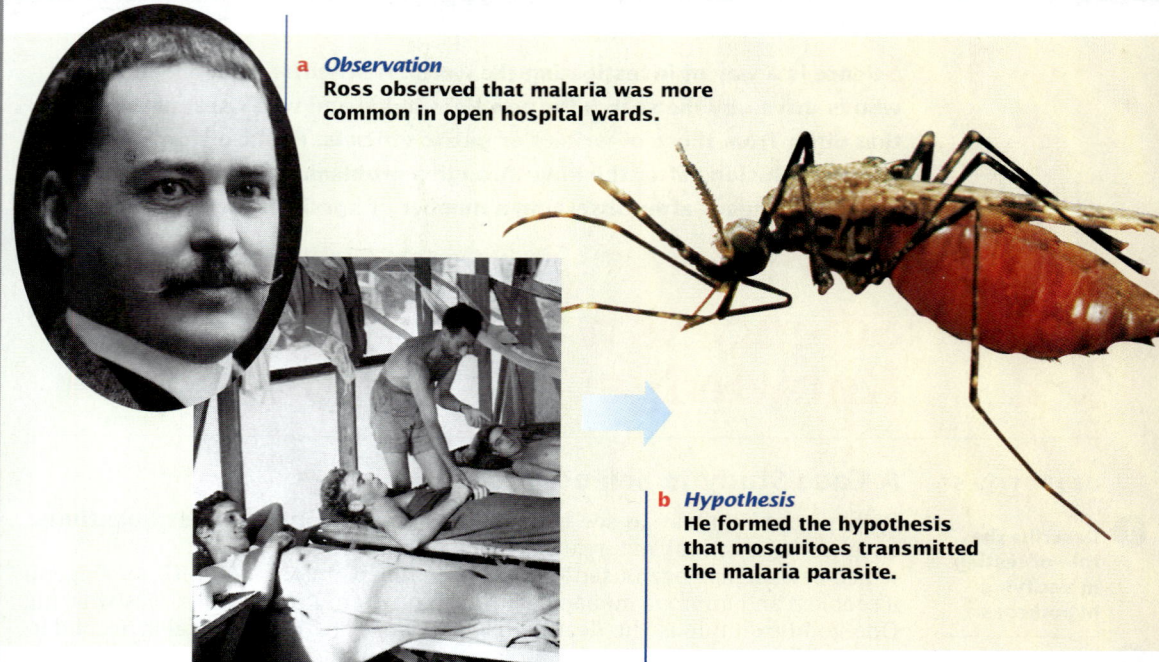

a *Observation*
Ross observed that malaria was more common in open hospital wards.

b *Hypothesis*
He formed the hypothesis that mosquitoes transmitted the malaria parasite.

Figure 1-6
Follow the steps of Ronald Ross's investigation of malaria.

disease in the open wards (those without screens or netting) than in wards with closed windows or screens. Ross wondered why people in open wards were much more likely to get malaria than those in closed wards.

Hypothesis: The basis of further investigation

Observing this pattern, Ross suggested an explanation for why people in open wards, like the one shown in **Figure 1-6a**, were more likely to get malaria. Such an explanation is called a hypothesis. A **hypothesis** is a testable explanation for an observation. Ross proposed that mosquitoes in the open wards might have spread the disease from patients with malaria to patients who did not have the disease. By observing the mosquitoes closely, Ross noted that they were the type known as *Anopheles*. Using this fact, Ross formulated a hypothesis. Ross's hypothesis was that *Anopheles* mosquitoes were spreading malaria from one patient to another.

Predictions: The framework for testing hypotheses

Ross knew that if his hypothesis were correct, he could reasonably expect several consequences. We call these expected consequences predictions. A **prediction** is what you expect to happen if a hypothesis is accurate. Ross predicted that *if* the *Anopheles* mosquitoes were spreading malaria (hypothesis), *then* mosquitoes that had bitten malaria patients and sucked up some of their blood would have picked up the *Plasmodium* parasite (prediction). Ross also predicted that parasites would be alive within the mosquito.

Testing under controlled conditions can verify predictions

The controlled test of a hypothesis is called an **experiment**. Ross carried out a type of experiment known as a control experiment. In a **control experiment**, a group that *has not been* exposed to the variable suspected of causing an effect is compared with one or more groups that *have been* exposed to the variable. The group not exposed to the variable is called a **control group** and serves as the standard for comparison. Since the suspected variable in Ross's experiment was exposure to malaria parasites from the blood of malaria victims, he compared mosquitoes that had fed on malaria patients with those that had fed on uninfected individuals.

12

Graphic Organizer

Use the following graphic organizer with the teaching strategy **Testing a Claim** on page 12.

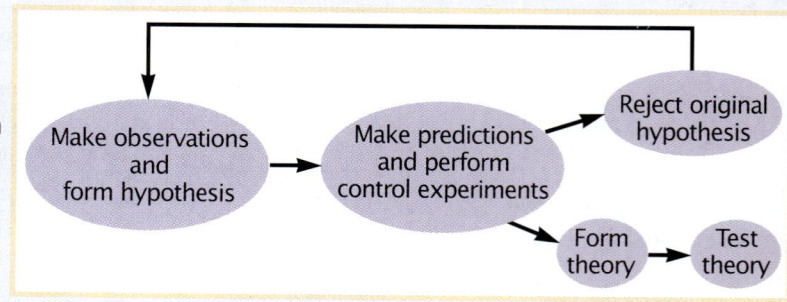

c Predictions
He predicted that only mosquitoes that had bitten malaria patients would carry the parasite, the small dark flecks visible below.

e Theory
Ross's findings were subjected to additional tests and were confirmed by other scientists.

d Control experiment
As a control experiment, Ross checked for the parasite in mosquitoes that had never bitten malaria patients.

Ross first looked for living malaria parasites in *Anopheles* mosquitoes that had fed on the blood of malaria patients. He carefully dissected each mosquito's stomach and found the live parasites. As a control group, Ross used mosquitoes that had not bitten someone with malaria. He checked to see if these mosquitoes also contained the parasites. He knew that if both groups of mosquitoes contained the parasites, then malaria patients could not possibly be the source of the parasites in the mosquitoes, and his hypothesis must be wrong. Gathering newly hatched mosquitoes that had not yet fed, he allowed them to mature and then fed them blood from people who didn't have malaria. When he examined the stomachs of these mosquitoes, he found no parasites. The control group of mosquitoes did not contain malaria parasites, confirming his hypothesis.

Theories: Explanations for observations
Ross reconfirmed and extended his hypothesis with later experiments. For instance, he suspected that the parasites must make their way from the mosquito's stomach to its salivary glands. In this way, the parasites would

be transferred with the mosquito's saliva to the next person bitten. Ross showed by careful dissection that the parasites spread through an infected mosquito's body and were indeed present in the salivary glands. Other scientists also conducted experiments that confirmed Ross's hypothesis. A collection of related hypotheses that have been tested and supported is called a theory. A **theory** is a unifying explanation for a broad range of observations. Theories can have a major effect on science when they tie many accepted hypotheses together into a unified concept. Ross's theory that malaria is transmitted from one person to another by *Anopheles* mosquitoes was an important milestone in medicine. The idea that malaria epidemics could be prevented by combating mosquitoes was first put forth in a letter written by Ross to the government of India in 1901. Before the end of that year, American army doctors had eliminated almost all malaria from Havana, Cuba—where malaria had been at an epidemic stage—by greatly reducing the mosquito population. Few advances in the history of medicine have been more dramatic.

13

Multicultural Perspective: Legends of the Bears

Legends of the Navajo, Chippewa, and Sioux Native Americans have told of bears teaching people to use herbs and roots for medicine. Scientists are now giving serious attention to these legends. Some tribes observed and described bears digging for roots and bulbs to eat. The Native Americans found that some of these roots could be used to treat certain ailments and fight infections and parasites. In some tribes, strong medicine is still called "bear medicine." Throughout the world, scientists are seeking the wisdom of indigenous peoples and observing the eating habits of animals to learn which plants hold medicinal value.

Theories
▲ Evaluating Conclusions
Theories form the foundation of biology. To a layperson, a theory seems like a "hunch." Hence the expression, "It's just a theory." But to a scientist, a theory is much more. List some examples on the board: the cell theory, the theory of evolution, the germ theory of disease, and the theory of heredity. Ask students why these are still considered theories as opposed to laws or facts. *Many hypotheses have not been thoroughly tested. Some of what we now accept may have to be discarded as new evidence comes to light.*

Life/Work Skills
Finding Information
▲ Forming an Opinion Supported by Sound Reasoning
portfolio Invite a scientist or lab assistant to speak to the class about the use of scientific methods in his or her research work. Students will find it interesting to learn that some scientific research projects take years to complete. If a guest speaker is not available, arrange telephone interviews with scientists. Students might want to obtain permission to make an audiotape of the interview. Have students write specific questions in advance, call and schedule the interview, turn in a written report, and share their results with the class. Provide students with the following list of questions to help them write their report: Are the scientists following scientific methodology? What is the cost of the research project? Who is funding the research, and why are they funding it? Who will be affected by the research outcome? What research would you like to see funded? Why is that important to you?

Key to Strategies
● Understanding Concepts (Tier I)
■ Applying Information (Tier II)
▲ Critical Thinking (Tier III)

Science Publications

■ Analyzing Methods

Show the class a science journal. Explain that some journals use reviewers, who carefully read the manuscript submitted for publication for scientific importance, appropriateness of methods, thoroughness, and accuracy. Only after repeated testing will the scientific world accept the findings. Have the class list reasons the reviewers might reject a scientist's work *(scientific methods were not followed, too few subjects in the experiment and control groups, invalid or outdated testing methods, the finding will probably not have much impact).*

Visual Strategy — Figure 1-7

▲ Determining Factual Accuracy

Have students work with reference books to discover the cartoon error. Then have students draw their own cartoon reflecting the necessary changes. *(Student cartoons should indicate that the female Anopheles mosquito carries Plasmodium.)*

Pasteur's Words

▲ Evaluating Viewpoints

In December 1854, at the inauguration of the Faculty of Science, Louis Pasteur said, "In the fields of observation, chance favors only the mind that is prepared." Ask students what he meant by that comment. *(Pasteur recognized that most people would pay little or no attention to many observations that might seem unimportant or trivial. A scientist must be cognizant of what is happening, or an opportunity for discovery may be missed.)* Have students write this quote on art paper and illustrate its meaning by drawing, painting, or making a collage from magazine pictures.

Figure 1-7
Cartoonist Gary Larson has a unique view of Ross's theory, but he has made an important biological error. Can you spot it?

Chronicle Features, 1981 Larson 8-26

"What a day! . . . I must have spread malaria across half the country."

Science requires continued verification of hypotheses

The essence of science is to reject any hypothesis not supported by observations and the results of control experiments. A new hypothesis is examined very closely to see what it predicts, and the predictions are then rigorously tested. If the predictions are not supported by the results of experiments or observations, the hypothesis is rejected. If they are confirmed, the hypothesis is subjected to further testing. One critical aspect of science is that a scientist's work is held up for review by other scientists. The validity of one's hypothesis is questioned by others until similar results are obtained from similar control experiments. This system of checking and rechecking hypotheses helps ensure that scientific reporting is factual and objective.

Hypotheses that do not explain observations are rejected

A scientist works by systematically showing that certain hypotheses are invalid, that is, that they are not consistent with the results of experiments. The results of all experiments are used to evaluate alternative hypotheses. An experiment is successful when it shows that one or more of the alternative hypotheses are inconsistent with observations. By conducting experiments, Ross was able to eliminate the hypothesis that mosquitoes *could* transmit the malaria parasite without biting malaria victims. He retained the hypothesis that if mosquitoes did bite malaria victims, then the mosquitoes could transmit the parasite. Scientific progress is often made in the same way a marble statue is made—by chipping away the unwanted bits.

Theories Have Limited Certainty

Theories are the solid foundation of science, that of which we are most certain. But in science there is no absolute certainty, no scientific "truth." The possibility always remains that future evidence will cause a theory to be revised or discarded. A scientist's acceptance of a theory is always provisional. For example, **Figure 1-8** describes how the accepted view of our solar system changed as new evidence became available.

The word *theory* is used differently by scientists than by the general public. To a scientist, a theory represents that of which he or she is most certain. To the general public, the word *theory* implies a lack of knowledge, a guess. How often have you heard someone say "It's only a theory" to imply lack of certainty? As you can imagine, confusion often results. In this text, the word *theory* will always be used in its scientific sense, as a generally accepted scientific principle.

Some theories are so strongly supported that the likelihood of their being rejected in the future is very small. Most of us would be willing to bet that the sun will rise in the east tomorrow, or that if an apple is dropped, it will fall. In physics, the theory of the atom is universally accepted, even though no one had seen an atom until recently. In biology, the theory of evolution by natural selection is so strongly supported by evidence that biologists accept it with as much certainty as physicists accept the theory of the atom. We will examine the theory of evolution in Chapter 10. This theory is very important to biologists because it provides the framework that unifies biology as a science.

14

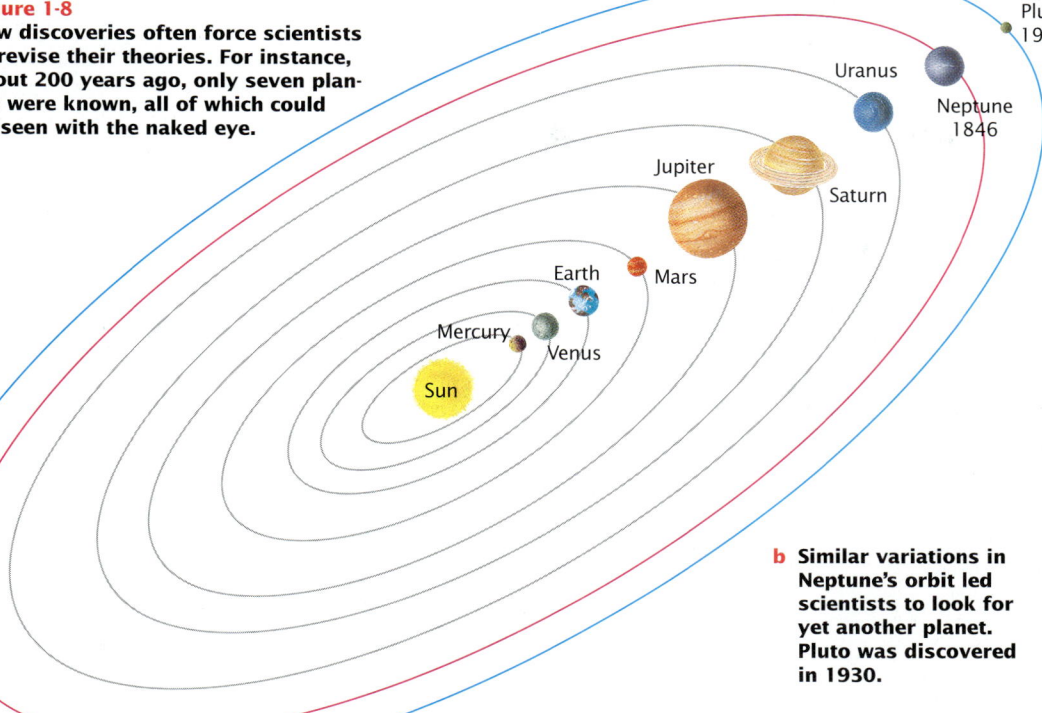

a A "wobble" in the orbit of Uranus led scientists to suspect that a planet existed beyond Uranus. That planet, discovered in 1846, was Neptune.

Figure 1-8
New discoveries often force scientists to revise their theories. For instance, about 200 years ago, only seven planets were known, all of which could be seen with the naked eye.

Pluto 1930
Uranus
Neptune 1846
Jupiter
Saturn
Earth
Mars
Mercury
Venus
Sun

b Similar variations in Neptune's orbit led scientists to look for yet another planet. Pluto was discovered in 1930.

Scientific method: the systematic study of a question or problem

It was once fashionable to claim that scientific progress was the result of applying a series of steps called "the scientific method." In this view, science is a sequence of logical "either/or" steps, each step rejecting one of two incompatible alternatives. Trial-and-error testing could inevitably lead one through a maze of uncertainty. If this view were true, a computer could be programmed to be a good scientist. But science is not done this way. If you ask successful scientists how they do their work, you will find that they design experiments with a good idea of the results they will get. Not just any hypothesis is tested—only a hunch or educated guess that is based on all the scientist knows and that allows his or her imagination full play. Because insight and imagination are so important in scientific progress, some scientists are better than others.

SECTION REVIEW

1. Under what conditions is a hypothesis supported?

2. Why was it necessary for Ross to examine the stomachs of mosquitoes that had not fed on blood from malaria patients?

3. Would Ross's hypothesis have been supported if the mosquitoes in the control group had contained malaria parasites? Explain your answer.

4. Write a sentence using *theory* in its scientific sense.

15

ANSWERS TO SECTION REVIEW

1 A hypothesis will be supported when it passes repeated testing under controlled conditions.

2 The mosquitoes that had not fed on the blood from malaria patients served as controls that gave Ross a standard for comparison.

3 No. The control-group mosquitoes had never bitten malaria patients, so people with malaria could not have been the source of the parasites in the mosquitoes.

4 The following is an example of a correct answer: I have a theory that if I study for the test, I will make a passing grade.

The Science of Biology 15

Preparation

Scheduling
See the **Lesson Planning Guide** on pages 3A and 3B for lecture, class-work, and assignment options for Section 1-3.

Phase Two
Teaching Strategies

Active READING
Technique: K-W-L
Have students choose one of the six themes presented in Section 1-3. Ask them to write short individual lists of all the things they **K**now (or think they know) about their chosen theme. When students have finished their lists, have them list things they **W**ant to know about this theme. Ask students to save their lists to find out what they **L**earned about this theme as they study biology. For more information about using the K-W-L technique, see Reading Strategies Worksheets in Holt BioSources Teaching Resources CD-ROM.

Life/Work Skills
Communicating

■ **Recognizing Patterns**
To introduce the theme of *Heredity*, ask for student volunteers to bring in photographs of family members to whom they are biologically related. Emphasize that all living things pass on instructions for development to their offspring. Have students display photographs and describe to the class any family resemblance. Before students make their presentation, remind them to stand straight with their chin up, projecting their voice to the people at the back of the room.

From the mountain of information scientists have collected about living things, general principles of particular importance have emerged. You will encounter these principles repeatedly as you explore the ideas in this text. They are the framework of biology, the skeleton that supports all you will learn.

1-3 Studying Biology

OBJECTIVES

1 List and describe the six major themes of biology.

2 Identify one way in which each theme relates to humans.

3 Relate evolution to natural selection.

Themes Unify Ideas

This text uses six unifying principles, or themes, as a framework for your study. These themes are introduced here, and you will see them repeatedly throughout the text. Your goal should be to understand how the many topics you study in biology are examples of these themes.

Theme 1: Cell Structure and Function

All organisms are composed of **cells**, tiny compartments surrounded by membranes. Your body has about 10 trillion cells. Some of these cells like the white blood cells shown in **Figure 1-9**, perform highly specialized functions. The complex chemical processes that occur within cells are much the same in all organisms, and all cells have the same basic structure. A covering called a membrane surrounds the cell and controls what information and materials enter and leave. An internal fluid and an internal framework give shape to the cell and support its other components. A central zone or a nucleus contains the cell's genes, which are coded within long complex molecules called DNA. Many cells contain specialized structures that carry out some of the cell's activities. Cellular activities are often influenced by outside molecules that attach to certain proteins in the cell's membrane. Much of a cell's biology is determined by the nature of the proteins in its membrane. You will learn much more about cellular processes in Chapters 3, 4, 5, and 6.

Figure 1-9
White blood cells recognize and destroy invading foreign cells, thus protecting the body from infection.

Theme 2: Stability and Homeostasis

Control is an essential aspect of life. All organisms must maintain a constant internal environment in order to function properly. For example, your body temperature must not vary by more than a few degrees. Your body has many mechanisms for maintaining **homeostasis**, a state of constant internal conditions. Some of these mechanisms involve circulating chemical signals called hormones; other mechanisms involve cells called neurons that carry electrical signals. Systems of neurons, called nervous systems, are capable of producing very complex behaviors, learning, and conscious thought.

16

Videodisc Resources
Holt Biology Videodiscs
Lesson 1-3: Studying Biology

Theme 3: Heredity

In organisms composed of many cells, such as humans, most of the cells are specialized, each performing distinct functions. For example, red blood cells carry oxygen, muscle cells contract, and nerve cells conduct electrical signals. All of the many different kinds of specialized cells, however, are descended from the same fertilized egg cell. As the cells grow and divide, their genes manage an orderly process of change called **development**. The process is controlled by genes and is the same in all humans.

You have probably noticed that children tend to resemble their parents. The transmission of characteristics from parents to their offspring is called **heredity**. Children resemble their parents because instructions for development are passed from parents to offspring. These instructions are in the form of genes. Sometimes "damage" to the genes occurs. These changes, called **mutations**, are usually harmful, but occasionally mutations help an organism to survive. For example, as you will learn in Chapter 10, a mutation in the gene for the blood protein hemoglobin produces resistance to malaria.

Theme 4: Evolution

Biologists have long suspected that life on Earth is the result of evolution. **Evolution** is inherited change in the characteristics of organisms over time. Living things are slowly changing and have apparently been changing since they first appeared on Earth. Charles Darwin proposed that this change is the result of **natural selection**. In natural selection, those organisms with favorable versions of genes are more likely to survive and reproduce. These favorable genes enable an organism to better meet the many challenges presented by its environment. Darwin's theory provides biology with a basis for understanding the diversity of life on Earth. The living things found on Earth today, including humans, resulted from a long history of organisms adjusting to a diverse and changing environment. A **species** is a group of organisms that look similar and can produce fertile offspring in their environment. Natural selection leads to changes in species over time.

Figure 1-11
The earliest known bird, like its modern relatives, had feathers.

World of Work

Paleontology

Show the class a fossil specimen as a way of highlighting the theme of evolution. Point out that paleontologists are scientists who study fossils. Have students investigate the role paleontologists play in our understanding of evolution. Have students use the library or on-line references to prepare a report on a fossil discovery. Ask students to include ideas on how the fossil contributes to our understanding of evolution. Students may be able to draw or photocopy a picture of the fossil to go in their report.

Interdependence

■ **Inferring Relationships**

Have students turn to page 257 and examine Figure 14-6, the illustration of a food web. Students should notice the interdependence in nature. Ask students to describe the relationship between two organisms shown in this figure. Have them predict how the removal of one organism would affect the others shown in this figure.

Demonstration

■ **Relating Concepts**

Show the class a leaf from a plant or tree. Point out that the leaf uses light energy from the sun to convert matter—carbon dioxide and water—into glucose and oxygen. Emphasize that the leaf is a highly organized structure for this process.

Key to Strategies
● **Understanding Concepts (Tier I)**
■ **Applying Information (Tier II)**
▲ **Critical Thinking (Tier III)**

Demonstration

● **Interpreting Data**

Materials: oral thermometer

To illustrate the theme of Stability and Homeostasis, ask a student to volunteer to have his or her body temperature monitored before and immediately after vigorous exercise. Human body temperature is not always 37°C (98.6°F). It fluctuates around this point. Mention that all animals must maintain their body temperature within a certain temperature range but have many different methods of doing so. The range of tolerance and method of control vary among animal groups. Ask students what cooling mechanism is being used by the volunteer during and after exercise. *(Students should observe perspiration and conclude that it helps cool the body.)*

Phase Three
Assessment Options

Closure

■ **Relating Concepts**

Place some budding *Hydra* in a small dish with *Daphnia,* and use an overhead projector to show students how the *Hydra* feed on *Daphnia.* Ask students which lesson themes are illustrated in what they observe.

SECTION REVIEW

Assign the *Section Review.*

Reteaching

Have students play a timed game in which one student tries to get his or her team to guess a particular theme of biology. The student can give clues but cannot use certain designated words. For example, if the theme is **heredity,** you might designate *heredity, genetics, traits, reproduction,* and *mutation* as words that cannot be given as clues.

Theme 5: Interdependence

Living things interact with each other and with the nonliving part of their environment in complex ways. Ecology is the study of these interactions. A biological community is a group of interacting organisms. Biological communities are highly structured. The species they contain are interdependent—they interact in ways that influence their survival. For example, owls must capture mice for food. Mice, in turn, must eat plants. Neither owls nor mice can survive without their food supply. The interdependence in biological communities is the result of a long process of evolution in which species have adjusted to each other. The complex web of interactions in a biological community is easily disrupted when the environment is polluted and individual species become extinct, as is happening in much of the world today.

Figure 1-12

All organisms interact with other organisms. For this mouse, its interaction with the owl is fatal.

Theme 6: Matter, Energy, and Organization

Living things are made of the same materials as the rest of the universe—atoms assembled into molecules. All of the physical principles that apply to stars and home computers also apply to you and to every other living creature. Living things differ from nonliving ones only in their degree of organization.

All organisms require energy to carry out life processes. Organisms use energy to grow and to carry out their activities. Without it, life soon stops. Almost all the energy that drives life on Earth is obtained from the sun. Plants capture the energy of sunlight and use it to make complex molecules in a process called photosynthesis. These molecules then serve as the source of fuel for animals that eat them. Maintaining the complexity of living organisms requires a constant input of energy. This energy flows from plants to plant-eating organisms to meat-eating organisms. The availability of energy is a major factor in limiting the size and complexity of biological communities.

SECTION REVIEW

1 Write a brief summary of the six themes presented in this section.

2 List one way you depend on other organisms.

3 How is your body temperature related to the theme of *Stability and Homeostasis*?

4 Give a brief definition of evolution.

ANSWERS TO
SECTION REVIEW

1 All organisms are composed of cells, small compartments surrounded by membranes. Heredity is the transmission of characteristics from parents to offspring. Organisms evolve, or change. All organisms are interdependent; they depend on other organisms. All organisms are organized to obtain the energy they need for their life processes. All organisms can maintain a constant internal environment.

2 Answers will vary but should indicate an understanding of the interdependency of living things.

3 The human body has several mechanisms (for example, sweating and shivering) to maintain a constant internal temperature, within limits, regardless of changes in the environment.

4 Evolution is the change in the genetic makeup of a species over a long period of time.

Highlights

Life is plentiful in this rain forest. A single tree may contain hundreds of species of insects.

	Key Terms	Summary
1-1 **Biology Today** Pollution is one of the many human-caused environmental problems we face today. 	science (p. 5) biology (p. 5) gene (p. 7)	• Biologists are combating infectious diseases. Some diseases have been conquered, but AIDS and malaria remain major killers. • Genetic disorders such as cystic fibrosis may be cured through the the transfer of normally functioning genes to affected individuals. • Humans are rapidly changing the environment, and the growing human population is straining the Earth's ability to support it.
1-2 **Science Is a Search for Knowledge**  Using scientific methods, Ronald Ross discovered that mosquitoes transmit the disease malaria.	hypothesis (p. 12) prediction (p. 12) experiment (p. 12) control experiment (p. 12) control group (p. 12) theory (p. 13)	• Scientific progress is made by posing hypotheses and testing their predictions. Verification of hypotheses is required before they are widely accepted. • Control experiments are important in testing hypotheses. Control groups are used for comparison with experimental groups. • A theory links well-supported hypotheses together in one concept. • All scientific theories can be overturned by new evidence.
1-3 **Studying Biology** All life is the product of evolution. 	cell (p. 16) homeostasis (p. 16) development (p. 17) heredity (p. 17) mutation (p. 17) evolution (p. 17) natural selection (p. 17) species (p. 17)	• All organisms are made of cells. • Offspring tend to resemble their parents because genetic information is passed from parents to offspring. • Charles Darwin proposed that living things evolve, or change, through the process of natural selection. • Organisms interact with and depend on other living things. • All living things are composed of atoms and require energy. • Organisms maintain stable internal conditions.

Alternative Assessment

Use a piece of cardboard to construct a maze within a shoe box. Place a marble inside the box, and seal the box. Have students use the scientific method to deduce the structure of the maze. Have them draw their hypothesis on paper, test their hypothesis, and make changes to their drawing until they are fairly certain they have it exactly like the cardboard maze.

Portfolio Assessment

Portfolio Assessment on page T39 provides options for building and evaluating student portfolios. Students and teachers can select items from the areas listed on page T39 for inclusion in a portfolio.

19

ANSWER TO CONCEPT MAP

The following is one possible answer to the Relating Concepts exercise on page 20.

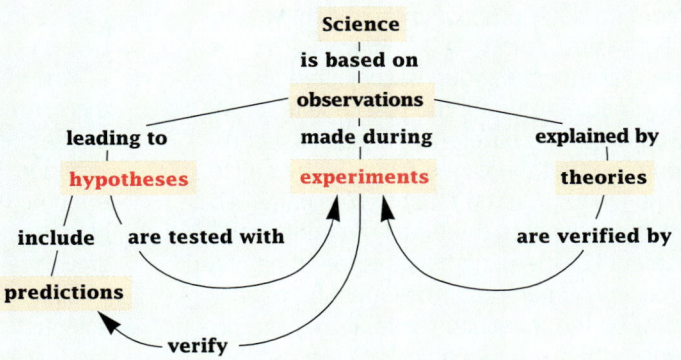

review

ANSWERS

Understanding Vocabulary

1. a. A hypothesis is a testable explanation for an observation. A prediction is what you expect to happen if a hypothesis is accurate. An experiment is the controlled test of a hypothesis.
b. Development is an orderly process of change that is controlled by genes. Heredity is the transmission of characteristics from parents to offspring. Mutations are changes that occur in genes.
c. Evolution is inherited change in the characteristics of organisms. Natural selection occurs when organisms with certain inherited traits survive and reproduce because they are better able to meet the challenges presented by the environment. A group of similar organisms that can produce fertile offspring make up a species.

2. a. Science is a way of investigating the world to form general rules about what causes things to happen. Biology is the science of life.
b. Genes are the "operating instructions" for the organism. Heredity is the transmission of genes from parents to offspring.
c. Malaria is an infectious disease caused by the parasite *Plasmodium*. AIDS is an infectious disease caused by HIV.

Understanding Concepts

3. Answer to concept map is shown on page 19.
4. Cystic fibrosis and muscular dystrophy are two genetic disorders. Scientists hope to cure these disorders by replacing the defective genes with normal genes.
5. The burning of coal, oil, and natural gas is adding large amounts of carbon dioxide to the atmosphere. As a result, global temperatures are rising.
6. By knowing the risks of certain behaviors, people can make

---

review

Understanding Vocabulary

1. Using each set of words below, write one or more sentences summarizing information learned in this chapter.
   a. hypothesis, prediction, experiment
   b. development, heredity, mutation
   c. evolution, natural selection, species

2. For each pair of terms, explain the differences in their meanings.
   a. science, biology
   b. gene, heredity
   c. malaria, AIDS

Understanding Concepts

3. **Relating Concepts** Copy the unfinished concept map below onto a sheet of paper. Then complete the concept map by writing the correct word or phrase in each oval containing a question mark.

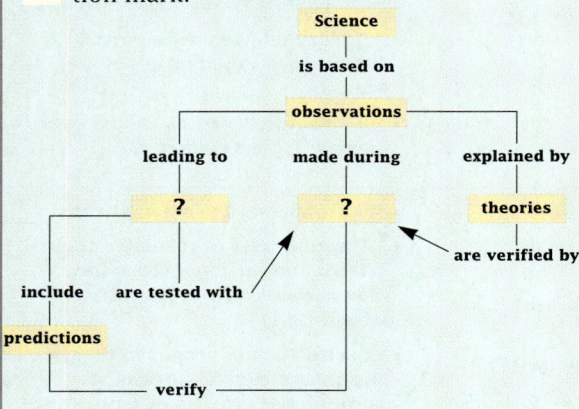

4. **Summarizing Information** Name two genetic disorders. What causes these disorders? Explain the new approach to curing genetic disorders that scientists are developing.

5. **Recognizing Relationships** How is the burning of coal, oil, and natural gas changing the atmosphere?

6. **Recognizing Relationships** Explain why knowledge of the relationships between cigarette smoking and lung cancer and between diet and heart disease are important.

7. **Analyzing Methods** Explain why it is important that the experimental group and the control group differ in only one way in an experiment.

8. **Analyzing Methods** After his initial series of experiments, Ross went on to show that the *Plasmodium* parasites move from the stomach of the mosquito to her salivary glands. Why was it necessary for Ross to make this demonstration?

9. **Analyzing Data** A scientist conducted an experiment to test which kind of fertilizer was the most effective. The graph below shows the data from the experiment. Plants in Group A and Group B received different kinds of fertilizer. Answer the following questions about the graph.

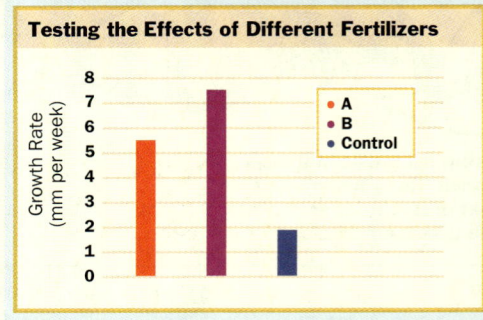

Testing the Effects of Different Fertilizers

a. Are both kinds of fertilizer effective? Explain your answer.
b. Which kind of fertilizer should the control group receive? Explain your answer.
c. Suppose that the plants in the Group B had been grown in full sunlight while the plants in the control group and in Group A had been grown partially in the shade. How would this influence the interpretation of the results?

10. **Identifying Concepts** Explain why a scientist is unlikely to say, "It's only a theory," when referring to a scientific principle.

11. **Summarizing Information** What is homeostasis? Give an example of homeostasis in your body.

---

informed decisions about their lifestyle and their health.

7. The experimental group is subjected to a single variable so that if the test results for the two groups are different, the scientist can conclude that the varied factor is the cause.

8. A mosquito picks up *Plasmodium* parasites when she ingests the blood of an infected person. For these parasites to be transmitted to a new human host, they must be passed on when the mosquito feeds. If they are present in the mosquito's salivary glands, they

can be injected into the wound when she bites.

9. a. Yes, both resulted in faster growth than in the control group.
b. The control group should not receive any fertilizer. The effectiveness of the two fertilizers can then be judged by comparing the growth rates in Groups A and B with the growth rate in the control group.
c. Since more than one variable exists, the scientist cannot make a determination about the fertilizers.

Interpreting Graphics

12. Look at the photograph below of a scientist at work. Based on your examination of the photo, write a hypothesis about what you think the scientist could be investigating. Then write a prediction about what you would expect to occur if the hypothesis is true.

Design an experiment to test the hypothesis you wrote above.

Reviewing Themes

13. *Interdependence*
You could not survive without other species. Identify at least two ways in which you depend on other species. Also identify two ways in which you affect other species.

14. *Stability and Homeostasis*
How do sweating, heavy breathing, and thirst after strenuous exercise help maintain homeostasis?

Thinking Critically

15. **Determining Factual Accuracy** The following is an argument for reducing the amount of money the government spends on medical research: "In 1900, three diseases—influenza, tuberculosis, and pneumonia—were the leading causes of death in the United States. Advances in medicine have completely eliminated these diseases from the United States and the rest of the world. Now the leading cause of death for Americans is accidents. Since accidents are preventible, our country can reduce the amount of money we spend on medical research." Identify two factual errors in this argument.

Life/Work Skills

16. **Working Cooperatively** Work in a group to set up a recycling project in your school. Find out ways to recycle materials such as paper, cardboard, aluminum cans, and plastic. Also design a program to reuse items such as books, containers from the cafeteria, packaging materials, and so forth. Explore methods of selling the recycled goods that you cannot use, and find out the processes that those goods go through to emerge as "new" materials.

17. **Communicating** Investigate one of the different fields of biology, such as botany, cell biology, evolutionary biology, microbiology, parasitology, ornithology, zoology, forestry, biochemistry, or bacteriology. Write a report about a scientist who works in one of these fields. What does he or she do? What kind of education does he or she have? Where does the scientist work? What salary ranges can be expected for careers in this field?

Activities and Projects

18. **History Connection** Edward Jenner conducted a daring experiment that led to the eradication of smallpox in the world. What was his hypothesis? What led him to formulate this hypothesis?

19. **Career Connection** Many careers rely on some biological knowledge. Interview people in the following professions and find out what they know about biology and why this knowledge is important to their job: greenhouse or nursery operator, high school athletic coach, swimming pool manager, school nurse, and wildlife illustrator or photographer.

Discovering Through Reading

20. Read the article "On the Brink: Hawaii's Vanishing Species" by Elizabeth Royte in *National Geographic*, September 1995, pages 2–37. Why has Hawaii become the endangered species capital of the United States?

environment. Plants make glucose with carbon dioxide we exhale.

14. After strenuous exercise, the body removes excess heat by sweating and acquires more oxygen by breathing heavily. Thirst then reminds the individual to replenish lost fluids.

Thinking Critically

15. The two errors are: These diseases have not been eliminated, and heart disease, not accidents, is the leading cause of death in the United States.

Life/Work Skill

16. Students should set up a recycling center that is sanitary, easy to maintain, and convenient to use. A used-book drop might be created for a local charitable organization. An art class might be recruited to use discarded items for an art project promoting reuse and recycling.

17. Reports will vary depending on the field chosen but should demonstrate neatness, organization, and attention to detail.

Activities and Projects

18. Jenner hypothesized that introducing material from a cowpox scab into a scratch would prevent the person from contracting smallpox. Jenner's treatment of milkmaids who had had cowpox led him to recognize that the milkmaids did not get smallpox.

19. Answers will vary but should reflect that knowledge of biology is helpful in many careers.

Discovering Through Reading

20. Students' answers should include the ecological damage of nonindigenous pigs, goats, rats, and mongooses, and the crowding out of native plant species by non-native plant species.

21

10. To a scientist, a theory is an explanation that is supported by large amounts of data. "Only a theory" implies uncertainty.

11. Homeostasis is a state of constant internal conditions. Body temperature cannot vary by more than a few degrees without causing serious damage or even death.

Interpreting Graphics

12. Answers will vary, but a possible hypothesis is that the fish are dying from toxic chemicals in the river. From the hypothesis, the scientist might predict that toxic chemicals will be found in tissue samples from the dead fish. Testing the hypothesis might involve comparing the chemical analysis of the dead fish with that of a healthy fish.

Reviewing Themes

13. Student answers will vary. We depend on other organisms for air, food, beverages, leather, cotton, wood, etc. We affect other organisms in many ways when we change the

2 | Discovering Life

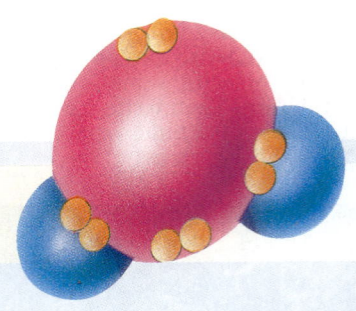

Lesson Planning Guide With Options for Block Scheduling

Lecture Concepts	Lesson Resources

2-1 What Is Life?

BLOCK ❶ (45 minutes)

1. To be considered living, something must reproduce, use energy, be composed of one or more cells, contain genetic information, and maintain a stable internal condition.

❶ Lecture Resources
- Determining Prior Knowledge
- Active Reading: L.I.N.K.
- Demonstration: Analyzing Methods
- Holt Biology Videodiscs Lesson 2-1

Classwork Options
- Quick Labs: Lab A2

Assignment Options
- Teaching Resources CD-ROM: Problem-Solving Worksheets 10

BLOCK ❷ (45 minutes)

2. Living things use energy in a process called metabolism.

3. Maintenance of a stable internal condition is called homeostasis.

❷ Lecture Resources
- Active Reading: Paired Reading
- Holt Biology Videodiscs Lesson 2–1

Classwork Options
- Closure: Applying Concepts
- Life/Work Skills: Selecting Technology

Assignment Options
- Reteaching
- Section Review
- Chapter Review, questions 1a, 4, 5, 6, 15, 19
- Directed Reading Worksheet

2-2 Basic Chemistry

BLOCK ❸ (45 minutes)

1. An atom consists of a core called a nucleus, which is surrounded by electrons.

2. The nucleus contains two kinds of particles: protons and neutrons.

3. Atoms combine with one another by forming bonds.

❸ Lecture Resources
- Visual Strategy: Figure 2-4
- Visual Strategy: Videodisc
- Teaching Transparencies: 2, 3, 4
- Holt Biology Videodiscs Lesson 2-2

Classwork Options
- Quick Labs: Lab A33

Assignment Options
- Teaching Resources CD-ROM: Supplemental Reading Guides 5

BLOCK ❹ (45 minutes)

4. An ionic bond forms when one atom loses one or more electrons and another atom gains one or more electrons.

5. A covalent bond forms when two atoms share electrons.

6. Both ionic and covalent bonds stabilize atoms in forming compounds.

❹ Lecture Resources
- Ionic vs. Molecular Compounds
- Visual Strategy: Videodisc
- Demonstration: Comparing Properties
- Teaching Transparencies: 1A, 2A, 3A
- Holt Biology Videodiscs Lesson 2-2

Classwork Options
- Closure: Recognizing Relationships

- Teaching Resources CD-ROM: Occupational Applications Worksheets 4

Assignment Options
- *Small Group* Reteaching
- Section Review
- Chapter Review, questions 1b, 2, 7, 8, 11, 14, 16, 23
- Directed Reading Worksheet

2-3 Molecules of Life

BLOCK ❺ (45 minutes)

1. Organic compounds contain carbon-carbon bonds.

2. Large covalent compounds are known as macromolecules.

3. Lipids are compounds that store energy.

❺ Lecture Resources
- Visual Strategy: Figure 2-9
- Visual Strategy: Videodisc
- Demonstration: Predicting Outcomes
- Holt Biology Videodiscs Lesson 2-3

Classwork Options
- Quick Labs: Lab A5

Assignment Options
- Macromolecules
- Teaching Resources CD-ROM: Reading Strategies Worksheets 10

Lecture Concepts

Lesson Resources

2-3 Molecules of Life, *continued*

BLOCK ⑥ (45 minutes)

4. Proteins are organic compounds that provide structure and serve as enzymes.

5. Nucleic acids are the organic compounds that contain the genetic information.

⑥ Lecture Resources
- ■ Visual Strategy: Figure 2-10a, 2-10b
- ■ Visual Strategy: Videodisc
- ■ Demonstration: Forming a Model
- ■ Demonstration: Identifying Structures
- ⊘ Holt Biology Videodiscs Lesson 2-3

Classwork Options
- ■ Reteaching
- ■ Closure: Relating Concepts

Assignment Options
- ■ Section Review
- ■ Chapter Review, questions 1c, 9, 10, 12, 13, 17, 18, 20, 21, 22, 24
- ■ Directed Reading Worksheet

Chapter Review and Assessment

BLOCK ⑦ (45 minutes)

Review
- ■ Reteaching Worksheet
- ■ Thinking Skills Worksheet
- ■ Vocabulary Development Worksheet
- ⊙ Language Development and Reading Comprehension Audio CD Program: Chapter 2

BLOCK ⑧ (45 minutes)

Assessment
- ■ Alternative Assessment, p. 35
- ■ Portfolio Assessment, p. T39

Chapter Test
- ■ Chapter 2 Test

Test Generator
- ⊙ Item bank for customizing Chapter Tests

Teaching Resources CD-ROM
- ⊙ Scoring Rubrics and Classroom Management Checklist

The Portfolio icon denotes items throughout the Teacher's Edition lesson wrap that may be selected for inclusion in student portfolios.

Holt Biology Videodiscs and *Concepts of Biology*

Holt Biology Videodiscs gives you a powerful tool for teaching, review, and assessment. For further information regarding the media on the videodiscs, see *Holt Biology Videodiscs Teacher's Correlation Guide to Holt Biology: Visualizing Life.*

Concepts of Biology adds interactive lesson plans and extensive tools for customization using CD-ROM technology.

Use the following topic from *Concepts of Biology* to help you teach this chapter:
Topic 3: The Chemistry of Life

Laboratory Planning

Holt BioSources Laboratory Program

Block 1: Quick Labs Lab A2: Comparing Living and Nonliving Things
Block 3: Quick Labs Lab A33: Reading Labels: Nutritional Information
Block 5: Quick Labs Lab A5: Interpreting Labels: Stored Food Energy

Determining Prior Knowledge

- Ask students what criteria they would use to distinguish between living and nonliving things.
- Have each student draw an atom and label its parts.
- Have students describe how any two atoms they have drawn might combine.
- Draw the structural formula for water. Ask students what information this structural formula provides.
- Prepare a table on the chalkboard with four headings: carbohydrates, lipids, proteins, and nucleic acids. Ask students to go to the board and write what they know about each kind of macromolecule under the appropriate heading.

Active READING

Technique: L.I.N.K.

Write the word *Life* on the chalkboard, and have students **L**ist on their own paper all the words, phrases, and ideas that they associate with the word *life*. After several minutes, ask the students to share one or two of their ideas as you record them. Facilitate a discussion in which students **I**nquire of each other or the teacher to clarify each of the ideas listed. After all discussion is completed, have students make **N**otes on paper of all they remember. Allow about one minute. Have them look over their notes to see what they **K**now about "life" based on experience and discussion.

REVIEW
- biological themes (Section 1-3)
- the term *cell* (Glossary)

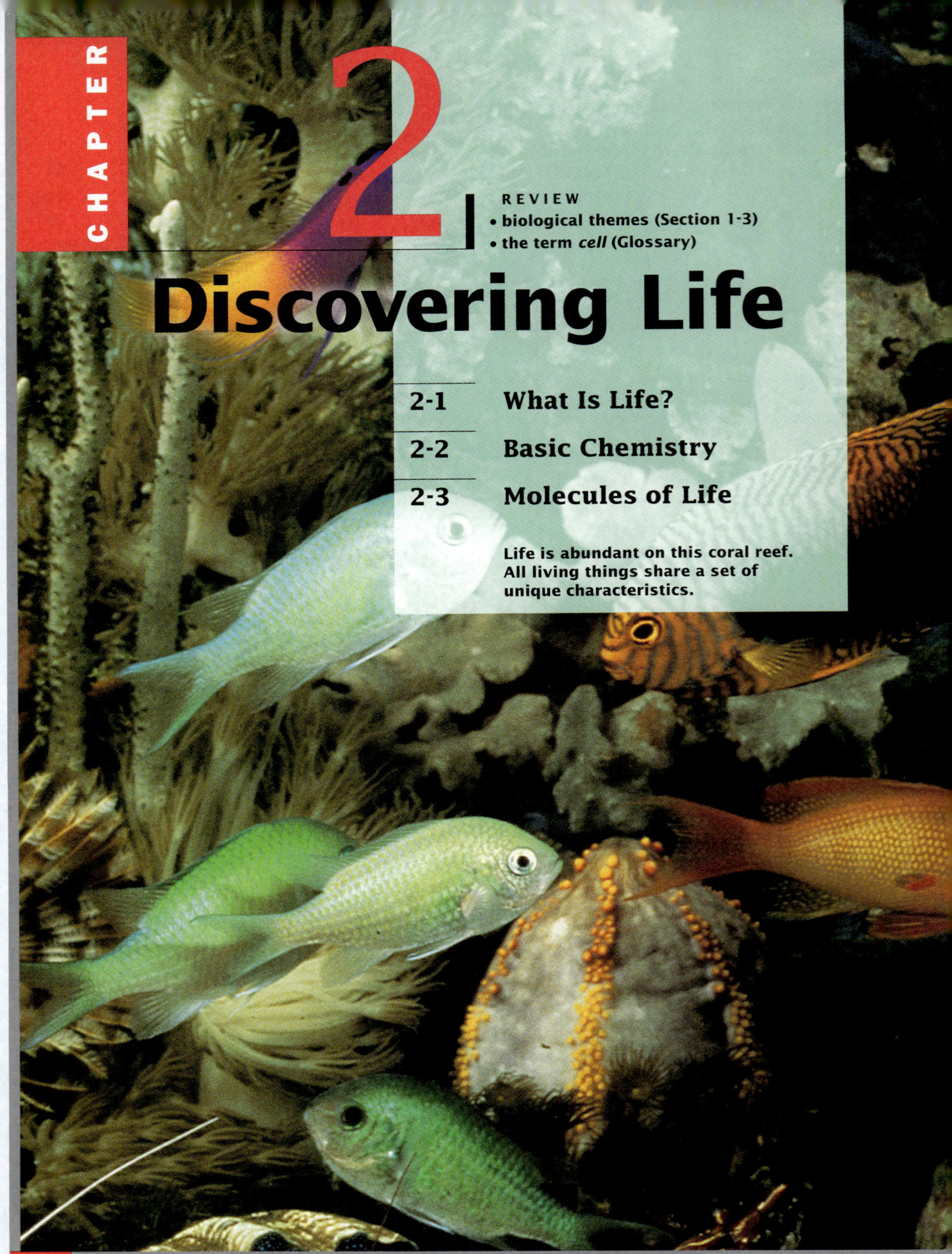

Discovering Life

2-1	**What Is Life?**
2-2	**Basic Chemistry**
2-3	**Molecules of Life**

Life is abundant on this coral reef. All living things share a set of unique characteristics.

22

Author's Rationale The chapter is devoted to defining what we mean by the term *alive*. After looking at the limitations of characteristics commonly thought of as defining life, the student is introduced to the importance of heredity as the key criterion. Since most life-defining characteristics are determined at the molecular level, some basic chemistry is introduced here. This information provides the framework needed to understand cellular processes in Chapters 3–5.

Biology is the study of life. But how can you tell living things from nonliving things? For instance, imagine that you are walking in the woods and you unexpectedly encounter a blob, like the one shown below, lying still on the forest floor. Is the blob alive? How would you decide? Make a list of the things you might do to determine whether the blob is alive.

2-1

What Is Life?

OBJECTIVES

1 **Explain the difficulty in defining life using only visually observable properties.**

2 **Describe five properties shared by all living organisms.**

3 **Relate the properties of life to the biological themes presented in Chapter 1.**

First Guesses at Defining Life

In making your list about the blob shown in **Figure 2-1**, the first thing you would probably look for would be movement.

Movement Almost all animals move around. Squirrels dash along tree branches, sharks knife through the water, and humans ride bicycles and run. However, movement from one place to another is not in itself a sure sign of life. A tree does not move about, for example, but it is alive. A cloud does move about, but it is not alive. Even if you could see the blob move on the ground in front of you, that would not be enough to tell you that the blob is alive.

Sensitivity So what should you do next? One thing you might do is poke the blob to see whether it responds. If you did that, you would be checking its **sensitivity**, its ability to respond to a stimulus (being poked).

Almost all organisms respond to stimuli. Deer flee from sounds that they associate with danger, and plants grow toward light. Air movement, sound, light, and temperature are all stimuli. But not every stimulus produces a visible response. Can you imagine getting a response from kicking a redwood tree? If the blob just sits there after you poke it, and the tree doesn't move after you kick it, that doesn't mean they are not alive. Sensitivity, while a better criterion than movement, is still not a good single characteristic to define life.

Figure 2-1
If you found this blob on the ground, would you think it was alive? How would you be able to tell? What are the characteristics of living things?

23

Phase One
Preparation

Scheduling
See the **Lesson Planning Guide** on pages 21A and 21B for lecture, classwork, and assignment options for Section 2-1.

Phase Two
Teaching Strategies

Active READING
Technique: Paired Reading
Give the students self-stick notes, and have them mark areas of difficulty as they read Section 2-1 silently. Have students use a question mark to signify an area that is unclear and a check mark to indicate understanding. Remind students to study the captions, charts, diagrams, and illustrations as they read. After completing the section, have students work with a partner to discuss what they did or did not understand. Their discussion should lead them to a better understanding of the text. Have students write their remaining questions on the board for a class discussion.

Key to Strategies
Teaching Strategies are keyed to three tiers of learning.

● **Understanding Concepts (Tier I)**
Content mastery and comprehension

■ **Applying Information (Tier II)**
Applying and analyzing content

▲ **Critical Thinking (Tier III)**
Practicing evaluative thinking

Discovering Life 23

Development The next thing you might do is watch the blob to see if it changes. You would be looking for some signs of development. Development is an orderly progression that leads to greater specialization.

Most organisms exhibit development. For instance, development is the process by which an acorn grows into an oak tree. You too are a product of the processes of development. You started life as a single cell too small to see. As you developed within your mother, some of your cells specialized to become nerve, muscle, and skin cells. But not all living things change markedly as they develop. Bacteria

Figure 2-2
If you watched the blob for some time, you might see it change shape.

simply grow and reproduce by splitting in half. Nor should all things that undergo orderly, progressive change be considered alive. The lines you see in rocks reflect the progressive, orderly laying down of material over a period of time, but the rock was never alive. The blob may or may not change as you watch it, but either way you cannot be sure if it is alive.

Complexity At this point you might walk up to the blob, pick it up, and examine it more closely to see how complex it is.

All living things are complex. Even the simplest bacterium contains many intricate structures. Complex organization is essential to life. However, complexity is not solely a characteristic of life. A computer is also complex, and so is a television, but they are not alive. So even though complexity is a necessary condition of life, the fact that the blob may seem complex when you examine it does not tell you that the blob is alive.

Death It might occur to you that the blob is the remains of a creature that was once alive but is now dead.

All living things die, but inanimate objects do not. Death is not the same thing as ceasing to function. A car that breaks down does not die. You may say, "The car died," but the now-broken car was never alive. Death is simply the termination of life. Unless one can detect life, death is a meaningless concept.

Life Has Five Characteristic Properties

You can now see that it is not so easy to determine whether something is alive. If you are going to determine whether the blob shown in **Figure 2-2** is alive, you will have to learn a great deal more about it. You will need to examine it more carefully to see how the blob resembles living things. All known organisms share certain general properties. These characteristics have been passed down from the very first organisms that evolved on Earth. It is by these properties that we recognize other living things—these properties define what we mean by *life*. If the blob displays these properties, it is alive.

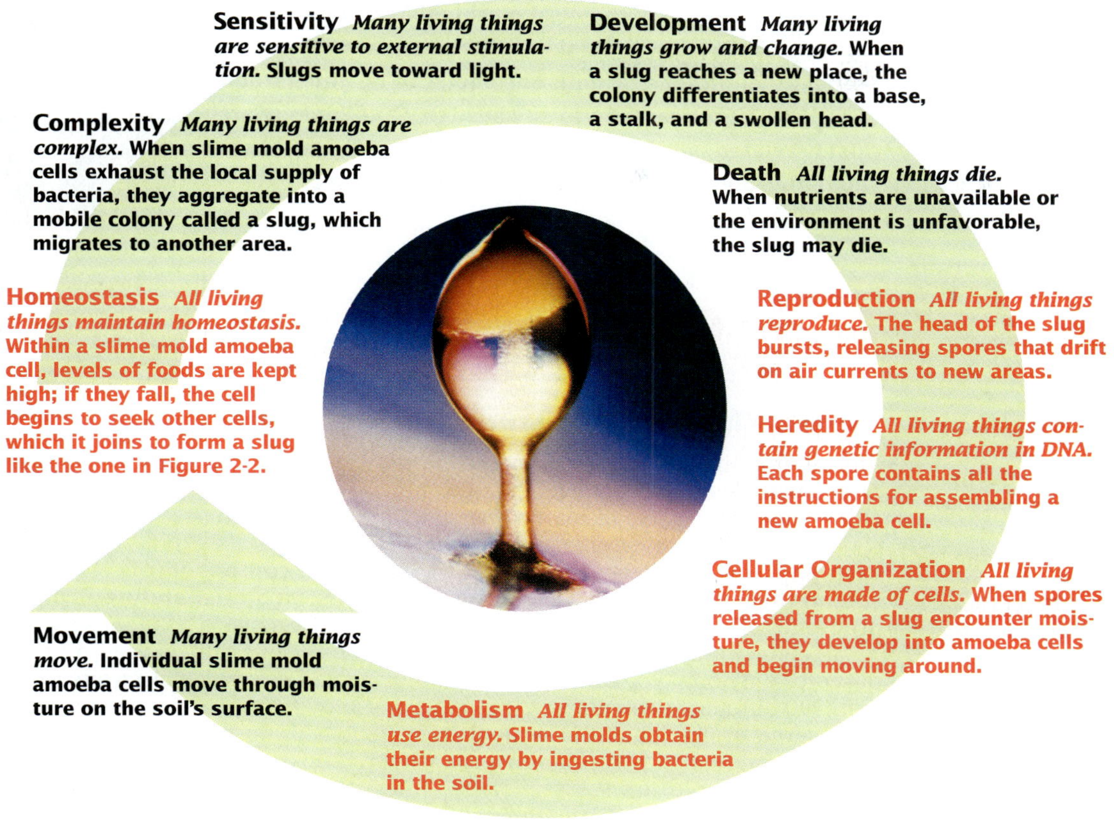

Sensitivity *Many living things are sensitive to external stimulation.* Slugs move toward light.

Complexity *Many living things are complex.* When slime mold amoeba cells exhaust the local supply of bacteria, they aggregate into a mobile colony called a slug, which migrates to another area.

Development *Many living things grow and change.* When a slug reaches a new place, the colony differentiates into a base, a stalk, and a swollen head.

Death *All living things die.* When nutrients are unavailable or the environment is unfavorable, the slug may die.

Homeostasis *All living things maintain homeostasis.* Within a slime mold amoeba cell, levels of foods are kept high; if they fall, the cell begins to seek other cells, which it joins to form a slug like the one in Figure 2-2.

Reproduction *All living things reproduce.* The head of the slug bursts, releasing spores that drift on air currents to new areas.

Heredity *All living things contain genetic information in DNA.* Each spore contains all the instructions for assembling a new amoeba cell.

Cellular Organization *All living things are made of cells.* When spores released from a slug encounter moisture, they develop into amoeba cells and begin moving around.

Movement *Many living things move.* Individual slime mold amoeba cells move through moisture on the soil's surface.

Metabolism *All living things use energy.* Slime molds obtain their energy by ingesting bacteria in the soil.

Figure 2-3
To be classified as a living thing, the blob must show the five characteristics listed in red type. The blob meets all the requirements for life. The figure also shows a summary of the first guesses about the blob in black type.

All living things are characterized by cellular organization, metabolism, reproduction, homeostasis, and heredity. Look at **Figure 2-3**. It shows how these characteristics apply to the blob, which is a living organism called a cellular slime mold. Living things use energy to grow and move in a process called *metabolism*. All living things must also maintain relatively stable internal conditions through a process called *homeostasis*. All living things contain genetic information. Through *reproduction*, organisms produce new organisms that are genetically similar, or sometimes identical,

to themselves. The transmission of genetic information from parent to offspring is called *heredity*.

The blob is alive because it has all five of these characteristics. These five properties define the core of your study of biology. Notice that the characteristics are closely related to the biological themes presented in Chapter 1. For example, the theme Stability and Homeostasis is related to the characteristic of homeostasis because homeostasis is defined as the stability of internal conditions. Keep these relationships in mind as you study biology.

SECTION REVIEW

① Why is it insufficient to use movement as a characteristic to define life?

② What are five properties that define life?

③ How is the slime mold dependent on other organisms in its surroundings?

④ Explain why a computer is not alive.

ANSWERS TO SECTION REVIEW

① Movement from place to place is not itself a sure sign of life. Some living things, such as plants, do not move, while some nonliving things, such as water and clouds, do move.

② All living things are characterized by cellular organization, metabolism, reproduction, homeostasis, and heredity.

③ The slime mold obtains energy by ingesting bacteria present in the soil.

④ A computer does not reproduce, contain genetic information, maintain homeostasis, or contain cells. The only characteristic it shares with living things is its complexity and use of energy.

Connection: *Chapter 1*

Characteristics of Life
Review the five characteristics shared by all living things as summarized in this figure. Have students discuss the relationship between these characteristics and the major themes presented in Chapter 1, pages 13–15. Obtain a course selection guide from a university. Have students relate some biology course titles to the themes of biology.

Phase Three
Assessment Options

Closure

■ **Applying Concepts**
Point out that viruses have only one characteristic of life—heredity. Show the class a picture of a virus, and describe its structure and how it reproduces. Ask students to consider the other characteristics of life and why they do not apply to the virus. *(It is not composed of a cell, cannot maintain homeostasis, and cannot reproduce by itself but must infect a host cell.)*

SECTION REVIEW
Assign the *Section Review*.

Reteaching

People have long wondered if life exists elsewhere in the universe. Tell students that they have been assigned the task of determining whether a specimen brought back by a space probe is living. Have each student write an experimental procedure to determine if the specimen is alive. Challenge students to read a science-fiction book and imagine their procedure being used on a nonhuman fictional character.

Key to Strategies
● Understanding Concepts (Tier I)
■ Applying Information (Tier II)
▲ Critical Thinking (Tier III)

Discovering Life   25

The human body is a chemical machine. Everything humans do, from the smashing stroke of a tennis player to the deepest thought of a scientist or poet, can be understood as a chemical process. Because chemistry and biology are closely related, a brief introduction to chemistry will help you better understand how living organisms function.

Phase One
Preparation

Scheduling
See the **Lesson Planning Guide** on pages 21A and 21B for lecture, classwork, and assignment options for Section 2-2.

Phase Two
Teaching Strategies

| Visual Strategy | Figure 2-4 |

● **Identifying Structures**
Have students locate the protons, neutrons, and electrons in this figure. Emphasize that electrons do not have distinct orbits like those of the planets circling the sun. Rather, electrons are found in a mathematically defined region of probability called an *electron cloud*.

| Visual Strategy | Videodisc |

■ **Recognizing Relationships**
To review the basic structure of an atom, use *Diagram—Atomic Structure 2: Unlabeled* in Chapter 2 Section 2-2 of *Holt Biology Videodiscs Teacher's Correlation Guide to Holt Biology: Visualizing Life.* Tell students that this is a model of a neon atom. Have students identify the nucleus *(B)*, electrons *(A)*, and energy levels *(C)*. Ask them to count the number of electrons in the atom *(10)*. Ask, based on this number, how many protons would be in the nucleus and why *(10, because the number of protons is equal to the number of electrons)*.

2-2

Basic Chemistry

OBJECTIVES

1 Describe the structure of an atom.

2 Identify the differences between atoms, elements, ions, and molecules.

3 Distinguish between covalent and ionic bonds, and explain how both form.

Atoms: The Basic Structural Units of Matter

All matter in the universe is composed of tiny particles called atoms. An **atom** is the smallest particle of matter that retains its chemical properties. For example, the smallest particle of carbon that still has all the chemical properties of carbon is a carbon atom.

An **element** is a substance composed of only one type of atom. More than 100 different elements have been discovered. Each element is symbolized by a one- or two-letter abbreviation. For example, iron's symbol is Fe, uranium's is U, and calcium's is Ca. Only 11 elements are common in living things. Over 99 percent of the atoms in your body are either nitrogen, N, oxygen, O, carbon, C, or hydrogen, H.

Atoms are composed of electrons, protons, and neutrons
An atom consists of a dense core called a nucleus surrounded by tiny moving particles called **electrons**. Electrons move about the nucleus. The nucleus contains two kinds of particles, protons and neutrons. Most of the interior of an atom is empty space. If the nucleus of an atom were the size of an apple, the nearest electron could be more than a mile away. **Figure 2-4** shows a highly simplified model of the structure of an atom.

Each proton in the nucleus has a positive charge, and the neutrons have no charge. Each electron has a negative charge. Atoms contain equal numbers of electrons and protons; therefore, atoms have no charge. Electrons move about the nucleus in different energy levels. The farther an electron is from the nucleus, the more energy the electron has.

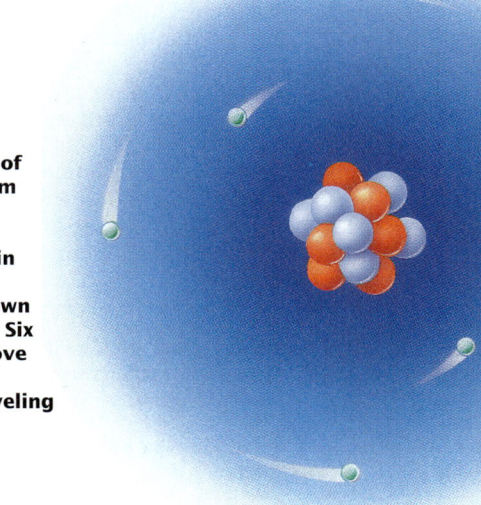

Figure 2-4
The nucleus of a carbon atom contains six neutrons, shown here in red, and six protons, shown here in blue. Six electrons move around the nucleus, traveling at very high speeds.

Videodisc Resources

Holt Biology Videodiscs
Lesson 2-2: Basic Chemistry

Figure 2-5

a Table salt, or sodium chloride, NaCl, is a crystal composed of ions of sodium and chloride held together by ionic bonds.

b At very high magnification, a crystal of salt looks like this.

c The salt crystal is held together by ionic bonds between positively charged sodium ions and negatively charged chloride ions.

d A sodium ion is positively charged because it has lost the single electron from its outer energy level. A chloride ion is negatively charged because it has gained an electron.

Formation of Bonds Stabilizes Atoms

When an atom reacts with other atoms, it gains, loses, or shares electrons. An atom that has gained or lost electrons is called an **ion**. If the ion has more protons than electrons, it is said to be positively charged. If the ion has more electrons than protons, it is said to be negatively charged. Ions with positive charges are electrically attracted to ions with negative charges.

The force holding two atoms or ions together is called a **chemical bond**. All chemical bonds involve interactions between electrons in the energy levels farthest from the nucleus. These outer electrons determine an atom's chemical behavior. In other words, the atom's outermost electrons determine its ability to react with other atoms. Atoms bond to fill their outer energy levels with electrons. A full outer energy level makes an atom chemically stable. Carbon, nitrogen, and oxygen require eight electrons to fill their outer energy levels. Since these atoms all have fewer than eight electrons in their outer energy levels, they form bonds to gain, lose, or share electrons.

An **ionic bond** is the force of attraction between oppositely charged ions. To form an ionic bond, one atom loses one or more electrons so that it has a full outer energy level. The other atom involved in bonding gains one or more electrons so that it too has a full outer energy level. **Figure 2-5** illustrates ionic bonding in table salt.

Molecules result from the formation of covalent bonds

A second type of chemical bond results when two atoms share one or more electrons. This type of chemical bond is called a **covalent bond**. A covalent bond is different from an ionic bond because electrons are *shared*, rather than lost or gained. For example, an atom of oxygen will form covalent bonds with two atoms of hydrogen. The result is a molecule of water.

Demonstration
● **Comparing Properties**
Materials: rock salt, paraffin, plastic knife, 2 empty beakers, 2 beakers of water
Show students samples of rock salt, an inorganic compound, and paraffin, an organic compound. Have students take notes in chart form while you demonstrate the properties of these substances. Use a plastic knife to show that the rock salt is brittle and hard, whereas the paraffin is soft and flexible. Place the substances in separate beakers of water to show that the rock salt dissolves easily but that the paraffin does not. Ask students which type of substance would make the best building material for living organisms *(organic, because it resists dissolving and breaking in a watery environment)* and which would be best for transporting dissolved compounds in living organisms *(inorganic, because it dissolves easily in water)*. The differences between these two substances are due to different bond types.

Ionic *vs.* Molecular Compounds
■ **Comparing Functions**
Compounds can be molecular or ionic. *Molecular* compounds are made up of individual, independent molecules held together by covalent bonds. Water (H_2O) is a good example of a molecular compound. *Ionic* compounds are in the form of extended crystals like the salt crystal shown in Figure 2-5c. A formula unit of NaCl, a single sodium ion–chloride ion pair, is almost never found alone in nature.

Matter of Fact: Dry Weight of Cells
Most students have heard that water makes up most of protoplasm (45 percent to 90 percent). They also will be familiar with the chemical formula of water and thus will be aware that carbon is not a component of water. Stress that more than one-half of the dry weight of cells is carbon.

Key to Strategies
● Understanding Concepts (Tier I)
■ Applying Information (Tier II)
▲ Critical Thinking (Tier III)

Assessment Options

Closure

■ **Recognizing Relationships**

Free radicals are unstable molecules that break down other molecules by "stealing" electrons. They may attack enzymes, proteins, and DNA, preventing normal cellular function. Have students research and prepare a report on current information about free radicals. Have them research natural free-radical inhibitors called antioxidants, such as vitamin E. Students might also find information about commercial uses of antioxidants, such as the use of vitamin E as a food preservative.

SECTION REVIEW

Assign the *Section Review*.

Reteaching

Assign students to cooperative groups of four. Have each group develop a concept map for this section and explain it to the rest of the class. Concept maps will vary, but they should show that electrons, protons, and neutrons make up atoms and that atoms form covalent or ionic bonds.

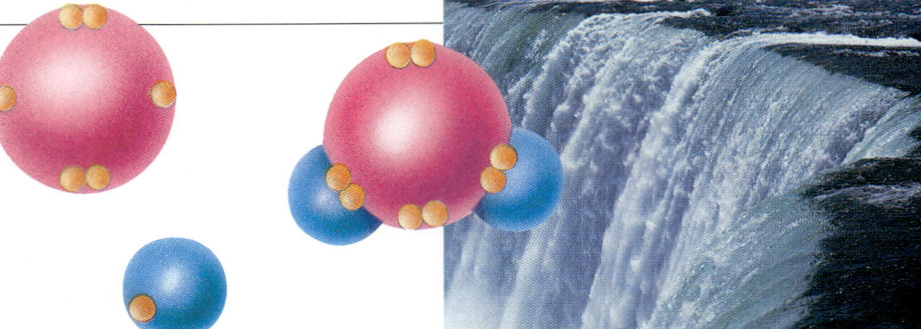

Figure 2-6

a An atom of oxygen has six electrons in its outer energy level and needs two more electrons to be stable.

b Hydrogen has one electron in its sole energy level, but it needs a total of two to fill this level.

c Water, H_2O, is composed of molecules. Because they share electrons, all three atoms in the molecule have complete outer energy levels.

A **molecule** is a group of atoms held together by covalent bonds. The force that holds these atoms together comes from the sharing of electrons. Most molecules are made of more than two atoms because most atoms must share electrons with more than one other atom to fill their outer energy levels. Oxygen atoms are able to form covalent bonds with two other atoms. Nitrogen atoms can form covalent bonds with up to three other atoms. Carbon atoms can form covalent bonds with as many as four different atoms.

The models in **Figure 2-6** show the shared electrons in a water molecule. Each hydrogen atom shares two electrons with the oxygen atom. A bond in which two electrons are shared is called a single bond. Atoms can also form covalent bonds in which two pairs of electrons are shared—called a double bond—or three pairs of electrons are shared—called a triple bond. Acetic acid, a component of vinegar, is an example of a molecule that contains a double bond. Three models of the structure of acetic acid are shown in **Figure 2-7**.

Figure 2-7
A molecule of acetic acid contains a double bond between one oxygen and one carbon atom. Its formula can be written as $C_2H_4O_2$.

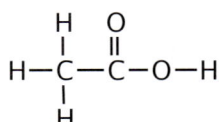

a A simple model of acetic acid shows its double bond.

b In the structural formula, a single line between atoms represents a single bond and a pair of lines represents a double bond.

c This space-filling model shows the three-dimensional shape of the molecule.

SECTION REVIEW

1 Describe the structure of an atom.

2 How do atoms differ from ions?

3 How are elements related to molecules?

4 How do covalent bonds differ from ionic bonds?

ANSWERS TO SECTION REVIEW

1 An atom consists of a nucleus that contains protons and neutrons and that has electrons circling it in various energy levels. A proton has a positive charge, an electron has a negative charge, and a neutron is neutral.

2 An atom is the smallest particle of matter that can retain its chemical properties. If an atom has gained or lost one or more electron, then it is an ion and has an electric charge.

3 A molecule is composed of atoms of one or more elements.

4 A covalent bond is formed when atoms share electrons. An ionic bond is formed between ions of opposite charge.

You have just learned how atoms combine to form molecules. Small molecules also join together to form very large and complex molecules that have important functions in living things. There are four types of these large molecules in your body. They are composed almost entirely of carbon, hydrogen, and oxygen. In this section you will learn the basic structure and function of each kind of large molecule.

Phase One
Preparation

Scheduling
See the **Lesson Planning Guide** on pages 21A and 21B for lecture, classwork, and assignment options for Section 2-3.

2-3 Molecules of Life

OBJECTIVES

1 Define sugars, and describe the process that occurs in the formation of polysaccharides.

2 Describe the properties of lipids.

3 Explain the factors that affect the three-dimensional structure of proteins.

4 Define nucleic acids, and describe their functions.

Organic Molecules Are Derived From Carbon

Of the 92 different kinds of atoms that occur naturally, carbon is the most closely associated with living things, including the many creatures living on the coral reef shown in **Figure 2-8**. In the last section, you read that carbon has four electrons in its outer energy level and that a carbon atom seeks to fill that energy level by sharing electrons with other atoms. Carbon atoms form long chains that are the backbone of many different kinds of molecules. Molecules with carbon-carbon bonds are called **organic molecules**.

Organic molecules join together to form more complex molecules

Just as atoms can be joined to form molecules, molecules can be linked together to form **macromolecules** *(MAHK roh MAWL uh kyools)*. All organisms are composed of four major classes of macro-

molecules: carbohydrates, lipids, proteins, and nucleic acids. Each class of macromolecule is composed of long chains of nearly identical subunits, and the different classes of macromolecules are distinguished primarily by the nature of the subunit they contain. The chemical bonds that link the subunit molecules together in macromolecules are the same kind of covalent bonds that hold atoms together in a molecule. The forming and breaking of bonds is called a **chemical reaction**.

Figure 2-8
Diamonds are pure carbon. Carbon-containing molecules are the primary components of living things, including the plants and animals that live on this coral reef.

Phase Two
Teaching Strategies

Visual Strategy | **Videodisc**

■ **Predicting Patterns**
Use *Step-Frame Sequence—Covalent Bonding in Methane* shown in Chapter 2 Section 2-3 of *Holt Biology Videodiscs Teacher's Correlation Guide to Holt Biology: Visualizing Life.* In the first frame, have students identify the carbon atom, the hydrogen atom, and the electrons in each atom. Move to the second frame, and have students explain the process by which each atom has completed its outer shell. *(The carbon atom shares electrons with four hydrogen atoms.)* For the third frame, have students compare the three-dimensional model with the dot diagram. *(Both diagrams show that hydrogen and carbon atoms are bonded. The dot diagram shows the relationship among the electrons of the five atoms; each dot represents a shared electron. The three-dimensional diagram shows the approximate placement of the hydrogen atoms around the carbon atom.)*

29

Figure 2-9
Starch and glycogen are macromolecules composed of glucose subunits (symbolized by a six-sided molecule). Starch, the carbohydrate found in corn, is chopped into glucose subunits and converted to glycogen when it is eaten by this worm.

Carbohydrates Are Energy Sources

A **carbohydrate** *(KAHR boh HEYE drayt)* is an organic macromolecule composed of carbon, hydrogen, and oxygen in a ratio of one carbon atom to two hydrogen atoms to one oxygen atom. Some carbohydrates, such as table sugar, are simple, small molecules. Other carbohydrates, like the starch in potatoes, exist as chains that are hundreds of subunits long. Carbohydrates contain many carbon-hydrogen bonds. They are well suited to be energy sources because their bonds store considerable energy.

Carbohydrates can be either simple or complex molecules

Among the simplest carbohydrates are sugars, small molecules that taste sweet. While sugars may have as few as three carbon atoms, the sugars involved in energy storage, like glucose, have six. These sugars have the formula $C_6H_{12}O_6$. Complex carbohydrates are made by linking individual sugars together to form long chains called polysaccharides. Large polysaccharides are insoluble in water; that is, they do not dissolve in water. They can be deposited in specific storage areas in a cell. This ability to store energy in the form of polysaccharides enables organisms to build up energy reserves.

Starch and glycogen are both complex carbohydrates

Starch is a polysaccharide composed of glucose subunits. Amylose is the simplest kind of starch. It exists as a long, unbranched chain of glucose molecules. Baking or boiling starchy plants such as potatoes and corn breaks these chains into shorter fragments that are soluble and can be taken up by the body.

Humans consume a great deal of carbohydrates; the seeds of rice, wheat, and corn supply about one-half of all the calories used by people. Animals store glucose in the form of long, branched chains called glycogen. **Figure 2-9** shows the structural differences between starch and glycogen.

Cellulose provides structural support

Many organisms use polysaccharides as structural molecules as well as for energy storage. Plants manufacture a polysaccharide called cellulose. Cellulose consists of glucose subunits linked in a way that most animals cannot break down. Cellulose forms the major part of the cell walls of plants. When you eat plants containing cellulose, it passes through your body undigested. This undigested cellulose is one kind of dietary fiber and is an important component of your diet. In contrast, cows and horses are able to digest the cellulose in plants. In their stomach or intestines, these animals have microorganisms that break down cellulose. You lack these microorganisms and would starve on a diet of grass.

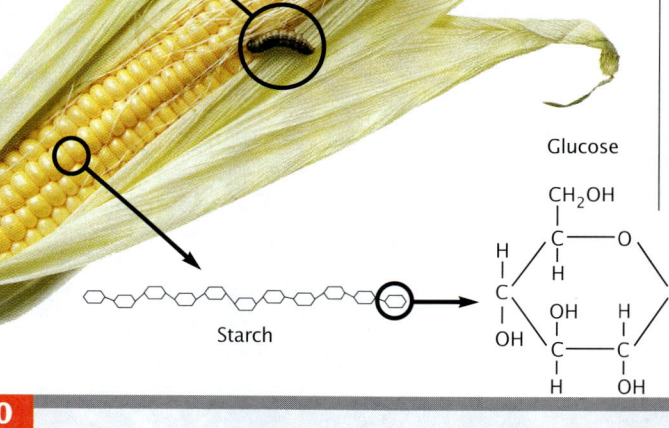

Glucose

Glycogen

Starch

Glucose

30

Matter of Fact: Benefits of Fiber

Dietary fiber from a variety of plants promotes health in many ways. Fiber promotes weight loss by enhancing satiety. It prevents constipation by attracting water into the digestive tract. Fiber prevents the formation of fecal stones, which can lead to appendicitis. The bulk that it creates exercises muscles of the intestinal wall, thus preventing diverticulitis. Fiber speeds up passage of foods, thus helping prevent exposure to cancer-causing agents. It binds with lipids, such as cholesterol, so that they are eliminated with the feces, and it promotes an even rise in blood glucose by slowing carbohydrate absorption.

Lipids Store Energy

A **lipid** (LIHP ihd) is an organic macromolecule that is not soluble (won't dissolve) in water, but is soluble (will dissolve) in oil. The most important lipids are fats, which are energy storage molecules. Fats have more carbon-hydrogen bonds than do carbohydrates. Therefore, a gram of fat contains more energy than a gram of carbohydrate. As

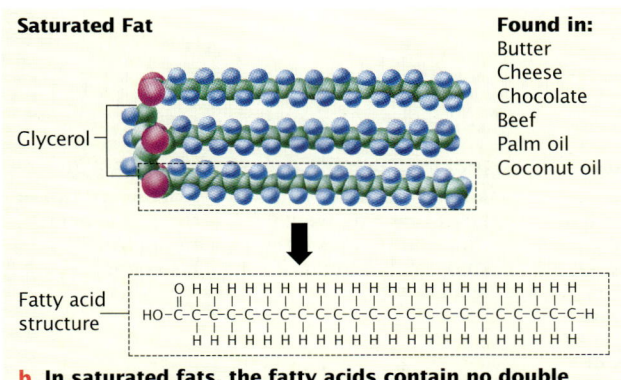

Glycerol — Fatty acid / Fatty acid / Fatty acid

Figure 2-10

a Fats are composed of two kinds of molecules: glycerol and fatty acids. Fats always contain three fatty-acid molecules.

Saturated Fat

Found in:
Butter
Cheese
Chocolate
Beef
Palm oil
Coconut oil

Glycerol

Fatty acid structure

b In saturated fats, the fatty acids contain no double bonds between carbon atoms. In this space-filling model, carbon is indicated by green balls, hydrogen by blue balls, and oxygen by red balls. The same color-coding holds for the next diagram.

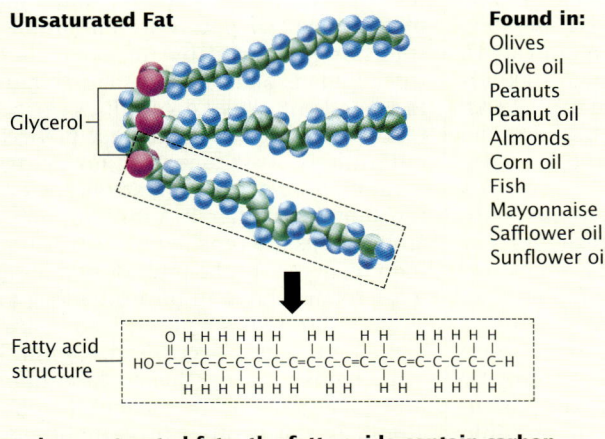

Unsaturated Fat

Found in:
Olives
Olive oil
Peanuts
Peanut oil
Almonds
Corn oil
Fish
Mayonnaise
Safflower oil
Sunflower oil

Glycerol

Fatty acid structure

c In unsaturated fats, the fatty acids contain carbon-carbon double bonds. As a result, the fatty-acid chains have kinks in them.

you can see in **Figure 2-10**, a fat molecule consists of fatty acids, which are long chains composed mainly of CH_2 units, joined to a molecule of glycerol, the backbone of the fat molecule. There are many kinds of fats, which differ in the kind of fatty acids attached to the glycerol molecule.

In addition to fats, there are many other types of lipids. Among them are steroids (STEHR oydz) and waxes. Steroids include the sex hormones and cholesterol. Earwax and beeswax are examples of waxes.

Fats can be saturated or unsaturated

There are two major categories of fats: saturated fats and unsaturated fats. As you can see in **Figure 2-10b**, most carbon atoms in a **saturated fat** are bonded to two hydrogen atoms. The carbon atoms are "saturated" with hydrogen atoms; that is, the carbon atoms are bonded to as many hydrogen atoms as possible. If some carbons within a fatty acid chain are linked by double bonds, kinks occur in the chain. This type of fat is called an **unsaturated fat**. At room temperature, unsaturated fats usually exist as liquids called oils. In contrast, most saturated fats are solid at room temperature. Palm oil and coconut oil are exceptions because they are liquid at room temperature. They are classified as saturated fats because they lack carbon-carbon double bonds. The amount of saturated fat in your diet has an important effect on your health. People who eat diets high in saturated fats are more likely to suffer from heart disease than are people whose diets are low in saturated fats. You will learn more about this topic in Chapter 34.

It is possible to make an oil into a solid fat through a chemical reaction that adds hydrogen to the carbons in the oil. The double bonds become single bonds. This is often done to the oils in peanut butter. The unsaturated peanut fats are converted to saturated fats so that they don't separate as oils while the jar sits on the store shelf.

31

Visual Strategy | **Figure 2-10a**

■ **Analyzing Information**
Have students compare the structural formula of a lipid with that of a carbohydrate in Figure 2-9. Ask them to point out a similarity (both contain C, H, and O) and a difference (a lipid contains much more C and H relative to O).

Visual Strategy | **Figure 2-10b**

▲ **Distinguishing Relevant Information**
Have students redraw the unsaturated fat illustrated in this figure to make it a saturated fat. Be sure students not only replace all carbon-carbon double bonds with single ones but also add the necessary hydrogen atoms.

Demonstration

■ **Predicting Outcomes**
Show a picture of a sea mammal, such as a seal. Point out that a thick layer of fat serves to insulate the animal against the cold water and is therefore appropriate for the cold-climate animal. Then show graphic diagrams or microscope-slide cross sections of a healthy artery and a clogged artery. Too much fat in the diet, especially saturated fat and cholesterol, causes *atherosclerosis*, a disease in which fatty molecules accumulate at the site of a small lesion, resulting in reduced blood flow. Ask students what effect reduced blood flow might have on a particular organ or muscle. *(There will be inadequate nutrients and an imbalance of oxygen and carbon dioxide, which can result in muscle fatigue, muscle damage, nerve damage, cramping, dizziness, unconsciousness, and death. If the blockage is in the heart, a heart attack might occur.)*

Key to Strategies
● **Understanding Concepts (Tier I)**
■ **Applying Information (Tier II)**
▲ **Critical Thinking (Tier III)**

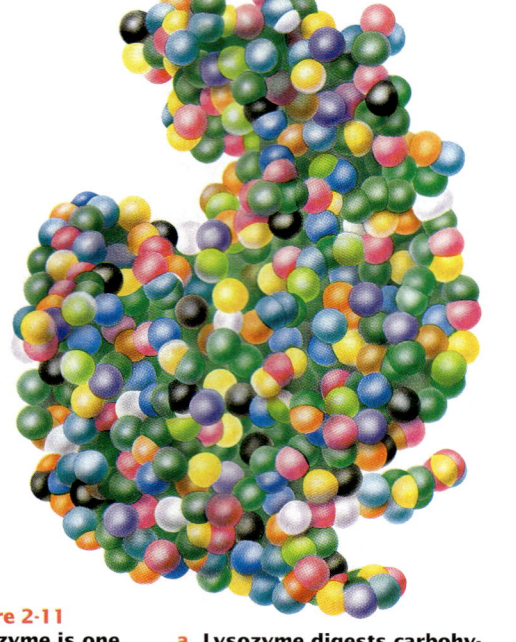
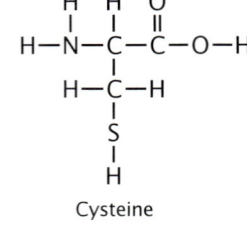

Cysteine

Leucine

Figure 2-11
Lysozyme is one of your body's defensive proteins. It is found in tears, sweat, saliva, mucus, and other body fluids. Lysozyme has a very specific function that is determined by its shape—it destroys bacteria.

a Lysozyme digests carbohydrates found in the outer coating of some kinds of bacteria. These carbohydrates fit into the groove at the upper left of the lysozyme molecule. Lysozyme cannot digest other kinds of molecules, such as proteins or fats, because they do not fit into this groove.

b If you could unfold and stretch out lysozyme, you would find that it is a single chain of 129 amino acids.

c Cysteine and leucine are two of the amino acids found in lysozyme.

Proteins Provide Structure and Increase Reaction Rate

A **protein** (PROH teen) is an organic macromolecule composed of long chains of subunits called amino acids. All living things use the same 20 kinds of amino acids to construct proteins. Proteins differ in the number of amino acids they contain and in the sequence in which the amino acids occur. As a consequence, there is an almost endless variety of possible proteins. For example, just consider how many different proteins containing 100 amino acids (a typical length for a protein) could be made by a cell. Since there are 20 amino acids that can potentially occupy each position in the chain, there are many trillions of possible proteins of this length.

The importance of proteins as biological molecules stems from their tendency to bend, twist, curl, and fold into complex shapes. A protein's function is determined by its particular three-dimensional shape, as illustrated in **Figure 2-11**. What determines a protein's shape? Its amino acid sequence determines its shape. Amino acids within a protein interact, attracting or repelling each other. In addition, some amino acids are repelled by water and tend to cluster in the interior of a protein. Thus, each kind of protein has a slightly different shape.

In some cases, two or more amino acid chains join together to form one functional protein. For instance, hemoglobin is the protein in your blood that transports oxygen. A molecule of hemoglobin contains four separate amino acid chains.

32

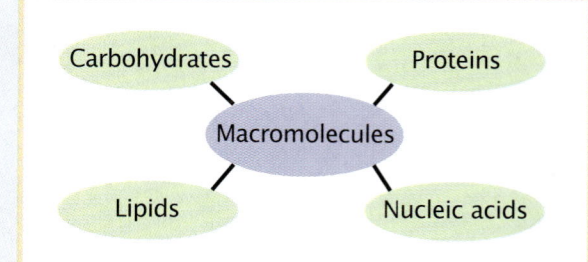

In the next few chapters, you will study various types of proteins. Pay particular attention to the shapes of these macromolecules because shape determines a protein's biological function.

Proteins function as structural molecules and enzymes
Proteins often play structural roles in organisms. Cartilage and tendons are made of a protein called collagen, which also gives strength to your skin and bones. A protein called keratin forms the horns of a rhinoceros and the feathers of birds, as well as your own hair.

Proteins play a second very important role in organisms—they act as enzymes. Enzymes increase the rate at which chemical reactions occur, such as those that take place during metabolism. Most of the chemical reactions necessary for growth, movement, and other body activities could not take place without enzymes. You will learn more about enzymes in Chapter 5.

Nucleic Acids Contain Genetic Information

The fourth major class of organic macromolecules is the **nucleic** *(noo CLAY ihk)* **acids**. There are two types of nucleic acids: DNA (deoxyribonucleic acid) and RNA (ribonucleic acid). Subunits of DNA and RNA are called **nucleotides** *(noo CLAY oh teyedz)*. In DNA, these nucleotides form a series of units called genes, which encode information concerning how a given organism will grow and develop. RNA is involved in making working copies of genes. These copies are used in assembling amino acids to make proteins.

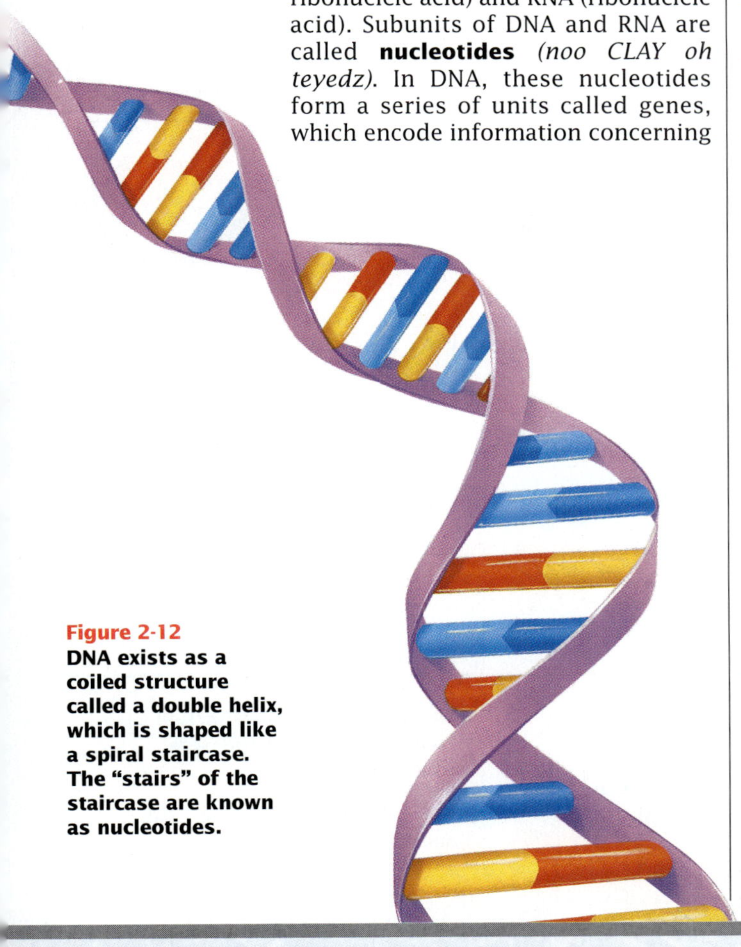

Figure 2-12
DNA exists as a coiled structure called a double helix, which is shaped like a spiral staircase. The "stairs" of the staircase are known as nucleotides.

DNA is a double helix
A DNA molecule consists of two interlocking, coil-shaped strands and resembles a spiral staircase. Chemists refer to this coiling structure as a double helix. **Figure 2-12** shows the structure of a DNA double helix. DNA encodes the sequences of all the cell's proteins, as well as information that determines when each protein is to be produced. In simple cells like bacteria, the DNA exists as a long molecule. But in complex cells like those of your body, the DNA folds and twists into compact bundles associated with proteins. These protein-DNA bundles are called **chromosomes** *(KROHM oh sohmz)*.

RNA helps in the synthesis of proteins
RNA molecules have a variety of shapes, depending on their function in the cell. RNA molecules that are associated with proteins serve as scaffolds for the assembly of all the different proteins in the cell. Other RNA molecules exist in the cell as long, single-stranded threads that carry DNA's message from one part of the cell to another. You will learn more about how DNA and RNA work together to build proteins in Chapter 8.

2-3 section

Visual Strategy Videodisc

■ **Forming Hypotheses**
Use *Video—Proteins/Nucleic Acids* (1 min 55 s) in Chapter 2 Section 2-3 of ***Holt Biology Videodiscs Teacher's Correlation Guide to Holt Biology: Visualizing Life.*** As students view the video, tell them to pay special attention to how amino acids join to form proteins. After viewing the video, review how the sequence and kinds of amino acids determine the shape of a protein. Have students hypothesize why it might be important for an organism to have proteins of different shapes. Lead students to realize that different shapes can do different jobs. Tell students that they will learn more about different proteins in Chapter 3.

Demonstration

● **Identifying Structures**
Take two red or black licorice whips that are 2–3 ft long. With the strands of licorice representing the sides of a ladder, add equally spaced rungs made of toothpicks. Finally, twist the top of the ladder to the right. The "rungs" represent nucleotide bases. The model may be kept until Chapter 8, where it can be used again. Ask students why DNA is important. *(DNA is the substance in which the hereditary information is stored.)*

Historical Perspective: Vitamin C and Scurvy

Vitamin C (ascorbic acid) is a six-carbon compound similar to glucose. A severe deficiency of this nutrient results in a condition called scurvy. Without ascorbic acid, collagen fails to form, causing connective tissue to degenerate and resulting in swelling, hemorrhaging, and eventually death. Scurvy has been known since ancient times and was once a common disease among sailors, who lived on salt beef and dry biscuits for weeks at a time. In 1753, the Scottish physician James Lind showed that eating citrus fruits would cure scurvy and that adding lime juice to the daily rations would prevent the disease. In 1795, the British Lords of the Admiralty began requiring all vessels to carry enough limes for each sailor to have a daily ration. This tradition resulted in English sailors being referred to as "limeys."

Key to Strategies
● Understanding Concepts (Tier I)
■ Applying Information (Tier II)
▲ Critical Thinking (Tier III)

Assessment Options

Closure

■ Relating Concepts

Bring some food labels to class to show students how they can check for carbohydrate, fat, and protein content in food. Have students review the four classes of macromolecules. Explain that because our bodies manufacture nucleic acid, it is not considered a nutrient. Have volunteers bring snacks for the class that have a caloric breakdown of near 60 percent carbohydrates, 12 percent proteins, and 28 percent fats. A nutrition book or packaged food labels could be used to find this information. Students can work in groups to plan their snack combinations.

SECTION REVIEW

Assign the *Section Review*.

Reteaching

Prepare a table on the board. Across the top, write the names of the four major types of organic compounds. Down the left side of the table, write *Elements present, Functions, Examples,* and *Special properties.* Have students fill in the necessary information.

Macromolecule Summary

The four basic macromolecules (carbohydrates, lipids, proteins, and nucleic acids) have the same fundamental structure. All four are composed of long chains of similar subunits. Using **Table 2-1** you can compare and contrast the structures and functions of these macromolecules.

Table 2-1 Classes of Macromolecules

Class	Typical Subunit	Roles	Examples
Carbohydrates	Sugar	Store energy	Starch, glycogen
		Structural components	Cellulose, chitin
Lipids	Fatty acid	Store energy	Body fat
		Form membranes	Cell membrane
		Steroid hormones	Testosterone
Proteins	Amino acid	Serve as enzymes	Lactase
		Structural components	Hair, cartilage
		Peptide hormones	Insulin
Nucleic Acids	Nucleotide	Store genetic information	DNA
		Direct production of proteins	RNA

Starch granules

Human fat cells

Hair

Chromosomes

SECTION REVIEW

1. What is the difference between a sugar and a polysaccharide?

2. What is the difference between saturated and unsaturated fats?

3. Why might a protein function incorrectly if its shape were changed?

4. Contrast the functions of DNA and RNA.

34

ANSWERS TO SECTION REVIEW

1. Polysaccharides consist of sugar molecules that are bonded together to form long chains.

2. In a saturated fat, all of the carbon-carbon bonds are single bonds, and each carbon atom is bonded to as many hydrogen atoms as it can "hold." In an unsaturated fat, some of the carbon-carbon bonds are double bonds, and not all of the carbon atoms "hold" as many hydrogen atoms as they can.

3. A protein and the molecule with which it reacts must fit together. Changing the shape of a protein would prevent it from fitting and thus would affect the function of that protein.

4. DNA contains the genetic code that determines the sequence of amino acids in a cell's proteins. RNA is involved in assembling the proteins.

2 Highlights

These seeds are the start of new life, but is a seed alive? Use the five properties of life to decide.

	Key Terms	Summary
2-1 **What Is Life?** 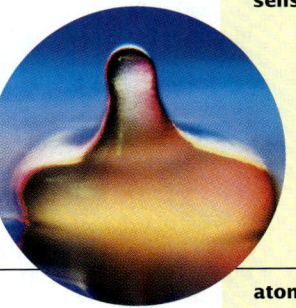 Is this blob alive? How would you go about answering this question?	sensitivity (p. 23)	• Some of the most obvious properties of life cannot be used alone to decide whether something is alive because these properties can also appear in nonliving things. • All living things have all five of these characteristics: cellular organization, metabolism, reproduction, homeostasis, and heredity.
2-2 **Basic Chemistry** 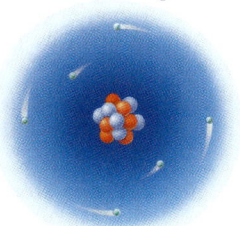 Atoms are the basic structural units of matter.	atom (p. 26) element (p. 26) electron (p. 26) ion (p. 27) chemical bond (p. 27) ionic bond (p. 27) covalent bond (p. 27) molecule (p. 28)	• There are more than 100 kinds of atoms. Each kind is known as an element. More than 99 percent of the atoms in your body are nitrogen, oxygen, carbon, or hydrogen. • An ionic bond is the attraction between ions with opposite charges. • A covalent bond is the attraction between atoms that share electrons. Molecules are groups of atoms held together by covalent bonds.
2-3 **Molecules of Life** Carbon is the primary chemical component of the macromolecules found in living things, including the plants and animals on this coral reef. 	organic molecule (p. 29) macromolecule (p. 29) chemical reaction (p. 29) carbohydrate (p. 30) lipid (p. 31) saturated fat (p. 31) unsaturated fat (p. 31) protein (p. 32) nucleic acid (p. 33) nucleotide (p. 33) chromosome (p. 33)	• Carbon is the most abundant element in living things. Molecules with carbon-carbon bonds are called organic compounds. • Organisms use carbohydrates to store energy and provide structural support. • Lipids are not soluble in water. Fats store more energy than carbohydrates because they have more carbon-hydrogen bonds. • The sequence of amino acids in a particular protein determines its shape and chemical properties. The shape of a particular protein determines its function. • Nucleic acids contain genetic information and direct protein production.

35

Alternative Assessment

Have students use common materials such as clay, string, wire, rubber bands, colored "pipe cleaners," licorice strands, toothpicks, and gumdrops to build models of carbohydrates, lipids, proteins, and nucleic acids.

Portfolio Assessment

Portfolio Assessment on page T39 provides options for building and evaluating student portfolios. Students and teachers can select items from the areas listed on page T39 for inclusion in a portfolio.

ANSWER TO CONCEPT MAP

The following is one possible answer to the Relating Concepts exercise on page 36.

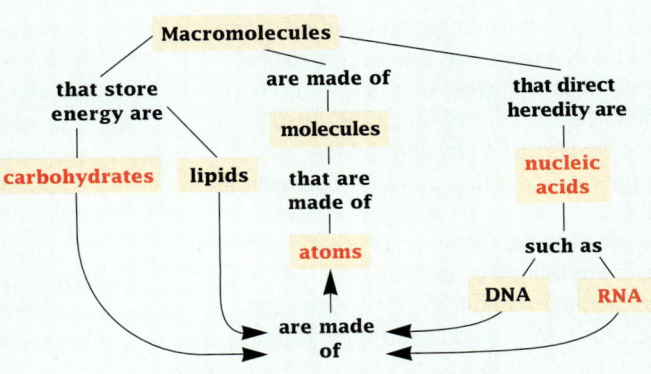

review

Understanding Vocabulary

1. a. Sensitivity, although a characteristic of many living things, is not a factor that helps determine if an organism is alive.
   b. Electrons, protons, and neutrons are all parts of an atom. A molecule is a group of similar or different atoms held together by covalent bonds.
   c. Carbohydrates, nucleic acids, proteins, and lipids are types of macromolecules—all of which contain carbon. Water is not a macromolecule and does not contain carbon.
2. a. An atom is the smallest particle of matter that retains its chemical properties. An element is a substance composed of only one type of atom.
   b. An ion is an atom that has gained or lost one or more electrons. A molecule is a group of atoms held together by covalent bonds.
   c. A covalent bond is formed when atoms share electrons. An ionic bond results when one atom loses one or more electrons and the other atom gains one or more.

Understanding Concepts

3. Answer to concept map is shown on page 35.
4. The visually observable characteristics of living things are sometimes observable in non-living things.
5. Human intestinal cell, tree. Each of the others is lacking one or more characteristics of life. A car cannot reproduce and is not made of cells. A dinosaur bone cannot reproduce or maintain homeostasis, and it no longer has a metabolism.
6. A slime-mold cell consumes bacteria. In response to food shortages, cells join together to form a mobile colony (a slug), which moves to a new habitat.
7. b

Understanding Vocabulary

1. Select the term that does not fit with the others and explain why.
   a. metabolism, reproduction, sensitivity, homeostasis, heredity
   b. proton, molecule, neutron, electron
   c. carbohydrate, nucleic acid, water, protein, lipid

2. For each pair of terms, explain the differences in their meanings.
   a. atoms, elements
   b. ions, molecules
   c. covalent bond, ionic bond

Understanding Concepts

3. **Relating Concepts** Copy the unfinished concept map below onto a sheet of paper. Then complete the concept map by writing the correct word or phrase in each oval that contains a question mark.

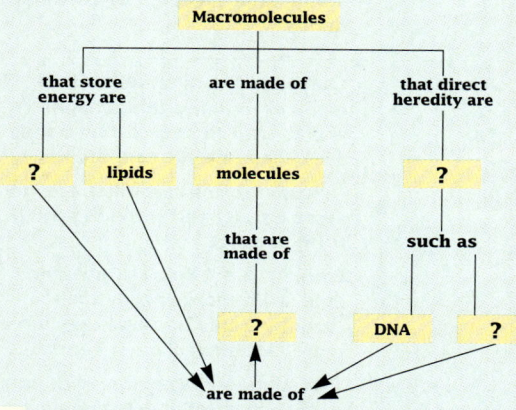

4. **Summarizing Information** Explain why using only visually observable properties is not sufficient to define life.

5. **Inferring Conclusions** Decide which of the following objects are alive: automobile, fossilized dinosaur bone, human intestinal cell, tree. Explain how you made your decisions.

6. **Recognizing Relationships** All living things need energy. How does a slime mold cell obtain energy? How does it respond to shortages of food?

7. **Comparing Structures** Which of the following statements about atoms and ions is true?
   a. An ion always has more electrons than an atom of the same element.
   b. An atom and ion of the same element always have the same number of protons.
   c. Ions are attracted to other ions with the same charge.

8. **Summarizing Information** List two differences between an ionic bond and a covalent bond. Give an example of a molecule that contains a covalent bond.

9. **Recognizing Relationships** Carbohydrate and lipid molecules both store energy. Explain why a lipid contains more energy per gram than a carbohydrate.

10. **Inferring Relationships** Describe two ways in which carbohydrates, proteins, lipids and nucleic acids are similar.

11. **Inferring Conclusions** On a recent Arctic expedition, a biochemist discovered an unknown substance. After performing several experiments, she determined that the substance had the following characteristics: contains carbon, hydrogen, and oxygen and is soluble in oil but not in water. What kind of substance did the biochemist discover? Explain your answer.

12. **Identifying Variables** What factors determine the three-dimensional shape of a protein molecule?

13. **BUILDING ON WHAT YOU HAVE LEARNED** As you learned in Chapter 1, all organisms require energy to carry out life processes. Because they need energy, all living things, including humans, must have ways to store the energy for when they need it. Where do humans get their energy? In what two ways do humans store energy?

---

8. Ionic bonds form between charged atoms, and no electrons are shared. Covalent bonds form between uncharged atoms, and one or more pairs of electrons are shared. Glucose contains covalent bonds.
9. A lipid molecule has more carbon-hydrogen bonds.
10. Proteins, carbohydrates, lipids, and nucleic acids are all made up of smaller, nearly identical subunits, and they all contain carbon.
11. The biochemist discovered a lipid. Lipids are made up of carbon-containing subunits called fatty acids, they store energy in carbon-hydrogen bonds, and they are soluble in oil but not in water.
12. A protein's shape is determined by the sequence of its amino acids. The amino acids within a protein interact with and attract each other. Some amino acids are repelled by water and move toward the interior of the molecule, causing the molecule to curl, twist, bend, or fold into a complex three-dimensional shape.

Interpreting Graphics

14. Examine the figure shown below.

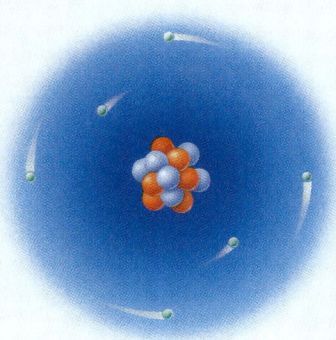

a. What kind of charge does a proton have? a neutron? an electron?
b. Where are the protons and neutrons located?

Reviewing Themes

15. **Stability and Homeostasis**
Describe the process of homeostasis and explain why it is one of the characteristics of all living things.

16. **Matter, Energy, and Organization**
What determines the chemical behavior of an atom?

Thinking Critically

17. **Justifying Conclusions** Why do football players and other athletes often consume a diet rich in complex carbohydrates while training?

18. **Recognizing Logical Inconsistencies** "Scientists know that the genetic information in a human cell is carried on the structures called chromosomes, which are found in the nucleus. Proteins are found in chromosomes, so proteins must be the genetic molecule." Explain the logical flaw in this argument.

19. **Justifying Conclusions** Movement is not a characteristic used to define life because some organisms don't move. All organisms eventually die, but death is not a defining characteristic of life either. Explain why death is not a good characteristic for defining life.

20. **Working Cooperatively** Work together with a classmate to research and write a report on kwashiorkor, a severe form of malnutrition that is caused by the lack of dietary protein. What are the symptoms of this condition? Include facts and examples to support your information.

Activities and Projects

21. **Health Connection** Today, many health experts and nutritionists warn people against consuming too much saturated fat. Use library references or information from an on-line database to compare the average daily diet of an adult living in the United States with that of a person living along the Mediterranean Sea (Greece, Italy, France, Portugal, or Spain) or in Japan. How do these diets differ in the amounts and kinds of fish, meat, fruits, vegetables, carbohydrates, and fats consumed daily? What effects do these dietary differences have on health?

22. **Career Connection: Dietitian** Dietitians provide information on proper nutrition. They know the chemical makeup of foods and the effects foods have on the human body. Use a handbook of nutrition to evaluate the nutritional content of the following three typical lunches: (1) cheeseburger, french fries, milk shake; (2) baked potato, sour cream, butter, cheddar cheese, soft drink; (3) pizza with cheese, pepperoni, mushrooms, soft drink.

23. **History Connection** Use references in your local or school library to investigate the research that lead to the discovery of the structure of an atom. Create a time line of the major events and the individuals responsible for the discoveries.

Discovering Through Reading

24. Read the article "The Facts About Fats" in *Consumer Reports*, May 1994, page 308. Describe two ways that excess fat in the diet can be harmful.

37

18. DNA is also found in chromosomes, so from this observation it cannot be concluded that proteins are the genetic material.

19. Death cannot be used to define life because death is defined as the permanent end of life. Life requires its own definition.

20. Kwashiorkor is common to developing countries in Africa and Asia and can be prevented by consuming adequate amounts of protein. Symptoms include a swollen belly, weakness, hair loss, and possible brain damage.

Activities and Projects

21. Answers will vary but should point out health benefits of diets that are low in saturated fats.

22. Students should recognize that all of the described lunches have a high fat content and are not well balanced. Each lunch can be made more nutritious by including foods from different food groups, especially fruits, vegetables, and grains, and by reducing the amount of fat.

23. Answers will vary, but reports might include scientists such as Democritus, Rudjer Boscovich, John Dalton, Joseph John Thomson, Ernest Rutherford, Niels Bohr, Louis de Broglie, James Chadwick, Murray Gell-Mann, and George Zweig. The time line might go as far back as 400 B.C. and span through the 1900s.

Discovering Through Reading

24. Excess fat can lead to obesity, diabetes, heart disease, high cholesterol levels, and plaque accumulation in the arteries.

---

13. Humans obtain energy from food and store energy as carbohydrates and fats.

Interpreting Graphics

14. a. A proton has a positive charge, a neutron has no charge, and an electron has a negative charge.
b. Protons and neutrons are located in the nucleus.

Reviewing Themes

15. Homeostasis is the process by which a living thing maintains relatively stable internal conditions. Living things use energy to maintain homeostasis as well as to grow and move.

16. An atom's chemical behavior is determined by the number of electrons found in its outer energy levels.

Thinking Critically

17. Football players and other athletes consume diets rich in complex carbohydrates because carbohydrates store large amounts of energy.

Objectives

- Describe the uses of DNA profiling.
- Summarize the process of gel electrophoresis.
- Recognize the potential conflicts that can arise regarding the use of DNA profiling and the privacy rights of an individual.

A Test for Huntington's Disease

▲ **Evaluating Viewpoints**

Huntington's disease is an inherited disease that causes a progressive, irreversible deterioration of the nervous system. Individuals who inherit the gene for Huntington's disease will inevitably develop the disease, which is incurable. Because the symptoms do not appear until middle age, individuals with Huntington's disease can become parents before the disease strikes, unknowingly passing the gene to some of their children. There is a test that will reveal the presence of the gene.

Ask students whether adult offspring of individuals with Huntington's disease should be required to undergo the test, and ask whether employers and insurers should be allowed to have access to the test results. Have students list arguments to support their viewpoint and then discuss the issue with a partner. After their discussion, suggest that students could use references available in the library or research an on-line database to find information supporting their viewpoint.

Genes Associated With Behaviors

■ **Predicting Outcomes**

Tell students that researchers have detected a partial genetic explanation for the human personality trait called "novelty seeking." Discuss with your students the issues that could arise as we begin to associate more genes with behaviors.

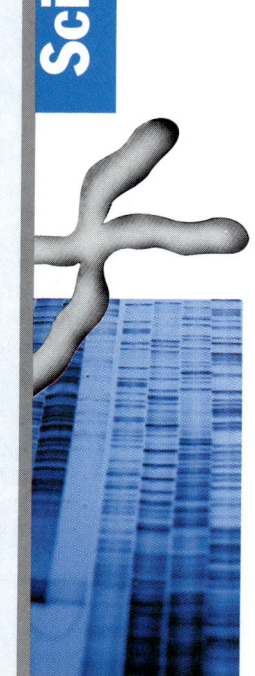

DNA Profiling: Promise or Peril?

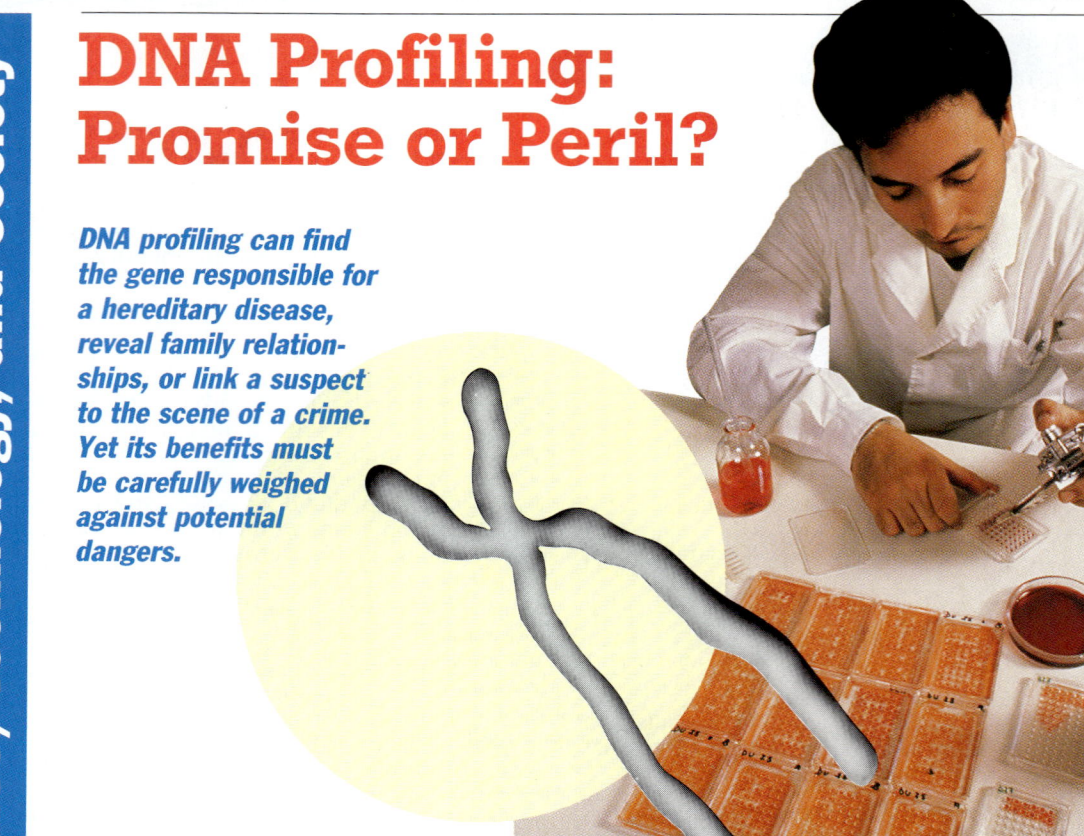

DNA profiling can find the gene responsible for a hereditary disease, reveal family relationships, or link a suspect to the scene of a crime. Yet its benefits must be carefully weighed against potential dangers.

38

DNA Takes the Witness Stand

Just as a bar code specifies a certain product, the patterns produced by a DNA sample are specific to each individual. A tiny sample of blood, semen, saliva, or bone at a crime scene provides a sufficient amount of DNA for analysis. The patterns obtained can be compared with the patterns of DNA in blood or tissue samples obtained from suspects. Because no two individuals have the same DNA pattern, every person has a unique "DNA fingerprint." This "DNA fingerprint" can be used to establish a link between a suspect and a crime scene.

Forecasting Disease

Using gel electrophoresis, researchers can identify the adult who carries a gene that causes a hereditary disease—such as cystic fibrosis, for example—or a newborn who has the disease. Sometimes the presence of a particular gene does not necessarily guarantee that the individual will have the disease. For example, a recently discovered gene increases an individual's risk of colon cancer. People who have this gene would be wise to have regular checkups, even though it is not certain that they will someday develop colon cancer.

Mapping Family Relationships

The ability of DNA profiling to reveal the base sequences of selected genes makes it an invaluable tool for studying the inheritance of these genes within a family. The characteristic DNA patterns are passed from one generation to the next and thus provide evidence that can be used to determine the identities of family members. In Argentina, DNA profiling has enabled children whose parents were abducted in 1977 by military security forces to be reunited with

ANSWERS TO ANALYZING THE ISSUES

1 Genetic profiling is not 100 percent foolproof. DNA samples can decompose or be contaminated with common substances (e.g., cleaning fluids, bacteria, chemicals, carpet dyes), which may affect results. Band shifting can cause differences in the pattern of DNA bands. Some skeptics question whether we know enough about population genetics to accurately predict the likelihood that a sample from one individual will match that of any other. Estimates of error rates in DNA profiling range from 1 in 30 million to 5 percent.

2 Students' answers should consider the fears and concerns of the communities and the victims' families as well as the privacy rights of the men. By requesting that these men voluntarily subject themselves to DNA testing, the police were able to eliminate everyone tested. Finally, information came to light about a villager who had paid someone else to give a blood sample in his name. A similar action in the United States probably would not be admissible in court because of the Fourth Amendment, which protects Americans against unlawful search and seizure.

their grandparents years later. Biologists studying animal populations have used DNA profiling to measure genetic variety, an important indicator of population diversity. Anthropologists studying ancient civilizations have performed a similar test using DNA from specimens that may be hundreds or even thousands of years old.

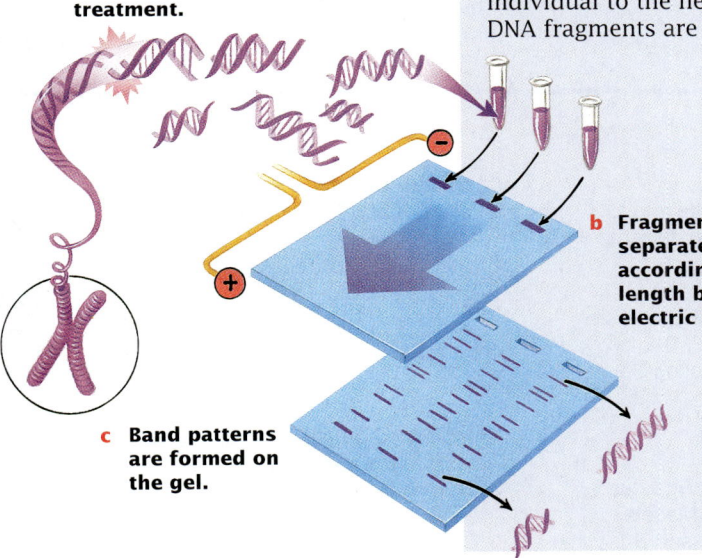

a DNA is fragmented by restriction enzyme treatment.

b Fragments are separated according to length by an electric charge.

c Band patterns are formed on the gel.

Technique

Gel Electrophoresis

Analysis of an individual's DNA begins with the use of restriction enzymes, which cut the DNA at specific base sequences, leaving fragments of various lengths. These fragments vary distinctively from one individual to the next. The DNA fragments are then placed on a bed of semi-solid gel. Electrodes at either end of the gel generate an electric current. The DNA, which is negatively charged, moves through the gel toward the positive electrode. Because the smaller DNA fragments move faster than the larger fragments, the separated fragments form a pattern of bands. This pattern, which looks similar to the barcode used by supermarkets, is an individual's DNA profile.

Applications: pinpointing genes responsible for hereditary diseases, confirming family relationships and individual identities, and studying the diversity of genes within populations

Users: medical geneticists, physicians, research biologists, forensic analysts

Analyzing the Issues

Is genetic testing foolproof?

1 Many scientists have warned that DNA profiles can be misinterpreted. Others caution that the possibility of human error must be recognized and urge the adoption of industry-wide quality control standards. Use references available in the library or research an on-line database, and write a report summarizing the ways in which DNA evidence can be altered or misused.

Should genetic testing be mandatory?

2 Read "DNA Profiling," in *National Geographic*, May 1992, pages 112–124. Do you think the police searching for Lynda Mann's killer were justified in requiring DNA profiling of the young men from nearby towns? Would a similar action in the United States violate the Fourth Amendment? Use references available in the library or research an on-line database to find information supporting your viewpoint. Write a report summarizing your conclusions.

Will genetic testing lead to discrimination?

3 Many fear that evidence linking genes with certain diseases opens the door for genetic discrimination. Should employers and insurers have access to an individual's DNA profile? What legislation exists to protect people against genetic discrimination? Write to the following organization for information:

The Council for Responsible Genetics
19 Garden Street
Cambridge, MA 02138

Who will have access to your genetic profile?

4 The Fourth Amendment to the United States Constitution protects citizens against unwarranted search and seizure. Could law enforcement officials order genetic testing of blood or tissue specimens previously collected for another purpose—such as for a medical exam—for comparison if they suspect that an individual has committed a crime? Use references available in the library or research an on-line database to learn more about the role of the Fourth Amendment.

39

What sort of discrimination—positive and negative—could be provoked by this sort of knowledge? Where do students think this discrimination might arise? Discuss how sports coaches, military and college recruiters, and employers might use this information.

Life/Work Skills
Finding and Organizing Information
Have students use references available in the library or research an on-line database to find information about the use of restriction fragment-length polymorphisms, or RFLPs, as genetic markers that signal the presence of disorder-causing mutations.

References

1. Angier, Natalie. "Researchers Link Obesity in Humans to Flaw in a Gene." *New York Times,* December 1, 1994.
2. Angier, Natalie. "Variant Gene Tied to a Love of New Thrills." *New York Times,* January 2, 1996.
3. Fischetti, Mark. "The Blossoming of Biotechnology." *Omni,* November 1992, 68–75.
4. Kiernan, Vincent. "U.S. Bans Gene Prejudice at Work." *New Scientist,* April 1995.
5. Lee, Thomas F. *Gene Future: The Promise and Perils of the New Biology.* New York: Plenum Press, 1993. 79–125.
6. Liebmann-Smith, Richard. "It's a (Blonde-Haired, Blue-Eyed, Even-Tempered, Ivy-Bound) Boy!" *New York Times Magazine,* February 7, 1993, 20–21.
7. Noonan, David. "Genes of War." *Discover,* October 1990, 46–52.

3 The Equal Employment Opportunity Commission (EEOC) has made genetic discrimination illegal in the United States, ruling that employers cannot terminate or refuse to hire an individual because of a genetic predisposition to an illness. This ruling is based on the Americans with Disabilities Act, which prohibits employers from discriminating against anyone who is regarded as disabled. Insurance companies, however, are exempt from the act and therefore are also exempt from the EEOC ruling.

4 Because DNA profiling provides the most precise identification possible at this time, various institutions have begun keeping records of DNA profiles. By 1990, seven states had insisted on DNA specimen collection from convicted felons. To help identify casualties, the U.S. Defense Department began compiling a DNA bank and required that all active-duty personnel submit to DNA profiling. In 1995, two U.S. Marines filed a class-action suit against the Defense Department, fearing that their DNA samples might be used without their knowledge or consent for research or criminal investigation.

3 | Cells

Lesson Planning Guide With Options for Block Scheduling

Lecture Concepts	Lesson Resources

3-1 At the Boundary of the Cell

BLOCK ❶ (45 minutes)

1. A cell is the smallest unit of life.
2. The cell membrane controls what enters and leaves the cell.

❶ Lecture Resources
- Determining Prior Knowledge
- Active Reading: Reading Organizer
- Visual Strategy: Figure 3-2
- Visual Strategy: Videodisc
- Demonstration: Forming a Hypothesis
- Teaching Transparencies: 8, 9
- Holt Biology Videodiscs Lesson 3-1

Classwork Options
- *Small Group* Demonstration: Summarizing Information
- Interactive Explorations Laboratory Manual: Lab E1

BLOCK ❷ (45 minutes)

3. As a cell grows, its volume increases more rapidly than its surface area.
4. As water molecules cluster together, non-polar lipid molecules of the cell membrane are forced into layers.

❷ Lecture Resources
- Visual Strategy: Videodisc
- Demonstration: Comparing Structures
- Demonstration: Evaluating Models
- Holt Biology Videodiscs Lesson 3-1

Classwork Options
- Reteaching
- Closure: Relating Concepts

Assignment Options
- Section Review
- Chapter Review, questions 1, 4, 5, 6, 7, 8, 9, 29
- Directed Reading Worksheet

3-2 Membrane Architecture

BLOCK ❸ (45 minutes)

1. The cell membrane consists of a phospholipid bilayer containing proteins and other molecules.
2. Each lipid layer consists of a polar head attracted to water and a nonpolar tail pushed away by water.
3. The nonpolar tails block the passage of polar molecules through the cell membrane.

❸ Lecture Resources
- The Cell Membrane
- Active Reading: Paired Summarizing
- Visual Strategy: Figure 3-8
- Holt Biology Videodiscs Lesson 3-2

Classwork Options
- Exploration 3A
- Teaching Resources CD-ROM: Basic Skills Worksheets 5

BLOCK ❹ (45 minutes)

4. The protein molecules serve as channels, receptors, and markers.
5. The proteins contain nonpolar amino acids that anchor the molecules to the nonpolar lipid tail region.
6. The proteins also contain polar amino acids that extend into the water inside and outside the cell.

❹ Lecture Resources
- Problem Solving
- Holt Biology Videodiscs Lesson 3-2

Classwork Options
- Closure: Inferring Conclusions

Assignment Options
- Reteaching
- Section Review
- Chapter Review, questions 10, 11, 12, 13, 18, 28
- Directed Reading Worksheet

3-3 Inside the Cell

BLOCK ❺ (45 minutes)

1. A eukaryotic cell is large, complex, and contains a nucleus. A prokaryotic cell is small, simple, and lacks a nucleus.
2. All cells have a cell membrane, cytoplasm, and ribosomes.
3. Only eukaryotic cells contain membrane-bound organelles.

❺ Lecture Resources
- Comparing Cell Types
- Active Reading: Reading Organizer
- Visual Strategy: Table 3-1
- Visual Strategy: Videodisc
- Demonstration: Comparing Substances
- Demonstration: Identifying Structures
- Holt Biology Videodiscs Lesson 3-3

Classwork Options
- Problem Solving
- Quick Labs: Lab A32

Assignment Options
- World of Work: Industry

KEY	
	■ Annotated Teacher's Edition
	■ Pupil's Edition
	■ Directed Reading Worksheets
	■ Vocabulary Development Worksheets
	■ Thinking Skills Worksheets
	■ Reteaching Worksheets
	■ Chapter Tests
	◉ Language Development and Reading Comprehension Audio CD Program

Holt BioSources
Laboratory Program
A Quick Labs
B Inquiry Skills Development
C Laboratory Techniques and Experimental Design
D Biotechnology
E Interactive Explorations in Biology Laboratory Manual

■ Teaching Transparencies
◉ Testing Resources CD-ROM
◉ Test Generator/Assessment Item

Holt Biology Technology
● Holt Biology Videodiscs

Lecture Concepts   Lesson Resources

3-3 Inside the Cell, continued

BLOCK ❻ (45 minutes)

4. Organelles help the cell perform the basic life functions of reproduction, energy use, and homeostasis.

5. Plant cells, unlike animal cells, have cell walls, vacuoles, and chloroplasts.

6. Details of cell structure have been observed with compound microscopes and electron microscopes.

❻ **Lecture Resources**
■ Visualizing Cells
■ Active Reading: K-W-L
■ Visual Strategy: Figures 3-13, 3-16
■ Demonstration: Predicting Outcomes
■ Demonstration: Identifying Functions
● Holt Biology Videodiscs Lesson 3-3
Classwork Options
■ Preparing SEM Specimen

■ Closure: Relating Concepts
▮ Inquiry Skills Development: Lab B2
Assignment Options
■ Reteaching
■ Section Review
■ Chapter Review, questions 2, 3, 14, 15, 16, 17, 19, 20, 21, 22, 23, 24, 25, 26, 27
■ Directed Reading Worksheet

Chapter Review and Assessment

BLOCK ❼ (45 minutes)
Review
■ Reteaching Worksheet
■ Thinking Skills Worksheet
■ Vocabulary Development Worksheet
◉ Language Development and Reading Comprehension Audio CD Program: Chapter 3

BLOCK ❽ (45 minutes)
Assessment
■ Alternative Assessment, p. 59
■ Portfolio Assessment, p. T39
Chapter Test
■ Chapter 3 Test
Test Generator
◉ Item bank for customizing Chapter Tests

Teaching Resources CD-ROM
◉ Scoring Rubrics and Classroom Management Checklist

The Portfolio icon denotes items throughout the Teacher's Edition lesson wrap that may be selected for inclusion in student portfolios.

Holt Biology Videodiscs and Concepts of Biology

Holt Biology Videodiscs gives you a powerful tool for teaching, review, and assessment. For further information regarding the media on the videodiscs, see **Holt Biology Videodiscs Teacher's Correlation Guide to Holt Biology: Visualizing Life.**

Concepts of Biology adds interactive lesson plans and extensive tools for customization using CD-ROM technology.

Use the following topic from **Concepts of Biology** to help you teach this chapter:
Topic 1: Cell Size

Laboratory Planning

Text
Materials and preparation instructions appear on the teacher's wrap accompanying each laboratory exercise.
Block 3: Exploration 3A: Observing Cells With a Microscope, p. 760

Holt BioSources Laboratory Program
Block 1: Interactive Explorations Laboratory Manual: Lab E1: Cell Size
Block 5: Quick Labs Lab A32: Relating Cell Structure to Function
Block 6: Inquiry Skills Development Lab B2: Cell Structures

Determining Prior Knowledge

- Have students draw a generalized cell and label any parts they can remember from previous course work.
- Inflate several balloons with different amounts of air. Have students identify the surface area and volume of each balloon. See if they can identify which measurement increases more rapidly as a balloon is inflated.
- Pour some oil and water into a beaker. Have students describe their observations and theorize why oil and water react this way.

Active READING

Technique: Reading Organizer

As students read Section 3-1, ask them to think about its organizational pattern and to identify a section of a previous chapter that had a similar structure. *(Section 1-1 had a similar organizational pattern.)* Have students create a reading organizer that represents the structure of the text. Have them compare their reading organizers, or have volunteers present their organizers to the class. For more information about reading organizers, see Reading Strategies Worksheets in Holt BioSources Teaching Resources CD-ROM.

CD-ROM Resources

Concepts of Biology
Topic 1: Cell Structure and Function

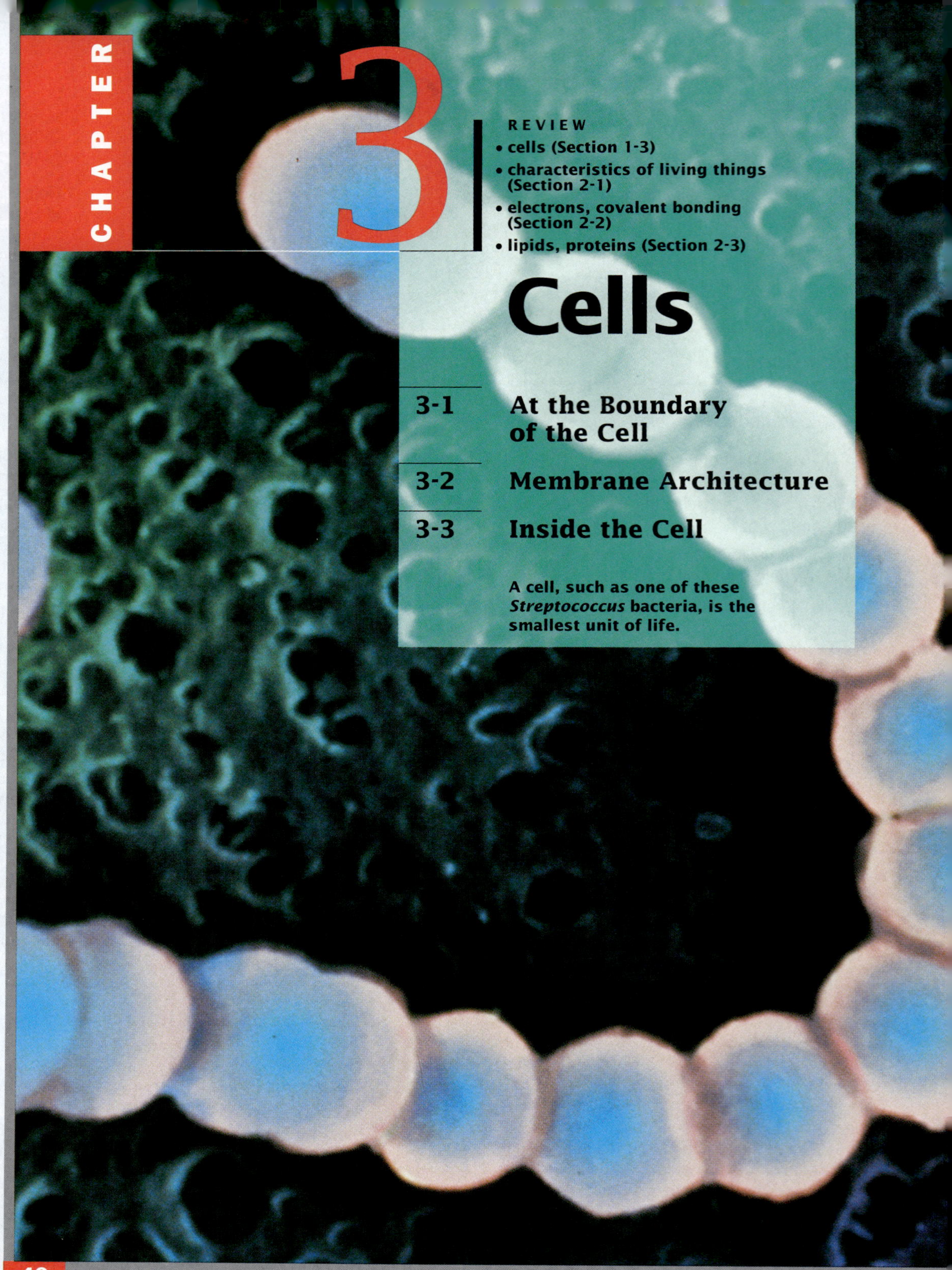

REVIEW
- cells (Section 1-3)
- characteristics of living things (Section 2-1)
- electrons, covalent bonding (Section 2-2)
- lipids, proteins (Section 2-3)

Cells

3-1	At the Boundary of the Cell
3-2	Membrane Architecture
3-3	Inside the Cell

A cell, such as one of these *Streptococcus* bacteria, is the smallest unit of life.

Author's Rationale   This chapter is critical for understanding important biological concepts in the rest of the text. It describes the architecture of the cell membrane and the characteristics that have made cells so successful. Surface-area-to-volume ratio is presented in detail because it is a useful concept that helps students understand cell size limitations in this chapter, as well as cell and tissue arrangements for specialized functions described in later chapters. The organizing role of water is presented here in the context of its most important function, rather than in isolation in a discussion of chemistry.

   By discussing the cell membrane as the key element that enables a cell to communicate with its environment, students learn about the challenges of multicellularity early in the book. The chapter closes with a study of the two different kinds of cells, emphasizing the advantages of compartmentalization, and some of the technology scientists have at hand to explore the microscopic world.

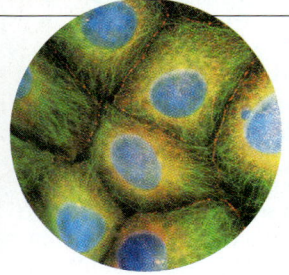

Your body is composed of trillions of cells. As long as these cells work normally, you are generally unaware of them. However, abnormal cell behavior can bring about changes such as these cancer cells. If we are ever to find cures for this deadly disease and others, we must first look closely at cells to understand how they function.

3-1 At the Boundary of the Cell

OBJECTIVES

1 Define the function of a cell membrane.

2 Explain why smaller cells function more efficiently than larger cells.

3 Distinguish between polar and nonpolar molecules.

4 Compare the interaction of water molecules with each other and with lipid molecules.

Cells: The Smallest Vessels of Life

Look at the organisms below and think about the characteristics you share with them. You, the squid, the earthworm, and all other living things are made of tiny compartments called cells. A **cell** is the smallest unit that can carry out all the activities necessary for life. Most microscopic organisms, such as the protist seen in **Figure 3-1**, are made up of a single cell.

In some ways, a cell is like a submarine. A submarine has a tough outer hull that seals the vessel and protects the equipment inside. Similarly, an outer surface called the **cell membrane** shields the delicate internal machinery of a cell. Like a submarine's hull, the cell membrane separates what is inside from what is outside. However, a cell membrane is more complex than the hull of a submarine. It must have "gates" that allow the raw materials needed by the cell to enter and that allow harmful waste products to exit promptly. Without this flow of materials, a cell would not be able to survive. By regulating what goes into and out of a cell, the cell membrane helps to maintain the internal environment of the cell.

Figure 3-1
Even though these organisms look very different, they share an important characteristic of life—they are made of cells.

Squid

Earthworm

Water lily

Protist

41

Phase One
Preparation

Scheduling
See the **Lesson Planning Guide** on pages 39A and 39B for lecture, classwork, and assignment options for Section 3-1.

Phase Two
Teaching Strategies

Connection: *Chapter 1*

Characteristics of Life
Have students list the six characteristics of life that the organisms shown in Figure 3-1 share.

Demonstration
■ **Forming a Hypothesis**
Materials: dialysis tubing, string, beaker, diluted Lugol's iodine solution

 Caution: Put on a lab apron, safety goggles, and disposable gloves. Lugol's iodine solution is poisonous; avoid contact with skin and eyes. Close one end of a small piece of dialysis tubing by tying it with string, and fill the tube with some diluted Lugol's iodine solution. Tie the other end of the tubing closed, and submerge the tube in a beaker of water. Compare the submerged sac to a cell, and ask students what the tubing represents *(the cell membrane)*. Have students describe their observations and hypothesize what is happening in the beaker. *(The dialysis tubing acts like a cell membrane, allowing substances like iodine to pass through.)*

Key to Strategies
Teaching Strategies are keyed to three tiers of learning.

● **Understanding Concepts (Tier I)**
Content mastery and comprehension

■ **Applying Information (Tier II)**
Applying and analyzing content

▲ **Critical Thinking (Tier III)**
Practicing evaluative thinking

Cells 41

What Limits the Size of a Cell?

The most obvious thing that can be said about cells is that they are very small. Although cell sizes vary (for example, the diameter of a human egg cell is about 14 times greater than that of a red blood cell), most cells are so small that you can see them only through a microscope. Study **Figure 3-2**. What factors do you think limit the size of a cell?

Cell parts cannot be too far from the cell membrane

Every bit of food and information needed by the cell must enter through the cell membrane. When cells are small, no part of their complex machinery lies too far from the area outside the cell. If a cell were larger, fewer of its interior structures could be near the cell membrane. That is bad for just the same reason that long supply lines are bad for an army—too many things could go wrong, and responses to information would be too slow. Thus, small cells work more efficiently because their "supply lines" are short.

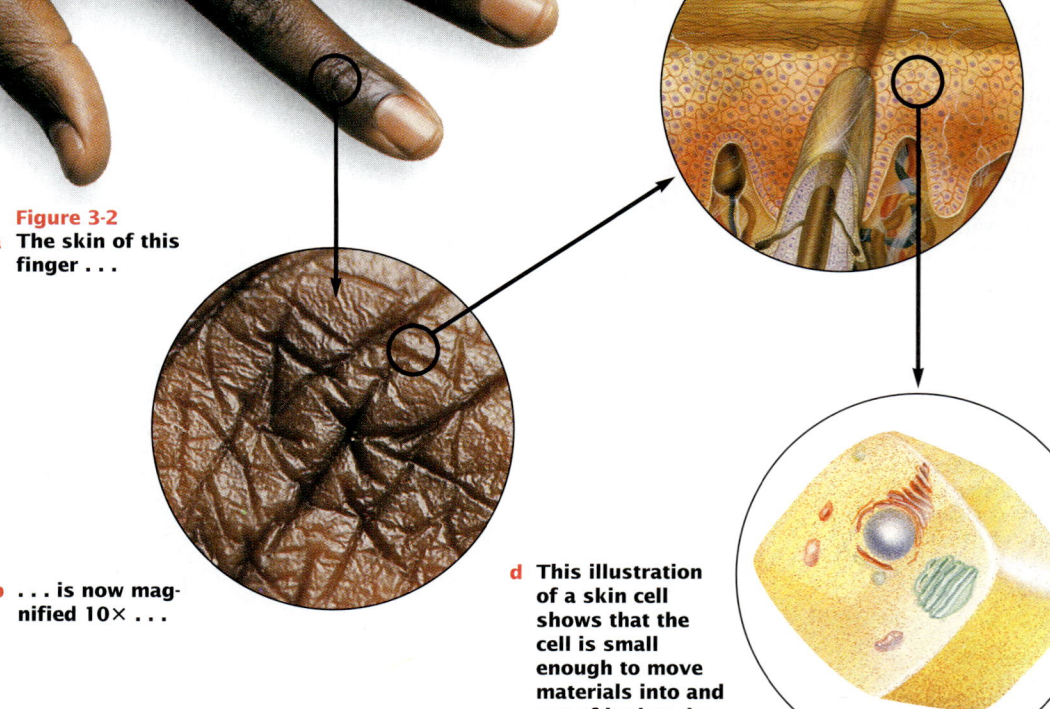

Figure 3-2

a **The skin of this finger . . .**

b **. . . is now magnified 10× . . .**

c **. . . and in this illustration you can see that the skin is a complex organ that is made of many different kinds of cells.**

d **This illustration of a skin cell shows that the cell is small enough to move materials into and out of its interior efficiently.**

42

Matter of Fact: Cell Size

To illustrate how small cells are, point out that the human body consists of approximately 100 trillion cells. To help students visualize the magnitude of 100 trillion, point out that a string 100 trillion inches long could be wrapped around the Earth more than 63,000 times, and that 100 trillion seconds is more than 3 million years. If someone handed you a dollar every second, it would take over 3 million years to accumulate 100 trillion dollars.

The Ratio of Surface Area to Volume in Cells

- The surface area of a cell is a measurement of the exterior of the cell.
- The volume is a measurement of the internal contents of the cell.

In this cell model, each side is 1 cm long.

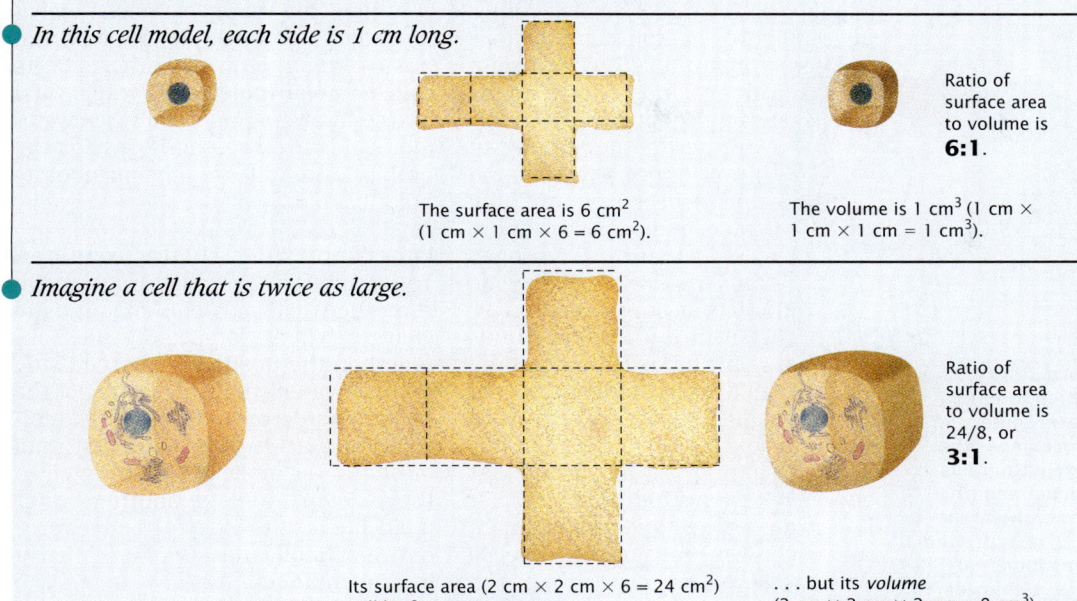

The surface area is 6 cm² (1 cm × 1 cm × 6 = 6 cm²).

The volume is 1 cm³ (1 cm × 1 cm × 1 cm = 1 cm³).

Ratio of surface area to volume is **6:1**.

Imagine a cell that is twice as large.

Its surface area (2 cm × 2 cm × 6 = 24 cm²) will be four times greater, . . .

. . . but its *volume* (2 cm × 2 cm × 2 cm = 8 cm³) will be eight times greater!

Ratio of surface area to volume is 24/8, or **3:1**.

Figure 3-3
As a cell gets larger, its volume increases faster than its surface area. A cell's surface area must be large enough to meet the needs of its volume.

A cell's volume increases faster than its surface area

As a cell grows, it takes in more food and creates more wastes. Since these substances must pass into and out of the "gates" in the cell membrane, the membrane must be large enough to service the cell's needs. As the cell grows, so does its membrane. But cells cannot grow indefinitely. So what limits cell size?

One factor is the relationship between the surface area and the volume of the cell. As a cell grows, its volume increases at a much faster rate than its surface area. A small cell, such as the one shown in the top row of **Figure 3-3**, has enough surface area to meet its needs. But a cell as large as the one shown in the bottom row might not. The ratio of a cell's surface area to its volume ultimately limits how large that cell can become. Cells cannot grow so large that their surface area becomes too small to take in enough food and remove enough wastes.

Water and the Cell

All cells are surrounded by water. Single-celled creatures swim in small ponds as well as in vast oceans. Even the cells of your body, such as blood cells or skin cells, are surrounded by a thin film of water. Water is present inside the cell too. All of the complex machinery inside the cell perform their functions in water. The cell membrane is shaped by the water found inside and outside of the cell. To understand how water can shape a cell membrane, you must first look closely at the structure of a water molecule.

Water is a polar molecule

The chemical formula for water is H_2O. A water molecule is made of two

43

Matter of Fact: A World of Water
Water is the most common liquid on Earth. Wherever water is found, life is also present. Water makes up 50 to 95 percent of the mass of organisms, with jellyfish being at the high end of that percentage range. In humans, water accounts for more than 65 percent of body mass.

Connection: *Chapter 2*

Covalent Bonds

Review covalent bond formation, emphasizing that atoms share electrons. Use a molecular model kit to build a water molecule, or draw its structure on the board. Ask students how many atoms are present (*3*) and how many covalent bonds are present (*2*).

Demonstration

● **Comparing Structures**
Materials: molecular model kit
Show the class models of H_2 and O_2. Point out that because the two atoms in each molecule are identical, they pull on the electrons with equal force and thus share them equally. Identify these molecules as nonpolar, and compare them with a polar molecule, such as a water molecule. Have students review the text description of a polar molecule.

Demonstration

▲ **Evaluating Models**
Materials: molecular model kit
Show the class models of CO_2. Ask students whether the molecule is polar or nonpolar. (*The molecule is nonpolar because both ends have the same net charge. As in water, each oxygen atom has a negative charge, but unlike a water molecule, the CO_2 molecule does not have opposite charges at opposite ends, and thus, no poles.*) Now draw the structure of a water molecule as it would be if the molecule were linear (H-O-H) and not bent, as shown in Figure 3-4. Ask students how this would affect the polar nature of a water molecule. (*If the water molecule were linear, it would be nonpolar.*)

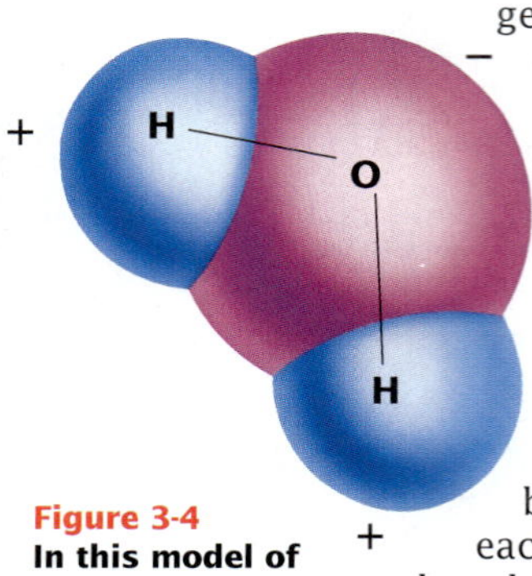

Figure 3-4
In this model of a water molecule, the area near the oxygen atom has a partial negative charge; the areas near the hydrogen atoms have partial positive charges.

hydrogen atoms and one oxygen atom that are bonded together. These bonds form when hydrogen and oxygen atoms share pairs of electrons.

Look at **Figure 3-4**. The lines between hydrogen atoms and the oxygen atom are used to represent covalent bonds. These bonds are actually pairs of electrons. Now here's the important thing about a water molecule: the oxygen atom attracts electrons more strongly than the hydrogen atoms do. Because oxygen attracts electrons so strongly, the electrons in the bonds between the oxygen atom and each hydrogen atom are not shared equally. They are more likely to be near the oxygen atom. Think of this unequal sharing as a tug of war between two atoms for the shared pair of electrons in the bond. In this tug of war, oxygen wins most of the time, so the shared electrons spend most of their time near the oxygen atom.

Because electrons have a negative charge, the oxygen part of the water molecule is slightly negative. The hydrogen atoms in the water molecule have slightly positive charges because electrons rarely spend their time near the positive hydrogen nuclei. We think of the oxygen side of the molecule as having a partial negative charge and the hydrogen side of the molecule as having a partial positive charge, as shown in **Figure 3-4**.

A molecule that has a partial negative charge on one side and a partial positive charge on the other side is called a **polar molecule**. These partial charges are very important when water molecules are together. Most of the properties of water are the result of its polarity.

Water molecules cluster together

You know that there is an attractive force between particles of opposite charge. When water molecules are together, the positively charged side of one water molecule attracts the negative side of another water molecule. The fact that the hydrogen atom of one water molecule is attracted to the oxygen atom of another water molecule results in an attractive force between molecules that is called a **hydrogen bond**.

Water molecules are at a lower energy state when they form hydrogen bonds with each other. Since all things tend toward lower energy, there is a natural tendency for water molecules to form hydrogen bonds. When forming hydrogen bonds, the water molecules will cluster together, as illustrated in **Figure 3-5**, creating a large number of bonds.

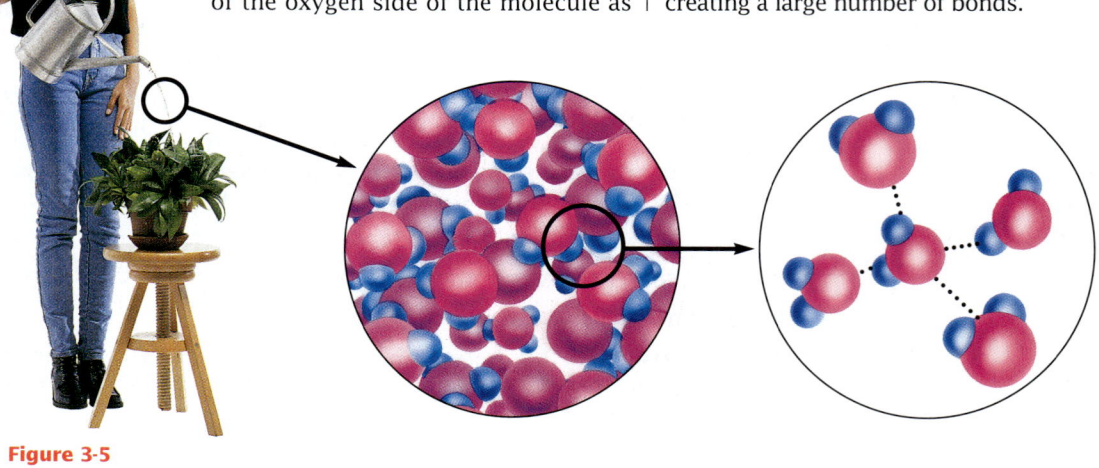

Figure 3-5
a **Water in its liquid state is composed of . . .**
b **. . . many rapidly moving water molecules.**
c **These water molecules form clusters due to the formation of hydrogen bonds.**

Water and the Cell Membrane

Now that you know something about the nature of water molecules, you can look more closely at how water shapes the cell membrane. The basic plan of the cell membrane begins with a sheet of lipids. You learned in Chapter 2 that lipids are molecules such as fats and oils. The interaction between water and lipids shapes the cell membrane.

Figure 3-6 shows what happens when oil is poured into a beaker of water and thoroughly mixed. Soon after mixing, small beads of oil form. Eventually the water and oil separate into two distinct layers. The water and oil won't stay mixed. Why? Water molecules start to cluster together because they form hydrogen bonds with each other. Unlike water, which is polar, lipids are **nonpolar molecules** because they have no negative and positive poles. Polar and nonpolar substances, like oil and water, will separate after being mixed. The oil, which is a nonpolar lipid, is not attracted to the water. Because the water molecules attract one another, the oil is pushed away. In this way, lipids interact only with each other. You can see the lipid and water layers in **Figure 3-6d**.

Figure 3-6

a **If you pour oil into a beaker of water . . .**

b **. . . and stir it thoroughly, . . .**

c **. . . the oil and water will separate because water is polar and oil is nonpolar.**

Lipid molecules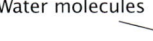

Water molecules

d **The force of water molecules pushing a sheet of lipids is the force that shapes a cell's membrane.**

SECTION REVIEW

1 What is the function of a cell membrane?

2 Why is it advantageous for a cell to grow only to a certain size and then divide into two smaller cells?

3 How does a polar molecule differ from a nonpolar molecule? Give an example of each molecule.

4 How do the properties of water help shape a cell membrane?

45

Visual Strategy Videodisc

■ **Relating Concepts**
Use *Photo—Lipid Insolubility* shown in Chapter 3 Section 3-1 of **Holt Biology Videodiscs Teacher's Correlation Guide to Holt Biology: Visualizing Life** to point out how water and oil separate into two distinct layers.

Phase Three
Assessment Options

Closure
● **Relating Concepts**
Fill a beaker with water, and gently place a needle on the surface. Ask students why the metal, which is denser than water, floats. (*The clustering of water molecules caused by hydrogen bonding results in a high surface tension that can support light objects.*)

SECTION REVIEW
Assign the *Section Review*.

Reteaching

  CAUTION: Put on lab apron, safety goggles, and disposable gloves. Lugol's iodine solution is poisonous; avoid contact with skin and eyes.
Cut a potato into three different-sized cubes. Drop each cube into a beaker containing diluted Lugol's iodine. When the iodine comes in contact with starch, a blue-black color appears. After five minutes, carefully remove each potato cube and slice the cubes in half. Have students explain their observations. (*The iodine will completely penetrate only the smallest cube. Students should realize that the movement of materials into a cell is affected by cell size.*)

ANSWERS TO SECTION REVIEW

1 The cell membrane controls which substances enter and exit the cell.

2 A smaller cell has a higher surface-area-to-volume ratio, which allows materials to reach the cell's interior more quickly than in a larger cell.

3 A polar molecule, such as water, has a negative charge at one end and a positive charge at the other, which results from the unequal sharing of electrons between the atoms. A nonpolar molecule, such as H_2 or O_2, does not have charged ends and shares electrons equally between atoms.

4 Polar water molecules cluster together and force the nonpolar lipid molecules in the membrane together, causing them to form layers.

Key to Strategies
● **Understanding Concepts (Tier I)**
■ **Applying Information (Tier II)**
▲ **Critical Thinking (Tier III)**

Phase One
Preparation

Scheduling
See the **Lesson Planning Guide** on pages 39A and 39B for lecture, classwork, and assignment options for Section 3-2.

Phase Two
Teaching Strategies

Active READING

Technique: Paired Summarizing
Pair each student with a partner. Have each student silently read pages 46 and 47. Then have one student, the "Reteller," orally summarize the text from memory. The other student, the "Listener," should listen to the retelling without interrupting (except with requests for clarification) and be prepared to point out any inaccuracies in the summary and add any ideas that were left out. Students should work together during this final clarification process and may refer to the text if needed. Have students switch roles and repeat this activity after reading pages 48 and 49.

Health Connection

Cholesterol
Many students may have the misconception that cholesterol presents a health risk in the body. Explain that cholesterol is an important structural component of the cell membrane. Cholesterol molecules form part of the nonpolar "tail" region of the membrane. Emphasize that cholesterol creates a health risk when it is present in high levels in the blood, where it builds up in arteries and obstructs blood flow.

Proteins determine most of the functional characteristics of a cell membrane. If a cell's proteins are defective, the cell's function may be impaired, which can have devastating effects. For example, scientists have found that a single faulty gene encodes for a defective protein that causes the deadly disease cystic fibrosis. If scientists can correct the protein, they may be able to cure the disease.

3-2 Membrane Architecture

OBJECTIVES

1 Illustrate the arrangement of phospholipids in a lipid bilayer.

2 Describe two characteristics of a lipid bilayer.

3 Describe the functions of proteins in the cell membrane.

4 Explain how proteins stay anchored in the cell membrane.

Structure of the Lipid Bilayer

Recall that the cell membrane is not just an envelope enclosing the contents of a cell. It is more like a security guard controlling the flow of materials into an official building. In order to understand how a cell membrane exercises this control, you must first take a look at its structure.

The basic building block of the cell membrane is a kind of lipid molecule called a **phospholipid**, which has both polar and nonpolar regions. As you can see in **Figure 3-7a**, a phospholipid is an unusual-looking molecule: a short "head" is joined to two long "tails." The head of a phospholipid contains phosphorus and nitrogen, which make it polar. Therefore, the head is attracted to water. The long tails of a phospholipid molecule are nonpolar, however, so water molecules tend to push them away.

Water can interact with the polar heads and repel the nonpolar lipid tails best if the phospholipids are aligned in two layers, as shown in **Figure 3-7b**. This double layer of phospholipids forms a flexible **lipid bilayer**, which is shown in **Figure 3-7c**. Notice that the polar heads of the phospholipids point toward the water inside and outside the cell. The tails are buried in the interior of the membrane, directing themselves away from the water.

Figure 3-7
a This phospholipid molecule . . .

b . . . is part of a lipid bilayer.

c The lipid bilayer forms the framework of the cell membrane.

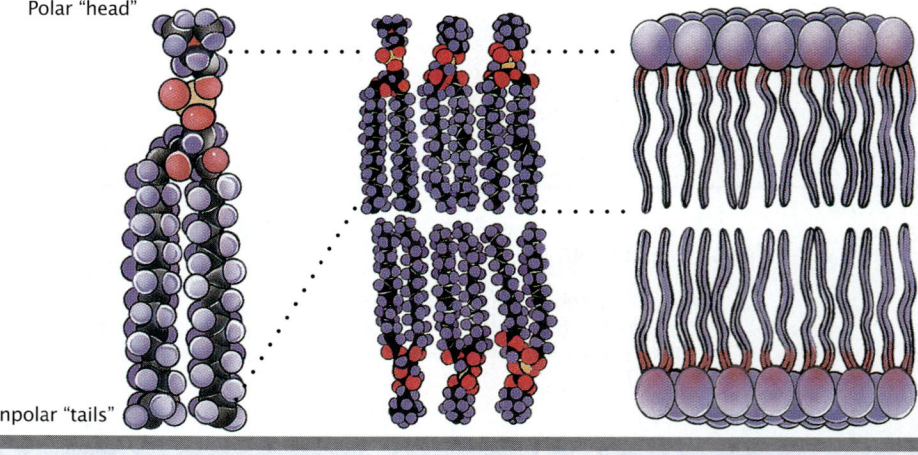

Polar "head"

Nonpolar "tails"

Videodisc Resources

Holt Biology Videodiscs
Lesson 3-2: Membrane Architecture

Characteristics of the Lipid Bilayer

Evolution

All cells have a cell membrane constructed of a lipid bilayer. What does this suggest about evolutionary relationships among living things?

Lipid bilayers stop polar molecules

The lipid bilayers found in cell membranes have two important characteristics. One important characteristic is that most polar molecules cannot go across it. Polar molecules are attracted to the water inside the cell or to the water outside. However, they cannot interact with the nonpolar tails of the phospholipids within the lipid bilayer. The result is that the interior part of the cell membrane acts as a barrier to polar molecules. But most food molecules and other substances needed by the cell are polar. So the cell must have a way of allowing these molecules across. If the cell membrane were made only of a lipid bilayer, there would be no way for food and other things to pass into and out of the cell.

The solution is to have passageways through the barrier. The cell membrane has passageways made of proteins, such as those shown in **Figure 3-7d**. By making "gates" that can open and shut in the lipid bilayer, proteins enable the passageways to regulate precisely the substances that go into and out of cells. You will see later that cell membrane proteins have other roles, too.

Lipid bilayers are fluid

A second important characteristic of lipid bilayers is that their phospholipid and protein molecules are not rigidly fixed in place. These molecules move about like rubber life preservers floating on the surface of a swimming pool. The lipid bilayer is fluid.

Because they are not fixed in place, the phospholipid and protein molecules that make up the cell membrane can shift from one region of the cell membrane to another. This is important because cell membranes can be structured to fit the needs of different cell types.

d The lipid bilayer and its associated proteins make up the cell membrane.

Marker protein

Receptor protein

Channel protein

47

Theme Answer
Evolution
All cell membranes, including those surrounding various organelles, have the same basic composition: 40 percent lipid and 60 percent protein. However, the types of lipids and proteins vary not only among cells from different organisms but also within the cells of the same organism. A common structural arrangement, such as the lipid bilayer, points to an evolutionary relationship among all organisms. The variations in composition indicate adaptations by different organisms (and different cells) to their environments.

The Cell Membrane
■ **Drawing Analogies**

Ask students to list analogies that illustrate the cell membrane's ability to control which substances enter and exit the cell. *(Analogies may include a toll gate, an airport security gate, a stadium gate, and a fence gate.)*

Art Connection
Fluid Mosaic Model
Present a picture of a piece of art that consists of mosaic tiles. Ask students to study Figure 3-7d and then explain why the structure of the cell membrane is referred to as the fluid mosaic model. *(Like a mosaic, the cell membrane has a design consisting of a repetitive pattern, the phospholipid molecules in the lipid bilayer, interspersed with pieces of various shapes and styles, the proteins.)*

Multicultural Perspective: Protein channels

In 1991 two German scientists, Erwin Neher and Bert Sakmann, received the Nobel Prize for Medicine and Physiology for their work on how protein channels control the passage of ions into and out of the cell. Their research may lead to the development of drug molecules designed to enter cells through these channels and treat certain diseases.

Key to Strategies
● **Understanding Concepts (Tier I)**
■ **Applying Information (Tier II)**
▲ **Critical Thinking (Tier III)**

Problem Solving

■ **Forming a Model**
Materials: toothpicks, large marshmallows, drinking-straw segments, jelly beans, tape
Present materials to the class and challenge students in small groups to design a model of the cell membrane based on Figures 3-7 through 3-10. *(Connect two rows of marshmallows with toothpicks to represent the lipid bilayer. Poke several straws of different diameters through the marshmallows to represent protein channels. Embed jelly beans into the marshmallows to represent receptor proteins. Make small flags out of tape and toothpicks, and stick these into the marshmallows to represent marker proteins.)* Have each group present its model to the rest of the class.

Visual Strategy Figure 3-8

● **Identifying Structures**
Point out that cystic fibrosis, the disorder described in the section opener, is caused by a defective channel protein. A healthy version of the channel protein pumps chloride ions across the cell membrane. When this protein is defective, transport of chloride ions is impaired and the ions accumulate outside the cell, leading to the collecting of thick mucus on the surface of cells in the digestive and respiratory systems.

Roles of Cell Membrane Proteins

If you were able to peer at the surface of a cell, it would look like a smooth sea of phospholipids interrupted by proteins sticking out from the surface, some like boulders, others like tall trees. Proteins that protrude from the cell membrane may serve as channels, receptors, or markers.

Channels allow some molecules to pass through the membrane

Channels through a cell membrane are formed by doughnut-shaped proteins, as you can see in **Figure 3-8**. Many molecules and ions that are needed by the cell cross the membrane through these passageways. However, these channels are like locked doors—only people with a key can enter. In the same way, each channel will admit only certain molecules.

Receptors transfer information

Receptor proteins in the cell membrane are shaped like boulders, as shown in **Figure 3-9**. Receptors convey information from the external environment into the cell. The part of the receptor that sticks out from the cell membrane has a specific shape. Only molecules with the right shape can fit into these receptors. When a molecule and its receptor are locked together, a change occurs to the part of the receptor that faces inside the cell. This change triggers responses inside the cell.

Markers help identify cells

Cell surface markers are elongated proteins, often with short chains of carbohydrates attached, as you can see in **Figure 3-10**. These proteins are the "name tags" of the cell. Every cell of your body has markers on its surface saying that it is a part of you and nothing else. These markers organized your first body tissues before you were born. As you developed and new tissues and organs were formed, these markers directed your cells to their proper locations. In Chapter 4, you will learn how cell surface markers help a cell interact with its environment.

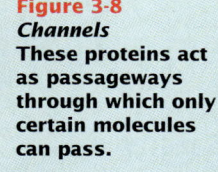

Figure 3-9
Receptors
These proteins transmit information into the cell by reacting to certain other molecules.

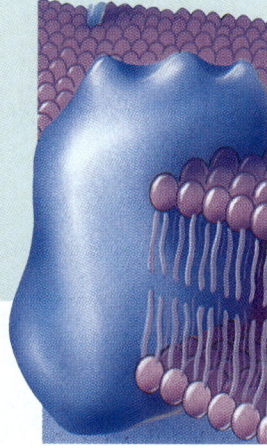

Figure 3-8
Channels
These proteins act as passageways through which only certain molecules can pass.

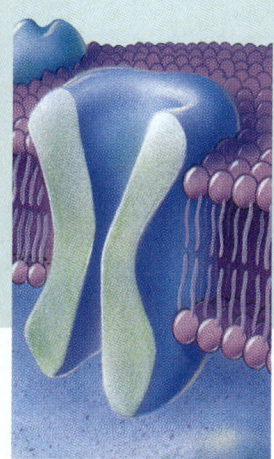

Figure 3-10
Markers
These proteins are the "name tags" of cells, giving each an identity.

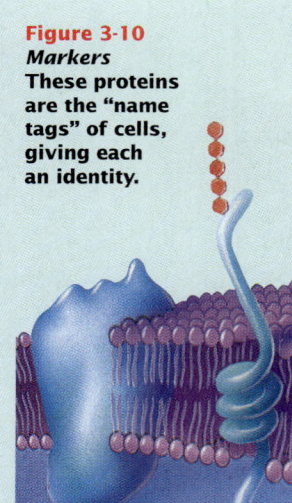

48

Historical Perspective: Naming the Cell

In 1665, at a meeting of scientists in London, England, Robert Hooke decided to present the compound microscope he had built to discuss a simple question: Why does cork float? After cutting a very thin slice of cork with his pocket knife, Hooke had scientists observe sections through his microscope. The walls surrounding the air spaces reminded Hooke of the small rooms in a monastery, which are called cells. Referring to each space as a cell, Hooke introduced the term into the vocabulary of science.

Protein Structure and the Cell Membrane

Recall from Chapter 2 that proteins are molecules made of subunits called amino acids. Proteins in the cell membrane can serve as channels, receptors, or markers. How are proteins able to play such different roles? And how do proteins, which can be polar molecules, fit into the inner nonpolar region of the lipid bilayer? To answer these questions, take a closer look at the structure of protein.

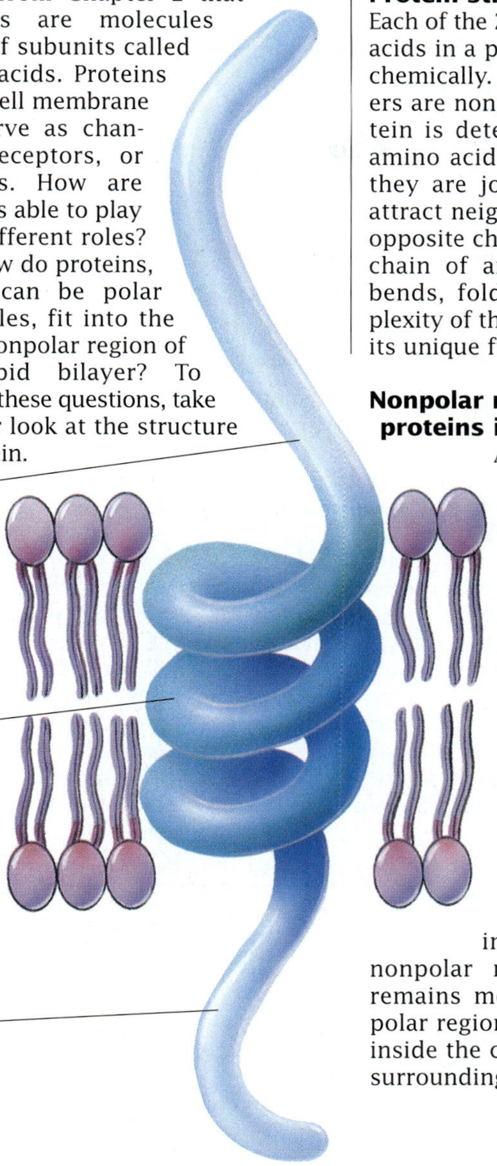

Figure 3-11
a **The amino acids in this region of the protein are mostly polar. Therefore, this polar region is compatible with the water outside the cell.**
b **The amino acids in this region of the protein are mostly nonpolar. Therefore, this region is compatible with the nonpolar area in the center of the bilayer.**
c **This region is also polar and is compatible with the water inside the cell.**

Protein structure is variable

Each of the 20 different kinds of amino acids in a protein is slightly different chemically. Some are polar, while others are nonpolar. The shape of a protein is determined by its particular amino acids and the order in which they are joined. Some amino acids attract neighboring amino acids with opposite charges. As a result, a single chain of amino acids in a protein bends, folds, and twists. The complexity of the shape gives each protein its unique function.

Nonpolar regions anchor proteins in the membrane

A protein that fits into a cell membrane has three basic sections, which are pointed out in **Figure 3-11**. The two end sections contain many polar amino acids that form hydrogen bonds with water. However, the middle section is made of many nonpolar amino acids. This nonpolar coil fits into the nonpolar interior of the lipid bilayer, allowing the protein to float in the membrane like a ship at sea. The protein is anchored into the membrane by this nonpolar region, but the protein remains mobile. The protein's nonpolar region prevents it from sinking inside the cell or floating off into the surrounding water.

SECTION REVIEW

1. **How do phospholipids interact with water to form a lipid bilayer?**
2. **Why is a lipid bilayer said to be fluid? What is the importance of this property?**
3. **Explain three roles proteins play in cell membranes.**
4. **How does a protein stay anchored in a cell membrane?**

Connection: *Chapter 2*

Amino Acids
Have students describe the structure of an amino acid. Be sure they are aware that a protein consists of a long chain of amino acids linked together with covalent bonds and folded into a specific shape.

Phase Three
Assessment Options

Closure

■ **Inferring Conclusions**
List the following cells on the board: red blood cell, brain cell, kidney cell, and tongue cell. Ask students to hypothesize which type of protein (channel, receptor, or marker) would be most common in the membrane of each cell type. Have students provide a reason for their choice. *(Possible answers include red blood cell—marker proteins that make up the blood group antigens; brain cell—receptor proteins for transferring information; kidney cell—channel proteins to filter wastes from the blood; tongue cell—receptor proteins for detecting food molecules.)*

SECTION REVIEW

Assign the *Section Review.*

Reteaching

Have students select an object visible from outside of their house that could serve as a model for either the lipid bilayer or a protein of a cell membrane. Have them defend their analogy. *(Examples might include a wall as the lipid bilayer, a door or window as a channel protein, a TV antenna or satellite dish as a receptor, or a nameplate as a marker protein.)*

ANSWERS TO SECTION REVIEW

1. The long nonpolar "tails" of a phospholipid molecule are repelled by water molecules and align to point inward, toward each other. The polar "heads" are attracted to water molecules and align to face outward, toward the water.
2. The lipid bilayer is fluid because the phospholipids are not rigidly fixed in place, lending flexibility to the cell membrane.
3. Proteins in the cell membrane can serve as channels, receptors, or markers.
4. The nonpolar region of the protein anchors the molecule to the nonpolar interior of the lipid bilayer.

Key to Strategies
● Understanding Concepts (Tier I)
■ Applying Information (Tier II)
▲ Critical Thinking (Tier III)

Scheduling

See the **Lesson Planning Guide** on pages 39A and 39B for lecture, classwork, and assignment options for Section 3-3.

Phase Two
Teaching Strategies

Active READING

Technique: Reading Organizer
As students read about organelles on pages 51 and 52, have them create a descriptive reading organizer. Students should design the descriptive organizer to identify and describe the organelles explained in the text.

Visual Strategy Table 3-1

● **Interpreting Tables**
Have students identify similarities *(cell membrane and cytoplasm)* and differences *(size and complexity of organization)* between the *Chilodenella* and the bacterium. Have students refer to the information listed in Table 3-1.

Comparing Cell Types

● **Forming a Model**
Have students make a **Graphic Organizer** similar to the one on page 51 that illustrates the differences between prokaryotes and eukaryotes. Have them include examples of each cell type.

Have you ever had a case of strep throat? If so, your cells were under attack by bacteria. Bacteria are single-celled organisms. Bacterial cells are very different from your cells, but they are nevertheless the ancestors of your cells. How do bacterial cells differ from your cells, and how did bacteria evolve into the kind of cells that make up your body?

3-3 Inside the Cell

OBJECTIVES

1 Distinguish between eukaryotic cells and prokaryotic cells.

2 Relate the success of eukaryotes to the presence of organelles.

3 Describe a theory that explains the evolution of eukaryotic cells.

4 Compare three types of microscopes commonly used by biologists.

Two Types of Cells

All cells can be divided into two large categories. A eukaryotic *(yoo KAR ee oht ik)* cell is a large, complex cell that contains a membrane-bound compartment called a **nucleus**. The nucleus contains DNA within chromosomes. Organisms with eukaryotic cells are called **eukaryotes** *(yoo KAR ee ohtz)*. A prokaryotic cell, or **prokaryote** *(pro KAR ee oht)*, is a very small, simple cell that lacks a nucleus. Its DNA is a single, circular molecule that is not enclosed in a membrane-bound compartment. Prokaryotic organisms, or prokaryotes, are ancient life-forms. Fossils of the oldest cells on Earth reveal that prokaryotes existed 3.5 billion years ago. Although bacteria are the only living prokaryotes, they are the most numerous of all living things. Every other living organism is a eukaryotic organism, or eukaryote. Compare a few of the general characteristics of these two cell types in **Table 3-1**.

Eukaryotes and prokaryotes share several characteristics. Both kinds of cells have a cell membrane. They also contain a mostly fluid internal environment called the **cytoplasm** *(SYT uh plaz uhm)*. They both also contain **ribosomes** *(RY buh sohmz)*, structures on which proteins are made.

Table 3-1
a **This bacterium, *Streptococcus pneumoniae*, is an example of a prokaryotic cell. It has been magnified approximately 40,000 times in this micrograph.**

Table 3-1 Two Cell Types

Prokaryote	Eukaryote
No nucleus	Nucleus
No membrane-bound organelles	Many organelles
Most 1–10 μm in size	Many 2–1,000 μm in size
Evolved 3.5 billion years ago	Evolved 1.5 billion years ago
Only bacteria	All other cells

b **This protist, *Chilodonella*, is an example of a eukaryotic cell. It has been magnified 150 times in this micrograph.**

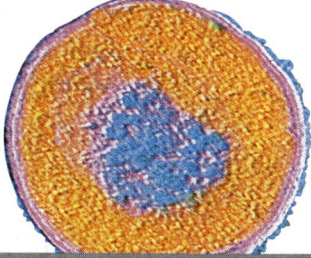

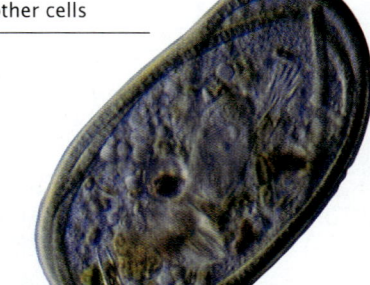

50

Videodisc Resources

Holt Biology Videodiscs
Lesson 3-3: Inside the Cell

Eukaryotic Cells Have Compartments

The nucleus is not the only compartment inside a eukaryotic cell. The cytoplasm consists of an aqueous space called the **cytosol** *(SYT uh sohl)* and a variety of structures known as organelles. Each **organelle** is a specialized compartment that carries out one or more specific functions. Some organelles supply energy to other parts of the cell, while some use energy to make molecules. Other organelles package these products for delivery to other sites in the cell or outside the cell. Many organelles, such as the nucleus, are bound by membranes. You can see a variety of organelles in the cell in **Figure 3-12**.

How do organelles benefit a eukaryotic cell? Imagine if you had to attend class in a building without internal walls. How would you get any work done if the gymnasium, cafeteria, library, and office were in the same room? The organelles of a eukaryotic cell are like the many separate rooms in a building. The separate compartments allow specialized activities to be restricted to particular places.

Organelles contribute to the specialization of eukaryotic cells

The organelles in a eukaryotic cell are continuously working, moving, reproducing, and disappearing. Networks of these busy cellular components enable eukaryotic cells to specialize and perform different functions.

Think about the different kinds of cells that make up your body. A muscle cell in your leg must be able to contract quickly. Therefore, it contains a greater number of energy-converting organelles than a bone cell contains. Likewise, the striped, pulsating cells in your heart are very different from the

Nucleus
Cytosol
Organelles

Figure 3-12
One way that a eukaryotic cell differs from a prokaryotic cell is that they contain organelles, specialized compartments that carry out specific functions.

boxlike cells that make up the layers of skin covering your hand. And these skin cells differ greatly from the nerve cells that send electrical signals from your brain throughout your body. Other examples of specialized eukaryotic cells include gland cells, which secrete life-sustaining substances, and sperm cells, which need to be able to move to perform their job.

Keep in mind that all of the cells in your body originated from a single fertilized egg cell. As these cells divided, they changed in slightly different ways, becoming specialized for specific functions. Specialization enabled single-celled eukaryotes to evolve into multicellular organisms capable of surviving in a variety of environments.

51

Graphic Organizer

Use the following graphic organizer with the teaching strategy **Comparing Cell Types** on page 50.

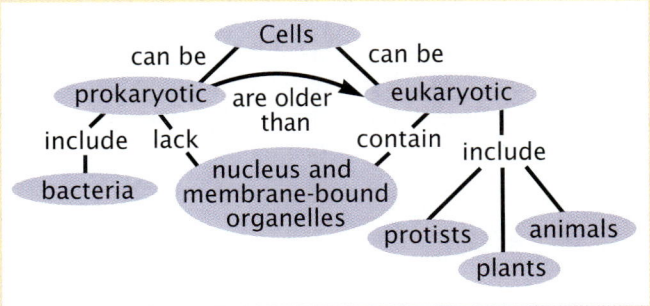

Organelles: A Cell's Laborers

Like all living things, cells perform basic functions of life. Cells use energy, cells maintain homeostasis, and cells reproduce. Like the cell's nucleus, the other organelles in a eukaryotic cell are specialized membrane-bound compartments whose contents are separated from other parts of the cytoplasm. Isolated from the hustle and bustle of the rest of the cell, each organelle stands ready to perform a specific task. The coordinated activities of the different organelles enable cells to go about the business of living. *A Closer Look: Eukaryotic Cell*, on page 53, highlights the major organelles in the eukaryotic cell.

The nucleus directs cell activities
The nucleus directs cell activities and serves as the storage center for the cell's DNA. Much like wearing two layers of clothing, the nucleus is encased in a double membrane called the nuclear envelope. The cell's activities are regulated by molecules that pass into and out of the nucleus through the nuclear envelope. How do they get through? Scattered over the surface of the nuclear envelope are shallow pits called nuclear pores, which provide passageways for these molecules.

Cells manufacture and release energy
By now you are aware that the life of a cell is not a restful one. Your cells are always at work. Where do they get the energy to perform all of life's tasks? The energy that drives a cell's activities is converted within organelles called **mitochondria** *(myt uh KAHN dree uh)*. These organelles are specialized to convert energy stored in food. The number of mitochondria in most cells varies. A muscle cell in your heart, which may pump more than 70 times per minute, can contain thousands of mitochondria. A mature red blood cell has none.

The significant differences between you and plants is the source of the food processed by mitochondria for your energy. How do plants provide their mitochondria with food molecules? Plant cells contain **chloroplasts**, organelles that have the amazing ability to make chemical energy in the form of sugars, using air, water, and the energy from sunlight. This process is called photosynthesis. Chloroplasts are found mostly in algae, such as seaweed, and in green plants.

Cells maintain homeostasis
In order for a cell to function properly, supplies must be transported from one part of a cell to another. In a bacterium, materials move about at random. In eukaryotic cells, some of the molecular traffic is directed by an extensive system of membranes called the **endoplasmic reticulum** *(ehn duh PLAZ mihk rih TIHK yuh luhm)*, or ER. Weaving in sheets throughout the cell, the ER creates a series of channels that acts as a highway system through the cytoplasm. This system of internal compartments is a fundamental distinction between eukaryotes and their prokaryote ancestors.

The cell manufactures many proteins and lipids on the surface of the ER. Some of these are used within the cell to replace damaged parts. Other products, such as digestive enzymes and hormones, are exported from the cell. Those proteins and lipids destined for export are enclosed within vesicles that bud off from the ER surface. These molecules are then transported to another organelle called the **Golgi** *(GOHL jee)* **apparatus** (named after Camillo Golgi, the scientist who first described them). The Golgi apparatus is the cell's packaging and distribution center. It puts the finishing touches on molecules and releases them in the membrane-wrapped vesicles. Substances packaged in this way can be sent to different cellular compartments or exported from the cell. Some vesicles fuse with the cell membrane, releasing their contents outside the cell.

52

Matter of Fact: Mitochondria
Point out that muscle cells aren't the only types of cells that have high-energy requirements. For example, a liver cell has about 2,500 mitochondria, which make up about 25 percent of the cell's volume. This high number of mitochondria reflects the many jobs the liver cell performs and the high level of energy it requires.

Eukaryotic Cell

Eukaryotic cells contain DNA within the nucleus and have membrane-bound organelles. Eukaryotes evolved approximately 1.5 billion years ago.

A Closer Look

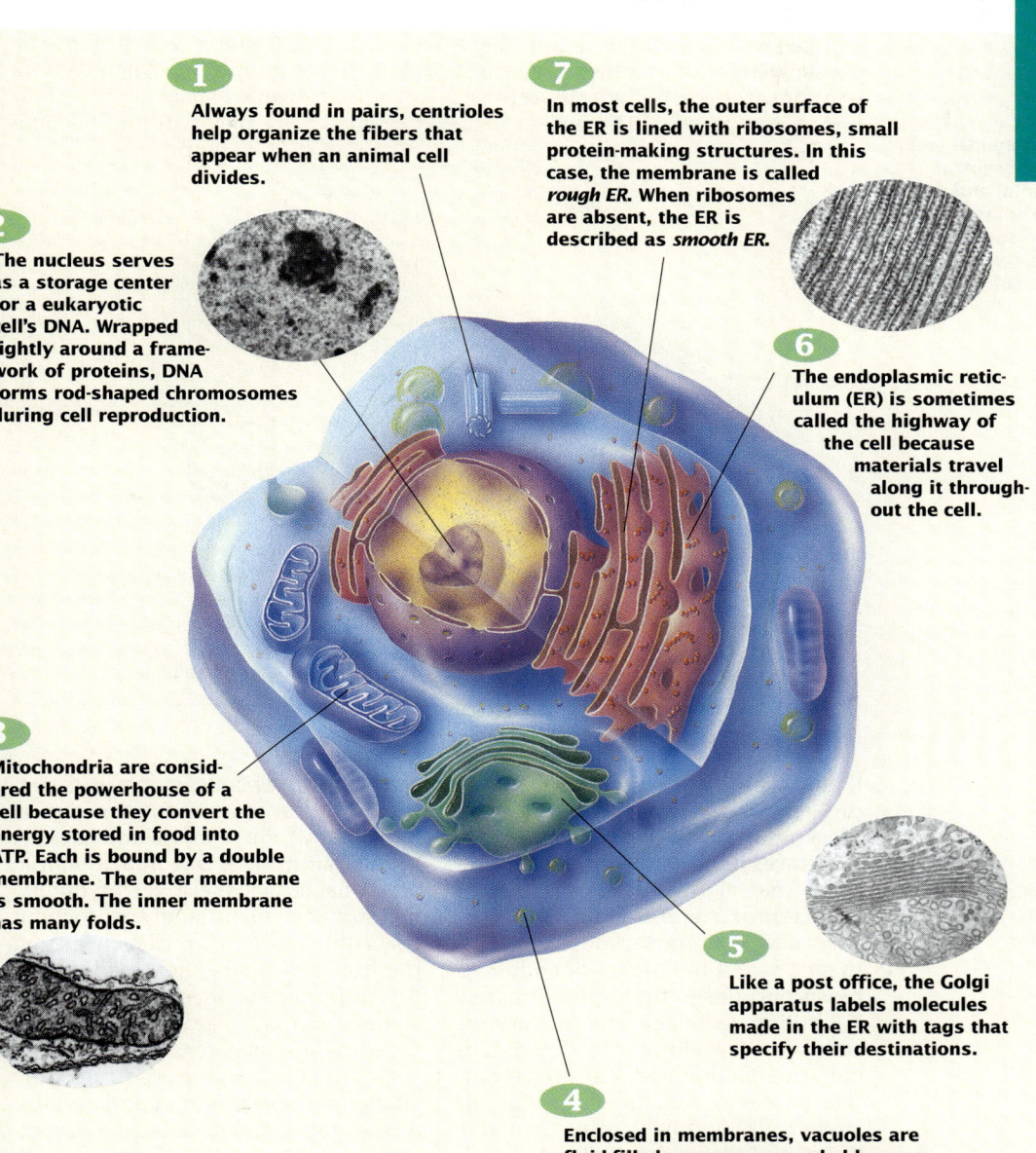

1 Always found in pairs, centrioles help organize the fibers that appear when an animal cell divides.

2 The nucleus serves as a storage center for a eukaryotic cell's DNA. Wrapped tightly around a framework of proteins, DNA forms rod-shaped chromosomes during cell reproduction.

3 Mitochondria are considered the powerhouse of a cell because they convert the energy stored in food into ATP. Each is bound by a double membrane. The outer membrane is smooth. The inner membrane has many folds.

4 Enclosed in membranes, vacuoles are fluid-filled spaces surrounded by membranes. Vacuoles function in digestion, storage, support, and water balance.

5 Like a post office, the Golgi apparatus labels molecules made in the ER with tags that specify their destinations.

6 The endoplasmic reticulum (ER) is sometimes called the highway of the cell because materials travel along it throughout the cell.

7 In most cells, the outer surface of the ER is lined with ribosomes, small protein-making structures. In this case, the membrane is called *rough ER*. When ribosomes are absent, the ER is described as *smooth ER*.

section 3-3

Visual Strategy Figure 3-13

● Identifying Structures

Ask students to identify the characteristics this plant cell shares with an animal cell *(vacuole, mitochondria, nucleus, endoplasmic reticulum, and cell membrane).*

Demonstration

■ Predicting Outcomes

Materials: *Elodea,* microprojector, 5% salt solution, forceps

Prepare a wet-mount slide of *Elodea.* As students observe, place a drop of 5% salt solution next to the coverslip and draw the solution to the *Elodea* by placing a piece of dry paper towel at the opposite edge of the coverslip. Ask students to describe the effects of a high salt solution on plant cells. *(Students should describe the shrinking of cell organelles, especially vacuoles.)*

Connection: *Chapter 2*

Definition of Life

Point out that both mitochondria and chloroplasts divide to produce new organelles. Ask students what characteristic of life these organelles display *(reproduction).*

Plant Cells Differ From Animal Cells

Although all eukaryotic cells contain a nucleus and organelles, not all cells contain the same organelles. For example, many green-plant cells contain chloroplasts. Because they face environmental challenges that other organisms don't, plants have additional organelles and cell structures. As you can see in **Figure 3-13**, plants have a **cell wall**, a thick outer layer that contains the carbohydrate cellulose and protein. The cell wall gives strength and rigidity to the cell. Although vacuoles are found in both animal and plant cells, they are often more highly developed in plant cells. Plant cells store waste products, nutrients, and water in large centrally located vacuoles that may occupy between 30 and 90 percent of the cell's volume. The pressure exerted by the stored water helps the plant to stand upright. When its vacuoles lack water, a plant may wilt and become limp.

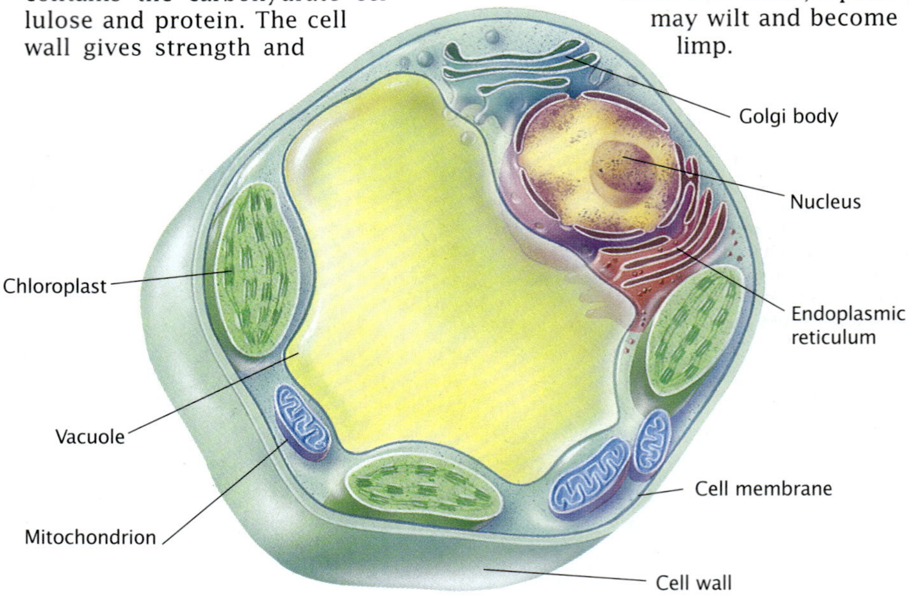

Figure 3-13
A strong cell wall, a large central vacuole, and chloroplasts that make sugar set plant cells apart from animal cells.

The Origin of Eukaryotic Cells

If one of the main differences between prokaryotic and eukaryotic cells is the presence of organelles, how did these structures arise? Most biologists now think that at least two organelles—mitochondria and chloroplasts—are descendants of prokaryotic cells. This theory, called the theory of endosymbiosis, proposes that approximately 1.5 billion years ago tiny prokaryotic cells were "swallowed" by larger cells but were not digested. The prokaryotic "trespassers" remained inside the larger cells, gradually losing their ability to live independently. The two cells formed a partnership—the trespassers became organelles, thus forming the first eukaryotic cells.

The theory of endosymbiosis is supported by several pieces of evidence. First, many mitochondria and bacteria are similar in size. Like mitochondria, some bacteria have a set of double membranes. Surprisingly, mitochondria contain their own ribosomes and their own chromosomes, evidence of their past self-reliance. Their chromosomes are circular strands of DNA, like those of prokaryotes. And the ribosomes in mitochondria are structurally similar to those found in prokaryotes. Also, some organelles divide in a manner similar to bacteria. According to the theory of endosymbiosis, bacteria capable of photosynthesis gave rise to chloroplasts found in plants and algae.

Community Connection: Water Balance and Agriculture

Assign students to research the effects recent weather patterns might have had on the local and global economies, especially the agricultural sector. Suggest that they research topics such as droughts, floods, and acid rain. If possible, consider inviting a local individual such as a county extension agent to speak to one of your classes or to respond to requests for interviews from some of your students.

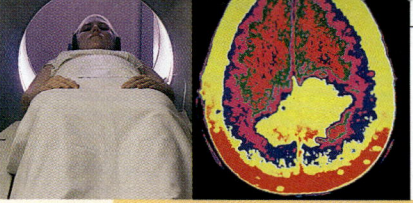

Science Technology

What would it be like to . . .

- perform cutting-edge research and investigations?
- have the expertise to work in hospitals, industry, or education?

These are just a few of the opportunities open to people who work in the field of science technology.

Science Technology: What Is It?

Science technology encompasses the tools, equipment, and procedures used in science and medicine. A science technician is skilled in carrying out specialized procedures and techniques, usually under the supervision of a scientist or doctor. In hospitals, technicians do laboratory work or handle sophisticated diagnostic equipment. In industry, technicians are involved in production of pharmaceutical products, food processing, and manufactured goods.

Science/Math Career Preparation

High school
- Biology
- Chemistry
- Math

College
- Depends on area of specialization; varies from a 2-year to a 4-year degree

Employment Outlook

As scientific investigations grow more complex, technicians will be needed to use practical skills, new technologies, and analytical methods.

Career Focus: Phyllis Stout

Technician at a Biological Supplies Company

"I can't remember a time in my life when I wasn't interested in science. I loved my high school biology classes, especially lab work. After I graduated, I began working at Ward's Natural Science, Inc. as a clerk filling orders. Soon, an opportunity to advance came along and for six months I trained to prepare and assemble skeletons. One of my projects involved preparing a bison skeleton for a college in Canada."

What I Do: "A few years later, I trained to work in the microscope-slide department preparing slides in all stages of production. Preparing a microscope slide is meticulous but fulfilling work. After slicing the tissues of a specimen, I stain it using one of many different dyes and techniques. It is then mounted on a glass slide and protected with a coverslip. Last year, I helped prepare over 200,000 slides that were distributed to students all over the world."

To Find Out More

1 For further information, write to:
American Society for
  Clinical Laboratory Science
7910 Woodmont Ave.
Suite 530
Bethesda, MD 20814

2 Visit your school counselor to find out which colleges and universities offer programs for science technicians. Review the prerequisites and course requirements. Make a poster showing the range of job opportunities in this field.

3 Find articles that describe a recent advance in medical technology. Prepare a report that describes the technology and the circumstances under which it is used.

Career Opportunities

Understanding Technology

1. Have students brainstorm ideas about the following questions:
If you wanted a career in science technology...

- what kind of personality traits would be essential?
- which subjects should you study in high school? in college?
- what kinds of extracurricular activities should you pursue?
- what kind of practical experience should you gain?
- what kind of issues or current events would interest you?

2. In small groups, have students choose a technological achievement in science (i.e., electron microscopy, DNA fingerprinting, etc.) and create a timeline that traces its development from its earliest uses to today. Each group can then present its findings and teach other students about important developments in technology.

3. In small groups, have students select a familiar piece of equipment or machinery and write descriptions and instructions for its proper use. Prepare them for this activity by distributing various kinds of manuals and catalogues for review and discussing guidelines for formatting the text.

55

Viewing the Cell

The existence of cells became known only after microscopes were developed in the 1600s. Our knowledge of cell structure is the result of better and more powerful microscopes. Each kind of microscope has its own strengths and limitations. Scientists have learned which microscopes can give the most information about the objects they are examining.

Two concepts are important when using a microscope to examine a specimen: magnification and resolution. **Magnification** is the microscope's ability to make an object appear larger. **Resolution** is its capacity to distinguish different objects that are close to one another.

A compound microscope uses two lenses to magnify cells

A microscope that has two lenses is called a compound microscope, shown in **Figure 3-14a**. A typical compound microscope has a light source that shines light up through the specimen, the object being examined. Light passes through the objective lens and then through the eyepiece. The image you see is magnified by both lenses. Total magnification is determined by multiplying the magnification of one lens by that of the other. If your microscope has an eyepiece lens that magnifies 10 times and an objective lens that magnifies 40 times, the specimen appears 400 times larger than it actually is.

When you look at a living cell through a compound microscope, it appears transparent, with slight variations in thickness and density. Contrast is often obtained by slicing the samples of living materials into very thin sections and staining the cells being studied. Since parts of the cell differ in their abilities to soak up various dyes, it is possible to use different stains to make specific cell structures stand out from each other. Looking at a cell this way has disadvantages—only one slice of cell can be seen, and, of course, the cells prepared in this manner die. **Figure 3-14b** shows a micrograph of a *Paramecium* magnified 100 times under a compound microscope. A micrograph is a photograph of an object as seen through a microscope.

Figure 3-14
a In a compound light microscope, light passes through a specimen and is bent and directed through the eyepiece.

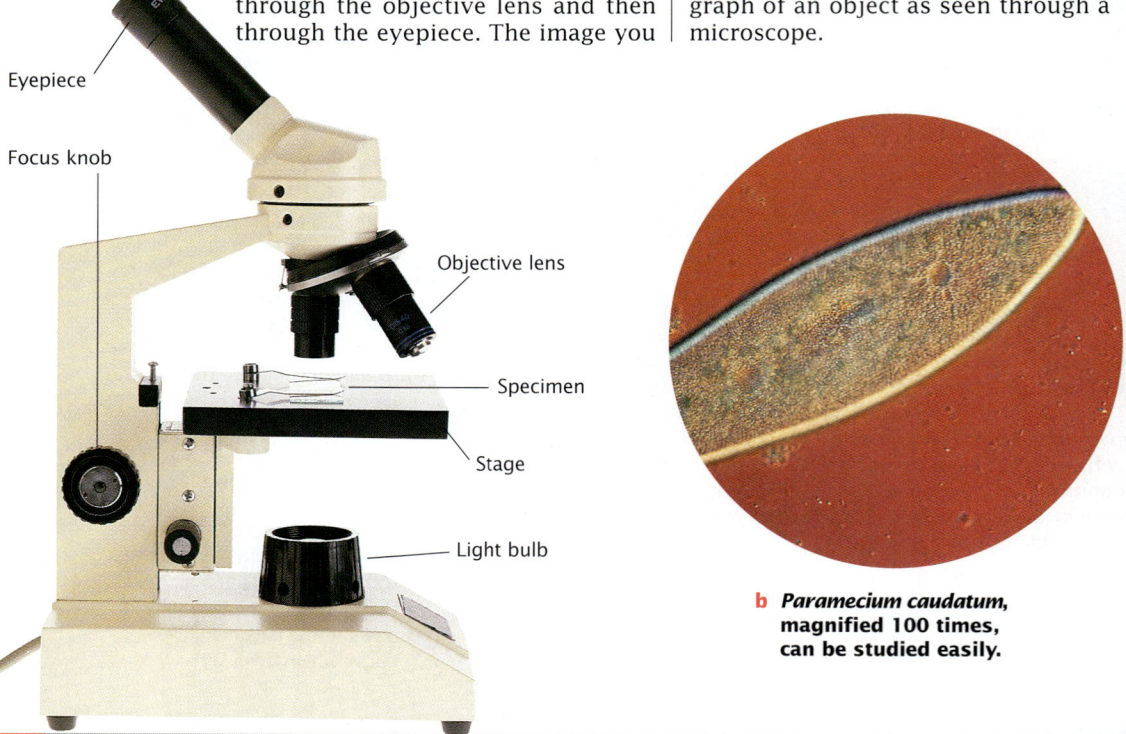

Eyepiece

Focus knob

Objective lens

Specimen

Stage

Light bulb

b *Paramecium caudatum,* magnified 100 times, can be studied easily.

Matter of Fact: A Simple Microscope

A magnifying lens can be considered a simple (single-lens) microscope. In fact, 300 years ago, Dutch scientist Anton van Leeuwenhoek used a small, simple lens to observe a variety of protists. Using this crude microscope, he also observed sperm cells. Using similar methods to study sperm, other scientists claimed they could see a miniature human inside each cell. This tiny form was thought to be a miniature version of the future adult.

Electron microscopes use a beam of electrons to reveal detail

Because light has wavelike characteristics, there is a limit to the size of objects that can be viewed as a sharp, focused image. Practically speaking, a bacterium with a diameter of 0.5 μm is about the smallest living thing that can be distinguished using a good mass-produced light microscope. In the early part of the twentieth century, physicists showed that an accelerated beam of electrons has wavelike properties similar to those of light. This discovery made possible a breakthrough in microscopy, the electron microscope. Electron microscopes show details not visible with light microscopes. However, they are very expensive and hence much less available than light microscopes. Also, specimens must be elaborately prepared before they can be viewed.

The transmission electron microscope (TEM) uses a beam of electrons instead of light to form images, as illustrated in **Figure 3-15a**. The specimen being examined must be sliced into extremely thin sections to allow the electrons to pass through and strike a photographic plate. These sections are treated with stains that block electrons, making details visible. The image produced is called a transmission electron micrograph. It offers very high magnification and resolution, but it does not give information about the three-dimensional shape of the specimen, as you can see in **Figure 3-15b**. Because specimens must be sliced and stained, it is impossible to view living cells with a TEM.

Preparing SEM Specimen

▲ **Evaluating Viewpoints**

Tell students that to prepare a cell for the scanning electron microscope, small pieces of tissue are coated with heavy metal salts that solidify the cell's protein, killing the cell. Ask students why they think the use of SEMs initially met strong resistance from traditional cell biologists. *(The preparation changed the material of the cell to such an extent that the biologists could not be sure of what they were viewing. Verification of the cellular structures by other means quieted the opposition.)*

Figure 3-15

a **In a transmission electron microscope, electrons pass through a specimen and form an image on a piece of film.**

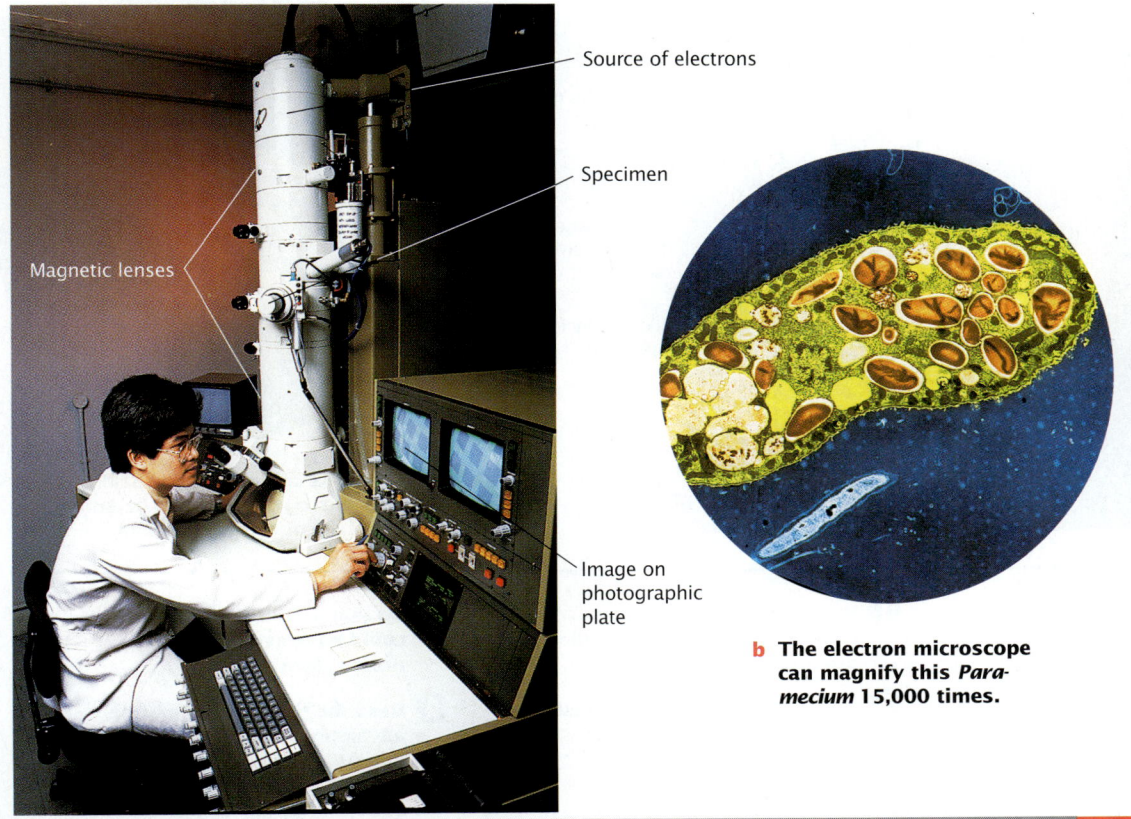

Source of electrons

Specimen

Magnetic lenses

Image on photographic plate

b **The electron microscope can magnify this *Paramecium* 15,000 times.**

Historical Perspective: Development of the Electron Microscope

The transmission electron microscope was independently invented in 1931 by two Germans, Ernst Ruska and Rheinhold Ruedenberg, but it was not until 1933 that Ruska built the first electron microscope that was more powerful (12,000×) than a light microscope. The first electron microscope did not become commercially available until 1935, in England. In 1945, Albert Claude, a Belgian-born American, first began electron microscope studies of the cell and discovered the endoplasmic reticulum and the details of the mitochondrion. Claude won the Nobel Prize in 1974 for his discoveries.

Key to Strategies
- ● **Understanding Concepts (Tier I)**
- ■ **Applying Information (Tier II)**
- ▲ **Critical Thinking (Tier III)**

Visual Strategy — Figure 3-16

■ Analyzing Information

Have students compare Figure 3-15 with Figure 3-16. Ask them to describe the kind of information a scientist can obtain through a SEM that is not available through a TEM. *(A SEM provides vivid three-dimensional images, whereas a TEM provides only two-dimensional views of the object being studied.)*

Visualizing Cells

■ Comparing Structures

Have students design a graphic organizer that illustrates the similarities and differences between the microscopes discussed in the text.

Phase Three

Assessment Options

Closure

■ Relating Concepts

Have students assemble a collage of photographs that represent the various cell organelles. *(Examples might include a computer for a nucleus, highways for the endoplasmic reticulum, and a post office for the Golgi body. Have students explain the reasons for each of their choices.)*

SECTION REVIEW

Assign the *Section Review*.

Reteaching

Prepare a table for students to complete. Across the top, place the headings Prokaryotic cell, Animal cell, and Plant cell. Down the left-hand side, write the names of the organelles covered in this section. Have students indicate in which cell(s) these organelles are present and describe their function.

The scanning electron microscope (SEM), shown in **Figure 3-16a**, enables biologists to see the surface of the specimen being studied. Specimens are not sliced, but are placed on a small metal cylinder and coated with a very thin layer of metal. A beam of electrons moves back and forth across the specimen in a manner similar to the electron beam in a television tube. The electrons do not pass through the specimen but instead bounce off its surface, forming an image that can be viewed on a video screen, as seen in **Figure 3-16b**. Because electrons bounce off molecules of gas in the air, the specimen must be viewed in a vacuum chamber. Therefore, living cells cannot be viewed with the SEM.

Micrographs made with electron microscopes are always black and white. This is because the beam of electrons is only one wavelength. The electrons strike film that detects the presence or absence of electrons—light or dark. To enhance cellular detail, color can be added when the film is developed.

A recent development in electron microscopy is the scanning tunneling microscope (STM). It uses an ultrafine, electron-emitting probe that systematically skims the surface of the object, moving up and down to accommodate the contours of the specimen. These movements are used by a computer to reconstruct an image of the specimen's surface. The STM can be used to view living cells.

Figure 3-16

a In a scanning electron microscope, a beam of electrons moves across a specimen and forms an image that is detected and displayed on a video screen.

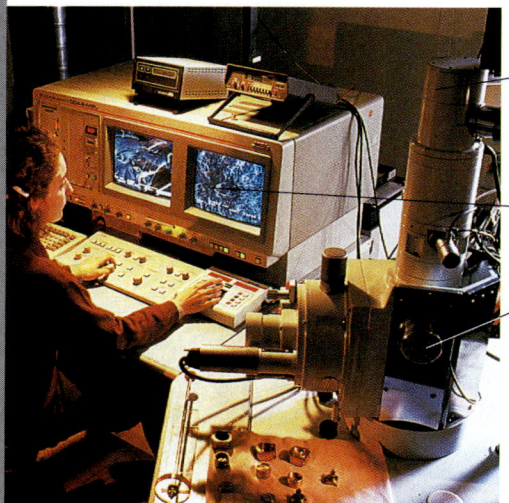

Source of electrons

Image on video screen

Specimen

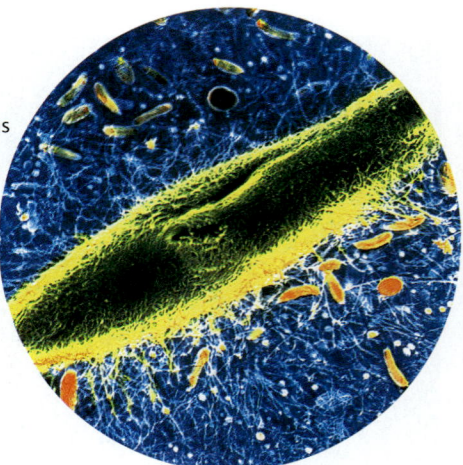

b This color-enhanced SEM micrograph shows the surface of the *Paramecium.*

SECTION REVIEW

1 How could you determine whether an unidentified cell was prokaryotic or eukaryotic?

2 How have organelles enabled eukaryotic cells to become successful?

3 Do you think that eukaryotes could have evolved without prokaryotes? Explain.

4 Describe the benefits and disadvantages of using an electron microscope to study how substances enter a cell.

ANSWERS TO SECTION REVIEW

1 If the cell contained organelles, then it would be eukaryotic. If not, then it would be prokaryotic.

2 Organelles function as specialized compartments, making a eukaryotic cell much more efficient than a prokaryotic cell.

3 Eukaryotes could have evolved without prokaryotes, but the process might have taken a lot longer because organelles would have to have been built "from scratch" rather than simply being "swallowed up."

4 An electron microscope will reveal the fine details of how substances enter the cell, but it will not allow scientists to study the process as it occurs because live cells cannot be viewed.

3 | Highlights

In about two years, this boy has grown from a single cell to more than a trillion cells.

	Key Terms	Summary
3-1 **At the Boundary of the Cell** The cell is the fundamental unit of life. 	cell (p. 41) cell membrane (p. 41) polar molecule (p. 44) hydrogen bond (p. 44) nonpolar molecule (p. 45)	• A cell is the smallest unit of life. • Smaller cells function more efficiently than larger cells. • Water molecules attract each other and help shape the cell membrane.
3-2 **Membrane Architecture** The cell membrane is the interface between a cell and its environment. 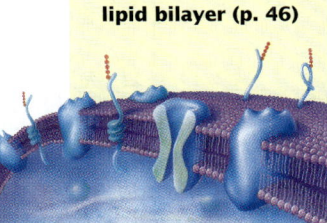	phospholipid (p. 46) lipid bilayer (p. 46)	• The cell membrane is a flexible bilayer made of phospholipids, proteins, and other molecules. • Protein in the cell membrane serve many purposes. Some enable molecules to enter and exit the cell, some enable cells to communicate with their environments, and some identify cells.
3-3 **Inside the Cell**  A eukaryotic cell contains many membrane-bound compartments called organelles. Each organelle carries out specific functions.	nucleus (p. 50) prokaryote (p. 50) eukaryote (p. 50) cytoplasm (p. 50) ribosome (p. 50) cytosol (p. 51) organelle (p. 51) mitochondrion (p. 52) chloroplast (p. 52) endoplasmic reticulum (p. 52) Golgi apparatus (p. 52) cell wall (p. 54) magnification (p. 56) resolution (p. 56)	• All cells have DNA and cytoplasm. • A eukaryotic cell has a nucleus and other membrane-bound organelles, whereas a prokaryotic cell does not. • Organelles are compartments that carry out life-supporting activities. Their presence enables eukaryotic cells to become specialized for specific functions. • Evidence shows that organelles arose from prokaryotic trespassers in larger cells. • Unlike animal cells, plant cells have cell walls, vacuoles, and chloroplasts. • A compound microscope can magnify a specimen according to the multiplication of the power of its two lenses. • An electron microscope uses beams of electrons to form images magnified up to 200,000 times.

Alternative Assessment

As a review technique, have students formulate questions and answers about the material covered in this chapter and use them for playing a trivia-type game.

Portfolio Assessment

Portfolio Assessment on page T39 provides options for building and evaluating student portfolios. Students and teachers can select items from the areas listed on page T39 for inclusion in a portfolio.

59

ANSWER TO CONCEPT MAP

The following is one possible answer to the Relating Concepts exercise on page 60.

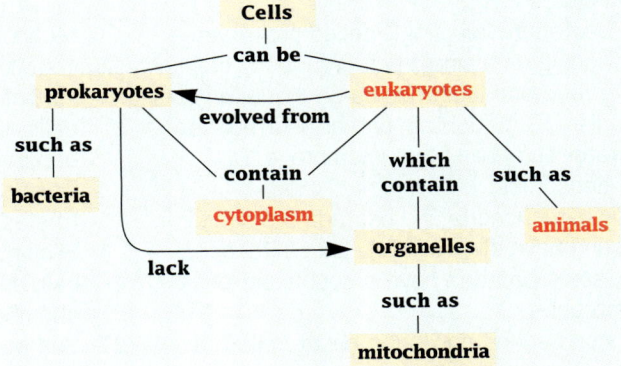

review

ANSWERS

Understanding Vocabulary

1. a. A cell wall surrounds the cell membrane of a plant cell. A cell membrane, found in all cells, is a lipid bilayer that separates a cell's interior from its environment.
   b. A polar molecule has a partial positive charge on one side and a partial negative charge on the other. A nonpolar molecule has no negative or positive sides.
   c. A eukaryote has cells that have membrane-bound nuclei and organelles, and have their DNA in chromosomes. A prokaryote is a single cell that lacks a nucleus and membrane-bound organelles, and has a single circle of DNA.
   d. Cytoplasm is the entire fluid environment within a cell, including the organelles. Cytosol refers to the aqueous portion of the cytoplasm.

2. a. lipid
   b. chromosome
   c. mitochondria

Understanding Concepts

3. Concept map answer is shown on page 59.
4. Like a submarine hull, the cell membrane separates and protects the internal parts of the cell from the external environment. However, it is flexible and allows substances to enter and exit the cell.
5. Substances would be unable to enter or exit the cell.
6. With a high surface-area-to-volume ratio, a small cell has organelles close to the cell membrane, where supplies and wastes can quickly enter and leave the cell.
7. See Figures 3-5 and 3-6.
8. See page 47.
9. See page 47.
10. See Figure 3-11.
11. This statement illustrates a cell's dependence on its lipid bilayer for protection from its environment and its dependence on membrane proteins for communication with its environment.

Understanding Vocabulary

1. For each pair of terms, explain the differences in their meanings.
   a. cell wall, cell membrane
   b. polar molecule, nonpolar molecule
   c. prokaryote, eukaryote
   d. cytoplasm, cytosol

2. For each set of terms, complete the analogy.
   a. polar molecule : water :: nonpolar molecule : _____
   b. prokaryotic cell : circle of DNA :: eukaryotic cell : _____
   c. protein manufacture : ribosomes :: extract energy stored in food : _____

Understanding Concepts

3. **Relating Concepts** Copy the unfinished concept map below onto a sheet of paper. Then complete the concept map by writing the correct word or phrase in each box containing a question mark.

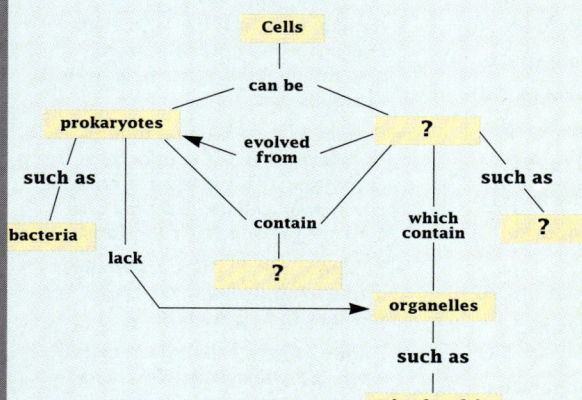

4. **Comparing Functions** In what ways is a cell membrane similar to and different from the hull of a submarine?

5. **Inferring Conclusions** How would a cell be affected if the cell membrane were completely solid and watertight?

6. **Recognizing Relationships** What are the advantages of being composed of many small cells instead of a few large ones?

7. **Inferring Relationships** Compare how water molecules interact with each other with how they interact with lipid molecules. Include an illustration with your answer.

8. **Comparing Structures** Describe how the structure of the lipid bilayer that makes up the cell membrane acts as a barrier to polar molecules.

9. **Summarizing Data** Describe two characteristics of a lipid bilayer. Explain how each characteristic affects the cell membrane.

10. **Comparing Structures** Explain how the structure of a protein enables it to fit in the cell membrane. Include an illustration with your answer.

11. **Inferring Relationships** Explain the following statement: Each cell is a prisoner of its lipid bilayer.

12. **Recognizing Relationships** Describe the functions of three cell membrane protein types. How does the structure of each kind of protein suit its function?

13. **Comparing Structures** In what ways does a bacterium swimming in a pond differ from a cell in your body? How is it similar?

14. **Summarizing Information** Describe two kinds of evidence that suggest eukaryotes evolved from prokaryotes.

15. **Drawing Conclusions** Although cells were first discovered during the 1660s, how would you explain the fact that most of our knowledge about cell structure and function has occurred within the last 50 years?

16. **Drawing Conclusions** Which kind of microscope would you use to study living cells: a compound microscope, a transmission electron microscope, or a scanning electron microscope? Support your answer.

17. **BUILDING ON WHAT YOU HAVE LEARNED** Name five organelles found in cells, and describe how each organelle enables the cell to display the properties of life as they are described in Chapter 2.

12. See Figures 3-8, 3-9, and 3-10.
13. The bacterium is a single-celled prokaryote, functioning as a single unit. Your body cell is eukaryotic and functions as part of a larger organism. Both contain and are surrounded by water and have a cell membrane, DNA, and ribosomes.
14. Many mitochondria and bacteria are similar in size and have circular DNA. Like mitochondria, some bacteria have a double set of membranes.
15. Our increase in knowledge about cells is a result of advancements in scientific technology.
16. You would use a compound microscope or a scanning tunneling microscope. Some living cells, such as protists and bacteria, can be observed in prepared live mounts under a compound microscope. An STM can be used to study the surface of a living specimen. Slicing a cell to view under a TEM kills the cell, as does viewing the cell in a vacuum chamber for a SEM.
17. See page 53.

Interpreting Graphics

18. In the illustration below, identify the polar heads and the nonpolar tails in the lipid bilayer. How many layers make up the cell membrane? Why are the layers aligned in the manner shown? Describe the pathway that molecules and ions would take to get across the cell membrane.

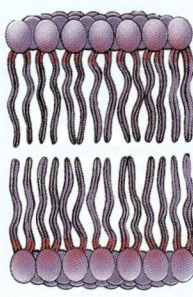

Reviewing Themes

19. *Cell Structure and Function*
How do chloroplasts and mitochondria function in the capture and release of energy within the cell?

20. *Evolution*
Describe the theory of endosymbiosis, and list three types of evidence that support it. How does this theory support the theme of evolution?

Thinking Critically

21. **Distinguishing Relevant Information** To determine if an automobile had been involved in a hit-and-run accident, police scientists took samples from matter ground into a smashed fender. They discovered that the material had cell walls and chloroplasts. Had the automobile hit anyone? Explain your answer.

22. **Evaluating Results** A scientist decides to remove one particular kind of organelle from a eukaryotic cell to see if the cell can survive without it. The scientist chooses to remove all mitochondria from the cell. The cell subsequently dies. Explain the probable reason.

23. **Recognizing Logical Inconsistencies** Suppose in the future that cell biologists were able to add any type of organelle or cell structure to any kind of living cell. Would you encourage a scientist to add cell walls to animal cells? Explain your answer.

Life/Work Skills

24. **Finding Information** Many careers require and use knowledge about cell structure and function. Use library references or search an on-line database to research careers such as that of an electron microscopist. What kinds of special equipment and materials do people in these careers use? What kind of educational background and training do jobs in this area require?

25. **Using Technology** Electron microscopes make it possible to see viruses, bacterial cells, and other small organisms in amazing detail. Find references that show details of microorganism structures discovered during the last 20 years. Make a table listing the kinds of organisms and the structures revealed.

Activities and Projects

26. **Unit Focus** Use library references, search an on-line database, or use an electronic encyclopedia to investigate the progress that has been made in gene therapy. Create an illustrated poster depicting at least 25 genetic disorders that doctors are seeking to cure. Include information about research and the technology used to carry out the research.

27. **Health Connection** Work together with some of your classmates to research and prepare a report on the differences between normal human cells and cancer cells. Find out about the differences in cell structure, reproduction rate, and metabolism. Find out how these differences are exploited to create cancer therapy drugs. Make a poster to go along with your report.

28. **Art Connection** Before photographs were commonly used in biology, drawings of cells and organisms were the most accurate way to share information. Describe the benefits and disadvantages of using art instead of a photograph.

Discovering Through Reading

29. Read the article "Crucibles in the Cell" in *Discover*, January 1995, pages 90–91. What new cellular organelles have been discovered and what are their functions? How are they thought to be involved in disease?

Thinking Critically

21. Since cell walls and chloroplasts are found in plants and not in animals, the car most likely hit a tree.

22. The cell died because it was unable to obtain energy.

23. Adding cell walls to animal cells would render the cells rigid, making it difficult for animals to move.

Life/Work Skills

24. Students' research should yield a variety of technology used by professionals such as biochemists, doctors, research assistants, etc.

25. Students' tables should list organisms and structures discovered during the last 20 years.

Activities and Projects

26. Posters will vary but should include current methods for research and technology.

27. Students should mention that cancer cells often have cellular structures different from normal cells, divide at a faster rate, and have abnormal metabolic rates. They often respond to stimuli and chemicals differently than do normal cells.

28. Hand-drawn art enables the artist to highlight features, show perspectives, and reflect observations, and costs little to produce. However, drawings can be biased or inaccurate.

Discovering Through Reading

29. CPLs (compartments for peptide loading) and caveolae. CPLs are compartments where processed antigen is joined to HLA proteins for immune stimulation; caveolae are transport vesicles that move extracellular materials into or through cells. CPLs are involved in immune responses, and caveolae are probably involved in thickening of the arteries, diabetes, muscular dystrophy, and cancer.

61

Interpreting Graphics

18. Polar heads point outward; nonpolar lipid tails face inward. The cell membrane consists of two layers of phospholipids. The alignment is due to the polarity of the structures; polar heads are attracted to water, while the nonpolar tails are repelled by water. The cell membrane contains proteins, through which many molecules and ions can pass.

Reviewing Themes

19. Chloroplasts capture energy in sunlight to make food. Mitochondria convert the energy stored in food to a form that can be used by the cell.

20. Approximately 1.5 billion years ago, prokaryotic cells were swallowed by larger cells, remained inside the larger cells, and gradually lost their ability to live independently.

4 | The Living Cell

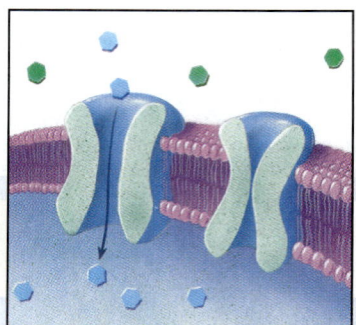

Lesson Planning Guide With Options for Block Scheduling

Lecture Concepts	Lesson Resources

4-1 How Cells Communicate

BLOCK ❶ (45 minutes)

1. The cells in a multicellular organism must communicate with one another.
2. Proteins in the cell membrane are able to transmit messages from cell to cell.

❶ Lecture Resources
- Determining Prior Knowledge
- Active Reading: Brainstorming
- Holt Biology Videodiscs Lesson 4-1

Assignment Options
- World of Work: Nutrition

BLOCK ❷ (45 minutes)

3. Proteins form voltage-sensitive channels that control the passage of ions through the cell membrane.
4. Proteins known as receptors enable the cell membrane to sense chemical signals.

❷ Lecture Resources
- Visual Strategy: Figure 4-1
- Visual Strategy: Videodisc
- Teaching Transparencies: 6A, 7A
- Holt Biology Videodiscs Lesson 4-1

Classwork Options
- Exploration 4A

BLOCK ❸ (45 minutes)

5. Proteins known as cell surface markers establish a cell's identity, so it will recognize foreign cells.
6. Cell surface markers specify what kind of cell it will be, and how it will function.

❸ Lecture Resources
- Visual Strategy: Figure 4-2
- Visual Strategy: Videodisc
- Demonstration: Analyzing Probabilities
- Holt Biology Videodiscs Lesson 4-1

Classwork Options
- Closure: Inferring Relationships

Assignment Options
- Reteaching
- Section Review
- Chapter Review, questions 1, 4, 5, 6, 8, 9, 16, 17, 19, 20, 21, 23, 25, 27
- Directed Reading Worksheet

4-2 Movement of Substances Into and Out of Cells

BLOCK ❹ (45 minutes)

1. Diffusion is the movement of molecules from a region of high concentration to a region of lower concentration until they are evenly distributed.

❹ Lecture Resources
- Problem Solving, p. 68
- Visual Strategy: Videodisc
- Demonstration: Interpreting Observations
- Holt Biology Videodiscs Lesson 4-2

Classwork Options
- Quick Labs: Lab A4

BLOCK ❺ (45 minutes)

2. Osmosis is the diffusion of water through a cell membrane.

❺ Lecture Resources
- Demonstration: Evaluating Results
- Teaching Transparencies: 5, 6
- Holt Biology Videodiscs Lesson 4-2

Classwork Options
- Inquiry Skills Development: Lab B3

Assignment Options
- Teaching Resources CD-ROM: Supplemental Reading Guides 2

BLOCK ❻ (45 minutes)

3. Water inside a cell creates osmotic pressure by pushing against the cell membrane and the cell wall.
4. The cell can control what enters and leaves by selective transport processes called facilitated diffusion and active transport.

❻ Lecture Resources
- Problem Solving, p. 70
- Active Reading: Paired Reading
- Visual Strategy: Figure 4-9
- Visual Strategy: Videodisc
- Teaching Transparencies: 10, 11
- Holt Biology Videodiscs Lesson 4-2

Classwork Options
- Life/Work Skills: Finding Information
- Closure: Recognizing Relationships

Assignment Options
- Reteaching
- Section Review
- Chapter Review, questions 2, 3, 7, 10, 11, 12, 13, 14, 15, 18, 22, 24, 26
- Directed Reading Worksheet

Lecture Concepts   Lesson Resources

Chapter Review and Assessment

BLOCK 7 (45 minutes)

Review
- ■ Reteaching Worksheet
- ■ Thinking Skills Worksheet
- ■ Vocabulary Development Worksheet
- ⊙ Language Development and Reading Comprehension Audio CD Program: Chapter 4

BLOCK 8 (45 minutes)

Assessment
- ■ Alternative Assessment, p. 73
- ■ Portfolio Assessment, p. T39

Chapter Test
- ■ Chapter 4 Test

Test Generator
- ⊙ Item bank for customizing Chapter Tests
- ⊙ Performance-Based Assessment: Diffusion Through a Cell Membrane

Teaching Resources CD-ROM
- ⊙ Scoring Rubrics and Classroom Management Checklist

The Portfolio icon denotes items throughout the Teacher's Edition lesson wrap that may be selected for inclusion in student portfolios.

Holt Biology Videodiscs and Concepts of Biology

Holt Biology Videodiscs gives you a powerful tool for teaching, review, and assessment. For further information regarding the media on the videodiscs, see **Holt Biology Videodiscs Teacher's Correlation Guide to Holt Biology: Visualizing Life.**

Concepts of Biology adds interactive lesson plans and extensive tools for customization using CD-ROM technology.

Use the following topic from **Concepts of Biology** to help you teach this chapter:
Topic 1: Cell Structure and Function

Laboratory Planning

Text

Materials and preparation instructions appear on the teacher's wrap accompanying each laboratory exercise.

Block 2: Exploration 4A: Modeling the Action of a Cell Membrane, p. 762

Holt BioSources Laboratory Program

Block 4: Quick Labs Lab A4: Demonstrating Diffusion
Block 5: Inquiry Skills Development Lab B3: Diffusion and Cell Membranes

Determining Prior Knowledge

- Ask students to name and describe the functions of the three major types of cell-membrane proteins discussed in Chapter 3.
- Open a bottle of perfume or after-shave lotion. Have students explain what is happening to the molecules in the bottle.
- Display wilted and crisp celery stalks. Ask students to describe their observations and hypothesize why the stalks look different.

Active READING

Technique: Brainstorming

Have students survey the first page of Section 4-1, noting the title, sub-headings, objectives, boldface terms, captions, and illustrations. Have them formulate a hypothesis about the topic of this section. Read the first page aloud and ask students to refine their hypothesis. Have students survey the rest of Section 4-1. Students should begin forming a mental model of the structure of Section 4-1 and deciding on a graphic organizer that fits the structure of the text. Have two or three students discuss their preliminary mental models.

CD-ROM Resources

Concepts of Biology

Topic 1: Cell Structure and Function

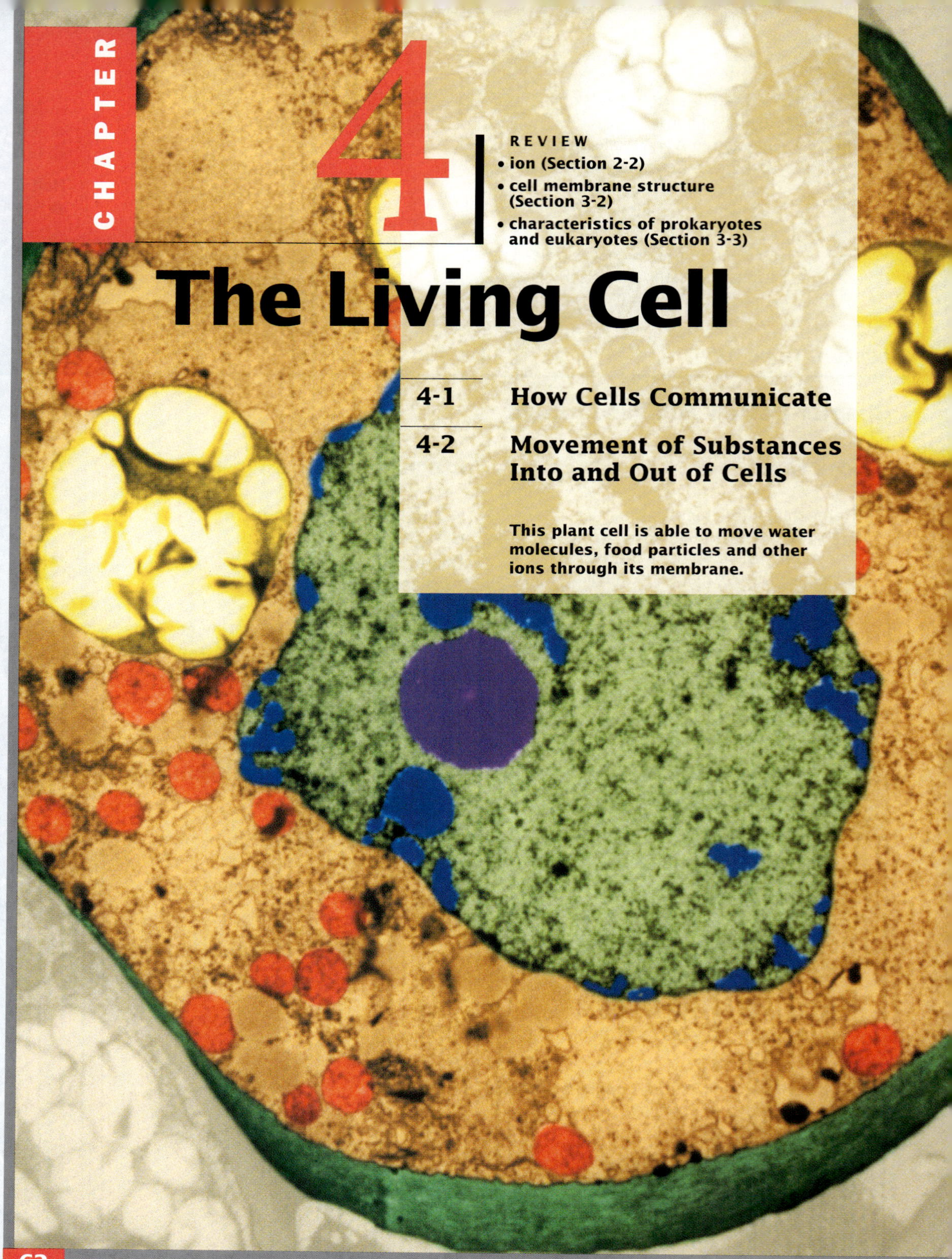

REVIEW
- ion (Section 2-2)
- cell membrane structure (Section 3-2)
- characteristics of prokaryotes and eukaryotes (Section 3-3)

The Living Cell

4-1	**How Cells Communicate**
4-2	**Movement of Substances Into and Out of Cells**

This plant cell is able to move water molecules, food particles and other ions through its membrane.

62

Author's Rationale Of the many cellular activities that might be considered, three are particularly important:
- transporting materials across the cell membrane
- transmitting and receiving information
- obtaining energy

The focus will be on explaining how these processes work, rather than on describing the component parts. Proton pumps are introduced because of the key roles they play in the flow of energy and because of their importance to future chapters.

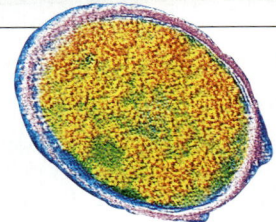

Like all living things, a cell, like this bacterium, needs information about its environment. In the same way that your senses enable you to see, hear, and feel things in your world, proteins in a plasma membrane connect a cell to its surroundings. These proteins are the cell's avenues of communication.

4-1 How Cells Communicate

OBJECTIVES

1 Recognize the importance of cell communication in multicellular organisms.

2 Describe two ways receptor proteins transmit information.

3 Explain how an electrical signal affects a voltage-sensitive channel.

4 Evaluate the role of cell surface markers in the human body.

Cell Communication in Multicellular Organisms

A significant difference between your cells and the cells of bacteria and most protists has to do with communication. Your cells are able to "talk" to one another because they have the ability to send and receive information. These "conversations" are essential for all **multicellular organisms** (such as animals and plants), which are made of many cells. They enable all of your cells to coordinate their behavior so that your body functions as a whole rather than as individual cells. The information that a cell receives from its neighbors allows it to determine its position in the body, to adjust its metabolism to suit its particular function, and to grow and divide at the proper time. Without communication, multicellular life would not be

possible. **Figure 4-1** shows a stage of development in which communication among cells ensures their correct position in the organism's future shape.

Figure 4-1
a This starfish embryo (magnified 1700 times) is only hours old, but its cells are already communicating with each other to find their proper position in the developing individual.

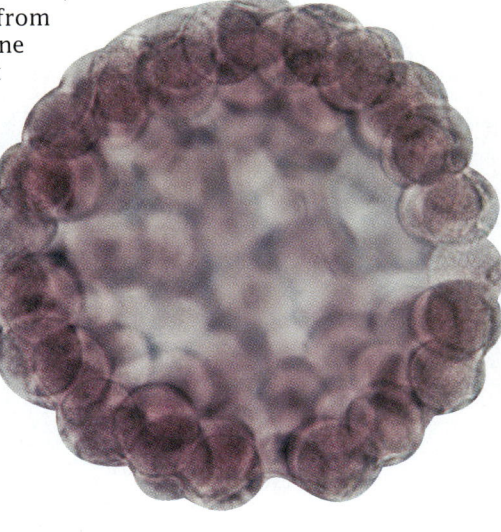

b This communication ensures that the embryo will grow into its normal adult form shown here approximately 1/3 actual size.

63

Videodisc Resources

Holt Biology Videodiscs
Lesson 4-1: How Cells Communicate

Phase One
Preparation

Scheduling
See the **Lesson Planning Guide** on pages 61A and 61B for lecture, classwork, and assignment options for Section 4-1.

Phase Two
Teaching Strategies

Visual Strategy | Figure 4-1

■ Inferring Conclusions
Point out that cell communication continues to be essential in the adult organism. Explain that in humans, a disease called multiple sclerosis results from the breakdown of myelin, an insulating sheet that surrounds a portion of nerve cells. Without myelin, nerve cells have difficulty responding to cellular messages. Ask students what kind of symptoms a person with multiple sclerosis might experience (*muscle weakness, paralysis*).

Sports Connection
Communication
To help students develop an appreciation for cell communication, have them discuss how athletes and coaches communicate during a sporting event. Be sure they are aware of the various modes used: speaking, writing, and hand signaling. Have them describe a specific example of what happens when such communication breaks down.

Key to Strategies
Teaching Strategies are keyed to three tiers of learning.

● **Understanding Concepts (Tier I)**
Content mastery and comprehension

■ **Applying Information (Tier II)**
Applying and analyzing content

▲ **Critical Thinking (Tier III)**
Practicing evaluative thinking

Visual Strategy — Videodisc

Inferring Relationships
Review with students the structure of the cell membrane. Use *Illustration—Cell Membrane: Unlabeled* shown in Chapter 4 Section 4-1 of ***Holt Biology Videodiscs Teacher's Correlation Guide to Holt Biology: Visualizing Life.*** Have students identify each structure and its function. *(A: marker proteins distinguish the cell from every other cell; B: channel proteins allow certain molecules to pass through the cell membrane; C: receptor proteins convey information from the environment to the cell.)* Then have students write one or two sentences for each structure, explaining how they think its function might be important to the cell. *(Accept any reasonable answer that indicates an understanding of the function of each structure.)*

Mathematics Connection

Receptor Proteins
The information that passes into a cell when a receptor protein binds to a signal molecule is amplified many times. For example, the binding of a few adrenalin molecules to their receptors in a liver cell membrane activates an estimated 25 million molecules of the enzyme that breaks down glycogen into glucose. As a result of the binding of these few adrenalin molecules, several grams of glucose are released into the blood.

Visual Strategy — Figure 4-2

Interpreting Graphics
Have students note the structural changes that occur in the receptor protein when it binds with glucagon. Have them describe the activities that take place in the cell once these changes take place. (*The second messenger molecule can activates cyclic AMP, which in turn causes glucose to be released into the blood.)*

Figure 4-2

a **Your body keeps you energized even when you don't have time for a meal. When your blood-sugar levels are low, cells in your pancreas release the hormone glucagon.**

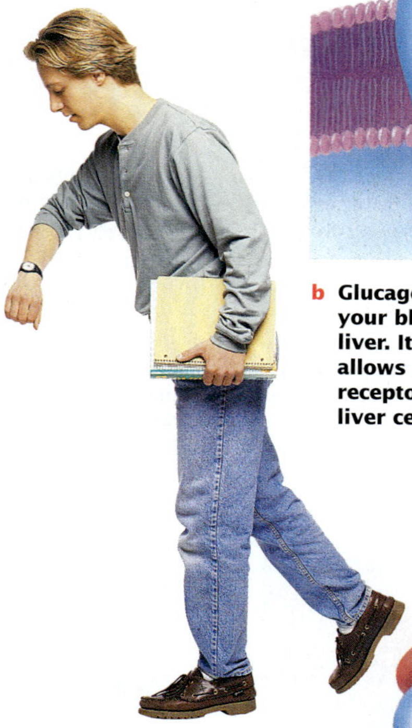

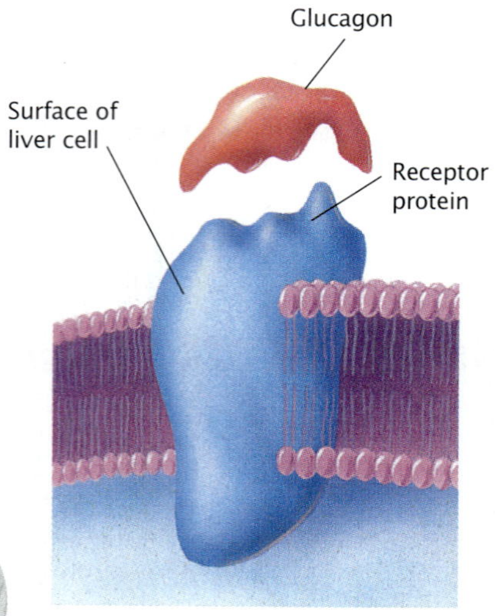

b **Glucagon travels through your bloodstream to your liver. Its unique shape allows it to bind to specific receptors on the surface of liver cells.**

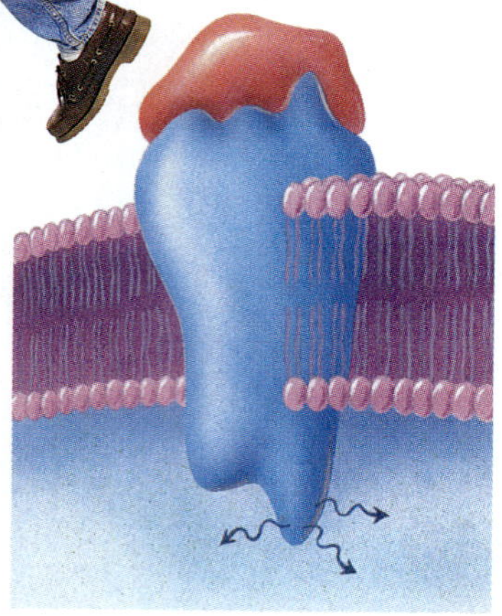

c **The binding of glucagon to its receptor activates a second messenger molecule inside the cell. The second messenger relays glucagon's important message to an enzyme inside the cell, which causes blood-sugar levels to rise.**

Receptors Transmit Information

Cells in your body are constantly bombarded with news sent by other cells. This information is in the form of chemical signals. The chemical signals that a cell responds to are determined by the cell's **receptor proteins**. Some receptor proteins are located on the cell's surface and function like tiny antennas, transmitting information from the world outside the cell to its interior. Other receptor proteins are located in the cell's interior.

Some receptors work outside the cell

Most receptor proteins extend through the cell's membrane. This enables a chemical signal that can't pass through the membrane to send a message into a cell. For example, a hormone is a chemical signal that acts as a messenger. Many hormones made of proteins cannot penetrate the lipid bilayer of the cell membrane. In order to deliver their messages, these hormones must bind to surface receptor proteins. One such hormone is glucagon. Glucagon is made in your pancreas and released when your blood-sugar levels are low. It travels to your liver through your bloodstream, carrying its urgent message. When glucagon reaches the liver, it causes liver cells to release stored supplies of sugar, which restores blood-sugar levels to normal.

How do receptor proteins deliver glucagon's message? **Figure 4-2** illustrates the action of glucagon. When glucagon reaches the liver, it binds to receptor proteins on the surface of liver cells. This binding causes the receptor proteins to send the message inside the cell. Glucagon's message is transferred to a second messenger, just as one runner passes a baton to the next runner in a relay race. In this case, the second messenger is a compound called cyclic AMP, which triggers an enzyme that causes the release of stored sugar. As a result, blood-sugar levels rise.

Matter of Fact: Evolutionary Evidence

A number of hormones in humans, including glucagon, insulin, and somatostatin, have been found in a wide variety of organisms, including fruit flies, earthworms, fungi, bacteria, and protists. Their functions in these organisms are not understood. However, their presence is another piece of evidence that points to an evolutionary relationship among all organisms.

Some receptors work inside the cell

Unlike protein hormones, hydrophobic hormones are able to deliver their message by passing through the lipid bilayer of the cell's membrane. These hormones bind to receptor proteins located inside the cell rather than on its surface. Once the hormone and receptor bind, they travel as a unit to the cell's DNA. This unit has the right shape to bind to a particular gene and trigger the production of a new protein. The new protein will then influence chemical activity in the cell and play a vital role in metabolism or development. Examples of hormones that use these receptors are thyroxin, hormones that regulate the body's metabolic rate, and estrogen and testosterone, hormones responsible for the development and maintenance of sexual characteristics.

Some Channels Can Respond to Electricity

Some cells are specialized for conducting information from one cell to another. For example, your nervous system, shown in **Figure 4-3**, is made up of cells that can respond to electrical signals carried by ions. These cells are studded with **voltage-sensitive channels**, proteins that are embedded in the cell membrane. **Figure 4-4** illustrates how voltage-sensitive channels work. Each channel is lined with charged amino acids. At one end of the channel is a gate that is usually closed. However, when ions carrying an electrical signal arrive, the gate flips open and allows the ions to enter the cell. Voltage-sensitive channels are important because they allow electrical signals to travel along nerves as fast as 100 m/s. Without them, your brain and nerves couldn't function, as you'll see in Chapter 30.

Figure 4-3
Nerve cells called neurons carry electrical signals throughout the body.

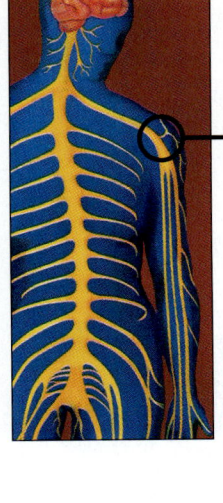

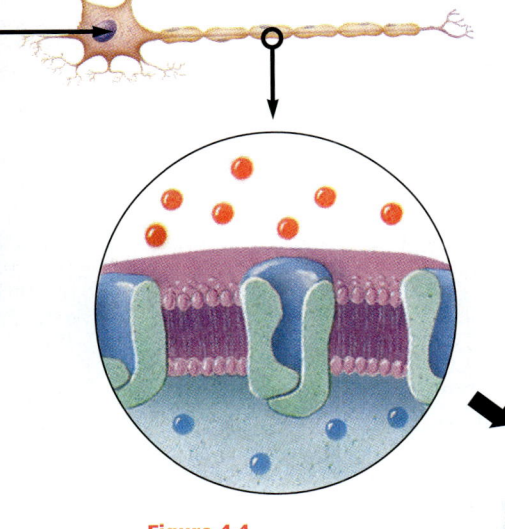

b But when additional ions upset the balance, the voltage-sensitive channels spring open and ions pass through.

Figure 4-4
a Voltage-sensitive channels are embedded in the cell membrane of a neuron. When the concentration of ions is balanced on both sides of the membrane, the channels are closed.

65

Matter of Fact: Calcium Channel Blockers

Calcium channel blockers are drugs that inhibit the flow of calcium through voltage-sensitive channels in heart cells and smooth muscle cells in blood vessels. This action accounts for their effects of lowering blood pressure, relieving chest pain (angina), and stabilizing certain abnormal heart rhythms. Calcium channel blockers are the most widely prescribed medication in the United States; approximately 87 million prescriptions were filled in 1994 for an estimated 6 million people suffering from high blood pressure and heart ailments.

Demonstration

■ **Analyzing Probabilities**
Materials: a deck of playing cards
Many people think that only surface markers that determine blood type are considered for an organ transplant. Explain that many types of markers must be evaluated, especially those on white blood cells. To illustrate how the problem of finding a suitable donor is greatly magnified as the number of markers increases, deal 13 students 4 cards each. Tell them to first assume that only one marker is important. Inform them that anyone holding a card with a diamond would make a suitable donor-recipient combination. Chances are that many students will meet this criterion. Now tell them that two markers are needed. Thus, only students holding a diamond and an ace would make a suitable combination. Students should see a drastic drop in the number of possible donor-recipient combinations.

Phase Three
Assessment Options

Closure

■ **Inferring Relationships**
Ask students why communication is more important for the members of a football team than for the double partners of a tennis team. Have them relate this analogy to the need for cellular communication in multicellular organisms. *(Like a team with many players, an organism composed of many cells has a greater need for coordination in order to function as a single unit.)*

SECTION REVIEW
Assign the *Section Review.*

Reteaching

Have students create analogies that compare the structures of cell communication to common objects or appliances.

Markers Identify Cells

Just as an athlete wears a uniform bearing a name and number, a cell displays specific proteins that identify its "team" and "position." These unique sets of membrane proteins are called **cell surface markers**. Why should a cell spend energy making these markers? Cell surface markers distinguish your cells from other cells, enabling your immune system to recognize and destroy uninvited guests, such as harmful bacteria. Cell surface markers are also used during early development to determine a cell's fate—whether it will become a blood cell, a muscle cell, or a kidney cell.

The uniqueness of an individual's cell surface markers explains why organ donors and recipients must be carefully matched. The doctors who operated on the organ transplant patient shown in **Figure 4-5** had to be sure that the donated heart was a good match before they attempted a transplant. A good match can be defined as two organs that share many of the same identifying proteins on the surface of their cells. As with all proteins, the structure of cell surface markers is determined by genes. If the donor and recipient are related, a successful match is likely. However, cell surface markers are unique, so perfect matches occur only between identical twins. Most organ recipients must therefore take medication to suppress the immune system, which could identify the transplanted organ as an invader and attack it.

Figure 4-5
a This man's heart transplant was successful because the cell surface markers on his cells closely match the cell surface markers on the donor's heart.

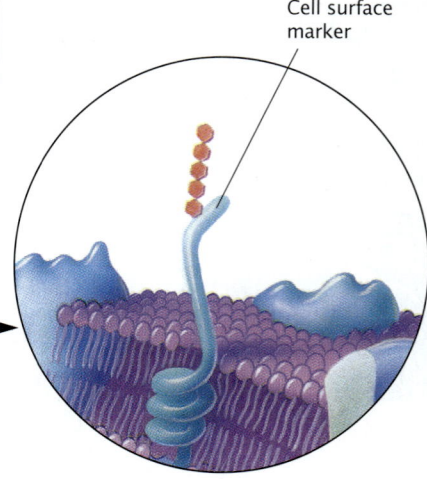

Cell surface marker

b Human heart   **c** Heart cells   **d** Cell membrane of a heart cell

SECTION REVIEW

1 Why is cellular communication essential for multicellular organisms?

2 In what two ways do receptor proteins affect cellular activity?

3 How do voltage-sensitive channels respond to electrical signals?

4 Why are protein markers important when matching organ donors to recipients?

66

ANSWERS TO SECTION REVIEW

1 Without such communication, the cells would not work in a coordinated fashion and function as a single unit.

2 Some receptor proteins work outside the cell by binding to a chemical signal and transmitting the message into the cell. Others work inside the cell by carrying the signal to the nucleus.

3 Electrical signals open the voltage-sensitive channels so that ions can pass through the cell membrane.

4 If the protein markers do not match, then the recipient's body will reject the transplanted organ.

On a hot day or after a hard workout, you might reach for a cold sports drink. This type of beverage contains water and ions to replenish what your body lost through perspiration. These ions enter your cells through protein channels. In this section you will take a close look at how cells take in substances and discard wastes.

4-2

Movement of Substances Into and Out of Cells

OBJECTIVES

1 Describe diffusion and osmosis.

2 Distinguish facilitated diffusion from active transport.

3 Explain how the sodium-potassium pump transports ions.

4 Describe how large substances can enter and exit cells.

Diffusion and Osmosis

In addition to communicating, cells move water molecules, food particles, and other ions through their membranes. Some molecules, such as water, pass through most membranes freely. Other molecules rely on help from proteins in the plasma membrane.

Diffusion mixes molecules

Look at **Figure 4-6**, which shows a few drops of dye solution that have been placed onto a layer of gelatin in a beaker. What is happening? Within an hour, molecules of dye have begun to move into the gelatin.

The mixing of two substances by the random motion of molecules is called **diffusion**. As shown in **Figure 4-6**, molecules diffuse from a region where their concentration is high (the drops of dye) to a region where their concentration is low (the gelatin). Diffusion stops when the two kinds of molecules are evenly dispersed.

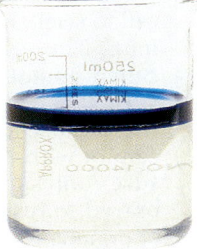

Figure 4-6
a The leisurely pace of diffusion can be demonstrated by placing a few drops of food coloring onto a layer of gelatin.

b In an hour, the food coloring will begin to slowly diffuse.

c Hours later, molecules of food coloring have diffused still further throughout the gelatin.

67

Videodisc Resources

Holt Biology Videodiscs
Lesson 4-2: Movement of Substances Into and Out of Cells

Phase One
Preparation

Scheduling
See the **Lesson Planning Guide** on pages 61A and 61B for lecture, classwork, and assignment options for Section 4-2.

Phase Two
Teaching Strategies

Demonstration
● **Interpreting Observations**
Materials: beakers containing gelatin, a dark food coloring
Perform the demonstration shown in Figure 4-6 by preparing several beakers of gelatin and adding a few drops of a dark food coloring. Have students explain their observations as the food coloring diffuses through the gelatin. (Changes may not be noticeable for several hours.) Make sure students understand that the random motion of molecules continues even when the food coloring is evenly dispersed.

Key to Strategies
● Understanding Concepts (Tier I)
■ Applying Information (Tier II)
▲ Critical Thinking (Tier III)

The Living Cell **67**

Demonstration

▲ **Evaluating Results**

Materials: beaker, dialysis tubing (or plastic bag), water (distilled or deionized), salt, sugar, gelatin

Add 5 g of salt, 5 g of sugar, and 5 g of gelatin to 200 mL of water, and heat until all solutes dissolve. Allow the solution to cool, and pour a measured volume into a piece of dialysis tubing or a plastic bag. Seal the contents, and submerge it in a beaker of water. The next day, remove the tubing or bag. Collect the contents and measure its volume. Have students explain why the volume changed. *(Water moved into the dialysis tubing by osmosis.)* Relate the results to the text describing why there is often a net movement of water into a cell.

Problem Solving

■ **Proposing Solutions**

Ask students to propose a way to restore the osmotic pressure in the plant cell illustrated in Figure 4-5b. *(Add a high concentration of water to the cell's environment. Water will then move into the cell.)*

Theme Answer

Cell Structure and Function

Osmosis allows a cell to absorb water needed for its metabolic process.

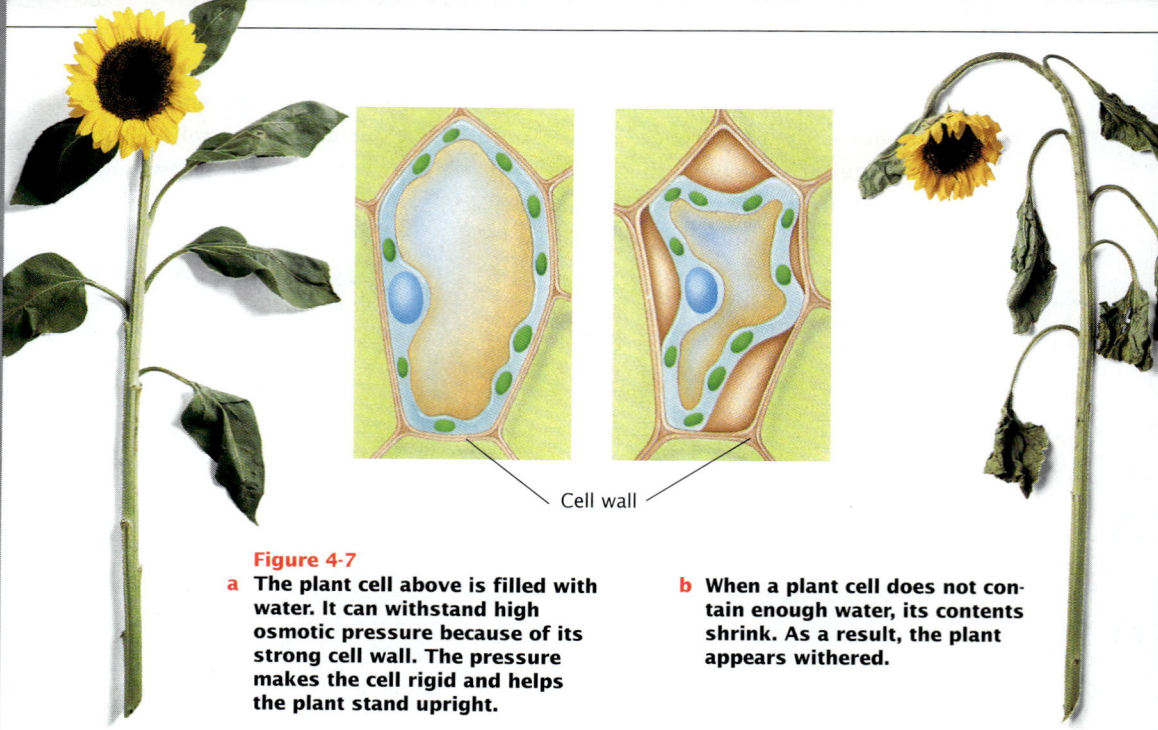

Cell wall

Figure 4-7

a The plant cell above is filled with water. It can withstand high osmotic pressure because of its strong cell wall. The pressure makes the cell rigid and helps the plant stand upright.

b When a plant cell does not contain enough water, its contents shrink. As a result, the plant appears withered.

Water passes through membranes by osmosis

Water enters and leaves living cells by diffusing across cell membranes. As you learned in Chapter 3, certain molecules can pass through a cell membrane, but others cannot. Because water molecules are very small, they are able to slip freely through the tiny gaps in the lipid bilayer of a cell membrane. Water molecules constantly move back and forth across cell membranes. This free motion of water has a very important consequence—it enables cells to absorb water.

The diffusion of water across a membrane, such as the cell membrane, is called **osmosis** *(ahz MOH sihs)*. As water enters a cell by osmosis, the water molecules move from an area of higher concentration to an area of lower concentration. Cells also contain sugars, proteins, and other substances. Therefore, the concentration of water outside the cell is usually greater than the concentration of water inside the cell. As a result, cells tend to continually gain water by osmosis.

Water in a cell creates osmotic pressure

When water enters a cell, it causes the cell to swell, much as air inflates a balloon. This force creates a pressure called **osmotic** *(ahz MAH tihk)* **pressure**. If osmotic pressure is very high, it can cause a cell to burst. Most cells cannot withstand high osmotic pressure unless their membranes are braced to resist swelling. Many kinds of organisms, such as the plant in **Figure 4-7**, have cell walls to support their cells and prevent them from bursting.

How do organisms without cell walls keep from bursting? Many single-celled organisms, such as paramecia, have organelles that pump excess water out of the cell. In multicellular animals, a balance exists between the concentration of fluids inside and outside the cells. In your body, for example, the concentrations of salts, sugars, and other ions are about the same inside cells as in the fluids surrounding them. Thus, water enters the cells of the body at the same rate that it leaves.

Cell Structure and Function

How does osmosis enable a cell to respond to changes within an organism?

Matter of Fact: Living in the Sea

Point out that most unicellular organisms that live in salt water have an internal water concentration equal to that of their environment. Thus, unlike freshwater paramecia, they lack organelles specialized for pumping out excess water.

Channels and Pumps Provide Selective Transport

Unlike water molecules, many substances cannot easily pass through the cell membrane. Molecules such as sugars and proteins are often too large to slip through the gaps between the phospholipids. In addition, these molecules are often polar and cannot pass through the nonpolar region of the lipid bilayer. To move into and out of cells, polar molecules and ions use channels and pumps embedded in the cell membrane. These structures are made of protein. Protein channels are shown in **Figure 4-8**.

The transport of specific substances by means of protein channels and pumps is called **selective transport**. This form of transport is said to be selective because channels and pumps enable only certain substances to pass into or out of a cell. By using selective transport, a cell can control the substances that enter and leave. There are two kinds of selective transport: facilitated diffusion and active transport.

Facilitated diffusion is toll-free

The simplest selective transport channels are similar to tunnels. As long as a molecule or ion can fit, it is free to pass through the channel in either direction, as shown in **Figure 4-8**. These channels allow each kind of molecule or ion to diffuse toward the side of the cell where it is least concentrated. Eventually, diffusion balances the concentrations of that molecule or ion on both sides of the membrane. This form of selective transport is called **facilitated diffusion** because the channels assist, or facilitate, the diffusion of substances. The movement of substances is caused by their different concentrations inside and outside the cell. Therefore, a cell does not have to expend energy to obtain these substances. Many ions, such as potassium ions, enter the cell using facilitated diffusion. Potassium ions help maintain the proper balance of electrical charges inside and outside of the cell.

Figure 4-8

a **Ahhhh! There is nothing like the taste of a good thirst quencher after a tough workout. Have you ever wondered how the cells of your body replenish nutrients?**

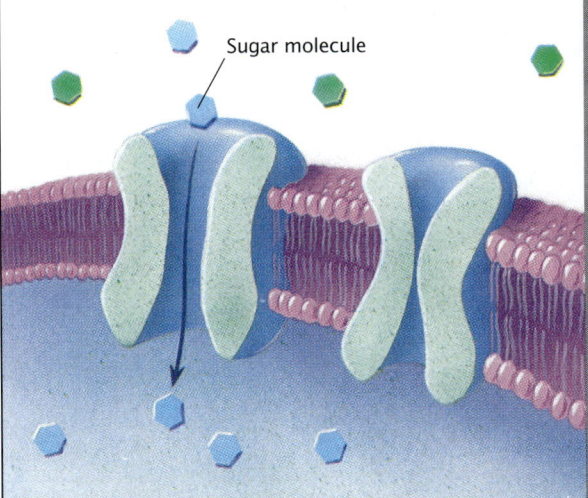

Sugar molecule

b **Your bloodstream carries minerals and sugars to your body's cells. If the molecule has a certain shape, it can freely enter the cell through protein channels.**

69

Community Connection: Dialysis

To illustrate the importance of molecular transport across membranes, invite a technician from a local dialysis center to speak to the class about the techniques used to clean wastes from the blood when an individual's kidneys are unable to function properly.

Active READING

Technique: Paired Reading
Pair each student with a partner, and have each student read pages 70 and 71 silently. As they read, have them note passages they understand with a check mark and passages they do not understand with a question mark. Then have partners discuss what they did and did not understand.

Visual Strategy   Figure 4-9

● **Interpreting Graphics**

Lead students through each step of the illustration. In Figure 4-9a, point out the three sodium ions inside the cell. In Figure 4-9b, have students observe that these sodium ions are moving through the channel protein. Have them note that the change in shape of the channel protein allows potassium ions to move into receptor sites on the cell membrane surface. In Figure 4-9c, the sodium ions are pumped out of the cell as the potassium ions are moved into the cell. In Figure 4-9d, the potassium ions are released into the cell. Be sure students recognize that in both cases the ions moved against a concentration gradient. Have students make a **Graphic Organizer** similar to the one at the bottom of the page to illustrate the flow of ions.

Problem Solving

■ **Predicting Outcomes**
Studies have shown that each complete pumping sequence results in three sodium ions being moved out of the cell, while two potassium ions are transported into the cell. Ask students how many potassium ions are pumped into a cell in just 1 second. *(In just 1 second, some 300 sodium ions are pumped out. Thus, some 200 potassium ions must be pumped into the cell every second.)*

Active-transport moves molecules in one direction
If all selective transport occurred by means of channels, all kinds of molecules and ions would simply diffuse into or out of a cell. In fact, this is not the case. Unlike channels, selective-transport pumps allow molecules and ions to pass in only one direction. Like turnstiles at a stadium, pumps admit certain molecules and ions into the cell but do not let them out. This strategy enables a cell to stockpile certain substances in far greater concentrations than they occur outside the cell.

In order to operate pumps, a cell must use some of its energy to change the shape of the pump protein. The cell also uses energy to move a substance across the cell membrane to a region of higher concentration. Therefore, the operation of pumps is called **active transport**. Active transport plays a critical role in moving many important materials, such as sugars and amino acids. Almost all of the active transport in animal cells is carried out by only two kinds of pumps: the sodium-potassium pump and proton pumps.

The sodium-potassium pump enables your cells to conduct nerve impulses
Without sodium-potassium pumps, you and most other animals would be immobile lumps. As you can see in Figure 4-9, the **sodium-potassium pump** moves sodium ions out of cells and potassium ions into cells. In just 1 second, each channel can transport more than 300 sodium ions out of a cell. This flow of ions is vital for restoring a balance needed to keep a nerve cell functioning. More than one-third of all the energy expended by your body's cells is spent driving the sodium-potassium pump.

Sodium-potassium pumps also help transport sugars and amino acids into your cells. When a few sodium ions remain in the cell, facilitated diffusion channels in the cell membrane allow sodium ions to rush back into the cell. Because so many sodium ions rush back in through these channels, large numbers of partner molecules are pulled through as well, even if they are already present in high concentrations within the cell. The cell-membrane channels that admit sodium ions and their partners are called coupled channels.

A proton pump is the key to cell metabolism
Cells rely on proton pumps to move protons across membranes. Just as the sodium-potassium pump causes a buildup of sodium ions outside the cell, the **proton pump** expels protons, causing large numbers of protons to accumulate on one side of a membrane. The protons then diffuse back into the cell through certain channels.

Figure 4-9
The sodium-potassium pump moves sodium ions out of cells and potassium ions into cells.

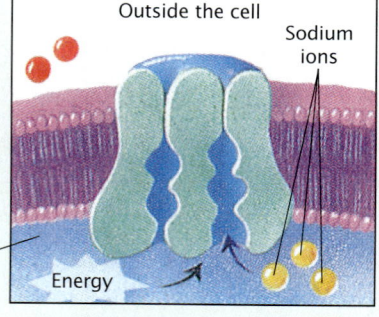

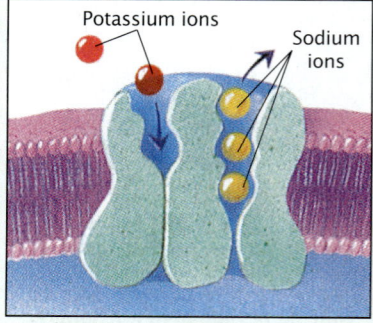

a Sodium ions within the cell fit precisely into receptor sites on the protein channel.

b The channel changes shape, pumping the sodium ions across the membrane. Potassium ions outside the cell move into receptor sites.

Graphic Organizer

Use the following graphic organizer with **Visual Strategy Figure 4-9** on page 70.

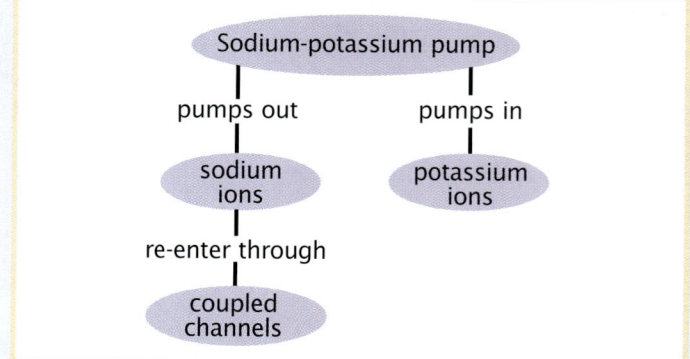

Proton pumps are an important mechanism in cell metabolism, as you will learn in Chapter 5. Proton pumps depend on chemical or light energy to function. In green plants, a proton pump enables cells to convert light energy into chemical energy. Another proton pump enables your cells to transform energy obtained from the food you eat into chemical energy you can use.

Defective channel proteins can be lethal

A cell's proteins are built according to genetic instructions that evolved millions of years ago and that have stood the test of time. Any changes in a protein's structure can alter or impair its function and, in turn, threaten the cell's normal activities. The effects can be devastating. Consider, for example, the disorder known as cystic fibrosis. Cystic fibrosis causes the body to produce very thick mucus, which builds up in the lungs, pancreas, and liver. As a result, people with cystic fibrosis have extreme difficulty breathing, and they cannot produce the enzymes needed to completely digest food. The thick mucus also coats the hairlike projections that line air passages and inhibits their sweeping motion. Without the cleansing effect of the hairs, harmful bacteria and debris remain in

the lungs and increase the chances of infection.

What causes cystic fibrosis? Research into its cause reads like a detective story. A key clue was that people with cystic fibrosis have very salty sweat, an indication of abnormally high levels of sodium and chloride ions. This salt imbalance is what causes thick mucus to accumulate in a patient's lungs—the high levels of salt in the cells draw water out of the mucus, causing it to thicken.

The level of salt within a cell is determined by the movement of sodium and chloride ions across the cell membrane. These ions pass through protein channels embedded in the cell membrane. Tests of cystic fibrosis patients revealed that their cells are unable to export chloride ions. For some reason their chloride channels do not work.

Searching for the genes that encode chloride channels, researchers eventually isolated the gene that causes cystic fibrosis. Normally, this gene encodes a protein channel that helps move chloride ions out of the cell. In cystic fibrosis patients, the gene encodes for a misshapen protein channel that cannot function properly. In Chapter 9, you will read how this information could yield new methods of treatment and a possible cure for cystic fibrosis patients.

Chemistry Connection
Protons
Inform students that the simplest element is a form of hydrogen called hydrogen-1. It consists of just one proton and one electron. The protons that are moved by proton pumps come from hydrogen atoms whose electrons have been removed.

Life/Work Skills
Finding Information
■ **Analyzing Data**

Have students search the library or an on-line database to obtain information on cystic fibrosis. Have them organize their information by writing a short report. The following questions may be useful in getting them started:
• How common is cystic fibrosis in various ethnic groups?
• How does cystic fibrosis affect a person's lifestyle?
• How is cystic fibrosis treated?
• What have scientists done in an attempt to cure cystic fibrosis?
Students may also want to contact the Cystic Fibrosis Foundation by writing to 185 Silas Deane Highway, Wethersfield, CT 06109 or by calling 1-800-841-2828.

Visual Strategy | Videodisc
● **Organizing Information**
Use *Illustration—Passive and Active Transport* shown in Chapter 4 Section 4-2 of *Holt Biology Videodiscs Teacher's Correlation Guide to Holt Biology: Visualizing Life.* Have students use the information in the illustration to make a chart that compares and contrasts the processes shown.

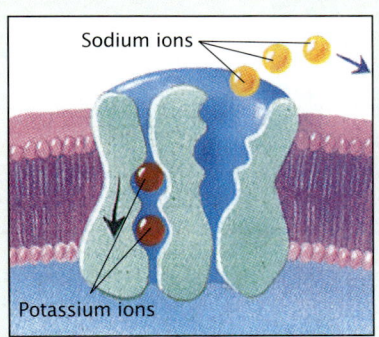
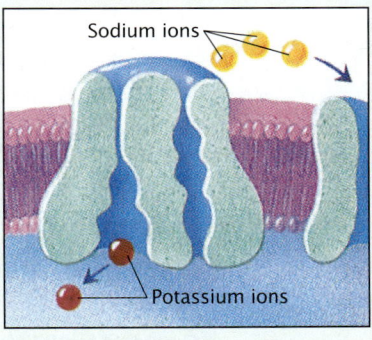

c Sodium ions are released and cannot reenter through this channel. At the same time, potassium ions are pumped across the channel into the cell.

d Potassium ions are released inside the cell. Sodium ions outside the cell, along with sugar molecules, later enter the cell through coupled channels.

71

Matter of Fact: Cystic Fibrosis
Cystic fibrosis is the most common genetic disease among Caucasians, affecting some 30,000 people in the United States. In addition, approximately 12 million (1 in 20) people are carriers, possessing one allele for the disease.

Key to Strategies
● Understanding Concepts (Tier I)
■ Applying Information (Tier II)
▲ Critical Thinking (Tier III)

Moving Large Particles

Matter, Energy, and Organization

What would happen to a cell if its membrane were solid and impenetrable?

Sometimes particles enter a cell without actually crossing the membrane. For example, some single-celled eukaryotes take in food particles by engulfing them with armlike extensions, as shown in **Figure 4-10**. When the edges of the extensions meet, they fuse together, capturing the particle within a sac inside the cell. The process of bringing particles into a cell using extensions of the membrane is called **endocytosis**. The engulfed material can consist of particles or liquid. In a reverse process, called **exocytosis**, material within sacs inside the cell is discharged from the cell. Exocytosis releases secretions and wastes from the cell.

Figure 4-10
a **In the process of endocytosis, armlike extensions of the cell reach out to surround and engulf particles that are too large to pass through the plasma membrane.**

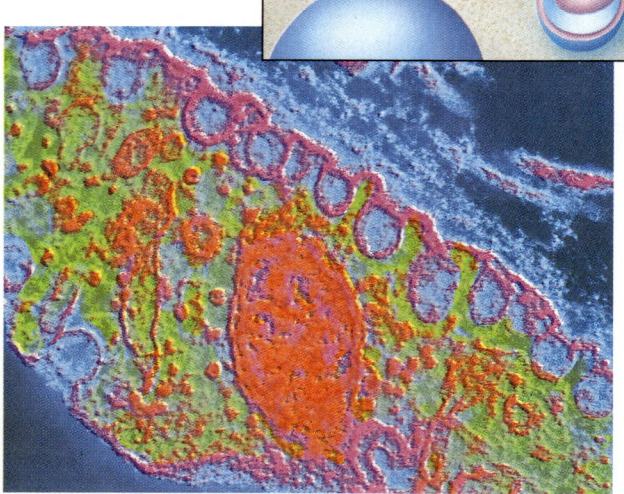

b **In the process of exocytosis, a sac of cellular waste inside the cell fuses with the plasma membrane and empties its contents outside the cell.**

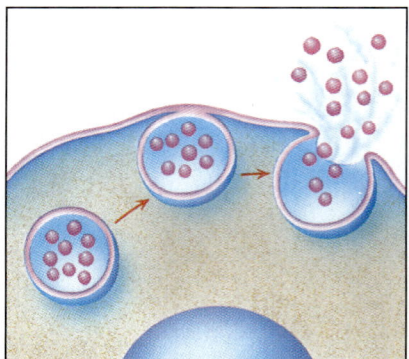

c **In this blood capillary, materials outside the capillary are engulfed and taken in.**

SECTION REVIEW

1 What occurs in the processes of osmosis and diffusion?

2 What distinguishes facilitated diffusion from active transport?

3 What is the function of the sodium-potassium pump? How does it work?

4 How can a cell take in particles too large to cross its membrane?

72

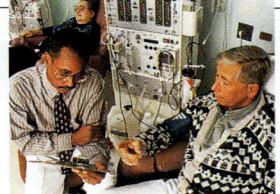

Kidney dialysis uses an artificial membrane to filter toxins out of the blood.

	Key Terms	Summary
4-1 **How Cells Communicate** Chemical signals like glucagon bind to receptor proteins on the cell's surface to send a message to its interior. 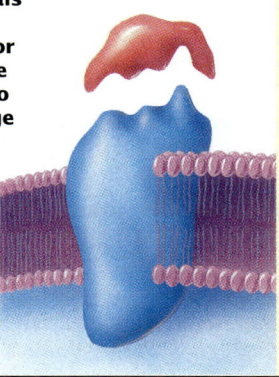	multicellular organism (p. 63) receptor protein (p. 64) voltage-sensitive channel (p. 65) cell surface marker (p. 66)	• Multicellular organisms could not exist without cell-to-cell communication. • Proteins embedded in the surface of the cell and within the cell's cytoplasm are capable of transmitting messages carried by other molecules. • Some proteins are able to respond to electrical currents. • Other proteins identify a cell as belonging to a specific individual.
4-2 **Movement of Substances Into and Out of Cells**  A strong cell wall prevents this plant cell from bursting from osmotic pressure.	diffusion (p. 67) osmosis (p. 68) osmotic pressure (p. 68) selective transport (p. 69) facilitated diffusion (p. 69) active transport (p. 70) sodium-potassium pump (p. 70) proton pump (p. 70) endocytosis (p. 72) exocytosis (p. 72)	• Some substances enter a cell by diffusion, the movement of molecules from a higher to a lower concentration. • Water enters and leaves a cell by osmosis, the diffusion of water across a cell membrane. • Selective transport and facilitated diffusion do not require energy to move substances into cells. Active transport requires energy and can move substances to a region of higher concentration. • Larger particles are moved into and out of a cell by endocytosis and exocytosis.

73

Alternative Assessment

Divide the class into cooperative work groups of four students each. Have each group construct a cross-word puzzle with clues, using the terms introduced in this chapter. Make copies of all the puzzles, and have each group try to complete the puzzles.

Portfolio Assessment

Portfolio Assessment on page T39 provides options for building and evaluating student portfolios. Students and teachers can select items from the areas listed on page T39 for inclusion in a portfolio.

ANSWER TO
CONCEPT MAP

The following is one possible answer to the Relating Concepts exercise on page 74.

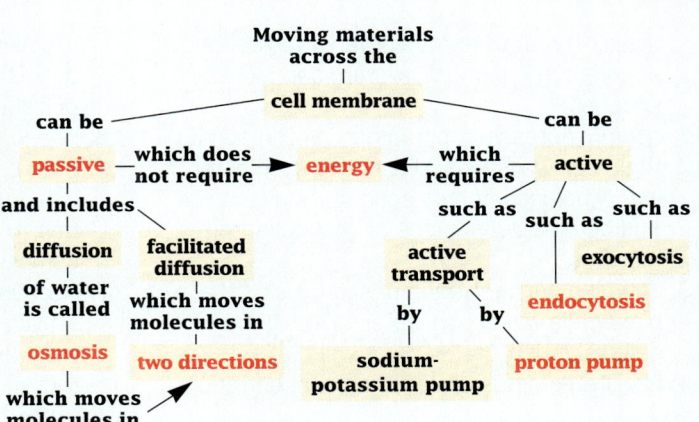

Understanding Vocabulary

1. a. Diffusion is the random movement of molecules from an area of higher concentration to one of lower concentration; osmosis is the diffusion of water across a membrane.
b. In facilitated diffusion, substances are transported without using the cell's energy. In active transport, a cell uses energy to move substances.
c. See page 72.

2. a. These three structures enable a cell to communicate with other cells and its environment. See pages 64–66.
b. Active transport requires energy to move substances. The sodium-potassium pump moves sodium ions out of cells and potassium ions into cells. The proton pump moves protons across the cell membrane and allows cells to transform energy in food into energy a cell can use to perform work.

Understanding Concepts

3. Answer to concept map is found on page 73.

4. Cellular communication enables cells to coordinate their behavior so that they function as a single organism rather than as individual cells.

5. See Figure 4-4 on page 65.

6. See Figure 4-2 on page 64.

7. Insulin molecules have a specific shape that can bind to receptors in the cell membrane. The binding causes the receptor to change shape and send a message into the cell to take in and store excess sugar.

8. Cells in multicellular organisms have the ability to send and receive signals, which enables them to coordinate reactions that affect the entire organism.

9. See pages 64 and 65.

10. If the cell surface markers of the donor do not match those of the recipient, the recipient's immune system will

---

Understanding Vocabulary

1. For each pair of terms, explain the difference in their meanings.
   a. diffusion, osmosis
   b. facilitated diffusion, active transport
   c. endocytosis, exocytosis

2. Using each set of words below, write one or more sentences summarizing information learned in this chapter.
   a. receptor protein, voltage-sensitive channel, cell surface marker
   b. active transport, sodium-potassium pump, proton pump

Understanding Concepts

3. **Relating Concepts** Copy the unfinished concept map below onto a sheet of paper. Then complete the concept map by writing the correct word or phrase in each oval containing a question mark.

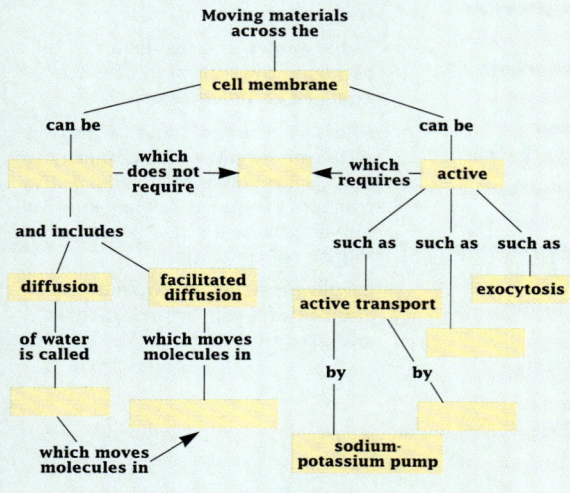

4. **Inferring Relationships** Explain why it is important for cells to communicate with one another.

5. **Summarizing Information** Explain how voltage-sensitive channels work and why they are important.

---

6. **Comparing Structures and Functions** Where are the two kinds of receptor proteins located? How does each type of receptor protein function?

7. **Predicting Outcomes** Insulin, a hormone that regulates the level of sugar in your blood, reacts with receptor proteins in much the same way as glucagon. Based on what you know about the way glucagon reacts with receptor proteins, describe how insulin sends a message to a cell that it should take in and store extra sugar.

8. **Recognizing Relationships** Explain the importance of the relationship between cellular communication and multicellularity.

9. **Summarizing Information** Describe how cells communicate using both chemical and electrical signals.

10. **Recognizing Relationships** How do cell surface markers affect the success of organ transplants? What can be done to increase the success of organ transplants?

11. **Identifying Functions** What are two active transport mechanisms that enable cells to store certain substances?

12. **Comparing Structures** Compare the methods by which plant and animal cells keep from bursting due to osmotic pressure.

13. **Analyzing Results** People sometimes sprinkle salt on weeds growing through cracks in their sidewalks and driveways. Based on what you know about osmosis, explain why salt would kill the weeds.

14. **Analyzing Methods** Compare the processes of facilitated diffusion and active transport. In what ways are they alike? In what ways are they different?

15. **Identifying Functions** Describe two functions of the sodium-potassium pump.

16. **Comparing Processes** Compare the similarities and differences between diffusion and osmosis.

17. **BUILDING ON WHAT YOU HAVE LEARNED** How does the molecular structure of water enable it to interact with sugars, proteins, and other polar molecules within the cell?

---

attack the transplanted organ. Medication to suppress the immune system can increase success.

11. sodium-potassium pump and proton pump

12. Rigid cell walls keep plant cells from bursting. A balance of fluid concentrations inside and outside cells keeps animal cells from bursting.

13. The high concentration of salt outside the plant cells will cause water to leave the cells. The dehydrated plant will die.

14. Facilitated diffusion relies on concentration gradients and does not require energy; active transport moves molecules to regions of higher concentration, which requires energy.

15. See Figure 4-9 on pages 70 and 71.

16. Both processes involve the movement of molecules from areas of higher concentration to areas of lower concentration. In osmosis, water moves across a membrane.

17. Because they are polar, water molecules attract and bond with other polar molecules, such as sugars, proteins, and other important molecules in the cell.

Interpreting Graphics

18. Study the drawing of the sodium-potassium pump shown below. Label the structures in the diagram by matching each letter in the list below to a numbered structure. Describe what happens when a sodium ion moves into a receptor site on the protein channel.

    a. sodium ions
    b. protein channel
    c. lipid bilayer
    d. potassium ions

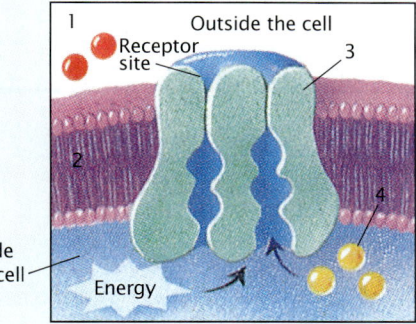

Reviewing Themes

19. *Cell Structure and Function*
Predict what would happen if red blood cells and plant cells were each placed in containers of distilled water.

20. *Heredity*
Your friend needs a kidney transplant. Explain why the best source for a donated kidney would be from your friend's identical twin brother.

Thinking Critically

21. **Evaluating Results** A scientist takes skin cells from a frog and a human and places them both in an 0.8 percent salt solution. He was later surprised to find that the frog cells had swollen and burst and that the human cells had shrunk. Based on what you know about osmosis, how would you explain these results?

22. **Evaluating an Argument** How would you respond to someone who says that both osmosis and active transport can occur in a dead cell? Use examples from the chapter to support your response.

Life/Work Skills

23. **Finding Information** When a person's kidneys fail to remove wastes, that person may need to undergo kidney dialysis—the artificial filtering of blood. Consult references in your library to find out how membranes are used in kidney dialysis machines, how frequently dialysis is performed, and what costs are involved. Summarize your findings in a presentation to your class.

24. **Working Cooperatively** Because it involves a defect in cell membrane channel proteins, the disease cystic fibrosis affects the body in many ways. Treatments involve overcoming the various effects of the disease. Work in cooperative teams to research the ways in which cystic fibrosis damages the body. Identify which organs are likeliest to be severely affected by the disease and describe treatments that combat the effects of cystic fibrosis on each organ. Work with the other members of your team to present your findings to your class.

Activities and Projects

25. **Health Connection** Find out how disinfectants, such as alcohol, are able to kill disease-causing bacteria. What part of the bacterial cell is affected by disinfectants? Summarize your findings in a report that includes other methods used to destroy bacteria.

Discovering Through Reading

26. Read the article "The Early Days of Transplantation" by Thomas E. Starzl in *Journal of the American Medical Association*, December 1994, page 1705. What is the single most important case in the history of transplantation? Explain your answer.

27. Read the article "Biology on Ice" by Wallace Ravven in *Discover*, August 1994, pages 36–41. Why would it be beneficial to be able to freeze human organs prior to transplanting them? What damage does freezing and thawing do to an organ? What are two ways to prevent the formation of ice crystals when freezing tissues?

Human cells had a lower concentration of salt and a higher concentration of water than the solution. As a result, water moved out of the cell and the cell shrank.

22. Osmosis can occur in a dead cell because it can occur without energy. Active transport, however, can occur only in a living cell because it requires energy.

Life/Work Skills

23. Students' findings should describe current techniques and costs of dialysis.

24. Reports will vary but should discuss damage to lungs, pancreas, and liver.

Activities and Projects

25. Answers will vary. Disinfectants work by disrupting a cell's membrane.

Discovering Through Reading

26. Answers may vary, but according to Starzl, the most important case is the 1959 transplant of a kidney between dizygotic twins. Previous transplant successes had been limited to identical twins.

27. Freezing organs would greatly extend the time an organ is viable for transplantation after it is removed from a donor. However, freezing causes ice crystals to rip vessels, dehydrate cells, and destroy vital proteins. Melting ice crystals deform cells by squeezing them into tighter and tighter spaces.

75

---

be at risk for bursting from osmotic pressure. However, the plant cell's rigid cell wall would keep it intact.

20. Answers will vary but should discuss the importance of matching cell surface markers.

Interpreting Graphics

18. a—4, b—3, c—2, d—1; Sodium ions enter the receptor site, the protein channel changes shape allowing the potassium ions to enter the cell and the sodium ions to leave the cell.

Reviewing Themes

19. Water molecules would be at a higher concentration outside both cells and would enter them by osmosis. The red blood cell would

Thinking Critically

21. Frog cells have a higher concentration of salt and a lower concentration of water molecules than the solution. As a result, water entered the cell and caused it to burst.

5 | Energy and Life

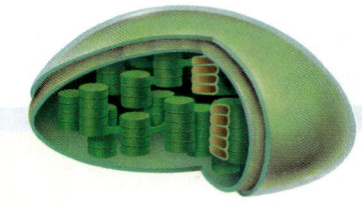

Lesson Planning Guide With Options for Block Scheduling

Lecture Concepts	Lesson Resources

5-1 Cells and Chemistry

BLOCK ❶ (45 minutes)

1. A chemical reaction involves the making or breaking of bonds between atoms.

2. Chemical reactions store or release energy.

3. Enzymes provide the energy required to start chemical reactions.

❶ Lecture Resources
- Determining Prior Knowledge
- Active Reading: Brainstorming
- Visual Strategy: Videodisc
- Demonstration: Analyzing Information
- Demonstration: Interpreting Graphs
- Teaching Transparencies: 8A, 9A, 11A
- Holt Biology Videodiscs Lesson 5-1

Classwork Options
- Exploration 5A

Assignment Options
- Teaching Resources CD-ROM: Occupational Applications Worksheets 6

BLOCK ❷ (45 minutes)

5. Enzymes are proteins with specific sites where substrates bind.

6. Enzyme activity is affected by changes in temperature, pH, or concentration.

❷ Lecture Resources
- Visual Strategy: Figure 5-3
- Visual Strategy: Videodisc
- Demonstration: Constructing Models
- Holt Biology Videodiscs Lesson 5-1

Classwork Options
- Closure: Organizing Information
- Investigation 5B

Assignment Options
- Reteaching
- Section Review
- Chapter Review, questions 1a, 2a, 5, 7, 8, 9, 28
- Directed Reading Worksheet

5-2 Cells and Energy

BLOCK ❸ and ❹ (45 minutes each)

1. Cells use energy to perform all life functions.

2. Cells release energy in small, gradual steps.

3. Cells use energy stored in ATP to drive chemical reactions.

4. Photosynthesis and respiration are responsible for flow of energy.

❸ Lecture Resources
- Active Reading: Paired Summarizing
- Visual Strategy: Figures 5-7, 5-9, 5-10
- Teaching Transparencies: 12, 16, 20
- Holt Biology Videodiscs Lesson 5-2

Classwork Options
- Problem Solving

❹ Small Group Reteaching
- Closure: Analyzing Relationships

Assignment Options
- Section Review
- Chapter Review, questions 2b, 6, 26, 27, 29
- Directed Reading Worksheet

5-3 Photosynthesis

BLOCK ❺ (45 minutes)

1. Photosynthesis uses light energy to manufacture carbohydrates from carbon dioxide.

2. The first photosynthesizing organisms evolved about 3 billion years ago.

3. Light energy from the sun energizes electrons in chlorophyll during photosynthesis.

❺ Lecture Resources
- Active Reading: Brainstorming
- Active Reading: Reading Organizer
- Visual Strategy: Figure 5-12
- Demonstration: Recognizing Relationships
- Teaching Transparencies: 19, 22
- Holt Biology Videodiscs Lesson 5-3

Classwork Options
- Photosynthesis
- Interactive Exploration 5C

Assignment Options
- Decision Making

BLOCK ❻ (45 minutes)

4. Energy in excited electrons is used to make ATP and NADPH in photosynthesis.

5. ATP and NADPH are used to convert carbon dioxide into carbohydrates in photosynthesis.

❻ Lecture Resources
- Visual Strategy: Figure 5-14
- Demonstration: Determining the Validity of a Claim
- Teaching Transparencies: 17, 18
- Holt Biology Videodiscs Lesson 5-3

Classwork Options
- Reteaching
- Closure: Identifying Variables

Assignment Options
- Section Review
- Chapter Review, questions 1c, 10, 11, 12, 13, 14, 19, 20, 21, 25, 26
- Directed Reading Worksheet

Lecture Concepts   ## Lesson Resources

5-4 Cellular Respiration

BLOCK ⑦ (45 minutes)

1. Cellular respiration is the process of releasing energy stored in organic molecules.
2. Glycolysis is the process by which glucose is broken down into pyruvic acid and ATP is made.
3. Fermentation is the process by which pyruvic acid is converted into alcohol or lactic acid.

⑦ Lecture Resources
- ■ Yeast Enzymes
- ■ Active Reading: Anticipation Guide
- ■ Visual Strategy: Videodisc
- ◫ Teaching Transparencies: 21, 23
- ◉ Holt Biology Videodiscs Lesson 5-4

Classwork Options

▲ Laboratory Techniques and Experimental Design: Lab C7

BLOCK ⑧ (45 minutes)

4. Oxidative respiration is the process by which pyruvic acid is broken down, enters the Krebs cycle, and yields ATP, NADH, and CO_2.
5. The breakdown of glucose yields 36 ATPs.

⑧ Lecture Resources
- ■ Exchanging Gases
- ■ Visual Strategy: Figure 5-18, 5-19b
- ◉ Holt Biology Videodiscs Lesson 5-4

Classwork Options
- ■ *Small Group* Reteaching
- ■ Closure: Relating Concepts

Assignment Options
- ■ Respiration
- ■ Section Review
- ■ Chapter Review, questions 1b, 2c, 3, 4, 15, 16, 17, 18, 22, 23, 24
- ■ Directed Reading Worksheet

Chapter Review and Assessment

BLOCK ⑨ (45 minutes)

Review
- ■ Reteaching Worksheet
- ■ Thinking Skills Worksheet
- ■ Vocabulary Development Worksheet
- ◎ Language Development and Reading Comprehension Audio CD Program: Chapter 5

BLOCK ⑩ (45 minutes)

Assessment
- ■ Alternative Assessment, p. 95
- ■ Portfolio Assessment, p. T39

Chapter Test
- ■ Chapter 5 Test

Test Generator
- ◎ Item bank for customizing Chapter Tests

Teaching Resources CD-ROM
- ◎ Scoring Rubrics and Classroom Management Checklist

 The Portfolio icon denotes items throughout the Teacher's Edition lesson wrap that may be selected for inclusion in student portfolios.

Holt Biology Videodiscs and *Concepts of Biology*

Holt Biology Videodiscs gives you a powerful tool for teaching, review, and assessment. For further information regarding the media on the videodiscs, see *Holt Biology Videodiscs Teacher's Correlation Guide to Holt Biology: Visualizing Life.*

Concepts of Biology adds interactive lesson plans and extensive tools for customization using CD-ROM technology.

Use the following topic from *Concepts of Biology* to help you teach this chapter:

Topic 4: Energy and Enzymes
Topic 5: Photosynthesis and Cellular Respiration

Laboratory Planning

Text

Materials and preparation instructions appear on the teacher's wrap accompanying each laboratory exercise.

Block 1: Exploration 5A: Measuring the Rate of a Process, p. 764

Block 2: Investigation 5B: Measuring the Rate of a Process: Falling Bread, p. 766

Block 5: Interactive Exploration 5C: Photosynthesis, p. 768

Holt BioSources Laboratory Program

Block 7: Laboratory Techniques and Experimental Design Lab C7: Measuring the Release of Energy From Sucrose

Determining Prior Knowledge

- Use an apple as a focal point for determining what students know about photosynthesis. Ask students what process produced the carbohydrates that are stored in the apple. Ask students what the tree needs to be able to produce its fruit. Ask students to name an important byproduct released by the tree.
- Again, focus on the apple. Ask students how foods supply the energy they need. Have them describe life processes that are fueled by this energy.
- Have students recall a time when physical activity caused them to become slightly winded or tired. You may want to take them out for a brisk walk to demonstrate this point.

Active READING

Technique: Brainstorming

Write "things needed to sustain life" on the chalkboard. Ask students to consider what is really needed to sustain living things. Have two student volunteers quickly list on the board all the responses from the class. (Students should include water, food, oxygen, carbon dioxide, shelter, and clothing, but they may identify many less-necessary items that are important to them, such as music, television, cars, etc.) Emphasize that in Chapter 5 they will learn about the chemical needs of living things. Remind students to be on the lookout for things on their list.

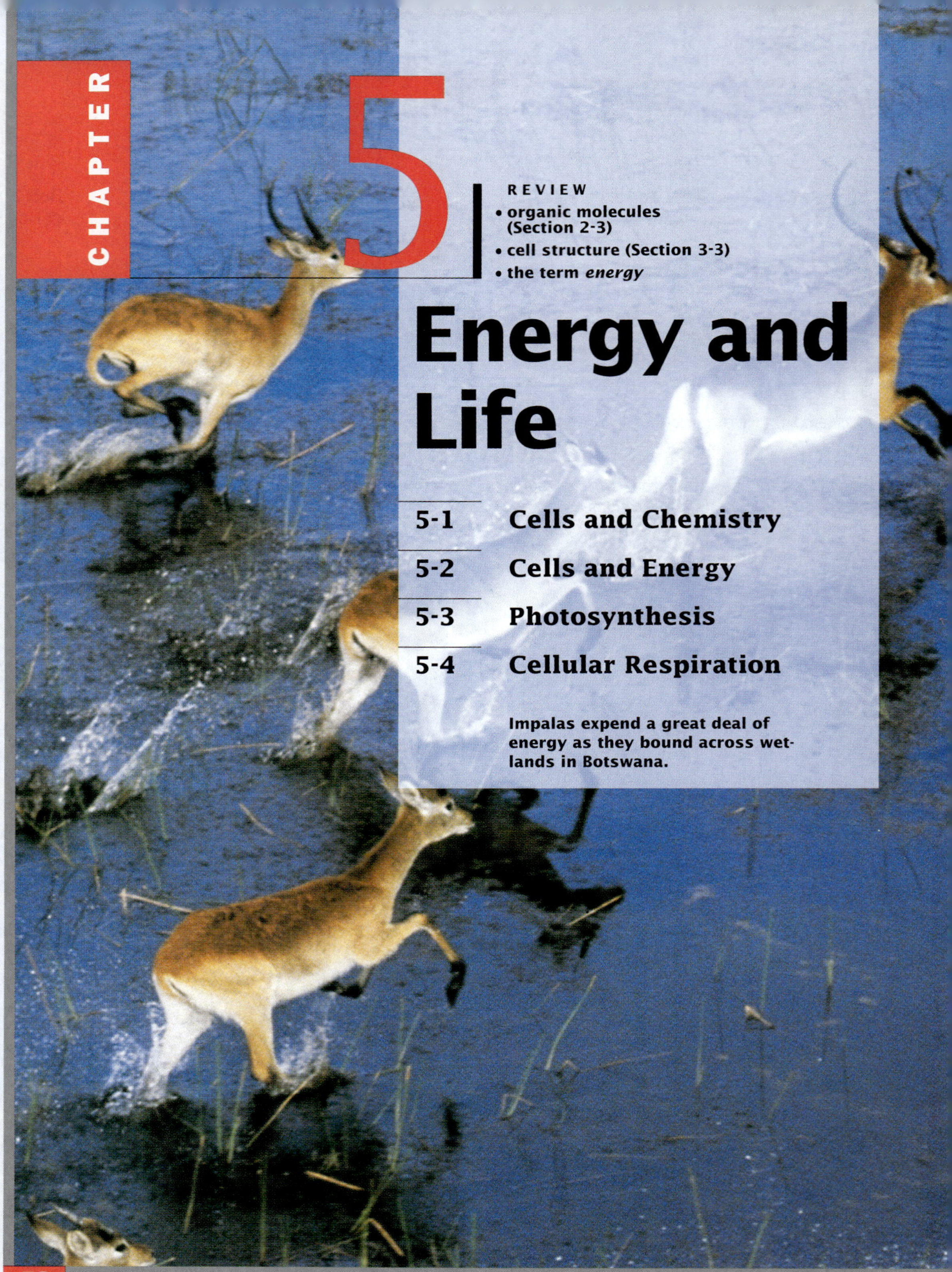

CD-ROM Resources

Concepts of Biology

Topic 4: Energy and Enzymes

Topic 5: Photosynthesis and Cellular Respiration

CHAPTER **5**

REVIEW
- organic molecules (Section 2-3)
- cell structure (Section 3-3)
- the term *energy*

Energy and Life

5-1 **Cells and Chemistry**

5-2 **Cells and Energy**

5-3 **Photosynthesis**

5-4 **Cellular Respiration**

Impalas expend a great deal of energy as they bound across wetlands in Botswana.

76

Author's Rationale In this chapter, students are given an overview of metabolism without a lot of chemical terminology. The answers to three simple questions summarize this chapter.

- How does energy flow through the living world?
- How do plants capture energy from the sun?
- How do we obtain this energy when we eat plants (or the animals that ate plants)?

Students will need to master the idea that energy-boosted electrons moving from one molecule to another are being used to drive proton pumps and make ATP.

Just as mechanical engineers study car engines to learn how cars run, scientists study cells to understand how living things work. Like cars, living things are complex machines, full of delicate details, and driven by chemical energy. To understand how your body works, you must look "under the hood" at the chemical "machinery" in your cells.

5-1 Cells and Chemistry

OBJECTIVES

1 Distinguish chemical reactions that absorb energy from those that release energy.

2 Describe the role of activation energy in chemical reactions.

3 Describe how an enzyme interacts with its substrate.

4 Analyze the role of enzymes in cells.

Chemical Reactions in Living Things

Fizzing test tubes are not the only places where chemical reactions occur. Chemical reactions within cells drive all the activities associated with life. During chemical reactions, atoms of the reactants (starting materials) are rearranged to form the products (ending materials). Chemical reactions are written in the following form:

$$\text{reactants} \longrightarrow \text{products}$$

In your cells, chemical reactions rearrange the atoms in glucose molecules, making new products and releasing energy. A potato, like the one in **Figure 5-1a**, is an excellent food because it is crammed with starch (long chains of glucose molecules). In plant cells, chemical reactions that absorb energy make glucose and other organic molecules that plants use for energy and growth.

Figure 5-1

a When you eat a potato, chemical reactions in your mouth and small intestine convert starch into glucose. Other reactions break down glucose and release energy that your body uses to do work.

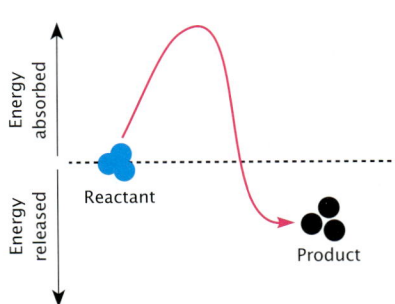

b This graph represents the breakdown of glucose. Notice that energy is released as the reaction's product forms.

77

Videodisc Resources

Holt Biology Videodiscs
Lesson 5-1: Cells and Chemistry

Phase One
Preparation

Scheduling
See the **Lesson Planning Guide** on pages 75A and 75B for lecture, classwork, and assignment options for Section 5-1.

Phase Two
Teaching Strategies

Demonstration

■ **Analyzing Information**
Materials: crackers or bread
Provide each student with a cracker or piece of bread. Have the students chew until they notice the sweet taste resulting from the digestion of starch (the reactant) into sugar (the product). Ask students what substance is responsible for this chemical reaction that is occurring in their mouth *(saliva)*. Explain to students that saliva contains chemicals called enzymes, which begin the chemical breakdown of starchy foods.

Key to Strategies
Teaching Strategies are keyed to three tiers of learning.

● **Understanding Concepts (Tier I)**
Content mastery and comprehension

■ **Applying Information (Tier II)**
Applying and analyzing content

▲ **Critical Thinking (Tier III)**
Practicing evaluative thinking

Energy and Life 77

Activate an instant warm pack and cold pack according to the instructions. Pass both packs around the class so that students can feel the contrasting temperatures. Point out that the activation of each type of pack initiates a chemical reaction. In the case of the heat pack, the chemical reaction that occurs releases energy. This energy raises the temperature of the surrounding solution, making the pack feel warm. Relate this to Figure 5-1b, in which the products have less energy than the reactants. The energy that was "lost" was given off as heat energy. The reverse happens with a cold pack. In this case, the chemical reaction absorbs energy from the water, causing the temperature of the solution to drop. Relate this to Figure 5-2b, in which the products have more energy than the reactants.

Connection: *Chapter 2*

Covalent Bonds
Review the basic chemistry of covalent bond formation. Point out that most chemical reactions occurring in living things involve either the making or breaking of covalent bonds. Write the formulas for carbon dioxide, water, and glucose on the board. Emphasize the importance of these molecules in the metabolism of living things.

Chemical reactions can release or absorb energy
The graph shown in **Figure 5-1b** on the previous page represents a chemical reaction that releases energy. The breakdown of glucose is an example of this type of chemical reaction. Your cells use the energy released during the breakdown of glucose to make proteins and the other organic molecules that make up your body.

Chemical reactions that build macromolecules such as proteins absorb energy. A chemical reaction that absorbs energy is represented by the graph in **Figure 5-2b**. The formation of glucose in a potato plant is an example of a chemical reaction that absorbs energy.

At any moment, thousands of chemical reactions are going on in every cell of an organism's body—a living symphony of chemistry. Collectively, all of the chemical reactions occurring in an organism are called **metabolism** (*muh TAB uh liz uhm*).

Figure 5-2
a **This potato plant uses energy from light to form the chemical bonds of glucose.**

Chemical reactions need some energy to get started
The heat from a flame ignites the logs in a campfire. The spark from a spark plug causes the gasoline in an engine to ignite. In both of these cases, an input of energy is used to start a chemical reaction. The energy needed to start a chemical reaction is called **activation energy**. Think of a boulder that you want to roll down a hill. To get it rolling downhill, you must first give it a push. Activation energy is simply a chemical push that gets a chemical reaction going.

Even if a chemical reaction releases energy, activation energy must still be supplied before that reaction can occur. For example, the combustion of gasoline provides the energy needed to power an automobile. But only after the key is turned in the ignition will sparks from the spark plugs ignite the gasoline in the engine's cylinders. The sparks provide the activation energy that triggers the burning of gasoline.

Enzymes lower activation energy for chemical reactions
Like engines, cells consume fuel. The burning of gasoline fuel in an engine requires a spark or high temperature to get the reaction going fast enough to power a car. Most chemical reactions that happen in cells also require very high temperatures in order to proceed fast enough to keep a cell alive. Such high temperatures kill most cells.

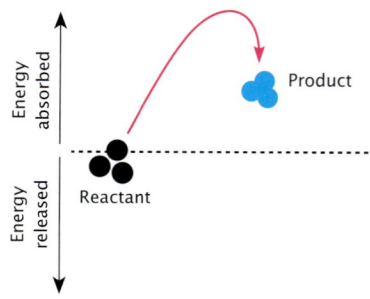

b **This graph represents the making of glucose. Notice that energy is absorbed as the reaction's product forms.**

Historical Perspective: Activation Energy

In 1937, the *Hindenburg,* an airship that was inflated with highly explosive hydrogen gas, exploded as it was about to land in New Jersey. For some still-unknown reason, the airship blew up when something provided the activation energy that sparked the violent reaction of hydrogen gas with atmospheric oxygen. Some believe the activation energy came from a spark produced by an atmospheric discharge. Others suspect the work of saboteurs.

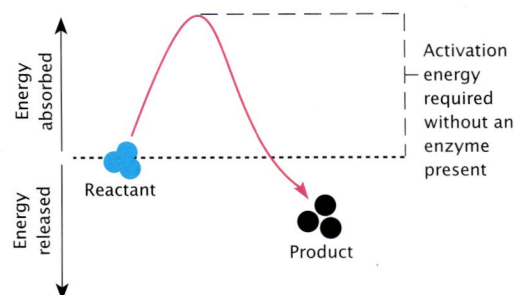

Figure 5-3

a Activation energy must be supplied for most chemical reactions to occur.

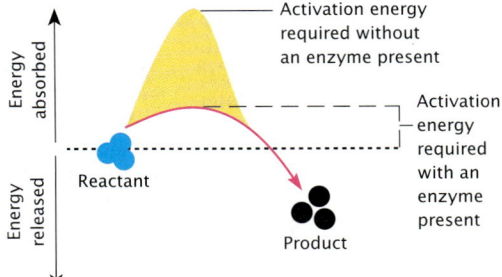

b Enzymes lower the amount of activation energy required to start a chemical reaction.

Fortunately, the chemical reactions in cells occur quickly and at relatively low temperatures through the action of enzymes. As you read in Chapter 2, **enzymes** are proteins that can hasten a chemical reaction. How do enzymes increase the speed of a reaction?

A chemical reaction could proceed faster if less energy were needed to get it started. Think about the activation energy needed to roll a heavy boulder over a hill. One way to reduce the amount of energy necessary would be to reduce the hill's size. Once the boulder is at the top of the hill, digging away some of the ground in front of the boulder would reduce the amount of energy needed to send it rolling downhill. In a sense, using an enzyme in a reaction is like lowering the top of the hill. Enzymes cause reactions to occur with less activation energy, as shown in **Figure 5-3**.

Enzymes are biological catalysts. A **catalyst** makes a chemical reaction proceed faster, but it is not used up by the reaction. An enzyme-catalyzed reaction is faster because it has a lower activation energy than does an uncatalyzed reaction.

Actions of Biological Catalysts

To understand the importance of enzymes, consider how your blood picks up carbon dioxide and delivers it to your lungs to be exhaled. Carbon dioxide is a waste product that will poison the body if it is not continuously removed. When carbon dioxide is converted to carbonic acid, it can be safely carried within the bloodstream. However, the chemical reaction that converts carbon dioxide to carbonic acid is very slow. In a given volume of water, only 200 molecules of carbonic acid form in an hour.

Fortunately, an enzyme called carbonic anhydrase is present in the blood. This enzyme increases the rate of this reaction to form 600,000 molecules of carbonic acid every second. The enzyme, shown in **Figure 5-4**, accelerates the reaction rate about 10 million times! Without carbonic anhydrase, your blood would quickly become poisoned with carbon dioxide.

Figure 5-4

This is a computerized, three-dimensional model of a molecule of carbonic anhydrase, an enzyme that enables your blood to remove carbon dioxide quickly. The colors represent different amino acids that make up the enzyme.

Historical Perspective: Jokichi Takamine

Jokichi Takamine, a Japanese chemist who was educated in the United States, was the first to separate diastase (a starch-hydrolyzing enzyme). His discovery facilitated commercial production of the enzyme. He was also the first to isolate pure adrenaline.

Theme Answer

Stability and Homeostasis
By controlling the kinds and amounts of enzymes present in a cell, the body can control the chemical reactions that take place in it.

Visual Strategy | Videodisc

● **Interpreting Graphics**
Review the interaction of an enzyme and substrate while showing *Step-Frame Sequence—Enzyme and Substrate* shown in Chapter 5 Section 5-1 of **Holt Biology Videodiscs Teacher's Correlation Guide to Holt Biology: Visualizing Life.** Guide students through each step, identifying the structures and summarizing the process. Next, show *Diagram—Enzyme/Substrate: Unlabeled.* Have students copy the diagram and label the substrate, enzyme, and active sites.

Demonstration

■ **Constructing Models**
Materials: a lock, keys, gloves
Show students a lock and several keys, only one of which will open the lock. Tell them that Emil Fischer, a German chemist, suggested in 1894 that enzymes and substrates work like a lock and key. Try to open the lock with the various keys. Only the key that fits correctly works. This "lock-and-key" model was accepted for many years until the "induced-fit" model replaced it. To show students how scientists today think enzymes function, show the class several gloves, only one of which fits your hand. Tell students that scientists think that an enzyme and its substrate work more like a hand and a glove. In this model, the enzyme does not have a rigid shape. Instead, the enzyme undergoes a slight change in shape as the substrate enters the active site. But as with the lock-and-key model, the substrate must have a certain shape to enter the active site. As it enters, the enzyme and substrate fit together snugly.

Stability and Homeostasis

A conductor controls the music of an orchestra by dictating when each instrument plays. How is this similar to the way your body controls chemical reactions?

Enzymes speed reactions by binding with specific molecules

How does an enzyme work? An enzyme binds to a specific molecule (or molecules) and stresses the bonds of that molecule in a way that makes a reaction more likely to occur. The molecule on which the enzyme acts is called a **substrate** (*SUHB strayt*).

The key to an enzyme's activity is its shape. Typically, an enzyme is a large protein that consists of a folded chain of hundreds of amino acids. Each enzyme has one or more deep folds on its surface. These folds form pockets called **active sites**. As you can see in **Figure 5-5**, an enzyme's substrate will fit into an active site just as your feet fit comfortably into your favorite pair of sneakers.

An enzyme makes a reaction proceed more quickly by lowering activation energy in one of two ways. When a substrate molecule binds to the active site of an enzyme, the molecule is held close to a certain part of the enzyme's surface. The enzyme may put a strain on a particular chemical bond in the substrate molecule and thus make the bond more likely to break. An enzyme may also encourage the formation of a bond between two substrates by binding to both substrates and holding them near each other. When the reaction is complete, the products of the reaction are released, and the enzyme is ready to combine with an identical substrate molecule.

Because an enzyme must have a precise shape in order to work correctly, a cell can control an enzyme's activity by altering the enzyme's shape. The shapes of many enzymes can be altered by binding "signal" molecules to their surfaces. The new shape produced by binding the signal molecule acts to turn the enzyme "on" or "off."

Cells have thousands of different enzymes

A cell contains thousands of different kinds of enzymes, each promoting a different chemical reaction. Not all cells contain the same enzymes. As you read this page, the chemical reactions going on in a nerve cell in your eye are very different from the chemical reactions in one of your red blood cells because the two kinds of cells contain different enzymes. The enzymes active at any one time in a cell determine what happens in that cell, just as traffic lights control the flow of traffic in a city.

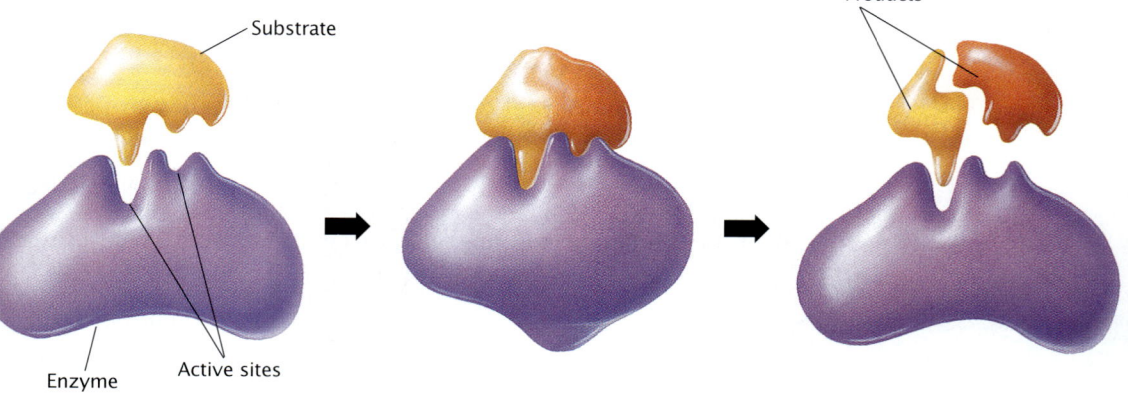

Figure 5-5

a **Enzymes lower the activation energy of a reaction. Here an enzyme is about to bind with its substrate.**

b **The enzyme binds to the substrate, stressing a particular bond and lowering the activation energy needed to break the bond.**

c **When the products of the reaction are released, the enzyme returns to its original shape and is ready to combine with another substrate molecule.**

Matter of Fact: Coenzymes

Vitamins are important in the diet because they serve as coenzymes, small nonprotein molecules that work with enzymes to promote enzyme activity. Many coenzymes have B vitamins as part of their structure. The B vitamins play an important part in the release of energy from food.

Figure 5-6
In some animals, enzymes that control pigmentation are active only at certain temperatures.

a The darker parts of the Siamese cat are also the cooler regions of its body. This is because the enzyme catalyzing the formation of the dark pigment is more active in cooler temperatures.

b Similarly, the fur of the adult northern seal is dark because the enzyme that catalyzes pigment formation is more active in cold arctic temperatures. The newborn seal is white because the enzyme was less active in the warmer temperatures inside its mother's body.

Heat, acidity, and enzyme concentration affect enzymes

Each enzyme functions best within a certain temperature range. When temperatures become too low or too high, reaction rates decrease sharply. For instance, many enzymes in your body shut down when you have a high fever. If the internal body temperature of a human being were to reach 44°C (112°F), many enzymes would be destroyed, and the individual would probably die. For additional examples of how enzymes are affected by temperature, look at **Figure 5-6**. How does temperature affect the pigmentation of the Siamese cat and the northern seal?

Another factor influencing enzyme activity is acidity (the strength of the acids in body fluids). When an organism's acidity is too high or too low, most enzymes cease to function properly. One exception, however, is the enzyme pepsin, which functions in the stomach's highly acidic environment.

Finally, the rate of an enzyme-catalyzed reaction is affected by the concentration of the enzyme and the substrate. The rate of a chemical reaction in the body, for example, can be accelerated by increasing the concentration of the enzyme necessary to catalyze that reaction. This is how your body controls its development.

SECTION REVIEW

1 How does the outcome of a chemical reaction that absorbs energy differ from one that releases energy?

2 What is activation energy, and how does it relate to cell metabolism?

3 Explain how an enzyme can increase the rate of a chemical reaction.

4 Why do you think it is advantageous for the human body to have many different enzymes?

ANSWERS TO SECTION REVIEW

1 When a chemical reaction absorbs energy, the products have more energy than the reactants. When a chemical reaction releases energy, the products have less energy than the reactants.

2 Activation energy is the energy needed to start a chemical reaction. All the reactions that make up metabolism require activation energy.

3 An enzyme can increase the rate of reaction by bringing reactants together and reducing the amount of activation energy required to start the reaction.

4 The many different reactions that occur in the body require many different enzymes.

Phase Three
Assessment Options

Closure

● **Organizing Information**
Use the Active Reading strategy below to summarize information from the lesson.

Active READING

Technique: Reading Organizer
Have students complete a spider map to help them identify the characteristics of enzymes described in Section 5-1. *(Students' organizers will vary but should include the following points: enzymes lower the activation energy required; enzymes are affected by heat, acidity, and enzyme concentration; enzymes speed up chemical reactions; enzymes are made up of amino acids, etc.)*

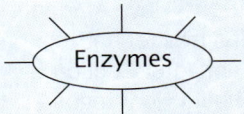

Enzymes

SECTION REVIEW
Assign the *Section Review.*

Reteaching

Students often get the impression that because there are thousands of different enzymes, if one were missing or damaged the effect would be insignificant. Have students use the library to locate information on galactosemia and phenylketonuria (PKU). *(Galactosemia is a disease among infants caused by a lack of the enzyme needed to convert galactose to glucose. Phenylketonuria is another disease among infants; it is caused by the lack of the enzyme needed to convert the amino acid phenylalanine to the amino acid tyrosine.)*

Key to Strategies
● **Understanding Concepts (Tier I)**
■ **Applying Information (Tier II)**
▲ **Critical Thinking (Tier III)**

Energy and Life 81

Scheduling

See the **Lesson Planning Guide** on pages 75A and 75B for lecture, classwork, and assignment options for Section 5-2.

Phase Two
Teaching Strategies

Active READING

Technique: Paired Summarizing
Have students read silently the first page of Section 5-2. Then assign partners and have one student, the "reteller," summarize orally what has been read while the other student, the "listener," listens to the retelling. The listener should point out inaccuracies and add ideas that were left out. Have students alternate roles and repeat this process for each page of Section 5-2. Students should work together during a final clarification process, referring to the text as needed.

Visual Strategy | Figure 5-7

■ **Relating Concepts**
Ask students why a doctor might prescribe bed rest for someone who is sick. (*Energy is needed by the immune system to produce more cells like the one shown in Figure 5-7. Too much physical activity during illness might slow the body's defensive actions and repair processes.*)

If you stopped eating, you would eventually die. Why? Because the food you eat provides the energy needed for life. All of the properties by which we define life—growth, movement, sensitivity, and reproduction—use energy. Just as logs must be continually supplied to a campfire to keep the fire burning, energy must be continually supplied to living cells to keep life going.

5-2 Cells and Energy

OBJECTIVES

1. **Explain how cells use energy.**

2. **Compare the way a fire releases energy from fuel with the way a cell releases energy from fuel.**

3. **Describe the role played by ATP in cells.**

4. **Recognize the path of energy between plants and animals in the living world.**

How Cells Use Energy

Living cells use energy to do all those things that require work. One of the most obvious of these is movement. Some bacteria and protozoans swim about, propelling themselves through fluids by rapidly spinning flagella. Cells also use energy to change their shape. White blood cells, for example, must extend and retract their cell membranes when they engulf invading bacteria in the bloodstream, as shown in **Figure 5-7.** Metabolism, which includes tasks such as manufacturing cellular components and repairing cellular structures, requires great quantities of energy. Cells also need energy to transport food and other nutrients into the cell and to expel wastes.

Cells release energy in a series of small steps

Perhaps you have heard that jogging or some other exercise "burns" a lot of calories. The word *burn* is often used to describe what happens when your cells release stored energy from food.

Obviously the "burning" of food in living cells differs from the burning of logs in a campfire. When logs burn, the energy stored in wood is released in a single reaction as heat and light. But this is not what happens in cells. Instead, energy stored in food molecules is released at each step in a series of enzyme-catalyzed chemical reactions, as shown in **Figure 5-8.** The product of one chemical reaction is a reactant in the next reaction.

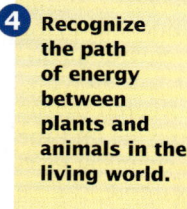

White blood cells

Bacterium

Figure 5-7
This electron micrograph shows a bacterium being engulfed by a human white blood cell. The white blood cell uses energy when changing its shape.

82

Videodisc Resources
Holt Biology Videodiscs
Lesson 5-2: Cells and Energy

Figure 5-8
Energy is released from starch through a series of enzyme-catalyzed chemical reactions. The product of one reaction becomes the reactant of the next. Energy is released by each reaction.

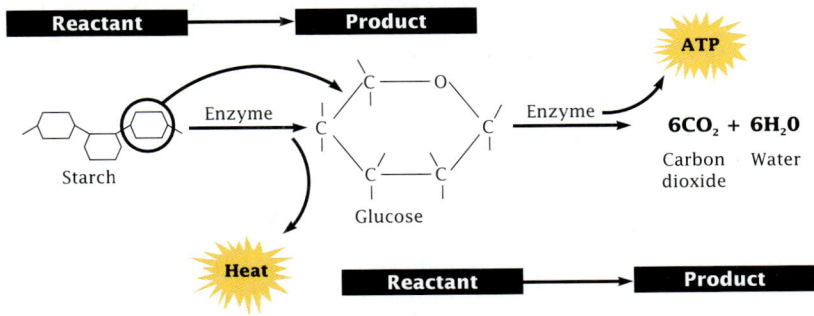

Cells transfer energy from food to a molecule called ATP

When living cells break down molecules, some of the energy released from the molecules is in the form of heat. The rest of the energy is stored temporarily in molecules of adenosine triphosphate, or **ATP**, as shown in **Figure 5-8**. Like the money you use to pay for your needs, ATP is a portable form of "energy currency" inside of cells. ATP molecules deliver energy to wherever it is needed in a cell.

As **Figure 5-9** shows, ATP contains three phosphate groups. The term *triphosphate* means "three phosphate groups." When the outer phosphate group of ATP is removed, ADP (adenosine diphosphate) is formed. The term *diphosphate* means "two phosphate groups." The reaction that forms ADP

from ATP releases energy in a way that enables cells to use the energy. The following equation summarizes this reaction:

$$ATP \xrightarrow{H_2O} ADP + P + energy$$

In cells, almost all chemical reactions that absorb energy require less energy than is released by the removal of a phosphate group from ATP. Therefore, ATP is able to drive most of a cell's activities.

Cells use ATP to drive many chemical reactions

A steady supply of ATP is necessary to ensure that a cell can perform all the tasks essential for life. Making molecules, for example, uses energy. The reactions that build new molecules cannot begin until something supplies the energy needed by the reaction. That something, as you have probably guessed, is ATP.

The energy released from the breakdown of ATP can provide energy for other reactions. When a reaction that absorbs energy in a cell is driven by the conversion of ATP to ADP, it is called a coupled reaction. Coupled reactions occur often during metabolism.

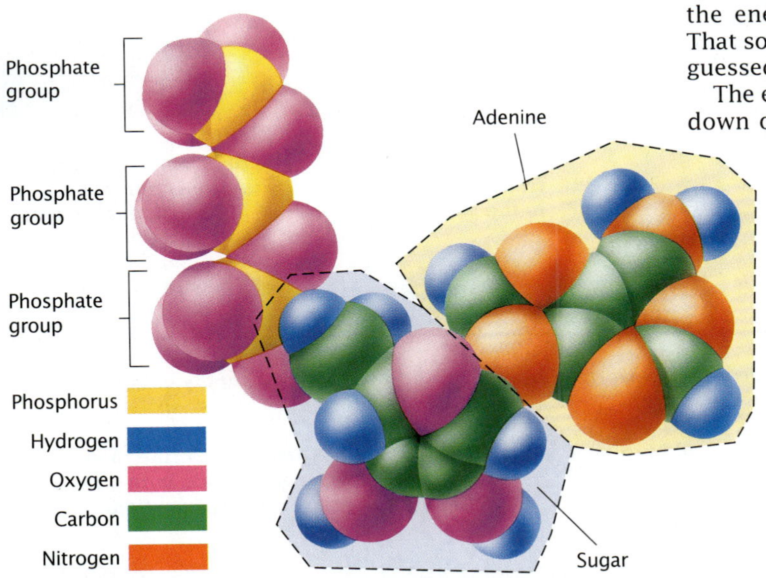

Phosphate group
Phosphate group
Phosphate group

Phosphorus
Hydrogen
Oxygen
Carbon
Nitrogen

Adenine

Sugar

Figure 5-9
An ATP molecule is made of a sugar, adenine, and a chain made of three phosphate groups. Energy is released when the outermost phosphate group is removed.

83

Problem Solving

■ **Forming a Hypothesis**
Give students the following situation: A racehorse jockey followed a low-calorie diet to make the weight for her class during each of several racing seasons. She noticed that she gained more during each consecutive off-season even though her calorie intake was consistent with the previous off-season. Have students work in cooperative groups to research possible causes and solutions. Resources on diet and nutrition should provide information about the body's metabolic responses to low-calorie diets and fasting. Ask students to hypothesize about the reason for the jockey's increasing off-season gain and suggest actions that might correct the problem. *(Students should ascertain that the jockey's weight gain is probably due to a reduced metabolic rate that occurred because the body conserves energy for survival. Because it is the off-season, the jockey's activity level has probably decreased. Possible solutions should include an increase in physical activity during the off season, and if the jockey decides to diet, only a mild calorie reduction of about 250 calories a day would be necessary with the increased activity.)*

Visual Strategy Figure 5-9

● **Interpreting Graphics**
Have students identify where the bond in ATP is broken to produce ADP. *(Students should indicate that the phosphate group at the end of the chain is removed.)*

Matter of Fact: Cyanide

Cyanide is a deadly poison that disrupts the metabolic pathway by inactivating an enzyme important to metabolism and preventing the tissues from using oxygen. When energy and materials cannot be passed through the system, the cells die. Ingesting less than 3 g of cyanide can result in death in a short amount of time.

Key to Strategies
● **Understanding Concepts (Tier I)**
■ **Applying Information (Tier II)**
▲ **Critical Thinking (Tier III)**

Visual Strategy   Figure 5-10

■ Relating Concepts
Explain to students that the transfer of energy continues beyond this illustration. When the carnivore dies, microbes will benefit. But the microbes themselves will be consumed by soil dwellers, which will be consumed by some other animal, and so on. Large amounts of energy escape in the form of heat with each transfer.

Phase Three
Assessment Options

Closure
● **Analyzing Relationships**
Assign students to cooperative work groups. Have each group create a display that shows the transfer of energy from the sun throughout the living world. Students may decide to assemble a collage of photographs or drawings, create a computer-generated display, or produce a video.

SECTION REVIEW
Assign the *Section Review.*

Reteaching
Have students work with a partner to prepare a concept map summarizing the main ideas discussed in this section.

Energy Flow in the Living World

Almost all of the energy needed for life comes ultimately from the sun, which shines continuously on Earth. Plants, algae, and some bacteria capture energy directly from sunlight and use that energy to produce ATP, energy-storing carbohydrates, and other types of organic molecules. This process is called **photosynthesis** *(foh toh SIHN thuh sihs)*. Organisms that cannot capture energy directly from sunlight get the energy for life by consuming food, which contains carbohydrates and other organic molecules.

All living things use a process called **cellular respiration** to obtain energy from carbohydrates and other organic molecules. During cellular respiration, energy that was stored in organic molecules is used to make the ATP needed for life processes.

Energy from the sun flows in connected pathways throughout the living world. You can see one such pathway in **Figure 5-10**. The energy-absorbing chemical reactions of photosynthesis capture energy from sunlight and transform it into chemical energy. Some of that chemical energy is transferred when one organism eats another. The energy-releasing reactions of cellular respiration enable living things to use that chemical energy to do work. You will learn more about the processes of photosynthesis and cellular respiration in Sections 5-3 and 5-4.

Figure 5-10
a **Light energy streaming from the sun . . .**

b **. . . is converted into carbohydrates by plants.**

c **When an animal eats plants, it gets energy from the carbohydrates in the plants.**

d **And when that animal is eaten by another animal, energy that originated in the sun is again transferred.**

SECTION REVIEW

1 What life activities performed by cells require energy?

2 Why doesn't a cell burn up as it releases energy from organic molecules?

3 How does ATP supply energy for the cell?

4 Compare and contrast the roles of plants and animals in the flow of energy in the living world.

84

ANSWERS TO SECTION REVIEW

1 Cells require energy for movement, growth, metabolism, transporting nutrients into the cell, and eliminating wastes.

2 The cell releases energy in small, gradual steps, thus preventing the sudden and explosive release of energy that could occur in one giant step.

3 When the bond between the second and third phosphate groups of ATP is broken, ATP becomes ADP. This reaction releases energy.

4 Plants use the sun's energy to produce carbohydrates. The carbohydrates provide energy for plant-consuming animals. These animals may be eaten by other animals, providing them with energy.

Have you ever eaten beef enchiladas? The beef came from a cow that ate grass. Other parts of the enchiladas came directly from plants. With few exceptions, you end up with plants (or some other photosynthetic organism) if you trace your food back to its origin. Clearly, you depend on plants for food, as do all plant eaters and organisms that eat plant eaters. The energy in that food came from sunlight.

5-3 Photosynthesis

OBJECTIVES

1 **Describe** how photosynthetic organisms use energy from light to make organic molecules and oxygen.

2 **Explain** how plant cells use the ATP and NADPH that forms during photosynthesis.

3 **Analyze** the roles of electrons and protons in photosynthesis.

4 **Summarize** the three stages of photosynthesis.

Harnessing the Sun's Energy

Each day, the light energy that reaches Earth equals the energy released by the explosions of about 1 million atomic bombs. Plants, algae, and some bacteria capture about 1 percent of that energy and convert it to chemical energy through photosynthesis. During photosynthesis, energy captured from sunlight is used to obtain electrons, which carry the energy through a series of chemical reactions.

Photosynthesis has three stages

In the first stage of photosynthesis, energy is captured from light. During the second stage, the energy is used to make ATP and an energy-carrying compound called NADPH. During the third stage, the ATP and NADPH are used to power the manufacture of energy-rich carbohydrates using CO_2 from the air.

This method of photosynthesis evolved among ancient bacteria more than 3 billion years ago. Today, all plants and algae use this type of photosynthesis. During the process, electrons are obtained by removing hydrogen atoms from water (H_2O) molecules, and oxygen (O_2) molecules are released, as you can see in **Figure 5-11**. Earth's atmosphere is now rich in oxygen gas because of the oxygen released by photosynthesis.

Figure 5-11
In bright light, scores of tiny bubbles appear on the leaves of this water plant. The bubbles contain oxygen gas that is produced through the process of photosynthesis.

85

Videodisc Resources

Holt Biology Videodiscs
Lesson 5-3: Photosynthesis

Phase One
Preparation

Scheduling
See the **Lesson Planning Guide** on pages 75A and 75B for lecture, classwork, and assignment options for Section 5-3.

Phase Two
Teaching Strategies

Active READING

Technique: Brainstorming
Write "photosynthesis" on the chalkboard or overhead projector. Explain to students that the prefix *photo* comes from the Greek word *photo,* which means *light*. Work with students to generate a list of words that include the prefix *photo*. (*Some examples include photocopy, photograph, photon, photogenic, and photojournalism.*) Explain to students that *synthesis* is the putting together of parts to build a whole. Ask students to read Section 5-3 and think about why the process described is called *photosynthesis*. (*Light energy is used by plants to build organic molecules from inorganic molecules.*)

Demonstration

■ **Recognizing Relationships**
Materials: a light-powered calculator
The photovoltaic cells in the calculator are made of semiconductor materials. When light shines on a solar cell, electrons are given off, producing a current in a circuit connected to the cell. Show the class a light-powered calculator, and ask them what it has in common with photosynthesis. (*Light provides the energy needed to run both the calculator and photosynthesis.*)

Key to Strategies
● **Understanding Concepts (Tier I)**
■ **Applying Information (Tier II)**
▲ **Critical Thinking (Tier III)**

Technique: Reading Organizer

Explain to students that writers often use cue words in titles and headings to signal the organizational structure of the text that follows. Have students scan the headings on pages 86–89 to find words that signal sequential organization (*Stage 1, Stage 2, Stage 3*). Then have students read the section silently and note cue words in the body of the text that indicate a sequential pattern. *(Possible answers include* when, after, series, steps, *and* before.*)*

Visual Strategy | Figure 5-12

● **Interpreting Graphics**

Ask students which portion of the electromagnetic spectrum shown in this figure has the longest wavelengths *(radio waves, because they have the least energy)* and which portion has the shortest wavelengths *(gamma rays, because they have the most energy).* Have students tap a slow rhythm and then a fast rhythm on their desk. Ask them which rhythm required more energy. *(A fast beat requires more energy than a slow beat.)* Use this analogy to explain that high-energy rays have short wavelengths and low-energy rays have long wavelengths.

Decision Making

▲ **Evaluating Viewpoints**

High-energy electromagnetic waves can be damaging to human tissues. Ultraviolet waves are responsible for premature aging of the skin and skin cancer. This type of radiation is given off by the sun and sunlamps. Have students use library references or interview a dermatologist to find out about the risks involved with UV exposure. Have students write a report on their findings and discuss their personal decisions concerning tanning.

Stage 1: Capturing Light Energy

Now that you know plants use energy from light for photosynthesis, you might be wondering where the energy is in light. Light is a form of electromagnetic radiation, which is energy transmitted by special waves. When the sun shines on you, your body is bombarded by all types of radiation emitted from the sun.

The amount of energy transmitted by an electromagnetic wave depends on its wavelength—shorter wavelengths have more energy than longer wavelengths. Some wavelengths of electromagnetic radiation, such as those in X rays and ultraviolet light, carry a large amount of energy. Other wavelengths, such as those in radio waves, carry very little energy. Our eyes detect only wavelengths that carry intermediate amounts of energy. These wavelengths make up "visible" light, as shown in **Figure 5-12**. Plants absorb mostly blue and red light and reflect much of what is left of the visible light, which is why most plants look green.

Certain molecules absorb light

How can a leaf or a human eye "choose" which colors of light to absorb? Certain molecules within these structures are able to absorb particular wavelengths of light. Molecules that absorb light are called **pigments**. Your eyes contain a pigment called retinal, which absorbs all wavelengths of visible light. Insect eyes contain a pigment that absorbs wavelengths with more energy than those absorbed

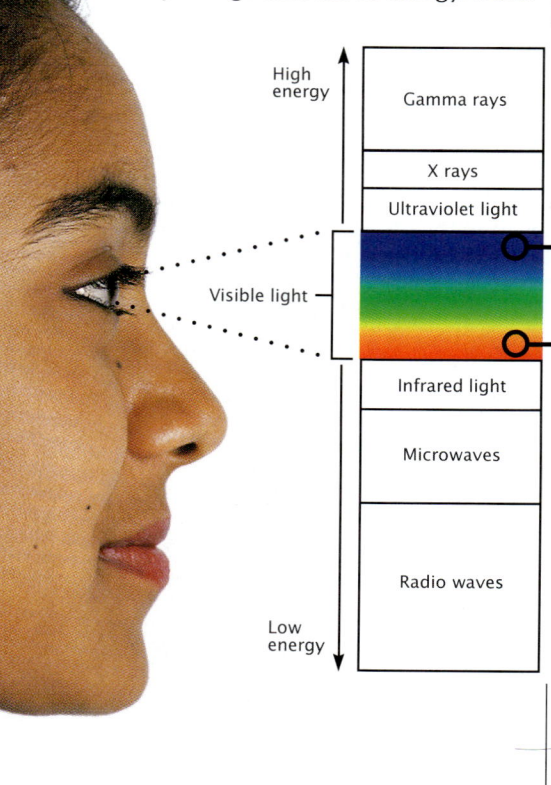

by retinal, so insects can see ultraviolet light that humans cannot see.

When a pigment absorbs light, electrons of certain atoms in the pigment molecules are boosted to a higher energy level. Energy transferred from the light to the electrons causes this move. Just as climbing to the next rung of a ladder requires you to raise your foot an exact distance, boosting an electron requires an exact amount of energy. Therefore, a particular kind of pigment can absorb only wavelengths with the appropriate amount of energy.

Figure 5-12
The entire range of wavelengths of electromagnetic radiation, from low-energy radio waves to high-energy gamma rays, is called the electromagnetic spectrum. Visible light is the portion of the spectrum that humans can see.

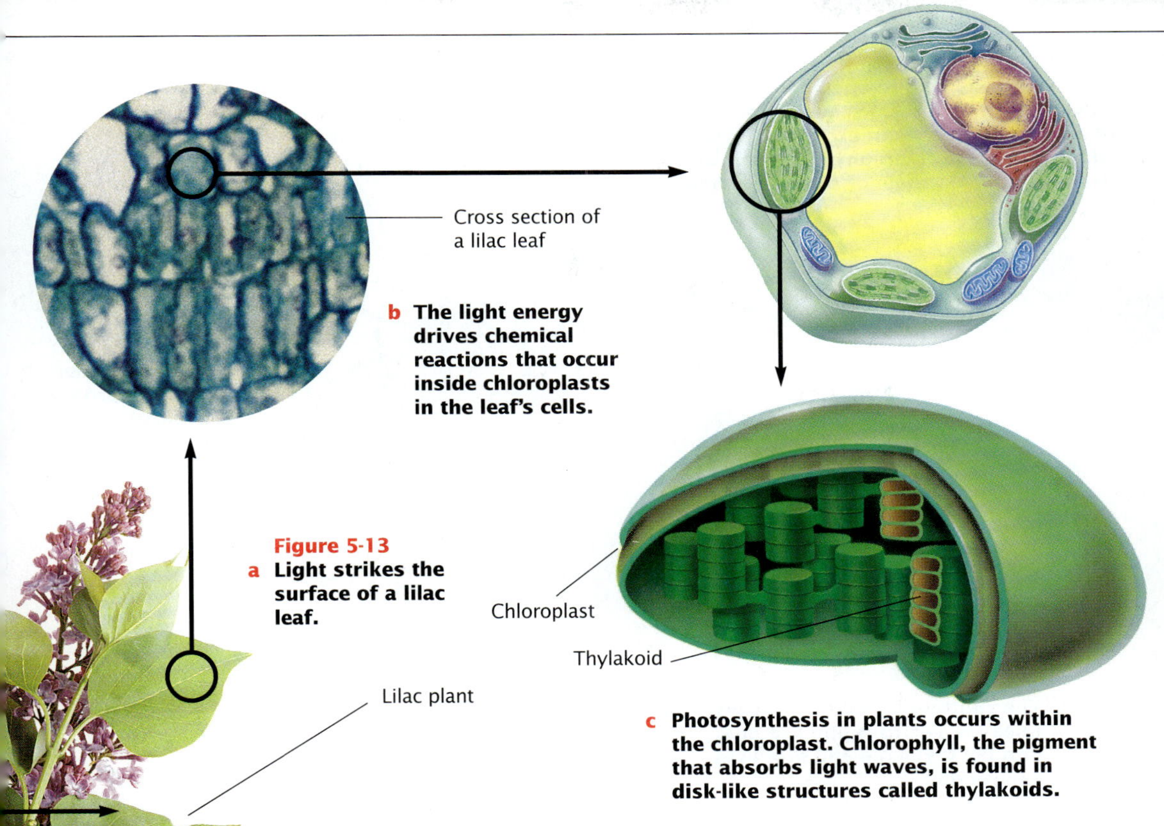

Cross section of a lilac leaf

b The light energy drives chemical reactions that occur inside chloroplasts in the leaf's cells.

Figure 5-13
a Light strikes the surface of a lilac leaf.

Chloroplast

Thylakoid

Lilac plant

c Photosynthesis in plants occurs within the chloroplast. Chlorophyll, the pigment that absorbs light waves, is found in disk-like structures called thylakoids.

Chlorophyll and other pigments capture light energy

The major pigment in plants is **chlorophyll**, which absorbs mainly red and blue light and reflects green light. Plants also contain other pigments that help in gathering energy for photosynthesis. These pigments, called carotenoids, absorb slightly different wavelengths of light and reflect colors such as yellow and orange. In most leaves, the green reflected by chlorophyll covers up the colors reflected by other pigments. Chlorophyll, however, breaks down in cold temperatures, enabling the colors of the carotenoids to be seen in the yellow and orange leaves of autumn.

Where are the pigments for photosynthesis located? Look at the structure of the leaf seen in **Figure 5-13**. Chlorophyll and the other pigments that assist in photosynthesis are found within the chloroplasts of plant cells.

Inside the chloroplasts, chlorophyll molecules are contained within the disk-like membrane structures called thylakoids.

When light strikes the thylakoids in a chloroplast, electrons within certain chlorophyll molecules are boosted to a higher energy level. These "excited" (boosted) electrons jump from their chlorophyll molecules to a nearby protein molecule in the thylakoid membrane. Each excited electron is then passed through the membrane from one electron-accepting molecule to another, like a ball being passed down a line of people.

Before excited electrons can leave their chlorophyll molecules, the electrons must be replaced by other electrons. Water supplies these electrons. Plants obtain electrons from water by splitting water molecules, H_2O. As water molecules split, chlorophyll takes the electrons from the hydrogen atoms, leaving protons. The remaining oxygen atoms combine to form oxygen gas.

87

Community Connection: Tourism

Check with a local travel agent for information about autumn tours for viewing the changing colors of leaves throughout the United States. They may be able to provide posters or travel brochures to help you illustrate how the tourism industry benefits from nature. Ask about local tourist attractions that involve plants or animals.

Visual Strategy **Figure 5-14**

● **Interpreting Graphics**
Lead students through stages 1 and 2 of photosynthesis with the illustrations in this figure. Emphasize that photosynthesis would come to a grinding halt if the electrons removed from chlorophyll were not replaced. Have students identify the source of these replacement electrons *(water)*. Point out that water also serves as the source of oxygen. Although it is not used in photosynthesis, it is crucial to respiration, as they will see in the next section. Be sure they can identify the two products made in stage 2 *(ATP and NADPH)*.

Theme Answer
Cell Structure and Function
Protein channels in the thylakoid membrane use the energy from protons passing through the membrane to add a phosphate group to ADP to make ATP, one of the two chemical compounds needed for the next stage of photosynthesis.

Chemistry Connection
Electron + Proton = Hydrogen
Remind students that the simplest form of hydrogen consists of an electron and a nucleus with one proton. This will help them understand why NADP$^+$ plus a proton forms NADPH.

Figure 5-14

a Photosynthesis begins when light strikes a chlorophyll molecule in the membrane of a thylakoid. The light excites an electron, which leaves the chlorophyll molecule and passes through a chain of electron carriers.

b The energy carried by the electron powers the movement of protons into the thylakoid.

c When light strikes a second chlorophyll molecule, it excites an electron that passes through another chain of electron carriers. The electron and a proton are joined to NADP$^+$, forming NADPH.

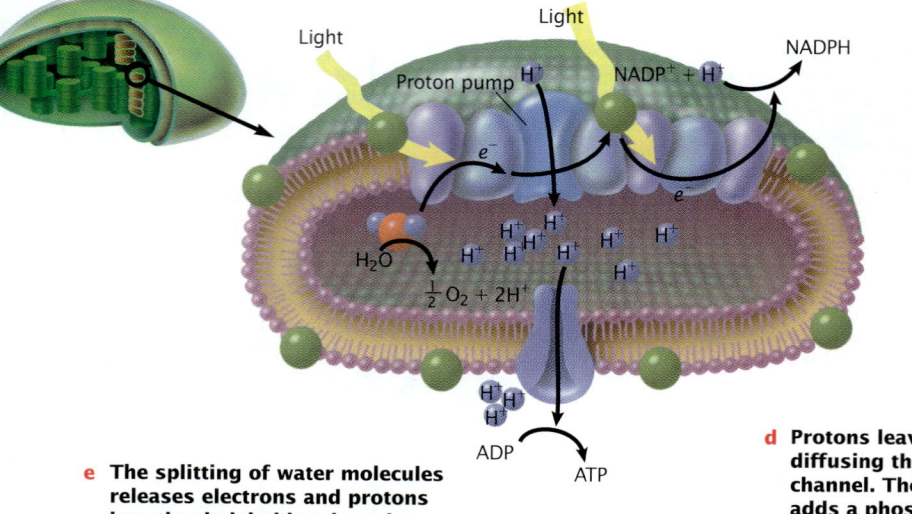

d Protons leave a thylakoid by diffusing through a protein channel. The force of their exit adds a phosphate group to ADP, forming ATP.

e The splitting of water molecules releases electrons and protons into the thylakoid and produces oxygen gas.

Stage 2: Using Light Energy to Make ATP and NADPH

Just as the action of a football game depends on moving the ball down the field, energy flow in cells depends on passing excited electrons from one carrier to another. This movement of excited electrons transfers the energy contained in those electrons from carrier to carrier as well. Follow the path taken by excited electrons in stage 2 of photosynthesis in **Figure 5-14**. The journey begins when chlorophyll absorbs light and loses an electron, as **Figure 5-14a** indicates. This electron is replaced by an electron from water, as **Figure 5-14e** indicates.

Cell Structure and Function

How does the structure of the thylakoid enable plants to capture light energy and transform it into chemical energy?

ATP is made when protons flow through a protein channel
Each excited electron from chlorophyll loses some of its energy as it passes through a series of carriers in a thylakoid membrane. This energy is used to pump protons across the membrane and into the interior of the thylakoid, as **Figure 5-14b** indicates. Protons are pumped inward until the thylakoid is "bursting at the seams." These protons are driven by diffusion through the only available exits, protein channels like the one in **Figure 5-14d**. These channels use the force of protons exiting a thylakoid to add a phosphate group to an ADP molecule, making ATP.

Additional light energy is absorbed to make NADPH
After the energy of excited electrons is used to make ATP, the electrons are accepted by other chlorophyll molecules. These molecules absorb more light, which excites some of their electrons. The excited electrons pass through another series of electron carriers. Finally, these electrons are attached to an electron acceptor called NADP$^+$, forming the energy carrier NADPH. These steps are pointed out by **Figure 5-14c**. The ATP and NADPH generated in stage 2 help power stage 3 of photosynthesis—the building of carbohydrates.

Stage 3: Building Carbohydrates

In the final stage of photosynthesis, carbon atoms are captured from carbon dioxide in the air and used to make organic molecules, which store energy. A series of reactions called the Calvin cycle produces organic molecules that can be used to assemble more complex organic molecules, such as the carbohydrates, lipids, and proteins needed for energy and growth. Because this series of reactions also regenerates its starting molecule, it forms a cycle. The Calvin cycle, which is summarized in **Figure 5-15**, is named for Melvin Calvin, the American biochemist who worked out the series of reactions in the cycle. The energy to fuel the Calvin cycle comes from the ATP and NADPH made during stage 2 of photosynthesis.

The many steps in the overall process of photosynthesis are often represented by the following single equation:

$$6CO_2 + 6H_2O \xrightarrow{\text{(light)}} C_6H_{12}O_6 + 6O_2$$

However, this equation does not show how photosynthesis happens. It merely says that 6 carbon dioxide molecules, 6 water molecules, and light are needed to form one 6-carbon organic molecule and 6 molecules of oxygen.

Plants use the organic molecules they produce during photosynthesis for their life processes. For example, sugar made in the leaves of a potato plant can be used to make cellulose for building new cell walls. Some of the sugar is stored as starch in the potato tuber. The plant may later break down the starch to make the ATP needed for energy, as you will see in Section 5-4.

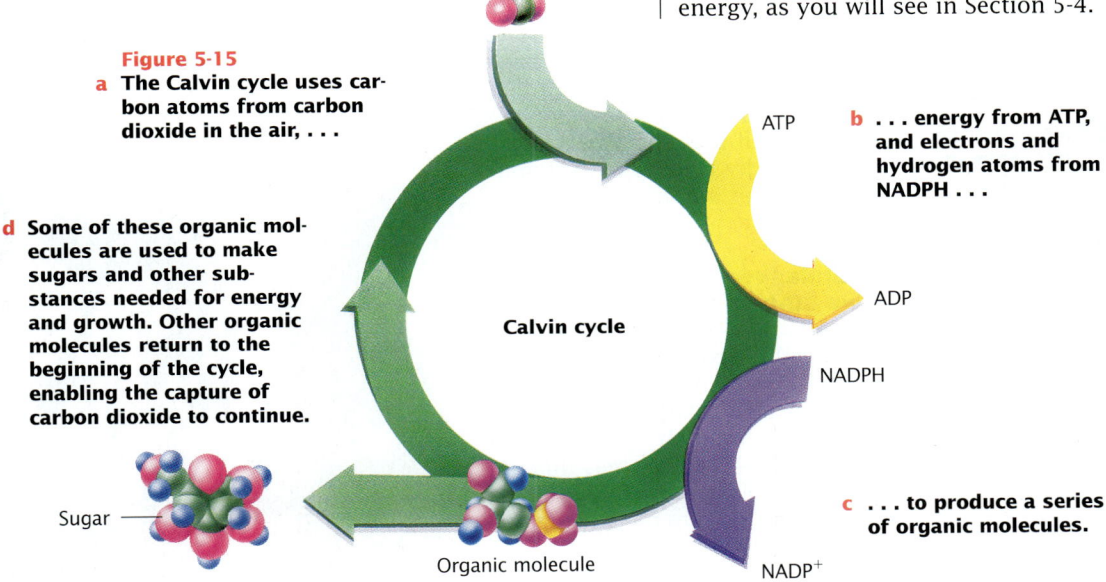

Figure 5-15

a The Calvin cycle uses carbon atoms from carbon dioxide in the air, . . .

CO₂

ATP

b . . . energy from ATP, and electrons and hydrogen atoms from NADPH . . .

ADP

Calvin cycle

NADPH

d Some of these organic molecules are used to make sugars and other substances needed for energy and growth. Other organic molecules return to the beginning of the cycle, enabling the capture of carbon dioxide to continue.

c . . . to produce a series of organic molecules.

Sugar

Organic molecule

NADP⁺

SECTION REVIEW

1. How is the energy in light captured by photosynthetic organisms?

2. What is the general role played by both ATP and NADPH during photosynthesis?

3. How are electrons and protons used during the photosynthetic process?

4. How does stage 2 of photosynthesis depend on stage 1? How does stage 3 depend on stage 2?

89

Active READING

Technique: Discussion
After students have read Section 5-3, ask the following questions to help stimulate discussion:
1. What role does light play in photosynthesis? *(Light provides energy for the reactions.)*
2. What chemical elements are involved in photosynthesis? *(C, H, O, N, P)*
3. What are the final products of photosynthesis? *(Products include all of the organic molecules made by the photosynthetic organism.)*

Phase Three
Assessment Options

Closure
● **Identifying Variables**
Have students list three factors that would increase the rate of photosynthesis. Have them identify what stage of photosynthesis each factor would affect. *(Examples might include increasing light intensity, which would affect stage 1; providing more water, which would affect stage 2; or increasing the CO₂ concentration, which would affect stage 3.)*

SECTION REVIEW
Assign the *Section Review*.

Reteaching
Have students examine *Figure 5-15* to answer the following questions: (1) What molecule goes into the Calvin cycle? *(CO₂)*, (2) What molecule comes out of the Calvin cycle? *(a 3-carbon organic molecule that can be used to make sugar)*, (3) What molecules are needed to keep the Calvin cycle operating? *(CO₂, ATP, and NADPH)*

A N S W E R S TO SECTION REVIEW

1. During stage 1 of photosynthesis, chlorophyll molecules absorb light energy, causing electrons to become excited and to jump from the chlorophyll molecules to the protein molecules in the thylakoid membrane.

2. Both ATP and NADPH are used to power stage 3, the building of carbohydrates in the Calvin cycle.

3. Electrons carry the energy that chlorophyll absorbs from light through the stages of photosynthesis. Protons are used in the synthesis of ATP and NADPH.

4. The electrons that are "excited" in stage 1 are used in stage 2 to make ATP and NADPH. The ATP and NADPH made in stage 2 are used to drive the Calvin cycle in stage 3.

Key to Strategies
● Understanding Concepts (Tier I)
■ Applying Information (Tier II)
▲ Critical Thinking (Tier III)

Scheduling

See the **Lesson Planning Guide** on pages 75A and 75B for lecture, classwork, and assignment options for Section 5-4.

Phase Two
Teaching Strategies

Active READING

● **Technique: Anticipation Guide**
Write the following statements on the chalkboard:

1. Living things do not need oxygen to get energy from organic molecules.
2. It is unlikely that humans will ever run a 2-minute mile.

Ask students to think about each statement and decide whether they agree or disagree. Ask volunteers with differing views to share the reasons for their opinions. After reading the section, ask volunteers to discuss with the class how their opinions changed or stayed the same as a result of their reading. Students should point to specific passages in the text that support their reasoning. Then have students read the section to see if their opinions are changed.

Exchanging Gases

■ **Recognizing Relationships**
Point out that during oxidative respiration, oxygen is used and carbon dioxide is produced as a byproduct. The body needs a continuous supply of oxygen and an elimination process for excess carbon dioxide. In humans, this exchange of gases is accomplished by the circulatory and respiratory systems, which will be covered in more detail in Chapter 32.

Although a plant produces carbohydrates only in cells with chloroplasts, all cells of the plant use these carbohydrates for energy. In both plants and animals—indeed, in almost all organisms—the energy for living is obtained by recycling the carbohydrate molecules produced by photosynthesis. The energy in these molecules is released in cellular respiration.

5-4 Cellular Respiration

Releasing Energy From Organic Molecules

OBJECTIVES

❶ **Explain the role of cellular respiration in making energy available to living things.**

❷ **Contrast fermentation with oxidative respiration.**

❸ **State the role of oxygen in oxidative respiration.**

❹ **Explain how feedback inhibition regulates ATP production.**

You have seen how energy from the sun is converted into chemical energy by photosynthesis. The chemical energy is stored in organic molecules such as carbohydrates. Living things such as those seen in **Figure 5-16** release energy from carbohydrates and other organic molecules through the process of cellular respiration. This energy is used to power chemical reactions in cells. The first result of cellular respiration is the formation of ATP. As you will see, the amount of ATP produced by cellular respiration depends on whether oxygen is present.

Cellular respiration has two stages
The first stage of cellular respiration is called **glycolysis** (*gly KAHL uh sihs*). Glycolysis happens in the cytoplasm of cells and does not require oxygen. It is an ancient energy-extracting process thought to have evolved more than 3 billion years ago, when no oxygen gas existed in Earth's atmosphere.

In most living things, a second stage of cellular respiration, called **oxidative respiration**, follows glycolysis. Oxidative respiration, which requires oxygen, happens within mitochondria. It is far more effective than glycolysis at recovering energy from organic molecules. Oxidative respiration is the method by which most living cells get the majority of their energy.

Figure 5-16
The plants that this cow is eating obtained energy from the sun. In turn, the plants provide the cow with the energy it needs to carry out its life activities. Both plants and animals use the process of cellular respiration to release energy stored in organic molecules.

90

Videodisc Resources
Holt Biology Videodiscs
Lesson 5-4: Cellular Respiration

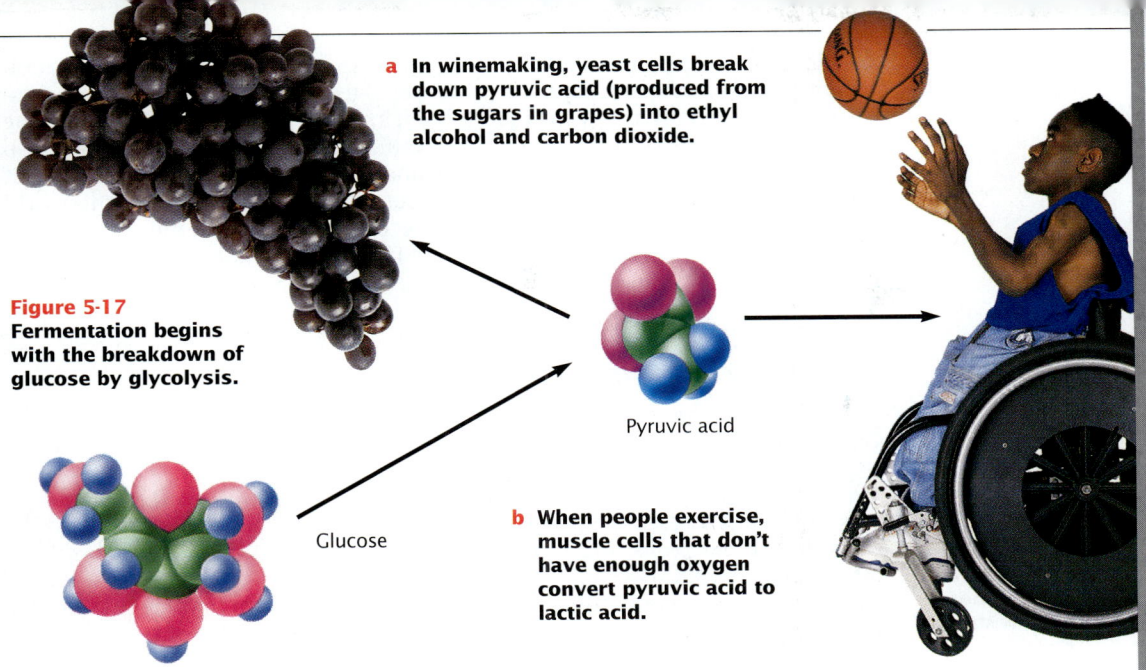

a In winemaking, yeast cells break down pyruvic acid (produced from the sugars in grapes) into ethyl alcohol and carbon dioxide.

Figure 5-17
Fermentation begins with the breakdown of glucose by glycolysis.

Pyruvic acid

Glucose

b When people exercise, muscle cells that don't have enough oxygen convert pyruvic acid to lactic acid.

Stage 1: Glycolysis

Glycolysis is one of the oldest biological processes we know. Ancient bacteria used it to make the ATP needed to drive chemical reactions within their cells. Today, every living thing, including you, still uses glycolysis.

Glycolysis breaks down glucose into smaller molecules

The word *glycolysis* means "the splitting of glucose." In a series of reactions, one molecule of glucose is split into two smaller molecules of a compound called **pyruvic** *(py ROO vihk)* **acid**. Although cells must use some ATP to begin glycolysis, the process produces a little more ATP than it uses. For each molecule of glucose that enters glycolysis, a cell gains two molecules of ATP.

During glycolysis, electrons carried on hydrogen atoms are stripped from glucose molecules. The electrons and hydrogen atoms are donated to an electron acceptor called NAD^+, forming the energy carrier NADH. For glycolysis to continue, however, electrons donated to NAD^+ to form NADH must be donated to some other organic molecule. This process frees the NAD^+ to accept more electrons and hydrogen atoms from glycolysis. Thus, glycolysis is followed by another set of reactions—either fermentation or oxidative respiration. The pyruvic acid molecules made during glycolysis still contain energy, but they cannot be broken down further to release energy if no oxygen is present.

Fermentation occurs in the absence of oxygen

The incomplete breakdown of organic compounds in the absence of oxygen is called **fermentation**. Like glycolysis, fermentation evolved before Earth's atmosphere contained oxygen and does not use oxygen. Today, cells still use fermentation to produce small amounts of ATP when oxygen is not available.

During fermentation, the electrons and hydrogen atoms carried by NADH are attached to pyruvic acid molecules. This process regenerates NAD^+, which enables glycolysis to continue. In some organisms, pyruvic acid is broken down into carbon dioxide and ethyl alcohol (ethanol), which is the alcohol in beer and wine. In other organisms, pyruvic acid is converted to lactic acid. These two types of fermentation are summarized in **Figure 5-17**.

Energy and Life

Health Connection

Aerobics

Ask a physical education teacher to discuss the advantages of aerobic exercise. Also have the teacher discuss what is meant by the popular term *hitting the wall,* an experience that marathon runners and other athletes occasionally encounter. During long-distance events, oxygen supply may become inadequate for aerobic pathways, so the body will use glycogen stored in the muscles. "Hitting the wall" occurs when the athlete depletes the glycogen stores. There is a substantial decrease in muscle performance because the body must produce energy from fat. Energy production from fat occurs at about half the rate of energy production from glucose.

Connection: *Chapter 3*

Mitochondria

Remind students that mitochondria are the organelles in eukaryotic cells with the special function of releasing energy stored in food. They are more numerous in muscle cells, which use large amounts of energy, and less numerous in bone cells, which use less energy.

Visual Strategy   Figure 5-18

■ **Calculating Efficiency**

Take students through the steps of glycolysis, fermentation, and cellular respiration. Point out how many ATPs are produced in oxidative respiration (36 ATPs), and calculate how many times more efficient oxidative respiration is than glycolysis *(36 ATPs/2 ATPs = 18 times more efficient).*

Lactic acid forms in muscles during vigorous exercise

Pyruvic acid is converted into lactic acid in your muscles when they are forced to operate without enough oxygen, such as during vigorous exercise. This process enables glycolysis to continue in your muscles as long as the glucose supply lasts. Blood circulation removes excess lactic acid from muscles. But when lactic acid cannot be removed quickly enough, it builds up and your muscles get tired. Because of the buildup of lactic acid, the world record for running a mile (just under 4 minutes) has not been beaten.

Stage 2: Oxidative Respiration

When Earth's atmosphere grew rich in oxygen, an alternative to fermentation became possible. Oxidative respiration, which happens within mitochondria, was this alternative. In the presence of oxygen, the electrons and hydrogen atoms carried by NADH can ultimately be attached to oxygen atoms instead of to pyruvic acid molecules.

Oxidative respiration involves chemical reactions that make much more ATP than is made by fermentation. **Figure 5-18** compares the results of fermentation and oxidative respiration. The complete breakdown of glucose through oxidative respiration can be summarized by the following equation:

$$C_6H_{12}O_6 + 6O_2 \longrightarrow$$
$$6CO_2 + 6H_2O + 36ATP$$

As with the summary equation for photosynthesis, this equation does not show how cellular respiration happens. It merely indicates that the complete breakdown of a glucose molecule uses 6 oxygen atoms and forms 6 carbon dioxide molecules, 6 water molecules, and as many as 36 ATP molecules.

Figure 5-18

a **Both cellular respiration and fermentation begin with glycolysis, in which glucose is broken down into pyruvic acid and two ATP molecules are released.**

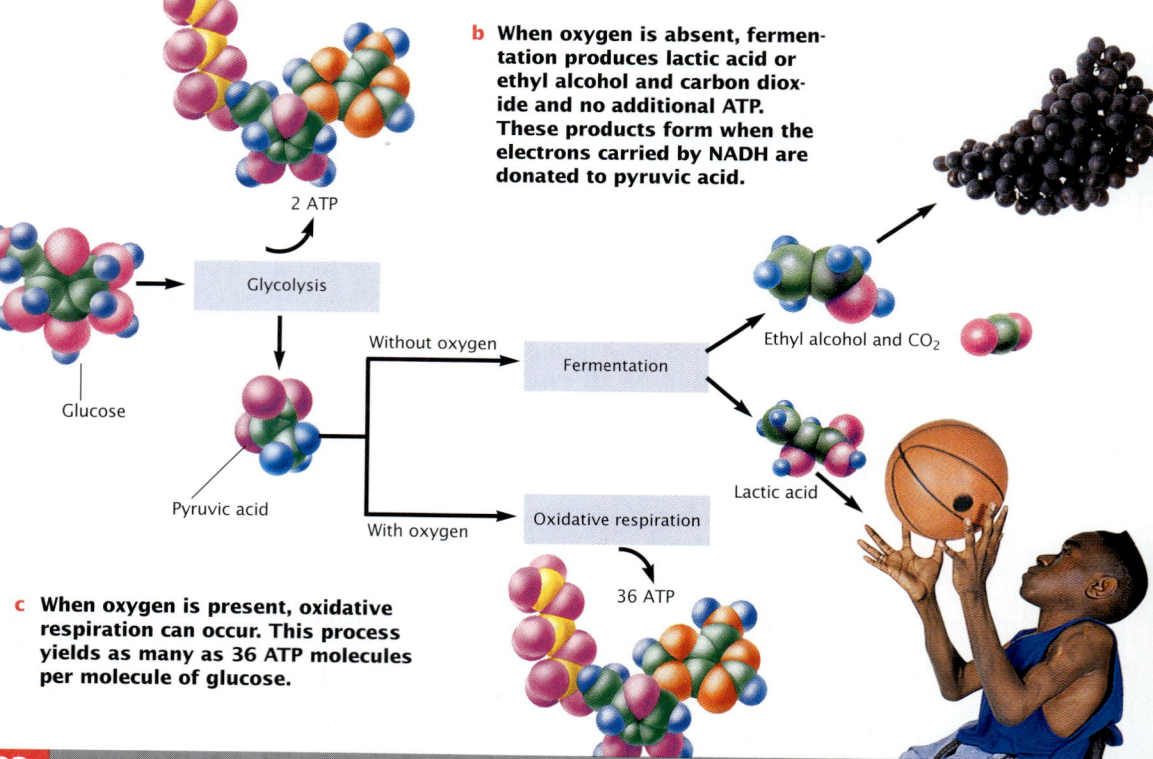

b **When oxygen is absent, fermentation produces lactic acid or ethyl alcohol and carbon dioxide and no additional ATP. These products form when the electrons carried by NADH are donated to pyruvic acid.**

c **When oxygen is present, oxidative respiration can occur. This process yields as many as 36 ATP molecules per molecule of glucose.**

92

Matter of Fact: Huntington's Disease

Lactic acid appears to be the first biochemical indication for Huntington's disease. The inherited disease causes neuron damage and leads to a decline in cognitive and physical functions. High levels of lactic acid were found in the occipital cortex of 23 of 24 patients with the disease. The cells are apparently unable to use oxidative respiration, so they use glycolysis to make ATP. This leads to a buildup of lactic acid. The cause of the disease is still unknown, and no treatment stops the progression.

Pyruvic acid   CO₂

NADH

NAD⁺

Two-carbon fragment

b If ATP is needed, the two-carbon fragment enters the Krebs cycle. It joins with a four-carbon sugar. Additional reactions produce carbon dioxide and ATP as they regenerate the starting material.

ATP

a Prior to the Krebs cycle, each pyruvic acid molecule is broken down into a two-carbon fragment and a carbon dioxide molecule. An electron is donated to NAD⁺, forming NADH.

Krebs cycle

NAD⁺

c NADH formed during the Krebs cycle takes electrons and hydrogen atoms to an electron transport chain. ATP is generated, and the electrons and hydrogen atoms join with oxygen to form water (H_2O).

ADP

NADH

Electron transport chain

ATP + H_2O

CO₂

Figure 5-19
Oxidative respiration occurs in two major steps: the Krebs cycle and the electron transport chain.

Oxidative respiration picks up where glycolysis leaves off

Figure 5-19 summarizes the major events of oxidative respiration. Inside the mitochondria, a carbon atom is removed from each pyruvic acid molecule produced by glycolysis. This reaction frees electrons that carry energy and releases carbon dioxide molecules. The electrons and a hydrogen atom combine with NAD⁺, forming NADH (another carrier of electrons and hydrogen atoms). The NADH will be used at the end of oxidative respiration. After the two reactions, only a two-carbon fragment remains, as you can see in **Figure 5-19a**. If a cell has enough ATP, the two-carbon fragment is used in reactions that produce fat, which stores energy. If the cell needs ATP, the two-carbon fragment will continue on to the next step of oxidative respiration.

The Krebs cycle yields ATP, NADH, and carbon dioxide

Two-carbon fragments produced by the removal of carbon atoms from pyruvic acid enter a series of reactions called the Krebs cycle. This cycle was named for Sir Hans Krebs, the biochemist whose work in the 1930s revealed how the reactions work. During the Krebs cycle, summarized in **Figure 5-19b**, two carbon dioxide molecules, one ATP molecule, and more

NADH molecules are made. The cycle also regenerates its starting molecule, enabling another two-carbon fragment to enter the cycle.

The electron transport chain makes more ATP

The electrons carried by molecules of NADH formed during the Krebs cycle are passed through a series of proteins in the membranes within mitochondria. This series of proteins, called the electron transport chain, uses the energy of these electrons to pump protons across the membrane. As in photosynthesis, protons become highly concentrated on one side of the membrane. The protons pass back through the membrane by diffusing through a protein channel. This movement of protons supplies the energy needed to attach a phosphate group to an ADP molecule, making ATP.

As **Figure 5-19c** shows, the protons and spent electrons from NADH are joined to oxygen at the end of the electron transport chain, forming water. Oxidative respiration requires oxygen because the electrons stripped from pyruvic acid must have a final home. Energy cannot be extracted from pyruvic acid without oxygen to accept spent electrons. Otherwise, the electron transport chain would become "clogged" with electrons.

93

Graphic Organizer

Use the following graphic organizer with the teaching strategy **Respiration** on page 93.

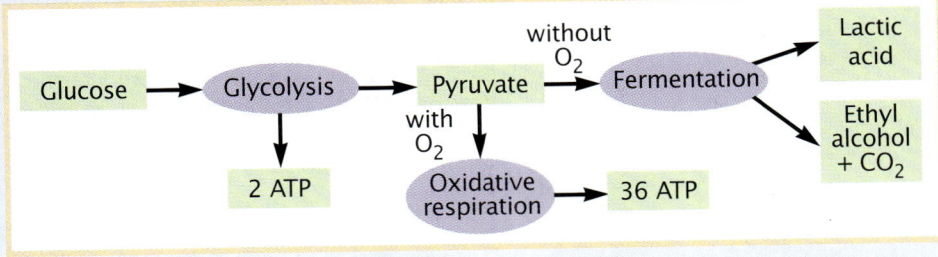

Glucose → Glycolysis → Pyruvate → without O_2 → Fermentation → Lactic acid / Ethyl alcohol + CO₂
Glycolysis → 2 ATP
Pyruvate → with O_2 → Oxidative respiration → 36 ATP

Theme Answer

Stability and Homeostasis

When the temperature gets to the upper level set on the thermostat, the furnace shuts off, just as a high level of a product can shut off an enzyme in feedback inhibition.

Phase Three

Assessment Options

Closure

■ **Relating Concepts**

Doctors often recommend exercise for people who lack energy. Have students review the molecular makeup of fats. When carbohydrates are not available, the cells can continue to carry on respiration by oxidizing fats stored in the body. Fat is best used for fuel during moderately intensive exercise such as long walks. If the exercise is too strenuous, the body starts using glycogen, which is quickly depleted, leaving the person with muscle fatigue. Take the class out for a walk while you review the process of respiration. Explain to students that conditioned muscles oxidize fat faster than unconditioned muscles, so regular exercise can help a person feel energetic.

SECTION REVIEW

Assign the *Section Review.*

Reteaching

Have students work in cooperative groups to develop an artistic display that summarizes how photosynthesis and cellular respiration are related. Encourage students to illustrate ways that plants store excess starch and sugar. Student displays will vary but should represent an overview of how energy is passed from the sun to plants and from plants to animals.

Stability and Homeostasis

How does the regulation of cellular respiration resemble a thermostat controlling the temperature in your home?

Regulating Cellular Respiration

The rate of cellular respiration slows down when your body's cells have enough ATP. But what signals each mitochondrion to slow down ATP production? The control works through a process called feedback inhibition. **Feedback inhibition** is the slowing or stopping of an early reaction in a series of reactions, caused by high levels of the end product of the process.

How does feedback inhibition work? Key reactions that occur early in glycolysis and the Krebs cycle are catalyzed by enzymes that have a second, "regulatory" active site. This site is the same shape as an ATP molecule, as shown in **Figure 5-20**.

When the ATP level in the cell is high, ATP molecules will likely bind to the regulatory site. The binding of ATP to this site causes the enzyme to change its shape to better accommodate the fit. This new shape makes the enzyme inactive. High levels of ATP thus shut down the cell's production of ATP. Like the engine of a car, your energy-producing machinery operates only when you step on the gas.

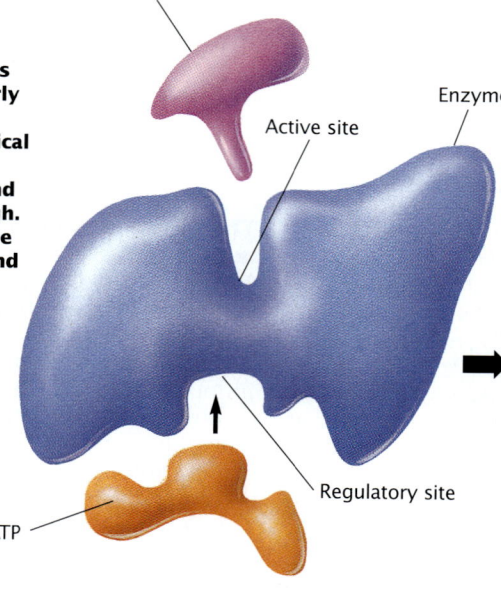
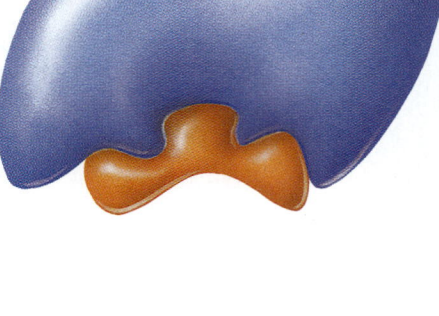

Figure 5-20
Feedback inhibition slows or stops an early reaction in a series of chemical reactions when levels of the end product are high. Molecules of the end product bind to an enzyme's regulatory site.

Substrate

Enzyme

Active site

Regulatory site

ATP

a When there is excess ATP in a cell, ATP binds to the regulatory site of an enzyme.

b The enzyme then changes shape. The active site is no longer able to catalyze its usual reaction, and no more ATP is made.

SECTION REVIEW

1. How is cellular respiration important for living cells?

2. How do fermentation and oxidative respiration differ?

3. Why is oxidative respiration unable to occur without oxygen?

4. Explain how feedback inhibition enables cellular respiration to slow down when supplies of ATP are sufficient.

ANSWERS TO
SECTION REVIEW

1. Cellular respiration provides the energy for all life processes.

2. During oxidative respiration, more ATP is produced than during fermentation.

3. During oxidative respiration, electrons and hydrogen atoms are attached to oxygen atoms. Without oxygen to accept spent electrons, the electron transport chain would become "clogged" with electrons.

4. ATP can fit into the regulatory site of an enzyme that is important to ATP production. If excess ATP is available, it will bind to this enzyme, causing a shape change so that it can no longer catalyze the production of ATP.

5 Highlights

Grass is the mainstay of this cow's diet. Using what you've learned, can you explain the link between sunlight and dairy products?

	Key Terms	Summary
5-1 **Cells and Chemistry**  Enzymes, such as carbonic anhydrase, hasten chemical reactions.	metabolism (p. 78) activation energy (p. 78) enzyme (p. 79) catalyst (p. 79) substrate (p. 80) active site (p. 80)	• The energy needed for life is absorbed and released through chemical reactions. • Enzymes make chemical reactions occur rapidly enough to sustain life. • Enzymes act on specific substrates. Enzyme activity is affected by heat, acidity, and substrate concentration.
5-2 **Cells and Energy**  Many living things depend on energy stored in plants.	ATP (p. 83) photosynthesis (p. 84) cellular respiration (p. 84)	• The energy for life is released gradually through a series of chemical reactions. • The energy released is stored temporarily in a molecule called adenosine triphosphate, or ATP. • Photosynthesis captures energy needed for life from light. • Cellular respiration releases energy stored in organic molecules.
5-3 **Photosynthesis** 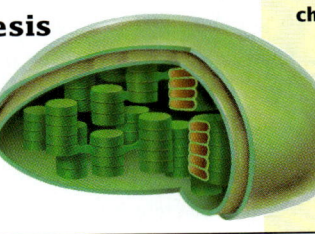 Photosynthesis begins when light strikes a chloroplast.	pigment (p. 86) chlorophyll (p. 87)	• Photosynthesis involves a complicated series of chemical reactions. • Plants, algae, and some bacteria contain the pigment chlorophyll. • Light striking chlorophyll boosts electrons to higher energy levels. As electrons pass through a series of reactions, their energy is used to produce organic molecules.
5-4 **Cellular Respiration** 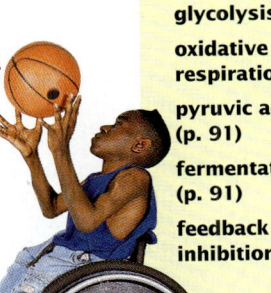 Cellular respiration releases the energy necessary to carry out life activities.	glycolysis (p. 90) oxidative respiration (p. 90) pyruvic acid (p. 91) fermentation (p. 91) feedback inhibition (p. 94)	• Living things obtain energy from organic molecules through cellular respiration. • In the absence of oxygen, fermentation converts the pyruvic acid from glycolysis to lactic acid or ethyl alcohol. With oxygen present, the Krebs cycle and the electron transport chain produce most of the ATP needed for life. • Feedback inhibition controls the reactions of cellular respiration.

95

Alternative Assessment

Have each student write a question on an index card based on the information presented in this chapter. Have the students record an answer for their question on a second index card. Have students trade question cards with a partner and answer their partner's question. Then have them confer with each other about their answers. Encourage students to refer to the text to settle any disagreements.

Portfolio Assessment

Portfolio Assessment on page T39 provides options for building and evaluating students portfolios. Students and teachers can select items from the areas listed on page T39 for inclusion in a portfolio.

ANSWER TO CONCEPT MAP

The following is one possible answer to the Relating Concepts exercise on page 96.

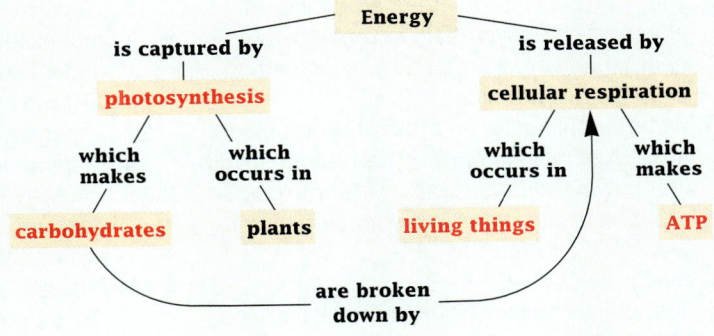

Understanding Vocabulary

1. a. unchanged
   b. two phosphate groups
   c. releases energy
2. a. Reactants are the starting materials, and products are the ending materials.
   b. Enzymes speed reaction rates. A substrate is a molecule to which an enzyme binds.
   c. Glycolysis breaks down a glucose molecule into two molecules of pyruvic acid. Fermentation converts pyruvic acid to lactic acid or ethyl alcohol and carbon dioxide.

Understanding Concepts

3. Answer to concept map is shown on page 95.
4. The chemical reaction that produces glucose absorbs energy. The chemical reaction that breaks down glucose releases energy.
5. Enzyme activity is reduced or stopped in frozen food, so decaying is prevented.
6. Only certain keys with specific shapes will fit in a lock; likewise, only one or very few substrates with specific shapes will bind with each enzyme.
7. Without enzymes, most chemical reactions inside a cell would require high, damaging temperatures.
8. Chemical reactions that are catalyzed by enzymes require less activation energy. Student graphs should resemble those on page 79.
9. Cells use energy for all their functions that require work, including movement, manufacturing new cellular components, transporting food into the cell, and removing wastes.
10. ATP, or adenosine triphosphate, is a molecule in the cell that contains energy and delivers energy to wherever it is needed in a cell.
11. Chlorophyll absorbs light energy that will be converted to chemical energy.

Understanding Vocabulary

1. For each set of terms, complete the analogy.
   a. reactants : changed :: enzyme : _____
   b. ATP : three phosphate groups :: ADP : _____
   c. photosynthesis : stores energy :: cellular respiration : _____

2. For each pair of terms, explain the differences in their meanings.
   a. reactants, products
   b. substrate, enzyme
   c. glycolysis, fermentation

Understanding Concepts

3. **Relating Concepts** Copy the unfinished concept map below onto a sheet of paper. Then complete the concept map by writing the correct word or phrase in each box containing a question mark.

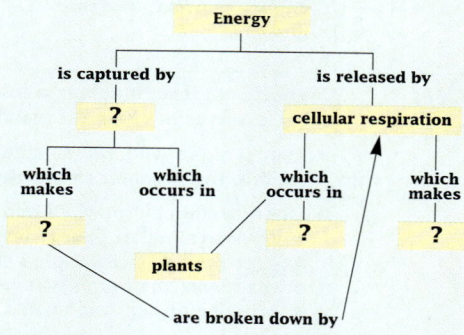

4. **Comparing Functions** In terms of energy, how does a chemical reaction that produces glucose compare with a chemical reaction that breaks down glucose?

5. **Inferring Conclusions** Temperature affects how quickly an enzyme reacts. How might freezing food affect the enzyme activity of organisms that cause food to decay?

6. **Comparing Structures and Functions** How is the interaction of a lock and key similar to the interaction of an enzyme and its substrate?

---

7. **Inferring Relationships** Explain why enzymes are needed to control chemical reactions within cells.

8. **Organizing Information** Describe the difference in the amount of activation energy required to start a chemical reaction with an enzyme and without an enzyme. Include a graph to illustrate your answer.

9. **Summarizing Information** Explain how cells use energy. Give two examples.

10. **Inferring Relationships** What is ATP? Why is it important to a cell?

11. **Interpreting Processes** Describe the role of chlorophyll in photosynthesis.

12. **Recognizing Relationships** How do plant cells use the ATP and NADPH that forms during the second phase of photosynthesis?

13. **Relating Concepts** What is the role of water in photosynthesis? What happens to the protons after the electrons are removed?

14. **Organizing Information** Indicate at which stage of photosynthesis each event occurs: (a) ATP is made when protons flow through a protein channel, (b) electrons within chlorophyll molecules are boosted to a higher energy level, (c) electrons are used to make NADPH, (d) carbon atoms are captured from carbon dioxide in the air and used to make organic molecules that store energy.

15. **Inferring Conclusions** Do plants perform cellular respiration? Support your answer.

16. **Evaluating Outcomes** Which process is more efficient—fermentation or oxidative respiration? Justify your answer.

17. **Summarizing Information** Describe the net gain of ATP molecules from one glucose molecule by glycolysis, fermentation, and oxidative respiration.

18. **Inferring Relationships** How does feedback inhibition control the rate of cellular respiration?

19. **BUILDING ON WHAT YOU HAVE LEARNED** In Chapter 3 you read about proton pumps. How does a proton pump function during photosynthesis? How does a proton pump function during oxidative respiration?

---

12. The ATP and NADPH are used during the third phase of photosynthesis to manufacture energy-rich carbohydrates by using carbon dioxide from the air.
13. Water supplies the electrons that replace those lost by chlorophyll. The protons (hydrogen nuclei) released when water molecules are broken apart can join with an electron and NADP$^+$ to form NADPH.
14. a—2, b—1, c—2, d—3
15. Yes, plants make ATP in stems, roots, and developing seeds.

16. Oxidative respiration yields as many as 36 molecules of ATP from one molecule of glucose. Fermentation results in no net gain of ATP molecules.
17. glycolysis—2, fermentation—0, oxidative respiration—as many as 36
18. Excess ATP molecules bind to sites on enzymes, preventing the enzymes from catalyzing the reactions.
19. A proton pump in the thylakoid membrane moves protons into a chloroplast, where they collect. The protons then diffuse out of the

Interpreting Graphics

20. Scientists have discovered that the rate of photosynthesis is affected by both the intensity of light and temperature. Study the following two graphs, and then answer the questions below.

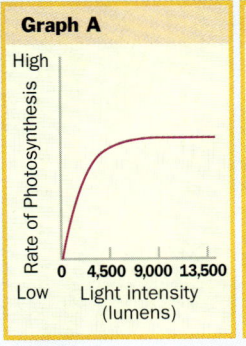
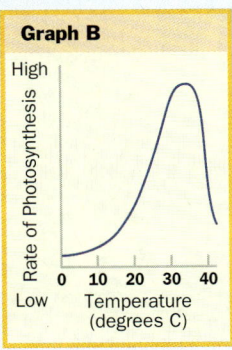

Graph A — Rate of Photosynthesis (Low to High) vs. Light intensity (lumens): 0, 4,500, 9,000, 13,500

Graph B — Rate of Photosynthesis (Low to High) vs. Temperature (degrees C): 0, 10, 20, 30, 40

a. At what light intensity does the rate of photosynthesis level off?
b. In what range of temperatures does the rate of photosynthesis increase?

Reviewing Themes

21. *Evolution*
How did the appearance of a new kind of photosynthesis about 3 billion years ago change Earth's atmosphere?

22. *Evolution*
What evidence suggests that glycolysis is a more ancient process than oxidative respiration?

23. *Stability and Homeostasis*
After strenuous exercise, an athlete often has sore muscles and breathes heavily. How does this muscle soreness and heavy breathing relate to the production of lactic acid by fermentation?

Thinking Critically

24. **Distinguishing Relevant Information** Scientists have recently discovered a cellular substance that has a shape and structure very similar to that of pyruvic acid. How might the presence of this substance in a cell affect the process of oxidative respiration?

25. **Justifying Conclusions** Would being able to photosynthesize eliminate humans' need to eat food? Why or why not?

Life/Work Skills

26. **Finding Information** Today, scientists know a great deal about the chemical processes of photosynthesis. Prior to the seventeenth century, however, scientists knew very little about how plants manufactured organic compounds. Use library references or search an on-line database to find information about the discoveries that led to the understanding of the process of photosynthesis. Look up the contributions made by English clergyman and chemist Joseph Priestley, Dutch physician and naturalist Jan Ingenhousz, Swiss chemist Nicolas de Saussure, German physicist Julius Robert von Mayer, and American biochemist Melvin Calvin. Summarize your findings in a poster or written report.

Activities and Projects

27. **Health Connection** Use library references or interview a medical specialist to find out about enzyme deficiency disorders in humans such as phenylketonuria (PKU) and alkaptonuria. Write a report that describes the symptoms and cause of the disorder, based on enzyme function. For PKU, also include information about how this disorder can be treated.

28. **Social Studies Connection** Yogurt is a fermented dairy product with an unusual history. Use library resources to find out how fermentation has been used in the production of yogurt and other commodities, such as cheese, soybean products, and beverages. Also find out which regions of the world are the largest producers of these commodities. Show these regions on a map of the world. Summarize your findings in a written report.

Discovering Through Reading

29. Read the article "When Science Imitates Nature: Using Artificial Photosynthesis to Harness Solar Energy" by Hunter Whitney in *Omni*, May 1994, page 25. What was Giacomo Ciamician's dream? Describe one obstacle that scientists have not yet been able to overcome in perfecting artificial photosynthesis.

Thinking Critically

24. The substance might attach to the active site of an enzyme and prevent the breakdown of glucose.

25. Humans would still need to consume food for the inorganic nutrients they need.

Life/Work Skills

26. Reports will vary but should discuss the discoveries that have led us to our current understanding of photosynthesis.

Activities and Projects

27. Reports will vary. PKU occurs when the body fails to produce the enzyme that breaks down phenylalanine. Alkaptonuria occurs when the body fails to produce the enzyme needed to break down alkapton.

28. Answers will vary. Students should find that fermentation plays many commercial roles.

Discovery Through Reading

29. Ciamician's dream was to eliminate the burning of fuels, and instead provide power for society through contained systems that perform photosynthesis. Scientists have been able to develop a photosynthetic molecule that functions well when it can move around in a liquid but ceases to function in a solid, which would be a more practical fuel source than a liquid.

chloroplast through a protein channel. Proton pumps in the inner mitochondrial membrane move protons out of the inner chamber of the mitochondrion, where they collect. The protons then diffuse back into the inner chamber through protein channels. The force of the moving protons is used to make ATP by adding a phosphate group to ADP.

Interpreting Graphics

20. a. 4,500 lumens
b. 10–30°C

Reviewing Themes

21. Oxygen was released as a byproduct. Earth's atmosphere became rich in oxygen gas.

22. All organisms use glycolysis, which could have taken place in the early atmosphere since it requires no oxygen.

23. Soreness could be due to the lack of oxygen and the accumulation of lactic acid in the muscle. Heavy breathing returns oxygen to muscle cells and enables the conversion of lactic acid back to pyruvic acid.

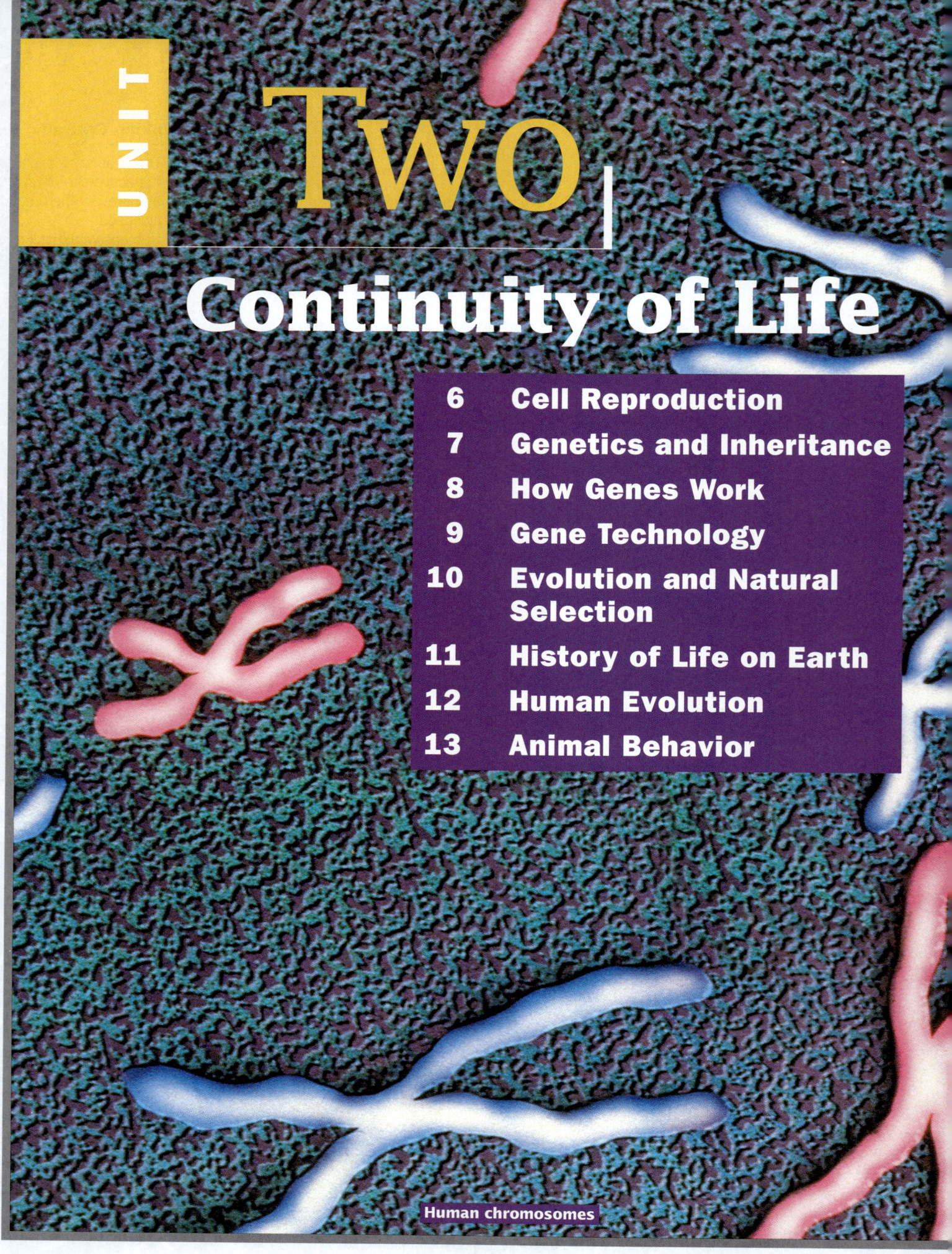

Human chromosomes

YOUR GENETIC COMPUTER

When you use a computer to type a paper, each letter is translated into a unique code that the computer reads. Using 0s and 1s, thousands of character combinations are made. But these numbers are small compared with the millions of instructions made from the four nucleotides that are repeated in your DNA.

Disorderly Conduct

Genes made of these nucleotides copy and transfer codes that determine how your body is built and how it works. Sometimes a gene gets damaged—part of the code is left out or changed. Called mutations, these changes can cause genetic disorders or uncontrolled cell division leading to cancer.

Knowing the Code

Scientists who study gene sequencing now know the code for many genes in the body. Gene technology is being used to pinpoint and correct errors in existing code and to identify factors that trigger mutations. Techniques such as gene transference are no longer science fiction but are scientific reality.

LOOKING AHEAD

- How are genes passed from parent to child? See **A Closer Look: Meiosis,** page 111.
- How can mutations enable a species to change over time? See page 127.
- How can knowledge of genetics help people make personal decisions? See **Career Opportunities: Genetic Counseling,** page 131.
- What benefits could you receive because of gene technology? See **Science, Technology, and Society: What Is the Future of Genetic Engineering?** pages 170–171.

6 | Cell Reproduction

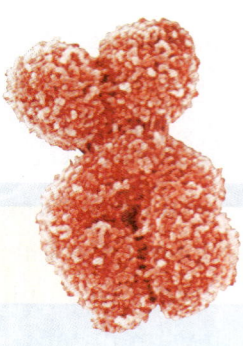

Lesson Planning Guide With Options for Block Scheduling

Lecture Concepts	**Lesson Resources**	

6-1 Chromosomes

BLOCK ❶ (45 minutes)

1. DNA may exist as very long threads known as chromatin or in the form of condensed bodies called chromosomes.

❶ Lecture Resources
- Determining Prior Knowledge
- Active Reading: Anticipation Guide
- Holt Biology Videodiscs Lesson 6-1

Classwork Options
- Demonstration: Inferring Conclusions

BLOCK ❷ (45 minutes)

2. Most cells in an organism contain the diploid (2*n*) number of chromosomes, but sex cells (gametes) contain the haploid (*n*) number of chromosomes.

❷ Lecture Resources
- Sex Chromosomes
- Visual Strategy: Videodisc
- Demonstration: Identifying Structures
- Holt Biology Videodiscs Lesson 6-1

Classwork Options
- Closure: Predicting Outcomes
- Exploration 6A

Assignment Options
- Reteaching
- Section Review
- Chapter Review, questions 1a, 2a, 4, 5, 7, 8, 20, 27, 28
- Directed Reading Worksheet

6-2 Mitosis and Cell Division

BLOCK ❸ (45 minutes)

1. When the cells of any organism divide, the genetic information in the chromosomes must be passed on to each new cell.

2. The process by which the nucleus divides in eukaryotic cells is called mitosis. The process by which the cell divides in eukaryotes is called cytokinesis.

❸ Lecture Resources
- Phases of Interphase
- Active Reading: Reading Organizer
- Visual Strategies: Figure 6-4
- Visual Strategy: Videodisc
- Demonstration: Recognizing Relationships
- Teaching Transparencies: 24
- Holt Biology Videodiscs Lesson 6-2

Classwork Options
- Modeling Mitosis and Cell Division
- Inquiry Skills Development: Lab B5

Assignment Options
- Life/Work Skills: Finding Information

BLOCK ❹ (45 minutes)

3. Mitosis and cytokinesis make up the cell cycle, which involves growth and division.

4. A malfunction of the cell cycle may result in cancer.

❹ Lecture Resources
- Controlling the Cell Cycle
- Visual Strategy: Videodisc
- Holt Biology Videodiscs Lesson 6-2

Classwork Options
- World of Work: Cancer Specialists
- Closure: Relating Concepts
- Laboratory Techniques and Experimental Design: Lab C9

Assignment Options
- *Small Group* Reteaching
- Section Review
- Chapter Review, questions 1b, 2b, 6, 9, 10, 11, 12, 13, 14, 15, 19, 21
- Directed Reading Worksheet

6-3 How Gametes Form—Meiosis

BLOCK ❺ (45 minutes)

1. A gamete is a sex cell and can be either a sperm or an egg cell.

2. Meiosis is the process by which gametes obtain the haploid number of chromosomes. It involves two cell divisions.

❺ Lecture Resources
- Active Reading: Reading Organizer
- Active Reading: Anticipation Guide
- Visual Strategies: Figure 6-7
- Visual Strategy: Videodisc
- Holt Biology Videodiscs Lesson 6-3

Classwork Options
- Laboratory Techniques and Experimental Design: Lab C11

Lecture Concepts

Lesson Resources

6-3 How Gametes Form—Meiosis, *continued*

BLOCK ⑥ (45 minutes)

3. Crossing-over during meiosis results in the production of new chromosome combinations.

⑥ Lecture Resources
■ Visual Strategy: Videodisc
⬛ Teaching Transparencies: 27, 28, 29A
⊙ Holt Biology Videodiscs Lesson 6-3

Classwork Options
■ Modeling Meiosis
■ Closure: Predicting Patterns
■ Interactive Exploration 6C

Assignment Options
■ *Small Group* Reteaching
■ Section Review
■ Chapter Review, questions 1c, 2c, 3, 16, 17, 18, 22, 23, 24, 25, 26, 30
■ Directed Reading Worksheet

Chapter Review and Assessment

BLOCK ⑦ (45 minutes)

Review
■ Reteaching Worksheet
■ Thinking Skills Worksheet
■ Vocabulary Development Worksheet
⊙ Language Development and Reading Comprehension Audio CD Program: Chapter 6

BLOCK ⑧ (45 minutes)

Assessment
■ Alternative Assessment, p. 113
■ Portfolio Assessment, p. T39

Chapter Test
■ Chapter 6 Test

Test Generator
⊙ Item bank for customizing Chapter Tests

Teaching Resources CD-ROM
⊙ Scoring Rubrics and Classroom Management Checklist

The Portfolio icon denotes items throughout the Teacher's Edition lesson wrap that may be selected for inclusion in student portfolios.

Holt Biology Videodiscs and *Concepts of Biology*

Holt Biology Videodiscs gives you a powerful tool for teaching, review, and assessment. For further information regarding the media on the videodiscs, see ***Holt Biology Videodiscs Teacher's Correlation Guide to Holt Biology: Visualizing Life.***

Concepts of Biology adds interactive lesson plans and extensive tools for customization using CD-ROM technology.

Use the following topic from ***Concepts of Biology*** to help you teach this chapter:
Topic 2: Cell Division

Laboratory Planning

Text

Materials and preparation instructions appear on the teacher's wrap accompanying each laboratory exercise.

Block 2: Exploration 6A: Modeling Mitosis and the Cell Cycle, p. 774
Block 6: Interactive Exploration 6C: Meiosis: Down Syndrome, p. 772

Holt BioSources Laboratory Program

Block 3: Inquiry Skills Development Lab B5: Mitosis
Block 4: Laboratory Techniques and Experimental Design Lab C9: Preparing a Root Tip Squash
Block 5: Laboratory Techniques and Experimental Design Lab C11: Modeling Meiosis

CHAPTER 6

Determining Prior Knowledge

- Ask students to explain the relationship between heredity and chromosomes.
- Ask students if they know the number of cells in the human body. Have students explain how the one cell that began their lives produced the trillions of cells that compose their bodies today.
- Have students explain why the chromosome number in a mature sex cell must be different from that found in any other cell in that organism.

Active READING

Technique: Anticipation Guide
Write the following statements on the board:

- Chromosomes from females determine the sex of humans.
- Every human cell contains 46 chromosomes.
- Normal healthy cells cannot become cancerous cells.

Give students a minute to decide whether they agree or disagree with each statement. Ask volunteers to share their responses. Have students save their responses for the Active Reading on page 112.

CD-ROM Resources

Concepts of Biology
Topic 2: Cell Division

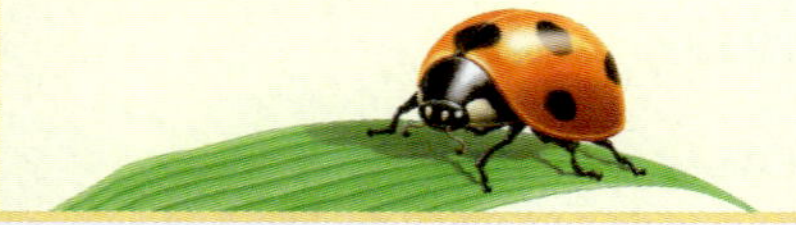

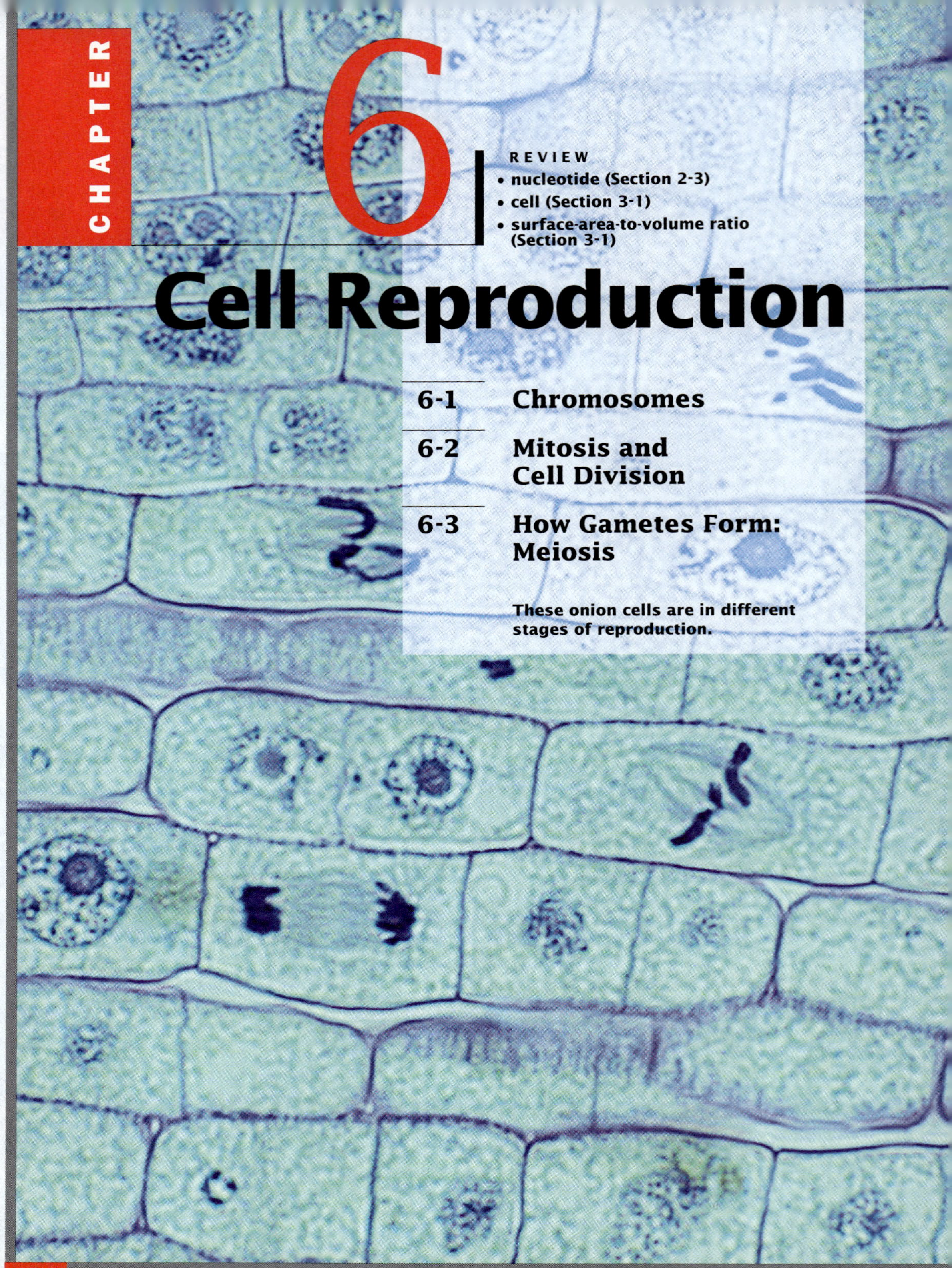

CHAPTER 6

REVIEW
- nucleotide (Section 2-3)
- cell (Section 3-1)
- surface-area-to-volume ratio (Section 3-1)

Cell Reproduction

These onion cells are in different stages of reproduction.

100

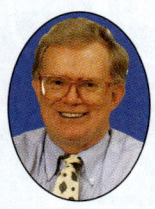

Author's Rationale This chapter provides a close look at cell reproduction, with an emphasis on hereditary information. First students are introduced to chromosomes, the cell's library of genetic material. Then they will study mitosis and how duplicate sets of chromosomes are passed to new cells during cell division. The chapter closes with an examination of how gametes form through meiosis and how a cell's chromosome number is reduced by half before being sorted to new cells. Students will end the chapter with an introduction to the concepts of diploid and haploid, which they will encounter later in the text.

A key concept developed in the chapter is the cell cycle and its regulation of cell growth and division. Students learn that cancer can result when the genes that restrain cell division become mutated.

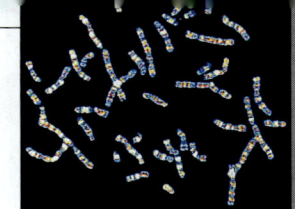

A typical chromosome in your body contains thousands of genes. Each gene is a segment of DNA that codes for a particular trait. This information was used to assemble tissues and organs while you were an embryo. Now the information regulates the functions of the billions of cells in your body.

6-1 Chromosomes

OBJECTIVES

1 Define *chromatin*.

2 Describe the structure of a chromosome.

3 Distinguish between diploid and haploid cells.

4 Explain the significance of sex chromosomes.

Chromosome Structure

The growth and development of your cells are carefully controlled by a set of instructions found inside the cell nucleus. This set of instructions, encoded in long molecules of DNA, is what determines that you are a human and not a different kind of organism, such as a housefly or a carrot. Molecules of DNA might look like strands of spaghetti piled on a plate, but on closer inspection you can see that they are more than a tangled mass. These

long molecules are wound around chunks of protein. When cells divide, this material is tightly compacted, creating bodies of DNA and protein called **chromosomes**, as shown in **Figure 6-1**.

DNA coils to form a chromosome
In the century since their discovery, we have learned a great deal about the structure and function of chromosomes. Eukaryotic chromosomes are made of **chromatin** (*KROH muh tihn*), a complex of DNA and protein. The DNA of a chromosome exists as one very long double-stranded thread that curls up tightly to form a compact rod-shaped body. A typical human chromosome contains about half a billion (5×10^8) nucleotides in its thread of DNA. If the strand of DNA from a single chromosome were laid out in a straight line, it would be about 5 cm (2 in.) long. This is much too long to fit into a cell. But when the strand is wound around proteins, it can be compacted into a smaller, more manageable structure, just as a piece of thread can be neatly stored by wrapping it around a wooden spool. The complex structure of a chromosome is shown in *A Closer Look: Chromosome*, on the next page.

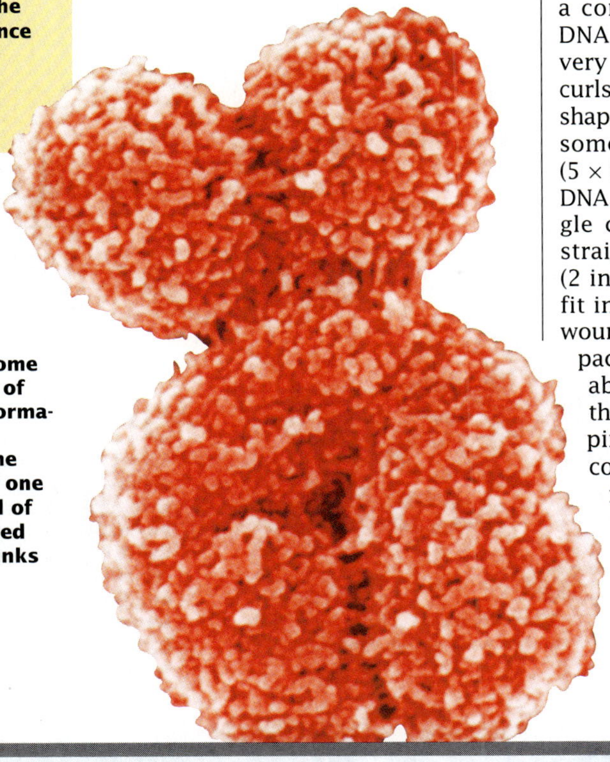

Figure 6-1
A chromosome is a library of genetic information. Each chromosome consists of one long strand of DNA wrapped around chunks of protein.

101

Videodisc Resources

Holt Biology Videodiscs

Lesson 6-1: Chromosomes

6-1

Phase One
Preparation

Scheduling
See the **Lesson Planning Guide** on pages 99A and 99B for lecture, classwork, and assignment options for Section 6-1.

Phase Two
Teaching Strategies

Connection: *Chapter 2*

Nucleic Acids
Remind students that DNA is one of two types of nucleic acids in a cell. Ask them to name the other nucleic acid *(RNA)*. Remind students that both nucleic acids play a part in building proteins.

Demonstration
● **Identifying Structures**
Use a microprojector or video camera setup to show the class a cross section of an onion root tip. The cells in this region undergo repeated mitotic divisions, and this slide, therefore, provides many opportunities for viewing chromosomes. First point out chromosomes that are clearly visible. Next identify cells where they are not visible and ask students to hypothesize where the chromosomes might be. *(The chromosomes have not yet condensed and are in the form of chromatin.)*

Key to Strategies
Teaching Strategies are keyed to three tiers of learning.

● **Understanding Concepts (Tier I)**
Content mastery and comprehension

■ **Applying Information (Tier II)**
Applying and analyzing content

▲ **Critical Thinking (Tier III)**
Practicing evaluative thinking

Cell Reproduction   101

A Closer Look

Demonstration

▲ Inferring Conclusions

Prepare students for understanding the behavior of chromosomes in the upcoming lessons about mitosis and meiosis. Provide each student with an identical numbered set of instructions for assembling or using a product. Have students take turns reading each step in the instructions until they recognize that each of them has a complete set of instructions to assemble or use a product. Then distribute another set of instructions to each student. This time, omit the even-numbered steps from the instructions given to female students and the odd-numbered steps from those given to male students. Have the class read and compare the instructions until they realize that each sex has only one-half of the information needed to produce a final product. Have students hypothesize how their lists compare to the behavior of chromosomes during mitosis in Section 6-2 and during meiosis in Section 6-3.

Visual Strategy · Videodisc

■ Recognizing Relationships

Use *Illustration—Chromosome Numbers* shown in Chapter 6 Section 6-1 of *Holt Biology Videodiscs Teacher's Correlation Guide to Holt Biology: Visualizing Life.* Have students compare chromosome numbers for different species. Lead students to an understanding that the number of chromosomes for an organism does not directly relate to the organism's complexity. For example, the amoeba has 50 chromosomes, while the alligator, a more complex organism, has only 32.

102

Chromosome

In eukaryotes, chromosomes are contained in the nucleus. Each chromosome contains one long DNA molecule in which two parallel strands are twisted like a spiral staircase.

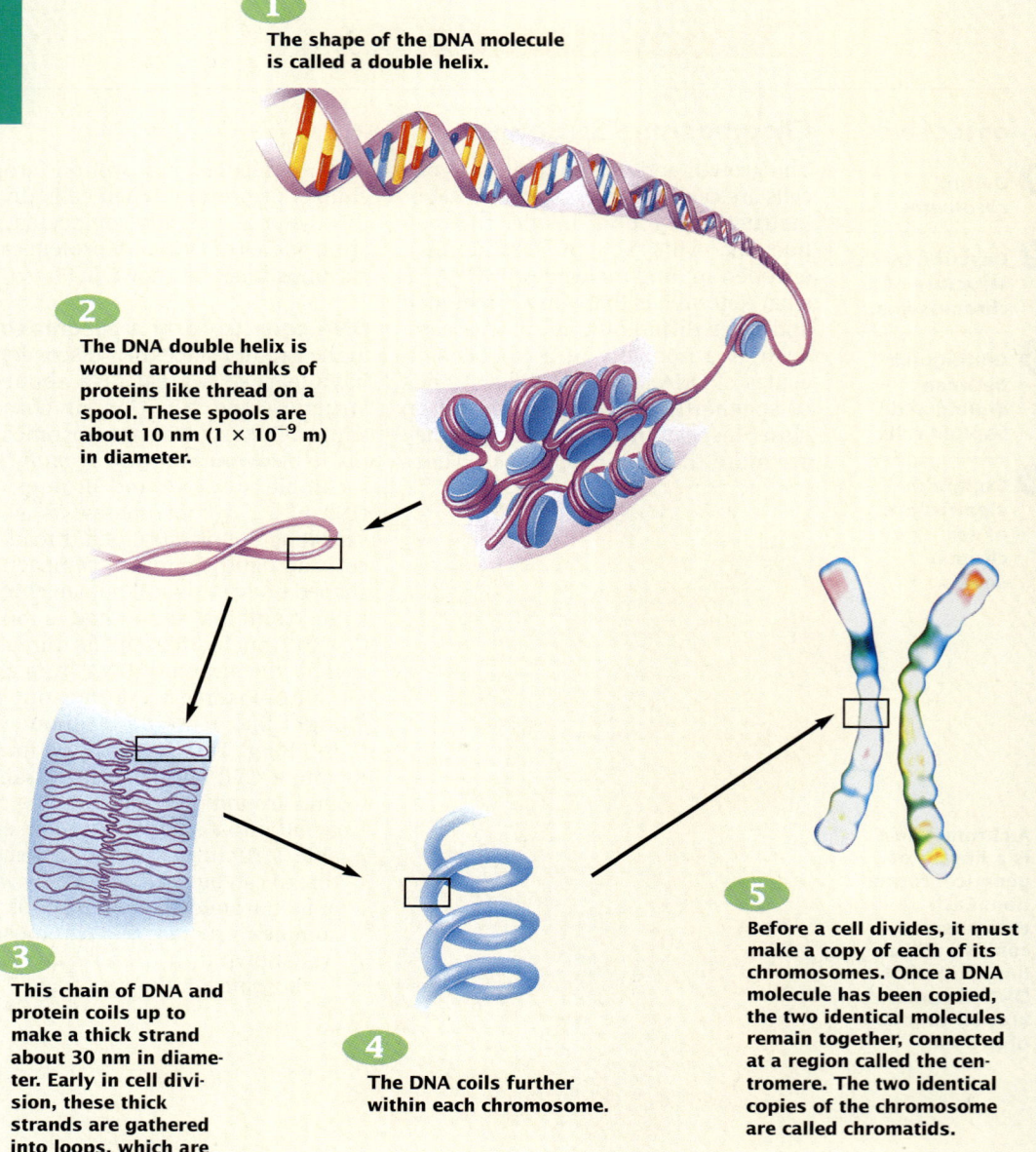

1 The shape of the DNA molecule is called a double helix.

2 The DNA double helix is wound around chunks of proteins like thread on a spool. These spools are about 10 nm (1×10^{-9} m) in diameter.

3 This chain of DNA and protein coils up to make a thick strand about 30 nm in diameter. Early in cell division, these thick strands are gathered into loops, which are wound like a corkscrew.

4 The DNA coils further within each chromosome.

5 Before a cell divides, it must make a copy of each of its chromosomes. Once a DNA molecule has been copied, the two identical molecules remain together, connected at a region called the centromere. The two identical copies of the chromosome are called chromatids.

Chromosome Number

The chromosomes contained within a cell can be extracted and stained to reveal the set of chromosomes. A set of chromosomes is called a **karyotype** *(KAH ree oh typ)*. If you could look inside almost any cell in your body, you would find 46 chromosomes that are similar to those in the karyotype shown in **Figure 6-2**. Sorted by size and shape, your chromosomes can be arranged into 23 pairs. The two members of each pair look very similar. In fact, they are almost identical copies of each other, containing the same genes in the same order. When a human cell contains 23 pairs of chromosomes, it is said to be **diploid** *(DIH ployd)*. Practically all the cells that make up your body are diploid. By contrast, the chromosomes in your gametes (eggs or sperm) occur singly. These cells, which contain only one copy of each chromosome, are said to be **haploid** *(HAHY ployd)*. The symbol commonly used for the diploid number is $2n$, and that used for the haploid number is n. For example, in humans, $2n = 46$ and $n = 23$.

Sex chromosomes determine whether you are male or female

One of your 23 pairs of chromosomes determines whether you are male or female. These chromosomes are called **sex chromosomes** and are designated as X and Y. If you are female, you have two X chromosomes. If you are male, you have one X chromosome and a smaller Y chromosome. Because females have two X chromosomes, they can only produce eggs that contain an X chromosome. Males, however, can produce sperm that contains either an X or a Y chromosome. Thus, if you're female, you've received an X chromosome from your father. If you're male, you've inherited your father's Y chromosome. Study the karyotype in **Figure 6-2**. Do these chromosomes belong to a male or to a female? The members of each pair of sex chromosomes are separated during a process called meiosis *(my OH sihs)*, which you will learn about later in this chapter.

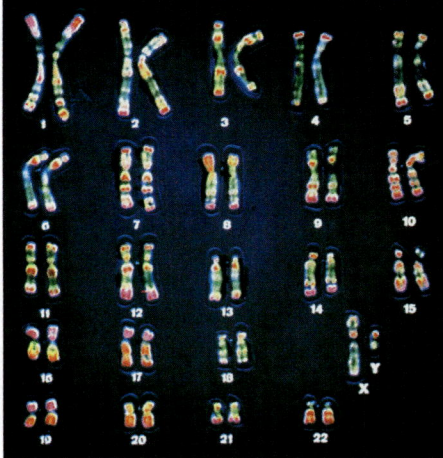

Figure 6-2

a **Like this human white blood cell, almost every cell in the human body . . .**

b **. . . contains 46 chromosomes. They occur in 23 pairs whose members have similar shapes, sizes, and information.**

SECTION REVIEW

1 **At what point does chromatin coil up to form a chromosome?**

2 **What do you think would happen to DNA if it were not wrapped around proteins?**

3 **Which cells in your body are diploid? How many chromosomes do they have?**

4 **What are sex chromosomes? Which sex chromosomes do your cells contain?**

103

Sex Chromosomes

■ **Recognizing Patterns**

Prevent students from developing the misconception that an XX combination is always a female and an XY is always a male. Point out that in other species, such as birds, moths, and butterflies, males have the XX combination, while females have only one X. The Y chromosome may or may not be present.

Phase Three

Assessment Options

Closure

■ **Predicting Outcomes**

On the board, prepare a table with two headings: Diploid Number and Haploid Number. Place numbers at random under only one of the headings, and have students complete the table.

SECTION REVIEW

Assign the *Section Review*.

Reteaching

Inform students that the first human karyotype was prepared in the 1920s and that for more than 30 years afterward, scientists believed that the diploid number of human cells was 48. Not until better techniques became available in the 1950s did scientists realize that the diploid number was actually 46.

A N S W E R S TO
SECTION REVIEW

1 Chromosomes form when a cell is preparing to divide.

2 The DNA would be loose and fragile and would be open to attack by enzymes.

3 Most cells in the human body (except for sperm and eggs) are diploid with 46 chromosomes.

4 The sex chromosomes are a pair of chromosomes that determine an organism's sex. In humans, a female is XX, while a male is XY.

Key to Strategies
● **Understanding Concepts (Tier I)**
■ **Applying Information (Tier II)**
▲ **Critical Thinking (Tier III)**

Scheduling

See the **Lesson Planning Guide** on pages 99A and 99B for lecture, classwork, and assignment options for Section 6-2.

Connection: *Chapter 3*

Prokaryotic Cells

Review the structure of a prokaryotic cell by referring students to Table 3-1 on page 50. This will enable students to associate the uncomplicated nature of prokaryotic cell division with the cell's structural simplicity.

Mathematics Connection

Prokaryotic Chromosomes

Although prokaryotic chromosomes are simple in structure, they are still impressive in size, especially compared with the size of the cell that contains them. For example, if the chromosome in *E. coli* were fully extended, it would measure 1 mm in length. The cell itself is only .002 mm in length. Have students calculate how much longer the *E. coli's* chromosome is than its "body" length is *(1/.002 = 500 times longer)*.

Active READING

Technique: Reading Organizer
Have students create a reading organizer to compare reproduction in prokaryotic cells and eukaryotic cells.

As cells busily carry out the functions of life, they grow and develop. You learned in Chapter 3 that cells operate most efficiently when they have a high surface-area-to-volume ratio. When most cells reach a certain size, they either stop growing or divide into two cells. Cell reproduction is essential for the growth and development of an organism.

6-2 Mitosis and Cell Division

OBJECTIVES

1 Describe cell reproduction in bacteria and eukaryotes.

2 Summarize the events of mitosis and cytokinesis.

3 Define *cell cycle.* Describe a cell's activities during interphase.

4 Explain how cancer arises.

Cell Reproduction Differs in Bacteria and Eukaryotes

When a cell reaches a certain size, it will either stop growing or divide. Because chromosomes carry an organism's genetic information, they must be transmitted in an orderly fashion during cell reproduction. Just as a contractor needs a complete blueprint to build a house, many cells need a complete set of genetic information in order to function. If a cell is to divide and produce two new healthy cells, it must first copy the genetic information contained within its chromosomes. Then, as the cell divides, each new cell will receive a complete copy of the genetic information. As you will see, the process of cell division in bacteria is different from that in eukaryotic cells.

Bacteria simply split

In bacteria, the process of cell division appears fairly simple. First a bacterium becomes larger. Then its single circle of DNA attaches to the inner surface of the cell membrane and makes a copy of itself. The copy of the chromosome attaches to a different part of the inner wall of the bacterium. Next, new membrane and wall materials begin to form between the two chromosomes, near the middle of the cell. The long cell pinches inward at this point, and eventually the cell is split into two cells. Each cell contains a circle of DNA and is an independent, living bacterium. This process is illustrated in **Figure 6-3**.

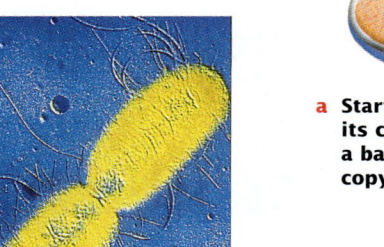

Figure 6-3
This bacterium is dividing. The process will be completed in about 20 minutes.

a Starting at one point of its circular chromosome, a bacterium makes a copy of its DNA.

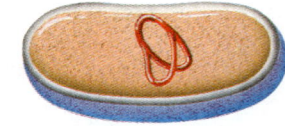

b Side by side, the two copies of hereditary information attach to the inner wall of the bacterium.

c A new membrane and cell wall form between the DNA copies, gradually pinching inward.

d Eventually, the cell is split into two cells. Each cell contains its own DNA and is a distinct living bacterium.

104

Videodisc Resources

Holt Biology Videodiscs
Lesson 6-2: Mitosis and Cell Division

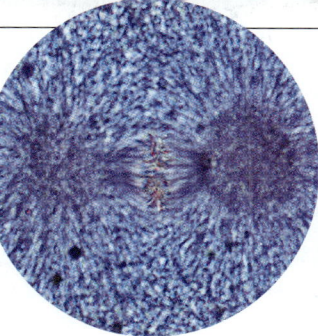

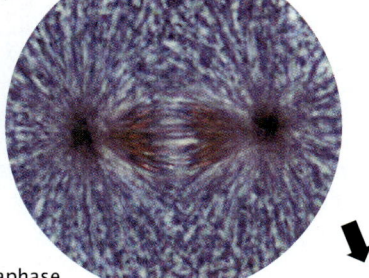

Metaphase   Anaphase

Prophase

Figure 6-4
During mitosis, copies of chromosomes are divided into two equal sets. What do you think is happening to the chromosomes of this cell in each photo?

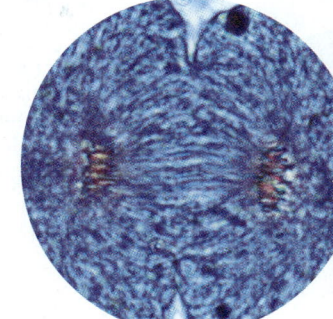

Telophase

How Eukaryotic Nuclei Divide: Mitosis

Eukaryotic cells carry far more DNA than prokaryotic cells. During cell division, the DNA in eukaryotic cells is packaged into tightly wound chromosomes. Cell division plays a major role in the development and maintenance of the tissues of eukaryotic organisms. Look at your hand and try to imagine how many millions of cells divided to form your skin, bones, tendons, and the actively growing regions of your nails.

A typical human cell contains 46 chromosomes. Eukaryotic chromosomes are contained within the nucleus. Because eukaryotic cells have more DNA than prokaryotic cells have, and because the DNA is confined within a nucleus, eukaryotic cell division is quite different from bacterial cell division. First each chromosome must be copied exactly. Then the chromosomes must be sorted out precisely so that each new cell gets a complete set. Finally the cell itself can divide in half.

Two processes have evolved that enable eukaryotic cells to divide suc- cessfully: mitosis and cell division. **Mitosis** *(my TOH sihs)* is the process by which the nucleus of a eukaryotic cell divides to form two nuclei, each containing a complete set of the cell's chromosomes. Mitosis can be broken down into four distinct phases: prophase, metaphase, anaphase, and telophase. These steps are shown in **Figure 6-4**.

In many cells, mitosis is followed by cell division, also called **cytokinesis** *(syt oh kuh NEE sihs)*. During cell division, the cell divides into two cells, each with its own nucleus. Plant cells, which have strong cell walls that resist being pinched in like the membranes of animal cells, form a new cell wall in the center of the cell. This new cell wall divides the cell in half, like a partition dividing a room.

The end result of mitosis and cytokinesis is two cells with the same genetic information, where only one cell existed before. To follow the events of eukaryotic cell division, study the steps in *A Closer Look: Mitosis and Cell Division*, on the next page.

105

Historical Perspective: Chromosomes

Ever since the German scientist Walther Flemming identified chromosomes in 1879, they have been studied intensely. One intriguing discovery stemmed from Barbara McClintock's work with corn. McClintock showed that nonhomologous chromosomes undergo recombination. The importance of her research was not recognized for many years. In 1983, she was awarded the Nobel Prize in Medicine and Physiology, becoming the first woman to win an unshared prize in this category.

A Closer Look

Modeling Mitosis and Cell Division

■ Designing a Model

1. Divide the class into six groups, and have each group be responsible for one of the six stages of mitosis and cell division. Distribute modeling clay to each group. Explain that each group is to create a visual model of their stage of mitosis and cell division. Tell students that a basic style must be consistent for each model so that the models can be arranged and viewed as a whole.

2. Allow groups to work independently to form ideas before convening to discuss styles. Then have them meet to establish style guidelines.

3. Schedule a time for students to complete their models. Be sure to include time for drying, painting, and other related tasks.

4. When models are finished, have groups meet to describe the stage depicted in their model. Then have the groups arrange models in the proper sequence of mitosis and cell division.

5. Have students assess the accuracy of the models individually and as a whole.

Visual Strategy   Videodisc

● **Interpreting Graphics**

To review the stages of mitosis, use the unlabeled diagrams from *Gallery—Stages of Mitosis* shown in Chapter 6 Section 6-2 of **Holt Biology Videodiscs Teacher's Correlation Guide to Holt Biology: Visualizing Life.** Show the images in a random order. Have students identify each stage of mitosis and describe what is happening.

Mitosis and Cell Division

In mitosis, eukaryotic cell nuclei divide to form two nuclei, each containing a complete set of the cell's chromosomes. Follow the events as this animal cell undergoes mitosis.

1
DNA Replication
Chromosomes are not yet visible because they are extended and uncoiled. The DNA of each chromosome is copied. Each chromosome consists of two identical strands.

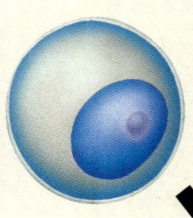

2
Prophase
Mitosis begins. The chromosomes coil into short, fat rods. The nuclear envelope breaks up. A network of protein cables called spindle fibers assembles across the cell.

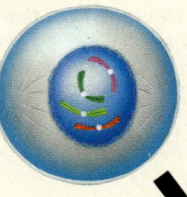

3
Metaphase
Chromosomes attach to the spindle fibers and line up in the center of the cell.

6
Cytokinesis
The cytoplasm is pinched in half, forming two new cells. Each new cell contains identical DNA. After growth and replication, these cells may divide again.

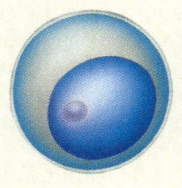
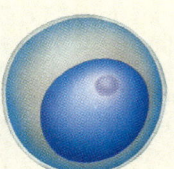

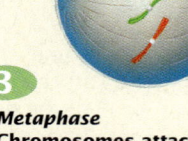

4
Anaphase
Each chromosome separates from its identical copy. Chromosomes are reeled to opposite sides of the cell. The spindle fibers begin to break down.

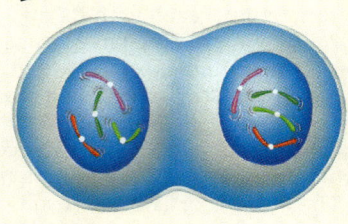

5
Telophase
Each side of the cell now has a complete set of chromosomes. A nuclear envelope forms around each new set of chromosomes. The chromosomes uncoil so that proteins can be built. The spindle fibers disappear.

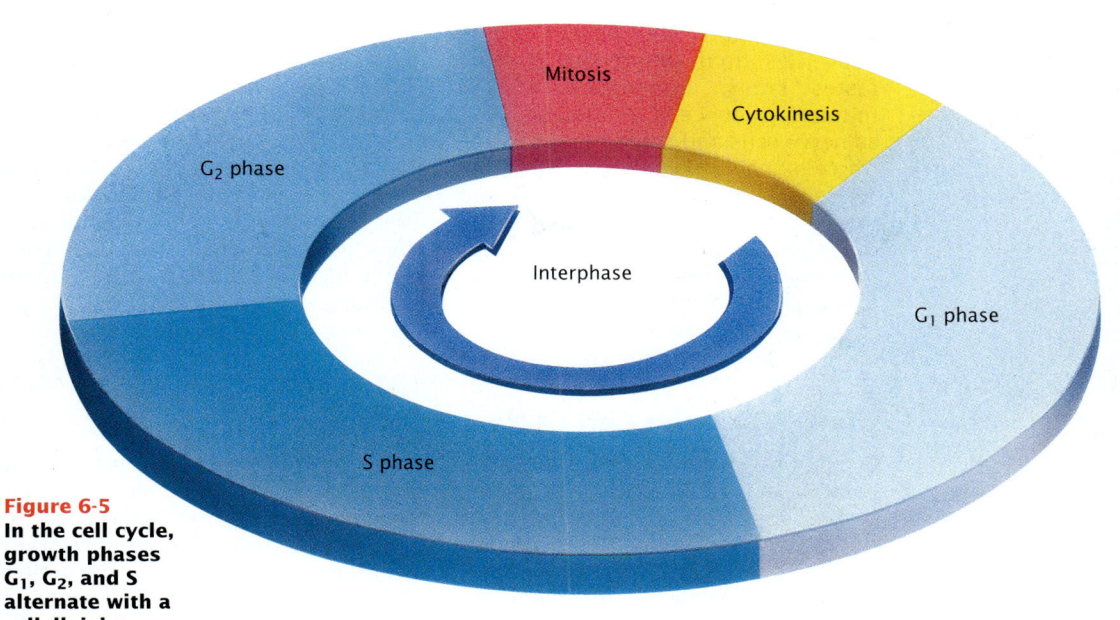

Figure 6-5
In the cell cycle, growth phases G_1, G_2, and S alternate with a cell-division phase (mitosis and cytokinesis).

The Cell Cycle

Mitosis and cytokinesis are just small portions of a cell's life span. Most of a cell's lifetime is spent growing. This cycle of growth and division is called the **cell cycle**. For convenience, the cell cycle is divided into the five phases shown in **Figure 6-5**. Identify the phases of the cell cycle as you follow a typical cell through its life.

Interphase is the most active part of the cell cycle

A newly formed cell begins its life by undergoing a period of growth and activity called interphase. During interphase, the new cell is hard at work carrying out the tasks of life: taking in food, converting energy, discarding wastes, growing, and differentiating. In addition, it is making copies of its genetic material and duplicating its organelles.

Interphase occurs in three distinct stages. First there is a gap in the cell cycle, designated the G_1 phase (G_1 stands for first gap). During this phase, the cell undergoes intense growth. In fact, the cells of many organisms spend most of their lives in this phase.

Next the cell may enter the S phase (*S* stands for synthesis) of the cycle. During this phase, the cell makes a precise copy of the DNA molecule in each of its chromosomes. Once copied, the two identical molecules remain together, joined by the centromere. The S phase is followed by another gap in the cycle, called the G_2 phase, the final stage of interphase. Here, the cell continues to grow and begins to make preparations for cell division. The cell is also busy duplicating its organelles.

Once the G_2 phase is finished, the cell has successfully completed interphase. It now enters the M phase (mitosis). During this phase the two copies of each chromosome are separated. When the cell reaches the final phase of the cell cycle, the C phase (cytokinesis), it divides in half and becomes two new, identical cells.

Cell cycle lengths differ among cell types

The time it takes to complete a cell cycle varies greatly among organisms. In plants, it usually lasts between 10 and 30 hours. In animals, the cell cycle

Phases of Interphase

■ **Organizing Information**
Have students use Figure 6-5 and the information on this page to construct a **Graphic Organizer** that illustrates the stages of interphase. Use arrows between the phases, pointing to the right, to indicate the sequence of events.

Demonstration

● **Recognizing Relationships**
Show the class either a model or photograph of a human brain. Point out that once the human brain is formed, the nerve cells do not divide again. These cell are arrested in the G_1 phase. Next, display either a model or photograph of a human bone. Point out that red blood cells are produced by specialized cells found in the red marrow of bones. An average red blood cell lives for about 120 days. New blood cells must be constantly produced to replace those that die. In fact, every second, approximately 2 million new red blood cells are produced by cell divisions occurring in the bone marrow. Cells in the marrow, unlike those in the brain, continue to pass through repeated cell cycles throughout a person's life.

Mathematics Connection

Cell Division
Every second, approximately 25 million cells are produced by mitosis in the human body. Have students calculate the number of cells produced by mitosis in a day *(25 million/second × 60 seconds × 60 minutes × 24 hours = 2.16 trillion cells/day).*

Graphic Organizer

Use the following graphic organizer with the teaching strategy **Phases of Interphase** on page 107.

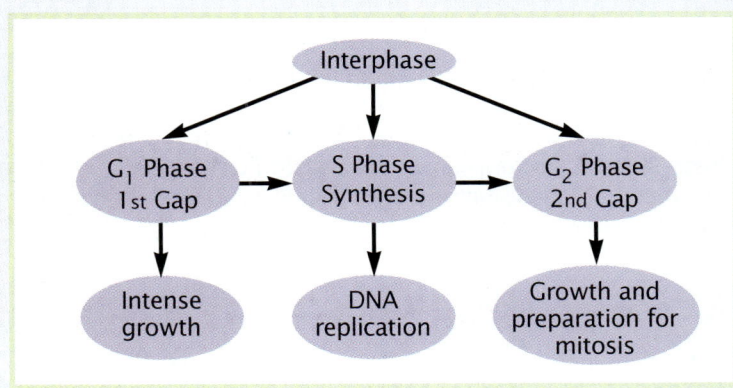

Key to Strategies
● Understanding Concepts (Tier I)
■ Applying Information (Tier II)
▲ Critical Thinking (Tier III)

Cell Reproduction 107

Life/Work Skills
Finding Information
● **Summarizing Information**

Cell death is a focus of current research. Much of this work has been in studying the tips of chromosomes, known as telomeres. Telomeres are thought to play a time-keeping role by telling the cell how old it is. Scientists have determined that telomeres are shaved down slightly every time a cell divides. When the telomere reaches a certain length, the cell may lose its ability to divide. Have students conduct a library or on-line search to find out what scientists have recently uncovered about telomeres and their association with cell division and cancer. Have each student prepare a brief written report as a way of organizing the information.

Controlling the Cell Cycle
■ **Recognizing Relationships**
Ask students why a cell would have both cyclins to stimulate mitosis and growth factors to block mitosis. *(Having both a positive and negative control is much more efficient than having only one or the other. Point out that a car has both kinds of control—an accelerator and a brake.)*

Health Connection
Cancer
Students may have the misconception that there are only a few types of cancer. Point out that the human body has at least 200 different cell types, each of which can become cancerous. Thus, there are at least 200 different types of cancer.

---

can take between 18 and 24 hours, but it may be much shorter. Embryonic fruit flies hold the record for the fastest known animal cell cycle—8 minutes. Some cells in humans, such as nerve cells and some types of muscle cells, never complete a cell cycle. These cells remain in the G_1 phase and typically never divide again. On the other hand, skin cells and cells in your intestine divide almost continuously.

No cell lives forever. Cells appear to be programmed to undergo only so many divisions and then die, as if following a plan written into their genes. For example, when human cells are cultured in a laboratory, they divide about 50 times and then die. Even cells that are thawed after being frozen for years under laboratory conditions die after reaching a certain number of divisions. Perhaps cells in your body contain hidden "hourglasses" whose grains of sand are cell divisions.

Controlling the Cell Cycle

Some of the most intriguing questions in biology surround the cell cycle. One of them has challenged scientists since the discovery of cells—What controls a cell's cycle? Not until very recently have scientists begun to unlock the secrets of the cell cycle.

Using new techniques to identify and trace the movements of cell proteins, researchers have discovered that animal cells use a class of proteins called cyclins to help control different phases of the cell cycle. For example, S-cyclin helps stimulate DNA replication in the S phase. M-cyclin helps trigger mitosis. Cyclins are influenced by another class of proteins, called growth factors. Growth factors supervise and monitor a cell's progress through the phases of the cell cycle. For example, some growth factors direct a cell to enter a phase by triggering genes that make specific cyclins. Other growth factors restrain a cell's growth by blocking the action of cyclins. The joint efforts of proteins like these help keep a cell's cycle in check and prevent unnecessary cell division.

Cancer arises from a faulty cell cycle
The mechanisms controlling the cell cycle occasionally become damaged and fail. The effects can be disastrous. Without such regulation, a cell begins to grow and divide without restraint, like the cell in **Figure 6-6a**. The result is a clump of cells called a **tumor**, as shown in **Figure 6-6b**. A tumor may stay in the

Figure 6-6
a **This epithelial cell (×110) has a faulty cell cycle and has grown large and misshapen.**

b **A tumor forms when a single cell divides at an uncontrolled rate.**

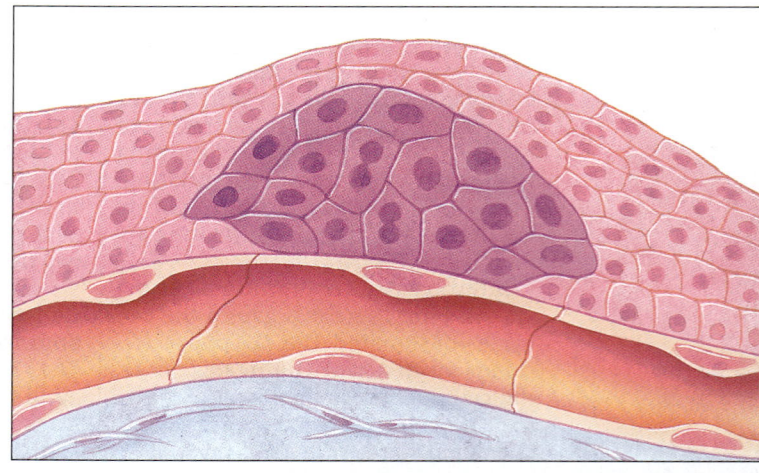

Community Connection: Cancer-Related Issues

Have students search the library and on-line services for news and information about current cancer-related issues. Relevant topics include research in and treatments for breast and prostate cancers. Have students discuss their findings and create a list of questions about items that interest them. Invite a cancer specialist to class to talk about these issues and answer students' questions. Request that the specialist include information about how students can reduce their risk of developing cancer.

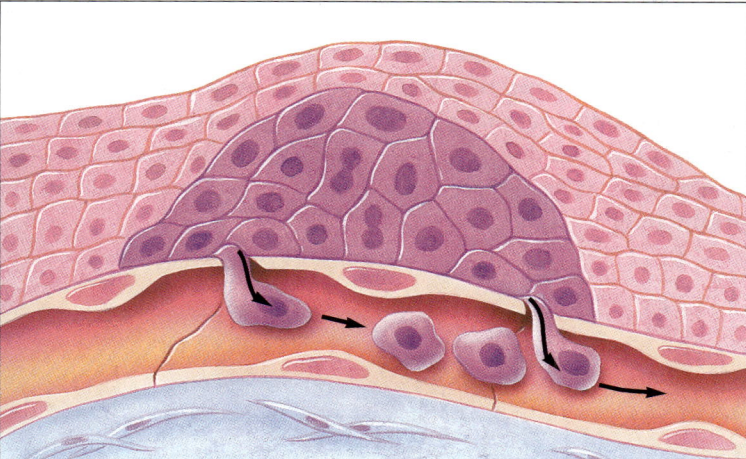

c **Cells from the tumor may break away and spread to other parts of the body.**

region in which it originally formed. In this case the tumor is usually harmless and is described as benign *(bee NEYN)*. Or, as shown in **Figure 6-6c**, it may continue to grow and invade other tissues, in which case the tumor is described as cancerous. **Cancer** is a term used to describe a disease characterized by uncontrolled cell division and growth. In essence, cancer results from a malfunction of the cell cycle.

A faulty cell cycle can produce many changes in a cell, making it significantly different from a normal one. For example, a cancer cell is typically very round, making it more mobile than a normal cell. And unlike a normal cell, which can usually only grow on a solid surface, a cancer cell can also grow in liquids. A cancer cell also has abnormal proteins and lipids in its outer membrane, which may prevent it from reacting to signals in its environment.

How does a normal, healthy cell become a life-threatening cancer cell? It isn't easy. Several independent changes

must accumulate in the cell, such as loss of regulated cell division. In addition, the cell must be able to maneuver around and break through protective membranes in tissues. It also needs to establish a foothold in other tissues and to maintain a supply of oxygen and nutrients.

What causes these changes in a cell? By examining many cancers, scientists have discovered that cancer cells have defects in the genes regulating cell division. The cell cycle is regulated in several ways, and all must be damaged for cancer to occur. A change in a gene is called **mutation**. Because changes to genes usually occur in body tissues such as lungs or skin, cancer-causing mutations are usually not hereditary. Occasionally cell-cycle control genes become mutated in eggs and sperm, leading to an increased likelihood of developing cancer later in life.

Factors that are suspected of contributing to the development of cancer include environmental agents such as radiation and cancer-causing chemicals present in cigarette smoke. This is why some of the more significant risk factors are linked to lifestyle, including the use of tobacco products and exposure to ultraviolet (UV) radiation. Recently there has been a great deal of interest in the effects of diet and obesity on cancer rate. Although it is impossible to avoid exposure to all risk factors, it is prudent to minimize or eliminate exposure to those that you *can* control, particularly smoking.

World of Work

Cancer Specialists

 Have small groups of students prepare a report about a person whose occupation deals with cancer. Possibilities include a research scientist looking for the cause of a particular type of cancer, an oncologist specializing in the treatment of cancer, a geneticist probing the hereditary basis of cancer, and a hospice worker dealing with cancer patients. Students can check local hospitals and support agencies or contact the National Cancer Institute, 9000 Rockville Pike, Bethesda, MD 20892.

Phase Three

Assessment Options

Closure

■ **Relating Concepts**
Have students hypothesize about the amounts of ATP required by a cell undergoing mitosis. *(The events of mitosis—including the duplication and movement of chromosomes, the duplication of organelles, the pinching in of the cell membrane, and the formation of a cell wall—have a high energy requirement that is supplied by ATP.)*

SECTION REVIEW

Assign the *Section Review.*

Reteaching

Assign students to cooperative work groups. Provide each group with colored pipe cleaners or crayons. Have them design models for the various stages of mitosis for a cell in which $2n = 4$.

SECTION REVIEW

1 How is cell division in bacteria similar to that in eukaryotes? How does it differ?

2 How does mitosis ensure that a new cell resembles its parent cell?

3 What is the cell cycle? Are the cell cycles of all organisms the same? Explain.

4 What is cancer? What are some of the factors that may cause a cell to become cancerous?

109

ANSWERS TO SECTION REVIEW

1 In both bacteria and eukaryotes, a chromosome is duplicated and one copy is passed to each new cell. However, in eukaryotes, mitosis is a more complicated process because these contain more DNA (and therefore chromosomes).

2 During mitosis, the parent cell's set of genetic instructions is copied exactly, thus ensuring that each new cell receives the same information.

3 The cell cycle consists of the growth and division stages of a cell. The stages of the cell cycle are the same for all organisms; however, the length of each stage varies among organisms and even between cell types within an organism.

4 Cancer is uncontrolled cell division. Factors that may cause cancer include viruses, certain genes, environmental agents such as chemicals and radiation, and dietary habits.

Key to Strategies
● **Understanding Concepts (Tier I)**
■ **Applying Information (Tier II)**
▲ **Critical Thinking (Tier III)**

Cell Reproduction 109

6-3

Phase One
Preparation

Scheduling

See the **Lesson Planning Guide** on pages 99A and 99B for lecture, classwork, and assignment options for Section 6-3.

Phase Two
Teaching Strategies

Visual Strategy **Figure 6-7**

● **Interpreting Graphics**

Ask students what the chromosome number would be in the fertilized egg cell shown in this figure if the gametes were diploid *(92)*. Ask them to hypothesize about the consequences of having fertilized cells that contain this number of chromosomes. *(If the fertilized egg contained 92 chromosomes, it would not develop normally and it certainly would not become the child shown in this figure.)*

Active READING

Technique: Reading Organizer

Point out to students that they have already encountered two reading organizers in this chapter. Ask students if they can spot the reading organizers provided. *(One depicts mitosis and cell division; the other depicts the cell cycle.)* See if students can locate a reading organizer in Section 6-3. Have them identify the types of organizers in this chapter and explain why these are appropriate graphic representations of the text.

As you have seen, mitosis serves to maintain the constant number of chromosomes in a cell. The two new cells produced by mitosis are genetically identical to the parent cell. Although some organisms are able to use mitosis and cell division to reproduce, most multicellular organisms use another type of nuclear division to produce specialized cells for reproduction.

6-3 How Gametes Form: Meiosis

OBJECTIVES

❶ **Define** *gamete*, **and state its function in sexual reproduction.**

❷ **Explain how meiosis maintains chromosome number throughout generations.**

❸ **Summarize the events of meiosis.**

❹ **Define** *crossing-over*, **and explain its impact on evolution.**

Figure 6-7
Most of your life cycle is spent as a diploid organism. Only certain cells—gametes—are haploid.

Making Haploid Cells

At the beginning of this chapter, you learned that most of your cells are diploid and have 46 chromosomes. Gametes are the exception; they are haploid and have 23 chromosomes. A **gamete** is a reproductive cell—an egg or a sperm. Gametes are found only in organisms that reproduce sexually, as do most animals. In sexual reproduction, two gametes fuse to form the first cell of a new individual, as shown in **Figure 6-7**. If gametes were diploid instead of haploid, the new individual would have twice as many chromosomes as its parents. Imagine how this number would continue to increase with each new generation.

Gametes are formed by a type of nuclear division called meiosis *(my OH sihs)*. **Meiosis** is a two-stage form of nuclear division in which the chromosome number is halved. The first meiotic division (meiosis I) reduces the number of chromosomes by half. The second meiotic division (meiosis II) separates identical copies of chromosomes. Like mitosis, meiosis is usually followed by cell division. Study the details of meiosis in *A Closer Look: Meiosis*, on the next page.

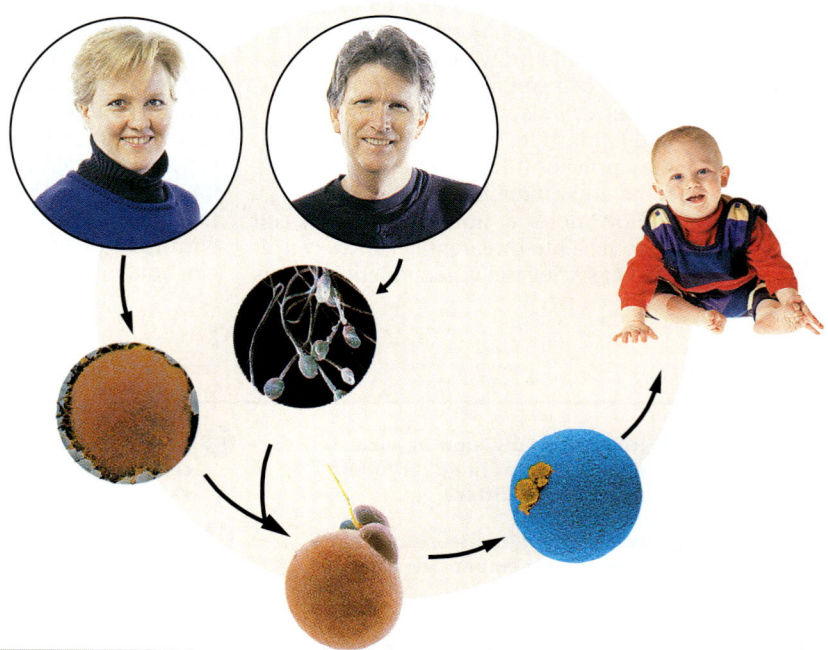

Videodisc Resources

Holt Biology Videodiscs
Lesson 6-3: How Gametes Form: Meiosis

Meiosis

In meiosis, eukaryotes produce reproductive cells that contain one-half as many chromosomes as the parent cell.

A Closer Look

1 The diploid (2*n*) cell nuclei shown here each have four chromosomes. One member of each chromosome pair is from one parent; the other is from the other parent.

2 First the amount of DNA doubles. Then the similar chromosomes pair with one another. Occasionally, paired chromosomes will exchange segments in a process called crossing-over.

3 The first meiotic division (meiosis I) separates the members of each pair of chromosomes. Meiosis I reduces the number of chromosomes in the cell by one-half.

4 The second meiotic division (meiosis II) separates the two copies of each chromosome (the chromatids). Cell division now occurs, producing four haploid (*n*) cells.

5 During sperm formation, the four cells containing these nuclei develop heads and tails. During egg formation, only one of the cells containing these nuclei becomes a mature egg; the other three cells usually die.

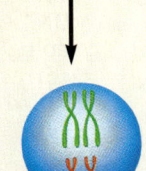
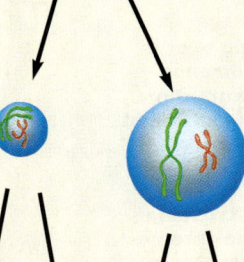
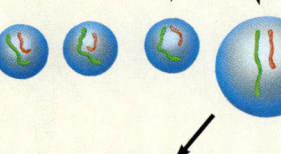
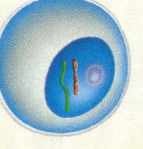
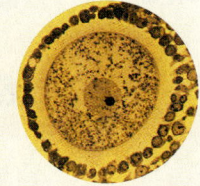

Modeling Meiosis

■ **Designing a Model**

Repeat the modeling activity that students completed for *A Closer Look: Mitosis and Cell Division* on page 106. Have students compare final models of meiosis with those made to illustrate mitosis and identify points where chromosome behavior differs.

Visual Strategy   Videodisc

■ **Analyzing Information**

Use *Video—Meiosis* shown in Chapter 6 Section 6-3 of ***Holt Biology Videodiscs Teacher's Correlation Guide to Holt Biology: Visualizing Life*** to help students understand how genetic variability is produced. As students view the video, have them note ways in which genetic variability is increased during meiosis and fertilization *(crossing-over, random separation of chromosomes, and random fertilization by one of many sperm).* Discuss with students whether they think genetic variation might be important to a species and why.

The Importance of Crossing-Over

When two haploid gametes unite in fertilization, the resulting cell is diploid. It received one of each type of chromosome from the egg of the female parent and one of each type from the sperm of the male parent. During the first division of meiosis, the two members of each chromosome pair move together and line up side by side. Proteins hold the two pairs of chromosomes so closely together that they appear indistinguishable.

While paired together, the chromosomes may exchange segments of DNA, as the two chromosomes are doing in **Figure 6-8**. This exchange of corresponding segments of DNA is called **crossing-over**. The importance of crossing-over lies in its consequences: the two sets of chromosomes are no longer identical. Each chromosome now contains genetic material from each parent.

From the perspective of evolution, crossing-over has an enormous impact. Exchanging segments of DNA between the members of a pair of chromosomes results in new combinations of genes in particular gametes, just as shuffling a deck of cards generates new combinations of cards dealt in a hand. These new combinations of genes act as one source of variation within a species. It is this sort of genetic variation that is necessary for natural selection to occur.

Figure 6-8
Crossing-over is a phenomenon that occurs during meiosis, when pairs of chromosomes are held tightly together. During crossing-over, the chromosomes exchange segments of DNA.

SECTION REVIEW

① What is a gamete? What is its role in organisms that reproduce sexually?

② Why will meiosis ensure that offspring have the same chromosome number as parents?

③ What is the result of meiosis I? of meiosis II?

④ What is crossing-over? What is its influence on evolution?

112

ANSWERS TO SECTION REVIEW

① A gamete is a sex cell, either a sperm or an egg. In sexual reproduction, a sperm cell and an egg cell fuse to form the first cell of a new individual.

② Meiosis reduces the chromosome number in each gamete from $2n$ to n. Thus, at fertilization, the $2n$ number will be restored.

③ Meiosis I produces haploid cells. Meiosis II simply separates the two copies of each chromosome (like mitosis).

④ Crossing-over involves the exchange of corresponding segments of chromosome pairs. The new combinations of genetic material provide the variation needed for evolution.

Highlights

These identical twins grew from the same fertilized egg cell, which separated into two independent cells after its first division.

	Key Terms	Summary
6-1 Chromosomes 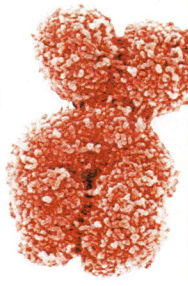 Chromosomes are composed of DNA and associated proteins.	chromosome (p. 101) chromatin (p. 101) karyotype (p. 103) diploid (p. 103) haploid (p. 103) sex chromosome (p. 103)	• Chromosomes carry genetic information from parent to offspring. • A eukaryotic chromosome is made of DNA wrapped around protein. A prokaryotic chromosome is a single circle of DNA. • Before a eukaryotic cell divides, a chromosome condenses into a compact rod-shaped body that can be easily moved around the cell.
6-2 Mitosis and Cell Division 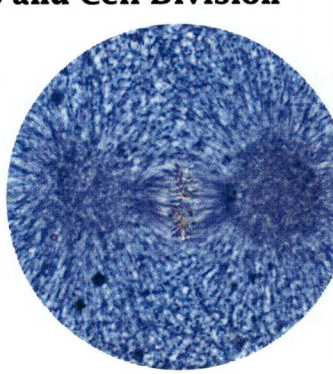 This cell is in the middle of mitosis; its chromosomes have been copied and are preparing to separate.	mitosis (p. 105) cytokinesis (p. 105) cell cycle (p. 107) tumor (p. 108) cancer (p. 109) mutation (p. 109)	• Before it can divide, a cell must make a copy of its DNA. • Bacteria divide by splitting in half. Eukaryotic cells divide through mitosis (division of the nucleus) followed by cytokinesis (division of the cytoplasm). • In mitosis, the nucleus of a cell is divided into two nuclei, each with the same number of chromosomes as the parent cell. In cytokinesis, the cytoplasm forms two distinct cells. • A cell undergoes an interval of growth and division called the cell cycle. • Cancer is a life-threatening disease that results from unregulated cell growth.
6-3 How Gametes Form: Meiosis   Meiosis results in the formation of haploid gametes: eggs or sperm.	gamete (p. 110) meiosis (p. 110) crossing-over (p. 112)	• A gamete is a haploid reproductive cell, such as an egg or a sperm cell. • Meiosis is a type of nuclear division that reduces the number of chromosomes in a cell by half. • Crossing-over is the exchange of segments of DNA between homologous chromosomes. It is a source of genetic variation.

113

Highlights

Alternative Assessment

Have students design a concept map that relates the two forms of cell division to the human life cycle. Be sure they include the terms *haploid, diploid, mitosis, meiosis,* and *gamete.*

Portfolio Assessment

Portfolio Assessment on page T39 provides options for building and evaluating student portfolios. Students and teachers can select items from the areas listed on page T39 for inclusion in a portfolio.

ANSWER TO CONCEPT MAP

The following is one possible answer to the Relating Concepts exercise on page 114.

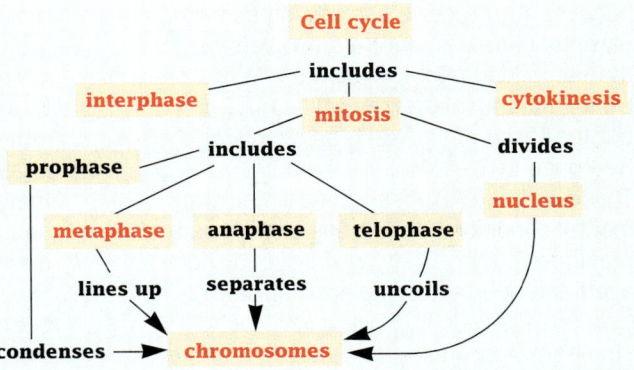

Cell Reproduction   113

review
ANSWERS

Understanding Vocabulary

1. a. diploid
   b. male
   c. cytokinesis
2. a. Chromatin is a complex of DNA and proteins that condenses to form chromosomes. The collection of chromosomes in a cell is called a karyotype.
   b. Mitosis consists of four stages: prophase, metaphase, anaphase, and telophase. (See page 106 for the events of the four stages.)
   c. Mitosis, cytokinesis, and interphase are all parts of the cell cycle. During interphase, the longest part of the cell cycle, the cell is growing and duplicating its genetic material.

Understanding Concepts

3. Concept map answer is shown on page 113.
4. Chromatin is a complex of DNA and proteins that condenses prior to cell division to form a compact, rod-shaped body called a chromosome.
5. Prior to cell division, the strand of DNA is duplicated. The two copies remain attached at one point on the chromosome and resemble a small butterfly.
6. Cytokinesis is the division of a cell to form two new cells. In animal cells, the cytoplasm pinches in half; in plant cells, a new cell wall splits the cell in two.
7. Sex chromosomes carry genes that determine an individual's sex.
8. The father's sperm determines the sex of the child because it can contribute one of two different sex chromosomes—an X or a Y.
9. By copying the genetic information within the chromosomes, each new cell will receive a complete copy of genetic information, ensuring that it will function properly.
10. See page 105 for details.
11. See page 106 for details.
12. Homologous chromosomes, found in eukaryotic cells

review

CHAPTER 6

Understanding Vocabulary

1. For each pair of terms, complete the analogy.
   a. 23 chromosomes : haploid :: 46 chromosomes : _____
   b. XX chromosomes : female :: XY chromosomes : _____
   c. nuclear division : mitosis :: cell division : _____

2. Using each set of words below, write one or more sentences summarizing information learned in this chapter.
   a. chromatin, chromosomes, karyotype
   b. prophase, metaphase, anaphase, telophase
   c. mitosis, cytokinesis, cell cycle, interphase

Understanding Concepts

3. **Relating Concepts** Construct a concept map that describes cell division. Try to include the following terms in your map: cell cycle, interphase, nucleus, chromosomes, cytokinesis, mitosis, and metaphase.

4. **Identifying Structures** What is chromatin? How does its appearance change before a cell divides?

5. **Comparing Structures** How does the shape of a chromosome change prior to cell division?

6. **Comparing Processes** What is cytokinesis? How does it differ in plant and animal cells?

7. **Recognizing Relationships** What are sex chromosomes? Why are they significant in cell reproduction?

8. **Summarizing Data** Who determines the sex of a child—the mother or the father? Explain your answer.

9. **Relating Conclusions** Why must a cell make a copy of the genetic information contained within its chromosomes before it divides?

10. **Summarizing Information** Describe what happens during each of these stages of mitosis: prophase, metaphase, anaphase, telophase.

11. **Identifying Functions** Describe the events that result in the formation of two complete nuclei in a eukaryotic cell. What usually happens, following division of eukaryotic nuclei in most cells?

12. **Recognizing Relationships** What are homologous chromosomes? Are they present in prokaryotic or eukaryotic cells?

13. **Organizing Information** What happens to a cell during interphase? Summarize the events that take place during the G_1 phase, the S phase, and the G_2 phase. Explain why interphase is the most active part of the cell cycle.

14. **Comparing Functions** Why do you think it is important for some cells in your body, such as skin cells and those that line your intestine, to have shortened cell cycles and divide almost continuously?

15. **Comparing Structures** Describe three ways cancer cells are different from normal cells.

16. **Summarizing Information** What is a gamete? How does it function in sexual reproduction?

17. **Inferring Conclusions** Why is meiosis sometimes called reduction division?

18. **Analyzing Results** If you are observing a dividing living cell and you see homologous chromosomes paired along the equator of the cell, are you observing mitosis or meiosis? Which stage of nuclear division is occurring?

19. **BUILDING ON WHAT YOU HAVE LEARNED** In Chapter 3 you learned that the surface-area-to-volume ratio in a cell is very important to the cell's survival. Based on what you know about that relationship, explain this statement: When a cell reaches a certain size, it will either stop growing or it will divide.

because they receive chromosomes from two parents instead of one, are two versions of the same kind of chromosome.

13. During interphase, a new cell is busy carrying out the tasks of life, such as taking in food. See page 107.
14. These cells are exposed to harsh environmental conditions and strong chemicals that break down food. They are frequently damaged and need to be replaced quickly.
15. Cancer cells typically have a very round shape, making them more mobile than normal cells. Unlike normal cells, which usually grow on solid surfaces, cancer cells can grow in liquids such as blood and lymph. They also have abnormal proteins and lipids in their outer cell membrane.
16. A gamete is a sex cell—an egg or a sperm—that contains the haploid number of chromosomes. When gametes fuse, the diploid number of chromosomes is restored.
17. The chromosome number in each cell has been reduced by half.

Interpreting Graphics

20. Look at the figure below of the human life cycle. Indicate the number of chromosomes at each stage of the life cycle.

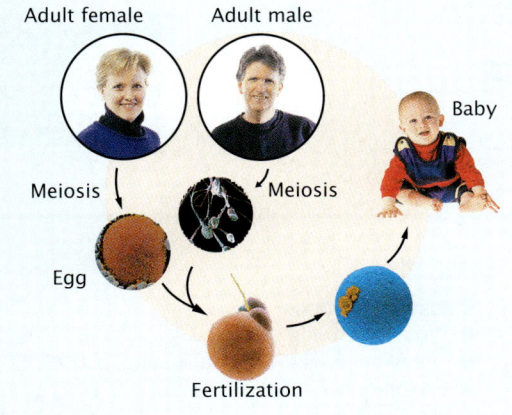

Adult female   Adult male

Baby

Meiosis   Meiosis

Egg

Fertilization

Reviewing Themes

21. *Heredity*
    How does mitosis promote genetic consistency?

22. *Evolution*
    Bacteria simply split, but eukaryotic cells reproduce by mitosis. How has the evolution of mitosis in eukaryotic cells aided their reproduction?

23. *Evolution*
    How does crossing-over during meiosis contribute to genetic diversity?

Thinking Critically

24. **Distinguishing Fact From Opinion** A classmate, after studying the cell cycle, concluded that the same cell goes through the cell cycle more than once. Do you agree or disagree? Support your answer.

25. **Evaluating Results** A genetic engineer was conducting studies on a plant with a haploid number of 12. After two gametes were joined together, the offspring had 36 chromosomes. What do you think happened to cause this result?

Life/Work Skills

26. **Applying Technology** Physicians may offer the use of amniocentesis or chorionic villus sampling to women who are pregnant. Investigate how these procedures are performed, and what technology is required. With a classmate, research the information that can be obtained by these two methods.

27. **Communicating** Research the link between cigarette smoking and different kinds of cancer. Communicate your results to your classmates by making an oral presentation that is supported by graphics, such as photos, charts, or graphs that show the number of cancer cases over a period of time.

Activities and Projects

28. **Career Connection: Cytotechnologist** A cytotechnologist is a person trained to observe abnormalities in cells that might indicate cancer or some other disease. Use library references to find out about becoming a cytotechnologist. What kind of equipment do cytotechnologists use? Where do they work? What kind of and how much education is required? Prepare a written report summarizing your findings.

Discovering Through Reading

29. Read the article "Strange Genes" in *Discover*, January 1996, p. 33. What is the "werewolf syndrome"? What common disorders are geneticists hoping to alleviate?

30. Read the article "By a Thousand Cuts" by Lori Oliwenstein in *Discover*, February 1993, pages 24–25. What is cellular senescence? What are telomeres? What happens to the telomeres each time a cell divides? What is the function of the enzyme telomerase, and how does its function contribute to cells becoming cancer cells?

31. Read the article "Stopping Cancer in Its Tracks" by J. Madeleine Nash in *Time*, April 25, 1994, pages 54–61. How does the gene p53 stop the formation of tumors?

115

Thinking Critically

24. A cell goes through the cell cycle only once. If the cell does not divide, it remains in one of the phases, such as interphase. If the cell divides, two new cells are formed.

25. Answers will vary, but students should speculate that cytokinesis did not occur during meiosis for some of the gametes.

Life/Work Skills

26. Students should describe the techniques physicians use to obtain tissues that yield a fetus's genetic information.

27. Students should indicate that the number of lung and throat cancer cases as a result of smoking increases over time.

Activities and Projects

28. Students should describe a cytotechnician's career path and working conditions.

Discovery Through Reading

29. Werewolf syndrome, or congenital generalized hypertrichosis, causes thick hair to sprout on the upper body and all parts of the face (nose, cheeks, forehead, and eyelids) of affected males. Some of the common disorders that geneticists are hoping to alleviate are cancer, Alzheimer's, and diabetes.

30. Cellular senescence is the number of times a cell will divide before it dies. Telomores protect the ends of chromosomes and prevent breakage. Telomeres are shaved down every time a cell divides and apparently signal a cell to stop dividing. Telomerase adds nucleotides that are lost. It may play a role in cancer cells by removing the signal to stop dividing.

31. The gene p53 monitors DNA during cell division. If cells become damaged, p53 activates other genes that cause the cell to self-destruct.

18. You are observing metaphase in meiosis I.
19. When a cell reaches an optimum size for the surface-area-to-volume ratio, the cell will stop growing and will divide.

Interpreting Graphics

20. Adult: 46; Egg and sperm: 23; Fertilization: 46; Baby: 46

Reviewing Themes

21. The two new cells resulting from mitosis have chromosomes that are identical to one another and to the original cell.
22. Mitosis increases the chance that both cells will receive complete sets of chromosomes.
23. See page 112.

7 | Genetics and Inheritance

	S	s
S	SS	Ss
s	Ss	ss

Lesson Planning Guide With Options for Block Scheduling

Lecture Concepts	Lesson Resources

7-1 The Work of Gregor Mendel

BLOCK 1 (45 minutes)

1. Gregor Mendel discovered the basic principles of heredity from his analysis of crosses using garden peas.

2. Mendel's experiments were carefully designed, meticulously executed, and mathematically analyzed.

1 Lecture Resources
- Determining Prior Knowledge
- Active Reading: K-W-L
- Visual Strategy: Figure 7-2
- Demonstration: Recognizing Relationships
- Teaching Transparencies: 25, 26
- Holt Biology Videodiscs Lesson 7-1

Classwork Options
- Problem Solving
- Life/Work Skills: Communicating, p. 121
- Exploration 7A

Assignment Options
- Mendel's Journal
- World of Work: Animal Breeding
- Teaching Resources CD-ROM: Portfolio Project 3

BLOCK 2 (45 minutes)

3. Mendel reasoned that each of the seven traits he studied was controlled by two factors, which today are known as alleles.

4. Mendel's findings are summarized in the law of segregation and the law of independent assortment.

2 Lecture Resources
- Unexpected Traits
- Visual Strategy: 7-3, 7-4, Table 7-1
- Holt Biology Videodiscs Lesson 7-1

Classwork Options
- Life/Work Skills: Communicating, p. 122
- Closure: Identifying Variables
- Quick Labs: Lab A6

Assignment Options
- Reteaching
- Section Review
- Chapter Review, questions 1, 2, 5, 6, 7, 19
- Directed Reading Worksheet
- Teaching Resources CD-ROM: Portfolio Projects—Genetics Project

7-2 Patterns of Inheritance

BLOCK 3 (45 minutes)

1. Probability can predict the likely outcome of a cross. A Punnett square is a mathematical model used to show the possible results of a cross.

2. A monohybrid cross involves the inheritance of a single gene with two alleles.

3 Lecture Resources
- Visual Strategy: Figure 7-6
- Visual Strategy: Videodisc
- Teaching Transparencies: 29, 30
- Holt Biology Videodiscs Lesson 7-2

Classwork Options
- World of Work: Agricultural Science
- Investigation 7B

Assignment Options
- Independent Assortment
- Teaching Resources CD-ROM: Supplemental Reading Guides 3

BLOCK 4 (45 minutes)

3. A dihybrid cross involves the inheritance of two genes, each with two alleles.

4. Some traits are controlled by complex patterns of inheritance, and other traits are controlled by more than one gene.

4 Lecture Resources
- Breeding Snapdragons
- Teaching Transparencies: 31, 32
- Holt Biology Videodiscs Lesson 7-2

Classwork Options
- Closure: Organizing Information
- Interactive Exploration 7C

Assignment Options
- Reteaching
- Section Review
- Chapter Review, questions 8, 9, 10, 11, 12, 13, 14, 15, 16, 18, 21
- Directed Reading Worksheet

7-3 Human Genetic Disorders

BLOCK 5 (45 minutes)

1. A mutation is any change in the genetic information of an organism.

2. Mutations are rare and can have a helpful, harmful, or neutral effect on an organism.

5 Lecture Resources
- Hemophilia Treatments
- Visual Strategy: Figures 7-11, 7-15
- Teaching Transparencies: 30A
- Holt Biology Videodiscs Lesson 7-3

Classwork Options
- Laboratory Techniques and Experimental Design: Lab C12

Assignment Options
- Life/Work Skills: Being a Team Member
- Teaching Resources CD-ROM: Problem-Solving Worksheets 3

Lecture Concepts

Lesson Resources

7-3 Human Genetic Disorders, *continued*

BLOCK ❻ (45 minutes)

3. Genetic disorders in humans originally brought about by a change in genetic information include cystic fibrosis, sickle cell anemia, hemophilia, and Down syndrome.

❻ Lecture Resources
- ■ Pedigree Key
- ■ Building a Pedigree
- ■ Active Reading: Reading Organizer
- ■ Visual Strategy: Figure 7-16
- ⬛ Teaching Transparencies: 38
- ⊙ Holt Biology Videodiscs Lesson 7-3

Classwork Options
- ■ *Small Group* Reteaching
- ■ Closure: Organizing Information

Laboratory Techniques and Experimental Design: Lab C13

Assignment Options
- ■ Section Review
- ■ Chapter Review, questions 3, 17, 20, 22, 23, 24, 25
- ■ Directed Reading Worksheet

Chapter Review and Assessment

BLOCK ❼ (45 minutes)

Review
- ■ Reteaching Worksheet
- ■ Thinking Skills Worksheet
- ■ Vocabulary Development Worksheet
- ⊙ Language Development and Reading Comprehension Audio CD Program: Chapter 7

BLOCK ❽ (45 minutes)

Assessment
- ■ Alternative Assessment, p. 133
- ■ Portfolio Assessment, p. T39

Chapter Test
- ■ Chapter 7 Test

Test Generator
- ⊙ Item bank for customizing Chapter Tests
- ⊙ Performance-Based Assessment: Identifying Dominant and Recessive Traits

Teaching Resources CD-ROM
- ⊙ Scoring Rubrics and Classroom Management Checklist

The Portfolio icon denotes items throughout the Teacher's Edition lesson wrap that may be selected for inclusion in student portfolios.

Holt Biology Videodiscs and *Concepts of Biology*

Holt Biology Videodiscs gives you a powerful tool for teaching, review, and assessment. For further information regarding the media on the videodiscs, see **Holt Biology Videodiscs Teacher's Correlation Guide to Holt Biology: Visualizing Life.**

Concepts of Biology adds interactive lesson plans and extensive tools for customization using CD-ROM technology.

Use the following topic from **Concepts of Biology** to help you teach this chapter:
Topic 6: Fundamentals of Genetics

Laboratory Planning

Text

Materials and preparation instructions appear on the teacher's wrap accompanying each laboratory exercise.

Block 1: Exploration 7A: ABO Blood Typing, p. 774

Block 3: Investigation 7B: ABO Blood Typing—Hospital Mix-up, p. 776

Block 4: Interactive Exploration 7C: Cystic Fibrosis, p. 778

Holt BioSources Laboratory Program

Block 2: Quick Labs Lab A6: Interpreting Information in a Pedigree

Block 5: Laboratory Techniques and Experimental Design Lab C12: Analyzing Corn Genetics

Block 6: Laboratory Techniques and Experimental Design Lab C13: Preparing Tissue for Karyotyping

CHAPTER 7

Determining Prior Knowledge

- Ask students for examples of traits that are inherited. Encourage them to find examples from a variety of organisms.
- Have students explain how traits are passed from one generation to the next.
- Ask students to define the term *gene*.
- Have students identify the location, the products, and the purpose of meiosis in humans.
- Review chromosome activity during meiosis. Ask students to compare meiosis with mitosis.

Active READING

Technique: K-W-L
Before students read this chapter, have them write short individual lists of all the things they already **K**now (or think they know) about inheritance. When students have finished their lists, ask them to contribute their entries to a group list on the chalkboard or on the overhead projector. Then have students list things they **W**ant to know about inheritance. Have students save their lists for later use in Active Reading on page 132.

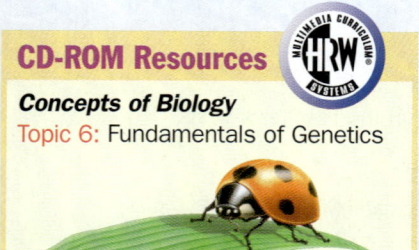

CD-ROM Resources

Concepts of Biology
Topic 6: Fundamentals of Genetics

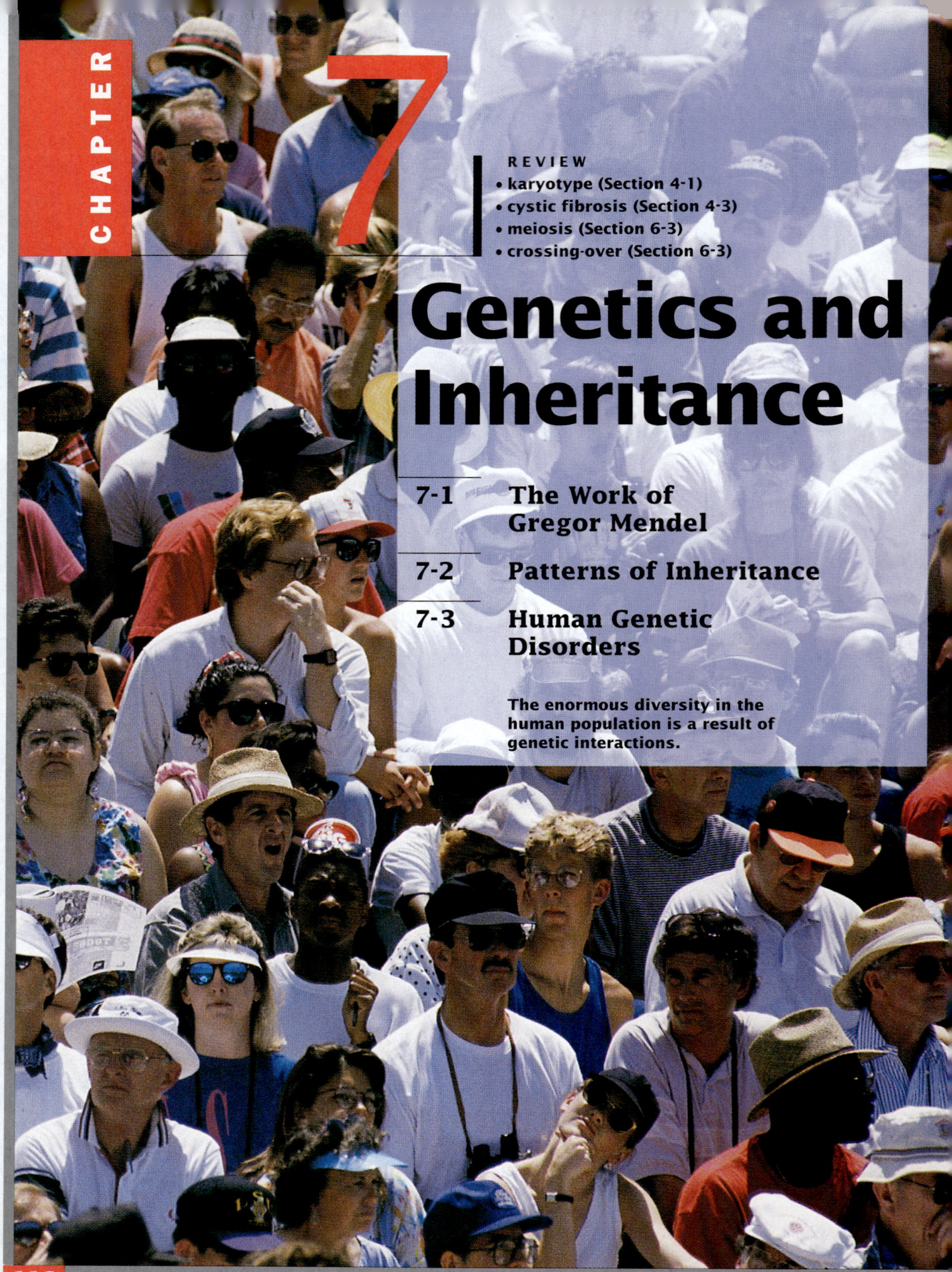

CHAPTER 7

REVIEW
- karyotype (Section 4-1)
- cystic fibrosis (Section 4-3)
- meiosis (Section 6-3)
- crossing-over (Section 6-3)

Genetics and Inheritance

The enormous diversity in the human population is a result of genetic interactions.

116

Author's Rationale This chapter reviews Mendel's garden-pea experiments to help students understand heredity as gene segregation. Dihybrid crosses and other patterns of inheritance are then introduced to help students appreciate some of the complexities of inheritance. The chapter closes with a discussion of mutations, genetic disorders, and genetic counseling.

The key lesson of this chapter is that heredity—the most important criterion of life—is not mysterious. It can be explained by simple mechanisms and should be clearly understood in order for students to be biologically literate.

Try to recall the last news story about genetics that you read or heard. Did it describe a new kind of genetically altered food or drink now available in grocery stores? Did it hail the discovery of a gene linked to cancer? Such stories are becoming commonplace these days. However, the events leading up to our current knowledge are not much older than your great-grandparents.

GENETICALLY NEW TOMATO WILL IT SELL? —
A Genetic I ...
Genetists Report Breakthrough in New Food Crops
Companies Push for New Genetic Crops

7-1 The Work of Gregor Mendel

OBJECTIVES

1 Outline the garden-pea experiments performed by Gregor Mendel.

2 Explain how Mendel's approach enabled him to reach his conclusions.

3 Define the following terms: gene, allele, dominant, recessive, homozygous, heterozygous, genotype, and phenotype.

4 Relate Mendel's two laws of inheritance to the behavior of chromosomes during meiosis.

Gregor Mendel and the Garden Pea

The scientific study of heredity is called **genetics** (*juh NEHT ihks*). Its story begins in the 1860s in the gardens of a monastery in Brünn, Austria (which is now Brno in the Czech Republic). There, a monk named Gregor Mendel, shown in **Figure 7-1**, was performing a series of experiments on ordinary garden peas, *Pisum sativum*. Trained in the sciences and mathematics, Mendel was curious about patterns of heredity and was studying traits in generations of pea plants. Like others before him, he had noticed that when a pea plant with purple flowers was bred, or crossed, with a pea plant with white flowers, all the offspring had purple flowers. Then, if two of these purple-flowered offspring were crossed, the white flowers reappeared in some of the pea plants in the next generation.

Earlier researchers had tried to unravel this mystery of heredity in garden peas. Mendel repeated their efforts but added an important twist—he used a mathematical approach and counted the number of kinds of offspring in each generation of pea plant. Quantitative approaches to science—those that include measuring and counting—were just becoming popular in Europe, so Mendel was on the cutting edge of research.

You might be wondering why Mendel and others studied the garden pea. The garden pea is a good subject for genetic study. These small, delicate vines are easy to grow, produce large numbers of offspring, and mature quickly. Garden-pea plants also have their male and female reproductive parts enclosed in the same flower, as shown in **Figure 7-1b**. This meant that Mendel could allow a flower to fertilize itself through a process called self-fertilization. Or he could intervene and transfer the pollen from one flower to another flower on a different plant, a process called cross-fertilization.

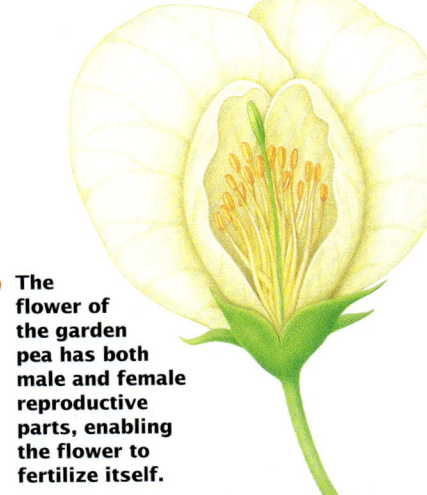

Figure 7-1
a Modern genetics began with the garden-pea experiments performed by Gregor Mendel in the 1860s.

b The flower of the garden pea has both male and female reproductive parts, enabling the flower to fertilize itself.

117

Phase One
Preparation

Scheduling
See the **Lesson Planning Guide** on pages 115A and 115B for lecture, classwork, and assignment options for Section 7-1.

Phase Two
Teaching Strategies

Demonstration
■ **Recognizing Relationships**
Have students bring old photographs of parents or siblings to class. Ask them to match the names of fellow students with the photographs of their family members. Once the students have matched the photographs to their classmates, show the pictures individually and ask the matching student to stand. Ask students to identify how the two are similar as well as how they are different. Once students have completed the activity, ask them to identify the strategies they used to match the family members. Ask students to identify techniques they think modern scientists would use to find a family connection.

Videodisc Resources

Holt Biology Videodiscs
Lesson 7-1: The Work of Gregor Mendel

Key to Strategies
Teaching Strategies are keyed to three tiers of learning.

● **Understanding Concepts (Tier I)**
Content mastery and comprehension

■ **Applying Information (Tier II)**
Applying and analyzing content

▲ **Critical Thinking (Tier III)**
Practicing evaluative thinking

Visual Strategy   Figure 7-2

● **Summarizing Information**
Walk students through the three steps of Mendel's experiments. Check for understanding of the term *pure-breeding* by having students identify the step in which Mendel used such plants. To personalize the steps of Mendel's experiments, ask students to identify P, F_1, and F_2 generations using their own family as an example.

Problem Solving

■ **Analyzing Methods**
Have students review the scientific methods discussed in Chapter 1 Section 1-2. Then have students apply these methods to Mendel's discoveries about heredity. Students' reports should summarize the hypothesis, predictions, and control experiments that Mendel used to support his theory.

Mendel's Journal

▲ **Justifying Conclusions**

Have students write journal pages that represent comments Mendel could have written in a journal as he did his research. Students should put themselves in the place of Mendel and write as they think he would have written in his own journal. Use Mendel's experimental observations to justify the conclusions he reached.

Mendel's Experiments

Mendel carried out his experiments with garden peas in three steps, illustrated below in **Figure 7-2**.

Step 1
First Mendel produced pure-breeding strains of pea plants. He did this by allowing a population of pea plants to self-fertilize for many generations. He then collected and grew the seeds from these plants. These seeds gave rise to offspring that produced only one form of a particular trait. For example, the purple-flowering strain produced only purple flowers and the white-flowering strain produced only white flowers. Mendel called these pure-breeding offspring the parental generation, or, in abbreviated form, P generation.

Step 2
Next Mendel crossed the two different varieties in the P generation. For example, he took pollen from the anthers of purple flowers and placed it on the stigmas of white flowers. He then collected and grew the seeds from these plants. Mendel called the offspring that grew from the seeds the first filial generation, or F_1 generation for short. In the F_1 generation, Mendel found only purple flowers. White flowers did not appear.

Step 3
Finally Mendel allowed the F_1 generation plants to self-fertilize. As before, he grew the seeds. He called the offspring produced by these seeds the second filial generation, or F_2 generation for short. After noticing that white flowers reappeared in the F_2 generation, Mendel applied his mathematical approach. Out of the 929 F_2 individuals, he counted 705 plants with purple flowers and 224 plants with white flowers. He calculated that approximately three-fourths of the F_2 plants had purple flowers, a 3:1 ratio.

Mendel studied more than flower color in garden peas. He studied other traits that, like the purple and white flower color, appeared in contrasting forms. Several of these traits are listed in **Table 7-1**. For each pair of traits, Mendel counted the number of F_2 individuals exhibiting contrasting forms of each trait.

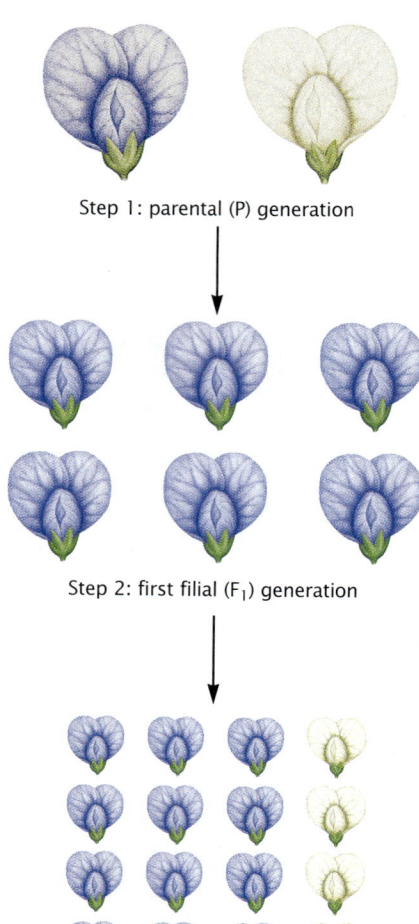

Step 1: parental (P) generation

Step 2: first filial (F_1) generation

Step 3: second filial (F_2) generation

Figure 7-2
Mendel's garden-pea experiments consisted of three steps, each of which involved either self-fertilization or cross-fertilization.

Table 7-1 Contrasting Traits in Pea Plants

Trait	Contrasting forms of traits		F₂ generation ratio
Flower color	Purple	White	705:224
Seed color	Yellow	Green	6,022:2,001
Seed shape	Round	Wrinkled	5,474:1,850
Pod color	Green	Yellow	428:152

Mendel developed a model to explain his results

Each time Mendel counted the number of F₂ individuals exhibiting contrasting forms of a trait, he obtained a 3:1 ratio. Surely this ratio must mean something important. To explain his results, Mendel came up with a simple model, a set of rules that could be used to accurately predict patterns of heredity. These rules summarize Mendel's ideas about inheritance.

1. Parents transmit information about traits to their offspring. Mendel called this information "factors."

2. Each individual has two factors for each trait, one from each parent. The two factors may or may not have the same information. If the two factors do have the same information (for example, if both have information for purple flowers), the individual is said to be **homozygous** (hoh muh ZY guhs) for the trait. If the two factors have different information (for example, one factor codes for purple flowers and the other for white flowers), the individual is said to be **heterozygous** (heht uh roh ZY guhs).

3. The alternative forms of a factor are called **alleles** (uh LEELS). The many alleles that an organism possesses make up its **genotype** (JEE nuh typ). An organism's physical appearance, which is determined by its alleles, is called its **phenotype** (FEE nuh typ).

4. An individual possesses two alleles for each trait. One allele is contributed by the female parent, and the other is contributed by the male parent. The two alleles in each pair are not affected by each other. They are passed on when an individual matures and produces gametes (eggs and sperm). During the formation of gametes, the paired alleles segregate (separate) randomly so that a gamete receives a copy of one allele or the other.

5. The presence of an allele does not ensure that the trait will be expressed in the individual that carries it. In heterozygous individuals, only the **dominant** allele achieves expression. The **recessive** allele is present but remains unexpressed. In Mendel's F₁ generation, purple flower color was caused by a dominant allele. For every pair of contrasting forms of a trait—tall versus short, or green seeds versus yellow seeds—the allele for one form of the trait was always dominant and the allele for the other form of the trait was always recessive.

Unexpected Traits
■ Analyzing Results
A greenhouse manager raising sweet peas notices that unlike the plants she has had in other years, some of the flowers this year are white. Previously, the pea flowers have been purple. What explanation would account for this difference in the plants? Have students suggest answers. Tell them that the information on this page might provide some insight. At the end of this chapter, pose this question again. (Instead of buying the more expensive F₁ hybrid seeds as she did in the past, she decided to save money and plant pea seeds from the crop she harvested the previous year. Her plants were the F₂ generation, which shows a 3:1 ratio of purple to white flowers.)

Visual Strategy   Table 7-1
● Interpreting Graphics
Use this table to expand students' understanding of Mendel's research. For each trait, have students identify the contrasting forms that Mendel crossed. Then have them analyze the ratios to determine which trait was self-pollinated to produce the F₂ generation.

Life/Work Skills
Finding Information
● Organizing Data
Tell students that Table 7-1 illustrates only four of the seven traits that Mendel studied during his experiments. Have students research the other three traits that interested Mendel, and then have them add this information to Table 7-1 on a separate sheet of paper.

Key to Strategies
● Understanding Concepts (Tier I)
■ Applying Information (Tier II)
▲ Critical Thinking (Tier III)

Genetics and Inheritance   119

Theme Answer

Heredity

The parents could be heterozygous for the trait and both contribute the recessive gene.

Visual Strategy Figure 7-3

● **Interpreting Graphics**

Have students identify the genotypes and phenotypes of the offspring in Figure 7-3. Have them identify the haploid gametes in the Punnett square and describe the process that produces these cells. (*Students should describe the events of meiosis.*) Then have them name the process that restores the diploid number to the offspring (*fertilization*). Ask students which step of Mendel's research is illustrated in this figure (*Step 2*).

World of Work

Animal Breeding

The beef industry is using selective breeding techniques to develop beef products with reduced fat content. Ask students to contact local agricultural extension agents (both home economics and agriculture) or to write to the National Association of Animal Breeders (Box 1033, Columbia, MO 65205) to find answers to the following questions:

• What are some additional desirable traits that have been created or enhanced through the use of selective breeding? What are some undesirable traits that have been reduced or eliminated?

• What are some breeding systems that animal breeders use to improve domestic animals?

Heredity

Explain how a form of a trait that appears in both parents could be absent from their children.

Figure 7-3
This Punnett square illustrates a cross between two true-breeding varieties of garden pea plants. This was Step 2 of Mendel's experiment.

1 **Each gamete, whether male or female, contains a single allele for flower color.**

2 **The eggs produced by this flower . . .**

3 **. . . can only have a w allele because the plant is ww.**

Visualizing Mendel's Model

Mendel's model can be understood easily by diagramming Mendel's crosses. For example, consider Mendel's cross of parental (P) purple-flowering pea plants with parental white-flowering pea plants. For the sake of convenience, letters are used to represent alleles. The recessive allele is represented by the lower case letter "w" (for "white"), and the dominant allele is represented by the corresponding upper case letter "W." A plant that is true-breeding for the recessive white flower color would be designated "ww," and a plant that is true-breeding for the dominant purple flower color would be designated "WW." A heterozygote would be designated "Ww."

A simple diagram called a Punnett square can help you visualize crosses. Named for the British geneticist Reginald Punnett, a Punnett square is also a handy device for predicting the results of a cross.

In a Punnett square, the symbols for all the possible alleles carried by male gametes (sperm) are arranged along the top of the square, while all the possible alleles carried by the female gametes (eggs) are shown along the left side. By combining the symbol for an allele carried by a male gamete with the symbol for the allele carried by the female gamete, all the possible gamete combinations can be predicted, as shown in **Figure 7-3**.

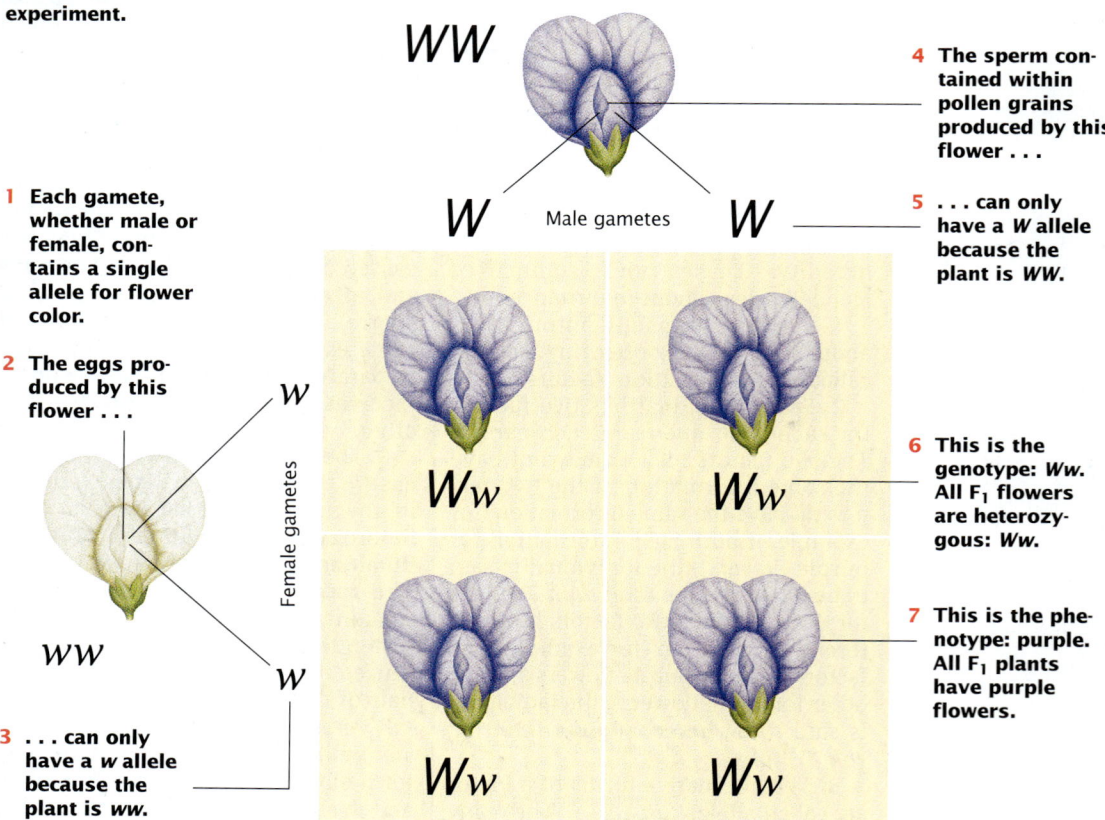

4 **The sperm contained within pollen grains produced by this flower . . .**

5 **. . . can only have a W allele because the plant is WW.**

6 **This is the genotype: Ww. All F₁ flowers are heterozygous: Ww.**

7 **This is the phenotype: purple. All F₁ plants have purple flowers.**

Crossing two heterozygous plants

When heterozygous (Ww) F_1 individuals with purple flowers are allowed to self-fertilize, what will the resulting F_2 individuals be like? Let's predict what we would expect to find using Mendel's rules. To make a prediction, consider what scientists call **probability**. Probability is simply the likelihood that something will happen. For example, when you toss a coin, the probability that the coin will land with "heads" up is 50 percent, or one-half, because the coin, is just as likely to fall showing "tails." Similarly, because of the segregation of alleles, the probability that an egg or sperm cell in one of Mendel's heterozygous F_1 pea plants (Ww) will contain the allele W is 50 percent, or one-half, just as in a coin toss. Obviously, the reverse is also true: the probability that a gamete will contain the allele w is also 50 percent or one-half.

Figure 7-4
This Punnett square illustrates a cross between two heterozygous F_1 individuals. This was Step 3 of Mendel's experiment.

Study the Punnett square for a cross involving two purple-flowered heterozygous plants (Ww) shown in **Figure 7-4.** In this particular cross, one-half of the male and female gametes carry the allele for purple flowers (W). The other one half of the gametes carry the allele for white flowers (w). You can see that Mendel's model clearly predicts that 75 percent of the F_2 generation will have purple flowers and 25 percent will have white flowers, a 3:1 ratio. The Punnett square also shows the genotypes found in the F_2 generation. Twenty-five percent of the F_2 is homozygous (ww) with white flowers, 50 percent heterozygous (Ww) with purple flowers, and the remaining 25 percent is homozygous (WW) with purple flowers. The 3:1 ratio Mendel had repeatedly observed is the expression of an underlying 1:2:1 ratio of genotypes in which the heterozygotes look like one of the homozygotes.

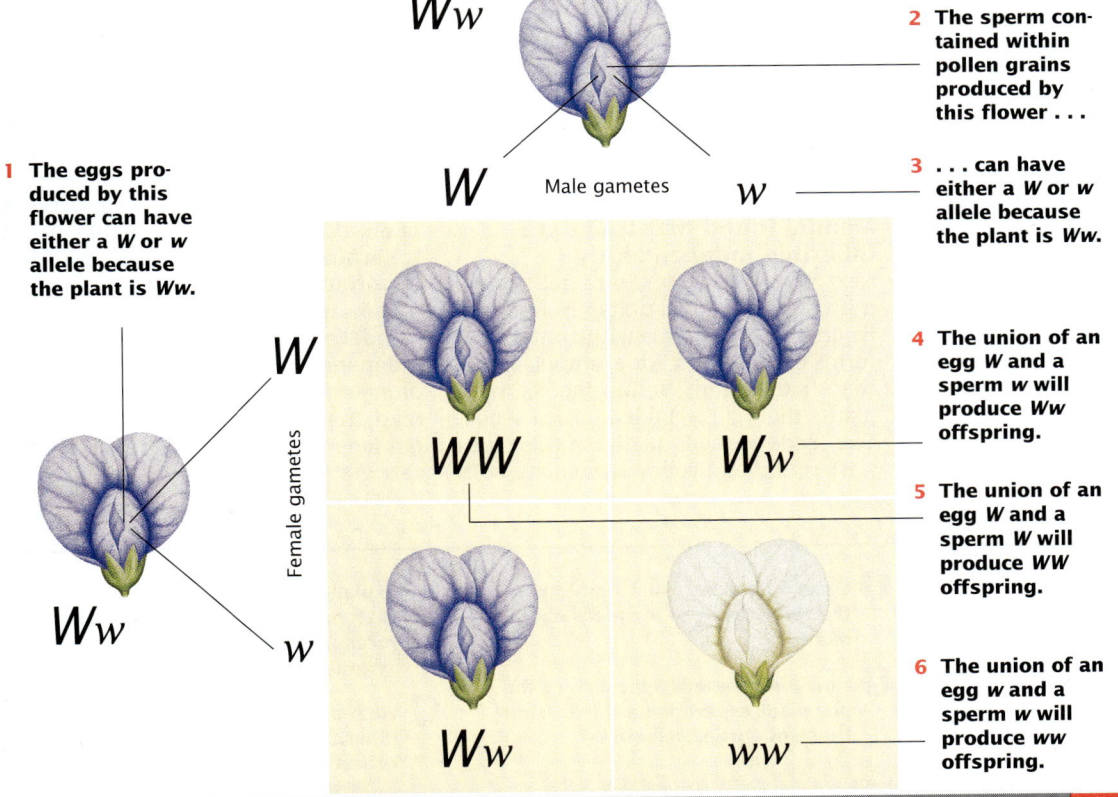

1 The eggs produced by this flower can have either a *W* or *w* allele because the plant is *Ww*.

2 The sperm contained within pollen grains produced by this flower . . .

3 . . . can have either a *W* or *w* allele because the plant is *Ww*.

4 The union of an egg *W* and a sperm *w* will produce *Ww* offspring.

5 The union of an egg *W* and a sperm *W* will produce *WW* offspring.

6 The union of an egg *w* and a sperm *w* will produce *ww* offspring.

Male gametes

Female gametes

Visual Strategy   **Figure 7-4**

● **Interpreting Graphics**
Have students identify the genotypes and phenotypes of the offspring shown in Figure 7-4 and state them as ratios. Ask students to compare this Punnett square with the one shown in Figure 7-3. Ask students which step of Mendel's research is illustrated in Figure 7-4. *(Step 3).*

Mathematics Connection
Probability and Genetics
Compare the probability involved in tossing a coin with that of the segregation of the two alleles shown in Figure 7-4. Ask students how many heads and tails are expected if a coin is flipped 100 times. Ask them what numbers they may actually obtain. Emphasize that observed results often differ from predicted ones, although the deviations should be minor. Relate this to the number of gametes containing the *W* allele and the number of those containing the *w* allele, if 100 gametes are produced by each heterozygous F_1 plant in Figure 7-4.

Life/Work Skills
Communicating
■ **Applying Information**
Have students design a persuasive advertisement that would have attracted someone like Mendel to purchase these peas for genetic research. Students should select a medium (newspaper, magazine, radio, television, or computer) for their advertisement.

Key to Strategies
● Understanding Concepts (Tier I)
■ Applying Information (Tier II)
▲ Critical Thinking (Tier III)

Genetics and Inheritance 121

Evolution
How does the law of independent assortment provide a source of variation from one generation to the next?

Mendel's Conclusions

Studying the results of his crosses, Mendel realized that in each case one form of each trait did not appear in the F_1 generation. The missing form of each trait then reappeared in approximately one-fourth of the plants in the F_2 generation. Every F_2 generation consisted of the contrasting trait forms in an approximate 3:1 ratio. Surely, this ratio was significant.

Mendel saw that these results could be explained if a pea plant had two hereditary factors for each trait. He concluded that a plant receives one hereditary factor from one parent and the other factor from the other parent. In turn, the plant passes on one of its two factors to each of its offspring. Today this conclusion is referred to as Mendel's first law, or the law of segregation. The law of segregation describes the behavior of chromosomes during meiosis, when homologous chromosomes and then chromatids are separated.

> **The law of segregation states that the members of each pair of alleles separate when gametes are formed. A gamete will receive one allele or the other.**

Mendel found that traits are inherited independently
Next Mendel wondered, Are traits transmitted as individual units? To find out, he crossed pea plants with contrasting forms of two traits: for example, plants that had round, yellow seeds with plants that had wrinkled, green seeds. The seeds of the F_1 plants of this cross were round and yellow, which are both dominant traits. When these plants self-fertilized, the F_2 generation had four different phenotypes: 315 had round, yellow seeds, 101 had wrinkled, yellow seeds, 108 had round, green seeds, and 32 had wrinkled, green seeds. Mendel calculated that these numbers represent a 9:3:3:1 ratio. These results told him that the genes for two different traits—seed color and seed form—don't necessarily stay together. Half of the time they separate and join in new combinations. This idea is the basis for Mendel's second law, the law of independent assortment.

> **The law of independent assortment states that two or more pairs of alleles segregate independently of one another during gamete formation.**

The law of independent assortment reflects the way homologous chromosomes pair up in the middle of the cell during meiosis I. This law applies to traits whose genes are found on different pairs of homologous chromosomes or far apart on the same chromosome pair. (Keep in mind that chromosomes had not yet been discovered in Mendel's time.)

Mendel published his results in 1866. Unfortunately, his paper failed to arouse much interest, and the importance of his work was not recognized. In 1900, sixteen years after Mendel's death, several investigators independently rediscovered Mendel's pioneering paper. Scientists soon realized that chromosomes, discovered not long before Mendel's death, are the carriers of heredity.

SECTION REVIEW

❶ Draw a flowchart that highlights the three steps of Mendel's experiments.

❷ How did Mendel's approach to the pea-plant experiments differ from those of earlier scientists?

❸ Explain the difference between each pair: gene, allele; dominant, recessive; homozygous, heterozygous; genotype, phenotype.

❹ What are Mendel's two laws of inheritance? How do these laws reflect the events of meiosis?

For more than half a century after Mendel's work was rediscovered, scientists sought a deeper understanding of genetics. Soon they discovered that most traits follow patterns of inheritance far more complex than those proposed by Mendel. Since then, genetics has moved to the forefront of scientific research.

7-2 Patterns of Inheritance

OBJECTIVES

1 Recognize the relationship between the laws of probability and inheritance.

2 Use a Punnett square to predict the outcome of a cross.

3 Describe three other factors that influence inheritance.

Predicting the Outcome of a Cross

Most of Mendel's conclusions are based on the fact that genes combine according to the rules of probability. When a pea plant reproduces, its pair of alleles for each gene segregate into separate cells during meiosis. As a result, the probability that an egg or a sperm cell will contain one or the other allele is 50 percent or one-half.

A simple Punnett square neatly illustrates a monohybrid (*mah noh HY brihd*) cross, which is a cross focusing on only one trait, such as flower color. **Figure 7-5** shows a monohybrid cross between a homozygous purple-flowering plant and a homozygous white-flowering plant and reveals the possible offspring.

Figure 7-5
This Punnett square illustrates a monohybrid cross between a homozygous purple-flowering plant and a homozygous white-flowering plant.

1 This purple flower is homozygous dominant: *WW*. Each gamete it produces has a *W* allele.

2 This white flower is homozygous recessive: *ww*. Each gamete it produces has a *w* allele.

3 All the offspring of this cross have purple flowers. Their genotype is *Ww*.

123

Videodisc Resources

Holt Biology Videodiscs
Lesson 7-2: Patterns of Inheritance

Phase One
Preparation

Scheduling
See the **Lesson Planning Guide** on pages 115A and 115B for lecture, classwork, and assignment options for Section 7-2.

Phase Two
Teaching Strategies

Visual Strategy | **Videodisc**

● **Interpreting Graphics**
Use the step-frame sequences shown in Chapter 7 Section 7-2 of *Holt Biology Videodisc Teacher's Correlation Guide to Holt Biology: Visualizing Life* to explain how a Punnett square is useful in predicting the results of a cross. Guide students through the diagram. Remind students that these images visually summarize Steps 1 and 2 of Mendel's research, which was described on page 118.

Key to Strategies
● Understanding Concepts (Tier I)
■ Applying Information (Tier II)
▲ Critical Thinking (Tier III)

Applying Information

Ask students how we know that the two parental plants can produce four different gametes. *(Mendel's law of independent assortment states that during gamete formation, pairs of alleles separate independently.)* Encourage students to brainstorm about what the independent assortment of the alleles suggests about the location of the alleles shown in the figure. *(Because the alleles separate independently, they are located on different chromosomes or far apart on the same chromosome.)*

Independent Assortment

● Forming a Model

Have students make a **Graphic Organizer** similar to the one at the bottom of this page to demonstrate the law of independent assortment. Ask students to illustrate their graphic organizers with at least one example showing the inheritance of two pairs of contrasting traits, and ask them to write a brief explanation.

Figure 7-6
This Punnett square illustrates a dihybrid cross between two heterozygous plants that have yellow, round peas. Four phenotypes will be found among the offspring of this cross. Mendel calculated a 9:3:3:1 ratio of these phenotypes.

Visualizing a Dihybrid Cross

The Punnett square in **Figure 7-6** illustrates a dihybrid (dy HY brihd) cross. A dihybrid cross shows two traits of interest. Notice that the Punnett square for a dihybrid cross contains 16 boxes. These additional boxes are necessary to account for all possible gene combinations.

To illustrate a dihybrid cross, reconstruct one of Mendel's experiments, in which he studied the inheritance of two traits. Mendel crossed plants that were homozygous for yellow, round seeds with plants that were homozygous for green, wrinkled seeds. The F$_1$ generation offspring produced yellow and round seeds, indicating that these were the dominant traits. Thus, let Y = yellow and y = green, and R = round and r = wrinkled. When these seeds were grown into plants that were allowed to self-fertilize, the offspring shown in **Figure 7-6** resulted. Recall Mendel's law of independent assortment, which states that members of pairs of alleles segregate independently into gametes. This means that each plant shown in **Figure 7-6** can produce four kinds of gametes, which are arranged along the top and the left side of the Punnett square. When the boxes of the Punnett square are filled, each box will hold four symbols. How many phenotypes are shown among the offspring of the dihybrid cross in **Figure 7-6**?

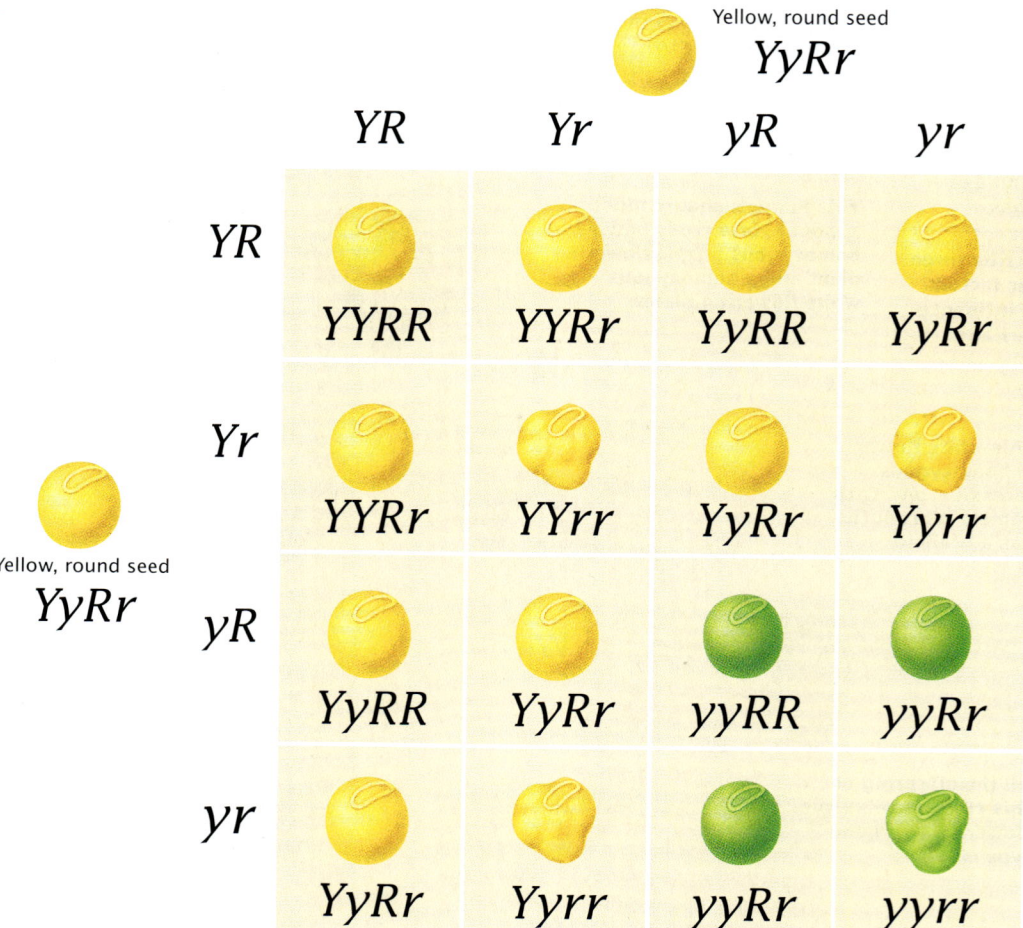

Graphic Organizer

Use the following graphic organizer with the teaching strategy **Independent Assortment** on page 124.

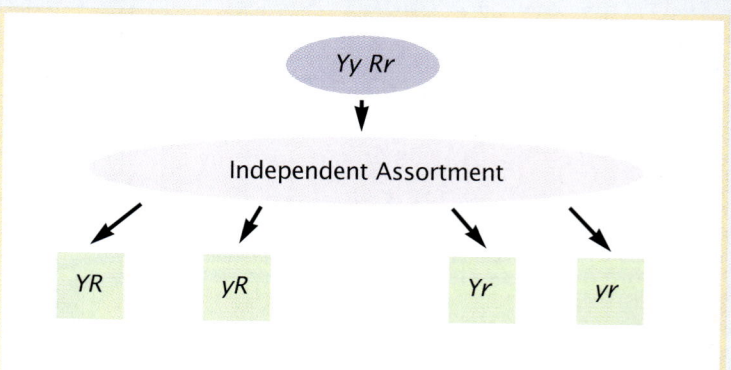

Other Factors That Influence Heredity

Since Mendel's time, scientists have discovered many genes that do not follow the simple pattern of inheritance described by Mendel. Most of the time, genes exhibit more complex patterns of inheritance, such as those described below.

Two traits appear to blend in incomplete dominance

In many cases, an individual has a trait that appears to be an intermediate form of the traits displayed by the two parents. This phenomenon is called incomplete dominance. An example of incomplete dominance is found in snapdragons. A cross between a red-flowered snapdragon and a white-flowered snapdragon will result in offspring with pink flowers, as shown in **Figure 7-7**. As dominant traits in snapdragons, red flowers and white flowers are homozygous. Pink flowers are heterozygous. Heterozygous flowers are pink because they are unable to produce enough red pigment to make their petals appear red.

Figure 7-7
When red-flowering snapdragons are crossed with white-flowering snapdragons, the offspring will produce pink flowers, an example of incomplete dominance.

Figure 7-8
The roan coat of this horse consists of both red hairs and white hairs, a result of codominance.

Two traits are fully displayed in codominance

In some cases, both genes in a heterozygote are fully expressed, a phenomenon called codominance. Codominance can affect coat color in horses. When a horse that is homozygous for red coat color is crossed with a horse that is homozygous for white coat color, the offspring are heterozygous and have roan coats. A roan coat is one in which the color is a mixture of two colors, such as red hairs mixed with white hairs, as shown in **Figure 7-8**.

Varieties of a trait arise from multiple alleles

Some traits are controlled by genes that have more than two alleles. In such cases, a trait is said to be controlled by multiple alleles. Combinations of any two of these alleles can produce different phenotypes. An example of multiple alleles can be seen in the human ABO blood groups. The four blood groups are governed by three alleles—I^A, I^B, and i. Recall that a person can have only two alleles for any gene. **Table 7-2** shows the possible phenotypes and genotypes of human ABO blood groups.

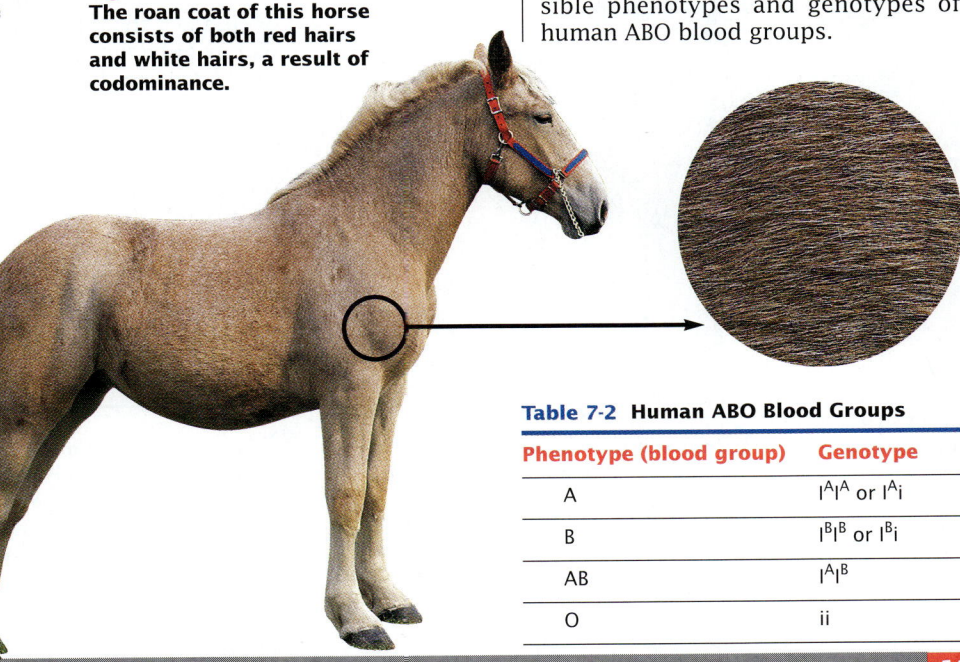

Table 7-2 Human ABO Blood Groups

Phenotype (blood group)	Genotype
A	$I^A I^A$ or $I^A i$
B	$I^B I^B$ or $I^B i$
AB	$I^A I^B$
O	ii

Matter of Fact: Mendelian Inheritance
Mendel's work with garden-pea plants showed that the traits he studied are controlled by single genes. In humans, single-factor inheritance has been found in about 600 recessively inherited traits and in such dominant conditions as Huntington's chorea and Marfan's syndrome. However, many more diseases are determined by polygenic inheritance, which involves several genes. Common diseases that are governed by polygenic inheritance include cleft lip and palate, schizophrenia, hypertension, and diabetes. These types of traits do not exhibit the single gene inheritance patterns studied by Mendel.

Phase Three
Assessment Options

Closure
● **Organizing Information**
Use the Active Reading strategy below to organize information from the lesson.

Active READING

Technique: Reading Organizer
Have students use the following reading organizer to compare monohybrid crosses with dihybrid crosses:

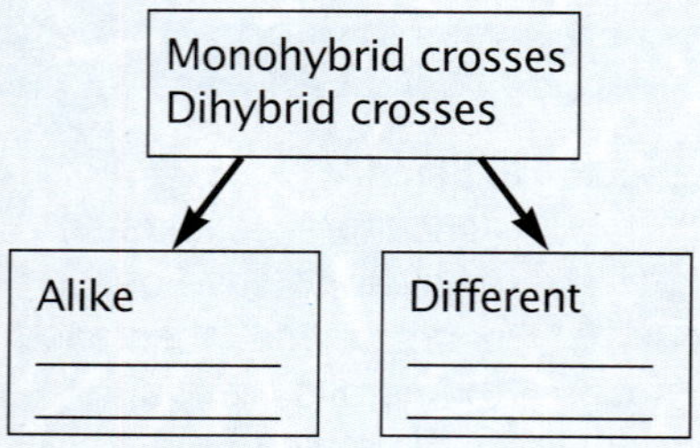

Monohybrid crosses
Dihybrid crosses

Alike _____

Different _____

SECTION REVIEW
Assign the *Section Review.*

Reteaching
Write the following genotypes on the board: (1) *WW,* (2) *Ww,* and (3) *ww.* Pair each student with a partner. Assign two of the genotypes to one partner. Assign a different pair of genotypes to the other partner. Have students construct a Punnett square showing a cross between their assigned genotypes. Students should express the phenotypes and genotypes among the offspring as ratios. When students have completed their work, have them share their results with their partners.

Figure 7-9
Many of your distinguishing features—your height, weight, and skin color—are examples of polygenic traits, which are influenced by many pairs of genes.

Figure 7-10
a **Conditions in the environment can affect an organism's genes and therefore its appearance. The arctic fox's red coat enables it to blend into the summer background, . . .**

b . . . while in winter the fox blends into the snowy landscape.

Some traits are controlled by many genes

The term polygenic is used to describe a trait that is controlled by more than one pair of genes. The genes for a polygenic trait may be scattered along the same chromosome or located on different chromosomes. Due to independent assortment and crossing-over, many different combinations appear among the offspring. Each combination influences the trait to a different degree. Familiar examples of polygenic traits in humans include height, weight, body build, and hair and skin color, as shown in **Figure 7-9**. Characteristics such as these all have degrees of intermediate conditions between one extreme and the other.

Gene expression can be affected by environmental conditions

An individual's phenotype often depends on surrounding environmental conditions. For example, the color of an arctic fox is affected by temperature. During the warm temperatures of summer, the fox produces enzymes that manufacture pigments. These pigments darken the fox's coat to a reddish brown, as shown in **Figure 7-10a**, enabling the fox to blend into the summer landscape. But during the cold winter these enzymes do not function. As a result, the fox has a white coat that blends into the snowy background, as shown in **Figure 7-10b**.

SECTION REVIEW

1. Explain the role of probability in understanding inheritance.

2. Construct a Punnett square to predict the offspring of a cross between a tall pea plant *(TT)* and a short pea plant *(tt).*

3. Cross two of the offspring from the cross just completed in (2) above. Construct a Punnett square to predict the kinds of offspring that could result from this cross.

126

ANSWERS TO SECTION REVIEW

1. Probability is the likelihood that something will happen.

2. The Punnett square should reflect phenotypic and genotypic ratios of 4 tall *(Tt)*:0 short *(tt)* among the offspring.

3. The Punnett square should show a cross between two individuals, each with the genotype *Tt.* Offspring of this cross should exhibit a phenotypic ratio of 3 tall: 1 short and a genotypic ratio of 1*TT*: 2*Tt*: 1*tt.*

Many genes in human populations code for metabolic processes that are far more important than characteristics such as hair color and eye color. Some of the most devastating human disorders are caused by rare genes that are the result of genetic mutations. Many of these genes are passed from parent to child in patterns of inheritance described by Mendel.

7-3 Human Genetic Disorders

OBJECTIVES

1 Explain what mutations are and how they can affect an organism.

2 Describe the patterns of inheritance for three genetic disorders.

3 Explain a technique used to identify people at risk of passing genetic disorders to their children.

4 Discuss the possibilities that exist for curing genetic disorders.

Mutations Are Changes in Genes

In order to develop and function properly, your body requires specific proteins that are built according to instructions in your genes. In some cases, genes are sometimes damaged or copied incorrectly. A change in a gene is called a **mutation** *(myoo TAY shuhn)*. Mutations are a source of the variation a species needs in order to adapt to changing conditions and thus to evolve over time. A mutation's effect can vary. Most mutations are harmful or neutral, such as the one shown in **Figure 7-11**. Since mutations change genes at random, the chance that a mutation will improve an individual is very slim. For instance, imagine that you randomly changed a part of a blueprint for the construction of an airplane. Some changes, such as the color of the passenger seats, would not matter. Other changes, such as the size of the jet engines, are more serious.

Most mutations are recessive

Most mutations are recessive and therefore are not expressed in the heterozygous condition. Although mutations are rare, everyone is probably heterozygous for a number of genetic mutations. It is unlikely, however, that a person who is heterozygous for a recessive mutation will mate with someone who is heterozygous for the same mutation. Therefore, there is little chance that his or her offspring would be homozygous for the recessive mutation, which could be a harmful and unfortunate condition.

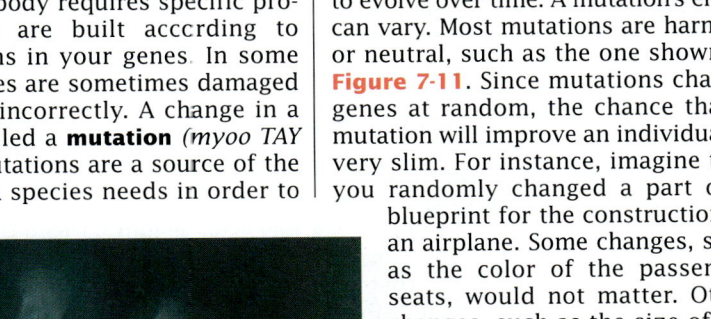

Figure 7-11
A genetic mutation causes some humans to have six toes, as shown in this X ray.

127

Videodisc Resources

Holt Biology Videodiscs
Lesson 7-3: Human Genetic Disorders

Phase One
Preparation

Scheduling
See the **Lesson Planning Guide** on pages 115A and 115B for lecture, classwork, and assignment options for Section 7-3.

Phase Two
Teaching Strategies

Visual Strategy	Figure 7-11

■ **Inferring Conclusions**
Use this figure to point out two important features of mutations: (1) although phenotypically visible here, not all mutations result in a phenotypic expression, and (2) mutations need not be harmful. Have students provide an example in which a mutation might be beneficial to an organism.

Key to Strategies
● **Understanding Concepts (Tier I)**
■ **Applying Information (Tier II)**
▲ **Critical Thinking (Tier III)**

1	2	3	4	5	6	7	8	9	10	11	12	13	14

Connection: *Chapter 4*

Cell Membrane Proteins

To determine how much students recall about protein channels and their role in cystic fibrosis, ask them how cell membrane proteins control the interaction of the cell with its environment.

Health Connection

Hemophilia and HIV

Hemophilia is currently manageable with the addition of blood-clotting factors (collected from donated blood) to a hemophiliac's blood. Tell students that the United States blood supply was contaminated with HIV during the period from 1977 to 1985. Ask students what effect the HIV-contaminated blood supply has had on the hemophilic community. *(The Centers for Disease Control and Prevention report that the effect on hemophiliacs was devastating. Currently, more than 10,000 hemophiliacs, or 70 to 90 percent of the severe cases in the United States, are HIV positive.)*

Hemophilia Treatments

▲ **Evaluating Alternatives**

Have students research the use of technology in the treatment of hemophilia. Students should examine current treatment technologies and rank them according to their efficacy, cost, and availability. Have students prepare a report or presentation summarizing their findings.

Figure 7-12
The chromosomes highlighted in blue play a role in the genetic disorders described on these pages. Staining techniques reveal the unique banding patterns, shown above, that help researchers identify each chromosome.

	F	f
F	FF	Ff
f	Ff	ff

Figure 7-13
Cystic fibrosis is caused by a recessive gene on chromosome 7. If both parents carry a copy of the cystic fibrosis gene (*f*), their child has a one-in-four chance of developing the disease.

Genetic Disorders

Particular mutations have established a foothold in human populations. The harmful effects that some mutations produce are called **genetic disorders**. Many genetic disorders are the result of mutations in a single gene in one of the 46 human chromosomes, shown in **Figure 7-12**. In most cases, a genetic disorder is recessive. A person with a recessive genetic disorder has inherited a defective gene from both parents. Other genetic disorders are caused by dominant alleles. A single copy of the defective gene is enough to cause the disease.

Cystic fibrosis is caused by a faulty transport protein

Cystic fibrosis is a recessive genetic disorder caused by a mutation in a gene that codes for a protein responsible for transporting chloride ions. In the homozygous condition, this mutation causes cells in the respiratory system and in the digestive system to produce misshapen chloride transport proteins that are unable to function properly. In these individuals, such as the girl shown in **Figure 7-13**, mucus accumulates in the lungs and pancreas, clogging ducts needed for these organs to function properly. People with cystic fibrosis have difficulty breathing and cannot properly digest their food. Most of the current treatments for cystic fibrosis relieve the symptoms of the disease but do not cure it.

Researchers have isolated the mutated gene that causes cystic fibrosis. Isolation of the gene has led to the possibility of gene transfer therapy, in which a healthy copy of the mutated gene is transferred into the lungs of cystic fibrosis patients to cure the disease.

Sickle cell anemia results from faulty hemoglobin

Sickle cell anemia is a recessive genetic disorder caused by a mutation in a gene that codes for hemoglobin, the protein in red blood cells that transports oxygen throughout the body. In the homozygous condition, this mutation causes the body to build an abnormal form of hemoglobin. When the faulty hemoglobin is inside a red blood cell, it gives the cell a deformed, sickle-shaped appearance, as shown in **Figure 7-14**. The sickled cells get caught in small blood vessels and restrict blood flow to tissues. The sickled cells are also very fragile and break down easily. This leaves the person with significantly fewer red blood cells than average, a condition called anemia. Symptoms of sickle cell anemia include fatigue, headaches, muscle cramps, and sometimes kidney or heart failure.

The sickle cell mutation in the hemoglobin gene apparently first arose in central Africa centuries ago. Up to 45 percent of the population in central Africa is heterozygous for the sickle cell gene. Evolution has favored the sickle cell gene in central Africa because heterozygous people are more resistant to malaria, a deadly tropical disease caused by parasites in red blood cells.

Figure 7-14
Sickle cell anemia is caused by a recessive gene on chromosome 11. If each parent carries a copy of the sickle cell gene, there is a one-in-four chance that their child will have sickle cell anemia.

	S	s
S	SS	Ss
s	Ss	ss

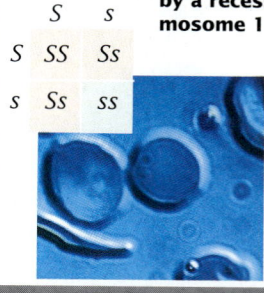

128

Multicultural Perspective: Understanding Sickle Cell Anemia

Working with limited laboratory facilities but a strong determination to fight the disease that was killing their friends and families, Dr. Angela Ferguson and Dr. Roland Scott published a paper on sickle cell anemia in the 1940s. Dr. Scott, known as a pioneer of sickle cell anemia research, is the founder and former director of Howard University's Center for Sickle Cell Anemia Research. Dr. Ferguson was an associate professor of pediatrics at Howard University. In 1970, she was listed in *Who's Who of American Women*.

	X	Y
X	XX	XY
X^H	X^HX	X^HY

Figure 7-15
A mother who carries the gene for hemophilia may pass it on to her sons and daughters. However, only the sons who inherit the gene will develop the disorder. With proper treatment, hemophiliacs, like this boy, can lead active lives.

Hemophilia results from a faulty blood-clotting protein

Hemophilia is a recessive genetic disorder caused by a mutation on the X chromosome. This mutation causes the body to build a defective form of a protein needed to clot blood. Usually when body tissues are cut, the blood in the immediate area of the cut forms a clot that seals the wound. In an individual with hemophilia, such as the boy in **Figure 7-15**, small cuts are difficult to heal and internal bleeding can be fatal. Long-term sufferers are susceptible to serious arthritis, arising from bleeding in joint cavities, and other disorders. Fortunately, treatments are available, such as injections of the correct form of the faulty protein.

The proteins involved in blood clotting are encoded in dozens of genes. Two of these genes are found on the X chromosome. Any male who inherits a mutant copy of either gene will develop hemophilia because his other sex chromosome, a Y chromosome, lacks a gene for the blood-clotting protein. A pattern of heredity in which traits are transmitted by genes located on the X chromosome is called **sex-linked inheritance**. Traits that are determined by genes located on the X chromosome are said to be sex-linked traits.

Down syndrome arises from three copies of chromosome 21

Down syndrome is an example of a genetic disorder caused by an extra chromosome. Whereas most people have two copies of each chromosome, individuals with Down syndrome have three copies of chromosome 21, as shown in **Figure 7-16**. The features that characterize Down syndrome include extra folds in the upper eyelids, a broad and somewhat flattened nose, short stature, and, most important, varying degrees of mental retardation. These characteristics were first described in 1866 by a researcher named J. Langdon Down. Although people with Down syndrome are physically challenged, they are able to lead active lives and to make positive contributions to society.

Down syndrome occurs in about 1 of every 1,000 births. This syndrome is much more common among children born to older mothers. In mothers older than 45, the risk is as high as 1 in 16 births. Pregnant women over the age of 35 are usually informed of medical procedures in which fetal cells are extracted and used to prepare a fetal karyotype. In one technique, amniocentesis, a small amount of the fluid surrounding the fetus is removed and fetal cells are collected. In another technique, chorionic villi sampling, a tiny piece of embryonic membrane is removed. In addition to Down syndrome, a fetal karyotype can reveal hemophilia, sickle cell anemia, and cystic fibrosis.

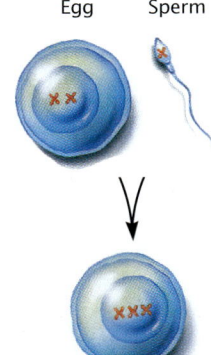

Egg   Sperm

Zygote

Figure 7-16
When chromosome 21 fails to separate properly during meiosis in either parent, the child can receive three copies of the chromosome, a condition that causes Down syndrome.

129

Historical Perspective: Hemophilia and the Royalty of Europe

Ask students to name some possible genetic reasons for the high frequency of hemophilia among members of Queen Victoria's family and other royal families throughout Europe. Explain that Queen Victoria was a carrier of sex-linked hemophilia. Because members of the European nobility usually married among themselves as a practice of forming alliances, the hemophilia gene was passed via Queen Victoria's daughters to the Russian, German, and Spanish royal families, increasing the frequency of the recessive allele among European nobility.

Visual Strategy Figure 7-15

■ **Predicting Outcomes**
Most students will have difficulty understanding the reason for the superscript H. Inform them that the female carries one allele for hemophilia and is shown having the genotype X^HX. The male is normal and is XY. Review the phenotypes for each of the children. Ask students what the odds are of this couple having a son with hemophilia.

Visual Strategy Figure 7-16

■ **Interpreting Graphics**
Point out that the zygote should contain only two copies of chromosome 21 but in fact has three. Have students review **A Closer Look: Meiosis** on page 111 to see how chromosome pairs separate normally in the first meiotic division. Sometimes, however, they don't. If it is chromosome pair 21, then Down syndrome results.

Life/Work Skills
Being a Team Member

● **Summarizing Information**
Assign students to cooperative groups. Have each group research a genetic disorder and design an informative brochure, videotape, or audiotape about the disorder. Set guidelines on information you expect the students to include, such as symptoms, causes, prognosis, and support groups, and emphasize the importance of using colors and illustrations that would interest prospective readers. Encourage students to work together to designate individual responsibilities and to work cooperatively to allocate the time and resources required to accomplish the task.

Key to Strategies
● Understanding Concepts (Tier I)
■ Applying Information (Tier II)
▲ Critical Thinking (Tier III)

Active READING

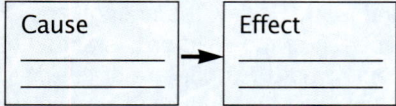
Pedigree Key

■ **Predicting Outcomes**
Before teaching students to interpret a pedigree, introduce the symbols for male (square), female (circle), afflicted (shaded), and normal (not shaded) individuals. Once students are comfortable with the meanings of the symbols, have them interpret the pedigree in Figure 7-17.

Building a Pedigree

■ **Forming a Model**

Have students research history books to construct a pedigree showing the spread of hemophilia throughout the royal families of Europe, beginning with Queen Victoria. Students should note how the disease was spread to other countries by marriages among nobility.

Figure 7-17
a Two boys in this family have hemophilia, but no one else does. How can this happen?

Genetic Counseling and Gene Therapy

Most genetic disorders are caused by recessive genes. Therefore, a gene that causes a genetic disorder could be present but not expressed in a person who is heterozygous for that gene. These heterozygous individuals are said to be carriers for the disorder. How can a person find out if he or she is a carrier for a genetic disorder? If one family member is affected by a genetic disorder, it may be possible that other family members are heterozygous for the disorder. In these cases, physicians may recommend genetic counseling to family members who wish to find out if they are at risk of having children with a genetic disorder. In some cases, a genetic counselor can prepare a family **pedigree** *(PEHD uh gree)*, a record that shows inheritance patterns over several generations, as shown in **Figure 7-17**. Noting relatives with a genetic disorder enables a genetic counselor to determine an individual's chances of being a carrier for that disorder. With such information, a person can decide whether or not to have children.

b This pedigree shows that the mother carries the gene for hemophilia (shaded), and that two of her sons have received this gene.

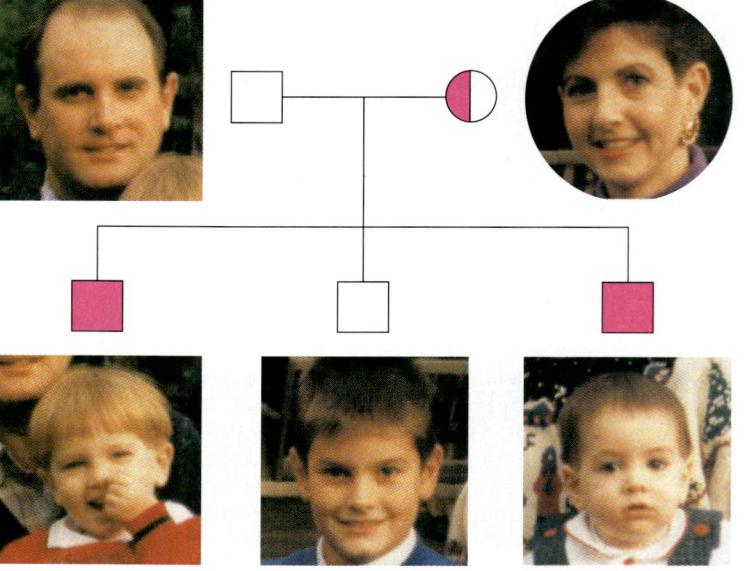

Community Connection: Animal Breeder

Invite a local animal breeder to speak to your class. Possible speakers could be breeders of dogs, cats, horses, birds, or any livestock. Have the guest discuss traits that are desirable, traits that are undesirable, and the reasons for these distinctions. Students may be interested in the market values of animals with certain traits. Ask the breeder to bring photographs of the animals so the students can see some of the traits being discussed.

Genetic Counseling

What would it be like to . . .

- educate people and families about inherited diseases?

- play a significant role in bringing healthy children into the world?

These are just a few of the opportunities open to people who work in the field of genetic counseling.

Genetic Counseling: What Is It?

Genetic counseling is a service for people seeking information about a possible genetic disorder or disease that has affected one or more relatives. Might it affect them or their children? What treatment is available? In responding to such questions, a genetic counselor provides information that could help individuals make important decisions about having children.

Career Focus: Diana Punales-Morejon

Genetic Counselor at a medical center in New York

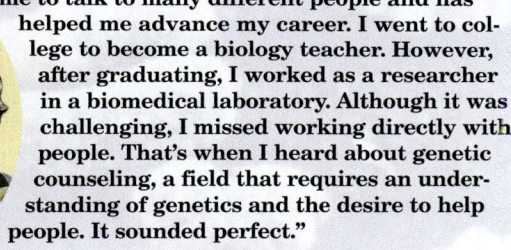

"I was born in Cuba and didn't learn to speak English until the first grade. Learning another language was difficult but worth the effort. Being bilingual enables me to talk to many different people and has helped me advance my career. I went to college to become a biology teacher. However, after graduating, I worked as a researcher in a biomedical laboratory. Although it was challenging, I missed working directly with people. That's when I heard about genetic counseling, a field that requires an understanding of genetics and the desire to help people. It sounded perfect."

What I Do: "As a genetic counselor, I advise people who are at risk of having children with genetic disorders or birth defects. I answer questions, explain common misconceptions, and administer tests that detect genetic disorders in fetuses. One of my favorite things about being a genetic counselor is telling an expecting couple that their child will be healthy. However, it's never easy telling a couple that tests show their child will be affected with a genetic disorder. Dealing with these sensitive matters is difficult, but it can be one of the most rewarding things about my job."

Science/Math Career Preparation

High school
- Biology
- Chemistry
- Physics

College
- Biology
- Genetics
- Chemistry
- Psychology

Graduate school
- Master's degree is recommended

Employment Outlook

As our knowledge about human genetics and reproductive technologies grows more sophisticated, the demand for genetic counselors will quickly increase.

To Find Out More

1 Write for more information:
Is a Career in Genetic Counseling in Your Future?
National Society of Genetic Counselors
233 Canterbury Drive
Wallingford, PA 19086

Solving the Puzzle: Careers in Genetics
The Genetics Society of America & The American Society of Human Genetics
9650 Rockville Pike
Bethesda, MD 20814-3998

2 Visit your school counselor and library to find out what colleges and universities offer programs in genetic counseling. Review the prerequisites and course requirements. Make a poster showing the range of job opportunities in this field.

131

Career Opportunities

Organizing and Presenting Information

1. Have students brainstorm ideas about the following questions:

If you wanted a career in genetic counseling...

- what kind of personality traits would be essential?
- which subjects should you study in high school? in college?
- what kind of extracurricular activities should you pursue?
- what kind of practical experience should you gain?
- what kind of issues would interest you?

2. In small groups, have students research a specific genetic disorder, using appropriate sources (library, on-line databases, or field research). Have each group deliver an oral presentation that includes overhead transparencies.

3. Using the research from the preceding activity, have each group produce a written report that includes graphics illustrating how the faulty genetic information affects proteins and enzymes, disrupts a biochemical pathway, and produces the disorder or disease. Then have groups meet to "publish" their papers in a journal devoted to genetic counseling.

Assessment Options

Closure

● **Organizing Information**
Use the Active Reading strategy below to help students summarize their knowledge.

Active READING

Technique: K-W-L
Tell students to return to the lists of things they **W**ant to know about inheritance, which they created using the K-W-L active reading technique on page 116. Have them place check marks next to the questions that they are now able to answer. Students should finish by making a list of what they have **L**earned. Conclude by asking students the following:

• Which questions are still unanswered?

• What new questions do you have?

You may wish to assign projects that require students to research their unanswered questions.

SECTION REVIEW

Assign the *Section Review*.

Reteaching

Have students work with a partner to prepare a concept map summarizing the different patterns of inheritance exhibited by the genetic diseases discussed in this section.

Finding Cures for Genetic Disorders

Most genetic disorders cannot be cured. However, therapy is available for some genetic disorders if they are diagnosed early enough. For example, phenylketonuria (PKU) is a recessive disorder in which affected individuals lack an enzyme that converts the amino acid phenylalanine into the amino acid tyrosine. In these individuals, phenylalanine builds up in the body, leading to mental retardation. If PKU is diagnosed shortly after birth, the infant can be placed on a low-phenylalanine diet. Such a diet ensures that the infant gets enough phenylalanine to make proteins but not enough to cause damage. The patient must stay on the diet as directed in order to control the levels of phenylalanine. Because this genetic disorder is easily detected after birth by inexpensive laboratory tests, many states have extensive screening programs to check newborns for PKU.

Techniques in genetic engineering can make it possible to cure genetic disorders by replacing copies of defective genes with copies of healthy ones. One of the first gene therapy attempts involved two young girls, shown in **Figure 7-18**, who suffered from an immune-system disorder caused by a defective gene. The defective gene failed to produce an important immune-system enzyme. Doctors took bone marrow cells from the girls and replaced the defective gene with a normal copy. Later, after the genetically engineered cells were returned to the girls' bones, they began to produce the missing enzyme. Five years after their gene therapy, the girls are doing well, although they are still on medication. Doctors monitor them closely, looking for signs that the gene therapy was effective. Unfortunately, gene therapy as a simple and foolproof cure for a disorder is still in the future.

Figure 7-18
Ashanthi DeSilva (left) and Cynthia Cutshall (right) were among the first patients to receive gene therapy.

SECTION REVIEW

1 What is a mutation? Why are most mutations recessive?

2 Create a table that contains information about three genetic disorders.

3 Describe a technique used to identify people at risk of passing genetic disorders to their children.

4 How are genetic engineering techniques providing hope for people with genetic disorders?

132

ANSWERS TO **SECTION REVIEW**

1 A mutation is a change in a gene. Since most mutations are harmful, most are also recessive; a recessive mutation is likely to have no phenotypic effect among heterozygotes because it will be overshadowed by the effects of the corresponding dominant (i.e., normal) allele.

2 Answers will vary but should reflect an accurate understanding of the disorders discussed in this section.

3 Students should describe the technique of pedigree analysis.

4 Genetic engineering could make it possible to replace copies of defective genes with copies of healthy genes. One successful example of genetic engineering involved replacing a defective gene that failed to produce an immune system enzyme with a normal copy of the gene.

7 | Highlights

These children are brothers. Even though they have the same parents, they look very different from each other.

	Key Terms	Summary
7-1 **The Work of Gregor Mendel**  Mendel unlocked the secrets of heredity by studying pea plants.	genetics (p. 117) homozygous (p. 119) heterozygous (p. 119) allele (p. 119) genotype (p. 119) phenotype (p. 119) dominant (p. 119) recessive (p. 119) probability (p. 121)	• Gregor Mendel's experiments with pea plants marked the beginning of genetics. • Using a mathematical approach, Mendel concluded that each trait is governed by two factors, one of which is received from each parent. An individual passes either one of its factors to each of its offspring. • Mendel's ideas about heredity can now be interpreted using modern genetic terminology. • Mendel's laws of inheritance reflect the events of meiosis.
7-2 **Patterns of Inheritance** Patterns of heredity are passed from generation to generation. 		• Probability and Punnett squares are two techniques used to predict the outcome of genetic crosses. • A monohybrid cross studies the inheritance of one trait. A dihybrid cross studies the inheritance of two traits. • The inheritance of most traits is complex and can be affected by many different influences.
7-3 **Human Genetic Disorders** Occasionally a harmless mutation causes a person to have six toes. 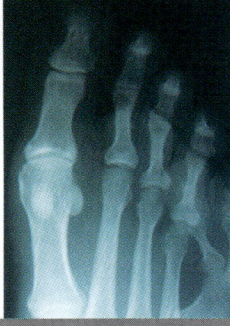	mutation (p. 127) genetic disorder (p. 128) sex-linked inheritance (p. 129) pedigree (p. 130)	• A change in a gene, called a mutation, can cause inherited diseases called genetic disorders. • Examples of genetic disorders include cystic fibrosis, sickle cell anemia, hemophilia, and Down syndrome. • Genetic counseling can help identify people at risk of having children with genetic disorders. • Therapies are available to treat some genetic disorders, if they are diagnosed early enough.

Alternative Assessment

Assign students to cooperative work groups. Have each group develop a genetics problem based on the information developed in this chapter. Students can use Section Review questions 2 and 3 on page 126 as models. Collect the problems, write them down on the board, and have each group work on the solutions.

Portfolio Assessment

Portfolio Assessment on page T39 provides options for building and evaluating student portfolios. Students and teachers can select items from the areas listed on page T39 for inclusion in a portfolio.

133

ANSWER TO CONCEPT MAP

The following is one possible answer to the Relating Concepts exercise on page 134.

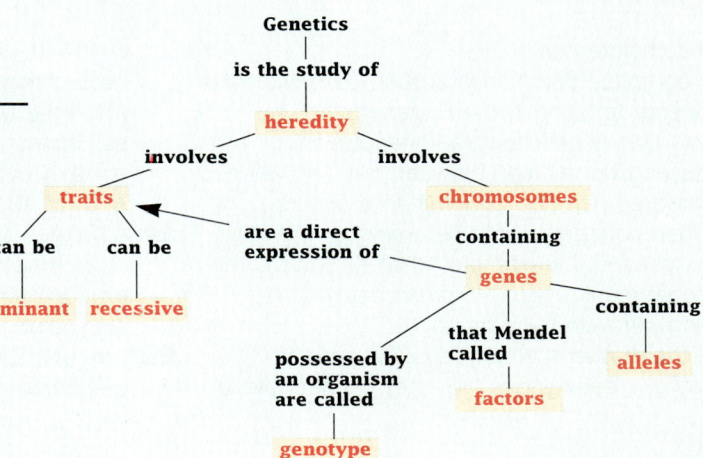

Understanding Vocabulary

1. a. The parental, or P, generation are the organisms that are crossed to produce the first filial, or F_1, generation.
b. A gene is a segment of DNA that carries the instructions for a specific trait. An allele is one of two or more forms of a gene.
c. When an individual has two different alleles for a trait, the dominant trait is expressed. The recessive trait is not expressed.
2. a. evolution
b. two or more pairs of alleles
c. dihybrid cross

Understanding Concepts

3. Answer to concept map is found on page 133.
4. See page 118.
5. See page 122.
6. Mendel hypothesized that a pea plant has two hereditary factors for each trait. He then hypothesized that a plant receives one hereditary factor from one parent and the other factor from the other parent.
7. Probability is the likelihood that something will happen. Because the two alleles for a trait segregate into gametes during meiosis, the probability that an egg or a sperm will receive one of these two alleles is 1/2.
8. A mutation is a change in a gene. Mutations are not often expressed in a heterozygote because most mutations are recessive.
9. Both the male and the female rabbits would have brown fur, and both would be homozygous recessive *(bb)*.
10. When the weather is warm, enzymes in the arctic fox make pigments that turn the coat reddish brown. These enzymes do not function during winter, so the fox's coat appears white.
11. No, because pink flowers are the result of a cross between red-flowered and white-flowered snapdragons, an example of

---

review

Understanding Vocabulary

1. For each pair of terms, explain the differences in their meanings.
 a. parental generation, filial generation
 b. gene, allele
 c. dominant, recessive

2. For each set of terms, complete the analogy.
 a. Mendel : heredity :: Darwin : _____
 b. segregation : one pair of alleles :: independent assortment : _____
 c. one trait : monohybrid cross :: two traits : _____

Understanding Concepts

3. **Relating Concepts** Construct a concept map describing the study of genetics. Try to include the following terms in your concept map: chromosomes, factors, traits, dominant, recessive, genotype, alleles, and heredity.

4. **Organizing Information** Identify the three steps of Mendel's experiments with garden-pea plants. Summarize the events and results of each step. In your answer, include a diagram that shows the passage of traits from one generation to the next.

5. **Summarizing Information** Contrast Mendel's two laws: the law of segregation and the law of independent assortment. Explain how these two laws relate to the behaviors of chromosomes during meiosis.

6. **Inferring Conclusions** How did Mendel explain the results of his experiments that led to the law of segregation?

7. **Inferring Relationships** What is probability? Explain why the probability that an egg or a sperm cell will contain one or the other allele for each gene is 1/2.

8. **Summarizing Information** What is a mutation? Explain why mutations are seldom expressed in a heterozygous individual.

---

9. **Predicting Outcomes** In rabbits, the allele for black fur *(B)* is dominant over the allele for brown fur *(b)*. In order for all the offspring to have brown fur, what would the genotype and phenotype of the male and female parents have to be? Draw a Punnett square to support your answer.

10. **Inferring Relationships** How does the environment affect this organism's phenotype?

11. **Predicting Outcomes** A plant breeder wants to produce only pink snapdragons. Can he do so by crossing pink snapdragons and white snapdragons? Explain your answer.

12. **Comparing Functions** Compare incomplete dominance with codominance. Give an example of each pattern of heredity.

13. **Identifying Variables** Is it possible for a woman with type AB blood and a man with type B blood to have a child with type O blood? What possible blood types can their children have? Use a Punnett square to support your answer.

14. **Summarizing Information** What is a polygenetic trait? Give an example.

15. **Inferring Relationships** In Japanese four o'clocks, red flowers show incomplete dominance with white flowers. What color flowers will offspring in the F_1 generation have? Explain your answer. Give the genotypes for the three types of flowers.

16. **Predicting Outcomes** A rough-coated male guinea pig is crossed with a homozygous smooth-coated female *(rr)*. Their offspring are rough-coated and smooth-coated in a 1:1 ratio. Use a Punnett square to calculate the genotype of the male parent.

17. **BUILDING ON WHAT YOU HAVE LEARNED** Based on what you learned in Chapter 6 about the formation of male and female gametes, explain sex inheritance in humans.

---

incomplete dominance.

12. Incomplete dominance occurs when two traits appear to blend in the F_1 generation. An example is pink-flowered snapdragons produced from a cross between red- and white-flowered parents. Codominance occurs when both genes in a heterozygote are fully expressed, for example, when a roan-colored horse results from the cross between red- and white-coated parents.

13. If the mother's genotype is $I^A I^B$ and the father's genotype is $I^B I^B$, they cannot have a

child with blood type O. However, they could have children with blood type A or blood type AB. If the father's genotype is $I^B i$, the couple still cannot have a child with blood type O, but they could have children with blood types A, B, or AB.

14. A polygenic trait is one that is controlled by more than one pair of genes. Examples include human height, weight, and hair and skin color.

15. Like snapdragons, the flowers of the F_1 generation will be pink. The genotypes are red

Interpreting Graphics

18. The Punnett square below shows the cross between two parents heterozygous for two traits. In watermelons, the allele for solid green color *(G)* is dominant over the allele for striped pattern *(g)*. Short shape *(S)* is dominant over long shape *(s)*.

a. What are the genotype and phenotype of each parent?
b. What are the genotype and phenotype of the offspring in block *a*? in block *b*?
c. How many different genotypes are possible among the offspring of this cross?
d. How many different phenotypes are found among the offspring? What is the phenotypic ratio?

		GgSs		
	GS	*Gs*	*gS*	*gs*
GS	*GGSS*	*GGSs*	*GgSS*	*GgSs*
Gs	(a)	*GGss*	*GgSs*	*Ggss*
gS	*GgSS*	(b)	*ggSS*	*ggSs*
gs	*GgSs*	*Ggss*	*ggSs*	*ggss*

(left label: *GgSs*)

Reviewing Themes

19. *Heredity*
Two tall pea plants are crossed. Both plants are heterozygous *(Tt)* for height. How does this information help you predict the genotypic and phenotypic ratios for the offspring?

20. *Evolution*
Explain how mutations contribute to the evolution of a species over time.

Thinking Critically

21. Evaluating Conclusions The offspring of two short-tailed cats exhibit the following phenotypic ratio: 1 tailless:2 short tail:1 long tail. Based on this information, their owner has concluded that tail length is an example of incomplete dominance. Is the owner correct? Include a Punnett square to support your answer.

Life/Work Skills

22. Finding Information Colorblindness in humans is an example of sex-linked inheritance. Use references to find out about the different kinds of colorblindness and how this disorder is inherited. Draw Punnett squares to illustrate your findings.

Activities and Projects

23. History Connection The genetic disorder hemophilia was important to European history because it occurred in certain powerful royal families that were descendants of Queen Victoria. Queen Victoria was heterozygous for the trait and passed the disorder to her children and grandchildren. Research the presence of hemophilia in Queen Victoria's family. Draw a human pedigree that shows how this disorder was passed from generation to generation.

24. Mathematics Connection Probability and the law of independent assortment also apply to games of chance. Many states have lottery drawings in which a person selects five numbers from the numbers 1 to 20. To win, all five numbers must match the randomly selected winning numbers. Imagine that balls numbered from 1 to 20 are placed in a jar. Your chances of matching any number in the jar, say 7, are 1 chance in 20 chances. If you have two identical jars, the chance of drawing a 7 from each jar is $1/20 \times 1/20 = 1/400$, or 1 in 400 chances. If you had five identical jars, what is the chance that the numbers 3, 9, 12, 13, and 18 would be selected—in that order?

Discovering Through Reading

25. Read the article "Micro Gets Macro" by Josie Glausiusz in *Discover*, November 1995, page 40. What are microsatellites, and how are they used by gene mappers?

26. Read the article "Ascent of the Dog" by Rosie Mestel in *Discover*, October 1994, pages 90–98. How does Jasper Rine hope to study the inheritance of traits among different breeds of dogs?

135

square to show that the genotypic ratio is 1:2:1 and the phenotypic ratio is 3:1.

20. Mutations act as a source for the variation that is needed for a species to adapt to changing conditions.

Thinking Critically

21. This example illustrates codominant inheritance. Both parents are heterozygous.

Life/Work Skills

22. Answers will vary. Punnett squares should indicate that colorblindness is a recessive trait carried on the X chromosome.

Activities and Projects

23. Because hemophilia is an example of X-linked inheritance, it is expressed mostly in males. Queen Victoria passed the disorder to her son. Hemophilia also appeared in the sons of three of Queen Victoria's daughters.

24. The answer is $1/20 \times 1/20 \times 1/20 \times 1/20 \times 1/20 = 1/3,200,000$.

Discovering Through Reading

25. Microsatellites are strings of repetitious DNA, with each string consisting of a repeating sequence of two to five nucleotides. Gene mappers use microsatellites as readily distinguishable landmarks.

26. Rine and his colleagues will map each dog's DNA in an effort to link specific characteristics of each animal to unique DNA sequences in that animal's DNA.

---

flowers *(RR)*, white flowers *(WW)*, and pink flowers *(RW)*.

16. The male is heterozygous *(Rr)*.

17. The sex of a child is determined by whether the father's sperm contains an X or Y chromosome. The mother can only give an X, so she has no influence on the sex of the child.

Interpreting Graphics

18. a. Male parent genotype: GgSs; phenotype: green and short. Female parent genotype: GgSs; phenotype: green and short.

b. Block a genotype: GGSs; phenotype: green, short. Block b genotype:GgSs; phenotype: green, short.
c. 9 possible genotypes: GGSS, GGSs, Ggss, GgSS, GgSs, Ggss, ggSS, ggSs, ggss.
d. 4 possible phenotypes; ratio is 9 green short: 3 green long: 3 striped short: 1 striped long.

Reviewing Themes

19. This information can be used in a Punnett

Lesson Planning Guide With Options for Block Scheduling

Lecture Concepts

Lesson Resources

8-1 Understanding DNA

BLOCK ❶ (45 minutes)

1. A series of experiments, starting with the work of Frederick Griffith in 1928, has shown that DNA is the genetic material.

2. In the 1950s, James Watson and Francis Crick determined that the structure of the DNA molecule consists of a double helix.

❶ Lecture Resources
- Determining Prior Knowledge
- Protein or DNA?
- Active Reading: K-W-L
- Visual Strategy: Figure 8-1
- Visual Strategy: Videodisc
- Teaching Transparencies: 33
- Holt Biology Videodiscs Lesson 8-1

Classwork Options
- Laboratory Techniques and Experimental Design: Lab C14

Assignment Options
- Hershey and Chase's Experiment
- Teaching Resources CD-ROM: Supplemental Reading Guides 6

BLOCK ❷ (45 minutes)

3. The DNA molecule can make a copy of itself in a process called replication.

❷ Lecture Resources
- Active Reading: K-W-L
- Teaching Transparencies: 25A
- Holt Biology Videodiscs Lesson 8-1

Classwork Options
- Chargaff's Rule
- Closure: Sequencing Events

Assignment Options
- Reteaching
- Section Review
- Chapter Review, questions 1a, 2a, 4, 5, 6, 7, 8, 9, 10, 11, 29
- Directed Reading Worksheet

8-2 How Proteins Are Made

BLOCK ❸ (45 minutes)

1. DNA directs the synthesis of RNA in a process called transcription. RNA directs the synthesis of proteins in a process called translation.

2. Three types of RNA are involved in protein synthesis: messenger RNA (mRNA), transfer RNA (tRNA), and ribosomal RNA (rRNA).

❸ Lecture Resources
- Replication and Transcription Enzymes
- Active Reading: Brainstorming
- Visual Strategy: Figure 8-6
- Visual Strategy: Videodisc
- Demonstration: Predicting Outcomes
- Teaching Transparencies: 34, 35, 36
- Holt Biology Videodiscs Lesson 8-1

Classwork Options
- Biotechnology: Lab D2

Assignment Options
- Life/Work Skills: Communicating

BLOCK ❹ (45 minutes)

3. The genetic information in DNA is transcribed into mRNA as a triplet combination known as a codon. The mRNA codon is matched by a triplet combination in the tRNA known as an anticodon. The codon-anticodon match determines which amino acid is inserted into the protein being synthesized on the ribosomes.

4. The genetic code in DNA is universal because a particular codon specifies the same amino acid in all organisms.

❹ Lecture Resources
- Visual Strategy: Videodisc
- Demonstration: Identifying Structures
- Teaching Transparencies: 37
- Holt Biology Videodiscs Lesson 8-2

Classwork Options
- Demonstration: Predicting Outcomes, p. 144
- Reteaching

- Closure: Recognizing Relationships
- Exploration 8A

Assignment Options
- Demonstration: Predicting Outcomes, p. 145
- Section Review
- Chapter Review, questions 1b, 2b, 3, 13, 14, 15, 16, 20, 21, 22, 28
- Directed Reading Worksheet

8-3 Regulating Gene Expression

BLOCK ❺ (45 minutes)

1. In prokaryotes, a repressor protein attaches to DNA and switches off genes by preventing transcription.

2. An inducer turns on genes by combining with the repressor so that it can no longer attach to the DNA and inhibit transcription.

❺ Lecture Resources
- Demonstration: Interpreting a Model
- Teaching Transparencies: 27A
- Holt Biology Videodiscs Lesson 8-3

Classwork Options
- Interactive Explorations Laboratory Manual: Lab E4

Assignment Options
- World of Work: Protein Chemist

Lecture Concepts

Lesson Resources

8-3 Regulating Gene Expression, *continued*

BLOCK ❻ (45 minutes)

3. An activator facilitates transcription by helping the DNA unwind and allowing RNA polymerase to bind to the DNA.

4. In eukaryotes, the DNA contains intron and exon regions. Exons are the regions that code for proteins.

5. Transposons are genes that can move from one location in a chromosome to another.

❻ Lecture Resources
- ■ Reteaching
- ■ Closure: Evaluating Information
- 🗋 Teaching Transparencies: 26A
- ⊘ Holt Biology Videodiscs Lesson 8-3

Classwork Options
- 🗋 Inquiry Skills Development: Lab B6

Assignment Options
- ■ Section Review
- ■ Chapter Review, questions 1c, 2c, 17, 18, 19, 23, 24, 25, 26, 27, 30, 31
- ■ Directed Reading Worksheet

Chapter Review and Assessment

BLOCK ❼ (45 minutes)

Review
- ■ Reteaching Worksheet
- ■ Thinking Skills Worksheet
- ■ Vocabulary Development Worksheet
- ◎ Language Development and Reading Comprehension Audio CD Program: Chapter 8

BLOCK ❽ (45 minutes)

Assessment
- ■ Alternative Assessment, p. 149
- ■ Portfolio Assessment, p. T39

Chapter Test
- ■ Chapter 8 Test

Test Generator
- ◎ Item bank for customizing Chapter Tests

Teaching Resources CD-ROM
- ◎ Scoring Rubrics and Classroom Management Checklist

The Portfolio icon denotes items throughout the Teacher's Edition lesson wrap that may be selected for inclusion in student portfolios.

Holt Biology Videodiscs and *Concepts of Biology*

Holt Biology Videodiscs gives you a powerful tool for teaching, review, and assessment. For further information regarding the media on the videodiscs, see ***Holt Biology Videodiscs Teacher's Correlation Guide to Holt Biology: Visualizing Life.***

Concepts of Biology adds interactive lesson plans and extensive tools for customization using CD-ROM technology.

Use the following topic from ***Concepts of Biology*** to help you teach this chapter:
Topic 7: How Genes Work

Laboratory Planning

Text
Materials and preparation instructions appear on the teacher's wrap accompanying each laboratory exercise.
Block 4: Exploration 8A: Modeling the Effect of a Mutation, p. 780

Holt BioSources Laboratory Program
Block 1: Laboratory Techniques and Experimental Design Lab C14: Karyotyping
Block 3: Biotechnology Lab D2: Laboratory Techniques: Extracting DNA
Block 5: Interactive Explorations Laboratory Manual Lab E4: Gene Regulation
Block 6: Inquiry Skills Development Lab B6: Effect of Environment on Gene Expression

Determining Prior Knowledge

- Have students recall the structure of proteins and nucleic acids, as described in Chapter 2.
- Have students explain the following statement: DNA contains the genetic code.
- Ask students to explain how a newly formed cell gets the genetic information it needs to function.

Active READING

Technique: K-W-L

Before students read this chapter, have them write short individual lists of all the things they already **K**now (or think they know) about DNA. When students have finished their lists, ask them to contribute their entries to a group list on the board or on the overhead. Then have students list the things they **W**ant to know about DNA. Have students save their lists for later use in Active Reading on page 140.

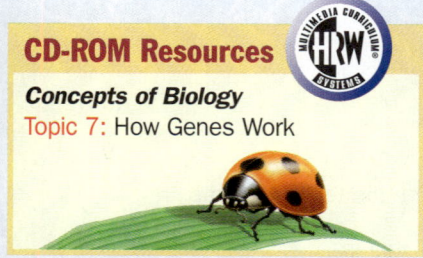

CD-ROM Resources

Concepts of Biology
Topic 7: How Genes Work

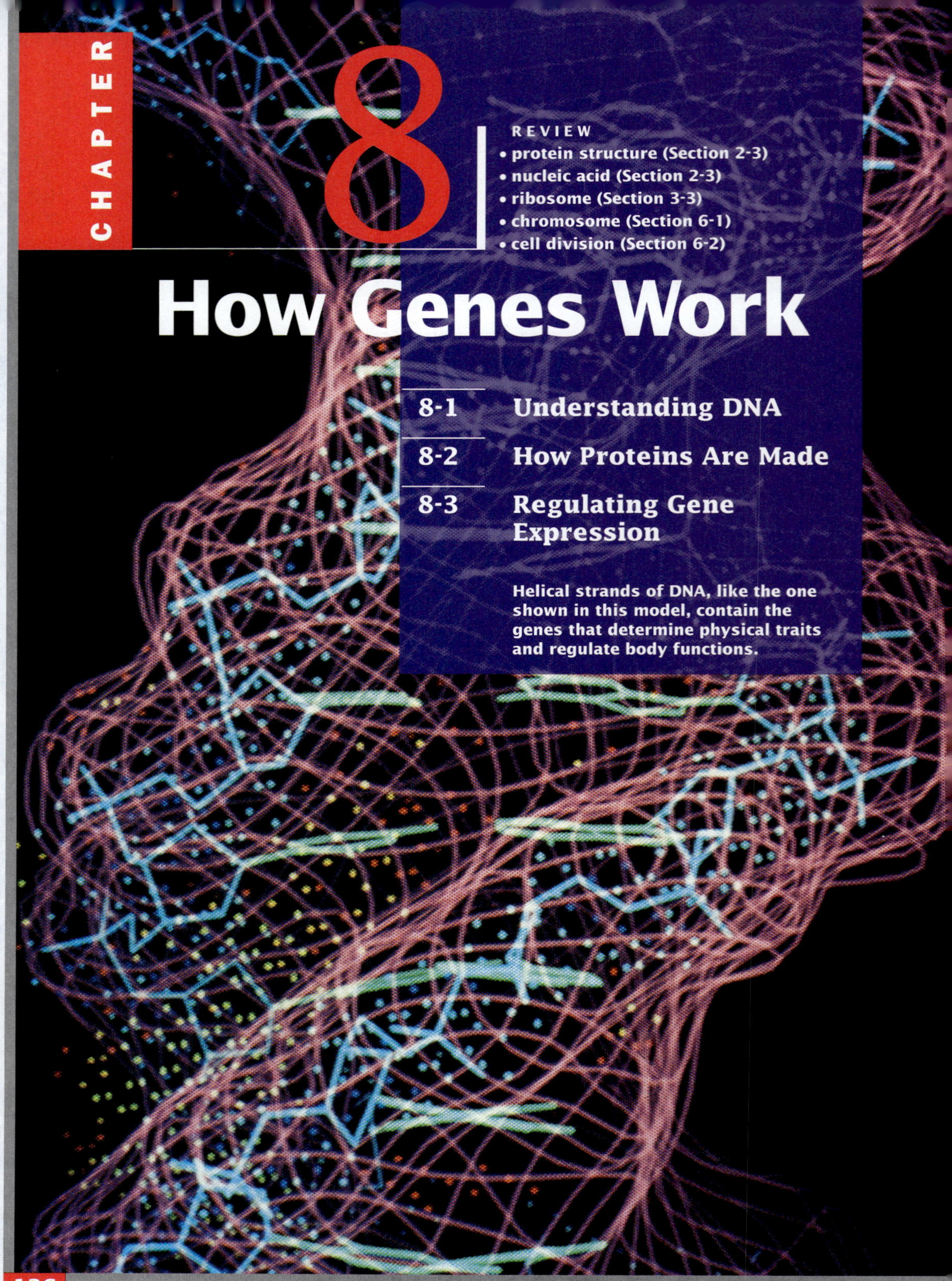

CHAPTER

8

REVIEW
- protein structure (Section 2-3)
- nucleic acid (Section 2-3)
- ribosome (Section 3-3)
- chromosome (Section 6-1)
- cell division (Section 6-2)

How Genes Work

Helical strands of DNA, like the one shown in this model, contain the genes that determine physical traits and regulate body functions.

Author's Rationale   This chapter describes how DNA encodes information about proteins, how that information is passed to ribosomes, and how ribosomes use it to assemble proteins. The key element of this chapter is the explanation of how cells control the process of gene expression. Students also learn about the genetic code and its universality among nearly all living organisms.

Mendel showed that traits are passed from parents to off-spring in the form of discrete packages of genetic material that sort independently of each other. Then scientists set out to determine how a gene actually operates.

8-1 Understanding DNA

OBJECTIVES

1 List the events that led scientists to identify the genetic material.

2 Summarize how scientists determined the structure of DNA.

3 Describe the structure of the DNA molecule.

4 Summarize the process of DNA replication.

How Scientists Identified the Genetic Material

Scientists set out to identify the chemical substances in chromosomes that store and transmit genetic traits. Was it DNA or protein? Answers came from medical studies involving two forms, or strains, of the bacterium *Pneumococcus.* One strain is **virulent** (*VEER yoo luhnt*), or disease-causing, and causes pneumonia. The other strain is nonvirulent, or harmless.

Griffith studies bacteria

In 1928 in London, a bacteriologist named Frederick Griffith was working out a way to identify two strains of *Pneumococcus.* He found that one strain formed rough colonies in a petri dish. The other strain formed smooth colonies. To determine which bacteria were virulent, he injected the two different strains into mice. The bacteria from the smooth colonies were virulent and killed mice **(Figure 8-1a)**. The

bacteria from the rough colonies were nonvirulent and didn't harm the mice **(Figure 8-1b)**.

Griffith found that if he killed the virulent bacteria with heat, they lost their ability to cause disease in mice **(Figure 8-1c)**. However, heat-killed virulent bacteria (now made harmless) mixed with nonvirulent bacteria (also harmless) had deadly results. Mice injected with these two seemingly harmless bacterial strains became ill and died **(Figure 8-1d)**. Furthermore, when Griffith examined bacteria taken from the dead mice, he found living virulent bacteria even though the only living bacteria that had been injected were the nonvirulent ones. Nonvirulent bacteria had changed to virulent bacteria by taking in something from the virulent bacteria. Griffith had discovered **transformation**, a process in which a bacterium takes up foreign DNA.

Figure 8-1
Griffith's experiment showed that nonvirulent bacteria could acquire the ability to cause disease from virulent bacteria.

c Virulent bacteria killed with heat did not harm mice.

d A mixture of nonvirulent bacteria and heat-killed virulent bacteria killed mice.

a Virulent bacteria from smooth colonies killed mice.

b Nonvirulent bacteria from rough colonies did not harm mice.

137

Videodisc Resources

Holt Biology Videodiscs
Lesson 8-1: Understanding DNA

Phase One
Preparation

Scheduling
See the **Lesson Planning Guide** on pages 135A and 135B for lecture, classwork, and assignment options for Section 8-1.

Phase Two
Teaching Strategies

Visual Strategy   Figure 8-1

■ **Analyzing Results**
Lead students through each of the four illustrations depicting Griffith's experiment. Ask them why Griffith may have been puzzled by the results of his experiment. Explain that he thought he had made an error in the procedures and therefore repeated the experiment many times. Each time, the results were the same. Ask students why Griffith concluded that the living virulent bacteria he found in the dead mice had come from the living nonvirulent bacteria that were in the mixture.

Key to Strategies
Teaching Strategies are keyed to three tiers of learning.

● **Understanding Concepts (Tier I)**
Content mastery and comprehension

■ **Applying Information (Tier II)**
Applying and analyzing content

▲ **Critical Thinking (Tier III)**
Practicing evaluative thinking

Protein or DNA?

▲ **Forming Opinions by Sound Reasoning**

Explain to students that many scientists were reluctant to accept the results of experiments that suggested DNA was the hereditary material. Ask students to explain why most scientists initially thought that the hereditary material was protein, not DNA. Prepare them for this task by having them consider the structures of both proteins and DNA. *(Students should recall that proteins are made from 20 different amino acids that can be combined in a variety of ways. DNA, on the other hand, has a relatively simple structure that consists basically of four nucleotide bases. Scientists reasoned that the complex processes involved in heredity must be controlled by a complex molecule—protein rather than DNA.)*

Hershey and Chase's Experiment

● **Summarizing Information**

Have students design a **Graphic Organizer** like the one shown at the bottom of the page to summarize Hershey and Chase's experiment. Have them include a paragraph that explains how the experiment proved that DNA is the genetic material.

Avery identifies the agent of transformation

In 1944 in New York, a biologist named Oswald Avery was very interested in Griffith's discovery. Avery wanted to identify the substance that made the nonvirulent bacteria become virulent. Was this substance DNA or protein? Avery and two colleagues modified Griffith's experiment. They extracted DNA from bacteria in smooth colonies and added it to bacteria in rough colonies. Some of the bacteria that grew from this mixture formed smooth colonies.

In a separate experiment, Avery found that when he added protein-destroying enzymes to bacteria, transformation still occurred. However, when DNA-destroying enzymes were added to bacteria, transformation did not occur. Avery's work provided clear evidence that DNA was the genetic material in these bacteria.

Figure 8-2

a Hershey and Chase used radioactive elements to label the DNA and the protein coats of viruses.

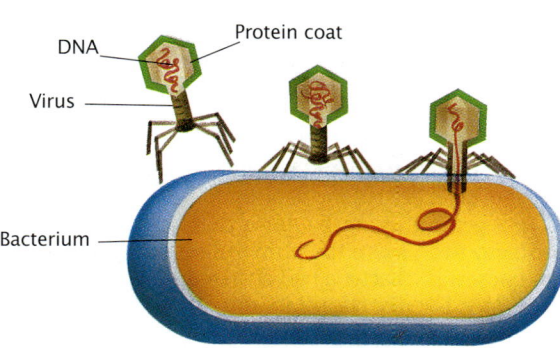

DNA
Protein coat
Virus
Bacterium

b They infected bacteria with the radioactive viruses. When sufficient time had passed, Hershey and Chase used a blender to detach the remains of the viruses.

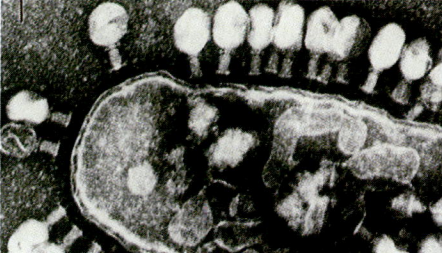

c After examining the remains, Hershey and Chase found that DNA, not protein, was injected into the cell.

Hershey and Chase confirm that DNA is the genetic material

At first, Avery's results were not widely appreciated. Many biologists were reluctant to give up the idea that protein was the genetic material. In 1952, however, Alfred Hershey and Martha Chase, two scientists at Cold Spring Harbor Laboratory on Long Island, New York, performed an experiment using viruses that infect bacteria. These viruses attach to the surfaces of bacteria and inject their hereditary information into the cells like tiny hypodermic needles. Once inside the bacteria, this hereditary information directs the production of hundreds of new viruses. When the new viruses are mature, they burst out of the infected bacteria and attack new cells. These bacteria-infecting viruses have a very simple structure: a core of DNA surrounded by a protein coat.

To identify the hereditary material, Hershey and Chase did two experiments using viruses with radioactive labels, as summarized in **Figure 8-2**. One experiment used viruses with radioactive sulfur (^{35}S), and one used viruses with radioactive phosphorus (^{32}P). Hershey and Chase used one kind of virus to infect one batch of bacteria and the other kind of virus to infect another batch of bacteria. After allowing enough time for the viruses to attach to the bacteria and inject their genetic material, Hershey and Chase put the two batches of bacteria separately into an ordinary food blender to detach the protein coats. When they examined the remains of the bacteria infected by the ^{35}S-labeled viruses, they found the protein outside the bacteria, but it was not found in any of the new viruses that resulted from this infection. When they examined the remains of the bacteria infected by the ^{32}P-labeled viruses, they found the DNA inside the bacteria as well as in the new viruses that resulted from this infection. The conclusion was undeniable—DNA is the hereditary material.

138

Graphic Organizer

Use the following graphic organizer with **Hershey and Chase's Experiment** on page 138.

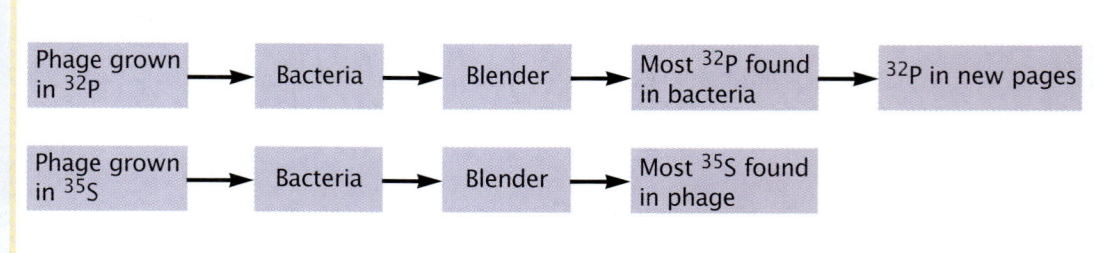

Phage grown in ^{32}P → Bacteria → Blender → Most ^{32}P found in bacteria → ^{32}P in new pages

Phage grown in ^{35}S → Bacteria → Blender → Most ^{35}S found in phage

How Scientists Determined the Structure of DNA

Scientists knew that DNA was composed of subunits called **nucleotides** (*NOO klee oh tydz*). A nucleotide has three parts: a sugar called deoxyribose, a phosphate group, and a base. The sugar and phosphate group are the same in every nucleotide, but the base can be one of four kinds. The two larger bases, adenine and guanine, are called **purines** (*PYUR eenz*). The two smaller bases, cytosine and thymine, are called **pyrimidines** (*py RIHM uh deenz*)

In 1949 Erwin Chargaff, a biochemist working at Columbia University in New York City, made a key discovery about the structure of DNA by analyzing DNA samples from different organisms. He found that the amount of adenine in a DNA molecule always equals the amount of thymine (A = T). Likewise, the amount of guanine always equals the amount of cytosine (G = C). These observations, now known as Chargaff's rules, suggested a regularity in the composition of DNA.

The value of Chargaff's rules became clear when Rosalind Franklin, a chemist working at King's College in London, began studying the structure of DNA using X-ray diffraction. Franklin's X-ray diffraction images, one of which is shown in **Figure 8-3**, suggested that the DNA molecule resembles a tightly coiled spring, a shape called a helix.

Watson and Crick build a model showing DNA's structure

In the early 1950s a young American scientist, James Watson, went to Cambridge, England, on a research fellowship. At Cavendish Laboratories he worked with Francis Crick, a British physicist interested in DNA. Together, Watson and Crick attempted to construct a model of DNA. They applied the clues provided by Chargaff's rules and Franklin's X-ray diffraction studies. Using brass and wire models of the bases, sugars, and phosphate groups, Watson and Crick deduced that the structure of the DNA molecule is a **double helix**, a spiral staircase composed of two strands of nucleotides whose bases face each other. The double helix is held together by weak hydrogen bonds between the bases. Adenine can form hydrogen bonds only with thymine, and guanine can form hydrogen bonds only with cytosine. **Figure 8-4** shows the structure of DNA. Francis Crick and James Watson were awarded the Nobel Prize in 1962 for their development of this model.

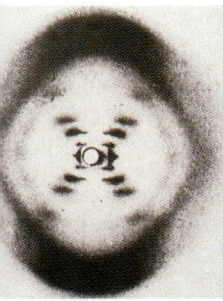

Figure 8-3
This X-ray diffraction photograph taken by Rosalind Franklin provided evidence that DNA was shaped like a helix.

Figure 8-4
a An organism's hereditary information is contained in its chromosomes. Each chromosome is made of a long DNA molecule.

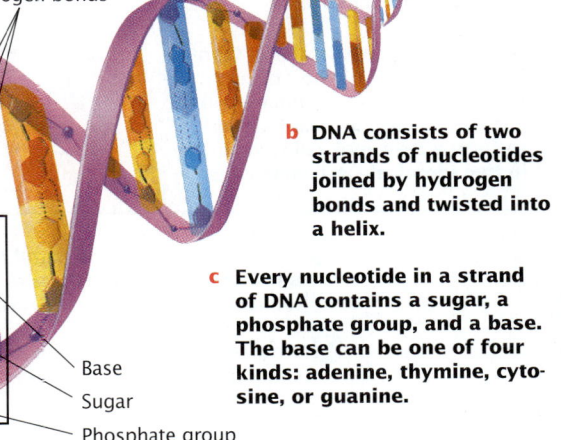

Adenine
Thymine
Guanine
Cytosine
Hydrogen bonds
Base
Sugar
Phosphate group

b DNA consists of two strands of nucleotides joined by hydrogen bonds and twisted into a helix.

c Every nucleotide in a strand of DNA contains a sugar, a phosphate group, and a base. The base can be one of four kinds: adenine, thymine, cytosine, or guanine.

139

Historical Perspective: Rosalind Franklin

Although Franklin's X-ray diffraction photograph was crucial to solving the puzzle of the structure of DNA, she never received the credit that Watson and Crick did. She died from cancer at age 37, before her accomplishments were fully recognized.

Chargaff's Rule
■ **Analyzing Data**
Place the following information on the board to illustrate Chargaff's rule:

	A	T	G	C
Animals				
human	30.4	30.1	19.6	19.9
sheep	29.3	28.3	21.4	21.0
sea urchin	32.8	32.1	17.7	17.3
salmon	29.7	29.1	20.8	20.4
Plants				
wheat	27.3	27.1	22.7	22.8
Bacteria				
E. coli	24.7	23.6	26.0	25.7
Viruses				
lambda	21.3	22.9	28.6	27.2

Tell students that the values in the table represent the percentage of each nucleotide base found in an organism's DNA. The A-T and G-C percentages are not exactly equal because of the experimental error involved in measuring the amounts of nucleotide bases present in an organism's DNA. Ask students to draw conclusions about the percentages and ratios of purines and pyrimidines among various organisms. (*Students can conclude that the DNA in these organisms follows Chargaff's rule, that the percentages of A-T and G-C vary among organisms, and that the ratio of purines to pyrimidines is 1:1.*)

Visual Strategy   Videodisc

■ **Recognizing Relationships**
Use *Video–DNA: Replication* shown in Chapter 8 Section 8-1 of **Holt Biology Videodiscs Teacher's Correlation Guide to Holt Biology: Visualizing Life** to introduce replication on page 140. Instruct students to pay close attention to the nucleotide pairing. Then show *Step-Frame–DNA: Replication* and have students identify the nucleotides and predict the base sequence that will appear on the complementary strand.

Key to Strategies
● **Understanding Concepts (Tier I)**
■ **Applying Information (Tier II)**
▲ **Critical Thinking (Tier III)**

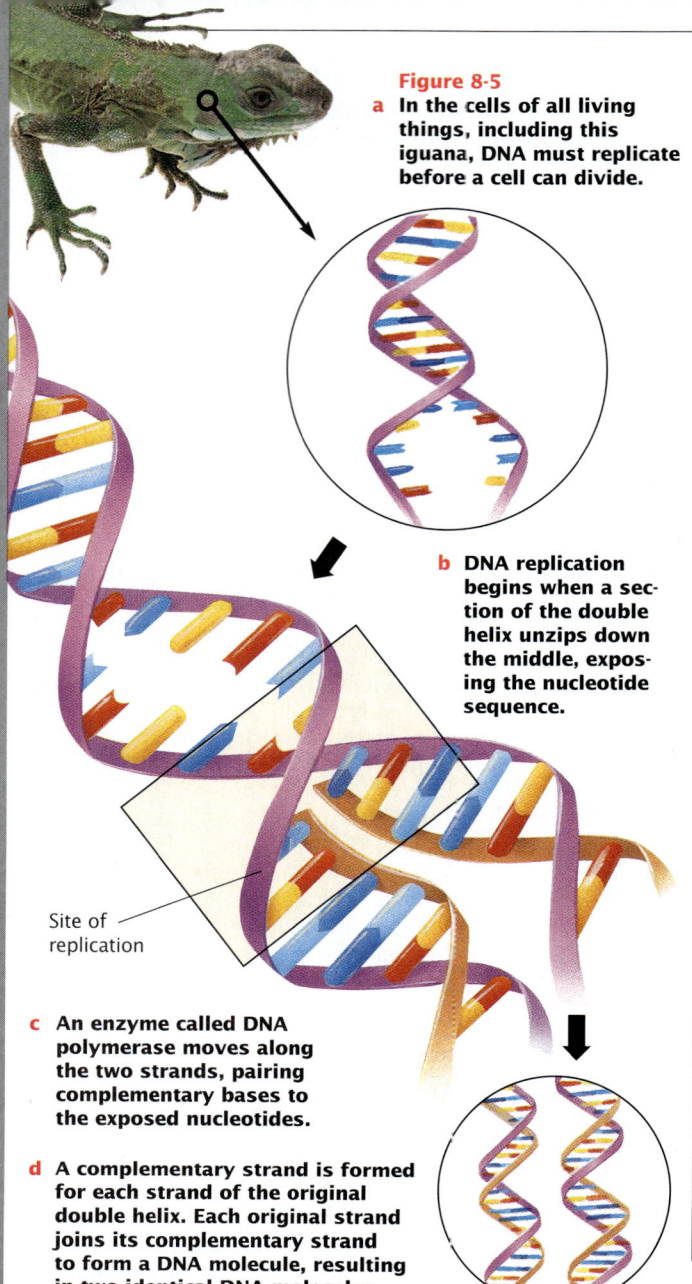

Figure 8-5

a In the cells of all living things, including this iguana, DNA must replicate before a cell can divide.

b DNA replication begins when a section of the double helix unzips down the middle, exposing the nucleotide sequence.

Site of replication

c An enzyme called DNA polymerase moves along the two strands, pairing complementary bases to the exposed nucleotides.

d A complementary strand is formed for each strand of the original double helix. Each original strand joins its complementary strand to form a DNA molecule, resulting in two identical DNA molecules.

How DNA Is Copied

Before a cell can successfully divide, its genetic information must be copied precisely. The process of copying DNA is called **replication**. To be successful, a model of DNA must be able to explain how replication could take place. Watson and Crick's double helix model readily suggested a mechanism. According to their model, the two strands of the double helix are complementary to each other; that is, the sequence of bases on one strand determines the sequence of bases on the other strand. For example, if the sequence of one strand of a DNA molecule is ATTGCAT, the sequence of the partner strand *must* be TAACGTA. Watson and Crick pointed out that if the two strands of the DNA molecule were separated, each strand would expose all of the necessary information to build two identical strands.

The actual process of replication, illustrated in **Figure 8-5**, is complex and requires the assistance of several enzymes. One enzyme is responsible for breaking the hydrogen bonds between base pairs and untwisting the two strands. Other enzymes work to shuttle the correct complementary nucleotides to the exposed strands. Replication occurs simultaneously at many points along a single human DNA molecule.

Replication preserves the sequence of bases in an organism's DNA. However, mutations can occur. Some mutations arise when a base is accidentally inserted or left out during replication. Other mutations are caused by **mutagens**, environmental agents such as ultraviolet light and chemicals that can alter the structure of DNA.

SECTION REVIEW

1 What did Griffith, Avery, and Hershey and Chase contribute to identifying the genetic material?

2 What evidence did Watson and Crick use to deduce the structure of DNA?

3 What are the restrictions on the pairing of the four different nucleotide bases in the double helix?

4 How does replication ensure that identical copies of DNA are made?

140

How is the information in DNA used? Scientists now know that DNA directs the construction of proteins. Proteins help determine the structure of cells and increase the rates of chemical reactions, such as those that occur during metabolism and photosynthesis.

8-2 How Proteins Are Made

OBJECTIVES

❶ Summarize the process of gene expression.

❷ Describe how RNA is made.

❸ Explain why the genetic code is said to be universal.

❹ Explain the relationships among codons, anticodons, and amino acids.

The Transfer of Genetic Information

Once scientists understood the structure of DNA, they were able to study how a specific protein is built from information found in the DNA of one gene. Scientists now know that DNA is used as a blueprint to make a similar molecule called **ribonucleic acid**, or RNA for short. This RNA molecule then directs the formation of proteins. **Gene expression** is the use of the genetic information in DNA to make proteins. Gene expression takes place in two stages. The first stage is called **transcription**. During transcription, an RNA copy of a gene is made. During **translation**, the second stage of gene expression, three different kinds of RNA work together to assemble amino acids into a protein molecule. The process of gene expression is summarized in **Figure 8-6**.

Through gene expression, the information encoded in DNA directs all cellular activities. For example, when you eat carbohydrates, such as those found in a bowl of cereal or a slice of bread, certain genes direct the production of a protein called insulin. Insulin helps your body maintain its blood-sugar level. Other genes direct the production of thousands of other structural proteins and enzymes.

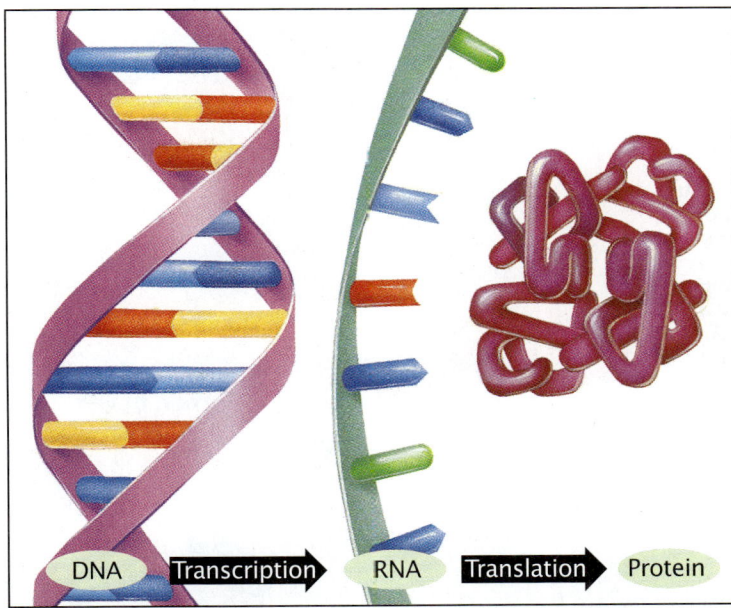

Figure 8-6
During gene expression, the information in DNA is used to assemble proteins.

DNA → Transcription → RNA → Translation → Protein

141

Phase One
Preparation

Scheduling
See the **Lesson Planning Guide** on pages 135A and 135B for lecture, classwork, and assignment options for Section 8-2.

Phase Two
Teaching Strategies

Active READING

Technique: Brainstorming
Tell students that the first page of Section 8-2 provides an overview of the contents of the section and hints at the organizational pattern of the section. Pair each student with a partner. Have each pair of students read the first page of the section aloud, sharing the reading equally. Then ask students to answer the following questions:
• What is the subject of this section?
• What passages or words led you to this conclusion?
• How will this section be organized?
• What words or sentences support this conclusion?

Visual Strategy | **Figure 8-6**

● **Comparing Functions**
Use Figure 8-6 to emphasize the importance of proteins in determining an organism's individuality. Many organisms have the same carbohydrates and lipids, although not necessarily in the same amounts. However, no two individuals (except clones and identical twins) have the same combination of proteins. Thus, organisms are unique because of their proteins, which are determined by the genetic code contained in DNA.

Key to Strategies
● Understanding Concepts (Tier I)
■ Applying Information (Tier II)
▲ Critical Thinking (Tier III)

How Genes Work   141

142   Chapter 8

Demonstration
■ Predicting Outcomes
Have each student write a sequence of 18 bases that might be found in a segment of a DNA molecule. Then instruct them to transcribe this sequence into a strand of RNA. Make sure that each A in DNA has been correctly transcribed into the complementary U in the mRNA. Have students keep their sequences for later use, when they will examine how translation operates.

Replication and Transcription Enzymes
■ Interpreting Data
Inform students that cells contain less DNA polymerase (used for replication) than they do RNA polymerase (used for transcription). Ask students to explain these data. *(An organism needs more protein than it does DNA. Proteins are required for life-sustaining metabolic processes and structural components, whereas DNA is needed only as a blueprint.)*

Visual Strategy   Videodisc
■ Recognizing Relationships
Use *Video–DNA-RNA Transcription* shown in Chapter 8 Section 8-2 of *Holt Biology Videodiscs Teacher's Correlation Guide to Holt Biology: Visualizing Life* to introduce the concept of transcription. Continue by using *Step-Frame Sequence–Transcription.* Afterward, have students compare and contrast replication and transcription.

How DNA Makes RNA

Transcription is the process by which genetic information encoded in DNA is transferred to an RNA molecule. Genetic information must be copied because DNA cannot leave the nucleus. Just as an architect protects building plans from loss or damage by keeping them in a central place, your cells protect genetic information by keeping the DNA safe within the nucleus. Instead of sending out the DNA, copies of genes are sent out into the cell to direct the assembly of proteins. These working copies of genes are single strands of RNA.

RNA is chemically similar to DNA except that its sugar, ribose, has an additional oxygen atom, and the base thymine (T) is replaced by a structurally similar base called uracil (U). RNA occurs in three different forms. Figure 8-7 shows transcription of one form of RNA, messenger RNA (mRNA). Just as monks once copied manuscripts by faithfully transcribing each letter, enzymes in your cells' nuclei make mRNA copies of your genes by copying their nucleotides.

Like DNA replication, transcription is a complex process that requires the help of enzymes. Transcription begins when the enzyme RNA polymerase binds to a region of DNA called a promoter. Once bound to a promoter, the RNA polymerase unwinds the double helix and separates a section of the two DNA strands. As shown in Figure 8-7, RNA polymerase moves along one strand of the DNA like a train on a track. As it proceeds, complementary base-pairing takes place between the DNA strand and nucleotides. RNA polymerase joins these nucleotides one right after the other, forming a chain of single-stranded RNA. This process continues until a specific "stop" sequence in the DNA is reached. The polymerase then detaches from the DNA, and the RNA strand drifts free. In eukaryotes, after transcription of a gene is finished, the mRNA passes out of the nucleus and into the cytoplasm through pores in the nuclear membrane. There the second stage of gene expression, translation, takes place.

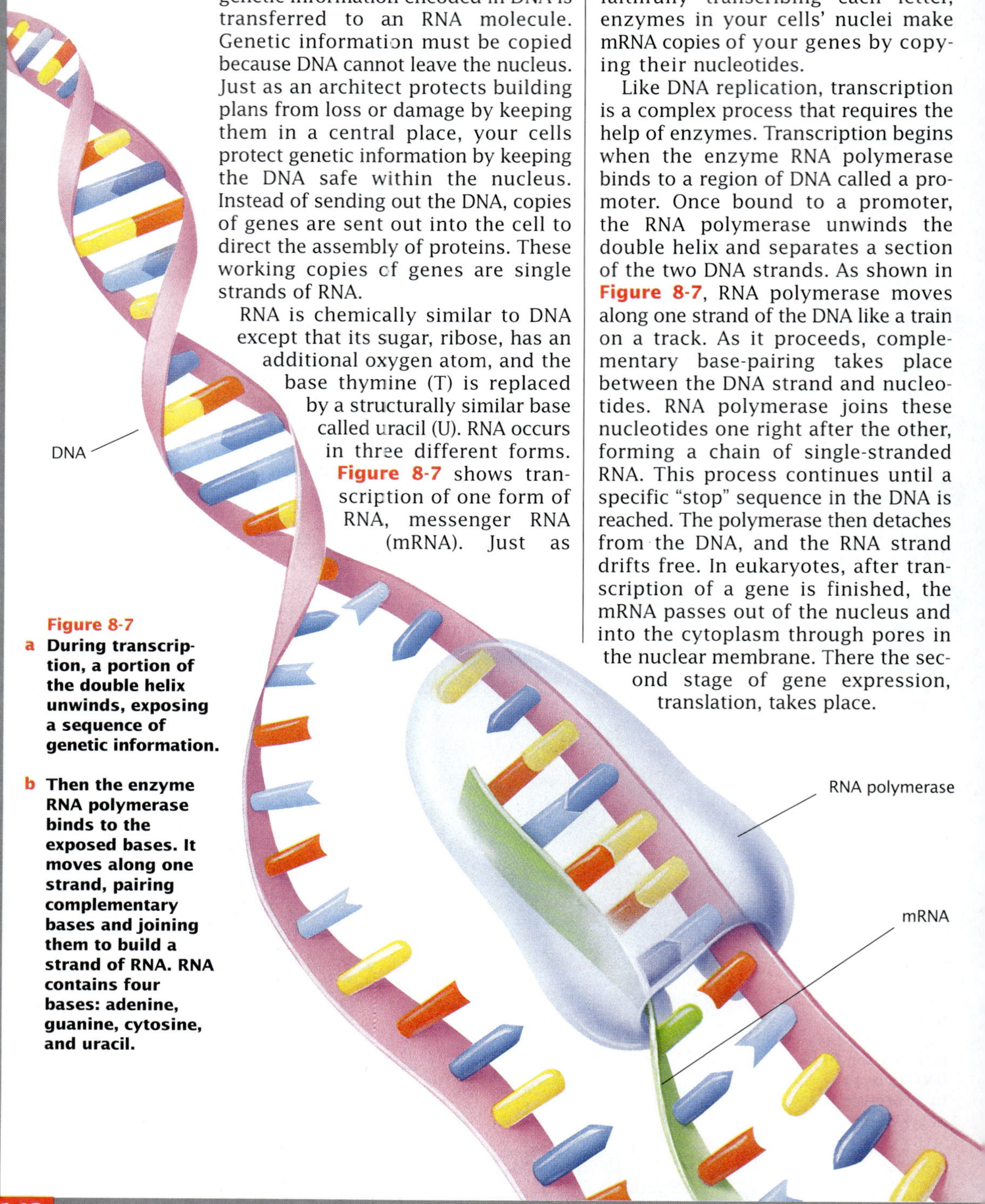

DNA

Figure 8-7
a During transcription, a portion of the double helix unwinds, exposing a sequence of genetic information.

b Then the enzyme RNA polymerase binds to the exposed bases. It moves along one strand, pairing complementary bases and joining them to build a strand of RNA. RNA contains four bases: adenine, guanine, cytosine, and uracil.

RNA polymerase

mRNA

142

Matter of Fact: Transcription
Only one strand of DNA serves as a template during transcription. The nontranscribed strand is called the "antisense" strand. The RNA that is synthesized is complementary (not identical) to the template strand and identical (with the exception of U substituting for T) to the "antisense" strand.

Figure 8-8
In the genetic code, each amino acid is coded for by three mRNA bases arranged in a specific sequence.

b The second base is at the top of the chart.

c The third base in the codon is found along the right side of the chart.

a The first base in a codon is found along the left side of the chart.

1st ↓	2nd → U	C	A	G	
U	Phenylalanine Phenylalanine Leucine Leucine	Serine Serine Serine Serine	Tyrosine Tyrosine *Stop* *Stop*	Cysteine Cysteine *Stop* Tryptophan	U C A G
C	Leucine Leucine Leucine Leucine	Proline Proline Proline Proline	Histidine Histidine Glutamine Glutamine	Arginine Arginine Arginine Arginine	U C A G
A	Isoleucine Isoleucine Isoleucine Methionine	Threonine Threonine Threonine Threonine	Asparagine Asparagine Lysine Lysine	Serine Serine Arginine Arginine	U C A G
G	Valine Valine Valine Valine	Alanine Alanine Alanine Alanine	Aspartic acid Aspartic acid Glutamic acid Glutamic acid	Glycine Glycine Glycine Glycine	U C A G

The Genetic Code

Evolution

How is the DNA of all organisms similar?

How is mRNA translated into the sequence of amino acids that make up proteins? How can the four nucleotide bases found in mRNA carry instructions to build the thousands of proteins your body needs? Every three nucleotides in mRNA specify a particular amino acid. Each nucleotide triplet in mRNA is called a **codon** (KOH dahn). The order of bases in a codon determines which amino acid will be added to a growing protein chain. In turn, the order of amino acids will determine the structure and function of a protein.

To learn more about how mRNA directs amino acids to join in a specific order, biologists performed laboratory experiments using artificial mRNA to direct protein production. An mRNA molecule that contained only the nucleotide uracil (U), for example, made a protein that consisted entirely of the amino acid phenylalanine. This information told scientists that the codon "UUU" codes for the amino acid phenylalanine. These experiments ulti-mately revealed the genetic code, which is shown in **Figure 8-8**. The **genetic code** is the correspondence between nucleotide triplets in DNA and the amino acids in proteins. Any of the four bases (U, C, A, G) found in mRNA can occur at any of the three positions of a codon. Thus, 64 different possible three-letter codons ($4 \times 4 \times 4 = 64$) are possible in the genetic code. Since there are 64 possible codons but only 20 different amino acids, more than one codon may specify a single amino acid. Codons known as "stop" codons specify the end of an amino-acid sequence.

The genetic code is the same in nearly all organisms, so it is said to be universal. For example, the code for phenylalanine is the same in bacteria and humans. The universality of the genetic code supports the view that the code had originated at least by the time bacteria evolved, over 3.5 billion years ago. The genetic code may be considered the oldest of languages.

Mathematics Connection
A Triplet Code
Have students explain why a genetic code consisting of either one base or two bases would not be effective. Prepare them for this activity by having them recall how many different amino acids are found in proteins. (Because 20 amino acids are used to synthesize proteins, a one- or two-base system would not provide enough combinations for the 20 different amino acids. Only 4^1, or 4, combinations are possible with a one-base code, while only 4^2, or 16, are possible with a two-base code. A three-base system provides 4^3, or 64, combinations and redundancy.)

Theme Answer
Evolution
The DNA in all organisms consists of the same four nucleotide bases, and the same triplet combination specifies the same amino acid in all organisms.

Life/Work Skills
Communicating

▲ **Justifying Conclusions**
Tell students to assume that they have encountered a person who has never heard of DNA. Assign four students to a cooperative work group. Have each group prepare a persuasive argument that DNA is the genetic code. Require that each group include at least four supporting statements.

Historical Perspective: DNA

DNA was first isolated in 1869, by a German physician named Friedrich Miescher. Miescher reported that the chemical substance he isolated from white blood cells was white, sugary, and slightly acidic. Because he found it only in the nuclei of these cells, he called it nuclein.

Key to Strategies
● Understanding Concepts (Tier I)
■ Applying Information (Tier II)
▲ Critical Thinking (Tier III)

Connection: *Chapter 3*

Protein Synthesis
Review the roles that ribosomes, the endoplasmic reticulum, and Golgi bodies play in eukaryotic cells.

Visual Strategy | Videodisc

● **Identifying Functions**
Use *Video–Protein Synthesis: Translation* shown in Chapter 8 Section 8-2 of **Holt Biology Videodiscs Teacher's Correlation Guide to Holt Biology: Visualizing Life** to introduce students to the concept of translation. Instruct students to pay close attention to the roles of mRNA and tRNA. After viewing the video, have students formulate descriptions of each kind of RNA.

Demonstration

● **Identifying Structures**
Materials: licorice strands, large paper clips, paper
Divide the class into groups of three students, and distribute the materials to each group. Challenge the groups to develop a model of translation using the materials and their hands. Have each group present its model to the class. *(One possible model is as follows: One student places a fist into the palm of another student's hands to represent the ribosome. A licorice strand, representing the mRNA, is draped over the fist. A large paper clip is bent into a clover-leaf shape, representing the tRNA, and a piece of paper, cut to represent an amino acid, is attached to one end. Finally, a flattened end of the paper clip is attached to the licorice.)*

Demonstration

■ **Predicting Outcomes**
Using the 18-base sequence previously transcribed to RNA (on page 142), have students divide the sequence into codons. Then have them write down the sequence of the anticodons to see how mRNA and tRNA interact during translation.

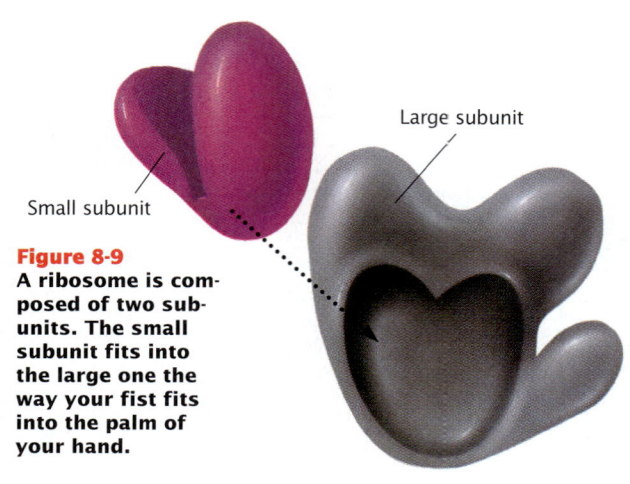

Small subunit

Large subunit

Figure 8-9
A ribosome is composed of two subunits. The small subunit fits into the large one the way your fist fits into the palm of your hand.

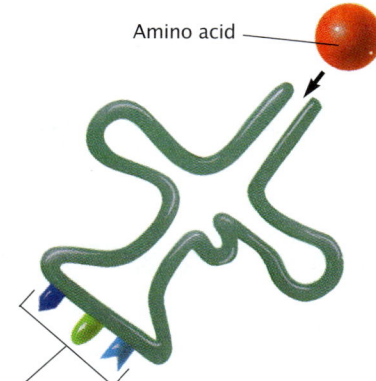

Amino acid

Anticodon

Figure 8-10
A transfer RNA molecule is a chain of RNA about 80 nucleotides long, folded into a compact shape. At one end of the molecule is a three-nucleotide sequence called the anticodon. At the opposite end is an amino acid.

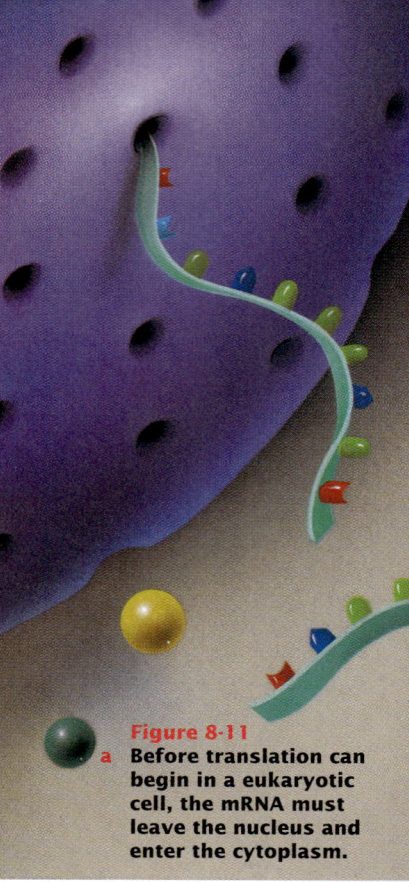

Figure 8-11
a Before translation can begin in a eukaryotic cell, the mRNA must leave the nucleus and enter the cytoplasm.

How RNA Makes Proteins

Translation is the process by which the genetic message is deciphered. During translation, the mRNA works with two other types of RNA to build proteins by joining amino acids. Translation occurs on ribosomes, which are complex organelles that contain a special kind of RNA called ribosomal RNA (rRNA). **Figure 8-9** shows that each ribosome consists of two subunits. During translation, an mRNA molecule passes between the two subunits of a ribosome.

Translation begins when mRNA binds to a specific site on the small ribosomal subunit. The large ribosomal subunit attaches to form a complete ribosome with a strand of mRNA

running through it. Just as factories use blueprints to direct the assembly of cars, ribosomes use mRNA to direct the assembly of proteins.

The pocket, or dent, in the small ribosomal subunit has just the right shape to bind a third kind of RNA molecule, transfer RNA (tRNA), shown in **Figure 8-10**. Transfer RNA carries amino acids to the ribosome. On one end of the transfer RNA molecule is a three-nucleotide sequence called an **anticodon**. Anticodons are complementary to mRNA codons.

Like the address on an envelope, the anticodon ensures that an amino acid is delivered to its proper "address" on the mRNA as a protein is being assem-

144

Community Connection: Proteins In the Diet

Have students investigate different kinds of diets (local, regional, popular, fad) with regard to proteins. As an alternative, have students visit a health-food store and collect information about dietary supplements that supposedly help the body build proteins more effectively.

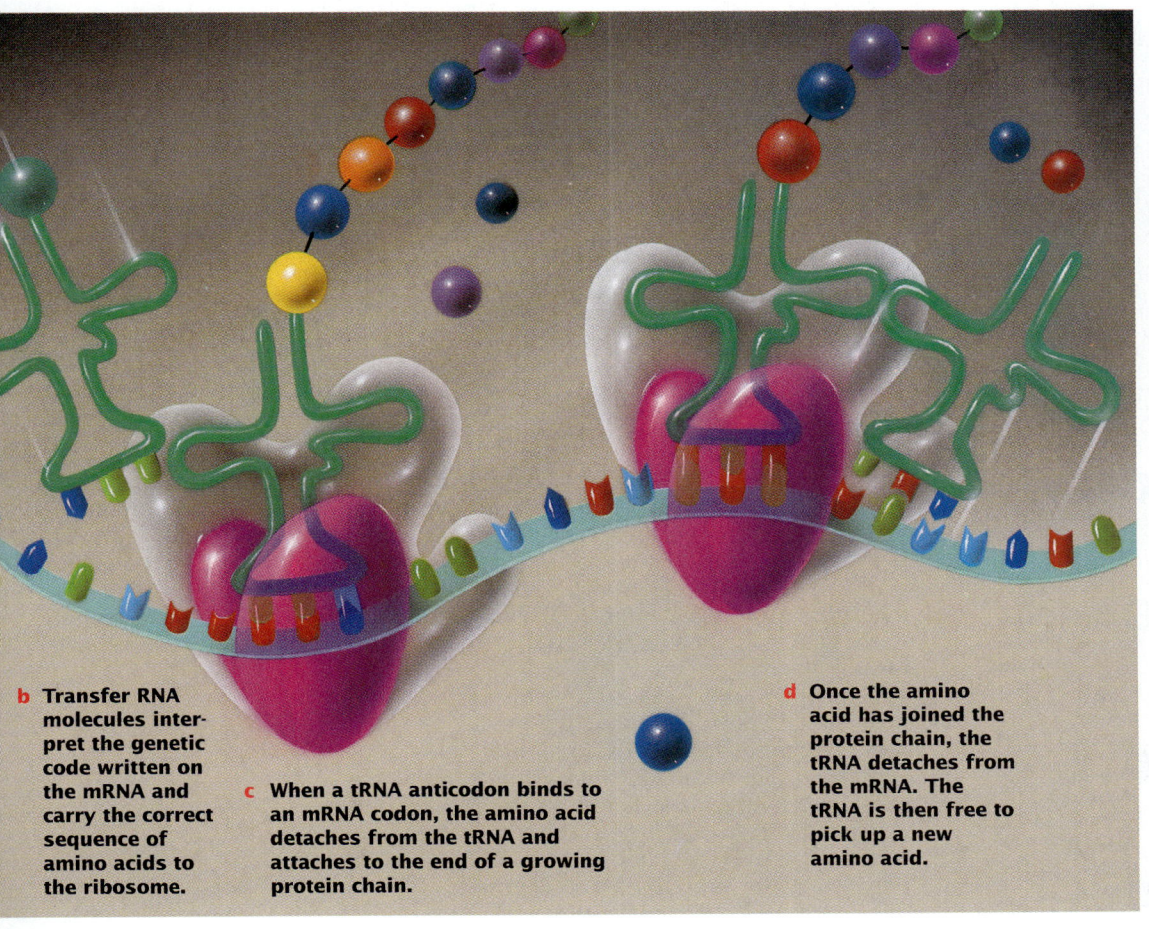

b Transfer RNA molecules interpret the genetic code written on the mRNA and carry the correct sequence of amino acids to the ribosome.

c When a tRNA anticodon binds to an mRNA codon, the amino acid detaches from the tRNA and attaches to the end of a growing protein chain.

d Once the amino acid has joined the protein chain, the tRNA detaches from the mRNA. The tRNA is then free to pick up a new amino acid.

bled. And just as a mail carrier checks the address before delivering a letter, so the small ribosomal subunit checks the tRNA anticodon to see that it is complementary to the mRNA codon.

As the mRNA passes along the ribosome, one tRNA after another is selected to match the sequence of mRNA codons. Amino acids are added to the growing protein chain until the end of the mRNA sequence is reached as seen in **Figure 8-11**. At this point, a "stop" codon is encountered for which there is no corresponding anticodon on any tRNA molecule. With nothing to fit into the tRNA site, the ribosome complex falls apart and the newly assembled protein is released into the cell. A cell's cytoplasm contains thousands of protein-making ribosomes.

SECTION REVIEW

1 Outline the path taken by the genetic information as proteins are made.

2 How does a cell make RNA?

3 What is the genetic code? Why is it said to be universal?

4 How do codons and anticodons interact to build proteins? How will a mutation that causes the codon UGU to be changed to UGG affect the amino-acid sequence specified by a strand of mRNA?

145

ANSWERS TO SECTION REVIEW

1 See Figure 8-6 on page 141.

2 See Figure 8-7 on page 142.

3 The genetic code is the correspondence between nucleotide triplets in DNA and the amino acids in proteins. The genetic code is the same in nearly all organisms, so it is said to be universal.

4 See Figure 8-11 on page 144. Changing the codon UGU to UGG will cause the amino acid cysteine to be replaced by the amino acid tryptophan.

Demonstration
■ **Predicting Outcomes**
Tell students to take out the sheets on which they had formed codon-anticodon pairings. Have them refer to Figure 8-8 on page 143 and replace each anticodon with the name of the amino acid that will be inserted.

Phase Three
Assessment Options

Closure
■ **Recognizing Relationships**
Write a sequence of three amino acids on the board. Have students refer to Figure 8-8 to write an mRNA sequence that could code for these amino acids. Then have them write the appropriate DNA sequence. Compare several responses to show students that more than one sequence of DNA bases can code for the same sequence of amino acids.

SECTION REVIEW
Assign the *Section Review*.

Reteaching
Write a nine-base DNA sequence on the board. Have students transcribe this sequence into mRNA and then translate it into the amino acid sequence. Next, change any one of the original nine bases, and have students repeat the process to see how transcription and translation would be affected by these "mutations."

Key to Strategies
● Understanding Concepts (Tier I)
■ Applying Information (Tier II)
▲ Critical Thinking (Tier III)

Scheduling
See the **Lesson Planning Guide** on pages 135A and 135B for lecture, classwork, and assignment options for Section 8-3.

Phase Two
Teaching Strategies

Demonstration
● **Interpreting a Model**
Run the flat side of a chalkboard eraser along the edge of a meterstick. Inform students that the meterstick represents a segment of a DNA molecule and the eraser represents RNA polymerase. Wrap a piece of clay around the meterstick, and tell the class that it represents a repressor protein. Point out how the repressor blocks RNA polymerase from moving along the DNA molecule. Use a different color of clay to represent the inducer. Attach it to the repressor, and have the two fall off the DNA. Ask students what will happen now that the repressor is no longer attached to the DNA. Relate this demonstration of gene regulation to the illustrations in Figure 8-12.

The translation of a gene into a protein is only part of gene expression. Every cell must also be able to regulate the use of particular genes. Just as a conductor controls when the different instruments in an orchestra play, a cell determines when particular genes are transcribed by controlling when genes are switched "on" and "off."

8-3 Regulating Gene Expression

OBJECTIVES

1 Explain why cells must regulate gene expression.

2 Summarize how a gene can be switched off and on.

3 Distinguish between exons and introns.

4 Explain how transposons affect gene expression.

Switching Genes On and Off
Cells control the expression of their genes by determining when individual genes are to be transcribed. Each gene possesses special regulatory sites, which act as points of control. Specific regulatory proteins within the cell bind to these sites, switching transcription of the gene on or off.

The best understood regulatory mechanisms are those used by bacteria. Some genes in bacteria are expressed nearly all the time, while others are rarely used. Genes that are expressed only occasionally are said to be switched off. They are transcribed only when the proteins are needed. In these genes, transcription cannot occur because a large molecule called a **repressor protein** is bound to the DNA in front of the genes, as shown in **Figure 8-12a**. The repressor protein blocks transcription by preventing the RNA polymerase from moving along the gene. If someone placed a brick wall between your chair and desk, you could not begin your work until the wall was removed. In the same way, transcription cannot begin until the repressor protein is removed.

Transcription begins when an inducer is present
For transcription to begin, molecules called **inducers** must bind to the repressor protein. The binding causes the repressor protein to change its

shape so that it no longer fits the DNA. As a result, the repressor protein falls off, removing the barrier to transcription. When this happens, the gene is switched on.

In bacteria, gene expression controls the digestion of lactose, the sugar

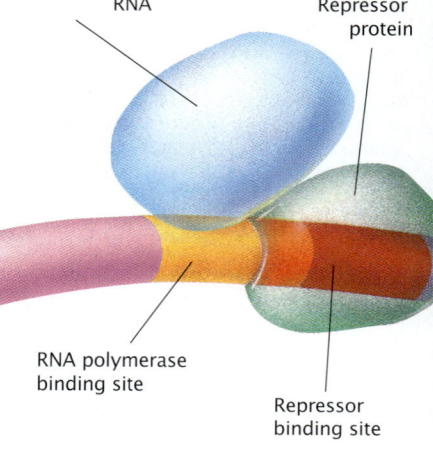

RNA

Repressor protein

RNA polymerase binding site

Repressor binding site

Figure 8-12
a A repressor protein is bound to DNA, blocking RNA polymerase from its binding site and preventing transcription.

Videodisc Resources

Holt Biology Videodiscs
Lesson 8-3: Regulating Gene Expression

Cell Structure and Function

What processes

provide a cell

with the proteins

it needs to function

properly?

found in milk. When a bacterium encounters lactose, the lactose acts as an inducer by binding to the repressor protein and altering its shape. The altered repressor protein then detaches from the DNA molecule, which allows the RNA polymerase to transcribe the genes needed to produce the enzyme responsible for digesting lactose.

Activators help DNA unwind

Because RNA polymerase binds to only one strand of the DNA double helix, it is necessary that the DNA molecule partially unwind to expose the bases at the promoter site. In many genes, this unwinding cannot take place without the help of a regulatory protein called an activator. An activator binds to the DNA in this region and helps it unwind. Cells are able to switch genes "off" by binding signal molecules to the activator protein. This prevents the activator from binding to the DNA molecules. As a result, the double helix cannot unwind and the genes cannot be transcribed.

Activators enable a cell to carry out a second level of control. When a bacterium already has plenty of energy, the level of another signal molecule—a special "I-need-sugar" signal molecule—decreases. Without being prodded by this signal molecule, the activator protein cannot bind to the DNA molecule's unwinding site. As a result, the

genes are not transcribed, even though the repressor protein is not blocking the RNA polymerase.

Eukaryotic cells have many ways to regulate genes

Gene regulation is more complex in humans and other eukaryotic organisms than in bacteria, even though the same basic mechanisms are used. Because a nuclear envelope physically separates transcription from translation in a eukaryotic cell, more opportunities for regulating gene expression exist. Scientists have found mechanisms that occur after mRNA leaves the nucleus and after translation, when the protein is functional.

As in bacteria, most gene regulation in eukaryotes works by controlling the onset of transcription. However, eukaryotic cells employ a more flexible system. The decoding of each gene is controlled by proteins called transcription factors. Transcription factors help arrange polymerases in the correct position on the promoter. A gene can be influenced by many different factors. Sometimes one kind of transcription factor has several forms that bind to regions of DNA called enhancers. An enhancer is a sequence of DNA located thousands of nucleotide bases away from the promoter. When the strand of DNA is looped in the correct manner, factors bound to enhancers are able to activate factors bound to the promoter.

Genes for digesting

Repressor protein

RNA polymerase

Inducer

b When an inducer is present, it binds to the repressor protein and changes its shape. As a result, the repressor protein falls off the DNA, enabling RNA polymerase to bind to the DNA strand and begin transcribing genes.

147

Matter of Fact: Eukaryotic DNA vs. Prokaryotic DNA

Eukaryotes have more DNA in their chromosomes than do prokaryotes, with their single chromosome consisting of just one double helix. For example, a human cell typically has about 1,750 times the amount of DNA that is found in a bacterial cell. But the salamander has the largest amount of DNA per haploid cell, with slightly more than 20 times the amount present in a human haploid cell.

Assessment Options

Closure

▲ **Evaluating Information**

Inform students that each person is capable of making millions of different antibodies, which are protein molecules, and explain that the human genome does not have millions of genes to code for these antibodies. Have students consider how their genetic information can be manipulated to produce this vast array of antibodies. *(The variety of antibody molecules humans produce is the result of the rearrangement of gene fragments, a phenomenon similar to transposons but on a larger scale. Segments containing several genes that code for a portion of the antibody are actually moved to a new place on the chromosome as each white blood cell develops. This rearrangement is known to occur only in the immune system.)*

SECTION REVIEW

Assign the *Section Review*.

Reteaching

Review how mitosis produces daughter cells containing the same number and kind of chromosomes as the parent cell. Emphasize that the 100 trillion cells in an adult human must therefore contain the same genetic information because they were the result of mitotic divisions. Discuss how genes must be turned on and off in different ways in the various types of cells to produce a normal adult. For example, the genes for making hemoglobin, present in all cells, should function only in maturing red blood cells and no others.

Architecture of the Gene

While it is tempting to think of a gene as a single, uninterrupted stretch of DNA that codes for proteins, this simple arrangement occurs only in bacteria. In eukaryotes, a gene contains a series of sequences called exons and introns. **Exons** are the portions of a gene that actually get translated into proteins. They are interrupted by noncoding portions of the DNA called **introns**. In most genes, the introns far outweigh the protein-encoding exons. In fact, in most cases, less than 10 percent of a human gene consists of exons. Like cars on a rural highway, exons are scattered here and there within genes. Introns are separated from exons during transcription.

Figure 8-13
Barbara McClintock received a Nobel Prize in 1983 for her discovery of transposons in corn.

Exons play a role in evolution

How could such a complicated system have survived the process of natural selection? The answer is that it adds evolutionary flexibility. Each exon encodes a different part of a protein. One exon may influence which molecules an enzyme is able to recognize, while another may determine whether a protein will respond to particular signal molecules. By possessing introns and exons, cells can shuffle exons between genes and create new combinations. Natural selection probably favored the intron-exon system of organization because it enables cells to manufacture many different proteins by juggling exons between genes. The many thousands of proteins that occur in human cells appear to have arisen from only a few thousand exons!

Genes can jump to new locations

A few genes in chromosomes have the ability to move from one location in the chromosome to another. These genes are known as **transposons** (*tranz POH zahnz*). Once every few thousand cell divisions, a transposon jumps to a new location in the same chromosome or in a different chromosome. Transposons often inactivate the genes they jump into, creating mutations. Barbara McClintock, a geneticist working in the Cold Spring Harbor Laboratory on Long Island, New York, discovered transposons during her studies of corn. The spotted and streaked patterns seen in the corn in **Figure 8-13** result from the interactions of transposons that control its kernel pigments.

SECTION REVIEW

1 How do repressor proteins and inducer molecules affect transcription?

2 How do activator proteins help RNA polymerase bind to a strand of DNA?

3 How do the arrangements of genes differ in bacteria and eukaryotes?

4 What effect do transposons have on other genes?

ANSWERS TO SECTION REVIEW

1 A repressor protein inhibits transcription by blocking RNA polymerase from moving along the DNA molecule. An inducer molecule binds to the repressor and changes its shape so that it detaches from the DNA molecule. As a result, RNA polymerase can move along DNA and transcribe the message.

2 Activator proteins help unwind the two strands of the DNA molecule, which allows RNA polymerase to bind.

3 In bacteria, the genes occur as a linear segment of DNA. In eukaryotes, genes consist of a series of segments called exons (coding) and introns (noncoding).

4 Transposons can inactivate the genes they jump into, which can lead to mutations.

Highlights

Watson and Crick built this model of DNA in 1953.

Highlights

8 chapter

Alternative Assessment

Have students construct a graphic organizer to summarize what they have learned about genes.

Portfolio Assessment

Portfolio Assessment on page T39 provides options for building and evaluating students' portfolios. Students and teachers can select items from the areas listed on page T39 for inclusion in a portfolio.

	Key Terms	Summary
8-1 **Understanding DNA** It took scientists many years to prove that DNA is the genetic material. 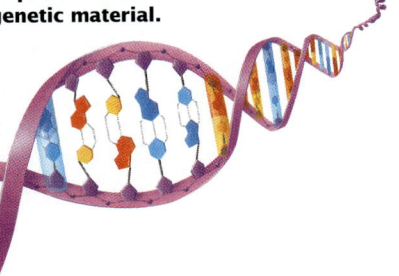	virulent (p. 137) transformation (p. 137) nucleotide (p. 139) purine (p. 139) pyrimidine (p. 139) double helix (p. 139) replication (p. 140) mutagen (p. 140)	• Griffith, Avery, and Hershey and Chase performed experiments that helped show that DNA is the hereditary material. • DNA is composed of subunits called nucleotides. Each nucleotide contains a sugar, a phosphate group, and one of four bases. • Watson and Crick showed that the DNA molecule is a double helix. • Before cell division, DNA copies itself in a process called replication. The DNA separates into two strands, and new complementary bases attach to the exposed base.
8-2 **How Proteins Are Made**  Proteins are made when amino acids are assembled by mRNA and tRNA molecules at a ribosome.	ribonucleic acid (p. 141) gene expression (p. 141) transcription (p. 141) translation (p. 141) codon (p. 143) genetic code (p. 143) anticodon (p. 144)	• During transcription, the genetic message from DNA is transferred to RNA. • During translation, RNA directs the production of specific proteins encoded by genes. • Each group of three nucleotides in mRNA is called a codon. Codons specify amino acids. • A three-nucleotide sequence on a tRNA molecule is called an anticodon. Anticodons complement the nucleotide sequence in mRNA codons.
8-3 **Regulating Gene Expression** Cells can control gene activity. When an inducer binds to the repressor molecule, it falls from the DNA, allowing transcription to begin.	repressor protein (p. 146) inducer (p. 146) exon (p. 148) intron (p. 148) transposon (p. 148)	• In prokaryotes, transcription is regulated by repressor proteins. A repressor protein blocks RNA polymerase from transcribing a gene. • In eukaryotes, genes are fragmented. Exons are the portions of a gene that are translated into proteins. Introns are noncoding regions of DNA. • Transposons are genes that can jump to new locations in chromosomes.

149

ANSWER TO CONCEPT MAP

The following is one possible answer to the Relating Concepts exercise on page 150.

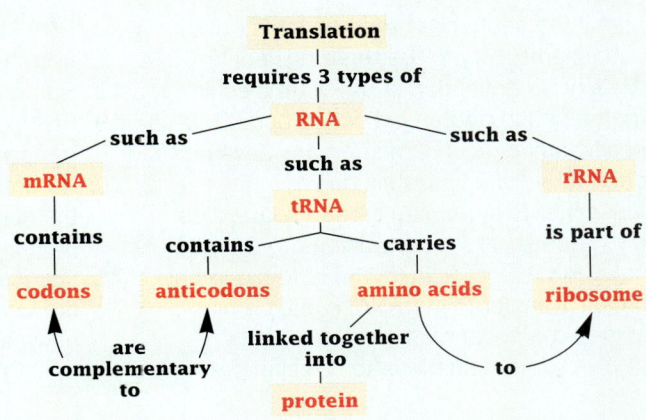

Understanding Vocabulary

1. a. A gene is a segment of DNA that codes for a particular protein. See page 139.
   b. See page 141.
   c. A repressor protein binds to DNA and prevents RNA polymerase from transcribing a gene. An inducer binds to a repressor protein, causing it to detach from the DNA.
2. a. transforming agent
   b. replication
   c. RNA

Understanding Concepts

3. Concept map answer is shown on page 149.
4. The nonvirulent strains became virulent by transformation, the process in which a bacterium incorporates foreign DNA.
5. They saw that when protein-destroying enzymes were added to bacteria, transformation still occurred; when DNA-destroying enzymes were added, it did not occur.
6. See Figure 8-2 on page 138.
7. A nucleotide consists of a sugar, a phosphate group, and a base.
8. See page 139.
9. Chargaff's rules state that in DNA, the amounts of adenine and guanine are always equal, as are the amounts of guanine and cytosine.
10. Franklin studied the structure of DNA using X-ray diffraction and found that the DNA molecule resembled a tightly coiled shape called a helix.
11. The genetic code has existed since the first life-forms evolved, over 3.5 billion years ago.
12. Because guanine bonds with cytosine and adenine bonds with thymine, the complementary sequence would be A A T G C G A T.
13. See page 141.
14. See Figures 8-7 on page 142 and 8-11 on page 144 for details about both processes.
15. A codon in a segment of mRNA consists of three nucleotide

---

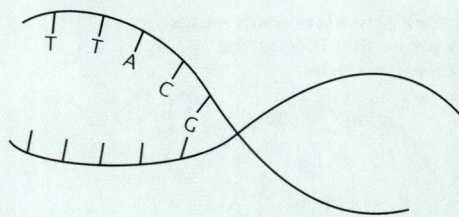

Understanding Vocabulary

1. For each pair of words, explain the differences in their meanings.
   a. gene, nucleotide
   b. transcription, translation
   c. repression protein, inducer
2. For each set of terms, complete the analogy.
   a. Griffith : transformation :: Avery : _____
   b. process in which a bacterium takes up foreign DNA : transformation :: process of copying DNA : _____
   c. thymine : DNA :: uracil : _____

Understanding Concepts

3. **Relating Concepts** Construct a concept map describing the process of translation. Try to use the following terms in your map: codons, rRNA, tRNA, amino acids, RNA, ribosome, anticodons, mRNA, and protein.
4. **Inferring Conclusions** In Frederick Griffith's experiments, how did nonvirulent strains of *Pneumococcus* bacteria become virulent?
5. **Relating Conclusions** Describe how Oswald Avery and his associates determined that DNA is the genetic material in cells.
6. **Summarizing Information** Summarize the experiments of Hershey and Chase that confirmed DNA as the genetic material.
7. **Identifying Structures** What are the three parts of a nucleotide?
8. **Comparing Structures** What are purines? pyrimidines? Give an example of each.
9. **Summarizing Information** Summarize Chargaff's rules.
10. **Inferring Relationships** What contribution did Rosalind Franklin make toward discovering the structure of DNA?
11. **Relating Conclusions** Why is the genetic code considered to be the oldest of languages?

150

---

12. **Predicting Patterns** What would be the complementary base sequence for the following sequence of bases on an unzipped strand of DNA: T T A C G C T A? Explain your answer.

13. **Organizing Information** What is gene expression? Identify and describe the two stages of gene expression.
14. **Inferring Relationships** Where and how do the processes of transcription and translation each occur?
15. **Summarizing Information** Explain how codons specify a particular amino acid.
16. **Comparing Functions** What are the names and the roles of the three types of RNA? Where in the cell does each type of RNA function?
17. **Identifying Functions** What is a repressor protein? How does it prevent transcription?
18. **Identifying Structures** What are promoters, activators, and enhancers? Where is each located on a gene?
19. **Inferring Conclusions** How would the operation of RNA polymerase be affected if the repressor protein were not bound to the proper site on a gene?
20. **Summarizing Information** Describe what happens when a "stop" codon is encountered during protein assembly.
21. **BUILDING ON WHAT YOU LEARNED** In Chapter 6 you learned about mitosis and cell division. Why is it important that DNA replication occur before mitosis and cell division?

---

bases. The sequence of the codon's bases is complementary to the three nucleotide bases of an anticodon in a tRNA molecule. When a codon and an anticodon bond, the specific amino acid carried on the tRNA is added to a growing protein chain.

16. Messenger RNA (mRNA) carries sequences of nucleotides from the nucleus to the ribosome. Ribosomal RNA (rRNA) is found in ribosomes. Transfer RNA (tRNA) carries amino acids to the ribosomes.
17. A repressor protein binds to a region on a DNA strand and prevents RNA polymerase from transcribing a gene.
18. See pages 146 and 147.
19. RNA polymerase would not be blocked from transcribing the gene.
20. No anticodon matches the "stop" codon, so the ribosome complex falls apart and the protein is released into the cell.
21. Replication must occur first to ensure that the DNA copies can be distributed to the two new cells.

Interpreting Graphics

22. The figure below shows the events of translation. Recall that translation follows transcription and is the process by which a protein molecule is assembled according to the mRNA code.

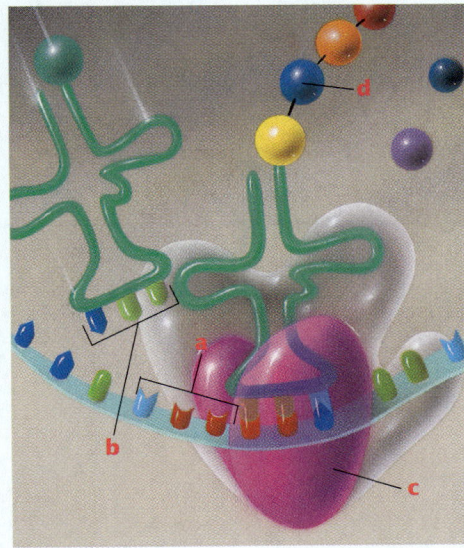

a. What does *a* represent in the model?
b. Part *c* represents the organelle inside the cell where translation occurs. What is the name of this organelle?
c. What is the relationship between *a* and *b* during translation?
d. What structure is represented by *d*?

Reviewing Themes

23. *Evolution*
How does the genetic code support the theory that all organisms have a common ancestry?

24. *Evolution*
How does natural selection favor the intron-exon system of organization within chromosomes?

Thinking Critically

25. **Distinguishing Relevant Information** After messenger RNA has assisted in the formation of necessary proteins within the cell, it breaks down into free-floating nucleotides. What problems would occur inside the cell if mRNA did not break down after protein synthesis?

26. **Finding Information** Find out more about Barbara McClintock, who received a Nobel Prize in 1983 for her discovery of transposons in corn. Write a report about her life and include when she began to study the "jumping" gene that causes irregular coloration in corn.

27. **Communicating Effectively** Find out the genetic link between "mad cow disease" and similar diseases that afflict humans. What are prions? Why are prions considered to be very different from bacteria and viruses that cause disease? How do prions cause disease? Report to your class on your findings.

Activities and Projects

28. **Language Arts Connection** As you learned in this chapter, proteins are compounds that consist of one or more chains of amino acids. Do library research to find the origin of the word *protein* and to determine why it is used to describe amino-acid chains.

29. **Unit Focus** Read J. D. Watson's book *The Double Helix*, which provides a day-by-day account of how he and Crick developed the double-helix model of DNA. Write a book report, and share your favorite passages from Watson's book with your classmates.

Discovering Through Reading

30. Read the article "Gene Defects and Therapies: An Update on the Expanding Nature of Science," in *American Biology Teacher*, February 1995, pages 70–75. What will dissection of the human genome lead to? What approaches do geneticists want to use in treating hereditary and medical diseases?

31. Read "Hidden Costs of a Clean Inheritance," in *New Scientist*, May 1994, pages 14–15. What is germ-line therapy? What do scientists think its therapeutic value will be? What outcomes do its critics fear?

32. Read "Artificial RNA Enzymes: Big and Fast," in *Science News*, July 22, 1995, page 53. What are ribozymes? What is a catalytic domain? How did Bartel and Szostak create molecular test-tube evolution? Why did researchers try to create ribozymes?

151

Science (1970) and the Rosenthal Award (1978).
27. Answers will vary depending on the resources available.

Activities and Projects

28. *Protein* is derived from the Greek *proteios,* meaning "first." The word well describes chemical compounds consisting of one or more amino acid chains because they rank first among the substances of life.
29. Answers will vary.

Discovering Through Reading

30. The molecular dissection of the human genome will lead to the construction of physical and cytogenic maps of the genome. A three-pronged approach is currently being developed. The first approach is determining the abnormalities in the genes and the changes in the resulting proteins. The second is finding ways of correcting the DNA or protein and incorporating them into cells. The third is developing chemical treatments for genetic and medical disorders.

31. Germ-line therapy, the altering of DNA in the sperm or egg, would change the genetic makeup of the child. The therapy could be used to prevent a child from being born with a defective gene. Critics say that parents will be making choices for children who do not yet exist. Others argue that the side effects of the therapy might not show up for decades.

32. Ribozymes are RNA molecules that can function as enzymes, catalyzing chemical reactions. A catalytic domain is a group of nucleotides that help a ribozyme chemically bond to target RNA. In vitro evolution was achieved by adding mutations with each new generation of RNA molecules. To determine if a world of RNA could have existed at one time.

Interpreting Graphics

22. a. Part *a* represents a codon.
b. Part *c* is the ribosome.
c. Parts *a* and *b* are complementary.
d. Part *d* is a growing amino acid chain.

Reviewing Themes

23. The genetic code is universal for almost all organisms, from bacteria to humans.
24. Cells are able to make many kinds of proteins by juggling exons between genes.

Thinking Critically

25. The cell may continue making the protein encoded in the mRNA. This would use up the cell's energy and interfere with other cellular functions.

26. McClintock began her studies of transposons almost 40 years ago when she was crossing strains of multicolored kernel corn. She also won the National Medal of

9 | Gene Technology

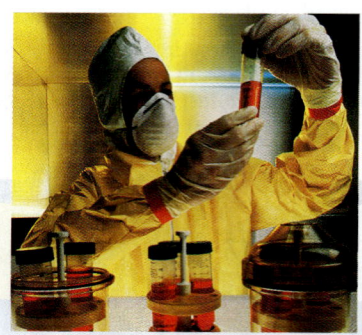

Lesson Planning Guide With Options for Block Scheduling

Lecture Concepts	Lesson Resources

9-1 The Revolution in Genetics

BLOCK ❶ (45 minutes)

1. Genetic engineering is the transfer of genes between the organisms of two different species to produce a recombinant DNA.

2. Restriction enzymes are used to cleave the DNAs of two different organisms.

3. The DNAs are combined to form the recombinant DNA.

❶ Lecture Resources
- ■ Determining Prior Knowledge
- ■ Active Reading: Anticipation Guide
- ■ Visual Strategy: Videodisc
- n Demonstration: Identifying Structures
- ■ Teaching Transparencies: 39, 40
- ● Holt Biology Videodiscs Lesson 9-1

Classwork Options
- ■ Recombinant DNA
- ■ Demonstration: Identifying Structures
- ⚗ Quick Labs: Lab A8

BLOCK ❷ (45 minutes)

4. The recombinant DNA is inserted into target cells that are cloned.

5. Target cells are examined to see if the particular gene of interest in the recombinant DNA is functioning.

❷ Lecture Resources
- ■ Visual Strategy: Figure 9-4
- ■ Visual Strategy: Videodisc
- ● Holt Biology Videodiscs Lesson 9-1

Classwork Options
- ■ Closure: Inferring Relationships

Assignment Options
- ■ Reteaching
- ■ Section Review
- ■ Chapter Review, questions 1a, 1b, 2a, 4, 5, 6, 7, 8, 9, 10, 11
- ■ Directed Reading Worksheet

9-2 Transforming Agriculture

BLOCK ❸ (45 minutes)

1. The Ti plasmid has been used to insert specific genes into plants.

❸ Lecture Resources
- ■ Nitrogen Fixation
- ■ Active Reading: Reader Response Logs
- ● Holt Biology Videodiscs Lesson 9-2

Classwork Options
- ⚗ Biotechnology : Lab D6

Assignment Options
- ■ Life/Work Skills: Finding Information

BLOCK ❹ (45 minutes)

2. Genetic engineering experiments have produced crop plants that are resistant to weed-killers and insects, bacteria that can convert nitrogen into a usable form, and larger and more productive livestock.

❹ Lecture Resources
- ■ Visual Strategy: Figure 9-8
- ■ Teaching Transparencies: 41
- ● Holt Biology Videodiscs Lesson 9-2

Classwork Options
- ■ Closure: Crop Rotation
- ⚗ Interactive Explorations Laboratory Manual: Lab E5

Assignment Options
- ■ Reteaching
- ■ Section Review
- ■ Chapter Review, questions 1c, 2b, 12, 13, 14, 16, 20, 23, 26
- ■ Directed Reading Worksheet

9-3 Advances in Medicine

BLOCK ❺ (45 minutes)

1. Genetic engineering experiments have produced bacteria capable of synthesizing insulin and other proteins of medical value to humans.

2. Genetic engineering experiments have produced vaccines designed to protect against certain viral diseases, including herpes and hepatitis.

❺ Lecture Resources
- ■ Decision Making
- ■ Visual Strategy: Figure 9-12
- ■ Teaching Transparencies: 32A
- ● Holt Biology Videodiscs Lesson 9-3

Classwork Options
- ⚗ Inquiry Skills Development: Lab B7

Assignment Options
- ■ Human Gene Therapy

Lecture Concepts

Lesson Resources

9-3 Advances in Medicine, *continued*

BLOCK ⑥ (45 minutes)

3. Genetic engineering experiments have introduced certain genes into humans with the eventual goal of curing inherited disorders and treating cancer.

4. Experiments are currently in progress to determine the nucleotide base sequence for every human gene.

⑥ Lecture Resources
- ■ DNA Fingerprinting
- ▮ Teaching Transparencies: 33A
- ◉ Holt Biology Videodiscs Lesson 9-3

Classwork Options
- ■ Closure: Recognizing Differences
- ■ Exploration 9A

Assignment Options
- ■ Reteaching
- ■ Section Review
- ■ Chapter Review, questions 2c, 3, 15, 18, 19, 21, 22, 24, 25, 27, 28
- ■ Directed Reading Worksheet

Chapter Review and Assessment

BLOCK ⑦ (45 minutes)
Review
- ■ Reteaching Worksheet
- ■ Thinking Skills Worksheet
- ■ Vocabulary Development Worksheet
- ◎ Language Development and Reading Comprehension Audio CD Program: Chapter 9

BLOCK ⑧ (45 minutes)
Assessment
- ■ Alternative Assessment, p. 167
- ■ Portfolio Assessment, p. T39

Chapter Test
- ■ Chapter 9 Test

Test Generator
- ◎ Item bank for customizing Chapter Tests

Teaching Resources CD-ROM
- ◎ Scoring Rubrics and Classroom Management Checklist

The Portfolio icon denotes items throughout the Teacher's Edition lesson wrap that may be selected for inclusion in student portfolios.

Holt Biology Videodiscs and *Concepts of Biology*

Holt Biology Videodiscs gives you a powerful tool for teaching, review, and assessment. For further information regarding the media on the videodiscs, see *Holt Biology Videodiscs Teacher's Correlation Guide to Holt Biology: Visualizing Life.*

Concepts of Biology adds interactive lesson plans and extensive tools for customization using CD-ROM technology.

Use the following topic from *Concepts of Biology* to help you teach this chapter:
Topic 7: How Genes Work

Laboratory Planning

Text
Materials and preparation instructions appear on the teacher's wrap accompanying each laboratory exercise.
Block 6: Exploration 9A: Separating DNA With Gel Electrophoresis, p. 782

Holt BioSources Laboratory Program
Block 1: Quick Labs Lab A8: Making a Genetic Engineering Model
Block 3: Biotechnology Lab D6: Laboratory Techniques: DNA Fragment Analysis
Block 4: Interactive Explorations Laboratory Manual Lab E5: Heredity in Families
Block 5: Inquiry Skills Development Lab B7: Gene Expression

Determining Prior Knowledge

- Genetic technology has received much attention from the media in the past several years. Have students discuss any reports they may have read in the news or seen on TV.
- Ask students why scientists follow certain precautions and restrictions when conducting genetic-engineering experiments.
- Ask students what kind of vaccinations they have received. Ask them to explain how vaccines are prepared.

Active READING

Technique: Anticipation Guide
Write the following statements on the chalkboard or an overhead transparency:

1. Using genetic engineering, scientists are making certain plants more resistant to disease.
2. Using genetic engineering, scientists are making a growing number of pharmaceutical products.
3. Every organism has a unique set of DNA.

Have students decide if they agree or disagree with each statement. Ask volunteers to share their opinions with the rest of the class. Have students read the chapter to see if their opinions are changed, validated, or contradicted.

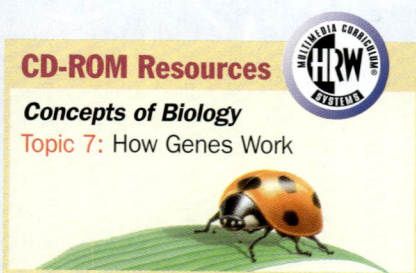

CD-ROM Resources

Concepts of Biology
Topic 7: How Genes Work

9

REVIEW
- DNA structure (Section 8-1)
- replication (Section 8-1)
- protein synthesis (Section 8-2)

Gene Technology

9-1	**The Revolution in Genetics**
9-2	**Transforming Agriculture**
9-3	**Advances in Medicine**

Analysis of DNA can reveal DNA sequence differences among several samples.

Author's Rationale This chapter explains the key concepts of genetic engineering from an insider's perspective. These concepts are then applied by looking at three areas in which genetic engineering has been important: agriculture, medicine, and mapping the human genome. Understanding this chapter is essential for developing scientific literacy and for honing decision-making skills used for considering issues that involve genetic technologies.

The basic mechanisms of gene expression have been understood since the 1950s. Since then, scientists, like this one, have worked to transfer genes under laboratory conditions. In order to perform effective gene transfers, they needed to be able to transfer genes in a controlled fashion. Within the last 20 years, scientists have successfully developed the technology that has made gene transfers common.

9-1 The Revolution in Genetics

OBJECTIVES

1 Outline the genetic engineering experiment performed by Cohen and Boyer.

2 Explain the four stages involved in a gene transfer experiment.

3 Describe how scientists use restriction enzymes.

4 Summarize some of the uses of genetic engineering.

What Is Genetic Engineering?

In 1973 Stanley Cohen and Herbert Boyer, two geneticists at the University of California at San Francisco, began an experiment that would revolutionize genetics. Cohen and Boyer set out to insert a gene from an African clawed frog into a bacterium. They were hoping that the bacterium would then make the molecule encoded by the frog gene.

To begin their experiment, Cohen and Boyer isolated the gene that coded for frog ribosomal RNA. Then they added that gene to bacterial DNA. This procedure produced the first living cells that had DNA from a foreign organism added to their own DNA. **Recombinant DNA** is a molecule formed when fragments of DNA from two or more different organisms are spliced together in a laboratory. Did the bacteria with the recombinant DNA use the frog gene? Yes! The genetically engineered bacteria produced frog rRNA, just as Cohen and Boyer had hoped. **Figure 9-1** outlines the stages of their experiment.

This experiment ushered in a new age in biology, one that explores the possibilities of moving genes from one organism to another. Over a period of 20 years, the increasing ability of researchers to transfer DNA from one organism into another has revolutionized genetics. **Genetic engineering** is the process of moving genes from the chromosomes of one organism to those of another. Today, for example, specific genes from human chromosomes can be routinely transferred into bacteria.

Figure 9-1

a Using an African clawed frog as their experimental organism, . . .

b . . . Cohen and Boyer isolated an rRNA gene from one of its chromosomes . . .

c . . . and inserted the gene into a bacterium. The bacterium then produced frog rRNA.

 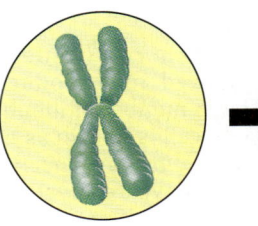 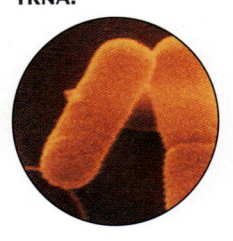

153

Videodisc Resources

Holt Biology Videodiscs

Lesson 9-1: The Revolution in Genetics

Phase One
Preparation

Scheduling

See the **Lesson Planning Guide** on pages 151A and 151B for lecture, classwork, and assignment options for Section 9-1.

Phase Two
Teaching Strategies

Visual Strategy — Videodisc

■ **Analyzing Information**
Introduce the chapter by using *Video—Genetic Engineering* shown in Chapter 9 Section 1 in **Holt Biology Videodiscs Teacher's Correlation Guide to Holt Biology: Visualizing Life.** Afterward, have students note the practical applications and ethical dilemmas of genetic engineering. Then discuss their importance.

Visual Strategy — Videodisc

■ **Relating Concepts**
Use *Step-Frame Sequence—Genetically Engineered Frogs* shown in Chapter 9 Section 1 in **Holt Biology Videodiscs Teacher's Correlation Guide to Holt Biology: Visualizing Life** to review the experiment of Cohen and Boyer. As students review each frame, have volunteers use their own words to summarize the information. Be sure students can identify the structures shown in each frame and that they understand the significance of the genes for resistance to tetracycline.

Key to Strategies

Teaching Strategies are keyed to three tiers of learning.

● **Understanding Concepts (Tier I)**
Content mastery and comprehension

■ **Applying Information (Tier II)**
Applying and analyzing content

▲ **Critical Thinking (Tier III)**
Practicing evaluative thinking

Demonstration

● **Identifying Structures**
Materials: Velcro strips, scissors
Distribute the materials to small groups of students. Challenge them to use these materials to design a model that demonstrates the first stage of the Cohen and Boyer experiment, as shown in Figure 9-2. *(Attach two Velcro strips to represent two strands of frog DNA. Use scissors to make two staggered cuts that represent where EcoRI would cut the different strands.)* Have groups present their models to the rest of the class and identify the "sticky ends" in both the DNA segments. Save the strips to use with the Demonstration described on page 155.

Recombinant DNA

■ **Predicting Outcomes**
Write the following DNA sequence on the chalkboard: GAATTC. Have students copy this sequence and write the complementary sequence *(CTTAAG)*. Inform students that *Eco*RI cleaves DNA between the nucleotide bases A and G. Have students add arrows to their drawings to indicate where *Eco*RI would cleave each DNA strand.

G⇓AATTC

CTTAA⇑G

Next, have students redraw the strands to show how the DNA has been cleaved, and ask them to label the "sticky ends."

Figure 9-2

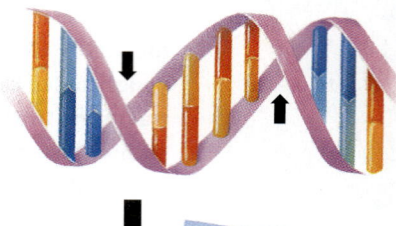

a **In the first stage of their experiment, Cohen and Boyer obtained chromosomes from a frog . . .**

b **. . . and treated them with a restriction enzyme called *Eco*RI, which recognizes a specific sequence of bases in DNA and cuts each strand when the sequence occurs.**

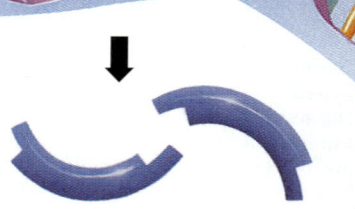

c **These cuts resulted in fragments of DNA with single-stranded tails, or "sticky ends."**

How to Move a Gene From One Organism to Another

If you were a scientist working in a genetic engineering lab, how would you go about moving a gene? First you would need to find a source chromosome that contains the gene you wish to isolate. Next you would need to select a target cell into which the gene could be moved. And finally, you would need to figure out a way to transfer the isolated gene into the target cell. Every gene transfer experiment is performed in four distinct stages:

1. *Cleaving DNA* The source chromosome is cut into fragments of DNA.
2. *Producing recombinant DNA* The DNA fragments containing the desired gene are inserted into viral or bacterial DNA. The recombinant DNA is then allowed to infect target cells.
3. *Cloning cells* Infected cells are allowed to reproduce. Growing a large number of identical cells from one cell is known as **cloning**.
4. *Screening target cells* Target cells that have received the particular gene of interest are isolated.

Each of these stages will be explained in greater detail using the Cohen-Boyer experiment as an example.

Enzymes cut DNA into pieces with sticky ends

The first stage in any genetic engineering experiment involves cutting the source chromosome into fragments to isolate the gene you wish to transfer. In their experiment, Cohen and Boyer used chromosomes from *Xenopus laevis*, the African clawed frog.

To cut the frog DNA, Cohen and Boyer used special enzymes called **restriction enzymes**, as shown in **Figure 9-2**. Restriction enzymes recognize and bind to specific short sequences of nucleotide bases and then cut the DNA at a specific site within that sequence. There are hundreds of these enzymes, each of which cuts at a specific sequence. Cohen and Boyer used a restriction enzyme called *Eco*RI, which cuts DNA whenever it encounters the sequence CTTAAG. The sequence of the opposite strand is GAATTC, the same sequence written backward.

Matter of Fact: Restriction Enzymes

The restriction enzyme *Eco*RI was first isolated in the early 1970s. Since then, more than 200 restriction enzymes have been isolated, making it possible to cleave a DNA molecule at more than 90 specific sites. These enzymes function as immune systems in bacteria, where they attack the foreign DNA from either viruses or other bacterial strains.

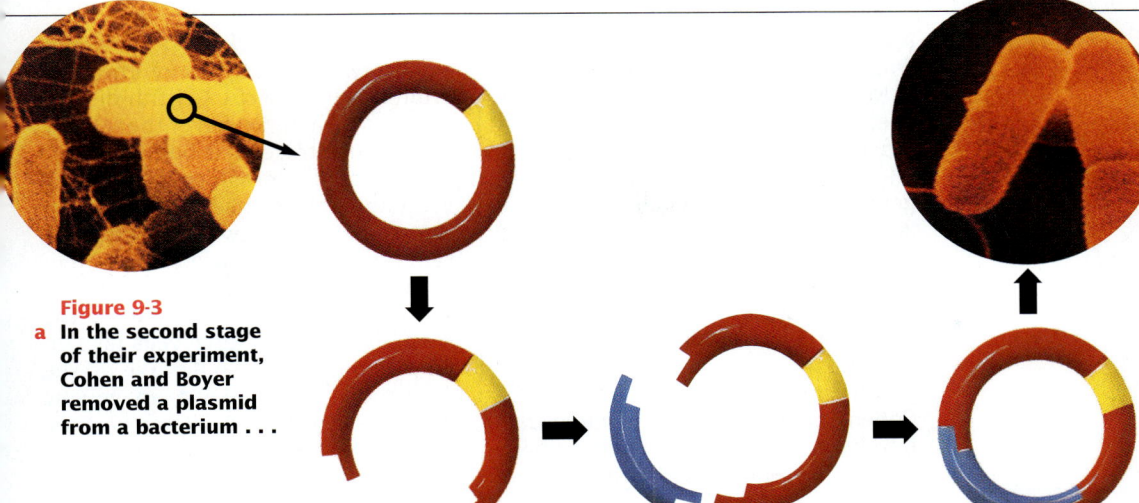

Figure 9-3

a In the second stage of their experiment, Cohen and Boyer removed a plasmid from a bacterium . . .

b . . . and treated it with the restriction enzyme *Eco*RI. The enzyme cut the plasmid, leaving sticky ends.

c Then they mixed the frog DNA with the plasmid. The fragments and the plasmid had complementary sticky ends that paired together like pieces of a puzzle.

d The resulting recombinant DNA molecules were used as vectors to infect bacterial cells.

Evolution

What evidence revealed by gene technology suggests that all organisms are related?

Note that restriction enzymes do not make a straight cut through both strands of DNA. Instead, the cut is off-set a few bases. For example, in the sequence CTTAAG, *Eco*RI cuts each strand between the A and G, a site four bases apart on both strands, creating DNA fragments with single-stranded "sticky ends." One of the fragments that Cohen and Boyer cleaved from the frog DNA contained the rRNA gene that they wanted to transfer.

Because the two single-stranded sticky ends have complementary sequences, they can pair back up and seal the break (which is why they are called sticky), *or they can pair with any other DNA fragment cut by the same enzyme.* DNA cut by the restriction enzyme *Eco*RI can be joined to DNA from any other organism that has also been cut by *Eco*RI because they have complementary sticky ends. At this point, the DNA segments are held together by hydrogen bonds between complementary nucleotide bases. The bound fragments are then treated with an enzyme called ligase, which seals the breaks in the DNA molecule.

DNA fragments are inserted into a vector

Cohen and Boyer had to figure out a way to get a fragment of frog DNA into a bacterial cell. They used **plasmids**, which are small, circular DNA molecules found in the cytoplasm of bacteria. Plasmids are independent from the bacterial chromosome but can carry genes necessary for the cell's survival, as you will see in a moment. After isolating plasmids from bacterial cells, Cohen and Boyer exposed them to the restriction enzyme *Eco*RI. Because each plasmid had only one sequence that *Eco*RI could recognize, it was cut in only one place. As a result, the plasmids opened up with the same sticky ends as the frog DNA fragments.

Now Cohen and Boyer mixed the frog DNA fragments and the cut plasmids. Because all the sticky ends were complementary, they joined in a variety of combinations. Cohen and Boyer hoped that a fragment of frog DNA would join with a cut plasmid and then reform as a circular molecule, as shown in **Figure 9-3**. This combination would serve as a delivery agent called

155

Demonstration

● **Identifying Structures**
Materials: Velcro strips (different color from strips used for Demonstration on page 154), Velcro model of frog DNA, scissors, stapler

Distribute the materials to small groups of students. Challenge them to use these materials to design a model that demonstrates the second stage of the Cohen and Boyer experiment, as shown in Figure 9-3. *(Attach the two strips, and staple them end to end to form a circle. Cut the circle to form sticky ends. Combine this plasmid model with the frog DNA model made in the Demonstration on page 154.)* Have groups present their models and describe how the frog DNA is inserted into the plasmid.

Theme Answer
Evolution
Restriction enzymes cleave at specific sites along a DNA molecule regardless of the source of the DNA. This fact is another piece of evidence pointing to the universality of DNA, indicating an evolutionary relationship among all organisms.

Matter of Fact: pSC101

Although the names of genetic engineering tools sound nonsensical, they are carefully devised. For example, the plasmid Cohen and Boyer used in their experiment is named pSC101. The *p* stands for *plasmid,* the letters *SC* are Stanley Cohen's initials, and the *101* signifies that it was the 101st plasmid they isolated from bacteria.

Key to Strategies
● **Understanding Concepts (Tier I)**
■ **Applying Information (Tier II)**
▲ **Critical Thinking (Tier III)**

Mathematics Connection

Vectors

Plasmids are useful as vectors for DNA segments up to 20,000 nucleotide bases in length. A plasmid tends to eliminate segments that are longer. To deliver a longer recombinant DNA molecule, scientists use specially modified viruses called cosmids. As a vector, a cosmid is capable of carrying recombinant DNA segments 2 times longer than those inserted into plasmids. Have students calculate the length of the DNA fragment that can be delivered by a cosmid (*up to 40,000 bases in length*).

Connection: *Chapter 4*

Cell Division

Ask students to explain how the recombinant DNA is cloned. (*Students should recall that when a bacterial cell divides, its genetic information is copied so that each newly formed cell receives an exact copy of the original chromosome. Thus, all the DNA is cloned.*)

Visual Strategy   Figure 9-4

● **Interpreting Graphics**

Ask students to explain why the number of bacteria shown growing in the culture in Figure 9-4 successively decreases. (*Bacteria that do not contain the gene for tetracycline resistance will not survive to grow in the culture illustrated in Figure 9-4b. Of these, only the bacteria that contain the frog rRNA gene will be detected in the culture illustrated in Figure 9-4c.*)

---

a **vector**. The vector would carry the frog rRNA gene into a bacterial cell.

Not just any fragment of DNA can be used as a vector. To be useful, a vector must have a gene for replication. This allows the DNA to be copied once it gets into a new cell. The vector Cohen and Boyer sought also contained another critical gene—one that made the cell resistant to the antibiotic tetracycline. This gene would be important during the screening stage of the experiment.

After mixing the fragments, how did Cohen and Boyer insert the molecules into bacterial cells? Recall the experiments of Frederick Griffith, the bac-teriologist who worked with virulent and nonvirulent strains of the bacterium *Pneumococcus*. Griffith discovered that bacteria have the ability to take up extracellular bits of DNA, a process called transformation. Gene technology makes use of transformation. Cohen and Boyer knew that if bacterial cells are placed in an environment containing plasmids, with special treatment, a few will take up the plasmids. When bacterial cells take up the plasmids, they would take up the new gene as well. Today many genetic engineers also use viruses as vectors. The DNA in these viruses can be manipulated like plasmids, placed back into viruses, and then used to infect cells.

Bacterial cells with plasmids are cloned

In the third stage of their experiment, Cohen and Boyer let the bacterial cells reproduce. As the bacteria reproduced, the plasmids inside the cells made many identical copies of themselves, called clones. Because each plasmid carried different fragments of DNA, thousands of different clones were produced. Such clones are sometimes referred to as a gene library. The entire gene library had to be searched to find the one clone that contained the desired gene.

Cells are screened to locate the desired gene

In the fourth stage of their experiment, Cohen and Boyer needed a way to eliminate bacterial cells that hadn't taken up plasmids. Recall that they used plasmids that contained a gene for resistance to the antibiotic tetracycline. By growing the bacterial cells in dishes that contained the antibiotic tetracycline, Cohen and Boyer ensured that a cell lacking a plasmid would die. This screening procedure, illustrated in **Figure 9-4a** and **b**, left cells that at least contained plasmids.

Now Cohen and Boyer were faced with a more difficult problem—locating the cells that contained plasmids with the frog rRNA. Remember, a plasmid could consist of any number of combinations of DNA fragments.

Figure 9-4
a **In the final stages of their genetic engineering experiment, Cohen and Boyer grew bacteria in dishes that contained the antibiotic tetracycline.**

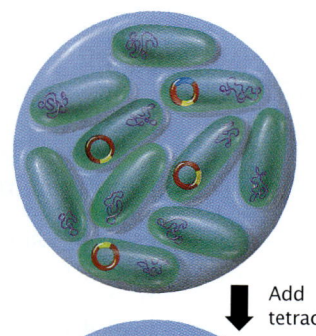

Add tetracycline

b **Only bacteria that contained the plasmids with the genes for resistance to tetracycline survived.**

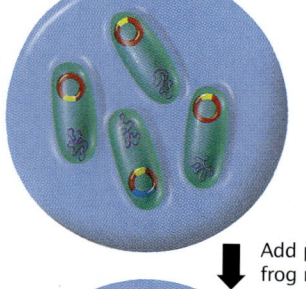

Add pure frog rRNA

c **Some of these plasmids also possessed the gene for frog rRNA. Cohen and Boyer then used radioactive probes to locate the cells that had taken up the gene.**

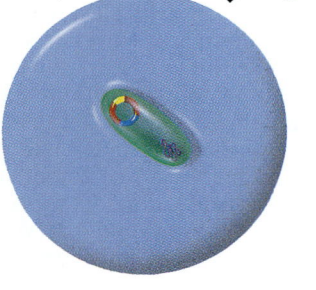

Community Connection: Gene Technology: A Source of Controversy

portfolio

When genetic engineering became a reality in the 1970s, scientists were concerned about the potential dangers of producing new strains of pathogenic organisms. They called for a voluntary moratorium on such work until guidelines could be established.

A strict protocol for working with recombinant DNA was first developed at a scientific conference held in 1975 in Asilomar, California. The problems that concerned scientists never developed, but over 20 years later, some people are still opposed to genetic engineering. Have students explore the controversy surrounding recombinant DNA technology. For example, some people believe that organisms containing recombinant DNA should never be introduced into nature, as when crops are sprayed with bacteria genetically engineered to prevent frost. Have students discuss their findings.

They began with what they knew—somewhere in the colonies of bacteria was a gene for frog rRNA. If they made a short single strand of radioactive frog rRNA, they could use it as an indicator or probe to find the gene. Patient searching revealed a colony with cells containing DNA that bound to the radioactive frog rRNA. These are the cells they sought—bacterial cells that carried the frog gene. **Figure 9-4c** illustrates the final step of the screening procedure.

Safety Considerations

Genetic engineering techniques are now being used for a wide variety of commercial applications. Like any new technology, genetic engineering and its products have been sources of controversy. Critics have raised questions about potential risks and hazards.

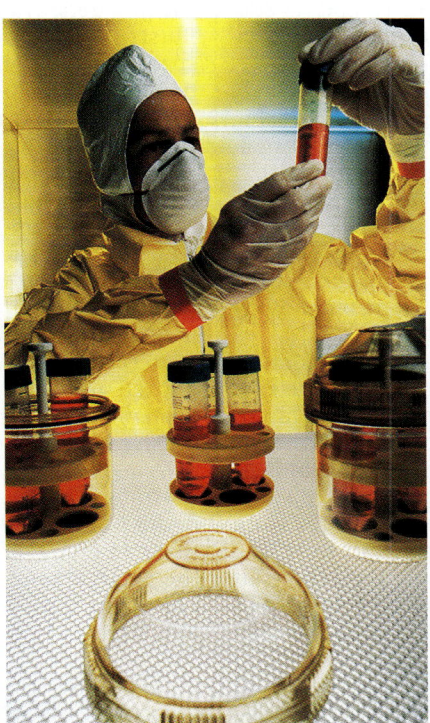

Some question the safety of certain procedures. Others worry about the effects of genetically engineered organisms on the environment. For example, certain bacteria have been engineered to break down contaminants in water and soil. Could these bacteria have an adverse effect on the environment at some time in the future? Or could bacteria be genetically engineered to create new microorganisms for biological warfare?

Recognition of the possible undesirable effects has led to strict regulation of how gene engineering technology is used, as shown in **Figure 9-5**. Laboratories must be equipped with facilities to ensure physical containment of genetically engineered organisms. In addition, scientists follow strict rules stating that microorganisms used in genetic engineering should be incapable of surviving outside a laboratory. Use of these specialized strains of microorganisms, and the rigorous testing of their products, helps ensure that genetic engineering poses no threat to the natural environment.

Figure 9-5
The wearing of safety garb protects both the lab worker and the genetic samples, which could easily become contaminated by the bacteria, viruses, and enzymes on the worker's skin.

SECTION REVIEW

1 Describe the first experiment that successfully transferred a gene from a frog to a bacterium.

2 Define the term *genetic engineering*. List the four distinct stages involved in a gene transfer.

3 How are restriction enzymes used in gene transfer experiments?

4 How do scientists ensure that microorganisms used in genetic engineering experiments will not cause damage?

Assessment Options

Closure

■ **Inferring Relationships**
The first genetic-engineering experiments were conducted before restriction enzymes had been identified and isolated. Ask students why such experiments were known as "shotgun" procedures. (*Scientists were not sure where the enzymes they used would cleave the DNA molecule. In effect, these enzymes were like the pellets of a shotgun in that they could hit a wide range of sites.*)

SECTION REVIEW

Assign the *Section Review*.

Reteaching

Engineering can be defined as "the application of scientific principles to design, construct, and operate systems." Ask students if they consider the term *genetic engineering* appropriate and accurate for describing the techniques discussed in Section 9-1. (*The term accurately conveys the nature of the work. A genetic engineer designs an experiment by carefully choosing the right restriction enzymes and genes to be cloned, constructs a system by selecting the right organisms and vectors, and then operates the system to bring about the desired result.*)

ANSWERS TO SECTION REVIEW

1 See Figure 9-1 on page 153 for an explanation.

2 Genetic engineering is defined as the transfer of genes from the chromosomes of one organism to those of an unrelated organism. The four stages are (1) cleaving DNA, (2) producing recombinant DNA, (3) cloning target cells, and (4) screening target cells.

3 Restriction enzymes recognize and cleave specific sites along the DNA molecule, leaving fragments with sticky ends.

4 Scientists select target cells that cannot survive outside the laboratory. Strict guidelines control or prohibit potentially dangerous experiments.

Key to Strategies
● Understanding Concepts (Tier I)
■ Applying Information (Tier II)
▲ Critical Thinking (Tier III)

One of the greatest successes of genetic engineering has been the manipulation of genes in crop plants and livestock. Gene transfers have made crop plants more resistant to disease, herbicides, and insects. Genetic engineering has also been used to produce hormones that increase the efficiency of milk production in dairy cows and increase the growth rate of livestock.

9-2 Transforming Agriculture

OBJECTIVES

1. **Explain the role of the Ti plasmid in agricultural research.**

2. **Describe how herbicide-resistant genes in crop plants can benefit the environment.**

3. **Explain how genetic engineering techniques are used to improve crop yields.**

4. **Describe how gene transfers are used to make livestock more productive.**

Getting Genes Into Eukaryotic Cells

The gene transfer method used by Cohen and Boyer is useful for getting genes into bacterial cells, and its success has been far-reaching. For example, many kinds of human proteins used to make drugs are inexpensively manufactured in large amounts using bacteria. However, this method is ineffective for getting genes into eukaryotic cells because the vectors used cannot enter eukaryotic cells. How do scientists get desired genes into eukaryotic cells? Clearing this hurdle was essential before gene technology could be useful in agriculture.

One method that enabled scientists to transfer genes into plants uses a bacterium that causes a type of tumor in plants. This bacterium contains the Ti plasmid, a circular molecule of DNA that possesses the genes responsible for the tumor. When the bacterium containing the Ti plasmid infects a plant cell, the Ti plasmid inserts itself into the plant cell's chromosomes. To transform the Ti plasmid into an effective genetic engineering vehicle, scientists first remove the tumor-causing gene from the Ti plasmid, as illustrated in **Figure 9-6**. The vacant space in the now harmless plasmid can be filled by the desired gene. Unfortunately, bacteria carrying the Ti plasmid cannot be used to insert DNA into plants that produce cereal grains, such as corn, rice, and wheat.

Researchers are developing powerful new techniques for introducing useful genes into these plants, such as shooting the cells with a DNA particle gun. In this procedure, tiny metal pellets are coated with DNA that contains the desired gene. Using a shotgun mechanism, these pellets are "shot" into plant cells. Inside some of the plant cells, the DNA inserts itself into one of the chromosomes. When these plant cells divide, they produce a clone of cells that can give rise to a new plant with the desired gene. Recently, this technique has been used to insert genes into the DNA in chloroplasts.

Figure 9-6

a **One method of transferring genes into eukaryotic cells uses the Ti plasmid.**

b **The gene that causes tumors can be removed and replaced with a desired gene.**

c **When the plasmid is put back into a bacterium, the new gene is carried along when it infects a plant cell.**

Resistance to Herbicides

A recent improvement in agriculture has been the development of crop plants that are resistant to the chemical glyphosate, a powerful weed killer, or herbicide, that kills most actively growing plants. Glyphosate kills plants by destroying an enzyme needed to make certain amino acids. Scientists found a kind of bacterium in which this enzyme is resistant to glyphosate. They then isolated the gene that codes for the enzyme. Shooting the gene in like a bullet, they transferred the glyphosate-resistant gene into crop plants such as the wheat plant shown in **Figure 9-7**.

This advance is of great interest to farmers. The farmer simply treats a field with glyphosate, and all growing plants die except the crop, which is resistant to glyphosate. After it is applied, glyphosate is quickly broken down in the environment. Glyphosate is not harmful to humans because our bodies do not make the amino acids that glyphosate affects. These qualities make it a great improvement over most commercial herbicides, which can be highly toxic. In addition, much of the erosion of fertile topsoil could be prevented if cropland did not have to be intensively cultivated to remove weeds.

Figure 9-7
Scientists have made crop plants such as this wheat resistant to herbicides.

Nitrogen Fixation

Nitrogen is an element that plants must have to make proteins and DNA. The most abundant source of nitrogen in the environment is the atmospheric gas N_2. However, plants cannot obtain nitrogen from the air. Bacteria living in the roots of plants such as soybeans, peanuts, and clover convert N_2 gas from the atmosphere into a form that plants can use. **Figure 9-8** shows these bacteria. The process of converting nitrogen into a form that plants can use is called **nitrogen fixation**.

Because crops use nitrogen rapidly, most farmers add high-nitrogen fertilizers to the soil. Worldwide, farmers applied more than 65 million metric tons of nitrogen fertilizers in 1990. Since high-nitrogen fertilizers are costly, using them adds a considerable expense to a farmer's budget. Farming would be much cheaper if major crops such as wheat, rice, and corn could be genetically engineered to carry out nitrogen fixation. The bacterial genes for nitrogen fixation have been successfully inserted into plants. However, these genes do not seem to function properly in their new hosts. Many experiments are being performed to find a way to overcome this difficulty.

Figure 9-8
Nodules on the roots of this soybean plant contain populations of bacteria that convert nitrogen to a form the plant can use.

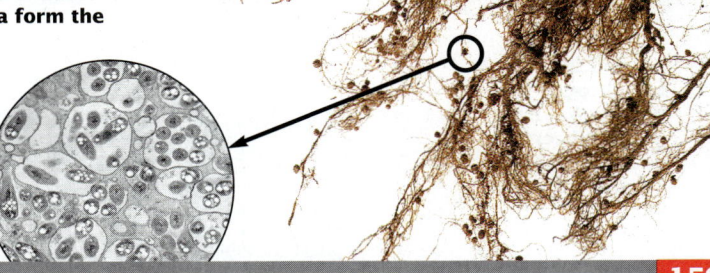

159

Community Connection: Organic Gardens

Organic farmers do not use synthetic chemicals, but instead depend on natural herbicides and pesticides. Invite an organic gardener (or someone familiar with the subject) to speak with the class about the practices such gardeners follow and the products they use. Have students use what they learn from the speaker to prepare a written report describing the differences between a typical farmer who uses synthetic pesticides and herbicides, an organic farmer, and a biotech farmer who uses genetically engineered products. Afterward, have students discuss their opinions about the various agricultural products and which ones they would prefer.

Life/Work Skills
Finding Information
● **Summarizing Facts**

Cotton plants are important crops because their fibers are used throughout the world to make cloth. They could not survive for long without the help of chemical pesticides. Scientists are looking for alternatives to using these chemicals. Have students check on-line references for information about genetic-engineering experiments currently being conducted with cotton plants. Students may also contact Cotton Incorporated, 4505 Creedmoor Road, Raleigh, NC 27612.

Resistance to Insects

Genetic engineering techniques can also make crops resistant to destructive insects, such as the locust and other pests. Resistant crops would not need to be sprayed with insecticides, which are expensive and can be harmful to the environment. Today more than 40 percent of all chemical insecticides are used to kill insects that eat cotton plants. Biologists have produced cotton plants that are resistant to these pests so that insecticides are not needed.

One successful approach to making plants resistant to insects uses bacteria that produce enzymes which kill destructive caterpillars.

When the genes coding for these enzymes are inserted into tomato plants, for example, the new enzymes make the plants highly toxic to tomato hornworms. Hornworms that eat any of the tomato plants quickly die.

Many pests attack the roots of important plants. To combat these pests, genetic engineers are introducing the same insect-killing enzyme into a bacterium that colonizes the roots of crop plants. If an insect eats these roots, it will consume the bacteria and be killed. **Figure 9-9** shows how genetic engineering could improve a cotton plant.

Figure 9-9
Plants, such as this cotton plant, could be genetically engineered . . .

a . . . to produce an enzyme that kills pests so that highly toxic pesticides would not be needed, . . .

b . . . to resist glyphosate so that highly toxic herbicides would not be needed, . . .

c . . . and to carry out nitrogen fixation so that nitrogen fertilizers would not need to be added to the soil.

160

Matter of Fact: The Ti Plasmid

The large Ti (tumor-inducing) plasmid consists of approximately 200,000 base pairs. Found in a common soil bacterium, the Ti plasmid causes crown gall disease when it is incorporated into a plant cell's DNA. The incorporation of the Ti plasmid into the plant cell's DNA is the only known naturally occurring recombination between prokaryotic and eukaryotic cells.

Figure 9-10
These cows produce more milk after being injected with genetically engineered growth hormone.

Genetic Engineering in Livestock

Genetic engineering can also produce bigger, more productive livestock. For example, injecting growth hormone, genetically engineered in bacteria, into dairy cows, such as the ones shown in **Figure 9-10**, increases their milk production. The milk is no different from milk produced by other cows. Bovine growth hormone is the natural signal that increases milk production in cows. In this case, the hormone is used in higher amounts than occur naturally.

Prior to the development of genetic engineering, growth hormone was extracted from the pituitary glands of dead cows. Today the hormone is obtained in the laboratory using genetic engineering. The gene containing the instructions for producing growth hormone has been introduced into bacteria. These bacteria produce growth hormone, which is then injected into cows.

Biologists have introduced extra copies of the genes that code for growth hormones into the chromosomes of cows and hogs. These attempts are likely to create new, leaner, fast-growing cattle and hogs.

Phase Three
Assessment Options

Closure

■ **Analyzing Information**
Crop rotation involves alternating the kind of crops grown in a field from year to year. For example, one year a farmer grows a crop of nitrogen-fixing, or leguminous, plants such as soybeans. The following season, the farmer sows the same field with nonleguminous plants such as corn. Ask students why farmers throughout the world have been following such a practice for hundreds of years. *(By rotating crops, a farmer will not need to use as much nitrogen-rich fertilizer because the leguminous plants will replenish the usable nitrogen in the soil.)* Ask students how genetic engineering could help change this practice. *(Genetically engineered crops could fix their own nitrogen.)*

SECTION REVIEW
Assign the *Section Review*.

Reteaching

Although thousands of plants have been identified as edible, modern agriculture utilizes just a few crops. Have students list these crops. Have each student select one from the list and research how that crop is being genetically engineered. Students can use the library, check on-line references, or contact the American Society of Agronomy, 667 South Segoe Road, Madison, WI 53711.

SECTION REVIEW

1. How is the Ti plasmid used to insert genes into plant cells? What are its shortcomings as a genetic engineering tool?

2. How can genetic engineering make crop plants resistant to glyphosate?

3. How can genetic engineering reduce the use of insecticides?

4. What effects can genetic engineering have on livestock?

161

ANSWERS TO **SECTION REVIEW**

1. Refer to Figure 9-6 for an explanation. The Ti plasmid cannot be used as a vector for inserting genes into plants that produce grains.

2. Genetic engineers have inserted weedkiller-resistant genes from bacteria into certain crop plants.

3. Genetic engineers have inserted genes that produce insect-killing enzymes into the DNA of certain crops.

4. Genetic engineers have developed products that make livestock grow leaner, faster, and more productive.

Key to Strategies
● Understanding Concepts (Tier I)
■ Applying Information (Tier II)
▲ Critical Thinking (Tier III)

Much of the excitement surrounding genetic engineering has focused on its potential to aid in preventing and curing illnesses. Major advances have been made in the production of proteins that can treat illnesses, in the development of new vaccines to combat diseases, and in the replacement of defective genes with healthy ones.

9-3 Advances in Medicine

OBJECTIVES

1 **Describe how transferring human genes into bacteria can benefit human health.**

2 **Explain how gene transfers could be used to combat genetic disorders.**

3 **Describe three uses of DNA profiling.**

4 **Summarize the goals of the Human Genome Project and the ethical issues it raises.**

Making Miracle Drugs

Many human illnesses occur because our bodies fail to make critical proteins. One example of such an illness is diabetes. In one form of diabetes, a person cannot make a protein called insulin. As a result, they cannot regulate the levels of sugar in their blood. Diabetes can be treated if the body is supplied with insulin.

Until recently, it was not practical to use proteins as drugs. The body contains only small amounts of proteins such as insulin, making them difficult and expensive to obtain. In most cases, proteins had to be obtained from tissues of cows or pigs. Now genetic engineering can be used to provide large quantities of proteins in a short period of time. Genes that produce medically important proteins can be inserted into bacteria. Because bacteria can be easily grown in bulk, large amounts of the desired protein can be inexpensively prepared. **Figure 9-11** shows how genetic engineering is used to produce insulin.

Some proteins now being produced by genetically engineered bacteria dissolve blood clots, helping to prevent heart attacks and strokes. Genetically engineered bacteria are also used to produce proteins that prevent high blood pressure and that help regulate kidney function. Genetically engineered vaccines that are safer and less expensive than traditional vaccines are also being produced.

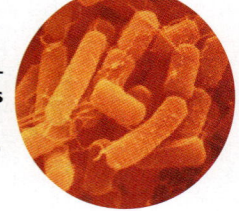

Figure 9-11

a To manufacture large amounts of insulin, scientists insert the gene for insulin into a bacterial plasmid.

b Bacteria containing the plasmids are cloned and produce insulin.

c The insulin can be collected and used to treat diabetics like this young man.

Figure 9-12

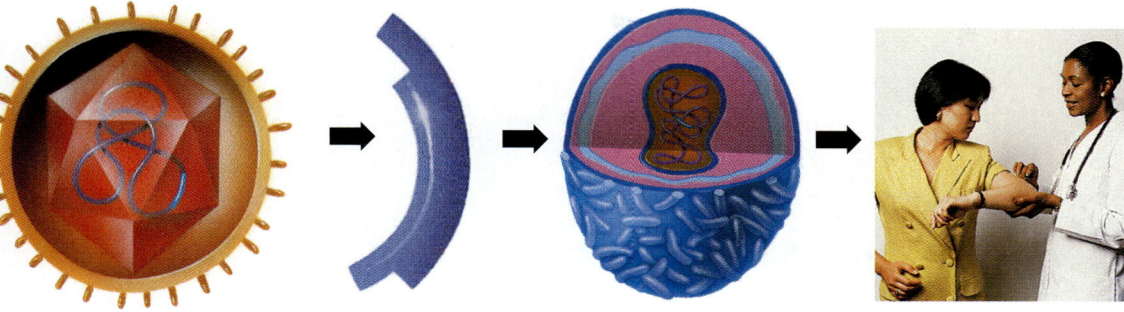

a	b	c	d
To produce a vaccine against genital herpes, the virus that causes genital herpes is obtained from the cells of an infected person.	A DNA fragment containing the gene that codes for the herpes surface protein . . .	. . . is inserted into a harmless cowpox virus. The gene causes the virus to make the herpes surface proteins.	A person injected with the engineered virus containing the desired gene can make antibodies against the genital herpes virus.

Making Vaccines

A **vaccine** is a harmless version of a disease-causing microbe (bacterium or virus) injected into animals or people so that their immune systems will develop defenses against the disease. The injected version serves as a model for the body, which responds by making defensive proteins called **antibodies**. If a vaccinated animal is exposed to the disease-causing microbe, it will immediately begin large-scale production of microbe-attacking antibodies. The antibodies will stop the growth of the microbe before the disease can develop.

Traditionally, vaccines have been prepared either by killing the microbe or by preventing its growth. This ensures that injecting a vaccine into your body will not make you sick. The problem with this approach is that any failure in the killing or weakening of the disease-causing microbe can result in the disease being introduced into the very patients in need of protection. While the majority of such vaccines are extremely safe, a tiny percentage of vaccinated individuals contract the disease from the vaccine. This small, but real, danger is one reason why rabies vaccines are administered only when a person has actually been bitten by an animal suspected of carrying rabies.

Harmless microbes can be made into vaccines

Using genetic engineering techniques, genes from disease-causing microbes can be inserted into harmless bacteria or viruses. These harmless microbes can be used to stimulate your body to make disease-attacking antibodies. For example, a vaccine against the genital herpes virus, which produces small blisters on the genitals, has been made using genetic engineering techniques, as shown in **Figure 9-12**. Genes that encode the surface proteins of the herpes virus are inserted into a harmless virus. This viral vector carries the genes "piggyback" into the human body, stimulating the person's immune system to make protective antibodies against the virus. Individuals who are injected with the vaccine are able to fight infections from the herpes simplex virus type 2.

Genetically engineered vaccines also offer hope for other diseases. A vaccine against the hepatitis B virus, which causes a fatal inflammation of the liver, is also available. Scientists are also working to produce a vaccine that will protect people against malaria. Transmitted by mosquitoes, malaria affected more than 500 million people worldwide in 1994.

163

Decision Making
▲ **Evaluating Viewpoints**

The fact that a tiny percentage of individuals contract a disease from the vaccine has been used as an argument against certain vaccination programs. For example, some people take the position that polio vaccinations should be halted because the chances of contracting polio from the vaccine are greater than the chances of contracting the disease in nature. Have students select a particular disease for which people are presently vaccinated and examine any alternatives that are available. Have them analyze each alternative and then select the one they would recommend. For example, in the case of polio, alternatives could include a strict quarantine for afflicted individuals and a public education program about the disease. A student may select the latter as the better alternative because it does not interfere with anyone's lifestyle.

Visual Strategy | **Figure 9-12**

● **Interpreting Graphics**
Remind students that protein markers establish the identity of a cell or virus. A protein marker must be recognized as foreign by an infected individual, whose body then mounts an immune response. Ask students what would happen if the DNA fragment shown in Figure 9-12b did not produce a surface protein. *(The immune system of the infected individual would not "see" the invading virus and thus would not mount an immune response.)*

Historical Perspective: Vaccinations

Louis Pasteur's development of a rabies vaccine in 1884 provided the basis for most modern vaccines. He used the term *vaccination* in recognition of the work performed by the English doctor Edward Jenner in 1798. Jenner observed that milkmaids who contracted cowpox, a mild disease in farm animals, never contracted smallpox. At the time, smallpox afflicted 95 percent of the population, killing 10 percent of those who contracted the disease. Many survivors were blinded and disfigured with scars. Jenner inoculated a boy with fluid from a milkmaid's cowpox sore. He subsequently inoculated the boy with fluid from a smallpox sore. The boy survived and never developed smallpox. Jenner called his process *vaccination,* from the Latin word *vacca,* meaning "cow."

Key to Strategies
● Understanding Concepts (Tier I)
■ Applying Information (Tier II)
▲ Critical Thinking (Tier III)

Connection: *Chapter 7*

Patterns of Heredity
Use a Punnett square to review how a child can be born with a disease carried by a recessive gene if both parents carry one copy of this gene. Ask what percentage of these parents' children can be expected to inherit the disease (25 percent).

Theme Answer

Heredity
The genetic alteration would not be passed on to her children because it did not affect her egg cells, which represent her contribution to her offspring.

Human Gene Therapy

● **Relating Concepts**
Have students make a **Graphic Organizer** similar to the one at the bottom of this page to show how genetic engineering is used to treat human diseases.

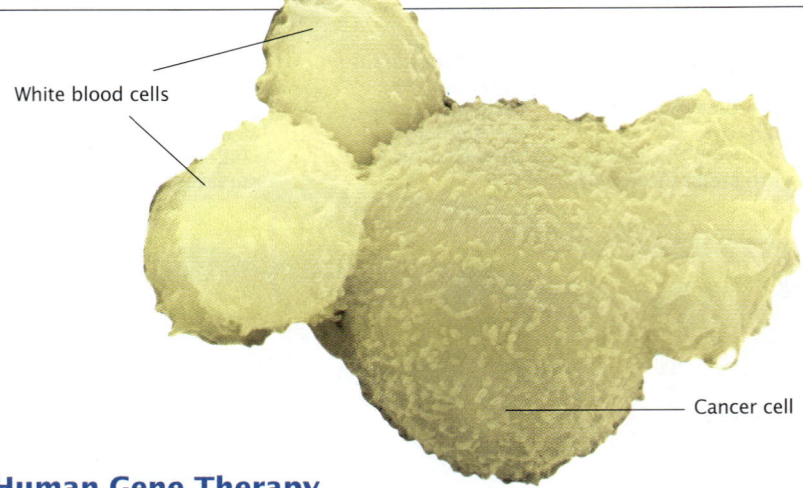

Figure 9-13
White blood cells containing tumor necrosis factor are attacking this cancer cell.

White blood cells

Cancer cell

Human Gene Therapy

Heredity

If a woman with genetically altered bone-marrow cells has children, will the genetic change be passed on to them?

Most human genetic diseases are due to an individual's lack of a normally functioning copy of a particular gene. The problem usually arises when both of the individual's parents contribute defective copies of a gene. One obvious way to cure such disorders is to give the person a working copy of the defective gene. Until recently, this approach was not practical for three reasons. First, the defective gene was difficult to identify and isolate. Second, it was hard to transfer a "healthy" copy into the cells of body tissues that use it. Finally, it was necessary to find a way to keep the altered cells or their offspring alive in the body for a long time. With genetic engineering, it is now possible to overcome these difficulties. Gene transfers are being attempted as a way of combating a variety of genetic disorders, including cystic fibrosis and muscular dystrophy.

Human gene therapy may prove successful

In 1995, doctors reported that the first three infants to undergo gene therapy appeared to be responding to the treatment. In 1993, the newborns were given a gene that they were missing at birth. People born without this gene develop a fatal blood disease. In the therapy, doctors inserted the gene into certain blood cells taken from the newborns' umbilical cord. These cells were then injected into the infants' bloodstream. The hope was that the genetically engineered cells would produce the missing blood factor that would protect them from the disease. Two years later, the children are found to be producing a blood factor necessary for survival.

However, it is too soon to declare the children entirely cured of the disease. They are also being treated with medication, so doctors are unable to tell whether the drug or the gene therapy is keeping the children alive. While it is too early to say the technique has been completely successful, the signs are positive. If the technique works over the long run, it might be used to treat common blood disorders like hemophilia and sickle cell anemia, as well as diseases like AIDS.

Human gene transfers may also help in the battle against cancer

All humans have white blood cells that secrete a protein called TNF (tumor necrosis factor) into the blood. TNF attacks and kills cancer cells like the one shown in **Figure 9-13**. Unfortunately, TNF cannot work unless it encounters a cancer cell. This does not often happen. Recently, genetic engineers developed a way to add the gene encoding TNF to a kind of white blood cell that is effective at locating cancer cells but not effective at harming them. Armed with this new TNF weapon, however, these white blood cells will become more like cruise missiles homing in on cancer cells.

164

Graphic Organizer

Use the following graphic organizer with the teaching strategy **Human Gene Therapy** on page 164.

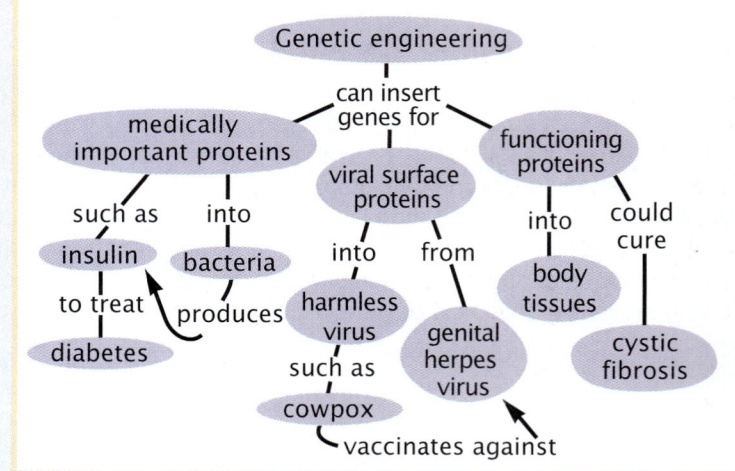

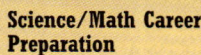

Biotechnology

What would it be like to . . .

- search the rain forest for new medicines?
- study the effects of chemicals on living cells?
- design new foods and drugs?

These are just a few of the daily adventures experienced by people working in the field of biotechnology.

Biotechnology: What Is It?

Biotechnologists work in areas such as developing drugs, using enzymes and catalysts to increase the yields of reactions, and developing chemical and genetic engineering processes that are safe for the environment. Advances in the field of biotechnology have resulted in the production of synthetic hormones and in crops that are tastier, that are more disease resistant, and that have a longer shelf life.

Career Focus: Dr. Eloy Rodriguez

Biochemist at Cornell University, Ithaca, New York

"It was a good thing that I ignored a school counselor's advice to go to technical school, which was standard advice for many minority students at the time. I grew up in Hidalgo County, Texas, the county with the lowest average income per person in the country. When I was a young boy, my grandfather would take me on long walks through nearby fields, where he taught me everything he knew about the different plants and insects we found there. Ever since then, I have been fascinated by the life around me. I have made this passion my career."

What I Do: "I have helped develop a new scientific discipline called zoopharmacognosy—the chemistry of plants that are used medicinally by animals. One plant that I studied in the rain forest of Africa is used by wild chimpanzees to remove parasites. By studying the plant's chemicals, I discovered a drug that is effective against human intestinal parasites, fungi that cause skin infections, and possibly cancer."

Science/Math Career Preparation

High School
- Chemistry
- Physics
- Calculus

College
- Chemistry/biochemistry
- Molecular biology
- Statistics
- Genetics
- Organic chemistry
- Physics
- Anatomy and physiology

Graduate
- Master's degree is suggested

Employment Outlook:
Accelerated growth in this field is predicted as the number of research areas in biotechnology increases.

To Find Out More

1 For further information, write to:
American Society for Biochemistry and Molecular Biology
9650 Rockville Pike
Bethesda, MD 20014

2 See your school counselor to find out what colleges and universities offer programs in biotechnology. Review the prerequisites and course requirements. Make a poster showing the range of job opportunities in this field.

Find articles that describe how new drugs and enzymes are created using computers. Prepare a report for your class.

The rosy periwinkle is the source of two

165

Career Opportunities

Writing a Résumé

1. Have the class brainstorm ideas to the following questions:

If you wanted a career in biotechnology...

- what kind of personality traits would be essential?
- which subjects should you study in high school? in college?
- what kind of extracurricular activities should you pursue?
- what kind of practical experience should you gain?

Write student responses on the board or on the overhead projector.

2. Collect and distribute newspapers and periodicals that contain advertisements for jobs in biotechnology. In small groups, have students browse ads and select one. Instruct each group to write down all the information needed to apply for the position described in the ad (name and address of company, description of position, desired qualifications, etc.).

3. In small groups, have students use the information collected in Steps 1 and 2 to write a one-page résumé responding to their chosen advertisement. Present the basic format for writing a résumé. Have groups trade résumés and critique each group's efforts.

Identifying Sequences in Genes

The knowledge that restriction enzymes cut DNA at specific sites has produced powerful tools that have great effects beyond the biological sciences. Because every person's DNA is unique, analysis of DNA from tissues can identify an individual. In this procedure, DNA samples are taken from the blood of a person suspected of committing a crime and from a tissue sample (such as blood, semen, or bone) found at the scene of the crime. Then the DNA in each sample is treated and developed to produce a piece of film characterized by columns of short black bands. This pattern of bands is a **DNA fingerprint**. If the patterns of bands match, an individual can be positively identified.

These techniques for DNA analysis can link a suspect to a crime, confirm family relationships, and identify the remains of deceased individuals. DNA analysis is also valuable for identifying the genes that cause genetic disorders. Alleles for Huntington's disease, sickle cell anemia, and a number of other genetic disorders can now be detected in this way.

Figure 9-14
In 1995 biologists successfully sequenced all the genes in the bacterium *Haemophilus influenzae*, which causes bacterial meningitis. This is one of the first bacteria to be completely sequenced and biologists hope to use this "blueprint" to develop a vaccine.

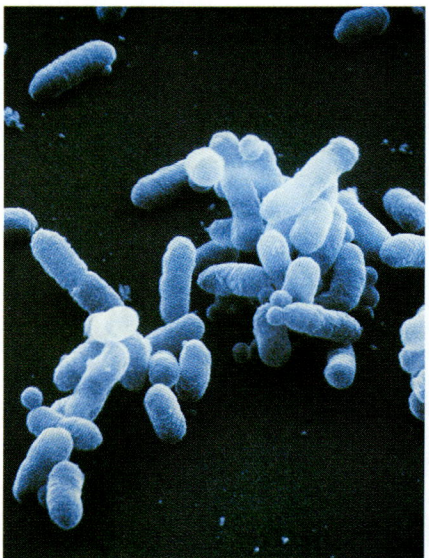

DNA can be copied in a test tube
In 1985, Kary B. Mullis, a biochemist working for a biotechnology corporation in California, discovered a simple way to make unlimited copies of a gene. This process is known as polymerase chain reaction (PCR). The starting materials for PCR include a fragment of DNA, DNA polymerase, and a supply of the four nucleotides—adenine, thymine, guanine, and cytosine. When these ingredients are heated in a test tube, millions of copies of the molecule can be made in just a few hours. PCR has revolutionized biological research.

Scientists are mapping the human genome
Gene sequencing is the process of determining the order of nucleotide bases within a gene. Gene sequencing has been successfully completed on several species of bacteria, including *Haemophilus influenzae*, shown in **Figure 9-14**. Genetic engineers are attempting to locate, catalog, and sequence every gene on the 23 human chromosomes. Biologists call the entire collection of genes the **human genome**. The effort to sequence every human gene is called the Human Genome Project. Because the human genome contains approximately 3 billion nucleotides, the project is not a small one. This international project was launched in 1990 and is expected to cost several billion dollars.

SECTION REVIEW

1. Explain how genetic engineering can be useful in the treatment of human illnesses such as diabetes.

2. How could human genetic therapy cure genetic disorders such as cystic fibrosis?

3. Describe how genetic engineering techniques could be used to help determine a suspected criminal's innocence or guilt.

4. What are the goals of the Human Genome Project?

166

Highlights

Gene therapy offers hope for patients with genetic disorders, such as this child with cystic fibrosis.

Key Terms	Summary
9-1 **The Revolution in Genetics**  Bacterial plasmids make genetic engineering possible.	recombinant DNA (p. 153) genetic engineering (p. 153) cloning (p. 154) restriction enzyme (p. 154) plasmid (p. 155) vector (p. 156)	• Over the last 20 years, genetic engineers have learned how to transfer genes from one organism to another. • Every gene transfer starts by cleaving DNA into small fragments using restriction enzymes. • Fragments containing the desired gene are then transferred to a target cell using a vector. • After removing uninfected cells, scientists search for cells that have taken up the desired gene.
9-2 **Transforming Agriculture** Cows injected with genetically engineered growth hormone produce more milk. 	nitrogen fixation (p. 159)	• Genetic engineers have manipulated the genes of certain kinds of crop plants to make these plants resistant to herbicides and destructive pests. • Genetic engineers are looking for a way to transfer genes for nitrogen fixation into crop plants. • Adding genetically engineered bovine growth hormone to the diet of livestock increases milk production in dairy cows and increases the weight of cattle and hogs.
9-3 **Advances in Medicine** 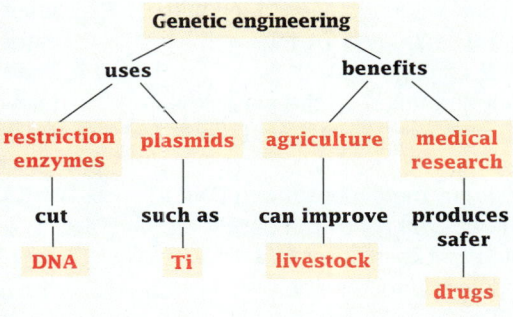 Scientists hope to use genetic engineering to treat diseases like cancer.	vaccine (p. 163) antibody (p. 163) DNA fingerprint (p. 166) human genome (p. 166)	• Genetic engineering techniques can be used to manufacture proteins, such as insulin, and vaccines. • Some human genetic disorders are being treated by inserting copies of healthy genes into individuals lacking them. • Scientists use DNA fingerprinting to reveal DNA patterns that vary from one individual to the next. • The Human Genome Project seeks to locate, catalog, and record the nucleotide base sequence of every human gene.

Alternative Assessment

Assign students to cooperative work groups. Have each group develop a board game called Human Genome Project. Tell students that they are free to choose the format of the game and the way in which the winner is determined. Suggest that they model their game format on existing board games or TV game shows. Emphasize that any questions used in the game must be based on information covered in this chapter.

Portfolio Assessment

Portfolio Assessment on page T39 provides options for building and evaluating students' portfolios. Students and teachers can select items from the areas listed on page T39 for inclusion in a portfolio.

167

ANSWER TO CONCEPT MAP

The following is one possible answer to the Relating Concepts exercise on page 168.

Genetic engineering

uses — benefits

restriction enzymes — plasmids — agriculture — medical research

cut → DNA

such as → Ti

can improve → livestock

produces safer → drugs

review

Understanding Vocabulary

1. For each pair of terms, explain the difference in their meanings.
   a. recombinant DNA, restriction enzyme
   b. vector, plasmid
   c. glyphosate, nitrogen fixation

2. Using each set of words below, write one or more sentences summarizing information learned in this chapter.
   a. genetic engineering, cloning, restriction enzyme
   b. plasmid, vector, recombinant DNA, *Eco*RI
   c. gene sequencing, human genome, DNA fingerprint

Understanding Concepts

3. **Relating Concepts** Construct a concept map describing genetic engineering. Try to include the following terms in your map: plasmids, livestock, DNA, medical research, drugs, agriculture, restriction enzymes, and Ti.

4. **Inferring Relationships** What is recombinant DNA? How did Cohen and Boyer recombine DNA in bacteria?

5. **Inferring Conclusions** Explain why Cohen and Boyer's experiments ushered in a "new age" of biology.

6. **Predicting Outcomes** How did Cohen and Boyer use their knowledge of transformation to predict that bacteria would take up plasmids containing recombinant DNA?

7. **Identifying Functions** What is the function of the enzyme ligase in forming recombinant DNA?

8. **Identifying Structure and Function** What are plasmids? How do they function in the formation of recombinant DNA?

9. **Applying Information** You are a paleontologist with experience in using DNA fingerprinting techniques. A colleague has discovered a fossilized bone that contains small amounts of DNA. What method will yield sufficient genetic material for DNA analysis?

10. **Interpreting Graphs** The following graph shows the results of an experiment with populations of natural and engineered bacteria, both of which were able to convert a harmful chemical to harmless byproducts. Each population had 40 mL of the chemical added on the first day. The graph shows how much of the chemical remained after almost three days. Approximately how much of the chemical did each population of bacteria convert by the end of the test?

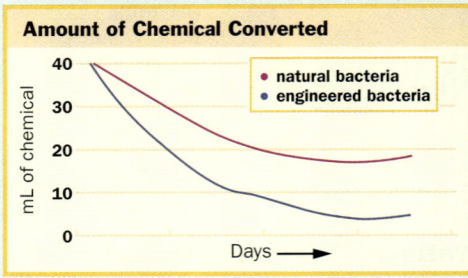

Amount of Chemical Converted
- natural bacteria
- engineered bacteria

(y-axis: mL of chemical, 0–40; x-axis: Days)

11. **Identifying Functions** How does a restriction enzyme, such as *Eco*RI, create DNA fragments with "sticky" ends?

12. **Recognizing Relationships** How did the bacterial cell's resistance to the antibiotic tetracycline contribute to the results of Cohen and Boyer's experiments?

13. **Identifying Functions** Explain how scientists introduce genes into plants in which the Ti plasmid cannot be used.

14. **Inferring Conclusions** How can herbicide-resistant genes in crop plants benefit the environment? Give an example.

15. **Summarizing Information** Describe two ways that genetic engineers are attempting to make plants resistant to insects.

16. **Identifying Functions** Identify two types of genetically engineered medicine, and tell what each type does.

17. **BUILDING ON WHAT YOU HAVE LEARNED** In Chapter 8 you learned about the double-helix model of DNA that was first constructed by Watson and Crick. How did Watson and Crick's model of DNA lead to genetic engineering?

Answers

Understanding Vocabulary

1. a. Recombinant DNA is made of DNA fragments from unrelated organisms; a restriction enzyme cleaves DNA into fragments.
   b. A vector is a vehicle for transporting a gene into a cell; a plasmid is a circular piece of DNA capable of replicating.
   c. Glyphosate, an herbicide, kills plants by destroying an enzyme that they need to make certain amino acids; nitrogen fixation is the process of converting elemental nitrogen into a form that plants can use.

2. Answers will vary.
   a. See pages 153–154.
   b. See pages 154–156.
   c. See page 166.

Understanding Concepts

3. Concept map answer is shown on page 167.

4. Recombinant DNA forms when fragments of DNA from two or more organisms are joined in the laboratory. Cohen and Boyer isolated the rRNA gene from a frog cell and inserted it into a bacterium.

5. Scientists now have the ability to engineer organisms to produce new proteins.

6. In transformation, bacteria take up bits of extracellular DNA. When bacteria are placed in an environment containing plasmids, a few cells will take in the molecules.

7. Ligase seals together two DNA fragments.

8. A plasmid is a circular DNA molecule found in bacteria. When cut by *Eco*RI, a plasmid opens and has the same sticky ends as a DNA fragment cut by the same enzyme. When joined with one of these DNA fragments, the plasmid closes and can be used as a vector to carry the fragment into a cell.

9. PCR method will yield sufficient DNA for analysis.

10. Engineered bacteria consumed 35 mL and natural bacteria consumed 21 mL.

11. See Figure 9-2 on page 154.

12. Only cells that had taken up the plasmid survived. Some of these cells also had the transferred gene.

13. Scientists coat tiny metal pellets with DNA containing the desired gene. The pellets are then shot into plant cells, where the DNA inserts itself into a chromosome.

14. See page 159.

15. See Figure 9-9 on page 160.

16. Insulin maintains blood sugar level and vaccines protect us against disease.

17. Their model provided scientists with the knowledge they needed to be able to transfer genetic material.

Interpreting Graphics

18. a. d, a, c, b
    b. a: inserting gene into plasmid; b: bacteria containing the plasmid are cloned; c: target cells are screened; d: DNA sequence is cut by restriction enzyme

Interpreting Graphics

18. The figures below show four distinct stages of a gene transfer experiment.

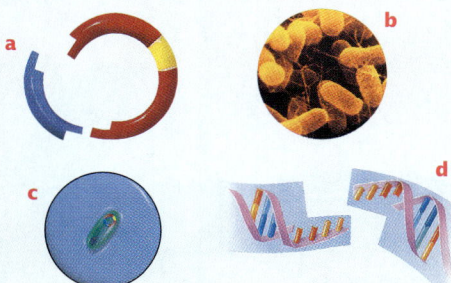

a. How should the figures be ordered to show the proper sequence of events?
b. What is occurring in each step of the illustration?

Reviewing Themes

19. **Heredity**
How are organisms produced by genetic engineering different from organisms produced by sexual reproduction?

20. **Evolution**
Natural selection is a process of evolution in which the members of a population who are best able to adapt to their environment survive and produce offspring. How is natural selection affected by genetic engineering?

21. **Interdependence**
Why would farmers be interested in genetically engineered crop plants that are resistant to the herbicide glyphosate?

Thinking Critically

22. **Evaluating Opinions** The federal government of the United States has strict regulations that require researchers to contain genetically engineered organisms inside a laboratory and to ensure that the organisms could not survive outside the laboratory if they did escape. Why do you think the government has these strict regulations?

23. **Distinguishing Fact From Opinion** A judge presiding over a highly publicized murder trial dismissed the prosecution's request to admit DNA fingerprints as evidence, calling it "unproven scientific mumbo-jumbo." Do you agree with the judge? Explain your answer.

Life/Work Skills

24. **Finding Information** Use library references or search an on-line database to find out about American plant breeder Luther Burbank and the work he did on mass selection. Prepare a visual summary of your findings to share with your class.

25. **Working Cooperatively** Hold a debate with your classmates regarding the safety questions raised by the potential release of genetically engineered plants, bacteria, and animals into the environment.

Activities and Projects

26. **Agriculture Connection** Search an on-line data base to find out about vegetable vaccines. Researchers at Texas A & M University are testing genetically-engineered potatoes containing a vaccine that they hope will protect people from common gut infections. What are some of the advantages of these vegetable vaccines?

27. **Economics Connection** Use library references or contact seed companies to find out how customer demand for new plants and seeds is met.

Discovering Through Reading

28. Read the article "The New Science of Identity" by Cassandra Franklin-Barbajosa in *National Geographic*, May 1992, pages 112–124. Summarize five ways DNA fingerprinting is being used today to answer questions about identity and heredity.

29. Read the article "Invasion of the Shapechangers" by Stephen Day in *New Scientist*, October 1995, pages 30–35. What are Hox genes? How are scientists manipulating these genes? What do they hope to discover from them?

30. Read the article "Swallowing *Shigella*" by John Travis in *Science News*, May 11, 1996, pages 302–303. What is the third vaccine revolution? What are the alternatives to using *Shigella* as a vaccine carrier? How do DNA vaccines work?

31. Read the article "Computing with DNA" by Ivars Peterson in *Science News*, July 13, 1996, pages 26–27. What advantages and disadvantages do DNA-based computers have? What proposals have been made to cope with errors?

169

Life/Work Skills

24. Luther Burbank hand-selected "parents" with desirable characteristics from large populations of fruits, flowers, vegetables, and grains. He developed more than 800 new plant varieties, including seedless grapes and the spineless cactus.
25. Topics for debate will vary.

Activities and Projects

26. Students may explain that such vaccines would be easily produced and administered.
27. Students may cite marketing and research strategies.

Discovering Through Reading

28. Students should cite examples in forensics, zoology, genealogy, tissue and organ matching, and evolutionary biology.
29. Scientists are manipulating *Hox* genes, primitive genes for body plans, in attempts to recreate and study the evolution of development.
30. DNA vaccines represent the third-generation revolution. Alternatives include microscopic spheres of a biopolymer called PLG and cochleates—lipid-based structures. DNA vaccines enter host cells and induce production of foreign proteins, thus mimicking infected cells and inducing a strong immune response.
31. Advantages include speed, memory capacity, and energy efficiency. Disadvantages include the error-prone nature of the system and imperfect separation or extraction techniques. Proposals include using a "sticker" model of DNA (short DNA fragments) or using DNA strands that are attached to the test tube.

Reviewing Themes

19. Genetically engineered organisms have DNA that is combined in a laboratory using specific tools, not during fertilization.
20. Genetic engineering enables unlikely combinations of genes that might not have formed under naturally occurring selective pressure.
21. Farmers could use glyphosate to kill weeds and reduce erosion by reducing the need to plow.

Thinking Critically

22. Students should reason that safety is an important issue surrounding these experiments.
23. Answers will vary, but students can point out that a match of DNA fingerprints from two different samples has only one explanation—that the prints are from the same person.

Science, Technology, and Society

Objectives

- Review the concepts of genetic engineering and recombinant DNA technology.
- Consider the goals that genetic engineering can achieve.
- Investigate the problems and controversies surrounding gene technology.

Commercialization of Genetics

▲ Evaluating Viewpoints

Can a scientist or a company own a gene and the information it encodes? Have students use references in the library or search an on-line database to investigate the U.S. Supreme Court's ruling on the patenting of genes and the controversies that surround this topic. How does the U.S. Patent Office decide what should and should not be patented? What about the rights of the people whose DNA is used in genetic research? Should these people be entitled to royalties? Discuss these and related issues with your class.

Controversies Surrounding Genetically Engineered Food

■ Predicting Outcomes

Have students use references in the library or search an on-line database to find information about genetically engineered food products currently available in the marketplace. Discuss with your class reasons for the controversies surrounding food products such as Flavr Savr tomatoes and milk from bST-treated cows. Why have other products, such as herbicide- and disease-resistant strains of wheat, been exempt from such public scrutiny? Have students find and compare examples of media coverage of these products. Should all genetically engineered foods be labeled? Discuss the consequences that could occur if the FDA decides to require labeling of all food products developed through genetic engineering.

What Is the Future of Genetic Engineering?

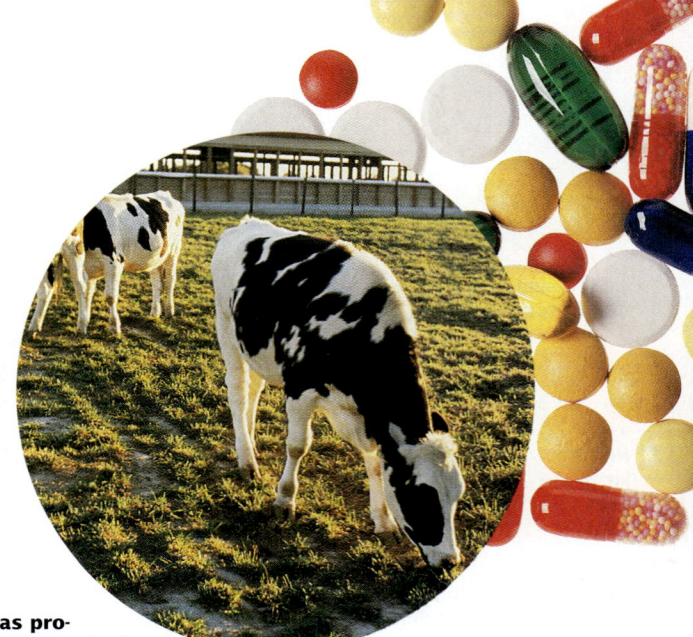

From food to pharmaceuticals, genetic engineering is affecting our lives. Science and industry are eager to explore the possibilities of this revolutionary technology. Will society be responsible enough to handle the powerful tools that science has developed?

Genetic engineering has produced many useful pharmaceutical and agricultural products.

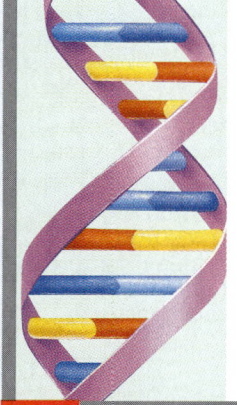

Joining Genes

Every living organism has genes made of DNA. Genes contain the information to build proteins, the structurally and metabolically important molecules required for all life processes. In genetic engineering, a gene from one organism is spliced into the DNA of another organism, where it builds a protein that wasn't there before.

Genetic Engineering at Work

Since its development over 20 years ago, genetic engineering has yielded many useful pharmaceutical and agricultural products. Today, bacteria are routinely turned into microscopic factories that produce large supplies of medically important human proteins, such as insulin and growth hormone. Genetically engineered drugs now offer hope for treating diseases such as cys-

tic fibrosis and cancer. Every year, agriculturally important plants, animals, and bacteria are given new genes that increase crop yield, enhance the nutritional value of food, increase productivity, and reduce the need for toxic pesticides and herbicides.

What Will the Future Bring?

What can we expect from genetic engineering in the future? Agriculture can continue to look forward to the development of new varieties of crops that are resistant to herbicides, insects, viruses, and changes in temperature. For example, in 1995, the United States government approved commercial use of a variety of corn that contains genes from the bacterium *Bacillus thuringiensis*. When these genes are expressed, they produce high levels of a protein that is

---

ANSWERS TO **ANALYZING THE ISSUES**

1 Answers will vary. Students should discover that genetic engineering research in humans presents many complicated and controversial issues, such as the patenting of human cells, the value and monitoring of eugenics, and the safety of gene therapy. Students should realize that guidelines, though they exist, will be constantly refined and updated in the years to come.

2 Through their research, students should learn that the United States Department of Agriculture (USDA), the Food and Drug Administration (FDA), the Environmental Protection Agency (EPA), and most state governments closely monitor and regulate the development and testing of genetically engineered products. Students should conclude that consumers should stay informed and decide for themselves if a product, whether genetically engineered or not, is right for them.

toxic to major pests such as corn borers and corn earworms.

Scientists are also now working on new vaccines called DNA vaccines. These vaccines contain a portion of the DNA from an organism that causes disease. Once injected into a host, the host's cells take up the DNA and express the foreign proteins on their surface—just as occurs in a natural infection, but without causing disease. This stimulates the host's immune system to provide protection against the disease. It is hoped that these vaccines will someday be able to protect us against allergies and against diseases such as AIDS and malaria.

In a test tube, strands of a DNA sample are separated by heat. Using nucleotides as building blocks, DNA polymerase makes a complementary copy of the DNA. Once a copy is made, the DNA strands are separated by heat, and each strand is copied again.

Technique

Polymerase Chain Reaction (PCR)

PCR is used to make exact copies of a sample of DNA. The DNA sample to be copied is placed in a test tube with short pieces of DNA called primers, a surplus of nucleotides, and the enzyme DNA polymerase. First the two DNA strands in the sample are separated by heating the sample to a high temperature (typically 94°C). Then the temperature is lowered, and the primers form complementary base pairs with the DNA sample. DNA polymerase then uses the sur-plus nucleotides to form the new strand of DNA. The temperature is raised again so that the strands will separate, and the cycle begins again. By repeating this many times, huge amounts of DNA can be made from a very small sample.

Applications: locating and cloning genes from an organism, diagnosing genetic diseases, and producing large amounts of DNA for research or for use in crime investigations

User: research biologists, forensic analysts, medical geneticists

Starting materials for PCR include:

DNA

+ DNA polymerase
+ Nucleotides

2 copies → 4 copies → 8 copies → 16 copies

Analyzing the Issues

Should genetic engineering research include humans?

1 Do ethical guidelines exist to help scientists determine what kinds of human genetic research should be permitted? Do library research or use an on-line database to find out. Describe additional guidelines that you would propose.

Is genetic engineering safe?

2 Use library references and on-line databases to learn about the regulations that govern genetic engineering. Design and distribute a questionnaire that examines your classmates' knowledge of the safety of genetic engineering.

Can gene therapy become a reality?

3 Many of the early results of human gene therapy have been disappointing. Read "Promises, Promises," in *Newsweek*, October 9, 1995, pages 60–62. What kind of obstacles must be overcome if gene therapy is to succeed?

Do genetically engineered foods pose health risks?

4 Find out what genetically engineered foods are currently available in the marketplace. How are new genetically engineered food products tested to ensure their safety?

3 Technological obstacles include getting the correct DNA into the target cells and getting the gene to express itself. Such obstacles put a halt to initial gene therapy trials for cystic fibrosis, in which the viruses used to transfer the gene produced an inflammatory response. Recently, an NIH committee on gene therapy suggested that such NIH-funded research be confined to lab animals until more details of the technology are determined.

4 Examples of products that are currently available include the Flavr Savr tomato, a genetically engineered tomato with a longer shelf life, and bovine somatotropin (bST), a genetically engineered hormone that increases milk production in dairy cows. Students can find details about testing such products by visiting the Web site for Animal and Plant Health Inspection Services (APHIS), a branch of the USDA, at http://www.aphis.usda.gov.

Science, Technology, and Society

CONTINUED

Life/Work Skills

Finding and Organizing Information

Advances in genetic engineering techniques are innovating the medical and agricultural industries. Encourage students to keep abreast of developments in these fields. Have them use references in the library or search an on-line database to collect information about current topics and issues in genetic engineering. Have them work in cooperative groups to summarize, organize, and publish this information in a quarterly newsletter. Allow students time each month to update their newsletters.

References

1. Anderson, W. French. "Gene Therapy." *Scientific American,* vol. 273, 124–128.

2. Berg, Paul and Maxine Singer. "The Recombinant DNA Controversy: Twenty Years Later." *Bio/Technology,* vol. 13, 1132–1134.

3. Council on Scientific Affairs, American Medical Association. "Biotechnology and the American Agricultural Industry." *Journal of the American Medical Association,* vol. 265, 1429–1436.

4. Miller, Henry. "Labeling of 'Biotech Foods' in No Free Lunch." *Bio/Technology,* vol. 13, 1510.

5. Stix, Gary. "A Recombinant Feast." *Scientific American,* vol. 272, no. 3, 38–40.

6. Suzuki, David and Peter Knudtson. *Genethics: The Clash Between the New Genetics and Human Values.* Cambridge: Harvard University Press, 1989.

10 | Evolution and Natural Selection

Lesson Planning Guide With Options for Block Scheduling

Lecture Concepts	Lesson Resources

10-1 Charles Darwin

BLOCK ❶ (45 minutes)
1. Evolution is the change in species over time.
2. In 1859, Charles Darwin proposed the theory of natural selection to explain how evolution occurs.

❶ **Lecture Resources**
- Determining Prior Knowledge
- Active Reading: Brainstorming
- Teaching Transparencies: 44, 52
- Holt Biology Videodiscs Lesson 10-1

Classwork Options
- Darwin's Finches

Assignment Options
- Teaching Resources CD-ROM: Supplemental Reading Guides 1

BLOCK ❷ (45 minutes)
3. Natural selection is the process in which organisms adapt to their environment, survive, and reproduce to a greater extent than those organisms that are not as well adapted.
4. Darwin used the finches of the Galapagos Islands as an example of how natural selection operates.

❷ **Lecture Resources**
- Changes in Finch Population
- Active Reading: Reader Response Logs
- Visual Strategy: Videodisc
- Holt Biology Videodiscs Lesson 10-1

Classwork Options
- Closure: Predicting Outcomes

Assignment Options
- Reteaching
- Section Review
- Chapter Review, questions 1a, 2a, 4, 5, 8, 20, 22
- Directed Reading Worksheet

10-2 The Evidence for Evolution

BLOCK ❸ (45 minutes)
1. Evidence for evolution comes from the fossil record, including examples of gradual change over time.
2. Radioactive dating is used to determine the age of fossils.

❸ **Lecture Resources**
- The Origin of Species
- Active Reading: Reading Organizer
- Visual Strategy: Figure 10-4
- Demonstration: Interpreting Graphs
- Teaching Transparencies: 45, 48, 49
- Holt Biology Videodiscs Lesson 10-2

Classwork Options
- Inquiry Skills Development: Lab B8

Assignment Options
- Evidence of Evolution

BLOCK ❹ (45 minutes)
3. Evidence for evolution comes from a study of homologous structures in different organisms.
4. Evidence for evolution comes from vestigial structures, comparative embryology, and comparative biochemistry.

❹ **Lecture Resources**
- Evolutionary Relationships
- Visual Strategy: Figures 10-5, 10-6
- Visual Strategy: Videodisc
- Teaching Transparencies: 50, 51
- Holt Biology Videodiscs Lesson 10-2

Classwork Options
- Closure: Organizing Information
- Exploration 10A

Assignment Options
- Reteaching
- Section Review
- Chapter Review, questions 1b, 2b, 7, 9, 17, 21, 23
- Directed Reading Worksheet

10-3 Natural Selection

BLOCK ❺ (45 minutes)
1. The process of natural selection is driven by several conditions: genetic variation in the population; a constant struggle for survival (selection pressure); and lower survival rate, and thus reproduction, of less well-adapted species.
2. Natural selection results in genetic change and adaptation to the environment.

❺ **Lecture Resources**
- Active Reading: Paired Summarizing
- Visual Strategy: Tables 10-1, 10-2
- Demonstration: Recognizing Relationships
- Teaching Transparencies: 63
- Holt Biology Videodiscs Lesson 10-3

Classwork Options
- Laboratory Techniques and Experimental Design: Lab C17

Assignment Options
- World of Work: Field Biologist

Lecture Concepts

Lesson Resources

10-3 Natural Selection, *continued*

BLOCK ❻ (45 minutes)

3. The peppered moths in England provide an example of how natural selection operates.

4. Scientists have recently proposed that evolution can occur at an irregular rate in a process known as punctuated equilibrium.

❻ Lecture Resources
- ■ Divergence
- ■ Visual Strategy: Figures 10-10, 10-11
- ■ Visual Strategy: Videodisc
- ■ Demonstration: Recognizing Patterns
- ⊟ Teaching Transparencies: 43A
- ⊘ Holt Biology Videodiscs Lesson 10-3

Classwork Options
- ■ Closure: Forming Hypotheses
- ⚗ Incuiry Skills Development: Lab B9

Assignment Options
- ■ Reteaching
- ■ Section Review
- ■ Chapter Review, questions 1c, 2c, 3, 6, 10, 11, 13, 14, 15, 16, 18, 19
- ■ Directed Reading Worksheet

Chapter Review and Assessment

BLOCK ❼ (45 minutes)
Review
- ■ Reteaching Worksheet
- ■ Thinking Skills Worksheet
- ■ Vocabulary Development Worksheet
- ⊙ Language Development and Reading Comprehension Audio CD Program: Chapter 10

BLOCK ❽ (45 minutes)
Assessment
- ■ Alternative Assessment, p. 187
- ■ Portfolio Assessment, p. T39

Chapter Test
- ■ Chapter 10 Test

Test Generator
- ⊙ Item bank for customizing Chapter Tests

Teaching Resources CD-ROM
- ⊙ Scoring Rubrics and Classroom Management Checklist

The Portfolio icon denotes items throughout the Teacher's Edition lesson wrap that may be selected for inclusion in student portfolios.

Holt Biology Videodiscs and *Concepts of Biology*

Holt Biology Videodiscs gives you a powerful tool for teaching, review, and assessment. For further information regarding the media on the videodiscs, see **Holt Biology Videodiscs Teacher's Correlation Guide to Holt Biology: Visualizing Life.**

Concepts of Biology adds interactive lesson plans and extensive tools for customization using CD-ROM technology.

Use the following topic from **Concepts of Biology** to help you teach this chapter:
Topic 8: Evolution and Natural Selection

Laboratory Planning

Text
Materials and preparation instructions appear on the teacher's wrap accompanying each laboratory exercise.

Block 4: Exploration 10A: Analyzing Variation Within a Species, p. 786

Holt BioSources Laboratory Program
Block 3: Inquiry Skills Development Lab B8: Fossil Study
Block 5: Laboratory Techniques and Experimental Design Lab C17: Analyzing Blood Serum to Determine Evolutionary Relationships
Block 6: Inquiry Skills Development Lab B9: Peppered Moth Survey

Determining Prior Knowledge

- Have students discuss what the term *evolution* means to them. Ask the students questions about the types of organisms subject to evolution, the time required for evolutionary change, and the evidence that scientists rely on to explain the evolutionary process.
- Show the class a fossil or a picture of one. Ask how fossils can help scientists learn about evolution.
- Show students a photograph of an animal in its natural habitat, for example, a polar bear in the Arctic. Ask students to describe the adaptations that enable an animal to survive in its environment. Have students hypothesize what might happen to the animal if its environment were to suddenly undergo a drastic change.

Active READING

Technique: Brainstorming

Write the word *evolution* on the overhead projector or chalkboard. Have students create a list of words and phrases that relate to this subject. Encourage all students to contribute at least one idea. Afterward, tell students they will be reading about the theory of evolution and some of its supporting evidence.

CD-ROM Resources

Concepts of Biology
Topic 8: Evolution and Natural Selection

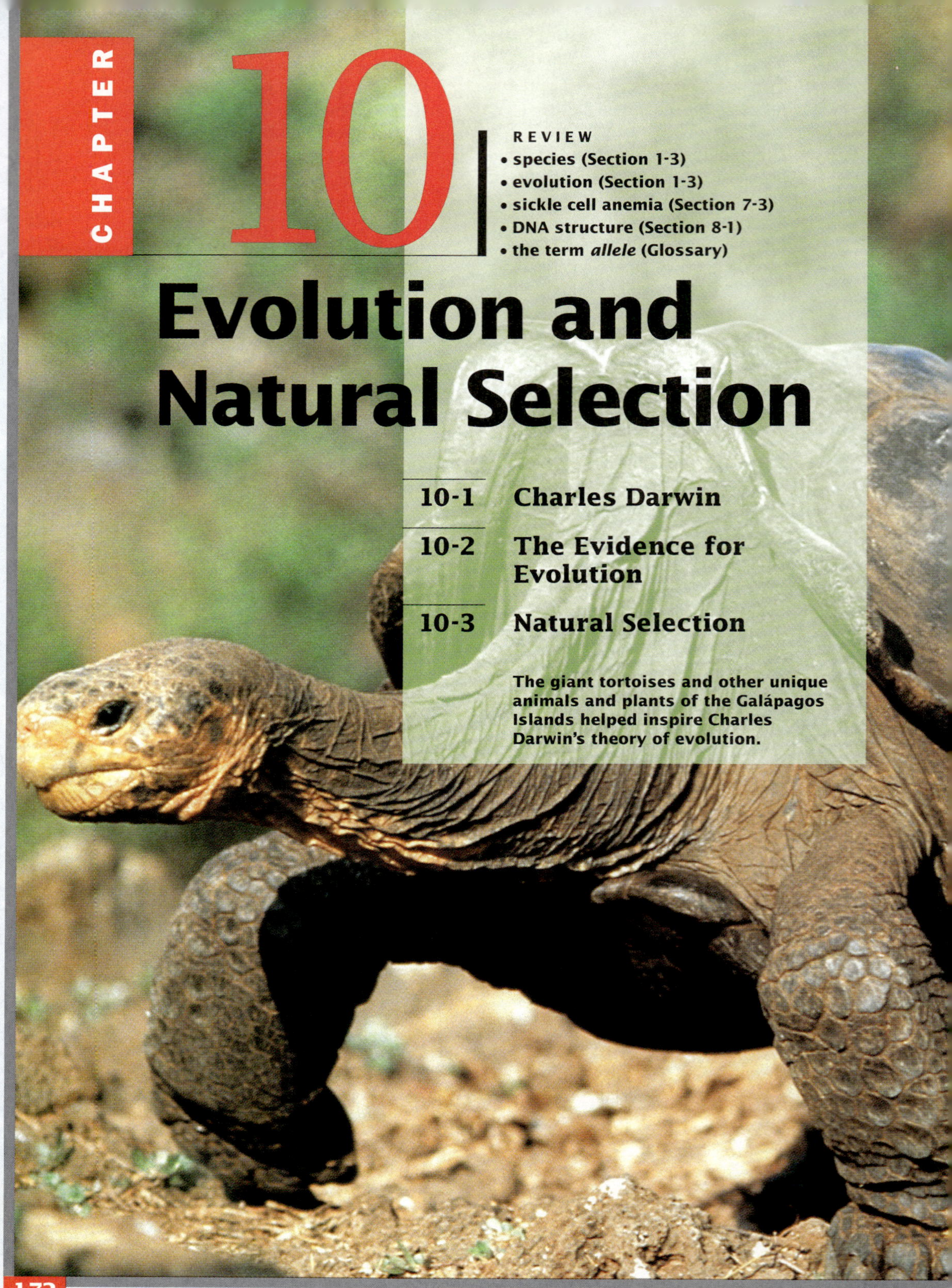

REVIEW
- species (Section 1-3)
- evolution (Section 1-3)
- sickle cell anemia (Section 7-3)
- DNA structure (Section 8-1)
- the term *allele* (Glossary)

Evolution and Natural Selection

10-1   **Charles Darwin**

10-2   **The Evidence for Evolution**

10-3   **Natural Selection**

The giant tortoises and other unique animals and plants of the Galápagos Islands helped inspire Charles Darwin's theory of evolution.

172

Author's Rationale   Evolution is the fundamental unifying theme of biology. This chapter plays a key role in advancing students' understanding of the principles they studied in previous chapters. Assuming that students will perceive evolution as a source of controversy, I begin the chapter with an objective presentation of the evidence. The text focuses first on the observation that evolution has occurred; it then proceeds with Darwin's reasoning that natural selection provides the mechanism that drives evolution.

The Earth is rich in life. About 1.5 million species have been named, and millions more are thought to exist. Where did all of these species come from? Was each species separately created, or can species change and give rise to other species? It was not until 1859, through the work of Charles Darwin, that convincing answers were provided to these questions.

10-1 Charles Darwin

OBJECTIVES

1. **Summarize Darwin's beliefs about the origin of species before he sailed around the world.**

2. **Identify two observations from Darwin's voyage that led him to question his beliefs.**

3. **Describe the two major ideas Darwin put forth in *The Origin of Species*.**

Voyage of the *Beagle*

On December 27, 1831, H.M.S. *Beagle* sailed from England to survey the coast of South America. On board as the ship's unpaid naturalist was Charles Darwin, a 22-year-old who had just graduated from Cambridge University. Darwin's observations during his five years at sea have changed the way we think of ourselves and our world.

The son of a wealthy doctor, Darwin was not an attentive student, spending more time outdoors than in school. As a medical student in Edinburgh, he was horrified by operations, which were performed without anesthetic. For two years Darwin skipped lectures to spend time collecting biological specimens. In desperation, his father sent him to Cambridge University to train to be a minister. After graduating from Cambridge in 1831, Darwin was recommended by one of his professors for the position on the *Beagle*. Follow the voyage of the *Beagle* in **Figure 10-1**.

Figure 10-1

Below you can see the course of the *Beagle*, the ship in which Darwin sailed around the world. On this voyage, Darwin collected thousands of specimens of plants, animals, and fossils.

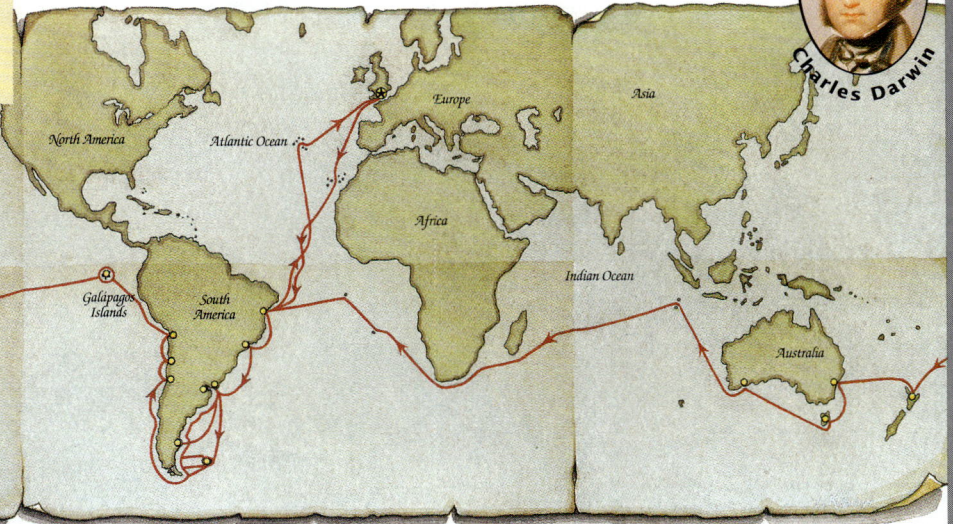

Charles Darwin

173

10-1

Phase One
Preparation

Scheduling

See the **Lesson Planning Guide** on pages 171A and 171B for lecture, classwork, and assignment options for Section 10-1.

Phase Two
Teaching Strategies

Visual Strategy | **Videodisc**

■ **Relating Concepts**

To introduce the chapter, use *Video—Evidence for Evolution* (5 min 25 s) shown in Chapter 10 Section 10-1 of **Holt Biology Videodiscs Teacher's Correlation Guide to Holt Biology: Visualizing Life.** Tell students to note the observations Darwin made to develop his theory of evolution by natural selection. Then discuss the questions on the final frame of the video: Why are isolated island chains good places to observe the effects of evolution? *(Answers should indicate that because populations on islands are isolated, each population changes to adapt to the particular environment on each island.)*

Videodisc Resources

Holt Biology Videodiscs
Lesson 10-1: Charles Darwin

Key to Strategies
Teaching Strategies are keyed to three tiers of learning

● **Understanding Concepts (Tier I)**
Content mastery and comprehension

■ **Applying Information (Tier II)**
Applying and analyzing content

▲ **Critical Thinking (Tier III)**
Practicing evaluative thinking

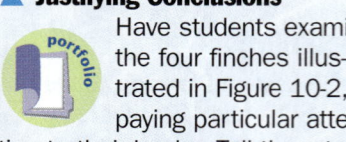

Darwin's Finches

▲ **Justifying Conclusions**

Have students examine the four finches illustrated in Figure 10-2, paying particular attention to their beaks. Tell them to imagine themselves in Darwin's place as he studied these birds. Then have them write journal pages that Darwin could have written as he later examined his notes about the finches to understand the mechanism of evolution.

Active READING

Technique: Reader Response Logs

Students may already hold opinions about the origin of species. So that students can make personal responses to the concepts presented in Chapter 10, have them create a Reader Response Log. Remind students to divide their paper in half. On the left side of the paper, have them copy a word, phrase, or passage from the text. On the right side, have them write their reactions, thoughts, or questions regarding the entries on the left side of the paper.

Changes in Finch Population

■ **Predicting Outcomes**

In 1977, the Galápagos Islands suffered a severe drought. Plants that produced small, soft seeds were devastated. In turn, a species of finch that fed on these seeds was similarly affected. As its source of food became depleted, this finch population declined by 85 percent. Ask students to describe the type of finch that would have been able to survive this drought. *(Only birds with beaks strong enough to crack large, hard seeds survived.)* As a result, the composition of this species changed so that the average body and beak size of its members increased dramatically. The situation was reversed in 1983, when heavy rains prevailed.

When the *Beagle* sailed from England, Darwin, like nearly all scientists of his time, accepted the view that God was responsible for the creation of all species of organisms. According to this view, God designed each species of animal and plant to match its habitat. This explained why, for example, polar bears, which live in a very cold climate, have white fur for camouflage and a thick layer of insulating fat beneath the skin. In addition, most scientists thought that species were unchanging.

During his journey, Darwin often left the ship to collect specimens of animals, plants, and fossils. He made careful observations and recorded them in a journal. What Darwin saw on his voyage led him to doubt the idea that species were constant.

Darwin's Finches

Figure 10-2
The blue-black grassquit (inset), native to the Pacific coast from Mexico to Chile, is thought to be very similar or identical to the ancestor of the Galápagos finches (below). Darwin attributed the differences in bill size and feeding habits among these finches to evolution that occurred after their ancestor migrated to the Galápagos Islands.

Darwin repeatedly saw patterns in how kinds of animals and plants differed, patterns suggesting that species changed over time and gave rise to new species. On the Galápagos Islands, 1,000 km (600 mi) from the coast of Ecuador, Darwin collected several species of finches. All of these species were similar, but each was specialized to catch food in a different way, as shown by the different shapes of the birds' bills in **Figure 10-2**. Some species had thick, sturdy bills for cracking open tough seeds. Others had slender bills for catching insects.

All of the species of finches closely resembled one species of South American finch. In fact, all of the plants and animals of the Galápagos Islands were very similar to those of the nearby coast of South America. If each one of these plants and animals had been created to match the habitat on the Galápagos Islands, why did they not resemble the plants and animals of islands with similar environments that lie off the coast of Africa? Why did they instead resemble those of the adjacent South American continent? Darwin felt that the simplest explanation was that a few organisms from South America must have migrated to the Galápagos Islands in the past. These few kinds of animals and plants then changed over the years that they lived in their new home, giving rise to many new species. Change in species over time is known as evolution.

a The woodpecker finch captures insects with its grasping bill.

b The crushing bill of the large ground finch enables it to feed on seeds.

c The cactus finch uses its probing bill to feed on cactuses.

174

Community Connection: Ecotourism

Ecotourism is a growing industry that is thriving in once-remote areas of the world. Although this new industry is providing a much-needed economic boost to many developing regions of the world, it is also threatening ecosystems that had been spared the adverse effects of human presence until recently. Have students search the library or an on-line database for information about ecotourism. Have them look for specific information about ecotourism in the Galápagos Islands and how it is affecting the fragile environment. Then have students debate whether ecotourism should be encouraged, restricted, or prohibited.

Figure 10-3
In 1859 Darwin published his famous book, *The Origin of Species*. He accomplished much of his work in his study at Down House in Kent, England (above right). Darwin is shown at age 73 (above).

Alfred Russel Wallace

Darwin's Mechanism for Evolution

Darwin returned to England in 1836. He got married and wrote several books. He accomplished much of his work in Down House in Kent, England, shown in **Figure 10-3**. For 20 years, Darwin gathered evidence supporting his ideas about evolution, but he did not publish them. Then in 1858 another biologist, Alfred Russel Wallace, sent Darwin an essay that presented these same ideas. This prompted Darwin to finally publish his work.

When Darwin's book *On the Origin of Species by Means of Natural Selection* appeared in November of 1859, it stirred up great controversy. Darwin's conclusion that species changed over time and gave rise to new species contradicted the prevailing beliefs that God created all species and that species did not change. Furthermore, the implication that apes were close relatives of humans was unacceptable to many people.

In *The Origin of Species*, as the book is commonly known, Darwin not only presented much evidence that evolution occurred but also proposed that natural selection was its mechanism. Organisms with traits well suited to an environment are more likely to survive and produce more offspring than organisms without these favorable traits. This process is called **natural selection**.

Because Darwin presented a mechanism as well as evidence for evolution, his arguments were compelling. His views were soon accepted by biologists around the world. Since the discovery of Mendel's ideas about genetics in the early 1900s, genetic principles have been added to Darwin's ideas, forming the modern theory of evolution.

SECTION REVIEW

1. What were Darwin's views about the origin of species before he sailed on the *Beagle*?

2. Describe two observations Darwin made on his voyage that led him to doubt these views.

3. Explain the two major ideas in *The Origin of Species*.

4. How did Darwin explain the similarities and differences between the species of Galápagos finches?

175

ANSWERS TO SECTION REVIEW

1. Before his voyage, Darwin accepted the commonly held view that each organism was designed by God to match its habitat.

2. Darwin's observations of the finches found on the Galápagos Islands and the fossils he collected led him to doubt his early views.

3. The book describes evidence supporting evolution and describes how the idea of natural selection explains the mechanism of evolution.

4. Darwin felt that a few finches had migrated to the Galápagos Islands and then changed over the years they lived there, giving rise to many species.

Connection: *Chapter 1*

Evolution: Fact or Theory?
Emphasize that evolution is considered a scientific fact, as documented by several lines of evidence that will be discussed in Section 10-2. Point out that natural selection is a theory Darwin proposed to describe how evolution occurs. Evidence that supports Darwin's theory will be covered in Section 10-3.

Phase Three
Assessment Options

Closure

■ **Predicting Outcomes**
Have students explain what would happen to the cactus finch shown in Figure 10-2c if a drought occurred on the Galápagos Islands. (*This species should thrive because it feeds on cactus, a plant that would be least affected by a drought.*)

SECTION REVIEW

Assign the *Section Review.*

Reteaching

 *portfolio*

Point out that Alfred R. Wallace, like Darwin, traveled extensively and collected many specimens. While in Malaya (now Indonesia), Wallace wrote a 20-page paper describing his idea about how evolution occurred and sent it to Darwin, asking him to evaluate it and perhaps submit it for publication. Have students imagine themselves in Darwin's study, as pictured in Figure 10-3, as he read Wallace's paper. Ask students to write a letter that Darwin could have written to Wallace in response.

Key to Strategies
● **Understanding Concepts (Tier I)**
■ **Applying Information (Tier II)**
▲ **Critical Thinking (Tier III)**

Scheduling

See the **Lesson Planning Guide** on pages 171A and 171B for lecture, classwork, and assignment options for Section 10-2.

Active READING

Technique: Reading Organizer
As students read Section 10-2, have them devise a descriptive reading organizer that details the evidence for evolution. For more information about reading organizers, see Reading Strategies Worksheets in Holt BioSources Teaching Resources CD-ROM.

Demonstration

● **Interpreting Graphs**
Materials: 100 pennies, large container with cover
Place 100 pennies in a large, covered container. Shake the container several times, and remove the cover. Remove all the coins that have the "head" side of the coin turned upward. Record the number of pennies removed and the number of those remaining. Repeat the process until no pennies are left in the container, remembering to remove the coins showing the "head" side. Have students devise a graph in which they plot the number of remaining pennies on the *x*-axis and the number of times the container is shaken on the *y*-axis. Have them plot a similar graph of the decay of carbon-14 as described in the text. In this case, have them plot grams of carbon-14 remaining on the *x*-axis and years on the *y*-axis. Have students compare the two graphs.

Much of what you have read so far in this book was unknown to Darwin when he wrote *The Origin of Species*. The nucleic acids DNA and RNA had not been discovered. Mendel's genetic experiments were unpublished. These and other discoveries, such as this fossil of an insect trapped in amber, have since contributed additional evidence for evolution.

10-2 The Evidence for Evolution

OBJECTIVES

1 Describe the conditions necessary for fossils to form.

2 List one example from the fossil record indicating that evolution has occurred.

3 Explain how comparisons of organisms can reveal evidence of evolution.

4 Describe the important evidence for evolution found in proteins and DNA.

Understanding the Fossil Record

More than a century has passed since Darwin's death in 1882. During this period, a great deal of new evidence has accumulated supporting the theory of evolution, much of it far stronger than that available to Darwin and his contemporaries. This evidence has come from a variety of sources, including studies of fossils, comparisons of the structures of organisms, and the rapidly expanding knowledge about DNA and proteins.

Fossils are any traces of dead organisms

What are fossils? Most people think of fossils as shells or old bones. Actually, fossils are any traces of dead organisms. Tracks of dinosaurs, footprints of human ancestors, insects trapped in sticky tree sap, impressions of leaves or skin, and animals buried in tar are all fossils. For fossils to form, very special conditions are necessary. If a skeleton or shell is to fossilize, for example, the dead animal must be buried by sediment. Burial usually occurs on the ocean floor, in swamps, in mud, or in tar pits. Calcium in the bone or in the shell is slowly replaced by other, harder minerals. Unless the sediment is very fine and no oxygen is present to promote decay, soft tissues, such as those found in skin or muscle, do not fossilize. Thus, the fossil record provides only a glimpse into life's history.

How Fossils Are Dated

Since the late 1940s scientists have been able to determine the ages of rocks and fossils by measuring the amount of radioactive decay, or breakdown, of radioactive atoms in the rock. A radioactive atom contains an unstable combination of protons and neutrons. Since it is unstable, a radioactive atom will eventually change into a more stable atom of another element. For example, carbon-14, a rare form of carbon found in tiny amounts in living things, decays into nitrogen. The term **half-life** describes how long it takes for one-half of the radioactive atoms in a sample to decay. For example, the half-life of carbon-14 is 5,730 years. Thus, a sample that initially contained 12 g of carbon-14 will have 6 g of carbon-14 left after 5,730 years and 3 g of carbon-14 left after 11,460 years. Since carbon-14 decays relatively rapidly, other isotopes with longer half-lives are more often used to date fossils.

Because the rate of decay of a radioactive element is constant, scientists can use the amount of radioactive element remaining in a rock or fossil to determine its age. This technique is called **radioactive dating**.

Evolution can be a very slow process; the transformation of one

Videodisc Resources

Holt Biology Videodiscs
Lesson 10-2: The Evidence for Evolution

Stability and Homeostasis

Explain why the evolution of one species from another can be considered an instance of instability.

Figure 10-4
Recent fossil discoveries have revealed some of the steps in the evolution of whales.

species into another by natural selection requires thousands of years. Using radioactive dating, scientists have determined that the Earth is about 4.5 billion years old, ancient enough for all species to have been formed through evolution.

Transitional forms link new species to old

Because new species form from existing species, Darwin predicted that transitional forms, intermediate stages between older and newer species, would be found in the fossil record. When *The Origin of Species* was published, no intermediates had been found. Darwin recognized that this was a weakness in his argument. But

there are now many good examples of evolutionary transitions. For instance, modern whales are the descendants of four-legged land animals that are also the ancestors of horses and cows. As you can see in **Figure 10-4**, fossil intermediates between modern whales and their 60-million-year-old ancestor reveal a history of slow transformation. Over time, the hind limbs became smaller and smaller, until eventually they were lost entirely. Modern whales have a pelvis, but no rear legs are attached to it. A detailed picture of whale evolution is emerging from fossil finds, making it clear that a progressive reduction in the hind limbs was a central feature of whale evolution.

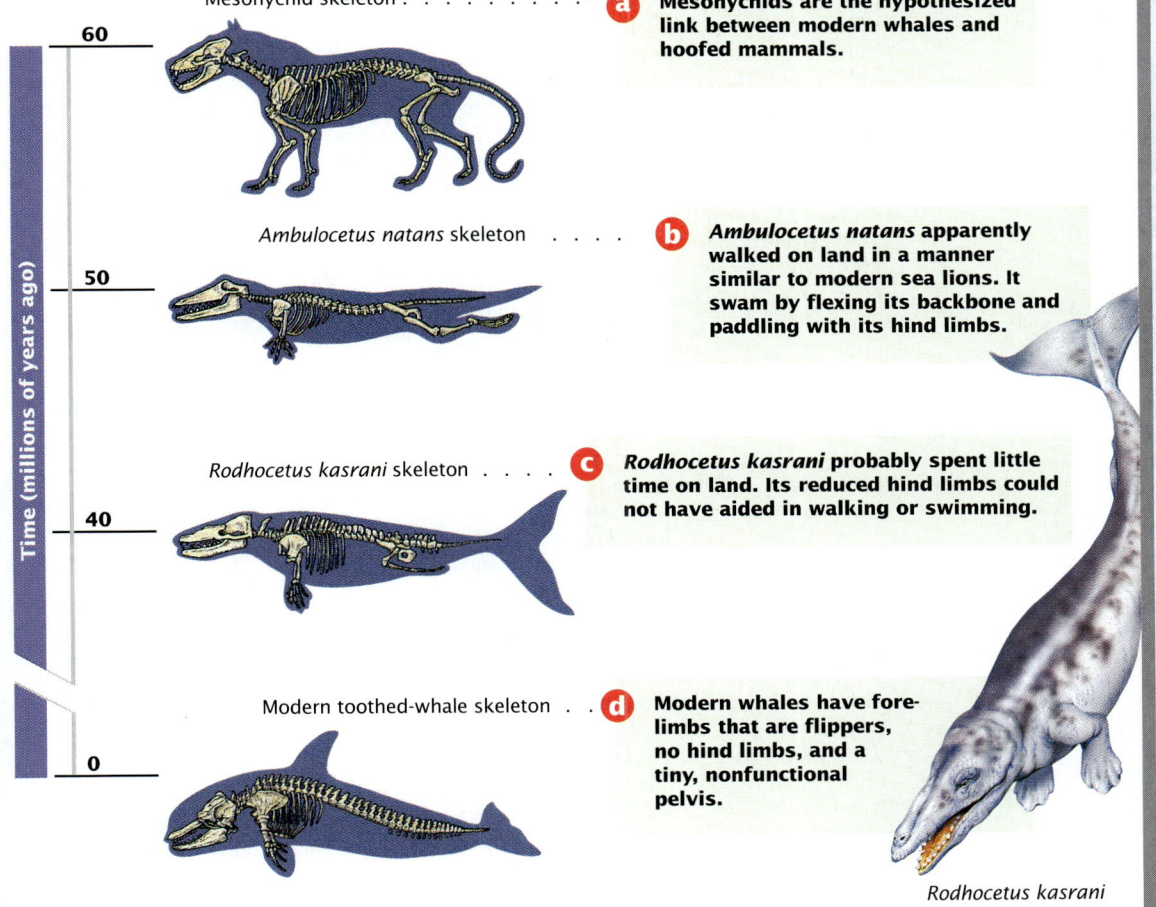

Mesonychid skeleton . . . .
a Mesonychids are the hypothesized link between modern whales and hoofed mammals.

Ambulocetus natans skeleton . . . .
b *Ambulocetus natans* apparently walked on land in a manner similar to modern sea lions. It swam by flexing its backbone and paddling with its hind limbs.

Rodhocetus kasrani skeleton . . . .
c *Rodhocetus kasrani* probably spent little time on land. Its reduced hind limbs could not have aided in walking or swimming.

Modern toothed-whale skeleton . .
d Modern whales have forelimbs that are flippers, no hind limbs, and a tiny, nonfunctional pelvis.

Time (millions of years ago): 60, 50, 40, 0

Rodhocetus kasrani

177

Matter of Fact: Radioactive Isotope Half-Lives

The following radioactive isotopes have longer half-lives than carbon-14: uranium-235 (700 million years); potassium-40 (1.25 billion years); and uranium-238 (4.5 billion years).

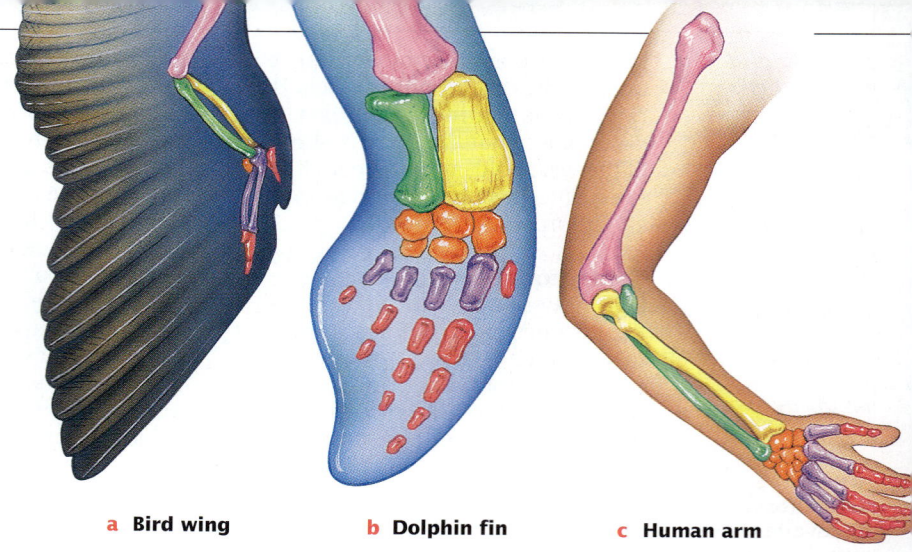

Figure 10-5
The bones in the front limbs of a bird, a dolphin, and a human are homologous structures. Homologous bones are shown in the same color on each diagram.

a **Bird wing**   b **Dolphin fin**   c **Human arm**

■ **Relating Concepts**

Ask students to identify the common structural features shared by the front limbs of these three animals. Use this figure to compare homologous and analogous structures. Have students use references to describe what analogous structures are. (*Analogous structures have similar functions but different evolutionary origins, such as the wings of an insect and the wings of a bird.*)

Evolutionary Relationships

■ **Recognizing Relationships**

Homologous structures, such as those shown in Figure 10-5, are helpful for determining the evolutionary relationship between different species. Such structures point to a common ancestry. Point out that in addition to the three species shown in this figure, crocodiles, whales, horses, and bats also have forelimbs with the same number, placement, and order of bones.

● **Comparing Structures**

Point out that snakes also have a vestigial pelvis. Ask what this similarity suggests. (*The presence of a similar vestigial structure in both whales and snakes points to a common ancestry.*) Have students identify vestigial structures in humans. (*Most will name the appendix. Other vestigial structures include the tailbone, pointed canine teeth, muscles to move the ears, and a nictitating membrane on the eye.*)

Evidence of Evolution

■ **Relating Concepts**

Have students design a **Graphic Organizer** that describes two kinds of physical traits that can be used to support the theory of evolution.

Comparing Organisms

Comparing the way organisms are put together provides important evidence for evolution. Your arm appears quite different from the wing of a bird or the front fin of a dolphin. Yet if you examine **Figure 10-5**, you can see that the position and order of bones in these limbs are very similar. Biologists say that these three limbs are homologous. **Homologous structures** are structures that share a common ancestry. Homologous structures are similar because they are modified versions of structures that occurred in a common ancestor. Although suited for flying, swimming, and grasping, the limbs of the animals above are modified versions of the front fins of their common fish ancestor.

Vestigial structures are clues to evolutionary origins
If you were designing a submarine, would you include a set of wheels in your design? Of course not. Wheels would serve no function on a submarine. However, structures without function are found in living things. A whale propels itself with its powerful tail

and has no need for hind limbs or the pelvis to which they attach. Nevertheless, whales still have a reduced pelvis that serves no apparent function, as shown in **Figure 10-6**. Structures with no function are known as **vestigial structures**. Vestigial structures are remnants of an organism's evolutionary past. The whale's pelvis is evidence of its evolution from four-legged, land-dwelling mammals.

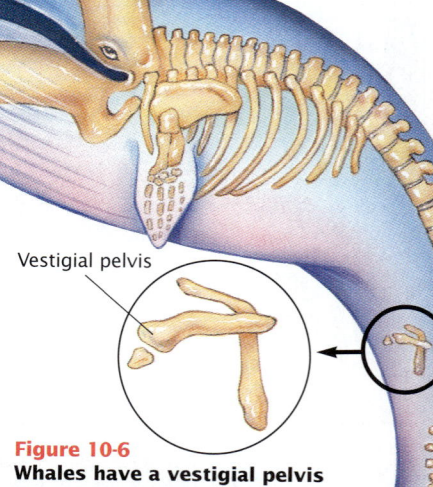

Vestigial pelvis

Figure 10-6
Whales have a vestigial pelvis that serves no apparent function. This pelvis is a remnant of the whale's evolutionary past.

Graphic Organizer

Use the following graphic organizer with the teaching strategy **Evidence of Evolution** on page 178.

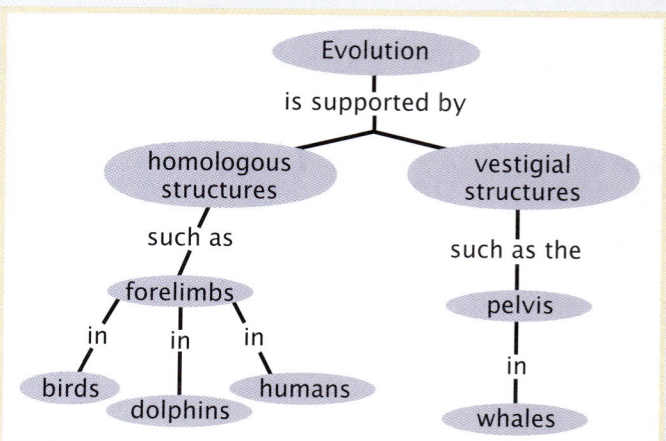

Evolution

is supported by

homologous structures   vestigial structures

such as   such as the

forelimbs   pelvis

in   in   in   in

birds   dolphins   humans   whales

Developmental patterns show evolutionary relationships

Much of our evolutionary history can be seen in the way human embryos develop. Early in development, human embryos and embryos of all other vertebrates are strikingly similar, as shown in **Figure 10-7**. In later stages of development, a human embryo develops a coat of fine fur. The similarity of these early developmental forms strongly suggests that the process of development has evolved. New instructions on how to grow have been added to old instructions inherited from ancestors.

Figure 10-7
The five-week-old human embryo (a) and the four-day-old chicken embryo (b) each have a bony tail and gill pouches similar to those of fishes.

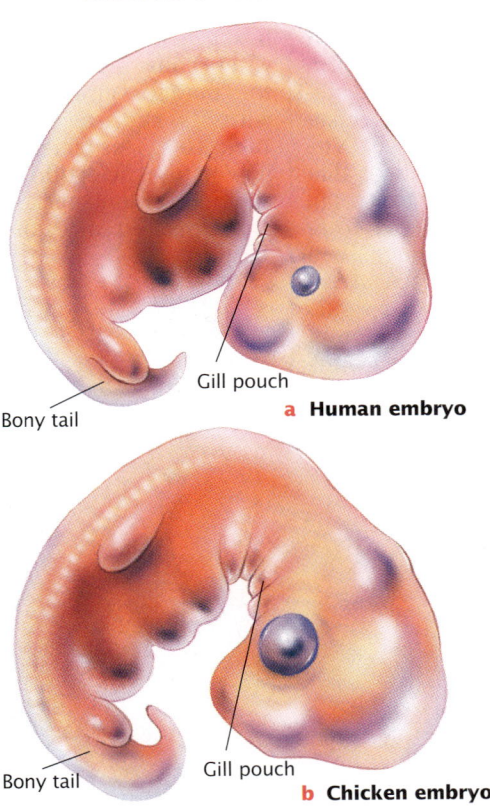

Gill pouch

Bony tail

a Human embryo

Gill pouch

Bony tail

b Chicken embryo

DNA and proteins contain evidence of evolution

Although complete fossil histories for living organisms are rare, an organism's history is written in the sequence of nucleotides making up its DNA. If species have changed over time, their genes also should have changed. The theory of evolution predicts that genes will accumulate more alterations in their nucleotide sequences over time. Thus, if we compare the genes of several species, closely related species will show more similarities in nucleotide sequences than will distantly related species. Closely related species also will show more similarities in the amino acid sequences in their proteins. This is because the amino acid sequence in a protein reflects the nucleotide sequence of the gene coding for that protein.

For example, to see how closely related chimpanzees, dogs, and rattlesnakes are to humans, scientists examined the sequence of amino acids in the protein cytochrome *c*, an essential participant in cellular respiration. They found that human cytochrome *c* and chimp cytochrome *c* are identical in all 104 amino acids. This high degree of similarity indicates our very close kinship to chimpanzees. A dog's cytochrome *c* differs from human cytochrome *c* in 13 amino acids, indicating that dogs are fairly distant relatives. But dogs are more closely related to us than are rattlesnakes, whose cytochrome *c* differs from ours in 20 amino acids. In most cases, the evolutionary relationships indicated by DNA or protein sequences confirm those suggested by comparative anatomy and by developmental patterns.

SECTION REVIEW

1 Why is it unlikely that you will be fossilized?

2 Explain why transitional species, such as the ancestors of modern whales, are crucial evidence for evolution.

3 How does the whale's vestigial pelvis provide evidence in support of evolution?

4 Explain how sequences of amino acids in proteins can be used to reveal relationships among organisms.

179

ANSWERS TO SECTION REVIEW

1 To become fossilized, an organism usually must be buried by sediment in slow-moving bodies of water, which is an unlikely situation for most humans.

2 Transitional species act as links that provide evidence of how an ancestral form evolved into a modern species.

3 The whale's vestigial pelvis is a remnant from an earlier life form and is evidence of its evolution from a four-legged, land-dwelling mammalian ancestor.

4 Closely related organisms have more similar DNA sequences and therefore more similar amino acid sequences in their proteins than do distantly related organisms.

Evolution and Natural Selection   **179**

Scheduling

See the **Lesson Planning Guide** on pages 171A and 171B for lecture, classwork, and assignment options for Section 10-3.

Phase Two
Teaching Strategies

Active READING

Technique: Paired Summarizing
Group students into pairs, and have them silently read about natural selection on pages 180–182. Then have one student, the "reteller," summarize how natural selection causes evolution, without referring to the text. The other student, the "listener," should listen to the retelling and point out any inaccuracies or ideas that have been left out. Students should work together during this final clarification process and refer to the text if needed. Have students alternate roles and repeat this process after reading about how species form on pages 184–185.

Has natural selection affected your life directly? Yes, because your body has been shaped by natural selection. For example, the ability of your eyes to focus, the way your hands grip objects, your upright posture, your large brain, the color of your hair, and numerous other characteristics are all results of evolution by natural selection.

10-3 Natural Selection

OBJECTIVES

1 **Describe how natural selection occurs.**

2 **Summarize the effects of natural selection on the peppered moth and on the sickle cell allele.**

3 **Describe how natural selection can lead to the formation of new species.**

4 **Contrast the hypotheses of punctuated equilibrium and gradualism.**

How Natural Selection Causes Evolution

Darwin not only demonstrated that evolution has occurred but also proposed its principal mechanism—natural selection. The key factor in natural selection is the environment. The environment presents challenges that individuals with particular traits can better overcome. Thus, the environment "selects" which organisms will survive and reproduce more often. Traits possessed by organisms successful at survival and reproduction are more likely to be transmitted to the next generation. These traits, therefore, will become more common. Compare the modern giraffe in **Figure 10-8** with its short-necked ancestors in **Table 10-1**. This table explains in detail how natural selection could drive the evolution of long-necked giraffes from short-necked ancestors.

Figure 10-8
How did giraffes evolve long necks? Natural selection is the mechanism by which their long necks probably evolved.

180

Videodisc Resources

Holt Biology Videodiscs
Lesson 10-3: Natural Selection

Table 10-1   The Process of Natural Selection

Step	Explanation	Example
Variation is the raw material for natural selection.	Every species contains genetic variation: individuals differ because they carry different alleles for certain traits. As you learned in Chapter 7, mutation is the source for new variation. In addition, sexual reproduction and crossing-over produce individuals with unique combinations of alleles.	Giraffes were born with alleles for varying neck lengths. Some had longer necks than others.
Living things face a constant struggle for existence.	Organisms produce more offspring than can survive. These offspring emerge into a hostile world where they must evade predators and compete with other individuals for limited supplies of food and living space.	Giraffes with longer necks could reach the leaves in tall trees. Those with shorter necks could not.
Only some individuals survive and reproduce.	Some individuals are better able to survive the challenges of life than others. Perhaps a particular allele makes them more drought tolerant, or more efficient, or more resistant to disease. These individuals are more likely to survive and produce offspring.	The giraffes with longer necks were better at getting food than were giraffes with shorter necks. Consequently, long-necked giraffes produced more offspring than did giraffes with short necks.
Natural selection results in genetic change.	Each generation consists of the offspring of individuals that successfully reproduced. Thus, it contains an increased proportion of individuals with traits that promote survival and reproduction than did the previous generation. The same is true for subsequent generations. Over time, the alleles for successful traits will increase in frequency, while alleles for traits that reduce the chances of survival and reproduction will decline in frequency.	Since more long-necked than short-necked giraffes were being born, long-necked giraffes became common, and short-necked giraffes became rare. The average neck length increased. Eventually, long-necked giraffes replaced short-necked giraffes.
Species adapt to their environment.	Selection tends to make a population better suited to its environment. The environment determines the direction of genetic change. An allele favored in one environment may not be favored in another.	Long-necked giraffes are well suited for browsing on the foliage of tall trees, which is out of the reach of most other animals.

181

Historical Perspective: Lamarck

Tell students that Darwin was not the first person to state that organisms evolve. In fact, his grandfather, Erasmus Darwin, had come to the same conclusion many years earlier. Another was Jean Baptiste Lamarck (1744–1829), who developed a different theory, known as the inheritance of acquired characteristics. Point out that although Lamarck's theory has been discredited, he did attempt to explain how evolution occurred some 50 years earlier than Darwin did. Have students use library and on-line references to obtain information about Lamarck and his ideas. Ask students to write a brief report summarizing their findings, and have them share it with their classmates.

Visual Strategy   Table 10-1

● **Interpreting Tables**

Lead students through each step of natural selection described in this table. Point out that the struggle for existence does not mean that organisms physically compete with one another, a misconception held by many students. Rather, it means that the best-adapted can survive and reproduce. In this case, only the giraffes with necks long enough to reach the food have the necessary adaptation.

Mathematics Connection

Overproduction

Not long after returning to England, Darwin read an essay by Thomas Malthus that was written in 1798. The essay warned that the human population was increasing so rapidly that it would soon be impossible to feed everyone. Darwin realized that Malthus's conclusion was true for all organisms, not just humans. In fact, Darwin did some calculations involving reproduction among elephants. He calculated that a pair of breeding elephants, which are among the slowest reproducers in the animal kingdom, would produce 19 million elephants in just 750 years. This was based on the assumption that all the offspring would live, survive a normal life span, and reproduce the normal number of offspring. Yet Darwin recognized that the average number of elephants remains fairly constant over the years. Obviously, as Darwin concluded, natural selection must be operating to keep the number constant from generation to generation.

Point out to students that survival is favored by natural selection only if it translates into increased reproduction. The genes of an individual who lives to old age but never reproduces will not be transmitted to the next generation.

Key to Strategies
● Understanding Concepts (Tier I)
■ Applying Information (Tier II)
▲ Critical Thinking (Tier III)

Evolution and Natural Selection   181

Field Biologist

Remind students that Darwin was a naturalist and field biologist. The study of peppered moths is another example of how biology is studied in the field rather than in a laboratory. Have students identify contemporary naturalists who are popular with the media. Then have them write a short biography on one of these naturalists, and have them include a summary of their work.

As an alternative assignment, students may report on a recently conducted field investigation on evolution. Inform students that they can explore a new fossil find, a report of a new species, an update on an endangered or extinct species, or a study revealing evolutionary relationships between different species. Be sure students include information about the purpose of the study, the field biologist's observations, and any conclusions.

Visual Strategy   Table 10-2

■ Making Predictions

Recently, England has introduced strict air-pollution control measures. Forests near industrial centers like Birmingham are once again becoming covered with lichens. Have students predict what Kettlewell would find today if he repeated the experiments described in this table. *(He would find more light-colored moths near Birmingham now that there are more lichen-covered trees.)*

Visual Strategy   Videodisc

■ Inferring Relationships

Show students the photo *Peppered Moths* in Chapter 10 Section 10-3 in *Holt Biology Videodiscs Teacher's Correlation Guide to Holt Biology: Visualizing Life.* Have students identify the organisms in the photo. Ask students what advantages the camouflaged moth has over the other moth.

182   Chapter 10

The Peppered Moth: Natural Selection in Action

Over many generations natural selection gradually changes a species in response to the demands of its environment. **Adaptation** is the process by which a species becomes better suited to its environment. The word *adaptation* can also refer to any change in a trait that increases the likelihood that an organism will survive or reproduce. For an example of natural selection's effects, look closely at the light and dark peppered moths in **Figure 10-9**. Until the 1850s, dark gray peppered moths were rare and were treasured by British butterfly and moth collectors. Almost all peppered moths were pale. Around 1850, however, dark peppered moths started to become more common, usually in heavily industrialized areas. By 1950, peppered moth populations living near industrial centers consisted almost entirely of dark individuals.

Why did the dark peppered moths become more common? Darwin's theory of evolution by natural selection suggests a hypothesis. The color change coincided with a great increase in the number of factories in England. Pale tree trunks were blackened by heavy pollution from these factories. Perhaps dark moths sitting on soot-darkened bark escaped being eaten by birds because it was hard for the birds to see the dark moths against the dark background. Light-colored moths, on the other hand, would have stood out against a dark background and would have been easily spotted by hungry birds. H.B.D. Kettlewell, a British biologist, tested this hypothesis in the late 1950s. **Table 10-2** describes Kettlewell's experiments.

Figure 10-9
Studies of light and dark peppered moths provide an example of adaptation.

Table 10-2   How Kettlewell Demonstrated Natural Selection in Peppered Moths

	What Kettlewell did	What Kettlewell found
Step 1	Kettlewell knew that coloration was an inherited trait. He raised large numbers of both light and dark moths in the laboratory. He released equal numbers of light and dark moths into a forest near Birmingham, England, where trees were blackened by soot. For identification, each of these moths was marked with a dot on the underside of its wings.	Kettlewell set out rings of traps to recapture moths that survived. He found that two-thirds of the recaptured moths were dark. More moths that matched the dark tree trunks had survived.
Step 2	Again using marked moths, Kettlewell released equal numbers of light and dark moths into an unpolluted forest in Dorset, England. Trees here were light gray, not black.	When Kettlewell set out traps, two-thirds of the moths that were recaptured were light. Again, more moths that matched the color of the tree trunks survived.
Step 3	Kettlewell set up hidden cameras in both forests to record the capture of moths by birds.	Films showed that birds were more likely to capture light moths on the dark trunks near Birmingham. In Dorset, birds were more likely to eat the dark moths, which were easily seen against the light trunks.

182

Matter of Fact: Industrial Melanism

The tendency for dark-colored individuals to replace light-colored individuals in forests near industrial areas is known as industrial melanism. Since the first report by Kettlewell, industrial melanism has been reported in 70 moth species in England and some 100 moth species found near Pittsburgh, Pennsylvania.

The Puzzle of Sickle Cell Anemia

Sickle cell anemia, as you learned in Chapter 7, is a hereditary disease that affects hemoglobin molecules, the proteins in human blood that carry oxygen. Defective hemoglobin molecules deform the red blood cells, as shown in **Figure 10-10**. People who are homozygous for the defective sickle cell allele have sickle cell anemia and often die at an early age. Heterozygous individuals, who have both a defective and a normal allele, are healthy. The disease is now known to have originated in central Africa, where 1 person in 100 is homozygous for the defective allele and thus has the disease. In the United States, however, only 1 African American out of every 500 has sickle cell anemia, and the disease is almost unknown in other races.

Why has natural selection not acted against the sickle cell allele in Africa and reduced its frequency? Why is this potentially fatal allele common there?

The sickle cell allele confers an unexpected advantage in Africa

The defective allele is common in central Africa because people who are heterozygous for the sickle cell allele are much less susceptible to malaria. Over 1 million people die of malaria each year, most of them in central Africa and tropical Asia.

In central Africa, the number of deaths from sickle cell anemia is far lower than would occur from malaria if heterozygous individuals were not malaria resistant. One in five individuals is heterozygous for the sickle cell allele and survives malaria. But only 1 person in 100 is homozygous for the allele and dies of anemia. Stated simply, natural selection has favored the sickle cell allele in central Africa because the payoff in survival of heterozygotes is greater than the price in death of homozygotes.

You can see that natural selection is acting on the sickle cell allele in opposite directions. On one hand, selection tends to eliminate the sickle cell allele because of its lethal effects on homozygotes. On the other hand, selection tends to favor the sickle cell allele because it protects heterozygotes from malaria. Biologists use the term **balancing selection** to refer to the situation in which two opposing selective forces affect the frequency of an allele in a population.

Selection does not favor the sickle cell allele in the United States

Why is the frequency of individuals who are homozygous for sickle cell anemia so much lower among African Americans? After all, most African Americans are descended from Africans who arrived in this country hundreds of years ago. While interbreeding has occurred, much of the answer lies in the distribution of malaria. Malaria is extremely rare in North America today. The protection against malaria that is associated with being heterozygous for the sickle cell allele offers no real advantage in the United States. As a result, the allele for sickle cell anemia has become far less common in the United States than it is in central Africa. Biologists call unopposed selection **directional selection**. Directional selection moves the frequency of a particular allele (and that of the trait the allele produces) in one direction.

a Oxygenated red blood cells

Increasing level of oxygen in the bloodstream

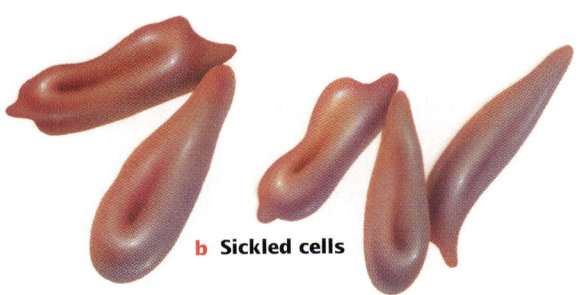

b Sickled cells

Figure 10-10
When oxygen levels in the blood are high, the red blood cells of people homozygous for the sickle cell allele appear normal (a). But when oxygen levels are low, some of their cells collapse into a sickle shape (b) and cannot function normally. In people heterozygous for the sickle cell allele, only a few red blood cells sickle at low oxygen levels. These individuals are malaria resistant.

183

Visual Strategy   Figure 10-11

■ **Recognizing Patterns**

Have students identify the regions of the United States in which the four races of sparrows have been found. Ask them if they can recognize a pattern between the geographic distribution and the various races. *(Many species, including the sparrow, exhibit North-South variations. For example, sparrows in the North have a large body size, which is advantageous for heat conservation. Conversely, those in the South have a smaller body size.)*

Demonstration

■ **Recognizing Patterns**

Have students review the definition of a species. Show students photographs of viceroy and monarch butterflies. Ask whether they are members of the same species. *(No, they are different species.)* Do the same with photographs of a horse and a donkey, pointing out that their offspring is a mule, which is sterile and therefore cannot be defined as a species.

How Species Form

Because natural selection favors changes that increase an organism's chances of surviving and reproducing, it will continuously shape a species to improve the fit between the species and its environment. Recall from Chapter 1 that a species is a group of individuals that can interbreed and produce fertile offspring but that cannot breed with any other such group. When populations of a species are found in several different kinds of environments, natural selection will act to make each population suited to its particular environment. Populations in different places thus become increasingly different, as each population becomes better suited to its particular environment.

Over time, separate populations of a species can eventually become quite distinct if their environments differ enough. These populations form what biologists call ecological races, as shown by the example of the seaside sparrows in **Figure 10-11**. **Ecological races** are populations of the same species that differ genetically because they have adapted to different living conditions.

Figure 10-11

a Dusky seaside sparrow
Ammodramus maritimus nigrescens
This ecological race is now extinct. The last individual died in captivity in 1987. This race occurred only near Merritt Island and the marshes of the St. John's River near Titusville, Florida. It differed from the other seaside sparrows in having a very dark gray back and a light, streaked breast.

b Gulf seaside sparrow
Ammodramus maritimus fisheri
This sparrow is found along the Gulf Coast, but not along the Atlantic Coast. It differs from other ecological races of seaside sparrows in its more orange color. Its range (shown in yellow) overlaps that of the seaside sparrow in Figure 10-11c.

184

Members of different ecological races are not yet different enough to belong to different species, but they have taken the first step. The differences among human races, while they may seem large to some of us, are actually very small in an evolutionary sense. Notice that each sparrow in **Figure 10-11** has a three-word scientific name; the third word of the name indicates a subspecies, a distinct group within a species.

Ecological races form new species

Ecological races often become increasingly different. The accumulation of differences between species or populations is called **divergence**. Divergence occurs because natural selection favors different survival strategies in different environments. Eventually, races can accumulate so many differences that biologists consider them separate species.

Divergence

■ **Analyzing Information**
Inform students that 13 species of finches are found on the 13 main volcanic masses that make up the Galápagos Islands. Ask students why islands such as the Galápagos favor divergence. *(Because each island differs geographically, the populations on each island face different selection pressures.)*

c **Seaside sparrow**
Ammodramus maritimus maritimus
This sparrow is widely distributed along the Atlantic and Gulf Coasts from Massachusetts to southern Texas. It is a common bird, noted for making "crash landings" into marsh grasses. This is by far the most common and widespread of the four ecological races of seaside sparrow. Its range is shown in pink.

d **Cape Sable seaside sparrow**
Ammodramus maritimus mirabilis
This olive green seaside sparrow is found only in Cape Sable, on the southwestern tip of Florida. It is a very local ecological race. No other type of seaside sparrow lives in the area.

185

Phase Three
Assessment Options

Closure

■ Forming Hypotheses

When the insecticide DDT was first introduced, it was considered a highly effective way to control insect pests, especially mosquitoes. Over time, however, DDT became increasingly less effective. In fact, many populations of insects are now resistant to DDT. Have students explain how natural selection acted in this case. *(Individual insects that were resistant to DDT when it was first used survived and passed on the genes for resistance to their offspring. Those that were not resistant died. As DDT was continually used, this process repeated itself, until only resistant insects remained.)* Ask students to use this information to explain the recent development of antibiotic-resistant pathogens.

SECTION REVIEW

Assign the *Section Review.*

Reteaching

Sharks and alligators are considered living fossils because they have changed little over millions of years. Have students suggest why these organisms have not evolved to any appreciable extent. *(Their environments have remained fairly constant; therefore, these organisms have remained adapted. No selection pressure has existed to favor one phenotype over another to cause the population to change.)*

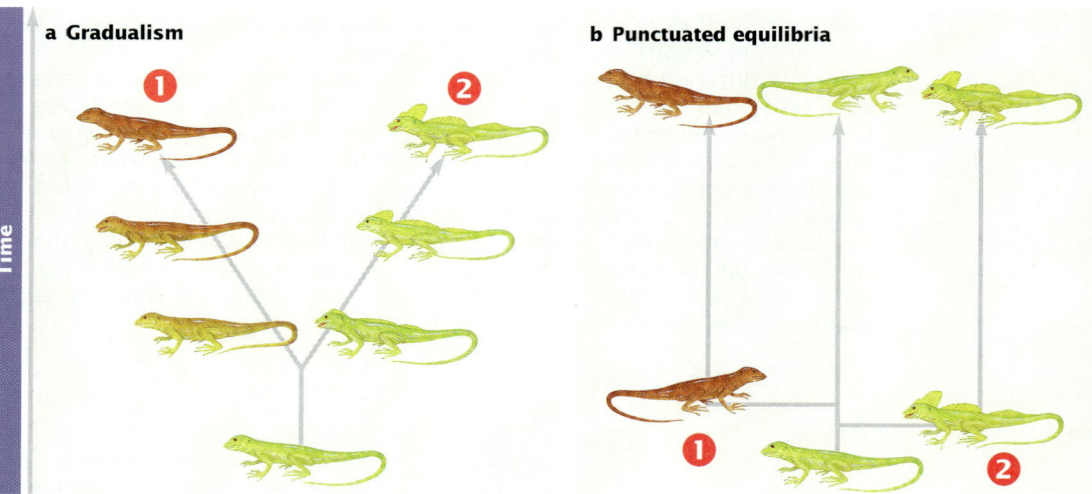

a Gradualism **b Punctuated equilibria**

Figure 10-12

a According to the hypothesis of gradualism, the differences between species 1 and 2 accumulated slowly over a long period of time.

b According to the punctuated equilibria hypothesis, the differences between the species evolved rapidly during the relatively short period of time in which the species were forming. After each species formed, it did not change for a long period of time.

Does Evolution Occur in Spurts?

Biologists are now engaged in a debate about the rate at which evolution proceeds. Following Darwin's lead, most biologists have assumed that species formation is a slow, gradual process that goes on all the time. The hypothesis that evolution occurs at a slow, constant rate is known as **gradualism**.

Recently, some biologists have challenged gradualism, arguing that species formation occurs rapidly after major environmental upheavals. (Keep in mind that a rapid occurrence in geological time lasts many thousands of years.) Short periods of rapid species formation have been followed by long periods during which little evolution occurred. The hypothesis that evolution occurs at such irregular rates is known as **punctuated equilibria**.

Punctuated equilibria predicts that the fossil record should be very discontinuous and that fossils should exhibit little evidence of change over long periods of time. Transitional forms should be rare because new species evolve so rapidly. Is this prediction supported by fossil evidence? There is considerable disagreement among biologists on this point. Some groups of organisms appear suddenly in the fossil record, as if they had evolved very rapidly, and then remain almost unchanged for millions of years. Other groups show gradual change. Compare these two hypotheses in **Figure 10-12**. Note that the disagreement about punctuated equilibria is a debate about the rate and regularity of evolution, not about whether evolution occurs.

SECTION REVIEW

1 Describe the steps of natural selection.

2 The British have instituted pollution controls on factories. How do you think this will affect the evolution of the peppered moth?

3 Describe how natural selection can lead to the formation of new species.

4 Contrast the hypothesis of punctuated equilibria with that of gradualism.

ANSWERS TO SECTION REVIEW

1 Refer to Table 10-1 on page 181.

2 Without soot in the atmosphere, trees will regain a lighter, more natural color, causing dark peppered moths to become more visible and therefore less common.

3 As a population of a species spreads throughout an environment, it is exposed to varying conditions. Over time, the separate populations become distinct and split into ecological races. Gradually, they can become so different from one another that they become two separate species.

4 Gradualism states that evolution occurs at a slow, steady rate. Punctuated equilibrium states that evolution occurs at an irregular rate—long steady periods of little or no change interrupted by short periods of rapid evolution.

Using radioactive dating, scientists found that this fossil of a duck-billed dinosaur skull is about 125 million years old.

	Key Terms	Summary
10-1 **Charles Darwin**  The observations of a young Charles Darwin changed our ideas about the world.	natural selection (p. 175)	• Darwin's observations during his voyage led him to doubt his beliefs about the origin of species. • Darwin proposed that new species formed by the slow transformation of existing species. • Darwin proposed that natural selection caused evolution. • Natural selection occurs because some organisms have traits that increase their ability to survive or produce offspring.
10-2 **The Evidence for Evolution**  Fossils show that modern whales evolved from land-dwelling animals with four limbs.	half-life (p. 176) radioactive dating (p. 176) homologous structure (p. 178) vestigial structure (p. 178)	• Fossils are preserved traces of dead organisms. Fossils form only under specific conditions. • Radioactive dating enables us to determine the ages of fossils. • The fossil record provides evidence that older species gave rise to more recent species. • Organisms with homologous structures share common ancestry. • Closely related organisms have more similarities in their DNA than do distantly related organisms.
10-3 **Natural Selection** 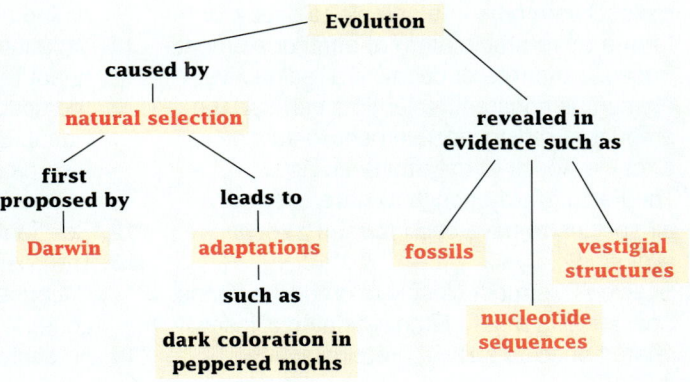 Dark peppered moths became increasingly common when pollution darkened forest trees in England.	adaptation (p. 182) balancing selection (p. 183) directional selection (p. 183) ecological race (p. 184) divergence (p. 185) gradualism (p. 186) punctuated equilibria (p. 186)	• Adaptation is the process by which organisms become better suited to their environments. • In response to the darkening of tree trunks by pollution, some peppered moth populations evolved from cream colored to dark gray. • In Africa, the sickle cell allele is favored because it produces resistance to malaria in heterozygotes. • Gradualism is the hypothesis that evolution occurs at a constant rate. Punctuated equilibria is the hypothesis that evolution occurs at an irregular rate.

Alternative Assessment

Humans have long exerted their own selection pressure: artificial selection. Humans have affected the evolution of many different organisms, especially plants and animals, by selecting which individuals breed. Have each student select such an organism and research its development through artificial selection. Students may want to contact either an animal breeder or plant breeder.

Portfolio Assessment

Portfolio Assessment on page T39 provides options for building and evaluating student portfolios. Students and teachers can select items from the areas listed on page T39 for inclusion in a portfolio.

187

ANSWER TO CONCEPT MAP

The following is one possible answer to the Relating Concepts exercise of page 188.

Evolution

caused by

revealed in evidence such as

natural selection

first proposed by

leads to

Darwin

adaptations

fossils

vestigial structures

such as

nucleotide sequences

dark coloration in peppered moths

Understanding Vocabulary

1. a. See pages 174–175.
   b. See page 178.
   c. See page 183.
2. a. A fossil is any trace of a dead organism. Scientists use the technique of radioactive dating to determine the age of a fossil by measuring the amount of a radioactive element in the sample.
   b. The environment is the key factor in natural selection, the process by which organisms with traits well suited, or adapted, to an environment will survive and reproduce in greater number than organisms less suited.
   c. Natural selection favors changes that increase an organism's chances of surviving and reproducing. As separate populations of a species continue to adapt to their environment, they can become quite different, forming ecological races. Through divergence, the accumulation of differences among species or populations, new species eventually emerge from ecological races.

Understanding Concepts

3. Concept map answer is shown on page 187.
4. Like nearly all scientists in the 1830s, Darwin accepted the view that God created new species of organisms and designed each species to match its habitat. After his voyage on the *Beagle,* Darwin had evidence to support his theory of natural selection as a mechanism for the origin of species, which he explained in his book *The Origin of Species.*
5. Darwin concluded that species changed over time and gave rise to new species. He also described natural selection as the mechanism that drives evolution.
6. See pages 174–175.
7. See page 176.
8. Half-life is the amount of time it takes for one-half of the

---

review

Understanding Vocabulary

1. For each pair of terms, explain the differences in their meanings.
   a. evolution, natural selection
   b. homologous structures, vestigial structures
   c. balancing selection, directional selection

2. Using each set of words, write one or more sentences summarizing information learned in this chapter.
   a. fossil, half-life, radioactive dating
   b. natural selection, environment, trait, adaptation, survival
   c. natural selection, ecological race, divergence, new species

Understanding Concepts

3. **Relating Concepts** Construct a concept map summarizing the study of evolution. Try to include the following terms in your concept map: Darwin, adaptation, fossils, natural selection, vestigial structures, and nucleotide sequences.

4. **Summarizing Information** Each species of Galápagos finch has a beak suited for eating a particular type of food. How would Darwin have explained this pattern before his voyage on the *Beagle?* How would he have explained it after writing the *Origin of Species?*

5. **Recognizing Patterns** The plants and animals of the Galápagos Islands closely resemble those of the South American mainland. What did Darwin conclude from this pattern of resemblance?

6. **Relating Concepts** Explain the difference between evolution and natural selection.

7. **Comparing Structures** What is a fossil? Give examples of three different kinds of fossils. Why are hard parts of organisms, such as bones and shells, more likely to be fossilized than soft parts, such as muscles and skin?

8. **Interpreting Processes** What does the term *half-life* mean? Explain the process of radioactive dating.

9. **Recognizing Relationships** The Earth is thought to be about 4.5 billion years old. Explain the importance of this information for the theory of evolution.

10. **Interpreting Data** Use the data in the table below to answer the following questions. Which species is most closely related to humans? Which species is most distantly related to humans? Explain your answers.

Species	Number of amino acid differences compared with human hemoglobin
Humans	0
Species A	17
Species B	39
Species C	8

11. **Recognizing Relationships** Why is variation among individuals so important for the process of natural selection? What are the main sources of this variation?

12. **Analyzing Methods** What was Kettlewell's hypothesis to explain the evolution of dark coloration in peppered moths? Describe the methods he used to test this hypothesis.

13. **Predicting Outcomes** Suppose that scientists discover an effective vaccine for the disease malaria. How would you expect the vaccine to affect the frequency of the sickle cell allele in central Africa over several generations? Explain your answer.

14. **Summarizing Information** What is an ecological race? How does an ecological race form? What is the relationship between an ecological race and a species?

15. **BUILDING ON WHAT YOU HAVE LEARNED** In Chapter 8 you learned that DNA is a molecule made up of the nucleotides that code for amino acids. What can biologists learn about two species by comparing their DNA sequences?

---

radioactive atoms in a sample to decay, or form a more stable atom of another element. Because the rate of decay of a radioactive element is constant, scientists can use the amount of radioactive element remaining in a rock or fossil to determine its age.
9. The Earth is old enough to have allowed all species to have been formed through evolution.
10. Species C is most closely related to humans. Species B is most distantly related. Closely related species show more similarities in

amino acid sequences in their proteins.
11. Variation allows more individuals to better adapt to selective pressure. Mutations are the source of new genetic variation in an individual. Sexual reproduction and crossing-over also produce individuals with unique combinations of alleles.
12. See Table 10-2 on page 182.
13. The allele frequency would decrease. Because the selective pressure would be gone.
14. An ecological race is a population of a

Interpreting Graphics

16. The graph below shows average shell length for three species of clams. The data begin with the first appearance of each species in the fossil record and end with the species' last appearance. Which hypothesis about evolutionary rates—gradualism or punctuated equilibria—do the data support? Explain your answer.

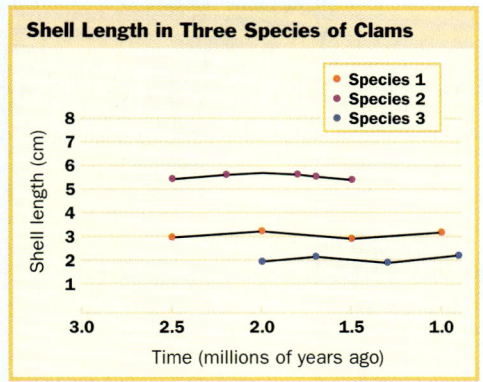

Shell Length in Three Species of Clams

- Species 1
- Species 2
- Species 3

Shell length (cm) / Time (millions of years ago)

Reviewing Themes

17. *Evolution*
The bones in the human arm are very similar to the bones in a bird's wing and a dolphin's flipper. What does this similarity in structure reveal about the ancestry of these animals?

18. *Evolution*
What is sickle cell anemia? What unexpected advantage do heterozygous individuals have in central Africa? Why don't heterozygotes have the same advantage in the United States?

Thinking Critically

19. **Evaluating an Argument** Here is a student's explanation of the evolution of the peppered moth. "At first, all peppered moths were light colored. When pollution began to darken the tree trunks, some light colored moths turned a little darker. These darker moths survived and passed on their darker coloration to their offspring. The offspring became even darker, and their offspring were darker still. This continued until all peppered moths matched the color of the tree trunks." What is wrong with this explanation?

Life/Work Skills

20. **Finding Information** Many species of destructive insects have evolved resistance to the pesticides once used to control them. Use references available in a library or search an on-line database to gather information about pesticide resistance in insects. Write a report that explains the causes of pesticide resistance, describes its costs to humans, and explains some of the alternative pest-control methods being researched.

Activities and Projects

21. **Career Connection: Paleontologist** A paleontologist is a scientist who excavates and studies fossils and other remains. Use library references or search an on-line database to find out what a paleontologist does in his or her day-to-day job. Where do most paleontologists work? What kind of educational background is required?

22. **Math Connection** Study the following table, which shows the half-lives of radioactive elements. Then answer the questions.
a. How old is a rock that has half the amount of uranium-238 that it originally had?
b. How old is a rock that has approximately one-quarter of the amount of potassium-40 that it originally had?

Radioactive isotope	Half-life	Stable product
Carbon-14	5,730 years	Carbon-12
Uranium-235	704 million years	Lead-207
Potassium-40	1.25 billion years	Argon-40
Uranium-238	4.5 billion years	Lead-206

Discovering Through Reading

23. Read the article "No Longer Human" by Lori Oliwenstein in *Discover*, December 1992, pages 34–35. What was the original source of HeLa cells, and how did they travel from lab to lab? Why do some researchers claim that HeLa cells have become a new species? What are the arguments against the cells being a new species?

advantageous for people in the United States.

Thinking Critically

19. The explanation is wrong in saying that the pollution turned light-colored moths darker and that this dark color was passed on to offspring. A correct explanation would describe natural selection as the mechanism behind the evolution of the peppered moth.

Life/Work Skills

20. Reports should describe the causes of pesticide resistance and the techniques being developed to combat damage and infestation.

Activities and Projects

21. Paleontologists often work for universities, museums, and large oil and construction companies. Most often, a Ph.D. is required for teaching and museum positions. Entry-level positions are sometimes available for individuals who have completed a course of study in biology, geology, or a related field at the community college level and who are willing to acquire some specialized training.

22. a. 4.5 billion years old
b. 2.5 billion years old

Discovering Through Reading

23. They were cancer cells removed from Henrietta Lacks in 1951. Some think the cells (*Helacyton gartleri*) have lost their connection to humans; they believe the cells are single-celled microbes because they have a different ecological niche than humans and because they behave like other microbial species. Others think the cells are not a new species because their survival is purely artificial.

species that differs genetically because it has adapted to different living conditions. They are early stages in the formation of a new species.

15. DNA sequences can be used to deduce the relationship between species.

Interpreting Graphics

16. Gradualism, because they evolved at a slow, constant rate.

Reviewing Themes

17. The structures are homologous; this indicates that the organisms share a common ancestry.

18. Sickle cell anemia is a hereditary disease that affects hemoglobin molecules in the blood, impairing their ability to carry oxygen. In homozygotes, the defective sickle cell allele has lethal results. In heterozygotes, the allele imparts resistance to malaria, which is advantageous for individuals in Africa but not

11 | History of Life on Earth

Lesson Planning Guide With Options for Block Scheduling

Lecture Concepts	Lesson Resources

11-1 Origin of Life

BLOCK ❶ (45 minutes)

1. The Earth was formed some 4.5 billion years ago.

2. Scientists think that life arose on Earth from nonliving matter approximately 3.5 billion years ago.

❶ Lecture Resources
- Determining Prior Knowledge
- Active Reading: Anticipation Guide
- Active Reading: Reading Organizer
- Visual Strategies: Figures 11-1, 11-2

- Teaching Transparencies: 46
- Holt Biology Videodiscs Lesson 11-1

Assignment Options
- Life/Work Skills: Finding Information

BLOCK ❷ (45 minutes)

3. Under primitive conditions, simple molecules formed the macromolecules found in living things.

4. RNA was probably the first genetic molecule that could replicate and catalyze reactions.

5. The first cells probably arose when membranes formed around aggregates of organic compounds.

❷ Lecture Resources
- Visual Strategy: Videodisc
- Demonstration: Recognizing Relationships
- Teaching Transparencies: 47
- Holt Biology Videodiscs Lesson 11-1

Classwork Options
- Closure: Justifying Conclusions

Assignment Options
- Reteaching
- Section Review
- Chapter Review, questions 1a, 2a, 3, 4, 5, 6, 18, 22
- Directed Reading Worksheet

11-2 Early Life in the Sea

BLOCK ❸ (45 minutes)

1. Bacteria are divided into two groups: eubacteria, the ancestors of modern bacteria, and archaebacteria, the ancestors of eukaryotes.

2. About 3 billion years ago, photosynthetic eubacteria began to release oxygen into the oceans and atmosphere.

3. About 1.5 billion years ago, the first eukaryotes evolved from bacteria.

4. Most of the major groups of animals evolved about 600 to 500 million years ago, during the Cambrian period.

❸ Lecture Resources
- Multicellularity
- Visual Strategy: Figure 11-6
- Holt Biology Videodiscs Lesson 11-2

Classwork Options
- Closure: Forming Hypotheses

Assignment Options
- Life/Work Skills: Communicating
- Reteaching
- Section Review
- Chapter Review, questions 1b, 7, 8, 9, 10, 21, 25
- Directed Reading Worksheet

11-3 Invasions of the Land

BLOCK ❹ (45 minutes)

1. The ozone layer developed about 400 million years ago, permitting life to move onto land.

2. Mycorrhizae, a partnership between plants and fungi, enabled the first living things to make the transition from water to land.

❹ Lecture Resources
- Mycorrhizae
- Active Reading: Reading Organizer
- Visual Strategy: Figure 11-10
- Demonstration: Forming a Hypothesis
- Holt Biology Videodiscs Lesson 11-3

Classwork Options
- Quick Labs: Lab A10

Assignment Options
- World of Work: Paleontologist

BLOCK ❺ (45 minutes)

3. Continental drift results from heat and pressure generated deep within the Earth.

4. Arthropods, especially insects, were the first animals to thrive on land.

❺ Lecture Resources
- Continental Drift
- Holt Biology Videodiscs Lesson 11-3

Classwork Options
- *Small Group* Reteaching
- Closure: Forming a Hypothesis

Assignment Options
- Section Review
- Chapter Review, questions 2b, 11, 13, 19, 20, 23, 24
- Directed Reading Worksheet

KEY

- ■ Annotated Teacher's Edition
- ■ Pupil's Edition
- ■ Directed Reading Worksheets
- ■ Vocabulary Development Worksheets
- ■ Thinking Skills Worksheets
- ■ Reteaching Worksheets
- ■ Chapter Tests
- ◉ Language Development and Reading Comprehension Audio CD Program

Holt BioSources
Laboratory Program
- A Quick Labs
- B Inquiry Skills Development
- C Laboratory Techniques and Experimental Design
- D Biotechnology
- E Interactive Explorations in Biology Laboratory Manual

- ■ Teaching Transparencies
- ◉ Testing Resources CD-ROM
- ◉ Test Generator/Assessment Item

Holt Biology Technology
- ◉ Holt Biology Videodiscs

Lecture Concepts

Lesson Resources

11-4 Parade of Vertebrates

BLOCK ❻ (45 minutes)

1. Vertebrates are organisms that possess a vertebral column or backbone.

2. The first vertebrates to evolve were jawless fishes.

❻ Lecture Resources
- ■ Visual Strategies: Figures 11-13, 11-15
- ■ Visual Strategy: Videodisc
- ■ Demonstration: Identifying Structures
- ◉ Holt Biology Videodiscs Lesson 11-4

Assignment Options
- ◉ Teaching Resources CD/ROM: Supplemental Reading Guides 4

BLOCK ❼ (45 minutes)

3. Other vertebrates to evolve were jawed fishes, sharks, bony fishes, amphibians, reptiles, mammals, and birds.

❼ Lecture Resources
- ■ Popular Portrayals of Dinosaurs
- ■ Amphibians
- ■ Form and Function
- ■ Demonstration: Analyzing Information
- ◉ Holt Biology Videodiscs Lesson 11-4

Classwork Options
- ■ Reteaching
- ■ Closure: Forming Hypotheses

Assignment Options
- ■ Section Review
- ■ Chapter Review, questions 1c, 2c, 14, 15, 16, 17, 26
- ■ Directed Reading Worksheet

Chapter Review and Assessment

BLOCK ❽ (45 minutes)
Review
- ■ Reteaching Worksheet
- ■ Thinking Skills Worksheet
- ■ Vocabulary Development Worksheet
- ◉ Language Development and Reading Comprehension Audio CD Program: Chapter 11

BLOCK ❾ (45 minutes)
Assessment
- ■ Alternative Assessment, p. 209
- ■ Portfolio Assessment, p. T39
Chapter Test
- ■ Chapter 11 Test
Test Generator
- ◉ Item bank for customizing Chapter Tests

Teaching Resources CD-ROM
- ◉ Scoring Rubrics and Classroom Management Checklist

  The Portfolio icon denotes items throughout the Teacher's Edition lesson wrap that may be selected for inclusion in student portfolios.

Holt Biology Videodiscs and *Concepts of Biology*

Holt Biology Videodiscs gives you a powerful tool for teaching, review, and assessment. For further information regarding the media on the videodiscs, see *Holt Biology Videodiscs Teacher's Correlation Guide to Holt Biology: Visualizing Life.*

Concepts of Biology adds interactive lesson plans and extensive tools for customization using CD-ROM technology.

Use the following topic from *Concepts of Biology* to help you teach this chapter:
Topic 9: Evolution of Life on Earth

Laboratory Planning

Holt BioSources Laboratory Program

Block 4: Quick Labs Lab A10: Analyzing Adaptation: Living on Land

Determining Prior Knowledge

- Have students suggest how the first life-form may have originated on Earth.
- Assign students to cooperative work groups of four students each. Have each group construct a model, draw a picture, assemble a collage, or create a computer-generated graphic that depicts their impression of the first life-form on Earth. Have each group discuss their representation with the class.
- Write the following words on the board: plant, insect, fish, amphibian, reptile, bird, mammal. Have students arrange these words to show their evolutionary relationships.

Active READING

Technique: Anticipation Guide

Write the following statements on the chalkboard or overhead:

1. Organic molecules can form spontaneously from inorganic materials.
2. Scientists have created life from nonlife in the laboratory.
3. The first living things to populate the Earth were arthropods, animals with hard shells, such as scorpions and insects.
4. Dinosaurs evolved from birds.

Give students time to form opinions about each statement. Have students discuss their opinions in small groups. Then have students read the chapter to see if their opinions are confirmed or changed in any way.

CD-ROM Resources

Concepts of Biology
Topic 9: Evolution of Life on Earth

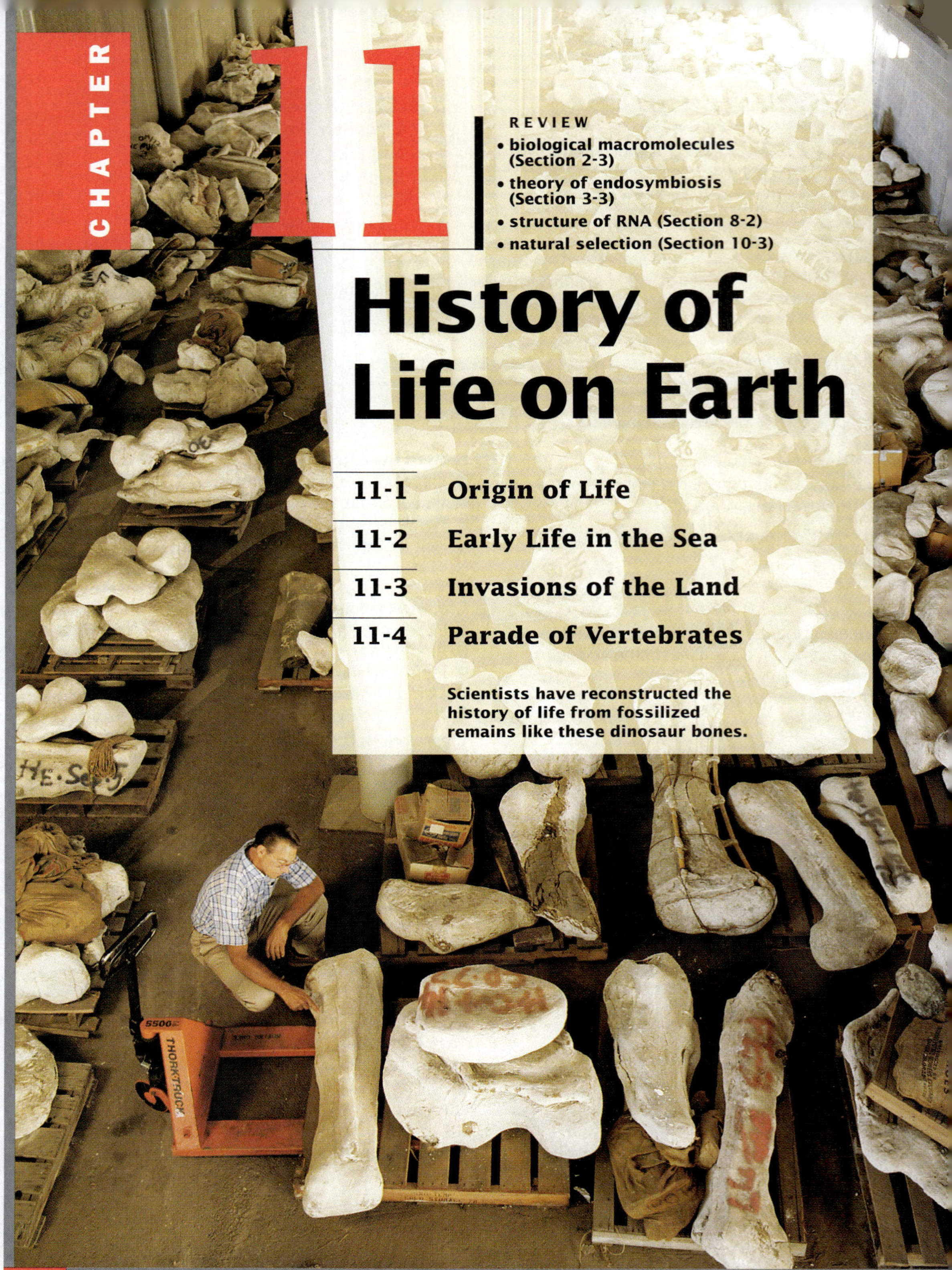

CHAPTER

11

REVIEW
- biological macromolecules (Section 2-3)
- theory of endosymbiosis (Section 3-3)
- structure of RNA (Section 8-2)
- natural selection (Section 10-3)

History of Life on Earth

11-1	**Origin of Life**
11-2	**Early Life in the Sea**
11-3	**Invasions of the Land**
11-4	**Parade of Vertebrates**

Scientists have reconstructed the history of life from fossilized remains like these dinosaur bones.

190

Author's Rationale This chapter tells the history of life on Earth. An overview describes how the major groups of organisms evolved. The advantage of the overview at this point in the text is that it provides students with a dynamic picture of life's diversity. Rather than seeing the Earth as a large zoo consisting of exhibits of unrelated animals, students come to view the diversity of all life-forms on Earth as the result of a long evolutionary process.

With life all around us, it is difficult to imagine a time when there was no life on Earth, when no plants grew and no fishes swam in the sea. The Earth is much older than life, however. The study of radioactive decay in rocks reveals that the Earth is some 4.5 billion years old, about 1 billion years older than the oldest fossils. Where did life come from?

11-1 Origin of Life

OBJECTIVES

1 Contrast the three explanations for the origin of life.

2 Describe the importance of the Miller-Urey experiment.

3 Summarize the reasons scientists think RNA, not DNA, was the first genetic material.

4 Describe how the first cells might have evolved.

How Did Life Begin?

There were no witnesses to the origin of life, and you cannot go back in time to see for yourself. In principle, there are at least three ways life could have begun:

1. *Extraterrestrial origin* Some scientists hypothesize that life originated on another planet outside our solar system. Life was then carried here on a meteorite or an asteroid and colonized the Earth. How life arose on other planets, if it did, is a question we cannot hope to answer soon.

2. *Creation* Many people believe that life was put on Earth by divine forces. In this view, common to many of the world's religions, the forces leading to life cannot be explained by science.

3. *Origin from nonliving matter* Most scientists think that life arose on Earth from inanimate matter. First, random events produced stable molecules that could reproduce themselves. Then natural selection favored changes in these molecules that increased their rate of reproduction, leading eventually to the first cell.

This chapter will examine the third option. The first two possibilities are not considered because they are not testable and thus fall outside the realm of science. The first step in the origin of life from nonliving matter is the origin of the Earth. The Earth formed about 4.5 billion years ago. Three steps in its formation are shown in **Figure 11-1**.

Figure 11-1
About 4.5 billion years ago, the Earth and the rest of the solar system condensed from a cloud of dust and debris. The Earth was initially uninhabitable because it was bombarded by debris left over from the formation of the solar system. About 4 billion years ago this bombardment tapered off, and the oceans formed shortly afterward.

191

Videodisc Resources

Holt Biology Videodiscs
Lesson 11-1: Origin of Life on Earth

Phase One
Preparation

Scheduling
See the **Lesson Planning Guide** on pages 189A and 189B for lecture, classwork, and assignment options for Section 11-1.

Phase Two
Teaching Strategies

Active READING

Technique: Reading Organizer
Read aloud the first page of Section 11-1. Then ask students to survey the rest of the section. Point out that students will read about the origin of molecules and the first cells. Have students read Section 11-1 individually, and then have them work in small groups to create a reading organizer that represents the structural patterns of the section. You may want to suggest a series-of-events chain as a possible reading organizer for this section.

Visual Strategy | Figure 11-1

■ **Forming a Model**
portfolio Tell students to imagine that they are "distant travelers" examining Earth 4 billion years ago, as it is shown in this figure. Have them write a journal entry or create a model (drawing, collage, painting, computer graphic, or any other artistic form) that describes what they might have seen as their spacecraft descended to take a closer look at Earth.

Key to Strategies
Teaching Strategies are keyed to three tiers of learning.

● **Understanding Concepts (Tier I)**
Content mastery and comprehension

■ **Applying Information (Tier II)**
Applying and analyzing content

▲ **Critical Thinking (Tier III)**
Practicing evaluative thinking

Earth Science Connection

Why Earth?

Earth appears to be the only planet in our solar system that supports life. Several factors make Earth unique in this regard: Earth has a moderate temperature because it is neither too close to nor too far from the sun; it has liquid water; and it is large enough to exert a gravitational pull to hold a protective atmosphere, but not so large that it produces a dense atmosphere that would block solar radiation needed for photosynthesis.

Visual Strategy Figure 11-2

Analyzing Information

Focus students' attention on the wording in Step 4: "Organic molecules could have formed . . ." Ask students why the sentence could not read "Organic molecules formed . . ." *(Students should recognize that Miller and Urey's experiment did not prove that organic molecules formed under such conditions some 3.5 billion years ago, only that they could have formed in such a manner. Only by observing their formation firsthand could one say that organic molecules formed in such a manner.)*

Origin of Life's Chemicals

For life to have arisen from nonliving matter on the early Earth, the chemicals that make up living things must have been present. Recall from Chapter 2 that all organisms are composed of the same four kinds of macromolecules: proteins, lipids, carbohydrates, and nucleic acids. But where did these macromolecules, the building blocks of life, come from?

In a letter to a friend, Charles Darwin speculated that life began in "a warm little pond." In the 1920s, the Russian scientist A. I. Oparin and the British geneticist J.B.S. Haldane independently proposed a more elaborate version of Darwin's idea. They suggested that the Earth's oceans once contained large amounts of simple molecules and that these molecules spontaneously came together to form the macromolecules that compose living things.

Oparin and Haldane proposed that the early Earth's atmosphere lacked oxygen. They believed that it was instead rich in nitrogen gas (N_2) and hydrogen-containing gases such as water vapor (H_2O), methane (CH_4), hydrogen gas (H_2), and ammonia (NH_3). Electrons in these gases would have been frequently pushed to higher energy levels by photons from the sun and by electrical energy from lightning. Today, such high-energy electrons are quickly soaked up by oxygen in the atmosphere (which is 21 percent oxygen gas) because oxygen atoms have a great attraction for such electrons. But early in Earth's history, there was no oxygen in the air, and a wealth of high-energy electrons would have been available to help form complex organic molecules.

Figure 11-2
The results of Miller and Urey's experiment were startling. Other scientists accepted these results, however, because of the careful planning and execution by the experimenters. Follow some of the steps in the experiment below.

Objective:
Determine whether organic molecules that make up living things could form under conditions found on early Earth.

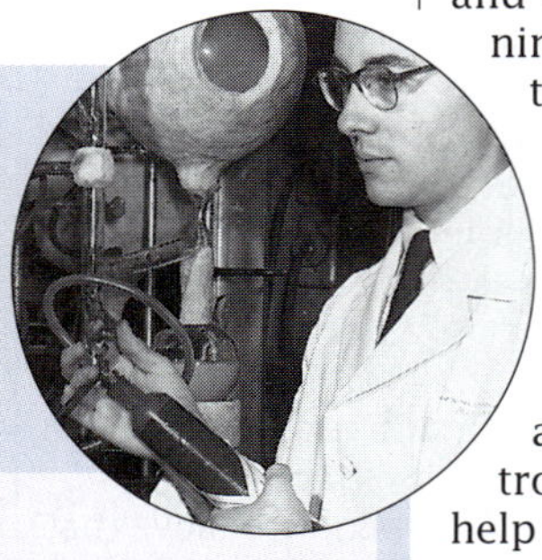

1 Methods:
- Mix molecules found in early atmosphere.
- Stimulate reactions with heat and electricity.
- Collect and analyze products of reactions.

2 Key Assumptions:
- Experiment matches conditions on early Earth—in temperature and chemical composition.
- Experiment has not been contaminated by bacteria, which could also produce organic molecules.

3 Results:
Complex mixture of organic molecules forms; contains amino acids.

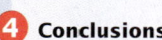

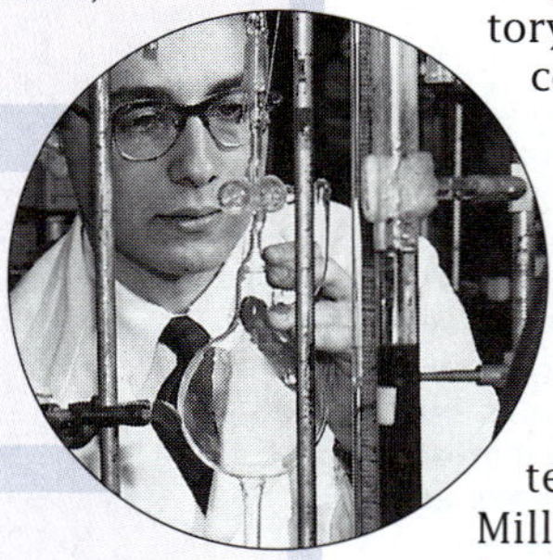

4 Conclusions:
Organic molecules could have formed on early Earth before life existed. Thus, a key step in the origin of life is possible.

Life's building blocks can form spontaneously

Oparin's and Haldane's hypothesis was first tested in 1953 by Stanley Miller and Harold Urey of the University of Chicago. Figure 11-2 explains the reasoning behind their experiment, and Figure 11-3 shows the laboratory setup they used to simulate conditions on the young Earth. The brownish mixture that resulted from this experiment contained a variety of organic molecules and, most important, six of the twenty amino acids that organisms use to make proteins. Similar experiments by Miller and other scientists have produced a variety of biologically important molecules, including many of the amino acids found in living things, nucleotides from DNA and RNA, lipids, carbohydrates, and ATP.

Historical Perspective: A Long Delay

Approximately 30 years elapsed between Oparin and Haldane's proposal and Miller and Urey's experiment. The delay was due to the effect of Louis Pasteur's conclusive proof that spontaneous generation does not occur. After spontaneous generation was disproven, scientists were quite reluctant to accept the view that a life-form could arise from nonliving matter. But, as it turned out, spontaneous generation has nothing in common with the origin of the first life-form other than the fact that a life-form arose from nonliving matter.

Figure 11-3
Stanley Miller and Harold Urey used an apparatus like this to simulate the conditions on the early Earth.

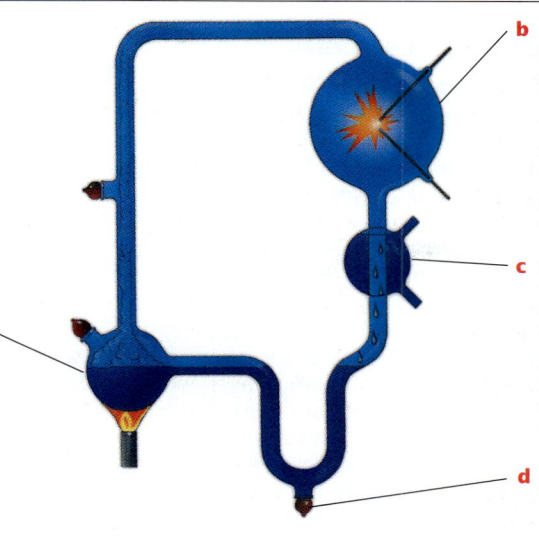

b **... the vessel representing the atmosphere. It contains a mixture of hydrogen gas, methane, ammonia, and water vapor. Sparks discharged into the mixture mimic the effects of lightning, stimulating reactions among the gases.**

c **Cold water circulates over the tubing, causing water vapor to condense, simulating rain. Thus, the products of any reactions in the "atmosphere" are carried back into the "ocean," where they can continue to react.**

a **This flask contains water and represents the ocean. Heating causes water to evaporate and move up a glass tube to ...**

d **Miller could remove samples for analysis through this valve.**

These experiments show that the components of the macromolecules found in living things could have formed spontaneously on the early Earth.

Recent discoveries suggest that life was present within a few hundred million years of Earth's origin. Also, the intense solar radiation reaching the Earth in the absence of oxygen would have depleted the ammonia and methane in the atmosphere. So there would have been less of these gases dissolved in the ocean than in Miller and Urey's experimental mixture. Some scientists now speculate that spontaneous processes like those in the Miller-Urey experiment may have occurred primarily within the tiny bubbles that are abundant at the ocean's surface. The bubbles would have concentrated the chemicals and thereby speeded the reactions. They also would have protected these reactions from solar radiation.

RNA was probably the first genetic molecule

Miller and Urey's experiment and other similar experiments show that the basic building blocks of life can assemble spontaneously. But there was still a long way to go before life could arise. How did amino acids join together to form the chains we call proteins? And how did nucleotides join to form long chains of DNA and RNA?

As you learned in Chapter 8, cells link amino acids together into proteins, but only according to instructions encoded in DNA and carried in RNA. Similarly, cells synthesize DNA and RNA, but only with the aid of enzymes, which are proteins. So how could proteins form without DNA and RNA, and vice versa?

Although nucleic acids are only produced by living things today, small chains of RNA will form spontaneously under conditions that were probably found on the early Earth. Also, Thomas Cech of the University of Colorado and Sidney Altman of Yale University have recently discovered that RNA molecules can catalyze chemical reactions. In your cells, for example, RNA molecules participate in the synthesis of other RNA molecules.

The discovery that RNA can act as a catalyst suggests the following hypothesis. First, RNA nucleotides formed from simple gas molecules. Nucleotides then assembled spontaneously into small chains. These small chains were able to catalyze chemical reactions, such as synthesis of protein, and were able to make copies of themselves. Once self-replicating molecules like these appear, natural selection and evolution are possible. Molecules that can replicate faster or more efficiently will become more common than slower-replicating or less-efficient molecules.

■ **Recognizing Relationships**
Use the step-frame sequence *Miller-Urey Experiment* shown in Chapter 11 Section 11-1 in *Holt Biology Videodiscs Teacher's Correlation Guide to Holt Biology: Visualizing Life* to review the experiment that Miller and Urey performed. Have students identify the purpose of the experiment. Ask why Miller and Urey chose those particular gases. Make sure students understand the importance of electricity in their model. Ask students to explain the significance of the presence of the amino acids in the dark mixture that formed. Then have students write a short paragraph explaining whether they think this experiment provides enough evidence to support the theory that the basic building blocks of life could have arisen spontaneously in the early seas.

Life/Work Skills
Finding Information

● **Summarizing Information**
portfolio The debate about where the first life-form arose has continued ever since Miller and Urey's experiment. Some have suggested that life originated in claylike material and not in a "primordial soup." Tell students to check library and on-line references to find information about possible locations of life's origins. Have them write a brief report and share their findings with their classmates.

Matter of Fact: Another Serendipitous Finding

The discovery of the catalytic property of RNA was a serendipitous finding. Cech was working with several systems, one of which was protein-free. Each system consisted of an RNA molecule from which an intron had to be excised. Such a process is dependent on enzymatic activity. Consequently, Cech did not expect to observe any catalytic activity in the protein-free system, so he was later surprised to find that the introns had been removed. A closer look at the system revealed that RNA was responsible, thereby proving that RNA has catalytic properties.

Key to Strategies
● Understanding Concepts (Tier I)
■ Applying Information (Tier II)
▲ Critical Thinking (Tier III)

History of Life on Earth 193

Origin of the First Cells

How did the first cells form? The crucial feature that separates the cell from its environment is the cell membrane, which contains lipids, as you learned in Chapter 3. If you mix a lipid such as oil with water, you can see an important lipid property: small spherical bubbles of oil appear in the water because the oil molecules do not mix with the water molecules. You can see a similar effect if you shake a bottle of oil and vinegar salad dressing, as shown in **Figure 11-4a.** Scientists think that tiny spheres of lipid may have been the first stage in the origin of the cell. When mixed with water, certain lipids will form a bubble or droplet that has a double-layered membrane much like the lipid bilayer of the cell membrane. **Figure 11-4b** shows some of these droplets.

The early oceans probably contained numerous small lipid droplets, each one forming and then dispersing. Over millions of years, droplets that could survive longer by taking in molecules and energy from their surroundings would have become more common than the here-today-gone-tomorrow kind. When a means arose to transfer this ability to "offspring" droplets, probably through self-replicating RNA, life had begun.

If RNA was the first genetic material, when did DNA evolve? Most scientists think DNA evolved after simple cells had arisen. The advantage of DNA over RNA as a genetic material may have been that DNA ensured the safety of the hereditary information by storing it in a central, protected location.

Our vision of the origin of life is incomplete. No scientist has been able to create life from nonlife in the laboratory. Yet many of the important steps that might have led to living cells have been worked out. Also remember that scientists have been performing experiments regarding the origin of life for fewer than 50 years. Simple molecules were combining in the ancient seas for millions of years before life resulted.

Figure 11-4
Recall from Chapter 3 that lipids, which are nonpolar molecules, will not mix with polar molecules such as water.

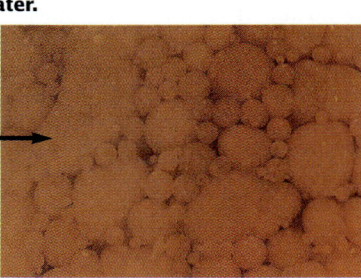 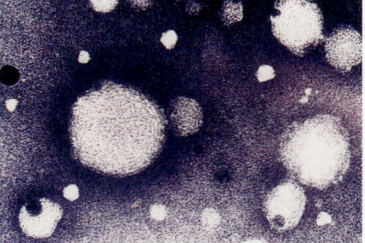

a In a bottle of oil-and-vinegar salad dressing, lipids cluster into droplets to minimize contact with water.

b Similar, but smaller, droplets form when lipids are combined with water in the laboratory.

SECTION REVIEW

1 Explain why the hypothesis that life arose from nonliving matter is a scientific hypothesis.

2 What were the results of the Miller-Urey experiment? Why was this experiment so important?

3 Describe the evidence that suggests RNA was the first genetic molecule.

4 Describe one hypothesis that explains how the cell membrane might have evolved.

ANSWERS TO SECTION REVIEW

1 It is a hypothesis because it is testable, as shown by the experiment conducted by Miller and Urey.

2 Some organic molecules were produced, including amino acids. This experiment showed that some of the basic building blocks of life can assemble spontaneously.

3 Two scientists discovered that RNA can catalyze chemical reactions.

4 The cell membrane may have evolved when lipids mixed with water and formed a double-layered lipid membrane, much like the modern cell membrane.

Soon after the Earth became hospitable to living things, life arose in the ancient seas. The first organisms to appear on the planet were bacteria. These early bacteria are the ancestors of modern bacteria and of all the many different kinds of organisms living today, including you.

11-2

Early Life in the Sea

OBJECTIVES

1 Recognize the great age of the Earth.

2 Compare and contrast the two major groups of bacteria.

3 Identify the major change in the early atmosphere caused by bacteria.

4 Describe the evolutionary relationships between prokaryotes and eukaryotes.

Earliest Life: Bacteria

Several independent studies estimate the Earth's age as 4.5 billion years. So far, no fossils have been found in the oldest known rocks, which are about 3.8 billion years old. The oldest fossils that have been discovered occur in 3.5-billion-year-old rocks that were once sediments on the ocean floor. The tiny fossils that have been found in these ancient rocks were bacteria.

Biologists separate the bacteria into two groups that differ in the composition of their cell walls and cell membranes and in the structure of some of their proteins. Because the differences between these two groups are so great, it is likely that they diverged early in the history of life. One group is the **eubacteria** (YOO bak TIHR ee ah), or "true bacteria," the most common bacteria today. Most living bacteria, including those that cause disease and decay, are eubacteria. Eukaryotic cells contain mitochondria and chloroplasts, which are probably descendants of ancient eubacteria.

Representatives of the second group of bacteria, the **archaebacteria** (AHR kee bak TIHR ee ah), or "ancient bacteria," are shown in **Figure 11-5**. Today most kinds of archaebacteria live in extreme environments such as very salty lakes, hot springs, and swamps. However, there are archaebacteria in your intestine and in the stomachs of sheep, cattle, and other hoofed mammals. The RNA polymerase (the enzyme that copies DNA into messen-

Figure 11-5
The archaebacterium *Sulfolobus* thrives at temperatures of up to 90°C (194°F). That is how it can live in this hot spring in Yellowstone National Park.

ger RNA) and ribosomes of archaebacteria are much more like those of eukaryotes than are those of eubacteria. Most biologists now think that archaebacteria are direct ancestors of eukaryotes.

Scheduling
See the **Lesson Planning Guide** on pages 189A and 189B for lecture, classwork, and assignment options for Section 11-2.

Connection: *Chapter 3*

Evolution of Eukaryotes
Remind students that scientists think certain bacterial "trespassers" became trapped inside other cells and gradually lost their independence. These bacteria evolved into mitochondria and chloroplasts.

Language Arts Connection

Thermoacidophiles
Refer students to Figure 11-5. Have them use a dictionary to decipher the meaning of the word *thermoacidophile* by examining its prefixes and suffix. (*Thermoacidophiles are bacteria that "love" [-phile] heat [thermo-] and an acidic environment [acido-].*)

195

Videodisc Resources

Holt Biology Videodiscs
Lesson 11-2: Early Life in the Sea

Key to Strategies
● Understanding Concepts (Tier I)
■ Applying Information (Tier II)
▲ Critical Thinking (Tier III)

Connection: *Chapter 5*

Photosynthesis

Cyanobacteria carry out photosynthesis much like plants do. However, they lack the chloroplasts found in plant cells. Instead, their photosynthetic pigments are found on folded membranes in the cytoplasm. These pigments include green chlorophyll and blue phycocyanin, which both give cyanobacteria their blue-green color.

Multicellularity

● Comparing Functions

Ask students if multicellularity has any evolutionary advantages or disadvantages. *(In a multicellular organism, cells can become specialized to perform different functions. Although this specialization leads to greater efficiency, it comes at a price. Cells become dependent on one another and thus are not self-sustaining units like those of a unicellular eukaryote.)*

Visual Strategy | **Figure 11-6**

● Organizing Data

Have students identify the six kingdoms shown in this figure. Emphasize that this grouping is not accepted by all scientists. In fact, no one grouping is satisfactory to all scientists. This reflects our lack of knowledge about complete evolutionary histories of all organisms. In addition, the classification system reflects human values. Some scientists are "groupers," who emphasize similarities among organisms and keep the number of kingdoms to a minimum. Others are "splitters," who focus on differences and thus propose systems with six or more kingdoms. Have students make a **Graphic Organizer** that illustrates the evolution of six separate kingdoms.

Though small, bacteria changed the atmosphere

The modern atmosphere is about 21 percent oxygen. Where did this oxygen come from, since the early Earth's atmosphere lacked oxygen? It was produced by bacteria. About 3 billion years ago, a group of photosynthetic eubacteria known as **cyanobacteria** *(sy uh noh bak TIHR ee ah)* evolved. By carrying out photosynthesis, cyanobacteria released oxygen gas into the oceans. After hundreds of millions of years, when the waters of the ancient oceans had soaked up all the oxygen they could hold, the oxygen produced by photosynthesis began to bubble out of the oceans and into the air. Over the billions of years that followed, more and more oxygen was added to the air until the modern composition of the atmosphere was achieved. As you will see in the following section, this change in the atmosphere had an important influence on the course of evolution.

Dawn of the Eukaryotes

For about 2 billion years, bacteria were the only living things on Earth. About 1.5 billion years ago, the first eukaryotic cells evolved from bacteria. Fossils of early eukaryotes show that they were much larger than bacteria and that they had internal membranes.

Based on evolutionary relationships, biologists classify living things into six great kingdoms: eubacteria, archaebacteria, protists, plants, animals, and fungi. Study the representatives of these six groups in **Figure 11-6**. Archaebacteria and eubacteria are prokaryotic. Of the four eukaryotic kingdoms, the most diverse by far is the kingdom that first arose from bacteria, the protists. Protists are important to the history of life because they are the ancestors of the three other eukaryotic kingdoms. Some protists and most members of the other three eukaryotic kingdoms are made of many cells. Having more than one cell is known as **multicellularity**. Multicellularity is a relatively recent evolutionary event. The first known fossils of multicellular organisms are found in 630-million-year-old rocks, which are nearly 1 billion years younger than the first eukaryotes. These early multicellular organisms were animals that did not have hard shells or bones and, as a result, were not well preserved as fossils. Many appeared to have been very flat and thin, like pancakes, and they probably floated on the surface of the ancient seas.

Figure 11-6
This diagram shows the evolutionary relationships among the six kingdoms of organisms.

Eubacteria are prokaryotes. Eubacteria are found in great numbers in nearly all habitats on Earth.

Eubacteria

Archaebacteria are also prokaryotes. They are more closely related to eukaryotes than are eubacteria.

Archaebacteria

Many protists are single-celled. Some, such as seaweed, are made of many cells.

Protista

All plants are multicellular.

Plantae

All animals are multicellular.

Animalia

Most fungi are multicellular.

Fungi

Graphic Organizer

Use the following graphic organizer with the teaching strategy **Visual Strategy Figure 11-6** on page 196.

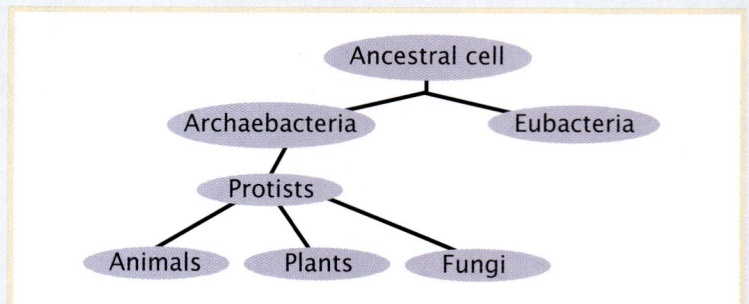

Ancestral cell — Archaebacteria — Eubacteria — Protists — Animals — Plants — Fungi

Figure 11-7
This artist's rendition shows some of the unusual Burgess Shale animals. Since these animals are known only from fossils, their true coloration is unknown.

Life Blooms in the Ancient Seas

The appearance of multicellular animals led to a great blossoming of life in the Earth's oceans. Almost all of the major groups of multicellular organisms that survive today, except plants, originated during a very short period of time, from about 550 million years ago to about 500 million years ago, a time period known as the Cambrian period.

Biologists further divide each kingdom into major groups called **phyla** (singular, phylum). Among the important animal phyla are mollusks (including snails, slugs, clams, and octopuses), sponges, and arthropods (including insects, crabs, lobsters, and spiders). Almost all of the major animal phyla that exist today evolved during the Cambrian period.

Animals unlike any living today also originated during the Cambrian. A rich collection of Cambrian fossils has been discovered on a rocky mountain slope in eastern British Columbia, Canada, in a rock formation called the Burgess Shale. There you can see the remains of many bizarre "oddball" animals that are members of extinct phyla, such as those illustrated in **Figure 11-7**. For unknown reasons, many of the phyla represented in the Burgess Shale became extinct before the end of the Cambrian period.

Large numbers of species die out during mass extinctions

At least five times during the history of life, a large percentage of existing species have become extinct within a short period of time. These large extinction events are called **mass extinctions**. The first well-documented mass extinction occurred about 440 million years ago, some 60 million years after the end of the Cambrian period. Scientists are not sure what caused most of these mass extinctions.

SECTION REVIEW

1. A human lifetime is about 75 years. Calculate the number of human lifetimes in 4.5 billion years.

2. Identify two differences between eubacteria and archaebacteria.

3. Describe how cyanobacteria changed the composition of the atmosphere.

4. Explain why the following statement is true: A human cell is descended from both eubacteria and archaebacteria.

197

ANSWERS TO SECTION REVIEW

1. 60 million lifetimes

2. They differ in the composition of their cell wall and cell membrane and in the structure of some of their proteins.

3. Cyanobacteria carried out photosynthesis, releasing oxygen into the seas. After the seas became saturated with oxygen, the gas began to bubble out into the atmosphere. As a result, the composition of the atmosphere changed.

4. A human cell is a eukaryotic cell. Eukaryotic cells are thought to have evolved when eubacterial trespassers invaded larger archaebacterial cells and established a symbiotic relationship.

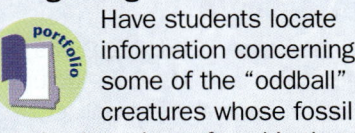

Scheduling

See the **Lesson Planning Guide** on pages 189A and 189B for lecture, classwork, and assignment options for Section 11-3.

Active READING

Technique: Reading Organizer

Point out that Section 11-3 is organized in a chronological pattern. Before students read this section, have students survey the subheadings and identify words that hint at the chronological structure of the chapter. As students read the text, have them note key words that signal the sequential structure.

Health Connection

Ozone

When present in the lower atmosphere, ozone is a pollutant that can cause smog and affect health. However, in the stratosphere, ozone forms a thin blanket that absorbs ultraviolet radiation.

What was the Earth like 500 million years ago? It was very different from today's Earth. Even though the seas teemed with life, the dry land was uninhabited, as it had been for the Earth's entire history. The great variety of terrestrial life that exists today evolved only in the last 400 million years.

11-3 Invasions of the Land

OBJECTIVES

1 Explain how ozone was critical to the development of life on Earth's surface.

2 Recognize how the relationship between plants and fungi enabled both to invade the land.

3 Identify the importance of flight in the evolution of insects.

4 Describe the role that insects and plants played in each other's evolutionary success.

The Importance of Ozone

Until just over 400 million years ago, there was no life on the dry, rocky surface of the land because high levels of ultraviolet light from the sun bombarded the Earth. Ultraviolet light damages DNA. So much ultraviolet light was reaching Earth that life could not survive out of water, which absorbs ultraviolet rays.

Life was able to move onto land because of a change in the atmosphere. Recall that photosynthesis carried out by cyanobacteria added oxygen gas to the atmosphere. As large amounts of oxygen diffused into the upper atmosphere, ultraviolet rays broke apart some of the oxygen molecules, which then recombined to form **ozone**. Ozone (O_3), shown in **Figure 11-8**, is a gas that has the remarkable and very fortunate property of absorbing ultraviolet radiation. In the upper atmosphere, ozone acted like a great shield, blocking out ultraviolet radiation. By about 400 million years ago, enough ozone had formed in the atmosphere to make the Earth's surface a safe place to live.

In this context, you can understand why so many people are worried about the ongoing destruction of Earth's ozone shield by industrial chemicals. You will learn more about the damage to the ozone layer in Chapter 16.

Figure 11-8

a Ozone, composed of three oxygen atoms, protects Earth's surface by absorbing ultraviolet radiation in the upper atmosphere.

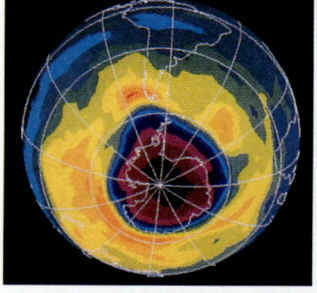

b The protective layer of ozone is being destroyed by industrial chemicals. The dark center of this satellite image indicates an area of very low ozone concentration over Antarctica.

198

Videodisc Resources

Holt Biology Videodiscs

Lesson 11-3: Invasions of the Land

Plants and Fungi Colonize Land

The first living things to populate the surface of the land were plants and fungi. Together, plants and fungi solved a particularly difficult challenge—surviving on bare rock. Each brought to this task a unique ability. Plants, which evolved from green algae, were able to carry out photosynthesis. However, they could not extract minerals from the soil-less, rocky surface of ancient Earth. Fungi, which evolved from protists, could not make sugars from sunlight but were adept at absorbing minerals.

The solution to the challenge of living on dry land was a unique biological partnership between plants and fungi called **mycorrhizae** (MY koh REYE zee). Mycorrhizae are close associations between the roots of plants and fungi. Fungi actually grow on or into the plant root and then branch out into rock or soil, as shown in **Figure 11-9**. The fungi provide the plant with minerals absorbed from rock or soil. The plant provides food to the fungi. This kind of "you-help-me-and-I-help-you" partnership is called **mutualism**. Fossils show that the earliest plants, which lived about 410 million years ago, had mycorrhizae. The partnership between plants and fungi continues today. Indeed, 80 percent of plant species have mycorrhizae associated with their roots.

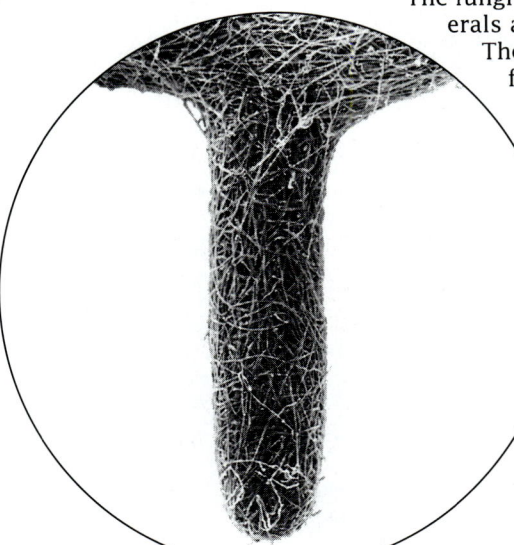

Figure 11-9

a Eighty percent of living plant species have mycorrhizae associated with their roots.

b This is a single branch root. The hairlike strands on the branch root are fungi, which help the plant absorb minerals in return for food from the plant.

Invasion of the Arthropods

The fossil record reveals that plants covered the surface of Earth within 80 million years of their initial invasion. Animals soon followed plants onto land. The first animals to leave the water were the arthropods, a kind of animal with a hard body covering and jointed legs. Crabs and lobsters are examples of existing aquatic arthropods. Some of the first arthropods to live on land resembled scorpions, carnivorous relatives of spiders with two large pincers on their front legs and a venomous stinger at the end of their tail. The arthropod invasion of the land and other major events in Earth's history are illustrated in **Figure 11-10** on the following pages.

199

Mycorrhizae

■ **Inferring Relationships**

Inform students that mycorrhizae are most common in plants growing in nutrient-poor soil. Have students explain this observation. (*Mycorrhizae enable the plants to thrive in such soil because they absorb whatever minerals are available and pass them on to the plants.*)

Demonstration

■ **Forming a Hypothesis**

Materials: specimens or photographs of various arthropods

Point out that nearly 80 percent of the known animal species are arthropods. Have students examine the specimens or photographs and hypothesize what features enabled arthropods to invade the land with such great success. (*Their rapid and prolific reproductive rate enabled them to populate an area quickly. Their exoskeleton served as protection.*)

Community Connection: Paleontologist

Invite a paleontologist to class to discuss the biological history of the local community and surrounding area. If possible, arrange a field trip so that students can visit and study the sites discussed in class.

Key to Strategies

● Understanding Concepts (Tier I)

■ Applying Information (Tier II)

▲ Critical Thinking (Tier III)

● **Interpreting Graphics**

Students may have difficulty understanding the time line of Earth's history as illustrated in this figure. This analogy may provide some perspective. Draw a time line on the board representing 24 hours. Place an arrow at 12:01 A.M. to indicate when the Earth was formed. Place additional arrows at the following points: 5 A.M., when the first bacteria appeared; 4 P.M., when the first eukaryotes appeared; 10 P.M., when life first appeared on land; 11:40 P.M., when the dinosaurs became extinct; and 11:59 P.M., when the first human appeared.

Figure 11-10

Scientists have pieced together a detailed picture of the history of life from the fossil record. The upper timeline illustrates some of the major events in the history of life on Earth. The timeline below shows a more detailed view of the events of the last 550 million years.

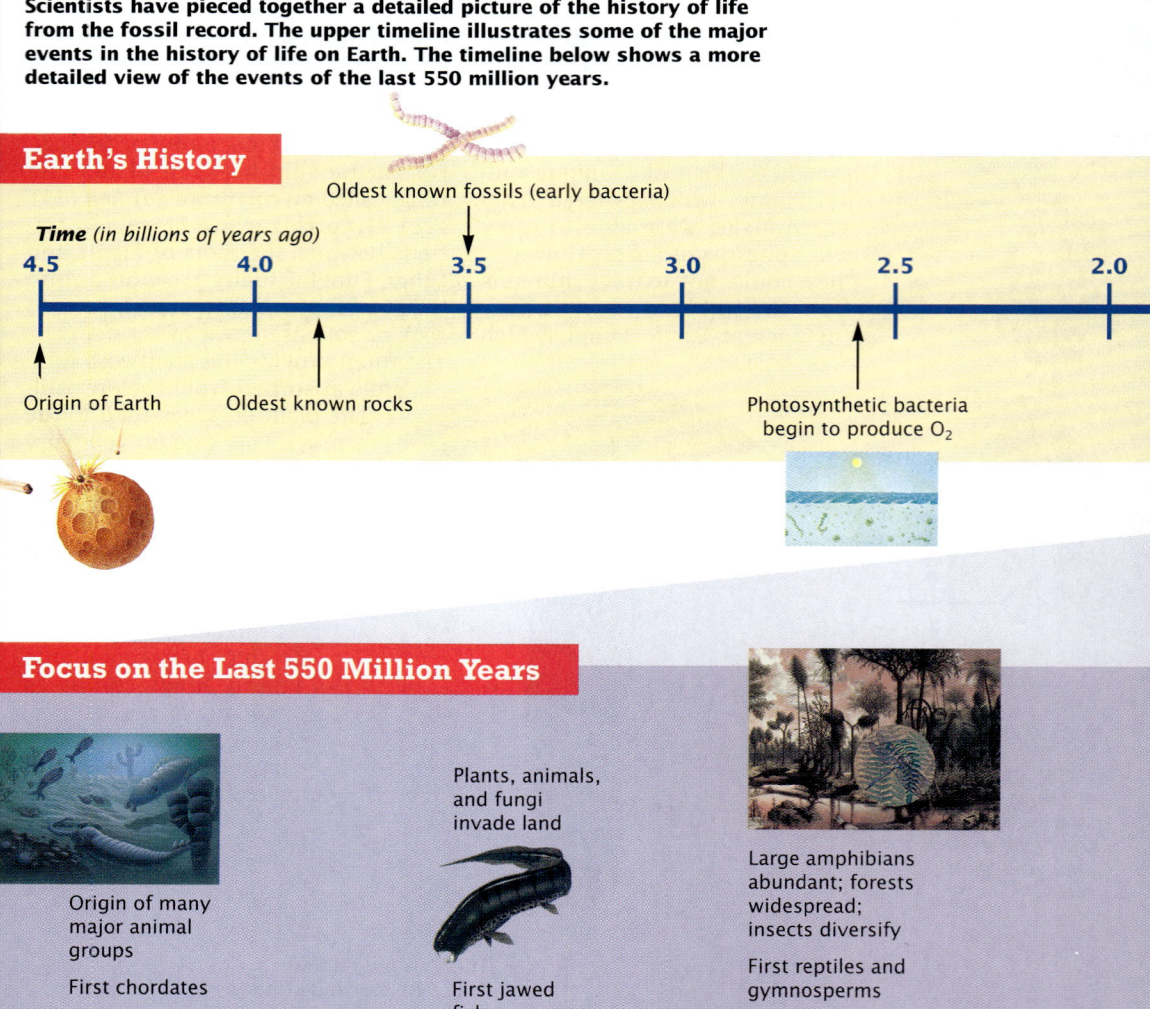

Earth's History

Oldest known fossils (early bacteria)

Time (in billions of years ago)

4.5   4.0   3.5   3.0   2.5   2.0

Origin of Earth   Oldest known rocks

Photosynthetic bacteria begin to produce O_2

Focus on the Last 550 Million Years

Plants, animals, and fungi invade land

Large amphibians abundant; forests widespread; insects diversify

First reptiles and gymnosperms

Origin of many major animal groups

First chordates

First jawed fishes

550   500   450   400   350   300   250

| Cambrian | Ordovician | ★ Silurian | Devonian ★ | Carboniferous | Permian | ★ |

Time (in millions of years ago)
★ = mass extinction

Earliest vertebrates (jawless fishes) and invertebrates diversify

Diversification of bony fishes

Origin of amphibians, insects, and ferns

Diversification of reptiles

Largest of all mass extinctions at end of period

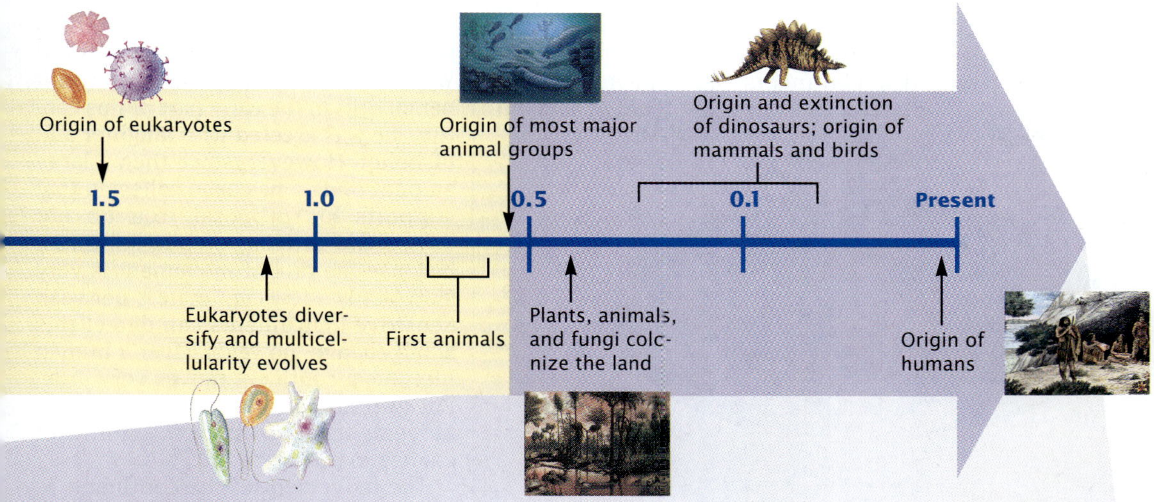

Origin of eukaryotes

1.5

Origin of most major
animal groups

1.0

0.5

Origin and extinction
of dinosaurs; origin of
mammals and birds

0.1   Present

Eukaryotes diver-
sify and multicel-
lularity evolves

First animals

Plants, animals,
and fungi colc-
nize the land

Origin of
humans

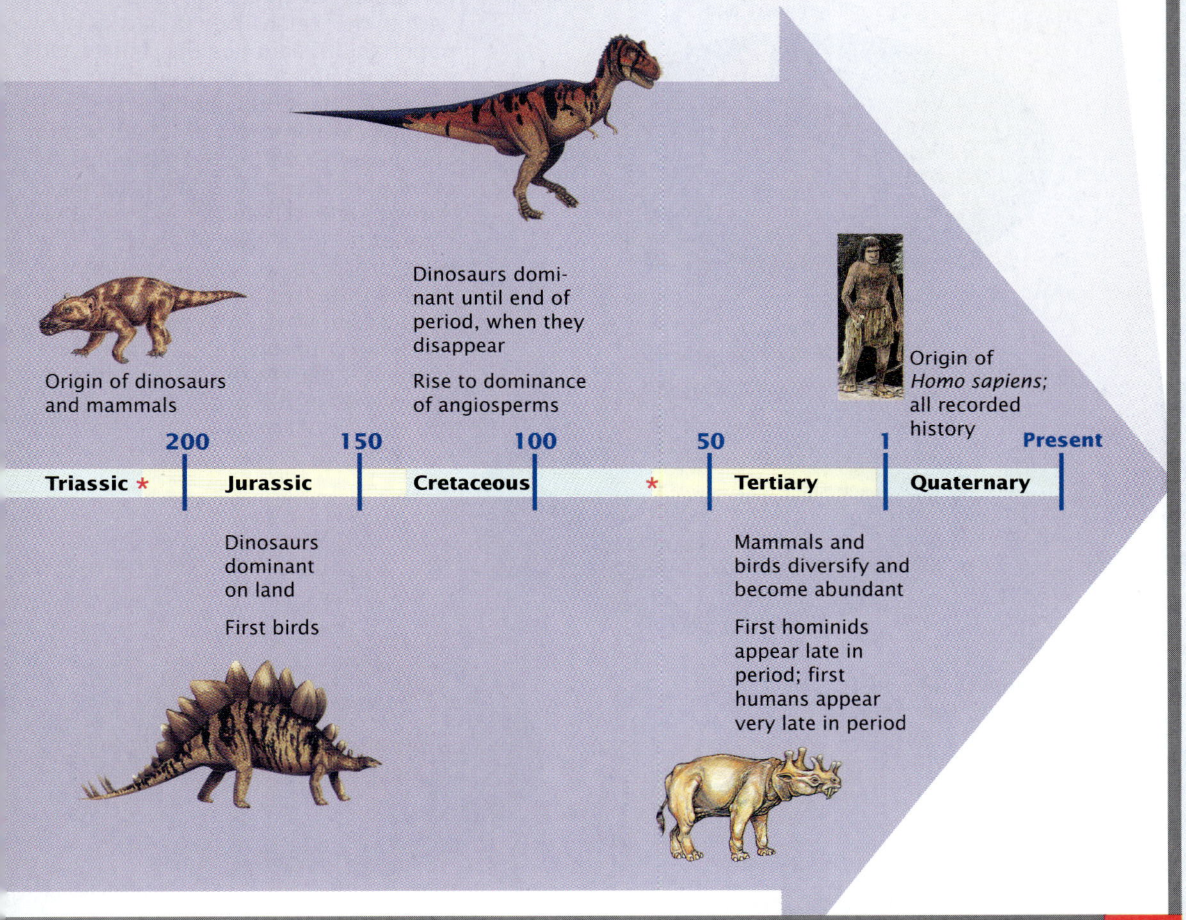

Origin of dinosaurs
and mammals

Dinosaurs domi-
nant until end of
period, when they
disappear

Rise to dominance
of angiosperms

Origin of
Homo sapiens;
all recorded
history

200   150   100   50   1   Present

| Triassic * | Jurassic | Cretaceous | * | Tertiary | Quaternary |

Dinosaurs
dominant
on land

First birds

Mammals and
birds diversify and
become abundant

First hominids
appear late in
period; first
humans appear
very late in period

World of Work

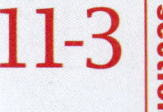

Paleontologist

Paleontology is the study
of fossil and ancient life-
forms. Have students
assume the role of a
paleontologist and select one
period in Earth's last 550 million
years. Tell them to use library and
on-line references to obtain information about the organisms that
lived during this period. In their
role as a paleontologist, students
should select one organism, explain
the adaptations that enabled the
organism to thrive, and explain the
factors that could have contributed
to its extinction.

201

Key to Strategies

● Understanding Concepts (Tier I)
■ Applying Information (Tier II)
▲ Critical Thinking (Tier III)

Continental Drift

■ Analyzing Data

Inform students that a team of American scientists in the early 1980s discovered a fossil of a marsupial in Antarctica, the first fossil of a land mammal ever found there. Today, marsupials are found in South America, North America, and Australia, but not in Antarctica. Ask students how the distribution of marsupials today compared with their distribution in the past supports the theory of continental drift. As a hint, tell students to refer to Figure 11-11. *(The finding of a marsupial fossil in Antarctica, and their absence today, supports the current theory that marsupials migrated from South America across Antarctica and into Australia when all the continents were connected as shown in the top illustration of Figure 11-11.)*

The Drifting Continents

When the first plants and animals colonized the land, the world was very different. One of the most significant differences is shown in **Figure 11-11**—the continents were not in the same positions as they are today. The continents have been slowly moving for at least the last 2 billion years, and they continue to move. This movement is called **continental drift**. When Alfred Wegener proposed the idea of continental drift in the early part of this century, he was greeted with laughter and disbelief. However, since then a large amount of data has been collected that supports his proposal. You do not notice the drifting of our continent because the rate of movement is very slow—only a few centimeters per year. Sensitive instruments can detect this small change, however. Over a human lifetime, a continent moves very little. But over millions of years, these small movements add up to a significant change in position.

The movement of the continents is driven by heat and pressure deep within the Earth, but it had a very important influence on the climate and on the inhabitants of the planet. For instance, about 300 million years ago, all the continents joined together into one massive continent. Following this event, the swamps that had been widespread were replaced by drier environments. Relatives of today's pine trees prospered in the dry conditions because they were able to deal with shortages of water. Water-loving plants that had thrived in swamps were unable to tolerate the dry conditions, however, and they disappeared.

385 million years ago

265 million years ago

175 million years ago

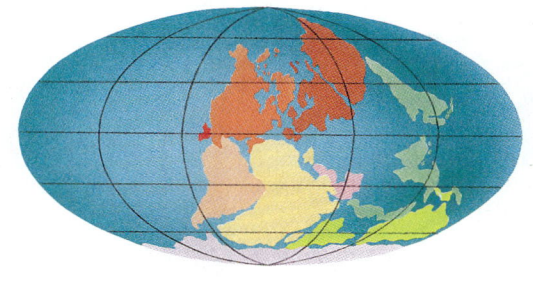

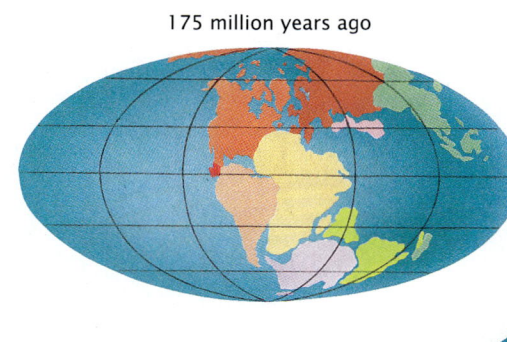

Present

Figure 11-11
The continents change position very slowly. Four stages in the movement of the continents are shown here.

Matter of Fact: Pangaea

The supercontinent that is believed to have existed some 200 million years ago is known as Pangaea. For decades, scientists rejected Wegener's hypothesis about the existence of Pangaea primarily because of the thick crust below the ocean floor. They reasoned that such a crust would make it impossible for continents to move. The discovery of tectonic plates, which slide around the surface of the Earth, made scientists take another look at Wegener's work.

Insects Were the First Flying Animals

Interdependence

Is the relationship between insects and flowering plants a case of mutualism? Why or why not?

From the initial arthropod invaders of the land, a unique kind of terrestrial arthropod soon evolved—insects. Insects, such as the dragonfly in **Figure 11-12**, would eventually become the largest and most diverse group of animals ever. Today there are more than 200 million individual insects alive at any one time for each person on Earth. In addition, more than half of the animal species discovered so far are insects. What is special about the insects? From fossils, we know that insects were the first animals to evolve wings.

Flying opened up the world's entire surface to insects, enabling individual insects to patrol the countryside in search of food, mates, or nesting sites. A flying insect can also transport objects long distances. Plants with flowers have benefited from this ability. With sweet nectars or other food, the flower of a plant attracts insects. When the insect lands on the flower, pollen containing the plant's male gametes is brushed onto the insect. After the insect has finished feeding, it flies off, carrying pollen that will pollinate other flowers of the same species that the insect visits. The relationship between insects and flowering plants has been an important factor in the evolution of both groups for well over 100 million years.

Figure 11-12
About 370 million years ago, forests might have looked like the one illustrated here. Some dragonflies that lived at this time, although similar in structure to modern dragonflies, had wingspans of more than 1 m (3 ft).

SECTION REVIEW

1. Why is ozone important for life on dry land?
2. Explain how plants and fungi were able to move onto land together.
3. What advantages does a flying insect have over a non-flying insect?
4. Describe the relationship between insects and flowering plants.

203

ANSWERS TO SECTION REVIEW

1. Ozone blocks much of the ultraviolet light from the sun, which would otherwise damage and destroy DNA, making life on land difficult or even impossible.
2. Their mutualistic relationship enabled plants and fungi to move onto land together. The plants provided fungi with food, while the fungi absorbed minerals from the rocks and soil for the plants to use.
3. A flying insect can seek out distant territories for food, potential mates, and shelter.
4. Insects are the pollinators for flowering plants, which in turn provide food for the insects.

Theme Answer
Interdependence
Yes. Mutualism is a symbiotic relationship in which all participating species benefit. Certain species of insects are attracted by certain species of flowering plants that offer sweet nectars or other nutrients. Insects that land on the plants are brushed with pollen (the male gametes). After feeding, the insects move on to other plants, carrying pollen to a stigma (female reproductive structure) on another plant.

Phase Three
Assessment Options

Closure
Forming a Hypothesis
Have students examine Figure 11-12. Ask them to suggest a hypothesis as to why modern-day dragonflies no longer have wingspans of more than 1 m. *(Students might suggest that such a wingspan was an adaptation when insects first colonized the land, but that such a large wingspan became detrimental once other organisms, including predators, made their appearance on land. In fact, a shorter wingspan would be an adaptation under such circumstances, making the dragonfly less visible to its predators.)*

SECTION REVIEW
Assign the *Section Review*.

Reteaching

Assign students to cooperative work groups of four. Have each group design a hypothetical animal that would be well adapted for making the transition from ocean to land. Have each group describe their organism and its adaptations to the rest of the class.

Key to Strategies
● **Understanding Concepts (Tier I)**
■ **Applying Information (Tier II)**
▲ **Critical Thinking (Tier III)**

History of Life on Earth 203

Scheduling

See the **Lesson Planning Guide** on pages 189A and 189B for lecture, classwork, and assignment options for Section 11-4.

Phase Two
Teaching Strategies

| Visual Strategy | Figure 11-13 |

● **Identifying Structures**

Have students locate the mouth on the lamprey shown in this figure. Point out that some species of lampreys are parasites. They obtain food by attaching to their prey and using their tongue to scrape a hole in their victim's flesh. Lampreys then suck the blood and other body fluids from their victims. The majority of lampreys, however, are detritus feeders.

| Visual Strategy | Videodisc |

● **Summarizing Information**

Use the *video—Evolution of Vertebrates* (5 min 45s) shown in Chapter 11 Section 11-4 of *Holt Biology Videodiscs Teacher's Correlation Guide to Holt Biology: Visualizing Life* to introduce students to the evolution of vertebrates. Have students identify the following adaptations: jaws; four-chambered heart; waterproof eggs; dry, waterproof skin; endothermic heat regulation; hollow bones; and courtship rituals. Have students relate each adaptation to at least one group of vertebrates. Then discuss how each adaptation helps vertebrates survive in different environments.

Think of a common animal. Was the animal you thought of a horse? an elephant? a guppy? a cat? The animal you thought of was probably a vertebrate. Vertebrates are the animals most familiar to us, not only because we are vertebrates but also because all land animals bigger than your fist are vertebrates.

11-4 Parade of Vertebrates

OBJECTIVES

❶ Identify the defining characteristic of vertebrates.

❷ List three adaptations that enabled amphibians to colonize land.

❸ Describe some of the reptilian features for life on land.

❹ Identify three differences between mammals and reptiles.

Animals With Backbones

Along with the organisms you saw in **Figure 11-7**, the Burgess Shale also contains fossils of a 5 cm (2 in.) worm-like animal that is the earliest known chordate. Members of this phylum have a flexible rod of cartilage known as a **notochord** that extends along the back. In most living chordates, the notochord exists for only a short time during early embryonic development and is then replaced by the vertebral column, or backbone. Chordates with a vertebral column are called **vertebrates**.

The first vertebrates lacked jaws

The earliest vertebrates, which appeared about 500 million years ago, were jawless fishes with bony skeletons. These small fishes appear to have fed in a head-down position, with their fins helping to keep them upright while they sucked up organic particles from the bottom. For about 100 million years, jawless fishes were the only vertebrates. Today, only two groups of jawless fishes remain. These are the eel-like, parasitic lampreys and the scavenging hagfishes. Two examples of jawless fishes are shown in **Figure 11-13**.

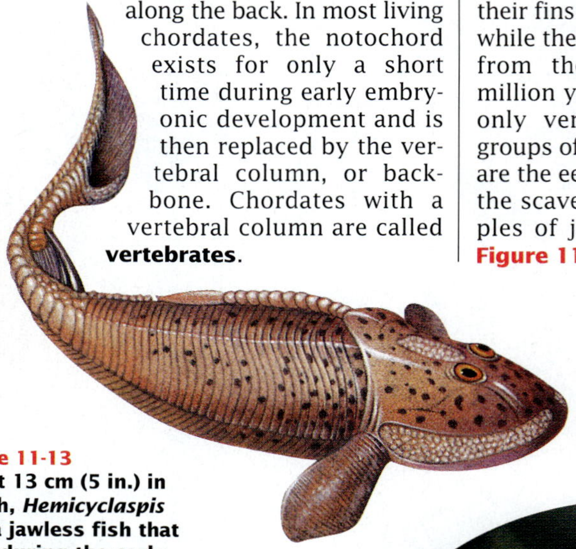

Figure 11-13
a About 13 cm (5 in.) in length, *Hemicyclaspis* was a jawless fish that lived during the early Devonian period, about 400 million years ago.

b This lamprey is a modern-day jawless fish. It attaches to other fishes with its suckerlike mouth and feeds on their flesh and blood.

204

Videodisc Resources

Holt Biology Videodiscs
Lesson 11-4: Parade of Vertebrates

Figure 11-14
Like modern sharks, the early shark _Cladoselache_ was a predator. It grew to 1.8 m (6 ft) in length and lived about 360 million years ago.

Jaws evolved about 400 million years ago

Scientists know that the first fishes with jaws evolved approximately 400 million years ago. These jawed fishes rapidly replaced the jawless fishes in the oceans. Jaws enabled fishes to bite instead of suck and thus become efficient predators. Early jawed fishes dominated the seas for 50 million years before being replaced by swifter swimmers, the sharks and bony fishes.

Shark skeletons are not made of bone

From the early jawed fishes evolved a group of very efficient predators, the sharks. Shark skeletons are made of cartilage rather than bone, making sharks lighter and more buoyant than the early jawed fishes. Sharks also have large, strong, mobile fins, which allow them to swim fast and to change their direction quickly in the water. The first sharks evolved about 400 million years ago. **Figure 11-14** illustrates one of the early sharks.

Bony fishes are versatile and abundant

Sharks have been largely replaced by more versatile fishes, the bony fishes. Today's bony fishes include trout, catfish, perch, bass, guppies, salmon, and most other familiar fishes. Almost one-half of all living vertebrate species are bony fishes. As their name indicates, bony fishes have a skeleton of bone instead of cartilage. This very successful and diverse group first appeared more than 400 million years ago. **Figure 11-15** shows one modern bony fish.

Although bony fishes are now abundant in both fresh water and salt water, they probably first appeared in fresh water. The early bony fishes were small and had gills to absorb oxygen from water and lungs to absorb oxygen from the air. In the ancestors of most modern bony fishes, lungs evolved into the swim bladder, a gas-filled sac used to regulate buoyancy. Amphibians and all other land-dwelling vertebrates are the descendants of some of the early air-breathing bony fishes.

Figure 11-15
Pink salmon are among the few bony fishes that can live in both salt water and fresh water.

Demonstration

● **Identifying Structures**

Show the class a balloon, and ask what part of the early bony fish it could represent. _(Students should recognize that it could represent the air sacs.)_ Point out that in most of these fishes, the air sacs evolved into the air or swim bladder that serves as a flotation device, enabling the fish to ascend and descend in the water. Demonstrate this buoyancy by inflating the balloon and raising it. Point out that as a fish fills its air sac with gases from its bloodstream, the fish rises in the water.

Visual Strategy   **Figure 11-15**

■ **Recognizing Relationships**

Ask students why salmon live in both fresh and salt water. As a hint, ask why salmon swim upstream. _(Salmon spend most of their lives in salt water but swim to fresh water to spawn.)_ Point out that some eels follow a similar migratory pattern. But eels may spend many years swimming from the Sargasso Sea, where they spawn, to the freshwater rivers and lakes of North America.

Key to Strategies
● **Understanding Concepts (Tier I)**
■ **Applying Information (Tier II)**
▲ **Critical Thinking (Tier III)**

Amphibians

Amphibians, though adapted to life on land, reproduce in moist environments

The first vertebrates on land were amphibians, which evolved from bony fishes about 350 million years ago.

Three crucial adaptations enabled amphibians to become successful on land. First, amphibians absorb oxygen from the air with lungs. Second, in amphibians, blood flows from the heart to the lungs, where it picks up oxygen. The blood then returns to the heart to be repumped throughout the body. In a fish, by contrast, the heart pumps blood to the gills to absorb oxygen, but the blood does not return to the heart for repumping. Thus, in an amphibian, oxygen-rich blood flows more rapidly to the muscles and organs than it does in a fish. Third, amphibians walk on four sturdy limbs, which evolved from the fins of their fish ancestors.

Although they live on land, amphibians constantly lose water through their moist skins, through which they also absorb oxygen. Hence they generally must remain in moist places. Most amphibians also must lay their eggs in water or in moist environments. Modern amphibians include toads, salamanders, and frogs, such as the tree frog in **Figure 11-16**.

Figure 11-16
The tropical red-eyed tree frog has suction pads on its toes, enabling it to cling to vertical surfaces.

Figure 11-17
Dimetrodon's sharp "steak-knife" teeth reveal that it was a predator. The large "sail" along the back may have helped regulate body temperature. Relatives of dimetrodon were the ancestors of mammals.

Reptiles reproduce out of water

Unlike amphibians, reptiles thrive in dry climates because their skin and their eggs are largely watertight. Examples of living reptiles include snakes, lizards, turtles, and crocodiles.

Reptiles evolved from amphibians about 300 million years ago. During the following 50 million years, these earliest reptiles gave rise to a variety of forms, such as *Dimetrodon*, shown in **Figure 11-17**. Reptiles gradually replaced the amphibians as the dominant land vertebrates. Reptiles enjoyed a special advantage over amphibians during this period, because dry conditions were widespread. About 240 million years ago, at the end of the Permian period, another mass extinction occurred. Scientists estimate that about 96 percent of all species became extinct.

Those reptiles lucky enough to survive found themselves in a world full of food that no one else was eating and space that was no longer occupied by others. A great burst of evolution occurred among the reptiles. The most famous and most impressive reptiles, the dinosaurs, arose about 220 million years ago, soon after the Permian mass extinction. You can read more about the dinosaurs in the *Tour of a Dinosaur* on page 207.

Dinosaur

Brachiosaurus is the largest dinosaur for which a complete skeleton has been assembled. Its fossils were first discovered in East Africa in 1907 and have also been found in western North America. Brachiosaurus lived during the Jurassic period, which lasted from 213 million to 144 million years ago.

The nostrils of *Brachiosaurus* were on top of its head.

Its simple teeth suggest that *Brachiosaurus* fed on plants.

A long, flexible neck was characteristic of sauropods. Each of the 15 neck vertebrae of *Brachiosaurus* was as long as 1 m (3 ft).

Habitat
Brachiosaurus lived on land and fed on the foliage of tall trees, like modern giraffes do.

Evolutionary Relationships
Dinosaurs are classified into two major groups based on the structure of the pelvis: the lizard-hipped dinosaurs (including *Brachiosaurus*) and the bird-hipped dinosaurs. Within the lizard-hipped dinosaurs, *Brachiosaurus* belongs to a group known as sauropods, which includes the largest land animals that have ever lived. Other sauropods are *Diplodocus* and *Apatosaurus*.

Brachiosaurus's tracks show a narrow stance, telling us that its legs were positioned beneath its body (unlike the legs of modern reptiles) and directly supported its immense weight. Since these tracks show no marks of a dragging tail, *Brachiosaurus* probably held its tail off the ground as it walked.

Size
From nose to tip of tail, *Brachiosaurus* was about 23 m (75 ft) long. It was about 12.5 m (41 ft) tall, as high as a four-story building. If you stood next to its skeleton in a museum, you would not even reach its knee. *Brachiosaurus* weighed about 73,000 kg (80 tons), about as much as 1,000 people.

207

Tour

Form and Function
● **Recognizing Patterns**
Have students describe the evidence that suggests *Brachiosaurus* ate plants. *(It had simple teeth.)* Show students a picture of a lizard, and ask them how its stance compares with that of a mammal such as a dog? *(The lizard's limbs jut out from the sides of the body, while the dog's are directly below the body.)* Ask students what evidence suggests that *Brachiosaurus's* limbs were positioned beneath its body, like a dog's? *(Fossilized tracks indicate a narrow stance.)*

Popular Portrayals of Dinosaurs
■ **Recognizing Relationships**
Ask students to cite examples of how the entertainment industry portrays dinosaurs. Then ask them to use what they have learned about dinosaurs to explain the inaccuracies of such portrayals. *(Students may describe portrayals of dinosaurs as huge, stupid, sluggish beasts or quixotic, sentimental, performing puppets.)* These perceptions are increasingly at odds with modern research. Emphasize that dinosaurs were not ill-adapted monstrosities doomed to extinction once the "superior" mammals came on the scene. For one thing, mammals and dinosaurs appeared almost simultaneously. But it was dinosaurs that diversified rapidly, while mammals remained small and mainly nocturnal until the extinction of the dinosaurs. For enrichment, have students investigate the perceptions of dinosaurs reflected in books such as *Digging Dinosaurs,* by John Horner and James Gorman.

Evolution

What effect did the extinction of the dinosaurs have on the evolution of mammals?

Mammals have hair and produce milk

Mammals appeared at about the same time as the dinosaurs. Mammals, such as the zebras shown in **Figure 11-18**, are animals with hair that produce milk to feed their young.

Another feature of mammals is the four-chambered heart. This type of heart is more efficient than the three-chambered heart found in most living reptiles. Mammals are also **endotherms**. Endotherms are able to regulate their body temperature through internal mechanisms. **Ectotherms**, on the other hand, cannot regulate their temperature internally and must absorb heat from their surroundings. Living reptiles and amphibians are ectotherms.

For more than 150 million years, mammals and dinosaurs coexisted. During this time, mammals were small and did not evolve into many species.

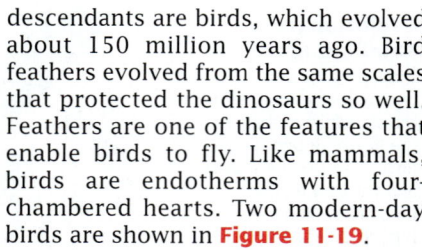

Figure 11-19

a Hummingbirds, such as this bee hummingbird, are among the smallest birds. Some are only 5 cm (2 in.) long.

b The ostrich is the largest bird, standing almost 1.8 m (6 ft) tall. Although the ostrich cannot fly, it has feathers like all other birds.

Figure 11-18
All mammals, including these zebras, produce milk to feed their young.

Birds are the descendants of dinosaurs

Although dinosaurs are extinct, descendants of small, insect-eating dinosaurs are still with us today. These descendants are birds, which evolved about 150 million years ago. Bird feathers evolved from the same scales that protected the dinosaurs so well. Feathers are one of the features that enable birds to fly. Like mammals, birds are endotherms with four-chambered hearts. Two modern-day birds are shown in **Figure 11-19**.

Birds, mammals, and dinosaurs coexisted until the mass extinction 65 million years ago, in which about two-thirds of land animals, including the dinosaurs, became extinct. The post-dinosaur world offered many opportunities for evolution. In response, mammals and birds diverged rapidly and filled the nearly empty world.

SECTION REVIEW

1 Explain why you are considered a vertebrate.

2 Describe three adaptations that enable amphibians to live on land.

3 Compare the reptilian adaptations for living on land with the adaptations of amphibians.

4 Describe two differences between mammals and reptiles.

11 Highlights

There are many stars
similar to the sun in our
galaxy. Could life exist
on another planet?

	Key Terms	Summary
11-1 Origin of Life  Lipids may have formed protective coatings around the earliest molecules.		• Life arose from nonliving matter present on the early Earth. • Miller and Urey showed that simple molecules could react to form some of life's building blocks. • RNA can catalyze chemical reactions. • RNA was the first self-replicating molecule. DNA evolved later.
11-2 Early Life in the Sea 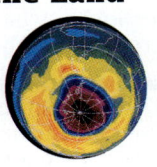 Archaebacteria are thought to be the direct ancestors of eukaryotes.	eubacteria (p. 195) archaebacteria (p. 195) cyanobacteria (p. 196) multicellularity (p. 196) phylum (p. 197) mass extinction (p. 197)	• The Earth is 4.5 billion years old. • The oldest fossils are 3.5-billion-year-old bacteria. Eukaryotes evolved from prokaryotes about 1.5 billion years ago. • Multicellular organisms arose about 630 million years ago. • There have been at least five mass extinctions that wiped out many of the Earth's inhabitants.
11-3 Invasions of the Land 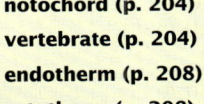 Ozone made it possible for life to move onto land. The thinning of the ozone layer is threatening all life.	ozone (p. 198) mycorrhizae (p. 199) mutualism (p. 199) continental drift (p. 202)	• By 400 million years ago, enough ozone had formed to make life on land possible. • Plants and fungi invaded the land about 400 million years ago. • Arthropods, including insects, followed plants and fungi onto land.
11-4 Parade of Vertebrates Birds are the descendants of the dinosaurs.	notochord (p. 204) vertebrate (p. 204) endotherm (p. 208) ectotherm (p. 208)	• Chordates have a rod of cartilage called the notochord that runs along the back. • In most vertebrates, the vertebral column replaces the notochord. • Vertebrates include sharks, bony fishes, amphibians, reptiles, birds, and mammals. • The first vertebrates were fishes without jaws. • The dinosaurs died out about 65 million years ago.

209

Alternative Assessment

Have each student prepare a blank bingo card with 25 squares, labeling the center one *FREE*. Write 24 terms, names, or short phrases from this chapter on the board. Have students place each term in one of the squares on their bingo card at random. Next have students cross out the appropriate box each time a definition is read or a clue is provided. Have students yell "bingo" whenever a horizontal or vertical line is completed.

Portfolio Assessment

Portfolio Assessment on page T39 provides options for building and evaluating student portfolios. Students and teachers can select items from the areas listed on page T39 for inclusion in a portfolio.

ANSWER TO CONCEPT MAP

The following is one possible answer to the Relating Concepts exercise on page 210.

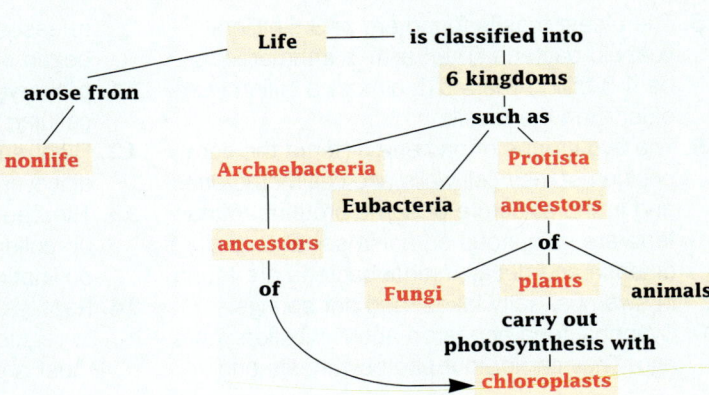

review

Understanding Vocabulary

1. a. eubacteria
   b. arthropods
   c. birds

2. a. The eubacteria is a group that contains most living bacteria. The archaebacteria is a group that differs biochemically from eubacteria and that probably gave rise to eukaryotes.
   b. Mutualism is a partnership between two organisms that both benefit from the relationship. Mycorrhizae is a unique mutualistic partnership between fungi and the roots of plants.
   c. A notochord is a flexible rod of cartilage found in chordates. Chordates with a bony vertebral column are vertebrates.

Understanding Concepts

3. Answer to concept map can be found on page 209.

4. The three explanations for the origin of life are (1) extraterrestrial origin, which states that life began on another planet and was carried to Earth by a meteorite or asteroid; (2) creationism, which states that life was created and put on Earth by divine forces; and (3) origin from nonliving matter, which states that life arose from inanimate matter that formed molecules that could reproduce. This final explanation falls within the realm of science because it can be tested.

5. They proposed that the Earth's early atmosphere lacked oxygen but was rich in nitrogen gas, water vapor, methane, hydrogen gas, and ammonia.

6. Cech and Altman discovered that RNA molecules can catalyze chemical reactions, which suggests that RNA was the first molecule to assemble and synthesize other molecules successfully.

7. When mixed with water, certain lipids will form a droplet that has a double-layered membrane similar to the lipid bilayer of a cell's membrane.

Understanding Vocabulary

1. For each set of terms, complete the analogy.
   a. ancestors of eukaryotes : archaebacteria :: ancestors of mitochondria and chloroplasts : _____
   b. first life on land : plants and fungi :: first animals on land : _____
   c. evolved from fishes : amphibians :: evolved from dinosaurs : _____

2. For each pair of terms, explain the differences in their meanings.
   a. eubacteria, archaebacteria
   b. mycorrhizae, mutualism
   c. notochord, vertebrate

Understanding Concepts

3. **Relating Concepts** Construct a concept map describing life's origin and earliest forms. Try to include the following terms in your map: non-life, Protista, Archaebacteria, plants, chloroplasts, Fungi, ancestors, and kingdoms.

4. **Summarizing Information** Describe the three explanations for the origin of life. Why is only one explanation considered within the realm of science?

5. **Recognizing Relationships** According to Oparin and Haldane, what was the atmosphere of the early Earth composed of?

6. **Interpreting Processes** What is the importance of Thomas Cech's and Sidney Altman's work to understanding the origins of life on Earth?

7. **Summarizing Information** What characteristic of lipids may have allowed the cell membrane to form?

8. **Summarizing Information** How old is the Earth? How old are the oldest known fossils? What type of organisms are represented by these fossils?

9. **Comparing Structures** Identify two differences between archaebacteria and eubacteria. Where could you find examples of eubacteria? of archaebacteria?

10. **Recognizing Relationships** When did cyanobacteria first appear? What important effect did they have on the environment of the early Earth?

11. **Organizing Information** Copy the unfinished table below onto a sheet of paper. Then fill in the blanks in each column.

	Prokaryotic or eukaryotic	Unicellular or multicellular
Archaebacteria		unicellular
Eubacteria	prokaryotic	
Protista		
Fungi		multicellular
Plantae		multicellular
Animalia	eukaryotic	

12. **Identifying Functions** Describe some of the benefits of flight for an insect.

13. **Recognizing Relationships** When a bee visits the flower of a plant, how does the bee benefit? What does the plant gain?

14. **Recognizing Relationships** Explain why reptiles are absent from extremely cold environments, such as northern Alaska, that are inhabited by mammals and birds.

15. **Analyzing Conclusions** What makes a vertebrate different from other animals?

16. **Organizing Information** Arrange the following animals in the correct order in which they first appeared on Earth: Include a key characteristic about each animal in your list.
   a. reptiles
   b. arthropods
   c. bony fishes
   d. jawless fishes
   e. insects
   f. mammals
   g. amphibians
   h. birds

17. **BUILDING ON WHAT YOU HAVE LEARNED** As you learned in Chapter 2, all living things make proteins from the same 20 kinds of amino acids. Explain how this fact supports the idea that all life shares a common ancestor.

8. The oldest fossils found are of 3.5-billion-year-old bacteria. The Earth is estimated to be 4.5 billion years old, almost a billion years older than the fossils.

9. The two groups of bacteria differ in the composition of their cell walls and cell membranes and in the structure of some proteins. Eubacteria are ubiquitous organisms that cause disease and decay; archaebacteria are found in swamps, salty lakes, and hot springs.

10. Cyanobacteria appeared about 3 billion years ago. They carried out photosynthesis and released oxygen gas into the oceans; it began bubbling out into the air.

11. prokaryotic; unicellular; eukaryotic, many unicellular; eukaryotic; eukaryotic; multicellular

12. Flight enables insects to travel to new sites, discover new sources of food, and find mates.

13. The bee gets nectar as food, and it picks up pollen and carries it to other flowers for pollination.

14. Reptiles are ectotherms. They are unable to regulate their temperature internally and must absorb heat from their surroundings.

Interpreting Graphics

18. The diagram below shows the apparatus used by Miller and Urey in their 1953 experiment.

  a. What is the purpose of discharging electricity into the flask labeled *c*?

  b. Why was it important for Miller and Urey to sterilize the apparatus to kill any bacteria in it?

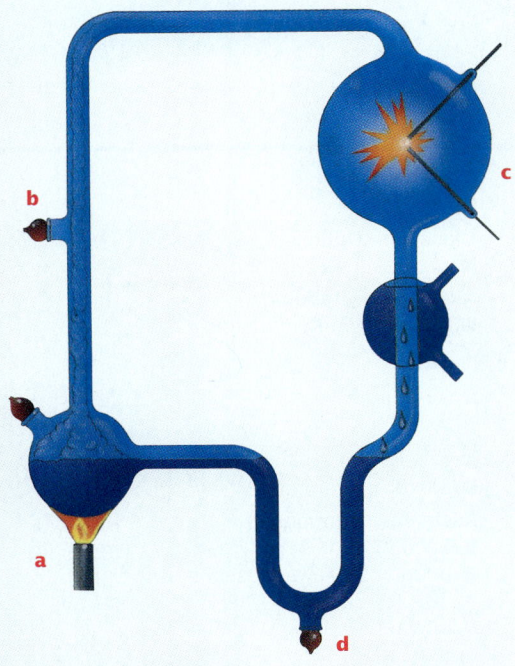

Reviewing Themes

19. *Evolution*
Why are amphibians sometimes called transitional land-dwellers?

20. *Interdependence*
What are mycorrhizae? What does each partner gain from this relationship? What role did mycorrhizae play in the colonization of land?

Thinking Critically

21. **Distinguishing Fact From Opinion** In an ongoing debate with environmentalists, a politician stated, "The thinning ozone layer does not affect life on Earth." Explain the error in the politician's statement.

22. **Finding Information** Scientists have determined the past positions of the continents, but how will the Earth look millions of years from now if the continents continue to move in the same direction and at the same rate? Use library references or search an on-line database to find information about the projected positions of the continents. Draw maps that show how the Earth is expected to look 5 million, 10 million, and 50 million years from now. Share what you have learned with your class.

23. **Using Technology** Radioactive dating is one technique for determining the age of a fossil or artifact. Some others are electron spin resonance and thermoluminescence. Use library resources or search an on-line database to find out more about these methods of dating fossils. Find out how each method is carried out. What are the advantages of each method? What are the limitations of each method? Prepare a report that summarizes what you have learned.

Activities and Projects

24. **Language Arts Connection** *Saurus* is the Greek word for lizard. Find out what the names of these dinosaurs mean: *Brontosaurus, Tyrannosaurus, Stegosaurus, Gorgosaurus*. How does each dinosaur's name reflect its habits and structure? Why do scientists no longer use the name *Brontosaurus*?

Discovering Through Reading

25. Read the article "The Origin of Life" by Anthony Mellersh in *Natural History*, June 1994 (vol. 103, no. 6), pages 10–13. What two characteristics of RNA suggest that it might have been the first living molecule?

26. Read the article "Nesting Dinosaur Discovered in Mongolia," in *Science News*, January 6, 1996, page 7. Why is the fossil discovered by Mark Norell and his colleagues significant? What does *Oviraptor*'s name mean? Why did its discoverers give it this name? How have recent discoveries changed scientists' view of *Oviraptor*?

Their skin must remain moist, and they must lay their eggs in water or moist places.

20. Mycorrhizae are close associations between the roots of plants and fungi. The fungi provide the plant with minerals, and the plant provides the fungi with food. Mycorrhizae provided a solution to the challenge of living on dry land.

Thinking Critically

21. The ozone layer absorbs ultraviolet radiation from the sun. Without it, the radiation would reach the Earth, where it would damage DNA in living organisms.

22. Answers will vary, but students' maps should accurately reflect predicted changes in the continents' positions on Earth.

23. Answers will vary, but students' reports should summarize the methods, advantages, and limitations of the two techniques.

Activities and Projects

24. *Brontosaurus* means "thunder lizard," which hints at its great size (30 tons). (*Brontosaurus* is now called *Apatosaurus* because this was the first name given to the genus.) *Tyrannosaurus* means "tyrant lizard," which is an appropriate description of the large, fierce predator. *Stegosaurus* means "roof or thatch lizard," which describes the plates on its back. *Gorgosaurus* is named for Gorgons, three hideous mythical monsters.

Discovering Through Reading

25. RNA can replicate itself, and it can also act as a catalyst.

26. The fossil is strong evidence that *Oviraptor* ("egg stealer") cared for its own eggs and that birds descended from dinosaurs such as *Oviraptor*.

Therefore, they cannot live in very cold climates.

15. A vertebrate is an animal with a vertebral column, or backbone.

16. The correct order is b, d, e, c, g, a, f, h. Characteristics will vary.

17. It is unlikely that all living things would use the same 20 amino acids if they had multiple origins.

Interpreting Graphics

18. a. The discharged electricity simulated lightning.

b. In order for the experiment to be successful, there could be no organisms in the apparatus that could be a source of organic molecules.

Reviewing Themes

19. Even though amphibians spend time on land, they are dependent on the water for survival.

12 | Human Evolution

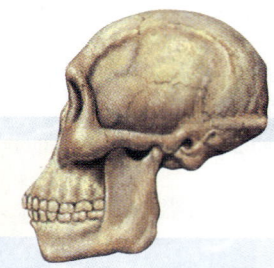

Lesson Planning Guide With Options for Block Scheduling

Lecture Concepts	Lesson Resources

12-1 Primates

BLOCK ❶ (45 minutes)

1. Primates are mammals that have opposable thumbs, binocular vision, and large brains.
2. Prosimians, the first primates to evolve, are small, furry, nocturnal animals that live in trees.

❶ **Lecture Resources**
- ■ Determining Prior Knowledge
- ■ Active Reading: Brainstorming
- ■ Visual Strategy: Videodisc
- ■ Demonstration: Comparing Abilities, p. 213
- 🔒 Teaching Transparencies: 53, 56
- ● Holt Biology Videodiscs Lesson 12-1

Classwork Options
- ■ Contrasting the Groups of Primates

Assignment Options
- ■ World of Work: Primatologist

BLOCK ❷ (45 minutes)

3. Anthropoids, which include monkeys, apes, and humans, are primates that evolved after prosimians and that possess large brains and color vision.
4. Humans and chimpanzees shared a common ancestry as recently as 5 million years ago.

❷ **Lecture Resources**
- ■ Visual Strategy: Figure 12-6
- ■ Demonstration: Comparing Abilities, p. 214
- 🔒 Teaching Transparencies: 54, 55
- ● Holt Biology Videodiscs Lesson 12-1

Classwork Options
- ■ Reteaching

- ■ *Small Group* Demonstration: Analyzing Data
- ■ Closure: Interpreting Viewpoints

Assignment Options
- ■ Section Review
- ■ Chapter Review, questions 1a, 2a, 4, 5, 6, 20, 21, 22
- ■ Directed Reading Worksheet

12-2 Evolutionary Origin of Humans

BLOCK ❸ (45 minutes)

1. Humans and their ancestors are known as hominids.
2. Hominid fossils are rare because there were few early hominids and their fossils are buried in rock formations.

❸ **Lecture Resources**
- ■ Genetic Similarity
- ■ Active Reading: Reading Organizer
- ■ Visual Strategy: Table 12-2
- ■ Demonstration: Interpreting Information
- 🔒 Teaching Transparencies: 62
- ● Holt Biology Videodiscs Lesson 12-2

Classwork Options
- 🧪 Laboratory Techniques and Experimental Design: Lab C19

BLOCK ❹ (45 minutes)

3. Compared with other primates, hominids displayed bipedal locomotion, had larger brains, and had smaller jaws and teeth.
4. The first hominids were the australopithecines, which appeared some 3.5 million years ago.

❹ **Lecture Resources**
- ■ Visual Strategy: Figures 12-8, 12-11
- ● Holt Biology Videodiscs Lesson 12-2

Classwork Options
- ■ Life/Work Skills: Being a Team Member
- ■ Reteaching
- ■ Closure: Summarizing Information

Assignment Options
- ■ Section Review
- ■ Chapter Review, questions 1b, 2b, 7, 9, 10, 14, 19, 23, 24
- ■ Directed Reading Worksheet

12-3 The First Humans

BLOCK ❺ (45 minutes)

1. Modern humans belong to the genus and species *Homo sapiens,* a descendant of *Homo erectus,* which evolved from *Homo habilis.*
2. *Homo habilis* had a large brain and used crude stone tools.
3. *Homo erectus* was the first hominid to use specialized tools, hunt, build shelters, and form social groups.

❺ **Lecture Resources**
- ■ Fossils
- ■ The Tools of Early Humans
- ■ Does Brain Size Equate to Intelligence?
- ■ Visual Strategy: Figure 12-13
- ● Holt Biology Videodiscs Lesson 12-3

Classwork Options
- ■ Life/Work Skills: Finding Information

Assignment Options
- ■ Problem Solving

Lecture Concepts

Lesson Resources

12-3 The First Humans, *continued*

BLOCK 6 (45 minutes)

4. *Homo sapiens* first appeared in Africa and then spread to the rest of the world.

5. Neanderthals were the first *Homo sapiens* to evolve in Europe, and they were replaced by humans migrating from Africa.

6 Lecture Resources
- The Caring Neanderthals
- Teaching Transparencies: 57
- Holt Biology Videodiscs Lesson 12-3

Classwork Options
- Reteaching
- Closure: Summarizing Information

Assignment Options
- Life/Work Skills: Finding Information
- Section Review
- Chapter Review, questions 1c, 2c, 3, 8, 11, 12, 13, 15, 16, 17, 18
- Directed Reading Worksheet

Chapter Review and Assessment

BLOCK 7 (45 minutes)
- Reteaching Worksheet
- Thinking Skills Worksheet
- Vocabulary Development Worksheet
- Language Development and Reading Comprehension Audio CD Program: Chapter 12

BLOCK 8 (45 minutes)
Assessment
- Alternative Assessment, p. 229
- Portfolio Assessment, p. T39

Chapter Test
- Chapter 12 Test

Test Generator
- Item bank for customizing Chapter Tests

Teaching Resources CD-ROM
- Scoring Rubrics and Classroom Management Checklist

The Portfolio icon denotes items throughout the Teacher's Edition lesson wrap that may be selected for inclusion in student portfolios.

Holt Biology Videodiscs and Concepts of Biology

Holt Biology Videodiscs gives you a powerful tool for teaching, review, and assessment. For further information regarding the media on the videodiscs, see **Holt Biology Videodiscs Teacher's Correlation Guide to Holt Biology: Visualizing Life.**

Concepts of Biology adds interactive lesson plans and extensive tools for customization using CD-ROM technology.

Use the following topic from **Concepts of Biology** to help you teach this chapter:
Topic 9: Evolution of Life on Earth

Laboratory Planning

Holt BioSources Laboratory Program
Block 3: Laboratory Techniques and Experimental Design Lab C19: Analyzing Amino Acid Sequences to Determine Evolutionary Relationships

12

Determining Prior Knowledge

- Ask students to describe the steps of natural selection and explain how it causes evolution.
- Have students explain how scientists use nucleotide sequences in DNA and amino acid sequences in proteins to infer evolutionary relationships.
- Write the following words on the board: gorilla, chimpanzee, orangutan, and human. Ask students to name similarities and differences between these organisms.

Active READING

Technique: Brainstorming

Before students begin this chapter, explain that the focus of the chapter is on primates and human evolution. Work with the class as a whole to create a list of characteristics that identify primates. Write the list on the chalkboard or the overhead. After you have created the list, have students check the list. Have students add to the list any additional characteristics they find in the chapter.

CD-ROM Resources

Concepts of Biology

Topic 9: Evolution of Life on Earth

REVIEW
- DNA structure (Section 8-1)
- use of DNA and proteins to study evolution (Section 10-2)
- radioactive dating (Section 10-2)
- natural selection (Section 10-3)

Human Evolution

Early humans drew these images deep in a French cave about 20,000 years ago.

212

Author's Rationale   Human evolution is the part of the evolution story that is of most interest to students. This chapter provides in-depth treatment of the major fossil finds, where they occurred, who found them, and how they were interpreted. Students will see firsthand how science works. Although the origin of humans is a highly controversial subject, it is the best-known part of the evolution story.

In 1871 Darwin published a second controversial book, *The Descent of Man*. In this book, he argued that humans were the product of evolution and were most closely related to the African apes—the gorilla and the chimpanzee. Although little fossil evidence existed in 1871 to support Darwin's case, numerous fossil discoveries made since Darwin's death, such as the skull shown at left, strongly support his hypothesis.

12-1 Primates

OBJECTIVES

1 List two distinctive features of primates.

2 Describe one adaptation of modern prosimians to nighttime activity.

3 Identify two differences between monkeys and prosimians.

4 Recognize the close evolutionary relationship between humans and apes.

Evolution of Primates

Look closely at your hand. You have five flexible fingers. Animals with five flexible fingers are called **primates**. Monkeys, apes, and humans are examples of primates. All primates are mammals, animals that have hair and nurse their offspring with milk. Primates most likely evolved from small, insect-eating, rodentlike mammals that lived about 60 million years ago.

Like nearly all of today's primates, the earliest primates dwelt in trees. Natural selection favored traits that enabled these early primates to capture insects while scampering through the trees. Unlike rodents, which have clawed feet, primates have grasping hands and feet. Primates can grip objects, hang from branches, and seize food. Some primates can even use tools. Compare your hand with the primate hands shown in **Figure 12-1**. The hand of a primate can grasp an object because it has an **opposable thumb**. An opposable thumb stands out at an angle from the other fingers and can be bent toward them to grip an object. All primates except for humans also have opposable big toes.

Phase Two
Teaching Strategies

Demonstration

● **Comparing Abilities**
Demonstrate the importance of the opposable thumb by having students try to pick up objects such as pencils, pieces of paper, and paper clips without using their thumbs. Also have them try to write their name, open a door, and undo a button. Then have students repeat these tasks using their thumbs, and have them describe how the thumb makes each task easier.

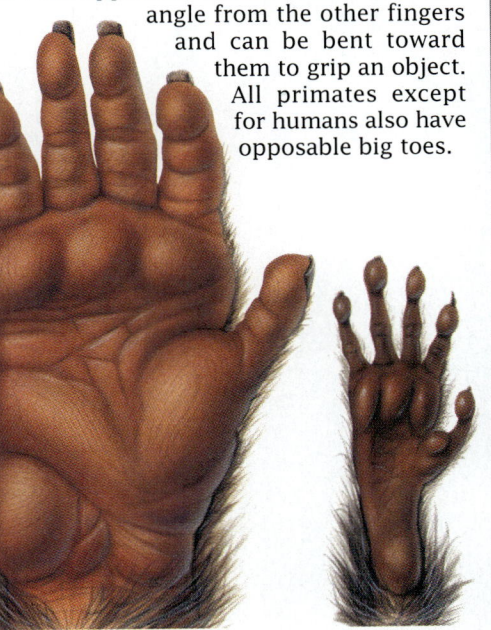

Figure 12-1
Primates have five flexible fingers on each hand.

a Chimpanzee hand   b Baboon hand   c Lemur hand

213

Videodisc Resources

Holt Biology Videodiscs

Lesson 12-1: Primates

Key to Strategies
Teaching Strategies are keyed to three tiers of learning.

● **Understanding Concepts (Tier I)**
Content mastery and comprehension

■ **Applying Information (Tier II)**
Applying and analyzing content

▲ **Critical Thinking (Tier III)**
Practicing evaluative thinking

Human Evolution   213

Demonstration

● Comparing Abilities

Have students work in pairs to test their binocular vision. They are to take turns holding two pencils, each at a different distance, in front of their partner. Tell them to hold the pencils so that their partner can clearly see both of them. With both eyes open, the other student should attempt to grab the pencil that is farther away, using just the thumb and forefinger. Repeat this process several times, changing the pencils' distance with each trial. Then have students test their ability to perform the same task with one eye closed. *(Students should have more difficulty grasping the pencils with one eye closed because they lack binocular vision.)*

Social Studies Connection

Last Refuges for Prosimians

Have students locate Madagascar on a world map. In addition to lorises and lemurs, modern prosimians also include tarsiers, which are found only in the Philippines, Indonesia, and Malaysia. Have students also locate these areas on the map.

Visual Strategy | Videodisc

● Observing Differences

Use *Video—Primates* (3 min 35 s) in Chapter 12 Section 12-1 of **Holt Biology Videodiscs Teacher's Correlation Guide to Holt Biology: Visualizing Life** to introduce students to some of today's primates. After students have viewed the video, have them write a brief description of each type of primate shown in the video.

Figure 12-2
The large eyes of this loris reveal that it is a nighttime hunter. Native to India, Sri Lanka, and Southeast Asia, lorises creep slowly through the trees, hunting insects and small animals. They grow to about 25 cm (10 in.) in length.

214

Another adaptation for living in trees is the position of the eyes in the skull. The eyes of rats and squirrels are in the sides of their heads. The fields of vision of their eyes do not overlap. The eyes of primates, in contrast, are located in the front of the head, like the eyes of the loris in **Figure 12-2**. Each eye of a primate sees a slightly different view of the same scene. The brain merges the two views in perceiving the distances to objects. This type of vision is called **binocular vision**. The ability to judge distance is advantageous when jumping from one branch to another or when stalking prey.

Other mammals, such as cats, have binocular vision, but only primates have both binocular vision and grasping hands. These features require an enlarged brain to process information from the eyes and to coordinate hand movements. Large brains and increased intelligence have become hallmarks of the primates.

Prosimians were the first primates

The first primates were **prosimians** (meaning "before monkeys"). Fossils 30 million to 40 million years old show that prosimians were common in North America, Europe, Asia, and Africa. Only a few species of prosimians, such as the loris shown in **Figure 12-2**, survive today. Many of these surviving species are nighttime hunters. You can tell by the disproportionately large size of their eyes. Large eyes are necessary to capture what little light is available at night or in dark forests. All 24 surviving species of lemurs, cat-sized prosimians with long tails for balancing, live on Madagascar, an island about 400 km (250 mi) off the east coast of Africa. Today the native vegetation of Madagascar is being rapidly destroyed by an expanding human population. As the lemurs' forest home disappears, many of these unique prosimians may become extinct in the wild.

Anthropoids Are Day-Active Primates

About 35 million to 40 million years ago, a revolutionary change occurred in how primates lived—they became active during daytime. How do we know this change occurred? Fossil skulls of primates that lived at this time have much smaller eye sockets than do earlier prosimian skulls, suggesting that they were active during the day. The new day-active primates were **anthropoids**. Monkeys, apes, and humans are the existing anthropoids.

Since daytime activity places different demands on the eye, many changes in eye design probably evolved at this time. One of these changes was the development of color vision. Of course, we can't actually examine 35-million-year-old anthropoid eyes to learn if they could see color. Soft tissues such as those of the eye are rarely preserved as fossils. Instead, we infer that early anthropoids had color vision because all living anthropoids see color. Therefore, color vision probably arose early in anthropoid history.

The brains of anthropoids are larger than prosimian brains. Larger brain size seems to be associated with the more complicated behavior patterns of anthropoids. Anthropoids replaced prosimians rather rapidly. In the fossil record, prosimian fossils become rare

Figure 12-4
This spider monkey, like many other New World monkeys, has a long tail that functions as a limb for grasping branches.

as anthropoid fossils become common. Scientists don't know exactly why prosimians declined while anthropoids became more abundant, but they suspect that the larger brains and color vision of anthropoids contributed to their success.

Monkeys have complex social interactions

Monkeys are anthropoids with tails. Two groups of monkeys occur today. Old World monkeys, such as the baboons in **Figure 12-3**, live in Asia and Africa. New World monkeys, such as the spider monkey in **Figure 12-4**, inhabit Central America and South America. Monkeys feed mainly on fruits and leaves rather than on insects. They live in groups in which complex social interactions occur. Monkeys tend to care for their young for a longer time than most other mammals, except for humans and apes. This long period of dependency seems to be necessary for the development of the large brains of monkeys, apes, and humans.

Figure 12-3
Monkeys, such as the adult baboon (below left), take care of their young for a longer time than do most other mammals.

215

Connection: *Chapter 11*

Continental Drift

The separation of the New World and Old World monkeys took place when the continents of South America and Africa drifted apart about 25 to 35 million years ago. The separation resulted in different selection pressures. Originally confined to living in trees, the Old World monkeys evolved in an environment that permitted them to move to the ground. On the other hand, New World monkeys remained arboreal.

Demonstration

■ **Analyzing Data**
Materials: watch with a second hand
Assign students to a cooperative group of four. Have each group select a name for their hypothetical organism. Draw a long sequence of DNA bases on the board, and inform students that this represents the genetic information of the common ancestor of all their organisms. Have each group copy the sequence on paper. Inform students that spontaneous mutations to DNA occur at a constant rate. Tell students that every 15 seconds, each group is to randomly change one base in their DNA sequence, but have the groups start their "molecular clocks" at different times. After 3 or 4 minutes, instruct all groups to stop their clocks. Have each group compare the DNA sequence of their organism with the DNA sequence of the common ancestor to examine their similarities and differences. Have students construct a diagram to show the evolutionary history of the common ancestor and their hypothetical organisms, based on a comparison of the DNA.

Key to Strategies
● **Understanding Concepts (Tier I)**
■ **Applying Information (Tier II)**
▲ **Critical Thinking (Tier III)**

World of Work

Primatologist

Students may be familiar with the behavioral studies of gorillas conducted by Dian Fossey in Rwanda, especially if they saw the movie *Gorillas in the Mist*. Two other famous primatologists are Jane Goodall, who observed chimpanzees in Tanzania, and Birute Galdikas, who studied orangutans in Borneo. Have students select one of these scientists and use library resources or an on-line database to research her life and career. Have students write a short biography of their subject that includes information about how she became interested in primates, her training, and how she began her career.

Contrasting the Groups of Primates

● **Comparing Functions**

Have students make a **Graphic Organizer** like the one shown at the bottom of this page. They should complete the chart by putting marks in the appropriate blanks. Answers are shown in the completed graphic organizer at the bottom of the page.

Apes

Unlike monkeys, apes lack tails. Apes also have larger brains than monkeys. The existing apes are the gibbons, the orangutans, the gorillas, the bonobos *(BAHN uh bohs)*, and the chimpanzees. With their large brains, apes are capable of learning a greater variety of behaviors than any mammal except human beings. Once common, apes are rare today. Their natural forest habitat has largely disappeared as the growing human population has cleared woodland to make way for farms. Modern apes are confined to relatively small areas in Africa and Asia. No apes have ever been native to North America or South America.

DNA sequences reveal our close kinship to chimpanzees

Modern apes are not our direct ancestors. Humans share a common ancestor with the living apes, but the apes from which humans descended are extinct. Nevertheless, much can be

learned about our own evolution by studying the modern apes, such as the chimpanzees in **Figure 12-5** below. For example, studies of DNA and protein sequences have revealed a great deal about the relationships among the living apes and about their relationship to humans. You learned in Chapter 10 how differences in nucleotide sequences in DNA and differences in amino acid sequences in proteins can be used to determine evolutionary relationships. If the average rates of change in these sequences are known, it is possible to calculate approximately when evolutionary divergences occurred. When DNA from apes and humans is compared, gibbon DNA shows the greatest number of differences in nucleotide sequence. Scientists think the species that gave rise to gibbons diverged from the common ancestor of humans and the other apes about 10 million years ago, as shown in **Figure 12-6**. The next ape to evolve, the ancestor of the orangutan, split off approximately 8 million years ago.

Humans shared a common ancestor with gorillas, chimpanzees, and bonobos until about 7 million years ago. At this time, the gorilla's ancestor diverged from the common ancestor of chimpanzees, bonobos, and humans. The ancestor of humans did not begin to diverge from the ancestor of chimpanzees and bonobos until about 5 million years ago. Because this divergence began so recently, the genes of humans and chimpanzees have not had time to accumulate many differences. Overall, the nucleotide sequences of human and chimpanzee genes differ by only about 1.6 percent. As a result, most of the proteins encoded by your genes are very similar or even identical to the corresponding proteins in a chimpanzee.

Figure 12-5
The physical structure, DNA sequences, and protein sequences of humans are more similar to those of bonobos and chimpanzees, such as this female and her offspring, than to those of any other living species.

216

Graphic Organizer

Use the following graphic organizer with the teaching strategy **Contrasting the Groups of Primates** on page 216.

Type of primate	Grasping hands	Binocular vision	Color vision	Tail	Upright walking	Uses tools
Prosimians	X	X		X		
Monkeys	X	X	X	X		
Apes	X	X	X			X
Humans	X	X	X		X	X

| Gibbons | Orangutan | Gorilla | Bonobo | Chimpanzee | Humans |

Millions of years ago

0
2
4
6
8
10

Figure 12-6
This evolutionary tree shows the close relationship between humans and apes. Going back in time, . . .

a . . . humans shared a common ancestor with chimpanzees and bonobos until about 5 million years ago.

b About 7 million years ago the gorilla's ancestor diverged from the ancestor of chimpanzees, bonobos, and humans.

c The ancestor of orangutans diverged about 8 million years ago. The ancestors of gibbons diverged from the other apes earlier, about 10 million years ago.

SECTION REVIEW

1 Describe two distinctive primate features.

2 How could you distinguish the skulls of day-active primates from those of night-active primates?

3 Contrast the characteristics of monkeys with those of prosimians.

4 Which apes are most distantly related to humans? Explain your answer.

217

ANSWERS TO SECTION REVIEW

1 Possible answers include a highly developed brain, opposable thumbs, grasping hands, and binocular vision.

2 The eye sockets of night-active primates are much larger than those of day-active primates.

3 Prosimians lack color vision and have smaller brains than do monkeys. Monkeys are day-active and prosimians are not.

4 Refer to Figure 12-6 on page 217.

Visual Strategy | **Figure 12-6**

● **Interpreting Graphics**
Use this figure to reinforce the fact that Darwin never stated that humans evolved from modern apes. Rather, modern apes and humans share a common ancestor. Ask students to identify the closest relative of the chimpanzee *(the bonobo).*

Phase Three
Assessment Options

Closure

▲ **Interpreting Viewpoints**
Read students the following passage from Darwin's *Descent of Man.* "Thus we have given to man a pedigree of prodigious length, but not, it may be said, of noble quality. The world . . . appears as if it had long been preparing for the advent of man: and this, in one sense is strictly true, for he owes his birth to a long line of progenitors. If any single link in this chain had never existed, man would not have been exactly what he is now." Ask students to interpret this passage. *(The evolution of humans can be traced through a long chain to the origin of the first living things. If any ancestors in this chain had not evolved, modern humans would not be the same.)*

SECTION REVIEW
Assign the *Section Review.*

Reteaching
Show students *Gallery—Primate Diversity* in Chapter 12 Section 12-1 of *Holt Biology Videodiscs Teacher's Correlation Guide to Holt Biology: Visualizing Life.* Have students identify the group (prosimians, monkeys, or apes) to which each primate belongs. Ask students to point out one difference between each group and humans.

Key to Strategies
● Understanding Concepts (Tier I)
■ Applying Information (Tier II)
▲ Critical Thinking (Tier III)

Human Evolution 217

Scheduling

See the **Lesson Planning Guide** on pages 211A and 211B for lecture, classwork, and assignment options for Section 12-2.

Genetic Similarity

▲ **Justifying Conclusions**

Human cytochrome *c* and chimpanzee cytochrome *c* are identical in all 104 amino acids. Human hemoglobin and chimpanzee hemoglobin differ in only 1 of 573 amino acids. Have students explain how these two facts can be reconciled with the observation that human and chimpanzee DNA differ in nucleotide sequence by about 1.6 percent. *(The difference of 1.6 percent is an average for the entire genome, so individual genes can differ by more or less than this value. Also, because one amino acid can be coded for by several codons, two genes can have different nucleotide sequences and still code for the same protein.)*

Connection: *Chapter 10*

Sickle Cell Anemia

Underscore how a 1.6 percent genetic difference can have a large impact by reminding students that a single-base substitution in DNA is the cause of sickle cell anemia, an often fatal disease. This is the result of altering only one of the many billions of nucleotide bases that make up the human genome.

Writing, sculpting, and dialing a telephone—these are just three of the many tasks you can do with your hands. Your hands are free to do these tasks because you walk on two legs instead of on four. Upright walking was one of the first adaptations to evolve among our ancestors after the human and chimpanzee lines diverged about 5 million years ago.

12-2
Evolutionary Origins of Humans

OBJECTIVES

❶ **Contrast the characteristics of chimpanzees with those of humans.**

❷ **List three reasons why hominid fossils are rare.**

❸ **Describe evidence that human ancestors walked upright before their brains enlarged.**

❹ **Compare and contrast australopithecines with modern humans.**

Searching for the Fossil Relatives of Humans

No one could mistake a human for a chimpanzee, despite their 98.4 percent genetic similarity. That 1.6 percent genetic difference—accumulated in the 5 million years since the lines that gave rise to humans and chimps began to separate—results in substantial differences in physical appearance. The chimp is covered with long hair, and its skull, teeth, limbs, and feet also differ from those of a human. Moreover, chimps walk on four legs, while humans walk on two. The earliest primates to walk upright diverged from the chimpanzee line about 5 million years ago. Very little is known about these ancient human ancestors. Scientists like the Leakey family, shown in **Figure 12-7**, dig into the fossil record to find out what these early relatives were like. Humans and their closest fossil relatives are known as **hominids** (*HAHM uh nihdz*).

Figure 12-7
For more than 60 years, members of the Leakey family have been searching for fossils in East Africa.

Videodisc Resources

Holt Biology Videodiscs
Lesson 12-2: Evolutionary Origins of Humans

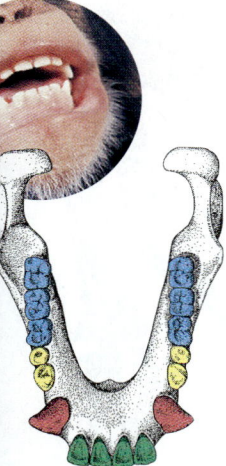

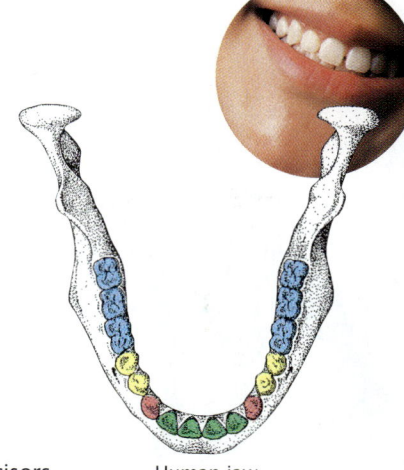

Table 12-1 Comparison of Chimpanzee and Human Jaws

Chimpanzee	Human
U-shaped tooth arrangement; molars in two parallel rows	Arc-shaped tooth arrangement; molars not parallel
Space between incisors and canines	No space between incisors and canines
Relatively long canines	Short canines

Chimpanzee jaw ● Molars ● Premolars ● Canines ● Incisors Human jaw

Hominid fossils are rare and hard to find

As you learned in Chapter 10, fossils do not form very often. Conditions have to be right, or a dead body will simply decay, leaving no evidence of what it looked like. Not surprisingly, scientists searching for hominid fossils face many difficulties. Until the development of agriculture about 10,000 years ago, hominids seem to have been rare. For example, early hominids left few footprints relative to other animals. Add to this difficulty the fact that only individuals that died on the shores of a lake or swamp or that fell into a mud pit would be covered by sediment, a necessary step in fossilization. Furthermore, fossils that formed 3 million to 5 million years ago are embedded within rock formations deep in the ground. These fossils can be found only if the rock formation is exposed by wind, water, or earth movements. Once exposed, however, fossils are quickly destroyed by erosion. Since most hominid fossils are only fragments, scientists must reassemble them like pieces of a jigsaw puzzle.

How can the age of a fossil be determined? Only fossils less than about 40,000 years old can be dated directly with radioactive dating. And we cannot usually date the rock in which the fossil is found, because fossil-bearing rock is composed of little bits of rock broken off from other rocks. Therefore, radioactive dating would yield the age of the original rock that broke into bits, not the rock that formed much later around the fossil. So how do scientists find the age of a fossil? First, they know that volcanic rock can be dated with great accuracy. If a nearby volcano erupted within a few thousand years of the time when the fossil was deposited, scientists can date the rock that formed as a result of the eruption. A fossil embedded nearby can be said to have a similar age.

How are hominid fossils recognized?

Despite the difficulties, scientists have discovered many hominid fossils. Once a fossil is discovered, how can a scientist tell if it is from a hominid or some other kind of animal? After all, fossils don't come with name tags. Identification is possible because different kinds of animals exhibit different details of structure. For instance, hominid jaws and teeth are quite different from those of chimpanzees, as shown in **Table 12-1**. Other structural differences are apparent in the skull, spine, pelvis, and other bones, as you will soon see. Only by painstaking comparisons can scientists distinguish hominid fossils from those of apes or other animals.

219

Community Connection: The Human Jaw

Ask a local dentist to speak to the class about the human jaw, focusing on how the four kinds of teeth are adapted for different functions. Have the dentist compare the human jaw with that of other organisms, especially animals with which students are familiar, such as dogs and cats. Also ask the dentist to discuss some common dental problems in modern humans. Have students speculate on how early hominids might have dealt with these problems.

Demonstration

● **Interpreting Information**
Materials: a jigsaw puzzle
To show students the difficulties involved in interpreting fossil fragments, display only a small percentage of the pieces of a jigsaw puzzle and ask students to determine what the entire puzzle looks like. Show how the task becomes progressively easier as more and more puzzle pieces (fossil fragments) are added.

Connection: *Chapter 10*

Radioactive Dating

Review how radioactive dating is used to determine the age of a fossil. Point out that carbon-14 is useful for determining the age of very recent hominid fossils (less than about 50,000 years old) because of its relatively short half-life (5,730 years).

Active READING

Technique: Reading Organizer
Students need an organizational framework to help them remember the hominids discussed in the last two sections of this chapter. Have students make a chart with these column headings: Which Hominid? Who Discovered It? Where Was It Discovered? When Was It Discovered? For each species of hominid mentioned in the next two sections, have students answer as many of these questions as possible. Caution students that the text may not provide all the information needed to complete the chart. Students should indicate missing information on their charts. For more information about reading organizers, see Reading Strategies Worksheets in Holt BioSources Teaching Resources CD-ROM.

Key to Strategies
● **Understanding Concepts (Tier I)**
■ **Applying Information (Tier II)**
▲ **Critical Thinking (Tier III)**

● **Interpreting Graphics**

Review the characteristics that distinguish gorillas from australopithecines. Have students trace the gorilla's spine to see the C-shaped curve and trace the hominid's spine to see the S-shaped curve. Point out the location where the spinal cord enters the skull, emphasizing that its location in hominids allowed the head to be balanced on top of the spinal cord. In fossils, the location of this opening reveals whether the primate walked upright. Inform students that the first australopithecines were only about 1–1.5 m (3.5–5 ft) tall, even when standing upright, and weighed about 25 kg (55 lb).

Connection: *Chapter 3*

Surface Area and Volume
Review the differences between surface area and volume. Inform students that a modern human's brain is characterized not only by a larger volume but also by a much greater surface area. Show students an illustration of the human brain, and point out the folds of the cerebral cortex. These folds greatly increase the surface area of the human brain without affecting the volume that this portion of the brain occupies.

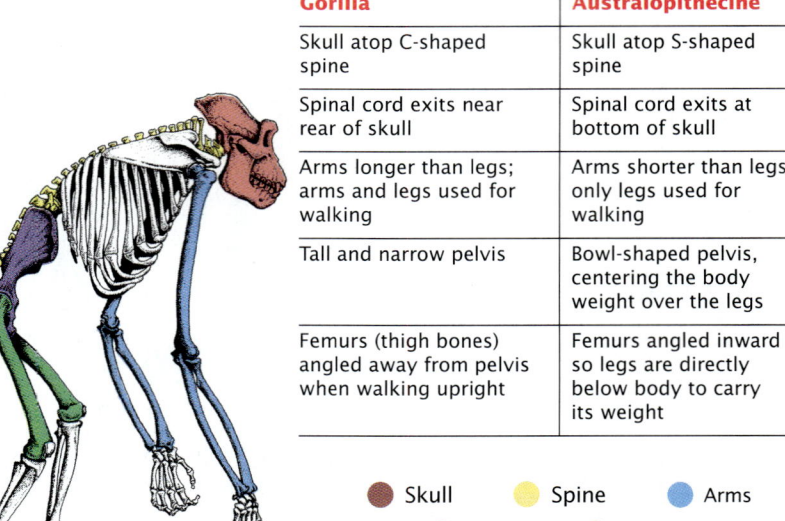

Gorilla

Table 12-2 Comparison of Gorilla and Australopithecine Skeletons

Gorilla	Australopithecine
Skull atop C-shaped spine	Skull atop S-shaped spine
Spinal cord exits near rear of skull	Spinal cord exits at bottom of skull
Arms longer than legs; arms and legs used for walking	Arms shorter than legs; only legs used for walking
Tall and narrow pelvis	Bowl-shaped pelvis, centering the body weight over the legs
Femurs (thigh bones) angled away from pelvis when walking upright	Femurs angled inward so legs are directly below body to carry its weight

● Skull   ● Spine   ● Arms
● Pelvis   ● Femurs

Australopithecine

Characteristics of the Earliest Hominids

If you were looking for early hominid fossils, where would you search? In 1871 Charles Darwin considered this question and decided that Africa was the most likely place to find these fossils. How did he reach this conclusion? Darwin reasoned that because the closest relatives of humans, the chimpanzees and gorillas, lived in Africa, humans probably evolved there too.

As Darwin predicted, fossils of the earliest hominids were uncovered in eastern and southern Africa. Ranging in age from more than 4 million years old to 1 million years old, these fossils represent species that evolved after the human line split off from the line leading to chimpanzees and bonobos.

At least six species of these early hominids have been discovered, all belonging to the genus *Australopithecus*. Members of this genus are called australopithecines *(aw stray loh PIHTH uh seenz)*. Even the earliest australopithecines show clear differences in structure from apes.

Australopithecines walked upright

Australopithecines were **bipedal**—that is, they walked upright on two legs. In fact, upright walking is a characteristic of all hominids. Although apes can walk upright for short distances, they do so with an awkward, waddling gait. How do we know that australopithecines that died millions of years ago walked upright? Comparisons of australopithecine skeletons with those of apes such as the gorilla have revealed how they walked, as shown in **Table 12-2**.

Most australopithecines also had larger brains than apes have. A chimp's brain occupies a volume of about 400 cm^3 (24 in.^{3}), about the size of an orange. Australopithecine brains were slightly larger, ranging from 400 to 550 cm^3 (24–34 in.^{3}). Though larger than an ape's brain, australopithecine brains were still much smaller than the brains of modern humans, which average 1,350 cm^3 (83 in.^{3}), about the size of a small melon.

220

Branches of the Hominid Evolutionary Tree

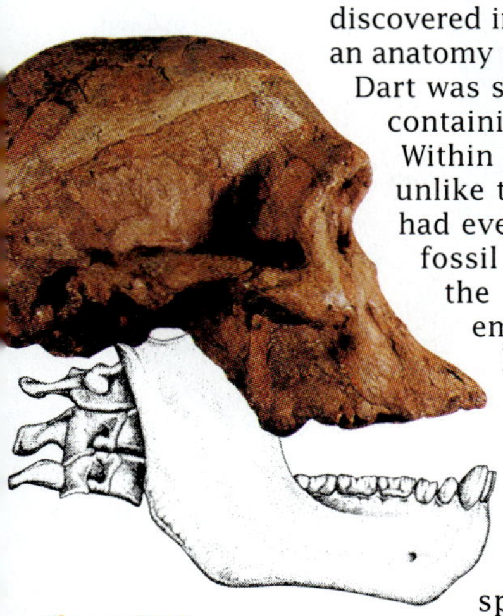

The first australopithecine fossil was discovered in 1924 by Raymond Dart, an anatomy professor in South Africa. Dart was sent a shipment of fossil-containing rock from a quarry. Within this rock was a skull unlike the skull of any ape Dart had ever seen. One detail of the fossil riveted Dart's attention: the rock in which it was embedded was from a geological formation thought to be at least a million years old. At that time, the oldest reported hominid fossils were only 500,000 years old.

Dart named the new species *Australopithecus africanus*, which means "southern ape from Africa." (This name is unfortunate, since we no longer think *Australopithecus* was an ape.) Dart argued that *A. africanus* was the direct ancestor of humans, the long-sought "missing link" between apes and humans. Most scientists at the time dismissed Dart's discovery as the skull of a young ape. Yet many *A. africanus* fossils have been discovered since 1924, and we now know that this species was a hominid, not an ape. **Figure 12-8** shows a skull of *A. africanus*. This species had jaws that are more rounded than those of an ape and teeth that resemble those of a human. The brain of *A. africanus* was larger than the brain of an ape, about 440 cm^3 (27 in.^{3}). *Australopithecus africanus* was bipedal and existed from 2.5 million to 3 million years ago. Whether *A. africanus* was a direct ancestor of humans is still a matter for debate.

Figure 12-8
The spinal cord of *A. africanus* exited from the bottom of its skull, indicating that this hominid walked upright. This species lived about 2.5 million to 3 million years ago. (The lower jaw and spine have been added by an illustrator.)

Figure 12-9
The footprints below show that bipedal hominids had evolved by about 3.5 million years ago.

Another important find was the footprints of a group of bipedal animals that walked across wet volcanic ash about 3.5 million years ago in what is now northern Tanzania. The footprints, shown in **Figure 12-9**, were preserved when the ash hardened. They reveal small but very humanlike feet, lacking the ape's opposable toe. Our ancestors or very close relatives were walking upright only 1.5 million years after diverging from the chimpanzee line.

Other australopithecines have been discovered

A stockier kind of australopithecine was unearthed in South Africa in 1938. Called *A. robustus*, this species had massive teeth and jaws. In 1959 Mary Leakey discovered the even more solidly built *A. boisei*, shown in **Figure 12-10**, in Tanzania. Nicknamed "nutcracker man" because of its massive jaws, *A. boisei* had a large, bony ridge running along the crest of its skull to anchor powerful jaw muscles. Excavations in 1985 turned up yet another australopithecine, a massively boned species resembling *A. boisei*.

Figure 12-10
Australopithecus boisei's skull had a massive jaw (illustrated below) and a bony ridge along its crest.

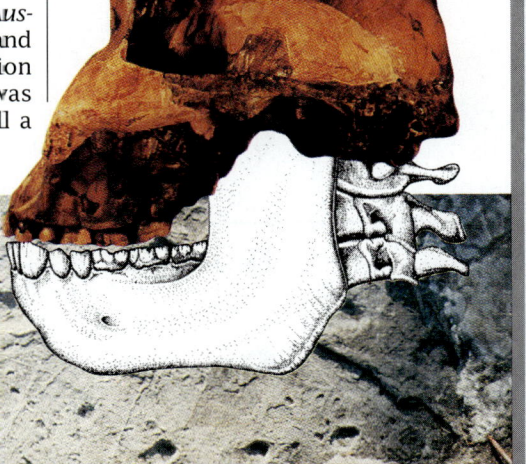

Visual Strategy Figure 12-8

● **Comparing Structures**
Have students compare the *A. africanus* jaw illustrated in this figure with the chimpanzee and human jaws shown in Table 12-1 on page 219. Ask students which two of these three species are more closely related, as evidenced by the structural similarities of their jaws. *(Even though the jaw of A. africanus is shown in profile, while those of the chimpanzee and human are shown in top view, students should be able to notice that both A. africanus and humans have short canines and have no space between their incisors and canines.)*

Language Arts Connection

Australis, one of the roots of the word *australopithecine,* means "southern." Point out to students that the same root is found in the word *Australia.* Have students locate Australia on a world map and explain why this name is apt.

Life/Work Skills
Being a Team Member

■ **Developing Methods**
Assign each student to one of four cooperative groups. Show students a model of a human skull, and assign them the task of determining the brain capacity of the skull. Each group should develop a method for measuring brain capacity, and then a student representative of each group should present the method to the rest of the class. Class members should critique the methods devised by the other groups.

Historical Perspective: The Piltdown Man Hoax

One reason that most scientists of Raymond Dart's day rejected his contention that *Australopithecus africanus* was in the human lineage was that another, very human-looking fossil had been unearthed about a decade before—the famous Piltdown man from southeastern England. The skull fragments of Piltdown man indicated a very large brain, but the jaw was very much like an ape's. In the 1950s, Piltdown man was revealed to be a hoax. The skull fragments were from a modern human skull that had been stained to simulate the effects of aging. The jaw came from an orangutan, and the teeth had been filed to make them appear less apelike. The hoaxer may finally have been conclusively identified. In the early 1990s, bone fragments stained in the same manner as the Piltdown fossils were found in a trunk belonging to Martin Hinton, a zoology curator at the British Museum at the time the Piltdown fossils were discovered.

Key to Strategies
● **Understanding Concepts (Tier I)**
■ **Applying Information (Tier II)**
▲ **Critical Thinking (Tier III)**

Theme Answer

Evolution

The assumption is made that australopithecines were still covered by hair, as are the modern apes, and that the largely hairless condition of modern humans had not yet evolved.

Visual Strategy Figure 12-11

● **Interpreting Graphics**

Use this figure to point out some of the difficulties in identifying and interpreting human fossils. Lucy's skeleton is the most complete of an early hominid, yet it is only 40 percent complete. Have students identify some of the parts of the skeleton that are missing *(the feet and hands, the lower left leg, the upper right leg, and much of the skull).*

Phase Three

Assessment Options

Closure

● **Summarizing Information**

Have students prepare a list of similarities between apes and australopithecines and between humans and australopithecines. *(Like apes, australopithecines had large jaws, protruding faces, and a relatively small brain. Like humans, australopithecines walked upright, had relatively short arms and relatively long legs, and had an S-shaped spine.)*

SECTION REVIEW

Assign the *Section Review.*

Reteaching

Prepare a table on the chalkboard. Across the top, write the following names: *A. afarensis, A. africanus, A. robustus,* and *A. boisei.* Down the left side, write *skull features, jaw features, brain size,* and *additional features.* Have students fill in the appropriate information.

Evolution

Reconstructions of Lucy usually show her as covered with hair, like an ape. What assumptions about evolution are made by showing Lucy in this way?

Figure 12-11
Because major portions of Lucy's limb bones and pelvis were preserved, scientists were able to determine that she walked upright.

Discovery of the oldest hominids

In 1974 Donald Johanson went to the Afar Desert of Ethiopia in search of early hominid fossils. There he found the most complete, best preserved skeleton of a prehuman hominid ever discovered. Nicknamed "Lucy," the skeleton was over 40 percent complete, as shown in **Figure 12-11**. Lucy was found to be nearly 3 million years old. Johanson assigned the skeleton the scientific name *Australopithecus afarensis.* Since the discovery of Lucy, many other fossils of *A. afarensis,* some over 3.5 million years old, have been unearthed in Ethiopia and Tanzania.

What do we know about Lucy's species? A reconstruction of how a living *A. afarensis* individual might have looked is shown in **Figure 12-12.** Lucy herself was small by modern standards, just over 1 m (3 ft 6 in.) tall. Other *A. afarensis* specimens range up to 1.5 m (5 ft) tall, with males much larger than females. The shape of Lucy's pelvis indicates that she was female, and the inward angle of her femur shows that she walked upright. Despite being bipedal, *A. afarensis* was quite apelike in many respects.

Figure 12-12
This reconstruction illustrates how Lucy might have looked 3 million years ago.

With a protruding face and fairly large jaws, an *A. afarensis* skull resembles a chimpanzee skull more than a human skull. In size, *A. afarensis* teeth are intermediate between most ape and human teeth. For instance, the canines of *A. afarensis* were shorter than those of apes, but still longer than human canines. Most important, the brain of *A. afarensis* was only about 400 cm^3 (24 in.^{3}), the size of a chimpanzee brain. Johanson's discovery demonstrated that hominids walked upright before they evolved brains larger than those of apes.

Australopithecus afarensis is no longer the oldest known hominid. In 1995, a team led by Meave Leakey and Alan Walker discovered fossils of a hominid species that lived about 4 million years ago. Though only fragmentary, these fossils indicate a species that walked upright but had an apelike jaw. Leakey and Walker have named their find *Australopithecus anamensis.*

SECTION REVIEW

1 Identify four structural differences that distinguish humans from apes.

2 Describe three difficulties you might face in trying to find hominid fossils.

3 Evaluate: "During human evolution, upright posture and large brain size evolved at the same time."

4 Describe three differences between *A. afarensis* and modern humans.

ANSWERS TO SECTION REVIEW

1 Refer to Table 12-2 on page 220.

2 Hominid fossils are rare, often fragmentary, and usually buried deep within rock formations.

3 This statement is false. As an example, *A. afarensis* walked upright but had an ape-sized brain.

4 *A. afarensis* was small in stature and had a protruding face, fairly large jaws, a relatively small brain, and medium-sized canines.

Because of your large, complex brain, you are able to read this book, whereas a chimpanzee is not. Your brain is about three times larger than a chimp's brain and more than twice the size of the largest australopithecine brain. Large brains are a characteristic of our genus, *Homo*, and are responsible for our complex culture.

Phase One
Preparation

Scheduling
See the **Lesson Planning Guide** on pages 211A and 211B for lecture, classwork, and assignment options for Section 12-3.

12-3 The First Humans

OBJECTIVES

1 List the two key characteristics of *Homo habilis*.

2 Contrast the skeletal features of *Homo habilis* with those of *Homo erectus*.

3 Summarize the evidence that *Homo sapiens* evolved in Africa.

4 Describe evidence that Neanderthals had a complex culture.

Evolution of the Genus *Homo*

Modern humans belong to the species *Homo sapiens*, the third and only surviving species of the genus *Homo*. All members of this genus are called humans. About 2 million years ago, the first member of our genus, *Homo habilis*, evolved from australopithecine ancestors. Between 1.8 million and 1.5 million years ago, *Homo habilis* was replaced by its larger-brained descend-ant, *Homo erectus*. In turn, *H. erectus* gave way to its even larger-brained descendant, *H. sapiens*.

There are many hypotheses describing which australopithecines gave rise to humans. **Figure 12-13** shows two hypotheses. Most researchers think that *Australopithecus afarensis* is the ancestor of all later hominids, including ourselves.

Phase Two
Teaching Strategies

| Visual Strategy | Figure 12-13 |

● **Interpreting Graphics**
According to either hypothesis illustrated in this figure, three hominid species coexisted at one time. Ask students to identify them. (*Australopithecus boisei* and *A. robustus* coexisted with *Homo habilis.*)

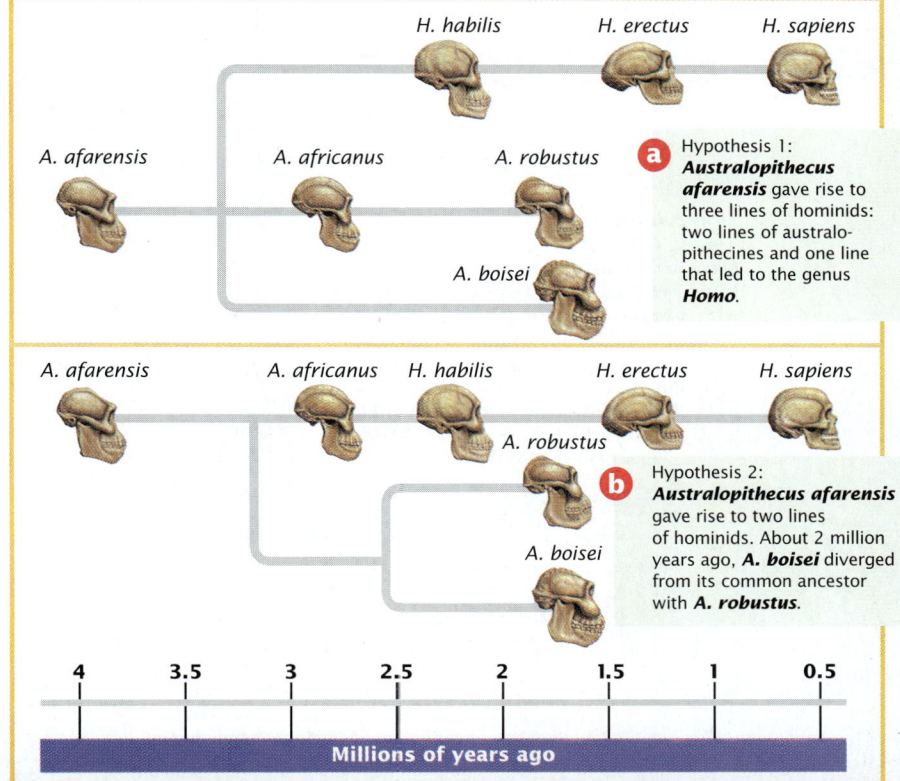

H. habilis   H. erectus   H. sapiens

A. afarensis   A. africanus   A. robustus

a Hypothesis 1: *Australopithecus afarensis* gave rise to three lines of hominids: two lines of australopithecines and one line that led to the genus *Homo*.

A. boisei

A. afarensis   A. africanus   H. habilis   H. erectus   H. sapiens

A. robustus

b Hypothesis 2: *Australopithecus afarensis* gave rise to two lines of hominids. About 2 million years ago, **A. boisei** diverged from its common ancestor with **A. robustus**.

A. boisei

4   3.5   3   2.5   2   1.5   1   0.5

Millions of years ago

Figure 12-13
These evolutionary trees show two hypotheses of how *Homo sapiens* evolved from australopithecines.

223

Videodisc Resources

Holt Biology Videodiscs
Lesson 12-3: The First Humans

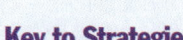

Key to Strategies
● Understanding Concepts (Tier I)
■ Applying Information (Tier II)
▲ Critical Thinking (Tier III)

Fossils

● Comparing Structures

Point out the difficulty in comparing fossil specimens to determine whether a new species has in fact been discovered. For example, the skull of *H. habilis,* shown in Figure 12-14a, was reconstructed from some 300 fossil fragments that Richard Leakey found. This skull, known by its museum catalog number of KNM-ER 1470, was the most convincing piece of evidence that Leakey uncovered to support the classification of *Homo habilis* in the genus *Homo* rather than in the genus *Australopithecus.*

The Tools of Early Humans

● Comparing Species

Inform students that the tools made by *Homo habilis* were crude by modern standards and included only a few types. In fact, to a layperson many of these tools would look like ordinary rocks. However, close examination of these tools reveals purposeful shaping of the rock. With *H. erectus,* the number of tool types increased to about a dozen, and many of the tools had characteristic shapes. For example, teardrop-shaped hand axes are often found at sites where *H. erectus* lived. Both species may have made tools or other artifacts out of materials such as wood, skins, or grass, but such objects are very unlikely to be preserved.

Does Brain Size Equate to Intelligence?

■ Analyzing Information

Inform students that an increase in brain size and complexity is a trend in human evolution. This expansion of the brain clearly made possible the tool-using and communication abilities of modern humans. However, caution students that there is no evidence that brain size is correlated to intelligence within our species. In other words, people with bigger brains are not necessarily more intelligent.

Our African Origins

Since the publication of Darwin's *Descent of Man* in 1871, scientists have spread over the globe in search of fossil remains that tell the story of the origin of humans. Scientists have unearthed fossils, tools, and other remains belonging to *Homo habilis* and *H. erectus* the ancestors of our species. Look at the map in **Figure 12-14** to see where many of these finds were discovered.

Homo habilis evolved in Africa

The earliest fossils of *H. habilis* have been discovered in East Africa. These fossils are about 2 million years old. *Homo habilis* is known for its large brain; the brain of one specimen is about 775 cm^3 (47 in.^{3}), nearly twice the size of Lucy's brain. *Homo habilis* fossils have been found alongside crude, stone tools. Most scientists think that *H. habilis* fashioned and used these tools for hunting and scraping. *Homo habilis* existed from about 2 million to 1.5 million years ago, when it was replaced by *H. erectus.*

Homo erectus migrated out of Africa

Homo erectus was a larger species than *H. habilis*—about 1.5 m (5 ft) tall. It also had a large brain (about 1,000 cm^3, or 61 in.^{3}) and walked erect.

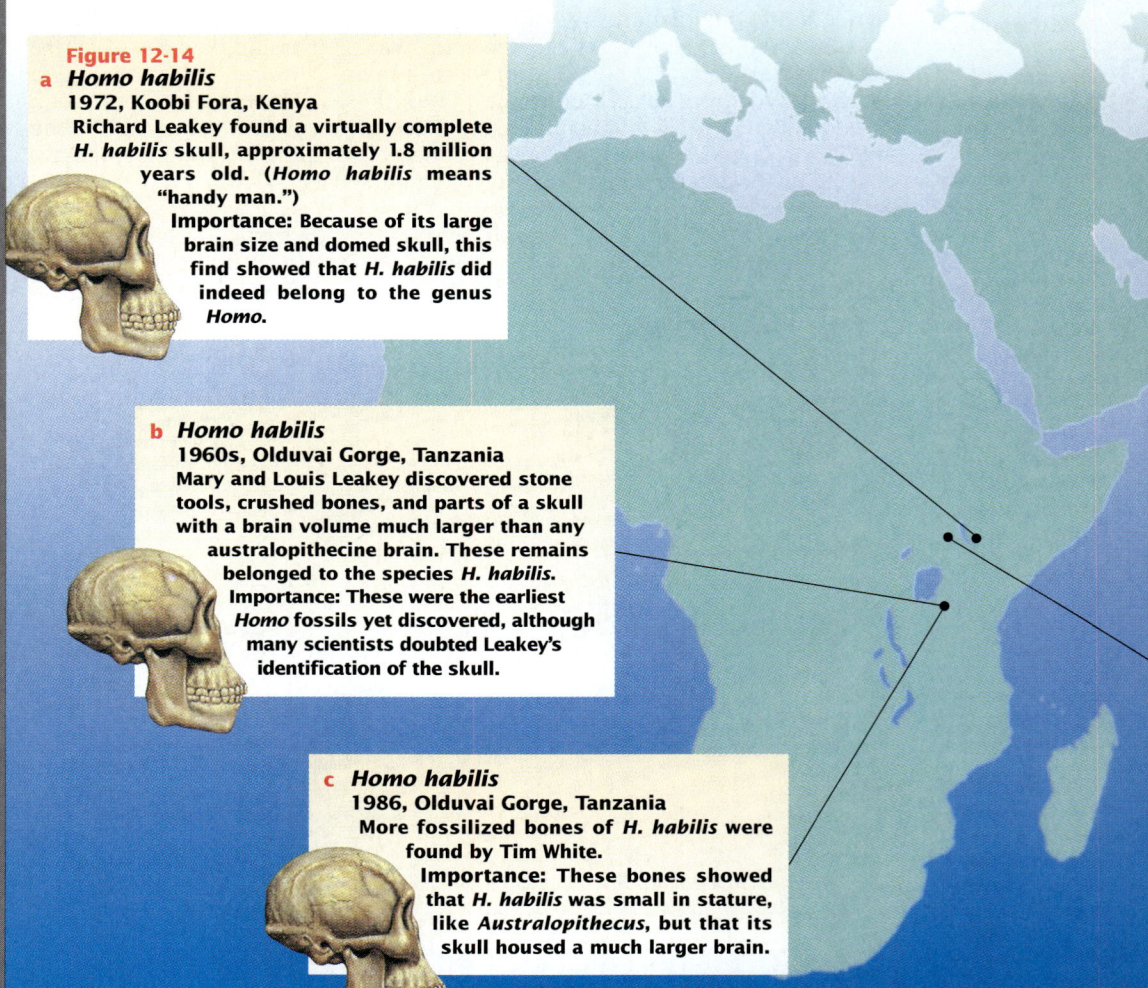

Figure 12-14

a Homo habilis
1972, Koobi Fora, Kenya
Richard Leakey found a virtually complete *H. habilis* skull, approximately 1.8 million years old. (**Homo habilis** means "handy man.")
Importance: Because of its large brain size and domed skull, this find showed that *H. habilis* did indeed belong to the genus *Homo.*

b Homo habilis
1960s, Olduvai Gorge, Tanzania
Mary and Louis Leakey discovered stone tools, crushed bones, and parts of a skull with a brain volume much larger than any australopithecine brain. These remains belonged to the species *H. habilis.*
Importance: These were the earliest *Homo* fossils yet discovered, although many scientists doubted Leakey's identification of the skull.

c Homo habilis
1986, Olduvai Gorge, Tanzania
More fossilized bones of *H. habilis* were found by Tim White.
Importance: These bones showed that *H. habilis* was small in stature, like *Australopithecus,* but that its skull housed a much larger brain.

Matter of Fact: Louis Leakey's Influence

Louis Leakey influenced many areas of anthropology. He and his second wife, Mary, made many significant discoveries of hominid fossils and tools, and Mary continued this work after Louis's death in 1972. Their son Richard also became a prominent paleontologist and was head of the Kenya Wildlife Service from 1989 to 1994. He now rarely takes part in fossil digs because he lost both legs in an airplane accident in 1993. Richard's wife, Meave, continues to search for fossils and recently discovered the oldest known hominid fossils. Louis Leakey also encouraged Jane Goodall, Dian Fossey, and Birute Galdikas to begin their pioneering studies of apes.

Where did *H. erectus* originate? Since its immediate ancestor, *H. habilis*, lived in Africa, it should come as no surprise that the earliest *H. erectus* skulls have been found in Africa. *Homo erectus* first evolved in Africa about 1.8 million years ago. Its appearance marked the beginning of an expansion of human populations across the globe. Far more successful than *H. habilis*, *H. erectus* quickly became widespread and abundant in Africa and had migrated into Asia and Europe by at least 1 million years ago.

Homo erectus probably lived in small groups of 20 to 50 individuals. We know how these early humans lived because scientists have found the remains of their living places. Some *Homo erectus* groups lived in caves, and there is some evidence that they also built crude wooden shelters. They successfully hunted large animals, butchered them using flint and bone tools, and cooked them over fires. *Homo erectus* living sites in China contain the remains of horses, bears, elephants, deer, and rhinoceroses. *Homo erectus* survived for more than 1 million years, longer than any other species of human. These very adaptable humans disappeared in Africa and Europe only about 300,000 years ago, while modern humans were evolving. Interestingly, *H. erectus* may have survived much longer in Asia, until about 250,000 years ago. *Homo erectus* was clearly our immediate ancestor. From the neck down, we are almost identical to this early human.

Social Studies Connection

The Social Life of *Homo erectus*

Fossil evidence suggests that *H. erectus* was the first species to use specialized tools, to hunt, to build shelters, to cook with fire, and to live in large groups. It is not known whether these early humans were capable of speech, but they must have had some means of communicating with one another. Their skills enabled them to migrate out of Africa to parts of Europe and Asia.

d **Homo erectus**
1927–1938, Peking (now Beijing), China
Scientists unearthed a *Homo erectus* skull that closely resembled Java Man's skull (found in 1890). It was nicknamed "Peking Man." Several other well-preserved skulls, together with lower jaws and other bones, crude stone tools, and the ashes of campfires, were also discovered.
Importance: These finds showed that both Java Man and Peking Man belonged to the same species, *H. erectus*.

e **Homo erectus**
1890, Java (now Indonesia)
Physician Eugene Dubois discovered the top of a skull that could house a brain much larger than any ape's brain. It belonged to *Homo erectus* and was nicknamed "Java Man."
Importance: Java Man's skull proved to be older than any other hominid fossils discovered up to that time.

f **Homo erectus**
1984, Lake Turkana, Kenya
Scientists discovered a nearly complete skeleton of *Homo erectus*, dated at about 1.5 million years old (1 million years older than the skulls found in Java and Peking).
Importance: The age of this fossil suggested that *H. erectus* first evolved in Africa.

225

Key to Strategies

● Understanding Concepts (Tier I)

■ Applying Information (Tier II)

▲ Critical Thinking (Tier III)

Connection: *Chapter 3*

Mitochondrial DNA

Ask students to explain why mitochondria contain DNA. (*Students should recall that eukaryotic cells contain mitochondria, which are believed to be descendants of ancient eubacteria. As eubacteria, these cells would have contained their own genetic information in the form of DNA.*) Also ask students why mitochondrial DNA is inherited only from the mother. (*Sperm contribute no mitochondria to the fertilized egg. All mitochondria in the egg therefore must come from the mother.*)

Life/Work Skills
Finding Information
● **Summarizing Facts**

There are two main hypotheses for the origin of modern *Homo sapiens*. According to advocates of the multiregional hypothesis, several geographically separate groups of *Homo erectus* evolved more or less simultaneously into *Homo sapiens*. According to the out-of-Africa hypothesis, modern *H. sapiens* appeared in Africa and spread to the rest of the world. Divide the class into two groups, and assign one hypothesis to each group. Students should use library resources or an on-line database to gather information about their hypothesis. Arrange a classroom debate in which both groups present the case for their hypothesis.

Problem Solving
■ **Analyzing Conclusions**

Have students use a pedigree to answer this question: From which great-grandparent did you inherit your mitochondrial DNA?

Figure 12-15
Scientists disagree about how and when different racial groups, some of which are represented by the people above, evolved.

The Origin of *Homo sapiens*

Scientists have long debated the issue of where *Homo sapiens* evolved. Some scientists argue that our species evolved simultaneously from different groups of *H. erectus* that lived in different areas of the Old World. According to these scientists, the differences among racial groups, such as among the young people in **Figure 12-15**, reflect the descent of each racial group from a different population of *H. erectus*. In contrast, other scientists contend that our species evolved in one place, in Africa, and then spread to the rest of the world. Therefore, the unique characteristics of each race represent adaptations to local conditions that arose after our species migrated out of Africa.

Recently, scientists studying DNA within human mitochondria have added fuel to the fire of this controversy. They examined the mitochondrial DNA sequences in people from all over the world. The human races evolved only recently, and there has not been enough time for many differences in their mitochondrial DNA sequences to accumulate. Since DNA accumulates mutations over time, the oldest DNA should show the largest number of mutations. It turns out that the greatest number of different mitochondrial DNA sequences occur among modern Africans. This result suggests that humans have been living in Africa longer than on any other continent and that *Homo sapiens* originated in Africa.

A clearer analysis is possible using DNA from the chromosomes in the nucleus. Some segments of nuclear DNA are far more variable than mitochondrial DNA. When a variable segment of DNA from human chromosome 12 was analyzed in 1996, a clear pattern emerged. A total of 24 different versions of this segment were found. Twenty-one of these versions were found in Africans; only three versions were found in Europeans, and only two were found in Asians and Native Americans. Although these new data strongly support the African origin of *Homo sapiens*, this conclusion is still quite controversial, and there is no firm consensus among researchers as to where our species originated.

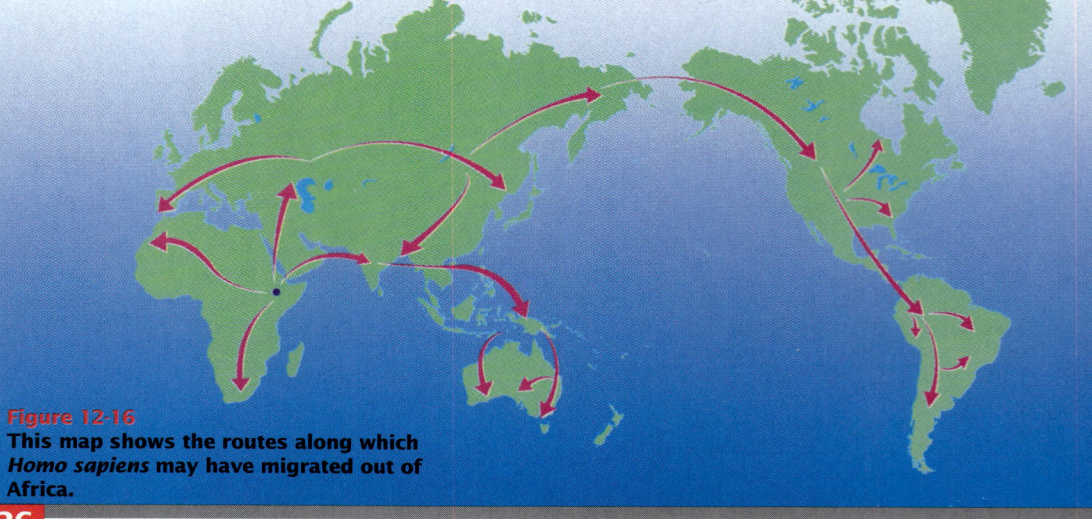

Figure 12-16
This map shows the routes along which *Homo sapiens* may have migrated out of Africa.

226

Historical Perspective: The Mitochondrial Eve Hypothesis

In 1987, a team of scientists led by Allan Wilson of the University of California at Berkeley presented what seemed to be powerful evidence for the out-of-Africa hypothesis. Wilson's group collected mitochondrial DNA from people around the world and used the samples to construct a phylogenetic tree of our species. They concluded that modern humans originated in Africa fairly recently (about 200,000 years ago) and that all humans alive today are descendants of one female, whimsically named Mitochondrial Eve, who lived in Africa about 200,000 years ago. These startling results caught the attention of the popular press and the general public. In 1992, the conclusions of the Berkeley group were shown to have been based on incorrect use of the computer program that created the phylogeny.

Figure 12-17
Fossil evidence shows that Neanderthals had a complex culture. They hunted, built shelters for their families, buried their dead, and made a variety of tools.

Neanderthals were the first *Homo sapiens* in Europe

Homo sapiens first appeared in Europe about 130,000 years ago. The first fossil of one of these individuals was found in 1856 in the Neander Valley of Germany. Hence, these early humans were called Neanderthals (*nee AN dur THALZ*; the word *thal* means "valley" in Old German). By 70,000 years ago, Neanderthals were common in Europe and in parts of the Middle East. They made diverse stone tools, including scrapers, spearheads, and hand axes. Neanderthals were more powerfully built, shorter, and stockier than humans today. Their skulls were massive, with protruding faces and bony brow ridges. Their brains were even larger than those of modern humans. They lived in huts, caves, or open-air sites, as shown in **Figure 12-17**. Neanderthals took care of their injured and sick and buried their dead, often placing food and weapons with the dead bodies. Such attention to the dead suggests that Neanderthals may have believed in a life after death. This is the first evidence of the kind of symbolic thought processes that are characteristic of modern humans.

Modern *Homo sapiens* evolved in Africa and replaced the Neanderthals

A new version of *Homo sapiens* essentially identical to modern humans appeared in Africa at least 100,000 years ago. By about 40,000 years ago, these modern humans had migrated out of Africa and had replaced the Neanderthals of southwest Asia. The modern humans then spread across Europe, coexisting and possibly interbreeding with Neanderthals.

By about 34,000 years ago, the Neanderthals had disappeared. The modern humans that replaced them had skulls identical to those of present-day humans. In fact, one of these early modern humans would look just like you or me (groomed and wearing modern clothes, of course).

These modern humans used tools made of bone, horn, and stone, some of which are shown in **Figure 12-18**. Their preserved camps and burial grounds show that they had complex

The Caring Neanderthals

● **Recognizing Relationships**

How do scientists know that Neanderthals cared for their sick and injured? Neanderthal skeletons have been found with healed broken bones. The fractures probably incapacitated the individuals, so they must have been cared for by others until their bones healed. Furthermore, an adult male skeleton was found with severe deformities that probably made the individual dependent on others for his entire life. Ask students to describe how an archaeologist of the future might determine how our civilization treats the sick and injured.

Life/Work Skills
Finding Information

▲ **Evaluating Viewpoints**

What happened to the Neanderthals is still a mystery. They may have interbred with modern humans or may have simply gone extinct. Have students use library resources or search an on-line database to find information about the fate of the Neanderthals. Students should write a report in which they present and evaluate the competing theories on this topic.

Multicultural Perspective: Genetic Differences Among Human Populations

The frequencies of many alleles differ among populations. One well-studied example is the A, B, and O blood group alleles. This chart shows the A-B-O frequencies for several populations.

Population	Frequency of A	Frequency of B	Frequency of O
Caucasians (United States)	0.258	0.070	0.673
Blacks (United States)	0.168	0.131	0.701
Asians (China)	0.181	0.158	0.662
American Indians (Peru)	0.073	0.158	0.662

Key to Strategies
● **Understanding Concepts (Tier I)**
■ **Applying Information (Tier II)**
▲ **Critical Thinking (Tier III)**

Mathematics Connection

Human Population Growth
Have students assume that the human population has grown steadily for the last 10,000 years. Have students calculate the average growth rate of the human population over the last 10,000 years, using a current population of 6 billion ((6,000,000,000–3,000,000)/10,000 = 599,700 people/year).

Phase Three
Assessment Options

Closure

● **Summarizing Information**
After students have read the chapter, pair each student with a partner. Without referring to the text, one student in each group should orally summarize the account of the origins of humans presented in Section 12-3. The other student should listen to the retelling without interruption (except to request clarification) and be prepared to point out any inaccuracies in the summary. The listener should also be prepared to add any ideas that were left out. Students should work together during this final clarification process and may refer to the text if needed.

SECTION REVIEW
Assign the *Section Review*.

Reteaching
Assume that a nearly complete fossil skeleton has just been found. Ask students what evidence they would need to justify the claim that the fossil was an early member of *Homo sapiens,* rather than a member of a different species. *(The fossil should include a skull with characteristics shared by modern humans: a large cranial capacity, relatively small teeth, and less-prominent brow ridges. Students may also suggest that tools and other artifacts would be useful in classifying the specimen as H. sapiens.)*

Figure 12-18
Modern *Homo sapiens* used these stone tools about 10,000 years ago.

Figure 12-19
The painting below was discovered in a cave in Lascaux, France, about 50 years ago. It was painted by *Homo sapiens* individuals 17,000 to 20,000 years ago.

social organization. And the shape of certain regions of the skull suggests that modern *H. sapiens* had full language capabilities.

At the time anatomically modern *H. sapiens* moved into Europe, the world was cooler than it is now. A huge sheet of ice extended from the Arctic into northern Europe; southern Europe was covered with grasslands inhabited by large herds of grazing animals. Modern *H. sapiens* painted pictures of these animals deep within caves throughout Europe, as shown in **Figure 12-19**. Modern *H. sapiens* eventually spread throughout Asia and Australia and entered North America, which they reached at least 13,000 years ago. At that time, a land bridge connected Siberia and Alaska, and it was possible to walk from Asia to North America. By 10,000 years ago, about 3 million people lived throughout the entire world.

Like all other living things, humans are the product of evolution. Our evolution has been marked by a progressive increase in brain size. As a result, humans are the only animal able to make complex tools, a capability that has enabled us to change the world around us. Although other animals are capable of conceptual thought, we humans have extended this ability until it has become the hallmark of our species. We use symbolic language and can use words to shape concepts out of experience. This ability has led to the accumulation of knowledge that can be transmitted from one generation to the next. Thus, we have what no other animal has ever had, cultural evolution. Through culture, we have found ways to mold our environment to our needs. We control our biological future in a way never before possible—an exciting potential, but one that carries weighty responsibility.

SECTION REVIEW

1. Identify two characteristics of *Homo habilis.*
2. Contrast two features of the skeletons of *Homo habilis* and *Homo erectus.*
3. How does mitochondrial DNA analysis support the hypothesis that *Homo sapiens* evolved in Africa?
4. Describe some of the cultural traits of Neanderthals.

ANSWERS TO SECTION REVIEW

1. *Homo habilis* had a large brain (approximately 775 cm³) and a dome-shaped skull. They were the first hominids to make stone tools.

2. *Homo erectus* had a larger brain and was taller than *Homo habilis.*

3. Scientists have analyzed the mitochondrial DNA from people on all continents. The oldest DNA should show the largest number of mutations or differences. Such differences are found among modern Africans, supporting the hypothesis that *Homo sapiens* first evolved in Africa.

4. Their cultural traits included the following: using stone tools; living in huts, caves, or open-air sites; caring for their sick and injured; and burying their dead.

"I don't know what it means, but I like the look of it."

	Key Terms	Summary
12-1 Primates  Many New World monkeys, such as this spider monkey, have long tails that can be used as an extra limb.	primate (p. 213) opposable thumb (p. 213) binocular vision (p. 214) prosimian (p. 214) anthropoid (p. 215)	• Prosimians, monkeys, apes, and humans are primates. They have opposable thumbs and binocular vision. • The first primates were prosimians. • Anthropoids evolved about 35 million to 40 million years ago. Apes, monkeys, and humans are anthropoids. • Humans are most closely related to chimpanzees and bonobos. The DNA nucleotide sequences of humans and chimpanzees differ by 1.6 percent.
12-2 Evolutionary Origins of Humans Because of its massive jaws, *Australopithecus boisei* was nicknamed "nutcracker man."	hominid (p. 218) bipedal (p. 220)	• Humans and their closest fossil relatives are known as hominids. • Fossils show that upright walking evolved soon after the evolutionary line leading to modern humans diverged from the line leading to chimpanzees. • *Australopithecus afarensis* walked upright but had an ape-sized brain.
12-3 The First Humans Neanderthals hunted, built shelters, cared for their sick, and buried their dead. 		• The genus *Homo* evolved about 2 million years ago in Africa. The first member of our genus was *Homo habilis*. • *Homo habilis* was later replaced by *Homo erectus*. *Homo erectus* migrated out of Africa to Europe and Asia. • Analysis of mitochondrial and nuclear DNA suggests that *Homo sapiens* evolved in Africa. • Modern *Homo sapiens* evolved in Africa at least 100,000 years ago and migrated to Europe about 40,000 years ago.

Alternative Assessment

Have students devise some method of demonstrating the differences in brain size among the various species of *Australopithecus* and *Homo*. Possibilities include building life-sized models in clay, filling large containers with water (with the volume of water representing the hominid's brain size), and stacking cubes on top of one another (with each cube representing the volume of the hominid's brain).

Portfolio Assessment

Portfolio Assessment on page T39 provides options for building and evaluating student portfolios. Students and teachers can select items from the areas listed on page T39 for inclusion in a portfolio.

229

ANSWER TO CONCEPT MAP

The following is one possible answer to the Relating Concepts exercise on page 230.

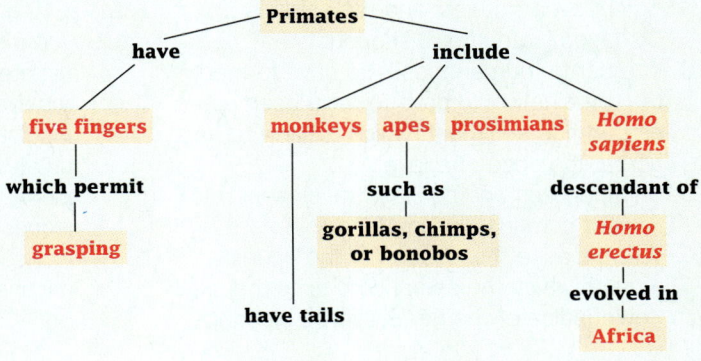

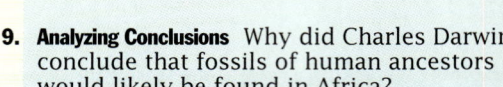

Understanding Vocabulary

1. a. All except the baboon are apes.
b. All except the lemur are anthropoids.
c. All describe *Homo erectus* except for "brain about 400 cm³ (29 in.³)."

2. a. Prosimians lack color vision and are more closely related to the early primates than any other group. All primates except the prosimians are anthropoids. All anthropoids have color vision.
b. Old World monkeys live in Asia and Africa, while New World monkeys live in Central America and South America.
c. *Homo habilis* was the first human and was the direct descendant of australopithecines. *Homo erectus* is the descendant of *H. habilis*, had a larger brain, used more complex tools, and moved out of Africa to Asia and Europe.

Understanding Concepts

3. Concept map answer is shown on page 229.

4. Primates have grasping hands and binocular vision. Binocular vision gives primates the ability to judge distance, which allows them to move from branch to branch and to hunt. Grasping hands are suited for gripping branches and seizing prey.

5. Nocturnal animals often have large eyes for receiving as much light as possible.

6. A completed chart is shown below.

	Prosimians	Monkeys
Opposable thumb	Yes	Yes
Binocular vision	Yes	Yes
Tail	Yes	Yes
Color vision	No	Yes

7. The chimp's spinal cord exits the skull near the back, not the bottom; the arms are longer than the legs; the pelvis doesn't center the body's

---

Understanding Vocabulary

1. Identify the word or phrase that does not fit the pattern, and explain why.
   a. baboon, chimpanzee, gorilla, gibbon
   b. anthropoid, *Homo sapiens*, gorilla, lemur
   c. migrated to Europe and Asia, walked erect, controlled fire, brain about 400 cm³ (29 in.³)

2. For each pair of terms, explain the differences in their meanings.
   a. prosimian, anthropoid
   b. Old World monkeys, New World monkeys
   c. *Homo habilis*, *Homo erectus*

Understanding Concepts

3. **Relating Concepts** Construct a concept map describing primates. Try to include the following terms in your concept map: monkeys, five fingers, prosimians, apes, grasping, *Homo erectus*, *Homo sapiens*, and Africa.

4. **Summarizing Information** Describe two characteristics that make primates unique. How are these characteristics advantageous for living in trees?

5. **Recognizing Relationships** The eyes of an ocelot are relatively large in relation to the size of its head. What might the large eyes of an ocelot suggest about this animal?

6. **Summarizing Information** Copy the following chart onto a sheet of paper. Then fill in the blanks in the chart.

	Prosimians	Monkeys
Opposable thumb		Yes
Binocular vision		
Tail	Yes	
Color vision	No	

7. **Comparing Structures** What features of a chimpanzee's skeleton indicate that chimps cannot walk upright like humans?

8. **Analyzing Methods** Lucy's skeleton was found on the shore of an ancient lake. Explain why this is a likely place to find fossils.

---

9. **Analyzing Conclusions** Why did Charles Darwin conclude that fossils of human ancestors would likely be found in Africa?

10. **Summarizing Information** Suppose that Donald Johanson had found only Lucy's skull. From just this evidence, could he conclude that she walked upright? Explain your answer.

11. **Comparing Structures** Match the hominid species in the first column with its description in the second column.
   a. *Australopithecus afarensis*
   b. *Australopithecus anamensis*
   c. *Homo habilis*
   d. *Homo erectus*
   e. *Homo sapiens*

   1. migrated to North America
   2. had a chimpanzee-sized brain
   3. first hominid to use fire
   4. oldest known hominid
   5. had a brain of about 775 cm³

12. **Comparing Hypotheses** What are the two hypotheses for the origin of *Homo sapiens*? How does evidence from DNA sequences support the "African origins" hypothesis?

13. **Sequencing Information** Put the following hominid species in correct evolutionary order: *Homo erectus, Australopithecus anamensis, Homo habilis, Australopithecus afarensis, Homo sapiens.*

14. **Analyzing Conclusions** Chimpanzees sometimes strip the leaves from a twig and use it as a tool to capture termites. How does the way a chimpanzee uses a tool compare to the way humans use tools?

15. **Summarizing Information** Where did the Neanderthals live? How do they differ from modern *Homo sapiens*? Describe what is known about the culture of the Neanderthals.

16. **BUILDING ON WHAT YOU HAVE LEARNED** Based on what you learned about fossils in Chapter 10, explain how scientists could have made mistakes in some of their conclusions about human evolution.

---

weight over the legs; and the spine is C-shaped instead of S-shaped.

8. In order for human fossils to have formed, the remains would have to have been covered in fine sediment, which is likely to happen at the edge of a lake.

9. Chimpanzees and gorillas, the closest relatives of humans, live in Africa.

10. Yes, because the location of the opening through which the spinal cord exits the skull would indicate whether Lucy was bipedal.

11. a. 2, b. 4, c. 5, d. 3, e. 1

12. *Homo sapiens* originated in Africa and migrated to the other continents, or *H. sapiens* evolved in several areas of the world from populations of *H. erectus*. Because DNA accumulates mutations over time, the oldest DNA should have the greatest number of different sequences. The greatest number of mitochondrial sequence versions are found among Africans.

Interpreting Graphics

17. Look at the evolutionary tree below.

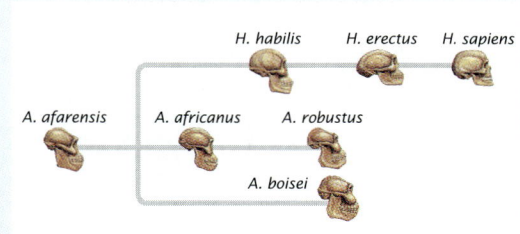

H. habilis   H. erectus   H. sapiens

A. afarensis   A. africanus   A. robustus

A. boisei

  a. Which species is the common ancestor of all the other species?
  b. Which species is the direct ancestor of *A. robustus*?
  c. Which species exists today?

Reviewing Themes

18. *Interdependence*
Describe two instances in which human actions are negatively affecting wild primates.

19. *Evolution*
The DNA nucleotide sequences of chimpanzees and humans differ by only 1.6 percent. The DNA sequences of gorillas differ from those of humans by about 2.3 percent. What do these differences reveal about the evolutionary relationship among these primates?

Thinking Critically

20. **Distinguishing Relevant Information** Here is a scientist's hypothesis about the evolution of upright walking in hominids. "About 5 million years ago, the climate was warming, causing forests to transform into grasslands. Some primates began to spend less time in trees and more time on the ground. Ground-dwelling primates that could stand upright could gather more food because their hands were free. The primates that remained in the trees had grasping hands. Over time, upright primates left more offspring than primates that walked on all fours." Which information is irrelevant to the evolution of upright walking? Justify your answer.

Life/Work Skills

21. **Using Technology** You and your classmates are in charge of specimens at a natural history museum. A university professor, who has returned from a successful dig revealing the bones of three new species of dinosaur, wishes to present your museum with two entire skeletons. This would be a valuable asset and would bring many people and more money to the museum. The professor, however, wants you to transport and clean the fossils. Investigate the techniques paleontologists use to transport and clean valuable specimens so that they can be studied, displayed, and preserved. Check the library for the information you need, and send a report to the museum director about your plans.

Activities and Projects

22. **Health Connection** The cause of 80 percent of human backaches cannot be diagnosed. Some scientists and doctors have suggested that back problems are the result of strain caused by upright posture. Use references available in a library or search an on-line database to gather information about health problems caused or aggravated by our upright posture. In addition to back pain, consider other common problems, such as bunions, fallen arches, and knee injuries. Prepare a poster summarizing what you have learned.

23. **Career Connection: Museum Technician** Museum technicians are professionals who work in museums and help to prepare, maintain, and install exhibits, including fossil exhibits of dinosaurs and other organisms. Find out what a museum technician does on a day-to-day basis and what kind of educational background is required. For information, write to the American Association of Museums, 1005 Thomas Jefferson Street NW, Washington, DC 20007.

Discovering Through Reading

24. Read the article "The Farthest Horizon: The Dawn of Humans" by Meave Leakey in *National Geographic*, September 1995, pages 38–51. What evidence from fragments of leg bones discovered at the Kanapoi site suggest that this hominid, *Australopithecus anamensis*, walked upright?

231

Reviewing Themes

18. Humans are destroying the native vegetation of Madagascar. Humans are also clearing the forests in which apes live.
19. The differences indicate that humans are more closely related to chimpanzees than to gorillas.

Thinking Critically

20. The irrelevant statement concerns the grasping hands of arboreal primates. All primates have grasping hands, so this characteristic cannot have differentiated bipedal primates from arboreal primates.

Life/Work Skills

21. To protect fragile fossils, exposed portions of the fossil are wrapped in layers of cloth soaked with wet plaster. After the plaster hardens, the fossils can be safely extracted from the rock and transported to the lab. The plaster is removed, and technicians use electric grinding tools and fine picks to remove any remaining rock. Fossils enclosed in limestone may be soaked in a weak acid solution to dissolve the limestone but not the fossil.

Activities and Projects

22. Answers will vary, but students should address the causes of these problems, the symptoms, and any possible treatments or cures.
23. Museum technicians prepare, install, and maintain exhibits and work closely with a curator. Many have bachelor's degrees or have completed specialized training programs.

Discovering Through Reading

24. The top part of the tibia is shaped like a hominid's tibia, not like an ape's. Also, the bottom part of the tibia has an enlarged flange that absorbs some of the stress of upright walking.

13. *Australopithecus anamensis, A. afarensis, Homo habilis, H. erectus, H. sapiens*
14. Chimpanzees can make simple tools for simple jobs, but they cannot make the diverse and complex tools that humans make.
15. Neanderthals lived in Europe and the Middle East. Neanderthals were shorter, stockier, and more powerfully built than modern humans. They had heavy skulls with massive brow ridges, and their brains were larger than those of modern humans.

16. Because fossils are often fragmentary, key features of fossils may be missing. The relationships of species known only from fossils may therefore be difficult to determine. Fossilization is unlikely, so some species may not be represented by fossils. Also, key fossils may not yet have been discovered.

Interpreting Graphics

17. a. *Australopithecus afarensis*
    b. *A. africanus*
    c. *Homo sapiens*

13 | Animal Behavior

Lesson Planning Guide With Options for Block Scheduling

Lecture Concepts	Lesson Resources

13-1 Evolution of Behavior

BLOCK ❶ (45 minutes)
1. A study of behavior includes asking both "how" and "why" questions.
2. Natural selection favors a behavior that benefits an individual member of a species.

❶ Lecture Resources
- ■ Determining Prior Knowledge
- ■ "How" and "Why" Questions in Biology
- ■ Active Reading: Brainstorming
- ■ Visual Strategy: Figure 13-2
- ⊘ Holt Biology Videodiscs Lesson 13-1

Classwork Options
- ⚗ Inquiry Skills Development: Lab B27

Assignment Options
- ⊙ Teaching Resources CD-ROM: Supplemental Reading Guides 8

BLOCK ❷ (45 minutes)
3. A specific behavior is the product of heredity and the environment.

❷ Lecture Resources
- ■ Alternative Hypotheses for Cub-Killing Behavior
- ■ Visual Strategies: Figure 13-3
- ⊘ Holt Biology Videodiscs Lesson 13-1

Classwork Options
- ■ Pavlov's Experiments
- ■ *Small Group* Learning in Pets
- ⚗ Quick Labs: Lab A24

BLOCK ❸ (45 minutes)
4. Learning is a behavior that is modified by experience.

❸ Lecture Resources
- ■ Instincts vs. Learning: A False Dichotomy
- ■ Imprinting
- ■ Visual Strategies: Figure 13-8
- ⊘ Holt Biology Videodiscs Lesson 13-1

Classwork Options
- ■ Closure: Summarizing Information

Assignment Options
- ■ Reteaching
- ■ Section Review
- ■ Chapter Review, questions 1a, 1b, 2, 4, 5, 6, 7, 8, 9, 17, 19, 21, 23
- ■ Directed Reading Worksheet

13-2 Kinds of Behavior

BLOCK ❹ (45 minutes)
1. Animals communicate in a variety of ways that include all five senses.
2. Humans communicate with the use of complex symbolic language.

❹ Lecture Resources
- ■ Active Reading: Reading Organizer
- ■ Visual Strategy: Table 13-1
- ■ Demonstration: Recognizing Relationships
- ⊘ Holt Biology Videodiscs Lesson 13-2

Classwork Options
- ⚗ Laboratory Techniques and Experimental Design: Lab C20

Assignment Options
- ■ Life/Work Skills: Communicating
- ⊙ Teaching Resources CD-ROM: Occupational Applications Worksheets 15

BLOCK ❺ (45 minutes)
3. Communication is important in the selection of a mate.

❺ Lecture Resources
- ■ Choosing a Mate
- ■ Visual Strategies: Figure 13-12
- ■ Visual Strategy: Videodisc
- ⊘ Holt Biology Videodiscs Lesson 13-2

Classwork Options
- ⚗ Laboratory Techniques and Experimental Design: Lab C21

BLOCK ❻ (45 minutes)
4. Kin selection is an example of altruism.

❻ Lecture Resources
- ■ Sexual Selection and Human Evolution
- ■ Honeybee Society
- ■ Visual Strategies: Figure 13-15
- ⊘ Holt Biology Videodiscs Lesson 13-2

Classwork Options
- ■ Understanding Social Behavior
- ■ Closure: Recognizing Relationships

Assignment Options
- ■ *Small Group* Reteaching
- ■ Section Review
- ■ Chapter Review, questions 1c, 3, 10, 11, 12, 13, 14, 15, 16, 18, 20, 22, 24
- ■ Directed Reading Worksheet

KEY

- ■ Annotated Teacher's Edition
- ■ Pupil's Edition
- ■ Directed Reading Worksheets
- ■ Vocabulary Development Worksheets
- ■ Thinking Skills Worksheets
- ■ Reteaching Worksheets
- ■ Chapter Tests
- ◉ Language Development and Reading Comprehension Audio CD Program

Holt BioSources
🧪 **Laboratory Program**
- A Quick Labs
- B Inquiry Skills Development
- C Laboratory Techniques and Experimental Design
- D Biotechnology
- E Interactive Explorations in Biology Laboratory Manual

- 📑 Teaching Transparencies
- ◉ Testing Resources CD-ROM
- ◉ Test Generator/Assessment Item

Holt Biology Technology
- ⬤ Holt Biology Videodiscs

Lecture Concepts   Lesson Resources

Chapter Review and Assessment

BLOCK ❼ (45 minutes)
Review
- ■ Reteaching Worksheet
- ■ Thinking Skills Worksheet
- ■ Vocabulary Development Worksheet
- ◉ Language Development and Reading Comprehension Audio CD Program: Chapter 13

BLOCK ❽ (45 minutes)
Assessment
- ■ Alternative Assessment, p. 247
- ■ Portfolio Assessment, p. T39

Chapter Test
- ■ Chapter 13 Test

Test Generator
- ◉ Item bank for customizing Chapter Tests

Teaching Resources CD-ROM
- ◉ Scoring Rubrics and Classroom Management Checklist

The Portfolio icon denotes items throughout the Teacher's Edition lesson wrap that may be selected for inclusion in student portfolios.

Holt Biology Videodiscs and *Concepts of Biology*

Holt Biology Videodiscs gives you a powerful tool for teaching, review, and assessment. For further information regarding the media on the videodiscs, see **Holt Biology Videodiscs Teacher's Correlation Guide to Holt Biology: Visualizing Life.**

Concepts of Biology adds interactive lesson plans and extensive tools for customization using CD-ROM technology.

Use the following topic from **Concepts of Biology** to help you teach this chapter:
Topic 18: Invertebrate Diversity

Laboratory Planning

Holt BioSources Laboratory Program

Block 1: Inquiry Skills Development Lab B27: Schooling Behavior in Fishes
Block 2: Quick Labs Lab A24: Observing Insect Behavior
Block 4: Laboratory Techniques and Experimental Design Lab C20: Observing Animal Behavior
Block 5: Laboratory Techniques and Experimental Design Lab C21: Observing Animal Behavior—Grant Application

Determining Prior Knowledge

- Ask students to draw on their experiences with pets or other domesticated animals to make a list of some examples of animal behaviors. Have students explain what they think the stimulus is for each behavior, and ask them to speculate about the function of each behavior.
- Ask students to explain the steps of natural selection, using the evolution of the peppered moth as an example.
- Have students describe what they know about learning and the inheritance of behavior.

Active READING

Technique: Brainstorming

Before students begin this chapter, read aloud the introduction at the top of page 233. Remind students that in Chapter 10 they learned about the relationship between natural selection and evolution. Have a student summarize natural selection for the class. Then ask students to think about how natural selection might affect behavior. Discuss why certain behaviors, such as those mentioned in the introduction, might exist and how natural selection might help maintain those behaviors. Have students read to confirm their ideas.

CD-ROM Resources

Concepts of Biology
Topic 18: Invertebrate Diversity

REVIEW
- testing hypotheses (Section 1-2)
- meiosis (Section 6-2)
- natural selection (Section 10-3)

Animal Behavior

13-1   Evolution of Behavior

13-2   Kinds of Behavior

Male bighorn sheep fight for control of groups of females by charging each other and butting heads.

232

Author's Rationale In this chapter we examine how genes and learning interact to shape behavior. We learn from the behavior of animals that behaviors can be inherited and can be acted on by natural selection. Behaviors, however, are not determined by genes alone. Learning also influences behavior in important ways. Looking at different kinds of behavior among animals reinforces the idea that behaviors evolved to better adapt particular animals to their way of life. The study of behavior is one of the areas of biology in which scientists often disagree. As an example, this chapter examines ideas on how cooperative behaviors might have evolved.

A squirrel buries a nut. A lizard spreads its collar of skin when threatened. A hungry baby cries. These are examples of animal behavior. Over the last few decades, scientists have greatly increased their understanding of animal behavior by considering it from an evolutionary perspective.

13-1 Evolution of Behavior

Phase One
Preparation

Scheduling

See the **Lesson Planning Guide** on pages 231A and 231B for lecture, classwork, and assignment options for Section 13-1.

OBJECTIVES

1 Distinguish between "how" and "why" questions about behavior.

2 Explain how natural selection affects behavior.

3 Describe a case in which learning helps shape a behavior.

4 Explain the importance of Tryon's experiment on learning in rats.

What Is Behavior, and How Is It Studied?

A **behavior** is an action or series of actions performed by an animal in response to a stimulus. The stimulus might be something in the environment, such as a sound, a smell, or a subtle change in the facial expression of another individual. The stimulus can also be the internal state of the animal, such as whether it has recently eaten. Behavior is crucial to an animal's survival because it is often the first response to a change in the environment.

Scientists studying behavior investigate two kinds of questions—"how" questions and "why" questions. "How" questions are about the mechanisms of the behavior within the animal—how the behavior is triggered, controlled, and performed. For instance, consider a squirrel burying a nut, as shown in **Figure 13-1**. "How" questions about this behavior include "How does a squirrel select which nuts to bury?" and "How does it choose where to bury

nuts?" A scientist seeking to answer the first question might offer nuts of different kinds and sizes to a squirrel to see which it prefers.

Answering the "how" questions provides only a partial understanding of a behavior. Scientists also must answer the "why" questions. "Why" questions concern the reasons the behavior exists. "Why do squirrels bury nuts?" is an example of a "why" question about behavior. **Figure 13-1** lists some "how" questions and some "why" questions about the squirrel's behavior. The Dutch biologist Niko Tinbergen, who received the Nobel Prize in 1973 for his work on behavior, emphasized that "why" questions are really questions about the evolution of behavior. To explain why a behavior exists, it is necessary to understand why the behavior evolved and why it is maintained in the species. Therefore, it is necessary to learn how natural selection acts on the behavior.

Figure 13-1
Gaining a full understanding of a behavior requires answering "how" questions, which concern the behavior's mechanisms, and "why" questions, which concern its evolution.

How?
• How does a squirrel select which nuts to bury?
• How does a squirrel choose where to bury nuts?
• How does this behavior develop?
• What environmental conditions affect the performance of the behavior?

Why?
• What advantage does a squirrel gain from burying nuts?
• What is the evolutionary history of this behavior?

233

Phase Two
Teaching Strategies

"How" and "Why" Questions in Biology

■ **Recognizing Relationships**
Inform students that scientists seek to answer "how" and "why" questions in all areas of biology. For example, geneticists have learned much about how meiosis occurs—how the chromosomes line up and separate, and how cytokinesis occurs. But they are also interested in why meiosis occurs and what benefits it brings to the organism. Ask students to come up with some "how" and "why" questions about subjects they studied in previous chapters. Ask students to provide answers to their questions.

Language Arts Connection
Ethology
The study of behavior is known as ethology, from the Greek word *ethos,* meaning "character" or "custom."

Videodisc Resources

Holt Biology Videodiscs
Lesson 13-1: Evolution of Behavior

Key to Strategies
Teaching Strategies are keyed to three tiers of learning.

● **Understanding Concepts (Tier I)**
Content mastery and comprehension

■ **Applying Information (Tier II)**
Applying and analyzing content

▲ **Critical Thinking (Tier III)**
Practicing evaluative thinking

How Natural Selection Shapes Behavior

In Chapter 10 you learned how natural selection causes evolution. Recall that natural selection favors features that improve the likelihood that an individual will survive and reproduce. Over time, features that are advantageous become more common, while disadvantageous features become less common and may disappear.

To see how an understanding of natural selection can help answer a "why" question about behavior, it helps to consider a real example. In East Africa, lions live in small groups called prides. Each pride contains several adult females, several youngsters (called cubs), and one or more adult males. The adult males, which are usually brothers or other relatives, dominate the pride and father all the cubs. They also defend the pride against other males. A group of males usually can control a pride for only a couple of years before being forced out by younger males. When this happens, the new males often kill all the young cubs in the pride. Why do the new males behave in this way?

To explain why this behavior exists, you need to know how a male lion benefits from performing the behavior. Consider a male lion who has just taken over a pride. Because he likely will be in the pride for only a few years before he is forced out by a younger male, he has a very short time in which to reproduce. But female lions with cubs will not breed until their cubs are grown, which may take more than two years. If a female's cubs die, however, she will mate again almost immediately. These observations suggest the evolutionary hypothesis for cub-killing behavior explained in **Figure 13-2**.

Note that this explanation does not imply that male lions are aware that they are killing the offspring of other males or that they somehow calculate how they will benefit from performing this behavior.

Figure 13-2
After taking over a pride, a male lion usually kills the young cubs in the pride. This diagram shows one hypothesis of how this behavior benefits the male lion.

Hypothesis
A new male lion kills the young cubs in the pride so that . . .

. . . female lions will mate with him and have his offspring.

Predictions
• Male lions that kill young cubs after taking over a pride have more offspring than males that let cubs live.
• Males are unlikely to kill cubs after they have been in residence in a pride for several months—they would be killing their own offspring.

Historical Perspective: Nobel Prizes for Behavior

There is no Nobel Prize for ecology, evolutionary biology, or behavior. However, four scientists who studied behavior have received Nobel Prizes in the category of physiology or medicine. The first was the Russian scientist Ivan Pavlov, who is famous for his experiments on learning in dogs. Pavlov received his award in 1904. In 1973, Karl von Frisch and Konrad Lorenz, both of Austria, and Niko Tinbergen, from the Netherlands, were honored for their pioneering studies of behavior.

Natural selection favors traits that benefit individuals

Most scientists now agree that natural selection favors traits that contribute to the survival and reproduction of individuals. The idea that natural selection favors traits that benefit groups or species is most often expressed as the claim that a trait has evolved because it "ensures the survival of the species." The cub-killing behavior of lions and many other behaviors show that this belief is false. The actions of male lions increase the already high death rate among cubs and actually reduce the likelihood that the species will survive. Because natural selection favors traits that benefit individuals, an animal usually will behave in ways that are most likely to ensure its own survival and increase its likelihood of reproducing.

The Genetic Basis of Behavior

Do genes determine behavior, or do animals learn how to behave from experience? Over the last century, this question has been very controversial. Some scientists argued that most behaviors were genetically programmed and appeared in the same form in different individuals of a species. Other scientists claimed that behaviors were shaped by an animal's experience, not controlled by its genes. The conflict between these two views is largely settled now. Many studies have shown that both heredity and learning play significant roles, often interacting to shape the final behavior.

Behaviors can be inherited

From years of observation and experimentation, biologists have learned that many kinds of animal behaviors are influenced by genes. One behavior demonstrated to have a genetic basis is nest building in lovebirds. These small parrots construct their nests from vegetation that they collect and carry back to the nesting site. One species, Fischer's lovebird, carries its nesting material in its beak. A second, closely related species, the peach-faced lovebird, carries its nesting material in the feathers near its tail.

In the 1960s, biologist William Dilger created hybrids by crossing peach-faced lovebirds with Fischer's lovebirds. As you can see in **Figure 13-3**, the hybrids' nesting behavior resembled the behaviors of both their parents. Though the hybrids usually tried to place nesting material in their feathers, they were rarely successful and usually ended up carrying the nesting material in their beak.

Figure 13-3
William Dilger crossed individuals of two lovebird species and showed that nest-building behavior in these birds has a genetic basis. The hybrid offspring exhibited behaviors of both their parents.

Fischer's lovebird   Peach-faced lovebird

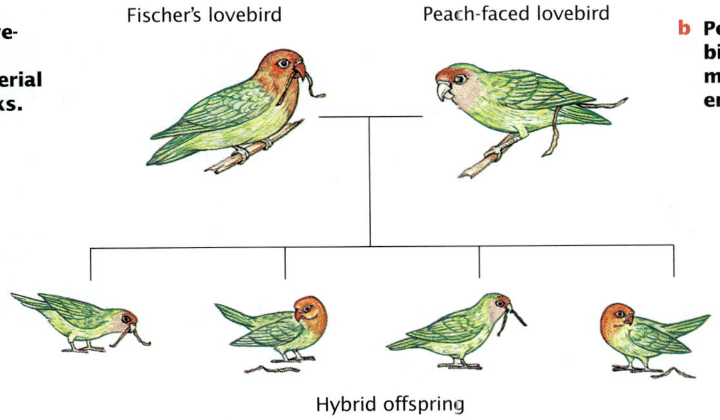

a Fischer's lovebirds carry nesting material in their beaks.

b Peach-faced lovebirds carry nesting material in the feathers near their tail.

c Hybrids of these two species try to insert nesting material into the feathers near their tail, but they usually don't succeed and must carry the material in their beaks.

Hybrid offspring

235

Instincts vs. Learning: A False Dichotomy

■ **Recognizing Relationships**
Ask students to describe what they have heard about the so-called nature versus nurture debate. After eliciting student answers, describe the outlines of this long-standing debate. Extreme "nature" advocates claim that behavior is instinctive, a word they have defined as meaning "genetically programmed and not subject to modification by experience." The views of extreme "nurture" proponents are the opposite—all behaviors are the result of an animal's experience. Inform students that the truth lies somewhere between these extreme views. All of an animal's behaviors are controlled by its nervous system, which develops under the influence of its genes and its environment. Therefore, all behaviors are the result of the interaction between genes and the environment, and it is inaccurate to speak of behaviors as being either genetic or environmental.

Visual Strategy   **Figure 13-3**

● **Interpreting Graphics**
Have students contrast this diagram with the pedigree from Chapter 7, shown on page 130. Point out that Figure 13-3 shows a cross between two individuals of different species, while the pedigree in Chapter 7 shows a cross between two individuals of the same species.

Multicultural Perspective: Australian Aborigines

To the early European colonists of Australia, the technology of the Aborigines indicated a very primitive people. The Aborigines could produce only a limited variety of tools because they did not know how to mine, smelt, or work metal. They had to rely on hunting and gathering because they did not practice agriculture. Most groups did not wear clothes, even in winter. The largest "structures" they created were piles of discarded shells. However, as the Europeans soon learned, the Aborigines compensated for their technological "deficiencies" with a deep and detailed knowledge of their environment, which allowed them to survive in areas where European explorers and settlers perished. In particular, the Aborigines were experts on the behavior of animals, and they used this knowledge to help capture game and to find water in dry areas.

Key to Strategies
● Understanding Concepts (Tier I)
■ Applying Information (Tier II)
▲ Critical Thinking (Tier III)

Connection: *Chapter 10*

Genetic Variation

Remind students that inherited variation is essential in order for natural selection to occur. Ask students to explain how Cade's procedure was analogous to natural selection. *(He caused genetic changes in the two groups of crickets by selecting which individuals would reproduce.)*

Imprinting

■ **Recognizing Relationships**

Explain to students what is meant by the term *critical period*. The critical period is the time period in the life of an individual in which imprinting occurs, establishing a relationship that can last a lifetime. For example, if the goslings shown in Figure 13-5 had seen Lorenz at some time other than during their critical period, they would not have behaved as they did. Goslings also apparently learn to recognize members of their species during this critical period. As adults, Lorenz's geese would have tried to mate with humans, preferring them to members of their own species.

Figure 13-4
How long a male cricket sings is controlled genetically. In William Cade's experiment, crickets in the initial group varied in how long they sang. By allowing only the males that sang for the greatest or least amount of time to breed, Cade produced two distinct groups.

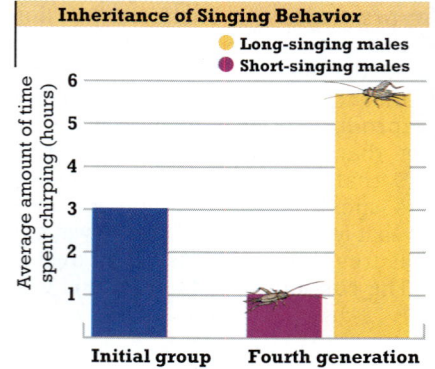

Inheritance of Singing Behavior

● Long-singing males
● Short-singing males

Average amount of time spent chirping (hours)

Initial group   Fourth generation

Another behavior that has a genetic basis is chirping in crickets. Males chirp to attract females. Biologist William Cade noticed that males differed in how much time they spent chirping per night. Some males did not chirp at all, some chirped for just a few hours, and a few chirped for almost the entire night. To determine whether this difference in behavior was inherited, Cade selected two groups of crickets. One group consisted of the males that spent the most time chirping. The second group contained the males that spent the least amount of time chirping. He allowed males in both groups to mate and then examined their male offspring. Of these offspring, only the extreme individuals (the males that sang for the longest and shortest times) were permitted to mate. Cade continued this procedure through four generations of crickets. As you can see in **Figure 13-4**, by the fourth generation the two groups differed significantly in the amount of time they chirped. Because this behavioral difference was transmitted from one generation to the next, it clearly had a genetic basis.

Learned Behaviors Are Modified by Experience

Behaviors can be influenced by genes. But to what degree can behavior be modified by experience? The development of behaviors through experience is called **learning**. In many animals, learning is very important in determining the final shape of a behavior. For example, young geese and ducks follow their mother as she leads them to water, helps them find food, and keeps them out of danger. However, a duckling or gosling must learn to recognize its mother. This type of learning is called **imprinting**. Nobel Prize–winning animal behaviorist Konrad Lorenz discovered that imprinting takes place during a short period following hatching. During this period, the young birds will learn to follow any object—including toy wagons, boxes, and balloons—that they are associated with. When Lorenz raised a group of newly hatched goslings by hand, he found that young birds will even imprint on humans. **Figure 13-5** shows Konrad Lorenz leading his "family" of goslings. Once the young birds had imprinted onto Lorenz, they preferred to follow him, even when given the opportunity to follow a member of their own species.

Figure 13-5
These goslings followed Konrad Lorenz as if he were their mother.

Community Connection: Psychologist

Invite a psychologist from either your school or your community to speak to the class about his or her work in behavior modification. Have the speaker describe the various methods and strategies psychologists employ to get people to modify their behavior. Ask the speaker to cite specific examples without violating confidentiality.

Figure 13-6
In Ivan Pavlov's experiments, dogs learned to associate the ringing of a bell with food. They would salivate each time the bell rang, whether food was present or not.

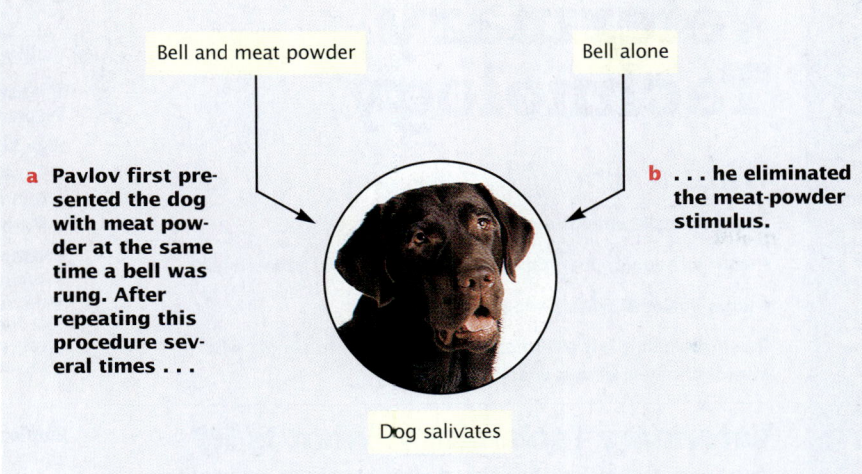

Bell and meat powder

Bell alone

a Pavlov first presented the dog with meat powder at the same time a bell was rung. After repeating this procedure several times . . .

b . . . he eliminated the meat-powder stimulus.

Dog salivates

One of the most famous studies of learning is Russian psychologist Ivan Pavlov's work on salivation behavior in dogs, which he carried out in the late 1890s and early 1900s. **Figure 13-6** is an overview of Pavlov's methods. If meat powder (stimulus) is presented to a hungry dog, the dog will salivate (response). Pavlov also presented the dog with a second, unrelated stimulus—a ringing bell—at the same time that meat powder was blown into the dog's mouth. As expected, the dog salivated. After repeated trials, the dog would salivate in response to the bell alone, having learned to associate the unrelated stimulus (the ringing of the bell) with the meat stimulus.

In another famous set of experiments, the American psychologist B. F. Skinner studied learning in rats by placing them in a "Skinner box," illustrated in **Figure 13-7**. Once inside, the rat would explore the box. Occasionally, it would accidentally press a lever, and a pellet of food would appear. At first, the rat would ignore the lever and continue to move about, but it soon learned to press the lever to obtain food. When it was hungry, it would spend all of its time pushing the lever. This sort of trial-and-error learning is of major importance to most vertebrates.

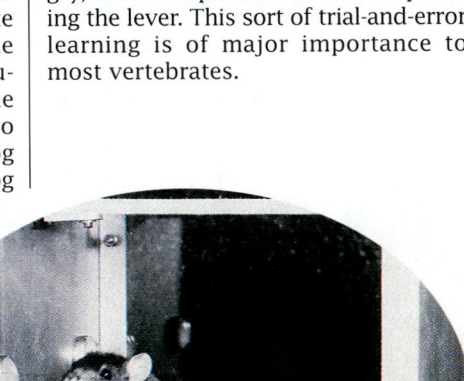

Figure 13-7
When the rat presses the lever it has its paw on, it receives a reward of food. A rat placed in this Skinner box quickly learns to press the lever when it is hungry.

237

Learning in Pets

■ **Designing an Experiment**

Divide the class into two-person teams, and have each group design an experiment to test the ability of a pet to learn a new behavior. Suggest some possibilities, such as teaching a dog a new behavior or having a mouse perform some sort of activity to obtain food. Encourage students to test different conditions to determine if one method is more successful. For example, a dog that performs a certain behavioral response can be rewarded with food. In a second conditioning experiment, the same dog can be rewarded with petting when it exhibits the desired response. Students can then compare the learning time with the type of reward. If students plan to carry out their experiments, be sure they treat any animals in a humane manner. Guidelines for working with vertebrates can be obtained from the National Association of Biology Teachers, 11250 Roger Bacon Drive, Reston, Virginia 22090. Have students write a report describing their plans and the results of their experiments.

Pavlov's Experiments

■ **Applying Information**
Pavlov's dogs initially would salivate only in response to the meat-powder stimulus. Salivation is an unconditioned response, meaning it occurs automatically and does not have to be learned. Remind students that they show a similar behavior when they sense food. Ask students to speculate about what the function of this response might be. *(Salivation prepares the mouth to receive food by lubricating the mouth and increasing the concentration of digestive enzymes, which are found in saliva.)*

Key to Strategies
● Understanding Concepts (Tier I)
■ Applying Information (Tier II)
▲ Critical Thinking (Tier III)

Animal Behavior 237

Exploring a Career

1. Have students brainstorm ideas about the following questions:

If you wanted a career in veterinary technology...

- what kind of personality traits would be essential?
- which subjects should you study in high school? in college?
- what kinds of extracurricular activities should you pursue?
- what kind of practical experience should you gain?
- what kind of issues would interest you?

2. Pose the following situation: You are the head veterinary technician for a small group of veterinarians who are planning to build a new clinic. They have asked you to help design the layout of the new building. In small groups, have students consider the daily operations of a veterinarian and design a layout for the clinic. Afterward, have groups transfer their layouts to overhead transparencies and describe their ideas to the class.

3. A veterinary technician has opened a pet-sitting and dog-walking service. In small groups, have students create a brochure that describes the company's services and fees. Prepare students for this activity by distributing and reviewing examples of brochures. Then have students brainstorm ideas about how to appeal to potential customers.

Career Opportunities

Veterinary Technology

What it would be like to . . .

- help animals without attending veterinarian school?
- work in a zoo, a pharmaceutical company, or a research lab?
- run a business while caring for animals?

These are just a few of the opportunities open to people who work in the field of veterinary technology.

Veterinary Technology: What Is It?

Veterinary technicians are knowledgeable about animal life processes and assist in the care and handling of animal patients. They play important supportive roles in diagnostic, medical, and surgical procedures. Veterinary technicians are also skilled in routine laboratory and clinical procedures. Many work in private veterinary practices where they may also help out in the office.

Career Focus: Jennifer Dusek
Veterinary technician at a veterinary clinic

"I've loved animals for as long as I can remember. I was always bringing home hurt animals—birds, chickens, squirrels, dogs, and even a pig. When I was in high school, I helped out at a veterinary clinic feeding animals and cleaning kennels. It's a good way to get experience, and vets are always happy to have the help. I looked into becoming a veterinarian but didn't feel comfortable with the amount of school required. I wanted practical training. I heard about a vocational school that offered courses in veterinary technology, so I enrolled."

What I Do: "Today I'm a manager of a veterinary clinic, where I've been working for 10 years. As a veterinary technician I'm responsible for a variety of duties, from monitoring a patient during surgery to taking X rays. For me, every day is busy, exciting, and truly rewarding. I also work in a wildlife rehabilitation center nursing injured animals back to health. I visit elementary schools and bring one or two animals along. The kids love learning about animals, especially when they get to use the stethoscope to listen to the animals' hearts."

Science/Math Career Preparation

High School
- Biology
- Chemistry
- Math

Vocational School/College
- Two-year associate's degree at a school accredited by the American Veterinary Medical Association

Employment Outlook:
The ever-broadening scope of veterinary medicine has created a shortage of trained veterinary technicians. Also, as the number of family pets rises, the demand for veterinary technicians is increasing quickly.

To Find Out More

1 For further information, write to:
American Veterinary Medical Association
930 N. Meachum Road
Schaumburg, IL 60172

2 Many states require veterinary technicians to be registered or certified. Find out the specific registration provisions in your state.

3 See your school counselor to find out what colleges and institutions offer programs for veterinary technicians. Review the prerequisites and course requirements. Make a poster showing the range of job opportunities in this field.

238

Genes and Learning Interact to Shape Behaviors

Most behavioral biologists have come to think that animal behavior has both learned and genetic components. An example is provided by a famous 1940s experiment by the biologist Robert Tryon. Tryon studied rats' ability to find their way through a maze with many blind alleys and only one exit, where a reward of food awaited. It took awhile, as false avenues were tried and rejected, but eventually some individuals learned to finish the maze while making few incorrect turns. Other rats never seemed to learn the correct path. Tryon bred the "maze-bright" rats with one another, establishing a colony from the fast learners. He also established a "maze-dull" colony by breeding the slowest-learning rats with each other. He then tested the offspring in each colony to see how quickly they learned the maze. The offspring of maze-bright rats learned even more quickly than their parents had, while the offspring of maze-dull parents were even poorer at maze learning. After Tryon repeated this procedure over several generations, two behaviorally distinct types of rats with very different maze-learning ability resulted, as shown in **Figure 13-8**. Clearly, the ability to learn the maze was to some degree hereditary, controlled by genes passed from parent to offspring. It is important to note that the genes were specific for this particular behavior. When Tryon tested the ability of the two groups of rats to complete a different kind of maze, he found no difference between maze-dull and maze-bright rats.

Figure 13-8
In rats, the ability to learn a maze is at least partly inherited.

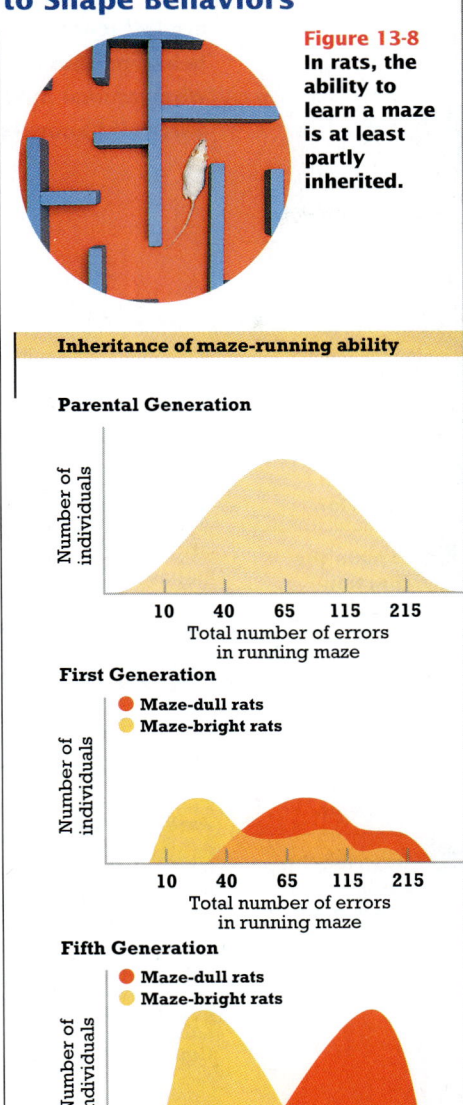
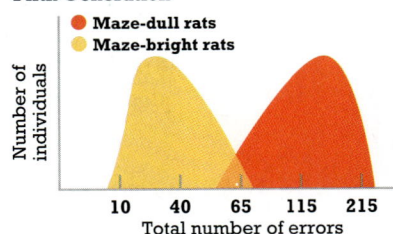

Inheritance of maze-running ability

Parental Generation

First Generation
● Maze-dull rats
● Maze-bright rats

Fifth Generation
● Maze-dull rats
● Maze-bright rats

Visual Strategy Figure 13-8

■ **Recognizing Relationships**
Ask students to compare Tryon's methods with Cade's methods, described on page 236, and to explain the similarities and differences between the experiments of these two scientists. Also emphasize that Tryon was not breeding for general intelligence in his rats. The maze-bright rats were much better at negotiating one kind of maze, but they were no better than the maze-dull rats at finding their way through a different kind of maze.

Phase Three
Assessment Options

Closure
● **Summarizing Information**
Have students observe the behavior of a pet or other animal and write a report describing their observations. In their reports, students should describe the behaviors of their subject and the social context for each behavior. Students should also explain the function of each behavior they observe.

SECTION REVIEW
Assign the Section Review.

Reteaching
Have students select any behavior that has been described in this section, and ask them to write a list of "why" and "how" questions that a scientist could ask about that particular behavior. (Students could ask, "Why does a gosling follow any object shortly after hatching?" and "How does this behavior change, if at all, over time?")

SECTION REVIEW

① Propose a hypothesis to explain why squirrels bury nuts. How would you test your hypothesis?

② Construct an argument to explain why female lions do not kill their cubs when new males take over a pride.

③ What is imprinting?

④ Describe Tryon's experiment, and explain how it shows the interaction between genes and learning.

239

ANSWERS TO SECTION REVIEW

① Answers will vary. Most students will hypothesize that squirrels bury nuts to use during times of food scarcity. One way to test this hypothesis is to see if squirrels dig out the nuts during such times.

② Answers will vary. Some students might suggest that the female does not kill her cubs because this behavior will not benefit her in any way.

③ Imprinting is a behavioral pattern that an animal learns during a very short period in its early life.

④ Tryon tested the ability of rats to learn to complete a maze. He bred fast learners with other fast learners and slow learners with other slow learners. The offspring of the fast learners learned the maze even faster than their parents, while the offspring of the slow learners were even poorer at learning the maze than their parents. These similarities indicated that the ability to learn the maze was at least partly inherited.

Key to Strategies
● Understanding Concepts (Tier I)
■ Applying Information (Tier II)
▲ Critical Thinking (Tier III)

Scheduling

See the **Lesson Planning Guide** on pages 231A and 231B for lecture, classwork, and assignment options for Section 13-2.

Phase Two
Teaching Strategies

Visual Strategy   Table 13-1

● **Interpreting Graphics**
Have students refer to the types of behavior listed in this table and categorize the two specific behaviors of squirrels that are described in the text ("digs a hole" and "runs to shelter"). *(The former is an example of a foraging behavior, while the latter can be categorized as a defensive behavior.)*

Active READING

Technique: Reading Organizer
Have students make a chart with the following headings: Parental Care, Courtship Behavior, Defensive Behavior, Foraging Behavior, Migratory Behavior, Territorial Behavior. As students read this section, they should assign each behavior mentioned in the text to one of the categories on their chart. Inform students that some behaviors will not fit into any of the categories, so it will not be possible to classify all the behaviors described in this section. For more information about reading organizers, see Reading Strategies Worksheets in Holt BioSources Teaching Resources CD-ROM.

Most biologists have concluded that many aspects of animal behavior are influenced by genes. Because natural selection acts on genes, animal behavior should be, at least to some extent, the result of evolution. When animal behavior is studied in nature, behaviors characteristic of particular animals are, by and large, suited to their way of life.

13-2   Kinds of Behavior

OBJECTIVES

❶ **List three types of behavior.**

❷ **Explain the function of animal signals.**

❸ **Summarize how sexual selection affects the evolution of behavior.**

❹ **Describe the evolution of altruism by kin selection.**

Categories of Behavior

Behavior is an animal's most immediate way of dealing with its environment. Because the environment is complex and can change rapidly, most animals have several different kinds of behavior, each suited to a particular situation. For instance, a squirrel may perform one kind of behavior when it finds a nut on the ground—it digs a hole. It performs a completely different behavior when a snake approaches—it runs for shelter—because digging a hole would not help it escape from the snake. Biologists have classified the behaviors animals perform into several broad categories. **Table 13-1** lists some of these categories and gives an example of each. The rest of this section examines some kinds of animal behavior in more detail.

Table 13-1 Some Types of Animal Behaviors

Type of behavior	Function	Example
Parental care	Ensure survival of young	This robin is feeding an insect to its offspring.
Courtship behavior	Attract a mate	The peacock spreads his large, brightly colored tail to attract females.
Defensive behavior	Protect individual from predators	A hognose snake flips onto its back and plays dead when threatened.

Videodisc Resources

Holt Biology Videodiscs
Lesson 13-2: Kinds of Behavior

Foraging behavior	Locate, obtain, and consume food 	A sea otter opens mussels and clams by smashing them against a rock it carries on its chest.
Migratory behavior	Move to a more suitable environment for living or reproduction	Monarch butterflies migrate thousands of kilometers, from the United States to central Mexico. 
Territorial behavior	Protect a resource for exclusive use	These wolves belong to a pack that defends its territory from other packs. 

Evolution

Many songbirds migrate north in the spring and south in the fall. Identify some benefits and costs of this behavior.

How Animals Communicate

If you approach an unfamiliar dog and it growls, you know that it may bite if you come any closer. You have responded to a signal given by the dog. Animals use signals to influence the behavior of other animals. A signal can be a posture, call, movement, scent, color, or facial expression. Animals send and receive signals through all of the senses familiar to us—sight, hearing, smell, touch, and taste. Some fishes communicate through a sense we do not have—sensitivity to weak electrical fields.

Natural selection has shaped animal signals so that they reach the intended receiver efficiently and stimulate a response. To be transmitted efficiently, a signal must be able to travel through the environment from sender to receiver. A signal must also be recognizable to the receiver, or it won't have any effect on behavior. When a male frog like the one shown in **Figure 13-9** seeks to attract a mate, he emits a loud call. This signal is a very effective way to reach female frogs. The call carries a long distance, reaching even far-off females. At night, when many frogs are active, visual signals such as colors and movements are visible from only a short distance away and would therefore be much less effective at attracting a mate.

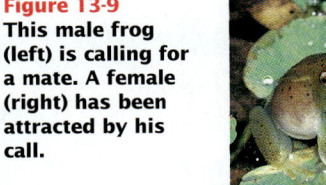

Figure 13-9
This male frog (left) is calling for a mate. A female (right) has been attracted by his call.

241

Demonstration

■ **Recognizing Relationships**
Materials: a gypsy moth trap or other insect trap

Show the class a gypsy moth trap. Inform students that the chemicals some animals use to communicate with are known as pheromones. The "bait" used in the trap is an example of a pheromone. One female gypsy moth emits only about one-millionth of a gram of pheromone. Yet this small amount is sufficient to attract males that are several kilometers downwind. We humans exploit the male moth's vigorous response to even tiny amounts of the female's pheromone to help control gypsy moths, which are destructive pests of trees.

Language Arts Connection

Learning Language
How fast do children learn language? Steven Pinker, a linguist at the Massachusetts Institute of Technology, estimates that the average six-year-old knows about 13,000 words. By the time that child graduates from high school, he or she will know about 60,000 words, according to Pinker.

Figure 13-10
Animals communicate in many ways. Here are three examples.

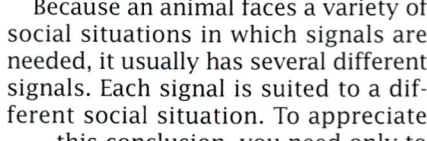

a **A male sparrow sings to attract females and to warn other males against entering his territory.**

b **When scout ants find food, they lay down a chemical trail that leads other members of the nest to the food. These ants are following such a trail.**

Because an animal faces a variety of social situations in which signals are needed, it usually has several different signals. Each signal is suited to a different social situation. To appreciate this conclusion, you need only to think about your own behavior. Would you try to attract the attention of someone far down the street with subtle facial expressions and whispers? Of course not. You would probably shout and perhaps wave your arms over your head. However, these signals wouldn't be suitable for a face-to-face conversation with a friend. **Figure 13-10** shows several examples of animal signals and describes their functions.

Humans communicate with complex symbolic language

Among animals, vocal communication is most developed in the primates. Many primates have a "vocabulary" that allows individuals to communicate the identity of specific predators, such as eagles, leopards, and snakes. Chimpanzees and gorillas can learn to recognize and use a large number of symbols to communicate abstract concepts. They cannot talk, however, because they cannot produce the sounds of speech. Furthermore, the ability to assemble symbols into new sentences requires very complex brain structure, a complexity that has evolved only in humans.

Language develops at an early age in humans. Human infants learn language by trial and error during the "babbling baby" phase of childhood. Humans learn a particular language while young. Children who have not heard certain consonant sounds as infants usually cannot distinguish or produce them as adults. That is why most Americans never master the throaty French \r\, whereas speakers of French typically replace the English \th\ with \z\ or \s\. Children quickly and effortlessly learn a vocabulary of thousands of words. This rapid-learning ability seems to be genetically programmed.

Although language is the primary form of human communication, much evidence suggests that odor and other nonverbal signals (body language) may also be important. Think of how much you learn by a quick look at the expression on the face of another person. Among humans, many forms of communication may occur simultaneously.

c **Using rhythmic head bobs and pulsations of their throat fan, male anoles signal to other members of their species.**

Matter of Fact: Animal Odors

Many animals use chemicals to mark their territories. Examples include deer, which release chemicals through glands in their hooves; dogs and cats, which release chemicals in their urine; and male antelopes, which mark twigs with compounds secreted by glands near their eyes.

Choosing a Mate

When ready to mate, animals produce signals to communicate with potential partners. Each species usually produces a unique courtship signal. This helps ensure that individuals don't mate with individuals of another species. For example, the flash patterns of fireflies are coded for species identity. A female recognizes males of her own species by the number of flashes in his pattern, and she will ignore any male with a different flash pattern. The chemical produced by a female silk moth attracts only males of her own species. Many species of insects, amphibians, and birds produce unique sounds or songs to attract mates. A white-crowned sparrow will respond to the song of another white-crowned sparrow, but totally ignore the song of a song sparrow.

Selection of a mate involves much more than just finding an individual of the same species. Females, and to a lesser extent males, are often very selective about which potential partner they mate with. Female frogs, for instance, have been observed "shopping around" among calling males. A female will sit near a male, listen to his call for several minutes, and then move on to another male and listen to his call. She may evaluate several males before choosing one (usually the largest) with which to mate.

Mate choice can drive evolution

What characteristics do animals use in choosing a mate? When Charles Darwin considered this question more than a century ago, he made an important discovery about evolution. Darwin noticed that males often had extreme characteristics that they used in their courtship displays. Take, for example, a widowbird, shown in **Figure 13-11**. During the breeding season, the male widowbird grows an extremely long tail, up to 0.5 m (19 in.) in length. The female bird, also shown

in **Figure 13-11**, has a short tail, only about 7 cm (3 in.) long. How has this difference between the sexes evolved? The long tail of the male widowbird cannot be essential for survival, since the female bird survives quite well without it. In fact, the male's long tail probably reduces his chances of survival by making him more visible to predators.

Figure 13-11
The tail of the male widowbird (top) can be more than three times his body length. The female (left) has a short tail.

Choosing a Mate

■ Inferring Relationships
Students have probably seen a movie that includes a tropical rain forest or jungle scene. Such a scene is often accompanied by a sound track that includes a variety of animal sounds. Ask students why animals living in such an environment often use sound as a form of communication. *(The dense foliage makes visual communication difficult, but it does not interfere as much with the perception of sound.)*

Connection: *Chapter 6*

Parental Investment in Gametes
As a general rule, females are the choosier sex when it comes to selecting a mate. Why is this so? Biologists explain this difference by noting that a female produces much larger gametes than a male—a human egg is about 195,000 times larger than a human sperm, for example—and therefore cannot produce as many gametes. A sensible "strategy" for a female, then, is to produce a few high-quality offspring, each of which receives a large amount of her investment. One way to improve the quality of her offspring is to be selective about her mate, choosing the one that provides the most for her offspring.

Connection: *Chapter 10*

Natural Selection and the Widowbird's Tail
Ask students to explain why extreme male traits like the widowbird's tail were such a problem to Darwin's theory that he felt it necessary to propose an additional mechanism to explain their evolution. *(Darwin could not see how a trait that reduced the likelihood of survival could have evolved through natural selection.)* Emphasize to students that sexual selection is a form of natural selection.

Key to Strategies
● Understanding Concepts (Tier I)
■ Applying Information (Tier II)
▲ Critical Thinking (Tier III)

Animal Behavior   243

243

▲ **Evaluating Hypotheses**

An alternative hypothesis for the presence of antlers on male deer is that antlers serve as defensive weapons. This hypothesis is bolstered by the observation that deer sometimes use their antlers to fend off predators such as cougars. Ask students to critique this hypothesis. *(If antlers evolved solely as defensive weapons, female deer would also probably have antlers. Also, male deer shed their antlers after the mating season, and it is unlikely that an animal would jettison its primary defense for part of the year.)*

Sexual Selection and Human Evolution

● **Identifying Functions**

Is sexual selection responsible for any human traits? One trait likely to have evolved through sexual selection is the beard in males. Another likely candidate is the difference in size between the sexes; although not as pronounced as in gorillas, the difference is still significant. On average, human males are 8 percent taller and 20 percent heavier than females. Jared Diamond, an evolutionary biologist at UCLA, believes that many of the differences among the human races are due to sexual selection, not natural selection. For example, many scientists argue that dark skin coloration evolved among people living in the tropics as a protection against ultraviolet light from the sun. People living at higher latitudes, the argument goes, have lighter skin because they are exposed to less ultraviolet radiation. Diamond points out that American Indians living in tropical regions of South America do not have very dark skin, while Aborigines living in the temperate regions of Australia do have very dark skin. Also, he notes that skin cancer causes few deaths compared with infectious diseases and therefore would not be a strong selective force.

Darwin recognized that such traits could have evolved if they helped males attract mates. He proposed the mechanism of **sexual selection** to account for the evolution of traits like the widowbird's tail. Sexual selection is an evolutionary mechanism in which traits that enhance the ability of individuals to acquire mates increase in frequency. Even traits that have a negative effect on survival can evolve in this way, provided that their benefits to reproduction are high enough. For example, the long tail of the male widowbird probably evolved because males with this trait were able to attract more mates than males with short tails. Even though long-tailed males were more likely to be captured by predators, they still fathered more offspring than short-tailed males because of their greater attractiveness to females.

What kinds of traits are advantageous for acquiring mates? Because males usually compete among themselves for the chance to mate with a female, sexual selection has often favored traits that make males more intimidating or better at combat. Examples of such traits are large body size, antlers of deer, manes of lions, and horns of bighorn sheep. **Figure 13-12** shows several examples of male traits favored by sexual selection. Competition among males can also take subtle forms. A male can gain a reproductive advantage over other males by interfering with their reproduction. In some species of worms, butterflies, and snakes, for instance, the male seals the female's reproductive tract after mating so that no other males can mate with her.

Figure 13-12
What characteristics are favored by sexual selection? Three examples are shown below.

a A large rack of antlers helps a male deer intimidate rivals and attract mates.

b Swordtails are common aquarium fish. Females prefer males with longer swords attached to the tail.

c Gorillas live in groups of many females dominated by one large adult male. The dominant male, known as a silverback, must be large to fight off attacks by other males. Males, on average, are 50 percent larger than females.

Figure 13-13
Young scrub jays often will help their parents raise offspring. This is an example of altruism.

Figure 13-14
This honeybee is performing an extremely altruistic behavior for the benefit of her hive. She is stinging an attacker, even though this will result in her death.

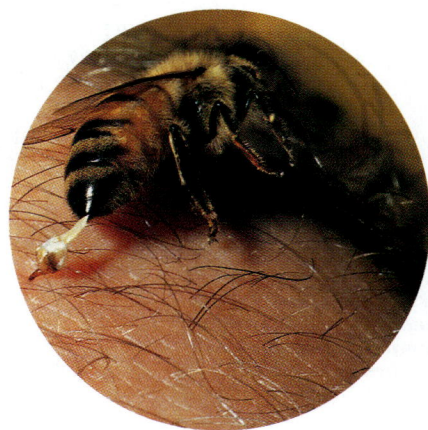

The Evolution of Self-Sacrificing Behavior

When a young scrub jay reaches maturity, it may not leave its parents' nest and begin to have its own offspring, as do young birds in most other species. Instead, the young scrub jay, shown in **Figure 13-13**, often remains with its parents and helps them raise additional offspring. This behavior is an example of altruism. **Altruism** is self-sacrificing behavior. Altruism is often thought of as heroic human behavior, such as jumping into a river to save a drowning person. But altruism is not limited to humans; it occurs in many other kinds of animals. In many species it is an important aspect of cooperation on which the survival of the whole group depends. The social insects (ants, bees, wasps, and termites) exhibit extreme forms of altruism. Most of the individuals in a beehive are female workers that never reproduce. They care for and defend the only female that does reproduce, the queen, and help raise her offspring. If the hive is attacked, the workers sacrifice themselves to protect the hive, as shown in **Figure 13-14**.

Altruism usually occurs among relatives

How can altruism evolve? How can a trait producing an altruistic behavior be passed from generation to generation if individuals that have the trait never leave any offspring? The most widely accepted answer was proposed by the British biologist W. D. Hamilton

245

Understanding Social Behavior

■ **Inferring Conclusions**
To help students understand the different possible categories of social behavior, have them make a **Graphic Organizer** like the one at the bottom of the page. Students should complete the chart by writing the words *negative* or *positive* in each blank.

Honeybee Society

■ **Recognizing Relationships**
Point out that the queen bee releases pheromones to keep her position in the hive. These pheromones inhibit ovarian development in the worker bees, thus preventing them from becoming potential rivals.

Visual Strategy | Videodisc

■ **Forming Hypotheses**
To introduce the concept of altruism, use *Video—Honeybee Society* (1 min 30 s) in Chapter 13 Section 13-2 of *Holt Biology Videodiscs Teacher's Correlation Guide to Holt Biology: Visualizing Life.* Tell students to pay close attention to the roles of the queen, workers, and drones. After viewing the video, work with students to develop a list of "how" and "why" questions similar to those developed for the squirrel shown on page 233. When the lists are completed, ask students to study the "why" questions carefully and to form hypotheses about why these behaviors evolved and why they are maintained. *(Accept any reasonable answers.)* Then show *Video—Kin Selection in Bees* (2 min 25 s) in Chapter 13 Section 13-2 of *Holt Biology Videodiscs Teacher's Correlation Guide to Holt Biology: Visualizing Life.* Have students compare their hypotheses with the explanation given in the video.

Graphic Organizer

Use the following graphic organizer with the teaching strategy **Understanding Social Behavior** on page 245.

Type of behavior	Effect on donor	Effect on recipient
Altruism	**negative**	**positive**
Self-serving	**positive**	**negative**
Cooperative	**positive**	**positive**
Spiteful	**negative**	**negative**

Key to Strategies
● **Understanding Concepts (Tier I)**
■ **Applying Information (Tier II)**
▲ **Critical Thinking (Tier III)**

Visual Strategy Figure 13-15

■ **Predicting Outcomes**

Scientists have suggested that one reason a young scrub jay remains near its parents' nest is the lack of an available territory for the bird to occupy. Ask students to predict what would happen if a territory were to become available. *(The scrub jay probably would leave its parents' nest. In fact, scientists have observed that this is what occurs if a territory does become available.)*

Phase Three
Assessment Options

Closure

■ **Recognizing Relationships**

Ask students to describe the relationship between two organisms that practice a type of behavior that scientists have termed "reciprocal altruism." *(One organism performs an altruistic act in expectation that the favor will be returned. Such acts of reciprocal altruism have been observed between members of the same species and between organisms of different species.)*

SECTION REVIEW

Assign the *Section Review*.

Reteaching

Assign four students to a cooperative work group. Have each group describe examples of human behaviors that can be classified into the categories of behavior listed in Table 13-1. Ask students to highlight those behaviors that can be classified in two or more categories.

---

in 1964. This mechanism is called **kin selection**. Kin selection occurs when an individual helps relatives (kin) reproduce rather than producing its own offspring. **Figure 13-15** explains the logic underlying kin selection. To understand kin selection, you need to think about meiosis and sexual reproduction. Hamilton realized that relatives share genes in common because of the way gametes form during meiosis and join together during sexual reproduction. Recall that each gamete (sperm or egg) contains only one-half the normal number of chromosomes. One gamete from the male parent joins with one gamete from the female parent to form the fertilized egg, which develops into a new individual. As a result, one-half of an individual's genes come from its mother and one-half come from its father. In other words,

each individual shares one-half of its genes with each parent. Other relatives also share genes. On average, each individual shares one-half of its genes with a full brother or sister, and one-fourth of its genes with an uncle, aunt, half brother, or half sister. The more distantly related two individuals are, the fewer genes they share.

Because relatives have genes in common, an individual can sometimes transmit more copies of its genes to the next generation by helping relatives reproduce than by producing its own offspring. Kin selection explains why worker bees do not reproduce and even give up their lives for the benefit of the hive. They are helping the queen, who is their mother, reproduce. It also explains why a scrub jay would remain with its parents and help raise its brothers and sisters.

Figure 13-15
Each *X* in this pedigree of a scrub jay family represents a chromosome. For simplicity, only one pair of chromosomes for each individual is shown here.

a A young scrub jay can pass on its genes, symbolized as the red and blue chromosomes, by having its own offspring . . .

b . . . or by remaining at its parents' nest and helping raise their offspring, its brothers and sisters.

SECTION REVIEW

1 What is the function of territoriality?

2 List three human nonverbal signals, and describe their functions.

3 Explain how sexual selection accounts for the long tail of the widowbird.

4 Why is the evolution of altruism a puzzle? How does kin selection help solve this puzzle?

ANSWERS TO
SECTION REVIEW

1 Territoriality protects a resource for exclusive use by the individual or group of organisms inhabiting that territory.

2 Answers will vary, but students should describe three gestures, postures, or movements and their presumed meanings. For example, a shrug is an expression of uncertainty.

3 Their long tails make them more attractive to female widowbirds, thus enabling them to father more offspring.

4 The question is, How can altruism evolve if the individuals that have this trait never leave any offspring? The answer can be found in the relatives of the organism practicing altruism. By helping relatives reproduce, the organism can sometimes transmit more copies of its genes to the next generation.

"Ernie! Look what you're doing—take those shoes off!"

Animal Misbehavior

	Key Terms	Summary
13-1 **Evolution of Behavior**	behavior (p. 233) learning (p. 236) imprinting (p. 236)	• Biologists ask two kinds of questions about behavior. "How" questions concern what stimulates a behavior, how it is controlled, and how it is performed. "Why" questions are about why a behavior exists. • Behaviors contribute to an animal's survival and reproduction. Behaviors evolve through natural selection. • Natural selection favors behaviors that are beneficial to individuals. • Learning is the alteration of behavior by experience. Genes and learning interact to shape behavior.
13-2 **Kinds of Behavior**	sexual selection (p. 244) altruism (p. 245) kin selection (p. 246)	• Animals use signals to communicate. Signals can be movements, colors, scents, calls, electrical impulses, or physical contact. • Darwin proposed that traits enabling an individual to attract more mates will evolve, even if they have a negative impact on survival. He called this evolutionary mechanism sexual selection. • Altruism is self-sacrificing behavior. W. D. Hamilton showed that altruism directed toward relatives can be favored by natural selection.

Lions live in cooperative groups called prides.

Female swordtails prefer males with long swords on their tail.

Alternative Assessment

Insect societies, like those of humans, exhibit complex behavioral patterns. Have students use library and on-line references to obtain information about a behavioral pattern exhibited by a particular social insect. Have them prepare a brief written report and share their findings with their classmates.

Portfolio Assessment

Portfolio Assessment on page T39 provides options for building and evaluating student portfolios. Students and teachers can select items from the areas listed on page T39 for inclusion in a portfolio.

247

ANSWER TO
CONCEPT MAP

The following is one possible answer to the Relating Concepts exercise on page 248.

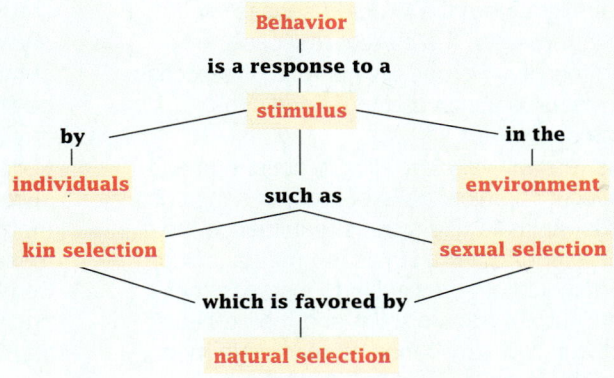

Behavior
is a response to a
stimulus
by — in the
individuals — environment
such as
kin selection — sexual selection
which is favored by
natural selection

review

ANSWERS

Understanding Vocabulary

1. a. In kin selection an animal doesn't reproduce; instead, it helps a relative reproduce. Traits that help attract mates are favored in sexual selection.
b. A behavior is an action by an animal. A stimulus is the factor that triggers behavior.
c. Territoriality is the control of an area or resource. Altruism is self-sacrificing behavior that benefits another.

2. a. rats
b. evolution
c. salivation

Understanding Concepts

3. Concept map answer is shown on page 247.

4. Gulls that remove eggshells lose fewer chicks, and this trait is successfully passed on.

5. "What feature of the eggshell stimulates removal behavior?" "How does the gull remove the eggshell from the nest?" "How does this behavior benefit the gull?" "How did this behavior originate?"

6. He timed male cricket chirping and found that it varied several hours. He selected males that chirped longest and shortest times, allowed them to breed, and evaluated the chirping of their male offspring. He continued this procedure through four generations, producing two distinct chirping groups that differed by nearly 5 hours. Because the difference in chirping was transmitted to offspring, Cade concluded that it had a genetic basis.

7. No, because the two groups did not differ in their ability to complete other mazes.

8. Trial-and-error is accidentally finding the right solution to a problem. For example, a rat in a Skinner box may put its paw on a lever that releases food. The rat will learn to acquire food by pressing the lever. This gives an animal flexibility and allows it to learn responses that are appropriate. The ani-

Understanding Vocabulary

1. For each pair of terms, explain the differences in their meanings.
   a. kin selection, sexual selection
   b. behavior, stimulus
   c. territoriality, altruism

2. For each set of terms, complete the analogy.
   a. Pavlov : dogs :: Tryon : _____
   b. "how" question : mechanisms :: "why" question : _____
   c. stimulus : meat powder :: response : _____

Understanding Concepts

3. **Relating Concepts** Construct a concept map describing animal behavior. Try to use the following terms in your map: behavior, stimulus, natural selection, environment, individuals, kin selection, sexual selection.

4. **Inferring Conclusions** In his studies of black-headed gulls, Niko Tinbergen observed that the gulls removed the empty shells from the nest after the chicks had hatched. Gulls that did not remove the empty shells from the nest lost more chicks to predators. The white inside part of the eggshell attracted predators to the camouflaged nest. Explain how natural selection might favor the removal of empty shells from the nest.

5. **Summarizing Information** List two "how" questions and two "why" questions about the behavior described in question 4.

6. **Recognizing Relationships** Explain William Cade's experiment on crickets. What evidence led him to conclude that the duration of singing in crickets had a genetic basis?

7. **Analyzing Methods** Could Tryon have concluded that the maze-bright rats were better at all kinds of learning than the maze-dull rats? Explain your conclusion.

8. **Inferring Relationships** What is trial-and-error learning? Give one example. Explain how trial-and-error learning can be beneficial to an animal. What are some of the possible drawbacks of trial-and-error learning?

9. **Analyzing Relationships** Assume that natural selection acts on the behavior of territoriality. Identify some of the possible advantages of defending a territory in spite of the fact that doing so consumes energy and increases the risk of injury.

10. **Comparing Functions** Give three examples of different types of animal signals. Explain the function of animal signals in terms of natural selection.

11. **Inferring Relationships** Based on your personal observations of dogs, describe some of the signals dogs use when they meet another dog and when they meet their owner. How do you think these signals influence the behavior of the other dog and the owner?

12. **Summarizing Information** What is sexual selection? Describe how it affects the evolution of behavior.

13. **Comparing Functions** Describe the kinds of male traits that are advantageous for acquiring mates. Give three examples.

14. **Analyzing Methods** A scientist is studying sexual selection in widowbirds. He captures several male widowbirds, cuts off part of their long tail, and releases the birds. He finds that these males mate with half as many females as males that weren't captured. He concludes that female widowbirds prefer males with longer tails. What is an alternative explanation for this observation? How can the scientist alter his experiment to determine which explanation is correct?

15. **Recognizing Relationships** What is altruistic behavior? Give an example of altruistic behavior. Describe W. D. Hamilton's explanation for the evolution of altruistic behavior.

16. **BUILDING WHAT YOU HAVE LEARNED** In Chapter 10 you learned how natural selection causes evolution. Summarize the mechanism of natural selection and explain why behaviors are just as important to survival and reproduction as physical features are.

---

mal might learn the wrong response, or it might not learn the correct response.

9. Territoriality gives an animal exclusive access to resources such as food, living sites, mates, or water.

10. Answers will vary: growling in dogs, human speech, chemical trails of ants, or songs of birds. Animals use signals to influence the behavior of other animals, so natural selection should act on signals to increase their efficiency of transmission and their efficacy.

11. Answers will vary. When strange dogs meet,

they often exchange signals such as barks and a raised tail to determine which dog is dominant. Around its owner, a dog signals to be fed or petted by wagging its tail or barking.

12. It is an evolutionary mechanism in which traits that increase an individual's mating success are favored. The frequency of traits that improve mating success rise, even if these traits decrease the survival rates.

13. Combat-oriented and mate-attracting traits are favored, such as large body size in gorillas, antlers in deer, long tails in widowbirds,

Interpreting Graphics

17. The illustrations below show a chimpanzee that was placed in a room for the first time. Notice the boxes in the room and the bananas hanging over the chimp's head. The type of behavior exhibited by the chimpanzee is called insight.

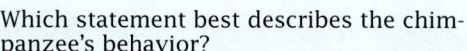

Which statement best describes the chimpanzee's behavior?

a. The chimpanzee stacked boxes to reach the bananas based on past experience.
b. The chimpanzee learned to stack the boxes to reach the bananas.
c. The chimpanzee figured out how to reach the bananas by trial and error.

Explain why you chose the statement you did.

Reviewing Themes

18. *Homeostasis and Stability*
How does a dog's behavior on a hot day help it control its body temperature?

Thinking Critically

19. **Recognizing Logical Inconsistencies** "A child's behavior closely resembles the behavior of its parents. Therefore, most human behaviors are genetically controlled." Explain the logical flaw in this argument.

Life/Work Skills

20. **Working Cooperatively** Prepare a chart with your classmates. On one side list some of the behavior patterns you have read about in this chapter. Now think about human behaviors that are similar to the animal behaviors you just listed. Can you think of an example of human territoriality? human aggression? Think about whether your behavior changes when you are in a group, or with just a few friends. How do you behave with a large group of people you don't know? How are some of our reactions and behaviors similar to the ones you have read about in this chapter?

Activities and Projects

21. **Career Connection: Psychologist** A psychologist studies human behavior and helps people improve their mental health. Find out what a psychologist does on a daily basis. What kind of educational background is required? Where do psychologists usually work?

22. **Art Connection** Honeybees have a sophisticated form of communication many people call the "honeybee dance." Use library references or an on-line database to research how honeybees dance to communicate. Make posters that summarize the honeybee dance. Share the posters with your classmates.

Discovering Through Reading

23. Read the article "Leafcutters: Gardeners of the Ant World" by Mark W. Moffett in *National Geographic*, July 1995, pages 98–111. Explain the ant's relationship with fungi. What positive effect do leafcutter ants have on their environment?

24. Read the article "Scent of a Man" by Sarah Richardson in *Discover*, February 1996, pages 26–27. What are the functions of MHC genes? How did the women in Claus Wedekind's experiment respond to the different T-shirts? How might this response have been favored by natural selection?

249

and-error learning requires repeated responses to a stimulus to learn the correct behavior.

Reviewing Themes

18. To stay cool, a dog seeks out shade and minimizes its movement. It also pants to create evaporative cooling.

Thinking Critically

19. A child may have learned how to behave by imitating its parents.

Life/Work Skills

20. Answers will vary. Students should identify as many human behaviors as possible.

Activities and Projects

21. Counseling patients and helping them with behavioral or mental problems, or research on human behavior. Work places include schools, hospitals, government agencies, and universities. Master's degrees in psychology are common.
22. The round dance consists of circular motions, and the waggle dance resembles a figure eight. Posters should describe how the dance relates the direction and distance to food.

Discovering Through Reading

23. The ants cultivate fungus on leaves to eat it. Native plant species, such as palms, grow from abandoned, collapsed mounds.
24. They help recognize foreign cells and bacteria. They preferred the T-shirts from men with dissimilar MHC genes. It may be a means to prevent inbreeding or increase MHC diversity in offspring. Higher-diversity MHC genes recognize more microorganisms. Couples with similar MHC genes have reduced fertility.

and the swords of swordtails.
14. Capture and handling may have caused abnormal behavior in the widowbirds. Include a control group of captured and manipulated males, whose tails are not cut off or are cut off and then reattached.
15. It is one animal sacrificing itself for another. Examples will vary. Altruistic behavior could evolve if it were directed toward relatives, who share genes with the performer. Therefore, some of the performer's genes can still be transmitted to future generations.

16. Features that improve survival and reproduction are naturally selected. Beneficial features become more common; deleterious features occur less often and may vanish. An animal's behaviors allow it to perform the tasks necessary to survive and procreate.

Interpreting Graphics

17. b. The chimpanzee "recognized" the problem and figured out a solution. It could not have learned this solution before, because it had not seen this problem before. Trial-

Three

The Environment

A GLOBAL GREENHOUSE

Whatever your home address, your universal address is Earth. Each day, CO_2 and other gases in the air above Earth trap most of the sunlight that pours down, allowing the Earth to remain warm enough to sustain life. As the CO_2 admits sunlight and retains heat, it works like a greenhouse!

A World of Convenience

Inside the global greenhouse, you and your family enjoy the conveniences of electronic communication and entertainment, public and private transportation, and a broad array of appliances and labor-saving devices. Ever greater amounts of coal, oil, wood, and other hydrocarbons are burned each time someone flips a switch.

An Uncertain Future

The burning of these common hydrocarbon fuels releases more CO_2 into Earth's atmosphere. As CO_2 levels rise, it's like raising Earth's thermostat—more heat is retained. Scientists predict that Earth's temperature might increase as much in 100 years as it has since the last ice age!

LOOKING AHEAD

- What might someone like Carmen Cid do for you or your future children? See **Career Opportunities: Environmental Science,** page 267.
- How might you and other life-forms be affected if the Earth gets much warmer? See page 293.
- How can you help solve environmental problems? See pages 301–304.
- How can the loss of atmospheric ozone be slowed? See **Science, Technology, and Society: Can the Ozone Layer Be Saved?** pages 308–309.

14 | Ecosystems

Lesson Planning Guide With Options for Block Scheduling

Lecture Concepts	Lesson Resources	

14-1 What Is an Ecosystem?

BLOCK ❶ (45 minutes)

1. Ecology is the study of the relationships between organisms and their environment.

2. An ecosystem is a self-sustaining community and system of habitats.

❶ Lecture Resources
- Determining Prior Knowledge
- Active Reading: Prediction Guide
- Visual Strategy: Figures 14-2, 14-3
- Demonstration: Identifying Functions
- Teaching Transparencies: 82
- Holt Biology Videodiscs Lesson 14-1

Classwork Options
- Rain-Forest Products
- Teaching Resources CD-ROM: Occupational Applications Worksheets 7
- Exploration 14A

Assignment Options
- Environmental Problems
- Life/Work Skills: Being a Team Member

BLOCK ❷ (45 minutes)

3. Food chains and food webs are models that describe energy flow through an ecosystem.

4. An ecological pyramid is a model that shows the amount of energy present at each level within a food chain.

❷ Lecture Resources
- Visual Strategy: Figures 14-4, 14-5, 14-6
- Teaching Transparencies: 84, 85, 67, 68, 69, 77
- Holt Biology Videodiscs Lesson 14-1

Classwork Options
- Closure: Recognizing Relationships
- Quick Labs: Lab A12

Assignment Options
- Reteaching
- Section Review
- Chapter Review, questions 1, 2, 3, 4, 5, 6, 7, 8, 9, 17, 19
- Directed Reading Worksheet

14-2 Cycles Within Ecosystems

BLOCK ❸ (45 minutes)

1. Materials, including nitrogen, water, and carbon, are passed through ecosystems in delicate cycles.

❸ Lecture Resources
- Active Reading: Paired Reading
- Visual Strategy: Figures 14-8, 14-10
- Waste Management
- Teaching Transparencies: 73
- Holt Biology Videodiscs Lesson 14-2

Classwork Options
- Inquiry Skills Development: Lab B10

Assignment Options
- Teaching Resources CD-ROM: Occupational Applications Worksheets 16

BLOCK ❹ (45 minutes)

2. The burning of fossil fuels is upsetting the carbon cycle and warming the atmosphere in a phenomenon known as the greenhouse effect.

❹ Lecture Resources
- Visual Strategy: Figure 14-11
- Teaching Transparencies: 71, 72
- Holt Biology Videodiscs Lesson 14-2

Classwork Options
- Closure: Relating Concepts
- Laboratory Techniques and Experimental Design: Lab C22

Assignment Options
- Reteaching
- Section Review
- Chapter Review, questions 10, 11, 12, 20, 21, 22, 23
- Directed Reading Worksheet

14-3 Kinds of Ecosystems

BLOCK ❺ (45 minutes)

1. Freshwater ecosystems include lakes, ponds, and rivers.

2. The major types of terrestrial ecosystems are tropical rain forest, savanna, desert, temperate grassland, deciduous forest, coniferous forest, and tundra.

❺ Lecture Resources
- Terrestrial Ecosystems
- Visual Strategy: Videodisc
- Demonstration: Observing Organisms
- Teaching Transparencies: 65
- Holt Biology Videodiscs Lesson 14-3

Classwork Options
- Life/Work Skills: Communicating

Assignment Options
- Life/Work Skills: Finding Information

Lecture Concepts

Lesson Resources

14-3 Kinds of Ecosystems, *continued*

BLOCK ❻ (45 minutes)
3. Ocean ecosystems include shallow ocean waters, open ocean surfaces, and deep ocean waters.

❻ Lecture Resources
■ Hydrothermal Vent
■ Visual Strategy: Figure 14-13
■ Teaching Transparencies: 79
⊘ Holt Biology Videodiscs Lesson 14-3
Classwork Options
■ Reteaching
■ Closure: Summarizing Information

Assignment Options
■ Section Review
■ Chapter Review, questions 13, 14, 15, 16, 18, 24
■ Directed Reading Worksheet

Chapter Review and Assessment

BLOCK ❼ (45 minutes)
Review
■ Reteaching Worksheet
■ Thinking Skills Worksheet
■ Vocabulary Development Worksheet
⊙ Language Development and Reading Comprehension Audio CD Program: Chapter 14

BLOCK ❽ (45 minutes)
Assessment
■ Alternative Assessment, p. 269
■ Portfolio Assessment, p. T39
Chapter Test
■ Chapter 14 Test
Test Generator
⊙ Item bank for customizing Chapter Tests

Teaching Resources CD-ROM
⊙ Scoring Rubrics and Classroom Management Checklist

The Portfolio icon denotes items throughout the Teacher's Edition lesson wrap that may be selected for inclusion in student portfolios.

Holt Biology Videodiscs and *Concepts of Biology*

Holt Biology Videodiscs gives you a powerful tool for teaching, review, and assessment. For further information regarding the media on the videodiscs, see *Holt Biology Videodiscs Teacher's Correlation Guide to Holt Biology: Visualizing Life.*

Concepts of Biology adds interactive lesson plans and extensive tools for customization using CD-ROM technology.

Use the following topic from **Concepts of Biology** to help you teach this chapter:
Topic 10: Ecosystem Structure and Function

Laboratory Planning

Text
Materials and preparation instructions appear on the teacher's wrap accompanying each laboratory exercise.
Block 1: Exploration 14A: Modeling an Ecosystem, p. 788

Holt BioSources Laboratory Program
Block 2: Quick Labs Lab A12: Making a Food Web
Block 3: Inquiry Skills Development Lab B10: Ecology Scavenger Hunt
Block 4: Laboratory Techniques and Experimental Design Lab C22: Examining Owl Pellets

Determining Prior Knowledge

- Have students provide examples of environmental problems of global concern. What are we doing to solve these problems?
- Display a diagram of a simple food web (grass, mosquito, mouse, bat, snake). Ask students what it represents. Ask them to identify producers, herbivores, carnivores, direction of energy flow, and what habitat is represented by this model.
- Ask students to discuss how carbon or water might move through an ecosystem. Ask them to define a cycle.
- Show students a picture of a greenhouse. Have them explain how the air inside is warmed. Ask them what traps the heat inside. Ask them what the greenhouse effect is.

Active READING

● **Technique: Prediction Guide**

Before students begin this chapter, write the following statements on the chalkboard or overhead.

1. The most important factor determining how many and what kinds of organisms live in an ecosystem is the amount of water available.
2. There is more energy stored in plants than in heterotrophs in an ecosystem.
3. The extinction of one species in an ecosystem can impact all other species.

Let the students think a minute about each statement and decide if they agree with it. Have students read the chapter to see if their opinions are confirmed.

CD-ROM Resources

Concepts of Biology
Topic 10: Ecosystem Structure and Function

CHAPTER **14**

REVIEW
- metabolism (Section 5-1)
- photosynthesis (Section 5-3)
- cellular respiration (Section 5-4)

Ecosystems

14-1 What Is an Ecosystem?

14-2 Cycles Within Ecosystems

14-3 Kinds of Ecosystems

This desert vegetation is growing in Organ Pipe Cactus National Monument, Arizona.

252

Author's Rationale   To study the environment from an issues perspective, a thorough knowledge of ecosystems is necessary. This chapter explains how ecosystems function as dynamic machines that cycle nutrients and process energy—two major biological themes. The chapter ends with the role that the climate plays in shaping the characteristics of each type of ecosystem.

You cannot pick up a newspaper today without seeing news about the environment. Environmental issues are important because we all have to live in a world we seem to be destroying. We need detailed knowledge of how the world works so that we can prevent further abuse to our planet and perhaps begin to repair the damage we have already done.

14-1 What Is an Ecosystem?

OBJECTIVES

1 Identify the components of an ecosystem.

2 Discuss the flow of energy through ecosystems.

3 Identify the different trophic levels in an ecosystem.

4 Explain why ecosystems can contain only a few trophic levels.

State of Our World

Nearly 6 billion humans live on Earth. Scientists estimate that at least 10 million other species share the world with us. Yet we seem to be rapidly destroying our planet's ability to support us and its other inhabitants. Here are a few changes humans will make to the Earth *in the next year.* About 17 million hectares (40 million acres) of forest will be burned down or cut, like the forest shown in **Figure 14-1**. That is an area almost as large as the state of Washington. The world's human population will increase by about 88 million people, an amount nearly equal to the population of Mexico. Most of these 88 million people will be born in the world's poorest countries. Worldwide, there are already nearly 500 million people who are not adequately nourished.

For centuries people have believed that the environment was there for them to use as they saw fit. But today's environmental problems teach us that the environment is not a passive stage on which we can act as we please. Rather, we share the environment with other organisms, resulting in a complex network of interactions on which we all depend. Changes made to the environment can have serious consequences, not all of which are predictable.

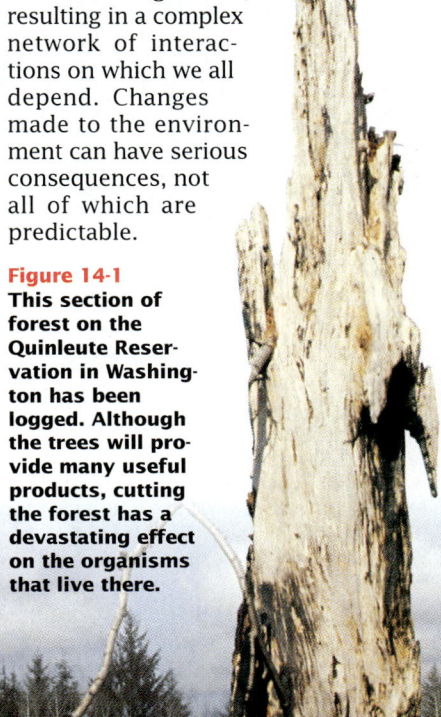

Figure 14-1
This section of forest on the Quinleute Reservation in Washington has been logged. Although the trees will provide many useful products, cutting the forest has a devastating effect on the organisms that live there.

253

Phase One
Preparation

Scheduling
See the **Lesson Planning Guide** on pages 251A and 251B for lecture, classwork, and assignment options for Section 14-1.

Phase Two
Teaching Strategy

Environmental Problems
■ **Relating Concepts**
Ask students to bring in newspaper or magazine articles about current environmental problems. Have each student summarize each article, stating both the problem and the possible solution. Ask the student to identify the parts of an ecosystem that are affected by the problem. Then have students form cooperative groups. Have each group choose a problem it considers to be the most significant. Have each group create a posterboard exhibit summarizing the problem and its effects on all levels of organisms in the environment. Encourage students to find relationships among the different groups of problems and explain how they interact.

Key to Strategies
Teaching Strategies are keyed to three tiers of learning.
● **Understanding Concepts (Tier I)**
Content mastery and comprehension
■ **Applying Information (Tier II)**
Applying and analyzing content
▲ **Critical Thinking (Tier III)**
Practicing evaluative thinking

Figure 14-2
The inhabitants of this soil ecosystem include earthworms, insects, snakes, moles, bacteria, and a variety of plants and fungi.

Ecology and Ecosystems

In 1866, the German biologist Ernst Haeckel gave a name to the study of how organisms fit into their environment. He called it **ecology**, from the Greek words *oikos*, meaning "house, place where one lives," and *logos*, meaning "study of." Ecology, then, is the study of the "house" in which we live. Most of our environmental problems could be avoided if we treated the world in which we live the same way we treat our own homes.

Ecology is the study of the interactions of organisms with one another and with their physical environment. The organisms that live in a particular place, such as a forest, are known as a **community**. Ecologists, the scientists who specialize in ecology, call the physical location of a community its **habitat**. You can think of a habitat as a neighborhood and of a community as the residents of the neighborhood. The sum of the community and habitat is called an ecological system, or ecosystem. An **ecosystem** is a self-sustaining collection of organisms and their physical environment.

Imagine that you could collect every organism living in an ecosystem. **Figure 14-2** shows just some of the inhabitants of a soil ecosystem. If you visited a tropical rain forest, you could collect many more species than occur in this soil ecosystem. As many as 100 species of trees can be found in a patch of South American rain forest about the size of two football fields. The **diversity** of an ecosystem is a measure of the number of species living there. Tropical rain forests are the most diverse terrestrial ecosystems.

Matter of Fact: Species Diversity

A single acre in New Hampshire may have 8 species of trees, while the same amount of land in a tropical rain forest may have 120.

Figure 14-3
An ecological model can predict how an ecosystem, such as this pond, responds to disturbance.

Why Study Ecology?

You study ecology because you need to know about the place in which you live. If you are going to prevent pollution, conserve resources, and help preserve the world for your children to live in, then you need to know how your world works—just as you need to study how any complex machine works in order to keep it running properly. Do you think a car would run for long if its owner had no idea of the need for water, oil, and gasoline? Remember that there is a fundamental difference between a car and an ecosystem, however. A car that receives no care from its owner will eventually break down. Ecosystems, on the other hand, normally function without human tending. But some ecosystems now require our help because we have caused them great damage.

Ecosystems are very complex

It is very difficult to understand how an ecosystem works because it can contain hundreds or even thousands of interacting species. Nevertheless, you can gain a basic understanding of how an ecosystem works by asking two questions: Where does the energy come from that is needed by particular animals and plants? and How do organisms in ecosystems acquire adequate amounts of the minerals and other inorganic substances they need?

Answering these questions will give you a pretty good idea of how an ecosystem normally works. You will then be in a position to ask how an ecosystem might be expected to respond to a disturbance. To make such predictions, ecologists build a model, a simplified version of the ecosystem. An ecosystem model consists of a series of hypotheses that describe how the ecosystem functions: how energy moves through the ecosystem, how species interact, and so on. In some cases, ecologists express their models as mathematical equations and then solve these equations for various situations. **Figure 14-3** is a schematic representation of an ecological model.

Because ecosystems are so complex, no model can consider all of the factors that affect an ecosystem. Nevertheless, seeing what happens to the ecosystem model when a variable is changed helps ecologists predict what might happen if some component of the real ecosystem were altered. If, for example, one species in an ecosystem becomes extinct or the amount of available energy declines, an ecological model can help scientists predict the possible consequences. Ecological models may allow you to look into the future, but your vision can be only as accurate as the information and assumptions used to build the model.

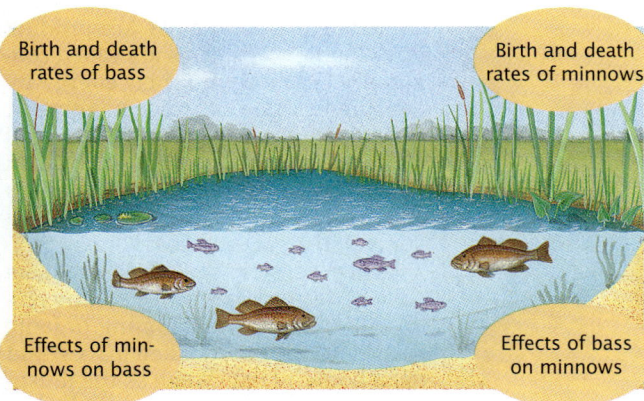

a A scientist making a model of this ecosystem might consider the factors shown in the yellow ovals.

Birth and death rates of bass

Birth and death rates of minnows

Effects of minnows on bass

Effects of bass on minnows

b The model predicts that a disturbance, such as a disease that affects minnows, would cause the number of bass to decrease.

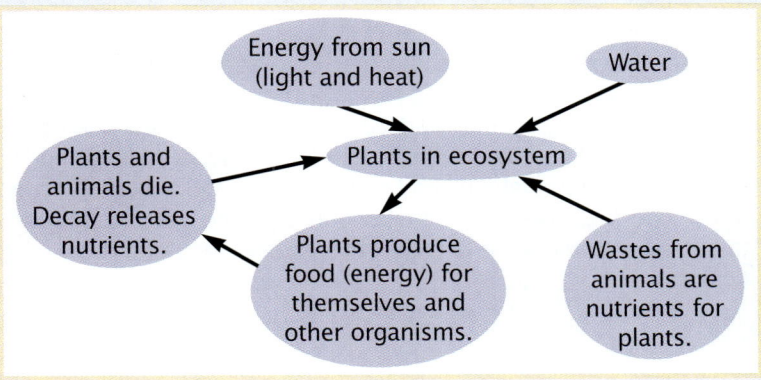

Energy from sun (light and heat)

Water

Plants in ecosystem

Plants and animals die. Decay releases nutrients.

Plants produce food (energy) for themselves and other organisms.

Wastes from animals are nutrients for plants.

Connection: *Chapter 5*

Photosynthesis

Review the major features of photosynthesis and cellular respiration so that students can appreciate the role of producers in a food chain. Point out the circularity of CO_2 and O_2 in photosynthesis and cellular respiration.

Visual Strategy Figure 14-4

● **Interpreting Graphics**
Have students identify the producers and consumers in the food chain. *(The algae are producers, while whale, seal, cod, and krill are consumers).* Have students describe what would happen if all the cod were removed from this particular ecosystem by fishermen. *(The krill population would increase for a time, at the algae's expense).* Ask students why killer whales would have more than one kind of prey? *(If the number of leopard seals decreased, killer whales would starve unless they had alternative food sources. Some kinds of organisms are extreme specialists and feed on only one kind of prey.)*

Visual Strategy Figure 14-5

● **Identifying Relationships**
Remind students that mushrooms are heterotrophic fungi. Point out that by breaking down dead organisms and organic material, decomposers return nutrients to the soil to be reused by other members of the ecosystem. Ask the students how they benefit by decomposers recycling nutrients in the environment. *(Some students will say that they eat some fungi, while others will recognize that they eat either the producers that use the recycled nutrients or the consumers that eat those producers.)*

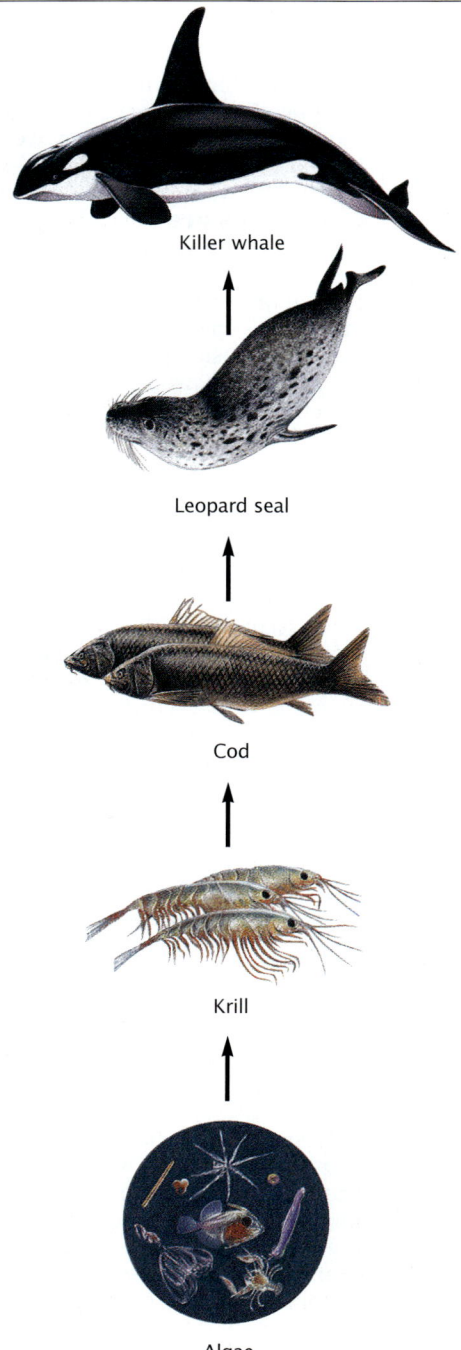

Killer whale

Leopard seal

Cod

Krill

Algae

Figure 14-4
This food chain shows a path of energy transfer in an ocean ecosystem. Algae, which are photosynthetic, are the producers in this ecosystem. Krill, cod, leopard seals, and killer whales are consumers.

256

Energy in Ecosystems

An ecosystem needs energy because its living members use energy. A flower blooming, a squirrel running along a tree branch, a worm burrowing through the soil—every action of even the tiniest creature requires energy. The most important factor determining how many and what kinds of organisms live in an ecosystem is the amount of energy available.

How do the organisms in an ecosystem obtain energy? Life exists because organisms called **producers** take in energy from their surroundings and store it in complex molecules. Nearly all producers are photosynthetic; they capture the sun's energy to synthesize carbohydrates. Plants, some bacteria, and algae are producers. All other organisms are called **consumers**. They obtain their energy by consuming other organisms. Animals, most protists and bacteria, and all fungi are consumers. The food chain in **Figure 14-4** shows how energy is transferred from producers to consumers in an ocean ecosystem.

Each ecosystem contains consumers called **decomposers**. Decomposers obtain energy by consuming organic wastes (feces, urine, fallen leaves) and dead bodies. Fungi, such as the mushrooms shown in **Figure 14-5**, and some species of bacteria, are decomposers.

Figure 14-5
These scarlet waxy cap mushrooms are decomposers.

Matter of Fact: Florida Everglades

Florida's Everglades, once considered an eyesore and a breeding ground for mosquitoes and alligators, is now recognized as a regional resource. The Everglades were once drained for farmland, but we now know that the Everglades are a unique estuarine ecosystem. This ecosystem contains dozens of species of rare birds as well as the endangered Florida panther. Agricultural pollution is destroying offshore coral reefs and fish and is hurting commercial and recreational fishing. Most important, fresh water that should sink into the underground aquifer is instead rushing out to sea as a result of the shrinking Everglades. Today, laws are being proposed to reverse past policies.

Interdependence

If pollution drastically reduced the number of algae in the food web shown below, would killer whales be affected? Explain.

Energy flows from producers to consumers

To follow the movement of energy through an ecosystem, ecologists assign each organism to a **trophic** (feeding) **level**. All members of a trophic level are the same number of energy-transferring steps away from the sun. Producers, such as plants, are in the first trophic level. Plants and other organisms that make their own food are called **autotrophs**. Animals that eat plants are in the second trophic level. Animals that feed on plant eaters are in the third trophic level.

Creatures in the second trophic level are **herbivores** (plant eaters). Cows, caterpillars, elephants, and ducks are herbivores. All organisms at the third trophic level or above are **carnivores**

(flesh eaters). Carnivores at the third level feed on herbivores, while carnivores above the third trophic level feed on other carnivores. Tigers, hawks, weasels, pelicans, and killer whales are carnivores. Some animals cannot be classified as either carnivores or herbivores. **Omnivores**, such as bears and humans, eat both plants and animals. Because they cannot make their own food, organisms in trophic levels above the first trophic level are **heterotrophs**.

Most animals feed at more than one trophic level and feed on several different species at each trophic level. As shown in **Figure 14-6**, energy moves through an ecosystem in a complex network of feeding relationships called a food web. Notice that the food chain in **Figure 14-4** is just one part of this food web.

Figure 14-6
This food web shows how energy flows through an ocean ecosystem as one organism is eaten by another.

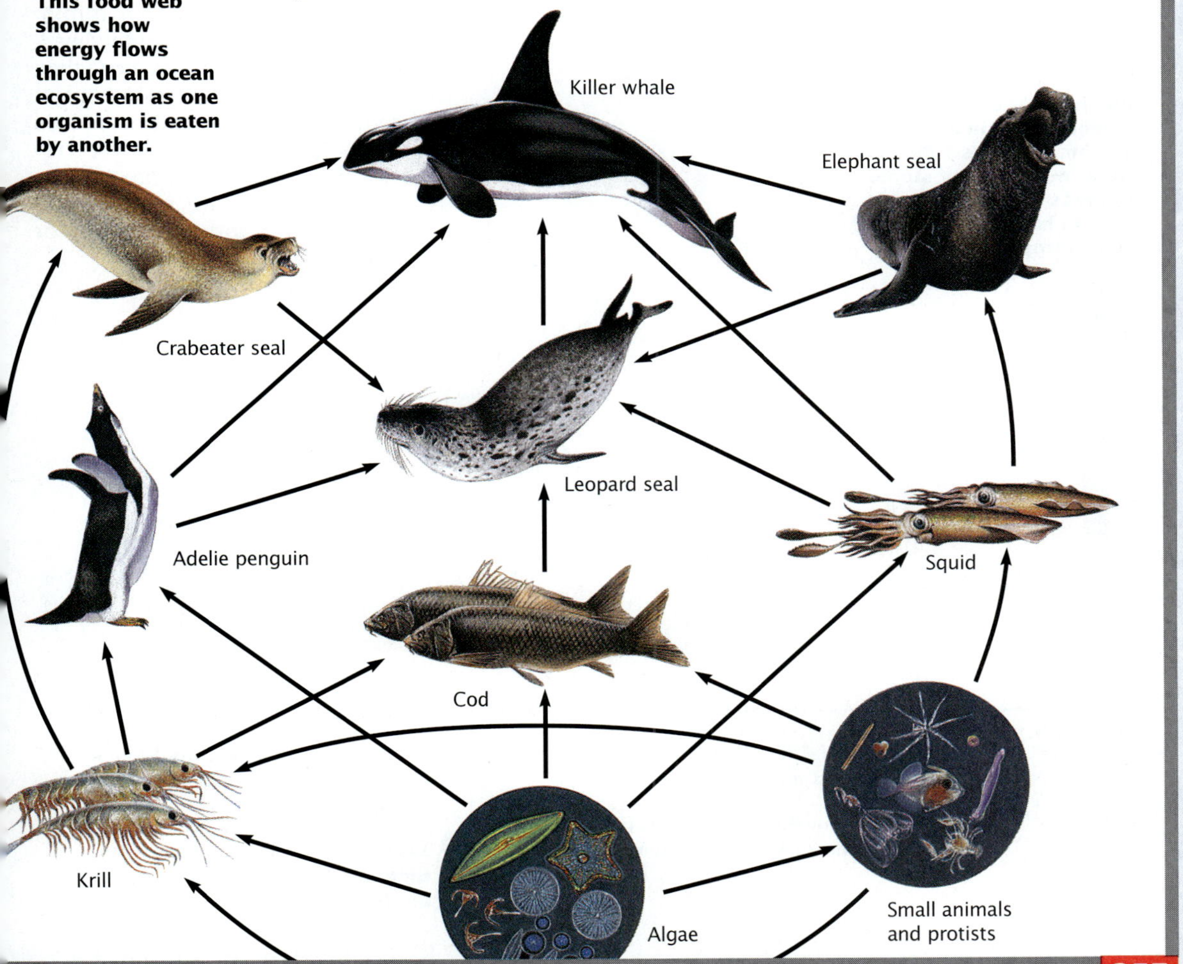

Killer whale

Elephant seal

Crabeater seal

Leopard seal

Adelie penguin

Squid

Cod

Krill

Algae

Small animals and protists

257

Matter of Fact: Geoengineering

In July 1988, John Martin of the Moss Landing Marine Lab in California suggested that iron was a limited resource for algal growth in deep oceans. In 1993, Kenneth Coale and his associates of Moss Landing Marine Lab added iron to the Pacific ocean near the Galapagos Islands and briefly produced an algal bloom. The zooplankton rapidly consumed the algae, thus ending the bloom. In 1995, a second attempt was made at adding iron to the ocean, but this time it was added slowly over several days, to avoid predation of algae by zooplankton. Scientists estimated that 1 ton of iron resulted in the removal of 10,000 tons of CO_2 from the air. While some scientists think this could be a solution to global warming, others worry that a large algal bloom could cause anaerobic conditions in the water that would generate another greenhouse gas—methane.

Matter, Energy, and Organization

More food would be available for the growing human population if humans did not eat meat. Explain why.

How Many Trophic Levels Can an Ecosystem Contain?

A plant absorbs energy from the sun and uses it to make carbohydrates such as cellulose, the major component of cell walls. Only about one-half of the energy captured by a plant becomes part of the plant body, however. Part of the remaining energy is stored in ATP made during cellular respiration. Most of the remaining energy escapes as heat. Similar losses of energy occur at each trophic level of an ecosystem.

In the 1950s, the ecologist Howard Odum determined how much energy was present at each trophic level in a Florida stream ecosystem. He captured animals and plants, measured their energy content, and built a model of how energy passed through the ecosystem. Odum found that when a herbivore eats a plant, only about 10 percent of the energy present in the plant's molecules ends up in the herbivore's molecules. The other 90 percent of the energy is "lost," some as the cost of doing work (breathing, moving, chewing) and much more as heat. Likewise, when a carnivore eats the herbivore, only 10 percent of the energy in the herbivore goes toward making carnivore molecules. At each trophic level, the energy stored in the organisms is about one-tenth that of the level below it.

One way ecologists show the declining amount of energy at higher trophic levels is by drawing a diagram called an ecological pyramid, shown in **Figure 14-7**. Because energy diminishes at each successive trophic level, few ecosystems can contain more than five trophic levels. Also, organisms at higher trophic levels tend to be less numerous than those at lower trophic levels. On the African plains, for instance, there are about 1,000 zebras, gazelles, and wildebeest for each lion.

Figure 14-7
This ecological pyramid shows the amount of energy (indicated by red numbers) at each of four trophic levels in an ecosystem. There is 1,000 times more energy stored in grass at the first level than in hawks at the fourth trophic level.

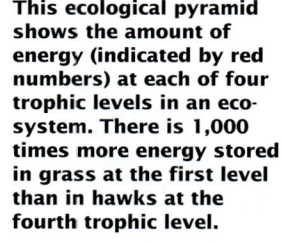

Trophic Level

4 10

3 100

2 1,000

1 10,000

SECTION REVIEW

❶ **What is the difference between a habitat and a community?**

❷ **Explain the important role producers play in ecosystems.**

❸ **In which trophic level would you place humans? Explain your answer.**

❹ **Suggest an explanation for why there are fewer lions than zebras on the African plains.**

Newspapers, aluminum cans, plastic bottles, and many other products can be recycled and used again. Likewise, the physical components of an ecosystem are used again and again. Ecologists call this continual reuse "cycling." Materials that cycle within ecosystems include nitrogen, water, and carbon.

14-2 Cycles Within Ecosystems

OBJECTIVES

1 Describe the results of Bormann and Likens's experiments.

2 Describe how nitrogen and water are recycled within ecosystems.

3 Explain the role of plants in the cycling of materials within ecosystems.

4 Trace the pathway of carbon between living organisms and the environment.

Nutrient Cycles

Unlike energy, which flows through an ecosystem, nutrients such as calcium and nitrogen circulate within an ecosystem. To study how nutrients cycle, a team of scientists led by ecologists Herbert Bormann and Gene Likens carried out studies at Hubbard Brook in New Hampshire beginning in the 1960s. Bormann and Likens wanted to determine if rainwater removed nutrients from ecosystems. They built small dams so that they could measure how much water left the ecosystem in the stream at the base of the valley. They found that water leaving the ecosystem contained few nutrients. They concluded that the trees very efficiently prevented nutrients from leaving the ecosystem.

Having built an ecological model, Bormann and Likens were able to make predictions about what would happen if the ecosystem were disturbed. For example, they knew that nutrients such as calcium were held by the trees of the forest. Their ecological model predicted that much more calcium would be lost if the trees were cut down.

Bormann and Likens test their model of nutrient cycling

To test their ecological model, Bormann and Likens cut the trees and vegetation from one portion of the forest. For several years they monitored the levels of calcium and other nutrients in the water that drained from the forest into Hubbard Brook. The ecosystem lost the ability to retain nutrients. The runoff of calcium, for example, was six times greater than it had been before the trees were cut, as shown in **Figure 14-8**. Other studies have confirmed that minerals and other nutrients pass from organisms to their habitat and back again in delicate cycles that are easily disturbed.

Figure 14-8
Herbert Bormann and Gene Likens found that removing the vegetation from an ecosystem greatly reduced its ability to recycle nutrients such as calcium.

Forest Uncut

Rate of calcium loss

Forest Cut

Rate of calcium loss

259

Videodisc Resources

Holt Biology Videodiscs

Lesson 14-2: Cycles Within Ecosystems

14-2

Phase One
Preparation

Scheduling
See the **Lesson Planning Guide** on pages 251A and 251B for lecture, classwork, and assignment options for Section 14-2.

Phase Two
Teaching Strategies

Waste Management
● **Organizing Information**

Discuss with students the similarity between nutrient cycling by nature and waste recycling by humans. Arrange for the class to visit a solid-waste management or recycling center. Students should expect to learn how material is treated, how the solids are processed, and how the product is used. Students should be prepared to interview the personnel, and they may want to produce a videotape of their visit or write a report. They could prepare a persuasive argument to convince other students to recycle. They should include segments on each aspect described above.

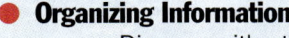

Visual Strategy | Figure 14-8

■ **Analyzing Information**
Have the students explain why the rate of calcium loss is higher in the cut forest. *(Trees extract calcium from soil and store it, thus keeping it in the habitat. If the trees are cut, then calcium can be eroded out of the area.)*

Key to Strategies
● **Understanding Concepts (Tier I)**
■ **Applying Information (Tier II)**
▲ **Critical Thinking (Tier III)**

Active READING

Technique: Paired Reading

Pair each student with a partner. Have one student read about the nitrogen cycle silently. As they read, have them make a check mark on a sticky note next to the passages they understand and a question mark next to passages they find confusing. After they finish reading, ask one student to summarize what he or she understood, referring to the text when needed. The second student should add anything omitted. The second student should continue the discussion by pointing out passages that he or she did not understand. The first reader should help the second with ideas that were unclear and discuss passages that he or she did not understand. Both readers should then work together to come to an understanding of the passages that neither understood. Have them create a list of questions to ask the class. Have students repeat this process for the water and carbon cycles.

Connection: *Chapter 9*

Gene Technology

Review how genetic engineering is being used to develop crops that will carry out nitrogen fixation without the help of symbiotic bacteria.

Bacteria play a key role in the nitrogen cycle

Organisms must have nitrogen to produce proteins and nucleic acids. **Figure 14-9** shows how nitrogen cycles through an ecosystem in the northeastern United States. As you learned in Chapter 9, most living things cannot use the nitrogen gas in the air. The two nitrogen atoms of a molecule of nitrogen gas are held together by a strong chemical bond that is difficult to break. The variety of life found on Earth is possible only because a few kinds of bacteria have enzymes that can break this strong bond. Nitrogen atoms are then free to bond with hydrogen atoms to form ammonia molecules. Conversion of nitrogen gas to ammonia is called **nitrogen fixation**. Ammonia is a form of nitrogen that plants can absorb and use to make proteins. Since animals cannot absorb nitrogen from the soil, they must obtain nitrogen by eating plants or other animals.

Nitrogen-fixing bacteria live in the soil or within the roots of plants such as peas, clover, alfalfa, beans, and alder trees. Because nitrogen is such an important nutrient, the growth of plants in ecosystems is often severely limited by shortages of nitrogen in the soil.

When an organism dies, the nitrogen in its body is released by decomposers. Animal wastes, such as dung and urine, and plant materials, such as leaves and bark, also contain nitrogen. These materials are also broken down by decomposers. Thus, decomposers play a vital role in ecosystems by returning nitrogen to the soil. Some kinds of bacteria absorb nitrogen compounds from the soil and convert them to nitrogen gas, thereby completing the nitrogen cycle.

Figure 14-9
White-tailed deer and alder play important roles in the nitrogen cycle of an ecosystem found in the northeastern United States.

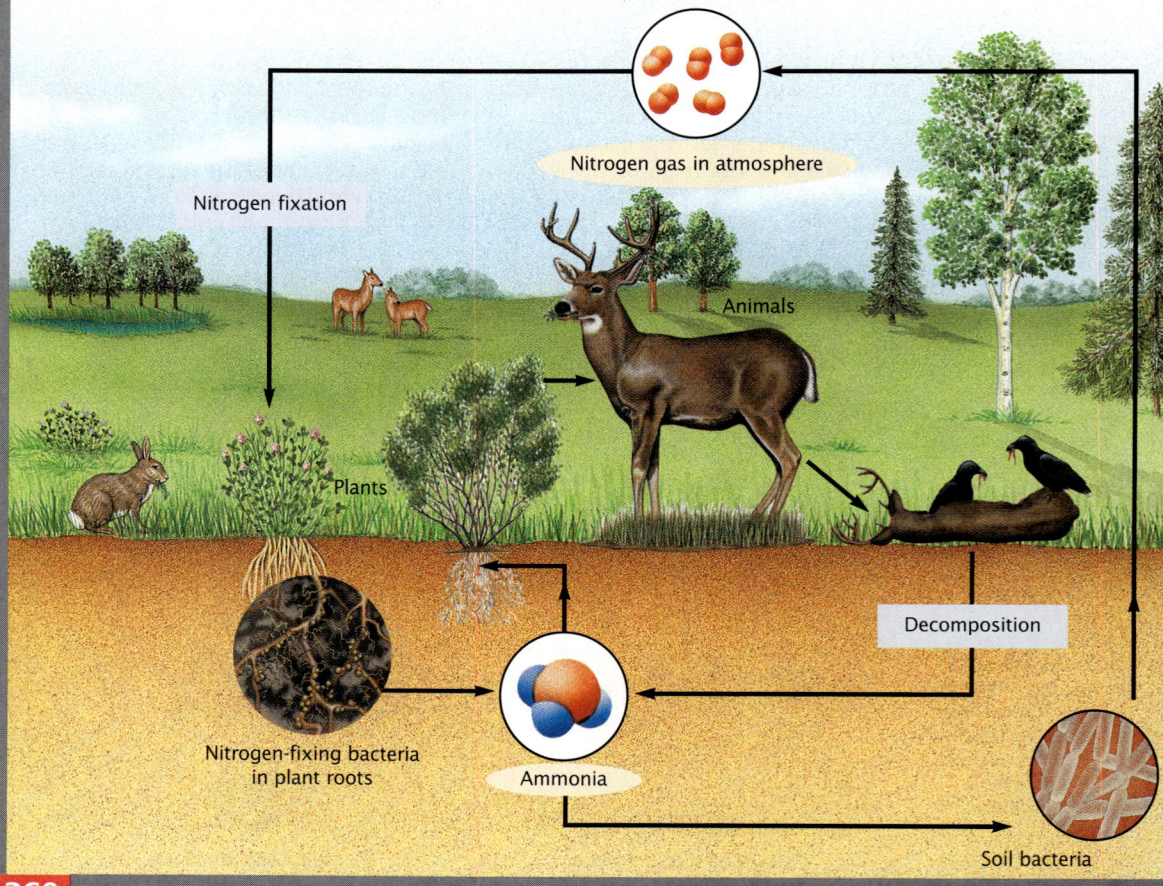

Nitrogen gas in atmosphere

Nitrogen fixation

Animals

Plants

Nitrogen-fixing bacteria in plant roots

Ammonia

Decomposition

Soil bacteria

Matter of Fact: Ecological Impact

The greatest impact of cutting down trees in the Hubbard Brook ecosystem was seen in the nitrogen cycle. In the undisturbed forest areas, the ecosystem accumulated nitrogen at the rate of about 2 kg (5.5 lb) per hectare (about 2.5 acres) per year. Where the trees had been cut, nitrogen was lost from the soil at the rate of about 120 kg per hectare (about 650 lb per acre) per year.

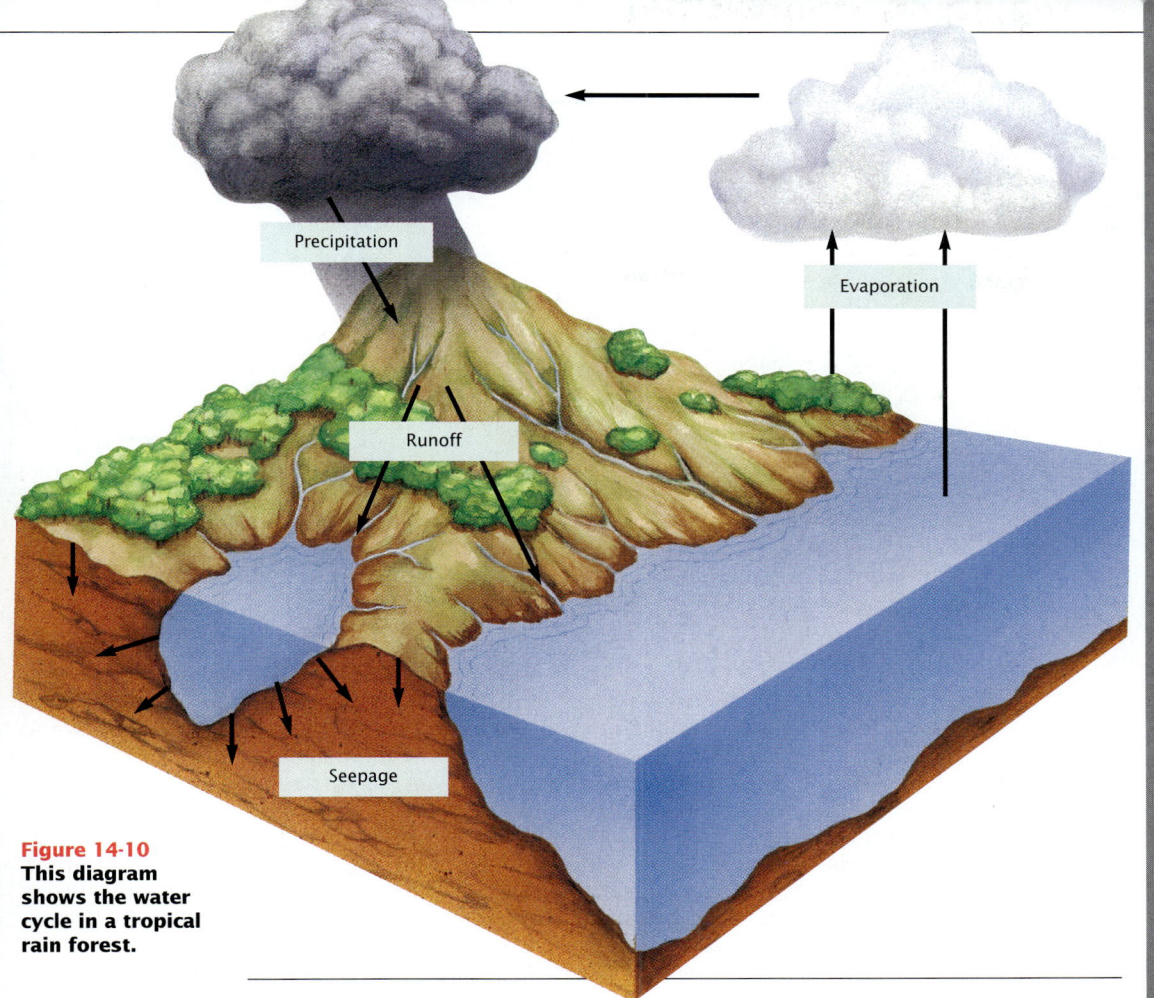

Figure 14-10
This diagram shows the water cycle in a tropical rain forest.

Visual Strategy   Figure 14-10

● **Interpreting Graphs**
Explain to students that the driving force behind the water cycle is the sun. Most of the water returned to the atmosphere by evaporation comes from the oceans.

Language Arts Connection

Food Web Essay
American naturalist John Muir said, "When we try to pick out anything by itself we find it hitched to everything else in the universe." Have students explain what Muir meant, using their knowledge of food webs and nutrient cycles.

Water Cycle

Water is perhaps the most important nonliving component of an ecosystem. To a large degree, availability of water determines the diversity of organisms in an ecosystem. For example, fewer species live in the desert, where there is little water, than in the tropical rain forest, where water is plentiful. Water is constantly cycling within ecosystems. The water cycle is illustrated in **Figure 14-10**.

Plants play an important role in the water cycle

In tropical rain forests, where there are dense concentrations of trees and other plants, more than 90 percent of the moisture that enters the ecosystem passes through plants and evaporates from their leaves. In a very real sense, these plants create their own rain.

When forests are cut down, the water cycle is broken. Moisture cannot be returned to the atmosphere by plants. Instead, water drains into streams and rivers and eventually flows into the ocean. Moreover, without protection from the roots of trees and other plants, the soil is easily carried away by runoff. As a result, nutrient cycles also are broken. Because neither water nor nutrients can cycle in a forest ecosystem after the trees are cut down, extensive cutting can convert lush forests into deserts. Tragically, such a transformation is presently occurring in many tropical rain forests.

Multicultural Perspective: Old-Fashioned Recycling

In many cultures it is not unusual for farmers to use dung and urine as fertilizer for their crops. Although this form of recycling is performed in the United States, the use of human waste is fairly uncommon and unsanitary. Parasites, viruses, and bacteria, which can be pathogenic, are likely to find their way back into the food chain and infect new individuals who consume the produce. In developing countries, where recycling of human waste is common, care must be taken to cleanse fresh produce thoroughly before eating, because a lettuce leaf might harbor dysentery, tapeworms, or hookworms. In the United States, dung from horses and cows is likely to become garden fertilizer.

Key to Strategies
● **Understanding Concepts (Tier I)**
■ **Applying Information (Tier II)**
▲ **Critical Thinking (Tier III)**

▲ **Evaluating Results**

Because combustion adds more CO_2 to the atmosphere than plants can use, the carbon cycle is no longer balanced. CO_2 levels are higher than they have been in 160,000 years. Ask students what this does to our global temperatures. *(Increased CO_2 causes more heat to be absorbed in our atmosphere. If temperatures rise too high, the climatic changes might have a devastating effect on agriculture.)*

Phase Three

Assessment Options

Closure

■ **Relating Concepts**

Using components found in Figure 14-11, have students diagram how oxygen cycles through an ecosystem. Ask students how the oxygen cycle relates photosynthesis to respiration? *(The oxygen cycle is a summary of two processes, showing how oxygen is taken up by respiration and given off by photosynthesis.)*

SECTION REVIEW

Assign the *Section Review.*

Reteaching

Have students develop concept maps for each of the cycles in this section. *(Answers will vary but should include the key concepts of each nutrient cycle and the names of representative organisms. Students should show that they understand how the cycles are balanced.)*

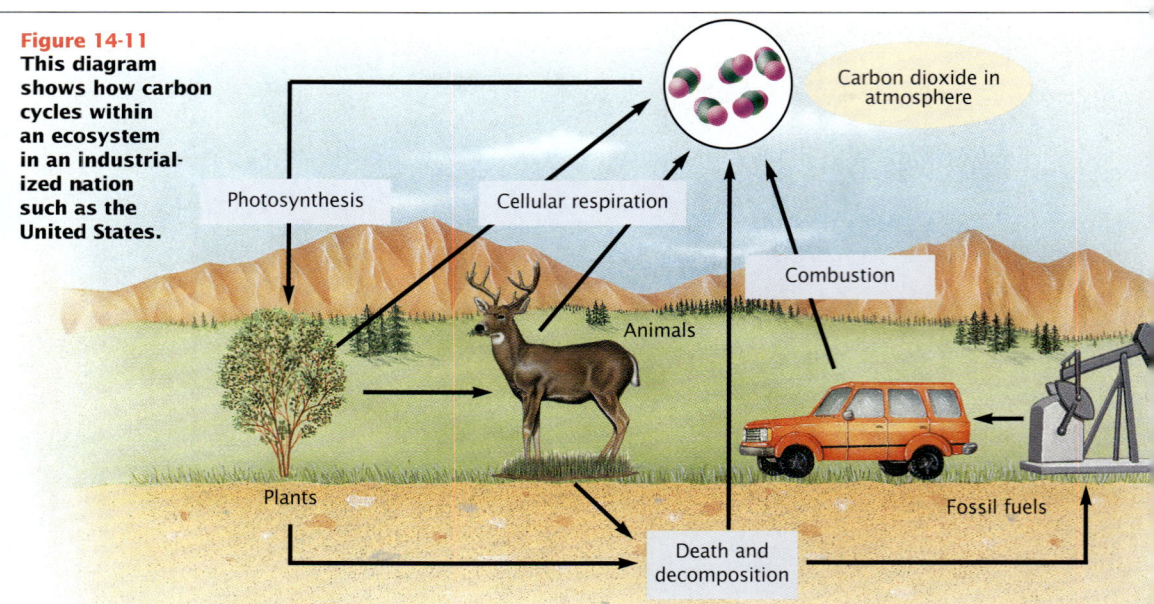

Figure 14-11
This diagram shows how carbon cycles within an ecosystem in an industrialized nation such as the United States.

Photosynthesis   Cellular respiration   Combustion   Carbon dioxide in atmosphere   Animals   Plants   Fossil fuels   Death and decomposition

Carbon Cycle

Like water, carbon also cycles between the nonliving environment and organisms. The Earth's atmosphere contains carbon in the form of carbon dioxide. Plants use carbon dioxide to build organic molecules during photosynthesis. Consumers obtain energy-rich molecules that contain carbon by eating plants or other animals. As these molecules are broken down, carbon dioxide is produced and released into the Earth's atmosphere. Cellular respiration by decomposers and photosynthetic organisms also returns carbon dioxide to the atmosphere. **Figure 14-11** shows how carbon cycles within an ecosystem.

Humans are overloading the carbon cycle

Large amounts of carbon are tied up in wood and may stay trapped there for hundreds of years, returning to the atmosphere only when the wood decomposes or is burned. Over millions of years, organisms that become buried in sediment may be gradually transformed into fossil fuels such as coal, oil, and natural gas. The carbon originally trapped by these organisms is not released back into the atmosphere until fossil fuels are burned. By burning large amounts of fossil fuels, humans are increasing the concentration of carbon dioxide in the atmosphere. Carbon dioxide traps heat from the sun within the atmosphere, much like glass panes trap the sun's heat in a greenhouse. The ability of gases such as carbon dioxide to retain the sun's heat, and in so doing to warm the atmosphere, is called the **greenhouse effect**. You will learn more about the greenhouse effect in Chapter 16.

SECTION REVIEW

1. Explain the significance of Bormann and Likens's experiments at Hubbard Brook.

2. Explain the role of nitrogen-fixing bacteria in the nitrogen cycle.

3. How does deforestation affect the water cycle?

4. Describe how human interference in the carbon cycle may be causing an increase in global temperatures.

262

ANSWERS TO SECTION REVIEW

1. Bormann and Likens showed that trees keep nutrients in an ecosystem by withdrawing them from the soil and preventing their loss in runoff. Disturbing the ecosystem disrupts these cycles.

2. These bacteria transform unusable nitrogen gas into ammonia that can be absorbed and used by plants to make proteins and nucleic acids.

3. Deforestation reduces evaporation from plants, so less water is returned to the air. Without plants, runoff increases, often carrying away soil and nutrients and disturbing other cycles that depend on the presence of the trees.

4. By burning fossil fuels, humans are increasing the levels of CO_2 in the atmosphere. Since CO_2 traps the sun's heat, increased temperatures may result.

All ecosystems are connected. The destruction of the rain forests in Brazil, for example, will affect you and everyone else in the world. If humans are going to take action to preserve the world for future generations, it is important that we understand what the major ecosystems of the world are like and how they function.

14-3 Kinds of Ecosystems

OBJECTIVES

1 Identify the importance of plankton in freshwater ecosystems.

2 Identify the factors that determine the type of ecosystem found in a particular area.

3 Contrast the seven major biomes.

4 Identify the major ocean ecosystems.

Freshwater Ecosystems

Freshwater ecosystems include lakes, ponds, and rivers. These ecosystems are very limited in area. Inland lakes cover 1.8 percent of the Earth's surface, and rivers and streams cover about 0.3 percent. Although small in total area, freshwater ecosystems support a rich array of life, including fishes, amphibians, insects, turtles, crocodiles, and many plants. A diverse biological community of microscopic organisms called **plankton** lives near the surface of lakes and ponds. Plankton contain photosynthetic organisms that are the base of aquatic food webs. All freshwater habitats are strongly connected to land ecosystems. Nutrients flow from terrestrial ecosystems into freshwater ecosystems. In addition, many land animals come to the water to feed, drink, or reproduce. **Figure 14-12** shows a freshwater ecosystem.

Ponds and lakes usually have three zones in which organisms occur: a shallow "edge" zone, an open-water surface zone, and, in deep lakes and ponds, a deep-water zone to which little light penetrates.

Figure 14-12
Freshwater ecosystems, such as this pond, support a variety of plants and animals.

263

Videodisc Resources

Holt Biology Videodiscs

Lesson 14-3: Kinds of Ecosystems

Ecosystems 263

Terrestrial Ecosystems

● Classifying Biomes

Lead the students through the descriptive information on the various biomes. Be sure to point out the different climates for each biome. Use the information to dispel misconceptions that many students have. Tell students that deserts are not just biomes that have low yearly precipitation. Point out that what marks a desert as unique is the low level of available water and that what little water does fall evaporates quickly. Larger animals are not found only in the warmer biomes. Although elephants are large, endotherms, as a general rule, tend to be much larger in colder climates. Larger animals have a smaller surface-area-to-volume ratio, thus reducing their heat loss. Remind students about the relationship between surface area and volume as a cell gets larger (see Chapter 3). Remind students that the tundra is not lifeless; although the vegetation supports a limited number of animal species, migrating visitors, including flies, make their appearance during the warm season.

Demonstration

● Observing Organisms

Conduct a field trip to study a freshwater ecosystem. Have students collect specimens. While most specimens can be examined on-site, return a few to class for further examination. They can be kept in a freshwater aquarium. Macroinvertebrates can be used to monitor the water quality of a river. Certain organisms, such as leeches, tolerate poor water, while other invertebrates, such as dobsonfly larvae and dragonfly nymphs, live in clean water. Contact a local water conservation group. These groups can provide introductions to mentors and supply students with literature and an appropriate database to use when collecting macroinvertebrates.

Terrestrial Ecosystems

Major biological communities that occur over wide areas on land are called **biomes**. The seven major biomes are (1) tropical rain forests, (2) savannas, (3) deserts, (4) temperate grasslands, (5) deciduous forests, (6) coniferous forests, and (7) tundra. These biomes differ remarkably from one another because they evolved in areas that have very different physical characteristics. The kinds of animals and plants that live in a biome depend on the physical nature of the habitat: the soils, the terrain, and the climate. The following boxes contain information about the seven major biomes.

Tropical Rain Forests

● Climate:
Warm and moist, with little variation in either rainfall or temperature

● Yearly precipitation:
250 cm (100 in.)

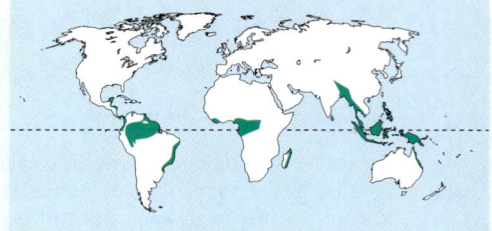

Tropical rain forests have more species than any other biome, probably containing at least half of the Earth's species of land-dwelling organisms. In a single square mile (just over 2.5 km^2) of tropical rain forest in Peru or Brazil, there may be 1,500 or more species of butterflies, twice the total number of butterfly species found in the United States and Canada combined. Although tropical rain forests are noted for lush growth, they exist mainly on quite infertile soils. Most of the nutrients are held within the plants themselves. Today tropical rain forests are being destroyed so rapidly that most will be gone within 40 years. Their destruction will lead to the extinction of large numbers of species.

Savannas

● Climate:
Hot, with alternating wet and dry seasons

● Yearly precipitation:
90–150 cm (36–60 in.)

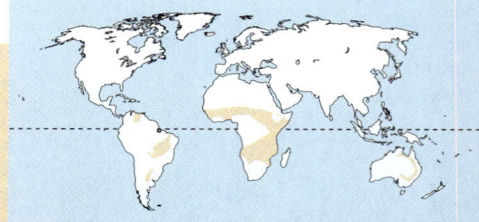

The world's great dry grasslands, called savannas, are found in tropical areas that have relatively low annual precipitation or prolonged annual dry seasons. There are wider extremes in temperature during the year in savannas than in tropical rain forests, and there is seasonal drought. These factors have led to the evolution of an open landscape with widely spaced trees. The huge herds of grazing mammals and their predators that inhabit the savannas of Africa are well known and spectacular. Typical inhabitants of the African savanna are lions, cheetahs, zebras, rhinoceroses, and gazelles.

264

Matter of Fact: Rain-Forest Soils

American biologist E. O. Wilson estimates that more than 44.1 mi^2 of rain forest are destroyed each hour. Infertile soils add to the problem when rain forests are destroyed—in fact, it takes 20 years to develop enough topsoil on former rain-forest land to support crops for 1 year. It takes 1,000 years for a pioneer rain-forest community to form. For example, the forest surrounding the ancient capital of Angkor, in Cambodia, is structurally different from older forests in the same area. Angkor was abandoned in 1431. In his book *Diversity of Life,* Wilson wrote that in some areas of the world, the soil is so poor the forest might never regenerate without human help.

Deserts

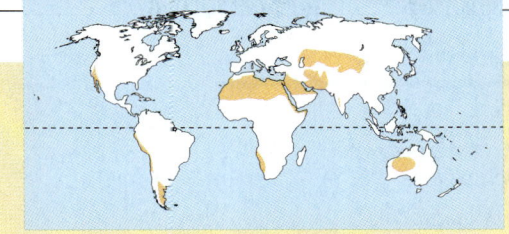

- Climate:
  Very dry, often hot
- Yearly precipitation:
  20 cm (8 in.)

Deserts receive very little precipitation. The scarcity of water is the major factor influencing the lives of desert inhabitants. Desert organisms often have features that enable them to conserve water. For instance, many desert plants have waxy coatings on their leaves to reduce the loss of water through evaporation. In desert regions, vegetation is characteristically sparse. Less than 5 percent of North America is desert. Inhabitants of North American deserts include roadrunners, kangaroo rats, kit foxes, creosote bushes, and saguaro cactuses.

Temperate Grasslands

- Climate:
  Dry, hot summers and cold winters
- Yearly precipitation:
  10–60 cm (4–24 in.)

Temperate grasslands once covered much of the interior of North America and were widespread in Europe, Asia, and South America. Much of the rich agricultural land in the United States and Canada was once covered by prairie, another name for temperate grassland. Temperate grasslands are often populated by herds of grazing mammals. In North America, the prairies were once inhabited by huge herds of bison.

Temperate Deciduous Forests

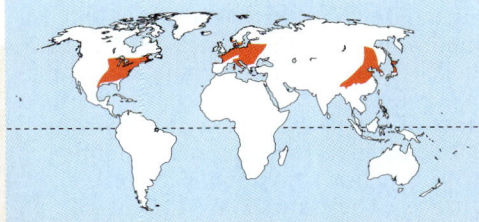

- Climate:
  Warm summers and cool to cold winters
- Yearly precipitation:
  75–250 cm (30–100 in.)

Relatively mild climates and plentiful rainfall promote the growth of deciduous forests (deciduous trees shed their leaves all at once in the fall). Precipitation in temperate deciduous forests is usually distributed fairly evenly throughout the year. In North America, deciduous forests are home to deer, bears, beavers, and raccoons. The trees are hardwoods such as oak, hickory, and beech, and shrubs and herbs grow on the forest floor.

265

Multicultural Perspective: The Neem Tree

In India, the neem tree provides so many useful products that it has been called "the village pharmacy." Its leaves are used to make medicinal teas and insect repellents. Juice from the tree is used to treat skin problems, and the twigs are used to clean teeth.

Life/Work Skills
Finding Information

▲ **Distinguishing Fact From Fiction**

We may have destroyed as much as 50 percent of our wetlands before we passed laws to protect them. To introduce students to the legal and political sides of conservation, have them interview a member of a local wetlands commission. They might ask such questions as the following: Why are wetlands valuable to us? What levels of government regulate wetland use? Are federal regulations equally appropriate in all parts of the country? How are conflicts between landowners and conservationists resolved? Have students consolidate what they learn from the interview by writing a newspaper-style article about the topic. Remind them to be objective and to avoid a biased and emotional response.

Life/Work Skills
Communicating

● **Summarizing Information**

Have students create an advertisement that points out the "best" features of a specific biome. Take the talents of the students into consideration in making assignments. For example, a student who is good in art can be placed on the same team with someone who writes well, because ads should consist of both textual and artistic components. Present a realistic scenario that will stimulate creativity. Students might be asked to develop ads for the travel industry, or they could pitch their ad to potential inhabitants of the biome, such as producers or herbivores. Successful advertisements should be visually and emotionally appealing and should show a significant understanding of the primary characteristics of the biome.

Key to Strategies
● **Understanding Concepts (Tier I)**
■ **Applying Information (Tier II)**
▲ **Critical Thinking (Tier III)**

Connection: *Chapter 10*

Biomes as Selective Pressure

Ask students to choose an organism that lives in a specific biome. Have them identify the ecological characteristics to which the species of organism has had to adapt. *(Accept any reasonable answer that connects the unique characteristics of a biome with the unique characteristics of the animal living in that biome. For example, the desert-dwelling kangaroo rat produces a minimal amount of urine, thereby conserving water. Evergreen trees of the coniferous forests are triangle-shaped so that each needle, or leaf, can receive maximum sunlight for optimum levels of photosynthesis during the relatively short growing season. Students should realize that evolution is a response to ecological pressures on a population. Organisms possess particular characteristics, or adaptations, because those characteristics enable the organism to survive in its particular habitat.)*

Hydrothermal Vent

■ **Recognizing Relationships**

Have students draw a food web for a hydrothermal vent community. An example of this **Graphic Organizer** is shown below. Students should consult the library for information about the types of organisms found in these habitats. *(They will find that chemoautotrophic bacteria oxidize reduced sulfur compounds as an energy source and fix carbon dioxide into organic compounds.)*

Coniferous Forests

- **Climate:**
  Cool, short summers and cold, long winters
- **Yearly precipitation:**
  20–60 cm (8–24 in.)

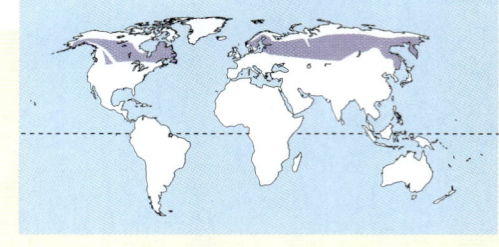

Cold, wet climates provide ideal conditions for conifers, needle-leaved evergreens such as pine trees. The coniferous forest biome is one of the largest on Earth. Winters in coniferous forests are long and cold, and most of the precipitation falls in the summer. Marshes, lakes, and ponds are common and are fringed by willows or birches. Most of the few species of trees tend to occur in dense stands of one or only a few species. Many large mammals live in this biome, including herbivores such as elk, moose, and deer. Carnivores of coniferous forests include wolves, bears, lynxes, and wolverines.

Tundra

- **Climate:**
  Cold, long winters and cool, short summers, with little precipitation
- **Yearly precipitation:**
  25 cm (10 in.)

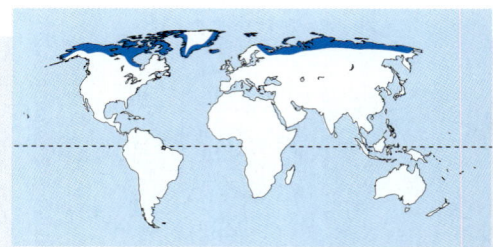

Between the coniferous forests and the permanent ice surrounding the North Pole lies the tundra. This open, wind-swept biome covers one-fifth of the Earth's land surface. Annual precipitation is low, and water is unavailable for most of the year because it is frozen. The ground is usually permanently frozen within 1 m (about 3 ft) of the surface. The tundra is a land of grasses, sedges, dwarf willows, and mosses. Animals living here include foxes, lemmings, owls, and caribou.

266

Graphic Organizer

Use the following graphic organizer with the teaching strategy **Hydrothermal Vent** on page 266.

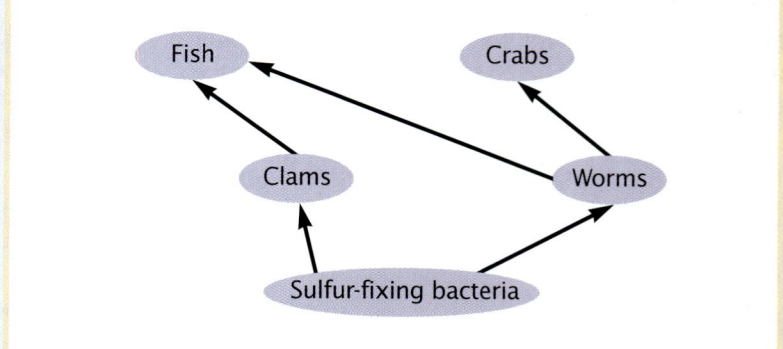

Environmental Science

What would it be like to . . .

- preserve places of great natural beauty for future generations?
- diagnose "sick" ecosystems and prescribe treatments to help restore their health?

These are just a few of the opportunities open to people who work in the field of environmental science.

Environmental Science: What Is It?

Environmental science focuses on one aspect of the natural world. For example, ecology and forestry are specialized environmental subjects, as are oceanography, geology, and meteorology. Traditionally, environmental scientists have worked as researchers or teachers. But today, exciting opportunities are opening for environmental scientists in many industries and businesses.

Career Focus: Dr. Carmen Cid

Ecologist at Eastern Connecticut State University

"I've been interested in biology ever since I was a little girl living in Cuba. My interest intensified in high school in New York, thanks to my high school biology teacher. We were a tough audience of inner-city teenagers, but she demanded our respect and cooperation. In college, I fell in love with the outdoors. Most of the time, class was held in nearby woods and wetlands. Having always lived in large, crowded cities, this class gave me my first opportunity to visit the unspoiled environment of a forest. My attitude toward nature changed when I began studying plants as living, growing, competing organisms."

What I Do: "Being an ecologist is like being a detective—you need to study a scene, search for clues, and test your ideas with investigations. I design experiments to discover how different species coexist in a forest. One project examined a species of short-lived annual plant that grew in patches throughout forests. Why did they grow in isolated, scattered clusters? Once I discovered the answers to such questions, I could solve the puzzle of species interaction in the forest."

Science/Math Career Preparation

High school
- Biology
- Chemistry

College
- Courses vary according to field of specialization

Graduate school
- Master's degree is suggested

Employment Outlook:

As concerns about pollution and threatened plant and animal species heighten, opportunities in environmental science will increase significantly.

To Find Out More

1 For further information, write to:
Ecological Society of America
Center for Environmental Studies
Arizona State University,
Tempe, AZ 85287-3211

2 Visit your school counselor to find out what universities offer programs in environmental science. Review the prerequisites. Make a poster showing the range of job opportunities in this field.

3 Find articles that describe an environmental issue being debated in your community. Prepare a report that describes the area in conflict and causes for concern. With your class, make a list of suggestions to help solve the problem.

267

Career Opportunities

Exploring Opportunities

- Use this feature to discuss the potential impact women and minorities can have in all areas of biology. Ask students to brainstorm about ways to encourage young people to enter careers in the sciences.

- This feature can also be used to discuss the difficulties Dr. Cid may have faced when she moved to Brooklyn, New York from Havana, Cuba. Ask students who have been in a similar situation to share their experience.

Discussion

Guide a discussion by posing the following questions:

1. What factors in Dr. Cid's background led her to study biology and then ecology? *(Dr. Cid had been interested in biology since she was a little girl, and she had a demanding and dedicated teacher in high school. Dr. Cid grew up in a large, crowded city and was overwhelmed by the woods and wetlands she visited while in college.)*

2. Why does Dr. Cid compare ecology to being a detective? *(The two jobs are both investigatory in nature. She must use clues that she finds in order to determine the interactions of a species in a forest.)*

● **Comparing Functions**

Lead students through the descriptive information on the ocean ecosystems. After describing each region of the ocean, point out that the ocean really consists of three different, but interdependent, regions. Materials produced in shallow ocean water, for example, can be carried to the open ocean by currents. Some organisms, such as the flounder, spend their early life in estuaries and then swim out to the oceans. The perpetual rain of detritus from the surface of the open ocean provides nutrients to the deep ocean food chains.

Phase Three

Assessment Options

Closure

● **Summarizing Information**

Ask students what characteristics of a tropical rain forest make it a suitable home for so many different species of plants and animals. *(Answers will vary; biologists are still debating this question. Rainforest producers have a high level of productivity and are able to support large and complicated food webs. In addition, the rain forest offers many different kinds of habitats. Some organisms, such as the giant cockroach, live on the forest floor and eat decaying plant matter, while other organisms are adapted to the forest canopy and spend their entire life there.)*

SECTION REVIEW

Assign the *Section Review.*

Reteaching

Show students pictures of various biomes. Ask them to identify each one and to discuss its characteristics.

Ocean Ecosystems

Nearly three-quarters of the Earth's surface is covered by ocean. Three types of ocean ecosystems are shown in **Figure 14-13**. Shallow ocean waters are small in area but contain most of the ocean's diversity. Many fishes swim in the open ocean surface, feeding on plankton. Photosynthetic plankton account for about 40 percent of all photosynthesis on Earth. There is increasing evidence that pollution is harming photosynthetic plankton. If significant numbers of these organisms are destroyed, the oxygen you breathe will be slowly depleted from the Earth's atmosphere. The deep ocean waters are cold and dark. Among the few residents of the deep ocean are some of the most bizarre organisms found on Earth. Many organisms in the deep ocean have light-producing body parts that they use to attract mates or lure prey. Because photosynthesis cannot occur in the deep ocean, most of these organisms prey on other deep-sea residents or scavenge the dead bodies of organisms that have drifted down from above.

Figure 14-13
Each type of ocean ecosystem supports different kinds of organisms. This representation is not drawn to scale.

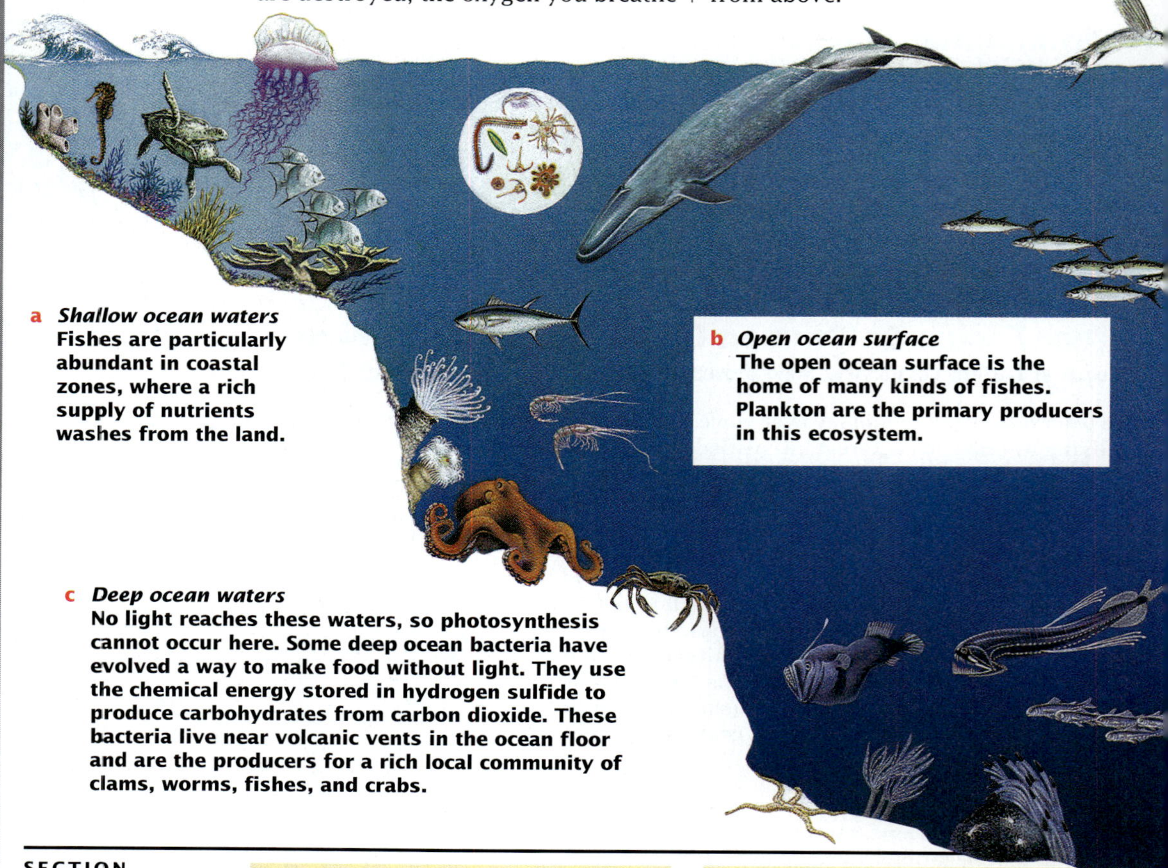

a **Shallow ocean waters**
Fishes are particularly abundant in coastal zones, where a rich supply of nutrients washes from the land.

b **Open ocean surface**
The open ocean surface is the home of many kinds of fishes. Plankton are the primary producers in this ecosystem.

c **Deep ocean waters**
No light reaches these waters, so photosynthesis cannot occur here. Some deep ocean bacteria have evolved a way to make food without light. They use the chemical energy stored in hydrogen sulfide to produce carbohydrates from carbon dioxide. These bacteria live near volcanic vents in the ocean floor and are the producers for a rich local community of clams, worms, fishes, and crabs.

SECTION REVIEW

1 What role do plankton play in a freshwater ecosystem?

2 List two reasons why tropical rain forests do not occur in the United States.

3 Name two biomes that occur where there is very little precipitation.

4 Describe how organisms living deep in the ocean obtain their food.

ANSWERS TO SECTION REVIEW

1 Plankton, as photosynthetic organisms, are the base of aquatic food webs.

2 Variations in temperature and smaller amounts of precipitation do not allow such a forest to exist.

3 Possible answers are deserts, temperate grasslands, tundra, and coniferous forests.

4 They obtain their food through predation, scavenging, and bacterial producers.

Highlights

If the tropical rain forests disappear, so will this butterfly from Trinidad.

	Key Terms	Summary
14-1 **What Is an Ecosystem?** Decomposers, such as these mushrooms, are an important part of every ecosystem. 	ecology (p. 254) community (p. 254) habitat (p. 254) ecosystem (p. 254) diversity (p. 254) producer (p. 256) consumer (p. 256) decomposer (p. 256) trophic level (p. 257) autotroph (p. 257) herbivore (p. 257) carnivore (p. 257) omnivore (p. 257) heterotroph (p. 257)	• Ecology is the study of how living things fit into their environment. • An ecosystem is a group of interacting organisms and their physical environment. • Producers capture energy and store it in complex molecules. Consumers obtain energy by feeding on producers or other consumers. Decomposers eat dead organisms, animal wastes, fallen leaves, twigs, and other debris. • Autotrophs, such as plants, are organisms that make their own food. Heterotrophs cannot make their own food and must obtain it by eating other organisms.
14-2 **Cycles Within Ecosystems** Plants play an important role in the water cycle. 	nitrogen fixation (p. 260) greenhouse effect (p. 262)	• Materials such as water, nitrogen, and carbon move through ecosystems in cycles. • Some bacteria absorb nitrogen gas and convert it to ammonia. The process of transforming nitrogen gas into ammonia is known as nitrogen fixation. • The burning of fossil fuels releases large amounts of carbon dioxide into the atmosphere. Carbon dioxide in the atmosphere retains heat from the sun, a phenomenon known as the greenhouse effect.
14-3 **Kinds of Ecosystems** The tundra is one of the seven major biomes. 	plankton (p. 263) biome (p. 264)	• Photosynthetic plankton are the basis of the food web in aquatic ecosystems. • On land, there are seven major types of communities, which are called biomes. • There are three major types of ecosystems found in the ocean.

269

Remind students that most paleontologists believe the extinction of dinosaurs, 65 millions years ago, was caused by a large meteorite that crashed into the Earth and raised a cloud of dust. This dust may have cut off sunlight and resulted in the death of many plants, and consequently of dinosaurs as well. Ask students to draw up a scenario of what life on Earth would be like if we were suddenly struck by a large meteorite and were faced with several months without sunlight. Students should address the problem ecologically and should indicate what would happen to the various food webs. *(Accept any answer that demonstrates the student's understanding of the interconnected nature of species in a habitat and how disturbances of a habitat can have negative or even disastrous effects. Most important, the students should demonstrate how the death of producers would cause all other organisms to face possible extinction.)*

Portfolio Assessment

Portfolio Assessment on page T39 provides options for building and evaluating student portfolios. Students and teachers can select items from the areas listed on page T39 for inclusion in a portfolio.

ANSWER TO CONCEPT MAP

The following is one possible answer to the Relating Concepts exercise on page 270.

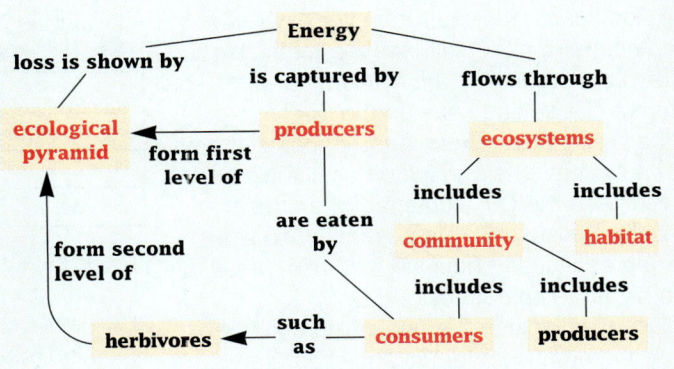

review

ANSWERS

Understanding Vocabulary

1. a. *Producers* are autotrophs; the others are heterotrophs.
   b. *Energy* does not cycle within ecosystems.
   c. *Photosynthesis* does not add CO_2 to the atmosphere.
2. a. *habitat*
   b. *heterotrophs*
   c. *trophic level*

Understanding Concepts

3. Answer to concept map is shown on page 269.
4. An ecosystem is a self-sustaining collection of organisms and the physical location in which they live.
5. An ecosystem model consists of a series of hypotheses that describe how the ecosystem functions. Models are used to predict how an ecosystem will behave if conditions change.
6. Producers harvest energy from the habitat, while consumers get energy from producers or other consumers. Grass is a producer, and deer are consumers.
7. Plants would be consumed. Mice could not find seeds to eat and would have to move or die. The snake and raptor would also be forced to move or die because of a lack of prey.
8. The amount of energy transferred to the next trophic level is only about 10 percent; the rest is lost to heat or in work obtaining the energy. Thus, there isn't enough energy available in the highest trophic level to support an additional level.
9. The control group showed how the ecosystem normally functioned.
10. The leaf falls and decays by bacterial action, and the nitrogen in the leaf becomes ammonia. The ammonia is then further broken down by other bacteria to produce nitrogen.
11. Plants absorb the water and then allow it to evaporate through their leaves. This

Understanding Vocabulary

1. For each set of terms, identify the term that does not fit and explain why.
   a. producers, consumers, herbivores, omnivores
   b. water, energy, carbon, nitrogen
   c. photosynthesis, cellular respiration, decomposition, combustion
2. For each set of terms, complete the analogy.
   a. organisms that live in a particular place : community :: physical location of a community : _____
   b. Plants and other organisms that make their own food : autotrophs :: organisms that cannot make their own food : _____
   c. movement of energy through an ecosystem in a complex network of feeding relationships : food web :: a group of organisms whose energy sources are the same number of steps away from the sun : _____

Understanding Concepts

3. **Relating Concepts** Construct a concept map that describes energy flow in ecosystems. Try to include the following terms in your concept map: ecological pyramid, producers, community, ecosystems, habitat, consumers.
4. **Identifying Components** What is an ecosystem? Describe its two basic components.
5. **Summarizing Information** What is an ecological model? How are ecological models used by ecologists?
6. **Comparing Functions** Differentiate between the roles of producers and consumers in the transfer of energy in an ecosystem. Give an example of each type of organism.
7. **Inferring Conclusions** Figure 14-7 shows an ecological pyramid for a very simple ecosystem. Suppose that sheep were introduced into this ecosystem. Explain some possible effects of this introduction on each species in the ecosystem.

8. **Recognizing Relationships** Explain why most ecosystems usually can contain no more than five trophic levels.
9. **Analyzing Methods** Bormann and Likens first determined how efficiently nutrients were recycled in an undisturbed ecosystem. Explain how this ecosystem served as a control group for their experiment.
10. **Organizing Information** Imagine an atom of nitrogen that is in a protein in the leaf of a plant. Trace the steps of the nitrogen cycle this atom must pass through in order to reach the atmosphere.
11. **Recognizing Relationships** What role do plants play in the water cycle in a tropical rain forest? How do the plants affect the climate of the forest?
12. **Summarizing Information** What is the greenhouse effect? How has the burning of fossil fuels changed the atmosphere? What is the consequence of this change?
13. **Recognizing Relationships** Evaluate this statement: Photosynthetic plankton play the same role in aquatic ecosystems as plants do in terrestrial ecosystems.
14. **Summarizing Information** Copy the following table onto a sheet of paper. Complete the table by filling in the missing entries.

Biome	Annual precipitation	Found in United States?
Tropical rain forest		
	10–60 cm	Yes
Desert		
	90–150 cm	No

15. **Recognizing Relationships** What effect do photosynthetic marine plankton have on the composition of the atmosphere?
16. **BUILDING ON WHAT YOU HAVE LEARNED** In Chapter 5 you learned about photosynthesis and cellular respiration. Using what you learned in this chapter, explain this observation about the carbon cycle. Plants produce and use carbon dioxide, while animals only produce carbon dioxide.

action keeps the water from washing away nutrients from the soil, and the roots also keep the soil intact. The evaporated water forms clouds and rains on the forest.

12. The greenhouse effect is the trapping of heat in a system. The burning of fossil fuels has increased the CO_2 content of the atmosphere. Because CO_2 is a greenhouse gas, the greenhouse effect will increase, resulting in higher temperatures.
13. Because plankton are photosynthetic, they are the producers for aquatic ecosystems,

just as plants are for terrestrial ecosystems.

14.

	250 cm	No
Temperate		
	20 cm	Yes
Savannas		

15. They absorb CO_2 from the atmosphere and produce O_2.
16. Plants consume CO_2 in photosynthesis but also release it through respiration.

Interpreting Graphics

17. Look at the food chain of a marine ecosystem shown below.
    a. What is the producer in this ecosystem?
    b. Which trophic level is the killer whale in?
    c. Which organism should be least common? Explain your answer.

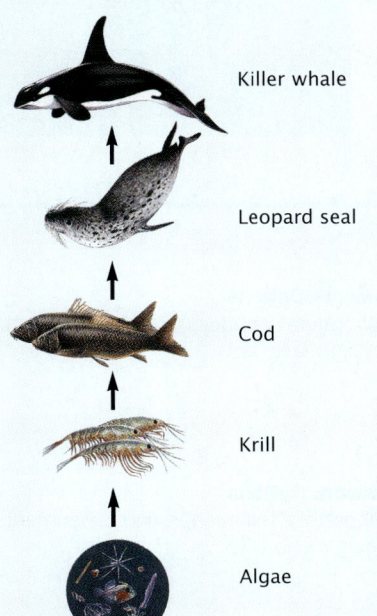

Killer whale

Leopard seal

Cod

Krill

Algae

Reviewing Themes

18. **Interdependence**
    If destruction of tropical rain forests continues at its present rate, most of the world's rain forests will be gone within 40 years. What are two likely effects of the destruction of tropical rain forests?

Thinking Critically

19. **Evaluating Methods** Ecologist often use models to help them understand ecosystems. What is a model? Why are models useful to ecologists? What are some possible drawbacks of models?

Life/Work Skills

20. **Finding Information** In the last few decades, scientists have noticed dramatic declines in the populations of some kinds of amphibians. Use library resources or search an on-line database to find out more about disappearing amphibians. What amphibians are affected, and where do they live? What are some of the hypothesized causes of the decline in amphibian populations? Write a report that summarizes what you have learned.

21. **Using Technology** Computer mapping, remote sensing, and satellite imaging are important tools for evaluating the health of the environment. Use library references or search an on-line database to find out how these technologies are helping scientists monitor the environment. What agencies or businesses would require the kind of information that these technologies provide? Write a report that summarizes your findings. Try to find a map created by one of these methods that shows an area around your city or town.

Activities and Projects

22. **Math Connection** Scientists introduced a breeding pair of one species into an ecosystem. This species doubles its population size every year. Another species, native to the ecosystem, maintains its numbers at 500 individuals from one year to the next. How many years will it take for the introduced species to outnumber the native species?

Discovering Through Reading

23. Read the article "Why Trees Need Birds" by Sharon Begley in *National Wildlife*, August/September 1995, pages 42–45. What idea did Robert Marquis and Christopher Whelan set out to test? Describe their experiments. What is the importance of their discovery? What are the two main explanations for the decreasing numbers of some songbirds?

24. Read the article "Collapse of a Food Chain" by Kathy A. Svitil in *Discover*, July 1995, pages 36–37. What is the cause of fewer fish and birds in California's coastal waters? What is the cause of the decline in the zooplankton population?

271

ecosystem were altered. Models may not be accurate, depending on the data and assumptions that are used.

Life/Work Skills

20. frogs; near wetlands and bodies of water. Habitat destruction, pollution, natural population fluctuations, and UV irradiation may be responsible for the population decline.

21. Students should point out that conservation groups use computer mapping to determine the size of ecosystems. This information, along with data on wildlife population size, can help determine the health of an ecosystem and pinpoint problems.

Activities and Projects

22. 8 years

Discovering Through Reading

23. If consumers could positively influence the well-being of a producer. They wrapped trees in nets to keep the birds away from them. As controls, they monitored trees that birds had access to, and they sprayed another tree for insects but kept the tree wrapped in a net. They found that birds can keep the populations of trees healthy by consuming the insects that directly affect trees. A decrease in the songbird's wintering grounds in Central and South America and a fragmentation of their habitat, which has led to increased predation of the birds.

24. Fewer nutrients in the ocean led to a decline in the amount of phytoplankton, which are eaten by zooplankton, which are eaten by fish, which are eaten by birds. Fewer phytoplankton (producers) results in fewer zooplankton, fish, and birds (consumers).

Heterotrophs release it back into the atmosphere through respiration. Heterotrophs have no Calvin cycle and cannot fix CO_2.

Interpreting Graphics

17. a. algae
    b. fifth trophic level
    c. Killer whales, because they are at the top of the food chain. More organisms from the lower trophic levels are required to support them, and they are therefore going to be less numerous.

Reviewing Themes

18. Higher levels of extinction will result because of the loss of habitat; rapid soil erosion will result from the lack of trees to keep the soil in place; the loss of so much plant life could result in an increased greenhouse effect.

Thinking Critically

19. A model is a series of hypotheses that describe how an ecosystem works. It helps ecologists predict what might happen if the

15 | How Ecosystems Change

Lesson Planning Guide With Options for Block Scheduling

Lecture Concepts	Lesson Resources	

15-1 Interactions Within Ecosystems

BLOCK ❶ (45 minutes)

1. Species evolve in response to environmental challenges, including those posed by other organisms.

❶ Lecture Resources
- Determining Prior Knowledge
- Active Reading: Brainstorming
- Demonstration: Identifying Functions
- Demonstration: Identifying Structures
- Holt Biology Videodiscs Lesson 15-1

Classwork Options
- Laboratory Techniques and Experimental Design: Lab C24

BLOCK ❷ (45 minutes)

2. Coevolution is the process in which two or more species evolve in response to one another.

3. Examples of coevolution include the interactions between flowering plants and their animal pollinators and between plants and herbivores.

❷ Lecture Resources
- Coevolution
- Active Reading: Reading Organizer
- Visual Strategy: Videodisc
- Holt Biology Videodiscs Lesson 15-1

Classwork Options
- Laboratory Techniques and Experimental Design: Lab C23

BLOCK ❸ (45 minutes)

4. Relationships between two or more species include parasitism, mutualism, and commensalism.

❸ Lecture Resources
- Floral Defense
- Demonstration: Recognizing Relationships
- Holt Biology Videodiscs Lesson 15-1

Classwork Options
- Reteaching
- Closure: Evaluating an Argument

Assignment Options
- Section Review
- Chapter Review, questions 1a, 4, 5, 6, 7, 8, 9, 10, 19, 21, 22, 23
- Directed Reading Worksheet

15-2 Ecosystem Development and Change

BLOCK ❹ (45 minutes)

1. A niche is the role an organism plays in its ecosystem.

2. Different species sharing resources tend to evolve reduced competition.

❹ Lecture Resources
- Who Benefits and Who Loses in Species Interactions?
- Visual Strategy: Figure 15-9
- Demonstration: Comparing Functions
- Teaching Transparencies: 86, 87
- Holt Biology Videodiscs Lesson 15-2

Classwork Options
- Investigation 15A

Assignment Options
- Life/Work Skills: Finding Information

BLOCK ❺ (45 minutes)

3. Ecosystems develop by succession, in which a progression of species replacements takes place.

❺ Lecture Resources
- Stability in Nature
- Visual Strategy: Figure 15-10
- Demonstration: Observing Succession
- Teaching Transparencies: 70, 80
- Holt Biology Videodiscs Lesson 15-2

Classwork Options
- Decision Making

BLOCK ❻ (45 minutes)

4. The diversity of species within an ecosystem is related to the size of the ecosystem and its latitude.

❻ Lecture Resources
- Visual Strategy: Figure 15-2, Table 15-1
- Teaching Transparencies: 83
- Holt Biology Videodiscs Lesson 15-2

Classwork Options
- Closure: Predicting Outcomes

Assignment Options
- Reteaching
- Section Review
- Chapter Review, questions 1b, 1c, 2, 3, 12, 13, 14, 15, 16, 17, 18, 20, 24
- Directed Reading Worksheet

Chapter Review and Assessment

BLOCK 7 (45 minutes)

Review
- Reteaching Worksheet
- Thinking Skills Worksheet
- Vocabulary Development Worksheet
- Language Development and Reading Comprehension Audio CD Program: Chapter 15

BLOCK 8 (45 minutes)

Assessment
- Alternative Assessment, p. 285
- Portfolio Assessment, p. T39

Chapter Test
- Chapter 15 Test

Test Generator
- Item bank for customizing Chapter Tests: Testing Pond Water for Carbon Dioxide

Teaching Resources CD-ROM
- Scoring Rubrics and Classroom Management Checklist

The Portfolio icon denotes items throughout the Teacher's Edition lesson wrap that may be selected for inclusion in student portfolios.

Holt Biology Videodiscs and Concepts of Biology

Holt Biology Videodiscs gives you a powerful tool for teaching, review, and assessment. For further information regarding the media on the videodiscs, see **Holt Biology Videodiscs Teacher's Correlation Guide to Holt Biology: Visualizing Life.**

Concepts of Biology adds interactive lesson plans and extensive tools for customization using CD-ROM technology.

Use the following topic from **Concepts of Biology** to help you teach this chapter:

Topic 10: Ecosystem Structure and Function

Laboratory Planning

Text

Materials and preparation instructions appear on the teacher's wrap accompanying each laboratory exercise.

Block 3: Investigation 15A: Modeling an Ecosystem: Fertilizer Dilemma, p. 790

Holt BioSources Laboratory Program

Block 1: Laboratory Techniques and Experimental Design Lab C24: Mapping Biotic Factors in the Environment

Block 2: Laboratory Techniques and Experimental Design Lab C23: Examining Owl Pellets—NW v. SE

Determining Prior Knowledge

- Show students a plant in bloom and a cactus. Have them explain how the flowering plant has adapted to promote reproduction. Ask how the plant and its pollinators have adjusted to each other. Have students describe the challenges that are imposed on the cactus by its habitat. Ask how the cactus has adapted to favor its survival.
- Have students name as many parasites as possible. Have them determine what these organisms have in common.
- Show the class a short videotape of a volcanic eruption. Have students describe what might happen to the local ecosystem after the eruption.
- Have students describe one specific example of how humans have had a negative impact on the environment.

Active READING

Technique: Brainstorming

Before students begin reading, explain that they will be reading about ecosystems, the complex networks of interactions between species. Read the first two paragraphs of the chapter to the class. Then work with the class to create a list of other interactions among species. Ask them to identify the larger ecosystems in which these interactions take place. Discuss with students why ecosystems might change. Tell students that as they read, they will discover more about species interactions within ecosystems and about why ecosystems change.

CD-ROM Resources

Concepts of Biology

Topic 10: Ecosystem Structure and Function

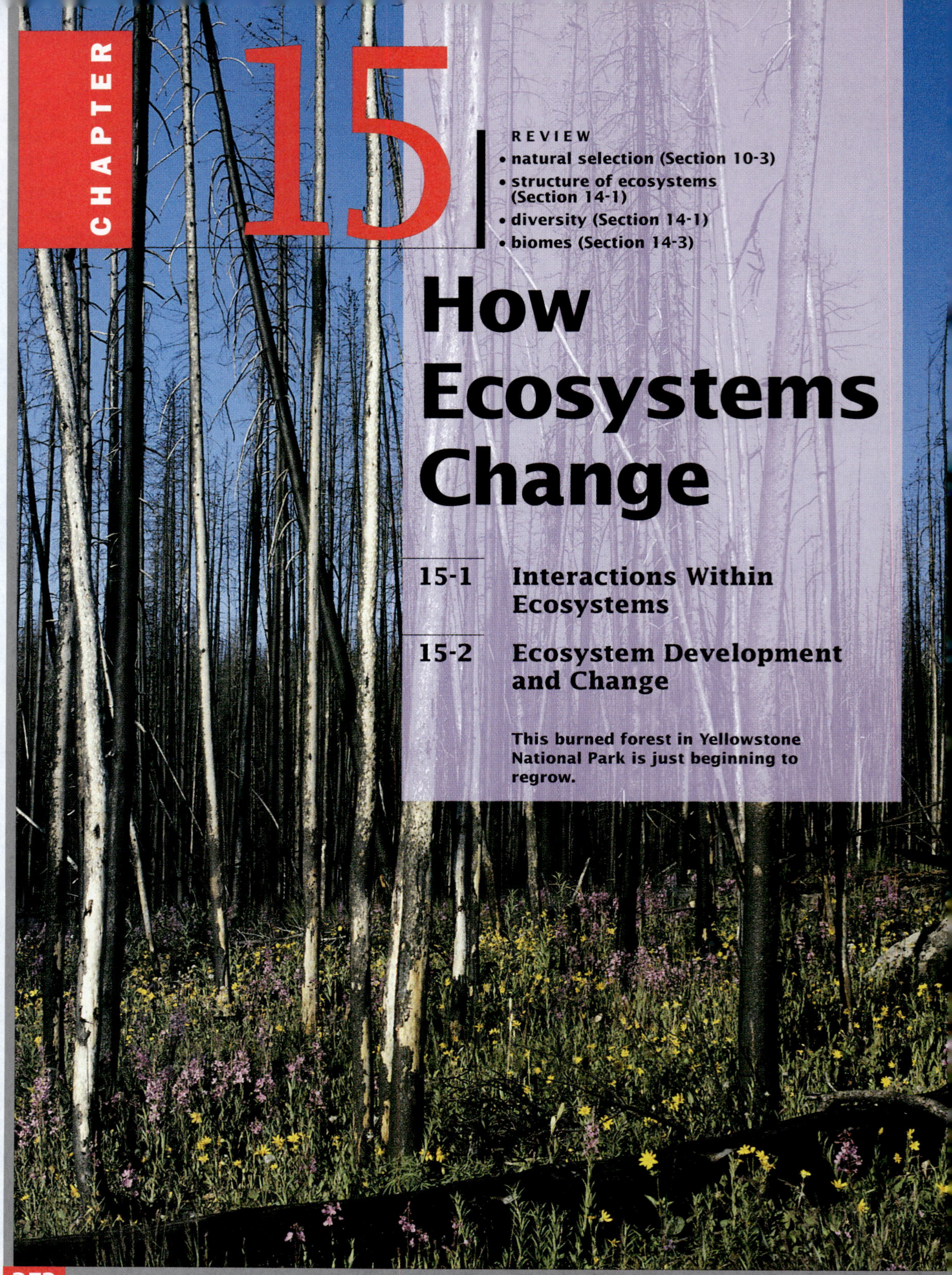

REVIEW
- natural selection (Section 10-3)
- structure of ecosystems (Section 14-1)
- diversity (Section 14-1)
- biomes (Section 14-3)

How Ecosystems Change

| 15-1 | Interactions Within Ecosystems |
| 15-2 | Ecosystem Development and Change |

This burned forest in Yellowstone National Park is just beginning to regrow.

272

Author's Rationale This chapter focuses on the key issue in ecology today—how ecosystems respond to disruptions. Students learn what factors tend to make an ecosystem more stable. They recognize how humans have an impact on and disrupt the natural order of an ecosystem. This chapter outlines principles that will shape a student's thinking on environmental issues for years to come, and as such it is a highly relevant part of his or her study of biology.

Every ecosystem on Earth, whether it is frozen tundra or tropical rain forest, is a complex network of interacting species. To preserve the Earth's fast-disappearing ecosystems, it is essential to understand the nature of these interactions and how they are shaped by natural selection and the physical environment.

15-1 Interactions Within Ecosystems

OBJECTIVES

1 Recognize the role of coevolution in shaping the structure of ecosystems.

2 Relate the characteristics of flowers to the coevolution of flowering plants with insects.

3 Describe how plants and herbivores have coevolved.

4 Contrast parasitism, mutualism, and commensalism.

Evolution and Ecosystems

Species evolve in response to the challenges posed by their environments. As a result, animals, plants, and other organisms in an ecosystem have characteristics that fine-tune them for living where they do. For example, many plants in desert ecosystems have thick, waxy coatings on their leaves that help them retain water. For the same reason, desert animals often hide underground during the hottest part of the day; an animal's behavior is just as much an adaptation to its environment as are its physical characteristics.

An organism's survival and reproduction also depend on interactions with other living members of its ecosystem, including members of other species. **Figure 15-1** shows an interaction between members of two species of fish. Species evolve not only in response to the physical environment but also in response to other species. For instance, many plant species have evolved tough leaves that protect them against being eaten by herbivores. Of course herbivores evolve too, and many have evolved flatter, larger teeth that are better suited to grinding the very tough leaves they eat. Cows and horses have teeth such as these. **Coevolution** occurs when two or more species evolve in response to each other.

Figure 15-1
The cleaner wrasse removes parasites from the gills and mouths of larger fish. The wrasse benefits by gaining a food source, and the fish it cleans benefit by having harmful parasites removed.

273

Videodisc Resources

Holt Biology Videodiscs
Lesson 15-1: Interactions Within Ecosystems

Coevolution

■ Analyzing Information

The yucca plant can be pollinated only by the yucca moth. As the yucca moth lays its eggs in the ovary, it pollinates the plant. The ovary becomes a seed pod, and the larvae eat some of the seed pods as they grow. Ask students if this evolutionary strategy is sound. *(The risks of coevolution are real. If the yucca moth were to become extinct, the yucca plant would disappear, too.)*

Demonstration

● Identifying Structures

Show students photographs or specimens of orchids, snapdragons, and irises. Point out their deep nectar-secreting structures, the unusual platforms on which only certain pollinators can land, and the traps that increase the likelihood of pollination. These flowering plants attract only certain pollinators that are efficient and precise in their job.

Figure 15-2
The odor of this giant *Rafflesia* flower attracts flies. The flies will pollinate it and then transfer pollen from this flower to another *Rafflesia* flower.

Coevolution Shapes Species Interactions

Coevolution shapes the many ways that animals and plants interact within ecosystems, creating a complex web of interactions among the organisms in each ecosystem. For example, producers, herbivores, and carnivores in a mature forest ecosystem have adjusted to one another over long periods of evolutionary time.

One of the most dramatic examples of coevolution is the side-by-side evolution of flowering plants with insects. Plants are immobile and cannot actively search for mates. Instead of moving to seek a mate, many species of flowering plants rely on animals to transport their male gametes, which are located within grains of pollen. Insects are attracted to a plant's flowers by their colors, odors, and the food that they provide, which is usually sweet nectar. As the insect feeds, pollen attaches to its body. After feeding at the flowers of one individual, the pollen-covered insect flies to flowers of another individual. At this next feeding stop, some of the insect's load of pollen may be rubbed onto the female reproductive structures of the flowers. Fertilization is now able to take place. Animals that carry pollen from flower to flower are known as pollinators.

Within each species of flowering plant, those individuals that are better at attracting pollinators will leave more offspring. Thus, the attractive features of each species of flowering plant have evolved to match the preferences of its pollinators. For instance, bees cannot see the color red, and plant species pollinated by bees rarely have red flowers. Bee-pollinated flowers are usually yellow or blue. The *Rafflesia* flower in **Figure 15-2** is pollinated by flies that feed on dead organisms. To attract its pollinators, this flower releases a scent that has been described as resembling the stench of rotting flesh.

Pollinators, in turn, have evolved traits that enable certain species to specialize on particular species of flowers when seeking nectar. Some kinds of honeysuckles are pollinated by hawk moths and produce nectar at the bottom of very long, tube-shaped flowers. Hawk moths can reach the bottom of the flower with their long tongue.

274

Matter of Fact: Malaria and Coevolution

In 1991, British parasitologist Adrian V. S. Hill announced that he had found evidence of coevolution between humans and the malaria parasite *Plasmodium falciparum*. He found two genes that protect people from malaria by encoding for the production of proteins that aid in the recognition of infected cells. These genes are most common in human populations that live in areas where malaria is prevalent. Hill concluded that these genes might have evolved in response to the pressure exerted by malaria.

Avoiding Being Eaten: Plants and Herbivores

Being eaten is not beneficial for plants. Herbivores can kill plants by feeding on them, just as carnivores kill their prey. Therefore, characteristics that enable plants to protect themselves from herbivores are favored by natural selection. The biological structures of many of the Earth's ecosystems have been determined largely by the ways plants avoid being eaten and herbivores succeed in eating them.

Plants defend themselves from herbivores

Touch the stem of a rosebush and you might experience a familiar plant defense against herbivores. Many species of plants, such as roses and the cactus in **Figure 15-3**, employ physical defenses such as thorns, prickles, sticky hairs, and tough leaves. The most crucial plant defenses, however, are chemical. Virtually all plant species produce chemicals that protect them against herbivores. Some of these defensive chemicals are poisons that kill the animal that eats the plant, while other chemicals simply make the plant taste bad. Most herbivores learn to avoid plants that have defensive chemicals. Anyone who has broken out in a rash from contact with poison ivy, shown in **Figure 15-4**, has been the victim of plant chemical defenses. Poison ivy produces a substance that causes severe blistering in many people.

As a rule, each group of closely related plant species has a unique battery of chemical defenses. The plants of the mustard family, for instance, produce a group of defensive chemicals called mustard oils. Mustard oils are the source of the pungent aromas and tastes characteristic of such plants as mustard, cabbage, radish, capers, and horseradish. The same tastes that we enjoy signal the presence of chemicals that are toxic to many groups of insects.

Many herbivores overcome plant defenses

Over time, some herbivores have evolved ways to overcome the chemical defenses of plants. Because different plant species produce different chemicals, coevolution has resulted in a very specialized pattern of feeding; certain kinds of herbivores feed exclusively on particular kinds of plants.

Cabbage butterflies provide a good example of how counteractive measures have evolved in response to the chemical defenses of plants. Although most insects avoid plants of the mustard family, the caterpillars of cabbage butterflies eat these plants voraciously. These caterpillars are able to eat plants of the mustard family because they have evolved the ability to break down mustard oils into harmless chemicals. As a result of this evolutionary breakthrough, cabbage butterflies have been able to use a new food resource—plants of the mustard family—without competition from other insect herbivores.

Figure 15-3
The spines of this golden barrel cactus protect it from herbivores.

Figure 15-4
If you touch the leaves of poison ivy, chances are good that you'll get a rash from the chemicals on their surface.

275

Health Connection
Plant Chemicals
Some of the chemicals that plants produce as a defensive mechanism include nicotine, caffeine, curare, mescaline, cocaine, opium, and tetrahydrocannabinol (the active ingredient of marijuana). Though toxic in large doses, curare is administered in small doses to surgical patients to relax their muscles.

Floral Defense
● **Identifying Functions**
Show a geranium to students, and ask what function the trichosomes, or hairs, might have. (The trichosomes of the desert thistle contain allergenic chemicals that repel many herbivores.)

Visual Strategy | Videodisc

■ **Recognizing Relationships**
Use *Step-Frame Sequence— Introduced Species: Kudzu,* shown on Chapter 15 Section 15-1 of **Holt Biology Videodiscs Teacher's Correlation Guide to Holt Biology: Visualizing Life.** Show the first frame, and tell students that kudzu is a Japanese vine that was introduced in the southeastern United States to help control soil erosion. Proceed to frame 2, and explain that because kudzu has no natural predators or diseases in the United States, its growth has gone unchecked. Now it is a destructive weed, covering hills, trees, and utility poles. The vine is confined to the southern United States. Have students use what they know about ecological relationships to suggest solutions to the problem. (Accept any reasonable suggestions.)

Matter of Fact: Chemical Defenses

Some plants, such as the common fern, *Polypodium vulgare,* produce an ecdysone-like substance that profoundly disturbs the growth cycle of insects that go through incomplete metamorphosis. In one test, for example, a locust that had eaten *Polypodium* molted to produce a nymph with two heads. This kind of long-term defense would reduce the number of individuals capable of reproducing, thereby reducing the number of herbivores.

Key to Strategies
● **Understanding Concepts (Tier I)**
■ **Applying Information (Tier II)**
▲ **Critical Thinking (Tier III)**

Theme Answer

Evolution

The rabbits varied in their ability to resist the myxoma virus. Those with high resistance survived and passed this ability on to their offspring. Consequently, the frequency of resistant rabbits rapidly increased.

Connection: *Chapter 1*

Malaria

Review how Ronald Ross discovered that mosquitoes were responsible for transmitting malaria.

Active READING

Technique: Reading Organizer

Have students work in small groups to create a reading organizer that compares and contrasts the three types of symbiosis. Ask one person from each group to present the group's reading organizer to the class. For more information about reading organizers, see Reading Strategies Worksheets in Holt BioSources Teaching Resources CD-ROM.

Demonstration

■ Recognizing Relationships Mutualism

Pass around a sealed jar containing termites and wood. Point out that protozoans called *Mixotricha* living in the digestive tracts of the termites digest the cellulose in the wood, providing the termites with nutrients. The termites provide the protozoans with food and a home. The degree of mutualism becomes even more involved when we consider that these protozoans are propelled by symbiotic spirochetes that are aligned along their surface.

Three Types of Close Species Interactions

Three types of species interactions involve particularly close relationships among the participants. **Symbiosis** is a close, long-term association between two or more species. The three types of symbiotic relationships are parasitism, mutualism, and commensalism.

Parasites and their hosts coevolve

Worldwide, between 200 million and 300 million people suffer from malaria. People who have malaria play host to a single-celled parasite that was injected into their blood by the bite of a mosquito. Parasites obtain nutrition by feeding on their host. How is a parasite different from a predator? A parasite usually does not kill its host, and it is usually smaller than the organism on which it feeds. The relationship between a parasite and its host is called **parasitism**.

Both host and parasite can coevolve in response to each other. In 1859, 12 rabbits were introduced to Australia. No rabbits occur naturally on the Australian continent. By the 1940s there were millions of rabbits swarming the countryside. To control the rabbit population, the Australian government introduced the viral disease myxomatosis *(mihk suh muh TOH suhs)* from South America. At first, myxomatosis was very deadly to the rabbits. In some areas, more than 90 percent of the rabbits were killed by the virus, and nearly all infected individuals died. Soon, however, scientists monitoring the introduction noticed that the disease was becoming less deadly.

Tests on the rabbits and the virus showed that both were evolving. Because rabbits resistant to myxomatosis were more likely to survive and reproduce, the rabbit population contained a greater proportion of resistant individuals after each generation. Also, instead of becoming more deadly to overcome the rabbit's resistance, the virus had actually become less virulent, or deadly. If a virus kills its host rabbit too quickly, that rabbit cannot spread the virus to other rabbits. A virus that "allows" its hosts to live longer is able to infect more hosts. However, some recent evidence suggests that the virus's virulence may be increasing.

All parties benefit in mutualism

Not all coevolution involves antagonistic relationships, such as those between plants and herbivores or between parasites and their hosts. **Mutualism** is a symbiotic relationship in which all participating species benefit. For example, a lichen, such as the British soldier lichen in **Figure 15-5**, is a mutualistic partnership between a fungus and a green alga or a cyanobacterium. The fungus absorbs nutrients for both partners from the surface on which the lichen is growing. The alga or cyanobacterium carries out photosynthesis to provide food for itself and its fungal partner. Mycorrhizae, which you read about in Chapter 11, are mutualistic associations between plants and fungi. In Chapter 14, you learned about

Evolution

Variation is essential for natural selection. What role did variation play in the long-term survival of rabbits in Australia?

Figure 15-5
The British soldier lichen is composed of a fungus and an alga living in a mutualistic partnership.

Alga

Fungus

Matter of Fact: Normal Flora

The so-called normal flora of vertebrate intestinal tracts are actually symbiotic protozoa, yeasts, and bacteria. They provide a hostile environment to pathogenic organisms. These genera include bacteria *(Bacteroides* and *Escherichia),* yeasts *(Candida* and *Torulopsis),* and protozoa *(Entamoeba, Balantidium,* and *Trichomonas).* In ruminant animals, such as cows and deer, they aid the host in digestion of food. Without these normal flora, many multicellular organisms would find it difficult to digest their food.

Figure 15-6
Stinging anemones (the yellow, flowerlike objects) live on the claws of this female boxing crab. She guards herself and the red eggs she is carrying by using the anemones like boxing gloves, jabbing them at attacking predators. This is an example of a commensal relationship.

the relationship between nitrogen-fixing bacteria and the roots of plants such as peas and beans. These bacteria provide the plants with a source of nitrogen. In exchange, the nitrogen-fixing bacteria receive a place to live (swellings on the plant roots) and sugars produced by the plant.

Mutualism also has played an important role in the coevolution of humans and the microbes that live in our intestines. Within the human large intestine live immense colonies of the bacterium *Escherichia coli*. These bacteria have ready access to food while providing us with vitamin K, which is necessary for blood to clot. Animals that lack these bacteria, such as birds, must consume food that contains the necessary amounts of vitamin K.

Commensalism is taking without harming

Commensalism is an ecological relationship in which one species benefits and the other is not obviously affected. A very intriguing example of commensalism is the boxing crab, which is described in **Figure 15-6**. The crab benefits from the protection anemones provide, and the anemones apparently are not harmed or helped.

The crusty growths seen on the back of the gray whale in **Figure 15-7** are actually small animals called barnacles. Barnacles hitch a ride on the whale. In doing so, they gain protection from predators and transportation to new sources of food (tiny animals they filter from the water). Apparently, the whale neither benefits nor is harmed by the presence of barnacles.

Figure 15-7
Barnacles on this gray whale have found a safe way to obtain food by riding on the whale's back. The whale does not seem to be harmed or helped by the presence of barnacles.

SECTION REVIEW

1 Describe one example of coevolution.

2 Do you think that the drab flowers of some grasses and trees are pollinated by insects? Explain.

3 How have caterpillars and their food plants coevolved?

4 How could you determine whether the relationship between two species is mutualism or commensalism?

277

15-1 section

Phase Three
Assessment Options

Closure

▲ **Evaluating an Argument**
"Disease usually results from inconclusive negotiations for symbiosis, an overstepping of the line by one side or the other.... [There] is nothing to be gained, in an evolutionary sense, by the capacity to cause illness or death." Ask students: What do you think Lewis Thomas meant when he wrote this in his essay "Germs" in *The Lives of a Cell*? *(Students should realize that the goal of parasitism is not the death of the host—it is to be passed on to other hosts. Many diseases, but not all, that were initially lethal, such as syphilis, may become attenuated over time, giving both the parasite and the host a chance to live.)*

SECTION REVIEW
Assign the *Section Review.*

Reteaching
Have students imagine that they are on an expedition to a tropical rain forest when they suddenly come upon a very strange-looking organism. On closer examination, they discover that there are actually two organisms attached to one another. Have students describe how they would determine what kind of symbiotic relationship these organisms share. *(Students should examine whether one organism feeds on the other, whether both benefit, or whether one benefits and the other is unaffected by the relationship.)*

ANSWERS TO
SECTION REVIEW

1 Answers will vary. Students should suggest species that have evolved in response to other living members of their ecosystem.

2 No. These plants are pollinated by wind. They do not need to produce colorful flowers to attract a pollinator.

3 Plants evolved poisonous chemicals that deter caterpillars. In response, caterpillars have evolved the ability to detoxify the defensive chemicals of their food plants.

4 By separating the organisms and looking for evidence that indicates that they suffer from the separation, the relationship can be determined.

Key to Strategies
● Understanding Concepts (Tier I)
■ Applying Information (Tier II)
▲ Critical Thinking (Tier III)

How Ecosystems Change 277

Scheduling
See the **Lesson Planning Guide** on pages 271A and 271B for lecture, classwork, and assignment options for Section 15-2.

Demonstration

● **Comparing Functions**
Tell students that the difference between a habitat and a niche can be illustrated with an analogy. Their house or apartment is their habitat. What they do in their habitat is their niche. Show students a picture of a house, and tell them that this represents a habitat. Tell them that a family of four occupies the house— a father, a mother, a teenage girl, and a baby boy. Have them describe what possible niche (role) each might play. *(The teenage girl, for example, might be a high school senior who works part time, takes care of her baby brother when her mother works, likes Italian food, and enjoys playing board games with her family.)* What is each person's fundamental niche? *(The baby prefers room temperatures, demands food when hungry, eats baby foods, and is incapable of finding his own food.)*

Our effect on the environment now extends to all parts of the globe, to every living thing in the world. Whether the world's ecosystems can survive depends on how they respond to human interference. The relationships among organisms in an ecosystem determine how the ecosystem responds to change.

15-2

Ecosystem Development and Change

OBJECTIVES

❶ **Describe the components of an organism's niche.**

❷ **Describe the process of succession.**

❸ **Relate the stability of an ecosystem to its diversity, and explain two factors that affect diversity.**

❹ **Explain the three main ways that humans disrupt ecosystems.**

Ecosystem Lifestyles

Changes are a natural part of the history of any ecosystem. However, to save ecosystems threatened by human interference, it is essential to first understand that every organism in an ecosystem plays a role in the ecosystem. An organism might be prey for one species and predator of another. The sum of an organism's interactions with its physical environment and with other organisms is its **niche**.

A niche describes how an organism lives, its role in the ecosystem. A niche can be described as the position a species occupies in the movement of energy through the ecosystem. The niche of grass growing in a meadow, for example, is that of producer, while the niche of deer that eat the grass is that of herbivore. The niche of an organism also includes the climate it prefers, the time of day it feeds, the time of year it reproduces, what it likes to eat, and where it finds its food. Each species in an ecosystem, like the jaguar shown in **Figure 15-8**, has a unique niche. The total niche that an organism could potentially use within an ecosystem is that organism's **fundamental niche**.

Figure 15-8
Every organism has a niche, or role, in its ecosystem. The jaguar's niche includes all the ways it interacts with its environment. This diagram shows just three aspects of the jaguar's niche.

Time of activity
Jaguars hunt by day and by night.

Diet
Jaguars feed on mammals, fish, and turtles.

Reproduction
Jaguars give birth between June and August.

278

Videodisc Resources

Holt Biology Videodiscs
Lesson 15-2: Ecosystem Development and Change

Figure 15-9

a The barnacle *Chthamalus stellatus* can live in both shallow and deep water on a rocky coast. These areas are its fundamental niche.

b The barnacle *Balanus balanoides* prefers to live in deep water, which is its fundamental niche.

c When the two barnacles live together, *Chthamalus* is restricted to shallow water, its realized niche. What is the realized niche of *Balanus*?

15-2 section

Visual Strategy Figure 15-9

Have students hypothesize what would happen to *Chthamalus* in Figure 15-9c if all of the *Balanus* barnacles were removed. What then would constitute *Chthamalus*'s realized niche? (*Chthamalus would be found in both shallow and deep water. Its realized niche would expand.*)

Who Benefits and Who Loses in Species Interactions?

● **Organizing Information**

Have students create a **Graphic Organizer** like the one at the bottom of the page. It should summarize the effects of each type of species interaction on the participants. Students should indicate benefit with a "+," harm with a "−," and no effect with a "0." A completed Graphic Organizer is shown below.

Competing Organisms Coevolve

Sometimes organisms are unable to occupy their entire fundamental niche because another species already occupies part of it. Along the coast of Scotland, for example, the barnacle *Chthamalus* is able to live on rocks in both shallow and deep water. It is not usually found in deep water, but another species of barnacle, *Balanus*, does live at these depths, as shown in **Figure 15-9**. In the 1950s, ecologist Joseph Connell demonstrated that this pattern was the result of competition between the two species. *Balanus* individuals grow faster and are larger as adults. Connell showed that *Chthamalus* individuals could live on rocks in deep water if he removed nearby *Balanus* individuals. If *Balanus* individuals were not removed, they grew over *Chthamalus* individuals or crowded them off the surface of the rocks.

Situations in which two or more organisms attempt to use the same scarce resource are called **competition**. The two kinds of barnacles in Connell's experiment competed for living space. Competition often prevents an organism from occupying all of its fundamental niche. That part of a fundamental niche that an organism actually occupies as a direct result of competition is called its **realized niche**. The fundamental niche of the barnacle *Chthamalus* extended down to deep water. Its realized niche was restricted by competition to shallow water.

Competition can cause changes in an ecosystem

If two species compete intensely for the same resource, one species usually wins. The losing species may be eliminated from the ecosystem. The process in which one species is outcompeted and dies out within an ecosystem is called **competitive exclusion**. Competitive exclusion is rare in most ecosystems, however, because natural selection tends to favor evolutionary changes that decrease competition. As a result, competing species reduce their use of common resources, and their niches become less similar.

In the 1950s the Princeton ecologist Robert MacArthur showed how potential competitors often compete very little because of subtle differences in their niches. MacArthur studied five species of warblers (small insect-eating songbirds) that fed in the same spruce trees. Each species spent most of its time feeding in a different part of the tree and concentrated on a different part of the available resources. As a result, competition among the species was reduced. The result of this pattern of resource use is that the ecosystem supports many more ways of life, which makes the ecosystem more complex.

279

Graphic Organizer

Use this Graphic Organizer with the teaching strategy **Who Benefits and Who Loses in Species Interactions?** on page 279.

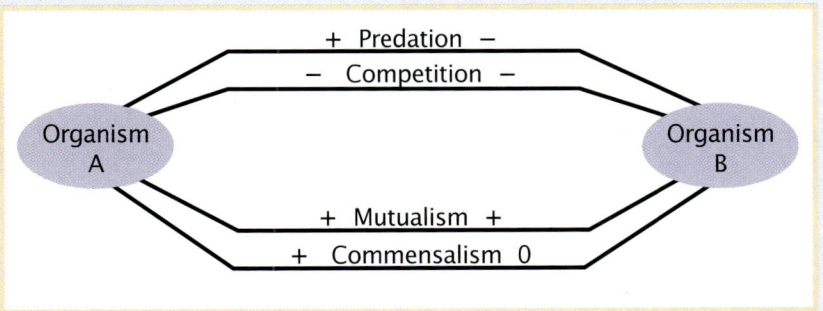

Key to Strategies

● Understanding Concepts (Tier I)

■ Applying Information (Tier II)

▲ Critical Thinking (Tier III)

How Ecosystems Change 279

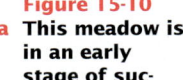
Competition and Ecosystem Development

Competition plays an important role in how ecosystems develop. The role of competition in the development of ecosystems is most easily seen when a serious disruption creates a new habitat. New habitats are formed when a volcano forms a new island, when a glacier recedes and exposes bare soil, or when a fire burns all the vegetation in an area. In every case scientists have been able to study, the empty habitat is quickly occupied. The first organisms to move into a burned patch of forest are small, fast-growing plants—you would probably call them "weeds." On bare rock, the early "settlers" are mosses and lichens, which are able to eke out a living under harsh conditions.

Competition drives change in a developing ecosystem

The initial colonists do not remain in the ecosystem very long, however, because their pioneering efforts soon make the habitat more hospitable. As a result of this improvement, later arrivals soon outcompete and replace the original inhabitants. This second wave of immigrants is replaced in turn by still other species that are better able to survive in the new environment. As the ecosystem matures, niches become more and more finely subdivided, and species become more and more interdependent. Hence, the diversity of the ecosystem usually increases as the ecosystem matures.

The regular progression of species replacement in a developing ecosystem is called **succession**. When succession takes place on land where there was no previous growth, it is called **primary succession**. When it occurs in areas where there has been previous growth, such as in abandoned fields or forest clearings, it is called **secondary succession**. **Figure 15-10** shows an example of secondary succession. Succession does not continue indefinitely. Eventually, if the ecosystem is undisturbed for a long time, a community that is resistant to change results. Although no two episodes of succession are exactly alike, the progression of species replacement tends to result in similar communities developing in similar physical conditions. That is why biomes such as tropical rain forests are so similar wherever they occur.

Figure 15-10
a This meadow is in an early stage of succession.

b Later in succession, trees and shrubs move in.

c After many years, a forest of deciduous trees becomes established.

Ecosystem Stability

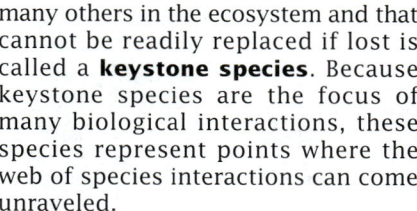

Why does succession stop? The last stage in a series of successional stages is able to absorb disruption without major change better than its predecessors could. Early successional stages, for instance, are easily changed by the invasion of new species. In contrast, the final stage of succession is able to resist invasion by potential competitors. The ability of an ecosystem to resist change in the face of disturbance is known as **stability**. During succession, early stages show low stability, later stages are more stable, and the final community is the most stable.

Figure 15-11
a The sea star in the photograph above is prying open a mussel. The sea star is a keystone species in a 15-species ecosystem that was studied by Robert Paine.

What factors promote stability?

What makes some ecosystems more stable than others? Most ecologists now agree that more diverse ecosystems tend to be more stable than less diverse ecosystems. A more diverse ecosystem contains a more complex web of interactions among species than a less diverse ecosystem does. Alternate links in the web of species interactions are more likely to be available to compensate for disruptions such as the loss of a species.

Even ecosystems that are very diverse contain points of vulnerability, however. A species whose niche affects many others in the ecosystem and that cannot be readily replaced if lost is called a **keystone species**. Because keystone species are the focus of many biological interactions, these species represent points where the web of species interactions can come unraveled.

In the 1960s, ecologist Robert Paine of the University of Washington discovered an excellent example of a keystone species. Paine worked on a 15-species ecosystem along the Washington coast. As described in **Figure 15-11**, when he removed all the sea stars from this ecosystem, one species of mussel that the sea star ate began to thrive and outcompeted many other species in the ecosystem. The number of species in this ecosystem fell from 15 to 8. The sea star in Paine's ecosystem was a keystone species.

To preserve natural ecosystems, it is essential to promote their biological diversity. It is very important to realize that diverse ecosystems can be damaged if key species are lost.

b When the sea stars were removed, the mussels thrived. They out-competed other inhabitants of the ecosystem, thereby reducing the total number of species in the ecosystem from 15 to 8.

281

Demonstration

● **Observing Succession**
Materials: 1 pint pasteurized whole milk and pH strips
Forest succession proceeds too slowly for it to be observed directly, but succession can be easily demonstrated with milk. Maintain whole milk at 37°C. The initial culture represents the pioneer community. As the milk spoils, students can see the pH drop, due first to fermentation and later to decomposition. The populations of microorganisms also undergo successive changes and can be identified by shape and size. Streptococci appear first. They convert lactose to lactic acid. Eventually, the culture becomes so acidic that the growth of streptococci becomes inhibited. Lactobacilli become the next dominant species. They convert the remaining lactose to lactic acid, causing the pH to drop even further and eventually making the environment unsuitable for themselves. The acid sours the milk and denatures, or curdles, proteins. Yeasts and molds move in and convert the acid into non-acid products. The appearance of *Bacillus* marks the stage of milk succession when protein is the only available nutrient. This bacterium metabolizes protein and raises the pH as ammonia is produced. Students can conclude that the very presence of an organism causes a habitat to change.

Stability in Nature

● **Comparing Systems**
The replacement of species by other species during succession leads to a community that is the most stable. Point out that stability is a characteristic of all levels in nature—from chemical bonds that form when atoms combine with one another to the final community in an ecosystem undergoing succession.

Key to Strategies
● Understanding Concepts (Tier I)
■ Applying Information (Tier II)
▲ Critical Thinking (Tier III)

Why Are Some Ecosystems More Diverse Than Others?

What determines the diversity of an ecosystem? Two key factors are important: the size of the ecosystem and its latitude (distance from the equator).

Larger ecosystems support more species

Ecosystems that occupy large areas and are not subdivided into isolated patches will usually contain a wider variety of physical habitats than small ecosystems. Large ecosystems therefore usually support more species than small ecosystems, as shown in **Figure 15-12**. Geography often acts to restrict the size of an ecosystem. An island forest can be only as big as the island. Even on the continents, terrain or human activity can limit the size of an ecosystem. A river can isolate the inhabitants on one side from those on the other side, and so can a road or a fence. These divisions have little effect on organisms that can readily cross them (for example, eagles that fly over fences), but they serve to isolate organisms that cannot (deer that are unable to jump high fences).

Reducing the area of an ecosystem reduces the variety of physical habitats it contains. Thus, the number of species the ecosystem can support declines. Today human activity is causing ecosystems to shrink or disappear, resulting in the extinction of many species.

Figure 15-12
Larger ecosystems generally support more species.

a In the Caribbean, more species of reptiles and amphibians live on large islands like Cuba than on smaller islands like Jamaica.

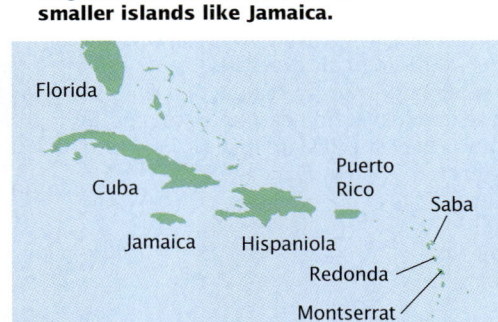

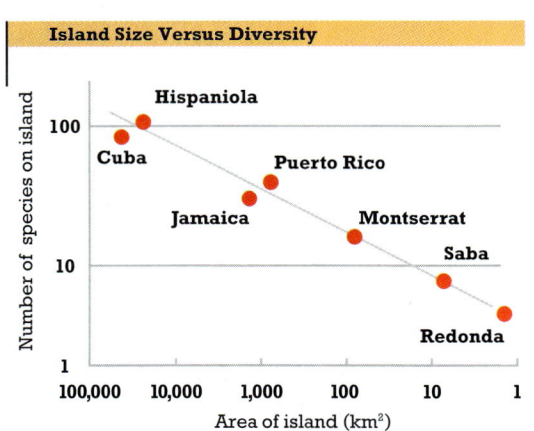

Island Size Versus Diversity

b The knight anole is one of the Cuban species.

Table 15-1 The Effects of Latitude on Diversity

Latitude	Number of bird species	Location
70° N	26	Northern Alaska
30° N	153	Southwest Texas
10° N	600	Central America

Visual Strategy Table 15-1

■ **Predicting Patterns**

Have students identify the latitudes where species diversity would be the greatest and the least. Have students hypothesize what would happen to the diversity of species at increasing altitudes within a particular latitude. *(The greatest diversity is found along the equator. Increases in altitude have much the same effect as an increase in latitude. For example, although Kilimanjaro is located near the equator, it snows at the top of the mountain while temperatures on the plains below may exceed 40°C, so species diversity decreases as you travel up the mountain.)*

Latitude affects diversity

Latitude has a great influence on the diversity of ecosystems because both moisture and temperature vary with distance from the equator. For example, as you can see in **Table 15-1**, there are almost 30 times more bird species in Central America than there are in Alaska.

The tropics, the regions closest to the equator, have the highest species diversity for two reasons. First, latitude helps determine the length of the growing season. The greater the amount of food produced by plants and other producers, the more consumers an ecosystem can support. In the tropics, where ample sunlight, warm temperatures, and generous rainfall occur throughout the year, the growing season never ends.

Second, latitude plays a major role in determining climatic stability. The tropical climate does not vary much from season to season or from year to year. The unchanging physical conditions in the tropics have provided a long evolutionary window for specialized relationships to coevolve. In temperate or arctic regions, by contrast, weather can vary a great deal from one year to the next and does vary from season to season. Conditions do not usually persist long enough for coevolution to foster as many relationships as in the tropics.

283

Matter of Fact: Smog

One of the most recognizable effects of human activity on the planetary ecosystem is the presence of smog. Smog is a thick smoke that is formed by the action of sunlight on automotive and industrial exhaust. Smog is a serious problem that can have dangerous consequences for humans. In 1948, 20 people died and 6,000 people became ill in Donora, Pennsylvania, because of smog. In London in 1952, 4,000 people died in five days as a result of smog. Smog also kills plants and destroys buildings and statues. Effective control of pollution controls smog.

Key to Strategies

● Understanding Concepts (Tier I)

■ Applying Information (Tier II)

▲ Critical Thinking (Tier III)

How Humans Disrupt Ecosystems

The most important single influence on natural ecosystems today is human activity. Humans are disturbing ecosystems on a greater scale and to a greater degree than ever before. Humans alter ecosystems in three principal ways: by disrupting the physical habitat, by decreasing species diversity, and by destroying interactions among species.

Ever since humans learned to grow crops, about 10,000 years ago, natural habitats have been altered and replaced with habitats of human construction. Forests are cut down, swamps are drained and filled, and rivers are diverted, all to make room for buildings, parking lots, roads, and farms. Now humans are changing not only local habitats but the whole globe. Burning of fossil fuels releases carbon dioxide, leading to a warmer climate worldwide. At the same time, industrial chemicals are destroying the Earth's ozone shield. These human-caused changes reduce the ability of natural habitats to support living things.

Altering habitats in drastic ways often eliminates native organisms that have evolved to fit the natural habitats. For instance, conversion of forest to farmland or pasture reduces the number of species from hundreds or thousands to only a few. Similarly, massive logging of virgin forests followed by the planting of a single species of tree as a future lumber "crop" diminishes the diversity of forest ecosystems.

Intentionally or unintentionally, human actions often disrupt the kinds of species interactions that promote diversity. Removal of predators often reduces diversity, as you saw in the earlier keystone species example. The intentional or accidental introduction of exotic species from other parts of the world, such as the fire ants shown in **Figure 15-13**, can disrupt competitive balances that have coevolved among native species. Freed from the controls imposed by their natural predators and parasites, exotic species often easily outcompete native species and may drive them to extinction.

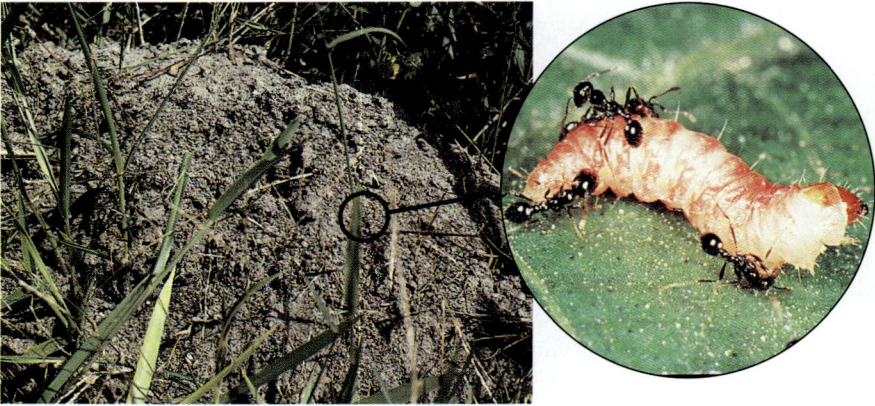

Figure 15-13
This is a fire-ant mound. Brazilian fire ants were accidentally introduced into Mobile, Alabama, in the 1920s. They are now found throughout the South. Fire ants are very aggressive, and they have had a serious negative impact on many native species.

SECTION REVIEW

❶ Describe the niche of humans.

❷ What features of weeds make them well suited for their role in early successional stages?

❸ Explain what makes high-diversity ecosystems more stable than low-diversity ecosystems.

❹ Why do introduced species often have an advantage over their native competitors?

Naturally occurring fires are part of the process of succession in many ecosystems.

	Key Terms	Summary
15-1 **Interactions Within Ecosystems**  This boxing crab has a commensal relationship with the anemones it is carrying.	coevolution (p. 273) symbiosis (p. 276) parasitism (p. 276) mutualism (p. 276) commensalism (p. 277)	• Species evolve in response to other living members of their ecosystems. This process, called coevolution, shapes the species interactions in an ecosystem. • Insects and flowers coevolve, as do plants and the herbivores that attempt to eat them. • A symbiosis is a close, long-term relationship between species. • In parasitism, one species (the parasite) lives on or in another species (the host). Mutualism is a symbiotic relationship in which all parties benefit. Commensalism is a relationship in which one species benefits and the other is neither helped nor harmed.
15-2 **Ecosystem Development and Change**  The sea star in the 15-species ecosystem studied by Robert Paine is an example of a keystone species.	niche (p. 278) fundamental niche (p. 278) competition (p. 279) realized niche (p. 279) competitive exclusion (p. 279) succession (p. 280) primary succession (p. 280) secondary succession (p. 280) stability (p. 281) keystone species (p. 281)	• An organism's niche is the sum of all its interactions in its environment, including interactions with other organisms. • Competition occurs when organisms attempt to use the same scarce resource. • Succession, the regular progression of species replacement in a developing ecosystem, is driven by competition. • Stability is the ability of an ecosystem to resist change. More diverse ecosystems tend to be more stable than less diverse ecosystems. • An ecosystem's diversity is partly determined by its latitude and its size. • Human activities disrupt ecosystems in three main ways: by altering natural habitats, by reducing species diversity, and by disrupting interactions among species.

285

Alternative Assessment

Tell students to imagine that they have been assigned to design a terrestrial biome for a giant space station. Tell them that they must choose one type of biome and must be careful to include a wide variety of organisms in order to keep the biome functioning for as long as possible. Have them write their design in the form of a report. *(Accept any answer that demonstrates their knowledge of the need for organisms to interact, the need for space, and the need for a variety of organisms that fill the niches of their ecosystems. They should list the problems that they will face and propose solutions. For example, a forest could be created with many shrubs, lots of plant eaters, a few small carnivores, and very few large carnivores because many organisms at lower trophic levels are required to support just a few organisms at higher trophic levels. Other problems to solve could involve space, weather, and even the composition of the atmosphere, such as carbon-oxygen cycling.)*

Portfolio Assessment

Portfolio Assessment on page T39 provides options for building and evaluating student portfolios. Students and teachers can select items from the areas listed on page T39 for inclusion in a portfolio.

ANSWER TO CONCEPT MAP

The following is one possible answer to the Relating Concepts exercise on page 286.

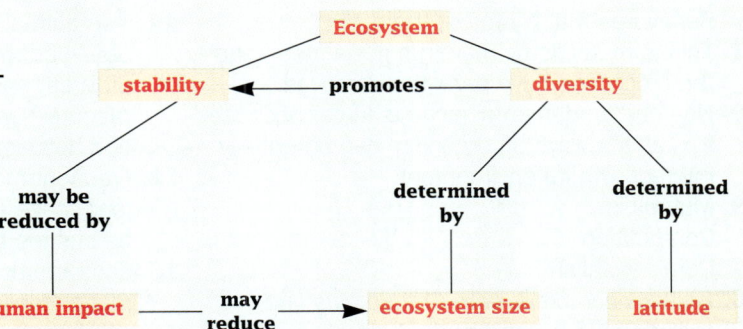

review

CHAPTER 15

Understanding Vocabulary

1. For each pair of terms, explain the differences in their meanings.
   a. parasitism, mutualism
   b. fundamental niche, realized niche
   c. competition, competitive exclusion

2. Using each set of terms below, write one or more sentences summarizing information learned in this chapter.
   a. symbiosis, benefit
   b. habitat, succession
   c. predation, competition

Understanding Concepts

3. **Relating Concepts** Construct a concept map that illustrates the relationship between stability and diversity in an ecosystem. Try to include the following terms in your concept map: ecosystem, diversity, stability, human impact, ecosystem size, and latitude.

4. **Summarizing Information** What is coevolution? Give an example of coevolution. How is coevolution different from evolution in response to the physical environment?

5. **Inferring Conclusions** Bee-pollinated flowers are rarely red, while bird-pollinated flowers often are. What does this fact indicate about the sensitivity of bees and birds to the color red? Explain your answer.

6. **Comparing Functions** Identify and describe two ways plants defend themselves from herbivores.

7. **Recognizing Relationships** Crocodile birds eat leeches and food particles from the mouths of crocodiles. What type of symbiosis is exhibited by this relationship? Explain your answer.

8. **Inferring Conclusions** Can an organism's realized niche be larger that its fundamental niche? Explain your answer.

9. **Organizing Information** Copy the chart below onto a separate sheet of paper. Complete the chart so that it summarizes the effects of the four kinds of species interactions on each participating species. Place a "+" (if the interaction is beneficial), a "–" (if the interaction is harmful), or a "0" (if the interaction is neutral) in each blank. The first row of the table has been completed for you.

Interaction	Effect on 1st species	Effect on 2nd species
Parasitism	+	–
Mutualism		
Competition		
Commensalism		

10. **Summarizing Information** What effect does *Balanus* have on *Chthamalus*? Does *Chthamalus* have any effect on *Balanus*? Explain your answer.

11. **Predicting Outcomes** Why would competition between two animals of the same species likely be more intense than competition between two animals of different species?

12. **Analyzing Information** A lawn is not a stable community, yet it usually does not undergo succession. Explain why.

13. **Recognizing Relationships** Explain two reasons why ecosystems in the tropics usually have more species than ecosystems in the temperate regions.

14. **Summarizing Information** What is a keystone species? Why is it particularly important to its ecosystem? Give an example of a keystone species.

15. **Inferring Conclusions** How are exotic species, such as fire ants, able to spread rapidly when introduced to a new environment?

16. **BUILDING ON WHAT YOU HAVE LEARNED** In Chapter 14 you learned that habitat is the physical location where an organism lives in an ecosystem. How does an organism's habitat differ from its niche?

Understanding Vocabulary

1. a. Parasitism is a type of symbiosis in which one organism benefits and the other is harmed. Mutualism is a type of symbiosis from which both parties benefit.
   b. An organism's fundamental niche is the total niche that it is potentially able to use, while an organism's realized niche is the one the organism actually occupies.
   c. Competition occurs when two or more organisms use the same resources. Competitive exclusion is the process in which one species is outcompeted and dies out in the ecosystem.

2. a. A symbiosis is a long-term relationship between two organisms during which one or both benefit.
   b. Succession is an event that describes the replacement of one set of organisms by another in a specific habitat.
   c. Competition between two species may involve the predation of another species by both competing predator species.

Understanding Concepts

3. See the concept map on the bottom of page 285.
4. Coevolution is the evolution of two or more species in response to each other. Many plants evolved tough leaves that protect them from being eaten by herbivores. Herbivores, such as horses and cows, however, have evolved larger, flatter teeth to better grind tough leaves. Coevolution is a response to another organism.
5. This indicates that bees are probably not attracted to the color red but birds are. This is because of the frequency of red color among flowers that are pollinated either by bees or birds.
6. Plants have thorns, which hurt herbivores that try to eat them, and they also have chemicals that either repel or kill herbivores that try to eat them.
7. This is mutualism. The birds get a meal, and the crocodiles have parasites removed.
8. No—the fundamental niche is larger because it is all the ways an organism can potentially interact with its environment.
9. Mutualism   +   +
   Competition   –   –
   Commensalism   +   0
10. *Balanus* competes with *Chthamalus* and excludes it from part of the habitat. *Chthamalus* has no effect on *Balanus.*
11. Two animals of the same species are, by definition, more similar than two animals of different species. Therefore, their use of resources will be more similar and competition between them will be more intense.
12. Frequent mowing keeps a lawn at the grassland stage and prevents other species, such as bushes and trees, from invading.
13. Ecosystems in the tropics have greater climatic stability and a longer growing season, which enables more organisms to grow.

Interpreting Graphics

17. The two graphs below summarize an experiment in which two types of single-celled organisms, *Paramecium aurelia* and *Paramecium caudatum*, were grown alone and together. Study the graphs and answer the question.

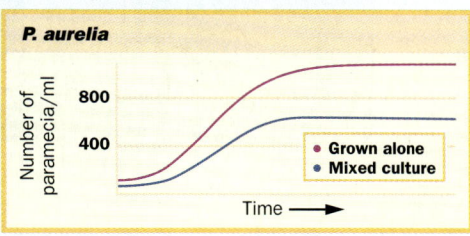

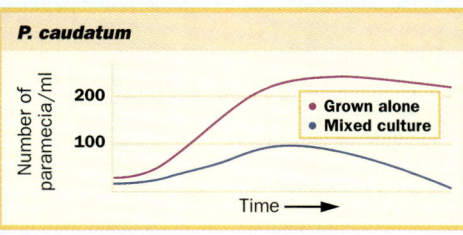

Which statement is most consistent with the data summarized in the graphs?

a. The two types of paramecium grew equally well alone and together.

b. The two types of paramecium competed for the same food source, causing the decline in the *P. caudatum* population.

c. *Paramecium aurelia* was unaffected when grown together with *P. caudatum*.

Reviewing Themes

18. *Evolution*
Why was the disease myxomatosis introduced into the Australian rabbit population? What evidence suggests that the virus that causes myxomatosis coevolved with the rabbits?

Thinking Critically

19. Evaluating Results A scientist studying termites discovered a single-celled organism living inside the termite's digestive system. When the scientist removed the organism from a group of termites, the termites and the single-celled organism died. What kind of relationship existed between termites and the single-celled organism? Explain your answer.

Life/Work Skills

20. Communicating Design a "wanted" poster that alerts the public to the problems caused by introduced, or exotic, species, such as the Brazilian fire ant. Include information about exotic species that are problems in your area. These species might include zebra mussels, purple loosestrife, or kudzu. Include a photo or drawing of the introduced species, information on how it damages the environment, where the organism comes from, and a summary of efforts to control it. Add any additional information that you think is interesting and important.

Activities and Projects

21. Unit Focus Study historical records and documents about the area where your town or city is located. What kind of environment existed there 300, 200, 100, and 50 years ago? What will the environment be like 100 years from now? Prepare a report to share your findings with your class.

22. Career Connection: Ecologist Use library references or talk to a career counselor to find out about becoming an ecologist. Ecologists study the relationships of living organisms to each other and to their physical environment. What kind of educational background is required? Where and for whom do ecologists work? For additional information, write to the Ecological Society of America, Department of Botany and Microbiology, Arizona State University, Tempe, AZ 85281.

Discovering Through Reading

23. Read the article "The Secret Life of Backyard Trees" by Kevin Krajick in *Discover*, November 1995, pages 92–101. What surprise did Neville Winchester discover the first time he climbed a tree in an old-growth forest?

24. Read the article "A New Ant on the Block" by Karen Schmidt in *New Scientist*, November 4, 1995, pages 28–31. How did Brazilian fire ants spread to the United States? What effects have they had on native organisms? What new control methods for fire ants are being researched?

287

began to decline, and the virus was found to be less virulent than it was originally. As a result, surviving rabbits were resistant to myxomatosis.

Thinking Critically

19. This is mutualism because both organisms needed one another to survive.

Life/Work Skills

20. Accept any reasonable answers. Students should demonstrate awareness of local problems created by exotic species, knowledge of efforts to control them, and an understanding of how these control methods take advantage of the exotic species' biology.

Activities and Projects

21. Students should state the percentage of developed land, types of industries and activities of that time, and ways it affected the environment. Reports should address whether current problems will have been dealt with and how.

22. Ecologists usually train in biology, microbiology, or zoology, and they usually pursue graduate degrees. They work at universities, foundations, or government agencies and are found anywhere in the world.

Discovering Through Reading

23. The canopies of old-growth forests supported diverse and numerous life-forms.

24. They came on a ship to Mobile, Alabama, in the 1930s. Fire ants destroy native ant species—reducing their population by 70 percent and reducing arthropod populations by 30 percent. They also attack birds in their nests, reptiles, rodents, and fawns. Plans are being made to introduce fire ants' natural predators, such as phorid flies, parasitic ants, and a microsporidial disease.

14. A keystone species is a species that affects many other species in an ecosystem and cannot be easily replaced if lost. It is important because its presence either helps or controls other species in that ecosystem. An example of a keystone species is the sea star, which in some habitats keeps mussels in check that would otherwise overwhelm and drive out other species in that ecosystem.

15. Exotic species do not have any naturally occurring predators or parasites and are thus able to outcompete the native species.

16. The niche includes the habitat along with the organism's role in the food web.

Interpreting Graphics

17. b

Reviewing Themes

18. Myxomatosis was introduced to kill an exotic species—the rabbit. After the initial introduction, the percentage of rabbits that died

16 | The Fragile Earth

Lesson Planning Guide With Options for Block Scheduling

Lecture Concepts	Lesson Resources

16-1 Planet Under Stress

BLOCK ❶ (45 minutes)

1. Pollution is the process during which substances potentially harmful to ecosystems are added to the environment.

❶ Lecture Resources
- Determining Prior Knowledge
- Interacting Systems
- Active Reading: Brainstorming
- Visual Strategy: Videodisc
- Demonstration: Interpreting Data
- Teaching Transparencies: 74, 81
- Holt Biology Videodiscs Lesson 16-1

Classwork Options
- Laboratory Techniques and Experimental Design: Lab C27

Assignment Options
- Teaching Resources CD-ROM: Supplemental Reading Guide 10

BLOCK ❷ (45 minutes)

2. Pollution has endangered our water supply, promoted acid precipitation in the atmosphere, and depleted the ozone layer.

❷ Lecture Resources
- Influencing the Atmosphere
- Visual Strategy: Videodisc
- Holt Biology Videodiscs Lesson 16-1

Classwork Options
- CFCs in the Home
- Closure: Predicting Outcomes

Assignment Options
- Reteaching
- Section Review
- Chapter Review, questions 1, 2a, 2b, 4, 5, 6, 7, 8, 9
- Directed Reading Worksheet

16-2 Meeting the Challenge

BLOCK ❸ (45 minutes)

1. Special laws have been enacted and pollution permits are now required for certain activities to help reduce pollution in the United States.

2. Nonrenewable energy resources include oil, coal, and natural gas. Renewable energy resources include solar energy and wind power.

❸ Lecture Resources
- Active Reading: Paired Summarizing
- Visual Strategy: Videodisc
- Demonstration: Measuring
- Holt Biology Videodiscs Lesson 16-2

Classwork Options
- Laboratory Techniques and Experimental Design: Lab C28

Assignment Options
- Teaching Resources CD-ROM: Problem-Solving Worksheets 6

BLOCK ❹ (45 minutes)

3. Three nonrenewable resources warrant immediate attention: fertile soil, groundwater supply, and existing species.

4. The growth of the human population is the major factor contributing to environmental pollution.

5. Increasing levels of carbon dioxide in the atmosphere may lead to global warming.

❹ Lecture Resources
- Erosion
- Visual Strategy: Figure 16-11
- Teaching Transparencies: 75, 76, 64A
- Holt Biology Videodiscs Lesson 16-2

Classwork Options
- Reteaching
- World of Work: Bacteriologist

- Closure: Predicting Outcomes
- Quick Labs: Lab A14

Assignment Options
- Section Review
- Chapter Review, questions 10, 11, 12, 13, 17
- Directed Reading Worksheet

16-3 Solving Environmental Problems

BLOCK ❺ (45 minutes)

1. Some efforts to solve environmental problems have been successful.

2. The five basic steps to solving an environmental problem are assessment, risk analysis, public education, political action, and follow-through.

❺ Lecture Resources
- Visual Strategy: Table 16-1
- Demonstration: Relating Concepts
- Holt Biology Videodiscs Lesson 16-3

Classwork Options
- Inquiry Skills Development: Lab B11

Assignment Options
- Life/Work Skills: Being a Team Member

Lecture Concepts   ## Lesson Resources

16-3 Solving Environmental Problems, *continued*

BLOCK 6 (45 minutes)

3. An individual can make a difference in solving an environmental problem.

6 Lecture Resources
- ■ Your Role in a Biological World
- ■ How to Save Energy
- ■ Active Reading: Discussion
- ⊙ Holt Biology Videodiscs Lesson 16-3

Classwork Options
- ■ Life/Work Skills: Finding Information

- ■ Closure: Determining the Validity of a Claim

Assignment Options
- ■ Reteaching
- ■ Section Review
- ■ Chapter Review, questions 3, 14, 15, 16, 18, 19, 20, 21, 22, 23
- ■ Directed Reading Worksheet

Chapter Review and Assessment

BLOCK 7 (45 minutes)
Review
- ■ Reteaching Worksheet
- ■ Thinking Skills Worksheet
- ■ Vocabulary Development Worksheet
- ⊙ Language Development and Reading Comprehension Audio CD Program: Chapter 16

BLOCK 8 (45 minutes)
Assessment
- ■ Alternative Assessment, p. 305
- ■ Portfolio Assessment, p. T39

Chapter Test
- ■ Chapter 16 Test

Test Generator
- ⊙ Item bank for customizing Chapter Tests
- ⊙ Performance-Based Assessment: Effect of Acid Rain on Trout Populations

Teaching Resources CD-ROM
- ⊙ Scoring Rubrics and Classroom Management Checklist

The Portfolio icon denotes items throughout the Teacher's Edition lesson wrap that may be selected for inclusion in student portfolios.

Holt Biology Videodiscs and *Concepts of Biology*

Holt Biology Videodiscs gives you a powerful tool for teaching, review, and assessment. For further information regarding the media on the videodiscs, see **Holt Biology Videodiscs Teacher's Correlation Guide to Holt Biology: Visualizing Life.**

Concepts of Biology adds interactive lesson plans and extensive tools for customization using CD-ROM technology.

Use the following topic from **Concepts of Biology** to help you teach this chapter:
Topic 11: Global Ecology

Laboratory Planning

Holt BioSources Laboratory Program

Block 1: Laboratory Techniques and Experimental Design Lab C27: Studying an Algal Bloom

Block 3: Laboratory Techniques and Experimental Design Lab C28: Studying an Algal Bloom—Phosphate Pollution

Block 4: Quick Labs Lab A14: Determining the Amount of Refuse

Block 5: Inquiry Skills Development Lab B11: Composting

CHAPTER 16

Determining Prior Knowledge

- Have students list different kinds of pollution. Ask them to provide examples of pollution in their local community and in areas they have visited, especially cities. Ask them to rate their examples from the most to least critical.
- Show students a piece of coal. Have them explain how it was formed, why it is called a fossil fuel, how it is used, and how it is contributing to atmospheric pollution.
- Show students a log. Have them discuss the benefits of wood as an energy source. Ask students to name concerns that have been raised about cutting forests for lumber and firewood.
- Have students discuss examples of how an individual can contribute to solving an environmental problem.

Active READING

Technique: Brainstorming
Most students will be familiar with or will have participated in efforts to preserve the environment. Working with the class as a whole, create a student-generated list of these efforts. Save the list for later use in Active Reading on page 304. Tell students that in Chapter 16 they will read about global environmental problems and the ways each student can help solve these problems.

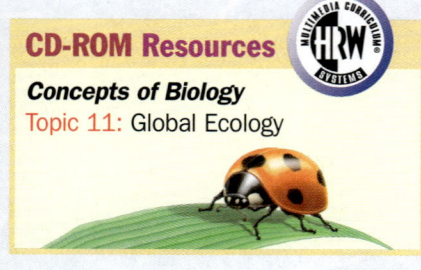

CD-ROM Resources

Concepts of Biology
Topic 11: Global Ecology

CHAPTER 16

REVIEW
- ozone (Section 11-2)
- ecological models (Section 14-1)
- carbon cycle (Section 14-2)
- how humans disrupt ecosystems (Section 15-2)

The Fragile Earth

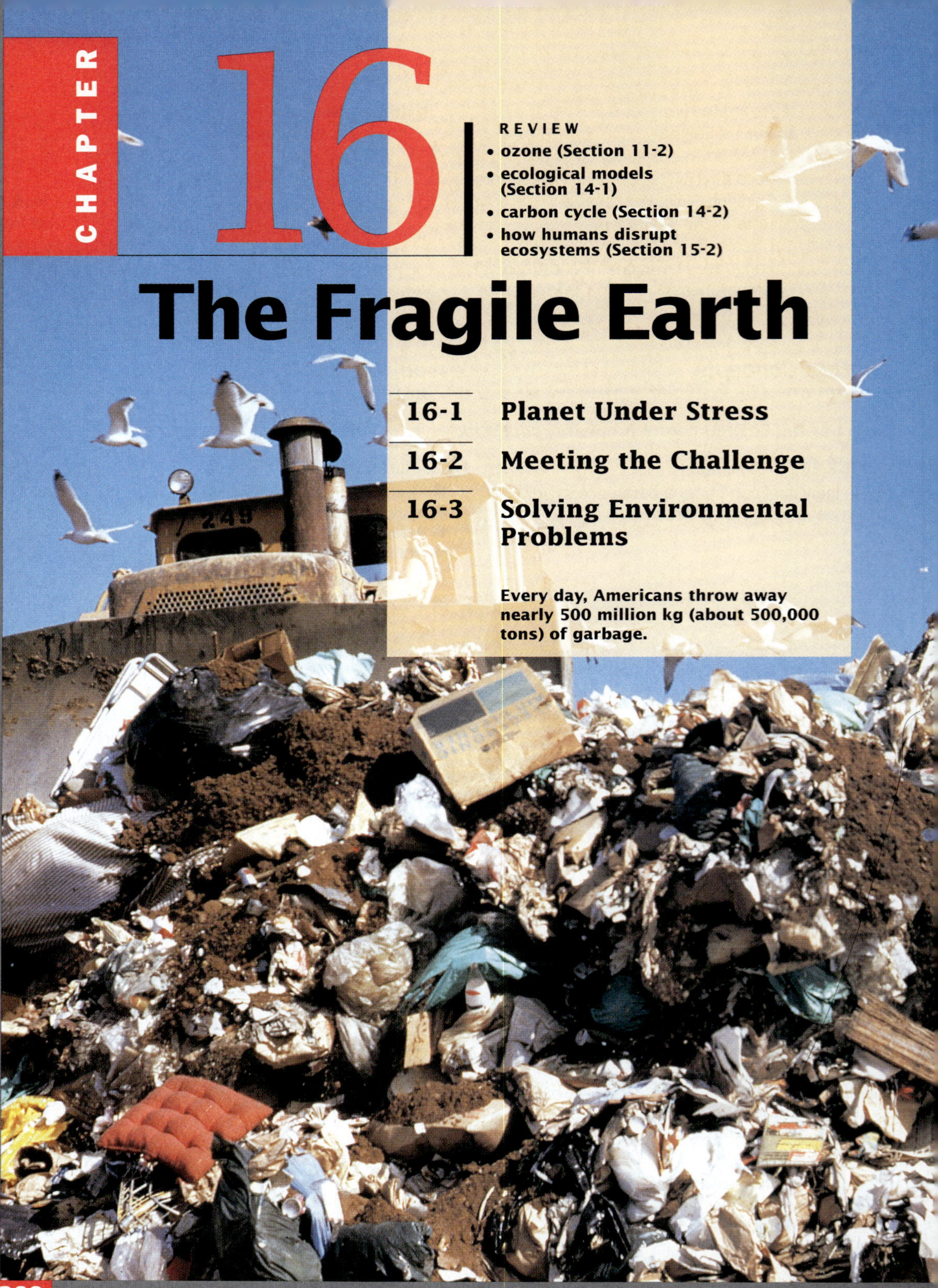

Every day, Americans throw away nearly 500 million kg (about 500,000 tons) of garbage.

288

Author's Rationale This final chapter in the unit focuses on today's major ecological problems. An explanation is given for how each problem arose, leading inevitably back to the world's exploding human population. The discussion of each problem focuses on developing reasonable solutions.

Imagine every plastic wrapper, cup, and container you have ever thrown away piled up beside you. All of this plastic is still in the environment. Plastics are just one of the many kinds of chemicals and other substances that humans are adding to ecosystems, sometimes with damaging effects to our health and the health of ecosystems.

16-1 Planet Under Stress

OBJECTIVES

1 List some ways that human health is affected by pollution.

2 Explain the cause and the effects of acid rain.

3 Identify the causes and effects of ozone depletion.

4 Describe why global temperatures are rising.

Humans Have Damaged the Environment

Our world is a patchwork of interconnected ecosystems. Because of this interdependence, damage done to any one ecosystem can have ill effects on others. Burning sulfur-rich coal in Missouri kills trees in Canada; dumping refrigerator coolants in California destroys atmospheric ozone over Antarctica and leads to higher rates of skin cancer in Paris. Biologists call such widespread effects on our world *global change.*

How much trash do you think you throw away? On average, each American tosses out almost 2 kg (4 lb) of unwanted paper, metals, glass, plastics, food, and other items *every day.* We cannot banish our wastes from existence—garbage does not just disappear when you haul it to the curb or drop it into a dumpster. We release our wastes into the environment—the water, the air, and the soil, as shown in **Figure 16-1**. **Pollution** is anything

potentially harmful that humans add to the environment. Automobile exhaust is an example of pollution, as are poisonous chemicals dumped into rivers and heat from the cooling towers of nuclear power plants. The substance added to the environment is called a pollutant. Automobile exhaust, for example, contains a variety of pollutants. Until recently, people felt that the environment could absorb and dilute pollution without suffering ill effects. It is now apparent that this was a mistaken belief.

Pollution can drastically damage the health of ecosystems as well as the health of human beings. Some pollutants are poisonous. Others are carcinogens. A **carcinogen** is a substance that causes cancer. Examples of carcinogens include industrial chemicals such as dioxin, benzene, and carbon tetrachloride (a solvent formerly used in dry cleaning).

Figure 16-1
The chemicals that these smokestacks are pouring into the air are pollutants.

289

Videodisc Resources

Holt Biology Videodiscs
Lesson 16-1: Planet Under Stress

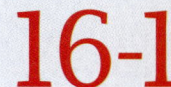

Phase One
Preparation

Scheduling
See the **Lesson Planning Guide** on pages 287A and 287B for lecture, classwork, and assignment options for Section 16-1.

Phase Two
Teaching Strategies

Visual Strategy   **Videodisc**

■ **Recognizing Relationships**
To introduce the chapter, use *Video—The Fragile Atmosphere* (4 min 40 s) shown in Chapter 16 Section 16-1 of **Holt Biology Videodiscs Teacher's Correlation Guide to Holt Biology: Visualizing Life.** After viewing the video, ask students how we are changing the Earth's atmosphere *(by releasing ozone-depleting chemicals, by global warming, and by acid rain).* Then have students use the information from the video to make a list of ways they might help protect the atmosphere *(by not using CFCs and by reducing fossil-fuel burning).* Have students keep their lists, and at the end of the chapter give students time to add other ideas.

Key to Strategies
Teaching Strategies are keyed to three tiers of learning.

● **Understanding Concepts (Tier I)**
Content mastery and comprehension

■ **Applying Information (Tier II)**
Applying and analyzing content

▲ **Critical Thinking (Tier III)**
Practicing evaluative thinking

Geography Connection

Help students develop their sense of geography. Use a world map to point out locations mentioned in the text. When possible, show how pollution from one site could affect neighboring areas.

Connection: *Chapter 14*

Freshwater Ecosystems

When rainfall washes chemicals, such as nitrogen-containing fertilizers, into bodies of water, a freshwater ecosystem can be seriously disrupted. For example, when large amounts of nitrates and phosphates are washed into a pond, they stimulate explosive growth of algae. Only the topmost algal layer receives enough light for photosynthesis, while the lower layers die and are decomposed by bacteria. These bacteria use up large amounts of dissolved oxygen, resulting in the death of organisms that require a high level of oxygen to survive.

Interacting Systems

● **Relating Concepts**

Ask students to discuss ecosystem interdependence by hypothesizing how damage to one ecosystem can affect other ecosystems. *(Destruction of the rain forest in South America can upset the nesting grounds of a migratory bird. If fewer birds migrate to North America, other organisms might be adversely affected by the loss of that population.)*

Pollution's Toll

Ecosystems cannot absorb chemical punishment indefinitely. Too much pollution disrupts the delicate and complex web of relationships that binds the world's ecosystems together. In eastern Europe, a century of unrestrained pollution has destroyed forests and rendered lakes nearly lifeless. Eighty percent of Poland's deep wells are polluted, and one-fourth of its soil is far too contaminated for safe farming. One-third of Bulgaria's forests are damaged or dying. Intensive efforts are underway to reverse this damage, but no one knows if they will succeed.

Figure 16-2
a **Oil that spilled from the *Exxon Valdez* (the larger ship in this photo) is visible as a dull film on the surface of the water.**

Pollution endangers our water supply

Humans need water for drinking, irrigation, and industry, yet we have a very casual attitude toward water pollution. Every day, wastes are poured down the sink, flushed down the toilet, or dumped into rivers and lakes without considering where they will end up.

b **This seabird was killed by oil that spilled from the *Exxon Valdez*. Thousands of other seabirds, sea otters, and other marine mammals were also killed.**

For instance, while putting out a fire in a chemical warehouse in Basel, Switzerland, in November 1986, firefighters washed 27 metric tons (30 tons) of mercury and pesticides into the Rhine River. A deadly wall of poisonous pollutants flowed down the Rhine, killing everything as it moved through Germany and Holland to the sea.

The poisoning of the Rhine is just one example of a worldwide problem. In 1989 an oil tanker, the *Exxon Valdez*, ran aground off the coast of Alaska. If the *Exxon Valdez* had been loaded no higher than the waterline, little oil would have spilled—but it was loaded much higher than that. The weight of the above-waterline oil forced thousands of tons of oil out of a rip in the ship's hull. The spilled oil fouled about 1,600 km (1,000 mi) of coastland and killed fishes, marine mammals, and birds. **Figure 16-2** shows the *Exxon Valdez*.

The high productivity of modern agriculture is based on the widespread use of insecticides to kill insect pests, herbicides to control weeds, and fertilizers to enrich the soil. Rainfall washes these chemicals, some of which are carcinogenic or toxic, into rivers, lakes, and the ocean. It is no coincidence that one of the highest rates of cancer in the United States is seen in the Mississippi Delta region. Here the river draining our country's agricultural heartland empties into the sea, carrying with it herbicides, insecticides, and industrial chemicals.

Acid rain threatens forests and lakes

Many coal-burning power plants use high-sulfur coal because it is cheap and plentiful. The smoke produced when high-sulfur coal is burned smells bad (like rotten eggs), blackens buildings, and kills local trees. Smokestacks more than 65 m (210 ft) tall were introduced as a way to burn high-sulfur coal without public outcry. The intent of those who designed plants with tall stacks was to release the sulfur-rich smoke high in the atmosphere, where winds would disperse and dilute it.

290

Historical Perspective: Acid Rain

A study performed in the Adirondack Mountains of New York between 1929 and 1937 found that only 4 percent of the lakes were acidic and had no fish life. A similar study of the same region in 1977 revealed that 51 percent of the lakes had a pH below 5.0 and that 90 percent of these acidic lakes had no signs of fish life. One storm in West Virginia dropped rain with a pH of 1.5. Because of the presence of CO_2, which dissolves from the air and hydrolyzes to form carbonic acid (H_2CO_3), normal rainwater has a pH of about 5.6. Acid rain is formed from the sulfur dioxide and nitrogen oxides released by automobile exhaust and burning coal.

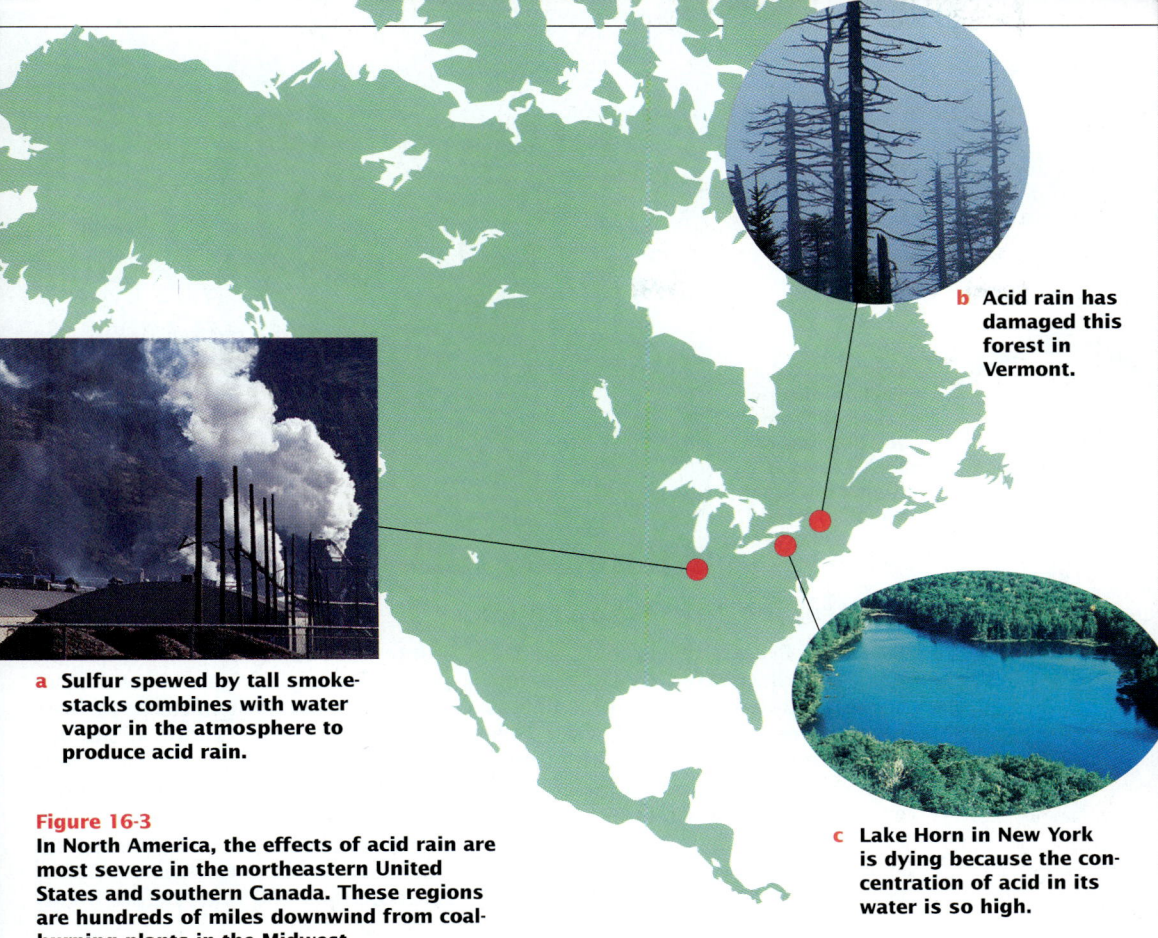

b Acid rain has damaged this forest in Vermont.

a Sulfur spewed by tall smokestacks combines with water vapor in the atmosphere to produce acid rain.

Figure 16-3
In North America, the effects of acid rain are most severe in the northeastern United States and southern Canada. These regions are hundreds of miles downwind from coal-burning plants in the Midwest.

c Lake Horn in New York is dying because the concentration of acid in its water is so high.

In the 1970s, it became clear to ecologists that tall stacks were not eliminating the problems of sulfur-rich coal, just exporting the ill effects elsewhere. In the upper atmosphere, sulfur released by smokestacks combines with water vapor to produce sulfuric acid. When the water vapor later condenses and falls back to the surface as rain or snow, it carries the sulfuric acid with it. Since moisture can travel great distances high in the atmosphere, the acid is far from its source when it falls. Beginning in the 1970s, ecologists reported that the lakes of Sweden were beginning to die. These lakes could no longer support life. Also dying were the trees of the great Black Forest of Germany. **Figure 16-3** shows some areas of North America damaged by acid rain.

What was causing lakes and forests to die? Scientists discovered that the rain in these areas was unusually acidic, a phenomenon called **acid rain** (although it is more correctly called acid precipitation, since snow can be acidic as well). When an **acid** is dissolved in water, the resulting solution has a higher concentration of hydrogen ions (H^+) than does pure water. Scientists describe the acidity of a solution using a logarithmic value called **pH**. A solution with a low pH has a high concentration of hydrogen ions. Rainwater normally has a pH value of 5.6. Pure water has a pH of 7.0. Rainfall in some areas of the northeastern United States, however, has a pH value of 3.8, almost 100 times more acidic than the typical value for the rest of the country.

291

Social Studies Connection

Emphasize that acid precipitation is a global threat. It has received more attention in recent years, but acid precipitation has been a concern since the turn of the century. A few years after a large copper smelter opened in Tennessee early in the 1900s, all the vegetation in a once-thriving nearby forest was dead. Early in the 1920s, the pH values for rain and snow in the Scandinavian countries also began to show a significant decrease, reflecting the increase in acidity.

Demonstration

● **Interpreting Data**
Materials: 200 mL beaker, 1 M HCl, pH meter (or pH strips)
Students often do not know the magnitude of the difference between two solutions that differ by only one pH unit. To demonstrate this difference, have students measure the pH of some water that has been previously adjusted to pH 6. Then take 10 mL of the water and add 90 mL of distilled water to it. Measure the pH to show that the tenfold dilution resulted in only a one-unit change on the pH scale. Students should realize that rainwater with a pH of 3.8 is almost 100 times as acidic as normal rainwater.

Influencing the Atmosphere

● **Organizing Information**
Have students construct a **graphic organizer,** similar to the one shown at the bottom of this page, that shows how human activities are disrupting the atmosphere.

Graphic Organizer

Use the following graphic organizer with the teaching strategy **Influencing the Atmosphere** on page 291.

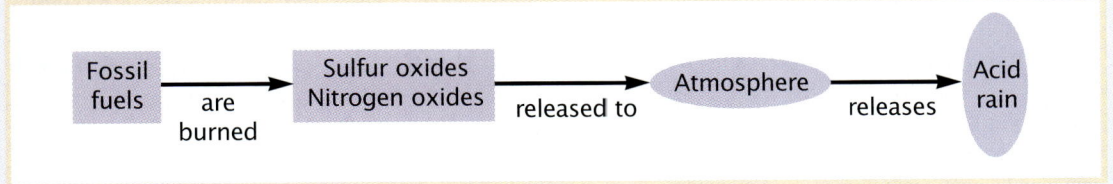

Fossil fuels → are burned → Sulfur oxides Nitrogen oxides → released to → Atmosphere → releases → Acid rain

Key to Strategies
● Understanding Concepts (Tier I)
■ Applying Information (Tier II)
▲ Critical Thinking (Tier III)

The Fragile Earth 291

CFCs in the Home
● **Organizing Data**
Have students prepare a list of items in their homes that release CFCs (*Styrofoam, paint solvents, old refrigerators, and air conditioners*).

Connection: *Chapter 5*

Enzymes
Review how enzymes remain unchanged after they have catalyzed a reaction so that students can understand that CFCs may catalyze reactions for more than 150 years before breaking down.

Connection: *Chapter 5*

UV Radiation
Tell students to review Figure 5-12 on page 86 to determine where ultraviolet light is located in the electromagnetic spectrum.

Connection: *Chapter 14*

UV Light and the Food Web
Remind students about the food web they studied in Chapter 14. Increased ultraviolet radiation in the Antarctic could have a far-reaching impact on that ecosystem, moving up from algae to the zooplankton that the krill eat, and on through a web that includes fish, sea birds, seals, whales, and dolphins.

1980

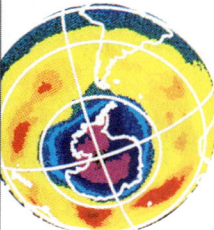
1989

1992

Figure 16-4
This series of images was taken by a satellite over the South Pole. The colors were added by computer and indicate the levels of ozone in the atmosphere. Black, purple, and blue indicate the lowest ozone levels. The ozone hole is visible as a blue or purple blotch in the center of each photo.

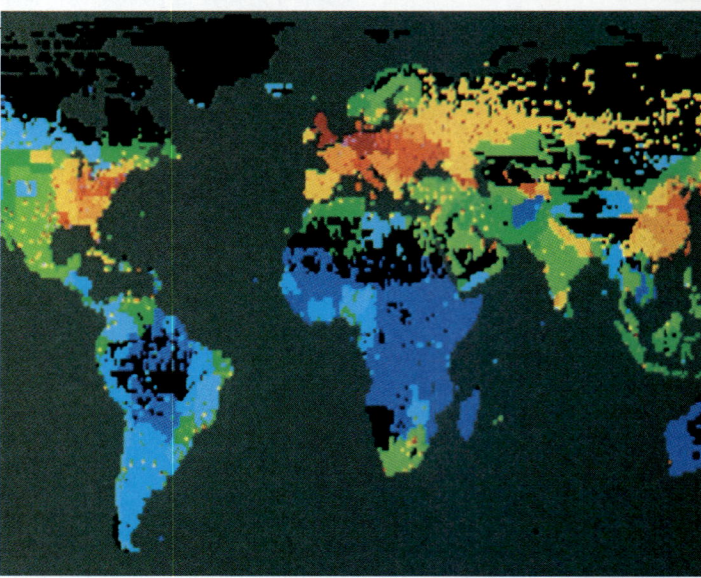

Figure 16-5a
Carbon dioxide released from the burning of fossil fuels is highest in areas shaded red and lowest in areas shaded blue.

Destroying the Ozone Layer

In 1985, British researchers in the Antarctic discovered that the ozone concentration over the South Pole was much lower than expected. A decrease in the amount of ozone in the upper atmosphere has caused a "hole" in the ozone layer, as shown in **Figure 16-4**. Currently, the ozone hole is about the size of North America and grows every year. Ozone destruction is occurring over areas other than Antarctica. A similar but smaller zone of very low ozone levels has appeared over the Arctic. And the ozone layer over most of the globe is thinning.

What is destroying the ozone? The major culprit is a class of chemicals that scientists once thought were harmless—**chlorofluorocarbons** (CFCs). Since their invention in the 1920s, CFCs have been manufactured for use as the coolant in refrigerators and air conditioners, as the propellant in aerosol cans, and as the foaming agent in the production of plastic-foam containers.

Eventually CFCs escaped into the atmosphere and accumulated there. High in the atmosphere, CFCs began to attack ozone molecules. Just as an enzyme carries out a reaction in your cells without being changed itself, so CFCs catalyze the conversion of ozone (O_3) into oxygen (O_2).

International agreements to ban the production of CFCs and several other ozone-destroying chemicals have been signed. But no one knows if the ban has come in time. The vast majority of CFCs produced have not yet reached the Earth's upper atmosphere. Furthermore, CFCs are long-lived molecules; some kinds can destroy ozone for more than 100 years before finally breaking down.

Ozone depletion leads to health problems
The ozone layer blocks ultraviolet (UV) radiation. Ozone depletion is frightening because exposure to high levels of UV radiation can cause severe health problems. In humans, exposure to UV radiation causes skin cancer and cataracts, an eye disorder that can lead to blindness if not treated. Experts estimate that each 1 percent drop in atmospheric ozone leads to a 3 percent increase in the incidence of skin cancer. Thus, the drop of just over 6 percent in ozone concentration that has already occurred is estimated to have caused an increase of as much as 18–20 percent in skin cancer. In addition, productivity of the ocean's plankton, the basis of all oceanic food webs, has declined as a result of increased levels of UV radiation.

292

Matter of Fact: Greenhouse Gases
Gases other than carbon dioxide also contribute to the greenhouse effect. These include methane, nitrous oxide, and CFCs. The atmospheric level of methane has doubled in the last 200 years as a result of the anaerobic bacterial decomposition of organic matter. This decomposing action has occurred mainly in rice paddies and in the digestive tracts of cattle and sheep. Students may be amused to learn that belching cattle and sheep are a source of greenhouse gases.

Global Warming

For more than 200 years, our industrial society has grown on a diet of cheap energy. Much of this energy has been obtained by the burning of fossil fuels. **Figure 16-5a** shows that most of the carbon dioxide released by burning fossil fuels comes from industrialized nations. When something is burned, its molecules are broken apart. They combine with oxygen, freeing energy as a result. Coal, oil, and natural gas are the remains of ancient organisms and are rich in carbon. When fossil fuels are burned, this carbon combines with oxygen to produce carbon dioxide. Centuries of fossil-fuel burning has released large quantities of carbon dioxide into the atmosphere.

Plants use carbon dioxide to make carbohydrates. Unfortunately, too much carbon dioxide is harmful. As you learned in Chapter 14, carbon dioxide absorbs solar energy, trapping heat in the atmosphere. That is one reason why the Earth is warm and the moon (which has no atmosphere) is

very cold. Most scientists think that the increased levels of carbon dioxide in the atmosphere are causing increases in global temperatures, or **global warming**. **Figure 16-5b** compares the release of carbon dioxide from all sources with the change in global temperatures. Today the average global temperature is about 0.6°C (1°F) higher than it was a century ago. Nearly all scientists think this temperature increase is the result of human modification of the atmosphere.

Global warming may have many serious consequences

Most scientists studying the problem expect the world's average annual temperature to rise 1.5–4.5°C (3–8°F) by the year 2100. Based on this, the city of Dallas, Texas, would have 78 days each year in which the temperature would be greater than 38°C (100°F), compared with only 19 such days currently.

That 1.5°C–4.5°C change is approximately equal to the temperature change from the last ice age, 15,000 years ago, until now. However, the change in temperature is now occurring over a period of less than 100 years. Obviously, this kind of climatic change will vastly change patterns of rainfall and temperature, which will have a major and unpredictable impact worldwide. Rising temperatures may cause partial melting of the polar ice-caps, which would raise sea levels and threaten many of the world's major cities with flooding.

Figure 16-5b
The blue line indicates change in average global temperature compared with the average from 1951–1980. The red line indicates carbon dioxide levels.

Carbon Dioxide Levels and Temperature

● Carbon dioxide level in atmosphere
● Change in average global temperature

Year	Carbon dioxide levels (parts per million)	Temperature change (°C)

Chart with x-axis Year (1960, 1965, 1970, 1975, 1980, 1985, 1990, 1994); left y-axis Carbon dioxide levels (parts per million): 315, 320, 325, 330, 335, 340, 345, 350, 355, 360; right y-axis Temperature change (°C): −.40, −.30, −.20, −.10, 0, +.10, +.20, +.30, +.40, +.50

SECTION REVIEW

1. Define *carcinogen*, and give one example.

2. Describe the cause of acid rain.

3. Explain two health effects of ozone depletion.

4. How does the destruction of tropical rain forests contribute to global warming?

ANSWERS TO SECTION REVIEW

1. A carcinogen is a substance that causes cancer. Examples may vary. Some possible answers are benzene, asbestos, and dioxin.

2. Sulfur oxides, released in smoke, combine with water vapor in the upper atmosphere to form acids (sulfuric or sulfurous). As the water vapor condenses, it falls in the form of acid rain or snow.

3. Loss of ozone results in increased ultraviolet radiation striking organisms on Earth. This can cause increases in skin cancer and the loss of oceanic producers such as plankton.

4. Deforestation destroys tropical vegetation, which absorbs large amounts of CO_2. In addition, tropical rain forests are often burned, quickly releasing CO_2 that would have been slowly released by decomposition.

Visual Strategy | Videodisc

● **Understanding Concepts**
To review the greenhouse effect, use *Illustration—Greenhouse Effect* shown on Chapter 16 Section 16-1 of *Holt Biology Videodiscs Teacher's Correlation Guide to Holt Biology: Visualizing Life.* Have students view the illustration, and ask them to identify the harmful gas given off by industry *(CO_2)*. Then have them explain how CO_2 causes the greenhouse effect. *(When CO_2 is released, it does not allow heat to escape. This in turn heats the atmosphere.)*

Phase Three
Assessment Options

Closure

■ **Predicting Outcomes**
Have students hypothesize which environmental concern will have the greatest impact on their community in the first decade of the twenty-first century, and have them explain their choice. *(Answers should include the problem as well as the consequences of not dealing with it. For example, if the community is located near a beach, then the rise in skin cancer caused by the loss of ozone could result in fewer people at the beach, and the community could suffer financially.)*

SECTION REVIEW
Assign the *Section Review.*

Reteaching
Have students prepare a movie script outline of an ecological disaster. Students should include environmental conditions as well as factual consequences of the disaster. *(Accept any well-reasoned scenarios that are based on fact.)*

Key to Strategies
● Understanding Concepts (Tier I)
■ Applying Information (Tier II)
▲ Critical Thinking (Tier III)

The Fragile Earth 293

Scheduling

See the **Lesson Planning Guide** on pages 287A and 287B for lecture, classwork, and assignment options for Section 16-2.

Active READING

Technique: Paired Summarizing

Pair students with a partner. Have each student read silently about reducing pollution and finding enough energy, on pages 294–295. Then have one student, the "reteller," orally summarize what has been read, without referring to the text. The other student, the "listener," should listen without interrupting (except for clarification) and be prepared to point out any inaccuracies in the summary and to add any ideas that were left out. Students should work together during this final clarification process and may refer to the text if needed. Have students switch roles and repeat this process after reading about conserving nonrenewable resources and population growth, on pages 296–299.

In the United States today, practically everyone, from individual citizens to large corporations, participates in recycling in some way. Seventy percent of the glass in every glass bottle was present in some previous glass container. As you will see in this section, recycling is just one way we are meeting the challenges posed by our environmental problems.

16-2   Meeting the Challenge

OBJECTIVES

1 Explain two ways pollution has been reduced in the United States.

2 Identify alternatives to fossil fuels, and describe some benefits of each.

3 Contrast nonrenewable resources with renewable resources.

4 Explain the causes and consequences of the human population explosion.

Reducing Pollution

The pattern of global change overwhelming our world is very disturbing. Human activities are placing severe stress on ecosystems worldwide, and we must quickly find ways to reduce the harmful impact. There are five areas in which it is particularly important to find solutions: reducing pollution, finding enough energy, preserving irreplaceable resources, curbing human population growth, and reducing consumption of natural resources.

Governments all around the world are now making serious efforts to reduce pollution. In some cases, such as CFC production, the efforts involve international agreements to reduce or stop production of the pollutant. In most cases, however, pollution problems are national or local and require action by individual governments. Individuals can also have an impact. The man shown in **Figure 16-6** hopes to improve the quality of the water he and his family drink.

Two approaches, both effective, have been taken to curb pollution in this country. The first approach is to pass laws limiting how much pollution can be released. In the last 20 years, laws have begun to significantly curb the spread of pollution by setting stiff standards for what can be released into the environment. All new cars must have effective catalytic converters to reduce the amount of pollution they release. Similarly, the Clean Air Act of 1990 requires that power plants install scrubbers on their smokestacks to restrict sulfur emissions.

A second approach to curbing pollution has been to directly increase the costs of polluting by placing a "tax" on pollution. These taxes, often imposed as "pollution permits," are becoming an increasingly important part of laws that regulate pollution. They are a key element of the 1990 Clean Air Act.

Figure 16-6
To solve our environmental problems, action is needed from both governments and individuals.

Videodisc Resources

Holt Biology Videodiscs
Lesson 16-2: Meeting the Challenge

Finding Enough Energy

Our dependence on fossil fuels has led to serious pollution problems and has resulted in rapid draining of fuel supplies. The known reserves of oil and natural gas will be nearly depleted by the middle of the next century. Fossil fuels are nonrenewable energy sources. **Nonrenewable resources** do not replenish themselves naturally, whereas **renewable resources** do. Trees are a renewable resource. New trees can be grown to replace those cut down.

Interdependence

Trees are a renewable resource, but a forest ecosystem is nonrenewable. Explain why.

Alternatives to fossil fuels do exist

Nuclear power—capturing the energy released when radioactive atoms break apart—is one alternative to fossil fuels. More than 70 percent of France's electricity is produced by nuclear power plants. For all its promise of plentiful energy, nuclear power presents three areas of concern that must be addressed if it is to provide energy for our future. These areas are safe operation, waste disposal, and security.

New nuclear power plant designs are much safer than those of the past. The best of these designs virtually eliminates the possibility of loss-of-coolant explosions, such as the one that occurred in 1986 at Chernobyl in Ukraine. Spent nuclear fuel is very radioactive, and the power plants themselves eventually wear out. Spent fuel and components of power plants will remain dangerously radioactive for thousands of years. For this reason, wastes must be disposed of in a safe manner, often by burying them in a remote location. Finally, security is an issue because spent nuclear fuel can be used to recover plutonium, which can be used to make atomic weapons.

It is important to develop alternatives to nonrenewable energy sources like oil, coal, and gas. Solar energy and wind power are two promising sources of energy that are not in limited supply.

Energy conservation can reduce reliance on fossil fuels

The most cost-effective way to meet our future energy needs is conservation, using energy more efficiently. As much as 75 percent of the electricity used in the United States and Canada is wasted through the use of inefficient appliances, according to scientists at the Lawrence Berkeley Laboratory in California. The use of highly efficient motors, lights, heaters, air conditioners, refrigerators, and light bulbs, like the one shown in **Figure 16-7**, could lead to large energy savings.

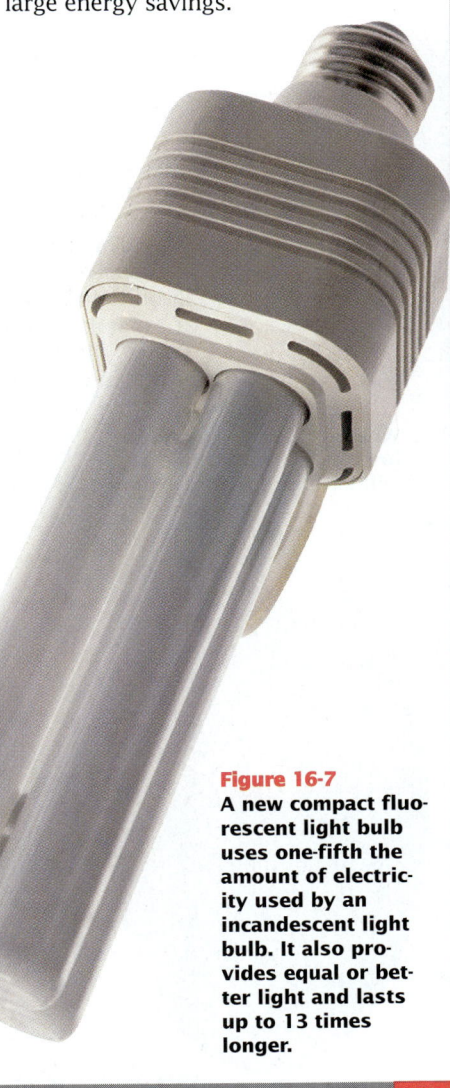

Figure 16-7
A new compact fluorescent light bulb uses one-fifth the amount of electricity used by an incandescent light bulb. It also provides equal or better light and lasts up to 13 times longer.

295

Matter of Fact: Nuclear Power

The first nuclear power plant in the United States went into operation in 1957. By 1994, nearly 40 years later, 22 percent of the nation's energy came from nuclear power. On a global scale, nuclear power accounted for only 12 percent of the world's energy supply, less than that supplied by hydroelectricity (24 percent).

Conserving Nonrenewable Resources

While a polluted stream can be cleaned up, no one can restore an extinct species. Worldwide, three sorts of nonrenewable resources merit particular attention.

Topsoil is the basis for agriculture

One of the great strengths of the United States over the last two centuries has been its strong agriculture. The United States has been able to grow extraordinary amounts of crops because of its particularly fertile soils. These soils have accumulated slowly during hundreds of thousands of years. Although it takes hundreds of years for an inch of topsoil to form, we are allowing topsoil to be lost at a rate of inches each decade. By intensively cultivating crops—repeatedly turning the soil over to eliminate weeds—we permit rain and wind to carry topsoil away. The world has lost one-fourth of its topsoil since 1950. Each year, nearly 22 billion metric tons (24 billion tons) of topsoil is blown or washed off the world's farmland. **Figure 16-8** shows how some farmers have implemented contour farming in an effort to prevent the erosion of topsoil. Another method of soil conservation, minimum till cultivation, is now practiced on more than half of the farmland in the United States. It greatly reduces the amount of soil lost to erosion.

Ground-water supplies are being depleted

A second resource that we are depleting is ground water. Ground water is water trapped beneath the soil, largely in porous rock. This water seeped into its underground reservoirs very slowly during the last 12,000 years. We use ground water in thousands of ways, especially for irrigating crops and in our homes. But we should not waste it, for it accumulates very slowly.

Today there is very little control over the use of ground water, and much of what is used is wasted to water lawns, wash cars, and run fountains. A great deal more ground water is inadvertently polluted by poor disposal of chemical wastes. Once pollution enters the ground water, there is no effective means of removing it.

Figure 16-8

a When trees and vegetation are cleared from land that will become a field, erosion can occur.

b In an effort to save land that has begun to erode, farmers can plant rows on different levels, or "contours."

c In the long run, contour farming limits erosion.

Matter of Fact: Water

Although the Earth has an abundant supply of water, more than 97 percent is salt water. In addition, nearly 75 percent of the Earth's fresh water is contained as ice or snow in the icecaps at the poles. With the average American using more than 300 L (80 gal) of water per day, the ground water supply is being seriously affected. Have students hypothesize what will happen to water consumption in the next decade. *(Water supplies will decrease as this country's population increases. Ground water supplies will decrease. In some areas, such as Long Island, salt water from the surrounding ocean will leach into the aquifers and contaminate the well water.)*

Figure 16-9

The rosy periwinkle, the neem tree, and the medicinal leech provide useful products. How many other undiscovered species have potential uses? We will never find out if these species go extinct before they can be studied.

a The rosy periwinkle of Madagascar is the source of two anticancer drugs.

b In India, the neem tree is known as the village pharmacy because it is the source of so many medicines and other useful products, including a treatment for skin disease and an insect repellent.

c Leeches may be disgusting to some people, but they produce a chemical that prevents blood from clotting. This chemical is now used in treating injuries and some diseases.

Species are disappearing

During the last 20 years, about half of the world's tropical rain forests have been destroyed—burned to make pasture and farmland or cut for timber. Each year the rate of loss increases; nearly 2,000 hectares (4,800 acres) of forest are cut each minute, an area larger than Indiana each year. At this rate, most of the world's rain forests will be gone in about 40 years. It is estimated that one-fifth or more of the world's species of animals and plants will become extinct, more than a million species lost, if the rain forests are destroyed.

Why saving species is important

As you learned in Chapter 15, removing even one species from an ecosystem can seriously disrupt the workings of that ecosystem. Moreover, as species disappear, so do our chances to learn about them and their potential benefits. Like burning a library without reading the books, we do not know what we are wasting. All we can be sure of is that we cannot retrieve it.

Many important and useful species are discovered each year. For instance, the rosy periwinkle, a plant native to Madagascar, has been used to develop two drugs used to treat leukemia, a type of cancer that affects white blood cells. A child with Hodgkin's disease (a form of leukemia) has a 90 percent chance of survival if treated with these drugs. Without the drugs, the child would have only a 5 percent chance of living.

With the advent of genetic engineering, scientists now have the ability to transfer desirable genes—ones that confer resistance to pests or spur more rapid growth—from one species to another. Genetic engineering could lead to major improvements in agriculture—but only if the vast library of genes contained in the world's species is there to be searched.

Figure 16-9 shows three useful species. No one knows how many other useful species have already disappeared or how many more will disappear if extinction continues at its present rate.

297

Connection: *Chapter 10*

Natural Selection

Remind students that extinction is a natural process. Organisms not adapted to their environment cannot survive and reproduce. As time passes, the species will become extinct. Fossil records reveal many species that have become extinct, including our own human ancestors, *Homo habilis* and *Homo erectus*. *Homo sapiens* has merely accelerated the rate at which the extinction of other species is occurring.

Social Studies Connection

Government Action

Tell students that the United States government has established an endangered species list. Ecosystems where such species live receive protective safeguards. Have students check to determine what local species are on this list. Also, instruct students to find out what local measures are being taken to save the species. (*Answers will vary but should include measures such as restriction of hunting, logging, and fishing; establishment of preserves and refuges; and captive-breeding programs.*)

Connection: *Chapter 9*

Genetic Engineering

Review how scientists produce recombinant DNA molecules by inserting the gene from one organism into the chromosomes of another organism.

Historical Perspective: Did Humans Cause the Ice-Age Extinctions?

The first humans to reach North America encountered an assortment of large mammalian species—three species of woolly mammoths, sabertooth cats, camels, antelopes, horses, and large ground sloths. Within 1,000 years, nearly all these species had disappeared. Did human hunters exterminate the large North American mammals? Yes, say some scientists. Harvard University's Edward O. Wilson said, "Mankind soon disposed of the large, the slow, and the tasty." Critics of this theory say that these extinctions coincided with large-scale climatic changes associated with the retreat of the glaciers at the end of the last ice age. Since both sides base their arguments on the same evidence, the debate remains unresolved.

Key to Strategies
- ● Understanding Concepts (Tier I)
- ■ Applying Information (Tier II)
- ▲ Critical Thinking (Tier III)

Mathematics Connection
Zero Population Growth
To stabilize population growth, the governments of many countries are promoting zero population growth, primarily by encouraging families to have no more than two children. Also, a country's immigration must equal its emigration in order to stabilize its population. However, many parents continue to have more than two children, especially in agricultural societies. Children grow to become laborers for the family. In some countries of Africa, children are expected to send a portion of their income to their parents, providing them with security in their old age. Impress upon the students that the issue of population control is often tied to complex cultural practices. Tell students that the population of the United States is currently about 265 million. Ask them what would happen to this country's population if each family had four children. *(While answers may vary, they should take into account the economic, social, and especially ecological effect of population growth. Effects would include increased water usage and waste water, the conversion of forests to cropland, and increased fossil-fuel burning.)*

The Deeper Problem: Population Growth

If we were to solve the many problems mentioned in this chapter, we would only buy time to address the fundamental problem: there are too many of us. **Figure 16-10** shows the growth of the world's human population over the last several thousand years.

Ten thousand years ago, when agriculture was first developed, there were about 3 million people on Earth, distributed over all the continents except Antarctica. As new, more dependable sources of food became available as a result of agriculture, the human population began to grow more rapidly.

What factors triggered the human population explosion?
A population will grow when the birth rate (number of births per thousand people per year) exceeds the death rate (number of deaths per thousand people per year). From the time agriculture was introduced, approximately 10,000 years ago, until about 1650, the birth rate was only slightly higher than the death rate. The result of this small difference was fairly slow population growth. With better sanitation and the improved medical care that began around 1650, the death rate plunged while the birth rate remained relatively constant. As a result, the human population began to grow more rapidly. By 1800, there were about 1 billion people on Earth, and the population reached 2 billion around 1930. The world population passed 5 billion people in early 1987 and will hit 6 billion before the year 2000.

Currently, the death rate (as a world average) is about 9 deaths per thousand people per year, and the birth rate is about 24 births per thousand people per year. The difference between these two figures yields an annual population growth rate of approximately 1.5 percent. This number may seem small, but it would lead to a doubling of the world's population in only 45 years. About 88 million more people are born each year than die. About 240,000 people are added to the world population each day, about 170 each minute. Our world cannot continue to support such growth over such a short period of time without sharply reducing the quality of life.

The human population continues to grow
Population growth is occurring most rapidly in the developing countries, a category that includes most of the countries in Asia, Africa, and Latin America. Population growth is much slower or has stopped in the industrialized countries, which include the United States, Japan, all the countries of Europe, Russia, Canada, New Zealand, and Australia. For example, Kenya's population is growing at about 3.3 percent per year. The United States population is growing by about 0.7 percent, and the populations of Germany and Russia are actually shrinking. **Figure 16-11** shows the current and projected populations of several countries.

Figure 16-10
In the past, the human population grew very slowly. Technology has increased the average life span and decreased infant mortality to the point where the human population can now double in just 45 years.

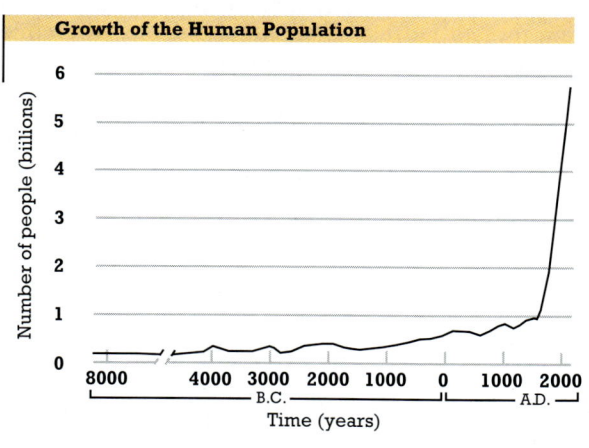

Growth of the Human Population

Multicultural Perspective: Population Control in China
China's population of 1.2 billion is the largest of any country. China has a very strict and controversial population control program, which rewards those who have small families and punishes those who have large families. Couples who agree to have only one child receive economic benefits, including higher salaries, more food, and better housing. One parent of families with two children must be sterilized. The program includes an intensive educational effort and free access to contraceptives. Between 1972 and 1985, China reduced its birth rate by nearly 50 percent.

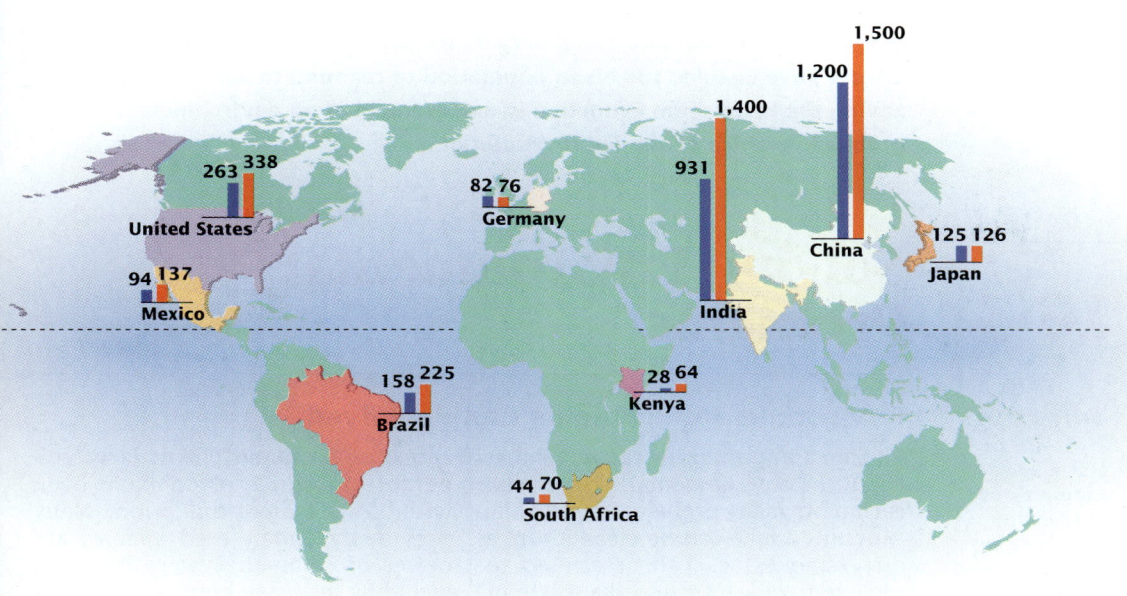

Figure 16-11
This chart shows the current population (blue bar) and projected population in 2025 (red bar) of selected countries. All values are in millions of people.

Many countries are devoting considerable attention to slowing the growth rates of their populations, and there are genuine signs of progress. For example, by encouraging families to have only two children, Thailand reduced its population growth rate from 3.2 percent to 2.4 percent between 1960 and 1994. In Mexico over the last 30 years, the average number of children per family has decreased from five to fewer than three.

The United Nations estimates that if these efforts continue, the world's population will peak by the middle of the twenty-first century at somewhere between 8 billion and 13 billion people. Can the Earth support this many people? Scientists agree that the world cannot support 5.8 billion people, its current population, if current resource consumption patterns continue. Finding ways to reduce consumption, improve technology, and restrain human population growth are the greatest tasks we will face in the coming years. The quality of life available for your children in the next century will depend to a large extent on our success.

Phase Three
Assessment Options

Closure

■ **Predicting Outcomes**
Have students discuss what resources would be conserved by implementing the following actions: taking a shorter hot shower, turning off the water while brushing their teeth, carpooling or riding a bicycle to school rather than driving a car, turning down the heat, recycling trash, and refusing to buy any products made from skins or other animal parts. *(Answers will vary but may include trees, fresh water, and fossil fuels.)*

SECTION REVIEW
Assign the *Section Review*.

Reteaching
Show the class a videotape that features efforts to reduce pollution, look for alternative energy sources, or control the world's population.

SECTION REVIEW

1 Describe two approaches that the United States government has taken to reduce pollution.

2 Explain two reasons why we should reduce our dependence on fossil fuels.

3 Give an example of a nonrenewable resource and a renewable resource.

4 What caused the rapid population growth that began around 1650?

`299`

ANSWERS TO SECTION REVIEW

1 laws that limit release of pollution; taxes on pollution, such as "pollution permits"

2 Fossil fuel supplies are limited and can be exhausted. Burning fossil fuels releases large amounts of pollution, including CO_2.

3 Renewable resources include trees, wind power, and solar energy. Nonrenewable resources include topsoil, ground water, fossil fuels, and living species.

4 Improved sanitation and medical care lowered the death rate. The birth rate remained constant and the population began to increase rapidly.

Key to Strategies
● Understanding Concepts (Tier I)
■ Applying Information (Tier II)
▲ Critical Thinking (Tier III)

Phase Two
Teaching Strategies

Chemistry Connection
Modifying CFCs
Industrial chemists have modified CFCs by replacing one chlorine or one fluorine atom with one hydrogen atom. Such a modified CFC degrades before it reaches the ozone layer. However, these modified CFCs have different physical properties, which prevent them from being used in older air conditioners and refrigerators. New machines were developed to accommodate the new refrigerants. Other non-CFC coolants include propane and butane.

Life/Work Skills
Communicating
▲ **Evaluating Viewpoints**
Present students with controversial questions, and ask them to defend their position. *(The following are examples of questions: Is it right for the government to require a company to reduce its pollution levels even if the company might then go bankrupt? Should people in one state be forced to pay to clean up their water in order to save fish that live downstream in another state?)*

300

When European settlers arrived in North America, 60 million to 125 million bison lived here. By 1889, only 85 bison remained. Conservation efforts have enabled the bison population to rebound to about 65,000. Saving the bison from extinction is one example of an environmental problem in which action led to a solution.

16-3
Solving Environmental Problems

OBJECTIVES

1. **List some examples of successful solutions to environmental problems.**
2. **List the five basic elements necessary to solve any environmental problem.**
3. **Recognize your role in solving environmental problems.**

Environmental Problems Can Be Solved

The most important fact to remember about the environmental crisis is that each of its many problems is solvable. A polluted lake can be cleaned up, a dirty smokestack can be altered to remove toxic gases, and the waste of key resources can be stopped. Solving each problem requires a clear understanding of the problem and a commitment to doing something about it. The extent to which American families recycle aluminum cans and newspapers shows that people want to become part of the solution rather than remaining part of the problem. Progress is being made. Newspapers carry success stories daily. In the United States since 1970, 18 national parks have been established. Forty-two million hectares (103 million acres) of land have been protected as wilderness, and 14 million hectares (34 million acres) of farmland particularly vulnerable to soil erosion have been withdrawn from production. Many previously endangered species are better off than they were in 1970, including the pronghorn antelope, the wild turkey, the bald eagle, and the peregrine falcon, which is shown in **Figure 16-12**.

Pollution control efforts have been particularly successful. Emissions of sulfur dioxide, carbon monoxide, and soot were 200 million tons in 1970, and they have been reduced by more than 30 percent. The release of some toxic chemicals into the environment (notably the insecticide DDT and carcinogens such as PCBs and dioxin) has been banned outright. The Environmental Protection Agency estimates that private firms and public agencies are spending more than $100 billion per year on pollution control, more than double the figure of 10 years ago and five times the figure of 1970. In the same period, the population of the United States increased by more than 60 million people and the number of cars grew by about 60 million vehicles. Had this progress not been made, environmental quality in the United States would almost certainly have declined dramatically.

Figure 16-12
By 1970, pesticides had reduced the number of peregrine falcons in the United States to less than 100. Today, because of government protection, there are more than 2,000 falcons in the lower 48 states alone.

Videodisc Resources
Holt Biology Videodiscs
Lesson 16-3: Solving Environmental Problems

Steps Toward Saving the Environment

There are five steps to solving an environmental problem: assessment, risk analysis, public education, political action, and follow-through. **Table 16-1** outlines these steps, using a lake damaged by pollution as an example.

Table 16-1 Steps Toward Solving an Environmental Problem

Step	Plan of action	What you can do
Assessment	Data must be collected and experiments performed in order for scientists to construct an ecological model of an ecosystem. The model predicts how the environment will respond to changes.	You can volunteer to test the water of a nearby lake to determine the degree of damage done by chemical pollution. You also can record changes in the numbers of animals and plants found in and around the lake.
Risk analysis	Using the ecological model, scientists can predict the effects of environmental intervention. Scientists will evaluate the potential for solving the environmental problem as well as the potential for any adverse effects of the proposed solution.	A local college or university can test the water samples that you collect. Scientists there can suggest ways to decrease the amounts of chemicals entering the lake.
Public education	When a clear choice can be made, the public must be informed. This involves explaining the problem in terms people can understand. Costs and expected results of each alternative should be presented and explained.	The people of your town or city will have to decide whether they are willing to pay for the ditches necessary to divert agricultural runoff from the lake. You could go to a city-council or town meeting and emphasize the importance of saving the lake.
Political action	The public, through its elected officials, selects a course of action and implements the plan. Individuals can have a major impact by exercising their right to vote. Many voters do not understand the magnitude of what they can achieve by writing letters and supporting special-interest groups.	It is important to start learning about environmental issues now so that you can make good decisions when you are old enough to vote. Voters in your town or city will need to ask themselves if the potential benefits of preventing water pollution are worth the costs.
Follow-through	The results of any action taken should be monitored carefully to see if the environmental problem is being solved and to evaluate and improve the initial assessment and modeling of the problem. We learn by doing.	If the town does agree to channel runoff water away from the lake, you can volunteer to continue collecting water samples. From these samples, scientists can determine how well the lake is recovering.

301

Historical Perspective: Auctioning Pollution Permits

The first auction of pollution permits in the United States was held in 1993. At this auction, some 150,000 permits were sold for over $21 million. The top buyer was California Power and Light, which spent $11.5 million for permits. Some public interest groups also bid in an effort to keep the pollution permits out of the hands of industry. Their efforts amounted to less than 1 percent of the bidding.

Your Role in a Biological World

■ Analyzing Information

Remind students that a knowledge of biology will be crucial in finding answers to the world's environmental problems. Ask students to pick out specific knowledge that they have gained in class and to discuss how it helps them understand a problem in the environment. *(Answers will vary, but students should logically apply previously gained knowledge to practical problems as they exist in our environment.)*

How to Save Energy

■ Inferring Conclusions

Ask students to suggest ways they can save energy. Introduce students to the notion that saving energy requires making choices and modifying habits. *(Answers will vary, but students will begin to realize that cleaning the Earth will require sacrificing some activities, such as "riding around," running the air conditioner at a very low temperature, or buying cars with large gas-guzzling motors.)*

Figure 16-13
These environmental organizations and magazines can provide more information on how to help the environment.

National Audubon Society
950 Third Avenue
New York, New York 10022
http://www.audubon.org/audubon/

World Wildlife Fund
1250 24th Street NW, Suite 500
Washington, D.C. 20037
http://www.envirolink.org:80/
orgs/wqed/wwf_home.html

Natural Resources Defense Council
1350 New York Avenue, NW
Suite 300
Washington, D.C. 20005
http://www.nrdc.org/nrdc/

What You Can Contribute

Can you help solve environmental problems? It may seem that the solutions to these problems are the responsibility of far-off scientists or government agencies. Not so. Your actions directly affect the environment. There are many simple and inexpensive ways you can help solve the environmental problems described in this chapter. Some ways are listed on the following pages. You can find out more from your teacher; from books and magazines; from local, state, and federal government agencies; and from local, national, and world environmental organizations. **Figure 16-13** shows some magazines that contain useful information and some environmental organizations you can contact.

Helping conserve energy

The United States consumes more energy than any other country. The United States consumes 25 percent of the world's energy but has less than 5 percent of the world's population. Nearly 90 percent of our energy is derived from nonrenewable fossil fuels—coal, oil, and natural gas. Extracting fossil fuels from the Earth causes significant environmental damage. Transporting and refining these fuels is also damaging, as the *Exxon Valdez* disaster shows. Burning fossil fuels for energy creates pollution; an automobile emits its own weight in pollutants each year. Global warming is a direct result of our massive appetite for fossil fuels.

Here are some ways you can reduce your consumption of energy.
- Turn off all lights and appliances when you leave a room.
- Set the water-heater temperature at 54°C (130°F).
- Use compact fluorescent light bulbs. Although more expensive to buy than incandescent bulbs, compact fluorescent bulbs use one-fourth as much energy and last 10 to 13 times longer. Thus, they save money in the long run.
- Reduce your use of automobiles. Ride a bike, walk, or take public transportation (buses or trains).
- If you drive a car, make sure the tires are properly inflated; this can increase fuel efficiency by 5 percent. A tuneup can increase fuel efficiency by 9 percent.

302

Matter of Fact: Other Sources of Pollution

Most people think industry is the primary cause of water pollution, but industry is not the only contributor. Agriculture has polluted over 160,000 km (100,000 mi) of river, while industry has been responsible for polluting nearly 25,600 km (16,000 mi). The runoff of silt, pesticides, and fertilizers from agricultural land constitutes the largest single source of water pollution.

Helping reduce pollution and waste

Each year, Americans generate 138 billion kilograms (153 million tons) of garbage. This mountain of trash is dumped into landfills or is burned, creating air pollution. Moreover, much of this waste could be reused or recycled. Here are some ways to help reduce waste and pollution.

- Recycle as much as possible. Aluminum products (cans, foil, and pie plates), glass containers, office and school paper, newspaper, and many kinds of plastic can be recycled. Many communities, school groups, and private organizations collect recyclable materials. Also, whenever possible, buy products that contain recycled material.
- Properly dispose of toxic and hazardous materials. These materials include many household products (insecticides, oven cleaner, furniture cleaners, oil-based paint), used automobile batteries, and used motor oil. To avoid contaminating ground water, no toxic or hazardous substance should be poured down the drain or thrown into the trash. Many communities will collect and properly dispose of your hazardous and toxic materials.

Helping save water

The Unites States is the world's biggest consumer of water. In many of the Western states, water is already in short supply. By the year 2000, most of the United States west of the Mississippi River is projected to face water shortages. Here are some ways you can reduce your water use.

- Turn off faucets and taps when not in use. Letting a faucet run while brushing your teeth wastes 11–19 L (3–5 gal.) per minute.
- One flush of the toilet uses 19–26 L (5–7 gal.). Fill a plastic bottle with water, and add a few stones for ballast. Placing the bottle in the toilet tank saves 4–8 L (1–2 gal.) per flush.
- Showers account for as much as 32 percent of home water use. Inexpensive, low-flow shower heads are easy to install, increase water pressure, and reduce shower-water use by 50 percent. Taking shorter showers also helps reduce water use.

Figure 16-14
Riding your bicycle for transportation helps save energy and reduce pollution.

Figure 16-15
By recycling newspapers, you can help reduce the amount of material added to your local landfill.

Life/Work Skills
Being a Team Member

● **Summarizing Facts**

Have your students create flyers to encourage others to conserve resources. *(Students might start with the following recommendations: turn off the water when you brush your teeth—letting water run can waste 32 to 40 liters (8 to 10 gallons), recycle your lunch bags, and drive 55 mph to increase your car's gas efficiency.)* Have students post the flyers around the school.

Life/Work Skills
Finding Information

● **Organizing Facts**

Have students use library resources to locate information concerning how an individual, group, or community solved an environmental problem. Ask each student to make an oral presentation to the class summarizing what he or she has learned. *(Answers will vary but students should show a well-reasoned approach to environmental problems, listing the problem, why it is a problem, and how the problem was solved.)*

Key to Strategies
- ● Understanding Concepts (Tier I)
- ■ Applying Information (Tier II)
- ▲ Critical Thinking (Tier III)

The Fragile Earth 303

Figure 16-16

a We can all do our part to solve the Earth's environmental problems. Members of a community transformed a vacant lot in New York City into a community garden.

b The garden was once similar to this vacant lot across the street.

Why Learning About Ecology Is Important

Interdependence

How can your decision to walk or ride a bike to school affect global temperatures?

Humans rely on the Earth's ecosystems for food and for all of the other materials on which our civilization depends. It has been said that we do not inherit the Earth from our parents but borrow it from our children. We must preserve for them a world in which they can live. Each of us can contribute to solving today's environmental problems. Although it may seem that your actions will have a very small effect, the cumulative efforts of large numbers of people can result in significant changes. For instance, the difference between the two photographs in **Figure 16-16** shows the impact that students like you can make by joining a community effort to improve your neighborhood.

The most important way you can contribute to solving environmental problems is to make a very serious effort to *understand* the environment. You cannot preserve what you do not understand. Although solving the world's environmental problems will take the efforts of many different kinds of people, including politicians, economists, and engineers, the issues are largely biological. Your knowledge of ecology is an essential tool that you will need in order to contribute to the effort.

SECTION REVIEW

1 Describe two examples of reductions in pollution that have occurred in the United States since 1970.

2 List the five essential steps to solving environmental problems.

3 Describe two things you can do to help save the environment.

4 Describe the advantages and disadvantages of using an ecological model to help plan a solution to an environmental problem.

304

Automobiles are a major source of the carbon dioxide that causes global warming.

	Key Terms	Summary
16-1 **Planet Under Stress**  Water pollution and acid rain threaten our water supply and the inhabitants of rivers, lakes, and streams.	pollution (p. 289) carcinogen (p. 289) acid rain (p. 291) acid (p. 291) pH (p. 291) chlorofluorocarbon (p. 292) global warming (p. 293)	• Human activities are causing changes to the entire planet. • Pollution is anything potentially harmful that humans add to ecosystems. • Sulfur-containing pollution from coal-burning plants mixes with water in the atmosphere, causing acid rain. Acid rain is killing forests and lakes. • The protective ozone shield that surrounds our planet is being destroyed by chemicals called chlorofluorocarbons. • The world's climate is warming as large amounts of carbon dioxide are released into the Earth's atmosphere.
16-2 **Meeting the Challenge** The neem tree is a source of medicines, insect repellents, and many other useful products. 	nonrenewable resource (p. 295) renewable resource (p. 295)	• Humans need to reduce pollution, ensure adequate energy supplies, and conserve nonrenewable resources. • Nuclear power is one alternative to fossil fuels, although there are significant safety problems associated with its use. • We must act now to save nonrenewable resources such as topsoil, ground water, and species diversity. • The exploding human population is the single greatest environmental problem.
16-3 **Solving Environmental Problems**  You can take action to improve the environment.		• Almost all environmental problems can be solved. • Every citizen can help by reducing consumption of resources and by learning about ecology.

305

Alternative Assessment

Have the class create a display entitled *The Fragile Earth*. Tell students that the objective of the display is to inform the rest of the school about the severity of the environmental issues raised in this chapter. Consequently, the display should cover a wide range of issues, provide specific information, and show how an individual can make a difference. Make arrangements to have the display exhibited in a common area for the entire student body to see. *(The display should present problems, consequences, and solutions.)*

Portfolio Assessment

Portfolio Assessment on page T39 provides options for building and evaluating student portfolios. Students and teachers can select items from the areas listed on page T39 for inclusion in a portfolio.

ANSWER TO CONCEPT MAP

The following is one possible answer to the Relating Concepts exercise on page 306.

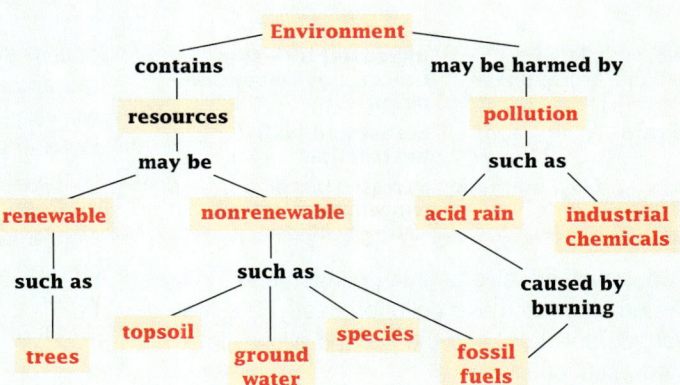

review
ANSWERS

Understanding Vocabulary

1. a. CO_2
b. global warming
c. nonrenewable

2. a. A pollutant is any potentially harmful substance that is added to the ecosystem. A carcinogen is a substance that causes cancer.
b. Ozone depletion is caused by chlorofluorocarbons in the atmosphere. Global warming is caused by increased CO_2 in the atmosphere.
c. Renewable resources replenish themselves naturally; nonrenewable resources do not.

Understanding Concepts

3. A possible answer for the Concept Map is shown on page 305.

4. They were intended to send the smoke from sulfur-rich coal high into the atmosphere, where it would be diluted and not offend people living nearby. No, because the sulfur oxides came back to the Earth in the form of acid rain.

5. Acid rain is formed by sulfur oxides from burned sulfur-rich coal that dissolves in raindrops to form sulfuric acid. It is most severe in the northeastern United States.

6. coolants in refrigerators and air conditioners, propellants in aerosol cans, and foaming agents in plastic-foam production

7. Because CFCs are catalysts and are not consumed by the reaction that destroys ozone, they can do much damage before ultraviolet light degrades them. CFCs in our lower atmosphere have not yet made it to the upper atmosphere where the protective ozone layer resides.

8. The greenhouse effect is a natural phenomenon that keeps the Earth's atmosphere heated, but global warming is excessive warming of the Earth due to the accumulation of CO_2.

Understanding Vocabulary

1. For each set of terms, complete the analogy.
a. acid rain : sulfuric acid :: global warming : _____
b. less atmospheric ozone : skin cancer :: more carbon dioxide : _____
c. tree : renewable :: gasoline : _____

2. For each pair of terms, explain the differences in their meanings.
a. pollutant, carcinogen
b. ozone depletion, global warming
c. renewable resources, nonrenewable resources

Understanding Concepts

3. **Relating Concepts** Construct a concept map that describes how humans can conserve the environment. Try to include the following terms in your concept map: environment, pollution, renewable, nonrenewable, acid rain, industrial chemicals, trees, topsoil, ground water, species, and fossil fuels.

4. **Recognizing Relationships** What problems were tall smokestacks designed to eliminate? Did they eliminate these problems? Explain why or why not.

5. **Recognizing Patterns** What is acid rain? Where in the United States is acid rain most severe?

6. **Summarizing Information** List three uses of CFCs.

7. **Analyzing Conclusions** Although production of CFCs is scheduled to stop by 2006, scientists think that CFCs will continue to destroy ozone for several decades afterward. Explain this prediction.

8. **Comparing Processes** What is the difference between the greenhouse effect and global warming? How are the two processes related?

9. **Organizing Information** Copy the following chart onto a separate piece of paper. Complete the chart by filling in the blanks.

Problem	Main cause	Consequence
Ozone depletion		
	Sulfuric acid	
Global warming		

10. **Summarizing Information** What two general approaches has the United States government taken to reduce pollution? How do these two approaches differ?

11. **Recognizing Relationships** How might widespread use of efficient appliances help reduce global warming? Give an example of one of these appliances.

12. **Contrasting Concepts** What is the difference between a renewable and a nonrenewable resource? Why is topsoil considered a nonrenewable resource?

13. **Interpreting Data** This chart shows the growth of the human population since 1800. How long did it take for the population to double from 1 billion to 2 billion? from 2 billion to 4 billion?

Population size	Year reached
1 billion	1800
2 billion	1930
3 billion	1960
4 billion	1975
5 billion	1987

14. **Summarizing Information** List three steps you can take to help reduce energy use. List three things you can do to help reduce pollution.

15. **BUILDING ON WHAT YOU HAVE LEARNED** In Chapter 14 you learned about ecological models. Explain how ecological models help scientists understand and plan solutions for environmental problems.

9.

Ozone depletion	**CFCs in atmosphere**	**Increased UV—skin cancer, phytoplankton death**
Acid rain	Sulfuric acid	**Forest and lake destruction**
Global warming	CO_2, methane	Increased global temperatures, possible icecap melting

10. It has passed laws to limit pollution and levied taxes to make pollution costly. The first forbids pollution, and the second allows limited pollution.

11. It would reduce energy demand and reduce coal or gas burning, which would reduce the amount of generated CO_2. Answers will vary—e.g., fluorescent light bulbs or low-energy computers.

12. Renewable resources can be renewed, such as trees, sunlight, wind, and ocean waves. Nonrenewable resources cannot be re-created, such as petroleum, some ground water, and topsoil. Because it takes hundreds of years to form an inch of topsoil.

Interpreting Graphics

16. A biologist interested in population growth conducted an experiment in which she grew yeast in a closed ecosystem. A closed ecosystem is one with only a limited amount of space and resources, including food. The illustrations below show how the population changed over a period of five days. Each dot represents a single yeast cell. Answer the following question about the data.

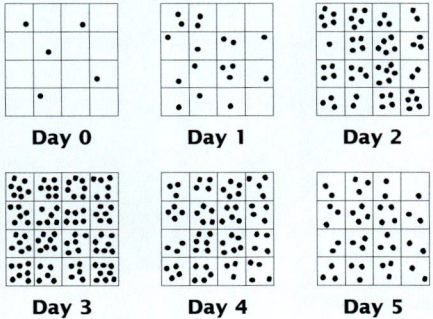

Day 0   Day 1   Day 2

Day 3   Day 4   Day 5

How do you think the population size will change between day 5 and day 10?

a. The population will drop slightly and then level off to the appropriate number of yeast cells for the ecosystem.

b. The population will drop slightly and then increase again as part of the natural cycle of yeast population.

c. The population size will decrease, possibly to 0, due to consumption of all available food and accumulation of wastes.

Explain your choice.

Reviewing Themes

17. **Interdependence**
Describe two ways people in the United States would benefit from helping to protect tropical rain forests.

Thinking Critically

18. **Recognizing Logical Inconsistencies** A candidate for mayor of a large city proposed that the city stop spending money to encourage people to ride public transportation. He argued that the money was no longer needed because air-pollution levels in the city had dropped significantly. His opponent disagreed. Identify a logical flaw in the candidate's argument that the opponent can use to support his case. What additional data might help voters decide who was right?

Life/Work Skills

19. **Finding Information** The oil spill from the *Exxon Valdez* is one of the largest environmental disasters in human history. Although immediate efforts to contain the oil and minimize the damage were somewhat successful, no one knows what the long-term effects of this disaster will be. Use library references or search an on-line database for information about the *Exxon Valdez* oil spill and its consequences. What continuing efforts are underway to monitor and correct long-term effects on wildlife and the environment?

20. **Communicating** Contact your state division of wildlife or natural resources. Find out which animals and plants in your state are on the endangered species list, and select one of the animals or plants to investigate. Find out all you can about the organism, such as where it lives, what it eats, its predators, its reproduction rate, and what efforts are being made to save it. Summarize your findings, including a photo or a drawing of the organism, in a poster to share with your class.

Activities and Projects

21. **Mathematics Connection** Obtain census records from your town or community for the last 100 years, or longer if possible. Summarize the figures on a bar graph to share with your class. Predict what the population will be in your community 50 years from now and 100 years from now. What factors helped you make your predictions?

Discovering Through Reading

22. Read the article "The Alarming Language of Pollution" by Daniel Glick in *National Wildlife*, April/May 1995, pages 38–45. What developmental effects do pollutants such as dioxins have on animals such as gulls and turtles?

23. Read the article "The Return of the Peregrine" by Frank Graham in *Audubon*, October 1995, pages 20 and 22. What effect did DDT have on peregrine falcons? Describe two steps taken to help protect the peregrine falcon.

307

Thinking Critically

18. Decreased use of public transportation will result in increased use of private cars, which will increase air pollution—the opposite of the desired effect. Air monitoring will prove this.

Life/Work Skills

19. Results will vary, but students should find articles about the long-term consequences of the spill and the effect it has had on other food webs indirectly associated with the Prince William Sound. They should also identify groups or programs that monitor the ecosystems in the Prince William Sound.

20. Answers will vary. Students should cite the name of a species, when it was placed on the endangered list, its habitat, possible food webs it is involved in, rate of reproduction, and efforts being made to save the species.

Activities and Projects

21. Answers will vary according to the population trends in your area, but charts should reflect the recent trends and possibly anticipate future economic expansions in your area that would cause the population to suddenly blossom.

Discovering Through Reading

22. DDT caused "feminization" of gull eggs, and PCBs caused turtles to develop with abnormal reproductive systems.

23. DDT caused the falcon eggs to be thin-shelled, and eggs either did not hatch or broke. DDT was banned, the birds were listed as endangered, and a peregrine falcon breeding program was established.

---

13. 130 years, 45 years

14. Answers will vary. Bicycling or walking instead of driving, turning off lights when not needed, raising the thermostat in the summer and lowering it in the winter, tuning up the car, or soundly insulating the home.

15. Scientists use modeling to explain how pollution is affecting the environment and to thereby convince politicians and the public of the need to take action. Modeling can also help provide solutions to ecological problems and predict long-term outcomes.

Interpreting Graphics

16. Answers will vary. Students should extrapolate from the history of the yeast's growth patterns and should also consider the variety of organisms in the ecosystem.

Reviewing Themes

17. By receiving products from the rain forest, such as fruits, nuts, and medicines, we also benefit from the CO_2-absorbing function, which reduces global warming.

Objectives

- Review the causes and consequences of thinning areas in the ozone layer.
- Consider the events leading to current regulations and solutions regarding the thinning ozone layer.
- Evaluate the effectiveness of these solutions.

Phasing Out Ozone-Depleting Substances

▲ **Distinguishing Relevant Information**

Title VI of the 1990 Clean Air Act (CAA) has provisions for repairing the damage to the ozone layer. Have students use references in the library or on the Internet to study sections of Title VI and its provisions. What are examples of ozone-depleting substances (ODSs)? What kinds of consumer products contain ODSs? Have students explain the term *ozone depletion potential* (ODP), and have them describe and give examples of Class I and Class II substances. What guidelines has the CAA established for phasing out the production and consumption of ODSs? Have students investigate these questions in cooperative groups and design visual presentations of their findings.

Handling Ozone-Depleting Substances

■ **Analyzing Information**

Title VI of the 1990 Clean Air Act also directs the United States Environmental Protection Agency (EPA) to create programs to protect the ozone layer. Such programs require the recycling of CFCs and the labeling of products containing ODSs; they also specify guidelines for servicing and disposing of automobile air conditioners and industrial and home refrigerators. In addition to using references in the library or on the Internet, have students contact local, state, and federal agencies for information about these requirements and guidelines.

Science, Technology, and Society

Can the Ozone Layer Be Saved?

Once the international community accepted the fact that the ozone hole was a direct result of human activity, solutions were sought to reverse the damage. But questions still remain: will these solutions work and can they be implemented in time?

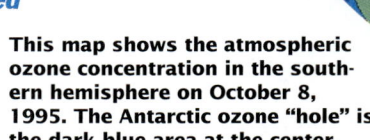

This map shows the atmospheric ozone concentration in the southern hemisphere on October 8, 1995. The Antarctic ozone "hole" is the dark blue area at the center.

The Problem

The ozone layer absorbs harmful ultraviolet radiation, preventing it from reaching the Earth's surface. The ozone "hole" is a thinning of the ozone layer over the Antarctic caused primarily by the release of synthetic chemicals called CFCs (chlorofluorocarbons). Further destruction of atmospheric ozone will cause extensive health and environmental problems.

A Study of Ozone Destruction

After the first reports of the ozone hole were published in 1985, an international meeting, called the Vienna Convention, initiated an effort to save the ozone layer. Ultimately, 130 nations pledged to reduce the use of CFCs, share information, and cooperate in monitoring the ozone hole through the United Nations–sponsored Intergovernmental Panel on Climate Change (IPCC). Because a great deal of information about ozone levels comes from satellites, NASA established the Ozone Trends Panel in 1986 to evaluate data collected during satellite studies and to recommend solutions to the problem of ozone destruction.

In 1986 and 1987, extensive research produced a clear picture not only of the size of the ozone hole, but the cause. Measurements of ozone and other gases were taken from balloons floating above the Antarctic, from airplanes flying through the hole, and from satellites orbiting the Earth. These measurements showed increasing amounts of chlorofluorocarbons, which contain chlorine. One chlorine atom can destroy 100,000 ozone molecules. The results were clear: CFCs and other synthetic chemicals were responsible for significant ozone destruction.

A Time for Action

In 1987, 149 countries approved the Montreal Protocol, an agreement calling for drastic reductions in CFC production. Additional meetings among climatologists, other scientists and policy makers in 1990 and 1992 amended the Montreal Protocol to require complete elimination of CFCs by the year 2000. Limits on other ozone-destroying chemicals were also imposed. Production of new CFCs in the United States ceased on January 1, 1996.

ANSWERS TO ANALYZING THE ISSUES

1. In 1970, Crutzen discovered that oxides of nitrogen, chlorine, sodium, and bromine were catalysts for ozone destruction. He also helped identify the role of polar stratospheric clouds in ozone depletion. In 1974, Molina and Rowland concluded that CFCs can be transported to the stratosphere, where, after being broken down by UV radiation, they can destroy ozone.

2. Replacements for CFCs include HCFCs (hydrochlorofluorocarbons), HFCs (hydrofluoro-carbons), and HCs (hydrocarbons). HCFCs contain chlorine but do not destroy ozone to the extent that CFCs do. HFCs do not destroy ozone but can contribute to global warming. HCs do not destroy ozone and have little impact on global warming, but they are flammable.

3. Russia is the largest country that is not complying with the Montreal Protocol. Other former Soviet republics and Mexico may be selling large amounts of CFCs on the black market. Pressure from the international community, may persuade these nations to stop manufacturing and using these chemicals.

The Good News...

Due to public outcry and boycotts, some reductions in CFC use occurred even before the Montreal Protocol took effect. Manufacturers stopped using CFCs in aerosol products, and many fast-food restaurants switched from foam containers, produced with CFCs, to paper wrappers.

Industrialized nations have developed alternatives to CFCs. Scientists predict that if the Montreal Protocol is strictly followed, the ozone hole will begin to repair itself after the turn of the century.

...And the Bad News

Some industries have stockpiled CFCs. Although production will cease, the use of CFCs will continue for some time. In addition, many countries, such as those of the former Soviet Union, might not comply with the Montreal Protocol and may continue to make CFCs indefinitely. This noncompliance has already created a black market for these chemicals. Large amounts of CFCs are smuggled from these countries into other countries, including the United States, and are sold illegally.

Technique

Climate Modeling

Atmospheric measurements of ozone-destroying chemicals and images of the ozone hole are gathered on a daily basis. These data are interpreted with computers in order to design models. A model seeks to provide answers to a "what if" scenario.

In climate modeling, computers analyze the data from satellites to predict our climate. The accuracy of climate modeling depends on the accuracy of the data gathered and our understanding of the complex environmental relationships among climate, land, and ocean. Scientists used such models to correctly predict the temperature changes caused by the eruption of Mount Pinatubo in the Philippines in 1991.

Applications: weather forecasting; monitoring, and predicting climate change; predicting future trends in environmental and human health problems

Users: meteorologists; epidemiologists; atmospheric, environmental and marine scientists

309

Analyzing the Issues

Why did CFC use stop only *after* the ozone hole formed?

1 Researchers predicted the destructive nature of CFCs long before the ozone layer was damaged. In 1995, the Nobel Prize in chemistry was awarded to Paul Crutzen, Mario Molina, and F. Sherwood Rowland for their work on ozone. Research what these scientists contributed to our understanding of the ozone hole.

Are the alternatives to CFCs safe?

2 The Montreal Protocol calls for the elimination of production of CFCs by the year 2000. Although CFC alternatives such as HFC-134a and HFC-23 do not destroy ozone, they may present different environmental problems. Research these alternatives and the risks involved with their use.

How can the Montreal Protocol be enforced?

3 To effectively reduce the hole in the ozone, we must stop the production of ozone-destroying chemicals on a global level. Several nations allow the continued production and use of CFCs. What countries are not complying with the Montreal Protocol? What could be done to encourage compliance?

How can existing supplies of CFCs be destroyed safely?

4 Because CFCs are chemically stable and unreactive, it is difficult to dispose of them in an environmentally friendly way. In January of 1996, a new method of eliminating CFCs was introduced. Read "CFCs Transformed Into Pillar of Salt," in the January, 1996 *Science News*, page 36. How does this method of CFC disposal work?

4 The technique, developed by J. Burdeniuc and R. H. Crabtree, involves exposing CFCs to sodium oxalate at 290°C, which converts the chemicals to $NaCl$, NaF, C, and CO_2. This method has potential for industrial-scale use.

Life/Work Skills
Communicating Effectively

In response to an increasing number of health problems arising from exposure to the sun's ultraviolet rays, the EPA, the Centers for Disease Control and Prevention (CDC), and the National Weather Service (NWS) have collaborated to develop a sun-awareness information program that features the Ultraviolet (UV) Index. The UV Index is the level of ultraviolet radiation predicted to occur in a particular area at noon the following day. Have students find out more about the UV Index. What are the Index's five categories? What factors affect an individual's exposure to ultraviolet rays? How is overexposure to these rays harmful? Have students present their findings in the form of a public-health message, such as a poster, pamphlet, or video.

References

1. Chipperfield, Martyn. "Satellite Maps Ozone Destroyer." *Nature,* vol. 362 (1993), 592–593.

2. Den Elaen, M.G.J.; R. J. Swart; and J. Rotmans. "Strengthening the Montreal Protocol: Does It Cool Down the Greenhouse?" *Science for the Total Environment,* vol. 113 (1992), 229–250.

3. Fisher, Marshall. *The Ozone Layer.* New York: Chelsea House Publishers, 1992.

4. Gay, Kathlyn. *Ozone.* New York: Franklin Watts, 1989.

5. Gibbs, W. Wayt. "The Treaty That Worked—Almost." *Scientific American,* September 1995, 18–19.

6. Kerr, Richard A. "Not Over the Arctic—For Now." *Science,* vol. 256 (1992), 734.

7. Lawler, Andrew. "Making Nice With the Nobelists." *Science,* vol. 270 (1995), 1291.

Four

Diversity of Life

Sheep grazing on South Island, New Zealand

The next time you eat, think about your food. Is it from a plant that received artificial fertilizer or one that was nourished with compost and mulch? Is it from an animal that was grazed on grass or from one that was fed a fortified formula?

Getting the Job Done

Farmers need high yields per acre and healthy crops and live-stock in order to feed millions of consumers like you. For decades, they turned exclusively to com-mercial fertilizers, herbicides, and pesticides to help them. Now some chemicals are suspected of fouling streams, polluting ground water, and endangering other forms of life.

Back to Basics

"Sustainable agriculture" is a form of agriculture that aims to improve the soil by cooperating with nature. It is helping some farmers achieve impressive yields with fewer chemicals and less machinery, and it is produc-ing healthier conditions for work-ers, plants, and beneficial bacteria and insects.

LOOKING AHEAD

- How do beneficial bacteria help cycle nutrients among plants, animals, and the soil? See page 336.
- What role can composting play to sustain trees, flowers, or crops? See page 423.
- How are new drugs to fight harmful bacteria and viruses being tested for human use? See **Science, Technology, and Society: New Drug Develop-ment—How Are New Drugs Tested?** pages 354–355.
- How might art and science work together to beautify an urban landscape? See **Career Opportunities: Landscape Architecture,** page 425.

17 | Classifying Living Things

Lesson Planning Guide With Options for Block Scheduling

| Lecture Concepts | Lesson Resources |

17-1 The Need for Naming

BLOCK ❶ (45 minutes)

1. Scientific names avoid the ambiguity and confusion created by an organism's common name.

❶ Lecture Resources
- Determining Prior Knowledge
- Active Reading: Brainstorming
- Visual Strategy: Figure 17-1
- Demonstration: Communicating
- Holt Biology Videodiscs Lesson 17-1

Classwork Options
- Inquiry Skills Development: Lab B12

Assignment Options
- World of Work: Taxonomy

BLOCK ❷ (45 minutes)

2. A scientific name consists of two words derived from Latin. The first word denotes the genus name, and the second denotes the species name.

❷ Lecture Resources
- Active Reading: Reading Organizer
- Visual Strategy: Table 17-1
- Demonstration: Recognizing Relationships
- Holt Biology Videodiscs Lesson 17-1

Classwork Options
- Closure: Relating Concepts

Assignment Options
- *Small Group* Reteaching
- Section Review
- Chapter Review, questions 1, 3, 4, 7, 8, 9, 11, 26
- Directed Reading Worksheet

17-2 Classification: Organizing Life

BLOCK ❸ (45 minutes)

1. Taxonomy is the science of classifying organisms.

2. Organisms are classified in a hierarchical system of seven levels: kingdom, phylum, class, order, family, genus, and species.

3. Classification of organisms reflects their evolutionary relationships.

❸ Lecture Resources
- Classifying Plane Figures
- Visual Strategy: Figures 17-6, 17-7
- Visual Strategy: Videodisc
- Demonstration: Identifying Structures
- Holt Biology Videodiscs Lesson 17-2

Classwork Options
- Name That Organism

BLOCK ❹ (45 minutes)

4. In classifying organisms, taxonomists use a variety of information, including evolutionary history, structural features, behavioral patterns, methods of reproduction, life cycles, patterns of development, and DNA similarities.

5. Phenetics and cladistics are methods of taxonomy.

6. A species is a group of organisms that are able to interbreed with each other to produce fertile offspring.

❹ Lecture Resources
- Species Determination
- Visual Strategy: Figures 17-8, 17-9
- Demonstration: Comparing Structures
- Holt Biology Videodiscs Lesson 17-2

Classwork Options
- Closure: Relating Concepts

Assignment Options
- *Small Group* Reteaching
- Section Review
- Chapter Review, questions 2, 5, 6, 12, 13, 14, 19, 20
- Directed Reading Worksheet

17-3 Six Kingdoms

BLOCK ❺ (45 minutes)

1. Linnaeus's two-kingdom system of classification did not enable taxonomists to make precise distinctions between major groups of animals.

2. Many organisms have some characteristics of both plants and animals.

❺ Lecture Resources
- Animal or Plant?
- Active Reading: Reading Organizer

Classwork Options
- Laboratory Techniques and Experimental Design: Lab C29

Assignment Options
- Life/Work Skills: Finding Information

Lecture Concepts

Lesson Resources

17-3 Six Kingdoms, *continued*

BLOCK ❻ (45 minutes)

3. All organisms can be placed into one of the six kingdoms: Archaebacteria, Eubacteria, Protista, Fungi, Plantae, or Animalia.

❻ Lecture Resources
- ■ Where Does It Belong?
- ⬜ Teaching Transparencies: 45A
- ⊘ Holt Biology Videodiscs Lesson 17-3

Classwork Options
- ■ Closure: Analyzing Information

Assignment Options
- ■ Reteaching
- ■ Section Review
- ■ Chapter Review, questions 10, 15, 16, 17, 21, 22, 23, 24, 25, 27
- ■ Directed Reading Worksheet

Chapter Review and Assessment

BLOCK ❼ (45 minutes)

Review
- ■ Reteaching Worksheet
- ■ Thinking Skills Worksheet
- ■ Vocabulary Development Worksheet
- ⊙ Language Development and Reading Comprehension Audio CD Program: Chapter 17

BLOCK ❽ (45 minutes)

Assessment
- ■ Alternative Assessment, p. 327
- ■ Portfolio Assessment, p. T39

Chapter Test
- ■ Chapter 17 Test

Test Generator
- ⊙ Item bank for customizing Chapter Tests

Teaching Resources CD-ROM
- ⊙ Scoring Rubrics and Classroom Management Checklist

The Portfolio icon denotes items throughout the Teacher's Edition lesson wrap that may be selected for inclusion in student portfolios.

Holt Biology Videodiscs and *Concepts of Biology*

Holt Biology Videodiscs gives you a powerful tool for teaching, review, and assessment. For further information regarding the media on the videodiscs, see *Holt Biology Videodiscs Teacher's Correlation Guide to Holt Biology: Visualizing Life.*

Concepts of Biology adds interactive lesson plans and extensive tools for customization using CD-ROM technology.

Use the following topic from **Concepts of Biology** to help you teach this chapter:
Topic 12: Classification of Life

Laboratory Planning

Holt BioSources Laboratory Program

Block 1: Inquiry Skills Development Lab B12: Classification

Block 5: Laboratory Techniques and Experimental Design Lab C29: Classifying Mysterious Organisms

CHAPTER

17

Determining Prior Knowledge

- Write the term *Homo sapiens* on the board. Ask students to name and identify this organism and to explain the importance of scientific names.
- Have students explain why a dog and cat belong to different species.
- Assemble and display a variety of objects found in the classroom, such as a beaker, a dissecting tray, a microscope, chalk, pipettes, etc. Have students develop a classification system to place the objects in various categories. Emphasize that they must have a rationale for their system.

Active READING

Technique: Brainstorming

Explain to students that we often categorize things or separate objects into fundamental classes. For example, as the text mentions, the products in a store are often organized into groups. Work with the class as a whole to come up with a list of other things that are categorized or organized into classes or groups. Some examples include books in a library, classified ads, and subjects in a school curriculum. After they have created a list, tell students that scientists have organized living things by groups and that this system of classification is the subject of Chapter 17.

CD-ROM Resources

Concepts of Biology
Topic 12: Classification of Life

Enoplotrupes sharpi—Thailand

Sternocera aequisignata—Thailand

REVIEW
- characteristics of living things (Section 2-1)
- natural selection (Section 10-1)
- six kingdoms (Section 11-2)

Sphingnotus miriabilis—Papua New Guinea

Classifying Living Things

Chrysocarabus auronitens—France

17-1	The Need for Naming
17-2	Classification: Organizing Life
17-3	Six Kingdoms

Scientists give each kind of organism on Earth a unique name.

Chrysotribax hispanus—France

Eupholus bennetti—Papua New Guinea

Chrysochroa buqueti—Malaysia

Euchroma gigantea—Brazil

Plusiotis gloriosa—USA

312

Author's Rationale This chapter provides the framework for principles designed to help students explore and understand biological diversity. It defines species and discloses methods taxonomists and biologists use to classify species into hierarchical systems. The use of analogies keeps the chapter interesting. Students develop an appreciation for the six-kingdom system as they observe difficulties in classifying living things into two kingdoms—Plantae and Animalia.

Do the words *inu, chien,* and *hund* mean anything to you? These are Japanese, French, and German words for "dog." Could you conduct a conversation about dogs with someone who spoke only one of these languages? Scientists—regardless of their native language—can communicate about dogs because they have the same name for the dog: *Canis familiaris.*

17-1 The Need for Naming

OBJECTIVES

1 Explain why scientists use scientific names instead of common names.

2 Describe the scientific system of naming organisms.

3 Explain why scientific names are in Latin.

4 Evaluate the role of Linnaeus in creating the modern system of naming organisms.

The Importance of Scientific Names

What do you and your classmates call the "bug" shown in **Figure 17-1**? You will probably have many common names for this animal, including sow bug, pill bug, wood louse, roly-poly, and potato bug. If some of your classmates are from other countries, you could collect an even longer list of names.

But if you ask a biologist to name this creature, you will receive only one answer: *Porcellio scaber.* Each kind of organism on Earth is assigned a unique two-word **scientific name**. *Porcellio scaber* is the scientific name of the animal shown below. *Homo sapiens*, which means "wise man," is our species' scientific name. All biologists, regardless of their native language, use scientific names when speaking or writing about organisms.

Most organisms also have common names. Why don't scientists use them?

Although adequate for everyday use, common names may be confusing in scientific communication. As you have seen, an organism can have more than one common name. In addition, science requires international cooperation and communication, and an organism rarely has the same name in different languages. Finally, one common name often refers to more than one kind of living thing. The plant we know as corn in North America is called maize in Great Britain. To a resident of Britain, corn is the plant we call wheat. When a biologist writes a scientific paper on *Zea mays*, however, other scientists know the subject of the paper is the American "corn" plant. Using scientific names enables scientists, no matter what language they speak, to exchange information about an organism and to be certain that they are referring to the same living thing.

Figure 17-1
These are some of the common names for this animal (240×). Scientists have assigned it a single scientific name: *Porcellio scaber.*

Sow bug

Roly-poly

Wood louse

Potato bug

Pill bug

313

Videodisc Resources

Holt Biology Videodiscs
Lesson 17-1: The Need for Naming

Scheduling
See the **Lesson Planning Guide** on pages 311A and 311B for lecture, classwork, and assignment options for Section 17-1.

Phase Two
Teaching Strategies

Demonstration
● **Communicating**
Show students a picture of *Felis concolor,* and ask them to name the animal. Answers may include mountain lion, puma, cougar, catamount, or panther. Emphasize that besides being ambiguous, common names can also be misleading. Ask students to give examples of misleading common names, e.g., starfish, sea horse, silverfish, horseshoe crab, and ringworm. Collect pictures of these and other apt organisms to help students identify animals with misleading names.

Visual Strategy | **Figure 17-1**

■ **Recognizing Relationships**
Have students examine a *Porcellio scaber* with a stereomicroscope. Have students use their observations to explain how the common names reflect the organism's physical nature. Have students find the meaning of the scientific name. Tell students this "bug" is a crustacean.

Key to Strategies
Teaching Strategies are keyed to three tiers of learning.

● **Understanding Concepts (Tier I)**
Content mastery and comprehension

■ **Applying Information (Tier II)**
Applying and analyzing content

▲ **Critical Thinking (Tier III)**
Practicing evaluative thinking

Classifying Living Things **313**

What's in a Scientific Name?

The first word in a scientific name describes the organism in a general way. The second word identifies the exact kind of living thing. We use a similar naming system in our everyday speech. For instance, your last name identifies your family, while your first name specifies exactly who you are.

The first word of a scientific name is the name of the **genus** *(JEE nuhs)* to which the organism belongs. (The plural of genus is *genera*.) A genus is a group of organisms that share major characteristics. For example, all oak trees produce acorns. Therefore, all oak trees are assigned to the genus *Quercus*, which means "oak" in Latin.

There are dozens of different kinds of oak trees. One kind is tall, while another is low and spreading. Leaves and acorns of different oak trees can vary in size and shape, as shown in **Table 17-1**. The second word in a scientific name identifies one particular kind of organism within the genus. For example, *Quercus rubra* is the red oak, and *Quercus phellos* is the willow oak. Scientists call each different kind of organism a **species** *(SPEE sheez)*. (The plural of species is *species*.) The correct name for an organism must include *both* parts of its scientific name. The red oak is properly called *Quercus rubra*, not just *rubra*.

Table 17-1 Comparison of Red Oak and Willow Oak

	Red oak	Willow oak
Genus name	*Quercus*	*Quercus*
Scientific name	*Quercus rubra*	*Quercus phellos*
Traits	Acorns about 25 mm (1 in.) long	Acorns about 15 mm (0.5 in.) long
	Common in open Northeastern forests; tolerant of city soot and cold temperatures	Popular shade tree found in the South; grows well in rich, moist soil
	Lobed leaves	Unlobed, narrow leaves

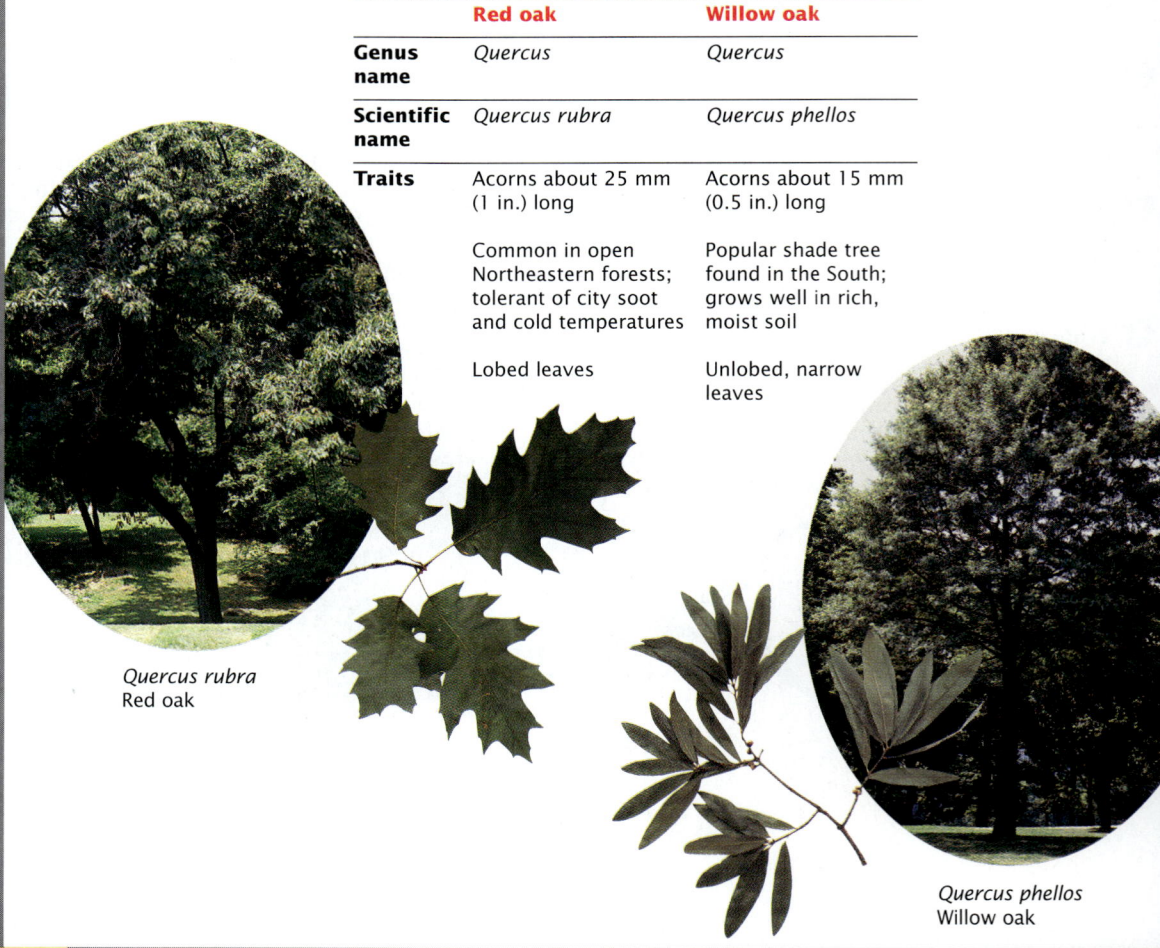

Quercus rubra
Red oak

Quercus phellos
Willow oak

314

Figure 17-2

a The second word of a scientific name is often descriptive of an organism or its distribution. The green anole lizard *Anolis carolinensis* and the chickadee *Parus carolinensis* are both found in North Carolina and South Carolina.

Scientific names must conform to a set of rules

The name given to a newly discovered species must conform to rigorous rules formulated by authorized groups of scientists. All scientific names must consist of Latin words or of terms constructed according to the rules of Latin grammar. Two different organisms cannot be assigned the same name. Because all members of a genus share their genus name, the second word in the name must be different. Only one member of the genus *Homo* can be given the name *sapiens*. Organisms in different genera cannot have the same genus name but can share the second word of their scientific names. For example, the green anole lizard *Anolis carolinensis* and the chickadee *Parus carolinensis*, shown in **Figure 17-2a**,

share the name *carolinensis* because they both occur in North Carolina and South Carolina.

When choosing a name for a species, biologists often pick a name that describes the appearance or distribution of an organism. One of the most vivid names belongs to the ferocious dinosaur *Tyrannosaurus rex*, shown in **Figure 17-2b**. *Tyrannosaurus rex* means "tyrant-lizard king," a fitting name for a carnivore with teeth 15 cm (6 in.) long. Sometimes scientific names are a tribute to the discoverer of a species or to an admired colleague or teacher of the discoverer. The frog *Rhinoderma darwinii*, shown in **Figure 17-2c**, the lizard *Liolaemus darwinii*, and the bird *Rhea darwinii* are three of the many species named to honor Charles Darwin.

b *Tyrannosaurus rex*, which means "tyrant-lizard king," was named for its enormous teeth and tremendous size. This dinosaur measured about 15 m (49 ft) in length.

c The frog *Rhinoderma darwinii* was named to honor Charles Darwin.

315

Language Arts Connection
Etymology

Assign students to cooperative work groups. Have each group select 10 organisms by their common names. Then tell students to find the scientific name for each organism and to conduct a word-root search for each scientific name. The *Dictionary of Word Roots* and the book *Combining Forms,* by Donald J. Borror, are excellent for this type of assignment. Each group will then report their findings to the entire class.

World of Work

Taxonomy

Taxonomists study, identify, and name organisms so that they can be properly classified. To do this, a taxonomist must pay careful attention to detail and must understand the relationships among various organisms. Some of the places a taxonomist might work are a university, a research laboratory, or a museum. Sometimes taxonomists travel to different parts of the world to study endangered species.

Taxonomists need a bachelor's degree with a strong background in the biological sciences.
For additional information, contact:
- American Society of Plant Taxonomists
  St. Mary's College
  Department of Biology
  Notre Dame, IN 46556
- American Association for Zoological Nomenclature
  c/o National Museum of Natural History
  MRC 163
  Smithsonian Institution
  Washington, D.C. 20560

Key to Strategies
- ● Understanding Concepts (Tier I)
- ■ Applying Information (Tier II)
- ▲ Critical Thinking (Tier III)

Classifying Living Things   315

Mathematics Connection

(a + b)²

In biology, the two-part naming system is called binomial nomenclature. In mathematics, $(a + b)^2$ represents a binomial expansion. Have students explain the meaning of both the biological and mathematical terms. *(The word* binomial *refers to a phrase or term consisting of two names or symbols. In mathematics, the binomial expansion will result in a polynomial, with two terms a and b. In biology, binomial nomenclature refers to a scientific name consisting of two words.)*

Phase Three
Assessment Options

Closure

■ Relating Concepts

Have students determine what is incorrect about each of the following "scientific names": spotted leopard *(common name)*; Tabanus b. *(species name missing)*; Acer Rubrum *(species name is capitalized)*; and lumbricus terrestris *(genus name is lowercased and names are not underlined).*

SECTION REVIEW

Assign the *Section Review.*

Reteaching

Assign students to cooperative groups of four. Have each group develop a concept map that summarizes what a scientific name is and justifies the use of a scientific-naming system. *(Maps will vary but should indicate an understanding that the system eases communication by standardizing the use of Latin and using binomial names, capitalized genus names, and lowercased species names.)*

Figure 17-3
If you asked scientists from around the world what they might call the animal in Figure 17-1, they would all agree on one name: *Porcellio scaber.*

'תחבית (*tah hah VEET*) or *Porcellio scaber*"
—Jacob Cohen, Molecular Evolution Biologist
Israel

Why are scientific names in Latin?

Why are scientific names written in a language that is no longer spoken? Why aren't they in English or Russian or Chinese? In the Middle Ages, when scientists began to name organisms, Latin was used in academic circles. Hence, scientists and other scholars found it easier to communicate with each other in Latin. Latin was the language of the scholar and was used for all spoken and written communication.

Although scientists no longer communicate with each other in Latin, it is easier and more logical to retain the Latin names for living things than to rename all 1.4 million known organisms in a more modern language. **Figure 17-3** shows how useful a Latin name can be when scientists from around the world communicate with each other.

Linnaeus devised the two-name system

The modern system of naming organisms was the brainchild of Swedish botanist Carl Linnaeus. In Linnaeus's day, organisms were given very long Latin names (sometimes more than 15 words), which were often changed according to the whims of particular scientists. Linnaeus assigned a standard, two-word Latin name to each organism known in his time.

Writing a scientific name is simple

When you write a scientific name, always capitalize the genus name. Begin the second word with a lower-case letter. Both parts of a scientific name are underlined or written in italics. The scientific name for humans can be written as either Homo sapiens or *Homo sapiens*. After the first use of the full scientific name, the genus name can be abbreviated as a single letter if the meaning is clear. For example, since *Homo sapiens* has just been mentioned, *H. sapiens* is acceptable.

"Cloporte *(klo PORT)* or *Porcellio scaber*"
—Paul Melançon, Chemist and biochemist
Canada

"Mangy sow bug or *Porcellio scaber*"
—Maria Alma Solis, Entomologist
United States

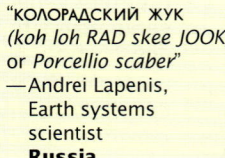

"КОЛОРАДСКИЙ ЖУК *(koh loh RAD skee JOOK)* or *Porcellio scaber*"
—Andrei Lapenis, Earth systems scientist
Russia

"Cucaracha *(koo kah RAH chah)* or *Porcellio scaber*"
—Ernest H. Williams, Jr., Marine biologist
—Lucy Bunkley-Williams, Microbiologist
Puerto Rico

SECTION REVIEW

1 List and explain the problems associated with using common names to identify living things.

2 Why is it necessary to use both words of a scientific name to correctly identify an organism?

3 Explain the advantages of using Latin for scientific names.

4 Evaluate the accuracy of this statement: "Linnaeus was the first scientist to give species Latin names."

ANSWERS TO SECTION REVIEW

1 An organism can have more than one common name, and different organisms can have the same common name. Both situations make it difficult for scientists to properly communicate with one another.

2 Some organisms can share a genus name—e.g., *Homo sapiens* and *Homo erectus*—or the second word of the species name—e.g., *Drosophila melanogaster* and *Thamnophis melanogaster*. Yet each organism will have a unique genus and species name.

3 Scientists can understand one another when speaking about the same organism. Changing the Latin names of the 1.5 million living organisms into a modern language would be difficult and illogical.

4 Linnaeus was the first to assign a standard two-word Latin name to organisms, but previous scientists had assigned Latin names to organisms.

Because sewing supplies in a sewing box are organized, you can go straight to the compartment where cotton thread is kept to find red cotton thread, instead of searching the entire box. Living things have been similarly organized by scientists, but not for convenience only. Living things are organized into groups to reflect evolutionary relationships.

17-2 Classification: Organizing Life

OBJECTIVES

❶ Describe the system scientists use to classify organisms.

❷ How does the classification of living things reflect their evolutionary history?

❸ Distinguish between the methods of classification used by taxonomists.

❹ Define the term *species*.

Classification of Living Things

Humans have classified organisms for thousands of years. The Greek philosopher Aristotle (384–322 B.C.) grouped animals by their physical similarities. Some of those groupings are still recognized today, such as the mammals. In the Middle Ages, herbalists used plants to treat disease, and they needed to identify which plants were poisonous and which could heal. Herbalists produced manuals of plant types, called "herbals," like the one shown in **Figure 17-4**. In herbals, plants were organized by their medicinal uses.

Today biologists classify organisms based on their physical, genetic, biochemical, and behavioral similarities. These similarities reveal evolutionary relationships. The classification of organisms is based on decisions made by many scientists using available information. Not all scientists agree on these classifications, and additional information or new technology can cause them to reevaluate their conclusions. The science of classifying living things is called **taxonomy**. Taxonomists are scientists who examine, classify, and argue about where organisms fit in a group.

The system of classification that biologists have developed over the 250 years since Linnaeus wrote his fundamental works is a hierarchical system. In a hierarchical system of classification, species are assigned to genera, genera are assigned to families, and

Figure 17-4
This page from a manual called a herbal was published in Turkey in the tenth century. The Greek text classifies the plant illustrated according to its medicinal uses.

families are assigned to groups of increasing size. A similar system is used in the U.S. Army. Each soldier belongs to a squad containing about nine soldiers. Four squads are organized into a platoon. Each platoon belongs to a company of about 150 people, and so on.

317

Phase One
Preparation

Scheduling

See the **Lesson Planning Guide** on pages 311A and 311B for lecture, classwork, and assignment options for Section 17-2.

Phase Two
Teaching Strategies

Social Studies Connection

Classification and Geography
List the seven classification groups on the board. Next to *kingdom* write *continent;* next to *phylum* write *country.* Have students provide the appropriate geographic descriptions (state, county, city, etc.) for the remaining classification groups. After the classification scheme is completed, have the students give an example of a continent, then a country on that continent, and so forth.

Videodisc Resources

Holt Biology Videodiscs
Lesson 17-2: Classification: Organizing Life

Key to Strategies
● Understanding Concepts (Tier I)
■ Applying Information (Tier II)
▲ Critical Thinking (Tier III)

Classifying Plane Figures

■ **Recognizing Relationships**

Have students prepare a **Graphic Organizer** to orient the following terms according to their relationships: triangle, hexagon, trapezoid, parallelogram, square, pentagon, rectangle, quadrilateral, and polygon. Ask the students to justify the rationale for their organizer. Suggest that the students begin by grouping the shapes according to their general concept, and then group them according to their more specific types.

Theme Answer

Evolution

In a biological hierarchy of classification, organisms are assigned to a group because they share distinctive characteristics with other members of that group. Organisms share distinctive characteristics because they are descended from a common ancestor. The more similarities two organisms share, the more recently their commonly shared ancestor lived.

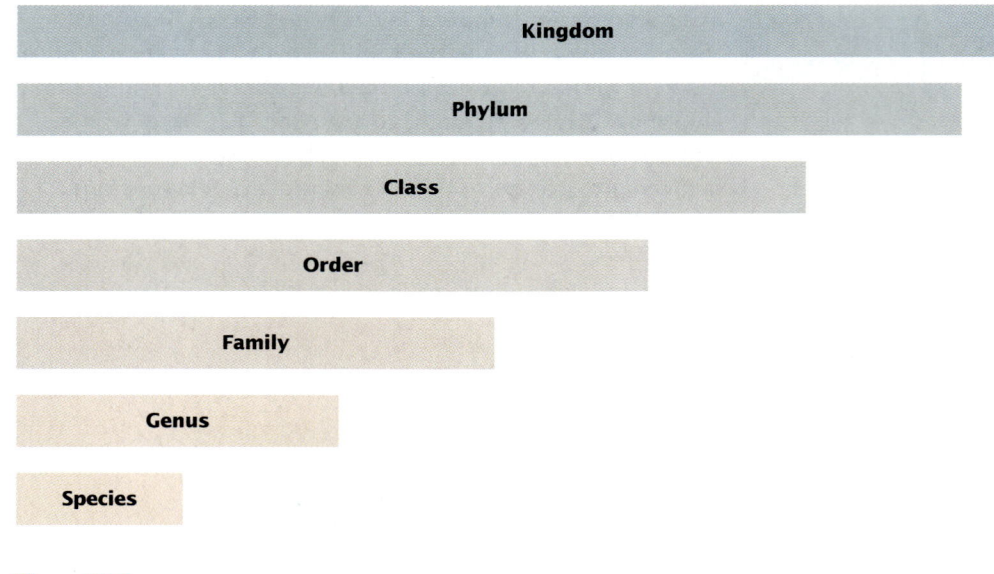

Figure 17-5
The biological hierarchy of classification is made of seven different levels.

Evolution

How is the

hierarchy of

classification

based on

evolutionary

relationships

among organisms?

Organisms are classified by similarity

In the army, soldiers are assigned to a group without regard to their appearance; there are no companies of only tall soldiers or of only blond soldiers, for instance. In a biological classification, however, organisms are assigned to a group because they share distinctive characteristics with the other members of that group. The biological hierarchy of classification has seven different levels: kingdom, phylum, class, order, family, genus, and species, as shown in **Figure 17-5**.

The smallest group in biological classification is the species. Similar species are collected into a genus. Similar genera are united into a **family**. Families that are alike are combined into an **order**. Similar orders are collected into a **class**. Classes are united into a **phylum** *(FEYE luhm)*. Finally, similar phyla are collected into a **kingdom**. The term *division* was formerly substituted for *phylum* in classifications of plants, bacteria, and fungi. **Table 17-2**, at right, illustrates the classification of our species, *Homo sapiens.*

The more classification categories two species share, the more traits they have in common. For instance, a house cat and a guppy belong to only two of the same categories: the kingdom Animalia and the phylum Chordata. The guppy and the cat both have bony skeletons, notochords, and nerve cords. But only the cat breathes with lungs, is covered with fur, walks on four legs, and nurses its young with milk. The guppy breathes with gills, has fins and scales, and does not nurse its young. The house cat, *Felis cattus*, and the mountain lion, *Felis concolor*, belong to six of the same classification categories: kingdom Animalia, phylum Chordata, class Mammalia, order Carnivora, family Felidae, and genus *Felis*.

If more specific groups are needed, the seven classification categories can be subdivided into smaller units. For example, the phylum Chordata includes all animals that develop notochords. The great majority of the members of Chordata also have backbones. To reflect this difference, animals with backbones are placed into their own subphylum—Vertebrata.

318

Matter of Fact: Early Classification

Aristotle classified dolphins with land creatures rather than with fish because he recognized that dolphins and mammals shared many characteristics, a fact overlooked by biologists for almost 2,000 years.

Table 17-2 The Classification of Modern Humans

	Homo sapiens	*Homo erectus*	*Australo-pithecus*	Gorilla	Elephant	Fish	Snake Sea star Earthworm Snail	

Kingdom
Animalia

Chordates, sea stars, earthworms, snails, jellyfish, sponges, clams, and insects are members of the kingdom Animalia.

Phylum
Chordata

Mammals, fishes, reptiles, birds, and amphibians are chordates, members of the phylum Chordata.

Class
Mammalia

Primates and elephants, along with cats, dogs, horses, kangaroos, whales, bats, seals, dolphins, and many others, belong to the class Mammalia.

Order
Primates

Members of the family Hominidae, along with prosimians, monkeys, and apes such as the gorilla, make up the order Primates.

Family
Hominidae

The family Hominidae includes the genus *Homo* and the extinct genus *Australopithecus*.

Genus
Homo

Homo sapiens belongs to the genus *Homo*, along with the extinct species *Homo habilis* and *Homo erectus*, which is shown here.

Species
Homo sapiens

Modern humans belong to the species *Homo sapiens*.

Name That Organism

● **Observing**
Give each student pictures of several organisms and a corresponding classification key. Have students use the classification key to identify the common and scientific names of each organism.

Visual Strategy Videodisc

▲ **Forming Opinions Supported by Sound Reasoning**
Use *Video—Convergent Evolution* (3 min 45 s) shown in Chapter 17 Section 17-2 of *Holt Biology Videodiscs Teacher's Correlation Guide to Holt Biology: Visualizing Life.* As students view the video, have them pay particular attention to the similarities and differences between the dolphin and the shark, and between the seal and the penguin. After viewing the video, ask students which they think is more useful—classifying according to evolutionary relationships or classifying by similar physical appearances. Have students support their opinions. *(Accept any opinions that show logical thinking and an understanding of the process of classification.)*

Multicultural Perspective: Different Cultures, Same Taxonomy

Are species natural units that are recognized by different cultures? Or are they artificial distinctions imposed on nature by Western scientists? It appears that the first is true. In 1928 Ernst Mayr, then a young ornithologist, traveled to New Guinea to collect bird specimens. Mayr found that the local Arfak people recognized 136 kinds of birds, just one less than he did. Moreover, Mayr and the Arfak recognized the same species except for two very similar species that the Arfak did not distinguish.

Key to Strategies
● **Understanding Concepts (Tier I)**
■ **Applying Information (Tier II)**
▲ **Critical Thinking (Tier III)**

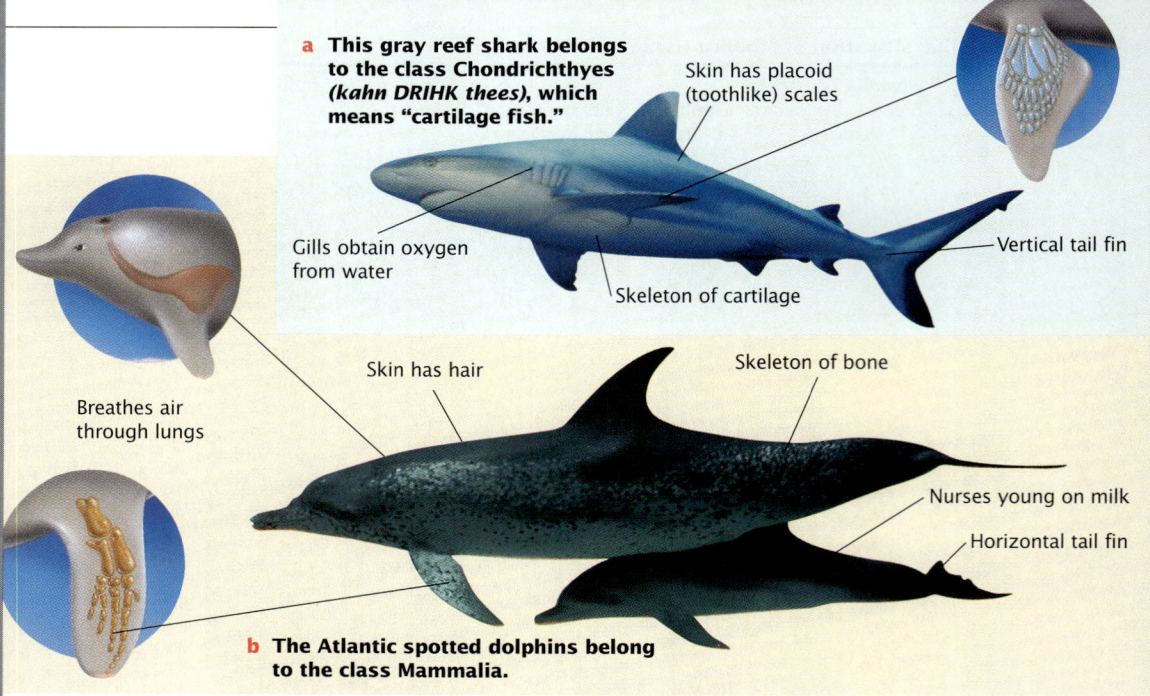

a This gray reef shark belongs to the class Chondrichthyes *(kahn DRIHK thees)*, which means "cartilage fish."

Skin has placoid (toothlike) scales

Gills obtain oxygen from water

Vertical tail fin

Skeleton of cartilage

Skin has hair

Skeleton of bone

Breathes air through lungs

Nurses young on milk

Horizontal tail fin

b The Atlantic spotted dolphins belong to the class Mammalia.

Figure 17-6
Although the shark and the dolphin look somewhat alike, they belong to different classes. This is an example of convergent evolution.

Classification and Evolution

The biological hierarchy of classification is based on the fact that different degrees of similarity exist among organisms. For instance, mountain lions more closely resemble house cats than do guppies. For Darwin, classification provided strong evidence supporting evolution. Organisms are similar because they descended from a common ancestor. The more similarities two organisms share, the more recently they shared a common ancestor. For instance, the ancestor of the house cat diverged from that of the mountain lion just a few million years ago. In contrast, the ancestor of guppies and the far-distant ancestor of cats diverged about 390 million years ago. Thus, the more classification categories two organisms share, the more closely related they are.

Similarity does not guarantee close relationship

Compare the two ocean-dwelling animals in **Figure 17-6**. Both have streamlined bodies, paddlelike fins, and flattened tails. Would you say these organisms are closely related? Many people classified both as "fish." Although both belong to the subphylum Vertebrata, they are now placed in different classes.

The shark and dolphin are an example of **convergent evolution**. In convergent evolution, organisms evolve similar structures independently, often because they live in similar habitats. Similar features that evolved through convergent evolution are known as **analogous structures**. Homologous structures, which you read about in Chapter 10, are similar because of common ancestry. Analogous structures are similar because of similar selection of two or more species.

Convergent evolution creates problems for scientists trying to classify species, because it means that similar appearance does not guarantee common ancestry. Taxonomists, therefore, view a classification as a hypothesis of relationships between organisms. Like any hypothesis, a classification can be tested against the available evidence and disproved or supported. Because the number of differences between sharks and dolphins far exceeds the number of similarities, it is easy to reject the hypothesis that these animals are close relatives.

320

Matter of Fact: Happy Anniversary!

While many species have been named after important scientists, it is a little-known fact that occasionally a scientist who discovers some new species will name the creature after a relative or friend. J. A. Sáenz of the University of Costa Rica discovered a new genus for the family Clathraceae (stinkhorn fungi). In the paper announcing this discovery, he wrote, "I dedicate this genus to my wife, Ligia, on our 24th wedding anniversary." The genus is called *Ligiella*.

Methods of Taxonomy

The example of the shark and dolphin illustrates the difficulty in determining which similarities will be useful when classifying an organism. There are two alternative methods of choosing which similarities are important. The first method is cladistics *(kluh DIHS tihks)*, from the Greek word *klados*, meaning "branch." The scientists who use cladistics seek to determine the order in which evolutionary lines diverged, or branched. To do so, they consider only a restricted set of characters of the organisms they want to classify. Organisms are assigned to a group because they share unique characters not found in any other organisms. These unique characters are called **derived characters**. For example, all species of mammals share the derived characters of hair and the ability to produce milk. Using patterns of shared derived characters, scientists construct branching diagrams called **cladograms**, which show the evolutionary relationships among groups of organisms. A cladogram of the major groups of plants is shown in **Figure 17-7**.

The second method for classifying organisms is phenetics *(fuh NEHT ihks)*. Scientists using phenetics consider as many characters of organisms as possible and classify organisms into groups based on overall degree of similarity. Phenetics does not attempt to reconstruct the relationships among organisms, just to produce groups that can be named.

Both cladistics and phenetics have drawbacks. Phenetic classifications do not always reveal the relationships among organisms. And while cladistics is able to reconstruct the sequence of evolutionary divergence, it does not reveal the amount of difference between groups.

The taxonomy used in this book and by many biologists reflects both overall similarity and the sequence of evolutionary divergence—a compromise between phenetics and cladistics.

Energy and Organization

How could methods of obtaining energy be used as derived characters in a cladogram of the six kingdoms?

Figure 17-7
This cladogram shows the evolutionary relationships among the selected phyla of plants. A derived character distinctive to each group is marked on the cladogram. These derived characters indicate the divergence of one group from the common ancestor shared with the others.

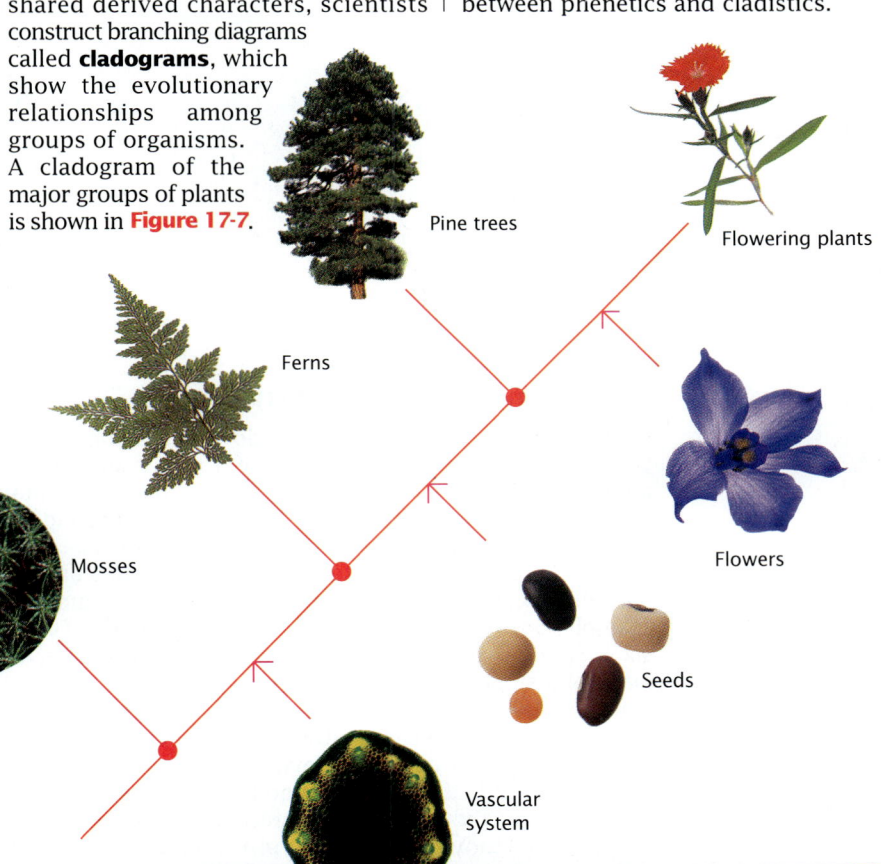

Pine trees

Flowering plants

Ferns

Flowers

Mosses

Seeds

Vascular system

321

Connection: *Chapter 8*

DNA

Review DNA's role as the carrier of genetic information. Emphasize that much of what taxonomists use to classify organisms—basic structures, reproductive patterns, life cycles, development from fertilization to adulthood—is controlled by DNA.

Visual Strategy   Figure 17-8

● **Interpreting Graphics**

Have students identify the two birds shown in this figure (other than the stork and New World vulture) whose DNA sequences are more similar and who are therefore more closely related than the others. Ask the students why the shoebills and pelicans are more closely related than are the storks and New World vultures. *(Their date of divergence is more recent.)*

Species Determination

▲ **Evaluating Viewpoints**

Have students further research the concept of a species. Ask students to evaluate the problems associated with this classification level. *(Students should note that a species is defined as a population of organisms that can breed with one another but not with other populations. Yet crossbreeding between organisms classified as different species is common among plants and animals.)* Then ask them about the role of genetic engineering in the formation of new species. *(Students may wonder if new species may be formed by introducing different genes into an organism.)* Ask students how the word *species* is interpreted in the Endangered Species Act. *(Hybrid animals and plants are considered species. If a parent is an endangered species and the hybrid resembles the endangered parent more closely than it resembles an intermediate, then it too is protected.)*

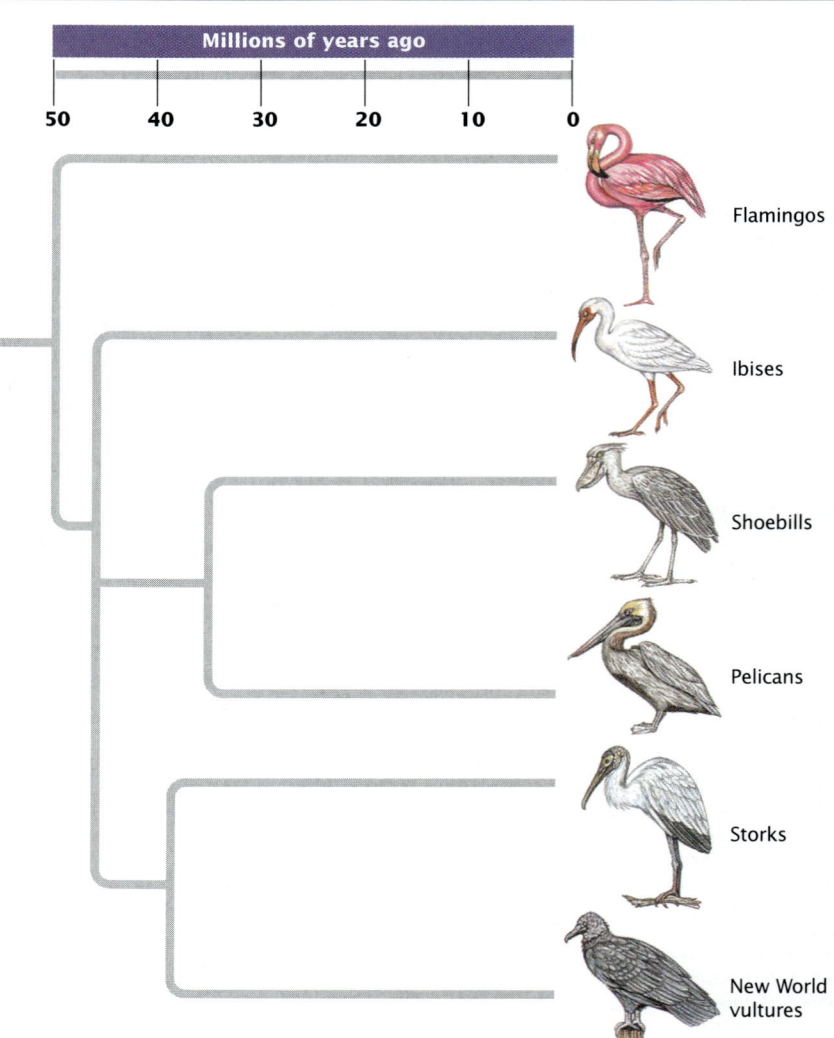

Figure 17-8
Comparison of the DNA sequences of these birds reveals their evolutionary relationships. For example, the DNA sequences of flamingos differ by the greatest amount. Their ancestor diverged from the other birds about 50 million years ago.

Taxonomy and Technology

What characteristics of organisms do you think might be useful for determining evolutionary relationships? As you might expect, biologists have traditionally compared the appearances of organisms in order to discover the relationships among them. For example, does the animal have four or six legs? Are the flowers of a plant made of a single tube or of many separate petals? Biologists also consider the behavioral patterns, methods of reproduction, life cycles, and development from fertilization to adulthood.

Technological advances have enabled biologists to study the genes that pro- duce the traits used to classify organisms. Taxonomists use techniques of molecular biology to compare the DNA nucleotide sequences of different organisms. Comparisons of DNA sequences are especially important for the taxonomist because mutations— changes in DNA—are random events. As time passes, more mutations tend to occur in the DNA of a particular species. Thus, DNA acts as a "molecular clock." As shown in **Figure 17-8**, the more similar the DNA sequences of two species, the more recently their common ancestor must have lived, and the more closely they are related.

What Is a Species?

Why do we say that house cats belong to one species while mountain lions belong to another? What is a species? In one sense, a species is just a level in the classification system to which scientists assign very similar organisms. But in a more profound sense, a species is the basic unit of evolution. Over time, species change and give rise to new species in a process known as speciation. Indirectly, speciation gives rise to new genera, new families—all of the so-called higher classification categories. A new genus, for example, is not produced by the transformation of all members of an existing genus. A new genus is formed when one species in the "old" genus accumulates enough changes to be considered not only a new species but also a member of a new genus.

Figure 17-9
The zebra and horse belong to the same genus *(Equus)* but are members of different species. When they mate, they produce sterile offspring, known as a "zebroid," like the one below.

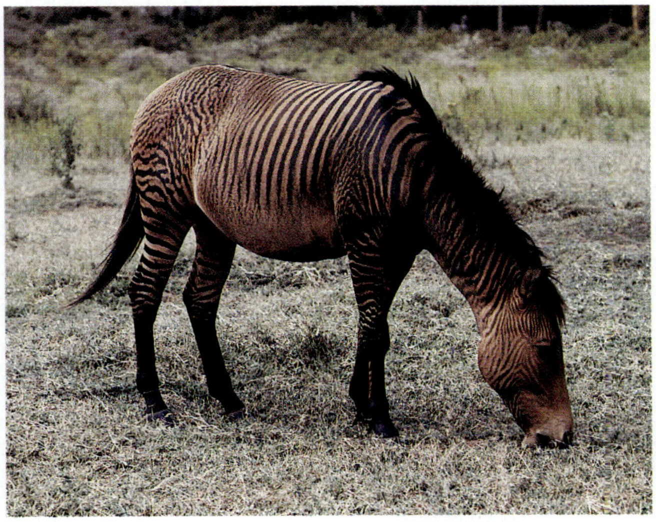

Biologists have traditionally defined a species as organisms that are able to interbreed with each other to produce fertile offspring and that usually do not reproduce with members of other groups. This definition works well for most animals. For example, the horse and the zebra belong to different species. Although they can mate, the resulting offspring, the "zebroid" shown in **Figure 17-9**, is sterile.

Reproductive barriers between species are not always perfect. Indeed, the traditional definition of species does not work nearly as well for plants because hybrids of different species are often fertile. **Hybrids** are offspring that result from interbreeding by individuals of different species. Coyotes, dogs, and wolves are all separate species in the genus *Canis.* Interbreeding between dogs, coyotes, and wolves produces fertile hybrids.

A species is a unique kind of organism

Despite these complications, the classification of organisms into species has worked fairly well. The word *species* means "kind" in Latin. Therefore, a species is basically a unique kind of organism. Members of a species share at least one inherited characteristic not found in other similar organisms. The characteristic that sets a species apart might be the shape of a leaf, beak, flower, or tooth. In sexually reproducing species, this distinctive characteristic is maintained from generation to generation because members of different species do not usually interbreed.

SECTION REVIEW

1. **Explain why two species in the same genus must also belong to the same family.**
2. **Explain how convergent evolution can make classification difficult.**
3. **Describe how cladistics classifies organisms.**
4. **Why aren't the breeds of domestic dogs considered separate species?**

17-2 section

Visual Strategy Figure 17-9

● **Comparing**

Tell students that when a horse and a donkey mate, the result is a sterile mule. Have students compare a mule with the zebroid shown in this figure. Ask if they would classify the horse and donkey as members of the same species; have them explain their rationale(s). *(They would not be considered the same species because their offspring are sterile.)*

Phase Three

Assessment Options

Closure

■ **Relating Concepts**

Have students provide examples from everyday situations in which some sort of classification system makes life easier. *(Answers could include books in a library, food in a store, grade level in school, and CDs in a music store.)* In each case, have them explain the rationale for their taxonomy.

SECTION REVIEW

Assign the *Section Review.*

Reteaching

Assign students to cooperative work groups. Take them to the school parking lot to make a list of cars; include make, model, and color. Have each group develop a taxonomy for all the cars.

ANSWERS TO SECTION REVIEW

1. Because the classification system is hierarchical, two organisms that belong to a classification category must also belong to the same categories higher in the hierarchy.
2. Through convergent evolution, organisms can have similar characteristics without being closely related. Such similarities complicate the task of defining groups of related organisms.
3. Cladistics identifies related organisms by shared, uniquely evolved, or derived characters. A cladistic classification is based on the derived evolutionary relationships.
4. Although they differ anatomically, different breeds of dog can interbreed.

Key to Strategies

● Understanding Concepts (Tier I)
■ Applying Information (Tier II)
▲ Critical Thinking (Tier III)

Preparation

Scheduling

See the **Lesson Planning Guide** on pages 311A and 311B for lecture, classwork, and assignment options for Section 17-3.

Active READING

Technique: Reading Organizer
As students read this chapter, ask them if they can spot the Reading Organizer provided by the author. You may want to tell them that they are looking for a comparison/contrast organizer *(Figure 17-11a on page 325, listing the characteristics of Archaebacteria and Eubacteria).*

Phase Two
Teaching Strategies

Animal or Plant?

■ **Relating Concepts**
Use a microprojector or a video-microscope to show the students live *Euglena*. Have them determine whether they would place this organism in kingdom Plantae (because it has chlorophyll), kingdom Animalia (because it moves), or neither (kingdom Protista).

The ability to move is probably one trait that you associate with animals, while the ability to photosynthesize is characteristic of plants. *Euglena* is a single-celled organism that is able to move and to perform photosynthesis. Is *Euglena* a plant or an animal? There are a number of organisms that cannot be categorized as animals or plants.

17-3 Six Kingdoms

OBJECTIVES

1. **Discuss the weaknesses of Linnaeus's two-kingdom classification system.**

2. **Differentiate between the six kingdoms of organisms.**

3. **Identify two characteristics of members in each of the six kingdoms.**

Six-Kingdom System

Following Linnaeus's lead, biologists of his time classified every living thing into either kingdom Plantae or kingdom Animalia. This seemed logical because most familiar organisms are either plants or animals. If it is green, has leaves, and is rooted in soil, it is a plant. If it is furry, slimy, or scaly and it runs, swims, crawls, or slithers, it is an animal. However, numerous living things do not quite fit either description. For example, where would a mushroom fit? It doesn't seem like an animal. On the other hand, is it a plant if it doesn't have leaves and isn't green?

If you had to fit a mushroom into one of the two kingdoms—Plantae or Animalia—you would most likely place it in kingdom Plantae. That is what Linnaeus did. After all, a mushroom does look a little like a plant. It grows in the soil and doesn't move from one place to another.

Does this mean that any organism that doesn't move from place to place is a plant? Sea anemones, such as the one in **Figure 17-10**, are organisms that are firmly attached to one spot and look like flowers. They eat other organisms, however, and are animals. Since Linnaeus's time, biologists have learned a great deal about the structure and function of living things. This information has enabled them to make increasingly precise distinctions among the major groups of organisms. Most biologists now use a six-kingdom system of classification. The six kingdoms are Archaebacteria, Eubacteria, Protista, Fungi, Plantae, and Animalia.

Figure 17-10
Like plants, sea anemones cannot move from place to place. However, they are classified as animals. They are heterotrophs, using tentacles to paralyze and capture small fishes.

Videodisc Resources

Holt Biology Videodiscs
Lesson 17-3: Six Kingdoms

Matter, Energy, and Organization

Which traits of bacteria are shared by all living things?

The Six Kingdoms of Living Things

All prokaryotes, also called bacteria, are in the kingdoms Archaebacteria *(ahr kee bak TIHR ee uh)* or Eubacteria *(yoo bak TIHR ee uh)*.

The bacteria represent the most ancient groups on Earth. They have adapted to almost every environment, including those with extremes of acidity, temperature, and salt content. In addition, bacteria have evolved more ways to obtain nutrients than have all eukaryotic organisms combined.

> **Bacteria**
> - are unicellular
> - lack cell nuclei
> - lack membrane-bound organelles
> - have more methods of obtaining nutrients than eukaryotes
> - are the oldest forms of life

Archaebacteria
- found in extreme environments
- gave rise to eukaryotes

Eubacteria
- common environments
- gave rise to eukaryotic cell organelles

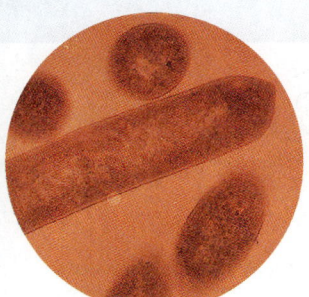

Figure 17-11
a Archaebacteria, like this one, have been found in extreme environments.

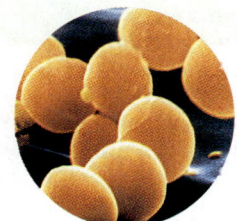

b These eubacteria can live on human skin and inside the human body.

All bacteria lack cell nuclei. Bacteria are 0.20 to 500 μm in size and exist in almost every place on Earth.

But during the last decade, studies of DNA have revealed such fundamental differences between the two groups of bacteria that many scientists now assign them to different kingdoms instead of simply the kingdom Monera. Monera used to comprise all bacteria.

It is now believed that these two very different groups evolved from a common ancestor about 4 billion years ago!

The archaebacteria, one of which can be seen in **Figure 17-11**, evolved before oxygen filled our atmosphere and now are found principally in extreme environments, obtaining energy from sulfur, salt, hydrogen, and carbon dioxide. Fewer than 100 species have been recognized so far, but recent research suggests that these bacteria exist in far larger numbers than was previously believed. Archaebacteria are believed to be the ancestors of the protists, the first eukaryotes.

The eubacteria, one of which is seen in **Figure 17-11**, contain most of the common bacteria that share our world. They are an extremely diverse group, containing both autotrophic and heterotrophic forms. Approximately 5,000 species have been characterized so far, but undoubtedly many more exist. Eubacteria are believed to be the ancestors of mitochondria and chloroplasts, organelles within eukaryotic cells.

Kingdom Protista is a catchall kingdom

All the multicellular eukaryotes not classified as plants, animals, or fungi are assigned to the kingdom Protista. Plants, animals, and fungi probably descended from ancient protists. One of the protists can be seen in **Figure 17-12**.

Protists include protozoa, such as *Amoeba* and *Paramecium*, and algae, such as seaweeds and kelps. Slime molds and water molds also belong to kingdom Protista.

Figure 17-12
This colony of Volvox (50×) belongs to the kingdom Protista.

Historical Perspective: Development of the Kingdom Classification

The German biologist Ernst Haeckel (1834–1919) is credited with naming kingdom Monera when he realized that bacteria are more primitive than plants and animals. Not knowing what to do with protists, he sometimes included them in kingdom Monera. The American biologist H. P. Copeland (1902–1968) suggested separating kingdom Monera into two. This idea was finally put into action by another American biologist, R. H. Whittaker (1920–1980), who not only supported the idea of kingdom Protista but also developed a kingdom of his own—kingdom Fungi.

Classifying Living Things **325**

Connection: *Chapter 5*

Photosynthesis

Review the major features of photosynthesis, the process carried out by most members of kingdom Plantae and by some protists and bacteria.

Where Does It Belong?

■ **Recognizing Relationships**

Show students pictures of living organisms. Include in your collection organisms that are unusual in appearance, such as the slime mold *Plasmodium*. Ask students to determine in what kingdom they would place these organisms.

Phase Three

Assessment Options

Closure

■ **Analyzing Information**

Place students in cooperative work groups. Give each group a list of 10 organisms. Next to each organism, list the kingdom to which it may or may not belong. Have students determine if the kingdom associated with the organism is correct. They must provide a reason for their choice.

SECTION REVIEW

Assign the *Section Review*.

Reteaching

Have students make a chart by filling in the name of the kingdoms in one column and the associated characteristics for that kingdom in the next column.

Kingdom Fungi contains the mushrooms

Mushrooms, yeast, and molds are members of the kingdom Fungi. Difficult to classify in a two-kingdom system, a mushroom, like the one in **Figure 17-13**, fits neatly into kingdom Fungi in the six-kingdom system. Instead of roots, stems, and leaves, fungi are made of thin filaments that penetrate the soil or decaying organisms, absorbing nutrients from them (absorption). Fungi do not contain chloroplasts and cannot make their own food by photosynthesis. Fungi are so different from all other living organisms that they are clearly best classified as a separate kingdom.

Figure 17-13
This mushroom belongs to the kingdom Fungi. It secretes enzymes that break down organic matter, which it then absorbs.

Kingdom Plantae contains multicellular photosynthetic organisms

This kingdom includes only terrestrial multicellular organisms that obtain their nutrients by photosynthesis. These are the organisms that most people would recognize as "plants," such as mosses, ferns (shown in **Figure 17-14**), flowers, and trees. Nearly all plants occur on dry land, but a few grow submerged in fresh water, and a very few grow at the edges of the

Figure 17-14
The leaves of this Dallas fern contain chloroplasts, which carry out photosynthesis.

sea. Plant cells have cell walls made of the polysaccharide cellulose. Because some green algae are so similar to plants in this and other features, they have been identified as the ancestral group for this kingdom.

Kingdom Animalia has about 1 million known species

The first members of this kingdom, like the demon stinger in **Figure 17-15**, evolved in the ocean. The largest number of animal phyla are still found only in the sea. Like plants and most fungi, organisms in kingdom Animalia are multicellular. Animals, however, do not photosynthesize. Their cells do not have cell walls. Nearly all animals have some kind of nervous system, although it might be a very simple one.

Figure 17-15
This demon stinger, which measures about 8 cm (4 in.) across, looks like a plant but belongs to kingdom Animalia. It hides in the sand in the South Pacific Ocean with only its mouth and eyes exposed. There it lies waiting for crabs and small fish to cross its path.

SECTION REVIEW

1 Explain why it would be difficult to classify a mushroom using the two-kingdom classification system.

2 How can you recognize an animal?

3 List two characteristics of protists.

4 What are two differences between plants and fungi? What are two characteristics they share?

ANSWERS TO **SECTION REVIEW**

1 Students should explain that mushrooms are not plants because they do not make their own food and that they are not animals because they do not move, do not ingest food, and have cell walls.

2 Animals are multicellular, eukaryotic, nonphotosynthetic organisms that lack cell walls, ingest food, and are capable of movement.

3 Protists are eukaryotes and may be either multicellular or unicellular and either photosynthetic or nonphotosynthetic.

4 Fungi do not have roots or chloroplasts, which prevents them from making their own food, while plants do have chloroplasts and roots. Both plants and fungi have nuclei and membrane-bound organelles.

Interbreeding among members of the genus *Canis* produces fertile hybrids, such as this hybrid of a dog and a wolf.

	Key Terms	Summary
17-1 **The Need for Naming**  The scientific name for the red oak is *Quercus rubra*.	scientific name (p. 313) genus (p. 314) species (p. 314)	• To ensure accurate communication of information, biologists assign a unique two-word scientific name in Latin to each organism. • The first word of a scientific name is the name of the genus to which the organism belongs. The first and second words identify the kind of organism within the genus. • The system of scientific names used today was developed by Linnaeus in the eighteenth century.
17-2 **Classification: Organizing Life**  In the Middle Ages, herbalists classified plants according to their medicinal uses.	taxonomy (p. 317) family (p. 318) order (p. 318) class (p. 318) phylum (p. 318) kingdom (p. 318) convergent evolution (p. 320) analogous structure (p. 320) derived character (p. 321) cladogram (p. 321) hybrid (p. 323)	• Scientists classify organisms into a hierarchical system of groups within groups. • Linnaeus classified organisms into groups according to their similarities. Since Darwin, some classifications have reflected the evolutionary relationships among organisms. • Analogous structures are similar but do not share a common ancestry. Convergent evolution is the evolution of similar structures in unrelated organisms. • A species is a group of organisms with unique characteristics.
17-3 **Six Kingdoms** The sea anemone is one example of an organism that looks like a plant but is classified as an animal. 		• Linnaeus classified all living things into either the plant kingdom or the animal kingdom. Today many biologists use a six-kingdom classification system. • The six kingdoms are Archaebacteria, Eubacteria, Protista, Fungi, Plantae, and Animalia.

Alternative Assessment

Use the names of the six kingdoms as the categories for a game. Assign students to cooperative work groups of four. Have each group develop acceptable questions and answers for all six categories. Arrange competitions by having two cooperative groups use the information developed by a third group. Competitors choose a category and select an answer at random from that category. A question must then be formulated by the competitor to match the answer. (The game is similar to a popular television game show).

Portfolio Assessment

Portfolio Assessment on page T39 provides options for building and evaluating student portfolios. Students and teachers can select items from the areas listed on page T39 for inclusion in a portfolio.

327

ANSWER TO CONCEPT MAP

The following is one possible answer to the Relating Concepts exercise on page 328.

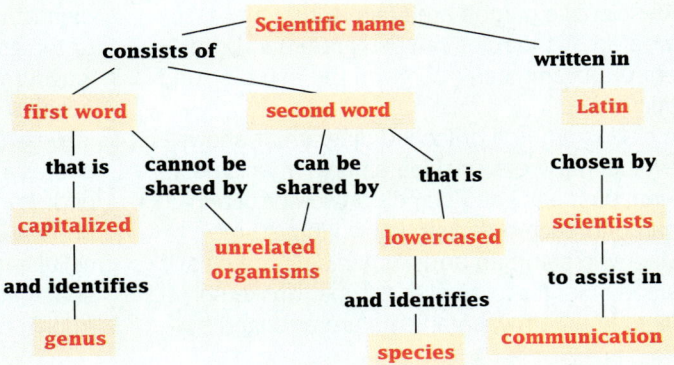

Understanding Vocabulary

1. a. Genus is the second most specific classification; species is the most specific. Both names are needed to identify the species.

b. Phylum is the second highest classification category for animals. Division, like a phylum, is used in plants, fungi, and bacteria.

c. analogous structures—similar features that evolved via convergent evolution; homologous structures—similar because of common ancestry

2. a. division

b. analogous structure

c. eubacteria

Understanding Concepts

3. Concept map answer is on page 327.

4. Organisms can have one or more common names; they rarely have the same name in different languages. And one name may refer to more than one kind of organism.

5. They're very similar because they share a genus. They may have been found in different areas. *O. californicus* is in California, and *O. fultoni* was perhaps discovered by someone named Fulton or near a town named Fulton.

6. It is true because the more traits that two organisms share, the more likely it is that they will be classified in the same categories. For example, dogs and wolves share many traits and are classified in the same kingdom, phylum, class, order, family, and genus, but they are different species.

7. The first part is the genus. The second plus the first identifies the species; for example, *Felis* is the genus of the house cat and the puma, but *Felis cattus* is the house cat.

8. Answers will vary but should include size, color, habitat, and maybe the name of the discoverer or someone who studied the organism.

review

Understanding Vocabulary

1. For each pair of terms, explain the differences in their meanings.
   a. genus, species
   b. phylum, division
   c. analogous structure, homologous structure

2. For each set of terms, complete the analogy.
   a. animal : phylum :: plant : _____
   b. common ancestry : homologous structure :: similar features evolved independently : _____
   c. ancestors of the first eukaryotes : archaebacteria :: ancestors of mitochondria and chloroplasts : _____

Understanding Concepts

3. **Relating Concepts** Construct a concept map that describes how a scientific name is written. Try to include the following terms in your map: scientific name, first word, second word, Latin, capitalized, genus, species, scientists, lowercase, communication, unrelated organisms.

4. **Organizing Information** Give three reasons why using an organism's common name is not clear enough for scientific communication.

5. **Comparing Relationships** What relationship can you guess when you see these names: *Oecanthus californicus* and *Oecanthus fultoni*?

6. **Inferring Conclusions** Determine whether the following statement is true or false: "The more classification categories two organisms share, the more traits they have in common." Explain your answer and give an example.

7. **Summarizing Information** What are the two parts of a scientific name? Give an example of each.

8. **Inferring Relationships** What kinds of information can you find out about an organism from its scientific name?

9. **Organizing Information** What are two rules that must always be followed when giving an organism a scientific name?

10. **Inferring Relationships** What is a cladogram? How does it help scientists classify organisms?

11. **Summarizing Information** Who was responsible for devising the two-name system of scientific names? Describe the contribution made by this individual.

12. **Comparing Relationships** How is the classification of living things similar to the way an army is organized? How is it different?

13. **Organizing Information** Arrange the following classification terms in order from least specific to most specific: family, genus, order, kingdom, species, class, phylum.

14. **Inferring Relationships** Look at the organisms below. Use the information in your chapter to assign as many appropriate biological terms as you can to each organism.

15. **Predicting Outcomes** What is convergent evolution? Explain why it can create problems for taxonomists.

16. **Summarizing Information** Name the six kingdoms of living organisms, and give at least two characteristics of each.

17. **BUILDING ON WHAT YOU HAVE LEARNED** Based on what you learned in Chapter 12, which pair of organisms—humans and chimpanzees or chimpanzees and prosimians—are more closely related?

---

9. All scientific names are Latin words or are created by the rules of Latin grammar. Different organisms can't be given the same scientific name.

10. A cladogram is a branched diagram. It shows evolutionary relationships among organisms.

11. Linnaeus; assigned standard two-word Latin name to each organism known in his time

12. Like soldiers in an army, organisms are classified in larger to smaller groups. Unlike soldiers in an army, organisms are arranged by distinctive characteristics shared by members of the group.

13. kingdom, phylum, class, order, family, genus, species

14. leaves: *Quercus phellos,* kingdom Plantae, photosynthetic multicellular organism
bird: *Parus carolinensis,* kingdom Animalia, phylum Chordata, nonphotosynthetic multicellular organism
sea anemone: kingdom Animalia, heterotrophic multicellular organism

Interpreting Graphics

18. Examine the cladogram shown below.

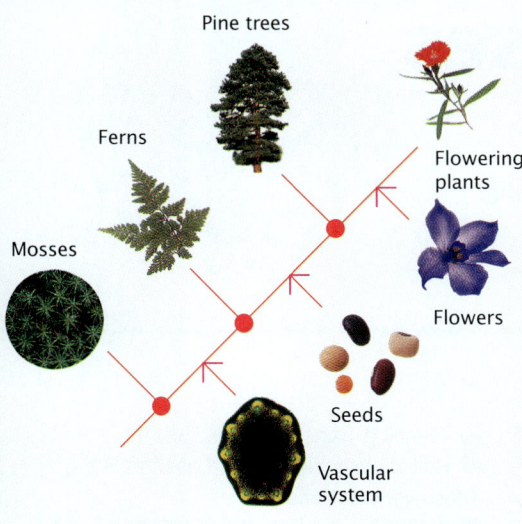

Pine trees

Ferns

Mosses

Flowering plants

Flowers

Seeds

Vascular system

a. What is the derived character possessed by ferns?
b. What derived characters are shared by pine trees and flowering plants?
c. Which type of plant is most ancient?
d. Which type of plant evolved most recently?
e. Which type of plant lacks a vascular system?

Reviewing Themes

19. *Heredity*
How does DNA act like a "molecular clock"?

20. *Evolution*
What features common to both the shark and the dolphin suggest that convergent evolution has occurred?

Thinking Critically

21. **Evaluating Viewpoints** Explain this statement: Diversity is the result of evolution; classification systems are the inventions of humans.

22. **Recognizing Verifiable Facts** In the laboratory, a scientist studied two identical-looking daisies that belonged to the genus *Aster*. The two plants produced fertile hybrids in the laboratory, but they never interbreed in nature because one plant flowers only in the spring and the other only in autumn. Are the plants the same species? Explain your answer. What could the scientist do to be certain about whether the plants are the same or different species?

Life/Work Skills

23. **Allocating Resources** You and your classmates have been allotted $500 to buy enough laboratory specimens to demonstrate the six kingdoms of life in a high school biology laboratory. Check scientific supply catalogs to get ideas of what is available and the prices of those items. Think about whether you would select prepared microscope slides, preserved specimens, or living organisms and about the advantages and drawbacks of each. Make a poster of your choices to "sell" your biology teacher on your ideas.

24. **Using Technology** Work with two or three of your classmates to develop a system of classification using computer software (spreadsheet or word processor) to organize your favorite books, movies, TV programs, sports teams, music, or performers. For each system of classification, include at least three levels of distinguishing characteristics. Make a poster of the classification system to share with your class.

Activities and Projects

25. **Language Arts Connections** A mnemonic is a code used to aid memory. In the mnemonic "King Philip came over from Geneva, Switzerland," the first letter of each word is the same as the first letter of each of the seven levels of classification. Design your own mnemonics to help you remember the six kingdoms and two characteristics of each.

26. **Reading Connection** Read the book *Life on Earth: A Natural History* by David Attenborough, which describes the diversity of life on Earth and how organisms relate to and interact with one another. Write a book report, and share with your class the ways in which some life-forms relate to their unique geographical habitats.

Discovering Through Reading

27. Read the article "Why Cladistics?" by Gaffney, Dingus, and Smith in *Natural History*, June 1995, pages 33–35. What did cladistics reveal about the evolution of birds? What does cladistic analysis reveal about the fossil record?

Reviewing Themes

19. As time passes, mutations tend to accumulate in the DNA of a particular species. Thus, if the DNA sequences of two species are more similar, then their common ancestor must have lived more recently and they are more closely related.

20. body shape, paddlelike fins, and flattened tails

Thinking Critically

21. Over time, the characteristics of organisms change, leading to diversity. Humans attempt to organize these characteristics by devising systems of classification.

22. Because the plants can form fertile hybrids, they are probably the same species. That they flower at different times of the year may indicate that they are evolving into different species. One would have to compare DNA nucleotide sequences of the plants to determine their relationship.

Life/Work Skills

23. Answers will vary. Students' answers should cover all six kingdoms and be within budget. Posters should justify their choices.

24. Answers will vary.

Activities and Projects

25. Answers will vary but should include all the details needed to classify organisms.

26. Answers will vary.

Discovering Through Reading

27. Cladistics revealed that birds evolved from a small carnivorous dinosaur like *Deinonychus* or *Velociraptor,* not from *Archaeopteryx,* as the geologic evidence indicated. The common ancestor had a hole in its hip sockets that allowed the legs to descend straight down from the body, enabling dinosaurs to stand erectly.

15. Convergent evolution occurs when organisms evolve similar features independently, often because they live in the same or similar habitats. Taxonomists have to look beyond physical characteristics to correctly classify organisms that have convergently evolved.

16. Archaebacteria—energy from sulfur, salt, or hydrogen, and CO_2; live in extreme environments; prokaryotic. Eubacteria—very diverse; mitochondria and chloroplast ancestors; prokaryotic. Protista—eukaryotic, mostly single-celled. Fungi—mostly multicellular, made of thin filaments, absorb rather than create food. Plantae—multicellular, photosynthetic, cell walls made of cellulose. Animalia—multicellular, no photosynthesis, no cell walls, nervous system.

17. humans and chimpanzees

Interpreting Graphics

18. a. vascular system; b. seeds; c. mosses; d. flowering plants; e. mosses

18 | Bacteria and Viruses

Lesson Planning Guide With Options for Block Scheduling

Lecture Concepts	Lesson Resources

18-1 Bacteria

BLOCK ❶ (45 minutes)

1. Bacteria have successfully colonized almost every place on Earth because of their rapid rate of cell division, protective mechanisms, and diversity of nutritional sources.

2. Bacteria are prokaryotic cells that lack certain cell structures found in eukaryotic cells.

❶ Lecture Resources
- ■ Determining Prior Knowledge
- ■ Active Reading: K-W-L
- ■ Active Reading: Paired Reading
- ■ Visual Strategy: Figure 18-1
- ■ Visual Strategy: Videodisc
- ■ Demonstration: Observing Morphology

- 🔖 Teaching Transparencies: 89, 91
- 💿 Holt Biology Videodiscs Lesson 18-1

Classwork Options
- ■ Bacterial Structure and Function

Assignment Options
- ⊙ Teaching Resources CD-ROM: Supplemental Reading Guides 9

BLOCK ❷ (45 minutes)

3. Special dyes are used to determine if bacteria are Gram-positive or Gram-negative. The difference between Gram-positive and Gram-negative bacteria is important in diagnosing and treating illnesses caused by bacteria.

4. Bacteria obtain energy by photosynthesis, chemosynthesis, or heterotrophic nutrition.

❷ Lecture Resources
- ■ Bacterial Membrane Function
- ■ Visual Strategy: Figure 18-3
- ■ Visual Strategy: Videodisc
- 🔖 Teaching Transparencies: 90, 88A
- 💿 Holt Biology Videodiscs Lesson 18-1

Classwork Options
- ■ Closure: Relating Concepts

- 🧪 Laboratory Techniques and Experimental Design: Lab C32

Assignment Options
- ■ Reteaching
- ■ Section Review
- ■ Chapter Review, questions 1, 7, 18, 22, 23, 24
- ■ Directed Reading Worksheet

18-2 How Bacteria Affect Humans

BLOCK ❸ (45 minutes)

1. Some bacteria are helpful because they cycle nutrients, fix nitrogen, and are useful in the preparation of certain foods and drugs.

2. Some bacteria are harmful because they cause diseases and are responsible for food poisoning.

❸ Lecture Resources
- ■ Importance of Bacteria
- ■ Active Reading: Paired Summarizing
- ■ Visual Strategy: Videodisc
- 🔖 Teaching Transparencies: 92
- 💿 Holt Biology Videodiscs Lesson 18-2

Classwork Options
- ■ Life/Work Skills: Being a Team Member
- ■ Exploration 18A

Assignment Options
- ■ Read All About It!
- ■ World of Work: Microbiology

BLOCK ❹ (45 minutes)

3. Harmful bacteria can be controlled by proper sanitation, good hygiene, temperature treatments, antibiotics, and vaccinations.

4. Bacteria develop resistance to antibiotics, making some infectious bacterial diseases difficult to cure.

❹ Lecture Resources
- ■ Problem Solving
- ■ Visual Strategy: Figures 18-10, 18-11
- ■ Visual Strategy: Videodisc
- 💿 Holt Biology Videodiscs Lesson 18-2

Classwork Options
- ■ Life/Work Skills: Finding Information
- ■ Closure: Forming a Hypothesis
- 🧪 Quick Labs: Lab A16

Assignment Options
- ■ Beneficial and Harmful Bacteria
- ■ Reteaching
- ■ Section Review
- ■ Chapter Review, questions 2, 8, 9, 10, 13, 19, 20
- ■ Directed Reading Worksheet

18-3 Viruses

BLOCK ❺ (45 minutes)

1. Viruses are small particles consisting of a nucleic acid core surrounded by a protein coat.

2. Viruses have genetic material and can evolve, but are not considered living because they are not made of cells, cannot use energy, and can reproduce only when inside living cells.

3. Viruses reproduce by invading a host cell where new virus particles are assembled.

❺ Lecture Resources
- ■ Vaccine Development
- ■ Active Reading: Reading Organizer
- ■ Visual Strategy: Figure 18-15
- ■ Visual Strategy: Videodisc
- ■ Demonstration: Comparing Structures
- 🔖 Teaching Transparencies: 93, 94, 95
- 💿 Holt Biology Videodiscs Lesson 18-3

Assignment Options
- ⊙ Teaching Resources CD-ROM: Supplemental Reading Guides 5

Lecture Concepts

Lesson Resources

18-3 Viruses, *continued*

BLOCK ⑥ (45 minutes)

4. Viruses cause many diseases, including AIDS, polio, rabies, influenza, and colds.

5. Vaccinations can protect an individual against certain viral diseases.

⑥ Lecture Resources
■ End of a Species
■ Active Reading: K-W-L
■ Teaching Transparencies: 96, 97
◉ Holt Biology Videodiscs Lesson 18-3

Classwork Options
■ The Polio Virus
■ Reteaching

■ Closure: Evaluating Situations
Assignment Options
■ Section Review
■ Chapter Review, questions 3, 4, 5, 6, 11, 12, 14, 16, 21
■ Directed Reading Worksheet

Chapter Review and Assessment

BLOCK ⑦ (45 minutes)
Review
■ Reteaching Worksheet
■ Thinking Skills Worksheet
■ Vocabulary Development Worksheet
◉ Language Development and Reading Comprehension Audio CD Program: Chapter 18

BLOCK ⑧ (45 minutes)
Assessment
■ Alternative Assessment, p. 351
■ Portfolio Assessment, p. T39
Chapter Test
■ Chapter 18 Test
Test Generator
◉ Item bank for customizing Chapter Tests

Teaching Resources CD-ROM
◉ Scoring Rubrics and Classroom Management Checklist

The Portfolio icon denotes items throughout the Teacher's Edition lesson wrap that may be selected for inclusion in student portfolios.

Holt Biology Videodiscs and *Concepts of Biology*

Holt Biology Videodiscs gives you a powerful tool for teaching, review, and assessment. For further information regarding the media on the videodiscs, see **Holt Biology Videodiscs Teacher's Correlation Guide to Holt Biology: Visualizing Life.**

Concepts of Biology adds interactive lesson plans and extensive tools for customization using CD-ROM technology.

Use the following topic from **Concepts of Biology** to help you teach this chapter:
Topic 13: Bacteria and Viruses

Laboratory Planning

Text

Materials and preparation instructions appear on the teacher's wrap accompanying each laboratory exercise.

Block 3: Investigation 18A: Culturing Bacteria: New Antibacterial Soap, p. 792

Holt BioSources Laboratory Program

Block 2: Laboratory Techniques and Experimental Design Lab C32: Gram Staining of Bacteria
Block 4: Quick Labs Lab A16: Using Bacteria to Make Food

Determining Prior Knowledge

- Have students explain why bacteria are prokaryotes.
- Show the class a container of yogurt, and ask what its connection is to bacteria. *(Bacteria turn the milk into yogurt.)*
- Ask how many students have had strep throat. Have them describe their experiences, especially any medical treatments they received. Ask students to state any other bacterial diseases they know of. *(Answers may include botulism, tuberculosis, diphtheria, pertussis, or whooping cough.)*
- Have students define an antibiotic *(a chemical that inhibits the biochemistry or growth of bacteria)* and list some examples *(streptomycin and penicillin).*
- Have students list the characteristic properties of life *(homeostasis, reproduction, DNA, cellular organization, and metabolism).*
- Ask students to name some viral diseases they know of *(AIDS, rabies, polio, and Ebola).*

Active READING

Technique: K-W-L

Before students read this chapter, have them write short individual lists of all the things they already **K**now (or that they have heard) about bacteria and viruses. When student have finished their lists, ask them to contribute their entries to a class list on the chalkboard or on the overhead. Then have students list things they **W**ant to know about bacteria and viruses. Have students save their lists for later use in *Active Reading* on page 349.

CD-ROM Resources

Concepts of Biology
Topic 13: Bacteria and Viruses

REVIEW
- prokaryotes (Section 3-3)
- cell division (Section 4-3)
- six kingdoms (Section 11-2)

Bacteria and Viruses

18-1	**Bacteria**
18-2	**How Bacteria Affect Humans**
18-3	**Viruses**

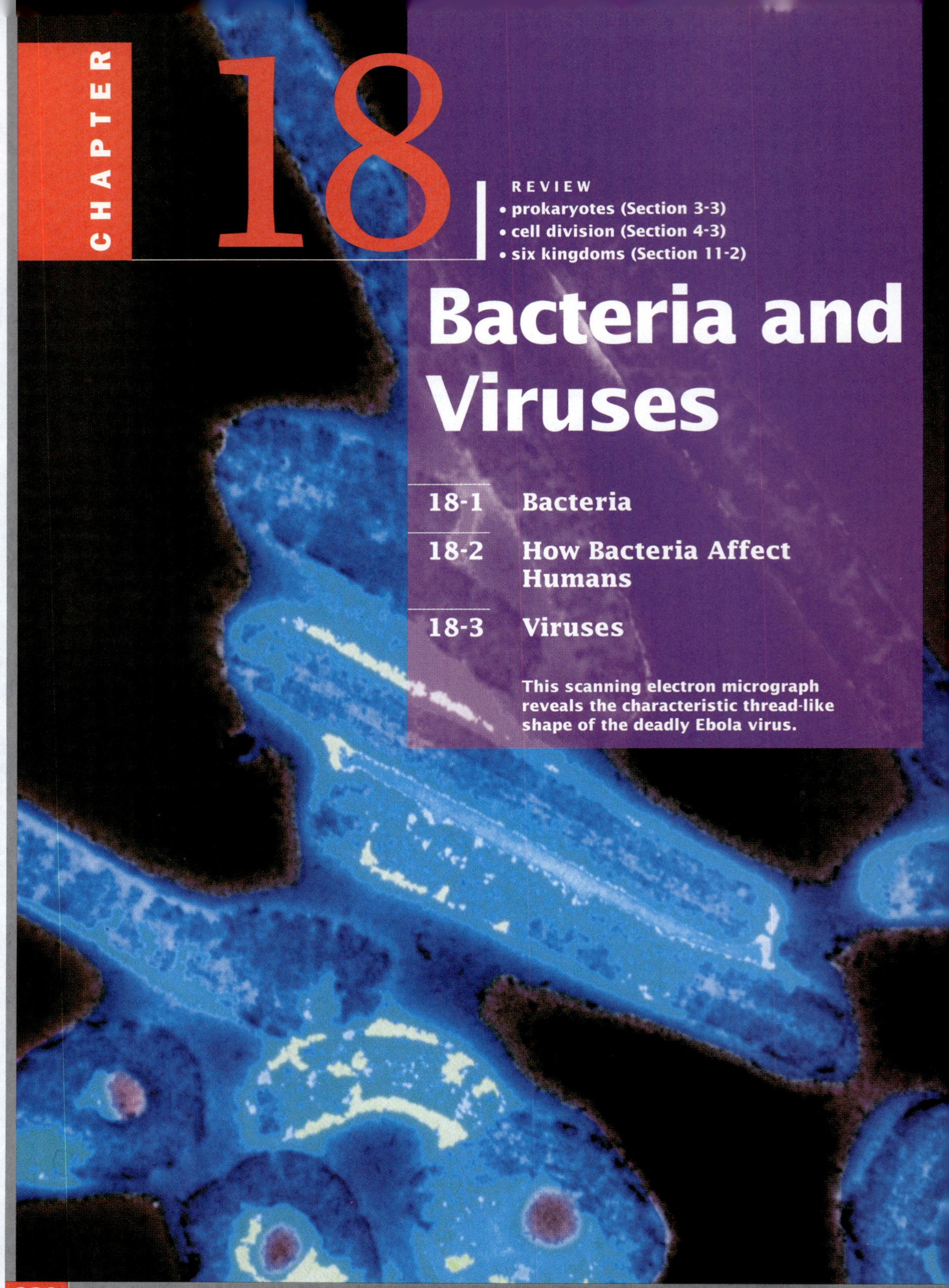

This scanning electron micrograph reveals the characteristic thread-like shape of the deadly Ebola virus.

330

Author's Rationale This chapter introduces the student to bacteria and viruses. The nature of bacteria is seen in their ability to survive in the most extreme environments and their effects on humans. The section on viruses focuses on their structure and on their ability to take over host cell machinery and produce other viruses. Vaccines are introduced in this chapter as a technological application of our knowledge of viruses and bacteria.

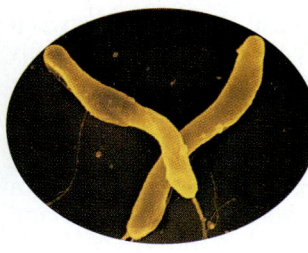

Although you do not see them, bacteria affect your life in many ways. In your large intestine, bacteria synthesize vitamin K, which is essential to good nutrition. Bacteria thrive in your mouth and may cause cavities in your teeth. Bacteria also cause many diseases, including cholera, typhus, pneumonia, sexually transmitted diseases, and tuberculosis.

18-1 Bacteria

OBJECTIVES

1 Draw the structure of a bacterial cell.

2 Differentiate between a bacterial cell and a eukaryotic cell.

3 Explain how bacteria reproduce.

4 Distinguish between the diverse ways bacteria obtain nutrition.

Bacteria Are Small and Successful

In many ways, bacteria are the most successful organisms on Earth. The earliest known fossils are of 3.5-billion-year-old bacteria, making them the oldest group of organisms. Today, bacteria can be found living almost everywhere on the globe, even in some very hostile habitats. Certain bacteria live beneath more than 400 m (1,200 ft) of ice in Antarctica, and others live near deep-sea volcanic vents where temperatures reach 360°C. Bacteria have even been found thriving miles below the Earth's surface. Bacteria also occur in great abundance. One gram (0.035 oz) of rich soil can contain about 2.5 billion bacteria.

It is obvious that bacteria are very small, otherwise you could see them without a microscope. To get an idea of how small bacteria are, look at **Figure 18-1**. A human red blood cell dwarfs the *Escherichia coli* bacterium that is normally found in the human intestine. If you made a chain of *E. coli* bacteria laid end to end, the chain would have to be more than 250 bacteria long just to be visible to the unaided eye.

Most species of bacteria are one of three different shapes: spherical, spiral, or rod-shaped. **Figure 18-1** clearly illustrates these shapes. *Streptococcus* bacteria that cause strep throat are spherical, for example. Spherical bacteria often link to form long chains of cells.

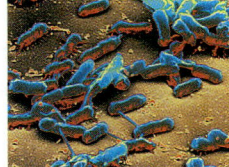

a **These rod-shaped bacteria, *Escherichia coli*, synthesize vitamin K.**

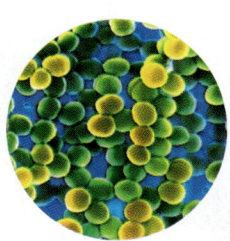

b **These spherical bacteria, *Staphylococcus aureus*, cause skin infections.**

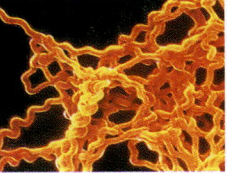

c **This spiral bacterium, *Leptospira* sp., can infect the liver or the brain.**

Figure 18-1
A human red blood cell (250×) is larger than the bacteria shown above and to the right.

331

Videodisc Resources

Holt Biology Videodiscs

Lesson 18-1: Bacteria

Phase One
Preparation

Scheduling
See the **Lesson Planning Guide** on pages 329A and 329B for lecture, classwork, and assignment options for Section 18-1.

Phase Two
Teaching Strategies

Visual Strategy **Figure 18-1**

■ **Recognizing Patterns**
Tell students that rod-shaped and spiral-shaped bacteria are called bacilli and spirillum, respectively, from the Latin for "little stick" and "spiral." Round-shaped bacteria are called cocci, from the Greek for "berry." The prefix *staphylo-* refers to a group.

Active READING

Technique: Paired Reading
Have pairs of students silently read the first part of the chapter. As they read, have them mark parts they don't understand. After students finish, ask one member of each team to summarize what he or she understood, referring to the text as needed. The listener should add anything omitted. The listener should continue the discussion by pointing out what he or she didn't understand. The first student should then help with ideas that were unclear and point out passages that he or she didn't understand. Partners should work together to clarify what wasn't clear and make questions for the class about unclear concepts.

Key to Strategies
Teaching Strategies are keyed to three tiers of learning.

● **Understanding Concepts (Tier I)**
Content mastery and comprehension

■ **Applying Information (Tier II)**
Applying and analyzing content

▲ **Critical Thinking (Tier III)**
Practicing evaluative thinking

Cell Structure and Function

How does the structure of the bacterial cell wall affect its susceptibility to antibiotics?

The structure of a bacterial cell is simple

All bacteria are prokaryotes, members of either the kingdom Archaebacteria or the kingdom Eubacteria. Recall from Chapter 3 that prokaryotes lack cell nuclei, chromosomes, and membrane-bound organelles, such as mitochondria, Golgi bodies, and chloroplasts. You can see the internal and external structure of a bacterial cell in the *Tour of a Bacterium* on the next page.

Bacteria have one of two kinds of cell walls

Like a cell from your body, a bacterial cell is enveloped by a cell membrane made of a double layer of lipids. Unlike your cells, bacterial cells have an outer cell wall composed of polysaccharides. In some bacteria, this cell wall is surrounded by yet another layer, which is made up of polysaccharides bound to molecules of lipid.

The chemical difference between these two types of bacterial cell walls is revealed using a special staining procedure called **Gram staining**. In this procedure, a series of dyes is added to a sample of bacteria as a microscope slide is being prepared. As shown in **Figure 18-2**, bacteria are either Gram-negative or Gram-positive. The difference between Gram-negative and Gram-positive bacteria is important in diagnosing and treating diseases caused by bacteria. Gram-negative bacteria are unaffected by many antibiotics, the drugs used to treat bacterial infections. These antibiotics cannot penetrate the additional layer outside the cell wall.

As you learned in Chapter 4, bacteria reproduce by splitting in two. Except for occasional mutations, each new cell is exactly like the parent cell. Genetic material in some cases is transferred from one bacterium to another, as in the case of **conjugation**. Conjugation does not increase the number of bacteria, but it does give them more genetic possibilities.

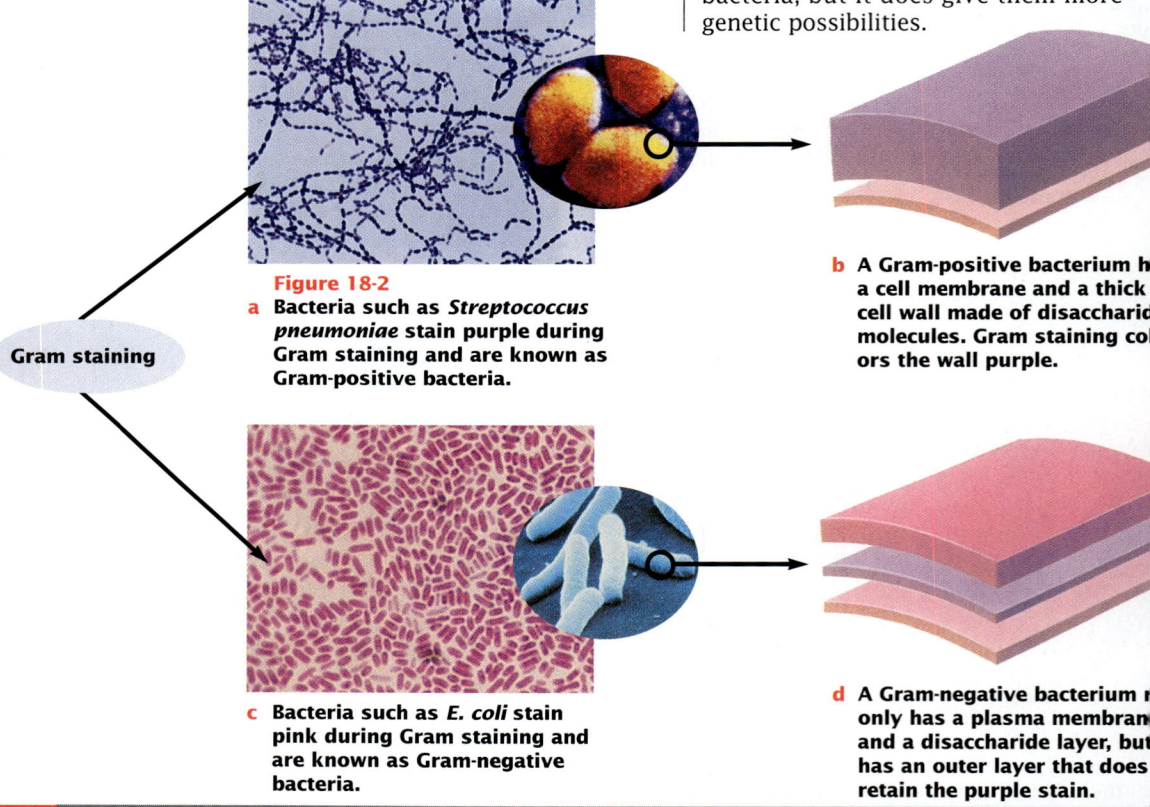

Gram staining

Figure 18-2

a Bacteria such as *Streptococcus pneumoniae* stain purple during Gram staining and are known as Gram-positive bacteria.

c Bacteria such as *E. coli* stain pink during Gram staining and are known as Gram-negative bacteria.

b A Gram-positive bacterium h▮ a cell membrane and a thick cell wall made of disaccharid▮ molecules. Gram staining col▮ ors the wall purple.

d A Gram-negative bacterium ▮ only has a plasma membran▮ and a disaccharide layer, bu▮ has an outer layer that does▮ retain the purple stain.

332

Historical Perspective: Black Death

The plague that spread through Europe in the fourteenth century killed more than 25 million people. Introduced by rats from the Black Sea region, it spread through trade routes to Europe. The disease is caused by the bacterium *Yersinia pestis* and is transmitted by fleas. It causes enlarged lymph nodes, called buboes—hence, the bubonic plague. Fever, pain, and necrosis, or blackening of the skin, can also occur. This last symptom gave us the name Black Death. Those suspected of being sick were quarantined. The term *quarantine* is from the Italian *quarantenaria,* meaning a period of 40 days, because sea voyagers to Sicily had to wait 40 days before coming ashore.

Bacterium

This bacterium, Escherichia coli, *is perhaps the most thoroughly studied organism in the world. It is used in genetic engineering and in studies of protein synthesis and the control of gene expression.*

Evolutionary Relationships
Bacteria are the oldest and most successful living organisms on Earth. Bacteria, which are prokaryotic cells, existed for 2 billion years before eukaryotic cells appeared. *E. coli* belongs to the kingdom Eubacteria.

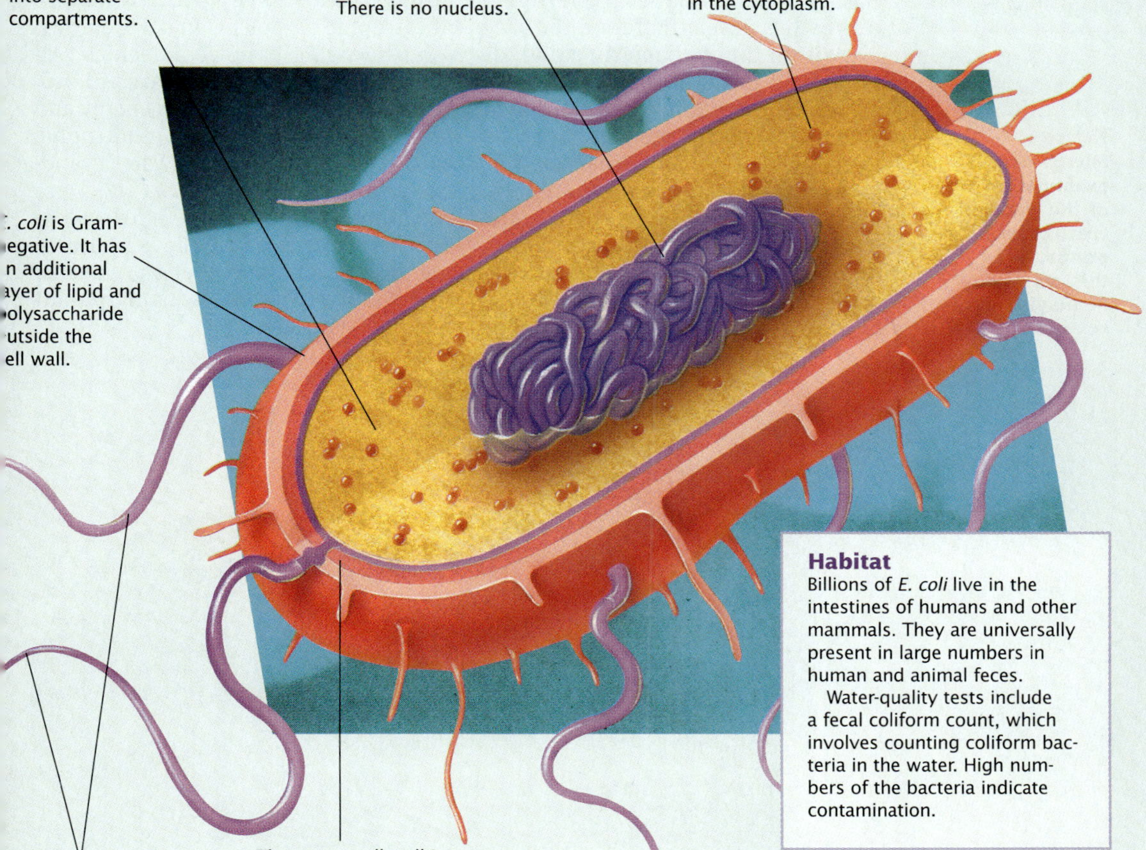

The cytoplasm is not divided into separate compartments.

All of the genes are located on a single molecule of DNA. There is no nucleus.

Proteins are made on ribosomes that float free in the cytoplasm.

. *coli* is Gram-negative. It has n additional ayer of lipid and olysaccharide utside the ell wall.

Habitat
Billions of *E. coli* live in the intestines of humans and other mammals. They are universally present in large numbers in human and animal feces.
 Water-quality tests include a fecal coliform count, which involves counting coliform bacteria in the water. High numbers of the bacteria indicate contamination.

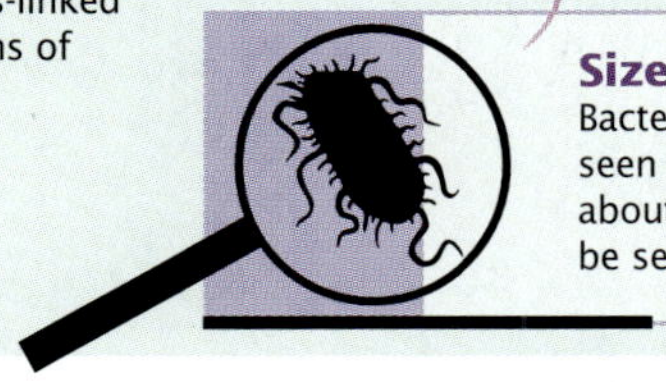

Flagella rotate like propellers to drive the cell through its environment.

The strong cell wall is a network of polysaccharides cross-linked by short chains of amino acids.

Size
Bacteria are single cells that are too small to be seen without a microscope. This one, *E. coli*, is about 1 μm in size. A line of 250 *E. coli* could just be seen by the naked eye.

333

Tour

Bacterial Membrane Function

■ **Inferring Relationships**
Given the theory that mitochondria were once independent organisms that fused with ancient prokaryotes, ask the students to infer where the enzymes for the Krebs cycle are located on bacteria. Remind students that mitochondria use their membrane to create energy. *(The enzymes are located on the bacterial cell membrane.)* Encourage students to speculate as to whether bacteria will ever fuse with other cells and become new "mitochondria."

Bacterial Structure and Function

● **Summarizing Information**
Have students make a **Graphic Organizer** with two rows. In the first column they should list the following structures: flagella, ribosomes, cell wall, DNA, and cell membrane. In the second column students should describe how each structure contributes to the function of a bacterium. An example of a completed organizer is at the bottom of the page.

Graphic Organizer

Use the following graphic organizer with the teaching strategy **Bacterial Structure and Function** on page 333.

Structure	Flagella	Ribosomes	Cell wall	DNA	Cell membrane
Function	Locomotion	Protein synthesis	Protection & structure	Direct cell function	Protection & transport

Theme Answer

Matter, Energy, and Organization

Bacteria are quite versatile in the ways they obtain nutrients. For instance, autotrophs carry out photosynthesis or chemosynthesis, and heterotrophs ingest organic materials. This versatility in obtaining energy is a major reason for their success in life.

Visual Strategy | Videodisc

● Summarizing Information

To review the bacterial reproduction process, use *Step-Frame Sequence—Cell Division in Bacteria* in Chapter 18 Section 18-1 of *Holt Biology Videodiscs Teacher's Correlation Guide to Holt Biology: Visualizing Life.* Show the first frame, and remind students that bacterial genes are located on a single molecule of DNA. Have students identify the DNA ring in the illustration. Proceed through the four frames, asking students to summarize what is happening in each frame. Discuss how the rapid rate of bacterial reproduction contributes to their success.

Connection: *Chapter 5*

Photosynthesis

Review the major features of photosynthesis that enable cells to convert light into chemical energy.

Visual Strategy | Figure 18-3

■ Relating Concepts

Tell students that the steps of photosynthesis in cyanobacteria are much the same as in eukaryotes. The prokaryotes, however, lack chloroplasts. Cyanobacterial chlorophyll is found folded on membranes in the cytoplasm called thylakoids. Additionally, cyanobacteria contain phycocyanin, a blue pigment, and phycoerythrin, a red pigment. These pigments also allow cyanobacteria to use different wavelengths of light for photosynthesis.

Matter, Energy, and Organization

Bacteria use many different energy sources. How does this enable them to live in a wide variety of places?

Figure 18-3

a **Microscopic examination of the water in freshwater ponds, like this one in Pennsylvania, reveals . . .**

Bacteria reproduce rapidly

Bacteria, unlike most other organisms, do not undergo mitosis or meiosis. Instead, a bacterium first duplicates its DNA so that there is enough DNA for two cells. Then the bacterium splits into two identical cells. Each cell receives one molecule of DNA and some cytoplasm, a process you saw in Chapter 4. Some kinds of bacteria are able to divide as many as five times in an hour. The time required for a cell to divide is called the generation time.

If you were to place a single bacterium into a culture dish containing an abundant supply of food, you could find more than 600,000 bacteria in the dish after only 4 hours. After 6 hours, the bacterial population of the dish could reach 476 million.

How Bacteria Obtain Nutrition

A glass of milk left out of the refrigerator provides a wealth of food for bacteria. Within hours, bacteria colonize the milk and break down its supply of sugar, causing the milk to curdle. Other species of bacteria feed on organic material in sewage. Still other species consume industrial products such as nylon and pesticides. Some bacteria are able to metabolize petroleum and may be used to clean oil spills. A major reason for the success of bacteria is the wide variety of foods they can use.

Some bacteria are autotrophs

Autotrophic organisms make their own food by using simple molecules. All autotrophic eukaryotes are photosynthetic: they capture solar energy and use it to make food. Many autotrophic bacteria, such as the freshwater cyanobacteria shown in **Figure 18-3**, are also photosynthetic. As you learned in Chapter 11, cyanobacteria were probably the first photosynthetic organisms to produce oxygen, starting about 3 billion years ago.

b **. . . that photosynthetic cyanobacteria such as these are a major component of the pond's ecosystem.**

334

Matter of Fact: Travertine

A famous travertine deposit is found around the Mammoth Hot Springs in Yellowstone National Park. Travertine is a rocklike substance that forms when cyanobacteria precipitate chalky, insoluble carbonate deposits. Cyanobacteria are found in abundance in these hot springs. Brilliantly colored streaks often form in the travertine.

Not all autotrophic bacteria are photosynthetic, however. In Chapter 14 you studied the communities that surround volcanic vents on the ocean floor, as shown in **Figure 18-4**. The organisms in these very deep ocean environments cannot perform photosynthesis because no light reaches them. Instead, these bacteria are able to use the energy stored in the inorganic compound hydrogen sulfide. Similarly, some kinds of soil-dwelling bacteria obtain energy from ammonia. And bacteria that live in swamps use methane. These bacteria use a process called **chemosynthesis** to make complex organic molecules from the energy in inorganic molecules. All chemosynthetic organisms are prokaryotes.

Heterotrophic bacteria are consumers

Most bacteria cannot make their own food and are therefore heterotrophs. Many feed on dead animals and animal wastes; dead plants; and fallen leaves, branches, and fruit. Other types of heterotrophic bacteria are parasites. Parasitic bacteria cause many diseases, as you will see later in the chapter.

Figure 18-4
a On the ocean floor, volcanic vents are surrounded by organisms that receive nourishment from . . .

b . . . large numbers of bacteria that are able to use the energy stored in hydrogen sulfide.

SECTION REVIEW

1. How does Gram staining help a doctor prescribe treatment for a bacterial infection?

2. List three structures found in a eukaryotic cell that are not present in a bacterial cell.

3. How do bacteria reproduce?

4. Name and explain the two ways in which autotrophic bacteria obtain energy.

ANSWERS TO SECTION REVIEW

1. The doctor must know if the bacteria causing the infection are Gram-negative or Gram positive before prescribing an antibiotic. Gram-negative bacteria are covered with an outer membrane layer and are unaffected by some antibiotics.

2. Answers may vary. Possible answers are a cell nucleus, linear chromosomes, and membrane-bound organelles such as lysosomes and vacuoles.

3. First the DNA is copied, and then the cell divides. A complete set of DNA is passed into each of the two daughter cells that are produced when the cell divides.

4. photosynthesis, which basically involves using light energy; and chemosynthesis, which involves harvesting the energy of inorganic molecules

Connection: *Chapter 14*

Nutrient Cycles
Review how heterotrophic bacteria function in cycling materials through the ecosystem.

Phase Three
Assessment Options

Closure

■ **Relating Concepts**
Halobacterium are quite similar in appearance to *E. coli*. But unlike *E. coli*, which thrive in the human intestine, *Halobacterium* grow best in very salty water like the Great Salt Lake and the Dead Sea. Have students describe what special adaptations *Halobacterium* might have to help them survive in such an environment. (*Their cell membranes are physiologically different since high salt concentrations normally disrupt membrane transport systems. Also, their enzymes require a high salt concentration for activity.*)

SECTION REVIEW
Assign the *Section Review.*

Reteaching
Have students compare prokaryotic cells with eukaryotic cells in terms of cell size (*prokaryotes are much smaller*), organelles (*prokaryotes lack a nucleus and other membrane-bound organelles*), reproduction (*prokaryotes reproduce by binary fission and eukaryotes by mitosis*), and nutrition (*prokaryotes obtain energy in a variety of ways; they may be heterotrophic, photosynthetic, or chemosynthetic, whereas eukaryotes do not obtain energy through chemosynthesis*).

Key to Strategies
● **Understanding Concepts (Tier I)**
■ **Applying Information (Tier II)**
▲ **Critical Thinking (Tier III)**

Bacteria and Viruses   335

The disease tuberculosis is caused by the bacterium *Mycobacterium tuberculosis*. Tuberculosis patients were once treated with streptomycin, an antibacterial drug that is produced by bacteria of the genus *Streptomyces*. This example shows how bacteria are both harmful and beneficial to humans.

Phase Two
Teaching Strategies

Importance of Bacteria

■ **Inferring Relationships**
Prepare a display consisting of actual items *(may include pickles, sauerkraut, cheese, yogurt, or root nodules of a bean plant)* and pictures *(may include photos of an oil spill, manmade snow, leprosy, or a tick)*. Have students attempt to determine how bacteria might be involved in the items on display. *(Pickles, sauerkraut, cheese, and yogurt are made with bacterial cultures; root nodules contain nitrogen-fixing bacteria; bacteria are being bioengineered to clean up oil spills; artificial snow is made from water and a powder containing dead* Pseudomonas syringae; *leprosy is caused by* Mycobacterium leprae; Ixodes dammini *is the vector for* Borrelia burgdorferi, *the bacteria that causes Lyme disease.)*

Active READING

▸ **Reading Technique: Paired Summarizing**
Pair the students. Have students read silently about bacterial diseases on pages 338–341. Have one student orally summarize what was read without referring to the text. The other student should listen without interruption (except to request clarification), state any inaccuracies in the summary, and add any ideas left out. Students should work together and may refer to the text if needed. Let students alternate roles and repeat the process after reading about how bacterial diseases are controlled, on pages 341–344.

18-2 How Bacteria Affect Humans

OBJECTIVES

1 **Describe three beneficial effects of bacteria.**

2 **List five human diseases caused by bacteria.**

3 **Summarize three ways to prevent bacterial diseases.**

4 **Evaluate the importance of antibiotics in fighting bacterial diseases.**

Beneficial Bacteria

Although you probably know that some bacteria can cause harm—such as when they destroy food or make you ill—you might not be fully aware of the tremendous benefits bacteria provide. For instance, bacteria maintain crucial links in nutrient cycles that make essential elements such as nitrogen and sulfur available to plants and, indirectly, to humans. Bacteria are also very important in the manufacture of food and life-saving drugs. Without bacteria, life as we know it could not exist.

Decomposers are nutrient recyclers
Try to imagine what life would be like if all the dead plants and animals in the world never decayed! Garbage and waste would pile up and every bit of land on Earth would be filled with material that could not be used and would never go away.

Recall from Chapter 14 that decomposers are organisms that return nutrients to the environment by breaking down organic matter, like the leaf litter shown in **Figure 18-5**. When a plant or animal dies, bacteria from the air and soil settle on the dead organism. The bacteria begin to grow, releasing carbon dioxide, water, nitrogen, phosphorus, and sulfur—nutrients that plants need in order to grow. Without decomposers, most of these nutrients would be locked away in the bodies of dead organisms.

Nitrogen-fixing bacteria enrich the soil
Because nitrogen is a component of proteins, plants cannot photosynthesize, grow, or reproduce without it. Much of the nitrogen available for plants is produced by nitrogen-fixing bacteria. Nitrogen-fixing bacteria transform atmospheric nitrogen, which cannot be absorbed by plants, into ammonia, a nitrogen compound that plants can absorb. No other organisms have this ability.

Nitrogen-fixing bacteria are found in the soil, in aquatic ecosystems, and within the roots of some plant species. The legumes, plants including the peas and beans, contain nitrogen-fixing bacteria in swellings on their roots. These bacteria enable legumes to grow in nitrogen-poor soils where other plants cannot.

Figure 18-5
Without decomposers, nutrients would not be recycled.

Multicultural Perspective: Yogurt

Plain yogurt was originally made by nomadic Middle Eastern tribes. The hot desert sun, aided by the gentle rocking of camel transportation, provided the perfect environment for making yogurt. Yogurt is made from milk that is curdled by two types of bacteria, *Lactobacillus bulgaricus* and *Streptococcus thermophilus*. Because yogurt is cultured, it is easier to digest than regular milk. Additionally, the bacteria in yogurt produce B vitamins in the intestine. Today, many Americans prefer to eat yogurt sweetened with fruit.

Helpful Bacteria

- *Fix nitrogen*
- *Recycle nutrients*

Figure 18-6
a **Without the billions of bacteria that share our world, life as we know it could not exist.**

- *Used to make certain foods and aid in digestion*
- *Clean up oil and toxic spills*
- *Used to make antibiotics, vitamins and drugs*
- *Used as natural pesticides*

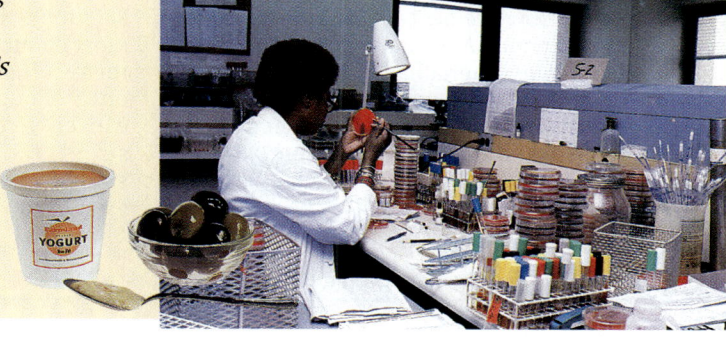

Harmful Bacteria

- *Cause disease*
- *Contaminate food*

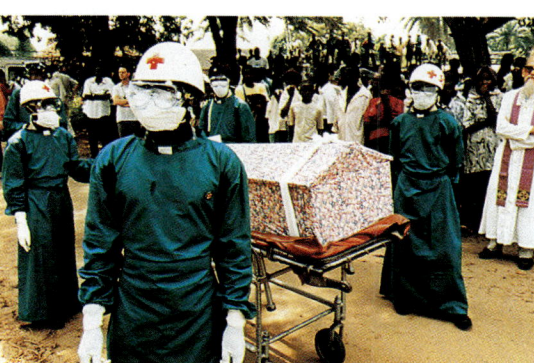

b **Unfortunately, bacteria do not always interact with humans in a helpful way.**

Interdependence

How would an ecosystem be affected if its nitrogen-fixing bacteria were destroyed?

Bacteria are used to manufacture food and drugs

When you eat yogurt or olives, you are eating food that is the product of bacterial decomposition. Humans have learned that decomposition is occasionally beneficial because it adds flavor to food. For example, bacteria convert cabbage and cucumbers into tangy sauerkraut and pickles.

Modern technology is taking advantage of the enormous genetic diversity among the bacteria. Using genetic engineering technology, biologists can now "reprogram" bacteria to manufacture any protein for which a gene has been isolated. For example, bacteria now produce most of the insulin needed by diabetics in the United States. Before genetic engineering, insulin had to be isolated from the pancreases of animals killed in slaughterhouses. Some of the other ways we are affected by bacteria are listed in **Figure 18-6**.

337

Connection: *Chapter 9*

Genetic Engineering
Review the process of genetic engineering with the students.

Life/Work Skills
Being a Team Member
- **Summarizing Information**

Divide the class into teams of 3 to 4 students each. Have each team use information from library materials and databases to find a bioengineered product. Approve each team's choice. Each team should include physical and chemical properties, importance, and availability of the product in its research. *(Some products include human insulin, gamma interferon, interleukin-2, human growth hormone, vitamin B_2, and cotton.)*

Theme Answer
Interdependence
Nitrogen-fixing bacteria provide nitrogen to plants. Without these bacteria, the amount of available nitrogen would fall. Compounds requiring nitrogen could not be produced. Plant growth would drop, and energy and nutrient availability in higher trophic levels would decline.

Visual Strategy **Videodisc**
- **Summarizing Information**
To review the Lyme disease infection process, use *Illustration—Lyme Disease* in Chapter 18 Section 18-2 of *Holt Biology Videodiscs Teacher's Correlation Guide to Holt Biology: Visualizing Life.* Explain that Lyme disease was first identified in 1975 and is found in almost every state. It is common among pets.

Key to Strategies
- Understanding Concepts (Tier I)
- Applying Information (Tier II)
- Critical Thinking (Tier III)

Historical Perspective: Unintended Collaboration

Alexander Fleming (1881–1955), winner of the Nobel Prize in 1945 for his discovery of penicillin, probably owed his success to the fact that an Irish mycologist was working with *Penicillium* one floor below his laboratory. Some *Penicillium* spores probably blew in an open window and contaminated his *Staphylococcus aureus* plates, resulting in the discovery of penicillin's antibiotic activity. Strange accidents happen frequently, but as Louis Pasteur once said, "In the fields of observation, chance favors only the prepared mind."

338

Health Connection
Infectious Diseases

Invite a medical microbiologist to speak to the class about some infectious bacterial diseases that have occurred in recent years. Be certain that information about symptoms, mode of transmission, available treatment, incidence and cure rate, and appropriate audio-visual materials will be included in the lecture.

Visual Strategy Table 18-1

■ **Inferring Conclusions**

Point out that most diseases listed in this table do not pose a significant health problem in the United States. Have students suggest reasons for this. (*Answers may include proper sanitation, better health care and preventative care, and availability of medicine.*)

Mathematics Connection
Counting Bacteria

Explain to the students that in theory each colony on a petri dish arose from a single bacterium and that bacteriologists use this understanding to count the number of bacteria in a sample. Tell the students that a 1 mL sample of bacterial solution was diluted 1,000 times in water and then a 1 mL sample was added to a petri dish. Twenty-four hours later, 38 colonies were counted. How many bacteria were in the original sample? (*38 × 1000 = 38,000 bacteria per mL*) How many bacteria would have been in the sample if the dilution factor had been only 250 and only a 0.1 mL sample had been put on the plate? (*38 × 10 × 250 = 95,000 bacteria per mL*)

Bacteria and Disease

Your body occasionally becomes a temporary home for parasitic bacteria, with serious effects—they cause disease or infection. A disease-causing agent is called a **pathogen**. Pathogenic bacteria are harmful because they damage their host's tissues. This damage results either from direct attacks on the host's cells or from poisonous substances called toxins that many bacteria release.

How are bacterial diseases actually transmitted? Each species of pathogenic bacteria has a characteristic way of being carried to new hosts: in water, in the air, in food, by insects, or by direct human contact. **Table 18-1** lists some bacterial diseases and their modes of transmission.

Bacteria cause tooth decay and ulcers

One of the most widespread of human diseases caused by bacteria is dental caries (decay leading to cavities), which arises in the film on our teeth. Diets high in sugar promote dental caries because the bacteria ferment the sugars into lactic acid. The acid causes a loss of calcium, followed by breakdown of the proteins in tooth enamel. Scientists have recently found that most common stomach ulcers are also the result of bacterial infection. It was once thought that excessive stress caused ulcers, but it is possible that stress creates an environment in the stomach that is beneficial to the bacteria's growth.

Table 18-1 Examples of Bacterial Diseases

Disease	Mode of transmission	Symptoms
Tuberculosis	Airborne water droplets	Fatigue, persistent cough, bleeding in lungs; can be fatal
Diphtheria	Airborne water droplets	Fever, sore throat, fatigue
Syphilis	Sexual contact	Lesions, CNS damage if untreated
Bubonic plague	Fleas	Swollen glands, bleeding under skin; often fatal
Typhus	Lice	Rash, chills, fever; often fatal
Tetanus	Wounds, skin breaks	Severe, prolonged muscle spasms
Cholera	Contaminated water	Severe diarrhea, vomiting; often fatal
Typhoid	Contaminated water and food	Headaches, fever, diarrhea, rash; often fatal
Leprosy	Personal contact	Nerve damage, skin lesions, tissue degeneration
Lyme disease	Ticks	Rash, pain, swelling in joints

Matter of Fact: Stomach Ulcers

The bacterium recently associated with the formation of some stomach ulcers is *Helicobacter pylori*, a spirochete. This bacterium colonizes the lower portion of the stomach, where there are fewer acid-producing cells. In addition, these bacteria also produce enzymes that buffer their microenvironment. Most individuals infected with *H. pylori* never develop symptoms. It is thought that immune responses, smoking, and age at the time of infection might play a role in the development of disease. An excellent article for more detailed information is "The Bacteria Behind Ulcers," by Martin J. Blaser, in *Scientific American,* February 1996.

Figure 18-7
Just in case the chicken you are preparing is contaminated with *Salmonella*, you should use hot, soapy water to wash the surfaces that have been touched by the raw chicken.

Food can be contaminated by bacteria

Although certain bacteria can produce yogurt and cheese, most bacteria in food are not helpful. Pathogenic bacteria can contaminate foods and cause food poisoning.

One of the most dangerous kinds of food poisoning is botulism, which is caused by a toxin released by the bacterium *Clostridium botulinum*. Consumption of less than one-millionth of a gram of this toxin causes paralysis and death. *C. botulinum* normally lives in the soil, but it can grow in canned foods that have not been properly sterilized. Because oxygen kills botulism bacteria, they cannot grow in fresh and frozen foods, which contain oxygen.

Another type of food poisoning is caused by *Salmonella* bacteria found in pork, eggs, poultry, and other foods. The symptoms of *Salmonella* food poisoning are diarrhea, vomiting, and abdominal cramps. A serious infection can cause dehydration, a drastic loss of water from the body. In the very young or in the elderly, severe dehydration can be fatal.

Food poisoning has also been linked to a newly discovered strain of the bacterium *Escherichia coli*. This bacterium normally lives in the intestines of mammals, including humans, and synthesizes vitamin K for us. The new strain of *E. coli*, however, has caused serious outbreaks of severe food poisoning and even death in people who unknowingly ate undercooked hamburgers from a fast-food restaurant. New regulations concerning cooking temperatures in restaurants make it safer to eat out.

Taking the following precautions can mean the difference between a good meal and a trip to the hospital: thaw frozen meats and poultry in the refrigerator or microwave; wash working surfaces, utensils, and hands with hot, soapy water after contact with raw meats, as shown in **Figure 18-7**; and, most important, cook meat thoroughly until there are no pink juices left.

Heat and cold help protect food from bacterial contamination

Bacterial contamination of food can be treated with either heat or cold. **Pasteurization** involves heating food to a temperature that kills most bacteria. Pasteurization eliminates the possibility of contracting diseases such as botulism from canned food or tuberculosis from milk.

Cooling food to a few degrees above freezing reduces bacterial contamination. Although bacteria are not killed, their rate of growth is greatly slowed. Most *Salmonella* infections are caused by food that has been left out of the refrigerator too long, allowing bacteria to grow to significant numbers.

339

Matter of Fact: Dystonia

Dystonia is an abnormal muscle rigidity that causes painful muscle spasms, unusually fixed postures, or strange movement patterns. It may affect only a certain area of the body or may be more generalized. Botulinum toxin has been used to treat certain dystonias since 1984. The toxin inhibits the release of acetylcholine from the neurons in the neuromuscular junction, allowing the muscles to relax. The toxin is administered by injection. The effects are noticeable within 3 to 5 days. The botulinum toxin treatment is effective for about 6 months, after which it has to be readministered.

Health Connection
Food Poisoning
Invite the school dietitian to speak to the class about food poisoning and what a person can do to prevent it.

Life/Work Skills
Finding Information

● **Organizing Information**
Assign students to cooperative groups of four. Have each team research a type of food poisoning and write a report. Be certain to assign some types not discussed in the book, such as *Staphylococcus aureus* and *Campylobacter jejuni.* Students should use reference books and databases to obtain basic background information and to find one example of a food-poisoning incident that occurred in recent years. The report should then be presented orally.

World of Work

Microbiology
The job of a microbiologist is a varied one. Some are responsible for the development of vaccines. Others are employed in the food industry, contributing to the production, development, and preservation of food products. Microbiologists are employed in hospitals, private industry, pharmaceutical companies, universities, and government agencies.

Ask students to do further reading on these careers in order to make a list of personal characteristics that a microbiologist should possess. (*Possible answers include the following: must be organized, detailed, able to tolerate microscope work, and able to work independently.*)

Key to Strategies
● Understanding Concepts (Tier I)
■ Applying Information (Tier II)
▲ Critical Thinking (Tier III)

Bacteria and Viruses   339

Problem Solving

▲ Distinguishing Relevant Information

Present the following situation to the students: Two people have come down with bacterial infections. One is suffering from food poisoning caused by *Clostridium botulinum*. The other person has contracted tuberculosis. Ask the students to evaluate the situation and suggest a possible course of treatment for each person. *(The person with tuberculosis should be given an appropriate antibiotic determined by the doctor. The person with botulism, however, should be given an antitoxin because this condition is caused by the toxin that the bacteria produce. Antibiotics are not effective against the toxin.)*

Beneficial and Harmful Bacteria

■ Forming a Model

Have students construct a **Graphic Organizer** similar to the one shown at the bottom of this page. Have them list instances in which bacteria are beneficial to humans, instances in which they are harmful to humans, and examples of how their adverse effects can be controlled. When students have completed this list, they should conclude that the beneficial uses outweigh the harmful ones.

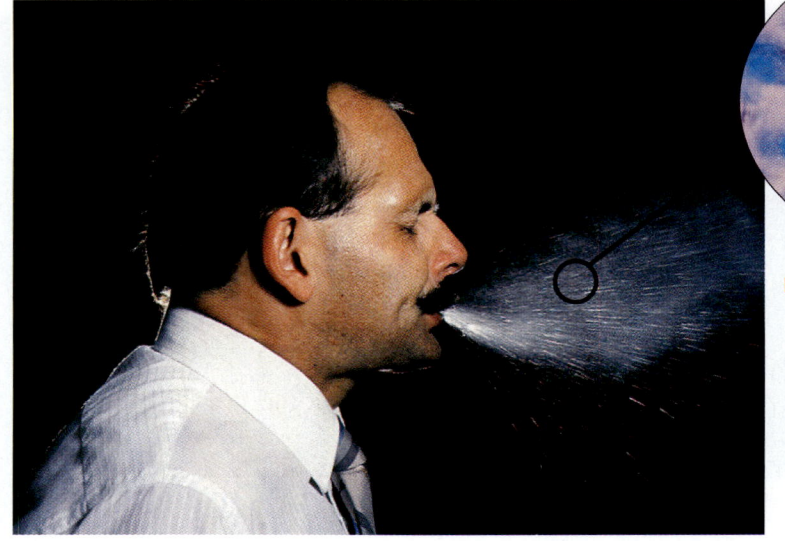

b This view shows the bacteria that can be found in a single water droplet of a sneeze. *Mycobacterium tuberculosis*, the bacterium that causes the disease tuberculosis, can be transmitted in airborne water droplets such as these.

Figure 18-8
a A sneeze sends thousands of bacteria into the air. Some of these bacteria may be pathogens.

Bacteria travel through the air

A sneeze or cough sprays out a shower of tiny droplets, as you can see in **Figure 18-8**. Visible in the circular photograph are some of the 10,000 to 100,000 bacteria carried in the droplets produced by a single sneeze. The bacteria that cause diphtheria, scarlet fever, whooping cough, and tuberculosis drift through the air in droplets such as these. Most airborne diseases affect the respiratory system of their victims.

By far the most serious airborne disease is tuberculosis (also called TB), caused by the bacterium *Mycobacterium tuberculosis*. Three million people die of this disease annually. In fact, for most of this century, TB has been the leading worldwide cause of death from a single infectious agent. In the 1970s and 1980s, TB was not a serious health problem in the United States. However, in the last decade there has been a marked increase in cases, many of which are resistant to the best available antituberculosis medications. Drug-resistant pneumonia is also on the rise.

Bacteria are carried by animals

Lyme disease is an example of a disease caused by a bacterium that lives inside several species of ticks. When an infected tick, like the one in

Figure 18-9, bites a human to feed on blood, the bacteria can be transferred to the human, who may then develop Lyme disease.

Ticks carrying the bacteria are spread by deer, rodents, and other mammals as well as by birds. The first symptom of Lyme disease is usually a red rash that begins at the site of the tick bite and spreads outward. If left untreated, muscle pains, joint inflammation, and, in advanced stages, brain damage can occur.

Lyme disease is treated with various antibiotics. With early treatment, a patient can be cured before any severe damage occurs. The best "cure" is prevention. Cover up when you journey into wooded, grassy, or brushy areas. Wear long sleeves and long pants tucked into socks. Remove any attached ticks according to a physician's instructions.

Figure 18-9
Deer ticks have eight legs and a flat body. Like lobsters, crabs, and insects, they have a hard outer covering that must be periodically shed as the animal grows.

Graphic Organizer

Use the following graphic organizer with the teaching strategy **Beneficial and Harmful Bacteria** on page 340.

Beneficial Effects	Harmful Effects	Methods of Control
Yogurt	Tetanus	Vaccine, antitoxin
Cheese	Salmonella food poisoning	Cook poultry, wash hands

Since ticks are unable to fly, they must wait for a host to wander close to them. They have poor vision and rely on their keen sense of smell. They are especially sensitive to carbon dioxide and butyric acid, a rancid-smelling chemical occurring on the skin of many animals, including humans. These substances immediately cause the hungry tick to move toward the odor. A biting tick injects its victim with not only the bacteria that cause Lyme disease, but with chemicals that suppress the victim's immune system.

Controlling Bacterial Diseases

Since the 1940s, when antibiotics like penicillin began to be widely used, most Americans have had little experience with serious bacterial diseases. Advances in medicine and sanitation have brought freedom from illnesses that had been commonplace for centuries.

Sanitation and hygiene help prevent bacterial diseases

Cholera is a serious disease transmitted through polluted water. Cholera bacteria produce a strong toxin that causes acute diarrhea and vomiting, which can lead to rapid dehydration. If untreated, this severe loss of water can be fatal within 24 hours. Cholera bacteria are spread in drinking water that has been contaminated by the feces of infected individuals. Any fish that are caught in contaminated water can also carry cholera bacteria. In 1991 a large cholera epidemic struck Peru and rapidly spread to the rest of South America and Central America, as shown in **Figure 18-10**. At least 1,700 people died in the first year of this devastating outbreak.

In the industrialized countries, drinking water is filtered and then purified with chlorine, a chemical that kills bacteria. Similarly, sewage is collected and treated to remove pathogens before it is discharged into rivers or the ocean. Thus, cholera, typhoid, and other diseases of contaminated water are almost unknown in the industrialized countries.

Unfortunately, these clean conditions are not characteristic of some of the developing countries. Because of

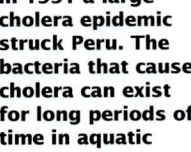

Figure 18-10
In 1991 a large cholera epidemic struck Peru. The bacteria that cause cholera can exist for long periods of time in aquatic environments, making contaminated water very dangerous. These Peruvian children are waiting for uncontaminated water to be brought to them.

341

Visual Strategy   Figure 18-10

■ **Relating Concepts**
Use this figure to point out that nearly 200 years elapsed between the discovery of bacteria and the germ theory of disease. Bacteria and other organisms were first seen and described by Anton van Leeuwenhoek, who worked with a simple microscope in the late 1600s. Not until the mid-1800s was the germ theory of disease accepted, as a result of the efforts of Louis Pasteur in France, Robert Koch in Germany, Joseph Lister in England, and Ignaz Semmelweis in Austria. Also emphasize the health problems that exist in developing countries. Compare these countries with developed countries, like the United States. Unsanitary conditions coupled with less-than-adequate medical care is a major problem in developing countries. Some students might question the use of chlorine in water treatment. Chlorine reacts with organic materials to form small amounts of chlorinated hydrocarbons, some of which are carcinogenic. Remind students that other treatments in existence are more expensive and that without chlorination we run the risk of drinking water that is contaminated with pathogenic microorganisms.

Community Connection: Water Purification

Arrange a guided tour of your local water-treatment facility. If possible, have them send you specific literature and an itinerary before the tour. Before the trip, discuss the types of diseases that are transmitted by water, and point out possible consequences of insufficient water and wastewater treatment. Also discuss the treatment methods employed by the facility. After the trip, ask the students to write a report about how wastewater is treated and what improvements they would make to the water-treatment system if they were water engineers.

Key to Strategies
● **Understanding Concepts (Tier I)**
■ **Applying Information (Tier II)**
▲ **Critical Thinking (Tier III)**

Connection: *Chapter 9*

Vaccines

Review how scientists manufacture vaccines with recombinant DNA technology.

● **Summarizing Information**

Review the steps of vaccine preparation. Tell students that, depending on the disease, bacterial vaccines can be composed of polysaccharides found in bacterial capsules, inactivated toxins, or killed or live attenuated bacteria. Inform students that new vaccines must undergo rigorous testing mandated by the Food and Drug Administration. An excellent article that summarizes vaccine testing is "How FDA Works to Ensure Vaccine Safety," in *FDA Consumer,* December 1995.

Figure 18-11
The preparation of vaccines involves inactivation of the disease-causing organism and its subsequent introduction into the body.

a Whooping cough vaccine is prepared by first culturing the bacteria responsible for whooping cough.

b The bacteria, *Bordetella pertussis,* are then killed using heat or chemicals.

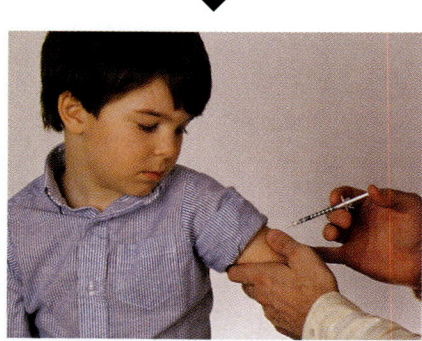

c The dead bacteria are purified and cleansed, and the vaccine is packaged.

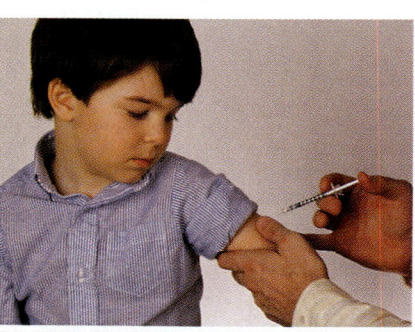

d The vaccine containing the dead bacteria is injected. This child's body will now produce antibodies that fight *Bordetella pertussis.*

poverty, many of these countries cannot provide clean drinking water for all of their citizens. In any nation, natural or human-caused disasters, such as floods, earthquakes, or wars, can destroy or interrupt water treatment. These situations create conditions that are ideal for water contamination. Each year about 25 million people around the world die from typhoid, cholera, and other diseases caused by contaminated water.

Vaccination stimulates the body's defenses

Preventing the contamination of food and drinking water are only two ways to protect yourself from infection. Vaccinating against disease is another way. Before you started school, you were probably vaccinated against bacterial diseases such as diphtheria, whooping cough, and tetanus. A **vaccine** is a solution that contains pathogens or their toxins that have been made harmless, usually by treatment with heat or chemicals or by genetic engineering. How does a vaccine protect you against pathogenic bacteria? As shown in **Figure 18-11**, a vaccine against whooping cough, for example, is a solution of whooping cough bacteria that have been killed with heat or chemicals. These dead bacteria cannot cause disease, but once inside your body they stimulate your immune system to make defenses against them. Once you have been vaccinated against whooping cough, your immune system has defenses ready to destroy any live whooping cough bacteria before they have a chance to make you ill. Scientists have learned that many vaccinations, such as those for diphtheria, tetanus, and whooping cough, require more than one dose. This is because our bodies require more stimulation from some vaccines in order to provide us with a strong defense against those diseases. So it is very important that all people receive their booster vaccinations on schedule to ensure protection against those disease-causing organisms. Scientists are trying to develop vaccines to protect us against diseases for which we currently do not have vaccines.

342

Figure 18-12
Alexander Fleming's discovery of penicillin is one of the most important medical milestones of the century. Millions of lives have been saved because of his observations. The fungus that produces penicillin is shown below.

Antibiotics are used to treat bacterial diseases

Before the 1940s, doctors had few treatments for bacterial diseases. Whether a patient recovered or died often depended more on the type of disease and the strength of the patient than it did on the efforts of the doctor. This grim situation changed because of a chance event in 1928. In that year, Alexander Fleming, the British physician shown in **Figure 18-12**, found a blue-green mold growing on one of his bacterial samples. At first Fleming was angry because his experiment had been contaminated. Before throwing out the sample, however, he noticed that bacteria did not grow near the mold. The mold was apparently releasing a chemical that was poisonous to bacteria. Fleming isolated this substance and

named it **penicillin**, after the *Penicillium* mold that produced it.

In the early 1940s, scientists following up on Fleming's discovery showed that penicillin was a very effective treatment for many bacterial diseases. Antibacterial drugs such as penicillin are called **antibiotics**. There have been many other antibiotics discovered since penicillin; tetracycline and streptomycin are two common examples. Some antibiotics prevent bacteria from making new cell walls. Unfortunately, antibiotics have been so successful in alleviating our illnesses that some doctors prescribe them when they are unnecessary. Most sore throats, upset stomachs, and other minor problems go away by themselves. Our own immune systems can usually deal with attacks very effectively.

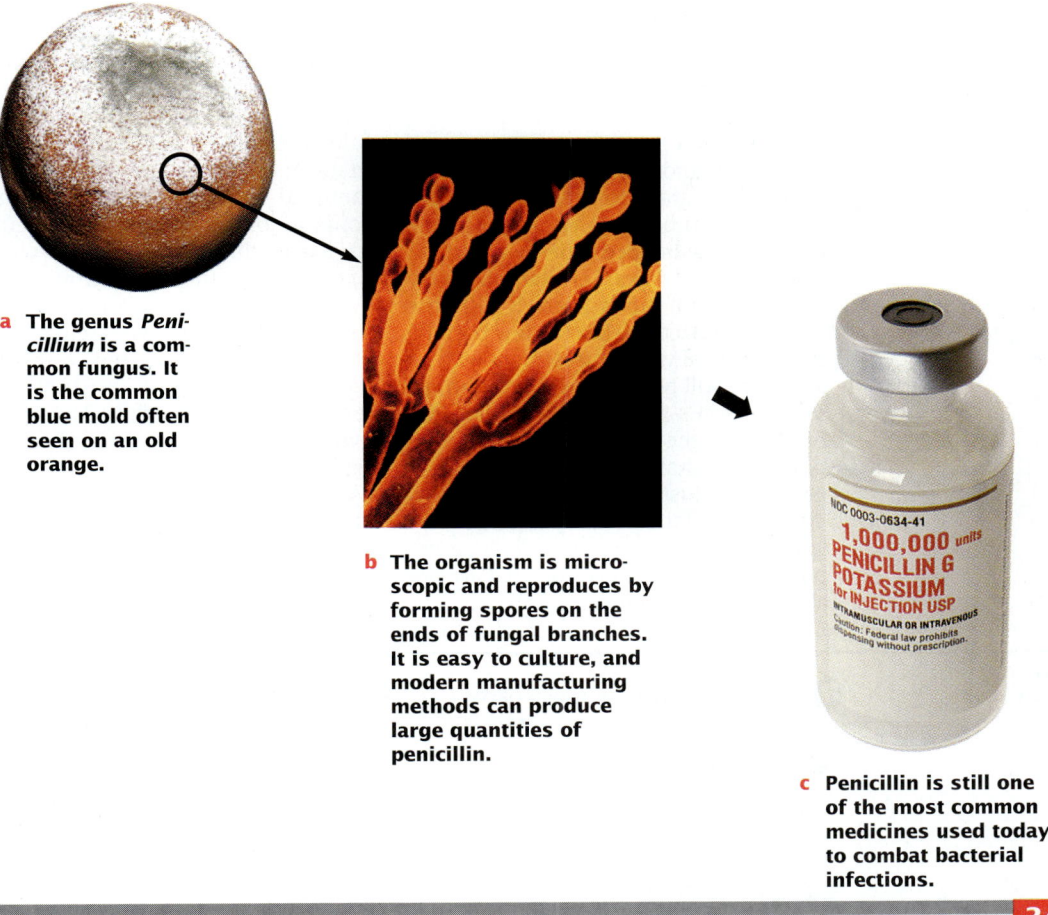

a The genus *Penicillium* is a common fungus. It is the common blue mold often seen on an old orange.

b The organism is microscopic and reproduces by forming spores on the ends of fungal branches. It is easy to culture, and modern manufacturing methods can produce large quantities of penicillin.

c Penicillin is still one of the most common medicines used today to combat bacterial infections.

343

Historical Perspective: Maggot Therapy

During World War I, before the age of antibiotics, American military doctor William Baer noticed that wounded soldiers whose wounds were infested with maggots recovered more quickly than those not so infested. Blowfly maggots consume the dead flesh, where bacteria grow and cause problems. After the war, Baer convinced the medical community of the value of maggots, and in the 1930s hundreds of hospitals used maggot therapy. With the introduction of sulfa drugs, maggot therapy ceased. With the recent rise of antibiotic-resistant bacteria, maggot therapy has begun a quiet renaissance, although squeamishness has slowed the growth of this "new" therapy.

Key to Strategies
● **Understanding Concepts (Tier I)**
■ **Applying Information (Tier II)**
▲ **Critical Thinking (Tier III)**

Phase Three
Assessment Options

Closure

■ **Forming a Hypothesis**

Have students hypothesize what would happen if all the bacteria in the world were destroyed. *(Answers should include that bacterial infections would be eliminated; certain foods, such as yogurt, cheese, and sauerkraut, could not be made; dead organisms could not be decomposed, eliminating nutrient recycling; and our intestinal tracts would suffer greatly from the lack of a microflora.)*

SECTION REVIEW

Assign the *Section Review*.

Reteaching

Have each student write a brief report on one bacterial disease. Providing a list of diseases may be helpful. The report should concentrate on a brief description of the disease, the organism that causes it, its incidence, and its treatment.

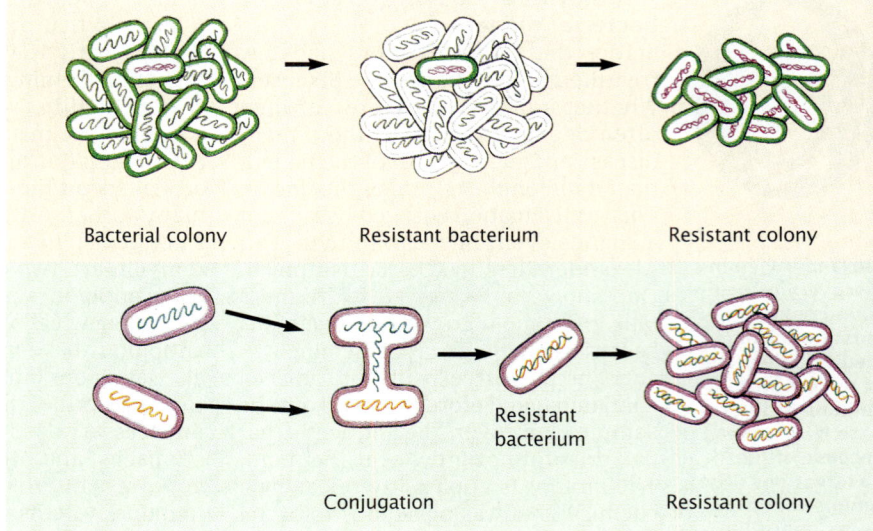

Figure 18-13
Bacteria acquire resistance through natural selection or by receiving the resistance gene through conjugation.

Bacterial colony   Resistant bacterium   Resistant colony

Resistant bacterium

Conjugation   Resistant colony

Bacteria are fighting back

Until the late 1980s, many scientists thought that we had conquered most infectious bacterial diseases and that the rest would soon be controlled. But bacteria have been here a long, long time. They reproduce rapidly, as we have seen, and they mutate. And they become resistant to the drugs we use against them by a variety of methods. **Antibiotic resistance** evolves in bacteria in a number of ways. For example, every time an antibiotic is used, it kills the majority of bacteria. But the few bacteria that remain alive after treatment with an antibiotic will reproduce, as you can see in **Figure 18-13**. These bacteria are resistant to the antibiotic, and they will pass along that resistance to the next generation. Just as we have seen insects develop resistance to pesticides, so bacteria have developed increasing numbers of resistant strains that are not affected by antibiotics.

Some cases of antibiotic resistance arise in patients who do not complete the full course of antibiotics prescribed by a physician. Without a full treatment, only the weaker bacteria are killed. Their stronger counterparts come back full force, and repeated antibiotic treatment encourages the rapid development of antibiotic-resistant strains. Some serious outbreaks of tuberculosis have been due to the failure of patients to complete antibiotic treatment.

Antibiotics have also been widely used by farmers, who learned that animals that were fed antibiotics gained more weight. Constantly challenged by antibiotics, the rapidly evolving bacteria give rise to new, resistant strains. Bacteria are the oldest and most successful group of organisms on Earth. Human beings are beginning to appreciate that the struggle to defeat disease-causing bacteria is going to be an ongoing battle.

SECTION REVIEW

1 Describe one way in which bacteria are used to treat a disease.

2 Name four diseases caused by bacteria. Identify the mode of transmission for each disease.

3 Explain why pasteurization is effective in preventing bacterial contamination.

4 Why is it important to finish the entire course of antibiotics prescribed by a physician?

344

ANSWERS TO SECTION REVIEW

1 Through genetic engineering, bacteria can be reprogrammed to manufacture many of the proteins for which a gene has been isolated; for example, bacteria are used to produce insulin to treat diabetes.

2 Answers will vary. See Table 18-1, page 338.

3 Pasteurization is effective because heating the food to a particular temperature for a set time will kill most bacteria.

4 When the full course of antibiotics is not finished, only the weaker bacteria are killed. The mildly resistant bacteria survive and may cause a recurrence of the disease. A repeated antibiotic treatment (if not finished) will then encourage the development of an antibiotic-resistant strain.

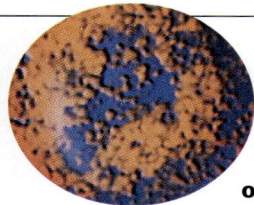

The World Health Organization estimates that more than 10 million people throughout the world are infected by HIV, the virus that causes AIDS. The number of infected people grows rapidly each year. Finding a cure for AIDS or a vaccine against HIV will require a clear understanding of what viruses are, how they reproduce, and how they affect their hosts.

18-3 Viruses

OBJECTIVES

1 Draw the structure of a virus.

2 Justify this statement: Viruses are not living organisms.

3 Describe viral reproduction.

4 List four diseases that are caused by viruses.

What Is a Virus?

Think back to the last time you had a cold or the flu. Did you ask the doctor for antibiotics to kill the flu or cold "bacteria" that were making you so miserable? Did the doctor explain that colds and flu are not caused by bacteria, so antibiotics would have no effect? Colds and flu are caused by **viruses**. Viruses are microscopic particles that invade the cells of plants, animals, fungi, and bacteria. Viruses often destroy the cells they invade.

Viruses are small, simple particles

If you could open a virus, what would you find inside? Would you find cyto-plasm, ribosomes, and mitochondria like you would find in one of your own cells? No, because a virus is not a cell. A typical virus, such as the polio virus shown in **Figure 18-14**, is composed of a core of genetic material surrounded by a protein "coat." The protein coat protects the genetic material and enables the virus to invade its host cell. The *Tour of a Virus* on the next page shows the structure of the human immunodeficiency virus (**HIV**). This virus causes acquired immune deficiency syndrome (**AIDS**).

In many viruses, DNA is the genetic material. Other viruses have RNA instead. The viruses that cause AIDS, polio, and the flu are RNA viruses. Viruses are parasitic and can reproduce only inside the cells of their hosts. Because viruses are so small, viral genetic material has room for only a few genes, usually only genes coding for the protein coat and for enzymes that enable the virus to take over its host cell.

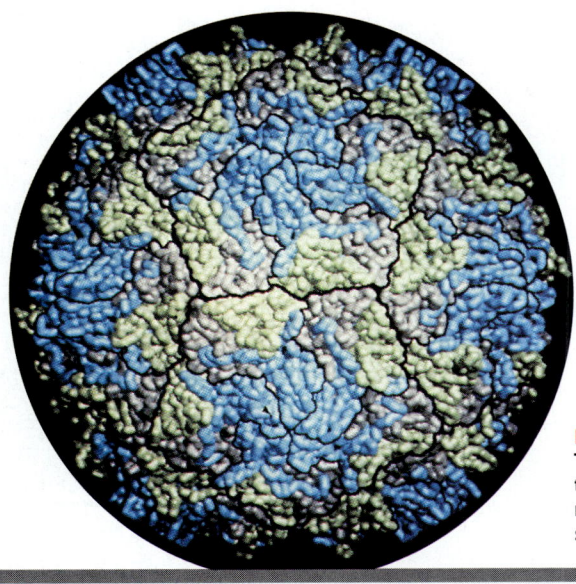

Figure 18-14
The computer-generated colors on this image of the polio virus represent the different proteins present on the surface of the virus.

345

Phase One
Preparation

Scheduling
See the **Lesson Planning Guide** on pages 329A and 329B for lecture, classwork, and assignment options for Section 18-3.

Active READING

Technique: Reading Organizer
As students read about viruses in Section 18-3, have them work in small groups to create a Spider Map Reading Organizer that identifies the characteristics of viruses.

Phase Two
Teaching Strategy

Connection: *Chapter 8*

Viruses
Review the experiments of Hershey and Chase.

Demonstration
● **Comparing Structures**
Show students various electron micrographs of viruses. Have them compare the structures of viruses and bacteria.

Historical Perspective: Viruses

Viruses were first detected 100 years ago when scientists were searching for something that they knew was smaller than bacteria and could cause a disease in tobacco plants. Known as tobacco mosaic disease, the disease caused the leaves to develop a patchwork of light- and dark-green areas. In the late 1800s, this disease was destroying the tobacco crop in Russia. In 1892, a Russian biologist, Dimitri Ivanowsky, discovered that whatever caused this disease was smaller than bacteria and was contagious. In 1935, an American biologist, Wendell Stanley, isolated the tobacco mosaic virus.

Key to Strategies
● Understanding Concepts (Tier I)
■ Applying Information (Tier II)
▲ Critical Thinking (Tier III)

Connections: *Chapter 8*

Backward Transcription

Review the process of transcription in Section 8-2 and ask why the term *reverse transcriptase* is an apt one to describe the enzyme that makes DNA from RNA. *(Cells start with DNA and then make RNA, from which they make protein. With reverse transcriptase, however, DNA is made from RNA. This is the reverse of normal transcription, hence the term* reverse transcriptase.*)*

Vaccine Development

▲ Evaluating Hypotheses

Explain to the students that virologists working on HIV have had great difficulty in developing a vaccine. Ask the students to imagine that they are research virologists trying to develop a vaccine for HIV. Ask them to look at the virus on page 346 and name parts of the virus that could perhaps be used as a basis for a vaccine. *(Answers will vary, but they should include structures that would be accessible by an immune response.)* When they are finished, tell them that HIV can periodically change its protein surface so that the immune system "sees" HIV as a new virus and thus has to react to the new proteins (see page 350). Ask them to critique their approach to vaccine development in light of this information.

Virus

The disease AIDS is caused by a virus called HIV, human immunodeficiency virus.

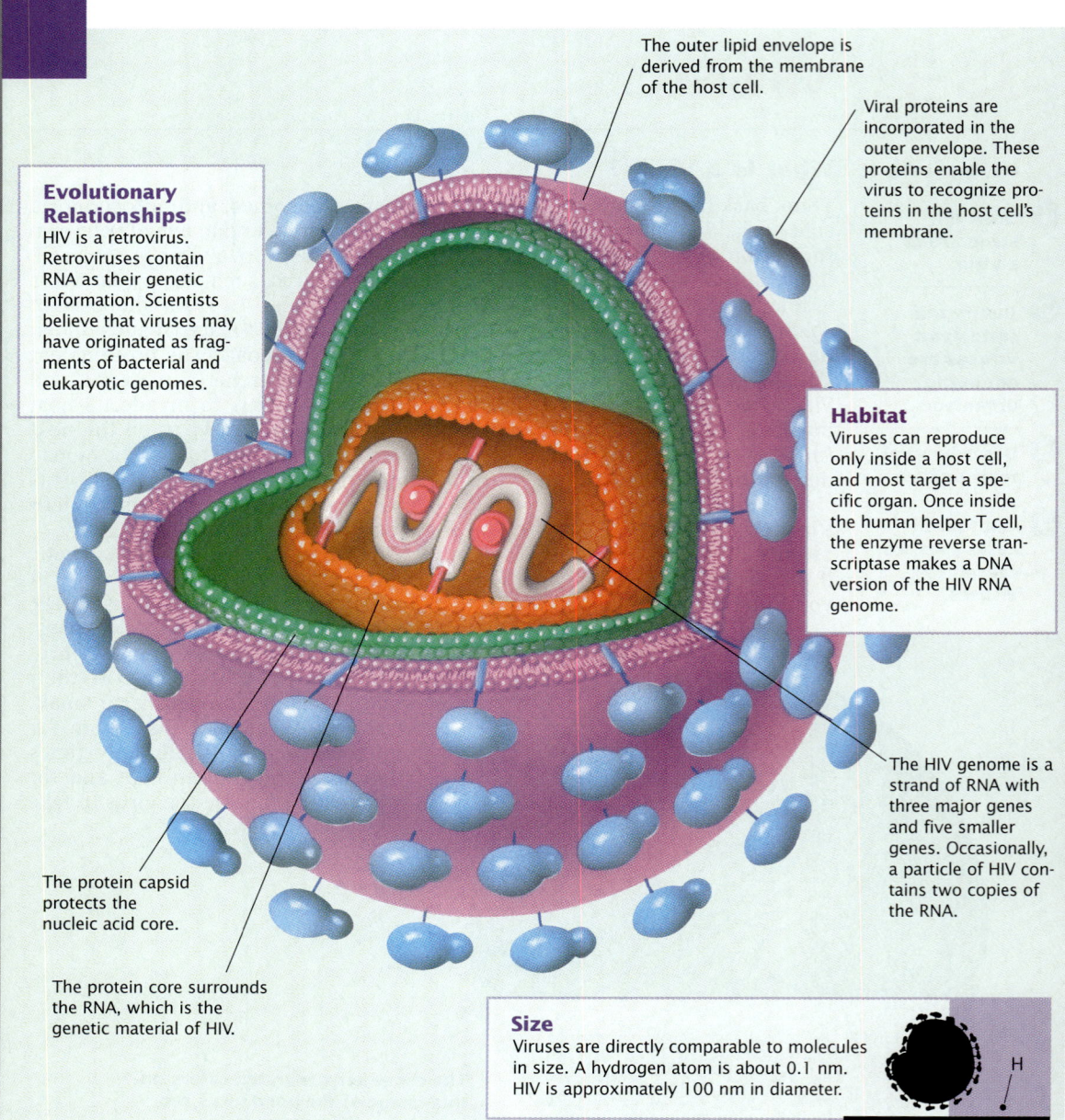

The outer lipid envelope is derived from the membrane of the host cell.

Viral proteins are incorporated in the outer envelope. These proteins enable the virus to recognize proteins in the host cell's membrane.

Evolutionary Relationships
HIV is a retrovirus. Retroviruses contain RNA as their genetic information. Scientists believe that viruses may have originated as fragments of bacterial and eukaryotic genomes.

Habitat
Viruses can reproduce only inside a host cell, and most target a specific organ. Once inside the human helper T cell, the enzyme reverse transcriptase makes a DNA version of the HIV RNA genome.

The HIV genome is a strand of RNA with three major genes and five smaller genes. Occasionally, a particle of HIV contains two copies of the RNA.

The protein capsid protects the nucleic acid core.

The protein core surrounds the RNA, which is the genetic material of HIV.

Size
Viruses are directly comparable to molecules in size. A hydrogen atom is about 0.1 nm. HIV is approximately 100 nm in diameter.

H

346

Multicultural Perspective: AIDS Highway

The road that runs from Kinshasa, Zaire, in West Africa to Mombasa, Kenya, in East Africa is sometimes called the AIDS highway. Scientists believe that HIV has been in the human population for many decades in Africa but that because of the lack of transportation, those individuals who had HIV almost never left their local area. As Africa has become more developed, travel has increased along with advances in transportation. War and prostitution have scattered HIV-infected individuals throughout villages along the highway. With them, the virus has traveled to the cities of Africa and then to the rest of the planet.

Viruses: living or nonliving?

Viruses do have some characteristics of living things. They have genetic material that is transmitted to future generations and that can change over time. Therefore, viruses are able to evolve. On the other hand, viruses lack three essential features of living things: they are not made of cells, they cannot make proteins by themselves, and they cannot use energy. Even though viruses can reproduce, they are able to do so only when inside living cells. Viruses are considered nonliving because they lack characteristics that biologists attribute to living things. Outside a host cell, a virus is an inert collection of chemicals. Nevertheless, because viruses are active inside living cells, the study of viruses is part of biology.

How Viruses Reproduce

To reproduce, a virus must insert its genetic material, which contains the instructions for making new viruses, into a host cell. This viral genetic material seizes control of its host cell and transforms it into a virus-making factory. All viruses reproduce by taking over the reproductive machinery of a cell. Follow how HIV reproduces in the example below.

HIV seizes control of host cells

HIV cannot infect a cell that it cannot enter. HIV is able to enter only those cells that have particular receptor proteins in their cell membranes. HIV recognizes these cells because the virus contains a protein that will bind to the receptor proteins on the cell membrane. You can think of the relationship between the viral protein and the cell membrane proteins as being like the relationship between a key and a lock. If the key (the viral protein) fits the lock (the cell proteins), then the cell is opened to invasion. Otherwise, the virus is locked out.

One host cell for HIV is a type of white blood cell known as the helper T cell. Helper T cells occur in the blood and in the lymphatic system. They play a very crucial role in the body's ability to fight infection. Follow the events that occur when HIV infects a helper T cell in **Figure 18-15**.

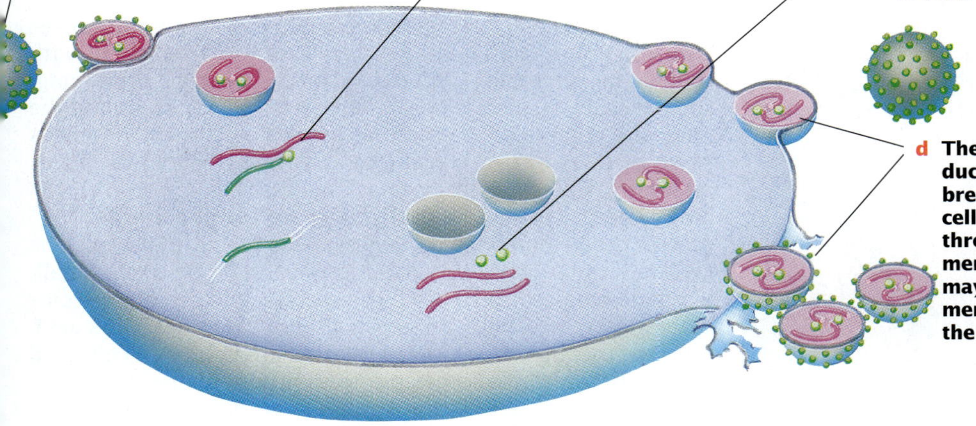

Figure 18-15
HIV enters a human helper T cell and then takes over the cell's machinery. The cell is directed to make HIV proteins and RNA. Newly made viruses then leave the cell and continue the cycle of infection.

a The knob-shaped proteins on the surface of the virus bind to specific receptor proteins on the cell's surface. The virus then enters the cell.

b Viral RNA is released into the cell. A viral enzyme, reverse transcriptase, makes a DNA copy of the virus's RNA.

c The cell then produces HIV proteins and genes. These assemble to form new viruses.

d The newly produced viruses may break out of the cell by budding through the cell membrane. Or they may burst the cell membrane, killing the cell.

347

Multicultural Perspective: Worldwide Fevers

Movies such as *Outbreak* gave people a good scare about viruses from Africa, but Africa is not the only place where there are deadly viruses. Many viruses throughout the world cause hemorrhagic diseases, including Machupo in Bolivia and Hantaan in Korea and much of Asia. In the United States, the Sin Nombre virus (Hanta-related) caused a series of deadly pneumonias in the Four Corners area of the Southwest. Hantavirus pneumonias throughout the United States give reason for concern. Hantavirus has also been implicated in kidney dysfunction in Antwerp, Amsterdam, and in other ailments in Europe. When it comes to disease, viruses recognize no cultural, racial, or language barriers.

Mathematics Connection
Viral Reproduction

A single virus that infects a bacterial cell can produce about 100 viruses in 20 minutes. Have students calculate how many viruses would exist 4 hours after a single virus infected one bacterium in a culture. (10^{24} *viruses; remember, the number of viruses increases by* 10^2 *every 20 minutes, and there are 12 lytic cycles in 4 hours*).

Visual Strategy — Videodiscs

■ **Recognizing Relationships**
Use *Video—Human Immunodeficiency Virus (HIV)* (3 min 5 s) in Chapter 18 Section 18-3 of *Holt Biology Videodiscs Teacher's Correlation Guide to Holt Biology: Visualizing Life* to discuss the structure and life cycle of HIV. As students view the video, tell them to pay special attention to the ways HIV depends on host cells. After viewing, point out that the virus was described as a parasite. Have students write a short paragraph explaining this. (*Responses should indicate that, like parasites, viruses need a host cell to survive.*)

Visual Strategy — Figure 18-15

● **Identifying Structures**
Review HIV as shown in *Tour of a Virus*. Use this figure to guide students through the process of viral infection of an animal cell. Point out the connection to Chapter 3 (Cells), in which cell surface receptors were discussed. Also compare and contrast the infection of an animal virus with a bacteriophage (Chapter 8, How Genes Work).

Key to Strategies
● Understanding Concepts (Tier I)
■ Applying Information (Tier II)
▲ Critical Thinking (Tier III)

The Polio Virus

▲ **Evaluating Viewpoints**

In 1954, Jonas Salk (1914–1995) developed the first polio vaccine from inactivated viruses. In the early 1960s, Albert Sabin (1906–1993) introduced his oral vaccine made from live viruses. Have students research the virus and the two vaccines in order to determine the advantages and disadvantages of each vaccine. For example, students will find that both vaccines prevent disease and induce IgG antibodies but differ in their ability to interrupt fecal-oral transmission, to induce IgA antibodies in the intestine, to interfere with viral replication in the gut, to revert to virulence, to cause disease in immunocompromised individuals, to provide long duration of immunity, to be administered easily, and to be stored without refrigeration.

Language Arts Connection

Bestsellers

Have students read either a fiction book (such as *The Andromeda Strain* by Michael Crichton) or nonfiction book (such as *The Hot Zone* by Richard Preston or *The Coming Plague* by Laurie Garrett) that deals with bacteria or viruses. Consult the criteria set by your school administration for assigned reading before giving this assignment. Work with a language arts teacher in your school to prepare a format for a book report in order to provide an interdisciplinary approach.

AIDS is fatal

HIV causes AIDS by killing helper T cells, which coordinate the body's defenses against pathogens. However, HIV may not begin to destroy large numbers of cells for a few months to over 10 years after infection. During this period, an infected person may experience only mild flulike symptoms or no symptoms at all. An infected person can transmit HIV to others during this period. Scientists now think that practically everyone infected with HIV will develop AIDS. Eventually, the virus begins to destroy a large percentage of an infected person's helper T cells. When the number of helper T cells has fallen to very low levels, the person is said to have AIDS. AIDS patients usually die of cancer or diseases a healthy immune system would defeat. You will read more about HIV transmission and AIDS prevention in Chapters 33 and 35.

Diseases Caused by Viruses

Figure 18-16
The telltale blotchy rash of measles has become relatively uncommon since the development of the measles vaccine.

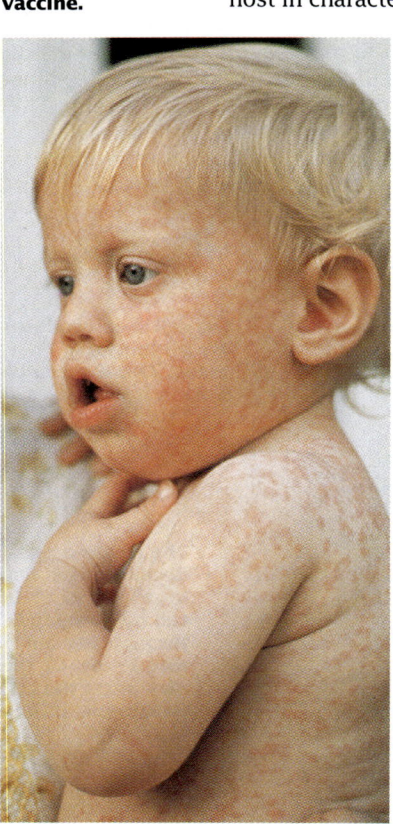

Viruses cause many serious human diseases in addition to AIDS, such as measles, shown in **Figure 18-16**, and influenza. Viruses also cause diseases in plants, insects, and even bacteria. Like pathogenic bacteria, pathogenic viruses are transmitted from host to host in characteristic ways. Some of the viral diseases listed in **Table 18-2** are airborne. A few, such as infectious hepatitis and polio, can spread through contaminated water. Insects also transport viruses. The yellow fever virus, common in tropical regions, is carried by mosquitoes.

There are defenses against viruses

Why don't physicians treat viral diseases such as colds, flu, and AIDS with antibiotics? Antibiotics work by interfering with cellular processes such as protein production or cell-wall synthesis, which do not occur in viruses. Moreover, because a virus uses its host cell for reproduction, it is very difficult to find any drugs that will destroy the virus without damaging the host.

A drug called azidothymidine (AZT) blocks an enzyme essential for DNA replication. Many AIDS patients are now being treated with AZT, which can prolong the lives of these patients. Unfortunately, AZT cannot cure AIDS; it only slows the course of the disease. Furthermore, AZT is very toxic and has numerous side effects.

Vaccination also protects against viral diseases

The only effective defense we now have against most viral diseases is a healthy immune system. Vaccination works to build up your immune system. Recall that vaccines against bacterial disease are composed of dead bacteria. But viruses are not "alive" and cannot be "killed." Instead, vaccines against viral diseases contain viruses made harmless by treatment with chemicals or by genetic engineering. These harmless viruses stimulate the immune system to create defenses against the harmful form of the virus.

Smallpox is no longer a killer

Eliminating smallpox from the world is vaccination's greatest triumph. Smallpox virus produced tiny pustules or sores (small "pox") on its victim's skin. These pustules developed scabs and often turned into permanent, disfiguring scars. Far worse, smallpox killed

Community Connection: Local Memories

Invite an older individual to speak to the class about personal memories of viral epidemics, such as St. Louis encephalitis, yellow fever, the influenza of 1918, polio, dengue fever, or smallpox. Ask them to tell students what it was like to live through those times of uncertainty.

Figure 18-17
Ali Maow Maalin, of Merka, Somalia, contracted smallpox in 1977 at the age of 23. His was the last known case of smallpox contracted outside a laboratory.

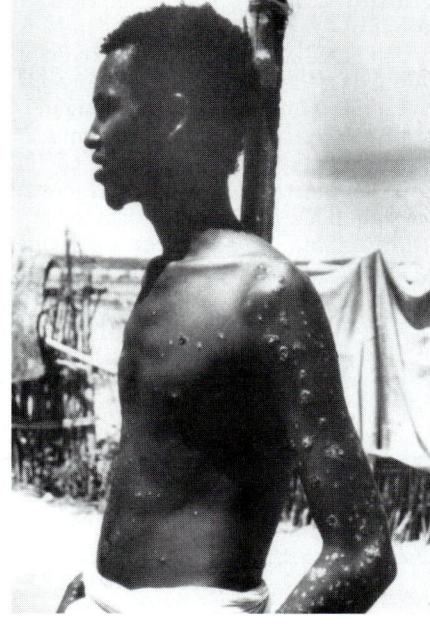

half of those who contracted it. Because smallpox was so deadly, cures and means of prevention were sought for centuries. A vaccine was discovered in 1796, and efforts to extend its use increased with time.

Finally, vaccination against smallpox became commonplace in industrialized countries. As a result, smallpox rapidly disappeared from these countries. The last case in the United States occurred in 1949. Because the disease persisted in some of the poorest nations, the World Health Organization launched a worldwide vaccination campaign against smallpox. In 1967, the year this campaign was launched, 10 million to 15 million cases of the disease occurred. Just 11 years later, smallpox had been eliminated. The last known person to contract smallpox outside a laboratory is shown in **Figure 18-17**.

Emerging viral diseases

Many viruses live in animals without causing apparent harm, but they cause diseases when they infect other animals or humans. Among the most dangerous of these are a group of filoviruses (*filo-* from the Greek word for "thread," and *viron* from the Latin word for "poison") that have produced outbreaks of hemorrhagic fever in regions of central Africa and other parts of the world that received animals imported from Africa. These viruses attack human connective tissue, leading to massive bleeding (hemorrhaging). With mortality rates ranging from 30 to 90 percent, these filoviruses are among the most lethal infectious agents known. The outbreak of Ebola virus in Zaire, shown in **Figure 18-18**, in the spring of 1995 was confined to a few villages and fortunately did not reach the nearby city of Kinshasa, which has a population of 4 million.

No one knows the identity of the central African animal that harbors the Ebola virus. It does not appear to be chimpanzees, because the virus kills them as well. It might be another primate, a mosquito, or even an elephant. Intensive efforts are being made to find the carrier so that an attempt can be made to control the disease. Filoviruses could be a very real threat to worldwide human health if they ever achieve widespread dissemination, as the AIDS virus has done.

Figure 18-18
Two boys waiting for the body of a relative at a cemetary in Kikwit, Zaire, in May 1995 try to protect themselves by covering their faces. Ebola virus killed over 200 people in central Africa before the epidemic ended.

End of a Species
▲ **Evaluating Viewpoints**
In 1978, a medical photographer in England died after being accidentally infected during smallpox destruction. Stocks of smallpox still exist at the Centers for Disease Control and Prevention in Atlanta, Georgia, and at the Institute for Viral Preparations in Moscow, Russia. June 30, 1999, has been set as the destruction date for these stocks. Cloned DNA fragments of the full genome of the virus exist in order to continue scientific research. These fragments are noninfectious and safe to handle. Some scientists would like to see the last of the viable virus destroyed, while other scientists maintain that it is important to keep the virus for further study. Ask the students if it is worth the risk to keep the virus alive. Ask them to defend their position.

Active READING
Technique: K-W-L
Tell students to return to the list that they created using the K-W-L technique on page 330. Have them check off the questions that they can now answer. Students should then make a list of what they've **L**earned. Conclude by asking the following:
• Which questions are still unanswered?
• What new questions do you have?
You may wish to have students research their unanswered questions.

349

Multicultural Perspective: Who Really Won the West

The early struggles between Europeans and Native Americans may well have been decided by disease. Spanish conqueror Hernán Cortés was aided in his conquest of the Aztecs by a smallpox epidemic that struck the Aztecs—smallpox had been unknown in the New World prior to the Europeans' arrival. Smallpox killed millions of Native Americans. Spanish chronicler Toribio Motolinía wrote that so many had died that they could not be buried—"They pulled down the houses over them in order to check the stench that rose from the dead bodies." Native Americans also died in great numbers in the northeastern United States, allowing Europeans to more easily establish their presence there.

Key to Strategies
● Understanding Concepts (Tier I)
■ Applying Information (Tier II)
▲ Critical Thinking (Tier III)

Theme Answer

Evolution

The development of a vaccine is based on the surface protein of the virus. If a virus changes those proteins, then the vaccine becomes ineffective. This is why influenza vaccines must be reformulated every year.

Connection: *Chapter 7*

Mutations

Remind students that a change in a gene is called a mutation. Review how a change in DNA will cause a change in RNA and, in turn, a change in the protein that is synthesized.

Phase Three

Assessment Options

Closure

▲ Evaluating Situations

Have students imagine that a viral epidemic has been declared in their community. Discuss what steps should be taken to control the epidemic and eventually eliminate it. *(Answers should include but not be limited to the following: virus must be identified; route of transmission must be determined in order to prevent spread of the disease; quarantine must be established if necessary; types of treatment and medication must be evaluated, selected, and applied.)*

SECTION REVIEW

Assign the *Section Review*.

Reteaching

Ask students why viruses cannot be grown on nutrient agar as bacteria are, but must be cultured in living tissues. *(Viruses cannot carry out the cellular functions necessary for growth; they can reproduce only in the cells of living tissues.)*

Evolution

Why is it difficult

for researchers to

develop effective

vaccines against

those viruses that

change the shapes

of their surface

proteins?

Vaccines do not protect against all viral diseases

Why has it been so difficult to develop a vaccine against HIV? And why do millions of us suffer from colds and flu each year? Unfortunately, vaccination is effective only against viruses with nonvarying proteins on their surfaces, proteins that remain unchanged generation after generation. Smallpox virus, measles virus, and polio virus have surface proteins that remain the same from one viral generation to the next. HIV, cold viruses, and flu viruses, however, have surface proteins whose genes mutate often. As a result, the shape of these surface proteins often changes over just a few generations. Such a change produces a form of virus not recognized by the immune system. Although you can be vaccinated against influenza, each kind of influenza vaccine produces immunity against just one form, or strain, of the virus. That is why a person vaccinated against the flu can get the flu many times in a lifetime, each time from a different strain. Of all the changeable viruses, HIV changes most rapidly. **Table 18-2** lists some common viral diseases.

Table 18-2 Examples of Viral Diseases

Disease	Transmitted by	Symptoms
Chickenpox	Airborne	Rash, fever
Measles	Airborne	Blotchy rash, high fever, congestion in nose and throat
Rabies	Bite of infected animal	Fever, paralysis; fatal unless treated
Rubella (German measles)	Airborne	Rash, swollen glands
Mumps	Airborne	Swollen salivary glands
Influenza (flu)	Airborne	Headache, muscle aches, sore throat, cough; historically, one of the great "killer" diseases
Smallpox	Airborne	High fever, pustules on skin; often fatal; now extinct
Infectious hepatitis	Contaminated food or water	Fever, chills, nausea, swollen liver, jaundice, pain in the joints
Polio	Contaminated food or water	Headache, stiff neck, possible paralysis
Yellow fever	Mosquitoes	Nausea, fever, aches, liver cell destruction; can be fatal
AIDS	Sexual contact, contaminated blood products, contaminated hypodermic needles and syringes	Immune system failure; fatal
Hemorrhagic fever: Ebola virus	Sexual contact, contact with blood or other body fluids	Fever, epithelial cell destruction, massive hemorrhaging; often fatal

SECTION REVIEW

1 Draw a virus and label its parts.

2 Describe three ways in which viruses differ from living cells.

3 How does a virus reproduce?

4 Explain why a vaccination against influenza will not give you life-long protection against the flu.

ANSWERS TO SECTION REVIEW

1 See *Tour* of a Virus, page 346.

2 Viruses are not made up of cells; they cannot make proteins by themselves; they cannot use energy.

3 A virus reproduces by entering a host cell and taking over the reproductive machinery of that cell. New viruses are then assembled and released from the cell.

4 Influenza viruses mutate rapidly. Hence, the proteins on their outer surface change rapidly. The body does not immediately recognize the "new" viruses as pathogens that it has been vaccinated against. These viruses can therefore cause disease.

Highlights

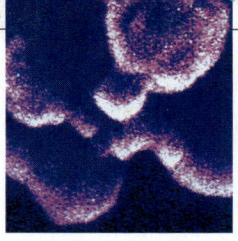

These are human immuno-deficiency viruses seen through a scanning electron microscope.

	Key Terms	Summary
18-1 **Bacteria** Unlike eukaryotic cells, bacterial cells do not have a nucleus. 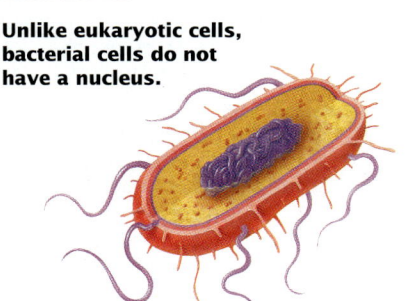	Gram staining (p. 332) conjugation (p. 332) chemosynthesis (p. 335)	• Bacteria, the oldest group of organisms on Earth, have cells much smaller than those of eukaryotes. • Most bacteria are spherical, spiral, or rod-shaped, and they have one of two types of cell walls. • Bacterial cells lack membrane-bound organelles and chromosomes. They have ribosomes, cytoplasm, and one molecule of DNA. • The kingdoms Archaebacteria and Eubacteria contain autotrophs and heterotrophs.
18-2 **How Bacteria Affect Humans** The discovery of penicillin by Alexander Fleming is one of the great scientific and medical achievements of this century. 	pathogen (p. 338) pasteurization (p. 339) vaccine (p. 342) penicillin (p. 343) antibiotic (p. 343) antibiotic resistance (p. 344)	• Beneficial bacteria include decomposers and nitrogen-fixing bacteria. Bacteria also make certain foods and drugs. • Vaccines help the body's immune system resist infection, thereby reducing the incidence of many bacterial diseases. • Antibiotics are antibacterial drugs. Alexander Fleming discovered the first antibiotic, penicillin, in 1928. • Overuse of antibiotics has encouraged the development of resistant bacteria.
18-3 **Viruses** Viruses are responsible for many diseases, including polio, herpes, AIDS, and the common cold. 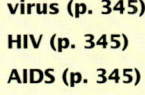	virus (p. 345) HIV (p. 345) AIDS (p. 345)	• Viruses are not considered living organisms. They are small particles that invade cells. • Viruses consist of RNA or DNA surrounded by a coat of protein. • A virus can only reproduce by controlling a cell. • Emerging viruses such as HIV and Ebola virus can appear and disappear without warning or can become a long-term world health problem.

351

Alternative Assessment

Scientists have recently discovered two types of particles, viroids and prions (from proteinaceous, infectious particles), that are even smaller than viruses. Viroids have been identified as the cause of several diseases in plants. Have students use library resources to obtain information about these two particles, and have them prepare a brief oral report to share with the class. *(Viroids consist only of a short chain of naked RNA; prions consist of a glycoprotein, but the DNA that codes for this glycoprotein is not found in the host cell. Prions are believed to be responsible for several animal diseases, including bovine spongiform encephalopathy [mad cow disease], scrapie [in sheep], and kuru [in humans]. Creutzfeldt-Jakob disease is suspected by some to be caused by a prion, but this theory is not yet widely accepted.)*

Portfolio Assessment

Portfolio Assessment on page T39 provides options for building and evaluating student portfolios. Students and teachers can select items from the areas listed on page T39 for inclusion in a portfolio.

A N S W E R TO CONCEPT MAP

The following is one possible answer to the Relating Concepts exercise on page 352.

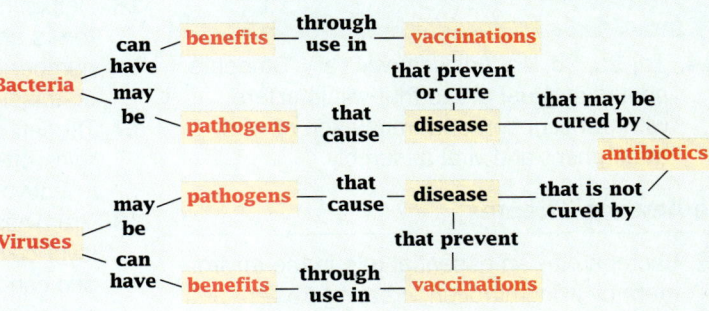

Understanding Vocabulary

1. a. nonliving
   b. heat
   c. helpful
2. Answers will vary.

Understanding Concepts

3. Concept map answer is shown on page 351.
4. Virus and bacteria. Bacteria have flagella, ribosomes, cytoplasm, and a cell wall and membrane. Viruses are smaller and have no cytoplasm, ribosomes, or flagella. They are microscopic and have no nuclear membrane or organelles.
5. A vaccine is made of attenuated or killed virus or bacteria and stimulates the immune system to respond against specific nonself molecules. When you are exposed to a "live" virus or bacteria, an effective response is made.
6. No, AZT only slows the replication of HIV.
7. Antibiotics interfere with cellular processes that do not occur in viruses.
8. Tuberculosis has increased among the poor and in immunocompromised people. Treatment for TB takes months to complete; patients who do not take their full course of medication are in danger of developing resistant strains of TB.
9. Antibiotics kill bacteria, but some bacteria may contain mutations that protect them from certain antibiotics. When other bacteria are killed, these protected bacteria reproduce, passing on the antibiotic resistance to future generations of bacteria.
10. See Figure 18-6, page 337.
11. a-2, b-4, c-1, d-6, e-3, f-7, g-5
12. metabolism, cellular organization and homeostasis
13. c

Understanding Vocabulary

1. For each set of terms, complete the analogy.
   a. bacteria : living :: viruses : _____
   b. refrigeration : cold :: pasteurization : _____
   c. pathogen : harmful :: vaccine : _____

2. Using each set of words below, write one or more sentences summarizing information learned in this chapter.
   a. cell walls, Gram staining, diseases, bacteria
   b. heterotrophic, nutrition, photosynthetic, bacteria, autotrophic, chemosynthesis
   c. bacterial diseases, pasteurization, vaccine, sanitation, hygiene

Understanding Concepts

3.  **Relating Concepts** Construct a concept map describing the relationships of bacteria and viruses to diseases. Use as many terms as necessary from the vocabulary list. Try to include the following terms in your map: bacteria, viruses, pathogen, antibiotics, benefits, and vaccination.

4. **Comparing Structures** Look at the two representations below. What are they? How do their structures differ? How are they the same?

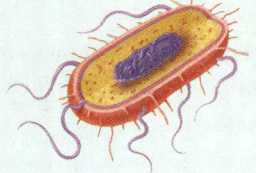

5. **Interpreting Conclusions** How can a vaccine protect you against a disease?

6. **Applying Information** The synthetic drug AZT is used by many people who have AIDS. Does AZT cure AIDS? Explain your answer.

7. **Analyzing Conclusions** Explain why antibiotics work against bacterial diseases but not against viral diseases.

8. **Summarizing Information** Explain why tuberculosis is once again becoming a serious concern to public-health officials.

9. **Analyzing Functions** Describe the process by which bacteria develop resistance to antibiotics.

10. **Recognizing Relationships** Even though bacteria can be very harmful to humans, they are also essential to life. Explain why

11. **Inferring Relationships** Match each term on the left with the most appropriate term on the right. After you have matched them, explain the relationships between them.

    a. *Escherichia coli*   1. Lyme disease
    b. HIV   2. vitamin K
    c. ticks   3. photosynthetic
    d. conjugation   4. AIDS
    e. autotrophic eukaryotes 5. immunization
    f. bacterial decomposition 6. genetic exchange
    g. vaccination   7. pickles

12. **BUILDING ON WHAT YOU HAVE LEARNED** Which of the five properties of life described in Chapter 2 would have to be changed before the viruses could be considered alive?

13. **Interpreting Data** Lab technicians routinely test for the presence of *E. coli* to ensure that municipal water supplies are not polluted by sewage. The number of *E. coli* bacteria found in water samples may indicate the amount of sewage present in the water.

Three-Year Fecal Coliform Averages (bacterial colonies per 100 mL of water)			
	1992	1993	1994
Site 1	15	13	12
Site 2	5	16	35
Site 3	88	92	6

Which statement is most consistent with the data?

a. The water at Site 1 is safe to drink.
b. The amount of sewage decreased each year at Sites 1, 2, and 3.
c. In 1993, a factory at Site 3 was fined for releasing untreated sewage.
d. Water samples collected from Site 1 contain the largest amounts of sewage.

14. 1d, 2a, 3c, 4b. Answers will vary. Students should suggest drugs that will interfere with transcription and translation or with attachment and viral assembly.

Reviewing Themes

15. Bacteria play an essential role in the environment by fixing nitrogen, creating oxygen, and releasing nutrients from decomposing dead organisms.

16. Helper T cells coordinate the immune system's attack on pathogens. Reduction in their number impairs the body's ability to resist disease.

17. The influenza virus changes its surface proteins often, and it is difficult to make an effective vaccine for all strains.

18. Gram-negative bacteria have an additional layer covering the cell wall, which the antibiotic can't penetrate, so these bacteria are not affected.

Interpreting Graphics

14. Examine the figure shown below..Match each numbered event in the figure with the sentence that best describes it.

   a. Viral DNA is injected into the host cell.
   b. Viruses are released.
   c. New viruses are made.
   d. A virus attaches to the host cell surface.

Arrange the events in the correct sequence. Using your imagination, describe some ways in which a drug or vaccine could affect events shown in the figure below.

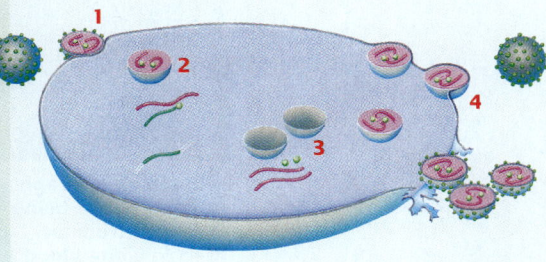

Reviewing Themes

15. *Interdependence*
Even though bacteria can be very harmful to humans, they are also essential to life as we know it. Explain why.

16. *Interdependence*
HIV attacks and destroys helper T cells. How does having fewer helper T cells affect the human immune system?

17. *Evolution*
Hundreds of thousands of people get flu shots each year. Yet many of them still get the flu. Why are flu shots often ineffective?

18. *Cell Structure and Function*
How do the cell walls of Gram-positive bacteria differ from those of Gram-negative bacteria? How does this difference affect the effectiveness of antibiotics used to treat bacterial infections?

Thinking Critically

19. Distinguishing Fact From Opinion A reporter wrote, "The ongoing development of new antibiotics means that humans will soon be free of bacterial diseases." Explain the error that the reporter has made.

Life/Work Skills

20. Applying Technology Farm managers have discovered that mixing low doses of antibiotics into cattle feed makes animals grow larger. Biologists claim that this practice encourages the development of resistant strains of bacteria. In your opinion, is this use of antibiotics justified? Use references available in a library or search an on-line database to write a report summarizing your opinion. Include facts and examples to support your conclusions.

Activities and Projects

21. Social Studies Connection The global flu epidemic of 1918–1919 claimed 20 million lives. Use references available in a library or search an on-line database to find resources for writing a short description of the steps taken to prevent further epidemics. How long was it before another epidemic occurred? How did it differ from that in 1919?

22. Career Connection: Microbiological Technician Technicians in this field study bacteria, fungi, and viruses and their relationships to disease, agriculture, genetic engineering, and pollution. Use references in the library or search an on-line database to discover the many job possibilities in this area.

23. Health Connection Make a poster showing a list of behaviors that could reduce the spread of colds and flu in your school. Write to the Association for Practitioners in Infection Control, 505 East Hawley, Mundelein, IL 60060, for more information about the importance of hand washing and other sanitation issues mandated for those who work in the food industry.

Discovering Through Reading

24. Read the article "Revenge of the Killer Microbes" in *Time*, September 12, 1994, pages 63–69. Describe four human behaviors that have encouraged the development of antibiotic-resistant bacteria.

Activities and Projects

21. Vaccines have been developed in anticipation of the new strains of influenza and then distributed. The next great pandemic was the 1957–1958 Asian flu epidemic. Deaths were greatly reduced because of the availability of antibiotics to treat secondary pulmonary infections.

22. Reports will vary depending on the profession selected.

23. Behaviors such as washing your hands, staying home when you are sick, covering your mouth when you sneeze or cough, and cleaning surfaces such as door knobs could significantly reduce the spread of colds and flu.

Discovering Through Reading

24. Widespread and sometimes reckless overuse of antibiotics has favored the spread of strains of antibiotic-resistant bacteria; increased mobility in our society has aided the spread of many diseases; disruption of ecosystems has exposed us to predation by new viruses; poverty and homelessness, along with drug addiction, overcrowding, and the increased numbers of HIV-positive people in the population, have all contributed to the spread of "killer microbes."

353

Thinking Critically

19. Realistically, the medical profession has always been just a step ahead of bacterial resistance, which is rising sharply and shows no sign of lessening.

Life/Work Skills

20. Reports should be indicative of sufficient research and thought on the student's part. They should include statements of thoroughly examined positions on both sides and careful consideration of all positions in drawing conclusions.

Objectives

- Summarize the phases of a new drug study.
- Describe how experiments for testing a new drug are designed.
- Discuss new FDA guidelines for expediting the availability of certain new drugs.

Accelerated Drug Studies

▲ **Developing Informed Opinions**

During the past decade, the medical and health-care communities have seen an increased demand for early access to promising new therapies. Discuss with your class how the Food and Drug Administration (FDA) has responded to this demand by raising the following questions: What is the FDA's role and responsibility in new-drug development? What are the standard procedures for drug approval? Should these procedures apply to all drugs? Under what circumstances does the FDA allow access to a therapy before it is formally approved?

Have students use references in the library or on the Internet to research the history of a rapidly approved drug, such as the drug AZT, which was approved by the FDA in March 1987 after only three and a half months of testing. Encourage students to debate the advantages and shortcomings of accelerated drug studies. Have them write an editorial that could be submitted to a local newspaper or could be read on public radio.

The Nature of Research

● **Evaluating Viewpoints**

Biological and pharmaceutical research is a complicated, time-consuming, and costly process with results that usually could not have been predicted. The majority of chemicals tested as possible new drugs turn out to be either unsafe or ineffective. Scientific literature citing medical progress is full of accounts of false starts, accidental discoveries, and challenges to be overcome. Have students explore the nature of research in the pharmaceutical industry. How long can

Science, Technology, and Society

New Drug Development—How Are New Drugs Tested?

What happens when you or a family member is seriously ill? If you're lucky, a drug is available to treat the illness or disease. A streamlined Food and Drug Administration approval process now allows new drugs that offer the promise of saving lives to reach the market faster.

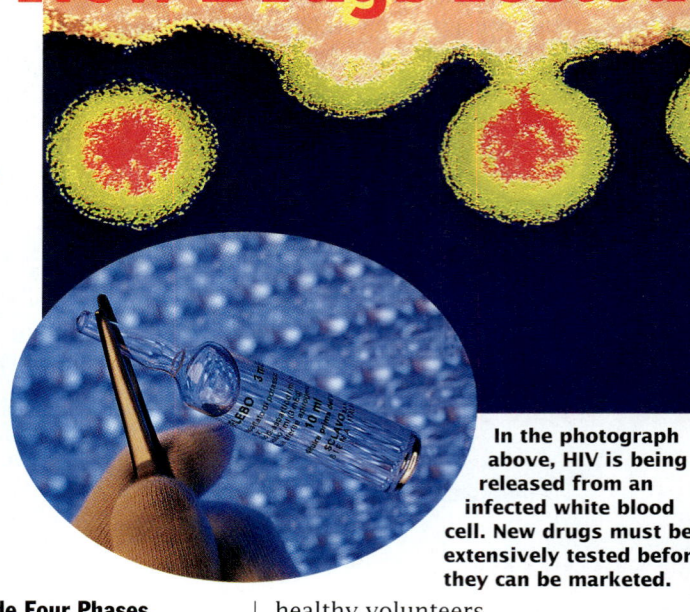

In the photograph above, HIV is being released from an infected white blood cell. New drugs must be extensively tested before they can be marketed.

Drug Studies Include Four Phases

Before a new drug can be sold, its sponsor—a pharmaceutical company, a research organization, or a public or private agency—must first conduct studies to show that the drug is safe and effective. The results of these studies are submitted to the Food and Drug Administration (FDA) for approval. If the FDA determines that the drug is both safe and effective, the drug may then be approved for sale. The FDA currently requires drugs to be tested in four phases, each designed to answer specific questions about the drug.

Is the drug safe to use on humans? During Phase I, investigators seek to answer questions about how the drug is absorbed and excreted by the body and seek to discover what effects (including short-term side effects) various doses of the drug have on the body. Investigators also determine the minimum effective dosage, the amount of the drug that is effective yet does not produce undesirable side effects. Phase I testing involves only a few individuals, usually

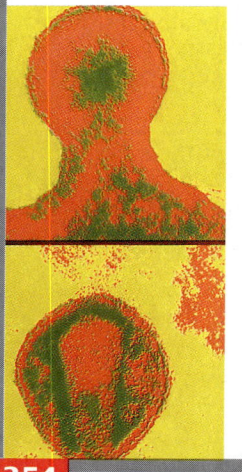

354

healthy volunteers.

Does the drug work? If Phase I testing does not reveal unacceptable safety problems, Phase II testing can begin. Investigators look to see if the drug is effective in treating the disease or condition for which it is intended. Researchers also seek to discover if the drug has short-term side effects. These side effects may be very harmful, so it is important to know exactly what they are before many people use the drug.

How effective is the drug? By the time a drug reaches Phase III, researchers have shown that the drug does have a therapeutic effect. Phase III tests involve large numbers of people (usually several hundred individuals) who have the condition against which the drug is effective. These tests measure the extent of the drug's effectiveness and help determine what fraction of the population is helped by the drug. In some cases, Phase III testing may also examine the consequences of long-term use of the drug. After the drug has gained FDA approval, Phase IV studies evaluate

ANSWERS TO **ANALYZING THE ISSUES**

① Thalidomide, a sedative once prescribed to pregnant women to prevent morning sickness, was later found to cause severe birth defects. It was never marketed in the United States and has been used as a defense for stringent United States drug regulations. Lately, however, the drug has been extensively studied in autoimmune disease research and is making a comeback as a medication for a number of AIDS-related conditions.

② Students should find information about the controversy over whether it is ethical to give placebos to seriously ill patients when a promising experimental therapy exists. Some critics believe all patients should be given the experimental drug since it offers some hope. Others believe such a practice would make it impossible to learn if the experimental drug has any more effect than no treatment at all. Many drug study experimental designs reduce or eliminate the objections to giving placebos to some patients by stopping the study early if positive (or negative) effects of the drug are demonstrated.

the drug's long-term effectiveness. Phase IV studies are sometimes referred to as post-marketing studies. Phase IV studies obtain information from large numbers of individuals who are using the drug as directed by their physicians.

Accelerated Studies Speed Drug Availability

Testing a new drug from Phase I to Phase IV, can take more than ten years. When a new drug offers hope to patients with otherwise untreatable, life-threatening diseases, new FDA guidelines can provide access to the drug before it has received full FDA approval. In each case, the benefits of early use must be carefully weighed against the threat of potential dangers, and patients using the drug must be carefully monitored. If the drug is found to be ineffective or dangerous, it can then be removed from the market.

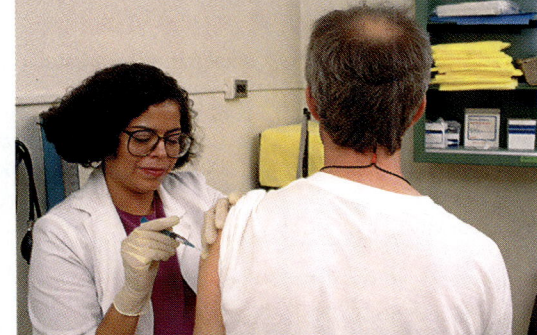

In most drug studies, some participants are given a placebo instead of the drug. The use of a placebo enables researchers to ensure that effects are due solely to the drug.

Technique

Experimental Design

Before a new drug study can begin, the Food and Drug Administration must approve its experimental design. The study must include two groups of individuals: a group that receives the drug and a control group that does not. Instead of taking the medication containing the drug, the control group is instead given a placebo *(pluh SEE boh)*. The placebo is identical to the medication in every way except one—it does not contain the drug.

To ensure valid results, drug studies are often conducted as double-blind studies. In a double-blind study, neither the doctors nor the patients know who receives the drug and who receives the placebo. Double-blind studies eliminate bias, the tendency of individuals to lean towards a particular conclusion based upon what they know. The removal of bias reduces the likelihood that a positive drug response could be due solely to a patient's wishful thinking.

Applications: Knowledge of experimental design is required by research scientists in many areas.

Users: Medical researchers, biostatisticians, marketing researchers

it take to find and develop a new drug? How has the nature of the team of scientists engaged in finding new drugs changed over the years? What purposes do animal studies serve in investigating a potential new therapy? Have students research the development of an approved drug and design a time line that highlights points of progress. Each time line should be accompanied by a report that describes the drug's development and that portrays research as an evolutionary process.

World of Work

Pharmacist

Once a drug is approved, a patient gains access to it through a physician and a local pharmacy. Have students use references in the library or search an on-line database to research the procedures and guidelines for distributing therapies that have been approved and marketed. Topics they should research include generic versus name-brand drugs, over-the-counter versus prescription drugs, and the ways in which doctors and pharmacists learn about new products. Invite a local pharmacist to class to discuss these and related topics and to answer questions students may have about this career.

References

1. Byar, David P., et al. "Design Considerations for AIDS Trials." *New England Journal of Medicine,* November 8, 1990, 1343–1348.
2. Department of Health, Food and Drug Administration. *"From Test Tube to Patient: New Drug Development in the United States."* FDA Consumer, 1990.
3. Kessler, David A. and Karyn L. Feiden. "Faster Evaluation of Vital Drugs." *Scientific American,* March 1995, 48–54.

Analyzing the Issues

Why is it important that a new drug be thoroughly tested?

1. Research the use of the drug thalidomide in Europe in the early 1960s. For what purpose was the drug prescribed? What happened when the drug was taken by pregnant women? How do the consequences of thalidomide use support the need for drug testing?

When a new drug is tested, should *all* test participants be given the drug?

2. If a potential new drug is known to improve survival, should Phase II tests omit the use of placebos? Use references available in the library or research an on-line database to find information supporting your viewpoint. Write a report summarizing the benefits and drawbacks of using placebos.

Are study participants informed of potential risks and benefits?

3. By law, before individuals can participate in a drug study, they must give their informed consent, indicating that they are willingly participants and that they understand the purpose of the study. What facts do you think participants in a new drug study should know before they agree to participate in the study?

How does the cost of drug testing influence which drugs are developed?

4. The Orphan Drug Act passed by the United States Congress in 1983 has helped to ensure that certain drugs will be developed and brought to market. What is an "orphan drug"? How did the Orphan Drug Act encourage pharmaceutical companies to develop orphan drugs?

3. Patients who are thinking about enrolling in a drug study should research the legitimacy of the study's investigator, the institution, and the drug being studied. They should ask to see the informed consent form and insist on speaking with an authority who can explain the project in plain, understandable language. They should be wary about signing anything that waives their rights if they are harmed during the course of the study.

4. An orphan drug is a medication for a rare disease. The Orphan Drug Act fosters the development of such drugs by granting pharmaceutical companies special privileges to make the approval of orphan drugs cheaper and faster, such as tax credits, exceptions to clinical-research guidelines, and access to research grants. Drugs that have been developed as orphan drugs include cyclosporine (an immune-system suppressant used to prevent organ-transplant rejection) and desmopressin (a drug used to treat some cases of hemophilia).

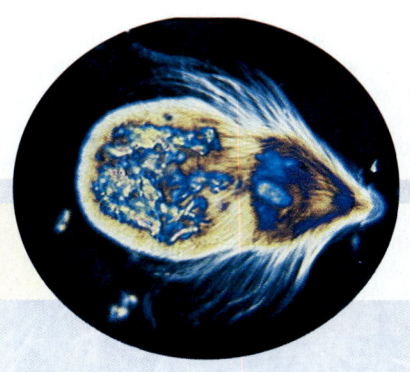

Lesson Planning Guide With Options for Block Scheduling

Lecture Concepts	Lesson Resources

19-1 What Is a Protist?

BLOCK ❶ (45 minutes)

1. The kingdom Protista contains nearly all of the single-celled eukaryotes.

2. Many protists are capable of movement and of sensing and responding to their environment.

❶ Lecture Resources
- ■ Determining Prior Knowledge
- ■ Active Reading: L.I.N.K.
- ■ Visual Strategy: Videodisc
- ■ Teaching Transparencies: 99, 100, 89A, 90A
- ● Holt Biology Videodiscs Lesson 19-1

Classwork Options
- ■ Food-Getting in the Amoeba
- ■ Exploration 19A

BLOCK ❷ (45 minutes)

3. Protists reproduce both sexually and asexually.

4. Protists are descended from prokaryotes and gave rise to plants, animals, and fungi.

❷ Lecture Resources
- ■ Active Reading: Reading Organizer
- ■ Demonstration: Comparing Structures
- ■ Teaching Transparencies: 98
- ● Holt Biology Videodiscs Lesson 19-1

Classwork Options
- ■ Closure: Inferring Conclusions

Assignment Options
- ■ Reteaching
- ■ Section Review
- ■ Chapter Review, questions 1, 4, 5, 9, 13
- ■ Directed Reading Worksheet

19-2 Protist Diversity

BLOCK ❸ (45 minutes)

1. The members of the kingdom Protista exhibit a greater variety of sizes and structures than do members of any other kingdom.

2. Protista is the only kingdom that contains both autotrophs and heterotrophs.

❸ Lecture Resources
- ■ Visual Strategy: Figure 19-7
- ■ Demonstration: Comparing Structures
- ● Holt Biology Videodiscs Lesson 19-2

Classwork Options
- ▲ Quick Labs: Lab A17

Assignment Options
- ■ Ideal Environment
- ■ Problem Solving

BLOCK ❹ (45 minutes)

3. Autotrophic protists called algae form the base of the aquatic food web.

4. Heterotrophic protists are very diverse and play many different ecological roles.

❹ Lecture Resources
- ■ Active Reading: Reading Organizer
- ■ Teaching Transparencies: 103, 104, 105
- ● Holt Biology Videodiscs Lesson 19-2

Classwork Options
- ■ Protist Diversity
- ■ Closure: Relating Concepts

Assignment Options
- ■ *Small Group* Reteaching
- ■ World of Work: Limnologist
- ■ Section Review
- ■ Chapter Review, questions 7, 8, 10, 15, 16, 19, 22, 23, 30
- ■ Directed Reading Worksheet

19-3 Diseases Caused by Protists

BLOCK ❺ (45 minutes)

1. Malaria kills more than one million people per year and is a leading cause of death among children in tropical countries.

2. Protozoans transmitted by mosquitoes cause malaria.

❺ Lecture Resources
- ■ Active Reading: Paired Reading
- ■ Visual Strategy: Figure 19-13
- ■ Teaching Transparencies: 101
- ● Holt Biology Videodiscs Lesson 19-3

Classwork Options
- ▲ Inquiry Skills Development: Lab B14

Lecture Concepts

Lesson Resources

19-3 Diseases Caused by Protists, *continued*

BLOCK 6 (45 minutes)

3. Malaria can be treated by taking drugs that inhibit the growth of the protozoa, and it can be prevented by reducing the size of mosquito populations.

4. Protists are responsible for causing many diseases in humans.

6 Lecture Resources
■ Teaching Transparencies: 102
◉ Holt Biology Videodiscs Lesson 19-3
Classwork Options
■ Life/Work Skills: Finding Information
■ Closure: Recognizing Relationships

Assignment Options
■ *Small Group* Reteaching
■ Section Review
■ Chapter Review, questions 2, 3, 6, 11, 12, 14, 17, 18, 20, 21, 24, 25, 26, 27, 28, 29, 31
■ Directed Reading Worksheet

Chapter Review and Assessment

BLOCK 7 (45 minutes)
Review
■ Reteaching Worksheet
■ Thinking Skills Worksheet
■ Vocabulary Development Worksheet
◉ Language Development and Reading Comprehension Audio CD Program: Chapter 19

BLOCK 8 (45 minutes)
Assessment
■ Alternative Assessment, p. 369
■ Portfolio Assessment, p. T39
Chapter Test
■ Chapter 19 Test
Test Generator
◉ Item bank for customizing Chapter Tests
◉ Performance-Based Assessment: Fermentation by Yeast

Teaching Resources CD-ROM
◉ Scoring Rubrics and Classroom Management Checklist

The Portfolio icon denotes items throughout the Teacher's Edition lesson wrap that may be selected for inclusion in student portfolios.

Holt Biology Videodiscs and *Concepts of Biology*

Holt Biology Videodiscs gives you a powerful tool for teaching, review, and assessment. For further information regarding the media on the videodiscs, see *Holt Biology Videodiscs Teacher's Correlation Guide to Holt Biology: Visualizing Life.*

Concepts of Biology adds interactive lesson plans and extensive tools for customization using CD-ROM technology.

Use the following topic from *Concepts of Biology* to help you teach this chapter:
Topic 14: Protists and Fungi

Laboratory Planning

Text
Materials and preparation instructions appear on the teacher's wrap accompanying each laboratory exercise.
Block 1: Exploration 19A: Observing the Behavior of Protists, p. 794

Holt BioSources Laboratory Program
Block 3: Quick Labs Lab A17: Observing Protists
Block 5: Inquiry Skills Development Lab B14: Protists—A Comparison

Determining Prior Knowledge

- Have students describe the major features of the kingdom Protista and distinguish between autotrophs and heterotrophs.
- Show students a photograph, slide, or overhead transparency of a protozoan, such as a paramecium or an amoeba. Have them identify as many cell structures and organelles as possible.
- Name some diseases caused by protists, such as malaria, sleeping sickness, and amoebic dysentery. Ask students to discuss what they know about these diseases.

Active READING

Technique: L.I.N.K.

Write the work *Protist* on the chalkboard, and have students **L**ist on their own paper all the words, phrases, and ideas that they associate with the word *protist*. After several minutes, ask the students to share one or two of their ideas as you record them. Facilitate a discussion in which students **I**nquire of each other or the teacher to clarify each of the ideas listed. After all discussion is completed, have students make **N**otes on paper of all they remember. Allow about one minute. Have them look over their notes to see what they **K**now about "protists" based on experience and discussion.

CD-ROM Resources

Concepts of Biology
Topic 14: Protists and Fungi

REVIEW
- evolution of protists (Section 11-2)
- autotrophs and heterotrophs (Section 14-1)
- archaebacteria and eubacteria (Section 17-3)
- the terms *endocytosis, exocytosis,* and *conjugation* (Glossary)

Protists

19-1   **What Is a Protist?**

19-2   **Protist Diversity**

19-3   **Diseases Caused by Protists**

Diatoms are single-celled algae, which form a large part of both marine and freshwater plankton.

356

Author's Rationale   This chapter focuses on the diversity of the kingdom Protista and the methods by which protists obtain energy. The kingdom Protista is a sort of catchall kingdom, containing organisms that vary in size, structure, manner of movement, and mode of reproduction. Students review the basic characteristics of living cells and gain an understanding of the advantages of multicellularity. This chapter also covers the role of photosynthetic protists and their importance in an ecosystem. The relevance of this chapter becomes apparent as students explore the benefits of protists as well as the diseases they cause.

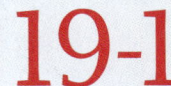

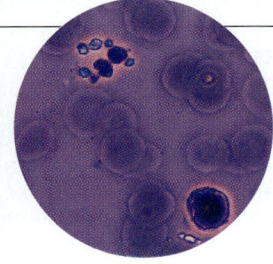

Did you know that malaria, a disease caused by a parasitic protist, currently infects up to 500 million human beings? Malaria kills more than 1 million people each year. Other protists cause sleeping sickness, dysentery, and giardiasis. Like bacteria and viruses, protists exert major influences on humans.

19-1 What Is a Protist?

OBJECTIVES

1 Identify the characteristics shared by all members of the kingdom Protista.

2 Describe the evolutionary relationship between bacteria and protists.

3 Summarize the relationships of protists to the other three eukaryotic kingdoms.

Characteristics of Protists

If you examine a drop of pond water under a microscope, you might see, swimming on the slide, a tiny one-celled organism called *Euglena*, shown in **Figure 19-1**. To which kingdom does *Euglena* belong? It cannot be a member of the kingdoms Archaebacteria or Eubacteria because it has organelles and a nucleus. Its lack of a cell wall and its ability to move suggest that *Euglena* might be an animal—but it is single-celled, and all animals are multicellular. Also, if you look carefully, you can see that this *Euglena* has chloroplasts; it is photosynthetic. Scientists place organisms such as *Euglena* into the kingdom Protista. The kingdom Protista contains nearly all of the single-celled eukaryotes as well as multicellular algae.

Protists have complex cells

Like all protists, *Euglena* is eukaryotic. Its nucleus, which contains chromosomes, is separated from the

cytoplasm by a membrane. Also, membrane-bound organelles, such as chloroplasts and mitochondria, are found in the cell's cytoplasm. Chloroplasts occur in autotrophic protists, such as *Euglena*, but they are lacking in heterotrophic protists. *Euglena* has the unique ability to shift between being autotrophic and heterotrophic. In abundant light, *Euglena* produces its own nutrients. When light is scarce, *Euglena* feeds on bacteria and smaller protists. Most protists, however, are either autotrophs or heterotrophs.

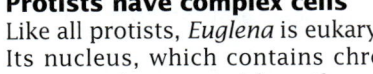

Figure 19-1
This photomicrograph of *Euglena* shows that it is a single cell. Is *Euglena* a bacterium, a plant, a fungus, an animal, or a protist?

357

Videodisc Resources

Holt Biology Videodiscs

Lesson 19-1: What Is a Protist?

Scheduling
See the **Lesson Planning Guide** on pages 355A and 355B for lecture, classwork, and assignment options for Section 19-1.

Phase Two
Teaching Strategies

Visual Strategy	Videodisc

● **Summarizing Information**
To introduce the chapter, use *Video—The World of Protists* (4 min 20 s) shown in Chapter 19 Section 19-1 of **Holt Biology Videodiscs Teacher's Correlation Guide to Holt Biology: Visualizing Life.** Before viewing the video, have students identify from Chapter 2 the characteristics that are essential for life *(cellular organization, metabolism, reproduction, homeostasis, and heredity).* As students view the video, direct them to note how single-celled organisms can carry out these life functions. Have students use a chart to record this information. After viewing the video, discuss examples that students noted.

Key to Strategies
Teaching Strategies are keyed to three tiers of learning.

● **Understanding Concepts (Tier I)**
Content mastery and comprehension

■ **Applying Information (Tier II)**
Applying and analyzing content

▲ **Critical Thinking (Tier III)**
Practicing evaluative thinking

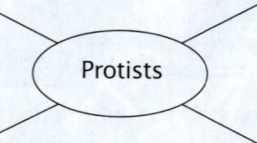
Figure 19-2
Euglena (180×) moves with the aid of a whip-like flagellum.

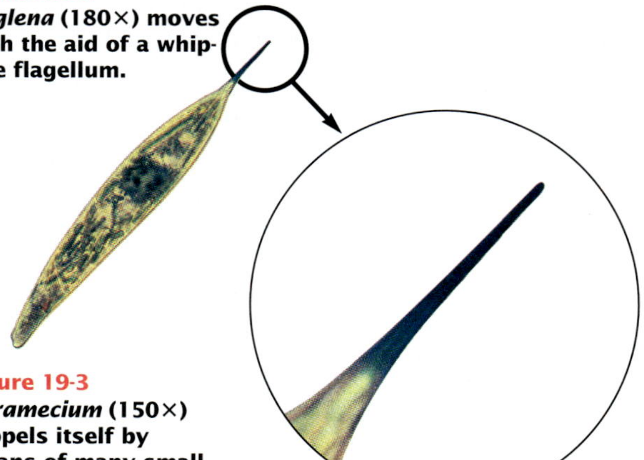

Figure 19-3
Paramecium (150×) propels itself by means of many small cilia located on its surface.

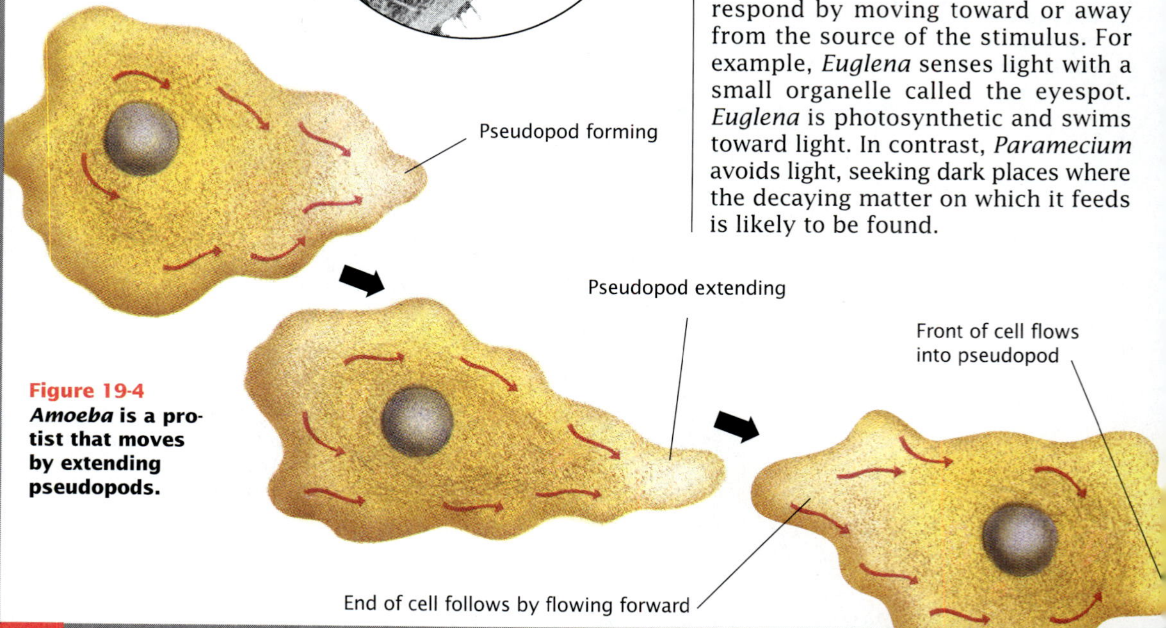

Figure 19-4
Amoeba is a protist that moves by extending pseudopods.

Pseudopod forming

Pseudopod extending

Front of cell flows into pseudopod

End of cell follows by flowing forward

Many protists are capable of movement

Euglena swims about powered by a flagellum, as shown in **Figure 19-2**. Cilia, which cover the *Paramecium* in **Figure 19-3**, and flagella are hairlike projections that produce movement and consist of similar internal microtubule structures. Unlike the bacterial flagellum, the eukaryotic flagellum does not spin like a propeller. Instead, it lashes back and forth like a whip. *Paramecium*, the protist in **Figure 19-3**, is covered with thousands of tiny hairlike projections called **cilia**. Cilia beat back and forth like miniature boat oars to propel *Paramecium* forward or backward.

Amoeba, shown in **Figure 19-4**, moves and feeds using fingerlike, flowing extensions of the cell body called **pseudopods**, or "false feet." To move, *Amoeba* first extends a pseudopod. Then, as its cytoplasm streams into the pseudopod, the rest of the cell flows along behind. *Amoeba* moving in this manner resembles a raindrop slowly running down a window.

Protists can sense and respond to their environment

Most protists can detect stimuli such as light, touch, and chemicals. They respond by moving toward or away from the source of the stimulus. For example, *Euglena* senses light with a small organelle called the eyespot. *Euglena* is photosynthetic and swims toward light. In contrast, *Paramecium* avoids light, seeking dark places where the decaying matter on which it feeds is likely to be found.

358

Matter of Fact: White Cliffs of Dover

Foraminiferans are marine protozoans that secrete calcium shells. These shells have many chambers arrayed in a spiral shape much like a tiny snail. Long, thin projections of cytoplasm extend through the pores in the shells to aid in swimming and food capture. When the foraminiferans die, their calcium shells sink to the ocean floor. These shells accumulate over millions of years, forming huge limestone deposits like the White Cliffs of Dover, in England. Have students locate Dover on a map.

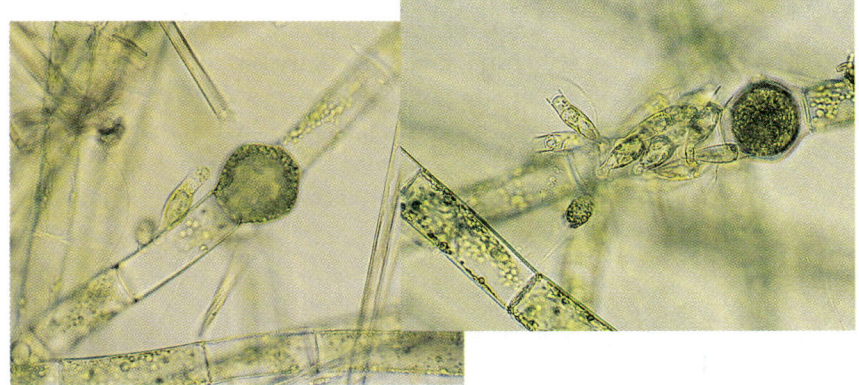

Figure 19-5
Oedogonium is a green alga that can reproduce sexually, producing sperm and eggs, and asexually.

Protists reproduce both asexually and sexually

As you read in Chapter 18, bacterial reproduction is usually a very simple process: bacteria simply split in two. This is a form of asexual reproduction. No genetic material is exchanged. Bacteria use conjugation to exchange genetic information. Sexual reproduction as a method of exchanging genetic material first evolved among the protists. Many protists, including *Euglena*, reproduce by the asexual process of mitosis alone. *Paramecium* and others can use both conjugation and mitosis. Other protists, such as the green alga *Oedogonium*, shown in **Figure 19-5**, can produce sperm and egg cells and reproduce sexually. Flagellated sperm released into the water swim to the egg. *Oedogonium* can also reproduce asexually.

Many protists that are capable of sexual reproduction use this method in times of environmental stress, such as when there is a shortage of nutrients.

Evolutionary Relationships Among Protists

Eukaryotes are descended from prokaryotes, but in two different ways. First, the eukaryotic cell itself arose through modification and elaboration of an ancestral archaebacteria. Second, ancestral eubacteria gave rise to two of the organelles that exist within the eukaryotic cell. Mitochondria evolved from heterotrophic eubacteria, whereas chloroplasts evolved from autotrophic eubacteria. Thus, a protist such as *Euglena*, which has both mitochondria and chloroplasts, is a union of three evolutionary lines.

Most protists live in a water environment. As you learned in Chapter 17, protists are the ancestors of the three major multicellular eukaryotic kingdoms. Over time, plants evolved from autotrophic protists, whereas animals and fungi descended from different heterotrophic protists. Multicellularity, involving coordination and interaction among specialized cells, also evolved independently in different groups of protists at different times.

SECTION REVIEW

1. Describe the structural differences between a bacterial and a protistan cell.

2. Contrast bacterial reproduction with reproduction in protists.

3. Summarize the ways in which protists are related to bacteria.

4. Draw a diagram showing the evolutionary relationship of plants, animals, and fungi to protists.

359

Connection: *Chapter 4*

Mitosis
Review mitosis as a process in which eukaryotic cells divide.

Phase Three
Assessment Options

Closure

■ **Inferring Conclusions**

Sporozoans are animal-like protists that do not move by means of either cilia, flagella, or pseudopods. Have students suggest an answer to the following question: Since sporozoans cannot move and are heterotrophic, how can they obtain their food? *(Since sporozoans cannot trap their food, they live as parasites. Sporozoans reproduce by sporelike structures. These structures penetrate host cells in order to obtain nutrients. An example of a sporozoan is* Plasmodium, *which causes malaria.)*

SECTION REVIEW
Assign the *Section Review*.

Reteaching

Have students make illustrated flash cards for *Euglena, Paramecium,* and *Amoeba.* Each flash card should have a labeled drawing of the organism on one side and a list of characteristics on the other side. Have students add cards and information to the collection as they study additional protists in this chapter.

A N S W E R S TO
SECTION REVIEW

1. A protist cell has a membrane-bound nucleus with chromosomes and membrane-bound organelles such as chloroplasts and mitochondria. A bacterial cell does not have a nucleus, membrane-bound organelles, or chromosomes.

2. In bacterial reproduction, the DNA is copied and then the cell divides. Many protists reproduce only by mitosis. Others carry out both mitosis and meiosis. Both bacteria and some protists can exchange genetic material by means of conjugation.

3. Eukaryotes are descended from bacteria in two ways. First, eukaryotic cells arose through modification and elaboration of an ancestral archaebacteria. Second, other eubacteria gave rise to mitochondria and chloroplasts.

4. One possible answer is found in Figure 11-6 on page 196.

Key to Strategies
● Understanding Concepts (Tier I)
■ Applying Information (Tier II)
▲ Critical Thinking (Tier III)

Scheduling

See the **Lesson Planning Guide** on pages 355A and 355B for lecture, classwork, and assignment options for Section 19-2.

Demonstration

● **Comparing Structures**

Display photographs, live specimens, and preserved specimens of various protists. The display might include *Amoeba, Paramecium,* diatoms, desmids, *Volvox, Spirogyra,* dinoflagellates, sea lettuce, *Sargassum,* and slime molds. As students identify them, point out how diverse protists are. Have students sketch the organisms and compare their size and structures.

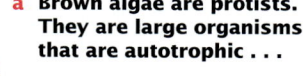

Look for carrageenan in the list of ingredients of yogurt, ice cream, and other dairy products. It is added to these foods and to paints and cosmetics to create a smooth texture. Carrageenan is a jellylike material that is extracted from the cell walls of a red alga, like the organism known as Irish moss, and is one of many products we obtain from protists.

19-2 Protist Diversity

OBJECTIVES

1 Compare the variations in shape, size, and method of obtaining energy among protists.

2 Evaluate the role that autotrophic protists play in ecosystems.

3 Recognize the evolutionary connection between green algae and plants.

4 Identify three kinds of heterotrophic protists.

Classification of the Protists

Look at the two dissimilar organisms in **Figure 19-6**. **Figures 19-6a** and **19-6b** show a brown alga that is a type of seaweed. Brown algae are multicellular and autotrophic. The creature in **Figure 19-6c** is *Didinium*. It is single-celled and heterotrophic. *Didinium* is so small that it cannot be seen without a microscope. Both of these organisms are classified as protists. The members of the kingdom Protista exhibit a greater variety of sizes and structures than do the members of any other kingdom.

Great diversity is also found in protist metabolism. Among the eukaryotic kingdoms, Protista is the only one that includes both heterotrophs and autotrophs. Autotrophic protists, including both unicellular and multicellular forms, are photosynthetic, as are plants. Heterotrophic protists, such as *Paramecium* and *Amoeba,* obtain their energy by consuming other organisms or by parasitism. You can see the structure of a heterotrophic protist in the *Tour of a Protist* on the next page.

Separating the protists into autotrophs and heterotrophs is an artificial classification that does not show the complexity of their evolutionary relationships. Because of the diversity in kingdom Protista, biologists disagree on how many phyla it should contain.

a Brown algae are protists. They are large organisms that are autotrophic . . .

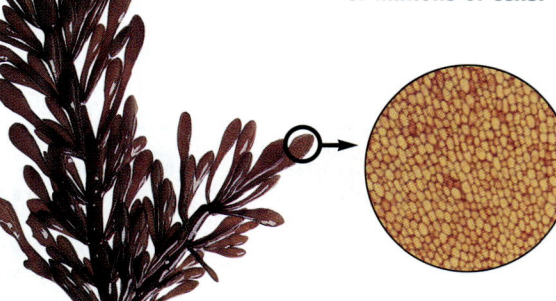

Figure 19-6
Although these two organisms look very different, they are both members of the kingdom Protista.

b . . . and are composed of millions of cells.

c *Didinium* (150×), also a protist, is unicellular and heterotrophic.

Videodisc Resources

Holt Biology Videodiscs

Lesson 19-2: Protist Diversity

Protist

Paramecium is a kind of protist called a ciliate. It is covered with tiny, hairlike structures called cilia, which move it through the water.

Tour

Connection: *Chapter 4*

Osmosis

Ask students to look at Chapter 4 Section 4-2 to review how substances pass through the cell membrane. Ask them what causes *Paramecium* to absorb water. *(The internal fluids have a higher salt concentration than the environment does.)*

Ideal Environment

▲ Distinguishing Relevant Information

Tell students that pollution can damage the cilia of a paramecium. Pollution can also impair the organism's ability to maintain water balance and to acquire nutrients. Have students use the information in the chapter and in this feature to write a description of an ideal environment for a paramecium. *(Answers will vary but should include a food source and a freshwater environment that will allow a paramecium to maintain homeostasis.)*

Active READING

Technique: Reading Organizer
Have students make a compare/contrast matrix describing ingestion of food in amoebas and paramecia. For more information about reading organizers, see Reading Strategies Worksheets in Holt BioSources Teaching Resources CD-ROM.

Evolutionary Relationships

Paramecium is a member of the kingdom Protista. This kingdom descended from the bacteria. Plants, animals, and fungi are the descendants of different protist ancestors.

Paramecium has two nuclei. The macronucleus contains fragmented chromosomes that are used in routine cellular functions, and it divides by pinching in two. Paramecia exchange genetic information with each other by a method called conjugation.

The micronucleus contains the cell's chromosomes, and it divides by mitosis.

Paramecium absorbs water by osmosis. Excess water is squeezed back out by contractile vacuoles.

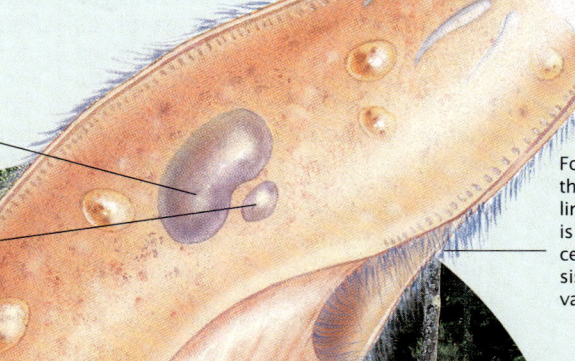

Food is ingested through a cilia-lined gullet and is taken into the cell by endocytosis within a food vacuole.

Habitat
Paramecium lives in freshwater streams and ponds.

Paramecium ejects wastes by exocytosis.

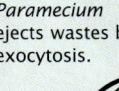

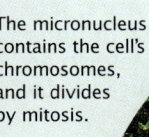 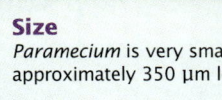

Size
Paramecium is very small, approximately 350 µm long.

1 mm

361

Connection: *Chapter 14*

Food Webs
Have students refer to Figure 14-6 on page 257 to review how algae form the base of this oceanic ecosystem.

Visual Strategy   **Figure 19-7**

● **Comparing Structures**
Have students examine the diatoms in Figure 19-7a, *Porphyra* in Figure 19-7b, and *Fucus* in Figure 19-7c. Students should note the difference in structure in each algae. Emphasize that though the algae are photosynthetic, not all are green. In addition to chlorophyll, the brown algae contain the pigment fucoxanthin, and the red algae contain the pigment phycobilins. *Fucus* has gas-filled structures called bladders that allow it to float.

Biotechnology Connection

Agar
The red algae *Gelidium* is used in the production of agar, a substance that has the consistency of gelatin. Agar is used in laboratories as a culture medium for the growth of bacteria. Various nutrients are added to the agar to promote the growth of specific bacteria as well as the growth of plant and animal cells. Agar is used in making capsules for medicine, as a base for cosmetics, as a gelling agent in desserts, and as an agent to retain moistness in bakery products. A highly refined agar is a major component of agarose, the powder used in gels for electrophoresis. Show students a petri dish containing agar.

Autotrophic Protists

Do you think anything you did today involved autotrophic protists? Before you answer "no" without hesitation, consider these activities. Did you drive or ride in a car? Did you eat ice cream, cheese, or yogurt? Did you eat fish or other seafood? Autotrophic protists or their products are involved in all of these activities. Autotrophic protists are often called algae (*AL jee*). Despite being grouped under one name, not all kinds of algae are closely related.

Although they can be found in moist soil, on damp rocks, and on the shady sides of trees, most species of algae live in fresh water or salt water, as shown in **Figure 19-7**. Algae serve the same ecological function in aquatic ecosystems as plants serve in terrestrial ones. Algae also produce about one-third of the oxygen in the atmosphere. They form the base of the aquatic food web, directly or indirectly providing food for all aquatic consumers. Thus, fishes, whales, and humans depend on algae for the food they eat and the air they breathe.

Figure 19-7
Autotrophic protists are found in the open ocean, along the shore, and in freshwater habitats. They range from unicellular to multicellular, yet all are photosynthetic.

Most kinds of algae are unicellular

Unicellular algae are one part of a community of aquatic organisms called plankton. The organisms found in plankton float near the surface in fresh water or salt water. Heterotrophic bacteria, fish larvae, crustaceans, and heterotrophic protists are also considered part of the plankton. Photosynthetic plankton are called **phytoplankton** (*fy tuh PLANK tuhn*), which means "plant plankton."

Phytoplankton require light for photosynthesis, so they usually are found near the surface. A wide variety of adaptations help them stay afloat. Some beat their flagella and "tread water." Others have fins and spines that act as water wings. Others store extra food as oil, which buoys them up near the surface. When algae full of oil die and sink to the bottom, they can be buried. Over millions of years, heat and pressure within the Earth transform the oil from the algae into crude-oil deposits. The gasoline used today

a Microscopic algae, like this diatom, serve as food for many marine animals.

b Red algae, such as this *Porphyra*, often are attached to rocks at the edge of the sea.

c Brown algae, such as *Fucus*, grow on rocks exposed at low tide.

362

Historical Perspective: Sargasso Sea

The name of this sea is derived from floating masses of the brown algae *Sargassum natans*. This algae reproduces by fragmenting into small pieces. Each piece grows and fragments again. These fragments cover millions of square miles of ocean between the Azores and the Bahamas, forming the Sargasso Sea. Nautical lore tells of ship graveyards consisting of vessels trapped in the thick mat of algae. However, these masses of algae pose no problems for sailing ships. The area was avoided because it lies within the wind-sparse horse latitudes. Have students locate this area on a map.

Figure 19-8
Red tides (above) happen when large numbers of dinoflagellates, like the *Gonyaulax* seen above, experience massive population explosions in marine waters. This protist contains a toxin that becomes concentrated in the tissues of shellfish and kills fish and marine mammals.

was formed partly from the remains of algae that died millions of years ago.

Look at the object in **Figure 19-7a**. It may look like a hubcap or jewelry, but it is the remains of aquatic algae called diatoms. Diatoms form intricately patterned shells made of silica, a glasslike substance. When diatoms die, their shells settle to the ocean floor. Humans harvest fossilized deposits of these shells to make detergents, fertilizers, paint removers, and insulators.

If you visit the beach, you might experience a dangerous effect of marine algae. Occasionally the ocean turns reddish, and thousands of dead fishes, seabirds, turtles, and dolphins wash up onto the beach. These "red tides," seen in **Figure 19-8**, are caused by phytoplankton known as dinoflagellates *(deye noh FLAJ uh lihtz)*. Population explosions of certain species of dinoflagellates occur irregularly in coastal areas. The dinoflagellates release toxins that are poisonous to vertebrates. Because fishes and shellfish concentrate toxic secretions in their internal organs, authorities place restrictions on taking fish or shellfish during red tides.

Many green, all brown, and most red algae are multicellular

There are three groups of multicellular algae—the green, brown, and red algae. The brown algae and the red algae are commonly called "sea-weeds." You might have seen algae like the ones in **Figure 19-7b** and **19-7c** attached to rocks at low tide or washed up on a beach.

Green algae, like pond scum, are distinguished by photosynthetic pigments, by their use of starch to store food, and by their unique form of cell division. Plants share these characteristics with some green algae. Therefore, scientists think that these green algae are the ancestors of the plant kingdom.

Kelp is a brown alga that often grows in dense stands or thick floating mats. Kelp "forests" occur off the coast of California. The Sargasso Sea, an area of the Atlantic Ocean east of Florida, is so thick with floating sargassum weed, another brown alga, that early European explorers feared their sailing ships could be trapped there (an unreasonable fear, it turns out).

Red algae tend to be smaller and less spectacular than the brown algae. Distinctive photosynthetic pigments give red algae their color. These same pigments enable some species to photosynthesize in waters more than 200 m (650 ft) deep, where there is little light.

Red and green algae are harvested for many uses. *Porphyra*, one of the red algae, is particularly popular in Japan and China, where it is known as *nori*. Nori is cultivated as a crop on coastal algae "farms."

Problem Solving
■ Forming a Hypothesis

Propose the following situation to the students: A once clear lake has now become ridden with a mat of dense algae. The fish and other aquatic life are dying. Have students evaluate this situation in terms of possible causes for this algal bloom and reasons for death of aquatic life. *(This algal bloom may be due to nitrate or phosphate pollution from either sewage or runoff from fertilized soil. Fertilizer and septic runoff contain nitrogen and phosphorus, which fertilize the water. A thick mat of algae results. Aquatic plant life below this mat will die because the plants cannot receive the sunlight they need. When the algae die, bacterial decomposers proliferate, resulting in the depletion of oxygen in the water. In turn, oxygen-dependent organisms suffocate. Eventually the algae will die because their supply of carbon dioxide is no longer available.)*

World of Work

Limnology

Dr. Ruth Patrick, a limnologist, has invented a device called a diatometer that is used to identify particular types of diatoms. Have students use reference books to investigate the field of limnology. Their findings should include a career description, the educational requirements, and the personal qualifications an individual in this field should possess.

Multicultural Perspective: Algae as a Food Source

Algae have been used as a food source by people for hundreds of years. In Japan, the brown algae, such as *Laminaria,* are eaten raw, jellied, or baked into breads. The red algae, including dulse, laver or *nori,* and Irish moss (which is not a moss), are eaten fresh, dried, or toasted. Green algae, such as sea lettuce, are used in soups and salads and as garnishes for meat and fish. The Japanese not only have harvested these wild algae but also have farmed them for over 300 years. Show students some sushi that has an algae wrapper around the rice. Various types of dried algae can be purchased at an Asian market or health-food store.

Key to Strategies

● **Understanding Concepts (Tier I)**
■ **Applying Information (Tier II)**
▲ **Critical Thinking (Tier III)**

Agriculture Connection

Agriculture Connection

Potato Blight

A new, more virulent form of the blight that was responsible for the Irish potato famine of 1845–1847 threatens current potato crops. It is resistant to the fungicide used against late blight in the United States. The disease threatens a major food source because potatoes are widely grown and consumed throughout the world. Currently, scientists are working with wild potatoes to produce new disease-resistant varieties of potatoes.

Protist Diversity

● **Organizing Information**

Have students prepare a **Graphic Organizer,** like the one at the bottom of the page, that compares heterotrophic and autotrophic protists.

Heterotrophic Protists

The word *carnivore* brings to mind fierce, sharp-toothed animals like lions, tigers, wolves, and sharks, and the word *herbivore* makes you think of plodding creatures like cows and sheep. You don't normally think of tiny one-celled protists as carnivores and herbivores, but most heterotrophic protists play one of these two ecological roles. In the plankton, for example, some heterotrophic protists "graze" on phytoplankton, and others prey on these grazers. Other heterotrophic protists are parasites or decomposers.

Slime molds and water molds superficially resemble fungi

If you look carefully through moist, decaying leaves on a forest floor, you might find a brightly-colored plasmodial slime mold, such as the one shown in **Figure 19-9a.** Such an organism spends much of its life as a mass of streaming material that moves through damp environments in the forest feeding on small particles of organic matter. If food or moisture becomes scarce, the streaming mass produces black spore-bearing bodies like those shown in **Figure 19-9a.** These spores can survive many years.

If your ancestors arrived in the United States from Ireland in the 1840s, they were probably fleeing the effects of a heterotrophic protist. From 1845 to 1847, a famine in Ireland killed more than 1 million people and forced another 3 million to emigrate; most came to the United States. This famine occurred because the potato crop (the staple of the Irish diet) was almost wiped out by an outbreak of late blight. Late blight is a disease caused by *Phytophthora infestans*, a protist that is a water mold, shown in **Figure 19-9b.**

Years ago, slime and water molds were placed in the kingdom Fungi. Now we know they are unrelated to the fungi and have different cell walls, composition, and structure.

Figure 19-9
Heterotrophic protists are extremely diverse. Two very different species are shown below.

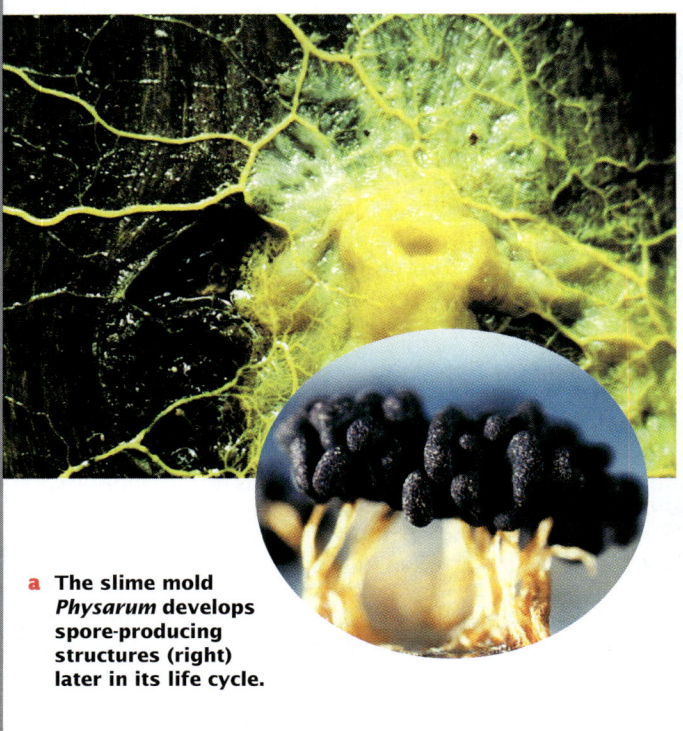

a The slime mold *Physarum* develops spore-producing structures (right) later in its life cycle.

b Water molds are microscopic organisms. The water mold *Phytophthora infestans*, which causes late blight of potatoes, has profoundly influenced history.

Potato plant

364

Graphic Organizer

Use this graphic organizer with the teaching strategy **Protist Diversity** on page 364.

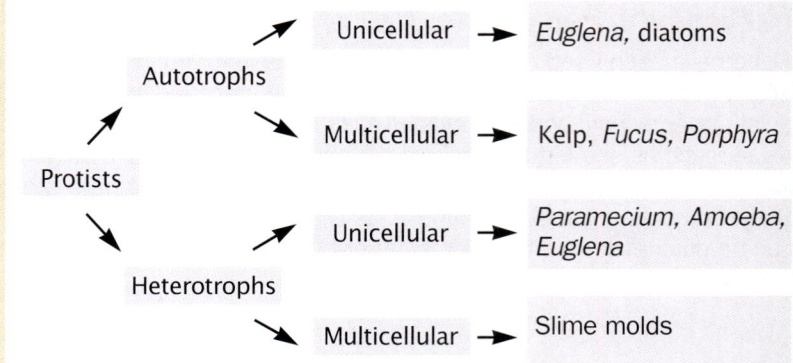

Protists

Autotrophs
- Unicellular → *Euglena*, diatoms
- Multicellular → Kelp, *Fucus, Porphyra*

Heterotrophs
- Unicellular → *Paramecium, Amoeba, Euglena*
- Multicellular → Slime molds

Figure 19-10
Trichonympha (right) is a zoomastigote that lives in the digestive system of insects like this termite (above), making it possible for the termite to eat wood.

Protists include the ancestors of animals

About 300 years ago, scientists using the first microscopes saw what appeared to be tiny animals darting about in drops of water. They called these organisms protozoa, which means "first animals." Biologists now classify these organisms as protists and believe they are related to the ancestors of modern animals.

The ancestor of animals probably belonged to a group of protists known as the zoomastigotes *(ZOH mast ih gohtz)*. Zoomastigotes are one-celled, heterotrophic protists with at least one flagellum. Some zoomastigotes, such as the *Trichonympha* illustrated in **Figure 19-10**, are covered with flagella. If your house has ever been attacked by termites, you can blame *Trichonympha*. Without these protists living in their intestines, termites could not digest wood.

Paramecium and *Didinium*, shown in **Figure 19-11**, are members of a group of protists called ciliates. Ciliates are covered with numerous cilia, which function in locomotion and feeding. In some ciliates, the cilia have fused to form sheets that function as mouths or teeth.

Not all groups of protists are closely related. Indeed, based on recent molecular analysis of DNA, some biologists argue that ciliates are so different from all other protists that they should be placed in a separate kingdom of their own.

Figure 19-11
One protist, *Didinium*, attacks and swallows another protist, *Paramecium*, under a scanning electron microscope.

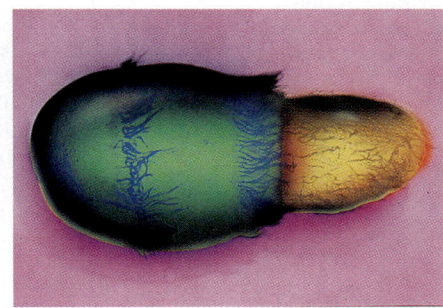

SECTION REVIEW

1. Explain why the statement "All protists are microscopic" is untrue.

2. Summarize the importance of algae in aquatic ecosystems.

3. Describe two pieces of evidence indicating that plants evolved from green algae.

4. Name two kinds of heterotrophic protists.

365

ANSWERS TO SECTION REVIEW

1. Many red, brown, and green algae are microscopic, while some brown algae reach 100 m (320 ft) in length.

2. Algae form the base of the aquatic food web, directly or indirectly supplying food for all aquatic consumers. Algae also produce large amounts of oxygen.

3. Green algae and plants have the same photosynthetic pigments in their chloroplasts, store food as starch, and have a unique form of cell division.

4. Possible answers include slime molds, water molds, *Amoeba*, and *Paramecium*.

In central Africa, a protist transmitted by the bite of a large fly, the tsetse fly, causes the disease sleeping sickness. This disease is often fatal to humans and domestic animals such as cattle, sheep, and pigs. Livestock cannot be raised in much of central Africa because of the presence of sleeping sickness.

19-3 Diseases Caused by Protists

Protists and Disease

Although many protists do not affect the health of human beings, millions of people are infected by, and die from, various protist-caused diseases each year. Disease-causing protists are transmitted mainly by insects and contaminated water.

Malaria is the great killer

Currently, from 300 million to 500 million people are infected with malaria. This disease kills more than 1 million people each year, making it one of the most serious human diseases. It is a leading cause of death among young children in tropical countries. This disease has affected the evolution of our species. As you learned in Chapter 10, the allele for sickle cell hemoglobin, a mutant form of hemoglobin, is prevalent in malaria-prone areas of Africa. This mutant hemoglobin produces resistance to the parasite that causes malaria.

A parasitic protozoan causes malaria

Malaria is caused by protozoa of the genus *Plasmodium*, which has a very complex life cycle. *Plasmodium* is carried between human hosts by mosquitoes, particularly mosquitoes of the genus *Anopheles*, shown in **Figure 19-12**. When a female mosquito feeds, she injects saliva into the wound to prevent her victim's blood from clotting. The mosquito's saliva transfers *Plasmodium* into the human bloodstream. (Male mosquitoes do not spread the disease because they feed on nectar instead of blood.) Once in the blood, the *Plasmodium* parasites are carried to the liver, where they reproduce. They then reenter the bloodstream, penetrate the red blood cells, and reproduce again. Every 48 or 72 hours, depending on the species of *Plasmodium*, a new generation of parasites bursts out of infected red blood cells, as shown in

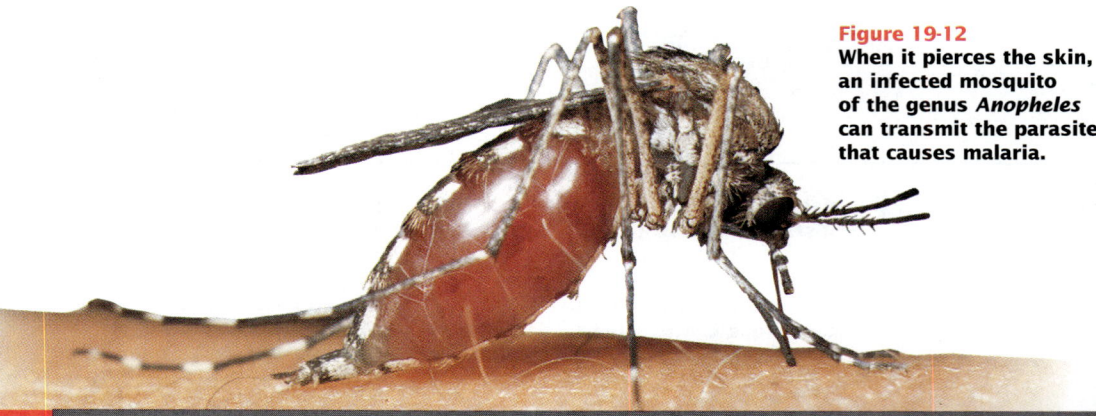

Figure 19-12
When it pierces the skin, an infected mosquito of the genus *Anopheles* can transmit the parasite that causes malaria.

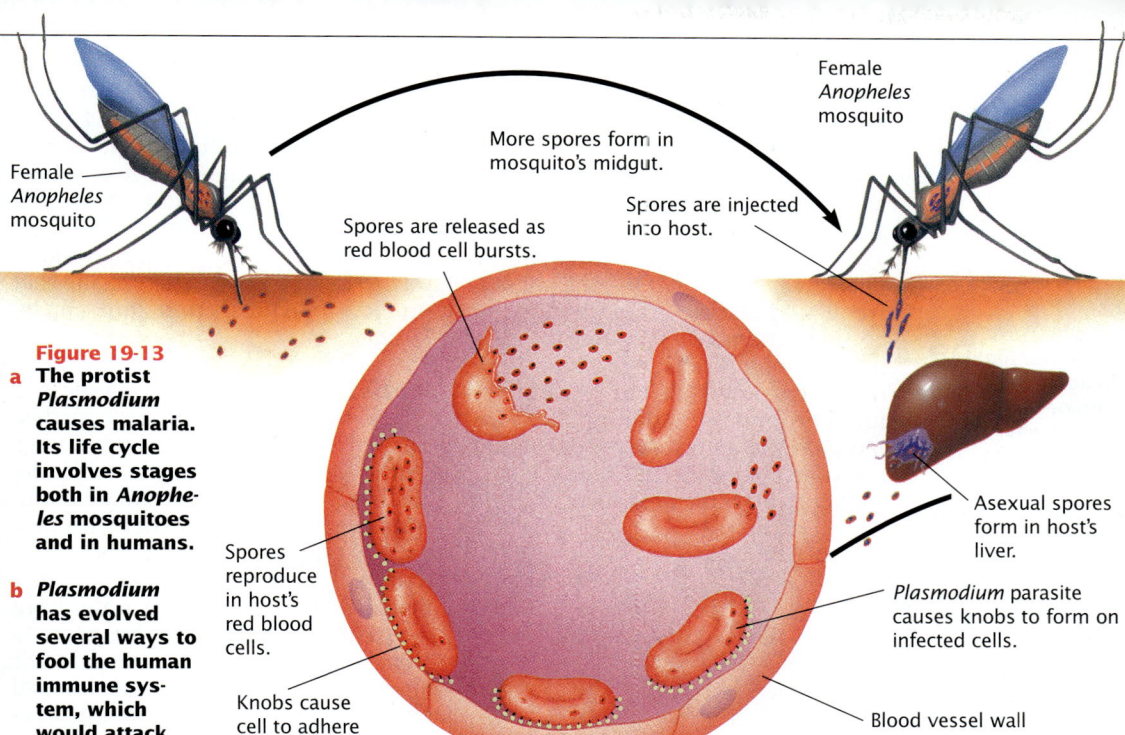

Female
Anopheles
mosquito

Female
Anopheles
mosquito

More spores form in
mosquito's midgut.

Spores are injected
into host.

Spores are released as
red blood cell bursts.

Asexual spores
form in host's
liver.

Plasmodium parasite
causes knobs to form on
infected cells.

Spores
reproduce
in host's
red blood
cells.

Knobs cause
cell to adhere
to vessel wall.

Blood vessel wall

Figure 19-13

a The protist *Plasmodium* causes malaria. Its life cycle involves stages both in *Anopheles* mosquitoes and in humans.

b *Plasmodium* has evolved several ways to fool the human immune system, which would attack and kill it. The parasites change the proteins on an infected cell's surface every few generations to keep them invisible to the body's defenses.

Figure 19-13, and invades other red blood cells. Each of these outbreaks can destroy up to 40 percent of the host's red blood cells.

Female mosquitoes acquire *Plasmodium* when they bite infected humans. *Plasmodium* does not make the mosquito ill, so she is able to fly off and transmit the parasite to other humans.

The symptoms of malaria follow a cycle that corresponds to the reproduction of *Plasmodium* in the blood. When the parasites emerge from the blood cells, the host experiences high fever, delirium, and sweating. Severe chills follow the fever and can last until the next outbreak. Malaria sometimes weakens its victims so much that they die from other infections. Also, the drastic loss of blood cells causes anemia and can result in fatal brain or kidney damage.

Malaria was hit hard by treatment and prevention programs
In the 1600s, quinine, a bitter chemical derived from the bark of a tropical tree, was found to reduce the symptoms of malaria, although it did not always cure the disease. Derivatives of quinine, such as chloroquine and primaquine, are used today to treat and prevent malaria. If you travel to the tropics, you will probably have to take regular doses of one of these drugs to prevent malaria.

One way to reduce the number of cases of malaria is to reduce the size of mosquito populations. To control *Anopheles* mosquitoes, swamps and ditches where mosquitoes breed were drained. Powerful insecticides such as DDT were applied to kill mosquitoes. Through these two measures, malaria has been eradicated from the southern United States and southern Europe, where the disease was common until the 1940s. The World Health Organization introduced similar mosquito population control measures into parts of Africa and South America. Initially, these programs greatly reduced the worldwide incidence of malaria. Some optimists predicted the elimination of the deadly disease.

367

Connection: *Chapter 10*

Natural Selection and DDT Resistance
Have students explain how repeated use of an insecticide such as DDT will bring about a change in the mosquito population. *(DDT resistant individuals will survive and produce resistant offspring, so the insecticide will eventually be ineffective.)*

Visual Strategy Figure 19-13

● **Interpreting Graphics**
Use this figure to point out that malaria has killed more people than any other infectious disease in history. During World War II, more people died from malaria than were killed in battle. Also inform students that scientists are attempting to develop a vaccine for malaria. One problem is that the parasite changes the antigens on its cell surface during different stages of its life cycle.

Connection: *Chapter 16*

Food Chains and DDT
Remind students that DDT use has been banned in the United States because it accumulates in the tissues of organisms as it passes through the food chain. Review how some organisms, such as the bald eagle, were affected before and have been affected since the banning of DDT. *(Before the ban, the shells of the eggs were so thin that many broke, and the unhatched chicks died. The eagle is now making a comeback.)*

Multicultural Perspective: Malaria Vaccine

Dr. Manuel Patarroyo, a Colombian biochemist and physician, has developed an unorthodox, synthetic malaria vaccine called SPf66. This vaccine is made from malaria proteins chemically linked together. The antibodies that it induces recognize the real malaria parasites rather than just the vaccine's synthetic proteins. Trials have shown that the vaccine offers some amount of prevention against malaria infections, including those carried by the drug-resistant parasites. At first, scientists were skeptical about the vaccine because it originated from research in a small country and its preparation was unusual. However, the World Health Organization is calling for further research.

Key to Strategies
● Understanding Concepts (Tier I)
■ Applying Information (Tier II)
▲ Critical Thinking (Tier III)

Life/Work Skills
Finding Information
■ **Relating Concepts**

Many protozoans are human parasites. Have each student use reference books and databases to prepare a brief report on such a protozoan and a disease associated with it. The report should include the name of the disease, the organism responsible for infection, the method of infection, the symptoms of the disease, the short- or long-term effects, the treatment, areas where the organism is found, a summary of its life cycle, and a picture of the organism.

Phase Three
Assessment Options

Closure
■ **Recognizing Relationships**

The disease primary amoebic meningencephalitis (PAM) is caused by an amoeba that lives at the bottom of swimming holes and lakes. The amoeba enters the body with water that is inhaled through the nose. Once inside the nasal passages, the amoeba travels to the brain. Almost immediately, headaches and fever develop. Death usually occurs within 48 hours. Fortunately, the disease is rare. Ask students to suggest ways to avoid becoming infected with this organism. (*Answers might include wearing a nose clip when swimming and avoiding contact with water that might be contaminated.*)

SECTION REVIEW

Assign the *Section Review.*

Reteaching

Have students work in cooperative groups to illustrate the life cycles of several disease-causing protists. Students should use library references to find the information.

Malaria struck back

Malaria has not been eliminated. In fact, the number of cases has been increasing since the mid-1970s. Human efforts to combat the disease have been thwarted by evolutionary advances in both the *Plasmodium* parasite and the *Anopheles* mosquito. As you saw in **Figure 19-13**, the parasite frequently changes the protein knob configurations on the surfaces of infected blood cells, effectively making them invisible to the body's immune system. Additionally, *Plasmodium* parasites have developed resistance to some of the drugs that traditionally controlled them.

Figure 19-14
This computer model shows the regions of the world where malaria does occur.

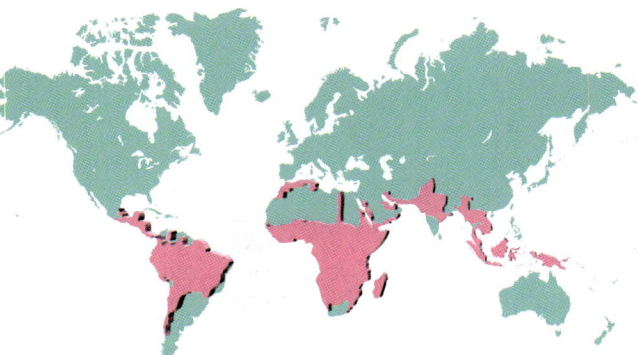

In many areas, mosquitoes have evolved resistance to insecticides. People are therefore exploring other methods of mosquito control, such as importing fish that eat large numbers of larval mosquitoes and investigating ways to fight mosquitoes with their natural enemies. Efforts are also underway to develop a malaria vaccine that protects individuals from infection by *Plasmodium*.

Protists cause many diseases

In the less industrialized countries, one in five people have been infected with malaria, dysentery, or sleeping sickness. In the industrialized countries, we have little contact with protists that can kill us. Protists may make us sick if our water treatment facility breaks down or if we drink water from a stream contaminated by protists from the feces of infected humans or animals. But for us, a disease caused by protists is an oddity, not an everyday possibility. **Figure 19-14** shows how widespread malaria is in the world now. However, because of predicted climate changes, the range of disease-causing insects could increase. Examples of diseases caused by protists are listed in **Table 19-1**.

Table 19-1   Human Diseases Caused by Protists

Disease	Host	Organism
Amoebic dysentery	Humans	*Entamoeba*
Malaria	Humans	*Plasmodium*
Toxoplasmosis	Humans, cats	*Toxoplasma*
Giardiasis	Humans	*Giardia*
Sleeping sickness	Humans, tsetse flies	*Trypanosoma*
Chagas' disease	Humans, kissing bugs	*Trypanosoma*
Leishmaniasis	Humans, sand flies	*Leishmania*

SECTION REVIEW

1 Why might the use of mosquito netting in malaria-prone areas decrease the number of malaria cases?

2 Describe two methods by which the incidence of malaria was reduced.

3 Explain why malaria has not been eliminated despite intense efforts to do so.

4 What are three human diseases caused by protists?

368

ANSWERS TO SECTION REVIEW

1 The netting protects humans from mosquitoes.

2 Applying insecticide and draining wet areas help reduce mosquito populations. Drugs such as chloroquine are taken to prevent infection.

3 Malaria continues to be a problem because mosquitoes have developed resistance to many insecticides, and *Plasmodium* has developed immunity to drugs that have been used to control it.

4 Answers will vary but should include three diseases from Table 19-1 on page 368.

Shirts on fire...
NOW IT'S OUT!

Amoeba and other protists are remarkably sensitive to their environments.

Humor at its lowest form.

	Key Terms	Summary
19-1 **What Is a Protist?** *Euglena* is a unicellular protist that is photosynthetic.	cilia (p. 358) pseudopod (p. 358)	• The kingdom Protista contains the eukaryotes that are not plants, animals, or fungi. • Both mitosis and meiosis occur among protists. • Protists descended from bacteria. Plants, animals, and fungi are the descendants of different protist ancestors.
19-2 **Protist Diversity** *Trichonympha* is a single-celled protist that lives in the guts of termites and digests wood.	phytoplankton (p. 362)	• The kingdom Protista is the most diverse eukaryotic kingdom. • Both autotrophs and heterotrophs are included among the protists. • Most protists are unicellular, but some are multicellular. • Green algae are the ancestors of plants. • Zoomastigotes are probably the ancestors of animals.
19-3 **Diseases Caused by Protists** The female *Anopheles* mosquito carries a protist called *Plasmodium*, which causes malaria.		• Malaria is a disease caused by a parasitic protozoan in the genus *Plasmodium*. About 300 million to 500 million people are currently infected with the malaria parasite. • *Plasmodium* is transmitted by mosquitoes, especially species in the genus *Anopheles*. • Intense efforts to eliminate malaria initially showed promise. These efforts have failed to eliminate malaria because of the evolution of drug resistance in the *Plasmodium* parasite and pesticide resistance in mosquitoes. • Other protists cause amoebic dysentery, giardiasis, and sleeping sickness.

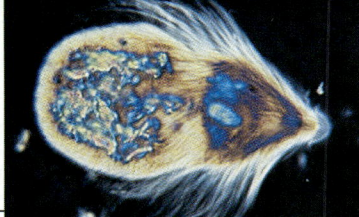

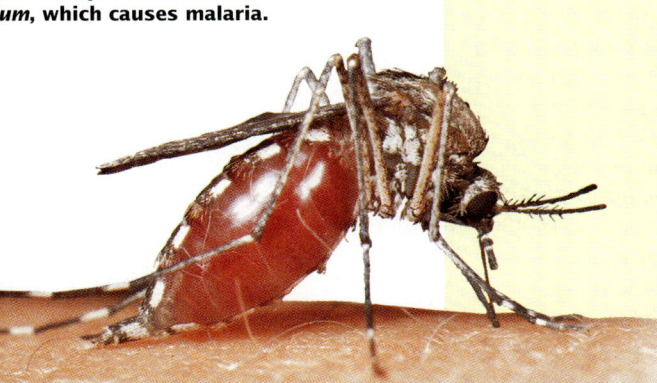

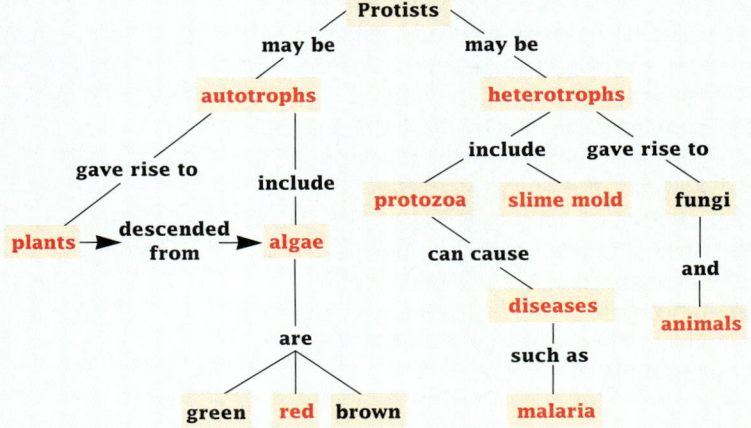

369

Alternative Assessment

Have students refer to the **Tour** of a Protist, on page 361. Using information provided on this page as well as in Chapters 3 and 4, have students write an essay with the title "Paramecium: A Small but Complex Protist." Tell students they may use any other chapter in the book as well as library resources to obtain additional information.

Portfolio Assessment

Portfolio Assessment on page T39 provides options for building and evaluating student portfolios. Students and teachers can select items from the areas listed on page T39 for inclusion in a portfolio.

ANSWER TO
CONCEPT MAP

The following is one possible answer to the Relating Concepts exercise on page 370.

Protists
— may be → **autotrophs**
— may be → **heterotrophs**

autotrophs — gave rise to → **plants**
plants — descended from → **algae**
autotrophs — include → **algae**
algae — are → green **red** brown

heterotrophs — include → **protozoa** **slime mold**
heterotrophs — gave rise to → **fungi**
protozoa — can cause → **diseases**
diseases — such as → **malaria**
fungi — and → **animals**

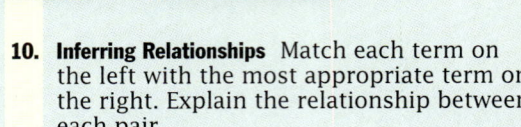

review

Understanding Vocabulary

1. a. *E. coli* is a single-celled, prokaryotic bacteria. The other terms fit the definition of kingdom Protista.

b. Flagella, pseudopods, and cilia are structures that provide locomotion. Algae is a living organism.

c. *Salmonella* is a bacteria; kelp, *Amoeba,* and slime molds are protists.

2. a. Red tides occur when there is a population explosion of certain types of dinoflagellates that release toxins.

b. *Euglena,* though capable of a heterotrophic lifestyle, can also obtain nutrients by photosynthesis because it contains chloroplasts.

c. Kingdom Protista contains organisms that are widely diverse, such as the microscopic *Paramecium* and algae 100 m long.

Understanding Concepts

3. Concept map answer is shown on page 369.

4. Kingdom Protista contains organisms that do not fit neatly into the other kingdoms.

5. *Euglena* is able to be autotrophic in the presence of light and heterotrophic in the absence of light.

6. The water mold *Phytophthora infestans* wiped out the Irish potato crops and caused a famine that drove millions of people from Ireland in the 1840s.

7. Brown algae is multicellular and photosynthetic like a plant, but it has different photosynthetic pigments in its chloroplasts.

8. Both structures function to provide locomotion.

9. *Euglena* moves toward light and uses the light to make its own nutrients. *Paramecium* moves away from the light to locations where food such as bacteria and other protists are more likely to be found.

10. a—3, b—4, c—2, d—1, e—5

Understanding Vocabulary

1. Identify the word or phrase that does not fit the pattern and explain why.

a. eukaryotic, chloroplasts, single-celled, multicelled, *Escherichia coli*

b. flagella, pseudopods, cilia, algae

c. kelp, *Amoeba, Salmonella,* slime mold

2. Using the words below, write one or more sentences summarizing information learned in this chapter.

a. red tides, dinoflagellate, population explosion, toxins

b. *Euglena,* nutrients, chloroplasts, heterotrophic

c. *Paramecium,* protists, microscopic, algae 100 m long

Understanding Concepts

3. **Relating Concepts** Construct a concept map describing the protists. Try to include the following terms in your map: algae, red, malaria, protozoa, slime mold, autotrophs, plants, diseases, heterotrophs, animals.

4. **Inferring Relationships** The kingdom Protista is sometimes called a catchall kingdom. What does this term mean, and why is it used?

5. **Evaluating Information** What characteristic of the protist *Euglena* makes it unusual among both the protists and other organisms?

6. **Predicting Outcomes** Describe how one protist caused the major immigration of many people to the United States.

7. **Applying Information** How is a brown alga similar to a plant? How is it different?

8. **Inferring Conclusions** Explain why the *Euglena*'s flagellum and the *Paramecium*'s cilia are homologous structures.

9. **Predicting Outcomes** Describe two ways in which protists react to their environment, and explain what each reaction reveals about their way of obtaining nutrients.

370

10. **Inferring Relationships** Match each term on the left with the most appropriate term on the right. Explain the relationship between each pair.

a. flagellum
b. light
c. *Trichonympha*
d. cilia
e. *Plasmodium*

1. *Paramecium*
2. termites
3. *Euglena*
4. phytoplankton
5. *Anopheles*

11. **Recognizing Relationships** Describe the symptoms of malaria and relate them to what is happening inside the individual who is infected with the disease.

12. **Summarizing Information** Explain why blood cells damaged by *Plasmodium* are not swept away to the spleen for destruction, as are other damaged red blood cells.

13. **Comparing Structures** Draw and label a bacterial cell and a protistan cell.

14. **Summarizing Information** Name five diseases caused by protists.

15. **Identifying Functions** Explain why red algae, which obtain nutrients by photosynthesizing, can exist at depths in the ocean where little light is able to penetrate.

16. **Summarizing Functions** By what methods do protists reproduce? How do they exchange genetic information?

17. **Inferring Relationships** Why have the major diseases AIDS and malaria been so hard to combat?

18. **Inferring Relationships** Describe the characteristics of slime molds and water molds that have sometimes caused them to be classified with the fungi. Describe how they are different from fungi.

19. **Comparing Structures** Describe the methods of locomotion used by the structures flagella, pseudopodia, and cilia.

20. **BUILDING ON WHAT YOU HAVE LEARNED** Based on what you learned about bacteria and viruses in Chapter 18, explain five ways that bacteria, viruses, and protists help humanity, and explain five ways that they harm us.

11. When the parasite emerges from the blood cells, the host experiences high fever, delirium, and sweating. Severe chills follow and can last until the next outbreak.

12. Blood cells infected by *Plasmodium* grow special protein knobs that anchor them to the walls of the blood vessels.

13. Drawings will vary. See pages 333 and 361.

14. malaria, Chagas' disease, African sleeping sickness, giardiasis, amoebic dysentery

15. Red algae contain distinctive pigments that enable them to photosynthesize with very little light.

16. Protists reproduce by mitosis and meiosis and exchange genetic information by a process called conjugation.

17. AIDS and malaria do not usually kill their hosts immediately, giving infected people opportunities to spread the disease. HIV and *Plasmodium* evolve rapidly, thereby thwarting efforts to control them. HIV's surface proteins evolve quickly, complicating the task of developing a vaccine. Malaria has been difficult to eradicate due to evolutionary advances that make the protist resistant to

Interpreting Graphics

21. Examine the figure shown below.

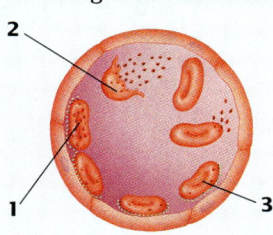

Match each numbered event in the figure with the sentence that best describes it.
a. *Plasmodium* causes protein knobs to form on the surface of infected red blood cells.
b. An infected *Anopheles* mosquito bites a human being.
c. Spores reproduce in a host's red blood cell.
d. Spores are released as the red blood cell bursts.

Arrange the events described above, in the correct sequence. Using your imagination, describe some ways in which a drug or vaccine could affect events shown in the figure above.

Reviewing Themes

22. *Evolution*
In what ways are protists related to bacteria?

23. *Interdependence*
Describe the role of autotrophic protists in the environment. What other living organisms depend on them?

24. *Interdependence*
Trichonympha is a protist that lives in the guts of termites. Explain how this has been a favorable situation for the termite and an unfavorable one for humans.

Thinking Critically

25. **Evaluating Arguments** A classmate says, "Holes in the ozone layer that allow more radiation to reach the Earth's surface can't have any effect on phytoplankton." Do you agree or disagree with this statement? Explain your reasoning.

Life/Work Skills

26. **Communicating** You are in charge of a public health service in a seaside community. You are informed by the authorities that a red tide has occurred along your coast. What information would you want to communicate to tourists and others in your community? Research red tides, and learn about the possible health complications they can cause. Make a presentation before your class as if you were addressing the city council, and answer any questions they might have.

27. **Applying Technology** If you were in charge of trying to control the mosquito population in a small town and knew that repeated applications of the same pesticide kill fewer and fewer mosquitoes, what other alternatives would you recommend? What other information would you need to have before proposing alternatives?

Activities and Projects

28. **Health Connection** Create a poster outlining the many diseases caused by protists in the world. What medical efforts are being made to treat and control these diseases?

29. **History Connection** Do research in the library or search an on-line database to investigate the early attempts to describe and control malaria. What did people think caused malaria before Ross made his discoveries?

Discovering Through Reading

30. Read the article "Malaria Vaccine Raises a Dilemma" in *Science*, January 1995, pages 320–323. What have the clinical trials shown that has caused the research community to be divided in their endorsement of the vaccine?

31. Read the article "Super Vaccine Crawls Out of the Slime" in *New Scientist*, June 1994. How are researchers growing genetic material in a slime mold? Why are they using this method instead of cloning genes by conventional methods? Why are the cells of slime molds better to work with?

heterotrophic eubacteria, and chloroplasts evolved from autotrophic eubacteria.

23. Autotrophic protists produce about one-third of the oxygen in the atmosphere and form the base of the aquatic food web. All animals depend on them directly or indirectly for food and oxygen.

24. *Trichonympha* enables the termite to digest wood. Unfortunately, termites damage wood structures.

Thinking Critically

25. Answers will vary. Students should support their answer with ideas from Unit 2, Continuity of Life; Unit 3, The Environment; and Chapter 19, Protists.

Life/Work Skills

26. Answers will vary. Students might suggest that people avoid consuming fish that have been swimming in red tide areas.

27. Answers will vary. Students might recommend natural controls which require knowledge about the mosquito's life cycle and natural enemies.

Activities and Projects

28. Posters will vary. Students might begin by researching the diseases listed in Table 19-1, on page 368.

29. Answers will vary but might discuss the belief that it was carried by "bad air."

Discovering Through Reading

30. Answers will vary but should discuss the effectiveness of the vaccine compared to traditional antimalaria tools.

31. The cells of slime mold are more like animal cells, are cheaper, and reproduce quickly.

the drugs used to control it, and due to the resistance of mosquitoes to pesticides.

18. Slime molds and water molds resemble fungi but have either cellulose cell walls or no cell walls. Fungi have cell walls made of chitin.

19. A flagellum lashes back and forth like a whip. Cilia move like boat oars. Cytoplasm streams out to form structures called pseudopodia.

20. Answers will vary. Protists and bacteria often cause disease. But they play an important part in the ecosystem, some enrich the soil, some form the base of the food chain, autotrophic protists release oxygen into the atmosphere, and many have industrial uses.

Interpreting Graphics

21. 1—a, 2—d, 3—c; b, c, a, d; drugs and vaccines usually affect the function of the protein knobs.

Reviewing Themes

22. The eukaryotic cell arose from an ancestral archaebacteria. Mitochondria evolved from

20 | Fungi and Plants

Lesson Planning Guide With Options for Block Scheduling

Lecture Concepts	Lesson Resources

20-1 Fungi

BLOCK ① (45 minutes)

1. Fungi are heterotrophic eukaryotes. Most fungi are multicellular and terrestrial.

2. The body of a multicellular fungus is composed of hyphae, and the cell wall contains chitin.

3. Fungi reproduce asexually and sexually and are characterized by their method of reproduction.

① Lecture Resources
- Determining Prior Knowledge
- Fungus Variety
- Active Reading: Anticipation Guide
- Active Reading: Reading Organizer
- Visual Strategy: Figure 20-1
- Visual Strategy: Videodisc
- Demonstration: Identifying Functions
- Holt Biology Videodiscs Lesson 20-1

Classwork Options
- Laboratory Techniques and Experimental Design: Lab C34

Assignment Options
- World of Work: Growing Mushroom

BLOCK ② (45 minutes)

4. There are four groups of fungi: zygomycetes, ascomycetes, basidiomycetes, and deuteromycetes.

5. The major role of fungi is to act as decomposers.

6. Although some fungi are beneficial, many cause diseases in plants and animals.

② Lecture Resources
- Hyphae
- Active Reading: Paired Summarizing
- Visual Strategy: Figure 20-6
- Visual Strategy: Videodisc
- Teaching Transparencies: 106, 107, 108, 109, 110, 111
- Holt Biology Videodiscs Lesson 20-1

Classwork Options
- Life/Work Skills: Finding Information
- Closure: Identifying Variables

Assignment Options
- *Small Group* Reteaching
- Section Review
- Chapter Review, questions 1a, 2a, 4, 5, 6, 7, 8, 9, 10, 20, 25, 27, 29
- Directed Reading Worksheet

20-2 Early Land Plants

BLOCK ③ (45 minutes)

1. The first land plants had no vascular tissues or seeds.

2. Club mosses, horsetails, and ferns were among the first plants to evolve vascular tissue.

③ Lecture Resources
- Active Reading: Reading Organizer
- Visual Strategy: Figure 20-11
- Visual Strategy: Videodisc
- Teaching Transparencies: 117
- Holt Biology Videodiscs Lesson 20-2

Classwork Options
- Terrarium Construction
- Quick Labs: Lab A18

BLOCK ④ (45 minutes)

3. Mosses, horsetails, and ferns do not produce seeds.

4. Land plants alternate generations from a haploid gametophyte to a diploid sporophyte.

④ Lecture Resources
- Active Reading: Reading Organizer
- Teaching Transparencies: 118
- Holt Biology Videodiscs Lesson 20-2

Classwork Options
- Closure: Relating Concepts

Assignment Options
- Reteaching
- Section Review
- Chapter Review, questions 1b, 2b, 11, 12, 13, 14, 21, 26
- Directed Reading Worksheet

20-3 Seed Plants

BLOCK ⑤ (45 minutes)

1. Seeds, pollen, cones, flowers, and vascular tissue allow seed plants to fully adapt to dry land conditions.

⑤ Lecture Resources
- Plant Survival
- Visual Strategy: Figure 20-12
- Visual Strategy: Videodisc
- Teaching Transparencies: 114, 133
- Holt Biology Videodiscs Lesson 20-3

Classwork Options
- World of Work: Paleobotanist
- Quick Labs: Lab A20

Assignment Options
- This Land

KEY

- ■ Annotated Teacher's Edition
- ■ Pupil's Edition
- ■ Directed Reading Worksheets
- ■ Vocabulary Development Worksheets
- ■ Thinking Skills Worksheets
- ■ Reteaching Worksheets
- ■ Chapter Tests
- ◉ Language Development and Reading Comprehension Audio CD Program

Holt BioSources
🧪 **Laboratory Program**
- A Quick Labs
- B Inquiry Skills Development
- C Laboratory Techniques and Experimental Design
- D Biotechnology
- E Interactive Explorations in Biology Laboratory Manual

- 🔖 Teaching Transparencies
- ◉ Testing Resources CD-ROM
- ◉ Test Generator/Assessment Item

Holt Biology Technology
- ◉ Holt Biology Videodiscs

Lecture Concepts

Lesson Resources

20-3 Seed Plants, *continued*

BLOCK ❻ (45 minutes)

2. Seed plant embryos have leaflike structures called cotyledons that store food or absorb food stored elsewhere in the seed.

3. The two groups of seed plants are the gymnosperms, which produce naked seeds in cones, and the angiosperms, which surround the seed with a fruit.

❻ Lecture Resources
- ■ Visual Strategy: Videodisc
- 🔖 Teaching Transparencies: 115
- ◉ Holt Biology Videodiscs Lesson 20-3

Classwork Options
- ■ Closure: Relating Concepts

Assignment Options
- ■ Reteaching
- ■ Section Review
- ■ Chapter Review, questions 1c, 2c, 3, 15, 16, 17, 18, 19, 22, 23, 24, 28
- ■ Directed Reading Worksheet

Chapter Review and Assessment

BLOCK ❼ (45 minutes)
Review
- ■ Reteaching Worksheet
- ■ Thinking Skills Worksheet
- ■ Vocabulary Development Worksheet
- ◉ Language Development and Reading Comprehension Audio CD Program: Chapter 20

BLOCK ❽ (45 minutes)
Assessment
- ■ Alternative Assessment, p. 387
- ■ Portfolio Assessment, p. T39

Chapter Test
- ■ Chapter 20 Test

Test Generator
- ◉ Item bank for customizing Chapter Tests

Teaching Resources CD-ROM
- ◉ Scoring Rubrics and Classroom Management Checklist

The Portfolio icon denotes items throughout the Teacher's Edition lesson wrap that may be selected for inclusion in student portfolios.

Holt Biology Videodiscs and *Concepts of Biology*

Holt Biology Videodiscs gives you a powerful tool for teaching, review, and assessment. For further information regarding the media on the videodiscs, see *Holt Biology Videodiscs Teacher's Correlation Guide to Holt Biology: Visualizing Life.*

Concepts of Biology adds interactive lesson plans and extensive tools for customization using CD-ROM technology.

Use the following topic from *Concepts of Biology* to help you teach this chapter:
Topic 14: Protists and Fungi
Topic 15: Plant Evolution

Laboratory Planning

Holt BioSources Laboratory Program

Block 1: Laboratory Techniques and Experimental Design Lab C34: Limiting Fungal Growth
Block 3: Quick Labs Lab A18: Comparing Plant Adaptations
Block 5: Quick Labs Lab A20: Relating Root Structure to Function

CHAPTER 20

Determining Prior Knowledge

- Have students explain why mushrooms are not considered plants.
- Have students describe fungi they have seen on food, moist surfaces, tree trunks, or soil.
- Show students examples of the following: moss, algae, a mushroom, an evergreen, and a flowering plant. Have them point out similarities and differences.
- Show students a piece of fruit and a pine cone. Have them compare and discuss the structure and function of both.
- Have students describe what they know about how a seed develops into a plant.

Active READING

Technique: Anticipation Guide
Before students begin this chapter, write the following statements on the chalkboard or the overhead:

1. Fungi are more closely related to plants than to animals.
2. Most fungi are beneficial to other organisms.
3. Almost all of our food is derived directly or indirectly from flowering plants.

Give students a minute or two to think about each statement and decide whether they agree or disagree with it. Ask volunteers to share the reasons for their opinions with the class. Have students read the chapter to see if their opinions are confirmed or changed in any way.

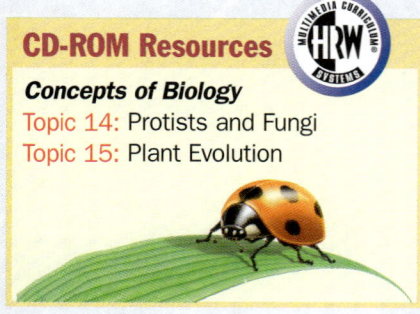

CD-ROM Resources

Concepts of Biology
Topic 14: Protists and Fungi
Topic 15: Plant Evolution

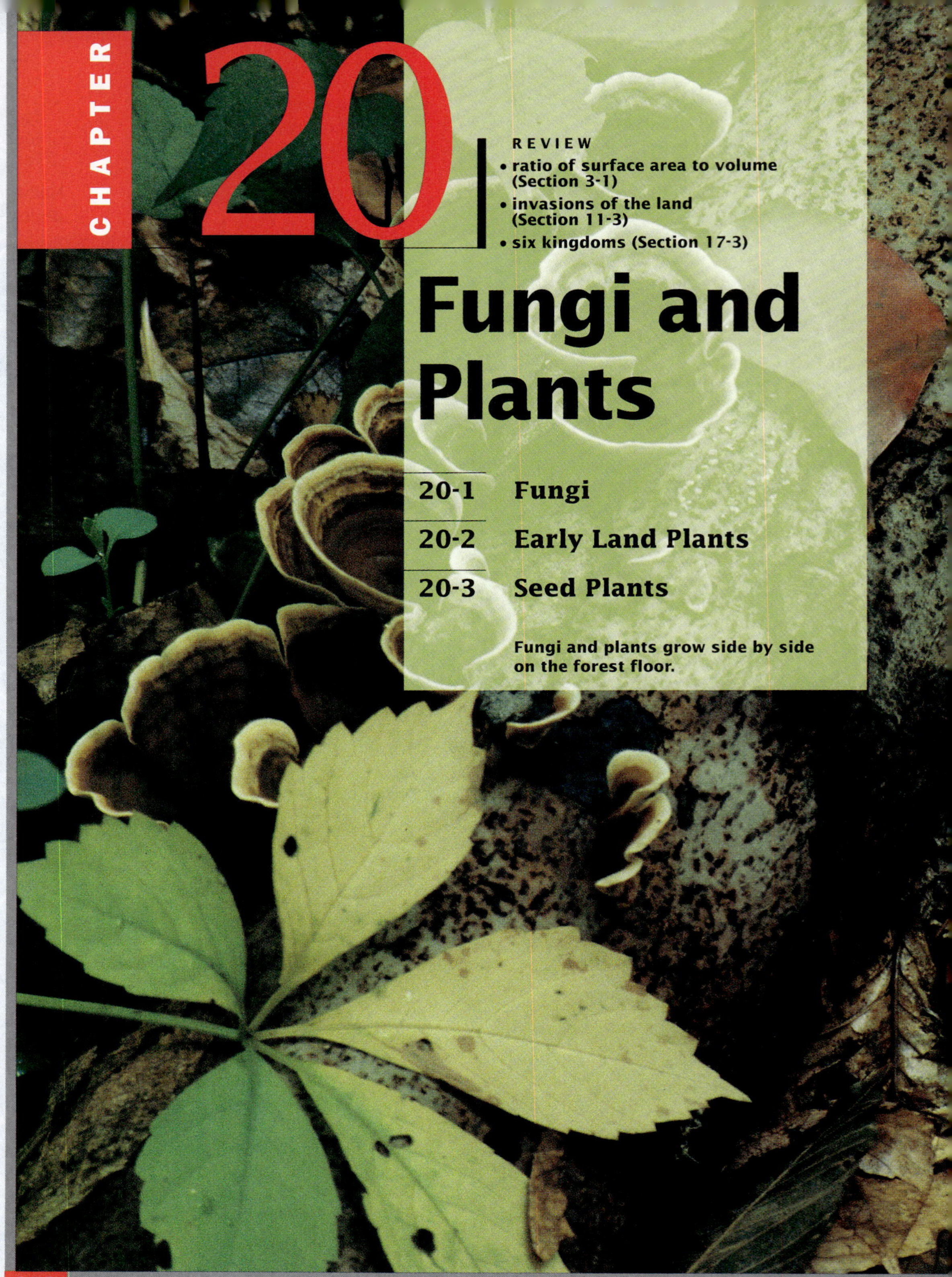

CHAPTER 20

REVIEW
- ratio of surface area to volume (Section 3-1)
- invasions of the land (Section 11-3)
- six kingdoms (Section 17-3)

Fungi and Plants

Fungi and plants grow side by side on the forest floor.

Author's Rationale The evolutionary story of plants begins with the introduction of fungi. The first plants were able to invade land through symbiosis with fungi. The relationship involved plants as the providers of food, through photosynthesis, and fungi as the providers of inorganic nutrients, extracted from the ground. The chapter covers the parade of successful adaptations of plants.

Fungi and the algal ancestors of plants were the first eukaryotes to invade land from the sea. Like the bracket fungi on this tree trunk, most fungi are terrestrial, as are the majority of plants. The primary role of fungi in the environment is to decompose organic matter; this is also the role of many bacteria. Fungi also affect human life by causing disease as well as by providing us with food and medicine.

20-1 Fungi

OBJECTIVES

1 Identify the characteristics shared by most fungi.

2 Describe how fungi obtain nutrients.

3 Differentiate among the four groups of fungi.

4 Relate characteristics of fungi to their ecologic and economic importance.

Characteristics of Fungi

The kingdom Fungi (*FUHN jy*) is a group of eukaryotic organisms, most of which are multicellular. Little is known about the origins of fungi. The oldest fossils that have been identified as fungi are 450–500 million years old. Fungi have many unique features, which strongly suggests that they are not closely related to any other kingdom of organisms.

Biologists once placed fungi in the plant kingdom, probably because many fungi seem to be more plant-like than animal-like. Most fungi are immobile, grow at both ends, and appear to be "rooted" like plants. However, fungi are as different from plants as they are from other living things. Compare familiar fungi, such as those in **Figure 20-1**, with a familiar plant. Careful study reveals several characteristics that distinguish fungi from plants.

b . . . to this poisonous fly agaric mushroom . . .

c . . . to these single-celled yeasts.

Figure 20-1
Fungi exist in many forms, . . .

a . . . from the mold growing on these strawberries . . .

373

Videodisc Resources

Holt Biology Videodiscs
Lesson 20-1: Fungi

Phase One
Preparation

Scheduling
See the **Lesson Planning Guide** on pages 371A and 371B for lecture, classwork, and assignment options for Section 20-1.

Phase Two
Teaching Strategies

Active READING

Technique: Reading Organizer
Before students read about the kinds of fungi, point out to students that Table 20-1 on page 376 is a reading organizer that visually represents the structure of this portion of the text. As students read about the four kinds of fungi, see if they can locate the information that appears in Table 20-1 within the body of the text.

Visual Strategy | **Figure 20-1**

● **Comparing Structures**
Have students compare these fungi and list similarities and differences. *(Answers will vary but may include the following: some are unicellular like the yeast, some are harmful like the mold, and some are poisonous. All mushrooms are heterotrophic. The fly agaric mushroom is poisonous.)*

Key to Strategies
Teaching Strategies are keyed to three tiers of learning.

● **Understanding Concepts (Tier I)**
Content mastery and comprehension

■ **Applying Information (Tier II)**
Applying and analyzing content

▲ **Critical Thinking (Tier III)**
Practicing evaluative thinking

Fungi and Plants 373

● **Interpreting Graphics**
Use *Illustration—Fungus Structure* shown in Chapter 20 Section 20-1 of **Holt Biology Videodiscs Teacher's Correlation Guide to Holt Biology: Visualizing Life** to discuss the structure of a mushroom. Have students point out the hyphae that make up the mycelium, the septa, and the holes in the septa. Remind students that all parts of the mushroom are made of the same kind of cell.

Demonstration

● **Identifying Functions**
Show students two different kinds of multicellular fungi, such as a mold and a mushroom. Even though their appearance is different, they are both composed of hyphae. Make a wet mount of each, and use a videomicroscope to demonstrate this to the students.

Fungus Variety

■ **Relating Concepts**
Have students read the article "Mushroom Mania" in *Natural History,* April 1996, pages 32–35. The article is about a mushroom festival that is an annual event in Telluride, Colorado. But more important, mycorrhizal mushrooms and a variety of others are discussed. Slime molds are also included, as are problems that occur in classification.

Hyphae

● **Identifying Functions**

Have students create a **Graphic Organizer** to summarize the structure and functions of hyphae. Students' organizers will vary but should be similar to the one at the bottom of this page.

Fungi are heterotrophs
One obvious difference between fungi and plants is their color; fungi are not green like the leaves of plants. Certain parts of plants appear green because they contain chlorophyll, which enables them to capture energy from sunlight. Plants use that energy to make organic molecules from inorganic materials. As a result, plants are autotrophs (organisms that capture energy and make organic molecules from inorganic materials). Fungi do not contain chlorophyll and cannot capture energy from sunlight. As a result, fungi are heterotrophs (organisms that get energy and organic molecules by obtaining food from their surroundings).

The bodies of multicellular fungi consist of filaments
Unlike the bodies of most plants, which consist of many types of cells arranged in tissues, the body of a fungus consists of similar-looking cells arranged in long slender filaments. The filaments that make up the body of a fungus are called **hyphae** *(HY fee)*. Each hypha is a long string of individual cells that are separated by walls called septa. The septa of many kinds of fungi have holes in them. These holes enable the cytoplasm and nuclei of the cells in a hypha to flow from cell to cell. As hyphae grow, they branch repeatedly and form a tangled mass called a **mycelium** *(my SEE lee uhm).* Yeasts, which are unicellular fungi, do not form either hyphae or a mycelium.

Often, the only parts of a fungus that you can see are its reproductive structures. This is the case with the *Aspergillus* mold seen on the fruit in **Figure 20-2**. The black fuzz that you recognize as the mold is a mass of reproductive structures. Most of the mycelium of the fungus lies within the fruit. In another type of fungi, some of the hyphae in the mycelium weave tightly together to form a mushroom, which is also a reproductive structure.

Cell walls of fungi contain chitin
The cells of fungi have cell walls made of a polysaccharide called **chitin** *(KY tihn)*. This tough material is also found in the exoskeletons of insects and other arthropods. Cells of plants, on the other hand, have cell walls made of cellulose, a different polysaccharide. Chitin is more resistant to decomposition by bacteria than is cellulose.

Figure 20-2
The parts of a fungus that you normally see are reproductive structures.

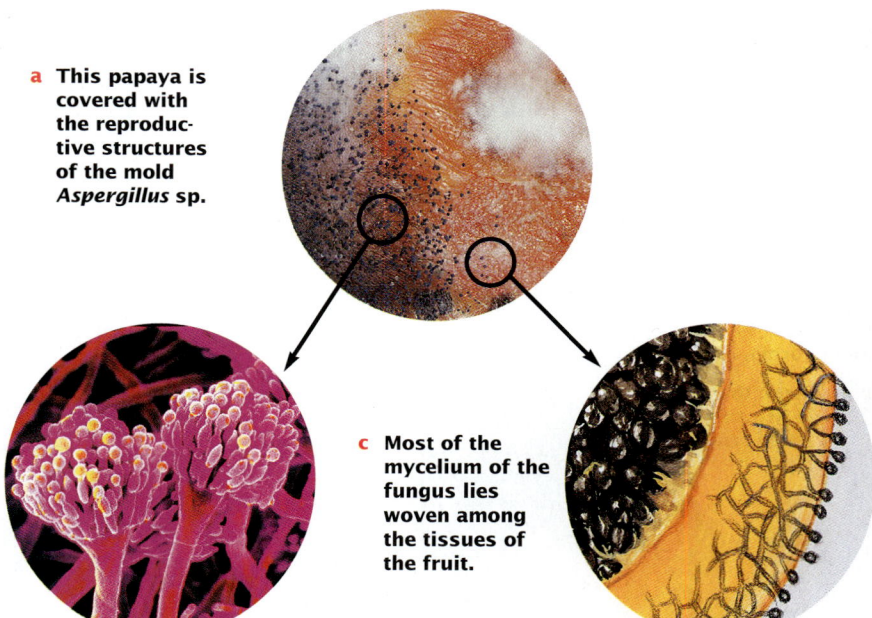

a **This papaya is covered with the reproductive structures of the mold *Aspergillus* sp.**

b **The black fuzz consists of fungal spores produced by these structures.**

c **Most of the mycelium of the fungus lies woven among the tissues of the fruit.**

374

Graphic Organizer

Use the following graphic organizer with the teaching strategy **Hyphae** on page 374.

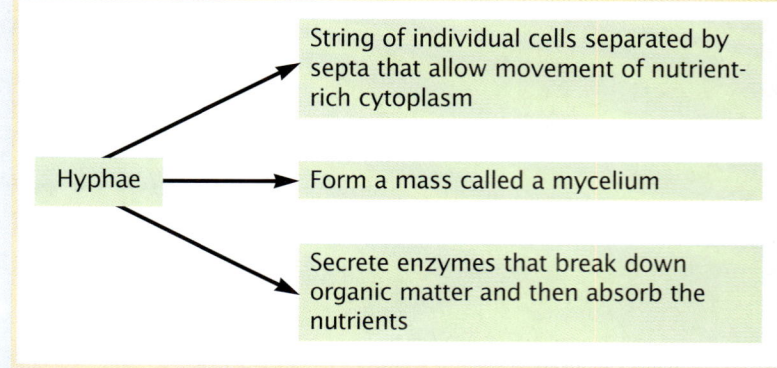

Hyphae → String of individual cells separated by septa that allow movement of nutrient-rich cytoplasm

Hyphae → Form a mass called a mycelium

Hyphae → Secrete enzymes that break down organic matter and then absorb the nutrients

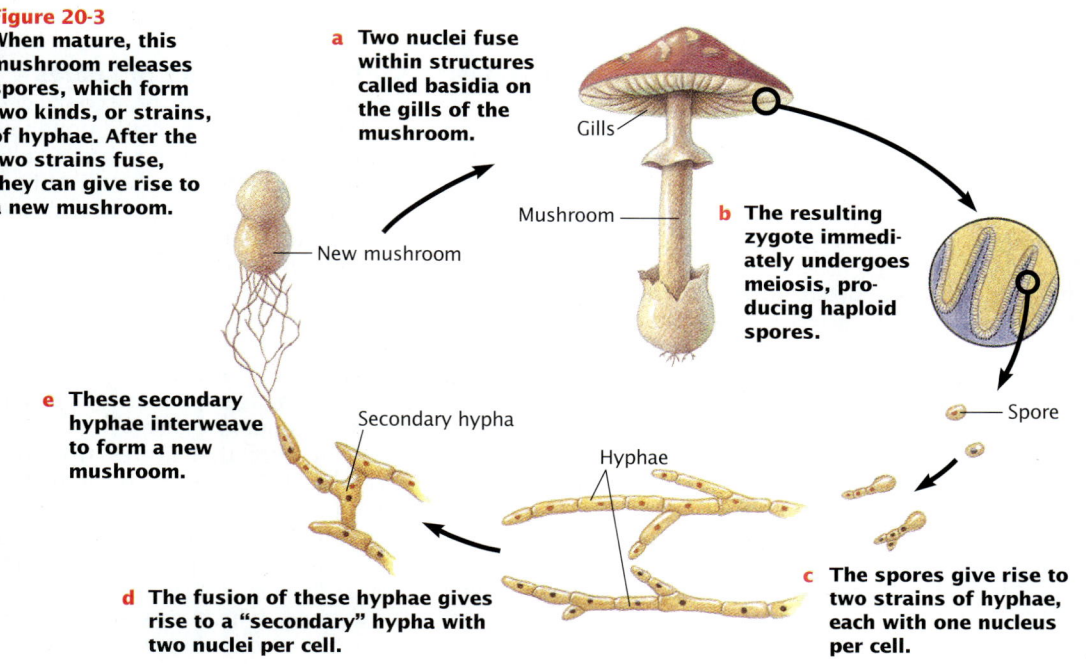

Figure 20-3
When mature, this mushroom releases spores, which form two kinds, or strains, of hyphae. After the two strains fuse, they can give rise to a new mushroom.

a Two nuclei fuse within structures called basidia on the gills of the mushroom.

Gills

Mushroom

New mushroom

b The resulting zygote immediately undergoes meiosis, producing haploid spores.

e These secondary hyphae interweave to form a new mushroom.

Secondary hypha

Hyphae

Spore

d The fusion of these hyphae gives rise to a "secondary" hypha with two nuclei per cell.

c The spores give rise to two strains of hyphae, each with one nucleus per cell.

Mathematics Connection
Counting Spores
A mushroom was found to have 12,750 spores on one side of one gill. If there were 160 gills on that mushroom, how many spores would there be? *(12,750 spores × 2 sides of gill × 160 gills = 4,080,000 spores)* Ask students why the large number of spores is inconsistent with the relatively small number of mushrooms. *(Most spores will not encounter conditions suitable for growth.)*

Theme Answer
Interdependence
Fungi and bacteria are the decomposers in the biosphere. They break down organic matter from dead plants, providing nutrients for the living plants.

Fungi digest food outside their bodies
You have seen mold growing on bread and fruit. Fungi use these items for food just as you do. Some fungi attack living plants and animals to obtain nutrients, while others attack dead organisms. Both methods provide fungi with a rich supply of nutrients (organic molecules, water, and minerals).

A fungus growing on a food source is digesting the food and absorbing nutrients. Like most animals, you digest food within your digestive system. However, fungi digest food outside their bodies. As the hyphae of a fungus spread through a food source, they secrete enzymes that break down organic matter. The hyphae then absorb the nutrients. The mycelium of a fungus may consist of many meters of hyphae. As a result, fungi have a very high ratio of surface area to volume and are efficient feeders.

Most fungi reproduce by spores
If you examine part of a patch of mold or mildew with a microscope, you will probably see many hyphae that are tipped with clusters or short strings of tiny, beadlike spheres. These tiny structures are reproductive cells called **spores**. A fungal spore can develop into a new individual.

Most fungal spores are well adapted to life on land. They can withstand dry conditions and a wide range of temperatures. Some fungal spores are light and easily carried to new sites by air currents, while others are sticky and cling to animals that carry them to new places. When a fungal spore lands on a food source with enough moisture, the spore rapidly grows into a hypha. If conditions remain favorable, the hypha continues to grow and branches repeatedly, forming a mycelium.

Fungi produce spores by both asexual and sexual reproduction. During asexual reproduction, spores form by cell division at the tips of certain hyphae. Sexual reproduction involves the combining of genetic materials from two strains of a fungus. In mushrooms, for example, this combining occurs just before a mushroom's stalk and cap develops. Spores are produced in gills, which are found under the cap of the mushroom. The spores are shed when the cap opens like an umbrella. The life cycle of a mushroom is shown in **Figure 20-3**.

Interdependence

How do the fungi and plants in a forest depend on each other?

375

Matter of Fact: Sexual Reproduction in Molds
Molds reproduce sexually when contact occurs between hyphae from two genetically different molds, called mating strains. The mating strains are called plus (+) and minus (–) rather than male and female, because they have identical shapes and functions.

Key to Strategies
● Understanding Concepts (Tier I)
■ Applying Information (Tier II)
▲ Critical Thinking (Tier III)

Biotechnology Connection
The Human Genome

American geneticists are in the process of mapping the genetic information found on the 23 pairs of human chromosomes. The work is so complicated that nine different laboratories are involved in the 12-year plan. However, Dr. Daniel Cohen, of the Center for the Study of Human Polymorphism, in Paris, has developed a procedure that should allow the French to complete the task two years ahead of the Americans. His procedure involves slicing the sets of chromosomes into thousands of pieces and putting each piece into a genetically manipulated yeast cell. These cells can make thousands of copies of the human DNA pieces, which will then be analyzed. One drawback is that some of these pieces also contain yeast DNA. Even so, this will speed the search for gene identification. Cohen intends to donate his gene map to the United Nations as a gift to the world.

Kinds of Fungi

Fungi are divided into three groups, according to the structures they possess for sexual reproduction. Fungi in which sexual reproduction is rare, or has not been observed, are placed in a fourth group. The four groups of fungi are summarized in **Table 20-1**.

Bread molds form structures called zygosporangia

You may have had unpleasant experiences with bread molds, which belong to the smallest group of fungi—the zygomycetes *(zy goh MY seets)*. This group includes the mold *Rhizopus stolonifer*, which frequently grows on bread. Other zygomycetes live on the decaying plant or animal matter in soil. During sexual reproduction, zygomycetes form a zygosporangium, which is a thick-walled reproductive structure that can remain dormant for months. When conditions are favorable, spore-producing stalks grow from the zygosporangium. When the spores reach maturity, they are often picked up by the wind and blown about.

Sac fungi form sacs of spores

Without the sac fungi, or ascomycetes *(as coh MY seets)*, you could not enjoy many baked foods, such as bread, rolls, and pizza. On the other hand, without sac fungi, many ornamental and food plants, such as boxwood, crape myrtles, cucumbers, and squash, would not be attacked by powdery mildews. In addition to the powdery mildews, the ascomycetes include yeasts, morels, truffles, and the *Penicillium* molds that produce the strong flavors of Camembert and Roquefort cheese.

The feature that unites the ascomycetes is the saclike reproductive structure that forms after genetic materials fuse together during sexual reproduction (the prefix *asco* means "sac"). Spores are produced inside these sacs, which eventually burst open. The spores of some ascomycetes are thrown as far as 30 cm (12 in.). Many species of fungi resemble ascomycetes but have not been observed to reproduce sexually. These species are placed in the fourth group of fungi.

Table 20-1 Groups of Fungi

Group	Sexual Reproduction	Examples	
Zygomycetes	Spores are produced on stalks that grow from a structure called a zygosporangium	Some of the black molds on bread and other foods	*Rhizopus stolonifer* on bread
Ascomycetes	Spores are produced in saclike reproductive structures	Yeast, mildews, morels, and truffles; fungi that cause Dutch elm disease and chestnut blight	Powdery mildew
Basidiomycetes	Spores form at tips of clublike reproductive structures	Toadstools, puffballs, mushrooms, bracket fungi, rusts, and smuts	*Amanita muscaria* mushroom
Deuteromycetes	Unusual, rare, or not observed	Many common molds; molds that produce antibiotics, and many disease-causing fungi	*Penicillium* sp.

376

Historical Perspective: Ergotism

Ergotism, a disease that results when grain infected with the ergot fungus is harvested and milled, was common in Europe in the Middle Ages, where it was known as St. Anthony's Fire. In 1722, the cavalry of Peter the Great was inflicted with ergotism just as the czar was about to conquer Turkey. Ergot contains several alkaloids that cause seizures and hysteria. In the past, victims of ergotism were sometimes accused of being witches.

Club fungi produce spores on clublike structures

Most organisms you call mushrooms belong to a third group of fungi, the basidiomycetes *(buh sid ee oh MY seets)*. This is the largest group of fungi and also includes bracket fungi, toadstools, puffballs, rusts, and smuts. These fungi form reproductive structures shaped like wooden bats, or clubs (the prefix *basidio* means "little club"). The clublike structures develop under the caps of mushrooms or under the "shelves" of bracket fungi. Spores form on the tips of the clubs. Many club fungi live on dead organisms.

Some fungi have no known form of sexual reproduction

Fungi with no known method of sexual reproduction are placed in a group called the deuteromycetes *(doot uh roh MY seets)*. This group is also known as the Fungi Imperfecti. Some of these fungi have great economic importance. *Penicillium notatum* produces the antibiotic penicillin. Two species of *Aspergillus* are used to ferment soy beans in the production of soy sauce. In addition, deuteromycetes cause many fruits and vegetables to rot, and they cause human skin diseases such as athlete's foot.

Fungi in Nature

There are very few places on land that at least one species of fungi does not call home. Carried by air currents, fungal spores may land almost anywhere. Thus, many molds and mushrooms seem to spring up wherever there is the right amount of food and moisture.

Although some fungi cause diseases of plants and animals, most fungi are beneficial to other organisms. Fungi decompose organic wastes and the remains of dead plants and animals, returning nutrients such as nitrogen and phosphorus to the soil. Imagine what the world would look like if fungi did not exist! Fungi are also key components in two important types of mutualistic associations—mycorrhizae and lichens. Similar symbiotic associations played a crucial role in the invasion of land by life from the sea.

Fungi form mycorrhizae with plants

As you read in Chapter 11, many fungi grow on or within the roots of certain plants, in symbiotic associations called mycorrhizae *(my koh RY zee)*. Mycorrhizal fungi played a critical role in the successful colonization of land by plants. Many of the earliest known plants formed mycorrhizae with fungi. The fungi provided the plants with water and minerals, and the plants provided the fungi with photosynthetically produced food.

One type of mycorrhizal fungus is shown in **Figure 20-4**. Recently, researchers have discovered that the destruction of mycorrhizal fungi by acid rain is playing a key role in the deaths of many forests. Without mycorrhizae, most forest trees are unable to absorb minerals from soil.

Figure 20-4
a These tiny mushrooms, which grow under ponderosa pine trees, are reproductive structures of a mycorrhizal fungus.

b Underground, the hyphae of this fungus surround and penetrate the roots of the trees.

377

Historical Perspective: Sourdough

Sourdough bread may be the oldest of all breads, dating back to 4000 B.C. Sourdough was very important to the pioneers and prospectors who traveled west seeking gold in the nineteenth century. The sourdough starter was something to be guarded, nursed, and bequeathed in one's will. Making a fresh batch of yeast on demand was not always possible. The sourdough starter is a self-perpetuating yeast mixture made by combining flour, sugar, and water. The ingredients would be combined at night, and in the morning a small amount would be removed and set aside, and the rest would be used for baking. That small amount could then be saved for later use.

Fungi and Plants   377

Active READING

Technique: Paired Summarizing

Have students read silently Fungi in Nature on pages 377 and 378. Assign partners and have one student, the "reteller," summarize orally what has been read while the other student, the "listener," listens to the retelling. The listener should point out inaccuracies and add ideas that were left out. Have students alternate roles and repeat this process for each paragraph. Students should work together during a final clarification process, referring to the text as needed.

Connection: *Chapter 16*

Environmental Indicator

Point out that lichens are one of the first groups of organisms to suffer from airborne contaminants. Detecting air quality with lichens is less costly than using electronic gauges. Lichens were used to prove that the air over Lake Superior's Isle Royale contained high levels of sulfur dioxide. Lichens were also used following the Chernobyl disaster to pinpoint the most seriously contaminated areas.

Life/Work Skills
Finding Information

■ **Recognizing Relationships**

Fungi can be both harmful and beneficial to a variety of living things. Have each student investigate and write a report about fungi in agriculture or biotechnology. Some topics to consider are the following: fungal insecticides, fungal herbicides; fungi that cause plant diseases and fungi that fight plant diseases; human diseases caused by fungi, bioremediation; antibiotics; gene cloning; food processing; cultivation of fungi for food; enzyme technology; alcoholic beverage production; industrial alcohol production; and citric acid production.

Figure 20-5
Lichens are able to survive in extremely harsh environments. Chemicals released by these lichens help begin the breakdown of rock into soil.

Fungi form lichens with algae and cyanobacteria

If you have ever visited a rocky seacoast or a forest, you may have noticed rocks or logs with crusty orange, yellow, or gray-green patches, like those shown in **Figure 20-5**. These patches are lichens. A **lichen** (*LY kuhn*) is a mutualistic association between a fungus and either a green alga or a cyanobacterium. The fungus absorbs

water and other nutrients from the environment. The alga uses these nutrients for photosynthesis. In turn, the alga produces organic molecules that the fungus uses as food.

Lichens can live in very harsh environments. For instance, they live in deserts and on the highest mountains. The secret to a lichen's success in a harsh environment seems to be its ability to dry out very quickly. When it is dry, a lichen is less likely to be damaged by very hot or very cold temperatures. Today, many lichens play an important role in ecosystems as pioneers, the first organisms to inhabit bare rock.

Because they absorb water and nutrients from the air, lichens are extremely susceptible to air pollution. For example, lichens are usually absent in and around cities, where automobile traffic and industrial activity produce pollutants that destroy chlorophyll. As a result, the alga or cyanobacterium of a lichen cannot photosynthesize for itself or for the fungus. Because of this sensitivity, scientists use lichens as indicators of air quality.

Fungi and Humans

Fungi benefit humans in many ways. Take the unicellular yeasts, for example. You could not enjoy freshly baked bread or pizza without *Saccharomyces cerevisiae*, better known as baker's yeast. Yeast cells break down sugar into carbon dioxide and alcohol when oxygen is in short supply. These substances enable us to make bread and alcoholic beverages. However, the greatest effect of fungi on humans is as disease-causing and decay-causing organisms.

Fungi cause diseases in humans and crop plants

Fungi cause many diseases in humans. Some examples of fungal diseases that you may be familiar with are ringworm and athlete's foot. These common skin diseases are caused by deuteromycetes.

Histoplasmosis is a serious and sometimes fatal disease that is caused by the ascomycete *Histoplasma capsulatum*. This fungus grows in bird and bat droppings. When its spores are inhaled, they infect the lungs. New spores produced in the lungs may spread and infect the liver, central nervous system, and other internal organs. Many people also suffer from allergies caused by fungi.

Every year, farmers lose billions of dollars in crops due to the effects of fungal diseases. Powdery mildews, leaf spots, stem and root rots, sooty molds, rusts, and smuts are common names for several types of fungal diseases that affect crop plants. Fungal diseases also destroy millions of dollars of forest trees that provide us with lumber, paper, and many other products.

378

Multicultural Perspective: Lichens

Lichens have been used to make dyes by the Greeks, Romans, and Native Americans. The lichen dye industry thrived in Europe for many centuries. Today lichens are used in the manufacture of Scottish tweeds and East Indian cotton fabrics. In China, lichens are used to make an antibiotic.

After harvest, millions of dollars of fruits, vegetables, and grains are destroyed by fungi that cause them to rot. As a result, growers and shipping companies must spend a great deal of money to treat or ship these crops in airtight or refrigerated containers to protect them. Molds such as *Rhizopus*, *Penicillium*, and *Aspergillus* commonly cause unpreserved foods to rot.

Fungi provide medically valuable compounds

Some of the same fungi that are harmful to organisms also have beneficial properties. As you read in Chapter 18, Alexander Fleming discovered the antibiotic effects of the fungus *Penicillium notatum* in 1928. Fleming's accidental discovery, shown in **Figure 20-6**, led to the development of the world's most widely used antibiotic—penicillin.

Other fungi have helped revolutionize the field of medicine. In 1972, the Swiss immunologist Jean Borel found a type of fungus that produces a substance capable of suppressing the immune system's response to transplanted organs. This substance, called cyclosporine, opened up a new frontier in surgery. Before it became available in 1979, fewer than half of all kidney transplants were successful. Now, with the widespread use of cyclosporine, the success rate has risen to 90 percent.

Yeasts are now popular subjects for genetic engineering. Although bacteria are excellent subjects for genetic engineering, they are prokaryotes. Yeast cells, which are eukaryotes, are more suitable models for developing genetic engineering techniques for plants and animals, which are also eukaryotes. Research with yeast may lead to new and innovative treatments for diseases such as cancer and AIDS.

Figure 20-6
In 1928, Alexander Fleming discovered that *Penicillium notatum* killed bacteria. Ten years later, the drug penicillin was purified. Penicillin is effective in curing several bacterial diseases, including pneumonia, scarlet fever, diphtheria, and many others.

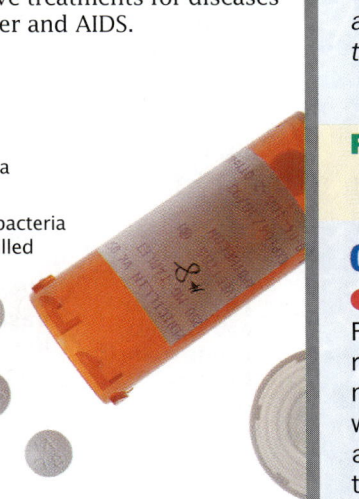

a *Penicillium* with spores

b *Penicillium* killing bacteria in Fleming's original petri dish

Colony of bacteria

Area where bacteria have been killed

Penicillium

c The drug penicillin

SECTION REVIEW

1. Describe four characteristics shared by all fungi.

2. How do fungi obtain nutrients?

3. Compare and contrast the methods of reproduction found in the four groups of fungi.

4. How might life on Earth be different if all fungi were to suddenly disappear from this planet?

379

ANSWERS TO SECTION REVIEW

1. Fungi are eukaryotes, are heterotrophic, have a chitin cell wall, and can be found almost anywhere that moisture and nutrients are available.

2. Fungi secrete enzymes that break down organic matter, which they absorb through the cell walls of their hyphae.

3. The spores of the basidiomycetes are produced in clublike structures, those of the ascomycetes are produced in a saclike structure, and those of zygomycetes are produced in spore-producing stalks. Sexual reproduction is rare or not observed among the deuteromycetes.

4. Answers will vary but may include effects on forest ecosystems, food sources, drug availability, and commercial uses in foods and beverages.

Fungi and Plants 379

Phase One
Preparation

Scheduling
See the **Lesson Planning Guide** on pages 371A and 371B for lecture, classwork, and assignment options for Section 20-2.

Phase Two
Teaching Strategies

Social Studies Connection
Sphagnum Bandages
During World War II in France, nurses ran out of cotton bandages. They discovered that a soft green plant found growing in the water at the edge of a nearby lake made a good substitute. Wounds bandaged with the plant became infected less frequently than those treated with the regular cotton bandages. The plant used was a species of sphagnum moss. This moss is water absorbing and has been shown to have antiseptic properties.

Active READING
Technique: Reading Organizer
Before students begin to read Sections 20-2 and 20-3, explain to them that these sections trace the evolution of plants. Have them survey these sections and identify any subtitles, headings, and captions that signal the topic of discussion. *(Examples include the following: Evolution of Vascular Plants, The first vascular plants did not produce seeds, Ferns were among the first vascular plants to evolve, and Pollen eliminates the need for water in sexual reproduction.)* As students read, ask them to locate other words in the body of the text that signal the sequential pattern.

Plants are another group of mostly terrestrial, multicellular, eukaryotic organisms. We take for granted their presence almost everywhere on Earth. Plants probably evolved from an ancient form of green algae that grew at the edges of bodies of water. These algae invaded the land about 400 million years ago. The successful occupation of the land by plants involved adaptation to dry conditions and cooperation with fungi.

20-2   Early Land Plants

OBJECTIVES

1 Describe the adaptations that enable plants to survive on land.

2 Define alternation of generations.

3 Distinguish nonvascular plants from vascular plants.

4 Relate characteristics of nonvascular and vascular plants to their habitats.

Characteristics of Plants

Plants are photosynthetic, like their ancestors, green algae. Unlike fungi, plants have cells with cell walls made of the polysaccharide cellulose. And unlike both fungi and algae, most plants have bodies made up of many types of cells arranged in tissues.

Before early plants could survive on land, they had to overcome three challenges. First, they had to avoid drying out. Second, they had to reproduce on land. And third, they had to obtain minerals from the rocky surface. Fossil remains of early land plants, such as the one in **Figure 20-7**, show how these challenges were met.

Most plants have vascular tissues
In order to grow very large, a multicellular organism must have a way to distribute water and nutrients to all parts of its body. Like you, plants have a system of internal tubes called **vascular tissue**, which conducts water and other nutrients. Plants that have vascular tissue are called vascular plants. Most of the plants you are familiar with—including roses, houseplants, grasses, oak trees, and ferns—are vascular plants.

a A waterproof, waxy coating *reduced water loss.*

b Spores were produced at the tips of stems. The spores grew if they landed in a spot covered by dew, enabling the plant to *reproduce with very little water.*

c The formation of mycorrhizae with fungi enabled the plant to *absorb minerals from soil.*

Figure 20-7
The early land plant *Rhynia* evolved with features that enabled it to overcome the environmental challenges of life on land. This illustrated reconstruction of *Rhynia* is based on fossil evidence.

380

Videodisc Resources
Holt Biology Videodiscs
Lesson 20-2: Early Land Plants

Figure 20-8
In a plant's life cycle, a haploid gametophyte alternates with a diploid sporophyte.

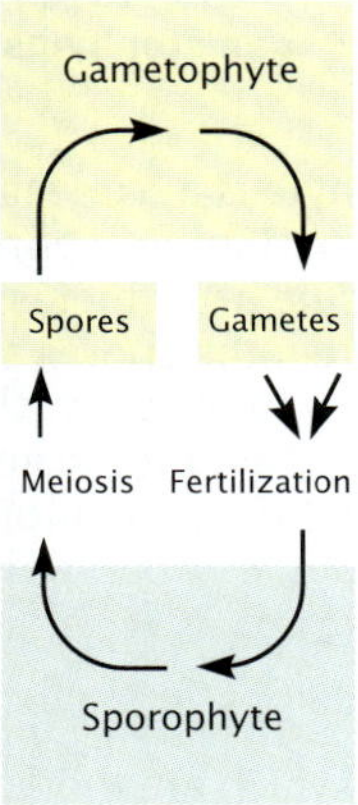

Gametophyte

Spores   Gametes

Meiosis   Fertilization

Sporophyte

However, some small plants, such as mosses, lack vascular tissue. Plants that lack vascular tissue are called nonvascular plants. Nonvascular plants, which live in moist environments, transport water and nutrients by osmosis and diffusion, much as algae do.

Plants have adaptations for survival in dry conditions

The waxy, waterproof layer that covers the surface of most plants is called the **cuticle**. The cuticle helps prevent a plant from drying out by reducing the evaporation of water from leaves and stems. Today, only one group of nonvascular plants lacks a cuticle.

Plants also produce reproductive structures that resist drying. All nonvascular plants and some vascular plants produce spores, tiny drought-resistant structures that can be carried to new locations by wind. Most vascular plants produce **seeds**, plant embryos that are surrounded by protective coats.

Haploid and diploid generations alternate in the plant life cycle

In plants, gametes are produced by a haploid form of the plant called the **gametophyte** (guh MEET uh fyt). When two gametes fuse they produce a diploid form, the **sporophyte** (SPOHR uh fyt). In most plants, this is the form you see. Some of the sporophyte's cells undergo meiosis, producing haploid spores. Each spore then develops into a haploid gametophyte. Thus, in a plant's life cycle, a haploid stage alternates with a diploid stage, as shown in **Figure 20-8**. This cycle is referred to as **alternation of generations**.

Nonvascular Plants

The first successful land plants had no vascular tissue or seeds. Nonvascular plants transport materials by osmosis and diffusion, so they need a large supply of water to survive. Because many of these plants produce sperm that must swim to an egg to fertilize it, they also need a film of water for sexual reproduction. For these reasons, most nonvascular plants—mosses, hornworts, and the liverworts shown in **Figure 20-9**—grow close to the ground in moist, shady environments such as forests and swampy shorelines.

Nonvascular plants are relatively small—nearly all are less than 20 cm (8 in.) tall, and most are less than 2.5 cm (1 in.) tall. Most are anchored by rootlike structures called rhizoids (REYE zoydz). The green, leaflike structures where photosynthesis occurs are only one or two cells thick. In most nonvascular plants, a waxy cuticle protects the upper surfaces of these structures. Water enters through pores on the lower surfaces, which are not covered by a cuticle.

Mosses are the most widespread nonvascular plants. Mosses often grow in dense carpets on forest floors and decaying logs or in cushionlike patches in sidewalk cracks. Most mosses grow in areas of high humidity, although some mosses are extremely drought-resistant.

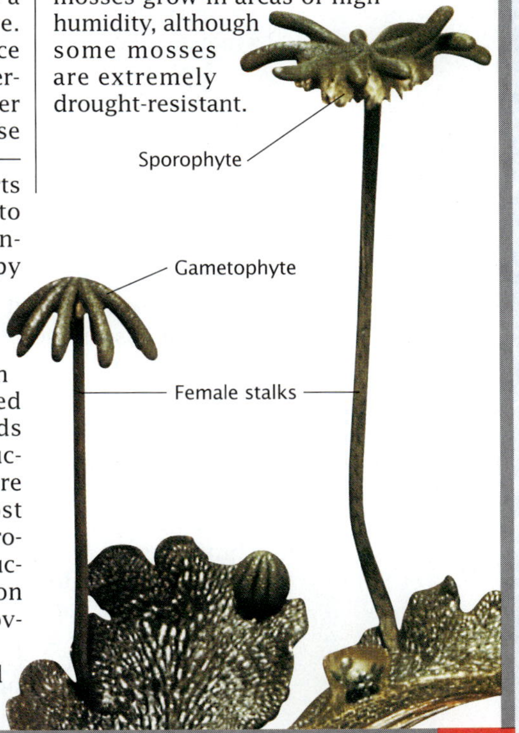

Sporophyte

Gametophyte

Female stalks

Figure 20-9
The gametophyte of the liverwort *Marchantia* produces gametes under separate, 2 cm high stalks. Very tiny sporophytes develop under the female stalks.

381

Terrarium Construction
■ **Relating Concepts**
Have students determine what features make mosses and liverworts suitable for terrarium life (lying close to the ground to absorb water and prevent crowding other inhabitants). Have the class assemble a terrarium to observe these features firsthand. Information about assembling a terrarium can be obtained from reference books or biological supply companies.

Connection: *Chapter 17*

Mistaken Identity
A variety of plantlike organisms are mistakenly called mosses. Examples include Irish moss, Spanish moss, and reindeer moss. Show photos of these examples, and reinforce the concept that common names can be very misleading. Irish moss is a red algae, Spanish moss is a flowering vascular plant, and reindeer moss is a lichen.

Visual Strategy   Videodisc

● **Interpreting Graphics**
Use *Illustration—Alternation of Generations* shown in Chapter 20 Section 20-2 of *Holt Biology Videodiscs Teacher's Correlation Guide to Holt Biology: Visualizing Life.* Have students use the graphic to summarize alternation of generations. Review with students the meaning of *haploid (having only one chromosome of a pair)* and *diploid (having a paired set of chromosomes).* Discuss the importance of spores producing gametophytes that are haploid. (When gametes combine, their haploid number ensures that the resulting sporophyte will have the correct number of chromosomes.)

Historical Perspective: Peat Bogs

Peat bogs that formed during the Carboniferous period were the first step in the formation of coal. The plants that lived in swampy areas died and fell into the boggy waters, where there was little oxygen and few decomposing bacteria. They were later subjected to pressure that caused them to harden and form coal. The major producer of a peat bog is a moss that belongs to the genus *Sphagnum*.

Key to Strategies
● Understanding Concepts (Tier I)
■ Applying Information (Tier II)
▲ Critical Thinking (Tier III)

Sporophyte

Gametophyte

b Moss sporophytes grow at the tips of the "leafy," green gametophytes.

Figure 20-10

a Mosses are often found in a moist, shady environment.

The gametophyte is the dominant form of nonvascular plants

A mat of moss, seen in **Figure 20-10a**, contains many individual plants growing close together. The soft, "leafy," green moss plant that is most familiar to you is the haploid gametophyte, which produces gametes by mitosis. Eggs and sperm form at the tips of separate gametophytes. Sperm have flagella and must swim to eggs. Therefore, to reproduce, mosses need a film of water that sperm can swim through. Fertilization can take place only when moisture covers the gametophytes.

A moss sporophyte grows from a fertilized egg, called a **zygote**. As a sporophyte develops, it takes nutrients from the gametophyte beneath it. A mature moss sporophyte is a bare stalk with a capsule on top. Haploid spores form within the capsule after meiosis. The capsule opens when the spores are mature, and wind carries away the spores. A spore will grow into a new gametophyte if it lands in a moist place. Moss gametophytes and sporophytes are seen in **Figure 20-10b**.

Mosses help form soil

Mosses are pioneers, which are the first organisms to grow in barren areas. Like lichens, mosses grow on bare rock and aid in soil formation. Once soil begins to form, mosses help prevent erosion by covering the soil. This soil enables other plants to become established.

The moss that is most important to humans is *Sphagnum*. Masses of *Sphagnum* form peat, an organic fuel used in Ireland, Canada, Siberia, and other northern regions. *Sphagnum* peat moss is widely used in potting soils and to improve garden soil.

Evolution of Vascular Plants

The more than 250,000 species of ferns, herbs, grasses, shrubs, and trees are vascular plants. These plants have vascular tissue that carries water, minerals, and products of photosynthesis throughout the plant. Vascular tissue enabled vascular plants to be larger and more complex than nonvascular plants. Vascular tissue can even carry nutrients from roots buried deep in the soil to treetops more than 80 m (262 ft) high. Larger size and greater complexity was a huge evolutionary advantage that enabled plants to extend their geographic range.

The first vascular plants did not produce seeds

The earliest vascular plants reproduced with drought-resistant spores instead of seeds. Today, the seedless vascular plants are represented by the club mosses, the horsetails, and the ferns. During the Carboniferous period, about 325 million years ago, club mosses and horsetails grew in dense forests of tall tree ferns that covered much of the land areas on Earth. Seedless vascular plants, such as ferns, still thrive in the tropical and temperate forests.

382

Ferns are the most successful seedless vascular plants

Ferns are by far the most familiar and abundant seedless vascular plants. Ferns have arched leaves called fronds. The fronds grow from thick underground stems with roots. Most ferns live in the moist regions of the tropics. Yet the ferns that inhabit deserts and areas north of the Arctic Circle show that some ferns have adapted to harsher climates.

The sporophyte is the dominant form of vascular plants

Like all vascular plants, ferns have a sporophyte that is much larger and more complex than the gameto-phyte. Spores form on the underside of fronds, in clusters of sporangia that resemble insect eggs. Mature spores are dispersed by wind. If a fern spore lands in a suitable environment, it grows into a fingernail-sized, heart-shaped gametophyte that is anchored to the soil by structures called rhizoids.

The gametophytes of ferns produce gametes in structures located on their lower surfaces. Like the nonvascular plants, ferns need a film of water to enable sperm to swim to eggs. The zygote that forms from the fusion of an egg and a sperm develops into a new sporophyte. As a fern sporophyte grows, it produces tightly coiled, new leaves called fiddleheads. Each fiddlehead unrolls into a frond. **Figure 20-11** shows a fern's life cycle.

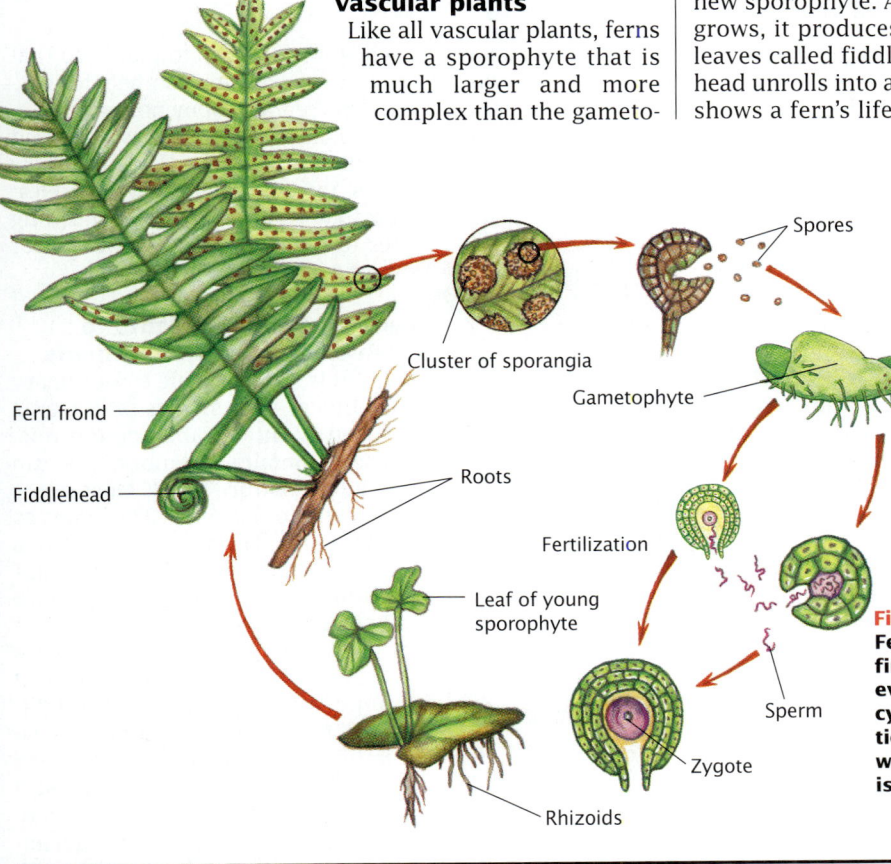

Fern frond
Fiddlehead
Roots
Cluster of sporangia
Gametophyte
Spores
Fertilization
Leaf of young sporophyte
Sperm
Zygote
Rhizoids

Figure 20-11
Ferns were among the first vascular plants to evolve. The fern life cycle involves alternation of generations, in which the sporophyte is the dominant phase.

SECTION REVIEW

1. What adaptations enabled plants to survive on land?

2. How do sporophytes differ from gametophytes?

3. How were vascular plants able to become so successful on land?

4. How do the methods of reproduction used by nonvascular and vascular plants determine the types of environments in which they can live?

383

ANSWERS TO SECTION REVIEW

1. A waxy cuticle, drought-resistant reproductive structures, and seed development have enabled plants to survive on land.

2. Sporophytes are diploid, whereas gametophytes are haploid.

3. These plants have vascular tissue that carries water, minerals, and the products of photosynthesis throughout the plant. This allows for plants to be larger in size compared with the nonvascular plants.

4. Nonvascular plants and vascular plants that reproduce using flagellated sperm must live in a moist environment. Plants that produce seeds do not require moisture.

The evolution of the seed was a critical step in the spread of plants across the land. A seed protects an embryonic plant from drying out. It also stores carbohydrates, fats, and proteins that a rapidly growing young plant uses as a source of energy and as building blocks for growth. Some seeds develop within fruits that help distribute them in a variety of ways.

Scheduling
See the **Lesson Planning Guide** on pages 371A and 371B for lecture, classwork, and assignment options for Section 20-3.

Visual Strategy | **Figure 20-12**

■ **Relating Concepts**
Explain that seeds are adapted for survival in a wide variety of climates. Emphasize that they can survive in a dormant state if conditions are unfavorable for growth. Have students propose an explanation of why seedlings appear after a forest has been destroyed by fire. *(Seeds withstand and often benefit from the high temperature. Fire removes the accumulated litter from the seed coat and in some cases opens the cones to release the seeds.)*

World of Work

Paleobotanist
The branch of paleontology that deals with fossil plants is paleobotany. In 1960, paleobotanists discovered that fossil structures believed to belong to two different plants actually belonged to one plant. Fossils were found that show *Callixylon* (thought to be a gymnosperm) and *Archaeopteris* (thought to be a fern) to be parts of the same plant. A new class of plants, called Progymnospermopsida, resulted. This fossil plant provides scientists with the evolutionary link between ferns and gymnosperms.

20-3 Seed Plants

OBJECTIVES

1 **Explain how the development of seeds enabled plants to be successful in more habitats.**

2 **Summarize the process of reproduction in gymnosperms.**

3 **Describe the role of flowers in the life cycle of angiosperms.**

4 **Identify several important families of angiosperms.**

Vascular Plants With Seeds

Although some early land plants such as ferns had vascular tissue, they were still confined to moist environments. In contrast, the plants with seeds were fully adapted to life on land and were able to live in dry places.

One of the evolutionary achievements of the seed plants is woody tissue, which lends strength to plants so that they can grow tall and compete for sunlight. Another development—more complex vascular tissue—enables water and nutrients to be carried to these new heights. Seed plants also developed features that freed them from needing water to reproduce—pollen, cones or flowers, and seeds.

Seeds enable seed plants to survive in harsh environments
The seed is a remarkable evolutionary development that enables seed plants to survive unfavorable conditions. Each seed contains an embryo that can grow into a mature plant. Most seeds contain stored nutrients. The embryos of flowering plants have structures called **cotyledons** *(kaht uh LEED uhnz)*. Cotyledons store food or help absorb food stored elsewhere in the seed.

A hard outer seed coat surrounds the embryo in a seed, protecting it from physical injury and drought. Because the seed coat provides protection from harsh conditions, a seed can lie dormant for years and still grow into a healthy plant when conditions improve. When a seed germinates (cracks open and starts to grow), the embryo first develops into a **seedling**, as shown in **Figure 20-12**.

Seeds may also help carry young plants away from their parents. For example, some seeds have hooks, feathery projections, or winglike projections that enable them to travel long distances on animals or with the wind.

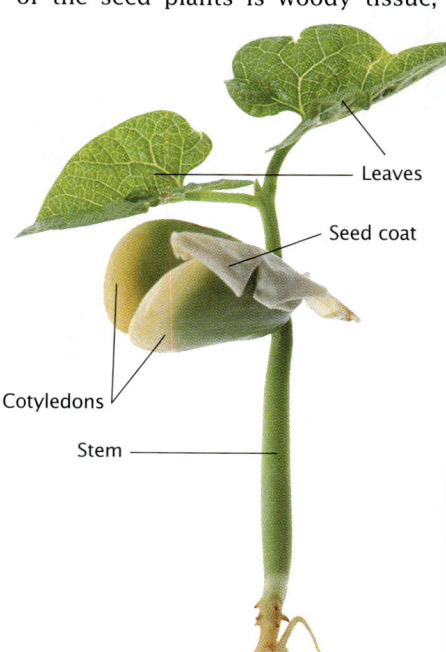

Leaves

Seed coat

Cotyledons

Stem

Roots

Figure 20-12
This bean seedling has just emerged from a seed. A seed is a storage container that houses a plant embryo. A tough outer seed coat protects the embryo from drying out. Food is stored in the cotyledons.

384

Videodisc Resources

Holt Biology Videodiscs
Lesson 23-3: Seed Plants

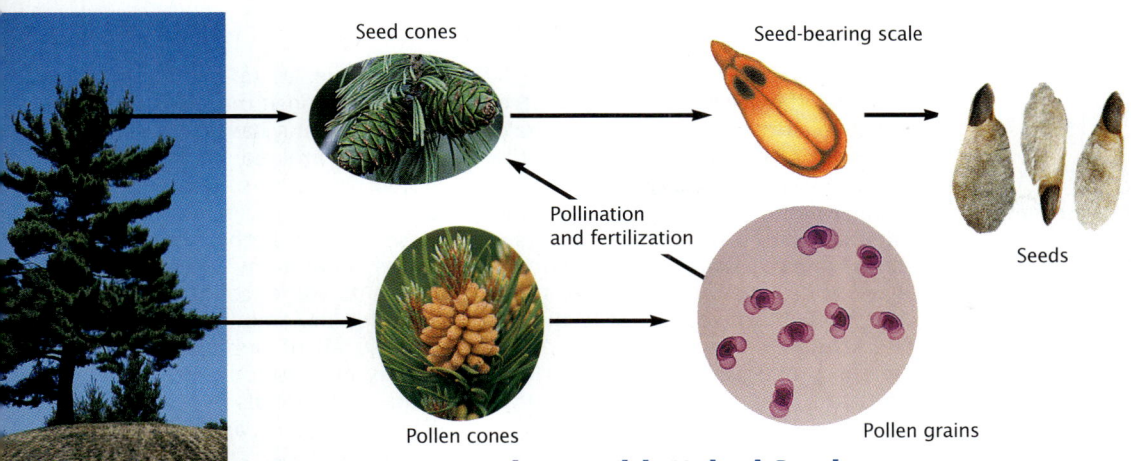

Seed cones   Seed-bearing scale

Pollination and fertilization

Seeds

Pollen cones   Pollen grains

Gymnosperms: Plants With Naked Seeds

Figure 20-13
A pine tree is a gymnosperm that produces both pollen cones and seed cones. After pollination, new seeds are formed and fall to the ground. There, they germinate to form a new tree.

Pine tree

Gymnosperms were among the first seed plants. The word *gymnosperm* combines the Greek words for "naked" and "seed." **Gymnosperms** (*JIHM noh spurmz*) are plants with seeds that do not develop within a fruit. The seeds of most gymnosperms form in **cones**, which are clusters of scales or modified leaves. Egg-bearing structures form on the surfaces of scales.

Most familiar gymnosperms—firs, junipers, pines, and spruces—are conifers (trees that produce seeds in cones). The redwoods of California and the bald cypresses in Southern swamps are also conifers. A conifer that grows in Nevada—a 5,000-year-old bristlecone pine—may be the world's oldest tree. Another conifer—a giant sequoia that grows in California and is named for General Sherman of the Civil War—is the world's biggest tree. This tree is more than 84 m (276 ft) tall and 31 m (102 ft) around its base. The palmlike cycads of the tropical climates and the ginkgo trees growing along city streets are also gymnosperms, but they are not conifers and do not produce cones.

Pollen eliminates the need for water in sexual reproduction

Unlike earlier plants, gymnosperms have an innovation that enables sperm to reach the eggs without swimming— pollen. **Pollen grains** are tiny male gametophytes that are portable, unlike the gametophytes of earlier plants.

Conifers produce two types of cones—female (seed) cones and male (pollen) cones. Each type of cone produces a different kind of spore by meiosis. The spores produced by female cones develop into female gametophytes, each of which contains an egg. The spores produced by male cones develop into pollen grains, each of which contains a sperm.

Gymnosperms are wind pollinated

Gymnosperms produce huge quantities of pollen. A pair of air sacs helps each pollen grain drift on the wind. Pollen grains often settle on the surface of ponds and lakes, where they form a sticky yellow layer. A few pollen grains settle onto the scales of female cones. The transfer of pollen from where it is produced to where the eggs are located is called **pollination**. Wind pollination is the transfer of pollen by the wind.

Within a female cone, a pollen grain completes its development and grows a slender tube that will deliver a sperm to a female gametophyte. Fertilization occurs when the sperm fuses with an egg, forming a zygote. The zygote becomes the embryo of a seed. Most pine seeds have thin, flat wings, which help catch air currents that carry the seeds to new areas. When conditions are favorable, the seeds will sprout. Reproduction in gymnosperms is summarized in **Figure 20-13**.

385

Matter of Fact: Old Trees

The bristlecone pines are the world's oldest living organisms. They are found in the White Mountains of eastern California and in the Snake Range on the central Nevada-Utah border. The standing trees are about 4,600 years old. The oldest, which was 4,900 years old, was cut down in 1964.

This Land
● **Organizing Information**
Provide each student with a back issue of *Natural History.* Have students read the regular feature "This Land." Then have them write a report about the plants discussed in the article. Reports should include descriptions of the plants' adaptations, drawings of the plants, and a map indicating the location of the plants' habitats.

Plant Survival
● **Identifying Variables**
Read aloud a few excerpts from *Plant Survival: Adapting to a Hostile World,* by Brian Capon. Students will learn about interesting adaptations that enable these plants to meet various environmental challenges. Have students discuss adaptations that have allowed plants to survive the intense heat and drought of deserts, freezing temperatures of the Arctic, and changing seasons of the northern forests.

Key to Strategies
● Understanding Concepts (Tier I)
■ Applying Information (Tier II)
▲ Critical Thinking (Tier III)

Theme Answer
Evolution
The fact that both gymnosperms and angiosperms produce seeds, have similar life cycles, and carry on pollination suggests a close evolutionary relationship.

Visual Strategy | Videodisc

■ Relating Concepts

To compare reproduction in mosses, ferns, gymnosperms, and angiosperms, use *Video—Plant Reproduction* (5 min) shown in Chapter 20 Section 20-3 of **Holt Biology Videodiscs Teacher's Correlation Guide to Holt Biology: Visualizing Life.** As students view the video, point out the evolutionary developments of flowering plants. After viewing the video, have students make a two-column chart stating the adaptation in one column and its advantage in the other.

Phase Three
Assessment Options

Closure
■ Relating Concepts
Have students use the following Active Reading strategy to review what they have learned.

Active READING

Technique: Anticipation Guide
Ask volunteers to discuss how their opinions formed in the Active Reading exercise on page 372 changed or stayed the same as a result of their reading. Students should point to specific passages in the text that support their reasoning.

SECTION REVIEW
Assign the *Section Review.*

Reteaching
Have students construct a crossword puzzle using the terms presented in this chapter.

Angiosperms: Flowering Plants

Evolution

What traits shared by angiosperms and gymnosperms suggest a close evolutionary relationship?

When you think of plants, you usually think of the seed plants that evolved most recently—angiosperms (*AN jee oh spurmz*). **Angiosperms** are plants that have flowers, which help ensure the transfer of sperm to eggs. The colors, shapes, and aromas of the flowers of many angiosperms attract particular insects, birds, or other animals, which carry pollen from one plant to another.

In contrast to gymnosperms, angiosperms produce seeds that are enclosed in fruits. Fruits protect seeds as they develop and also help disperse them.

For example, an animal that eats fruit may later deposit the seeds elsewhere.

Angiosperms have been extremely successful on land. Of the more than 250,000 species of vascular plants, about 235,000 species are angiosperms. These include herbs, grasses, vines, shrubs, and many trees—nearly all the plants you encounter daily. Some examples are shown in **Table 20-2.** Virtually all of our food is derived, directly or indirectly, from flowering plants. They are also valuable sources of timber, textiles, and medicines.

Table 20-2 Economically Important Families of Angiosperms

Families	Familiar examples
Liliaceae (lily)	daylily, tulip, asparagus, aloe vera
Poaceae (grass)	wheat, corn, rice, lawn grass
Lamiaceae (mint)	mint, rosemary, sage, coleus
Rosaceae (rose)	roses, apple, peach, plum
Fabaceae (legume)	beans, peas, peanut, acacias
Asteraceae (composite)	daisies, sunflowers, lettuce
Brassicaceae (mustard)	broccoli, turnip, cabbage

SECTION REVIEW

1 How do seeds enable plants to survive in the harsh environments of deserts and tundras?

2 How do the male gametes of gymnosperms reach the female gametes?

3 How do you think a flower that is wind pollinated might differ from a flower that is pollinated by insects?

4 What do the grass family and the legume family have in common?

ANSWERS TO SECTION REVIEW

1 The seed protects the plant embryo from these harsh conditions. The embryo inside can lie dormant and later grow into a healthy plant when conditions become more favorable.

2 After pollination, the male gametophyte grows a slender tube to deliver the sperm cell to the female gametophyte so that fertilization can occur.

3 A flower that is pollinated by insects will be brightly colored or fragrant, or both. A flower that is pollinated by the wind might be positioned on a tall slender stalk or high in a tree, where there is wind exposure.

4 Both are economically important as food sources.

CHAPTER

20 Highlights

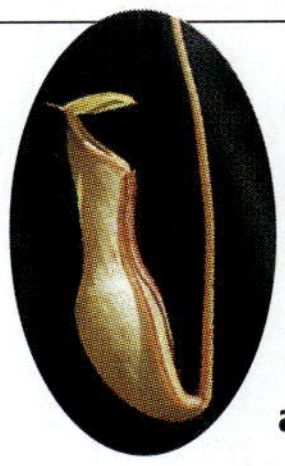

This pitcher plant is a vascular plant that traps insects within its leaves. Enzymes break down an insect's tissues, and the plant absorbs its nutrients.

	Key Terms	Summary
20-1 Fungi 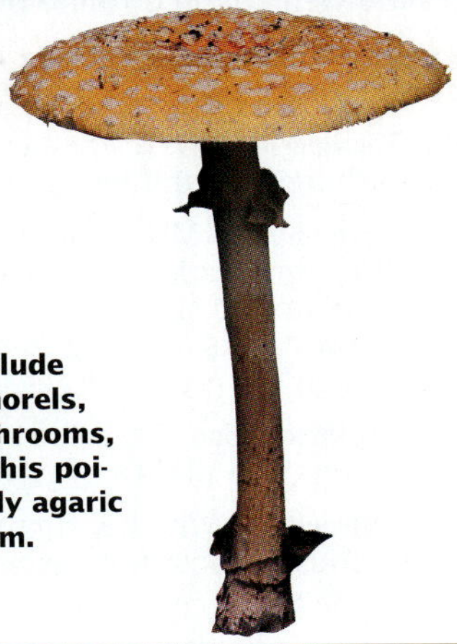 Fungi include molds, morels, and mushrooms, such as this poisonous fly agaric mushroom.	hypha (p. 374) mycelium (p. 374) chitin (p. 374) spore (p. 375) lichen (p. 378)	• Fungi are eukaryotic organisms made up of slender filaments called hyphae. Their cells have cell walls that contain chitin. • Fungi secrete enzymes that digest food outside their bodies, and then they absorb the nutrients. • Fungi are classified into three groups based on their sexual reproductive structures. Some fungi display no evidence of sexual reproduction and are placed into a fourth group. • While many fungi spoil food and cause disease, some are helpful to humans.
20-2 Early Land Plants 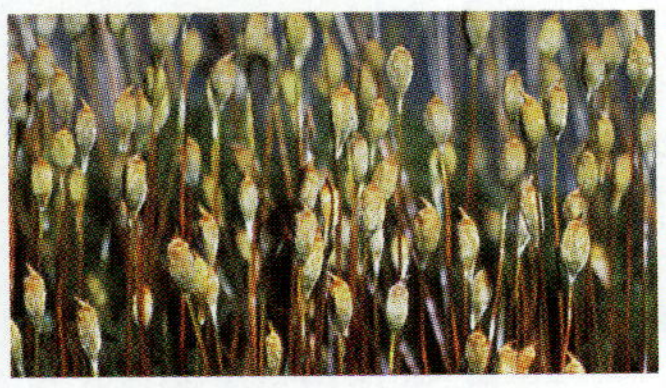 Mosses are the most widespread nonvascular plants. The mosses shown here are pioneers, which help break down bare rock into soil.	vascular tissue (p. 380) cuticle (p. 381) seed (p. 381) gametophyte (p. 381) sporophyte (p. 381) alternation of generations (p. 381) zygote (p. 382)	• Land plants have certain adaptations that enable them to live in a dry environment. These adaptations reduce water loss, move water and nutrients throughout the plant, and enable plants to reproduce in dry environments. • Land plants have a life cycle that involves alternation of generations between a haploid gametophyte and a diploid sporophyte. • Mosses and ferns, like their ancestors, the early land plants, are able to reproduce only when water is available for their sperm to swim through.
20-3 Seed Plants 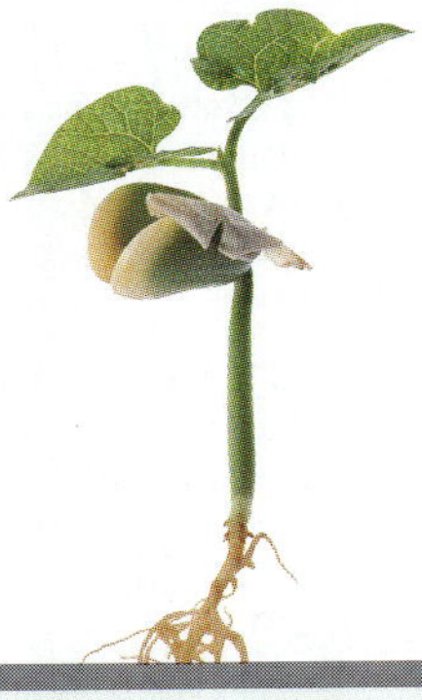 Angiosperms are the most recently evolved of the land plants. They are unique in that they produce flowers and fruits.	cotyledon (p. 384) seedling (p. 384) gymnosperm (p. 385) cone (p. 385) pollen grain (p. 385) pollination (p. 385) angiosperm (p. 386)	• Seed plants are able to reproduce without water for sperm to swim through. Seeds can survive for long periods of time in unfavorable environments. • Gymnosperms are seed plants that do not produce seeds within fruits. Most form seeds in cones. • Angiosperms are seed plants that have flowers and produce seeds within fruits.

387

Highlights 20 chapter

Alternative Assessment

Have students use the information in Chapter 20 to design a procedure for a question-and-answer game. Students may choose to model their game after a television game show or a trivia-type board game. Encourage students to write questions that vary in level of difficulty.

Portfolio Assessment

Portfolio Assessment on page T39 provides options for building and evaluating student portfolios. Students and teachers can select items from the areas listed on page T39 for inclusion in a portfolio.

ANSWER TO CONCEPT MAP

The following is one possible answer to the Relating Concepts exercise on page 388.

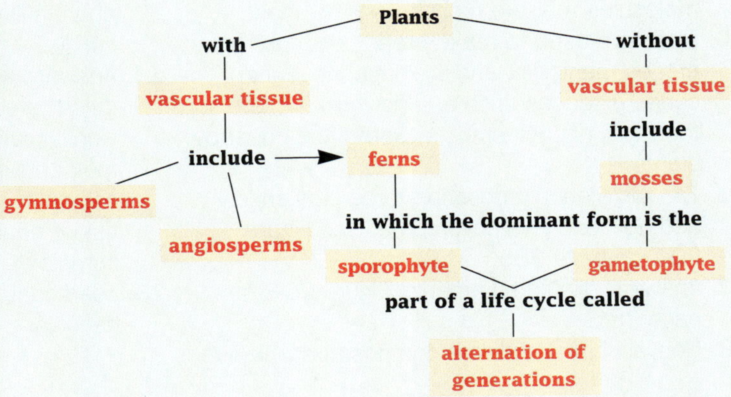

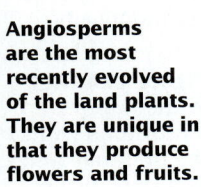

review

Understanding Vocabulary

1. a. autotroph
   b. sporophyte
   c. flower
2. a. Hyphae are the filaments that make up the body of a fungus. A mycelium is a tangled mass of branched hyphae.
   b. A mycorrhiza is a symbiotic relationship between fungi and plants, whereas a lichen is a symbiotic relationship between a fungus and either a green alga or a cyanobacterium.
   c. Nonvascular tissue uses osmosis and diffusion to transport materials; vascular tissue uses an internal system of interconnected tubes and vessels to transport materials throughout the plant.

Understanding Concepts

3. Answer to concept map is shown on page 387.
4. Most fungi have the following characteristics: multicellular, heterotrophs, lack chlorophyll, bodies made up of hyphae, cell walls of chitin, external digestion, reproduce by spores.
5. Fungi are "rooted" to the ground. Fungi are heterotrophs, lack chlorophyll, lack differentiation except among the reproductive cells, have cell walls of chitin not cellulose, and do not have alternation of generations.
6. Answers should summarize Table 20-1 on page 376.
7. Hyphae secrete enzymes that break down organic matter. The hyphae then absorb the nutrients.
8. Fungal spores can withstand dry conditions and a wide range of temperatures, they are light and easily carried by air currents or are sticky and cling to animals for transport, and they grow rapidly.
9. A lichen is the symbiotic relationship between a fungus and either a green alga or a cyanobacterium. The fungus absorbs water and nutrients. The alga uses the nutrients for photosynthesis to produce organic

Understanding Vocabulary

1. For each set of terms, complete the analogy.
   a. fungus : heterotroph :: plant : _____
   b. gamete-forming plant : gametophyte :: spore-forming plant : _____
   c. gymnosperms : cone :: angiosperms : _____

2. For each pair of terms, explain the difference in their meanings.
   a. hypha, mycelium
   b. mycorrhiza, lichen
   c. nonvascular, vascular

Understanding Concepts

3. 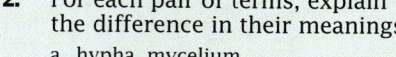 **Relating Concepts** Construct a concept map that differentiates between nonvascular and vascular plants. Try to include the following terms in your concept map: vascular tissue, gymnosperms, angiosperms, mosses, ferns, sporophyte, gametophyte, alternation of generations.

4. **Summarizing Information** What characteristics are shared by most fungi?

5. **Summarizing Information** Explain why fungi were once considered plants. What features distinguish fungi from plants?

6. **Identifying Structures** Identify the major group of fungi represented by each fungus below, and describe how each reproduces.

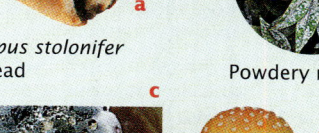

Rhizopus stolonifer on bread
a

Powdery mildew
b

c

d

Penicillium sp.

Amanita muscaria mushroom

7. **Describing Processes** Describe how fungi obtain nutrients.
8. **Inferring Relationships** Explain why fungal spores are well adapted to life on land.
9. **Recognizing Relationships** Describe the relationship that occurs in a lichen.
10. **Inferring Relationships** Describe how fungi can be both helpful and harmful to you.
11. **Organizing Information** Make a table in which you identify three challenges that plants had to overcome to survive on land, and describe how plants adapted to meet each challenge.
12. **Summarizing Information** Describe alternation of generations in a plant's life cycle.
13. **Identifying Structures** Which structures are characteristics of most nonvascular plants, such as mosses?
14. **Inferring Relationships** Differentiate between vascular and nonvascular plants in terms of size and transportation of water and nutrients. Relate the characteristics of each group to how successful the group is on land.
15. **Identifying Structures and Functions** List the three main parts of a seed, and describe the function of each part.
16. **Recognizing Relationships** How did seeds enable the seed plants to become so successful on land?
17. **Summarizing Information** Describe the process of reproduction in gymnosperms.
18. **Comparing Processes** Describe the ways in which gymnosperms and angiosperms distribute pollen. Which method of pollen distribution is more efficient?
19. **Summarizing Information** Identify at least three economically important families of angiosperms. Name a member of each family, and explain why it is economically important.
20. **BUILDING ON WHAT YOU HAVE LEARNED** In Chapter 14 you learned the importance of recycling minerals and nutrients within an ecosystem. Describe the role that fungi play in the recycling of materials in the environment.

molecules that the fungus uses for food.
10. Fungi are used to make bread, alcoholic beverages, penicillin, and cyclosporine. Fungi cause diseases such as ringworm, athlete's foot, and histoplasmosis. Some fungi destroy plants.
11. The table should describe three challenges and how each was overcome. See Figure 20-7 on page 380.
12. Answers should summarize Figure 20-8 on page 381.
13. Nonvascular plants are composed of rhizoids

and leaflike structures covered by a waxy cuticle.
14. Answers will vary but should include distinguishing characteristics of each type of plant. Nonvascular plants are small and grow in moist environments. Vascular plants are successful in dry environments. Their vascular tissue enables them to be larger and more complex.
15. seed coat protects embryo, embryo becomes new plant, cotyledon provides nutrients

review

Interpreting Graphics

21. Study the diagram below, and answer the following questions.
    a. What process is shown at A?
    b. What structures are produced at B?
    c. What structures are produced at C?
    d. What process takes place at D?
    e. Which plant in the life cycle is haploid?
    f. Which plant in the life cycle is diploid?

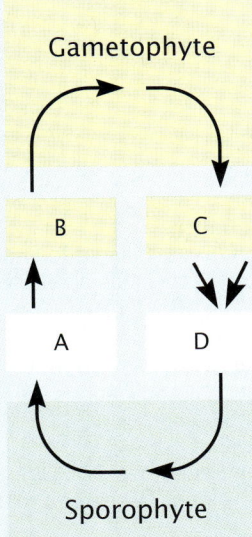

Gametophyte

B

C

A

D

Sporophyte

Reviewing Themes

22. **Heredity**
    Both gymnosperms and angiosperms require pollination. What, specifically, is accomplished by pollination? How is this event important to the reproduction of gymnosperms and angiosperms?

23. **Matter, Energy, and Organization**
    What energy source is used by the embryo in a seed before photosynthesis begins in the new plant?

Thinking Critically

24. **Predicting Outcomes** You want to grow some wildflower seeds that you have collected from the roadside. Why do you think including some of the soil from the original habitat is important to the survival of the plants that grow from the seeds?

Life/Work Skills

25. **Finding Information** Use library references or search an on-line database to find out about the importance of fungi as food or in the preparation or manufacture of food. You may want to investigate mushrooms eaten as food, fungi used to produce certain types of cheeses and soy sauce, fungi used in baking bread, and fungi used to produce wine. Summarize your findings in an oral report to the class.

26. **Communicating** Investigate the history and use of coal. How and when was coal formed? When did people first begin to use coal? Is coal still being formed today? Create a series of posters to summarize your findings for your classmates.

Activities and Projects

27. **Career Connection: Agriculture** Mushroom growers grow mushrooms to be sold as food in stores and restaurants. Some mushroom growers have large farms where they produce several kinds of common mushrooms. Other growers have small farms where they grow exotic or gourmet mushrooms on a small scale. Use library references or write to the Mushroom Growers Association, at 18 South Water Market, Chicago, IL 60608, to find out the kind of education and equipment necessary to become a mushroom grower.

28. **History/Economics Connection** Coniferous trees (gymnosperms) are among the oldest living organisms on Earth. The western parts of North America are home to some of the oldest and largest of these trees. Use library references or search an on-line database to find out about the historical distribution, age, size, and economic importance of trees such as pinyon pine, redwood, spruce, juniper, Douglas fir, and lodgepole pine. Prepare an oral and visual report of your findings to share with your class.

Discovering Through Reading

29. Read the article "A New Gold Rush Packs the Woods in Central Oregon" by Mike Pipske in *Smithsonian*, January 1994, pages 35–45. What are the causes of the "mushroom war"?

Reviewing Themes

22. The male gametophyte, the pollen grain, is transferred to the female gametophyte, where it delivers a sperm to the egg. Pollination results in the formation of seeds.
23. food stored in cotyledons

Thinking Critically

24. Mycorrhizae may help the plants thrive.

Life/Work Skills

25. Reports will vary but should include a variety of uses for fungi in the food industry.
26. Posters will vary but should include various facts about the use and history of coal.

Activities and Projects

27. Answers will vary depending on sources. Mushroom growers need to have a basic understanding of soil science and mycology.
28. Reports will vary but should discuss the history and distribution of the conifers.

Discovering Through Reading

29. Answers will vary but should include the environmental and economic controversy discussed in the article.

16. The seed provides food and protection for the embryo. Some seeds have special features that enable them to be transported to new habitats.
17. Answers will vary but should outline the steps in Figure 20-13 on page 385.
18. In gymnosperms, pollen is moved by wind, whereas animals transfer pollen in many angiosperms. Movement by animals is more efficient.
19. Answers will vary but should include the economic importance of three families from Table 20-2 on page 386.
20. They break down wastes and release nutrients.

Interpreting Graphics

21. a. meiosis
    b. spores
    c. gametes
    d. fertilization
    e. gametophyte
    f. sporophyte

Lesson Planning Guide With Options for Block Scheduling

Lecture Concepts	Lesson Resources

21-1 The Plant Body

BLOCK ❶ (45 minutes)

1. Roots anchor the plant in the soil and absorb water and minerals from the soil.

2. Shoots consist of stems and leaves. Stems support growth above ground and transport water and food between roots and leaves. Leaves are the primary sites of photosynthesis.

3. Plants consist of three types of tissue: vascular, ground, and dermal.

❶ Lecture Resources
- Determining Prior Knowledge
- Stomata
- Active Reading: K-W-L
- Visual Strategy: Figure 21-2
- Visual Strategy: Videodisc
- Demonstration: Recognizing Relationships
- Teaching Transparencies 119, 122, 116A, 117A, 118A, 119A, 120A
- Holt Videodiscs Lesson 21-1

Classwork Options
- Life/Work Skills: Being a Team Member
- Laboratory Techniques and Experimental Design: Lab C35

Assignment Options
- Teaching Resources CD-ROM: Occupational Applications Worksheets 3
- Teaching Resources CD-ROM: Portfolio Projects 2
- Teaching Resources CD-ROM: Portfolio Projects—Plant Research Project

BLOCK ❷ (45 minutes)

4. Vascular tissue is composed of xylem and phloem. Xylem transports water and minerals. Phloem transports sugar and other organic molecules.

5. Plants grow at regions of active cell divisions, called meristems.

6. There are two types of flowering plants: monocots and dicots.

❷ Lecture Resources
- Growth Rings
- Active Reading: Reading Organizer
- Demonstration: Identifying Functions
- Teaching Transparencies: 120, 121, 123, 124, 125
- Holt Biology Videodiscs Lesson 21-1

Classwork Options
- Closure: Summarizing Information

- Exploration 21A

Assignment Options
- Reteaching
- Section Review
- Chapter Review, questions 1a, 2a, 4, 5, 6, 7, 18, 26, 28
- Directed Reading Worksheet

21-2 How Plants Function

BLOCK ❸ (45 minutes)

1. Water moving in plants results from capillary action and the pull created by transpiration.

2. The transport of nutrients within phloem tissue is known as translocation.

❸ Lecture Resources
- Visual Strategy: Videodisc
- Teaching Transparencies: 126, 127
- Holt Biology Videodiscs Lesson 21-2

Classwork Options
- Inquiry Skills Development: Lab B17

Assignment Options
- Translocation and Transpiration

BLOCK ❹ (45 minutes)

3. Auxins affect growth in plant stems, gibberellin stimulates stem growth and causes some kinds of plants to sprout and flower, and ethylene causes fruits to ripen.

4. Temperature and length of darkness affect the growth and development of plants.

❹ Lecture Resources
- Visual Strategy: Videodisc
- Teaching Transparencies: 129, 130
- Holt Biology Videodiscs Lesson 21-2

Classwork Options
- Closure: Relating Concepts

Assignment Options
- *Small Group* Reteaching
- Section Review
- Chapter Review, questions 1b, 2b, 3, 8, 9, 10, 12, 19, 25
- Directed Reading Worksheet

21-3 Reproduction in Flowering Plants

BLOCK ❺ (45 minutes)

1. Flowers are the reproductive organs of the angiosperms. The stamen is the male part of the flower, and the pistil is the female part.

2. Pollination occurs when pollen is transferred to the pistil. Fertilization occurs when a sperm cell fuses with an egg cell. Pollination is necessary for fertilization to occur.

❺ Lecture Resources
- Active Reading: Paired Reading
- Rhizomes and Bulbs
- Visual Strategy: Figure 21-7
- Demonstration: Identifying Structures
- Teaching Transparencies: 116, 128
- Holt Biology Videodiscs Lesson 21-3

Classwork Options
- Inquiry Skills Development: Lab B15

Assignment Options
- World of Work: Botanist
- Life/Work Skills: Allocating Resources

Lecture Concepts   Lesson Resources

21-3 Reproduction in Flowering Plants, *continued*

BLOCK 6 (45 minutes)

3. In double fertilization, one sperm cell fuses with an egg cell to form the embryo, and a second sperm cell fuses with two nuclei to form nutritive tissue for the embryo.

4. After fertilization, the flower's ovary becomes the plant's fruit, and the ovule becomes the seed.

6 Lecture Resources
■ Time to Flower
■ Active Reading: K-W-L
■ Seed Dispersal
■ Visual Strategy: Figure 21-8c, 21-10
■ Demonstration: Comparing Structures
▯ Teaching Transparencies: 131, 132
⊘ Holt Biology Videodiscs Lesson 21-3
Classwork Options
■ Closure: Relating Concepts

▲ Inquiry Skills Development: Lab B16

Assignment Options
■ Reteaching
■ Section Review
■ Chapter Review, questions 1c, 2c, 11, 14, 15, 16, 17, 20, 21, 22, 23, 24, 27, 29
■ Directed Reading Worksheet

Chapter Review and Assessment

BLOCK 7 (45 minutes)
Review
■ Reteaching Worksheet
■ Thinking Skills Worksheet
■ Vocabulary Development Worksheet
⊙ Language Development and Reading Comprehension Audio CD Program: Chapter 21

BLOCK 8 (45 minutes)
Assessment
■ Alternative Assessment, p. 407
■ Portfolio Assessment, p. T39
Chapter Test
■ Chapter 21 Test
Test Generator
⊙ Item bank for customizing Chapter Tests

Teaching Resources CD-ROM
⊙ Scoring Rubrics and Classroom Management Checklist

The Portfolio icon denotes items throughout the Teacher's Edition lesson wrap that may be selected for inclusion in student portfolios.

Holt Biology Videodiscs and *Concepts of Biology*

Holt Biology Videodiscs gives you a powerful tool for teaching, review, and assessment. For further information regarding the media on the videodiscs, see **Holt Biology Videodiscs Teacher's Correlation Guide to Holt Biology: Visualizing Life.**

Concepts of Biology adds interactive lesson plans and extensive tools for customization using CD-ROM technology.

Use the following topic from **Concepts of Biology** to help you teach this chapter:
Topic 16: Plant Structure and Function

Laboratory Planning

Text

Materials and preparation instructions appear on the teacher's wrap accompanying each laboratory exercise.
Block 6: Exploration 21A: Altering Plant Growth With a Hormone, p. 798

Holt BioSources Laboratory Program

Block 1: Laboratory Techniques and Experimental Design Lab C35: Staining and Mounting Stem Cross-Sections
Block 3: Inquiry Skills Development Lab B17: Transpiration and Stem Structure
Block 5: Inquiry Skills Development Lab B15: Flower Structures
Block 6: Inquiry Skills Development Lab B16: Fruits and Seeds

Determining Prior Knowledge

- Have students state the function of the root, stem, and leaf of a plant.
- Have students explain the difference between pollination and fertilization.
- Display pictures of a variety of fruits and vegetables. Have students locate the seeds.
- Have students state some ways in which seeds might be dispersed.
- Have students explain where the fruit develops in a flowering plant. Have them explain the purpose of a fruit.

Active READING

Technique: K-W-L

Before students read this chapter, have them write short individual lists of all the things they already **K**now (or that they have heard or read) about plant growth and reproduction. Then have students list things they **W**ant to know about plant growth and reproduction. Have students save their lists for later use in Active Reading on page 406.

CD-ROM Resources

Concepts of Biology
Topic 16: Plant Structure and Function

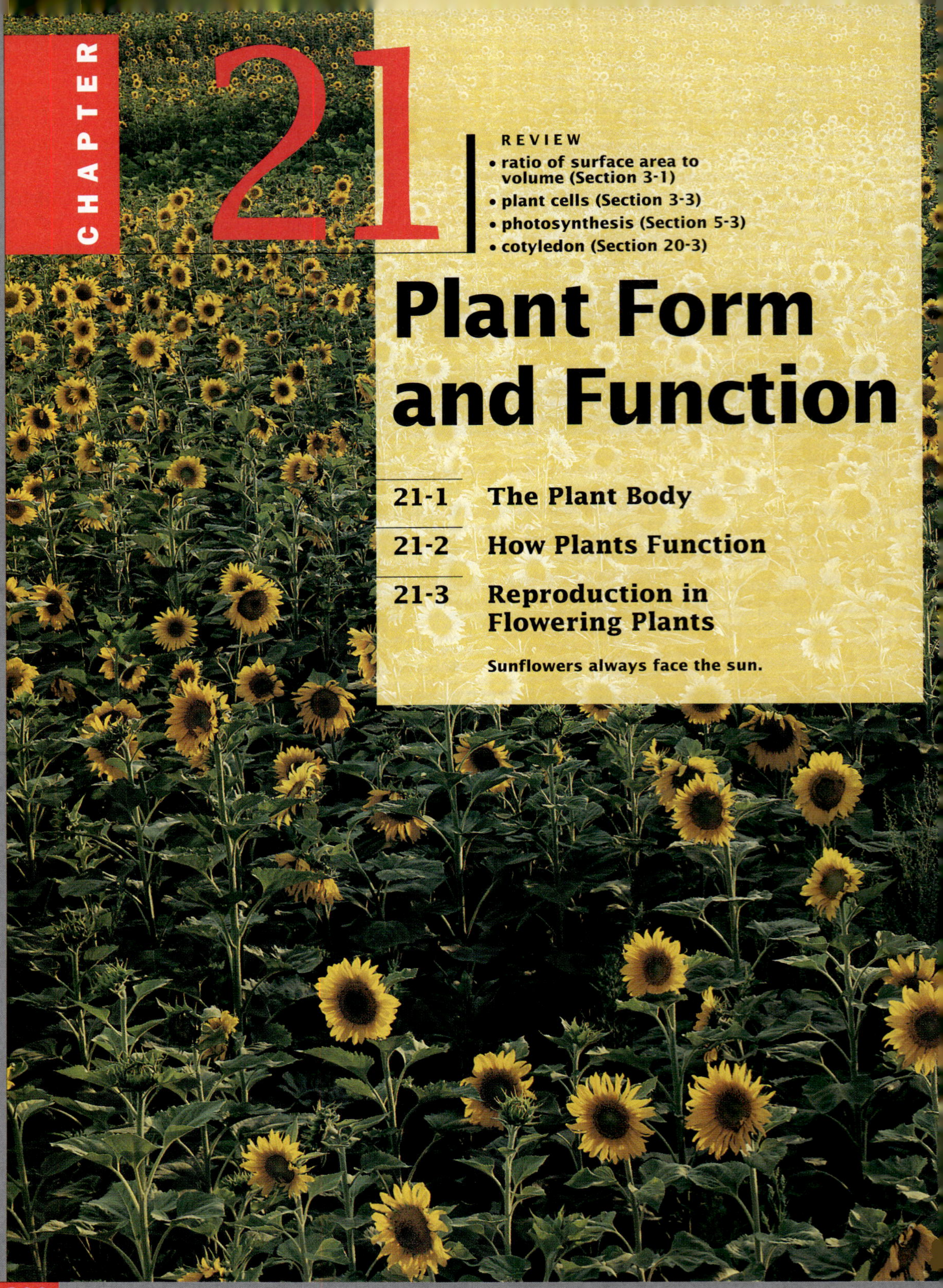

REVIEW
- ratio of surface area to volume (Section 3-1)
- plant cells (Section 3-3)
- photosynthesis (Section 5-3)
- cotyledon (Section 20-3)

Plant Form and Function

21-1	**The Plant Body**
21-2	**How Plants Function**
21-3	**Reproduction in Flowering Plants**

Sunflowers always face the sun.

Author's Rationale   This chapter is an overview of plant biology—how a plant's body is organized and how it works. Emphasis is placed on four key activities of plants: growth, photosynthesis, material transport, and reproduction. Structural details are de-emphasized so that you can focus your instruction on these plant processes. The coverage of each of the four plant activities, in effect, describes the organization of the plant body. These activities are splendid examples of structure dictating function.

A plant cannot move about and capture food as an animal can. Instead, a plant's structure enables it to obtain nutrients from its environment. Most vascular plants consist of roots, stems, and leaves. Roots anchor plants and absorb water and minerals. Stems hold leaves high, enabling them to capture light energy and to take in carbon dioxide that is used during photosynthesis.

21-1 The Plant Body

OBJECTIVES

1 Describe the structures and functions of roots and shoots.

2 Compare and contrast vascular tissue, ground tissue, and dermal tissue.

3 Describe the role of meristems in plant growth.

4 Distinguish between monocots and dicots.

Figure 21-1
This radish seedling's root has many root hairs, which greatly increase its surface area for absorption. A root cap protects the root tip, which contains a region of actively dividing cells called a meristem.

Roots

When a seed germinates, the first part of the seedling (young plant) to start growing is the root. **Figure 21-1** shows the root of a radish seedling. Roots are usually an underground part of a plant. They anchor the plant and absorb water and minerals from the soil. The roots of most plants grow no deeper than about 5 m (16 ft). However, the roots of some plants are very long. For example, mesquite trees have roots that can grow to more than 50 m (164 ft) long. Roots make up about one-third of the dry mass of a plant.

The roots of some plants have specialized functions

Roots often store nutrients. For example, carrots and sweet potatoes have roots that store large amounts of carbohydrates. Some plants have above-ground roots such as prop roots or aerial roots. Prop roots give additional support to plants such as corn. Aerial roots fasten plants such as orchids to trees and absorb water and minerals from the air and surrounding surfaces.

Roots grow from their tips

A thimble-like cluster of cells called the **root cap** covers and protects the tip of a root. Cell division within the root tip causes roots to grow from their tips. As a root grows longer, the outer cells of the root cap are sloughed off and replaced by new cells from underneath.

In most roots, the region above the root cap has many slender projections called **root hairs**. Root hairs are so tiny that they can penetrate the spaces between soil particles to obtain water and minerals. Each root hair is a projection from a single cell. Root hairs greatly increase the surface area of a root.

Root hairs

Meristem

Root cap

391

Videodisc Resources

Holt Biology Videodiscs
Lesson 21-1: The Plant Body

Phase One
Preparation

Scheduling
See the **Lesson Planning Guide** on pages 389A and 389B for lecture, classwork, and assignment options for Section 21-1.

Phase Two
Teaching Strategies

Active READING

Technique: Reading Organizer
Before students read Section 21-1, have them survey the subtitles, headings, captions, and words in boldface type. Ask students to identify the purpose of this section of the chapter. *(The purpose of this section is to describe the three major parts of the plant body: roots, shoots, and plant tissues.)* As students read Section 21-1, have them work individually or in small groups to create a descriptive reading organizer.

Demonstration

■ **Recognizing Relationships**
Germinate some radish seeds in a petri dish lined with filter paper about two days prior to starting this section. Have students view the root hairs using a stereomicroscope. Explain that root hairs are thin enough to grow between soil particles and absorb water and minerals, while the thicker roots anchor the plant.

Key to Strategies
Teaching Strategies are keyed to three tiers of learning.

● **Understanding Concepts (Tier I)**
Content mastery and comprehension

■ **Applying Information (Tier II)**
Applying and analyzing content

▲ **Critical Thinking (Tier III)**
Practicing evaluative thinking

Life/Work Skills
Being a Team Member

■ **Analyzing Information**

Divide the class into three groups. Assign one group the name "Roots," another "Stems," and the last "Leaves." Each student in a group is to report on a specialized organ within that group. Topics for the "Roots" group may include food storage roots, aerial roots, and pneumatophores. Topics for the "Stems" group may include stolons, bulbs, and tubers. Topics for the "Leaves" group may include tendrils, spines, and bracts. Each report should consist of a brief summary of the specialized plant organ and an illustration or photograph of the organ. Have students present their reports and display the pictures for the class.

Visual Strategy Figure 21-2

● **Identifying Structures**

Reinforce the concept of adaptation by walking students through this figure. If necessary, explain how these stems are an adaptive feature of the plant.

Figure 21-2
To survive in different environments, plants have evolved with different types of shoots.

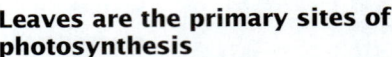

Shoots

The aboveground part of a plant is called the **shoot**. The shoots of most plants consist of leaves and stems and, in many cases, flowers and fruits. Leaves conduct photosynthesis. Stems support the leaves and enable them to receive sunlight. Compare the shoots of the plants shown in **Figure 21-2**.

Stems connect roots to leaves

The stems of a flowering plant support its leaves, flowers, and fruits, usually holding them off the ground. Stems also contain vascular tissue that transports substances between the roots and the leaves.

Stems vary greatly in shape and size from one plant species to another, as is evident when comparing the trunk of a redwood tree with a grass stalk. Some stems are adapted for storage. For example, cactuses can store a considerable amount of water inside their fleshy stems. Potatoes are underground stems that are swollen with nutrients stored as starch.

Leaves are the primary sites of photosynthesis

In Chapter 5, you learned that plants capture energy from sunlight and use it to make organic molecules through photosynthesis. Leaves are specialized to carry out photosynthesis. Most of the cells in a leaf are packed with chloroplasts, the chlorophyll-containing organelles where photosynthesis occurs.

Regardless of their size, most leaves are relatively thin and flat. This shape produces the highest ratio of surface area to volume. Thin, flat leaves help a plant efficiently capture the light energy and carbon dioxide needed for photosynthesis. A waxy outer layer called the cuticle prevents leaves from losing too much water and drying out. Carbon dioxide enters a leaf, and water and oxygen exit, through tiny pores called **stomata** *(STOH muh tuh)*. The singular of *stomata* is *stoma*.

Inside a leaf, there are layers of photosynthetic cells. Bundles of vascular tissue also run through a leaf. These bundles are the veins you see when you look at a leaf. Vascular tissue moves water and dissolved minerals to photosynthetic cells and carries away the products of photosynthesis. You can read more about leaves in *A Closer Look at a Leaf* on page 393.

a This pine tree has a woody stem that provides the support that is necessary for it to grow tall and compete with other trees for sunlight.

b This cactus has a fleshy stem that stores water, and it has spines (modified leaves) that reduce water loss and provide protection.

c The horizontal, green stems of this strawberry plant spread over the ground and ultimately may take root and establish a new plant.

392

Multicultural Perspective: Manioc

The staple crop of Brazil and many other tropical and subtropical countries is a perennial shrub called manioc, or cassava. Its starchy root contains cyanide, which must be processed out before the root is ground into flour and used for cooking. Processing methods are complex, labor intensive, and pose a risk of cyanide poisoning to processors. In Brazil, manioc meal, or "farofa," is served at most meals. Manioc is also used to make tapioca and beer in some cultures. There are bitter and sweet varieties with varying levels of toxicity. Worldwide, manioc feeds over 400 million people.

Leaf

A leaf is not as simple as it might first appear. It has an intricate architecture well suited to its function—photosynthesis.

Stoma

1 During photosynthesis, carbon dioxide enters, and oxygen and water exit, a leaf through openings called stomata.

2 Cells within the leaf that come into contact with these gases are rich with chloroplasts.

3 Each chloroplast is crammed with stacks of sacs called thylakoids, which contain chlorophyll.

4 When light strikes chlorophyll in a thylakoid membrane, energy is captured by an electron and used to pump protons inward. Diffusing back out, the protons power the making of ATP. The end products of photosynthesis provide the chemical energy and building blocks needed for the plant's life.

393

A Closer Look

Connection: *Chapter 5*

Pigments and Photosynthesis
Use this feature to review the role of chloroplasts in photosynthesis. Ask students to explain why the leaf in this feature is green. (The chlorophyll absorbs mainly red and blue light and reflects green light.)

Health Connection

Leaves We Eat
Leafy vegetables are an important source of nutrition. Most greens may be eaten cooked or raw. Many varieties are rich in beta carotene, vitamin C, folacin, calcium, iron, and other substances that help protect us against diseases. In general, darker leaves are more nutritious than lighter-colored leaves. Have students check references on nutrition for vitamin, mineral, and fiber content of a variety of leafy green vegetables.

Stomata

● **Identifying Structures**
Stomata are usually present in the lower epidermis of plants. However, some plants, like alfalfa, have stomata on both the upper and lower epidermis; some, such as the water lily, have stomata only on the upper epidermis; and submerged leaves of aquatic plants have no stomata. Ask students if leaves of rain-forest plants have more or fewer stomata per square centimeter of surface than leaves of cold-climate plants. *(Leaves of plants in colder, drier regions have fewer stomata.)*

Life/Work Skills

Finding Information
● **Interpreting Data**
Have students use library references to research CAM (crassulacean acid metabolism) photosynthesis. CAM plants, which are adapted to hot dry climates, include a variety of succulents and cactuses. Photosynthesis in these plants is modified so that the light reactions occur during the day with stomata closed.

394

Visual Strategy Videodisc

● **Identifying Structures**

To review the three types of tissue in vascular plants, use *Diagram— Plant Tissues: Unlabeled* shown in Chapter 21-1 of *Holt Biology Videodiscs Teacher's Correlation Guide to Holt Biology: Visualizing Life.* As you provide clues for each of the labeled parts, have students identify the part on the diagram and give its name. For example, you might give the clue "protects the plant from water loss," and students would reply, "B, epidermis."

Demonstration

● **Identifying Functions**

Slice a stalk of celery lengthwise to just below the leaves. Place the two halves in separate beakers, each containing a different color of water. Red and blue food coloring work best. Students should be able to see the veins in the leaves change color due to capillary action.

Growth Rings

■ **Relating Concepts**

Draw or obtain a cross section of a tree trunk in which the rings are not regular. Ask students to relate what the rings might indicate about the tree's history. *(Closely spaced rings usually indicate slow growth, possibly due to drought; rings that are closer together on one side than on the other indicate growth against an obstacle; and a dark slash indicates fire.)* Have students count the rings to estimate the age of the tree. Explain to students that scientists use an increment borer to extract a thin cylinder-shaped sample from a living tree to obtain this information.

Plant Tissues

The leaves, stems, and roots of plants are made of specialized tissues. The arrangement of the tissues in a non-woody stem is seen in **Figure 21-3a**.

Vascular plants have three basic types of tissue

Vascular tissue enables water, minerals, and the products of photosynthesis to move through the roots, stems, and leaves of a plant. Water and minerals flow through vascular tissue called **xylem** (ZY luhm). Sugars and other organic molecules move through vascular tissue called **phloem** (FLOH ehm).

Most of a plant is made of **ground tissue**, which surrounds the vascular tissue. Some types of ground-tissue cells store water or carbohydrates, while others have thickened walls that lend support to a plant. A plant's body is covered by a layer of flattened cells called the **epidermis**. These cells secrete the waxy cuticle that protects a plant from water loss.

New tissue forms in regions of actively dividing cells

Plants grow at regions of cell division called **meristems** (MEHR uh stemz).

One type of meristem is shown in **Figure 21-3b**. Every time a cell in the meristem divides, one cell remains in the meristem and the other cell becomes a specialized cell as it matures. Meristems at the tips of roots and shoots enable plants to grow in length. Growth that occurs by the lengthening of a plant's roots and shoots is called **primary growth**. Annuals—plants that die after one season of growth—may have only primary growth.

Woody plants—trees and shrubs—also have **secondary growth**, which causes plant bodies to thicken by producing new xylem and phloem. Secondary growth occurs in meristems that run like cylinders through stems. Wood consists mainly of layers of secondary xylem. Secondary phloem forms the inner part of bark. If a ring of bark is stripped from the trunk, a tree's roots will not receive the nutrients produced by photosynthesis, and the tree will die.

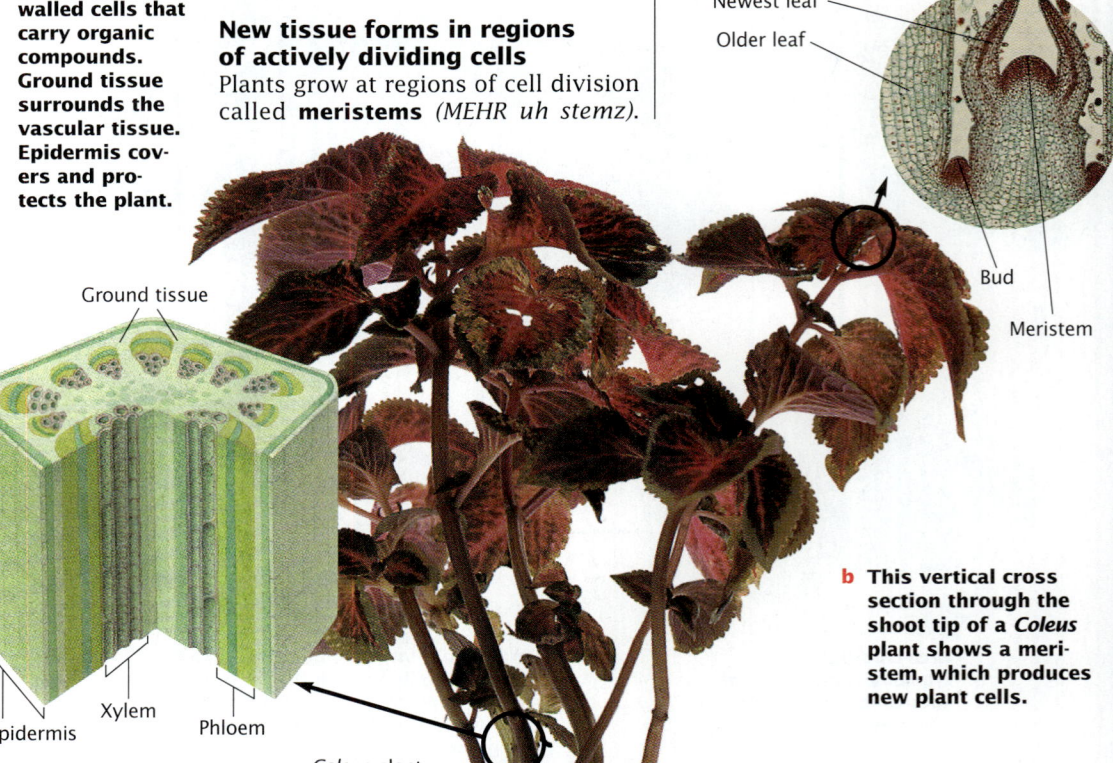

Figure 21-3

a The xylem of a *Coleus* plant is made of thick-walled cells that conduct water and minerals. The phloem contains thin-walled cells that carry organic compounds. Ground tissue surrounds the vascular tissue. Epidermis covers and protects the plant.

Ground tissue

Epidermis Xylem Phloem

Coleus plant

Newest leaf
Older leaf
Bud
Meristem

b This vertical cross section through the shoot tip of a *Coleus* plant shows a meristem, which produces new plant cells.

Matter of Fact: Incriminating Wood

In 1932, the infant son of Charles Lindbergh, the first person to fly solo across the Atlantic Ocean, was kidnapped and killed in Hopewell, New Jersey. The most damaging piece of evidence that led to the conviction of the suspect, Bruno Hauptmann, was a ladder used in the kidnapping. Arthur Koehler, a wood technologist, established by microscopic evidence that four types of wood were used in making the ladder. A detailed analysis of the grain and wood from one of the rungs was shown to match the floorboards from Hauptmann's attic. Hauptmann was executed for this crime in 1936.

Table 21-1 Summary of Differences Between Monocots and Dicots

Monocots (lily)	Dicots (hibiscus)
Embryos have one cotyledon.	Embryos have two cotyledons. — Cotyledons
Leaf veins are parallel.	Leaf veins are netlike.
Flower parts occur in threes or multiples of three.	Flower parts occur in fours or fives, or multiples of four or five.
Bundles of vascular tissue are scattered throughout ground tissue in the stem. Vascular tissue	Bundles of vascular tissue often form a ring within the ground tissue in the stem. Vascular tissue

Lily

Hibiscus

Monocots and Dicots

As you read in Chapter 20, the embryos of flowering plants have cotyledons. The number of cotyledons differs in the two great groups of flowering plants: monocots (about 65,000 species) and dicots (about 170,000 species). Monocots include grasses, palms, lilies, and orchids. The crop plants wheat, corn, rice, oats, rye, and barley are also monocots. Dicots include many familiar nonwoody plants, shrubs, trees, and cactuses. Monocots and dicots are similar in structure and function, but they differ in distinct ways. Evidence suggests that monocots evolved from primitive dicots. **Table 21-1** shows some of the characteristic differences between most monocots and dicots.

SECTION REVIEW

❶ **How do the functions of roots and shoots relate to their structures?**

❷ **What are the functions of vascular tissue, ground tissue, and epidermis?**

❸ **How do meristems enable a plant to grow?**

❹ **If you had neither flowers nor seeds to look at, how would you determine whether a plant is a monocot or a dicot?**

ANSWERS TO SECTION REVIEW

❶ Roots anchor the plant and absorb water and minerals from the soil. Shoots consist of stems and leaves. Stems support the leaves, enabling them to receive sunlight for photosynthesis. The vascular tissue in stems transports substances between the roots and leaves.

❷ Vascular tissue moves materials throughout the plant. Ground tissue stores and supports. The epidermis protects the plant from water loss.

❸ Plants grow at meristems. Meristems at the tips of roots and shoots allow the plant to increase in length because this is the place where cell division occurs.

❹ One could examine the leaves. The veins are parallel in a monocot and netlike in a dicot. A cross section of the stem could also be examined. In monocots the vascular tissue is scattered, and in dicots it forms a ring within the ground tissue.

Connection: *Chapter 17*

Taxonomy

Form cooperative groups of four students. Provide each group with a wide variety of leaves from plants that grow in your geographic region. Also give each group a taxonomic key or field guide. Have students identify as many specimens as possible.

Phase Three
Assessment Options

Closure

● **Summarizing Information**
Make a chart with the following column heads: *Structure* and *Function*. List the following titles down the left side of the chart as row heads: *Root, Root Hairs, Stem, Stoma, Leaf, Xylem, Phloem, Ground Tissue, Epidermis,* and *Meristem.* Have students complete the table by describing the structure and function of each part.

SECTION REVIEW
Assign the *Section Review.*

Reteaching

A spacecraft, whose mission may take many months, has a small environmental center on board. The crew needs plants for experimental purposes as well as supplemental food sources. What kinds of plants might the crew take with them? Have students list environmental requirements that must be considered for the plants *(amount of space, moisture, soils, fertilizers, air).* Then have students design, draw, and label a plant that might meet the needs of the scientists. Students should specify types of roots, stems, and leaves.

Key to Strategies
● Understanding Concepts (Tier I)
■ Applying Information (Tier II)
▲ Critical Thinking (Tier III)

Plant Form and Function   **395**

Scheduling

See the **Lesson Planning Guide** on pages 389A and 389B for lecture, classwork, and assignment options for Section 21-2.

Visual Strategy   Videodisc

● **Summarizing Information**
To introduce students to the processes by which materials move throughout plants, use *Video— Plant Transport* (2 min 40 s) shown in Chapter 21 Section 21-2 of *Holt Biology Videodiscs Teacher's Correlation Guide to Holt Biology: Visualizing Life.* Have students identify the processes and discuss how each moves materials. *(During osmosis, water moves by diffusion; capillary action results from adhesion between water molecules and sides of the plant's tubes; transpiration occurs as water evaporates from the leaves, drawing more water molecules up through the xylem; active transport moves carbohydrates produced in cells into the phloem.)*

Theme Answer

Cell Structure and Function

The long narrow tubes contained in xylem tissue are designed for capillarity. The water in these tubes is attracted to the xylem cells. As water evaporates from the leaves, other water molecules move up, since each water molecule pulls on the one below it.

Although a plant may not seem as complex as an animal, its internal structure is more complex than you might think. Its vascular system sends water, minerals, and organic compounds from one plant part to another. Like your body, a plant regulates its growth with hormones, chemicals that act as messengers to coordinate activities.

21-2   How Plants Function

OBJECTIVES

1 Describe how water and other nutrients move within xylem and phloem.

2 Relate plant growth patterns to the action of plant hormones.

3 Describe the ways in which a plant can respond to seasonal changes.

Cell Structure and Function

Explain how the structure of xylem enables the efficient transport of water and minerals.

How Nutrients Move Through Plants

In northern California, giant sequoia (redwood) trees can be up to 111 m (364 ft) tall. How do trees move water from roots deep in the soil up to branches and leaves at such heights? Water enters the roots of a plant by osmosis. But it takes more than just osmosis to move water up to the top of a tall tree!

Water is pushed and pulled through a plant

Several factors work together to move water through a plant. First, water continually enters a plant's roots by osmosis when enough water is present in the soil. The movement of more water into the roots pushes water into the xylem tissue that extends into the roots. Second, xylem cells form long narrow tubes. **Figure 21-4a** shows the xylem tissue of a plant's stem. The water in these tubes is attracted to the xylem cell walls. This attraction tends to pull water up the tubes. The movement of water up narrow tubes such as those in the xylem is called **capillary action**.

The major forces behind the movement of water in plants, however, are the attraction of water molecules for each other and the evaporation of water from leaves. As water evaporates from leaves, the water in the xylem moves upward because each water molecule pulls on those below it. Thus, the loss of water from leaves is responsible for the flow of water through a plant.

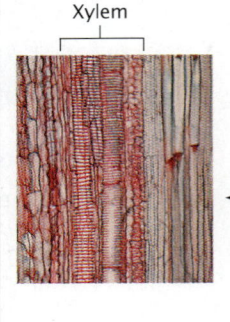

Figure 21-4

a Capillary action, attraction of water molecules, and loss of water from shoots cause water to move up a squash plant through xylem.

Xylem

Zucchini plant

Videodisc Resources

Holt Biology Videodiscs
Lesson 21-2: How Plants Function

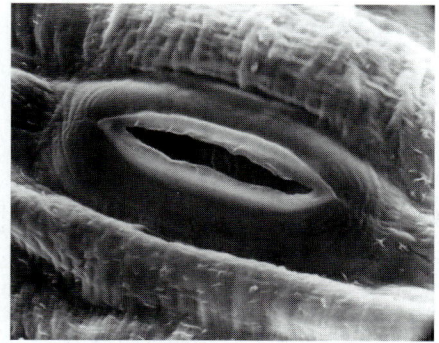

b Water is lost from the above-ground portion of the plant through the process of transpiration.

c Stomata on the surfaces of leaves open and close to regulate water loss.

Phloem

d Within phloem, organic molecules made during photosynthesis are transported throughout a plant by the process of translocation.

More than 90 percent of the water taken up by the roots of a plant is lost to the atmosphere as water vapor. The loss of water by a plant is called **transpiration**. Water is lost by a plant primarily through the stomata in its leaves, shown in **Figure 21-4b**. Water entering the plant's roots replaces the water lost through transpiration.

Stomata regulate water loss

The main way that plants control water loss is to close their stomata. Each stoma is formed by two pickle-shaped cells called guard cells. The structure of guard cells causes them to curve outward when they are swollen with water. As a pair of guard cells take in water, the stoma opens, as shown in **Figure 21-4c**. When the guard cells lose water, they collapse and the stoma closes. The stomata of a zucchini plant are open during the day and closed at night. Therefore, very little water is lost from its leaves at night.

Organic compounds are transported in another way

Organic compounds and some minerals move throughout a plant within the phloem. **Figure 21-4d** shows the phloem tissue from a plant. The contents of phloem cells are under great pressure. Yet individual molecules move within phloem tissue from areas of high concentration to areas of low concentration.

The transport of nutrients within phloem tissue is called **translocation**. Through translocation, organic molecules made in a plant's photosynthetic (green) parts move to other parts of the plant. Many organic molecules move to the actively growing regions of a plant. In some plants, such as carrots and potatoes, excess organic molecules accumulate in storage structures, where the molecules are converted to starch. When other parts of the plant need organic molecules, the starch molecules are broken down into smaller molecules and moved through the phloem. **Figure 21-4** summarizes the structures and processes that transport nutrients within a plant.

397

Language Arts Connection
Word Origin
Have students use a dictionary to find the origin of the term *stoma.* (Stoma *comes from the Greek word meaning "mouth."*)

Visual Strategy | Videodisc

● **Interpreting Graphics**
To help students understand the function of stomata, use *Illustration—Stomata: Open and Closed* shown in Chapter 21 Section 21-1 of *Holt Biology Videodiscs Teacher's Correlation Guide to Holt Biology: Visualizing Life.* Indicate the opening in the diagram on the left, and tell students that this is a stoma. Have students compare the size of this stoma with the size of the stoma in the illustration on the right. Indicate the arrows on each of the diagrams, and ask how they might explain the difference in the sizes of the stomata. (*In the illustration on the left, water has diffused into the guard cells, causing them to curve outward. In the illustration on the right, water has diffused out of the guard cells, and they have collapsed, closing the stoma.*)

Translocation and Transpiration
● **Organizing Information**
Have students prepare a **Graphic Organizer** similar to the one at the bottom of this page to compare translocation with transpiration.

Key to Strategies
● Understanding Concepts (Tier I)
■ Applying Information (Tier II)
▲ Critical Thinking (Tier III)

Graphic Organizer
Use the following graphic organizer with **Translocation and Transpiration** on page 397.

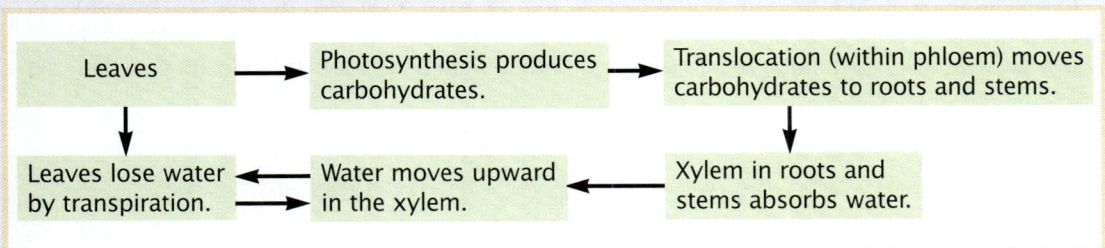

| Leaves | → | Photosynthesis produces carbohydrates. | → | Translocation (within phloem) moves carbohydrates to roots and stems. |

| Leaves lose water by transpiration. | ← | Water moves upward in the xylem. | ← | Xylem in roots and stems absorbs water. |

Factors Regulating Plant Growth

As a plant grows, leaves, stems, and reproductive structures form, and then seeds develop and mature. After they form, seeds usually remain dormant, or inactive, for a while. As a seed sprouts, the seedling's shoot grows up and its root grows down. Hormones control most of these events. Three examples of plant hormones are auxin (*AWK sihn*), gibberellin (*jihb uhr EHL ihn*), and ethylene.

Auxin stimulates the elongation of plant cells
Have you ever seen a plant bending toward light? Research has shown that this growth pattern occurs in many plants when auxin becomes more concentrated on the side of a stem away from the light's source. Auxin, which is produced in the tips of stems, causes cell walls to become more flexible. As a result, cells exposed to auxin grow longer. Auxin also stimulates root development; prevents the dropping of leaves, flowers, and fruits; and blocks the growth of buds along a stem.

If a stimulus causes auxin to concentrate on only one side of a stem, then the cells on that side will elongate more than the cells on the opposite side. As a result, the stem will bend away from the side where auxin is concentrated. Auxin causes a variety of growth responses that result in the bending of plants either toward or away from a stimulus such as light, gravitational pull, or touch. These growth responses are called **tropisms** (*TROH pihz uhmz*).

Gibberellin stimulates cell division and cell elongation
Gibberellin, which occurs naturally in plants, was named after the fungus *Gibberella*. In 1926, Japanese scientists reported that the stems of rice plants infected with the fungus grew abnormally long. A substance (gibberellin) extracted from the fungus caused the same effect in plants that were not infected by the fungus. Gibberellin not only greatly increases stem growth, as you can see in **Figure 21-5**, but also stimulates flower formation and the sprouting of seeds.

Ethylene stimulates fruit ripening
In ancient China, farmers ripened fruits in rooms that contained burning incense. Ethylene gas released by the burning of incense caused the ripening. Today ethylene is used commercially to ripen bananas, honeydew melons, and mangoes. These fruits are harvested when they are still green. In 1934, scientists discovered that fruits and other parts of a plant produce ethylene naturally. Ethylene also promotes the dropping of leaves, flowers, and fruits.

Figure 21-5
The plants on the right have greatly elongated stems because each was sprayed with water containing gibberellin. The plants on the left, which were sprayed with plain water, show normal development.

398

Historical Perspective: The Father of Botany

The first known botanical garden was founded by Aristotle in Athens, Greece. When he died, he willed his botanical garden to his pupil Theophrastus of Eresus. Theophrastus added to the knowledge he acquired from Aristotle. It is said that he wrote over 200 treatises. *The History of Plants* and *Causes of Plants* are considered to be the most important of all the treatises that have survived. His contributions to the field of botany were so great that Linnaeus gave him the title "Father of Botany."

Night Length and Flowering

Figure 21-6

a Irises are long-day plants, which bloom in early summer when nights are short and days are long.

● *Early summer*

Midnight · 6 P.M. · 6 A.M. · Noon

In the summer, when night length is shortest, . . .

. . . irises respond by producing flowers.

Poinsettias, which are short-day plants, do not bloom.

b Poinsettias are short-day plants, which bloom in late fall and early winter when nights are long and days are short.

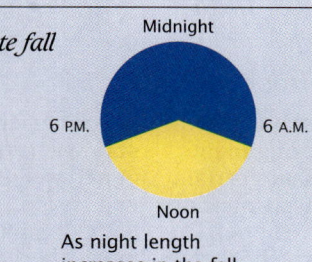

● *Late fall*

Midnight · 6 P.M. · 6 A.M. · Noon

As night length increases in the fall, . . .

. . . irises stop flowering.

Poinsettias respond to long nights (short days) by producing flowers.

Seasonal changes affect plant growth

The growth of many plants varies with the seasons. Different types of plants produce flowers at different times of the year. The seeds of some plants sprout in the spring, while the seeds of others sprout in the fall. Still other plants go through periods of inactivity, or dormancy. Chemicals other than hormones are responsible for many of these growth patterns.

The length of a night (daily period of darkness) affects the production of flowers by some plants, as **Figure 21-6** shows. These plants contain a pigment that senses the change from light to dark. This pigment also enables a plant to sense how long darkness lasts. Long-day (short-night) plants produce flowers only when the daily period of

darkness is less than a certain length. Short-day (long-night) plants produce flowers only when the daily period of darkness exceeds a certain length. Some plants, such as tomatoes, are not sensitive to darkness because they evolved in the tropics, where nights are virtually the same length all year.

In many plants, temperature affects flower or fruit production and the release of buds or seeds from a dormant state. For example, tomato plants will not produce fruit if nighttime temperatures are too high. Few varieties of apples are grown in southern regions of the United States because winters there are not cold enough for most varieties to produce fruit. Cold temperatures cause the breakdown of chemicals that cause dormancy in buds and seeds.

SECTION REVIEW

① Trace the path of water through a plant.

② How does the movement of water through a plant differ from the movement of organic molecules through a plant?

③ List three plant hormones, and describe their effects on plant development.

④ How can a change in season affect plant growth?

A N S W E R S TO
SECTION REVIEW

① Water enters the cells of the root by osmosis and travels up through xylem tissue by capillary action. Transpiration pulls water up through the plant.

② Water moves upward through the xylem tissue. Organic molecules move from where they were made by photosynthesis to different parts of the plant through phloem tissue.

③ Auxins cause the cell wall to become more flexible, allowing cell elongation. They also stimulate root development and prevent the dropping of leaves, flowers, and fruit. Gibberellin increases stem growth and stimulates flower formation and the sprouting of seeds. Ethylene hastens the ripening of fruits.

④ The length of darkness determines when plants bloom.

Plant Form and Function 399

Sepal

Petal

Flowering plants are the dominant group of plants on Earth today. While you may appreciate flowers for their decorative role, they are actually the visible evidence of a flowering plant's ability to reproduce sexually. Each flower helps ensure that a particular plant species will produce more of its own kind.

21-3 Reproduction in Flowering Plants

Architecture of a Flower

Figure 21-7 shows the sexual reproductive structure of flowering plants, the flower. Most flowers share certain basic features. They consist of four whorls, or circles, of parts. The sepals, which form the outermost whorl and are usually greenish, protect the flower bud. Just inside the sepals is a whorl of petals, which are often brightly colored to attract animal pollinators. The inner whorls of a flower produce the male and female gametophytes.

One inner whorl of a flower consists of **stamens** (STAY mehnz), the male parts of a flower. Pollen grains are produced in a structure called the anther, which is the top part of a stamen. The innermost whorl of a flower consists of one or more **pistils**, the female parts of a flower. The base of a pistil is called the ovary. Inside an ovary, eggs are produced within **ovules**. The tip of a pistil is called the stigma, the site where pollen sticks.

Figure 21-7
If you slice the flower of a lily in half, you can see all of its reproductive structures.

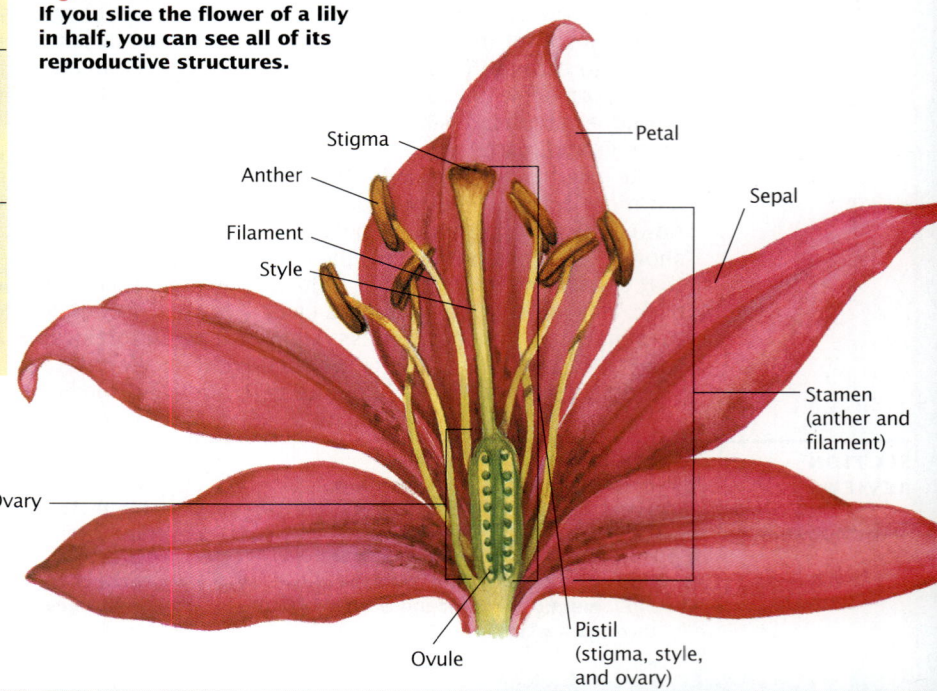

Stigma
Anther
Filament
Style
Petal
Sepal
Stamen (anther and filament)
Ovary
Ovule
Pistil (stigma, style, and ovary)

Iris

Iris virginica (Southern blue flag) has violet flowers that resemble cultivated irises. In Roman mythology, Iris was a goddess whose visible sign was a rainbow. The iris is named for its rainbow of colors. Iris flowers occur in many colors, from white to deep violet and yellow to reddish brown.

Iris flowers have parts in multiples of three. Three violet petals curve upward, while three petal-like sepals curve downward. The style branches into three flat, petal-like parts. The flower has three stamens, one under each branch of the style.

The long, narrow leaves exhibit parallel veins and form a sheath around each stem.

Evolutionary Relationships

Iris virginica is an angiosperm—a flowering plant. Iris flowers are adapted for attracting insect pollinators, in this case bees. While visiting flowers, bees seeking nectar transfer pollen from one flower to another. Irises are also monocots, as the structure of their leaves and flowers indicates.

Habitat

Iris virginica grows in wet meadows, marshes, and other moist places, such as forests and the edges of ponds and streams. Of the many native irises found in the United States, *I. virginica* has one of the widest distributions. It grows throughout the Southeast, as far west as Texas and as far north as Virginia and Missouri.

In addition to forming seeds, irises reproduce asexually from an underground stem called a rhizome. The plants are perennials—old shoots die each winter, and new shoots arise from the rhizome the next spring.

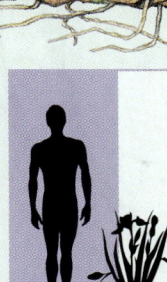

Size

The shoots of *I. virginica* can be up to 1 m (3 ft) tall. Leaves up to 76 cm (2.5 ft) long and up to 3.2 cm (1.2 in.) wide rise from ground level. Flowers with petal-like sepals that are 7.6 cm (3 in.) long crown stems that are 0.6–1.0 m (2–3 ft) tall. Irises often grow in extensive colonies. Some of the clumps in a colony may belong to a single plant. These clumps are connected by a common rhizome.

Tour

Connection: *Chapter 7*

Hybrid Crosses

Iris breeders have crossed diploid plants with tetraploid plants to enhance the color variation. The newest advance in iris breeding has been the introduction of *rebloom*. Breeders have successfully developed irises that will complete two or more growth cycles in one season.

Life/Work Skills
Allocating Resources
▲ **Distinguishing Relevant Information**

Have students write or call the American Iris Society at 8426 Vinevalley Drive, Sun Valley, CA 91352, phone 818-767-5512 to find out about breeding, classification, cultivation, exhibition, and history of irises. Check the local newspaper for information about flower competitions and exhibitions in your area. If possible, have students interview a judge about judging standards for irises.

Rhizomes and Bulbs
● **Comparing Structures**

Show students a tulip bulb and an iris rhizome. Ask students to discuss the adaptive advantages of these structures (*food storage and asexual reproduction*).

Pollination and Fertilization

For sexual reproduction to occur, pollen containing the male gametes must reach the stigma. Since flowering plants cannot move about to seek their mates, they must rely on other methods to move pollen. Pollination is the transfer of pollen grains from an anther to the stigma of a flower. Wind causes the pollination of the flowers of many plants, such as oaks and grasses. In many other plants, pollen falls from the anthers onto a stigma of the same flower, resulting in **self-pollination**. However, most flowering plants, from magnolias to orchids to the morning glory seen in **Figure 21-8**, depend on animals for pollination.

The flowers of plants pollinated by animals must attract pollinators. In Chapter 14 you learned that flowering plants and their pollinators have coevolved, or evolved in response to changes in each other. To attract pollinators, some flowers, such as the morning glory in **Figure 21-8b**, have attention-getting "advertisements"

such as brightly colored petals or scents. The flowers of many kinds of plants secrete a sugary liquid called nectar, which pollinators use as food. Pollen itself also serves as food for many pollinators.

As an animal explores a flower, pollen may stick to its body. When the animal visits another flower, it may inadvertently transfer some of this pollen to the stigma of that flower. By attracting animals, flowering plants can ensure **cross-pollination**, which is the transfer of pollen to another plant of the same species. Cross-pollination ensures genetic recombination and thus may produce more genetic variation than does self-pollination.

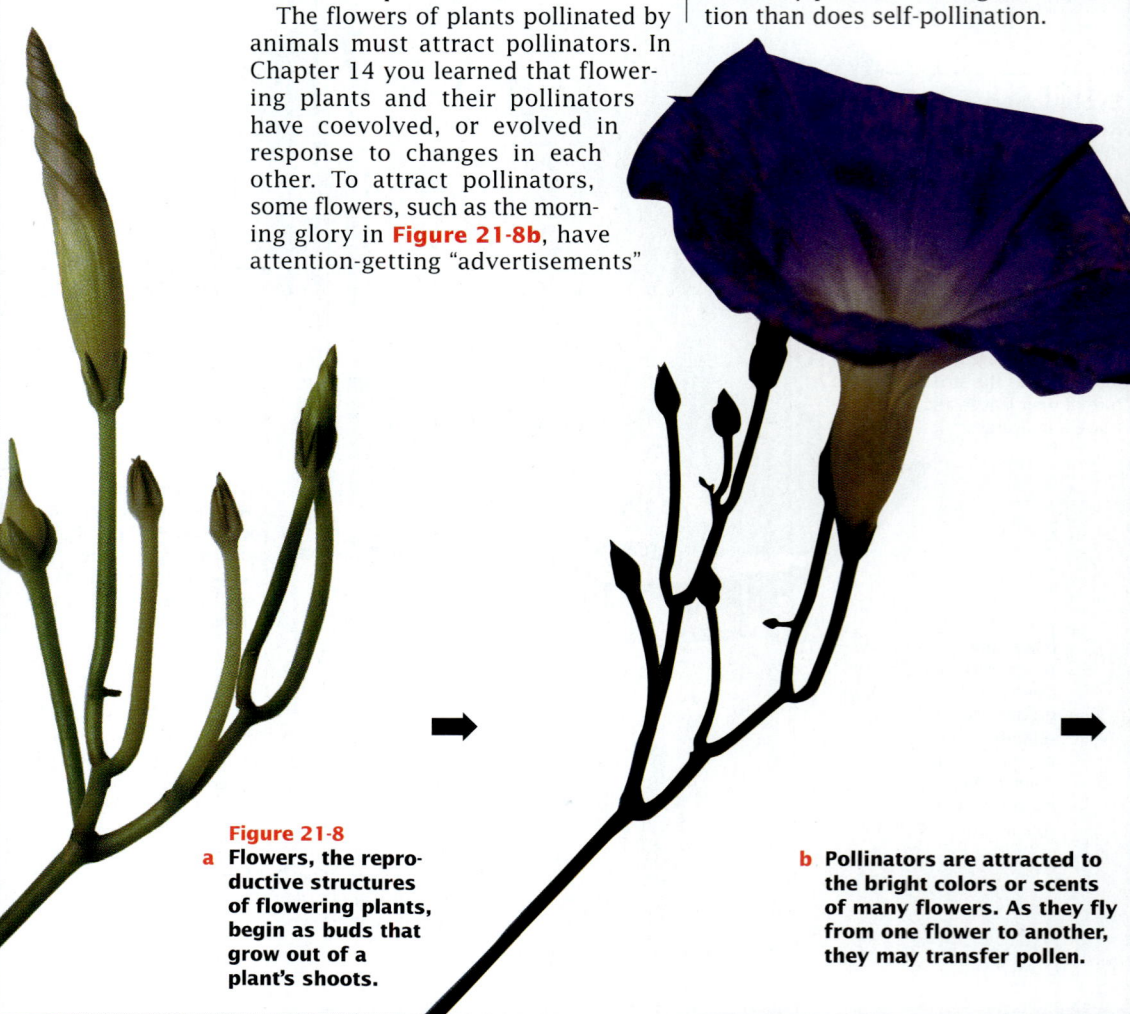

Figure 21-8
a Flowers, the reproductive structures of flowering plants, begin as buds that grow out of a plant's shoots.

b Pollinators are attracted to the bright colors or scents of many flowers. As they fly from one flower to another, they may transfer pollen.

402

Matter of Fact: Attracting Pollinators

Orchids have evolved highly elaborate ways of attracting pollinators. One species has a petal modified to resemble a female wasp. Male wasps try to mate with the "female wasp" and in the process pick up some pollen. In another species, the flower holds a small pool of water. When a bee tries to gather nectar, it falls into the water and can escape only through a narrow passageway that forces the bee to brush against the pollen-bearing anthers.

Fertilization in flowers occurs in two stages

After a pollen grain lands on the stigma of a flower, a pollen tube may grow through the style of the pistil and into an ovule, which contains an egg. The egg is one of eight haploid nuclei in an ovule. A pollen grain has two sperm that travel down the pollen tube, as shown in **Figure 21-8c**. One sperm fuses with the egg to form a zygote. The other sperm fuses with two other nuclei in the ovule to form a tissue that will be a source of nutrition for the embryo. This event, in which one sperm fuses with an egg and a second sperm fuses with two nuclei, is called **double fertilization**. Double fertilization has great survival value because it provides each generation with an initial source of nutrition.

Remember that pollination is not the equivalent of fertilization. Fertilization involves the union of egg and sperm and may not occur until weeks or months after pollination has taken place. Sometimes fertilization fails to occur after pollination.

Seeds and fruits form after fertilization

Fertilization causes rapid changes in a flower. The ovule develops into a seed, often with a tough coat protecting the plant embryo and its nutrient supply. As you read in Chapter 20, the development of the seed was a major factor in the success of plants on land. Seeds help plant species to survive in unfavorable environments.

As seeds develop, the ovary grows larger and develops into a fruit. A **fruit** is an enlarged ovary of a flowering plant. You can see the fruit of a morning glory plant in **Figure 21-8d**. Many "vegetables," including squash, green beans, tomatoes, and cucumbers are technically fruits. The development of an ovary into a fruit usually depends on whether fertilization has occurred. If the eggs go unfertilized, the ovary will normally wither and drop, along with the rest of the flower.

Some fruits lack seeds

Have you ever wondered why navel oranges and bananas are seedless? The ability of plants to develop fruits without the fertilization of eggs is called parthenocarpy *(pahr thuh noh KAHR pee)*. Seedless varieties of bananas, citrus fruits, and some grapes occur naturally. Parthenocarpy can be induced in plants such as tomatoes and watermelons by applications of auxin at certain stages in development.

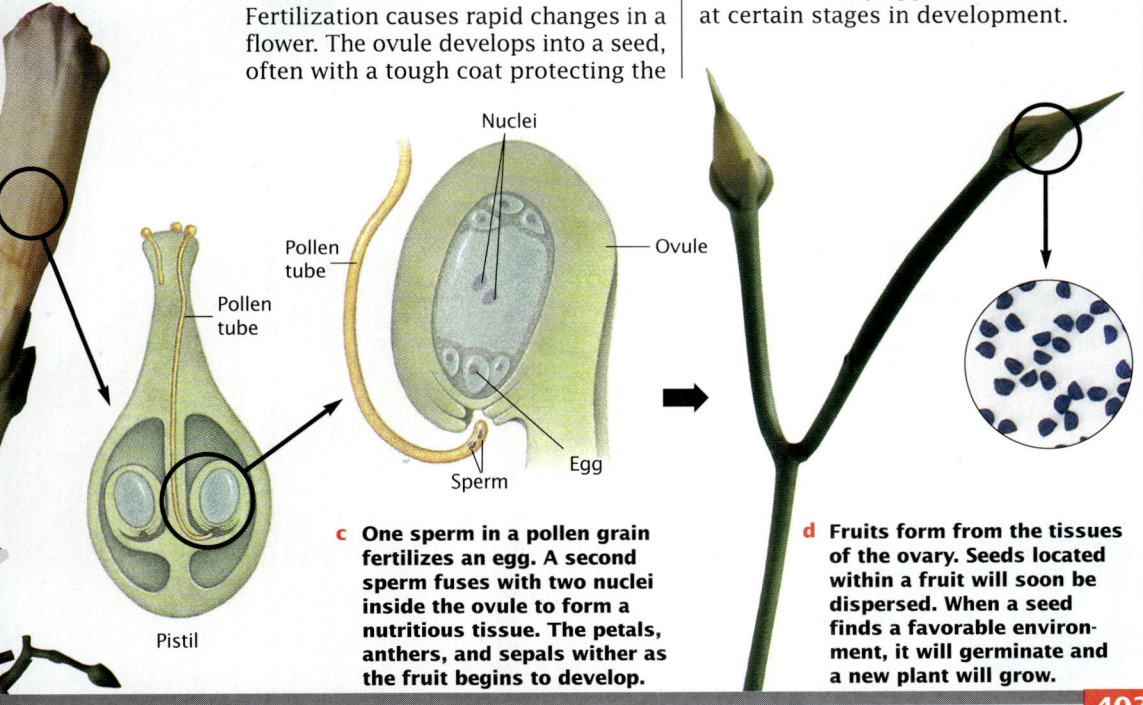

Nuclei

Pollen tube

Pollen tube

Ovule

Sperm

Egg

Pistil

c One sperm in a pollen grain fertilizes an egg. A second sperm fuses with two nuclei inside the ovule to form a nutritious tissue. The petals, anthers, and sepals wither as the fruit begins to develop.

d Fruits form from the tissues of the ovary. Seeds located within a fruit will soon be dispersed. When a seed finds a favorable environment, it will germinate and a new plant will grow.

403

Historical Perspective: Ancient Plant Breeding

Artificial pollination was practiced as early as 3500 B.C. by farmers in ancient Mesopotamia. These farmers noted that date palm trees were either male or female, and that if they brought clusters of staminate flowers in contact with pistillate flowers, fruit production was controlled. This ancient method of artificial pollination is still being used today.

Demonstration

● **Comparing Structures**

Prepare a display of different kinds of fruits. Include the following types: drupes (peaches); berries (tomatoes, grapes, and blueberries); pomes (apples); aggregates (strawberries); multiples (pineapples and figs); and dry fruits (beans and nuts). Obtain a botany book prior to this demonstration so that you can help students determine how the fruits are classified.

Seed Dispersal

■ **Inferring Relationships**

Collect specimens or pictures of various seeds. Display these to the students without telling them the names of the plants. Have students note the structure of each seed and suggest a means of dispersal *(such as wind or animals)*. Afterward tell students the name of each plant.

How Seeds Are Dispersed

Figure 21-9
Plant seeds are dispersed in a variety of ways. Several examples are shown below.

Once mature, seeds are ready to be dispersed. **Figure 21-9** shows how various types of seeds are dispersed. Some fruits, such as the plump, fleshy peaches, tomatoes, and watermelons you buy at the grocery store, are eaten by animals. When fleshy fruits ripen, their sugar content increases and the fruit becomes soft and juicy. Their colors often change from green to bright red, yellow, or orange. These changes, signs that the seeds are ripe and ready for dispersal, aid in catching the attention of hungry animals.

When fruits are eaten by birds or mammals, the seeds are spread by passing unharmed through the digestive tract. The success of sweet, colorful fruits as a method of seed dispersal is important in the coevolution of animals and flowering plants. Plants such as maple trees, tumbleweeds, and dandelions have extremely light fruits and seeds that can be carried by the wind. The fruits and seeds of many plants growing in or near water, like coconuts, are adapted for floating. Some fruits or seeds, such as burdocks, have hooks that attach them to the feathers, fur, or clothing of passing animals, giving the seed a free ride to a new home.

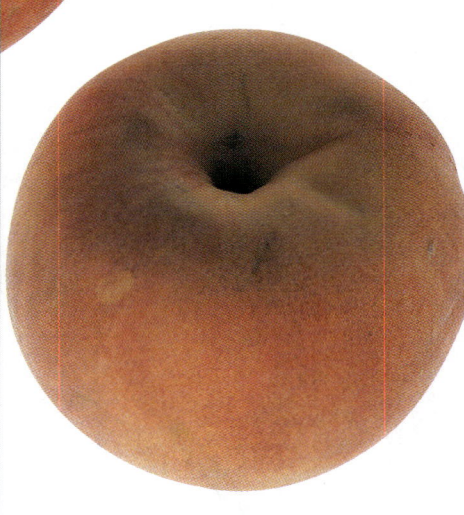
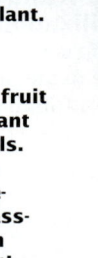

d Humans can disperse seeds too. Have you ever spit watermelon seeds on the ground? One of those seeds may have germinated and grown into a new watermelon plant.

c The succulent fruit of a tomato plant attracts animals. The seeds are deposited elsewhere after passing through an animal's digestive system.

a The sharp, tough coat of a peach pit cannot be eaten by animals. A new plant may germinate wherever the animal drops the pit.

b Squirrels and other animals carry seeds from one area to another.

404

Multicultural Perspective: Kola Nuts

Kola nuts are cultivated in the West Indies, West Africa, and South Africa. They are the fruits of several types of evergreen trees. People who live in African countries call the nuts *guru* or *goora* nuts and chew them like gum. Kola nuts are also used to make cola soft drinks and medicines. The nuts contain caffeine and theobromine. Caffeine is a stimulant, and theobromine is a toxic alkaloid.

e   Double samaras, the fruits of maples, spin in the wind like helicopter blades.

Demonstration

● **Identifying Structures**

Seven days before students read this section, place bean (dicot) and corn (monocot) seeds between moist paper towels in separate clear-plastic beverage cups. Prepare several setups. Label each cup. Have students observe the germination stages and growth of the seeds every day and record their observations in a journal. Discuss these changes when you discuss the topic of germination. You may wish to have students continue to write in their journals after you have concluded the chapter.

f   Wind carries the fruit of dandelions to new locations.

g   Tumbleweeds can sometimes be seen blowing across roads in the southwestern United States, dispersing their seeds along the way.

Time to Flower

■ **Inferring Conclusions**

Tell students that some plants have lengthy reproductive cycles. A plant grown from seed may take years to produce one flower. Gardeners often take advantage of asexual reproduction to produce colorful landscapes in one growing season. Have students use a seed catalog to discover which flowers can be propagated without seeds. Remind students that genetic variation results from seed production. Ask students to list reasons why a landscaper might prefer bulbs and rhizomes over seeds (*flowers in one growing season, predictable traits such as color and size*).

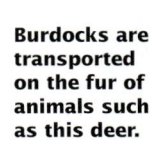

h   The fruit of a coconut palm can float from place to place.

i   Burdocks are transported on the fur of animals such as this deer.

Seeds resume growth by germinating

After they have formed, many seeds go through a period of decreased activity called dormancy. Their metabolic activity is greatly reduced. The length of time that a seed can be dormant and still grow into a plant varies. The record is held by a seed of the arctic tundra lupine. Seeds from this plant were found in a frozen animal burrow in the Canadian Yukon and were estimated to be 10,000 years old. When these seeds were planted, they sprouted in 48 hours.

In order to germinate, or begin growing into a new plant, seeds need a suitable environment. **Germination**, which is the sprouting of a seed, cannot take place until water and oxygen reach the embryo. Sometimes this involves cracking the seed coat. Some seeds are covered by seed coats that will not crack unless they are exposed to the heat of fire. Other seeds will germinate only after they have passed through the intestines of birds or mammals. After water and oxygen enter a seed, the embryo swells, grows, and breaks through the seed coat. The young plant that grows when a seed germinates is called a seedling.

405

Matter of Fact: Beans That Jump

A "jumping bean" is a seed of the spurge family grown in Central and South America that contains a moth larva. The jumping movements occur when the grub changes position with a jerk. The jumping bean is also known as the "bronco bean" or "leaper."

Key to Strategies
● Understanding Concepts (Tier I)
■ Applying Information (Tier II)
▲ Critical Thinking (Tier III)

Plant Form and Function   **405**

Plant Cell Growth and Differentiation

When an embryo starts to develop, all of its cells are identical. The cells have the same genes because they came from the same fertilized egg. Over time, hormones act on some cells but not others. The hormones turn some genes on and others off, causing the cells to differentiate, or become different from one another. Some of the cells become vascular tissue, while others become ground tissue or epidermis.

Even after they have differentiated, many kinds of plant cells retain the potential to form other types of cells. As illustrated in **Figure 21-10**, potato plants can grow from pieces of stem tissue. Each cell in the tissue contains all the genetic information needed to grow a new plant. Tissue culture is used in the commercial production of millions of orchids, houseplants, fruit plants, and landscape plants.

The ability of plant cells to differentiate into other specialized types of plant cells enables leaf and stem cuttings to form new roots. A single plant can be cut into many pieces that can grow into identical plants. Bananas and chrysanthemums are produced in this way. The ability of plant cells to differentiate into other cell types also makes it possible to attach, or graft, the stems or buds of one plant to another plant. Grafting and budding are used commercially to produce plants such as hybrid rosebushes and grapevines, and to produce citrus, peach, apple, and pecan trees.

Figure 21-10
The large-scale production of most vegetables by tissue culture is not economically feasible. The procedure is used commercially to grow potatoes that are free of viruses.

a **To grow a new potato plant by tissue culture, scientists first isolate tissue from the tip of the stem.**

b **The stem tissue is placed in a flask containing nutrients and hormones.**

c **A new plant then begins to grow in the culture flask.**

d **When the plant is large enough, it is planted in soil and allowed to grow to maturity.**

SECTION REVIEW

1 How does each part of a flower help a plant achieve sexual reproduction?

2 How does the process of pollination enable the process of fertilization to occur in plants?

3 A certain plant produces seeds within fruits that have many long, straight spines. Predict how this plant's seeds are dispersed.

4 What are some possible advantages of using tissue culture to reproduce plants?

406

Highlights

Rose hips, the fruit of a rose plant, are sometimes an ingredient of herbal tea.

	Key Terms	Summary
21-1 **The Plant Body** This strawberry plant has roots that anchor it and absorb water and minerals, and shoots that absorb light and perform photosynthesis. 	root cap (p. 391) root hairs (p. 391) shoot (p. 392) stoma (p. 392) xylem (p. 394) phloem (p. 394) ground tissue (p. 394) epidermis (p. 394) meristem (p. 394) primary growth (p. 394) secondary growth (p. 394)	• Roots absorb water and minerals. Shoots consist of stems and leaves. • Leaves are the main site of photosynthesis. Carbon dioxide enters a leaf, and water and oxygen exit, through the stomata. • Vascular tissue contains xylem and phloem. Xylem transports water and minerals. Phloem transports organic compounds. • Vascular tissue is found within ground tissue, which makes up most of a nonwoody plant. Epidermis covers the outside of a plant. • Regions of cell division are called meristems. Cell division in meristems increases the length and diameter of a plant.
21-2 **How Plants Function** Transpiration drives the uptake of water by a plant, while translocation distributes products of photosynthesis throughout a plant. 	capillary action (p. 396) transpiration (p. 397) translocation (p. 397) tropism (p. 398)	• The loss of water through transpiration helps to pull water through a plant. • Stomata in leaves open and close to regulate the amount of water lost through transpiration. • Plant growth and development is regulated by hormones. • Chemicals that sense light and temperature affect the growth and development of many plants.
21-3 **Reproduction in Flowering Plants** 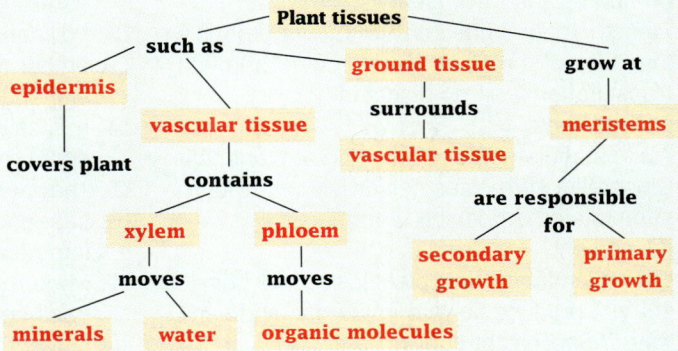 Flowers are one of several characteristics that have helped make flowering plants the dominant plants on Earth.	stamen (p. 400) pistil (p. 400) ovule (p. 400) self-pollination (p. 402) cross-pollination (p. 402) double fertilization (p. 403) fruit (p. 403) germination (p. 405)	• Flowers usually consist of sepals, petals, stamens that form pollen, and pistils that form ovules. • During fertilization in flowering plants, one sperm fuses with an egg to form an embryo, and another sperm fuses with two nuclei to form a nutritious tissue. • After fertilization, seeds develop within ovaries that become fruits. • Germination occurs when the embryo in a seed resumes growth under favorable conditions.

Alternative Assessment

Provide students with grocery-store produce ads from a newspaper. Ask them to cut out pictures of fruits and vegetables and to glue the pictures to notebook paper. Next to each picture, have students write a short paragraph about the plant structure. Paragraphs should include the biological function of the fruit or vegetable. Broccoli is a good example because students may not realize they are eating flower buds.

Portfolio Assessment

Portfolio Assessment on page T39 provides options for building and evaluating student portfolios. Students and teachers can select items from the areas listed on page T39 for inclusion in a portfolio.

407

ANSWER TO CONCEPT MAP

The following is one possible answer to the Relating Concepts exercise on page 408.

Plant tissues

such as

epidermis — covers plant

vascular tissue — contains

xylem — moves — minerals, water

phloem — moves — organic molecules

ground tissue — surrounds — vascular tissue

grow at — meristems — are responsible for — secondary growth, primary growth

review

ANSWERS

Understanding Vocabulary

1. a. transport water
   b. phloem
   c. different plant
2. a. The shoot, the aboveground part of the plant, includes the leaves and stems, which are the major site of photosynthesis.
   b. Water enters the vascular system of a plant through root hairs and moves into xylem cells, which form long narrow tubes and carry water to the leaves, where transpiration occurs.
   c. Pollen is produced on a part of the stamen called the anther and is transferred to the pistil. The sperm develop and move down to the ovary, where eggs are produced in ovules.

Understanding Concepts

3. Answer to concept map is found on page 407.
4. The primary functions of roots are to anchor a plant in the soil and to absorb water and minerals. The shoot is the aboveground part of the plant that includes the stem and enables the leaves to receive sunlight. Specialized roots store nutrients (carrots), fasten plants to aboveground structures (orchids), and give support to plants (corn).
5. A woody stem can support a large plant such as a tree. The cactus has a fleshy stem that stores water. Potatoes have underground stems that store nutrients.
6. Secondary growth produces new xylem and phloem and increases the width of a tree.
7. Monocots include lilies, grasses, and palms. Dicots include morning glories and many familiar shrubs and trees. Students should summarize the characteristics listed in Table 21-1 on page 395.
8. The major forces behind the movement of water in plants are the attraction of water molecules for each other and evap-

CHAPTER 21

review

Understanding Vocabulary

1. For each set of terms, complete the analogy.
   a. roots : absorb water :: stems : _____
   b. water transport : xylem :: sugar transport : _____
   c. self-pollination : same flower :: cross-pollination : _____

2. Using each set of words below, write one or more sentences summarizing information learned in this chapter.
   a. shoot, leaves, stem, photosynthesis
   b. water, root hairs, transpiration, xylem
   c. stamen, pollen, anther, pistil, ovary, ovule

Understanding Concepts

3. **Relating Concepts** Construct a concept map that describes the types of plant tissues and their functions. Try to include the following terms in your concept map: ground tissue, vascular tissue, xylem, phloem, meristem, minerals, water, organic molecules, epidermis, secondary growth, primary growth.

4. **Comparing Functions** What are the functions of roots? How do they differ from the functions of shoots? Describe three specialized functions of roots.

5. **Summarizing Information** Describe three functions of stems, and explain how stems are able to perform each function.

6. **Analyzing Information** When rings are counted to determine the age of a tree, is primary or secondary growth being measured? Explain your answer.

7. **Summarizing Information** Describe the characteristics of monocots and dicots, and give examples of each.

8. **Analyzing Processes** Describe the major forces behind the movement of water in plants.

9. **Recognizing Relationships** How might the rate of water movement within a plant differ between plants in cool, humid environments and those in hot, dry environments?

10. **Summarizing Information** Describe how plants respond to the hormones auxin, gibberellin, and ethylene.

11. **Reading Graphs** The seeds of certain conifers must experience cold temperatures before they will germinate. Using the graph below, what percent of seeds would germinate after a winter with only two cold months?

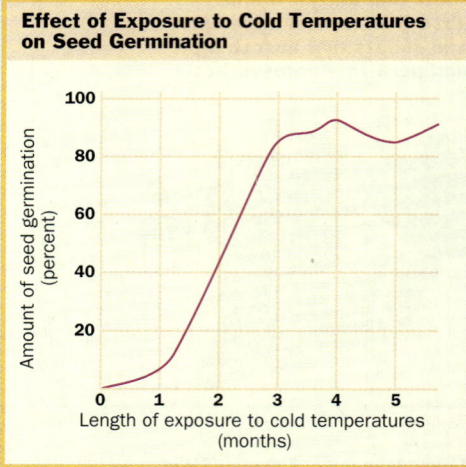

Effect of Exposure to Cold Temperatures on Seed Germination

Amount of seed germination (percent) vs. Length of exposure to cold temperatures (months)

12. **Relating Information** Give an example of a long-night plant and a short-night plant. At what time, or times, of the year would these plants normally produce flowers?

13. **Comparing Functions** Distinguish between pollination and fertilization in angiosperms.

14. **Inferring Relationships** Explain why the process of fertilization in angiosperms is called double fertilization.

15. **Summarizing Information** String beans, cucumbers, and squash are typically called vegetables. Why are they actually fruits?

16. **Inferring Relationships** Explain how the ability of a plant's cells to differentiate can be used to produce new plants.

17. **BUILDING ON WHAT YOU HAVE LEARNED** In Chapters 20 and 21 you read about the symbiotic associations between fungi and plants that are called mycorrhizae. Why do you think plants that develop mycorrhizae have fewer root hairs than plants without mycorrhizae?

408

oration of water from leaves.
9. Plants in cool, humid environments probably lose less of their total water content through transpiration than do plants in hot, dry environments.
10. Auxin stimulates the elongation of plant cells. Gibberellin stimulates cell division. Ethylene stimulates the ripening of fruit.
11. 41 percent
12. Long-night (short-day) plants, such as poinsettias, produce flowers in late fall and early winter. Short-night (long-day) plants, such as

asters, produce flowers in early summer.
13. Pollination is the transfer of pollen from anther to stigma. Fertilization is the joining of egg and sperm.
14. It is called double fertilization because two sperm are involved.
15. They are enlarged ovaries.
16. Leaf and stem cuttings form roots and grow into new plants.
17. Mycorrhizae reduce a plant's need for root hairs because they assist in transferring nutrients from the soil to the roots.

Interpreting Graphics

18. Study the photographs below. Identify each structure as belonging to a monocot or a dicot. For each response, write a sentence that explains why the structure belongs to a monocot or dicot.

Reviewing Themes

19. **Matter, Energy, and Organization**
Explain how the thin, flat structure of a leaf helps increase the efficiency of photosynthesis.

20. **Evolution**
Describe three features of flowering plants that suggest plants and their animal pollinators have coevolved.

21. **Heredity**
How does cross-pollination ensure genetic recombination?

22. **Evolution**
Explain why the development of the seed was a major factor in the success of plants.

Thinking Critically

23. **Evaluating Results** You put several seeds in a moist, airtight container and place the container in the dark. After a few days, you see that the seeds have germinated. After a few more days, you notice that the seedlings are dead. Explain your results.

24. **Evaluating Opinion** Your grandfather told you that if you hammer a nail into the trunk of a young tree, the nail will remain at the same height no matter how tall the tree grows. Do you think your grandfather is right or wrong? Support your answer.

Life/Work Skills

25. **Finding Information** Use library references or search an on-line database to find out about tree-ring dating. Find out what causes the rings that appear in a tree trunk and how differences in the sizes of the rings can indicate climatic conditions at the time the rings were made. What other kind of information about the environment can be determined by studying tree rings? Summarize your findings in a written report.

26. **Finding Information** Use library references or search an on-line database to find out about different kinds of plant movements, such as phototropism, thigmotropism, gravitropism, chemotropism, hydrotropism, and nastic movements. Prepare a poster with illustrations of the different kinds of plant movements to share with your class.

27. **Working Cooperatively** With two or three of your classmates, visit a wholesale plant grower. Orchid growers would be an excellent choice if one is in your area. Find out how tissue culture is used to reproduce different kinds of plants. Try to find out information on two methods of tissue culture that are not described in this chapter. Prepare an illustrated report of your findings to share with the class.

Activities and Projects

28. **Art Connection** Use library references or visit a local art museum or botanical garden to survey the different ways that flowers have been depicted by artists over the years. Look at flowers in paintings, tapestries, stained glass, quilts, sculptures, and porcelains. Compare how flowers are represented by Western artists, such as Claude Monet, Vincent van Gogh, Leonardo da Vinci, and Georgia O'Keeffe, with the ways they are represented by Japanese and Chinese artists.

Discovering Through Reading

29. Read the article "A Garden of Mutants" by Carol Fletcher in *Discover*, August 1995, pages 49–53. Why do botanists study genetics using the *Arabidopsis* plant? What is the MADS-box? What causes the flower mutations in *Arabidopsis*?

carbon dioxide prevented the plant from photosynthesizing.

24. Your grandfather is right. The height of a plant is an example of primary growth; its height is determined by growth at the tip of the stem, not at the base.

Life/Work Skills

25. Answers will vary, but students' reports might include that the wider rings form during growth seasons with abundant rainfall and adequate soil nutrients. Periods of drought are characterized by narrow rings. Scientists are also able to determine periods of volcanic activity and amounts of air pollution by studying tree rings.

26. Posters will vary but should accurately represent the kinds of plant movements.

27. Results will vary but might include additional information on the use of growth-stimulating chemicals, air layering, and different methods of vegetative propagation.

Activities and Projects

28. Results will vary. Students should be able to discuss the various styles of the artists.

Discovering Through Reading

29. *Arabidopsis* has the smallest known genome of any flowering plant; it also has very little repetitive DNA and requires little space or expertise to grow. Each of the three types of flower mutations was caused by the loss of a single class of gene.

409

Interpreting Graphics

18. Answers should be consistent with Table 21-1 on page 395.

Reviewing Themes

19. A thin leaf has a high ratio of surface area to volume.

20. Pollinators have an attraction for brightly colored petals or flower scents, and they feed on the nectar.

21. Cross-pollination ensures genetic recombination by transferring pollen from one plant to another.

22. Seeds enabled plant species to survive and reproduce in unfavorable environments.

Thinking Critically

23. Answers will vary but might include that the plant did not have an additional source of nutrients and water to continue growing and that the absence of sunlight and available

22 | Plants in Our Lives

Lesson Planning Guide With Options for Block Scheduling

Lecture Concepts	Lesson Resources

22-1 Uses of Plants

BLOCK ❶ (45 minutes)
1. Plants form the base of the food chain on which human survival depends.
2. Wheat, rice, corn, and oats are the fruits of cereal plants, which provide the most food to humans.

❶ Lecture Resources
- Determining Prior Knowledge
- Active Reading: Anticipation Guide
- Active Reading: Reading Organizer
- Demonstration: Analyzing Results
- Holt Biology Videodiscs Lesson 22-1

Classwork Options
- Exploration 22A

- Inquiry Skills Development: Lab B18

Assignment Options
- Problem Solving
- World of Work: Green Thumb Careers

BLOCK ❷ (45 minutes)
3. Roots, stems, and leaves of certain plants are also used as a food source.
4. Plants are used for many things such as fuel, paper making, medicine, and cloth.

❷ Lecture Resources
- Famine
- Active Reading: Reading Organizer
- Demonstration: Identifying Structures
- Teaching Transparencies: 112A
- Holt Biology Videodiscs Lesson 22-1

Classwork Options
- Tree Products
- *Small Group* Reteaching
- Closure: Relating Concepts

- Laboratory Techniques and Experimental Design: Lab C37

Assignment Options
- Life/Work Skills: Finding Information
- Section Review
- Chapter Review, questions 1, 2a, 2b, 4, 5, 6, 7, 8, 9, 10, 18, 22, 24, 26, 28
- Directed Reading Worksheet

22-2 Growing Plants

BLOCK ❸ (45 minutes)
1. In addition to carbon dioxide and water, plants need a number of mineral nutrients that are obtained from the soil.
2. Soil fertility is maintained by methods such as crop rotation, plowing crop residues back into the soil, adding fertilizer, and composting.

❸ Lecture Resources
- Soil Erosion
- Active Reading: K-W-L
- Active Reading: Paired Summarizing
- Visual Strategy: Figure 22-17
- Demonstration: Evaluating Results
- Holt Biology Videodiscs Lesson 22-2

Classwork Options
- Soil Fertility
- Laboratory Techniques and Experimental Design: Lab C38

Assignment Options
- Problem Solving, p. 424
- *Small Group* Hydroponics

BLOCK ❹ (45 minutes)
3. Several factors must be taken into consideration prior to planting, such as climate, soil conditions, and the size and shape of mature plants.
4. Plants must be maintained by doing such things as watering, fertilizing, pruning, and inspecting for disease.

❹ Lecture Resources
- Active Reading: Reading Organizer
- Demonstration: Identifying Functions
- Holt Biology Videodiscs Lesson 22-2

Classwork Options
- *Small Group* The Plant Doctor
- Life/Work Skills: Selecting Technology

Assignment Options
- Pruning

Lecture Concepts

Lesson Resources

22-3 Growing Plants, *continued*

BLOCK 5 (45 minutes)

5. Humans assist in plant evolution by selecting, breeding, and propagating plants with desirable characteristics.

6. Genetic engineering has been responsible for manipulating the nutritional and commercial characteristics of plants.

5 Lecture Resources
- Active Reading: Anticipation Guide
- Visual Strategy: Figure 22-21
- Visual Strategy: Videodisc
- Demonstration: Comparing Structures
- Holt Biology Videodiscs Lesson 22-2

Classwork Options
- Problem Solving, p. 429
- Closure: Inferring Relationships

Assignment Options
- *Small Group* Reteaching
- Section Review
- Chapter Review, questions 2c, 3, 11, 12, 13, 14, 15, 16, 17, 19, 20, 21, 23, 25, 27
- Directed Reading Worksheet

Chapter Review and Assessment

BLOCK 6 (45 minutes)
Review
- Reteaching Worksheet
- Thinking Skills Worksheet
- Vocabulary Development Worksheet
- Language Development and Reading Comprehension Audio CD Program: Chapter 22

BLOCK 7 (45 minutes)
Assessment
- Alternative Assessment, p. 431
- Portfolio Assessment, p. T39

Chapter Test
- Chapter 22 Test

Test Generator
- Item bank for customizing Chapter Tests
- Performance-Based Assessment: Testing Enzyme Activity in Seeds

Teaching Resources CD-ROM
- Scoring Rubrics and Classroom Management Checklist

The Portfolio icon denotes items throughout the Teacher's Edition lesson wrap that may be selected for inclusion in student portfolios.

Holt Biology Videodiscs and *Concepts of Biology*

Holt Biology Videodiscs gives you a powerful tool for teaching, review, and assessment. For further information regarding the media on the videodiscs, see *Holt Biology Videodiscs Teacher's Correlation Guide to Holt Biology: Visualizing Life.*

Concepts of Biology adds interactive lesson plans and extensive tools for customization using CD-ROM technology.

Use the following topic from *Concepts of Biology* to help you teach this chapter:
Topic 16: Plant Structure and Function

Laboratory Planning

Text
Materials and preparation instructions appear on the teacher's wrap accompanying each laboratory exercise.
Block 1: Exploration 22A: Identifying Nutrients in Foods, p. 800

Holt BioSources Laboratory Program
Block 1: Inquiry Skills Development Lab B18: Mineral Deficiencies in Plants
Block 2: Laboratory Techniques and Experimental Design Lab C37: Growing Plants in the Laboratory
Block 3: Laboratory Techniques and Experimental Design Lab C38: Growing Plants in the Laboratory—Fertilizer Problem

CHAPTER 22

Determining Prior Knowledge

- Have students identify objects in the room or on their bodies that are made from plant products.
- Ask students to state the cereal grasses that provide most of the world's food.
- Have students identify the parts of the plant that are used for food and give an example of each.
- Ask students what factors they would take into consideration when planting a garden. Also ask students how they would know if their plants were not healthy.
- Have students state the benefits of genetically engineered plants.

Active READING

Technique: Anticipation Guide
Before students begin this chapter, write the following statements on the chalkboard or the overhead projector:

1. Wood is the most valuable resource that people get from plants.
2. Most of the food that people eat comes from fruits.
3. Plants need only water and air to grow.

Ask students to decide whether they agree or disagree with each statement. Ask volunteers to share the reasons for their opinions. Have students read the chapter to see if their opinions are confirmed or changed.

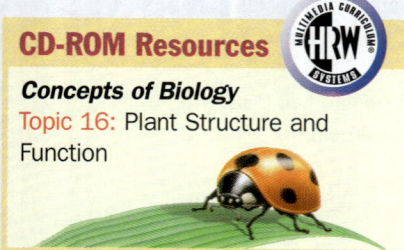

CD-ROM Resources

Concepts of Biology
Topic 16: Plant Structure and Function

CHAPTER 22

REVIEW
- **carbohydrates and proteins (Section 2-3)**
- **leaves, stems, and roots (Section 21-1)**
- **reproduction in flowering plants (Section 21-3)**

Plants in Our Lives

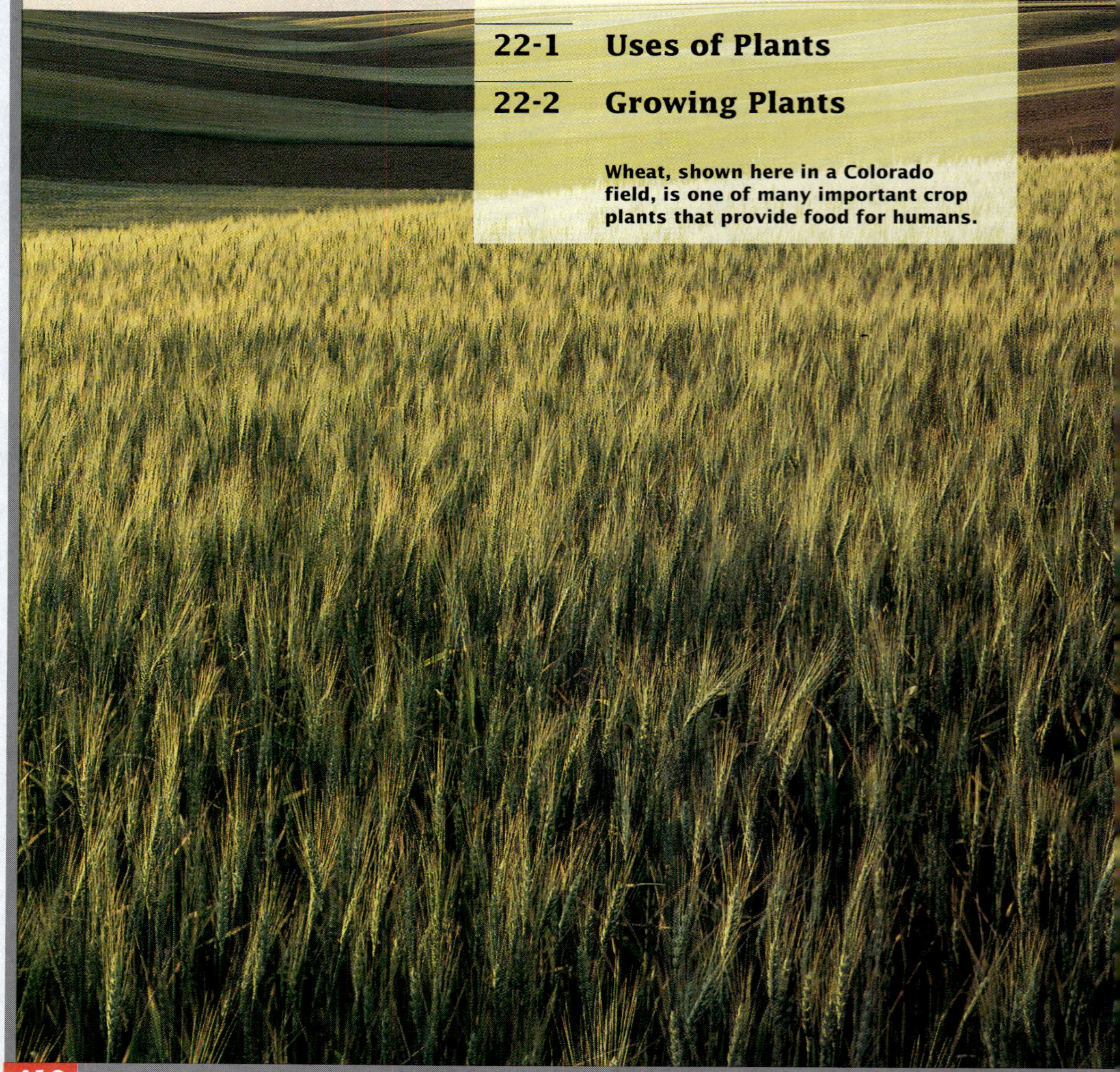

Wheat, shown here in a Colorado field, is one of many important crop plants that provide food for humans.

Author's Rationale In this chapter we first review the many ways that plants have an impact on our lives, focusing on plants as food. Grains like wheat, rice, and corn, for example, are an important part of the human diet. Wood, medicine, cloth, and rubber are but a few of the other uses considered. Then we consider how to grow a plant. Plants need water and nutrients, and often these nutrients must be supplied as fertilizer. Plants can be propagated in many ways, depending on the kind of plant. The key lesson learned in this chapter is that to grow plants successfully, you must identify and provide what the plant needs. Each plant has its own requirements for water, nutrients, soil, temperature, and light.

Plants are an essential part of our lives. You already know that plants produce oxygen. They also provide us with food; almost everything we eat comes from a plant or an animal that ate a plant. And plants provide us with many other useful products, such as wood, medicines, fibers for making cloth and paper, and rubber.

22-1 Uses of Plants

OBJECTIVES

1 **Describe the importance of cereal grains and legumes in the diet.**

2 **Identify the foods that come from plants as fruits, seeds, roots, stems, leaves, or flowers.**

3 **Describe several uses for wood.**

4 **Identify the plant sources of common medicines.**

5 **Name several plants that are natural sources of fibers and rubber.**

Important Grains

Did you know that most of the food people eat comes from fruits? As you read in Chapter 21, fruits are the parts of a flowering plant that contain the plant's seeds. When you think of fruits, you probably think of apples, oranges, and peaches. However, the fruits that provide the most food to humans come from the cereal grasses wheat, rice, corn, and oats. These grain crops occupy more than 70 percent of the world's farmland and provide about 60 percent of the calories eaten by humans, directly or indirectly. The map of the World in **Figure 22-1** shows the regions where wheat, rice, and corn are grown. The fruits of cereal grasses, which are called **grains**, are rich in carbohydrates, protein, vitamins, and dietary fiber. Grains are usually separated from their stalks and then ground into flour or meal and cooked.

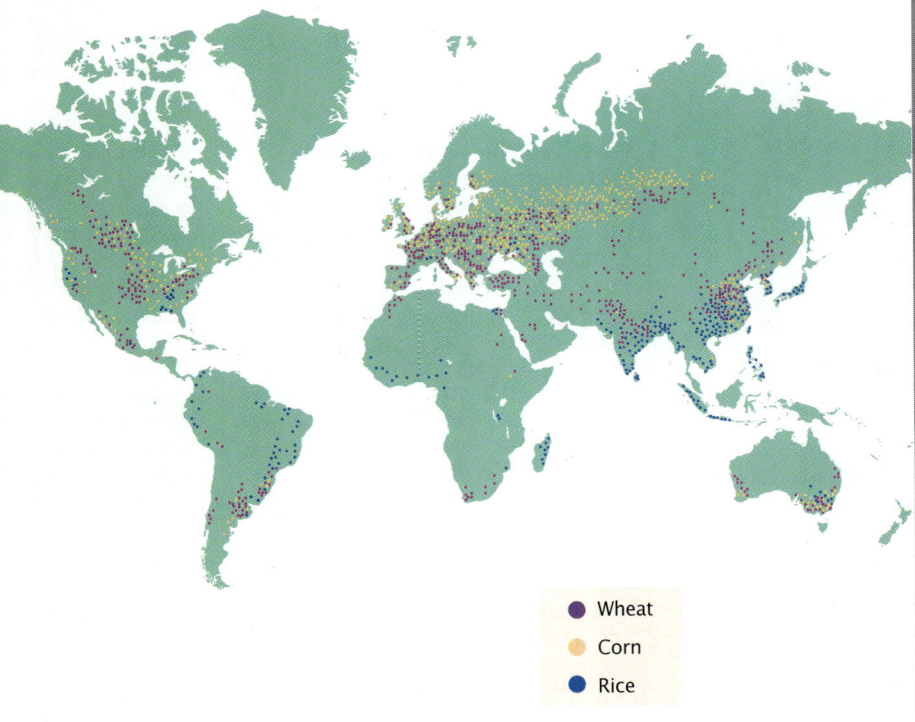

- Wheat
- Corn
- Rice

Figure 22-1
Wheat, rice, and corn are grown all over the world.

411

Videodisc Resources

Holt Biology Videodiscs
Lesson 22-1: Uses of Plants

Phase One
Preparation

Scheduling
See the **Lesson Planning Guide** on pages 409A and 409B for lecture, classwork, and assignment options for Section 22-1.

Phase Two
Teaching Strategies

Active READING
▶ **Technique: Reading Organizer**
As students read about wheat, rice, and corn, have them complete the following reading organizer to compare the important characteristics of each grain.

Important Grains		
Wheat	Rice	Corn

Geography Connection
The Fertile Crescent
The Fertile Crescent is the area of the Middle East where the earliest known civilizations began. This region extends from the Mediterranean Sea, south through the Tigris and Euphrates Valleys to the head of the Persian Gulf. The climate consists of dry summers and rainy winters. Cereals such as wheat, rye, barley, and oats were first cultivated in this area. Have students locate the Fertile Crescent on a world map.

Key to Strategies
Teaching Strategies are keyed to three tiers of learning.

● **Understanding Concepts (Tier I)**
Content mastery and comprehension

■ **Applying Information (Tier II)**
Applying and analyzing content

▲ **Critical Thinking (Tier III)**
Practicing evaluative thinking

Problem Solving
■ Relating Concepts

High-gluten varieties of wheat are used for making bread flour, and low-gluten varieties are used for making pasta flour. Gluten is a protein that helps trap bubbles of carbon dioxide during bread making. Therefore, high-gluten breads have a spongy texture. Some people have an inability to digest this protein completely. The result is malabsorption, which can lead to diarrhea, weight loss, vitamin deficiencies, anemia, and weakened bones. Have students research the problem and compose a list of foods to avoid and a list of foods that are gluten-free or very low in gluten. Students may want to check with a health-food store for wheat-bread substitutes such as spelt bread, rice crackers, and corn pasta.

Wheat bread

Tabbouleh

c Many foods are made from wheat.

Pasta

Bulgur

b The wheat plant is a grass that can grow up to 1.7 m (5 ft) tall.

Bran

Endosperm

Figure 22-2
a This section of a wheat kernel shows the starchy endosperm used in making white flour and the outer bran layer included in whole-wheat flour.

Wheat is the world's most widely grown plant

More than one-third of the people in the world depend on foods made from kernels (grains) of wheat. Wheat stalks and grains are shown in **Figure 22-2**. Long before the beginnings of agriculture, the people of the Middle East gathered and chewed kernels of wild wheat. Early farmers selected kernels from their best wheat plants for the next crop. Over time, this practice resulted in the development of improved varieties of wheat. About a century ago, scientists started using selective breeding to develop new kinds of wheat that are more productive and more resistant to cold temperatures, diseases, insects, and other stresses. The wheat that is grown today bears little resemblance to its wild ancestors.

In many areas of the world, wheat appears in some form at nearly every meal. Wheat flour is excellent for baking because it contains a mixture of proteins called gluten, which makes dough elastic. This elasticity enables dough containing yeast to rise. Yeast-risen dough is used to make a variety of breads and other baked goods. Pasta is made by mixing ground wheat and water to form a thick paste, which is then pressed into spaghetti and other shapes. In the Middle East, wheat kernels are also boiled or soaked and then pounded until they crack. The cracked pieces, which are called bulgur *(BUHL guhr)*, are then dried and used to prepare dishes such as tabbouleh, pilavi, or kisir. Pita, or pocket bread made from wheat flour, may accompany these meals. **Figure 22-2c** shows a variety of foods made from wheat.

Historical Perspective: Norman Borlaug

Norman Borlaug, who helped launch the Green Revolution, was awarded the Nobel Prize in 1970 for developing new strains of wheat in Mexico. This wheat was planted in 1944, and within 20 years Mexico had enough not only to feed its own people but also to export to other countries. India and Pakistan experienced similar successes. This high-yielding strain was produced from crosses with a dwarf variety from Japan.

Rice is one of the world's most important food crops

More than half of the people in the world eat rice as the main part of their meal. Rice is often grown in standing water, as seen in **Figure 22-3**. Therefore, rice is usually grown in moist regions, such as in the flood plains of rivers. The people of Southeast Asia probably gathered and ate wild rice thousands of years ago, but no one knows exactly when or where domesticated rice originated. China, India, or Indochina is probably where rice was first cultivated. Archaeologists have found evidence that people cultivated rice for food in southern China as early as 5000 B.C. From there, rice spread north to Japan.

Although low in protein, rice is an excellent source of carbohydrates. The nutrient-rich bran layers of rice grains are removed to make white rice, which has few vitamins. Brown rice, however, still contains the nutrient-rich bran layers on the outside of the kernel. **Table 22-1** shows the nutritional content of rice and wheat. In societies where people eat mainly white rice, vitamin-rich sauces such as soy sauce are added to the cooked rice to make meals more nutritious.

Rice is added to many processed foods, including breakfast cereals, soup, baby food, and flour. Breweries use broken rice grains to make mash, an ingredient used to make beer. In Japan, rice grains are used to make an alcoholic drink called sake (*SAHK ee*), or rice wine. But rice isn't just for eating and drinking. The outer coats of rice grains are used in products such as insulation and cement. Many people in Asia use the dried stalks of rice plants to thatch roofs and to make sandals, hats, and baskets.

Figure 22-3

a The rice plant is a grass that grows to heights of 80 to 180 cm (32 to 72 in.). When the rice is ripe, the plant turns golden yellow.

b Because rice requires a great deal of water, it is often grown in fields of standing water called paddies.

Table 22-1 Protein and Dietary Fiber

Grain (100 g)	Protein (g)	Fiber (g)
Brown rice	7.9	1.3
White rice	7.1	0.3
White wheat flour	10.3	0.3
Whole wheat flour	13.7	2.1

413

Multicultural Perspective: Shimenawa

Rice plays an important part in the customs of many cultures. For example, Japanese people place a *shimenawa*, a rice-straw rope, over an entrance to ward off evil. The largest *shimenawa* in the world hangs over the entrance to the Izumo Shinto shrine. That *shimenawa* weighs 6 metric tons. The Hindu consider rice the goddess of life and fertility. Pouring rice over someone's head is meant to bring the person prosperity and happiness. Students may be familiar with a similar custom, such as throwing rice at a wedding.

Health Connection

Pellagra

Pellagra is a nutritional-deficiency disease that is associated with a corn diet and is caused by a lack of the vitamin niacin. Although corn is rich in niacin, the niacin is in a bound form that the body cannot use. If the corn is first treated with lime water, as it is in Mexico before being used in certain dishes such as tortillas, then the niacin becomes available. Symptoms of pellagra include weakness, weight loss, lethargy, diarrhea, inflammation of the skin, and blisters. Treatment consists of doses of niacin and a high-protein diet rich in the amino acid tryptophan. The human body can convert tryptophan into niacin, so researchers are working to develop a strain of corn with substantially higher levels of tryptophan.

Agriculture Connection

Councils and Associations

Form cooperative groups of four students. Have each group compose a letter to an association that deals with a specific grain. The Encyclopedia of Associations, published by Gale Research, is a good source for this project. Students should request information on a specific topic. Possible topics include availability of genetically engineered varieties, farming methods, and pest control. Read the letters for content and accuracy before they are sent.

Corn is the most widely grown crop in the United States

Modern corn probably originated from *Zea mexicana*, a wild Mexican annual grass known as teosinte *(tee oh SIHN tee)*. Teosinte produces narrow female flower spikes that mature into "ears" with two rows of grains, as seen in **Figure 22-4a**. The grains of teosinte are covered by a hard case and are difficult to grind until they have been heated and popped like popcorn.

Corn was cultivated by the Aztecs of Mexico, the Mayas of Yucatan and Central America, and the Incas of South America. Columbus and other European explorers introduced corn to many areas of the world. The selective breeding of corn began more than 7,000 years ago in Mexico. American Indian farmers selected plants that produced "ears" with tender grains that could be eaten more easily than the hard teosinte grains. They also selected plants that produced ears with more rows of grains. The high-yield varieties of hybrid corn grown today, such as the one seen in **Figure 22-4b**, are made by crossing inbred strains of corn that each have a desirable trait.

Corn is more suited to the warm climate of the southern United States and Mexico than is wheat. As a result, corn is used to prepare many of the traditional components of the diets in these regions. Foods made from corn are seen in **Figure 22-4c**. Corn bread, corn pone, hominy, and grits are traditional components of the diet in the southeastern United States. Tortillas, which are served with many Mexican dishes, are a flattened, unleavened bread that is often prepared with corn meal. Corn is also used to produce corn syrup, margarine, cornstarch, cooking oil, and many industrial products. In addition, corn is one of the world's chief foods for domestic animals. Seventy percent of the United States corn crop is consumed by livestock.

Figure 22-4

a This ear of teosinte, which is the ancestor of modern corn, has two rows of grains.

Teosinte

Row of grains

b Large ears of tender corn are produced by modern hybrid corn plants.

Hybrid corn

Corn bread

c Corn tortillas and corn bread are foods made from corn.

Tortillas

414

Community Connection: Food From Plants

Invite a farmer or gardener to talk with students about vegetable production. Have the person point out to students that plants store excess starch, sugar, and other nutrients in fruits, pods, seeds, stems, roots, and leaves. Encourage the grower to bring samples of their products and to answer the following questions in their presentation: What do growers add to the soil? What can be done to increase the size of vegetables and fruits? How much water does the grower provide? What are some of the problems encountered in growing these foods? What kind of work is involved?

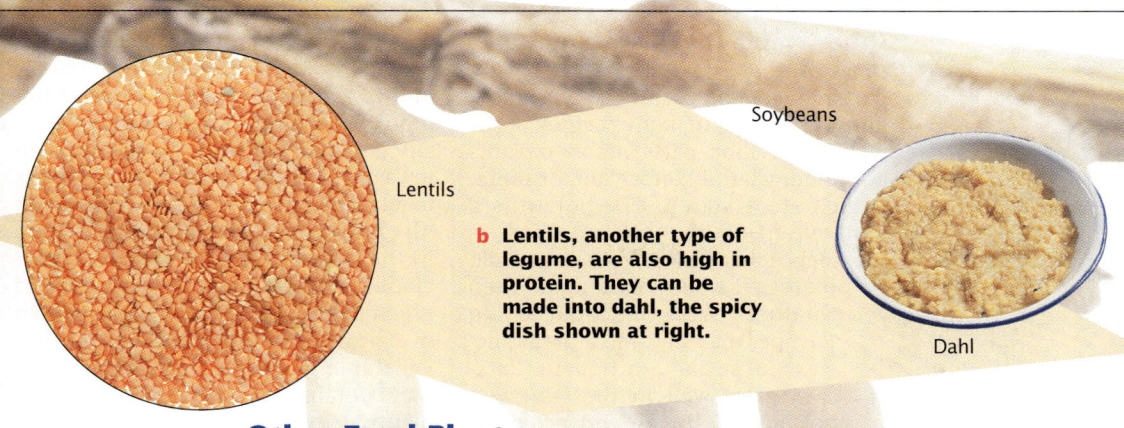

Soybeans

Lentils

b Lentils, another type of legume, are also high in protein. They can be made into dahl, the spicy dish shown at right.

Dahl

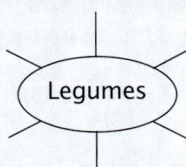
Other Food Plants

Although cereal grains provide most of the calories consumed by humans, they do not contain all of the nutrients you need for a healthy diet. They lack adequate amounts of some of the **essential amino acids**, which are the nine amino acids that are not made by the human body. Foods from other plants are rich sources of these amino acids, and they provide vitamins and minerals as well.

Legumes are high in protein

Legumes *(LEHG yooms)* are members of the pea (or bean) family. As you read in Chapter 9, many legumes host nitrogen-fixing bacteria in their roots. These bacteria provide legumes with extra nitrogen, which is a component of protein. The seeds of legumes have more protein than the seeds of most plants. They are also rich in essential amino acids that are scarce in grains. Many cultures eat combinations of grains and legumes, such as corn and beans, which provide ample amounts of all the essential amino acids.

Soybeans, shown in **Figure 22-5a**, were probably first cultivated in northeast China more than 3,000 years ago. Soybeans can be cooked and pressed into cakes called tofu, also known as bean curd or soybean cakes. Tofu has been the protein staple for people in eastern Asia for 2,000 years and is an important food for more than 1 billion people. Lentils are popular legumes in Egypt and India. They can be ground into flour or made into dahl, which is seen in **Figure 22-5b**.

Sugar comes from sugar cane and sugar beets

Sugar is by far the most important sweetener in the world today. Most of the sugar that you eat comes from sugar beets or sugar cane. Sugar beets have large fleshy roots, like carrots, in which they store sucrose. Sugar cane, seen in **Figure 22-6**, is a tall grass with sturdy stalks that have a large amount of juice containing sucrose. The juice is used to make table sugar and syrup. Sugar cane is thought to have been first used by people in the Far East. The process of producing sugar from sugar cane has been practiced in India since 3000 B.C. The sap was boiled to produce large and small lumps. Large lumps were called *khanda*, which may be the origin of the word *candy*. Small lumps were called *sakkara*, which may be the origin of the word *saccharine*.

Figure 22-6
This man is cutting stalks of sugar cane.

Figure 22-5
a Soybeans are very high in protein. They are used to make tofu, soy milk, cheese, and many types of meat substitutes.

Interdependence

How do humans benefit from the ability of plants to store the products of photosynthesis?

Historical Perspective: George Washington Carver

George Washington Carver (1864–1943) was a horticulturist whose agricultural research revolutionized the economy of the southern United States by encouraging farmers to grow more than just cotton. He urged farmers to grow sweet potatoes, peanuts, pecans, and soybeans. In 1896, the same year he received his master's degree at Iowa State Agricultural College, Carver was asked to head the Department of Agriculture at Tuskegee Institute in Alabama. It was there that he discovered more than 300 industrial products that could be made from the peanut, 100 that could be made from the sweet potato, and 75 that could be made from the pecan.

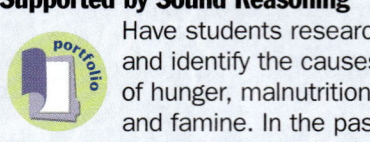

Famine

▲ **Forming Opinions Supported by Sound Reasoning**

Have students research and identify the causes of hunger, malnutrition, and famine. In the past 25 years alone, hunger and famine have been caused by droughts, floods, plant diseases, wars, slash-and-burn agriculture, chemical farming techniques, depleted soils, and plagues of insects. Have students write an opinion paper about what should be done to end this type of human suffering.

World of Work

Green Thumb Careers

A variety of interesting careers are available to plant lovers. They range from writing and photography to floriculture and herbal medicine. A book that covers this wide range of opportunities is *Careers for Plant Lovers and Other Green Thumb Types,* by Blythe Camenson. Encourage students to explore this book, especially if they like plants.

Cassava root

Figure 22-7
Cassava is a starchy root that can be prepared in much the same way as potatoes. In the United States, it is usually made into tapioca.

Tapioca pudding

Other staple foods are roots or stems

Potatoes are the dietary staple (most important food) in many regions of the world. The edible parts of potato plants are underground stems called **tubers**, which store starch. The potato is a native of South America. There is evidence that people in Chile ate wild potatoes 13,000 years ago. When potatoes were introduced in Europe, they became a great success, especially in Ireland. Potatoes grew well in the country's cool, moist climate and provided enough calories for an entire family. As you read in Chapter 19, a disease caused by the water mold *Phytophthora infestans* virtually destroyed the Irish potato crop in the mid-1840s. Yams, which are also tubers, are a food staple in many countries.

Some plants store food for the next season's growth in enlarged roots. Many of these roots are edible. For example, carrots have been grown as food in Europe for at least 2,000 years. Other important root crops include radishes, turnips, beets, sweet potatoes, and cassava, also called manioc. Cassava, shown in **Figure 22-7**, is the staple food of more than 500 million people around the world. It contributes more than one-third of the calories consumed in Africa.

Many vegetables are actually fruits

The term *vegetable* refers to an agricultural commodity, or product, that comes from a plant and is eaten with the main part of a meal. On the other hand, "fruits" are agricultural commodities that are sweet and are usually eaten as desserts. As you learned in Chapter 21, the term *fruit* also refers to a ripened ovary of a flowering plant. All of the "fruits" you eat are also fruits in the botanical sense. However, vegetables such as tomatoes, squash, and green beans are also fruits, as shown in **Figure 22-8**. How can you tell if a vegetable is also a fruit? Vegetables that contain seeds are the fruits of the plants that produce them.

Humans also eat the leaves or flowers of particular plants

The leaves of plants such as cabbage, parsley, spinach, chard, turnips, and lettuce are popular vegetables. Some forms of lettuce may have been cultivated as early as 4500 B.C. Lettuce is even depicted on Egyptian tombs. Other vegetables that you may have eaten are parts of leaves. Onion bulbs and garlic cloves consist of the fleshy bases of leaves, and celery is a petiole (leaf stalk). When you eat Brussels sprouts, you are eating leafy buds. When you eat broccoli, cauliflower, or artichokes, you are eating clusters of immature flowers.

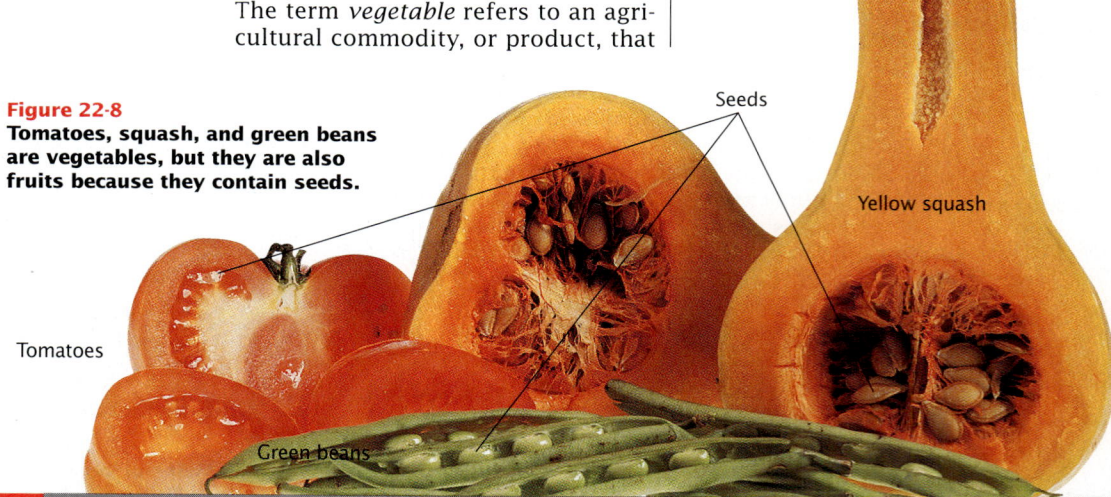

Figure 22-8
Tomatoes, squash, and green beans are vegetables, but they are also fruits because they contain seeds.

Seeds

Yellow squash

Tomatoes

Green beans

Matter of Fact: Garlic

Garlic was given daily to slaves building the Great Pyramid at Giza, in Egypt. To the Greeks, garlic was a protective herb that was left at crossroads to appease the underworld goddess Hecate. In World Wars I and II, garlic was used to treat infections. Recently, researchers have found that garlic contains a compound that activates enzymes in the liver to destroy aflatoxin, a carcinogen that is the leading cause of liver cancer. Garlic may also protect humans against carcinogens found in charcoal-broiled meats, polluted air, and cigarette smoke. Though researchers suggest that people eat garlic, it does have chemicals that irritate the intestines. Check for current recommended dosages, as they may change to reflect additional research.

Uses of Wood

After food and oxygen, wood is the most valuable resource that people get from plants. As you read in Chapter 21, many plants that live for many years have stems that get thicker each year. The thickening of stems results from the production of secondary xylem and phloem. **Wood** is secondary xylem.

Trees are harvested for lumber

Wood from trees that have been cut down and sawed into boards and planks is called **lumber**. Nearly three-fourths of the lumber in the United States is used for construction. The rest goes to factories that make products such as boxes, crates, toys, railroad cars, boats, and other items. Wood chips and sawdust are treated with chemicals to make wood pulp, which is used to make paper, rayon, and other products.

Some wood is used as fuel

Wood has been used as a fuel since prehistoric times. It is the main fuel in developing countries and for more than half of the people in the world. A family that uses wood for heating and cooking burns about a ton of wood each year. As a result, wood is being burned faster than

new trees can grow. In some African countries, wood is so scarce that the average family spends one-third of its income on wood.

Fuel can be made from wood chips through an experimental fermentation process. The wood chips are first treated with sulfuric acid to free cellulose and xylan, another polysaccharide. Additional enzyme treatments break these large compounds down into five- and six-carbon sugars. Finally, an assortment of bacteria and yeasts is added to ferment the sugars into ethanol.

Paper is one of our most important plant products

Cellulose fibers from plants are used to make paper. Papermaking fibers come from many different plants, such as cotton, bamboo, rice, sugar cane, and wheat. However, most paper is made from wood pulp. The process of making paper from wood pulp is summarized in **Figure 22-9**. Paper can be recycled and used to make new paper. But because it is expensive to remove inks and dyes from printed paper, the cost of recycling paper often exceeds the cost of making new paper from wood.

Figure 22-9
The papermaking process involves many steps.

b Wood chips are made into wood pulp.

c Huge rollers press the cellulose fibers from wood pulp into paper.

a Logs are ground into wood chips.

Tree Products

● **Organizing Information**
Have students make a **Graphic Organizer** similar to the one at the bottom of this page that illustrates the importance of trees. Have them use any of the vocabulary words contained in this section as well as any other words they may wish to include.

Recycling Paper

■ **Recognizing Relationships**
Stress the importance of paper recycling. The average American consumes more than 200 kg (600 lb) of wood per year in the form of lumber and paper used for packaging and advertisement. Recycling the country's Sunday newspapers could save an entire forest of 500,000 trees each week. Organize a visit to a paper-recycling plant. Prior to the visit, obtain information that will help students understand what is happening in the plant as they tour. Encourage students to ask questions during the tour.

417

Graphic Organizer

Use the following graphic organizer with the teaching strategy **Tree Products** on page 417.

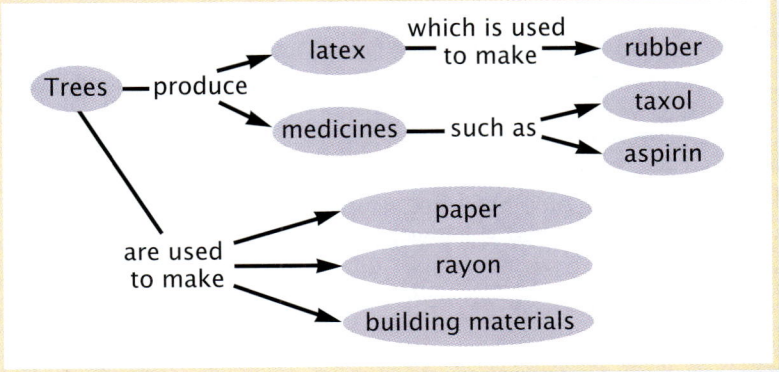

Key to Strategies
● Understanding Concepts (Tier I)
■ Applying Information (Tier II)
▲ Critical Thinking (Tier III)

Life/Work Skills
Finding Information

■ **Relating Concepts**

Some plants are used in the production of folk medicine and herbal remedies. Have students form cooperative groups of three. Each group is to report on a plant that is used for medicinal purposes. Students may choose from a variety of plants, including aloe, witch hazel, blackberry, camphor, ginger, echinacea, goldenseal, and garlic. Each group is to research the plant and find its scientific name, an illustration, a description, its habitat, its uses, and its side effects when used. Invite students to display their work.

Figure 22-10
An American Indian doctor (left) is teaching a Western doctor (right) about native Amazonian rain-forest plants that can be used to treat disease.

Medicines From Plants

People have always used plants to treat diseases and other ailments. Botany (the study of plants) was considered to be a branch of medicine until the mid-1800s. Doctors, such as the ones in **Figure 22-10**, continue to search for plants that may provide new treatments or cures for diseases such as cancer. Many familiar medicines, their original plant sources, and their uses are listed in **Table 22-2**. Some plants, such as the Pacific yew, nearly faced extinction as demand increased for the medicines made from them. Although the medicinal ingredients of most of these plants have been synthesized, most of these chemicals are still extracted from the plants that form them.

Table 22-2 Medicines Originally Derived From Plants

Name	Original source	Uses
aspirin	willow leaves and bark	relieves pain and reduces fever; is the world's most widely used drug
codeine	poppy fruits	relieves pain
digitalis	foxglove leaves	regulates irregular heartbeat
ephedrine	ephedra stems	relieves high blood pressure and symptoms of asthma and hay fever; acts as a decongestant
hydrocortisone	yam tubers	relieves symptoms of allergies and arthritis
quinine	cinchona tree bark	prevents malaria and relieves symptoms of malaria
reserpine	snakeroot roots	relieves high blood pressure and symptoms of schizophrenia
taxol	yew bark	reduces the size of cancerous tumors
vinblastine, vincristine	rosy periwinkle plants	used to treat cancers such as Hodgkin's disease and acute childhood leukemia

418

Community Connection: Arbor Day

In the United States and Canada, Arbor Day is celebrated to draw national attention to trees. *Arbor* is another word for *tree*. The idea for Arbor Day originated with Sterling Morton, a newspaperman who recognized that trees enrich the soil and help it hold water. On the first Arbor Day, the state of Nebraska offered prizes to people who planted the most trees. One million trees were planted in Nebraska on that day. After Morton's death, Arbor Day was celebrated on April 22, Morton's birthday. In California, Arbor Day is celebrated on Luther Burbank's birthday, March 7, because Burbank developed many new varieties of trees and plants.

Other Plant Products

Plants are an important source of fibers used to make clothing. Cloth has been made from cotton for centuries. Cotton thread is spun from the strong, fine fibers attached to cotton seeds, shown in **Figure 22-11**. Cotton is still the world's most important plant fiber. The stems of flax plants yield a softer, more durable fiber that is used to make a cloth known as linen. Although synthetic fibers now make up more than 30 percent of the world's fibers, natural fibers are still prized for their durability, comfort, and strength.

Turpentine is a colorless liquid solvent that is used to remove paint. This highly flammable substance is extracted from pine trees that grow in the southeastern United States. A vapor containing turpentine forms when pine trees are made into wood pulp. As the vapor cools, a liquid that contains turpentine forms. Turpentine is also used to make disinfectants, insecticides, medicines, and perfumes.

Rubber is one of the most important raw materials obtained from plants. Natural rubber is made from latex, which is a milky liquid produced by certain plants, such as trees of the genus *Hevea*. American Indians of South America made rubber balls and waterproof shoes from latex, which is shown in **Figure 22-12**. Today most natural rubber comes from plantations of rubber trees in Asia. Natural rubber is also made from the sap of a desert plant called guayule (*gwah YOO lee*), which is native to Texas and grown as a crop in the southwestern United States. Most of today's rubber, however, is manufactured from petroleum.

Figure 22-11
Fibers that encased seeds in cotton bolls (pods of the cotton plant) are being spun into thread by this Brazilian woman.

Figure 22-12
Latex is the milky sap of certain plants. These men are working with raw latex at a processing plant in Malaysia.

SECTION REVIEW

1. Why is it important to combine grains with other vegetables, such as legumes?

2. Identify each of the following as a fruit, seed, root, stem, leaf, or flower: broccoli, carrot, onion, corn, and potato.

3. What are three ways that people use wood?

4. Where were aspirin and taxol first obtained? How is each used?

5. What are two plant sources of fibers used to make cloth?

419

Plants in Our Lives 419

22-2

Scheduling

See the **Lesson Planning Guide** on pages 409A and 409B for lecture, classwork, and assignment options for Section 22-2.

Phase Two
Teaching Strategies

Active READING

Technique: K-W-L

Before students read Section 22-2, have them write short individual lists of all the things they already **K**now (or that they have heard) about how to grow plants. When students have finished their lists, ask them to contribute their entries to a class list on the chalkboard or on the overhead projector. Then have students list things they **W**ant to know about growing plants. After students finish the section, have them place check marks next to questions that they are now able to answer. Students should finish by making a list of what they've **L**earned. Conclude by asking students the following:
- Which questions are still unanswered?
- What new questions do you have?

Active READING

Technique: Paired Summarizing

Have students read silently about soils and plant growth on pages 420 and 421. Then assign partners and have one student, the "reteller," summarize orally what has been read while the other student, the "listener," listens to the retelling. The listener should point out inaccuracies and add ideas that were left out. Have students alternate roles and repeat this process for each page. Students should work together during a final clarification process, referring to the text as needed.

Fossils and art such as this Egyptian wall painting suggest that humans began cultivating plants between 7,000 and 9,000 years ago. Plants that furnish useful products are grown by farmers and horticulturists. Home gardeners grow plants outside and inside of their homes. Successful plant growers understand a plant's needs and provide for those needs.

22-2 Growing Plants

OBJECTIVES

1 Summarize the importance of soil to the growth of a plant.

2 Justify the use of well-adapted plants for landscapes and gardens.

3 Relate changes in the appearance of a plant to its health.

4 Describe five methods of vegetative propagation.

5 Compare and contrast traditional plant breeding with genetic engineering.

Soils and Plant Growth

Like you, plants require nutrients to grow. Plants obtain their nutrients from inorganic compounds such as carbon dioxide (CO_2) and water (H_2O). The carbon (C), oxygen (O), and hydrogen (H) in carbon dioxide and water are just three of the nutrients plants need. In Chapter 5, you learned that plants use the carbon, oxygen, and hydrogen from carbon dioxide and water in photosynthesis. But plants need more than just air and water to grow. Why do plants grow better in soil than they do in plain water? What is it about soil that helps plants grow?

Plants obtain nutrients from soil
The soil that surrounds a plant's roots, as seen in **Figure 22-13**, provides many of the nutrients that the plant needs. Roots take up these nutrients as they take up water. Plants require relatively large amounts of the nutrients nitrogen (N), phosphorus (P), potassium (K), calcium (Ca), sulfur (S), and magnesium (Mg). The nutrients that plants need in relatively large amounts are called **macronutrients**. Other nutrients, such as iron (Fe), chlorine (Cl), copper (Cu), manganese (Mn), zinc (Zn), and boron (B), are also critical to healthy plant growth, but they are needed only in tiny amounts. The nutrients that plants need in very small amounts are called **micronutrients**.

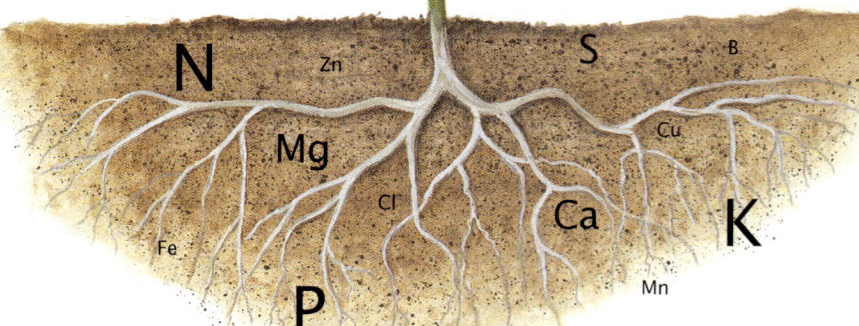

Figure 22-13
Most plants are anchored in soil by their roots. Soil provides nutrients such as water and a variety of macronutrients and micronutrients.

420

Videodisc Resources

Holt Biology Videodiscs
Lesson 22-2: Growing Plants

Soil is composed of rock particles and organic matter

Soil is a mixture of pieces of inorganic matter (weathered rock) and decaying organic matter. The rock particles in soil fall into three categories—sand, silt, or clay—based on their size. Sand grains are the largest soil particles, ranging from 2 mm (0.4 in.) to 20 μm (0.004 in.) in diameter. Silt particles range from about 20 μm (0.004 in.) to 2 μm (0.0004 in.) in diameter. Clay particles are the smallest soil particles, less than 2 μm (0.0004 in.) in diameter. If a soil is a mixture of sand, silt, and clay, it is called a **loam**. Most soils are loams. You can determine the amount of sand, silt, and clay in a soil by pouring the soil through a series of sieves with specific mesh sizes. **Figure 22-14** shows another way that soil can be analyzed to determine the types of soil particles it contains.

Soils also contain water, which is held in the air spaces between soil particles. As the size of soil particles decreases, the size of the air spaces between the particles also decreases. Therefore, sandy soils have large spaces between their particles, silty soils have medium-sized spaces, and clay soils have very small spaces.

Have you noticed that relatively few plants grow on sand dunes and on solid clay river banks? What is wrong with these soils? The size of the air spaces in a soil determines its capacity to hold water and air, as the graph

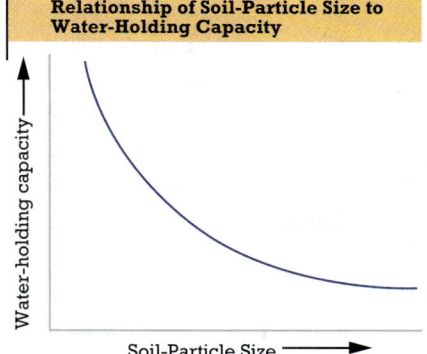

Relationship of Soil-Particle Size to Water-Holding Capacity

Water-holding capacity ⟶

Soil-Particle Size ⟶

Figure 22-15
This graph shows that the water-holding capacity of a soil increases as the soil-particle size decreases.

in **Figure 22-15** indicates. Sandy soils contain a lot of air but hold very little water. Clay soils hold a large amount of water when all of the spaces are filled but contain very little air as a result. Loams are generally the best soils for plant growth. A loam is packed loosely enough to contain ample air, which provides the oxygen needed by roots for cellular respiration, but tightly enough to hold sufficient water for plant growth.

The organic component of soil is called **humus** (hyoo muhs). It is a rich source of carbon, oxygen, nitrogen, and hydrogen for plants. Humus forms as bacteria and fungi in the soil decompose fallen leaves, dead organisms, and animal wastes. Earthworms and millipedes also consume and break down the remains of organisms. These burrowing animals work humus into a soil and aerate it (make tunnels that enable air to enter) at the same time.

Figure 22-14
One way to judge the composition of a soil is to make "soil balls."

a Sandy soils will not make a ball.

b Clay soils make balls that can be worked like modeling clay.

c Loams and silty soils make balls that readily fall apart.

421

Soil Erosion

■ Relating Concepts

Soil is formed by a weathering process that involves the breakdown of rock and minerals, whereas erosion is the physical movement of the soil from one place to another. Ask students to list direct and indirect causes of soil erosion. *(Possible answers are wind, flowing water, agriculture, logging, grazing, and human traffic that disturbs the vegetation and soil.)* Once these are listed, ask students what effect erosion has on the environment. *(Possible answers are loss of farmland and grazing areas, sediment pollution in lakes and streams, and decreased water quality.)* Ask students how they might remedy or prevent erosion. *(Answers may include contour farming, terracing, strip cropping, zoning, mulching hiking trails, and, for short-term solutions, fertilizing and irrigating.)*

Social Studies Connection
The Dust Bowl

The Dust Bowl comprised areas of Oklahoma, Texas, Colorado, New Mexico, and Kansas. In the early part of the twentieth century, mechanization allowed farmers to plow up the grass and plant crops such as wheat. Drought occurred between 1934 and 1937, leaving the area without the much-needed root systems of native grasses. The topsoil was blown away by strong winds. The majority of the population left the area. Farming was eventually made possible again with the help of government restoration projects.

Matter of Fact: Soil Color

The color of the soil helps indicate certain conditions. A dark brown or red soil usually indicates good drainage. Gray soil mixed with yellow or red indicates poor drainage. A black top layer indicates a high content of organic matter. Pale soil may mean that the topsoil has been removed. Soil that contains patches of different colors usually means the water table is near the surface during certain times of the year.

Key to Strategies
● Understanding Concepts (Tier I)
■ Applying Information (Tier II)
▲ Critical Thinking (Tier III)

422

Connection: *Chapter 14*

The Nitrogen Cycle
Ask students to discuss the role that nitrogen-fixing bacteria play in an ecosystem.

Soil Fertility

▲ **Evaluating Viewpoints**
Animal manure, although a highly effective organic fertilizer, is seldom used on a large-scale basis today. Ask students to list possible reasons for this. *(Motorized farm machinery has replaced working animals that would naturally add manure to the soil, and transporting manure to a farm is expensive.)* Commercial inorganic fertilizers—those that contain K, P, and N—are now widely used, but they have disadvantages. Ask students to name a few. *(Possible answers include that they do not add humus to the soil, they lack other important elements, and they decrease the porosity of the soil, which lowers the oxygen content and decreases water absorption.)*

Language Arts Connection

Children of the Dust Bowl

Obtain the nonfiction book *Children of the Dust Bowl.* Read aloud excerpts from the book, and discuss how the devastating erosion affected the children and their families. Show students current photographs of Oklahoma, and encourage them to discuss the importance of soil conservation programs.

b **Alfalfa plants host nitrogen-fixing bacteria in their roots, like many other legumes. These bacteria add nitrogen to the soil as the crop grows.**

Figure 22-16
a **This farmer is mowing a crop of alfalfa, which is a legume. The plants will be plowed into the soil as green manure, which adds humus to the soil.**

Cultivation practices help maintain soil fertility

Natural processes, such as decomposition and nitrogen fixation, continually add nutrients to the soil. However, plants can remove available nutrients from the soil around their roots more quickly than the nutrients can be replaced. The nutrients that plants take from the soil become part of the plants. These nutrients must be replaced if the soil is to maintain its **fertility**, or its ability to supply plants with nutrients. Many of the nutrients taken from the soil by plants are returned to the soil when the plants die and decay. However, few nutrients are returned to the soil when a crop is harvested. When another crop is planted in the same soil, there may not be enough nutrients in the soil for the crop to grow.

Over the centuries, farmers have developed many methods to help the soil maintain its fertility. For example, a farmer might grow corn in a field one year and soybeans the next year. Both crops remove nutrients from the soil, but the plants have different nutrient requirements, and therefore the soil does not lose the same nutrients two years in a row. Soybean plants even add nitrogen compounds to the soil. Alternating two or more crops in the same field from year to year is called **crop rotation**. Sometimes farmers do not grow a crop in a field for a year or two. This allows natural processes to rebuild the field's store of nutrients.

Other farming practices that help maintain soil fertility involve plowing under plant material left in fields. You can do the same thing in a lawn or garden by not removing grass clippings and dead leaves. Farmers often plow crop residues such as stems, roots, and leaves back into the soil. Occasionally farmers grow a crop not for harvest but strictly for plowing back into the field. Such a crop is called a **green manure**. Plowing under crop residues and green manure, as seen in **Figure 22-16**, adds organic matter to the soil. Decomposers in the soil do the rest, turning the residues and green manure into humus.

Matter of Fact: Soil

Soil scientists use the term *soil* to describe material that is capable of supporting plant growth. *Regolith* is the term reserved for infertile soil. *Dirt* is related to the word *defecate,* and it refers to an undesirable, filthy substance.

Fertilizers are applied to enhance soil fertility

A **fertilizer** is a substance that adds nutrients to soil. Farmers and home gardeners use fertilizers to replace the nutrients that are lost when crops, grass clippings, leaves, and other plant materials are harvested or discarded. The label on a fertilizer bag tells you which nutrients it provides. Look at the fertilizer label in **Figure 22-17**. The series of three numbers (5-10-5) indicates the percentage of available nitrogen (N), phosphorus (P), and potassium (K) that is provided by the fertilizer. This series of numbers is called the NPK rating.

Many different types of fertilizers are available. Complete fertilizers provide all of the nutrients that a plant might need. Special-purpose fertilizers are formulated for particular needs, such as stimulation of root growth or acidification of the soil. These fertilizers contain only one or two of the major nutrients. Chemical fertilizers are made from inorganic chemicals. They are sold in both liquid and dry forms. Some chemical fertilizers release their nutrients as soon as they are applied and are thus called quick-release fertilizers. Fertilizers that release their nutrients over a long period of time are called slow-release fertilizers.

Organic fertilizers contain organic material, such as composted manure (animal droppings), cottonseed meal, or sewage sludge. **Composting** involves mixing organic debris (such as grass clippings and table scraps) and allowing it to begin the process of decomposition. Not all organic materials are good fertilizers. Fresh manure, for example, contains only small amounts of usable nutrients (its NPK rating is typically about 1-1-1). Manure that has not been composted even competes with plants for available nitrogen. However, organic fertilizers also improve the water-holding capacity of soils and promote the growth of bacteria that help plants extract nutrients. Organic fertilizers are slow-release fertilizers because bacterial action releases their nutrients.

Plants can be grown without soil

One method of growing plants without soil is called **hydroponics**. This method involves growing plants in a nutrient solution (water plus nutrients). All of the macronutrients and micronutrients that plants obtain from soil must be included in the nutrient solution surrounding the plant roots. Many greenhouse tomatoes are grown using hydroponics.

N promotes overall plant growth.

P promotes root growth and flowering.

K regulates opening and closing of stomata.

Figure 22-17
The three large numbers on the label of this fertilizer bag show its NPK rating, which is the percentage of available nitrogen, phosphorus, and potassium in the fertilizer.

423

● **Interpreting Data**
Show students several labels from various fertilizers. Work with students to interpret the NPK rating on each label.

Hydroponics

● **Organizing Information**
Form cooperative groups consisting of three or four students. Have each group research the topic of hydroponics. Their research should include descriptions of how the plants are grown, supplemented with diagrams or pictures.

Community Connection: Composting

Many towns instruct residents on how to compost. Some garden centers sell composting containers designed for gardeners with limited space. These containers have special features that aid the process of decomposition. Have students attend a demonstration or do library research to find out about composting.

Key to Strategies
● **Understanding Concepts (Tier I)**
■ **Applying Information (Tier II)**
▲ **Critical Thinking (Tier III)**

Problem Solving

▲ **Justifying Conclusions**

Prepare a layout of a garden. Include important information, such as the dimensions, soil type, temperature, amount of rainfall, amount of sun, and wildlife. Form cooperative groups of four or five students. Inform them that they are the landscapers and that you want them to design a garden for you. Tell them they must consider things like cost, types of flowers (annuals, biennials, perennials), color combinations, appearance of flowers, and what the garden will look like during the different seasons. Give each group the layout and several gardening magazines and nursery catalogs. After they have designed your garden, ask each group to convince you that their choice of plants will work. *(The requirements of each plant the students chose must be compatible with information and expectations you gave them.)*

Choosing the Right Plants

Different kinds of plants thrive in different conditions: palm trees grow in the tropics, cacti grow in the desert, and spruce trees grow on cool mountain slopes. Some plants grow better in direct sunlight, while others grow better in shade.

Assess the conditions in your area and select suitable plants

Whether you are planting a field of tomatoes or a single plant, you must consider the conditions under which the plants will grow. For example, plants are adapted to certain ranges of temperature. Unless you grow plants in a greenhouse, you cannot protect plants from temperatures they cannot tolerate. Therefore, if you want to grow plants outside, particularly long-lived trees, shrubs, and perennials, you must plant varieties that are hardy (can survive) in your area. The map in **Figure 22-18** divides the United States into 10 *plant hardiness zones*, which are areas that share a similar climate. Seed packets and plant identification tags usually tell you the hardiness zones where a plant will do well. As a rule, you should grow plants that are rated for your zone.

Plants are also sensitive to the soil in which they grow.

Some plants require acidic soils, while others require alkaline soils. Some plants thrive in sandy soils, while others thrive in heavy clay. Again, it is best to grow plants that are suited to the soil in your area, but soils can be altered. Using a soil test kit, you can analyze a soil to determine its water-holding capacity and pH and to identify nutrient deficiencies. The soil can then be altered by adding organic matter or specific nutrients.

Consider the size and shape of mature plants

When planning a garden or a landscape, always plan ahead. An evergreen sapling may look great by the front door now, but what about when it gets to be two stories tall? Whether you plan to grow vegetables, flowers, shrubs, or trees, you must take into account what the full-grown plants will look like. Will the vines you want to plant have something to climb on? Will a tree or shrub crowd out or shade other plants when mature? Be particularly careful when planting trees. The limbs and roots of a large tree that is too close to a house can cause structural damage.

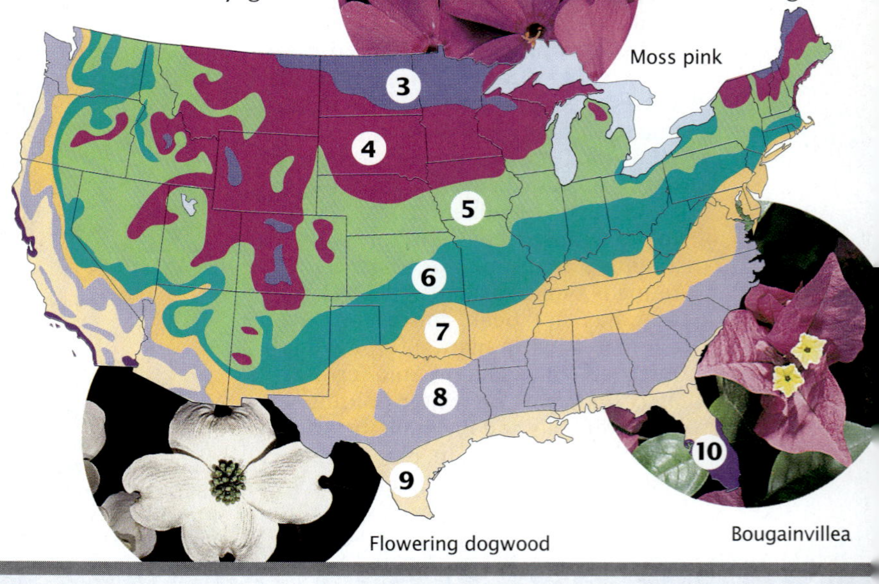

Figure 22-18
A map of plant hardiness zones was prepared by the United States Department of Agriculture (USDA). Moss pinks tolerate cold winters and grow well in zones 3–8. Flowering dogwoods are well adapted to zones 4–8. Bougainvilleas can survive the winters in zones 9 and 10 only.

Average Annual Minimum Temperatures in °C

zone 3	-40 to -30
zone 4	-30 to -20
zone 5	-20 to -10
zone 6	-10 to 0
zone 7	0 to 10
zone 8	10 to 20
zone 9	20 to 30
zone 10	30 to 40

Moss pink

Flowering dogwood

Bougainvillea

424

Matter of Fact: Moon's Influence on Planting

For centuries, gardeners have been using the phases of the moon and its position in the sky as a guide for planting. The annual *Farmer's Almanac* has a chart of the best times to plant, transplant, and kill plant pests, based on the moon's phases.

Landscape Architecture

What would it be like to . . .

- reclaim, rebuild, and reestablish the natural beauty of neglected, polluted sites in your community?

- plan and design gardens for private and public facilities?

These are just a few of the challenges faced by people working in the field of landscape architecture.

Landscape Architecture: What Is It?

A landscape architect seeks to enhance or restore an environment's natural balance and beauty. Many landscape architects work with architects and urban planners to design buildings, structures, and urban facilities for public use. Landscape architects also play an active role in education and conservation, working with foresters, biologists, and educators to preserve state and national parks, recreational sites, and wilderness areas.

Science/Math Career Preparation

High School
- Art
- Drafting
- Mathematics
- Biology
- Earth science

College
- Drawing and design
- Ecology
- Botany
- Geology

Employment Outlook
The demand for landscape architects will increase dramatically in response to rapid urbanization in all regions of the world.

Career Focus: Bob Murase
Landscape Architect in Portland, Oregon

"I would describe myself as an artist and craftsman. I've always been interested in art, especially drawing and sculpting. I had a part-time job helping a local mason build stone walls in San Francisco. This experience not only allowed me to use my imagination and develop my skills as an artist, but also taught me to appreciate the grand and subtle forms of natural beauty that surround us all. Through further, formal studies of the natural sciences, I've developed a keen understanding of the delicate balances in nature."

What I Do: "I went to college to study landscape architecture. Afterward I worked for a firm in San Francisco. When I felt I had enough experience and confidence, I started my own landscape architecture company. That was 15 years ago. Today I have the satisfaction of working with professionals on projects in many different parts of the world. We all have the same goal—to make the environment more pleasant and productive. I'm particularly excited about our work with teachers and students in a local school. We're helping them design real ecological projects that will benefit their communities now and in the future."

To Find Out More

1 For further information, write to:
American Society of Landscape Architects
4401 Connecticut Avenue NW
5th Floor
Washington, DC 20008

2 Visit your school counselor and library to find out which colleges and universities offer programs in landscape architecture. Review the prerequisites and course requirements. Make a poster showing the range of skills involved in this career.

3 Locate resources that contain sketches, photos, or graphics of landscape architecture. Evaluate the architect's design, and prepare a brief critique that explains how you would alter it.

Career Opportunities

Restoring Natural Beauty

1. Have students brainstorm ideas about the following questions:

If you wanted a career as a landscape architect...

- what kind of personality traits would be essential?
- which subjects should you study in high school? in college?
- what kinds of extracurricular activities should you pursue?
- what kind of practical experience should you gain?
- what kind of issues would interest you?

2. Have the class identify a neglected site in a local neighborhood. Have students visit the site and work together to construct a map of the area. Have them identify problems and possible solutions associated with the appearance and function of the site.

3. In small groups, have students determine the resources required to carry out the plans in the preceding activity. Have them investigate the costs required for improving the site. Have students develop a budget and schedule for the project.

425

Technique: Reading Organizer

Provide students with the worksheet titled "Series-of-Events Chain," found in Reading Strategies Worksheets in Holt BioSources Teaching Resources CD-ROM. Have students work in small groups to fill in the steps in planting and caring for plants.

Demonstration

▲ **Evaluating Results**

Bring in seed packets of several different flowers that are not compatible with each other because of their growth requirements. Prepare four sets of at least four seed packets. Divide the class into four groups, and give a set to each group. Tell students that these flowers were planted together in a garden but did not all germinate. You must supply the garden conditions of your choice to the class. Ask students to evaluate the situation. Students must consider factors such as sunlight, soil, and temperature requirements. Also point out other specific requirements, such as how to start the germination, when to transplant, and how to transplant.

Pruning

■ **Analyzing Data**

Assign each student a plant that needs annual pruning. Roses, azaleas, and peach trees are some examples. Have students find out how and when to prune the plants.

Planting and Caring for Plants

For specific instructions about planting and caring for your plants, ask for advice from someone at the garden store where you purchase the plants. Gardening books and seed packets also contain a wealth of information, such as when to plant, whether to start seeds in pots and then transplant, how plants should be spaced, and how to care for growing plants. Here are some general guidelines you can follow.

Prepare the soil before planting seeds or transplants

Soil preparation begins with plowing, turning, or raking the soil to break up hard clods. These procedures also add air to the soil, or aerate it. Loose soil is easier to dig in, and plant roots need air for healthy growth. You may also need to add nutrients to the soil. A complete fertilizer or a special-purpose fertilizer, such as an acidifying agent, can be applied before planting. Turning under composted organic matter also adds nutrients to the soil and improves its water-holding capacity.

Seeds and transplants should not be planted too deeply. Seeds should be planted no deeper than they are long. Tiny seeds should be barely dusted with soil. Transplants should be planted so that the top of the plant's root ball is at the surface of the soil when it is planted, as seen in **Figure 22-19**.

Pruning and thinning improve the growth of plants

Pruning, or trimming, a plant is more than just giving it a "hair cut" to make its appearance neater. Gardeners prune trees and shrubs to stimulate new growth, to encourage flowering, to remove dead or weak branches, and to shape them. Check with a garden store or a gardening book for advice on how and when to prune specific plants.

When plants are grown from seeds, the seeds are usually planted closer together than mature plants should be spaced to ensure that enough plants sprout. The instructions on a seed packet tell you how far apart the seeds should be planted and how far apart the mature plants should be. After the seeds sprout, thin the seedlings by removing some of them to achieve the proper amount of space between plants. When thinning, leave the stronger plants and remove the weaker ones.

Plants should be watered and fertilized when necessary

Your plants may need regular watering to thrive. As a rule, water plants when they show signs of wilting or when the soil around their roots feels dry 5 to 8 cm (2 to 3 in.) below the surface. A layer of **mulch** (bark chips or other organic matter) helps prevent evaporation of water from the soil. Some plants

Figure 22-19
When transplanting plants grown in pots, like this one, the hole you dig should be no deeper than the plant's root ball.

Table 22-3 Some Nutrient Deficiency Symptoms

Symptoms	Deficient nutrient
all leaves light green; lower leaves yellow	nitrogen (N)
leaves dark green or turning red or purple	phosphorus (P)
small spots of dead tissue at margins and between veins of older leaves	potassium (K)
new leaves of terminal buds hook-shaped; terminal buds die	calcium (Ca)
older leaves mottled, light green, or turning red; leaf margins curled up	magnesium (Mg)
young leaves wilted and light green with light green veins	sulfur (S)
young leaves wilted and light green with dark green veins	iron (Fe)

426

Matter of Fact: Garden Tips

A half cup of Epsom salts spread at the base of a climbing rose adds magnesium to the soil. Sprinkle crushed eggshells directly into the garden soil to add calcium. Work with the class to find more gardening tips. Check the library for magazines and books that contain gardening tips.

need applications of specific kinds of fertilizer for healthy growth. But unless you know that a plant has special needs, such as acidic soil, fertilize only when a plant shows signs that it is in need of certain nutrients. Some of these signs are listed in **Table 22-3**.

Watch for warning signs that a plant is unhealthy

Like humans, plants are attacked by viruses, bacteria, fungi, insects, and other parasites. If you notice the shoots of a plant turning yellow, developing spots, wilting, drying, or curling up, this could be an indication of a disease or an insect infestation. Some symptoms of disease and insect problems are shown in **Table 22-4**.

Once a problem has been identified, it can be treated. Plant diseases and insect pests can be controlled through the use of either chemical pesticides or natural techniques. For example, watering in the morning and pruning trees so that lawns and flower beds get more sunlight can help discourage disease-causing fungi. Many "biological controls," such as the one shown in **Figure 22-20**, are also very effective.

Figure 22-20 Ladybugs prey on insects that attack plants in your garden.

Table 22-4 Symptoms of Plant Diseases and Insect Infestations

Symptoms	Possible causes
black, gray, or white fuzzy patches on leaves; rounded target spots	fungi
leaves sticky, developing black patches; misshapen buds; buds that do not open; mottled, yellowed leaves with black specks and webs	sucking insects, mites
waxy bumps or fuzzy lumps	scale insects
young shoots chewed off just above the ground	snails, pill bugs
galls (hard lumps on leaves or swellings of stems)	gall-causing insects or bacteria
holes in leaves	caterpillars, pill bugs
plants wilted or having a blackened, watery area at the base of the stem	soil fungi or bacteria
plants small, misshapen, and yellowed	sucking insects, nematodes
wrinkled or curled leaves; leaves with angular spots or small pits	viruses

427

The Plant Doctor
▲ **Distinguishing Relevant Information**
Divide the class into cooperative groups of four students. Prepare a case study for each group in which a specific plant shows symptoms of disease, insect infestation, or nutrient deficiency. Have students use Tables 22-3 and 22-4 on pages 426 and 427 to form a diagnosis.

Life/Work Skills
Selecting Technology
▲ **Forming Opinions Supported by Sound Reasoning**
Prepare a list of brand-name pesticides commonly used in gardens. Include what the pesticide is used for, safety precautions, and the name of the chemical(s) contained in the product. Give groups of students case studies involving a garden pest that must be eliminated. Include information such as presence of pets, children, vegetables, and wildlife. The group is to choose a pesticide they think would be appropriate and give reasons for their choice. In some cases, more than one choice may be correct. Provide students with some gardening books that include natural pest-control methods. Have students attempt to find biological controls for the pest assigned to them. Discuss the advantages and disadvantages of both methods.

Matter of Fact: Companion Planting

Companion planting involves planting a specific plant with the plants you want to grow in your yard or garden. This companion plant will deter pests, improve soil, or increase the yield of your plant. For instance, planting mint between cabbage plants will discourage caterpillars (but plant mint in pots; it quickly becomes invasive). Plant nasturtiums next to zucchini. Aphids will attack these flowers and not your vegetables. Planting marigolds might keep the nematodes away from your vegetables. Sunflowers planted near cucumbers give the cucumbers shade. Always consult a good gardening book before planting your companion plants.

Key to Strategies
● **Understanding Concepts (Tier I)**
■ **Applying Information (Tier II)**
▲ **Critical Thinking (Tier III)**

Plant Propagation

Plant propagation is the growing of new plants from parent plants. Plants can be propagated by both sexual and asexual means. Growing plants from seeds is a sexual means of propagation because seeds result from sexual reproduction. Asexual propagation methods involve using a variety of vegetative (nonreproductive) plant parts, such as roots, stems, and leaves. Therefore, growing new plants from vegetative parts is called **vegetative propagation**. Several methods of vegetative propagation are shown in **Figure 22-21**.

Underground parts can be used for vegetative propagation

Underground parts of plants that can be used for vegetative propagation include bulbs, corms, rhizomes, roots, and tubers. Bulbs consist of the fleshy bases of leaves, whereas corms, rhizomes, and tubers are modified stems. Bulbs and corms divide naturally as they grow, forming many pieces that can each grow into a new plant. Many rhizomes, roots, and tubers can be cut into pieces with one or more buds that can grow into new shoots. Plants that are typically propagated from underground structures include caladiums, irises, daffodils, lilies, tulips, tuberous begonias, and potatoes.

Aboveground parts can be used for vegetative propagation

Have you ever clipped off a piece of a friend's English ivy and rooted it at home? People are often happy to share cuttings of houseplants such as airplane plants, philodendrons, pothos ivys, and African violets. Cuttings are

Figure 22-21
Plants are vegetatively propagated by many different methods.

Underground Plant Parts

● *Roots*

● *Bulbs*

● *Rhizomes*

● *Tubers*

a These daffodil bulbs have divided into several smaller bulbs, each of which will grow into a new plant.

b Each of the eyes of a potato contains a bud that can develop into a new plant.

Community Connection: Gardening

Many communities and their surrounding areas have garden clubs. Invite a speaker from the club to come to your class to discuss some aspect of gardening. Some suggestions for topics are sun versus shade; propagating new plants; and annuals, perennials, and biennials.

leaves or stems that are cut from a plant. Many fruit trees, ornamental trees, and shrubs are grown commercially from stem cuttings. Budding and grafting—which are used extensively to propagate fruit trees, pecan trees, grapevines, and hybrid roses—are specialized techniques that involve attaching the buds or stem cuttings of one plant to the stems of another plant. Tissue culture uses pieces of a plant's stem to produce large numbers of identical offspring. It is particularly important in the propagation of orchids, virus-free potatoes, and genetically engineered plants.

Plants are propagated sexually with seeds

Plants grown from seeds are usually slightly different from their parents because of genetic recombination. Therefore, propagating plants by seeds may not be desirable if a commercial grower or amateur gardener wants to produce large numbers of identical plants. In addition, propagating plants by seeds can be very slow because some plants require two or more growing seasons to produce seeds. Hybrids, which result from crossing genetically different individuals, are usually propagated from seeds.

Demonstration

● **Identifying Functions**

Two to three weeks prior to starting this section, plant some seeds of your choice. They may include herbs, flowers, and fruits. Have students observe the planting procedure. Students should observe that some seeds fail to germinate. Some plants are more successful when first germinated indoors and transplanted outdoors later, when they are better established and weather conditions are favorable.

Problem Solving

▲ **Forming Opinions Supported by Sound Reasoning**

Genetic engineering has produced many varieties of plants. Present the following situation to the students: If science had the capability to genetically engineer any plant, what plant would you like to see "changed"? Provide a sound reason for your answer. Who would benefit from the altered plant and why? Evaluate your hypothetical results.

Aboveground Plant Parts

● *Leaves*

● *Stems*

● *Bulbs*

c Tissue culture, which involves taking a small piece of tissue from a plant and placing it on a nutrient-rich medium, produces large numbers of identical plants.

d This young African violet plant grew from the stalk of the large leaf, a leaf cutting from a mature plant.

e A method of propagation called layering (covering part of a stem with soil) produced the roots on the stem of this dieffenbachia.

429

Matter of Fact: Naturally Colored Cotton

Biotechnology has now produced cotton plants with fibers that are different colors, including green, brown, blue, and red. These naturally colored fabrics do not fade like dyed fabrics when washed; in fact, they become darker. Naturally colored varieties have short fibers that are not machine spinnable. In an effort to improve the quality of the colored cotton, scientists are crossing the short-fibered, colored cotton with strains of high-quality, long-fibered cotton.

Key to Strategies
● **Understanding Concepts (Tier I)**
■ **Applying Information (Tier II)**
▲ **Critical Thinking (Tier III)**

Active READING

Technique: Anticipation Guide
Have students recall the Active Reading exercise on page 410. Ask volunteers to discuss how their opinions have changed or stayed the same. Students should point to specific passages in the text that support their reasoning.

Phase Three
Assessment Options

Closure

■ **Inferring Relationships**
Bonsai is the cultivation of dwarf versions of mature trees and shrubs in small pots. Some people take this up as a hobby, one that takes a lot of devotion and attention. The word *bonsai* comes from two Chinese characters—*bon* (tray) and *sai* (plant). Bonsai was practiced by the Chinese in approximately the third century B.C., but it was the Japanese Buddhist monks who perfected the art. Have students research how a bonsai is grown and maintained.

SECTION REVIEW

Assign the *Section Review.*

Reteaching

There are many household plants that function as air purifiers. Have students find the names of several houseplants and the pollutants they reportedly remove. *(Boston ferns reportedly remove formaldehyde, areca palm removes xylene, and the spider plant removes carbon monoxide.)*

Plant Breeding

Long before Mendel made his observations of pea plants, people had been observing plants and propagating those with desirable characteristics. As you read in Section 22-1, early farmers collected seeds from the best plants and used them to plant the next crop. By doing this repeatedly, they were practicing artificial selection. The practice of producing new varieties of plants through artificial selection is called **plant breeding**. Plant breeders use their knowledge of genetics and growing plants to produce improved varieties of plants.

Traditional methods of plant breeding, summarized in **Figure 22-22a**, begin with selecting parent plants that have one or more desirable characteristics, such as disease resistance and large fruit. Two desirable parents are then cross-pollinated, and their seeds are grown in a greenhouse or outdoors. Offspring that have the most desirable combination of the parental characteristics are then chosen to be the parents of the next generation. This process is repeated until a variety with all of the desired characteristics is produced.

While traditional plant-breeding methods are still widely used, genetic engineering can accomplish fantastic results in a laboratory in only a few weeks. Many new varieties of plants have been produced through genetic engineering. Some have been genetically engineered to be resistant to insects, diseases, drought, or herbicides. Others have been engineered to grow larger, resist rotting, or taste better. Still others have been engineered to produce proteins or other products that are needed by people with nutritional deficiencies. Genetic engineers have even produced a strain of cotton that has polyester-like qualities. Imagine a 100 percent cotton shirt that you would never have to iron!

Select parent plants
↓
Cross parent plants
↓
Grow offspring
↓
Screen offspring
↓
Select desirable offspring

Figure 22-22
a Many steps are involved in traditional plant breeding.

b This plant breeder is screening (exposing plants to a condition and selecting the ones with the desired response) rice seedlings for resistance to disease.

SECTION REVIEW

1. How is soil important to plants?

2. What may be the consequences of trying to grow plants in areas they are poorly adapted to?

3. How does a change in appearance indicate the health of a plant?

4. How can plants be propagated using vegetative parts from their shoots?

5. How are the results of traditional plant breeding different from the results of genetic engineering?

ANSWERS TO
SECTION REVIEW

1. Soil provides nutrients, water, and oxygen. Soil also anchors the plant.

2. Plants may fail to develop or may die.

3. Specific symptoms may indicate mineral deficiencies, insect infestations, or disease.

4. The shoots may be cut from the plant and allowed to root. Grafting can be used where the stem of one plant is attached to the stem of another plant, and tissue cultures can be used to produce large numbers of identical plants.

5. In genetic engineering, results are produced in a few weeks, whereas in traditional plant breeding, the results may take a year or more due to the number of cross-pollinations required.

Wheat, rice, and corn are eaten by people all over the world.

	Key Terms	Summary
22-1 **Uses of Plants** Many important products are made from wood. 	grain (p. 411) essential amino acid (p. 415) legume (p. 415) tuber (p. 416) wood (p. 417) lumber (p. 417)	• The most important foods are fruits called grains. • Legumes are high in protein and are often eaten with grains. • Plant parts that provide food include fruits, seeds, stems, roots, leaves, and flowers. • Sugar is produced from sugar cane and sugar beets. • Wood is a valuable source of lumber, fuel, paper, and rayon. • Many familiar drugs, such as aspirin and hydrocortisone, were first isolated from plants. • Important plant products include fibers, turpentine, and rubber.
22-2 **Growing Plants** People grow plants for a variety of purposes. 	macronutrient (p. 420) micronutrient (p. 420) loam (p. 421) humus (p. 421) fertility (p. 422) crop rotation (p. 422) green manure (p. 422) fertilizer (p. 423) composting (p. 423) hydroponics (p. 423) mulch (p. 426) vegetative propagation (p. 428) plant breeding (p. 430)	• Plants need relatively large amounts of macronutrients and relatively small amounts of micronutrients. • The best soils for growing plants are loams, which are a mixture of sand, silt, and clay particles. • Humus provides nutrients and helps soil hold moisture. • Farmers use fertilizers, crop rotation, and green manure to enhance soil fertility. • Knowledge of the local conditions and the needs of plants help people grow plants successfully. • Many plants are produced by vegetative propagation. • New plant varieties are produced by traditional plant breeding and by genetic engineering.

Alternative Assessment

Give each student a section of a newspaper or magazine that contains advertisements as well as news. Have each student make a list of all products advertised that are made from plants.

Portfolio Assessment

Portfolio Assessment on page T39 provides options for building and evaluating student portfolios. Students and teachers can select items from the areas listed on page T39 for inclusion in a portfolio.

ANSWER TO **CONCEPT MAP**

The following is one possible answer to the Relating Concepts exercise on page 432.

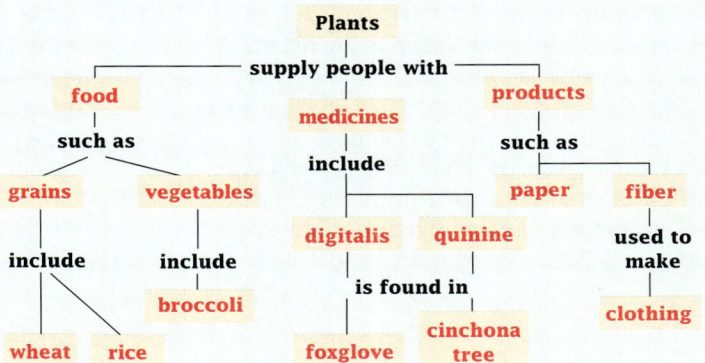

Understanding Vocabulary

1. a. A soybean is not a grain.
  b. Latex is not fibrous.
  c. Iron is a micronutrient.
2. a. tubers
  b. relieves pain
  c. vegetative propagation

Understanding Concepts

3. Answer to concept map is shown on page 431.
4. Grains are the fruits of cereal grasses. Wheat, rice, corn, and oats provide about 60 percent of the calories eaten by humans. They are a rich source of carbohydrates, proteins, vitamins, and dietary fiber.
5. a. fruit
  b. flower
  c. petiole (leaf stalk)
  d. seed
6. The legume and grain combination ensures adequate protein.
7. Potatoes and yams are underground stems called tubers. Carrots, beets, turnips, and cassava are some examples of roots.
8. Wood is used as fuel and can be processed to make building materials, paper, and rayon.
9. A mixture of wood pulp and water is poured onto a fine screen, where the fibers tangle into a mass. The mass is pressed between huge rollers and allowed to dry.
10. Answers will vary but should include examples from Table 22-2 on page 418.
11. Soil surrounds the roots and provides the nutrients needed for healthy growth. Soil also holds water and anchors the plant.
12. Water does not contain the nutrients needed by the plant.
13. Fertility of the soil is its ability to supply plants with nutrients and can be maintained by crop rotation, leaving a field unplanted for a year to rebuild its natural nutrients, or plowing under a crop to restore nutrients and organic matter to the soil.

review

Understanding Vocabulary

1. For each set of terms, choose the term that does not fit the pattern, and explain why.
  a. corn, wheat, soy beans, rice
  b. cotton, linen, wood, latex
  c. iron, nitrogen, phosphorus, sulfur
2. For each set of terms, complete the analogy.
  a. carrots and turnips : roots :: yams and potatoes : _____
  b. quinine : prevents malaria :: aspirin : _____
  c. seeds : sexual propagation :: bulbs : _____

Understanding Concepts

3.  **Relating Concepts** Construct a concept map that identifies the products people use from plants. Try to include the following terms in your concept map: food, medicines, products, grains, vegetables, digitalis, quinine, paper, fiber, wheat, rice, broccoli, foxglove, cinchona tree, and clothing.
4. **Summarizing Information** What are grains? Which grains provide about 60 percent of the calories eaten by humans? What nutrients do grains provide?
5. **Identifying Structures** Name the part of a plant represented by each of the following foods.

a

b

c

d

6. **Inferring Relationships** Why is a diet consisting of grains and legumes more nutritious than a diet consisting of grains alone?
7. **Summarizing Information** What are tubers? What two important foods are tubers? What are examples of other foods that are roots?
8. **Summarizing Information** Describe three primary uses of wood.
9. **Describing Processes** Describe the process of making paper.
10. **Summarizing Information** Identify three medicines derived originally from plants. Name the plant that the medicine comes from and the uses of the medicine.
11. **Understanding Functions** What is the function of soil in relation to plant growth?
12. **Inferring Relationships** Why do plants grow better in soil than they do in plain water?
13. **Summarizing Information** What is soil fertility? Describe three cultivation practices that help maintain soil fertility.
14. **Analyzing Methods** Explain why it is advantageous for gardeners and farmers to select and grow plants that are appropriate for their area.
15. **Interpreting Data** After carefully planning and planting your garden, you notice that some plants have waxy bumps, others have black and white patches on their leaves, and still others are small and misshapen with yellow leaves. What are the probable causes of these ailments?
16. **Summarizing Information** What is vegetative propagation? Describe five methods of propagating plants vegetatively.
17. **Recognizing Relationships** What is plant breeding? How do traditional methods of plant breeding compare with plant breeding by genetic engineering?
18. **BUILDING ON WHAT YOU HAVE LEARNED** In Chapter 16 you learned about several environmental problems. What environmental problems are associated with the burning of wood for cooking and heating?

14. Plants are adapted to certain ranges in temperature and are sensitive to conditions of the soil in which they live.
15. Possible causes include fungi, scale insects, sucking insects, and nematodes.
16. Vegetative propagation is the growing of new plants from vegetative parts of plants. Descriptions should be similar to those in Figure 22-21 on pages 428 and 429.

17. Plant breeding involves cross-pollinating parent plants that have desirable traits. The process is repeated until the desired characteristics are produced. New varieties can be produced in less time with genetic engineering.
18. Answers will vary but should include concerns about air pollution, global warming, and deforestation.

review

Interpreting Graphics

19. Study the graph shown below.

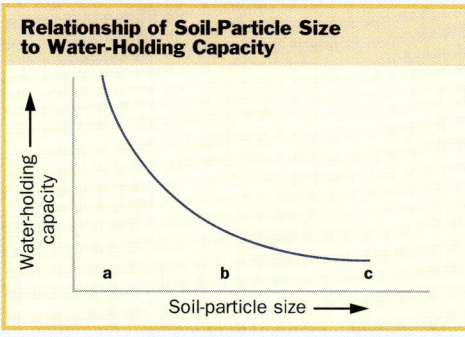

Relationship of Soil-Particle Size to Water-Holding Capacity

Water-holding capacity (vertical axis)
Soil-particle size → (horizontal axis)

a. What kind of soil is indicated by letter *a*? What is the relationship between this soil's ability to hold water and the size of its particles?
b. What kind of soil is indicated by letter *b*? What is the relationship between this soil's ability to hold water and the size of its particles?
c. What kind of soil is indicated by letter *c*? What is the relationship between this soil's ability to hold water and the size of its particles?

Reviewing Themes

20. Heredity
Modern wheat looks very different from its wild ancestors. What methods have been used to develop the varieties of wheat grown today?

21. Stability and Homeostasis
Describe several ways that farmers and agricultural scientists are striving to maintain adequate food supplies for growing populations.

Thinking Critically

22. Forming Opinions Assume that genetic engineers have been able to develop a cereal grass that produces nutritious grains and is also able to fix nitrogen from the soil in much the same way that a legume can. Of what advantage might the nitrogen-fixing characteristic be to a farmer?

23. Evaluating Results A gardener planted pole beans (beans that grow on tall, strong vines) too close to corn plants. As both plants grew, the beans intertwined around the corn stalks. The gardener also noticed that the corn plants yielded exceptionally large and numerous ears of corn. How would you explain these results?

Life/Work Skills

24. Allocating Resources For three days, record every paper product you use during the day. Include items such as newspaper, paper towels, notebook paper, and product packaging. Can any of these items be recycled? What is the advantage of recycling paper? Identify each product you list as recyclable or nonrecyclable. Write out several recommendations for reducing the amount of paper you use, and share these recommendations with your class.

25. Finding Information Use library references or search an on-line database to find out about Xeriscaping. In what parts of the country is this technique most appropriately used? What kinds of plants can be used in Xeriscape gardening? Prepare an illustrated report or informational posters to share with your class.

Activities and Projects

26. History Connection Use library references or search an on-line database to find out the ritual and economic importance of corn (maize) to early Mesoamerican cultures such as the Aztecs of central Mexico. How was the corn grown? What gods and rituals were associated with growing corn? How was corn used in the diet? Summarize your findings in an illustrated report to share with your class.

27. Unit Focus Use library references or search an on-line database to find out about some of the new varieties of plants that have been produced through genetic engineering. How will these varieties help reduce the amount of environmental pollution that results from agriculture? How might genetically engineered plants change methods of food preservation? Produce a poster that includes several genetically engineered plants and illustrates how these varieties might improve environmental and human health.

Discovering Through Reading

28. Read "A Farming Revolution: Sustainable Agriculture" by Verlyn Klinkenborg in *National Geographic*, December 1995, pages 60–89. What is sustainable agriculture? What do plants such as vetch, peas, and clover provide to farmers? What is a soil's tilth?

433

Thinking Critically

22. The cereal grass would not be dependent on legumes or fertilizers for nitrogen. Production would be less costly.

23. The gardener stumbled on the practice of companion planting. Beans made nitrogen available to the corn plants. The corn plants provided support for the vining bean plants, giving them maximum exposure to the light.

Life/Work Skills

24. Answers will vary depending on the individual's use of paper.

25. Answers will vary but should include information on soil analysis, efficient irrigation, appropriate plant selection, the use of mulches, and the reduction of fertilizers, pesticides, and maintenance.

Activities and Projects

26. Reports will vary but should include information about the Aztecs' use of corn as a staple food, a method of paying taxes, and an icon of worship.

27. Genetic engineering has the potential to produce plants that manufacture desirable chemicals, such as insect and fungus deterrents, as well as growth-enhancing nutrients. This could reduce the need for pesticides, fungicides, and fertilizer.

Discovering Through Reading

28. Sustainable agriculture is economically viable and environmentally sound farming. Vetch, peas, and clover naturally supply nitrogen to the soil, provide habitat for beneficial insects, hinder the emergence of competitive weeds, and prevent erosion. Tilth is the soil's texture, nutrients, and ability to hold water.

Interpreting Graphics

19. a. Clay soil has the smallest particles of any soil and very small air spaces between its particles. It holds water extremely well.
b. Silty soil has medium-sized particles with medium-sized air spaces between the particles. It holds water moderately well.
c. Sandy soil has the largest particles of any soil type and large air spaces between its particles. It has very poor water-holding capabilities.

Reviewing Themes

20. In early times, only seeds from the best plants were used for the next planting. Selective breeding and genetic engineering have been used to develop modern varieties.

21. Farmers and agricultural scientists are using fertilizers, rotating crops, and planting improved crop varieties. Agricultural scientists are improving the protein content of food through genetic engineering and breeding programs.

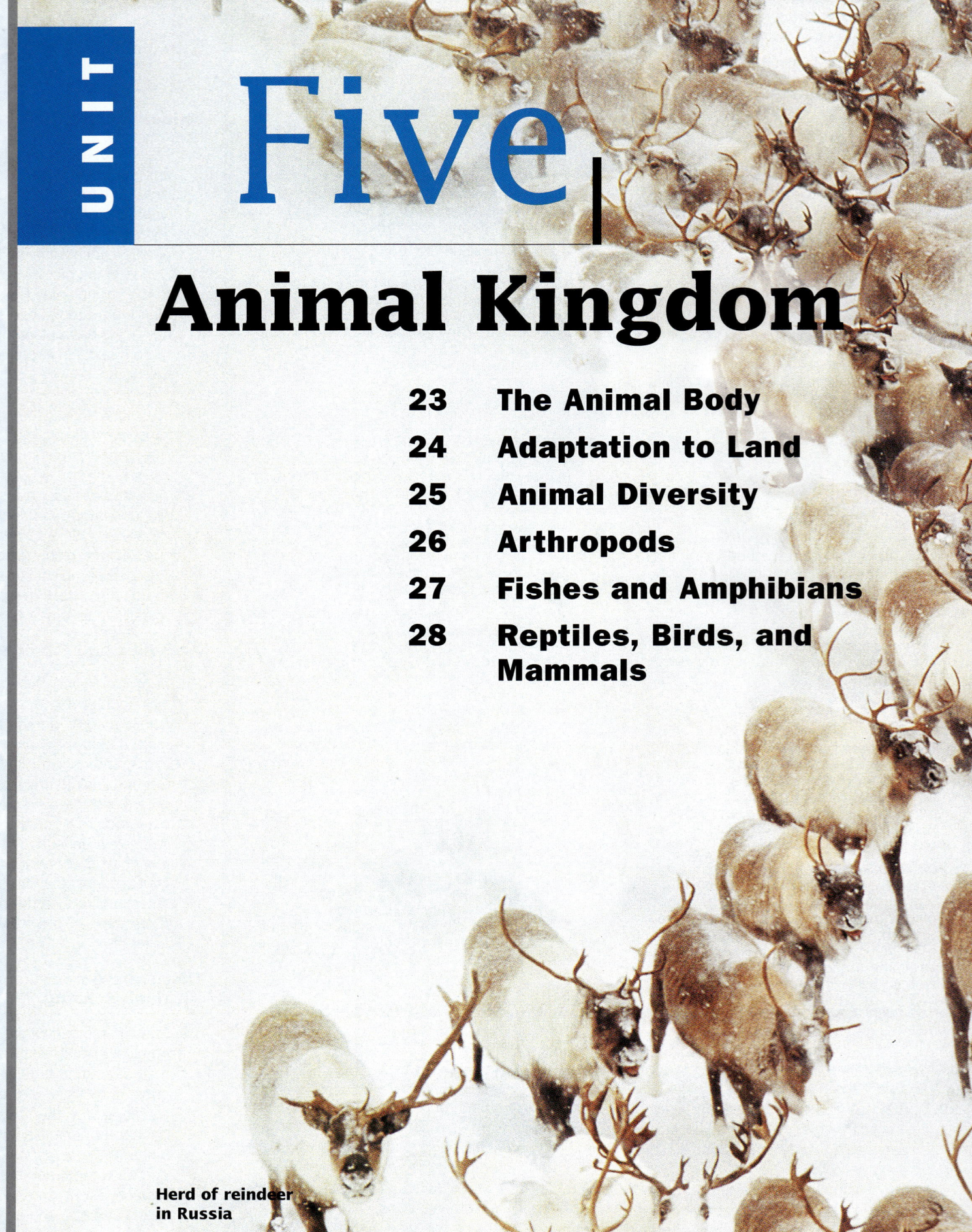

Animal Kingdom

Herd of reindeer in Russia

PLANS FOR SURVIVAL

Animal body plans first appeared millions of years ago and changed over time to ensure survival. About a million species of animals have since evolved. This wide diversity of animal life is the result of animal adaptations to a changing and challenging environment.

Human Right or Responsibility

The richness of diversity, however, is being threatened by humans striving to provide food, clothing, housing, and medicines for growing populations. Some industries remove animals from an environment. Other actions lead to habitat destruction, endangering or eliminating some species.

You Have a Say

What is lost when an endangered species, such as the spotted owl, becomes extinct? Some biologists believe that biological diversity is vital to long-term survival on Earth. Because of animal and plant diversity, ecosystems are able to recover after change occurs. Will your needs for food, clothing, shelter, and medicines allow ecosystem recovery or threaten it?

LOOKING AHEAD

- In which ways have animal body plans varied? See pages 439–454.
- How have mammals broken the tie to reproduction in water? See pages 472–474.
- What information can be gained by studying an indicator species? See **Science, Technology, and Society: Can One Species Tell All?** pages 498–499.
- How can the study of insects help humans? See **Career Opportunities: Entomology,** page 511.

23 | The Animal Body

Lesson Planning Guide With Options for Block Scheduling

Lecture Concepts	Lesson Resources

23-1 The Origin of Tissues

BLOCK ❶ (45 minutes)

1. All animals are heterotrophic and multicellular, and their cells do not have cell walls.

2. The body plan of an animal is its overall structure. Each body plan is successful for a certain lifestyle.

❶ Lecture Resources
- Determining Prior Knowledge
- Active Reading: Reading Organizer
- Active Reading: Brainstorming
- Visual Strategy: Figure 23-2
- Visual Strategy: Videodisc
- Demonstration: Comparing Structures

- Teaching Transparencies: 135, 143
- Holt Biology Biology Videodiscs Lesson 23-1

Classwork Options
- Inquiry Skills Development: Lab B23

BLOCK ❷ (45 minutes)

3. In multicellular organisms, cells can specialize. Tissues allow even more efficient functioning, as specialized cells work together in a coordinated way.

4. The body plan of most animals is symmetrical. They have a regular arrangement of body parts.

❷ Lecture Resources
- Active Reading: Summarizing
- Visual Strategy: Figures 23-3, 23-4
- Visual Strategy: Videodisc
- Teaching Transparencies: 144, 146
- Holt Biology Biology Videodiscs Lesson 23-1

Classwork Options
- Closure: Forming a Model

Assignment Options
- Reteaching
- Section Review
- Chapter Review, questions 1, 2, 5, 6, 7, 8, 9, 22, 28
- Directed Reading Worksheet

23-2 The Origin of Body Cavities

BLOCK ❸ (45 minutes)

1. Flatworms, roundworms, and mollusks are bilaterally symmetrical and cephalized.

2. The formation of mesoderm during gastrulation in these animals allows the development of organs.

3. Flatworms are acoelomates, organisms without a body cavity.

❸ Lecture Resources
- Two-Way or One-Way Gut
- Active Reading: Reading Organizer
- Demonstration: Recognizing Relationships
- Teaching Transparencies: 157, 158, 159
- Holt Biology Biology Videodiscs Lesson 23-2

Classwork Options
- What Are Organs?

Assignment Options
- Inquiry Skills Development: Lab B21

BLOCK ❹ (45 minutes)

4. Roundworms are pseudocoelomates, organisms that have a body cavity that develops between the mesoderm and the endoderm.

5. Mollusks are coelomates, organisms with a body cavity that forms within the mesoderm.

❹ Lecture Resources
- Mesoderm in Coelomates
- Demonstration: Identifying Structures
- Teaching Transparencies: 153, 155, 156
- Holt Biology Biology Videodiscs Lesson 23-2

Classwork Options
- *Small Group* Parasite-Host Specificity
- Closure: Identifying Structures

Assignment Options
- Reteaching
- Section Review
- Chapter Review, questions 3, 4, 15, 16, 17, 18, 20, 21, 23
- Directed Reading Worksheet

23-3 Four Innovations in Body Plan

BLOCK ❺ (45 minutes)

1. Annelids, such as earthworms and other segmented worms, were the first organisms to evolve a segmented body plan.

2. Arthropods, which include the insects, and chordates, which include the vertebrates, also have a segmented body plan.

❺ Lecture Resources
- Earthworm Segments
- Active Reading: Reading Organizer
- Visual Strategy: Figure 23-12
- Teaching Transparencies: 160, 161
- Holt Biology Videodiscs Lesson 23-3

Classwork Options
- Segmented Worms
- Comparing Annelids With Arthropods
- Inquiry Skills Development: Lab B22

Assignment Options
- Diversity in Arthropods

- ■ Annotated Teacher's Edition
- ■ Pupil's Edition
- ■ Directed Reading Worksheets
- ■ Vocabulary Development Worksheets
- ■ Thinking Skills Worksheets
- ■ Reteaching Worksheets
- ■ Chapter Tests
- ⊙ Language Development and Reading Comprehension Audio CD Program

Holt BioSources
Laboratory Program
- A Quick Labs
- B Inquiry Skills Development
- C Laboratory Techniques and Experimental Design
- D Biotechnology
- E Interactive Explorations in Biology Laboratory Manual

- ▮ Teaching Transparencies
- ⊙ Testing Resources CD-ROM
- ⊙ Test Generator/Assessment Item

Holt Biology Technology
- ⊙ Holt Biology Videodiscs

Lecture Concepts   Lesson Resources

23-3 Four Innovations in Body Plan, *continued*

BLOCK 6 (45 minutes)

3. Segmentation gave evolutionary rise to further specialization of body parts, because a change in an existing segment could give rise to a new kind of segment with a new function.

4. Chordates all share three characteristics at some time in their development: a notochord; a hollow, dorsal nerve cord; and pharyngeal slits.

6 Lecture Resources
- ■ Unscrambling the Groups
- ■ Grubs and Caterpillars
- ■ Visual Strategy: Videodisc
- ■ Demonstration: Identifying Functions
- ▮ Teaching Transparencies: 162, 163
- ⊙ Holt Biology Videodiscs Lesson 23-3

Classwork Options
- ■ Closure: Summarizing Information

Assignment Options
- ■ Reteaching
- ■ Section Review
- ■ Chapter Review, questions 10, 11, 12, 13, 14, 19, 24, 25, 26, 27
- ■ Directed Reading Worksheet

Chapter Review and Assessment

BLOCK 7 (45 minutes)
Review
- ■ Reteaching Worksheet
- ■ Thinking Skills Worksheet
- ■ Vocabulary Development Worksheet
- ⊙ Language Development and Reading Comprehension Audio CD Program: Chapter 23

BLOCK 8 (45 minutes)
Assessment
- ■ Alternative Assessment, p. 455
- ■ Portfolio Assessment, p. T39

Chapter Test
- ■ Chapter 23 Test

Test Generator
- ⊙ Item bank for customizing Chapter Tests
- ⊙ Performance-Based Assessment: Exploring Invertebrates

Teaching Resources CD-ROM
- ⊙ Scoring Rubrics and Classroom Management Checklist

The Portfolio icon denotes items throughout the Teacher's Edition lesson wrap that may be selected for inclusion in student portfolios.

Holt Biology Videodiscs and *Concepts of Biology*

Holt Biology Videodiscs gives you a powerful tool for teaching, review, and assessment. For further information regarding the media on the videodiscs, see *Holt Biology Videodiscs Teacher's Correlation Guide to Holt Biology: Visualizing Life.*

Concepts of Biology adds interactive lesson plans and extensive tools for customization using CD-ROM technology.

Use the following topic from *Concepts of Biology* to help you teach this chapter:
Topic 17: Animal Evolution
Topic 18: Invertebrate Diversity

Laboratory Planning

Holt BioSources Laboratory Program

Block 1: Inquiry Skills Development Lab B23: Live Earthworms
Block 3: Inquiry Skills Development Lab B21: Flatworm Behavior
Block 5: Inquiry Skills Development Lab B22: Earthworm Dissection

Determining Prior Knowledge

- Have students give examples of the various methods by which animals get their food. Ask students to explain what is meant by *heterotrophic*.
- Ask students to distinguish between cell membranes and cell walls.
- Display a wide variety of photos of the following animals: sponges, cnidarians, flatworms, roundworms, annelids, mollusks, arthropods, and vertebrates. Have students point out similarities and differences among the structures of the various animals.
- Ask students what comes to mind when they think of worms. Show them photos or preserved specimens of several different flatworms, roundworms, and annelids. Tell students that these animals actually belong to different major groups, or phyla, of animals. Have students group the photos in three categories and name the characteristics by which they grouped them.

Active READING

Technique: Reading Organizer
Have students survey the chapter, noting the headings, subheadings, illustrations, and boldface words in the text. Work with the class to create a list of the major headings in the chapter. Then discuss with students how the chapter is structured. Most students will agree that the chapter is organized sequentially; each body plan discussed has progressively more-complex adaptations.

CD-ROM Resources

Concepts of Biology
Topic 17: Animal Evolution
Topic 18: Invertebrate Diversity

CHAPTER

23

REVIEW
• natural selection (Section 10-3)
• animal evolution (Sections 11-3 and 11-4)
• classifying living things (Section 17-2)

The Animal Body

23-1	**The Origin of Tissues**
23-2	**Origin of Body Cavities**
23-3	**Four Innovations in Body Plan**

An elephant and her calf cross the Kenyan savanna. This chapter examines some of the milestones in animal evolution.

436

Author's Rationale This chapter is the core of the animal unit. It introduces animals by describing their evolutionary journey in terms of key adaptations. Though there are many animals to choose from, I chose those that serve to highlight both the progressive nature of animal evolution and the important role of key elements in body architecture. Each stage is highlighted by an Exploration and is linked to an overview of the phylum representing the stage. The intent of this chapter is to minimize detail and to emphasize the evolutionary processes that have produced the diversity that we see among animals today.

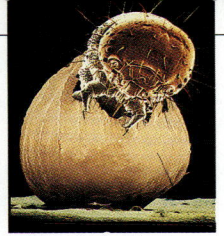

Animals, including the tobacco budworm shown at the left, occur in a great variety of sizes and shapes. This chapter describes the evolution of today's great diversity of animals in terms of a series of key adaptations in body architecture. These adaptations reveal both the cumulative nature of evolution and the importance of body design.

23-1 The Origin of Tissues

OBJECTIVES

1 List three characteristics of animals.

2 Recognize the advantage of multicellularity.

3 Identify the difference between tissues and specialized cells.

4 List three features found in cnidarians but not in sponges.

Animal Body Plans

What do the animals in **Figure 23-1** have in common? These animals, and all the other members of the kingdom Animalia, share three characteristics. First, all animals are heterotrophs that consume their food. Second, all animals are multicellular. Third, as you learned in Chapter 3, animal cells do not have cell walls.

Despite these similarities, it is obvious that the animals below differ in shape and structure. The **body plan** of an animal is its overall structure. You learned in Chapter 17 that animals evolved from heterotrophic protists. The first animals probably evolved from multicellular colonies of protists. In this chapter, you will see some of

Figure 23-1
These animals show part of the diversity of the kingdom Animalia.

437

Videodisc Resources

Holt Biology Videodiscs
Lesson 23-1: The Origin of Tissues

Phase One
Preparation

Scheduling
See the **Lesson Planning Guide** on pages 435A and 435B for lecture, classwork, and assignment options for Section 23-1.

Phase Two
Teaching Strategies

Active READING

Technique: Brainstorming
Read aloud pages 437–438. Then ask students to look at Figure 23-3 on page 439. Have them think about the body plan of a sponge in comparison with that of a human. Work with the class as a whole to create a list on the chalkboard of obvious similarities and differences in their physical structures. Then tell students that in Chapter 23 they will learn more about the role of evolution in animal structure. Save this list for the Closure activity on page 454.

Demonstration
● **Comparing Structures**
Show students photographs and preserved specimens of several animals with distinctly different body plans, for example, a sponge, a sea anemone, an octopus, a planarian, an earthworm, a bee, a sea star, and a human. Ask students to explain how the various structures are used by the animals. *(Answers will vary but might include feeding, defense, reproduction, movement, etc.)*

Key to Strategies
Teaching Strategies are keyed to three tiers of learning.

● **Understanding Concepts (Tier I)**
Content mastery and comprehension

■ **Applying Information (Tier II)**
Applying and analyzing content

▲ **Critical Thinking (Tier III)**
Practicing evaluative thinking

The Animal Body **437**

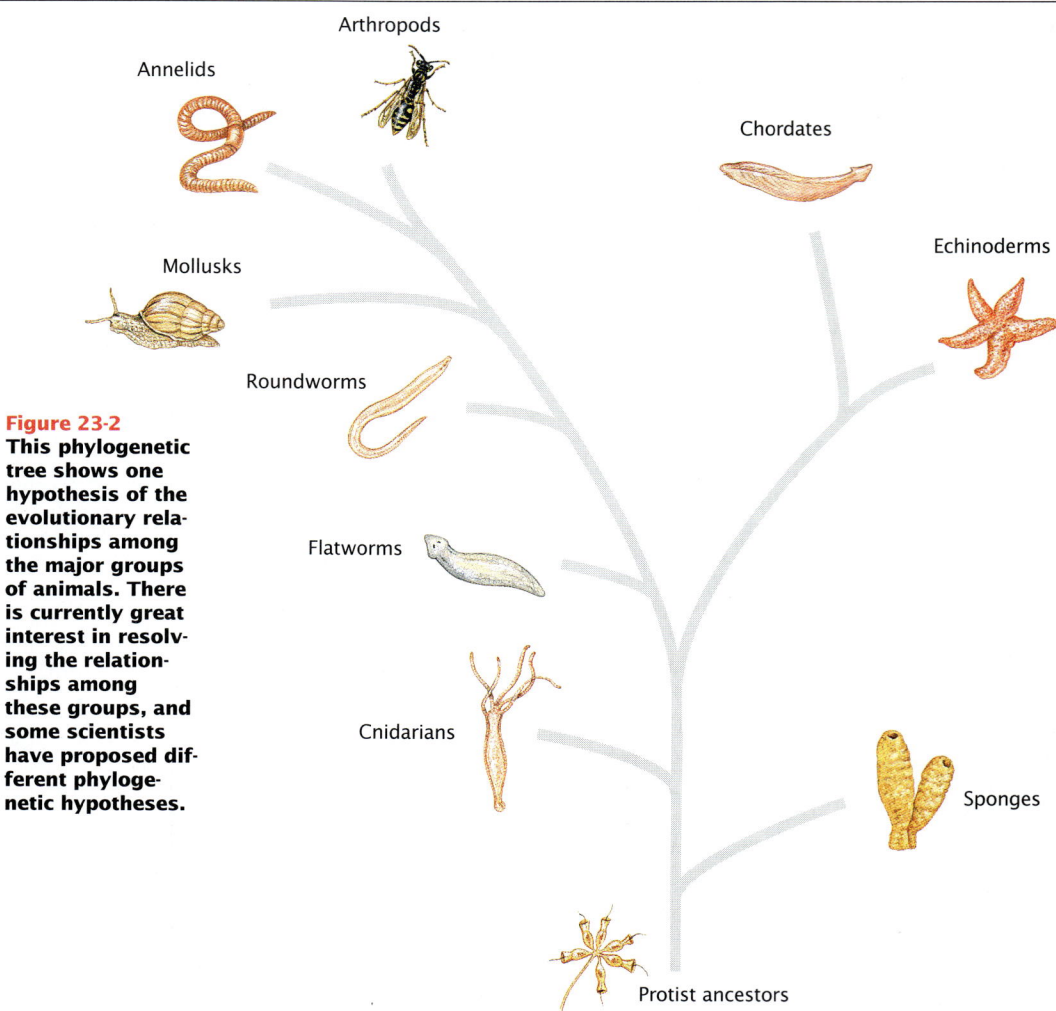

Arthropods

Annelids

Chordates

Echinoderms

Mollusks

Roundworms

Figure 23-2
This phylogenetic tree shows one hypothesis of the evolutionary relationships among the major groups of animals. There is currently great interest in resolving the relationships among these groups, and some scientists have proposed different phylogenetic hypotheses.

Flatworms

Cnidarians

Sponges

Protist ancestors

the diverse animal body plans that are descended from this protist ancestor. As you read the chapter, keep in mind that each body plan is the result of many additions and alterations to the body plans of earlier animals. The driving force for this process is natural selection, which favors changes in body plan that increase the likelihood of survival and reproduction.

This chapter traces the major evolutionary changes in animal body plans. The phylogenetic tree in **Figure 23-2** illustrates the relationships among the major groups of animals discussed in this chapter. Each group represents a unique body plan and is profiled in an **Exploration**. Keep in mind that the body

plan of an animal reflects the way it lives, how it functions in its environment. Changes in body plan often result in different body functions and entirely new ways of making a living. Each animal body plan is successful for a certain lifestyle. You might hear simple animals such as sponges described as "lower" or "primitive" animals, implying that the are somehow inferior to "higher" animals such as humans. This is not the case. Although sponges cannot fly, run, or think, they are well adapted for their particular way of life—clinging to rocks and filtering food particles from the water passing through their body. Sponges have been living this way for more than 500 million years.

438

Community Connection: Life With Humans

A variety of animals have adapted to life with humans and domestic animals. Animals are often attracted to food, water, nesting sights, and the absence of predators within the human community. Throughout the United States, we find examples of animals successfully adapted to urban or suburban life. Examples include the following: gulls, peregrine falcons, owls, rock doves, coyotes, rabbits, raccoons, squirrels, mice, chipmunks, opossums, turtles, lizards, snakes, roaches, ants, wasps, slugs, earthworms, nematodes, tapeworms, and many more. Work with students to create a list of animals that are adapted to life in their community.

Many Cells Instead of One: Sponges

As you learned in Chapter 11, animals belong to one of the three multicellular kingdoms of life. The most important advantage to multicellularity is the specialization of cells. Individual cells of an animal can specialize on a single task such as digestion or reproduction. Cell specialization enables division of labor among cells in an animal's body. Division of labor is advantageous because a specialized cell can carry out its task more effectively than a cell that must carry out many tasks.

Figure 23-3
Sponges are found in fresh water and salt water. All sponges, such as these tube sponges, have a simple body plan composed of specialized cells.

Sponges are simple, multicellular animals

Sponges, like the one shown in **Figure 23-3**, are members of the phylum Porifera. They demonstrate the advantages of cell specialization. A sponge extracts food and oxygen from the water flowing through its body. The **Exploration** below shows the simple body plan of a representative sponge. The outer layer of cells protects the sponge. Cells called choanocytes *(koh AN oh seyets)* line the internal chamber and produce water currents by beating their flagella. Choanocytes engulf and digest small organisms and small organic particles that are drawn into the sponge.

Although each of the sponge's different cell types is specialized to carry out one or more of the different functions needed for survival, there is very little coordination among cells. The flagella of choanocytes beat independently, for instance. Some sponges can even reassemble into a complete sponge after being forced through a fine silk mesh and separated into individual cells.

Exploration of a Sponge

Key Feature: Multicellularity
The cells of a sponge are not organized into tissues.

The sponge body plan is well suited for filtering small organisms from the water.

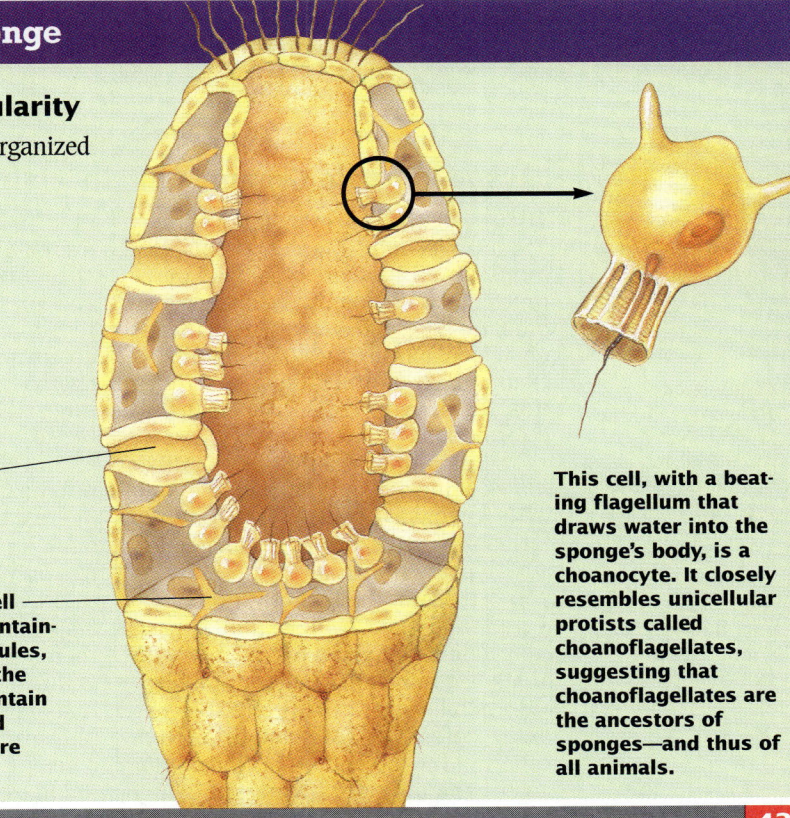

The body of a sponge is perforated by many tiny pores through which water enters the internal chamber.

Between the outer and inner cell layers is a jellylike material containing hard structures called spicules, which strengthen and protect the sponge. Most sponges also contain fibers of a tough protein called spongin. Some bath sponges are made of spongin.

This cell, with a beating flagellum that draws water into the sponge's body, is a choanocyte. It closely resembles unicellular protists called choanoflagellates, suggesting that choanoflagellates are the ancestors of sponges—and thus of all animals.

439

Matter of Fact: Commercial Uses of Sponges

Sponges have been used since ancient times as bath aids, cleaning tools, and even drinking vessels. When dried, the skeletons of certain species of sponge are soft and elastic, yet they are still capable of absorbing large amounts of water. Synthetic sponges have largely replaced natural sponges for household use.

440   **Chapter 23**

Visual Strategy — Figure 23-4

● Identifying Functions

Tell students that when one of the tentacles of the hydra is touched, all of the tentacles respond. Ask students to explain how this is evidence that the hydra has tissues. *(Nerve cells are working together to transmit information from the tentacle that was touched to the tentacles that respond.)* How does this response help the hydra capture food? *(If an organism that the hydra can eat touches one of the tentacles, all of the tentacles respond to draw the organism inside the hydra's body cavity.)*

Visual Strategy — Videodisc

■ Relating Concepts

Use *Photo—Aggregating Anemone* shown in Chapter 23 Section 23-1 of *Holt Biology Videodiscs Teacher's Correlation Guide to Holt Biology: Visualizing Life.* Tell students that this anemone lives in the intertidal zone of the northwest coast of North America. They reproduce by binary fission, producing populations of genetically identical clones. Tell students that although there is an advantage to producing a large number of the organisms in a short time, these genetically identical clones could be at a disadvantage. Have students write a paragraph explaining how disease and environmental change are greater threats to this genetically identical population than to a population that is genetically more diverse. *(The entire population of identical clones would be more likely to be killed off than a genetically diverse population in which some individuals had adaptations to help them survive.)*

Exploration of a Cnidarian

Key Features: Radial Symmetry, Extracellular Digestion, and Specialized Tissues

The cnidarian body is more complex than that of a sponge. The cells of *Hydra* are organized into *tissues.* The interior gut cavity is specialized for *extracellular digestion.* Unlike sponges, cnidarians are *radially symmetrical.*

Mouth

Jellylike middle layer

Gut tissue

Protective outer tissue

The tentacles and body have cells that contain small but very powerful "harpoons" called nematocysts.

Prey paralyzed by the stinging tentacles are drawn into the gut to be digested.

Gut

Hydra is a carnivore that captures prey with tentacles that ring the mouth.

A typical freshwater *Hydra* is about 1 cm (0.4 in.) or less in height.

The base of a *Hydra's* body is attached to a rock or plant.

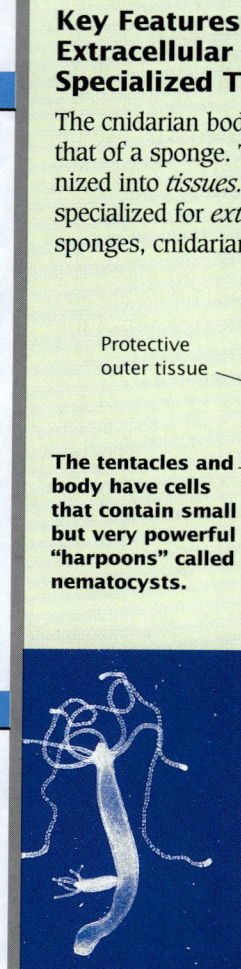

Figure 23-4
Hydra is a cnidarian carnivore. Anchored to rocks or plants, it captures its prey by stinging them with specialized structures in its tentacles. Cnidarians, unlike sponges, have tissues composed of specialized cells.

Tissues Enable Greater Cell Specialization: *Cnidarians*

Tissues are the first great innovation in the animal body plan. A **tissue** is a group of cells that are organized into a functional unit. Your body is composed of many types of tissues. The activities of cells in a tissue are coordinated. For example, cells in nervous tissue function together to collect and transmit information.

The phylum Cnidaria *(neye DAIR ee uh)* was one of the first groups of animals to have tissues. This phylum includes jellyfish, corals, sea anemones, and hydras, shown in **Figure 23-4**. As you can see in the **Exploration** above, a cnidarian *(neye DAIR ee uhn)* is basically a double-layered bag of cells with a jellylike substance between the layers. Each layer of cells is a tissue. The outer cell layer forms a protective covering for the cnidarian. This outer layer contains cells armed with sting- ing "harpoons" called nematocysts *(NEHM uh toh sihsts).* The inner layer is specialized for releasing digestive enzymes and absorbing nutrients from the digested food. This two-layered construction surrounds an inner chamber in which food is digested. An internal passage through which food passes while being digested is called a **gut**. In most animals, including humans, the gut is a long tube that begins at the mouth and ends at the anus. In cnidarians, however, the gut has only a single opening.

Extracellular digestion allows animals to consume organisms larger than themselves by taking pieces of those organisms into the body for digestion. A sponge has no gut and is able to eat only organisms small enough to be consumed by an individual cell in the lining of its internal cavity.

Matter of Fact: Sea-Bather's Eruption

Many swimmers and divers in tropical ocean waters develop a form of dermatitis known as sea-bather's eruption. Symptoms usually include red, rashlike bumps on the skin, but in severe cases, chills, fever, headache, and nausea may occur. The condition is caused by the larvae of a half-inch jellyfish known as the sea thimble. Researchers suspect that the larvae filter through clothing and stay pressed against the skin. Then rubbing or exposure to fresh water causes the nematocysts to fire. Scientists hope to develop a test that will indicate the presence of the larvae in sea water. Sea-bather's eruption is often mistakenly believed to be caused by "sea lice," which are actually crustaceans that parasitize fish.

Tissue layers form early in the development of the embryo

Figure 23-5 shows how the two-layered construction of a cnidarian is formed during the development of the embryo. This process of forming layers of cells is called **gastrulation** (gas troo LAY shuhn). Gastrulation takes place in the developing embryos of all animals except sponges. In humans, gastrulation occurs when the embryo is a little over one week old. The inner layer of cells formed by gastrulation is **endoderm**, meaning "inner skin." The outer layer of cells is **ectoderm**, meaning "outer skin."

The layers that result from gastrulation will produce all the tissues of the adult body. These layers develop into the same body structures in all animals. Endoderm always gives rise to the lining of the gut, and ectoderm always becomes the outer layer of skin and nervous tissue.

Figure 23-5
If you were to push on a tennis ball with your thumb, it would simulate what happens during the formation of the endoderm and ectoderm.

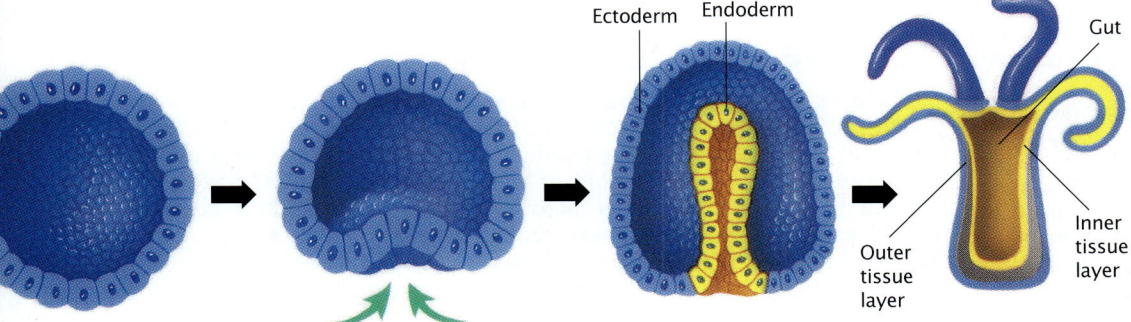

a A hollow ball of cells forms from continuous divisions of a single fertilized egg.

b Gastrulation begins when cell divisions force one surface inward.

c The inner layer of cells is the endoderm; the outer layer is the ectoderm.

d In *Hydra*, ectoderm forms the outer layer and nervous tissue, and endoderm forms the tissue that lines the gut.

Regularly Arranged Animals

Compare the shape of the cnidarian shown in the **Exploration** with the shape of the sponge shown in **Figure 23-3**. Most sponges are asymmetrical; they lack a regular arrangement of body parts. In contrast, cnidarians are symmetrical. A hydra's tentacles, for instance, seem to radiate from the body axis (an imaginary line through the center of the body) like spokes radiate from the hub of a wheel.

A test for symmetry is to imagine slicing the body along its axis. If such a slice produces approximate mirror-image body halves, then the animal is symmetrical. **Radial symmetry** is the wheel-like symmetry of hydras, sea anemones, jellyfish and their relatives. You will soon see that radial symmetry is very different from the type of symmetry shown by most other animals, including humans.

SECTION REVIEW

1 Explain why a protist such as *Amoeba* is not considered an animal, but a sponge is.

2 Why can a multicellular organism be more efficient than a unicellular one?

3 Why are the choanocytes of a sponge not considered a tissue?

4 List three differences between a sponge and a hydra.

441

The Animal Body 441

Phase Two
Teaching Strategies

Active READING

Technique: Reading Organizer
As students read Section 23-2, have them complete a series-of-events reading organizer to describe the adaptations in body plan for flatworms, roundworms, and mollusks. Organizers will vary but should summarize key features of each group.

Demonstration

■ **Recognizing Relationships**
Allow students to observe freshwater planaria. Ask them how they would identify the head of an unfamiliar animal. *(They will probably point out the location of the eyespots and the direction that the animal is traveling.)* Ask students to explain the relationship between the two. *(It is advantageous for sensory organs to be at the front of the animal so that the animal can get information about what is in front of it.)*

Although cnidarians have a few characteristics of animals you are familiar with, they probably still seem quite unusual to you. How many radially symmetrical animals have you seen today, for instance? Changes in symmetry and other aspects of the body plan eventually resulted in the more complicated animals that you are familiar with.

23-2 Origin of Body Cavities

OBJECTIVES

1. **Contrast the body plans of bilaterally and radially symmetrical animals.**

2. **List three structures derived from mesoderm.**

3. **Describe the advantage of a one-way gut.**

4. **Contrast the three kinds of body cavities.**

A Third Tissue Layer: Flatworms

Your body is neither radially symmetrical nor asymmetrical. You have two arms, two legs, two eyes, two kidneys, and two lungs—one member of each pair on the right side of your body and the other member of the pair on the left. The human body shows **bilateral symmetry**. (The word *bilateral* means "two sides.") Any animal with bilateral symmetry can be separated into nearly mirror-image halves by drawing an imaginary line lengthwise down the middle of the body, as shown in the flatworm in **Figure 23-6**. Like humans, most of the known species of animals are bilaterally symmetrical.

Look again at the hydra in the **Exploration** on page 440. Are you able to locate its head? Most bilaterally symmetrical animals have definite head and tail ends, but radially symmetrical animals such as cnidarians do not. **Cephalization** *(sehf uh lih ZAY shuhn)* is the evolution of a definite head end. Animals that have heads are often active and mobile, moving through their environment headfirst. It is advantageous for sensory organs to be concentrated in the head so that an animal can test for food, danger, hiding places, and mates as it enters new surroundings.

Figure 23-6
All flatworms are bilaterally symmetrical. If you were to cut this flatworm along the dotted line, the result would be two halves that are almost mirror images.

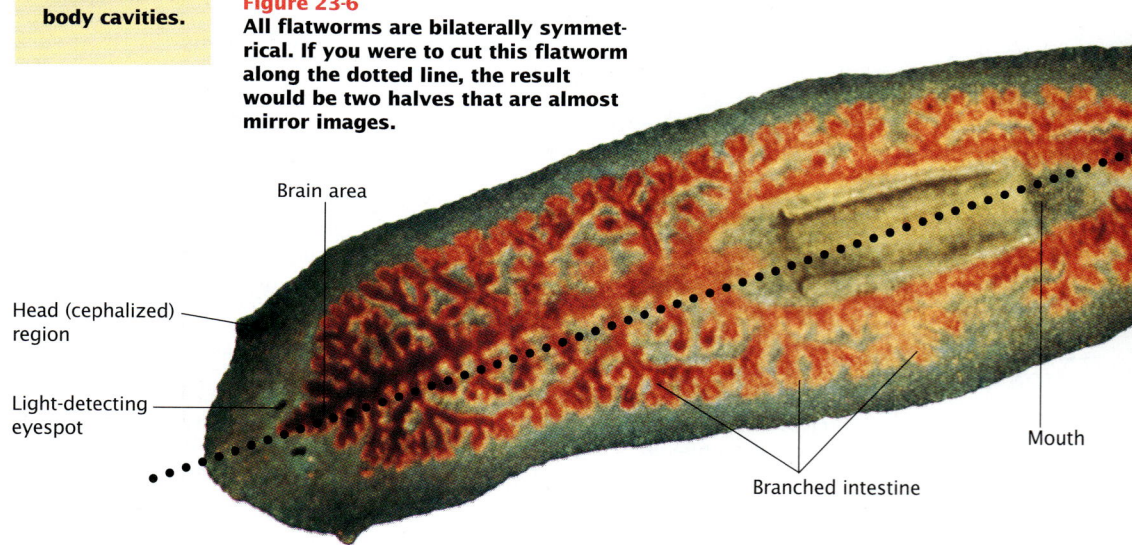

Brain area

Head (cephalized) region

Light-detecting eyespot

Branched intestine

Mouth

Videodisc Resources

Holt Biology Videodiscs
Lesson 23-2: Origin of Body Cavities

Interpreting and evaluating the information obtained by sensory organs requires a complex processing structure. Cephalization is usually accompanied by the evolution of a collection of nervous tissue at the front end of the animal—a brain or brainlike structure. A brain located near the sensory organs is advantageous because information can rapidly cross the short distance between brain and receptor. This enables an animal to respond quickly to stimulation.

Flatworms are bilaterally symmetrical and cephalized

Flatworms, members of the phylum Platyhelminthes *(plat ih hehl MIHN theez)*, are bilaterally symmetrical and cephalized. The dark spots on the head of the flatworm in **Figure 23-6** are eyespots that can detect light, but they cannot focus an image like your eyes can.

Flatworms have organs

Flatworms also have organs. **Organs** are collections of different kinds of tissue that are dedicated to one function. For instance, the heart of a vertebrate is made up of muscle tissue, connective tissue, and nervous tissue, all of which function together to pump blood. Organs are usually found as units in larger systems known as organ systems. An **organ system** is a group of interrelated organs that carries out one or a few essential body functions. A digestive system, for instance, breaks down food and absorbs nutrients, each organ playing a role in these processes.

Where do organs come from during development? During gastrulation, endoderm gives rise to the gut lining and ectoderm gives rise to nervous tissue and skin. A flatworm's body is more than these two simple kinds of tissue. In flatworms and all other major groups of animals that you will study in the rest of this chapter, a third tissue layer forms between the ectoderm and endoderm during gastrulation, as illustrated in **Figure 23-7**. This third layer is known as **mesoderm**, meaning "middle skin." Mesoderm develops into muscle, reproductive organs, and circulatory vessels.

Figure 23-7
In flatworms, the process of gastrulation gives rise to three types of tissue layers.

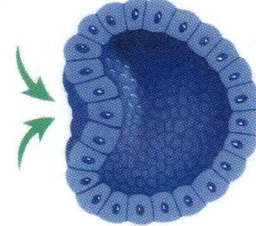

a   **After gastrulation begins, . . .**

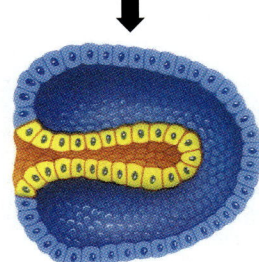

b   **. . . the endoderm and ectoderm form. Endoderm (yellow) gives rise to gut tissue. Ectoderm (blue) gives rise to nervous tissue and skin.**

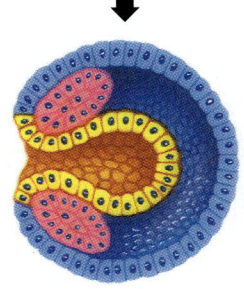

c   **The mesoderm forms in the space between the endoderm and the ectoderm. Mesoderm (red) gives rise to muscle, reproductive organs, and circulatory vessels.**

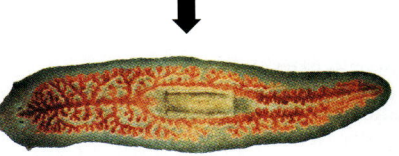

d   **The embryo eventually develops into an adult flatworm.**

443

Matter of Fact: Planarians

Planarians have extraordinary powers of regeneration. Any part of their body that is destroyed by injury can be replaced, and if a planarian is cut into two or more pieces, each piece eventually grows into a complete, new individual.

Parasite-Host Specificity
● **Comparing Functions**

Tell students that parasites are often restricted to one host genus or species. In general, a parasite with a direct life cycle is more species-specific than one with one or more intermediate hosts. Studies are continually revealing compatible hosts for parasites previously thought to be restricted to one host. Assign students to cooperative groups, and have them use library references to gather information about host specificity in roundworms and flatworms. Ask students to list scientific names of the parasites and their hosts.

Exploration of a Flatworm

Key Features: Internal Organs, Bilateral Symmetry, and Cephalization

The evolution of the mesoderm allowed the formation of *organs*. Flatworms, such as the liver fluke, have organs. Flatworms are *bilaterally symmetrical* and have a distinct *head* end. The body plan of the liver fluke is composed of solid layers of tissues surrounding a branched gut.

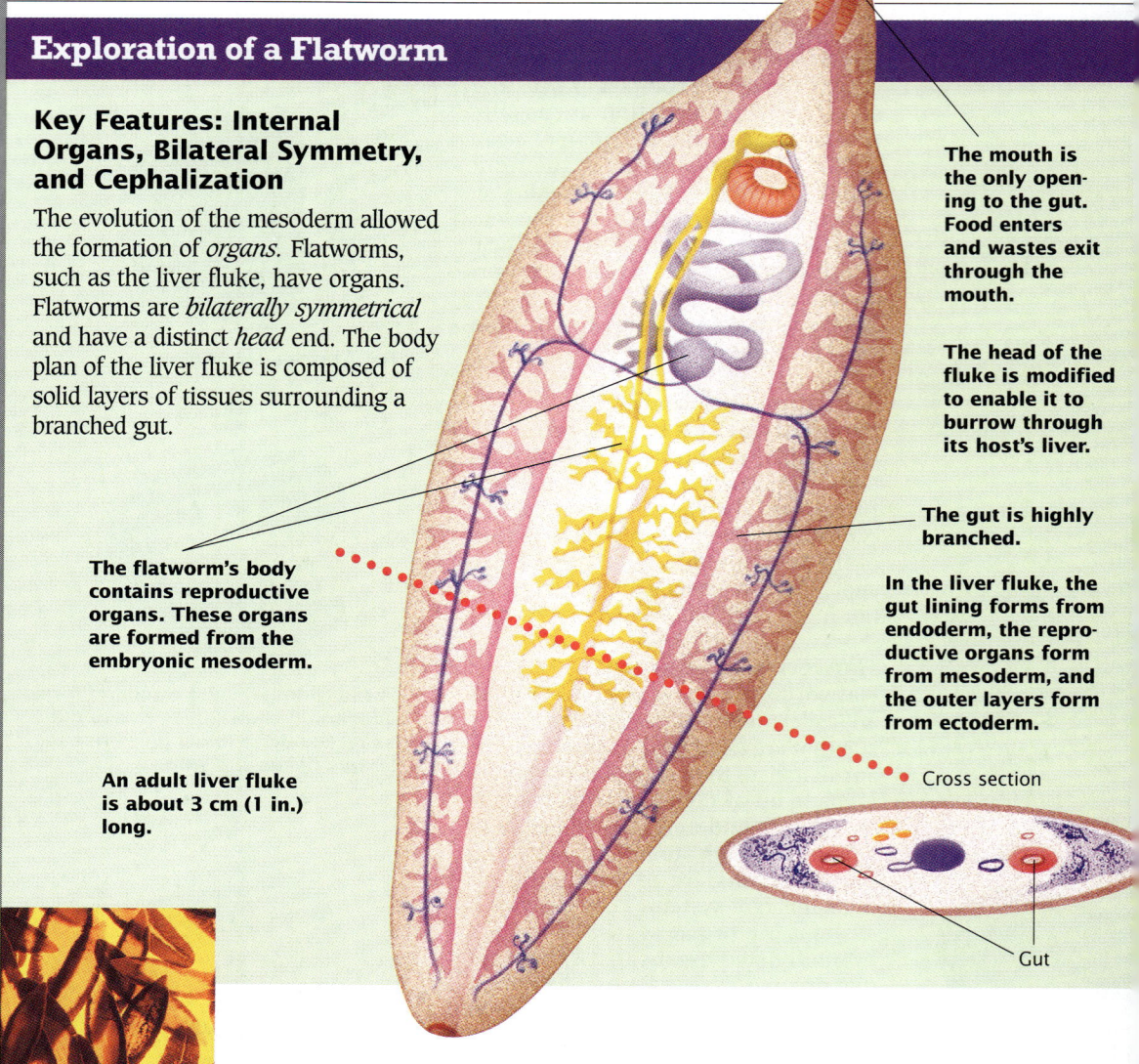

The mouth is the only opening to the gut. Food enters and wastes exit through the mouth.

The head of the fluke is modified to enable it to burrow through its host's liver.

The gut is highly branched.

In the liver fluke, the gut lining forms from endoderm, the reproductive organs form from mesoderm, and the outer layers form from ectoderm.

Cross section

Gut

The flatworm's body contains reproductive organs. These organs are formed from the embryonic mesoderm.

An adult liver fluke is about 3 cm (1 in.) long.

Figure 23-8
Liver flukes are parasitic flatworms. Their acoelomate body plan requires that they be thin in order to allow substances to pass easily to all organs.

Flatworms are solid worms

If you were to cut a flatworm in half across its body, as shown in the **Exploration** above, you would see that the gut is completely surrounded by tissue and organs. This solid body construction is termed **acoelomate** (*ay SEEL oh mayt*), meaning "without a body cavity."

Flatworms are thin because of their acoelomate body construction. Dissolved substances such as carbon dioxide, oxygen, and nutrients cannot diffuse rapidly through the solid bodies of flatworms, such as the liver flukes shown in **Figure 23-8**. Flatworms are small or thin (or both), which shortens the distance these substances must move. In addition, the gut of a flatworm is often branched so that it runs close to most of the tissues.

The guts of all flatworms have only one opening, the mouth. Because these animals consume food and eliminate wastes through the same opening, two-way movement of material occurs within the gut. The two-way gut is less efficient at extracting nutrients than is a one-way gut such as yours. If animals with an acoelomate body plan eat when food is already in the gut, newly consumed food can mix with partially digested food and wastes.

444

Matter of Fact: Protecting Our Pets

Internal parasites can pose a health threat to pets. Dogs and cats get tapeworms by ingesting fleas that carry tapeworm larvae. The pet owner will usually notice the tapeworm segments on the pet or in the pet's stool. Veterinarians can medicate the animal to kill the tapeworm, but as long as fleas are in the pet's environment, the problem will most likely reoccur. Pet owners may choose to use medication for their dog that, when used as directed, prevents heartworms, hookworms, roundworms, and whipworms.

A One-Way Gut and a Body Cavity: Roundworms

Figure 23-9
Roundworms, such as this nematode, have a body cavity, the pseudocoelom. The presence of the pseudocoelom means that roundworms are not packed with solid tissues as are flatworms. The pseudocoelom allows for more efficient diffusion of nutrients to body organs.

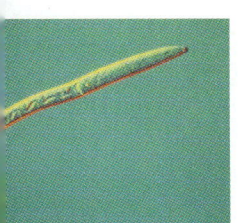

Roundworms (phylum Nematoda), or nematodes, such as *Caenorhabditis elegans* in **Figure 23-9**, have a cavity within the body and a one-way gut with two openings. Food is taken in through the mouth, and wastes are eliminated through an opening at the other end of the gut, the **anus**. This arrangement allows a one-way movement of food through the gut. Also, different regions of the digestive tube can be specialized for different digestive activities. The front part of the gut is adapted for ingesting food. The middle region breaks down food and absorbs nutrients. The last region expels waste products.

Specialization of different regions of the gut brings with it a potential problem, however. Since the absorption of nutrients occurs in only one part of the digestive tract, there must be some effective way of distributing those absorbed nutrients to other parts of the body. Roundworms have a fluid-filled cavity between the gut and the body wall, as illustrated in the **Exploration**. This body cavity is called a **pseudocoelom** (*SOO doh see luhm*), which means "false body cavity." This term is somewhat misleading. The cavity is real, but it differs from the body cavities of most other animals.

The pseudocoelom permits diffusion of nutrients and other dissolved substances over the short distances between tissues and organs. Diffusion is enhanced by body movements, which cause the fluid within the body cavity to move. Nevertheless, diffusion is a slow process. Pseudocoelomate animals must either be very small—most are less than 2.5 mm (0.1 in.) in length—or have body shapes that maintain short distances between organs and the body surface. For this reason, nematodes are usually thin and threadlike.

Exploration of a Roundworm

Key Feature: Body Cavity

The major body plan innovation in roundworms, such as this nematode, is the presence of a *body cavity* between the gut and the body wall. This cavity is the *pseudocoelom*. Animals with a body cavity are not constrained by a solid body as are flatworms. Nematode organs can form away from the gut because nutrients can diffuse through the new body cavity.

Nematode adults consist of very few cells. The nematode *Caenorhabditis elegans* has only 1,000 cells and is the only animal whose complete cellular anatomy is known.

This roundworm, like all terrestrial nematodes, must be small because organs have to be close to the pseudocoelom to receive diffused nutrients. Notice the presence of a mouth and an anus, indicating a one-way digestive tract.

Mouth

A cross section of a roundworm shows how the tissues are arranged around the pseudocoelom. The *body cavity* of a nematode separates the endoderm-lined gut from the rest of the body.

Muscles extend along the length of the worm's body, rather than encircling it.

Cross section

Pseudocoelom

Muscle tissue

Gut

Anus

Reproductive organs

445

Two-Way or One-Way Gut

● **Comparing Functions**

Flatworms have only one opening to the gut, while the roundworm has two. To help students understand the flatworm's two-way gut, ask them to imagine a full-service car wash with only one door. A set number of cars would enter through the door single file, be washed, and then exit by the same door. A more efficient car wash would have both an entrance and an exit, allowing a constant stream of cars to enter, be washed, and exit at the other end. In the same way, a roundworm, with its one-way gut, can eat, digest food, and eliminate wastes constantly.

Agriculture Connection

Nematodes

Show students a container of high-quality garden soil. Have them guess how many nematodes it might contain. Suggest as many as a million. Explain that nematodes are tiny organisms that are important in aerating the soil and in distributing organic and mineral nutrients. Some nematodes are harmful to plants, but many nematodes are helpful because they parasitize plant-eating insect larvae. Scientists are researching the possibility of using nematodes as biological controls for insect pests.

Key to Strategies
● **Understanding Concepts (Tier I)**
■ **Applying Information (Tier II)**
▲ **Critical Thinking (Tier III)**

Mesoderm in Coelomates

● **Identifying Structures**

Tell students that while pseudo-coelomates have muscles lining the body wall, coelomates have an advantage because they can have an additional layer of muscle surrounding individual organs. Ask students to name some human organs that contain their own muscle tissue and the functions of the organs' movements. *(Some examples might include the heart, which moves blood through the blood vessels; the digestive organs, which move food through the digestive tract; the ureters, which move urine from the kidneys to the bladder; and the blood vessels, which can dilate and constrict to circulate blood.)*

Figure 23-10
These cross sections show the differences between acoelomate, pseudo-coelomate, and coelomate body constructions.

A Better Body Cavity: Mollusks

A body cavity is advantageous in two main ways. First, because the organs lie within a fluid-filled cavity, they are insulated from the contractions of the muscles in the body wall. The organs can function independently of the movements of the animal. Food can be digested even while the animal is moving. The second advantage is that the digestive tract can coil up within the body cavity and be much longer than the animal. Your digestive tract is more than 8 m (26 ft) long. A longer digestive system allows food to be more completely digested and increases the efficiency of nutrient absorption.

Most animals with a body cavity have a coelom, or true body cavity. A **coelom** *(SEE luhm)* is a fluid-filled body cavity that lies completely within the mesoderm, as shown in **Figure 23-10**. The coelom separates the muscles of the body wall from the muscles that surround the gut. Animals that have a coelom are called coelomates *(SEE loh maytz)*. Why the coelom evolved is still a mystery. One suggestion is that it allows the mesoderm and endoderm to interact during embryonic development, producing specialized regions of the digestive tract.

In coelomates, as in flatworms, the gut tube is surrounded by solid tissue that is a barrier to rapid diffusion. This arrangement could limit the movement of nutrients, but most coelomates have a **circulatory system**, a network of blood-carrying vessels. The circulatory system brings nutrients and oxygen to the tissues and removes wastes and carbon dioxide. Blood is usually propelled through the circulatory system by contractions of one or more muscular hearts.

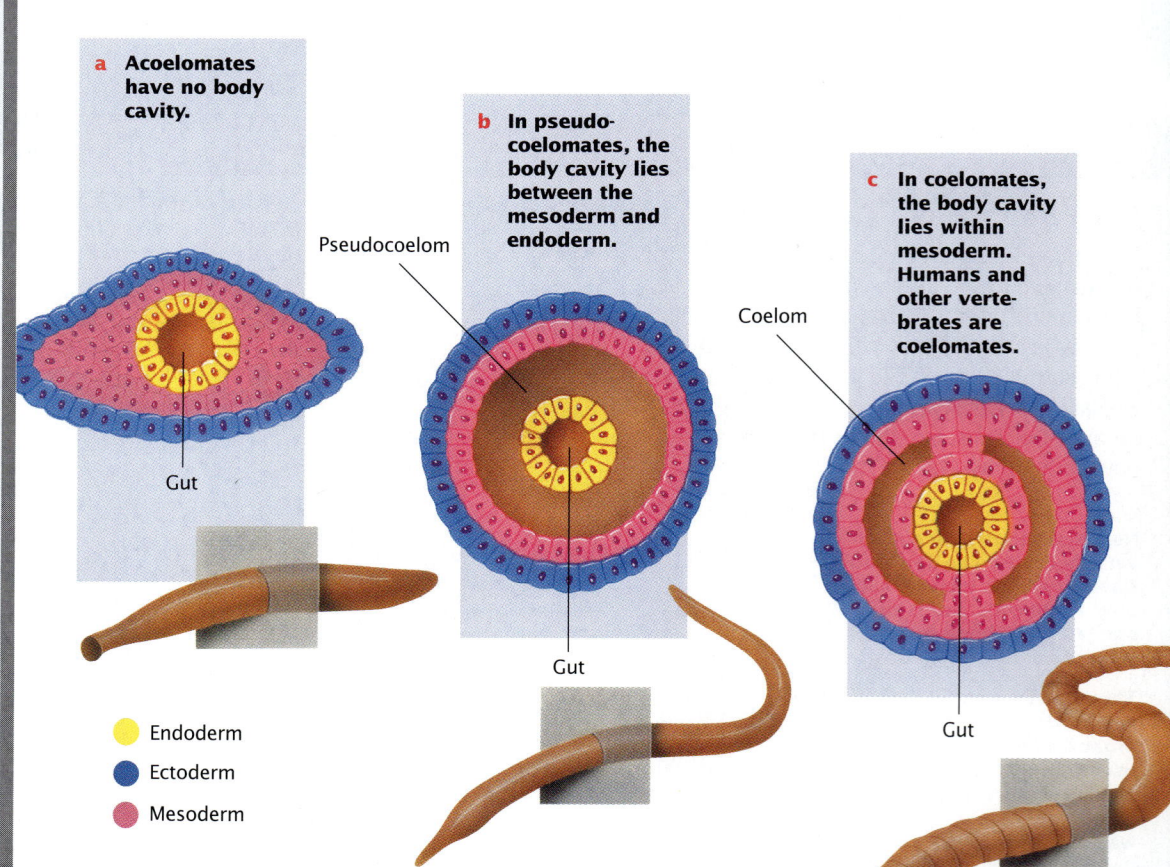

a **Acoelomates have no body cavity.**

b **In pseudo-coelomates, the body cavity lies between the mesoderm and endoderm.**

c **In coelomates, the body cavity lies within mesoderm. Humans and other vertebrates are coelomates.**

Pseudocoelom

Coelom

Gut

Gut

Gut

● Endoderm
● Ectoderm
● Mesoderm

446

Exploration of a Mollusk

Key Feature: Coelom

This snail is a mollusk. Mollusks have a *coelom* and a *circulatory system*. The coelom allows the gut to function independently from the muscles of the body wall and to be longer than the animal.

Heart

The mantle is a heavy fold of tissue wrapped around the central body mass like a cape.

Twisting and turning of the snail's body results in a complex internal anatomy. However, the basic body plan is one in which a coelom has developed within the mesoderm.

Reproductive organs

Foot

Gut

The mantle encloses a cavity between the shell and the central body mass. In aquatic snails, this cavity contains the gills, which absorb oxygen from water.

Within the mouth is a unique rasping tongue called the radula.

Eyes

Figure 23-11
This land snail is a mollusk.

Mollusks are coelomates with a circulatory system

Mollusks (phylum Mollusca) have a coelom and a circulatory system. Snails (such as the one in **Figure 23-11**), clams, squids, and mussels belong to this phylum. The mollusk body plan is illustrated in the **Exploration** above.

SECTION REVIEW

1 Explain the difference between bilateral symmetry and radial symmetry.

2 What structures in your body are derived from mesoderm?

3 Summarize the advantages of a one-way gut.

4 Diagram the two types of body cavities.

447

Phase Three
Assessment Options

Closure
● **Identifying Structures**
Show students a dissected fresh or preserved mollusk, such as a clam or oyster. Ask them to sketch the mollusk and label the following parts: shell, muscle, coelom, foot, gut, heart, and gills.

SECTION REVIEW
Assign the *Section Review*.

Reteaching
Have students make a chart with the following column heads: Flatworms, Roundworms, Mollusks, and Advantages. Have them list the following characteristics down the left side of the chart as row heads: Bilateral symmetry, Cephalization, Organs, Pseudocoelom, and Coelom. Have students then write in "yes" or "no" for each characteristic that the animal has and explain the advantages of the characteristic in the last column.

ANSWERS TO SECTION REVIEW

1 Bilateral symmetry is the arrangement of an organism's body parts so that one-half of the body is an approximate mirror image of the other half. Radial symmetry is the arrangement of body parts around the body axis.

2 Mesoderm tissue gives rise to muscle, reproductive organs, and circulatory vessels.

3 A one-way digestive tract allows different parts of the digestive tract to specialize in different functions. In a typical one-way digestive tract, the front part of the gut is specialized for ingesting food, the middle part for breaking down food and absorbing nutrients, and the last region for expelling wastes.

4 See Figure 23-10 on page 446.

Key to Strategies
● **Understanding Concepts (Tier I)**
■ **Applying Information (Tier II)**
▲ **Critical Thinking (Tier III)**

The Animal Body   447

There are more than 5 billion people on Earth. This figure may seem large, but it is tiny compared with the insect population. Scientists estimate that there are 200 million times more individual insects than humans alive today. Insects and humans belong to two of the most successful phyla of organisms—Arthropoda and Chordata.

23-3 Four Innovations in Body Plan

OBJECTIVES

1. **Contrast the body plan of segmented animals with that of non-segmented animals.**

2. **Compare the exoskeleton of arthropods with the endoskeleton of vertebrates.**

3. **Summarize the differences between protostomes and deuterostomes.**

4. **List two traits that reveal the relationship between chordates and echinoderms.**

Segmented Worms: Annelids

Look at the worm in **Figure 23-12**. This worm is made up of many similar units linked together like beads in a necklace. Animals showing **segmentation** are composed of repeated body units. Three very successful animal phyla are segmented: annelids (earthworms and their relatives), arthropods (insects, crustaceans, and spiders), and chordates (mostly vertebrates).

Can you point out an example of segmentation in your body? Don't be surprised if you cannot. In vertebrates, segments are not usually visible externally in adults but are apparent during embryonic development. Vertebrate

muscles develop from repeated blocks of tissue that occur in the embryo. Another example of segmentation is the vertebral column, which is a stack of very similar vertebrae.

What great advantage does segmentation provide? Its main advantage is the evolutionary flexibility it offers. A small change in an existing segment can produce a new kind of segment with a different function. As illustrated in the **Exploration of an Annelid** shown on the following page, some segments of the earthworm are modified for reproduction, and some are modified for feeding.

Figure 23-12
The bristle worm is an example of an annelid. Like the earthworm on the next page, its body is segmented. Specialized segments perform specific tasks.

448

Videodisc Resources

Holt Biology Videodiscs
Lesson 23-3: Four Innovations in Body Plan

Exploration of an Annelid

Key Feature: Segmentation

Annelids, such as this earthworm, have a body plan that consists of *segments*. Most segments are separated by partitions that cross the coelom. In each segment, parts of the excretory, circulatory, and nervous systems are repeated.

Gut

A cross section of the earthworm shows the gut and coelom.

Body wall

Coelom

A pair of excretory organs and a nerve center are located in each segment.

A small brain coordinates the activities of the segments.

Brain

Gut

Mouth

Excretory organ

Nerve cord

Blood vessels

Bristles called setae occur on each segment. Earthworms use setae as anchors while crawling.

Figure 23-13
The earthworm is an annelid. Members of this phylum have segmented bodies.

Annelids have segments that are specialized

Annelids (phylum Annelida), such as the earthworm in **Figure 23-13**, were among the first segmented animals to evolve. The earthworm body plan is shown in the **Exploration** above. The basic body plan of an annelid is a tube within a tube. The gut tube, which extends from mouth to anus, is suspended within the larger tube of the body wall. The coelom is the space between these tubes. It is divided internally between segments. This parti-

tioning limits diffusion of materials from segment to segment. However, a circulatory system overcomes this limitation by transporting materials between segments.

Segments near the front of an annelid are modified to house a small brain and sense organs. Each segment along the body is controlled by an individual nerve center. A nerve cord running along the underside of the worm connects these nerve centers to the brain so that all of the body's activities can be coordinated.

449

Earthworm Segments
● Identifying Structures
Have students use a hand lens to observe live earthworms, and ask them to find as many differences between the individual segments as they can. To increase their transparency, you may wish to culture the worms for a few days on an ordinary agar gel that has been perforated. As the worms eat the transparent agar and expel opaque dirt, their internal organs become visible.

Segmented Worms
● Comparing Structures
Prepare a display of dissected leech and earthworm specimens. Have students study the specimens to identify and compare homologous structures. Discuss the similarities and differences between earthworms and leeches.

Health Connection
Medicinal Leeches
Doctors once kept a supply of medicinal leeches, *Hirudo medicinalis,* to draw off "bad" or excess blood from their patients. Today doctors sometimes use leeches to reduce accumulation of blood during plastic surgery and to remove necrotic (dead) blood when limbs are being reattached.

Historical Perspective: The Service of Earthworms

Charles Darwin (1809–1882), a British naturalist famous for his theories of evolution and natural selection, was fascinated with the ways that earthworms aerate and enrich soil. In his last botanical book, *The Formation of Vegetable Mould Through the Action of Worms,* Darwin noted the service of earthworms in recycling organic matter in soil. He observed that an earthworm could ingest its weight in soil each day, and that in one year the earthworms inhabiting one hectare could digest 22 to 40 metric tons of soil. The work was published only six months prior to Darwin's death and was called a pioneering study in quantifying ecology.

Key to Strategies
● Understanding Concepts (Tier I)
■ Applying Information (Tier II)
▲ Critical Thinking (Tier III)

Diversity in Arthropods

● **Comparing Structures**

Point out that in addition to insects, the arthropods also include lobsters, shrimp, crabs, spiders, sow bugs, centipedes and millipedes, ticks, mites, crayfish, and horseshoe crabs. Show photos of a variety of these different types of arthropods, and have students list characteristics that they have in common.

Comparing Annelids With Arthropods

■ **Analyzing Information**

Have students observe an earthworm and a millipede (either live or preserved specimens). Have students list their similarities, and then have them make a table showing how the presence or absence of certain characteristics (for example, an exoskeleton) identifies the earthworm as an annelid and the millipede as an arthropod.

Grubs and Caterpillars

● **Comparing Structures**

Many people mistake grubs and caterpillars for worms. Make sure students understand that grubs and caterpillars are not annelids. Explain that they are insects in larval stages and that they belong to the phylum Arthropoda.

Exploration of an Arthropod

Key Features: Jointed Appendages and Exoskeleton

Arthropods have a coelom, segmented bodies, and *jointed appendages*. The three body regions of an insect, such as this wasp, are the head, thorax, and abdomen. Each region is composed of a number of segments that fuse during development. The strong *exoskeleton* provides protection and an attachment point for muscles.

Like most insects, wasps have two pairs of wings, which are attached to the thorax.

A wasp is an insect. Like all arthropods, it has a segmented body and jointed appendages. This body plan has helped insects become one of the most successful animal groups.

Wings

Abdomen

Head

Stinger

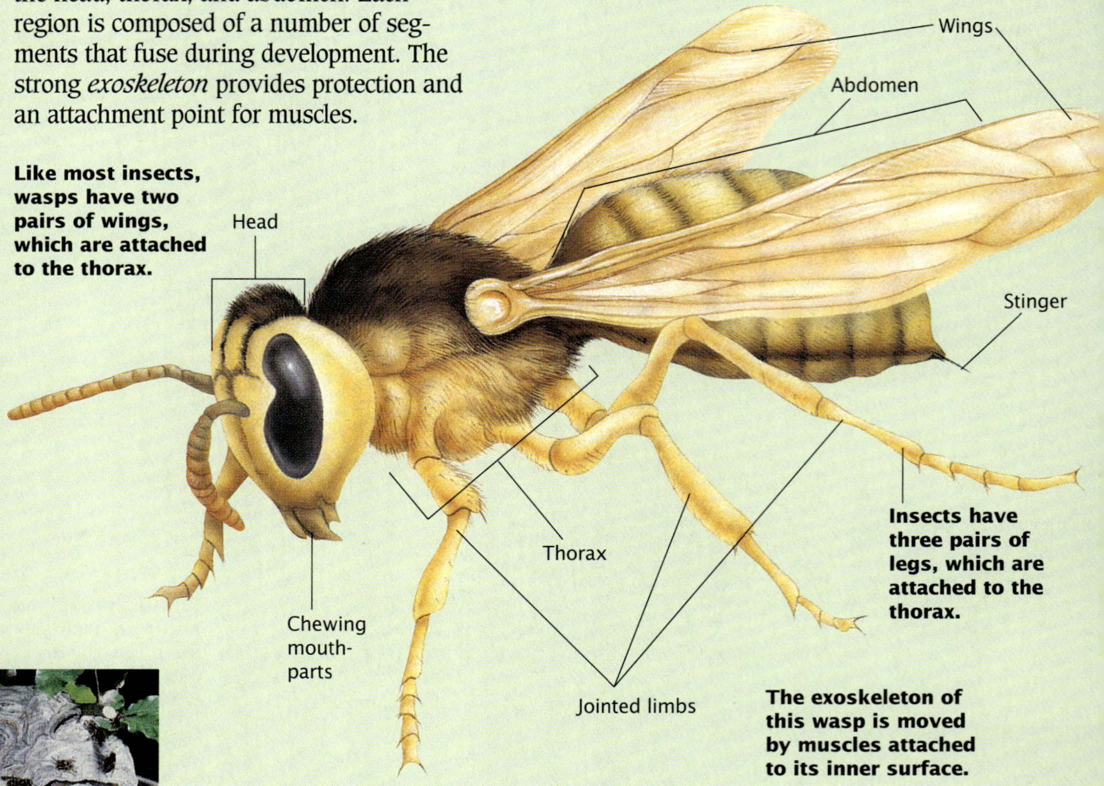

Insects have three pairs of legs, which are attached to the thorax.

Chewing mouth-parts

Thorax

Jointed limbs

The exoskeleton of this wasp is moved by muscles attached to its inner surface.

Figure 23-14
Wasps are highly social insects that build a nest where the colony lives and breeds. This nest is made of a paperlike material and may house hundreds of wasps.

Limbs and Skeletons: Arthropods

The name *arthropod* comes from the Greek words *arthros*, meaning "jointed," and *podes*, meaning "feet." The great success of arthropods, such as the wasps in **Figure 23-14**, is due largely to their jointed appendages. These appendages have evolved to perform a variety of tasks. Some appendages serve as limbs for walking or grasping. Others function as antennae for sensing the environment or as mouthparts for chewing, sucking, or poisoning prey. For example, a scorpion seizes and tears apart its prey with appendages that have been modified into large pincers capable of grasping and holding tightly.

Like annelids, the basic body plan of arthropods is segmented, as shown in the **Exploration** above. Individual segments of an arthropod often exist only during early development, however, and fuse into functional groups in adults. For example, caterpillars have

450

Evolution

Arthropods and chordates show segmentation. Many scientists think segmentation evolved independently in each group. What evidence supports this conclusion?

many obvious segments, while butterflies have only three main body units—head, thorax, and abdomen—each composed of several fused segments. Arthropods have an external skeleton, or **exoskeleton**. The arthropod exoskeleton is made of chitin *(KYT uhn)*, a tough polysaccharide, and protein. The muscles are internal to the skeleton and attach to its inner surface. As it grows, an arthropod periodically sheds its rigid exoskeleton. Many arthropods change their body form as they develop. A butterfly begins life as a wormlike caterpillar, later transforming into the flying adult. A silverfish, on the other hand, does not change as it matures; it merely grows larger.

Two Patterns of Development

Humans and the other chordates are more closely related to the echinoderms—the phylum that includes the sea star—than to the arthropods. At first glance, there seems to be little resemblance between humans and sea stars (often called starfish). Sea stars are radially symmetrical, as you can see in the **Exploration** on the next page. However, the embryos of chordates and echinoderms develop similarly.

In animals with mesoderm, except for echinoderms and chordates, the first opening that forms in the embryo during gastrulation eventually becomes the mouth. Animals that develop in this fashion are known as **protostomes**. The word *protostome* means "first mouth." In protostomes, the developmental fate of each cell of the early embryo is usually determined when that cell first appears.

Echinoderms and chordates are **deuterostomes**. The word *deuterostome* means "second mouth" and refers to the fact that the first opening in the embryo does not form the mouth—it becomes the anus of the adult animal. The mouth develops from an opening that appears later in development. In these animals, all the cells of the early embryo are identical. This means that any cell, if isolated early enough in development, can develop into a complete organism. **Figure 23-15** shows some protostomes and deuterostomes.

Figure 23-15
Below are examples of protostomes and deuterostomes. Recent studies using DNA nucleotide sequences support the division of the coelomates into these two groups.

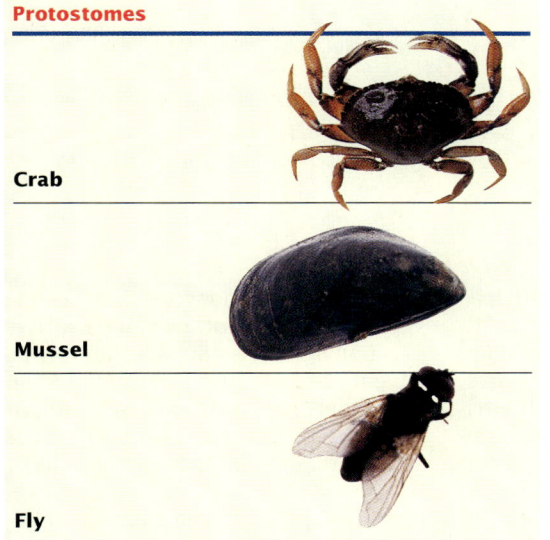

Protostomes

Crab

Mussel

Fly

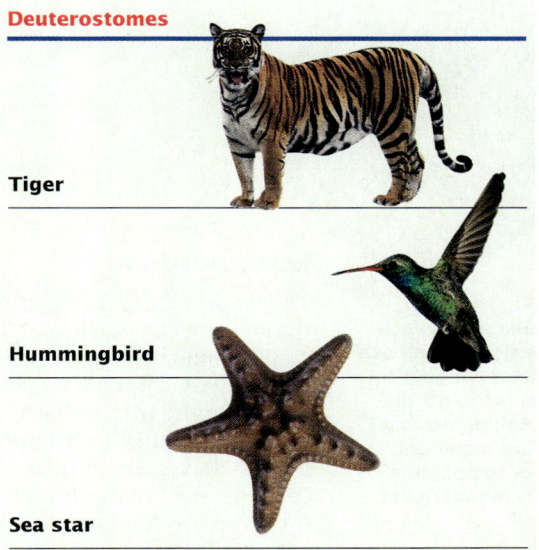

Deuterostomes

Tiger

Hummingbird

Sea star

Theme Answer

The protostomes, which include the arthropods, and the deuterostomes, which include the chordates, separated into two great evolutionary branches long before either group contained any members that were segmented. Therefore, segmentation must have evolved independently in the chordates and arthropods.

Social Studies Connection

Armor

Show students a picture of the armor worn by medieval knights, and ask them to imagine how it must have felt to wear it. Encourage students to think about how heavy the armor was and how it must have made moving around slow, clumsy, and difficult. Ask students to identify an important characteristic of insects that explains the ease with which they carry their armor. *(No insect is as large as a human being. In fact, most insects are very small. Only by keeping their size small can the disadvantages of an armor-like exoskeleton be overcome.)*

Key to Strategies
● **Understanding Concepts (Tier I)**
■ **Applying Information (Tier II)**
▲ **Critical Thinking (Tier III)**

Exploration of an Echinoderm

Key Features: Deuterostome Development and Endoskeleton

Echinoderms, such as this sea star, have coeloms and are deuterostomes. Sea stars are bilaterally symmetrical as larvae. As adults, they have five-part, radial symmetry and an *endoskeleton*. Sea stars move by means of a system of water-filled canals known as the water vascular system. The water vascular system causes tube feet on the bottom of the sea star to extend and retract.

Sea stars have a delicate skin stretched over a calcium-rich endoskeleton of spiny plates.

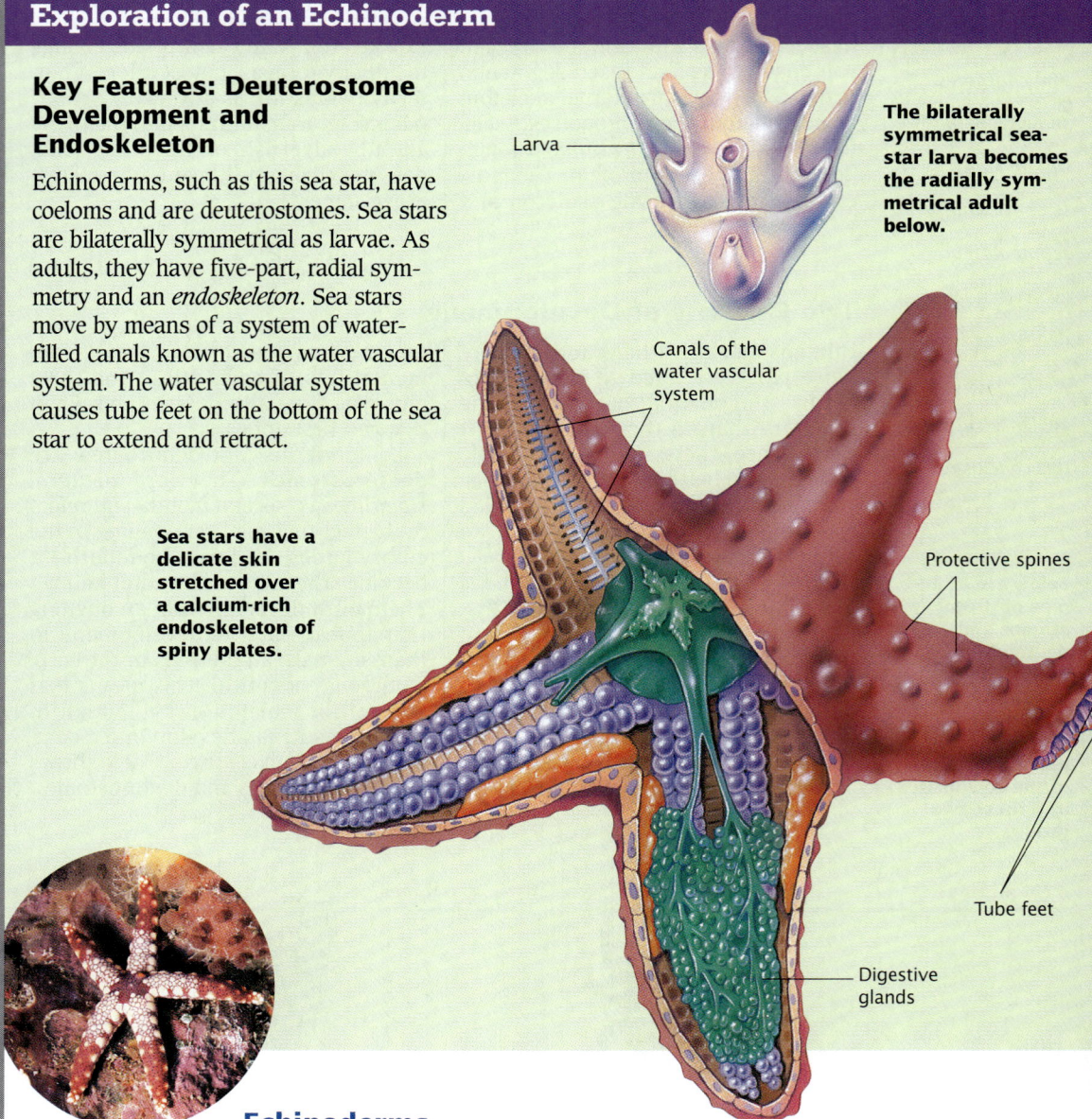

Larva

The bilaterally symmetrical sea-star larva becomes the radially symmetrical adult below.

Canals of the water vascular system

Protective spines

Tube feet

Digestive glands

Figure 23-16
Sea stars, such as this small sea star clinging to a ledge off the Philippine coast, are members of the phylum Echinodermata.

Echinoderms

The larvae of all echinoderms, such as the sea star in **Figure 23-16**, are bilaterally symmetrical and undergo a complex metamorphosis as they mature, transforming into radially symmetrical adults. Unlike arthropods, echinoderms have an internal skeleton composed of many bonelike plates. An internal skeleton is called an **endoskeleton**.

Most adult echinoderms, like the one shown in the **Exploration**, have a five-part body plan. As adults, echinoderms have no head or brain. The body of an echinoderm is controlled by a ring of nerves that branches into each of the arms. Although the arms are capable of complex movements, control of movement is not centralized as it is in bilaterally symmetrical animals.

452

Matter of Fact: Tube Feet

The tube feet of sea stars appear delicate, and it is easy to pull them one by one from an object to which they are attached. However, when they all pull together, they can exert tremendous force—enough to pull apart the valves of a clam. People who shell clams cannot open them by force. They must use a knife to cut the powerful muscle that holds the valves shut.

The Most Successful Deuterostomes: Chordates

Fishes, amphibians, reptiles, birds, and mammals are chordates, as is the lancelet shown in **Figure 23-17**. Lancelets do not resemble familiar chordates such as birds, dogs, or humans. Nonetheless, lancelets and all chordates share four key features:

1. dorsal (along the back) hollow nerve cord
2. dorsal supportive rod called the notochord
3. slits in the pharynx (the region of the digestive tract just behind the mouth) that connect the pharynx to the outside
4. a postanal tail—one that extends beyond the anus

This unique combination of characteristics can be seen in the lancelet shown in the **Exploration** below. All chordates have all four of these characteristics at some time during their lives. For example, humans have pharyngeal slits, a nerve cord, a tail, and a notochord as embryos. As adults, humans retain only the nerve cord and one pair of pharyngeal slits (which have become the external ear canals and the eustachian tubes that connect the throat to the middle ear).

In addition to these four principal characteristics, chordates have a number of other distinguishing features, such as a segmented body plan.

Figure 23-17
The lancelet is a chordate, a member of the same phylum as human beings. Although it does not resemble a human, the lancelet has characteristics that it shares with humans and all other chordates.

Exploration of a Lancelet

Key Feature: Notochord

The lancelet *Branchiostoma* is a chordate. It is a coelomate animal that has a *notochord*, pharyngeal slits, a postanal tail, and a dorsal nerve cord. The notochord persists throughout the life of *Branchiostoma*. In most other chordates, such as birds and humans, the notochord is replaced during embryonic development by the vertebral column.

The lancelet is modified for life as an ocean-dwelling bottom feeder. It takes in water through its mouth and passes it through its pharyngeal slits, filtering out small prey.

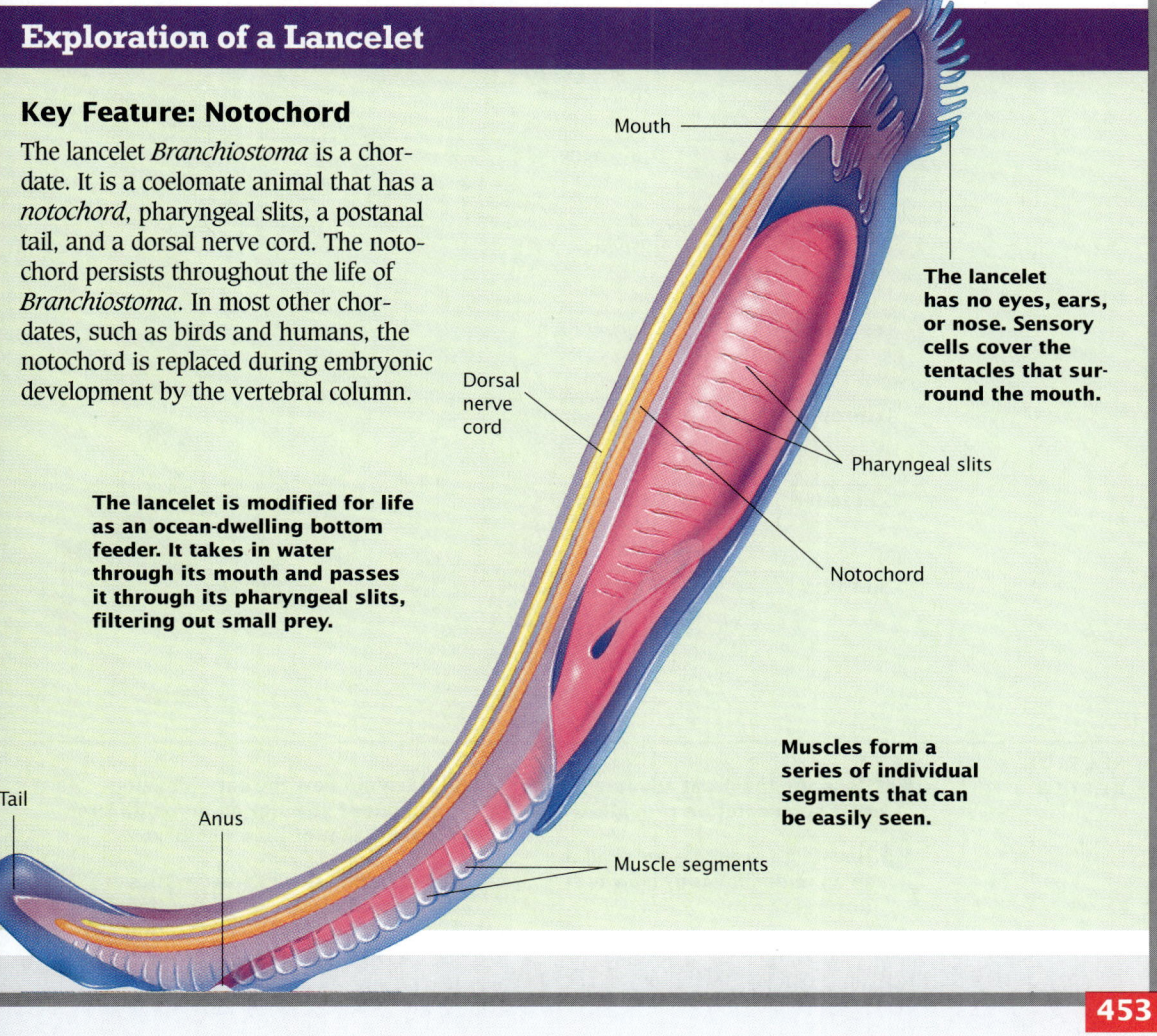

Mouth

The lancelet has no eyes, ears, or nose. Sensory cells cover the tentacles that surround the mouth.

Dorsal nerve cord

Pharyngeal slits

Notochord

Muscles form a series of individual segments that can be easily seen.

Tail

Anus

Muscle segments

453

Demonstration
● **Identifying Functions**
Materials: Two thin plastic bags and a drinking straw
Obtain two thin plastic bags, such as produce bags from a supermarket. Place a drinking straw lengthwise inside the bottom of one of the bags. Ask a volunteer to hold this bag upside down by the straw and to hold the other bag by the bottom of the bag. Now ask the volunteer to wave the bags back and forth to simulate a swimming motion. Tell students that the lancelet, a small filter feeder, moves by contracting muscles attached to a notochord. The notochord, forming a stiff rod along the back of the animal, is a tremendous advancement that greatly facilitates movement.

Unscrambling the Groups
● **Organizing Information**
Write a **Graphic Organizer** similar to the one located at the bottom of this page on the chalkboard or overhead projector, but leave out the names of the animal groups. Scramble the order of the animal groups and list them separately next to the organizer. Have a student come up to the board and write the correct animal group next to the feature "Multicellularity." Then ask the student to explain what the description means. Have different students come up and do the same until the organizer is complete.

Graphic Organizer

Use the following graphic organizer with the teaching strategy **Unscrambling the Groups** on page 453.

Animal group	Key features
Chordata	Improved skeleton
Echinodermata	Deuterostome development, endoskeleton
Arthropoda	Jointed appendages, exoskeleton
Annelida	Segmentation
Mollusca	Coelom
Nematoda	Body cavity
Platyhelminthes	Internal organs
Cnidaria	Symmetry, specialized tissues
Porifera	Multicellularity

Key to Strategies
● **Understanding Concepts (Tier I)**
■ **Applying Information (Tier II)**
▲ **Critical Thinking (Tier III)**

The Animal Body   453

Closure

● **Summarizing Information**
Use the Active Reading strategy below to help students summarize their knowledge.

Active **READING**

Technique: Discussion
Review the list that students created in the *Active Reading* exercise on page 437. Have students modify the list based on what they have learned from the chapter.

SECTION REVIEW

Assign the *Section Review.*

Reteaching

Have students write a short explanation of how each of the following modifications of basic animal body plans is advantageous to the animal: bilateral symmetry, cephalization, organs, organ systems, a one-way gut, a pseudocoelom, and a true coelom.

Vertebrates have a sturdy endoskeleton

Most chordates belong to the subphylum Vertebrata, the vertebrates. Fishes, amphibians, reptiles, birds, and mammals are vertebrates, but the lancelet is not. In most vertebrates, the notochord is replaced by the vertebral column during development.

Vertebrates also have an endoskeleton of bone or cartilage against which the muscles work. The vertebrate endoskeleton is lightweight and provides effective support.

Table 23-1 shows the changes in the animal body described in this chapter. You will read more about these groups in Chapters 24–28.

Table 23-1 The Animal Body: An Evolutionary Journey

Phylum	Key features	Typical organism	
Porifera	Multicellularity	Sponge	
Cnidaria	Radial symmetry Extracellular digestion Specialized tissues	Hydra	
Platyhelminthes	Internal organs Bilateral symmetry Cephalization	Liver fluke	
Nematoda	Body cavity	Nematode	
Mollusca	Coelom	Snail	
Annelida	Segmentation	Earthworm	
Arthropoda	Jointed appendages Exoskeleton	Wasp	
Echinodermata	Deuterostome development Endoskeleton	Sea star	
Chordata	Notochord	Lancelet	

SECTION REVIEW

1 Describe the great advantage that segmentation provides.

2 How is an exoskeleton similar to an endoskeleton? How is it different?

3 Explain how the early development of sea star embryos differs from that of insect embryos.

4 Describe two characteristics shared by sea stars and humans.

ANSWERS TO **SECTION REVIEW**

1 Its main advantage is its evolutionary flexibility. A small change in an existing segment can produce a new kind of segment with a different function.

2 They are similar in that they both provide support. They differ in location: an endoskeleton is internal, while an exoskeleton is external.

3 In an insect, the fate of each cell in the early embryo is usually determined when that cell first appears. In a sea star, all of the early cells of the embryo are identical.

4 Both are deuterostomes, and both have an endoskeleton.

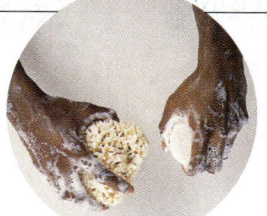

A natural sponge is the skeleton of a marine sponge.

	Key Terms	Summary
23-1 **The Origin of Tissues**  Sponges have a very simple body plan. They have no tissues, and most are asymmetrical.	body plan (p. 437) tissue (p. 440) gut (p. 440) gastrulation (p. 441) endoderm (p. 441) ectoderm (p. 441) radial symmetry (p. 441)	• Multicellularity enables individual cells to specialize on one or a few tasks. • Sponges are multicellular animals without tissues. Sponges filter small food particles from the water. • Cnidarians have two tissue layers and show radial symmetry.
23-2 **Origin of Body Cavities** 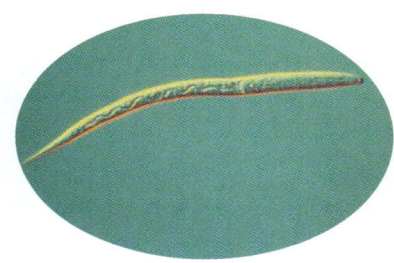 Nematodes have two openings to the gut, allowing for specialization of digestive activities.	bilateral symmetry (p. 442) cephalization (p. 442) organ (p. 443) organ system (p. 443) mesoderm (p. 443) acoelomate (p. 444) anus (p. 445) pseudocoelom (p. 445) coelom (p. 446) circulatory system (p. 446)	• Flatworms are bilaterally symmetrical and cephalized. • Nematodes have a one-way gut and a pseudocoelom, a cavity lying between the gut and the muscles of the body wall. • A coelom is a fluid-filled body cavity that lies within the mesoderm. Mollusks have a coelom and a circulatory system that distributes nutrients and oxygen to the tissues.
23-3 **Four Innovations in Body Plan** Arthropods have jointed appendages, a segmented body, and an exoskeleton. 	segmentation (p. 448) exoskeleton (p. 451) protostome (p. 451) deuterostome (p. 451) endoskeleton (p. 452)	• Annelids have a segmented body. Chordates and arthropods are also segmented. • An exoskeleton of chitin and protein, segmentation, and jointed appendages are characteristics of arthropods. • The embryos of echinoderms and chordates develop similarly. These two groups of animals are closely related.

Alternative Assessment

Have students make study cards from the information in Table 23-1 on page 454. Each card should represent one phylum and include key features of that phylum. Have students add the advantages for each key feature listed. Encourage students to use the key terms from the chapter when describing the characteristics of each group. Have students make a representative drawing for the phylum on the reverse side of each card. Have students use the cards with a study partner to review the chapter.

Portfolio Assessment

Portfolio Assessment on page T39 provides options for building and evaluating student portfolios. Students and teachers can select items from the areas listed on page T39 for inclusion in a portfolio.

455

ANSWER TO CONCEPT MAP

The following is one possible answer to the Relating Concepts exercise on page 456.

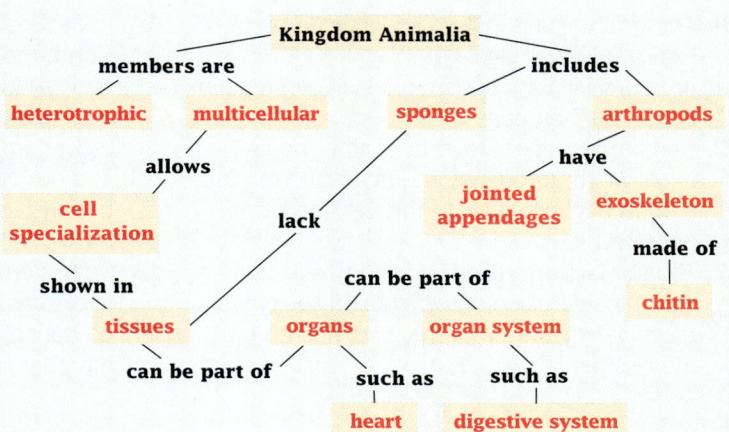

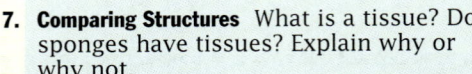
review

A N S W E R S

Understanding Vocabulary

1. a. Both are produced during gastrulation; the inner layer is called the endoderm and the outer layer is called the ectoderm.
   b. Radial symmetry is the arrangement of body parts around a central point. Bilateral symmetry is the arrangement of an organism's body parts so that a left and right half mirror each other.
   c. A tissue is composed of similar cells that perform a common function, while an organ is composed of different tissues that perform a single function.
2. a. cnidarian
   b. roundworm
   c. echinoderm

Understanding Concepts

3. Answer to Concept Map is found on page 455.
4. All animals are heterotrophic, multicellular, and lack cell walls.
5. Division of labor means that cells are specialized to perform specific tasks. A specialized cell can carry out one task more effectively than a cell that must carry out many tasks.
6. Both animals have tissue. The sea star is radially symmetrical.
7. A tissue is a group of similar cells coordinated for a particular function. Sponges do not have tissue. Their cells are specialized, but work independently.
8. Radially symmetrical animals have body parts arranged around a central axis. Bilaterally symmetrical animals have body parts that can be separated into two halves that are nearly mirror images. Examples will vary.
9. Proximity of the brain to the sense organs enables rapid information transfer from the sense organs to the brain, thus allowing a quick response.

---

review

Understanding Vocabulary

1. For each pair of terms, explain the difference in their meanings.
   a. endoderm, ectoderm
   b. radial symmetry, bilateral symmetry
   c. tissue, organ
2. For each set of terms, complete the analogy.
   a. asymmetrical : sponge :: radially symmetrical : _____
   b. acoelomate : flatworm :: pseudocoelomate : _____
   c. jointed appendages, exoskeleton : arthropod :: endoskeleton, radial symmetry as adult : _____

Understanding Concepts

3. **Relating Concepts** Construct a concept map that describes the characteristics of animals. Try to include the following terms in your concept map: heterotrophic, multicellular, cell specialization, tissues, organs, organ system, sponges, arthropods, jointed appendages, exoskeleton, chitin, heart, digestive system.
4. **Identifying Structures** What three characteristics do all animals have in common?
5. **Summarizing Information** What is meant by the phrase "division of labor"? Why is it advantageous for the cells of an animal to exhibit division of labor?
6. **Comparing Structures** Look at the figures below. Which animal has tissues? Which is radially symmetrical?

7. **Comparing Structures** What is a tissue? Do sponges have tissues? Explain why or why not.
8. **Comparing Structures** How do the body plans of radially and bilaterally symmetrical animals differ? Give an example of an animal with each kind of symmetry.
9. **Inferring Relationships** The brain and the sense organs in most bilaterally symmetrical animals are located in a head region. Why is this arrangement advantageous?
10. **Summarizing Information** Summarize the steps of gastrulation that lead to the formation of endoderm and ectoderm. What kinds of tissues do endoderm and ectoderm give rise to?
11. **Identifying Structures** What is mesoderm? What structures of an animal's body are derived from the mesoderm?
12. **Analyzing Functions** How does the movement of food in a nematode compare with the movement of food in a flatworm?
13. **Analyzing Functions** What similar problem do coelomates and acoelomates have? How do many coelomates overcome this problem?
14. **Contrasting Structures** Describe and contrast the two kinds of body cavities. Give an example of an animal with each kind of cavity.
15. **Comparing Structures and Functions** What are some of the functions of an exoskeleton? What are some limitations of an exoskeleton?
16. **Comparing Structures** Identify two traits that chordates and echinoderms have in common.
17. **Identifying Structures** What four features do all chordates have at some time during their lives?
18. **BUILDING ON WHAT YOU HAVE LEARNED** In Chapter 17 you learned about how organisms are classified. Combine your knowledge of classification systems with your knowledge of body cavity types to explain why earthworms and sand worms are grouped in the phylum Annelida but flatworms are not.

---

10. Answers will vary but should include steps in Figure 23-5 on page 441.
11. Answers will vary but should include steps in Figure 23-7 on page 443.
12. Nematodes ingest food through a mouth and expel waste through an anus. Flatworms take in food and expel waste through the same opening.
13. The gut is surrounded by solid tissue that slows the diffusion of nutrients. In coelomates, a circulatory system transports nutrients to the tissues.

14. In pseudocoelomates, such as the roundworm, the body cavity lies between the gut and the body wall. In coelomates, such as humans, the body cavity lies within the mesoderm.
15. The exoskeleton provides support and protection. As an arthropod grows, the exoskeleton has to be shed and replaced.
16. Both are deuterostomes and have endoskeletons.
17. dorsal hollow nerve cord, notochord, slits in the pharynx, postanal tail

Interpreting Graphics

19. Look at the diagrams below.

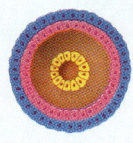

a. Identify each type of body plan shown above. Give an example of an animal with each type of body plan.
b. Describe the limitations and advantages of each type of body cavity.

Reviewing Themes

20. **Evolution**
What is segmentation? How does segmentation provide for evolutionary flexibility?

21. **Homeostasis**
Explain how the circulatory system of an animal helps maintain homeostasis.

Thinking Critically

22. **Forming Opinions Based on Sound Reasoning** As you learned in the chapter, radially symmetrical animals such as echinoderms and cnidarians are not found on land. However, bilaterally symmetrical animals live on land and in water. Propose a hypothesis to explain why radially symmetrical animals are not well suited to life on land.

23. **Recognizing Verifiable Conclusions** A scientist discovers a new species of animal living in a mountain lake. The animal is bilaterally symmetrical and is definitely segmented. It has no eyes and seems to feed on decaying material. The scientist tentatively classifies the animal as a chordate. Is this classification valid? Explain your answer.

Life/Work Skills

24. **Working Cooperatively** Work with two or three of your classmates. Create a chart that you can use in this chapter and in Chapters 24–28 to summarize and organize the characteristics of the different kinds of animals you will study. Include information such as appearance, habitat, type of symmetry, digestion and feeding habits, reproduction, and interactions with humans. On your chart, include room for illustrations of the various animals.

25. **Allocating Resources** Imagine that you are in charge of a large city aquarium. Explain how you would spend a donation given to you by a conservation-minded citizen who wants his money to further the cause of conserving and protecting aquatic and marine wildlife. Decide how much money is being donated. Would you spend some on education programs? Would you purchase new specimens? Make a poster presentation of your choices to convince your benefactor and board of directors.

Activities and Projects

26. **Art Connection** Use three different colors of modeling clay, or any other material, to construct models that show the formation of endoderm and ectoderm as a result of gastrulation and the formation of endoderm, ectoderm, and mesoderm as a result of gastrulation. Also make models that show the three major body plans: acoelomate, pseudocoelomate, and coelomate. Share your models with your class.

27. **Health Connection** Hookworms are parasitic roundworms that infect humans. Look for information in your local library or in an on-line database about the symptoms associated with hookworm infection. What can humans do to prevent becoming infected?

Discovering Through Reading

28. Read the article "Do Lions Purr?" by Doug Stewart in *National Wildlife*, August/September 1995, pages 30–38. Do lions purr? Why do flamingos stand on one leg?

Thinking Critically

22. Answers will vary. Students might suggest that movement on land would be slow and awkward, leaving the organisms vulnerable to predators.

23. It could be a chordate, but the scientist has not established the presence of the four key features of chordates.

24. Charts will vary but should summarize the main characteristics of the different kinds of animals.

25. Presentations will vary but should demonstrate a knowledge of aquatic and marine wildlife needs.

Activities and Projects

26. Models will vary but should represent the stages of gastrulation and the three major body plans of animals.

27. Sanitary sewage disposal and shoes help prevent hookworm infection.

Discovering Through Reading

28. Lions do not purr. They do not have the necessary delicate bones connecting the tongue to the base of the skull. Flamingos most likely tuck one leg to keep it warm.

18. Earthworms and sandworms are segmented and have a coelom and a circulatory system. Flatworms do not have a coelom or a circulatory system. They have a two-way gut and are not segmented.

Interpreting Graphics

19. a. See Figure 23-10 on page 446. Examples will vary.
b. Answers should include a discussion of size limitations and slow diffusion of dissolved substances in acoelomates and pseudocoelomates. Most coelomates have a circulatory system that carries dissolved substances.

Reviewing Themes

20. Segmentation, a body plan composed of repeated body units, enables segments to evolve different functions.

21. The circulatory system evens out the temperatures and concentrations of dissolved materials in the body.

Lesson Planning Guide With Options for Block Scheduling

Lecture Concepts	Lesson Resources

24-1 Leaving the Sea

BLOCK ❶ (45 minutes)

1. Almost all of the animal phyla are represented among land animals. Sponges, cnidarians, and echinoderms are found only in aquatic environments.

2. Arthropods and vertebrates are the most successful land animals.

❶ Lecture Resources
- Determining Prior Knowledge
- Ocean Emigration
- Active Reading: Anticipation Guide
- Demonstration: Comparing Functions
- Holt Biology Videodiscs Lesson 24-1

Classwork Options
- Inquiry Skills Development: Lab B24

Assignment Options
- Homologous Structures

BLOCK ❷ (45 minutes)

3. Skeletons enable land animals to hold up their bodies against gravity, and flexible limbs allow animals to move across land.

4. Sound waves make smaller pressure changes in air than in water. As animals moved to land, they adapted new ways of hearing.

❷ Lecture Resources
- Active Reading: Reading Organizer
- Demonstration: Inferring Relationships
- Teaching Transparencies: 167
- Holt Biology Videodiscs Lesson 24-1

Classwork Options
- Reteaching
- Demonstration: Forming a Model
- Closure: Predicting Outcomes

Assignment Options
- Section Review
- Chapter Review, questions 2a, 2b, 4, 5, 20, 21, 24
- Directed Reading Worksheet

24-2 Staying Moist in a Dry World

BLOCK ❸ (45 minutes)

1. A problem faced by animals on land is the loss of body water through evaporation.

2. Aquatic arthropods and vertebrates exchange gases through gills. On land, insects exchange gases through tracheae, and vertebrates exchange gases in lungs.

❸ Lecture Resources
- What If a Frog's Skin Dries Out?
- Watertight Skin
- Active Reading: Reading Organizer
- Active Reading: Paired Reading
- Teaching Transparencies: 166, 172
- Holt Biology Videodiscs Lesson 24-2

Classwork Options
- Exploration 24A

Assignment Options
- Gas Exchange
- Increasing Surface Area

BLOCK ❹ (45 minutes)

3. Terrestrial vertebrates have a double-loop circulatory system that carries blood through the lungs and other body tissues.

4. In vertebrates, kidneys remove wastes and regulate the salt and water content of the body.

❹ Lecture Resources
- Avian Lungs vs. Mammalian Lungs
- Flying Mammals
- Removing Wastes Two Ways
- Visual Strategy: Figures 24-10, 24-11
- Visual Strategy: Videodisc
- Teaching Transparencies: 183
- Holt Biology Videodiscs Lesson 24-2

Classwork Options
- Closure: Relating Concepts

- Teaching Resources CD-ROM: Problem-Solving Worksheets 7

Assignment Options
- Reteaching
- Section Review
- Chapter Review, questions 1a, 1b, 2c, 6, 7, 8, 9, 10, 11, 12, 13, 14, 15, 18, 22
- Directed Reading Worksheet

24-3 Four Innovations in Body Plan

BLOCK ❺ (45 minutes)

1. Amphibians and fishes produce eggs without shells that are fertilized externally.

2. Most land animals produce watertight eggs that are fertilized internally.

❺ Lecture Resources
- How Many Eggs?
- Active Reading: Reading Organizer
- Visual Strategy: Videodisc
- Demonstration: Relating Functions
- Holt Biology Videodiscs Lesson 24-3

Classwork Options
- Amniotes

Assignment Options
- Life/Work Skills: Being a Team Member

Lecture Concepts   Lesson Resources

24-3 Four Innovations in Body Plan, *continued*

BLOCK ⑥ (45 minutes)

3. Development in placental mammals is completed within the mother's body.

⑥ Lecture Resources
- ■ Active Reading: Anticipation Guide
- ◉ Holt Biology Videodiscs Lesson 24-3

Classwork Options
- ■ Closure: Summarizing Information

Assignment Options
- ■ Reteaching
- ■ Section Review
- ■ Chapter Review, questions 1c, 3, 16, 17, 19, 23, 25, 26, 27, 28
- ■ Directed Reading Worksheet

Chapter Review and Assessment

BLOCK ❼ (45 minutes)

Review
- ■ Reteaching Worksheet
- ■ Thinking Skills Worksheet
- ■ Vocabulary Development Worksheet
- ◎ Language Development and Reading Comprehension Audio CD Program: Chapter 24

BLOCK ❽ (45 minutes)

Assessment
- ■ Alternative Assessment, p. 475
- ■ Portfolio Assessment, p. T39

Chapter Test
- ■ Chapter 24 Test

Test Generator
- ◎ Item bank for customizing Chapter Tests
- ◎ Performance-Based Assessment: The Challenge of Water Retention

Teaching Resources CD-ROM
- ◎ Scoring Rubrics and Classroom Management Checklist

The Portfolio icon denotes items throughout the Teacher's Edition lesson wrap that may be selected for inclusion in student portfolios.

Holt Biology Videodiscs and *Concepts of Biology*

Holt Biology Videodiscs gives you a powerful tool for teaching, review, and assessment. For further information regarding the media on the videodiscs, see ***Holt Biology Videodiscs Teacher's Correlation Guide to Holt Biology: Visualizing Life.***

Concepts of Biology adds interactive lesson plans and extensive tools for customization using CD-ROM technology.

Use the following topic from ***Concepts of Biology*** to help you teach this chapter:

Topic 19: Evolutionary Trends in Vertebrates

Laboratory Planning

Text

Materials and preparation instructions appear on the teacher's wrap accompanying each laboratory exercise.

Block 3: Exploration 24A: Modeling the Action of a Kidney, p. 804

Holt BioSources Laboratory Program

Block 1: Inquiry Skills Development Lab B24: Snails

Determining Prior Knowledge

- Have students imagine how the first land animal might have looked and draw a picture of it.
- Have students explain the problems that aquatic animals would have to face when moving to a terrestrial environment.
- Have students explain why it is important for land animals to lay eggs that resist drying.

Active **READING**

Technique: Anticipation Guide

Before students begin this chapter, write the following statements on the chalkboard or overhead projector:

1. All major changes in animals' body plans took place in the sea.

2. The majority of the water you lose each day is lost through sweat.

3. External fertilization is fertilization that takes place outside the body of either parent; it is rare on land.

Ask students to decide whether they agree or disagree with each statement. Ask volunteers to share the reasons for their opinions. Have students read the chapter to see if their opinions are confirmed or changed.

CD-ROM Resources

Concepts of Biology
Topic 19: Evolutionary Trends in Vertebrates

REVIEW
- diffusion (Section 4-2)
- ozone layer (Section 11-3)
- innovations in body plan (Section 23-3)
- the terms *endoskeleton* and *exoskeleton* (Glossary)

Adaptation to Land

24-1   Leaving the Sea

24-2   Staying Moist in a Dry World

24-3   Reproducing on Land

These caribou are feeding in Denali National Park in Alaska.

458

Author's Rationale   Continuing the evolutionary journey, this chapter highlights key adaptations that led to the invasion of land by animals. Each adaptation illustrates the link between structure and function, and students will see that there may be more than one adaptive solution to a problem. The focus is on how adaptation has driven progressive evolutionary change. This permits students to see themselves as part of the larger evolutionary picture. This lesson is far more important than the details of the adaptations, which are treated as stories rather than taxonomic details.

Life arose in the sea and stayed there for more than 3 billion years, until a protective shield of ozone formed in the upper atmosphere. Without this shield, animals like this frog could not live on land. The requirements for living on land are very different from those for living in the sea. In this chapter, you will examine some key problems animals faced in moving onto land.

Phase One
Preparation

Scheduling
See the **Lesson Planning Guide** on pages 457A and 457B for lecture, classwork, and assignment options for Section 24-1.

24-1 Leaving the Sea

OBJECTIVES

1 List some animal groups that successfully made the transition to life on land.

2 Explain the importance of the skeleton to arthropods and vertebrates that live on land.

3 Describe the evolution of amphibian limbs from the fins of lobe-finned fishes.

4 Relate the structure of the vertebrate ear to the differences between air and water.

Which Animals Live on Land?

The animal body evolved over many millions of years in the sea. All of the major changes in body plan you read about in Chapter 23 took place in the sea. But the evolutionary journey of animals did not end there.

From the sea, animals invaded the land. Of the major animal phyla, only sponges, cnidarians, and echinoderms —groups of animals that pump water through their bodies—were left behind. Some members of every other major phylum can be found on land.

Flatworms, nematodes, and annelids burrow through the soil, and snails creep over damp ground at night. These animals, however, are found mainly in moist habitats. Only two groups of animals—arthropods and vertebrates—have members that are fully adapted to life on dry land. How animals such as the lizard shown in **Figure 24-1** evolved ways to survive the many challenges of living out of water is one of biology's most fascinating stories.

Phase Two
Teaching Strategies

Active READING
Technique: Reading Organizer
As students read about how animals adapted to land, have them complete two spider-map reading organizers for this section. One spider map should include details about adaptations that support the body, and the second spider map should include details about how animals hear airborne sounds.

Ocean Emigration
● **Interpreting Conclusions**
Why did some animals leave the ocean and move onto land? Was the water an unfavorable environment? Ask students to make a table with the headings "Advantages" and "Disadvantages." Students should first list advantages and disadvantages of living in water and then list advantages and disadvantages of living on land. Students should realize that there are many disadvantages to living on land, but that advantages such as less competition, new food sources, fewer predators, and more room may have outweighed the disadvantages for the first terrestrial organisms.

Figure 24-1
The thorny devil is a small lizard that lives in Australia. Its adaptations for water conservation enable it to live in very dry and harsh environments.

459

Videodisc Resources

Holt Biology Videodiscs
Lesson 24-1: Leaving the Sea

Key to Strategies
Teaching Strategies are keyed to three tiers of learning.

● **Understanding Concepts (Tier I)**
Content mastery and comprehension

■ **Applying Information (Tier II)**
Applying and analyzing content

▲ **Critical Thinking (Tier III)**
Practicing evaluative thinking

Homologous Structures

● **Comparing Structures**

Obtain line drawings similar to those shown in Figure 24-2 on page 460 that show the limb bones of a variety of vertebrates, including several amphibians, reptiles, birds, and mammals. Include familiar animals such as cows, horses, dogs, and cats, and include drawings of the human arm and leg. Have students color-code the drawings for the equivalent bones in each drawing. For example, all of the humerus bones (or equivalents) would be the same color. Ask students to compare the locations of the knee and ankle on a human leg with the locations of similar joints on a dog or horse, and to compare the human arm to a bird wing. Discuss how the arrangement of the bones affects movement. Point out the unusual number of digits on each limb of *Ichthyostega*—7. Some other early amphibians had 8 digits on each limb.

Demonstration

● **Comparing Functions**

Materials: Salamander, lizard, aquarium, terrarium

Have students observe a salamander swimming in an aquarium. Suggest that they observe its movements from above and then from the side as it swims. Have students describe their observations. Place the salamander in a terrarium, and have students again observe the animal from above and from the side. Ask students if the salamander had difficulty walking on land. What impeded its movement? Next, place a lizard in the terrarium. Ask how the lizard's movement differs from that of the salamander. Ask students to compare their own legs with those of the salamander and the lizard and explain how the differences in structure relate to differences in movement.

Figure 24-2
Several changes in limb structure took place as terrestrial vertebrates evolved from aquatic vertebrates.

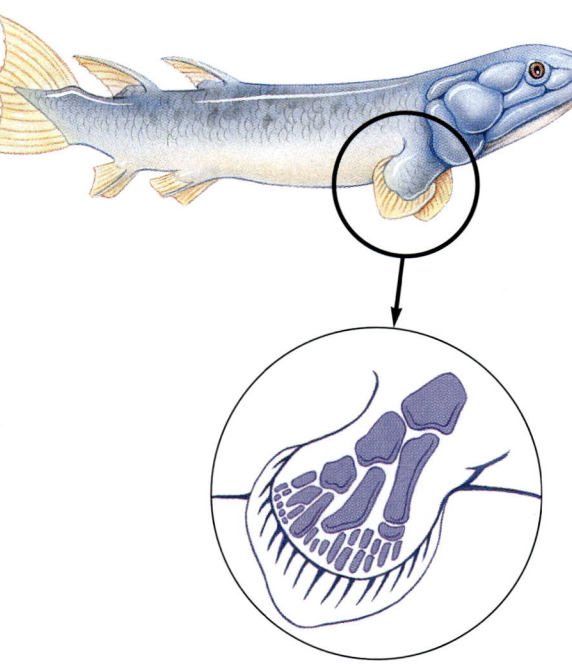

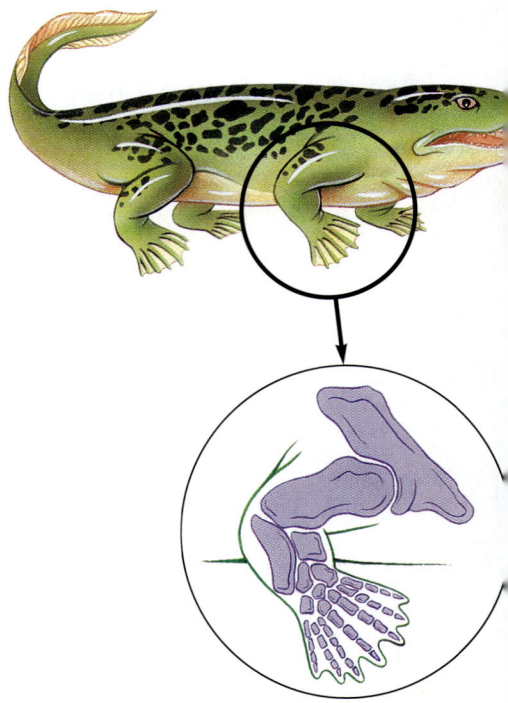

a Scientists think that lobe-finned fishes were the ancestors of the earliest land vertebrates. The drawing above shows the bones in the fin of an extinct lobe-finned fish.

b The earliest known land vertebrate is the amphibian *Ichthyostega*, which lived about 350 million years ago. It had four sturdy legs. Like its fish ancestors, it had a tail fin and some bony scales.

Supporting the Body

Water is about 1,000 times denser than air. Because of water's density, you can float on your back in a pool. For some aquatic animals, water provides much of the support necessary to keep their bodies from collapsing under the pull of gravity. That is why a jellyfish stranded on the beach cannot maintain its shape.

A variety of adaptations were necessary in order for animals that left the sea to overcome the loss of physical support. In nematodes and earthworms, the body cavity is filled with fluid under pressure, which helps to stiffen the body. In arthropods and vertebrates, support of the body is largely taken over by the skeleton. A land animal's skeleton holds up its body against gravity much like beams and girders hold up a skyscraper.

Limbs play an important role in supporting vertebrates on land. When a terrestrial animal is standing, its legs bear the entire weight of its body. In this way, legs function like the pillars that hold up the roof of a building. Unlike pillars, however, animal legs have flexible joints that enable them to move.

In both arthropods and vertebrates, legs evolved from limbs adapted for movement in water. **Figure 24-2a–b** illustrates the evolution of amphibian limbs from the fins of fishes. Recall from Chapter 11 that amphibians, the

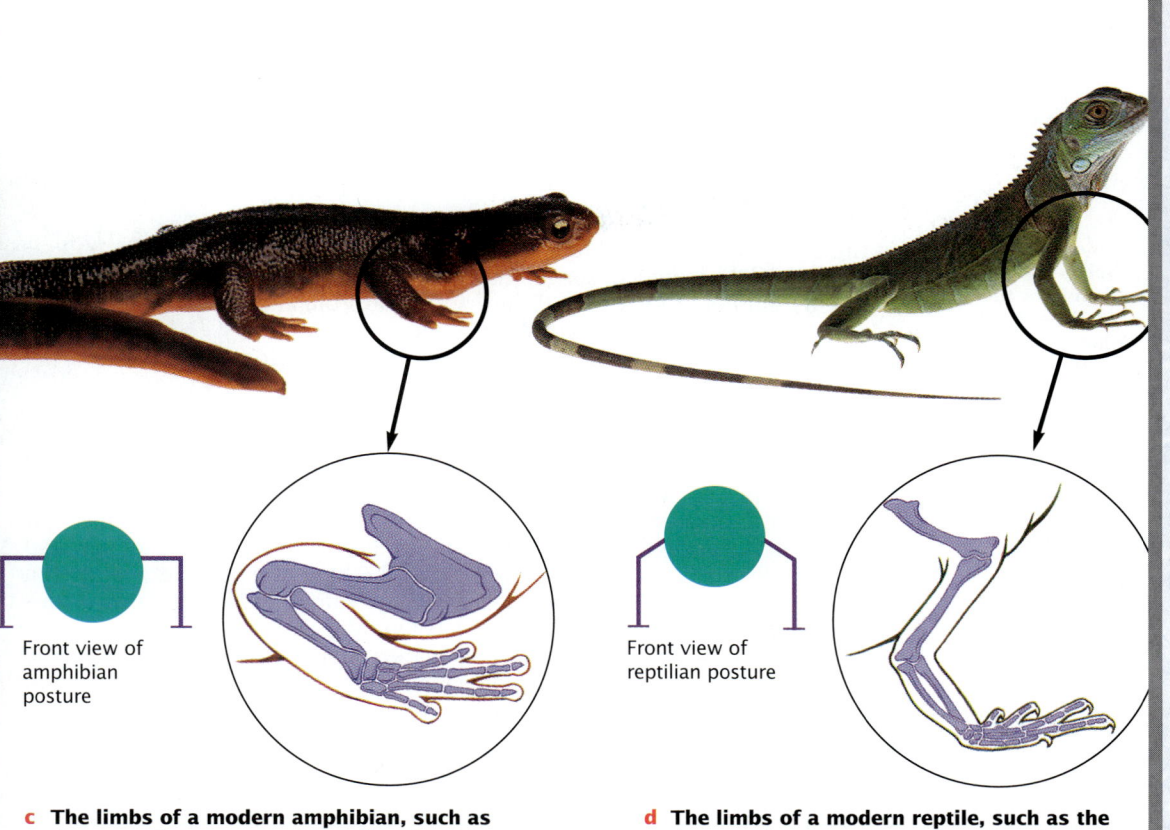

Front view of amphibian posture

Front view of reptilian posture

c **The limbs of a modern amphibian, such as the newt above, are positioned at the sides of its body. When the newt walks on land, its belly drags on the ground.**

d **The limbs of a modern reptile, such as the iguana above, are located partway beneath its body. These limbs are able to carry greater body weight than amphibian limbs, and they help reptiles run faster.**

first vertebrates on land, evolved from fishes. The limbs of amphibians are homologous to fins of fishes. However, most fishes have thin, paddlelike fins that would be useless for supporting and moving an animal on land. As you can see in **Figure 24-2a–b**, the arrangement and structure of bones in the limb of an early amphibian are similar to those in the fin of a lobe-finned fish. Because of these similarities, scientists think the first amphibians were descendants of the lobe-finned fishes, a group whose modern members include the coelacanth and the lungfishes.

Compare the posture of the amphibian in **Figure 24-2c** with that of the reptile in **Figure 24-2d**. Amphibian limbs are short and join the body horizontally; an amphibian's belly drags on the ground as it walks. The limbs of living reptiles are positioned slightly beneath the body. Limbs positioned in this way support more body weight than do the limbs of amphibians. The limbs of birds and mammals are positioned directly beneath the body, raising the belly well off the ground. Compared with reptilian and amphibian limbs, limbs located directly beneath the body support the animal's weight more effectively. They also enable the animal to run faster and, by elevating the head, help it locate food and be alert to danger.

461

Matter of Fact: Walking Catfish

The walking catfish pushes itself along the ground with its tail, using its strong pectoral fins to lift the front of its body. This catfish has gills, but it also has a special breathing organ tucked in a pocket behind its gills that allows it to breathe air. Walking catfish often come ashore at night to feed. Walking catfish were introduced to southern Florida from tropical Asia in the 1960s.

Lateral line

Demonstration

■ **Forming a Model**
Materials: One-gallon plastic milk jugs, plastic spoons
Allow students to experience for themselves the difference between sound conduction in air and sound conduction in water. Fill several one-gallon plastic milk jugs with water. Have students work in pairs, and have one student press his or her ear tightly against the milk jug while the other student lightly scrapes the opposite side of the jug with a plastic spoon. Then have the first student move his or her ear away from the jug while the second student continues scraping. Ask students to describe the difference in the sounds they heard.

Phase Three

Assessment Options

Closure

■ **Predicting Outcomes**
Have students speculate about future evolutionary trends in animals that may cause changes in the animals' physical appearance. Have students explain their reasoning. Remind students about the re-adaptation of cetaceans—whales and dolphins—to aquatic living.

SECTION REVIEW

Assign the *Section Review.*

Reteaching

Provide the class with specimens of a fish and a terrestrial mammal. A goldfish and a hamster are good choices. If live animals are not available, provide pictures of any fish and any terrestrial mammal from nature books or magazines. Have students suggest how each is adapted to its habitat. Ask students to describe how the fish would have to change before it could live on land and how the mammal would have to change before it could live in the water.

Figure 24-3
Fishes can sense sounds or the movements of other fishes with a row of pressure-sensitive cells called the lateral line.

Figure 24-4
Many mammals, such as this fox, can point their ears in the direction of a sound to pinpoint where the sound is coming from.

Hearing Airborne Sounds

In the ocean, whales are able to communicate with low-pitched "songs" that travel as far as 200 km (125 mi) because water is much denser than air. The denser the medium through which sound travels, the faster and farther the sound can travel.

Water's density makes detecting sound in water easier than doing so on land. Most species of fishes can hear. In addition, fishes are able to sense physical disturbances in the water, such as those caused by the swimming movements of nearby fishes, with their **lateral line** system. The lateral line is a row of pressure-sensitive cells that lies within a fluid-filled canal. One network of canals runs down each side of the fish. The lateral line is shown in **Figure 24-3**.

In air, the pressure changes caused by sound are much smaller because of air's lower density. Terrestrial animals have evolved structures that amplify airborne sounds so that they are detectable.

The ear is the sound-amplifying system of land vertebrates. In mammals, such as the fox in **Figure 24-4**, the eardrum and three small bones amplify sound waves and transmit them to the inner ear, where sounds are detected. In salamanders and snakes, sound is conducted to the inner ear entirely through bones of the jaw and skull. These animals rely more on ground vibrations (which transmit low-frequency sounds even better than water) than on airborne sounds. You will learn more about the workings of the ear in Chapter 30.

Insects can hear well, but they evolved different solutions to the challenges of hearing in air. Some insects detect sounds with sensitive hairs on their legs, body, or head. Others have eardrum-like structures on their body or legs. Crickets, for instance, hear the songs of other crickets through membranes on their front pair of legs, as you can see in **Figure 24-5**.

Figure 24-5
Crickets hear the songs of other crickets through membranes on their front pair of legs.

Hearing mechanism

SECTION REVIEW

① Which major groups of animals are not found on land?

② Describe the role of the skeleton in the life of a terrestrial animal.

③ What evidence suggests that amphibian limbs evolved from the fins of lobe-finned fishes?

④ Compare sound transmission in air with sound transmission in water.

462

ANSWERS TO **SECTION REVIEW**

① sponges, cnidarians, and echinoderms

② The skeleton provides support by holding the body up against gravity.

③ The arrangement and structure of bones in the limbs of early amphibians are similar to those of the fins of lobe-finned fishes.

④ Sound travels faster and farther in water than in air because water is denser.

Conserving body water is one of the greatest challenges of living on land. When animals first moved onto land, they faced the risk of losing excessive amounts of water through evaporation. Many terrestrial arthropods and vertebrates evolved traits that enabled them to conserve body water.

24-2 Staying Moist in a Dry World

OBJECTIVES

1 Recognize the role of the exoskeleton in preventing water loss.

2 Contrast the skin of amphibians with that of reptiles.

3 Summarize the evolution of lungs.

4 Describe two ways animals conserve water while ridding themselves of wastes.

Watertight Skin

If you leave a wet towel in the sun, what happens to it? The towel dries through evaporation. Since an animal's body is about 70 percent water, an animal on land is like a wet towel. Its cells are full of water and, like the fibers of the wet towel, are surrounded by water. Like the towel, an animal on land is in danger of drying out through evaporation. Losing even small amounts of body water can be dangerous. Losing 15–20 percent of the water in your body would be fatal. How do terrestrial animals limit their loss of water? In this section you will examine some of the adaptations that enable animals like the desert ants shown in **Figure 24-6** to exist on dry land.

Arthropods and vertebrates have waterproof coatings

What would happen if you sealed a wet towel inside a plastic bag? Because the bag is waterproof, water could no longer escape from the towel into the atmosphere. For the same reason, sandwiches stay moist when they are sealed in sandwich bags. Similarly, the bodies of arthropods and vertebrates are wrapped in a watertight coating. In arthropods, this coating is the exoskeleton. In vertebrates, it is the skin.

Recall from Chapter 23 that the arthropod exoskeleton is a stiff outer coat composed of chitin and protein. In addition to providing protection and physical support, the exoskeleton prevents water from leaving the terrestrial arthropod's body. Especially in spiders and insects, the outer layer of the exoskeleton contains waxes that enhance the waterproofing effect of the exoskeleton.

Figure 24-6
These ants are able to live in the desert because of their many adaptations for preventing water loss. You will read about some of these adaptations in this section.

463

Videodisc Resources

Holt Biology Videodiscs

Lesson 24-2: Staying Moist in a Dry World

Phase One
Preparation

Scheduling
See the **Lesson Planning Guide** on pages 457A and 457B for lecture, classwork, and assignment options for Section 24-2.

Phase Two
Teaching Strategies

Active READING

Technique: Reading Organizer
Explain to students that in Section 24-2 they will read about adaptations that help animals on land conserve water. Have students read the introduction at the top of the page and survey the section, noting the headings and subheadings and any words in boldface type. Then ask student volunteers to list some of the traits that will be described. Students' lists might include watertight skin, lungs, tracheae, book lungs, kidneys, and Malpighian tubules. Students should read to discover more about these adaptations.

What If a Frog's Skin Dries Out?

■ **Analyzing Methods**
Ask students what they think would happen to a frog that allowed its skin to dry out. (*The frog's body tissues would dehydrate, resulting in the frog's death.*) Ask students to list things that a frog can do to make sure its skin stays moist. List their suggestions. (*Answers may include sitting in water, hiding in the shade, burrowing into the damp earth, burying itself in mud, or living in a place that is almost always wet, such as a swamp or marsh.*)

Key to Strategies
● Understanding Concepts (Tier I)
■ Applying Information (Tier II)
▲ Critical Thinking (Tier III)

Adaptation to Land   463

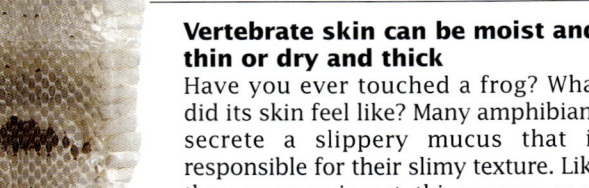

Active READING

Technique: Paired Reading
Give the students self-stick notes, and have them read Section 24-2 silently. Have students place notes with question marks beside passages that are unclear and notes with check marks to indicate passages they understand. Remind students to study the captions, charts, diagrams, and illustrations as they read. After completing the section, have students work with a partner to discuss what they did or did not understand. Their discussion should lead them to a better understanding of the text. Have students write their remaining questions on the board for a class discussion. Have students repeat this process as they read about gas exchange and the removal of wastes.

Figure 24-7
Reptiles have dry, scaly skin that is watertight. The skin of a banded rock rattlesnake is shown above.

Vertebrate skin can be moist and thin or dry and thick

Have you ever touched a frog? What did its skin feel like? Many amphibians secrete a slippery mucus that is responsible for their slimy texture. Like the wax on an insect, this mucous coating helps limit evaporation. Despite this mucous coating, the skins of amphibians are not watertight. As you will see in Chapter 27, amphibians absorb oxygen and release carbon dioxide directly through their skin. To do this, their skin must be moist and thin. Therefore, to keep from drying out, most amphibians must remain in water or in moist environments.

A reptile is not slimy like an amphibian. Reptilian skin is dry and covered with tough scales, as shown in **Figure 24-7**. A watertight skin of scales was a significant evolutionary step, completely freeing reptiles from the necessity of living in a wet or moist environment. Mammals and birds, which evolved from reptiles, also have skin that is dry and relatively watertight. As you might expect, mammals, birds, and reptiles do not exchange gases through their skin.

Gas Exchange

You breathe about 12 times each minute. From the perspective of water conservation, breathing is very costly. About 300 mL (9 oz) of water evaporates from your lungs each day. You breathe, despite the water loss, because breathing is essential for gas exchange. Gas exchange is the process of absorbing oxygen from the environment and ridding the body of carbon dioxide. This "swap" of molecules is necessary for all animals because they require oxygen to carry out cellular respiration and because they make carbon dioxide as a waste product.

Gas exchange occurs by diffusion, which you learned about in Chapter 4. Oxygen diffuses through the cell membrane into the cell, and carbon dioxide diffuses out. Because diffusion works well only over short distances, cells must either be close to the environment or have gases carried to and away from them. Recall from Chapter 23 that flatworms and nematodes cannot be thick because diffusion alone carries oxygen to their innermost tissues. Chordates, arthropods, mollusks, echinoderms, and some annelids can be larger because they have evolved ways to transport oxygen to the cells deep within their body.

Gills are structures for gas exchange in an aquatic environment. Aquatic arthropods, fishes, and amphibian larvae have gills. Amphibian larvae have external gills. The gills of crabs and many of their aquatic arthropod relatives are located in chambers behind the head, as shown in **Figure 24-8**. The gills of fishes also lie directly behind the head, as you can see in **Figure 24-9**.

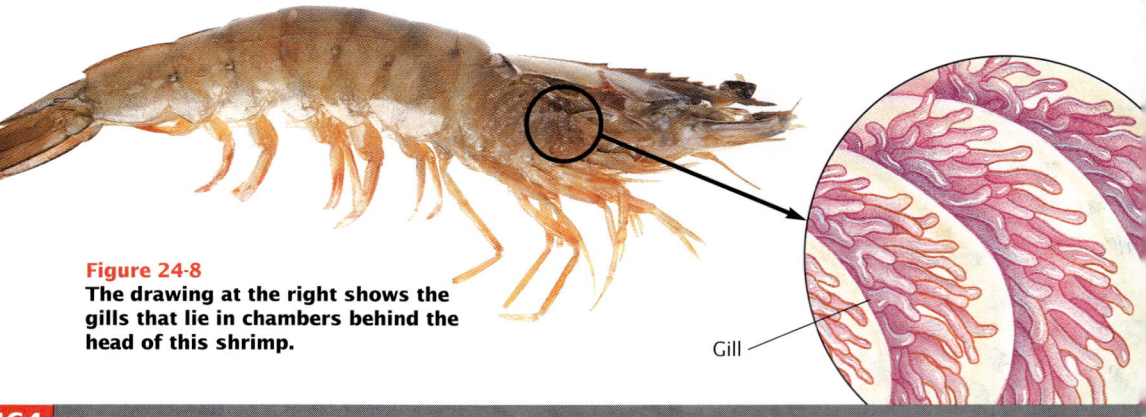

Figure 24-8
The drawing at the right shows the gills that lie in chambers behind the head of this shrimp.

Gill

Figure 24-9
A fish's gills are located directly behind its head. In the gills, oxygen enters the blood and carbon dioxide leaves.

Water flow

Oxygenated blood for body (red)

Deoxygenated blood from heart (blue)

Gill filament

Water flow

a Gills are made of thin filaments that provide a large surface area for gas exchange. Water enters the mouth, flows over the gills, and exits behind the head. In the process, . . .

Oxygenated blood (red)

Deoxygenated blood (blue)

b . . . oxygen-poor blood picks up oxygen from the water and releases carbon dioxide. Because water and blood flow in opposite directions, diffusion is particularly efficient.

Blood vessels

Blood flow

Water flow

Connection: *Chapter 5*

Cellular Respiration
Ask students to explain the relationship between the presence of oxygen in cells and the amount of energy released from nutrient molecules. Ask students to describe the types of animals that would need to circulate large amounts of oxygen to their cells. Students should realize that large, active animals with a constant, warm body temperature need more oxygen than small, sluggish animals whose body temperature is determined largely by the temperature of the surroundings.

How do gills work?
A fish's gills, shown in **Figure 24-9**, are composed of numerous small filaments, each with many small, disk-shaped units. These filaments provide a large surface area for gas exchange. Small blood vessels carry blood just beneath the surface of the gill filaments. The fish pumps water over its gills by sucking in water and then expelling it through an opening behind the head. As water flows over the gill filaments and between the disk-shaped units, diffusion occurs. Oxygen passes from the water to the blood, and carbon dioxide passes from the blood to the water.

Gills would collapse on land
Why do fishes suffocate when stranded on land, even though air contains far more oxygen than water? A fish's delicate gills would collapse if not supported by water. Even if the gills could be prevented from collapsing, they would quickly dry out in air. In terrestrial vertebrates, respiratory membranes deep within the body have replaced gills. These respiratory membranes line the interior surfaces of sacs called lungs.

465

Matter of Fact: Eutrophication

Because fish obtain oxygen from the water that passes over their gills, having sufficient oxygen dissolved in the water where they live is crucial to their survival. Phosphates that enter lakes from human waste, livestock waste, and detergents act as "fertilizers" for cyanobacteria, algae, and aquatic plants. The rapid growth of these organisms can form dense mats of green scum on the water's surface, preventing gas exchange. When the organisms die, bacteria that feed on the decaying organic matter use up so much of the oxygen in the water that fish begin to suffocate. This process is called eutrophication. The process occurs naturally over geologic time, but it is often accelerated by human activities.

Key to Strategies
● Understanding Concepts (Tier I)
■ Applying Information (Tier II)
▲ Critical Thinking (Tier III)

Adaptation to Land   **465**

Visual Strategy Figure 24-10

● **Interpreting Graphics**
Use this figure to compare the circulation of fish with that of amphibians. Which system is single and which is double? *(The fish system is single, and the amphibian system is double.)* Why does the amphibian need an extra loop in its circulation? *(It has to send blood to lungs.)* List a variety of vertebrates, and have individual students say whether the animal has a double circulatory system or a single circulatory system. If students have trouble, ask them whether the animal has gills or lungs.

Vertebrate Lungs

How does gas exchange occur in the lungs? Vertebrate lungs are lined with moist, thin tissues through which gas exchange occurs. A network of fine blood vessels called capillaries runs close to this lining. Oxygen-rich air is brought into the lungs by inhalation. Oxygen diffuses through the lining of the lungs into the capillaries. At the same time, carbon dioxide moves from the capillaries into the air in the lungs. Exhalation expels the "used" air from the lungs. You can follow the evolution of vertebrate lungs in the *Evolution of the Lung* feature on pages 468–469.

Terrestrial vertebrates have a double-loop circulatory system

In fishes, the heart pumps blood to the gills, where the blood picks up oxygen before flowing to the rest of the body. This creates the "single-loop" system shown in **Figure 24-10a**. The capillar-ies of the gills are narrow, so they present a great deal of resistance to blood flow. As a result, the flow of blood loses much of its force as it passes through the gills. Circulation from the gills to the rest of the body is sluggish.

The fine capillaries of an amphibian's lung also slow down blood flow. In amphibians, however, the blood returns to the heart for repumping before circulating to the body's tissues. In effect, there are two circulatory systems here: blood flowing from the heart to the lungs and back, and blood flowing from the heart to the body and back. This type of dual circulatory system is found in all terrestrial vertebrates. It carries oxygenated blood through the body much more rapidly than does the circulatory system of fishes. **Figure 24-10b** illustrates the "double-loop" circulation of a typical amphibian.

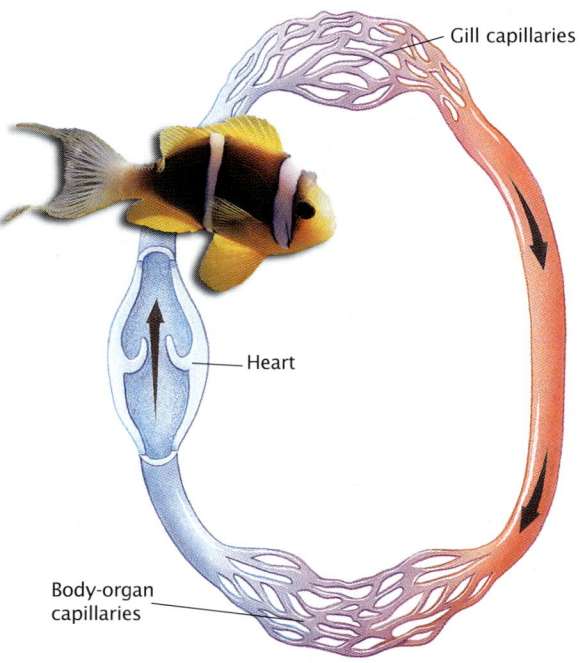

Gill capillaries

Heart

Body-organ capillaries

Figure 24-10

a In fishes, the heart pumps blood to the gills, where it picks up oxygen. The oxygenated blood then flows to the rest of the body.

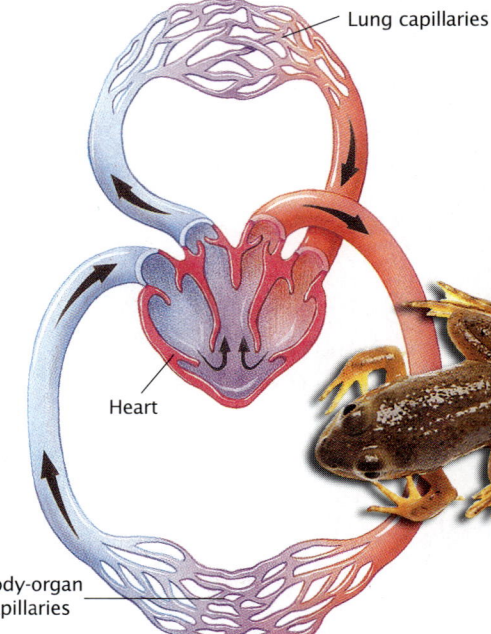

Lung capillaries

Heart

Body-organ capillaries

b In amphibians and other land vertebrates, the heart first pumps blood to the lungs, where it picks up oxygen. The oxygenated blood returns to the heart to be pumped to the rest of the body.

Matter of Fact: Genetic Variation Today

Differences among the hearts of different species of vertebrates may seem to have magically arisen from nowhere, but the genetic variability that provides raw material for natural selection is with us today. There are many variations even in the human heart, from the location and size of blood vessels to the orientation and function of structures. Genetic changes are usually not beneficial, however. Many of these variations are identified as congenital defects of the human heart.

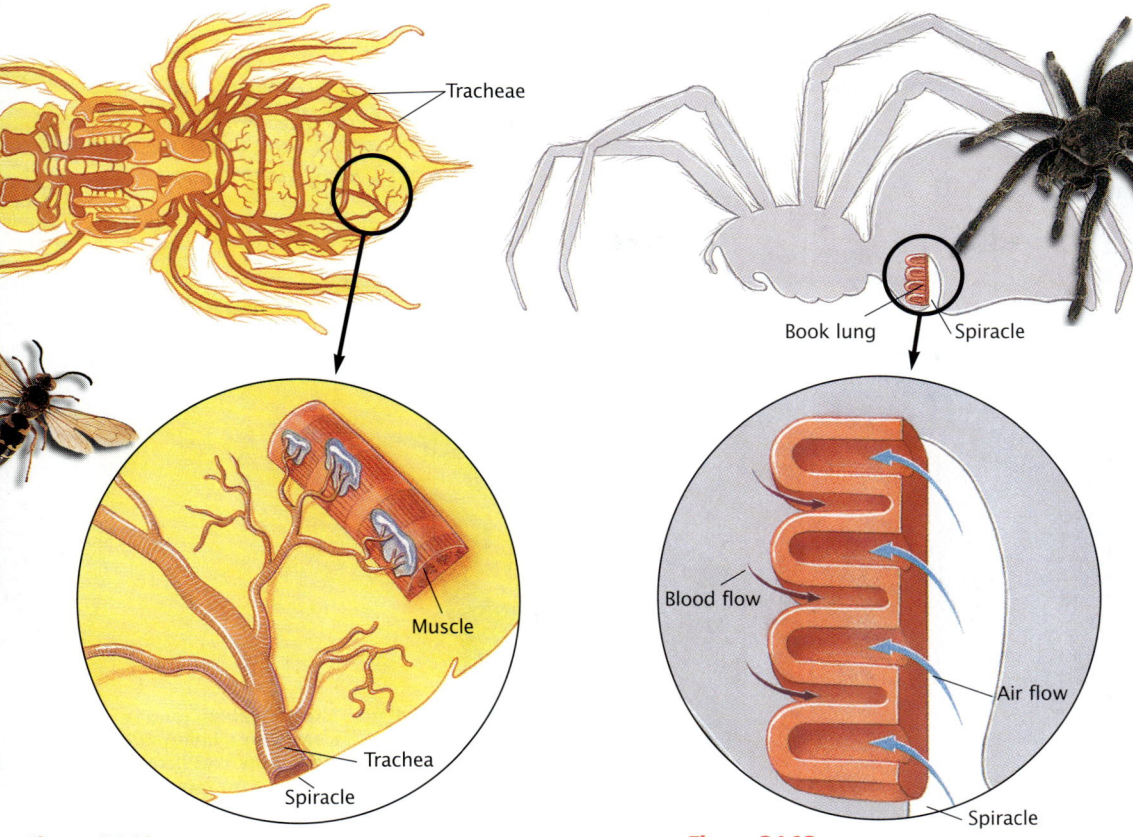

Figure 24-11
Tracheae leading into an insect's body from pores on the surface deliver oxygen directly to the cells and transport carbon dioxide to the outside of the body.

Figure 24-12
In many spiders, oxygen is absorbed through book lungs. The many folds of the book lungs provide a large surface area through which diffusion can occur.

How Terrestrial Arthropods Breathe

Land-dwelling arthropods, which are much smaller than most vertebrates, evolved different gas exchange systems. Insects breathe through **tracheae** *(TRAY kee ee)*. Tracheae (singular, trachea) are tubes that lead into an insect's body cavity from pores called spiracles in the surface of the exoskeleton, as shown in **Figure 24-11**. Each trachea branches and rebranches, penetrating deep into the body. The tips of the tiny branches carry oxygen directly to cells where it is needed. They also allow carbon dioxide to exit. This system is very efficient in small organisms, and it supports the very active lifestyles of most insects. In an insect, oxygen passes directly from the air in the tracheae to the tissues. In your body, oxygen is first transferred to blood cells in the lungs and is then carried to the tissues by blood. Insect blood does not transport oxygen.

Many spiders breathe through **book lungs**. As shown in **Figure 24-12**, book lungs are highly folded sacs that are located inside the body and that open to the outside through a spiracle. Air moves into the sacs, where it is moistened so the oxygen in the air can dissolve and pass into the blood. Having respiratory membranes inside the body allows the surface where gas exchange occurs to remain moist without losing large amounts of water to evaporation.

467

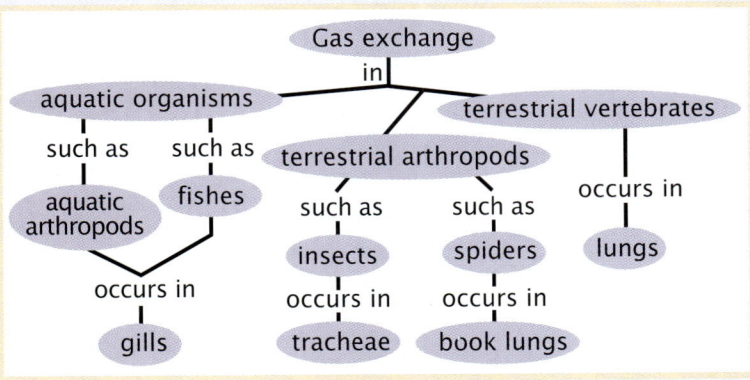

Increasing Surface Area

■ Forming a Model

To help students visualize how compartmentalization increases surface area, have them use graph paper to create a model of a lung. Have students cut out six 5 cm × 5 cm pieces of graph paper. They should tape five pieces together to form a cube without a top, representing a lung. Have students calculate the internal surface area of this "lung" *(125 cm²)*. They should then insert the sixth piece so that it divides the cube in half. Now have them calculate the internal surface area of this subdivided "lung" *(175 cm²)*. Simply dividing this model lung into two compartments increased its surface area by 40 percent. Inform students that their lungs are essentially hollow bags divided into more than 150 million compartments.

Size Limitation

■ Relating Concepts

An alternative way to increase the interior surface area of the lungs is to increase the overall size of the lungs. Ask students to explain why lung evolution did not follow this pathway. *(Lung size is limited by the size of the thoracic cavity, which contains the lungs. Thus, the surface area of the lungs can expand much more through interior subdivision than through increased size.)*

Watertight Skin

■ Recognizing Relationships

Many species of amphibians absorb oxygen through their skin, which is moist and is served by many blood vessels. Why can't reptiles, birds, and mammals supplement their oxygen intake by absorbing it through the skin? *(Reptiles, birds, and mammals have dry, watertight skin through which gases cannot diffuse.)*

The Lung

Lungs first evolved in early fishes. Early bony fishes with lungs were the ancestors of amphibians. Lungs provide land vertebrates with a large surface area where gas exchange can occur in a moist environment.

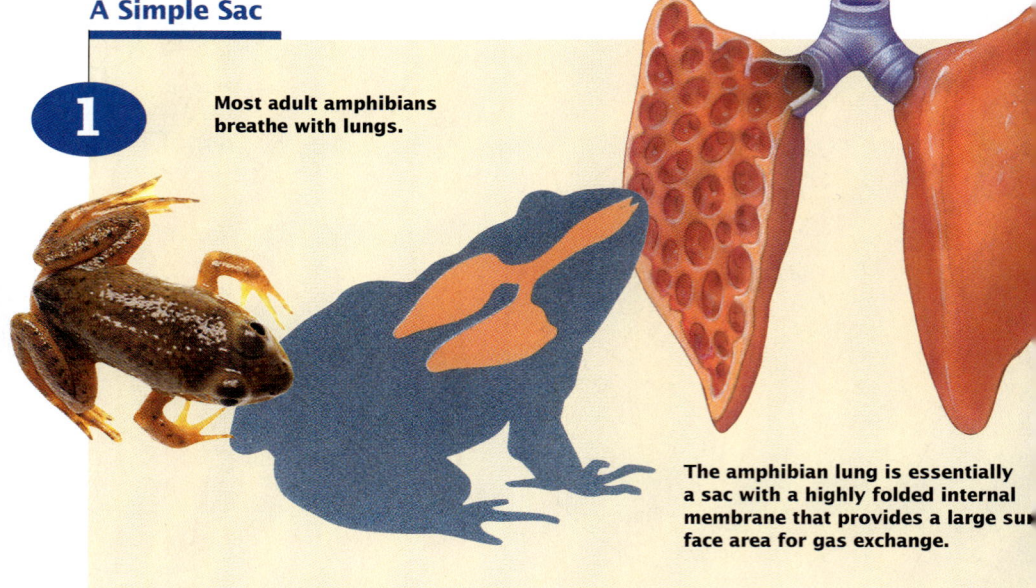

A Simple Sac

1 Most adult amphibians breathe with lungs.

The amphibian lung is essentially a sac with a highly folded internal membrane that provides a large surface area for gas exchange.

Increased Surface Area

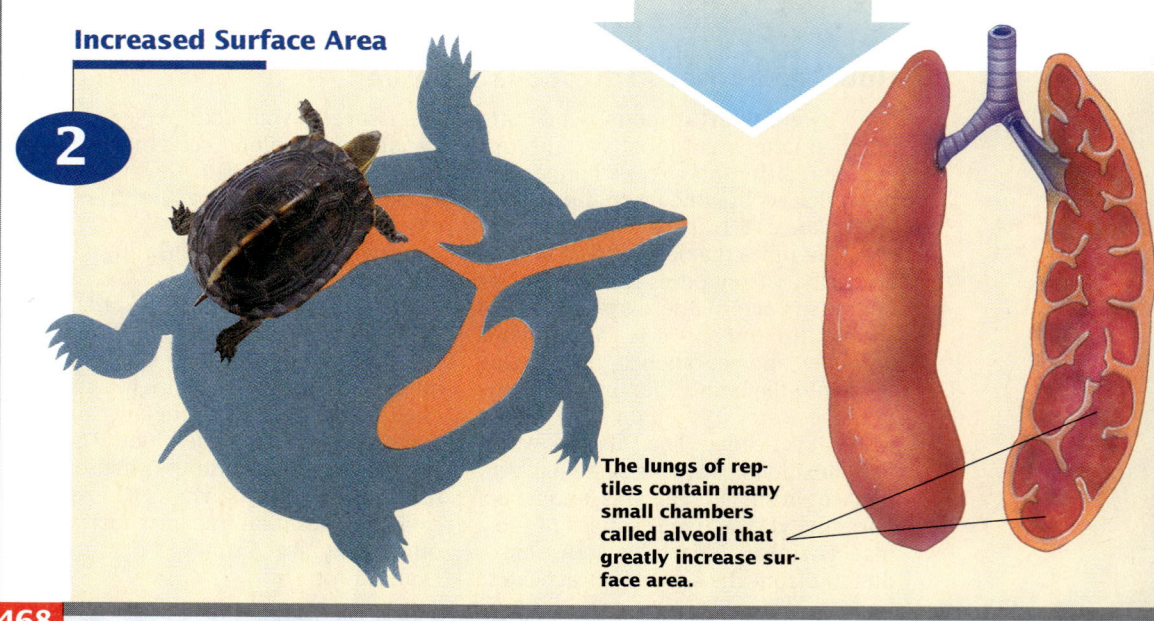

2

The lungs of reptiles contain many small chambers called alveoli that greatly increase surface area.

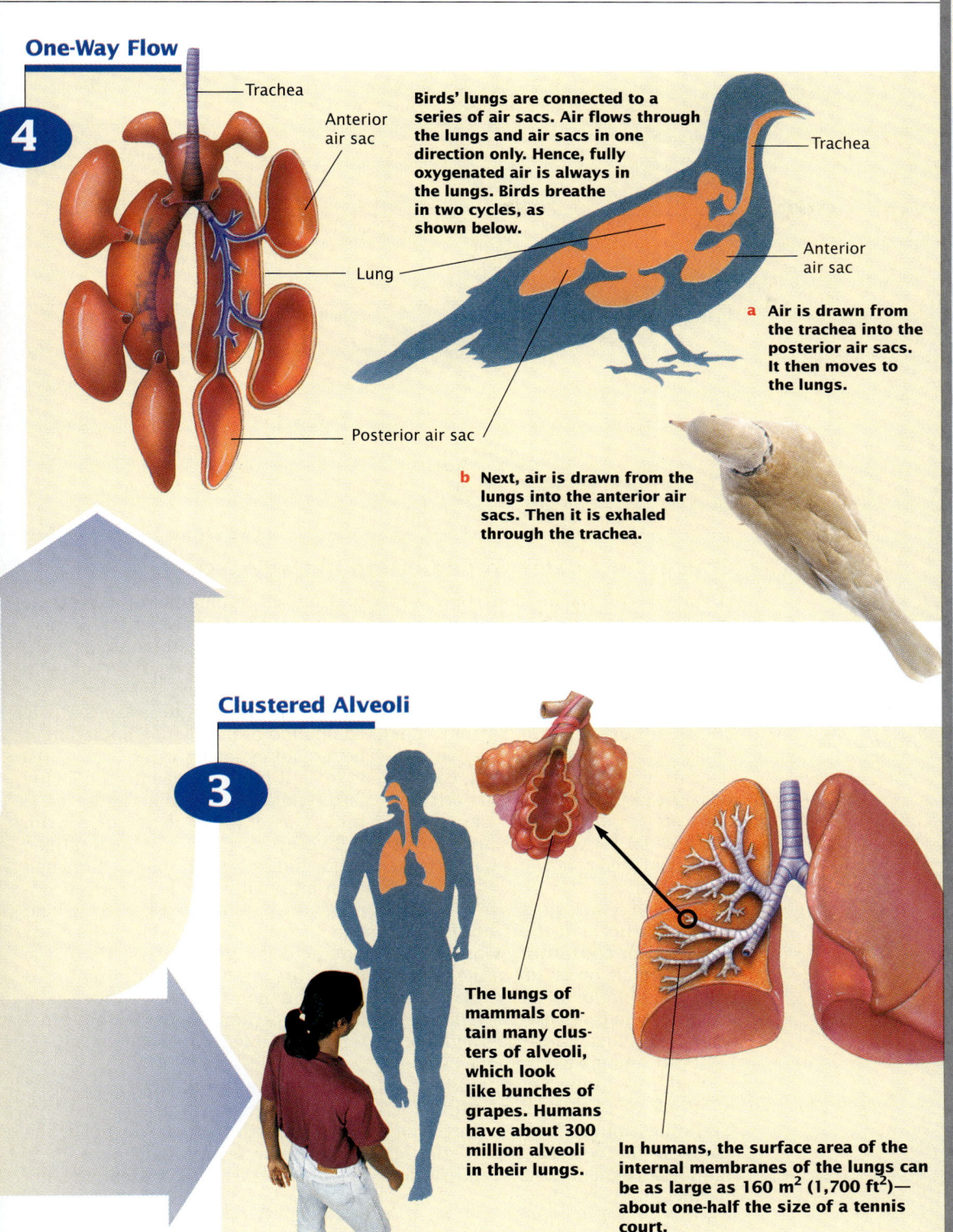

One-Way Flow

4

Trachea

Anterior air sac

Lung

Posterior air sac

Birds' lungs are connected to a series of air sacs. Air flows through the lungs and air sacs in one direction only. Hence, fully oxygenated air is always in the lungs. Birds breathe in two cycles, as shown below.

Trachea

Anterior air sac

a Air is drawn from the trachea into the posterior air sacs. It then moves to the lungs.

b Next, air is drawn from the lungs into the anterior air sacs. Then it is exhaled through the trachea.

Clustered Alveoli

3

The lungs of mammals contain many clusters of alveoli, which look like bunches of grapes. Humans have about 300 million alveoli in their lungs.

In humans, the surface area of the internal membranes of the lungs can be as large as 160 m^2 (1,700 ft^2)—about one-half the size of a tennis court.

469

Evolutionary Journey

Avian Lungs vs. Mammalian Lungs

● **Comparing Structures**

Ask students to point out two differences between a bird's lungs and a mammal's lungs. They should identify the attached air sacs and the one-way flow of air as two unique characteristics of avian lungs. Help students understand how this system allows the one-way flow of air by drawing a diagram of the avian respiratory system on the board. With colored chalk, trace the flow of a volume of air through this system. Air is drawn into the posterior air sacs, moves through the lungs to the anterior air sacs, and then is exhaled. Compare the avian system with that of a mammal, in which air is drawn in at inhalation and expelled at exhalation. Inform students that the respiratory system of a bird keeps oxygenated air in the lungs at all times. In mammals, by contrast, after exhalation the lungs contain just enough air to prevent them from collapsing. Very little gas exchange occurs until inhalation brings fresh air into the lungs.

Flying Mammals

■ **Forming a Hypothesis**

Bats flap their wings less often than birds do and spend more time gliding. Ask students to consider what they know about the lung structure of mammals and birds, and to hypothesize about the difference in bats' flying technique. *(Bats do not have the super-efficient lungs characteristic of birds, and they cannot obtain enough oxygen to flap their wings continually.)*

Theme Answer

Stability and Homeostasis

Kidneys help land animals maintain homeostasis by removing nitrogen-containing wastes from the blood and by regulating the amount of water and salt in the body.

Removing Wastes Two Ways

● **Comparing Structures**

Have students draw a simple diagram that shows how wastes are removed from blood while water, nutrients, and salts are reclaimed in the kidney. Have students draw a similar diagram for Malpighian tubules. Diagrams should show water, wastes, nutrients, and salts moving from the blood to the Malpighian tubules and then into the gut, where water, nutrients, and salts are separated from wastes and returned to the body tissues.

Health Connection

Urinalysis

Obtain a blank urinalysis form from a clinic, and have students study the list of substances that are measured by this test. Help students identify the nitrogen-containing wastes listed on the form. Point out the electrolytes that are measured by urinalysis, and explain that these are components of the various salts that kidneys help to keep in balance in our body fluids. You may wish to explain the roles of some of the electrolytes. For example, sodium and potassium are essential to the transmission of nerve impulses, and calcium is used in muscle contraction. Ask students to explain why a urinalysis is a routine part of a medical examination.

Table 24-1 Nitrogen-Containing Wastes

Type	Structure (nitrogen in orange)	Solubility in water	Found in
Ammonia		Soluble	Most aquatic animals
Urea		Soluble	Amphibians, mammals
Uric acid		Insoluble	Insects, reptiles, birds
Guanine		Insoluble	Spiders

Conserving Water While Getting Rid of Wastes

Despite its covering of skin, your body is not completely watertight. Every day you lose about 2.5 L (2.4 qt) of water—about 2 percent of the total amount of water in your body. How does that much water escape each day? About 300 mL (9 oz) evaporates from your lungs. Another 500 mL (15 oz) evaporates from your skin as sweat, cooling you in the process. The majority of the water you lose each day, about 1.5 L (45 oz), is excreted as urine. Urine carries nitrogen-containing wastes from your body.

Animals must rid their bodies of nitrogen-containing wastes

When animals break down the amino acids found in foods that contain protein, nitrogen is released as ammonia. Ammonia is toxic to animals and must be quickly eliminated from the body in very dilute form. Since the water required for dilution is plentiful for freshwater animals, they excrete their nitrogen directly as highly dilute ammonia. Land animals and some marine animals, however, cannot afford to lose so much body water. Instead, they spend some energy converting the ammonia to less toxic forms that need less water for dilution.

In vertebrates, ammonia is converted into one of two different compounds in the liver. Most mammals excrete nitrogen as **urea**, a less toxic compound of nitrogen. Elimination of urea requires some water because urea is toxic if highly concentrated. Many birds and reptiles (and insects) excrete their waste nitrogen as **uric acid**. Unlike urea, uric acid is a nontoxic solid, and can therefore be eliminated with minimal water loss. (Bird droppings are a combination of uric acid and feces.) Once produced, urea or uric acid is released by cells of the liver into the blood and is removed from the blood by the kidneys. The nitrogen-containing wastes are illustrated in **Table 24-1**.

Kidneys are blood filters

The kidneys of vertebrates remove wastes from the blood and regulate the amount of water and salts in the body. Blood circulates in the vertebrate body under pressure, and the kidneys act as filters. As blood flows through the kidneys, its pressure forces water and

Stability and Homeostasis

What role do the

kidneys play in

homeostasis?

Matter of Fact: Kangaroo Rats

Kangaroo rats survive in desert environments without drinking any water at all. They obtain 10 percent of their water from the food they eat. The other 90 percent of their water is supplied by metabolic water—water formed by cellular respiration. In addition, kangaroo rats conserve water by producing urine that is three to five times more concentrated than human urine.

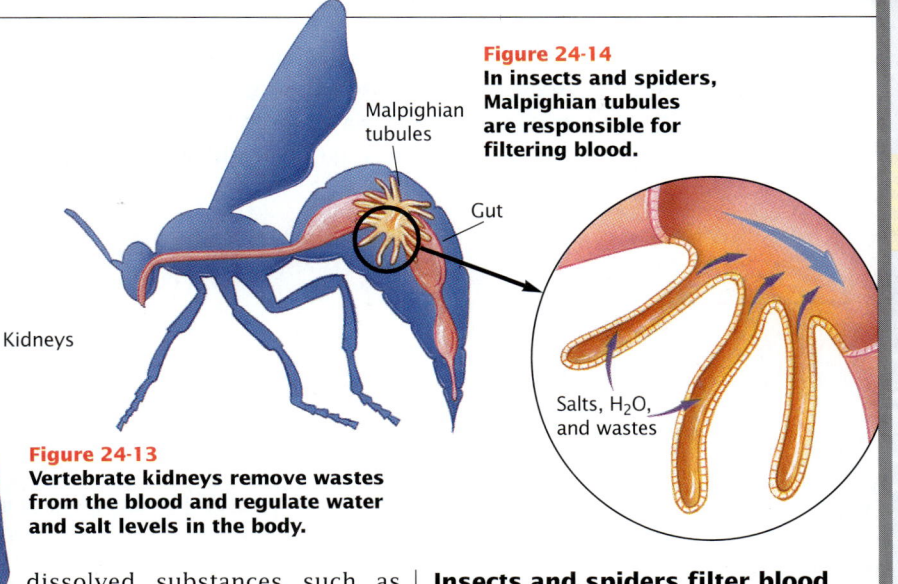

Figure 24-14
In insects and spiders, Malpighian tubules are responsible for filtering blood.

Malpighian tubules

Gut

Salts, H$_2$O, and wastes

Figure 24-13
Vertebrate kidneys remove wastes from the blood and regulate water and salt levels in the body.

Kidneys

dissolved substances such as sodium, potassium, chloride, glucose, urea, and wastes from blood vessels into a series of coiled tubes. Proteins and blood cells remain behind in the blood. Thus, the kidneys are pressure filters, as is the oil filter in a car. Vertebrate kidneys are shown in **Figure 24-13**.

Most of the filtered substances are useful to the body, and it would be wasteful to discard them. Instead they are reabsorbed back into the bloodstream. Reabsorption is very selective. Urea, wastes, and some water are not reabsorbed; they pass out of the body as urine. The body regulates how much water is reabsorbed and can control how much water leaves the body in the urine. If you drink a large amount of water, your brain senses an increase in blood pressure and releases hormones that cause the kidneys to reabsorb less water. As a result, you produce more urine.

Insects and spiders filter blood through Malpighian tubules
Since blood does not circulate under pressure in insects and spiders, these terrestrial animals do not have pressure-filter kidneys. The organs responsible for filtering blood in insects and spiders are the **Malpighian** (mal PIHG ee uhn) **tubules**, shown in **Figure 24-14**. Salts are actively transported from the blood into the Malpighian tubules. The high concentration of salts in the Malpighian tubules *draws* water from the blood. Wastes also move into the tubules. The contents of the Malpighian tubules are released into the gut, where useful salts such as potassium are reabsorbed. Water follows the salts by osmosis. Wastes such as uric acid and guanine are not reabsorbed and remain in the gut as a nearly dry paste that is excreted with the feces. This system enables insects and spiders to conserve water and contributes to their success on land.

Assessment Options

Closure

■ **Relating Concepts**

portfolio

Have students work in small cooperative groups to prepare illustrated tables on poster board that show how the skeletal, integumentary, circulatory, respiratory, and excretory systems of each group of animals are adapted to water, land, or both.

SECTION REVIEW

Assign *Section Review*.

Reteaching

Have students write a description of an adaptation to a terrestrial environment for each of the following systems: skeletal, integumentary, circulatory, respiratory, and excretory. Examples include adult amphibian limbs, reptilian scales, and amniotic eggs. Have students briefly explain their answers.

SECTION REVIEW

1 How would the exoskeleton of a land arthropod probably be different from that of an aquatic arthropod? Explain.

2 Contrast the amount of evaporation from amphibian skins with that from reptilian skins.

3 Describe the differences between amphibian lungs and mammalian lungs.

4 List two adaptations that enable land vertebrates to get rid of wastes while still conserving water.

471

ANSWERS TO SECTION REVIEW

1 The exoskeleton of land arthropods is covered by a waxy coating that prevents water loss. Aquatic arthropods lack this coating. The exoskeleton of land arthropods is also heavier than aquatic arthropods.

2 Water and gases pass through amphibian skin, so amphibians must stay in moist environments. Reptilian skin is dry and covered with tough scales, preventing water loss.

3 An amphibian lung is a sac with an internal membrane that is folded to increase surface area. The mammalian lung contains millions of tiny air sacs, or alveoli, which greatly increase surface area.

4 The liver converts ammonia into a less toxic compound of nitrogen—either urea or uric acid. Vertebrate kidneys remove wastes from the blood and regulate water levels in the body.

Key to Strategies
● Understanding Concepts (Tier I)
■ Applying Information (Tier II)
▲ Critical Thinking (Tier III)

Scheduling

See the **Lesson Planning Guide** on pages 457A and 457B for lecture, classwork, and assignment options for Section 24-3.

Phase Two
Teaching Strategies

Life/Work Skills
Being a Team Member

● **Comparing Functions**

Have students work in small groups to create displays that compare and contrast internal and external fertilization involving eggs with shells and eggs without shells. Have a spokesperson from each group present the group's project to the class.

How Many Eggs?

■ **Predicting Outcomes**

Tell students that animals that reproduce by external fertilization usually produce a large number of eggs. A frog, for example, may lay hundreds of eggs, while sea stars and sea urchins release millions into the sea. On the other hand, animals that reproduce by internal fertilization usually produce fewer eggs—a dozen or less per clutch is typical for many birds. Ask students to list reasons for this relationship between the type of fertilization and the number of eggs produced. *(Reasons should focus on the probability of the offspring surviving to reproductive age. Soft, externally fertilized eggs are vulnerable to predators. Only a fraction of the offspring will survive. Hard shells and parental care ensure a higher survival rate among internally fertilized eggs, so fewer eggs are needed.)*

Reproducing on land is very different from reproducing in water. Animals must protect their gametes and eggs from drying out. In this section, you will see some of the adaptations that make it possible for terrestrial animals like this wildebeest to reproduce far from water.

24-3 Reproducing on Land

OBJECTIVES

① **Recognize the advantages of internal fertilization for land animals.**

② **Compare a reptilian egg with an amphibian egg.**

③ **Summarize two advantages of the placental mammals' pattern of development.**

Internal Fertilization

The frogs that you see in **Figure 24-15** may have traveled miles to breed in the water. The behavior of these frogs reflects the strong ties between amphibians and water. Most amphibians must reproduce in water or in damp environments. Insects, mammals, birds, and reptiles have broken the reproductive tie to water.

An egg and a sperm must unite in a moist environment. For many aquatic animals, including most fishes, finding a moist environment is easy: they release their gametes into the surrounding water. Fertilization takes place outside the body of either parent. This type of fertilization is called **external fertilization**. External fertilization is rare on land because both the sperm and the egg could dry out and die.

Figure 24-15
The male frog (behind) grasps the female frog and fertilizes her eggs as they are released. Each egg is enclosed in a jellylike coating that is freely permeable to water. These eggs would quickly dry out if laid on land.

472

Videodisc Resources

Holt Biology Videodiscs
Lesson 24-3: Reproducing on Land

Most terrestrial animals reproduce by internal fertilization

How did terrestrial animals overcome the limitations of external fertilization? Recall that each animal carries its own supply of water inside its body. Therefore, if gametes can be transferred directly from the body of one individual to the body of another, the risk that gametes will dry out disappears. In almost all land animals, including flatworms, roundworms, annelids, mollusks, arthropods, reptiles, birds, and mammals, the male deposits his sperm directly inside the female. Fertilization occurs inside the female's body. This type of fertilization is called **internal fertilization**. Most amphibians lack the capability for internal fertilization. They reproduce by external fertilization, as did their fish ancestors. Now you can see one reason why amphibians, such as toads, must return to water to reproduce.

If you go to a pond a few days after toads breed, you will find that the water contains strings of small, round eggs, like those shown in **Figure 24-15**. These eggs are the second reason that most

amphibians must reproduce in water or moist places. The embryonic toad develops within the egg, which has a jellylike coating. This coating is freely permeable to carbon dioxide, oxygen, and water. Amphibian eggs removed from moisture soon dry out and die.

The eggs of reptiles and birds are watertight

Unlike amphibian embryos, the embryos of reptiles are surrounded by a watertight protective membrane called the **chorion** (KAWR ee ahn). The chorion is impermeable to water, but it does permit oxygen to enter the egg and carbon dioxide to leave. Lying within the chorion is another membrane, the **amnion** (AM nee ahn). The amnion encloses the embryo within a watery environment, as shown in **Figure 24-16**. This kind of egg is called an **amniotic egg**. Amniotic eggs evolved first in reptiles and are also found in birds and mammals. In the eggs of reptiles and birds, a nutrient-rich yolk supplies nutrition to the developing embryo. A tough shell surrounds and protects the eggs of all birds, most reptiles, and three species of egg-laying mammals.

Like the eggs of birds and reptiles, the eggs of most terrestrial arthropods are watertight and very yolky, providing nutrients for the young during development. Arthropod eggs are usually either thick-walled and resistant to drying or are encased in some sort of waxy protective covering.

Figure 24-16
The eggs of birds and reptiles, such as the turtle shown below, have a watertight protective coating called the chorion and an internal membrane called the amnion, which encloses the embryo in a watery environment.

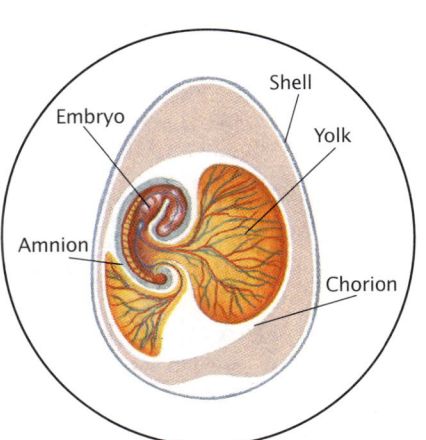

Shell
Embryo
Yolk
Amnion
Chorion

473

Matter of Fact: Egg Shells

How can a bird egg inside its hard shell be fertilized? Internal fertilization occurs before the shell is formed. After fertilization, as the egg moves through the oviduct, albumin (egg white) is deposited around the egg. Next, a fibrous shell membrane covers the albumin, and finally a hard shell of calcium salts covers the egg. It takes about 24 hours after the egg is released into the oviduct, where it may or may not be fertilized, for the shell to be completed and the egg to be ready for laying.

Amniotes

■ **Comparing Structures**

Show students a detailed drawing of a developing placental mammal that includes the embryo, the embryonic membranes (amnion and chorion), the umbilical cord, and the placenta. Have students compare the drawing with Figure 24-17. Ask students to list the structures that are characteristic of birds (*eggshell, albumin, large yolk*), those that are characteristic of placental mammals (*placenta, umbilical cord, rudimentary yolk sac*), and those that are found in both birds and placental mammals (*developing embryo, amnion, and chorion*).

Active READING

● **Technique: Anticipation Guide**

Ask volunteers to discuss how opinions they formed in the Active Reading exercise on page 458 changed or stayed the same after their reading. Students should point to specific passages in the text that support their reasoning.

Phase Three
Assessment Options

Closure

● **Summarizing Information**

Review what students know about the development, birth, and parental care of puppies and kittens; the laying, incubating, and hatching of birds; and the laying and hatching of frog eggs. Ask them to describe the advantages of each strategy.

SECTION REVIEW

Assign the *Section Review*.

Reteaching

Provide students with descriptions of fictional animals. Include their habitat and way of life. Have students infer the best type of fertilization and development for the imaginary animals and have them defend their choices.

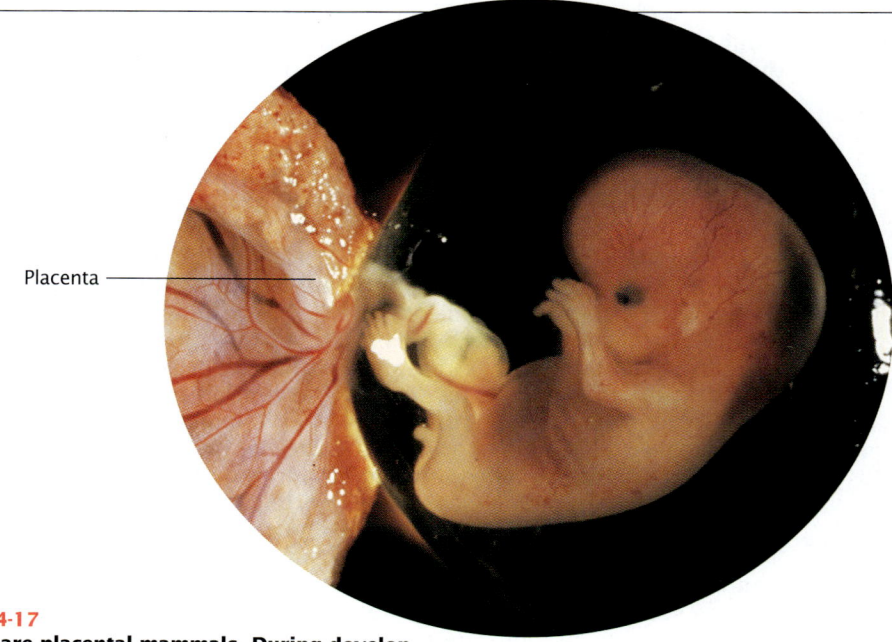

Placenta

Figure 24-17
Humans are placental mammals. During development, the embryo receives nourishment and eliminates wastes through the placenta.

Eggs Without Shells

Once the egg of a reptile or bird has been laid, the parent cannot provide further nourishment to the offspring until it hatches. Furthermore, the egg is exposed to environmental hazards such as predators and extremes of temperature.

Except for platypuses and echidnas (*ee KIHD nuhz*), mammals do not lay eggs. Instead, their eggs develop until birth inside the mother's body. No shell forms around the egg. Among marsupial mammals, such as kangaroos and opossums, birth occurs very early, and the offspring matures in the mother's pouch, nourished by suckling her milk.

Among placental mammals (mice and humans, for instance), birth occurs much later, when development is essentially complete. A human embryo develops for nine months inside its mother. During its development, the embryo of a placental mammal is nourished by the mother through a unique structure called the **placenta** (*pluh SEHN tuh*), which is shown in **Figure 24-17**. The placenta is made of embryonic and maternal membranes. Nutrients and oxygen move from mother to embryo through the placenta, while carbon dioxide and other wastes leave the embryo.

SECTION REVIEW

1 Why isn't external fertilization an effective way to reproduce on dry land?

2 Describe the advantages of the shelled egg over the amphibian egg.

3 Describe two hazards faced by reptilian eggs but not by eggs of placental mammals.

4 What are some disadvantages of the placental mammals' pattern of development?

ANSWERS TO SECTION REVIEW

1 In air, the sperm and eggs would dry out and die.

2 Amphibian eggs have a jellylike coating that loses moisture easily, so amphibians must lay their eggs in water or moist areas. Birds and reptiles can lay their watertight eggs in a greater variety of places.

3 Answers will vary. Students may suggest that reptilian parents cannot provide further nourishment to the unhatched offspring and that the egg is exposed to environmental hazards, such as predators and temperature extremes.

4 Answers may vary. Students may suggest that the developing offspring is completely dependent on the mother before birth. Any injury to the mother or poisonous substances she ingests could damage the offspring. If she dies, the offspring dies. This method of development also puts greater demands on the mother, possibly jeopardizing her survival.

"Gee, evolution is slow."

	Key Terms	Summary
24-1 **Leaving the Sea** Reptiles have limbs partway beneath their bodies to support their weight more effectively. 	lateral line (p. 462)	• Life on land places different demands on animals than life in water. • The most successful land groups are the arthropods and the vertebrates. Both of these groups have sturdy skeletons that support their bodies out of water. They also have strong, flexible limbs for moving on land. • The high density of water makes sound easy to detect. Land animals hear well only with an amplifying system, such as the ear.
24-2 **Staying Moist in a Dry World** Amphibian blood is pumped through a "double-loop" circulatory system. 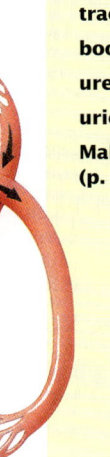	gill (p. 464) trachea (p. 467) book lung (p. 467) urea (p. 470) uric acid (p. 470) Malpighian tubule (p. 471)	• The exoskeleton of arthropods serves as a barrier to evaporation. Birds, reptiles, and mammals minimize water loss by means of their watertight skin. • Animals must obtain oxygen and release carbon dioxide. In land vertebrates, this gas exchange occurs in the lungs. In insects, tracheae carry oxygen. • The breakdown of amino acids produces the toxic byproduct ammonia. Aquatic animals excrete dilute ammonia. Terrestrial animals transform ammonia into urea or uric acid, which is eliminated with less water loss.
24-3 **Reproducing on Land** Reptilian eggs have a protective shell and a watery internal environment. 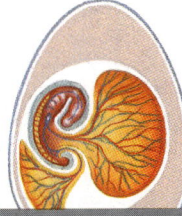	external fertilization (p. 472) internal fertilization (p. 473) chorion (p. 473) amnion (p. 473) amniotic egg (p. 473) placenta (p. 474)	• Most amphibians reproduce in water by external fertilization. Most other land animals reproduce by internal fertilization. • The eggs of reptiles, birds, and mammals are surrounded by watertight membranes. In most mammals, development is completed within the mother's body.

475

Alternative Assessment

Have students make a summary concept map based on the information found on this page. Encourage students to include transition linkages between the key terms.

Portfolio Assessment

Portfolio Assessment on page T39 provides options for building and evaluating student portfolios. Students and teachers can select items from the areas listed on page T39 for inclusion in a portfolio.

ANSWER TO CONCEPT MAP

The following is one possible answer to the Relating Concepts exercise on page 476.

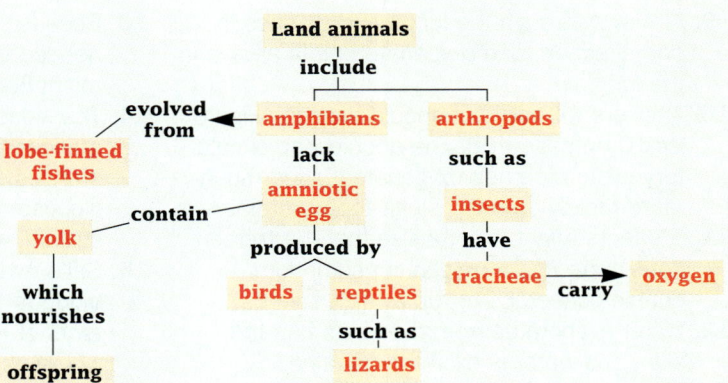

review
ANSWERS

Understanding Vocabulary

1. a. Kidneys are not gas-exchange structures.
b. Blood is not a nitrogen-containing waste excreted by animals.
c. Malpighian tubules are not a component of the amniotic egg.

2. a. The lateral line is a row of pressure-sensitive cells that allow a fish to sense physical disturbances. The ear is the sound-amplifying system of a land vertebrate.
b. The exoskeleton prevents water loss and provides support and protection. Scales provide a watertight covering that allows reptiles to live away from water.
c. Insects breathe through tracheae that lead to the body cavity from spiracles located on their surface. Spiders breathe through book lungs, highly folded sacs inside the body that open to the outside through a spiracle.

Understanding Concepts

3. Answer to concept map is shown on page 475.
4. Reptilian limbs are positioned slightly beneath the body. They allow reptiles to run faster, and they support more body weight than the limbs of amphibians.
5. As the density of a medium increases, the speed and distance traveled by sound also increase. Land animals have structures that amplify airborne sounds.
6. Arthropods have a stiff outer coat composed of chitin and protein. Amphibians secrete a slippery mucous coating over the skin. Reptiles have watertight skin covered with scales.
7. As a fish pumps water over its gills, diffusion occurs. Oxygen passes into the blood, and carbon dioxide passes to the water.
8. Water provides the support and moisture required for gills to function.

---

review

Understanding Vocabulary

1. For each list of terms, identify the one that does not fit the pattern and explain why.
a. kidneys, lungs, trachea, gills
b. blood, ammonia, urea, uric acid
c. chorion, amnion, shell, Malpighian tubules

2. For each pair of terms, explain the differences in their meanings.
a. lateral line, ear
b. exoskeleton, scales
c. trachea, book lungs

Understanding Concepts

3. **Relating Concepts** Construct a concept map that describes the adaptation of animals to life on land and the characteristics that allow them to live on land successfully. Try to include the following terms in your concept map: lobe-finned fishes, amphibians, arthropods, amniotic egg, yolk, birds, reptiles, insects, trachea, oxygen, lizards.

4. **Analyzing Structures** Compare the position of limbs in amphibians with that in reptiles. What advantages result from the arrangement shown by reptiles?

5. **Analyzing Relationships** Explain the relationship between the density of a medium and the speed and distance that sound travels through it. What is the consequence of this relationship for land animals?

6. **Comparing Structures** Arthropods and vertebrates prevent water loss by having waterproof coatings. How do the coatings of arthropods, amphibians, and reptiles differ?

7. **Identifying Processes** What is gas exchange? How does gas exchange occur in the gills of a fish?

8. **Analyzing Structures** Explain why the gills of fishes don't function out of water.

---

9. **Recognizing Relationships** What features contribute to the high efficiency of a bird's respiratory system?

10. **Comparing Structures** Compare the circulatory system of a fish with that of an amphibian. What is the advantage of the amphibian circulatory system?

11. **Interpreting Graphs** Cheetahs are the fastest land animals. Biologists were interested in learning how the lung size and oxygen consumption of cheetahs differed from those of other cats of similar size. This graph shows the results of their study. Form a hypothesis relating the rate of oxygen consumption in cheetahs to their running performance.

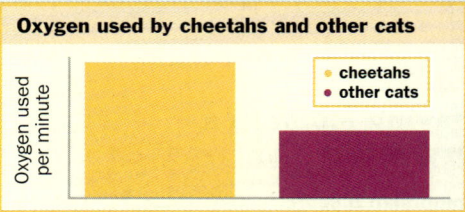

Oxygen used by cheetahs and other cats

- cheetahs
- other cats

Oxygen used per minute

12. **Summarizing Information** Identify three ways that water is lost from the human body.

13. **Predicting Outcomes** Fishes eliminate nitrogen-containing wastes as ammonia. What complications might result if land animals also eliminated waste in this form?

14. **Identifying Functions** Describe how kidneys enable a mammal to remove wastes and to regulate how much water is retained by the body.

15. **Analyzing Processes** Describe how insects and spiders filter blood to remove wastes.

16. **Recognizing Relationships** Explain why most amphibians must reproduce in water or moist environments.

17. **Summarizing Information** Describe two advantages of development in a placental mammal.

18. **BUILDING ON WHAT YOU HAVE LEARNED** In Chapter 4, you learned about diffusion. What role does diffusion play in the exchange of gases in the gills of fishes?

---

9. Air flows through the lungs and air sacs in one direction, and oxygenated air is always in the lungs.
10. Answers will vary but should describe Figure 24-10 on page 466. The double-loop circulatory system carries oxygenated blood much more rapidly than the single-loop system.
11. Students might hypothesize that the tremendous capacity for oxygen consumption enables cheetahs to run at high speeds.
12. Water evaporates from the lungs and the skin, and water is excreted as urine.

13. Because of the large amount of water needed to dilute ammonia, the land animals might become dehydrated.
14. The kidney filters waste and useful substances from the blood. The useful substances, such as potassium, chloride, and glucose, are reabsorbed into the bloodstream, while the waste—urea—is removed.
15. Salts, wastes, and water move from the blood to the Malpighian tubules. The contents of the tubules are released into the gut, where useful compounds are reabsorbed.

Interpreting Graphics

19. Look at the figure below.

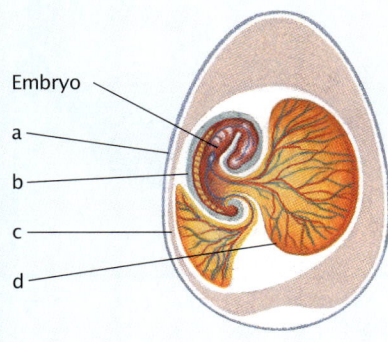

Embryo
a
b
c
d

a. What kind of egg is shown in the figure above? Identify the parts of the egg, and describe the function of each part.
b. What animals lay this kind of egg?
c. What evolutionary advantage does an egg of this type have over an amphibian egg?

Reviewing Themes

20. **Evolution**
What evidence has led scientists to conclude that the earliest land vertebrates evolved from lobe-finned fishes?

21. **Evolution**
Of what significance was the evolution of a watertight skin to reptiles?

22. **Matter, Energy, and Organization**
Land animals use energy to convert ammonia into urea or uric acid. What do these animals gain from this conversion?

Thinking Critically

23. **Determining Factual Accuracy** Explain the factual inaccuracies in the following statements: Amphibians evolved from sharks around 350 million years ago. Amphibians lay jellylike eggs in which the embryo is surrounded by an amnion and a chorion. Most amphibians have a moist skin through which they absorb oxygen.

Life/Work Skills

24. **Finding Information** Use library references or search an on-line database to research the fishes called mudskippers (*Boleophthalmus pectinirostris* is one species). Find out the unusual behaviors of male mudskippers that take them out of the water to reproduce and feed. Prepare an illustrated report of your findings to share with your class.

25. **Working Cooperatively** Work together with a partner to make models of a typical amniotic egg and a typical amphibian egg. Use modeling clay, paper, or other materials to make your models. Use library references to find out more detailed information about the structure of these two types of eggs. Write a report about the adaptations exhibited by each kind of egg.

Activities and Projects

26. **Art Connection** Draw a picture of a fictional animal that is adapted for survival in one of the seven biomes studied in Chapter 14. Write a description of how the animal reproduces, breathes, and eliminates wastes.

27. **History Connection** In 1938 a South African fisherman caught a strange type of fish. Scientists later identified it as a kind of lobe-finned fish called a coelacanth. Use library references or search an on-line database to find out the historical significance of this discovery. Write a report on the characteristics of coelacanths that indicate they are close relatives of modern amphibians.

Discovering Through Reading

28. Read the article "Coming Onto the Land" by Carl Zimmer in *Discover*, June 1995, pages 118–127. What is important about the discovery of *Acanthostega*? What evidence about the way the first land animals moved has been revealed by *Acanthostega*?

477

Reviewing Themes

20. similarities in limb bones
21. Watertight skin allowed for living in a dry habitat.
22. reduces water loss during elimination of wastes

Thinking Critically

23. Amphibians probably evolved from lobe-finned fishes. Amphibians do not lay amniotic eggs. The last statement is true.

Life/Work Skills

24. Drawings and descriptions will vary but should include details about the male mudskipper's behavior. Male mudskippers are able to breath air through lungs and to crawl onto mud flats to attract females and mate. One species can climb plants at the water's edge to feed on insects and other small animals.
25. Models and reports will vary but should accurately represent each type of egg.

Activities and Projects

26. Drawings and descriptions of the animal will vary but should include adaptive features for the selected biome.
27. Reports will vary but should compare adaptive features of modern coelacanths and extinct coelacanths.

Discovering Through Reading

28. Answers will vary but should include evidence that indicates *Acanthostega* was an underwater tetrapod.

Waste remains in the gut as a dry paste and is excreted with feces.

16. Fertilization takes place outside the body, and gametes must stay moist to survive. The eggs are vulnerable to drying.
17. The mother's body provides protection, nourishment, waste removal, and gas exchange for the developing young.
18. The difference in the concentration of molecules causes the molecules to diffuse into or out of the capillary.

Interpreting Graphics

19. a. amniotic egg; (a) shell—protection, (b) amnion—encloses the embryo within a watery environment, (c) chorion—prevents water loss but allows gas exchange, (d) yolk—provides nutrients
b. reptiles, birds, and three species of mammals
c. Amniotic eggs can survive dry conditions.

Animal Diversity

Lesson Planning Guide With Options for Block Scheduling

Lecture Concepts	Lesson Resources

25-1 Sponges, Cnidarians, and Simple Worms

BLOCK ❶ (45 minutes)

1. Sponges attach to rocks and filter water for food and oxygen, and they can reproduce both sexually and asexually. The skeletons of sponges are made of hard spicules or tough spongin.

2. Cnidarians include corals, jellyfish, sea anemones, and hydras. They have tentacles with stinging nematocysts, and many take two different body forms, the polyp and the medusa, during their life cycles.

❶ Lecture Resources
- Determining Prior Knowledge
- Active Reading: K-W-L
- Active Reading: Paired Summarizing
- Visual Strategy: Videodisc
- Demonstration: Identifying Structures
- Teaching Transparencies: 149, 150
- Holt Biology Videodiscs Lesson 25-1

Classwork Options
- Mathematics Connection
- Demonstration: Identifying Structures

Assignment Options
- World of Work: Biomedicine
- Teaching Resources CD-ROM: Supplemental Reading Guides 7

BLOCK ❷ (45 minutes)

3. Most species of flatworms are parasites that attack a wide variety of hosts and that can reproduce sexually or asexually by regeneration.

4. Roundworms are abundant in the environment. Some species of roundworms are parasites that damage crops or infect livestock or humans.

❷ Lecture Resources
- Prey Paralysis
- Visual Strategy: Figure 25-6
- Demonstration: Analyzing Data
- Teaching Transparencies: 154, 137A
- Holt Biology Videodiscs Lesson 25-1

Classwork Options
- Dog Parasites
- Closure: Organizing Data

Assignment Options
- Worms
- Reteaching
- Section Review
- Chapter Review, questions 1, 4, 5, 6, 7, 8, 19, 23
- Directed Reading Worksheet

25-2 Mollusks, Annelids, and Arthropods

BLOCK ❸ (45 minutes)

1. Mollusks include gastropods (slugs and snails), bivalves (oysters, mussels, clams, and scallops), and cephalopods (octopuses, squid, and nautiluses).

2. Mollusks have soft bodies covered with a fleshy fold called the mantle, which in most mollusks secretes a hard shell. The muscular foot of the mollusk allows it to burrow and move.

❸ Lecture Resources
- Mollusks on the Menu
- Self Defense
- Active Reading: Reading Organizer
- Demonstration: Comparing Structures
- Holt Biology Videodiscs Lesson 25-2

Classwork Options
- Quick Labs: Lab A23

Assignment Options
- The Octopus's Reputation
- Life/Work Skills: Finding Information, p. 488

BLOCK ❹ (45 minutes)

3. Annelids are segmented worms. Modifications of the segments allow specialized functions in different parts of the annelid body.

4. Earthworms play an essential role in maintaining the fertility of the soil. Leeches are often parasitic.

5. A million different species of arthropods have been described, and many more remain to be discovered.

❹ Lecture Resources
- An Earthworm Myth
- Visual Strategy: Figure 25-18
- Holt Biology Videodiscs Lesson 25-2

Classwork Options
- Life/Work Skills: Finding Information, p. 491
- Closure: Forming a Hypothesis

Assignment Options
- Reteaching
- Section Review
- Chapter Review, questions 2, 3, 9, 10, 11, 12, 13, 14, 20, 21, 22, 25
- Directed Reading Worksheet

Lecture Concepts

Lesson Resources

25-3 Echinoderms and Chordates

BLOCK ❺ (45 minutes)

1. Sea stars, sea cucumbers, sand dollars, and sea urchins are echinoderms. Echinoderms have five-part radial symmetry, a water vascular system, and no excretory system.

2. Chordates include the tunicates, lancelets, and vertebrates. All chordates share deuterostome development and four basic features: a notochord, a dorsal nerve cord, a postanal tail, and pharyngeal slits.

❺ Lecture Resources
- ■ Swimming Stars
- ■ Active Reading: K-W-L
- ⊘ Holt Biology Videodiscs Lesson 25-3

Classwork Options
- ■ Closure: Relating Concepts

Assignment Options
- ■ Reteaching
- ■ Section Review
- ■ Chapter Review, questions 15, 16, 17, 18, 24, 26, 27
- ■ Directed Reading Worksheet

Chapter Review and Assessment

BLOCK ❻ (45 minutes)
Review
- ■ Reteaching Worksheet
- ■ Thinking Skills Worksheet
- ■ Vocabulary Development Worksheet
- ⊙ Language Development and Reading Comprehension Audio CD Program: Chapter 25

BLOCK ❼ (45 minutes)
Assessment
- ■ Alternative Assessment, p. 495
- ■ Portfolio Assessment, p. T39

Chapter Test
- ■ Chapter 25 Test

Test Generator
- ⊙ Item bank for customizing Chapter Tests

Teaching Resources CD-ROM
- ⊙ Scoring Rubrics and Classroom Management Checklist

 The Portfolio icon denotes items throughout the Teacher's Edition lesson wrap that may be selected for inclusion in student portfolios.

Holt Biology Videodiscs and *Concepts of Biology*

Holt Biology Videodiscs gives you a powerful tool for teaching, review, and assessment. For further information regarding the media on the videodiscs, see **Holt Biology Videodiscs Teacher's Correlation Guide to Holt Biology: Visualizing Life.**

Concepts of Biology adds interactive lesson plans and extensive tools for customization using CD-ROM technology.

Use the following topic from **Concepts of Biology** to help you teach this chapter:

Topic 19: Evolutionary Trends in Vertebrates
Topic 18: Invertebrate Diversity

Laboratory Planning

Holt BioSources Laboratory Program

Block 3: Quick Labs Lab A23: Observing Some Major Animal Groups

Determining Prior Knowledge

- Ask students if a starfish (sea star) is really a fish.
- Display a variety of photos of invertebrates discussed in this chapter, and ask students to identify the animal groups to which each belongs.
- Ask students to identify which of the animal groups discussed in this chapter show the following characteristics: tissues, a body cavity, segmentation, jointed limbs, and adaptations to living on land.
- Show students a dried sponge, a piece of coral, a seashell or snail shell, and an insect exoskeleton. Ask students to describe how the living animal is different from its dried remains.

Active READING

Technique: K-W-L

Before students read the chapter, display a list of the following phyla: sponges, cnidarians, flatworms, roundworms, mollusks, annelids, arthropods, echinoderms, and chordates. Have students make lists of all the things that they already **K**now about the members of each phylum. Have them work together to form a class list. Then have each student list things they **W**ant to know about animals in these phyla. Have students save their lists for later use in Active Reading on page 494.

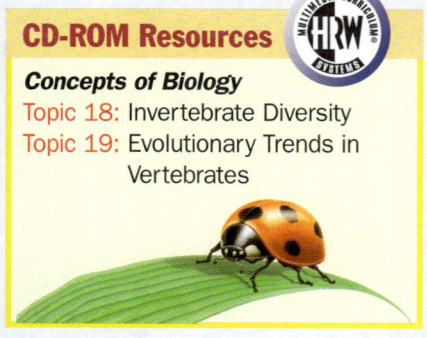

CD-ROM Resources

Concepts of Biology

Topic 18: Invertebrate Diversity
Topic 19: Evolutionary Trends in Vertebrates

CHAPTER

25

REVIEW
- animal tissues (Section 23-1)
- origin of body cavities (Section 23-2)
- innovations in body plan (Section 23-3)

Animal Diversity

This colorful nudibranch is a mollusk that lives in the Indian and Pacific Oceans.

Author's Rationale Students arrive at this chapter with a broad knowledge of the major evolutionary differences within the animal kingdom. In this chapter, students look at animals from a taxonomic perspective. The background that students acquired in earlier chapters will make it easier for them to understand the details of this chapter. Each animal group is treated similarly for easy comparison.

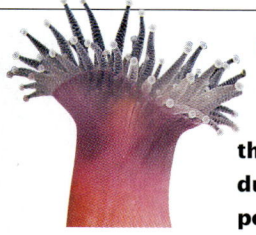

Chapter 23 told the story of the evolution of animal body architecture. In this chapter, you will return to the major phyla of animals for a longer visit. You will discover where some of these animals—such as the sea anemone at the left—live, how they feed, and how they reproduce. You will also learn how some of these animals affect humans, both positively and negatively.

25-1 Sponges, Cnidarians, and Simple Worms

OBJECTIVES

1 Contrast the way of life of a sponge with that of a cnidarian.

2 Compare the polyp stage of the cnidarian life cycle with the medusa stage.

3 Describe the life cycle of the beef tapeworm.

4 List two parasitic nematodes that can live in humans.

Figure 25-1
Sponges vary greatly in size, shape, and color. This purple tube sponge was photographed in the ocean surrounding Bonaire, an island in the Caribbean Sea.

Sponges

Sponges are probably most familiar to you as absorbent pads used for wiping up spills or cleaning dishes. The sponges you buy in the store are usually manufactured, not derived from the animals known as sponges. There are more than 9,000 species of sponges (phylum Porifera), most of which are marine. About 150 species live in fresh water. An adult sponge, like the one in **Figure 25-1**, spends its life attached to a hard surface. For this reason, it was not until 1765 that zoologists realized that sponges are animals, not plants. Most sponges are asymmetrical and grow to conform to the surface on which they live.

A sponge's body is perforated by holes (Porifera means "pore-bearer") that lead to an inner water chamber. Sponges pump water through these pores and expel it through a large opening at the top of the chamber. The water current flowing through the sponge's body carries in food particles and oxygen and carries out wastes.

As you learned in Chapter 23, between the inner and outer layer of many sponges is a jellylike layer. Embedded within this layer is a network of hard structures called **spicules**, a mesh of the tough protein spongin, or both. Spicules and spongin form the skeleton of the sponge. Large sponges with spongin skeletons (and few or no spicules) have been harvested for centuries because their

dried skeletons will soak up water and release it when squeezed. Most of the sponges you can buy today are copies of this spongin mesh manufactured from plastic or cellulose.

479

Videodisc Resources

Holt Biology Videodiscs
Lesson 25-1: Sponges, Cnidarians, and Simple Worms

Scheduling
See the **Lesson Planning Guide** on pages 477A and 477B for lecture, classwork, and assignment options for Section 25-1.

Phase Two
Teaching Strategies

Demonstration

● **Identifying Structures**
Pass around a small, dried natural sponge, and ask students what part of the sponge they are examining *(the skeleton)*. Ask students what this sponge's skeleton is made of *(spongin)* and how it is different from other sponge skeletons *(many sponges have skeletons made of sharp spicules)*. Have students explain why sponges with skeletons made of spicules are not used for washing *(spicules are not absorbent and would scratch skin or other surfaces being cleaned)*.

Active READING

Technique: Paired Summarizing
Have students read silently about the sponges and cnidarians on pages 479–481. Assign partners, and have one student summarize orally what he or she has read while the other student listens. The listener should then point out inaccuracies and add ideas that were left out. Students should work together during a final clarification process, referring to the text as needed.

Key to Strategies
Teaching Strategies are keyed to three tiers of learning.

● **Understanding Concepts (Tier I)**
Content mastery and comprehension

■ **Applying Information (Tier II)**
Applying and analyzing content

▲ **Critical Thinking (Tier III)**
Practicing evaluative thinking

Animal Diversity 479

Art Connection

Sponge Model

Caution: Students should use caution when working with sharp objects.

Provide students with three colors of modeling clay, and ask them to make a model of a sponge. Each color of clay should represent a layer of the body wall of the sponge. Models should include as many structural features as possible, including incurrent pores, the osculum, and choanocytes. Students may want to use various objects such as paper clips and pushpins to represent parts of the sponge.

Mathematics Connection

How Much Water Can a Sponge Sponge?

Tell students that a sponge that is 10 cm tall and 1 cm in diameter pumps 22.5 L of water through its body every day. To give students a sense of how much water this is, have them make a life-sized clay model of the sponge and display it next to a 3 L soda bottle. Ask students to calculate the number of bottles it would take to hold the amount of water circulated by the sponge in a day *(22.5 L ÷ 3 L/bottle = 7.5 bottles)*. Then ask students to calculate the amount of water that the sponge circulates in a year *(22.5 L × 365 days = 8212.5 L/year)*. How many bottles would it take to hold that amount of water? *(8212.5 L/year ÷ 3 L/bottle = 2737.5 bottles)* Have students display their calculations with the sponge model.

Sponges reproduce sexually and asexually

Most sponges are able to reproduce asexually. In some sponges, new individuals bud from the parent; in others, the parent sponge breaks into many fragments, and each fragment grows into a new sponge. Sponges can also reproduce sexually, as illustrated in **Figure 25-2**.

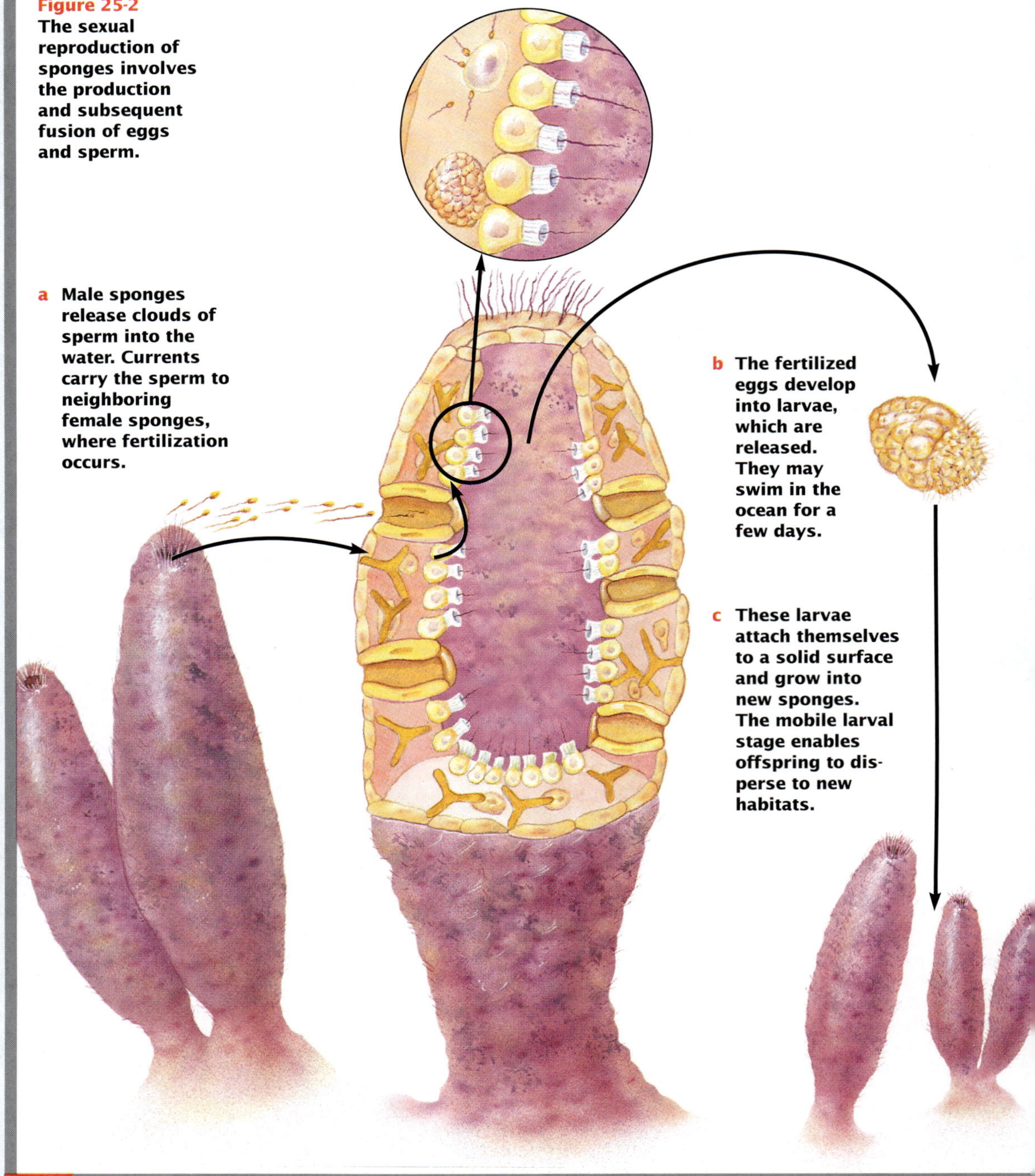

Figure 25-2
The sexual reproduction of sponges involves the production and subsequent fusion of eggs and sperm.

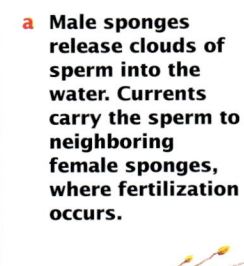

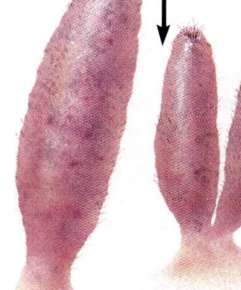

a Male sponges release clouds of sperm into the water. Currents carry the sperm to neighboring female sponges, where fertilization occurs.

b The fertilized eggs develop into larvae, which are released. They may swim in the ocean for a few days.

c These larvae attach themselves to a solid surface and grow into new sponges. The mobile larval stage enables offspring to disperse to new habitats.

Matter of Fact: Gemmules

When a marine environment becomes too cold or dry, some freshwater sponges ensure their survival by forming gemmules. These clusters of sponge cells are encased in a protective coat with a supply of food, so the cell clusters are able to survive even if the rest of the parent sponge dies. The cell clusters are able to grow into new sponges when conditions improve.

Cnidarians: Jellyfish and Relatives

Corals, jellyfish, sea anemones, and hydras are members of the phylum Cnidaria. The name *cnidaria* comes from the Greek word meaning "nettle" and refers to the stinging structures that are characteristic of these animals.

Cnidarians have a gut with only one opening to the outside. This opening is surrounded by a ring of tentacles used to capture food and defend against predators. Cells in the tentacles and outer body surface are armed with stinging, harpoon-like structures called **nematocysts** (*NEHM uh toh sihsts*). The projectile fired by a nematocyst contains toxins that can cause paralysis.

Most cnidarians are harmless to people. If you touch the tentacles of a sea anemone, you will feel a sticky sensation as its short projectiles barely pierce your skin. A few jellyfish and corals, however, have very potent toxins that cause a painful, burning rash. The stings of the tropical sea wasp jellyfish can be fatal. To protect against their stings, Australian surfers sometimes wear pantyhose when in the water.

Many cnidarians have two distinct life stages

In Chapter 20 you learned about alternation of generations in plants. Like plants, many cnidarians have two different body forms during their life cycle, as illustrated in **Figure 25-3**. The two forms are called the **polyp** stage and the **medusa** (plural, medusae), or jellyfish, stage. Polyps generally live attached to a hard surface. Sea anemones, hydras, and corals are polyps.

Not all cnidarians go through both polyp and medusa stages. Some remain as either a polyp or medusa throughout their lives. You can read more about cnidarians in the *Tour of a Jellyfish* on page 482.

Figure 25-3
The life cycle of a typical cnidarian involves two different body forms.

a Polyps bud to produce more polyps and, in some cnidarians, to produce the medusa stage of the life cycle.

b Medusae, or jellyfish, drift about with water currents or swim by pulsing their umbrella-shaped bodies. They release sperm and eggs into the water, where fertilization occurs.

c After fertilization, the embryo develops into a larva, . . .

d . . . which eventually settles to the bottom and becomes another polyp, thus completing the life cycle.

481

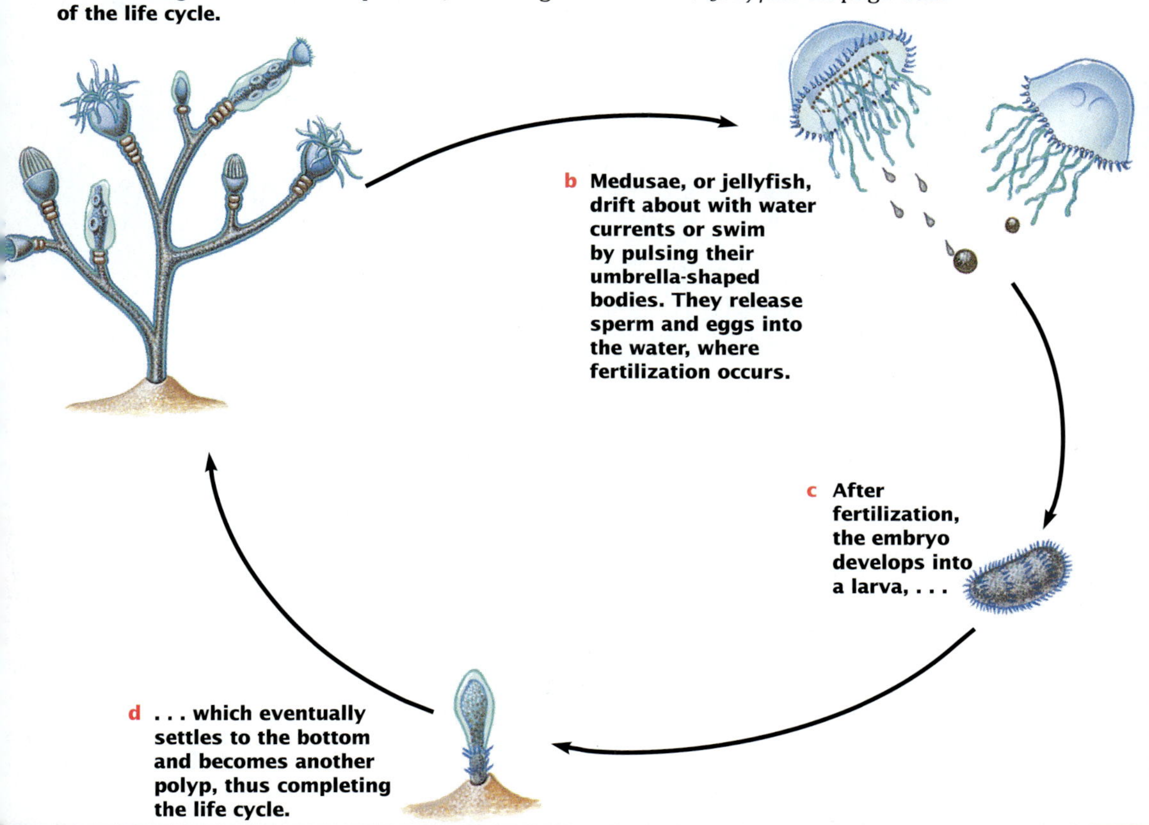

Matter of Fact: Borrowed Defenses

Some nudibranches, or sea slugs, feed on cnidarians and save the untriggered nematocysts within their own bodies. When other animals try to eat the nudibranches, they trigger the nematocysts. As a result, the predators learn to avoid encounters with the painful mollusks.

Tour

World of Work

Biomedicine

Spacelab experiments have used jellyfish polyps to study physiological changes that occur when animals develop in different gravitational environments. Jellyfish polyps were used because of their small size and quick development. Experimental results suggest that microgravity interferes with the development of the neuromuscular or nervous system in certain jellyfish.

Physics Connection

Jet Propulsion

Many aquatic animals can propel themselves by forcefully expelling water from their body. Explain to students that the jellyfish's movement is slow but efficient. Have students use library references to learn more about jet propulsion. Tell students that some mollusks use this propulsion system to produce a short burst of speed, which enables them to escape predators. A squid can produce a dramatic burst that propels its body out of the water and 50 ft away from its predator. You may want to demonstrate this type of movement by releasing an air-filled balloon in the classroom.

Connection: *Chapter 16*

In Costa Rica, strips of blue plastic doused with pesticides are used to protect developing bananas from insects. Because the strips of plastic are not reused or recycled, they are often carelessly discarded and end up as litter throughout the countryside. Many of these strips of blue plastic travel from the inland waterways to the coast. Leatherback sea turtles prey on jellyfish, which look very similar to blue plastic floating on the surface. These turtles have been known to mistake the plastic for jellyfish and choke on the plastic.

Jellyfish

The moon jelly is a common jellyfish. Like all cnidarians, the moon jelly has a body composed of two main layers of cells and a gut with only one opening to the outside.

Habitat
Moon jellies live close to the surface near the shore. In the United States, they are found on the Pacific, Atlantic, and Gulf coasts.

The moon jelly has a bell-shaped body. A muscular ring around the margin of the bell contracts rhythmically to propel the animal through the water.

Size
A large moon jelly can be 41 cm (16 in.) in diameter.

Moon jellies feed on small animals that become trapped in sticky mucus on the underside of the body. Beating cilia carry the prey to the mouth.

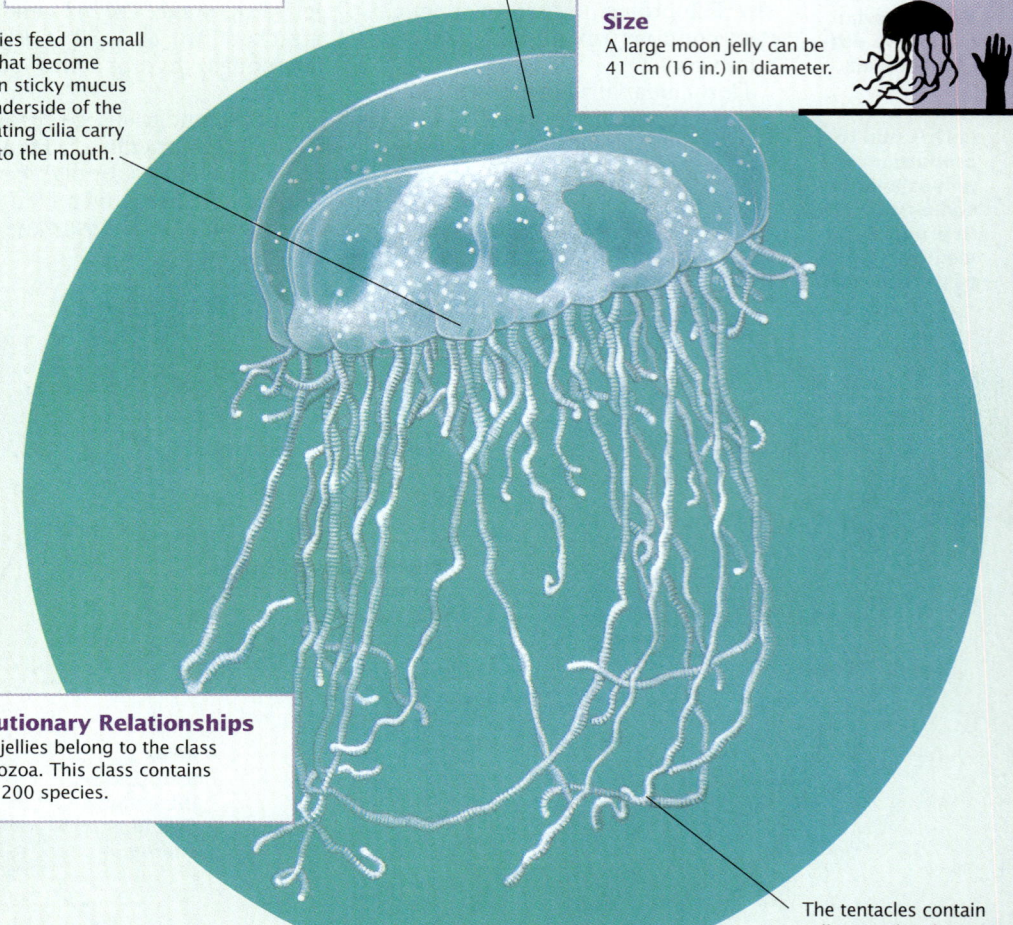

Evolutionary Relationships
Moon jellies belong to the class Scyphozoa. This class contains about 200 species.

The tentacles contain cells armed with stinging structures, which are used for defense. The stings of the moon jelly are harmless to humans.

482

Flatworms

There are about 20,000 species of flatworms (phylum Platyhelminthes). Most free-living flatworms, such as planarians, are aquatic. They are common in shallow oceans, usually in protected habitats. Freshwater flatworms often reside in gravel or under sunken objects. A few species live on land, but always in very damp areas. The flatworm body is soft and unprotected against predators and dehydration.

Flatworms can reproduce asexually by regeneration

If you cut a planarian in half, either lengthwise or across the body, each half will regrow into a complete worm. This ability to regrow lost parts is called regeneration. Many free-living flatworms can reproduce asexually through regeneration. Scientists are very interested in understanding how flatworms regenerate, and they hope to apply this information to humans. Humans can regenerate some damaged parts, such as growing new skin after

a cut or scrape. But human abilities to regenerate are far less dramatic than those of flatworms.

Flatworms also reproduce sexually. Most species are **hermaphrodites**. Hermaphrodites *(huhr MAHF roh deyets)* contain both male and female reproductive systems. During mating, two flatworms exchange sperm so that the eggs of both flatworms are fertilized. A flatworm usually does not fertilize its own eggs.

Most flatworms are parasites

Most species of flatworms are parasitic, infesting a variety of hosts, including humans. Nearly 300 million people are afflicted with the disease schistosomiasis *(shihs tuh soh MEYE uh sihs)*. Each year schistosomiasis kills approximately 800,000 people in Asia, Africa, Latin America, and the Middle East. Microscopic flatworms in the genus *Schistosoma* cause this deadly disease. **Figure 25-4** shows the life cycle of *Schistosoma*.

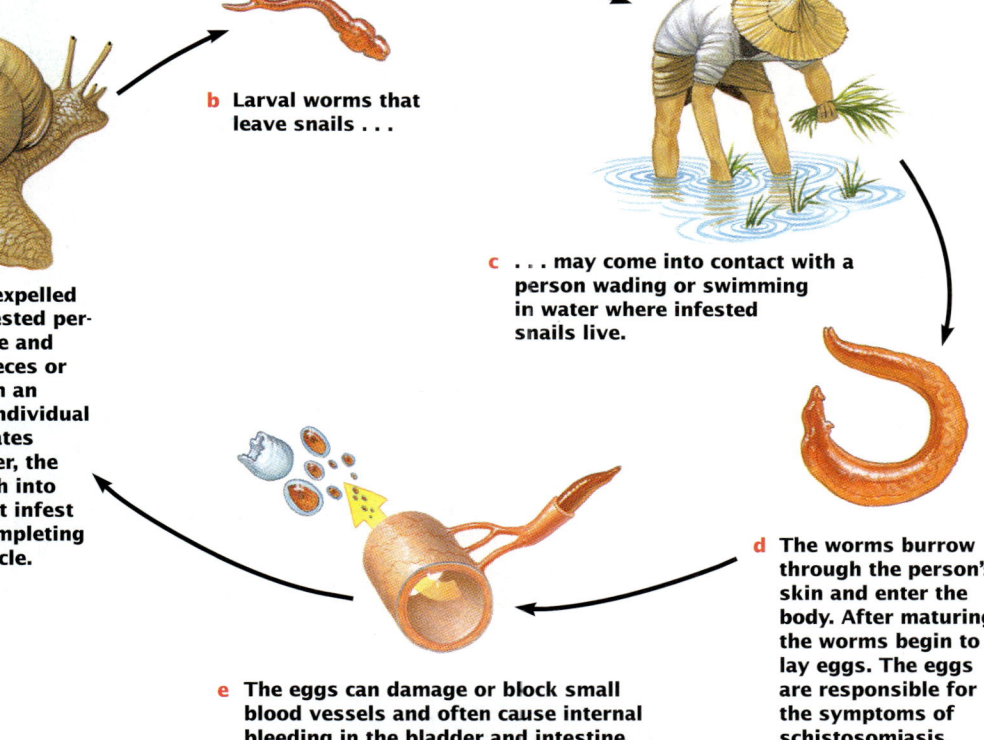

Figure 25-4

a **After hatching, *Schistosoma* larvae invade freshwater snails.**

b **Larval worms that leave snails . . .**

c **. . . may come into contact with a person wading or swimming in water where infested snails live.**

d **The worms burrow through the person's skin and enter the body. After maturing, the worms begin to lay eggs. The eggs are responsible for the symptoms of schistosomiasis.**

e **The eggs can damage or block small blood vessels and often cause internal bleeding in the bladder and intestine.**

Eggs are expelled in the infested person's urine and feces. If feces or urine from an infested individual contaminates fresh water, the eggs hatch into larvae that infest snails, completing the life cycle.

483

Visual Strategy Figure 25-6

● **Analyzing Information**
Ask students to study the diagram and identify the points in the tapeworm's life cycle where the cycle of infection can be broken. Ask students what public health measures could be taken at each point to reduce tapeworm infection in humans and livestock. *(Students may suggest the use of drugs to kill the tapeworms that have infected humans and cattle, adequate sewage treatment to ensure that eggs are not spread by human feces, and education efforts to inform people that meat must be thoroughly cooked.)*

Figure 25-5
The hooks on the head of the beef tapeworm can be thrust out and buried in the wall of its host's intestine.

In addition to *Schistosoma*, parasitic flatworms include flukes, which attack the liver or lungs, and tapeworms. The head of the beef tapeworm, which commonly infests humans, is shown in **Figure 25-5**. These parasites can grow to more than 10 m (30 ft) in length. Follow the tapeworm's life cycle in **Figure 25-6**.

Tapeworms are so specialized for a parasitic way of life that they do not have a digestive system. Nutrients from the host's digested food are absorbed directly through the tapeworm's skin. The beef tapeworm often causes no symptoms, but it may cause pain, discomfort, nausea, and abdominal swelling.

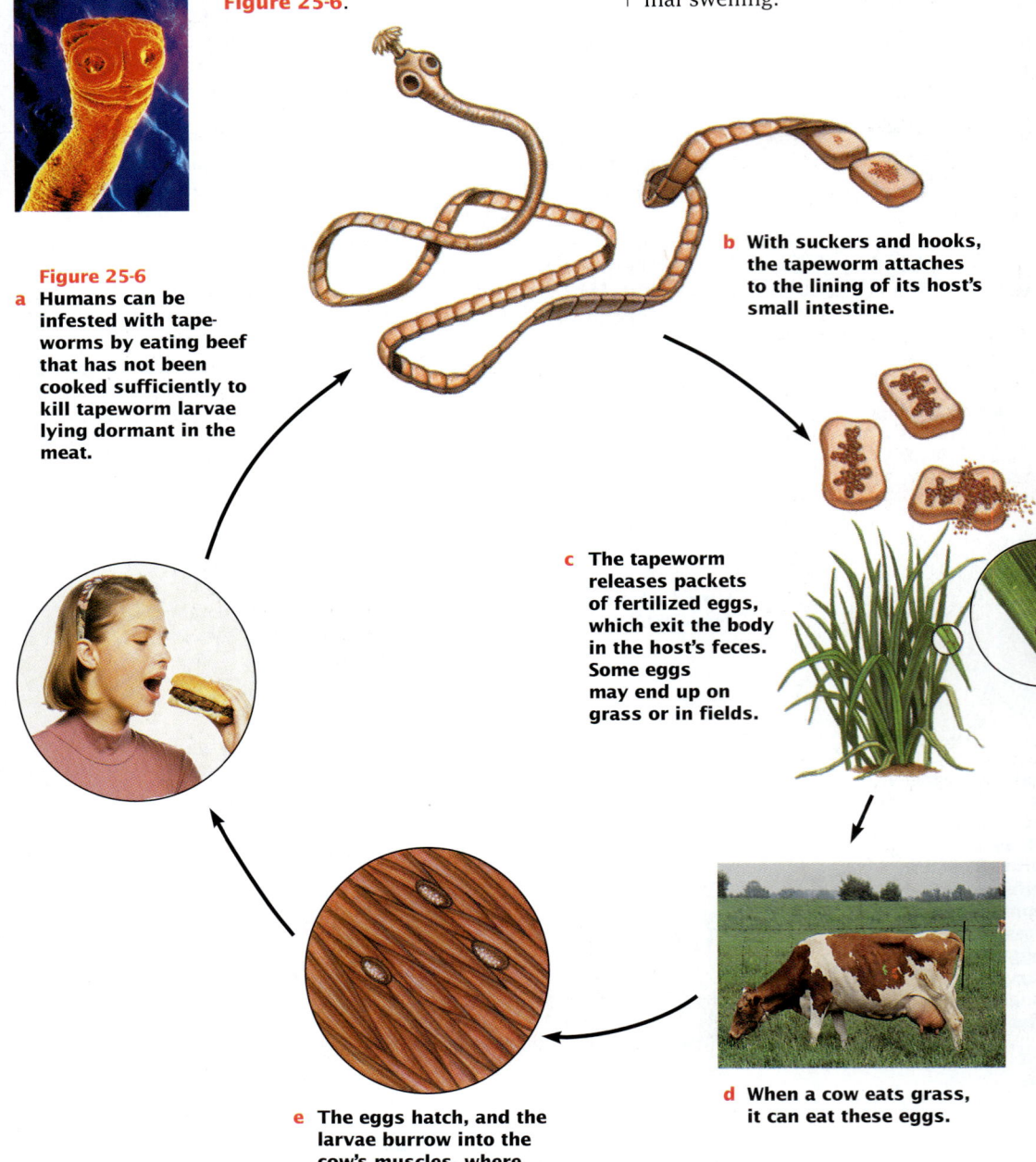

Figure 25-6
a **Humans can be infested with tapeworms by eating beef that has not been cooked sufficiently to kill tapeworm larvae lying dormant in the meat.**

b **With suckers and hooks, the tapeworm attaches to the lining of its host's small intestine.**

c **The tapeworm releases packets of fertilized eggs, which exit the body in the host's feces. Some eggs may end up on grass or in fields.**

d **When a cow eats grass, it can eat these eggs.**

e **The eggs hatch, and the larvae burrow into the cow's muscles, where they become dormant.**

484

Matter of Fact: Surfactants Against Worms

In laboratory tests, soaplike molecules have been used to destroy the surface membrane of the rat tapeworm. Without the surface membrane, the tapeworm has no protection against the digestive enzymes of the rat. In limited tests, scientists found that the compound affected the tapeworms but not the rats. The surfactant study may lead to new, inexpensive deworming medicines that could be made available to developing countries.

Roundworms

Roundworms, or nematodes (phylum Nematoda), are extremely abundant; a single spadeful of soil can contain more than 1 million individual nematodes. The great abundance of nematodes was illustrated by one very patient zoologist who counted 90,000 nematodes in a single rotting apple. One specimen of nematode is found only in the damp felt coasters under beer mugs in a few eastern European towns. Now *that* is specialization. Nematodes also occur in all aquatic environments and in the bodies of plants and animals as parasites. As shown in **Figure 25-7**, roundworms are shaped like thick threads that are tapered at both ends. In fact, without a microscope it is difficult to tell one end from the other. The name *roundworm* comes from the fact that the body is circular when viewed in cross section.

The sexes are separate in nearly all roundworms, and the males are often smaller than the females. After mating, the female secretes a tough case around each fertilized egg and deposits the eggs in the environment, where development takes place. Many parasitic roundworms have complex life cycles, regularly passing from one host to another.

Nematodes play an important role in research on genetics and development. Scientists have learned the complete cellular structure for the nematode *Caenorhabditis elegans*, which has only about 1,000 cells. In addition, scientists are close to identifying the locations of all of the approximately 10,000 genes of this nematode.

Some nematodes cause disease

Nematodes are known to infest virtually all kinds of animals and plants, and some cause millions of dollars of damage each year to livestock and crops. For instance, puppies and adult dogs often must be "wormed," or treated with drugs to kill parasitic nematodes such as the intestinal roundworm *Ascaris*. Heavy infestations of *Ascaris* can be fatal to puppies. *Ascaris* also infests livestock and humans. **Figure 25-8** shows *Ascaris suum*, which infests pigs.

Figure 25-7
Although most nematodes are similar in form, they vary in size. The smallest are about 0.2 mm (0.008 in.) long. This photograph of a predatory nematode has been magnified more than 2,000 times.

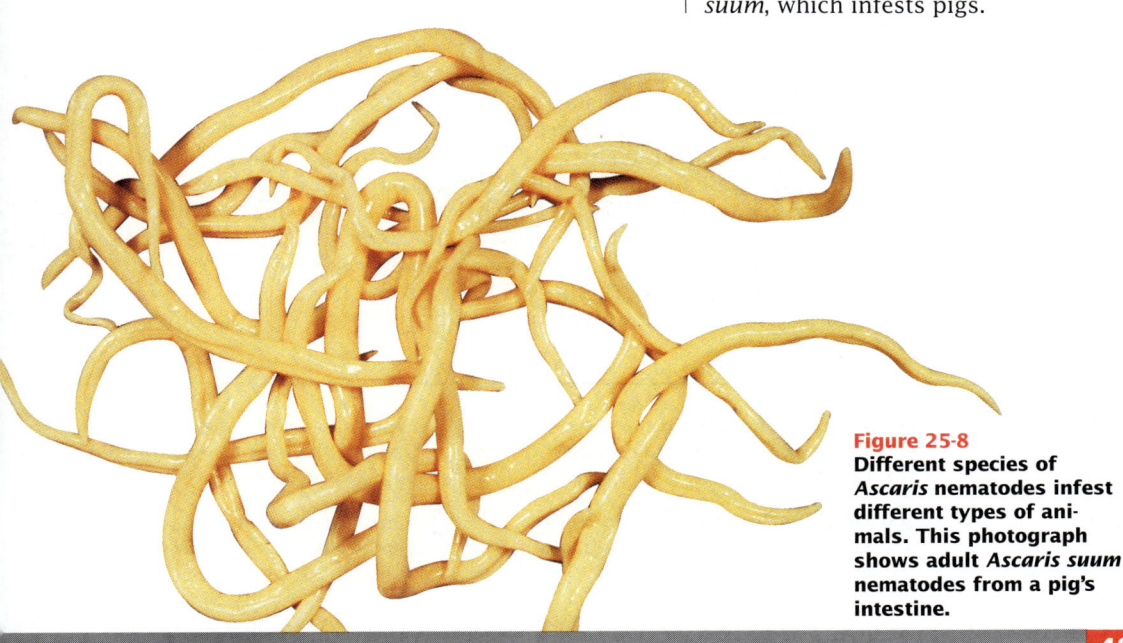

Figure 25-8
Different species of *Ascaris* nematodes infest different types of animals. This photograph shows adult *Ascaris suum* nematodes from a pig's intestine.

485

Agriculture Connection
Resistant Seeds
When you buy seeds or plants for your garden, they are sometimes marked with the letters *V, F,* or *N.* The *N* stands for "nematode resistant." Since some species of nematodes can cause serious crop damage, it is sometimes necessary to breed plants that are resistant to them. (*V* stands for virus resistant, and *F* stands for fungus resistant.)

Dog Parasites
■ **Recognizing Relationships**
Show students a preserved dog heart that is infected with heartworms. Depending on the number of worms living in a dog's heart, the disease may become life threatening. Veterinarians now prescribe medication that protects dogs from heartworms, roundworms, hookworms, and whipworms. Heartworm prevention is administered on a regular schedule according to the dog's body weight. Ask students to discuss how dog behaviors and other circumstances make them vulnerable to worm parasites. (*Answers will vary but might include the following: sniffing, eating, or chewing contaminated objects; exposure to insect carriers such as fleas and mosquitoes; and walking in contaminated soil.*) Encourage students to call a local veterinarian for answers to specific questions about pet parasites.

Worms
● **Organizing Information**
Have students prepare a **Graphic Organizer**, similar to the one at the bottom of this page, that identifies the characteristics that flatworms and roundworms have in common and the characteristics that are unique to each group.

Graphic Organizer

Use the following graphic organizer with the teaching strategy **Worms** on page 485.

Characteristics	Flatworms	Roundworms
Live in damp or wet environment	yes	yes
Capable of asexual reproduction	yes	no
Most are hermaphrodites	yes	no
Most are parasites	yes	yes
Body appears circular in cross section	no	yes

Key to Strategies
● **Understanding Concepts (Tier I)**
■ **Applying Information (Tier II)**
▲ **Critical Thinking (Tier III)**

Health Connection

Hookworms

Hookworms are parasitic roundworms that infect the host by burrowing through the skin. Once inside the host, they travel to the lungs, up the trachea, and down the esophagus after they are swallowed. The larvae then pass through the stomach and into the intestine, where they mature, attach to the wall, and suck blood. Eggs shed in the feces can contaminate the soil, upon which another potential host may walk. In the United States, education, public health laws, and sewage treatment systems have greatly reduced the incidence of intestinal parasites in humans. Hookworms are still a common health threat to dogs, but treatment and prevention are available through veterinarians.

Phase Three
Assessment Options

Closure

● **Organizing Data**

Have students make study cards that list the major characteristics of each of the invertebrate groups discussed in this section. Students should make drawings to illustrate the characteristics for each group.

SECTION REVIEW

Assign the *Section Review.*

Reteaching

Ask students to describe the life cycle of each of the following: sponges, cnidarians, flatworms, and roundworms.

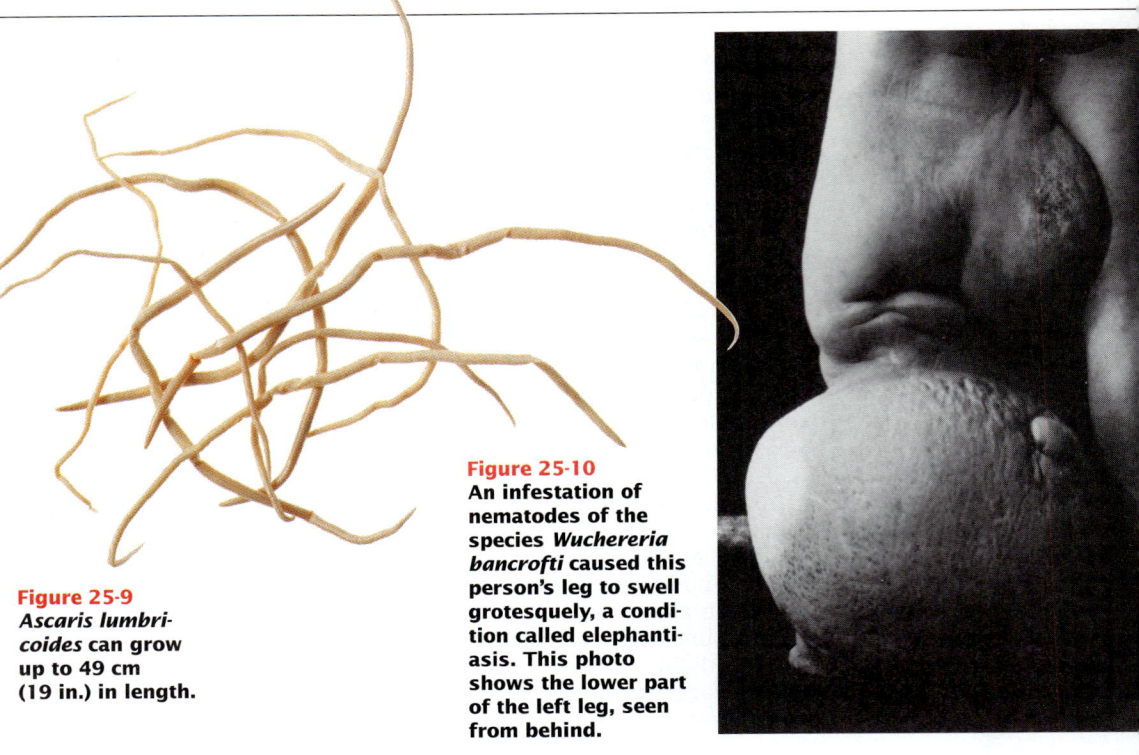

Figure 25-9
Ascaris lumbricoides can grow up to 49 cm (19 in.) in length.

Figure 25-10
An infestation of nematodes of the species *Wuchereria bancrofti* caused this person's leg to swell grotesquely, a condition called elephantiasis. This photo shows the lower part of the left leg, seen from behind.

About 50 species of nematodes parasitize humans. Almost 1 billion people are infested with the nematode *Ascaris lumbricoides*, shown in **Figure 25-9**. This nematode spends its adult life inside the intestine of its host. Large numbers of adult nematodes in the intestine can cause pain and intestinal blockage. Because juvenile worms bore through the tissues of the lungs, an infestation of *A. lumbricoides* can also lead to pneumonia.

Each day a female *A. lumbricoides* lays as many as 200,000 eggs, which pass out of her host in feces. These eggs are very durable and can survive in the soil for 10 years. The life cycle continues when a person consumes the nematode's eggs. This occurs when uncooked vegetables are eaten or when dirty hands are not properly washed before meals. *Ascaris lumbricoides* infections occur mainly in areas where sanitary facilities are poor or where human feces are used as fertilizer.

In tropical regions of Africa and Asia the nematode *Wuchereria bancrofti* causes the disease known as filariasis *(fihl uh REYE uh sihs)*. These nematodes are parasites of the circulatory system. They can clog lymphatic vessels, causing fluid accumulation, skin thickening, and extreme swelling. This condition, known as elephantiasis, is shown in **Figure 25-10**. Filariasis is transmitted by mosquitoes.

SECTION REVIEW

❶ Distinguish between the ways in which sponges and cnidarians capture food.

❷ Diagram the life cycle of a cnidarian that goes through polyp and medusa stages.

❸ Explain two ways that infestations of the beef tapeworm could be prevented.

❹ Name two examples of parasitic nematodes that can infest humans.

ANSWERS TO
SECTION REVIEW

❶ Sponges filter nutrients from water passing through their body. Cnidarians capture food with tentacles armed with nematocysts.

❷ Diagrams will vary but should include the stages outlined in Figure 25-3 on page 481.

❸ Students should suggest eating beef that has been thoroughly cooked, and ensuring proper sewage treatment and disposal.

❹ *Ascaris lumbricoides* and *Wuchereria bancrofti* can infest humans.

Chances are good that you have never seen a nematode or flatworm. In this section, you will learn about mollusks, annelids, and arthropods, three groups of animals that are probably more familiar to you. You can find members of these groups crawling in a field or garden, burrowing in the soil, flying overhead, or sitting on your plate as part of your evening meal.

25-2
Mollusks, Annelids, and Arthropods

OBJECTIVES

1 Identify the three main classes of mollusks.

2 Summarize the evolutionary advantages of segmentation.

3 Describe two ways annelids affect humans.

4 List five kinds of arthropods.

Mollusks

If you visit a shop where fresh seafood is sold, look for some of these mollusks: clams, scallops, mussels, squids, octopuses, and oysters. With more than 50,000 living species, the phylum Mollusca is the second largest animal phylum on Earth, exceeded in size only by the phylum Arthropoda, which includes insects, spiders, and crustaceans. **Figure 25-11** shows two types of mollusks that are often eaten by humans. A shell is a feature of many mollusks. The shell (or shells) provides protection for the body and a solid structure for muscle attach-ment. The rest of the body is soft; in fact, the name *mollusk* comes from the Latin word for "soft." All mollusk shells are lined with and secreted by a fleshy fold of tissue called the mantle. Another characteristic of mollusks is a muscular foot. Among mollusks, the foot has evolved to perform several functions, including locomotion and burrowing.

Mollusks were one of the earliest groups of animals to evolve efficient excretory organs, the nephridia. **Nephridia** *(nee FRIHD ee uh)* are small tubules that collect wastes from the body fluids and discharge them from the body.

Figure 25-11
Scallops (above) and razor clams (right) are two examples of aquatic mollusks.

487

Phase One
Preparation

Scheduling
See the **Lesson Planning Guide** on pages 477A and 477B for lecture, classwork, and assignment options for Section 25-2.

Phase Two
Teaching Strategies

Mollusks on the Menu
■ **Recognizing Relationships**
Ask managers of several local seafood restaurants to donate copies of their menus to your class. Ask students to identify which of the dishes contain mollusks. *(Possible examples include clams, oysters, scallops, and mussels. In some regions, students may also find abalone, octopus, and squid or calamari.)* Menus at some restaurants might include a variety of terrestrial snail called escargot. Ask students to identify menu items that are arthropods. *(Possible examples include shrimp, crabs, lobsters, and crayfish.)*

Videodisc Resources

Holt Biology Videodiscs
Lesson 25-2: Mollusks, Annelids, and Arthropods

Key to Strategies
● Understanding Concepts (Tier I)
■ Applying Information (Tier II)
▲ Critical Thinking (Tier III)

Active READING

Technique: Reading Organizer
Have students use the Compare/Contrast Matrix worksheet to organize the characteristics of mollusks and annelids. This worksheet can be found in Reading Strategies Worksheets in Holt BioSources Teaching Resources CD-ROM.

Demonstration

● **Comparing Structures**
Materials: a variety of shells of gastropods and bivalves, cuttlebones
Have students bring mollusk shells to class, and add shells that you have collected. Be sure that "cuttlebones" and ordinary garden-snail shells are included. Explain that the cuttlebone is a remnant shell from a cuttlefish, which is a type of cephalopod. Assign students to cooperative groups, and provide each group with an assortment of shells. Have students work together to make a dichotomous key for classifying their shells. Have each group prepare a report explaining how their key reflects what they have learned about the different types of mollusks.

Geology Connection

Fossils in Limestone
Provide students with pieces of fossiliferous limestone. Point out the mollusk shapes embedded in the rock. Ask students to explain how the mollusks became part of the rock. (*The shells were deposited at the same time as the sediments.*)

Life/Work Skills

Finding Information

● **Interpreting Conclusions**

Studies indicate that octopuses can be trained and that they learn by observation. Have students use library references to research the latest findings on the learning abilities of octopuses.

Slugs and snails are gastropods
Slugs and snails, which you often see in a garden or aquarium, belong to the class Gastropoda. Gastropods are the most diverse group of mollusks. They are found in the ocean, in fresh water, and on land. Snails and slugs move by creeping along slowly on a muscular foot. The shell, when present, is often brightly colored and is usually coiled.

Just inside the mouth of gastropods and some other mollusks is a unique feeding organ called the **radula** (*RAJ oo lah*). The radula, shown in **Figure 25-12**, is a flexible structure that is covered by rows of teeth, like a carpenter's file. The radula is used to scrape free small particles of food. In some predatory mollusks, the radula is a sharp fang that is used to stab prey and inject venom.

Figure 25-12

a A snail's shell is made of layers of calcium carbonate. The shell forms a protective barrier against predators.

b This shows an enlargement of the surface of the radula. The radula consists primarily of chitin and is covered with rows of pointed, backward-curving teeth.

Oysters, mussels, clams, and scallops are bivalves
If you are a fan of oysters, mussels, scallops, or clam chowder, you have enjoyed the delicate taste of bivalves (class Bivalvia). Some of these animals are of great value, supporting commercial harvesting industries around the world.

Bivalves have two shells. Unlike other mollusks, bivalves feed by filtering small particles from the water. They lack a radula. Most bivalves are sedentary, and some, such as oysters and mussels, permanently attach themselves to hard surfaces as adults. The foot is wedge-shaped and is used for digging in sand or mud or for secreting tough attachment threads.

Squids, octopuses, and nautiluses are cephalopods
In contrast to the bivalves and gastropods, the cephalopods (class Cephalopoda) are active and can be fast swimmers. Squids, octopuses, and nautiluses are examples of cephalopods. *Tour of a Mollusk* on page 489 profiles one kind of octopus.

Cephalopods are mobile marine predators that are known for their well-developed nervous system. Their body form reflects their active habits. Except for nautiluses, cephalopods have reduced shells or no shell at all. The body of a cephalopod includes the head, tentacles or "arms," and a large, fleshy mantle. **Figure 25-13** shows an example of a cephalopod. The mantle

Figure 25-13
The California market squid is a mollusk that lives in the Pacific Ocean.

Multicultural Perspective: Shells
Mollusk shells have served many different functions in various cultures, especially as ornaments in jewelry and crafts. In addition to their usefulness as decorations, these shells have been used for several practical purposes. Phoenicians and Romans used murex sea snails to make a purple dye for coloring fabric. Native Americans carved large clamshells into wampum beads and used other shells as money. Filipinos cut thin placuna oyster shells to fit into wooden frames as window panes.

Mollusk

The white-spotted octopus is a bottom-dwelling mollusk found in tropical oceans. Unlike snails, clams, mussels, and most other familiar mollusks, octopuses have no external shell. All octopuses have eight arms.

Size
A large adult white-spotted octopus can be 1 m (39 in.) in total length, including the arms.

An ink sac produces dark ink that can be expelled to confuse enemies.

Octopuses swim by forcefully expelling water from the mantle cavity—a sort of jet propulsion.

Most mollusks have a large muscular foot that is used for burrowing or crawling. In cephalopods, the foot has been modified into numerous arms. The eight arms of an octopus have sucking disks for seizing prey such as crabs or other mollusks.

Habitat
White-spotted octopuses live on coral reefs, where they can find abundant food and places to hide. They are found in tropical waters worldwide.

Evolutionary Relationships
Octopuses belong to the class Cephalopoda. This group of about 600 species also includes squids and nautiluses. All cephalopods have many arms, which they use to capture prey.

489

Tour

Connection: *Chapter 15*

Beer Bottle Lairs
A species of octopus common to the Pacific coast was found to be inhabiting beer bottles in Puget Sound. Eight beer bottles were found, each containing an octopus of the species *Octopus rubescens*. In areas with few lair sights, human trash may contribute to an increase in population of the species. Ask students to discuss long-range effects this could have on the Puget Sound ecosystem.

Self-Defense
● **Identifying Functions**
Octopuses are preyed on by sea lions, seals, dogfish, larger octopuses, and humans. Fortunately, they have developed several highly effective defense mechanisms. Octopuses can expel a burst of water through their siphon and jet to safety. They can also release a cloud of dark, noxious ink through the siphon, which confuses the attacker. Octopuses have no bones, so they can squeeze into small crevices for shelter. They can change the color and texture of their skin for camouflage among rocks and coral. Some species have developed the coloration of poisonous animals; predators may mistake them for a harmful species and stay away. Octopuses have keen eyesight, which helps them see predators at great distances. If part of an octopus's tentacle is lost to a predator, it will grow back.

The Octopus's Reputation
▲ **Distinguishing Fact From Fiction**
Ask students to recall a fictional octopus, such as the wicked Ursula in Disney's version of *The Little Mermaid*. Some students may be familiar with Ian Fleming's short story "Octopussy," in which the character Major Dexter Smythe attempts to befriend a venomous octopus. To help students get a more realistic view of octopus behavior, have them read "Octopus Swan Song," an article in the October 1994 issue of *Sea Frontiers*.

An Earthworm Myth
■ **Analyzing Conclusions**
Tell students that earthworms were once thought to "rain down" from the skies during downpours, or "worm weather." Ask students to suggest a more likely reason why earthworms are often seen on streets and sidewalks during heavy rains. *(When water fills their burrows, earthworms are forced to the surface for air.)*

is thick and muscular. It covers the internal organs and a large mantle cavity. A tubelike siphon derived from the foot serves as an outlet for water leaving the mantle cavity. When the mantle muscles contract, water is rapidly forced out of the siphon, allowing these animals to move by what is essentially jet propulsion. This is the usual manner of movement in squids. Octopuses use this method of movement to escape predators.

Annelids: Segmented Worms

The 15,000 or so species of segmented worms (phylum Annelida) include earthworms, leeches, and a host of marine species such as tube worms, feather dusters, and the clam worm shown in **Figure 25-14**.

Figure 25-14
Each body segment of this clam worm, found on Long Island, New York, has lateral flaps that function as gills.

The segmented body of annelids has allowed the evolution of tremendous diversity in the phylum. Since the segments or groups of segments can be operated somewhat independently, different regions of the body can be specialized for different functions.

Such specializations include the suckers of leeches, localized reproductive organs in earthworms, and tube-secreting segments in certain marine worms. **Figure 25-15** describes some of the functions of the specialized segments in an earthworm.

Earthworms feed by sucking in soil and decaying matter. Organic material is digested, and wastes are eliminated as castings, smooth blobs of soil that you can see at the entrances to earthworm burrows. Charles Darwin calculated that a single earthworm could eat its own weight in soil every day. The action of earthworms is beneficial to plants because it breaks up and aerates the soil and because castings are rich in nutrients.

b Segments in one part of the worm can contract while those in another part elongate. Alternating contraction and elongation propel the earthworm forward.

Figure 25-15
Segmentation is a feature of annelids. The body of an earthworm can have more than 100 segments.

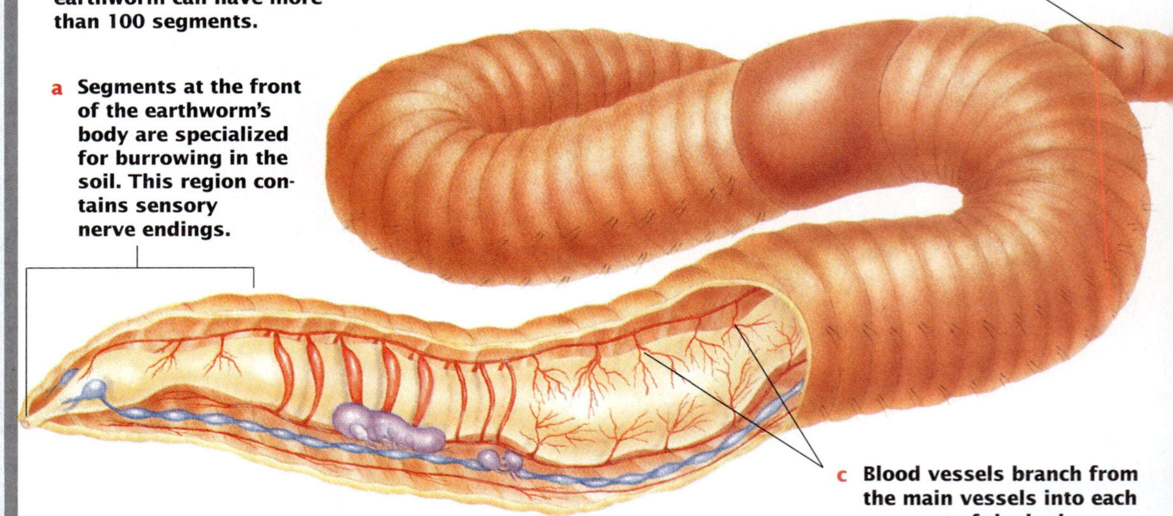

a Segments at the front of the earthworm's body are specialized for burrowing in the soil. This region contains sensory nerve endings.

c Blood vessels branch from the main vessels into each segment of the body.

Historical Perspective: Darwin's Earthworms

Charles Darwin was fascinated by earthworms. His last book was titled *The Formation of Vegetable Mould Through the Action of Worms*. Darwin calculated that 1 hectare (2.5 acres) of soil might contain 155,000 earthworms. These worms, he said, could bring 18 tons of soil to the surface in a year, and in 20 years they could build a new layer of soil 11 cm (3 in.) thick.

Figure 25-16
The body of this aquatic leech is segmented, just like the body of an earthworm.

Some leeches are parasitic annelids

Externally, leeches are distinct from the other annelids. The body is somewhat flattened and not quite as worm-like as an earthworm's body, as you can see in **Figure 25-16**. Some leeches are scavengers or predators. Many leech species are at least part-time parasites. They feed on other animals, usually vertebrates. Suckers on the front and back of the leech enable it to attach to its host.

Parasitic leeches use enzymes or three sharp, bladelike teeth to make an opening in the host's skin through which blood is sucked. Some leeches release proteins into the host that prevent blood from clotting and ending their meal. Scientists have isolated one of the proteins produced by leeches. This protein is being used in research on blood clotting. Another leech protein has been effective in treating lung cancer. Some leeches secrete a local anesthetic, so the host is not even aware that it is providing a meal for the leech.

For centuries, leeches were used to "bleed" sick patients because people believed that excess blood caused disease. This practice fell out of favor when scientists showed that viruses, bacteria, and other microorganisms cause disease. Recently leeches have made a medical comeback. The large blood-sucking leech *Hirudo medicinalis* is used by modern physicians to liquefy blood clots and to remove blood from bruises and severely damaged tissue.

Arthropods: The Most Abundant Animals

Arthropods (phylum Arthropoda) dominate virtually all habitats, both in numbers of individuals and in numbers of species. About 1 million species of arthropods have been described. Some specialists believe that as many as 30 million species still remain to be discovered.

As you learned in Chapter 23, arthropods have a segmented body that is covered by an exoskeleton of chitin. Most important, they have jointed appendages. The phylum Arthropoda includes a variety of familiar animals, including those shown in **Figure 25-17**. Spiders, insects, centipedes, scorpions, shrimp, crabs, and lobsters all belong to the phylum

Figure 25-17
a The praying mantis (above) and honeybees (right) are beneficial insects that are common throughout the United States.

b This tarantula is native to Asia.

491

Matter of Fact: Eye of a Fly

The common housefly has approximately 4,000 image-forming elements in each eye. These elements are called *ommatidia.* Each one consists of a lens or cornea, a crystalline cone, and a sensory region. A fly's eyes are excellent motion detectors.

Figure 25-18
Beetles, butterflies, ticks, scorpions, and centipedes are all arthropods.

Arthropoda. Stop for a moment to consider the many ways in which arthropods affect our lives. Lobsters, crabs, and shrimp are sources of food. Some insects are serious pests of food crops and cause millions of dollars in damage each year. Other insects are extremely beneficial as pollinators of crop plants. Still others are parasites. Malaria and African sleeping sickness, two of the world's most serious diseases, are transmitted by insects.

Look at the arthropods shown in **Figure 25-18**. These photos show just a tiny sample of the variety within this phylum. You will read much more about arthropods and their importance to humans in Chapter 26.

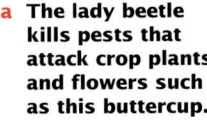

a The lady beetle kills pests that attack crop plants and flowers such as this buttercup.

b The giant centipede is found in Texas.

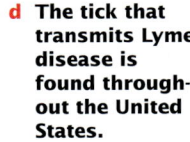

c The scorpion *Pandinus imperoitor* is found in Africa.

d The tick that transmits Lyme disease is found throughout the United States.

e Most monarch butterflies live in the United States during the summer and migrate to Mexico or South America in the winter.

SECTION REVIEW

1 Name the major classes of mollusks. Give an example of each.

2 What are the advantages of a segmented body?

3 Why would the fertility of a farmer's field decline if all of the earthworms were removed from the soil?

4 Name five different kinds of arthropods.

Echinoderms and chordates belong to a fundamentally different evolutionary line from the annelids, mollusks, and arthropods. Echinoderms and chordates are deuterostomes, which are distinguished from the groups you studied in the other sections of this chapter by differences in their embryonic development.

Phase One
Preparation

Scheduling
See the **Lesson Planning Guide** on pages 477A and 477B for lecture, classwork, and assignment options for Section 25-3.

25-3 Echinoderms and Chordates

OBJECTIVES

1 Identify three kinds of echinoderms.

2 List two characteristics of animals in the phylum Echinodermata.

3 Contrast the three subphyla of chordates.

Echinoderms: Sea Stars and Their Relatives

Sea stars, sea cucumbers, sand dollars, and sea urchins are echinoderms (phylum Echinodermata). As adults, nearly all echinoderms show a five-part radial symmetry: parts of the body radiate from its center like the arms of a five-pointed star, as shown in **Figure 25-19**. The sand dollar shown in **Figure 25-20** also has five-part body symmetry, but it is less obvious.

In addition to radial symmetry, echinoderms have a **water vascular system**. As you learned in Chapter 23, the water vascular system is a complex arrangement of fluid-filled tubes that operates the tube feet on the animal's lower surface. The water vascular system functions in locomotion, feeding, and gas exchange.

Echinoderms have no excretory organs and thus have no efficient means of regulating water balance. That is one reason echinoderms are restricted to marine habitats. Most of these animals obtain oxygen by diffusion through thin parts of the body surface or through the walls of the tube feet. Internal distribution of oxygen and nutrients occurs mainly by circulation of fluid within the coelom.

Figure 25-19
Many sea stars are brightly colored. This stubby-armed sea star is found in New Guinea's Mandang Harbor.

Figure 25-20
This endoskeleton of a sand dollar shows the five-part radial symmetry found in all echinoderms.

Phase Two
Teaching Strategies

Swimming Stars
● **Observing Functions**
Students often assume that a sea star is always rigid. Show students a nature video, possibly one filmed at a coral reef, that contains footage of sea stars swimming and feeding. Point out the grace and flexibility of sea stars.

493

Videodisc Resources

Holt Biology Videodiscs
Lesson 25-3: Echinoderms and Chordates

Active READING

Technique: Reading Organizer

Have students work individually or in pairs to create a reading organizer that describes the three subphyla that make up the phylum Chordata.

Phase Three
Assessment Options

Closure

■ **Relating Concepts**

Use the following Active Reading exercise to review the concepts in this chapter.

Active READING

Technique: K-W-L

Tell students to return to their "**W**ant to know lists" from the Active Reading exercise on page 479. Have them place check marks next to questions that they are now able to answer. Students should finish by making a list of what they have **L**earned. Conclude by asking students the following questions:

• Which questions are still unanswered?
• What new questions do you have?

Have students use library references to answer any remaining questions.

SECTION REVIEW

Assign the *Section Review.*

Reteaching

Point out that although most chordates are vertebrates, tunicates and lancelets are invertebrates. Ask students why vertebrates are classified with lancelets and tunicates. *(They have a notochord, a dorsal nerve cord, a postanal tail, and pharyngeal slits.)*

Chordates

Like echinoderms, chordates (members of the phylum Chordata) are deuterostomes. Recall that all chordates share four features: a notochord, a dorsal nerve cord, a post-anal tail, and pharyngeal slits. Three subphyla make up the phylum Chordata.

Tunicates lose some chordate characteristics

Most adult tunicates, or sea squirts (subphylum Urochordata), live attached to rocks or the sea floor, as shown in **Figure 25-21**. Like sponges, these tunicates obtain food by filtering particles of food from the water. They secrete a leathery or jellylike covering composed of a substance similar to cellulose. This outer body layer is known as a tunic, hence the name of the group. During development, urochordates go through a free-swimming larval stage. During this stage the four chordate features are apparent. Adult tunicates retain only the pharyngeal slits.

Figure 25-21
Unlike their larval form, these adult tunicates are not free-swimming.

Figure 25-22
Unlike tunicates, lancelets retain all of their chordate characteristics throughout their lives.

Lancelets retain their chordate features throughout their lives

Lancelets (subphylum Cephalochordata) are usually less than 5 cm (2 in.) long. **Figure 25-22** shows the lancelet *Branchiostoma*. Lancelets bury their tails in sand or mud and keep their heads exposed in the overlying water. As water enters the mouth, tentacles around the mouth exclude large particles. The water passes into the pharynx, where food is trapped in the mucus-covered lining. The water then exits through the pharyngeal slits.

Vertebrates have backbones

With 42,500 species, the vertebrates (subphylum Vertebrata) compose the largest and most successful group of chordates. Much of this success is due to the increased complexity of many organ systems and the internal skeleton. A distinguishing feature of the vertebrates is the vertebral column, for which the group was named. Fishes, amphibians, reptiles, birds, and mammals (including humans) are members of this very diverse subphylum.

SECTION REVIEW

❶ List three echinoderms.

❷ Describe two characteristics of echinoderms.

❸ What feature distinguishes the vertebrates from the other subphyla of chordates?

ANSWERS TO SECTION REVIEW

❶ Students may suggest sea stars, sand dollars, sea urchins, and sea cucumbers.

❷ Echinoderms have five-part radial symmetry and a water vascular system.

❸ Vertebrates have a vertebral column, or backbone.

Many bivalves are important sources of food for humans.

	Key Terms	Summary
25-1 **Sponges, Cnidarians, and Simple Worms** 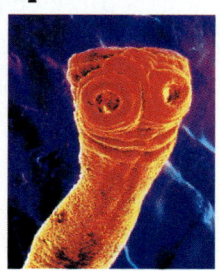 Structures on the head of this tapeworm allow it to attach to the intestinal wall of its host.	spicule (p. 479) nematocyst (p. 481) polyp (p. 481) medusa (p. 481) hermaphrodite (p. 483)	• Sponges live attached to rocks. They filter food from the water. • Jellyfish, hydras, corals, and sea anemones are cnidarians. Cnidarians are characterized by stinging nematocysts. • Many flatworms are parasites. Parasitic flatworms of humans include the beef tapeworm and *Schistosoma*, which causes the disease schistosomiasis. • Roundworms, or nematodes, are among the most abundant organisms. Some nematodes are parasites.
25-2 **Mollusks, Annelids, and Arthropods**  Snails belong to the class Gastropoda, one of the three major groups of mollusks.	nephridium (p. 487) radula (p. 488)	• Clams, mussels, snails, slugs, octopuses, and squids are mollusks. • Most mollusks have a protective shell and feed by using a rasping structure called a radula. • The three main classes of mollusks are Gastropoda, Bivalvia, and Cephalopoda. • Earthworms, leeches, and certain marine worms belong to the phylum Annelida, the segmented worms. • Most of the known species of animals are arthropods.
25-3 **Echinoderms and Chordates** 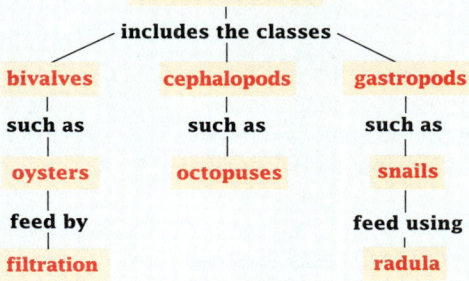 This sea star is an echinoderm. Like you, sea stars are deuterostomes.	water vascular system (p. 493)	• Echinoderms and chordates are deuterostomes. • Echinoderms have a five-part radial symmetry. They also have a water vascular system that operates their tube feet. • The three main groups of chordates are tunicates, lancelets, and vertebrates. You are a vertebrate.

Alternative Assessment

Divide students into three groups to represent each section of this chapter. Then divide each group into pairs of students. Have each pair of students make up questions of varying levels of difficulty for a trivia game. Play the game as a review using the students' questions.

Portfolio Assessment

Portfolio Assessment on page T39 provides options for building and evaluating student portfolios. Students and teachers can select items from the areas listed on page T39 for inclusion in a portfolio.

A N S W E R TO CONCEPT MAP

The following is one possible answer to the Relating Concepts exercise on page 496.

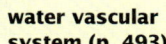

Phylum Mollusca

— includes the classes —

bivalves   cephalopods   gastropods

such as   such as   such as

oysters   octopuses   snails

feed by   feed using

filtration   radula

Understanding Vocabulary

1. a. attached
   b. *Wuchereria*
   c. segmented
2. a. Sponges belong to the phylum Porifera, not Cnidaria.
   b. A planarian belongs to the phylum Platyhelminthes, not Mollusca.
   c. Lancelets are not worms.

Understanding Concepts

3. Concept map answer is on page 495.
4. The mobile larvae are free to disperse to new habitats.
5. Both are aquatic. Sponges spend their adult life attached to a hard surface. Adult cnidarians are free-swimming. A sponge's body is perforated by holes that lead to an inner water chamber. Cnidarians have a gut with one opening to the outside.
6. During the polyp stage of the life cycle, the cnidarian is attached to a solid surface. The polyp stage of some cnidarians produces free-swimming medusas, or jellyfish, that drift with the water currents and release sperm and eggs.
7. Nematocysts are discharged and pierce the swimmer's skin. In the skin, they release a toxin that causes irritation.
8. Beef tapeworm larva have a dormant stage in the muscle tissue of cattle. Dormant tapeworm larvae could infect a person who eats the meat.
9. Answers will vary but might include specialized segments for burrowing.
10. Students might suggest sewage treatment or elimination of the snails. People could wear protective gear such as wading boots or avoid swimming in infected areas.
11.

Cephalopods	No	Aquatic	Octopuses
Gastropods	Usually	Aquatic and land	Snails
Bivalves	Yes, 2	Aquatic	Razor clam

Understanding Vocabulary

1. For each set of terms, complete the analogy.
   a. medusa : free-floating :: polyp : ____
   b. schistosomiasis : *Schistosoma* :: filariasis : ____
   c. flatworms : unsegmented :: annelids : ____
2. For each list of terms, identify the one that does not fit the pattern and explain why.
   a. coral, jellyfish, sea anemone, sponge
   b. octopus, planarian, scallop, snail
   c. leech, *Ascaris*, *Schistosoma*, lancelet

Understanding Concepts

3. **Relating Concepts** Construct a concept map that identifies and describes the characteristics of the three main classes of mollusks. Try to include the following terms in your concept map: phylum Mollusca, bivalves, cephalopods, gastropods, radula, oysters, octopuses, snails, and filtration.
4. **Inferring Conclusions** Considering that an adult sponge does not move from place to place, how can a population of sponges move to a different area?
5. **Comparing Structures** How are the adult stages of sponges and sea anemones similar? How are they different?
6. **Comparing Structures** How do the polyp stage and the medusa stage of the cnidarian life cycle differ?
7. **Identifying Structures** When a swimmer is stung by a jellyfish, what causes the pain felt by the swimmer?
8. **Recognizing Relationships** Explain how eating an inadequately cooked hamburger or steak puts you at risk of infestation by the beef tapeworm.
9. **Identifying Structures** Give an example of segmentation in an earthworm. How does the earthworm benefit from segmentation?

10. **Recognizing Relationships** Suggest two points at which the life cycle of *Schistosoma* could be interrupted, thus preventing infestations in humans. Describe the actions necessary to interrupt the life cycle at each point.
11. **Summarizing Information** Copy the following table onto a separate sheet of paper. Complete the table by filling in the blanks.

	Shell present?	Habitat	Example
Cephalopods		Aquatic	
Gastropods	Usually		
Bivalves			Razor clam

12. **Recognizing Relationships** How does an earthworm affect the soil? How do humans benefit from these activities?
13. **Summarizing Information** Describe two chemicals produced by leeches. What are the functions of these chemicals? How do doctors use leeches in modern medicine.
14. **Identifying Structures** Which of the following are not characteristics of arthropods: segmentation, endoskeleton of chitin, notochord, radial symmetry, jointed appendages?
15. **Identifying Structures** Describe the main characteristics of animals in the phylum Echinodermata.
16. **Organizing Information** What are the three subphyla in the phylum Chordata? What are the characteristics of each subphylum?
17. **Summarizing Information** If only adult forms were considered, would sea squirts be classified as chordates?
18. **BUILDING ON WHAT YOU HAVE LEARNED** In Chapter 20, you learned about alternation of generations in plants. Alternation of generations is also a characteristic of many members of the animal kingdom. Name one animal that exhibits alternation of generations, and describe the body form for each stage of its life cycle.

12. Earthworms aerate and fertilize the soil in which plants are grown, increasing crop yields.
13. Leeches produce proteins that can be used to prevent clotting and fight lung cancer. Physicians use them to liquefy and remove clotted blood from bruises and severely damaged tissues.
14. radial symmetry
15. water vascular system and radial symmetry
16. Urochordata—larvae that have all three chordate features, adults retain only the pharyngeal slits; Cephalochordata—marine organisms that retain all their chordate characteristics throughout their lives; Vertebrata—complex animals with organ systems, an internal skeleton, and a vertebral column
17. No, the notochord and nerve cord are missing.
18. Cnidarians have a polyp stage and a medusa stage. The polyp lives attached to a hard surface, and the medusa drifts or swims by pulsing its umbrella-shaped body.

Interpreting Graphics

19. Look at the graph below, which shows the number of cases of malaria and schistosomiasis in four areas.

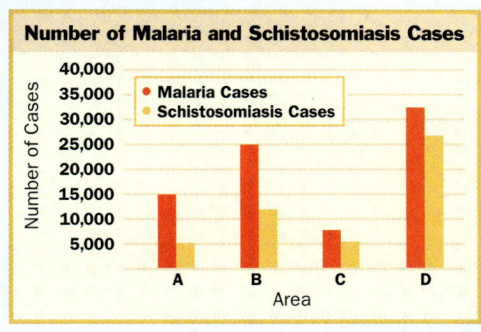

Number of Malaria and Schistosomiasis Cases

Which of the following statements is best supported by the data?

a. Malaria and schistosomiasis are caused by the same organism.
b. There are more cases of malaria in areas that have few cases of schistosomiasis.
c. Malaria cases outnumber schistosomiasis cases in each area.
d. Spraying for mosquitoes would reduce the number of cases of schistosomiasis.

Reviewing Themes

20. *Interdependence*
Explain how the life cycle of *Schistosoma* is dependent on snails.

21. *Homeostasis and Stability*
What are nephridia? What function do they perform? How have they contributed to the ability of some mollusks to live on land?

Thinking Critically

22. **Distinguishing Relevant Information** All cephalopods are aquatic, while some gastropods are terrestrial. Which of the following statements could help explain this difference?

a. Cephalopods move by expelling water from their mantle cavity.
b. Both groups have nephridia
c. Gastropods often have a shell.
d. Cephalopods have much larger brains than do gastropods.

Explain your answer.

Life/Work Skills

23. **Communicating** Many professionals, such as surgeons and cosmetologists, prefer to use natural sponges rather than manufactured ones. Find out how natural sponges are collected and prepared for use. Present an oral report of your findings to your class.

24. **Working Cooperatively** The class Turbellaria in the phylum Platyhelminthes contains about 3,000 different species. Form a group with three or four of your classmates. Each of you should research a different species of turbellarian. Draw accurate, color pictures of the species. Find out the animal's common and scientific names, its habitat, the part of the world in which it lives, how it feeds and reproduces, and how it protects itself from predators. Present your work to your class.

Activities and Projects

25. **Economics Connection** Use library references to find out about the economic importance of mollusks. Research the importance of mollusks as food. Also investigate the economic impact of plant destruction caused by snails. Investigate the uses of shells and the economic importance of shell collecting. Prepare a written report of your findings.

26. **Art Connection** Many people collect shells as a hobby. Ask friends and relatives if they have a shell collection that you can see. Many natural history museums and aquariums have extensive shell collections. If you cannot see a shell collection, consult a field guide to shells or a reference such as *The LaRousse Guide to Shells of the World*, by A.P.H. Oliver. Select five of your favorite shells. Make life-sized color drawings of each shell. Under each drawing, give the common and scientific name of the mollusk, its habitat, and in what part of the world the mollusk lives. Share your drawings with your class.

Discovering Through Reading

27. Read the article "The Mussels' Message" by William Stolzenburg in *Nature Conservancy*, November/December 1992, pages 17–23. What effect did building a dam on the Tennessee River have on mussel populations in Muscle Shoals?

24. Results will vary depending on the species selected. Students should discover that most marine turbellarians are very colorful and well adapted to their environment.

Activities and Projects

25. Mollusks such as oysters, clams, mussels, squids, and octopuses are important food sources for humans and other animals. An infestation of snails can quickly destroy a field of food crops. Mollusk shells are used to make jewelry and other decorative items.

26. Reports and drawings will vary depending on the species selected.

Discovering Through Reading

27. The dam buried the mussels' gravel beds under deep, cold water and smothering silt. Only 30 of the area's original 63 species still survive.

Interpreting Graphics

19. c

Reviewing Themes

20. A larval stage of *Schistosoma* involves freshwater snails.

21. Nephridia are small tubes that collect and discharge waste while conserving fluids. This efficient excretory organ reduces the amount of water needed to eliminate wastes.

Thinking Critically

22. a; Cephalopods depend on water for movement.

Life/Work Skills

23. Reports will vary. Natural sponges are collected from shallow marine waters and allowed to dry naturally. They are cleaned, sorted, sterilized if necessary, and sold for distribution.

Objectives

- Explain how scientists can use a single species as an indicator of an environment's health.
- Describe the types of information that an indicator species can reveal.
- Discuss the techniques researchers use to track animals in their natural habitat.

Become a Birdwatcher

■ **Developing Skills**

The number and diversity of birds in a community are usually good indicators of the surrounding environment's health. Help students develop skills that will increase their awareness of their community's birds and natural habitats by encouraging them to participate in one or more of the following activities:

- If possible, make arrangements with colleagues or parent volunteers to build bird feeders, birdhouses, and nest boxes. Have students find publications that include dimensions and diagrams, or have them design their own plans and specifications.
- Have students set up bird feeders or birdhouses in a location that can be easily observed. Instruct students to visit these sites on a weekly basis and to document the activities in an observation log. Information may include the number and type of birds that visit the sites.
- Plan a class trip to a nearby park or wildlife refuge to observe birds in their natural habitat. Teach students how to use field guides to identify local and migratory species. Have students develop a list of species that live in or visit their area, and instruct them to mark down sitings as they occur.
- Have students contact the local or regional office of the National Audubon Society for information about the organization's migratory-bird campaign, "Birds in Balance: International Action to Save Bird Habitat." Visit the Audubon Society's web site at http://www.audubon.org. for more information.

Can One Species Tell All?

Researchers sometimes use a single species to determine the health of an entire ecosystem. Studying a single species is convenient and relatively inexpensive, and it can give scientists valuable information about what is happening in an ecosystem.

The golden-cheeked warbler is just one of many endangered species whose existence is threatened by habitat destruction.

Using Indicator Species

A single species, called an indicator species, can provide an enormous amount of information about an ecosystem. Careful observation of the species' characteristics, including population size, appearance, behavior, reproductive health, and feeding habits, can help scientists evaluate the overall health of the ecosystem.

Ecosystems are sometimes exposed to stressful changes, such as climate shifts, immigration of new species, pollution, and deforestation. The response of the indicator species to these changes can be used to predict how other species will react and what long-term effects may result.

Predictors of Environmental Health

Consider Buchman's warbler, a migratory songbird that once made its summer home throughout the southeastern United States. The warblers used the forests in Cuba as their winter nesting site. Several decades ago, these forests were destroyed in order to plant sugar cane. No Buchman's warbler has been seen since the 1960s, and the species is assumed to be extinct. Is the fate of the Buchman's warbler an early predictor of the fate of other songbirds?

From the 1960s to the 1980s, the number of migratory songbirds in the United States decreased by 50 percent due to loss of habitat. These birds spend the winter months in tropical forests extending from Mexico to Argentina. If tropical forests continue to be logged, some experts think these forests may vanish in the next 50 years. With this habitat destruction, are the more than 250 species of songbirds facing the same fate as the Buchman's warbler?

Bioindicators Point to Pollution

Species that are used to predict changes for an entire ecosystem are called bioindicators. Samples taken from these species can be analyzed for levels of pollution, diversity, reproductive health, and disease.

Pollutants appear to be harming vertebrates worldwide. A growing concern among scientists is the presence of chemicals in the environment that mimic hormones. A large number of substances have been suggested as possible sources of these chemicals, including certain adhesives, plastics,

❶ Good characteristics for an indicator species include a large population size and an abundant habitat within the ecosystem. The choice of a species depends on the environment and on the specific problem being investigated. The list of characteristics would be specific to the particular area being studied.

❷ Researchers speculate that habitat destruction, pollution, and excessive exposure to ultraviolet radiation are all playing a role in the decline of amphibian populations in the wild. The loss of these organisms will be not only a loss of esthetically and behaviorally appealing creatures, but also an indicator of the environment's failing health.

❸ Answers will vary, but students should cite examples of environmental problems that exist in their community, such as rapid urban growth or declining air and water quality. They should explain how indicator species, such as birds, would be affected by the problems they described.

insecticides, and solvents. Animals that have been exposed to these agents—alligators in Florida, rainbow trout in Europe, and many others—show disrupted reproductive systems.

Human health may be affected by these pollutants too. Some studies suggest that sperm counts are declining worldwide and that incidences of endometriosis and testicular cancer are rising.

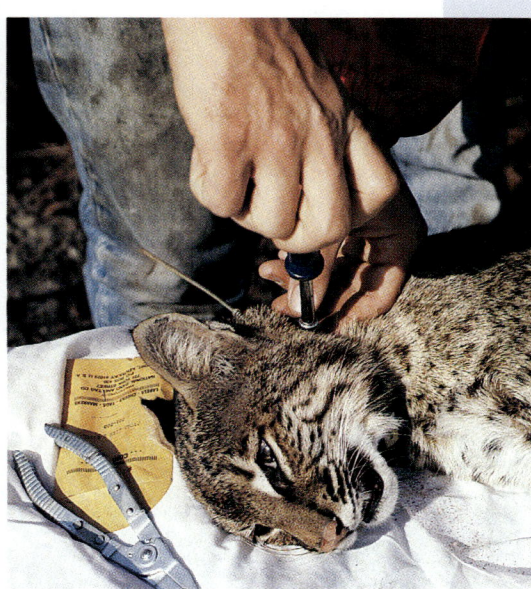

Technique

Electronic Identification for Animals

Scientists often track specific animals to study migration patterns or mating habits. This requires that the animals be tagged for identification. Identification tags, radio collars, metal bands, and tattoos are methods of tagging animals.

A new method of tagging involves implanting a small electronic device under an animal's skin. This device, called a transponder, is as small as a grain of rice, can't be broken or lost, and never needs new batteries. A computer chip inside the transponder contains an identification number that can be easily scanned, just like barcodes on products in a supermarket. Computers store information about the animal, allowing scientists to track its movements and behavior. Transponders have been used to track rattlesnakes in the American desert, hammerhead sharks in the Gulf of Mexico, and animals such as wolves and big cats that are reintroduced into environments where they once flourished.

Applications: tracking animal migrations in the wild, identifying lost pets, locating individual animals in wildlife preserves

Users: environmental scientists, wildlife trackers, and veterinarians

This sedated bobcat in Cumberland Islands, Georgia, is being fitted with a radio-tracking collar.

Analyzing the Issues

What makes a species a good indicator?

① List the characteristics that are desirable in an indicator species. Compare your ideas with those of other students in the class. Does everyone agree? Could some characteristics be desirable in some indicator species but detrimental in others?

Can information about an indicator species be applied to an entire ecosystem?

② Read "The Puzzle of Declining Amphibian Populations" by Andrew Blaustein in the April 1995 issue of *Scientific American*, pages 52–57. What possible effect on humans could the disappearance of frogs predict?

How can your community use an indicator species?

③ Consider the area in which you live. Do any potential environmental problems exist? Is your community recovering from an environmental threat? How could a local species provide information about the health of your ecosystem?

Can indicator species predict short-term damage?

④ Read "Red Tides" by Donald M. Anderson in the August 1994 issue of *Scientific American*, pages 62–68. What species would be a good indicator of the presence of organisms that cause red tide? Is it possible to stop red tides or prevent humans from being affected?

499

④ The red tide itself may be an indicator of future problems. Deaths among species such as mollusks and small, algae-consuming fish can be good bioindicators for the presence of the red tide. If the threat of red tide could be detected early, fishermen could avoid these regions. The complex causes of the red tide make it difficult to predict. Scientific studies have shown that red tides are increasing as coastal pollution worsens.

• Invite a representative from a local wildlife-rescue organization to class to discuss how to care for injured birds.

Measuring Public Awareness

▲ **Evaluating Opinions**

Have students design and conduct a survey that measures their community's awareness and gathers opinions about current environmental management strategies. Students should include questions that will reveal the community's understanding of important terminology, such as *biodiversity, threatened species, endangered species, indicator species,* and *extinct species.* Encourage students to seek out a variety of people from the community—from students of all ages to business people such as farmers, real estate developers, and home builders to senior citizens. Have students evaluate the results of their survey in a report that describes the community's understanding and awareness of the environment. Discuss with the class how the responses reflect the public's attitudes toward nature. Have students suggest ways to educate the public about important environmental issues.

References

1. Anderson, D. M. "Red Tides." *Scientific American,* August 1994, 62–68.
2. Brown, B. E. and J. C. Ogden. "Coral Bleaching." *Scientific American,* January 1993, 64–70.
3. Marcovecchio, J. E.; M. S. Gerpe; R. O. Bastida; D. H. Rodriguez; and S. G. Moron. "Environmental Contamination and Marine Mammals in Coastal Waters From Argentina: An Overview." *Science of the Total Environment,* vol. 154 (1994), 141–151.
4. Terborgh, J. "Why American Songbirds Are Vanishing." *Scientific American,* May 1992, 98–104.

Lesson Planning Guide With Options for Block Scheduling

Lecture Concepts	*Lesson Resources*

26-1 Spiders and Their Relatives

BLOCK ❶ (45 minutes)

1. Arachnids include spiders, scorpions, ticks, and mites.

2. Arachnids have two body regions, the cephalothorax and the abdomen; four pairs of legs; and specialized appendages at the front of the body.

3. Spider silk is used to capture prey, to protect young, to line burrows, and to provide a safety line.

❶ Lecture Resources
- Determining Prior Knowledge
- Active Reading: Anticipation Guide
- Active Reading: Reading Organizer
- Visual Strategy: Figure 26-1
- Teaching Transparencies: 140
- Holt Biology Videodiscs Lesson 26-1

Classwork Options
- Varieties of Silk
- Exploration 26A

Assignment Options
- Spider Web Journal

BLOCK ❷ (45 minutes)

4. The chelicerae of scorpions have been adapted as pincers. Scorpions use a stinger.

5. Ticks and mites are parasites that can carry disease.

6. The horseshoe crab is not a crab. It is an ancient arthropod that survives today.

❷ Lecture Resources
- Horseshoe Crabs and Vision
- Visual Strategy: Figures 26-5, 26-8
- Teaching Transparencies: 134A
- Holt Biology Videodiscs Lesson 26-1

Classwork Options
- Closure: Organizing Information

Assignment Options
- Reteaching
- Section Review
- Chapter Review, questions 1a, 4, 5, 6, 18, 23
- Directed Reading Worksheet

26-2 Insects, Millipedes, and Centipedes

BLOCK ❸ (45 minutes)

1. Insects have three main body parts—the head, the thorax, and the abdomen.

2. Most insects go through a metamorphosis as they develop.

❸ Lecture Resources
- Insect Characteristics
- Raising Butterflies
- Active Reading: Reading Organizer
- Visual Strategy: Videodisc
- Demonstration: Observing Functions
- Holt Biology Videodiscs Lesson 26-2

Classwork Options
- Environmentally Sensitive Pest Control

Assignment Options
- Insect Collections
- Incomplete and Complete Metamorphosis
- Life/Work Skills: Being a Team Member

BLOCK ❹ (45 minutes)

3. Ants, bees, wasps, and termites are social insects, with a division of labor among members of the society.

4. Millipedes and centipedes are closely related to insects. Millipedes feed on decaying plants, while centipedes are predators that kill their prey with venom.

❹ Lecture Resources
- Cooperation Versus Competition
- Vanishing Beehives
- Visual Strategy: Figure 24-15
- Visual Strategy: Videodisc
- Teaching Transparencies: 137, 135A, 136A
- Holt Biology Videodiscs Lesson 26-2

Classwork Options
- Fire Ant Control

- Closure: Relating Concepts
- Laboratory Techniques and Experimental Design: Lab C39

Assignment Options
- Reteaching
- Section Review
- Chapter Review, questions 1b, 2a, 7, 8, 9, 10, 11, 15, 17, 19, 20, 21, 22
- Directed Reading Worksheet

26-3 Crustaceans

BLOCK ❺ (45 minutes)

1. Crustaceans include lobsters, crayfish, crabs, shrimp, prawns, barnacles, and pill bugs. Crustaceans live in aquatic habitats, except for pill bugs.

2. Crustaceans typically have bodies divided into two major parts: the cephalothorax and the abdomen.

❺ Lecture Resources
- Visual Strategy: Figure 26-17
- Demonstration: Comparing Structures
- Holt Biology Videodiscs Lesson 26-3

Classwork Options
- *Small Group* Writing Questions
- Life/Work Skills: Communicating
- Inquiry Skills Development: Lab B25

Assignment Options
- Crustacean Diversity

KEY
- ■ Annotated Teacher's Edition
- ■ Pupil's Edition
- ■ Directed Reading Worksheets
- ■ Vocabulary Development Worksheets
- ■ Thinking Skills Worksheets
- ■ Reteaching Worksheets
- ■ Chapter Tests
- ◉ Language Development and Reading Comprehension Audio CD Program

Holt BioSources
Laboratory Program
- A Quick Labs
- B Inquiry Skills Development
- C Laboratory Techniques and Experimental Design
- D Biotechnology
- E Interactive Explorations in Biology Laboratory Manual

- 📷 Teaching Transparencies
- ◉ Testing Resources CD-ROM
- ◉ Test Generator/Assessment Item

Holt Biology Technology
- ◉ Holt Biology Videodiscs

Lecture Concepts

Lesson Resources

26-3 Crustaceans, *continued*

BLOCK ❻ (45 minutes)

3. Lobsters, shrimp, crabs, and crayfish are decapods with five pairs of feet.

4. Copepods, tiny crustaceans that live in oceans and fresh water, form a vital link in the ocean's food web.

❻ Lecture Resources
- ■ Isopods: Terrestrial Crustaceans
- ■ Active Reading: Anticipation Guide
- ■ Demonstration: Identifying Structures
- ◉ Holt Biology Videodiscs Lesson 26-3

Classwork Options
- ■ Ocean Food Webs
- ■ Closure: Forming a Model

Assignment Options
- ■ Reteaching
- ■ Section Review
- ■ Chapter Review, questions 1c, 2c, 3, 12, 13, 14, 16
- ■ Directed Reading Worksheet

Chapter Review and Assessment

BLOCK ❼ (45 minutes)
Review
- ■ Reteaching Worksheet
- ■ Thinking Skills Worksheet
- ■ Vocabulary Development Worksheet
- ◉ Language Development and Reading Comprehension Audio CD Program: Chapter 26

BLOCK ❽ (45 minutes)
Assessment
- ■ Alternative Assessment, p. 519
- ■ Portfolio Assessment, p. T39

Chapter Test
- ■ Chapter 26 Test

Test Generator
- ◉ Item bank for customizing Chapter Tests
- ◉ Performance-Based Assessment: Exploring Invertebrates

Teaching Resources CD-ROM
- ◉ Scoring Rubrics and Classroom Management Checklist

 The Portfolio icon denotes items throughout the Teacher's Edition lesson wrap that may be selected for inclusion in student portfolios.

Holt Biology Videodiscs and *Concepts of Biology*

Holt Biology Videodiscs gives you a powerful tool for teaching, review, and assessment. For further information regarding the media on the videodiscs, see ***Holt Biology Videodiscs Teacher's Correlation Guide to Holt Biology: Visualizing Life.***

Concepts of Biology adds interactive lesson plans and extensive tools for customization using CD-ROM technology.

Use the following topic from ***Concepts of Biology*** to help you teach this chapter:
Topic 18: Invertebrate Diversity

Laboratory Planning

Text

Materials and preparation instructions appear on the teacher's wrap accompanying each laboratory exercise.

Block 1: Exploration 26A: Classifying Insects, p. 806

Holt BioSources Laboratory Program

Block 4: Laboratory Techniques and Experimental Design Lab C39: Response in the Fruit Fly

Block 5: Inquiry Skills Development Lab B25: Crayfish Dissection

Determining Prior Knowledge

- Have students name different types of arthropods. Ask them to identify the characteristics that arthropods share, such as an exoskeleton, jointed appendages, and segmented bodies.
- Have students draw an insect and a spider. Use these drawings to highlight the differences between the two types of organisms, such as the number of legs and the number of body regions.
- Have students brainstorm about why spiders make webs.
- Have students name different types of crustaceans and describe where these organisms live.

Active READING

Technique: Anticipation Guide

Before students read this chapter, have them consider the following statements:

- Most spiders are harmful to humans.
- In most insect species, the form that emerges from the egg does not look like the adult form.
- Crustaceans cannot survive on land.

Allow students time to decide if they agree with each statement. Have volunteers share their opinions with the class. Then have students read the chapter to see whether their opinions are confirmed or changed.

CD-ROM Resources

Concepts of Biology
Topic 18: Invertebrate Diversity

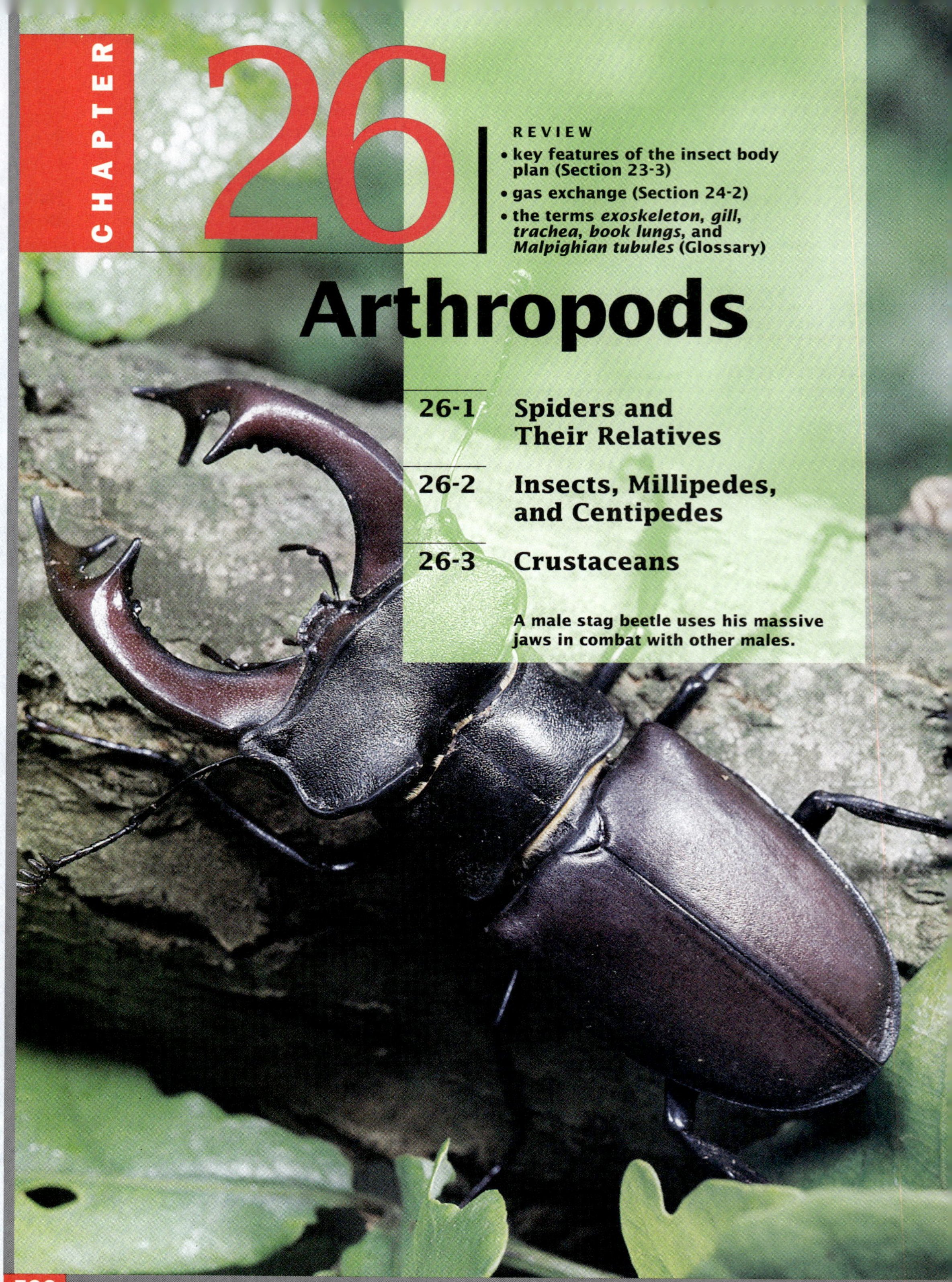

REVIEW
- key features of the insect body plan (Section 23-3)
- gas exchange (Section 24-2)
- the terms *exoskeleton, gill, trachea, book lungs,* and *Malpighian tubules* (Glossary)

Arthropods

26-1   **Spiders and Their Relatives**

26-2   **Insects, Millipedes, and Centipedes**

26-3   **Crustaceans**

A male stag beetle uses his massive jaws in combat with other males.

500

Author's Rationale   This chapter presents the story of arthropods, the largest and most diverse group of animals. It focuses on the adaptations that have contributed to the arthropods' success. Students learn to recognize the characteristics that distinguish the major types of arthropods: arachnids, insects, and crustaceans. They also realize that arthropods' abilities to both help and harm humans make them an ecologically and economically important group.

This spider is an arthropod. There are about 1 million named species of arthropods, far more species than belong to any other phylum. Arthropods have a great impact on humans and on world ecology. There are three major groups of living arthropods—spiders and their relatives, insects and their relatives, and crustaceans.

26-1 Spiders and Their Relatives

OBJECTIVES

1 Describe the functions of chelicerae and pedipalps in spiders.

2 Explain three ways spiders use silk.

3 List two arachnids that directly affect people.

Characteristics of Arachnids

What do you see when you look closely at a spider like the tarantula shown in **Figure 26-1**? One of the spider's key features is the pair of appendages called **chelicerae** *(kuh LIHS uh ree)*. Chelicerae, which are located at the front of a spider's body, are the hallmark of spiders and their relatives, including scorpions, mites, and ticks. Chelicerae are used for feeding. The chelicerae of spiders are poison-delivering fangs. A second pair of appendages, known as **pedipalps**, lies just behind the chelicerae. Pedipalps are used to capture and manipulate prey and for courtship displays and mating.

Spiders, scorpions, mites, and ticks are **arachnids** *(uh RAK nihdz)*, members of the class Arachnida. Remember from Chapter 23 that segmentation is a characteristic of the arthropods. In arachnids, the body segments are fused to form two main body regions: the cephalothorax *(sehf uh luh THAWR aks)* and the abdomen. Arachnids have four pairs of legs, which are attached to the cephalothorax.

Spinneret

Abdomen

Cephalothorax

Chelicerae

Pedipalps

Figure 26-1
This tarantula is one of the world's largest spiders. Tarantulas and all other arachnids have chelicerae.

501

Videodisc Resources

Holt Biology Videodiscs
Lesson 26-1: Spiders and Their Relatives

Phase One
Preparation

Scheduling
See the **Lesson Planning Guide** on pages 499A and 499B for lecture, classwork, and assignment options for Section 26-1.

Phase Two
Teaching Strategies

Visual Strategy **Figure 26-1**

● **Comparing Structures**
Have students study Figure 26-1 and identify the two key appendages and two body regions that characterize arachnids *(cephalothorax and abdomen; chelicerae and pedipalps)*. Display photographs of various spiders, scorpions, ticks, and mites. Have students identify these arachnoid characteristics in each photograph.

Active READING

Technique: Reading Organizer
Have students read pages 501 and 502. Afterward, discuss what type of reading organizer best represents this portion of the text. *(Students might suggest a descriptive reading organizer.)* After students reach a consensus, work with the class to design and complete the reading organizer.

Key to Strategies
Teaching Strategies are keyed to three tiers of learning.

● **Understanding Concepts (Tier I)**
Content mastery and comprehension

■ **Applying Information (Tier II)**
Applying and analyzing content

▲ **Critical Thinking (Tier III)**
Practicing evaluative thinking

Varieties of Silk

■ Inferring Conclusions

Explain that many spiders spin at least two different types of silk threads. Dry threads are used to form the web's radial framework; sticky threads are arranged in a spiral around the radial threads. Ask students what advantage a spider gains by spinning both dry and sticky threads. *(Students may reason that spiders avoid becoming trapped in their webs by walking on the dry radial threads.)* Have students find information about types of silk that other types of spiders spin.

Language Arts Connection

Arachne

Have students trace the etymology of the word *arachnid*. Students should discover that arachnids are named for Arachne, a weaver in Greek mythology. Arachne boastfully challenged the goddess Athena to a weaving contest and produced a beautiful tapestry. Athena was so enraged by Arachne's skill that she changed Arachne into a spider.

Spiders

There are about 35,000 named species of spiders. While a few live in fresh water, the majority are land dwellers. Indeed, spiders are thought to have been among the first arthropods to successfully colonize the land. Spiders are predators, feeding on nearly any other animal of manageable size.

Spiders have several adaptations that contribute to their success. First, they have efficient organs of excretion and water balance, so they can rid their bodies of wastes while still conserving precious water. Second, many spiders are able to breathe air by using book lungs. Recall from Chapter 24 that book lungs allow air to come close to the spider's blood in a humid chamber where gas exchange occurs. Third, nearly all spiders produce poison. The chelicerae of spiders are fangs equipped with poison glands. Fourth, and perhaps most important, spiders have the ability to produce silk threads, which they use in a great variety of ways.

Silk and fangs are a deadly combination

You may have watched a spider building its web. At the end of a spider's abdomen are small nozzle-like structures called **spinnerets**. Spinnerets direct the flow of silk from silk-producing glands in the abdomen. Spiders can produce different kinds of silk threads in various diameters.

Spider silk is composed of a complex structural protein that is produced in the glands as a liquid. As the liquid silk flows out through holes in the spinnerets, it solidifies into the threads that make up the web. As illustrated in **Figure 26-2**, spiders spin many different types of webs.

Figure 26-2
Spiders have many different kinds of specialized webs that enable them to catch their prey. Some spiders build webs in high tree branches, while others build horizontal sheet webs that catch insects that drop from above or are carried by the wind. Some spiders build silk-lined burrows beneath the ground. These spiders extend threads that act as trip lines around the burrow entrance. Then they sit inside, waiting for an unsuspecting insect to become entangled.

Spider silk is elastic and extremely strong, about as strong as a nylon thread of the same diameter. Spiders use silk for many purposes. Threads are used as safety lines when spiders dangle from branches or drop to the ground. Many spiders also use silk to line their nests or burrows, to wrap prey, or to fashion cocoons for their young. Some newly hatched spiderlings spin long, thin threads with which they ride the winds over great distances.

A spider's web is a sticky trap to ensnare prey. Constructing a web is a complex architectural feat that requires several steps. When an insect strikes the web and struggles, the spider is alerted by the threads' vibrations. The spider then rushes to the victim, bites it, and injects poison and digestive enzymes. The ability to stun or kill the prey quickly with poison from the chelicerae is a great advantage. It saves the spider from having to wrestle with large or potentially dangerous prey, such as bees and wasps. The spider shown in **Figure 26-3** has captured a bee in its web.

Although nearly all spiders produce poison, only about 20 kinds are considered dangerous to people. Two such species are found in the United States: the American black widow spider and the brown recluse spider, both shown in **Figure 26-4**. Most spiders are more beneficial than harmful to humans. They are the world's champion pest controllers, consuming millions of insects in their daily activities. Many of these insects are agricultural pests.

Spiders have courtship rituals

Spiders are usually solitary animals. When they do seek a mate, it is important that males and females of the same species be able to recognize each other. The male is usually smaller than the female and could easily be mistaken for a meal if some signal did not identify

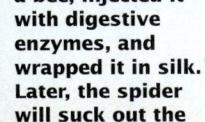

Figure 26-3
This *Argiope* spider has captured a bee, injected it with digestive enzymes, and wrapped it in silk. Later, the spider will suck out the liquefied tissues of the bee and discard the carcass.

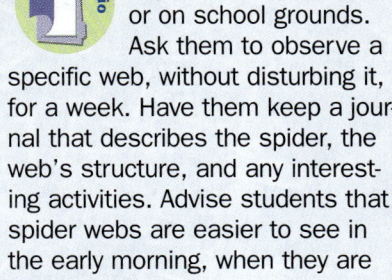

Figure 26-4
a The American black widow spider is most common in the southern United States. The bite of the female injects a powerful venom that acts on the victim's nervous system.

b The brown recluse spider can be recognized by the violin shape on its upper cephalothorax. Brown recluse spiders live in dark places such as basements and woodpiles. Their venom causes tissue damage in the area of the bite.

him to his prospective partner. Spiders have evolved complex behaviors that ensure successful mating and fertilization of the female's eggs.

Mating behavior in the black widow spider provides an example of the dangers a male spider faces. As the male approaches the web of a female, he drums a specific rhythm on the strands of the web to alert the female that he is a potential mate and not a meal. If he vibrates the female's web inappropriately, she will kill and eat him. After mating, the female sometimes kills the male anyway, wrapping and saving him for her offspring's first dinner.

Spider Web Journal
■ **Reporting Information**

portfolio

Have students locate spider webs in their yard or on school grounds.
Ask them to observe a specific web, without disturbing it, for a week. Have them keep a journal that describes the spider, the web's structure, and any interesting activities. Advise students that spider webs are easier to see in the early morning, when they are covered with dew.

Health Connection
Spider Bites
Have students search the library or an on-line database for information about poisonous spiders around the world, such as the Australian funnel-web spider, whose bite can be lethal if left untreated. Have students describe the spider and its habitat, the symptoms caused by the spider's bite, and the measures a person should take if bitten.

Matter of Fact: Nursery-Web Spiders

As its name implies, the nursery-web spider uses its web to protect its young, not to trap prey. An aggressive predator, the nursery-web spider hunts for fish, which can sometimes weigh four times as much as the spider, and drags it out of the water. Nursery-web spiders are unique in that they can swim underwater and build rafts from which to search for prey.

Key to Strategies
● Understanding Concepts (Tier I)
■ Applying Information (Tier II)
▲ Critical Thinking (Tier III)

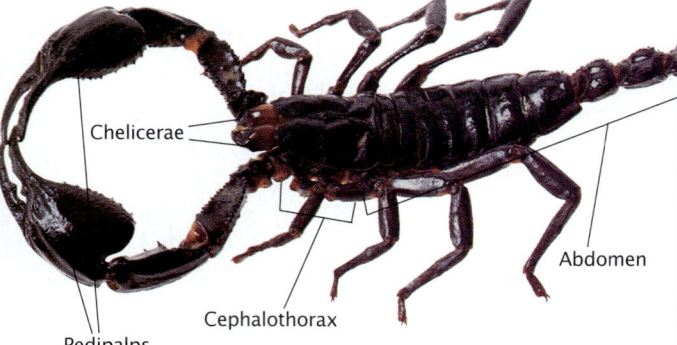

Stinger

Chelicerae

Cephalothorax

Pedipalps

Abdomen

● **Describing Functions**

Point out that a scorpion's stinger is located at its tail end, the end opposite from its eyes and pincers. Ask students to describe how a scorpion captures prey and injects it with venom. *(The scorpion seizes the prey in its pincers, arches its abdomen over its back, and injects the venom in its stinger into the victim.)* Ask them why this technique for injecting venom is more efficient than backing into the prey. *(If the scorpion could not see or hold the prey while injecting the venom, the prey would probably escape.)*

Health Connection

Checking for Ticks

Remind students that they should check themselves for ticks (especially in their hair and clothing) when hiking or working outdoors in an area where ticks are found. Suggest that they use a full-length mirror to check their backs or that they ask a friend for help. Have students find information that describes the recommended methods for successfully removing a tick from themselves or from a pet.

■ **Inferring Conclusions**

Ask students why horseshoe crabs are considered relatives of spiders and scorpions, and have them speculate about how they got their common name. Inform them that horseshoe crabs can grow to 78 cm (20 in.) long. They are not aggressive, and they defend themselves by hiding in their shells. Horseshoe crabs breathe air, so they can be seen along coastlines, especially in the northeastern United States.

Figure 26-5
This African scorpion is about 18 cm (7 in.) long. Scorpions found in the United States range from 5 to 13 cm (2 to 5 in.) in length.

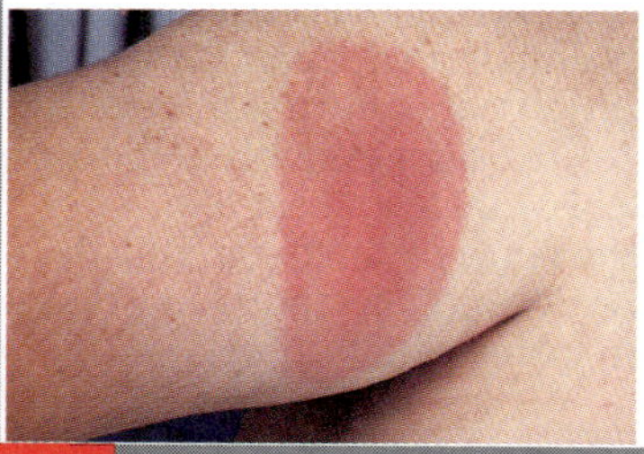

Figure 26-6
Lyme disease is caused by a bacterium that is transmitted by the bite of the deer tick. About one-half of the people infected with Lyme disease develop this "bull's-eye" rash within a few days of being bitten.

Other Arachnids

Relatives of scorpions were the first arthropods to invade land, more than 400 million years ago. Today's scorpions share many of the adaptations that enable spiders to survive on land, including book lungs and efficient excretory and water-conserving organs. Unlike the poison-injecting chelicerae of spiders, scorpions' chelicerae are ripping claws. Their pedipalps have evolved into enlarged pincers used to capture prey. Scorpions feed mostly on insects. As you can see in **Figure 26-5**, the scorpion's stinger is found at the tip of its abdomen. While the scorpion holds its victim in its pincers, it brings its abdomen forward to jab into the prey and then tears the prey into pieces.

Scorpions live in the warmer regions of the world. About 20 scorpion species are found in the United States, mostly in the Southwest. Scorpions hide during the day and hunt at night. Although a scorpion's sting is painful, it is rarely lethal to humans. Like spiders, scorpions perform elaborate mating rituals.

Most mites and ticks are parasites

If dust makes you sneeze, you may not be reacting to the dust itself, but to the tiny mites found in the dust. Over 30,000 species of mites and ticks have been described. A number of these species are free-living on land or in water, but many are parasites on the bodies of other animals. The free-living forms are mostly scavengers or predators on other tiny creatures.

If you have done much camping or hiking in brushy terrain, chances are you have spent some time removing ticks from your body. Most ticks are bloodsuckers that are parasites on vertebrates. Their sharp chelicerae are specialized for slicing skin. Although normally quite small, some ticks can swell to 3 cm (just over 1 in.) in length after a full meal of blood. Ticks transmit Lyme disease and Rocky Mountain spotted fever to humans, and they transmit Texas cattle fever to livestock. **Figure 26-6** shows the rash that usually occurs a few days after a person has been bitten by a tick that carried Lyme disease.

Mites, such as the red water mite in **Figure 26-7**, are much more diverse than ticks. They parasitize virtually all groups of animals and many plants. The incredible specialization of mites is shown by two species, *Demodex folliculorum* and *D. brevis*. *Demodex folliculorum* lives only in hair follicles,

Figure 26-7
The red water mite is an active swimmer. The larval stages of water mites may be parasites on insects or fishes.

and *D. brevis* lives only in oil glands of the human forehead. Mites have serious direct and indirect effects on humans. Many, such as chiggers, punch holes in the skin and cause severe itching. Mites also carry viruses that plague food crops, such as mosaic viruses of rye and wheat. The red-legged mite and the winter grain mite both feed on stored crops, destroying many tons of grain each year. Other mites cause feather loss in birds, decreased wool production in sheep, and mange in dogs. If you find yourself itching a bit after reading this section, don't be alarmed; we are all hosts to some of these parasites.

Horseshoe Crabs

Figure 26-8
Horseshoe crabs are not really crabs. They are more closely related to spiders and scorpions than to crabs.

Horseshoe crabs, such as the one shown in **Figure 26-8**, are arthropods that have changed little in 200 million years. There are only five species of horseshoe crabs today. They live in shallow parts of the oceans, where they plow through sandy bottoms and use their clawlike legs to grasp small animals on which they feed. They also eat dead animals.

Horseshoe crabs have chelicerae but are not arachnids. They are closely related to the extinct giant "water scorpions," or eurypterids, such as the one shown in **Figure 26-9**. Eurypterids lived from about 500 million years ago until about 300 million years ago.

SECTION REVIEW

① What functions do pedipalps serve in spiders?

② Describe two ways spiders use silk, other than for building webs.

③ Describe one way your life is affected positively by arachnids.

④ How do arachnids negatively affect humans?

505

ANSWERS TO SECTION REVIEW

① Pedipalps are used for capturing prey, and for courtship displays and mating.

② Spiders use silk threads to line their nest or burrows, to wrap prey, to fashion cocoons for their young, to aid in riding the winds over long distances, and to provide safety lines.

③ Students might point out that spiders help control populations of insects that are considered agricultural pests.

④ Students might point out that scorpions and some spiders, such as the brown recluse and the black widow, can inflict painful stings and bites; ticks can spread disease, such as Lyme disease; and mites feed on stored grain, and carry viruses that harm crops and may also adversely affect birds, sheep, and dogs.

Horseshoe Crabs and Vision
▲ **Evaluating Methods**
Horseshoe crabs are frequently used in research at the Marine Biological Laboratory in Woods Hole, Massachusetts. Tell students that scientists have learned a great deal about human vision by studying the horseshoe crab's multifaceted eyes. Ask students to suggest reasons why scientists would study an unusual animal like the horseshoe crab to learn about human vision. *(Horseshoe crabs are ancient and fairly simple organisms, so it is easier for researchers to study the basics of vision.)*

Phase Three
Assessment Options

Closure
■ **Organizing Information**
Have each student make a table titled *"Arachnids"* with the following headings: *Basic Structure, Function of Chelicerae, Food Sources, Specialized Structures,* and *Effects on Humans.* The left column of the table should be labeled *Spiders, Scorpions, Ticks,* and *Mites.* Have students work in cooperative groups to complete their tables.

SECTION REVIEW
Assign the *Section Review.*

Reteaching
Have students study photos or preserved specimens of arachnids. Ask students to identify each organism as a spider, a scorpion, a tick, or a mite, and have them explain the reasons for their identifications.

Key to Strategies
● Understanding Concepts (Tier I)
■ Applying Information (Tier II)
▲ Critical Thinking (Tier III)

Scheduling

See the **Lesson Planning Guide** on pages 499A and 499B for lecture, classwork, and assignment options for Section 26-2.

Phase Two
Teaching Strategies

Visual Strategy Videodisc

● **Summarizing Information**
Have students explore the reasons for the large diversity of insects. First, use *Gallery—Insects* shown in Chapter 26 Section 26-2 in **Holt Biology Videodiscs Teacher's Correlation Guide to Holt Biology: Visualizing Life** to provide some examples of insect diversity. Tell students that in terms of the number of individuals and diversity, insects are the most successful group of organisms. Have students brainstorm reasons for such diversity. Then show *Video—Insect Societies,* and have students note reasons for insects' success. *(Segmented bodies and multistage life cycles allow for many adaptations; societies allow for specialization of physical form and behavior.)*

Active READING

Technique: Reading Organizer
Read page 506 aloud to students. Then work with the class as a whole to create a reading organizer that describes the characteristics of insects. Have students read on to discover more about these diverse animals.

At this moment, there are over 200 million times more insects than humans living on Earth. Also, the number of insect species is far greater than the number of other animal species. In fact, there are more species of beetles than species of all non-insect animals combined. Insects and their close relatives, the millipedes and centipedes, have mandibles instead of chelicerae.

26-2 Insects, Millipedes, and Centipedes

OBJECTIVES

1. **Contrast the anatomy of spiders with that of insects.**

2. **Distinguish between incomplete and complete metamorphosis.**

3. **Describe five ways that insects affect your life.**

4. **Identify two differences between millipedes and centipedes.**

Insects

Like other arthropods, insects are segmented. In insects, the segments have fused into three body regions: the head, the thorax, and the abdomen, as shown in **Figure 26-10**.

A hallmark of insects is the diversity of the specialized appendages attached to their heads. Unlike arachnids, insects have antennae, appendages specialized for sensing the environment. Insect mouthparts are also extremely varied, enabling insects to feed on a greater variety of foods than other arthropods. Instead of chelicerae, insects have jaws called **mandibles**. They also have mouthparts that resemble the pedipalps of spiders. The mouthparts of arachnids are relatively simple when compared with those of insects, which often have evolved into highly specialized shapes for grinding, scraping, piercing, and sucking.

Insect legs have also evolved into a variety of shapes. The legs of beetles are modified for walking, while the legs of grasshoppers are adapted for jumping. The legs of some lice are suited for clinging to their host's hair.

Like other terrestrial arthropods, insects have evolved mechanisms for gas exchange and water conservation. Insect tracheae are extremely efficient in delivering oxygen directly to the body's cells. Insects have a thick, waxy exoskeleton that prevents water loss. Their Malpighian tubules enable them to excrete nitrogenous wastes with little loss of water. **Table 26-1** shows some of the major orders of insects. You can read more about a specific insect, the two-spotted lady beetle, in *Tour of an Insect* on page 508.

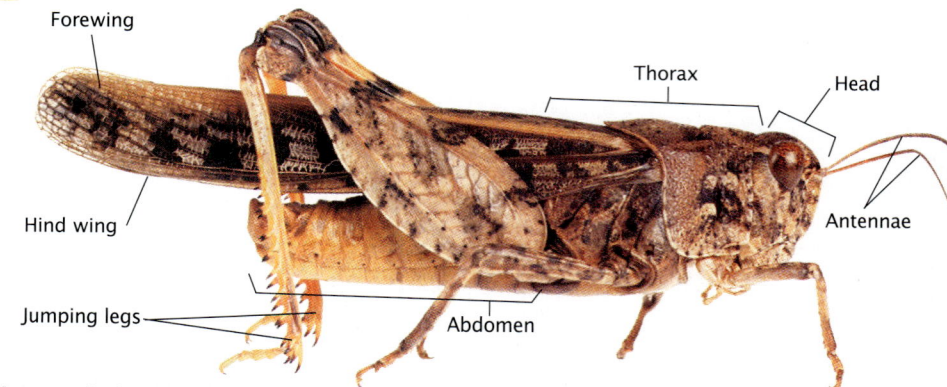

Forewing · Thorax · Head · Hind wing · Antennae · Jumping legs · Abdomen

Figure 26-10
The bodies of all insects, including this grasshopper, consist of three distinct regions: head, thorax, and abdomen. Three pairs of legs are attached to the thorax. Most insects have wings, which are also attached to the thorax. The evolution of wings was a major reason for the diversification of insects.

Videodisc Resources

Holt Biology Videodiscs
Lesson 26-2: Insects, Millipedes, and Centipedes

Table 26-1 Major Orders of Insects

Order	Number of named species	Description	Examples	
Coleoptera "Sheath-winged"	350,000	Two pairs of wings (front pair covers transparent hind pair); heavy, armored exoskeleton; biting and chewing mouthparts; complete metamorphosis	Beetles, weevils	
Diptera "Two-winged"	150,000	Transparent front wings; hind wings reduced to knobby balancing organs; sucking, piercing, and lapping mouthparts; complete metamorphosis	Flies, mosquitoes	
Hymenoptera "Membrane-winged"	125,000	Two pairs of transparent wings; mobile head; well-developed eyes; chewing and sucking mouthparts; stinging; many species social; complete metamorphosis	Ants, bees, wasps	
Lepidoptera "Scale-winged"	120,000	Two pairs of broad, scaly wings; hairy bodies; tubelike sucking mouthparts; complete metamorphosis	Butterflies, moths	
Hemiptera "Half-winged"	35,000	Two pairs of wings or wingless; piercing, sucking mouthparts; incomplete metamorphosis	Giant water bug, bedbug, chinch bug	
Orthoptera "Straight-winged"	20,000	Two pairs of wings or wingless; biting and chewing mouthparts in adults; incomplete metamorphosis	Grasshoppers, crickets, katydids	
Odonata "Toothed"	5,000	Two pairs of transparent wings; chewing mouthparts; incomplete metamorphosis	Dragonflies, damselflies	
Isoptera "Equal-winged"	2,000	Two pairs of wings, but some stages are wingless; chewing mouthparts; social insects with division of labor; incomplete metamorphosis	Termites	
Siphonaptera "Tube-wingless"	1,700	Small, wingless, flattened body; piercing and sucking mouthparts; jumping legs; complete metamorphosis	Fleas	

507

Demonstration

■ **Observing Functions**
Materials: Live grasshoppers, insect jars, food supply (leaves or grass)

Organize students into cooperative groups and provide each group with a live grasshopper to observe. Have each group gather data about the following: how the grasshopper eats, the movement of its abdomen as it breathes, its leg movements as it jumps, and characteristics that the grasshopper has in common with other insects. Have each group use their data to write a report that describes the structures and functions involved in these movements.

Insect Characteristics

■ **Relating Concepts**
Have students design a **Graphic Organizer** that describes the characteristics and functions of the insect body's three regions.

Life/Work Skills
Being a Team member

● **Organizing Information**

Divide the class into nine groups, and assign each group one of the insect orders listed in Table 26-1. Have the groups research their insect order and prepare an illustrated presentation for the class. Ask students to include the names of several local species and places where each can be found.

Graphic Organizer

Use the following graphic organizer with the teaching strategy **Insect Characteristics** on page 507.

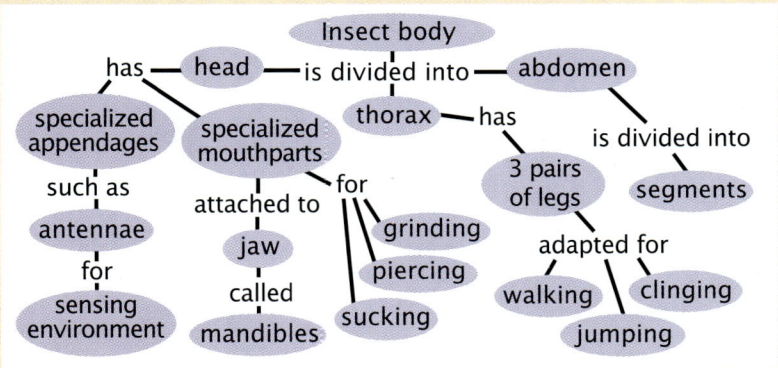

Key to Strategies
● **Understanding Concepts (Tier I)**
■ **Applying Information (Tier II)**
▲ **Critical Thinking (Tier III)**

Environmentally Sensitive Pest Control

▲ Evaluating Results

Have students search the library or an on-line database to find information about the use of lady beetles and other organisms to manage pests in the home garden as well as in commercial agriculture. Suggest that students contact retail suppliers for detailed information. Then have students evaluate the long-term benefits of this practice.

Insect Collections

■ Choosing Methods

Display insect collections, if available. In cooperative groups, have students discuss how they would carry out the task of producing such a collection and what valuable information they would expect it to yield.

Insect

Almost one-half of the named species of insects are beetles. The lady beetle is often called ladybug or ladybird beetle. There are more than 400 species of lady beetles in the United States. This species is the two-spotted lady beetle, which is common in northern parts of the United States.

Beetles, as well as most other insects, are characterized by three distinct body regions: head, thorax (to which legs and wings attach), and abdomen.

Like most insects, beetles have two pairs of wings. In beetles, the first pair is hardened and serves to protect the delicate second pair, which is used for flying.

Habitat
The lady beetle is often found on plants on which aphids, its main food, are living.

Insects have compound eyes, which are made up of many individual units. Each unit forms an image of part of the visual field. This type of eye is very good at detecting motion.

Evolutionary Relationships
Lady beetles and other beetles belong to the order Coleoptera, the largest order of insects. There are over 350,000 named species of beetles, far more than all vertebrates combined.

The jaws of the lady beetle are adapted for chewing. Lady beetles feed on other insects, including harmful pests like aphids and scale insects. Lady beetles are beneficial because of the large number of insects they eat—a single larva can eat 400 aphids.

There are 10 pairs of spiracles along each side of the abdomen. Spiracles allow air into a network of tubules that carry oxygen throughout the body.

Size
The two-spotted lady beetle is about 5 mm (0.2 in.) long.

Most insects change their body form as they mature

Spiders, scorpions, mites, and ticks all undergo **direct development**. In this kind of development, a miniature copy of the adult form hatches from the egg. Some species of insects also undergo direct development.

Most insects, however, hatch as a form that is not like the adult. As it grows, the young insect changes to become more and more like its parents. Each of these changes is called a **metamorphosis** (*meht uh MAWR fuh sihs*). If the metamorphosis into the adult form involves a series of gradual changes, it is called **incomplete metamorphosis**. Insects that undergo incomplete metamorphosis include grasshoppers, dragonflies, mayflies, and cockroaches. In this type of development, the insect that emerges from the egg is called a **nymph** (*NIHMF*).

The nymph is a smaller version of the adult insect, similar in structure but without wings or mature reproductive organs.

In **complete metamorphosis**, illustrated in **Figure 26-11**, the immature form usually does not resemble the adult. When the egg of an insect hatches, an immature form called a larva emerges. The larva cannot fly. It feeds and grows until ready to transform into an adult. When the larval stage is complete, the insect enters a stage called the pupa (*PYOO puh*) or, in butterflies, the chrysalis (*KRIHS uh lihs*). Many pupae form a covering around themselves. This covering may develop from the larva's "skin," or it may be a cocoon of silk. During this stage, most insects remain immobile while larval tissues and organs are replaced with new tissues and organs. At the end of the pupal stage, a fully formed, mature adult emerges.

About 90 percent of insect species

a Egg

b Larva (caterpillar)

d Adult butterfly about to emerge

c Chrysalis

Figure 26-11
The life cycle of the monarch butterfly illustrates complete metamorphosis.

e Adult butterfly

509

Graphic Organizer

Use the following graphic organizer with the teaching strategy **Incomplete and Complete Metamorphosis** on page 509.

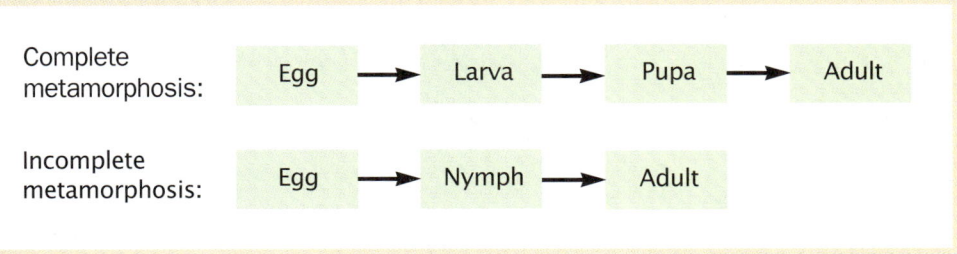

Complete metamorphosis: Egg → Larva → Pupa → Adult

Incomplete metamorphosis: Egg → Nymph → Adult

Raising Butterflies

● **Observing Patterns**
Materials: butterfly larvae, insect jar, food for larvae (leaves)

Obtain butterfly larvae (caterpillars) that will grow into adult butterflies within one to three weeks, such as painted lady butterflies. Or, if possible, have students bring in caterpillars that they have found feeding on garden plants. Place the larvae in insect jars with a food supply (fresh leaves). Tell students that they will be responsible for supplying the caterpillars with fresh leaves every day. Have students keep a daily journal that describes the caterpillars' development and activities. In a few weeks, have students release the adult butterflies outdoors.

Visual Strategy | **Videodisc**

■ **Recognizing Relationships**
Use *Illustration—Metamorphosis* shown in Chapter 26 Section 26-2 of *Holt Biology Videodiscs Teacher's Correlation Guide to Holt Biology: Visualizing Life* to illustrate metamorphosis in insects. First, discuss incomplete metamorphosis in the grasshopper. Point out that a young grasshopper resembles a miniature adult grasshopper and that both forms eat the same kind of food. Next, discuss complete metamorphosis in the butterfly. Explain that a butterfly eats different kinds of food during each stage of its development.

Incomplete and Complete Metamorphosis

■ **Relating Concepts**
Have students prepare a **Graphic Organizer** that compares incomplete metamorphosis with complete metamorphosis.

Key to Strategies
● **Understanding Concepts (Tier I)**
■ **Applying Information (Tier II)**
▲ **Critical Thinking (Tier III)**

Arthropods 509

Cooperation Versus Competition

■ **Analyzing Relationships**
Have students determine the advantages of division of labor in social insects, such as bees and ants. Then have them compare these benefits with those of insects that live solitary lives, such as butterflies and grasshoppers.

Figure 26-12
a A termite nest usually has a single queen that lays all the eggs. A nest of termites may contain as many as 5 million individuals.

b Worker termites search for food, which they supply to the queen, king, and soldiers.

undergo complete metamorphosis, including flies, beetles, ants, bees, wasps, butterflies, and moths.

What is the evolutionary advantage of the complicated insect life cycle? During the life cycle, the various stages not only are physically different from each other but also are ecologically different. As a result, at different times in its life a single animal can exploit different habitats and different food resources. For example, a leaf-chewing caterpillar will eventually transform into a nectar-drinking butterfly. This ecological separation of young from adults eliminates competition between the two phases of the life cycle.

Ants, bees, wasps, and termites live in complex societies

Ants, termites, and certain kinds of bees and wasps are highly social. These insects live in highly organized societies of related individuals, with division of labor among the society

members. Different individuals serve the group by performing different functions. In a termite colony, workers gather food, tend offspring, and excavate the tunnels and chambers of the colony. Soldiers, as the name implies, defend the colony against attack. Enlarged jaws and heads enable them to carry out this role. Soldiers and workers are sterile. Only the king and queen of the colony reproduce. The role played by an individual in the colony is its caste. **Figure 26-12** shows representatives of the four castes of a termite colony.

d The king termite fertilizes all the eggs laid by the queen.

c Soldier termites guard the passages in the nest and the covered trails that radiate out from the nest.

Community Connection: Destructive Pests

Invite a pest-control authority to class to discuss the problems and risks associated with termites and other common household pests, such as ants and cockroaches. Ask the visitor to explain when such insects are considered a hazard. Have students ask questions about new methods used to control pests and about how to avoid infestations.

Entomology

What would it be like to . . .

- devise new methods to control pests in agriculture and urban settings?
- engineer new ways to control and prevent deadly epidemics?

These are just a few of the opportunities open to people who work in the field of entomology.

Entomology: What Is It?

Entomology is a branch of zoology concerned with the study of insects and other arthropods. Many entomologists are affiliated with universities as teachers and researchers in classification, ecology, and behavior, increasing our knowledge of insects. Entomologists are recruited in industries that produce useful products, including honey, beeswax, and silk. Some entomologists seek new ways to prevent and treat persistent arthropod-borne diseases, such as malaria, bubonic plague, and sleeping sickness.

Employment Outlook

Entomology is a field with many potential applications. Insects have become so numerous and economically important that opportunities for entomologists will increase.

Career Focus: Entomologist
Dr. Genaro Lopez
Entomologist at University of Texas, Brownsville

"When I was young, I saw science as a means of escape from everyday life. I spent a lot of time outdoors. I always looked forward to my science classes in school. Although neither of my parents finished high school, they encouraged me to go to college.

"Naturally in college I studied science. I became very active in the zoology department. In addition to working in a mammal museum, I traveled to the tropics in Colombia to study bats and to mountains in Mexico to collect other animals and plants."

What I Do: "During the summer, I work as a consultant urban entomologist for a pest-control company. Every year, they fumigate large apartment complexes in New York City, Miami, and Los Angeles. As their Hispanic spokesperson, I explain procedures and precautions to the residents and the media.

"During the rest of the year, I teach biology at a university while carrying out research. I have a long term project studying populations of tiger beetles that inhabit the lower Laguna Madre in Texas."

To Find Out More

1. For further information, write to:
Entomological Society of America
9301 Annapolis Road
Lanham, MD 20706-3115

2. Visit your school counselor or library to find out what colleges and universities offer programs in entomology. Review the prerequisites and course requirements. Make a poster showing the range of job opportunities in this field.

3. Find articles that discuss how insects are used to control pests in agriculture. Prepare a report for your class.

Career Opportunities

Setting Up a Business

1. Have the class brainstorm ideas to the following questions:

If you wanted a career in entomology…

- what kind of personality traits would be essential?
- which subjects should you study in high school? in college?
- what kind of extracurricular activities should you pursue?
- what kind of practical experience should you gain?
- what kind of issues would interest you?

   Write students' responses on the chalkboard or overhead projector.

2. Assign students to small groups and explain that each group will be setting up a business whose product depends on the work of insects. Allow students time to brainstorm ideas for their businesses. Possibilities include honey-making, silk-making, or fruit-growing industries. Suggest alternatives, such as pest control and agricultural services.

3. Have students determine what they should know before setting up a business. For example, where will the business be located, where will the start-up money come from, who will use the product or services, how much will the product or services cost, and how will the business be advertised? Each group should devise a business plan based on answers to these questions.

511

Setting Up a Business, continued

4. Direct each group to contact local officials to find out the procedures for setting up a business in the community. Discuss these findings in class.

5. Have each group present its business venture to the rest of the class. Tell students that their peers will evaluate their efforts and predict whether the venture will be a success.

Fire Ant Control

▲ **Evaluating Methods**

Insects can be controlled by using chemicals that interfere with the insects' reproductive cycles. Ask students to describe advantages and disadvantages of using these types of chemicals rather than insecticides. *(Although adults continue to do damage, they will not be able to produce offspring.)* Have students consult an organic gardening store to find out what products are on the market and how they work against insect pests.

Figure 26-13
Many species of insects are harmful to humans. The three species shown below are particularly harmful.

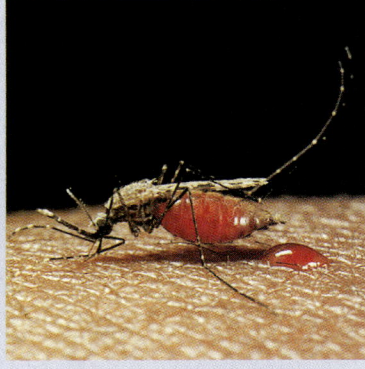

c Brazilian fire ants were accidentally introduced into the United States in the 1920s. These aggressive ants have largely replaced some native ant species.

b *Anopheles* mosquitoes transmit malaria. About 250 million people currently suffer from this disease. About 1 million people will die from malaria this year.

a Each year, boll weevils cause billions of dollars in damage to cotton plants in the United States. Even worse, they have evolved resistance to many of the insecticides used to control them.

Some insects are harmful

Imagine a world without insects. You might at first imagine a better world without many of the pests that spread disease and destroy crops. While some insects are merely nuisances, others cause billions of dollars of crop losses each year. These insects either eat the plants or transmit diseases to plants. **Figure 26-13** shows several insects that adversely affect humans. The use of pesticides to control insect pests is only partially effective, since many harmful insects have evolved resistance to pesticides. Also, many pesticides are toxic or carcinogenic to humans and other organisms.

Insects destroy our homes and transmit diseases to humans, livestock, and wildlife. In Africa, biting flies transmit African river blindness and sleeping sickness. Fleas carry bubonic plague and were responsible for transmitting this disease throughout Europe, Asia, and Northern Africa in the fourteenth century. Fleas also serve as an intermediate host for dog and cat tapeworms. Mosquitoes transmit not only malaria but also yellow fever, dengue fever, and encephalitis. Lice transmit typhus. You might want to look back at the tables of human diseases in Chapters 18 and 19 and count how many of these diseases are transmitted by insects.

Some insects are beneficial

In spite of these distasteful and often fatal consequences of sharing the planet with insects, humans benefit from insects in many ways. Important crops such as apples, cherries, pears,

Historical Perspective: Fear of Insects

As a child, Dr. May Roberta Berenbaum was terrified of insects. When she attended Yale University, she was determined to overcome her fear of insects and enrolled in a course about terrestrial arthropods. Today, Dr. Berenbaum is the head of the entomology department at the University of Illinois and has founded several programs to promote learning about insects, including an annual Insect Fear Film Festival, a radio commentary called *Those Amazing Insects,* and two books, *Ninety-Nine Gnats, Nits, and Nibblers* and *Ninety-Nine More Maggots, Mites, and Munchers.* Dr. Berenbaum has won several awards for her research. She teaches some of the most popular courses at the University of Illinois and was recently elected to the National Academy of Sciences.

Figure 26-14
These are three of the many species of insects that are beneficial to humans.

b Silk is produced by the caterpillars of the silk moth.

a Bees, such as these honeybees, pollinate the flowers of many important plants, including apple trees, cherry trees, cucumbers, and squash.

c Lady beetles feed on herbivorous insects, such as aphids and scale insects, and help control their populations.

carrots, cotton, and oranges depend on insects for pollination. The food supply for humans would be much lower without insect pollinators. Humans also harvest a variety of insect products. For example, silk is spun by the caterpillars of silk moths. Bees, in addition to their important role as pollinators, produce honey and beeswax. And insects are eaten by humans in some parts of the world. For example, Australian aborigines consider the larvae of certain large beetles to be delicacies.

Predatory and parasitic insects are important checks on the populations of many kinds of destructive insects. For instance, lady beetles consume large numbers of aphids, which are important pests of many crops, including cabbage, cucumbers, wheat, grapes, and apples. Farmers often use predatory or parasitic insects as an alternative to chemical pesticides. Scientists are currently searching for parasites that could be used to control Brazilian fire ants. These ants have spread throughout the South since their accidental introduction into the United States, despite an intensive and expensive effort to control them. However, one group of small flies that parasitizes fire ants in their natural habitat has shown promise in preliminary tests.

Perhaps most important, insects provide vital links in the food webs of nearly every ecosystem on Earth. Many freshwater fishes—trout, for example—feed on insects and insect larvae. Many birds, bats, amphibians, small reptiles, and small mammals eat insects. **Figure 26-14** shows some beneficial insects.

513

Vanishing Beehives

■ **Applying Information**
Tell students that many beekeepers have threatened to close their hives upon the arrival of the "killer bees," or Africanized bees, in their area. In addition, the widespread use of pesticide sprays has resulted in the loss of beehives. Have students discuss the effects the loss of these hives might have on consumers. *(Since bees are needed to pollinate many crops, reduced agricultural production and higher prices would be a consequence of the loss of beehives.)* Tell students that some farmers have to rent mobile beehives to pollinate their crops.

Agricultural Connection
Silk
Tell students that silk is made today with cultivated silkworms, usually the caterpillar *Bombyx mori*. The female lays 300 to 500 eggs on special paper provided by silk farmers. When fully grown, the silkworms spin a cocoon made of one continuous silk thread, in which the silkworm will develop into a pupa and then emerge as a moth. Silk farmers do not allow most pupas to become moths because a moth will shatter the silk cocoon as it emerges. Instead, farmers kill most pupa and process the silk cocoons. First the cocoon is unwound, and the threads are strengthened by several processes. Then the thread is dyed and woven into fabric.

Multicultural Perspective: Crickets
In Japan and other parts of Asia, crickets were once treated as pets and were considered a delightful source of musical and artistic pleasure. Favorite pet crickets were often given elaborate cages and beautiful porcelain water dishes. Some cricket owners even tickled their crickets with delicate hand-carved brushes to encourage the insect's chirping.

Key to Strategies
● Understanding Concepts (Tier I)
■ Applying Information (Tier II)
▲ Critical Thinking (Tier III)

■ **Comparing Structures**

Have students compare the millipede shown in Figure 24-15 with the centipede shown in Figure 26-16. Explain that millipedes have stink glands and more than 30 body segments, and that they use the legs on their seventh segment for mating. They protect themselves by curling their bodies so the hard plates of their back cover their leg-bearing surface. Centipedes can have as many as 173 pairs of legs or as few as 15. They feed on insects that they capture and poison with special claws. They are capable of killing small animals but are usually not harmful to humans, although their bite may be painful. Explain that both millipedes and centipedes are found in dark, moist environments, such as damp cellars, meadows, and gardens.

Phase Three

Assessment Options

Closure

● **Relating Concepts**

Have students design a graphic organizer that describes insect development, social structure, and effects on humans.

SECTION REVIEW

Assign the Section Review.

Reteaching

Have students create a mural that depicts the diversity of insects they have learned about in this chapter.

Millipedes and Centipedes

Figure 26-15
This giant tropical millipede is 25 cm (10 in.) long.

Elongated and multilegged, millipedes and centipedes scarcely resemble six-legged insects. However, centipedes, millipedes, and insects all share the same fundamental head structure.

The name *millipede* means "thousand feet," although no millipede really has that many feet. The segments of the long, wormlike millipede in **Figure 26-15** appear to bear two pairs of legs each. In fact, pairs of segments are fused together, giving this misleading impression. The 10,000 or so known species of millipedes are herbivores, feeding mostly on decaying plant material. They are common inhabitants of forest floors.

Centipedes (the name means "hundred feet") have one pair of walking legs on each body segment. Worldwide, there are about 2,500 known species of centipedes. Unlike millipedes, centipedes are predators. The centipede shown in **Figure 26-16** feeds on worms and arthropods. A few large tropical centipedes kill and eat animals as large as frogs and lizards. In centipedes, the first pair of limbs has evolved into large clawlike structures that are used to grasp prey and to inject a strong venom. The venom of most species of centipedes is usually not life threatening to people, but it can cause pain and swelling.

Figure 26-16
This desert centipede is about 12 cm (5 in.) long. It is found in the southwestern United States.

SECTION REVIEW

❶ **Describe two differences between a spider and an insect.**

❷ **Compare the metamorphosis of grasshoppers with that of butterflies.**

❸ **How do some insects benefit crop plants?**

❹ **How do the diets of millipedes and centipedes differ?**

ANSWERS TO **SECTION REVIEW**

❶ Insects have antennae specialized for sensing the environment and arachnids do not. Instead of chelicerae, insects have mandibles for grinding, scraping, piercing, or sucking, depending on the insect and the shape of the mandible.

❷ Butterflies undergo complete metamorphosis, whereas grasshoppers undergo incomplete metamorphosis. In complete metamorphosis,

the newly hatched young pass through a series of stages before they assume the adult form. In incomplete metamorphosis, the young resemble the adults except they lack wings and mature reproductive organs.

❸ Insects pollinate many crops and feed on other insects that are crop pests.

❹ Millipedes are herbivores, feeding mostly on decaying plant material. Centipedes are predators; they feed on other animals.

Although insects are very abundant on land, relatively few species of insects are aquatic. Of the arthropods, crustaceans such as crabs, lobsters, and shrimp are common ocean inhabitants. Crustaceans are also important in freshwater ecosystems. Only a few species of crustaceans live on land.

26-3 Crustaceans

OBJECTIVES

1 Identify three kinds of crustaceans.

2 List three differences between crustaceans and insects.

3 Describe the importance of crustaceans to the ecology of the sea.

Crustaceans Are Successful Aquatic Arthropods

Lobsters, crabs, shrimp, prawns, barnacles, and pill bugs are crustaceans, members of the subphylum Crustacea. The roughly 30,000 named species of crustaceans are even more varied in body form than are the insects. They range in size from microscopic forms that drift in the sea to huge lobsters.

Crustaceans have appendages for many kinds of locomotion—swimming, crawling, burrowing, and even jumping. They also have specialized appendages for sensing the environment, mating, brooding eggs and embryos, feeding, gas exchange, attracting mates, and defense. Like insects, crustaceans have mandibles. **Figure 26-17** shows some of the specialized appendages of a crayfish.

With very few exceptions (like pill bugs, which you saw in Chapter 17), crustaceans have not been able to successfully invade the land. Crustaceans never evolved several of the key adaptations that are crucial to survival on land. The exoskeleton of crustaceans is heavier and less watertight than that of insects, so they face problems of water loss. Recall also that insects have very efficient excretory and water-balance organs, called Malpighian tubules, that help them get rid of wastes while conserving water. Crustacean excretory organs are far less efficient in accomplishing these functions. Perhaps most important, crustaceans have gills. Although gills are very efficient under water, they collapse in air. You can read more about crustaceans in *Tour of a Crustacean* on page 516.

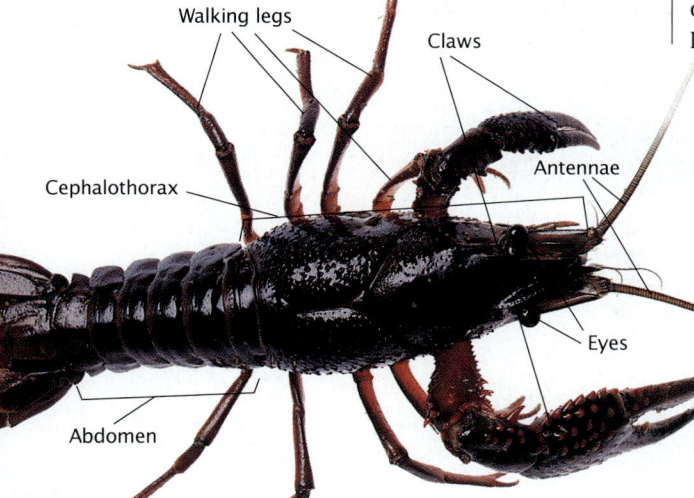

Walking legs

Claws

Antennae

Cephalothorax

Eyes

Abdomen

Figure 26-17
Crustaceans have thick calcium-rich exoskeletons that are generally much heavier than those of insects and spiders. Without the buoyancy of water, some large crustaceans cannot support their weight and therefore cannot move around on dry land.

515

Videodisc Resources

Holt Biology Videodiscs
Lesson 26-3: Crustaceans

Scheduling
See the **Lesson Planning Guide** on pages 499A and 499B for lecture, classwork, and assignment options for Section 26-3.

Demonstration
● **Comparing Structures**
Obtain several whole crustaceans (with heads), such as shrimp or crayfish, from a supermarket or seafood shop. In cooperative groups, have students study one of the crustaceans and compare it with Figure 26-17. Ask a member of each group to point out the crustacean's external structures. After the demonstration, have students wash their hands thoroughly with soap.

Visual Strategy | **Figure 26-17**

■ **Inferring Conclusions**
Have students study the body structure of the crayfish shown in this figure and speculate how it defends itself.

Key to Strategies
● Understanding Concepts (Tier I)
■ Applying Information (Tier II)
▲ Critical Thinking (Tier III)

Arthropods 515

Life/Work Skills
Communicating

● **Organizing Information**
Have students review the characteristics of arthropods. Then, in cooperative groups, have them make a list of the similarities and differences between the lady beetle on page 508 and the lobster on page 516.

Writing Questions

■ **Analyzing Information**
In cooperative groups, have students formulate at least five questions about the characteristics, adaptations, or behavior of crustaceans and other arthropods. Encourage groups to write a variety of types of questions (true/false; multiple choice; fill-in-the-blank). Then have groups take turns quizzing the rest of the class. Afterward, have students evaluate the kinds of questions they heard and determine which ones effectively tested their knowledge.

Crustacean

The northern lobster is a crustacean that lives along the eastern coast of North America from Labrador, Canada, to Virginia. All crustaceans are covered by a protective exoskeleton that is composed of chitin and protein.

Lobsters and other crustaceans are the only arthropods with two pairs of antennae.

The first pair of legs is modified into a pair of massive pincers, which are used to crush shellfish and slice the flesh of fish.

Habitat
Northern lobsters prefer rocky habitats. They live in both shallow water and deep water.

Evolutionary Relationships
Lobsters, crabs, crayfish, and shrimp belong to the order Decapoda. All of these crustaceans have five pairs of legs.

Periodically, lobsters molt, shedding their hard exoskeleton so that their body can grow larger.

Size
Large northern lobsters can be 86 cm (34 in.) long and weigh 20 kg (45 lb).

516

Crustacean Diversity

Lobsters, shrimp, crabs, and crayfish are all **decapods**. They have five pairs of thoracic legs (the name *decapod* means "ten feet"). The first pair of legs is often an enlarged set of claws used for food gathering and for defense, as you can see in **Figure 26-18**. Lobsters, shrimp, and crayfish all resemble one another in that the abdomen is large and muscular.

At first glance, barnacles don't look very much like other crustaceans or even other arthropods. However, as larvae they clearly resemble their crustacean relatives. As adults, barnacles live inside the walls of their calcium shells, which are attached to solid objects like rocks, pilings, ships' hulls, and even whales. If you look along almost any rocky seashore, you will probably find two different kinds of barnacles. Acorn, or volcano, barnacles have their shells cemented directly to the rock on which they live. The second kind, goose barnacles, sit atop a fleshy stalk, which is attached to the rock.

Pill bugs and their relatives are called isopods, which means "equal feet." They have seven pairs of similar walking legs. They are closely related to another group of crustaceans called amphipods. The name *amphipod* refers to having two different kinds of feet. If you turn over a stone along a beach or lake shore, you are sure to find some examples of amphipods. Beach hoppers, for instance, are very common on sandy coastlines. Often, you can find these animals by looking for their burrows or by turning over piles of seaweed lying on the sand.

Figure 26-18
Crustaceans exhibit a wide variety of body forms. They have many different kinds of appendages.

a This shrimp uses its legs to bury itself in the sand when a predator approaches.

b There are about 6,000 species of amphipods. Most species are aquatic.

c These common acorn barnacles feed by extending their feathery legs into the water to trap small food particles.

d Pill bugs are isopods that are often found under rotting logs in forests throughout the continental United States.

e The abdomen of a crab is small and is folded beneath the cephalothorax. Crabs can be found along most coastlines throughout the world.

517

Crustacean Diversity

● **Organizing Information**
Have students design a Graphic Organizer similar to the one at the bottom of this page that shows the kinds of organisms classified as crustaceans.

Demonstration

● **Identifying Structures**
Materials: brine-shrimp eggs, small aquarium, aquarium bubbler, yeast
Brine shrimp, often advertised as "sea monkeys," are crustaceans that are easy to raise in the classroom. Brine-shrimp eggs can be found in most pet shops. Put the shrimp eggs in a small aquarium with dechlorinated water and an aquarium bubbler. Brine shrimp may be fed a sprinkle of yeast after they hatch. Have students view these organisms using a hand lens or a low-power microscope and describe the characteristics that make them crustaceans. Also, have students determine these organisms' position in an aquatic food web.

Isopods: Terrestrial Crustaceans

■ **Designing an Experiment**
Isopods are unusual crustaceans because they are adapted to living on land. Ask students to design an experiment to determine whether pill bugs prefer a moist or dry environment, or whether they do not have a preference. Tell students that isopods breathe using gills that must be kept moist.

Graphic Organizer

Use the following graphic organizer with the teaching strategy **Crustacean Diversity** on page 517.

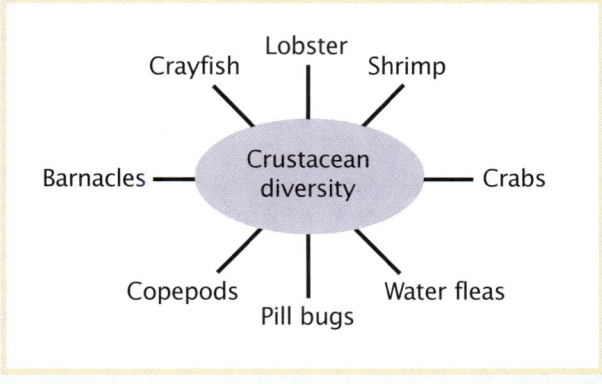

Crayfish — Lobster — Shrimp — Crabs — Water fleas — Pill bugs — Copepods — Barnacles — **Crustacean diversity**

Key to Strategies
● Understanding Concepts (Tier I)
■ Applying Information (Tier II)
▲ Critical Thinking (Tier III)

Arthropods 517

Ocean Food Webs

■ **Applying Information**

Have students search the library or an on-line database to find out the names of a variety of marine organisms that feed on copepods. Students should then find out which animals prey on the copepod feeders, and so on, up the food chain to the top predators. Have students draw a food web that shows the relationships between these organisms and then write a paragraph explaining the sequence of events that would occur if all of the copepods died.

Active READING

Technique: Anticipation Guide

Ask volunteers to discuss whether the opinions they formed in the Active Reading exercise on page 500 changed as a result of their reading. Students should support their reasoning with specific passages from the text.

Phase Three

Assessment Options

Closure

■ **Forming a Model**

Have students brainstorm ideas about the ecological and economical importance of crustaceans. Write their ideas on the board, then have them design a concept map based on this information.

SECTION REVIEW

Assign *Section Review.*

Reteaching

Show students photographs of a lobster and of a water flea, and ask them to identify the similarities and differences between the two animals.

Figure 26-19
Large numbers of *Daphnia* can be found in almost any sample of water taken from a nutrient-rich lake or pond. There are nearly 400 species of *Daphnia* in freshwater environments. They range from 0.2 to 3 mm (0.008 to 0.1 in.) in length.

Among the most important crustaceans in freshwater environments are the so-called water fleas, or cladocerans *(kluh DAHS uhr uhns)*, like *Daphnia*, shown in **Figure 26-19**. *Daphnia* feed on phytoplankton (photosynthetic plankton). In high concentrations, water fleas consume huge quantities of photosynthetic organisms and in turn are fed upon by small predators such as young fishes. In many freshwater habitats, these little crustaceans are a vital link between the producers and the rest of the food web.

Look at the photograph in **Figure 26-20**. This tiny crustacean is very important in marine ecosystems. It is a **copepod** *(KOH puh pahd)*. While some kinds of copepods live on the sea bottom, and a few are parasitic, the vast majority are part of the zooplankton, the heterotrophic organisms that feed on phytoplankton. Copepods occur both in the sea and in fresh water, often in incredibly high concentrations. Their abundance follows the seasonal changes in concentrations of phytoplankton. Like water fleas in lakes, copepods link the ocean's photosynthetic life to the rest of the ocean's food web. Copepods are consumed by a variety of small predators, which are eaten by larger predators, and so on. Virtually all animal life in the open sea depends on the copepods, either directly or indirectly. Although humans do not eat copepods directly, our sources of food from the ocean would disappear without the copepods.

Figure 26-20
Although most copepods are pale and transparent, some species are brilliant red, orange, purple, blue, or black. Most copepods are less than 10 mm (0.4 in.) long.

SECTION REVIEW

① **Name three kinds of crustaceans.**

② **Describe three differences between insects and crustaceans.**

③ **How would the ecology of the sea and the human food supply be affected if all crustaceans died?**

④ **Explain the advantages and disadvantages of an exoskeleton.**

518

ANSWERS TO SECTION REVIEW

① Possible answers include lobsters, crayfish, crabs, shrimp, prawns, barnacles, and pill bugs.

② The exoskeletons of crustaceans are heavier and less watertight than those of insects. Insects have Malpighian tubules to help them get rid of waste and conserve water. The crustacean excretory system is less efficient. Crustaceans have gills; insects do not.

③ Without crustaceans such as crayfish, shrimp, and crabs, the human food supply would dwindle considerably. The loss of copepods would break a crucial ecological link between phytoplankton and predators.

④ Exoskeletons provide protection and prevent water loss. However, an exoskeleton is relatively heavy. Animals with exoskeletons must either be relatively small, like the insects, or live in water, which provides support for the weight of the exoskeleton, like the crustaceans.

This pray-
ing mantis
is lying in
wait for fly-
ing insects.

Alternative Assessment

Have students make a concept map that shows the similarities and differences between the following different types of arthropods: arachnids, insects, millipedes and centipedes, and crustaceans.

Portfolio Assessment

Portfolio Assessment on page T39 provides options for building and evaluating student portfolios. Students and teachers can select items from the areas listed on T39 for inclusion in a portfolio.

	Key Terms	Summary
26-1 **Spiders and Their Relatives**  Spiders and their relatives are characterized by chelicerae.	chelicera (p. 501) arachnid (p. 501) pedipalp (p. 501) spinneret (p. 502)	• Spiders, scorpions, mites, ticks, and horseshoe crabs have chelicerae, a specialized pair of appendages at the front of the body. They have two main body units: the cephalothorax and the abdomen. Spiders, scorpions, mites, and ticks are arachnids. • The chelicerae of spiders are poison-delivering fangs. Spiders use silk to spin safety lines, to line burrows, to protect the young, and to trap food. • Scorpions' chelicerae are adapted for tearing prey. The pedipalps of scorpions are pincers for grasping prey. • Many ticks and mites are parasites. Some transmit diseases to humans and domestic animals.
26-2 **Insects, Millipedes, and Centipedes**  There are more species of insects on Earth than any other group of animals.	mandible (p. 506) direct development (p. 509) metamorphosis (p. 509) incomplete metamorphosis (p. 509) nymph (p. 509) complete metamorphosis (p. 509)	• Insects have three main body units: the head (with three sets of mouthparts), the thorax (with three sets of legs), and the abdomen. • Insect development usually involves either complete or incomplete metamorphosis. • Millipedes have two pairs of legs per segment and feed on decaying matter. Centipedes have only one pair of legs per segment and are predators.
26-3 **Crustaceans**  Most crustaceans live in or close to the ocean.	decapod (p. 517) copepod (p. 518)	• Crabs, lobsters, shrimp, pill bugs, and barnacles are crustaceans, subphylum Crustacea. Most crustaceans are aquatic. • The crustaceans known as copepods are extremely important links in marine food webs.

519

ANSWER TO
CONCEPT MAP

The following is one possible answer to the Relating Concepts exercise on page 520.

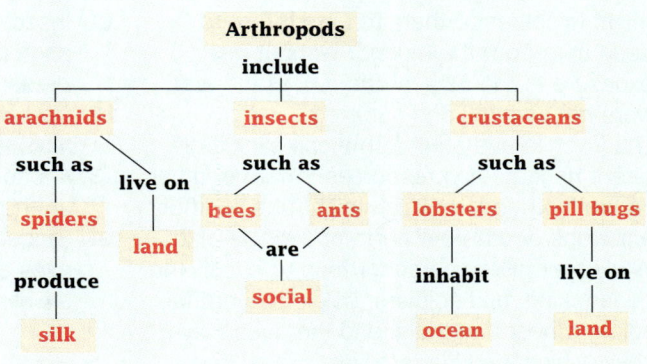

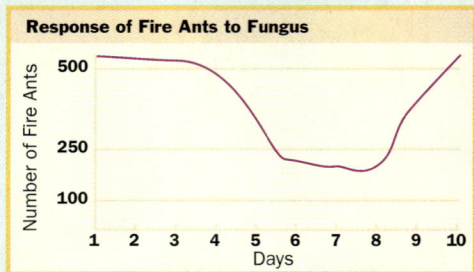

Understanding Vocabulary

1. a. pedipalps
   b. gills
   c. fleas
2. a. A spider is an arachnid with chelicerae, two body segments, and four pairs of legs. An insect is an arthropod with mandibles (instead of chelicerae), three body regions, and antennae.
   b. In incomplete metamorphosis, the immature form gradually changes into the adult form. In complete metamorphosis, the immature form undergoes distinct stages before it becomes an adult.
   c. Most crustaceans are aquatic arthropods with gills; most arachnids are terrestrial arthropods with book lungs.

Understanding Concepts

3. Concept map answer is shown on page 519.
4. In spiders, the chelicerae are poison-delivering fangs; in scorpions, the chelicerae are ripping claws. Scorpions capture prey with their large pedipalps, and then flip their abdomen forward to jab their stinger into the prey.
5. Spiders are arachnids with chelicerae modified as poison-delivering fangs, two body segments (the cephalothorax and abdomen), and four pairs of legs attached to the cephalothorax. Other arachnids include mites, which can trigger allergic reactions in humans, and ticks, which can transmit Lyme disease and Rocky Mountain spotted fever to humans. Both are parasitic.
6. When a spider has ensnared prey in its sticky silk web, it bites the victim, injecting poison and digestive enzymes, and then sucks out the liquefied tissues.
7. The arthropod has three body segments, so it is most likely an insect.
8. On Day 6, less than half (250) of the ants remained. Students

Understanding Vocabulary

1. For each set of terms, complete the analogy.
   a. first appendages : chelicerae :: second appendages : _____
   b. insects : tracheae :: crustaceans : _____
   c. Lyme disease : ticks :: bubonic plague : _____
2. For each pair of terms, explain the differences in their meanings.
   a. spider, insect
   b. incomplete metamorphosis, complete metamorphosis
   c. crustacean, arachnid

Understanding Concepts

3. **Relating Concepts** Construct a concept map that identifies the three major groups of arthropods and gives characteristics of each. Try to include the following terms in your concept map: arachnids, insects, crustaceans, spiders, silk, bees, ants, social, lobsters, ocean, pill bugs, land.
4. **Comparing Structures** How do the chelicerae and pedipalps of spiders compare with those of scorpions? How do scorpions capture their prey? How are their pedipalps and chelicerae adapted for this task?
5. **Identifying Structures** Identify three physical characteristics of animals classified as spiders. Name two kinds of arachnids that are not spiders. Describe two ways that the arachnids you chose affect humans.
6. **Summarizing Information** Spiders are predators but have no teeth or jaws. How do they capture their prey? How do they obtain nutrients from their prey?
7. **Inferring Conclusions** An unknown arthropod is found. It has three body segments, one pair of antennae, and three pairs of walking legs. What kind of arthropod is it? Explain how you arrived at this conclusion.

8. **Forming Hypotheses** A scientist knew that a particular fungus was known to kill fire ants. Using 500 ants, he set up an experimental mound with a glass window, through which he could watch the ants inside the mound. On Day 1 he introduced the fungus. By Day 6 how many ants were left? Propose a hypothesis to explain this result. How would you test your hypothesis?

Response of Fire Ants to Fungus

(graph: x-axis labeled "Days" from 1 to 10; y-axis labeled "Number of Fire Ants" with values 100, 250, 500)

9. **Recognizing Relationships** The different stages of an insect that undergoes complete metamorphosis are both anatomically and ecologically different. How is this beneficial for the insect? How does this pose a problem for the farmer on whose crops the insect feeds?
10. **Analyzing Information** Identify the four castes in a termite colony and describe the role of each.
11. **Recognizing Relationships** What are two ways that insects benefit humans?
12. **Summarizing Information** Which of the following are not crustaceans: shrimp, crayfish, horseshoe crab, scorpion, wasp, water flea, tick?
13. **Identifying Functions** A lobster's heavy exoskeleton cannot grow with the animal. How does a lobster grow?
14. **BUILDING ON WHAT YOU HAVE LEARNED** In Chapter 24, you learned that terrestrial animals have many adaptations that enable them to live on land. How are the eggs of many arthropods well suited for survival on land?

might hypothesize that fire ants removed the dead ants from the mound. Without daily exposure to the fungus, the rest of the ants were not infected and survived.
9. The juvenile and adult forms can exploit different habitats and resources. A farmer must control both forms, which might attack different crops or different parts of a single plant.
10. Worker termites search for food to supply the queen, king, and soldiers; soldiers guard the colony's nest and trails; and the queen lays eggs, which the king fertilizes.

11. Insects pollinate many crops, such as apples and oranges, and control agricultural pests by predation.
12. Horseshoe crabs, scorpions, wasps, and ticks are not crustaceans.
13. A lobster periodically sheds its exoskeleton so that its body can grow larger.
14. Students should suggest that arthropods' eggs are usually microscopic and encased in a watertight covering.

Interpreting Graphics

15. Look at the photograph of the arthropod below.

a. What kind of arthropod is this animal?
b. Explain the adaptations that enable this arthropod to conserve water, capture prey, and defend itself.

Reviewing Themes

16. *Interdepence*
How do humans depend on copepods?

17. *Evolution*
Some species of insects can produce a new generation every few weeks. How does such rapid reproduction affect their ability to evolve resistance to pesticides?

Thinking Critically

18. **Recognizing Logical Inconsistencies** A neighbor was recently complaining about the increased number of insects around her house. At the same time, she was removing every spider web and killing every spider she saw. What is wrong with the neighbor's attempt to control insects?

19. **Evaluating Proposals** To help control a species of scale insect that feeds on orange trees, a scientist proposes introducing a parasitic wasp from Australia. You are asked to help evaluate the proposal. What are some of the biological issues that you should consider before making your decision? What non-biological issues might you consider?

Life/Work Skills

20. **Allocating Resources** Working as a group, plan how you would spend a budget of $5,000 to eradicate fire ants on the grounds of a school in the South. This budget must last for three years, so you will have to think about long-term effectiveness. How well have chemical pesticides worked to kill fire ants in other places? What other methods have been tried, and how successful were they? Investigate these questions before you decide how to spend your budget. Prepare a report or poster presentation to inform the school board of the positive and negative aspects and the costs of the methods you have researched.

Activities and Projects

21. **Health Connection** Head lice are sometimes a problem in schools. Do library research or search an on-line database to discover the symptoms of lice infestation and to learn what can be done to stop the spread of head lice. Summarize your findings in a written report.

22. **History Connection** Ancient Egyptians worshiped the sun and held sacred the scarab beetle, *Scarabaeus saber*, as a symbol of immortality. Use library references or search an on-line database to find out about scarab beetles and their historical importance to Egyptians. Also research the importance of scarab beetles in Chinese history and folklore. Prepare a written report of your findings.

Discovering Through Reading

23. The entire March 1995 issue of *Natural History* is devoted to arachnids. Read the article "Webs of Deceit" by Catherine L. Craig on pages 33–35. How do the number and kinds of silk produced by a tarantula compare with those produced by spiders in the Araneoidea superfamily? How might the color of the golden orb spider's web be an advantage in capturing prey?

521

Thinking Critically

18. The neighbor should have encouraged the presence of spiders, which consume many insects.
19. Answers will vary. Students should show concern about the wasp's effects on other insects and organisms, and they should question whether the proposal is cost-effective.

Life/Work Skills

20. Students' reports and posters should include information such as cost of implementation, longevity of treatment, and potential effects on the environment.

Activities and Projects

21. Symptoms include an itching scalp and a rash on the neck. The spread of head lice can be prevented by not sharing combs, brushes, or clothing with other people. The lice can be treated by using a medicated shampoo.
22. Scarab beetles, which number more than 12,000 species and can be as long as 15 cm (6 in.), make up the family Scarabaeidae in the insect order Coleoptera. Because of the insect's characteristic horns, ancient Egyptians and Chinese depicted the beetle in amulets, seals, and rings, which also came to be known as scarabs.

Discovering Through Reading

23. Tarantulas spin a single kind of silk, which is used to line the spider's burrow and encase its eggs. Araneoidea spiders, in contrast, produce up to eight different kinds of silk that are used to wrap eggs, spin retreats, and lay safety lines. Because many flowers pollinated by bees are yellow, the bright yellow webs spun by the golden orb spider might attract bees, thus ensuring the spider frequent meals.

Interpreting Graphics

15. a. The animal is a scorpion, an arachnid with an exoskeleton fused into two body regions, four pairs of jointed appendages, well-developed chelicerae, and pedipalps.
b. Its exoskeleton and organs enable it to conserve water. The pedipalps, the chelicerae, and the stinger allow it to capture prey and defend itself.

Reviewing Themes

16. The majority of copepods, tiny aquatic crustaceans, are part of the zooplankton. They link the ocean's photosynthetic life to the rest of the food web, which supplies humans with a large amount of food.
17. Insects that survive the initial application of the pesticide are resistant. When they reproduce, they pass this resistance to their offspring. After several generations, a new strain of the insect immune to the pesticide's effects is quickly established.

27 Fishes and Amphibians

Lesson Planning Guide With Options for Block Scheduling

Lecture Concepts	Lesson Resources

27-1 Jawless Fishes and Cartilaginous Fishes

BLOCK ❶ (45 minutes)

1. The first vertebrates to evolve were jawless fishes, or agnathans. Agnathans living today include the lampreys and the hagfishes.
2. Agnathans have gill pouches, a skeleton of cartilage and bone, and a notochord.
3. Lampreys are parasites that attach to other fishes. Hagfishes are scavengers.

❶ Lecture Resources
- Determining Prior Knowledge
- Extinction and Survival
- Active Reading: K-W-L
- Active Reading: Reading Organizer
- Visual Strategy: Figure 27-1
- Demonstration: Forming Opinions Supported by Sound Reasoning

- Teaching Transparencies: 164
- Holt Biology Videodiscs Lesson 27-1

Classwork Options
- Get a Grip
- Quick Labs: Lab A25
- Quick Labs: Lab A34

BLOCK ❷ (45 minutes)

4. Jaws are believed to have evolved from one or more gill arches present in jawless fishes.
5. Sharks, skates, and rays have jaws, gill slits, teeth that move forward to replace lost teeth, skeletons made of cartilage, and sandpaper-like skin.

❷ Lecture Resources
- Visual Strategy: Figure 27-6
- Visual Strategy: Videodisc
- Demonstration: Comparing Structures
- Holt Biology Videodiscs Lesson 27-1

Classwork Options
- Closure: Recognizing Patterns

Assignment Options
- Reteaching
- Section Review
- Chapter Review, questions 1a, 2a, 4, 5, 6, 7, 8, 9, 21
- Directed Reading Worksheet

27-2 Bony Fishes

BLOCK ❸ (45 minutes)

1. Bony fishes have skeletons made largely of bone instead of cartilage, and they are covered with scales formed of bone.
2. The gills of bony fishes are covered by a hard plate called the operculum.
3. Most bony fishes have a gas-filled sac called a swim bladder.

❸ Lecture Resources
- Active Reading: Reading Organizer
- Visual Strategy: Table 27-1
- Demonstration: Comparing Structures
- Teaching Transparencies: 165, 168
- Holt Biology Videodiscs Lesson 27-2

Classwork Options
- Inquiry Skills Development Lab B26: Perch Dissection

Assignment Options
- Adaptations of Fishes

BLOCK ❹ (45 minutes)

4. In almost all bony fishes, fertilization and development occur outside the female's body.
5. There are two major groups of bony fishes: the ray-finned fishes and the lobe-finned fishes.
6. Lungfishes are the closest living relatives of the amphibians.

❹ Lecture Resources
- Fish and Scuba Divers
- Teaching Transparencies: 138A, 139A, 140A
- Holt Biology Videodiscs Lesson 27-2

Classwork Options
- Comparing Fishes
- Closure: Recognizing Patterns

Assignment Options
- Reteaching
- Section Review
- Chapter Review, questions 1b, 2b, 10, 11, 12, 13, 22, 24
- Directed Reading Worksheet

27-3 Amphibians

BLOCK ❺ (45 minutes)

1. Amphibians, which include frogs, toads, salamanders, and caecilians, were the first terrestrial vertebrates.
2. Most amphibians have lungs, and also exchange gases across their moist skin. Amphibians live in moist environments to keep their skin moist.

❺ Lecture Resources
- Moving to the Land
- Active Reading: Summarizing
- Visual Strategy: Videodisc
- Demonstration: Identifying Structures
- Teaching Transparencies: 169
- Holt Biology Videodiscs Lesson 27-3

Classwork Options
- Gas Exchange
- Protection of the Eggs
- Inquiry Skills Development: Lab B28

Assignment Options
- Disappearing Frogs

Lecture Concepts

Lesson Resources

27-3 Amphibians, *continued*

BLOCK 6 (45 minutes)

3. Amphibians have a double-loop circulatory system that is more efficient than the single-loop circulatory system of fishes.

4. Amphibians must return to water to lay their eggs, which hatch into aquatic larvae. Most amphibians then metamorphose into the terrestrial adult form.

6 Lecture Resources
- Amphibian Differences
- Active Reading: K-W-L
- Teaching Transparencies: 170
- Holt Biology Videodiscs Lesson 27-3

Classwork Options
- Closure: Understanding Concepts

Assignment Options
- Reteaching
- Section Review
- Chapter Review, questions 1c, 2c, 3, 14, 15, 16, 17, 18, 19, 20, 23
- Directed Reading Worksheet

Chapter Review and Assessment

BLOCK 7 (45 minutes)
Review
- Reteaching Worksheet
- Thinking Skills Worksheet
- Vocabulary Development Worksheet
- Language Development and Reading Comprehension Audio CD Program: Chapter 27

BLOCK 8 (45 minutes)
Assessment
- Alternative Assessment, p. 537
- Portfolio Assessment, p. T39

Chapter Test
- Chapter 27 Test

Test Generator
- Item bank for customizing Chapter Tests

Teaching Resources CD-ROM
- Scoring Rubrics and Classroom Management Checklist

The Portfolio icon denotes items throughout the Teacher's Edition lesson wrap that may be selected for inclusion in student portfolios.

Holt Biology Videodiscs and *Concepts of Biology*

Holt Biology Videodiscs gives you a powerful tool for teaching, review, and assessment. For further information regarding the media on the videodiscs, see **Holt Biology Videodiscs Teacher's Correlation Guide to Holt Biology: Visualizing Life.**

Concepts of Biology adds interactive lesson plans and extensive tools for customization using CD-ROM technology.

Use the following topic from **Concepts of Biology** to help you teach this chapter:
Topic 20: Vertebrate Diversity

Laboratory Planning

Holt BioSources Laboratory Program

Block 1: Quick Labs Lab A25: Observing a Frog
Block 1: Quick Labs Lab A34: Culturing Frog Embryos
Block 3: Inquiry Skills Development Lab B26: Perch Dissection
Block 5: Inquiry Skills Development Lab B28: Frog Dissection

Determining Prior Knowledge

- Ask students to explain why whales and dolphins are not fishes.
- Ask students to name and describe as many fishes as possible that illustrate extremes of size, shape, color, and way of life.
- Ask students if they can describe ways in which sharks are different from other fishes.
- Have students draw a storyboard of the life cycle of a frog.
- Ask students to describe differences in the habitats and lifestyles of tadpoles and frogs or toads.
- Have students explain the differences between frogs and toads.

Active READING

Technique: K-W-L

Before students read the chapter, have them make short individual lists of all the things they already **K**now about fishes. When students have finished their lists, ask them to contribute their entries to a class list on the board or overhead. Then have students list things they **W**ant to know about fishes. Have students save their lists for later use in Active Reading on page 536.

CD-ROM Resources

Concepts of Biology
Topic 20: Vertebrate Diversity

REVIEW
- **characteristics of chordates (Section 23-3)**
- **characteristics of vertebrates (Section 23-3)**
- **evolution of the amphibian heart (Section 24-2)**

Fishes and Amphibians

27-1 Jawless Fishes and Cartilaginous Fishes

27-2 Bony Fishes

27-3 Amphibians

Amphibians, such as these red-eyed tree frogs, thrive in the moist conditions of tropical rain forests.

522

Author's Rationale Fishes were the first vertebrates and are by far the most diverse of the vertebrates. Half of all vertebrate species are fishes. Fish diversity is presented as a fascinating evolutionary story. Amphibians are presented in the same chapter because they have parallels to fishes. This organization gives students a clearer view of the many changes that occurred during the evolutionary transition to land. In some ways an amphibian closely resembles a fish with feet: it is still adapted to a water environment. But in other ways it has been radically transformed.

You and most of the animals you commonly see are vertebrates. As you learned in Chapter 11, vertebrates are chordates that have a vertebral column, or spine. The first vertebrates evolved more than 500 million years ago. There are approximately 40,000 species of vertebrates today, and about half of them are fishes, including the great white shark shown at the left.

27-1 Jawless Fishes and Cartilaginous Fishes

OBJECTIVES

1 List three characteristics of agnathans.

2 Describe how a lamprey feeds.

3 Describe how jaws are thought to have evolved.

4 Contrast sharks and rays with agnathans.

The First Fishes: Class Agnatha

The first vertebrates evolved about 500 million years ago. They were jawless fishes belonging to the class Agnatha (*Agnatha* means "without jaws"). Thick bony plates covered the bodies of these ancient agnathans (*AG na thuns*), as you can see in **Figure 27-1**. Bone and cartilage first evolved in this group of fishes. Agnathans were an abundant and diverse group for about 150 million years, until they were largely replaced by jawed fishes about 360 million years ago. Only 81 species of agnathans exist today.

The living agnathans are the lampreys and hagfishes, which are shown on the next page. These eel-like creatures have scaleless, slimy skin and lack paired fins. Their skeleton is mostly composed of cartilage, and there is no well-developed vertebral column. The notochord, which is replaced by vertebrae in most vertebrates, functions as the major support structure in adult lampreys and hagfishes. The gills of agnathans lie within pouches that branch from the pharynx. Water exits these pouches through several openings behind the head.

Figure 27-1
Drepanaspis was an agnathan that fed on the bottom of the ocean. Its gaping mouth did not have jaws. This bizarre fish became extinct about 360 million years ago.

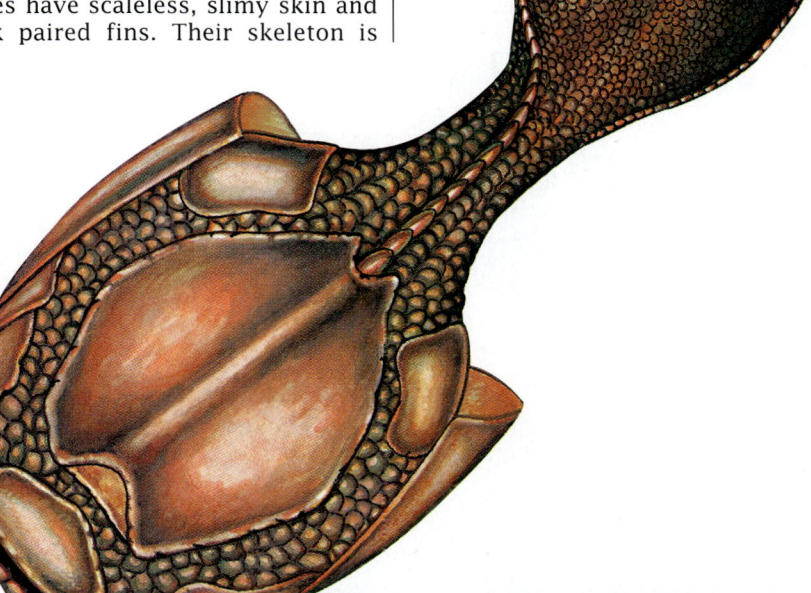

523

Videodisc Resources

Holt Biology Videodiscs
Lesson 27-1: Jawless Fishes and Cartilaginous Fishes

Phase One
Preparation

Scheduling

See the **Lesson Planning Guide** on pages 521A and 521B for lecture, classwork, and assignment options for Section 27-1.

Phase Two
Teaching Strategies

Active READING

Technique: Reading Organizer
Explain to students that the authors of the text have organized this chapter chronologically, presenting the various classes of fishes in evolutionary sequence. Have students survey the headings and subheadings in the first section of the chapter and note the words that signal this organizational structure. (Examples include "The First Fishes" and "Evolution of Jaws.") As students read, have them identify key words or phrases in the body of the text that also signal the sequential structure.

Visual Strategy **Figure 27-1**

● **Comparing Structures**
Have students study the figure and point out the obvious differences between this extinct agnathan and fishes living today. (*Students may identify the bony plates on the agnathan, rather than the scales they are more familiar with. Students may also point out features of bony fishes that this agnathan lacks, such as paired fins and the operculum.*)

Key to Strategies
Teaching Strategies are keyed to three tiers of learning.

● **Understanding Concepts (Tier I)**
Content mastery and comprehension

■ **Applying Information (Tier II)**
Applying and analyzing content

▲ **Critical Thinking (Tier III)**
Practicing evaluative thinking

Extinction and Survival

■ **Inferring Conclusions**
Tell students that for almost 100 million years, until the evolution of jawed fishes, the agnathans were the only vertebrates. Except for the lampreys and hagfishes, all of the major groups of agnathans are now extinct. Ask students to speculate about why most agnathans became extinct and why lampreys and hagfishes survived. *(Fishes with jaws were probably more efficient at obtaining food and outcompeted the agnathans. As parasites and scavengers, the lampreys and hagfishes have specific eating habits that may have minimized competition.)*

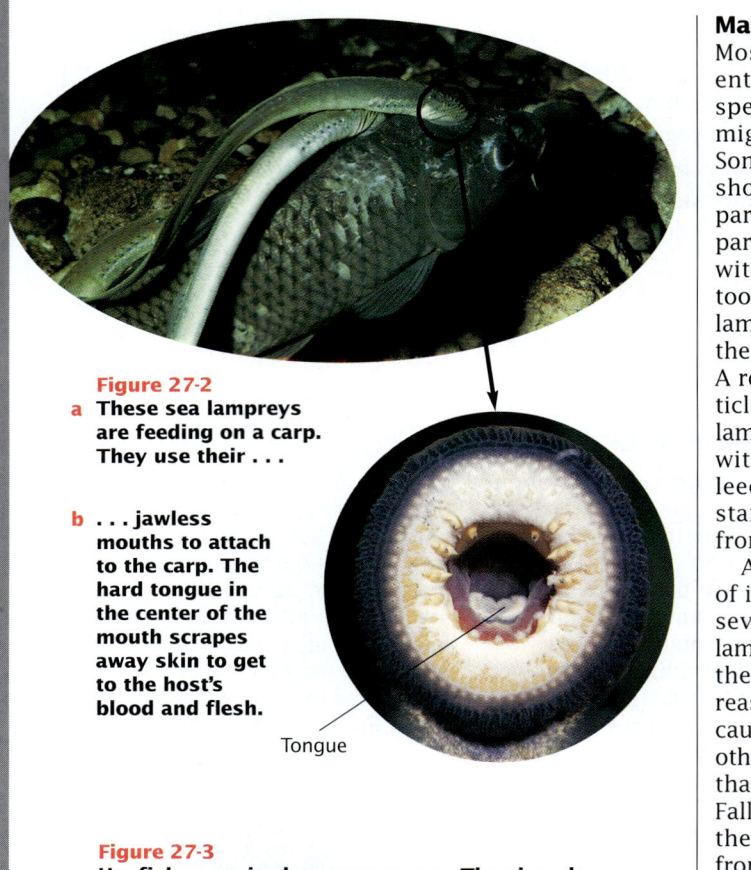

Figure 27-2

a These sea lampreys are feeding on a carp. They use their . . .

b . . . jawless mouths to attach to the carp. The hard tongue in the center of the mouth scrapes away skin to get to the host's blood and flesh.

Tongue

Figure 27-3
Hagfishes are jawless scavengers. They invade the bodies of dying or dead animals and feed on the internal organs.

Many lampreys are parasites
Most kinds of lampreys spend their entire lives in fresh water. A few species live in the sea as adults but migrate into fresh water to breed. Some lampreys, like the sea lampreys shown in **Figure 27-2**, are external parasites that feed on other fishes. A parasitic lamprey's mouth is recessed within a funnel-like structure. Sharp toothlike hooks in the funnel help the lamprey attach to its host. The rim of the funnel functions as a suction cup. A rough tongue scrapes off small particles of the host's skin and flesh. The lamprey sucks in these particles along with the host's blood. Like some leeches, the lamprey secretes a substance that prevents its host's blood from clotting.

After a lamprey has fed, it drops off of its host. Damage to the host can be severe since the wound left by the lamprey may become infected or cause the host to bleed to death. For this reason, large lamprey populations can cause great damage to populations of other fishes. For instance, when a canal that allowed ships to bypass Niagara Falls was deepened in the early 1900s, the ocean lamprey was able to move from the Atlantic Ocean into the upper Great Lakes. By the 1940s and 1950s, this lamprey was abundant enough to cause a serious decline in the commercial and sport fishing industries of the Great Lakes. Lamprey populations were eventually reduced by treating the Great Lakes with poisons toxic to lamprey larvae.

Hagfishes are scavengers
Hagfishes, such as the one in **Figure 27-3**, are scavengers that generally feed on dead or dying animals, such as large invertebrates or other fishes. When a hagfish locates a potential meal, it enters the body of the other animal by squirming in through the gill openings, the mouth, or the anus. Once inside, it feeds on the internal organs of the animal, biting with jawlike folds of muscle that close side to side.

Matter of Fact: Hagfishes

Hagfishes are bottom dwellers that live only in cold ocean water. They are sometimes called slime eels because they have mucus-secreting glands all over their bodies. They produce so much mucus that, when agitated, one hagfish can turn a bucket of water into a jellylike substance within minutes. Hagfishes have both male and female organs. They may produce eggs one season and sperm the next. Eggs are fertilized externally. Young hagfishes hatch from the eggs as miniature versions of the adult.

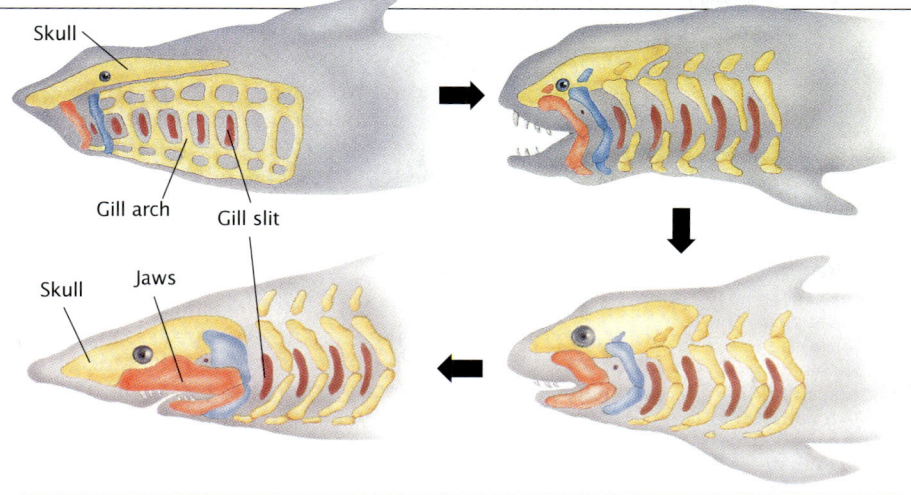

Figure 27-4
The jaw is an evolutionary modification of the first pair of gill arches that were present in ancient jawless fishes.

Skull

Gill arch   Gill slit

Skull   Jaws

Evolution of Jaws

Because they lack jaws, agnathans can eat only food that can be sucked into their mouths. Apart from the agnathans, all vertebrates have movable jaws. Animals with jaws can exploit a much wider range of foods than can jawless animals. Scientists think that jaws evolved from one or more of the gill arches that support the pharynx in agnathans, possibly in the way shown in **Figure 27-4**.

The earliest jawed fishes were acanthodians (*uh KAN thoh dee uhns*), members of the class Acanthodii. Although superficially resembling sharks, the acanthodians, or "spiny fishes," had a bony internal skeleton and were definitely not sharks. Acanthodians evolved about 435 million years ago. Another group of early jawed fishes was the placoderms (*PLAK uh durms*), class Placodermi, which evolved about 400 million years ago. Placoderms (meaning "plate skin") were armored with heavy, bony

plates and had strong jaws, as in the predator *Dunkleosteus*, illustrated in **Figure 27-5**. Both placoderms and acanthodians show a characteristic found in most other jawed vertebrates—paired appendages, in this case paired fins. Placoderms and acanthodians diversified rapidly. Perhaps because of jaws and paired fins, these fishes largely replaced the agnathans. Lampreys and hagfishes may have survived because of their specialized feeding habits. The placoderms became extinct about 345 million years ago, and the acanthodians died out about 270 million years ago. Scientists do not know why these once-diverse groups became extinct.

Figure 27-5
Dunkleosteus, a placoderm that was a predator in the ancient seas, might have looked like this drawing. Its skull and jaws were over 65 cm (2 ft) long.

525

Demonstration

▲ **Forming Opinions Supported by Sound Reasoning**
Materials: an assortment of pliers and suction bulbs; items such as screws, nuts, bottle caps, plastic forks and spoons, paper and plastic cups, etc.

portfolio

Have students form collaborative groups, and give each group a pair of pliers and a suction bulb. Have students experiment at picking up various objects with the pliers and the bulb. Students should then prepare reports describing how efficient each tool was at picking up and manipulating each of the objects. The report should conclude with a discussion of what type of fish is represented by the pliers (*jawed*) and by the bulb (*jawless*) and what advantage was gained by the evolution of jaws.

Get a Grip

■ **Relating Concepts**
The strongest muscles in a human, ounce for ounce, are the jaw muscles. Humans are not alone as vertebrates with strong jaws. We belong to a subphylum that is full of animals with grasping, tearing, and crushing mouths. Challenge students to name vertebrates that humans fear, or that are sometimes depicted as villains in books or movies. Write their suggestions on the board, and then ask students to identify which ones are scary because of their frightening teeth and jaws. (*Student suggestions might include animals such as sharks, bears, wolves, tigers, or snakes.*)

Matter of Fact: The Age of Fishes

The Devonian period began about 410 million years ago and lasted approximately 50 million years. During this period of time, sometimes called the Age of Fishes, fishes rapidly became abundant and diverse. By the end of the Devonian period, most of the jawless fishes were extinct. The placoderms survived into the next period, but they too eventually became extinct.

Key to Strategies
● **Understanding Concepts (Tier I)**
■ **Applying Information (Tier II)**
▲ **Critical Thinking (Tier III)**

Fishes and Amphibians   525

■ Recognizing Relationships

Have students study the figure and contrast the body shapes of the shark and the stingray. Ask students to identify differences in the structure of the head, the location of the eyes, the placement and shape of the fins, and the general body shape. Ask students to relate the body shape of each fish to the location where each is usually found. (*Because of its flattened body shape, the ray is more likely to be found resting on the ocean bottom in shallow water.*)

Demonstration

● Comparing Structures

Show students a shark's jaw or a photograph of one. Point out the hinged jaw and how the teeth are arranged in rows, with newer teeth replacing the older teeth as they are lost.

■ Relating Concepts

Use *Illustration—Placoid Scales* shown in Chapter 27 Section 27-1 of *Holt Biology Videodiscs Teacher's Correlation Guide to Holt Biology: Visualizing Life.* Point out the similarity in structure between the shark scale and the tooth. Explain that, like human teeth, each shark scale has a pulp cavity surrounded by a layer of dentine covered with enamel. Tell students that in most sharks these scales are slanted toward the tail. If students were to rub the shark from its head to its tail, the skin would feel almost smooth, but if they were to rub in the opposite direction in some species, they could actually cut through the skin on their hands. Ask students to suggest what evolutionary advantage sharks might have with this type of scale. (*The scales would provide a means of protection for the shark.*)

Sharks and Rays: Class Chondrichthyes

Soon after placoderms appeared, another group of jawed fishes arose, the class Chondrichthyes *(kahn DRIHK thees)*. The modern members of this class are the sharks, skates, and rays. Unlike the bony skeletons of acanthodians, the skeletons of sharks and rays are composed of a flexible substance called cartilage *(KAHRT'l ihj)*. Chondrichthyes means "cartilage fishes." There are about 850 living species of cartilaginous fishes, the vast majority of which live in salt water. **Figure 27-6** shows a shark and a ray.

If you were to touch a shark or ray, you would notice rough, sandpaper-like skin. This texture results from the many small scales that are embedded in the skin. As shown in **Figure 27-6b**, shark scales are very similar to shark teeth. The mouth of a cartilaginous fish includes upper and lower jaws, generally armed with rows of hard teeth. As teeth in the outer row are lost or broken, they are replaced by others that move up from the row behind.

The gills of sharks and rays open to the outside through a series of slits, as shown in **Figure 27-6c**. One gill slit, the spiracle, opens directly to the outside on the side or top of the head. Water can be brought to the pharynx through the spiracle and then expelled through the gill slits. This arrangement not only frees the mouth for feeding but also enables sharks and rays to lie on the bottom of the ocean and draw water in through the spiracle rather than the mouth, which would also bring in sediment.

Figure 27-6

a **Sharks, skates, and rays have two sets of paired fins: pectoral fins and pelvic fins. The dorsal fin (on the back) and the caudal fin (the tail) are unpaired. This ray has no dorsal fin, but its pectoral fins are greatly enlarged into a pair of large, winglike fins.**

Blue spotted stingray

Caudal fin

Dorsal fin

Pectoral fin

Blue shark

Pelvic fin

Shark tooth

b **The scales of a shark's skin are very similar to its teeth, though much smaller.**

Shark skin

Matter of Fact: Man-Eaters?

Movies such as *Jaws* have given many people the impression that all sharks are man-eaters. Of the 370 known species of sharks, only 27 have attacked humans. One expert estimates that the chances of being attacked by a shark are equal to the chances of being struck by lightning.

How sharks detect and capture prey

Evolution

Why is it advantageous for a shark to be able to replace lost teeth throughout its life?

Most sharks and rays are carnivores. Although sharks have a reputation for being man-eaters, only a few species of sharks are dangerous to humans. Three well-developed senses enable sharks and rays to detect their prey. First, they have an acute sense of smell. Second, they have the ability to sense electric currents in water. This sense is particularly useful in detecting the small electric currents generated by the muscle movements of animals. The electric ray *Torpedo* is also able to produce a powerful electric current, which it uses to deter predators and to stun prey. Third, sharks and rays have a lateral line system. As you learned in Chapter 24, the lateral line system is composed of pressure-sensitive cells that lie within canals along the sides of a fish.

Lateral line

Spiracle

Gill slit

c The gill openings of a shark open directly to the outside. Water is taken in through the mouth or spiracle, passes over the gills, and then exits through the gill slits.

Changes in pressure caused by a fish or other animal swimming nearby can be detected by the cells in the lateral line.

Given the variety of shapes and sizes of cartilaginous fishes, it is not surprising that they exhibit a variety of feeding methods. Like the largest whales, the largest shark (the whale shark) and the largest ray (the manta ray) feed on plankton. The whale shark may exceed 13 m (45 ft) in length, and the manta ray can have a "fin span" of nearly 6 m (20 ft). In both the whale shark and the manta ray, the mouth is filled with a hard mesh that is used to trap tiny organisms. Both of these large animals cruise the oceans and filter small animals from the water.

Sharks and rays have internal fertilization

The pelvic fins of male cartilaginous fishes are modified into a pair of claspers, which are used to transfer sperm to the female during mating. Thus, fertilization in these animals is internal. Skates, rays, and some sharks lay eggs. The extremely yolky fertilized eggs are usually housed in an elaborate leathery case. Many species of sharks do not lay eggs. Instead, the female keeps the yolky eggs inside her body until they hatch, and the young sharks are born alive. In some sharks, the female provides nutrients to her developing young through a membranous sac somewhat like the placenta.

Theme Answer

Evolution

A shark's teeth are adapted to its feeding habits. Struggles that ensue while trying to capture prey can cause the loss of teeth. If sharks could not grow new teeth, they would starve. A single shark may grow more than 20,000 teeth in its lifetime.

Phase Three

Assessment Options

Closure

■ **Recognizing Patterns**

Form cooperative groups of four students. Have each group make a table comparing characteristics of each type of fish that they have studied in this section. Have them leave room for the bony fishes, which they will study in the next section. Across the top of their tables, they should write *Body Shape, Placement of Fins, Gill Type and Location, Sense Organs,* and *Feeding Habits.* Down the left side they should write *Lampreys, Hagfishes, Sharks,* and *Rays.* Have individual students copy the completed table and save it for use with Section 27-2.

SECTION REVIEW

Assign the *Section Review.*

Reteaching

Ask students to make a list of shark characteristics that they would look for if they were given a preserved fish and were told to determine whether it was a shark or another kind of fish. (*Possible answers include the following: torpedo-like body shape, jaws, skeleton made of cartilage, sandpaper-like skin, gill slits open to the outside, and a spiracle on the top or side of the head.*)

Key to Strategies
● **Understanding Concepts (Tier I)**
■ **Applying Information (Tier II)**
▲ **Critical Thinking (Tier III)**

SECTION REVIEW

1 Identify two characteristics of agnathans.

2 Explain two adaptations that enable some lampreys to be external parasites of fishes.

3 Explain how the absence of jaws limits what a jawless fish can eat.

4 Describe two differences between sharks and lampreys.

ANSWERS TO **SECTION REVIEW**

1 Possible answers include the following: no jaws or paired fins, a skeleton composed mostly of cartilage, no well-developed vertebral column, gills that lie within pouches that branch from the pharynx. Modern agnathans are eel-like, with slimy skin. Extinct agnathans were a diverse group, with bodies covered by thick, bony plates.

2 Sharp, toothlike hooks around a funnel-like mouth enable the lamprey to attach to its

host. The lamprey also has a rough tongue that scrapes off the host's skin and flesh.

3 Jawless fishes can only eat food that can be sucked into their mouth. Jawed fishes can bite and tear their food.

4 Possible answers include the following: sharks have upper and lower jaws, while lampreys are jawless; sharks have rough skin, while lampreys have slimy skin; sharks have paired fins, while lampreys do not; and sharks have gill slits, while lampreys do not.

Phase One
Preparation

Scheduling

See the **Lesson Planning Guide** on pages 521A and 521B for lecture, classwork, and assignment options for Section 27-2.

Phase Two
Teaching Strategies

Active READING

Technique: Reading Organizer

As students read about bony fishes on pages 528–529, have them complete the following compare/contrast reading organizer.

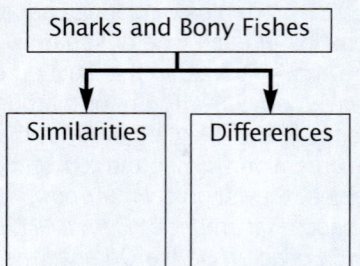

Sharks and Bony Fishes

Similarities — Differences

Of the nearly 22,000 living species of fishes, 21,000 species are bony fishes. Bony fishes evolved about 400 million years ago and are one of evolution's greatest success stories. The bony fishes alive today include familiar animals such as trout, bass, perch, tuna, swordfish, guppies, catfish, bluefish, mackerel, and cod.

27-2 Bony Fishes

OBJECTIVES

1 Identify three differences between bony fishes and sharks.

2 Describe the importance of the swim bladder for bony fishes.

3 Summarize the importance of lobe-finned fishes in the evolution of land vertebrates.

Structure of a Bony Fish

Bony fishes belong to the class Osteichthyes *(ahs tee IHK thees)*, which means "bone fish." What are the differences between sharks and bony fishes? As shown in **Figure 27-7**, most bony fishes have a skeleton composed largely of bone and are covered by scales formed of bone. These scales are very different from the toothlike scales of sharks and rays, as you can see by comparing **Figure 27-7a** with **Figure 27-6b**. The gills of bony fishes are housed in a common chamber on each side of the head. Each chamber is covered by a hard plate called the operculum *(oh PUR kyoo luhm)*. The

Figure 27-7

a The scales of bony fishes are usually made of bone. They are not toothlike, as are the scales of a shark.

b The bones of this bony fish are evident in this 40-million-year-old fossil.

Operculum
Gills

c The gills of bony fishes are covered by a protective plate, the operculum. Gills provide a large surface area for the rapid uptake of oxygen and the release of carbon dioxide.

528

Videodisc Resources

Holt Biology Videodiscs

Lesson 27-2: Bony Fishes

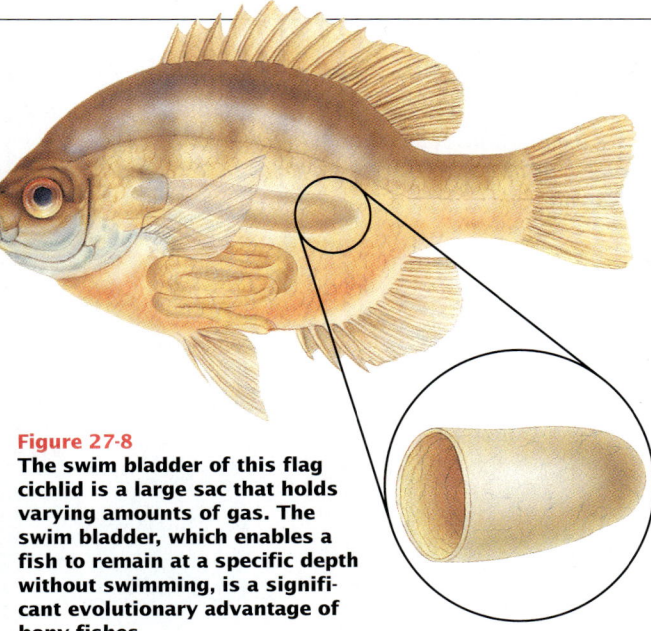

Figure 27-8
The swim bladder of this flag cichlid is a large sac that holds varying amounts of gas. The swim bladder, which enables a fish to remain at a specific depth without swimming, is a significant evolutionary advantage of bony fishes.

upper tail lobe is larger than the lower lobe in sharks, but the lobes are more symmetrical in bony fishes.

A critical difference between bony fishes and sharks is the presence of a **swim bladder** in most bony fishes. This gas-filled sac, shown in the cutaway view in **Figure 27-8**, gives the fish buoyancy. By regulating the amount of gas in the swim bladder, a fish can adjust its buoyant density. Thus, the fish can remain at a particular depth without expending energy through swimming. Although a shark's oil-rich liver gives it some buoyancy, a shark is denser than water and will sink if it stops swimming.

Like sharks, bony fishes sense pressure changes in water with a lateral line system. Vision is also an important sense for most bony fishes. Most bony fishes have color vision. The bright colors of many fishes, such as those in **Figure 27-9**, serve as signals to potential mates and rivals. Fishes living in different environments are sensitive to

Figure 27-9
The coloration of these glassy sweepers allows members of the species to easily recognize one another, which is especially important for schooling and mating.

different colors. For instance, fishes that live at moderate depths often are more sensitive to blue light than to red light; red light is absorbed by the ocean, so little red light penetrates to the depths inhabited by these fishes.

Many species of bony fishes can detect electric fields. The knife fishes of South America produce their own weak electric fields. Knife fishes detect disturbances in their fields, which can be caused by rocks or other objects, by prey or predators, or by other fishes of the same species. Knife fishes live in silty streams where vision is limited. They use their electric fields to navigate, to find prey, to avoid predators, and to signal to other members of their species.

Most bony fishes lay eggs
In almost all bony fishes, fertilization and development occur outside the female's body. The eggs and sperm of bony fishes are typically released into the water or into a nest fashioned by the parents. In live-bearing fishes, such as guppies, mollies, and swordtails, the male transfers his sperm directly to the female via a modified fin near his tail. Fertilization is internal, and the young develop inside the female. You can read more about fishes in the *Tour of a Fish* on the next page.

529

Demonstration
● **Comparing Structures**
Display a variety of live fishes in an aquarium. The aquarium could contain freshwater tropical fish or local native fishes such as trout, sunfish, bass, or bluegill that have been caught by your students for display. You might also wish to set up a saltwater aquarium for saltwater tropical fish. Encourage the students to observe the structure, movement, and behavior of the fish. Ask students to point out similarities in the fishes' shape, number and location of fins, movement, and respiration rate.

Connection: *Chapter 4*

Osmotic Balance
The body fluids of freshwater fish are more concentrated than the water in which they live, so water tends to flow into their cells by osmosis. To maintain homeostasis, these fish must excrete large amounts of dilute urine and replace lost salts by absorbing solutes from the water. Saltwater fish have the opposite problem. Their body fluids are less concentrated than sea water, so water tends to flow out of their cells. To maintain homeostasis, they must drink large quantities of sea water and get rid of the excess salt that they take in with the sea water through special salt-secreting cells.

Fish and Scuba Divers
● **Comparing Structures**
A swim bladder works the same way as a scuba diver's buoyancy compensator. Invite a trained scuba diver to demonstrate how he or she changes depth by regulating the gas in a buoyancy compensator.

Multicultural Perspective: Fish in Asia—Art and Food
Asian people have celebrated the elegant beauty of carp and goldfish for many centuries. Elaborately decorated fishbowls and kites with carp designs can be found throughout China, Japan, and Korea, as can serene water gardens with fish swimming among the willows and water lilies. Even a fish dinner becomes a celebration of beauty, as Asian chefs strive to create works of edible art.

Key to Strategies
● **Understanding Concepts (Tier I)**
■ **Applying Information (Tier II)**
▲ **Critical Thinking (Tier III)**

Mathematics Connection

How Many Survive?

Salmon return to the stream in which they hatched to spawn. During spawning, females lay from 2,000 to 10,000 eggs. The young salmon hatch and make their way to the sea. Most of them perish during this journey—a Canadian study reported that less than 1 percent of hatchlings return to spawn. Have students calculate the range of how many newly hatched salmon from each female survive to spawn (2,000 × 0.01 = 20, and 10,000 × 0.01 = 100, so between 20 and 100 hatchlings from each female survive to spawn).

Adaptations of Fishes

🔴 **Summarizing Information**

Many of the salmon's (or any fish's) adaptations make life in the water possible. Using the information in this section and the **Tour,** have students make a table with two columns. In the first column they should list the following adaptations: gills, slimy surface, swim bladders, sense of smell. In the second column, students should describe a function of each adaptation.

Mathematics Connection

How Fast Can Salmon Swim?

Salmon and other fish can swim no faster than 10 body lengths per second. Using the information in the **Tour,** have students calculate how fast a 20 cm salmon can swim (10 body lengths per second × 20 cm = 2 m per second).

Fish

The sockeye salmon is a bony fish. It lives in the northern Pacific Ocean and in lakes, streams, and rivers in North America and northern Asia. Like other bony fishes, it has a skeleton made of bone. The sockeye salmon also has a swim bladder, a gas-filled sac that allows the fish to adjust its buoyancy.

Habitat
Sockeye salmon live in the ocean and in fresh water. Salmon hatch in fresh water. The young migrate to the sea, where they mature. Adult salmon live in the ocean but return to the stream in which they hatched to reproduce.

Most scientists think that salmon locate their native river or stream by using their sense of smell.

Evolutionary Relationships
Sockeye salmon belong to the family Salmonidae. This family contains the salmon and trout.

The "slimy" surface of a fish reduces friction from water by more than 66 percent.

All fishes have gills composed of tiny filaments that are richly supplied with blood.

Bony fishes have paired pectoral and pelvic fins.

Size
Large sockeye salmon can reach 84 cm (33 in.) in length and weigh nearly 7 kg (15 lb).

Major Groups of Bony Fishes

Look carefully at the fins of the salmon shown in the *Tour of a Fish* on page 530. Salmon belong to the group of bony fishes known as the ray-finned fishes. All but seven species of modern-day bony fishes are **ray-finned fishes**. In these fishes, the fins are fan-shaped and are supported by thin, bony rays. Ray-finned fishes are the most successful and diverse group of vertebrates.

The other group of bony fishes is the **lobe-finned fishes**. In this group, the fins are fleshy and are supported by central bones. The existing lobe-finned fishes are six species of

lungfishes and one species of **coelacanth** *(SEE luh kanth)*. **Table 27-1** lists the major groups of fishes.

As their name suggests, lungfishes have functional lungs. These fishes live in Africa, South America, and Australia. A lungfish from Africa is shown in **Figure 27-10**. Some lungfishes

Figure 27-10
Lungfishes, like this African lungfish, have fleshy, lobed fins. Lungs enable these fishes to live in water that is low in oxygen.

Table 27-1   Major Groups of Fishes

Class	Number of modern species	Description	Examples	
Agnatha	81	No jaws; no paired appendages	Lampreys, hagfishes	
Acanthodii	Extinct	Jaws; spiny, paired fins	Acanthodians	
Placodermi	Extinct	Jaws; paired fins; bony armor	Placoderms	
Chondrichthyes	850	Jaws; paired fins; skeleton of cartilage; no swim bladder; spiracle; internal fertilization	Sharks, skates, rays	
Osteichthyes	21,000	Jaws; paired fins supported by bony rays; bony skeleton; most have swim bladder	Ray-finned fishes	
	7	Jaws; paired lobed fins; bony skeleton; extinct forms are ancestors of amphibians	Lobe-finned fishes	

531

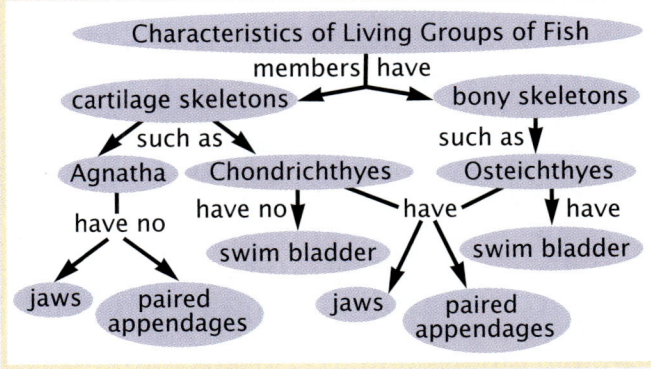

Figure 27-11
Latimeria chalumnae, the living species of coelacanth, was named to honor Marjorie Courtney-Latimer, a museum curator in South Africa. She recognized and preserved the first specimen of this species in 1938.

inhabit stagnant water that is low in oxygen. Other lungfishes live in ponds that dry up annually. Lungfishes survive these dry periods by burying themselves in mud at the bottom of the pond. Lungs enable these fishes to supplement their oxygen intake by breathing air.

The coelacanth, by contrast, inhabits deep ocean environments. Fossils of coelacanths from the time of the dinosaurs are common, but no coelacanth fossils younger than 80 million years old have been found. Coelacanths were thought to be extinct until a specimen was netted off the eastern coast of South Africa in 1938.

Figure 27-11 shows a coelacanth that was captured in deep water off the east coast of Africa.

Lobe-finned fishes are the ancestors of amphibians

Zoologists are convinced that land vertebrates evolved from lobe-finned fishes that are now extinct. Until recently, scientists thought that coelacanths, which have sturdier fins than lungfishes, were the closest living relatives of the amphibians. However, comparisons of mitochondrial DNA reported in 1990 suggest that lungfishes, not coelacanths, are the closest living relatives of modern amphibians.

SECTION REVIEW

1. How could you tell whether a fish was a shark or a bony fish?

2. Explain how a swim bladder enables a fish to conserve energy.

3. Describe two differences between ray-finned fishes and lobe-finned fishes.

4. Could legs have evolved from the fins of ray-finned fishes? Explain your answer.

The name *amphibian* is derived from the Greek words meaning "double" and "life." This name reflects the fact that although most amphibians are terrestrial, they must reproduce in water or in moist environments. Amphibians were the first vertebrates to walk on land. They evolved from lobe-finned fishes about 350 million years ago.

27-3 Amphibians

OBJECTIVES

1 Identify two characteristics that enabled amphibians to invade the land.

2 Describe the life cycle of a frog.

3 Describe the characteristics of the three orders of living amphibians.

The First Land Vertebrates

More than 4,300 species of amphibians exist today. Amphibians include frogs, toads, salamanders, and the wormlike, legless caecilians (see *SIHL ee uhns*). Two examples of amphibians are shown in **Figure 27-12** and **Figure 27-13**. As adults, amphibians are clearly different from fishes, showing many adaptations for life on land. Except for caecilians, all amphibians have legs. Most amphibians have lungs for gas exchange, although some salamanders lack lungs. Gas exchange also occurs across the thin, moist skin of most amphibians. The lack of a skin that is resistant to drying is one feature that limits most amphibians to moist environments.

Another difference between fishes and amphibians is evident in the amphibian circulatory system. Amphibians achieve more efficient circulation than fishes because of their double-loop circulatory system. As you saw in **Figure 24-10b** on page 466, a fish's heart pumps only deoxygenated blood,

Figure 27-13
This spotted newt is an amphibian. Limbs enable the newt to move on land.

Figure 27-12
The fire-bellied toad lives near slow-flowing rivers in the lowlands of central and eastern Europe. Although adapted to land, amphibians such as this toad must have access to a watery environment to reproduce.

533

Videodisc Resources

Holt Biology Videodiscs
Lesson 27-3: Amphibians

Phase One
Preparation

Scheduling
See the **Lesson Planning Guide** on pages 521A and 521B for lecture, classwork, and assignment options for Section 27-3.

Phase Two
Teaching Strategies

Active READING

Technique: Summarizing
After students read silently about amphibians, ask student volunteers to summarize what has been read without looking at the text. Other students should listen to the retellings without interrupting and be prepared to point out any inaccuracies in the summary and add any ideas that were left out. Students may refer to the text during this clarification process.

Moving to the Land

■ Relating Concepts
Remind students that there were plants and invertebrates living on land before the first vertebrates—amphibians—crawled out of the swamp. The earliest amphibian, *Ichthyostega,* is thought to have been a carnivore. Ask students to speculate on what its food might have been (*arthropods*).

Language Arts Connection

A Double Life
Amphibian means "double life." Ask students to explain why this is an appropriate name for these animals. (*Many amphibians begin their lives as aquatic tadpoles, and most live in a terrestrial habitat as adults.*)

Key to Strategies
● **Understanding Concepts (Tier I)**
■ **Applying Information (Tier II)**
▲ **Critical Thinking (Tier III)**

Gas Exchange

■ **Relating Concepts**

Tell students that although most amphibians have lungs, some species of salamanders exchange oxygen and carbon dioxide through gills, even as adults. Ask students where they would expect to find these amphibians and why *(in an aquatic environment because gills collapse in air)*. Tell students that some species of salamanders have neither lungs nor gills. Ask students to explain how these amphibians obtain oxygen and rid their bodies of carbon dioxide *(through their skins)*.

■ **Recognizing Relationships**

To introduce students to amphibians, use *Video—Amphibians* (1 min 15 s) shown in Chapter 27 Section 27-3 of **Holt Biology Videodiscs Teacher's Correlation Guide to Holt Biology: Visualizing Life.** Tell students to note how amphibians are tied to both land and water. Have students write a paragraph or two telling how the life cycle of a frog illustrates the evolution of amphibians from water-dwelling vertebrates to land-dwelling vertebrates. *(Fertilization and the early stages of development must take place in water. Tadpoles breathe with gills. Later, adult frogs live on land and breathe with lungs, but they must stay near water to keep their skin moist.)*

Demonstration

● **Identifying Structures**

Obtain tadpoles from a nearby pond or a biological supply company, and place them in an aquarium in the classroom so that students can observe metamorphosis in a frog. Have students observe the tadpoles daily, and ask them to determine what happens to a tadpole's tail. Does it fall off or is it reabsorbed? *(It is reabsorbed.)* If the tadpoles were obtained locally, return the adult frogs to the pond from which the tadpoles were taken.

---

sending it to the gills, where it picks up oxygen. When the blood reaches the gills, it slows down while passing through narrow capillaries. The amphibian heart, in contrast, pumps both deoxygenated and oxygenated blood. Deoxygenated blood returning from the body is sent back out by the heart to the lungs to absorb oxygen. This oxygen-rich blood, which also slows as it passes through the narrow capillaries of the lungs, returns to the heart to be pumped to the rest of the body. Thus, in amphibians blood is pumped to the body at higher pressures and faster rates of flow than in fishes. There is a new problem, however. Oxygenated blood partially mixes with deoxygenated blood in the single, undivided ventricle of the amphibian heart.

The Tie to Water

As you learned in Chapter 24, amphibians do not lay watertight eggs and so must reproduce in water or in moist environments. Many species of frogs and toads, for example, congregate in ponds during the spring in preparation for mating. The males generally arrive first and begin noisy mating calls that attract nearby females. You have probably heard the raucous symphony of male frogs on warm spring evenings. Once mating begins, the male grasps a female and holds her. While she releases eggs, he simultaneously releases sperm. Fertilization takes place externally. Follow the development of a frog in **Figure 27-14**. You can read more about frogs in *Tour of a Frog* on the next page.

Mating in some salamanders resembles that in frogs and toads. In most salamanders, however, fertilization occurs internally. After performing complex courtship behaviors to attract a female, the male deposits a packet of sperm on the ground or in the water. The female then draws the sperm packet into her reproductive opening. She later deposits the fertilized eggs in water or a moist area. Salamander larvae retain external gills until the time of metamorphosis. Other than that, they resemble their parents. All salamander larvae, like the adults, are carnivorous.

Figure 27-14

a The life cycle of a frog involves large-scale changes in body form. First a mass of eggs is laid in a wet or moist environment.

b The young tadpole emerges from the egg with external gills, which are later replaced by internal gills. After feeding and growing, the tadpole begins to transform into an adult frog.

c Dramatic changes occur in the tadpole. The tail and gills recede. Lungs and front and hind limbs grow. Feeding habits may also change. Herbivorous tadpoles change into carnivorous adults.

d By the time a tadpole becomes an adult frog, it has completely lost its tail and gills. Its lungs enable it to breathe air. The changes that transform a tadpole into an adult frog are called metamorphosis.

Frog

The red-eyed tree frog is an amphibian that lives in Central America and northern South America. Like most amphibians, the red-eyed tree frog has a moist, scaleless skin and passes through an aquatic tadpole phase during its development.

Adult frogs have powerful hind legs that are used for jumping. Adult frogs do not have a tail.

Habitat
As its name suggests, the red-eyed tree frog lives mainly in trees. It is found in tropical rain forests.

Evolutionary Relationships
Frogs belong to the order Anura. The name of this order is derived from the Greek words meaning "without a tail." Red-eyed tree frogs belong to the family Hylidae, which includes more than 500 species found in Asia, Europe, and the Americas.

Most amphibians lay jelly-like eggs that hatch into aquatic larvae. The female red-eyed tree frog attaches her eggs to vegetation that overhangs water. After hatching, the tadpoles drop into the water. They feed and grow for some time and then they undergo a complete metamorphosis into air-breathing frogs.

Size
Female red-eyed tree frogs average about 70 mm (2.8 in.) in length, not including the hind legs. Males are slightly smaller.

The red-eyed tree frog, like most frogs, is solitary except during the breeding season, when males call noisily to attract females.

535

Tour

Protection of the Eggs
● **Summarizing Information**

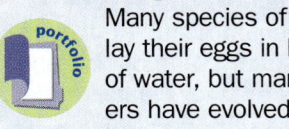

Many species of frogs lay their eggs in bodies of water, but many others have evolved ways to protect eggs laid out of water from desiccation. For instance, in several frog species (known as marsupial frogs), the females carry the eggs in a pouch on their back. South African tree frogs construct an arboreal foam nest in which the eggs develop and hatch. Using the information in this section and in the **Tour,** have students research some of the anuran adaptations for protecting their eggs from desiccation and predation.

Disappearing Frogs
■ **Analyzing Information**

Worldwide, populations of frogs and other amphibians have been declining dramatically in recent years. The declines are greater than can be explained by habitat destruction alone. Some scientists believe that because amphibians lay their eggs in shallow water, where they are exposed to direct sunlight, the thinning of the ozone layer may be contributing to the decline in frog numbers. As the ozone layer thins, more ultraviolet radiation reaches the Earth from the sun. Since UV rays are known to cause genetic damage, this could explain why frog eggs fail to develop and hatch. Have students research the apparent decline in amphibian populations. A good starting place is "Silence of the Frogs," in *The New York Times Magazine,* December 13, 1992, pages 36–39, 64, 66, and 76.

Amphibian Differences
● **Comparing Structures**
Using the information in this section and the **Tour,** have students identify two differences between frogs and salamanders and two differences between frogs and caecilians. *(Salamanders have tails and internal fertilization. Caecilians have no limbs and a little tail or no tail.)*

Active READING

Technique: K-W-L

Tell students to return to their lists of things they **W**ant to know about fishes, which they created using the K-W-L Active Reading on page 522. Have them place check marks next to questions that they are now able to answer. Students should finish by making a list of what they have **L**earned. Conclude by asking students the following questions:

- Which questions are still unanswered?
- What new questions do you have?

Phase Three

Assessment Options

Closure

● **Understanding Concepts**

Have students work in groups of four to prepare a poster showing the frog's life cycle. The poster should include drawings of each of the four stages of a frog's life. Next to each drawing, students should add a paragraph that explains what they have learned about this typical amphibian and how that relates to the drawing. For example, next to the drawing of frog eggs, the paragraph could explain how frog eggs are fertilized and where they are laid.

SECTION REVIEW

Assign the *Section Review.*

Reteaching

Have students make a list of amphibian characteristics that distinguish amphibians from fishes. *(Answers might include that amphibians have legs and lungs, can live on land, exchange gases through their skin, and have a double-loop circulatory system.)*

Kinds of Amphibians

Figure 27-15 shows a tropical burrowing amphibian called a caecilian. Caecilians are members of the order Gymnophiona (from the ancient Greek words for "naked" and "snakelike"). Caecilians burrow through the soil and feed on earthworms and other small animals.

Frogs and toads are **anurans**. They belong to the order Anura (meaning "without a tail" in Greek). This order is the largest amphibian order, containing over 3,800 species. As adults, frogs and toads are carnivores. They have large mouths, often with sticky tongues. The body form of adult frogs and toads is distinct—the hind legs are specialized for jumping, and there is no tail. Frogs and toads are found in a variety of habitats. Some species are completely aquatic, while others spend some time on land. Some species of frogs spend most of their adult lives in trees. Toads, which you might see in a garden or park, are mainly terrestrial, usually only returning to water to breed. The skin of a toad is dry and warty and is more resistant to evaporation than the skin of other amphibians.

Salamanders belong to the order Urodela (meaning "visible tail"). A salamander has a distinct head, trunk, and tail. The limbs are set at right angles to the body. Like frogs, toads, and caecilians, salamanders are carnivores. **Table 27-2** lists the three orders of living amphibians and their main characteristics.

Figure 27-15
Caecilians are limbless, one of their many adaptations for burrowing.

Table 27-2 Orders of Amphibians

Order	Number of modern species	Description	Examples
Gymnophiona	160	Wormlike body with no limbs; tail short or absent; restricted to tropics	Caecilians 
Anura	3,800+	No tail; hind limbs specialized for jumping; worldwide distribution	Frogs, toads 
Urodela	390	Body has distinct head, trunk, and tail; limbs set at right angles to body; distributed worldwide except Australia	Salamanders, newts 

SECTION REVIEW

1 Compare an amphibian with a bony fish. In what important ways are they different?

2 Describe the stages in the life cycle of a frog.

3 Name one representative of each amphibian order.

4 Form a hypothesis that explains why it is advantageous for caecilians to have no limbs.

536

ANSWERS TO SECTION REVIEW

1 Most amphibians have legs, while fish do not; amphibians breathe using lungs, while fish use gills for gas exchange; amphibians have a double-loop circulatory system that pumps both oxygenated and deoxygenated blood, while fish have a single-loop circulatory system that pumps only deoxygenated blood (to the gills).

2 The life cycle of the frog begins with an egg laid in a moist or wet environment. A tadpole with external gills emerges from the egg. The external gills are replaced by internal gills as the tadpole grows. The tail and gills recede, and lungs and limbs grow as the tadpole transforms into an adult frog.

3 Refer to Table 27-2 on page 536.

4 Students may suggest that the lack of limbs is advantageous to caecilians because they are burrowing animals and because their snakelike bodies enable them to enter smaller spaces than they could enter if they had limbs.

A male Darwin's frog carries developing offspring in his vocal sacs. Here, a young frog has just been released.

Alternative Assessment

Have students make a time line of the evolution of vertebrates from the first jawless fishes through amphibians. Next to each of the organisms listed on the time line, students should describe the new characteristics that arose in the organism through natural selection.

Portfolio Assessment

Portfolio Assessment on page T39 provides options for building and evaluating student portfolios. Students and teachers can select items from the areas listed on page T39 for inclusion in a portfolio.

	Key Terms	Summary
27-1 **Jawless Fishes and Cartilaginous Fishes**  Jawless fishes were the only vertebrates for over 150 million years.		• Jawless fishes were the first vertebrates to evolve. • The existing jawless fishes include lampreys, many of which are external parasites on other fishes, and hagfishes, which are scavengers. • Acanthodians were the first vertebrates with jaws. • Sharks and rays have skeletons of cartilage.
27-2 **Bony Fishes** 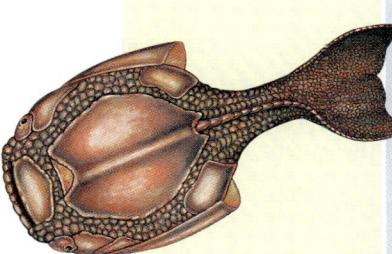 Most bony fishes are ray-finned fishes.	swim bladder (p. 529) ray-finned fishes (p. 531) lobe-finned fishes (p. 531) coelacanth (p. 531)	• Unlike sharks and rays, most bony fishes have skeletons of bone. • Bony fishes have a swim bladder, a gas-filled sac that helps them to maintain their level in the water. • Most bony fishes are ray-finned fishes. • A group of bony fishes known as the lobe-finned fishes are thought to be the closest relatives of the amphibians.
27-3 **Amphibians** Most amphibians, including this frog, must return to water to reproduce. 	anuran (p. 536)	• Amphibians were the first terrestrial vertebrates. • Frogs, toads, salamanders, and caecilians are amphibians. • Because their skins are not water-tight, most amphibians live in water or in damp environments. • Amphibian eggs are not water-tight and will dry out if not kept wet or moist. • Caecilians are legless, tropical amphibians. They burrow in moist soils and eat worms and other small animals. • Frogs and toads, the anurans, are adapted for jumping. • Salamanders have four limbs and a tail. They are carnivorous and have internal fertilization.

537

ANSWER TO CONCEPT MAP

The following is one possible answer to the Relating Concepts exercise on page 538.

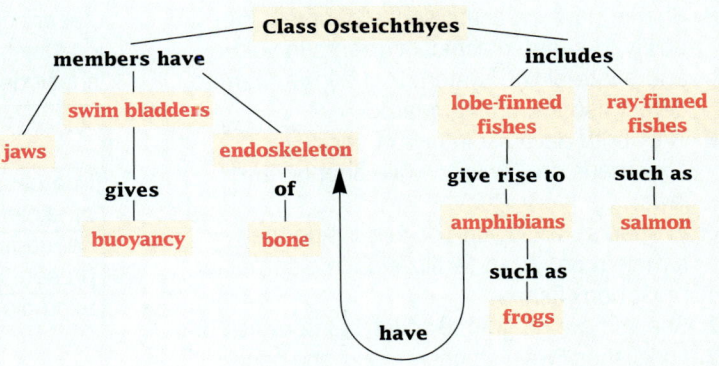

review

ANSWERS

Understanding Vocabulary

1. a. Agnatha
   b. Osteichthyes
   c. burrowing
2. a. Acanthodians do not fit the pattern; it is a primitive jawed fish. Lampreys and hagfishes are agnathans, or jawless fishes.
   b. Slimy skin does not fit the pattern; it is a characteristic of an agnathan. The other features are characteristics of cartilaginous fish in the class Chondrichthyes.
   c. Caecilian does not fit the pattern. All the others have limbs; caecilians do not.

Understanding Concepts

3. Concept map answer is on page 537.
4. *Agnathan* means "without jaws." The agnathans, or jawless fishes, are characterized by the absence of jaws, a skeleton composed mostly of cartilage instead of bone, and gills that lie within pouches that branch from the pharynx. The two main groups of modern agnathans are the lampreys and hagfishes.
5. The lateral line system in fish is a series of pressure-sensitive cells that lie within canals along the sides of the body. Changes in pressure can be detected, enabling the fish to locate prey or navigate within its school. The inner ear in terrestrial vertebrates most closely resembles the lateral line in function.
6. Sharp, toothlike hooks around a funnel-like mouth allows the lamprey to attach to its host. The lamprey also has a rough tongue that scrapes off the host's skin and flesh.
7. Scientists think that jaws evolved from one or more of the gill arches that support the pharynx in agnathans. Jaws enabled fishes and other animals to exploit many different food sources not available to jawless fishes.

---

review

Understanding Vocabulary

1. For each set of terms, complete the analogy.
   a. fishes with a swim bladder : Osteichthyes :: jawless fishes : _____
   b. skeleton of cartilage : Chondrichthyes :: skeleton of bone : _____
   c. frog : jumping :: caecilian : _____
2. For each list of terms, select the one that does not fit the others and explain why.
   a. agnathan, lamprey, hagfish, acanthodian
   b. internal fertilization, slimy skin, skeleton of cartilage, jaws
   c. frog, toad, coelacanth, newt, caecilian

Understanding Concepts

3. **Relating Concepts** Construct a concept map that identifies members of the class Osteichthyes and describes their characteristics. Try to include the following terms in your concept map: jaws, swim bladders, buoyancy, endoskeleton, bone, lobe-finned fishes, ray-finned fishes, amphibians, salmon, frogs.
4. **Identifying Structures** What does the term *agnathan* mean? What are three characteristics of agnathans? What are the two main groups of modern agnathans?
5. **Comparing Structures and Functions** What is the lateral line system? What function does it serve? What structure in terrestrial vertebrates most closely resembles the lateral line in function?
6. **Summarizing Information** Explain how parasitic lampreys obtain food.
7. **Comparing Functions** What structures in agnathans are thought to have given rise to jaws?
8. **Identifying Structures** Describe three senses that enable sharks to detect and capture their prey.
9. **Comparing Structures** Name one similarity and one difference between sharks and agnathans.

10. **Comparing Structures** How does fertilization in sharks differ from fertilization among most bony fishes?
11. **Comparing Functions** Explain why a shark will sink if it stops swimming. Why doesn't a bony fish have this same problem?
12. **Comparing Functions** How do the lungs of a lungfish help it survive? Why wouldn't lungs be useful for the living species of coelacanth?
13. **Summarizing Information** Copy the following table onto a separate sheet of paper. Complete the table by filling in the blanks.

	Agnathans	Sharks and rays	Bony fishes
Composition of skeleton		Cartilage	
Paired fins present?			Yes
Example	Hagfish		

14. **Recognizing Relationships** What characteristics enable amphibians to live on land? What characteristics require that most amphibians live in or near the water throughout their lives?
15. **Inferring Relationships** The populations of some species of amphibians have decreased dramatically in the last few decades. One hypothesized cause for this decline is acid rain. Explain one reason why amphibians might be more vulnerable to acid rain than reptiles are.
16. **Summarizing Information** Identify the characteristics of the three orders of amphibians. Give an example of an amphibian in each order.
17. **BUILDING ON WHAT YOU HAVE LEARNED** In Chapter 15 you learned about the evolutionary effects of competition. Using what you learned in that chapter, form a hypothesis to explain why the larvae of some amphibians feed on different foods from the adults. Name another group of animals in which this difference between larval and adult diets occurs.

---

8. Sharks have an acute sense of smell, the ability to sense electrical currents in water, and a lateral line system that allows them to detect fish swimming nearby.
9. They both have skeletons of cartilage. Agnathans are jawless while sharks have jaws.
10. In sharks, fertilization occurs inside the female's body, but fertilization is external in most bony fishes.
11. Sharks have no swim bladder, but bony fish do.
12. Lungfishes live in stagnant water and ponds that dry up annually. Lungs enable lungfishes to extract oxygen from the air. Coelacanths inhabit deep ocean environments.

13.

	Agnathans	Sharks and rays	Bony fishes
Composition of skeleton	Cartilage	Cartilage	Bone
Paired fins present?	No	Yes	Yes
Example	Hagfish	Blue shark	Salmon

Interpreting Graphics

18. Look at the photograph of the animal below.

 a. What kind of animal is shown in the photo? What characteristics enabled you to identify the animal?
 b. Describe the adaptations that enable this animal to live on land.

Reviewing Themes

19. *Evolution*
 Analysis of mitochondrial DNA indicates that lungfishes are the closest living relatives of amphibians. Identify one similarity in structure between lungfishes and amphibians.

Thinking Critically

20. **Determining Factual Accuracy** "The first fishes evolved about 200 million years ago. These fishes had no jaws and no paired fins and belonged to the class Chondrichthyes. Sharks, which appeared later, have paired fins, jaws, and a swim bladder, which they use to breathe air. Bony fishes are the descendants of sharks and the ancestors of amphibians. The first amphibians appeared about 360 million years ago. The three groups of amphibians alive today are the frogs and toads, the caecilians, and the lizards." Identify and correct any factual errors in this passage.

Life/Work Skills

21. **Finding Information** Use library references or search an on-line database to find out about some of the different species of sharks, such as hammerhead sharks, nurse sharks, basking sharks, great white sharks, gray reef sharks, "cookie cutter" sharks, bull sharks, tiger sharks, and whale sharks. Create a table that includes information about the scientific and common names of the sharks, their size, habitats, feeding habits, and unusual characteristics. Include illustrations of the sharks in your table. Share your findings with the class.

22. **Allocating Resources** Fish have been a primary source of food for humans around the world for thousands of years. Use library references or search an on-line database to research where the world's most productive fisheries are located and what kinds of fishes are harvested. Also explore the various techniques by which fish are collected. Investigate how changes in environmental conditions and increased demands by humans have affected the major fisheries of the world. Summarize your findings in a written report to your class.

Activities and Projects

23. **Language Arts Connection** Use library references to find out how amphibians are portrayed in literature. In Shakespeare's play *Macbeth*, the witches call for "eye of newt" and "toe of frog" as part of their mysterious concoctions. Children's fairy tales frequently mention kissing a frog and having it turn into a handsome prince. Collect several literary references to amphibians. Share your findings in an oral report to your class.

Discovering Through Reading

24. Read the article "Hammerhead City" by A. Peter Klimley in *Natural History*, October 1995, pages 33–38. How does a female hammerhead establish dominance within a school of sharks? Why do hammerhead sharks school near underwater mountains?

Reviewing Themes

19. Both have lungs to extract oxygen from the air, and both have moist skin.

Thinking Critically

20. The first fishes evolved 500 million years ago and belonged to the class Agnatha. Sharks have no swim bladder. Bony fishes are the descendants of the agnathans. The three groups of amphibians alive today are the frogs and toads, the caecilians, and the newts and salamanders.

Life/Work Skills

21. Results will vary depending on the resources available.
22. Results will vary depending on the resources available.

Activities and Projects

23. Results will vary depending on the resources available.

Discovering Through Reading

24. Female hammerhead sharks, which cluster at the school's center, establish and maintain their dominance by constantly fighting. Hammerhead sharks school near underwater mountains for reproduction; males can quickly locate and mate with dominant females. Large underwater mountains also serve as navigational centers for far-ranging feeding trips; the hammerheads navigate by following electromagnetic variations along the sea floor.

539

---

14. Lungs, a double-loop circulatory system, and sturdy limbs enable amphibians to live on land. Thin, moist skin and the need to reproduce in water keep amphibians in or near water for most of their lives.
15. Results will vary depending on the resources available.
16. Refer to Table 27-2 on page 536.
17. Students' answers will vary but should mention that the competition between the adult (carnivore) and larvae (herbivore) is reduced because they utilize different food sources.

Many insects reduce competition for food sources by utilizing different food sources as larvae (caterpillars) and as adults (butterflies).

Interpreting Graphics

18. a. This animal is an amphibian, specifically a newt. It has limbs and thin, moist skin.
 b. Adaptations that allow this animal to live on land include limbs, lungs, and double-loop circulation.

Lesson Planning Guide With Options for Block Scheduling

Lecture Concepts	Lesson Resources

28-1 Reptiles

BLOCK ① (45 minutes)

1. Reptiles are well adapted to life on land.
2. Reptiles are ectotherms. Their body temperature changes with their surroundings.

① Lecture Resources
- Determining Prior Knowledge
- Active Reading: Discussion
- Visual Strategy: Videodisc
- Demonstration: Identifying Structures
- Teaching Transparencies: 171, 173, 174
- Holt Biology Videodiscs Lesson 28-1

Classwork Options
- Life/Work Skills: Finding Information
- Quick Labs: Lab A22

Assignment Options
- Warmblooded Dinosaurs?
- Island Speciation

BLOCK ② (45 minutes)

3. Extinct reptiles include dinosaurs, ichthyosaurs, plesiosaurs, and pterosaurs.
4. Virtually all large animals became extinct about 65 million years ago.

② Lecture Resources
- Tied to Land
- Reptile Lands
- Active Reading: Reading Organizer
- Teaching Transparencies: 141A, 142A
- Holt Biology Videodiscs Lesson 28-1

Classwork Options
- Lizards and Snakes

- Closure: Determining the Validity of a Claim

Assignment Options
- Reteaching
- Section Review
- Chapter Review, questions 1a, 2a, 4, 5, 6, 7, 24, 25, 27, 29
- Directed Reading Worksheet

28-2 Birds

BLOCK ③ (45 minutes)

1. Birds evolved from reptiles, and they still share many characteristics.
2. Birds are the only animals that have feathers.

③ Lecture Resources
- Are Birds Reptiles?
- Demonstration: Comparing Structures
- Teaching Transparencies: 175, 176
- Holt Biology Videodiscs Lesson 28-2

Classwork Options
- Laboratory Techniques and Experimental Design: Lab C40

Assignment Options
- Life/Work Skills: Finding Information

BLOCK ④ (45 minutes)

3. Feathers, a lightweight skeleton, and endothermy enable a bird to fly.
4. The feet and beaks of birds are important in determining how birds are classified.

④ Lecture Resources
- Teaching Transparencies: 143A, 182
- Holt Biology Videodiscs Lesson 28-2

Classwork Options
- Life/Work Skills: Being a Team Member
- Closure: Relating Concepts

Assignment Options
- *Small Group* Reteaching
- Section Review
- Chapter Review, questions 1b, 2b, 8, 9, 10, 21, 22, 26, 28
- Directed Reading Worksheet

28-3 Introduction to Mammals

BLOCK ⑤ (45 minutes)

1. True mammals evolved from therapsids, have fur, and are able to produce milk.
2. Mammals took over ecological roles previously occupied by dinosaurs.

⑤ Lecture Resources
- How Long Ago?
- Best Adapted?
- Visual Strategy: Figure 28-17
- Teaching Transparencies: 177, 178
- Holt Biology Videodiscs Lesson 28-3

Classwork Options
- Teaching Resources CD-ROM: Occupational Applications Worksheets 1
- Investigation 28A

Assignment Options
- Life/Work Skills: Being a Team Member

BLOCK ⑥ (45 minutes)

3. Mammals are endotherms and can regulate their body temperature.
4. Monotremes lay eggs. Marsupials give birth to young that then develop in their mother's pouch. Placental mammals develop inside their mothers before birth.

⑥ Lecture Resources
- The Evolution of Mammals
- Active Reading: Reading Organizer
- Teaching Transparencies: 181
- Holt Biology Videodiscs Lesson 28-3

Classwork Options
- Closure: Organizing Information

Assignment Options
- Reteaching
- Section Review
- Chapter Review, questions 3, 11, 12, 13, 20, 23
- Directed Reading Worksheet

Lecture Concepts

Lesson Resources

28-4 Mammalian Adaptations

BLOCK ⑦ (45 minutes)

1. Mammalian hair functions as insulation, camouflage, sensory structures, and defense.

2. Horns are bone covered with keratin, and they are not shed. Antlers are also bone, and they are shed each year.

⑦ Lecture Resources
- ■ Gestation in the Mouse
- ■ Active Reading: Paired Reading
- ■ Demonstration: Comparing Functions
- ⊘ Holt Biology Videodiscs Lesson 28-4

Classwork Options
- ■ Parental Care in Mammals

BLOCK ⑧ (45 minutes)

3. Mammals may be herbivores, omnivores, or carnivores.

4. Among mammals, only bats are capable of powered flight.

⑧ Lecture Resources
- ■ Visual Strategy: Videodisc
- ⊘ Holt Biology Videodiscs Lesson 28-4

Classwork Options
- ■ Closure: Forming a Hypothesis
- ⚗ Inquiry Skills Development: Lab B29

Assignment Options
- ■ Reteaching
- ■ Section Review
- ■ Chapter Review, questions 1c, 2c, 14, 15, 16, 17, 18, 19
- ■ Directed Reading Worksheet

Chapter Review and Assessment

BLOCK ⑨ (45 minutes)

Review
- ■ Reteaching Worksheet
- ■ Thinking Skills Worksheet
- ■ Vocabulary Development Worksheet
- ⊙ Language Development and Reading Comprehension Audio CD Program: Chapter 28

BLOCK ⑩ (45 minutes)

Assessment
- ■ Alternative Assessment, p. 569
- ■ Portfolio Assessment, p. T39

Chapter Test
- ■ Chapter 28 Test

Test Generator
- ⊙ Item bank for customizing Chapter Tests

Teaching Resources CD-ROM
- ⊙ Scoring Rubrics and Classroom Management Checklist

The Portfolio icon denotes items throughout the Teacher's Edition lesson wrap that may be selected for inclusion in student portfolios.

Holt Biology Videodiscs and *Concepts of Biology*

Holt Biology Videodiscs gives you a powerful tool for teaching, review, and assessment. For further information regarding the media on the videodiscs, see **Holt Biology Videodiscs Teacher's Correlation Guide to Holt Biology: Visualizing Life.**

Concepts of Biology adds interactive lesson plans and extensive tools for customization using CD-ROM technology.

Use the following topic from **Concepts of Biology** to help you teach this chapter:
Topic 20: Vertebrate Diversity

Laboratory Planning

Text

Materials and preparation instructions appear on the teacher's wrap accompanying each laboratory exercise.

Block 5: Investigation 28A: Making a Cladogram—Wildlife Zoo, p. 808

Holt BioSources Laboratory Program

Block 1: Quick Labs Lab A22: Comparing Animal Eggs

Block 3: Laboratory Techniques and Experimental Design Lab C40: Conducting a Bird Survey

Block 8: Inquiry Skills Development Lab B29: Fetal Pig Dissection

Determining Prior Knowledge

- Randomly list characteristics of reptiles, birds, and mammals on the board or an overhead projector. Have students identify the type of animals described by each list.
- Ask students if reptiles are the only animals with scales. Have students describe the skin on the legs of birds.
- Have students identify which of these groups of animals lay eggs. Be prepared to discuss birds, egg-laying reptiles, and monotremes.
- Ask students if all birds can fly. Have students come up with ideas for functions of feathers other than to aid in flight.
- Have students explain the terms *endothermic* and *exothermic*.

Active READING

Technique: Discussion

Before students begin reading the chapter, have a student volunteer explain how the vertebrates they learned about in Chapter 27 were tied to the water. Tell students that in this chapter they will learn about the first vertebrates to fully adapt to life on land, the reptiles, and about their relatives, the birds and mammals.

CD-ROM Resources

Concepts of Biology
Topic 20: Vertebrate Diversity

CHAPTER

28

REVIEW
- placenta (Section 24-3)
- structure of the amniotic egg (Section 24-3)
- the terms *ectotherm* and *endotherm* (Glossary)

Reptiles, Birds, and Mammals

28-1	**Reptiles**
28-2	**Birds**
28-3	**Introduction to Mammals**
28-4	**Mammalian Adaptations**

The ringtail is one of more than 4,000 living species of mammals. It rests by day and hunts insects and other small animals by night.

540

Author's Rationale Reptiles, birds, and mammals are grouped together because they have successfully completed the transition to living on land. Their adaptations to the challenges of living out of water are somewhat similar. In addition, dinosaurs, though extinct, are given significant treatment here because they played an important role in the evolution of vertebrates by dominating the land for 200 million years.

Reptiles (class Reptilia) were the first fully terrestrial vertebrates. Their freedom from aquatic environments was made possible by several adaptations that made them and their eggs essentially watertight. Modern reptiles include snakes; lizards, like the iguana shown at left; turtles; crocodiles; and alligators. They represent the living members of a group that once dominated the land.

Phase One
Preparation

Scheduling
See the **Lesson Planning Guide** on pages 539A and 539B for lecture, classwork, and assignment options for Section 28-1.

28-1 Reptiles

OBJECTIVES

1. **Identify three adaptations that make reptiles well suited to terrestrial life.**

2. **Contrast ectothermy with endothermy.**

3. **Describe one hypothesis that explains the disappearance of the dinosaurs.**

4. **List the four orders of living reptiles.**

Reptilian Adaptations to Terrestrial Life

The skin of a reptile, contrary to what many people think, is not wet and slimy. Instead, reptilian skin is dry and covered with tough, hard, platelike scales, as shown in **Figure 28-1**. This dry skin forms a barrier to water loss in land environments. Reptilian skin is resistant to water loss because it contains large amounts of lipids and the protein keratin. Keratin is the tough, wear-resistant material that also composes your hair and fingernails and the feathers of birds. Unlike the scales of fishes, the scales of reptiles do not contain bone. In some reptiles, however, thick bony plates develop beneath the scales, such as those that form the shells of turtles.

Figure 28-1
This Philippine sail-finned lizard has dry, scaly skin that protects its body from drying out and from being cut or scratched while moving over the ground.

a **The scales on its back are rough, to protect against predators.**

b **The scales on its underside are tough but smooth, allowing the lizard to crawl more easily.**

541

Videodisc Resources

Holt Biology Videodiscs

Lesson 28-1: Reptiles

Phase Two
Teaching Strategies

Demonstration

● **Identifying Structures**
Allow students to observe an anole lizard. Students should note the difference in the scales on the back and sides of the lizard compared with those on its underbelly. As you closely supervise to ensure that the animal does not become stressed, allow some students to briefly touch or hold the lizard so that they can feel for themselves that reptiles are not slimy.

Active READING

Technique: Reading Organizer
As students read about reptilian adaptations to life on land, have them complete the following reading organizer. (Other parts of the organizer should include the amniotic egg, adaptations for water conservation, and circulatory system adaptations.)

Dry, scaly skin made up of lipids and keratin prevents water loss.

Reptilian adaptations to terrestrial life

Key to Strategies
Teaching Strategies are keyed to three tiers of learning.

● **Understanding Concepts (Tier I)**
Content mastery and comprehension

■ **Applying Information (Tier II)**
Applying and analyzing content

▲ **Critical Thinking (Tier III)**
Practicing evaluative thinking

Tied to Land

● Comparing Structures

Show students a picture of an aquatic reptile such as a turtle or a crocodile laying its eggs on land. The amniotic, shelled eggs of reptiles allowed the ancestors of reptiles to leave the water and freed them of the need to return to the water to reproduce, as amphibians must. Point out that just as most amphibians are tied to water for reproduction, egg-laying reptiles are tied to land.

Language Arts Connection

Reptiles

The term *reptile* is derived from the Latin word *repere,* meaning "to crawl."

Life/Work Skills

Finding Information

● Summarizing Information

Many people keep lizards or snakes as pets. Have students do research to determine how to care for a pet reptile. Students may consult library books, pet-store pamphlets, or magazines, or they may observe at zoo exhibits. Ask students to research how the trade in reptile pets is affecting wild populations and to name some reptiles that would not make good pets because their numbers are dwindling.

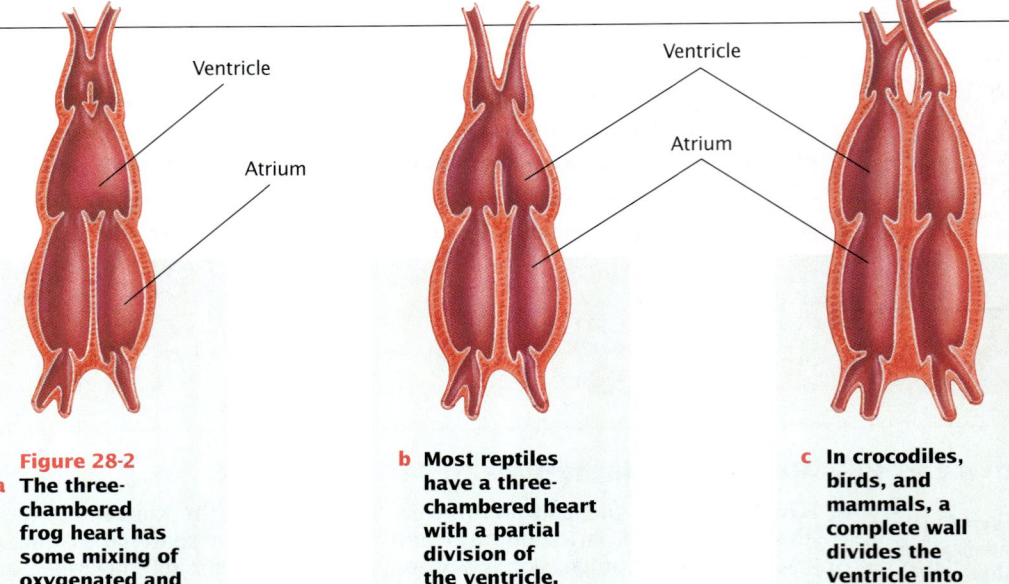

Ventricle

Atrium

Ventricle

Atrium

Figure 28-2
a **The three-chambered frog heart has some mixing of oxygenated and deoxygenated blood in the single ventricle.**

b **Most reptiles have a three-chambered heart with a partial division of the ventricle. Blood mixing is reduced.**

c **In crocodiles, birds, and mammals, a complete wall divides the ventricle into two chambers. Oxygenated and deoxygenated blood cannot mix.**

An important adaptation of reptiles to life on dry land is the amniotic egg, which is resistant to water loss. As you learned in Chapter 24, the reptilian egg protects the vulnerable embryo and provides for its needs as it develops. Since the amniotic egg contains its own supply of water, reptiles need not travel to water to reproduce.

You read about another reptilian adaptation for water conservation in Chapter 24. Reptiles excrete nitrogenous waste as uric acid, a form that requires very little water for dilution. Reptile urine contains so little water that it is a paste rather than a liquid.

The circulatory system of reptiles helps them meet the increased energy demands of an active terrestrial lifestyle. Recall that in the heart of an amphibian, such as the frog heart shown in **Figure 28-2a**, oxygenated and deoxygenated blood can mix in the single ventricle. In the hearts of all reptiles except crocodiles and alligators, by contrast, the ventricle is partially divided by a wall of tissue that reduces the amount of blood mixing, as shown in **Figure 28-2b**. In crocodiles, alligators, birds, and mammals, this partition is complete, as you can see in **Figure 28-2c**.

Are reptiles "coldblooded"?

Drive along a desert road on a warm morning and you may see lizards basking in the sun. Lizards and other reptiles, such as the snakes in **Figure 28-3**, raise their body temperature by absorbing heat from their surroundings. Like fishes and amphibians,

Matter of Fact: Finding Land for Eggs

Some sea turtles undertake long migrations to find beaches on which to lay their eggs. Green turtles migrate more than 2,000 km (1,250 mi) from the waters off Brazil to Ascension Island in the central Atlantic Ocean. A female green turtle will lay her eggs on the same beach where she hatched, but it is not known how she finds the correct beach.

reptiles are ectotherms. The metabolism of an ectotherm is too slow to produce enough heat to warm its body. Instead, ectotherms must absorb heat from their surroundings. Birds and mammals, in contrast, are endotherms. Their rapid metabolism produces large amounts of heat, some of which is used to maintain a high, relatively constant body temperature.

Throughout the day, the body temperature of an ectotherm often follows the temperature of its surroundings. Body temperature falls at night, when the air is cool. In the morning, many reptiles seek sunny places, letting the sun's rays warm their bodies. Once warmed, many reptiles maintain a high and relatively constant body temperature by moving into and out of the sunshine, their bodies warming and cooling, as described in **Figure 28-4**. You might hear ectotherms called "coldblooded," but this description is inaccurate. On warm days, some desert lizards have body temperatures higher than yours.

An ectotherm's slow metabolism limits where it can live and what activities it can perform. For instance, endotherms such as birds and mammals can sustain activity for longer periods of time than can reptiles and amphibians. Birds and mammals can also be active on colder days and live in colder climates than can reptiles and amphibians. But there is a high cost to endothermy—it requires large amounts of food. A mouse must eat about 10 times as much food as a similarly sized lizard. You can read more about reptiles in *Tour of a Lizard* on page 544.

Figure 28-3
These red-sided garter snakes are emerging from their den, where they have spent the winter. By clustering together, they are able to conserve heat.

Figure 28-4
a Heat exchange is very important for ectotherms. This spiny lizard is warmed by heat from the rock on which it sits and by sunlight.

b During the hottest part of the day, the lizard may retreat into the shade to lower its body temperature.

543

Visual Strategy | Videodisc

■ **Relating Concepts**
Use *Table—Body Temperature in Reptiles* shown in Chapter 28 Section 28-1 of *Holt Biology Videodiscs Teacher's Correlation Guide to Holt Biology: Visualizing Life* to help students understand why reptiles are not as widespread as some other vertebrates. Have students study the graph and note the temperature ranges for each animal. Point out that none of the animals represented in the graph live in temperatures much lower than 10°C (50°F) and that all but the tuataras have temperatures that are quite warm. Tell students that all these animals are ectotherms and that they depend on the environment to heat their bodies. Ask students how these temperature ranges help explain why ectothermic animals such as the alligator are not found in cold climates. *(The environmental temperature would not be high enough to sufficiently raise the animal's temperature to sustain life.)*

Visual Strategy | Figure 28-3

▲ **Recognizing Relationships**
Have students study the photograph and then ask them to explain how forming a group is advantageous for these snakes. *(The snakes are able to stay warm enough to survive the winter months.)* Have students brainstorm to come up with ideas of how forming a group can be advantageous for other types of animals. *(Possible answers might include the following: animals in groups are less vulnerable to predators; some animals share in caring for the young; social insects gain efficiency by dividing tasks such as food-gathering, reproduction, and defense; etc.)*

Key to Strategies
● Understanding Concepts (Tier I)
■ Applying Information (Tier II)
▲ Critical Thinking (Tier III)

Tour

Island Speciation

■ Relating Concepts

Lizards are found on all continents except Antarctica, but they are most abundant in the deserts and tropics. The lizard shown here is a day gecko from Madagascar. Unlike this species, which is active in the daytime, most geckos are nocturnal. Have students research Madagascar's unusual flora and fauna, which evolved during the island's long isolation. Have them concentrate on the reptiles of the island. Students can refer to Chapter 10 and library resources for information about evolution on islands.

Reptile Lands

■ Inferring Relationships

Have students brainstorm to name as many vertebrates as they can that live in very cold climates, such as in Canada and Alaska. Then have students name as many vertebrates as they can that live in a hot climate like that found in the American Southwest. Ask students to classify each animal they named as an amphibian, a reptile, a bird, or a mammal. Ask students to explain why most of the reptiles they named were found in the hot climate while most of the vertebrates found in the cold climates are birds or mammals. *(Because reptiles are ectotherms, their body temperature reflects their surroundings; it is difficult for them to retain enough warmth to maintain life in very cold temperatures. Endotherms, such as birds and mammals, can generate sufficient heat in a cold climate to stay warm.)*

Lizard

The largest group of reptiles today is the lizards. This day gecko is a lizard that lives on the islands of Mauritius and Madagascar in the Indian Ocean. Day geckos are unusual among lizards because they feed on nectar from flowers as well as on insects.

Size
Adult day geckos range from 10 to 15 cm (4 to 7 in.) in total length.

All reptiles have dry, tough, scaly skin. The outer layer of scales is shed periodically.

The day gecko has adhesive pads on its toes that allow it to climb vertical surfaces and even to walk on glass.

Habitat
Day geckos are tree dwellers.

The day gecko, like most reptiles, lays eggs with a protective shell. Reptilian eggs do not dry out when exposed to air.

Many lizards drop their tails when seized by a predator. The tail regrows in several weeks.

Evolutionary Relationships
Lizards belong to the suborder Sauria, which contains about 3,000 species. Day geckos belong to the family Gekkonidae. Most geckos are active at night, but nearly all day geckos are active during the day.

544

Figure 28-5
This phylogenetic tree shows the relationships among some of the major vertebrate groups that evolved from the early reptiles.

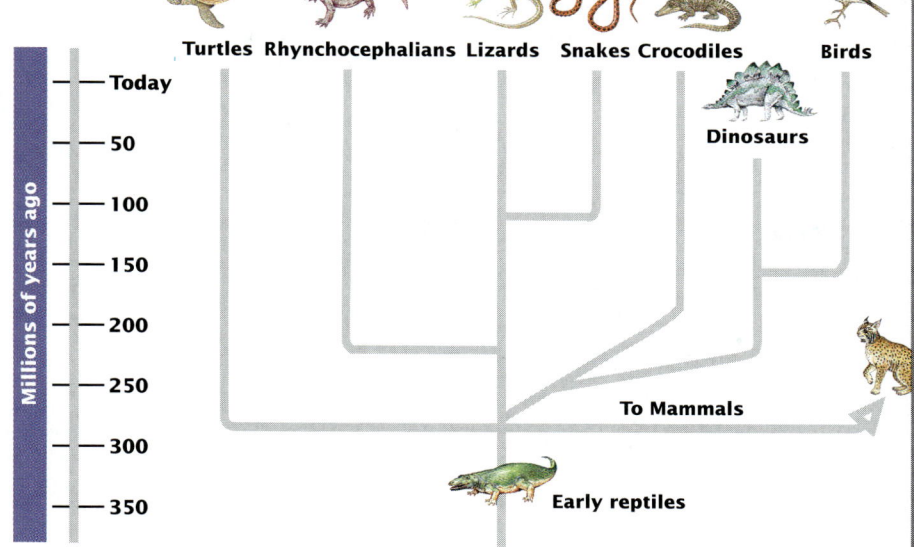

Turtles Rhynchocephalians Lizards Snakes Crocodiles Birds

Dinosaurs

Millions of years ago

— Today

— 50

— 100

— 150

— 200

— 250

— 300

— 350

To Mammals

Early reptiles

Figure 28-6
The 2 m (6 ft 6 in.) *Ichthyosaurus* gave birth to live young. The 2.3 m (7 ft 6 in.) body of *Plesiosaurus* was adapted for maneuverability to catch fish. Both existed during the Jurassic period.

The Age of Reptiles

The first reptiles evolved about 320 million years ago, when the world was entering a dry period. Well suited to dry conditions, reptiles diversified rapidly after their initial appearance, giving rise not only to the ancestors of modern reptiles but also to the wide variety of dinosaurs and other reptiles that were the dominant animals on Earth for over 170 million years. The period of reptilian dominance, which lasted from about 250 million to 65 million years ago, is called the Age

of Reptiles. The evolutionary relationships of the reptiles and their descendants are shown in **Figure 28-5**.

Two groups of reptiles, shown in **Figure 28-6**, inhabited the oceans while the dinosaurs lived on land. Ichthyosaurs *(IHK thee oh sawrs)* were fully adapted for an aquatic existence. Ichthyosaurs ("fish lizards" in Greek) resembled dolphins, having a pointed snout, streamlined body, paddlelike fins, and a flattened tail. Plesiosaurs *(PLEE see oh sawrs)* had barrel-shaped

Ichthyosaurus

Plesiosaurus

545

Warmblooded Dinosaurs?
▲ **Evaluating Hypotheses**

portfolio

Have students do library research to determine whether dinosaurs were ectotherms, like present-day reptiles, or endotherms, like modern birds and mammals. The question is a controversial one, with no clear answer yet. In their reports, students should state which scientific theorists they think have made the strongest case.

Language Arts Connection
Dinosaur Extinction
Form cooperative student groups of four. Have students read "The March Toward Extinction" in the June 1989 issue of *National Geographic* (pages 662–669). Have group members discuss the causes of extinction described in the article and relate them to how dinosaurs are believed to have become extinct. Have them speculate about why other reptilian groups present at the time of dinosaurs did not also become extinct.

Key to Strategies
● **Understanding Concepts (Tier I)**
■ **Applying Information (Tier II)**
▲ **Critical Thinking (Tier III)**

Connection: *Chapter 14*

Diversity and Niche

The diversity among different phylogenetic groups is related to their habitat and niche. Ask students to speculate about why there were so many species of dinosaurs.

Mathematics Connection

Calculating Scale

Body lengths are given in the text for two dinosaurs, *Brachiosaurus* (23 m) and *Stegosaurus* (6 m). Other lengths can be found in reference books. Have students bring toys or models of dinosaurs from home to measure. Calculate the scale of the model or toy dinosaur by using the length of the toy in centimeters as the numerator of a fraction and the length of the real animal in centimeters as the denominator, then reduce the fraction. For example, a 25 cm toy *Stegosaurus* would be a 1/24-scale model of a real *Stegosaurus* (the fraction 25/600 reduced to 1/24).

bodies with paddlelike fins. Plesiosaurs and ichthyosaurs probably fed on fish.

Dinosaurs, meaning "terrible lizards" in Greek, evolved from reptiles that were only 0.5 m to 1 m (1.5 ft to 3 ft) in length. Among the dinosaurs were the largest land animals, such as the herbivores *Apatosaurus*, *Diplodocus*, and *Brachiosaurus*. *Brachiosaurus* was about 23 m (75 ft) long and about 17 m (56 ft) tall. The dinosaurs also included the largest land carnivore, *Tyrannosaurus rex*. This great predator was over 5 m (16 ft) tall when standing on its hind legs. Dinosaurs were very diverse in size and shape. You can see a sampling of this diversity in **Figure 28-7**.

Pterosaurs were the first vertebrates to fly

No reptiles can fly today, but one group of flying reptiles existed alongside the dinosaurs—the pterosaurs *(TEHR oh sawrs)*, such as *Rhamphorhynchus* shown in **Figure 28-8**.

Figure 28-8
Pterosaurs, such as *Rhamphorhynchus*, were the first group of vertebrates to evolve the ability to fly. They evolved 75 million years before the first birds.

These reptiles were flying 75 million years before the first birds. During the 160 million years they existed, pterosaurs were a diverse group. Some were as small as a sparrow. Others had wingspans of 11 m (35 ft), greater than the wingspan of many small airplanes.

Figure 28-7
The popular conception of dinosaurs is of huge lumbering animals like *Stegosaurus*, which was 6 m (20 ft) long and weighed up to 1,500 kg (2 tons). But many dinosaurs, such as *Struthiomimus*, were small and fast. Although the dinosaurs shown here did not all exist at the same time, this illustration shows some of the great diversity among dinosaurs.

Tyrannosaurus rex

Diplodocus

Protoceratops

Deinonychus

Matter of Fact: The First Bird

Many students think that modern birds evolved from pterodactyls, extinct flying reptiles. However, fossils of pterodactyls show a wing structure unlike that of any living birds. The first known bird was *Archaeopteryx,* which probably evolved from other reptiles, not from pterodactyls.

How did the dinosaurs become extinct?

Dinosaurs, pterosaurs, plesiosaurs, and virtually all other land and sea animals larger than a small dog abruptly became extinct about 65 million years ago. Although this mass extinction is clearly recorded in the fossil record, its cause is not fully understood. One formerly popular hypothesis is that the Earth entered a time of significant cooling 65 million years ago. According to this hypothesis, dinosaurs were unable to maintain sufficiently high body temperatures to survive.

The most widely accepted hypothesis today was proposed in 1980 by the Nobel Prize–winning physicist Luis Alvarez, his son Walter, and several other scientists. These scientists proposed that the Earth was struck by a very large meteorite about the time the dinosaurs disappeared. In rocks of that age, Alvarez and other scientists discovered a layer of iridium (an element very rare on Earth but common in meteorites) and bits of melted rock that exhibit stress fractures characteristic of blast damage. The impact point of the meteorite appears to have been in northern Yucatan, Mexico. A collision between the Earth and a large meteorite would have raised thick dust clouds that could have blocked out sunlight for a time, perhaps for months. A reduction in the amount of sunlight reaching Earth's surface would have adversely affected plant life and might have caused large-scale climatic changes. Though evidence for a meteorite impact is strong, whether such an impact caused this mass extinction is still not established. The controversy over the end of the Age of Reptiles is still far from settled.

Brachiosaurus

Pachycephalosaurus

Stegosaurus

Struthiomimus

547

Matter of Fact: Name Change

One of the first dinosaurs children learn to identify is *Brontosaurus*. The accepted name for this dinosaur genus is *Apatosaurus*. In the late 1800s, paleontologist O. C. Marsh named both genera based on fragmentary fossils. Later research showed the two genera to be the same. By the rules of priority, the first name that Marsh coined—*Apatosaurus*—was applied to the genus. *Apatosaurus* means "deceptive lizard," a much less evocative name than *Brontosaurus,* which means "thunder lizard."

The Survivors

The mass extinction 65 million years ago spared four groups of reptiles: lizards and snakes (order Squamata), turtles and tortoises (order Testudines), crocodiles and alligators (order Crocodylia), and the tuataras (order Rhynchocephalia).

Of these four groups, alligators, such as the one in **Figure 28-9**, and crocodiles are the most closely related to dinosaurs. Twenty-two species of crocodiles and alligators live in tropical and subtropical regions of the world. Two species, the American alligator and the American crocodile, occur in the United States. Crocodiles and alligators lead a largely aquatic life, feeding on aquatic animals such as fishes and turtles and on terrestrial animals that come to drink or feed in the water. Crocodiles and alligators have been hunted intensely for their hides, which are used to make handbags, shoes, and other leather products. Because of overhunting and habitat destruction, 12 species of crocodiles are now endangered.

All turtles, such as the box turtle shown in **Figure 28-10a**, have a shell. A turtle's shell is composed of bony plates that are fused together. The vertebrae and ribs are fused to the interior of the shell, as shown in **Figure 28-10b**. Turtles lack teeth but have a sharp beak. Most turtles spend some of their

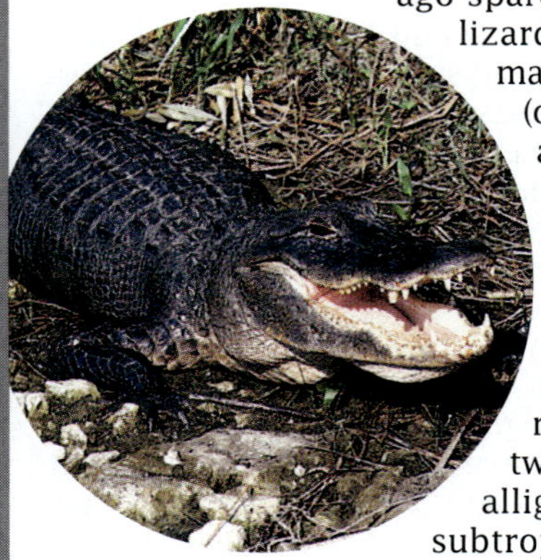

Figure 28-9
The American alligator and other crocodilians differ from other reptiles in having a four-chambered heart. All crocodilians are carnivores, and all lay eggs.

Vertebrae

b A turtle's shell is formed from plates of bone. The backbone runs along the underside of the shell.

Figure 28-10
a This Chinese box turtle is just one of 250 species of turtles and tortoises. Although some turtles live in water, they must deposit their eggs on dry land.

Multicultural Perspective: The Indian King Cobra

This snake is not only one of the deadliest reptiles but also one of the most fascinating to the people of India. In a tradition that goes back at least 2,000 years, the Indians compare areas of energy located throughout the human body, collectively called *kundalini* ("coiled one"), to a cobra. The Indians teach that this energy, like its cobra counterpart, must be treated with respect. A popular yoga exercise position is called the Cobra.

Figure 28-11
This is one of the two species of tuataras. The name *tuatara* means "spiny crest."

time in water. Extreme examples are the sea turtles, which leave the ocean only to lay their eggs. The limbs of sea turtles are flattened and paddlelike for steering and propulsion in the ocean. Tortoises, on the other hand, are almost completely terrestrial and have heavy limbs for walking.

The tuatara shown in **Figure 28-11** is a member of one of the two surviving species in the order Rhynchocephalia. The lizardlike tuataras closely resemble their relatives that were common 150 million years ago. Tuataras live only on a few of the smaller islands of New Zealand.

Snakes and lizards belong to the largest order of reptiles, order Squamata. There are about 6,000 species of snakes and lizards, and they live on every continent except Antarctica. All snakes lack limbs, movable eyelids, and external ears. Snakes are carnivores and can feed on animals much larger than themselves. A snake's jaw has five joints

(your jaw has only one), which give the jaw great flexibility. This flexibility enables the snake to engulf prey several times its own diameter, as shown in **Figure 28-12**. Most snakes are nonpoisonous, but a few species can deliver a poisonous bite. Rattlesnakes, coral snakes, copperheads, and cobras are examples of poisonous snakes.

Figure 28-12
The structure of the snake's jaw and the flexible nature of its skin and skeleton allow the snake to eat animals larger in diameter than its own body. It may take this snake an hour or more to swallow its prey.

a **After suffocating its prey by constriction, . . .**

b **. . . the snake begins the long process of swallowing.**

549

Demonstration
● **Identifying Structures**
If one of your students has a pet snake, ask if he or she is willing to let the class observe the snake's feeding behavior. If so, have the student bring the hungry snake to class, along with the snake's usual meal (such as a mouse). Many students are afraid of snakes. Be aware of these feelings as you display the animal in the classroom.

Visual Strategy **Figure 28-12**

■ **Relating Concepts**
Have students study the figure, and then have them imagine swallowing an object larger than the diameter of their head—a basketball, for example. Have students feel their own jaws move to determine which parts are movable and which parts are not. Students should note that their jaws can move only at the joints where the jaw articulates with the skull. Ask students how many joints are found in the jaw of a snake *(five).*

Demonstration
● **Identifying Variables**
Have students use a globe or atlas to locate New Zealand. Tell students that before humans colonized New Zealand, tuataras lived on both of the main islands (North Island and South Island). Humans and the animals they introduced to the islands have eliminated tuataras from all but a few of the small islands.

Historical Perspective: New Zealand's Disappearing Flora and Fauna

New Zealand separated from Australia about 80 million years ago. During this long isolation, a variety of unique plants and animals evolved in New Zealand, including tuataras, huge flightless birds called moas, kauri trees, and kiwis. The first Polynesian settlers, who probably arrived around the eighth century, began the destruction of this unique flora and fauna. By the time Europeans sighted New Zealand in the 1640s, all 12 species of moas had been hunted to extinction. European settlers expanded and accelerated the assault on the environment. Today, over 50 percent of the native species of birds have disappeared from New Zealand, and many of the remaining species are endangered.

Key to Strategies
● Understanding Concepts (Tier I)
■ Applying Information (Tier II)
▲ Critical Thinking (Tier III)

Lizards and Snakes

■ Recognizing Relationships

Ask students to make two lists side by side on the same sheet of paper. One list should itemize all of the characteristics of lizards, while the other should itemize all of the characteristics of snakes. Remind students to include characteristics of all reptiles on their lists. Then have students draw lines connecting identical characteristics on both lists. Have students use their lists to write a paragraph titled "Comparing and Contrasting Lizards and Snakes."

Active READING

Technique: Reading Organizer

Point out to students that the tables provided on pages 550, 556, and 562 are reading organizers that are designed to help students review what they learned in each section of the chapter and to provide additional information to complement what they learned. Remind students to read and review the tables provided after they finish each section of the chapter.

Unlike snakes, most lizards have four limbs and external ears. Lizards are most abundant in the tropics and in deserts. Most species are carnivorous, feeding on insects, small mammals, or other lizards. A few species are herbivorous. Only two species of lizards are poisonous: the Gila monster of the southwestern United States and northern Mexico, shown in **Figure 28-13**, and the Mexican beaded lizard of southern Mexico and Guatemala. **Table 28-1** summarizes the major orders of reptiles.

Figure 28-13
The glands that produce the Gila monster's poison are located in the lower jaw. The lizards chew it into their victims.

Table 28-1 Orders of Reptiles

Order	Number of living species	Description	Examples
Ornithischia	Extinct	Mostly plant-eating dinosaurs with two pelvic bones facing backward, as in a bird's pelvis; hole in the skull in front of eye socket; legs positioned beneath the body; over 150 genera	*Triceratops, Ankylosaurus, Iguanodon* *Stegosaurus*
Saurischia	Extinct	Flesh-eating and plant-eating dinosaurs with one pelvic bone facing forward and the other facing backward, as in a lizard's pelvis; terrestrial; three or sometimes five toes; hole in skull in front of eye socket; legs positioned beneath body; over 200 genera	*Allosaurus, Apatosaurus, Brachiosaurus* *Tyrannosaurus rex*
Pterosauria	Extinct	Flying reptiles with wings of skin between fourth finger and body; wingspan of early (Jurassic) *Rhamphorhynchus* was typically 60 cm (2 ft), and wingspan of later (Cretaceous) *Pteranodon* was over 7.5 m (25 ft)	*Pteranodon, Pterodactylus, Quetzalcoatlus* *Rhamphorynchus*
Plesiosauria	Extinct	Marine reptiles with very large paddle-shaped fins, a barrel shaped body, and long jaws with sharp teeth; some had a snakelike neck twice as long as the body; others had a short neck and elongated skull	*Peloneustes, Elasmosaurus, Kronosaurus* *Plesiosaurus*

550

Matter of Fact: Lizard Diversity

Lizards appeared in the late Jurassic period, about 150 million years ago. Common present-day lizards include iguanas, chameleons, geckos, horned lizards (often mistakenly called "horned toads"), and anoles. Most lizards are small, measuring less than 30 cm (1 ft) in length. The largest lizards belong to the Monitor family. The largest of these is the Komodo dragon of Indonesia, which reaches 3 m (10 ft) in length.

Ichthyosauria	Extinct	Marine reptiles with streamlined bodies up to 3 m (10 ft) in length; the four legs modified into balancing fins; apparently fast swimmers, with many body similarities to modern fishes such as tuna or mackerel	*Ichthyosaurus*
Squamata suborder Sauria	3,000	Lizards; limbs set at right angles to body; dry skin of scales; socketless teeth; heart with partially divided ventricle; most species are terrestrial, but a few are at least partially aquatic	Anoles, geckos, horned lizards
Squamata suborder Serpentes	2,500	Snakes; no legs; scaly skin is shed periodically; socketless teeth; heart with partially divided ventricle; no external ear openings; most species are terrestrial, but a few are aquatic	Rattlesnakes, garter snakes
Testudines	250	Body encased in shell of bony plates; sharp, horny jaw edges without teeth; vertebrae and ribs fused to shell; terrestrial and aquatic species	Turtles, tortoises, terrapins
Crocodylia	22	Four-chambered heart; extended jaw with socketed teeth; five digits on forelimbs, four digits on hind limbs; live near or in water	Crocodiles, alligators
Rhynchocephalia	2	Sole survivors of a group that largely disappeared about 100 million years ago. Skull like those of early Permian reptiles; fused, wedgelike, socketless teeth; terrestrial	Tuataras

SECTION REVIEW

1. **Describe two adaptations to land shown by reptiles.**

2. **What is one disadvantage of endothermy?**

3. **What evidence indicates that a meteorite collided with Earth about the time the dinosaurs became extinct?**

4. **List a representative of each of the four living orders of reptiles.**

551

ANSWERS TO SECTION REVIEW

1. Answers should include two of the following: skin containing keratin and lipid that resists water loss; amniotic eggs; excretion of wastes as uric acid, which requires little water for dilution; and a partially or fully divided ventricle of the heart that reduces or prevents mixing of oxygenated and deoxygenated blood.

2. Endotherms require large amounts of food to generate heat to keep their body temperature constant.

3. In rock layers laid down at the time of the extinction of the dinosaurs, a thin layer of iridium—rare on Earth but common in meteorites—is found. The layer also contains bits of melted rock with stress fractures typical of blast damage.

4. Refer to Table 28-1 on pages 550–551.

Language Arts Connection
Orders of Reptiles

Language Arts Connection
Orders of Reptiles
Divide students into five groups for cooperative learning. Assign each group one of the orders or suborders of living reptiles, as shown in Table 28-1. Have the groups make lists of facts about their assigned order that would be of interest to students throughout the school. Then have them design and produce a display about their assigned order of reptiles and display them in a hallway display case.

Phase Three
Assessment Options

Closure
▲ **Determining the Validity of a Claim**
Reptiles are sometimes portrayed in literature and horror movies as evil. Have students discuss facts that they have learned in this section that support or refute these portrayals.

SECTION REVIEW
Assign the *Section Review*.

Reteaching

Have your class pretend that your school is preparing a desert exhibit and is deciding whether to place reptiles or amphibians in the exhibit. Have each student write a letter to the exhibit committee recommending a particular reptile for the exhibit, describing in detail how well-adapted the animal is for a warm-terrestrial environment compared with an amphibian. Though different students will recommend different reptiles, all students should describe similar characteristics, such as watertight eggs, watertight skin, and an efficient excretory system and heart.

Key to Strategies
● Understanding Concepts (Tier I)
■ Applying Information (Tier II)
▲ Critical Thinking (Tier III)

Reptiles, Birds, and Mammals   551

Phase One
Preparation

Scheduling
See the **Lesson Planning Guide** on pages 539A and 539B for lecture, classwork, and assignment options for Section 28-2.

Phase Two
Teaching Strategies

Visual Strategy **Figure 28-14**

● **Identifying Structures**
Have students study the photograph and point out the fossil imprints of the feathers (*visible radiating from the wing bones and also stretching out from the tail*). Tell students that fossils of this type are rare because only this fine limestone would preserve the delicate imprints of feathers. Ask students to identify the structure that they would not be likely to find on a modern bird (*the long tail*).

Are Birds Reptiles?

▲ **Evaluating Viewpoints**
To cladists, birds are reptiles because the cladistic classification system only accepts groups that contain all the descendants of a common ancestor. Birds evolved from dinosaurs, so they must be included in the same group as the dinosaurs—reptiles. To other biologists, the unique features of birds, such as the feathers, justify placing them in a group of their own. Have students debate the question, "Are birds reptiles?"

552

Although the dinosaurs died out 65 million years ago at the end of the Cretaceous period, their descendants, the birds, survived. Today birds are the most diverse group of land vertebrates, with nearly 10,000 species. All birds have feathers, and almost all birds are capable of powered, sustained flight.

28-2 Birds

OBJECTIVES

❶ **List two similarities between birds and reptiles.**

❷ **Identify two differences between birds and reptiles.**

❸ **Identify two functions of feathers.**

❹ **Describe two bird adaptations, other than feathers, for flight.**

Birds Evolved From Reptiles

Birds (class Aves) evolved more than 150 million years ago. The oldest known fossils of birds were found in fine limestone in Bavaria. These specimens were named *Archaeopteryx*, which means "ancient wing." *Archaeopteryx* shared many characteristics with the small dinosaurs from which it evolved, including teeth in sockets and a long, bony tail. But as you can easily see in **Figure 28-14**, *Archaeopteryx* had feathers, a characteristic unique to birds.

Modern birds lack teeth and have only a vestigial tail, but they still retain many reptilian characteristics. For instance, birds lay amniotic eggs, although the shell of a bird's egg is hard rather than leathery. Scales are also present on the feet and lower legs of birds.

Feathers are unique to birds
Feathers have replaced scales as the body covering of birds. Feathers are flexible, strong structures that can be regrown—they make an excellent wing for flying. Feathers provide most of the surface area of a bird's wing. A bird can change the surface area of its wing and alter its flight patterns by spreading or collapsing its wing feathers and the wing itself.

Like wing feathers, a bird's tail feathers can be spread or collapsed, changing their effective surface area. Tail feathers can also be used for braking and steering during flight. Watch the movement of the tail of a bird in flight and during landing to see some of the actions of these feathers.

Figure 28-14
Archaeopteryx lithographica was about the size of a pigeon.

Videodisc Resources

Holt Biology Videodiscs
Lesson 28-2: Birds

As shown in **Figure 28-15**, birds have two major types of feathers. Most of a bird's feathers are **contour feathers**. These feathers cover the body of the bird and give the wings and tail their shape. Contour feathers also insulate against heat loss. Fine **down feathers** growing underneath or among the contour feathers are specialized for insulation. The down feathers of geese and eider ducks are used in sleeping bags because they are a lightweight, effective insulation.

Bird skeletons are lightweight

The skeleton of a bird is adapted for flight. The bones are thin and hollow. Many are reinforced by internal struts, like the wings of an airplane. The breastbone, or sternum, is large and has a keel, providing solid anchorage for some of the large flight muscles.

Bird wings are modified forelimbs. The bones of the forelimbs fully support and move the wings. The finger bones are very tiny, but the arm and hand bones are long, providing strength and enabling complex movements of the wings. As you learned in Chapter 10, the bones of a bird's wing are homologous to the bones of your arm and hand.

Birds are endothermic and active

Flight is an energy-demanding activity. Birds, like mammals, are endothermic. Their rapid metabolism provides the energy needed for flight. In addition, birds have a four-chambered heart with separate circulatory loops to the lungs and to the body. Therefore, oxygen-rich blood is rapidly delivered to tissues where it is needed, without mixing with deoxygenated blood. Respiration in birds is very efficient because their system of air sacs permits air to flow in only one direction through the lungs, as explained in Chapter 24. You can read more about birds in the *Tour of a Bird* on page 555.

Figure 28-15

a Contour feathers and down feathers have different functions. Down feathers serve primarily as insulation. Contour feathers provide insulation and help the bird with steering and balance.

Vane

Shaft

b The individual filaments, or barbs, of a contour feather are linked together by hooked barbules to form a continuous surface, thereby decreasing wind resistance.

Barbules

Barbs

c Most feathers are shed every year during molting.

d Down feathers trap air, which helps maintain the bird's constant, high body temperature.

Quill

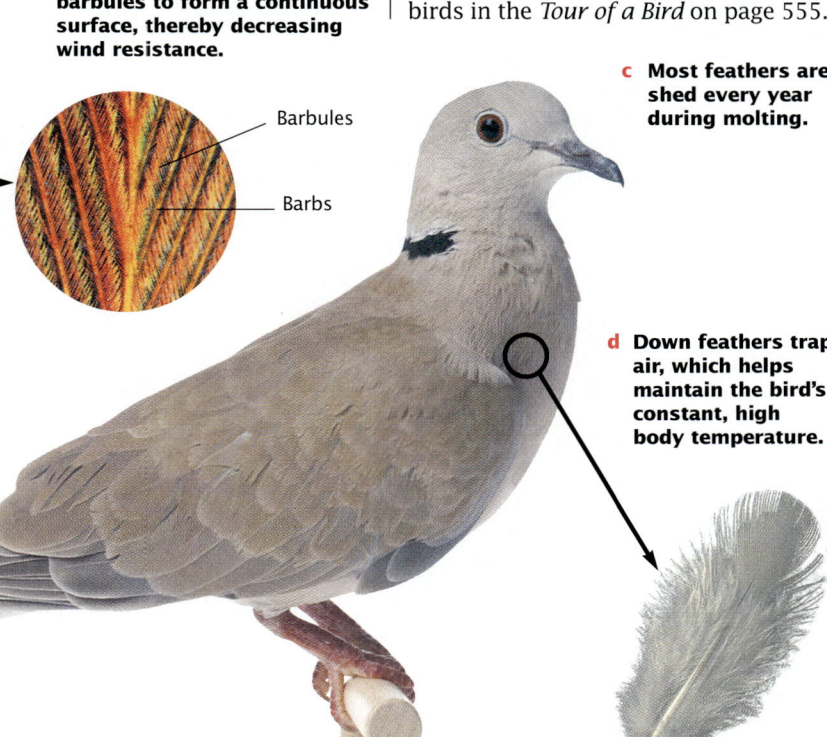

553

Matter of Fact: Feathers and Bones

Do all birds have the same number of feathers? No. Whistling swans often have more than 25,000 feathers, whereas ruby-throated hummingbirds have as few as 950 feathers. Because a bird's bones are very light, a bird's feathers typically weigh more than its bones.

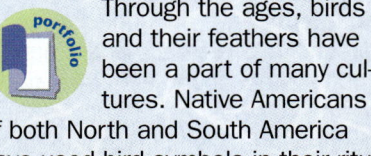

Excess Baggage?

■ **Forming a Hypothesis**
Tell students that the reproductive organs of some songbirds get smaller during long migratory flights and then enlarge again after they arrive at their mating and nesting grounds. Ask students how this temporary change in the bird's anatomy might benefit the bird. *(Any change that reduces the body weight of the bird will reduce the amount of energy required for the long flight.)*

Connection: *Chapter 13*

Bird Migration

There is an interaction of inheritance and learning in bird migration. Birds have an innate directional preference and a nervous system "odometer" that tells them when they have reached their destination. This is evident in some species when young birds leave earlier than their parents on the migratory trek. If adults and young are picked up along their migratory route and taken to an area away from the migratory route, the adults will fly back to the place where they spent their last winter. The young, however, will continue in the direction they were traveling when captured, for the amount of miles left on their "odometer."

How Birds Fly

Birds must overcome gravity in order to achieve and maintain flight. The wing is the feature that enables birds (and airplanes) to fly. An upward force known as lift is generated when air passes across the surface of a wing. Lift is produced when the pressure of the air passing over the top of the wing is less than that of the air passing under the wing. This pressure difference can be created in two ways. First, the wing can be arched. Second, the front edge of the wing can be held higher than the back edge, increasing what is called the angle of attack.

Lift is produced only when air is moving across the wing, either when the wind blows toward the bird or when the bird travels forward. Since wind direction and speed are unpredictable, efficient flight demands that birds generate force to propel themselves forward. This forward force is known as thrust. Birds typically move forward by beating their wings. Thrust is produced largely by the downstroke during flapping of the wings.

Active flight requires strong muscles to raise and lower the wings. The muscles that power the wings of birds during flight attach to the sternum, or breastbone. The sternum of a bird that flies is large and keeled, like the hull of a boat, to accommodate these large muscles.

There are different kinds of flight among birds

Birds fly in a variety of ways. The most common method is called flapping flight. It is also the most energy-demanding form of flight. The bird must actively lower and raise the wings in a complex twisting pattern that produces both lift and forward thrust.

If you watch birds in the air, you will notice that not all of them flap their wings all of the time. The simplest form of nonflapping flight is gliding. A bird always loses altitude as it glides because gravity overcomes the lift provided by its forward descent. Birds dropping from treetops to the ground often do so by simple gliding; it requires very little energy.

Some birds exhibit a different kind of nonflapping flight called soaring, which allows them to overcome gravity and stay aloft for long periods while using little energy. Soaring birds, such as the tern in **Figure 28-16**, are generally large-bodied and have relatively small flight muscles. The large body results in forward momentum once the bird is flying, thus maintaining lift. It is this ability to maintain lift that makes soaring different from simple gliding.

Figure 28-16
This soaring Caspian tern is a member of the gull family and is the largest North American tern.

554

Matter of Fact: Long-Distance Fliers

The arctic tern migrates from its nesting grounds near the North Pole to its wintering grounds near the South Pole. Some migratory birds fly nonstop on their migrations, sometimes flying hundreds of miles. Other birds stop to restock their fat reserves, then take off again in two or three days. Birds are incredible flying machines. It is obvious why their skeletons are so spongy—to reduce air freight!

Bird

The cedar waxwing is a common bird throughout North America. All modern birds have forelimbs modified into wings, are covered with feathers, feed with a horny beak, and lay hard-shelled eggs.

Size
Cedar waxwings reach a maximum length of 18 cm (7 in.).

Birds are endotherms. The body temperatures of birds range from 40°C to 42°C (104°F to 108°F), higher than the lethal limit for many mammals.

The bones of birds are laced with air cavities, making them light and strong at the same time. The skeleton of a bird typically weighs less than its feathers.

Feathers evolved from reptilian scales. Most birds molt, or shed their feathers, at least once a year. In most birds, however, only a few feathers are shed at a time.

The cedar waxwing, like all flying birds, has a keeled sternum to which powerful flight muscles are attached.

Like many birds, the cedar waxwing migrates seasonally. In the spring, cedar waxwings fly north. Some birds spend the summer as far north as Alaska and northern Canada. In the fall, cedar waxwings migrate south and spend the winter in warmer areas, sometimes as far south as Panama.

Habitat
Cedar waxwings prefer wooded areas in which berries, their favorite food, are plentiful. They will live in areas disturbed by human activities, such as fields and orchards.

Evolutionary Relationships
Birds are the descendants of dinosaurs. The close relationship between birds and dinosaurs prompted Thomas Huxley, a colleague of Darwin, to call birds "glorified reptiles." Cedar waxwings belong to the order Passeriformes, the largest order of birds. This order, commonly called "songbirds," contains more than 5,000 species.

555

Tour

Cedar Waxwing Adaptations
● **Summarizing Information**

Many of the cedar waxwing's adaptations help make flight possible. Have students make a table with two columns. In the first column they should list the following adaptations: feathers, hollow bones, keeled sternum, rapid metabolism. In the second column students should describe how each adaptation contributes to flight.

Behaviors of Cedar Waxwings
● **Making Observations**

Use a field guide or ornithology book to show students the extensive range of the cedar waxwing. Though cedar waxwings sometimes migrate as far south as Panama, they often spend their winters in the United States. Because they commonly live in residential areas and form large flocks, these birds are easily located and observed. Have students look for cedar waxwings in their neighborhood. Students who encounter cedar waxwings should observe them carefully, noting what the birds eat, where they roost, what other species of birds they interact with, and any other behaviors of interest. Have students present their observations to the class.

Life/Work Skills
Finding Information
● **Summarizing Information**

Have students research the "disappearing songbird" phenomenon and write a report summarizing what they have learned. In their reports, students should describe the evidence of population declines, the causes of these declines, and possible remedies.

Demonstration

■ **Recognizing Relationships**

Show students a photograph of a bat with its wings extended, such as Figure 28-26 later in this chapter, and show them a model or a photograph of a bird skeleton. Ask students if a bird could fly without its feathers—bats are able to fly without feathers! Students should point out that the feathers make up most of the surface area of a bird's wing, while the hand bones of the bat are greatly elongated with a thin layer of skin stretched between them.

Preening

■ **Forming a Hypothesis**

Students who have pet birds or who have observed wild birds around their homes or school may have noticed birds preening their feathers. Ask students to hypothesize about why birds spend so much time on this activity. *(Preening smooths the feathers and spreads oil to keep them waterproof.)*

Major Orders of Birds

You can often tell a great deal about the habits and food of a bird by examining its beak and feet. For instance, carnivorous birds, such as eagles, have curved talons for seizing prey and a sharp beak for tearing apart their meal. The beaks of seed-eating birds, such as finches, are short, thick, seed crushers. What birds are common in your neighborhood? What sorts of adaptations do they show? Twenty-eight orders of living birds have been described. **Table 28-2** lists 16 of the most common orders of birds and shows an example of each. Pay particular attention to the feet and beaks of these birds.

Table 28-2 Major Orders of Birds

Order	Number of living species	Description	Examples	
Passeriformes	5,276	Songbirds; perching feet; well-developed vocal organs; dependent young; largest bird order, containing 60 percent of all bird species	Sparrows, robins, warblers, crows, starlings, mockingbirds	
Apodiformes	428	Small bodies, short legs, rapid wing beat; hummingbirds are the smallest birds	Hummingbirds, swifts	
Piciformes	383	Sharp, chisel-like bills for pounding through wood in search of insects; grasping feet	Woodpeckers, toucans, honeyguides	
Psittaciformes	340	Well-developed vocal organs; large powerful bills for crushing seeds	Parrots, cockatoos	
Charadriiformes	331	Shorebirds; typically with long, slender, probing bills and long, stiltlike legs	Gulls, terns, plovers, auks, sandpipers	
Columbiformes	303	Stout bodies; perching feet	Pigeons, doves	
Falconiformes	288	Birds of prey; day-active carnivores; sharp pointed beaks for tearing flesh; keen vision; strong fliers	Eagles, hawks, falcons, vultures	
Galliformes	268	Rounded bodies; often limited flying ability	Chickens, quail, grouse, pheasants	

Matter of Fact: Honeyguides

In Africa, a bird called the honeyguide has a mutualistic relationship with the honey badger. The bird's call alerts the badger to a beehive and actually leads the badger to the hive. The badger tears apart the hive, leaving a supply of food for the honeyguide. Humans also follow the honeyguide to find beehives and perform the same service for the bird that the badger does.

Order	Number of Species	Characteristics	Examples	
Gruiformes	209	Marsh dwellers; diverse body shapes; long, stiltlike legs	Rails, coots, bitterns, cranes	
Anseriformes	150	Waterfowl; webbed toes; broad bill with filtering ridges at margins	Swans, geese, ducks	
Ciconiiformes	114	Long-legged waders; often with large bodies	Storks, herons, ibises	
Strigiformes	146	Nocturnal birds of prey; large eyes; powerful beaks and feet	Owls	
Procellariiformes	104	Sea birds; tube-shaped bills; many can fly for long periods of time	Albatrosses, petrels	
Sphenisciformes	18	Marine; flightless; confined to Southern Hemisphere; thick coat of insulating feathers; wings modified as paddles for swift swimming	Penguins	
Apterygiformes	3	Small and flightless; long probing bill; keen sense of smell; found only in New Zealand	Kiwis	
Struthioniformes	1	Large; flightless; only two toes; long, strong running legs	Ostrich	

SECTION REVIEW

1 What evidence indicates that birds evolved from reptiles?

2 Name two differences between a lizard and a bird.

3 Ostriches have feathers but cannot fly. What functions do feathers perform for an ostrich?

4 List two features of the bird's skeleton that make it well suited for flight.

557

ANSWERS TO SECTION REVIEW

1 Like reptiles, birds lay amniotic eggs. Scales similar to those found on the skin of reptiles are present on the lower legs and feet of birds.

2 Students' answers should include two of the following: a bird has feathers, while a lizard does not; the bones of a bird are thin and hollow, unlike a lizard's bones; a bird is endothermic, while a lizard is ectothermic; a bird has a four-chambered heart with the ventricle completely divided, while the heart of a lizard has only a partially divided ventricle.

3 Feathers are used by birds not only to fly but also to insulate against heat loss.

4 The following are possible answers: thin, hollow bones with air pockets; the sternum is large and has a keel for solid anchorage of large flight muscles; forelimb bones that support and move the wings.

Life/Work Skills
Being a Team Member
● **Organizing Information**
Divide students into cooperative groups. Assign half the groups to study Table 28-2 and identify 10 orders of birds that have distinctive and characteristic beak shapes. Each group should prepare a report listing the orders they identified, the beak structure, and the feeding habits of each order. Assign the other groups a similar task based on the structure of feet and legs.

Phase Three
Assessment Options

Closure
■ **Relating Concepts**
Obtain a recording of birdcalls, and play the songs of local species for the class. Have students try to identify the calls. Point out that birds use the calls for species recognition. Ask students to suggest reasons why species recognition is important to birds, and list their suggestions on the board.

SECTION REVIEW
Assign the *Section Review.*

Reteaching
Organize students into cooperative learning groups, and assign each group a particular feeding strategy and habitat where birds are found. Have each group use a field guide to identify five species of birds that share the assigned feeding strategy and habitat. Students should then use drawings or written descriptions to demonstrate the similarities in beaks, feet, and behavior among birds with similar lifestyles. Have a member of each group share the group's findings with the entire class.

Key to Strategies
● Understanding Concepts (Tier I)
■ Applying Information (Tier II)
▲ Critical Thinking (Tier III)

Reptiles, Birds, and Mammals 557

Scheduling

See the **Lesson Planning Guide** on pages 539A and 539B for lecture, classwork, and assignment options for Section 28-3.

How Long Ago?

● **Organizing Information**
Have students make a time line showing the following: the time the therapsids lived, the time the dinosaurs lived, the time that mammals other than humans have lived, the mass extinction at the end of the Cretaceous period, and the time that humans have lived.

Visual Strategy   Figure 28-17

■ **Recognizing Relationships**
Ask students to study the drawing of *Eozostrodon* and to infer whether this early mammal was nocturnal or diurnal. *(Most scientists believe that* Eozostrodon *was nocturnal because its large eyes are typical among nocturnal animals such as owls.)*

You are a mammal. So are many of the animals that humans eat, use as work animals, and keep as pets. All mammals have hair or fur on their bodies, a characteristic not found in any other kind of modern animal. Mammals are also endothermic, like birds. Female mammals produce milk with which they nurse their offspring.

28-3   Introduction to Mammals

OBJECTIVES

❶ **List the unique characteristics of mammals.**

❷ **Identify two features of monotremes.**

❸ **Contrast the pattern of development of marsupials with that of placental mammals.**

Origin of Mammals

Mammals (class Mammalia) arose from early reptiles called therapsids *(thuh RAP sihdz),* one of which is illustrated in **Figure 28-17a**. The fossil record provides a well-documented transition between these reptiles and mammals, with fossil forms ranging from reptiles with a few mammalian characteristics to true mammals. The first mammals appeared about 220 million years ago, just as the first dinosaurs were evolving. Early mammals, such as the *Eozostrodon* shown in **Figure 28-17b**, were small (about the size of mice), fed on insects, and lived in trees. Their relatively large eye sockets suggest that they were active at night. These early mammals had a jaw composed of only one bone, a characteristic that distinguishes them from the therapsids, which had a jaw composed of several bones. Two of the bones in the therapsid jaw became part of the chain of bones that transmits sound in the middle ear of mammals.

Figure 28-17

a   *Cynognathus* is a therapsid that lived about 250 million years ago. It was about as large as a medium-sized dog. Some therapsids lived in cold climates and may have had hair. The jaw of a therapsid is composed of several bones, while a mammal's jaw is a single bone.

b   *Eozostrodon* was a typical early mammal. It was about 18 cm (5 in.) long and lived about 215 million years ago.

Videodisc Resources

Holt Biology Videodiscs
Lesson 28-3: Introduction to Mammals

For over 150 million years, while the dinosaurs flourished, mammals were a minor group that changed little. Mammalian fossils from this time are very rare, indicating that mammals were not abundant. At the end of the Cretaceous period, 65 million years ago, the dinosaurs and many other kinds of aquatic and land-dwelling animals became extinct, but the mammals survived. In the time since the dinosaurs disappeared, mammals have diversified and have taken over many of the ecological roles once occupied by dinosaurs. Mammals reached their maximum diversity about 15 million years ago. At that time, tropical conditions existed over much of the world. During the last 15 million years, world climates have cooled and the area covered by tropical rain forests has decreased, causing a decline in the number of mammalian species. Today, human activities such as overhunting and habitat modification threaten many species of mammals.

Mammalian Characteristics

Mammals are distinguished by two characteristics: the presence of hair or fur on the body and the ability to produce milk. Even the apparently naked whales and dolphins grow sensitive bristles on their snouts. Evolution of fur and the ability to regulate body temperature through metabolism enabled mammals to inhabit colder environments than could be tolerated by ectothermic reptiles and amphibians.

Like birds, mammals have a four-chambered heart. There is no mixing of deoxygenated and oxygenated blood in the heart.

Female mammals have **mammary glands** that secrete milk. Newborn mammals, which are born without teeth, suckle this rich milk until they are able to feed on their own. **Figure 28-18** summarizes some of the key characteristics of mammals.

Figure 28-18
This cheetah shows the main characteristics of mammals.

Four-chambered heart
The cheetah's heart has four chambers—two atria and two ventricles.

Endothermic metabolism
The cheetah maintains a high and constant body temperature.

Fur
The cheetah is covered with a coat of fur. Its coloration and pattern help conceal her from predators and potential prey.

Mammary glands
The cheetah feeds her young nutrient-rich milk produced by her mammary glands.

559

Best Adapted?
▲ **Evaluating Viewpoints**
Read students the following quotation from paleontologist Robert T. Bakker: "Dinosaurs suppressed the evolutionary potential of mammals, not the other way around." Ask students to identify the common viewpoint of dinosaurs versus mammals that Bakker was trying to counter. *(Many people think that mammals survived because they were superior to dinosaurs and therefore destined to take over the dinosaurs' ecological niches. Bakker thinks that mammals were able to spread into many niches only because a stroke of bad luck wiped out the dinosaurs, which until then had been successful and well-adapted.)*

Mammal Diversity
● **Comparing Structures**
Show students photographs of a variety of mammals, such as a whale, seal, bat, horse, cow, cat, dog, giraffe, kangaroo, platypus, mole, and donkey. If possible, also show them anatomical drawings of these animals. (You may be able to borrow an anatomy book from a veterinarian.) Ask students to identify features found in all of these mammals.

Matter of Fact: Milk Is More Than Food

Mammalian milk is a rich source of food, but it contains other substances that also affect the lives of young mammals. Milk contains antibodies to all of the infectious organisms that the mother has been exposed to or immunized against in her lifetime. As she passes these antibodies to her young, the young mammal is protected from the diseases caused by these organisms as long as it nurses. On the other hand, some microorganisms also can be passed from mother to offspring through milk. Pollutants in the environment may also end up in mother's milk. Ask students if they know of other substances that are passed from mother to infant through milk. *(Caffeine is a good example. Many nursing mothers find that if they drink caffeine-containing drinks, their babies are restless and do not sleep well.)*

Key to Strategies
● Understanding Concepts (Tier I)
■ Applying Information (Tier II)
▲ Critical Thinking (Tier III)

Reptiles, Birds, and Mammals **559**

Geography Connection

The Placental Mammals of Australia and New Guinea

Australia and New Guinea once were part of the southern super-continent of Gondwana, whose other components were Africa, South America, Antarctica, and the Indian subcontinent. Gondwana began to fragment about 100 million years ago, during the Cretaceous period. Australia and New Guinea separated from the other continents about 50 million years ago. Placental mammals apparently did not reach Australia and New Guinea before the land masses separated from the other continents, although marsupials and monotremes were present then. Placental mammals found in Australia and New Guinea today are descendants of placental mammals that came to these regions only recently.

Active READING

Technique: Reading Organizer
Have students work in small groups to create a reading organizer that describes the characteristics of the three types of mammals. Have a spokesperson from each group present the group's reading organizer to the class.

Egg-Laying Mammals: The Monotremes

Imagine an egg-laying, furry animal with a large bill and webbed feet. Such an animal exists in Australia—the duck-bill platypus. The platypus and two species of echidnas (*ee KIHD nuhs*), or spiny anteaters, are the only living **monotremes**. A platypus and an echidna are shown in **Figure 28-19a** and **b**. Although they are mammals, monotremes have some reptilian characteristics. They lay shelled eggs, and the structure of their pelvis is very similar to that of the early reptiles. Also like reptiles, monotremes have a single opening through which feces, urine, and reproductive products leave the body. Scientists think monotremes resemble the early mammals more closely than do any other living mammals.

In addition to their reptilian features, monotremes have both defining mammalian features: fur and functional mammary glands. Young monotremes drink their mother's milk after they hatch from eggs. Because of their strange mouths and the absence of

b This species of echidna can be found in New Guinea and Australia. It uses its long nose to root for insects and other small animals.

well-developed nipples on the females, the young cannot suckle. Instead, the milk oozes onto the mother's fur and the young lap it up with their tongues.

The platypus is a good swimmer. It uses its bill much as a duck does, rooting in the mud for worms and other soft-bodied animals. Echidnas have very strong, sharp claws, which they use for burrowing and digging for insects. The echidna probes for insects, especially ants and termites, with its long snout.

Among living mammals, only monotremes lay eggs. In the rest of the mammals, the offspring are born after developing for some time inside the mother. **Marsupials**, such as kangaroos, koalas, and opossums, carry the offspring internally for only a short time. The young are born at an early developmental stage and finish developing in a pouch on the mother's abdomen. In contrast, the offspring of **placental mammals** remain inside their mother until development is essentially complete. They are nourished through a structure known as the placenta, which was described in Chapter 24. Dogs, cats, cows, horses, humans, and most other mammals are placental mammals.

Figure 28-19
a The platypus, about half the size of a house cat, is a mammal that lays eggs. The young are nourished by milk from the mother's mammary glands.

560

Historical Perspective: The Platypus Hoax?

When the first specimens of the platypus arrived in Europe in the 1790s, the scientists who examined them suspected a hoax. The platypus seemed to be composed of parts of two different animals. Like mammals, it had hair, a single jawbone, and three middle-ear bones. But it also had a duck's bill. When scientists could find no evidence of stitching or tampering, they concluded that the platypus, however odd, was indeed a mammal. Because the reproductive tract of the platypus was similar to a bird's, it was suspected that the platypus was oviparous, but that was not conclusively established until 1883, when platypus eggs were discovered.

Pouched Mammals: The Marsupials

The major difference between marsupials and placental mammals is their pattern of embryonic development. In marsupials, the fertilized egg is surrounded by a shell membrane, but no shell forms around the egg. During most of its early development the marsupial embryo is nourished by the abundant yolk within the egg. Shortly before birth, the shell membrane is lost and a short-lived placenta forms. Still early in its development, the baby marsupial is born. Newborn marsupials emerge hairless and tiny, as you can see in **Figure 28-20**. Smaller than your thumbnail, they must crawl to the pouch, where they can nurse.

Marsupials evolved not long before placental mammals, about 100 million years ago. Today, all but about 20 of the species of marsupials live in New Guinea and Australia, where there are relatively few species of placental mammals. Marsupials in Australia and New Guinea have diversified to fill ecological positions occupied by placental mammals elsewhere in the world. For example, some species of large kangaroos are the Australian grazers, playing the ecological role that antelope, horses, and buffalo perform elsewhere. The only marsupial native to the United States is the Virginia opossum.

Humans have had a negative impact on the unique marsupials of Australia and New Guinea. Humans introduced placental mammals, including dogs, cats, sheep, foxes, and rabbits, that prey on native marsupials or compete with them for food. The negative impact of humans has intensified since European settlers arrived in Australia about 200 years ago.

Figure 28-20

a **This newborn opossum has crawled to its mother's pouch and is nursing.**

b **After several months, the young opossums are able to grasp the hair on their mother's back.**

Natural Selection at Birth
■ **Inferring Relationships**
Marsupial newborns are so underdeveloped that they have not yet formed hind limbs and must crawl to their mother's pouch using their forelimbs. They find their way to the pouch by using their sense of smell. A female marsupial may give birth to more babies than she has nipples. Because each newborn attaches to a nipple and stays attached to it while it completes its development, any newborn that does not get a nipple dies. Ask students to describe the qualities in newborns that would enhance their chances of survival. *(Their sense of smell must be keen enough to find the pouch. They must have strong forelimbs to crawl to the pouch, and they must be able to crawl quickly. In addition, chance—in the form of birth order—may affect their survival.)*

The Evolution of Mammals
■ **Recognizing Relationships**
Have students create a cladogram **Graphic Organizer**, similar to the one at the bottom of this page, that shows the relationships among monotremes, marsupials, and placental mammals. Then have students locate the positions on the cladogram at which the following structures originated: hair, mammary glands, live birth, placenta. A completed cladogram is shown below.

561

Graphic Organizer
Use the following graphic organizer with the teaching strategy **The Evolution of Mammals** on page 561.

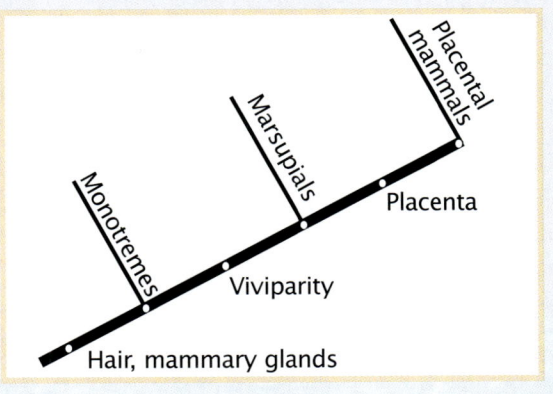

Key to Strategies
● **Understanding Concepts (Tier I)**
■ **Applying Information (Tier II)**
▲ **Critical Thinking (Tier III)**

Life/Work Skills

Being a Team Member
● **Summarizing Information**
Assign students to cooperative work groups of two or three. Assign each group an order from Table 28-3 on page 562. Have each group become experts on their order by researching a pertinent area of interest relating to the assigned order. For example, groups could research migratory habits, if any; general physical and behavioral characteristics; feeding habits; mode of living; and significance of the order to humans or to the biosphere. Group members should compile their findings in a group report and present it to the class.

Mathematics Connection

Mouse Populations
A field mouse always gives birth to a litter of eight, half of which are always female. All of the females, at sexual maturity, give birth at three months of age (and every three months after that) to a litter of eight, half of which also are female. Their average life span is two years. To survive, each mouse needs 1 m² (3.3 ft²) of grass.

A pair of adult field mice—a male and a pregnant female—arrive, floating on a log, at a grassy island. The island is the size of a football field, or 91 m × 49 m (299 ft × 160 ft). The day after they arrive, the female gives birth. There are no predators on the island, and the mice and their descendants survive until the island can no longer provide enough space and food.

How many field mice are there after three months? after six months? after nine months? When can the island no longer support the entire population of mice? *(After three months, 50; after six months, 250; after nine months, 1,550. The island [with an area of 4,459 m², or 14,665 ft²] will no longer have enough space for the mice before the end of the first year, when 7,050 mice are present.)*

True Placental Mammals

Mammals that produce a true placenta, through which the embryos are nourished for their entire development, are called placental mammals. The majority of mammal species, including humans, are placental mammals. Placental mammals are very diverse, ranging in size from 1.5 g (0.05 oz) bats to 100,000 kg (110 ton) whales. Today, placental mammals are found on all continents except Antarctica. They live in a variety of habitats, from hot, moist rain forests to the frigid tundra. They have also invaded the air and returned to the sea. There are more than 4,000 species of placental mammals. **Table 28-3** describes 12 of the 19 orders of modern-day placental mammals.

Table 28-3 Major Orders of Placental Mammals

Order	Number of living species	Description	Examples
Rodentia	1,814	Herbivores with chisel-like incisor teeth that grow continuously; typically small	Squirrels, rats, mice, beavers, porcupines
Chiroptera	986	The only flying mammals; elongated fingers support a thin wing membrane; mainly fruit or insect eaters; many fly at night, navigating by sonar	Bats
Insectivora	390	Small, chiefly night-active mammals; feed on insects; sharp-snouted; spend most of their time underground; the most primitive placental mammals	Moles, shrews, hedgehogs
Carnivora	240	Land-living predators; teeth adapted for seizing prey and shearing flesh; no native families in Australia	Dogs, bears, cats, wolves, otters, weasels
Primates	233	Largely tree dwellers; binocular vision and an opposable thumb; large brains; the end product of a line that branched off early from other mammals; retains many primitive characteristics	Prosimians, apes, monkeys, humans

Artiodactyla	211	Hoofed mammals with two or four toes; large herbivores; most are grass eaters	Sheep, pigs, cattle, deer, giraffes
Cetacea	79	Aquatic; streamlined bodies; front limbs modified into broad flippers; no hind limbs; nostrils are blowholes on top of head; hairless except on muzzle	Whales, dolphins, porpoises
Lagomorpha	69	Rodentlike mammals with four upper incisors, rather than the two seen in rodents; hind legs often longer than forelegs, an adaptation for jumping	Rabbits, hares, pikas
Pinnipedia	34	Marine carnivores with limbs modified for swimming; feed mainly on fish	Seals, sea lions, walruses
Edentata	30	Mostly insect eaters; many are toothless, but some have degenerate, peglike teeth	Sloths, anteaters, armadillos
Perissodactyla	17	Hoofed mammals with one or three toes; herbivores with teeth adapted for chewing	Horses, zebras, rhinoceroses, tapirs
Proboscidea	2	Enormous herbivores with long trunks; two upper incisors elongated as tusks; the largest living land animals	Elephants

SECTION REVIEW

1. Why are monotremes classified as mammals even though they lay eggs?

2. List two differences between monotremes and other mammals.

3. Describe two differences between reproduction in marsupials and that in placental mammals.

4. What are two advantages of the placental pattern of development over the marsupial pattern?

563

Phase Three
Assessment Options

Closure
● **Organizing Information**
Have students develop a concept map that distinguishes among the three types of mammals, based on the development of their young.

SECTION REVIEW
Assign the *Section Review*.

Reteaching
Show students pictures of different placental mammals. Have them classify these mammals according to the orders described in Table 28-3. Include pictures of as many kinds of mammals as possible, preferably in their native habitats. Include some nonmammals—birds, fish, or lizards—to test students' understanding.

ANSWERS TO SECTION REVIEW

1. Monotremes have the two defining characteristics of mammals—hair and mammary glands.

2. Students' answers will vary. Refer to the information on page 560.

3. Students' answers should include two of the following: in marsupials a shell membrane forms around the fertilized egg (though no shell forms), while in placental mammals it does not; the embryos of placental mammals are nourished through the placenta throughout their development before birth; marsupials develop inside the mother for only a short time and then finish developing in a pouch on the mother's abdomen, while placental mammals remain inside their mothers until development is essentially complete.

4. The embryo is better nourished by a placenta and better protected within the mother's body during its most vulnerable period of development.

Key to Strategies
● Understanding Concepts (Tier I)
■ Applying Information (Tier II)
▲ Critical Thinking (Tier III)

Scheduling

See the **Lesson Planning Guide** on pages 539A and 539B for lecture, classwork, and assignment options for Section 28-4.

Phase Two
Teaching Strategies

Demonstration

● **Comparing Functions**

Ask students if they have pets, such as dogs or cats, that require regular brushing. If so, ask the students to bring in samples of both guard hairs and hairs from the animal's undercoat. Allow all of the students in the class to observe the differences in the two types of hairs with a microscope.

Demonstration

● **Comparing Structures**

Allow students to observe hooves. Pet stores often sell cow hooves for dogs to chew. A butcher shop or meat market may be able to provide you with pigs' feet with the hooves still attached. Have students compare the animal hooves with their own fingernails.

Although there are fewer species of mammals than reptiles, mammals thrive in a far greater variety of habitats and show a greater variety of sizes and shapes than do reptiles. In this section, you will learn about some of the unique adaptations of mammals that suit them to their wide range of habitats and ways of life.

28-4 Mammalian Adaptations

OBJECTIVES

① **Identify three functions of hair.**

② **List two mammalian structures that contain keratin.**

③ **Contrast the teeth of herbivores with those of carnivores.**

④ **Describe how bats navigate in the dark.**

Hair Has Many Functions

All mammals have hair, including the seemingly hairless whales and dolphins. A hair extends from a bulblike structure known as a hair follicle, which lies below the surface of the skin. Hair is composed mainly of air spaces and dead cells filled with the protein keratin.

Most mammals are covered by a coat of hair, shown in **Figure 28-21**. Two different types of hair make up this coat. **Guard hairs** are the long, thick outer hairs responsible for the coat's color. Between the guard hairs grows a dense coat of **underhair**, consisting of thinner, shorter hairs. You can see the underhair of a dog or cat by brushing back the guard hairs with your hand.

What are the functions of hair? One of its functions is insulating against heat loss. Endothermic animals such as mammals often maintain body temperatures higher than the temperature of their surroundings and so tend to lose body heat. The dense underhair coat of many mammals reduces the amount of body heat that escapes, performing the same function as a sweater that you wear on cold days.

Another function of hair is camouflage. The coloration and pattern of a mammal's coat usually match its environment. Hairs also function as sensory structures. The whiskers of cats and dogs are stiff hairs that are sensitive to touch. Mammals that are active at night or that live underground often rely on their whiskers to locate prey or to avoid colliding with objects. Hair can also serve as a defensive weapon. For instance, porcupines and hedgehogs protect themselves with long, sharp, stiff hairs.

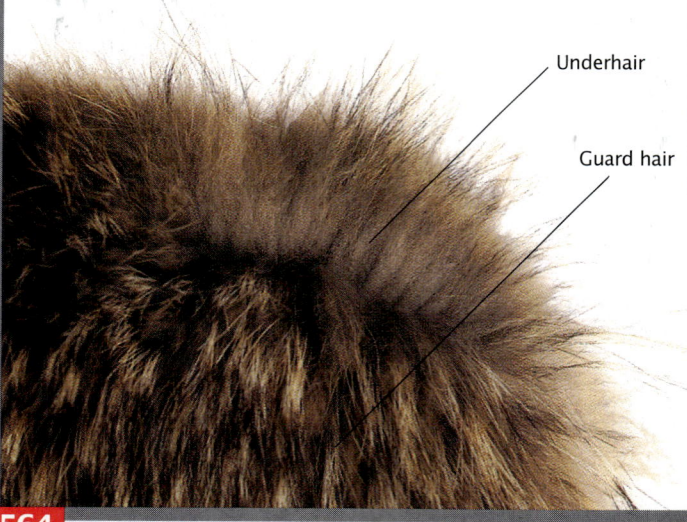

Underhair

Guard hair

Figure 28-21
All mammals have fur, which functions primarily as insulation. Underhair and guard hair aid in this function.

Videodisc Resources

Holt Biology Videodiscs
Lesson 28-4: Mammalian Adaptations

Claws, Hooves, Horns, and Antlers

Keratin is a versatile protein that is a component of many mammalian structures. For example, it is found in claws, fingernails, and hooves. Hooves, such as the zebra's hoof shown in **Figure 28-22**, are specialized pads on the toes of horses, cattle, sheep, antelopes, and other running mammals. In addition, the horns of cattle, sheep, and antelopes are composed of a core of bone surrounded by a sheath of keratin. The bony core is attached to the skull, and the horn is not shed. The horns of rhinoceroses are made of hairlike fibers of keratin that are compacted into a very hard structure.

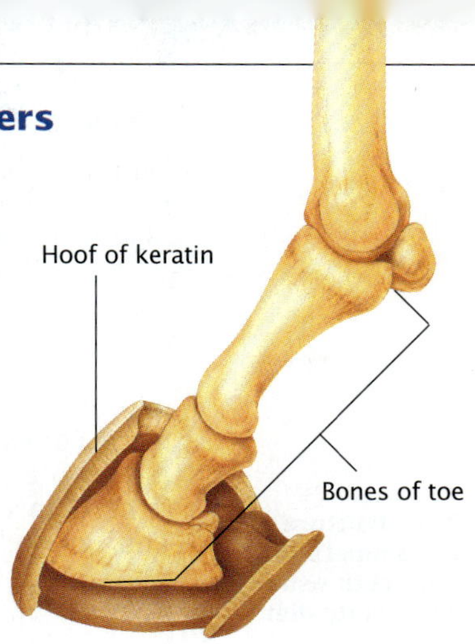

Figure 28-22
A zebra's foot is modified so that the zebra actually walks on a single toe that is covered with a hoof made of keratin.

Deer grow and shed a set of antlers each year. Deer antlers, which are grown only by males, are made of bone and have no keratin sheath. While growing, antlers are covered by a thin layer of skin known as velvet. The velvet dies and is scraped off when the antlers are fully grown. The male deer uses his antlers to attract females and to combat other males. After the breeding season, the male sheds his antlers. Some examples of horns and antlers are shown in **Figure 28-23**.

Figure 28-23
a **The hollow horns of the South African springbok are kept throughout life. Males use their horns to fight with other males.**

b **The antlers of the mule deer are used for combat and to attract females. They drop off every winter and regrow during the spring and summer.**

565

Multicultural Perspective: Animal Bones as Jewelry

Indigenous people in Brazil often wear jewelry made of animal bones, claws, teeth, and feathers. Jaguar claws, for example, are used in necklaces. The brightly colored feathers of the toucan are used in earrings.

28-4 section

Active READING

Technique: Paired Reading
Pair each student with a partner. Have each student silently read about mammalian adaptations. As students read, have them place a check mark on a sticky note next to passages they understand and a question mark on a sticky note next to passages they find confusing or have questions about. After students finish reading, ask one student to summarize what he or she understood, referring to the text as needed. The second student should add anything that the first student omitted. The second student should then continue the discussion by pointing out the passages that he or she did not understand. The first reader should then help the second student with the ideas that were unclear and discuss the passages that he or she did not understand. Both readers should then work together to come to an understanding of the passages they both did not understand. Have them create a list of questions to pose to the class about the ideas or passages that are still unclear after their discussion.

Demonstration

● **Comparing Structures**
Allow students to handle both bones and antlers in order to feel for themselves that antlers are made of bone. A deer or elk hunter may be willing to lend your class a mounted head or a rack of antlers, while a butcher shop can provide bones. Because animals shed their antlers, you may be able to find antlers on the ground in wooded areas. You can also sometimes find the bones of wild animals while hiking in the woods. (Federal and state parks do not usually permit the removal of such items from the park.)

Key to Strategies
● Understanding Concepts (Tier I)
■ Applying Information (Tier II)
▲ Critical Thinking (Tier III)

Reptiles, Birds, and Mammals 565

Food and Feeding

Mammals feed on a variety of foods. Horses, giraffes, antelopes, and elephants are herbivores. Lions, wolves, seals, and sperm whales are carnivores. The blue whale, the largest animal, filters small crustaceans from the ocean. It is usually possible to determine a mammal's diet by examining its teeth. For example, look at the skull of the coyote (a carnivore) and the deer (a herbivore) shown in **Figure 28-24**. The coyote's long canine teeth are suited for biting and holding prey. Its premolar and molar teeth are triangular and sharp for shearing off chunks of flesh. The deer's canines, in contrast, are small. It clips off mouthfuls of plants with its flat incisors. The deer's molars are large, and their surfaces are covered with ridges that form an effective grinding surface for breaking up tough plant tissues.

Cellulose is the major component of plant cell walls and is thus a major constituent of the plant body. Mammals do not have enzymes that can digest cellulose. Herbivorous mammals rely on a mutualistic partnership with bacteria and protists that can produce cellulose-splitting enzymes. Mammals such as cows, buffaloes, antelopes, goats, deer, and giraffes have huge four-chambered stomachs that function as storage and fermentation vats. The first chamber is the largest and holds a large population of bacteria and protists. When the animal swallows, chewed plant material passes into this chamber. Bacteria and protists partly digest the material, which is then regurgitated and chewed again. A cow chewing its cud is rechewing this partly digested food. After another thorough grinding, the cud is swallowed and further digested in the stomach. It then passes from the stomach into the intestines.

Rodents, horses, elephants, and rabbits are herbivores but have relatively small stomachs that lack mutualistic microorganisms. These animals do not chew a cud. Bacteria that aid in digestion live in a pouch that branches off the large intestine.

Even with these complex adaptations for breaking down cellulose, a mouthful of plants is less nutritious than a mouthful of flesh. Herbivores must consume large amounts of plant material to gain sufficient nutrition. An elephant eats 135–150 kg (300–400 lb) of food per day. You can read more about mammalian adaptations in the *Tour of a Mammal* on page 567.

Figure 28-24
The structure of a mammal's jaw and teeth usually reveals its diet.

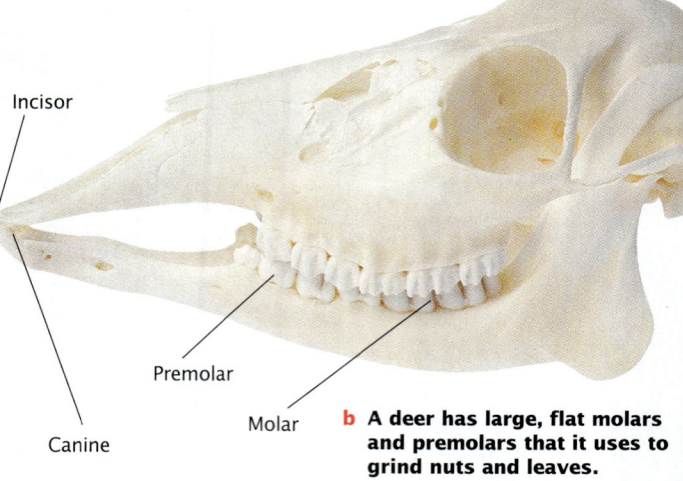

Incisor
Premolar
Molar
Canine

a A coyote has long canines to seize prey and sharp molars and premolars to cut flesh.

Incisor
Premolar
Molar
Canine

b A deer has large, flat molars and premolars that it uses to grind nuts and leaves.

566

Matter of Fact: Rodent Teeth

Rodents are known for their gnawing, accomplished by incisors in both jaws. These teeth grow continuously, but because they rub against each other when the rodent gnaws, they are kept at a constant length. Rodents are the best mammalian nest builders and the most efficient food handlers.

Mammal

The deer mouse is one of the most common and widespread mammals in the United States. It is found in most of the continental United States. Like all mammals, deer mice have hair, and the females feed their young with milk.

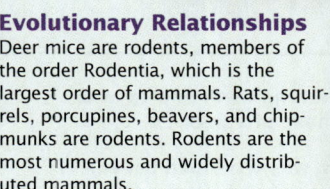

Size
The deer mouse ranges from 120 to 230 mm (about 5 in. to 9 in.) in length, including its tail. It weighs from 18 to 35 g (0.67 to 1.25 oz).

All mammals are endotherms. Per gram of body mass, a mouse consumes five times as much food as a dog. Smaller mammals, such as the deer mouse, must eat more to remain active because they lose much more heat due to their greater surface-area-to-volume ratio.

Whiskers are sensory hairs that enable the mouse to detect nearby objects in the dark.

The chisel-like incisors of rodents grow continually, an adaptation for gnawing. A mammal's teeth are replaced only once during its lifetime, unlike the teeth of a reptile, which are replaced continually throughout its life.

Habitat
Because it is such a widespread species, the deer mouse lives in many habitats. It prefers dry areas, such as forests and grasslands. It nests in burrows, fallen logs, and rock piles and in buildings in rural areas.

Evolutionary Relationships
Deer mice are rodents, members of the order Rodentia, which is the largest order of mammals. Rats, squirrels, porcupines, beavers, and chipmunks are rodents. Rodents are the most numerous and widely distributed mammals.

567

Tour

Gestation in the Mouse
■ **Recognizing Relationships**
The gestation period of a mouse is about 21 days, whereas the gestation period of a moose is about 8 months. Have students imagine that they are scientists looking for a laboratory animal for experiments dealing with mammalian development and heredity. Which animal would they select for their experiments? Have them explain their choice. *(Choosing the mouse would allow more experiments to be done in a shorter period of time.)*

Parental Care in Mammals
■ **Inferring Relationships**
Some mammal species must care for their young for many years until the young reach maturity and can survive on their own. This pattern of rearing young has advantages over the way reptiles rear their young. Longer periods of parental care offer the young food, protection, and time to learn necessary survival skills. Ask students to list some of the disadvantages of this pattern of rearing young, compared with the reptilian pattern. *(Students' answers will vary. Answers may include greater expenditures of time and energy and fewer offspring produced.)*

The Cost of Endothermy
■ **Inferring Relationships**
Mammals are endotherms, and they metabolically regulate their body temperature. Using the information in this section and the **Tour**, have students speculate on why a mouse must eat more food per gram of body mass than a dog. *(A mouse is smaller and therefore has a higher surface-to-body ratio than a dog does. A mouse loses heat more rapidly than a dog does and must compensate by having a higher metabolism.)*

Phase Three
Assessment Options

Closure

■ **Forming a Hypothesis**

Ask students to come up with as many common phrases as possible that refer to mammals. Such phrases might include "blind as a bat," "dog-tired," "quiet as a mouse," etc. Write the suggestions on the board and discuss whether the phrases accurately describe what the students know about these animals. If students decide the phrases are not accurate, ask them to hypothesize why these phrases are so widely used. For example, since bats hunt at night, people may have thought that bats did not need vision.

SECTION REVIEW

Assign the *Section Review*.

Reteaching

Have students design a mammal to fit a particular habitat. Tell them to draw this fictional mammal and to describe any particular anatomical or physiological adaptation that would enable it to successfully survive and reproduce. Provide the students with information such as habitat restrictions, whether the mammal is nocturnal or diurnal, and the habits of some of its predators.

Flying Mammals

Bats are the only mammals capable of powered flight. Like the wings of birds, the wings of bats are modified forelimbs. The bat wing is a leathery membrane of skin and muscle supported by the bones of four fingers. The membrane attaches to the side of the body and to the hind leg (and to the tail in some bats). When resting, most bats prefer to hang by their feet, as shown in **Figure 28-25**.

Contrary to popular belief, not all bats emerge only at night. The so-called flying foxes, for instance, feed on fruit during the day. Most bats, however, are active at dusk or at night. Some eat fish and frogs, which they pluck from the water's surface. Others feed on nectar from flowers or prey on small mammals, including other bats. Vampire bats of Central America and South America drink blood from large mammals. Flying insects are the main food source for most nocturnal bats. Since few birds fly at night, bats have almost exclusive access to this rich food supply.

Figure 28-25
Many bats, such as this California leaf-nosed bat, are social animals. They roost together in groups of thousands, and some species hunt cooperatively.

How do bats navigate in the dark?

How can bats fly in dark caves and hunt their food at dusk or even at night? Do bats have particularly sensitive vision? Or do they use another sense to find their way around? Late in the eighteenth century, the Italian scientist Lazzaro Spallanzani showed that a blinded bat could fly and capture flying insects. However, when Spallanzani plugged the ears of the bat, it was unable to navigate and collided with objects. Spallanzani concluded that bats "hear" their way through the world. It was not until the late 1930s that bats' ability to "fly blind" was explained.

Bats have evolved a sonar system that functions much like the sonar devices used by ships to locate underwater objects. As a bat flies, it emits extremely high pitched sounds that are outside our range of hearing. These high-frequency pulses are emitted through the mouth or, in some cases, through the nose. The sound waves reflect from obstacles or flying insects, and the bat hears the echo. Through sophisticated processing of this echo within its brain, a bat can determine not only the direction of an object but also the distance to the object. This sonar system enables bats to navigate and to capture their prey at night, as shown in **Figure 28-26**.

Figure 28-26
This bat used its sonar to catch a moth in midair in the dark.

SECTION REVIEW

1. List two functions of hair.

2. Name two keratin-containing structures on your body.

3. Contrast the teeth of a coyote with those of a deer.

4. Explain why a blinded bat can catch prey but a deafened one cannot.

ANSWERS TO SECTION REVIEW

1. Hair acts as insulation, sensory structures, defensive weapons, and camouflage.

2. Both the hair and nails contain keratin.

3. Coyotes have long canine teeth suited for biting and capturing prey. Their premolars and molars are triangular and sharp for tearing flesh. In contrast, deer have large flat molars covered with ridges for grinding and breaking plant tissue.

4. Bats often hunt in darkness and navigate more by hearing the echoes of their high-pitched cries than by sight.

"Well, of course I did it in cold blood, you idiot! ...I'm a reptile!"

Alternative Assessment

Arrange for a "Bring a Photo of Your Pet Day" for students who have pet reptiles, birds, or mammals. Display the photos on the class bulletin board, and have each student write down three questions about the various pets. Have students read their questions aloud, and have the pet owners answer the questions.

Portfolio Assessment

Portfolio Assessment on page T39 provides options for building and evaluating student portfolios. Students and teachers can select items from the areas listed on page T39 for inclusion in a portfolio.

	Key Terms	Summary
28-1 Reptiles Reptiles control their body temperature through their behavior. 		• Reptiles have dry, largely watertight skin and are ectotherms. Most species lay watertight eggs. • Reptiles evolved about 320 million years ago. • Pterosaurs were the only reptiles that evolved the ability to fly. • Dinosaurs became extinct about 65 million years ago. • The surviving reptiles include crocodiles and alligators, turtles, tuataras, lizards, and snakes.
28-2 Birds Some birds may have more than 25,000 feathers on their body.	contour feather (p. 553) down feather (p. 553)	• The first birds evolved more than 150 million years ago. • All birds have feathers, are endothermic, and lay eggs. • Birds have down feathers and contour feathers. • The skeletons of birds are lightweight. The bones are hollow and thin.
28-3 Introduction to Mammals Mammals, such as these cheetahs, receive nourishment from their mother's mammary glands while young. 	mammary gland (p. 559) monotreme (p. 560) marsupial (p. 560) placental mammal (p. 560)	• Mammals evolved from reptiles about 220 million years ago. • Mammals have hair and are endothermic. Female mammals have mammary glands. • Monotremes are mammals that lay eggs. • Marsupial mammals are born early in development and complete their development in the mother's pouch. • Placental mammals nourish their young through the placenta.
28-4 Mammalian Adaptations The skull of a coyote has long canines and strong jaws.	guard hair (p. 564) underhair (p. 564)	• Hair serves as insulation, as camouflage, as a sensory structure, and as a defense. • Bats are the only flying mammals. Bats are able to navigate and capture prey in the dark by means of a sonar system.

569

ANSWER TO CONCEPT MAP

The following is one possible answer to the Relating Concepts exercise on page 570.

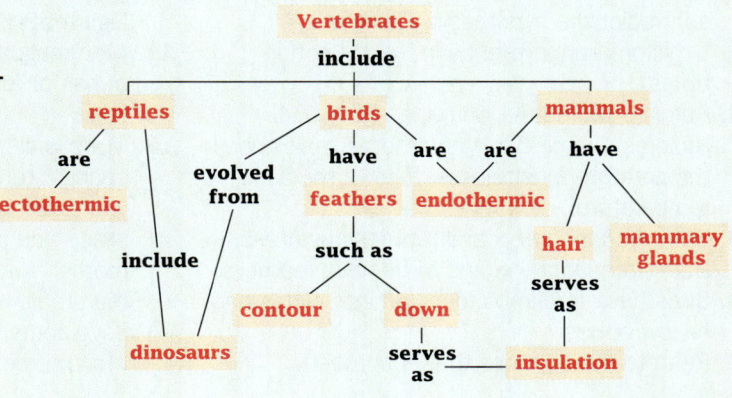

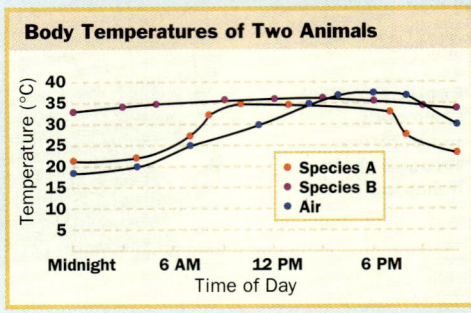

Understanding Vocabulary

1. a. An endotherm's body temperature does not fluctuate with the temperature of its surroundings. An ectotherm's body temperature follows the temperature of its surroundings.
b. Contour feathers give shape to the wings and tail and are used in flight; they provide some insulation. Down feathers are specialized for insulation and grow between and underneath the contour feathers.
c. Monotremes are mammals that have features similar to reptiles, including single openings for waste and reproduction, and young that hatch from eggs. Marsupials are mammals whose young move to their mother's pouch during early development.

2. a. All of these reptiles lived on Earth during the Age of Reptiles, 250 to 65 million years ago. Ichthyosaurs and plesiosaurs lived in the oceans. Dinosaurs lived on land. Pterosaurs were the first vertebrates to fly.
b. See page 554.
c. Refer to the captions that accompany Figure 28-18 on page 559.

Understanding Concepts

3. Concept Map answer is on page 569.

4. Reptilian skin is dry and covered with scales. Amphibian skin is usually moist and lacks scales. Amphibian eggs need to remain moist, while reptilian eggs are amniotic and resistant to water loss.

5. Alvarez proposed that a large meteorite struck the Earth about the time the dinosaurs became extinct (about 65 million years ago) and that the resulting dust clouds blocked the sun. Reduced sunlight caused the plants on which the dinosaurs fed to die, thus starving the dinosaurs into extinction. The new fossils

---

review

Understanding Vocabulary

1. For each pair of terms, explain the difference in their meanings.
   a. endotherm, ectotherm
   b. contour feathers, down feathers
   c. monotremes, marsupials

2. Using each set of words below, write one or more sentences summarizing information learned in this chapter.
   a. ichthyosaur, plesiosaur, dinosaur, pterosaur
   b. flapping flight, gliding, soaring
   c. hair, mammary glands, endothermic, four-chambered heart

Understanding Concepts

3. **Relating Concepts** Construct a concept map that describes the characteristics of the three vertebrate groups described in this chapter. Try to include the following terms in your concept map: vertebrate, reptiles, birds, mammals, ectothermic, endothermic, feathers, hair, mammary glands, dinosaurs, contour, down, and insulation.

4. **Comparing Structures** How does the skin of a reptile differ from the skin of an amphibian? Describe the differences between the eggs of amphibians and the eggs of reptiles.

5. **Analyzing Information** Suppose that some new dinosaur fossils are discovered. Radioactive dating shows that these fossils are 60 million years old. Do these fossils support or contradict the hypothesis that the dinosaurs became extinct because a meteorite struck the Earth? Explain your answer.

6. **Summarizing Information** List the four orders of living reptiles and give the main characteristics of each. Give an example of an animal in each order.

---

7. **Analyzing Data** The graph below shows how the body temperatures of two animals change over the day. Which animal is probably an ectotherm? Explain your answer.

Body Temperatures of Two Animals

Temperature (°C): 40, 35, 30, 25, 20, 15, 10, 5

● Species A
● Species B
● Air

Midnight   6 AM   12 PM   6 PM
Time of Day

8. **Recognizing Relationships** Early specimens of *Archaeopteryx* were misidentified as reptiles. What characteristics does *Archaeopteryx* share with reptiles? What features does it share with modern birds?

9. **Comparing Structures** Describe two ways the skeleton of a bird is modified for flight.

10. **Comparing Structures** How were the early mammals different from therapsids?

11. **Identifying Structures** Identify the two characteristics that make mammals unique.

12. **Comparing Functions** Contrast the pattern of development of marsupials with that of placental mammals. What makes monotremes unique among living mammals?

13. **Identifying Functions** Describe three functions of hair.

14. **Comparing Functions and Structures** How are underhair and down feathers alike? How are they different?

15. **Identifying Structures** Name three structures of your body that contain keratin.

16. **Comparing Structures** How could you tell if a mammalian skull was that of a herbivore or a carnivore?

17. **Recognizing Relationships** Explain how a bat is able to locate a flying insect on a dark night.

18. **BUILDING ON WHAT YOU HAVE LEARNED** In Chapter 18 you learned about bacteria. How are bacteria beneficial to herbivorous mammals?

---

contradict the hypothesis. There is a 5-million-year difference in the extinction times.

6. Refer to Table 28-1 on pages 550–551.

7. Species A is probably an ectotherm. Its body temperature most closely follows the air temperature.

8. Both *Archaeopteryx* and reptiles have tails. Both *Archaeopteryx* and birds have feathers.

9. Birds have forelimbs modified into wings and hollow bones.

10. Refer to the captions that accompany

Figure 28-17 on page 558.

11. Mammals are distinguished by the presence of hair or fur and by the ability to produce milk.

12. Marsupials, such as kangaroos, carry the offspring internally for only a short time. The young are born at an early developmental stage and finish developing in a pouch on the mother's abdomen. In contrast, placental mammals remain inside the mother until development is essentially complete. Monotremes lay shelled eggs, have a pelvis

Interpreting Graphics

19. Examine the animals pictured below.

a.
b.
c.

a. Identify the class to which each animal belongs.
b. Which animal is ectothermic?
c. In which animal is the ventricle of the heart incompletely divided?

Reviewing Themes

20. *Evolution*
Pterosaurs had a large, keeled breastbone. What might this feature indicate about how pterosaurs flew? Explain your answer.

21. *Evolution*
What evidence suggests that reptiles and birds have a common ancestor?

22. *Interdependence*
Explain the impact that humans have had on the survival of marsupials in Australia and New Guinea.

Thinking Critically

23. **Justifying Conclusions** When a female leatherback turtle comes up on the beach to lay her eggs, she first digs a deep hole, lays her eggs, and covers them with sand. Then she crawls about 100 m and digs another hole. This time she lays no eggs but covers the hole with sand anyway. Suggest a hypothesis to explain this behavior. Describe how you could test your hypothesis.

Life/Work Skills

24. **Finding Information** Use library references or search an on-line database to find out about the different ways that snakes move. Prepare an illustrated written report to share your findings with your class.

25. **Working Cooperatively** Working with two or three of your classmates, use library references and field guides to find out what kinds of birds are common in your area. Find out what the birds eat and what kind of shelter they require. Design and build a birdhouse appropriate for a particular bird in your area. Also design and build a bird feeder for the same bird. Place the house and feeder where they can be easily observed. Keep a journal of your observations to share with your class.

Activities and Projects

26. **Literature Connection** Throughout history, reptiles have been portrayed in literature as evil and dangerous monsters. Read fairy tales, folk tales, and other stories, and compile a list of the ways that reptiles are portrayed. Then use library references or search an on-line database to provide evidence to support or disprove these portrayals.

27. **Language Arts Connection** Use library references to look up common phrases that refer to characteristics of animals, such as "happy as a lark," "sings like a bird," "eats like a bird," "blind as a bat," and "dog tired." Are these phrases based on fact? Compile a list of phrases and information about their accuracy to share with the class.

Discovering Through Reading

28. Read the article "The Private Lives of Pit Vipers" by Michael Lipske in *National Wildlife*, August/September 1995, pages 14–20. Describe the function of the pits located behind the nostrils of all pit vipers. How frequently do blacktail rattlesnakes eat during a year? Describe one way that pit vipers have benefited medicine.

571

Interpreting Graphics

19. a. Reptilia, Aves, Mammalia
b. the turtle
c. the turtle

Reviewing Themes

20. Strong muscles to raise and lower the wings are required for active flight. The muscles that power the wings attach to a large sternum that bears a large keel. Thus, pterosaurs probably had the large muscles necessary for powered flight.
21. Both lay amniotic eggs and have scales.
22. See page 561.

Thinking Critically

23. Answers will vary, but students should suggest that the digging of empty holes may be a protective behavior to distract predators from the eggs.

Life/Work Skills

24. Results will vary depending on the resources available.
25. Results will vary depending on the resources available, location, time of year, and birds selected.

Activities and Projects

26. Results will vary depending on the resources available.
27. Results will vary depending on the resources available.

Discovering Through Reading

28. The pits contain organs that detect heat, helping the snake locate warmblooded prey, primarily rodents, in darkness. Blacktails eat only about 10 times a year. From the deadly venom of the jararaca, a pit viper of Brazil and Argentina, scientists have been able to synthesize a compound used in the treatment of high blood pressure.

---

similar to that of early reptiles, and have a single opening through which feces, urine, and reproductive products leave the body.
13. Hair insulates against heat loss, provides camouflage, and functions as a sensory structure.
14. Both serve to insulate the body of endotherms. Underhair is found on mammals, while birds have down feathers.
15. Skin, hair, and nails
16. Examine the teeth. A herbivore would have flat incisors and molars that are flat with

ridges. A carnivore would have long, sharp canine teeth and sharp, triangular-shaped molars. Refer to Figure 28-24 on page 566.
17. A bat uses a type of sonar, emitting high-pitched sound waves that bounce off insects, enabling the bat to determine the exact location of the insect.
18. Bacteria live in the animal's stomach, where they digest the cellulose in the plants that the animal has eaten.

Six

Human Life

A white blood cell devours invading bacteria

VIRUSES AND YOU

When you get a cold or the flu, a virus is trying to take over your cells as it spreads throughout your body. A few days after the virus invades, you begin to feel ill. Though colds and flu are uncomfortable, few healthy people die from them because the body's immune system battles viruses and other pathogens that cause disease.

A Deadly Virus

The virus that causes AIDS is another story. It can hide in the body for months or years before it produces any signs of illness. But all that time the virus is destroying the ability of the immune system to protect the body from other pathogens. That is why this virus is known as the human immunodeficiency virus (HIV).

A Profound Challenge

HIV mutates rapidly, disguising itself as a slightly different virus with each mutation. This rapid mutation makes the development of vaccines or treatments a challenge. Because the virus is now spreading most rapidly through sexual contact between men and women, it will be very difficult to eliminate.

LOOKING AHEAD

- How does the immune system usually fight off invasions by a virus? How does HIV disable the immune system? See pages 683–691.
- How frequently is AIDS affecting people aged 15–24? See page 693.
- What other pathogens are transmitted in the same ways as HIV? How can the risk of HIV infection be reduced? See pages 737–740.
- Why should health-care costs for the elderly be of concern to you? See **Science, Technology, and Society: Who Pays the Bill for Growing Old?** pages 716–717.

29 | The Human Body

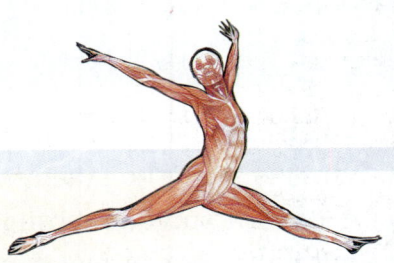

Lesson Planning Guide With Options for Block Scheduling

Lecture Concepts   **Lesson Resources**

29-1 An Inside View of the Human Body

BLOCK ❶ (45 minutes)

1. Cells that share a common structure and function form tissues.

2. The human body contains four types of tissue: epithelial, muscle, nerve, and connective.

❶ **Lecture Resources**
- Determining Prior Knowledge
- Tissues
- Nervous Tissue
- Active Reading: K-W-L
- Visual Strategy: Figures 29-1, 29-2

- Teaching Transparencies: 189
- Holt Biology Videodiscs Lesson 29-1

Classwork Options
- Interactive Exploration 29A

BLOCK ❷ (45 minutes)

3. Tissues that share a common function form organs.

4. Organs that share a common function form systems.

❷ **Lecture Resources**
- Hierarchy of Structure
- Visual Strategy: Figure 29-3
- Teaching Transparencies: 187
- Holt Biology Videodiscs Lesson 29-1

Classwork Options
- Closure: Recognizing Structures
- Quick Labs: Lab A9

Assignment Options
- Reteaching
- Section Review
- Chapter Review, questions 1a, 2a, 4, 26, 27
- Directed Reading Worksheet

29-2 Skin

BLOCK ❸ (45 minutes)

1. The skin is composed of two layers: an outer epidermis and an underlying dermis.

2. The dermis contains epithelial, muscle, nerve, and connective tissues.

❸ **Lecture Resources**
- Active Reading: Reading Organizer
- Visual Strategy: Figures 29-4, 29-5
- Visual Strategy: Videodisc
- Teaching Transparencies: 188
- Holt Biology Videodiscs Lesson 29-2

Classwork Options
- Epidermis
- Hair
- Inquiry Skills Development: Lab B30

Assignment Options
- Life/Work Skills: Selecting Technology

BLOCK ❹ (45 minutes)

3. The epidermis is made entirely of epithelial tissue containing melanin and hair follicles.

4. Skin disorders include acne and skin cancer.

❹ **Lecture Resources**
- Severe Sunburn
- Visual Strategy: Figure 29-7
- Holt Biology Videodiscs Lesson 29-2

Classwork Options
- Closure: Recognizing Relationships

Assignment Options
- *Small Group* Reteaching
- Section Review
- Chapter Review, questions 1b, 2b, 8, 9, 10, 11, 12, 20, 22, 23, 29, 30
- Directed Reading Worksheet

29-3 Bones

BLOCK ❺ (45 minutes)

1. Bones are dynamic structures that are continuously being broken down and repaired.

2. As a human embryo develops, minerals harden most of the cartilage, which is gradually replaced by bone.

❺ **Lecture Resources**
- Active Reading: Paired Reading
- Visual Strategy: Figures 29-11, 29-12
- Visual Strategy: Videodisc
- Demonstration: Identifying Structures
- Teaching Transparencies: 186
- Holt Biology Videodiscs Lesson 29-3

Classwork Options
- Quick Labs: A27

BLOCK ❻ (45 minutes)

3. All the bones in the body form the skeleton, which supports the body, enables it to move, and protects internal organs.

4. Bones meet at joints and are held together by ligaments, which can become sprained when stretched too far.

❻ **Lecture Resources**
- Visual Strategy: Figures 29-13, 29-14, 29-15, 29-16
- Visual Strategy: Videodisc
- Demonstration: Identifying Structures
- Demonstration: Comparing Structures
- Teaching Transparencies: 184, 185, 198
- Holt Biology Videodiscs Lesson 29-3

Classwork Options
- Reteaching
- Closure: Justifying Conclusions
- Quick Labs: Lab A26

Assignment Options
- Section Review
- Chapter Review, questions 1c, 13, 14, 16, 17
- Directed Reading Worksheet

Lecture Concepts

Lesson Resources

29-4 Muscles

BLOCK ⑦ (45 minutes)
1. The three major types of muscle include skeletal muscle, smooth muscle, and cardiac muscle.
2. Movement of bones requires two sets of muscles, and tendons that connect muscles to bone.

⑦ Lecture Resources
- ■ Active Reading: Reading Organizer
- ■ Visual Strategy: Figures 29-18, 29-20
- ■ Visual Strategy: Videodisc
- ■ Demonstration: Comparing Structures
- ■ Demonstration: Recognizing Patterns
- 🔒 Teaching Transparencies: 190, 192, 193
- 🔘 Holt Biology Videodiscs Lesson 29-4

Classwork Options
🔒 Laboratory Techniques and Experimental Design: Lab C41
Assignment Options
- ■ World of Work: Physiastry

BLOCK ⑧ (45 minutes)
3. Strength, flexibility, and endurance can be increased by exercise and physical activity. Different kinds of exercise, aerobic and anaerobic, affect muscles and use energy in different ways.
4. Use of anabolic steroids to increase muscle size may produce serious side effects.

⑧ Lecture Resources
- ■ Muscle Cell Subunits
- ■ Muscle Protein Functions
- ■ Active Reading: K-W-L
- ■ Demonstration: Comparing Structures
- 🔘 Holt Biology Videodiscs Lesson 29-4

Classwork Options
- ■ Reteaching
- ■ Closure: Analyzing Information

Assignment Options
- ■ Section Review
- ■ Chapter Review, questions 2c, 3, 5, 6, 7, 15, 18, 19, 21, 24, 25, 28
- ■ Directed Reading Worksheet

Chapter Review and Assessment

BLOCK ⑨ (45 minutes)
Review
- ■ Reteaching Worksheet
- ■ Thinking Skills Worksheet
- ■ Vocabulary Development Worksheet
- ◉ Language Development and Reading Comprehension Audio CD Program: Chapter 29

BLOCK ⑩ (45 minutes)
Assessment
- ■ Alternative Assessment, p. 597
- ■ Portfolio Assessment, p. T39
Chapter Test
- ■ Chapter 29 Test
Test Generator
- ◉ Item bank for customizing Chapter Tests

Teaching Resources CD-ROM
- ◉ Scoring Rubrics and Classroom Management Checklist

The Portfolio icon denotes items throughout the Teacher's Edition lesson wrap that may be selected for inclusion in student portfolios.

Holt Biology Videodiscs and *Concepts of Biology*

Holt Biology Videodiscs gives you a powerful tool for teaching, review, and assessment. For further information regarding the media on the videodiscs, see *Holt Biology Videodiscs Teacher's Correlation Guide to Holt Biology: Visualizing Life.*

Concepts of Biology adds interactive lesson plans and extensive tools for customization using CD-ROM technology.

Use the following topic from *Concepts of Biology* to help you teach this chapter:

Topic 21: Body Systems

Laboratory Planning

Text
Materials and preparation instructions appear on the teacher's wrap accompanying each laboratory exercise.

Block 1: Interactive Exploration 29A: Life Span and Lifestyle, p. 810

Holt BioSources Laboratory Program

Block 2: Quick Labs Lab A9: Comparing Observations of Body Parts
Block 3: Inquiry Skills Development Lab B30: Touch Receptors in the Skin
Block 5: Quick Labs Lab A27: Comparing Skeletal Joints
Block 6: Quick Labs Lab A26: Vertebrate Skeletons
Block 7: Laboratory Techniques and Experimental Design Lab C41: Evaluating Muscle Exhaustion

CHAPTER 29

Determining Prior Knowledge

- Ask students how we are different from other animals.
- Ask students why dogs and chickens pant but do not sweat, and why people and horses pant and sweat.
- Have students define and explain the differences between an *exoskeleton* and an *endoskeleton.* What benefits do we gain by having an endoskeleton?
- Ask if any student has had a sprain, fracture, or pulled muscle. Have each student describe what happened and how the injury was treated.
- Have students demonstrate different forms of movement (bending over, swinging an imaginary bat at a ball, sitting down, smiling, etc.) in various activities. Ask what muscles are used in each type of movement.

Active READING

Technique: K-W-L
Before students begin this chapter, divide the class into three groups. Have one group create a list of all the things they **K**now about skin; the second group should create a list of all the things they **K**now about bones; and the third group should create a list of all the things they **K**now about muscles. When the groups finish their lists, ask the spokesperson(s) to contribute his or her group's entries to class lists on the board or the overhead. Then have students individually list things they **W**ant to know about skin, bones, or muscles. Have students save their lists for later use in Active Reading on page 596.

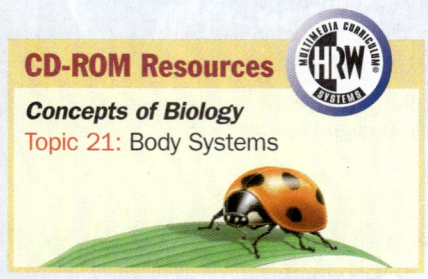

CD-ROM Resources

Concepts of Biology
Topic 21: Body Systems

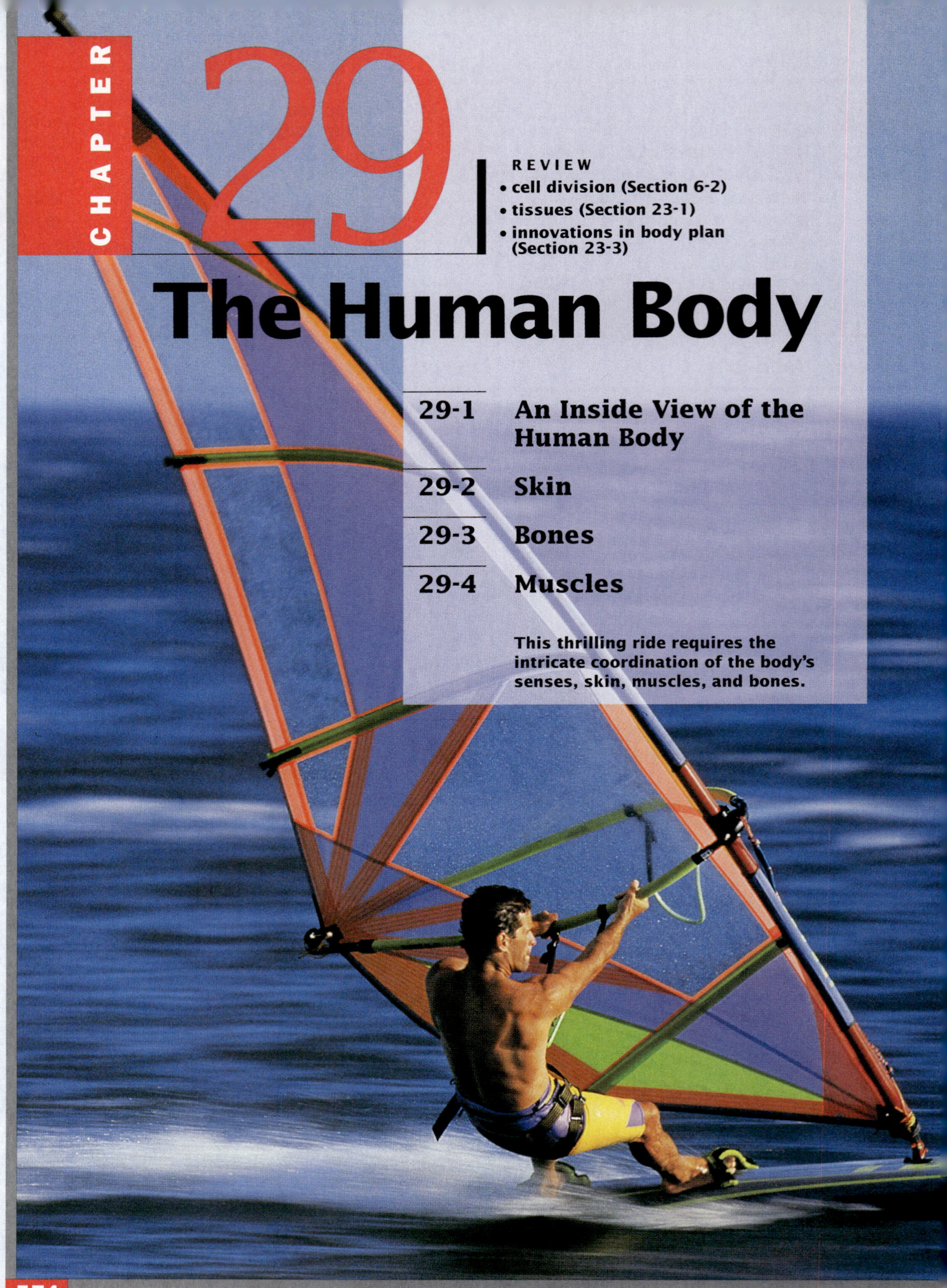

CHAPTER 29

REVIEW
- cell division (Section 6-2)
- tissues (Section 23-1)
- innovations in body plan (Section 23-3)

The Human Body

This thrilling ride requires the intricate coordination of the body's senses, skin, muscles, and bones.

574

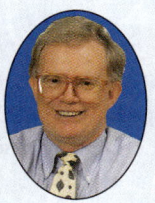

Author's Rationale This chapter introduces the unit covering body form from an organizational point of view. The first section lays out the basic architecture using the ideas developed in Unit 5 (particularly Chapter 21). The four tissue types should be covered briefly in making the point of how a tissue's characteristics match its function. The last two sections cover systems most closely associated with body form: bones and muscles.

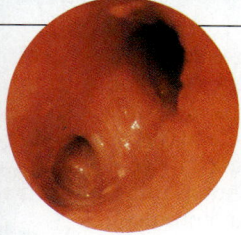

Your body consists of many specialized tissues, such as those seen in this view of the body's airway to the left lung. These tissues, each made of specialized cells, are arranged differently in each part of your body. This process of specialization and arrangement began before you were born, when a single cell began to divide.

29-1

An Inside View of the Human Body

OBJECTIVES

1 Explain the roles of the four kinds of tissues in the human body.

2 Classify connective tissue into three types, and name common examples.

3 Identify three organ systems that protect or support the body.

Similar Cells Form Tissues

All of the trillions of cells in the human body arise from a single cell—the fertilized egg. The first few cells that form by cell division after fertilization look alike. Soon, however, the new cells become specialized to carry out particular tasks.

As cells specialize, they begin to group together to form tissues. A **tissue** is a group of similar cells that work together to perform a specific function, such as movement or protection. Your body contains four types of tissue—epithelial tissue, muscle tissue, nervous tissue, and connective tissue, as shown in **Figure 29-1**.

Epithelial tissue covers and protects

Epithelial *(ehp uh THEE lee uhl)* **tissue** is made of tightly connected cells that are arranged in flat sheets, often only a few cells thick. Just as canvas protects machinery that must be stored outdoors, epithelial tissue prevents damage to the cells that lie beneath it. Skin is an example of epithelial tissue. Epithelial tissue also lines spaces within the body and covers the inner and outer surfaces of your internal organs.

Some epithelial tissue has an entirely different function. This epithelial tissue forms exocrine glands. An exocrine gland is a cell or group of cells that produces and releases secretions onto a body surface. One type of exocrine gland in your skin secretes sweat, which helps cool your body. Exocrine glands in the lining of your digestive system produce enzymes that digest food.

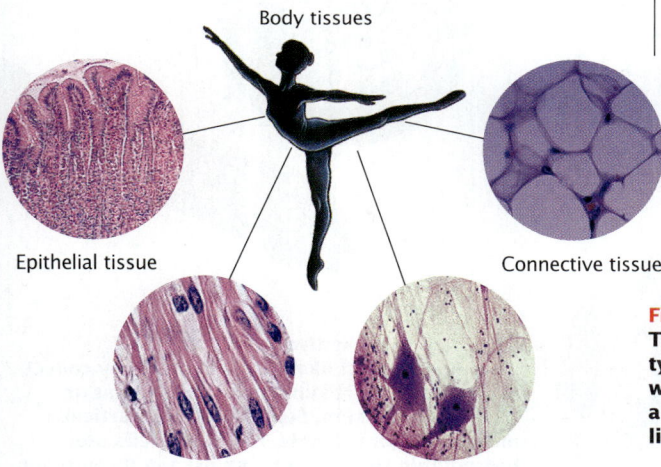

Body tissues

Epithelial tissue

Connective tissue

Muscle tissue

Nervous tissue

Figure 29-1
The human body is made of four types of tissue, shown at left. All work together to make the body a functional unit capable of all life activities.

575

Videodisc Resources

Holt Biology Videodiscs

Lesson 29-1: An Inside View of the Human Body

29-1

Preparation

Scheduling

See the **Lesson Planning Guide** on pages 573A and 573B for lecture, classwork, and assignment options for Section 29-1.

Phase Two

Teaching Strategies

Visual Strategy | **Figure 29-1**

● **Summarizing Information**
The four primary tissue types form the "fabric" of the body. If you have to assign one term to categorize each tissue type, use the following: *covering* (epithelium), *support* (connective), *movement* (muscle), and *control* (nervous).

Tissues

● **Observing Differences**
Use overhead transparencies or a microprojector and prepared slides to allow students to visualize the arrangement and structures of epithelial, connective, muscle, and nervous tissue cells.

Nervous Tissue

■ **Relating Concepts**
Show the class a piece of telephone or fiber optics cable. Point out that a nerve is actually a bundle of many neuron parts—usually hundreds or even thousands. Just like the individual wires in a telephone cable, each neuron is capable of transmitting a separate message.

Key to Strategies

Teaching Strategies are keyed to three tiers of learning.

● **Understanding Concepts (Tier I)**
Content mastery and comprehension

■ **Applying Information (Tier II)**
Applying and analyzing content

▲ **Critical Thinking (Tier III)**
Practicing evaluative thinking

Visual Strategy | Figure 29-2

■ Relating Concepts
Use this figure to reinforce a major difference between connective tissue and the other three types; it contains relatively few cells and is formed mostly from cell products like fibers and fluid. Students should understand that connective tissue is the most widely distributed tissue in the body since it joins, supports, and protects the other types.

Visual Strategy | Figure 29-3

▲ Critical Thinking
Ask students to identify the organ systems this dancer is using. (*The dancer is obviously using the skeletal, muscular, cardiovascular, and nervous systems. Less obvious are the respiratory, endocrine, lymphatic, and integumentary systems.*) What are the organs in each system? (*Within the skeletal system are the bones; in the muscular system the muscles; in the cardiovascular system the heart and blood vessels; and in the nervous system the brain, spinal cord, and nerves.*) What tissues compose each organ? (*The tissues used are epithelial, connective, muscle, and nervous.*)

Hierarchy of Structure

● Summarizing Information
Using the information in this chapter and in previous chapters, have the students make a **Graphic Organizer** in which they summarize the hierarchy of structural levels. Remind students that each level is built upon the previous level.

Muscle tissue moves the body
Have you ever awakened with sore muscles? If so, you probably became aware of how often you use those particular muscles. **Muscle tissue** moves the parts of your body. Even when you are sitting still, muscles are at work maintaining your posture, moving food through your digestive system, and moving blood through your heart.

Muscle tissue is made of cells that contract and then relax to return to their usual length. Another characteristic of muscle tissue is that it responds to electrical stimulation. Electrical signals control when a muscle will contract or relax.

Nervous tissue sends electrical signals through the body
As you walk up a flight of stairs, the electrical signals that cause the muscles in your legs to contract are produced by nerve tissue. **Nervous tissue** is found in your brain, nerves, and sense organs. It contains cells called neurons that generate electrical impulses and transfer the impulses to other cells. Neurons have long extensions that carry electrical impulses long distances. Nervous tissue also contains other cells that nourish and protect the neurons that carry the electrical signals.

Connective tissue joins, supports, and transports
Connective-tissue cells are spaced farther apart than cells of most other tissues. **Connective tissue** actually contains few cells. Some connective tissues are fluids; others are more like crystals. There are three types of connective tissue: defensive, structural, and sequestering. Sequestering tissues store, or "sequester," particular compounds. Defensive tissue defends the body; structural tissue supports it. **Figure 29-2** describes these types of connective tissue and gives examples of each.

Figure 29-2
The graceful leap of a dancer depends on many types of tissue, including muscle, nervous, and epithelial tissues. Examples of these tissues and all three types of connective tissue are shown below and to the right.

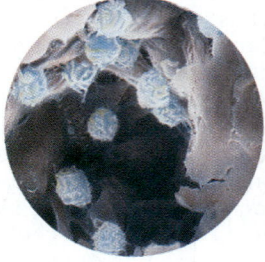

a *Defensive connective tissue*
Defensive connective tissue defends the body from invaders. This kind of tissue circulates in the blood, protecting the body from harm. White blood cells are a common example.

b *Structural connective tissue*
This tissue gives the body its support. Bone and softer connective tissues like cartilage, ligaments, tendons, and fibroblasts are examples. Fibroblasts secrete the protein strands that help wounds heal.

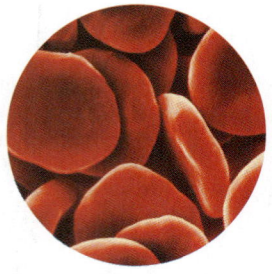

c *Sequestering connective tissue*
These tissues act like storehouses. They collect and store specific substances such as fat or melanin in the skin. Some transport particular molecules. For example, red blood cells store hemoglobin for transporting oxygen throughout the body.

576

Graphic Organizer
Use the following graphic organizer with the teaching strategy **Hierarchy of Structure** on page 576.

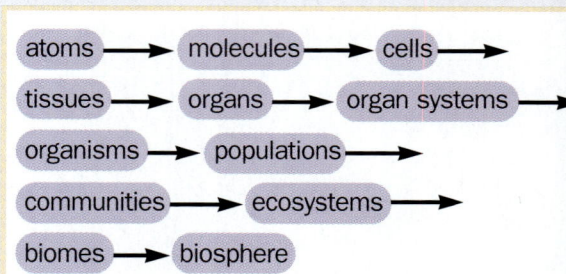

atoms → molecules → cells →
tissues → organs → organ systems →
organisms → populations →
communities → ecosystems →
biomes → biosphere

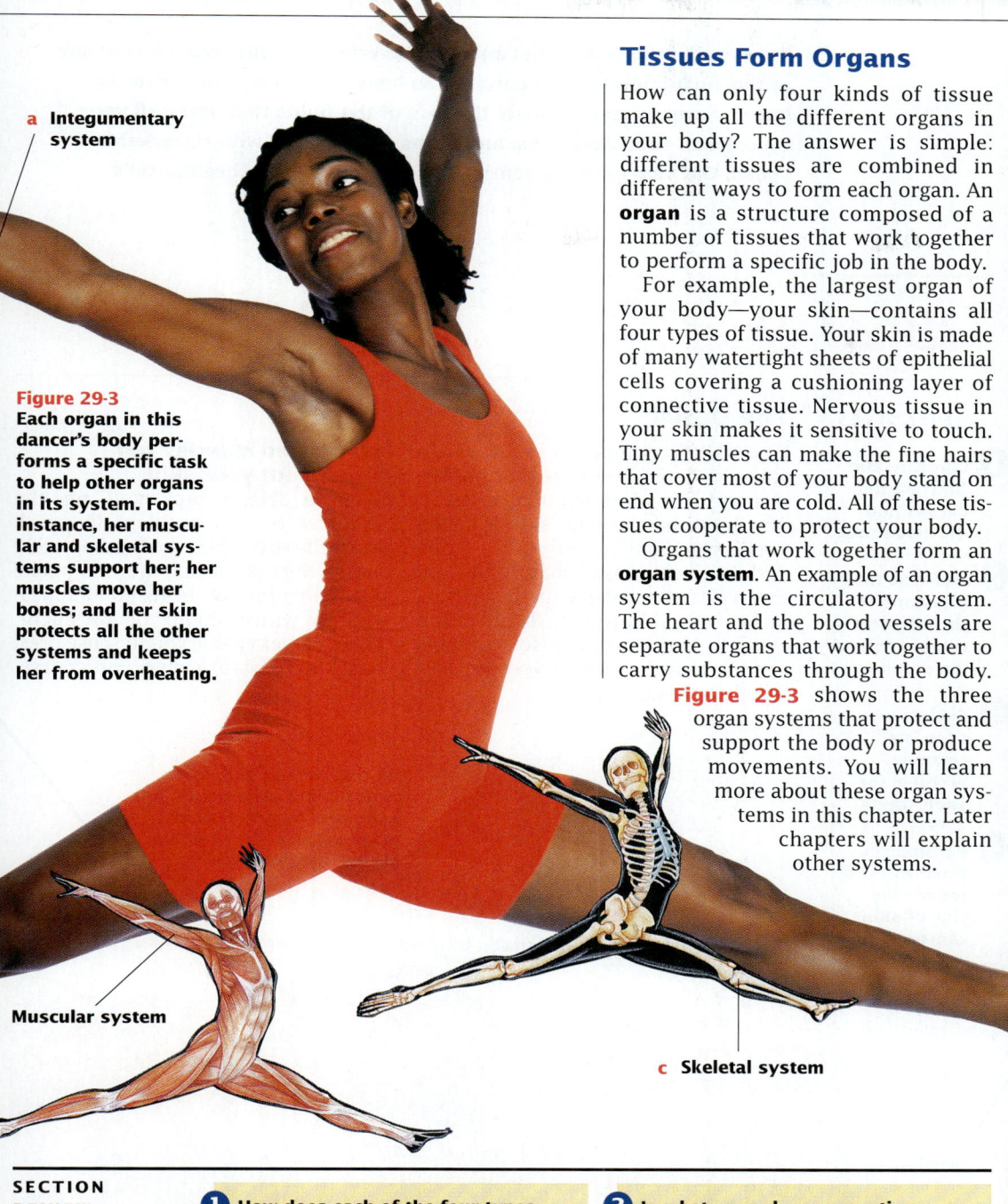

a **Integumentary system**

Figure 29-3
Each organ in this dancer's body performs a specific task to help other organs in its system. For instance, her muscular and skeletal systems support her; her muscles move her bones; and her skin protects all the other systems and keeps her from overheating.

b **Muscular system**

c **Skeletal system**

Tissues Form Organs

How can only four kinds of tissue make up all the different organs in your body? The answer is simple: different tissues are combined in different ways to form each organ. An **organ** is a structure composed of a number of tissues that work together to perform a specific job in the body.

For example, the largest organ of your body—your skin—contains all four types of tissue. Your skin is made of many watertight sheets of epithelial cells covering a cushioning layer of connective tissue. Nervous tissue in your skin makes it sensitive to touch. Tiny muscles can make the fine hairs that cover most of your body stand on end when you are cold. All of these tissues cooperate to protect your body.

Organs that work together form an **organ system**. An example of an organ system is the circulatory system. The heart and the blood vessels are separate organs that work together to carry substances through the body.

Figure 29-3 shows the three organ systems that protect and support the body or produce movements. You will learn more about these organ systems in this chapter. Later chapters will explain other systems.

577

SECTION REVIEW

1 How does each of the four types of tissue function in the human body?

2 How might a disease that slowly destroys nerve cells affect muscle tissue in the body?

3 In what ways does connective tissue help the body?

4 How do organ systems protect and support the human body?

Phase Three
Assessment Options

Closure
■ **Recognizing Relationships**
Have students list body parts that surgeons have transplanted in humans. Have them identify whether the part is a tissue or organ. Their list may include organs such as the heart, kidney, liver, lung, skin, and pancreas and tissues such as blood, bone marrow, cornea, lens, and bone.
Have students recognize that screening cell and tissue type before an organ and tissue transplant is vital in order to avoid transplant rejection. Students will recognize how unique and individual we all are when they study the immune system later in biology. Have students recognize that screening also checks for infectious agents such as viruses and bacteria.

SECTION REVIEW
Assign the *Section Review*.

Reteaching
Use an overhead transparency or microprojector to review with students the four tissue types. Have them identify each type.
Have the students make a flowchart on the board to list the organ systems, the organs that compose each system, and the tissue types that compose each organ.

ANSWERS TO
SECTION REVIEW

1 The four tissue types function as follows: *covering and protection* (epithelium); *support, transport, defend, and connect* (connective); *movement and support* (muscle); and *control by electrical signals* (nervous).

2 Muscles would not receive signals to contract. Over time, muscle tissue would begin to atrophy through disuse.

3 Connective tissue defends the body from invaders, gives support, and acts like a storehouse.

4 The example used in Figure 29-3 on page 577 illustrates that the skin protects and that the muscular and skeletal systems support and move the body.

Key to Strategies
● **Understanding Concepts (Tier I)**
■ **Applying Information (Tier II)**
▲ **Critical Thinking (Tier III)**

Scheduling

See the **Lesson Planning Guide** on pages 573A and 573B for lecture, classwork, and assignment options for Section 29-2.

Phase Two
Teaching Strategies

Visual Strategy   Figure 29-4

■ **Applying Information**

Instruct students to identify examples of the four tissue types illustrated in this figure. Have them calculate the relative thickness of the dermis and epidermis by using a metric ruler to measure each of the layers shown in this figure.

Active READING

Technique: Reading Organizer

As students read about the dermis, have them complete the following descriptive reading organizer. In addition to the information already covered by the dermis organizer, the following concepts should also be included: muscles that pull hair upright (goose bumps), blood vessels that carry nutrients, and sweat glands that cool the body.

Dermis

Nerves sense pressure, temperature, and pain

Skin is a lot more than just an outer covering. It is the largest—and one of the most important—organs of the body. It cushions and protects internal organs and prevents the loss of the fluids that bathe all your cells. Small cuts, abrasions, and burns are repaired with remarkable speed. Old skin cells are continually replaced by new, healthy cells.

29-2   Skin

OBJECTIVES

1 Compare and contrast the dermis and the epidermis.

2 Describe the functions of the different components of the dermis.

3 Explain why acne is a common problem for adolescents.

4 Recommend three ways to reduce the risk of skin cancer.

The Dermis

Your skin is composed of two main parts: an outer layer called the **epidermis** and an underlying, thicker layer. This inner part of your skin is called the **dermis**. Shown in **Figure 29-4**, the dermis is composed mainly of connective tissue. Fibers in the dermis make your skin tough, flexible, and elastic. The dermis also contains nerves, muscles, blood vessels, hair follicles and glands.

Nerves and muscles run throughout your skin

When a friend taps you on the shoulder or you accidentally prick yourself with a pin, you immediately react. Nerves in the dermis make it possible for you to respond appropriately with a "hello" or an "ouch." These nerves enable you to sense pressure, temperature, and, of course, pain.

Figure 29-4
On the surface, skin looks uniform. But underneath, it is a complex organ made of blood vessels, nerve fibers, glands, and muscles.

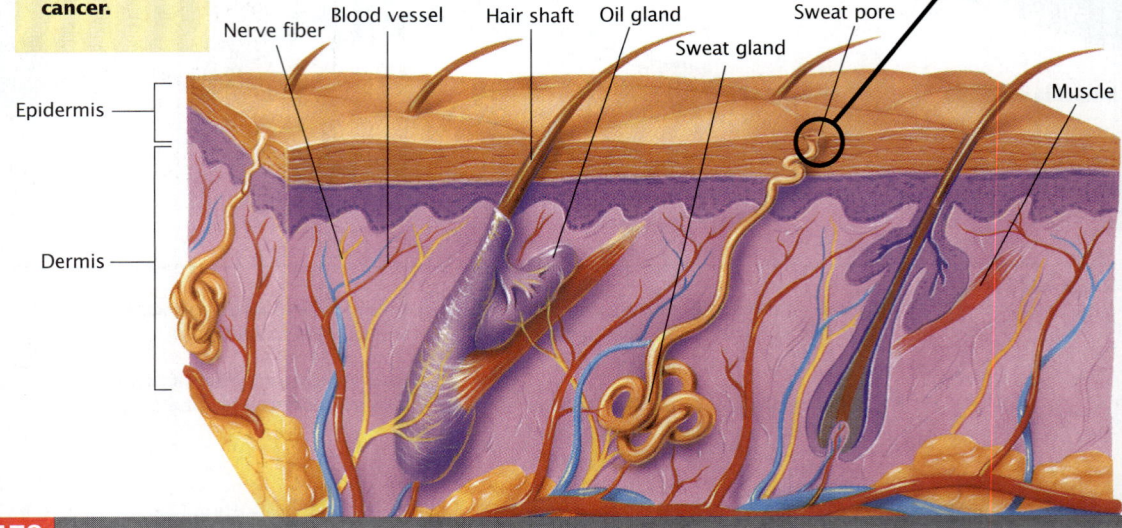

Nerve fiber   Blood vessel   Hair shaft   Oil gland   Sweat pore   Sweat gland   Muscle

Epidermis

Dermis

578

Videodisc Resources

Holt Biology Videodiscs
Lesson 29-2: Skin

Figure 29-5
The evaporation of sweat from the surface of your skin helps cool your body during and after a tough workout.

Stability and Homeostasis

How does sweating enable the human body to maintain homeostasis?

Your dermis also has tiny muscles that are attached to the hairs in your skin. When you are cold or afraid, the muscles contract, pulling the hairs upright. This same process happens in the skin of other mammals. The fur of a cat, for instance, will stand up when the cat is threatened by a dog, making the cat look larger and more dangerous. When the cat is cold, its fur fluffs up and traps more air near its body. Because trapped air is a good insulator, this helps the cat stay warm. The muscles in your skin behave just like those of a cat. However, because you don't have fur, you just get goose bumps—a leftover from our evolutionary past.

Blood vessels carry nourishment, remove wastes, and cool the body

Your skin, like all other living parts of your body, requires nourishment to live. This nourishment is supplied by blood that courses through tiny blood vessels in the dermis. In addition to carrying nutrients, the blood in these vessels carries away waste products and helps regulate body temperature. Blood radiates heat into the air as it passes near the surface of the skin. If your body becomes too hot, the tiny blood vessels enlarge, allowing more blood to flow through the dermis near the body surface. This increased flow of blood is easy to see in light-skinned people as their skin becomes reddish during strenuous exercise.

Sweat glands assist in cooling

Sweat is another way that your body removes excess heat. Your skin contains about 100 sweat glands per square centimeter. The evaporation of sweat from the surface of your skin removes heat much more efficiently than simply radiating heat from the blood into the air. Without sweat, you would have great difficulty cooling your body on a hot day or after exercising like the person in **Figure 29-5**.

Not all sweat is the same. Most sweat is about 99 percent water, mixed with small amounts of salts, acids, and waste products. However, the sweat from certain sweat glands, called apocrine glands, also contains proteins and fatty acids. These substances provide a rich source of food for bacteria that live on the skin. The waste products of these bacteria give sweat an unpleasant odor, particularly when a person's diet is high in protein and fats from animal sources. Most apocrine glands are located in the armpits and groin area. You have probably noticed that sweat glands are activated by nervousness or stress, even in cool temperatures.

579

Matter of Fact: Your Touch Receptors

You can take a crude measure of the surface area served by a single neuron by using a two-point compass (the kind used to draw circles) and the forearm of a blindfolded student. Lightly touch the forearm of the student with either one or two points of the compass in a random pattern. The compass should be set at different distances. People vary in receptor sensitivity from 1/4 mm to more than 22 mm apart. The distance at which the volunteer correctly answers whether he or she is being touched with one point or two 50 percent of the time is the distance apart of his or her touch receptors.

Epidermis

■ Analyzing Data

Have students use a stereomicroscope to examine the epidermis of their hands. Have them identify any skin marks, including moles, freckles, and birthmarks. Point out that most skin marks are formed from patches of pigment. Some birthmarks are the result of a collection of small blood vessels in an area. Tell students to examine their fingerprints. Point out that fingerprints are caused by ridges and indentations formed by the interlocking of the dermis and epidermis.

Hair

● Identifying Variables

Use a microprojector to show a variety of hair samples that have been carefully removed from student volunteers. Have the class compare the texture, thickness, and coloration of the hairs.

Connection: *Chapter 6*

Mitosis

Have students name the type of cell division responsible for producing new skin cells. Point out that a complete "surface armor" is generated approximately every 27 days by mitotic divisions in the lower epidermis.

The Epidermis

Not all of your skin is alive. The outermost layer of your skin is made of layers of dead cells. These cells were formed two to four weeks earlier as new epithelial cells in the innermost layer of the epidermis, a region called the basal layer. After the cells are formed, they are pushed outward by new cells forming underneath. As they move outward, many cells become flattened and begin to make a water-insoluble protein called keratin. The epithelial cells also move farther from the nutrients that diffuse from the blood flowing through the dermis. When the cells are pushed too far from their nutrient supply and are filled with keratin, they die. The dead epithelial cells become part of the skin's "surface armor," absorbing the wear and tear of life until each cell is eventually shed to make way for its replacement. The dead epidermal cells, shown in **Figure 29-6a**, are packed with the waterproof protein called keratin and are ready to be shed. Keratin works with the oil glands in the dermis to waterproof your skin. It also prevents the loss of water by evaporation from your skin and body.

Hair and nails are dead cells

A strand of hair is made of dead, keratin-filled cells that overlap like roof shingles, as shown in **Figure 29-6b**. Hairs grow from specialized epidermal structures called hair follicles. Each hair on your head grows for several years before its follicle enters a resting phase for a few months. While the follicle is dormant, the hair falls out. The length of time that a hair follicle is active before the hair falls out is a genetic trait. If you have inherited a short cycle of hair growth, you will never be able to grow very long hair, no matter how carefully you care for it.

Like hair, nails are also produced by specialized epidermal cells, as described in **Figure 29-6c**.

Inner epidermal cells are very alive

The inner layer of living epidermal cells is one of the most active regions of cell division in the body, even though the epidermis is the thinnest layer of skin on your body. Actually, there are many layers of cells and many shapes. As the cells migrate to the upper surface, some change shape. Some cells assume new roles. Other cells adapt for protection.

Most of the living epidermal cells sit on the basement membrane of the epithelium and produce all of the new epidermal cells. These are called basal

Figure 29-6

a This SEM of the epidermis reveals that by the time a skin cell is shed, it is a dead, flattened scale made of keratin.

b The center of each hair is filled with melanin and air bubbles. Dark hair contains more melanin than blond hair.

c In nails, new cells are produced in the white half-moons. These cells fill with keratin as they push cells that were produced earlier toward the free edge of the nail.

Matter of Fact: Rate of Hair Growth

Hair grows at different rates in different regions of the body. The growth rate also differs with age and sex, but it will average a growth of 2 mm per week. Hair follicles go through cycles that average 4 years of growth followed by several months of inactivity. With the beginning of a new active growth cycle, the old hair is pushed out (if it has not fallen out already). Out of more than 100,000 hairs, only about 50 hairs a day are lost. Several factors can increase hair loss. These include dietary factors, high fever, stress, drugs, radiation, and some hormonal factors related to pregnancy.

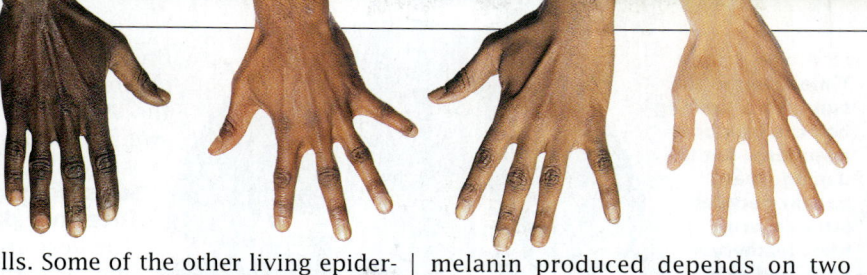
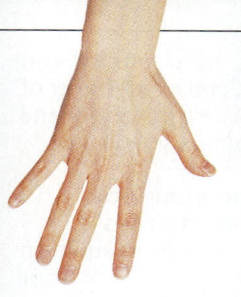

Figure 29-7
Variety in skin colors is caused by the pigment melanin. The amount of melanin varies from person to person.

cells. Some of the other living epidermal cells store chemicals known as provitamins, which are activated by sunlight to form vitamin D. Fifteen minutes of sun exposure two to three times a week activates this vitamin, which helps to calcify and harden your bones. Still other living epidermal cells in the innermost layer produce the pigments that give skin its color.

Pigments color the skin and help protect it

Human skin color ranges from pale pink to almost blue-black. Skin is mainly colored by cells that produce a brown pigment called **melanin** (MEHL uh nihn). These cells are found in the lowest epidermal layer. The amount of melanin produced depends on two things. First, melanin concentration is a genetic trait that varies from person to person. For example, melanin is missing in the skin of albinos but is abundant in black skin. Second, the amount of melanin in the skin depends on the length of time one is exposed to ultraviolet radiation. Ultraviolet radiation activates melanin to produce a darker coloration, commonly called a "tan." The longer you are exposed to the sun, the darker your melanin becomes. This darkening prevents you from further burning. Melanin, then, provides some protection from the sun's rays. **Figure 29-7** shows a variety of people with different levels of melanin.

Skin Disorders

Your skin is the most exposed part of your body. It serves as a protective barrier. Nevertheless, skin can be, and often is, damaged. The damage may be minor—a blister, an insect bite, or a small cut. Other damage is more serious, as in the case of skin cancer. Your skin may also be affected by changes within your body, by microbes, and by physical and chemical hazards in the environment.

Oil glands, heredity, and bacteria interact to produce acne

Oil glands in your skin produce oils and release them into nearby hair follicles. Normally the amount of oil produced is just enough to waterproof your hair and to seal moisture in the skin. However, high levels of sex hormones produced during adolescence increase oil production in these glands. The oil may combine with cellular debris and bacteria to clog follicles, resulting in the skin eruptions that are so common during the teen years.

Not all skin eruptions are diagnosed as acne. Some eruptions, known as whiteheads, are merely the build-up of oil. If a whitehead is invaded by bacteria and then exposed to air, it darkens and forms a blackhead. If the oil builds up or if the area is squeezed to the point that the oil gland actually bursts, the area around the gland becomes red and inflamed. The pimple that forms is evidence that the body is fighting the tissue damage and the invading bacteria.

Heredity determines the amount of oil and hormones produced. Most acne cures itself over a few months or a couple of years, but proper cleansing and daily skin care will certainly reduce the conditions leading to bacterial infections, whether or not acne is diagnosed.

581

Historical Perspective: Avicenna (Persian)

Avicenna (Ibn Sina), a philosopher and physician from Persia (now called Iran), wrote *The Canon of Medicine* about 1030. It stood as the standard reference of medical knowledge for 500 years.

Visual Strategy **Figure 29-7**

■ **Inferring Relationships**
Use this figure to discuss the following factors that affect skin color: (1) Melanin amount and kind (yellow, brown, or black) in the epidermis; (2) Carotene amount—an orange-yellow pigment found in abundance in carrots and other deep orange, yellow, or leafy green vegetables. Carotene is a precursor for vitamin D production along with melanin in the epidermis when exposed to the ultraviolet rays of the sun; (3) The amount of oxygen bound to hemoglobin (pigment in red blood cells) in the dermal blood vessels. Ask students how many skin tones are possible, given three tints and a variety of amounts. (*There are three basic types with infinite variations.*)

Health Connection
Abnormal Skin Pigmentation
Ask students about harmless changes in pigmentation, such as (1) moles—small dark areas of skin composed of dense collections of melanin, (2) vitiligo—pale irregular patches of skin, often symmetrically placed (the patches may grow, shrink, or stay the same size), and (3) chloasma—hormonal changes that cause darker areas of skin, particularly on the neck and face.

Health Connection
Cancer
Contact the American Cancer Society or a local health maintenance organization for free cards containing photographs of the three skin cancer types and the warning signs that accompany their development. Similar photographs are available through biological supply houses and in the *Family Medical Guide* of the American Medical Association.

Key to Strategies
● Understanding Concepts (Tier I)
■ Applying Information (Tier II)
▲ Critical Thinking (Tier III)

Severe Sunburn

■ **Analyzing Information**

Show the class a photograph of a person with severe sunburn. Remind students that melanin offers some protection by absorbing ultraviolet rays. However, melanin cannot absorb all of them. Ultraviolet rays penetrate into the skin, where they damage enzymes, destroy blood vessels, and even kill cells. Sun poisoning occurs when toxic materials from dead skin cells enter the bloodstream. Discuss how sunscreen products with different numerical ratings provide varying degrees of protection.

Life/Work Skills
Selecting Technology

■ **Relating Concepts**

Scientists have developed artificial skin for use in cases of severe skin burns. This artificial skin is temporarily useful while allowing skin grafts time to grow. Have students suggest several features scientists most likely incorporated into the design of this artificial skin.

Health Connection
Classification of Burns

The classification system used to describe the severity of burns is based on the number of tissue layers involved. First-degree burns (sunburn) result in minor discomfort and reddening of the skin. The surface of the epidermis may peel in one to three days and tissue damage is minimal. Second-degree burns (sunburn, fire, or chemical burn) result in the destruction of the epidermis, with some damage to the dermis, sweat glands, hair follicles, and oil glands. Blisters, pain, generalized swelling, and fluid loss occur, and scarring is common, but the skin can regenerate. Third-degree burns result in the complete destruction of the epidermis and dermis. Destruction can even extend to underlying muscles and bones. Third-degree burns are insensitive to pain immediately following injury because the nerve endings have been destroyed. Fluid loss is a very serious problem.

Figure 29-8
Time spent in the sun or in a tanning bed can produce deep tans. But the damage may appear decades later as wrinkles, leathery skin, and skin cancers.

Figure 29-9
SPF stands for sun protection factor. The SPF number indicates the product's ability to block UVB rays only. It tells you how much longer you can stay in the sun without burning in relation to when you would burn without protection. Broad-spectrum sunblocks of SPF 15 or greater may give the best protection from both UVA and UVB rays.

Skin changes are linked to ultraviolet radiation

Many changes occur in the skin after exposure to ultraviolet radiation. This form of radiation, often called black light, is invisible to the human eye and is produced by the sun's rays or by lamps that produce certain wavelengths of light. Radiation of this kind affects only the layers of the epidermis because the rays have low penetrating power.

Ultraviolet rays are classed as ultraviolet A rays (UVA) and ultraviolet B rays (UVB). UVB rays burn the skin. This is one of the first signs that one has been exposed to the sun too long. UVA rays, on the other hand, result in deeper "tanning" without burning; there is no warning that overexposure has occurred.

Overexposure to sunlight or tanning devices also results in a thickening of the skin, more rapid skin aging (including a loss of elasticity and greater wrinkling), and even cancer of the skin. **Figure 29-8** shows a scene where skin is commonly damaged.

Sunscreens and sunblocks filter out damaging rays

The best protection from sunburn and overexposure is reducing your exposure to ultraviolet rays and remaining covered when you are in the sun. You can reduce your exposure to ultraviolet radiation by doing the following:

- Stay out of the sun between 10 A.M. and 3 P.M.
- Cover up with hats, UV-filtering eyeglasses, and clothes when outdoors.
- Take care even on cloudy days. You can still burn.
- Avoid tanning beds and lamps.

Protection from overexposure can be achieved by using sunscreens and sunblocks. A product's ability to block ultraviolet light is rated by its SPF value. SPF stands for sun protection factor. Sunscreens block the shorter UVB rays, which can burn the skin. Sunblocks also block the UVA rays, which damage the deeper layers of the epidermis without burning.

Information on a product's label will indicate if the product blocks both UVA and UVB rays. Look for chemicals containing a mineral like titanium or zinc. These chemical combinations shield the skin from UVA rays and are found in products called broad-spectrum blocking agents. **Figure 29-9** illustrates the different SPF values found in lotions and creams and describes what each value means. A sunblock with an SPF of at least 15 is recommended. Reapply often because sweating and swimming wash the product away.

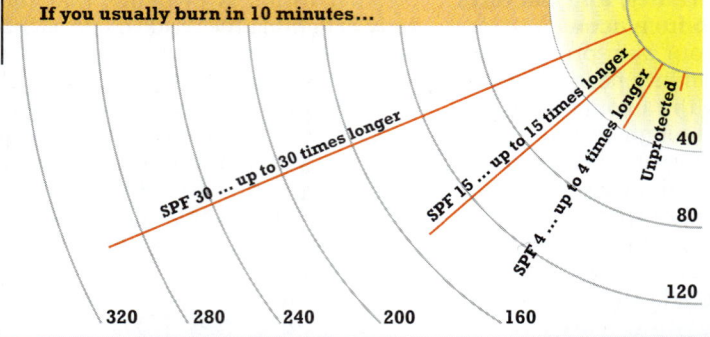

If you usually burn in 10 minutes...

SPF 30 ... up to 30 times longer
SPF 15 ... up to 15 times longer
SPF 4 ... up to 4 times longer
Unprotected

40
80
120

320 280 240 200 160

If you usually burn after 10 minutes in the sun, you can stay in the sun for up to 40 minutes (up to four times longer) by using a sunblock with an SPF of 4.

Figure 29-10
Moles exhibit characteristics that can be monitored by using the ABCD rule for dangerous changes that may signal skin cancer.

A—Asymmetry

B—Border irregularities

C—Color changes and differences

D—Diameter increases

a This is a normal mole. Each half matches the other.

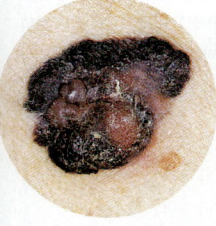

b This mole has two halves that do not match, a characteristic called asymmetry.

Changes in epithelial cells give rise to skin cancers

Continued exposure to ultraviolet light can trigger cellular mutations in DNA, which can then cause cells to lose the ability to stop dividing. This uncontrolled cell division may produce tumors, which can spread to other parts of the body and are then called cancers.

The danger of a particular skin cancer depends on the type of epidermal cell that becomes cancerous. The most common skin cancers have a very high cure rate when detected early. These include cancers that usually form around the ears or on the face in the basal cells of the epidermis. Once thought of as a disease of middle-aged or older people, basal cell cancer is being seen more often among younger people. This rise in the rate of basal cell cancer is believed to be primarily due to sunbathing, especially as more of the Earth's ozone layer is destroyed.

A second type of cancer begins in the flattened cells of the epidermis on sun-exposed areas or within skin lesions like scars or burns. Some of these cancers begin as flat, scaly, reddish patches on the skin, an indication that the skin has been damaged. These cancers are more invasive than the previous kind and are more likely to spread, although they are not as common as the first kind.

About 1 percent of all cancers begin in the melanin-producing cells. Called malignant **melanomas**, these cancers account for 75 percent of the deaths from skin cancers. Certain types of moles make it more likely that a person will develop a melanoma. **Figure 29-10** describes the difference between a melanoma and an ordinary mole.

Checking moles, spots, and birthmarks monthly is recommended. If these areas change or if patches of red, scaly skin are found, a doctor should be consulted.

Sunburn before age 18 increases risk of skin cancer later in life

What you do now as a teen affects how your skin may change in the future. Your risk for skin cancer and melanoma is higher if you

- experienced a severe, blistering sunburn before age 18,
- have used or now use tanning beds or sunlamps,
- sunbathe or work in the sun,
- have naturally blond, red, or light-brown hair,
- have freckled or fair skin, or
- wear sunscreen less than half of the time outdoors.

Knowing how ultraviolet radiation affects skin and how to reduce exposure may help you to maintain your skin's homeostasis.

A faulty gene may allow skin cancer to develop

The body cells contain a gene called p53 that acts as a tumor suppressor. This gene is believed to be activated in normal skin cells when UV light damages the cells' DNA. Following the damage, the p53 gene directs the injured cells to "commit suicide." As the cells die, they are shed from the skin. It appears, though, that repeated exposure to the sun damages the p53 gene. When a damaged p53 gene gets zapped with UV light, it does not direct cells to die as it normally would. Instead, the cells with damaged DNA continue to survive and divide. Eventually they may become pre-malignant skin patches that can later form cancer.

SECTION REVIEW

1. Which part of the skin has the simpler structure, the dermis or the epidermis? Explain your answer.

2. What do nerves, blood vessels, glands, and connective tissue contribute to the skin?

3. How could keeping your skin very clean help minimize the effects of acne?

4. What factors increase a person's risk of developing skin cancer?

583

Scheduling

See the **Lesson Planning Guide** on pages 573A and 573B for lecture, classwork, and assignment options for Section 29-3.

Visual Strategy   **Figure 29-11**

● **Summarizing Information**
Point out that the adult body (206 bones) has fewer bones than a human at birth (about 270 bones). As in the case of the skull, many bones fuse together during growth.

Active READING

Technique: Paired Reading
Less proficient readers may benefit from the paired reading strategy in this part of the chapter. Pair each student with a partner. Have each student read about bone structure and growth silently. As students read, have them place a check mark on a sticky note next to passages they understand and a question mark on a sticky note next to passages they find confusing or have questions about. After students finish reading, ask one student to summarize what he or she understood, referring to the text when needed. The second student should add anything omitted. The second student should then continue the discussion by pointing out the passages that he or she did not understand. The first reader should help the second with ideas that were unclear and discuss passages that he or she did not understand. Both readers should then work together to come to an understanding of all the passages. Have them create a list of questions to pose to the class about ideas or passages that are still unclear after their discussion. Have students repeat this process as they read about the skeleton.

You may think of your skeleton as just a rigid framework of bone that enables you to sit, stand, or run. Bone itself may appear as lifeless as rock. However, bone is in fact a dynamic connective tissue made of living cells. Throughout your life, these cells continue to produce the many fibers and minerals that fill the spaces between the cells.

29-3 Bones

OBJECTIVES

① Draw a diagram of a typical long bone, and identify changes in bone from infancy to old age.

② Differentiate a fracture from a sprain.

③ Discuss the causes and effects of osteoporosis.

④ Compare the actions of five types of joints in your body, and explain the movement that each permits.

Bone Structure and Growth

Throughout your childhood and adolescence, bone cells build more and more bone as your body grows. Compare the size and shape of the infant's skull with that of the adult's skull in **Figure 29-11**. Even in adults, specialized bone cells continue to break down and rebuild bone tissue. For example, the bone tissue at the end of the thighbone where it joins the knee is completely replaced every six months.

Four minerals are built into the bone cells to make bones strong. These minerals—calcium, phosphorus, magnesium, and manganese—also regulate an amazing variety of activities in your body. For example, nerves and muscles cannot work without the proper balance of calcium and magnesium. Bones act as a warehouse for storing calcium and phosphorus. And even though the body stores a very small amount of manganese, some of the highest concentrations of manganese are stored in bone. The storage and release of minerals, especially calcium, in your bones help maintain a precise level of minerals inside your body.

The human body contains bones of all shapes and sizes. The long bones of your arms and legs are shaped like cylinders. Curved, flat plates of bone form the part of the skull that protects your brain. Wrists and ankles contain many small bones that look like pebbles, and bones of the face and spine have unusual, irregular shapes.

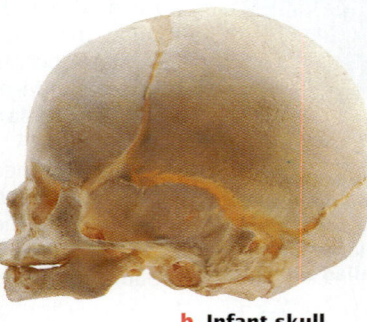

b Infant skull

Figure 29-11
The skull of an infant has more separate bones than that of an adult. As the child grows, many of these bones will fuse together. The "channels" you see in the infant skull will disappear by the age of four.

a Adult human skull

Videodisc Resources

Holt Biology Videodiscs
Lesson 29-3: Bones

Bone growth begins with cartilage

Bone growth begins long before birth. The basic shape of a long bone, such as an arm bone, is first formed in cartilage. Later, the cartilage cells begin to be replaced by cells that form bone. While you are growing, long bones still have a region of cartilage near each end that allows bones to grow longer. When you reach your adult size, these regions, too, are converted to bone. **Figure 29-12** shows a cross section of the femur in the thigh, a typical long bone. The outer layer of a long bone consists mainly of minerals and mature bone cells "trapped" by the minerals that they have deposited. To form this dense outer layer, bone cells deposit minerals in concentric rings, leaving a canal in the center of each group of rings. Each canal contains a small blood vessel that carries nutrients to the bone cells.

Inside the ends of a long bone are bone cells and minerals with large spaces in between, like a sponge. These spaces, and the entire center of the long middle part of the bone, are filled with **marrow**. The marrow inside long bones produces blood cells in newborns. As you get older, this marrow gradually changes its job to storing fat. In adults, most blood cells are produced in the marrow of flat bones like the sternum, or breastbone.

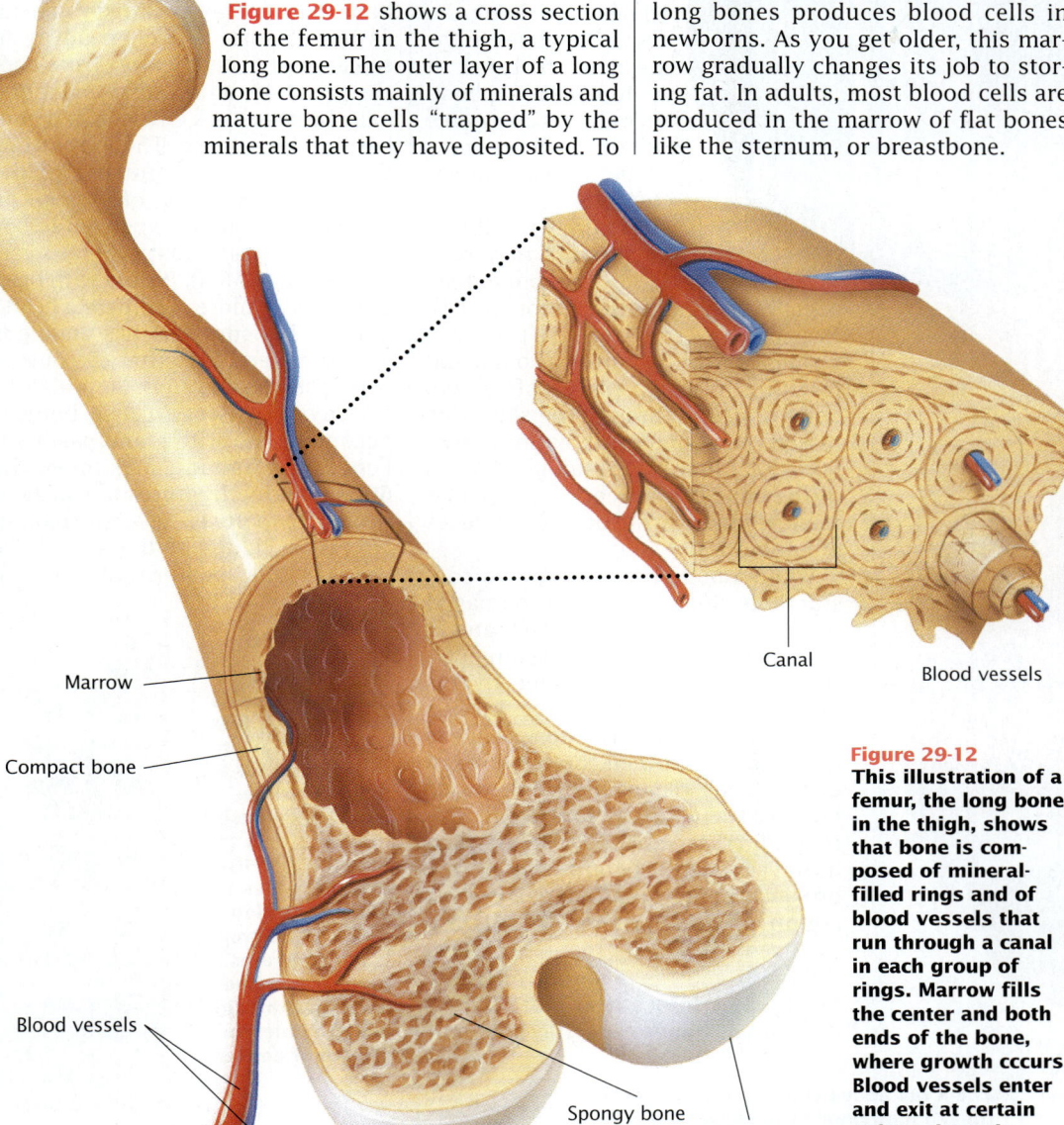

Marrow

Compact bone

Blood vessels

Spongy bone

Cartilage

Canal

Blood vessels

Figure 29-12
This illustration of a femur, the long bone in the thigh, shows that bone is composed of mineral-filled rings and of blood vessels that run through a canal in each group of rings. Marrow fills the center and both ends of the bone, where growth occurs. Blood vessels enter and exit at certain points along the bone.

585

Historical Perspective: Dr. Louis Tompkins Wright

Dr. Louis Tompkins Wright (physician) was a pioneer in science. He developed a method of surgery for fractures of the knee joint and invented a brace for patients with head and spine injuries. Dr. Wright was one of the first African American graduates of Harvard Medical School. He was the first African American doctor to be appointed to a municipal hospital position in New York City.

● **Identifying Structures**
CAUTION: Wear safety goggles, lab apron, and gloves.

Have students crack open the long bone from a well-cooked chicken leg and use a stereomicroscope to examine its structure. Other types of long bones may be obtained from the meat department at a supermarket. Students should be able to observe the compact bone of the shaft and the spongy bone and red bone marrow of the ends.

Visual Strategy | Figure 29-12

■ **Relating Concepts**
Point out that in newborns, the marrow in long bones is red (from producing blood cells), but that in adults, most of the marrow is yellow (from storing fat). Have students relate this structural change to the functional changes that occur in long bones as a person ages.

Visual Strategy | Videodisc

■ **Recognizing Relationships**
Use *Diagram—Bone Anatomy: Unlabeled* shown in Chapter 29 Section 29-3 of *Holt Biology Videodiscs Teacher's Correlation Guide to Holt Biology: Visualizing Life.* Have students identify and describe each labeled structure in as much detail as possible. Write their responses on the board. Then ask students to use the information to explain how the bone is well adapted to the work it does. *(Students might answer that the hard compact bone on the outside of the bone gives it strength. The less compact structure of the spongy bone and marrow-filled center makes the bone lighter.)*

Key to Strategies
● **Understanding Concepts (Tier I)**
■ **Applying Information (Tier II)**
▲ **Critical Thinking (Tier III)**

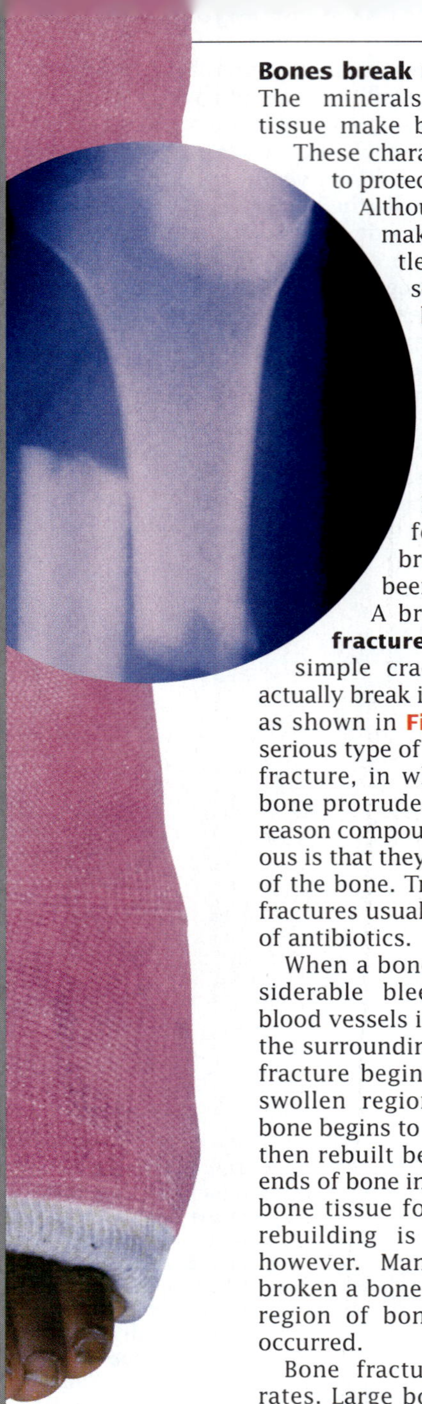

Bones break under stress
The minerals deposited in bone tissue make bones hard and rigid. These characteristics enable bone to protect and support the body. Although the fibers in bones make them much less brittle than a piece of chalk, severe stress placed on a bone may cause it to break. For example, certain types of falls while snow skiing can cause the bones in the lower leg to break at the top of the ski boot. In contact sports like football, a bone may break because a limb has been twisted.

A broken bone is called a **fracture**. A fracture may be a simple crack, or the bone may actually break into two or more pieces, as shown in **Figure 29-13**. The most serious type of fracture is a compound fracture, in which pieces of broken bone protrude through the skin. One reason compound fractures are so serious is that they may result in infection of the bone. Treatment of compound fractures usually includes large doses of antibiotics.

When a bone breaks, there is considerable bleeding from damaged blood vessels in the bone itself and in the surrounding tissues. Healing of a fracture begins as the blood in this swollen region around the broken bone begins to clot. The bone tissue is then rebuilt between the two broken ends of bone in much the same way as bone tissue forms before birth. The rebuilding is not always perfect, however. Many people who have broken a bone can still feel a thicker region of bone where the fracture occurred.

Bone fractures heal at different rates. Large bones heal more slowly than small bones, and the bones of young people heal more quickly than those of older people. Holding the broken ends close to each other and keeping them completely still speeds healing of bones. This is why bone fractures are often treated by encasing the fractured bone in a cast.

Osteoporosis causes bones to become brittle
As bones grow longer, they also grow thicker and denser. In young adults, bone density stays relatively constant as bone tissue is broken down and replaced at a steady rate. From about the age of 40, bone replacement gradually becomes less efficient, and bones become less dense. The loss of bone density that may eventually result is called **osteoporosis** *(ahs tee oh puh ROH sihs)*. About 5–10 percent of bone mass is normally lost every 10 years after the age of 40. People with osteoporosis lose more. Compare a healthy bone with a bone that has undergone severe mineral loss after the onset of osteoporosis, shown in **Figure 29-14**.

Osteoporosis can cause bones to become light, brittle, and easily broken. In the United States, more than 600,000 bone fractures a year result from osteoporosis. Severe osteoporosis in the bones of the spine often changes the posture of very old

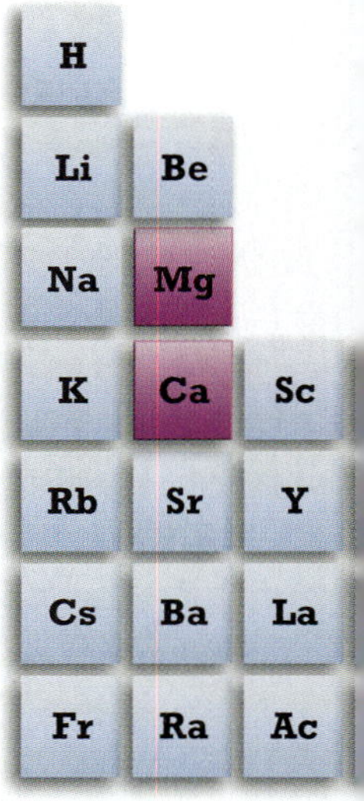

Figure 29-13
The X ray above shows a fracture of the tibia, a long bone in the lower leg. This fracture can be repaired without surgery by setting the fracture with a cast.

Figure 29-14
You may think that osteoporosis is something that you won't have to think about for a long time. However, bone density increases only to the mid-30s. After that, increases in bone mass slow down, while bone loss accelerates. Regular exercise and a healthy diet will promote the growth of denser bone.

H		
Li	Be	
Na	Mg	
K	Ca	Sc
Rb	Sr	Y
Cs	Ba	La
Fr	Ra	Ac

Matter of Fact: Callus Tissue
After a fracture, a bone usually bleeds, becomes inflamed, and then forms a bony framework called a callus around the injury. The callus tissue stabilizes the bone fragments and thus aids in the long healing and remodeling process. The callus is the "bump" that can sometimes be felt for months after the bone has healed.

people. Although both men and women lose bone as they age, women are at a greater risk for osteoporosis for two reasons. First, women's bones are usually smaller and lighter than men's bones. Therefore, the loss of the same amount of bone in a woman and a man results in thin, fragile bones in the woman, while the man's bones might still be quite strong. Second, the production of female sex hormones declines rapidly during menopause. Because sex hormones help to maintain bone density, this decline in hormone production increases the rate of bone loss.

Researchers have found that exercise can increase the amount of minerals deposited in bone. For people in their teens and twenties, regular exercise and a nutritious diet that includes a balance of all minerals, including calcium and magnesium, can actually increase bone density. For older people, regular exercise can slow the bone loss that can lead to osteoporosis. That's good news for the tennis player in **Figure 29-14**. Other factors that increase the amount of calcium available to the body and that increase bone density include adequate dietary protein, vitamin D, and digestive acids in the stomach.

Visual Strategy   Figure 29-14

■ **Recognizing Relationships**
Have students explain why the bone in Figure 29-14d is less dense than the one shown in 29-14c. Point out that people with osteoporosis become noticeably shorter. Although the body does not shrink, mineral loss causes bones to soften, allowing these bones to become more compressed. Ask students why milk and other dairy products, especially when consumed during the formative years, can help prevent osteoporosis later in life.

Demonstration

■ **Relating Concepts**
CAUTION: Wear safety goggles, lab apron, and gloves.

Demonstrate how calcium affects the rigidity of bones. Soak several chicken bones in vinegar (a dilute acid) for at least two weeks. Explain that vinegar dissolves the calcium phosphate that helps provide bones with their strength and rigidity. Have students contrast how easily they bend compared with chicken bones that have been soaked in water for an equal amount of time.

Health Connection

A Healthful Diet

Have students research and list foods that are high in calcium and minerals. Have them put together a daily menu that would reduce the likelihood of developing osteoporosis. Factors contributing to osteoporosis are a diet poor in calcium and protein, a lack of vitamin D, smoking, and a lack of weight-bearing exercise. A good diet can include calcium, vitamin D sources, milk and milk products, leafy green vegetables, eggs, and fish.

Key to Strategies
● Understanding Concepts (Tier I)
■ Applying Information (Tier II)
▲ Critical Thinking (Tier III)

a This woman is over 60 years old and is still very active. Regular exercise at any age can slow the bone loss that leads to osteoporosis.

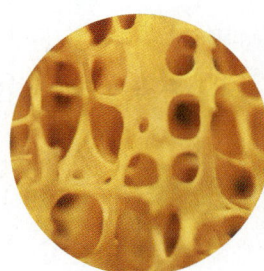

c In healthy bone tissue (magnified 10× in this photograph) minerals are continuously replaced, so the bone remains strong.

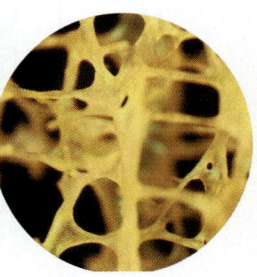

d After the onset of osteoporosis, minerals are not replaced as rapidly. As a result, bones become brittle and can break easily.

																	He
								B	C	N	O	F	Ne
								Al	Si	P	S	Cl	Ar
Mn	Fe	Co	Ni		Zn	Ga	Ge	As	Se	Br	Kr
Tc	Ru	Rh			Cd	In	Sn	Sb	Te	I	Xe
Re	Os	Ir	Pt	Au	Hg	Tl	Pb	Bi	Po	At	Rn
Uns	Uno	Une

b The elements highlighted in the periodic table represent the four primary minerals built into strong, healthy bones. Eating foods that provide these minerals will help to prevent osteoporosis.

587

Figure 29-15

Visual Strategy

● Comparing Structures

Point out that the vertebrae are separated by disks of cartilage that serve as cushions. A slipped disk occurs when a disk protrudes and presses on nerves. A disk may even break. This condition, known as a ruptured disk, can cause severe pain and even lead to paralysis. Point out that the bottom two pairs of ribs, unlike the others, are not attached to the sternum. These two pairs are known as floating ribs. Also point out that some people are born without one or two floating ribs.

Connection: *Chapter 12*

Hominids

Remind students that upright walking is a characteristic shared only by hominids. Apes can also walk upright, but only for short distances since their pelvic girdles do not permit true bipedalism. The spine of a human baby forms a continuous convex curve like that of an ape, and as we begin walking we develop two concave curves in our convex spine so that we can balance without effort. Point out to students how much effort it takes a baby to begin walking.

Visual Strategy · Videodisc

● Interpreting Graphics

Introduce the types of joints using the illustrations of the various joints shown in Chapter 29 Section 29-3 of *Holt Biology Videodiscs Teacher's Correlation Guide to Holt Biology: Visualizing Life.* For each type of joint, have students use the mechanical diagram to write a paragraph explaining how the joint allows movement.

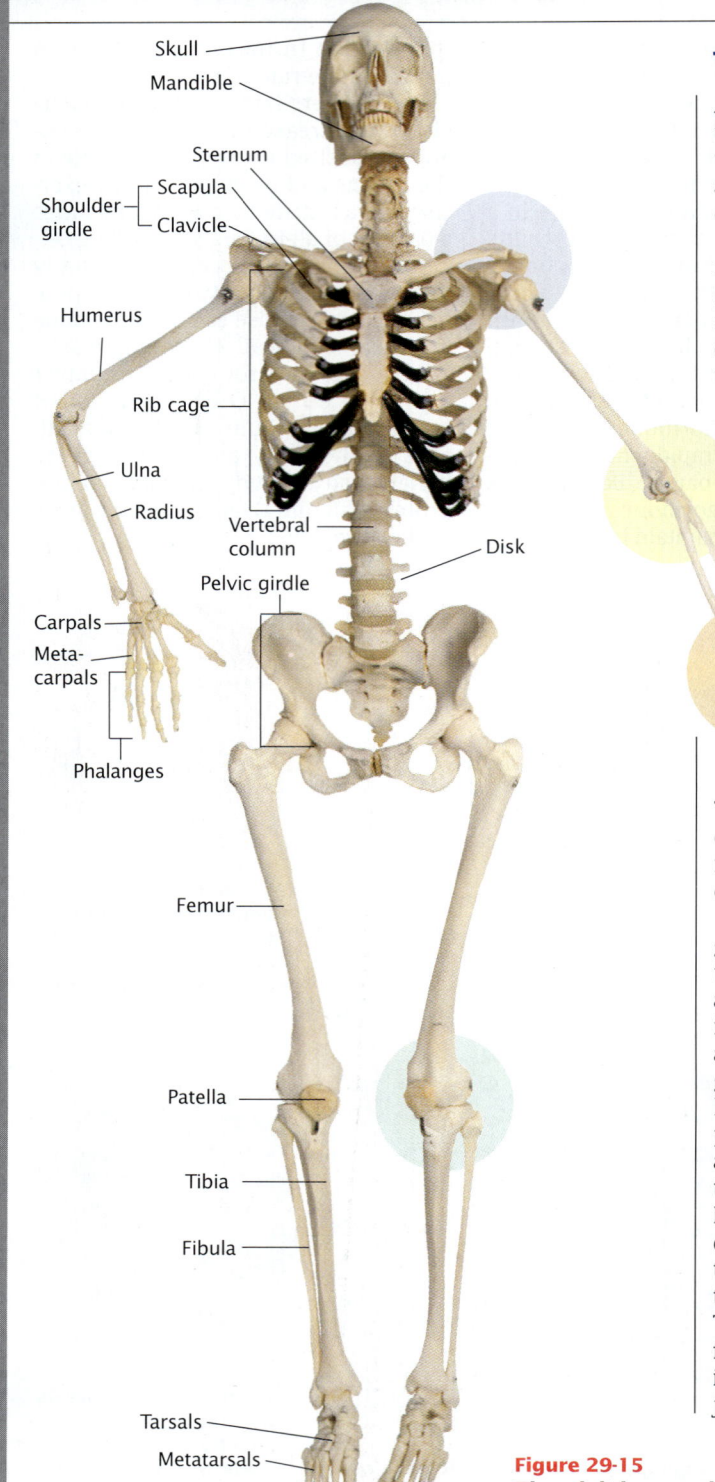

Skull
Mandible
Sternum
Scapula
Shoulder girdle
Clavicle
Humerus
Rib cage
Ulna
Radius
Vertebral column
Disk
Pelvic girdle
Carpals
Meta-carpals
Phalanges
Femur
Patella
Tibia
Fibula
Tarsals
Metatarsals
Phalanges

588

The Skeleton

All of the bones in the body make up the skeleton. The skeleton supports the body's weight, enables it to move, and protects many of its internal organs.

A typical human skeleton is shown in **Figure 29-15**. The central part of the skeleton consists of the skull, spine, sternum, and ribs. The skull consists of many fused bones that protect the brain and form the shape of the face. The lower jaw, the mandible, is the only bone of the skull that moves easily and visibly. The spine is made up of vertebrae that support the trunk and allow flexibility. In between the vertebrae are fluid-filled disks. These disks act as shock absorbers and prevent the vertebrae from rubbing against one another. The vertebrae surround and protect the spinal cord. Attached to the spine are 12 sets of ribs. The ribs protect the heart, lungs, and other organs in the chest cavity. Some ribs are attached to the sternum by cartilage.

Two frameworks of bone, called girdles, connect the arms and legs to the central skeleton. The legs are attached to the pelvic girdle. The clavicle and scapula (shoulder blade) move as a unit and are called the shoulder girdle. The attachment between the humerus and the clavicle is the only point of attachment between the arms and the main skeleton. This permits the arms and shoulders to move freely. In contrast, hipbones in the pelvic girdle attach directly to the lower part of the spine, enabling the hips and legs to bear the full weight of the body. This is why the legs cannot move as freely as the arms. The colored circles in **Figure 29-15** match those of specific joints in **Figure 29-16**.

Figure 29-15
The adult human skeleton has 206 bones. Several major bones are identified in this skeleton.

Historical Perspective: Dr. Augustus A. White III

Dr. Augustus A. White, an orthopedic surgeon and educator, specialized in the research of fracture healing and the spine. As a professor of orthopedic surgery at Yale Medical School, Dr. White assisted in the establishment of the first orthopedic biomechanic laboratory. He wrote more than 100 scientific publications, books, and articles. His most noted work is *The Clinical Biomechanics of the Spine.*

Figure 29-16

A joint is where two or more bones connect. Some examples of joints are shown here, along with the kinds of movement they allow. The wires, screws, and bolts holding these bones together represent the ligaments in the body.

a Suture joint
The skull is virtually immovable, shifting unseen in its own unique rhythm. Fusion of its bones prohibits other movement.

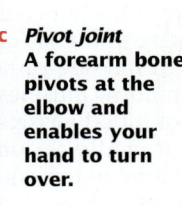

b Ball-and-socket joint
The shoulder enables your arm to move freely in all directions.

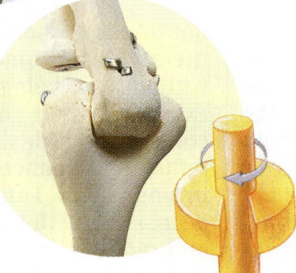

c Pivot joint
A forearm bone pivots at the elbow and enables your hand to turn over.

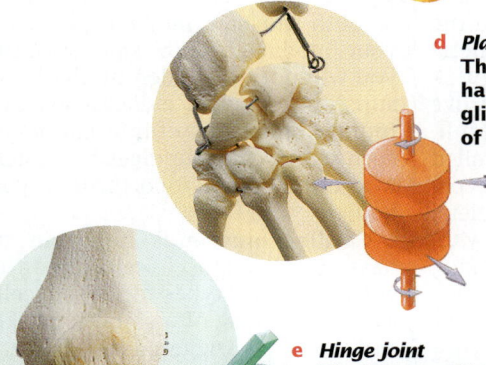

d Plane joint
The lower arm has bones that glide over those of the hand.

e Hinge joint
The knee enables you to flex and extend your lower leg.

Bones fit together with joints

The place where two or more bones connect is called a **joint**. Joints vary greatly in their flexibility. For example, the shoulder and hip can be moved in many directions, but the joints in your spinal column can move only slightly. Some examples of joints are shown in **Figure 29-16**.

Bones are joined to each other by strong elastic bands of connective tissue called **ligaments**. Although ligaments are very elastic, there is a limit to how far they can stretch. When ligaments are stretched too far, the injury that results is called a **sprain**. If the ligament is actually torn by overstretching, it will not heal and must be repaired surgically.

The hip is a particularly complex joint where the leg is attached to the pelvic girdle. Because of the upright posture of humans, the hip must support the body's full weight and allow leg movement in all directions. Many ligaments are needed to connect the pelvic and leg bones to one another at this joint and to make the joint as stable as possible. Proper placement of the pelvis and knees plus strong ligaments and muscles are necessary to prevent injury to the back and knees when lifting heavy objects.

SECTION REVIEW

1. Draw a diagram of a typical long bone, and label the dense bone, spongy bone, marrow, and blood vessels.

2. How do fractures and sprains differ?

3. What actions can you take now to prevent osteoporosis later in life?

4. Identify five different types of joints in your body, and give an example of each.

589

ANSWERS TO SECTION REVIEW

1. Students should use Figure 29-12 on page 585 as a model for their drawings.

2. A fracture is a broken bone, whereas a sprain is the overstretching of a ligament.

3. Students should suggest regular exercise and a balanced diet that includes plenty of calcium.

4. Suture joints are found between the bones of the skull and do not allow any movement to take place. The ball-and-socket joints allow movement in all directions. Two examples are the hip and shoulder joints. The pivot joints allow rotation around a pivot point. One of the bones of the forearm (radius) pivots at the elbow around another bone of the forearm (ulna). The plane joints allow only side-to-side and back-and-forth movements. Some examples are the joints between the bones of the wrist, the arch of the foot, and the collarbone and sternum. The hinge joints allow movement in one direction, usually flexion and extension. Some examples are the knee, elbow, and ankle.

Scheduling

See the **Lesson Planning Guide** on pages 573A and 573B for lecture, classwork, and assignment options for Section 29-4.

Phase Two
Teaching Strategies

Active READING

Technique: Reading Organizer
Have students work individually to create a reading organizer that compares and contrasts the three types of muscles.

Demonstration

● **Comparing Structures**
Use a microprojector to show students prepared slides of the three types of muscle. Have students describe similarities and differences.

Demonstration

■ **Recognizing Patterns**
How does the macroscopic consistency of meat change because of its microscopic structure? Have students compare eating and slicing steak, heart, and organ meat. *(Students' answers will vary but may include the following: (1) striated muscles are in bundles— steak is cut "across the grain" for tenderness, (2) cardiac muscle has the texture of steak without the bundles, and (3) liver has no striations and no "grain.")*

Large, powerful muscles in the legs can propel an athlete high enough to slam-dunk a basketball or fast enough to run 100 m (328 ft) in less than 10 seconds. Smaller muscles enable your eyes to read the words on this page. A smile or a frown would not be possible without the action of more than a dozen muscles beneath the skin of your face.

29-4 Muscles

OBJECTIVES

① Compare and contrast the three types of muscles.

② Explain how muscles work to move a bone.

③ Describe how different forms of exercise affect muscles.

④ Discuss the negative effects of taking anabolic steroids.

The Actions of Muscles

Your body has more than 600 muscles, each containing thousands of muscle cells. A muscle can move a part of the body when electrical signals cause the muscle cells to contract and change in length. For most of the muscles in your body, these electrical signals are provided by nerves. After contracting, a muscle relaxes and returns to its original length until the next signal.

Skeletal muscle is attached to the bones of the skeleton. When skeletal muscles like those in **Figure 29-17** contract, bones move, and actions like walking, grasping, or bending result. Skeletal muscles are sometimes called voluntary muscles because you can control their actions. You also use skeletal muscles for activities that happen without your thinking about them, such as blinking or maintaining your posture. However, you can consciously control these actions at any time.

Unlike skeletal muscle, **smooth muscle** is usually not under conscious control. Most of the actions of smooth muscle occur without your being aware of them. For example, when you go outside on a cold, sunny day, smooth muscles reduce the diameter of blood vessels in your skin. This automatic action decreases the flow of blood to the skin and reduces the amount of heat that your body loses. At the same time, smooth muscles in your eye cause your pupils to become smaller so that you will not be blinded by the bright sunshine. Smooth muscles are also found in the walls of internal organs such as those in your digestive system, where they move food through your body.

Cardiac muscle is found in the heart. Cardiac muscle cells are different from other types of muscle cells. The contraction of a smooth or skeletal muscle is triggered by an electrical signal from a nerve. However, cardiac muscle cells are "self-starters"—they generate their own electrical signals that cause them to contract. Nerves to the heart can control how fast the heart beats, but cardiac muscle will contract even if these nerves are cut. Connections among the muscle cells coordinate the contractions of the individual cells. This causes the entire heart to beat as the cells contract together. **Figure 29-18** on the next page shows the three types of muscle tissue and their functions in the human body.

Figure 29-17
Skeletal muscles move your skeleton about, making it possible to do leaps like this.

590

Videodisc Resources

Holt Biology Videodiscs
Lesson 29-4: Muscles

Making Your Skeleton Move

A skeletal muscle can move a bone like the one in your thigh by pulling on it. When the muscle contracts, it pulls on the bone to which it is attached. No muscle can push a bone; muscles can only pull on bones.

Muscle pairs work together

Moving a bone requires the cooperation of at least two sets of muscles. Pairs of muscles run parallel to each other on either side of a bone in the skeleton. Why are two sets of muscles needed to move a bone? When a muscle pulls on a bone, it moves the bone in one direction. Because the muscle cannot push on the bone, another muscle is needed to pull the bone in the opposite direction. Contracting one set of muscles while relaxing the other set can cause a particular bone to move and decreases the joint angle. Contracting the other set of muscles while relaxing the first set causes the joint angle to increase once again. **Figure 29-18d–e** shows how the main pair of muscles that control the human elbow works.

What would happen if both sets of muscles contracted and shortened at the same time? Under normal circumstances, the bone would not move because the muscles would be pulling in opposite directions at the same time. However, large muscles in your legs are so powerful that if all of the muscles contracted strongly at the same time, they could break a bone. This is prevented by a nerve message sent from one set of muscles to the other. When one set contracts, the other set is signaled to relax. An intricately coordinated sequence of muscle contractions and relaxations alternately bends and straightens the hips, knees, and ankles, allowing you to walk or run smoothly.

Figure 29-18
The human body contains three main types of muscle tissue that move different parts of the body.

a Skeletal muscle enables bones to move.

b Cardiac muscle causes the heart to beat.

c Smooth muscle moves food through digestive organs and makes other internal organs "work."

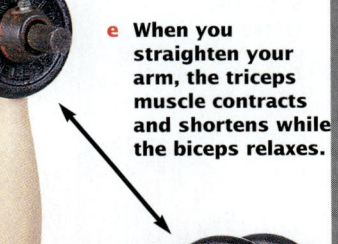

d When you bend your elbow, the biceps—a skeletal muscle in the front of your upper arm—contracts and shortens. The triceps muscle in the back of your upper arm relaxes.

e When you straighten your arm, the triceps muscle contracts and shortens while the biceps relaxes.

591

Tendons attach muscles to bones

Muscles, are connected to bones by **tendons**. For example, the biceps muscle in your arm is attached by tendons to a bone in your shoulder and to another bone in your forearm. Tendons are made of the same tough, elastic connective tissue as ligaments. The difference between tendons and ligaments is that ligaments connect a bone to another bone, while tendons connect a muscle to a bone.

Sometimes the distance between a muscle and the bone to which it is attached is quite long. When you bend your fingers, you are actually contracting muscles in your forearm. There are no muscles in your fingers—only long tendons that extend from muscles in your forearm to the bones in your fingers. Move your fingers and watch the muscles in your forearm move.

Skeletal muscle cells have light and dark bands

Each of your skeletal muscles contains many bundles of long, thin muscle cells, as shown in **Figure 29-19**. When stained and viewed with a microscope, muscle cells show alternating dark and light bands in repeating units called sarcomeres *(SAR kuh mihrz)*.

Two types of protein threads—actin and myosin—make up the dark and light bands within each sarcomere. These protein threads are arranged so that they can slide past each other.

When a muscle cell receives an electrical signal from a neuron, the sets of actin and myosin threads slide past one another, and the entire muscle cell shortens. You can read more about actin and myosin in *A Closer Look at Skeletal Muscle* on page 593.

Nerves send messages to muscles to generate force

If the muscles in your arms contracted with the same force when picking up a pencil as when picking up a bowling ball, the pencil would probably go flying to the ceiling. How does a muscle create just enough force to perform a particular job?

The contraction of each muscle cell generates a certain amount of force that pulls on the bone. But not every muscle cell contracts at once. Signals from the nervous system make a muscle generate more force by contracting more muscle cells. When you pick up a pencil, a small percentage of muscle cells in each muscle contract. But when you pick up a bowling ball, more muscle cells contract in order to provide enough force to lift the ball.

Your nervous system constantly sends signals to some of the muscle cells in all of your muscles, even when you are not moving. As one set of cells tires, signals are sent to another set, so your skeletal muscles are always partly contracted. This constant, partial contraction of your muscles is known as muscle tone. Muscle tone maintains your posture.

Figure 29-19
These photos show the relaxation and contraction of the frontalis muscle of the forehead.

a **When the muscle is relaxed, threads of actin and myosin are at rest, side by side in parallel stacks.**

b **When the muscle contracts, the threads of actin and myosin slide past each other and the muscle shortens.**

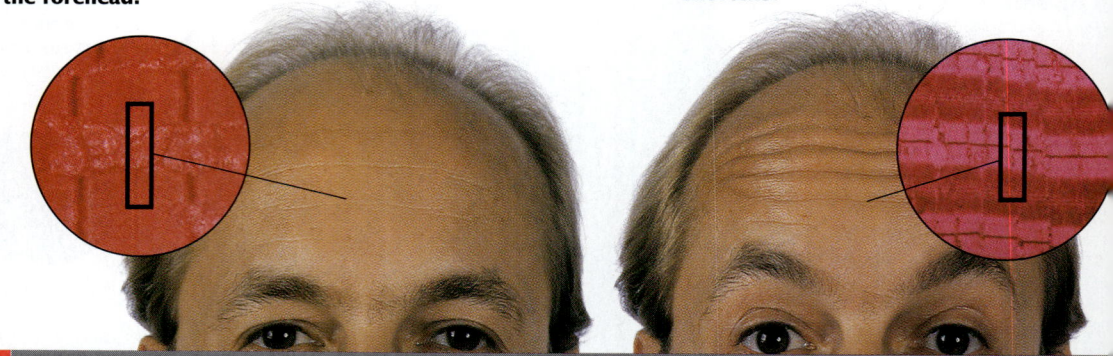

Skeletal Muscle

Vertebrates have three kinds of muscle cells: smooth muscle cells that are organized into sheets, cardiac muscle cells that form a lattice, and striated muscle cells (also called skeletal muscle cells) that appear to be striped.

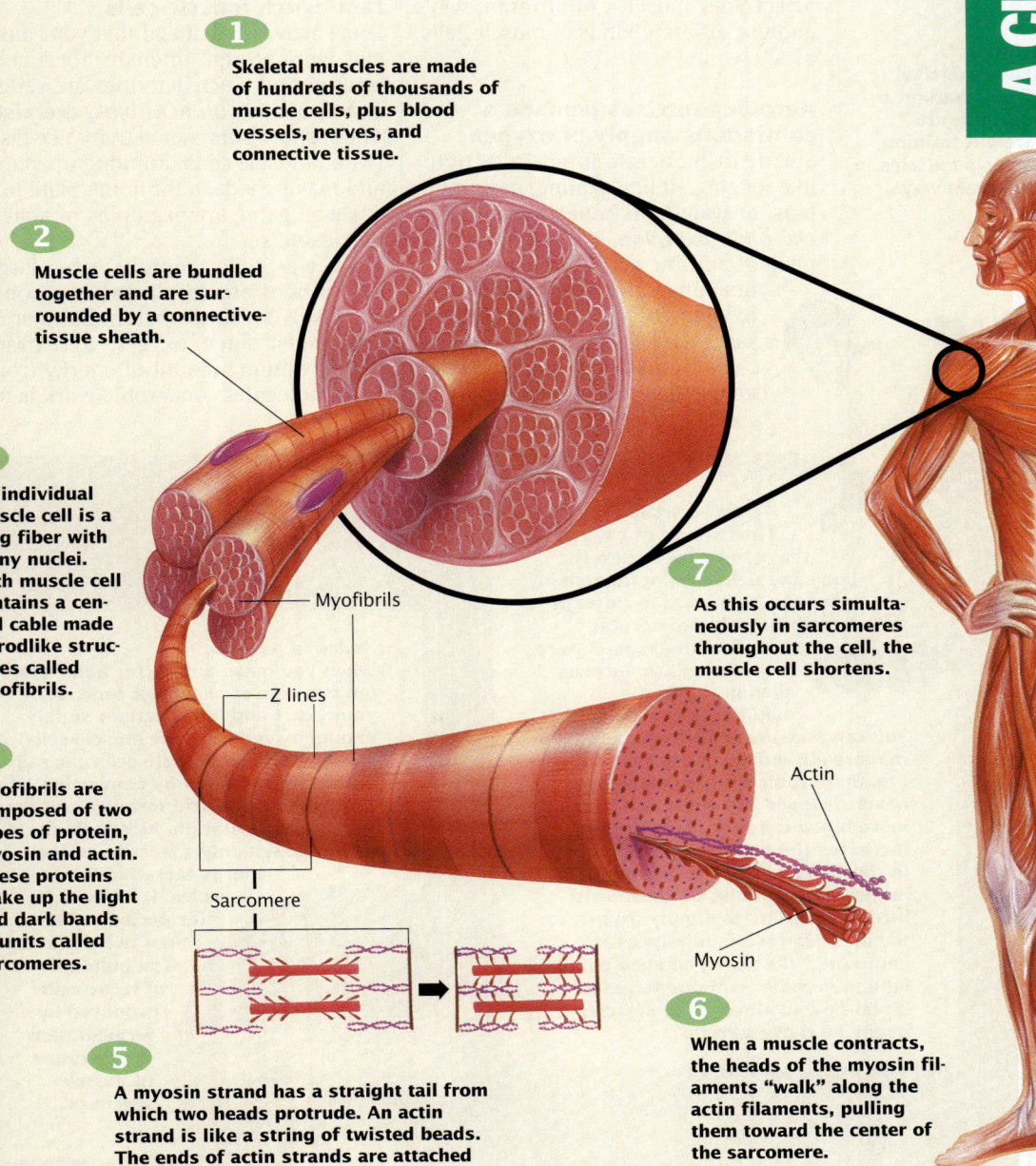

1 Skeletal muscles are made of hundreds of thousands of muscle cells, plus blood vessels, nerves, and connective tissue.

2 Muscle cells are bundled together and are surrounded by a connective-tissue sheath.

3 An individual muscle cell is a long fiber with many nuclei. Each muscle cell contains a central cable made of rodlike structures called myofibrils.

4 Myofibrils are composed of two types of protein, myosin and actin. These proteins make up the light and dark bands in units called sarcomeres.

5 A myosin strand has a straight tail from which two heads protrude. An actin strand is like a string of twisted beads. The ends of actin strands are attached to Z lines.

6 When a muscle contracts, the heads of the myosin filaments "walk" along the actin filaments, pulling them toward the center of the sarcomere.

7 As this occurs simultaneously in sarcomeres throughout the cell, the muscle cell shortens.

Myofibrils

Z lines

Sarcomere

Actin

Myosin

593

A Closer Look

Connection: *Chapter 5*

Cellular Respiration

This feature can be used to review cellular respiration in Chapter 5. Begin this review by asking students how the cells in a skeletal muscle would get their energy if they were working to lift a weight. Then ask students how the cells in a skeletal muscle would get their energy if they were working to swim across the English Channel. *(Review the major features of cellular respiration, emphasizing the energy amounts generated in aerobic respiration versus anaerobic respiration.)*

Muscle Cell Subunits

● **Identifying Structures**

List the units that compose a skeletal muscle, beginning with the protein molecules. *(Actin and myosin make up sarcomeres. Myofibrils are bundled together and surrounded by a connective tissue sheath. Hundreds of thousands of these bundles make up a skeletal muscle.)*

Muscle Protein Functions

■ **Relating Concepts**

Describe what happens to myosin and actin filaments when a muscle contracts. *(When a muscle contracts, the heads of the myosin filaments "walk" along the actin filaments, pulling them toward the center of the sarcomere.)*

What Exercise Does for Muscles

Muscles are structured to move and to do work. When muscles are not used, they fatigue easily, and over time they harden, become smaller, and lose strength. Most people can increase their strength, flexibility, and endurance through physical activity and exercise. Different kinds of exercise affect your muscles in different ways and use different kinds of muscle cells, as shown in **Figure 29-20**.

Figure 29-20
Each exercise, from skating to sprinting to weight training, affects muscles in different ways.

Aerobic exercises demand a continuous supply of oxygen

Steady or moderate-intensity activity like jogging, in-line skating, swimming laps, or walking is called **aerobic** *(ehr OH bihk)* **exercise**. The slow, steady pace of aerobic activity ensures that your lungs and heart can deliver oxygen to your muscles at the same rate at which the muscle cells are using it. Your muscles can use this continuous supply of oxygen to extract the maximum amount of energy from food molecules and to continue the activity for as long as 20 minutes or more. **Figure 29-20a** describes some of the benefits of aerobic exercise.

Anaerobic exercises use fast-twitch muscle cells

Some activities demand that your muscles work at high intensity for a very brief period. Such activities are called **anaerobic** *(an uh ROH bihk)* **exercise**. These short bursts of activity use fast-twitch muscle cells. Running up stairs and making a dash for home plate in a baseball game are examples of anaerobic exercise.

Muscle cells rapidly use large amounts of energy during anaerobic exercise. As you learned in Chapter 5, cells must have oxygen to extract the maximum amount of energy from food molecules. Anaerobic work is so

a *Aerobic exercise*
The amount of oxygen that can be taken into the body and delivered to the muscles can be increased through aerobic training. Aerobic means "with oxygen." Aerobic training strengthens the lungs and the diaphragm muscle so that you can take deeper breaths and take in more air and oxygen with each breath. Aerobic training makes the heart stronger and enables it to pump more blood in fewer beats. It also increases the number of capillaries in the muscles and the number of mitochondria in muscle cells. This increased ability to supply oxygen to the muscles results in increased endurance, the ability to keep going longer. Aerobic training increases blood flow to all working muscles in any kind of exercise.

b *Anaerobic exercise*
When you make a dash for home plate (an example of anaerobic exercise), your heart and lungs cannot supply enough oxygen to your muscle cells. Without oxygen, muscle cells can still obtain some energy by converting glucose to lactic acid through glycolysis and fermentation. Although glycolysis releases only a fraction of the energy stored in food molecules, it works well for periods of less than two minutes. The buildup of lactic acid produced by fermentation is one cause of muscle soreness.

intense that there's no time to take in enough oxygen in the short time that the work lasts. See **Figure 29-20b** for an explanation of how the needed energy is supplied for this form of activity.

After you stop anaerobic exercise, your body needs extra oxygen to burn up the excess lactic acid and return your energy reserves to normal. This need for extra oxygen is called oxygen debt. Oxygen debt is the reason you must breathe rapidly and deeply for a few minutes after a hard run.

Resistance exercises increase muscle size and strength

Aerobic exercise will increase the size and strength of your skeletal muscles somewhat, but it mostly strengthens the heart and lungs. To significantly increase the size or the strength of your skeletal muscles, resistance exercises are the most effective form of exercise. **Resistance exercises** are those that require muscles to over-come the resistance (weight) of another object. Overcoming your own body weight by doing chin-ups or push-ups and overcoming the resistance provided by free weights, weight machines, or rubber tubing are examples of resistance training. You can read more about resistance training in **Figure 29-20c**.

Skeletal muscle cells can be fast-twitch or slow-twitch

Every skeletal muscle in your body contains two types of muscle cells. Fast-twitch muscle cells are called into action when a person, such as a pole-vaulter, requires speed and quick movements over a short period. Slow-twitch muscle cells respond more slowly but do not tire as quickly as fast-twitch muscle cells. Slow-twitch muscles are used for activities, such as cycling, that require endurance. You can read more about fast- and slow-twitch muscles in **Figure 29-20d**.

c *Resistance exercise*
Resistance training increases both muscle strength and muscle endurance. Unlike free weights, rubber tubing places the muscle under constant resistance throughout the range of motion and is especially useful for rehabilitation after injury. Regular resistance training helps to increase bone mass and also strengthens the abdominal muscles necessary for a healthy back. As you get older, it becomes more important to include resistance training in your exercise routine. Your daily tasks become easier as you increase or maintain your strength.

d *Fast- and slow-twitch muscles*
The number of fast- and slow-twitch muscle cells that a person has is primarily an inherited trait that does not change with moderate exercise. Researchers measured the numbers of fast- and slow-twitch muscle cells in different athletes. Sprinters, jumpers, and weight lifters had a high number of fast-twitch muscle cells. Long distance runners and cyclists had more slow-twitch muscle cells.

595

Demonstration
● **Comparing Structures**
Show students pieces of white and dark chicken meat, or ask students to name the parts of a chicken that are white or dark meat. Explain to them that mammals have fast-twitch muscle fibers ("white meat") and slow-twitch muscle fibers ("dark meat") and that our muscle groups are mixtures of these types of muscle fibers. Gallinaceous birds like chickens have dark slow-twitch muscles in the legs (for walking around all day and perching) and white fast-twitch muscles in the breast meat (for short explosive bursts of flying). In contrast, geese have dark slow-twitch muscles in the breast meat (for long endurance flying). Dark meat is dark because it contains large amounts of an oxygen-carrying molecule called myoglobin (a red pigment related to hemoglobin). White meat lacks large amounts of myoglobin.

Visual Strategy | **Figure 29-20**

■ **Recognizing Relationships**
Tell students that the average human has a 50-50 distribution of fast-twitch and slow-twitch muscles. However, muscles of long-distance runners and swimmers average 80 percent slow-twitch, while those of sprinters and weight lifters average about 75 percent fast-twitch. Have students discuss which type of muscle would be best for each of the following players on a football team: tackle, running back, and quarterback.

Matter of Fact: Gravity and Muscles

One important function of muscles is to maintain muscle tone that counteracts the force of gravity on our skeleton. Exercise physiologists in the former Soviet Union have found that the zero-gravity environment of space promotes a loss of muscle tone. Some cosmonauts returning from space had to be carried around for months before their normal muscle tone returned. To avoid this problem, cosmonauts on later missions imitated the effects of gravity on postural muscles by pulling on resistance machines.

Key to Strategies
● Understanding Concepts (Tier I)
■ Applying Information (Tier II)
▲ Critical Thinking (Tier III)

Technique: K-W-L

Tell students to return to the lists of things they **W**ant to know that they created using the K-W-L Active Reading on page 574. Have them place check marks next to questions that they are now able to answer. Students should finish by making a list of what they've **L**earned. Conclude by asking students the following questions:

• Which questions are still unanswered?

• What new questions do you have?

Phase Three
Assessment Options

Closure

■ **Analyzing Information**

Have students research and submit a brief oral or written report about muscular dystrophy, which is characterized by the gradual wasting of skeletal muscle. *(A report should include the following: muscular dystrophy as a group of muscle-destroying diseases, muscle enlargement due to fat and connective tissue deposition, and muscle fiber atrophy.)*

SECTION REVIEW

Assign the *Section Review.*

Reteaching

Assign students to cooperative groups of four. Have each group develop a concept map for this section. *(Concept maps will vary but may show the structure, locations, and functions of skeletal, smooth, or cardiac muscle. Other maps may show the relationships of tendons to bone, striations to muscle type, nerve stimulation of each of the three muscle types, the difference between fast-twitch and slow-twitch muscle cells, or the difference between anaerobic and aerobic exercise.)*

Anabolic steroids are dangerous

Some people are tempted to experiment with anabolic steroids to increase the size of their muscles. Anabolic steroids are powerful synthetic compounds that chemically resemble the male sex hormone, testosterone. The use of steroids may produce serious side effects and health problems, as summarized in **Figure 29-21**.

When anabolic steroids are used before the skeleton matures completely, as in a teenager, the steroids stop the bones from growing. Remember that a bone grows from its soft ends, the regions called growth plates. Steroids cause premature closure of these growth plates. When the plates close, the once-soft cartilage begins to turn into bone earlier than it should. The bones stop growing, while the muscles continue to get larger. The body never reaches adult height and may look distorted. These and other symptoms of steroid use may not be reversible.

Some males who use anabolic steroids develop female-like breasts and shriveled testes. Females who use these chemicals may develop facial hair, deepening of the voice, and male-pattern baldness. The long-term risks to health are often greater than any benefits that might be gotten from the use of steroids.

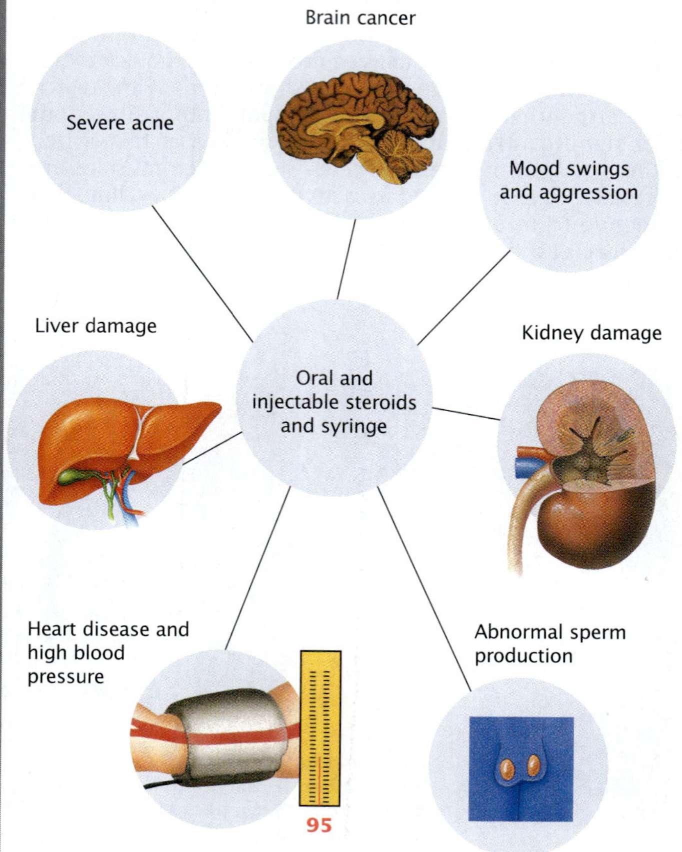

Overuse causes muscle injuries

Overusing muscles by exercising too much or without proper conditioning can lead to muscle injury. A muscle strain, commonly called a "pulled muscle," is the overstretching or even tearing of a muscle. Muscle strain may occur when a muscle is overused or not properly warmed up or when proper form is not used. Muscles are made of collagen and elastin fibers. Elastin stretches; collagen does not. When a muscle heals after a tear, its elastin is replaced by collagen. Then the muscle doesn't stretch as well as it once did. Tendons, as well as muscles, can get injured from overuse. Tendinitis is the painful inflammation of a tendon caused by too much friction or stress on the tendon.

Figure 29-21
The use of anabolic steroids poses a threat to numerous body systems. Both physical and psychological health may be affected.

Brain cancer

Severe acne

Mood swings and aggression

Liver damage

Kidney damage

Oral and injectable steroids and syringe

Heart disease and high blood pressure

Abnormal sperm production

95

SECTION REVIEW

1. Describe the three main types of muscle.

2. How might your ability to move your arm be affected by an injury to the biceps muscle? to the triceps muscle?

3. If you wanted to increase your endurance, which kind of exercise would be most effective?

4. Describe how anabolic steroids damage bones, and identify three other disadvantages of steroid use.

ANSWERS TO SECTION REVIEW

1. The three types of muscle are (1) skeletal muscle, which is attached to the bone and moves the bone, (2) smooth muscle, found in the walls of internal organs, where it can change the shape and size of the organ, and (3) cardiac muscle, found in the heart, where it causes the heart to contract.

2. Students should suggest that injury to the biceps muscle would affect bending the arm.

Injury to the triceps muscle would affect straightening or stretching the arm.

3. Aerobic exercise would be the most effective exercise to increase endurance.

4. Taking anabolic steroids causes the bones to stop growing prematurely and may result in a distorted body shape. Anabolic steroid use can also cause severe acne, heart disease and high blood pressure, liver and kidney damage, brain cancer, abnormal sperm production in males, and aggression and mood swings.

CHAPTER
29 | Highlights

Aerobic exercise, such as cross-country skiing, increases oxygen flow to the muscles.

	Key Terms	Summary
29-1 **An Inside Look at the Human Body** 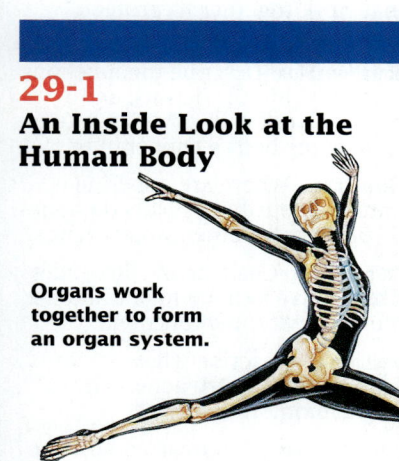 Organs work together to form an organ system.	tissue (p. 575) epithelial tissue (p. 575) muscle tissue (p. 576) nerve tissue (p. 576) connective tissue (p. 576) organ (p. 577) organ system (p. 577)	• Specialized cells are organized into groups called tissues. • The four types of tissue in the body are epithelial (for protection), muscle (for movement), nervous (for communication), and connective (for support and transportation). • Tissues work together to form organs. • Organs work together to form organ systems.
29-2 **Skin**  Dead skin cells flake off and are replaced.	epidermis (p. 578) dermis (p. 578) melanin (p. 581) melanomas (p. 583)	• Skin protects the body and aids in elimination. • Several skin layers contain a variety of cells, living and dead.
29-3 **Bones** 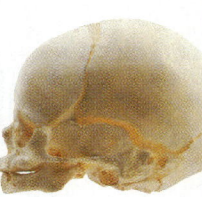 As you grow, bone cells build more bone tissue.	marrow (p. 585) fracture (p. 586) osteoporosis (p. 586) joint (p. 589) ligament (p. 589) sprain (p. 589)	• Bone is a living tissue made of cells that deposit minerals. • Marrow is important in blood cell production and fat storage. • The skeleton's joints are held in place by ligaments, which connect bone to bone.
29-4 **Muscles**  Exercise helps increase endurance, muscle strength, agility, and joint flexibility.	skeletal muscle (p. 590) smooth muscle (p. 590) cardiac muscle (p. 590) tendons (p. 592) aerobic exercise (p. 594) anaerobic exercise (p. 594) resistance exercise (p. 595)	• The three basic types of muscle tissue are skeletal muscle, smooth muscle, and cardiac muscle. • Moving a bone requires two sets of muscles working in opposition. • Muscles attach to bones directly by means of tendons. • Muscle action depends on the sliding action of protein threads (actin and myosin). • Three types of exercise (aerobic, anaerobic, and resistance) make different demands on muscles.

597

Alternate Assessment

Assign students to cooperative groups of four. Have each group develop a crossword puzzle for this chapter, including the clues for all the words in the puzzle. Then have the groups challenge one another to solve each other's puzzles.

Portfolio Assessment

Portfolio Assessment on page T39 provides options for building and evaluating student portfolios. Students and teachers can select items from the areas listed on page T39 for inclusion in a portfolio.

ANSWER TO CONCEPT MAP

The following is one possible answer to the Relating Concepts exercise on page 598.

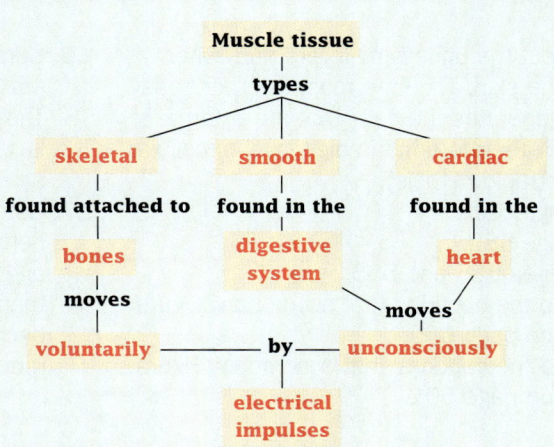

review

ANSWERS

Understanding Vocabulary

1. a. nervous tissue
   b. epidermis
   c. sprain
2. a. See pages 575 and 577.
   b. See page 580.
   c. Refer to the captions that accompany Figure 29-18 on page 591.

Understanding Concepts

3. Concept map answer on page 597.
4. Refer to the captions that accompany Figure 29-2 on page 576.
5. All four tissue types are found in the skin. Your skin is made of epithelial tissue covering a cushioning layer of connective tissue. Nervous tissue makes your skin sensitive to touch. Tiny muscles make the fine hairs in your skin stand on end when you are cold. These four kinds of tissues in your skin cooperate to protect your body. There are only two tissue types in bone (connective tissue and nervous tissue). There are three tissue types in muscles (muscle tissue, connective tissue, and nervous tissue).
6. It is safe to exercise when the temperature and humidity are in the Safe zone. Outdoor exercise is dangerous and should be avoided when the temperature and humidity are in the Danger zone and/or the Cancel zone.
7. Refer to the caption that accompanies Figure 29-3 on page 577.
8. See page 579.
9. Most apocrine glands are located in the armpits and groin. These glands produce proteins and fatty acids on which bacteria feed. The waste products of bacteria produce an odor.
10. The outermost layer of the epidermis is made up of dead cells that originated (through mitosis) at the innermost layer. The many layers of dead cells of the outermost layer function

---

CHAPTER 29

review

Understanding Vocabulary

1. For each set of terms, complete the analogy.
   a. cartilage : connective tissue :: sense organs : _____
   b. contains blood vessels : dermis :: contains melanin : _____
   c. broken bone : fracture :: ligament injury : _____
2. Using each set of words below, write one or more sentences summarizing information learned in this chapter.
   a. tissue, organ, circulatory system
   b. epidermis, keratin, melanin, hair follicles
   c. skeletal muscle, smooth muscle, cardiac muscle

Understanding Concepts

3. **Relating Concepts** Construct a concept map that identifies the three types of muscle tissue and their characteristics. Include these terms: cardiac, smooth, skeletal, heart, digestive system, bones, unconsciously, voluntarily, electrical impulses.
4. **Identifying Functions** Describe the functions of the three types of connective tissue, and give examples of each.
5. **Organizing Information** Describe how the different types of tissue work together in the skin, bones, and muscles. Give examples of each.
6. **Inferring Relationships** According to the graph below, under what outdoor conditions is it safe to exercise? When is outdoor exercise dangerous or to be avoided?

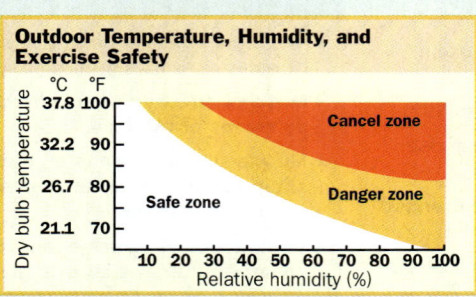

Outdoor Temperature, Humidity, and Exercise Safety

7. **Identifying Functions** Identify the organ systems that work together to protect, support, and move the body.
8. **Identifying Relationships** Describe the functions of blood vessels within the dermis, and explain how they work with other structures there to regulate the body's temperature.
9. **Identifying Structures** Where are apocrine glands located in your body? How do apocrine glands differ from other sweat glands?
10. **Organizing Information** Characterize the epidermal layers by relative location to one another, level of cellular activity, and function.
11. **Inferring Conclusions** Describe what causes the pimples associated with acne. Why is this condition common in teens?
12. **Recognizing Relationships** Summarize how the sun's rays contribute to the development of skin cancer, and explain how you can protect yourself from sun damage.
13. **Inferring Relationships** Describe how a bone grows, ages, breaks, and heals.
14. **Summarizing Information** Identify five kinds of joints in the human skeleton. Describe the movement allowed by each joint, and give an example of each.
15. **Identifying Structures** Classify the muscles of the body into three types, and describe each type's primary function.
16. **Analyzing Information** How are sprains and fractures alike? How are they different?
17. **Inferring Relationships** How does the term *osteoporosis* describe changes in mature bones? What causes these changes?
18. **Summarizing Information** Compare the effects of anaerobic exercise, aerobic exercise, and resistance exercise on the body.
19. **Inferring Relationships** Describe the results of using anabolic steroids before the skeleton matures completely.
20. **BUILDING ON WHAT YOU HAVE LEARNED** As you learned in Chapter 16, scientists have noted a reduction in the Earth's ozone layer. How is the destruction of this layer related to an increase in the number of warnings to use sunscreens and to avoid the midday sun?

598

---

to protect the underlying layers and waterproof the skin. The innermost layer, or basal layer, generates the cells that are external to it, and it therefore has a high level of cellular activity (rapid mitosis).

11. See page 581.
12. See page 582.
13. See pages 585 and 586.
14. Refer to the captions that accompany Figure 29-16 on page 589.
15. Refer to the captions that accompany Figure 29-17 on page 591.

16. Sprains and fractures are similar in that they are both traumas to the skeletal system. They are different in that a fracture is a broken bone, whereas a sprain is the overstretching of a ligament.
17. Osteoporosis results from a loss in bone density. There is a normal loss in density with age, but people with osteoporosis lose more than normal. Some possible causes are the decline in the levels of the female sex hormones with age, lack of regular exercise, and

598   Chapter 29

Interpreting Graphics

21. Look at the photo of the athlete below.

a. How can you tell that this person has just finished exercising?
b. Which sweat glands are responsible for the pattern of sweat shown here?

Reviewing Themes

22. *Evolution*
What do goose bumps reveal about our evolutionary past?

23. *Heredity*
Explain why some people are never able to grow long hair.

Thinking Critically

24. **Justifying Conclusions** In some countries, potential athletes have been selected for particular sports at a very young age based on the percentages of fast-twitch and slow-twitch muscle cells in their bodies. If an examination of muscle tissue from the leg reveals that athlete A has fewer fast-twitch muscle cells than athlete B, which athlete would be chosen for training as a marathon runner? Explain your answer.

25. **Inferring Relationships** Why are two sets of muscles required to move a bone?

Life/Work Skills

26. **Using Technology** Search the Internet to find information about the Visible Human Project, which was conducted to create a detailed, computerized atlas of the human body. The project produced computer-generated, three-dimensional models of a human male (the "Visible Man") and a human female (the "Visible Woman"). Find out how the images were created and how they might be used. Information about the Visible Human Project is also available on CD-ROM.

Activities and Projects

27. **Reading Connection** Study the beautifully illustrated book *The Incredible Machine*, by the National Geographic Society (1986). Read a chapter of your choice, such as "The Powerful River," which is about the circulatory system, and prepare a written report on information in the chapter that interested you.

28. **Health Connection** Use library references or search an on-line database to find out about muscular disorders such as muscular dystrophy and myasthenia gravis. What are the symptoms of these conditions? What are the causes? Obtain photos of some famous people who have suffered from these disorders, and share their stories with your classmates.

Discovering Through Reading

29. Read the article "Saving Face: Yes, You Can Prevent Wrinkles and Even Get Rid of Some You've Got" by Patricia Long in *Health*, November/December 1994, pages 56–63. When do men get facial wrinkles? When do women get them? Why?

30. Read the article, "Saving Burn Victims" from *Discover*, Volume 15, Issue 9. September 1994, pages 16–18. Why are third degree burns so dangerous? From what kind of tissue do fibroblasts make new skin?

599

skin pulls the hair upright. The hair in this position provides warmth. But since humans have little or no hair over most of the body, the contraction of muscles in the skin causes goose bumps.

23. See page 580.

Thinking Critically

24. Athlete A would have been chosen for training as a marathon runner because she has a greater percentage of slow-twitch muscles. Slow-twitch muscles are needed for the endurance associated with running a marathon.

25. Muscles cannot push on a bone. For movement to occur when a muscle contracts and pulls on a bone, another muscle is needed to pull the bone in the opposite direction after the contraction.

Life/Work Skills

26. Encourage students to find out about the project on the Internet; downloading information requires long periods of time and sizable amounts of computer memory. The best way to look at the images is on CD-ROM.

Activities and Projects

27. Results will vary depending on which chapter was read.
28. Results will vary depending on resources available.

Discovering Through Reading

29. Most men begin to get facial wrinkles in their forties, about 10 years later than women; men get fewer wrinkles because their skin is thicker and doesn't fold in on itself.
30. Third degree burns extend to the dermis. This destroys the protective function of the epidermis and leaves the body defenseless against infection. Fibroblasts help to regenerate the dermis.

inadequate diet (calcium, vitamin D, and protein).
18. Refer to the captions that accompany Figure 29-20 on pages 594–595.
19. Refer to the **Answers to Section Review** for Section 29-4, page 596, number 4.
20. The ozone protects the Earth from harmful ultraviolet rays. Without the protection provided by the ozone, more cases of skin cancer are very likely.

Interpreting Graphics

21. a. The person has sweat on his body and the face is flushed.
b. The apocrine glands, which are located in the armpits. The evaporation of sweat helps to cool the body quickly.

Reviewing Themes

22. In our evolutionary ancestors, as in most mammals, the contraction of muscles in the

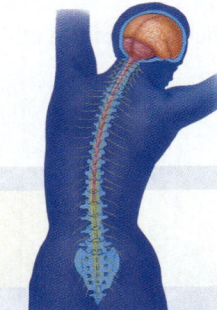

Lesson Planning Guide With Options for Block Scheduling

Lecture Concepts	**Lesson Resources**

30-1 Nervous Impulses

BLOCK ① (45 minutes)

1. A nerve cell (neuron) consists of a cell body, dendrites, and an axon.

2. A nerve impulse involves the movement of sodium and potassium ions across the cell membrane of a neuron.

3. When not conducting an impulse, a neuron exhibits a resting potential.

① Lecture Resources
- ■ Determining Prior Knowledge
- ■ Active Reading: Anticipation Guide
- ■ Visual Strategy: Figures 30-2, 30-3
- ■ Visual Strategy: Videodisc
- ■ Demonstration: Comparing Structures
- ■ Demonstration: Observing Relationships
- 🔒 Teaching Transparencies: 194, 195
- 🌀 Holt Biology Videodiscs Lesson 30-1

Classwork Options
- ■ Interactive Exploration 30B

Assignment Options
- ⊙ Teaching Resources CD-ROM: Occupational Applications Worksheets 14

BLOCK ② (45 minutes)

4. Neurotransmitters carry impulses from one neuron to another across a synapse.

5. Many drugs, including opium and alcohol, interfere with neurotransmitters.

6. Some neurotransmitters move from nerves to muscles, where they trigger contractions.

② Lecture Resources
- ■ Producing Chemicals Economically
- ■ Visual Strategy: Figures 30-4, 30-5, 30-7, Table 30-1
- ■ Visual Strategy: Videodisc
- ■ Demonstration: Comparing Structures
- 🔒 Teaching Transparencies: 233, 234
- 🌀 Holt Biology Videodiscs Lesson 30-1

Classwork Options
- ■ Demonstration: Relating Concepts
- ■ Closure: Summarizing Information

Assignment Options
- ■ Reteaching
- ■ Section Review
- ■ Chapter Review, questions 2a, 2b, 4, 5, 6, 7, 8, 9, 10, 21, 25
- ■ Directed Reading Worksheet

30-2 The Nervous System

BLOCK ③ (45 minutes)

1. The central nervous system consists of the brain and spinal cord.

2. The three main parts of the brain are the cerebrum, cerebellum, and brain stem.

3. The spinal cord transmits impulses to and from the brain.

③ Lecture Resources
- ■ Active Reading: Reading Organizer
- ■ Visual Strategy: Figure 30-10
- ■ Visual Strategy: Videodisc
- ■ Demonstration: Recognizing Relationships
- 🔒 Teaching Transparencies: 196, 197, 199
- 🌀 Holt Biology Videodiscs Lesson 30-2

Classwork Options
- ■ Demonstration: Categorize and Compare
- ■ Exploration 30A

Assignment Options
- ■ Health Connection "Brain Dead"

BLOCK ④ (45 minutes)

4. The peripheral nervous system consists of all the nerves outside the brain and spinal cord.

5. A reflex is an involuntary response to a stimulus.

6. The peripheral nervous system contains the autonomic nervous system, which controls involuntary body actions.

④ Lecture Resources
- ■ Brain Size and Body Mass
- ■ Peripheral Nervous System Neurons
- ■ Visual Strategy: Figures 30-13, 30-14
- ■ Visual Strategy: Videodisc
- ■ Demonstration: Relating Concepts
- 🌀 Holt Biology Videodiscs Lesson 30-2

Classwork Options
- ■ Brain Size and Intelligence
- ■ Closure: Organizing Information

Assignment Options
- ■ Reteaching
- ■ Section Review
- ■ Chapter Review, questions 1a, 2c, 11, 12, 13, 14, 15, 20, 22, 23, 24, 27
- ■ Directed Reading Worksheet

30-3 The Sense Organs

BLOCK ⑤ (45 minutes)

1. Sensory neurons detect stimuli and send impulses to the central nervous system.

2. Sensory neurons in the inner ear help us hear and maintain balance.

⑤ Lecture Resources
- ■ Active Reading: Paired Summarizing
- ■ Visual Strategy: Figures 30-15, 30-16
- ■ Demonstration: Comparing Structures
- 🔒 Teaching Transparencies: 200, 201
- 🌀 Holt Biology Videodiscs Lesson 30-3

Classwork Options
- ■ Demonstration: Analyzing Information
- ⚗ Inquiry Skills Development: Lab B31

Lecture Concepts

Lesson Resources

30-3 The Sense Organs, *continued*

BLOCK ❻ (45 minutes)

3. Sensory neurons in the eye help us see colors, and small details and movements.

4. Sensory neurons in the tongue help up distinguish sweet, sour, bitter, and salty tastes.

❻ Lecture Resources
- ■ Active Reading: Closure with Anticipation Guide
- ■ Demonstration: Identifying Variables
- ■ Teaching Transparencies: 202, 203
- ◉ Holt Biology Videodiscs Lesson 30-3

Classwork Options
- ■ Demonstration: Identifying Structures
- ■ Closure: Organizing Information

Assignment Options
- ■ *Small Group* Reteaching
- ■ Section Review
- ■ Chapter Review, questions 1b, 1c, 3, 16, 17, 18, 19, 26, 28, 29
- ■ Directed Reading Worksheet

Chapter Review and Assessment

BLOCK ❼ (45 minutes)
Review
- ■ Reteaching Worksheet
- ■ Thinking Skills Worksheet
- ■ Vocabulary Development Worksheet
- ◉ Language Development and Reading Comprehension Audio CD Program: Chapter 30

BLOCK ❽ (45 minutes)
Assessment
- ■ Alternative Assessment, p. 627
- ■ Portfolio Assessment, p. T39

Chapter Test
- ■ Chapter 30 Test

Test Generator
- ◉ Item bank for customizing Chapter Tests

Teaching Resources CD-ROM
- ◉ Scoring Rubrics and Classroom Management Checklist

 The Portfolio icon denotes items throughout the Teacher's Edition lesson wrap that may be selected for inclusion in student portfolios.

Holt Biology Videodiscs and *Concepts of Biology*

Holt Biology Videodiscs gives you a powerful tool for teaching, review, and assessment. For further information regarding the media on the videodiscs, see **Holt Biology Videodiscs Teacher's Correlation Guide to Holt Biology: Visualizing Life.**

Concepts of Biology adds interactive lesson plans and extensive tools for customization using CD-ROM technology.

Use the following topic from **Concepts of Biology** to help you teach this chapter:

Topic 24: Nervous and Endocrine Systems
Topic 25: Drugs and the Human Body

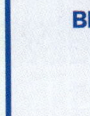

Laboratory Planning

Text

Materials and preparation instructions appear on the teacher's wrap accompanying each laboratory exercise.

Block 1: Interactive Exploration 30B: Drug Addiction, p. 814
Block 3: Exploration 30A: Determining the Effect of Drugs on Heart Rate, p. 812

Holt BioSources Laboratory Program

Block 5: Inquiry Skills Development Lab B31: Exploring Vision

Determining Prior Knowledge

- Ask students to brainstorm about the functions of the nervous system. Write their responses on the board or overhead. Categorize the responses into the following: (1) Monitoring the internal and external environments (sensory), (2) Coordinating bodily activities (motor), and (3) Incorporating experiences into memory.
- Have students compare the nervous systems of different animals, including the size of the brain in relation to the size of the body, the amount of "wrinkles" on the surface of the brain, and the varied sizes of specialized parts of the brain.

Active READING

Technique: Anticipation Guide

Before students begin this chapter, write the following statements on the board or the overhead:
1. Addiction is purely a psychological response to drug use.
2. Reflexes occur before the brain is aware of any danger.
3. Prolonged exposure to loud noise can cause permanent hearing loss.

Give students a minute or two to think about each statement and decide whether they agree or disagree with it. Ask volunteers with differing views about each statement to share the reasons for their opinions with the class. Have students read the chapter to see if their opinions are confirmed or if they are changed in any way. Have students save their lists for use in Active Reading on page 626.

CD-ROM Resources

Concepts of Biology
Topic 24: Nervous and Endocrine Systems
Topic 25: Drugs and the Human Body

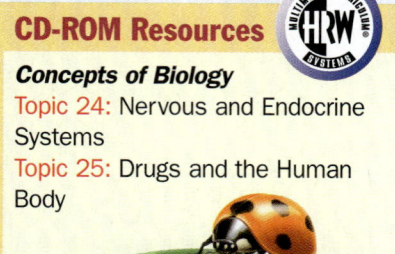

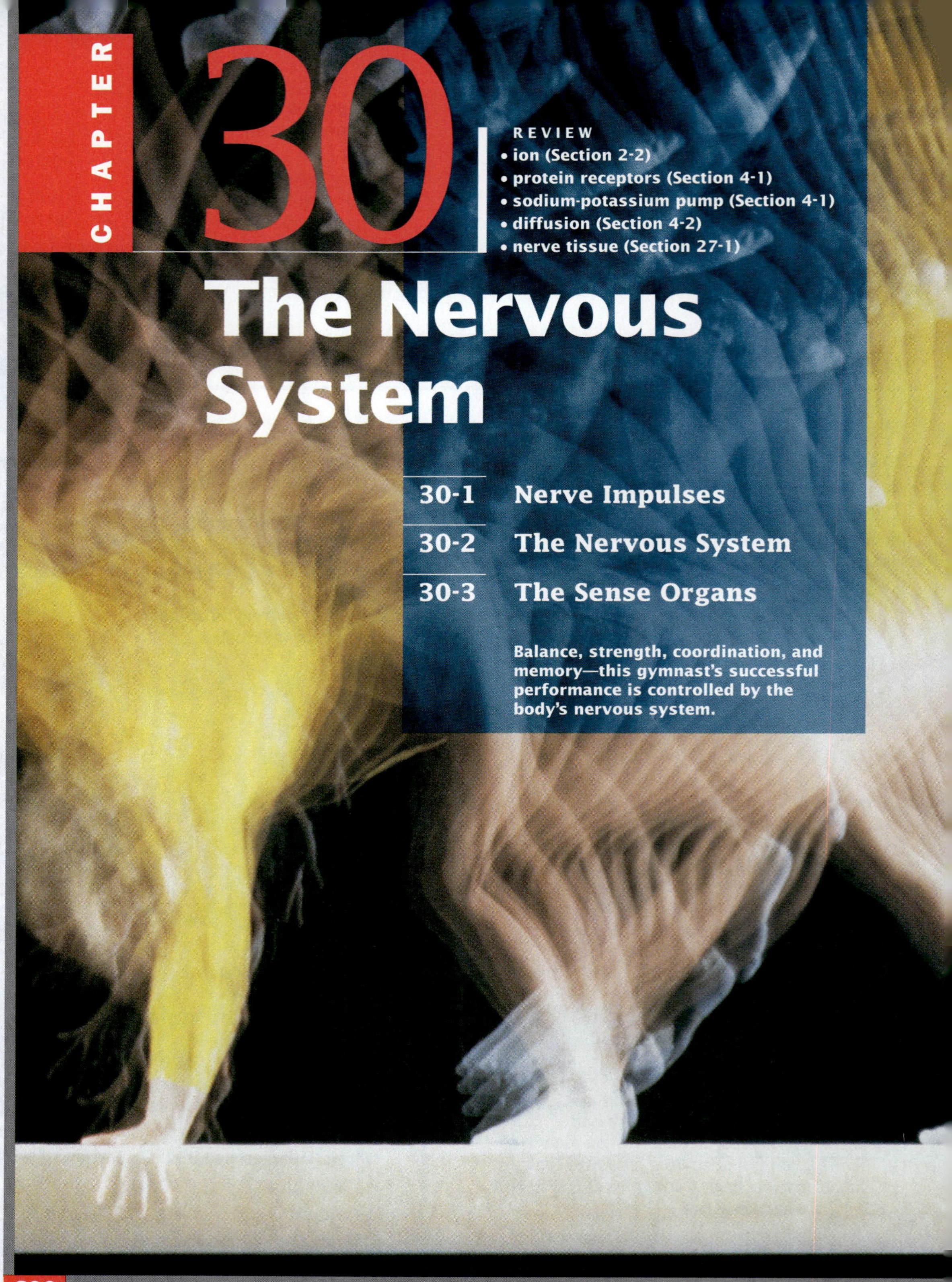

CHAPTER

30

REVIEW
- ion (Section 2-2)
- protein receptors (Section 4-1)
- sodium-potassium pump (Section 4-1)
- diffusion (Section 4-2)
- nerve tissue (Section 27-1)

The Nervous System

Balance, strength, coordination, and memory—this gymnast's successful performance is controlled by the body's nervous system.

Author's Rationale   The nervous system may be the most difficult body system for students to understand. Yet its overall importance is such that it cannot be skipped. Here I focus on describing how it works by looking at how membrane channels create nerve impulses. Anatomy of the nervous system is presented as an overview, and instructional time should not be bogged down with anatomical details. Integrated into the chapter are the actions of drugs, which in many cases mimic the action of natural neuromodulators and neurotransmitters. One intent of this chapter is to show students in very concrete terms the consequences of taking dangerous drugs. In this context, alcohol and nicotine are treated as addictive drugs.

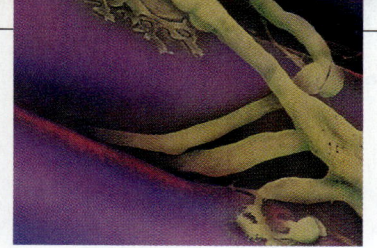

When you touch a hot stove, your hand instantly jerks back because of a message from your spinal cord. When you swat a fly, the muscles of your arm contract quickly because of a message from your brain. These messages travel along nerves, which are bundles of cells that carry electrical signals throughout your body.

30-1 Nerve Impulses

OBJECTIVES

❶ **Describe the basic structure of a neuron.**

❷ **Summarize the changes that occur in a neuron during a nerve impulse.**

❸ **Explain how a nerve impulse is carried across a synapse.**

❹ **Describe addiction in terms of a neuron's membrane.**

Structure of a Neuron

Nerve cells, or **neurons** *(NOO rahnz)*, are specialized for conducting information. Bundles of neurons form thin cables called **nerves**. Like electrical cables running through a town, nerves form a communications network that extends throughout your body, including organs like your skin, eyes, and stomach.

There are many types of neurons, all with structures that reflect their particular roles. However, all neurons have the same basic architecture. A typical neuron, shown in **Figure 30-1**, consists of an enlarged region called the cell body, which contains the nucleus and organelles. The cell body generally receives information at short, branched extensions called **dendrites** *(DEHN dryts)*. Typically, a neuron has many dendrites, which enables it to receive input from thousands of other cells. From the cell body, information is transmitted to other cells by long fibers called **axons**. In contrast to its high number of dendrites, a neuron usually has only one axon. The tip of the axon often branches into short knobs so that a single neuron can pass information to many other cells.

Figure 30-1
Neurons, or nerve cells, are specialized to receive information and send it to other cells in other parts of the body.

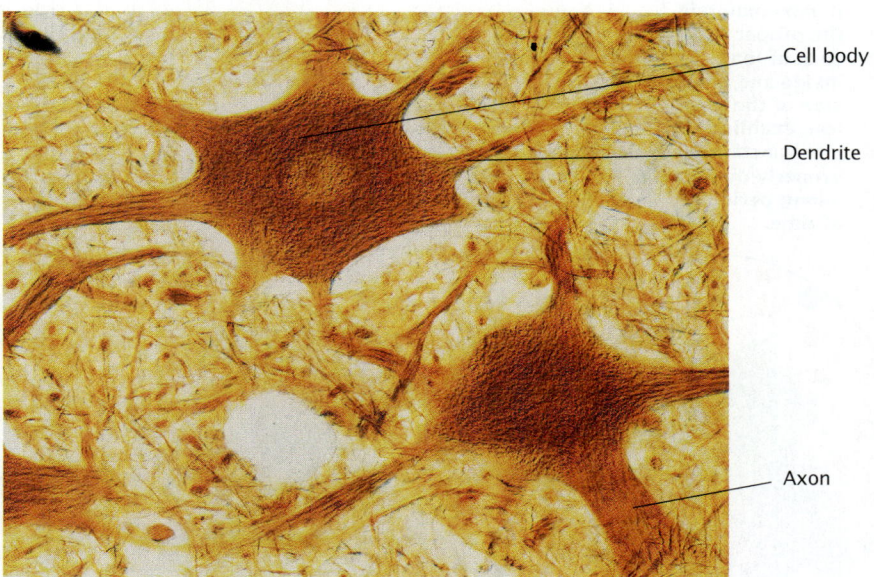

— Cell body

— Dendrite

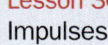

— Axon

Videodisc Resources

Holt Biology Videodiscs
Lesson 30-1: Nerve Impulses

Demonstration

● **Comparing Structures**
Tell students that most of the cell bodies of neurons involved in controlling muscle movement are located in the spinal cord. Consequently, axons must extend all the way from the spinal cord to the muscles they innervate. Demonstrate how long an axon can be by measuring the distance from a student's spine—at a point just below the neck—to the fingertips, and from the base of the spine to the toe.

Demonstration

● **Observing Relationships**
Arrange to have a physics teacher give a simple demonstration to the class on how electrodes conduct electrical activity detectable by a voltmeter or an oscilloscope. The electrical activity observed will be similar to the activity that can be observed when electrodes are attached to the skin in an electrocardiogram (ECG), electroencephalogram (EEG), or electromyogram (EMG).

Key to Strategies
Teaching Strategies are keyed to three tiers of learning.

● **Understanding Concepts (Tier I)**
Content mastery and comprehension

■ **Applying Information (Tier II)**
Applying and analyzing content

▲ **Critical Thinking (Tier III)**
Practicing evaluative thinking

Connection: *Chapter 2*

Electrons and Ions
Remind students that electrons are the negatively charged particles that move around the nucleus of an atom and that ions are atoms that have either a positive (lost an electron or electrons) or a negative (gained an electron or electrons) charge.

■ **Recognizing Relationships**
Have students locate where sodium and potassium ions would be concentrated in Figure 30-2b. Have them identify where both the resting and action potentials would be found in each of the three phases that are shown. Be sure students realize that the resting potential is restored with the help of the sodium-potassium pump, which reestablishes the original ion gradients. Point out that about 10 times as many sodium ions are found outside the membrane as are found inside, and that about 30 times as many potassium ions are present inside as outside. However, since the membrane keeps the positively charged sodium outside and the negatively charged organic ions inside, the outside of the membrane has a slight positive charge that registers as the resting potential of the neuron.

Connection: *Chapter 4*

Sodium-Potassium Pump
Refer students to figures in Chapter 4 to review how sodium and potassium ions are actively pumped across the cell membrane.

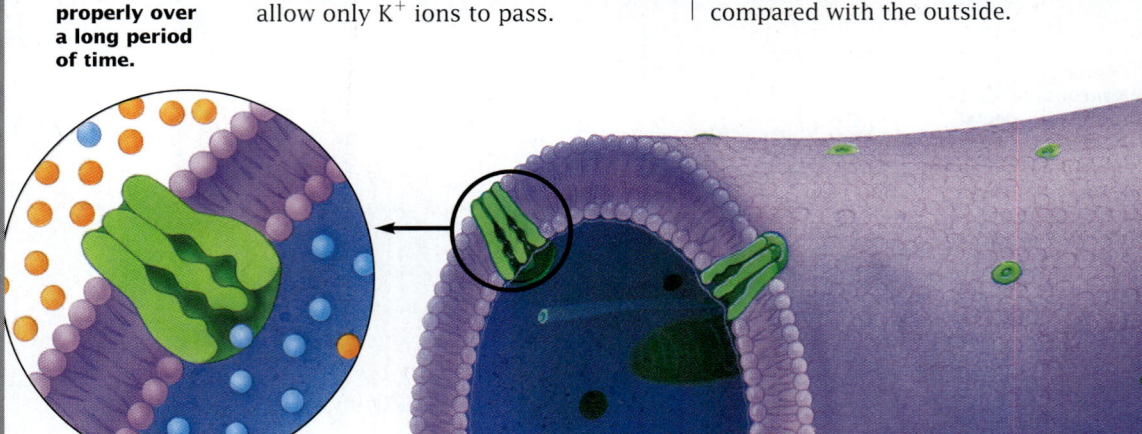

Transmission of Nerve Impulses

More than a century ago scientists discovered that a nerve impulse involves electrical changes in a neuron. Further investigations led to the current model of nerve-impulse transmission. This model explains the electrical changes as differences in concentrations of two ions—sodium (Na^+) and potassium (K^+).

The key to the transmission of nerve impulses lies in a neuron's membrane. The membrane of a neuron is studded with protein channels called voltage-gated channels. These channels open and close in response to changes in voltage (electrical charge) across the membrane. They are ion specific—some allow only Na^+ ions to pass through the membrane, while others allow only K^+ ions to pass.

What do ions, membranes, and channels have to do with nerve impulses, like the ones traveling from eyes to brain as you read? Look at a neuron that is not sending an impulse, one that is "at rest." When a neuron is at rest, its voltage-gated channels are closed. Inside the concentration of Na^+ ions is low, and the concentration of K^+ ions is high. Outside the neuron, the concentration of Na^+ ions is high, and the concentration of K^+ ions is low. The unequal distribution of ions, illustrated in **Figure 30-2a**, results in a difference in voltage across the cell membrane called the resting potential. During resting potential, the inside of the cell has a negative charge (about −70 millivolts) compared with the outside.

c Sodium-potassium pumps maintain the proper balance of ions inside and outside of the neuron, enabling it to function properly over a long period of time.

602

Matter of Fact: Referred Pain

Referred pains are those pain stimuli coming from internal organs that are perceived as coming from the surface of the body. Referred pain is important in clinical diagnoses. For example, inadequate oxygenation of the heart muscle often results in pain being referred to the chest wall and shoulder (angina pectoris), and reflux of gastric juice into the esophagus causes a sensation of intense discomfort, known as heartburn, in the thorax.

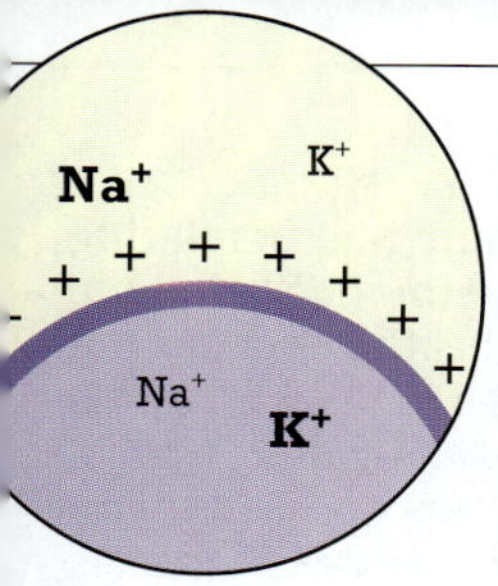

Figure 30-2

a *Resting potential* **The concentration of sodium ions is much greater outside the cell, and the concentration of potassium ions is greater inside the cell.**

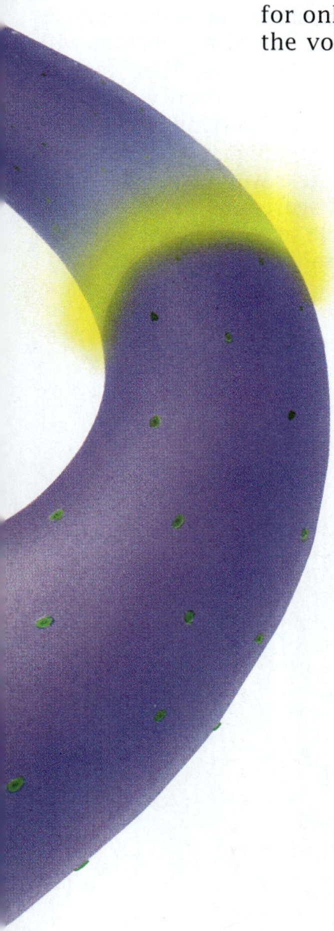

A nerve impulse begins when membrane voltage is reversed

When a neuron is stimulated, such as by light, odor, a pinch, or a mild electric shock, its membrane undergoes a change. For a fraction of a second, the voltage-gated channels in the membrane open, allowing Na^+ ions to pass through. Powered by diffusion and attracted by negative charges inside the cell, Na^+ ions rush across the membrane into the cell. The inward rush of Na^+ ions is so great that, for a moment, the inside of the neuron becomes positively charged (+35 millivolts) compared with the outside. This sudden reversal of electrical charge across the neuron membrane is called an action potential, illustrated in **Figure 30-2b**.

The inward rush of Na^+ ions lasts for only half of a millisecond before the voltage-gated channels close. At the same moment, other voltage-gated channels open, allowing K^+ ions to pass through. As a result, K^+ ions rush out of the cell, powered by diffusion and repelled by the momentarily high positive charge inside the cell. This exit of K^+ ions restores the cell to resting potential.

One action potential triggers another action potential

During an action potential, the voltage across a small patch of membrane is reversed. This change in voltage causes nearby voltage-gated Na^+ ion channels to open, triggering an action potential in another region of the membrane. Likewise, this action potential triggers another one farther along the axon and continues like a chain of falling dominoes. In short, a nerve impulse is a series of action potentials flowing along a neuron.

A neuron must maintain the balance of ions

If a nerve impulse involves an inward flow of Na^+ ions and an outward flow of K^+ ions, how does a neuron restore its original balance of ions? After an impulse passes, diffusion restores the balance between Na^+ ions outside of the cell and K^+ ions inside. This balance is maintained by sodium-potassium pumps, which actively transport sodium ions out of the cell and potassium ions into the cell, as shown in **Figure 30-2c**. Without the action of the sodium-potassium pump, a neuron would lose its ability to conduct impulses.

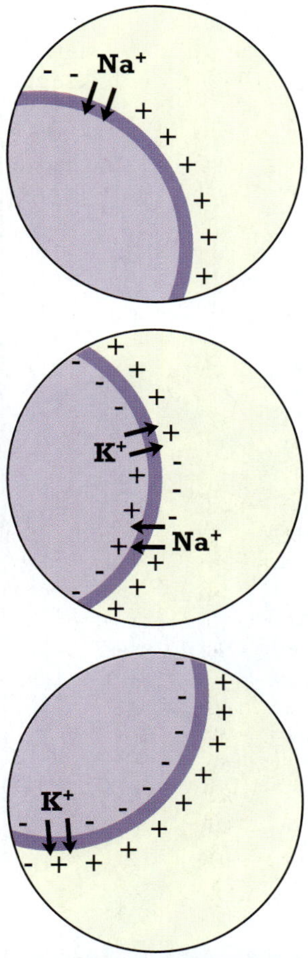

b *Action potential* **Sodium ions rush into the cell through voltage-gated channels, upsetting the resting potential. Potassium ions rush out of the cell through other channels, restoring the voltage.**

Visual Strategy Videodisc

● **Summarizing Information**
As an introduction to nerve impulses, use *Video—Nerve Impulses* (1 min 15 s) shown in Chapter 30 Section 30-1 of ***Holt Biology Videodiscs Teacher's Correlation Guide to Holt Biology: Visualizing Life.*** As students view the video, have them note each step in the transmission of a nerve impulse. After viewing the video, review the steps with the class, writing the steps on the board in the correct order.

Demonstration

■ **Relating Concepts**
Prepare three types of signs to distribute to each of your students: several labeled "sodium" with a "+" sign; others marked "potassium" with a "+" sign; and some marked "protein" with a "−" sign. Divide the room in half to represent the cell membrane of a neuron. Place most students with the sodium signs on the "outside" of the membrane and most of those with the other two signs on the "inside." Compare this situation to the resting potential of a neuron. Tell the class that the neuron has been stimulated, and have them demonstrate how the impulse is transmitted both during and after the action potential. Be sure that students with "−" signs remain "inside" the membrane; point out that the inside of the cell becomes more positive because of the inward flow of "+" (sodium) ions.

Matter of Fact: Squid Axons

The squid (*Loligo* sp.) was one of the first organisms used to measure the resting potential of a neuron. Because of its large, long axons that innervate muscles responsible for expelling water from the body cavity, the squid makes an ideal specimen for studies in nerve physiology. Some of the axons are 1 mm in diameter.

Key to Strategies
● Understanding Concepts (Tier I)
■ Applying Information (Tier II)
▲ Critical Thinking (Tier III)

Theme Answer

Theme Answer

Evolution

Myelin sheaths enable nerve impulses to be transmitted more rapidly. Evolution has taken two paths in regard to conduction velocity in axons: thin axons (1 to 20 μm in diameter), as in mammals with myelin sheaths and velocities from 6 to 120 m/s; and thick axons (1 mm in diameter), as in the squid without myelin sheaths and velocities to 20 m/s.

Health Connection

Multiple Sclerosis

Multiple sclerosis is an autoimmune disease that results from the actions of the immune system against the myelin sheaths of the nervous system. A protein in the myelin sheaths is attacked. As a result, the myelin sheaths in the brain and spinal cord become sclerotic and hard. This causes a short-circuiting of nerve impulses and poor impulse conductivity. Sometimes the symptoms disappear altogether, but sometimes they return after periods of remission. Current therapies include injections of beta interferon and ingestion of bovine myelin.

Visual Strategy | **Figure 30-3**

■ **Recognizing Relationships**

Have students use this figure to describe how the impulse "hops" along a myelinated axon. Have them explain what happens to the movement of ions across portions of the cell membranes that are covered with myelin. Students should realize that these portions of membrane do not undergo an action potential and consequently do not have to expend energy in actively pumping sodium and potassium ions to reestablish a resting potential.

Speeding Up Nerve Impulses

Evolution

Why are myelin sheaths considered an evolutionary advancement?

Humans and other vertebrates have neurons that run from the brain and spinal cord directly to muscles. Such neurons have very long axons—imagine a single axon stretching 5 m (16 ft) from a giraffe's spine to its foot! It takes time for a nerve impulse to travel the length of a long axon; this can have dangerous consequences. For example, a giraffe would be in trouble if the information traveling from its brain to the muscles in its legs were slower than a hungry, charging lion. Similarly, you could severely burn your hand on a hot stove if the message to remove it were slow in reaching your spinal cord.

Humans, giraffes, and other vertebrates have specialized nerve cells that speed up nerve impulses. These cells have fatty membranes that are wrapped around axons, forming an insulating layer called a **myelin** (MY uh lihn) **sheath**. A myelin sheath is not continuous, as you can see in **Figure 30-3**. It is interrupted by gaps called nodes, which are sites of exposed cell membrane. When a nerve impulse travels along a myelinated axon, it "jumps" from node to node. Because fewer action potentials need to be produced, a nerve impulse travels faster along an axon with a myelin sheath.

The importance of myelin sheaths becomes evident in people who suffer from a disease called multiple sclerosis. Multiple sclerosis destroys large patches of myelin around neurons in the brain and spinal cord. Without the insulating layer, normal nerve impulses are impaired. The disease begins with temporary symptoms that include weakened limbs, blurred vision, and slurred speech. The symptoms usually disappear spontaneously but return in repeated attacks with increasing severity. As the disease progresses, a person with multiple sclerosis is left weak and severely disabled.

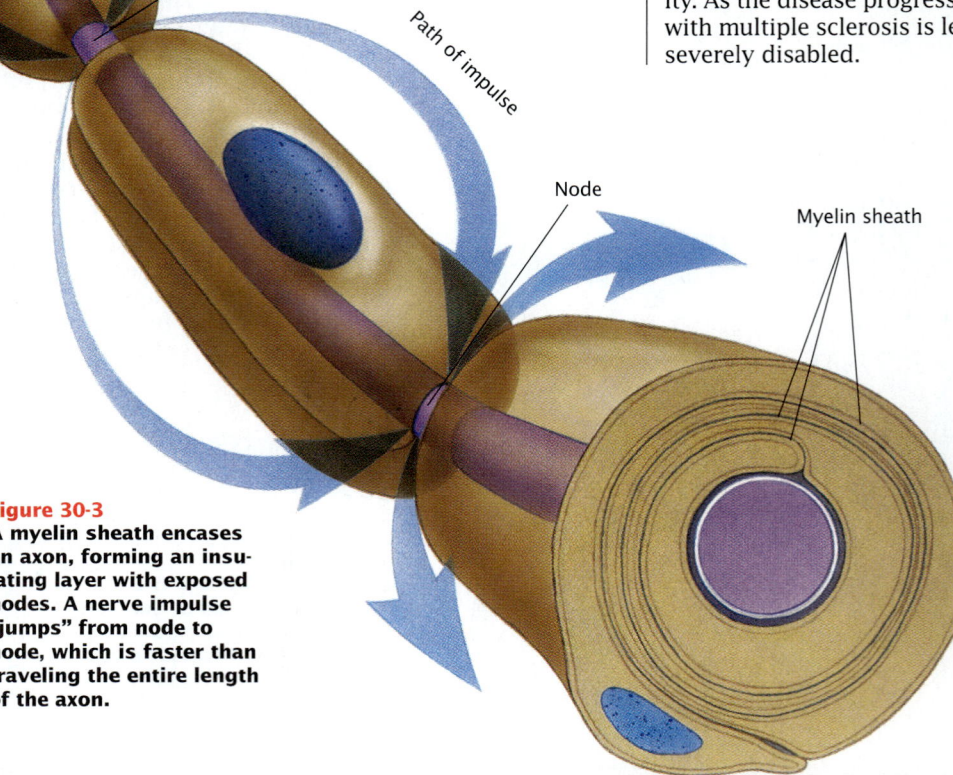

Node

Path of impulse

Path of impulse

Node

Myelin sheath

Figure 30-3
A myelin sheath encases an axon, forming an insulating layer with exposed nodes. A nerve impulse "jumps" from node to node, which is faster than traveling the entire length of the axon.

604

Transmission Across Synapses

A nerve impulse can travel only so far along a cell membrane before it reaches the end of the axon. In most cases, neurons do not touch each other directly. They are separated by a tiny gap called a **synapse** (SIHN aps), shown in **Figure 30-4**. Usually, the axon of one neuron forms a synapse with the dendrites or cell body of another neuron. Since the end portion of an axon may be branched, a single axon may form synapses with many other neurons.

When a nerve impulse reaches the end of an axon, it must cross the synapse if the message is to continue. In most cases, an action potential is unable to "jump" from one neuron to another. Instead, the impulse is carried across the synapse by chemical messengers called **neurotransmitters**. Neurotransmitters are contained in tiny sacs in the end of the axon. When a nerve impulse reaches the end of the axon, the sacs empty the neurotransmitters into the synapse, as shown in **Figure 30-4**. The neurotransmitters diffuse across the synapse and bind to receptors in the membrane of the adjacent neuron. This binding opens the gates of channel proteins in the neuron membrane, which allows specific ions to pass through the membrane in either direction. Ionic movement across the membrane triggers (or, in some cases, inhibits) an action potential.

After a neurotransmitter has carried an impulse across a synapse, it must be removed. Otherwise, it would remain in the synapse, stimulating a neuron indefinitely. How are spent neurotransmitters removed from a synapse? Some simply diffuse away, while others are absorbed by the axon and reused later. Still others are destroyed by specific enzymes.

Figure 30-4
Neurons come very close to each other but usually never touch. They are separated by a tiny gap called a synapse.

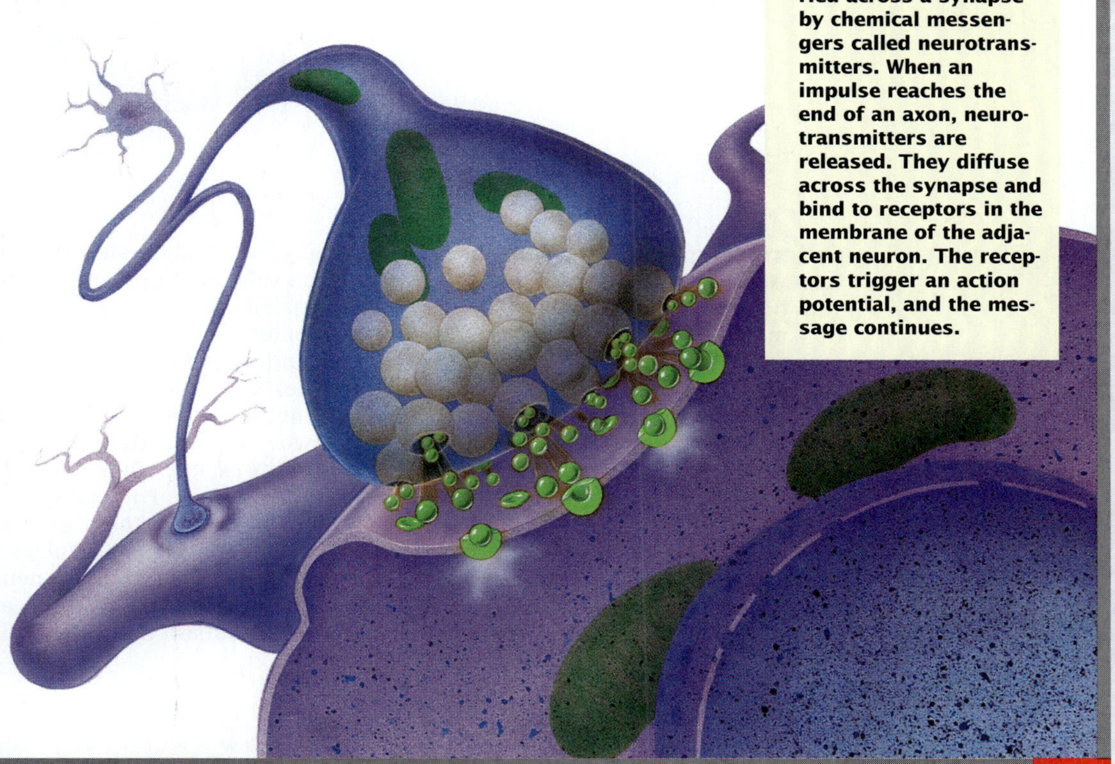

b A nerve impulse is carried across a synapse by chemical messengers called neurotransmitters. When an impulse reaches the end of an axon, neurotransmitters are released. They diffuse across the synapse and bind to receptors in the membrane of the adjacent neuron. The receptors trigger an action potential, and the message continues.

605

Visual Strategy Figure 30-4

● **Identifying Structures**
Use this figure to illustrate how an impulse is transmitted across a synapse. Have students identify the end of the axon with its neurotransmitter sacs and the dendrite with its cell membrane receptors. Point out that the amount of neurotransmitter released is related to the rate at which impulses reach the end of the axon—the stronger the stimulus, the faster and more often impulses arrive. Tell students that synapses control the direction an impulse can travel. Neurotransmitters are released only at the ends of axons, and they then travel to adjacent dendrites, cell bodies, and even other axons. Thus, an impulse can travel in only one direction across a synapse.

Mathematics Connection
How Many Neurons?
Each axon may have one or more synapses with as many as a 1,000 other neurons. Have the class calculate how many neurons could be stimulated if each of these 1,000 neurons forms synapses with another 1,000 neurons. Students should readily see how quickly and widely an impulse can travel. In reality, some of these synapses are excitatory, while others are inhibitory. Each neuron "evaluates" the total, averages the input, and responds accordingly. For example, if the overall total is excitatory, the neuron transmits the impulse to its neighbor.

Matter of Fact: Neurotransmitters and Mood

Extremely small amounts of neurotransmitters underlie all of our moods, from ecstasy to depression. Norepinephrine and dopamine make us feel good. If these neurotransmitters are low, we feel depressed. Endorphins and enkephalins block pain signals. They increase during physical stress, and runners who experience the increase in neurotransmitter refer to the sensation as a "runner's high." Substance P is released in the presence of capsaicin (a chemical irritant in hot peppers) and enhances the sensation of pain. Our neurotransmitters react to hormonal levels that react to physical stressors, such as our environment and thoughts. You can literally have an "attitude" that can affect your health.

Key to Strategies
● Understanding Concepts (Tier I)
■ Applying Information (Tier II)
▲ Critical Thinking (Tier III)

Connection: *Chapter 3*

Receptor Proteins

Review how molecules with the right shape can trigger receptor proteins on the surface of the cell membrane to convey information from the world outside the cell to the inside of the cell. The binding of opium and morphine to brain cell receptors led scientists to the discovery of chemicals known as endorphins, compounds produced naturally to help alleviate pain. Have students discuss what opium, morphine, and endorphins must have in common in order to bind to the same receptors. *(Opium, morphine, and endorphins must have parts of their molecules shaped similarly.)*

Visual Strategy | Figure 30-5

● **Communicating Knowledge**
Ask students if any of them have ever been given a drug that interferes with pain messages. Most students have probably received a local anesthetic when having a tooth cavity filled or a cut sutured.

Active READING

Technique: Reading Hint
Point out to students that the illustrations on pages 601, 602, 604, and 606 have been provided to help them process the more complex concepts presented in the first section of this chapter. Remind students to review these illustrations and the captions tied to them after they read the text.

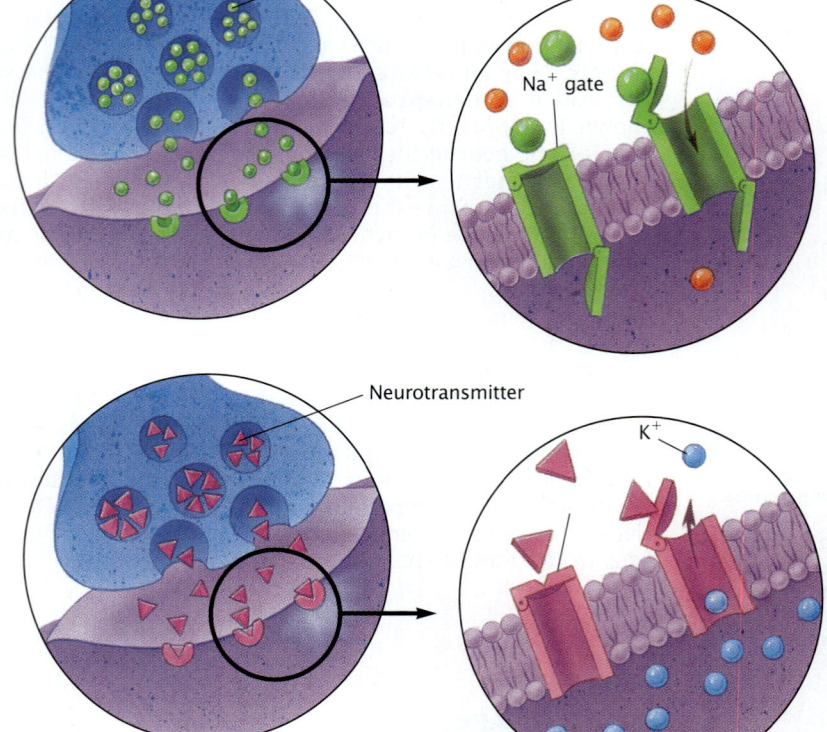

Figure 30-5

a Dopamine is an example of a neurotransmitter that excites nerve impulses. When it crosses a synapse, it opens sodium gates.

Neurotransmitter

Na⁺ gate

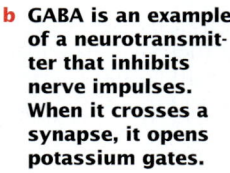

b GABA is an example of a neurotransmitter that inhibits nerve impulses. When it crosses a synapse, it opens potassium gates.

Neurotransmitter

K⁺

Different types of neurotransmitters produce different effects

Your body produces a variety of neurotransmitters. A neurotransmitter called acetylcholine binds to receptors in the membranes of muscle cells. This triggers an action potential, making the muscle fiber contract. Many drugs that cause paralysis work by affecting acetylcholine receptors. For example, molecules of a drug called curare, used to poison arrow tips, have the same shape as acetylcholine. Curare binds to the acetylcholine receptors, permanently blocking all nerve impulses, which leads to death. Insecticides and nerve gas are lethal because they contain molecules that prevent enzymes from breaking down acetylcholine. As a result, muscles become permanently active, and the affected animal eventually dies.

In general, neurotransmitters fall into two classes, depending on whether they excite or inhibit impulses across the synapse. For example, the neurotransmitters serotonin and dopamine both act to excite impulses, as illustrated in **Figure 30-5a**. A neurotransmitter abbreviated as GABA acts to inhibit impulses, as illustrated in **Figure 30-5b**.

Drugs and the Nervous System

Recent investigations have found that certain disorders, such as schizophrenia and severe clinical depression, are triggered by malfunctions of neurotransmitters and receptors. This research has yielded new ways to use chemicals to treat certain emotional disorders. It has also revealed new, intriguing information about how drugs affect the nervous system, reinforcing the dangers of their use.

In the broadest sense, a drug is a chemical that can alter biological structures and functions of tissues in your body. A class of drugs called psychoactive drugs alters tissues in the nervous system, which often makes these drugs addictive. Addiction to psychoactive drugs is a biological response that involves drug molecules and receptors in neuron membranes. In effect, addiction is the body's attempt to cope with the chemical disruption that a drug causes in a synapse.

To understand the nature of drug addiction, keep in mind how neurons communicate with one another. Recall that when a nerve impulse reaches the end of an axon, neurotransmitters are released, cross the synapse, and bind to receptors on the adjacent neuron, triggering an impulse. Psychoactive drugs interfere with this activity in the synapse. For example, certain drugs have chemical structures similar to those of a particular neurotransmitter. When a molecule of one of these drugs reaches a neuron, it may bind to receptors for that neurotransmitter. The result is that the neuron reacts as if the neurotransmitter were present. This is how drugs such as morphine and heroin work. Other drugs prevent a neurotransmitter from being destroyed or recycled, as shown in **Figure 30-6**.

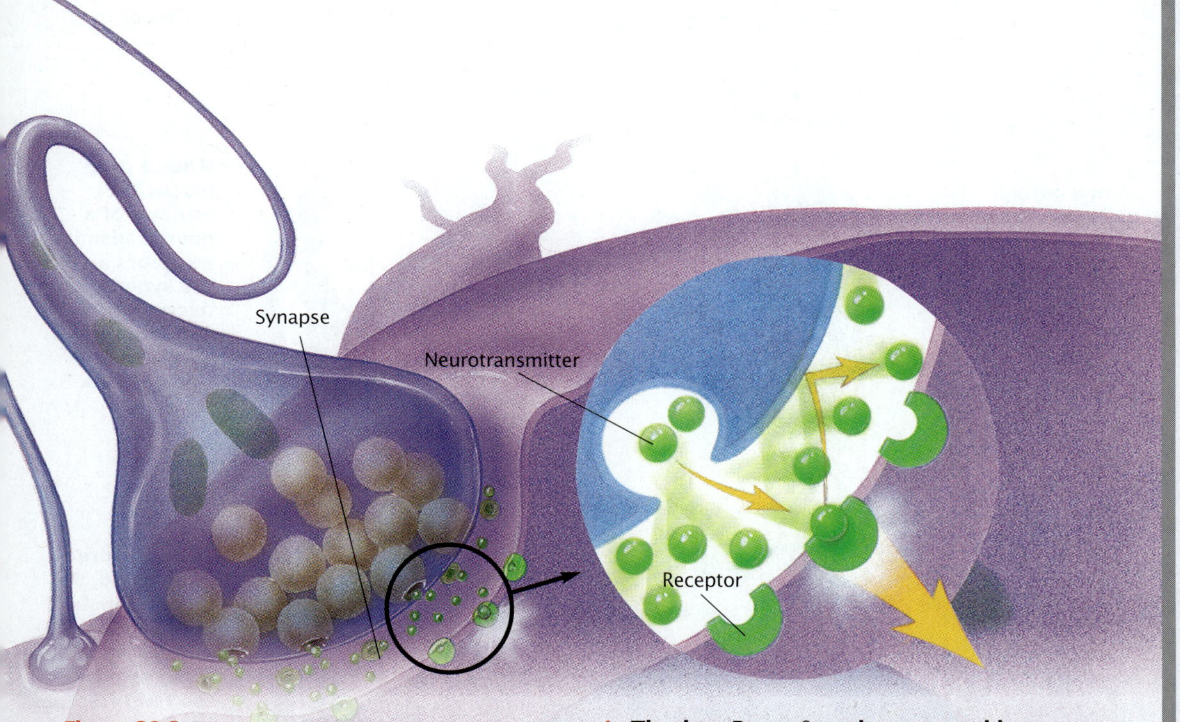

Energy and Life

Why is the term resting potential misleading when describing a neuron's cell membrane?

Figure 30-6
a Depression can result from a shortage of the neurotransmitter serotonin (green spheres).

Labels: Synapse, Neurotransmitter, Receptor

b The drug Prozac® works as an antidepressant because it blocks reabsorption of serotonin from the synapse, thus increasing the level of the neurotransmitter.

607

Graphic Organizer

Use the following graphic organizer with the teaching strategy **Producing Chemicals Economically** on page 607.

Tyrosine ⟶ L-dopa ⟶ Dopamine ⟶ Norepinephrine ⟶ Epinephrine

Theme Answer
Energy and Life
The term *resting potential* is misleading because there is actually a lot of activity going on. Ions are constantly being transported and diffused across the membrane.

Connection: *Chapter 2*
Enzymes
Remind students that an enzyme binds to a specific molecule (its substrate) in such a way as to make a reaction more likely to occur. Have students identify the substrate in Figure 30-6. Show the complex interactions that can occur in a synapse. The antidepressant drug binds and inhibits the enzyme, which consequently can no longer bind and break down serotonin (its substrate).

Producing Chemicals Economically
■ **Recognizing Relationships**
With the class, discuss ways in which the body has evolved conservative means of producing the myriad chemicals it needs. One example is the way in which many neurotransmitters are simply intermediates in a metabolic pathway, as the **Graphic Organizer** shown at the bottom of the page illustrates. Here the amino acid tyrosine is the common starting point for each of the neurotransmitters shown. A single enzyme converts tyrosine to L-dopa, which can in turn be transformed into dopamine by a different enzyme, and so on, finally ending with epinephrine (adrenaline). Each of the intermediates may function as an independent neurotransmitter or enter the conduit to produce another neurotransmitter later in the pathway.

Key to Strategies
● Understanding Concepts (Tier I)
■ Applying Information (Tier II)
▲ Critical Thinking (Tier III)

The Nervous System   607

Demonstration

● **Comparing Structures**
Refer students to Figure 30-7. Use a small marble and some clay to simulate addiction. Begin by flattening two pieces of clay. Then use a marble to make depressions in both pieces, making significantly more depressions in one piece than in the other. Show the class both pieces of clay and ask which would represent the surface of a neuron in a person addicted to a psychoactive drug. Students should recognize that the one with fewer depressions (receptors) represents a desensitized neuron from an addict. Emphasize that fewer receptors are needed since so many neurotransmitters are present for longer periods of time.

Visual Strategy   Figure 30-7

■ **Recognizing Relationships**
Emphasize that addiction is biological as well as psychological. Have students explain the relationship between the psychological effects of drugs and the decreased number of receptors.

Addiction is caused by a change in the number of receptors

When a neuron is exposed to a signal for a prolonged period of time, it tends to lose its ability to respond to the stimulus with its original intensity. For example, when you put on a wristwatch, you soon become used to wearing it and forget that it is there. Neurons are particularly affected by prolonged exposure to a signal. When neurotransmitters remain in a synapse for a prolonged period of time, a neuron will respond by building fewer receptors for its membrane. This feedback mechanism enables a cell to adjust its number of receptors to match levels of a neurotransmitter.

This feedback mechanism is illustrated in **Figure 30-7**. In this figure, a drug that blocks the removal of neurotransmitter molecules is present in a synapse. As a result, large amounts of the neurotransmitter remain in the synapse for a long time. In response, the neuron produces fewer receptors, creating a less sensitive neuron.

This change in the number of receptors is one of the physiological changes that occur in chemical dependence. As long as the use of the same dosage of the drug continues, large amounts of neurotransmitter molecules remain in the synapse. But when the drug is absent, neurotransmitter molecules can again be removed, and the level of neurotransmitters in the synapse declines. However, the neuron now has too few receptors to receive information. In the absence of the drug, the neuron is unable to function normally until it restores its original number of receptors, which takes time. In drug-treatment programs, a drug is sometimes withdrawn slowly to allow the number of receptors to adjust gradually, thus minimizing withdrawal symptoms such as anxiety, depression, and strong cravings for the drug. As you can see, addiction is not simply a psychological state that can be overcome by willpower; addiction is a physiological dependency caused by a change in the number of receptors.

Neurotransmitter

Figure 30-7
a **In a normal synapse, neurotransmitters are rapidly reabsorbed.**

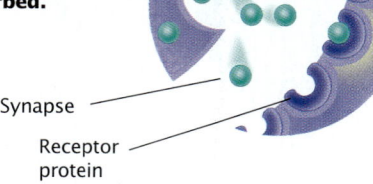
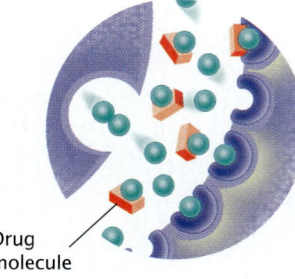

Synapse

Receptor protein

Drug molecule

b **When a drug blocks the removal of a neurotransmitter, receptors across the synapse are overstimulated by the excess neurotransmitters.**

c **The neuron responds by reducing the number of receptors.**

d **When the drug is removed, the excess supply of neurotransmitters dwindles. Now there are too few receptors in the synapse to receive the message.**

608

Multicultural Perspective: Dr. Emmeline Edwards

Dr. Emmeline Edwards, an African American who grew up in Haiti, studies the role that neurochemicals play in coping with stress. Information gained from her research can be applied toward the development of drugs for treating human depression. Dr. Edwards works at the department of psychiatry at the State University of New York in Stony Brook.

Psychoactive drugs affect neurons in a variety of ways

Most psychoactive drugs affect the nervous system by regulating activity at the synapse. For example, narcotics are powerful drugs derived from a species of poppy called *Papaver somniferum*. When this substance is prepared in the form of drugs such as opium, morphine, or heroin, it can be used to relieve pain or induce sleep. Narcotics function by imitating enkephalins, a natural pain reliever produced in your body. Enkephalins open potassium channels in spinal neurons, which blocks pain messages from traveling to the brain. Cocaine is another highly addictive psychoactive drug. It is extracted from the leaves of coca plants that grow in the mountains of South America. In the body, cocaine blocks the reabsorption of dopamine, a neurotransmitter that helps send pleasure messages to the brain. The dopamine trapped in the synapse continually stimulates neurons, producing an intense euphoria. Cocaine can also cause agitation, paranoia and severe depression. The mode of action of these and several other drugs are summarized in **Table 30-1**.

Table 30-1 Drug Actions and Effects

Drug	Mode of action	Effects
Nicotine (found in tobacco products such as cigarettes, chewing tobacco, and snuff)	Stimulants; mimic the effects of acetylcholine, a neurotransmitter that stimulates skeletal muscles	Contains highly mutagenic substances; highly addictive
Cocaine, crack (made from leaves of coca plants)	Stimulants; prevent reabsorption of dopamine, causing overstimulation of nerve pathways leading to regions of the brain that interpret pleasure	Highly addictive; can be fatal
Amphetamines, caffeine	Stimulants; stimulate the release of noradrenaline, a neurotransmitter that constricts blood vessels and elevates levels of blood glucose	Irregular heartbeat, high blood pressure, stomach disorders, exhaustion, violent behavior
Barbiturates, tranquilizers, phencyclidine hydrochloride (PCP)	Depressants; interact with GABA, a neurotransmitter that inhibits nerve impulses	Drowsiness, depression, emotional instability; especially dangerous when mixed with alcohol use
Narcotics (opium, morphine, heroin)	Mimic the effects of enkephalins, chemicals that act as natural pain relievers in your body	Extreme anxiety, tremors, drowsiness
Marijuana	At different dose levels it can produce sedative or hallucinatory effects.	Lung damage, loss of motivation, short-term memory loss
Hallucinogens	Inhibit the action of the neurotransmitter serotonin	Dangerous hallucinations, unpredictable behavior
Inhalants	Depressants; depress the central nervous system and tend to slow down the function of the brain and spinal cord	Hallucinations; permanent brain, kidney, and liver damage; can be fatal

609

The Nervous System   **609**

Connection: *Chapter 5*

Fermentation

Review how yeast and some other microorganisms, in the absence of oxygen, convert organic compounds such as glucose into ethyl alcohol. Ask students what glucose is converted to by human muscle cells in the absence of oxygen *(lactic acid)*.

Connection: *Chapter 3*

The Lipid Bilayer

Remind students that a double layer of phospholipids form a tough, yet flexible, lipid bilayer in the cell membrane.

Phase Three
Assessment Options

Closure

● Summarizing Information

Have students take turns lightly tapping each other's leg slightly below the knee. If possible, have them use a rubber-headed hammer borrowed from the school nurse or the anatomy and physiology class. Have students write a brief report summarizing their observation. Tell them that their report must include the following terms: dendrite, axon, neurotransmitter, synapse, resting potential, action potential, motor neuron, sensory neuron, spinal cord, acetylcholine, and nerve-muscle (neuromuscular) junction.

SECTION REVIEW

Assign the *Section Review*.

Reteaching

On the board or overhead, list the major concepts that were presented in Section 30-1. Have the class review pages 600–610 to identify examples that can be used to illustrate each of these concepts.

Alcohol changes the shape of receptors

Of all the psychoactive drugs, alcohol (ethanol) is one of the most widely used and abused. Alcohol is a product of fermentation; wine is made from fermented grapes, and beer from fermented grain. Both have been consumed for centuries.

Alcohol is known for its ability to reduce inhibitions and produce a sense of well-being. Unfortunately, consuming alcohol can alter both judgment and reaction time, a condition described as being "drunk." Every year, many high school students are killed in automobile accidents caused by drunken driving, making alcohol a dangerous drug in more ways than one.

Figure 30-8
This young woman, like many other Americans, is seeking help to overcome her addiction to alcohol.

Alcohol is an unusual psychoactive drug. Unlike narcotics and cocaine, it does not bind to receptors. Instead, research has shown that alcohol is able to alter the structure of the cell membrane, producing changes in the shapes of receptors. An altered receptor may become more sensitive to a stimulus or may be, in effect, switched off. As you can imagine, a change in a receptor can affect normal brain function in complicated ways. Alcohol also blocks nerves that repress the region of the brain responsible for feelings of pleasure and exhilaration.

Addiction to alcohol, or alcoholism, is the major drug-abuse problem in the United States. People who drink excessively over long periods of time can develop serious health problems. For example, many alcoholics suffer from a vitamin deficiency because they do not eat properly when drinking heavily. This can lead to malnutrition, abnormalities in the circulatory system, and inflammation of the stomach lining. In addition, alcohol is readily converted to energy, preventing the body from breaking down other nutrients, such as sugars, amino acids, and fatty acids. These nutrients are stored as fat in the liver. After years of drinking, liver cells become clogged with fat and die. If heavy drinking continues, a liver condition called cirrhosis may develop. In cirrhosis, liver cells are replaced with useless scar tissue, and the liver gradually shrinks into a small, hard mass, and can no longer function normally. Overcoming an addiction to alcohol can require physical, mental and emotional support, which a group such as the one seen in **Figure 30-8** can help to provide.

SECTION REVIEW

1 How does the structure of a neuron suit its function?

2 Devise a table that summarizes the events of a nerve impulse.

3 What role do neurotransmitters play in nerve-impulse transmission?

4 How do psychoactive drugs cause addiction?

ANSWERS TO SECTION REVIEW

1 Refer to Figures 30-1 and 30-2. The cell body with its dendrites is well suited for "collecting" information. The axon as an extension of the cell body serves to transmit messages over long distances.

2 The table should include in sequential order the events of a nerve impulse. Refer to the information on page 603 and the captions that accompany Figure 30-2 on page 603.

3 Neurotransmitters are chemical messengers that diffuse across the synapse and bind to receptors in the membrane of the cell on the other side, passing the signal to that cell.

4 Refer to the captions that accompany Figure 30-7 on page 608.

Signals from nerve cells enable you to play a piano, throw a baseball, write in your notebook, or just sit and think. A highly developed brain coordinates activities and enables you to learn, imagine, remember, and reason. The complex system that coordinates and controls body functions is the nervous system.

30-2   The Nervous System

OBJECTIVES

1 Describe the functions of the two main parts of the nervous system.

2 Discuss the functions of four parts of the brain.

3 Describe two types of technology used to study the brain.

4 Explain the roles of the peripheral nervous system.

Organization of the Human Nervous System

You can think of your nervous system as having two main parts. Your **central nervous system** consists of your brain and spinal cord. It is your control center, organizing all incoming and outgoing information. Your brain and spinal cord are connected to the rest of your body by nerves that make up the **peripheral nervous system**. The sensory neurons and the motor neurons that compose the peripheral nervous system act as independent communications pathways in that each monitors

a different part of the body. The organization of the human nervous system is summarized in **Figure 30-9**.

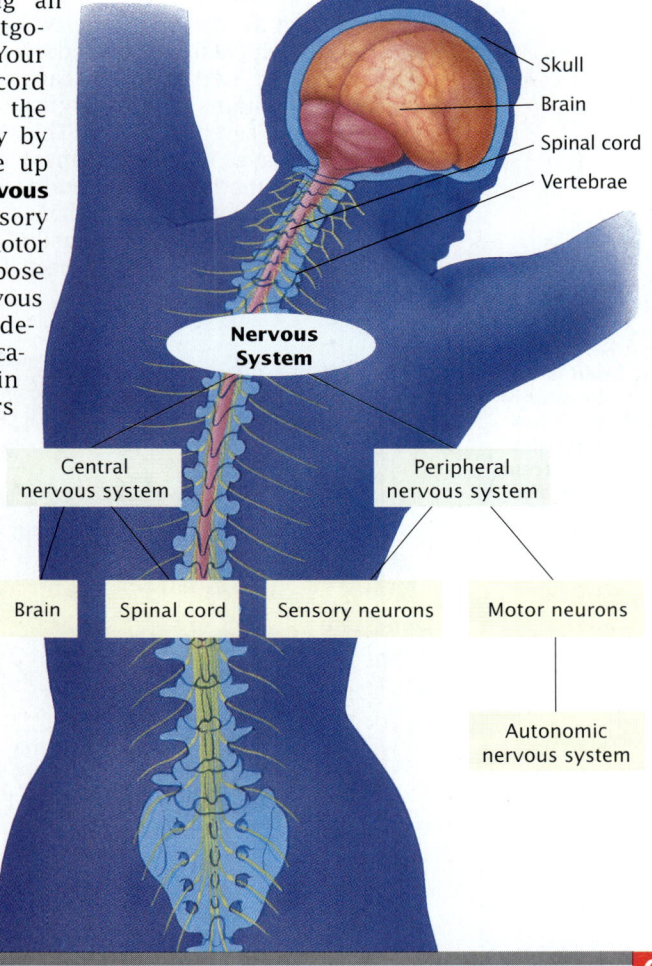

Nervous System

Central nervous system — Peripheral nervous system

Brain | Spinal cord | Sensory neurons | Motor neurons

Autonomic nervous system

Skull
Brain
Spinal cord
Vertebrae

Figure 30-9
The human nervous system can be organized into different categories based on functions. The fragile organs of the central nervous system are protected by the vertebrae and the skull.

Videodisc Resources

Holt Biology Videodiscs
Lesson 30-2: The Nervous System

Phase One
Preparation

Scheduling
See the **Lesson Planning Guide** on pages 599A and 599B for lecture, classwork, and assignment options for Section 30-2.

Phase Two
Teaching Strategies

Active **READING**

Technique: Reading Organizer
As students read about the central nervous system, have them complete the following reading organizer describing the main structures in the central nervous system. Other boxes in the organizer should include information from the captions that accompany Figure 30-10 on page 612.

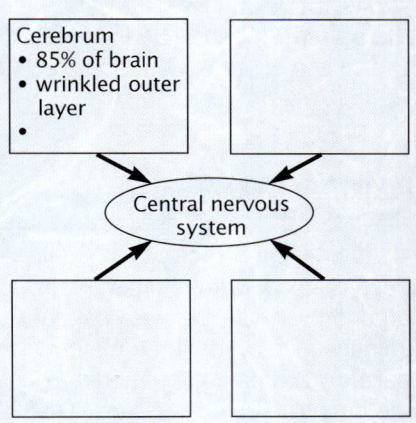

Cerebrum
• 85% of brain
• wrinkled outer layer
•

Central nervous system

Key to Strategies
● Understanding Concepts (Tier I)
■ Applying Information (Tier II)
▲ Critical Thinking (Tier III)

The Central Nervous System

At any given time of the day, your brain and spinal cord are being bombarded with information from sensory organs and receptors located throughout your body. After sorting this vast amount of information, they issue commands to your muscles, glands, and organs. Here is a brief look at some important structures found in the central nervous system.

The cerebrum is the control center of the brain

In the average adult, the brain is one of the largest organs of the body, weighing about 1,500 g (approximately 3 lb). About 85 percent of the weight of the brain is made up of the **cerebrum** *(suh REE bruhm)*, the familiar, wrinkled outer layer shown in **Figure 30-10a**. The cerebrum is divided into two hemispheres, which are connected by a large band of nerve fibers. Each hemisphere contains an outer gray layer called the cerebral cortex. This 2–4 mm thick layer handles the most sophisticated functions of the brain, from processing visual images to thinking and planning. Because it is easily accessible, the cerebral cortex has been extensively studied, and some parts have been mapped in great detail. Underlying the cerebral cortex is a region of white matter that relays information to the cortex.

The cerebellum coordinates muscle movements

Tucked beneath the rear of the cerebrum is the cauliflower-shaped structure called the **cerebellum** *(sehr uh BEHL uhm)*, shown in **Figure 30-10c**. The cerebellum is essential for coordination of movement. Damage to the cerebellum causes uncoordination and tremors. During the course of vertebrate evolution, the cerebellum has increased in size and complexity in many animals. While well developed in mammals, it is even more developed in birds. Birds maneuver through the air, which requires complicated feats of balance that most mammals never have to face. Imagine the coordination, balance, and control needed to land on a branch or fence post at precisely the right moment. You can learn more about the differences among vertebrate brains in the *Evolution of the Brain* on pages 616 and 617.

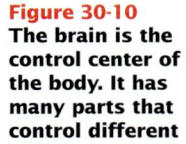

Figure 30-10
The brain is the control center of the body. It has many parts that control different body functions.

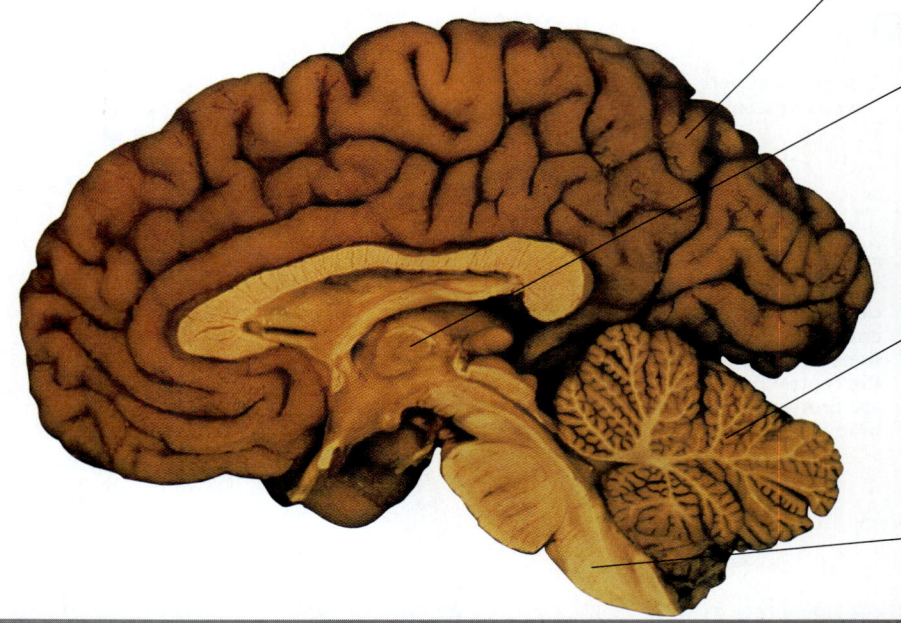

The brain stem controls essential body processes

Underneath the cerebrum lies the brain stem, a stalklike structure buried deep in the brain. The brain stem, shown in **Figure 30-10d**, contains nerves that control vital life processes such as breathing, swallowing, and digestion as well as heart rate and blood pressure. Many nerves that control muscles in the body cross in the brain stem. Thus, damage to one side of the brain above the crossover causes weakness or paralysis on the opposite side of the body.

An extremely important network of nerves called the reticular formation also runs through the brain stem. The reticular formation is the brain's arousal system; it activates other parts of the brain with appropriate information. Consisting of nerves running to and from the brain, the reticular formation "listens to" the messages entering and leaving. It then selects which messages to enhance and which to suppress. In a very real way, it "decides" what you will be aware of. Your reticular formation enables you to sleep through repetitive noises such as traffic yet awaken when an alarm clock rings.

The brain stem also contains the **hypothalamus**, shown in **Figure 30-10b**, the body's center for emotions and instincts. Scientists have identified areas in the hypothalamus that control hunger, thirst, body temperature, water balance, and blood pressure as well as sexual desire, pleasure, hostility, and pain.

The spinal cord shuttles information between the body and brain

Messages from the body and brain run up and down the spinal cord. The spinal cord is a cable of nerve tissue that extends from the brain stem. Like the brain, the spinal cord contains gray matter, which forms a column down the center of the cord. A layer of white matter surrounds the column. The spinal cord is surrounded and protected by the backbone, a tunnel of bone formed by the rings of the vertebrae. Injuries to the spinal cord can result in pain, numbness, or paralysis in limbs and extremities.

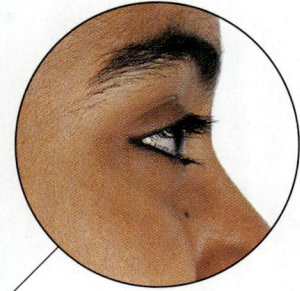

a The cerebrum is the center of intellect, memory, language, and consciousness. It receives information from this girl's eye and translates it into a meaningful image.

b The hypothalamus controls your body's homeostasis, maintaining functions such as body temperature and water balance. It also regulates hunger and thirst and tells this girl it is time to eat lunch.

c The cerebellum is responsible for smooth, coordinated body movements. It helps this gymnast maintain posture, muscle tone, and equilibrium.

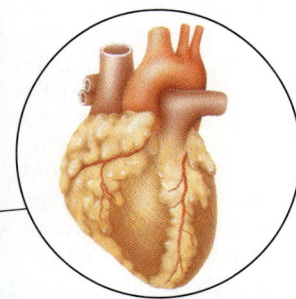

d The brain stem regulates vital body processes that you do not consciously control, such as heartbeat, respiration, and blood pressure.

613

Connection: *Chapter 12*

Early Hominids

Dispel any misconception that modern *Homo sapiens* have the largest brain of any human in history. Remind students that Neanderthals had larger brains than those of some modern humans. Obviously, brain size is not related to intelligence. The brain of modern humans is much more convoluted than that of the extinct Neanderthals, suggesting that the number of convolutions might be related to intelligence. The relative size of the brain in relation to the rest of the body may be a better indicator of intelligence. Whales and porpoises have brains larger than those of humans. When differences in body size are factored out, humans have the largest brains in relation to the rest of the body.

Health Connection

Meningitis

Remind students that the brain is encased in the skull. In addition, the brain is covered by tough protective membranes known as meninges. Inflammation of these meninges, brought about by bacteria or viruses, is known as meningitis and can be fatal if not treated.

Health Connection

"Brain Dead"

When no electrical activity in the brain—especially in the region of the brain stem—can be registered, a person is declared "brain dead." In such cases, the vital body processes controlled unconsciously by the brain stem must be sustained by a life-support system. Students might be interested in researching the legal definition of death in the different states and countries. Each student could be assigned one state, for example.

Key to Strategies
- ● Understanding Concepts (Tier I)
- ■ Applying Information (Tier II)
- ▲ Critical Thinking (Tier III)

The Nervous System   613

Demonstration

● **Categorize and Compare**

Provide each student with a photograph or drawing of a scene filled with detailed information. Have them study the graphic closely for several minutes, put it aside, and immediately list as many details as they can recall from memory. Without letting them see the graphic again, ask them several days later to prepare another list. Have each student compare the two lists to contrast the amount of information stored in short-term and long-term memories.

Health Connection

Psychosomatic Illnesses

Medical scientists think psychosomatic illnesses may be mediated by the hypothalamus because of its connections to the autonomic nervous system and its control of emotions. Many stress-related illnesses, such as ulcers, asthma, and high blood pressure, are clearly connected to hypothalamic functions.

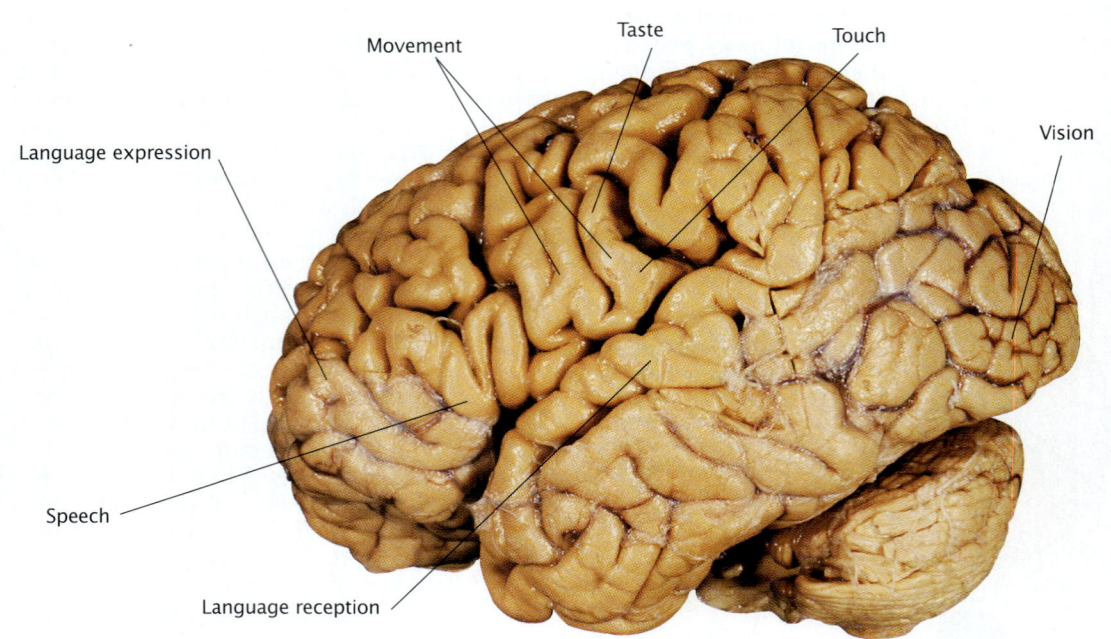

Figure 30-11
Advances in technologies are giving scientists new information about the exact position of many sites controlling the brain's processing.

Mapping the Brain

For centuries, people have been intrigued by the mysteries of the brain. In recent years science has taken great strides toward unraveling its secrets. Advances in technologies are now giving scientists the opportunity to probe deeply into the living tissues of the brain and to construct a blueprint of its functions, such as the map shown in **Figure 30-11**.

Learning and memory are related brain functions

Learning and memory are brain functions that are especially well developed in humans. Learning occurs when two or more pieces of information are linked into a pattern of connections between neurons. The repeated stimulation of this pattern of neurons results in memory. Almost every memory you have is made of different patterns of connections. Many overlapping patterns are stored together, so a single stimulus can cause a flood of memories, which you may have noticed if you've ever caught yourself "daydreaming."

Memory lasts for different lengths of time. When you take notes in class, you often remember what you hear only long enough to write it down. This is short-term memory, which can last from a few seconds to a few hours. You use your short-term memory for things like remembering to run an errand or cramming for a test. If information is stored for any length of time, it is transferred to long-term memory. Here it may remain for life.

Language is processed in the left hemisphere

Although scientists have learned a lot about language processing in the brain, much remains a mystery. Research has indicated that the human brain is already wired at birth with the nerve pathways necessary for language. Language processing is very complex, involving several regions in the left hemisphere. People with brain damage display a variety of unusual language problems. Some have trouble using and understanding nouns, while others have the same difficulties with verbs. Some can understand language but are unable to produce it. Still others can produce language but cannot understand what they hear.

How scientists study the brain

Scientists and researchers are able to study the brain by using technology that has become increasingly sophisticated over the years. The invention of the computerized axial tomography (CAT) in the early 1960s marked an important era in brain research. When undergoing a CAT scan, a patient is placed on a table that slides into a large tube. Inside the tube, a weak X-ray beam rotates around a person's head. Electronic sensors pick up the emerging rays and feed them into a computer, where they are integrated into a single image. This image can be viewed on a video screen and photographed. CAT scans are used to locate brain tumors, blood clots, and areas of cerebral damage.

Other new technologies used to study the brain and other organs have yielded diagnostic and investigative advances. In magnetic resonance imaging (MRI), a patient is placed in an intense magnetic field that stimulates the protons in the brain to resonate or vibrate and emit radio frequency pulses. This information is transformed into images such as the one shown in **Figure 30-12a**. These images reveal different tissue characteristics of the brain.

Positron emission tomography (PET) reveals tissue structure as well as biochemical activity in the brain. In a PET scan, a patient is injected with glucose (the main energy source for brain activity) that has been prepared with radioactive labels. The labels emit radioactive particles called positrons, which are detected by the PET scanner. Computer processing produces colored images, as shown in **Figure 30-12b**, that indicate a region of activity in the brain. PET scans can be used to diagnose brain tumors and strokes as well as mental illnesses such as Alzheimer's disease and schizophrenia. It is also being used to study how the brain processes language and the ways it constructs images from both memory and imagination.

All of these techniques have advantages and disadvantages, depending on which region and activity of the brain is being studied. Such noninvasive methods for studying the living brain has enabled researchers to probe the brain in ways never before possible.

Figure 30-12

a Magnetic resonance imaging (MRI) creates images of brain anatomy and can image the entire body in as little as 18 seconds.

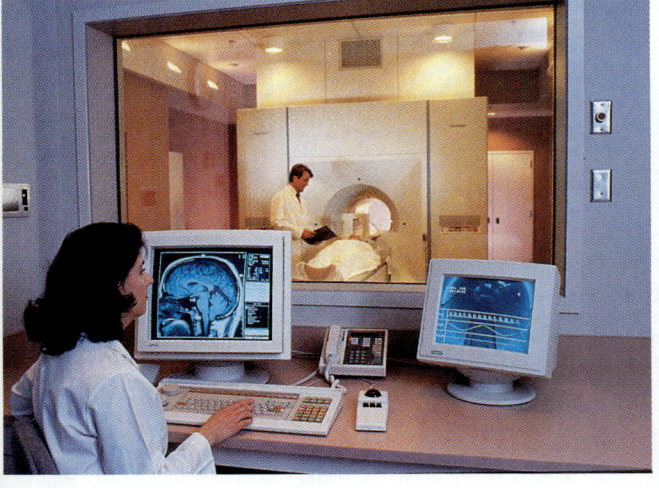

b Computer processing produces colored images such as this brain scan, which enable us to learn more than ever before. For example, this brain scan reveals the presence of a tumor, shown here in red.

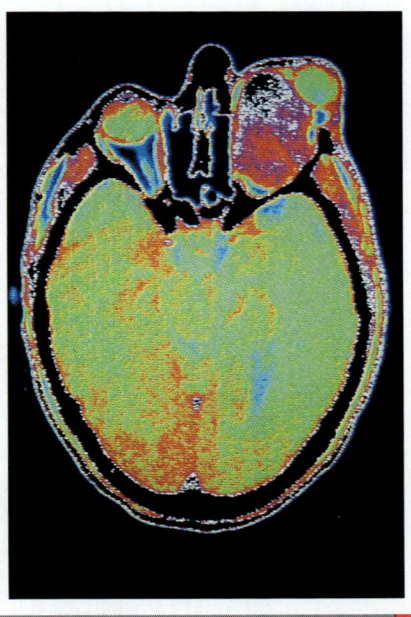

Biotechnology Connection

Medical Technology

Have students prepare reports on different medical procedures such as computerized axial tomography, magnetic resonance imaging, and positron emission tomography. They should describe how the procedure works and what disease or syndrome the procedure can help diagnose. Have students compile a list of the different -ologies in medicine and tell what each discipline entails. *(For example: cardiology—the study of the heart; gastroenterology—the study of the digestive system; or endocrinology—the study of the endocrine system.)*

Visual Strategy | Videodisc

■ **Recognizing Relationships**
Use *Illustration—Sensory Homunculus* shown in Chapter 30 Section 30-2 of **Holt Biology Videodiscs Teacher's Correlation Guide to Holt Biology: Visualizing Life.** Before showing the illustration, ask students if they think the brain pays equal attention to all the stimuli it receives. Then show the illustration and explain that it consists of two images. The image on the right shows a cross section of the sensory area of the cerebral cortex, indicating which area of the cortex receives input from which body part. The left image shows a human figure proportioned according to the amount of cerebral cortex that is devoted to sensory input from each body part. Point out the exaggerated size of the head, hands, and feet. Ask students to suggest why a large part of the cerebral cortex is concerned with these areas. *(Students might suggest that these areas have the most sensory neurons and receive the most information.)*

Key to Strategies
● **Understanding Concepts (Tier I)**
■ **Applying Information (Tier II)**
▲ **Critical Thinking (Tier III)**

615

The Nervous System 615

Evolutionary Journey

Brain Size and Body Mass

■ Relating Concepts

The human brain is not the largest in absolute size; whales and elephants have bigger brains. But humans do have the largest brains per kilogram of body mass. Our large, complex brains exemplify three trends in the evolution of the brain. The first trend is toward increased size, especially among birds and mammals. A 1 kg (2.2 lb) mammal will have a much larger brain than a 1 kg (2.2 lb) fish or reptile. The second trend is toward increasing specialization of brain regions. The third trend is toward increasing size and complexity of the cerebrum. This trend is most apparent in humans, in which the cerebrum accounts for 85 percent of the brain's mass.

Brain Size and Intelligence

■ Recognizing Relationships

Differences in brain size obviously account for some of the differences in intelligence between species. Large-brained chimpanzees can use tools, while pea-size-brained mice cannot. But do brain size differences explain differences in intelligence between members of the same species? Did Einstein, Shakespeare, and Darwin have exceptionally large brains? Have students research the debate over the connection between brain size and intelligence.

The Brain

Every vertebrate brain has a forebrain, a midbrain, and a hindbrain. As land vertebrates have evolved, the forebrain has become increasingly dominant.

● Cerebrum   ● Midbrain   ● Hindbrain

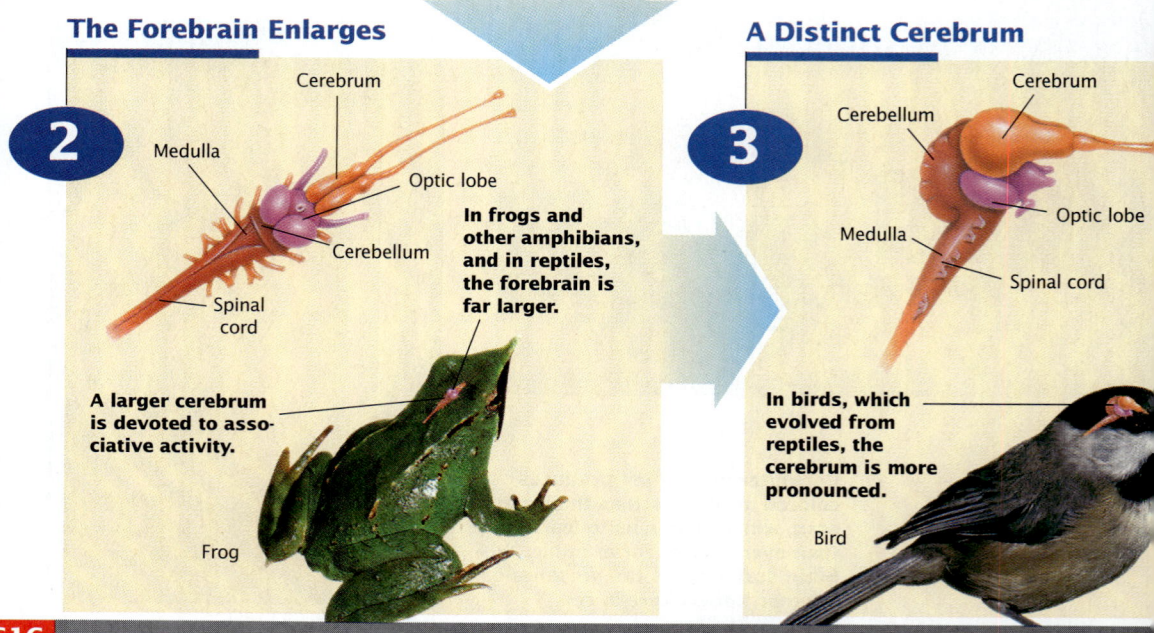

A Dominant Hindbrain

1 In sharks and other fishes, the principal part of the brain is the hindbrain, which is devoted largely to coordinating motor reflexes.

The rest of the brain serves mainly to process sensory information.

Cerebrum · Optic lobe · Cerebellum · Spinal cord · Medulla · Shark

The Forebrain Enlarges

2 In frogs and other amphibians, and in reptiles, the forebrain is far larger.

A larger cerebrum is devoted to associative activity.

Cerebrum · Medulla · Optic lobe · Cerebellum · Spinal cord · Frog

A Distinct Cerebrum

3 In birds, which evolved from reptiles, the cerebrum is more pronounced.

Cerebrum · Cerebellum · Optic lobe · Medulla · Spinal cord · Bird

Evolutionary Journey

A Powerful Cerebrum

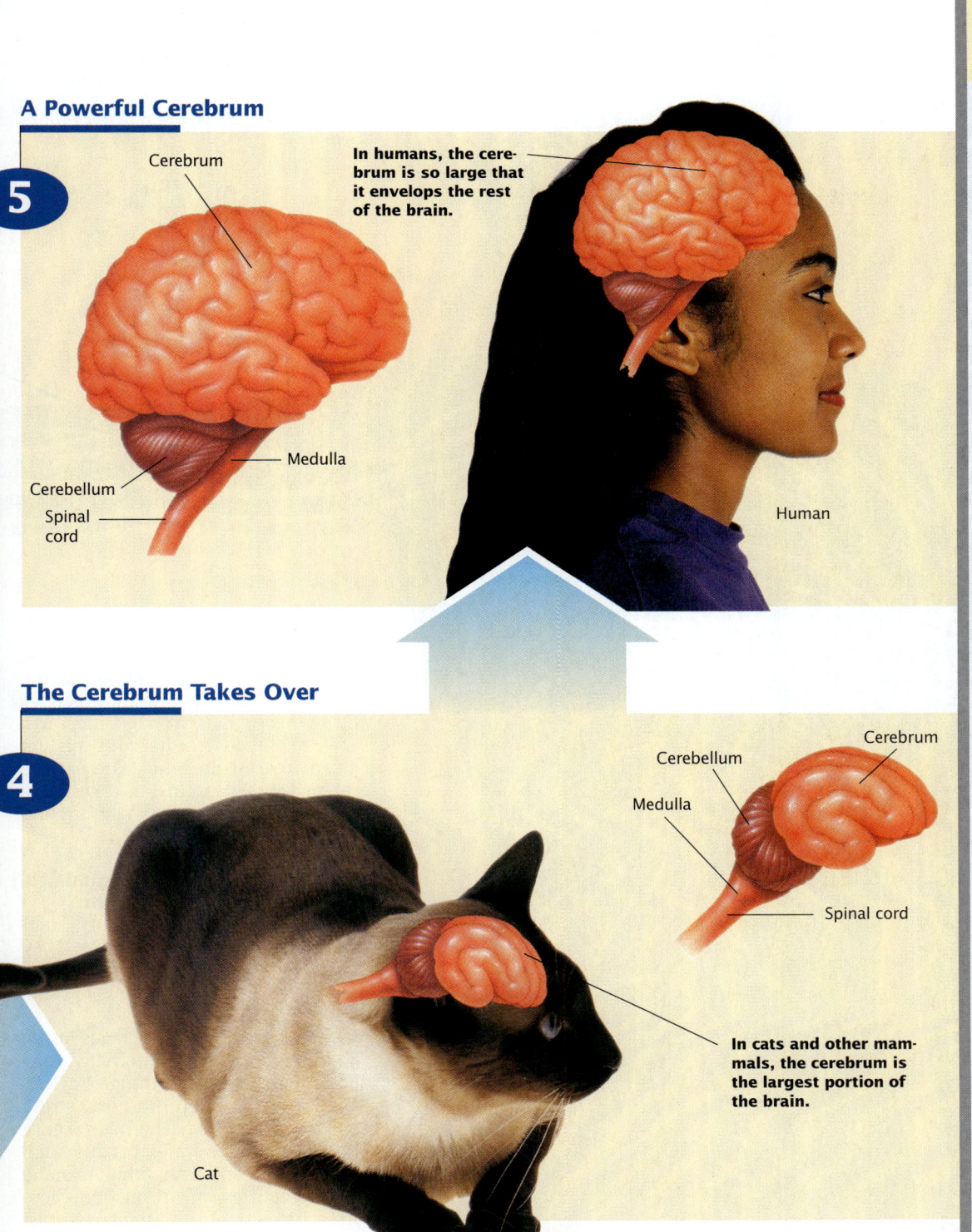

5

Cerebrum

In humans, the cerebrum is so large that it envelops the rest of the brain.

Medulla

Cerebellum

Spinal cord

Human

The Cerebrum Takes Over

4

Cerebrum

Cerebellum

Medulla

Spinal cord

In cats and other mammals, the cerebrum is the largest portion of the brain.

Cat

Brain Functional Regions

● **Identifying Function**

Identify the functions of the cerebrum and cerebellum. *(The cerebrum's functions are interpreting sensory data, learning, association, and—in humans—language, memory, and conscious thought. The cerebellum coordinates movement.)*

Birds have a large, complex cerebellum. Explain why. *(The cerebellum must be complex to organize the complicated motions of flight.)*

Sensory Region Size

■ **Recognizing Relationships**

In a shrew's brain, the olfactory region of the brain is very large—about the size of the rest of the brain. What does this indicate about the importance of the sense of smell to the shrew? *(The size of a brain region devoted to a particular sense indicates the importance of that sense to the animal. For a shrew, smell is the most important sense.)*

How would the size of the olfactory region of the human brain compare with the size of the visual region? *(For humans, sight is much more important than smell; thus, the visual region is much larger.)*

● **Identifying Structures**

Use this figure to have students trace the path that an impulse takes along a sensory neuron to the spinal cord, and from the spinal cord out to a motor neuron. Emphasize that most nerves, like the ones shown in this figure, contain both sensory and motor neurons running side by side. Students should not develop the misconception that the two types of neurons must be structurally separate.

■ **Predicting Outcomes**

To illustrate the different types of receptors in the skin, use *Illustration—Skin Receptors* shown in Chapter 30 Section 30-2 of **Holt Biology Videodiscs Teacher's Correlation Guide to Holt Biology: Visualizing Life.** Have students identify the different kinds of receptors in the illustration and note the difference in the structure of each. Then ask students to choose one kind of receptor and write a few short paragraphs telling what their life would be like if their skin did not contain that kind of receptor.

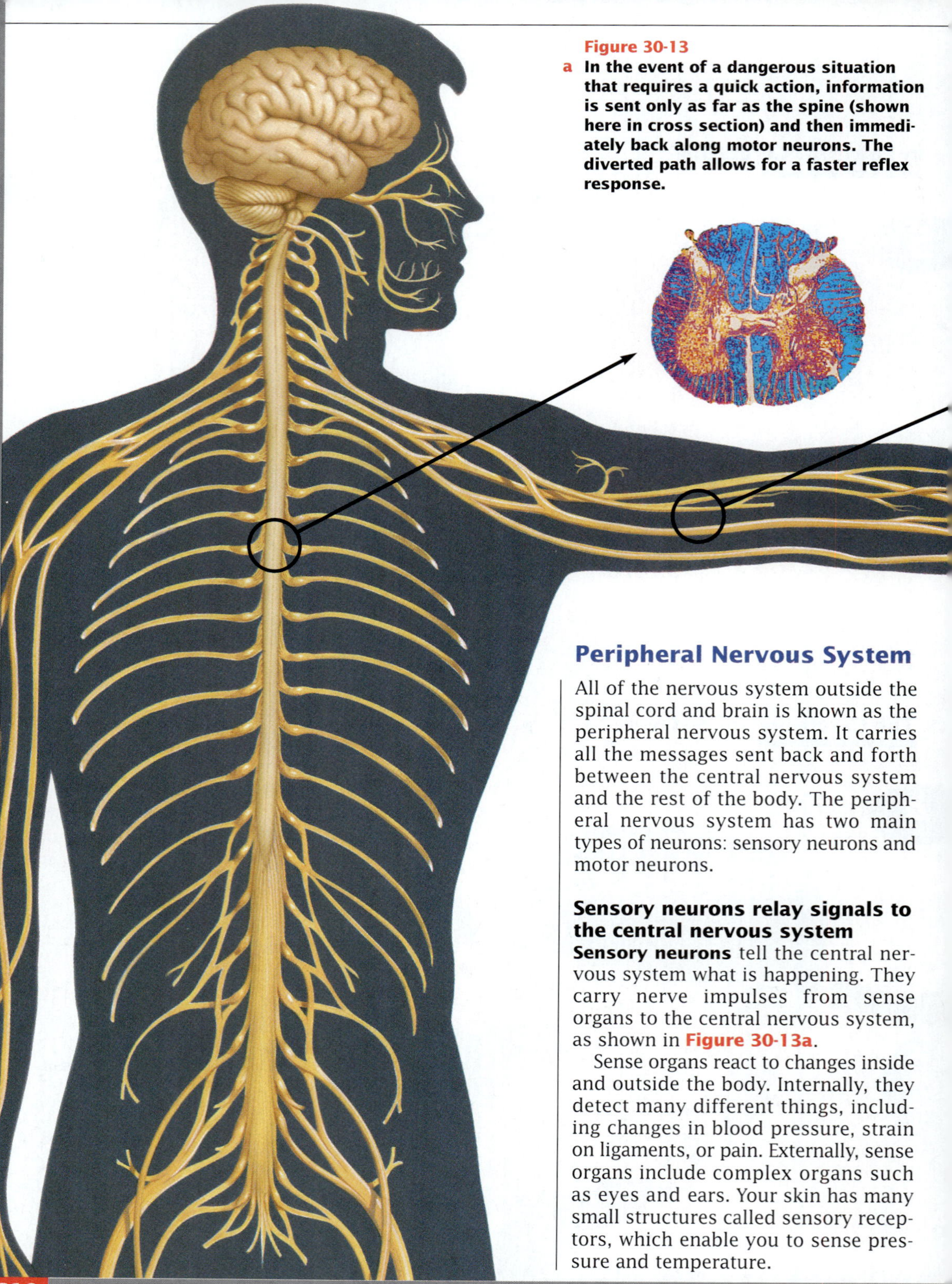

Figure 30-13

a In the event of a dangerous situation that requires a quick action, information is sent only as far as the spine (shown here in cross section) and then immediately back along motor neurons. The diverted path allows for a faster reflex response.

Peripheral Nervous System

All of the nervous system outside the spinal cord and brain is known as the peripheral nervous system. It carries all the messages sent back and forth between the central nervous system and the rest of the body. The peripheral nervous system has two main types of neurons: sensory neurons and motor neurons.

Sensory neurons relay signals to the central nervous system

Sensory neurons tell the central nervous system what is happening. They carry nerve impulses from sense organs to the central nervous system, as shown in **Figure 30-13a**.

Sense organs react to changes inside and outside the body. Internally, they detect many different things, including changes in blood pressure, strain on ligaments, or pain. Externally, sense organs include complex organs such as eyes and ears. Your skin has many small structures called sensory receptors, which enable you to sense pressure and temperature.

Multicultural Perspective: Acupuncture

Acupuncture, a traditional way of treating pain and disease, originated in China but has been used by the Japanese, Koreans, and Vietnamese. In acupuncture, needles are inserted into various parts of the body. Chinese philosophers believe that an imbalance occurs between yin and yang, causing pain and disease. Some believe that acupuncture works because needles inserted along certain lines of the body connect the body's organs in a certain way and influence organ functions. Others believe that acupuncture works by increasing the brain's production of natural painkillers, endorphins. Some believe that acupuncture works through the nervous system by triggering signals that interrupt pain messages sent to the brain.

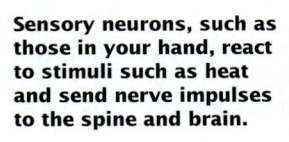

b After the brain has received this information, it sends a signal back to the motor neurons, telling them to react in a particular way.

c Sensory neurons, such as those in your hand, react to stimuli such as heat and send nerve impulses to the spine and brain.

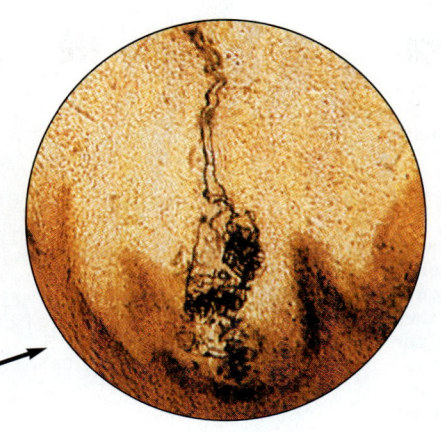

Visual Strategy   Figure 30-13

● **Identifying Functions**
Use this figure to have students trace the path an impulse takes in a reflex. Point out that although the brain is not involved in bringing about the response, it is involved in interpreting the stimulus. For example, the brain does not send a signal for the person to remove his or her hand from a hot radiator, but it does make the person aware of the subsequent pain.

Peripheral Nervous System Neurons

● **Comparing Functions**
Have students create a Graphic Organizer similar to the one at the bottom of this page to demonstrate the difference between the two types of neurons in the peripheral nervous system.

Demonstration

■ **Relating Concepts**
Without warning, produce a loud noise in class. Have students explain how a reflex was responsible for their reactions.

Motor neurons deliver information to muscles and glands

Motor neurons are partners of sensory neurons. Motor neurons carry information from the central nervous system to a muscle or gland, as shown in **Figure 30-13**. They act on the information delivered by the sensory neurons. If your eyes see a runaway truck speeding toward you, the central nervous system sends messages through motor neurons to glands that secrete adrenaline. The adrenaline increases your heartbeat and breathing rate. The central nervous system also sends messages through motor neurons to many muscles, which contract and get the body out of there—fast!

In each segment of the spine, sensory nerves go into the cord and motor nerves come out of it. The motor nerves control most of the muscles below the head. This is why injuries to the spinal cord often paralyze the lower part of the body. A muscle is paralyzed and cannot move if its motor neurons are damaged.

Reflexes enable you to act quickly

All animals have the ability to act particularly quickly at times of danger. These sudden, involuntary movements are reflexes. A **reflex** produces a rapid motor response to a stimulus because the sensory neuron synapses directly with a motor neuron. The escape reaction of a cockroach is a reflex. A good example in humans is a reflex that protects the eye. If anything, such as an insect or a cloud of dust, approaches the eye, the eyelid blinks closed even before we realize what has happened. The reflex occurs before the cerebrum is aware that the eye is in danger.

Reflexes involve few neurons and are therefore very fast. Many reflexes never reach the brain. The nerve impulse travels only as far as the spinal cord, as indicated in **Figure 30-13**. If you step on something sharp, your leg jerks away from the danger. The prick causes nerve impulses in sensory neurons. These neurons synapse in the spinal cord with motor neurons that cause the leg to pull away.

619

Graphic Organizer

Use the following graphic organizer with the teaching strategy **Peripheral Nervous System Neurons** on page 619.

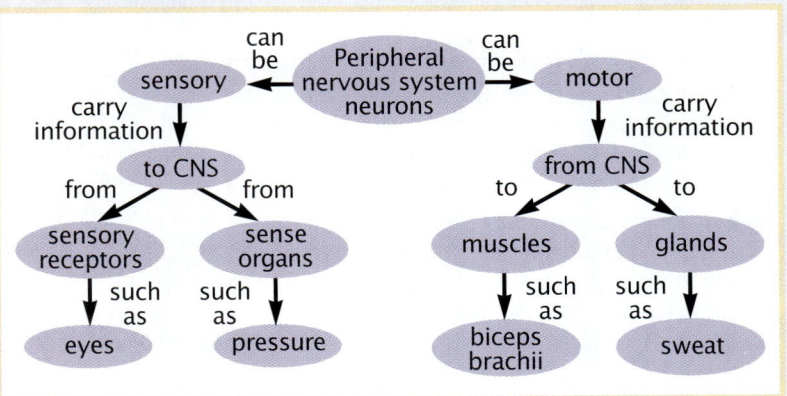

Key to Strategies
● **Understanding Concepts (Tier I)**
■ **Applying Information (Tier II)**
▲ **Critical Thinking (Tier III)**

The Nervous System   **619**

Demonstration

● Comparing Functions

Show the class a photograph of an automobile. Discuss how the car accelerates and slows down. Have students compare these actions to the workings of the autonomic nervous system—one division acts as the accelerator, and the other acts as the brake. Underscore the efficiency of such an arrangement by pointing out that although a car can slow down without a brake, the consequences might be disastrous.

Visual Strategy   Figure 30-14

■ Predicting Outcomes

Have students describe what the electrocardiogram shown in this figure might look like if the person were awake and active. *(Student answers will vary. Examples include more waveforms per second or taller waveforms.)*

Phase Three
Assessment Options

Closure

● Organizing Information

Assign students to cooperative groups of four. Have each group develop a plan that would help transfer the information in this section from short-term to long-term memory.

SECTION REVIEW

Assign the *Section Review.*

Reteaching

Present a case in which a person suffers a stroke resulting in brain damage to the right portion of the cerebrum. Have students discuss how this person might be affected. *(Sensations from the left side of the body and motor activity on the left side of the body would be affected.)*

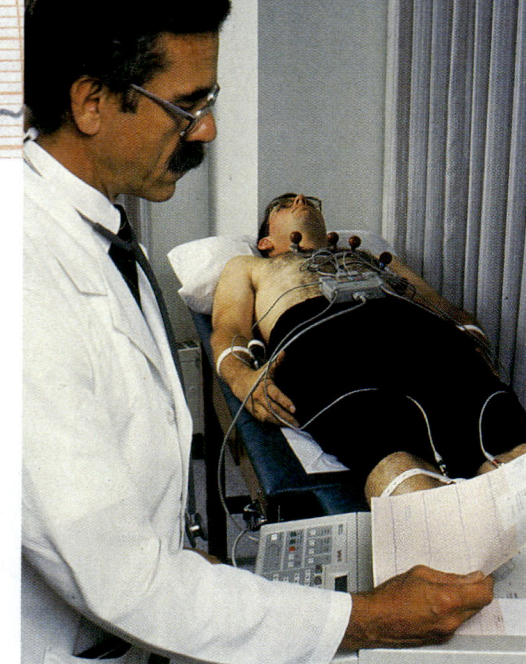

Figure 30-14
a This man may appear inactive, but his brain is busy maintaining his vital body functions.

b The beating of his heart, recorded on an electrocardiogram, is controlled by the autonomic nervous system, which is still active even when you are asleep.

The autonomic nervous system controls internal organs

Some motor neurons are active all the time, even when the body is asleep. These neurons carry messages from the central nervous system that keep the body going even when it is not active. These are the neurons of the **autonomic nervous system**. The autonomic nervous system carries messages to muscles and glands that usually work without our notice. For example, these muscles and glands control the blood pressure and the movement of food through the digestive system even during sleep, as shown in **Figure 30-14**.

The autonomic nervous system enables the central nervous system to govern most of the body's homeostasis. It helps regulate heartbeat and helps control muscle contraction in the walls of the blood vessels and in the digestive, urinary, and reproductive tracts. It also helps stimulate glands to secrete tears, mucus, and digestive enzymes.

One division of the autonomic nervous system dominates in times of stress. It controls the "fight-or-flight" reaction, increasing blood pressure, heart rate, breathing rate, and blood flow to the muscles. Another division of the autonomic nervous system has the opposite effect. It conserves energy by slowing the heartbeat and breathing rate and by promoting digestion and elimination.

Although the autonomic nervous system can carry out its tasks automatically, it is not completely independent of voluntary control. For instance, breathing is controlled by the autonomic nervous system, but one can decide to stop breathing for a short time. However, any voluntary control of the autonomic nervous system that endangers life disturbs homeostasis of the brain tissue, causing unconsciousness. The autonomic nervous system then takes over again and restores normal functions. This is why you cannot hold your breath indefinitely.

SECTION REVIEW

1 What are the functions of the two main parts of the nervous system?

2 Draw a sketch of a human brain and label four main parts. Explain the major functions of each part.

3 How is technology enabling scientists to learn more about the brain?

4 Compare two different roles of the peripheral nervous system.

620

ANSWERS TO SECTION REVIEW

1 The central nervous system is the control center. The peripheral nervous system carries messages back and forth between the central nervous system and the body.

2 Students should use Figure 30-10 on page 612 as a model for their drawings and should use the captions that accompany the figure to explain the major functions of each part.

3 New technologies enable scientists to study brain structure and function in noninvasive ways.

4 Sensory neurons deliver information to the CNS, and the motor neurons carry information to act upon muscles and glands away from the CNS.

Vivid reports about your environment stream into your brain through your eyes, ears, skin, nose, and mouth. The fact is, there are more than a dozen different types of sensory cells that detect changes outside and inside your body. Together, they help you interact with the world that surrounds you.

30-3 The Sense Organs

OBJECTIVES

1 Describe four different receptors that are found throughout your body.

2 Explain two functions of the inner ear.

3 Explain how humans perceive vision.

4 Explain how taste and smell are sensed.

Sensory Receptors

All information about your surrounding environment and the conditions within your body enters your brain through specialized cells called sensory receptors. There are many different kinds of sensory receptors in your body. There are receptors that detect and respond to internal changes, such as when your skin feels temperature changes or pain. Sensory receptors in your blood vessels respond to changes in blood pressure. Sensory receptors in your muscles are responsible for reflexes such as the knee jerk. **Table 30-2** lists several kinds of sensory receptors that your body uses to keep its internal environment constant. To provide information about the external environment, you also have sensory receptors associated with specialized cells and tissues. These form **sensory organs** such as your ears, eyes, nose, and tongue. The sensory receptors in your ears and eyes respond to sound and light to provide you with hearing and vision. The sensory receptors in your tongue and nose respond to particular types of molecules to produce the sensations of smell and taste.

Table 30-2 Sensory Receptors

Respond to internal stimuli	Stimulus	Location	Process
Heat receptor and cold receptor	Temperature changes	Skin and hypothalamus	Changes in temperature alter activity of ion channels
Nociceptor	Pain	In all tissues and organs except brain	Changes in temperature and pressure open membrane channels
Mechanoreceptor	Pressure	Skin surface	Changes in pressure deform membrane
Stretch receptor	Pressure; muscle contractions	Wrapped around muscle fibers	Motion of muscle fibers changes membrane
Respond to external stimuli			
Specialized structures of inner ear	Position and motion; sound	Inner ear	Cilia on cell membranes respond
Taste bud cell	Dissolved chemicals	Tongue	Bind to specific receptors in cell membranes
Olfactory neuron	Scents	Nasal passages	Bind to specific receptors in cell membranes
Rod and cone cell	Light	Retina of eye	Initiates process of focusing and visual processing

621

Videodisc Resources

Holt Biology Videodiscs
Lesson 30-3: The Sense Organs

30-3

Phase One
Preparation

Scheduling
See the **Lesson Planning Guide** on pages 599A and 599B for lecture, classwork, and assignment options for Section 30-3.

Phase Two
Teaching Strategies

Demonstration
■ **Analyzing Information**
Darken the room. Have students close their eyes while gently tapping or pressing a fingertip against the corner of their eyes. Ask which part of their brain "saw stars." Point out to students that they are not really "seeing" anything. Ask what this phenomenon tells them about the sense of sight. *(The eyes receive information that is sent via nerve impulses to the brain, which analyzes and interprets it.)*

Key to Strategies
● Understanding Concepts (Tier I)
■ Applying Information (Tier II)
▲ Critical Thinking (Tier III)

The Nervous System   621

Receptors in the Ear

Your ear is really two sense organs in one. It not only detects sound waves but also establishes equilibrium—your sense of position.

The receptor cells that establish equilibrium are located in the fluid-filled semicircular canals and chambers in your inner ear, shown in **Figure 30-15**. Each canal and chamber contains a bed of receptor cells. Each receptor cell has a protruding bundle of hairs. The hairs are covered with a jellylike layer, shown in **Figure 30-15c**, that contains tiny embedded mineral crystals. This layer has the ability to move over the bed of receptor cells. When you change the position of your head or your speed of motion, like the girl in **Figure 30-15a**, the jellylike layer, along with the minerals, slides over the hairs and bends them. This sends signals to the brain, which enables you to determine and adjust, if necessary, your position in space.

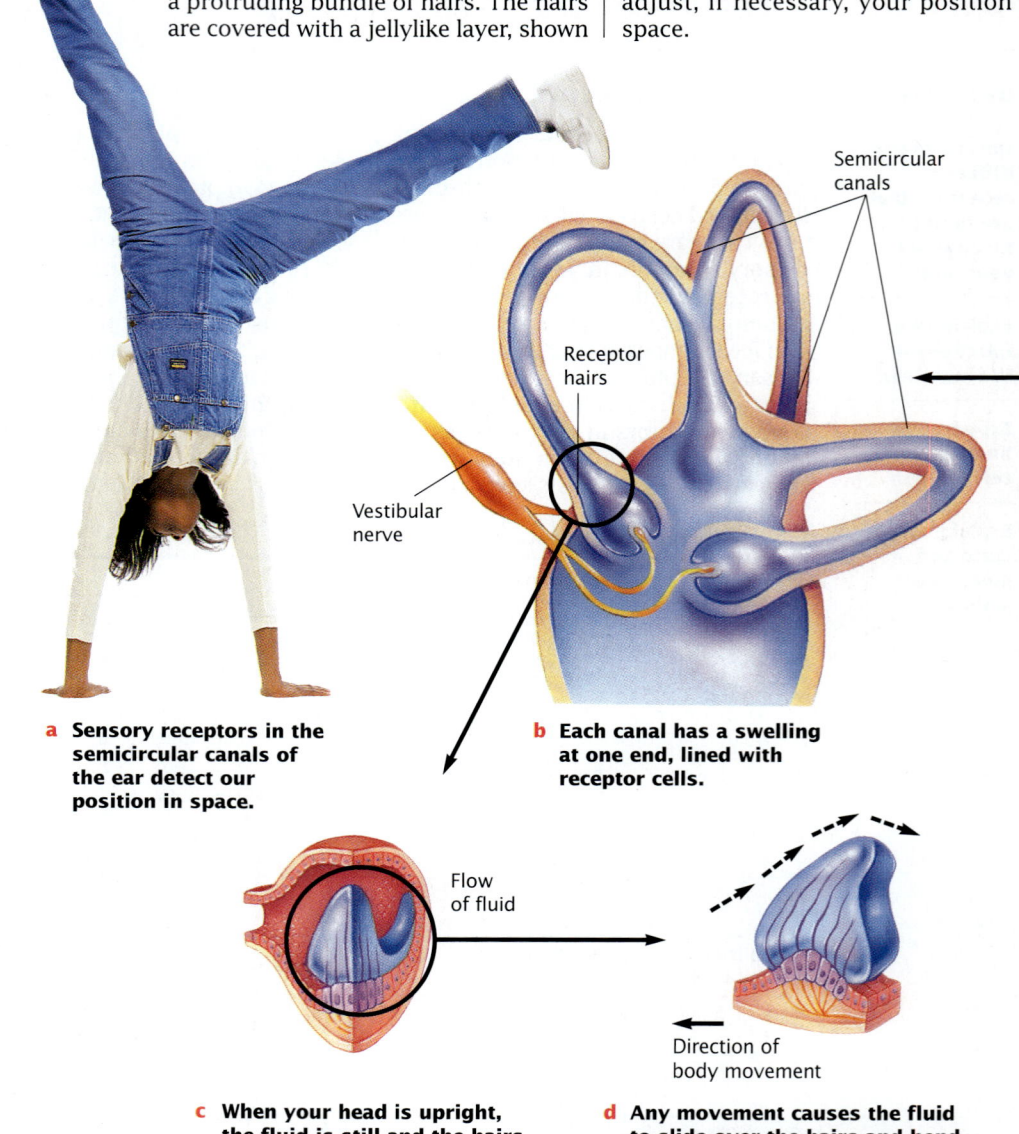

Semicircular canals

Receptor hairs

Vestibular nerve

a Sensory receptors in the semicircular canals of the ear detect our position in space.

b Each canal has a swelling at one end, lined with receptor cells.

Flow of fluid

c When your head is upright, the fluid is still and the hairs are straight.

Direction of body movement

d Any movement causes the fluid to slide over the hairs and bend them in the opposite direction.

The inner ear also senses sound waves

Look again at the structure of the inner ear in **Figure 30-15**. The cuplike outer ear helps capture sound waves in the air and funnel them into the ear canal. The waves strike the eardrum, causing it to vibrate. These vibrations pass through three small bones that stretch across a cavity inside the ear. One of these bones presses against a snail-shaped structure called the cochlea, shown in **Figure 30-15g**. The cochlea is the organ of hearing. It contains fluid-filled canals that are lined with hair cells. The hair cells project into an overhanging membrane. When vibrations are carried through the cochlea,

the hair cells vibrate, moving the hairs up and down against the membrane. As the hairs strike the overhanging membrane, they are bent. This sends signals through the cochlea, as shown in **Figure 30-15g**, and then to the brain, where they are interpreted as sound.

The hairs of the receptor cells are delicate and can be sheared off from forceful vibrations such as those from loud music. Because the hairs cannot grow back, prolonged exposure to loud noise can result in permanent hearing loss. Also, as humans get older, they tend to lose more and more hair cells, which is why some older adults may not hear very well.

Figure 30-15
In the inner ear, there are two kinds of sensory receptors that enable us to hear and maintain our balance.

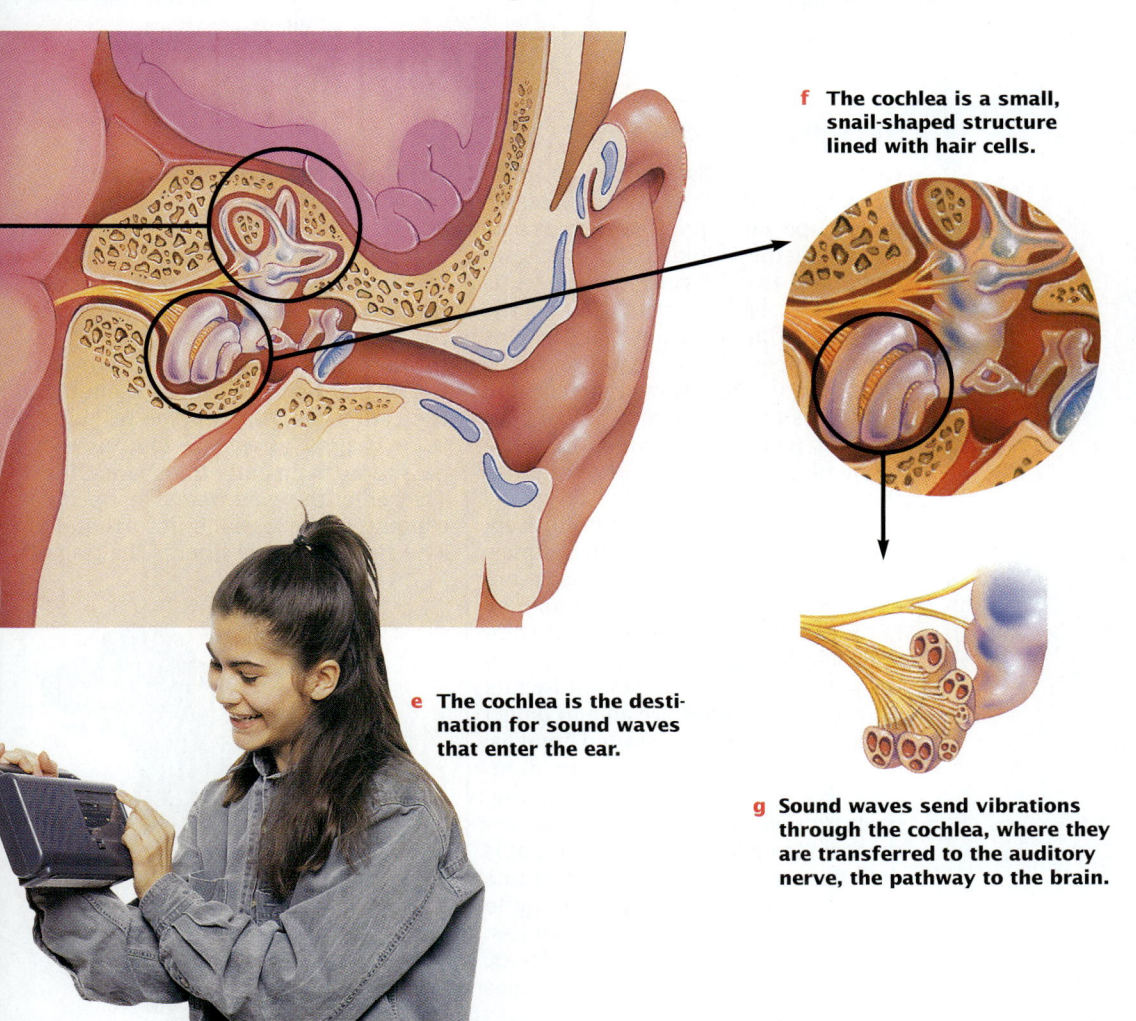

f The cochlea is a small, snail-shaped structure lined with hair cells.

e The cochlea is the destination for sound waves that enter the ear.

g Sound waves send vibrations through the cochlea, where they are transferred to the auditory nerve, the pathway to the brain.

■ Inferring Relationships

Point out how the three semicircular canals lie at right angles to each other (in the three dimensions of space or three planes of the body). Have students discuss how a person's sense of balance would be affected if the three canals were oriented in the same plane. *(The person would only be able to maintain balance on one plane.)*

Health Connection

Motion Sickness

Ask students to recall a time when they experienced motion sickness. Select volunteers to describe their experience and to explain why they think they became sick. After discussing possible causes, explain to them that motion sickness may be due to a sensory input mismatch. For example, if you are reading a book in a moving car, your eyes tell your brain that your body is fixed in reference to a stationary environment (the car). But as the car moves forward, impulses from the inner ear disagree with the visual information. The discrepancy between signals may cause excessive salivation, sweating, pallor, hyperventilation, nausea, and vomiting. Some motion-sickness medications work by depressing the signals from the inner ear.

Key to Strategies
● Understanding Concepts (Tier I)
■ Applying Information (Tier II)
▲ Critical Thinking (Tier III)

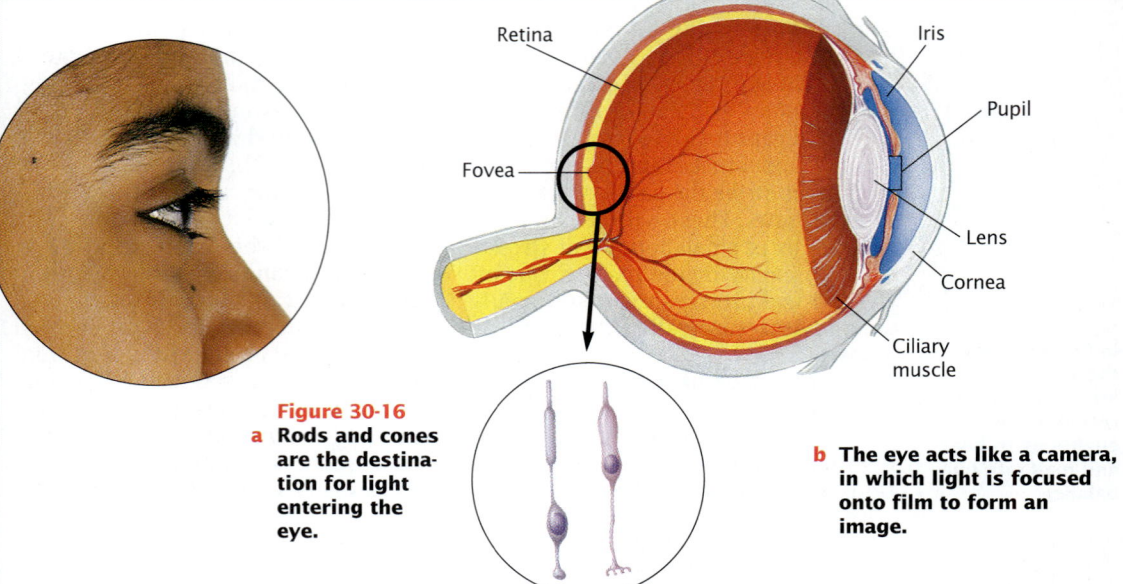

Figure 30-16

a Rods and cones are the destination for light entering the eye.

b The eye acts like a camera, in which light is focused onto film to form an image.

Receptors in the Eye

Almost all animals respond to light. Even some single-celled organisms have a special region that serves as a light detector. Humans and other animals have two eyes, each of which is a complex sense organ that is the starting point of vision. Both eyes contain specialized receptor cells, called photoreceptors, that contain light-sensitive pigments. The energy in light produces changes in these pigments, triggering a nerve impulse that travels to the brain.

You have two types of photoreceptor in your eyes—rods and cones, shown in **Figure 30-16a**. **Rods** are extremely sensitive and function only in dim light. They cannot detect color and therefore generate coarse, grainy images like those of black-and-white photographs. **Cones** are able to detect color and generate detailed images. Both rods and cones contain light-sensitive pigments. In rods, the pigment is called rhodopsin, which is synthesized from vitamin A. A diet that is deficient in vitamin A can result in a short supply of rhodopsin, leading to a condition called night blindness. Important sources of vitamin A include green and yellow fruits and vegetables and dairy products.

Light waves must be focused onto the retina

Rods and cones are packed close together in a layer called the **retina**, which covers the surface of the back of the eye. Before light waves can strike rods and cones, they must travel through a series of transparent materials that bend and focus them onto the retina. As you can see in **Figure 30-16b**, light waves are bent as they pass through an outer transparent film. They enter the eye through an opening called the pupil, which is surrounded by a ring of muscle fibers. The ring of

muscles fibers is able to contract and relax in different configurations, thus regulating the amount of light that enters the eye.

Suspended behind the pupil is an elastic, almond-shaped disk called the lens. Its elasticity is necessary for bending and focusing different angles of light waves that enter the eye. For example, when you are looking at a distant object (one more than 6 m away), light waves are traveling parallel to one another. They require little bending, if any, in order to strike the retina. As a result, the lens stretches, exerting little influence on the angle of incoming light waves. However, when you are viewing an object at close range, light waves are traveling at sharp angles to one another. In order to strike the retina, they must be bent and focused. Your lens accomplishes this by becoming thicker and rounder, which bends the incoming light rays.

Finally the light waves strike the retina, stimulating the rods and cones. Nerve impulses travel along the optic nerve to the brain, where they are interpreted as meaningful images, as shown in **Figure 30-16c.**

Perception varies among animals
Humans and other primates have excellent color vision, which is unusual for mammals. Most mammals evolved as nocturnal animals and thus have eyes that are adapted for vision in dim light. Their retinas contain only rods, making them extremely sensitive to shades of gray. Humans are not the only animals that can see color, however. Apparently many fishes and reptiles, as well as most birds, have color vision. Many insects also have color vision, an important adaptation for those that feed on flowers. In addition, many insects and other animals can detect ultraviolet light, but humans cannot.

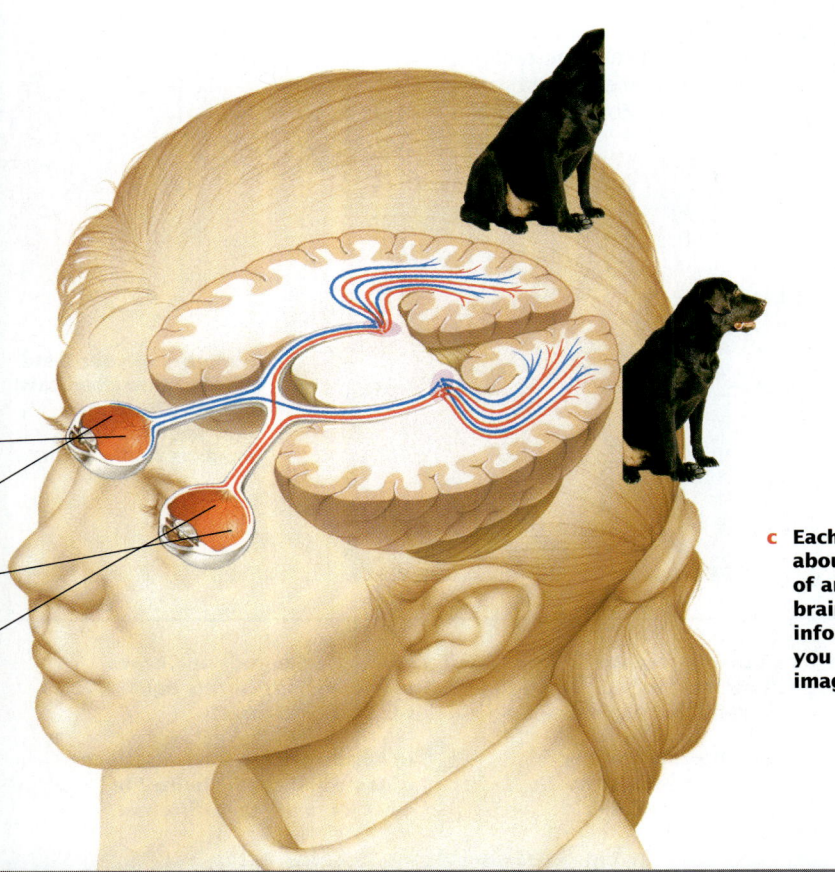

c Each eye receives about three-quarters of an image. The brain combines this information so that you see the entire image.

Demonstration
● **Summarizing Information**
Show the class a picture of a hawk. Point out that the fovea of the human eye has about 150,000 cones per square millimeter, whereas the hawk has nearly 1 million per square millimeter. Hawks consequently have a visual acuity that is about eight times greater than that of humans. Have students hypothesize the evolutionary advantage of this sharpened acuity.

Health Connection
Glaucoma
Glaucoma is an eye disease in which increased pressure inside the eye causes damage to the retina and the optic nerve. The cause of the increased pressure is a buildup of the aqueous humor, which presses the lens inward. Glaucoma is the second most common cause of blindness.

Key to Strategies
● **Understanding Concepts (Tier I)**
■ **Applying Information (Tier II)**
▲ **Critical Thinking (Tier III)**

The Nervous System   625

Receptors for Taste and Smell

Have you ever tried to describe the flavors and aromas of your favorite meal? If so, you have probably realized that your senses of taste and smell are very much alike. The receptor cells for taste and smell are both stimulated by particular chemicals. Your receptor cells for taste are located in taste buds that line the upper surface of your tongue, as shown in **Figure 30-17**. Receptor cells that detect smell are located in the wall of the upper part of your nasal cavity. Before chemicals can stimulate either kind of receptor cell, they must pass through a film of liquid coating the membranes in your mouth and nose. One reason you cannot taste food when you have a cold is that your nasal passages are inflamed and coated with mucus, rendering your smell receptors inoperable.

Humans have four basic taste senses: sweet, sour, salty, and bitter. Receptor cells for these basic tastes are in different areas of the tongue. Most chemicals stimulate two or more types to varying degrees. The sensation described as taste is produced by the blending of four basic senses in different intensities. Incidentally, the "hot" sensations of foods such as chili peppers is detected by pain receptors, not taste receptors.

While there appear to be four basic types of taste receptors, research shows that there may be more than 1,000 different receptors for smell. Most animals depend on their sense of smell to a far greater extent than humans. Certain insects, invertebrates, and mammals release scents that contain information about their species and sex. Their sense of smell can also be used to locate food, recognize family members, and mark territory, which you may have encountered if you've ever walked a dog.

c **Receptors in your taste buds react to chemicals in food. These reactions send nerve impulses to the brain.**

Figure 30-17

a **Taste buds in your tongue enable you to sense taste, like the sour bite of a lemon.**

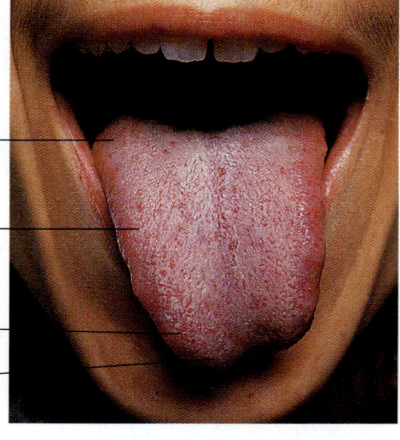

b **Your tongue contains receptors that detect four basic tastes.**

Bitter

Sour

Salty

Sweet

SECTION REVIEW

1. What is a sensory receptor? Describe four receptors that help your body maintain homeostasis.

2. What are two functions of the inner ear? Describe the structures responsible for these functions.

3. What roles do rods and cones play in vision? How is light focused onto them?

4. In what ways are the sensations of taste and smell similar? In what ways are they different?

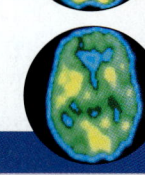
Positron emission tomography (PET) scans are useful for detecting activity in the brain. These scans compare deoxyglucose levels in a normal (top) and a clinically depressed (bottom) person.

	Key Terms	Summary
30-1 **Nerve Impulses** 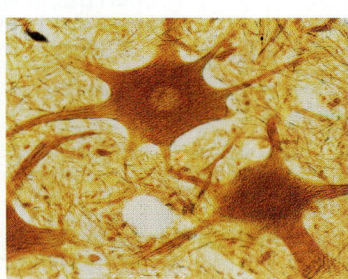 Neurons are the basic units of the nervous system. They conduct electrical information throughout your body.	neuron (p. 601) nerve (p. 601) dendrite (p. 601) axon (p. 601) myelin sheath (p. 604) synapse (p. 605) neurotransmitter (p. 605)	• A neuron is a cell specialized for conducting electrical information. • A nerve impulse is an action potential traveling along a neuron. During an action potential the balance of sodium and potassium on both sides of the membrane is briefly changed. • Myelin sheaths speed up nerve impulses, which jump from node to node instead of traveling the full length of the axon. • Neurons communicate with each other by sending neurotransmitters across synapses. • Drugs affect a neuron's membrane and cause addiction by altering the number of receptors.
30-2 **The Nervous System** 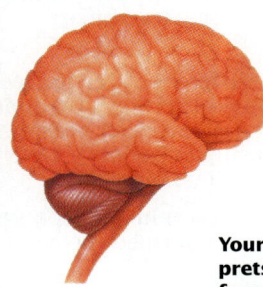 Your brain interprets messages from sensory neurons into meaningful information.	central nervous system (p. 611) peripheral nervous system (p. 611) cerebrum (p. 612) cerebellum (p. 612) hypothalamus (p. 613) sensory neuron (p. 618) reflex (p. 619) autonomic nervous system (p. 620)	• The central nervous system consists of the brain and spinal cord. Its main functions are to sort incoming information and to send messages to the body. • The brain is the subject of intense research using new technologies. • The peripheral nervous system consists of nerves that run throughout the body. • The autonomic nervous system regulates involuntary functions and is always active.
30-3 **The Sense Organs**  Your eyes contain light-sensitive cells called rods and cones.	sensory organ (p. 621) rod (p. 624) cone (p. 624) retina (p. 624)	• Different receptors in the ear establish equilibrium and detect sound waves. • Receptors in the eye detect light, enabling you to see.

627

Alternative Assessment

Have students formulate questions from the chapter for playing a trivia game as a review technique.

Portfolio Assessment

Portfolio Assessment on page T39 provides options for building and evaluating student portfolios. Students and teachers can select items from the areas listed on page T39 for inclusion in a portfolio.

ANSWER TO CONCEPT MAP

The following is one possible answer to the Relating Concepts exercise on page 628.

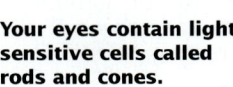

Nervous system
has divisions called

central nervous system ← sends signals to → peripheral nervous system

is composed of

spinal cord | brain

is composed of

sensory neurons | motor neurons

produces rapid responses called

contain

gray matter

receives signals from

has a division called

is composed of

many never reach the

reflexes

autonomic N.S.

many travel only as far as

Understanding Vocabulary

1. a. Reflex is not a part of the brain.
   b. Cochlea is a part of the ear.
   c. Neuron is not a form of energy that sensory receptors react to.
2. a. nerve
   b. axon
   c. cerebellum

Understanding Concepts

3. A possible answer to the concept map is shown on page 627.
4. Refer to Figure 30-1 and the information on page 601.
5. Refer to Figure 30-2 and the information on page 602.
6. Refer to the caption that accompanies Figure 30-2b on page 603. The upward slope represents the inward flow of sodium ions. The downward slope represents the outward flow of potassium ions. The portion of the graph below −70mV represents an excess outward flow of potassium ions. After the action potential, sodium-potassium pumps restore the resting membrane potential of −70mV.
7. Refer to the captions that accompany Figures 30-2a and 30-2b on page 603.
8. Psychoactive drugs are a class of drugs that alter tissues in the nervous system. Refer to Table 30-1 on page 609 for the modes of action and effects.
9. Refer to the captions that accompany Figure 30-7 on page 608.
10. Addiction to alcohol, or alcoholism, can cause vitamin deficiency, malnutrition, abnormalities in the circulatory system, inflammation of the stomach lining, accumulation of fats in the liver, and cirrhosis of the liver.
11. Refer to the captions that accompany Figure 30-10 on page 612.
12. The brain stem controls heart rate and breathing. A blow to the back of the skull could

---

review

CHAPTER 30

Understanding Vocabulary

1. For each list of terms, identify the one that does not fit the pattern and describe why it does not fit.
   a. cerebellum, cerebrum, reflex, brain stem
   b. pupil, retina, cochlea, iris
   c. chemical, sound, light, neuron
2. For each set of terms, complete the analogy.
   a. cell composed of dendrites and axons : neuron :: bundles of neurons that form network : _____
   b. incoming message : dendrite :: outgoing message : _____
   c. control center : cerebrum :: muscle coordination : _____

Understanding Concepts

3. **Relating Concepts** Construct a concept map that describes the structure and functions of the two main parts of the nervous system. Try to include the following terms in your concept map: central nervous system, peripheral nervous system, spinal cord, brain, sensory neurons, motor neurons, gray matter, autonomic nervous system, reflexes.
4. **Identifying Structures and Functions** Describe the parts and functions of a neuron.
5. **Identifying Structures** What is a voltage-gated channel? How does it function in the transmission of a nerve impulse?
6. **Reading Graphs** Look at the graph below. The curve was obtained when a neuron was stimulated by an electrode. Explain the shape of the curve in terms of changes in the concentration of ions inside and outside the cell.

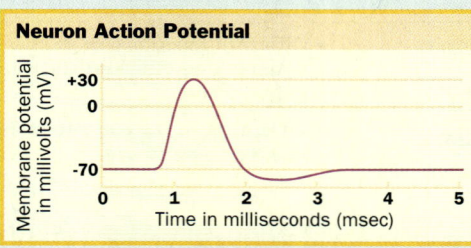

Neuron Action Potential

---

7. **Comparing Functions** Compare the concentration of sodium (Na^+) and potassium (K^+) ions both inside and outside the cell during the resting potential and during the action potential.
8. **Inferring Relationships** What is a psychoactive drug? Describe two ways that psychoactive drugs affect the way that neurons communicate with each other. Give examples.
9. **Analyzing Processes** Describe the feedback mechanism that results in addiction.
10. **Recognizing Relationships** Describe some of the long-term health problems associated with addiction to alcohol.
11. **Comparing Functions** Identify and compare the functions of the three main parts of the brain.
12. **Predicting Outcomes** Why is a blow to the back of the skull near the brain stem extremely dangerous?
13. **Summarizing Information** Describe two types of technology used to study the brain.
14. **Inferring Relationships** What is a reflex? How does a reflex enable you to act quickly?
15. **Identifying Functions** What is the autonomic nervous system? Describe its primary function.
16. **Inferring Conclusions** Sufferers of vertigo feel dizzy and disoriented in certain situations, such as when they are on a roller coaster. What is the relationship between vertigo and the semicircular canal?
17. **Predicting Outcomes** How would a person be affected if an accident damaged the hairs inside the cochlea?
18. **Comparing Functions** Differentiate between the two types of photoreceptors.
19. **Analyzing Information** How are the senses of taste and smell similar? How are they different?
20. **BUILDING ON WHAT YOU HAVE LEARNED** You learned about sodium-potassium pumps in Chapter 4. How do sodium-potassium pumps in a neuron's cell membrane achieve resting potential?

---

damage the brain stem and interfere with these vital processes.
13. Student answers will vary but should reflect the information on page 615.
14. A reflex is a sudden, involuntary movement. A reflex produces a rapid motor response to a stimulus because the sensory neuron synapses directly to a motor neuron.
15. The autonomic nervous system consists of motor neurons that are active all the time. These neurons carry messages from the central nervous system that keep the body going

even when it is not active and keep the body functioning without our noticing.
16. The semicircular canals contain receptor cells that enable a person to sense the body's position in space. Damage to them can result in vertigo.
17. His or her ability to hear would be impaired.
18. Refer to the **Answers to Section Review** for Section 30-3, page 626, number 3.
19. Refer to the **Answers to Section Review** for Section 30-3, page 626, number 4.

Interpreting Graphics

21. Study the figure below and answer the questions that follow.

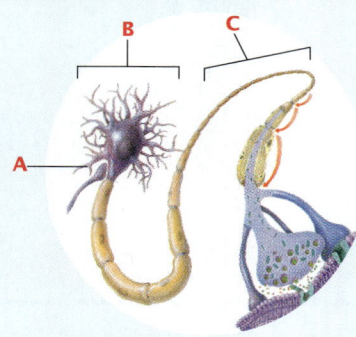

a. What kind of cell is shown in the figure? What evidence do you have for your decision?
b. What part of the cell is labeled *A*? What is its function?
c. What part of the cell is labeled *B*? What is its function?
d. What part of the cell is labeled *C*? What is its function?
e. Which part of the cell would be damaged by multiple sclerosis? What is the name of this structure?

Reviewing Themes

22. *Evolution*
What are the three main parts of every vertebrate brain? How do these parts compare in a shark, a frog, a bird, and a cat?

23. *Stability and Homeostasis*
A child may try to hold his breath during a tantrum. How does the autonomic nervous system prevent damage to the body in this situation?

Thinking Critically

24. **Recognizing Verifiable Conclusions** Epilepsy is a condition that affects one out of every 200 people in the United States. In a healthy human, brain cells produce small bursts of impulses in varying patterns. In a person with epilepsy, large numbers of brain cells occasionally send rapid bursts of impulses simultaneously, causing the person to have convulsions. How would you explain these symptoms? Why do you think the symptoms go away after only a short period of time?

Life/Work Skills

25. **Finding Information** Use library references or search an on-line database to find out about the different types of drugs and how they affect the nervous system. Investigate specific drugs that are classified as stimulants (amphetamines), depressants (barbiturates), and hallucinogens. Summarize your findings in an oral report to the class.

26. **Using Technology** Contact a local library or search an on-line database to observe sample images of the brain produced by one of the technologies described in this chapter, such as MRI or PET. Invite a physician or technician to class to describe the components of the images and what they reveal about the brain. Also ask about how the procedure is done and about the time and costs involved.

Activities and Projects

27. **Health Connection** Depression is a mental disorder that affects approximately 8 million people in the United States. Use library references or search an on-line database to find out about the symptoms, causes, and treatments of depression. Summarize your findings in a written report.

28. **Career Connection: Optometrist** Optometrists are professionals who provide and adjust eyeglasses and contact lenses for people with vision problems. Use library references or search an on-line database to find out what kind of education and specialized training is required to become an optometrist. Where do most optometrists work? For additional information, write to The American Optometry Association, 243 North Lindbergh Boulevard, St. Louis, Missouri 63141-7851.

Discovering Through Reading

29. Read the article "Scientists Explain Eight Wonders of the Human Brain" by Trina Chang in *American Health*, June 1995, pages 68–71. Why is handwriting unique? Why do some people have perfect pitch?

629

In frogs, the forebrain is the largest part and is devoted to associative activity. In birds, the cerebrum is the largest part of the brain. In a cat and other mammals, including humans, the cerebrum is the largest portion of the brain.

23. Functioning of the autonomic nervous system will cause the child to pass out, restoring involuntary control of breathing.

Thinking Critically

24. Answers will vary but should indicate that the repeated rapid impulses reach the muscles and cause sudden and violent contractions. Because the impulses are so rapid, the supply of neurotransmitters at the synapse is used up quickly, and the impulses stop.

Life/Work Skills

25. Results will vary depending on local resources.
26. Results will vary depending on local resources.

Activities and Projects

27. Results will vary depending on local resources.
28. Results will vary depending on local resources.

Discovering Through Reading

29. Handwriting is unique because of the way a person thinks about how the written letters should look, how the nerves carry impulses from the brain to the muscles, how a person holds the pen or pencil, and how fast a person writes. Perfect pitch is the result of the way a person processes a sound through different brain circuits.

---

20. Refer to Figure 30-2c and the information on page 603.

Interpreting Graphics

21. a. The cell is a neuron. It is identified by its unique structure, which consists of a cell body, an axon, and dendrites.
b. *A* is a dendrite; it receives messages from other cells.
c. *B* is the cell body that contains the nucleus of the cell; the cell body receives and sends information.
d. *C* is an axon; it sends messages to other cells.
e. The myelin sheath of the axon would be damaged by multiple sclerosis.

Reviewing Themes

22. All vertebrate brains have a forebrain, a midbrain, and a hindbrain. In a shark, the midbrain is the principal part of the brain; it coordinates motor reflexes, while the rest of the brain processes sensory information.

31 | Hormones

Lesson Planning Guide With Options for Block Scheduling

Lecture Concepts	Lesson Resources

31-1 What Hormones Do

BLOCK ❶ (45 minutes)

1. The endocrine system consists of glands that secrete hormones into the bloodstream.

2. Hormones and nerve impulses enable a person to respond to stimuli.

3. Hormones take longer to bring about a response, but their effects last longer than those brought about by nerve impulses.

❶ Lecture Resources
- Determining Prior Knowledge
- Active Reading: K-W-L
- Visual Strategy: Figures 31-1, 31-2
- Demonstration: Summarizing Information
- 🔒 Teaching Transparencies: 204, 205
- 💿 Holt Biology Videodiscs Lesson 31-1

Classwork Options
- The Endocrine-Nervous System Linkage

BLOCK ❷ (45 minutes)

4. Hormones and nerves work together to form the neuroendocrine system.

5. The pituitary gland secretes a number of hormones that regulate other endocrine glands.

6. The endocrine system operates on the principle of negative feedback.

❷ Lecture Resources
- Active Reading: Reading Organizer
- Visual Strategy: Figures 31-3, 31-4, 31-5
- Visual Strategy: Videodisc
- Demonstration: Comparing Structures
- Demonstration: Identifying Functions
- 🔒 Teaching Transparencies: 209, 230
- 💿 Holt Biology Videodiscs Lesson 31-1

Classwork Options
- Closure: Inferring Relationships

Assignment Options
- Reteaching
- Section Review
- Chapter Review, questions 1a, 2a, 4, 5, 6, 7, 8, 11, 24, 26
- Directed Reading Worksheet

31-2 How Hormones Work

BLOCK ❸ (45 minutes)

1. Steroid hormones bind with receptor proteins inside the cell cytoplasm, forming a complex that then attaches to the DNA, where it activates specific genes.

2. Peptide hormones bind with appropriate receptor proteins on the cell membrane, activating the formation of cyclic AMP which acts as a second messenger inside the cell.

❸ Lecture Resources
- Visual Strategy: Figures 31-6, 31-7, 31-8
- 🔒 Teaching Transparencies: 206, 207, 229, 231
- 💿 Holt Biology Videodiscs Lesson 31-2

Classwork Options
- Closure: Forming a Hypothesis
- Investigation 31A

Assignment Options
- Reteaching
- Section Review
- Chapter Review, questions 1b, 2b, 9, 20, 21, 22, 23, 25
- Directed Reading Worksheet

31-3 Glands and Their Functions

BLOCK ❹ (45 minutes)

1. The adrenal glands produce hormones that help the body react to sudden crises and deal with long-term stress.

2. The thyroid gland produces thyroxin, a hormone that regulates the body's metabolism.

3. Too much thyroxin results in an increased metabolic rate, leading to a condition known as Graves' disease.

❹ Lecture Resources
- Active Reading: Reading Organizer
- Visual Strategy: Figures 31-11, 31-12
- Demonstration: Comparing Functions
- Demonstration: Comparing Structures
- 🔒 Teaching Transparencies: 194A, 195A
- 💿 Holt Biology Videodiscs Lesson 31-3

Classwork Options
- Active Reading: Summarizing

Lecture Concepts

Lesson Resources

31-3 Glands and Their Functions, *continued*

BLOCK ❺ (45 minutes)

4. Too little thyroxin results in a decreased metabolic rate, which can lead to a condition of goiter or hypothyroidism.

5. The pancreas produces two hormones, insulin and glucagon, that regulate blood glucose level.

6. Examples of other hormones include the sex hormones, produced by the gonads; melatonin, produced by the pineal glands; and prostaglandins, produced by all cells in the body.

❺ Lecture Resources
■ Active Reading: K-W-L
■ Visual Strategy: Figures 31-13, 31-14, 31-15; Tables 31-1, 31-2
■ Visual Strategy: Videodisc
◉ Holt Biology Videodiscs Lesson 31-3

Classwork Options
■ Closure: Summarizing Information

Assignment Options
■ *Small Group* Reteaching
■ Section Review
■ Chapter Review, questions 1c, 2c, 3, 10, 12, 13, 14, 15, 16, 17, 18, 19
■ Directed Reading Worksheet

Chapter Review and Assessment

BLOCK ❻ (45 minutes)
Review
■ Reteaching Worksheet
■ Thinking Skills Worksheet
■ Vocabulary Development Worksheet
◉ Language Development and Reading Comprehension Audio CD Program: Chapter 31

BLOCK ❼ (45 minutes)
Assessment
■ Alternative Assessment, p. 647
■ Portfolio Assessment, p. T39
Chapter Test
■ Chapter 31 Test
Test Generator
◉ Item bank for customizing Chapter Tests

Teaching Resources CD-ROM
◉ Scoring Rubrics and Classroom Management Checklist

Management Checklist
The Portfolio icon denotes items throughout the Teacher's Edition lesson wrap that may be selected for inclusion in student portfolios.

Holt Biology Videodiscs and *Concepts of Biology*

Holt Biology Videodiscs gives you a powerful tool for teaching, review, and assessment. For further information regarding the media on the videodiscs, see **Holt Biology Videodiscs Teacher's Correlation Guide to Holt Biology: Visualizing Life.**

Concepts of Biology adds interactive lesson plans and extensive tools for customization using CD-ROM technology.

Use the following topic from **Concepts of Biology** to help you teach this chapter:
Topic 24: Nervous and Endocrine System

Laboratory Planning

Text

Materials and preparation instructions appear on the teacher's wrap accompanying each laboratory exercise.

Block 3: Investigation 31A: Determining the Effect of Hormones—Polluted Well, p. 816

Determining Prior Knowledge

- Once students have been seated at the start of class, tell them that you have decided to give a surprise quiz on what was covered in yesterday's session. After they have had a chance to absorb what you have said, discuss what physiological changes their bodies underwent as they experienced this "stressful" situation. Discuss the "fight or flight" response that epinephrine provides for us.

- Ask if anyone has—or knows someone who has—diabetes. Discuss what they know about this disease.

- Show the class photographs of people who obviously have a permanent or temporary hormonal imbalance, for example, someone who is extremely short or tall or someone who is covered with excessive body hair.

Active READING

Technique: K-W-L

Before students read the chapter, have them make short individual lists of all the things they already **K**now about hormones. When students have finished their lists, ask them to contribute their entries to a class list on the board or the overhead. Then have students list things they **W**ant to know about hormones. Have students save their list for later use in Active Reading on page 646.

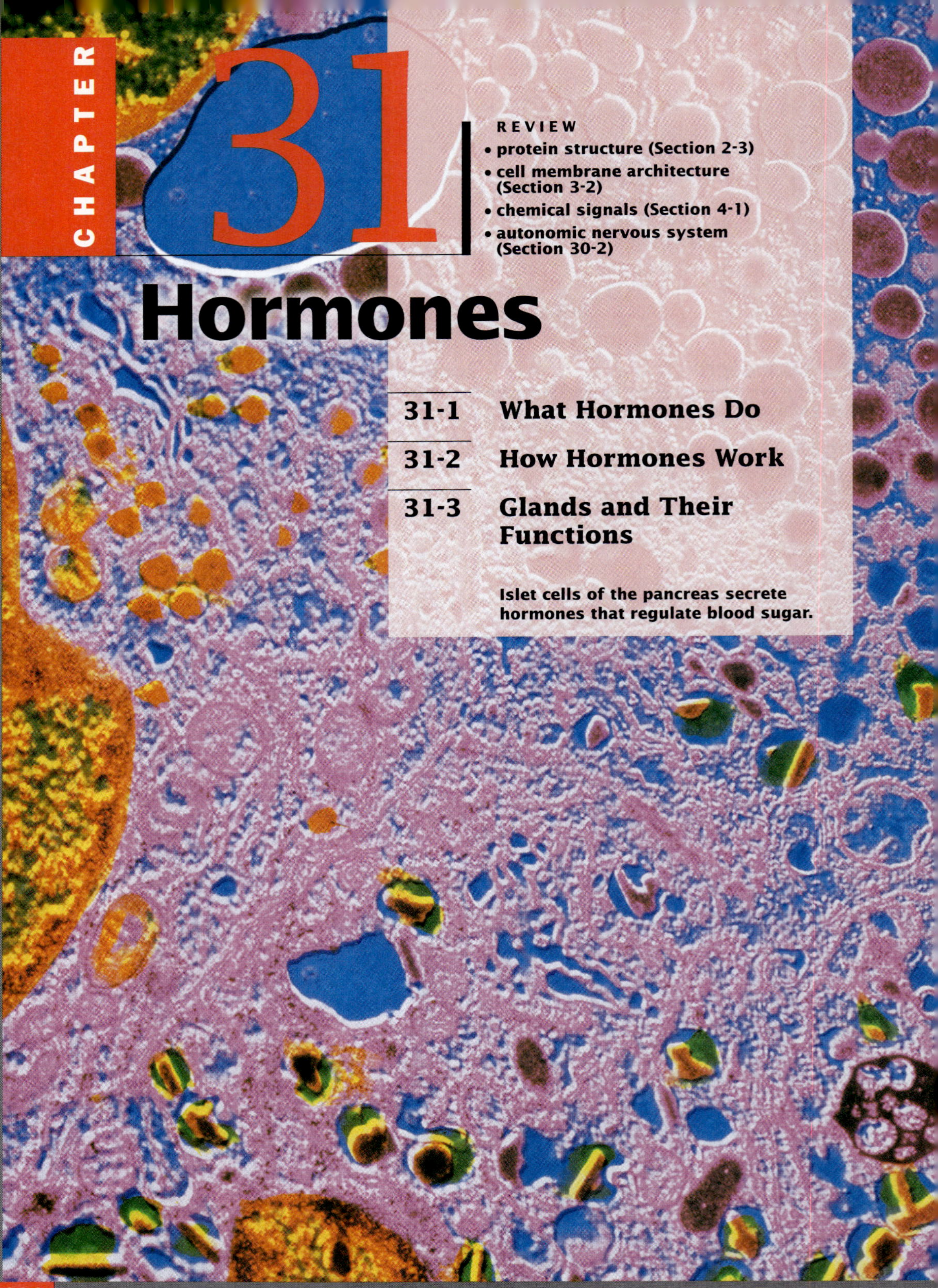

CHAPTER

31

REVIEW
- protein structure (Section 2-3)
- cell membrane architecture (Section 3-2)
- chemical signals (Section 4-1)
- autonomic nervous system (Section 30-2)

Hormones

31-1	**What Hormones Do**
31-2	**How Hormones Work**
31-3	**Glands and Their Functions**

Islet cells of the pancreas secrete hormones that regulate blood sugar.

Author's Rationale This chapter treats the endocrine system as an extension of the nervous system, while placing a strong emphasis on how hormones work. Students will learn what hormones do and how they do it.

After fighting a blazing fire for many hours, a firefighter nears exhaustion. Suddenly a wall collapses! The firefighter rushes to control the fiery debris. How? Chemical signals carried by the bloodstream ensure that the firefighter's body gets the extra oxygen and energy-supplying sugars needed to sustain peak performance until the crisis passes.

31-1   What Hormones Do

OBJECTIVES

1 Describe the major components of the endocrine system.

2 Summarize how the hypothalamus and pituitary gland work together to regulate body systems.

3 Explain the importance of feedback.

4 Analyze the relationship among chemicals involved in a negative-feedback loop.

Hormones: Chemical Signals

In the emergency described above, the signals traveling through the firefighter's blood are small molecules called hormones. A **hormone** is a chemical signal, made in one place and delivered (usually through the blood) to another, that regulates the body's activities. Various organs scattered throughout the body are sources of hormones. Organs that produce most of the hormones in your body are called **endocrine** (*EN duh krihn*) **glands**. The endocrine system is made up of the ductless endocrine glands and other organs, shown in **Figure 31-1**, that produce hormones. These other organs are part of other body systems as well.

Endocrine glands secrete hormones directly into the bloodstream. The hormones travel to a specific tissue or organ called a **target**. Once a hormone arrives at its target, the hormone will elicit a specific response. For example, some hormones speed up the heart. Others help digest food and enable the body to use the food as fuel. Without hormones,

humans would not grow or mature. Like the brain and nerves, hormones are essential to maintaining homeostasis. Often, two or more hormones work together to produce their effects.

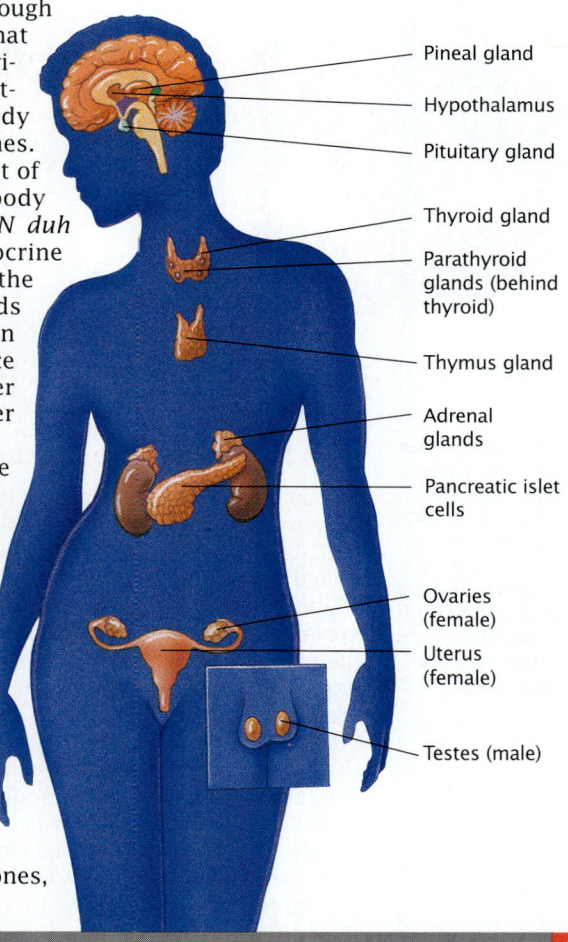

- Pineal gland
- Hypothalamus
- Pituitary gland
- Thyroid gland
- Parathyroid glands (behind thyroid)
- Thymus gland
- Adrenal glands
- Pancreatic islet cells
- Ovaries (female)
- Uterus (female)
- Testes (male)

Figure 31-1
The endocrine system regulates overall metabolism, growth, reproduction, and maintenance of homeostasis.

631

Videodisc Resources

Holt Biology Videodiscs

Lesson 31-1: What Hormones Do

Phase One
Preparation

Scheduling
See the **Lesson Planning Guide** on pages 629A and 629B for lecture, classwork, and assignment options for Section 31-1.

Phase Two
Teaching Strategies

Demonstration
● **Summarizing Information**
Have students working in pairs record each other's pulse and breathing rates a few minutes into the class period. Then have them think of something wonderfully exciting in their lives. Immediately afterward, have them again record their pulse and breathing rates. Ask: How did your pulse and breathing rates differ after the assignment? (*Both the pulse and breathing rates should be elevated.*) Tell students that hormones produced by the endocrine system are responsible for the changes that occurred in their pulse and breathing rates.

Visual Strategy   Figure 31-1
● **Comparing Structures**
Use this figure to point out how widely distributed the endocrine glands are in the body. Have students identify the parts of the brain illustrated in this figure so that they recognize the close association between the endocrine and nervous systems.

Key to Strategies
Teaching Strategies are keyed to three tiers of learning.

● **Understanding Concepts (Tier I)**
Content mastery and comprehension

■ **Applying Information (Tier II)**
Applying and analyzing content

▲ **Critical Thinking (Tier III)**
Practicing evaluative thinking

■ **Relating Concepts**

Use this figure to emphasize the autonomic nervous system's connection to the endocrine system. The autonomic nervous system stimulates, through nerve impulses, the secretion of epinephrine from the adrenal gland.

Connection: *Chapter 30*

The Hypothalamus

Review the location of the hypothalamus as described in Chapter 30. Emphasize its close association with the pituitary, as well as its role in the nervous system and in homeostasis.

Demonstration

● **Comparing Structures**

Show the class a diagram or overhead transparency of the brain, with the hypothalamus and pituitary gland clearly identified. Mention that the pituitary lies just beneath the hypothalamus and is directly influenced by the hypothalamus. The bloodstream carries hormones released by the hypothalamus that either stimulate or inhibit the pituitary gland.

The Endocrine–Nervous System Linkage

● **Comparing Functions**

Using the information on this page, have students make a **Graphic Organizer**—similar to the one at the bottom of this page—in which they contrast and compare the endocrine and nervous systems' activities in the homeostasis of the body. Ask students to include in their organizers the differences in both the speed of response and the length of action on the target organ.

The effects of hormones last longer than those of nerve impulses

Imagine that you start to cross a street. Suddenly a car speeds around the corner. Instantly, nerve impulses deliver the message "Danger!" from your eyes to your brain. The effect is immediate nervous control of one target cell at a time, spurring your body to action.

It takes your body just a moment to respond, but that brief moment is long compared to the nerves' rapid firing. Still, in a matter of seconds, hormones from your adrenal glands excite different target cells in several locations. Your heart pounds, and your blood pressure rises. Your skin sweats. Your muscles tense, and you sprint back to the curb—safe.

But, unlike the nerve impulses that have now ceased, some of the hormones that spurred you to action will affect you for 10 or 20 minutes. And when emergencies last for hours or days, other hormones are released. For reactions that occur over longer periods of time, like the changes of puberty leading to adulthood, hormones exert their influence over days, weeks, months, or even years.

Notice the shapes and colors used in **Figure 31-2**. You will see them used throughout this chapter to illustrate the nervous system, endocrine glands, target cells, and changes in tissue activity that occur as a result of hormones.

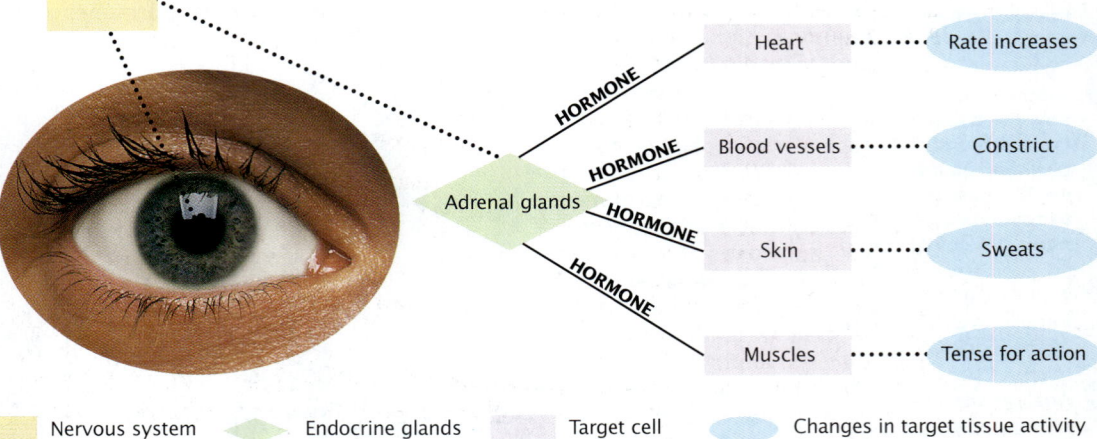

Figure 31-2
Hormones operate more slowly than the nervous system in controlling the body's operations, but notice how several target organs and activities may be affected by a single hormone.

The Hypothalamus-Pituitary Connection

The endocrine system and the nervous system are the two main control systems of the body. They are so closely linked that they often are considered a single system—the **neuroendocrine system**. In Chapter 30 you learned that the hypothalamus is the part of your brain that regulates body temperature, breathing, hunger, and thirst. Besides being a part of your nervous system, the hypothalamus also serves as the master switchboard of the endocrine system. Your hypothalamus is continuously checking conditions inside your body. Are you too hot or too cold? Are you running out of fuel? Are you in pain? If your internal environment starts to get out of balance, your hypothalamus can set things right again. In some cases, it acts like an endocrine gland itself, sending out commands in the form of hormones. In other cases, the hypothalamus sends messages instantaneously to other parts of the brain and to other glands in the body through direct neuron links. Together with hormones, these unique nerve transmissions are the hypothalmus's way of setting up a chain of command that allows it to control much of the activity of the endocrine system.

Graphic Organizer

Use the following graphic organizer with the teaching strategy **The Endocrine–Nervous System Linkage** on page 632.

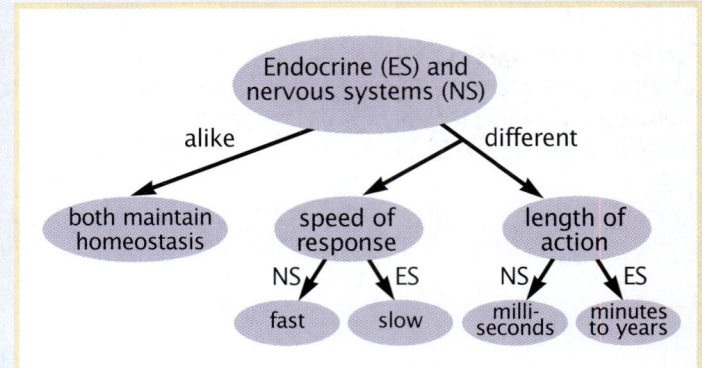

The pituitary gland secretes and stores hormones

All of the hormones produced by the hypothalamus move through a slender thread of tissue to the **pituitary** (*puh TOO uh tehr ee*) **gland**. The pituitary gland produces at least six different hormones in response to the hormones released from the hypothalamus. As described in **Figure 31-3a–b**, two of these hormones, growth hormone and prolactin, have direct effects on tissues in the body. Growth hormone, for instance, stimulates protein synthesis and cell division in target cells. It also profoundly influences the growth of cartilage and bone. Because these pituitary hormones are controlled by releasing hormones from the hypothalamus, the brain exercises direct control over the endocrine system.

Four of the hormones secreted by the pituitary gland control the activities of a number of other endocrine glands, such as the thyroid gland and the adrenal glands. Some of these glands are discussed in more detail later in this chapter.

The pituitary gland also stores hormones made in the hypothalamus. Two of these hormones, oxytocin (*ahk see TOHS ihn*) and antidiuretic hormone (ADH), discussed in **Figure 31-3c–d**, are released from the pituitary gland when needed by the body.

Figure 31-3
The pituitary gland was formerly called the "master gland" because so many of its hormones regulate other endocrine functions. Now the hypothalamus is considered to be the "master gland."

a *Growth hormone* stimulates general growth of the body, particularly of the skeleton. When too little growth hormone is produced, a condition called dwarfism can result. With too much growth hormone, a condition called giantism can occur.

b *Prolactin* causes glands in the mother's breasts to produce milk. Then the baby's nursing stimulates the release of oxytocin.

c *Oxytocin* aids in the release of milk from the mammary glands and also causes contractions of the uterus during and shortly after labor.

d *ADH* causes the kidneys to form more concentrated urine, thereby conserving water in the body.

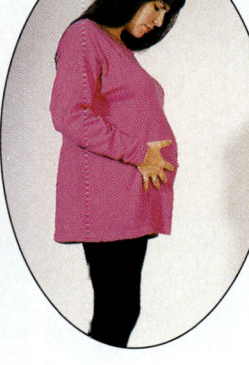

633

Multicultural Perspective: Choh Hao Li

Choh Hao Li, a Chinese American endocrinologist, isolated and identified five hormones of the pituitary gland. He discovered that the pituitary gland's growth hormone contains a chain of 256 amino acids. In 1970 he discovered a method for synthesizing the hormone, and he set the record for creating the largest synthesized protein molecule.

Figure 31-4
When you are cold, the hypothalamus sends signals to the pituitary gland, which signals the thyroid to produce thyroxine. Thyroxine speeds up metabolism until your body temperature rises slightly. Then the system shuts off.

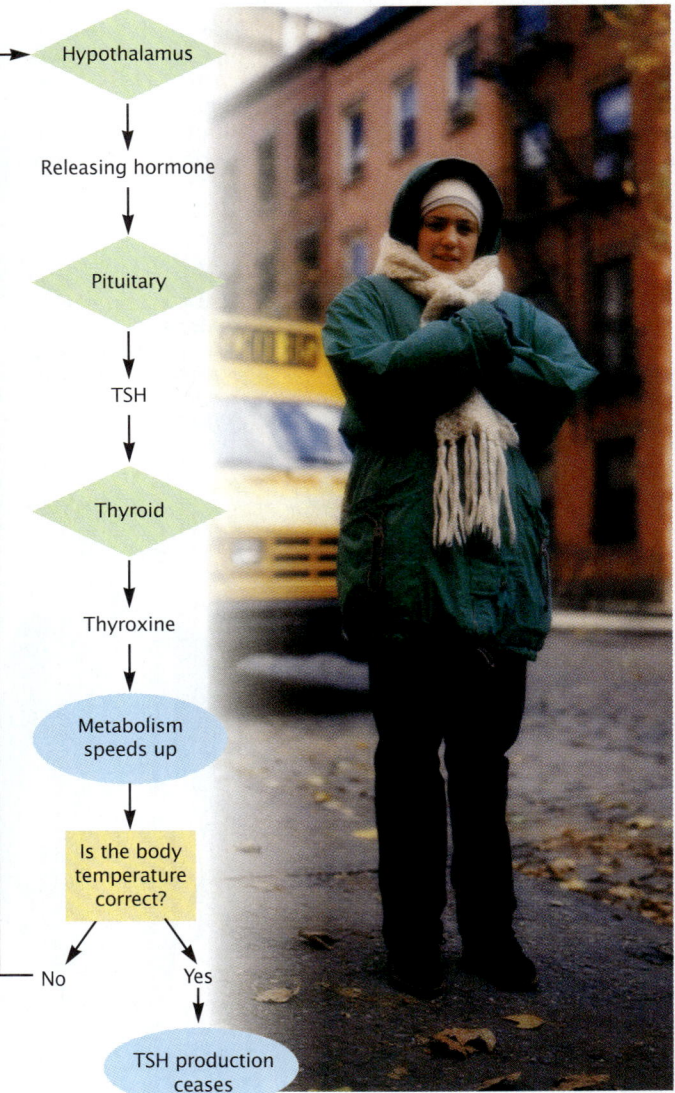

Regulating Hormone Release

The human body produces more than 40 hormones and must be able to regulate the release of these hormones. Although nerve impulses alone can increase or decrease hormone production, in many cases chemical signals, including hormones, regulate the activity of the endocrine system. These chemical signals are used as feedback by the endocrine system to regulate itself.

Feedback is a system for self-regulation. A feedback mechanism detects the amount of hormones already in circulation or the amount of other chemicals produced because of hormone action. After receiving feedback, the endocrine system adjusts the amount of hormones being made or released. If feedback stimulates the output of more hormone, it is called positive feedback. In contrast, a **negative feedback** system inhibits the production of more hormone. Most homeostatic control is accomplished by negative feedback, which is a fairly complex mechanism because hormones are never turned completely on or off. Sometimes more than one negative-feedback loop operates to control the rate of secretion and thus the levels of hormones in the blood. At other times, nervous stimulation, like that produced by the nursing infant on the previous page, regulates hormone secretion.

Thyroid hormones maintain body temperature

Imagine that you are waiting for a bus in cold, rainy weather. Your hypothalamus uses negative feedback to monitor your body temperature. Are you cold? If you are, neural adjustments will be made. Are you still cold? If you are, three hormones are released to help restore your body temperature. First, a hormone from the hypothalamus causes your pituitary gland to release thyroid stimulating hormone (TSH). TSH stimulates the thyroid gland to secrete two hormones. One of these is thyroxine, a hormone that speeds up your body's rate of metabolism. This is like turning up your internal furnace. When the feedback system senses that your temperature has returned to normal, it slows endocrine operations. The hypothalamus stops production of the releasing hormone. The pituitary reduces TSH secretion. In turn, the thyroid stops secreting thyroxine. This negative-feedback process is summarized in **Figure 31-4**.

634

Negative feedback also regulates blood calcium

You will remember that calcium is vital to bones, muscles, and nerves. Your bones are more than just support beams for your body; they are mineral reservoirs. More than 98 percent of your body's calcium is stored in your bones. Hormones control the level of calcium in the blood by controlling calcium's movement into and out of bone and other tissues.

Calcitonin from the thyroid gland lowers the level of calcium in the blood. Parathyroid hormone (PTH) from the parathyroid glands raises the level of calcium in the blood. **Figure 31-5** illustrates the negative-feedback loops that control the release of these hormones. If the level of calcium is too high, the thyroid gland secretes calcitonin, and blood calcium is lowered. When the level of calcium in the blood drops even slightly below normal, the parathyroid gland receives a message to secrete PTH. PTH causes the release of calcium from bone into the blood. What happens to calcium in the blood now? When the level of calcium in the blood rises to a normal level, the parathyroid glands halt production of PTH.

Figure 31-5
Blood calcium level is regulated by moving calcium into and out of storage. The major storage site for calcium is bone.

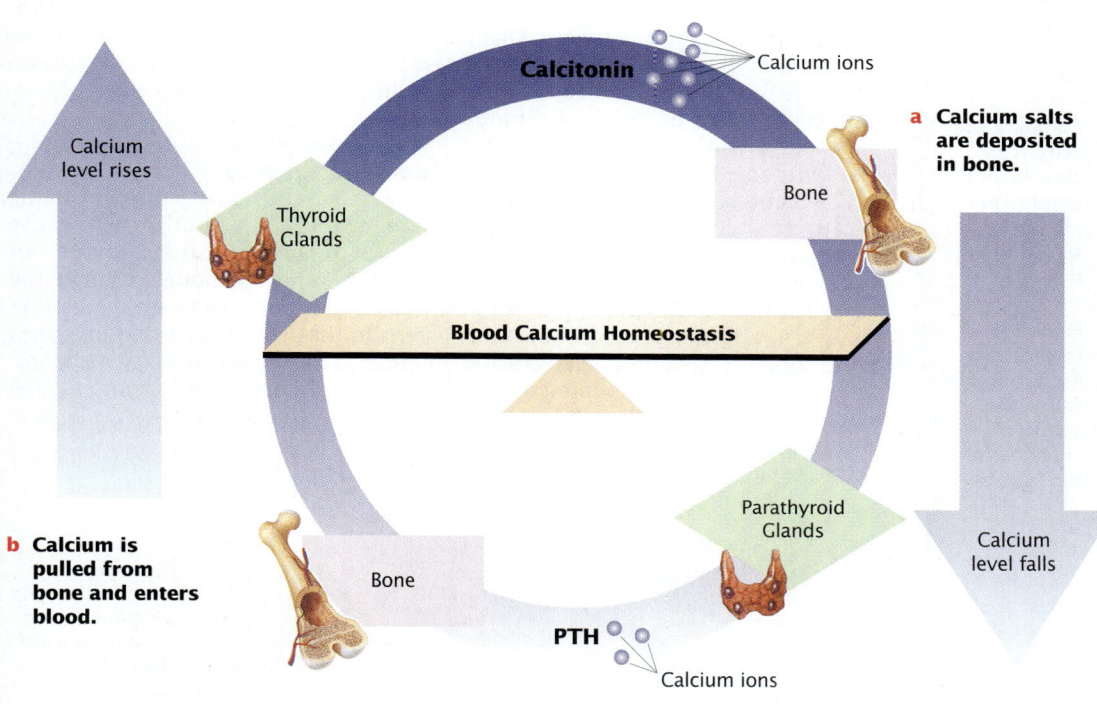

Calcitonin — Calcium ions

Calcium level rises

Thyroid Glands

a Calcium salts are deposited in bone.

Bone

Blood Calcium Homeostasis

b Calcium is pulled from bone and enters blood.

Bone

Parathyroid Glands

Calcium level falls

PTH

Calcium ions

SECTION REVIEW

1. Define the term *hormone*, and name four endocrine glands in the body.

2. Why are the nervous system and endocrine system often called the neuroendocrine system?

3. How does the body regulate the release of hormones?

4. What roles do the hormones calcitonin, PTH, and thyroxine play in homeostasis?

Phase One
Preparation

Scheduling

See the **Lesson Planning Guide** on pages 629A and 629B for lecture, classwork, and assignment options for Section 31-2.

Phase Two
Teaching Strategies

Visual Strategy Figure 31-6

● **Comparing Structures**
See if students recall which other class of organic compounds illustrated in this figure, besides protein, makes up the cell membrane. Have them compare the receptor protein's shape before the hormone binds to it with its shape after the hormone binds to it. Have the students review the cell membrane's architecture in Chapter 3.

Hormones are carried throughout the human body in the bloodstream. Only target cells actually respond to the message that has been sent. After a hormone arrives at its target, the hormone causes certain actions to occur. Two types of hormones cause changes in cells in different ways, as you will learn in this section.

31-2 How Hormones Work

OBJECTIVES

1 Describe how a target cell responds to a hormone.

2 Compare the actions of steroid and peptide hormones in affecting a target cell.

3 Explain how fewer than 50 hormones cause thousands of changes in the body.

Hormone Receptor Proteins

As you read in Chapter 4, the cell membrane contains receptor proteins. A receptor protein has a unique shape that will only hold a certain type of molecule. If a cell has a receptor protein that holds a particular hormone molecule, then the cell will respond to that hormone. For example, bone cells have receptor proteins that will hold parathyroid hormone molecules. A parathyroid hormone molecule will fit into one of these receptor proteins like a key fitting into a lock, as shown in **Figure 31-6**. Fitting the hormone molecule into the receptor changes the receptor's shape, like opening a lock, which causes the cell's activities to change. In this case, the bone cell will begin to break down the minerals stored in the bone so that calcium can be released. While many receptor proteins are located in the cell membrane, others are found inside the cytoplasm or in the nucleus of the cell.

Hormones affect enzymes in cells

How can the binding of a hormone molecule to a receptor protein cause drastic changes in the activities of a cell? Some hormones change the activity or amounts of enzymes present in that cell. Recall that enzymes initiate or speed up chemical reactions. When a hormone causes changes in the enzymes in a cell, it causes changes in the chemical reactions that occur inside the cell.

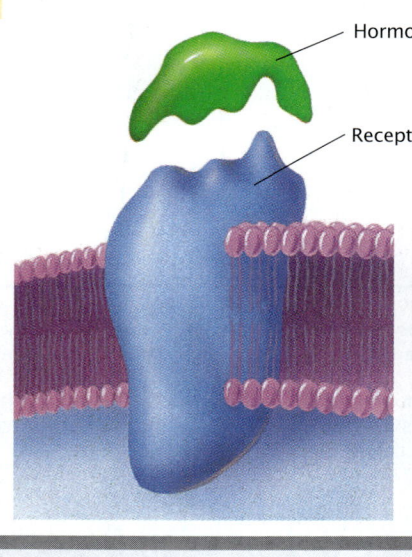
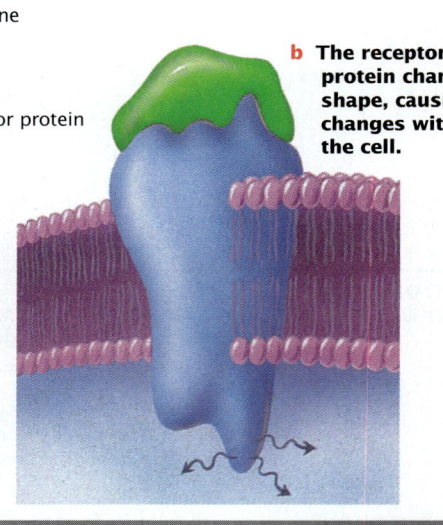

Hormone

Receptor protein

b The receptor protein changes shape, causing changes within the cell.

Figure 31-6
a When a hormone comes into contact with a cell membrane receptor protein that will hold it, the hormone binds to the receptor protein like a key fitting into a lock.

Videodisc Resources

Holt Biology Videodiscs
Lesson 31-2: How Hormones Work

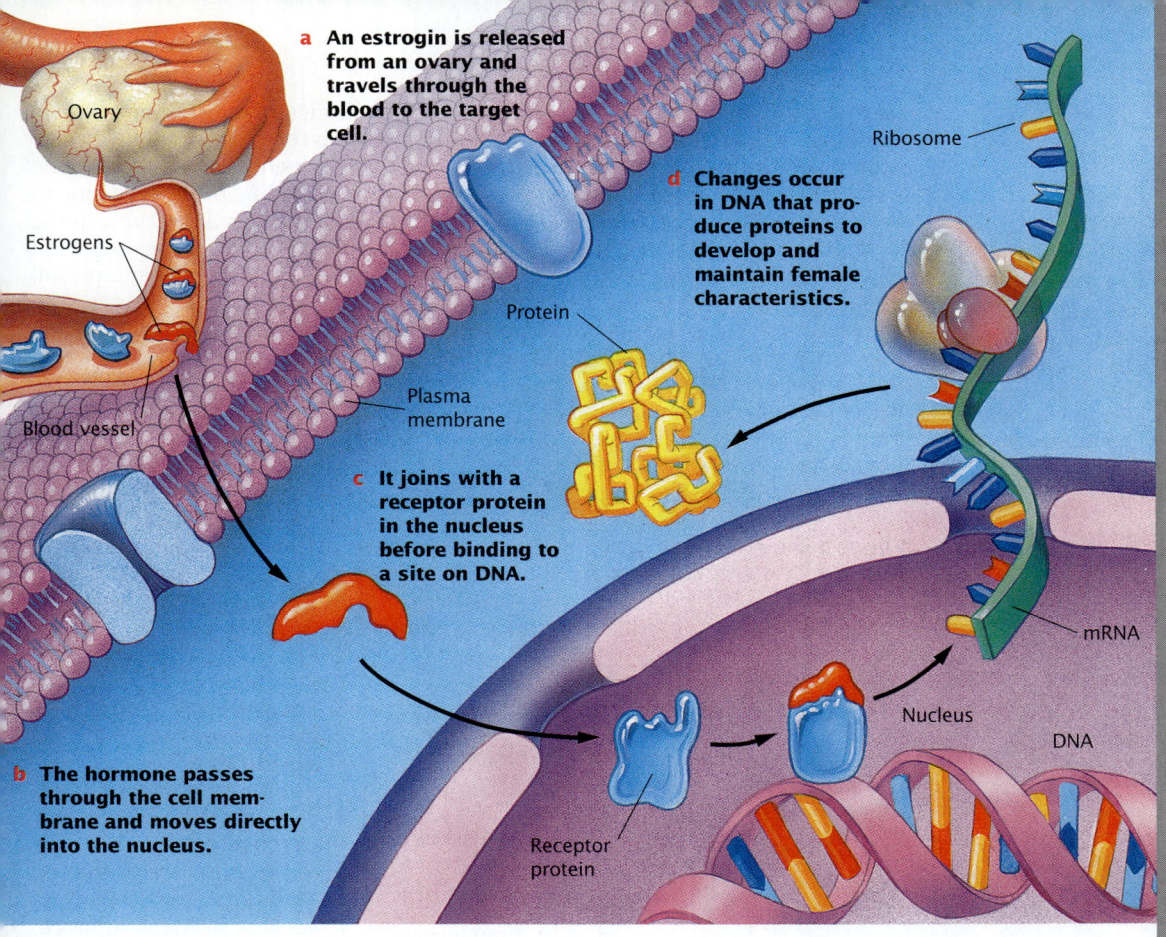

a An estrogin is released from an ovary and travels through the blood to the target cell.

Ovary

Estrogens

Blood vessel

Plasma membrane

Protein

Ribosome

d Changes occur in DNA that produce proteins to develop and maintain female characteristics.

c It joins with a receptor protein in the nucleus before binding to a site on DNA.

mRNA

Nucleus

DNA

b The hormone passes through the cell membrane and moves directly into the nucleus.

Receptor protein

Figure 31-7
The group of steroid hormones known as estrogens influence development of female sexual traits. The way these steroid hormones cause changes in cellular activity is described above.

Steroid Hormones

Hormones assembled from cholesterol are **steroid hormones**. Steroid hormones include the sex hormones and adrenal cortex hormones. All steroid hormones do their work inside the cell's nucleus, where they activate genes and trigger changes in chromosomes.

Steroid hormones pass through the cell membrane without help and enter the cytoplasm. Steroid hormones made in the adrenal cortex have receptors in the cytoplasm. Once bound to a receptor, the steroid hormone enters the cell's nucleus, where it binds to DNA and influences genes.

Receptors for most of the sex hormones reside in the cell's nucleus. After crossing the cell membrane, the sex hormone goes directly to the nucleus, where a receptor awaits. In the nucleus, the hormone and receptor bind first to one another, then to a site on DNA, as shown in **Figure 31-7**.

Steroid hormones switch genes on and off

Recall that every cell in your body (except sperm or egg cells) contains all of the genes that you inherited from your parents. However, different sets of genes are switched on or off in different types of cells. Steroid hormones operate some of these switches. Switching genes on or off alters a cell's enzyme activity. When the switch is on, enzyme activity, and thus protein synthesis, is in full swing. New proteins may then produce other receptors, proteins, or hormones, having far-reaching effects on the cell's metabolism.

Connection: *Chapter 3*

Polar and Nonpolar Molecules
Review how the lipid bilayer of the cell membrane inhibits polar molecules from entering the cell but does not pose any obstacle to nonpolar molecules, including steroid hormones.

Connection: *Chapter 5*

Enzymes
Remind students that the interaction between an enzyme and its substrate is much like that between a hormone and its receptor protein—the two must "fit together" in order to work.

Connection: *Chapter 8*

Regulating Gene Expression
Review how genes are switched on and off with the help of inducers and repressors to control gene expression. Have students discuss how steroid hormones function as inducers.

Visual Strategy | **Figure 31-7**

● **Identifying Functions**
Lead students through each of the steps illustrated in this figure so that they understand how steroid hormones activate certain genes. Discuss what would happen to these genes if the level of estrogen declined and eventually vanished.

Matter of Fact: Cholesterol Is Not All Bad

The most important steroid is cholesterol, which has earned a bad reputation for its role in arteriosclerosis but is absolutely essential to human survival. In fact, the body even synthesizes cholesterol in the liver, regardless of dietary intake. Cholesterol is not just a building block for the steroid hormones; it is found in cell membranes as well. Cholesterol is also the precursor to vitamin D.

Key to Strategies
● Understanding Concepts (Tier I)
■ Applying Information (Tier II)
▲ Critical Thinking (Tier III)

Peptide Hormones

Hormones made of chains of amino acids are called **peptide hormones**. Amino acids can be joined to form short and simple or long and complex peptides. Most hormones are peptide hormones. Recall that amino acids dissolve in water because both are polar molecules. However, the positive and negative charges on peptide hormones prevent them from passing through the lipid bilayer of a cell membrane to the cell's interior. Thus, peptide hormones and other polar hormones or neurotransmitters must send messages from outside the target cell.

Second messengers carry information into the cytoplasm
Because peptide hormones cannot enter the cell, they bind to receptors on the cell membrane. The hormone is the first messenger, carrying the message from the endocrine gland to the cell surface. Binding of the hormone to its receptor activates an enzyme in the cell membrane, which causes a second messenger to appear in the cytoplasm. The **second messenger** carries the message into the cytoplasm.

One of the most common second messengers is cyclic AMP. Cyclic AMP is made from ATP by an enzyme that removes two phosphate groups, forming AMP. The ends of the AMP join to form a circle. Second messengers such as cyclic AMP generally activate enzymes in the cytoplasm of target cells. **Figure 31-8** shows how the peptide hormone glucagon (*GLOO kuh gahn*) signals liver cells to release glucose into the blood.

Second messengers are hormone amplifiers
A single hormone molecule binding to a receptor in the cell membrane can result in the formation of many second messengers in the cytoplasm. Each second messenger, in turn, can activate many enzymes. Sometimes these enzymes activate other enzymes. This cascade of activity greatly amplifies the original signal, enabling each hormone molecule to have a tremendous effect inside a cell, even though it never actually enters the cell.

Figure 31-8
Liver cells have receptor proteins for the peptide hormone glucagon, which is made by the pancreas. Glucagon uses cyclic AMP as a second messenger to release glucose into the blood.

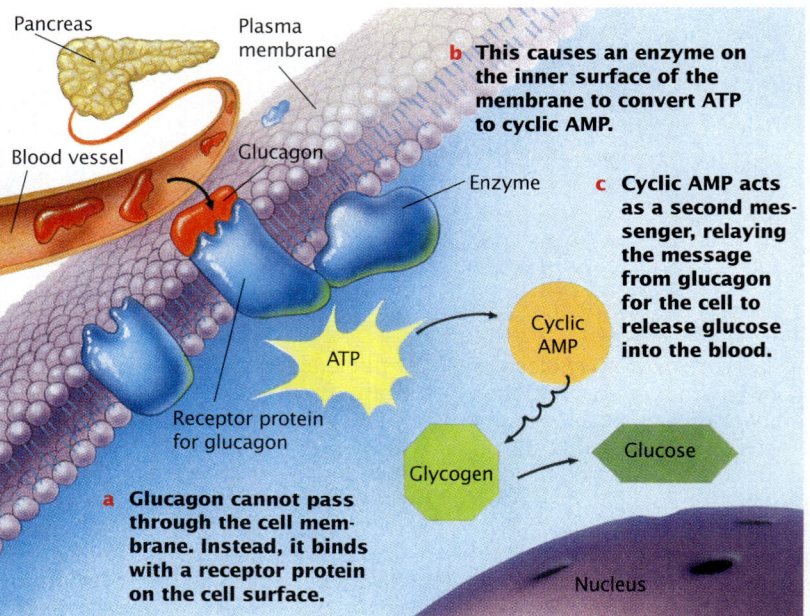

Pancreas

Plasma membrane

Blood vessel

Glucagon

Enzyme

Receptor protein for glucagon

ATP

Cyclic AMP

Glycogen

Glucose

Nucleus

b This causes an enzyme on the inner surface of the membrane to convert ATP to cyclic AMP.

c Cyclic AMP acts as a second messenger, relaying the message from glucagon for the cell to release glucose into the blood.

a Glucagon cannot pass through the cell membrane. Instead, it binds with a receptor protein on the cell surface.

SECTION REVIEW

1 How does a receptor protein respond to a hormone molecule?

2 Name the two ways that hormones affect enzymes.

3 How do the estrogens deliver a message to a target cell?

4 How does the hormone glucagon deliver a message to a target cell?

Your body functions depend on the delicate interaction between your endocrine system and your body tissues. The endocrine system orchestrates several processes used by the body to cope with stress, to regulate metabolism, to control blood sugar levels, to carry on respiration, and even to reproduce.

31-3 Glands and Their Functions

OBJECTIVES

1 Locate three major endocrine glands or organs, and identify the hormone(s) each produces.

2 Explain the effects of producing or administering too much or too little of a particular hormone.

3 Predict the effect of long-term stress on homeostasis.

4 Evaluate the advantages and disadvantages of inhibiting prostaglandin synthesis.

The Adrenal Glands

Fewer than 10 major endocrine glands and several other organs in the body produce dozens of different hormones. Six major hormones are produced by the **adrenal glands** alone. The adrenal glands are two almond-sized glands located on top of the kidneys. Each adrenal gland is two endocrine glands in one. The inner part of each adrenal gland is called the adrenal medulla, and the outer part is called the adrenal cortex.

The adrenal medulla helps the body react to a sudden crisis

The adrenal medulla is different from other glands because of the signal that activates it. Rather than being activated by hormones, the adrenal medulla is stimulated to release its hormones by nerves that run directly to it from the hypothalamus.

The adrenal medulla produces epinephrine *(ep ih NEF rihn)*, or adrenaline, and norepinephrine, or noradrenalin. These hormones work with the autonomic nervous system to produce the **"fight-or-flight" reaction** and are secreted in response to sudden stresses such as fear, anger, pain, or physical exertion. In a fraction of a second, the adrenal medulla can respond to any emergency that may arise, such as the scene in **Figure 31-9**. The heart beats faster, and blood flow increases to the heart and muscles. At the same time, respiration increases, and more oxygen is delivered throughout the body. In addition, blood pressure rises, sweating increases, and muscles become tense, ready for action. Because these changes help us to act quickly in times of sudden stress, it is also known as the alarm reaction phase of the "General Adaptation Syndrome," or GAS.

Figure 31-9
This is a famous movie scene. But if it were a real, life-threatening emergency, the adrenal medulla would secrete the hormone epinephrine. This hormone speeds up the heart rate and increases blood flow to the muscles.

639

Videodisc Resources

Holt Biology Videodiscs
Lesson 31-3: Glands and Their Functions

Phase One
Preparation

Scheduling
See the **Lesson Planning Guide** on pages 629A and 629B for lecture, classwork, and assignment options for Section 31-3.

Phase Two
Teaching Strategies

Demonstration
● **Comparing Functions**
Show students a photograph of a woman with a great deal of facial hair (the bearded lady in the circus). Point out that the adrenal cortex is also the source of androgens. A tumor in the adrenal cortex may result in the increased production of these sex hormones, enhancing the appearance of such male secondary sex characteristics as facial hair.

Health Connection

portfolio

Autoimmune Diseases
Have students prepare short reports on different autoimmune diseases, such as myasthenia gravis or rheumatoid arthritis, and present them to the class. Each student can do a different disease or a disease suspected of autoimmune initiation.

Key to Strategies
● **Understanding Concepts (Tier I)**
■ **Applying Information (Tier II)**
▲ **Critical Thinking (Tier III)**

Figure 31-10
Long-term stress and continued release of cortisol gradually threaten the homeostasis of the body. Long-term stress can be severe enough to cause death, but it is more likely to result in long-term adaptation or illness.

tation is called the resistance stage of adaptation.

In this second stage, cortisol is the steroid hormone that makes more energy available to the body, especially the brain. Cortisol causes the body to burn lean tissue (muscle) for energy. Its release increases the level of blood glucose so that the body increases in strength, endurance, and sensory response. In the alarm and resistance stages of adaptation, this effect helps you to adapt more efficiently. When stressful situations continue without relief, however, the body enters a state of chronic fatigue. Organs malfunction, and physical as well as mental burnout may result, signaling the third and final phase of the adaptation syndrome, the exhaustion stage.

Active READING

Technique: Reading Organizer
As students read about the adrenal glands on this and the previous page, have them complete the reading organizer below, which details the phases of the "General Adaptation Syndrome." *(Under the Alarm Reaction Stage, students should list the following: epinephrine and norepinephrine released, "fight-or-flight" reaction produced, heart rate increases, blood flow and pressure increase, and sweating increases. Under the Resistance Stage, students should list the following: cortisol secreted to produce more energy, increase in endurance and strength, and organ malfunction. Under the Exhaustion Stage, students should list the following: continued cortisol release results in immune system suppression, loss of bone mass, poor wound healing, and many other disorders.)*

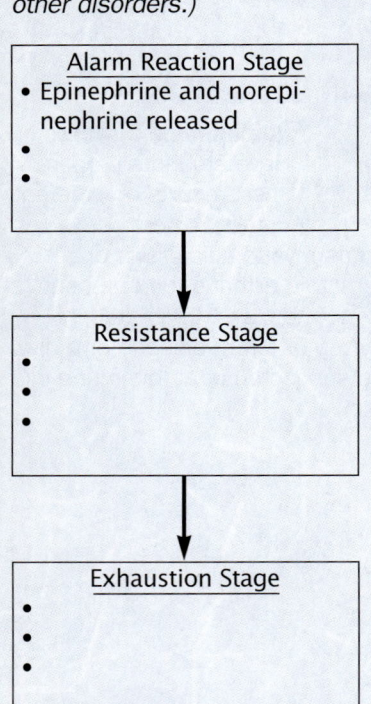

Alarm Reaction Stage
• Epinephrine and norepinephrine released
•
•

Resistance Stage
•
•
•

Exhaustion Stage
•
•
•

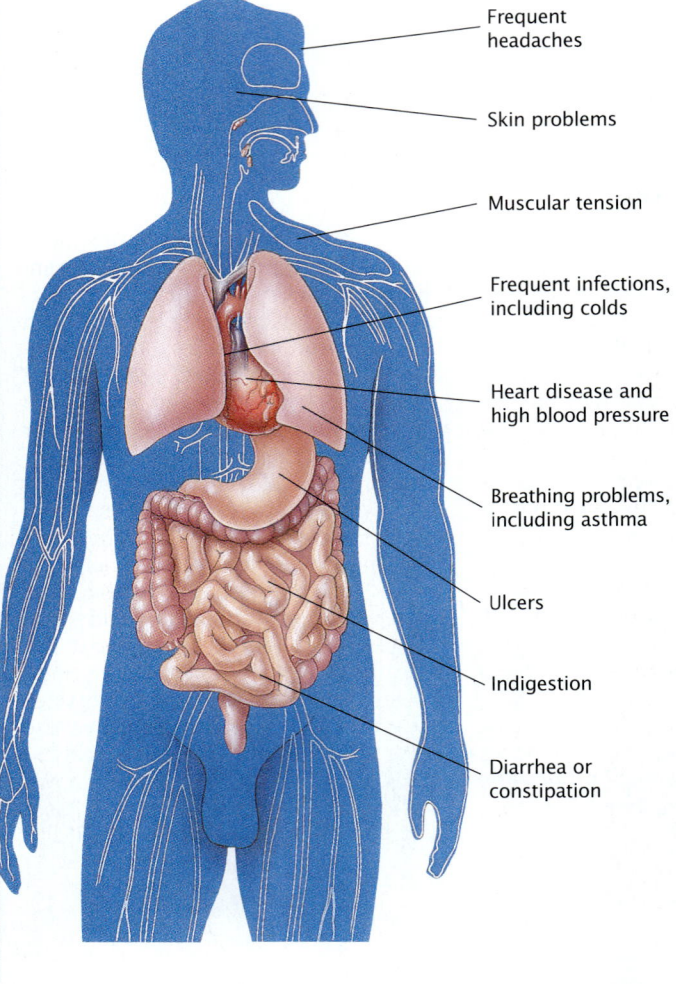

- Frequent headaches
- Skin problems
- Muscular tension
- Frequent infections, including colds
- Heart disease and high blood pressure
- Breathing problems, including asthma
- Ulcers
- Indigestion
- Diarrhea or constipation

The adrenal cortex helps the body deal with long-term stress

Once the alarm stage is over, the effects of epinephrine wear off within a few minutes. If the crisis continues for more than a few hours, however, other hormones produced by the adrenal cortex enable the body to adapt to stress for hours, days, or even weeks. This new period of adap-

Long-term exposure to steroid hormones weakens the immune system

When you are under stress for long periods of time, the continued release of cortisol has negative effects on your body's ability to defend itself. The immune system becomes suppressed, or weakened, and loses its ability to fight disease effectively. Immune suppression may play a role in the development of certain types of cancers and other health problems. For example, ulcers, bowel disorders, heart disease, high blood pressure, asthma, skin disorders, and even autoimmune diseases are linked to stress. Other side effects of continued release of cortisol include the loss of resistance to infections, loss of bone mass and muscle protein, and poor healing of wounds. Cortisone is similar to cortisol but is made in much smaller quantities by the body. Synthetically produced cortisone is injected, given orally, or used in cream form as an anti-inflammatory drug in the treatment of arthritis, joint injuries, and severe insect bites and other allergic responses. The prolonged use of cortisone or similar drugs can have the same negative effects as the continued release of cortisol. **Figure 31-10** illustrates a range of ways in which the body may adapt to long-term stress.

The Thyroid Gland

The thyroid gland is located in the neck, just below the Adam's apple. The thyroid gland releases thyroxine and other hormones containing iodine, which regulate the body's metabolic rate. Thyroid hormones are necessary for normal growth and development during childhood and for maintaining mental alertness in adults. Thyroid hormones also affect reproductive functions.

Too much thyroxine causes Graves' disease

Some common disorders of the endocrine system are caused by problems with the thyroid. If too much thyroxine is produced, the condition that results is called **hyperthyroidism**. One form of hyperthyroidism is Graves' disease. People with Graves' disease have a rapid, irregular heart rate, feel very nervous, and lose weight. Olympic gold medalist Gail Devers, pictured in **Figure 31-11**, began to experience the symptoms of Graves' disease just prior to the 1988 Summer Olympics. Most people with Graves' disease can lead normal, productive lives once they are treated.

Graves' disease seems to be caused by a malfunction of the immune system. Recall that hormones work by binding to receptor proteins, which causes changes in the activity of the cell. The binding of a hormone to receptor proteins in thyroid cells causes the thyroid gland to release thyroxine. In a person with Graves' disease, however, antibodies made by the immune system bind to these receptor proteins instead. As a result, the thyroid gland releases more hormone in the body even though too much is already present.

Graves' disease is usually treated with a dose of radioactive iodine. The iodine collects in the thyroid gland and, over the course of several months, slowly destroys thyroid tissue. It is hard to control just how much of the gland is destroyed, however, so the patient often makes too little thyroxine after the treatment. Thyroxine levels are then brought up to normal by taking pills containing the hormone.

Figure 31-11
In 1988, American sprinter Gail Devers experienced severe weight loss, uncontrollable shaking fits, and loss of vision in her left eye. Nearly two years later she was diagnosed with Graves' disease, a condition in which too much thyroxine is produced by the thyroid gland. With proper treatment, however, Devers went on to win the gold medal in the women's 100 m dash in the 1992 and 1996 Summer Olympics.

641

Figure 31-12

a **The lack of iodine in this woman's diet has caused her thyroid gland to swell, producing a goiter.**

b **A diet that includes adequate amounts of iodine, which is found in seafood and iodized table salt, can prevent a goiter from developing.**

Low levels of thyroxine cause hypothyroidism

The production of too little thyroxine is called **hypothyroidism**. Thyroid cells make thyroid hormones by attaching three or four iodine atoms to a large protein. Iodine comes from the diet, and the large protein is made and stored in the thyroid. When the diet contains little or no iodine, there is little to attach to the large protein. The negative-feedback loop that controls thyroxine production fails. More and more of the large protein is stored. The thyroid stays stimulated, trying unsuccessfully to make hormone. The thyroid gland swells with the growing store of protein, producing a **goiter** (GOY tuhr), shown in **Figure 31-12a**.

Iodine is found in foods like the ones shown in **Figure 31-12b**. People living near an ocean usually include seafood in their diets and rarely have thyroid problems caused by a lack of iodine. However, goiters used to be common in inland regions of the United States. Today, small amounts of iodine are added to plain table salt. But goiters are still common in developing countries, where they are considered a serious problem because of their effect on growth and brain development in children and on mental functions in adults.

Some people who get enough dietary iodine still suffer from hypothyroidism. Like those with Graves' disease, these people suffer from a misdirected attack by antibodies from their immune system. In this case, the damaged thyroid gland cannot produce adequate thyroxine.

Because the thyroid gland controls metabolic rate, people with too much thyroid hormone are thin. Sometimes being overweight is attributed to an "underactive thyroid." However, even very low thyroxine levels cause a weight gain of only 5–10 lbs, so being seriously overweight is not usually caused by low thyroxine levels.

642

Other Glands and Hormones

The hormones that are responsible for the development and maintenance of sexual characteristics are **sex hormones**. In males, a group of sex hormones called the androgens are produced by the testes. The most important of these is testosterone *(tehs TAHS tuh rohn)*. Anabolic steroids are synthetic androgens. In females, the ovaries produce two groups of sex hormones known as estrogens and progestins. The most abundant of these are estrogen *(EHS truh jehn)* and progesterone *(proh JEHS tuh rohn)*, respectively. Sex hormones affect sexual behavior.

The release of sex hormones is controlled by the hypothalamus and the pituitary gland. Males and females produce the same hormones in these glands, but the level of these hormones varies in males and in females. You will learn more about the sex hormones in Chapter 35.

Small glands produce hormones

Other endocrine glands release hormones. Specialized white blood cells called T-cells mature in the thymus gland because of thymosin, which stimulates T-cell development. Although the gland gets smaller after puberty, its role in adult immunity is still debated. You will learn more about T-cells in Chapter 33.

The pineal gland contains light-sensitive cells that mark changes in the length of days and nights. In some way not yet understood, the gland translates light information and then relates it to biological rhythms associated with reproduction. There is some reason to believe that melatonin may help to regulate the onset and ending of puberty. This gland, too, gets smaller with age, but it continues to function to a small degree in healthy adults. The functions of these glands and others are summarized in **Table 31-1**.

Table 31-1 Endocrine Glands, Organs, and Their Functions

Source	Hormone	Main target(s)	Effect(s)
Pineal gland	Melatonin	Gonads (indirectly)	Inhibits reproductive activities; stops functioning around onset of puberty
Parathyroid	Parathyroid hormone	Bone, kidney	Elevates calcium levels in blood
Thymus	Thymosin Other hormones	Lymphocytes	Plays role in immune response
Ovary	Estrogens	Female reproductive structures	Maturation of reproductive organs; influences egg maturation and release
	Progestins	Uterus, breasts	Prepares and maintains uterine lining for pregnancy; stimulates breast development
Testis	Testosterone	Male reproductive structures	Maturation of reproductive organs; influences sperm formation

643

Theme Answer

Stability and Homeostasis

Homeostasis is maintained by the active feedback mechanisms of our hormones. The feedback loop constantly monitors and adjusts our endocrine levels for optimum bodily function. Often our hormones act in opposition to one another. Insulin and glucagon work in opposition to maintain a certain level of glucose in the blood. Other hormones work synergistically. Estrogens and progesterone work together to prepare the uterus for the implantation of the embryo.

Demonstration

● Comparing Structures

Show the class a photograph of a girl and a boy in their early teenage years (puberty). Discuss which sex characteristics start to develop at this time in their lives. Point out that in females, sex hormones cause the enlargement of breasts, widening of hips, and acquisition of an additional layer of body fat, and that in males, they cause deepening of the voice, increased growth of body hair, and rapid growth.

Visual Strategy   Table 31-1

● Summarizing Information

Lead the students through the information in this table to complete their study of the endocrine glands.

Key to Strategies
● Understanding Concepts (Tier I)
■ Applying Information (Tier II)
▲ Critical Thinking (Tier III)

Figure 31-13
The hormone insulin lowers blood sugar levels after meals. The hormone glucagon raises blood sugar levels between meals. A balanced breakfast like #1 stabilizes blood sugar for the entire morning. A breakfast high in sugar like #2 produces the symptoms of low blood sugar soon after it's eaten.

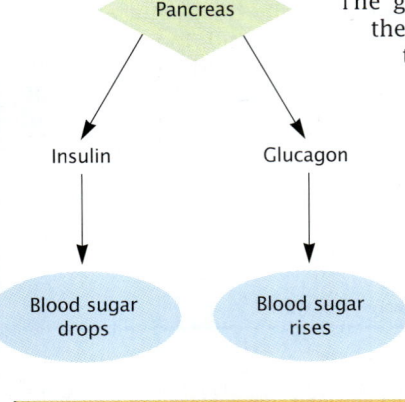

The Pancreas

The pancreas contains small clusters of hormone-secreting cells that help regulate how much glucose is dissolved in the blood. This **blood sugar**, as it is commonly called, circulates to all cells in the body, providing the energy needed to fuel all kinds of cellular activity. Two hormones from the pancreas work opposite one another to control blood sugar.

After you eat, enzymes break down the food you have eaten into amino acids, glucose, other simple sugars, and numerous other molecules that the body uses for fuel. The sugars pass through the walls of the small intestine and enter your bloodstream. Blood sugar level rises. The glucose molecules are then transported to all of the body's cells. The rise in blood sugar triggers release of insulin.

At the cell membrane, **insulin**, a peptide hormone, interacts with a receptor and helps glucose cross the membrane and enter the cytoplasm. Getting glucose into cells has the effect of lowering blood sugar. This is extremely important because high blood sugar can seriously upset homeostasis and even threaten life. After you have eaten, extra sugar not used by the cells is stored in the liver in the form of carbohydrate called glycogen or under the skin as fat.

If you haven't eaten for a while, your blood sugar level begins to fall. A different hormone, also made by the pancreas, helps you in this case. Glucagon raises the level of glucose in the blood. It does this by converting glycogen that has been stored in the liver into glucose, which the cells can use. This action, too, is important because low blood sugar can also upset homeostasis. Normal brain function requires a certain amount of glucose. If the level of sugar in the blood falls, the brain cannot get what it needs. Symptoms of lowered blood sugar may include nervousness, irritable mood, difficulty concentrating, weak or shaking muscles, and, frequently, headaches. The homeostatic control of blood sugar is shown in **Figure 31-13**.

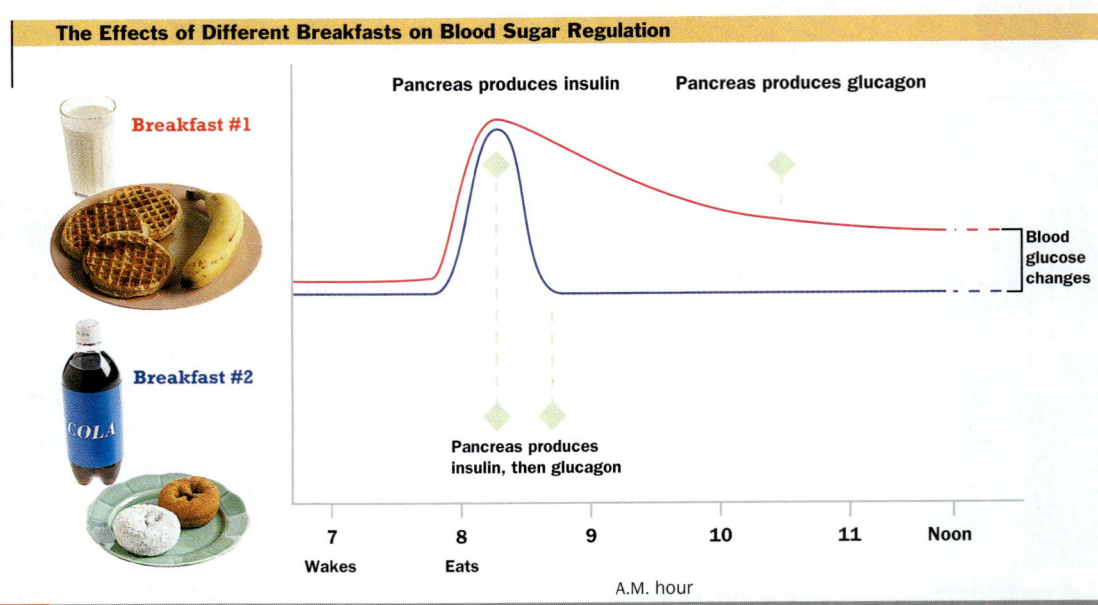

The Effects of Different Breakfasts on Blood Sugar Regulation

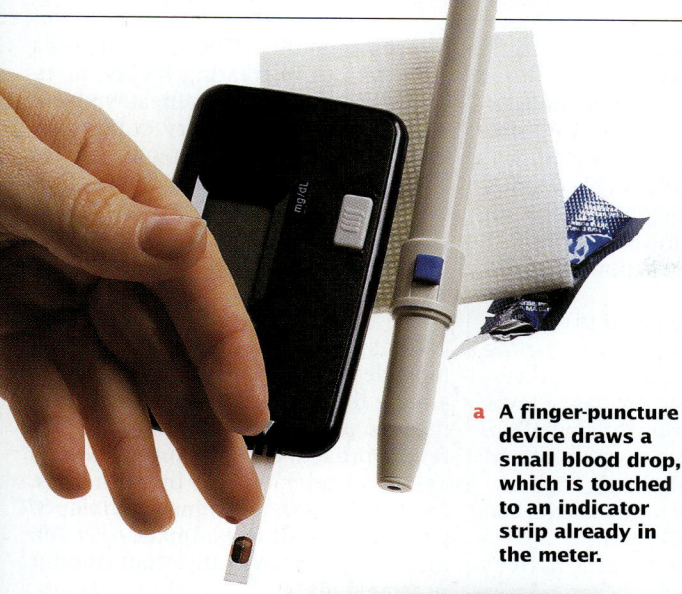

a A finger-puncture device draws a small blood drop, which is touched to an indicator strip already in the meter.

Figure 31-14
A glucose meter is used to monitor blood sugar level.

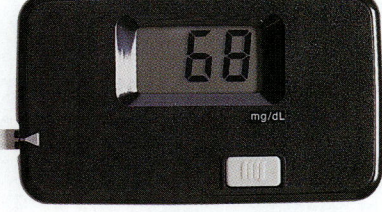

b The meter reads the strip and gives a glucose reading in 20–45 seconds.

Insulin plays a role in diabetes

Diabetes mellitus *(deye uh BEET eez muh LYT uhs)* is a disease that results from abnormally high blood sugar. Heredity, hormones, diet, and stress interact to produce different types of diabetes.

When a body makes little or no insulin, insulin-dependent diabetes mellitus (IDDM) is diagnosed. IDDM, also called Type I diabetes, usually develops in childhood or early adolescence. This form of diabetes requires daily injections of insulin. The amount of insulin given is determined by the calories taken in at each meal or snack.

When insulin is produced but glucose cannot enter cells, non-insulin dependent diabetes (NIDDM), or Type II diabetes, is diagnosed. NIDDM occurs when there are not enough insulin receptors on the cells, when the receptors are defective, or when too little insulin is produced. This form of diabetes accounts for about 95 percent of diabetics, and it usually occurs in adults over the age of 40. Obesity and inactivity contribute to the development of NIDDM, which can be prevented. Proper diet and aerobic exercise, which improves the cell's uptake of glucose, are used to manage the disease, although oral medicines may be used to lower blood sugar.

Uncontrolled blood sugar is dangerous for diabetics. When blood sugar rises but cannot enter cells, proteins and fats are burned for energy. Fat breakdown releases fatty acids and ketones into the bloodstream. Fatty acids release energy, but ketones are toxic and can disrupt heart rate, breathing, and brain activity if they are not excreted by the kidneys. Coma and death can follow. High blood sugar can result if diabetics eat or drink too much or fail to take their medication. When blood sugar is low, the brain cannot receive the glucose it needs. Dizziness, confusion, and fainting may result. Shock results if blood sugar drops too low. Blood sugar can get too low if a diabetic takes too much medication or does not eat regularly.

To prevent diabetic emergencies such as these, diabetics monitor their blood sugar several times a day. Glucose meters measure blood glucose and indicate if blood sugar is within the desired range. If needed, diabetics can adjust their caloric intake, their exercise, or their medication so that blood sugar stays within the normal range. **Figure 31-14** shows a glucose meter being used to monitor blood sugar, and **Table 31-2** summarizes the symptoms of IDDM and NIDDM.

Table 31-2 Warning Signs of Diabetes

Type I (IDDM)	Type II (NIDDM)
Frequent urination	Any of the Type I
Unusual thirst	symptoms
Extreme hunger	Frequent infections
Unusual weight loss	Blurred vision
Extreme fatigue	Cuts or bruises that
Irritability	are slow to heal
	Tingling or numbness in the hands or feet
	Recurring skin, gum, or bladder infections

645

Prostaglandins may cause fever and pain

A group of lipids called **prostaglandins** *(prahs tuh GLAN dihnz)* also function in the body as hormones. Prostaglandins are produced in small quantities by specialized cells in almost every part of the body. They act locally rather than traveling by blood to a distant site.

Prostaglandins help blood to clot and can raise blood pressure by causing the smooth muscle surrounding blood vessels to constrict. They also cause fever and increase pain during inflammation. Some cause the uterus to contract and start labor during childbirth. High levels of prostaglandins in the uterus can also cause menstrual cramps.

Aspirin and aspirin alternatives interfere with the synthesis and release of prostaglandins. These compounds are effective in treating fevers, menstrual cramps, headaches, muscle pains, and inflammatory conditions such as arthritis. However, only aspirin alternatives are recommended for children and teens. The use of aspirin is associated with Reye's syndrome, a potentially fatal disease of the liver and brain. Although many people are aware that young children should not take aspirin, they do not know that most deaths from Reye's syndrome are among teenagers. Aspirin alternatives include generic drugs such as ibuprofen, naproxen, and fenoprofen, which are sold under various brand names. **Figure 31-15** shows some examples of pain, fever, and inflammation, which may respond to drugs that inhibit prostaglandins.

Figure 31-15
Prostaglandins help produce fever, pain, and inflammation as part of the body's system of defense.

Joint injury with inflammation from overuse

Painful menstrual cramps

Chickenpox and fever

a Drugs that inhibit the production and release of prostaglandins can help reduce these symptoms.

b Aspirin alternatives are considered safer than aspirin for children and teens with viral infections, although many fevers respond well to ample fluids, calories, and rest, without medication.

SECTION REVIEW

1. Name three major endocrine glands in your body and the hormones they produce.

2. What occurs if the thyroid gland or the pancreas produces too much or too little hormone?

3. How does the fight-or-flight (alarm) reaction differ from the later stages of adaptation?

4. Why are aspirin and ibuprofen effective in treating headaches?

When the body produces too little growth hormone, dwarfism can result. When too much growth hormone is produced, giantism can occur.

	Key Terms	Summary
31-1 **What Hormones Do**  In a negative-feedback process, thyroxine speeds up metabolism, keeping body temperature constant.	hormone (p. 631) endocrine gland (p. 631) target (p. 631) neuroendocrine system (p. 632) pituitary gland (p. 633) feedback (p. 634) negative feedback (p. 634)	• Endocrine glands and other organs secrete hormones into the bloodstream. • The effects of the endocrine system are similar to those of the nervous system, but these effects usually occur more slowly and last longer. • The brain is connected directly to the endocrine system by the hypothalamus, which helps regulate the body's internal environment through the pituitary gland. • Feedback systems allow for endocrine self-regulation.
31-2 **How Hormones Work**  Hormones bind with receptors like keys fitting into locks.	steroid hormone (p. 637) peptide hormone (p. 638) second messenger (p. 638)	• Hormones travel throughout the body in the bloodstream. They affect only the appropriate target cells. • Steroid hormones pass through the cell membrane. Peptide hormones act from outside the cell by means of second messengers. • Hormones act by affecting the kinds or amounts of enzymes produced.
31-3 **Glands and Their Functions**  A treatable condition called Graves' disease causes the thyroid gland to produce too much thyroxine.	adrenal glands (p. 639) "fight or flight" reaction (p. 639) hyperthyroidism (p. 641) hypothyroidism (p. 642) goiter (p. 642) sex hormone (p. 643) blood sugar (p. 644) insulin (p. 644) diabetes mellitus (p. 645) prostaglandin (p. 646)	• Fewer than 10 endocrine glands produce dozens of hormones in the human body. • The adrenal medulla helps the body react quickly to crises. The adrenal cortex makes steroids that regulate energy levels and adaptation to long-term stress. • The thyroid gland regulates metabolism, while the pancreas regulates blood sugar. • Other hormones, made by smaller endocrine glands or by organs, also have powerful effects on their respective targets. • Hormone-like substances called prostaglandins act locally to regulate changes in the body.

Alternative Assessment

Have each student prepare a blank Bingo card with 25 squares, labeling the center one "FREE." Write 24 terms, names, or short phrases from this chapter on the board. Then instruct students to randomly place each term in one of the squares on their Bingo card. Instruct students to cross out the appropriate box each time a definition is read or a clue is provided. Have students yell "Bingo!" when either a horizontal or vertical line has been completed.

Portfolio Assessment

Portfolio Assessment on page T39 provides options for building and evaluating student portfolios. Students and teachers can select items from the areas listed on page T39 for inclusion in a portfolio.

647

ANSWER TO CONCEPT MAP

The following is one possible answer to the Relating Concepts exercise on page 648.

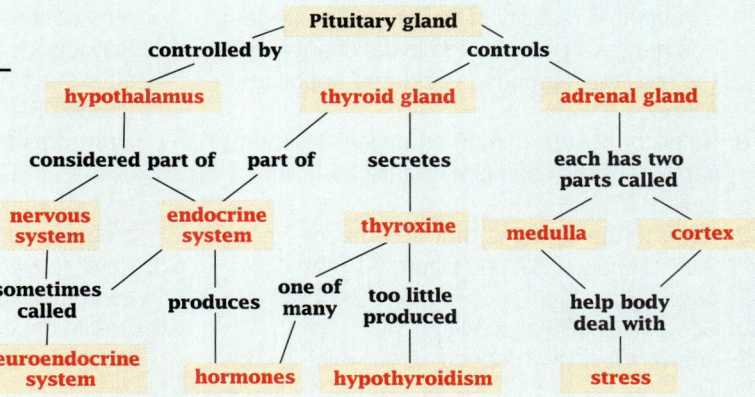

Understanding Vocabulary

1. a. hormones
b. steroid hormones
c. adrenal cortex

2. a. A hormone is a chemical produced by an endocrine gland that regulates the body's activities. Most hormones are produced by the endocrine system, which regulates overall metabolism, growth, reproduction, and maintenance of homeostasis. Hormones are carried in the blood to specific target tissues.
b. Prolactin causes glands in the mother's breasts to produce milk. Oxytocin is the hormone that causes contractions of the uterus during labor. ADH is a hormone that causes the kidneys to form more concentrated urine. These hormones are either produced or stored by the pituitary gland.
c. A peptide hormone is a chain of amino acids, which cannot pass through the cell membrane of a target cell. Binding of the hormone (the first messenger) to its receptor activates an enzyme in the cell membrane, which causes a second messenger to appear in the cytoplasm.

Understanding Concepts

3. Concept map answer is on page 647.

4. Refer to the information on page 631 and the captions that accompany Figure 31-1 on page 631.

5. Refer to the information on page 642 and the captions that accompany Figure 31-12 on page 642.

6. The hypothalamus is the part of the brain that regulates body temperature, breathing, hunger, and thirst. It functions as an endocrine gland by sending out commands in the form of hormones and by transmitting nerve impulses directly to other parts of the brain and other glands.

7. Negative feedback is the

Understanding Vocabulary

1. For each set of terms, complete the analogy.
a. short-term effects : nerve impulses :: long-term effects : _____
b. chains of amino acids : peptide hormones :: assembled from cholesterol : _____
c. epinephrine : adrenal medulla :: cortisol : _____

2. Using each set of words below, write one or more sentences summarizing information learned in this chapter.
a. hormone, endocrine gland, endocrine system, target
b. pituitary gland, prolactin, oxytocin, ADH
c. peptide hormone, target, first messenger, second messenger

Understanding Concepts

3. **Relating Concepts** Construct a concept map that describes the operation of the pituitary gland and its relationship to the rest of the endocrine system. Include the following terms in your concept map: hypothalamus, nervous system, endocrine system, neuroendocrine system, thyroid gland, thyroxine, hormones, adrenal gland, medulla, cortex, stress, and hypothyroidism.

4. **Summarizing Information** What is the function of the endocrine system? What components make up this system?

5. **Identifying Functions** Describe how thyroid cells produce thyroid hormones. What happens when iodine is in short supply?

6. **Recognizing Relationships** Describe the relationship between the hypothalamus and the pituitary gland.

7. **Recognizing Patterns** Explain the role of feedback systems. How does negative-feedback maintain homeostasis?

8. **Inferring Relationships** Describe how the binding of a hormone to a receptor protein changes the activities of a cell.

9. **Organizing Information** Identify the locations where steroid and peptide hormones are activated and ultimately exert their influence.

10. **Comparing Functions** Compare what happens to the body during the alarm-reaction phase of the general adaptation syndrome with what happens during the resistance phase. Identify which endocrine glands and hormones are involved in each phase.

11. **Summarizing Information** Identify three major endocrine glands. Describe where each gland is located and the major hormones produced by each.

12. **Reading Graphs** Look at the graph below. In males, the hormone testosterone regulates aggression and increases the rate at which glucose gets to the muscles. What is happening with baboon A and B? Can you relate this graph with any behavior?

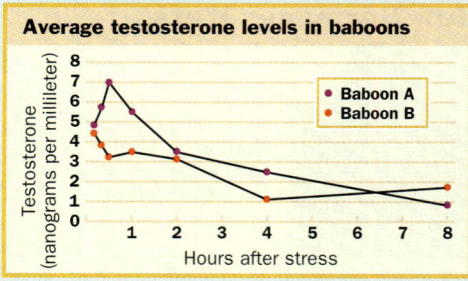

Average testosterone levels in baboons

13. **Recognizing Processes** Describe the relationship between the hormones glucagon and insulin in the regulation of blood sugar.

14. **Recognizing Relationships** Differentiate between the two types of diabetes mellitus. Describe the symptoms of each and how each is treated.

15. **Inferring Relationships** Why might prostaglandins be called "local" hormones?

16. **Analyzing Information** When might inhibiting prostaglandin synthesis be helpful? When might it be unwanted?

17. **BUILDING ON WHAT YOU HAVE LEARNED** In Chapter 30, you learned about neurotransmitters. How are the actions of hormones and neurotransmitters alike? How are they different?

---

regulation of activity of the endocrine system. It is negative because the initial change and the resulting responses occur as opposite actions.

8. Refer to the information on page 636 and the captions that accompany Figure 31-6 on page 636.

9. Refer to the captions that accompany Figure 31-7 on page 637 and Figure 31-8 on page 638.

10. See pages 639 and 640.

11. Answers will vary depending on which glands

are chosen.

12. Baboon A's testosterone level increased after stress and then decreased over time. Baboon B's testosterone level decreased after stress and then continued to decrease over time. Baboon A was probably aggressive and irritable after stress while Baboon B was probably submissive.

13. Refer to Figure 31-13 on page 644 and captions that accompany the figure.

14. Insulin dependent diabetes mellitus (IDDM) results when a person produces almost no

Interpreting Graphics

18. A scientist wanted to know the effects of thyroxine on tadpole growth. She placed three tadpoles in three different beakers of water. In one beaker she added 5 mL of thyroxine; in another beaker she added 10 mL of thyroxine. Nothing was added to the third beaker. She measured the length of the tadpoles every three days for three weeks. The results of her experiment are shown in the graph below.

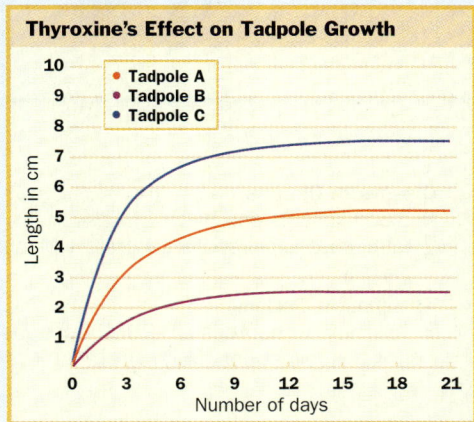

Thyroxine's Effect on Tadpole Growth

- Tadpole A
- Tadpole B
- Tadpole C

Length in cm / Number of days

a. Which line on the graph represents the tadpoles exposed to 10 mL of thyroxine? to no thyroxine? Explain your answer.
b. How would you verbally summarize the results of this experiment?

Reviewing Themes

19. *Stability and Homeostasis*
What are two ways that the hypothalamus helps the body maintain homeostasis?

20. *Matter, Energy, and Organization*
Describe the importance of "fit" between a receptor protein and a hormone.

Thinking Critically

21. **Distinguishing Relevant Information** After a medical examination, a person is found to be unable to move glucose, stored as glycogen, from the liver into the blood. Further tests show that glucagon levels are normal and so is the hormone itself. Why do you think glucagon is unable to carry out its function in this case?

Life/Work Skills

22. **Finding Information** Use library references or search an on-line database to find out about the hormonal causes of giantism and dwarfism. Research the tallest and shortest humans known. Prepare an illustrated report to share your findings with the class.

23. **Using Technology** Working with a group of your classmates, contact a reference librarian to find out about computer software programs such as SUPERDOC and PUFF. How are these programs used and by whom? What advantage is there for using such programs? Summarize your findings in a written report.

Activities and Projects

24. **Health Connection** Use library references or search an on-line database to find out about disorders of the endocrine system such as Addison's disease and Cushing's syndrome. Describe the symptoms and treatments for these and other disorders of the endocrine system. Summarize your findings in a written report to your class.

Discovering Through Reading

25. Read the article "Melatonin Mania" in *Newsweek*, November 1995, pages 60–63. What is melatonin? How do people think melatonin can affect their lives? What are the dangers of high doses of melatonin?

26. Read the article "A Chance to Be Taller," in *TIME*, January 8, 1990, page 70. As more and more synthetic hormones become available through technology, their use in healthy individuals raises questions. When a young person's height varies from that of most others of the same age, social and emotional problems may result. The synthesis in 1985 of human growth hormone (HGH), makes it possible to increase the height of normal, but short, children. With one or several friends, separate the issues into categories such as physical, financial, social, mental, and emotional concerns and present them to your class. After your presentation, develop a series of 8–12 questions to survey your classmates' opinions about the use of HGH.

to the highest levels of thyroxine; line A represents tadpoles exposed to no additional thyroxine. Thyroxine affects the rate of growth; an increased rate of growth indicates increased levels of thyroxine.
b. Increased levels of thyroxine increase the rate and level of growth in tadpoles.

Reviewing Themes

19. It can send out commands in the form of nerve signals or hormones.
20. Refer to the information on page 636 and the captions that accompany Figure 31-6 on page 636.

Thinking Critically

21. The problem could be caused by an insufficient number of, or incorrectly formed, receptor proteins in the cell membranes of cells in the liver.

Life/Work Skills

22. Answers will vary with the resources available.
23. Answers will vary with the resources available.

Activities and Projects

24. Answers will vary with the resources available.

Discovering Through Reading

25. Melatonin is a hormone that is secreted by the pineal gland when our eyes sense oncoming darkness. Melatonin is produced in abundance until puberty, when the amount produced drops off significantly. Melatonin helps keep the body "in sync" with the rhythms of the day and the season. It helps people sleep more soundly and may slow down the results of aging. Scientists do not know what the long-term effects of taking large amounts of melatonin might be.
26. Answers will vary.

---

insulin. Refer to Table 31-2 on page 645 for symptoms. It is treated by daily injections of insulin. Non-insulin dependent diabetes mellitus (NIDDM) has symptoms like those of IDDM. In this disease, the person produces insulin, but cells do not take in enough glucose. Weight control and regular physical activity are important for both the prevention and treatment of this type of diabetes.
15. Prostaglandins affect the cells in their immediate vicinity.
16. Inhibiting the production of prostaglandins

can reduce or eliminate pain; the downside of limiting production is that blood will not clot as quickly.
17. Both are released by a cell and change the behavior of another cell. They are different in that hormones carry a message over great distances in the body, while neurotransmitters carry a message from one cell to an immediate second cell.

Interpreting Graphics

18. a. Line C represents the tadpoles exposed

32 | Circulation and Respiration

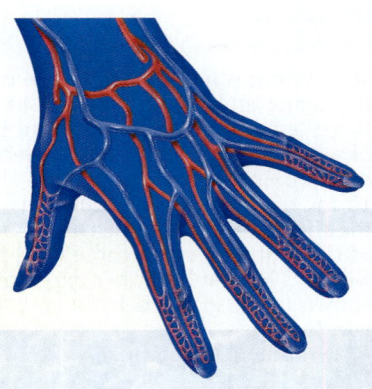

Lesson Planning Guide With Options for Block Scheduling

Lecture Concepts	Lesson Resources

32-1 Circulation

BLOCK ❶ (45 minutes)

1. The circulatory system transports materials, helps maintain body temperature, and protects the body from disease.

2. The blood is composed of plasma, red blood cells, white blood cells, and platelets.

3. Red blood cells contain hemoglobin, which transports oxygen. White blood cells defend the body against disease. Platelets control clotting.

❶ **Lecture Resources**
- ■ Determining Prior Knowledge
- ■ Active Reading: Reading Organizer
- ■ Visual Strategy: Figures 32-2, 32-2b, 32-3
- ■ Demonstration: Summarizing Information
- ■ Demonstration: Comparing Functions
- 🔒 Teaching Transparencies: 211, 212, 186A, 187A
- ● Holt Biology Videodiscs Lesson 32-1

Classwork Options
- ■ Blood Vessels and Heart Disease
- 🔺 Interactive Explorations Laboratory Manual: Lab E6

Assignment Options
- ⊙ Teaching Resources CD-ROM: Occupational Applications Worksheets 2

BLOCK ❷ (45 minutes)

4. Capillaries have walls that are only one cell thick, allowing substances to diffuse in and out of cells.

5. Marker proteins on red blood cells determine Rh factor and the major blood types: A, B, AB, and O.

6. The lymphatic system returns fluid and proteins to the blood.

❷ **Lecture Resources**
- ■ Drugs Used in Cardiovascular Disease
- ■ Visual Strategy: Figures 32-4, 32-5
- 🔒 Teaching Transparencies: 188A
- ● Holt Biology Videodiscs Lesson 32-1

Classwork Options
- ■ Closure: Relating Concepts
- 🔺 Laboratory Techniques and Experimental Design: Lab C42

Assignment Options
- ■ Reteaching
- ■ Section Review
- ■ Chapter Review, questions 1a, 2a, 4, 5, 6, 7, 8, 11, 26, 29
- ■ Directed Reading Worksheet

32-2 How Blood Flows

BLOCK ❸ (45 minutes)

1. The heart has right and left halves, and four chambers: two atria and two ventricles.

2. A group of specialized cells, known as the pacemaker, regulates the heart's beating.

3. Pulmonary circulation involves the transport of blood between the heart and lungs.

❸ **Lecture Resources**
- ■ Active Reading: Reading Organizer
- ■ Visual Strategy: Figures 32-6, 32-7, 32-8
- ■ Visual Strategy: Videodisc
- ■ Demonstration: Summarizing Information
- 🔒 Teaching Transparencies: 210, 213, 214
- ● Holt Biology Videodiscs Lesson 32-2

Classwork Options
- 🔺 Inquiry Skills Development: Lab B32

Assignment Options
- ⊙ Teaching Resources CD-ROM: Problem-Solving Worksheets 1

BLOCK ❹ (45 minutes)

4. Systemic circulation is the transport of blood between the heart and the rest of the body.

5. Blood pressure is a measure of the health of the circulatory system.

6. A chemical analysis of the blood provides information about an individual's health.

❹ **Lecture Resources**
- ■ Evolution of the Heart
- ■ Formed Elements of Blood
- ■ Active Reading: Paired Summarizing
- ■ Visual Strategy: Figures 32-9, 32-11
- ■ Visual Strategy: Videodisc
- ● Holt Biology Videodiscs Lesson 32-2

Classwork Options
- ■ Closure: Forming a Hypothesis

Assignment Options
- ■ *Small Group* Reteaching
- ■ Section Review
- ■ Chapter Review, questions 1b, 1c, 2b, 2c, 9, 12, 13, 14, 20, 21, 22, 24, 27
- ■ Directed Reading Worksheet

32-3 The Respiratory System

BLOCK ❺ (45 minutes)

1. Lungs take in air containing the oxygen needed for cellular respiration.

2. The diaphragm contracts and the rib cage moves up, causing inhalation. The diaphragm relaxes and the rib cage moves down, causing exhalation.

❺ **Lecture Resources**
- ■ Active Reading: Reading Aloud/Discussion
- ■ Visual Strategy: Figures 32-15, 32-16
- ■ Demonstration: Identifying Structures
- 🔒 Teaching Transparencies: 215
- ● Holt Biology Videodiscs Lesson 32-3

Classwork Options
- ■ Investigation 32A

Assignment Options
- ⊙ Teaching Resources CD-ROM: Occupational Applications Worksheets 12

KEY

- ■ Annotated Teacher's Edition
- ■ Pupil's Edition
- ■ Directed Reading Worksheets
- ■ Vocabulary Development Worksheets
- ■ Thinking Skills Worksheets
- ■ Reteaching Worksheets
- ■ Chapter Tests
- ◉ Language Development and Reading Comprehension Audio CD Program

Holt BioSources
Laboratory Program
- A Quick Labs
- B Inquiry Skills Development
- C Laboratory Techniques and Experimental Design
- D Biotechnology
- E Interactive Explorations in Biology Laboratory Manual

- Teaching Transparencies
- ◉ Testing Resources CD-ROM
- ◉ Test Generator/Assessment Item

Holt Biology Technology
- ⊘ Holt Biology Videodiscs

Lecture Concepts

Lesson Resources

32-3 The Respiratory System, *continued*

BLOCK ❻ (45 minutes)

3. Oxygen diffuses from the alveoli into the blood, where it is transported by hemoglobin in red blood cells. Carbon dioxide diffuses from cells into the blood, where it is transported by plasma. In the lungs, carbon dioxide diffuses from the blood into the alveoli to be exhaled.

4. Receptors in the brain are sensitive to the concentration of carbon dioxide in the blood and regulate the rate of breathing.

5. Respiratory disorders include asthma, emphysema, and lung cancer.

❻ Lecture Resources
- ■ Visual Strategy: Figure 32-17
- ■ Visual Strategy: Videodisc
- ■ Demonstration: Relating Concepts
- Teaching Transparencies: 217
- ⊘ Holt Biology Videodiscs Lesson 32-3

Classwork Options
- ■ Closure: Relating Concepts
- Quick Labs: Lab A31

Assignment Options
- ■ *Small Group* Reteaching
- ■ Section Review
- ■ Chapter Review, questions 3, 10, 15, 16, 17, 18, 19, 23, 25, 28
- ■ Directed Reading Worksheet

Chapter Review and Assessment

BLOCK ❼ (45 minutes)

Review
- ■ Reteaching Worksheet
- ■ Thinking Skills Worksheet
- ■ Vocabulary Development Worksheet
- ◉ Language Development and Reading Comprehension Audio CD Program: Chapter 32

BLOCK ❽ (45 minutes)

Assessment
- ■ Alternative Assessment, p. 675
- ■ Portfolio Assessment, p. T39

Chapter Test
- ■ Chapter 32 Test

Test Generator
- ◉ Item bank for customizing Chapter Tests

Teaching Resources CD-ROM
- ◉ Scoring Rubrics and Classroom Management Checklist

The Portfolio icon denotes items throughout the Teacher's Edition lesson wrap that may be selected for inclusion in student portfolios.

Holt Biology Videodiscs and *Concepts of Biology*

Holt Biology Videodiscs gives you a powerful tool for teaching, review, and assessment. For further information regarding the media on the videodiscs, see *Holt Biology Videodiscs Teacher's Correlation Guide to Holt Biology: Visualizing Life.*

Concepts of Biology adds interactive lesson plans and extensive tools for customization using CD-ROM technology.

Use the following topic from *Concepts of Biology* to help you teach this chapter:
Topic 22: Circulation and Respiration

Laboratory Planning

Text

Materials and preparation instructions appear on the teacher's wrap accompanying each laboratory exercise.

Block 5: Investigation 32A: Determining the Effect of Exercise—Dance Team, p. 818

Holt BioSources Laboratory Program

Block 1: Interactive Explorations Laboratory Manual: Lab E6: Hemoglobin

Block 2: Laboratory Techniques and Experimental Design Lab C42: Blood Typing

Block 3: Inquiry Skills Development Lab B32: Antigen-Antibody Interaction

Block 6: Quick Labs Lab A31: Determining Lung Capacity

Determining Prior Knowledge

- Use a microprojector to show the class an *Amoeba*, a *Paramecium*, or any other single-celled organism. Have students refer to Chapter 19 to explain why such an organism does not need a circulatory system. Review Chapter 23, which addresses the concept of terrestrial life and how terrestrial organisms developed a double circulatory system. Ask students to make a chart listing the advantages of a closed circulatory system.
- Ask students to list multicellular organisms without a closed circulatory system. Have students refer to Chapters 25 and 26 for information about multicellular organisms without closed circulatory systems. Ask students to compare organism size to circulatory and respiratory pathways.
- Ask students to identify the ways in which the circulatory and respiratory systems function in homeostasis.

Active READING

Technique: Discussion

Remind students that in Chapter 23 they learned about innovations in body plan. Ask students what phylum of animals was the first to develop a circulatory system. Discuss the advantages of a circulatory system. Tell students that in this chapter they will learn about the human circulatory system and its relationship with the respiratory system.

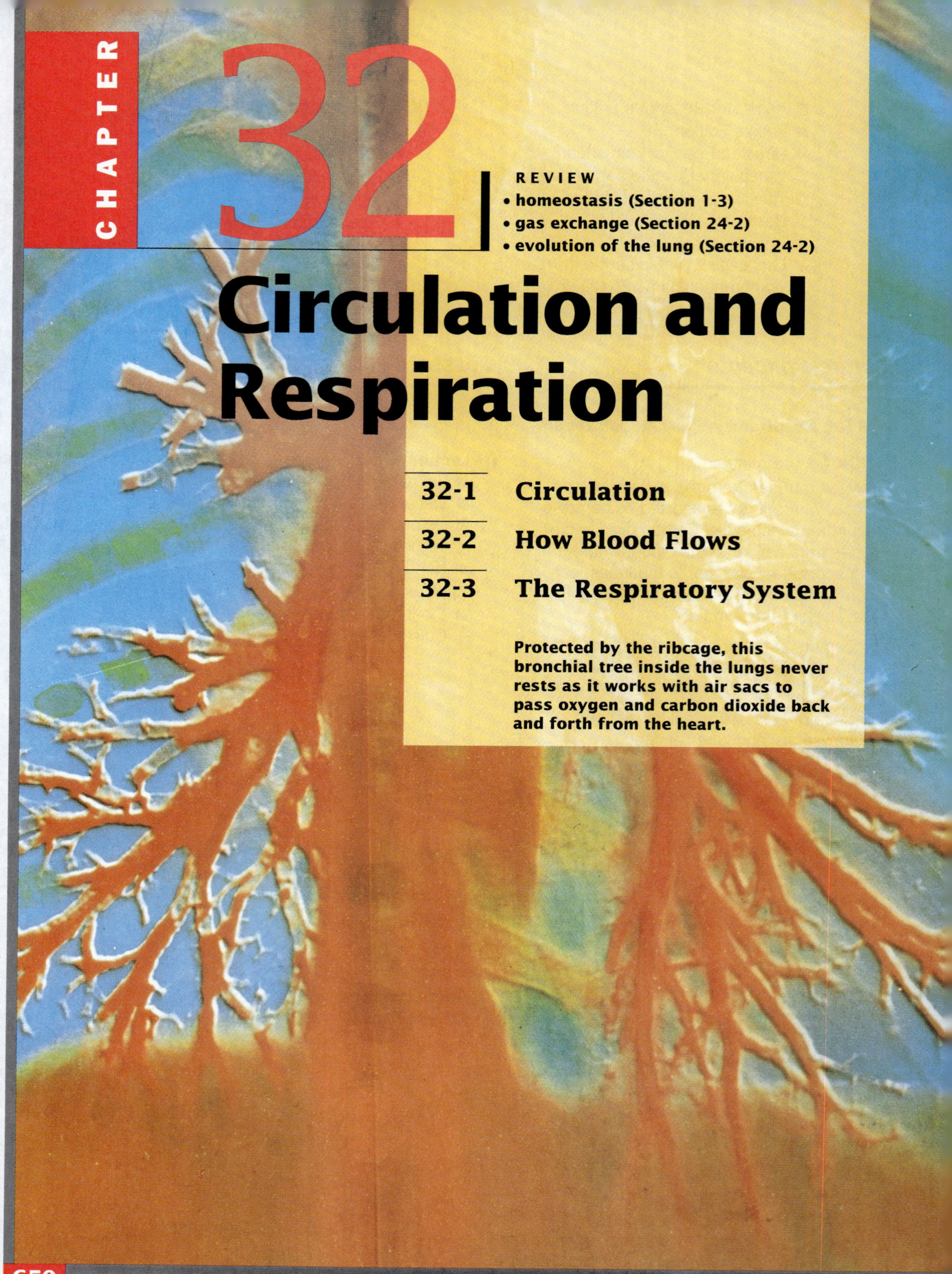

CD-ROM Resources

Concepts of Biology
Topic 22: Circulation and Respiration

REVIEW
- homeostasis (Section 1-3)
- gas exchange (Section 24-2)
- evolution of the lung (Section 24-2)

Circulation and Respiration

32-1	**Circulation**
32-2	**How Blood Flows**
32-3	**The Respiratory System**

Protected by the ribcage, this bronchial tree inside the lungs never rests as it works with air sacs to pass oxygen and carbon dioxide back and forth from the heart.

Author's Rationale   Circulation is treated as a basic physiological process. Each section of this chapter is devoted to one of the three elements: the piping, the pump, and the gas exchanger. The emphasis is on how structure leads to function. For example, why is it necessary for the atrium and the ventricle to be electrically insulated from one another, except for a narrow bridge of tissue? Health issues are introduced where appropriate.

Each lubb-dup of your beating heart can be seen as an up and down pair of spikes on an ekg strip. Inside your body, blood flows along a vast 60,000 mile highway, long enough to circle Earth two and a half times. With every beat, blood nourishes and cleanses the entire body, bringing life to all it touches.

32-1 Circulation

OBJECTIVES

1 Explain the three functions of circulation.

2 Describe the components of blood and identify their roles.

3 Explain the relationship between the three major types of blood vessels.

4 Contrast the role of the lymphatic system with that of general circulation.

Transporting Materials Through the Body

All living things must capture materials from their environment that enable them to carry on their life processes. Many bacteria, single-celled protists, and simpler multicellular animals live within a liquid environment, enabling materials to diffuse directly into and out of the organism through plasma membranes. However, larger animals with many cells stacked in layers, such as earthworms, armadillos, and humans, cannot rely solely on diffusion to supply needed materials and carry away wastes. In these organisms, a circulatory system transports oxygen, carbon dioxide, food molecules, hormones, and other materials to and from the cells of the body. In addition, the circulatory systems of mammals and birds help maintain their constant body temperatures. The circulatory system also carries cells that help protect the body from disease. All of these functions help the body maintain homeostasis. All are essential to survival.

Our modern understanding of the human circulatory system began with the work of the seventeenth-century English physician William Harvey, who demonstrated that blood circulates in one direction in a closed circuit throughout the body. An illustration of his experiment is shown in **Figure 32-1**.

Figure 32-1
In 1628, William Harvey demonstrated that blood travels from the heart to the body's limbs and then back again. If an arm is bound above the elbow, swellings appear in the lower arm. Harvey used this as evidence that blood flow back to the heart was slowed.

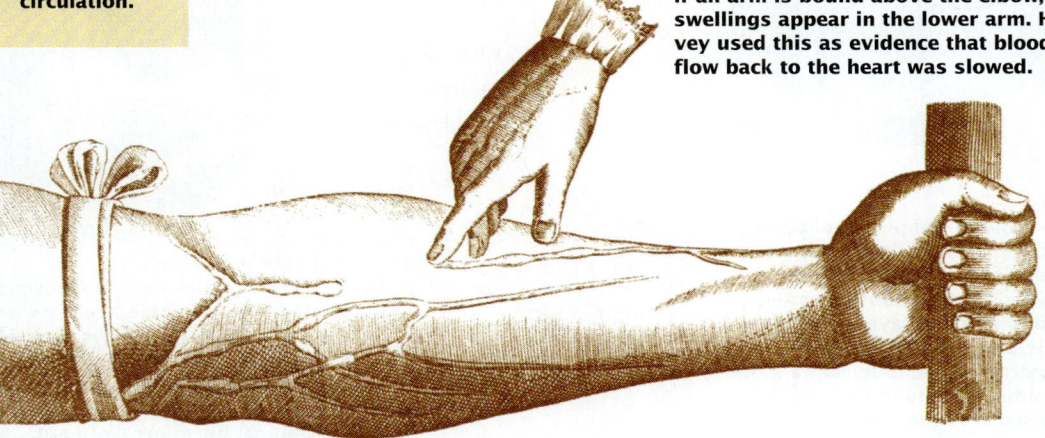

651

Videodisc Resources
Holt Biology Videodiscs
Lesson 32-1: Circulation

Phase One
Preparation

Scheduling
See the **Lesson Planning Guide** on pages 649A and 649B for lecture, classwork, and assignment options for Section 32-1.

Phase Two
Teaching Strategies

Language Arts Connection
William Harvey
This section offers an opportunity for an outside reading assignment. Check with the school librarian to obtain a description of William Harvey's work, and make it available for students to read. While reading about his experiments, students should develop an appreciation for Harvey's simple but brilliant scientific work.

Key to Strategies
Teaching Strategies are keyed to three tiers of learning.

● **Understanding Concepts (Tier I)**
Content mastery and comprehension

■ **Applying Information (Tier II)**
Applying and analyzing content

▲ **Critical Thinking (Tier III)**
Practicing evaluative thinking

Blood: A Liquid Tissue

Blood has been called the river of life. It is the tissue responsible for transporting nearly everything within the body. Among all the body's tissues, blood is the only liquid tissue. The material that makes blood a liquid is a protein-rich substance called **plasma** (PLAZ muh). Plasma is about 90 percent water and makes up approximately 55 percent of blood. The other 45 percent is made mostly of cells—red blood cells, white blood cells, and platelets.

Red blood cells carry oxygen to other body tissues
Most of the cells that make up blood are red blood cells. There are approximately 5 million red blood cells per cubic millimeter of blood! The main function of a **red blood cell** is to carry oxygen from the lungs to all cells of the body. Red blood cells also carry carbon dioxide from cells back to the lungs to be exhaled. The structure of a red blood cell is well suited to this function. As shown in **Figure 32-2a**, normal red blood cells are shaped like round cushions, squashed in the center. Red blood cells are filled with a protein called **hemoglobin**, an iron-containing molecule that gives blood its red color. Oxygen binds easily to the iron in hemoglobin, making red blood cells efficient oxygen carriers. A single red blood cell contains about 250 million hemoglobin molecules. Each red blood cell can carry about 1 billion molecules of oxygen.

Anemia (uh NEE mee uh) is a blood condition that results when there is an oxygen shortage in the cells of the body. Blood loss, too little hemoglobin, and not enough iron or certain vitamins can cause abnormalities in the shape, size, or color of red blood cells. Iron-deficiency anemia is common in young girls and women of childbearing age who lack adequate dietary or stored iron. Common symptoms include fatigue, stomach problems, broken and brittle nails, and paleness.

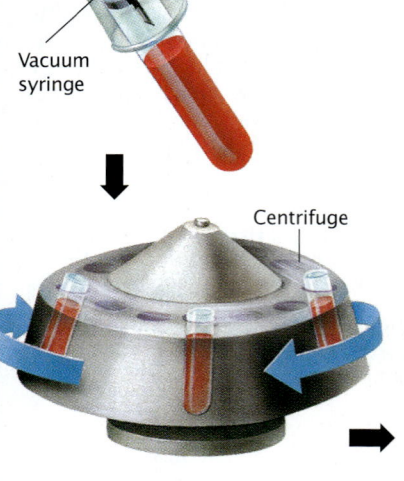

Vacuum syringe

Centrifuge

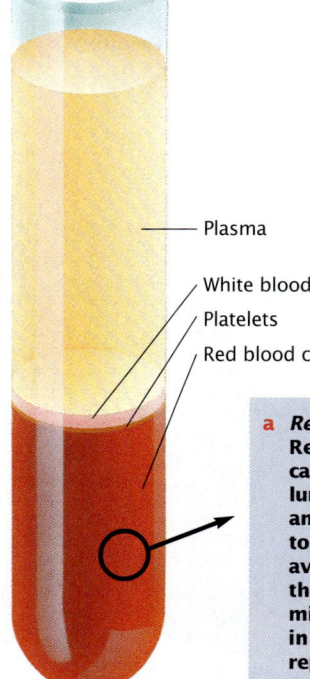

Plasma

White blood cells

Platelets

Red blood cells

Figure 32-2
After a blood sample is collected in a vacuum syringe, it is spun rapidly in a device called a centrifuge (above). This rotation forces the blood to settle in layers, with the heaviest cells (red blood cells) at the bottom of the tube, white blood cells and platelets in the middle, and plasma at the top.

a Red blood cells
Red blood cells carry oxygen from the lungs to all cells of the body and carry carbon dioxide back to the lungs to be exhaled. Each red blood cell has an average life span of only 120 days because they mature without a nucleus. About 2 million new red blood cells are produced in the bone marrow every second to replace those that die or are worn out.

652

Historical Perspective: Charles Richard Drew, M.D.
African American surgeon Dr. Charles Drew was born in Washington, D.C., in 1904 and received his M.D. from McGill University. Dr. Drew's work on blood plasma has helped to save countless lives. During World War II, Drew set up blood banks that served as models for the worldwide network of blood banks now operated by the American Red Cross and other agencies. Drew was also the first director of the blood plasma collection program of the American Red Cross.

White blood cells defend the body

White blood cells form a mobile army that protects the body against invading bacteria, viruses, or other foreign cells. White blood cells called macrophages *(MAK roh fayj iz)* act as a clean-up crew, scavenging worn-out or dead cells. While red blood cells are confined to the bloodstream, white blood cells are able to squeeze in and out of blood vessels. They move toward areas of tissue damage and infection in response to chemicals released by damaged cells. By following the chemical trail, macrophages are able to migrate to infected areas in the body, where they engulf and digest foreign cells.

As shown in **Figure 32-2b**, white blood cells are colorless and irregularly shaped. Most of them are manufactured and stored in bone marrow until needed by the body. Although they are larger than red blood cells, they are considerably less numerous; normally there are 4,000 to 11,000 white blood cells per cubic millimeter of blood. Whenever white blood cells are mobilized for action, the body speeds up their production so that twice the normal number may appear within a few hours. A white blood cell count over 11,000 generally indicates the presence of a bacterial or viral infection in the body.

Platelets help repair damaged blood vessels

Platelets are not really cells; they are fragments of large white blood cells formed within bone marrow. Each cubic millimeter of blood contains between 250,000 and 500,000 tiny platelets. Each platelet circulates for only three to eight days.

Platelets are essential for the clotting process that occurs when blood vessels are injured, as shown in **Figure 32-2c**. When you cut your finger, platelets make contact with the ends of the broken blood vessels. There, the platelets swell and stick to the injured surfaces as well as to each other. Certain platelets rupture and release a protein that triggers a series of reactions, resulting in the formation of a clot. The clot stops the bleeding and hardens into a patch over the injured area. In time, new cells grow and replace those that were damaged.

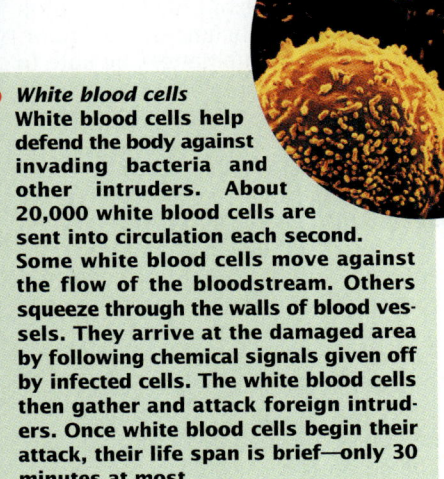

b *White blood cells*
White blood cells help defend the body against invading bacteria and other intruders. About 20,000 white blood cells are sent into circulation each second. Some white blood cells move against the flow of the bloodstream. Others squeeze through the walls of blood vessels. They arrive at the damaged area by following chemical signals given off by infected cells. The white blood cells then gather and attack foreign intruders. Once white blood cells begin their attack, their life span is brief—only 30 minutes at most.

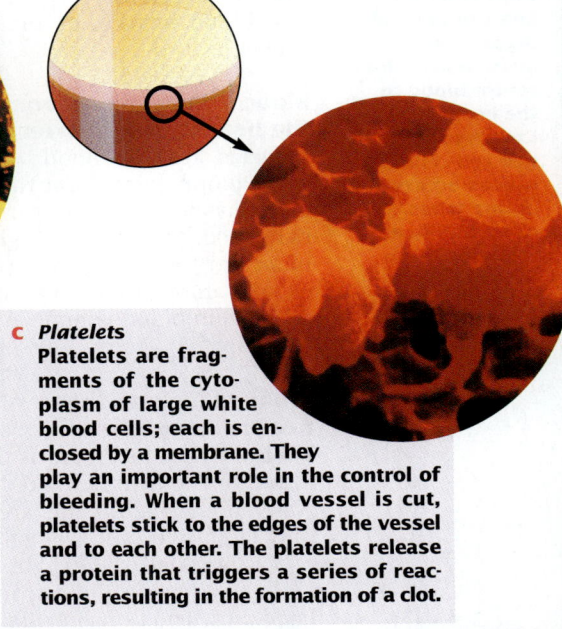

c *Platelets*
Platelets are fragments of the cytoplasm of large white blood cells; each is enclosed by a membrane. They play an important role in the control of bleeding. When a blood vessel is cut, platelets stick to the edges of the vessel and to each other. The platelets release a protein that triggers a series of reactions, resulting in the formation of a clot.

653

Demonstration

● Summarizing Information

Show students a photograph or transparency that illustrates the different kinds of white blood cells. Have students describe the differences that they detect among the various types of cells.

Visual Strategy   **Figure 32-2b**

● Identifying Structures

Review the process of endocytosis as discussed in Chapter 4. Explain how cells take in large particles, including foreign intruders. Point out that pus forms, in large part, from dead white blood cells after they have "eaten" infecting microorganisms.

Demonstration

● Comparing Functions

Show the class a picture of a man who has cut his face while shaving and has attempted to stop the bleeding by placing pieces of tissue on the nicks. Point out that platelets initiate a series of reactions that results in the formation of a mesh made of fine threads of proteins. The fine fibers that make up a tissue act like the protein threads, helping to form a clot to stop the bleeding.

Connection: *Chapter 7*

Hemophilia

Remind students that in hemophiliacs, the blood is slow to clot or does not clot at all. Explain that although hemophiliacs have platelets, they are missing a protein factor (known as factor VIII) that is crucial in converting fibrinogen to fibrin, the final step in the series of reactions leading to the formation of a clot.

Key to Strategies
- ● **Understanding Concepts (Tier I)**
- ■ **Applying Information (Tier II)**
- ▲ **Critical Thinking (Tier III)**

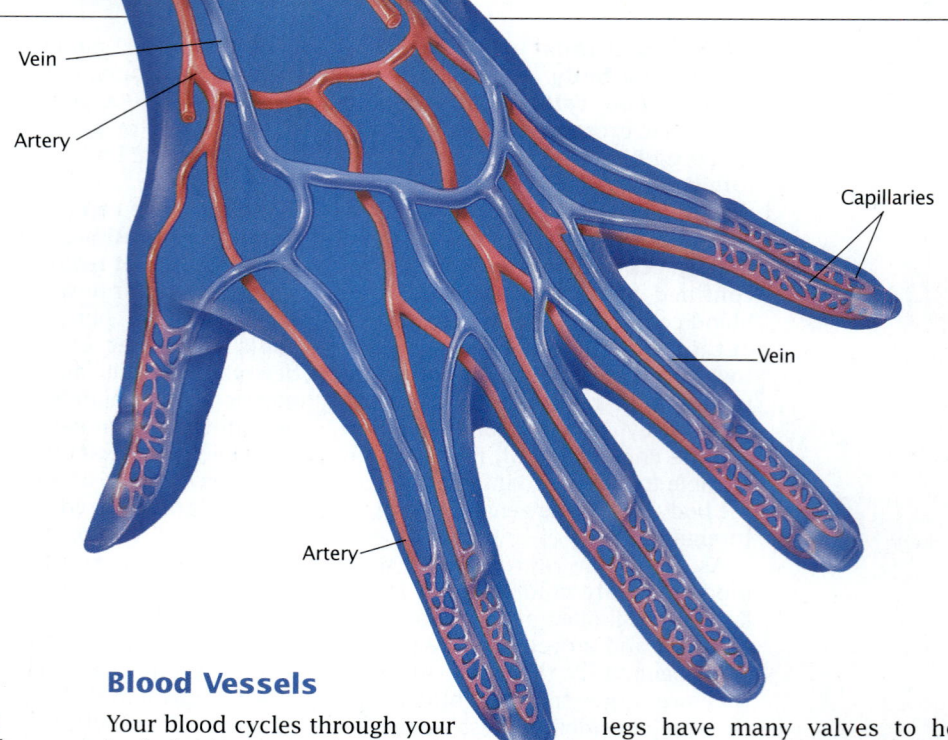

Vein

Artery

Capillaries

Vein

Artery

Visual Strategy Figure 32-3

● **Identifying Structures**

Have students trace the path blood follows in this figure. Be sure they understand that blood coming from the heart circulates as follows: artery → capillary → vein → back to heart.

Demonstration

● **Comparing Functions**

Show the class a picture of a person in a hospital bed. Ask why hospital workers try to get patients to walk, if only for a few minutes each day. Students should recognize that muscle movements squeeze the walls of veins, thus preventing blood from accumulating and clotting in parts of the body such as the legs.

Figure 32-3
Blood travels through all parts of the body (such as the hand above) in blood vessels. Arteries (red) carry blood away from the heart to the body's organs and tissues. Veins (blue) return blood to the heart. Exchange of oxygen and cellular wastes occurs in tiny tubes called capillaries (purple). These tubes form a network that connects arteries to veins.

Blood Vessels

Your blood cycles through your body 1,440 times a day, traveling through tubes called **blood vessels**. Blood vessels carry blood from the heart to the organs in the body and back again to the heart. They have flexible walls so that they can change diameter when more blood is needed. The blood vessels of the hand are shown in **Figure 32-3**.

Blood travels away from the heart through arteries

Arteries are the blood vessels that carry blood away from the heart. In most instances, arteries carry oxygen-rich blood. Arteries have highly elastic, muscular walls, enabling them to expand and contract to accommodate changes in blood volume as the heart pumps.

Blood travels to the heart through veins

Veins are the blood vessels that return blood to the heart. Unlike the artery walls, the walls of veins are thin and only slightly elastic. Veins have flaps of tissue called valves that open and close to prevent blood from flowing backward. The veins in your arms and legs have many valves to help return blood to the heart against the force of gravity. When valves do not work properly, blood tends to build up within the vein. The walls of the vein become stretched and twisted, causing a condition called varicose veins.

Materials are exchanged in the capillaries

Since the purpose of blood circulation is to transport substances, it is important that these substances be able to move from the blood into the surrounding cells. A network of tiny tubes called **capillaries** makes this transfer of substances possible. Their walls are only one cell thick, so substances are able to diffuse through them—oxygen and nutrients leave the blood and enter the fluid surrounding cells, and carbon dioxide and wastes from cells enter the blood in the capillary to be carried away. Networks of capillaries connect arteries to veins. Most capillaries are so narrow that blood cells must pass through them in single file. The structures of capillaries, arteries, and veins are shown in *A Closer Look at the Blood Vessels* on page 655.

654

Blood Vessels

Arteries, veins, and capillaries are the three main types of blood vessels in the human body. The walls of these vessels are well constructed for the passage of blood throughout the body.

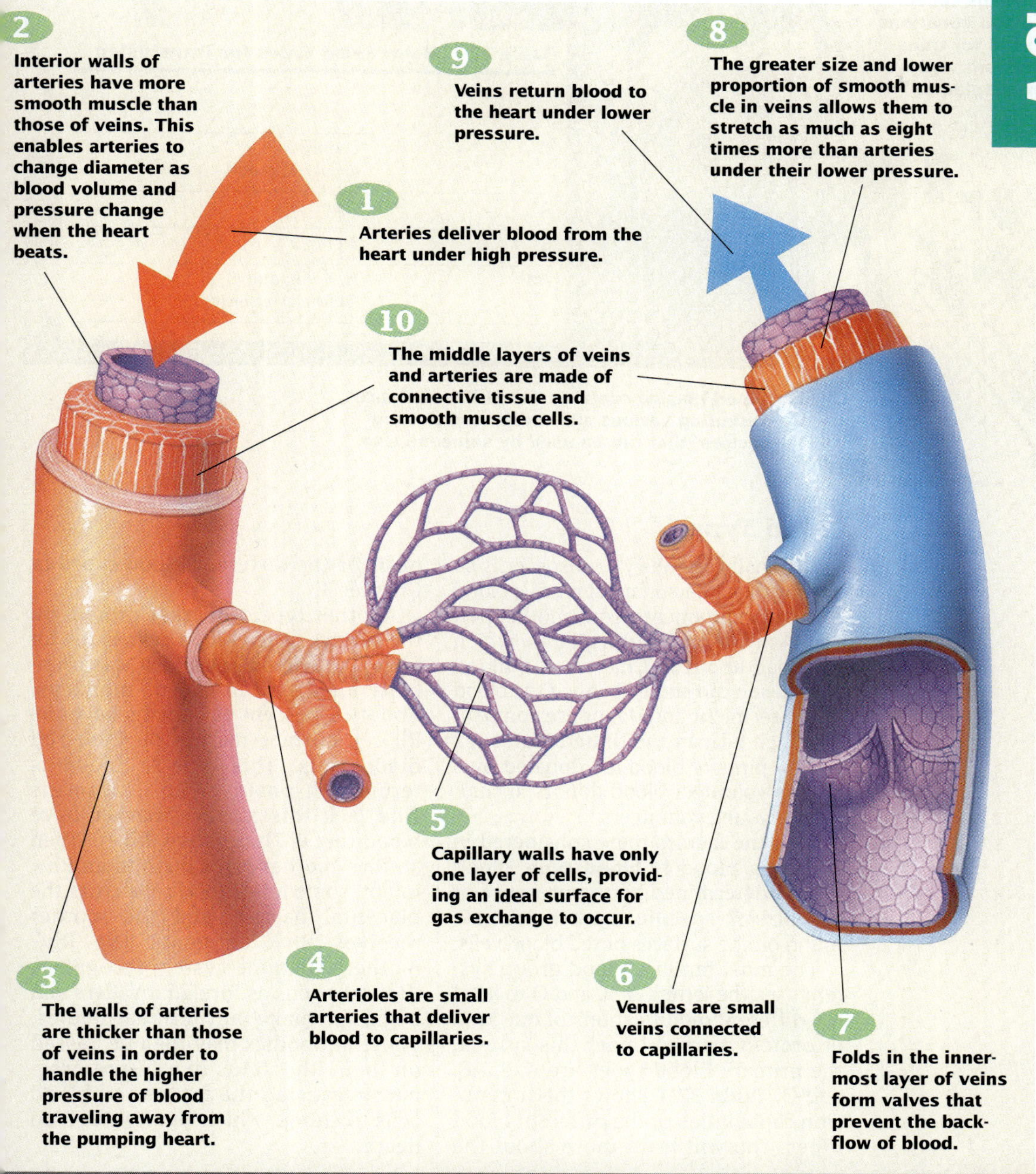

2 Interior walls of arteries have more smooth muscle than those of veins. This enables arteries to change diameter as blood volume and pressure change when the heart beats.

9 Veins return blood to the heart under lower pressure.

8 The greater size and lower proportion of smooth muscle in veins allows them to stretch as much as eight times more than arteries under their lower pressure.

1 Arteries deliver blood from the heart under high pressure.

10 The middle layers of veins and arteries are made of connective tissue and smooth muscle cells.

5 Capillary walls have only one layer of cells, providing an ideal surface for gas exchange to occur.

3 The walls of arteries are thicker than those of veins in order to handle the higher pressure of blood traveling away from the pumping heart.

4 Arterioles are small arteries that deliver blood to capillaries.

6 Venules are small veins connected to capillaries.

7 Folds in the innermost layer of veins form valves that prevent the backflow of blood.

655

A Closer Look

Blood Vessels and Heart Disease

■ **Recognizing Relationships**

Blood vessels are where many cardiovascular disorders originate. Use this fact as a foundation for a discussion about atherosclerosis and coronary artery spasms, two principal underlying causes of coronary artery disease. Hypertension, the most common disorder affecting the heart and blood vessels, can be explained at this time as well. Ask students to research the causes for these disorders, the dangers they pose, and the ways they can be prevented, treated, or cured.

Drugs Used in Cardiovascular Disease

● **Summarizing Information**

Students may be interested in learning about some of the drugs and techniques used in treating cardiovascular diseases. Present information about vasodilators (nitroglycerin), fibrinolytic drugs (streptokinase), inotropics (digitoxin), antiarrhythmics (quinidine and lidocaine), cholesterol-lowering agents (clofibrate), antihypertensives (diuretic drugs and beta blockers), and anticoagulates. Some surgical techniques to discuss include cardiac catheterization and open-heart surgery.

Blood Vessel Functions

● **Identifying Functions**

Guide a discussion by posing the following questions about blood vessels and their functions.

1. What are the three main types of blood vessels in the human body? *(arteries, veins, and capillaries)*

2. Capillaries have walls that are only one cell thick. How does this structure assist their function? *(It provides an ideal surface for gas exchange to occur.)*

3. How is the backflow of blood in veins prevented? *(Veins have folds of tissues called valves that prevent blood from flowing in the wrong direction.)*

● **Identifying Functions**

Blood transfusions have been accepted as a routine medical procedure for nearly 100 years. Prior to 1900, however, blood transfusions often led to serious complications and occasionally death. In the early 1900s, Karl Landsteiner discovered that sometimes the red blood cells taken from one member of his laboratory staff would clump when mixed with those taken from another lab worker. In other cases, two different blood samples would not clump. As a result, Landsteiner concluded that there were different categories of blood. Soon after, the four major blood types were determined.

Connection: *Chapter 7*

The Genetics of the Rh Factor

Inform students that a person with Rh-positive blood can be either homozygous dominant (+/+) or heterozygous (+/−). An Rh-negative person must be homozygous recessive (−/−). Have students use a Punnett square to demonstrate why there are no concerns during pregnancy about Rh factor if both parents are Rh negative.

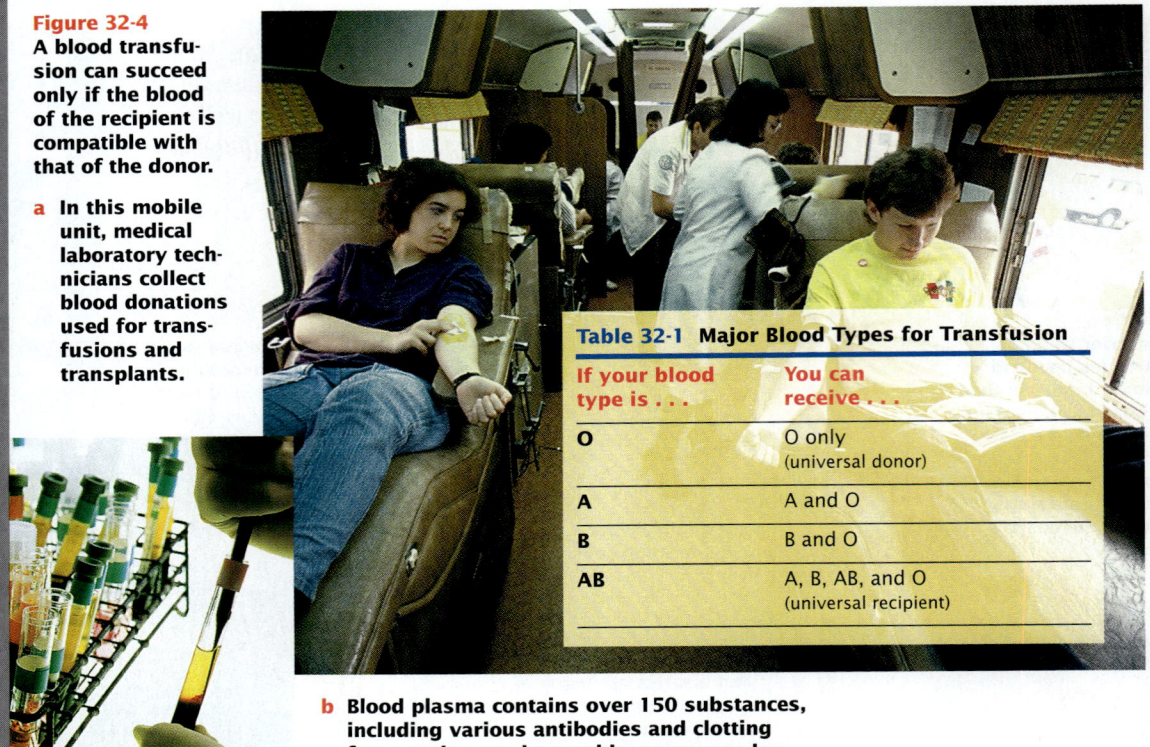

Figure 32-4
A blood transfusion can succeed only if the blood of the recipient is compatible with that of the donor.

a In this mobile unit, medical laboratory technicians collect blood donations used for transfusions and transplants.

Table 32-1 Major Blood Types for Transfusion

If your blood type is . . .	You can receive . . .
O	O only (universal donor)
A	A and O
B	B and O
AB	A, B, AB, and O (universal recipient)

b Blood plasma contains over 150 substances, including various antibodies and clotting factors, that can be used by someone else.

Blood Types

Occasionally an injury or disorder is so serious that a person must receive blood or blood components from another person. As with organ transplants, which you read about in Chapter 4, a blood transfusion can succeed only if the blood of the recipient and donor are compatible. Each year in the United States, 12 million pints of blood are donated by 8 million volunteer blood donors, including the young volunteers in **Figure 32-4**. Among the factors to be considered in matching blood is **blood type**. Blood type is determined by the presence or absence of specific marker proteins found on the surfaces of red blood cells.

The most familiar blood group system uses the letters A, B, and O to label the different modifications of one kind of protein marker. Under this system, the primary blood types are A, B, AB, and O. **Table 32-1** shows the transfusion capabilities of the different blood types. You will learn more about the basis of the different blood types in Chapter 33.

Another type of marker protein on the surface of red blood cells is the Rh factor, so named because it was originally identified in rhesus monkeys. About 85 percent of humans have the Rh cell surface marker on their red blood cells. This type of blood is termed Rh positive (Rh+). Humans who lack this surface marker have blood that is Rh negative (Rh−). When an Rh− mother gives birth to an Rh+ infant, some fetal blood cells cross the placental barrier, and the mother receives Rh+ antigens. The Rh− mother's immune system recognizes these antigens as foreign invaders and begins to make "anti-Rh" antibodies. These antibodies may then be passed on to an Rh+ fetus in a future pregnancy, causing the fetus's red blood cells to clump, which can lead to fetal death.

The Lymphatic System

All the cells in your body are bathed in a clear, watery fluid that moves materials between the capillaries and body cells. This fluid is formed from parts of the blood that diffuse out of capillaries—water, proteins, and other nutrients. If this fluid had no way of returning to the circulatory system, body tissues would soon become flooded and would swell up. At the same time, the constant loss of fluid from the blood would eventually drain the circulatory system. These excess fluids and proteins are returned to the blood by a system of vessels called the **lymphatic system**. Lymph nodes are located at various places along the lymphatic vessels, shown in **Figure 32-5**. Each lymph node contains many white blood cells that help defend the body against cancerous cells or disease-causing organisms. Lymph nodes also return water, proteins, and other nutrients to the blood.

Stability and Homeostasis

Explain why swollen lymph nodes are often considered a symptom of illness.

Lymph node

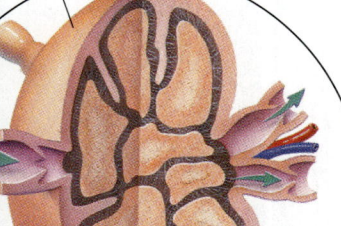

Figure 32-5

a **Lymph nodes about the size of small kidney beans are found in groups near veins.**

b **Enlarged lymph nodes in three sites (shown in white) can be felt by a health care professional.**

c **Lymph nodes filter foreign matter from the body's fluid and prevent cancerous cells and disease-causing agents from entering the bloodstream.**

SECTION REVIEW

1 **List three functions of the circulatory system.**

2 **Summarize the functions of the three cellular components of blood.**

3 **Distinguish between arteries and veins.**

4 **How does the lymphatic system help the body fight infection?**

657

Theme Answer

Stability and Homeostasis
Students should explain that swollen lymph nodes contain large numbers of white blood cells and immune system cells that are actively engulfing bacteria or virus particles. For this reason, the nodes become inflamed and tender.

Visual Strategy Figure 32-5

● **Identifying Structures**
Have students examine this figure to determine where lymph nodes are concentrated—for example, the abdomen, the armpits, and the groin. Point out that the tonsils and adenoids are made of lymphatic tissue.

Phase Three
Assessment Options

Closure

■ **Relating Concepts**
Have students explain why arteries are generally found far below the body's surface, why veins are located closer to the surface, and why capillaries are in close contact with every cell of the body.

SECTION REVIEW
Assign the *Section Review*.

Reteaching

Have students describe what the blood sample in the test tube in Figure 32-2 on page 652 might look like if it were taken from someone with either leukemia (cancer of the white blood cells) or an iron deficiency. *(With leukemia, the layer of white cells may be thicker. An iron deficiency may cause the layer of red cells to be shorter or lighter in color.)*

Key to Strategies
● Understanding Concepts (Tier I)
■ Applying Information (Tier II)
▲ Critical Thinking (Tier III)

ANSWERS TO SECTION REVIEW

1 The system transports vital materials throughout the body, maintains homeostasis, and protects the body against disease.

2 Refer to Figure 32-2 on pages 652–653. Red blood cells carry oxygen to other body cells, and they also carry some carbon dioxide. White blood cells help defend the body against invading bacteria and other intruders. Platelets play an important role in blood clotting.

3 Arteries are blood vessels that carry blood away from the heart, whereas veins are blood vessels that return blood to the heart.

4 Refer to Figure 32-5 on this page. The lymph system gathers and returns to the blood excess fluid and proteins that have filtered from the blood. In its travel back to the blood, the lymph fluid must pass through lymph nodes. The nodes filter foreign matter and prevent cancerous cells and disease-causing agents from entering the bloodstream.

Scheduling

See the **Lesson Planning Guide** on pages 649A and 649B for lecture, classwork, and assignment options for Section 32-2.

Phase Two
Teaching Strategies

Visual Strategy Videodisc

■ **Relating Concepts**
Use *Video—Inside the Heart* (2 min 45 s) shown in Chapter 32 Section 32-2 of *Holt Biology Videodiscs Teacher's Correlation Guide to Holt Biology: Visualizing Life* to introduce the lesson. Tell students to pay particular attention to the role of the valves in the heart as they view the video. After viewing the video, review the path of blood through the heart. Then tell students that some people have damaged heart valves that do not properly close. Ask students how this might affect the flow of blood. *(Blood could flow in the wrong direction in the heart.)* Ask how this backflow of blood might affect the individual. *(Possible answers: the blood would not contain enough oxygen and so the person might feel tired, or organs might become damaged.)*

Visual Strategy Figure 32-6

● **Comparing Functions**
Have students calculate how much blood their heart would pump while they rode a bicycle for 15 minutes. To dramatize the volume, fill a liter flask with water and ask how many flasks would be filled by their heart in that period of time. *(A possible answer is 35 L × 15 minutes = 525 L.)*

Blood could not meet the body's needs if it did not flow. Blood flows because the circulatory system includes a pump—the heart—that forces blood to move throughout the body. Keeping fit, not smoking, and eating foods low in saturated fats will reduce your risk of diseases affecting the heart and blood vessels.

32-2 How Blood Flows

OBJECTIVES

1 **Describe the structure of the heart.**

2 **Trace the two routes blood can take through the body.**

3 **Explain the significance of blood pressure, and explain how it is measured.**

4 **Summarize the value of a blood analysis in describing homeostasis.**

5 **Describe the causes and symptoms of two cardiovascular diseases.**

The Heart

The heart is a muscular organ that pumps blood throughout the body. When you are sitting still, your heart pumps about 5 L (5.3 qt) of blood each minute. If you are riding a bike, like the person in **Figure 32-6**, your heart may have to pump up to seven times that amount per minute.

Your heart is divided into left and right halves. The right half pumps blood to the lungs to pick up oxygen and release carbon dioxide. The left half of the heart pumps the oxygen-rich blood to the rest of the body—your head, arms, legs, and all the tissues and organs in between.

As shown in **Figure 32-7**, each half of the heart has an upper and a lower chamber. The upper chamber, called the **atrium**, receives blood coming into the heart. The lower chamber, called the **ventricle**, pumps blood out of the heart. The upper and lower chambers are separated from each other by flap-like valves that control the direction of the blood flow inside the heart. Blood flows into both atria at the same time, and the atria contract together. Similarly, the ventricles contract together. All this activity causes the heartbeat, a sound that is usually described as "lubb dup." The "lubb" sound relates to the closing of the valves that lead from the atrium to the ventricle. The "dup" comes very shortly afterward and is related to the closing of the valves between the ventricles and the arteries that lead to the lungs and the rest of the body.

Figure 32-6
When you are active, your heart pumps up to 35 L (37 qt) of blood each minute. That's seven times the amount your heart pumps when you are at rest.

Videodisc Resources

Holt Biology Videodiscs
Lesson 32-2: How Blood Flows

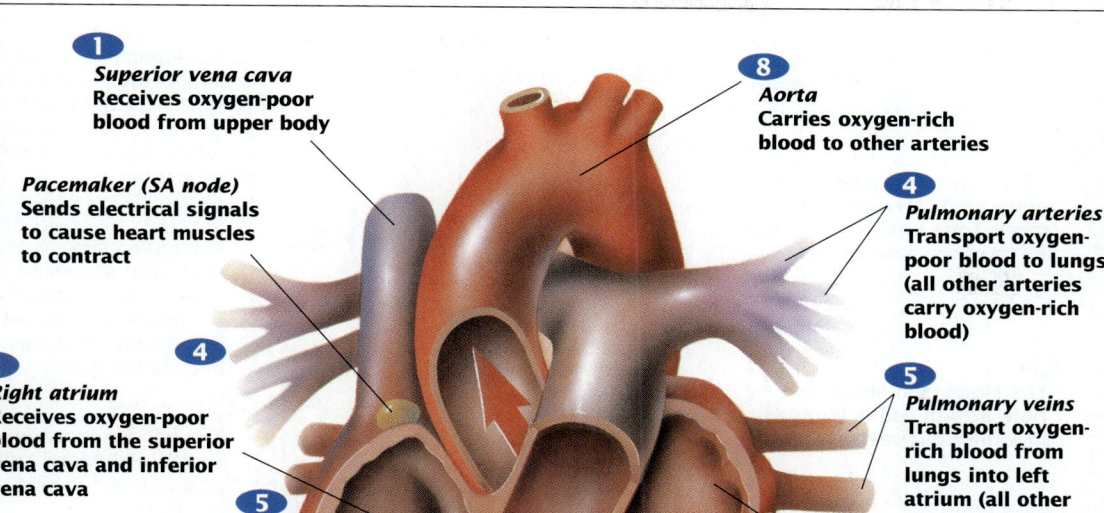

1 Superior vena cava
Receives oxygen-poor blood from upper body

Pacemaker (SA node)
Sends electrical signals to cause heart muscles to contract

2 Right atrium
Receives oxygen-poor blood from the superior vena cava and inferior vena cava

Tricuspid valve
Controls blood flow into right ventricle

3 Right ventricle
Channels oxygen-poor blood into the pulmonary arteries that lead to the lungs

1 Inferior vena cava
Receives oxygen-poor blood from lower body

8 Aorta
Carries oxygen-rich blood to other arteries

4 Pulmonary arteries
Transport oxygen-poor blood to lungs (all other arteries carry oxygen-rich blood)

5 Pulmonary veins
Transport oxygen-rich blood from lungs into left atrium (all other veins carry oxygen-poor blood)

6 Left atrium
Receives newly oxygenated blood from pulmonary veins

Bicuspid valve
Controls blood flow into left ventricle

7 Left ventricle
Pumps oxygen-rich blood into aorta

8 Descending aorta
Transports oxygen-rich blood to lower body

Figure 32-7
The human heart pumps oxygen-poor blood to the lungs and oxygen-rich blood to the rest of the body. The numbered steps above allow you to follow the flow of blood from its entry into the heart (1) to its exit from the heart (8).

The four-chambered human heart is shown in **Figure 32-7**. The *Evolution of the Heart* on pages 662–663 summarizes the evolution of the vertebrate heart.

What makes the heart beat?
The heartbeat originates in heart tissue. It begins to beat in the embryo, before any nerves connect it to the brain. It can continue to beat during transplant surgery, after all nerves have been cut. How is this possible?

Each heartbeat is started by the **pacemaker**, a small bundle of cells at the entrance to the right atrium. An electrical signal from the pacemaker, shown in **Figure 32-7**, travels through the heart muscles in the right and left atria, causing them to tighten, or contract. When the signal reaches the right and left ventricles, they also contract. These contractions cause the chambers to squeeze the blood through the heart and push it to other parts of the body.

659

Matter of Fact: The Heart
During an average lifetime, the heart beats some 2.5 billion times and pumps enough blood to fill about 2,000 swimming pools.

 Figure 32-7

Visual Strategy Figure 32-7

● **Comparing Structures**
Show the class a model or photograph of the human heart. Have them compare it with the one shown in this figure. Point out that in an anterior view of the heart, the right side of the heart is always shown on the left, as if the heart were in a person facing the viewer. Have students trace the path blood follows through the heart. Have them compare the thickness of the walls of the atria and ventricles and explain the reason for this difference.

Demonstration
■ **Recognizing Relationships**
Demonstrate how a stethoscope can be used to hear the sounds of a heartbeat. If stethoscopes are not part of the biology equipment, invite the school nurse to demonstrate. Have students identify which valves shown in Figure 32-7 make the "lubb" sound and which are responsible for the "dubb" sound. Inform students that heart murmurs are caused by blood leaking back through faulty heart valves. As the blood backs up, it produces a sloshy noise, heard as a heart murmur.

Health Connection
Irregular Heartbeat
Malfunctioning of the pacemaker (SA node) can result in a disorder known as fibrillation, a condition in which the heart contractions become irregular and rapid. In such cases, surgeons can implant an artificial pacemaker powered by batteries. This pacemaker operates by delivering electrical stimuli to the heart at regular intervals.

Key to Strategies
● Understanding Concepts (Tier I)
■ Applying Information (Tier II)
▲ Critical Thinking (Tier III)

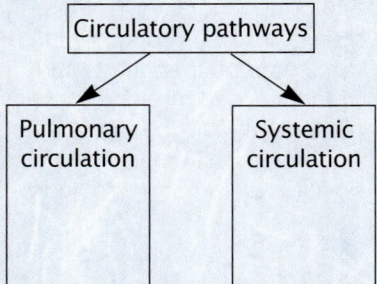
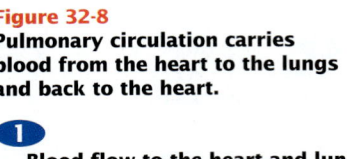

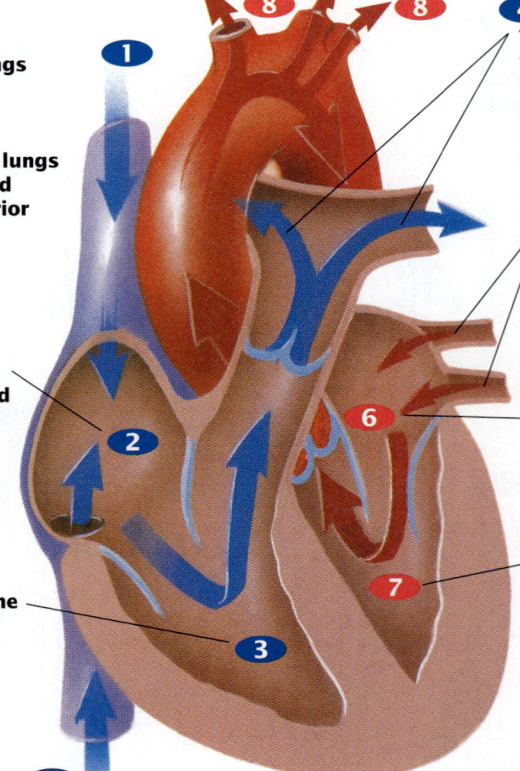

Figure 32-8
Pulmonary circulation carries blood from the heart to the lungs and back to the heart.

1 Blood flow to the heart and lungs begins as oxygen-poor blood travels from both the superior and inferior venae cavae.

2 The blood first enters the right atrium and is pumped into the right ventricle.

3 From the right ventricle, the blood is pumped through the pulmonary arteries.

4 The pulmonary arteries transport the blood to the lungs. There the blood picks up oxygen and gets rid of carbon dioxide and other wastes.

5 The pulmonary veins, not shown on other side, transport the newly oxygenated blood from the lungs back to the heart.

6 The left atrium receives oxygen-rich blood and pumps it to the next chamber.

7 The left ventricle is the final chamber through which blood flows.

8 The aorta pumps blood rich in oxygen to both sides of the body. The descending aorta is not shown here.

Circulatory Pathways

Your heart pumps blood through two major circulatory pathways. Pulmonary circulation, shown in **Figure 32-8**, carries blood from the heart to the lungs and back to the heart. The pathway of blood from the heart to other parts of the body is called systemic circulation.

Blood picks up oxygen and releases carbon dioxide in the lungs

Blood returning to the heart from the body is low in oxygen and high in carbon dioxide. This blood is pumped through the right side of the heart into arteries that lead to the lungs. These arteries, the pulmonary arteries, are the only arteries that carry oxygen-poor blood. As blood flows through the capillaries in the lungs, it picks up oxygen and gets rid of carbon dioxide. Leaving the lungs, the blood travels through veins, back to the heart. These veins, the pulmonary veins, are the only veins that carry oxygen-rich blood.

Systemic circulation carries blood from the heart to the rest of the body

Blood returning to the heart from the lungs is ready to deliver oxygen to the rest of the body. Notice in **Figure 32-8** that oxygen-rich blood is pumped through the left side of the heart and out the aorta, the largest artery in the body. From the aorta, blood flows to all parts of the body through a system of increasingly smaller arteries. Systemic circulation has three branches of special importance: the branch that carries blood to the heart, the branch that carries blood to the digestive tract and liver, and the branch that carries blood to and from the kidneys. Several of the major veins and arteries of systemic circulation are shown in **Figure 32-9**.

Matter of Fact: Causes of Death

The number of deaths due to heart attacks, hypertension, and strokes is greater than the number due to cancer and accidents combined.

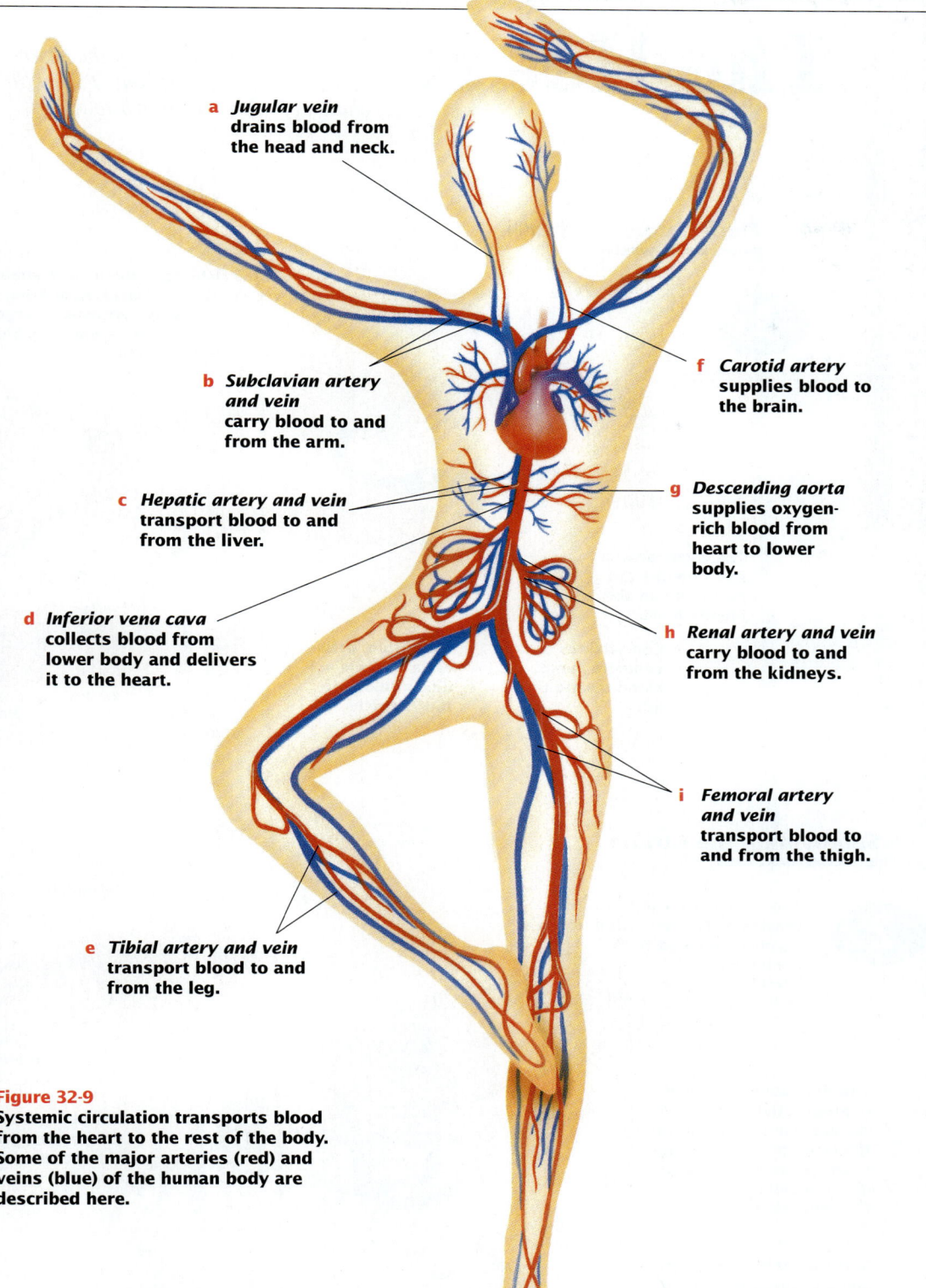

a *Jugular vein* drains blood from the head and neck.

b *Subclavian artery and vein* carry blood to and from the arm.

c *Hepatic artery and vein* transport blood to and from the liver.

d *Inferior vena cava* collects blood from lower body and delivers it to the heart.

e *Tibial artery and vein* transport blood to and from the leg.

f *Carotid artery* supplies blood to the brain.

g *Descending aorta* supplies oxygen-rich blood from heart to lower body.

h *Renal artery and vein* carry blood to and from the kidneys.

i *Femoral artery and vein* transport blood to and from the thigh.

Figure 32-9
Systemic circulation transports blood from the heart to the rest of the body. Some of the major arteries (red) and veins (blue) of the human body are described here.

661

Demonstration

● **Summarizing Information**

Ask a local physician or emergency medical technician (EMT) to show the class an electrocardiogram (ECG or EKG) and explain what it represents. If possible, have him or her take an ECG of a student volunteer. You might also have him or her exhibit contrasting abnormal electrocardiograms and discuss what is malfunctioning in each case.

Visual Strategy   Figure 32-9

● **Identifying Structures**

Instruct students to trace a drop of blood that travels from the brain to the leg, naming all the arteries and veins that are involved. Be sure that they describe how blood returning from the brain to the heart must first travel to the lungs and then back to the heart before beginning its voyage to the leg. Point out that if the person shown in this figure were an athlete engaging in the strenuous activity of dancing, the athlete's heart rate would climb rapidly, but so would the stroke volume—the amount of blood that passes through the heart with each beat. Although an unconditioned person's heart also beats faster during vigorous exercise, it does so with significantly less increase in stroke volume. Consequently, less blood is being pumped out to the body, causing him or her to tire more quickly.

Language Arts Connection

Coronary Disorders and the Heart

portfolio Have students bring in newspaper or magazine articles that deal with the heart, including articles about coronary disorders. Have each student write a summary of his or her article and make a brief report to the class at the conclusion of this lesson.

Key to Strategies

● Understanding Concepts (Tier I)
■ Applying Information (Tier II)
▲ Critical Thinking (Tier III)

Circulation and Respiration   **661**

Evolution of the Heart

● **Summarizing Information**

Have students summarize the following information by outlining the features of the fish, amphibian, reptile, bird, and mammal heart.

The evolution of the heart can be traced from the single-cycle heart of a fish to the two-cycle heart of amphibians, reptiles, birds, and mammals. In the fish, blood flows to the gills, where it picks up oxygen but also slows substantially while flowing through the narrow gill capillaries. Blood pressure falls about 50 percent in the gills. Consequently, delivery of oxygen to the tissues is relatively slow.

Adult amphibians have lungs, not gills, and two partially separated circulatory loops. Blood flows from the heart to the lungs and back through a new feature, the pulmonary circulation. The two components of pulmonary circulation are the pulmonary artery, which carries deoxygenated blood from the ventricle to the lungs, and the pulmonary vein, which carries the blood back to the heart. Because blood is repumped by the heart after slowing in the capillaries of the lungs, the blood pressure in the initial portion of the systemic circulation is about twice as high in an amphibian as in a fish. This arrangement creates a problem not found in the fish heart: mixing of deoxygenated blood and oxygenated blood in the ventricle.

In reptiles other than crocodiles, mixing is greatly reduced by a partial division of the ventricle. In crocodiles, birds, and mammals, this partition is complete, giving these animals a four-chambered heart.

The Heart

In vertebrates, contractions of the heart propel blood through the body. Follow the evolution of heart structure below.

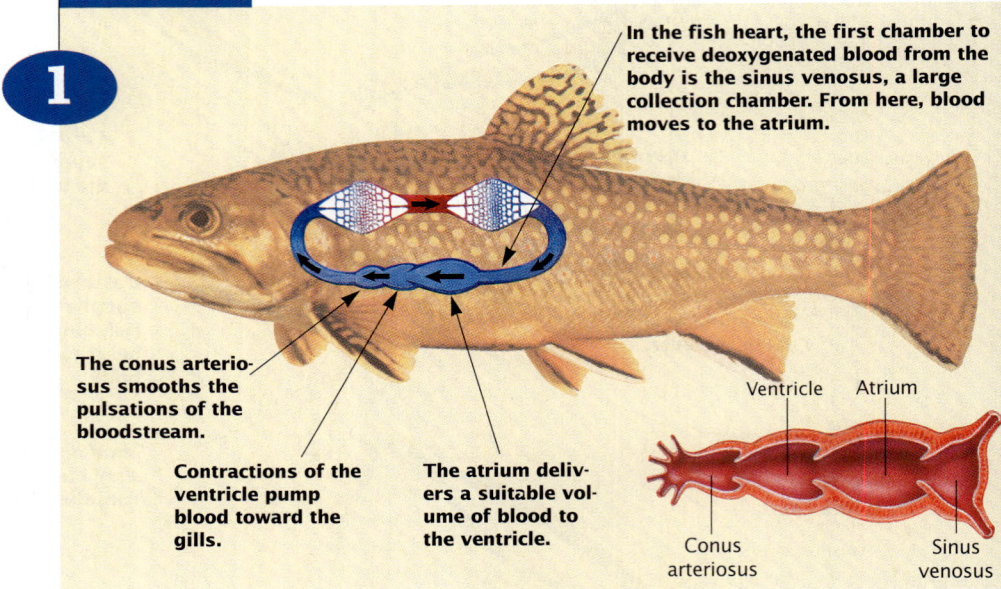

Four Simple Chambers

1

In the fish heart, the first chamber to receive deoxygenated blood from the body is the sinus venosus, a large collection chamber. From here, blood moves to the atrium.

The conus arteriosus smooths the pulsations of the bloodstream.

Contractions of the ventricle pump blood toward the gills.

The atrium delivers a suitable volume of blood to the ventricle.

Ventricle   Atrium

Conus arteriosus   Sinus venosus

Subdividing the Atrium

2

The atrium is divided into two chambers. The left atrium receives oxygenated blood from the lungs, sending it to the ventricle.

The right atrium receives deoxygenated blood from the body and pumps it into the ventricle. Some mixing of oxygenated and deoxygenated blood occurs in the ventricle.

In the amphibian heart, the sinus venosus is reduced in size.

The pulmonary vein carrying oxygenated blood enter the left atrium.

Atrium   Ventricle

Conus arteriosus

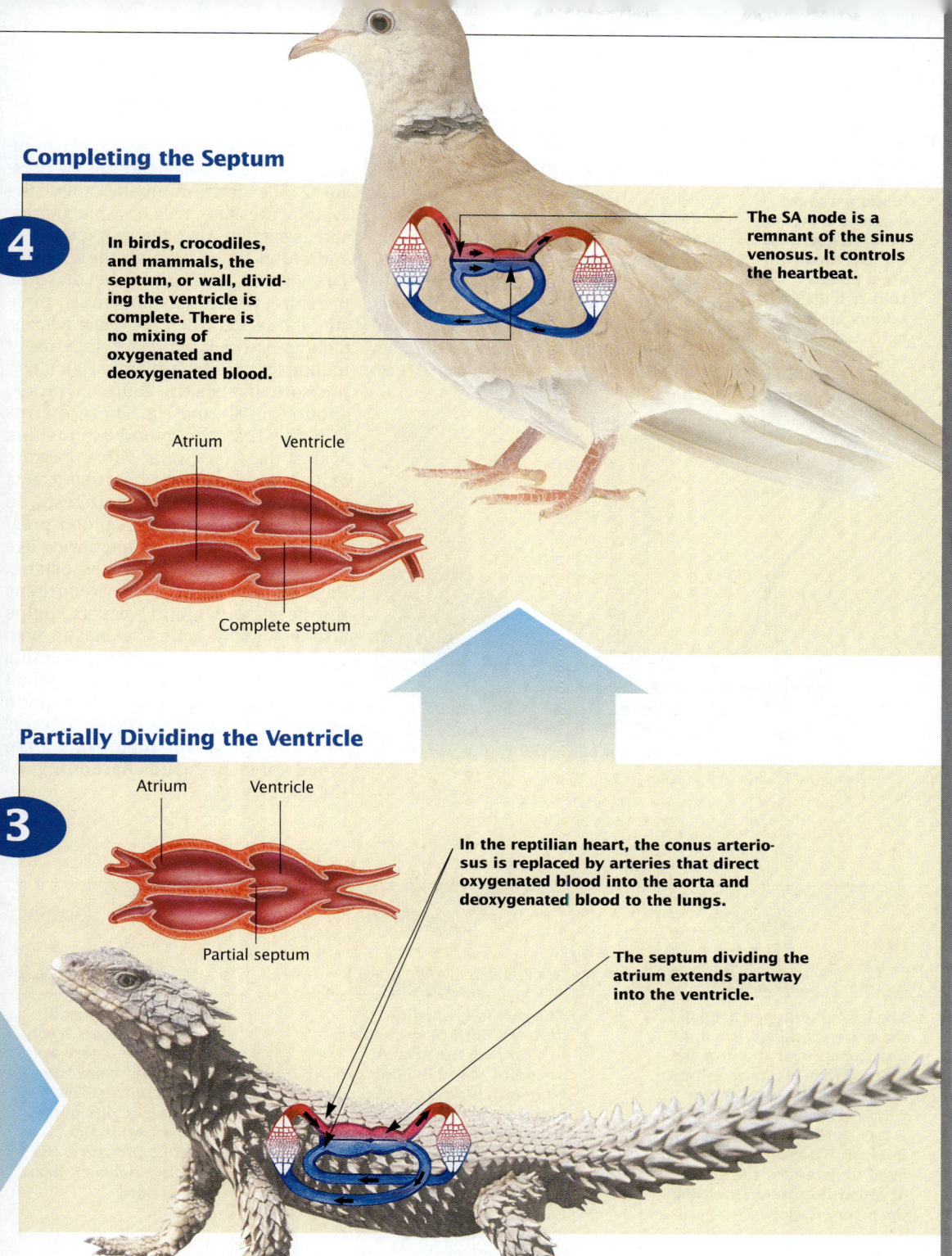

Completing the Septum

4

In birds, crocodiles, and mammals, the septum, or wall, dividing the ventricle is complete. There is no mixing of oxygenated and deoxygenated blood.

The SA node is a remnant of the sinus venosus. It controls the heartbeat.

Atrium   Ventricle

Complete septum

Partially Dividing the Ventricle

3

Atrium   Ventricle

Partial septum

In the reptilian heart, the conus arteriosus is replaced by arteries that direct oxygenated blood into the aorta and deoxygenated blood to the lungs.

The septum dividing the atrium extends partway into the ventricle.

663

Functional Parts of the Heart and Circulation

● **Identifying Functions**

Guide a discussion by posing the following questions about the heart.

1. In the mammalian heart, the left ventricle is much larger than the right. Explain this size disparity. *(The right ventricle only needs to generate enough pressure to send blood the short distance to the lungs and back. In contrast, the left ventricle must create enough pressure to circulate the blood throughout the body. The left ventricle must be stronger to generate the greater pressure, and so it is larger.)*

2. In embryonic mammals, the pulmonary artery is connected directly to the aorta through a structure known as the ductus arteriosus. The ductus arteriosus closes and ceases to function after birth. What is the function of the ductus arteriosus before birth? *(Since the embryo does not breathe until birth, blood need not flow to the lungs. The ductus arteriosus diverts blood from the pulmonary artery into the aorta.)*

Blood Pressure

Figure 32-10
A kit for measuring blood pressure includes a stethoscope, a cuff that can be filled with air, a hollow rubber bulb that pumps air into the cuff, and a gauge or hollow glass tube containing a column of mercury.

When the ventricles contract, blood is forced into the arteries, which exerts pressure on the walls of the blood vessel. This force is called **blood pressure**. When ventricles relax, the pressure decreases. The muscular, elastic walls of the arteries are able to adjust to the changing pressure. The elasticity helps maintain the pressure between heartbeats. This way blood is kept flowing through the body continuously. When you take your pulse, you are feeling the expansion and relaxation of an artery with each heartbeat.

How is blood pressure measured?

As described in **Figure 32-10**, two numbers are used to measure blood pressure. The first number, called the systolic pressure, tells how much pressure is exerted when the heart contracts and blood flows through the arteries. The second number is the diastolic pressure, which tells how much pressure is exerted when the heart relaxes. Blood pressure is expressed in terms of millimeters of mercury (mm Hg). Blood pressure in a healthy adult is typically about 120/80 mm Hg. These figures indicate that the blood is pushing against the artery walls with a pressure of 120 mm Hg as the heart contracts and 80 mm Hg as the heart rests. In industrialized countries, blood pressure steadily rises with increasing age as the arteries become less elastic. Regular aerobic activity strengthens the heart and blood vessels, helps arteries to stay somewhat elastic even with aging, and can minimize this expected rise in blood pressure. Blood pressure figures provide information about the conditions of the arteries and are useful in diagnosing high blood pressure and hardening of the arteries.

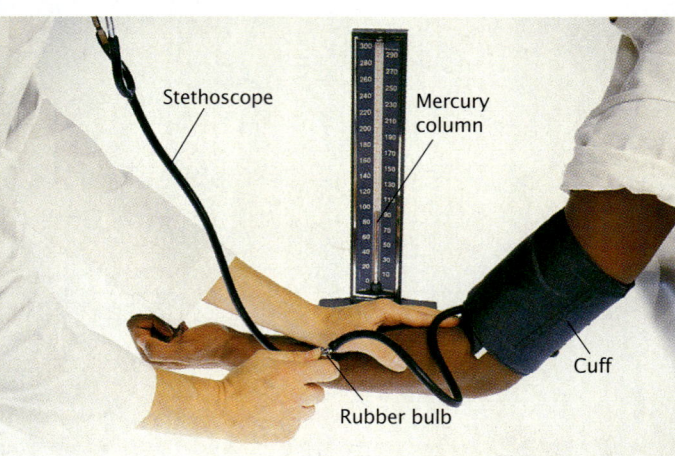

Stethoscope
Mercury column
Cuff
Rubber bulb

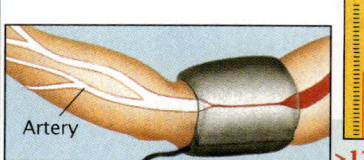

Artery
>120

a The cuff is wrapped around the patient's upper arm and positioned over the brachial artery. When the rubber bulb is pumped, air inflates the cuff. This squeezes the artery until no blood passes through. The stethoscope is used to listen for the sound of blood flow to ensure that the artery is closed.

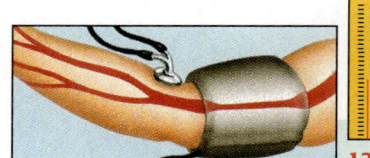

120

b The cuff is gradually deflated until blood begins to flow into the arm. A sound of blood pulsing can be heard, indicating that the blood pressure is greater than pressure exerted by the cuff. The pressure at this point (120 mm Hg) is the systolic pressure, which is read from the scale. Systolic pressure is exerted by contracting ventricles.

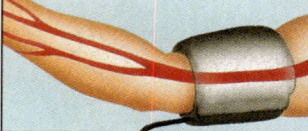

c The cuff is loosened until blood flows freely through the artery and the sounds below the cuff disappear. The pressure at this point (80 mm Hg) is the diastolic pressure, the pressure between heart contractions.

Pharmaceutical Industry

What would it be like to . . .

- help develop a drug that prevents or cures a disease?
- use experiences in business or health care to contribute to the health of people around the world?

These are just a few of the opportunities open to people who work in the pharmaceutical industry.

Pharmaceutical Industry: What Is It?

The pharmaceutical industry is made up of hundreds of companies that discover, develop, produce, and market drugs used for medicinal purposes. Since the widespread availability of antibiotics in the 1940s, the pharmaceutical industry has discovered thousands of new drugs that help cure diseases, prevent epidemics, and increase life expectancy. Most of the work in this industry focuses on researching and developing new drugs or new uses for existing drugs.

Science/Math Career Preparation

High School
- Biology
- Chemistry
- Mathematics

College
- Botany
- Zoology
- Anatomy and physiology
- Chemistry
- Biochemistry
- Biostatistics

Employment Outlook

Accelerated growth in the pharmaceutical industry is predicted as advances in technology increase.

Career Focus: Dora Duncan

Clinical Research Associate for Pharmaco International, Inc.

"When I was growing up, a woman had few career choices—she became either a teacher or a nurse. I chose nursing because I had always been interested in human biology and wanted to have an impact on people's lives. I was in nursing for 26 years, and I'm amazed how a nurse's image and role have changed. Nurses play a more active role in caring for patients, and have the ability to specialize in a diversity of areas in health care."

What I Do: "Today I'm using my experience in a different area—the pharmaceutical industry. I work for a contract research organization in the pharmaceutical industry as a clinical research associate. Before a new drug can be approved for sale and use, it must undergo a long series of tests to determine its safety and effectiveness. My job is to monitor these tests to ensure that they are conducted according to strict guidelines."

To Find Out More

1 For further information, write to:
Department of Health and
  Human Services
Public Health Service
Food and Drug
  Administration
5600 Fishers Lane
Rockville, MD 20857

2 Visit your school counselor and library to find out which colleges and universities offer training for careers in the pharmaceutical industry. Review the prerequisites and course requirements. Make a poster showing the types of careers that relate to this industry.

3 Find articles listing the procedures necessary before a new drug is approved by the Food and Drug Administration.

665

Career Opportunities

Using Resources

1. Have the class brainstorm ideas about the following questions:

If you wanted a career in the pharmaceutical industry...

- what kind of personality traits would be essential?
- which subjects should you study in high school? in college?
- what kinds of extracurricular activities should you pursue?
- what kind of practical experience should you gain?
- what kind of issues would interest you?

2.  Have students visit the US Food and Drug Administration (FDA) site on the Internet (http://www.fda.gov) to learn about CDER (the Center for Drug Evaluation and Research). Tell them to find information about guidelines for new-drug development. Then have the class meet to devise a flow-chart that highlights the steps involved in developing a new drug in the United States.

3. Have students use available resources to search for employment opportunities in the pharmaceutical and health-care industries. Encourage them to find as wide a variety of careers as possible. Have students collect reproductions of these advertisements to display in a section of the room or school devoted to career opportunities.

Active READING

Technique: Paired Summarizing

Pair each student with a partner. Have each student read silently about blood chemistry on page 666. Then have one student, the "reteller," summarize orally the first half of what has been read without referring to the text. The other student, the "listener," should listen to the retelling without interrupting (except for clarification) and be prepared to point out any inaccuracies in the summary and add any ideas that were left out. Students should work together during this final clarification process and may refer back to the text if needed. Have students switch roles and repeat this process with the second half of the text.

Demonstration

■ **Analyzing Data**

Refer to the test tube in Figure 32-2 on page 652. Have students estimate the amount of plasma compared with the amount of formed elements after centrifugation (this measurement is called a hematocrit). Ask students why the formed elements are on the bottom of the test tube and what types of cells are in the formed element portion of the blood. *(The formed elements of blood are denser than plasma. The formed elements of blood are red blood cells, white blood cells, and platelets. The platelets, however, are not cells.)* Use prepared slides of human blood and have students draw both red and white blood cells from their observations.

Formed Elements of Blood

● **Comparing Structures**

Using the information from pages 652 and 653 and from other sources, have students make a **Graphic Organizer** similar to the one at the bottom of this page in which they compare the formed elements of blood. Ask students to include in their organizers the number of each formed element in a cubic millimeter of whole blood.

Blood Chemistry

Blood is the fluid of life for the human body. As you have learned, the blood transports raw materials to cells so that they can carry on their necessary activities. Blood also removes wastes from cells so that they can continue their activities without interruption. Blood then transports these wastes to the lungs, skin, or kidneys for excretion so that the body does not experience a toxic buildup. In addition, blood maintains a fluid environment for cells. Water moves from the blood to spaces between the cells. The solids (salts, sugars, etc.) dissolved in that water must be kept at a proper concentration if the cells are to function properly. The blood regulates the amount of water by moving dissolved solids into and out of the spaces between the cells and into and out of the cells. Finally, blood contains weapons to protect the body from disease, from extreme changes in acidity, and from blood loss. The blood's ability to perform these vital functions depends on the kinds and concentration of substances in water, or depends on the blood's chemistry.

Changes in blood composition may indicate disease

Recall the composition of blood. There are three kinds of blood cells suspended in plasma. Most of your blood (about 85 percent) is circulating throughout your blood vessels at any given time. The rest of your blood is in your heart or lungs. The content of circulating blood is important to homeostasis. Medical science has established healthy ranges for the concentrations of solids and gases that are circulating in your blood. When these concentrations move outside the healthy range, it is an indication that the body is out of balance. Severe imbalances are termed "disease." How do we know when we are out of balance? One way is to perform a blood analysis on a sample of blood.

Blood drawn from an individual becomes a blood sample

A blood analysis is performed on a sample of blood drawn from the vein of an individual. Specialized collection tubes make it possible to keep the cells in suspension or to allow the cells to clot, yielding packed red cells. When the blood is allowed to clot at room temperature, the blood-clotting components form a netlike trap around the red cells, and a clot forms at the bottom of the tube. For certain types of blood analyses and for blood transfusions, it is necessary to prevent the blood from clotting, so an anticoagulant is added to the collection tube. The anticoagulant keeps the whole cells in suspension and yields a sample of whole blood for analysis.

A blood analysis can be simple or detailed

Performing a blood analysis is like looking inside the body without actually going inside. Sometimes the analysis is as simple as a complete blood count, or CBC, which is a count of the number of blood cells in a given volume of whole blood. Sometimes, when more detail is needed, the plasma is also analyzed.

In a CBC, a sample of whole blood is run through a specialized machine. The red blood cells are counted and analyzed for size, shape, and color. In addition, the different classes of white blood cells are identified, and the number of each class is counted. Finally, the platelets are counted. The general information learned from these counts is indicated in **Figure 32-11a–c**.

Remember that centrifuging the blood forces its components to settle in layers with a liquid portion called plasma at the top. The blood's plasma contains over 150 substances. The amount of each specific substance in circulation is vital to homeostasis. When the blood plasma is analyzed, a blood analysis provides more detail about the body's system of complex

Graphic Organizer

Use the following graphic organizer with the teaching strategy **Formed Elements of Blood** on page 666.

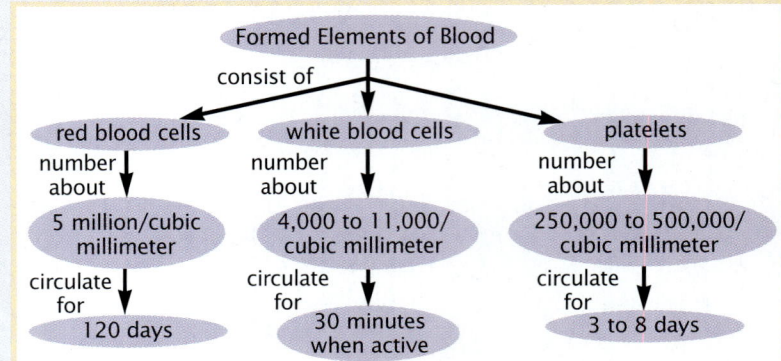

Formed Elements of Blood

consist of

red blood cells	white blood cells	platelets
number about	number about	number about
5 million/cubic millimeter	4,000 to 11,000/ cubic millimeter	250,000 to 500,000/ cubic millimeter
circulate for	circulate for	circulate for
120 days	30 minutes when active	3 to 8 days

interdependences that are required to maintain homeostasis. **Figure 32-11d** lists some of the substances that can be analyzed in plasma.

Analysis of blood lipids can be used to indicate disease risk

An analysis of blood lipids is becoming a routine part of annual health examinations. You have probably heard people talk about having their cholesterol checked. Cholesterol is a lipid that is an essential part of cell membranes and a starting compound for the manufacture of many substances, including sex hormones and vitamin D. But while the body needs cholesterol, it doesn't need some of the cholesterol compounds that collect in the blood vessels and the heart. These cholesterol compounds block the blood vessels and reduce blood flow. A blood analysis called a cardiac-risk profile reveals the presence of specific cholesterol compounds in the blood

and the amounts of each. The results of the cardiac-risk profile can be used to assess one's risk of developing diseases of the circulatory system. Cholesterol measurements are recommended for people 20 years of age and older.

The blood contains combination carrier molecules for cholesterol

Recall that plasma is primarily water and that lipids like cholesterol are soluble in oil, but not in water. How, then, does the body transport cholesterol in blood plasma, which is mostly water? The body uses a combination of lipid and protein to carry water-insoluble compounds like cholesterol. These lipid-protein carriers are called lipoproteins. When carrying cholesterol, a lipoprotein forms a lipoprotein-cholesterol complex. Sophisticated blood analyses can now measure the different kinds of lipoprotein-cholesterol complexes in the blood.

Figure 32-11
The most common blood analysis counts each of the blood cells in a sample of whole blood. Greater detail about homeostasis or disease can be learned by further analyzing the blood plasma.

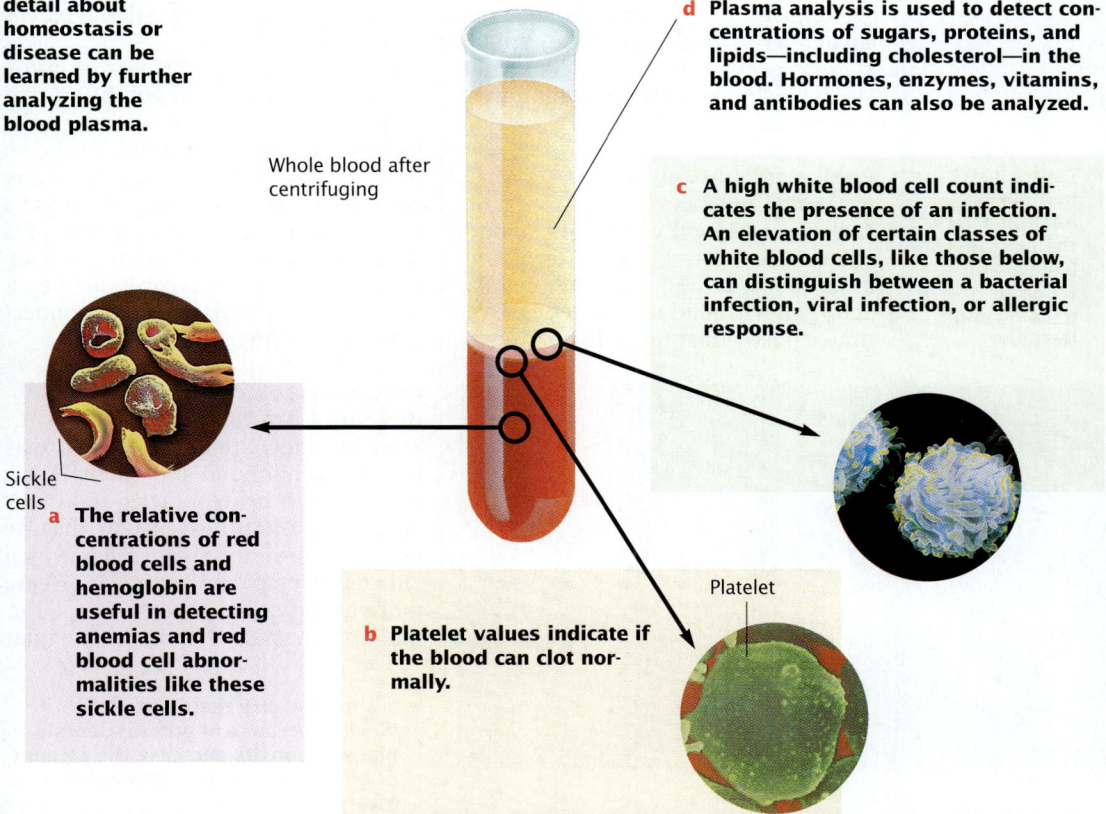

Whole blood after centrifuging

d Plasma analysis is used to detect concentrations of sugars, proteins, and lipids—including cholesterol—in the blood. Hormones, enzymes, vitamins, and antibodies can also be analyzed.

c A high white blood cell count indicates the presence of an infection. An elevation of certain classes of white blood cells, like those below, can distinguish between a bacterial infection, viral infection, or allergic response.

Sickle cells

a The relative concentrations of red blood cells and hemoglobin are useful in detecting anemias and red blood cell abnormalities like these sickle cells.

b Platelet values indicate if the blood can clot normally.

Platelet

Visual Strategy   Figure 32-11

■ **Analyzing Data**
Instruct students to consider the analysis of blood plasma as shown in this figure. Figure 32-11d discusses concentrations of sugars, proteins, and lipids. Ask students what high concentrations of each of these molecules can indicate. *(High blood glucose levels can indicate the pancreas is not producing enough insulin, high blood urea nitrogen (BUN) is a sign of reduced kidney function, increased bilirubin can indicate liver dysfunction, and high cholesterol levels can indicate an increased risk of cardiovascular disease.)*

Key to Strategies
● Understanding Concepts (Tier I)
■ Applying Information (Tier II)
▲ Critical Thinking (Tier III)

667

Circulation and Respiration   667

Stability and Homeostasis

How could

calcium deposits

in blood vessels

affect blood

pressure?

Blood analysis distinguishes good and bad cholesterol

Low-density lipoprotein (LDL) is the main cholesterol carrier in the blood, but cholesterol carried on LDL is readily deposited on the walls of arteries. As a result, LDL-cholesterol is often called "bad cholesterol."

On the other hand, cholesterol transported on high-density lipoprotein (HDL) is carried back to the liver for removal from the body. Because HDL-cholesterol is removed from body tissues, it is often referred to as "good cholesterol."

A cardiac-risk profile measures the amount of total cholesterol and HDL-cholesterol in the blood. In addition, it measures the amount of freely circulating lipids called triglycerides. From these measurements, the amount of LDL can then be calculated. **Table 32-2** gives the healthy ranges established by medical scientists for these blood lipids.

Table 32-2
Healthy Ranges for Blood Lipids

Lipid compound	mg/100 mL
Total cholesterol	130–200
HDL-cholesterol	
males	30–75
females	40–90
LDL-cholesterol	less than 130
Triglycerides	30–150

Diseases of the Heart and Blood Vessels

Diseases of the heart and blood vessels are referred to as **cardiovascular diseases**. Cardiovascular diseases are the leading cause of death in the United States, claiming about 1 million lives every year.

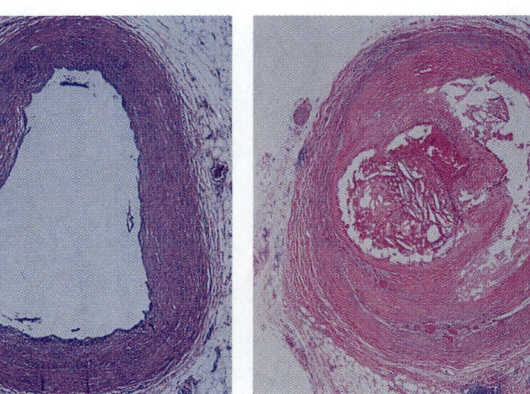

Figure 32-12
a **In a normal healthy artery, the passageway is clear for blood to pass through. However, . . .**

Plaque formation is a natural process
At birth, our blood vessels are smooth and unobstructed. Cholesterol and other fats, calcium, and other cellular debris slowly build up in arteries. Over time, these substances form a pasty mass called plaque *(plak)* that sticks to the artery walls. Plaque buildup blocks blood flow.

Atherosclerosis *(ATH uhr oh skluh ROH sihs)* is a medical condition that results when the blood-vessel walls become coated with plaque, as shown in **Figure 32-12b**. Tissues normally nourished by the blocked vessels become oxygen starved. A few cells begin to die. Over time, partial or complete blockages can occur in the heart, the brain, or the arteries that connect the heart to other tissues.

Cardiovascular disease develops gradually
Studies show that atherosclerosis begins in childhood and adolescence, even though heart attacks and other symptoms of cardiovascular disease may not appear for decades. Some individuals develop cardiovascular disease more quickly than others. Plaque formation is hastened by lack of regular

b **. . . in an artery that is partially blocked because of atherosclerosis, plaque deposits decrease the amount of blood that can flow through the artery.**

exercise, a diet high in saturated fats (dairy and meat fats, eggs, and hydrogenated vegetable oils), and cigarette smoke. High LDL and low HDL levels as well as high blood pressure also hasten plaque formation. Triglycerides are the most common fatty substance in the blood. About 95 percent of the lipids in our diets consist of triglycerides. Combined with cholesterol, triglycerides hasten plaque formation. Family history of cardiovascular disease is a critical factor for some people.

Blocked vessels starve tissues

When blood vessels are blocked, the pressure within them builds. When blood pressure against an artery wall remains higher than normal, a condition called **hypertension**, or high blood pressure, results. Because it has no warning symptoms, hypertension is often called the silent killer. High blood pressure is a key indicator of cardiovascular disease.

More obvious than hypertension, though, are the sudden emergencies that result when a heart stops or when part of the brain ceases to direct the body's functions. A heart attack results from a blockage that reduces the supply of blood to an area of heart muscle,

causing heart tissue to die. A stroke results from a blockage that reduces the supply of blood to an area of the brain, causing brain tissue to die. The severity of disability depends on how much of the heart muscle or the brain is damaged.

Blood lipids may indicate cardiovascular disease

More than half of the people who have heart attacks have normal total cholesterol levels. How can that be? Recall that there are good and bad cholesterol complexes in the blood. The *ratio* of total cholesterol to good cholesterol (total cholesterol divided by HDL) is more important than total cholesterol alone. Higher levels of good cholesterol lower the ratio. Lower ratios mean greater protection against cardiovascular disease.

Look at the picture and the lipid profile of the teen in **Figure 32-13**. How does her cardiac-risk profile shown in the figure compare with the healthy values for blood lipids in **Table 32-2**? Given her family history of high cholesterol and cardiovascular disease, what can she do to protect her heart and blood vessels?

Figure 32-13
This teen appears lean and healthy, but her cardiac-risk profile indicates factors that may hasten the development of plaque.

Blood lipid	Amount in mg/100 mL
Total cholesterol	210
HDL-cholesterol	40
Triglycerides	90
Calculated LDL	152

SECTION REVIEW

1 Describe the roles played by the left and right halves of the heart.

2 Compare and contrast systemic and pulmonary circulation.

3 What does a blood pressure of 120/80 mean?

4 What steps could you take to reduce your chances of developing cardiovascular disease?

Phase Three
Assessment Options

Closure

■ **Forming a Hypothesis**
Have students hypothesize where blood pressure would be the highest *(in the aorta as blood is leaving the left ventricle)* and where it would be the lowest *(in the vena cavae as blood is returning to the right atrium)*. Have them justify their choices.

SECTION REVIEW

Assign the *Section Review*.

Reteaching

Assign students to cooperative work groups of three. Have each group list features they would incorporate into the design of an artificial heart that could be used to replace a defective one.

A N S W E R S TO SECTION REVIEW

1 The right half of the heart pumps blood to the lungs to pick up oxygen and to release carbon dioxide. The left half pumps oxygen-rich blood to the rest of the body.

2 Refer to the captions for Figure 32-8 on page 660 and Figure 32-9 on page 661 for an explanation of the pulmonary and systemic circulations, respectively.

3 Students should suggest typical blood pressure in a healthy adult. Blood is pushing against the wall of an artery with a pressure of 120 mm Hg as the heart contracts and 70 mm Hg as the heart rests.

4 Students should suggest a healthful lifestyle that includes reducing the amount of animal fat, cholesterol, and salt in the diet; exercising more; and avoiding stress and drugs.

Key to Strategies
● Understanding Concepts (Tier I)
■ Applying Information (Tier II)
▲ Critical Thinking (Tier III)

Phase One
Preparation

Scheduling

See the **Lesson Planning Guide** on pages 649A and 649B for lecture, classwork, and assignment options for Section 32-3.

Phase Two
Teaching Strategies

Active **READING**

Technique: Reading Aloud/Discussion

Less-proficient readers will benefit from hearing the more detailed portions of Section 32-3 read aloud. Students should follow along in their textbooks as you read aloud. Have them mark with a sticky note any passages that they find confusing or that they do not understand. After you finish reading, the class should work together to come to an understanding of those passages that students found unclear or confusing.

How gases are exchanged in animals depends on the size of the animal. Very small animals can obtain oxygen and give off carbon dioxide directly through the plasma membranes of their outermost layer of cells. In contrast, larger animals have evolved special respiratory systems that provide a large surface area to exchange gases.

32-3 The Respiratory System

OBJECTIVES

1. **Explain how the diaphragm and rib muscles work to move air into and out of the lungs.**

2. **Describe the pathway by which oxygen from the air travels to a cell in the body.**

3. **Explain how your body regulates your breathing rate.**

4. **Describe three diseases of the respiratory system.**

Lungs and Breathing

Throughout this book, you have learned that most living organisms, like the soccer players in **Figure 32-14**, need to obtain oxygen from their environment and to remove carbon dioxide from their bodies. As you read in Chapter 5, oxygen is needed for cellular respiration, the chemical process that allows organisms to obtain energy from substances such as glucose. During aerobic respiration, carbon dioxide is produced as a waste product and must be removed from the cell. As you learned in Chapter 24, the evolution of lungs enables terrestrial animals to obtain oxygen from the atmosphere and release excess carbon dioxide.

Figure 32-14
On or off the soccer field, humans must obtain oxygen from the atmosphere and release excess carbon dioxide in the process of gas exchange.

Videodisc Resources

Holt Biology Videodiscs
Lesson 32-3: The Respiratory System

Figure 32-15

a Air taken in through the nose or mouth passes through the pharynx, larynx, and trachea into the many branches within the lungs. It soon reaches the alveoli, tiny sacs surrounded by capillaries through which gases are exchanged.

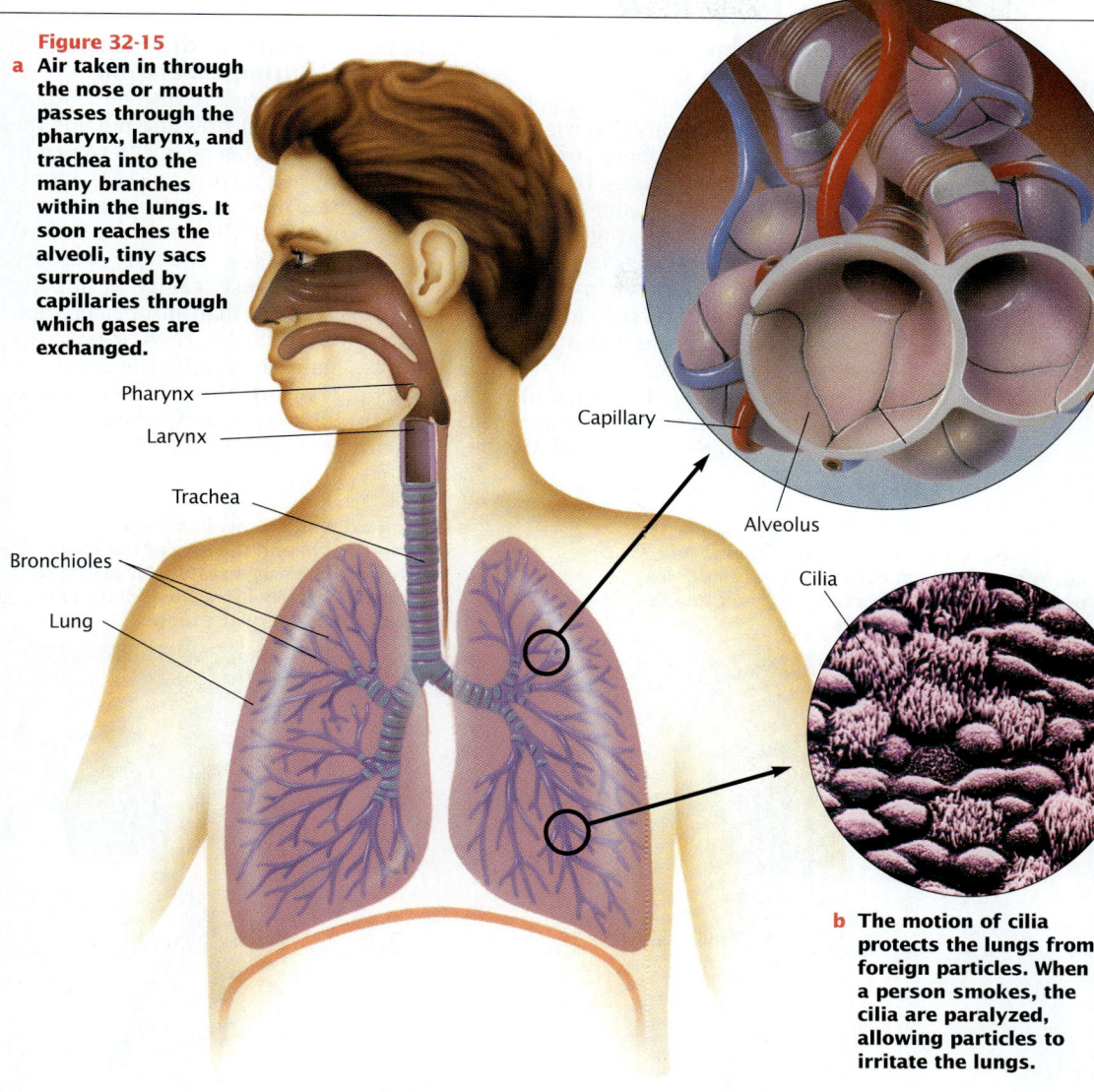

Pharynx
Larynx
Trachea
Bronchioles
Lung
Capillary
Alveolus
Cilia

b The motion of cilia protects the lungs from foreign particles. When a person smokes, the cilia are paralyzed, allowing particles to irritate the lungs.

● **Comparing Functions**

Discuss with students where the vocal cords would be found in this figure. Point out that sound is produced when air is forced through these cords. Also inform students that laryngitis is simply an inflammation of the vocal cords in which the cords lose their ability to vibrate. Hence, people "lose their voice."

Demonstration

● **Identifying Structures**

Have students gently rub their fingers up and down their throats to feel the rings of cartilage that prevent the trachea from collapsing.

Connection: *Chapter 4*

Diffusion

Point out that gases are exchanged between the air in the alveoli and the blood in the capillaries entirely by diffusion. Have students explain why a person breathes deeper and faster at higher altitudes, where there is decreased air pressure. *(At high altitudes, hemoglobin's affinity for oxygen is lower because of the lower partial pressure of oxygen. At 6,000 m [19,000 ft] the oxygen saturation of hemoglobin is only 67 percent, compared with 98 percent at sea level. One must become acclimatized over time to the low levels of oxygen.)*

Lungs contain branched tubes

Follow the passage of air through the respiratory system in **Figure 32-15**. Air enters the body through the nose or mouth and travels to the pharynx *(FAIR ihnks)*, a tube at the back of the nose and mouth. From the pharynx, air enters the voice box, or larynx *(LAR ihnks)*, and the windpipe, or trachea *(TRAY kee uh)*. These passageways are lined with tissues that warm and moisten incoming air. The lower end of the trachea divides into two branches, which divide many times into smaller branches of tubes called bronchioles *(BRAHNG kee ohlz)*. This branching network of tubes is lined with cilia, shown in **Figure 32-15b**, and a layer of protective mucus. The smallest of these tubes lead into **alveoli** *(al VEE uh leye)*, clusters of tiny air sacs. Gases enter and leave the circulatory system through the alveoli. Each alveolus is surrounded by a network of capillaries. Blood in these capillaries picks up oxygen from the alveoli and releases carbon dioxide to be exhaled. Each lung contains about 150 million alveoli, providing a surface area larger than that of a small house for gas exchange.

671

Key to Strategies

● Understanding Concepts (Tier I)
■ Applying Information (Tier II)
▲ Critical Thinking (Tier III)

Demonstration
■ Relating Concepts

Demonstrate how breathing works by making a model of the lungs and diaphragm. Attach a small, deflated balloon to one end of a short glass tube that is inserted through a one-holed rubber stopper. Use the stopper to plug the mouth of a bell jar, allowing the balloon to hang inside the jar. Use a rubber band to fasten a thin sheet of rubber over the mouth of the jar. Pull down on the rubber sheet and have students observe what happens to the balloon. Have students relate their observations to inhalation. Release the rubber sheet. Have them relate their observations to exhalation.

Visual Strategy Figure 32-16

● Comparing Structures

Use this figure to discuss lung capacity. Together the lungs can hold between 5 L and 6 L (about 1.5 gal) of air, which is the total lung capacity. However, a person normally inhales only about 0.5 L (0.13 gal), which is the same volume normally exhaled. Strenuous exercise can increase these values—it is possible to increase the capacity of a single breath to about 4.5 L (1.13 gal).

Inhalation involves muscle contraction in the chest

Breathing begins when the diaphragm, the dome-shaped muscle below the chest cavity, contracts and moves downward. The muscles between the ribs also contract, causing the rib cage to move up and out. Together, these muscle contractions cause the chest cavity to enlarge. When the chest expands, the air pressure in the chest cavity drops. Air pressure outside the body is then greater than that inside the chest, causing air to rush into the lungs to equalize the pressure. This part of breathing is called **inhalation**.

Muscles return to their relaxed position during exhalation

When the air pressure inside the lungs is equal to the air pressure outside the lungs, the muscles relax and return to their original positions. This movement, in turn, reduces the size of the chest cavity. As the size of the chest cavity decreases, the air pressure inside the chest cavity gradually becomes greater than air pressure outside the body. Air then leaves the lungs, again equalizing the pressure. This part of breathing is called **exhalation**. Inhalation and exhalation are illustrated in **Figure 32-16**.

Figure 32-16

a **During inhalation, the diaphragm contracts and moves down, and the rib cage moves up. When the chest expands as a result, air pressure in the chest cavity drops, causing air to rush into the lungs.**

b **During exhalation, the diaphragm relaxes and moves up, and the size of the chest cavity decreases as a result. Air pressure in the chest cavity increases, forcing air to be exhaled out of the lungs.**

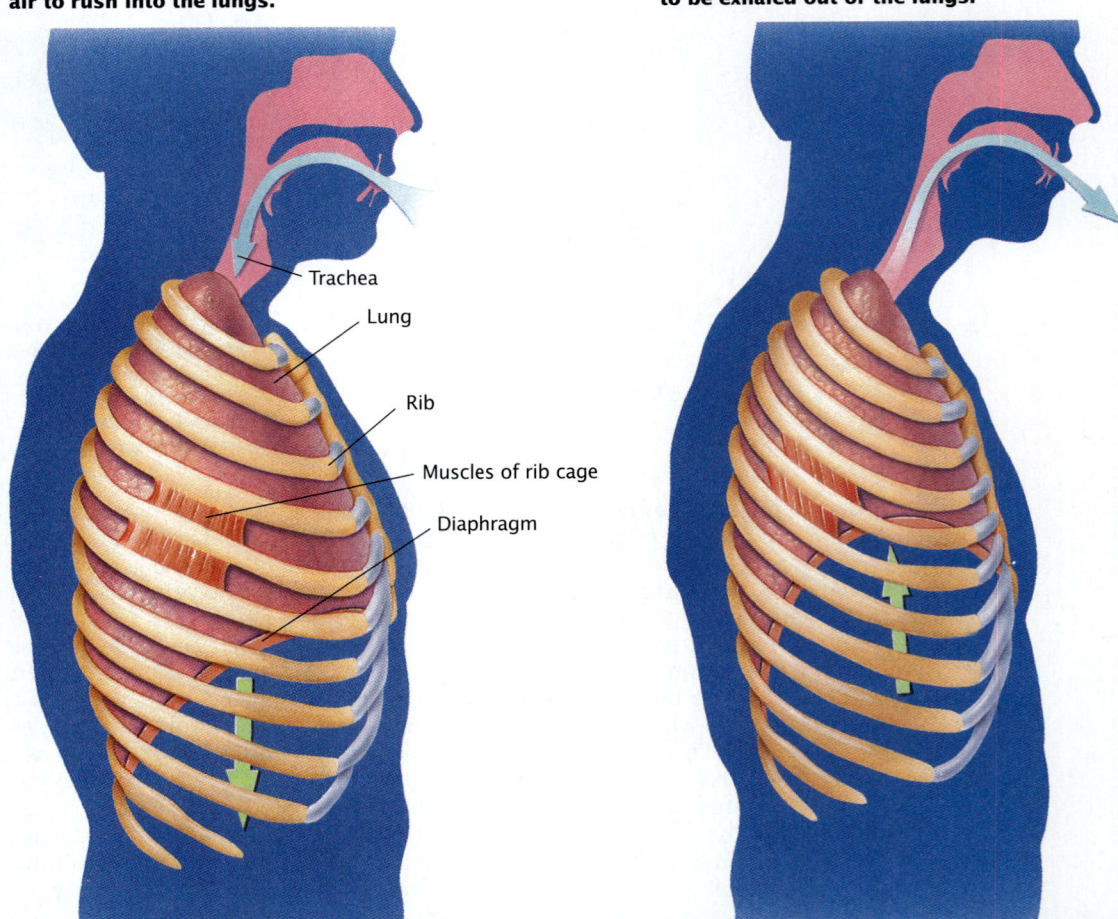

Trachea

Lung

Rib

Muscles of rib cage

Diaphragm

Figure 32-17
Follow the passage of carbon dioxide (CO_2) leaving body tissues (a) and being exhaled through the respiratory system (b) in the illustration below.

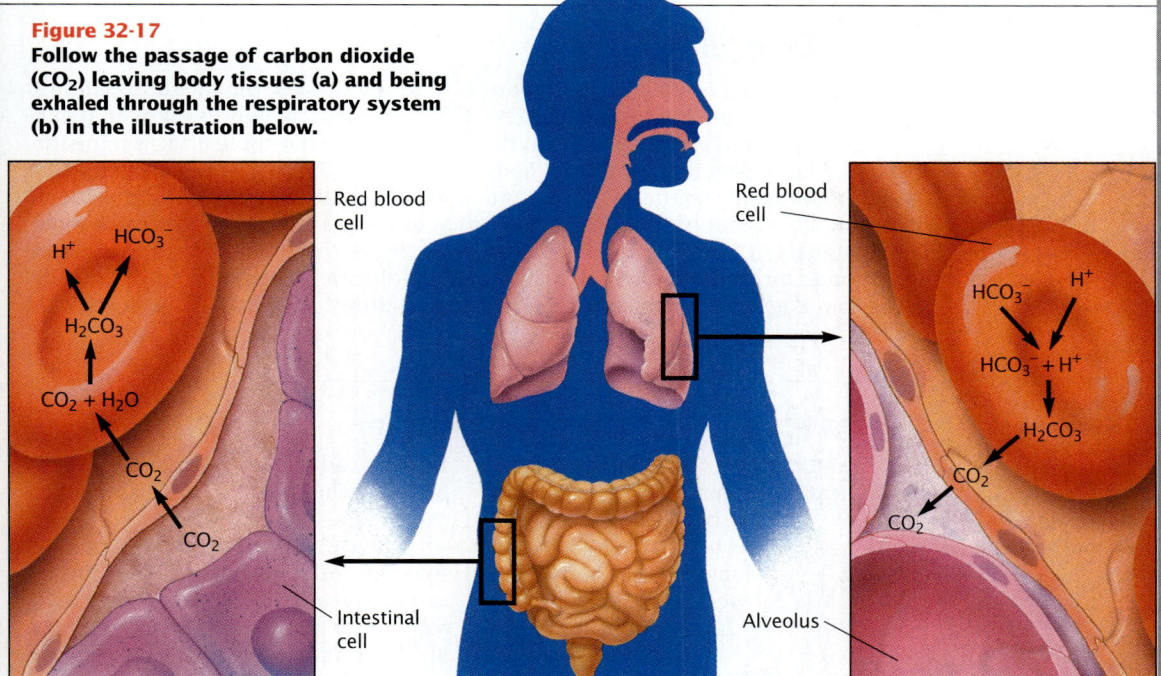

a **When CO_2 leaves cells of the intestines, it can enter red blood cells and combine with hemoglobin. Or it may combine with water to form carbonic acid, H_2CO_3, which breaks down to form hydrogen ions and bicarbonate ions.**

b **When blood reaches the lungs, the process is reversed, and CO_2 is released. The CO_2 diffuses from the blood into the alveoli in the lungs. From there, it is exhaled along with water vapor.**

Gas Exchange

The destination of the inhaled air is the alveoli, which are surrounded by capillaries. The tissue forming the walls of the alveoli and capillaries is only one cell thick. Gas exchange occurs when oxygen in the alveoli diffuses into the blood in the capillaries. In turn, the carbon dioxide in the blood diffuses into the air of the alveoli.

Oxygen binds to hemoglobin

In the blood, oxygen quickly binds with hemoglobin, the protein in red blood cells. Hemoglobin soaks up oxygen extremely effectively, which causes still more oxygen to enter red blood cells. The red blood cells then give up their oxygen to the cells of body tissues, where it is used in metabolism, the chemical activities of cells. As a result of metabolism, oxygen concentration in the body's cells is low, but carbon dioxide concentration is high.

Carbon dioxide is transported to the lungs to be exhaled

Carbon dioxide is a waste product that must be eliminated from cells. It is transported in the blood in three ways. About 5 percent of the carbon dioxide in the body dissolves in the plasma in blood. Another 25 percent enters the red blood cells and combines with hemoglobin. With help of an enzyme, the remaining 70 percent combines with water in the red blood cells to form carbonic acid, H_2CO_3. Because carbonic acid is unstable, hydrogen ions and bicarbonate ions quickly form, as shown in **Figure 32-17a**.

When blood reaches the lungs, chemical reactions occur that reverse the process, releasing carbon dioxide. As shown in **Figure 32-17b**, the carbon dioxide diffuses from the blood into the alveoli in the lungs. The carbon dioxide is exhaled with water vapor.

Visual Strategy   Figure 32-17

■ **Relating Concepts**
Use this figure to explain how carbon dioxide is transported by the blood, a process far more complex than the transport of oxygen. Avoid the misconception that oxygen is converted into carbon dioxide. The exact mechanism by which carbon dioxide is produced need not be discussed. Emphasize that it comes not from oxygen but from organic compounds from which a carbon atom and two oxygen atoms are removed during metabolism. Once students understand this point, lead them through Figure 32-17a and Figure 32-17b to show how most of the carbon dioxide is transported.

Health Connection

Carbon Monoxide Poisoning
Carbon monoxide, a poisonous gas contained in car exhaust, readily attaches to hemoglobin, preventing it from combining with oxygen. Consequently, a person exposed to sufficient amounts of this gas can die from suffocation. Point out that carbon monoxide, when combined with hemoglobin, produces a brighter red color than an oxygen-hemoglobin complex. Ask students why a person whose face is flushed and who is breathing heavily might be a victim of carbon monoxide inhalation.

Key to Strategies
● Understanding Concepts (Tier I)
■ Applying Information (Tier II)
▲ Critical Thinking (Tier III)

Regulation of Breathing

Receptors in the brain and circulatory system continuously monitor the levels of oxygen and carbon dioxide in the blood. These receptors enable the body to automatically regulate oxygen and carbon dioxide concentrations by sending signals to the brain. The brain responds by sending nerve signals to the diaphragm and rib muscles in order to speed or slow the rate of breathing. It may surprise you to know that carbon dioxide has more effect on breathing than does oxygen. For example, if the concentration of carbon dioxide in your blood increases, you breathe more deeply, ridding your body of excess carbon dioxide. When the carbon dioxide level drops, your breathing slows.

Figure 32-18
These posters, warning about some of the life-threatening illnesses associated with cigarette smoking, were designed by high school students.

Diseases of the Respiratory System

Respiratory diseases affect millions of Americans. **Asthma** *(AZ muh)* is a respiratory disease in which certain airways in the lungs become constricted because of sensitivity to certain stimuli. The narrowing of the airways reduces the efficiency of respiration, which decreases the amount of oxygen reaching body cells.

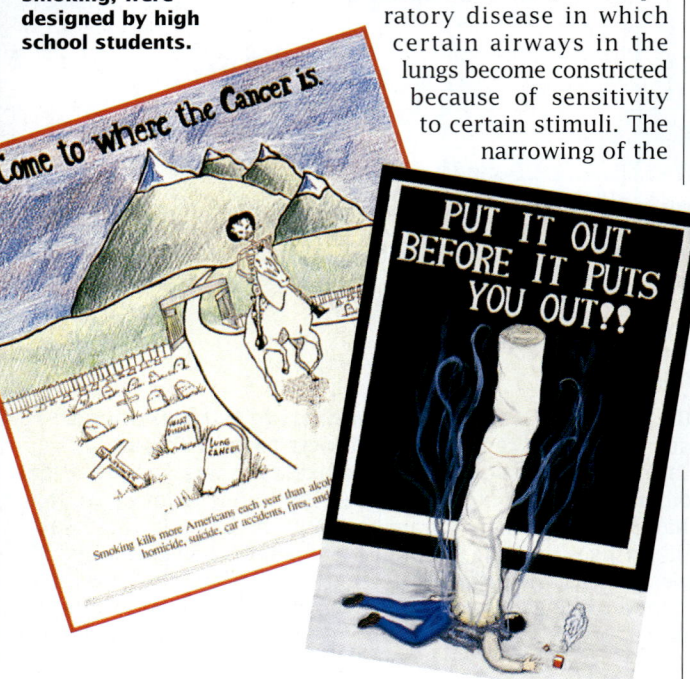

Cigarette smoking is harmful to both smokers and nonsmokers and is linked to emphysema and lung cancer, two respiratory diseases that claim millions of lives annually. Direct inhalation of smoke by the smoker, secondhand inhalation of the smoker's exhaled smoke by the nonsmoker, and inhalation of sidestream smoke from the smoker's burning cigarette by the nonsmoker—all increase the risk of developing emphysema and other serious respiratory diseases. In people who have **emphysema** *(em fuh SEE muh)*, the lung tissue loses its elasticity, greatly reducing the efficiency of gas exchange. In **lung cancer**, carcinogens present in tobacco smoke trigger the growth of cancerous cells in lung tissue. More than 90 percent of lung cancer patients are smokers, as suggested by the antismoking posters shown in **Figure 32-18**. Lung cancer has an extremely low cure rate. Fewer than 10 percent of its victims live more than five years after diagnosis.

SECTION REVIEW

1 What role do the diaphragm and rib muscles play in the processes of inhalation and exhalation?

2 How does the exchange of gases occur in the lungs?

3 When you exercise, you automatically begin to breathe faster. Explain how and why this occurs.

4 How do asthma and emphysema affect respiration?

674

ANSWERS TO **SECTION REVIEW**

1 Refer to Figure 32-16 on page 672. During inhalation, the chest cavity enlarges when the diaphragm and the muscles between the ribs contract. This lowers the pressure in the chest cavity and lungs, and air rushes into the lungs. During exhalation, the chest cavity decreases in size when the diaphragm and the muscles between the ribs relax. This raises the pressure in the chest cavity and lungs, and air is pushed out of the lungs.

2 Refer to Figure 32-17 on page 673.

3 Students should suggest that receptors in the brain and circulatory system continuously monitor the levels of oxygen and carbon dioxide in the blood. When a person exercises, the brain signals the body to breathe more deeply, ridding the body of excess carbon dioxide.

4 Asthma causes constriction or narrowing of airways, whereas emphysema causes the lung tissue to lose its elasticity. Both reduce the efficiency of respiration, decreasing the amount of oxygen in the blood.

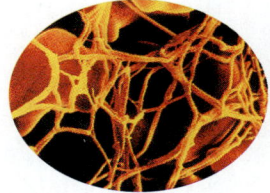

Strands of a protein called fibrin trap red and white blood cells. Soon a blood clot will form.

Alternative Assessment

Assign students to cooperative work groups of four. Have each group develop a word search puzzle based on the terms covered in this chapter. Tell students that the words can be spelled forward, backward, or on a diagonal. Collect the puzzles and distribute them to the other groups to solve.

Portfolio Assessment

Portfolio Assessment on page T39 provides options for building and evaluating student portfolios. Students and teachers can select items from the areas listed on page T39 for inclusion in a portfolio.

	Key Terms	Summary
32-1 **Circulation** 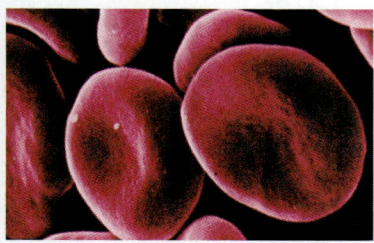 Red blood cells carry oxygen from the lungs to all cells of the body and carry carbon dioxide back to the lungs to be exhaled.	plasma (p. 652) red blood cell (p. 652) hemoglobin (p. 652) white blood cell (p. 653) platelet (p. 653) blood vessel (p. 654) artery (p. 654) vein (p. 654) capillary (p. 654) blood type (p. 656) lymphatic system (p. 657)	• The circulatory system transports materials to and from cells. • Blood consists of plasma, red blood cells that transport oxygen, white blood cells that protect against infection, and platelets that help clotting. • Blood types are defined by proteins on the surface of red blood cells. • Blood vessels include arteries that carry blood away from the heart, veins that carry blood back to the heart, and capillaries that connect the arteries to the veins. • The lymphatic system returns fluids back to the blood vessels.
32-2 **How Blood Flows** 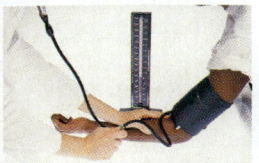 Blood pressure in a healthy adult is typically about 120/80 mm Hg.	atrium (p. 658) ventricle (p. 658) pacemaker (p. 659) blood pressure (p. 664) cardiovascular disease (p. 668) hypertension (p. 669)	• The heart has two sides: the right side moves blood to the lungs, and the left side moves blood to the rest of the body. • Blood pressure consists of a high value (systolic) when the heart contracts and a lower value (diastolic) when the heart rests. • Hypertension, or high blood pressure, is an example of a cardiovascular disease.
32-3 **The Respiratory System** The walls of the alveoli and the capillaries around them provide a large surface area for gas exchange. 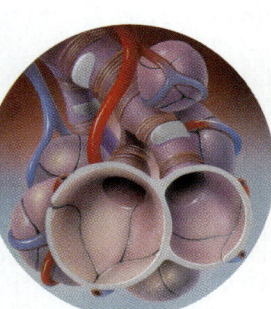	alveoli (p. 671) inhalation (p. 672) exhalation (p. 672) asthma (p. 674) emphysema (p. 674) lung cancer (p. 674)	• When the diaphragm and the rib muscles contract, enlarging the chest cavity, inhalation occurs. When the muscles relax, air is forced out and exhalation occurs. • Gas exchange occurs when oxygen in the alveoli diffuses into the blood in the capillaries. Carbon dioxide in the blood diffuses into the air of the alveoli. • Breathing is regulated mainly by the level of carbon dioxide detected in the blood. • Cigarette smoking is linked to emphysema and lung cancer.

675

ANSWER TO CONCEPT MAP

The following is one possible answer to the Relating Concepts exercise on page 676.

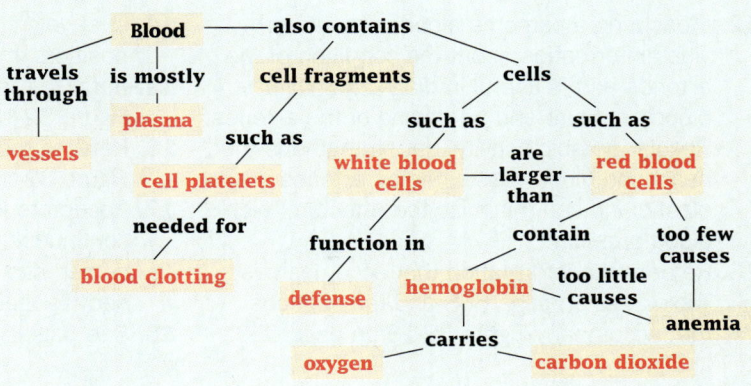

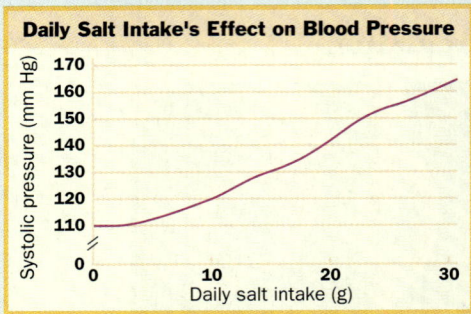

Understanding Vocabulary

1. a. See pages 652 and 653.
b. Heart attacks occur when an insufficient amount of blood reaches the heart and heart muscles begin to starve. Strokes occur when something blocks the path of oxygenated blood to the brain.
c. Refer to the captions that accompany Figure 32-10 on page 664.

2. a. platelets
b. white blood cells
c. aorta

Understanding Concepts

3. Concept Map answer is on page 675.

4. These organisms live within a liquid environment in which materials diffuse directly into and out of the organisms through plasma membranes.

5. It maintains homeostasis by controlling body temperature and carries white blood cells that help the body fight infections.

6. Refer to the captions that accompany Figure 32-2 on pages 652–653.

7. Refer to the captions that accompany Figure 32-2 on pages 652–653.

8. Refer to the captions that accompany Figure 32-3 on page 654. Arteries have highly elastic, muscular walls that enable them to expand and contract to accommodate changes in blood volume. Veins have thin and only slightly elastic walls; they also contain valves that prevent blood from flowing backward.

9. The increase in systolic blood pressure is directly proportional to salt intake.

10. Refer to the captions that accompany Figure 32-8 on page 660.

11. Refer to the captions that accompany Figure 32-5 on page 657. The circulatory system moves blood around the body for gas and nutrient exchange.

---

review

Understanding Vocabulary

1. For each pair of terms, explain the differences in their meanings.
   a. red blood cell, white blood cell
   b. heart attack, stroke
   c. systolic pressure, diastolic pressure

2. For each set of terms, complete the analogy.
   a. material that makes blood a liquid : plasma :: material that helps repair damaged blood vessels : _____
   b. confined to the bloodstream : red blood cells :: able to squeeze in and out of blood vessels : _____
   c. carries oxygen-poor blood from upper body : superior vena cava :: carries oxygen-rich blood to other arteries : _____

Understanding Concepts

3. **Relating Concepts** Construct a concept map that describes the structure and function of blood. Try to include the following terms in your concept map: vessels, plasma, cell platelets, white blood cells, red blood cells, hemoglobin, blood clotting, defense, oxygen, vessels, carbon dioxide.

4. **Identifying Functions** How do bacteria, single-celled protists, and simple multicellular animals transport materials from the environment throughout their bodies?

5. **Summarizing Information** The circulatory system transports oxygen, carbon dioxide, and hormones. What else does it do?

6. **Summarizing Information** Identify the main components of blood, and describe the function of each.

7. **Comparing Functions and Structures** How do red blood cells and white blood cells differ in terms of function, size, and number?

8. **Comparing Functions** What are the three main types of blood vessels and their functions? What characteristics of blood vessels allow them to adjust to different volumes of blood flow?

---

9. **Reading Graphs** Using the graph below, describe the relationship between the amount of table salt consumed daily and systolic blood pressure.

Daily Salt Intake's Effect on Blood Pressure

Systolic pressure (mm Hg): 170, 160, 150, 140, 130, 120, 110, 0

Daily salt intake (g): 0, 10, 20, 30

10. **Recognizing Patterns** Trace the path of blood during pulmonary circulation. Begin with oxygen-poor blood entering the heart.

11. **Comparing Functions** How does the lymphatic system assist the circulatory system? How do the operations of these two systems differ?

12. **Inferring Relationships** What kinds of information can be gained by measuring blood pressure? How can you help reduce high blood pressure?

13. **Inferring Relationships** Explain how an analysis of blood lipids can be used to indicate the risk of cardiovascular disease.

14. **Recognizing Relationships** Describe the factors that contribute to cardiovascular diseases.

15. **Summarizing Information** Describe the pathway of air as it travels through the respiratory system to a cell in the body.

16. **Analyzing Information** Describe the three ways that carbon dioxide is transported in the blood.

17. **Recognizing Relationships** Explain how your body regulates your breathing rate.

18. **Summarizing Information** Describe three diseases of the respiratory system.

19. **BUILDING ON WHAT YOU HAVE LEARNED** In Chapter 4 you learned about organ transplants. What role does blood type play in receiving organ transplants?

676

---

12. Measuring a person's blood pressure provides information about the condition of the arteries and is useful in diagnosing high blood pressure and hardening of the arteries. Regular aerobic activity that strengthens the heart and blood vessels helps arteries stay elastic and can minimize the effects of high blood pressure.

13. Refer to the information that accompanies Table 32-2 on page 668 and the captions that accompany Figure 32-13 on page 669.

14. Overweight, lack of exercise, genetic predisposition, improper diet, etc.

15. Refer to the captions that accompany Figure 32-15 on page 671.

16. Refer to the captions that accompany Figure 32-17 on page 673.

17. Receptors in the brain and circulatory system continuously monitor the levels of oxygen and carbon dioxide in the blood, enabling the body to regulate the breathing rate.

18. See page 674.

Interpreting Graphics

20. Look at the cross sections of the two coronary arteries below and answer the questions that follow.

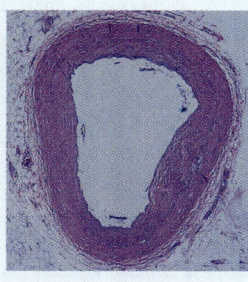

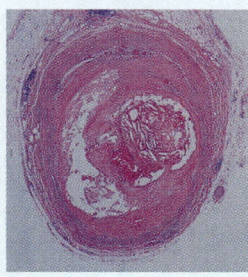

a. How are the two arteries different?
b. How can you explain the differences observed? What are the effects of the observed differences?

Reviewing Themes

21. *Cell Structure and Function*
Why can the four-chambered heart of mammals be thought of as two hearts in one?

22. *Homeostasis*
How can a blood analysis determine if the body is maintaining homeostasis?

23. *Evolution*
Explain why the vertebrate lung is considered an adaptation to terrestrial life.

Thinking Critically

24. **Recognizing Verifiable Conclusions** Endurance athletes, such as long-distance runners, often have larger hearts that can pump a greater volume of blood with each heart beat. How would these modifications help the heart respond to the demands placed on it by endurance activities?

Life/Work Skills

25. **Working Cooperatively** Work with a partner. Contact the local chapter of the American Lung Association to find out if certain diseases are more common in your area than in other parts of the country. Also contact the local chapter of the American Heart Association. Find out the warning signs of a heart attack and how to care for a heart attack victim until help arrives. Share your findings with your class.

26. **Using Technology** An electrocardiogram is a measurement and recording of the electrical activity of the heart. Contact a cardiac rehabilitation center or a cardiologist to find out about electrocardiograms. What kinds of information can be learned from this type of measurement? How are electrocardiograms taken?

Activities and Projects

27. **Mathematics Connection** Assume that the average heart beats 70 times per minute. How many times does the heart beat in a person who lives 75 years? Assume that the heart of an overweight person beats 10 additional times each minute. Explain why being overweight can strain the heart.

28. **Career Connection: Respiratory Therapist** A respiratory therapist, sometimes called an inhalation therapist, assists people with breathing problems by giving them respiratory treatment and life support. These patients might be suffering from asthma, bronchitis, emphysema, pneumonia, or other disease. Use library references or search an on-line database to find out about becoming a respiratory therapist. What are the educational and training requirements? For additional information, write to the American Association for Respiratory Therapy, 1720 Regal Row, Dallas, TX 75235.

Discovering Through Reading

29. Read the article "A Town With a Golden Gene" by Patricia Long in *Health*, January/February 1994, pages 60–66. What is unique about the people in Limone, Italy, who are called *portatori*? What are the benefits of high levels of HDL? Identify three things you can do to improve your various cholesterol levels.

respiratory membrane moist by being located inside the body, where the membrane is sheltered from the drying air.

Thinking Critically

24. The larger heart means stronger contractions and thus greater blood flow. The slower resting rate indicates greater efficiency. The increased circulation to the heart means more blood—thus more endurance—for the heart.

Life/Work Skills

25. Results will vary.
26. Answers will vary with the resources available.

Activities and Projects

27. In a person who lives 75 years, the heart beats 1,905,120,000 times. Beating just 10 more times an hour increases the number of beats per year by more than 15,000.
28. Answers will vary with the resources available.

Discovering Through Reading

29. *Portatori,* meaning "the carriers," carry a gene that alters a protein on the surface of HDL. Individuals who have this gene have extremely high levels of LDL and triglycerides and low levels of HDL in their blood, yet they remain very healthy and free of any kind of cardiovascular disease. These individuals also live to old age. HDL carries LDL (bad cholesterol) to the liver for disposal and causes platelets to be less sticky and therefore less likely to form clots in narrowed arteries. LDL levels can be lowered by eating a diet low in saturated fats; HDL levels can be raised by losing weight, not smoking, and drinking alcohol in moderation.

---

19. The plasma membranes of red blood cells are much like the plasma membranes of other body cells in that there are specific marker proteins on the surface of the membranes. Marker proteins must be closely matched (similar) from organ donor to organ recipient so that the recipient's immune system does not attack the donated organ.

Interpreting Graphics

20. a. Artery **(a)** is a normal artery. The other artery **(b)** is partially blocked.

b. In one artery **(a)**, the passage is clear and blood can flow. In the other artery **(b),** deposits decrease the amount of blood flow through the arteries.

Reviewing Themes

21. Refer to the captions that accompany Figure 32-7 on page 659.
22. Refer to the captions that accompany Figure 32-11 on page 667.
23. The lungs solve the problem of keeping the

Circulation and Respiration   677

33 | The Immune System

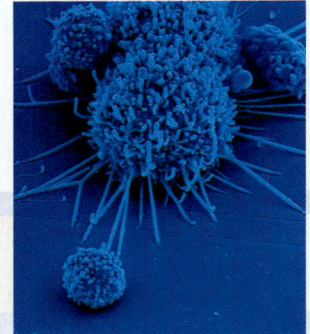

Lesson Planning Guide With Options for Block Scheduling

Lecture Concepts	Lesson Resources

33-1 The First Line of Defense

BLOCK ❶ (45 minutes)

1. The skin, tears, saliva, and mucous membranes act as physical and chemical barriers to pathogens.

2. An inflammatory response involves events designed to fight infection.

❶ Lecture Resources
- ■ Determining Prior Knowledge
- ■ The Inflammatory Response
- ■ Active Reading: Reading Organizer
- ■ Visual Strategy: Figures 33-1, 33-2
- 🔖 Teaching Transparencies: 235
- 💿 Holt Biology Videodiscs Lesson 33-1

Classwork Options
- 🧪 Laboratory Techniques and Experimental Design: Lab C43

Assignment Options
- ⊙ Teaching Resources CD-ROM: Occupational Applications Worksheets 10

BLOCK ❷ (45 minutes)

3. Macrophages play a crucial role in destroying pathogens and dead cells.

4. Marker proteins allow macrophages to recognize pathogens and other foreign substances.

5. Protein antigens on the membranes of red blood cells account for the various blood types.

❷ Lecture Resources
- ■ Active Reading: Summarizing
- ■ Visual Strategy: Figure 33-4
- ■ Visual Strategy: Videodisc
- 🔖 Teaching Transparencies: 189A
- 💿 Holt Biology Videodiscs Lesson 33-1

Classwork Options
- ■ Closure: Inferring Relationships

Assignment Options
- ■ *Small Group* Reteaching
- ■ Section Review
- ■ Chapter Review, questions 1a, 2a, 4, 5, 6, 8
- ■ Directed Reading Worksheet

33-2 The Immune Response

BLOCK ❸ (45 minutes)

1. Macrophages engulf invading pathogens that are recognized as being foreign.

2. Helper T cells release proteins that promote the division of killer T cells, and killer T cells destroy the pathogen. Suppressor T cells quell the immune response once the pathogen has been defeated.

❸ Lecture Resources
- ■ Active Reading: Paired Reading
- ■ Visual Strategy: Figures 33-7, 33-8
- ■ Visual Strategy: Videodisc
- ■ Demonstration: Summarizing Information
- 🔖 Teaching Transparencies: 236, 237
- 💿 Holt Biology Videodiscs Lesson 33-2

Classwork Options
- 🧪 Inquiry Skills Development: Lab B33

BLOCK ❹ (45 minutes)

3. B cells produce antibodies that bind pathogens to be destroyed by macrophages.

4. Memory B cells remain after the pathogen has been destroyed in case the same pathogen invades the body again.

5. Vaccines help develop memory B cells, thus arming the body against invasion by the pathogen.

❹ Lecture Resources
- ■ Visual Strategy: Figure 33-9, Table 33-2
- 🔖 Teaching Transparencies: 202A
- 💿 Holt Biology Videodiscs Lesson 33-2

Classwork Options
- ■ Closure: Forming a Hypothesis

Assignment Options
- ■ *Small Group* Reteaching
- ■ Section Review
- ■ Chapter Review, questions 1b, 1c, 2b, 2c, 7, 9, 10, 11, 12, 28
- ■ Directed Reading Worksheet

33-3 Immune System Failure

BLOCK ❺ (45 minutes)

1. An allergy involves the response by the immune system to a harmless antigen.

2. In an allergic reaction, mast cells release histamine, which causes capillaries to swell.

❺ Lecture Resources
- ■ Visual Strategy: Figures 33-13, 33-14, Table 33-3
- ■ Demonstration: Relating Structure to Function
- 💿 Holt Biology Videodiscs Lesson 33-3

Classwork Options
- ⊙ Teaching Resources CD-ROM: Basic Skills Worksheets 6

Lecture Concepts

Lesson Resources

33-3 Immune System Failure, *continued*

BLOCK ❻ (45 minutes)

3. In autoimmune disease, the immune system destroys its own body cells.

4. The immune system may fail to destroy cancer cells that arise from mutations or carcinogens.

5. The human immunodeficiency virus (HIV) destroys T cells, which results in autoimmune deficiency syndrome (AIDS).

❻ Lecture Resources
- ■ Active Reading: Reader Response Logs
- ■ Visual Strategy: Figures 33-15, 33-18, Table 33-4
- ■ Demonstration: Recognizing Relationships
- ■ Demonstration: Observing Relationships
- ⊙ Holt Biology Videodiscs Lesson 33-3

Classwork Options
- ■ Reteaching
- ■ Closure: Relating Concepts

Assignment Options
- ■ Section Review
- ■ Chapter Review, questions 3, 13, 14, 15, 16, 17, 18, 19, 20, 21, 22, 23, 24, 25, 26, 27, 29, 30
- ■ Directed Reading Worksheet

Chapter Review and Assessment

BLOCK ❼ (45 minutes)
Review
- ■ Reteaching Worksheet
- ■ Thinking Skills Worksheet
- ■ Vocabulary Development Worksheet
- ⊙ Language Development and Reading Comprehension Audio CD Program: Chapter 33

BLOCK ❽ (45 minutes)
Assessment
- ■ Alternative Assessment, p. 695
- ■ Portfolio Assessment, p. T39

Chapter Test
- ■ Chapter 33 Test

Test Generator
- ⊙ Item bank for customizing Chapter Tests

Teaching Resources CD-ROM
- ⊙ Scoring Rubrics and Classroom Management Checklist

The Portfolio icon denotes items throughout the Teacher's Edition lesson wrap that may be selected for inclusion in student portfolios.

Holt Biology Videodiscs and *Concepts of Biology*

Holt Biology Videodiscs gives you a powerful tool for teaching, review, and assessment. For further information regarding the media on the videodiscs, see ***Holt Biology Videodiscs Teacher's Correlation Guide to Holt Biology: Visualizing Life.***

Concepts of Biology adds interactive lesson plans and extensive tools for customization using CD-ROM technology.

Use the following topic from ***Concepts of Biology*** to help you teach this chapter:
Topic 22: Circulation and Respiration

Laboratory Planning

Holt BioSources Laboratory Program

Block 1: Laboratory Techniques and Experimental Design Lab C43: Blood Typing—Whodunit?

Block 3: Inquiry Skills Development Lab B33: Transmission of a Communicable Disease

Determining Prior Knowledge

- Have students use a magnifying glass or stereomicroscope to examine the skin on their hands. Refer them to Chapter 29. Have them explain how the skin functions to prevent pathogens from entering the body.
- Have students who have had chickenpox raise their hands. Have them keep their hands raised if they have had it more than once. Ask them to explain why most, if not all, hands went down in response to the second question.
- Have students review the concept of marker proteins on the surface of red blood cells. These proteins are responsible for the four major blood types—A, B, AB, and O—as well as the Rh factor. Ask how marker proteins might function in the immune response.

Active READING

Technique: Discussion

Most students will have heard or read about AIDS. Remind students that AIDS (Acquired Immune Deficiency Syndrome) is a syndrome in which the immune system, normally the body's defense against invading pathogens, cannot respond. When this defense system fails, the body is overwhelmed by invaders. Tell students that in this chapter they will learn about the body's powerful defense system and the effects of immune system failure.

CD-ROM Resources

Concepts of Biology
Topic 22: Circulation and Respiration

CHAPTER **33**

REVIEW
- **membrane marker protein** (Section 3-2)
- **viral reproduction** (Section 18-3)
- the term *pathogen* (Glossary)

The Immune System

33-1   First Line of Defense

33-2   The Immune Response

33-3   Immune System Failure

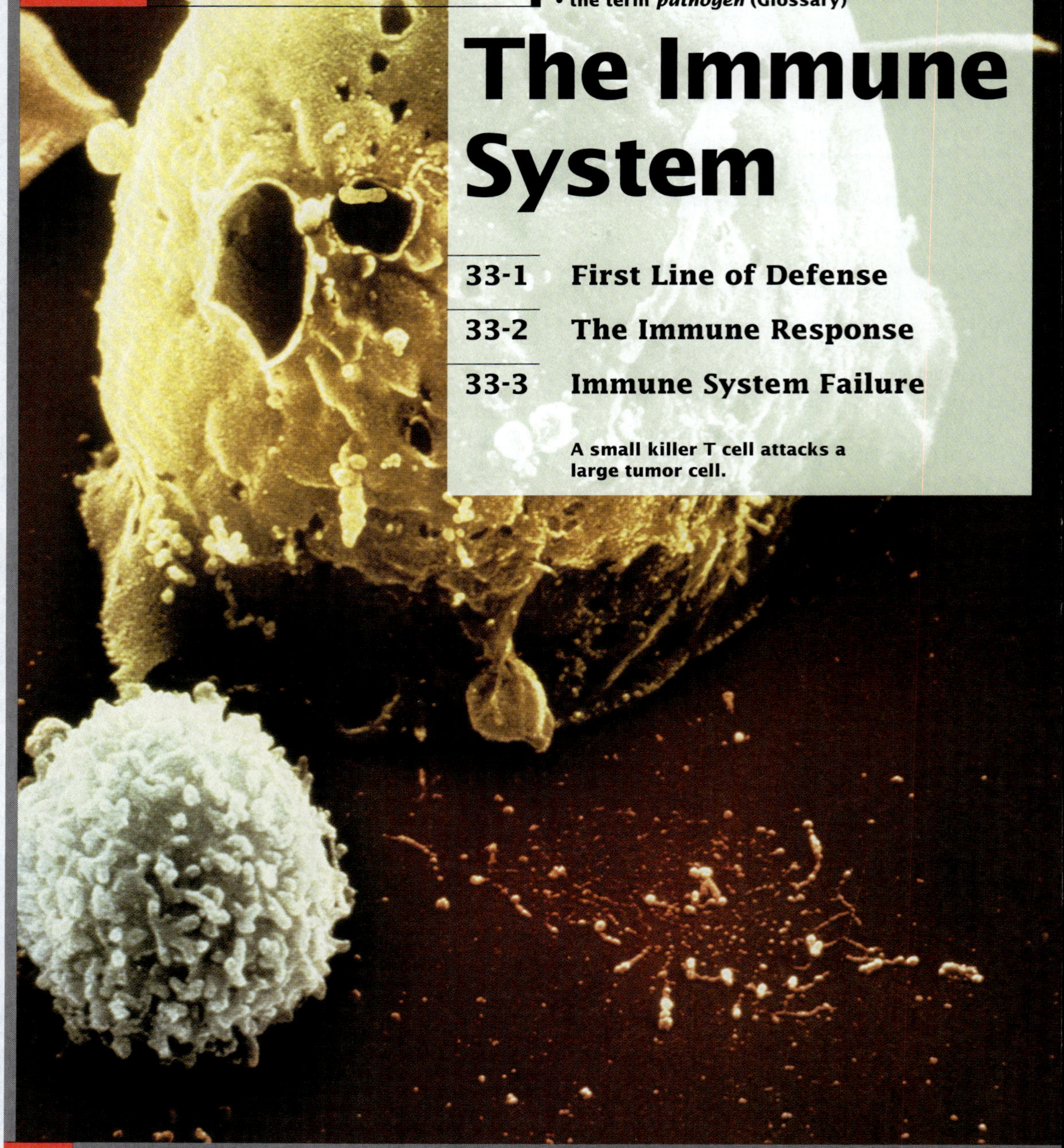

A small killer T cell attacks a large tumor cell.

Author's Rationale   The immune system is one of the most active areas of biological research. It is central to the fight against AIDS and many other diseases. While the immune system is complex, its workings can be explained in general terms to give students a basic understanding. Students are fascinated by the lengths to which the body goes to defend itself.

Your body is routinely surrounded by legions of would-be invaders: bacteria, viruses, protists, parasitic animals, and parasitic fungi. Yet you are usually well, because your body mobilizes cells like the yellow one at left to repel these pathogens. It defeats the few pathogens that manage to enter your body, using a powerful defense called the immune system.

33-1 First Line of Defense

Phase One
Preparation

Scheduling
See the **Lesson Planning Guide** on pages 677A and 677B for lecture, classwork, and assignment options for Section 33-1.

OBJECTIVES

1 Identify two types of defensive epithelial tissue, and describe how each works.

2 Summarize the reactions that make up the inflammatory response.

3 Describe how your body distinguishes its own cells from invading pathogens.

Keeping Pathogens Out

Most pathogens must enter the body to cause disease. Your skin functions as a wall to keep out foreign organisms, including viruses. As you learned in Chapter 29, skin is the body's dry, flexible covering. Cells of the outer layers of epidermis are continually being worn away and replaced by cells moving up from the lower layers of epidermis. In only 40 minutes, your body loses and replaces approximately 1 million skin cells. Such rapid replacement of body cells enables punctures or cuts to be sealed very quickly.

Skin not only acts as a barrier to pathogens but also engages in chemical warfare against them. Oils and sweat secreted by glands in the skin acidify its surface, creating an unfavorable environment for bacterial growth. In addition, sweat contains enzymes that digest the cell walls of certain bacteria.

Your body uses a different series of nonspecific defenses to guard the natural openings in your skin, such as the mouth, nostrils, eyes, vagina, urethra, and anus. These internal body surfaces that come into contact with the environment are covered with **mucous membranes**.

A mucous membrane is a moist epithelial layer that is impermeable to most pathogens. Mucous membranes line the nasal passages, mouth, lungs, digestive tract, urethra, and vagina. Mucous membranes contain glands that secrete mucus, a sticky fluid that traps pathogens. Pathogens inhaled into the respiratory tract become lodged in mucus and are swept up to the pharynx by cilia. They are then swallowed and pass into the stomach. Digestive enzymes and strong acids in the stomach destroy most pathogens that are swallowed.

Similar antibacterial enzymes are found in saliva and tears. **Figure 33-1** illustrates several nonspecific natural defenses used by the body to protect against invasion by disease-causing agents.

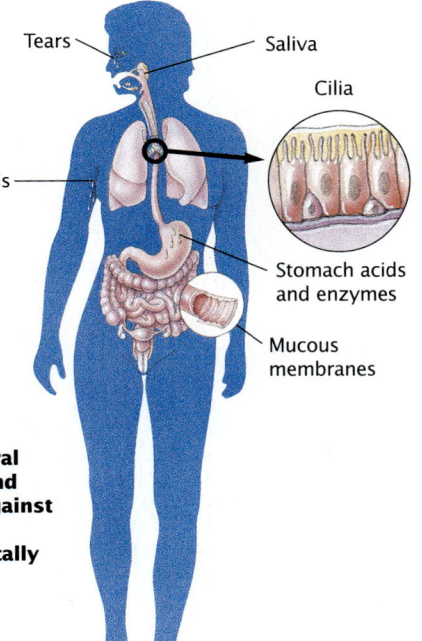

Tears — Saliva
Cilia
Sweat and oils
Stomach acids and enzymes
Mucous membranes

Figure 33-1
The body has a natural system of barriers and chemical defenses against invading agents. It responds nonspecifically to *any* microbe.

Phase Two
Teaching Strategies

Active READING

Technique: Reading Organizer
Most students will benefit from reading with an organizational structure in mind. Tell students that in this chapter they will read about the outer defenses of the body, about the inflammatory response used as a defense against small-scale infections, and, finally, about the body's immune response to large-scale infection.

Visual Strategy | Figure 33-1

● **Identifying Structures**
Have students create a table of the first lines of nonspecific defense as illustrated in Figure 33-1. Have students explain how each of these defenses traps or obstructs foreign invaders. *(The table should include the nonspecific barrier defenses: the physical barriers of skin and mucous membranes and the chemical barriers of skin oils and sweat that acidify the skin's surface, the stomach's digestive enzymes and strong acid that destroy most pathogens that are swallowed, and antibacterial enzymes in tears and saliva.)*

Key to Strategies
Teaching Strategies are keyed to three tiers of learning.

● **Understanding Concepts (Tier I)**
Content mastery and comprehension

■ **Applying Information (Tier II)**
Applying and analyzing content

▲ **Critical Thinking (Tier III)**
Practicing evaluative thinking

679

Videodisc Resources

Holt Biology Videodiscs
Lesson 33-1: First Line of Defense

Organizing the Defense

The outer defenses of the body may not always be successful in preventing pathogens or other foreign agents from entering. When the body's defensive barriers are broken, the body uses a variety of specialized white blood cells as defenders. White blood cells (**leukocytes**) are the "soldiers" of the immune system. Some white blood cells are best suited for short, minor invasions. These cells are known as **phagocytes**. Other white blood cells, known as **lymphocytes**, are specialized for longer, more serious invasions.

Phagocytes handle small-scale infections

A splinter in your fingertip is only a minor injury, even though pathogens can enter the puncture in your skin. Your body quickly activates a set of chemical and cellular defenses to destroy any invaders. Your finger gets red, swells, hurts, and feels hot. These are signs that your body is attacking

pathogens. Together these signs make up the **inflammatory response** to infection or injury, as shown in **Figure 33-2**. The inflammatory response is sufficiently powerful to repel most small-scale infections.

Phagocytes are crucial to the inflammatory response because they rapidly trap, consume, and completely destroy foreign material by phagocytosis. Some white blood cells, called natural killer cells, destroy your own infected cells. Phagocytes, dead cells, and pathogens are the components of pus. The presence of pus indicates that phagocytes are combating pathogens.

Several kinds of white blood cells use phagocytosis, but they continue to act repeatedly. This line of defense peaks within a day or two of the infection. If homeostasis is not restored, the body activates its main line of defense, a more powerful and specific response called the immune response.

Figure 33-2
When a splinter enters your finger, bacteria and viruses can gain access to your body. Your body initiates the inflammatory response to combat these pathogens.

a The inflammatory response is triggered when damaged or infected cells release chemical alarm signals.

b These signals cause more fluid than normal to leak out of capillaries near the injury; swelling results.

c Attracted by chemical alarm signals, white blood cells move from the blood into the injured area through the walls of swollen, leaky capillaries. White blood cells attack invading pathogens and consume dead and infected cells.

d Some cells responding to signals dilate blood vessels, causing more blood to flow in. The area reddens.

e The temperature of the area around the injury increases. Heat suppresses bacterial growth.

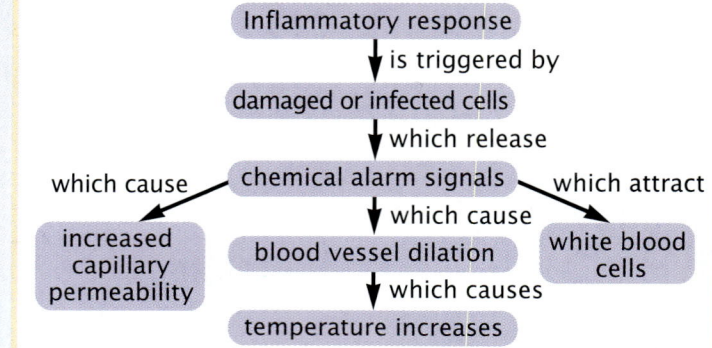

Figure 33-3

a The brief inflammatory response buys time so that the main line of defense can be recruited.

b The main immune response provides both short- and long-term defenses.

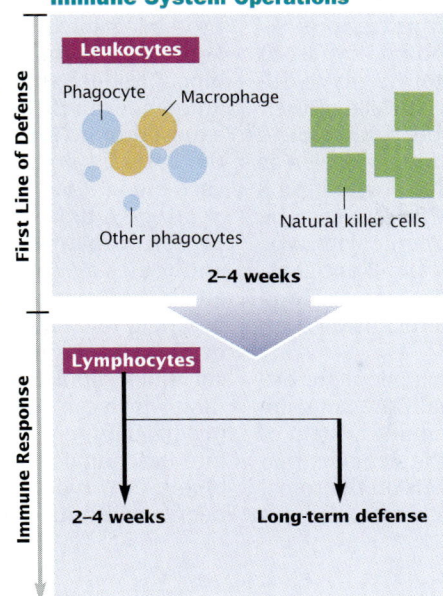

Immune System Operations

Leukocytes

Phagocyte   Macrophage

Other phagocytes

Natural killer cells

First Line of Defense

2–4 weeks

Immune Response

Lymphocytes

2–4 weeks   Long-term defense

A variety of other white blood cells help to defend the body

Phagocytes do well in short-term skirmishes like the splinter incident. But phagocytes alone cannot wage a long-term defense against specific agents that cause disease. For specific protection, the body uses a main line of defense, called the immune response, that involves recognition and then destruction. White blood cells called **macrophages** (*MAHK roh fayj ehz*) are used in this defense because they live longer than other leukocytes and can repeat their destructive actions many times. Macrophages and other phagocytes are joined in this longer battle by two other kinds of white blood cells called lymphocytes. Each of these white blood cells is a specialist in a particular field of defense. **Figure 33-3** shows the general classes of white blood cells involved in defending the body.

Antigen Recognition

Your white blood cells need to distinguish your body's cells from those of the enemy in order to defend your body successfully. Recall from Chapter 3 that there are marker proteins and receptor proteins in the cell membrane. Your marker proteins have a unique shape, which makes them different from marker proteins on cells of other humans and from marker proteins on the surface of disease-causing agents. Thus, marker proteins serve as identification tags. **Figure 33-4** illustrates marker proteins.

Marker proteins that differ from your own are identified as "non-self" by your white blood cells. Once they identify "non-self" cells, macrophages sound an alarm. How do they do that? When a macrophage battles an enemy, it uses phagocytosis, as other leukocytes do. But instead of destroying the enemy completely, the macrophage saves some of the invader's marker protein and moves it to its own surface as a "marker alert" for other white blood cells. Once alerted, receptor proteins of other white cells also recognize the material as "non-self."

The display and recognition of foreign marker proteins trigger the immune response. Marker proteins that trigger the immune response are called **antigens** (*AN tuh juhns*). Once antigens are displayed by macrophages and are identified as the enemy, the cells in your body bearing that antigen are marked as targets for elimination.

Figure 33-4

Because no two organisms have the same marker proteins, cells of the immune system are able to identify and destroy invading pathogens.

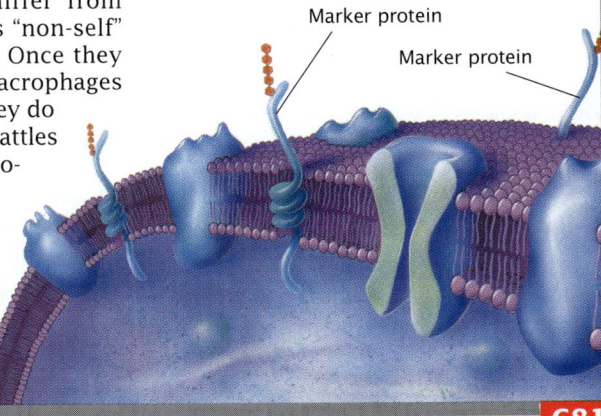

Marker protein

Marker protein

681

Visual Strategy   Figure 33-4

● **Identifying Structures**
Have students locate the marker proteins on this cell membrane. Point out that these proteins are known as antigens, which bring about a response by the host's phagocytes. Carbohydrates and nucleic acids can also function as antigens, but they generally do not bring about the same response as "foreign" proteins.

Visual Strategy   Videodisc

■ **Recognizing Relationships**
Use the *Illustration—Blood Cell Agglutination* shown in Chapter 33 Section 33-1 of *Holt Biology Videodiscs Teacher's Correlation Guide to Holt Biology: Visualizing Life.* Begin by having students compare the type O and type B blood samples shown at the top of the illustration. *(Type O has both anti-B and anti-A antibodies, but no A or B antigens. Type B has no antibodies, but has B antigens.)* Tell students that the illustration in the middle shows the results when both types of blood are mixed. Have students describe the results. *(The anti-B antibodies cause the type B blood cells to clump.)* Ask what effect giving the wrong type of blood during a transfusion might have on an individual. *(Blood could clump, causing blocked capillaries, organ damage, or death.)*

Historical Perspective: Sir Frank Macfarlane Burnet

Sir Frank Macfarlane Burnet was an Australian who advocated the clonal selection theory of immunology, the idea of *self* and *nonself*. Sir Macfarlane Burnet was elected to the Royal Society in 1942, received the Order of Merit in 1958, and was awarded the Nobel Prize for medicine in 1960. His book, *Natural History of Infectious Disease,* which is coauthored with David O. White, was published by Cambridge University Press in 1972.

Key to Strategies
● Understanding Concepts (Tier I)
■ Applying Information (Tier II)
▲ Critical Thinking (Tier III)

Phase Three

Phase Three
Assessment Options

Closure

■ Inferring Relationships

Drugs must be given to recipients of organ transplants to suppress their immune response. Have students explain why this is necessary and what precautions must be taken by transplant recipients. *(The drugs used in immunosuppressive therapy include cyclosporine, which is an immunosuppressant, and corticosteroids, which reduce inflammation. Precautions are necessary because the patient's immune-system activity will be lowered and will not be able to protect the patient from most infections.)*

SECTION REVIEW

Assign the *Section Review.*

Reteaching

Assign students to cooperative groups of three. Have each group write a comic sketch or draw cartoons to show how the first line of defense operates in protecting the body against pathogens. *(Sketches and drawings may depict the skin keeping out invaders, germs sticking to mucous membranes, phagocytes engulfing bacteria, and aspects of the inflammation response.)*

Antigen recognition is part of successful blood transfusions

People with different blood types, as you learned in Chapter 32, have different antigens on the surface of their red blood cells. People with type A blood have a marker protein known as the A antigen. Individuals with type B blood have a different marker protein, called the B antigen. People with type AB blood have both A and B antigens, while individuals with type O blood have neither A nor B antigens on their red blood cells.

Transfusions between people of different blood types usually are not compatible because the immune system of the recipient attacks the antigens that it recognizes as "non-self" in the transfused blood. The attack is carried out by antibodies. Antibodies are defensive proteins made by the immune system. For instance, individuals with type A blood produce antibodies against the B antigen, even if they have never been exposed to it. **Table 33-1** summarizes the antigens and antibodies found in each blood type.

If type A blood is transfused into a person with type B or type O blood, antibodies against the A antigen will attack the foreign red blood cells, causing them to clump together, as shown in **Figure 33-5**. Clumps of just 2–3 cells can block capillaries and cut off blood flow, which can be fatal. Clumping also occurs if type B blood is transfused into individuals with type A or type O blood, or if type AB blood is given to people with type O blood.

Figure 33-5
Some blood types are not compatible. When incompatible blood types are mixed, they form clumps (shown below) that prevent blood from circulating properly.

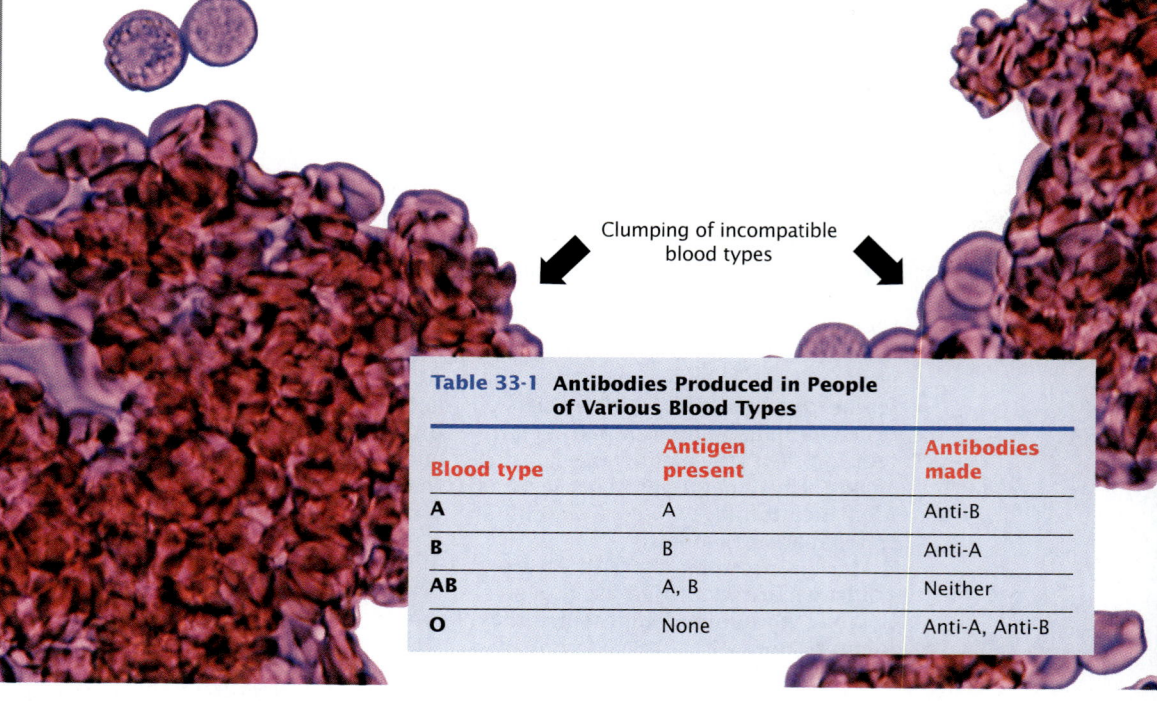

Clumping of incompatible blood types

Table 33-1 Antibodies Produced in People of Various Blood Types

Blood type	Antigen present	Antibodies made
A	A	Anti-B
B	B	Anti-A
AB	A, B	Neither
O	None	Anti-A, Anti-B

SECTION REVIEW

1 Describe the chemical and mechanical defenses of skin and mucous membranes.

2 Describe the defensive events that occur after a splinter enters your finger.

3 Contrast the first line of defense with the main line of defense.

4 Explain how white blood cells can distinguish your cells from those of invading pathogens or of incompatible blood.

682

ANSWERS TO SECTION REVIEW

1 Students should indicate that oil and sweat acidify the skin's surface, creating an unfavorable environment for some bacteria. In addition, sweat contains enzymes that digest the cell walls of certain bacteria. Mucous membranes are impermeable to most bacteria: Some contain antibacterial enzymes; others trap pathogens and transport them to areas for destruction.

2 Refer to the captions that accompany Figure 33-2 on page 680.

3 Refer to Figures 33-2 on page 680 and 33-3 on page 681.

4 Students should note that body cells carry certain marker proteins that enable the body to distinguish its own cells from invading pathogens.

The pain of a splinter does not compare to the suffering you endure when you have the flu. The symptoms of flu are more severe because influenza viruses break through your first line of defense. As you will see in this section, your body activates the main line of defense, called the immune response, that combats and defeats specific pathogens, including viruses.

Phase One
Preparation

Scheduling
See the **Lesson Planning Guide** on pages 677A and 677B for lecture, classwork, and assignment options for Section 33-2.

33-2 The Immune Response

OBJECTIVES

1 Identify the functions of helper T cells, killer T cells, and B cells.

2 Explain how fever helps to defeat pathogens.

3 Describe how the immune system protects against a pathogen's second attack.

4 Relate vaccines to the functioning of the immune system.

Main Line of Defense

The immune system consists of the defenses that your body uses to attack pathogens or other foreign agents that get past your first line of defense. For example, consider what happens when you get the flu. Influenza viruses are transmitted in small water droplets that are expelled when an infected person sneezes or coughs. If you inhale some of these droplets, influenza viruses can enter cells of the mucous membrane lining your respiratory tract. As you recall from Chapter 18, viruses seize control of their host cells and transform them into virus-producing factories. Influenza viruses take over and infect mucous-membrane cells. You feel sick because infected cells lining your respiratory tract are being destroyed by your own natural killer cells.

At this point during a case of flu, the viruses have the upper hand, but your body's defenses are beginning to fight back. As mentioned earlier, macrophages can engulf and consume the viruses. Macrophages then break down the viruses' surface proteins, capture fragments of the viral antigens, and display the antigens on their cell surface. This display serves as a victory banner, but, more important, it acts as an alert to other white blood cells, and it stimulates the immune system to carry out a full-blown immune response. The **immune response** is the immune system's main attack on a *specific* pathogen. Bacteria like the *E. coli* shown in **Figure 33-6** and other specific pathogens are also attacked by macrophages.

Figure 33-6
Macrophages attack foreign pathogens, such as viruses or the *E. coli* bacteria shown here. This macrophage's pseudopod is reaching out to retrieve the enemy for destruction.

Macrophage

Bacteria

Pseudopod of macrophage

Phase Two
Teaching Strategies

Demonstration

● **Summarizing Information**
Use a microprojector to show the class an amoeba. Have students compare the amoeba with the macrophage illustrated in Figure 33-6. Point out that a macrophage uses amoeboid movements to surround foreign cells and viruses. While some macrophages circulate, others remain stationary (for instance, in the spleen, liver, lungs, and lymph nodes), simply engulfing anything suspicious that passes by.

683

Videodisc Resources

Holt Biology Videodiscs
Lesson 33-2: The Immune Response

● **Comparing Structures**

Use this figure to explain the difference between helper T cells and killer T cells. The receptor sites on the killer T cells shown in Figures 33-7a and 33-7b are so specific that killer T cells can recognize the difference between healthy and diseased body cells. Emphasize that special proteins are produced once a helper T cell's receptors have combined with antigens presented by a macrophage. These proteins stimulate the division of killer T cells. Have students locate these killer T cells in Figure 33-7d.

Active READING

Technique: Paired Reading

Less proficient readers may benefit from the paired reading strategy as they study the actions of T cells and B cells. Pair each student with a partner. Have each student read pages 683–685 silently. As students read, have them place a check mark on a sticky note next to passages they understand and a question mark on a sticky note next to passages they find confusing or have questions about. After students finish reading, ask one student in each pair to summarize what he or she understood, referring to the text when needed. The second student should add anything omitted. The second student should then continue the discussion by pointing out the passages that he or she did not understand. The first reader should help the second with ideas that were unclear and then discuss passages that he or she did not understand. Both readers should then work together to come to an understanding of the passages they did not understand. Have them create a list of questions to pose to the class about ideas or passages that are still unclear after their discussion.

T Cells: Command and Attack

Figure 33-7
The immune response is activated when a macrophage that has consumed a pathogen, such as an influenza virus, comes into contact with a helper T cell and presents the captured antigens.

When a macrophage parades its victory banner of captured antigens, it sends an alarm to the immune system. This alarm activates **T-cell lymphocytes**. Some, called helper T cells, circulate in your blood and lymph. Helper T cells control the immune response and direct two kinds of lymphocytes at the same time—killer T cells and suppressor T cells. Suppressor T cells regulate the immune response, and some can even change into killer cells, which are the main "soldiers" of the immune response army.

Killer T cells carry specifically shaped receptor proteins on their cell membrane. These enable each killer T cell to recognize and bind to one specific antigen. Your body can respond to millions of different antigens because it manufactures millions of different types of T cells, each type bearing uniquely shaped proteins. When you have the flu, T cells that match the antigens of the influenza viruses in your body will be "called up" to fight.

Killer T cells destroy only infected cells. **Figure 33-7** describes the role of helper T cells and suppressor T cells.

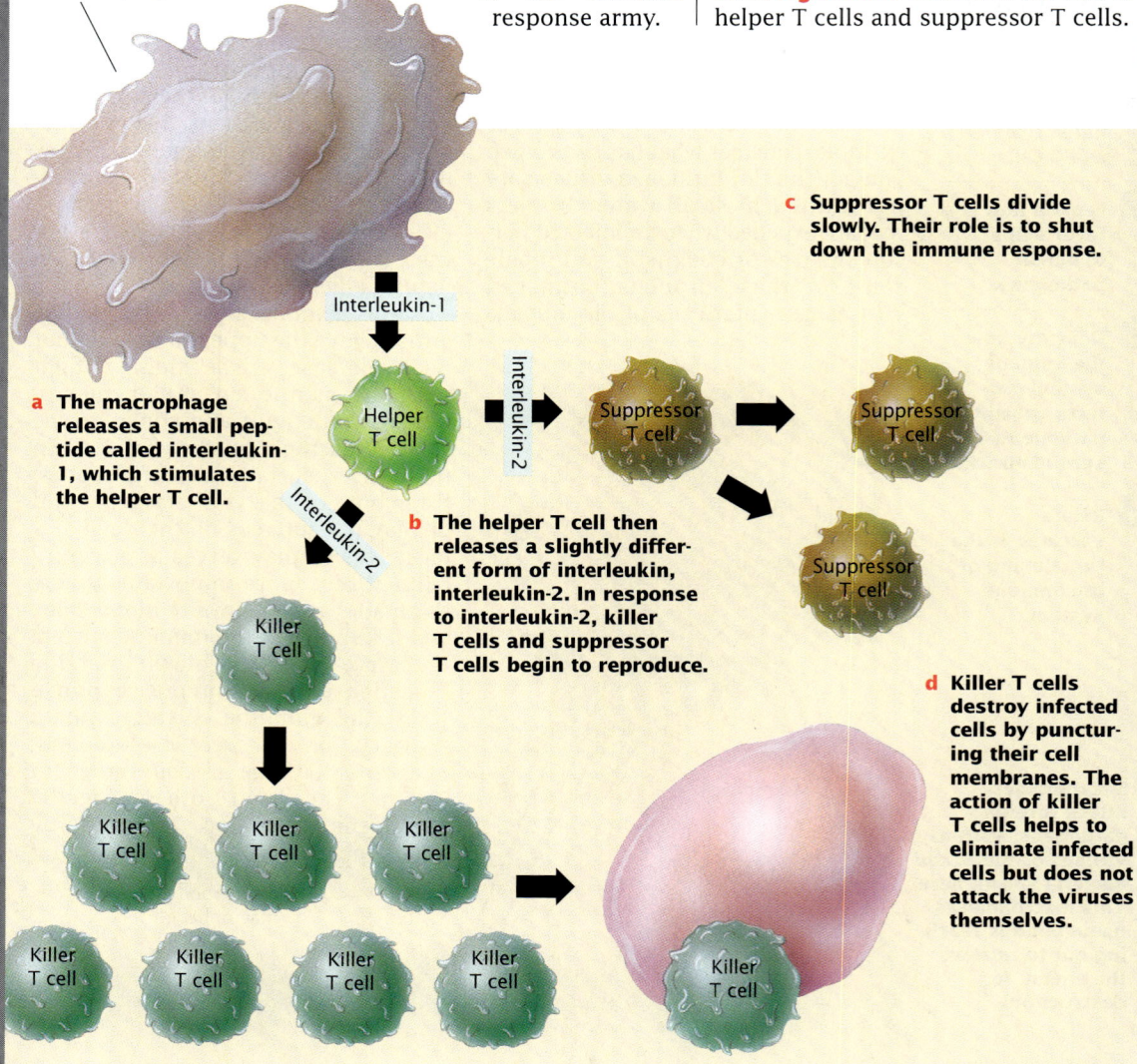

Macrophage

Interleukin-1

a The macrophage releases a small peptide called interleukin-1, which stimulates the helper T cell.

Helper T cell

Interleukin-2

Interleukin-2

b The helper T cell then releases a slightly different form of interleukin, interleukin-2. In response to interleukin-2, killer T cells and suppressor T cells begin to reproduce.

Suppressor T cell

Suppressor T cell

Suppressor T cell

c Suppressor T cells divide slowly. Their role is to shut down the immune response.

Killer T cell

Killer T cell   Killer T cell   Killer T cell

Killer T cell   Killer T cell   Killer T cell   Killer T cell

Killer T cell

d Killer T cells destroy infected cells by puncturing their cell membranes. The action of killer T cells helps to eliminate infected cells but does not attack the viruses themselves.

684

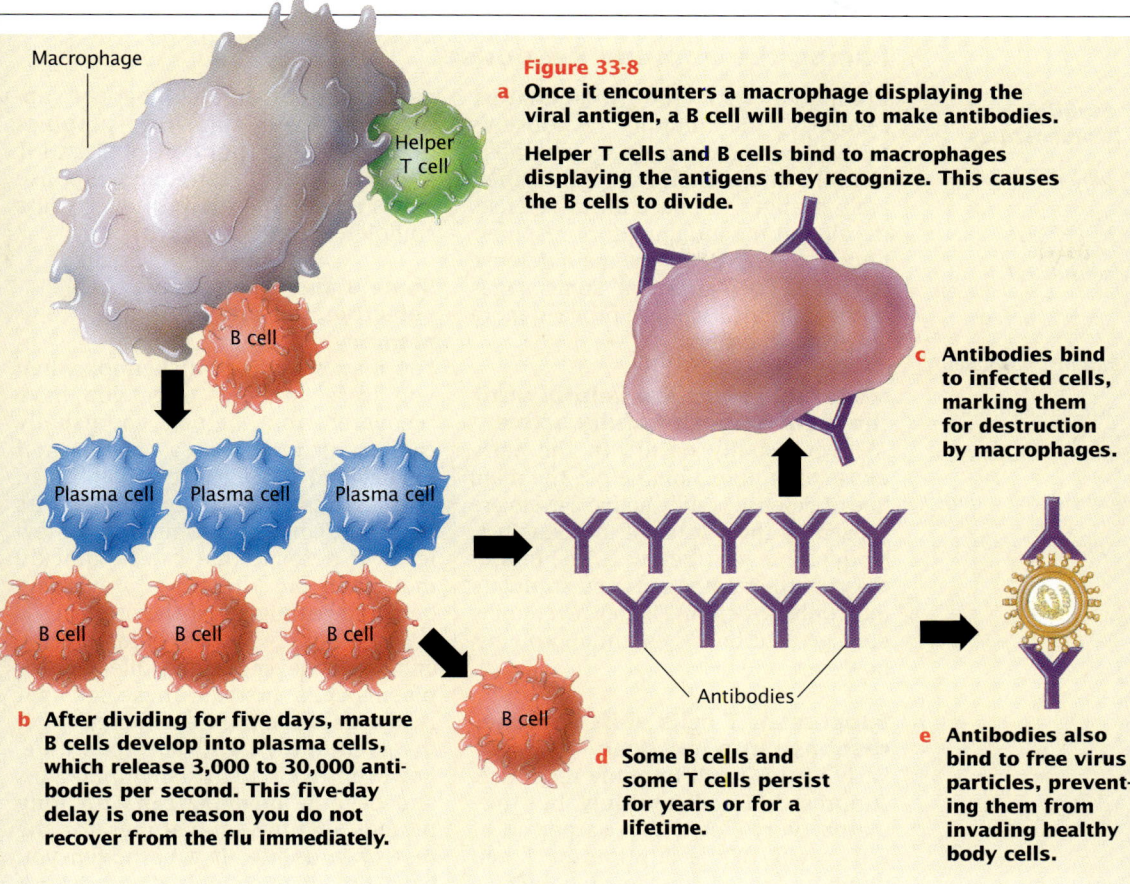

Macrophage

Helper T cell

Figure 33-8

a Once it encounters a macrophage displaying the viral antigen, a B cell will begin to make antibodies.

Helper T cells and B cells bind to macrophages displaying the antigens they recognize. This causes the B cells to divide.

B cell

Plasma cell   Plasma cell   Plasma cell

B cell   B cell   B cell

B cell

c Antibodies bind to infected cells, marking them for destruction by macrophages.

Antibodies

b After dividing for five days, mature B cells develop into plasma cells, which release 3,000 to 30,000 antibodies per second. This five-day delay is one reason you do not recover from the flu immediately.

d Some B cells and some T cells persist for years or for a lifetime.

e Antibodies also bind to free virus particles, preventing them from invading healthy body cells.

B Cells: Biological Warfare

Recall that killer T cells kill only infected cells. What happens to the invading pathogen or foreign agent? Other lymphocytes, called B cells, are deployed to attack the invaders. An assault by B cells is the other half of the attack commanded by helper T cells. Recall that antibodies are defensive proteins made by the immune system. B cells develop into plasma cells, which produce and release the **antibodies**. Antibodies recognize and bind to antigens on the surface of free-floating pathogens or to antigen fragments displayed by macrophages. Binding by antibodies does not kill a pathogen directly. Rather, it marks the pathogen for destruction by macrophages and phagocytes that are guided to enemy target cells coated with antibodies. Receptors on the surface of these macrophages and phagocytes react with the tail of specific antibodies, allowing them to secrete chemicals that destroy the enemy targets.

Your body makes millions of different types of **B cells**. Each type has a unique receptor protein on its membrane that will bind to one particular antigen. At any one time, millions of B cells are circulating in your blood and lymph but are not producing antibodies. Antibody production is turned on when B cells interact with antigen-displaying macrophages and helper T cells, as illustrated in **Figure 33-8**. Your body is capable of making millions of different antibodies. B cells become specialized plasma cells to manufacture only one chosen antibody of the millions possible. In this way, your body prepares defenses against a variety of potential invaders. Many will never be encountered.

Multicultural Perspective: Susumu Tonegawa

The first Japanese scientist to win the Nobel Prize in physiology and medicine, Dr. Susumu Tonegawa of the Massachusetts Institute of Technology has been studying T cells and B cells since the 1970s. He demonstrated that B cells produce a large diversity of antibodies by genetic rearrangement. Tonegawa also helped discover the structure of the T cell receptor and the mechanism by which a T cell recognizes a microbe.

The Immune System   685

Theme Answer

Stability and Homeostasis

The immune response is targeted toward pathogens it remembers. Memory cells continue to patrol the body's tissues, circulating through the blood and lymph for long periods of time and responding quickly against pathogens they recognize. The inflammatory response can inhibit the growth of pathogens and stimulate macrophage action, but the inflammatory response is not selective.

■ **Analyzing Data**

Have students explain why there are more antibodies present during the secondary immune response, as compared with the number involved in the primary response. Also have them explain why the variety of memory cells increases as one gets older. *(There are more cells available in the secondary response than in the primary response. With age, one is exposed to more antigens and acquires more antibodies.)*

Health Connection

Monoclonal Antibodies

Monoclonal antibodies are produced by cloning a single cell that has been obtained by fusing a B cell with a tumor cell. Known as a hybridoma, this new cell has properties of both parents—it divides forever (like a cancer cell) and it produces a specific antibody (like a B cell). The use of monoclonal antibodies is currently being studied as a way of focusing a massive attack on a particular pathogen, perhaps even killing cancer cells without harming normal cells.

Stability and Homeostasis

Why is the immune response considered a specific defense against pathogens, while the inflammatory response is considered a nonspecific defense?

Figure 33-9
The secondary immune response to a pathogen occurs much more quickly and produces more antibodies than the primary immune response.

Pacing the Immune Response

Compared with the inflammatory response, the immune response is fairly slow in defending against infection. But the immune system deliberately changes the pace of its defense. Recall that the inflammatory response bought time to allow the main defense to kick in. Even after that, some stages in the immune response proceed more slowly than others.

Moderate fevers are helpful until the main defense is fully active

A fever usually occurs in the early phase of an infection, before the main line of defense is fully active. Fevers are caused by the release of interleukin-1. Moderate fevers (below 103°F) inhibit the growth of pathogens and stimulate macrophage action. Higher fevers may damage your body's essential proteins, however.

Suppressor T cells shift immune response into low gear

Early in the T-cell immune response, suppressor T cells multiply, but they mature very slowly, over a period of 2–3 weeks. While suppressor T cell numbers are low, the heavy defensive action of T cells and B cells can take place. After two or more weeks, however, there are large numbers of suppressor T cells, and they suppress (inhibit) the production of B and T killer cells. The immune response slows down, although it never shuts completely off.

Some B and T cells have selective, yet vitally useful, memory

You may have had chickenpox when you were younger. Once you have recovered from the pox, you usually cannot catch this illness again, even if exposed to the virus that causes it. Your immune system "remembers" its battles. It continues to maintain a low level of defense that can be quickly mobilized to destroy previously defeated pathogens, if they return.

Some helper T cells, killer T cells, and B cells never become killer cells or plasma cells. Instead, these cells get ready for battle but never actually get involved in the fight. They continue, however, to circulate as lymphocytes and become **memory cells** for long periods of time—sometimes for the rest of your life. If a pathogen you have already encountered enters your body, memory cells recognize it and start to divide, quickly forming a new generation of antibody-producing cells. The antibodies generated by the new cells destroy the pathogen before you become ill; you are not even aware of the battle going on within your body. An immune response to a previously encountered pathogen is much faster than an initial immune response and produces many more antibodies than the first response, as shown in **Figure 33-9**. This later immune response is known as a **secondary immune response** because it occurs after the first exposure to a pathogen. The first exposure is known as the **primary immune response**.

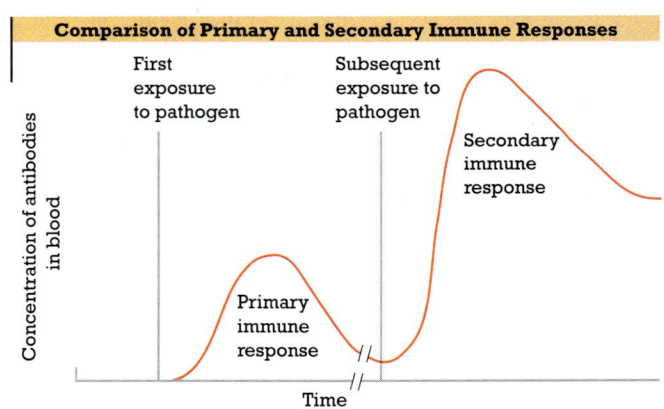

Comparison of Primary and Secondary Immune Responses

First exposure to pathogen

Subsequent exposure to pathogen

Secondary immune response

Primary immune response

Concentration of antibodies in blood

Time

Vaccination makes use of the immune system's "memory"

Many serious diseases can be prevented through vaccination, which you read about in Chapter 18. Vaccination triggers an immune response against a particular pathogen without causing the disease itself. Vaccines work because they contain antigens that have been stripped of their disease-causing abilities. For instance, vaccines for bacterial diseases usually contain bacteria killed by heat or chemical treatment. Mature B (plasma) cells respond to the antigens on the dead bacteria by producing antibodies. Similarly, viral vaccines stimulate the immune response with viruses made harmless by chemicals or genetic engineering.

The production of antibodies brings about **immunity**, or resistance to disease.

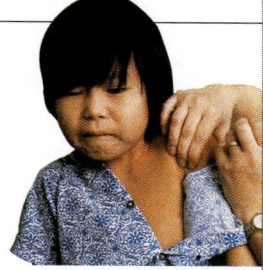

Figure 33-10
This child is receiving the vaccinations required before entering school.

Immunity as a result of vaccination is artificial compared with natural immunity, which results from having had the disease. Both types of immunity make use of the memory of T and B cells.

In many countries, children, like the girl in **Figure 33-10**, are routinely immunized against common childhood diseases, as identified in **Table 33-2**. Each year, more of the United States are requiring that newly developed vaccines for hepatitis B and chickenpox be given to children before they enter school. The immunity achieved from some vaccines lasts a lifetime, as with mumps, for example. Other vaccines, like the tetanus vaccine, require a "booster" shot from time to time to stimulate additional antibody production.

Vaccines aren't effective against rapidly evolving viruses

Genes that carry codes for the surface proteins of flu viruses mutate, or change, rapidly. Thus, the shapes of these surface proteins change frequently. Your body does not recognize viruses with altered surface proteins as the same viruses it has already successfully defeated or been vaccinated against. When these viruses invade your body, they provoke a new primary immune response, and you get sick again. This explains why you can catch the flu more than once.

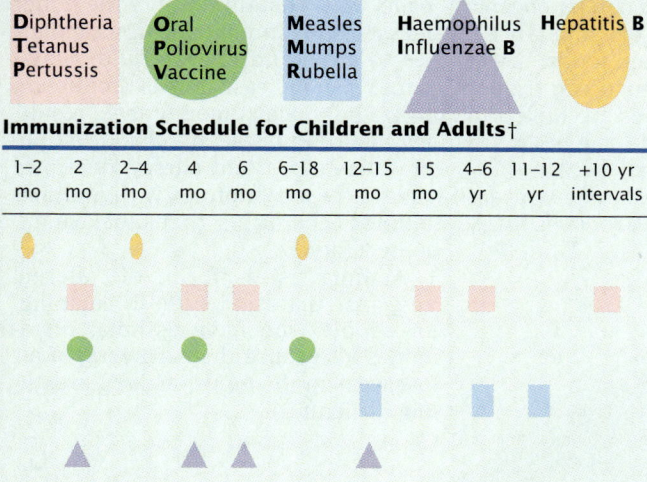

Table 33-2 Single Vaccines and Vaccine Combinations Used in Immunization

Diphtheria Tetanus Pertussis | Oral Poliovirus Vaccine | Measles Mumps Rubella | Haemophilus Influenzae B | Hepatitis B

Immunization Schedule for Children and Adults†

| 1–2 mo | 2 mo | 2–4 mo | 4 mo | 6 mo | 6–18 mo | 12–15 mo | 15 mo | 4–6 yr | 11–12 yr | +10 yr intervals |

†Immunization schedule as recommended by the American Academy of Pediatrics and the USPHS

SECTION REVIEW

1 Predict how the destruction of helper T cells would affect the immune response.

2 Contrast the roles of B cells and T cells in the immune response.

3 Explain the role of memory cells in the immune system.

4 What can you conclude about the surface proteins of viruses for which effective vaccines exist?

687

The Immune System   687

The immune system is a powerful weapon for self protection. But there are times when the immune system works in an unwanted fashion. Sometimes, the system may be overly sensitive and overreact to even mild stimulation. At other times, the body wages an immune assault against its own tissues.

33-3 Immune System Failure

OBJECTIVES

1. Describe the events of an allergic reaction.
2. Contrast cancer cells with normal cells.
3. Relate the symptoms of AIDS to the action of HIV.
4. Describe how HIV is transmitted.

Immune Overreaction

Petting a cat, smelling a flower, or walking into a dusty room can make some people miserable. In these individuals, these activities lead to sneezing, itchy nose and eyes, nasal congestion, and even difficulty in breathing. These are symptoms of an allergy. An **allergy** is an immune system response against a non-pathogenic antigen. A variety of substances, including pollen, certain foods, insect stings or bites, and dust, can trigger allergies. Dust allergies are linked to tiny mites, such as the one in **Figure 33-11**, that live on dust.

If you inhale pollen that you are allergic to, your body produces many more antibodies to the pollen antigen than it needs. These antibodies bind to the antigen and trigger a strong inflammatory response. This strong response causes the cells in the nasal passages to release a set of chemical messengers that includes **histamine** (*HIHS tuh meen*), as shown in **Figure 33-12** on page 689. Histamine and the other messengers stimulate nearby capillaries to swell and release fluid. Histamines also increase mucus production from the mucous membranes, resulting in a runny nose, nasal congestion, or watery eyes. Many allergy medicines relieve these symptoms with **antihistamines**, chemicals that block histamine action.

Asthma is a form of allergic response that can be life threatening. In people who have asthma, histamines also cause the narrowing of air passages in the lungs, making breathing difficult.

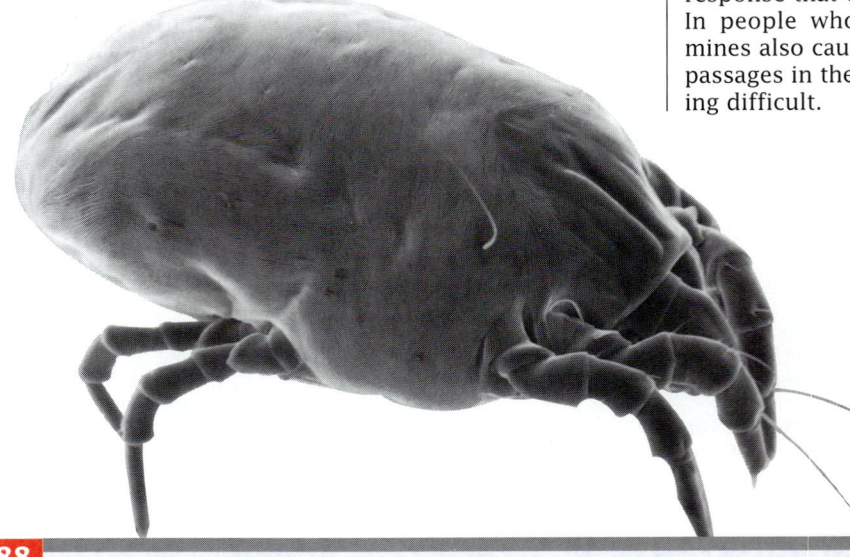

Figure 33-11
People with allergies to dust are actually allergic to the feces of the house-dust mite, which lives on dust particles. This photograph is magnified 300 times.

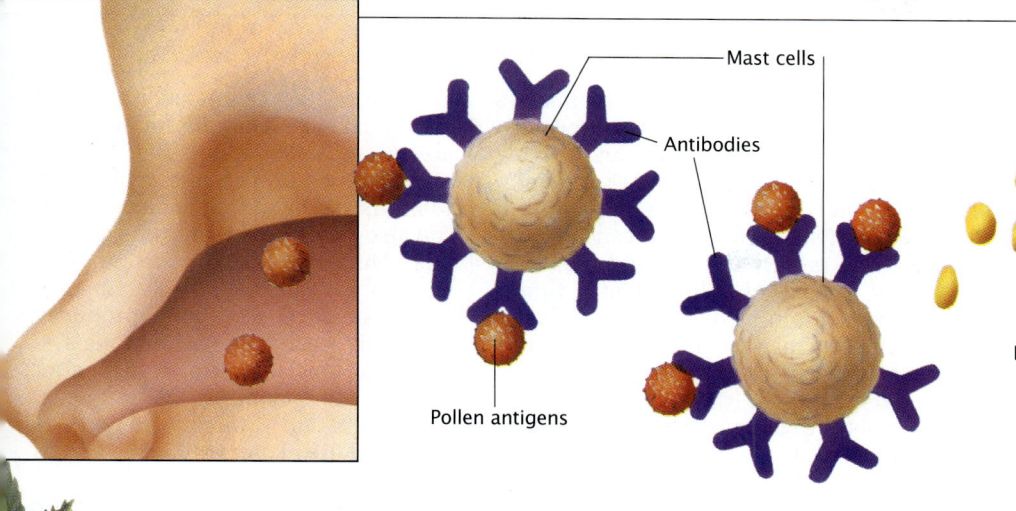

Source of pollen

Figure 33-12

Phase 1
When pollen from a plant enters the nose of a person who is allergic to it, pollen antigens attach to antibodies on the surface of the mast cells lining the nasal passages.

Phase 2
The binding of antibodies stimulates cells to release histamine and other chemicals that cause symptoms such as sneezing, runny nose, and itchy eyes.

Autoimmune diseases result when the body manufactures "anti-self" antibodies

Distinguishing self from non-self is the key ability of the cells of the immune system. In certain diseases, this ability breaks down, and the body attacks its own tissues. Such diseases are called **autoimmune diseases**. Multiple sclerosis is an autoimmune disease that usually strikes people between the ages of 20 and 40. In multiple sclerosis, the immune system attacks and destroys the insulating myelin sheath

that covers neurons. Degeneration of the myelin sheath interferes with transmission of nerve impulses, which eventually cannot travel at all. Voluntary functions, such as movement of the limbs, and involuntary functions, such as bladder control, are lost. Multiple sclerosis usually leads to paralysis and death. Scientists do not know what stimulates the immune system to attack myelin. Some other autoimmune diseases, the tissues or organs they affect, and their symptoms are listed in **Table 33-3**.

Table 33-3 Some Autoimmune Diseases

Disease	Areas affected	Symptoms
Systemic lupus erythematosus	Connective tissue, joints, kidney	Facial skin rash, painful joints, fever, fatigue, kidney problems, weight loss
Type 1 diabetes	Insulin-producing cells in pancreas	Excessive urine production, blurred vision, weight loss, fatigue, irritability
Graves' disease	Thyroid	Weakness, irritability, heat intolerance, increased sweating, weight loss, insomnia
Rheumatoid arthritis	Joints	Crippling inflammation of the joints

Connection: *Chapter 30*

Myelin and Nerve Impulses
Review how myelin wraps around the axon membrane, forming an insulating sheath. Remind students that the nerve impulse then "hops" between nodes found between the myelin sheaths, thereby speeding the transmission of the impulse.

Visual Strategy Table 33-3

● **Comparing Functions**
Lead the class through the survey of various autoimmune diseases listed in this table. When discussing the areas affected, be sure to review the functions of the structures listed: Chapter 29, connective tissues and joints; Chapter 34, kidneys; Chapter 31, pancreas and thyroid.

Key to Strategies
● **Understanding Concepts (Tier I)**
■ **Applying Information (Tier II)**
▲ **Critical Thinking (Tier III)**

The Immune System   689

Theme Answer

Evolution
Changes in the surface proteins of viruses prevent the immune system from recognizing the virus as one that has already been defeated or vaccinated against.

Connection: *Chapter 4*

How Cells Divide
Review how cells divide in mitosis. Remind students that cells appear to be programmed for a certain number of divisions, after which they die. Such is not the case with cancer cells, which continue to divide.

Visual Strategy Figure 33-13

● **Comparing Functions**
As a way of introducing the next section concerning AIDS, inform students that HIV selectively infects T cells. From what they understand from this figure, students should then be able to explain why cancer kills more AIDS patients than does any other disease. *(One of the functions of the immune system is to destroy cancer cells before they spread. If its activity is suppressed, cancer can spread.)*

Health Connection

Transplants and Cancer
Have students explain why transplant patients, who are given drugs to suppress their immune system, are more likely than others to develop cancer. *(The drugs used in immunosuppressive therapy decrease immune system activity. One of the functions of the immune system is to destroy cancer cells before they spread.)*

Cancer: Unrestrained Cell Division

Evolution

The protists that cause African sleeping sickness can rapidly change the antigens on their cell surfaces. Why is this an effective way to evade the immune system?

A major function of your immune system is to ward off cancer. Normally, cells in your body reproduce (divide) at a controlled rate. Cancer is a condition in which cells lose the ability to stop dividing. In benign cancers, cells divide rapidly but spread little, forming a mass of cells called a **tumor**. Unless tumors grow so large that they actually crush the internal organs, they are not usually fatal. In malignant cancers, however, the cells aggressively penetrate surrounding tissues. Cells of malignant cancers can even spread throughout the body via the lymph system and bloodstream. Because of the damage they cause to the tissues that they invade, malignant cancers are often fatal unless detected early.

Scientists think that the mutation of genes that regulate the cell division cycle initiates cancer. As you read in Chapter 14, a mutagenic agent that causes cancer is known as a carcinogen.

Carcinogens that can transform normal cells into cancer cells are found in cigarette smoke (smoking is a leading cause of lung cancer) and in a variety of industrial chemicals. Some viruses can also cause cells to become cancerous. Mutation also occurs spontaneously in your body all the time, so some cancer cells are being produced "naturally" each day. The immune system is on constant patrol, watching for surface changes on the body's cells. This constant watch, known as **immunological surveillance**, allows immune cells to identify and destroy these occasional cancer cells before they spread. **Figure 33-13** shows a T cell killing a cancer cell. Surveillance by the immune system is your body's primary defense against cancer. Among AIDS patients, who lack effective immune systems, cancer is one of the leading causes of death.

Figure 33-13

a When a killer T cell comes into contact with the cells of a tumor, it is able to recognize the tumor cells as enemies. Below you can see a killer T cell (upper right) that has bound to a tumor cell.

b The killer T cell releases proteins that disrupt the tumor cell's membrane. The damage results in osmotic imbalances within the cell's interior. The tumor cell below is "blebbing" prior to death.

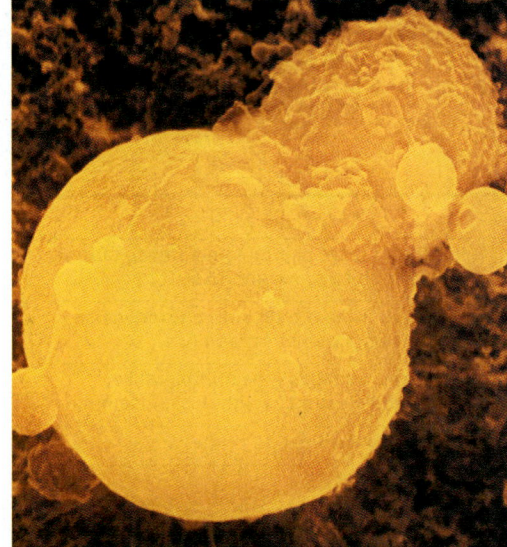
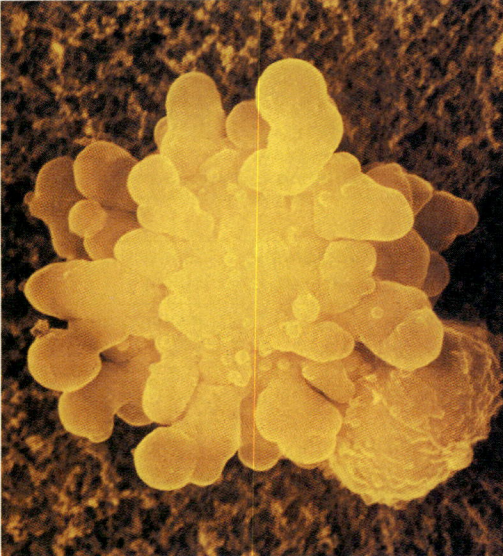

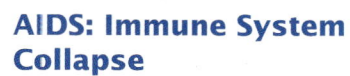

AIDS: Immune System Collapse

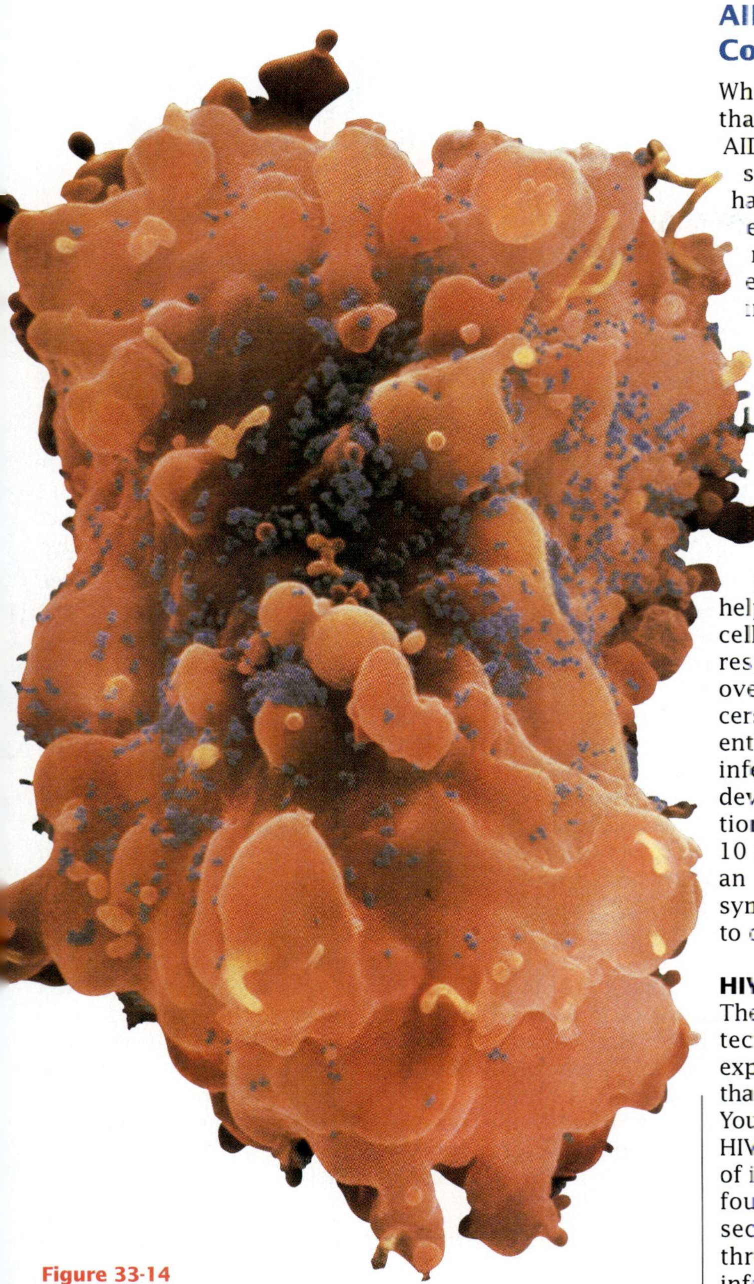

Figure 33-14
The blue particles in this scanning electron micrograph are particles of HIV. They have been produced in this infected helper T cell and are leaving the cell to infect other cells.

When this book was published, more than 300,000 Americans had died of AIDS (acquired immune deficiency syndrome) and more than 440,000 had the disease. Most are young. It is estimated that one out of every 92 men ages 27 to 39 and one out of every 250 people in general is infected.

HIV attacks and cripples the immune system. It invades macrophages and helper T cells, like the one shown in **Figure 33-14**. HIV transforms these cells into virus factories, killing large numbers of helper T cells. When the number of helper T cells in the blood has fallen to very low levels, a person is said to have AIDS. Without helper T cells to stimulate and direct B cells and killer T cells, the immune response cannot occur. The body is overwhelmed by pathogens and cancers that it normally could defeat. Scientists think that practically everyone infected with HIV will eventually develop AIDS. The time between infection and onset of AIDS can be 10 years or longer. During this time, an infected person with or without symptoms can still transmit the virus to others.

HIV is transmitted in body fluids

There is no cure for AIDS. You can protect yourself from AIDS by avoiding exposure to HIV. HIV is a fragile virus that cannot exist for long outside cells. You can get HIV only by contacting the HIV-infected blood cells or body fluids of infected individuals. Because HIV is found in both semen and vaginal secretions, you can contract HIV through sexual intercourse with an infected person; worldwide, most HIV infections are spread this way. The virus can be transmitted to either person during intercourse. Newer strains of HIV are more easily spread in this way. Use of a condom during sex reduces but does not eliminate the risk of getting HIV.

Visual Strategy Figure 33-14

● **Comparing Structures**
Point out to students that what they see happening to the T cell shown in this figure may be the result of an HIV infection that occurred several years earlier. One of the many puzzles about HIV concerns the dormancy of the virus. HIV can remain dormant for perhaps as long as 15 years before additional HIV particles leave an infected T cell.

Health Connection

The Difference Between HIV Infection and AIDS

A common misconception is that a person who is HIV positive has AIDS. In fact, AIDS is the last phase of a long HIV infection. A person is declared HIV positive when antibodies to HIV are found in his or her blood or tissues. However, an HIV-positive person may be healthy and disease-free for a decade or more after infection. During this asymptomatic stage, the HIV-positive person is fully infectious and can transmit the virus to others. AIDS is diagnosed when HIV has destroyed enough of the infected person's helper T cells that severe immune suppression occurs.

Historical Perspective: A Short History of AIDS

AIDS was first identified as a disease in 1981. Several mysterious deaths in the late 1970s and in 1980 were easily attributed to AIDS. However, using recently developed tests for HIV, scientists have been able to solve some unexplained deaths from previous decades. For instance, a British sailor who died in 1959 had an immune system that was apparently nonfunctional. His doctors saved tissue samples that, 30 years later, were found to contain HIV. Similar studies have implicated AIDS in the death of a Norwegian sailor in 1966.

Key to Strategies
- ● Understanding Concepts (Tier I)
- ■ Applying Information (Tier II)
- ▲ Critical Thinking (Tier III)

Figure 33-15
Anyone can be infected with HIV, regardless of age, sex, ethnic background, or sexual orientation. A person can be infected with the virus for 10 years or longer without knowing it.

Ryan White died of AIDS at the age of 18. His appearances before the United States Senate helped gain support and understanding for people with the disease. A major government funding act bears his name—the Ryan White Act.

Arthur Ashe, a professional tennis player, died in 1994 from an AIDS-related infection.

HIV can be transmitted when blood from an infected person is transferred to an uninfected person. People who inject drugs can be infected with HIV if they share or reuse needles or hypodermic syringes, both of which can be contaminated with blood carrying the virus. The majority of HIV infections in the United States in the late 1980s were transmitted in this manner.

In the late 1970s and early 1980s, many people contracted HIV by receiving blood transfusions from infected individuals. Many hemophiliacs, including Ryan White (one of the HIV-infected people shown in **Figure 33-15**), were infected by receiving blood clotting factor that had been isolated from blood of infected individuals. Since 1985, donated blood has been tested for the presence of HIV, so the likelihood of contracting HIV through blood transfusions or blood products is very low.

If a pregnant woman is infected, her fetus has about a one-in-three chance of being infected during the pregnancy. HIV can also be transmitted from mother to child in breast milk. **Table 33-4** summarizes the ways that HIV can be transmitted.

HIV is not transmitted through the air or on toilet seats. It cannot be contracted through casual contact, such as shaking hands, sharing food, or drinking from the same water fountain as an infected person. Although HIV is found in saliva, tears, and urine, it occurs there in very low concentrations. One drop of infected blood contains as many viruses as one quart of infected saliva. Scientists think that a large quantity of the virus must be received for infection to occur. You cannot catch HIV from the small amount of saliva exchanged when kissing. Biting arthropods, such as mosquitoes, bedbugs, fleas, and ticks, do not transmit HIV.

Table 33-4 Known Routes of HIV Transmission

- Vaginal, oral, or anal intercourse with an infected person
- Injecting drugs or other substances with hypodermic syringes or needles used by an infected individual
- Use of skin piercing equipment, such as tattooing needles, that has been used by an infected person
- From infected mother to fetus through the placenta; from infected mother to baby in breast milk
- Transfusions or injections of blood or blood products or organs donated from an infected person (Transmission rarely occurs by this route in the United States and other developed nations because blood is tested for the presence of HIV. It is still a common transmission route in the less developed countries, where such blood tests are often unavailable.)

After the death of her eight-year-old daughter in 1988, **Elizabeth Glaser**, herself infected, cofounded the Pediatric AIDS Foundation. Elizabeth died in 1994, leaving her husband and their second infected child, age 10.

Actor **Pedro Zamora** played one of the roommates on MTV's *Real World*. He died in 1994 at age 22.

AIDS has killed more than 300,000 Americans

As you can see in **Figure 33-16**, the number of AIDS cases and deaths have risen dramatically since 1981, when the disease was first described. American teenagers, such as those in **Figure 33-17**, are increasingly at risk of contracting HIV. More than 20 percent of all reported AIDS cases occur among people in their 20s. Given the average 10-year period before symptoms appear, the majority of these people were probably infected during their teenage years. In 1992, AIDS was the sixth leading cause of death among Americans between the ages of 15 and 24. In 1993, AIDS became the number one killer of people aged 25–44 in the United States. And AIDS is killing greater proportions of minority women and children than individuals from other groups. In 1993, AIDS became the fourth leading cause of death among women aged 25–44. Sexual intercourse of any kind—anal, oral, or vaginal—between males and females accounts for the greatest increase in AIDS cases in women in recent years.

Demonstration
● **Observing Relationships**
Show the class photographs of people holding hands, embracing, kissing, and engaging in other forms of physical contact. Point out that HIV is not spread by casual contact, nor is it spread by insects, such as mosquitoes.

Active READING

Technique: Reader Response Logs
To give students an opportunity to make a personal response to what they have read, have them make one or two entries in their reader response logs. Remind students to divide their paper in half. On the left side of the paper, have them copy a word, phrase, or passage from the text. On the right side, have them write reactions, thoughts, feelings, questions, or associations to what they wrote on the left side of the paper. Invite students to share their entries with a partner.

Figure 33-16
This graph shows the cumulative numbers of AIDS cases and deaths in the United States since 1981.

Figure 33-17
Anyone can get AIDS—even you.

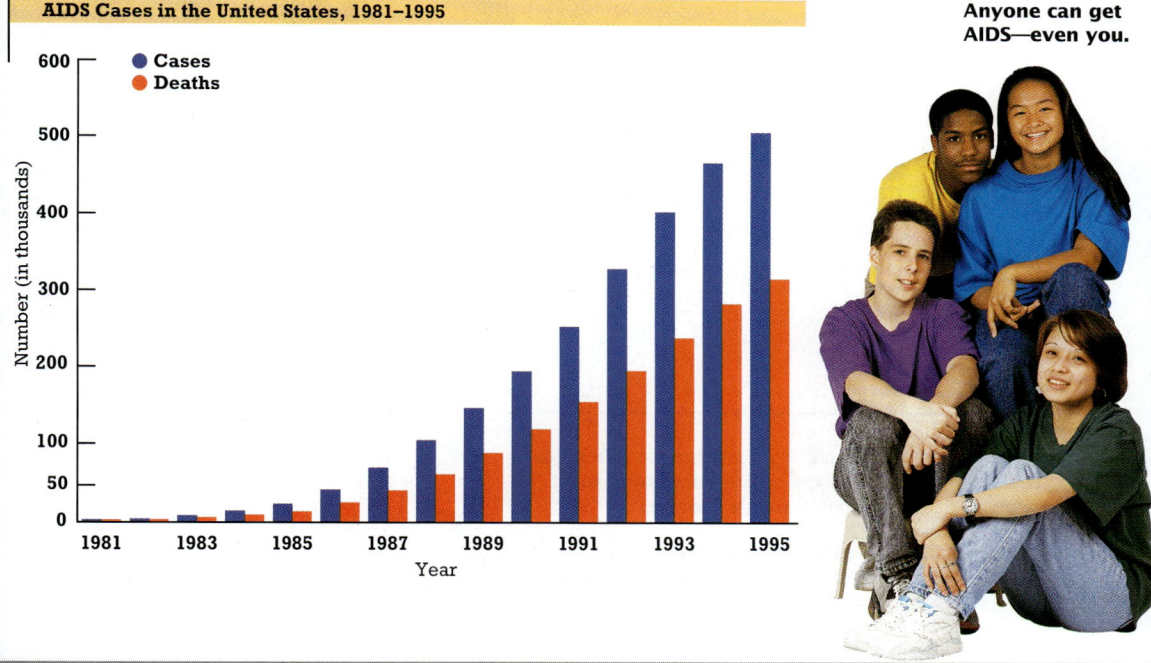

AIDS Cases in the United States, 1981–1995

● Cases
● Deaths

Number (in thousands)

600
500
400
300
200
100
50
0

1981 1983 1985 1987 1989 1991 1993 1995

Year

693

Key to Strategies
● **Understanding Concepts (Tier I)**
■ **Applying Information (Tier II)**
▲ **Critical Thinking (Tier III)**

The Immune System

Visual Strategy   Figure 33-18

● **Interpreting Graphs**
Have students examine and evaluate the percentage increase in the numbers of AIDS cases and AIDS-related deaths as shown in this figure.

Phase Three
Assessment Options

Closure
■ **Relating Concepts**
Assign students to cooperative work groups of three. Have each group prepare a poster that dramatizes the impact of AIDS and highlights ways to avoid contracting HIV. Arrange for the posters to be displayed for the rest of the school to see.

SECTION REVIEW
Assign the *Section Review.*

Reteaching
Invite a local physician or the school nurse to speak to the class about AIDS.

AIDS Is a Worldwide Disease

AIDS was first recognized as a disease in the United States. It has since been found in 163 countries. (The origin of the disease remains undetermined.) The World Health Organization estimates that by the year 2000 there will be 10 million cases of AIDS and that about 30 million people will be infected with HIV. Most of these cases will occur in the less-developed countries, where AIDS is now spreading rapidly. Each day, 6,000 people become infected with the virus, and the number of AIDS cases doubles every nine months in Nigeria alone. Currently, AIDS is one of the two biggest killers of women in Africa. **Figure 33-18** shows the projected increase in the number of people infected with HIV worldwide. AIDS is the final stage of HIV infection.

Figure 33-18
The World Health Organization (WHO) projects that 30 million people will be infected with HIV by the year 2000. WHO predicts that Africa and Asia will have the most infections and that the industrialized countries, the category that includes the United States, will have the fewest infections.

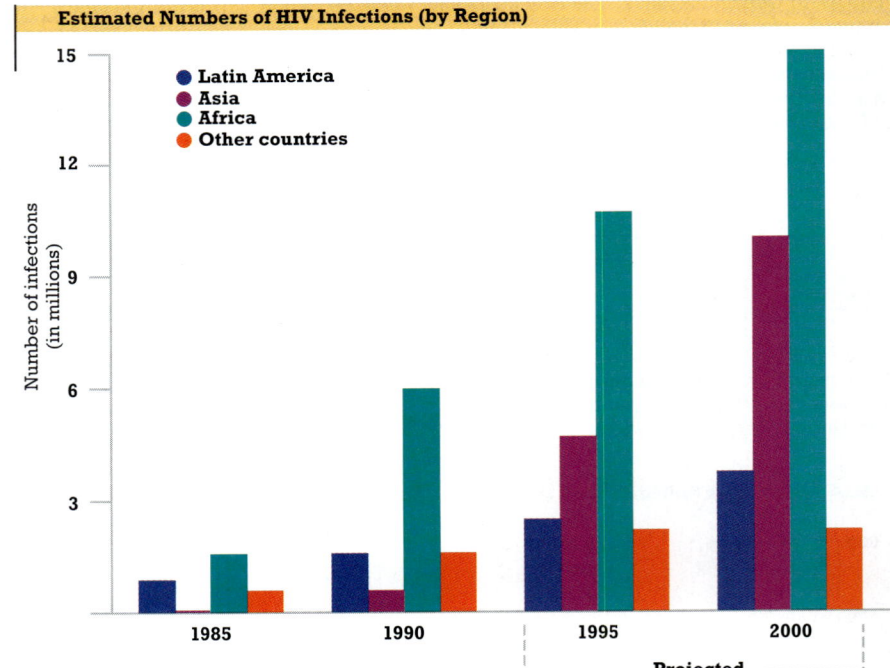

Estimated Numbers of HIV Infections (by Region)

SECTION REVIEW

1 Describe what happens when you are exposed to something to which you are allergic.

2 How are cancer cells different from normal cells?

3 Explain why AIDS patients are unable to fight infections.

4 List four ways HIV is transmitted.

ANSWERS TO
SECTION REVIEW

1 Refer to the captions that accompany Figure 33-12 on page 689.

2 Cancer cells lose their ability to stop dividing, whereas normal cells divide at a controlled rate.

3 AIDS patients have very low levels of helper T cells in their blood, making their immune systems unable to resist infections and cancers that healthy immune systems normally defeat.

4 HIV is transmitted in body fluids. HIV is spread by semen and vaginal secretions during sexual intercourse. It is also spread when blood from an infected person is transferred to an uninfected person. It can be transferred from a mother to her unborn child and to the child through breast milk. HIV can also spread through the use of skin-piercing equipment, such as tattooing needles.

Highlights

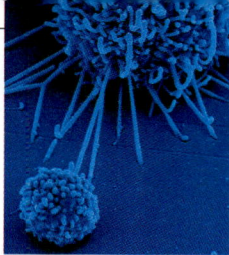

Killer T cells protect the body by destroying tumors, like the one in the lower left corner of the photograph.

Alternative Assessment

Have students formulate questions from the chapter to play a game similar to *Jeopardy* as a review technique.

Portfolio Assessment

Portfolio Assessment on page T39 provides options for building and evaluating student portfolios. Students and teachers can select items from the areas listed on page T39 for inclusion in a portfolio.

	Key Terms	Summary
33-1 **First Line of Defense** 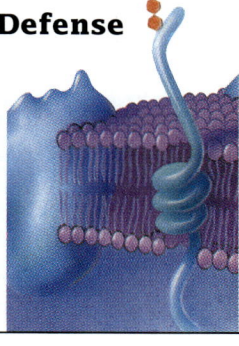 The immune system depends on marker proteins to distinguish self from foreign invaders.	mucous membrane (p. 679) leukocyte (p. 680) phagocyte (p. 680) lymphocyte (p. 680) inflammatory response (p. 680) macrophage (p. 681) antigen (p. 681)	• The body has several natural defenses for disabling pathogens. • Several kinds of white blood cells work together to defend the body. • Defensive cells and responses are suited for either short or long battles. • The display and recognition of marker proteins are critical to successful defense against invaders.
33-2 **The Immune Response** 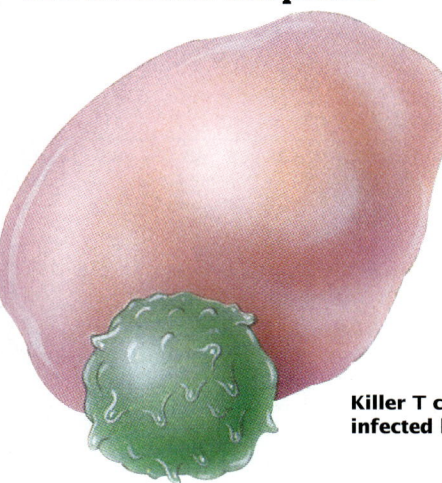 Killer T cells attack infected body cells.	immune response (p. 683) T-cell lymphocytes (p. 684) antibody (p. 685) B cell (p. 685) memory cell (p. 686) secondary immune response (p. 686) primary immune response (p. 686) immunity (p. 687)	• The immune response is used when pathogens get past the first line of defense. • It takes several days after invasion before the immune response is activated. • T cells command and regulate the immune response. Some T cells kill their own body's infected cells. • B cells are the main killers, attacking the enemy most directly. Some B cells become plasma cells and manufacture antibodies. • Long-term immunity results from the memories of enemies held by certain T cells and B cells.
33-3 **Immune System Failure** This house-dust mite is a source of misery for thousands of people who are allergic to dust. 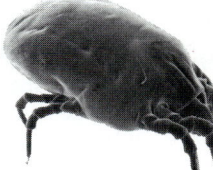	allergy (p. 688) histamine (p. 688) antihistamine (p. 688) autoimmune disease (p. 689) tumor (p. 690) immunological surveillance (p. 690)	• An allergy is a response to a non-pathogenic antigen. • Cancer is uncontrolled cell division. The immune system normally destroys cancer cells before they spread. • HIV causes the immune system to fail by invading and destroying helper T cells and macrophages.

695

ANSWER TO CONCEPT MAP

The following is one possible answer to the Relating Concepts exercise on page 696.

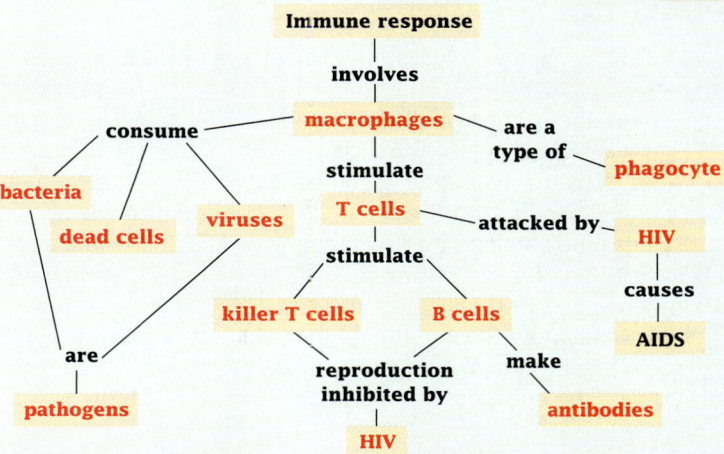

Understanding Vocabulary

1. a. The inflammatory response's symptoms include swelling, red coloration, and increased temperature. The immune response is the system's main attack on a specific pathogen.
b. Antigens are marker proteins that trigger an immune response; antibodies are defensive proteins made by the immune system that attack "nonself" antigens.
c. T cells activate and control the immune response and destroy cells showing viral antigens. B cells produce and release antibodies.

2. a. Mucous membranes, sweat, tears, and saliva are some of the body's nonspecific natural defenses.
b. Leukocytes are white blood cells involved in the inflammatory response. Lymphocytes and macrophages are white blood cells that are part of the immune response.
c. The immune response is the system's main attack on a specific pathogen. Macrophages engulf pathogens and display antigens on their cell surfaces. Macrophages secrete interleukin-1, which stimulates helper T cells.

Understanding Concepts

3. Concept Map answer is on page 695.

4. Refer to the **Answers to Section Review** for Section 33-1, page 682, number 1.

5. See page 679.

6. Refer to the captions that accompany Figure 33-2 on page 680.

7. The inflammatory response, which buys time with leukocytes, lasts about 24 hours, until the main line of defense, the immune response, can react with lymphocytes. Refer also to the captions that accompany Figure 33-3 on page 681.

8. Body cells carry certain marker proteins that enable the body

Understanding Vocabulary

1. For each pair of terms, explain the differences in their meanings.
   a. inflammatory response, immune response
   b. antigens, antibodies
   c. T cells, B cells

2. Using each set of words below, write one or more sentences summarizing information learned in this chapter.
   a. mucous membranes, sweat, tears, saliva
   b. leukocytes, lymphocytes, macrophages
   c. immune response, interleukin-1, pathogens, macrophage

Understanding Concepts

3. **Relating Concepts** Construct a concept map that describes an immune response. Include the following terms: macrophages, bacteria, dead cells, viruses, T cells, killer T cells, B cells, pathogens, HIV, phagocyte, antibodies.

4. **Identifying Structures and Functions** Describe how your skin defends your body.

5. **Identify Structures and Functions** Describe three nonspecific natural defenses that protect the body from invading microbes and pathogens.

6. **Summarizing Information** Describe the events that occur after a splinter enters your finger.

7. **Comparing Functions** Differentiate between the inflammatory response and the immune response in terms of duration of response and kinds of white cells involved.

8. **Inferring Relationships** Explain how white blood cells can distinguish your cells from those of invading pathogens.

9. **Inferring Relationships** What is the function of antibodies in the immune response?

10. **Summarizing Information** Summarize the steps leading to the production of antibodies by plasma cells that encounter a macrophage showing a viral antigen.

11. **Inferring Relationships** Identify the cells responsible for long-term immunity, and explain how they achieve it.

12. **Inferring Conclusions** What would be your chances of contracting German measles for a second time if memory cells lived only three months? Explain your answer.

13. **Inferring Conclusions** Explain why vaccines are not effective against viral diseases such as influenza and AIDS.

14. **Interpreting Graphs** Over time, people with AIDS become sicker and sicker, unable to fight infection. Look at the graph and explain why this occurs.

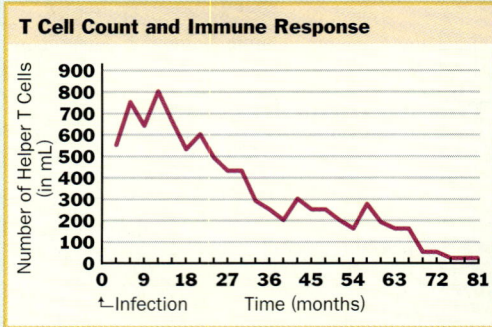

T Cell Count and Immune Response

(graph: Number of Helper T Cells (in mL) vs. Time (months); y-axis 0–900, x-axis 0, 9, 18, 27, 36, 45, 54, 63, 72, 81; ↑Infection)

15. **Summarizing Information** Describe the events of an allergic reaction.

16. **Recognizing Relationships** What happens to the immune system's ability to distinguish self from non-self cells in an autoimmune disease? Identify two autoimmune disease and their symptoms.

17. **Inferring Relationships** What causes normal cells to become cancer cells?

18. **Recognizing Relationships** What is AIDS? Why do people with AIDS die from bacterial and viral infections?

19. **Summarizing Information** Identify four routes by which HIV is transmitted.

20. **BUILDING ON WHAT YOU HAVE LEARNED** In Chapter 30 you learned about the function of myelin in the transmission of nerve impulses. How is myelin affected by the disease multiple sclerosis?

696

to distinguish its own cells from invading pathogens.

9. Refer to the captions that accompany Figure 33-8 on page 685.

10. Refer to the captions that accompany Figure 33-7 on page 684.

11. Refer to the captions that accompany Figure 33-8 on page 685.

12. If these cells lived only three months, the body would not recognize the pathogens and would respond as if the pathogens were invading the body for the first time.

13. Viruses mutate quickly, changing the shape of their surface proteins. When these viruses invade the body, they cause a new primary immune response, and the body becomes sick once again.

14. Helper T cells are some of the most important cells of the immune system. When their numbers are decreased, the whole immune system's activity is decreased.

15. Refer to the captions that accompany Figure 33-12 on page 689.

16. In an autoimmune disease, the body cannot

Interpreting Graphics

21. Study the diagram below.

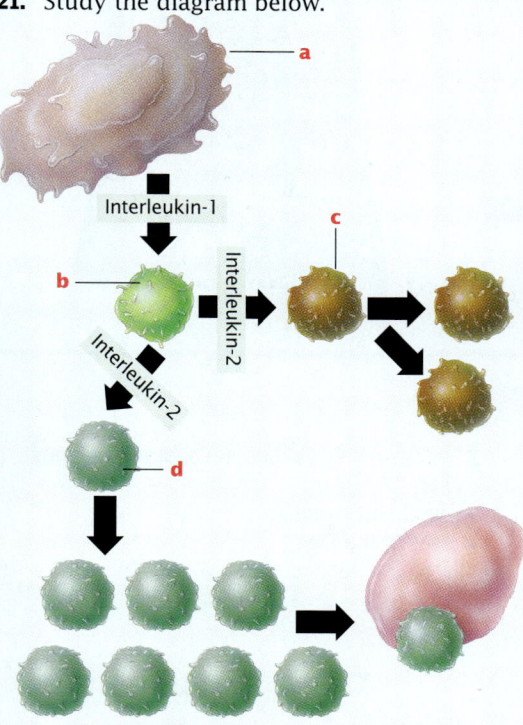

- a. Identify the cell labeled *a*. What is its function in the immune response?
- b. What is the function of the cells labeled *d*?
- c. Describe how HIV infection affects the process illustrated above.

Reviewing Themes

22. *Cell Structure and Function*
Long-term smoking causes paralysis of cilia lining the trachea. How would this affect the body's ability to repel pathogens?

23. *Stability and Homeostasis*
What symptoms are associated with an asthma attack? What effect would taking medicines that contain antihistamines have on the symptoms?

Thinking Critically

24. **Distinguishing Fact From Opinion** A newspaper columnist wrote "The ongoing fight against AIDS should be limited to only those people who are in high-risk groups, such as those people who abuse drugs." Comment on the effectiveness of this approach.

Life/Work Skills

25. **Finding Information** Use library references or search an on-line database to find out about the work of German physician Robert Koch. What did Koch contribute to the knowledge about the spread of disease? What are Koch's postulates? Summarize your findings in a written report.

26. **Allocating Resources** Every year billions of dollars are spent on research into the causes and treatment of tuberculosis. Use library references or search an on-line database to find out how much money is spent and by what agencies. How has the number of TB cases changed? What percentage of the money has been spent on testing, treatment, and education for prevention? Where is the bulk of the money currently being spent? Why? How has the amount of money spent changed over the last 10, 15, and 20 years? Summarize your findings in a series of graphs or charts.

Activities and Projects

27. **Health Connection** For decades, polio, or poliomyelitis, affected people around the world. This incurable disease causes pain, stiffness, paralysis, and eventually death. Use library references or search an on-line database to find out about Jonas Salk and the polio vaccine. How was the vaccine developed? How effective was it? What contribution did Albert Sabin make in the fight against polio? How common is polio today? Summarize your findings in a written report to your class.

28. **Geography Connection** According to the World Health Organization (WHO), the majority of future AIDS cases will occur in Africa, Asia, and South America. Look for information in your library about living conditions, medical care, and education in these areas and about their projected population growth. How might those conditions support WHO's projection?

Discovering Through Reading

29. Read the article "Our Immune System: The Wars Within" by Peter Jaret in *National Geographic*, June 1986, pages 702–735. Why is the AIDS virus so deadly? Explain why the analogy of the Trojan horse might be appropriate in describing HIV.

response.
b. Killer T cells destroy infected cells.
c. HIV invades macrophages and helper T cells, transforming them into virus factories.

Reviewing Themes

22. Without properly functioning cilia, pathogens will not be swept into the mouth, swallowed, and destroyed by digestive enzymes of the stomach.

23. Symptoms of an asthma attack include narrowing of the bronchioles in the lungs, which causes difficulty breathing, wheezing, and shortness of breath. Antihistamines will block the actions of the histamine, allowing the bronchioles to return to normal.

Thinking Critically

24. AIDS is a rapidly spreading disease that can infect any person from any group within society. Limiting the fight against AIDS to only certain groups would leave everyone else at risk.

Life/Work Skills

25. Results will vary depending on the resources available.
26. Results will vary depending on the resources available.

Activities and Projects

27. Results will vary depending on the resources available.
28. Results will vary depending on the resources available.

Discovering Through Reading

29. A virus is dangerous because it enters a human cell and makes it produce copies of itself, turning the cell into a "virus factory." One of the many puzzles about HIV is its period of dormancy. HIV can remain dormant for as long as 15 years before additional HIV particles leave an infected T cell.

distinguish "self" from "nonself." As a result, the immune system begins to attack and destroy healthy body cells. Students' answers should include two diseases and their symptoms from Table 33-3 on page 689.

17. Scientists think that spontaneous mutations (resulting from carcinogens such as cigarette smoke, industrial chemicals, and viruses) in the genes that regulate the cell-division cycle cause cancer.

18. Acquired Immune Deficiency Syndrome (AIDS) is caused by HIV, which attacks and cripples the immune system. The body is overwhelmed by pathogens and cancers that it normally could defeat.

19. Refer to Table 33-4 on page 692.

20. In multiple sclerosis, the immune system destroys the myelin, which affects the transmission of nerve impulses, thus leading to the loss of voluntary and involuntary muscle functions.

Interpreting Graphics

21. a. Macrophages activate an immune

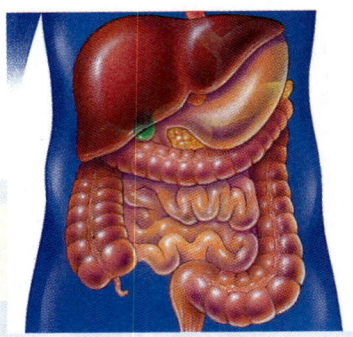

Lesson Planning Guide With Options for Block Scheduling

Lecture Concepts

Lesson Resources

34-1 Nutrition: What You Eat and Why

BLOCK ❶ (45 minutes)

1. Five nutrients essential to good health are carbohydrates, lipids, proteins, vitamins, and minerals.
2. Carbohydrates serve as the main source of energy for cells.
3. Proteins serve as the building blocks for growth and tissue repair.

❶ Lecture Resources
- Determining Prior Knowledge
- Active Reading: Prediction Guide
- Visual Strategy: Videodisc
- Demonstration: Summarizing Information
- Teaching Transparencies: 222, 190A
- Holt Biology Videodiscs Lesson 34-1

Classwork Options
- Demonstration: Interpreting Information

Interactive Explorations Laboratory Manual: Lab E7

Assignment Options
- Fats in the Diet
- Decision Making

BLOCK ❷ (45 minutes)

4. Vitamins are organic compounds needed in small amounts to help regulate body functions.
5. Two major eating disorders are anorexia nervosa and bulimia.

❷ Lecture Resources
- Active Reading: Reading Hint
- Visual Strategy: Figures 34-1, 34-2, 34-3
- Demonstration: Summarizing Information
- Teaching Transparencies: 191A, 192A
- Holt Biology Videodiscs Lesson 34-1

Classwork Options
- Closure: Recognizing Relationships

Laboratory Techniques and Experimental Design: Lab C46

Assignment Options
- Reteaching
- Section Review
- Chapter Review, questions 1a, 2a, 2b, 4, 5, 6, 7, 8, 9, 10, 22, 29
- Directed Reading Worksheet

34-2 The Digestive System

BLOCK ❸ (45 minutes)

1. Digestion begins in the mouth as enzymes in saliva break down complex carbohydrates.
2. Digestion continues in the stomach as pepsin and hydrochloric acid break down proteins.
3. Digestion is completed in the small intestine as food is broken into simple sugars, amino acids, and short chains of carbon and hydrogen molecules.

❸ Lecture Resources
- Active Reading: Reading Organizer
- Visual Strategy: Figure 34-5
- Visual Strategy: Videodisc
- Demonstration: Identifying Functions, p. 706
- Teaching Transparencies: 216, 219
- Holt Biology Videodiscs Lesson 34-2

Classwork Options
- Exploration 34A

Assignment Options
- Teaching Resources CD-ROM: Problem-Solving Worksheets 10

BLOCK ❹ (45 minutes)

4. Bile produced by the liver and enzymes secreted by the pancreas aid in digestion.
5. Nutrients are absorbed in the small intestine.
6. Undigested materials are compacted and eventually eliminated by the large intestine.

❹ Lecture Resources
- Visual Strategy: Figure 34-6, 34-7
- Demonstration: Identifying Functions, p. 707
- Teaching Transparencies: 193A
- Holt Biology Videodiscs Lesson 34-2

Classwork Options
- Closure: Recognizing Relationships
- Interactive Exploration 34C

Assignment Options
- *Small Group* Reteaching
- Section Review
- Chapter Review, questions 1b, 11, 12, 13, 14, 19, 20, 30, 31
- Directed Reading Worksheet

34-3 The Excretory System

BLOCK ❺ (45 minutes)

1. Urea is a waste excreted mainly by the kidneys.
2. Nephrons in the kidney filter the blood.
3. Urine formation involves both filtration and the reabsorption of certain substances.

❺ Lecture Resources
- Visual Strategy: Figures 34-8, 34-9
- Demonstration: Relating Structure to Function
- Teaching Transparencies: 218, 220
- Holt Biology Videodiscs Lesson 34-3

Classwork Options
- Exploration 34B
- Laboratory Techniques and Experimental Design: Lab C48

Lecture Concepts

Lesson Resources

34-3 The Excretory System, *continued*

BLOCK ⑥ (45 minutes)

4. ADH, a hormone produced by the hypothalamus, causes the excretion of a more concentrated urine.

5. Kidney disorders include kidney stones and kidney failure.

⑥ Lecture Resources
- ■ Active Reading: Prediction Guide
- ⬡ Teaching Transparencies: 221
- ⬭ Holt Biology Videodiscs Lesson 34-3

Classwork Options
- ■ Closure: Distinguishing Relevant Information

Assignment Options
- ■ Reteaching
- ■ Section Review
- ■ Chapter Review, questions 2c, 3, 15, 16, 17, 18, 21, 23
- ■ Directed Reading Worksheet

Chapter Review and Assessment

BLOCK ⑦ (45 minutes)

Review
- ■ Reteaching Worksheet
- ■ Thinking Skills Worksheet
- ■ Vocabulary Development Worksheet
- ◉ Language Development and Reading Comprehension Audio CD Program: Chapter 34

BLOCK ⑧ (45 minutes)

Assessment
- ■ Alternative Assessment, p. 713
- ■ Portfolio Assessment, p. T39

Chapter Test
- ■ Chapter 34 Test

Test Generator
- ◉ Item bank for customizing Chapter Tests
- ◉ Performance-Based Assessment: Testing Human Digestive Enzymes

Teaching Resources CD-ROM
- ◉ Scoring Rubrics and Classroom Management Checklist

The Portfolio icon denotes items throughout the Teacher's Edition lesson wrap that may be selected for inclusion in student portfolios.

Holt Biology Videodiscs and *Concepts of Biology*

Holt Biology Videodiscs gives you a powerful tool for teaching, review, and assessment. For further information regarding the media on the videodiscs, see ***Holt Biology Videodiscs Teacher's Correlation Guide to Holt Biology: Visualizing Life.***

Concepts of Biology adds interactive lesson plans and extensive tools for customization using CD-ROM technology.

Use the following topic from ***Concepts of Biology*** to help you teach this chapter:
Topic 23: Digestion and Excretion

Laboratory Planning

Text

Materials and preparation instructions appear on the teacher's wrap accompanying each laboratory exercise.

Block 3: Exploration 34A: Determining the Effect of pH on Protein, p. 820

Block 4: Interactive Exploration 34C: Thermodynamics, p. 824

Block 5: Exploration 34B: Conducting a Urinalysis, p. 822

Holt BioSources Laboratory Program

Block 2: Laboratory Techniques and Experimental Design Lab C46: Identifying Food Nutrients

Block 5: Laboratory Techniques and Experimental Design Lab C48: Urinalysis Testing

Holt Biology Supplements

Block 1: Interactive Explorations Laboratory Manual Lab E7: Diet and Weight Loss

Determining Prior Knowledge

- Display a potato, a piece of meat, and a stick of butter. Ask what organic compound makes up the bulk of each of these foods. Have students discuss what functions each of these compounds serve in the human body.
- Exhibit a model or overhead transparency of the human digestive system. Have students identify as many organs as possible and explain the role of each in the digestive process.
- Exhibit a model or overhead transparency of the human excretory system.

Active READING

Technique: Prediction Guide

Before students begin this chapter, write the following statements on the board or the overhead:

1. Fifty percent of your body's fuel should come from carbohydrates.
2. The majority of nutrients in food are released and absorbed in the stomach.
3. The kidneys and the liver both cleanse the blood of toxic substances.

Give students a minute or two to think about the statements listed above and decide whether they agree or disagree with each. Ask volunteers with differing views about each statement to share the reasons for their opinions with the class. Have students read the chapter to see if their opinions are confirmed or if they are changed in any way.

CD-ROM Resources

Concepts of Biology
Topic 23: Digestion and Excretion

CHAPTER 34

Digestion and Excretion

REVIEW
- organic molecules (Section 2-3)
- enzymes (Section 5-1)
- water conservation (Section 24-2)

34-1	**Nutrition: What You Eat and Why**
34-2	**The Digestive System**
34-3	**The Excretory System**

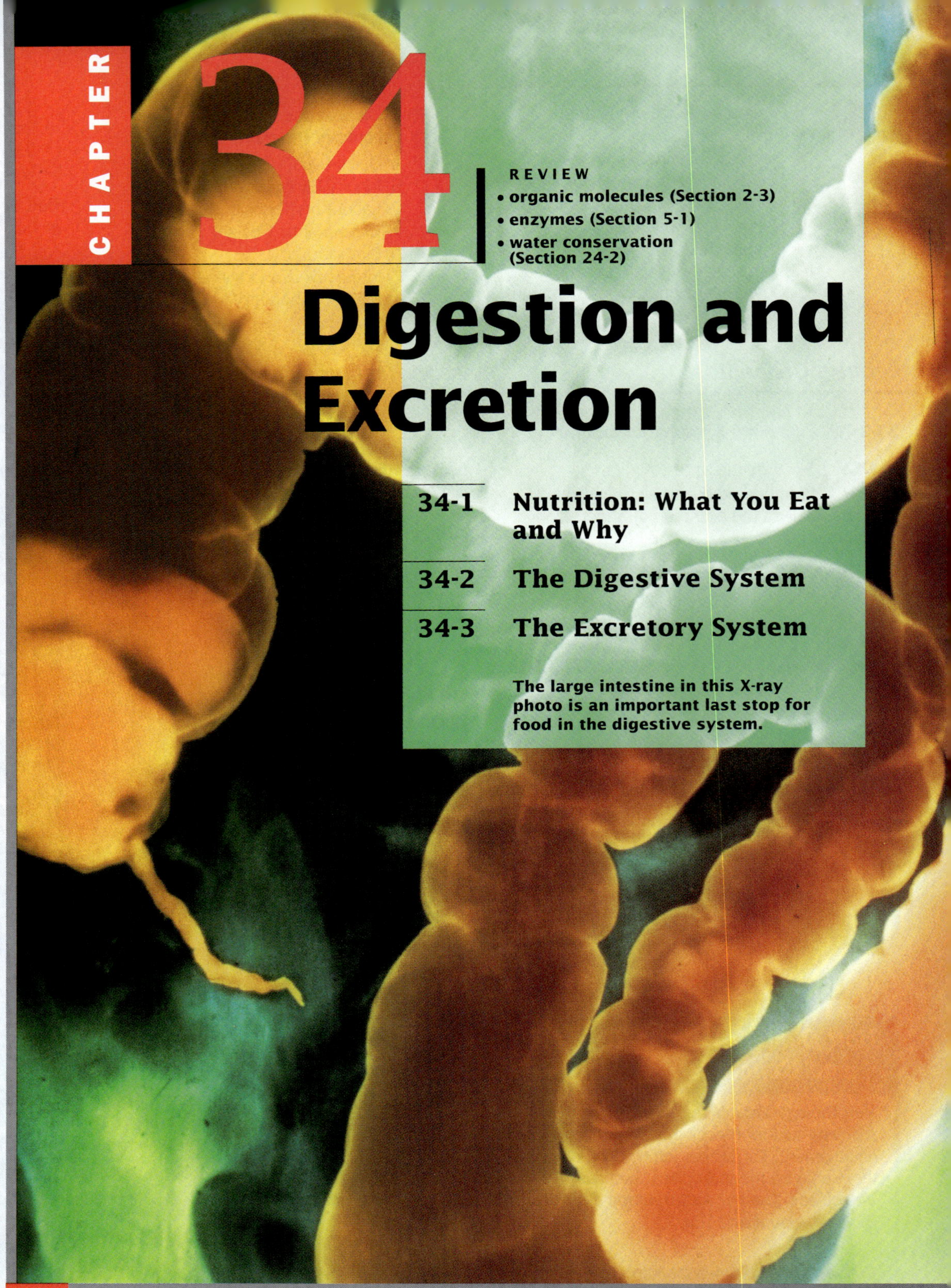

The large intestine in this X-ray photo is an important last stop for food in the digestive system.

698

Author's Rationale This chapter extends Chapter 32's description of how the body obtains and circulates nutrients. The liver and kidney are emphasized as organs that control sugar and water balance. The concept of homeostatic regulation of body function is critical to this chapter, and this theme should be the focus of instruction.

Animals cannot make their own food as plants do, so they must eat other organisms. Some animals, called carnivores, eat only other animals; others, called herbivores, eat only plants. But humans, like bears, are omnivores, eating both plants and animals.

34-1 Nutrition: What You Eat and Why

OBJECTIVES

① **Analyze the relationship between the six essential nutrients and the food pyramid.**

② **List two ways the body uses lipids, proteins, carbohydrates, water, minerals, and vitamins.**

③ **Discuss two factors that lead to nutritional problems in the United States.**

④ **Discuss the effects of the eating disorders anorexia nervosa and bulimia.**

Nutrition and Health

Historically, protein, mineral, and vitamin deficiencies were significant nutritional problems in both developed and developing countries. Today, too much food (overconsumption) and too little physical activity (sedentary lifestyle) are the two major factors leading to nutritional problems in the United States, although nutrient deficiencies still exist. Excess calories and fat lead to **obesity** and heart disease. Excess dietary fat has also been shown to increase the risk of breast and colon cancer. Too much protein harms the kidneys, and too much sodium is linked to high blood pressure. Too little fiber results in poor intestinal elimination and is linked to cancer of the large intestine (colon).

Nutrition is the science that studies how food affects the functions of living organisms. Proper nourishment is essential for healthy biological functioning. When the body does not receive the substances it needs, imbalances occur, biological processes are impaired, and diseases or death can result. Many of today's diets lead not only to inadequate nutrition but also to problems with digestion and elimination.

Essential nutrients are required for life

Food contains nutrients. You need several types of nutrients in your diet. To obtain energy, your body uses carbohydrates, lipids, and proteins as fuel nutrients. To regulate how your body uses energy from the fuel nutrients, your body needs water, minerals, and vitamins, which do not provide energy. From these six essential nutrients, your body gets all it needs in order to grow and to maintain and repair itself. Most of the food and beverages you consume provide a combination of the six nutrients. **Table 34-1** lists the nutrients required in the diet.

Table 34-1 Essential Nutrients

Fuel nutrients	Regulatory nutrients
Carbohydrates	Water
Protein	Minerals
Fats	Vitamins

699

Phase One
Preparation

Scheduling
See the **Lesson Planning Guide** on pages 697A and 697B for lecture, classwork, and assignment options for Section 34-1.

Phase Two
Teaching Strategies

Demonstration
● **Summarizing Information**
To help students organize the information they acquire from reading this section, have them prepare a table with the headings *Carbohydrates, Proteins, Lipids, Vitamins, Minerals,* and *Water.* Down the left side have them write *Functions in the Human Body, Food Sources,* and *Additional Comments.* Have students complete the table as they read this section.

Connection: *Chapter 5*

Cellular Respiration
Review how glucose is metabolized in aerobic respiration to produce ATP, which serves as the energy currency of the cell.

Videodisc Resources

Holt Biology Videodiscs

Lesson 34-1: Nutrition: What You Eat and Why

Key to Strategies
Teaching Strategies are keyed to three tiers of learning.

● **Understanding Concepts (Tier I)**
Content mastery and comprehension

■ **Applying Information (Tier II)**
Applying and analyzing content

▲ **Critical Thinking (Tier III)**
Practicing evaluative thinking

Digestion and Excretion   699

Figure 34-1
a The USDA Food Guide Pyramid serves as a guide for healthy eating. The placement of each food group reminds you which groups are needed in abundance and which ones should be eaten in smaller amounts.

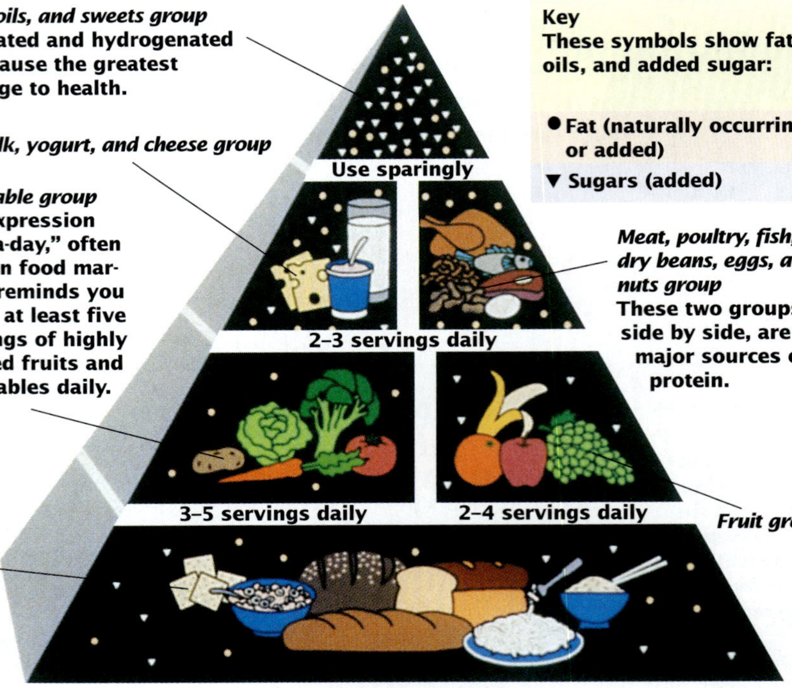

Fats, oils, and sweets group
Saturated and hydrogenated fats cause the greatest damage to health.

Milk, yogurt, and cheese group

Vegetable group
The expression "five-a-day," often seen in food markets, reminds you to eat at least five servings of highly colored fruits and vegetables daily.

Bread, cereal, rice, and pasta group
This group is the foundation of a healthy diet.

Key
These symbols show fats, oils, and added sugar:
● Fat (naturally occurring or added)
▼ Sugars (added)

Meat, poultry, fish, dry beans, eggs, and nuts group
These two groups, side by side, are the major sources of protein.

Fruit group

Use sparingly
2–3 servings daily
3–5 servings daily
2–4 servings daily
6–11 servings daily

Food Energy

b Each group of fuel nutrients should provide a specific percentage of the day's total calories.

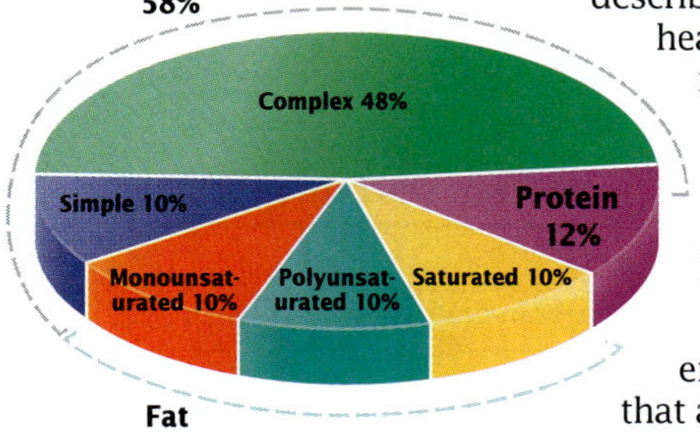

Carbohydrate 58%
Complex 48%
Simple 10%
Protein 12%
Monounsaturated 10%
Polyunsaturated 10%
Saturated 10%
Fat 30%

Energy stored in food is trapped in chemical bonds. When these bonds are broken in the body, the energy is released and then captured again in a form that the body can use. The amount of energy provided by the energy nutrients is measured in calories. A calorie is the unit of measurement used to describe the amount of heat energy that is released from food or that is used during physical activity. Three types of nutrients provide energy bonds that are useful to the human body.

Carbohydrates are the body's main source of fuel
Carbohydrates provide the most readily available energy for your body. More than half of your body's energy needs should come from those carbo-

hydrates classified as starches and sugars. Recall that glucose, a simple sugar, is the molecule that all of your cells use for energy. Glucose and other naturally occurring sugars are found in many foods, especially fruits, vegetables, and dairy foods. Simple sugars, such as glucose, are combined into longer chains to make complex carbohydrates called starches. Cereals, grains, seeds, and beans are examples of foods high in complex carbohydrates. **Figure 34-1** shows the USDA Food Guide Pyramid, a model for creating a healthful diet. Notice that carbohydrate foods are the foundation of a healthy diet. Other complex carbohydrates, such as cellulose, are components of plant tissues but are not digested by humans. These indigestible carbohydrates provide roughage, or fiber, in our diets. Fiber does not provide energy, but it is so important in the body that it is sometimes called the seventh essential nutrient. Whole grains, legumes, fruits, and vegetables are high in fiber.

Matter of Fact: High Fat and Seizure Free

Did you know that a diet high in fat (a ketogenic diet) can stop epileptic seizures in some children by forcing their bodies into ketosis? An example of such a meal is 14 g of melted butter, 50 g of heavy whipping cream, 14 g of chicken, 16 g of apple, and 30 g of sugar-free gelatin. By eliminating carbohydrates and sugars, the body is forced to fast metabolically. The ketones produced from burning fats in metabolism inhibit seizures. See the article "High Fat and Seizure Free" in the April 1995 *Johns Hopkins Magazine,* or call 410-955-9100 (JHU Pediatric Epilepsy Center).

Lipids store highly concentrated energy

Lipids such as fats (solid at room temperature) and oils (liquid at room temperature) are very concentrated energy sources. One gram of fat provides more than twice as much energy as one gram of carbohydrate or protein. Lipids in the body form the bilayer foundation of cell membranes and organelles; thus, they are vital to the life of cells. Fats in the diet act as a solvent for fat-soluble vitamins and essential fatty acids. Dietary fats also give a sense of satisfaction after eating, because they take a long time to digest.

Fats in the diet are classified according to their chemical makeup. Recall that saturated fats and too many calories from fat in the diet are linked to cardiovascular disease, obesity, and certain kinds of cancer. Saturated fats are found in animal fats and animal protein, coconut and palm oils, and vegetable oils that have been processed to be a solid at room temperature (hydrogenated). Monounsaturated fats are found in canola, olive, and peanut oils. Polyunsaturated fats are found in safflower, corn, soybean, and cottonseed oils, among others. Monounsaturated and polyunsaturated fats should each provide about 10 percent of the day's calories. Saturated fats should provide 10 percent or less of the day's calories. **Figure 34-2** shows a food label that provides information about calories and nutrients found in food.

Figure 34-2
"Nutrition Facts" is the title for the new food label required by law. The food label below helps consumers make food choices based on the nutrients that are most important to health.

1. *Serving size* is based on the amount of the food people usually eat. Label calculations are for one serving of the food.

2. *Total fat* displays the amount of all kinds of fat in the food.

3. *Total carbohydrate* shows the amounts of complex carbohydrates, fiber, and sugar.

Nutrition Facts

Serving Size ¾ cup (30g)
Servings Per Container About 14

Amount Per Serving	Corn Crunch	with ½ cup skim milk
Calories	120	160
Calories from Fat	15	20

	% Daily Value**	
Total Fat 2g*	3%	3%
Saturated Fat 0g	0%	0%
Cholesterol 0mg	0%	1%
Sodium 160mg	7%	9%
Potassium 65mg	2%	8%
Total Carbohydrate 25g	8%	10%
Dietary Fiber 3g		
Sugars 3g		
Other Carbohydrate 11g		
Protein 2g		

Vitamin A	15%	20%
Vitamin C	25%	25%
Calcium	2%	15%
Iron	25%	25%
Vitamin D	0%	10%
Thiamin	25%	30%
Riboflavin	25%	35%
Niacin	25%	25%
Vitamin B6	25%	25%
Folic Acid	25%	25%
Phosphorus	6%	20%
Zinc	25%	30%

*Amount in Cereal. A serving of cereal plus skim milk provides 2g fat, less 5mg cholesterol, 220mg sodium, 270mg potassium, 31g carbohydrate (19g sugars) and 6g protein.

**Percent Daily Values are based on a 2,000 calorie diet. Your daily values may be higher or lower depending on your calorie needs:

	Calories	2,000	2,500
Total Fat	Less than	65g	80g
Sat Fat	Less than	20g	25g
Cholesterol	Less than	300mg	300mg
Sodium	Less than	2,400mg	2,400mg
Potassium		3,500mg	3,500mg
Total Carbohydrate		300g	375g
Dietary Fiber		25g	30g

4. *Calories from fat* tells how many calories in the food come from fat.

5. *Cholesterol* and *sodium* amounts are also required on the label. A teaspoon of table salt contains about 2 g of sodium.

6. *Daily values* footnote lists the current nutrition recommendations for selected essential nutrients.

7. Some labels tell the approximate number of calories per gram of carbohydrate, fat, and protein.

Demonstration

● Summarizing Information

Obtain a list from a fast-food establishment that describes the nutritional content of its various food products. Have students describe a typical meal they might have at this restaurant. Then have them compare the nutritional content of this meal with some of the recommended guidelines given in Figure 34-1. As a follow-up activity, bring in several cans or packages of food. Have students determine from the labels the nutritional components of the food, and have them decide what part(s) of the food pyramid (Figure 34-1) that particular food fulfills.

Visual Strategy — Figure 34-2

● Interpreting Data

Have students discuss and explain what the seven parts of the new food labels mean. *(Student answers will vary.)*

Fats in the Diet

● Organizing Data

Using information about fats from this chapter and Chapter 2, have students make a **Graphic Organizer** similar to the one shown at the bottom of this page to illustrate the categories and examples of fats in the diet. Ask students to include the bonding between carbon atoms (from Chapter 2) and some dietary examples.

Graphic Organizer

Use the following graphic organizer with the teaching strategy **Fats in the Diet,** on page 701.

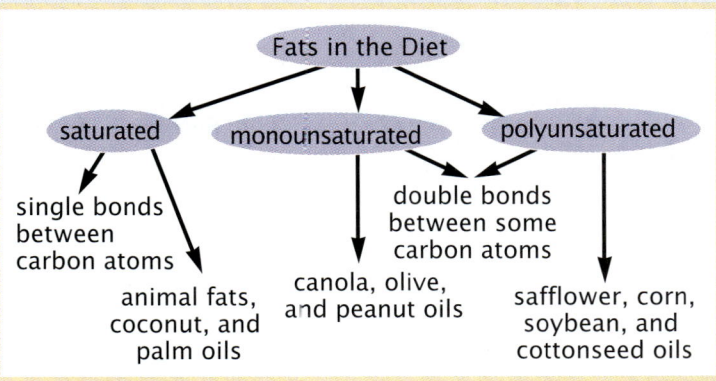

Key to Strategies

- ● Understanding Concepts (Tier I)
- ■ Applying Information (Tier II)
- ▲ Critical Thinking (Tier III)

Digestion and Excretion 701

Technique: Reading Hint

Tell students that the tables on pages 702 and 703 provide additional important material about minerals and vitamins. Remind them to review the tables after they read the main body of the text.

Decision Making

■ Analyzing Data

Have students make a list of protein food sources and note whether the food source is a "complete" or "incomplete" (all the basic amino acids or only partial) source of protein. Using the USDA Guide to Vegetarian Diets or your own knowledge, discuss the different types of vegetarian diets, such as (1) omitting only red meat, (2) omitting all "meat" but eating fish, (3) omitting all meat but eating animal products such as milk and eggs, and (4) omitting all meat and animal products. Have students create a meal of each type of "vegetarian" diet and decide if it is difficult or easy to obtain a nutritionally sound diet in each category.

Visual Strategy   Table 34-2

● Identifying Functions

Use the information in this table as a way of reviewing some points made about the human body in previous chapters. For example, a deficiency of calcium in later life can lead to osteoporosis (Chapter 29), a lack of iodine can cause goiter (Chapter 31), iron deficiency can result in anemia (Chapter 32), phosphorus is needed for bone growth (Chapter 29), and both potassium and sodium play key roles in nerve impulse conduction (Chapter 30).

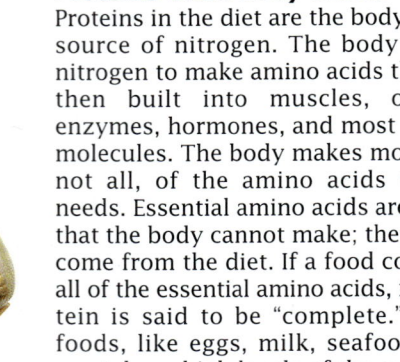

Corn:
calcium

Tomatoes:
potassium

Peas:
iron

Celery:
sodium

Proteins build body tissue

Proteins in the diet are the body's only source of nitrogen. The body needs nitrogen to make amino acids that are then built into muscles, organs, enzymes, hormones, and most carrier molecules. The body makes most, but not all, of the amino acids that it needs. Essential amino acids are those that the body cannot make; they must come from the diet. If a food contains all of the essential amino acids, its protein is said to be "complete." Some foods, like eggs, milk, seafood, and meat, have high levels of the essential amino acids. Other foods, such as legumes, grains, nuts, and seeds, have high levels of some essential amino acids and low levels of others. Vegetarians must plan their diets to get a balanced level of the essential amino acids. Foods can be combined to improve their amino acid balance. For instance, combinations like beans and rice or macaroni and cheese provide a more complete variety of protein than the individual foods would provide if eaten separately. Nutritious food combinations are staples in many cultures and complement each other's protein.

Regulatory Nutrients

The biological processes that release food energy are regulated by three kinds of nutrients that do not provide energy.

Water is the most vital nutrient

Water is the most vital nutrient, but its importance is often overlooked and its intake is often low. You can live for weeks without food, but you can live only a few days without water. Water acts as a lubricant, a solvent, and a coolant. Drinking one-half of an ounce of water daily for each pound of body weight will provide an adequate daily intake. You can monitor to see if you are drinking enough water throughout the day. When your water intake is adequate, your urine will be pale to almost clear in color.

Minerals are built into bone, essential compounds, and enzymes

Unlike other nutrients, **minerals** are inorganic compounds—they are not made by living things and must be obtained elsewhere. Plants absorb minerals from the water or soil, and animals get minerals by eating plants or plant-eating animals. Minerals are not broken down within the body. Some minerals, such as iron, copper, iodine, and zinc, are called trace elements because they are needed in very small amounts. Besides their use in body structure, specific minerals are required for the normal action of enzymes. Table 34-2 lists some minerals, their sources, and their functions.

Table 34-2 Important Minerals and Their Functions

Mineral	Function	Sources
Calcium	Needed for building bones and teeth; nerve and muscle function	Dairy products, legumes, dark green leafy vegetables
Iodine	Essential for production of thyroid hormone	Seafood, seaweed, spinach, iodized salt
Iron	Found in hemoglobin; needed for some enzymes	Meats, whole grains, legumes, dark green leafy vegetables
Potassium	Needed for normal metabolism; nerve and muscle function	Meats, poultry, fish, fruits, vegetables
Sodium	Essential for proper water balance in cells and tissues; bio-electrical conduction	Widely distributed in nature

Multicultural Perspective: The Western World

Inform students that Americans and Western Europeans suffer nutritional problems stemming from improper diets. For example, people in developed countries, on average, consume about 20 times more salt than their bodies need. Such excess salt may be associated with high blood pressure.

Whole-grain bread:
B-complex vitamins,
vitamins E, K

spinach:
carotenoids,
vitamins C, E, K

Tangerine:
vitamin C

Yellow
pepper:
carotenoids

Cheese:
vitamins A, B₂

Vitamins are needed in small amounts for regulation

Vitamins are organic substances needed by the body in very small amounts. Vitamins activate enzymes and regulate the release of energy in the body.

There are two classes of vitamins: those that are fat-soluble and those that are water-soluble. Fat-soluble vitamins, including vitamins A, D, E, and K, can accumulate in body fat and in the liver. Excessive amounts of these vitamins can be harmful. Plants provide substances called carotenoids that form vitamin A in the human body.

These substances are not toxic to the body, as excessive vitamin A can be.

Water-soluble vitamins, like vitamins B and C, are not stored in body tissue. Because these vitamins easily dissolve in water, any excess is excreted in urine. Therefore, regular, balanced sources of water-soluble vitamins must be available to prevent deficiencies. A varied diet containing foods from each of the groups in the food pyramid is recommended in order to provide adequate amounts of vitamins and minerals. **Table 34-3** lists some common vitamins and their sources, and explains their various functions.

Table 34-3 Some Important Vitamins and Their Functions

Vitamin	Function	Sources	Deficiency
Vitamin A (fat-soluble) Carotenoids	Maintains healthy eyes, skin, bones, teeth; keeps lining of digestive tract resistant to infection	Milk products, liver, bright fruit and vegetables and dark green leafy vegetables	Night blindness, impaired growth
Vitamin B₁ Thiamine (water-soluble)	Assists with conversion of carbohydrates to energy; normal appetite and digestion; nervous system function	Pork products, liver, legumes, enriched and whole-grain breads, cereals, nuts	Beriberi (inflamed nerves, muscle weakness, heart problems)
Vitamin B₂ Riboflavin (water-soluble)	Assists with nerve cell function; healthy appetite; release of energy from carbohydrates, protein, and fats	Dairy foods, eggs, whole-grain products, meat, dried beans, enriched breads, cereals, and pasta	Cheilosis (skin sores on nose and lips, sensitive eyes)
Vitamin B₃ Niacin (water-soluble)	Maintenance of normal metabolism, digestion, nerve function, energy release	Red meats, organ meats, fish, enriched breads and cereals, green vegetables	Pellagra (soreness of tongue and lips, diarrhea, irritability, and depression)
Vitamin B₁₂ (water-soluble)	Necessary for formation of red blood cells; normal cell function	Lean meats, liver, egg products, milk, cheese	Pernicious anemia, stunted growth
Vitamin C (water-soluble)	Needed for normal wound healing and the development of connective tissues, including those holding teeth	Citrus fruits, melons, green vegetables, potatoes	Scurvy (slow healing of wounds, bleeding gums, and loose teeth)
Vitamin D (fat-soluble)	Promotes normal growth; assists with calcium and phosphorus use in building bones and teeth	Fish-liver oils, fortified milk, liver, egg yolk, salmon, tuna	Rickets (inadequate growth of bones and teeth)
Vitamin E (fat-soluble)	Prevents destruction of red blood cells; needed for certain enzymes	Wheat germ, vegetable oils, legumes, nuts, dark green vegetables	Red blood cell rupture, causing anemia
Vitamin K (fat-soluble)	Assists with blood clotting	Leafy green vegetables and vegetable oils, tomatoes, potatoes	Slow blood clotting, hemorrhage

703

Connection: *Chapter 5*

Enzymes

Review the role of enzymes as biological catalysts. Point out that some enzymes cannot work unless they are first activated by coenzymes, which are often vitamins. Remind the students that enzymes can be reused many times. Have students explain why vitamins that function as coenzymes are needed in only small amounts. *(They can be reused many times.)*

Demonstration

● **Summarizing Information**

Pass a bottle of vitamin tablets around the class. Have students examine the label. Emphasize that taking too many fat-soluble vitamins can lead to health problems. For example, excessive amounts of vitamins A and D can cause disorders of the bones.

Visual Strategy | **Table 34-3**

● **Identifying Functions**

As students pass around the bottle of vitamin tablets, have them identify vitamins listed on the label but not listed on this table. List these additional vitamins on the board or overhead. Have students make Table 34-3 more complete by checking references to determine the function, sources, and deficiency information for each of the vitamins listed on the board or overhead.

Key to Strategies

● **Understanding Concepts (Tier I)**

■ **Applying Information (Tier II)**

▲ **Critical Thinking (Tier III)**

Eating Disorders

Millions of teens, afraid of gaining weight, are on weight-reducing diets. Unfortunately, obsessive dieting sometimes leads to eating disorders. Anorexia nervosa *(an oh RECK see ah ner VOH sah)* is an eating disorder in which afflicted people starve themselves. In contrast, bulimia *(byoo LEE mee uh)* is a disorder characterized by bingeing (consuming a large amount of food in a short time) and purging, either by self-induced vomiting or by taking laxatives, enemas, or diuretics (fluid pills).

Individuals with anorexia (such as the young woman in **Figure 34-3**) and bulimia have a distorted perception of their body and believe they are too fat. They see their eating behavior as a way to control their weight. The anorexic or bulimic is very secretive about eating. Those around them often do not know there is a problem. In addition, some anorexics and bulimics exercise obsessively. About 1 in 100 females between the ages of 12 and 18 are estimated to be anorexic. Between five to fifteen percent of people with eating disorders are male.

The metabolic changes caused by anorexia or bulimia are serious. Females may stop menstruating because they lose too much body fat and the level of sex hormones falls. Many anorexics never mature sexually. In addition, muscle mass and bone mass are lost, hair and skin become dry, and nails are brittle. Although bulimics may appear healthier than individuals with anorexia, bulimia leads to serious trauma to the lining of the mouth, stomach, and esophagus due to repeated vomiting. Tooth enamel may erode because of long-term exposure to stomach acids, and gums pull away from the teeth. Fatigue and muscle cramps are common because minerals are lost during purging. The binge-purge routine is characteristic of bulimia whether it occurs once a month or several times a day. At its most extreme, bulimia can lead to death by heart failure, stomach rupture, or kidney failure. Both anorexia and bulimia, however, can be managed with a combination of medical treatment, counseling, and family support.

"I got to be very thin, but I thought I looked normal. The disease persists to this day as a constant battle between my perception of my body and my common sense."
–Roxanne A.

Figure 34-3
Roxanne is a recovering anorexic. Today, she looks and feels healthy.

SECTION REVIEW

1. What are the six nutrients that the body requires for good health?

2. What roles do each of the six nutrients play in the body?

3. Which diseases are caused by nutrient deficiencies? by excesses?

4. What kind of damage can an eating disorder do to the body?

ANSWERS TO SECTION REVIEW

1. carbohydrates, proteins, lipids, vitamins, minerals, and water

2. Carbohydrates provide roughage and serve as the body's main source of energy; proteins provide essential amino acids and serve as the building blocks for tissue growth and repair; lipids store energy and serve as a major structural material for cells; vitamins regulate the production of energy and activate enzymes; minerals regulate body functions; and water is the basis of all metabolic activities—serving as a lubricant, the universal solvent, and a coolant.

3. Refer to page 699 and Table 34-3 on page 703.

4. Students should discuss anorexia nervosa and bulimia and the damage they do to the body, such as severe malnutrition, heart irregularities, ruptured stomach, kidney failure, and even death.

Pediatrics

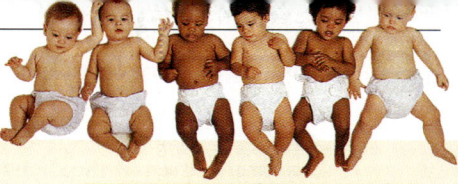

What would it be like to . . .

- diagnose and treat ailments and diseases in children?
- teach children about preventive medicine?
- contribute to the health of children in your community?

These are just a few of the daily adventures experienced by people working in the field of pediatrics.

Pediatrics: What Is It?

Pediatricians generally provide medical care for children from infancy through adolescence. In infants, a pediatrician is likely to encounter birth defects, infectious diseases, and problems arising from prematurity. In older children, a pediatrician is more likely to treat infectious diseases and injuries due to accidents. A regular task of a pediatrician is teaching children how to prevent, identify, and deal with health problems.

Science/Math Career Preparation

High school
- English
- Science

College
- Biology
- Chemistry
- Psychology

Medical school
- Biochemistry
- Physiology
- Anatomy
- Pathology

Employment Outlook

As the world population climbs, the need for pediatricians throughout the world will increase dramatically.

Career Focus: Dr. Cheryl Coldwater
Pediatrician

"As a child I had to spend a lot of time in the hospital because I was born with a birth defect—a broken leg that healed improperly in the womb. I wore a brace until I was six, at which point my leg was amputated. That way I could wear a prosthesis and have a greater range of movement.

"In high school, I volunteered in pediatrics in a hospital, weighing babies and helping nurses. I won't deny that medical school was hard work—long hours of intense study. However, working with patients was easy. That's what I like best about being a doctor—working with children."

What I Do: "As a pediatrician, I concentrate on preventive medicine. I discuss the importance of proper nutrition with young children. It's important for them to understand that learning to eat healthfully can prevent many kinds of health problems later. Other subjects I address include exercise, safety, and drugs and alcohol. Talking directly and frankly with children lets them know that there are adults other than their parents who care about them."

To Find Out More

1 For further information, write to:
American Academy of Pediatrics
141 N.W. Point Blvd.
P. O. Box 927
Elk Grove Village, IL 60009

2 Visit your school counselor and library to find out what colleges and universities offer programs in pediatrics. Review the prerequisites. Make a poster showing the range of job opportunities in this field.

3 Find articles that describe efforts of the Centers for Disease Control and the World Health Organization to develop immunization services worldwide. Prepare a report that convinces readers of the importance of immunization.

Career Opportunities

Making Informed Decisions

1. Have students brainstorm ideas about the following questions:

If you wanted a career in pediatrics...
- what kind of personality traits would be essential?
- which subjects should you study in high school? in college?
- what kinds of extracurricular activities should you pursue?
- what kind of practical experience should you gain?
- what kind of issues would interest you?

Write student responses on the board or on the overhead.

2. Pose the following situation: You are a pediatrician in a densely populated, multicultural community. You have just learned that the state government is trying to pass legislation that will cut funding for a health program that provides services for disadvantaged women and children. Write a letter to the editor of a local newspaper explaining why this legislation should not be passed.

3. Have small groups of students create a model of human population growth that includes factors that affect birth rate and infant mortality, such as education, nutrition, and availability of prenatal care and pediatricians.

Scheduling

See the **Lesson Planning Guide** on pages 697A and 697B for lecture, classwork, and assignment options for Section 34-2.

Visual Strategy Videodisc

■ Analyzing Information

To introduce the lesson, use *Video—Digestive System* (4 min 50 s) shown in Chapter 34 Section 34-2 of *Holt Biology Videodiscs Teacher's Correlation Guide to Holt Biology: Visualizing Life.* Before viewing the video, ask students where they think most digestion takes place. Have them write their answer on a sheet of paper. Tell students to watch the video to see if their answer is correct. After viewing the video, ask students to write a paragraph explaining whether they still agree with their original answer and why. *(Most digestion takes place in the small intestine.)*

Demonstration

● Identifying Functions

Pour approximately 1.25 L (2.6 pt) of water into a suitable container, and tell students that this represents the average amount of saliva each of them produces in one day.

Supplies of energy and building materials for the body exist only in potential forms in food. Whatever we eat must be processed into smaller pieces before it can be used by the body. Food undergoes this transformation in the digestive system, a hollow muscular tube where food is broken down and either absorbed or eliminated.

34-2 The Digestive System

OBJECTIVES

1 **List the main organs of the digestive system.**

2 **Identify the sites of digestion for each of the three fuel nutrients.**

3 **Describe the absorption of food from the digestive tract.**

4 **Explain the roles of the pancreas and liver in the digestive system.**

Digestion

Suppose you eat a taco for lunch. The taco is rich in the three kinds of fuel nutrients found in food. The tortilla and beans are made of complex carbohydrates. Proteins occur in the meat, cheese, corn, and beans. Fats are found in the meat and cheese. The taco also contains essential vitamins, minerals, water, and some fiber. When you eat the taco, however, the nutrient-containing substances found within it are too large for your body to use immediately. As the taco travels through your digestive system, a journey of more than 8 m (26 ft), it is crushed and churned, and the nutrients in it are broken down by various chemicals in order to release its store of energy and building materials. In short, it is digested.

Digestion begins in the mouth

Taking a bite of the taco, as shown in **Figure 34-4**, begins the process of digestion. As the food is chewed, it is broken apart so that it will be accessible to digestive enzymes. You have probably noticed that your mouth "waters" when you are hungry and you smell or see food (or sometimes just think of food). Salivary glands lying in and near the mouth increase their production of saliva before you eat, and saliva plays an important role in digestion. It moistens and lubricates food, making it easier to swallow. Saliva also contains an enzyme that begins to break down starches present in the food.

After being chewed, food is forced into the rest of the digestive tract by swallowing. The tongue and floor of the mouth rise, squeezing food into a muscular tube called the **esophagus**

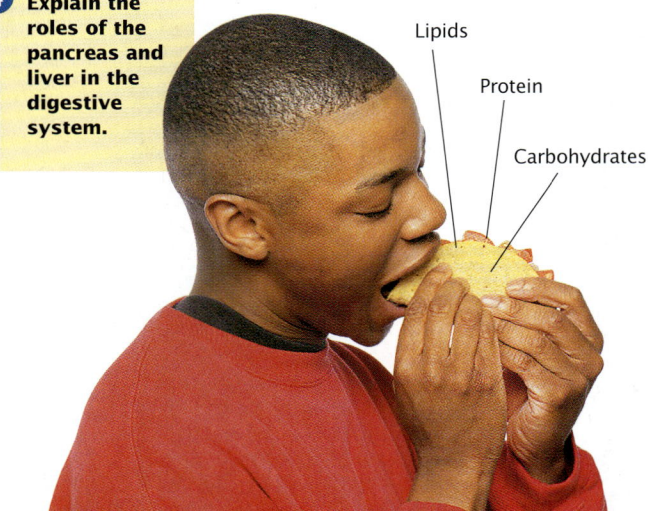

Lipids

Protein

Carbohydrates

Figure 34-4
Chewing not only makes a taco easier to swallow but also increases the surface area of the food so that digestive enzymes can come into contact with more of the food.

Videodisc Resources

Holt Biology Videodiscs
Lesson 34-2: The Digestive System

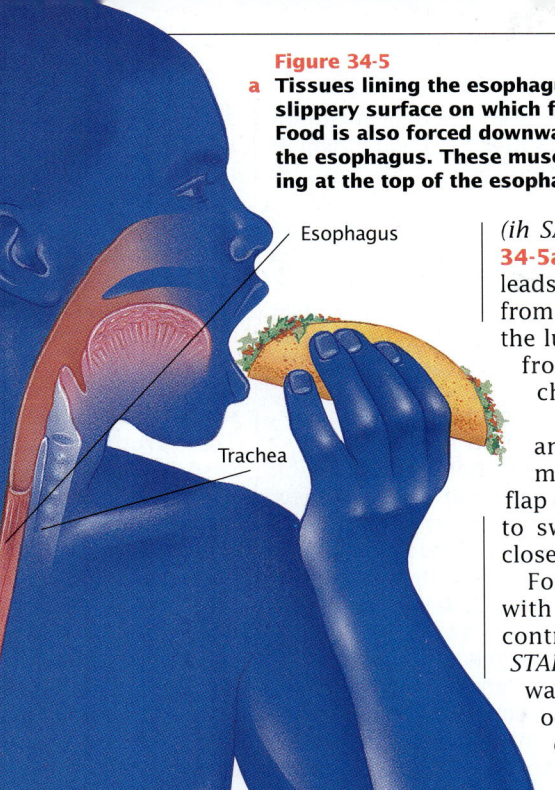

Figure 34-5

a Tissues lining the esophagus secrete mucus, forming a slippery surface on which food slides toward the stomach. Food is also forced downward by smooth muscles ringing the esophagus. These muscles contract in sequence, starting at the top of the esophagus and proceeding downward.

Esophagus

Trachea

Liver

b The stomach is a stretchable J-shaped bag where food is temporarily stored. The principal activity of the stomach is to begin the digestion of protein.

Pancreas

Gallbladder

Small intestine

Large intestine

Rectum

(ih SAHF uh guhs), shown in **Figure 34-5a**. A second tube, the trachea, leads to the lungs. What prevents food from going down the wrong tube into the lungs? As you swallow, touch the front of your neck just under your chin. You should feel the larynx (LAR ihnks), or voice box, slide up and then back down. The upward movement of the larynx causes a flap of tissue overhanging the trachea to swing down like a trapdoor and close off the trachea.

Food slides down the esophagus with the help of mucus and muscle contractions. **Peristalsis** (pehr uh STAHL sis) is the name given to this wavelike contraction, which also occurs in the stomach and the rest of the digestive tract. You can swallow food while standing on your head because of peristalsis.

Digestion continues in the stomach

After moving through the 25 cm (9.8 in.) length of the esophagus, the bite of food reaches the stomach, as shown in **Figure 34-5b**. The stomach can expand to 1-1.5 L (about 1.5 qts) of food, more than 50 times its empty volume. Cells in the stomach lining release concentrated hydrochloric acid (HCl). Consequently, stomach pH is between 1.5 and 2.5, easily strong enough to damage the stomach lining if it were not protected by a thick coating of mucus. Hydrochloric acid and **pepsin**, an enzyme present in the stomach during digestion, break proteins into small chains of amino acids. Agitating this mixture of food, acid, and enzymes are peristaltic waves that pulsate through the stomach's muscular walls. A small amount of lipid digestion takes place in the stomach by a lipase, an enzyme that breaks down lipids.

707

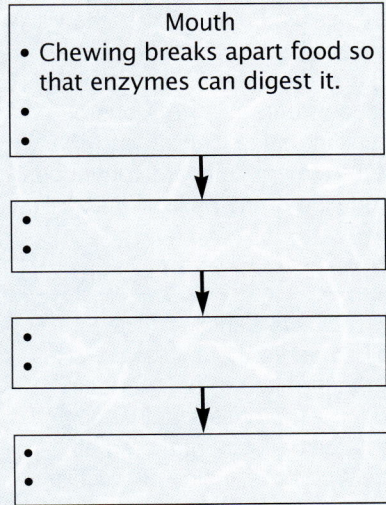

Matter of Fact: Absorption in the Stomach

Although partially digested, food is not absorbed by the stomach. However, both alcohol and aspirin are absorbed from the stomach directly into the bloodstream, accounting for their fast-acting effects on the body.

Activity in the Intestines

The swallowed bites of taco spend up to four hours in the stomach, where the food is reduced to a thin liquid. Most of the proteins in the taco are broken down in the stomach. Squeezed out of the stomach by peristalsis, the food then moves into the small intestine. Six meters (20 ft) of small intestine are tightly coiled within your abdomen.

The small intestine absorbs nutrients
The rest of digestion occurs in the entrance to the **small intestine**. The first 25 cm (9.8 in.) of the small intestine is known as the duodenum *(doo uh DEE nuhm)*, and it is here that the remaining carbohydrates and proteins are broken down. In adults, almost all lipids are digested in the small intestine. As in the stomach, peristalsis in the duodenum churns its contents.

The remaining 90 percent of the small intestine has a critical function: it absorbs the nutrients released by digestion and transfers them to the blood. Water is also absorbed. The small intestine is well adapted for absorption. In a cutaway view, the intestine looks as if it were lined with

shag carpeting, as shown in **Figure 34-6c**. The projections of the intestinal lining are **villi** (singular, villus). Each villus is coated with hairlike projections known as **microvilli**. With villi and microvilli, the total surface area available for absorption in the small intestine is about 300 m^2 (3,229 ft^2)—an area larger than a tennis court.

The pancreas and liver secrete digestive enzymes
The products of digestion are absorbed into the bloodstream during the three to six hours that food spends in the small intestine. Enzymes and chemicals secreted by the upper end of the small intestine cause additional food breakdown. Most of these secretions come from two organs, the **liver** and the **pancreas**. In Chapter 31 you studied the role of the pancreas in regulating blood sugar. The pancreas also secretes a variety of digestive enzymes. These enzymes break down carbohydrates into simple sugars. They also split proteins into amino acids, and fats into short chains of fatty acids. In addition, the pancreas secretes bicarbonate (the chemical found in antacids and baking soda),

Figure 34-6
a The small intestine is located in the lower abdomen.

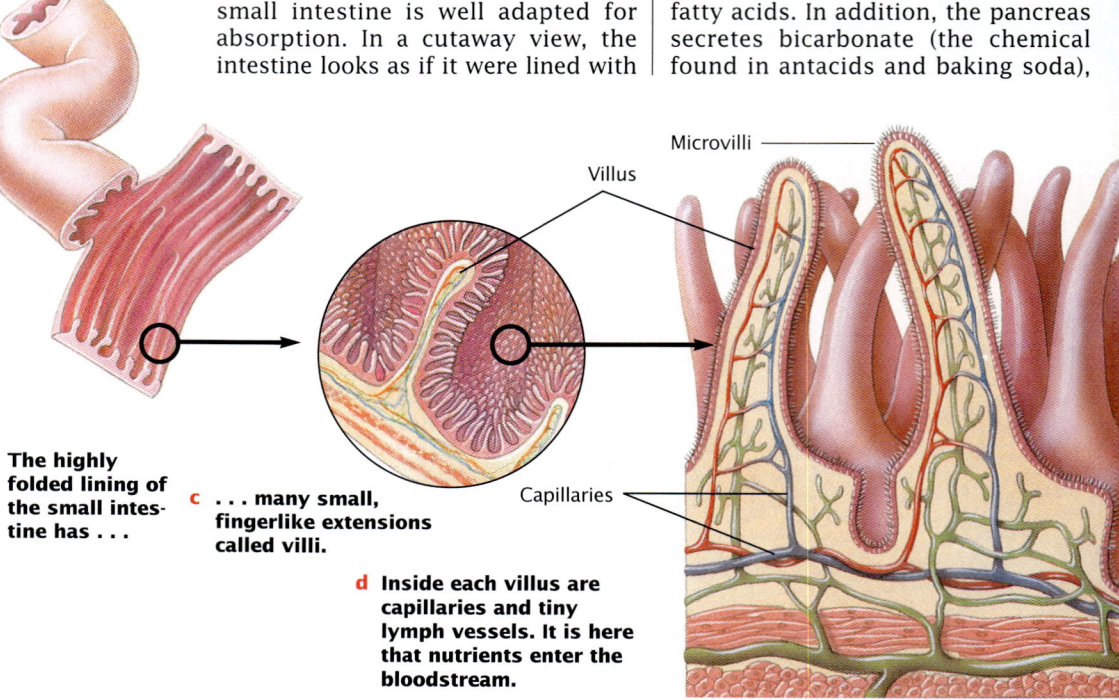

b The highly folded lining of the small intestine has . . .

c . . . many small, fingerlike extensions called villi.

d Inside each villus are capillaries and tiny lymph vessels. It is here that nutrients enter the bloodstream.

Microvilli

Villus

Capillaries

which helps neutralize the stomach acids so that lipid digestion can proceed and so that the acids do not digest the walls of the small intestine. When too much stomach acid is produced, the pancreas cannot form enough bicarbonate to compensate and acid begins to eat away the lining of the small intestine or stomach. Stress and certain foods (alcohol and coffee) or medications (aspirin) can cause the stomach to secrete excess acid.

Recall from Chapter 3 that fats are not soluble in water. Fat molecules avoid water and form small clusters or globules in the stomach. Your liver secretes bile, a greenish fluid that emulsifies fat globules so that they can be broken down and absorbed. The gall-bladder is a green muscular sac, attached to the liver, that stores bile until it is needed in the small intestine.

Nutrients are collected in the liver

After digested food molecules are absorbed into the bloodstream, they go first to the liver. The liver, shown in **Figure 34-7**, then sends these molecules into the rest of the bloodstream as needed. For example, when you eat a meal, the liver removes excess glucose from the blood and stores it as glycogen. When the level of glucose in the blood falls, glucagon causes the liver to release some of this glucose back into the blood. The liver also detoxifies many substances. For instance, it produces enzymes that break down drugs and alcohol.

The large intestine compacts wastes

Your lunch-time taco now is largely undigestible material such as cellulose. From the small intestine, what is left of the food now moves into the **large intestine**. The large intestine's role is to briefly store and compact this undigestible material and then, with the help of adequate dietary fiber and water, eliminate it. Some nutrients, including water, sodium, and vitamin K, are absorbed, and a number of B-vitamins and vitamin K are made in the large intestine. These vitamins are produced by the billions of beneficial bacteria living in the large intestine. In fact, the bacteria in the large intestine may play an important role in nourishing their host and in resisting disease.

After traveling the 1.5 m (5 ft) length of the large intestine, what remains of the taco passes out through the rectum and anus as feces. Feces contain undigested food, such as cellulose, and bacteria.

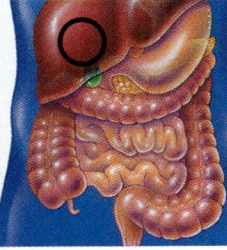

Figure 34-7
a **The liver, a football-sized organ, is located above and to the right of the stomach, just below the diaphragm.**

b **The liver produces bile, stores nutrients, regulates the level of blood sugar, and filters the blood.**

SECTION
REVIEW

1 What organs are needed to digest food?

2 Which nutrient is digested mainly in the stomach? in the small intestine?

3 How is the small intestine specialized for absorption?

4 How would digestion be affected if the pancreas or liver were damaged?

ANSWERS TO SECTION REVIEW

1 The mouth, stomach, and small intestines are needed to digest food.

2 Proteins are partially digested in the stomach and finally digested in the small intestines. Carbohydrates are mainly digested in the small intestines.

3 Students should suggest that the small intestine has numerous projections in its lining, called villi and microvilli, that carry out absorption.

4 Students should indicate that the pancreas and liver secrete digestive enzymes and that without them, proteins, fats, and carbohydrates could not be broken down.

Visual Strategy Figure 34-7

■ **Analyzing Data**
Show the class a piece of beef liver to underscore the highly vascularized nature of this organ. Point out that the liver is the largest internal organ, weighing about 1.5 kg (2.2 lb). Have students locate the gallbladder in this figure.

Phase Three
Assessment Options

Closure
■ **Recognizing Relationships**
Have students explain why people can live without their stomach or gallbladder but not without their liver or small intestine. *(The stomach does some of the digestion of proteins. However, one could live without it if properly prepared foods were eaten. The gallbladder stores and concentrates the bile received from the liver. The liver secretes bile, helps to regulate blood glucose, detoxifies drugs and alcohol, and produces many enzymes and plasma proteins. The small intestine does 90 percent of the absorption of food and water in the digestive system.)*

SECTION REVIEW
Assign the *Section Review*.

Reteaching
Assign students to cooperative work groups of three. Have each group develop a concept map for this section. *(The concept maps developed should include the structure, functions, and locations of the organs described in the section—mouth, esophagus, stomach, small intestine, pancreas, liver, and large intestine.)*

Key to Strategies
● **Understanding Concepts (Tier I)**
■ **Applying Information (Tier II)**
▲ **Critical Thinking (Tier III)**

Digestion and Excretion 709

Visual Strategy Figure 34-8

● **Comparing Functions**
Have students identify the two body systems shown in this figure so they can see the close association between the circulatory and excretory systems.

Demonstration

■ **Relating Structure to Function**
Obtain a pig or sheep kidney from a local butcher. Cut the kidney in half lengthwise. Have students identify the ammonia smell. Ask students how to cook a kidney. *(You must soak it in salt water to absorb the ammonia before cooking it.)*

Regulating the concentrations of substances in your body's fluids is essential. A slight rise in potassium levels in the blood can cause heart failure. But this rarely happens because the kidneys maintain the level of potassium and other substances within narrow limits. Kidneys also serve as filters to remove nitrogen-containing wastes from the blood.

34-3 The Excretory System

OBJECTIVES

1 **Explain how the kidneys determine what leaves the blood and what remains.**

2 **Describe the structure of a kidney nephron.**

3 **Compare and contrast the two stages of urine formation.**

4 **Explain how medical technology has helped people with kidney disorders.**

Kidney Form and Function

When the body breaks down amino acids, metabolic wastes—especially nitrogen compounds in the form of ammonia—are released. In Chapter 24 you read that land animals must rid their bodies of ammonia and other nitrogen-containing wastes. The body is able to make ammonia less poisonous by combining it with carbon dioxide in the liver to form a less toxic compound called urea. Urea enters the bloodstream and circulates throughout the body. Some urea is eliminated from the body through the skin as perspiration, which is a mixture of water, minerals, and urea. Most of the urea, however, is eliminated by the excretory system, illustrated in **Figure 34-8**.

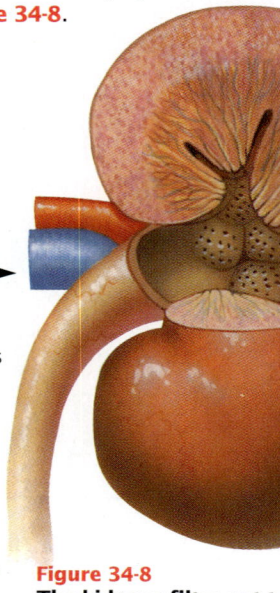

Kidneys

Ureter

Bladder

Urethra

Figure 34-8
The kidneys filter out toxins, urea, water, and mineral salts from the blood. These substances are then stored in the bladder as a liquid called urine until they are eliminated.

710

Videodisc Resources

Holt Biology Videodiscs
Lesson 34-3: The Excretory System

The kidneys clean the blood

Your **kidneys** are fist-sized organs located toward the back of your abdomen, about even with the bottom of the rib cage. The kidneys play a vital role in maintaining homeostasis; they remove urea and other wastes, regulate the amount of water in the blood, and adjust the concentrations of various substances in the blood. Because of their crucial function, the kidneys receive large amounts of blood. About one-fourth of the blood that your heart pumps every minute travels to the kidneys for cleaning.

Nephrons carry out the processes that form urine

Each kidney contains over 1 million blood-cleaning units called **nephrons** (*NEHF rahns*). A nephron, shown in **Figure 34-9**, is a tiny tube with a cup-shaped capsule at one end. The capsule surrounds a tight ball of capillaries. Substances in the blood inside the capillaries filter into the capsule. The substances then travel through the twists and loops in the nephron, forming urine, an amber-colored fluid that contains nitrogenous waste products and excess amounts of water and solutes.

Figure 34-9
a During filtration, blood pressure in the capillaries forces water, glucose, amino acids, and various salts through small pores in the capillaries and into the capsule of the nephron.

Urine Formation

The first stage of urine formation is called **filtration**, as shown in **Figure 34-9a**. During filtration, the blood cells, proteins, and other large solutes remain in the blood, while smaller solutes (such as glucose, salts, amino acids, and urea) and water are forced out of the blood.

Each day, about 180 L of fluid filter out of the blood and into the nephrons. Most of this fluid is absorbed back into the blood, leaving about 1 L of urine every day. The amount and content of urine varies, depending on what has been taken into the body.

b During reabsorption, water and solutes move out of the nephron and into the capillaries.

Reabsorption returns important substances to the blood

From the nephron capsule, the filtered fluid passes into the nephron, beginning **reabsorption**, the second process of urine formation, shown in **Figure 34-9b**. About 99 percent of the water, all of the glucose and amino acids, and many of the salts are reclaimed and sent back into your bloodstream. Water reabsorption is controlled by your hypothalamus. When your body needs to conserve water, the hypothalamus triggers the secretion of a hormone called ADH (antidiuretic hormone). ADH makes the ends of nephrons more permeable to water. As a result, more water is reabsorbed, and the urine leaving your body is more concentrated. When your body must get rid of excess water, the secretion of ADH is inhibited, and your urine is more dilute.

After reabsorption, the fluid remaining in the nephron tubes is urine. It is made up of water, urea, and various salts. Urine flows from each kidney into a slender tube called a ureter. It then flows into the urinary bladder, where it is stored. It leaves the body through a tube called the urethra, which leads to the outside of your body.

Mathematics Connection
How Much Blood?
The heart pumps about 5 L (2.6 gal) of blood per minute. Keeping in mind that one-fourth of this volume travels to the kidneys, have students calculate the volume of blood that is filtered each day. (5 L × 60 min × 24 h × 0.25 = 1800 L per day. About 55 percent of the 5 L of blood is plasma, and only 18 to 20 percent of the plasma, water, and small solutes are actually filtered out of the blood and into the nephron capsule. So 1800 L × 0.55 × 0.18 = 178.2 L per day.)

Visual Strategy | Figure 34-9

● **Comparing Functions**
To be sure students understand the close association between the circulatory and excretory systems, have them locate the vessels that carry blood to and from the kidney. Emphasize that kidneys clean the blood by removing urea, excess water, salt, acids, and wastes.

Connection: *Chapter 4*

Transport Mechanisms
Review how passive-transport processes account for the filtration of blood in the nephron. Have students locate where filtration occurs in the nephron shown in Figure 34-9. Review how active-transport processes account for the reabsorption of materials as urine passes through the nephron. Have students locate where reabsorption occurs in the nephron shown in Figure 34-9. Point out that because of active transport, the kidney has an extremely high energy requirement, even higher than that of the heart, when comparing their relative weights.

711

Historical Perspective: The First Organ Transplant
The first successful organ transplant was that of a kidney, performed in 1954. Since the donor and recipient were identical twins, rejection was not a problem.

Key to Strategies
● Understanding Concepts (Tier I)
■ Applying Information (Tier II)
▲ Critical Thinking (Tier III)

Digestion and Excretion 711

Active READING

Technique: Prediction Guide

Ask volunteers to discuss how the opinions they formed in the Active Reading exercise on page 698 changed or stayed the same as a result of their reading. Students should point to specific passages in the text that support their reasoning.

Phase Three
Assessment Options

Closure

▲ **Distinguishing Relevant Information**

Have students explain why high blood pressure, drinking plenty of fluids, and cold weather promote increased urine output, while low blood pressure, reduced intake of fluids, and hot weather favor decreased urine output. *(High blood pressure would increase the filtration pressure, drinking plenty of fluids would both raise the blood pressure and decrease the output of ADH, and cold weather would increase the metabolic rate and thus increase filtration. The converse would be true for the other situations.)*

SECTION REVIEW

Assign the *Section Review.*

Reteaching

Have students write a report on dehydration and the excretory system.

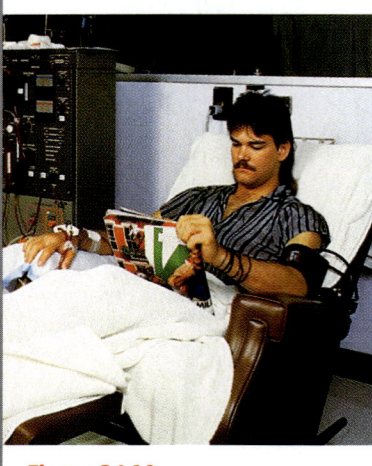

Figure 34-10
The kidney machine is an efficient device for filtering blood.

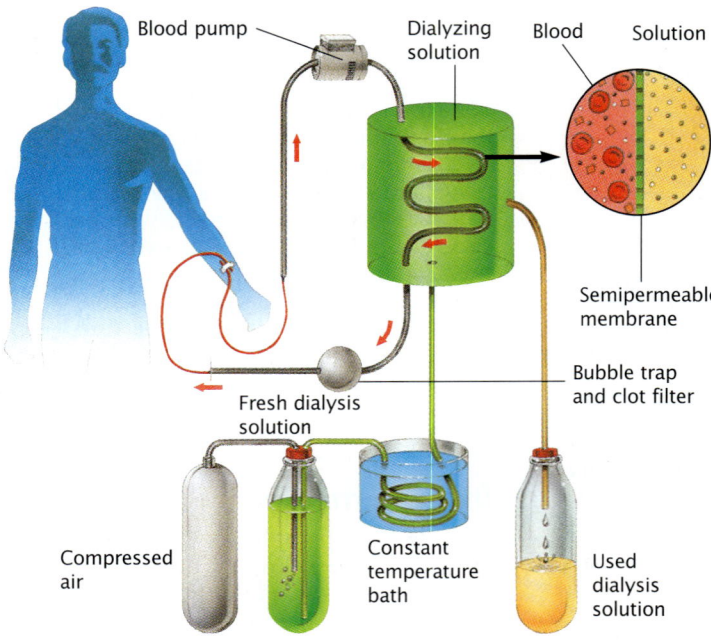

Blood pump · Dialyzing solution · Blood · Solution

Semipermeable membrane

Bubble trap and clot filter

Fresh dialysis solution

Compressed air · Constant temperature bath · Used dialysis solution

a Blood in a solution is passed through a membrane, where the wastes are removed.

b The blood is maintained at a constant temperature and pH so that it can be pumped back into the patient after it is filtered.

Kidney Disorders and Treatment

Stability and Homeostasis

Why might high-protein weight-loss diets contribute to the development of kidney stones?

An estimated 13 million people in the United States suffer from kidney disorders. One common disorder is the development of kidney stones. Kidney stones are deposits of uric or oxalic acid, calcium salts, and other substances that collect inside the kidney. The stones may become lodged in the urethra, the tube through which urine leaves the body, where they interfere with urine flow and cause pain. Kidney stones usually pass naturally from the body, but they can be eliminated by medical or surgical procedures.

When kidneys are unable to function, the blood must be artificially filtered. Filtering of the blood is called **hemodialysis**. The term *dialysis* refers to the use of a semipermeable membrane to separate large particles from smaller ones. The kidney machine shown in **Figure 34-10** can be used twice a week to filter the blood of patients with kidney disorders. A dialyzing solution is fed into the abdomen through a catheter, a small tube. The fluid is changed four times a day.

SECTION REVIEW

1. How do the kidneys help maintain homeostasis?

2. How are nephrons specialized for urine formation?

3. Which substances do nephrons filter out of the blood? Which are reabsorbed?

4. How does the process of hemodialysis work?

712

ANSWERS TO SECTION REVIEW

1. Students should indicate that kidneys remove urea and other wastes, regulate the amount of water in blood, and adjust the concentration of various substances in the blood.

2. The nephron is composed of a glomerulus, which allows the filtration of plasma, and a long epithelial tube, which selectively reabsorbs substances from the glomerular filtrate.

3. Students should indicate that the kidneys filter out toxins, urea, water, and mineral salts from the blood. About 99 percent of the water, all the glucose and amino acids, and many of the salts are reclaimed and sent back into the bloodstream.

4. In the process of hemodialysis, a patient's blood is passed through a semipermeable membrane that substitutes for the filtering action of the kidney. The wastes are removed from the blood in this manner, and the blood is returned to the patient's body.

Microvilli can be seen with the aid of a scanning electron microscope.

	Key Terms	Summary
34-1 **Nutrition: What You Eat and Why** Eating healthful foods is important for maintaining a healthy body.	obesity (p. 699) nutrition (p. 699) mineral (p. 702) vitamin (p. 703) anorexia nervosa (p. 704) bulimia (p. 704)	• A healthful diet includes carbohydrates and lipids (for fuel), proteins (for building tissues), vitamins, minerals, and water. • Too much food and too little activity lead to nutritional problems. • Anorexia nervosa and bulimia are eating disorders that can cause serious health problems.
34-2 **The Digestive System** Digestion is the process of breaking down food so that the body can absorb its nutrients.	esophagus (p. 706) peristalsis (p. 707) pepsin (p. 707) small intestine (p. 708) villi (p. 708) microvilli (p. 708) liver (p. 708) pancreas (p. 708) large intestine (p. 709)	• In the first stage of digestion, the teeth and saliva break down food and begin carbohydrate digestion. • In the stomach, proteins are broken down by pepsin. • Digestion is completed in the small intestine, where nutrients are absorbed. • The large intestine reabsorbs most of the water from the mass of undigested material left after the removal of nutrients in the small intestine. • The liver stores and regulates the levels of food molecules in the blood.
34-3 **The Excretory System** The kidneys are the filtering organs in the body, removing urea and other wastes from the blood.	kidney (p. 711) nephron (p. 711) filtration (p. 711) reabsorption (p. 711) hemodialysis (p. 712)	• The functional unit of the kidney is the nephron. • During filtration, water, glucose, amino acids, salts, and urea move out of the capillary and into the nephron. During reabsorption, water, glucose, amino acids, and many salts move out of the nephron and back into the bloodstream. • Some kidney disorders can be managed with hemodialysis, a process that uses a semipermeable membrane to simulate the filtering action of the kidney.

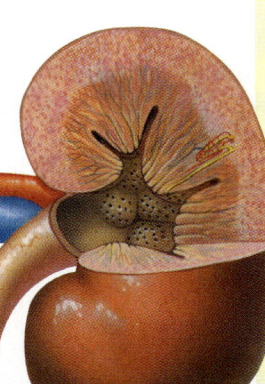

713

Alternative Assessment

Commercial diet programs are big business. They involve millions of people, who pay billions of dollars each year in hopes of gaining healthy eating habits while losing unwanted pounds. Have students research these commercial diet programs and report on how each claims to bring about weight loss. Encourage students to look for information on how these programs might affect either the digestive or excretory systems. For example, a high-protein diet places added stress on the liver, which must produce more urea as a result of increased nitrogen intake.

Portfolio Assessment

Portfolio Assessment on page T39 provides options for building and evaluating student portfolios. Students and teachers can select items from the areas listed on page T39 for inclusion in a portfolio.

ANSWER TO
CONCEPT MAP

The following is one possible answer to the Relating Concepts exercise on page 714.

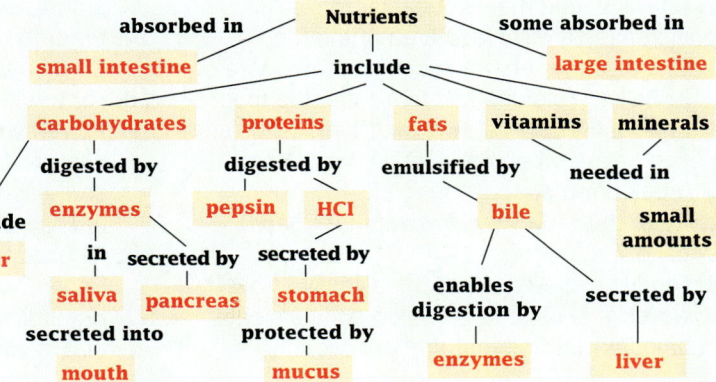

review

ANSWERS

Understanding Vocabulary

1. a. vitamins
   b. liver
   c. excretion
2. a. Fuel nutrients (carbohydrates, protein, and fats) provide energy to the body. Regulatory nutrients (water, minerals, and vitamins) help regulate how the body uses energy, but do not provide energy.
   b. Fat-soluble vitamins, such as A, D, E, and K, can accumulate in body fat and in the liver. Water-soluble vitamins, such as B and C, are not stored in body tissue.
   c. During filtration, small solutes and water are forced out of the blood. During reabsorption, about 99 percent of the water, all of the glucose and amino acids, and many of the salts are reclaimed and sent back into the bloodstream.

Understanding Concepts

3. Concept Map answer is on page 713.
4. See page 699.
5. The recommended daily percentages of fuel nutrients in the diet are as follows: carbohydrates—58 percent, fats—30 percent (10% each type), and proteins—12 percent.
6. Refer to the **Answers to Section Review** for Section 34-1, page 704, number 2.
7. Student drawings and number of daily servings from each pyramid level should resemble the Food Guide Pyramid shown in Figure 34-1 on page 700.
8. Refer to the captions that accompany Figure 34-2 on page 701.
9. Vegetarian foods have varying levels of essential amino acids. In order to obtain the correct amounts, vegetarians must combine foods like beans and rice.
10. Refer to the **Answers to Section Review** for Section 34-1, page 704, number 4.

---

review

Understanding Vocabulary

1. For each set of terms, complete the analogy.
   a. inorganic compounds : minerals :: organic substances : _____
   b. bicarbonate : pancreas :: bile : _____
   c. stomach and small intestine : digestion :: kidneys and large intestine : _____
2. For each pair of terms, explain the difference in their meanings.
   a. fuel nutrients, regulatory nutrients
   b. fat-soluble vitamins, water-soluble vitamins
   c. filtration, reabsorption

Understanding Concepts

3. **Relating Concepts** Construct a concept map that illustrates how the essential fuel nutrients are digested by the body. Include the following terms in your concept map: carbohydrates, proteins, fats, fiber, enzymes, saliva, mouth, pancreas, pepsin, HCl, stomach, mucus, bile, liver, small intestine, and large intestine.
4. **Identifying Relationships** What are the two major factors leading to nutritional problems today in the United States? What health problems are caused by these factors?
5. **Reading Graphs** Look at the pie chart below, showing the percentages of fuel nutrients recommended for our daily diet. What is incorrect in the chart?

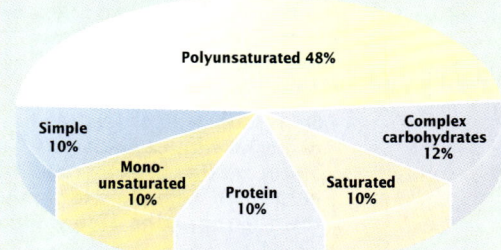

Polyunsaturated 48%
Simple 10%
Mono-unsaturated 10%
Protein 10%
Saturated 10%
Complex carbohydrates 12%

6. **Summarizing Information** List two ways that the body uses water, carbohydrates, fats, proteins, minerals, and vitamins.
7. **Summarizing Information** Draw the USDA Food Guide Pyramid, which serves as a guide for healthy eating. List the food groups at each level of the pyramid, the essential nutrients provided, and how many servings from each food group should be eaten daily.
8. **Distinguishing Relevant Information** How could you use the information from a food label to help you meet the food pyramid's recommendations?
9. **Inferring Relationships** Why must vegetarians plan their diets carefully?
10. **Inferring Relationships** Describe the physiological and metabolic changes that are caused by anorexia and bulimia.
11. **Identifying Functions** Describe the mechanical and chemical aspects of digestion that take place in the mouth.
12. **Summarizing Information** Describe the main organs of the digestive system, their location, and their function.
13. **Understanding Structures** Astronauts in space are often seen eating upside down. How is it possible for them to swallow and digest food in this inverted position?
14. **Identifying Structures and Functions** Explain how the structure of the small intestine enables it to absorb water and nutrients.
15. **Summarizing Information** How do the kidneys help to maintain homeostasis within the body? How does sweating contribute to elimination?
16. **Identifying Structures** Describe the structure of a nephron, and describe its involvement in the production of urine.
17. **Inferring Relationships** Discuss the similarities between natural and artificial dialysis.
18. **BUILDING ON WHAT YOU HAVE LEARNED** In Chapter 24 you learned about the different forms of nitrogen-containing wastes excreted by organisms. Why would it be a problem for humans to excrete ammonia rather than urea?

---

11. Chewing food makes it easier to swallow and increases the surface area of the food so that digestive enzymes can mix with more of it. Saliva moistens and lubricates the food, making it easier to swallow. Chemical digestion begins when enzymes in saliva begin to break down starches in food.
12. Refer to the **Review Answers** for Chapter 34, page 715, number 19.
13. Food is moved through the digestive tract by wavelike contractions (called peristalsis) of smooth muscles that ring the esophagus, stomach, and intestine.
14. Refer to the captions that accompany Figure 34-6 on page 708.
15. For the kidney, refer to the **Answers to Section Review** for Section 34-3, page 712, number 1. Sweat is 99 percent water, with some sodium chloride, some lactic acid, and traces of urea, uric acid, and ammonia.
16. Refer to the captions that accompany Figure 34-9 on page 711.
17. Hemodialysis is the artificial filtering of blood that is sometimes used when the kidneys are

Interpreting Graphics

19. Name the identified parts of the digestive tract, and describe the function of each.

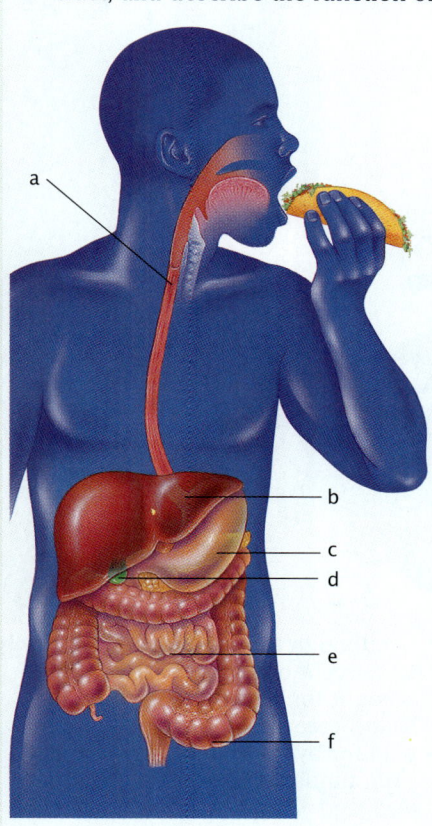

Reviewing Themes

20. *Cell Structure and Function*
Both chemical and mechanical processes are involved in digestion. Identify a chemical and a mechanical process that occur in one location, and describe how each aids digestion.

21. *Stability and Homeostasis*
How is water balance regulated in the human body?

Thinking Critically

22. **Evaluating Opinions** A friend trying to lose weight for several months now has just declared that he is now a "fruitarian"—one who eats nothing but fruits and fruit juices. Your friend is excited about this "healthy way to lose weight." How would you react to your friend's decision?

23. **Working Cooperatively** Work with a partner to collect labels from packaged and prepared foods. Study the nutritional information provided on the labels. Refer to the USDA Food Guide Pyramid on page 700. Collect enough appropriate labels to represent the proper number of servings from each group for one day. Arrange the labels as meals on a poster, and share your information with your class.

24. **Finding Information** Use library references or search an on-line database to find out about common disorders of the digestive system. Research the causes and symptoms of disorders such as ulcers, gastroenteritis, gallstones, pancreatitis, diverticulosis, and acid reflux. Summarize your findings in a written report.

Activities and Projects

25. **Career Connection: Dietitian** Dietitians are professionals who are trained in nutrition and who use dietary management to help patients maintain good health and prevent or manage disease. They may specialize in research, education, food service, or nutritional care of people of different age groups. Use library references or search an on-line database to find out about the requirements to become a clinical dietitian, a clinical nutritionist, a registered dietitian, and a dietetic assistant. Where do most dietitians work? To find out more, see the *Occupational Outlook Handbook* published by the U.S. Department of Labor and the *Health Careers Guidebook* published by the U.S. Department of Labor and the U.S. Department of Health and Human Services. You might also want to write to the American Dietetic Association at 216 West Jackson Boulevard, Suite 800, Chicago, IL 60606.

Discovering Through Reading

26. Read the article "Children of the Corn" in *Newsweek*, August 28, 1995, pages 60–62. What is the main reason that many teenagers become vegetarians? What is the leading problem facing teenage vegetarians? Could becoming a vegetarian be a warning sign of an eating disorder?

715

absorption and waste compaction occur in the large intestine (f).

Reviewing Themes

20. Student answers will vary depending on the location chosen.
21. See page 711.

Thinking Critically

22. A diet composed of only one type of food does not provide all the essential nutrients the body needs. Encourage your friend to include many fruits in his or her diet and to eat other types of food.

23. Results will vary depending on the labels selected. Make sure that students have the proper number of servings from each level of the Food Guide Pyramid.
24. Results will vary depending on resources.

Activities and Projects

25. Results will vary depending on the resources available.

Discovering Through Reading

26. Many teenagers become vegetarians because of their concern for animals. The leading problem facing teenage vegetarians is eating a proper, nutritious diet instead of junk food. Many young women who become anorexics begin losing weight by first becoming vegetarians. For this reason, a turn toward vegetarianism in teenagers is sometimes seen as an early warning for the eating disorder anorexia.

diseased, injured, or unable to function properly. Natural dialysis takes place in the nephron of the kidney.

18. Ammonia is very toxic to the body. A safe way to rid the body of ammonia is to excrete it into a watery environment or directly through the plasma membrane or skin. However, humans are not able to remove wastes from the body in this way.

19. The mouth is where food is crushed and broken into small pieces and acted on by juices secreted by the salivary glands. In the esophagus (a), food is moved to the stomach (c) by the action of smooth muscles. The stomach holds food while it is mixed by muscle action and broken down by HCl and pepsin secreted by the stomach lining. The liver (b) secretes bile into the intestine; bile breaks up fat globules. The gallbladder (d) stores bile. The pancreas secretes enzymes that break proteins into amino acids and bicarbonate to neutralize stomach acids. Absorption of nutrients occurs in the small intestine (e), and water

Objectives

- Explain why the percentage of elderly people in society is increasing.
- Discuss reasons for the high cost of health care for the elderly.
- Propose solutions for reducing health-care costs.
- Describe a technique that can be used to detect small tumors in the body.

Health-Care Options

■ Analyzing Information

Health-care costs are increasing rapidly, and the health-care insurance industry has responded by becoming more flexible and complex. In the past decade, millions of Americans have joined health maintenance organizations (HMOs) because of their low out-of-pocket costs and emphasis on preventive health care. Encourage students to start considering this important real-life issue by having them explore current trends in health-care options. Why is health insurance important? How do HMOs compare with other options, such as traditional health-insurance plans and preferred provider organizations (PPO)? What factors should an individual consider when choosing a health-care plan? Have students use references in the library, materials from local health-care providers, and information from an on-line database to research these questions. Invite a representative from a local health insurance agency to class to discuss these topics and other important issues related to health care.

Alternative Therapies: Plausible or Preposterous?

▲ Recognizing Verifiable Facts

Dissatisfied with the medical establishment, many Americans have been exploring alternative therapies, such as acupressure, acupuncture, Chinese medicine, chiropractic care, hypnotherapy, massage therapy, herbology, and reflexology. Have students form small groups to investigate a type of alternative therapy. Have them give a short

Science, Technology, and Society

Who Pays the Bill for Growing Old?

The population of the United States is growing older, and health-care bills for the elderly increase each year. How can we deal with this aging society?

716

A Mature Society

In 1900, less than 1 percent of our society was over the age of 65. By 1994, that figure had increased to 13 percent, and experts predict that by the year 2050, 25 percent of the population will be over 65. Why is our society aging so rapidly?

In 1900, one-third to one-half of all children died before their first birthday. Life expectancy was only 47 years. In a span of less than 100 years, many of the diseases that plagued humans have been controlled. Advances in medicine as well as improvements in housing, nutrition, and hygiene have increased life spans. Today, life expectancy is 82 years.

Caring for the Elderly

The elderly tend to have more health problems than younger people. Many of these problems are chronic, or long-term, illnesses, such as heart disease, stroke, cancer, and Alzheimer's disease. Many elderly people need professional nursing help or require expensive nursing-home care.

Although the elderly represent only 13 percent of the population, they account for about one-third of all health-care spending. Much of this is paid for by the federal government from funds such as Medicare and Medicaid. This money is supplied by taxpayers currently in the work force.

The High Cost of Health Care

Health-care costs have risen dramatically in the past few years. One reason is the use of high-tech procedures for diagnosing and treating illnesses. These procedures are perceived as the best in medical care, but they are not always cost effective (that is, they are not significantly better than less expensive alternatives). Today more than ever, people view high-quality health care as a right.

Quantity Versus Quality

The common use of life-extending procedures is an indication of how far medical discoveries have come. Even though doctors can help a person live longer, the quality of that life may be poor; a cancer patient may live two years longer but be in constant pain. Some feel we need to improve the quality of life rather than just extend it. Other recent studies seem to indicate that disease and disability rates are declining and that every year there is a smaller percentage of people unable to care for themselves.

Cutting the Costs

Many solutions have been proposed for reducing the cost of health care, especially for the elderly. Ideas include the following:

- providing more funds for in-home care
- preventing illnesses rather than just curing them
- using alternative, low-tech (and hence low cost) treatments

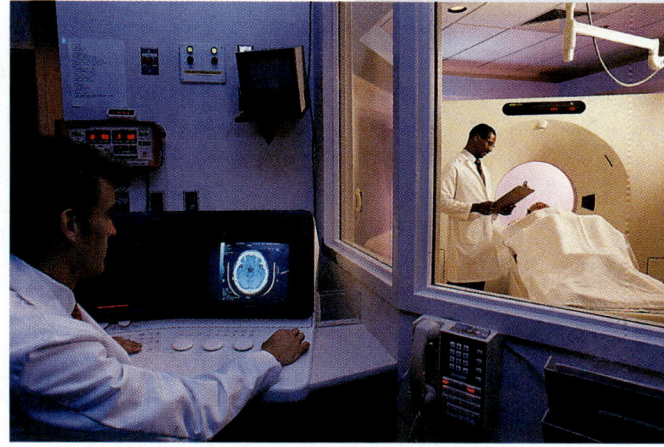

Technique

Computer Tomography (CT)
Many sophisticated, high-tech procedures are used for the diagnosis of illnesses rather than for treatment. One of these techniques, called computer tomography (CT), can find tumors in the body too small to be detected by other means. CT was such a major development in diagnostics that its inventors were awarded the Nobel Prize in 1979.

CT uses a combination of dyes, X rays, and computer images. The X-ray camera rotates completely around the patient to take pictures at all angles. A computer analyzes these pictures and creates a three-dimensional image of the region. If a tumor is found, the computer can measure its exact size, shape, and location.

The cost of CT rose by more than 400 percent in just a decade, making CT scans very expensive.

Applications: detecting small tumors in various organs; diagnosing tissue damage from head injuries, strokes, and arthritis; monitoring the effectiveness of treatments

Users: surgeons, oncologists (doctors who treat cancer patients), and X-ray technicians

Analyzing the Issues

1. What is a hospice?
Research the definition and history of the hospice movement. What services are offered by a hospice? What is the philosophy behind hospices? Present your findings to the rest of the class.

2. What solutions are there for funding health care?
The largest costs for the elderly are due to long-term care. Research the different solutions proposed for financing these health-care costs. What are some of the options? Describe the benefits and shortcomings of each option.

3. Does growing older mean growing sicker?
Read "The Oldest Old" by Thomas T. Perls in the January 1995 issue of *Scientific American*, pages 70–75. What does the author mean by "the oldest old," and what does he say about their health? How might the increasing numbers of the oldest old affect health-care costs in the future?

4. How can you increase your chances of staying healthy?
Doctors estimate that 70 percent of the illnesses they treat, such as lung cancer and heart disease, are preventable. Research lifestyles and habits that can help extend life span. Summarize your findings in a written report.

4. Answers will vary, but students should mention the benefits of a healthful diet, regular exercise, and routine examinations. Students should advise against developing habits such as cigarette smoking and excessive alcohol consumption.

presentation describing the therapy's philosophy, its methods of treatment, and the conditions it treats. Discuss with the class how these alternative therapies differ from conventional medical treatment. Which have been scientifically proven to be effective? How can patients safeguard themselves from quackery? Ask students which alternative therapies they have tried or would be willing to try. Could such therapies be used to reduce health-care costs? If so, should they be covered by health insurance?

Frontiers in Aging

Summarizing Information
Have students read the article "Older, Longer" in *Time*, Special Issue, Fall 1996, pages 76–80. What is the current average life expectancy in the United States? *(75.5 to 85 years)* What do some researchers predict this number will be in 80 years? *(about 100 years)* How have medical advances affected senior citizens' quality of life? *(There has been a decrease in the number of chronic disabilities, particularly those that affect sight and mobility.)* Have students summarize the studies that are investigating degeneration, senescence, and the effects of diet and of hormone therapy in the elderly.

References

1. Callahan, D. "Our Fear of Dying." *Newsweek,* October 4, 1993, 67.
2. Langone, John. "Alternative Therapies: Challenging the Mainstream." *Time,* Special Issue, Fall 1996, 40–43.
3. Leutwyler, K. "The Price of Prevention." *Scientific American,* April, 1995, 124–129.
4. Olshansky, S. J., B. S. Carnes, and C. K. Cassel. "The Aging of the Human Species." *Scientific American,* April 1993, 46–52.
5. Perls, T. T. "The Oldest Old." *Scientific American,* January 1995, 70–75.

717

35 | Reproduction and Development

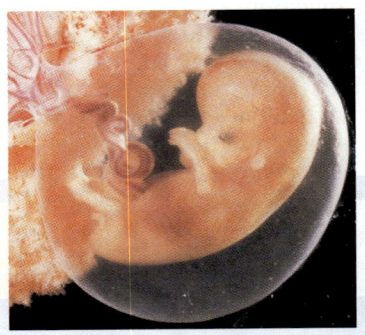

Lesson Planning Guide With Options for Block Scheduling

Lecture Concepts	Lesson Resources

35-1 The Male Reproductive System

BLOCK ❶ (45 minutes)

1. Sperm have a head region containing DNA and a tail region filled with mitochondria.

2. Sperm, produced in the testes, travel out of the body by passing through the epididymis, vas deferens, urethra, and finally the penis.

❶ Lecture Resources
- Determining Prior Knowledge
- Active Reading: Reading Organizer
- Visual Strategy: Figure 35-1
- Visual Strategy: Videodisc
- Teaching Transparencies: 224, 225
- Holt Biology Videodiscs Lesson 35-1

Classwork Options
- Visual Strategy: Figure 35-2

Assignment Options
- Teaching Resources CD-ROM: Occupational Applications 9

BLOCK ❷ (45 minutes)

3. Sperm and secretions from seminal vesicles and the prostate glands make up the semen.

4. Testosterone is a male hormone responsible for secondary sex characteristics.

❷ Lecture Resources
- Visual Strategy: Figures 35-4, 35-5
- Visual Strategy: Videodisc
- Teaching Transparencies: 232
- Holt Biology Videodiscs Lesson 35-1

Assignment Options
- Reteaching
- Section Review
- Chapter Review, questions 2a, 3, 4, 5
- Directed Reading Worksheet

35-2 The Female Reproductive System

BLOCK ❸ (45 minutes)

1. During the ovarian cycle, an egg matures in the ovary and is released during ovulation.

2. Both follicle stimulating hormone (FSH) and luteinizing hormone (LH) stimulate the maturation and ovulation of an egg.

❸ Lecture Resources
- Visual Strategy: Figure 35-6
- Visual Strategy: Videodisc
- Teaching Transparencies: 223
- Holt Biology Videodiscs Lesson 35-2

Classwork Options
- Visual Strategy: Figure 35-7, 35-8

BLOCK ❹ (45 minutes)

3. Estrogen prepares the uterus for possible implantation by a fertilized egg.

4. The menstrual (uterine) cycle involves changes in the uterus each month.

5. Menopause is the shutdown of the menstrual (uterine) and ovarian cycles.

❹ Lecture Resources
- Visual Strategy: Figure 35-9
- Visual Strategy: Videodisc
- Teaching Transparencies: 226
- Holt Biology Videodiscs Lesson 35-2

Classwork Options
- Reteaching
- Closure: Recognizing Relationships

Assignment Options
- Section Review
- Chapter Review, questions 1, 2b, 6, 7, 8, 9, 10, 21, 22, 23
- Directed Reading Worksheet

35-3 Fertilization and Development

BLOCK ❺ (45 minutes)

1. Sperm deposited in the vagina travel up the Fallopian tubes, where one may fertilize an egg.

2. The fertilized egg implants itself in the uterus.

3. A placenta exchanges nutrients and wastes between the fetus and mother.

❺ Lecture Resources
- Active Reading: Reading Organizer
- Visual Strategy: Figures 35-12, 35-13
- Demonstration: Comparing Structures
- Teaching Transparencies: 227, 228, 196A
- Holt Biology Videodiscs Lesson 35-3

Classwork Options
- Demonstration: Relating Concepts
- Inquiry Skills Development: Lab B34

BLOCK ❻ (45 minutes)

4. Viruses and drugs can pass from mother to fetus by way of the placenta.

5. Development is divided into three 3-month periods known as trimesters.

6. About 270 days following fertilization, labor begins, and birth follows.

❻ Lecture Resources
- Visual Strategy: Figures 35-14, 35-15
- Visual Strategy: Videodisc
- Demonstration: Comparing Structures
- Holt Biology Videodiscs Lesson 35-3

Classwork Options
- Fetal Alcohol Syndrome

Assignment Options
- Reteaching
- Section Review
- Chapter Review, questions 2c, 11, 12, 13, 14, 15, 16, 20, 24, 25, 26, 27
- Directed Reading Worksheet

Lecture Concepts   ## Lesson Resources

35-4 Sexually Transmitted Diseases

BLOCK 7 (45 minutes)
1. HIV can be transmitted through blood, semen, vaginal fluids, or the placenta.
2. Herpesvirus 2 produces painful blisters that form on the genitals.
3. Syphilis, gonorrhea, and chlamydia are bacterial diseases.

7 Lecture Resources
■ Active Reading: Reading Organizer
■ Visual Strategy: Figures 35-19, 35-20
🗍 Teaching Transparencies: 238
⊘ Holt Biology Videodiscs Lesson 35-4

Classwork Options
🗍 Laboratory Techniques and Experimental Design: Lab C44

BLOCK 8 (45 minutes)
4. Some sexually transmitted diseases can result in pelvic inflammatory disease (PID).
5. Ectopic pregnancy can be a consequence of PID.

8 Lecture Resources
■ Active Reading: Reading Organizer
⊘ Holt Biology Videodiscs Lesson 35-4
Classwork Options
■ Closure: Organizing Information

Assignment Options
■ Reteaching
■ Section Review
■ Chapter Review, questions 17, 18, 19, 28
■ Directed Reading Worksheet

Chapter Review and Assessment

BLOCK 9 (45 minutes)
Review
■ Reteaching Worksheet
■ Thinking Skills Worksheet
■ Vocabulary Development Worksheet
⊙ Language Development and Reading Comprehension Audio CD Program: Chapter 35

BLOCK 10 (45 minutes)
Assessment
■ Alternative Assessment, p. 741
■ Portfolio Assessment, p. T39
Chapter Test
■ Chapter 35 Test
Test Generator
⊙ Item bank for customizing Chapter Tests

Teaching Resources CD-ROM
⊙ Scoring Rubrics and Classroom Management Checklist

The Portfolio icon denotes items throughout the Teacher's Edition lesson wrap that may be selected for inclusion in student portfolios.

Holt Biology Videodiscs and Concepts of Biology

Holt Biology Videodiscs gives you a powerful tool for teaching, review, and assessment. For further information regarding the media on the videodiscs, see **Holt Biology Videodiscs Teacher's Correlation Guide to Holt Biology: Visualizing Life.**

Concepts of Biology adds interactive lesson plans and extensive tools for customization using CD-ROM technology.

Use the following topic from **Concepts of Biology** to help you teach this chapter:
Topic 26: Reproduction and Development

Laboratory Planning

Holt BioSources Laboratory Program
Block 5: Inquiry Skills Development Lab B34: Embryonic Development
Block 7: Laboratory Techniques and Experimental Design Lab C44: Blood Typing—Pregnancy and Hemolytic Disease

CHAPTER 35

Determining Prior Knowledge

- Display a model, photograph, or overhead transparency of the male and female reproductive systems. Have students identify as many organs as possible and describe their functions. Ask students the advantages of having such a reproductive system.
- Have students discuss how people generally react to individuals with a communicable disease. For example, ask how people react to someone with chickenpox. Compare this reaction with the way people might react to someone with AIDS, syphilis, or gonorrhea. Have the class discuss how these reactions affect the treatment and spread of these diseases.

Active READING

Technique: Reading Organizer
Tell students that the authors of the text have already provided two reading organizers in the chapter. Ask students if they can identify the reading organizers. *(Figure 35-3 and Figure 35-5 are graphic representations that visually represent the text.)* Have them identify what types of reading organizers are provided. *(Figure 35-3 is a series-of-events chain; Figure 35-5 is a cycle.)* Ask students to think about how original reading organizers that they created would differ from the ones in the textbook.

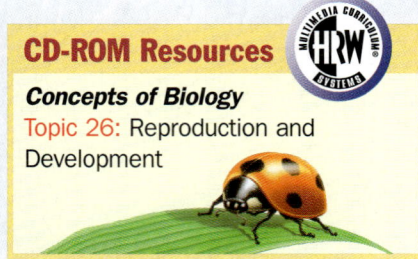

CD-ROM Resources

Concepts of Biology
Topic 26: Reproduction and Development

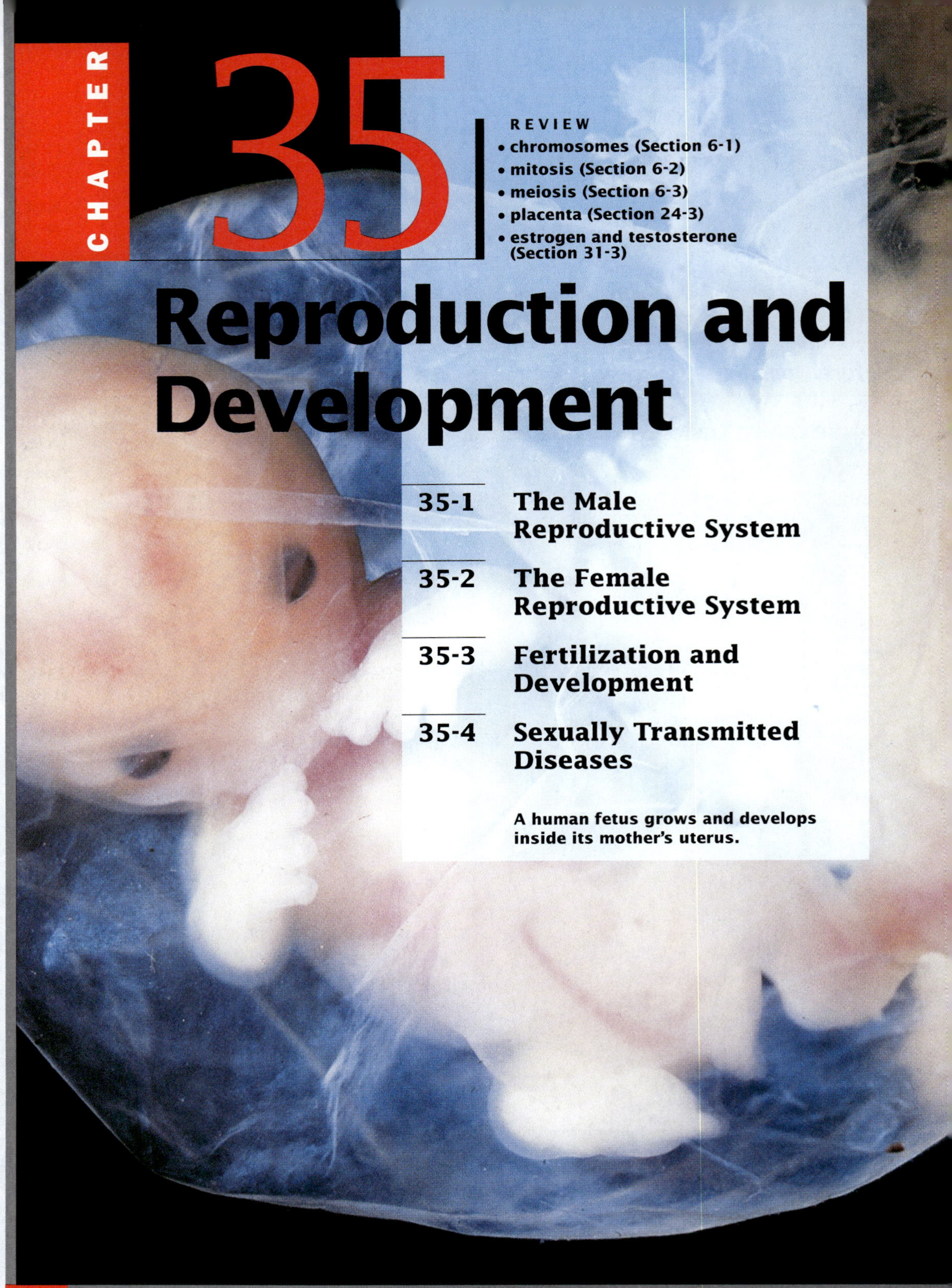

CHAPTER 35

REVIEW
- chromosomes (Section 6-1)
- mitosis (Section 6-2)
- meiosis (Section 6-3)
- placenta (Section 24-3)
- estrogen and testosterone (Section 31-3)

Reproduction and Development

A human fetus grows and develops inside its mother's uterus.

Author's Rationale Few subjects in biology are of more interest to students than reproduction. Our responsibility is to present factual information clearly and directly so that students can make informed decisions. The focus of the instruction should be on how the reproductive system works.

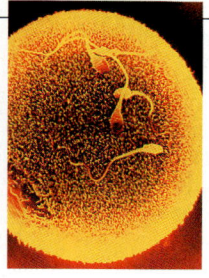

Both males and females produce specialized sex cells called gametes, which contain one-half of the genetic information needed to form a new individual. The role of the male reproductive system is to produce sperm, the male gametes, and to deliver them to the female gamete, the egg, so that fertilization can occur.

35-1 The Male Reproductive System

OBJECTIVES

1 Identify two features of sperm cells.

2 Trace the pathway of sperm from the testes to the outside of the body.

3 Describe how the hypothalamus regulates the functioning of the testes.

Structure of Sperm

A sexually mature human male produces millions of sperm each day. How are sperm cells different from other cells of the body? Recall from Chapter 6 that sperm are haploid. They have only one set of chromosomes instead of the two sets found in the body's other cells. The cells that give rise to sperm are initially diploid. These cells undergo meiosis, which reduces the number of chromosomes in the developing sperm cell by half.

After meiosis, a sperm matures for several weeks, becoming a highly specialized DNA delivery cell. As you can see in **Figure 35-1**, a sperm has a long tail and has discarded most of its cytoplasm and organelles. Mitochondria remain in the sperm cell, clustering around the top part of the tail. Mitochondria are "motors" for the sperm, providing energy for the tail to whip back and forth. A cap of digestive enzymes forms at the tip of the sperm's head. These enzymes enable the sperm to penetrate the egg.

Figure 35-1
a A sperm cell consists of a tail used for locomotion and a head that contains DNA.

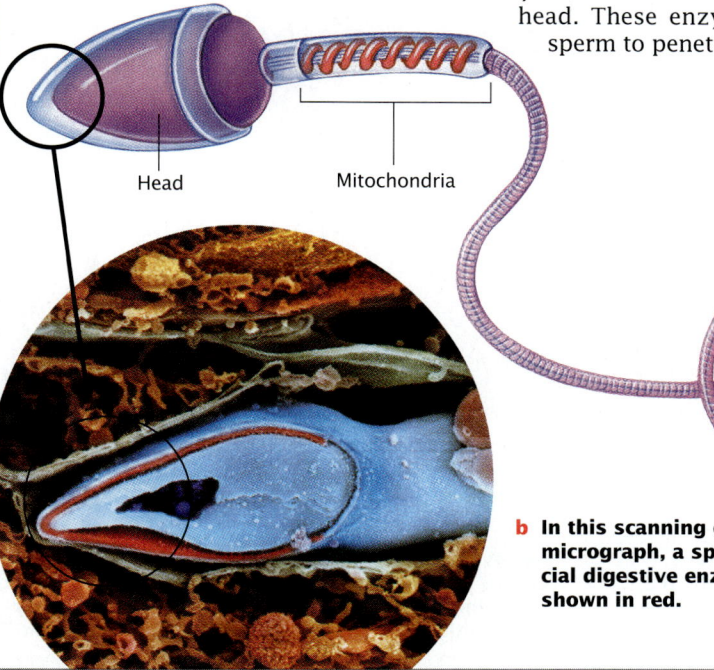

Head Mitochondria

b In this scanning electron micrograph, a sperm's special digestive enzymes are shown in red.

719

Phase One
Preparation

Scheduling
See the **Lesson Planning Guide** on pages 717A and 717B for lecture, classwork, and assignment options for Section 35-1.

Phase Two
Teaching Strategies

Visual Strategy **Figure 35-1**

● **Identifying Structures**
Tell students that a human male normally produces several hundred million sperm each day. Have students identify what part of the sperm shown in this figure must penetrate the egg. They should recognize that the head region, which contains DNA representing paternal genes, must be delivered into the egg.

Visual Strategy **Videodisc**

● **Summarizing Information**
To introduce the lesson, use *Video—Reproduction/Males* (1 min 20 s) shown in Chapter 35 Section 35-1 of *Holt Biology Videodiscs Teacher's Correlation Guide to Holt Biology: Visualizing Life.* Tell students to pay particular attention to the structure of sperm as they watch the video. After viewing the video, instruct students to make a diagram of a single sperm. Have them label the parts and indicate how each part helps the sperm cell reach and fertilize an egg.

Key to Strategies
Teaching Strategies are keyed to three tiers of learning.

● **Understanding Concepts (Tier I)**
Content mastery and comprehension

■ **Applying Information (Tier II)**
Applying and analyzing content

▲ **Critical Thinking (Tier III)**
Practicing evaluative thinking

Reproduction and Development **719**

Technique: Reading Hint

Remind students to review the diagrams and captions in Figure 35-2 and Figure 35-7. Both diagrams supplement the text by providing additional details about the male and female reproductive systems.

Visual Strategy Figure 35-2

● **Identifying Functions**

Discuss the major points made in this illustration. Have students trace the path traveled by sperm: testes → epididymis → vas deferens → urethra. Secretions from the seminal vesicle nourish the sperm, while those from the bulbourethral and prostate glands neutralize the acidic environment present in the female reproductive tract. Have students locate these glands in this figure. The testes lie outside the body cavity because a lower temperature is needed for sperm to mature (undergo meiosis) properly. Have students note the location of the testes in this figure. The urethra serves as a common exit for both urine and sperm. Have students trace how urine exits the body. Point out that during ejaculation, small muscles close off the urethra so that urine cannot exit at the same time as sperm.

The Path Traveled by Sperm

Sperm are produced in two oval-shaped organs called **testes** _(TEHS tees)_, or testicles. The testes are located in the scrotum, a loose sac hanging below the base of the penis. After sperm form, they mature and are stored temporarily in the **epididymis** _(ehp uh DIHD ih mihs)_, shown in **Figure 35-2**. The lower end of each epididymis gradually unwinds to become the **vas deferens** _(vas DEHF uh REHNZ)_.

Figure 35-2
The male reproductive system is a set of organs that produces and delivers sperm.

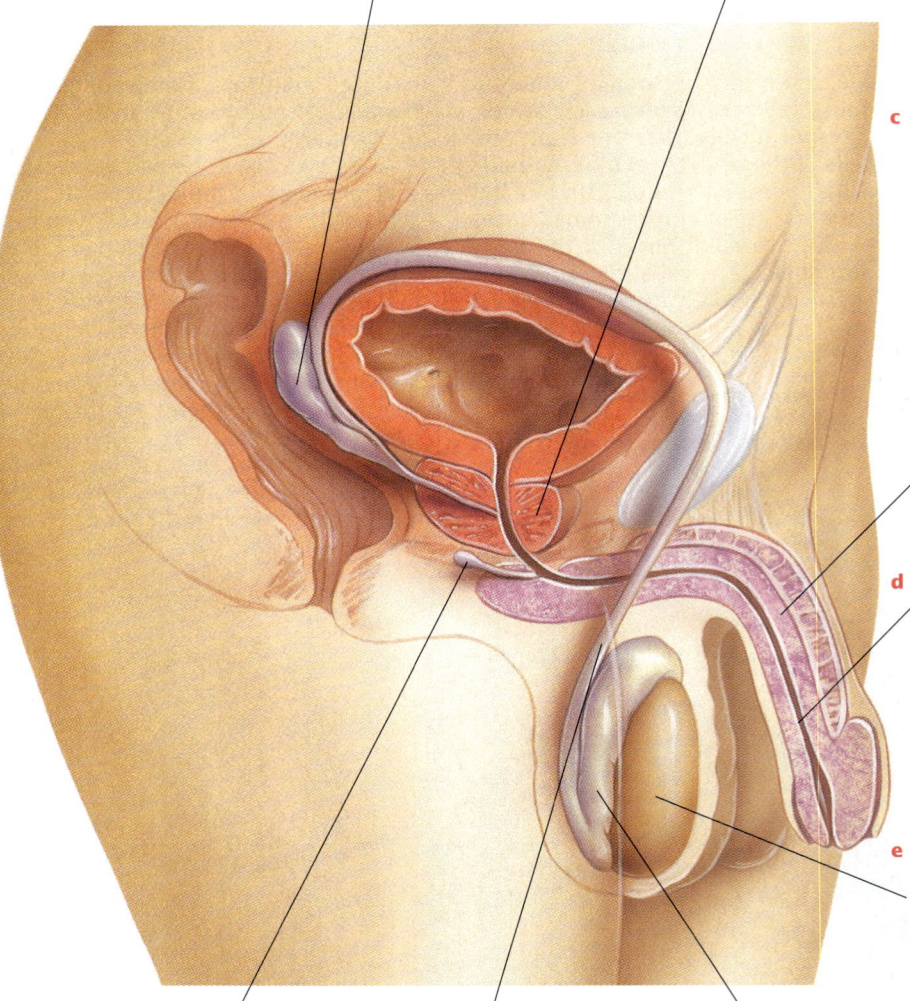

a The seminal vesicles produce fluid that nourishes sperm.

b The prostate gland secretes an alkaline fluid that counteracts the acids found in the male urethra and in the vagina of the female.

c When a male becomes sexually excited, blood accumulates in the penis, causing it to become firm and erect. The firmness of the erect penis makes it possible for the penis to be inserted into the vagina of the female.

d The urethra is the tube that carries urine from the bladder (center of picture) to the outside of the body. It also carries semen during ejaculation.

e Sperm production begins in each of the two testes at puberty and continues throughout life.

h The bulbourethral gland secretes an alkaline fluid that becomes part of the semen.

g The vas deferens passes over the urinary bladder, connecting the epididymis to the urethra.

f The epididymis is a coiled tube attached to the surface of each testis. If uncoiled, an epididymis would be about 6 m (20 ft) long.

720

For fertilization to occur, sperm first must be transferred from a male to a female. The penis is the male reproductive organ that delivers sperm to the body of the female. **Ejaculation** *(ee jak yoo LAY shuhn)* is the process by which sperm leave the male's body. The walls of the vas deferens contain a thick layer of smooth muscle. During ejaculation, rhythmic contractions of this smooth muscle propel sperm through the vas deferens. Sperm move from the vas deferens into a tube that leads into the urethra. During ejaculation, the tube from the bladder is closed off by a small valve. This valve keeps urine and semen separated and prevents urination during ejaculation. The path that sperm travel from the time they are produced to the time they are expelled during ejaculation is outlined in **Figure 35-3**.

Several glands add fluids to the sperm

As they travel through the vas deferens and urethra, sperm are bathed in fluids that are produced by glands along the route of travel. The seminal vesicles *(SEHM uh nuhl VEHS ih kuhlz)* are two small glands located near the bladder. The fluid produced by these glands nourishes the sperm. The bulbourethral *(buhl boh yoo REE thruhl)* gland is located just past the prostate *(PRAH stayt)* gland. Both glands secrete a thick, clear, alkaline fluid. These secretions mix with sperm to form **semen**. Semen is expelled from the penis during ejaculation. **Figure 35-4** shows sperm that have reached the uterus of a female.

If sperm cannot reach the egg, fertilization cannot occur. The surest way to prevent a pregnancy is to not have sexual intercourse. Blocking the path traveled by sperm can also prevent fertilization. One way to accomplish this is for a male to wear a latex rubber sheath called a condom whenever the penis is hard. If the condom is used properly and no semen leaks out, fertilization cannot occur because no sperm are deposited in the body of the female. If a male chooses to have no more children, he can have an operation called a vasectomy. During a vasectomy, a small incision is made in the scrotum. Each vas deferens is then cut and the ends are tied. A male who has had a vasectomy is sterile because the sperm's path to the outside of the body is blocked. Sperm are still produced, but they disintegrate in the epididymis.

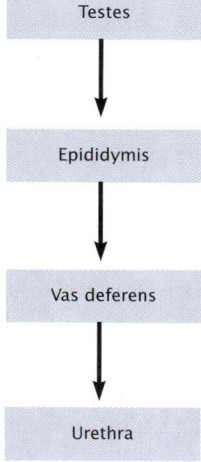

Figure 35-3
After sperm are produced in the testes, they are stored in the epididymis and vas deferens. As they pass out of a male's body during ejaculation, they pass through the vas deferens and urethra.

Testes

↓

Epididymis

↓

Vas deferens

↓

Urethra

Figure 35-4
As many as 350 million sperm, shown here in the uterus, are released into the vagina of the female during sexual intercourse. Sperm can live for as long as 3–5 days after being deposited within the female.

721

Matter of Fact: Vasectomy

A vasectomy does not have any significant effect on ejaculation because sperm account for only 1 percent of the total volume of the semen. Since male hormones are still produced, a vasectomy also does not affect secondary sex characteristics.

Visual Strategy — Videodisc

■ **Relating Concepts**
Review with students the formation of sperm during meiosis. Use *Illustration—Sperm Formation* shown in Chapter 35 Section 35-1 of *Holt Biology Videodiscs Teacher's Correlation Guide to Holt Biology: Visualizing Life.* Point out the diploid cell to the left in the illustration. Have students count the number of chromosomes (2 pairs). Elicit from students the following three steps in the illustration: (1) the chromosomes double; (2) the cell divides, producing two cells, each with the same number of chromosomes as the original cell; and (3) each cell divides again, producing four haploid sperm. Ask students why the final cell division is important. *(If the final division did not occur, the sperm would have a diploid number of chromosomes. When it combined with an egg, the resulting zygote would have a triploid number of chromosomes.)*

Health Connection

Prostate Problems

At birth, the prostate is about the size of an almond. During puberty, it doubles in size. It then stops growing. However, in most men 45 or older, the prostate again starts to enlarge as a result of hormonal activity. As the prostate continues to grow, it can squeeze the urethra, sometimes blocking the passage of urine out of the body.

Visual Strategy — Figure 35-4

● **Identifying Structures**
Tell students to identify the sperm (both the head and tail regions) in this figure. Have them hypothesize why a single ejaculation contains so many sperm.

Key to Strategies
● **Understanding Concepts (Tier I)**
■ **Applying Information (Tier II)**
▲ **Critical Thinking (Tier III)**

Connection: *Chapter 31*

Negative Feedback

Have students explain the principle of negative feedback. Remind them that the level of production of most hormones (with some exceptions such as oxytocin), and not just of testosterone, is controlled through negative feedback.

Visual Strategy Figure 35-5

● **Summarizing Functions**

Have students explain how this figure illustrates the negative-feedback control of testosterone. Point out that the production of testosterone is subject to factors other than GnRH. One such factor is stress, which has been shown in several studies to reduce testosterone production. In vertebrates other than humans, the production of testosterone can be responsive to daylight hours and temperature.

Phase Three
Assessment Options

Closure

■ **Recognizing Relationships**

Have students explain why sperm can survive for only about 48 hours once they enter the female reproductive tract (where the acidic fluid poses a hostile environment), yet survive much longer in the testes (where specialized cells and fluid nourish and protect them).

SECTION REVIEW

Assign the *Section Review*.

Reteaching

Show the class an overhead transparency of the male reproductive system. Have students identify the structure and function of the various parts.

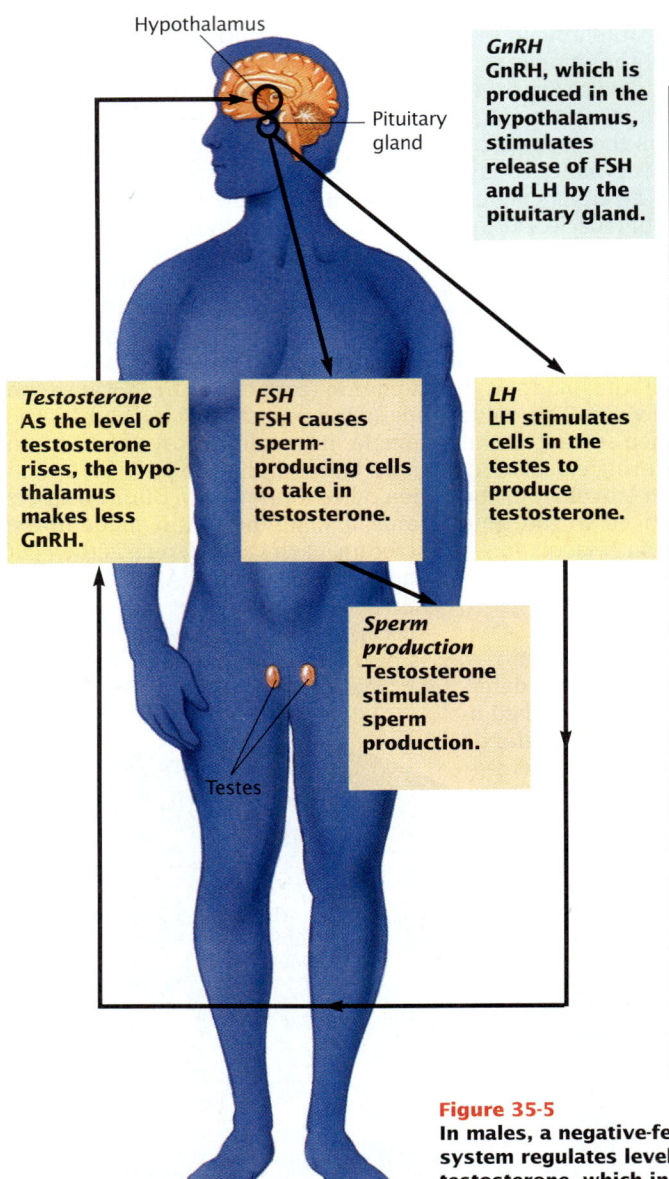

Hypothalamus

Pituitary gland

GnRH
GnRH, which is produced in the hypothalamus, stimulates release of FSH and LH by the pituitary gland.

Testosterone
As the level of testosterone rises, the hypothalamus makes less GnRH.

FSH
FSH causes sperm-producing cells to take in testosterone.

LH
LH stimulates cells in the testes to produce testosterone.

Sperm production
Testosterone stimulates sperm production.

Testes

Male Hormones and Reproduction

In addition to producing sperm, the testes also produce the male hormone testosterone. A male begins to make testosterone before birth. Testosterone causes an embryo to develop a penis and scrotum rather than female reproductive structures. At puberty, testosterone levels rise. These higher levels of testosterone cause the development of adult male characteristics, such as a beard, a low voice, and large muscles. Testosterone also stimulates sperm production. Production of sperm and testosterone are regulated by two pituitary hormones: luteinizing hormone (LH) and follicle-stimulating hormone (FSH).

The release of LH and FSH is controlled by a hormone from the hypothalamus. This hormone is called gonadotropin-releasing hormone, or GnRH for short. The hypothalamus is sensitive to testosterone levels in the blood. If the level of testosterone rises, the hypothalamus makes less GnRH. Thus, less LH and FSH are released, and less testosterone is produced by the testes. As the levels of testosterone fall, the hypothalamus begins to make more GnRH. More LH and FSH are released from the pituitary gland, and more testosterone is then produced by the testes. This negative feedback system maintains a nearly constant level of testosterone in the blood. The steps of this negative-feedback system are illustrated in **Figure 35-5**.

Figure 35-5
In males, a negative-feedback system regulates levels of testosterone, which in turn controls sperm production.

SECTION REVIEW

1 In what ways are sperm different from the body's other cells?

2 What is the function of fluids added to sperm as they travel from the epididymis?

3 Describe two functions of the testes.

4 What role does the hypothalamus play in sperm production?

ANSWERS TO SECTION REVIEW

1 Answers will vary. Possible answers might include the following: sperm are haploid; they are highly specialized DNA delivery cells; they have a flagellum; they have discarded most of their organelles and cytoplasm; their mitochondria cluster around the top part of the tail; a cap of digestive enzymes forms at the tip of their heads.

2 The fluids function to nourish the sperm, lubricate the vagina, protect the sperm from the acidity in the urethra and vagina, prevent the sperm from drying out, and protect the sperm from bacteria.

3 The testes produce sperm and the male hormone testosterone.

4 The hypothalamus produces a hormone called GnRH, which controls the release of two other hormones, LH and FSH. LH and FSH stimulate the production and uptake of testosterone, which stimulates sperm production.

The male contributes one set of chromosomes when the female's egg is fertilized. Once fertilization has occurred, the male's biological role is finished. In contrast, the female carries the developing fetus for about nine months, until birth. The female reproductive system thus must play two biological roles: making gametes and nourishing the fetus.

35-2 The Female Reproductive System

Phase One
Preparation

Scheduling
See the **Lesson Planning Guide** on pages 717A and 717B for lecture, classwork, and assignment options for Section 35-2.

Phase Two
Teaching Strategies

OBJECTIVES

1 Identify two differences between the male and female reproductive systems.

2 Compare and contrast sperm production with egg production.

3 Relate the events of the ovarian cycle to the levels of LH, FSH, and estrogens.

4 Describe the events of the uterine cycle.

Structure of the Female Reproductive System

Female gametes are called **ova** (singular, ovum), or eggs. The **ovaries** are the organs responsible for producing eggs. Ovaries are located in the lower part of the abdomen. An egg released from an ovary moves into a **fallopian tube**, which carries the egg into the uterus, as you can see in **Figure 35-6**. The **uterus** is a hollow, muscular organ about the shape and size of a small pear. During pregnancy, the uterus expands to many times its usual size.

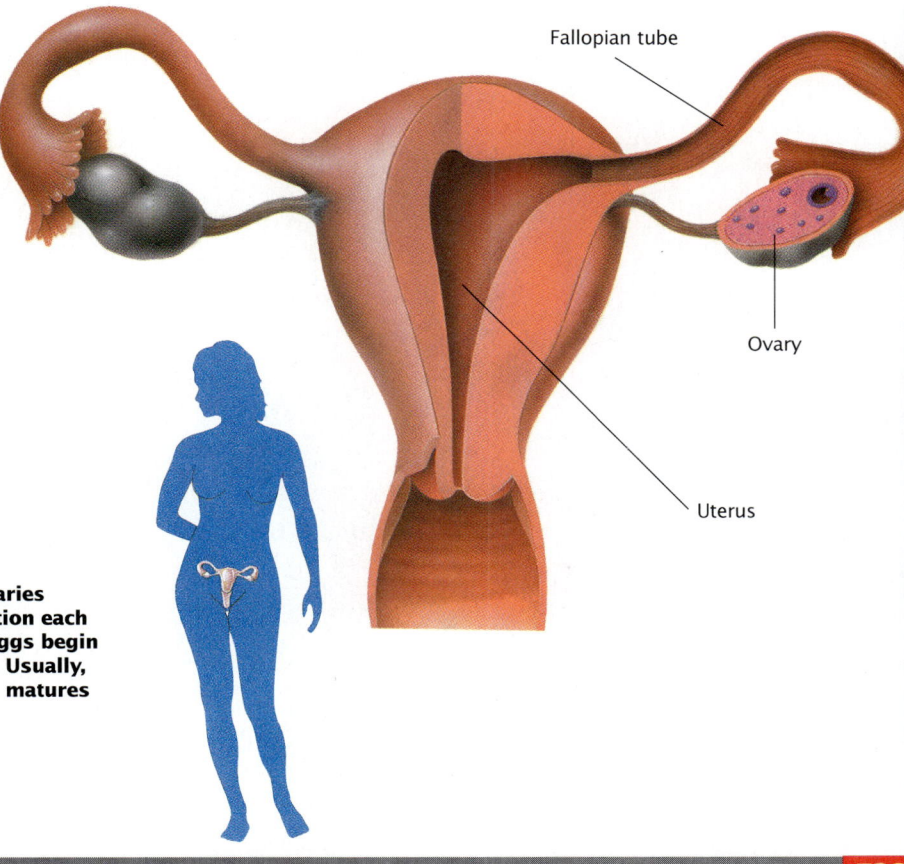

Fallopian tube

Ovary

Uterus

Figure 35-6
After puberty, the ovaries alternate egg production each month, and several eggs begin to grow in one ovary. Usually, though, only one egg matures each month.

Visual Strategy | **Videodisc**

● **Summarizing Information**
To introduce the lesson, use *Video—Reproduction: Females* (3 min 15 s) shown in Chapter 35 Section 35-2 of *Holt Biology Videodiscs Teacher's Correlation Guide to Holt Biology: Visualizing Life.* Tell students as they view the video to pay particular attention to the path of the egg through the female reproductive system. After viewing the video, have students describe the path of an egg *(ovaries, fallopian tube, uterus, vagina).* Ask students to identify in which of these organs fertilization takes place *(fallopian tube).*

Visual Strategy | **Figure 35-6**

● **Comparing Structures**
Have students locate where sperm enter the female reproductive system illustrated in this figure *(vagina).*

723

Videodisc Resources

Holt Biology Videodiscs
Lesson 35-2: The Female Reproductive System

Key to Strategies
● Understanding Concepts (Tier I)
■ Applying Information (Tier II)
▲ Critical Thinking (Tier III)

● **Identifying Functions**

Discuss the major points made in this illustration. Have students trace the path traveled by the egg: ovary → fallopian tube → uterus → vagina. Unlike in males, the urethra in females does not serve as a common exit for both urine and gametes. Have students trace how urine exits the body in a female. Point out that early in development, the embryonic female has a common opening for both the urinary and reproductive tracts. However, during fetal development, a separate opening for the reproductive system (the vagina) is formed.

Language Arts Connection

Cervix and Cervical Vertebrae

The word *cervix* means "neck" in Latin. Have students explain why this is an appropriate term for the ring of strong muscles located in the lower part of the uterus. *(Answers will vary but could include the similarity of the cervix to the neck of a bottle.)* Ask them where cervical vertebrae would be found. *(Cervical vertebrae are found in the part of the spine forming the neck.)*

Connection: *Chapter 6*

Meiosis

Remind students that meiosis is a type of nuclear division in which the chromosome number is halved. Ask why this is important for fertilization. *(If the chromosome number were not halved, the sperm or egg would have a diploid number of chromosomes. When it combined with an egg, the resulting zygote would have a triploid number of chromosomes.)*

Figure 35-7
The female reproductive system releases eggs and provides nourishment to a developing fetus.

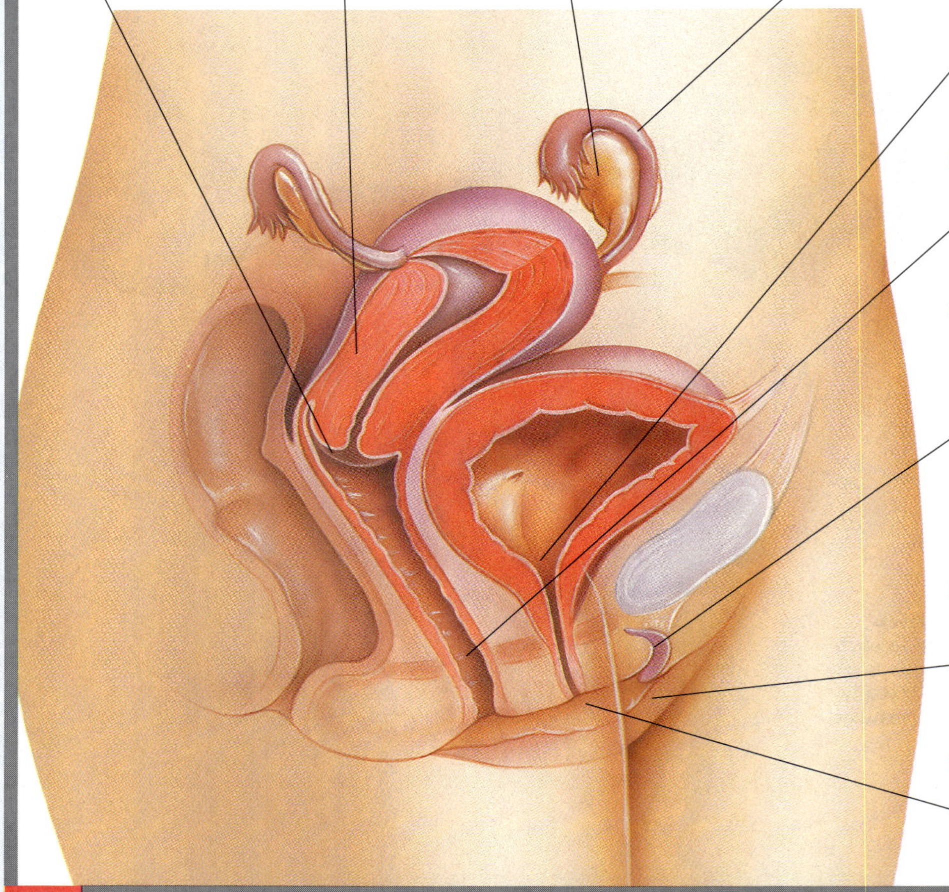

a This end of the cervix has a small opening through which sperm can enter. During childbirth, this opening dilates enough so that the infant can pass through.

b After fertilization, the embryo develops into a fetus inside the uterus.

c Ovaries are the site of egg production.

d Fertilization occurs in one of the fallopian tubes. The fertilized egg then travels to the uterus.

e The urethra carries urine from the bladder to the outside of the body but plays no role in reproduction.

f The vagina connects the uterus to the outside of the body.

g The clitoris is similar to the penis in that it also has the capacity to become erect. It is covered by a hood of skin that is connected to the labia.

h The two larger folds of skin between the thighs are called the labia majora.

i Inside the labia majora are two smaller folds called the labia minora.

The lower part of the uterus is a tubular ring of strong muscles known as the **cervix** *(SER vihks)*. As shown in **Figure 35-7**, the **vagina** *(vuh JEYE nuh)* is a muscular tube that receives the penis and any sperm ejaculated by a male during intercourse. The lower end of the vagina opens to the outside of the body, and the upper end connects to the cervix. During birth, the baby passes through the cervix and the vagina, also called the birth canal.

Pregnancy can be prevented by not allowing sperm to enter the opening in the cervix. A diaphragm is a shallow, round cup made of rubber that is placed inside the vagina to block the entrance to the cervix. A cervical cap is similar to a diaphragm but fits tightly over the cervix. A diaphragm or a cervical cap must be obtained from a doctor or health-care professional. Spermicidal creams, spermicidal jellies, vaginal suppositories, and spermicidal foams work by killing sperm in the vagina so that, in theory, no living sperm can enter the opening in the cervix (*spermicidal* means "sperm-killing"). Usually spermicides are used with a barrier such as a condom, diaphragm, or cervical cap. A barrier and spermicide used together are much more effective in preventing fertilization than either used by itself.

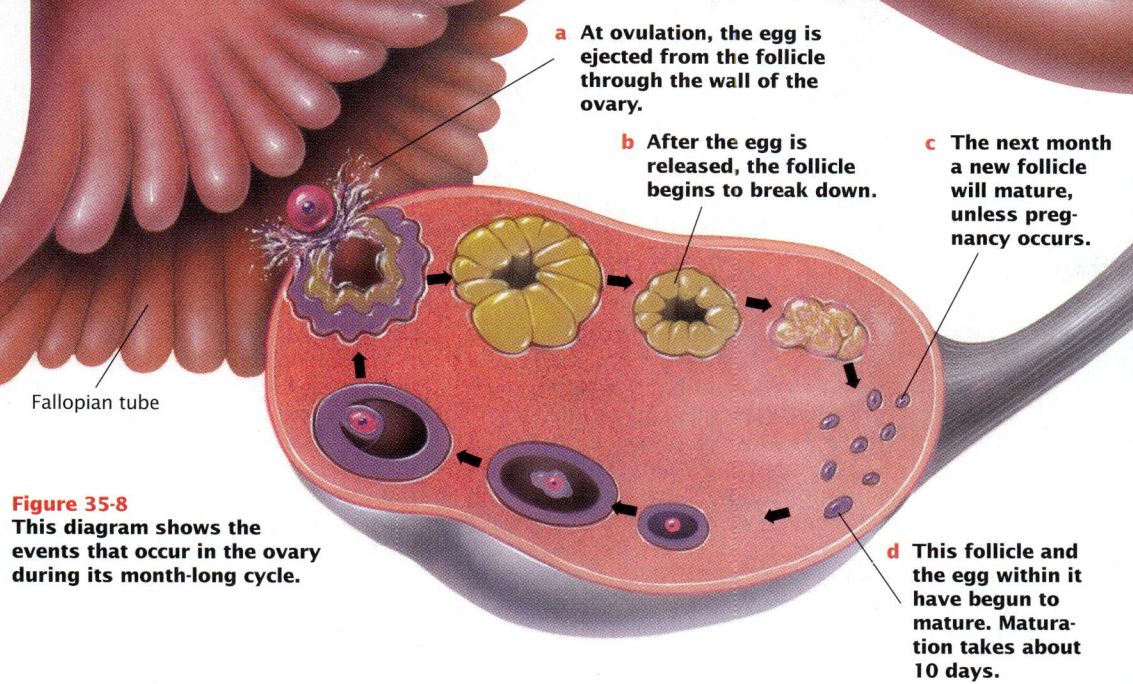

a At ovulation, the egg is ejected from the follicle through the wall of the ovary.

b After the egg is released, the follicle begins to break down.

c The next month a new follicle will mature, unless pregnancy occurs.

Fallopian tube

Figure 35-8
This diagram shows the events that occur in the ovary during its month-long cycle.

d This follicle and the egg within it have begun to mature. Maturation takes about 10 days.

Matter, Energy, and Organization

How are mature sperm and eggs different in size and structure?

The Female Reproductive Cycle

The two reproductive tasks of the female, making gametes and nourishing the fetus, are accomplished in two overlapping cycles—the ovarian cycle and the uterine cycle. Together these cycles allow for the maturation and release of female gametes (eggs) and for accommodation of the egg, whether fertilized or not. A delicate mix of hormones produces these changes in a sequence of events that is known as the **menstrual** *(MEHN struhl)* **cycle**.

The ovarian cycle prepares a mature egg for fertilization

Once a male has reached puberty, his testes continuously produce and release millions of sperm. In a female, however, egg release occurs only at a specific time once a month. The release of an egg from the ovary is called **ovulation** *(ahv yoo LAY shun)*. A female usually releases only one egg each month. If this egg is not fertilized, the ovaries prepare another egg for

release the next month. This cycle of activity in the ovaries is called the ovarian cycle.

Eggs begin to mature in the ovaries of a female while she is still in her mother's uterus. Thousands of her eggs grow and begin to undergo meiosis. Growth and meiosis stop before the eggs are completely mature, however. All of the eggs in the ovaries remain in this immature state until puberty. Several immature eggs are shown in **Figure 35-8**.

After puberty, follicle-stimulating hormone (FSH), released by the pituitary, signals several eggs to resume the process of maturation each month. The maturing eggs become large, highly complex cells, growing to be nearly 200,000 times larger than a sperm. Although many eggs begin to mature each month, usually only one egg completes the process and is released, as shown above. If two eggs mature, fraternal, or nonidentical, twins may result.

The egg matures within the follicle

Eggs grow inside a thin tissue sac called a **follicle** (FAHL ih kuhl), which is located in the ovary. A follicle also produces estrogens. At puberty, estrogens cause females to develop breasts and wider hips. Cells of a follicle produce larger amounts of progesterone and estrogens when an egg nears maturity. Progesterone causes the uterus to prepare to receive a fertilized egg. The high level of estrogen triggers the pituitary to release a burst of luteinizing hormone (LH). LH causes the egg to resume meiosis. Stimulated by high LH levels, the follicle ruptures, as shown in the previous figure, and the finger-like ends of the fallopian tube draw the egg into the tube where rhythmical contractions of its walls move the egg to the uterus.

An egg gradually disintegrates within 24 to 48 hours after its release from the ovary. For pregnancy to occur, fertilization must take place within the 12–24 hours after ovulation. If a woman chooses to have no more children, she can undergo tubal ligation, an operation in which the fallopian tubes are severed or tied.

Hormone levels change during the ovarian cycle

Estrogen level drops and progesterone level rises after ovulation. But the level of both hormones is enough to cause the pituitary gland to stop releasing LH and FSH. If no fertilized egg reaches the uterus, estrogen and progesterone levels fall even more, and FSH and LH levels rise again. Another egg will mature and be released. If fertilization occurs, however, estrogen and progesterone levels remain high. High levels of these hormones suppress the release of FSH and LH. Because no eggs mature, a woman does not ovulate or menstruate during pregnancy.

Prescription pills containing synthetic estrogen and progesterone prevent the egg from maturing. Use of these pills prevents pregnancy by keeping the levels of estrogen and progesterone at a steady level, as shown in **Figure 35-9**. The pituitary responds as if a pregnancy were in progress; it does not release FSH or LH. Since ovulation does not occur, pregnancy cannot take place.

The uterus waits for a fertilized egg

Like the ovaries, the uterus follows a monthly cycle. Each month, the uterus prepares to receive and nourish a fertilized egg, or **embryo**, in a cycle of changes called the uterine cycle.

As an egg matures in the follicle, the lining of the uterus grows thicker. Many tiny blood vessels grow into this thickened lining, which will provide a safe environment for an embryo. The progesterone produced just before ovulation causes the lining of the uterus to become spongy and rich in blood and nutrients. These changes prepare the uterus to receive an embryo four or five days after ovulation. It takes an embryo about this long to travel to the uterus. Most of the time, fertilization does not occur, and no embryo arrives.

The uterus sheds its lining when no fertilized egg arrives

Recall that the follicle produces less and less estrogen and progesterone as it breaks down. As the hormone levels fall, the blood vessels in the uterine lining begin to close and to break. Receiving little blood now, the cells of the uterine lining come loose from the inside of the uterus. Blood from the broken blood vessels helps to wash these cells out of the uterus. This mixture of blood and uterine cells is called

Figure 35-9
The graph below compares a woman's levels of estrogen and progesterone under normal conditions (solid lines) with her levels while she is using pills containing synthetic estrogen and progesterone (dotted lines).

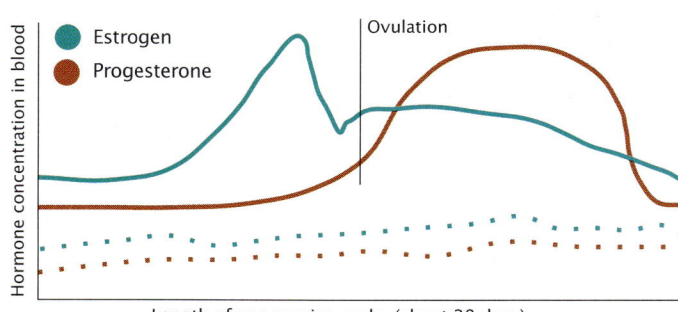

menstrual fluid. The passage of this fluid through the vagina and out of the body is called a menstrual period. It usually lasts from three to seven days. Changes in the uterine lining over the course of the uterine cycle are shown in **Figure 35-10**.

The average menstrual cycle is 28 days long. Women usually start their menstrual period 14 days after ovulation. The length of the first stage of the cycle, the period when the follicle is growing, differs from woman to woman. However, it is difficult to determine when ovulation occurs, especially in women with irregular menstrual cycles.

Some couples try to prevent pregnancy by abstaining from sexual intercourse around the time of ovulation. This approach, called the rhythm method, is not an effective means of preventing pregnancy because it is almost impossible to know when ovulation will occur. Also, sperm can survive in the female for two days or longer, so there are usually three or four days each month when fertilization is possible.

The menstrual cycle stops in middle age

Between the ages of 45 and 55, ovulation and menstruation stop. The shutdown of ovarian and uterine cycles is known as **menopause**. After menopause, a woman is no longer able to have children.

Figure 35-10
This graph shows the changes in uterine lining during the menstrual cycle.

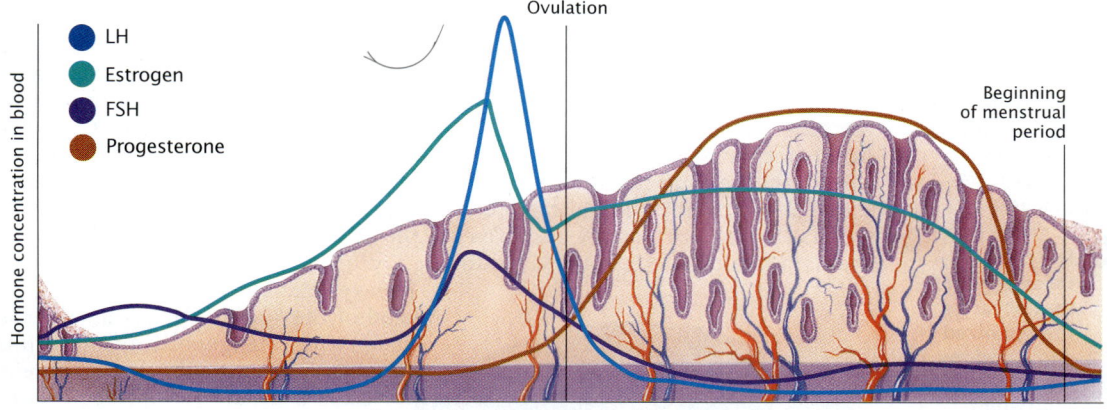

- LH
- Estrogen
- FSH
- Progesterone

Ovulation

Beginning of menstrual period

Hormone concentration in blood

Length of one menstrual cycle (about 28 days)

a During the first part of the menstrual cycle, blood vessels grow in the uterine lining as it thickens.

b The lining is ready to receive an embryo four or five days after the egg is released from the ovary.

c If no embryo arrives, blood vessels in the uterine lining break. Blood and cells from the uterine lining pass through the vagina during the menstrual period.

SECTION REVIEW

1 Trace the path of an egg through the female reproductive system.

2 Identify two differences between a sperm and an egg.

3 What role do hormones play in the uterine cycle?

4 Explain the role of progesterone in the uterine cycle.

727

1 The following is the the path traveled by the egg through the female reproductive system: ovary → fallopian tube → uterus → vagina. Also see Figure 35-7.

2 Answers may vary. The most obvious answers might indicate that sperm have flagella for movement and an oval-shaped head, whereas eggs are much larger and lack a tail. There are millions of sperm made per month, and usually one egg ovulates.

3 Hormones are the drivers of the cycle. They initiate and regulate.

4 Progesterone causes blood vessels in the uterus to enlarge, preparing the uterus to receive the embryo after the egg is released from the ovary.

Phase Three
Assessment Options

Closure
■ **Recognizing Relationships**
Ask the class why certain environmental factors, such as stress and prolonged strenuous exercise, can affect the female reproductive cycle. *(Students should realize that these can influence hormone levels, thus affecting the female reproductive cycle.)*

SECTION REVIEW
Assign the *Section Review*.

Reteaching
Have students simulate the complex events that occur during the uterine cycle by assuming the roles of the various hormones and structures that are involved. Begin by preparing the following labels: *hypothalamus, GnRH, pituitary, FSH, LH, ovary, follicle, egg, estrogen, progesterone,* and *uterus.* Give these labels to students, and lead them through a model of what happens during the uterine cycle. Begin with two students standing together. Have one student hold the *hypothalamus* label and the other hold the *GnRH* label. Have the *GnRH* student leave the hypothalamus student and move over to a student holding the *pituitary* label. In turn, the student with the *FSH* label, who had been standing alongside the student with the *pituitary* label, should walk to a student holding the *ovary* label. Have students orchestrate as many of the movements as possible. Have them explain what is happening at each step.

Key to Strategies
● **Understanding Concepts (Tier I)**
■ **Applying Information (Tier II)**
▲ **Critical Thinking (Tier III)**

Scheduling

See the **Lesson Planning Guide** on pages 717A and 717B for lecture, classwork, and assignment options for Section 35-3.

Demonstration

● **Comparing Structures**

Use a microprojector to show the class *Euglena* or other organisms propelled by a flagellum. Point out that the flagellum of a sperm functions in the same manner.

Demonstration

■ **Relating Concepts**

Have students place a 0.5 mm dot (about the size of a mechanical-pencil mark) at the top of a sheet of paper. Tell them to label the mark "14 days." Then have them draw a line about 1 mm in length below the dot and label it "18 days." Tell them to continue down the sheet in a similar manner, drawing lines 4, 8, 19, 38, and 63 mm in length and labeling them "4 weeks," "6.5 weeks," "9 weeks," "11 weeks," and "15 weeks," respectively. Tell students that these are the actual lengths of a developing human through the 15th week.

Before fertilization, a sperm and an egg are separate cells, each containing one-half of the information needed for the development of an embryo. During fertilization, gametes fuse into one cell containing all of the instructions needed to form a new individual. After fertilization, the embryo will grow and develop for about nine months inside its mother's uterus.

35-3 Fertilization and Development

OBJECTIVES

1. **Describe the process of fertilization.**

2. **Explain the process of implantation.**

3. **List three substances that can pass through the placenta.**

4. **Describe three changes that occur as the fertilized egg develops into a new individual.**

Fertilization: Fusion of Gametes

During ejaculation, 150 million to 350 million sperm are deposited just a few inches away from the fallopian tubes, in which **fertilization** can occur. Then a long and difficult journey begins. To reach the egg, a sperm must first pass through the small opening in the cervix. Then it must cross the uterus and swim up one of the fallopian tubes. The vast majority of ejaculated sperm never leave the vagina. Of the sperm that find the small opening to the cervix, many will be trapped in mucus that covers this opening. Over the next two days, sperm will gradu-ally free themselves from this mucus and start their journey across the uterus. Even if a mature egg is waiting in one of the fallopian tubes, half of the sperm will swim up the wrong tube.

Although only one sperm can fuse with the egg, many sperm can arrive at the egg at about the same time. The egg is surrounded by a protective layer of smaller cells. Enzymes in the heads of the sperm cells help loosen this layer of cells. Once a sperm reaches the surface of the egg, as shown in **Figure 35-11**, it leaves its tail behind. The genetic information inside the head of the sperm enters the egg and fuses with the genetic information inside the egg. A protective shield then forms around the egg to prevent other sperm from entering.

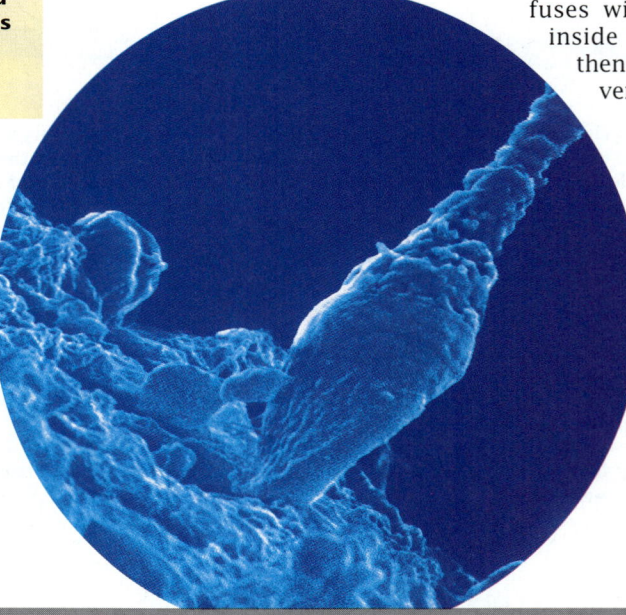

Figure 35-11
This sperm is penetrating an egg.

Videodisc Resources

Holt Biology Videodiscs

Lesson 35-3: Fertilization and Development

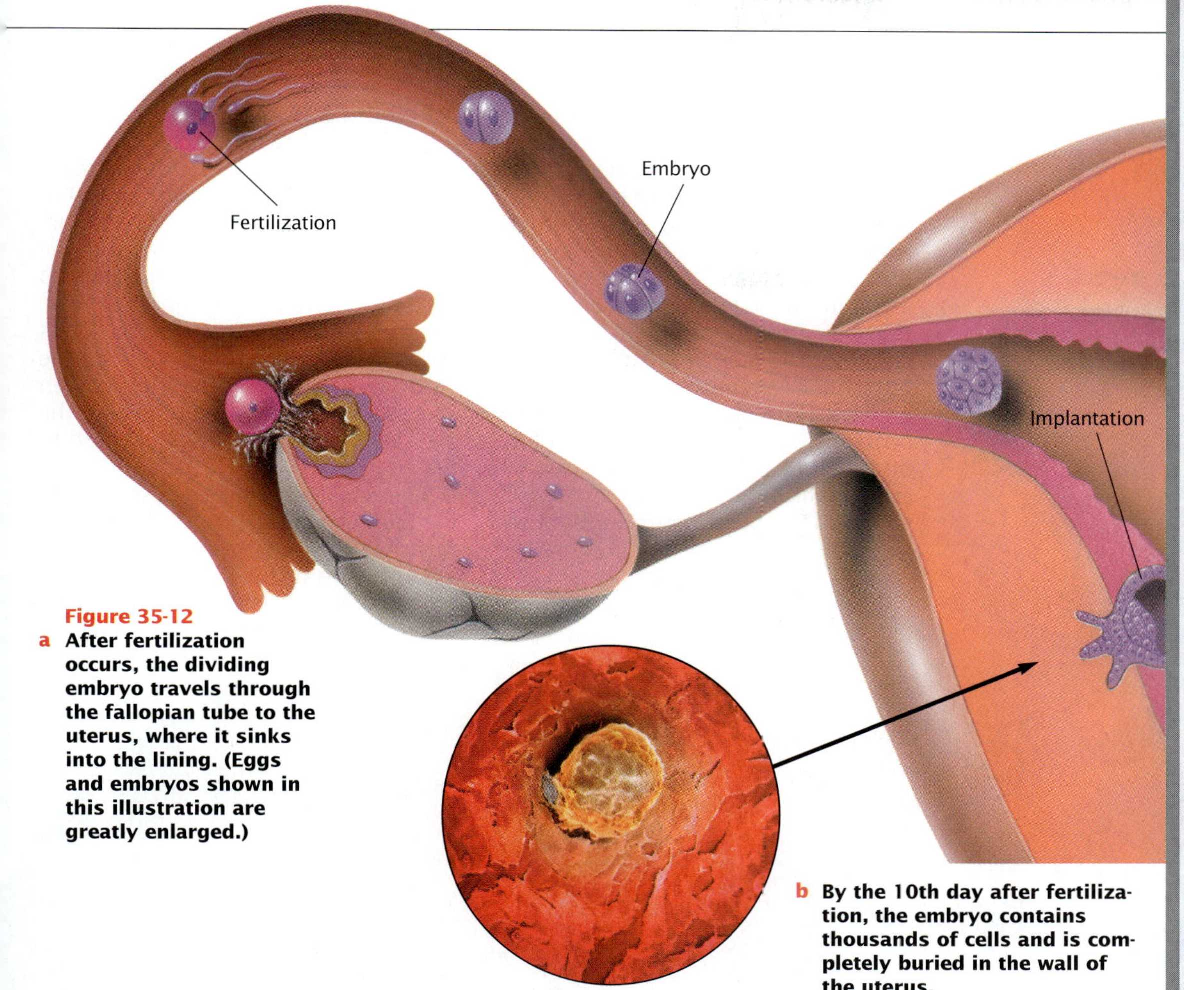

Fertilization

Embryo

Implantation

Figure 35-12

a **After fertilization occurs, the dividing embryo travels through the fallopian tube to the uterus, where it sinks into the lining. (Eggs and embryos shown in this illustration are greatly enlarged.)**

b **By the 10th day after fertilization, the embryo contains thousands of cells and is completely buried in the wall of the uterus.**

The Embryo Enters the Lining of the Uterus

Cell Structure and Function

Explain why a young girl can become pregnant even if she has not had her first menstrual period.

A newly fertilized egg is called a **zygote**. After the egg is fertilized, it continues to travel through the fallopian tube toward the uterus, as shown in **Figure 35-12**. After about 30 hours the zygote divides into two cells and is called an embryo. The cells of the embryo continue to divide by mitosis. (If the young embryo splits completely in two, identical twins will result.)

By the time the embryo reaches the uterus, about 4–5 days after fertilization, it is made up of a hundred or more cells. The embryo embeds itself in the soft, thickened uterine lining and then releases hormones to ensure that the thick lining of the uterus remains healthy and is not washed away by a menstrual period. The embryo's entry into the uterine wall is known as **implantation**. From the ninth week of development until birth, the developing embryo is called a **fetus**.

There are several ways for a female to determine whether she is pregnant. A missed menstrual period is one possible sign of pregnancy. A more accurate way of determining pregnancy is to test her blood or urine for the presence of the hormone produced by the embryo. By three weeks after fertilization, a pregnant woman will probably have enough of this hormone in her blood and urine to produce a positive test result. Doctors and health clinics are equipped to administer these tests, and they perform more reliable tests than those performed at home.

● **Comparing Structures**
Have students identify the ovary, fallopian tube, and uterus shown in this figure. Point out that if the first two cells of the zygote separate after the first mitotic division, and if each continues to develop normally, identical twins will result. Have students explain, based on their knowledge of mitosis, why these two individuals must be identical, rather then fraternal, twins. *(Their genetic composition is the same.)*

Active READING

Technique: Reading Organizer
Have students working in small groups create a reading organizer that represents the growth and development of the newly fertilized egg as it is described in the text. Remind students to include information from the graphs and illustrations provided on pages 733 and 734 in their reading organizers. Have a spokesperson from each group present the group's reading organizer to the class. *(The reading organizers developed should follow the sequence of events listed and illustrated in the text.)*

Theme Answer

Cell Structure and Function
Ovulation precedes a menstrual period. Therefore, a young girl must ovulate before her first menstrual period.

Matter of Fact: *In Vitro* Fertilization

If a male has a low sperm count, or if a female does not have enough hormones to ovulate or has a blocked fallopian tube, natural fertilization may be impossible. In such cases, the events that ordinarily happen in the oviduct can be caused in a culture dish in a process known as *in vitro* fertilization. In the process, hormones are given to the woman to ensure precise timing of ovulation. Within hours of ovulation, one or more eggs are surgically removed from the ovary and placed in a culture dish. Sperm taken from the male are then added. If the procedure is successful, one or more fertilized eggs are then implanted in the woman's uterus to complete development.

Key to Strategies
● **Understanding Concepts (Tier I)**
■ **Applying Information (Tier II)**
▲ **Critical Thinking (Tier III)**

The Placenta

As the embryo implants itself in the uterine wall, it uses up the raw materials that were stored in the egg. The body of the mother begins to transfer nutrients and oxygen to the embryo through the placenta, the two-layered, disk-shaped membrane that you read about in Chapter 23. The inner layer of the placenta is derived from the chorion *(KAWR ee ahn)* and forms the outermost membrane around the embryo. The outer layer of the placenta forms from the thickened lining of the mother's uterus. Cells from the embryo form the umbilical cord, which connects the placenta to the embryo.

Nutrients and oxygen pass from mother to child

As shown in **Figure 35-13**, the mother's part of the placenta forms pools of blood that bathe the outside of the embryo's blood vessels. Blood from the mother and the embryo come close to each other, but they do not mix. Oxygen and nutrients from the mother's blood pass through the walls of the embryo's blood vessels. The oxygen and nutrients then travel through the blood vessels in the umbilical cord to the embryo.

Since the embryo is enclosed within the mother's body, it cannot get rid of waste products on its own. Carbon dioxide and urea diffuse through the placenta into the mother's bloodstream and are eliminated by the mother's body.

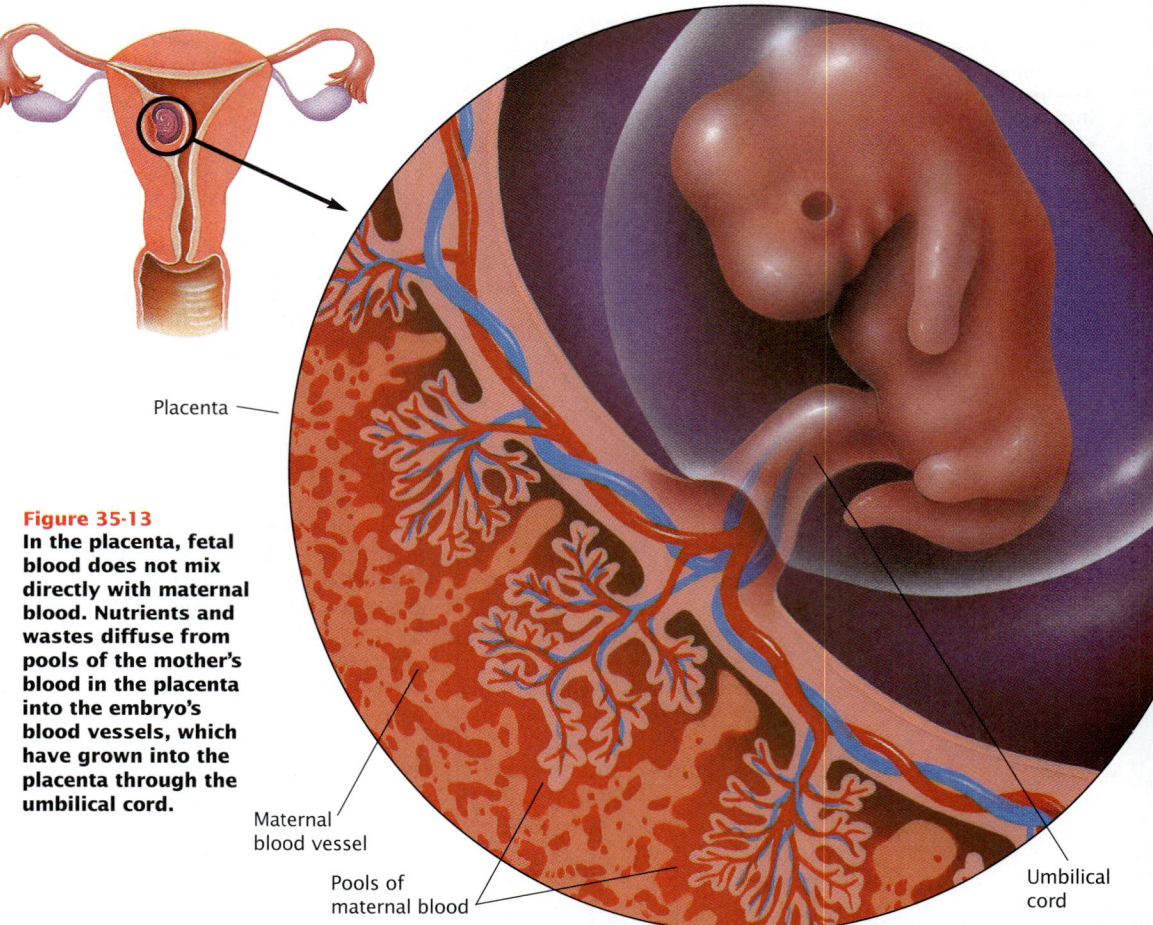

Placenta

Figure 35-13
In the placenta, fetal blood does not mix directly with maternal blood. Nutrients and wastes diffuse from pools of the mother's blood in the placenta into the embryo's blood vessels, which have grown into the placenta through the umbilical cord.

Maternal blood vessel

Pools of maternal blood

Umbilical cord

Drugs
Babies of mothers who use drugs during pregnancy are often born underweight. These babies can face a variety of medical complications. For this reason, no pregnant woman should take any drug without checking with her doctor first.

Nutrition and Exercise
Nutrition and exercise are important during pregnancy. A mother must provide all the nutrients that a fetus needs to develop normally. An undernourished mother will give birth to a smaller, less healthy baby.

Smoking
Smoking cigarettes decreases the amount of oxygen available to the growing fetus. Babies born to mothers who smoke heavily tend to be much smaller than the babies of nonsmokers. Babies of heavy smokers also face a much higher risk of complications after birth than the babies of nonsmokers.

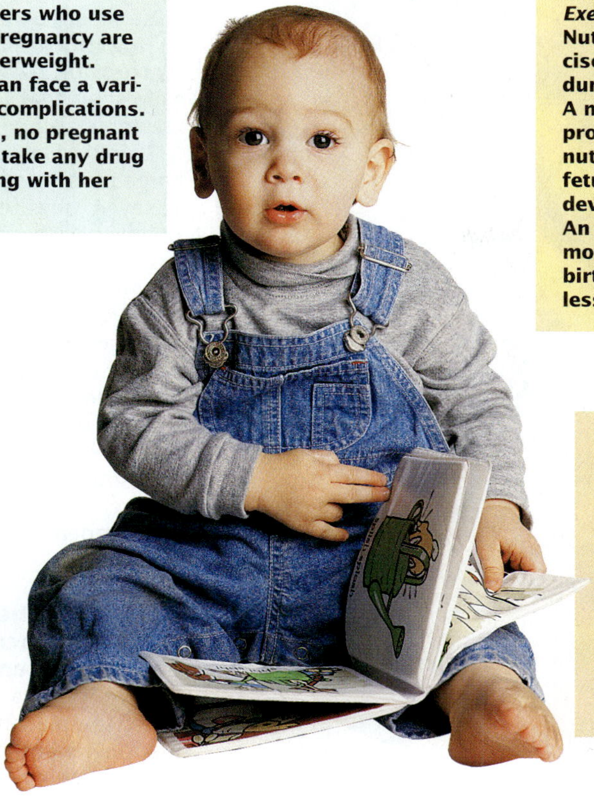

Alcohol
Women who drink alcohol during pregnancy may have babies with severe facial deformities and mental retardation. Most doctors think that even a small amount of alcohol may damage a fetus and therefore recommend that women do not drink at all during pregnancy.

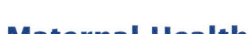

Figure 35-14 **This baby was born healthy because his mother was careful during pregnancy. She ate healthy foods, exercised regularly, and avoided drugs, including alcohol.**

Maternal Health

The health and activities of its mother influence whether an embryo develops normally. From the instant of fertilization, an embryo is vulnerable to damage. In the first three months of pregnancy, the major systems and organs are forming. In the last six months of pregnancy, a fetus grows and matures. As **Figure 35-14** indicates, the diet and behavior of a woman during her pregnancy can affect the mental and physical development of the child, before and even years after birth. Even when it is too early for a woman to suspect she is pregnant, her use of alcohol, nicotine, and other drugs—prescription drugs, over-the-counter drugs, or street drugs—can damage the embryo.

Radiation and certain diseases may damage the fetus

Chemicals and other agents that cause malformation to a fetus are called **teratogens** *(TUH rat oh jinz)*. All types of ionizing radiation, including X rays, and ultraviolet rays, are teratogens. Radiation is most damaging to cells undergoing rapid division, as fetal cells are. For this reason, a woman who suspects or knows she is pregnant should not undergo X rays.

Certain diseases can also harm a fetus. Rubella (German measles) causes birth defects in early pregnancy. Toxoplasmosis is caused by a protozoan that is transmitted by undercooked meat or by taking in food, water, or dust contaminated by an infected cat. Adults show no symptoms or only mild ones, but fetal infection is more severe and may result in brain or eye damage and sometimes death. Both rubella and toxoplasmosis pathogens can pass from the mother's blood, through the placenta, and into the blood of the fetus.

Historical Perspective: Thalidomide

Thalidomide, a sedative used by pregnant women in Europe in the 1960s as a remedy for morning sickness, caused deformities in the offspring, such as legs and arms resembling flippers, when taken during the limb-bud differentiation period (days 26 to 56).

Visual Strategy — Figure 35-14

■ **Analyzing Information**
Have students make a table outlining the effects of different teratogens on fetal development. Have one student put the table on the board and another lead a discussion comparing these effects.

Demonstration

● **Identifying Variables**
Invite the school nurse or health teacher to talk to the class about the effects of substance abuse during pregnancy. Have the speaker emphasize that in many cases, doctors do not know how much of a drug is necessary to harm a fetus. Consequently, a pregnant woman is best advised to avoid all unnecessary drugs, including alcohol and nicotine.

Connection: *Chapter 33*

The Immune System
The embryo, although a "foreign" entity in the body, is not attacked or rejected by the immune system of the mother. Somehow, in ways that are poorly understood, the embryo protects itself from immunological attack.

Key to Strategies
● Understanding Concepts (Tier I)
■ Applying Information (Tier II)
▲ Critical Thinking (Tier III)

■ Analyzing Information

Have students discuss the ethics of heavy alcohol consumption during pregnancy and the danger it poses to the health of the fetus. Tell your students that fetal alcohol syndrome (FAS) was first described in 1973 by researchers at the University of Washington and that all containers of liquor now carry warnings to pregnant women. These cautions have been mandatory only since 1989. If a woman had an FAS baby before 1989, should she be able to collect damages from alcohol manufacturers? *(Answers should be logical and should consider manufacturers' responsibilities to the public and the mother's responsibilities to the fetus.)*

Fetal Alcohol Syndrome

● Organizing Data

portfolio

Using information about fetal alcohol syndrome (FAS) from this chapter, have students make a **Graphic Organizer** similar to the one shown at the bottom of this page to illustrate the results of FAS. Ask students to write a report to summarize the physical and behavioral problems that result from FAS.

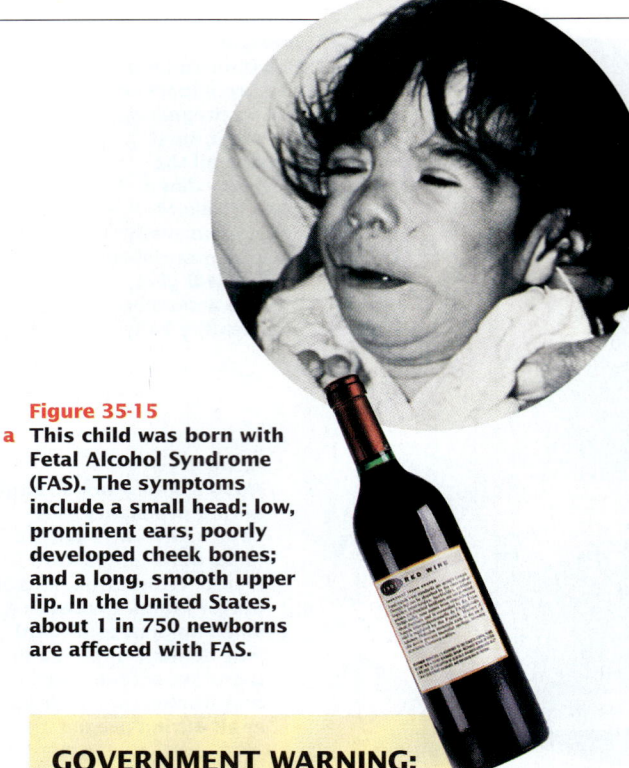

Figure 35-15

a This child was born with Fetal Alcohol Syndrome (FAS). The symptoms include a small head; low, prominent ears; poorly developed cheek bones; and a long, smooth upper lip. In the United States, about 1 in 750 newborns are affected with FAS.

GOVERNMENT WARNING:

ACCORDING TO THE SURGEON GENERAL, WOMEN SHOULD NOT DRINK ALCOHOLIC BEVERAGES DURING PREGNANCY BECAUSE OF THE RISK OF BIRTH DEFECTS.

b Warning labels now appear on all alcoholic beverage containers.

Alcohol can cause severe birth defects

Alcohol use is considered to be the main cause of preventable birth defects in the United States today. Heavy drinking can cause a variety of defects that are collectively called Fetal Alcohol Syndrome (FAS). FAS babies often have deformed faces like that of the infant shown in **Figure 35-15a**. They often are physically as well as mentally retarded, having

trouble with simple functions such as telling time or counting. The average IQ of children with FAS is 30–40 points below normal. The damage is non-treatable and permanent.

Drinking alcohol during the first three months of pregnancy can result in severe physical damage—malformed organs, misshapen spine, and impaired brain development. Drinking later in pregnancy often results in stunted physical growth, hyperactivity, brain damage, and behavioral problems long after the child is born. Because the brain develops throughout the nine months of pregnancy, fetal brain damage due to a pregnant woman's alcohol consumption can occur at any time. **Figure 35-15b** shows a warning label that appears on alcoholic beverage containers.

Many toxic chemicals and drugs cross the placenta and can damage the embryo

The stimulants nicotine and caffeine cross the placenta too. In addition to nicotine, many of the other chemicals in cigarette smoke cross the placenta. Women who smoke have more miscarriages than women who do not smoke. The more a woman smokes, the more problems she and her baby are likely to have. Compared with nonsmoking mothers, smoking mothers have smaller infants and more babies who die at or shortly after birth. Caffeine, on the other hand, damages chromosomes in animal cells before conception. Although the extent of the damage that caffeine causes to the human fetus is not yet clear, women are advised to reduce caffeine intake or to avoid caffeine completely, beginning early in pregnancy.

A growing problem in the United States is the increasing number of babies born to mothers who use crack cocaine during pregnancy. These "crack babies" have a very high risk of mental retardation, learning disabilities, and personality disorders. Other drugs, legal and illegal, also affect the fetus. Babies of mothers who are addicted to heroin or cocaine may themselves be addicted when born.

732

Graphic Organizer

Use the following graphic organizer with the teaching strategy **Fetal Alcohol Syndrome** on page 732.

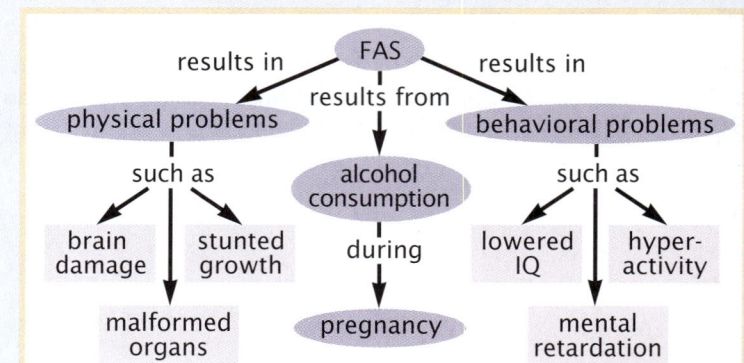

Growth and Development

Once the embryo implants in the uterus, it grows rapidly. It continues to grow for a period of about 40 weeks, or 240–300 days. The due date is calculated from the expectant mother's last menstrual period, but the fetus actually spends about 260 days in the uterus from fertilization to birth. Because only 5 percent of women deliver on their due dates, pregnancy is divided into three-month segments called **trimesters** that are used as guideposts to key events in the development of the embryo and fetus.

Figure 35-16

a **From conception through the second trimester, there is little outside evidence that the mother is pregnant.**

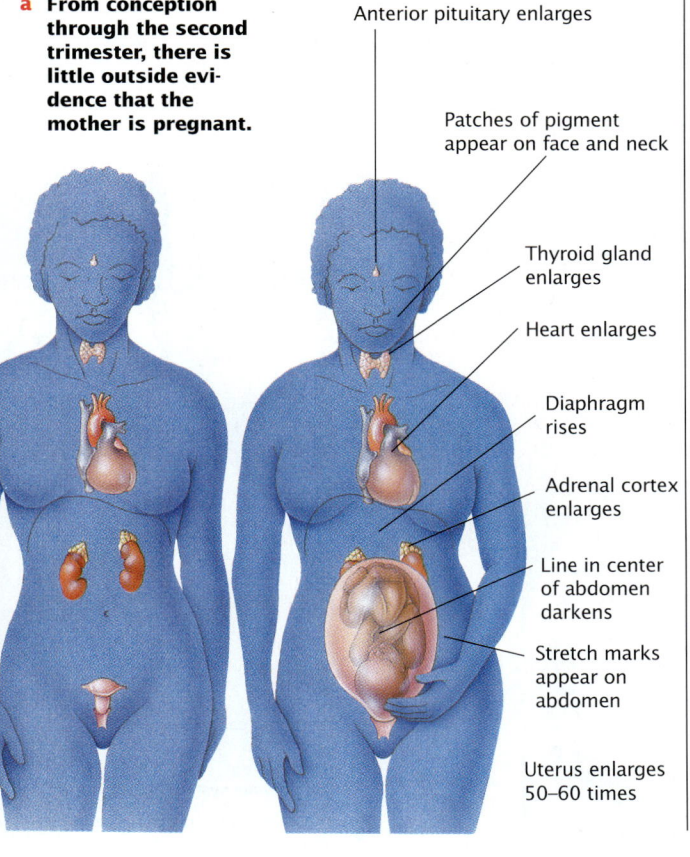

Anterior pituitary enlarges

Patches of pigment appear on face and neck

Thyroid gland enlarges

Heart enlarges

Diaphragm rises

Adrenal cortex enlarges

Line in center of abdomen darkens

Stretch marks appear on abdomen

Uterus enlarges 50–60 times

At conception

After 30 weeks

b **By the third trimester the fetus is growing rapidly. The mother's glands and organs have enlarged to take care of her and her fetus, and her pregnancy is obvious.**

Key events in fetal development and growth occur in each trimester

During the first trimester, very few changes occur in the mother's body, while the embryo is rapidly developing all of its major organ systems. By the end of the first trimester, all of the fetus's organ systems are in place. If damage occurs during the first trimester, significant birth defects may result, for this is the time that the embryo is most vulnerable.

At the beginning of the second trimester, changes in the mother's body are more noticeable as the fetus begins to make greater demands on the mother. Fetal organ systems are growing larger, the placenta is well established, and the circulatory systems for both mother and child are in full operation. **Figure 35-16** shows some of the changes that the mother's body experiences during pregnancy. Notice how certain organs and glands enlarge to handle a greater volume of blood, increased hormone secretion, and an increase in overall metabolism that supports rapid development and growth of cells, tissues, and organs. By the end of the second trimester, most of the fetus's development is complete.

Now growth of the fetus begins in earnest. The fetus gains the most weight in the last trimester. The fetus is refining respiratory and digestive organs, storing a fat layer, and gaining immunity from certain communicable diseases. Full-term infants (infants who stay within the mother for the full course of pregnancy) are much better equipped to survive outside the mother. Premature infants (those born before the 37th week of pregnancy) have problems related to immature organ systems, such as the lungs, kidneys, central nervous system, digestive organs, or liver.

733

Visual Strategy   Figure 35-16

● **Summarizing Information**
Have students make a chart outlining the changes that occur in the mother during pregnancy. (In addition to the information in this figure, the chart should include the changes that occur in the first, second, and third trimesters, which were discussed in the text.)

Health Connection

Diet and Vitamins

Recently, it has been discovered that an insufficiency of vitamin B_6 can put fetuses at risk for spina bifida and other nervous-system disorders. Mothers-to-be must make sure they are eating a balanced and healthy diet before conception so that their babies will be born healthy and whole. Oral contraceptives deplete the body's store of vitamin B_6, and a woman can therefore require up to 20 times the recommended daily dose.

Matter of Fact: The Father's Influence

Did you know that the habits of the father can also influence the development of the fetus? Exposure to radiation, lead, certain pesticides, marijuana, tobacco, cocaine, and excessive alcohol can lead to abnormal sperm that might be capable of fertilizing an egg. We also know that some common antibiotics, such as penicillin and tetracycline, can suppress sperm formation. See *U.S. News and World Report,* Dec. 14, 1992, pp. 94–96.

Key to Strategies

● Understanding Concepts (Tier I)
■ Applying Information (Tier II)
▲ Critical Thinking (Tier III)

● **Summarizing Information**

Have students make a chart outlining the changes that occur in the fetus during development in the first, second, and third trimesters of pregnancy. Lead students through these photographs so that they appreciate the dramatic changes that take place during development. Emphasize that most of the structural features form during the first trimester. Consequently, viral infections, such as German measles, have more serious consequences during this formative stage. During the second trimester, body structures become more refined. During the third trimester, more growth in body size takes place.

Demonstration

● **Comparing Structures**

During the first two to three weeks, the human embryo resembles the embryos of many other animals in their development. Show the class photographs or overhead transparencies of fish, amphibian, reptilian, avian, and human embryos at comparable stages of development. Have students identify similarities among the different embryos. Point out that such similarities are evidence suggesting a common ancestor.

Profound changes take place during the nine months of development

Figure 35-17
Key developmental events occur in each trimester of pregnancy. Follow the development and growth of zygote, embryo, and fetus over the course of nine months.

Four weeks after fertilization, the embryo is only about one-fourth of an inch long. The inner and outer cells that developed after fertilization have continued to expand and have formed a membrane that surrounds the embryo and is filled with fluid. In this liquid environment, the climate is controlled, and the embryo can grow freely without nearby tissues pressing on it. The fluid also cushions the embryo or fetus from bumping or jarring. To prevent the fetus from being overwhelmed by the fluid, a mucous plug fills its nose and part of its throat. At the end of 40 weeks, the fetus has grown to an average length of about 20 in. and a weight of about 7.25 lb. **Figure 35-17** will help you to follow the changes that occur during prenatal (before birth) development.

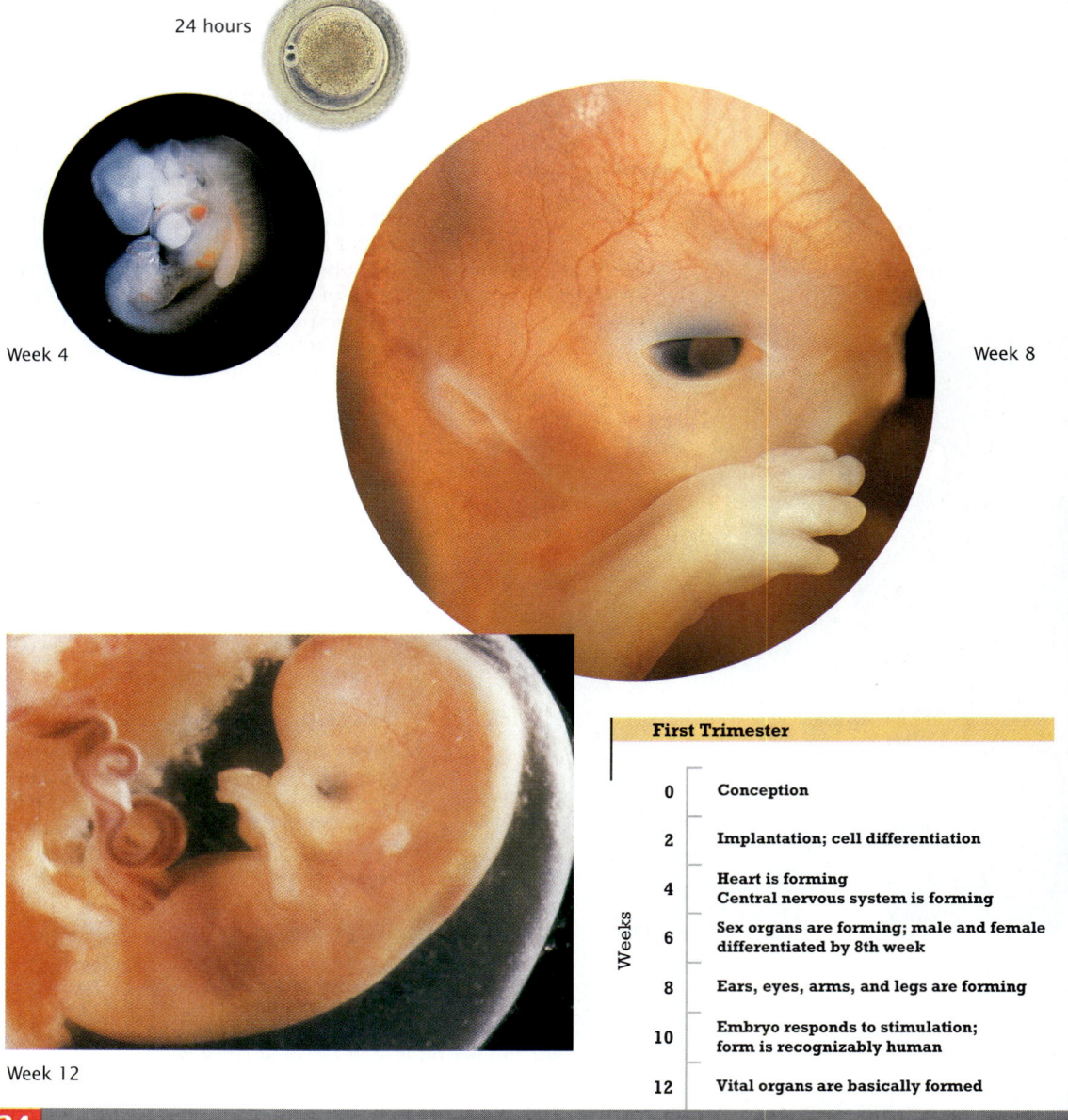

24 hours

Week 4

Week 8

Week 12

First Trimester	
0	Conception
2	Implantation; cell differentiation
4	Heart is forming Central nervous system is forming
6	Sex organs are forming; male and female differentiated by 8th week
8	Ears, eyes, arms, and legs are forming
10	Embryo responds to stimulation; form is recognizably human
12	Vital organs are basically formed

Weeks

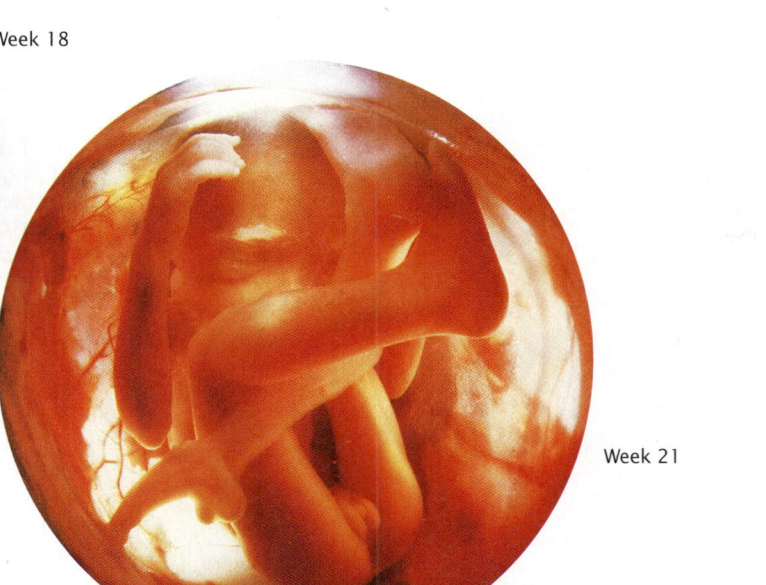

Week 18

Week 21

Week 22

Demonstration
● **Identifying Structures**
Have students put their fingers on their navel. Point out that the only evidence left of the umbilical cord is the navel. Once it is separated from the mother, a baby's umbilical cord is clamped, tied off, and cut. What remains on the baby slowly shrivels and falls off, leaving a scar known as the navel.

Second Trimester	
Weeks	
14	Circulatory system is operating
16	Mother can feel movements Fetus's sex organs are distinct
18	
20	Hair is forming on body and head
22	
24	Sucking movements; vigorous body movements; eyelashes and eyebrows appear; skin is thin, wrinkled, translucent

Third Trimester	
Weeks	
26	Eyes open Survival outside womb is possible
28	
30	Layer of fat starts forming beneath skin
32	Survival outside of womb is probable
34	
36	
38	Birth

735

Key to Strategies
● Understanding Concepts (Tier I)
■ Applying Information (Tier II)
▲ Critical Thinking (Tier III)

● **Summarizing Information**
Have students list in sequence the stages of childbirth using Figure 35-18 and the information in the text. *(The stages are: dilation of the cervix, movement of the baby into the vagina, delivery, the baby's first breath, separation of the placenta from the uterine wall, and the expulsion of the placenta and umbilical cord.)*

Phase Three
Assessment Options

Closure
● **Identifying Variables**
About 20 years ago, a number of pregnant women took a drug called thalidomide. Those who took this drug during the first trimester of pregnancy had babies with serious birth defects, including severely shortened arms and legs. Those who took this drug during the last trimester had normal babies. Have students explain the reason for this difference.

SECTION REVIEW
Assign the *Section Review*.

Reteaching
Show the class a videotape that describes the sequence of events from fertilization to birth.

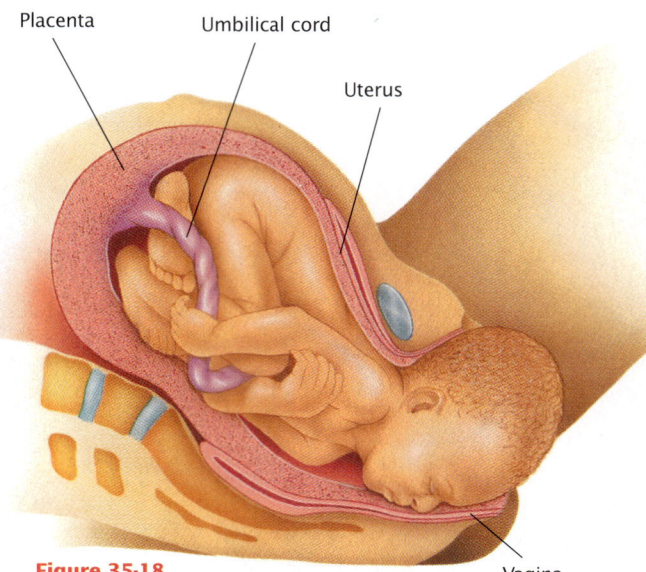

Placenta   Umbilical cord
Uterus
Vagina

Figure 35-18
a **During birth, the cervix is forced open and the baby is pushed out through the vagina.**

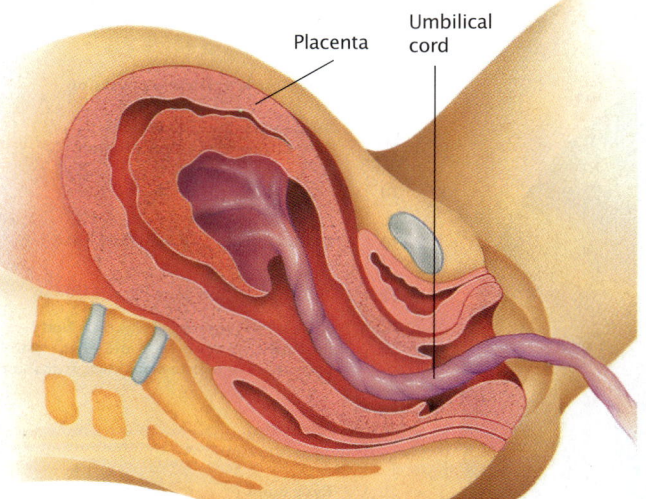

Placenta   Umbilical cord

b **Shortly after a child is born, fluid, blood, and the placenta are expelled from the uterus. This material is the afterbirth.**

Birth
About nine months after fertilization, the fetus is ready to be born. By this time, it has usually moved so that its head is against the cervix. Near the end of pregnancy, hormones cause muscles in the walls of the uterus to begin contracting. Weak, irregular contractions may occur for several weeks before birth. As the time for birth approaches, contractions become much stronger. They also start to come at regular intervals and closer together. This stage of pregnancy, when the uterus is contracting strongly enough to push the baby out of the mother's body, is called **labor**. Labor usually takes between 5 and 20 hours.

Contractions of the uterus press the fetus's head against the cervix, forcing it to open enough for the baby to pass through, as shown in **Figure 35-18**. The baby then passes through the vagina and out into the world. Within a few seconds the baby takes its first breath. The placenta separates from the wall of the uterus. A few minutes after the baby is born, the placenta and the umbilical cord are pushed out of the uterus, marking the final stage of birth. The process of childbirth is complete.

SECTION REVIEW

❶ **Explain why only one sperm fertilizes an egg.**

❷ **Describe the events of implantation.**

❸ **Describe two changes that occur in the fertilized egg before it is implanted in the uterus.**

❹ **Why can it be harmful to a fetus for its mother to use drugs, including alcohol, during pregnancy?**

ANSWERS TO SECTION REVIEW

❶ After the head of one sperm enters and fuses with the egg, a protective shield (a block to polyspermy) forms around the egg to prevent other sperm from entering.

❷ See Figure 35-12. After fertilization, the embryo travels to the uterus through the fallopian tube. By the 10th day after fertilization, the embryo is implanted in the uterine wall.

❸ First a protective shield forms around the egg. Then, after 30 hours, the fertilized egg cell divides into two cells and is called an embryo.

❹ Drugs such as alcohol can pass through the placenta and affect the mental and physical development of the child before and after birth.

Disease-causing bacteria and viruses travel from one host to another in characteristic ways. Some are carried in water, in air, or by insects, while others are transmitted by sexual contact. Diseases that can be spread from one person to another by sexual contact are called sexually transmitted diseases, or STDs.

35-4 Sexually Transmitted Diseases

Sexually Transmitted Viral Diseases

As you learned in Chapter 18, viruses cause many human diseases, including measles and influenza. In addition, viruses cause some sexually transmitted diseases, including AIDS, hepatitis B infection, papilloma virus infection, and genital herpes.

AIDS is a fatal viral disease

As you learned in Chapter 33, acquired immune deficiency syndrome (AIDS) is caused by the human immunodeficiency virus (HIV). AIDS patients, such as the man being examined in **Figure 35-19**, die from infections and cancers that their immune systems cannot fight.

HIV is present in blood, semen, and vaginal fluids of infected individuals and can be transmitted from one person to another during sexual intercourse. Anal intercourse, oral sex, and vaginal intercourse are each capable of transmitting HIV. Both females and males can get the virus from an infected partner during intercourse. Transmission of the virus can also occur anytime unsterilized needles are used. Sharing needles and syringes used for injecting drugs is the most common route of infection; however, tattoo needles and needles for piercing ears can also transmit the virus if not sterilized. In Africa, many cases of HIV have been transmitted through the reuse of needles in medical clinics. HIV can be transmitted from mother to infant across the placenta or in breast milk. About one-third of babies born to HIV-infected mothers are infected with the virus.

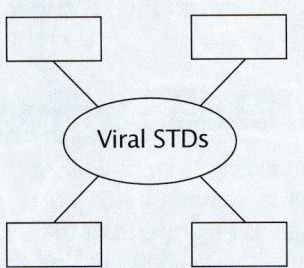

Figure 35-19
This California doctor is examining a patient with AIDS.

Videodisc Resources

Holt Biology Videodiscs
Lesson 35-4: Sexually Transmitted Diseases

Health Connection

Hepatitis

Remind students that there are estimated to be at least five forms of hepatitis; *hepatitis* means inflammation (*-itis*) of the liver (*hepat-*). It is a viral infection of the liver. Hepatitis A can be spread through contact, but once you recover, you have immunity to it. Hepatitis B is spread through needle punctures, tattooing, drug injections, blood transfusions, and sexual contact. Hepatitis C is similar to hepatitis B in transmission, but it cannot be identified in our blood supply and can lead to chronic active hepatitis. These diseases can cause liver failure and death. See the American Medical Association *Family Medical Guide* for more information.

Health Connection

Genital Herpes

Symptoms of genital herpes include painful, itching sores in or around the genitals. These sores usually appear between 2 and 20 days after exposure to the virus. They may last as long as three weeks. Other symptoms include a burning sensation during urination and a fever. Since the virus can spread to other parts of the body, an infected person is advised to not rub the affected area and to keep it dry.

Visual Strategy Figure 35-20

■ **Analyzing Information**
Tell students that these warts can spread to other parts of the body, such as the fingers, but that they spread more easily in moist and unhygienic conditions. If warts are neglected for many years, they may become malignant and cause cancer, so it is important to see a doctor for treatment. If medication does not work, warts can be removed in a physician's office. The doctor will probably take a blood sample to make sure the patient does not have syphilis, which causes a similar lesion.

A person can be infected with HIV for many years without knowing it. During this time, the infected person can spread the disease through sexual contact or by sharing needles and syringes. Although there is no cure for HIV or AIDS to date, HIV infection can be prevented. Abstaining from sexual intercourse and from the use of drugs of any kind are ways to eliminate exposure to HIV. Using a condom during sexual intercourse reduces but does not eliminate the risk of being exposed to HIV.

HBV infection is more common than HIV

Hepatitis B infection, caused by hepatitis B virus (HBV), can lead to serious liver damage, including cancer, in both infants and adults. Sexual contact is a major route of transmission, but drug users who share needles are also at risk for getting HBV. HBV can be transmitted from mother to child during pregnancy. Testing pregnant women for the HBV antigen is recommended, and infants born to mothers who test positive for the antigen should be immunized. The most commonly used vaccine in the United States is made using recombinant DNA technology.

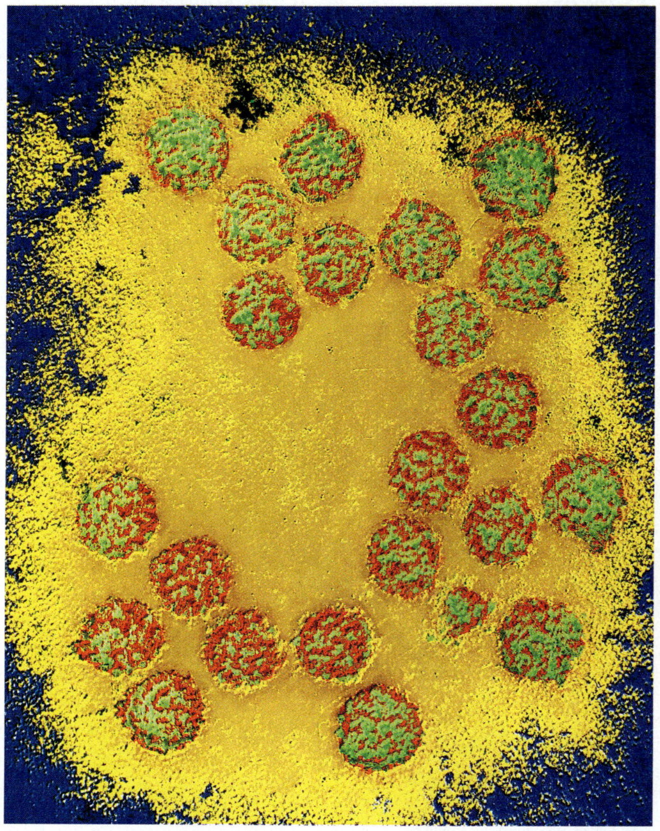

Genital herpes is also caused by a virus

Genital herpes is a sexually transmitted disease caused by herpes simplex virus (HSV). Two types of HSV can cause genital herpes: HSV-1 and HSV-2. About 80 percent of genital herpes is caused by HSV-2, which causes painful, recurring blisters and sores on the genitals, similar to the cold sores and fever blisters most commonly caused by HSV-1. Antiviral drugs can temporarily eliminate the blisters, but these drugs cannot eliminate the virus from the body. The virus is never completely destroyed by treatment; it remains dormant in the body and may recur at any time. The blisters transmit the infection to new hosts, including sex partners and infants delivered by vaginal birth from an infected mother. Infants infected in this manner may develop brain fever or infection of the membranes covering the brain or spinal cord.

Papilloma virus infection is the fastest growing STD

Human papilloma (*pap ih LOH mah*) virus (HPV), shown in **Figure 35-20**, causes today's fastest growing sexually transmitted disease, genital warts. HPV appears to play a role in cancers of the cervix, vagina, vulva, and penis as well. Even when warts and lesions are not seen or felt, viral particles are shed and transmitted through sexual contact. Having intercourse at an early age and having many sex partners over a lifetime greatly increase the risk of getting HPV. Some evidence suggests that up to 80% of the people exposed to the virus pick it up, although most will have no symptoms. There are many treatments, but no cures, for genital warts. A person carrying HPV may have it for life.

Figure 35-20
The human papilloma virus is the cause of today's fastest growing sexually transmitted disease, genital warts.

738

Sexually Transmitted Bacterial Diseases

Evolution

Strains of penicillin-resistant gonorrhea bacteria are becoming more common. How does penicillin resistance represent an adaptation by these bacteria?

Like viruses, bacteria cause many human diseases. Among these are sexually transmitted diseases such as syphilis, gonorrhea, and chlamydia. These sexually transmitted diseases, unlike those caused by viruses, can be treated with antibiotics.

Syphilis often goes unnoticed

Syphilis *(SIHF uh lihs)* is a serious disease that eventually afflicts the entire body if untreated. Although it can be cured with antibiotics, syphilis often is not diagnosed or treated because its early and later symptoms go unnoticed or ignored.

Two weeks to three months after infection, a small painless ulcer called a chancre *(SHAHNG kuhr)* appears on the genitals at the exact site of infection. Often the chancres are inside the vagina or rectum and are not seen.

Obvious chancres on the penis or labia may be ignored because they are painless. Weeks or months later, a rash that does not itch appears on the hands or feet along with fever, sore throat, or joint pains. Large, moist sores on the sex organs or mouth may develop. Like chancres, these sores are highly contagious, and the symptoms disappear without treatment. Sometimes unnoticed for years, the latent infection causes serious damage to the brain, spinal cord, and circulatory organs. The bacteria can cross the placenta and infect a fetus, usually after the fifth month of pregnancy. **Figure 35-21** shows the incidence of syphilis and gonorrhea among 15- to 19-year-olds. As cases of syphilis and gonorrhea have dropped over the years, cases of other sexually transmitted diseases have risen dramatically.

Gonorrhea can damage the reproductive organs

Gonorrhea *(gahn uh REE uh)* is another sexually transmitted disease that often goes untreated or ignored. Although antibiotics can cure the disease, some strains of gonorrhea are resistant to the more commonly used antibiotics, such as penicillin. Different antibiotics are required in the treatment of these resistant bacterial strains.

In males, gonorrhea bacteria usually cause painful urination and pus discharge from the penis. Untreated

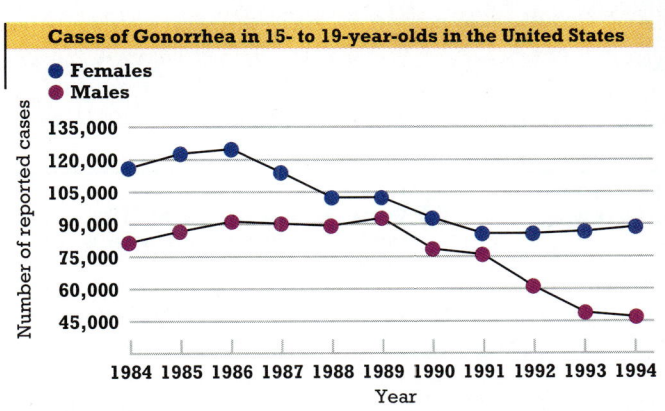

Cases of Syphilis in 15- to 19-year-olds in the United States

- ● Females
- ● Males

Figure 35-21
The incidence of syphilis and gonorrhea appears to be dropping in the teen population. This is not, however, a reliable picture. Many cases of both diseases are not reported, and many infected people never seek treatment.

Cases of Gonorrhea in 15- to 19-year-olds in the United States

- ● Females
- ● Males

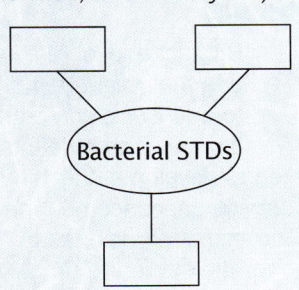
Multicultural Perspective: Dr. William Hinton

Dr. William Hinton, a pathologist and renowned authority on sexually transmitted diseases, developed the Hinton Test and the Damies-Hinton Test for the detection of syphilis. Hinton was the first African American professor to teach at Harvard Medical School.

gonorrhea can spread to the vas deferens, prostate, or testes. In females, the pathogen causes vaginal discharge but more often causes no symptoms. The disease can spread to the fallopian tubes and can affect the rectum, throat, or eyes as well. Infection of the male and female reproductive structures can cause scarring that results in infertility. Infants can be infected during birth, resulting in genital infections or eye infections that can lead to blindness.

Chlamydia is the most common sexually transmitted disease
Chlamydia *(kluh MIHD ee ah)* is the most common sexually transmitted disease in the United States, with up to 10 million new cases each year. The *Chlamydia* bacterium shown in **Figure 35-22** is usually transmitted through vaginal intercourse. The symptoms of chlamydia are similar to those of a mild case of gonorrhea: painful urination and a urethral discharge in males, and vaginal discharge and bleeding between menstrual periods in females. Chlamydia often produces no symptoms and goes unnoticed and undiagnosed. Untreated chlamydia can spread to the vas deferens and fallopian tubes and cause infertility. A baby born to a mother with chlamydia can be infected as it passes through the birth canal and may suffer eye or lung damage. Although gonorrhea and chlamydia often have no symptoms, routine laboratory tests available at hospitals and clinics can detect infections by either bacterium, and both partners should be treated simultaneously.

Untreated gonorrhea or chlamydia can cause pelvic inflammatory disease
Bacterial infection of the cervix, uterus, ovaries, and fallopian tubes is called pelvic inflammatory disease, or PID. PID is usually caused by gonorrhea or chlamydia bacteria that attach themselves to sperm and then move into the pelvic region. When the fallopian tubes are infected, scar tissue may form and close the tubes. If the tubes are closed, an egg can no longer be fertilized. PID is one of the most common causes of infertility in women.

Fallopian tubes that are damaged, but not completely closed, may allow sperm to reach the egg, but not allow the fertilized egg to reach the uterus. This is called an **ectopic pregnancy**. An ectopic pregnancy occurs when the embryo grows somewhere other than the uterus. An ectopic pregnancy in a fallopian tube can be life-threatening to a woman. As the embryo grows, it can cause the fallopian tube to rupture.

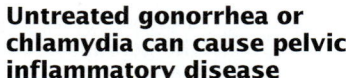

Figure 35-22
The bacterium that causes chlamydia, shown here in dark red, grows within cells of its human host. These bacteria are growing inside an infected woman's fallopian tubes.

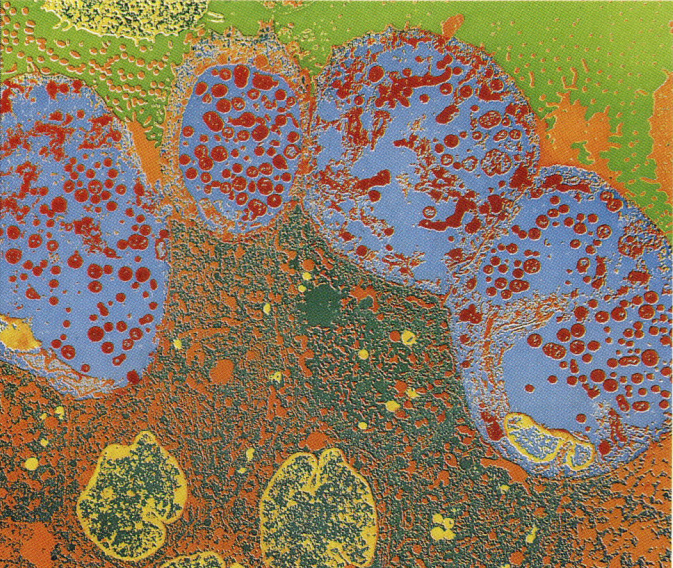

SECTION REVIEW

1. Describe three ways that STDs can be spread from one person to another.

2. List two ways to avoid HIV exposure and infection.

3. Describe three sexually transmitted diseases that are caused by bacteria and three caused by viruses.

4. Discuss the possible consequences of untreated gonorrhea or chlamydia.

ANSWERS TO
SECTION REVIEW

1. HIV can be transmitted by sexual intercourse, by sharing hypodermic needles, through body fluids, and from mother to child through the placenta.

2. Abstain from sexual intercourse and do not do drugs and share needles.

3. Bacterial—gonorrhea, chlamydia, syphilis. Viral—AIDS, herpes, hepatitis, papilloma (warts).

4. Untreated gonorrhea or chlamydia can cause pelvic inflammatory disease, which may cause infertility or ectopic pregnancies.

This young lady, not yet two years old, has much to learn before she can wear daddy's hat.

	Key Terms	Summary
35-1 **The Male Reproductive System** 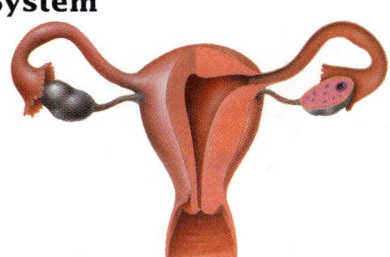 Millions of sperm are expelled by the male during ejaculation.	testes (p. 720) epididymis (p. 720) vas deferens (p. 720) ejaculation (p. 721) semen (p. 721)	• Sperm are produced in the testes, stored in the epididymis, and expelled during ejaculation. • Several hormones are responsible for sexual changes, including sperm production and release.
35-2 **The Female Reproductive System** 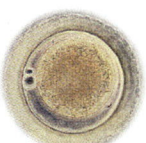 Usually, one egg is released from an ovary each month. If it is fertilized by a sperm, an embryo will develop.	ova (p. 723) ovaries (p. 723) fallopian tube (p. 723) uterus (p. 723) cervix (p. 724) vagina (p. 724) menstrual cycle (p. 725) ovulation (p. 725) follicle (p. 726) embryo (p. 726) menopause (p. 727)	• The release of an egg from an ovary is called ovulation. • Ovulation occurs once a month, about 14 days before the next menstrual period starts. • The ovarian cycle explains what happens in the ovary prior to and at ovulation. • The uterine cycle explains what happens in the uterus after ovulation and during menstruation.
35-3 **Fertilization and Development** The fetus will grow and develop for about nine months, until it is ready to be born.	fertilization (p. 728) zygote (p. 729) implantation (p. 729) fetus (p. 729) teratogens (p. 731) trimester (p. 733) labor (p. 736)	• Fertilization of an egg by sperm usually takes place in a fallopian tube. • Fertilization marks the start of pregnancy as the zygote moves to the uterus. • After implantation, the placenta is formed for fetal circulation. • Pregnancy is divided into trimesters. • Birth occurs about nine months after fertilization.
35-4 **Sexually Transmitted Diseases** In the United States, more than 500,000 new cases of genital herpes are reported each year.	chlamydia (p. 740) ectopic pregnancy (p. 740)	• Some STDs are treatable, some are curable, and some are deadly. • Untreated STDs can cause serious problems in both males and females.

741

Alternative Assessment

Assign students to cooperative work groups of four. Have each group develop a question to send to a newspaper advice columnist. Tell students that the question can deal with any topic covered in this chapter. Collect all of the questions and write them on the board. Have the groups write what their response to each question would be. Have them read what they wrote, one question at a time. Have groups critique the advice provided by others.

Portfolio Assessment

Portfolio Assessment on page T39 provides options for building and evaluating student portfolios. Students and teachers can select items from the areas listed on page T39 for inclusion in a portfolio.

ANSWER TO
CONCEPT MAP

The following is one possible answer to the Relating Concepts exercise on page 742.

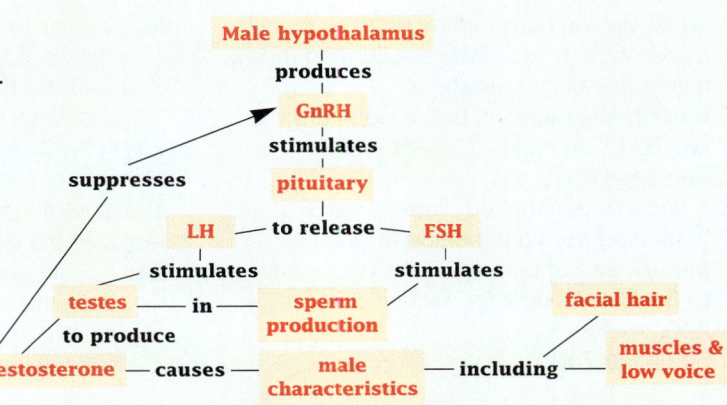

Male hypothalamus
produces
GnRH
stimulates
pituitary
suppresses
LH — to release — FSH
stimulates   stimulates
testes — in — sperm production
to produce
facial hair
testosterone — causes — male characteristics — including — muscles & low voice

Understanding Vocabulary

1. a. fallopian tubes are part of the female reproductive system
   b. epididymis is part of the male reproductive system
2. a. haploid
   b. ovaries
   c. implantation

Understanding Concepts

3. Concept Map answer on page 741.
4. Refer to the captions that accompany Figure 35-2 on page 720 and Figure 35-3 on page 721.
5. Prior to ejaculation, the bulbo-urethral glands discharge a few drops of colorless liquid, which pass through the urethra and neutralize the acid.
6. Both reproductive systems produce gametes, each contributing one set of chromosomes to a fertilized egg. The female produces eggs, or ova, instead of sperm and has a biological role after fertilization—carrying and nourishing the developing fetus until birth.
7. Refer to the captions that accompany Figure 35-10 on page 727.
8. See page 725.
9. It dissolves in the uterus.
10. Refer to the **Answers to Section Review** for Section 35-2, page 727, number 4.
11. See page 728.
12. Refer to the captions that accompany Figure 35-12 on page 729.
13. Oxygen and nutrients from the mother's blood diffuse through the walls of the embryo's blood vessels in the placenta. Waste products such as carbon dioxide and urea diffuse from the placenta into the mother's bloodstream and are eliminated by the mother's body.
14. See page 731.
15. Refer to the captions that accompany Figure 35-15 on page 732. Smoking cigarettes decreases the amount of oxygen available to the growing

Understanding Vocabulary

1. For each set of terms, choose the term that does not fit the pattern, and explain why.
   a. seminal vesicles, testes, urethra, fallopian tubes
   b. uterus, ovaries, epididymis, cervix
2. For each set of terms, complete the analogy.
   a. body cells of sexually mature male : diploid :: sperm cells : _____
   b. organs that produce sperm : testes :: organs that produce ova : _____
   c. the joining of an egg and sperm : fertilization :: an embryo's attachment to the uterine wall : _____

Understanding Concepts

3. **Relating Concepts** Construct a concept map that illustrates how the male hypothalamus regulates sperm production. Include the following terms: male hypothalamus, GnRH, pituitary, testes, LH, FSH, testosterone, sperm production, male characteristics, facial hair, muscles, and low voice.
4. **Identifying Functions** Trace the pathway of sperm from their production to their exit during ejaculation. Identify all important organs along the pathway.
5. **Inferring Relationships** Urine is acidic. After urine passes through the urethra, the urethra becomes acidic. How does the male body prevent sperm from being killed as they pass through the urethra?
6. **Comparing Structures and Functions** How are the male and female reproductive systems similar? In what two ways are they different?
7. **Organizing Information** Relate the rise, peak, and decline of four major hormones released during the menstrual cycle to the physiological events of ovulation, fertilization, implantation, and the onset of the menstrual period.
8. **Distinguishing Relevant Information** Explain why the menstrual cycle is better explained by an ovarian cycle and a uterine cycle.

9. **Predicting Outcomes** What happens to an egg if it is not fertilized within 24 hours after its release?
10. **Recognizing Relationships** Describe the role of progesterone in the uterine cycle.
11. **Summarizing Information** Describe the path a sperm must take to reach an egg. Also describe the events that occur once a sperm reaches the egg.
12. **Summarizing Information** Describe what happens to the egg between fertilization and implantation.
13. **Identifying Functions** List the substances that pass through the placenta and the direction in which they move.
14. **Predicting Outcomes** What are teratogens? What are some examples? How do they affect a developing fetus?
15. **Inferring Relationships** How can alcohol consumption by a pregnant woman affect the fetus she carries? How can smoking cigarettes during pregnancy affect a developing fetus?
16. **Organizing Information** Describe at least two major developmental events that occur in the fetus during each trimester of pregnancy.
17. **Inferring Relationships** What is AIDS? Identify three ways that the human immunodeficiency virus (HIV) is transmitted.
18. **Summarizing Information** What is a sexually transmitted disease? Describe two sexually transmitted diseases that are caused by viruses and two that are caused by bacteria.
19. **Inferring Relationships** What is pelvic inflammatory disease, or PID? How is it caused? What are the results of this disease?
20. **BUILDING ON WHAT YOU HAVE LEARNED** In Chapter 31 you learned about oxytocin and prolactin. What is the function of oxytocin-induced contractions during labor? after labor?

fetus. Babies born to mothers who smoke heavily tend to be much smaller and face a higher risk of complications.
16. Refer to the captions that accompany Figure 35-17 on pages 734 and 735.
17. See page 737.
18. A sexually transmitted disease, or STD, can be spread from one person to another through sexual contact. Refer to the **Answers to Section Review** for Section 35-4, page 740, number 4.
19. See page 740.

20. Oxytocin-induced contractions of the smooth muscle of the uterus push the baby out. After the birth, the contractions of the smooth muscle push out the placenta.

Interpreting Graphics

The illustration shows the changing hormone levels of the female reproductive cycle.
21. a. Estrogens. As the follicles grow, they produce increased amounts of estrogens. At point *b*, the increased amounts of estrogens act in a positive-feedback manner

Interpreting Graphics

21. Study the illustration below.

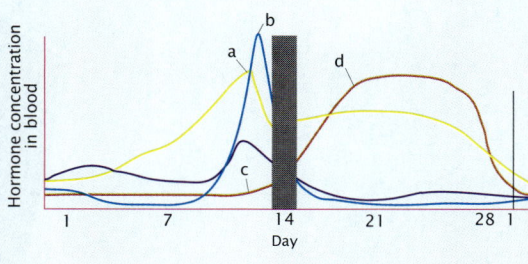

If day 1 indicates the start of the menstrual period,
a. What hormone is represented by the blue line? Support your answer. What primary event accompanies point *b*?
b. At which point, *a* or *c*, is the uterus stimulated to prepare for a fertilized egg? Support your answer. A gradual rise in which hormone is represented at this point?
c. What is point *a*'s relationship to point *b*?
d. If the egg were fertilized during this cycle, what would point *d* represent? Which hormone is primarily responsible for sustaining pregnancy, according to this graph?
e. What does the shaded area represent?

Reviewing Themes

22. *Cell Structure and Function*
Why does a woman who has undergone tubal ligation not get pregnant?

23. *Cell Structure and Function*
How are a vasectomy and a tubal ligation similar?

Thinking Critically

24. **Evaluating Results** In the early 1960s, many pregnant women took a tranquilizer called thalidomide. Women who took the tranquilizer during the first trimester of pregnancy gave birth to babies with serious limb deformities. Women who took the tranquilizer later in their pregnancies gave birth to normal babies. What does this information reveal about the sequence of development of the fetus?

Life/Work Skills

25. **Using Technology** Use library references or search an on-line database to find out about the technology used in the process of in vitro fertilization. Describe the process of in vitro fertilization. Who was the first baby born as a result of this process? Summarize your findings in a written report.

Activities and Projects

26. **Health Connection** Do library research on the use of ultrasound technology during pregnancy. What information can be learned about the fetus from this technology? Gather information from a community health-care provider about the cost of this technology in your area and when its use is recommended.

27. **Language Arts Connection** Do library research on folk tales and myths about the birth of human babies. One familiar myth is that babies are brought by the stork. Include modern myths. Summarize your findings in an oral report to share with your class.

Discovering Through Reading

28. Read the article "Prevent Sexually Transmitted Diseases" by Lauren Picker in *American Health*, October 1995, pages 62–66. Identify three sexually transmitted viral diseases that are incurable and whose numbers are on the rise. How do sexually transmitted diseases facilitate HIV's entry into the body? Describe two reasons women have a greater susceptibility than men to contract an STD. Identify five techniques to prevent sexually transmitted diseases.

743

Thinking Critically

24. Arms and legs are developed at an early stage of the pregnancy.

Life/Work Skills

25. Students' answers will vary depending on the resources available. The first baby born by this process was Louise Brown, who was born in England in 1978.

Activities and Projects

26. Students' answers will vary depending on the resources available.
27. Students' answers will vary but might mention babies being brought by the stork and found in gardens and cabbage patches.

Discovering Through Reading

28. Viral STDs include AIDS, genital warts (that may lead to cervical cancer), herpes, and hepatitis B. Herpes and syphilis cause sores or ulcers that facilitate HIV's entry into the body. Chlamydia and gonorrhea promote HIV infection, presumably allowing the virus to enter the body through the microscopic lesions they cause. Women have a larger genital surface to be infected by microbes; and during sex with an infected partner, the man's secretions are deposited directly into the woman's body. To avoid an STD, remain abstinent, be selective in choosing sexual partners, use condoms, be aware of subtle symptoms and changes in your body, be in a mutually monogamous relationship, and be tested on a periodic basis.

to cause LH release from the anterior pituitary.
b. At point *c,* the rising levels of progesterone cause the uterine lining to become spongy and rich in blood and nutrients.
c. At point *a,* the increased amounts of estrogens act in a positive-feedback manner to cause an LH surge (point *b*) from the anterior pituitary.
d. If fertilization occurred, point *d* would represent the beginning point from which progesterone levels would rise. Progesterone is primarily responsible for maintaining pregnancy.
e. Ovulation

Reviewing Themes

22. Ova cannot come down through the fallopian tubes.
23. They are both operations that cut or tie off tubes (fallopian tubes or vas deferens).

Teacher's notes

Lab Program Introduction

744

Nutrient	Indicator	Positive test (standard)	Negative test	Food sample
Sugar	Benedict's solution	Turns orange or brick red	Stays blue-green	
Starch	Lugol's iodine			
Protein	Biuret solution			
Lipid	Appearance on brown paper			

Additional information about the *Biology: Visualizing Life* lab program can be found on pages T28–T33.

What's So Special About This Lab Program?

Explorations *serve as technique builders by giving students practice with lab techniques and concepts. Each Exploration includes a detailed, step-by-step procedure, like many traditional labs. Unlike labs from other lab programs, however, Explorations are placed in the context of real-life occupational scenarios. A situation is described, and the students must solve the problem.*

1 Skills/Objectives
identifies the techniques to be learned and describes the expected accomplishments.

2 Materials
lists the items required to perform the lab.

3 Situation/Background
describes the real-life setting and provides additional information.

4 Prelab Preparation
defines the steps that must be taken before beginning the lab.

5 Procedure
is step-by-step instructions for doing the lab, including safety precautions and directions for clean-up and disposal.

6 Analysis
questions ask students to examine the techniques and skills they used in the lab and to interpret their findings.

7 Applications
questions require students to research a career related to the lab topic or to apply what they have learned to personal situations or other scientific settings.

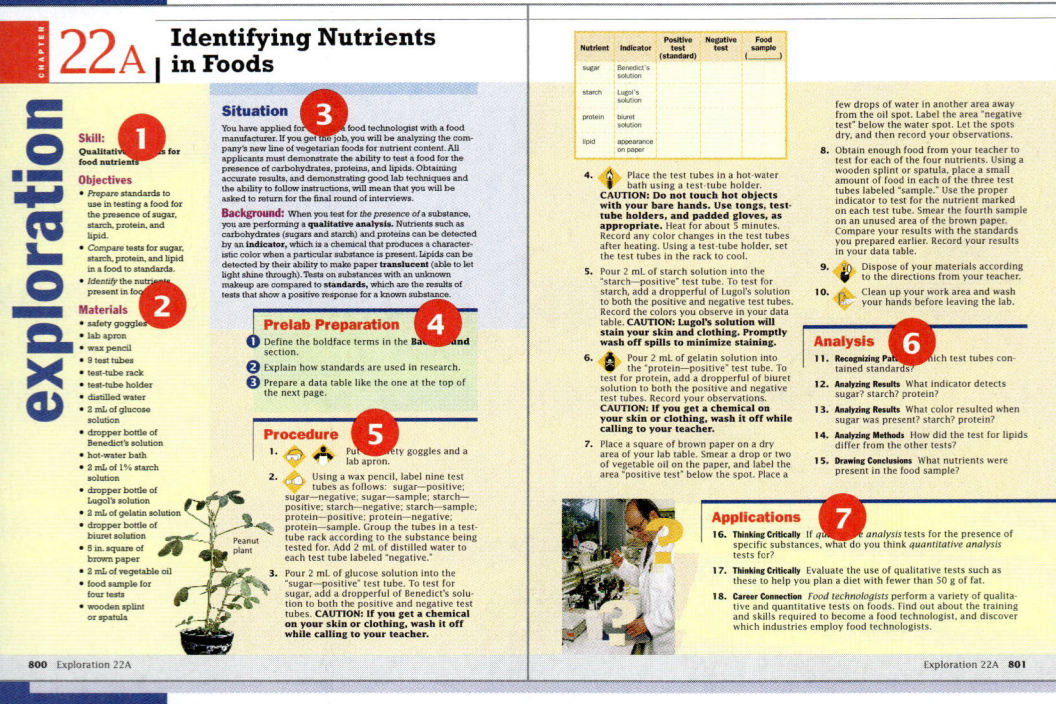

KEY BENEFITS

explorations

Students will
- learn practical lab skills and procedures.
- master fundamental concepts of biology.
- see biology in a real-world context.
- discover the role of biology in various careers.
- gain practice in the following life/work skills:
  - working as a member of a team
  - following directions

Investigations *invite students to join BioLogical Resources, Inc., a biological consulting firm. As employees, students are given a business letter from a "client" that outlines a problem, and a memo from their supervisor that offers suggestions and guidance. Based on the problem, students must devise a procedure, select supplies and equipment, and earn a profit for the firm.*

To ensure best results and minimal safety hazards, do not perform any Investigation without first performing its prerequisite Exploration, if there is one. Prerequisites are indicated at the beginning of each Investigation.

① Prerequisites/Review identifies Explorations that introduce procedures used and lists concepts students will need to know.

② The Business Letter poses a problem for students to solve.

③ Required Precautions lists the safety procedures students must follow.

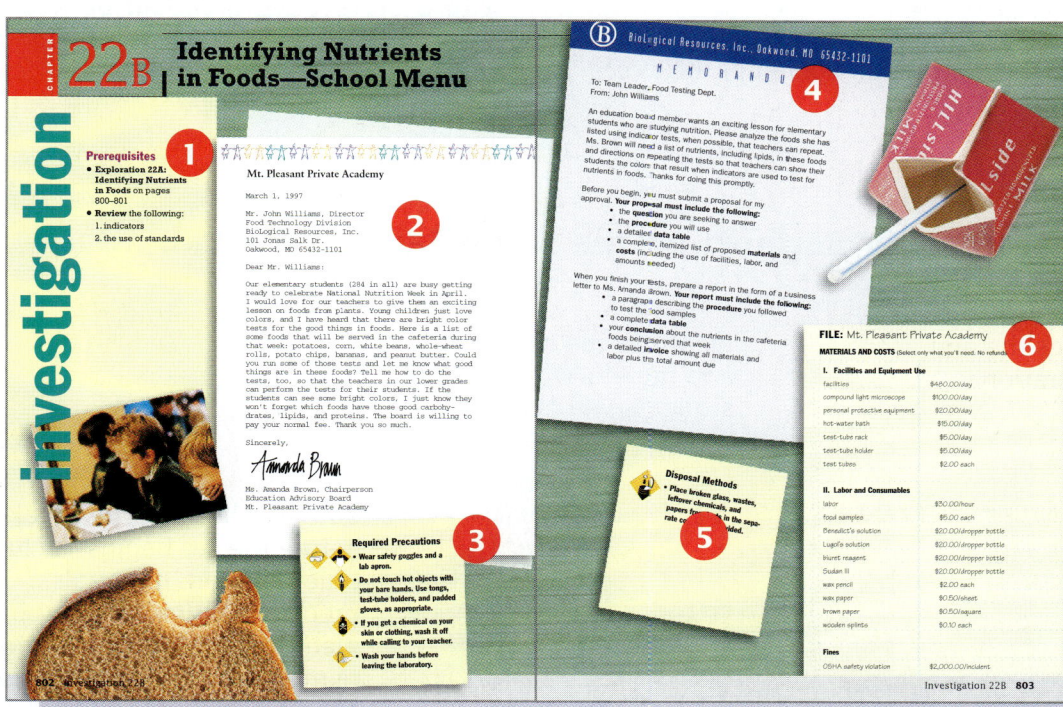

④ The Memorandum is a note from the supervisor directing the student to perform the work. Required elements for the *Initial Proposal* and the *Final Report* are clearly spelled out.

⑤ Disposal Methods provides instructions for the handling and removal of all materials used.

⑥ Materials and Costs includes non-essential items, forcing students to think carefully and request only what they need.

KEY BENEFITS

Students will
- use their knowledge of biological concepts to solve problems.
- practice lab skills and procedures.
- apply knowledge and skills from other disciplines, such as language arts (writing proposals and business letters) and mathematics (maintaining a budget, preparing an invoice).
- take responsibility for their own learning.

- gain practice in the following life/work skills:
  - communicating effectively
  - allocating resources wisely
  - selecting and applying technology
- practice decision-making and problem-solving.
- explore the role of biologists in creating new products, solving problems, and performing forensic analyses.

Explorations: Getting Started

Like labs you have used before, Explorations guide the student through a series of procedural steps. Along the way, students learn one or more key lab techniques, while learning the role of biology in the working world.

Before the Exploration

Assign the following tasks for students to complete before entering the lab:

1 Read the *Situation*, *Background*, and *Procedure* sections.

2 Complete the *Prelab Preparation* section. This ensures that students will
  - define key terms.
  - prepare one or more data tables according to the instructions given in the *Procedure* section.

3 Reread safety instructions within the Exploration. Review the safety information beginning on page 752.

4 You may want to give students a brief quiz on safety precautions or the procedure prior to beginning the Exploration. Only those with a perfect score should be allowed to proceed.

Complete Teacher Support on the Same Page as the Lab

(1) Purpose defines the aim of the Exploration.

(2) Instructional Goals identifies the concepts and the life/work skills that students will master.

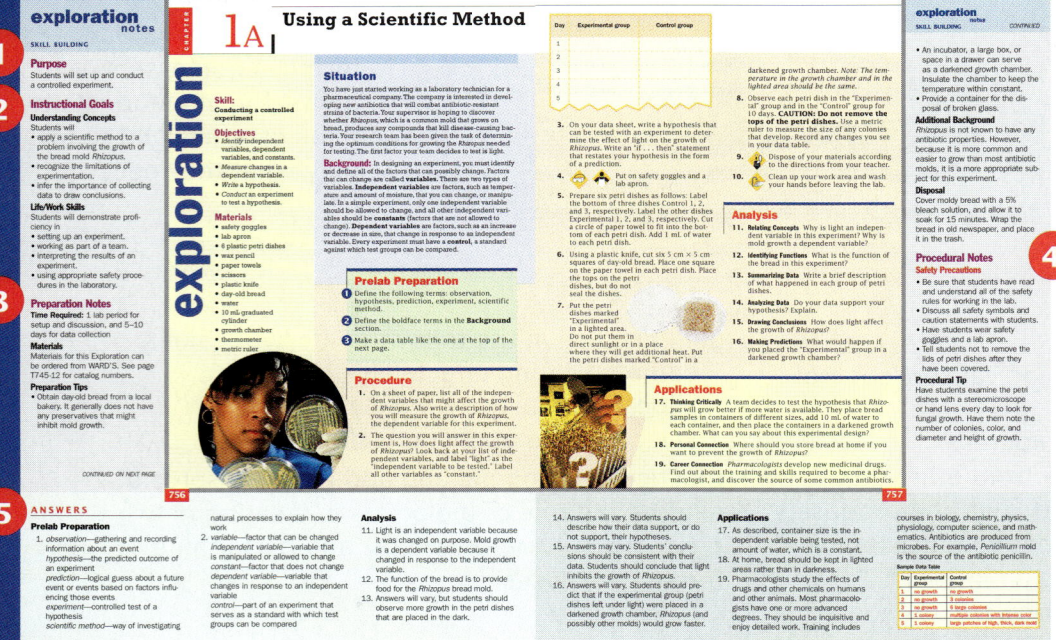

(3) Preparation Notes outlines the steps to be taken before the lab begins. Includes time required, materials, preparation tips, and disposal methods. **Prelab Discussion** reinforces the connection to the prerequisite Exploration.

(4) Procedural Notes lists safety precautions and offers classroom-tested strategies to help ensure success

(5) Answers provides responses for *Prelab Preparation*, *Analysis*, and *Application* items, plus completed data tables containing data that are representative of actual classroom results.

Assessment: Evaluating Explorations

After the Exploration, students should prepare a lab report with at least the following components:

- **Title**
- **Summary paragraph** describing the purpose and procedure
- **Data tables** and **observations** that are organized and comprehensive
- **Answers** to any of the *Analysis* and *Applications* questions you assign

Teaching Resources CD-ROM Includes Customizable Rubrics, Checklists, and Gowin's Vees

The **Holt BioSources Teaching Resources CD-ROM** includes *Scoring Rubrics* and *Classroom Management Checklists* to expand your assessment options. These rubrics will provide you with consistent, objective guidelines for monitoring and assessing student lab work. Laboratory-related rubrics and checklists include

- Introduction to Scoring Rubrics
- Specialized scoring rubrics for in-text Explorations and Investigations
- Student-Designed Experiments Rubric
- Informal Assessment Direct Observations Checklist
- Evaluating Laboratory Work

Plus specialized scoring rubrics for

- All labs in **Holt BioSources Lab Program (Quick Labs, Inquiry Skills Development, Laboratory Techniques and Experimental Design,** and **Biotechnology** lab manuals)

Complete instructions for using Gowin's Vee are also included for those who wish to experience the benefits of this powerful teaching tool.

- Vee Form Instructions—Teacher's Notes
- Teaching Students to Use the Vee
- Vee Form (a blank Vee form that students can use with any lab)
- Assessing Student-Constructed Vee Reports

The **Holt BioSources Teaching Resources CD-ROM** also includes two student worksheets that can help you emphasize the importance of safe lab behavior:

- Student Safety Contract
- Safety Quiz

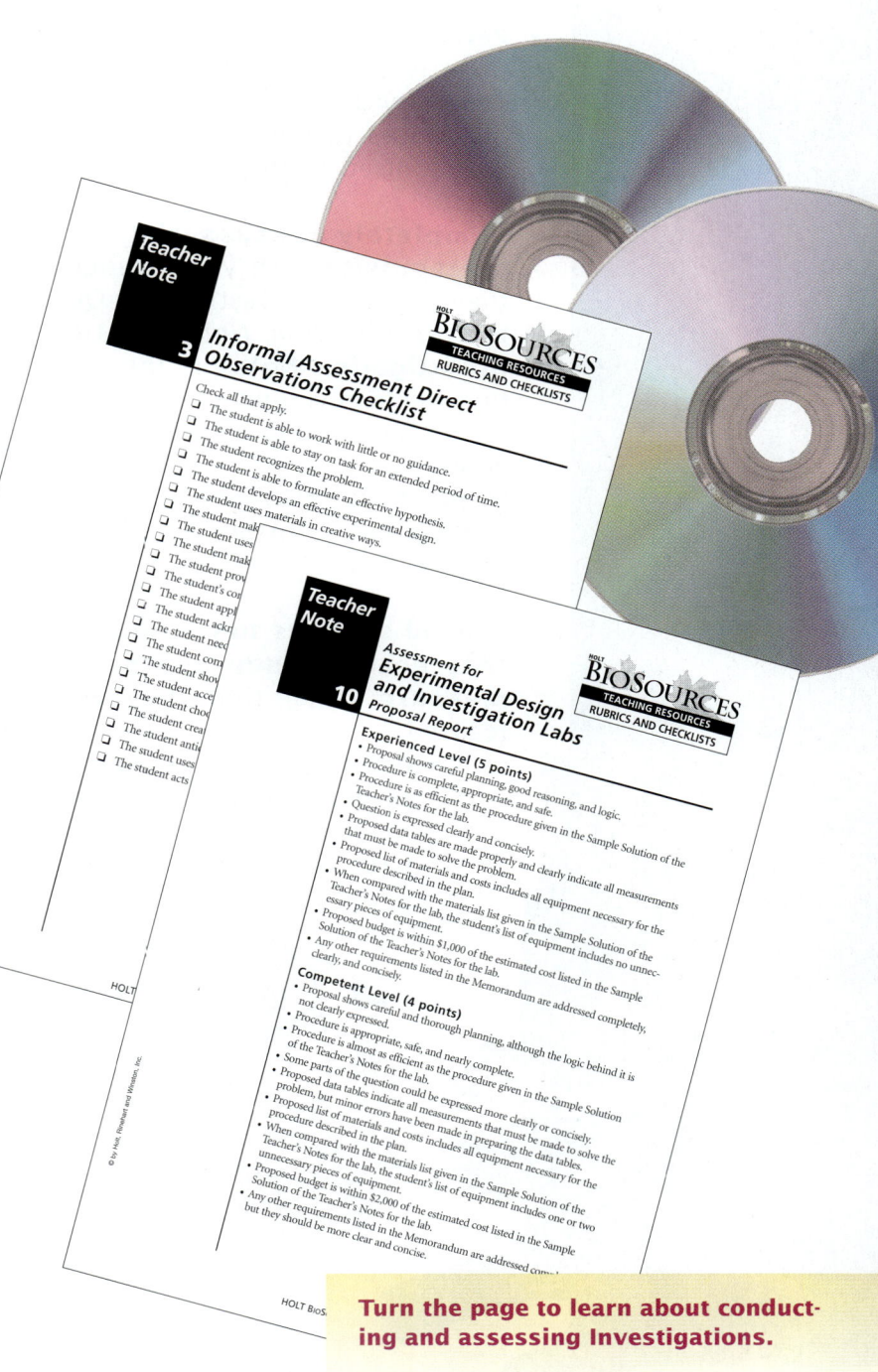

Turn the page to learn about conducting and assessing Investigations.

Investigations: Tips for Success

BioLogical Resources, Inc. Oakwood, MO 65432-1101

BioLogical Resources, Inc. Oakwood, MO 65432-1101

Caitlin Noonan

The Investigations require an approach different from most traditional labs. If your students have not worked independently in the past, they may initially feel uncomfortable when asked to propose a procedure for a self-directed lab. Be sure to take the following steps to help boost their confidence.

Before the Investigation

- **Perform the Exploration prerequisite** if there is one. Most Investigations are preceded by a prerequisite Exploration that introduces techniques or procedures that will be used in the subsequent Investigation.
- **Completely discuss the Exploration prerequisite** with your students before they begin the Investigation. Questions in the *Preparation Notes* section of the **Investigation Notes** in the teacher's edition will help you underscore the applicability of techniques or procedures learned earlier.
- **Suggest that students use materials and equipment similar to those in the Exploration** if they are not sure how to begin.
- **Remind students to concentrate on what they need to know and how they will measure it** so that they will remain focused.
    - **Point out that it is more important to understand** what is going on in the lab than to perform the exercise with excellent technique but no understanding.

- **Provide leading questions for students to consider** as they make their plans. Suggested questions are given in the *Preparation Notes* section of the **Investigation Notes** in the teacher's edition.
- **Hold a question-and-answer session** before students begin the lab.
- **Hint (don't tell) that some of the equipment and materials listed may be unnecessary.**
- **Remind students to check the Memorandum** in the Investigation for requirements for their *Initial Proposal* and *Final Report*.
- **Be thorough in helping students to develop their *Initial Proposal*,** as this will form the basis of their procedure. Each *Initial Proposal* should include the following:
    - the question(s) to be answered
    - the procedure to be used
    - at least one detailed data table
    - a list of proposed materials and costs

Emphasize that students cannot begin their procedure until you have approved their *Initial Proposal.*

Assessment: Evaluating Investigations

Because Investigations require that students design their own procedures and data tables, each *Initial Proposal* and *Final Report* will be unique. Students' *Initial Proposal* should include the elements listed above. Upon completion of the lab, students should report their findings in the form of a business letter to the client. An example of a completed invoice is shown on the next page.

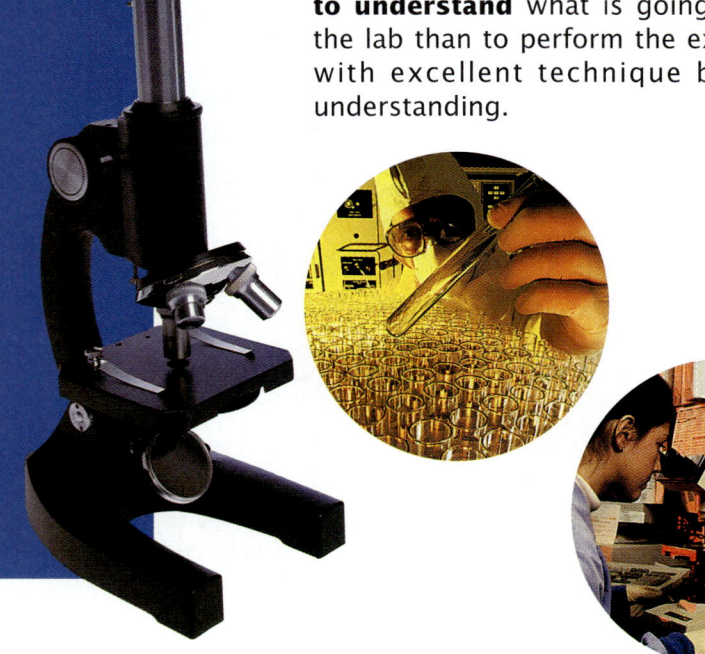

Complete Teacher Support Surrounds Each Investigation

(1) Purpose
defines the aim of the Investigation and will govern the design and execution of the students' experiments.

(2) Instructional Goals
identifies the concepts and life/work skills that students will master.

(3) Preparation Notes
outlines the steps to be taken before the lab begins. Includes time required, materials, preparation tips, and disposal methods.

(4) Procedural Notes
highlights things to remember during the Investigation, such as safety precautions and tips to ensure accurate measurements.

(5) Sample Solution
provides examples of all of the elements of the *Initial Proposal* and *Final Report*.

- **Question** forms the basis of the Investigation.
- **Proposed Procedure** can be compared with students' suggested plans to show discrepancies.
- **Materials** provides a concise list of items that each lab group should request.
- **Results/Conclusions** gives an accurate idea of possible student findings; includes representative completed data tables.
- **Estimated Cost of the Job** shows you approximately how much students should spend.

Students prepare an invoice for the client as part of the *Final Report*. Each invoice is an itemized list of the costs incurred from the experiment that students described in their approved *Initial Proposal*.

Invoices should group itemized costs in meaningful categories, such as *Facilities and Equipment Use*, and *Labor and Consumables*. Costs from fines for safety violations must be included. To remain "in business," students must show a profit.

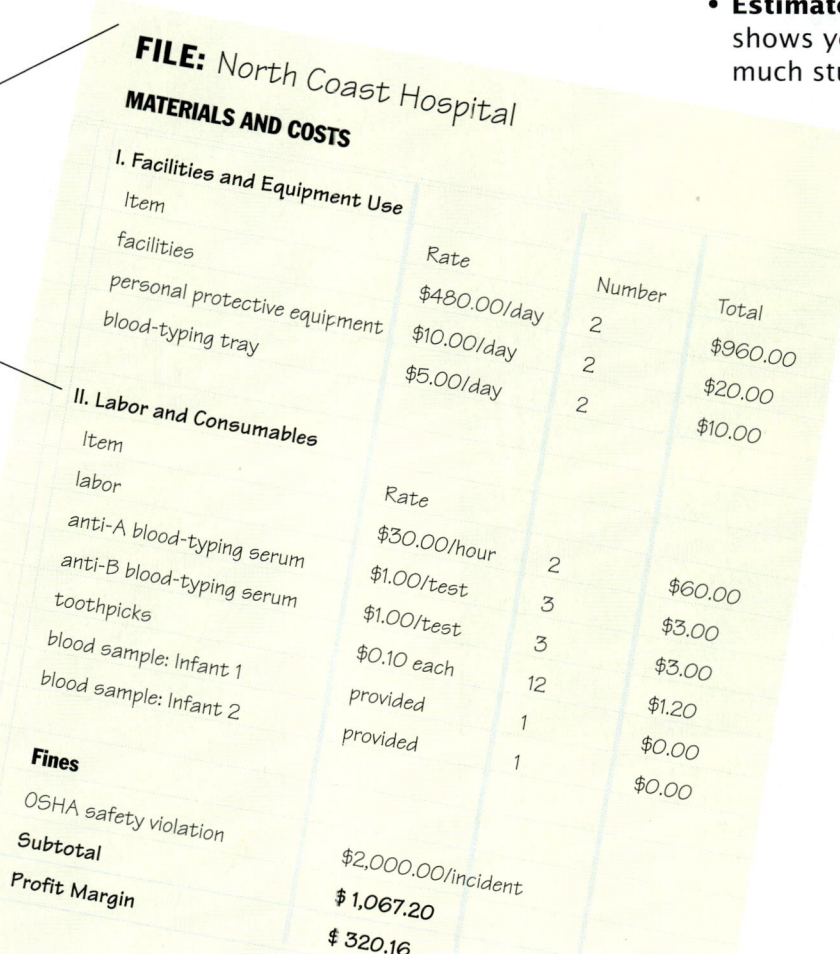

FILE: North Coast Hospital
MATERIALS AND COSTS

I. Facilities and Equipment Use

Item	Rate	Number	Total
facilities	$480.00/day	2	$960.00
personal protective equipment	$10.00/day	2	$20.00
blood-typing tray	$5.00/day	2	$10.00

II. Labor and Consumables

Item	Rate	Number	Total
labor	$30.00/hour	2	$60.00
anti-A blood-typing serum	$1.00/test	3	$3.00
anti-B blood-typing serum	$1.00/test	3	$3.00
toothpicks	$0.10 each	12	$1.20
blood sample: Infant 1	provided	1	$0.00
blood sample: Infant 2	provided	1	$0.00

Fines

OSHA safety violation	$2,000.00/incident	

Subtotal $ 1,067.20

Profit Margin $ 320.16

T745-6

Interactive Explorations: Using CD-ROM Technology

It's time for lab. How would you like to peer inside a chloroplast, watch a neuron respond to repeated doses of cocaine, or witness the cellular mechanism of cystic fibrosis? Now you can.

Navigating Through Interactive Explorations Is Simple—and Fun

Using CD-ROM technology, Interactive Explorations invite you and your students to

- predict the consequences of personal decisions in diet and lifestyle as the decades role by—in minutes.

- calculate the rate of receptor loss during sustained cocaine use—and recognize that addiction is governed by biology, not willpower.

- watch meiosis in motion—and see the occurrence of trisomy-21 increase with maternal age.

Now for the first time you and your students can harness the power of CD-ROM technology to study these and other difficult-to-observe phenomena in repeatable, controlled conditions.

The *Interactive Explorations in Biology: Human Biology* and *Interactive Explorations in Biology: Cell Biology and Genetics* CD-ROMs are easy to use. The Navigation palette described on page 751 makes access to all parts of the program as easy as a click of the mouse, and each Interactive Exploration has colorful, engaging graphics and control panels, which make it immediately interesting to the student. Audio narration is provided in both English and Spanish. Each Interactive Exploration also provides information about additional references and resources for further study.

Observe how drug use changes the nervous system, and adjust frequency and dosage.

Examine the effects of smoking, weight, exercise, and diet on life span, and then project the effects of these factors on your current lifestyle.

Watch photosynthesis occur—from inside a chloroplast!

Complete Teacher Support is Provided Where You Need it Most—At Point of Use

1 Purpose
describes the principal goal that will guide students through the lab exercise.

2 Instructional Goals
outlines the main points students will become familiar with during the exercise.

3 Preparation Notes
includes time required, tips to make sure students are well prepared, discussion topics related to the exercise, and additional helpful information.

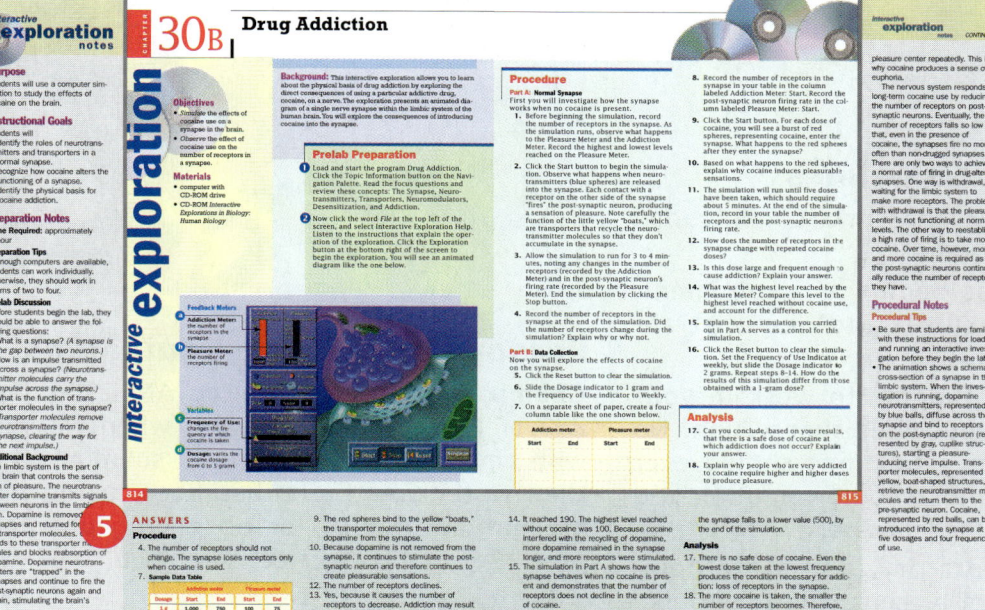

4 Procedural Notes
offers tips to ensure that, once underway, the lab will run smoothly.

5 Answers
provides answers for all questions, from the pre-lab stages to the *Analysis* questions and displays them right on the page for quick, easy reference; includes completed data tables.

KEY BENEFITS

Students will
- distinguish between qualitative and quantitative data.
- identify dependent and independent variables.
- hold or adjust one or more variables and then predict the consequences.
- evaluate the significance of their findings.
- understand biological phenomena as fluid processes instead of as series of static steps.

Teachers will
- enjoy the freedom and flexibility of scheduling offered by Interactive Explorations. Students using the Interactive Explorations can work
- individually or in small groups.
- at their own pace, repeating portions of an activity multiple times if needed.
- on their own when making up labs missed due to absence.

System Requirements

Interactive Explorations will play back off the CD-ROM directly; no installation onto your hard disk is necessary. Each CD is a hybrid disc, supporting either a PC or Macintosh® computer.

Recommended Macintosh System Requirements
- Macintosh LCIII or faster CPU
- Video card and monitor, capable of 256 colors, 640 x 480 resolution
- 8 MB of memory
- Double-speed CD-ROM drive
- Mouse
- System 7.1 or newer

Recommended PC System Requirements
- 486 PC, 25MHz PC
- VGA video card and monitor, capable of 256 colors, 640 × 480 resolution.
- 8 MB of memory
- SoundBlaster or compatible sound card
- External speakers
- Double-speed CD-ROM drive
- Mouse
- DOS 5.0 or newer
- Windows® 3.1

Running a Safe and Efficient Laboratory Program

General Safety Guidelines

1. Post laboratory rules in a conspicuous place in the laboratory.

2. Before the class begins an experiment, review safety rules, and demonstrate proper procedures.

3. Never permit students to work in your laboratory without your supervision. No unauthorized investigations should ever be conducted, nor should unauthorized materials be in the laboratory.

4. Lock your laboratory (and storeroom) when you are not present.

5. Clearly mark locations of eyewash stations, safety shower, fire extinguishers (ABC tri-class), chemical spill kit, first-aid kit, and fire blanket in the laboratory and storeroom. Check this safety equipment prior to conducting each investigation.

6. Post an evacuation diagram and procedures by every entrance to the laboratory.

7. Provide labeled disposal containers for glass, sharps, and waste chemical reagents.

8. Allow no food or beverages in the laboratory. Caution students to keep their hands away from their face and to wash hands with soap and water before leaving the laboratory.

9. Know the location of the master shut-off for laboratory circuits. Be sure that all outlets have correct polarity and have ground-fault interception. Polarity can be tested with an inexpensive (about $5) continuity tester available from most electronic hobby shops. All electrical equipment should have 3-prong plugs and 3-wire cords.

10. Follow prescribed procedures for any safety incident, including full documentation. Remind students that any safety incident, no matter how trivial, must be reported directly to you.

Personal Protective Equipment

Chemical goggles: (Meeting ANSI Standard Z87.1) These should be worn when working with any chemical or chemical solution other than water, heating substances, using any mechanical device, or observing physical processes that could eject an object.

Face shield: (Meeting ANSI Standard Z87.1) Use in combination with eye goggles when working with corrosives.

Contact lenses: The wearing of contact lenses for cosmetic reasons should be prohibited in the laboratory. If a student must wear contact lenses prescribed by a physician, that student should be instructed to wear eye-cup safety goggles meeting ANSI Standard Z87.1 (similar to swimmer's cup goggles).

Eye-wash station: The device must be capable of delivering a copious, gentle flow of water to both eyes for at least 15 minutes. Portable liquid supply devices are not satisfactory and should not be used. A plumbed-in fixture or a perforated spray head on the end of a hose attached to a plumbed-in outlet is suitable if it is designed for use as an eyewash fountain and meets ANSI Standard Z358.1 It must be within a 30-second walking distance from any spot in the room.

Safety shower: (Meeting ANSI Standard Z358.1) Location should be within a 30-second walking distance from any spot in the room. Students should be instructed in the use of the safety shower, which is to be used in the event of a fire or chemical splash on their body that cannot simply be washed off.

Gloves: Polyethylene, neoprene rubber, or disposable plastic may be used. Nitrile or butyl rubber gloves are recommended when handling corrosives.

Apron: Rubber-coated cloth or vinyl (nylon-coated) halter is recommended.

Emergency Preparedness

What would you do if a student dropped a liter bottle of concentrated sulfuric acid? RIGHT NOW? Plan how to react effectively BEFORE you need to.

1. Post the phone number of the regional poison control center, fire department, police, ambulance, and hospital on your telephone.
2. Practice fire and evacuation drills. Also have drills on what students MUST do if they are on fire or have chemical contact.
3. Assure that all personal and other safety equipment is available and tested frequently.
4. Compile an MSDS file for all chemicals. This reference resource should be readily available in case of a spill or other accident.
5. Provide for spill control procedures. Handle only those incidents that you feel comfortable in handling. Situations of greater severity should be handled by trained hazardous materials professionals.
6. Never allow students to fight fires or handle spills.
7. Be trained in first aid and basic life support (CPR) procedures. Have first-aid kits and spill kits readily available.
8. Fully document ANY INCIDENT that occurs.

Safety With Animals

It is recommended that teachers follow the *Guidelines for the Use of Live Animals*, which is established by the National Association of Biology Teachers. These guidelines are reproduced in the Teacher's Editions of *Holt BioSources Lab Program*

Quick Labs and *Inquiry Skills Development* lab manuals.

Safety in Handling Preserved Materials

The following practices are recommended when handling or dissecting any preserved specimen:

1. NEVER dissect road-kills or non-preserved slaughterhouse materials. Doing so increases the risk of infection.
2. Wear protective gloves and splash-proof safety goggles at all times when handling preserving fluids and preserved specimens and during dissection.
3. Wear lab aprons. Use of an old shirt or smock under the lab apron is recommended.
4. Conduct dissection activities in a well-ventilated area.
5. Do not allow preserving or body-cavity fluids to contact skin. Fixatives do not distinguish between living or dead tissues.

Biological supply firms use formalin-based fixatives of varying concentrations to initially fix zoological and botanical specimens. WARD'S Natural Science Establishment provides specimens that are freeze-dried and rehydrated in a 10% isopropyl alcohol solution. In these specimens, no other hazardous chemical is present.

Many suppliers provide fixed botanical materials in 50% glycerin.

Reduction of Free Formaldehyde

Currently, federal regulations mandate a permissible exposure level of 0.75 ppm for formaldehyde. Contact your supplier for an MSDS that details the amount of formaldehyde present and the gas-emitting characteristics of individual specimens.

Prewash specimens (in a loosely covered container) in running tap water for 1–4 hours to dilute the fixative. Formaldehyde may also be chemically bound (thereby reducing danger) by immersing washed specimens

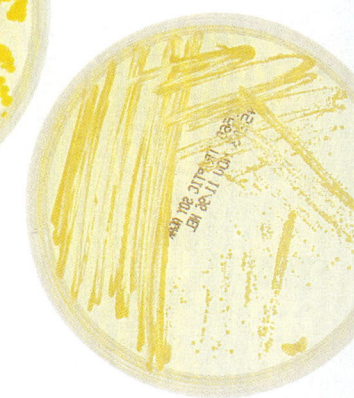

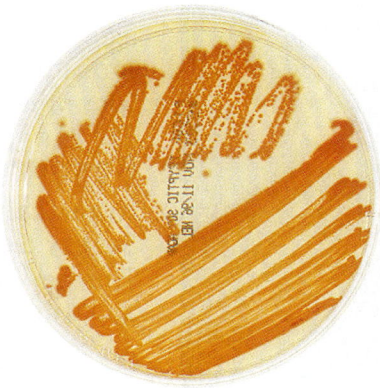

in a 0.5–1.0% potassium bisulfate solution overnight or by placing them in 1% phenoxyethanol holding solutions.

Safety With Microbes

Pathogenic (disease-causing) microorganisms are not appropriate investigational tools in the high school laboratory and should never be used.

Safety With Chemicals

Label student reagent containers with the substance's name and hazard class(es) (flammable, reactive, etc.).

Dispose of hazardous waste chemicals according to federal, state, and local regulations. Refer to the Material Safety Data Sheet for recommended disposal procedures.

Remove all sources of flames, sparks, and heat from the laboratory when any flammable material is being used.

continued

Material Safety Data Sheets

The purpose of a Material Safety Data Sheet (MSDS) is to provide readily accessible information on chemical substances commonly used in the science laboratory and in industry.

The MSDS should be kept on file and referred to BEFORE handling ANY chemical. The MSDS can also be used to instruct students on chemical hazards, to evaluate spill and disposal procedures, and to warn of incompatibility with other chemicals or mixtures.

Resources

American Chemical Society Health and Safety Service

This service will refer inquiries about health and safety to appropriate resources.

American Chemical Society (ACS)
1155 Sixteenth Street, N.W.
Washington, D.C. 20036
1-800-227-5558

Hazardous Materials Information Exchange (HMIX)

Sponsored by the Federal Emergency Management Agency and the U.S. Department of Transportation, HMIX can be accessed through an electronic bulletin board, and it provides information regarding instructional material and literature listings, hazardous materials, emergency procedures, and applicable laws and regulations. HMIX can be accessed by a personal computer having a modem. Dial (630) 252-3275. The service is available free of charge. You pay only for the telephone call. You can also call the HMIX hotline at 1-800-752-6367 for technical assistance.

Safety Information References

Gessner, G. H., ed. *Hawley's Condensed Chemical Dictionary*. 11th Ed. Van Nostrand Reinhold, 1987. (Revised by N. Irving Sax.)

A Guide to Information Sources Related to the Safety and Management of Laboratory Wastes from Secondary Schools. New York State Environmental Facilities Corp., 1985.

Lefevre, J.J. *The First Aid Manual for Chemical Accidents*. Dowdwen, 1989. (Revised by Shirley A. Conibeau.)

Pipitone, D., ed. *Safe Storage of Laboratory Chemicals, 2nd ed*. Wiley-Interscience, 1991.

Prudent Practices for Disposal of Chemicals from Laboratories. Committee on Hazardous Substances in the Laboratory, National Research Council, National Academy Press, 1983.

Prudent Practices for Handling Hazardous Chemicals from Laboratories. Committee on Hazardous Substances in the Laboratory, National Research Council, National Academy Press, 1981.

Strauss, H. and M. Kaufman, ed. *Handbook for Chemical Technicians*. McGraw-Hill, 1981.

WARD'S MSDS Users Guide. WARD'S, 1989.

Storing Chemicals

Never store chemicals alphabetically, as this greatly increases the risk of promoting a violent reaction.

Storage Suggestions

1. Always lock the storeroom and all cabinets when not in use.
2. Students should not be allowed in the storeroom and preparation area.
3. Avoid storing chemicals on the floor of the storeroom.
4. Do not store chemicals above eye level or on the top shelf in the storeroom.
5. Be sure shelf assemblies are firmly secured to the walls.
6. Provide anti-roll lips on all shelves.
7. Shelving should be constructed out of wood. Metal cabinets and shelves are easily corroded.
8. Avoid metal, adjustable shelf supports and clips. They can corrode, causing shelves to collapse.
9. Acids, flammables, poisons, and oxidizers should each be stored in their own locking storage cabinet.

Master Materials List

This materials list was prepared by WARD'S Natural Science, the exclusive science supplier for Holt, Rinehart and Winston's *Biology: Visualizing Life.* This list indicates all supplies needed to perform the in-text Explorations and Investigations. Items are listed alphabetically and are followed by the quantity, the WARD'S catalog number, and the lab number in which the material is used. Quantities indicate the number of items needed for each student team. For consumable items, quantities represent the cumulative amounts required to perform all of the labs listed here. *Local* means that the item should be available locally.

Biological Supplies (includes living organisms)

Item	Qty.	WARD'S No.	Lab
Amoeba proteus culture	1	87 M 0390	3A
Bacillus megaterium slide	1	90 M 0534	3A
Banana	2 g	Local	22B
Beans, white	2 g	Local	22B
Boiled egg white	18 cubes	Local	34A
Bread, day old	1 piece	Local	1A
Brewer's yeast, dry, 100 g	40 g	38 M 5830	1B, 5B
Brine shrimp (*Artemia*) eggs, vial	1.25 tsp	87 M 5102	1B
Corn	2 g	Local	22B
Daphnia magna, culture	9 *Daphnia*	87 M 5210	14A, 30A, 31A
Elodea, living, pkg. 10	6 plants	86 M 7500	5A, 14A, 15A
Escherichia coli culture	1 per class	85 M 0400	18A
Hydra slide (CS, LS)	1	92 M 0634	3A
Isopods (sow bug) culture	6 sow bugs	87 M 5520	14A
Leaves, "Plant A"	10	Local	10A
Leaves, "Plant B"	10	Local	10A
Myriophyllum, living, pkg. 10	1	86 M 7725	14A

Item	Qty.	WARD'S No.	Lab
Paramecium caudatum culture	1	87 M 1310	14A
Pinto bean seed, pkg. 1 lb	1 pkg. per class	86 M 8014	21A
Pond snails, living, pkg. 6	3 snails	87 M 4140	14A
Potato	2 g	Local	22B
Protozoa survey mixture, culture	1 per class	87 M 1618	19A
Rapid Radish seeds, pkg. 200	30 seeds	86 M 8021	14A
Spirogyra culture	1	86 M 0650	14A
Urine test strip, combination, pkg. 100	4 strips	14 M 4117	34B
Urine, artificial, 500 mL	5 mL	37 M 0100	34B
Urine, artificial w/albumin, 500 mL	5 mL	37 M 0105	34B
Urine, artificial w/glucose, 500 mL	5 mL	37 M 0104	34B
Urine, artificial w/ketone, 500 mL	5 mL	37 M 0102	34B
Vallisneria, corkscrew, living, pkg. 10	1 plant	86 M 7850	14A
Yeast, viable, pkg. 10 g	2 pkg.	88 M 0929	5B

Ordering Materials is Easy with WARD'S™ Software Ordering System

With **WARD'S** exclusive software-ordering system, specifically designed for use with *Biology: Visualizing Life,* you can order your materials and supplies quickly and easily. The system lists all required and supplemental materials—per lab group or class size—needed for every lab investigation in *Biology: Visualizing Life.* Call WARD'S at 1-800-962-2660 for your free copy.

- Click on the products you need and the software automatically creates your shopping list, keeping track of the materials ordered and their costs.
- A help window explains every function, making the program easy to use.
- Available for both Macintosh and IBM-compatible computers.

Service and Satisfaction

WARD'S technical staff is always available to answer your questions.

WARD'S Service Team

Toll-Free Phone:..1-800-962-2660
Toll-Free Fax:.. 1-800-635-8439
Internet Address:........................... http://www.wardsci.com
E-mail:................................. customer_service@wardsci.com

WARD'S Natural Science Establishment, Inc.
5100 West Henrietta Road
P.O. Box 92912
Rochester, New York 14692-9012

Chemicals and Media

Item	Qty.	WARD'S No.	Lab
3-Indoleacetic acid, 5 g	105 mL	39 M 1661	21A
Adrenaline (epinephrine) 1:10,000, 30 mL	1 drop	38 M 2052	31A
Agarose, prepared 0.8%, 200 mL	15 mL	88 M 1207	9A
*Bam*HI restriction enzyme, 50 µL	1 µL	85 M 1355	9A
Benedict's solution, qualitative, 1 L	23 mL	37 M 0701	4A, 22A, 22B
Biuret reagent, urea protein test, 120 mL	18 mL	37 M 0790	22A, 22B
Bromothymol blue 0.1% aqueous sol., 30 mL	224 mL	38 M 9105	5B, 32A
Bromothymol blue, aqueous solution, 500 mL	25 mL	38 M 9100	5A
DNA stain for gel electrophoresis, 500 mL	100 mL	38 M 9012	9A
Disinfectant, liquid household	1 mL	Local	18A
*Eco*RI restriction enzyme, 50 µL	1 µL	85 M 1356	9A
Ethyl alcohol (ethanol) anhydrous, 500 mL	3 drops	39 M 0273	30A
Food coloring, red, pkg. 4	1 bottle	15 M 0071	5A, 5B
Gelatin solution, 2%, pkg. makes 1 L	2 mL	37 M 9557	22A
Glucose solution 15%, 250 mL	12 mL	37 M 9000	4A, 22A
Glucose, monohydrate, 500 g	6 g	39 M 1457	5B
*Hind*III restriction enzyme, 50 µL	2 µL	85 M 1358	9A
Hydrochloric acid, 0.1 M, 1 L	15 mL	37 M 9561	34A
Isopropyl alcohol, 70% solution, 500 mL	1 oz	39 M 4917	18A

Item	Qty.	WARD'S No.	Lab
Lambda phage DNA, vial, 50 µL	42 µL	85 M 1330	9A
Loading dye, 6×, 5 mL	50 µ	38 M 9115	9A
Lugol's iodine solution, 3A, 4A, 22A, 500 mL	21 mL	39 M 1685	
			22B
Pancreatin, powder, 100 g	10–15 g per class	39 M 2728	34A
Pepsin, powder, (activity 1:3000), 25 g	4–6 g per class	39 M 2865	34A
Protist slowing agent: Detain, 0.5 oz	5 mL	37 M 7950	3A, 19A, 30A
Protist slowing agent: Detain 2, 0.5 oz	5 mL	37 M 7952	31A
Sea salts, synthetic, pkg. 25 oz	20 g	21 M 7353	1B
Simulated blood, unfiltered, 250 mL	20 mL	36 M 0039	24A
Sodium hydroxide, 0.1N, 1 L	15 mL	37 M 9562	34A
Sodium hypochlorite, reagent, 500 mL	10 mL	37 M 5558	18A
Starch solution (1%), 250 mL	32 mL	37 M 9001	4A, 22A
Sulfosalicylic acid 3%, 100 mL	5 mL	39 M 3205	34B
Tris-Borate-EDTA buffer, 10× Sol., 250 mL	1 bottle per class	37 M 0620	9A
Tryptic soy agar plates, pkg. 6	1	88 M 0925	18A
Tryptic soy agar, 125 mL bottle, pkg. 6	20 mL	88 M 1815	18A
Water, dechlorinated	1 L	Local	1B
Water, distilled, 1 gal	5 L per class	88 M 7005	9A, 18A, 21A, 22A, 22B, 24A, 32A, 34A

Laboratory Equipment

Item	Qty.	WARD'S No.	Lab
Apron, disposable polyethylene, box 100	1 per student	15 M 1050	1A, 1B, 3A, 4A, 5A, 5B, 7A, 7B, 9A, 14A, 15A, 18A, 21A, 22A, 22B, 24A, 30A, 31A, 34A, 34B
Balance, triple beam	1 per class	15 M 6057	1B
Beaker, low-form 100 mL Griffin	1	17 M 4020	15A, 30A, 31A
Beaker, low-form 150 mL Griffin	4	17 M 4030	32A
Beaker, low-form 250 mL Griffin	2	17 M 4040	4A, 24A
Beaker, low-form 400 mL Griffin	1	17 M 4050	5A
Beaker, low-form 50 mL Griffin	6	17 M 4010	18A

Item	Qty.	WARD'S No.	Lab
Beaker, low-form 600 mL Griffin	4	17 M 4060	1B, 4A, 5B, 9A, 22A, 22B, 34A
Borosilicate capillary tube, 1mm	12	17 M 0927	5B
Brush, *Drosophila*/ camel hair, pkg. 12	3	15 M 3846	21A
Bunsen burner, std. nat. gas	1	15 M 0612	14A, 18A
Capillary micropipets, pkg. 250	1	15 M 2096	9A
Capillary tube, melting point 100 m, vial 100	2	17 M 5020	19A
Clamp, Stoddard test tube, pkg. 6	1	15 M 0841	4A, 22A, 22B, 34A
Cotton, nonabsorbent, nonsterile, pkg. 1 lb	5	15 M 3828	21A
Cotton swab	1	Local	1B

Item	Qty.	WARD'S No.	Lab
Coverslip, 22 mm plastic, box 100	10	14 M 3555	3A, 14A, 15A, 19A, 30A, 31A
Culture tube, Pyrex 20 × 150 mm	5	17 M 1406	5A
Cup, plastic with lid, 9 oz, pkg. 25	5	18 M 3676	1B
DNA Electrophoresis System III (alternate)	1 per class	36 M 5103	9A
DNA fingerprinting	1 per class	36 M 5167	9A
Dialysis tubing, 15.9 mm diameter, 10-ft roll	one 6 in. piece	14 M 4516	24A
Dialysis tubing, 6.4 mm diameter, 100-ft roll	two 15 in. pieces	14 M 4510	4A
Dropping bottle, glass, 15 mL, pkg. 12	3	17 M 6018	22A, 22B
Dropping bottle, plastic, 15 mL, pkg. 12	1	18 M 1553	22A
Electrophoresis system, battery powered	1	36 M 5164	9A
Erlenmeyer flask, Pyrex 125 mL	5	17 M 2972	21A
Filter paper, medium grade, 9.0 cm, box	1 per class	15 M 2815	18A
Flower pot, plastic 3 in., pkg. 10	1 per class	20 M 2130	21A
Food Chemistry Module Kit	1 per class	36 M 2041	22A
Forceps, dissecting, medium	1	14 M 1001	18A, 34B
Gas lighter, flat file, pkg. 10	1	15 M 0683	18A
Glass disposal box, case 6	1 per classroom	18 M 1399	All
Glass tubing cutter, Griffin type	1	15 M 0611	5A
Gloves, disposable, medium, box 100	12 per student	15 M 1071	7A, 7B, 9A, 18A, 30A, 31A
Gloves, Heat Defier Kelnit cotton, pair	1	15 M 1095	9A
Graduated cylinder, 10 mL polypropylene	1	18 M 1705	1A, 1B, 4A, 34A, 34B
Graduated cylinder, 10 mL, glass	1	17 M 0170	15A
Graduated cylinder, 25 mL, polypropylene	1	18 M 1710	24A
Graduated cylinder, 25 mL, Pyrex	1	17 M 0826	18A
Graduated cylinder, 50 mL, polypropylene	1	18 M 1720	5B, 9A
Graduated cylinder, 100 mL, polypropylene	1	18 M 1730	21A
Graduated cylinder, 250 mL, polypropylene	1	18 M 1740	5A
Graduated cylinder, Pyrex 500 mL	1	17 M 0580	1B
Hot plate, Corning Pyroceram PC400	1	15 M 8055	4A, 22A, 22B, 34A
Incubator, all-purpose anhydric	1 per class	15 M 7531	1A
Incubator, lab	1 per class	15 M 0060	18A, 34A

Item	Qty.	WARD'S No.	Lab
Jar cap, white metal 53 mm	20	17 M 2133	26A
Jar, clear polystyrene, 2 oz, 53 mm	20	18 M 1632	26A
Knife, plastic	1	250 M 8128	1A
Lamp, clamp, with reflector	1 per class	36 M 4168	19A
Lens, Fresnel 2 1/8 in. × 3 1/4 in.	1	25 M 1350	1B
Lens tissue	4 sheets	15 M 8250	3A
Marker, black lab	1	15 M 3083	9A, 18A
Meter stick, maple	1	15 M 4065	6A
Metronome	1	Local	32A
Microcentrifuge tube rack	1	18 M 4205	9A
Microfuge tubes, 1.5 mL, pkg. 500	5	18 M 1361	9A
Microscope slide, qual. precleaned, pkg. 72	10	14 M 3500	3A, 14A, 15A, 19A
Microscope slide, single concavity, pkg. 12	1	14 M 3510	3A, 30A, 31A
Microscope	1	24 M 2310	3A, 14A, 15A, 19A, 30A, 31A
Model ecosystem from Exploration 14A	1	Local	15A
Modeling Kidney Action Lab, kit	1	36 M 0040	24A
Net, standard insect	1	10 M 0500	26A
Pen, black ink marking set, pkg. 4	1	18 M 2300	5A, 5B
Pen, black wax marker for glass	1	15 M 1155	1A, 1B, 4A, 14A, 15A, 21A, 22A, 22B, 24A, 34A, 34B
Petri dish, disposable 100 × 15 mm, pkg. 20	7	18 M 7101	1A, 18A
Petri dish, disposable 150 × 15 mm, pkg. 20	5	18 M 7100	1B
Pipet, glass dropping 3 in., pkg. 12	6	17 M 0230	1A, 3A, 4A, 5A, 19A, 22A, 30A, 31A
Pipet, graduated dropping, 2 mL	1	17 M 1706	1B
Pipet, nonsterile 6 in., pkg. 500	5	18 M 2971	14A, 15A, 32A, 34B
Rubber stopper, 1 hole, size 1, 1 lb	12	15 M 8481	5A, 5B
Ruler, 12 in. plastic	1	15 M 4655	8A
Ruler, 6 in. white vinylite	1	14 M 0810	1A, 4A, 5A, 5B, 9A, 10A, 21A, 34A
Ruler, clear vinyl		14 M 0811	3A
Ruler, metric & English, 12 in.	1	15 M 4650	20A
Safety goggles, regular	1 per student	15 M 3046	1A, 1B, 3A, 4A, 5A, 5B, 7A, 7B, 9A, 15A, 18A, 21A, 22A, 22B, 24A, 30A, 31A, 32A, 34A, 34B
Sand, fine white, pkg. 5 kg	2 in.	20 M 7425	14A

Item	Qty.	WARD'S No.	Lab
Scalpel, economy 1 1/2 in. blade	1	14 M 4320	21A
Scissors, 8 in.	1	15 M 9872	6A, 8A, 14A, 20A, 28A
Scissors, student econ. dissecting	1	14 M 0525	1A
Silicone culture gum, 1 oz	7 cm	37 M 9810	19A
Step stool	1	15 M 3510	32A
Stereomicroscope, widefield	1	24 M 4601	1B, 26A
Stir rods, 6 in. glass, pkg. 10	1	17 M 6005	5B
Stopper, black rubber, solid, size 1, 1 lb	3	15 M 8461	34B
Stopwatch, digital	1	15 M 0512	30A, 31A, 32A
Teasing needle, wood handle	1	14 M 0650	14A
Test-tube rack, 6-well LDPE	1	18 M 4231	4A, 5A

Item	Qty.	WARD'S No.	Lab
Test-tube rack, white plastic	1	18 M 4213	22A, 22B, 34A, 34B
Test-tube rack, white plastic	1	18 M 4214	5B
Test tube with rim, 15 × 125 mm Pyrex	21	17 M 0620	22A, 22B, 34A, 34B
Test tube with rim, 18 × 150 mm Pyrex	12	17 M 0640	4A, 5B
Thermometer, lab 1A, 5B, 15A, 34A	4	15 M 1416	
Tray, w/cover, 4 × 7 × 1 3/4 in.	1	18 M 0031	9A
Tubing, flint glass, 4 mm × 0.7 mm, 1 lb	five 6 cm pieces	17 M 0930	5A
Water bath	2 per class	14 M 5759	9A
Wood splints, 5 1/2 in., pkg. 500	8	14 M 0105	22A, 22B
Zipper bag, pkg. 50	1	18 M 6952	9A

Miscellaneous

Item	Qty.	WARD'S No.	Lab
A Field Guide to the Insects	1	32 M 0106	26A
Acetate, 8.5 × 11 in. sheet	1 per 2 teams	Local	8A
Alligator picture	1	Local	28A
Aluminum foil, 12 in. wide, roll 25 ft	1 m	15 M 1009	1B
Audubon Guide: *Insects & Spiders*	1	32 M 2101	26A
Box, cardboard	1	Local	1B
Cellophane, blue, 20 in.-wide, roll 100 ft	1 ft	14 M 8220	5A
Cellophane, clear, 20 in.-wide, roll 100 ft	1 ft	14 M 8225	5A
Cellophane, green, 20 in.-wide, roll 100 ft	1 ft	14 M 8210	5A
Cellophane, red, 20 in.-wide, roll 100 ft	1 ft	14 M 8200	5A
Cellophane, yellow, 20 in.-wide, roll 100 ft	1 ft	14 M 8215	5A
Cigarette tobacco, high-nicotine	1 cigarette per class	Local	30A
Clock, with second hand	1 per class	Local	4A, 30A, 31A, 32A
Coffee, with caffeine	3 drops	Local	30A
Diet pills, with PPA	3 drops	Local	30A
Display board, 48 × 32 in.	1 per	18 M 2105	28A
Food sample	10 mL	Local	22A
Frog picture	1	Local	28A
Glue, white, 4 oz	1	15 M 9806	20A, 26A, 28A
Gorilla picture	1	Local	28A
Graph paper, 5 squares/in., pkg. 100	2 sheets	15 M 3835	10A

Item	Qty.	WARD'S No.	Lab
Household detergent, liquid, 12 oz	1 mL	37 M 2268	18A
Index cards, 3 × 5 in. lined, pkg. 100	8	15 M 9807	8A
Lamprey picture	1	Local	28A
Magazine, gardening	3	Local	20A
Nail, 8d common, pkg. 36	1	15 M 9478	14A
Organic matter, dead	10 g	Local	14A
Paper	21 sheets	Local	20A, 26A, 28A
Paper bag, pkg. 50	eight 5 in. squares	18 M 6900	22A, 22B
Paper clips, pkg. 1000	41	15 M 9815	6A, 8A
Paper punch, one-hole	1	15 M 9810	18A, 19A
Paper towel, 100-sheet 2-ply roll	22 sheets	15 M 9844	1A, 3A, 9A, 18A, 30A, 31A, 34B
Paper, black construction, pkg. 50	2 sheets	15 M 9825	6A, 19A
Paper, blue construction, pkg. 50	1 sheet	15 M 9866	6A
Paper, green construction, pkg. 50	1 sheet	15 M 9867	6A
Paper, red construction, pkg. 50	1 sheet	15 M 9865	6A
Peanut butter	2 mL	Local	22B
Pencils, colored, pkg. 12	5 per	15 M 4690	26A, 28A
Pencils, Ticonderoga #2, box 12	1 per	15 M 9816	20A
Petroleum jelly	2 mL	Local	30A, 31A
Plant fertilizer, pkg. 2.75 g, makes 1 L	100 mL	20 M 6040	15A

Item	Qty.	WARD'S No.	Lab
Plastic wrap, 12 in. wide, roll 50 ft	four 12 in. squares	15 M 9858	32A
Plastic, 5 cm squares	2	Local	14A
Poster board, white, pkg. 5	2	15 M 9856	26A
Potato chips	2 g	Local	22B
Pushpins, assorted colors, box 100	37	15 M 0507	8A
Roll, bread	2 g	Local	22B
Salmon picture	1	Local	28A
Shark picture	1	Local	28A
Simulated ABO Blood Typing Lab, kit	1 per class	36 M 0022	7A, 7B
Soap, Betadine antiseptic, 16 oz	1 mL	15 M 9829	18A
Soap, liquid antibacterial	1 mL	18 M 1533	18A
Soap, liquid dishwashing	1 mL	Local	18A
Soap, liquid hand	1 mL	Local	18A
Soil, garden potting, bag 8 lb	2 bags per class	20 M 8306	14A, 21A
Strapping tape, roll 3/4 in. × 60 yd	3 ft	15 M 1980	14A

Item	Qty.	WARD'S No.	Lab
Straws, plastic wrapped, pkg. 500	42	15 M 9869	5A, 8A, 32A
String, pkg. 400 ft	2 1/2 m	15 M 9863	6A, 24A
String, colored	10 m	Local	28A
Tape, black vinyl electric, roll 66 ft	8 in.	15 M 5020	18A
Tape, cellophane, roll	1 roll	15 M 1957	5A, 6A
Tape, masking 3/4 in. × 60 yd roll, pkg. 3	1 roll	15 M 9828	8A
Tape, transparent w/dispenser	2 rolls per class	15 M 1959	8A, 9A
Tea, orange Pekoe	3 drops	Local	30A
Thread, nylon, 196 yd/spool, pkg. 3	four 10 cm pieces	15 M 9837	4A
Tiger picture	1	Local	28A
Toothpicks, round, box 800	1 box per class	15 M 9840	3A, 19A
Vegetable oil, 16 oz	2 mL	37 M 9540	22A
Wax paper, 12 in. wide, roll 75 ft	seven 12 in. squares	15 M 9857	22B
Yarn, red, 10 yd skein	10 m	15 M 2544	26A

Teacher's Guide Credits

List of Abbreviations

All photographs attributed to SP/Foca were taken by Sergio Purtell/Foca Co.

AA = Animals Animals; AT = Alexander & Turner; BPA = Biophoto Associates; BPS = BPS & Biological Photo Service; CM = Custom Medical; HS = Highlight Studios; KBI = Karapelou BioMedical Illustrations; KC = Kip Carter, M.S. certified medical illustrator; LPI = Lynne Prentice Illustration; MA = rep. Mattleson Associates, Ltd.; MMA = Margulies Medical Art; MHI = Mark Hallett Illustrations; PA = Peter Arnold, Inc.; PR = Photo Researchers; RWS = rep. Richard W. Salzman S.F., CA; SS = Studio Sloth

All Safety Symbols were designed by Michael Helfenbein/Evolution Design.

T1 (t) Peg Gerrity/HS; (c) SP/Foca; (b) John W. Karapelou/KBI; T2 SP/Foca; T3 (t,b) SP/Foca; T4 (c) SP/Foca; (b) Mark Hallet/MHI; (t) Deborah Daugherty/Laurie O'Keefe/HS; T5 European Space Agency/SPL/PR, Inc.; R. Margulies/MMA; T7 (t) E. Alexander/AT; (b) T. Narashima/SS; T8 (l) Daniel Kirk/BA; (b) Mark Hallet/MHI; T9 SP/Foca; T10 Laurie O'Keefe/HS; T11 (t) SP/Foca; (b) Peg Gerrity/HS; T12 (t) Wendy Smith-Griswold; (b) SP/Foca; T13 (t) SP/Foca; (b) Walter Stuart/RWS; T15 (bl) Lynne Prentice/LPI; (t) calculator permission of Texas Instruments; (bl) Lynne Prentice/LPI; (br) SP/Foca; T16 (tr) Walter Stuart/RWS; (l) Lynne Prentice/LPI; (r) David Beck/RMF; (r,b) SP/Foca; (l) Robert Margulies/MMA; (b) Kip Carter/KC; T17 (l) Kerry Klayman; (cl) Michael J. Balick/PA, Inc.; (cr) Carlos Goldin/SPL/PR, Inc.; (bl) BPS/Science Source/PR, Inc.; (bc) SP/Foca; T18 (tr) Ted Horowitz/ TSM; (tl) Michel Viard/PA, Inc.; (tl) SP/Foca; T19 (tl) Ralph A. Reinhold / Animals Animals ; (bl) @1992 /CM; (br) SP/Foca; T20 courtesy George Johnson; T21 SP/Foca; T22 courtesy George Johnson; T24 courtesy George Johnson; T26 SP/Foca; T27 (t,c,b) SP/Foca; T28 Ted Horowitz/ TSM; T30 (t,b) SP/Foca; T31 (t,b) SP/Foca; T32 (bl,br,c) SP/Foca; T34 Tim Fuller; T36 (t) SP/Foca; T38 SP/Foca; T40 SP/Foca; T41 SP/Foca; T745-3 (b) Peter Menzel/Boston Stock, Inc./PNI; T745-5 (c) Ted Horowitz/TSM; (l) SP/Foca; (r) Mark Gibson/Index Stock; T745-9 (b) SP/Foca; (tl, tr) SP/Foca; T745-10 SP/Foca; T745-11 SP/Foca

Lab Program Explorations

See **Explorations: Getting Started** on pages T745-3 and T745-4 for information about conducting and evaluating Explorations in your classroom.

Additional labs with the format used in Explorations can be found in the following **Holt BioSources Lab Program** laboratory manuals:

- **Laboratory Techniques and Experimental Design**
- **Biotechnology**

Complete listings of the lab titles found in each of these manuals appear on pages T32 and T33.

The **Holt BioSources Teaching Resources CD-ROM** includes customizable scoring rubrics to help you evaluate the **Explorations. The Holt BioSources Teaching Resources CD-ROM** also contains classroom-management checklists, a student safety contract and quiz, and basic skills worksheets and problem-solving worksheets that can help you reinforce skills needed for success in the laboratory. See pages T35 and T38 for additional information about the **Holt BioSources Teaching Resources CD-ROM.**

Using the Explorations

Each Exploration gives you an opportunity to practice techniques that are used in biological research by providing a step-by-step procedure for you to follow. You will use many of these techniques later in one or more Investigations.

Each Exploration Contains the Following Parts:

Skill identifies the technique you will learn.

Objectives tell you what you will be expected to accomplish.

Situation is the setting for the lab.

Background provides additional information you will need for the lab.

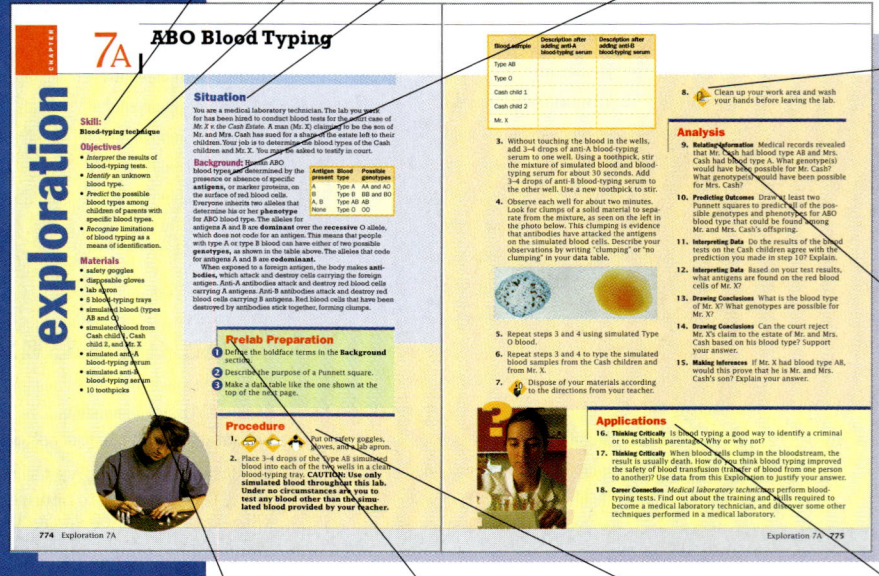

Procedure includes safety precautions and cleanup and disposal instructions.

Analysis items help you analyze the lab's techniques and your data to come to a conclusion.

Materials are the items you will need to do the lab.

Prelab Preparation items are things you should do before beginning the procedure.

Procedure is a step-by-step explanation for doing the lab.

Applications questions require you to apply what you have learned and direct you to research a career related to the lab's skills.

746

What You Should Do Before an Exploration

Preparation helps you work safely and efficiently. The day before a lab, be sure to complete the following steps.

- **Read the *Situation, Background, and Procedure*** to make sure you understand what you will do.
- **Read the safety information** that begins on page 752, as well as that provided in the lab procedure.
- **Complete the *Prelab Preparation* section** by defining the terms, answering the questions, and preparing data tables in your lab notebook.

What You Should Do After an Exploration

Most teachers require a lab report as a way of making sure that you understood what you were doing in the lab. Your teacher will give you specific details about how to organize the lab report. Most lab reports include the following information.

- **title** for the lab
- **summary paragraph** describing the purpose and procedure
- **data tables and observations** that are organized and comprehensive
- **answers** for the items in the Analysis and Applications sections

Tips for Success in the Lab

Whether you are doing an Exploration or an Investigation, you can take the following steps to help ensure success.

- **Read each lab twice** before you come to class.
- **Read and follow the safety precautions** in the lab and on pages 752–755.
- **Prepare a data table** before you come to class.
- **Record all data and observations immediately** in your data table or lab notebook.
- **Use appropriate units** whenever you record data.
- **Keep your lab table organized** and free of clutter.

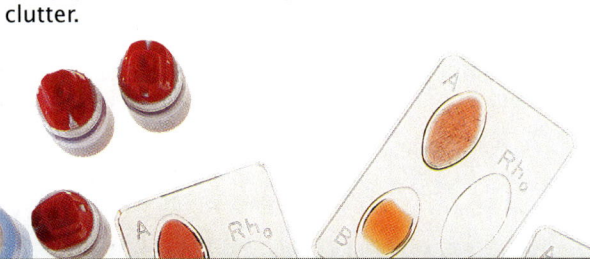

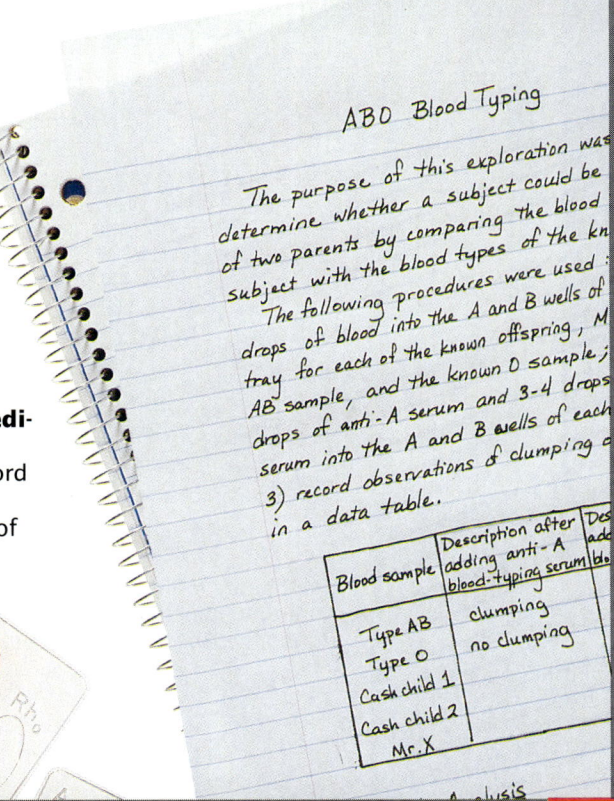

ABO Blood Typing

The purpose of this exploration was determine whether a subject could be of two parents by comparing the blood subject with the blood types of the kn

The following procedures were used: drops of blood into the A and B wells of tray for each of the known offspring, M AB sample, and the known O sample; drops of anti-A serum and 3-4 drops serum into the A and B wells of each 3) record observations of clumping in a data table.

Blood sample	Description after adding anti-A blood-typing serum	Des add blo
Type AB	clumping	
Type O	no clumping	
Cash child 1		
Cash child 2		
Mr. X		

Teacher's notes

The following components of the **Reference and Skills Appendix** will help prepare students for laboratory work:

Determining Mass and Temperature — pages 830–831

Graphing — pages 832–835

SI Measurement — pages 844–845

Interpreting Food Labels — pages 846–847

Each component contains **Practice Exercises** that you may wish to assign to students.

747

See **Investigations: Tips for Success** on pages T745-5 and T745-6 for information about conducting and evaluating Investigations in your classroom.

Additional labs with the format used in Investigations can be found in the following **Holt BioSources Lab Program** laboratory manuals:

- **Laboratory Techniques and Experimental Design**
- **Biotechnology**

Complete listings of the lab titles found in each of these manuals appear on pages T32 and T33.

Using the Investigations

Each Investigation requires you to assume the role of an employee in a biological consulting firm. You will develop your own procedure to solve a problem that has been presented to your company by a client. The procedures you develop will be based on the procedures and techniques you learned in previous Explorations. You must also decide what equipment to use for a project and manage expenses to earn a profit.

Each Investigation Contains the Following Parts:

Prerequisites tell you which Explorations contain procedures that apply to the Investigation and which concepts you will need to understand to complete the lab.

The **Letter** contains a request from a client to solve a problem or to do a project.

The **Memorandum** is a note from your supervisor directing you to perform the work requested by the client. The memorandum contains clues or directions that will help you design a successful experiment or project.

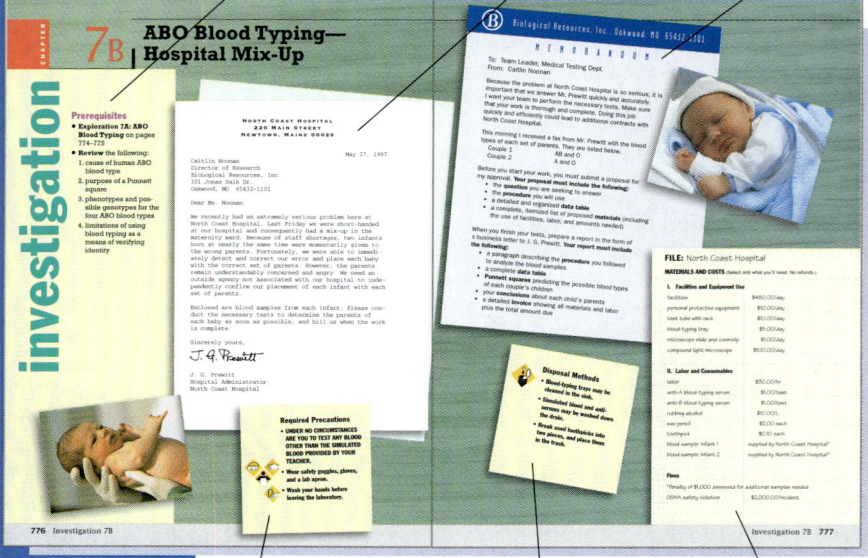

Required Precautions are the safety procedures you must follow during the lab.

Disposal Methods tell you how to dispose of the materials used.

Materials and Costs is a list of the services and items that might be needed to complete the work and the unit cost of each item. Select from this list only the services and items you will need to complete the project within your budget.

What You Should Do Before an Investigation

Before you will be allowed to work on an Investigation, you must turn in a proposal that includes the question to be answered, the procedure you will use, a complete and organized data table, and a list of all the required services and materials with their costs. Before you begin writing your proposal, follow these steps.

- **Read the Investigation thoroughly,** and jot down any clues you find that will help you successfully complete the lab.
- **Consider what you must measure or observe** to solve the problem.
- **Think about Explorations** you have done that required similar measurements and observations.
- **Imagine working through a procedure,** keeping track of each step and what equipment you will need.

What You Should Do After an Investigation

After you finish, organize a report as described in the Memorandum. The report can be in the form of a one- or two-page letter to the client plus an invoice showing how much you charged for each phase of the work and the total cost of the work. (Your teacher may have additional requirements for your report.) Carefully consider how to convey the information the client needs to know. In some cases, graphs and diagrams may communicate information better than words.

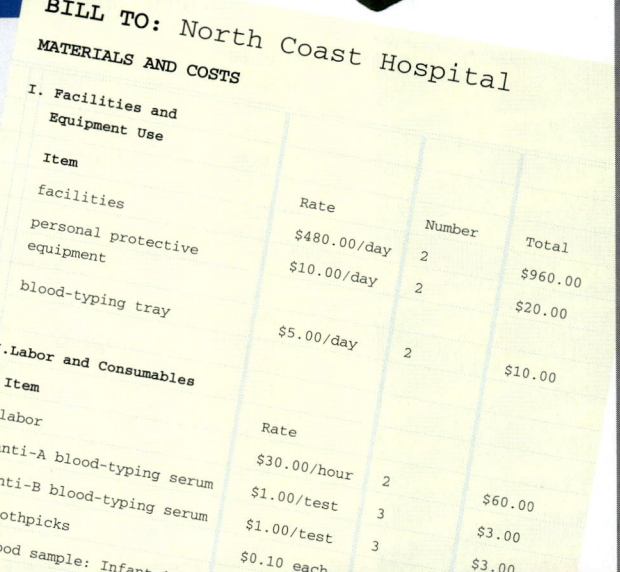

Biological Resources, Inc. Oakwood, MO 65▮▮ 1101

June 4, 1997

J. G. Prewitt
Hospital Administrator
North Coast Hospital
220 Main Street
Newtown, Maine 00020

Dear Mr. Prewitt,

We have completed the blood-typing tests as you reque▮ following procedures: 1) place 3-4 drops of Infant 1's ▮ two wells of a blood-typing tray; 2) add 3-4 drops of an▮ serum to one well and 3-4 drops of anti-B blood-typin▮ well; 3) stir the blood and typing serum in each well ▮ toothpick for 30 seconds; 4) observe each well for 2 ▮ observations in a data table; 5) repeat step 1–4 usi▮ 6) repeat steps 1–5 two more times; and 7) compa▮ Punnett squares completed for each couple. The P▮ below.

Couple 1
| A | B |

Couple 2
| A | A |

BILL TO: North Coast Hospital

MATERIALS AND COSTS

I. Facilities and Equipment Use

Item	Rate	Number	Total
facilities	$480.00/day	2	$960.00
personal protective equipment	$10.00/day	2	$20.00
blood-typing tray	$5.00/day	2	$10.00

II. Labor and Consumables

Item	Rate		
labor	$30.00/hour	2	$60.00
anti-A blood-typing serum	$1.00/test	3	$3.00
anti-B blood-typing serum	$1.00/test	3	$3.00
toothpicks	$0.10 each		
blood sample: Infant 1			

You may wish to extend the consulting-firm scenario that forms the basis of the **Investigations.** Students can be invited to do any of the following optional activities:

- Develop a plan for creating a business, including ideas for funding and potential clients.
- Fill out copies of business-loan forms from local banks.
- Design a logo, custom stationery, and a business card for the consulting firm.
- Create financial statements showing income, expenses, and profits.
- Fill out copies of governmental forms, such as incorporation papers or corporate registrations, business licenses, applications for lab permits or chemical licenses, etc.
- Develop a marketing campaign to reach new customers, and include costs. Students who are musically talented could write a theme or jingle for use in radio or television advertisements.
- Develop a plan for the use of any profits to reinvest in personnel, equipment, marketing, etc. (Some teachers allow lab groups that are profitable to become "venture capitalists," who loan money to lab groups that have made mistakes in planning their procedures and use of resources.)

749

See **Interactive Explorations: Using CD-ROM Technology** on pages T745-7 and T745-8 for information about conducting and evaluating Interactive Explorations in your classroom.

Additional information about **Interactive Explorations in Biology** can be found on pages T36 and T37.

Using the Interactive Explorations

Imagine that you could watch what happens within a plant cell during photosynthesis, or that you could observe how drug use changes the nervous system. You can't do these things in a conventional laboratory exercise, but you can in an Interactive Exploration.

Using the Disk *Interactive Explorations in Biology: Human Biology*

1. Obtain the CD-ROM *Interactive Explorations in Biology: Human Biology* from your teacher. Load the disk into the CD-ROM drive according to the instructions provided by your teacher.

2. An icon for the CD-ROM will appear on the screen. Click it, and then click the icon labeled "Start Explorations."

3. After a few moments, the title screen will appear. Click the button labeled "Menu" at the bottom right of the screen.

4. The computer will then display the menu screen, which lists all the Interactive Explorations on the disk. Select the Interactive Exploration you wish to run and click on its title.

5. After a few moments, the computer will display a screen containing a column of buttons along the right edge, as shown in **Figure 1**. This column is the Navigation Palette, and the buttons it contains allow you to access the various features found in each Interactive Exploration. To begin, click the top button on the column, labeled "Interactive Investigation."

6. If you have questions about an Interactive Exploration, you can play the instructions for operating the Interactive Exploration. Click the word *File* at the top of the screen, and select "Interactive Exploration Help." You may also refer to the User's Guide for additional information.

Using the Disk *Interactive Explorations in Biology: Cell Biology and Genetics*

1. Obtain the CD-ROM *Interactive Explorations in Biology: Cell Biology and Genetics* from your teacher. Load the disk into the CD-ROM drive according to the instructions provided by your teacher.

2. An icon for the CD-ROM will appear on the screen. Click it, and then click the icon labeled "Start Explorations."

3. After a few moments, the title screen will appear. Click the button labeled "Menu" at the bottom right of the screen.

4. The computer will then display the menu screen, which lists all the Interactive Explorations on the disk. Select the Interactive Exploration you wish to run and click on its title.

5. After a few moments, the computer will display the Interactive Exploration screen and play a short narration that describes the problem you will be studying. (To shut off this narration, select "Sound Off" from the Sound menu at the top right of the screen.) After this brief narration has played, the Interactive Exploration is ready to run.

6. If you have questions about an Interactive Exploration, you can play the instructions for operating the Interactive Exploration. Click the word *Help* at the top of the screen, and select "How to Use This Exploration" from the menu that appears. Clicking the Help button on the Navigation Palette will call up instructions on how to use the features of the Navigation Palette. You may also refer to the User's Guide.

Figure 1

Clicking the Navigation button at the bottom right of the screen calls up the Navigation Palette, a ribbon of 10 buttons, each with its own icon. The title of each button appears when you position the pointer on the icon. The buttons of the Navigation Palette allow you to navigate among features within the Interactive Exploration, to move to a different Interactive Exploration, or to quit entirely.

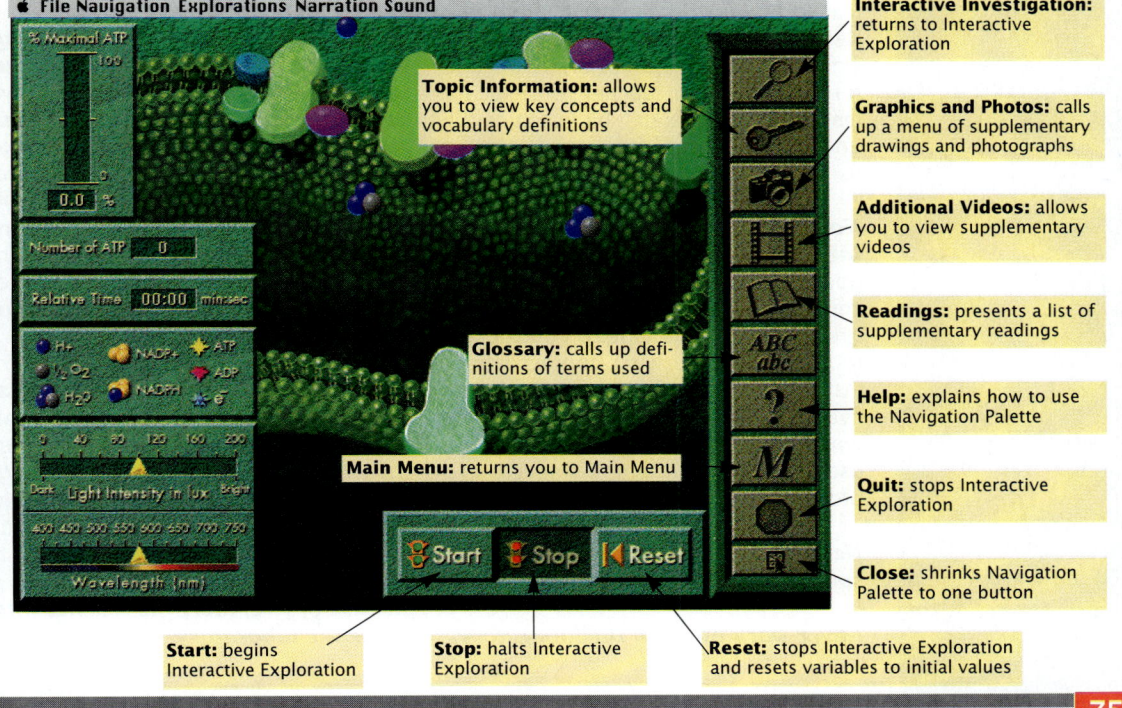

Navigation Palette

Topic Information: allows you to view key concepts and vocabulary definitions

Glossary: calls up definitions of terms used

Main Menu: returns you to Main Menu

Interactive Investigation: returns to Interactive Exploration

Graphics and Photos: calls up a menu of supplementary drawings and photographs

Additional Videos: allows you to view supplementary videos

Readings: presents a list of supplementary readings

Help: explains how to use the Navigation Palette

Quit: stops Interactive Exploration

Close: shrinks Navigation Palette to one button

Start: begins Interactive Exploration

Stop: halts Interactive Exploration

Reset: stops Interactive Exploration and resets variables to initial values

751

Frequently remind students that they are responsible for understanding and following the safety procedures discussed on this page and on pages 754–755. Students must be able to demonstrate that they understand the meaning of each of the 13 safety icons (and the safety procedures associated with each icon) introduced on these pages. These safety icons are used throughout the Explorations and Investigations in this book and throughout the lab activities found in **Holt BioSources Lab Program.** Students should recognize that each of the procedures associated with each safety icon must *always* be observed for *all* work in the laboratory. Help students understand and follow this guideline: **Whether or not the lab instructions remind you, all of these rules apply all of the time.**

Safe Laboratory Practices

It is your responsibility to protect yourself and other students by conducting yourself in a safe manner while in the laboratory. Familiarize yourself with the printed safety symbols—they indicate additional measures that you must take.

While in the Laboratory

Familiarize yourself with the investigation—especially safety issues—before entering the lab. Know the potential hazards of the materials, equipment, and procedures required. Ask the teacher to explain any parts you do not understand before you start.

Always wear a lab apron and safety goggles. Wear this equipment even if you are not working on an experiment at the time. Laboratories contain chemicals that can damage your clothing. Keep the apron strings tied. If your safety goggles cloud up, or are uncomfortable, ask your teacher for help. Try lengthening the strap a bit, washing the goggles with soap and warm water, or using an anti-fog spray.

No contact lenses are allowed in the lab. Even while you are wearing safety goggles, chemicals could get between contact lenses and your eyes and cause irreparable eye damage. If your doctor requires that you wear contact lenses instead of glasses, then you should wear eye-cup safety goggles in the lab. Ask your doctor or your teacher how to use this very important and special eye protection.

Never perform any experiment not specifically assigned by your teacher.

Never work alone in the laboratory.

Know the location of all safety and emergency equipment used in the laboratory. Examples include eyewash stations, safety blankets, safety shower, fire extinguisher, first aid kit, and chemical spill kit.

Know the location of the closest telephone. Be sure there is a posted list of emergency phone numbers, including poison control center, fire department, police, and ambulance.

Before beginning work: tie back long hair, roll up loose sleeves, and put on any required personal protective equipment as directed by your teacher. Avoid or confine loose clothing that could knock things over, catch on fire, or soak up chemical solutions. Remember that nylon and polyester fabrics burn and melt more readily than does cotton. Open-toed shoes or sandals offer no protection, and even cloth shoes are not a good idea in the laboratory.

Report any accident, incident, or hazard—no matter how trivial—to your teacher immediately. Any incident involving bleeding, burns, fainting, chemical exposure, or ingestion should also be reported immediately to your school nurse or school physician.

In case of fire, alert the teacher and leave the laboratory.

Horseplay and fooling around in the lab are very dangerous. NEVER be a clown in the laboratory.

Never consume food or drink, or apply cosmetics, in the laboratory. Never store food in the laboratory. Keep your hands away from your face. Wash your hands at the conclusion of each laboratory investigation and before leaving the laboratory. Remember that some hair-care products are highly flammable, even after application.

Keep your work area neat and uncluttered. Bring only books and other materials that are needed to conduct the experiment.

Clean your work area at the conclusion of the experiment as your teacher directs.

When Called for, Use These Safety Procedures:

 ### Eye Safety
Wear approved chemical safety goggles as directed. Goggles should always be worn in the laboratory, especially when you are working with a chemical or solution, heat source, mechanical device, or physical process.

In case of eye contact:
Go to an eyewash station immediately and flush your eyes (including under the eyelids) with running water for at least 15 minutes. Hold your eyelids open with your thumb and fingers, and roll your eyeball around. After starting to flush the eye, have another student notify your teacher or another adult in charge.

Wearing contact lenses for cosmetic reasons is prohibited in the laboratory. Liquids or gases can be drawn up under the contact lens and into the eye. If you must wear contacts prescribed by a physician, inform your teacher. You must wear approved eye-cup safety goggles.

Never look directly at the sun through any optical device or lens system, or reflect direct sunlight to illuminate a microscope. Such actions will concentrate light rays that will severely burn your retina, possibly causing blindness!

Electrical Supply
Never use equipment with frayed cords.

Make sure that electrical cords are taped to work surfaces. This will prevent tripping and will ensure that equipment can't be pulled off the table.

Never use electrical equipment around water, or with wet hands or clothing.

 ### Clothing Protection
Wear an apron or laboratory coat when working in the laboratory to prevent chemicals or chemical solutions from contacting skin or street clothes.

Animal Care
Do not touch or approach any animal in the wild. Be aware of poisonous or dangerous animals in any area where you will be doing outside fieldwork.

Always obtain your teacher's permission before bringing any animal (including pets) into the school building.

Handle animals only as your teacher directs. Mishandling or abuse of any animal will not be tolerated!

753

Teacher's notes

You may wish to use the following items found on the **Holt BioSources Teaching Resources CD-ROM** to emphasize the importance of lab safety and to check student understanding:

- **Student Safety Contract**
- **Student Safety Quiz**

See pages T35 and T38 for additional information about the **Holt BioSources Teaching Resources CD-ROM.**

---

continued

Sharp Object Safety

Use extreme care with all sharp instruments, such as scalpels, sharp probes, and knives.

Never use double-edged razor blades in the laboratory.

Never cut objects while holding them in your hand. Place objects on a suitable work surface.

Hygienic Care

Keep your hands away from your face and mouth.

Wash your hands thoroughly before leaving the laboratory.

Remove contaminated clothing immediately. If the spill is on your pants or somewhere else that will not fit under the sink faucet, use the safety shower. Remove the pants or other affected clothing while under the shower, and call your teacher. (It may be temporarily embarrassing to remove clothing in front of your classmates, but failing to flush that chemical off your skin could cause permanent damage.)

Launder contaminated clothing separately.

Use the proper technique demonstrated by your teacher when handling bacteria or similar microorganisms. Examine microorganism cultures (such as petri dishes) without opening them.

Return all stock and experimental cultures to your teacher for proper disposal.

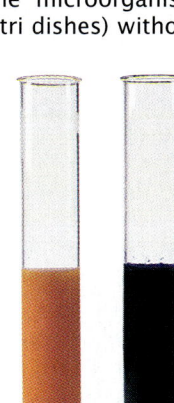

Chemical Safety

Always wear appropriate personal protective equipment. Eye goggles, gloves, and an apron or lab coat should always be worn when working with any chemical or chemical solution.

Never taste, touch, or smell any substance, or bring it close to your eyes, unless specifically told to do so by your teacher. If you are directed by your teacher to note the odor of a substance, do so by waving the fumes toward you with your hand. Never pipette any substance by mouth; use a suction bulb as directed by your teacher.

Always handle chemicals or chemical solutions with care. Check the label on the bottle and observe safety procedures. Never return unused chemicals or solutions to their containers. Return unused reagent bottles or containers to your teacher.

Never mix any chemical unless specifically told to do so by your teacher.

Never pour water into a strong acid or base. The mixture can produce heat and splatter. Remember this rhyme:
   Do as you oughta—
   Add acid (or base) to water.

Report any spill immediately to your teacher. Handle spills only if your teacher instructs you to do so.

Check for the presence of any source of flames, sparks, or heat (open flames, electric heating coils, etc.) before working with flammable liquids or gases.

Proper Waste Disposal

Clean and decontaminate all work surfaces and personal protective equipment as directed by your teacher.

Dispose of all sharp objects (such as broken glass) and other contaminated materials (biological or chemical) in special containers as directed by your teacher.

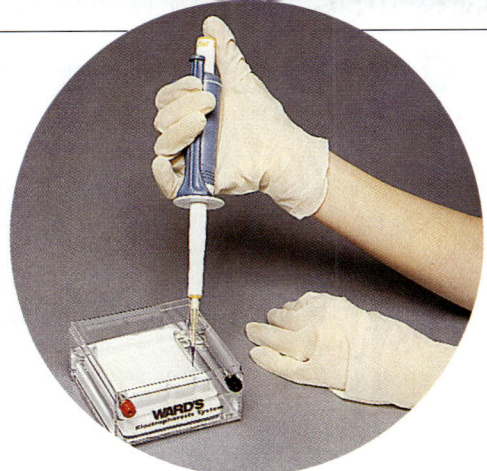

 Heating Safety
When heating chemicals or reagents in a test tube, never point the test tube toward anyone.

Use hot plates, not open flames. Be sure hot plates have an "On-Off" switch and indicator light. Never leave hot plates unattended, even for a minute. Never use alcohol lamps.

Know the location of laboratory fire extinguishers and fire blankets. Have ice readily available in case of burns or scalds.

Use tongs or appropriate insulated holders when heating objects. Heated objects often do not have the appearance of being hot. Never pick up an object with your hand unless you are certain it is cool.

Keep combustibles away from heat and other ignition sources.

 Hand Safety
Never cut objects while holding them in your hand.

Wear protective gloves when working with stains, chemicals, chemical solutions, or wild (unknown) plants.

 Glassware Safety
Inspect glassware before use; never use chipped or cracked glassware. Use borosilicate glass for heating.

Do not attempt to insert glass tubing into a rubber stopper without specific instruction from your teacher.

Always clean up broken glass by using tongs and/or a brush and dustpan. Discard the pieces in an appropriately labeled container.

 Safety With Gases
Never inhale any gas or vapor unless directed by your teacher.

Handle materials prone to emit vapors or gases in a well-ventilated area. This work should be done in an approved chemical fume hood.

 Plant Safety
Do not ingest any plant part used in the laboratory (especially seeds sold commercially). Do not rub any sap or plant juice in your eyes, on your skin, or on mucous membranes.

Wear protective gloves (disposable polyethylene gloves) when handling any wild plant.

Wash hands thoroughly after handling any plant or plant part (particularly seeds). Avoid touching your face and eyes.

Do not inhale or expose yourself to the smoke of any burning plant.

Do not pick wildflowers or other plants unless directed to do so by your teacher.

755

Purpose

Students will set up and conduct a controlled experiment.

Instructional Goals

Understanding Concepts

Students will
- apply a scientific method to a problem involving the growth of the bread mold *Rhizopus.*
- recognize the limitations of experimentation.
- infer the importance of collecting data to draw conclusions.

Life/Work Skills

Students will demonstrate proficiency in
- setting up an experiment.
- working as part of a team.
- interpreting the results of an experiment.
- using appropriate safety procedures in the laboratory.

Preparation Notes

Time Required: 1 lab period for setup and discussion, and 5–10 days for data collection

Materials

Materials for this Exploration can be ordered from WARD'S. See page T745-12 for catalog numbers.

Preparation Tips

- Obtain day-old bread from a local bakery. It generally does not have any preservatives that might inhibit mold growth.

CONTINUED ON NEXT PAGE

exploration

Skill:
Conducting a controlled experiment

Objectives
- *Identify* independent variables, dependent variables, and constants.
- *Measure* changes in a dependent variable.
- *Write* a hypothesis.
- *Conduct* an experiment to test a hypothesis.

Materials
- safety goggles
- lab apron
- 6 plastic petri dishes
- wax pencil
- paper towels
- scissors
- plastic knife
- day-old bread
- water
- 10 mL graduated cylinder
- growth chamber
- thermometer
- metric ruler

Situation

You have just started working as a laboratory technician for a pharmaceutical company. The company is interested in developing new antibiotics that will combat antibiotic-resistant strains of bacteria. Your supervisor is hoping to discover whether *Rhizopus*, which is a common mold that grows on bread, produces any compounds that kill disease-causing bacteria. Your research team has been given the task of determining the optimum conditions for growing the *Rhizopus* needed for testing. The first factor your team decides to test is light.

Background: In designing an experiment, you must identify and define all of the factors that can possibly change. Factors that can change are called **variables.** There are two types of variables. **Independent variables** are factors, such as temperature and amount of moisture, that you can change, or manipulate. In a simple experiment, only one independent variable should be allowed to change, and all other independent variables should be **constants** (factors that are not allowed to change). **Dependent variables** are factors, such as an increase or decrease in size, that change in response to an independent variable. Every experiment must have a **control,** a standard against which test groups can be compared.

Prelab Preparation

1. Define the following terms: observation, hypothesis, prediction, experiment, scientific method.
2. Define the boldface terms in the **Background** section.
3. Make a data table like the one at the top of the next page.

Procedure

1. On a sheet of paper, list all of the independent variables that might affect the growth of *Rhizopus*. Also write a description of how you will measure the growth of *Rhizopus*, the dependent variable for this experiment.

2. The question you will answer in this experiment is, How does light affect the growth of *Rhizopus*? Look back at your list of independent variables, and label "light" as the "independent variable to be tested." Label all other variables as "constant."

ANSWERS

Prelab Preparation

1. *observation*—gathering and recording information about an event

   hypothesis—the predicted outcome of an experiment

   prediction—logical guess about a future event or events based on factors influencing those events

   experiment—controlled test of a hypothesis

   scientific method—way of investigating natural processes to explain how they work

2. *variable*—factor that can be changed

   independent variable—variable that is manipulated or allowed to change

   constant—factor that does not change

   dependent variable—variable that changes in response to an independent variable

   control—part of an experiment that serves as a standard with which test groups can be compared

Analysis

11. Light is an independent variable because it was changed on purpose. Mold growth is a dependent variable because it changed in response to the independent variable.

12. The function of the bread is to provide food for the *Rhizopus* bread mold.

13. Answers will vary, but students should observe more growth in the petri dishes that are placed in the dark.

Day	Experimental group	Control group
1		
2		
3		
4		
5		

3. On your data sheet, write a hypothesis that can be tested with an experiment to determine the effect of light on the growth of *Rhizopus*. Write an "if . . . then" statement that restates your hypothesis in the form of a prediction.

4. Put on safety goggles and a lab apron.

5. Prepare six petri dishes as follows: Label the bottom of three dishes Control 1, 2, and 3, respectively. Label the other dishes Experimental 1, 2, and 3, respectively. Cut a circle of paper towel to fit into the bottom of each petri dish. Add 1 mL of water to each petri dish.

6. Using a plastic knife, cut six 5 cm × 5 cm squares of day-old bread. Place one square on the paper towel in each petri dish. Place the tops on the petri dishes, but do not seal the dishes.

7. Put the petri dishes marked "Experimental" in a lighted area. Do not put them in direct sunlight or in a place where they will get additional heat. Put the petri dishes marked "Control" in a darkened growth chamber. *Note: The temperature in the growth chamber and in the lighted area should be the same.*

8. Observe each petri dish in the "Experimental" group and in the "Control" group for 10 days. **CAUTION: Do not remove the tops of the petri dishes.** Use a metric ruler to measure the size of any colonies that develop. Record any changes you see in your data table.

9. Dispose of your materials according to the directions from your teacher.

10. Clean up your work area and wash your hands before leaving the lab.

Analysis

11. **Relating Concepts** Why is light an independent variable in this experiment? Why is mold growth a dependent variable?

12. **Identifying Functions** What is the function of the bread in this experiment?

13. **Summarizing Data** Write a brief description of what happened in each group of petri dishes.

14. **Analyzing Data** Do your data support your hypothesis? Explain.

15. **Drawing Conclusions** How does light affect the growth of *Rhizopus*?

16. **Making Predictions** What would happen if you placed the "Experimental" group in a darkened growth chamber?

Applications

17. **Thinking Critically** A team decides to test the hypothesis that *Rhizopus* will grow better if more water is available. They place bread samples in containers of different sizes, add 10 mL of water to each container, and then place the containers in a darkened growth chamber. What can you say about this experimental design?

18. **Personal Connection** Where should you store bread at home if you want to prevent the growth of *Rhizopus*?

19. **Career Connection** *Pharmacologists* develop new medicinal drugs. Find out about the training and skills required to become a pharmacologist, and discover the source of some common antibiotics.

- An incubator, a large box, or space in a drawer can serve as a darkened growth chamber. Insulate the chamber to keep the temperature within constant.
- Provide a container for the disposal of broken glass.

Additional Background
Rhizopus is not known to have any antibiotic properties. However, because it is more common and easier to grow than most antibiotic molds, it is a more appropriate subject for this experiment.

Disposal
Cover moldy bread with a 5% bleach solution, and allow it to soak for 15 minutes. Wrap the bread in old newspaper, and place it in the trash.

Procedural Notes
Safety Precautions
- Be sure that students have read and understand all of the safety rules for working in the lab.
- Discuss all safety symbols and caution statements with students.
- Have students wear safety goggles and a lab apron.
- Tell students not to remove the lids of petri dishes after they have been covered.

Procedural Tip
Have students examine the petri dishes with a stereomicroscope or hand lens every day to look for fungal growth. Have them note the number of colonies, color, and diameter and height of growth.

14. Answers will vary. Students should describe how their data support, or do not support, their hypotheses.

15. Answers may vary. Students' conclusions should be consistent with their data. Students should conclude that light inhibits the growth of *Rhizopus*.

16. Answers will vary. Students should predict that if the experimental group (petri dishes left under light) were placed in a darkened growth chamber, *Rhizopus* (and possibly other molds) would grow faster.

Applications
17. As described, container size is the independent variable being tested, not amount of water, which is a constant.

18. At home, bread should be kept in lighted areas rather than in darkness.

19. Pharmacologists study the effects of drugs and other chemicals on humans and other animals. Most pharmacologists have one or more advanced degrees. They should be inquisitive and enjoy detailed work. Training includes courses in biology, chemistry, physics, physiology, computer science, and mathematics. Antibiotics are produced from microbes. For example, *Penicillium* mold is the source of the antibiotic penicillin.

Sample Data Table

Day	Experimental group	Control group
1	no growth	no growth
2	no growth	3 colonies
3	no growth	6 large colonies
4	1 colony	multiple colonies with intense color
5	1 colony	large patches of high, thick, dark mold

Investigation notes

Purpose

Students will determine the ideal salt concentration for hatching brine shrimp.

Instructional Goals

Student Objectives

- Design and conduct an experiment.
- Collect and evaluate data.

Life/Work Skills

- setting up an experiment with a control
- selecting and using appropriate materials and techniques
- allocating resources
- acquiring, organizing, and interpreting data
- communicating effectively
- working as part of a team
- using appropriate safety procedures in the laboratory

Preparation Notes

Time Required: 1 lab period for setup and 20 minutes per day for 2–5 days for observations and data collection

Prelab Discussion

Review the procedure in Exploration 1A, and answer any questions students may have. Have students read Investigation 1B. Ask the following questions to guide their thinking:

- What does parts per thousand (ppt) mean? *(in a solution, the number of volume units of solute per 1000 volume units of solvent)*
- What will your independent variable be? *(the concentration of salt in the water)*
- What will your dependent variable be? *(the number of eggs that hatch)*
- How will you measure the dependent variable? *(counting hatched shrimp and eggs)*
- What are the constants in this experiment? *(volume of water, amount of eggs per container, water source)*

CONTINUED ON NEXT PAGE

Prerequisites

- **Exploration 1A: Using a Scientific Method** on pages 756–757
- **Review** the following:
  1. independent variable
  2. dependent variable
  3. control
  4. constant

Farmaquatics, Inc.

August 30, 1997

Caitlin Noonan
Director of Research
BioLogical Resources, Inc.
101 Jonas Salk Dr.
Oakwood, MO 65432-1101

Dear Ms. Noonan:

I have recently started a tropical-fish breeding company in Denver. I have extensive experience in raising and breeding fish but have always relied on others for food stocks, including brine shrimp for tropical fish. Because of the size of the operation, my staff will need to raise the brine shrimp for feeding.

I've heard that it is possible to increase the number of brine shrimp eggs that hatch by controlling the salt content of the water in the hatching containers, but I do not know the specifications. I need to know what salt concentration will enable the most brine shrimp to hatch.

Dr. Lamberton at the university told me of your new company and assured me that this is just the sort of problem you could handle. I wish to begin operating our facility as soon as possible. Please conduct the appropriate experiments to determine the optimal salt concentration for hatching brine shrimp. Bill us when you send your report.

Sincerely,

Arthur Beauchamp

Arthur Beauchamp
President
Farmaquatics, Inc.

Required Precautions

- Wear safety goggles and a lab apron.
- Do not touch or taste any solution or chemical used in the laboratory.
- Wash your hands before leaving the laboratory.

SAMPLE SOLUTION

Question

What is the optimal salt concentration for hatching brine shrimp?

Proposed Procedure

1. Prepare a data table.
2. Label five plastic-foam cups as follows: 0 ppt, 20 ppt, 40 ppt, 60 ppt, and 80 ppt.
3. Pour 200 mL of fresh, dechlorinated water into the cup marked 0 ppt.
4. Prepare 80 ppt, 60 ppt, 40 ppt, and 20 ppt solutions of sea salts. Pour 200 mL of each solution into the appropriately marked cups.
5. Carefully measure 0.1 g of brine shrimp eggs for each of the five cups. Pour the eggs into the labeled cups. Cover each cup with aluminum foil, and place the cups where they won't be disturbed.
6. Each day for 2–4 successive days, use a dropper to remove 0.5 mL of solution from each cup. Stir the solution in each cup before taking the sample. Place each solution into a clean petri dish, and examine it with a stereomicroscope or a hand lens. Count the numbers of eggs and hatched brine shrimp, and record the numbers in a data table. *Note: Do not return eggs or shrimp to the cups.*

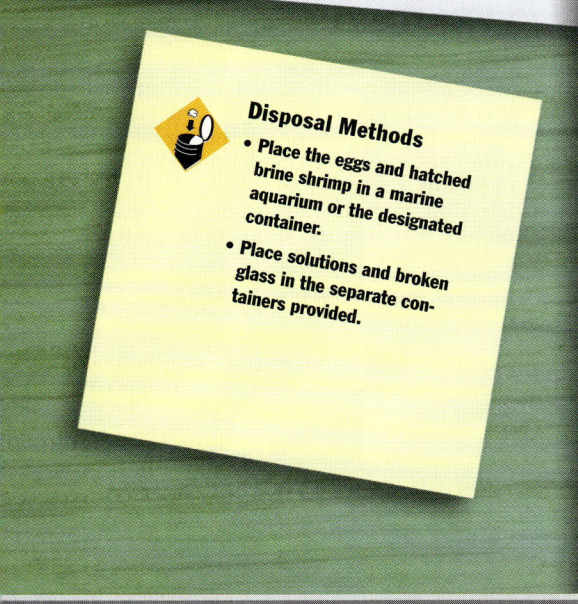

MEMORANDUM

BioLogical Resources, Inc., Oakwood, MO 65432-1101

To: Team Leader, Zoology Dept.
From: Caitlin Noonan

This could be a great first client for us! Good references from Mr. Beauchamp might bring us more business. Farmaquatics is relying on us to provide quick and accurate results about the optimal salt concentration for hatching brine shrimp. Test at least 5 different salt concentrations. Make sure that your work is thorough and accurate.

Last night I did some research on brine shrimp and found some potentially useful information:

- Brine shrimp live in tidal pools, estuaries, and salt lakes, where salt concentration may vary from 10 ppt to 60 ppt.
- Hatched brine shrimp and unhatched eggs can be collected with a clean cotton swab.

Before you start your work, you must submit a proposal for my approval. **Your proposal must include the following:**

- the **question** you are seeking to answer
- the **procedure** you will use
- a detailed **data table**
- a complete, itemized list of the proposed **materials** and **costs** (including the use of facilities, labor, and amounts needed)

When you finish your tests, prepare a report in the form of a business letter to Arthur Beauchamp. **Your report must include the following:**

- a paragraph describing the **procedure** you followed to determine the optimal salt concentration for hatching brine shrimp
- a complete **data table**
- your **conclusions** about the salt concentration that Mr. Beauchamp should use for hatching brine shrimp
- a detailed **invoice** showing all materials and labor plus the total amount due

Disposal Methods

- Place the eggs and hatched brine shrimp in a marine aquarium or the designated container.
- Place solutions and broken glass in the separate containers provided.

FILE: Farmaquatics, Inc.

MATERIALS AND COSTS (Select only what you'll need. No refunds.)

I. Facilities and Equipment Use

facilities	$480.00/day
personal protective equipment	$10.00/day
stereomicroscope or hand lens	$100.00/day
microscope slide and coverslip	$1.00/day
forceps	$5.00/day
dropper	$5.00/day
10 mL graduated cylinder	$10.00/day
balance	$10.00/day
beaker	$10.00/day

II. Labor and Consumables

labor	$30.00/hr
brine-shrimp eggs	$25.00/25 g package
dried yeast (brine-shrimp food)	$5.00/package
petri dishes	$5.00 each
wax pencil	$2.00 each
aluminum foil	$0.25/m
synthetic sea salts	$5.00/kg
dechlorinated water	$10.00/L
cotton swabs	$0.10 each
plastic foam cups	$1.00 each

Fines

OSHA safety violation	$2,000.00/incident

Materials

Materials for this Investigation can be purchased from WARD'S. See page T745-12 for catalog numbers. Provide the items in the "Materials and Costs" list on the pupil's page. Some of these items are distracters. See "Sample Solution" to estimate what each group will use.

Preparation Tips

- Results will be optimized by allowing salts to dissociate before introducing eggs and by using dechlorinated water. To dechlorinate water, aerate tap water by letting it stand for 24 hours.
- If you prepare solutions ahead of time, mix 40 g of sea salt with 490 mL of water and let it sit overnight. The next day, add 10 mL of dechlorinated water to make an 80 ppt solution. Then use the following table to prepare 60 ppt, 40 ppt, and 20 ppt solutions:

80 ppt solution	Dechlorinated water	Resulting solution
150 mL	50 mL	60 ppt
100 mL	100 mL	40 ppt
50 mL	150 mL	20 ppt

Disposal

- Place hatched brine shrimp in an aquarium.

Procedural Notes

Safety Precautions

- Discuss all safety symbols and required precautions with students.
- Have students wear safety goggles and a lab apron.

Procedural Tip

A temperature of about 27°C will promote the highest rate of hatching.

759

Materials (per lab group)

- safety goggles and lab aprons
- 1000 mL of dechlorinated water
- 5 plastic-foam cups
- wax pencil
- 1 m of aluminum foil
- 10 mL graduated cylinder
- balance
- 40 g of synthetic sea salts
- 2 large beakers
- 0.5 g of brine shrimp eggs
- eyedropper
- 5 petri dishes
- stereomicroscope or hand lens

Estimated Cost of the Job

$2,862.29 (for two students for four days). The invoice presented to the client should include a profit. See page T745-6 for an example of how to prepare an invoice.

Conclusions

Students should find that the optimal salt concentration for hatching brine shrimp is 40 ppt.

Results

Number of Hatched Brine Shrimp and Eggs Per 0.5 mL Sample

Cup	Salinity	Day 1 Number of eggs	Day 1 Number of shrimp	Day 2 Number of eggs	Day 2 Number of shrimp	Day 3 Number of eggs	Day 3 Number of shrimp
1	0 ppt	75	0	69	0	62	0
2	20 ppt	82	4	62	22	25	45
3	40 ppt	71	5	64	39	11	65
4	60 ppt	93	4	79	4	28	31
5	80 ppt	87	0	80	0	74	21

Purpose

Students will observe prokaryotic and eukaryotic cells and estimate their size.

Instructional Goals

Concepts

Students will

- apply principles of measurement and mathematics to estimate the size of cells.
- use knowledge of cell structure to categorize cells as prokaryotic or eukaryotic.

Life/Work Skills

Students will demonstrate proficiency in

- using a compound microscope.
- making wet-mount slides.
- staining cells.
- working as part of a team.
- using appropriate safety procedures in the laboratory.

Preparation Notes

Time Required: 50 to 65 minutes

Materials

Materials for this Exploration can be ordered from WARD'S. See page T745-12 for catalog numbers.

Preparation Tips

- Provide the following cultures and slides. Cover the labels.
  - *Amoeba proteus* culture (Organism A)
  - several stalks of *Elodea* (Organism B)
  - prepared slides of *Bacillus megaterium* (Organism C)
  - prepared slides of a hydra or a nematode (Organism D)

CONTINUED ON NEXT PAGE

exploration

Skills:

- **Using a compound microscope**
- **Making wet mounts**

Objectives

- *Make* wet mounts of cells.
- *Estimate* the size of cells.
- *Stain* cells.
- *Identify* cell structures.
- *Identify* a cell as eukaryotic or prokaryotic.

Materials

- safety goggles
- lab apron
- compound microscope
- lens paper
- transparent metric ruler
- depression slide
- microscope slide
- 2 coverslips
- culture of organism A
- medicine dropper
- DETAIN™, protist-slowing agent
- toothpick
- Lugol's solution (stain)
- paper towel
- leaf from organism B
- prepared slide of organism C
- prepared slide of organism D

Situation

You are a member of a biological research team that is studying the life in a polluted pond. You have been given samples of the organisms found in the pond. Your job is to observe the organisms with a compound microscope, determine the size of their cells, and categorize them as prokaryotic or eukaryotic.

Background: Cells are measured in micrometers (μm). There are 1000 μm in 1 mm. **Organelles** and other cell structures that can be seen with a compound microscope may include the **cell membranes, cell walls, nuclei,** and **chloroplasts.** Chemicals called **stains,** which are taken up by certain parts of cells, make cell structures more visible under a microscope.

Prelab Preparation

1. Define the boldface terms in the **Background** section.
2. List the characteristics of prokaryotic cells and eukaryotic cells.
3. Review the information about the care and use of a compound microscope in the Appendix.
4. Review the procedures for making a wet-mount slide in the Appendix.
5. Prepare a data table like the one at the top of the next page.

Procedure

1. Place a transparent metric ruler under the low power (LP) objective of a microscope. Focus the microscope on the scale of the ruler, and measure the diameter of the field of vision in millimeters. Record this number. Convert this measurement to micrometers by using the following equation:

$$\text{diameter in micrometers (μm)} = \text{diameter in millimeters (mm)} \times \frac{1000 \text{ μm}}{\text{mm}}$$

2. Calculate the diameter (in micrometers) of the field of vision under high power (HP) using the following formula:

$$\text{diameter (HP)} = \frac{\text{diameter (LP)} \times \text{mag. of LP objective}}{\text{mag. of HP objective}}$$

Record this number.

ANSWERS

Prelab Preparation

1. *organelle*—cell structure with a specific function
   cell membrane—membrane surrounding the cytoplasm of a cell
   cell wall—rigid covering that surrounds plant, algal, and fungal cells
   nucleus—organelle that contains DNA
   chloroplast—green organelle that contains chlorophyll and is the site of photosynthesis

   stain—chemical used to make cell structures more visible
2. *Prokaryotic cells* lack a nucleus and organelles. *Eukaryotic cells* have a membrane-bound nucleus and membrane-bound organelles.

Analysis

13. You cannot infer whether the cells (organisms) observed are alive or capable of moving.

14. Answers will vary. Students' paragraphs should note the size of cells, the types of organelles observed, and whether the organisms are composed of cells. Organism C has prokaryotic cells because the cells are so small and appear to lack organelles. Organisms A, B, and D have eukaryotic cells because the cells are larger and they have organelles.

Characteristics	Organisms			
	A	B	C	D
General observations				
Size (in μm)				
Cell membrane				
Cytoplasm				
Nucleus				
Chloroplast				
Cell wall				

3. To estimate the size of an object seen with a microscope, first estimate what fraction of the diameter of the field of vision that the object occupies (e.g., one-half, one-tenth). Then multiply the diameter you calculated in micrometers by that fraction. For example, if the field of vision's diameter is 400 μm and the object's estimated length is about one-tenth of that diameter, multiply the diameter by one-tenth to find the object's length (400 μm × 1/10 = 40 μm).

4. Using a medicine dropper, place some of the solution from the container marked "Organism A" into the well of a depression slide. Add one drop of DETAIN™ to this solution and stir with a toothpick. Place a coverslip over the well.

5. View the slide with the low-power objective of a microscope. Find one of the organisms and observe it.

6. Put on safety goggles and a lab apron. Place a drop of Lugol's solution at one edge of the coverslip. **CAUTION: Lugol's solution will stain your skin and clothing. Promptly wash off spills to minimize staining.**

Place a piece of paper towel at the opposite edge of the coverslip to draw the stain under the coverslip. Observe the organism.

7. Switch to high power, and continue observing the organism. Use the procedure in step 3 to estimate the size of the organism's cells. Draw what you see on a piece of paper. Label the visible cell structures. Describe this organism by completing the column for it in your data table.

8. Using a clean slide and coverslip, make a wet mount of a leaf from organism B. Repeat steps 5, 6, and 7 for this organism.

9. View a prepared slide of organism C under low power, and then repeat step 7.

10. View a prepared slide of organism D under low power, and then repeat step 7.

11. Dispose of your materials according to the directions from your teacher.

12. Clean up your work area and wash your hands before leaving the lab.

Analysis

13. Making Inferences What can you *not* infer about the organisms you observed on prepared slides?

14. Drawing Conclusions Your research team must summarize their findings in a report. Write a paragraph in which you describe organisms A, B, C, and D and explain why their cells are prokaryotic or eukaryotic.

Applications

15. Thinking Critically What was the purpose of adding a stain to the slides of organisms A and B?

16. Thinking Critically Biologists once classified all organisms into two kingdoms. Evaluate the accuracy of the two-kingdom system of classification on the basis of your observations.

17. Career Connection *Microscopists* prepare microscope slides of living cells and tissues. Find out about the training and skills required to become a microscopist, and discover some of the special techniques they must use.

761

- Lugol's solution can be purchased ready-made.
- Provide separate containers for the disposal of broken glass and materials stained with Lugol's solution.

Disposal
- Combine all wastes containing Lugol's solution. To this mixture, add a few drops of a strong acid, such as 1.0 M sulfuric acid (H_2SO_4), to make the mixture slightly acidic. Then slowly add 0.1 M sodium thiosulfate ($Na_2S_2O_3$) while stirring until the mixture loses its yellowish orange color. Pour the resulting mixture down the drain.

Procedural Notes
Safety Precautions
- Have students wear safety goggles and a lab apron.
- Discuss all safety symbols and caution statements with students.
- If students are using microscopes with mirrors, caution them not to look directly at the light reflected from the mirror.
- Tell students that they must wear safety goggles when working with Lugol's iodine solution because iodine can cause serious damage to their eyes.

Procedural Tips
- Allow students to take off their safety goggles when looking through the microscope.
- Have students use a scale of 1 μm = 1 cm when drawing cells.
- Have students record their field-of-vision data in a form similar to that shown below.
  Mag. of LP objective = _____ ×
  Mag. of HP objective = _____ ×
  Dia. of LP field of vision =
  _____ mm = _____ μm
  Dia. of HP field of vision =
  _____ μm
- Work through the following example: Suppose that a microscope has a 100× LP objective and a 430× HP objective. If you determine that the diameter of the LP field of vision is 1,500 μm, then
  $$\text{Dia. (HP)} = \frac{1,500 \text{ μm} \times 100}{430}$$
  $$= \frac{150,000 \text{ μm}}{430} = 349 \text{ μm.}$$

Applications
15. A stain is added to make colorless or transparent cell structures easier to see.
16. Answers will vary. Students should mention that there are fundamental differences in the cells of the organisms observed.
17. Microscopists usually earn at least a bachelor's degree and often earn a graduate degree. Courses include biology and chemistry. Microscopists must be patient, must be very detail oriented, and must have good eyesight and manual dexterity.

Sample Data

Characteristics	Organisms			
	A (*Amoeba*)	B (*Elodea*)	C (bacteria)	D (hydra)
General observations	Large, clear, moves slowly	many cells, boxlike shape, green	Very small, blue in color	many cells, clear, tube with tentacles
Size (in μm)	20 to 40 μm; can be up to 100 μm	10 to 20 μm	Too small to estimate size	5 to 10 mm
Cell membrane	yes	yes	yes (or no)	yes
Cytoplasm	yes	yes	yes	yes
Nucleus	yes	yes	no	yes
Chloroplast	no	yes	no	no
Cell wall	no	yes	no	no

Exploration 3A   761

Purpose

Students will determine whether a membrane is selectively permeable.

Instructional Goals

Understanding Concepts

Students will

• apply the principle of diffusion to the movement of molecules through dialysis-tubing membrane.

• recognize a color change as evidence of a chemical change.

Life/Work Skills

Students will demonstrate proficiency in

• determining the permeability of a membrane.

• using indicators to detect the presence of starch and glucose.

• working as part of a team.

• following directions.

• using appropriate safety procedures in the laboratory.

Preparation Notes

Time Required: two 50-minute periods

Materials

Materials for this Exploration can be ordered from WARD'S. See page T745-12 for catalog numbers.

Preparation Tips

• To prepare a 1% starch solution, add 1 g soluble starch to a small amount of cold water. Dilute to 100 mL with boiling water, and stir until dissolved. Cool before using. Do not store.

• To prepare a 15% glucose solution, dissolve 15 g of glucose to 100 mL of water.

• Benedict's solution can be purchased ready-made.

• Lugol's iodine solution can be purchased ready-made.

• Place indicator solutions in dropper bottles, or provide eye droppers or pipets for dispensing.

• Prepare separate containers for the disposal of the following: broken glass, wastes containing Lugol's solution, and wastes containing Benedict's solution.

CONTINUED ON NEXT PAGE

CHAPTER

exploration

4A | Modeling the Action of a Cell Membrane

Skill:

Using indicators to detect starch and sugar

Objectives

• *Demonstrate* the movement of molecules through a selectively permeable membrane.

• *Perform* the chemical tests that detect starch and sugar.

• *Collect* and *interpret* data.

Materials

• safety goggles
• lab apron
• wax pencil
• eight 18 × 150 mm test tubes
• test-tube rack
• 10 mL graduated cylinder
• starch solution
• glucose solution
• Lugol's iodine solution
• Benedict's solution
• test-tube holder
• boiling-water bath
• clock or timer
• two 250 mL beakers
• water
• two 15 cm pieces of dialysis tubing
• heavy-duty thread or string

Situation

A manufacturing company has asked you to test a new type of dialysis tubing. The company is concerned that the small gaps in the tubing membrane may be too large for the tubing to be selectively permeable. If it is not selectively permeable, the company will not be able to sell the tubing. Your job is to determine whether this tubing is selectively permeable.

Background: A **selectively permeable membrane** allows only certain particles to pass through it. **Dialysis tubing** is made of a membrane that is selectively permeable, like a cell membrane. It is used in **dialysis,** which is a process that filters soluble materials from blood. Small molecules, such as glucose, pass through dialysis-tubing membrane, while large molecules, such as starch, cannot. Starch and glucose can be detected with **indicators,** chemicals that change color in the presence of particular substances. **Lugol's iodine solution** indicates starch by turning blue-black. **Benedict's solution** indicates glucose by turning rusty red.

Prelab Preparation

1 Define the boldface terms in the **Background** section.

2 What is a selectively permeable membrane?

3 Prepare a data table like the one on the next page.

Procedure

1.  Put on safety goggles and a lab apron.

2. Using a wax pencil, label two clean test tubes "Glucose" and two "Starch." **CAUTION: Glassware is fragile. Notify your teacher promptly of any broken glass or cuts. Do not clean up broken glass or spills unless your teacher tells you to do so.**

3. Add 5 mL of starch solution to each test tube labeled "Starch." Add 5 mL of glucose solution to each test tube labeled "Glucose."

4. Perform a test for starch by adding 2 drops of Lugol's solution to one test tube labeled "Glucose" and one labeled "Starch." **CAUTION: Lugol's solution will stain your skin and clothing. Promptly wash**

ANSWERS

Prelab Preparation

1. *selectively permeable membrane*—membrane that allows some particles to pass through it but not others
dialysis tubing—tubing made of a thin selectively permeable membrane
dialysis—process of filtering soluble materials from the blood using dialysis tubing
indicator—a chemical used to show the presence of a particular substance
Lugol's iodine solution—indicator that

detects the presence of starch
Benedict's solution—indicator that detects the presence of glucose

Analysis

14. The water in Beaker 1 contains glucose, and the water in Beaker 2 contains no starch.

15. Answers will vary. Students should find that the dialysis tubing membrane is selectively permeable because starch did not pass through the membrane, while sugar did.

	Solution	Color after Lugol's test for starch	Color after Benedict's test for sugar
Initial tests	Glucose solution		
	Starch solution		
	Beaker 1 water		
	Beaker 2 water		
Final tests	Beaker 1 water		
	Beaker 2 water		

off spills to minimize staining. Record any color change in your data table.

5. ⚠ Perform a test for glucose by adding 10 drops of Benedict's solution to each of the remaining test tubes. Place the test tubes in a boiling-water bath for 5 minutes. **CAUTION: Do not touch hot objects with your bare hands. Use tongs, test-tube holders, and padded gloves, as appropriate.** Remove the test tubes from the water bath.

6. ⚠ Using a wax pencil, label a 250 mL beaker "Beaker 1—Glucose" and another 250 mL beaker "Beaker 2—Starch." Fill each beaker half full with water.

7. Label two test tubes "Beaker 1 water," and two test tubes "Beaker 2 water." Add 5 mL of water from the designated beaker to each test tube. Set the test tubes in a test-tube rack.

8. Obtain two 15 cm pieces of dialysis tubing from your teacher. Securely tie one end of a piece of dialysis tubing as shown in the photograph at right. Open the opposite end of the

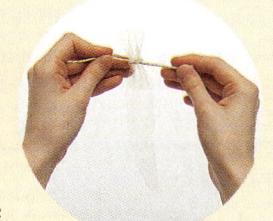

tubing, and pour glucose solution into the tubing until it is about two-thirds full. Using another piece of thread, tightly tie off the other end of the tubing to make a bag. Rinse the outside of the bag, and place it in the beaker labeled "Beaker 1—Glucose."

9. Make a second dialysis-tubing bag with starch solution. Rinse the outside of the bag, and place it in the beaker labeled "Beaker 2—Starch." Set the beakers aside.

10. Using the test tubes you labeled in step 7, repeat steps 4 and 5 to test the water from each beaker for the presence of starch and glucose. Record your results. Empty and clean the test tubes.

11. After 15 minutes, again test the water in the beakers for the presence of glucose and starch. Record your results.

12. ⚠ Dispose of your materials according to the directions from your teacher.

13. ⚠ Clean up your work area and wash your hands before leaving the lab.

Analysis

14. **Interpreting Data** What do your results suggest about the contents of the water in each beaker at the end of the experiment?

15. **Inferring Conclusions** What would you report to the manufacturing company about the permeability of their dialysis tubing? What evidence supports your conclusion?

Applications

16. **Thinking Critically** Why can dialysis tubing be used as a model for the cell membrane?

17. **Thinking Critically** How could you determine whether water from the beakers moved into the dialysis-tubing bags?

18. **Career Connection** *Hemodialysis technicians* perform kidney dialysis. Find out about the training and skills required to operate a hemodialysis machine, and discover how semipermeable membranes are used in these machines.

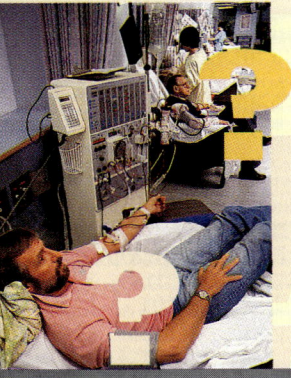

763

Applications

16. It is selectively permeable, like cell membranes.

17. The bags will be more turgid and will have a greater mass if they take on water.

18. Hemodialysis technicians must have a high-school education that includes courses in biology, chemistry, mathematics, and typing. Most hemodialysis technicians are trained in hospital programs. They should enjoy working with people and be able to read technical manuals and follow directions.

Sample Data

	Solution	Color after Lugol's test for starch	Color after Benedict's test for sugar
Initial tests	Glucose solution	yellowish orange	rusty red
	Starch solution	blue or blue-black	white
	Beaker 1 water	yellowish orange	colorless
	Beaker 2 water	yellowish orange	colorless
Final tests	Beaker 1 water	yellowish orange	rusty red
	Beaker 2 water	yellowish orange	colorless

Additional Background

Indicators produce a color change when added to certain solutions because of chemical reactions that produce new compounds. Iodine in Lugol's solution reacts with starch molecules to form a complex, which is blue. Cu(II) ions in Benedict's solution are reduced to Cu(I) ions by glucose, which is a reducing sugar.

Disposal

- Combine all wastes containing Benedict's solution. While stirring, slowly add 1 M sulfuric acid until the pH is between 5 and 6. Scour six 6d iron nails with steel wool until they shine. Immerse the nails in the acidified solution until all of the copper has precipitated. Filter the solution. Heat the nails and precipitate sufficiently to convert the copper precipitate and the copper on the nails into copper oxide. Let the nails and precipitate cool; then place them in the trash. Treat the filtrate with sufficient 1 M NaOH to bring the pH to from 8 to 10. Filter the liquid. Pour the filtrate down the drain. Let the precipitate dry, and place it in the trash.

- Combine all wastes containing Lugol's solution. To this mixture, add a few drops of a strong acid, such as 1.0 M sulfuric acid (H_2SO_4), to make the mixture slightly acidic. Then slowly add 0.1 M sodium thiosulfate ($Na_2S_2O_3$) while stirring until the mixture is colorless. Pour this solution down the drain.

Procedural Notes

Safety Precautions

- Have students wear safety goggles and a lab apron.
- Discuss all safety symbols and caution statements with students.
- Tell students that they must wear safety goggles when working with Lugol's iodone solution because iodine can cause serious damage to their eyes.
- Tell students that Benedict's solution contains copper ions, which are poisonous. This is one reason for the rules that prohibit touching or tasting chemicals used in the laboratory.

Exploration 4A   763

Purpose

Students will determine and compare rates of photosynthesis in different colors of light.

Instructional Goals

Understanding Concepts

Students will

- relate the production of a gas and a change in pH to evidence of a photosynthesis reaction.
- recognize that the color of light influences the rate of photosynthesis.

Life/Work Skills

Students will demonstrate proficiency in

- using an indicator to identify a chemical change.
- collecting and interpreting quantitative and qualitative data.
- communicating the results of lab tests.
- working as part of a team.
- using appropriate safety procedures in the laboratory.

Preparation Notes

Time Required: 1–2 lab periods

Materials

Materials for this Exploration can be ordered from WARD'S. See page T745-12 for catalog numbers.

Preparation Tips

- Order a 0.1% aqueous solution of bromothymol blue (BTB). To prepare a 0.1% aqueous solution of BTB, dissolve 0.5 g BTB powder in 500 mL distilled water. Add small amounts of sodium bicarbonate until the solution turns blue.

CONTINUED ON NEXT PAGE

CHAPTER

5A | Measuring the Rate of a Process

exploration

Skill:

Measuring the production of a gas

Objectives

- *Measure* the rate of photosynthesis.
- *Recognize* the relationship between color of light and the rate of photosynthesis.
- *Relate* a change in pH to evidence of photosynthesis.

Materials

- safety goggles
- lab apron
- 5 *Elodea* sprigs
- 5 large test tubes
- 5 one-hole stoppers with glass tubing
- water with food coloring
- fine-point marker
- test-tube rack
- 250 mL graduated cylinder
- 400 mL beaker
- 125 mL of water
- 25 mL of bromothymol blue solution
- soda straw
- colored cellophane (red, blue, green, yellow, and colorless)

764

Situation

You are an environmental engineer. A client wants to start a small retail garden center that will feature a greenhouse. Your client wants to use a bright color of plastic to cover the greenhouse for two reasons. First, bright colors are appealing to customers. Second, colored plastic will reduce the amount of light entering a greenhouse and will therefore keep the greenhouse cooler. Your client knows that the color of light affects the rate of photosynthesis. Your job is to determine which color of plastic will promote the highest rate of photosynthesis.

Background: Colored plastic acts as a **filter,** which permits a certain color of light to pass through it and absorbs the other colors. The color of a filter is due to the color of light it transmits (allows to pass through it). When carbon dioxide gas mixes with water, it reacts with the water to form a weak acid. Bromothymol blue is a **pH indicator** that is yellow in an acid solution and blue in a basic solution.

Prelab Preparation

1 Define the boldface terms in the **Background** section.

2 Write a chemical equation that summarizes photosynthesis. Underline the symbols for carbon dioxide gas and oxygen gas.

3 Describe how you will measure the rate of photosynthesis in this Exploration.

4 Prepare a data table like the one shown at the top of the next page.

Procedure

1. Put on safety goggles and a lab apron.

2. Prepare a solution containing 125 mL of water and 25 mL of bromothymol blue solution. Use a soda straw to blow your breath into the solution until the solution turns yellow. Move the straw through the solution as you blow. Fill five large test tubes, to within 3 cm of the top, with this solution. Place the test tubes in a test-tube rack. **CAUTION: Glassware is fragile. Notify your teacher promptly of any broken glass or cuts. Do not clean up broken glass or spills unless your teacher tells you to do so.**

ANSWERS

Prelab Preparation

1. *filter*—material that absorbs certain colors of light and transmits the color it appears to be
   pH indicator—chemical that can be used to determine the pH of a solution by observing its color at a particular pH

2. $6\underline{CO_2} + 6H_2O \longrightarrow C_6H_{12}O_6 + \underline{O_2}$

3. Measure the distance traveled by a drop of colored water in a glass tube.

Analysis

9. CO_2. The increase in CO_2 caused the BTB to change from blue to yellow.

10. the test tube covered in clear cellophane

11. BTB turns from yellow to blue as the pH of the solution becomes more alkaline, indicating that CO_2 has been removed from the water. If no color change occurs, then no CO_2 has been removed.

12. A pH change (color change) indicates that CO_2 has been removed from the solution by photosynthesis.

13. Students' rankings should be consistent with their data. This list should be as follows: clear, blue, red, yellow, and green.

14. The bubbles indicate the production of oxygen gas by photosynthesis.

15. blue

16. Plants will grow slower under any color of plastic, except green, because the rate of photosynthesis will not be as high when some colors of light are blocked.

Color of light	Distance	Starting color/pH	Ending color/pH
Blue			
Red			
Yellow			
Green			
White			

3. Obtain 5 stoppers into which glass tubing has been inserted. Place a tiny drop of water with food coloring in each glass tube, and position each drop just above the top of the stopper, as seen in the photo at right. Mark the top of each drop with a fine-point marker.

4. Select 5 healthy, green sprigs of *Elodea* that have been growing in bright light. Each sprig should be about 8 cm long. Immerse one sprig in each test tube. Close each test tube with a stopper and glass tube, as seen in the photo at right.

5. Wrap each test tube in a different color of cellophane. *Note: Use the same number of layers of cellophane for each test tube.* Put the test tubes in the test-tube rack, and place the rack under bright light. After 30 minutes, measure how far each drop of colored water moved in the glass tubes. Record your data.

6. Remove the cellophane from each test tube, and record the color of the solutions in the test tubes.

7. Dispose of your materials according to the directions from your teacher.

8. Clean up your work area and wash your hands before leaving the lab.

Analysis

9. **Relating Information** What substance in your breath caused bromothymol blue to turn yellow in step 1? Explain why the color change occurred.

10. **Relating Concepts** What is the control in this experiment?

11. **Interpreting Data** How would you explain any color change that occurred in the test tubes? If there were no color change in a test tube, how would you explain this result?

12. **Interpreting Data** How does a color change, or change in pH, indicate that photosynthesis has occurred?

13. **Summarizing Data** List the colors of the cellophane-covered test tubes in order from the fastest rate of photosynthesis to the slowest rate of photosynthesis.

14. **Making Inferences** What is indicated by the bubbles produced in the five test tubes?

15. **Drawing Conclusions** Which color of plastic (light) will enable the fastest rate of photosynthesis?

16. **Making Predictions** How will using colored plastic on the greenhouse affect the growth of the plants?

Applications

17. **Thinking Critically** What other experiments might you conduct to better advise your customer?

18. **Personal Connection** Incandescent light has a high percentage of red light, while fluorescent light has a high percentage of blue light. Which type of light would promote the highest rate of photosynthesis in houseplants? Explain.

19. **Career Connection** *Environmental engineers* study the effect of the environment on living things. Find out about the training and skills required to become an environmental engineer, and discover some of the types of work that they do.

765

Applications

17. Students could test how temperature in a greenhouse is affected by colored plastic, combinations of colored plastic, or different plastics of the same color but with different amounts of pigment.

18. Fluorescent lights should produce the greatest rate of photosynthesis because they produce the most blue light. A combination of fluorescent and incandescent lights would be even better.

19. Environmental engineers must earn a bachelor's degree, and most obtain one or more advanced degrees. They work for private industry and government, monitoring pollution and designing systems.

Sample Data

Color of cellophane	Distance	Starting color	Ending color	Beginning pH	Ending pH
Blue	22 mm	yellow	blue	6.0	>7.5
Red	20 mm	yellow	blue	6.0	>7.5
Yellow	5 mm	yellow	green	6.0	~7.0
Green	0	yellow	yellow	6.0	6.0
White	30 mm	yellow	blue	6.0	>7.5

- Before the lab, place *Elodea* stalks in water and under a light to make the cells use up available carbon dioxide (CO_2) and improve results.
- Assemble glass tubing and one-hole stoppers. To insert glass tubing into a one-hole stopper, first be sure that the ends of the tubing are fire-polished and that the outside diameter of the tubing is only slightly larger than the diameter of the hole in the stopper. Lubricate the hole in the stopper with glycerine or water. Then, wearing thick leather gloves or with both hands protected by multiple layers of cloth, gently insert the tubing into the hole without twisting or turning the tubing or stopper. Do not force the glass tubing; it can shatter.
- Provide a container for the disposal of broken glass.
- Provide a container of water for *Elodea* stalks.

Additional Background
BTB is a pH indicator that is blue in alkaline solutions and yellow in acidic solutions. As CO_2 is added to water containing BTB, a weak acid forms and the solution turns yellow. As CO_2 is removed and oxygen is added, the solution becomes alkaline and turns blue.

Disposal
- Pour solutions down the drain.

Procedural Notes
Safety Precautions

- Have students wear safety goggles and a lab apron.
- Discuss all safety symbols and caution statements with students.

Procedural Tip
Microcomputer Based Laboratory (MBL) probes can be used to measure changes in pH. Have each team collect data for one color of cellophane, and then help students compile data for the class before they complete the Analysis and Applications sections of the lab. Have students prepare test tubes using aquarium water instead of water containing BTB. Students should place a pH probe in the test tube, place the test tube under a bright light, and collect data for the desired length of time.

Investigation notes

Purpose

Students will investigate how temperature affects the rate of fermentation.

Instructional Goals

Student Objectives

- Recognize the relationship between temperature and the rate of fermentation.
- Relate volume of gas produced by a chemical process to the rate of the process.
- Relate a change in the pH of a solution to evidence of fermentation.

Life/Work Skills

- selecting and using appropriate materials and techniques
- allocating resources
- acquiring, organizing, and interpreting data
- working as part of a team
- using appropriate safety procedures in the laboratory

Preparation Notes

Time Required: 1–2 lab periods

Prelab Discussion

Review the concepts and procedures in Exploration 5A, and answer any questions students may have. Ask students the following questions to guide their thinking:

- What must be provided in order for a chemical process to occur? *(the reactants of the process)*
- What does yeast need to carry out fermentation? *(sugar and oxygen)*

Materials

Materials for this Investigation can be purchased from WARD'S. See page T745-12 for catalog numbers. Provide the items in the "Materials and Costs" list on the pupil's page. Some of these items are distracters. See "Sample Solution" to estimate what each group will use.

CONTINUED ON NEXT PAGE

5B | Measuring the Rate of a Process—Falling Bread

Prerequisites

- **Exploration 5A: Measuring the Rate of a Process** on pages 764–765
- **Review** the following:
  1. measuring the rate of a gas-producing process
  2. the reactants and products of fermentation

Windy Hill Bakery

Boston

December 30, 1997

John Williams, Director
Food Technology Division
BioLogical Resources, Inc.
101 Jonas Salk Dr.
Oakwood, MO 65432-1101

Dear Mr. Williams,

We are having a problem here at the bakery, and I hope you will be able to help us. Last week two batches of our bread failed to rise. Yesterday the problem occurred again.

As part of our continuous bread-making procedure, we mix together all of our ingredients except the flour. This mixture is called a broth. The yeast in the broth causes it to ferment. The fermentation process begins at room temperature. Flour is added at the last step, and then the dough is shaped into loaves and baked. Carbon dioxide gas produced by the yeast in the broth causes the bread to rise.

We suspect that our yeast supply may be bad. Dead yeast cells release an amino acid that affects the gluten in flour and prevents bread from rising. I am enclosing a sample of our yeast for you to test. It is very important that we know your results quickly. Please bill us when you send your report.

Very truly yours,

Simone Prevan

Simone Prevan
Windy Hill Bakery
Boston, MA

Required Precautions

- **Wear safety goggles and a lab apron.**
- **Glassware is fragile. Notify your teacher promptly of any broken glass or cuts.**
- If you get a chemical on your skin or clothing, wash it off while calling to your teacher.
- **Wash your hands before leaving the laboratory.**

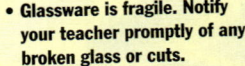

SAMPLE SOLUTION

Question

What temperature will enable the fastest rate of fermentation?

Proposed Procedure

1. Add 5 g of Yeast A and 10 mL of warm water to each of 4 test tubes. Stir gently with a glass rod. Then add 5 mL of glucose solution to each test tube, and stir. Finally, add 2 mL of BTB solution to each test tube. Label each test tube "A."

2. Repeat step 1 for Yeast B. Label each test tube "B."

3. Prepare a set of 4 test tubes by adding 15 mL of warm water, 5 mL of glucose solution, and 2 mL of BTB solution to each tube. Label each test tube "C."

4. Place a tiny drop of colored water in each of 12 glass tubes that have been inserted into rubber stoppers. Position each drop just above the top of the stopper. Mark the position of each drop with a fine-point marker.

5. Use ice and hot water in 500 mL beakers to make one water bath for each of the following temperatures: 10°C, 20°C, 30°C, and 40°C.

6. Place one each of test tubes A, B, and C in each water bath. Close each test tube with one of the stoppers. After 30 minutes, measure how far each drop of colored water moved in the capillary tubes. Record your data.

7. Record any color changes that occur in the test tubes.

MEMORANDUM

To: Team Leader, Food Testing Dept.
From: John Williams

This is our first big job in food technology. I phoned Ms. Prevan to assure her that we will deliver the results right away. She said that the bakery had recently tried to cut utility bills by lowering the temperature in the production area. This, not the yeast, may be the cause of their problem.

Please conduct the appropriate tests to compare the rate of fermentation by the bakery's yeast (Yeast A) with that of another sample of yeast (Yeast B). I also want you to test the rate of fermentation by the bakery's yeast at four different temperatures: 10°C, 20°C, 30°C, and 40°C.

Prepare yeast samples for testing by adding a measured amount of yeast to warm (not hot) water and stirring gently with a glass rod.

Before you start your work, you must submit a proposal for my approval. **Your proposal must include the following:**
- the **question** you are seeking to answer
- the **procedure** you will use
- a detailed **data table**
- a complete, itemized list of proposed **materials** and **costs** (including the use of facilities, labor, and amounts needed)

When you finish your tests, prepare a report in the form of a business letter to Simone Prevan. **Your report must include the following:**
- paragraph describing the **procedure** you followed to determine the rate of fermentation by the yeast
- a complete **data table**
- your **conclusions** about the bakery's yeast and how temperature affects the rate of fermentation by yeast
- a detailed **invoice** showing all materials and labor plus the total amount due

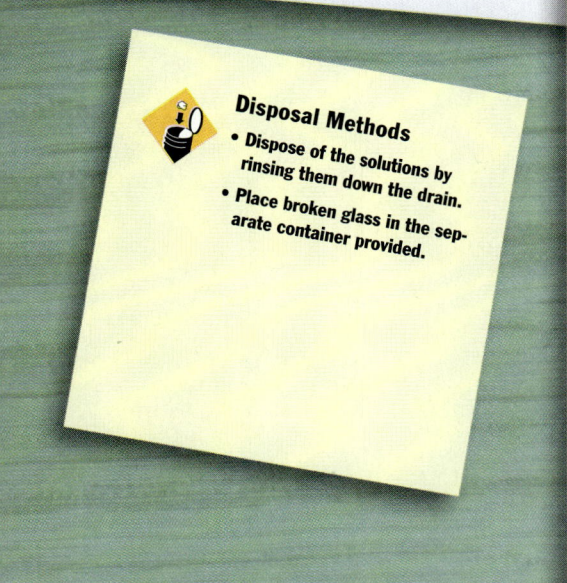

Disposal Methods
- Dispose of the solutions by rinsing them down the drain.
- Place broken glass in the separate container provided.

FILE: Windy Hill Bakery

MATERIALS AND COSTS (Select only what you'll need. No refunds.)

I. Facilities and Equipment Use

facilities	$480.00/day
personal protective equipment	$10.00/day
glass stirring rod	$1.00/day
stopper with glass tubing	$5.00/day
large test tube	$5.00/day
test-tube rack	$5.00/day
balance	$10.00/day
graduated cylinder	$10.00/day
beaker	$10.00/day
thermometer	$10.00/day

II. Labor and Consumables

labor	$30.00/hr
10% glucose solution	$0.10/mL
fine-point marker	$3.00 each
hot and cold tap water	$1.00/L
ice	$1.00/cup
bromothymol blue solution	$5.00/mL
food coloring	$2.00/bottle
Yeast A	no charge
Yeast B	$5.00/package

Fines

OSHA safety violation	$2,000.00/incident

Preparation Tips
- Purchase dried or fresh yeast. Most bakeries use fresh yeast in their breads. If you want students to discover that the bakery's yeast is bad, purchase inactive yeast sold as a dietary supplement and mix that with the dry or fresh yeast.
- Order a 0.1% aqueous solution of BTB. To prepare this solution, follow the directions on page 764.
- Prepare a 10% solution of glucose by diluting 100 g of powdered glucose in 1 L of water.
- Assemble stoppers and glass tubing according to the directions on page 765.
- Provide separate containers for the disposal of solutions and broken glass.

Disposal
- Solutions of BTB, sodium bicarbonate, and yeast may be rinsed down the drain.

Procedural Notes
Safety Precautions
- Have students wear safety goggles and a lab apron.
- Discuss all safety symbols and required precautions with students.

Procedural Tip
Microcomputer Based Laboratory (MBL) probes can be used to measure changes in pH. Have each team collect data for one type of yeast at one temperature, and then help students compile data for the class before they complete the lab. Students should place a pH probe in each test tube and then place the test tube in the water bath.

767

Materials (per lab group)
- personal protective equipment
- 1 glass stirring rod
- four 500 mL beakers
- 10% glucose (60 mL)
- 12 capillary tubes
- 12 large test tubes (25–30 mL)
- 12 one-hole rubber stoppers
- 50 mL graduated cylinder
- BTB solution (24 mL)
- warm tap water (140 mL)
- fine-point marker
- food coloring
- hot tap water (2 L)
- cup of ice
- test-tube rack
- thermometer
- 20 g of Yeast A (alternative source)
- 20 g of Yeast B (bakery's yeast)
- balance

Estimated Cost of the Job
$1,763.00 (for two students for two days). The invoice students present to the client should include a profit. See page T745-6 for an example of how to prepare an invoice.

Results
Students' results will vary, depending on the type of yeast you provide. Data tables should resemble those on page 765.

Conclusions
Generally the highest rate of fermentation is obtained between 20°C and 30°C. Students' data should support their conclusions.

Purpose

Students will use a computer simulation to study how varying the quantity and quality of light affects photosynthesis.

Instructional Goals

Students will
• determine how the rate of photosynthesis is affected by varying wavelength of light.
• determine how the rate of photosynthesis is affected by varying intensity of light.

Preparation Notes

Time Required: approximately 1 hour

Preparation Tips

If enough computers are available, students can work individually. Otherwise, they should work in teams of two to four.

Prelab Discussion

Before students begin the lab, they should be able to answer the following questions:

• What is chlorophyll? *(a green pigment, found in plants and other photosynthetic organisms, that absorbs some of the wavelengths of light in sunlight)*
• What is a chloroplast, and what function does it perform in a plant cell? *(A chloroplast is an organelle with a complex series of internal membranes. Chloroplasts are the site of photosynthesis.)*
• Describe the main steps of photosynthesis. *(Light energy is captured by pigments in the chloroplasts. This energy is used to make ATP and NADPH. NADPH and ATP, in turn, are used to make carbohydrates from carbon dioxide.)*
• Write the chemical equation for photosynthesis. *($6CO_2 + 6H_2O \longrightarrow C_6H_{12}O_6 + 6O_2$)*

CONTINUED ON NEXT PAGE

CHAPTER

5c Photosynthesis

interactive exploration

Objectives

• *Simulate* how the rate of photosynthesis is affected by variations in the intensity and wavelength of light.
• *Relate* the rate of photosynthesis to the production of ATP in a chloroplast.

Materials

• computer with CD-ROM drive
• CD-ROM *Interactive Explorations in Biology: Cell Biology and Genetics*
• graph paper

Background: Photosynthesis is the process in which plants, some bacteria, and some protists capture energy contained in sunlight and store it in carbohydrates. Recall that in photosynthesis, solar energy is first trapped and used to synthesize ATP and NADPH. ATP and NADPH are then used in making carbohydrates. This interactive exploration allows you to explore the effects that varying the intensity and wavelength of light have on the rate of ATP synthesis. The more ATP produced, the greater the amount of carbohydrate that can be synthesized.

Prelab Preparation

1 Load and start the program Photosynthesis. You will see an animated diagram of a chloroplast like the one below. Click the Navigation button, and then click the Topic Information button. Read the focus questions and review these concepts: Photons, Pigments, and The Action Spectrum of Photosynthesis.

2 Click the word *Help* at the top left of the screen, and select How to Use This Exploration. Listen to the instructions that explain the operation of the exploration. Click the Interactive Exploration button on the Navigation Palette to begin the exploration.

Feedback Meters

a **% Maximal ATP:** ratio of number of ATP molecules produced to the maximum number that can be produced

b **Number of ATP:** the number of ATP molecules that have been synthesized

c **Relative Time:** how long the investigation has been running

Variables

d **Light Intensity:** varies the amount of light

e **Wavelength of Light:** varies the wavelength of light

ANSWERS

Procedure

3. ATP is synthesized near the protein channel.

8. **Sample Data Table**

Light intensity (lux)	% Maximal ATP	Number of ATP
0	0	0
40	17	1
80	34	2
120	51	3
160	68	3
200	85	4

9. The wavelength is kept constant so that the effect of varying the light intensity can be evaluated.

14. **Sample Data Table**

Wavelength (nm)	% Maximal ATP	Number of ATP
400	65	3
450	15	1
500	7.5	1
550	15	1
600	20	1
650	85	4
700	5	1
750	3	1

Procedure

Part A: The Effect of Light Intensity on the Rate of Photosynthesis

You will first investigate how varying light intensity affects the rate of photosynthesis. Prepare a three-column table with the headings Light Intensity, % Maximal ATP, and Number of ATP. In the first column, list the following light intensities: 0, 40, 80, 120, 160, and 200 lux. Note on your table that the wavelength of light will be kept constant at 650 nm.

1. Click the word *Speed* at the top of the screen. Select Slow.

2. Click and slide the wavelength indicator to 650. Click and slide the light intensity indicator to 120 lux.

3. Click the Start button. Observe the protein channel at the bottom of the screen. What molecule is synthesized near this protein channel?

4. Allow the simulation to run for 30 seconds, as indicated on the relative time meter, then click the Stop button. In your table, record the % Maximal ATP and the Number of ATP molecules that were produced.

5. Click the Reset button, and then click and slide the light intensity indicator to 160 lux.

6. Click the Start button and allow the simulation to run for 30 seconds, as indicated on the relative time meter.

7. Click the Stop button and record the % Maximal ATP and Number of ATP in your table.

8. Continue testing until you have evaluated all the light intensities listed on your table.

9. Explain why the wavelength of light is kept constant in this series of steps.

Part B: Examining the Effect of Wavelength of Light on the Rate of Photosynthesis

10. Click the Reset button. Prepare another three-column table with the headings Wavelength, % Maximal ATP, and Number of ATP. In the first column, list the following wavelengths of light that you will test in this investigation: 400, 450, 500, 550, 600, 650, 700, and 750 nm.

11. Click and slide the light intensity indicator to 200 lux. Click and slide the wavelength of light indicator to 400 nanometers.

12. Click the Start button and allow the simulation to run for 30 seconds, as indicated on the relative time meter.

13. Click the Stop button and record the % Maximal ATP and Number of ATP in your data table.

14. Continue testing until you have evaluated all the wavelengths of light listed on your table.

15. Explain why you didn't vary the intensity of light in this part of the investigation.

Analysis

16. Prepare a bar graph that shows the % Maximal ATP on the *y*-axis and the intensity of light on the *x*-axis. Above each bar, indicate the number of ATP molecules produced.

17. What can you conclude about the effect of light intensity on the rate of photosynthesis? What assumption are you making when drawing your conclusion?

18. Prepare another bar graph, this time plotting the % Maximal ATP versus the wavelength of light (in nanometers). Again, above each bar indicate the number of ATP molecules synthesized.

19. Refer to your second graph. What wavelengths of light are most effective for photosynthesis? What wavelengths are least effective?

20. Which combination of wavelength and intensity of light would produce the highest rate of photosynthesis?

Additional Background

In the light-dependent reactions, chlorophyll and other photosynthetic pigments absorb photons of light, and electrons in these pigment molecules are raised to higher energy levels. These excited electrons are then passed through a series of electron acceptors and are ultimately used to make NADPH. ATP is also produced during the light-dependent reactions. ATP and NADPH are transferred to the Calvin cycle, in which carbohydrates are made from carbon dioxide. This exploration presents a cross section of a thylakoid membrane—the site of the light-dependent reactions—within the chloroplast of a cell. Students will manipulate the wavelength and intensity of light that falls on this chloroplast and observe the consequences on the rate of ATP production.

Procedural Notes

Procedural Tips

- Selecting *Slow Animation* from the *Speed* menu on the toolbar will allow students to follow the events occurring within the chloroplast.

769

15. It is kept constant so that only one variable is being evaluated at a time.

Analysis

16. **Sample Graph**

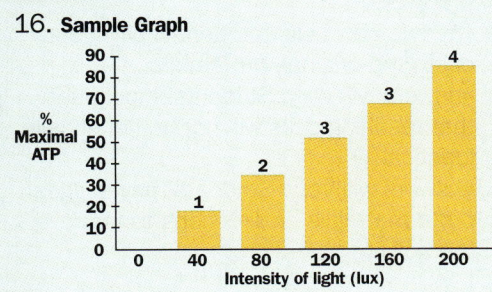

17. The rate of photosynthesis increases linearly with light intensity, assuming that the rate of photosynthesis is proportional to the rate of ATP formation.

18. **Sample Graph**

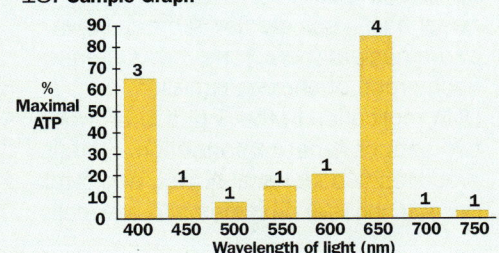

19. The most effective wavelengths are 400 nm and 650 nm. The least effective wavelength is 750 nm.

20. 650 nm at 200 lux

Purpose

Students will test a paper-and-string model of mitosis.

Instructional Goals

Understanding Concepts

Students will

- describe the events that occur in each phase of the cell cycle and mitosis in animal cells and plant cells.
- relate mitosis to cell reproduction and the cell cycle.

Life/Work Skills

Students will demonstrate proficiency in

- using a model to demonstrate a biological process.
- using appropriate safety procedures in the laboratory.

Preparation Notes

Time Required: 45 to 75 minutes

Materials

Materials for this Exploration can be ordered from WARD'S. See page T745-12 for catalog numbers.

Preparation Tip

Prior to the start of this lab, you may want to cut the string and index cards into the required lengths.

CONTINUED ON NEXT PAGE

exploration

CHAPTER

6A | Modeling Mitosis and the Cell Cycle

Skill:

Modeling a biological process

Objectives

- *Relate* cell reproduction to the cell cycle.
- *Model* the stages of mitosis in an animal cell.

Materials

- 1 piece of string (1 m long)
- 2 pieces of string (each 40 cm long)
- 4 strips (1 cm × 6 cm) of colored paper, 1 strip each of four different colors
- scissors
- 4 paper clips
- 8 pieces of string (each 10 cm long)
- transparent tape

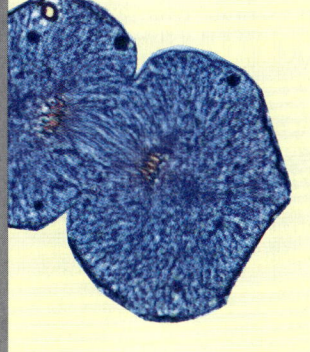

Situation

You are a science teacher who has been asked to test an activity that models mitosis and the cell cycle in animal cells. This activity will be part of a packet of instructional materials on cancer, which results when the cell cycle is disrupted. Your job is to evaluate whether the activity will help someone to visualize the stages of mitosis and the cell cycle.

Background: In science, a model is a hypothetical representation of an object or a process that can be used to study how the object or process works. Biologists use models to study many biological processes. You can use a model of an animal cell to study how mitosis occurs and to discover how errors in mitosis and the cell cycle might lead to cancer.

Prelab Preparation

1 List the five stages of the cell cycle, and describe the events that occur in each stage.

2 List the four stages of mitosis, and describe the events that occur in each stage.

3 Describe how mitosis and the cell cycle relate to cell reproduction.

4 Make a data table like the one at the top of the next page.

Procedure

1. Using a 1 m piece of string, make a circle on your lab table to represent the cell membrane of a cell. Using a 40 cm piece of string, make another circle inside of the "cell" to represent the nuclear membrane. Place 4 strips of paper (one of each color) inside the "nucleus" to represent chromosomes. The model you have built represents a cell in the G_1 phase. Record the number of "chromosomes" inside the "nucleus" in your data table.

2.  Use scissors to cut each paper strip in half lengthwise. The two pieces that result from each strip represent the two chromatids that make up a chromosome after replication. Use a paper clip to join the two strips of paper so that they form an X. Each paper clip represents a centromere.

ANSWERS

Prelab Preparation

1. G_1 *phase*—growth stage
   S phase—DNA replication stage
   G_2 *phase*—stage between replication and mitosis
   M phase—stage in which mitosis occurs
   C phase—stage in which the cytoplasm divides

2. *prophase*—the nuclear membrane disappears, and spindle fibers form
   metaphase—chromosomes line up across the center of a cell, and spindle fibers attach to the chromosomes
   anaphase—the spindle fibers contract and pull chromatids toward opposite poles of the cell
   telophase—spindle fibers break down, and a nuclear membrane forms around each group of chromosomes

3. DNA replication in the S phase provides two sets of genetic information, mitosis produces two identical nuclei, and cytokinesis (C phase) produces two new cells.

Analysis

10. Students modeled the dissolving of the nuclear membrane that occurs in prophase.

11. The two new cells are genetically identical to the original, but smaller.

12. Answers will vary. Students should see that resulting cells will not be genetically identical.

13. Answers will vary. Students may suggest other materials or directions to improve the activity.

Name of phase	Chromosome/chromatid number	Events
G₁ phase		
S phase		
G₂ phase		
M phase		
Prophase		
Metaphase		
Anaphase		
Telophase		
C phase		

3. You modeled the events of the S phase in step 2. Count the total number of "chromatids" (half-strips of paper) in the "nucleus," and record this number in your data table. The cell then enters the G₂ phase. Mitosis (the M phase) follows the G₂ phase.

4. Prophase Remove the "nuclear membrane." Place the 10 cm strings, which represent spindle fibers, inside the "cell" so that they look similar to those shown in the photo at right.

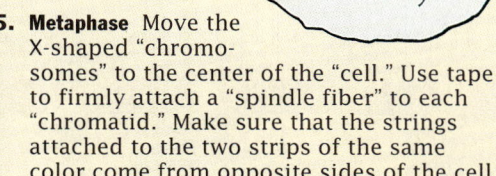

5. Metaphase Move the X-shaped "chromosomes" to the center of the "cell." Use tape to firmly attach a "spindle fiber" to each "chromatid." Make sure that the strings attached to the two strips of the same color come from opposite sides of the cell.

6. Anaphase Gather the loose ends of the strings on both sides of the cell, and pull the strings in opposite directions.

7. Telophase Untape the string from the paper strips. These half-strips of paper, which formerly represented chromatids, now represent chromosomes. Place one 40 cm string around each group of "chromosomes," forming two nuclei. Count the number of "chromosomes" in one of the new nuclei, and record this number in your data table. The C phase follows telophase.

8. Use the model to complete your data table.

9. Dispose of your materials according to the directions from your teacher.

Analysis

10. Relating Information What step in mitosis did you model when you removed the "nuclear membrane" in step 4?

11. Interpreting Results In what way are the two new cells that result from cell reproduction different from the original?

12. Predicting Outcomes Draw a line on one of the model chromatids. This line represents a mistake in the replication of a chromosome's DNA. How might such a mistake affect the outcome of cell reproduction?

13. Drawing Conclusions Evaluate this model's ability to help someone visualize animal cell reproduction.

Applications

14. Thinking Critically How can a model help someone understand a biological process?

15. Thinking Critically The G₁ phase is normally the longest phase of the cell cycle. A "tumor suppressor" gene holds a cell in the G₁ phase. Cancer results when this gene is defective. How do you think this defective gene affects the process of cell reproduction?

16. Career Connection *Cytologists* are scientists who study cells. Many cytologists are involved in cancer research. Find out about the training and skills required to become a cytologist, and discover where cytologists do their work.

771

exploration notes
SKILL BUILDING   CONTINUED

Additional Background
The process of mitosis is basically the same in all eukaryotic cells, with minor exceptions. Animal cells have spindle fibers that pull apart chromosomes during telophase. Plant cells lack spindle fibers. Two new animal cells separate when the cell membrane of the original cell pinches in two. Two new plant cells result when new sections of the cell wall and cell membrane have formed.

Disposal
none

Procedural Notes
Safety Precautions
• Discuss all safety symbols and caution statements with students.

Procedural Tips
• Make available to students the Animal & Plant Mitosis Smart Slides from WARD'S. This CD-ROM can be used in a variety of ways: (1) as a class demonstration prior to the start of the lab, (2) as a prelab activity, or (3) as a reference for students to access during the lab.
• Unit 1, *Cells, Energy, and Genetics,* in Holt's **Concepts of Biology** CD-ROM discs contains a video, "Mitosis and Cytokinesis," that shows the steps of mitosis for students to observe. Use this video to review the process of mitosis in both animal and plant cells.

Applications

14. Answers will vary. Students should relate visualizing a process to understanding it.

15. Answers will vary. Students should recognize that the rate of cell reproduction in cells with the defective gene would greatly increase.

16. Cytologists usually obtain a bachelor's degree in biology and a Ph.D. in cytology. Most cytologists work in university or medical laboratories. They must be very detail oriented.

Sample Data

Name of phase	Chromosome/chromatid number	Events
G₁ Phase	4	Cell growth and metabolism
S Phase	8	DNA replication occurs
G₂ Phase	8	Resting phase
Mitosis		Nucleus divides into two identical nuclei
Prophase	8	chromosomes shorten, nuclear membrane breaks down, spindle fibers form
Metaphase	8	chromosomes line up in cell center, spindle fibers attach to centromeres
Anaphase	8	spindle fibers contract and pull chromosomes to the poles
Telophase	8	spindle fibers break down, nuclear membrane forms, chromosomes lengthen
C Phase	4	cytoplasm divides, forming two new cells

6B Meiosis: Down Syndrome

Purpose

Students will use a computer simulation to determine whether parental age affects the probability of having a child with Down syndrome.

Instructional Goals

Students will

- observe the stages of a normal meiotic division and contrast them with the stages of a meiotic division in which nondisjunction occurs.
- evaluate whether the father's age affects the likelihood of having a child with Down syndrome.
- evaluate whether the mother's age affects the likelihood of having a child with Down syndrome.

Preparation Notes

Time Required: approximately 1 hour

Preparation Tips

If enough computers are available, students can work individually. Otherwise, they should work in teams of two to four.

Prelab Discussion

Before students begin the lab, they should be able to answer the following questions:

- What is meiosis? *(Meiosis is the process by which gametes are formed.)*
- How many chromosomes are found in a normal gamete? *(A normal gamete contains one of each kind of chromosome, or 23 chromosomes in total.)*
- Which cells in the body undergo meiosis? *(Only certain cells in the testes or ovaries undergo meiosis.)*
- What is nondisjunction? *(Nondisjunction is the failure of chromosomes to separate during meiosis.)*

CONTINUED ON NEXT PAGE

interactive exploration

Objectives

- *Compare* the events of a normal meiotic division with those resulting in Down syndrome.
- *Determine* the relationship between parental age and the likelihood that a child will have Down syndrome.

Materials

- computer with CD-ROM drive
- CD-ROM *Interactive Explorations in Biology: Cell Biology and Genetics*
- graph paper

Background: This interactive exploration allows you to explore the cause of Down syndrome, an inherited condition that results in mental retardation, short stature, stubby hands and feet, and a characteristic heavy eyefold. This condition is a consequence of nondisjunction, the failure of chromosomes to separate normally during meiosis. In this exploration, you will have the opportunity to examine how the age of each parent affects the events of meiosis.

Prelab Preparation

1. Load and start the program Meiosis: Down Syndrome. You will see an animated diagram like the one below. Click the Navigation button, and then click the Topic Information button. Read the focus questions and review these concepts: Ploidy, Meiosis, Aneuploidy, and Nondisjunction.

2. Now click the word *Help* at the top left of the screen, and select How to Use This Exploration. Listen to the instructions that explain the operation of the exploration. Click the Interactive Exploration button on the Navigation Palette to begin the exploration.

Feedback Meter

a **Incidence of Down Syndrome:** displays the frequency of Down syndrome births for the combination of parents chosen

Variables

b **Age of Mother:** allows you to set the mother's age

c **Age of Father:** allows you to set the father's age

ANSWERS

Procedure

4. Four gametes have formed.
6. One pair of sister chromatids fails to separate during the first meiotic division.

12. **Sample Data Table**

Parent Being Evaluated: Father	
Age of parent	Incidence of Down syndrome
25	0.70
30	0.70
35	0.70
40	0.70
45	0.70
50	0.70

The father's age apparently has no effect on the likelihood of having a child with Down syndrome because the incidence does not vary with the father's age.

Procedure

Part A: Normal Meiosis

First you will observe an animation showing the events of normal meiosis. For simplicity's sake, this animation shows only two pairs of chromosomes.

1. Click the Normal button to observe a simulation of normal meiosis.

2. Click the Detail button. Then click the Forward button (the one with the right-facing arrow) to progress through the eight steps of a normal meiotic division. As you view each step, read the caption and study the illustration.

3. Click the Close button.

4. Click the Start button to observe the same meiosis in continuous motion. How many gametes have formed when meiosis is complete?

Part B: Nondisjunction

Now you will observe an animation showing a meiotic division in which nondisjunction occurs.

5. Click the Nondisjunction button.

6. Click the Detail button. Then click the Forward button to observe nondisjunction. As you view each step, read the caption and study the illustration. What differences between normal meiosis and nondisjunction do you observe in frame 4?

7. Click the Close button.

8. Click the Start button to observe nondisjunction in continuous motion.

Part C: Determining the Effect of the Father's Age
Make a table like the one shown below.

Parent Being Evaluated: _____	
Age of parent	Incidence of Down syndrome

9. Click and slide the left-hand indicator so that the age of the mother is 25.

10. Click and slide the other indicator so that the age of the father is 25.

11. Click the Plot Point button. In your table, record the probability that these parents will have a child with Down syndrome, shown by the meter labeled Incidence of Down Syndrome per 1000 Live Births.

12. Repeat steps 10–11 five times, each time increasing the age of the father by 5 years. Make a graph of the age of the father versus the incidence of Down syndrome. What can you conclude about the effect of the father's age on the likelihood of having a child with Down syndrome?

Part D: Determining the Effect of the Mother's Age
Make a table like the one you made in Part C.

13. Click the Reset Graph button.

14. Click and slide the indicator so that the age of the father is 25.

15. Click and slide the indicator so that the age of the mother is 25.

16. Click the Plot Point button. In your table, record the Incidence of Down Syndrome per 1000 Live Births.

17. Repeat steps 15–16 five times, each time increasing the age of the mother by 5 years. Be sure to record the incidence of Down syndrome for each age. Make a graph of the mother's age versus the incidence of Down syndrome. What can you conclude about the effect of the mother's age on the likelihood of having a child with Down syndrome?

Analysis

18. In step 12, why did you hold the mother's age constant while varying the father's age?

19. In the United States, the age at which women have their first child has been increasing. How might this affect the incidence of Down syndrome?

Additional Background

Down syndrome is a disorder caused by the presence of an extra copy of chromosome 21. Down syndrome involves a variety of abnormalities, including reduced growth, a heavy eyefold, short hands, intestinal deformities, and heart defects. Although the severity of impairment varies, most individuals with Down syndrome also have some degree of mental retardation. The life expectancy for a child with Down syndrome is about 17 years.

In most cases, Down syndrome results from nondisjunction, the failure of chromosomes to separate during meiosis. The incidence of Down syndrome rises dramatically with the age of the mother. This age effect is thought to be due to the increasing amount of time the egg has remained in "suspended animation" within the mother's body. The older a woman is, the more time her eggs have had to accumulate genetic damage.

Procedural Notes
Procedural Tips

- Students may find the computer's graph of parental age versus incidence of Down syndrome confusing. Inform students that the meter labeled "Incidence of Down Syndrome per 1000 Live Births" that is located at the top left of the screen provides one value for the incidence of Down syndrome, given the ages of both parents. Students should use this value when recording their data.

773

17. **Sample Data Table**

Parent Being Evaluated: Mother	
Age of parent	Incidence of Down syndrome
25	0.70
30	1.22
35	3.38
40	12.3
45	56.0
50	145.0

The likelihood of having a child with Down syndrome rises with the mother's age.

Analysis

18. The mother's age was held constant so that the influence of the father's age could be evaluated.

19. This may lead to an increase in the frequency of children with Down syndrome.

Purpose

Students will use a laboratory test and knowledge of blood-type inheritance to determine a possible parent-child relationship.

Instructional Goals

Understanding Concepts

Students will

- apply principles of genetics to the inheritance of ABO blood types.
- recognize the limitations of using blood typing to determine relationship.
- infer the importance of blood typing to the practice of blood transfusion.

Life/Work Skills

Students will demonstrate proficiency in

- performing ABO blood-typing tests.
- interpreting the results of ABO blood-typing tests.
- working as part of a team.
- communicating the results of lab tests.
- using appropriate safety procedures in the laboratory.

Preparation Notes

Time Required: 1 lab period

Materials

Materials for this Exploration can be ordered from WARD'S. See page T745-12 for catalog numbers.

Preparation Tips

- Purchase simulated blood-typing kits from WARD'S. These kits include simulated blood, simulated typing sera, blood-typing trays, and plastic toothpicks.

CONTINUED ON NEXT PAGE

exploration

Skill:

Blood-typing technique

Objectives

- *Interpret* the results of blood-typing tests.
- *Identify* an unknown blood type.
- *Predict* the possible blood types among children of parents with specific blood types.
- *Recognize* limitations of blood typing as a means of identification.

Materials

- safety goggles
- disposable gloves
- lab apron
- 5 blood-typing trays
- simulated blood (types AB and O)
- simulated blood from Cash child 1, Cash child 2, and Mr. X
- simulated anti-A blood-typing serum
- simulated anti-B blood-typing serum
- 10 toothpicks

Situation

You are a medical laboratory technician. The lab you work for has been hired to conduct blood tests for the court case of *Mr. X v. the Cash Estate*. A man (Mr. X) claiming to be the son of Mr. and Mrs. Cash has sued for a share of the estate left to their children. Your job is to determine the blood types of the Cash children and Mr. X. You may be asked to testify in court.

Background: Human ABO blood types are determined by the presence or absence of specific **antigens,** or marker proteins, on the surface of red blood cells. Everyone inherits two alleles that determine his or her **phenotype** for ABO blood type. The alleles for antigens A and B are **dominant** over the **recessive** O allele, which does not code for an antigen. This means that people with type A or type B blood can have either of two possible **genotypes,** as shown in the table above. The alleles that code for antigens A and B are **codominant.**

When exposed to a foreign antigen, the body makes **antibodies,** which attack and destroy cells carrying the foreign antigen. Anti-A antibodies attack and destroy red blood cells carrying A antigens. Anti-B antibodies attack and destroy red blood cells carrying B antigens. Red blood cells that have been destroyed by antibodies stick together, forming clumps.

Antigen present	Blood type	Possible genotypes
A	Type A	AA and AO
B	Type B	BB and BO
A, B	Type AB	AB
None	Type O	OO

Prelab Preparation

1 Define the boldface terms in the **Background** section.

2 Describe the purpose of a Punnett square.

3 Make a data table like the one shown at the top of the next page.

Procedure

1. Put on safety goggles, gloves, and a lab apron.

2. Place 3–4 drops of the Type AB simulated blood into each of the two wells in a clean blood-typing tray. **CAUTION: Use only simulated blood throughout this lab. Under no circumstances are you to test any blood other than the simulated blood provided by your teacher.**

ANSWERS

Prelab Preparation

1. *antigen*—cell marker protein
   phenotype—physical expression of a genetic trait
   dominant—allele that is expressed whenever it is present
   recessive—allele that is not expressed when a dominant allele is present
   genotype—pair of alleles that determine a genetic trait
   codominant—condition where both alleles for a trait are expressed
   antibody—destroys foreign antigens

2. Punnett squares are used to determine the possible genotypes and phenotypes that may result from crosses.

Analysis

9. Mr. Cash could only have been genotype AB. Mrs. Cash could have been AA or AO.

10.

	A	B
A	AA	AB
O	AO	BO

or

	A	B
A	AA	AB
O	AA	AB

11. Yes. If Mrs. Cash were genotype AO, then both blood types A and B could occur among the Cashes' children.

12. none

13. Mr. X is Type O. The only possible genotype for Mr. X is OO.

14. Yes. It is not possible for Mr. and Mrs. Cash to have had a child with Type O blood.

15. No. It would only prove that it is possible for Mr. X to be their son.

Blood sample	Description after adding anti-A blood-typing serum	Description after adding anti-B blood-typing serum
Type AB		
Type O		
Cash child 1		
Cash child 2		
Mr. X		

3. Without touching the blood in the wells, add 3–4 drops of anti-A blood-typing serum to one well. Using a toothpick, stir the mixture of simulated blood and blood-typing serum for about 30 seconds. Add 3–4 drops of anti-B blood-typing serum to the other well. Use a new toothpick to stir.

4. Observe each well for about two minutes. Look for clumps of a solid material to separate from the mixture, as seen on the left in the photo below. This clumping is evidence that antibodies have attacked the antigens on the simulated blood cells. Describe your observations by writing "clumping" or "no clumping" in your data table.

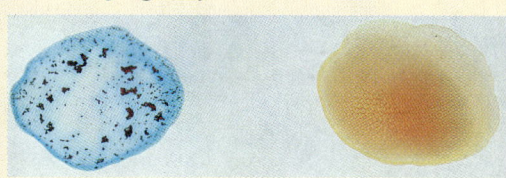

5. Repeat steps 3 and 4 using simulated Type O blood.

6. Repeat steps 3 and 4 to type the simulated blood samples from the Cash children and from Mr. X.

7. Dispose of your materials according to the directions from your teacher.

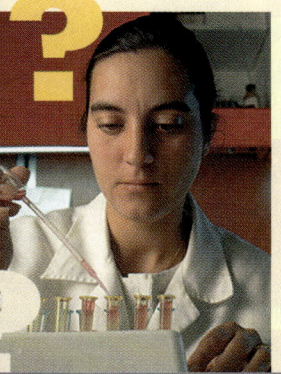

8. Clean up your work area and wash your hands before leaving the lab.

Analysis

9. **Relating Information** Medical records revealed that Mr. Cash had blood type AB and Mrs. Cash had blood type A. What genotype(s) would have been possible for Mr. Cash? What genotype(s) would have been possible for Mrs. Cash?

10. **Predicting Outcomes** Draw at least two Punnett squares to predict all of the possible genotypes and phenotypes for ABO blood type that could be found among Mr. and Mrs. Cash's offspring.

11. **Interpreting Data** Do the results of the blood tests on the Cash children agree with the prediction you made in step 10? Explain.

12. **Interpreting Data** Based on your test results, what antigens are found on the red blood cells of Mr. X?

13. **Drawing Conclusions** What is the blood type of Mr. X? What genotypes are possible for Mr. X?

14. **Drawing Conclusions** Can the court reject Mr. X's claim to the estate of Mr. and Mrs. Cash based on his blood type? Support your answer.

15. **Making Inferences** If Mr. X had blood type AB, would this prove that he is Mr. and Mrs. Cash's son? Explain your answer.

Applications

16. **Thinking Critically** Is blood typing a good way to identify a criminal or to establish parentage? Why or why not?

17. **Thinking Critically** When blood cells clump in the bloodstream, the result is usually death. How do you think blood typing improved the safety of blood transfusion (transfer of blood from one person to another)? Use data from this Exploration to justify your answer.

18. **Career Connection** *Medical laboratory technicians* perform blood-typing tests. Find out about the training and skills required to become a medical laboratory technician, and discover some other techniques performed in a medical laboratory.

exploration notes

SKILL BUILDING   CONTINUED

- Use simulated type A blood for Cash child 1 and simulated type B blood for Cash child 2.
- Use simulated type O blood for Mr. X.
- Prepare separate containers for the disposal of broken plastic trays and toothpicks.

Additional Background
Antigen-antibody interactions are part of the immune system. Antigens label a cell as belonging to or not belonging to an organism. Antibodies produced in response to the presence of a foreign antigen attack the foreign antigen, defending the body against invasion.

Disposal
- Simulated blood and typing sera may be washed down the drain.
- Broken typing trays and toothpicks may be placed in the trash.

Procedural Notes
Safety Precautions
- Have students wear safety goggles, gloves, and a lab apron.
- Discuss all safety symbols and caution statements with students.
- **DO NOT** allow students to test any blood other than the simulated blood you provide.
- Tell students that gloves provide protection from blood-borne pathogens and are necessary when working with body fluids.

Procedural Tip
Remind students to use a new toothpick for each test and to break used toothpicks in two before placing them in the designated container.

Applications

16. No. ABO blood type may be used to exclude someone, but it cannot confirm someone's identity or parentage.

17. Answers will vary. Students should recognize that blood typing increased the safety of blood transfusion because a patient's blood could be identified and the same blood type could be given to them. Students should provide an example based on their blood-typing data.

18. Medical laboratory technicians must be careful, organized, and analytical. They must complete at least a two-year college degree program emphasizing biology and chemistry and then must complete a technical-school program. Medical laboratory technicians use microscopes to examine body tissues and perform a variety of chemical tests on blood, urine, and other body fluids to help physicians assess the health of patients.

Sample Data

Blood sample	Description after adding anti-A serum	Description after adding anti-B serum
Type AB	clumping	clumping
Type O	no clumping	no clumping
Cash child 1	clumping	no clumping
Cash child 2	no clumping	clumping
Mr. X	no clumping	no clumping

Purpose

Students will use blood-typing tests to solve a problem involving the possible mix-up of two infants.

Instructional Goals

Student Objectives

- Determine the ABO blood type of simulated blood.
- Infer the identity of the parents of babies based on the results of blood-typing tests.
- Recognize the limitations of using blood typing to determine relationship.

Life/Work Skills

- performing ABO blood-typing tests
- selecting and using appropriate materials and techniques
- allocating resources
- acquiring, organizing, and interpreting data
- communicating effectively
- working as part of a team
- using appropriate safety procedures in the laboratory

Preparation Notes

Time Required: 1–2 lab periods

Prelab Discussion

Review the procedure in Exploration 7A, and answer any questions students may have. Remind them that they will use simulated blood. **Students should not attempt to perform these tests on real blood.** Ask students the following questions to guide their thinking:

- How are human blood types determined? *(by genes, which are inherited)*
- How can you identify an unknown blood type? *(perform a blood-typing test)*
- What materials will you need for the test? *(anti-A and anti-B blood-typing serum, blood-typing trays, and stirrers)*

CONTINUED ON NEXT PAGE

7B | ABO Blood Typing— Hospital Mix-Up

Prerequisites

- **Exploration 7A: ABO Blood Typing** on pages 774–775
- **Review** the following:
  1. cause of human ABO blood type
  2. purpose of a Punnett square
  3. phenotypes and possible genotypes for the four ABO blood types
  4. limitations of using blood typing as a means of verifying identity

---

NORTH COAST HOSPITAL
220 MAIN STREET
NEWTOWN, MAINE 00020

May 27, 1997

Caitlin Noonan
Director of Research
BioLogical Resources, Inc.
101 Jonas Salk Dr.
Oakwood, MO 65432-1101

Dear Ms. Noonan:

We recently had an extremely serious problem here at North Coast Hospital. Last Friday we were short-handed at our hospital and consequently had a mix-up in the maternity ward. Because of staff shortages, two infants born at nearly the same time were momentarily given to the wrong parents. Fortunately, we were able to immediately detect and correct our error and place each baby with the correct set of parents. However, the parents remain understandably concerned and angry. We need an outside agency not associated with our hospital to independently confirm our placement of each infant with each set of parents.

Enclosed are blood samples from each infant. Please conduct the necessary tests to determine the parents of each baby as soon as possible, and bill us when the work is complete.

Sincerely yours,

J. G. Prewitt

J. G. Prewitt
Hospital Administrator
North Coast Hospital

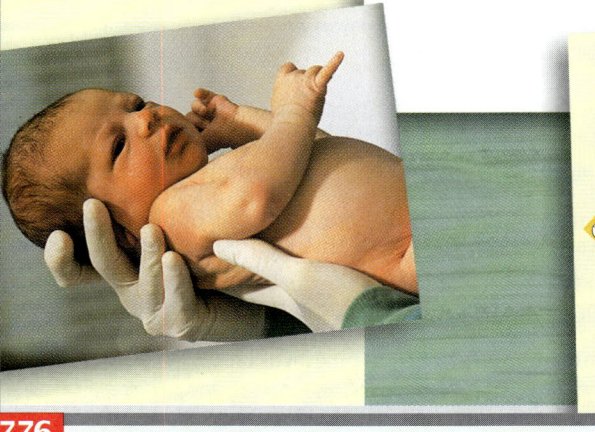

Required Precautions

- **UNDER NO CIRCUMSTANCES ARE YOU TO TEST ANY BLOOD OTHER THAN THE SIMULATED BLOOD PROVIDED BY YOUR TEACHER.**
- **Wear safety goggles, gloves, and a lab apron.**
- **Wash your hands before leaving the laboratory.**

776

SAMPLE SOLUTION

Proposed Procedure

1. Place 3–4 drops of Infant 1's blood in each of two wells of a blood-typing tray.
2. Add 3–4 drops of Anti-A blood-typing serum to one well and 3–4 drops of Anti-B serum to the other well.
3. Stir the blood and typing serum in each well with a separate toothpick.
4. Observe each well for 2 minutes, and record your observations in a data table.
5. Repeat steps 1–4 for Infant 2's blood.

6. Repeat steps 1–5 two more times.

Materials (per lab group)

- safety goggles, gloves, and lab aprons
- 2 blood-typing trays
- dropper bottle of simulated blood marked "Infant 1"
- dropper bottle of simulated blood marked "Infant 2"
- dropper bottle of simulated Anti-A serum
- dropper bottle of simulated Anti-B serum
- 12 toothpicks

Estimated Cost of the Job

$583.20 (for two students for one day and three tests of each infant's blood). The invoice students present to the client should include a profit. See page T745-6 for an example of how to prepare an invoice.

Results

Couple 1				Couple 2							
	A	B			A	A				A	O
O	AO	BO		O	AO	AO	or	O	AO	OO
O	AO	BO		O	AO	AO			O	AO	OO

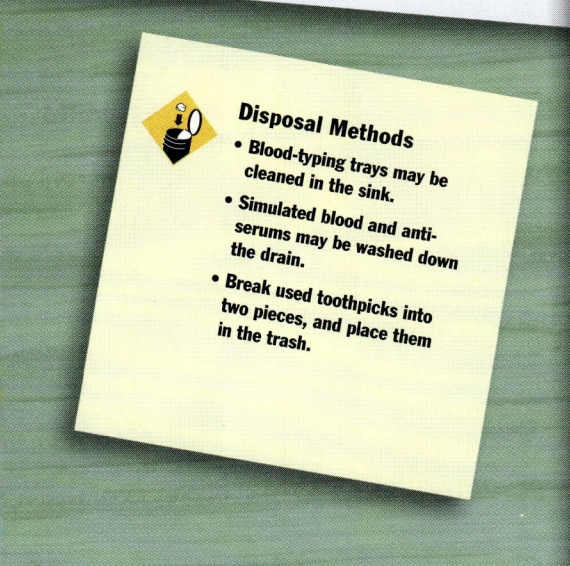

MEMORANDUM

B BIOLOGICAL RESOURCES, INC., OAKWOOD, MO 65432-1101

To: Team Leader, Medical Testing Dept.
From: Caitlin Noonan

Because the problem at North Coast Hospital is so serious, it is important that we answer Mr. Prewitt quickly and accurately. I want your team to perform the necessary tests. Make sure that your work is thorough and complete. Doing this job quickly and efficiently could lead to additional contracts with North Coast Hospital.

This morning I received a fax from Mr. Prewitt with the blood types of each set of parents. They are listed below.

Couple 1   AB and O
Couple 2   A and O

Before you start your work, you must submit a proposal for my approval. **Your proposal must include the following:**
- the **question** you are seeking to answer
- the **procedure** you will use
- a detailed and organized **data table**
- a complete, itemized list of proposed **materials** (including the use of facilities, labor, and amounts needed)

When you finish your tests, prepare a report in the form of a business letter to J. G. Prewitt. **Your report must include the following:**
- a paragraph describing the **procedure** you followed to analyze the blood samples
- a complete **data table**
- **Punnett squares** predicting the possible blood types of each couple's children
- your **conclusions** about each child's parents
- a detailed **invoice** showing all materials and labor plus the total amount due

Disposal Methods
- Blood-typing trays may be cleaned in the sink.
- Simulated blood and anti-serums may be washed down the drain.
- Break used toothpicks into two pieces, and place them in the trash.

FILE: North Coast Hospital

MATERIALS AND COSTS (Select only what you'll need. No refunds.)

I. Facilities and Equipment Use

facilities	$480.00/day
personal protective equipment	$10.00/day
test tube with rack	$10.00/day
blood-typing tray	$5.00/day
microscope slide and coverslip	$1.00/day
compound light microscope	$100.00/day

II. Labor and Consumables

labor	$30.00/hr
anti-A blood-typing serum	$1.00/test
anti-B blood-typing serum	$1.00/test
rubbing alcohol	$10.00/L
wax pencil	$2.00 each
toothpick	$0.10 each
blood sample: Infant 1	supplied by North Coast Hospital*
blood sample: Infant 2	supplied by North Coast Hospital*

Fines

*Penalty of $1,000 assessed for additional samples needed	
OSHA safety violation	$2,000.00/incident

777

Conclusions

Students should find that Infant 1 has type A blood and Infant 2 has type O blood. Infant 1 could be the child of either Couple 1 or Couple 2 because both can produce children with Type A blood. Infant 2 can only be the child of Couple 2 because only Couple 2 can produce children with Type O blood. Thus, Infant 1 is Couple 1's child, and Infant 2 is Couple 2's child.

Blood-Typing Results for Infants 1 and 2

Child	Reaction to Anti-A serum	Reaction to Anti-B serum	Blood type
Infant 1			
Trial 1	clumping	no clumping	A
Trial 2	clumping	no clumping	A
Trial 3	clumping	no clumping	A
Infant 2			
Trial 1	no clumping	no clumping	O
Trial 2	no clumping	no clumping	O
Trial 3	no clumping	no clumping	O

- Can you use blood typing to prove that a baby is the child of two parents? *(No.)* Explain. *(Everyone has one of only four different ABO blood types. Using genetic principles and blood typing, you can prove that a baby cannot be the child of two parents, or you can show that it is possible for a baby to be the child of two parents.)*
- What other information will help you solve this problem? *(knowing when and where the babies were born, and other genetic traits of the babies and parents)*

Materials
Materials for this Investigation can be purchased from WARD'S. See page T745-12 for catalog numbers. Provide the items in the "Materials and Costs" list on the pupil's page. Some of these items are distracters. See "Sample Solution" to estimate what each group will use.

Preparation Tips
- Prepare several dropper bottles each of simulated type A and type O blood. Label the simulated type A blood "Infant 1" and the simulated type O blood "Infant 2."
- Provide a separate container for the disposal of broken plastic trays and toothpicks.

Disposal
- Simulated blood and typing serum may be washed down the drains in lab sinks.
- Broken typing trays and stirrers may be placed in the trash.

Procedural Notes
Safety Precautions
- Discuss all safety symbols and required precautions with students.
- Have students wear safety goggles, gloves, and a lab apron.
- **DO NOT** allow students to test any blood other than the simulated blood you provide.

Procedural Tip
Advise students to stir the drops of simulated blood and blood-typing serum continuously for at least 30–60 seconds.

Interactive exploration notes

Purpose
Students will use a computer simulation to study the cellular basis for cystic fibrosis.

Instructional Goals
Students will
- identify the role of the CF protein.
- relate the function of the CF protein to the cell membrane's permeability to water and chloride ions.
- relate the symptoms of cystic fibrosis to the ability of chloride ions and water to cross the cell membrane.

Preparation Notes
Time Required: approximately 1 hour

Preparation Tips
If enough computers are available, students can work individually. Otherwise, they should work in teams of two to four.

Prelab Discussion
Before students begin the lab, they should be able to answer the following questions:
- What is cystic fibrosis? *(Cystic fibrosis is a fatal inherited disease in which large amounts of thick, sticky mucus are produced.)*
- How is cystic fibrosis inherited? *(It is caused by an autosomal recessive gene.)*
- What is the function of protein channels that pass through the membrane of a cell? *(These channels allow substances that cannot pass through the cell membrane to enter or leave the cell.)* CONTINUED ON NEXT PAGE

Interactive exploration

CHAPTER

7C Cystic Fibrosis

Objectives
- *Simulate* the effects of three different genotypes on the movement of water molecules and chloride ions through the cell membrane.
- *Relate* the symptoms of cystic fibrosis to the ability of water molecules and chloride ions to pass through the cell membrane.

Materials
- computer with CD-ROM drive
- CD-ROM *Interactive Explorations in Biology: Human Biology*

Background: Cystic fibrosis is a fatal genetic disease that results from the failure of chloride ions (Cl^-) to pass through the cell membrane. As a result, chloride ions accumulate inside the cells of the body. When this happens in the lungs, pancreas, and liver, mucus builds up on the lining of these organs. In this interactive exploration, you will explore how an individual's genotype affects the membrane proteins involved in transporting Cl^- ions through the cell membrane.

Prelab Preparation

1. Load and start the program Cystic Fibrosis. Click the Topic Information button on the Navigation palette. Read the focus questions and review these concepts: Transport Channels, Osmosis, Mutation, and Cystic Fibrosis.

2. Click the word *File* at the top left of the screen, and select Interactive Exploration Help. Listen to the instructions that explain the operation of the exploration. Click the Exploration button at the bottom right of the screen to begin the exploration. You will see an animated drawing like the one below.

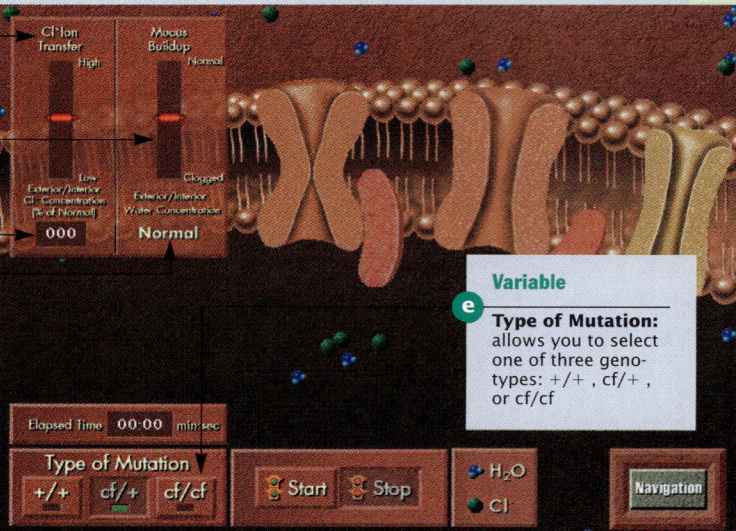

Feedback Meters

a. **Cl^- Ion Transfer:** the rate at which chloride ions move across the membrane

b. **Mucus Buildup:** how much mucus has accumulated on the cell

c. **Exterior/Interior Cl^- Concentration:** ratio of chloride ion concentration outside the cell to concentration inside the cell

d. **Exterior/Interior Water Concentration:** ratio of number of water molecules outside the cell to number inside the cell

Variable

e. **Type of Mutation:** allows you to select one of three genotypes: +/+ , cf/+ , or cf/cf

ANSWERS

Procedure
1. The phenotype is normal.
2. Water molecules move into and out of the cell through a protein channel. Chloride ions leave the cell through a protein channel but do not enter.
4. This person is also normal. The CF protein pivoted and closed off the chloride ion channel.
5. Fewer chloride ions leave the cell

because one of the chloride channels is blocked. As a result, more water molecules remain inside the cell. More mucus builds up on the cell's surface.

6. Chloride ions are at a higher concentration inside the cell. Water is also at a higher concentration inside the cell. In Part A, the chloride and water concentrations on each side of the membrane were equal because both chloride channels were open, and more chloride ions could move out of the cell.

7. This person has cystic fibrosis. Both CF proteins have changed position and closed off both chloride ion channels.
8. Chloride ions cannot leave the cell, and twice as many water molecules remain inside the cell as normal. The external surface of the cell becomes clogged with sticky mucus.
9. Inside the cell there are high concentrations of chloride ions and water. Outside the cell there are lower than normal concentrations of chloride ions and

Procedure

Create a table like the one below for recording your data.

Genotype	Exterior/ interior Cl⁻ concentration	Exterior/ interior water concentration	Mucus buildup
+/+			
cf/+			
cf/cf			

Part A: Two Normal Alleles (+/+)

First you will investigate how water molecules and Cl⁻ ions pass through the membranes of cells in individuals having two normal alleles.

1. Move the pointer to the Type of Mutation box and click the +/+ button. What is the phenotype of a person with this genotype? Note that water molecules and Cl⁻ ions are located outside the cell (the portion of the screen above the cell membrane) and inside the cell (the portion of the screen below the cell membrane). Also note the position of the two CF proteins in the cell membrane.

2. Click the Start button to begin the simulation. Allow the simulation to run for 3 to 4 minutes. Describe how water molecules pass through the cell membrane. How does this differ from the passage of Cl⁻ ions through the membrane?

3. Click the Stop button. In your table, record the Exterior/Interior Cl⁻ Concentration, the Exterior/Interior Water Concentration, and the amount of mucus buildup outside the cell membrane.

Part B: One Mutant Allele and One Normal Allele (cf/+)

4. Move the pointer to the Type of Mutation box and click the cf/+ button. What is the phenotype of a person with this genotype? Describe what happened to the CF protein shown on the left and how this has affected the Cl⁻ ion channel.

5. Click the Start button and allow the simulation to run for 3 to 4 minutes. Describe the changes in the way water molecules and Cl⁻ ions now move through the membrane. How will the change in the movement of water molecules and Cl⁻ ions affect the external surface of the cell?

6. Click the Stop button. In your table, record the same three variables as you did in step 3. On which side of the membrane are chloride ions at the higher concentration? On which side is water at the higher concentration? Compare the results to those you obtained in Part A, and explain any differences.

Part C: Two Mutant Alleles (cf/cf)

7. Move the pointer to the Type of Mutation box and click the cf/cf button. What is the phenotype of a person with this genotype? Describe what has happened to both CF membrane proteins and how this has affected the Cl⁻ ion channels.

8. Click the Start button and allow the simulation to run for 3 to 4 minutes. Describe the changes in the movement of water molecules and Cl⁻ ions through the membrane. How will the external surface of the cell be affected?

9. Click the Stop button. Describe the difference between the external and internal environments of the cell. In your table, record the same variables as you did in Steps 3 and 6. On which side of the membrane are chloride ions at the higher concentration? Compare the results with those you obtained in Parts A and B, and explain any differences.

Analysis

10. Why are the Cl⁻ ion channels, but not the water channels, called gated channels?

11. Explain why people with one normal allele and one mutant allele for cystic fibrosis have a normal life expectancy.

Additional Background

Cystic fibrosis is the most common genetic disease among Caucasians in the United States. About 1 in 2,500 Caucasian children born in the United States has cystic fibrosis, and about 1 in 20 adults is a carrier of the disease. Unusually thick and sticky mucus builds up in the liver, pancreas, lungs, and bronchial passages. This mucus may block delivery of pancreatic enzymes to the small intestine or disrupt liver function, but most deaths are the result of infections or damage to the lungs or bronchial passages. Recent advances in treatment have improved the prospects for cystic fibrosis patients, but the mortality rate is still high—about 90 percent of patients will die before reaching age 30.

The cystic fibrosis gene has been discovered and sequenced. The protein encoded by this gene apparently functions in the transportation of chloride ions across the cell membrane. Defects in the protein prevent chloride ions from leaving cells in the pancreas, liver, and lungs. Cells with abnormally high chloride ion concentrations will retain water, and this may account for the thick mucus that causes so many problems for cystic fibrosis patients.

Procedural Notes
Procedural Tips

- Remind students that the upper part of the screen (above the cell membrane) represents the outside of the cell and that the lower part of the screen represents the inside of the cell.

---

water and, as a result, a buildup of thick mucus. In this case, chloride ions cannot leave the cell because both channels are blocked. The cell retains water, causing the buildup of mucus outside the cell. This did not happen in Parts A and B because at least one chloride ion channel was open, and less water remained inside the cell.

Sample Data Table

Genotype	Exterior/interior water concentration	Exterior/interior water concentration	Mucus buildup
+/+	100%	normal	normal
cf/+	50%	normal	normal
cf/cf	20%	low	clogged

Analysis

10. Chloride ion channels are gated because they can be closed off by the CF protein. The water channel is not gated because it cannot be closed off.

11. Although chloride ions and water do accumulate in their cells, neither reaches abnormally high concentrations, and mucus does not build up.

CHAPTER

8A | Modeling the Effect of a Mutation

Purpose

Students will model the process of protein synthesis and the effect of the mutation that causes sickle cell anemia.

Instructional Goals

Understanding Concepts

Students will

- compare and contrast the structures of DNA and RNA molecules.
- compare proteins that result from normal DNA with proteins that result from a mutation.

Life/Work Skills

Students will demonstrate proficiency in

- using a model to demonstrate a biological process.
- following directions.
- working as part of a team.

Preparation Notes

Time Required: 2 class periods

Materials

Materials for this Exploration can be ordered from WARD'S. See page T745-12 for catalog numbers.

Preparation Tips

- Make sets of 8 tRNA/amino acid cards according to the table and instructions below:

Anticodon	Number	Amino acid
UUU	2	Lysine
GGU	2	Proline
CUC	3	Glutamic acid
CAC	1	Valine

For each set, cut four 3 × 5 index cards in half. On the top of each piece, draw three circles

CONTINUED ON NEXT PAGE

exploration

Skill:

Modeling a biological process: protein synthesis

Objectives

- *Compare* and *contrast* the structures and functions of DNA and RNA.
- *Use* a model to demonstrate how DNA directs protein synthesis.
- *Explain* how a mutation can affect a protein.

Materials

- masking tape
- metric ruler
- oval-shaped card marked "ribosome"
- 24 plastic soda-straw pieces of the same color
- 13 plastic soda-straw pieces of a different color
- 12 red (A) pushpins
- 10 green (G) pushpins
- 8 yellow (C) pushpins
- 6 clear (T) pushpins
- 1 blue (U) pushpin
- 37 paper clips
- set of 8 "tRNA/amino acid" cards
- scissors
- transparent tape
- piece of paper

Problem

You are a genetic counselor who has been asked to evaluate a hands-on activity that demonstrates the cause of sickle cell anemia. The activity models protein synthesis and the effect of a mutation on protein production. First you must perform the activity to see how it works.

Background: The process that uses the instructions in DNA to make proteins is called **protein synthesis.** The result of protein synthesis is a chain of **amino acids** that will become part of a protein. If a change, or **mutation,** occurs in a cell's DNA, a resulting protein may be defective. One such mutation causes a genetic blood disorder called **sickle cell anemia.** This disorder results from the production of abnormal **hemoglobin** molecules, which impair the blood's ability to carry oxygen.

Prelab Preparation

1. Define the boldface terms in the **Background** section.
2. Describe the events that occur during transcription and translation.
3. Describe the process of base pairing as it occurs in DNA and RNA.

Procedure

PART 1—DNA Structure

1. Using masking tape, mark off a 45 cm × 60 cm rectangle on your desk or lab table to represent the cell membrane of a cell. Within this rectangle, mark off a 20 cm × 45 cm rectangle to serve as the cell's nucleus. Place the clear plastic oval (ribosome) and the 8 tRNA/amino acid cards in the "cytoplasm" of your "cell."

2. Assemble the 24 soda-straw pieces of the same color, 24 paper clips, and 6 each of the red, clear, green, and yellow pushpins as shown in the photo at the top of the next page. To do this, insert a pushpin midway along the length of each soda-straw piece. **CAUTION: Pointed objects can cause injury.** Then push a paper clip into one end of each soda-straw piece until it touches the pushpin. The resulting structures represent DNA nucleotides. Each pushpin color represents a base.

ANSWERS

Prelab Preparation

1. *protein synthesis*—process that uses instructions in DNA to assemble amino acids into proteins
   amino acids—organic molecules that are the building blocks of proteins
   mutation—a change in the genetic material of an organism
   sickle cell anemia—disease caused by a mutation that produces defective hemoglobin molecules

hemoglobin—red pigment in red blood cells that transports oxygen

2. During transcription, one strand of a DNA molecule is used as a template (pattern) for assembling nucleotides into a strand of mRNA. During translation, an mRNA, which attaches to a ribosome, is used as a template to bring together amino acids, which are carried by tRNA molecules, in a particular order. The amino acids are joined to form a protein.

3. In base pairing among DNA and RNA nucleotides, cytosine always bonds with guanine, and adenine always bonds with either thymine (in DNA nucleotides) or uracil (in RNA nucleotides).

Analysis

13. DNA is double stranded; RNA is single stranded. DNA and RNA contain different sugars. DNA contains thymine; RNA contains uracil. DNA is only in the nucleus; RNA is in the nucleus and cytoplasm.

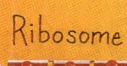

Ribosome

LYSINE

3. Use the 24 model DNA nucleotides to construct a strand of DNA inside your cell's "nucleus." First join two T "nucleotides" by inserting the paper clip of one into the open end of the other. Then, keeping the pushpins in a straight line, add 10 more "nucleotides" to make a strand of 12 "nucleotides" in the following order:

T—T—T—G—G—T—C—T—C—C—T—C

4. Using your DNA strand as a template, make the complementary DNA strand with the remaining "nucleotides." First pair the base in each "nucleotide" to a complementary base in the DNA strand, and then join the "nucleotides" as you did before.

PART 2—Transcription
5. Assemble the remaining soda-straw pieces, paper clips, and pushpins as before. These structures represent RNA nucleotides.

6. Using your first DNA strand as a template, construct a strand of mRNA. First separate the two DNA strands. Then pair the base in each mRNA "nucleotide" with a complementary base in your first DNA strand. *Note: Uracil (U) replaces thymine (T) in RNA and pairs with adenine (A).* Now join the RNA "nucleotides" to make a strand of mRNA.

7. Carefully move the mRNA strand from the nucleus to the ribosome in the cytoplasm.

PART 3—Translation
8. Starting at the red (A) end of the mRNA strand, place the "ribosome" above the first 3 bases. The 3 bases (AAA) make up a *codon*.

9. Match a tRNA/amino acid card to the codon, as shown in the photo above. To do this, pair the bases in the mRNA codon to the complementary set of 3 bases on a tRNA/amino acid card. These 3 tRNA bases (UUU) make up an *anticodon*. Move the "ribosome" to the next mRNA codon.

10. Repeat step 9 until all tRNA/amino acid cards have been matched to mRNA codons. Connect the amino-acid cards with tape. Then cut off the resulting amino-acid chain, tape it to a piece of paper, and label it "Fragment of Normal Human Hemoglobin."

PART 4—Effect of a Mutation
11. Repeat steps 3–10, using the following sequence of DNA nucleotides:

T—T—T—G—G—T—C—A—C—C—T—C

Label the resulting amino-acid chain "Fragment of Human Sickle Cell Hemoglobin."

12. Dispose of your materials according to the directions from your teacher.

Analysis

13. **Comparing Structures** Compare and contrast the structures of DNA and RNA.

14. **Inferring Relationships** How do the protein fragments you made differ? Explain this difference.

15. **Drawing Conclusions** Evaluate the effectiveness of this model in explaining what a mutation is.

Applications

16. **Critical Thinking** Can this model be used to explain the relationship between genes and proteins? Explain your answer.

17. **Critical Thinking** A person has been referred to you for genetic counseling. This person is concerned about contracting sickle cell anemia from a friend who has just been diagnosed with the disease. What would you tell your client about sickle cell anemia?

18. **Personal Connection** Research the effects of mutagens on DNA. Explain how you might protect yourself from the possible effects of a mutagen.

(about the size of the top of a pushpin) 3 cm apart, and write the letters for an anticodon. Use colored markers to fill in the circle above each letter as follows: A (red), T (none), G (green), C (yellow), and U (blue). At the bottom of each card, write the name of the corresponding amino acid. For example, tRNA molecules with a UUU anticodon carry the amino acid lysine.

• Cut the soda straws into 3 cm segments.

• Cut ovals (10 cm high and 13 cm long) from sheets of clear plastic. Label each oval "Ribosome."

Additional Background
Sugar (soda straw) and phosphate (paper clip) groups alternate along the backbone of a nucleic acid molecule. Thus, each chain of a DNA molecule has a sugar end and a phosphate end. To emulate actual DNA structure, the two strands of a DNA molecule should be arranged so that the two exposed paper clips fall at opposite ends of the molecule.

Sickle cell anemia is a genetic disorder caused by the production of defective hemoglobin molecules. Hemoglobin, the oxygen carrier in red blood cells, consists of 4 polypeptide chains (2 alpha chains and 2 beta chains). The mutation that produced the sickle cell allele occurred in the sixth triplet of the gene for the beta chain.

Disposal
Collect all materials for reuse.

Procedural Notes
Safety Precautions
• Discuss all safey symbols and caution statements with students.

14. The normal human hemoglobin fragment has glutamic acid where the sickle-cell fragment has valine. The difference was caused by a mutation.

15. Answers will vary. Students should explain how changes in the sequence of DNA nucleotides can result in a change in a sequence of amino acids.

Applications
16. Yes. The order of the nucleotides in a gene determines the order of the amino acids in a protein.

17. Sickle cell anemia is a hereditary disease that can only be passed from parents to a child.

18. Mutagens are agents, such as certain chemicals and radiation, that cause mutations. Avoiding exposure to mutagens will help prevent mutations. For example, ultraviolet radiation in sunlight is a mutagen that can cause skin cancer. Wearing sunscreen provides protection.

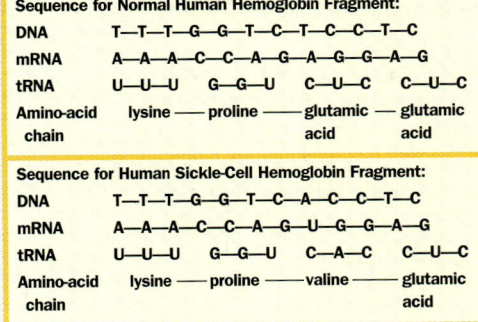

Sample Data

Sequence for Normal Human Hemoglobin Fragment:			
DNA	T—T—T—G—G—T—C—T—C—C—T—C		
mRNA	A—A—A—C—C—A—G—A—G—G—A—G		
tRNA	U—U—U G—G—U C—U—C C—U—C		
Amino-acid chain	lysine —— proline —— glutamic acid —— glutamic acid		

Sequence for Human Sickle-Cell Hemoglobin Fragment:			
DNA	T—T—T—G—G—T—C—A—C—C—T—C		
mRNA	A—A—A—C—C—A—G—U—G—G—A—G		
tRNA	U—U—U G—G—U C—A—C C—U—C		
Amino-acid chain	lysine —— proline —— valine —— glutamic acid		

Exploration 8A   781

Purpose

Students will cut Lambda bacteriophage DNA with restriction enzymes, prepare agarose gels, separate DNA fragments using gel electrophoresis, and analyze a gel to identify the restriction enzyme used to cut a DNA sample.

Instructional Goals

Understanding Concepts
Students will
- recognize the importance of restriction enzymes.
- relate the size of a DNA fragment to its rate of movement during gel electrophoresis.
- recognize the limitations of DNA analysis.

Life/Work Skills
Students will demonstrate proficiency in
- making a gel.
- conducting gel electrophoresis.
- staining a gel.
- interpreting the results of an experiment.
- working as part of a team.
- using appropriate safety procedures in the laboratory.

Preparation Notes

Time Required: 3–4 class periods

Materials
Materials for this Exploration can be ordered from WARD'S. See page T745-12 for catalog numbers.

Preparation Tips
- Purchase 0.125 µg/µL Lambda DNA.
- Prepare the following microtubes* for each group of students:
  - Microtube labeled "A"
  - Microtube labeled "B" with 1 µL *Hind*III
  - Microtube labeled "C" with 1 µL *Bam*HI
  - Microtube labeled "D" with 1 µL *Eco*RI
  - Microtube labeled "E" with 1 µL *Hind*III, 8 µL of Lambda DNA, and 1 µL of 10× restriction buffer for *Hind*III (unknown)
  - Microtube labeled "Lambda DNA" with 34 µL 0.125 µg/µL Lambda DNA

CONTINUED ON NEXT PAGE

---

exploration

CHAPTER

9A | Separating DNA With Gel Electrophoresis

Skill:
Gel electrophoresis

Objectives
- *Use* restriction enzymes to cut DNA.
- *Separate* DNA fragments of different sizes.
- *Identify* the restriction enzyme used to cut a sample of DNA.
- *Determine* the R_f of different DNA fragments.

Materials
- personal protective gear
- crushed ice
- ice bucket
- microtube rack
- microtube A—Uncut DNA
- microtube B—*Hind*III
- microtube C—*Bam*HI
- microtube D—*Eco*RI
- microtube E—Unknown
- permanent marker
- 0.5–10 µL micropipetter
- micropipetter tips
- 10× restriction buffer for each restriction enzyme
- 34 µL Lambda virus DNA
- 37°C water bath
- gel-casting tray
- 6-well gel comb
- 0.8% agarose
- hot mitt
- zipper-lock plastic bag
- 10 mL graduated cylinder
- 1× TBE buffer
- freezer
- 5 µL loading dye
- gel chamber and power supply
- WARD's DNA stain
- staining trays
- distilled water
- metric ruler

Situation

You have just started working as a forensic technician for a genetics lab that does **forensic analysis,** which is the analysis of materials for legal proceedings. You will be analyzing DNA for the lab. Your supervisor has given you a sample of DNA from the Lambda virus to use while you practice your technique. The Lambda virus is a **bacteriophage,** which is a virus that infects only bacteria. The DNA in the sample has been cut into pieces with an enzyme. Unfortunately, the sample did not get labeled. The DNA sample must be identified before your supervisor can use it in research. Your job is to determine which of several possible enzymes has cut the DNA.

Background: Cutting DNA into fragments is the first step in certain types of DNA analysis. The DNA is cut into fragments with a **restriction enzyme.** A restriction enzyme cuts DNA where a specific sequence of base pairs occurs. Each type of restriction enzyme cuts DNA at a different base-pair sequence. After a sample of DNA is cut by a restriction enzyme, the resulting DNA fragments are separated according to size by **gel electrophoresis** *(ee lehk troh foh REE sihs).* This process involves passing an electric current through a jellylike substance called a **gel.** The electric current causes one end of the gel to become negative and the other end to become positive.

A sample of cut DNA is placed in a **well** (depression) at the negative end of the gel. DNA has a negative charge and therefore flows toward the positive end of the gel during electrophoresis. Small DNA fragments move faster than larger fragments. After electrophoresis, the largest fragments are found closest to their wells, while the smallest fragments are found the farthest away. The distance that each fragment moves is used to calculate the R_f, or relative mobility, of a fragment. The R_f is used to calculate the number of base pairs in the fragment.

Prelab Preparation

1 Define the boldface terms in the **Situation** and **Background** sections.

2 Describe how gel electrophoresis moves DNA.

Procedure

Part 1—Cutting DNA

1. Wear safety goggles, gloves, and a lab apron.

ANSWERS

Prelab Preparation

1. *forensic analysis*—analysis of materials for legal proceedings
bacteriophage—virus that infects bacteria
restriction enzyme—specialized enzyme that breaks apart the bonds that hold DNA together at specific sites
gel electrophoresis—technique that uses an electric current to separate electrically charged substances by pulling them through a medium that is a gel

gel—jellylike medium used for the separation of substances by gel electrophoresis
well—depression in the end of a gel where solutions containing substances to be separated are placed
R_f—ratio of the distance a substance moves through a separation medium to the distance a reference substance (the loading dye) moves through the medium. It is a measure of the relative mobility of a substance in a separation medium.

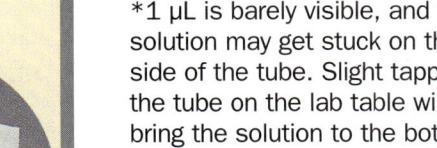

2. Fill an ice bucket with ice. Obtain one each of the following microtubes: A—Uncut DNA, B—*Hind*III, C—*Bam*HI, D—*Eco*RI, and E—Unknown. Microtubes B–D contain 1 µL of the indicated restriction enzyme. Place all microtubes in the ice. *Note: Restriction enzymes MUST be kept on ice until step 6.*

3. With a permanent marker, write the initials for everyone in your group ON THE TOP of microtubes A–E.

4. Set a micropipetter to 1 µL, and put a tip on the end of the micropipetter, as seen in the photo at right. Using a new tip for each microtube, add 1 µL of the corresponding 10× restriction buffer to each of microtubes B–D. Place the buffer on the side of the tube, as seen in the photo at right. *Note: DO NOT touch the micropipetter tips to the solutions in the microtubes.* **CAUTION: Report all spills to your teacher.**

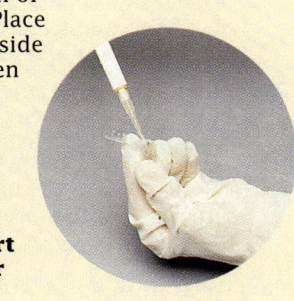

5. Reset the micropipetter to 8 µL. Using the micropipetter and a new tip for each microtube, add 8 µL of the Lambda virus DNA to the side of each of microtubes B–D. Gently tap each microtube on your lab table until the solutions are thoroughly mixed. *Note: Do not shake the microtubes!* Reset the micropipetter to 10 µL, and add 10 µL of Lambda DNA to microtube A.

6. Place all of the microtubes into a 37°C water bath. After 50–60 minutes, remove the microtubes from the water bath, and immediately put them into a freezer. If the class period ends before 50 minutes has passed, your teacher will give you further directions. While the restriction enzymes are working, prepare an agarose gel according to the directions in Part 2.

Part 2—Preparing an Agarose Gel

7. Set up a gel-casting tray, as seen in the photo at right, according to directions from your teacher. Place a gel comb in the grooves of the gel-casting tray. Make sure that the comb does not touch the bottom of the tray. If it does, get another gel comb and inform your teacher.

8. Write the names of the members of your group on a paper towel. Carry your tray to the table with the melted agarose, and place your tray on the paper towel.

9. ⚠ Using a hot mitt, pour melted 0.8% agarose into your gel-casting tray until the agarose reaches a depth of 3 mm. Make sure that the agarose spreads evenly throughout the tray. *Note: Do not move your gel tray before the agarose solidifies.*

10. Let the gel cool (about 20–30 minutes) until the agarose solidifies.

11. While the gel is cooling, write your name, the date, and your class period on a zipper-lock plastic bag. Pour 5 mL of 1× TBE buffer into the bag.

12. When the gel has solidified, carefully remove the gel comb by pulling it straight up, as shown in the photo at right. *Note: Do not wiggle the comb. This may tear the gel.* If the comb does not come up easily, pour a little 1× TBE buffer on the comb area. After removing the gel comb, open the plastic bag and carefully slide the gel tray into the bag. *Note: Do not remove the gel from the gel-casting tray.* Store the gel according to your teacher's instructions.

• Microtube labeled "loading dye" with 5 µL loading dye
*1 µL is barely visible, and the solution may get stuck on the side of the tube. Slight tapping of the tube on the lab table will help bring the solution to the bottom of the tube. **Always keep microtubes with enzymes on ice.** Microtubes come in a variety of colors. Students find it easier to keep microtubes separate if the tubes are different colors.

• Each restriction enzyme comes with the appropriate 10× restriction buffer. Keep the buffers on ice, and have students come to the supply table to get what they need. Tell students to be sure to add only the corresponding 10× restriction buffer to each of microtubes B, C, and D.

• To make 1× TBE buffer, dilute 250 mL of 10× TBE buffer to 2.5 L with distilled water.

• You can purchase ready-to-use 0.8% agarose and loading dye.

• To prepare 0.8% agarose, add 1.6 g of agarose to 200 mL of TBE buffer. Stir to suspend the agarose, and then heat on a hot plate or in a microwave oven until dissolved. Cover and keep in 65°C water bath until ready for use. Makes 200 mL. Unused agarose can be stored for several weeks under refrigeration.

• To prepare loading dye, dissolve 0.25 g bromophenol blue, 0.25 g xylene cyanol, 50.0 g sucrose, and 1.0 mL 1 M Tris (pH 8) in 60 mL distilled water. Dilute with distilled water to make a total volume of 100 mL.

CONTINUED ON NEXT PAGE

783

2. During gel electrophoresis, electricity runs through a gel. Since DNA is negatively charged, it is pulled toward the positive end of the gel.

Analysis

28. The DNA in microtube A serves as a control to determine what the Lambda DNA would look like uncut.

29. The fragments with the largest R_f values are located farthest from the wells.

30. Answers may vary. Some bands could appear darker because fragments similar in size may appear as one band. Both fragments together may stain darker.

31. The two samples that appear to have the same pattern of DNA bands are the *Hind*III (Sample B) and the unknown (Sample E).

32. *Hind*III cut the DNA in the unknown sample because the fragments of both samples produced the same pattern when separated by gel electrophoresis.

33. If DNA from different organisms (or even different individuals of the same species) were cut with the same restriction enzyme, the fragments would be different since the exact sequence of base pairs in the DNA would be different.

CONTINUED ON NEXT PAGE

- Provide a separate container for the disposal of the following: broken glass, microtubes, micropipets, and micropipetter tips.

Additional Background

DNA from the Lambda virus, which is a bacteriophage that can integrate itself with the chromosome of a bacterium such as *E. coli,* is used widely in genetic research. The Lambda virus's entire genome, which consists of about 48,500 base pairs, has been mapped. The restriction enzymes used in this experiment cut DNA at specific sequences of base pairs, which are shown in the table below.

Restriction enzyme	Base sequence cut
BamHI	G|GATCC CCTAG|G
HindIII	A|AGCTT TTCGA|A
EcoRI	G|AATTC CTTAA|G

Cutting Lambda virus DNA with *Hind*III produces the 8 DNA fragments shown below:

23,120	2,027	2,322	9,416
1	2	3	4
564*	125**	6,557	4,361
5	6	7	8

The numbers represent the number of base pairs in each fragment. *This fragment is typically not visible unless the gel is stained with ethidium bromide. **This fragment runs off the gel before the tracking dye reaches the end of the gel.

Disposal

- Follow the instructions on the WARD'S Material Safety and Data Sheets (MSDSs) for the disposal of solutions and dried gels.
- Paper towels and disposable gloves may be placed in the trash.

Procedural Notes
Safety Precautions

- Have students wear safety goggles, disposable gloves, and a lab apron.
- Discuss all safety symbols and caution statements with students.

CONTINUED ON NEXT PAGE

Exploration 9A, continued

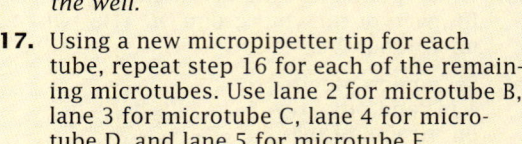

Part 3—Loading and Running a Gel

13. Retrieve your microtubes (A–E) and your gel. If the materials in the microtubes are frozen, hold each tube in your hand until the solutions thaw.

14. Set a micropipetter to 1 μL, and place a tip on the end. Add 1 μL, of loading dye to each microtube. *Note: Use a new tip for each microtube. Do not touch the bottom of the tube.* Gently tap each microtube on your lab table to thoroughly mix the solutions. *Do shake the microtubes.*

15. Remove your gel (still in the gel-casting tray) from the plastic bag, and place it in a gel chamber, as seen in the photo at right. Orient the gel so that the wells are closest to the BLACK wire, or anode.

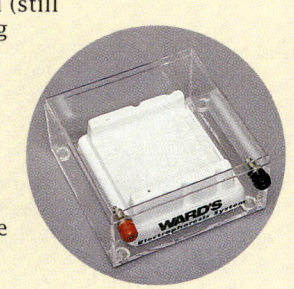

16. Set your micropipetter to 10 μL, and place a new tip on the end. Open microtube A, and remove 10 μL of solution. Carefully place the solution into the well in lane 1, as shown in the diagram below. To do this, place both elbows on the lab table, lean over the gel, and slowly lower the micro-

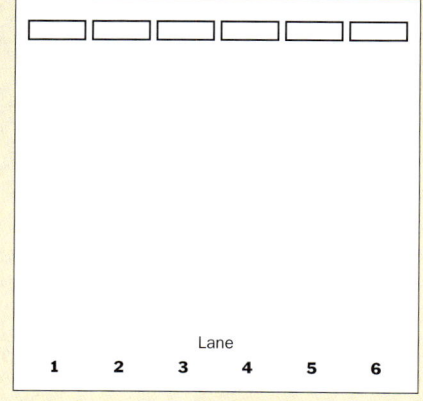

Lane

1   2   3   4   5   6

pipetter tip into the opening of the well before depressing the plunger, as seen in the photo at right. *Note: Do not jab the micropipetter tip through the bottom of the well.*

17. Using a new micropipetter tip for each tube, repeat step 16 for each of the remaining microtubes. Use lane 2 for microtube B, lane 3 for microtube C, lane 4 for microtube D, and lane 5 for microtube E.

18. Very slowly fill the gel chamber with 1× TBE buffer until the level of the buffer is approximately 1–2 mm above the surface of the gel.

19. Close the gel chamber and connect it to a power supply according to your teacher's instructions. **CAUTION: Follow all of the manufacturer's precautions regarding the use of this equipment.**

20. Allow an electric current to flow through the gel. You will see a blue line moving away from the wells. When the blue line is approximately 5 mm from the end of the gel, disconnect the power supply and remove the gel. Store the gel overnight in the plastic bag.

Part 4—Staining and Analyzing a Gel

21. To stain a gel, carefully place the gel (wells up) into a staining tray, as seen in the photo at right. Pour WARD's DNA stain into the staining tray until the gel is completely covered. Cover the staining tray, and label it with your initials. Allow the stain to sit for at least 2 hours. Next, carefully pour the stain into the sink drain, and flush it down the drain with water. *Note: Be careful. Do not let the stained gel break or slip out of the staining tray.*

Applications

34. The banding patterns that result when DNA from different individuals is cut by restriction enzymes and separated by gel electrophoresis should be different because everyone, except identical twins, has a different combination of genes. Therefore, the base sequences of their DNA will not be exactly the same.

35. Measures that prevent contamination of DNA samples include wearing gloves, changing micropipetter tips every time a new solution is added to a microtube, and not touching micropipetter tips to solutions in the microtubes or to the gels. It is important to prevent contamination while performing DNA analysis because any DNA from another source, including your hair or skin cells, could change the results and make the test inaccurate.

36. Forensic technicians must obtain at least a four-year college degree in science, emphasizing courses in biology, anatomy,

Lambda DNA Gel Analysis Data Table

Well 1 No enzyme		Well 2 HindIII		Well 3 BamHI		Well 4 EcoRI		Well 5 Unknown	
Distance (in mm)	R_f	Distance (in mm)	R_f	Distance (in mm)	R_f	Distance (in mm)	R_f	Distance (in mm)	R_f

22. To destain a gel, cover the gel with distilled water. *Note: Do not pour water directly over the gel. Pour water to one side of the gel.* Let the gel sit overnight (or at least 8–12 hours). After destaining the gel, the bands of DNA will appear as purple lines against a light background, as seen in the photo below.

23. Prepare a data table like the one on this page. Record your data in the table as you complete step 24.

24. Using a metric ruler, measure in millimeters the distance that each DNA fragment traveled from a well. Calculate the R_f for each fragment using the following equation:

$$R_f = \frac{\text{distance in mm that DNA fragment migrated}}{\text{distance in mm from well to the dye}}$$

25. Draw and label your stained gel on a piece of paper or in your lab notebook. Instead of drawing your gel, you may tape a photo of the gel or the dried gel to your report.

26. Dispose of your materials according to the directions from your teacher.

27. Clean up your work area and wash your hands before leaving the lab.

Analysis

28. Relating Concepts What is the purpose of testing the DNA in microtube A?

29. Analyzing Data Where on your gel were the fragments with the largest R_f values?

30. Analyzing Results Was the DNA in any of the bands darker than in others? What could account for this?

31. Interpreting Data Which two samples appear to have the same pattern of DNA bands?

32. Drawing Conclusions What restriction enzyme cut the DNA in the unknown sample? Justify your answer.

33. Predicting Outcomes In this lab, DNA from the *same* type of virus was cut with *different* restriction enzymes. What results would you expect from the gel electrophoresis of DNA from *different* organisms but cut by the *same* restriction enzyme?

Applications

34. Thinking Critically Would you expect different individuals to have the same or different patterns of DNA bands? Justify your answer.

35. Thinking Critically What are some measures that you took to prevent contamination of DNA samples during this lab? Why is it important to prevent contamination while performing DNA analysis?

36. Career Connection *Forensic technicians* perform DNA analysis on blood and hair samples taken from crime scenes. Find out about the training and skills required to become a forensic technician, and discover some of the types of tests that they perform.

785

physiology, and chemistry. They must have a logical mind, patience, an aptitude for scientific investigation, computer skills, and good writing skills. They should also be careful and persistent. Many forensic technicians work for law enforcement agencies, where they analyze fingerprints and other evidence from crime scenes. They work with microscopes, gas chromatographs, and other types of scientific instruments.

Sample Data Table

Well 1 No enzyme		Well 2* HindIII		Well 3 BamHI		Well 4 EcoRI		Well 5 * Unknown	
Distance in (mm)	R_f	Distance in (mm)	R_f	Distance in (mm)	R_f	Distance in (mm)	R_f	Distance in (mm)	R_f
10	.13	12	.15	19	.24	16	.21	12	.15
		22	.28	21	.27	24	.31	22	.28
		26	.33	25	.32	27	.35	26	.33
		28	.36	27	.35	29	.37	28	.36
		32	.41	29	.37	35	.45	32	.41
		44	.62					44	.62

*****Note:** Eight fragments should result from these digests, but samples may produce fewer than 8 lines. The two smallest fragments may migrate off the gel.

• Remind students to use chemicals only as directed and to carefully read the labels on containers of chemicals to be sure they have chosen the proper chemical.

• When using the WARD'S battery-powered gel chamber, use no more than five 9-volt batteries connected in series. Do not alter the electrical lead jacks to accommodate any power supply plugs. Do not use with any other power source. If another type of power supply is used, follow the safety instructions for the operation of that equipment.

Procedural Tips

• Prior to the lab, discuss with students the concept of gel electrophoresis—how it works and why.

• Tell students that an agarose gel contains agarose, a polysaccharide obtained from seaweed.

• Discuss with students how to analyze a gel. You may do this by placing a gel on an overhead projector and showing students how to recognize the bands and calculate R_f values.

• The appearance of the gels can be represented in several ways:
  1. DNA banding patterns can be drawn by students.
  2. Photos of gels can be taken after staining and can then be attached to a piece of paper.
  3. Gels can be dried on filter paper.

• There is a variety of equipment that can be used to perform gel electrophoresis. The equipment discussed in this lab is the micropipetter, the single-tray gel box, and a battery-operated power supply. Other types of equipment are available. Be sure that you discuss the equipment used in your classroom and that you instruct students to follow the safety instructions specifically for that equipment. **Model the proper use of all equipment for your students prior to the lab.**

Purpose

Students will collect and analyze numerical data to determine whether two plants belong to the same species.

Instructional Goals

Understanding Concepts
Students will

- recognize that variation exists within a species.
- apply mathematical principles to the analysis of numerical data.
- infer the relationship of two plants based on the size and shape of their leaves.

Life/Work Skills
Students will demonstrate proficiency in

- collecting numerical data.
- graphing the distribution of numerical data.
- determining the mean, median, and mode of a set of numbers.
- working as part of a team.

Preparation Notes

Time Required: 1–2 class periods

Materials
Materials for this exploration can be ordered from WARD'S. See page T745-12 for catalog numbers.

Preparation Tips
- Provide leaves from the same species or from two different species, depending on the results (trees are of the same species or trees are of two different species) you wish your class to obtain.

CONTINUED ON NEXT PAGE

exploration

Skills:
- **Taking numerical data**
- **Determining mean, median, and range**
- **Graphing data**

Objectives
- *Collect* numerical data on three characteristics of leaves.
- *Graph* the data for each characteristic.
- *Determine* the mean, median, and range of the data for each characteristic.
- *Compare* your data with the class data.
- *Infer* a possible relationship between two plants.

Materials
- 1 bag of leaves marked "Plant A"
- 1 bag of leaves marked "Plant B"
- metric ruler
- graph paper
- graphing calculator (optional)

786

Situation

You are a botanist who has been hired to study the plant life in a new park. To complete your study, you must identify (find the name of) a plant you found in the park. Normally you would use a *key* to identify an unknown plant. However, a plant key requires you to examine flowers, and the plant has no flowers at this time. The plant looks like one that you identified for the local school. You think the two plants might belong to the same species, so you take sample leaves from both plants to find out.

Background: The individuals of a **species** differ slightly in appearance. Many of these differences occur because of **genetic variation** (the different versions of the genes within a species). Some of these differences are caused by environmental factors, such as light, temperature, and moisture.

Numerical data (numbers obtained by counting and measuring) can be analyzed to determine how similar two individuals are. Graphing numerical data enables you to visualize the **range** (difference between largest and smallest value) and **frequency** (number of occurrences) of the numbers. To judge how similar the numbers are, their **distribution** (range and frequency) is compared with their **mean** (arithmetic average) and **median** (middle number in the range).

Prelab Preparation

1. Define the boldface terms in the **Background** section.
2. Prepare two data tables similar to the one at the top of the next page. Title one "Group Data" and the other "Class Data."

Procedure

1. Measure each leaf in the bags for Plant A and Plant B to determine its length and width (at the widest part) to the nearest tenth of a centimeter. *Note: Handle leaves carefully so that they do not break apart.* Record your measurements (numerical data) in your group's data table.

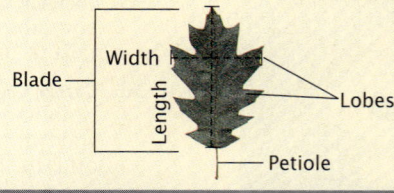

Blade — Width — Length — Lobes — Petiole

Prelab Preparation

1. *species*—group of organisms that are genetically alike
   genetic variation—differences between the individuals of a species that are due to different versions of genes
   numerical data—numbers obtained from counting or measuring characteristics
   range—difference between the largest and smallest values in a series of numbers

frequency—number of occurences
distribution—range and frequency of the numbers in a set of numerical data
mean—arithmetic average of a series of numbers
median—middle number in a series of numbers

Analysis

9. Answers will vary. The graphs for each characteristic should be similar.
10. Answers will vary.

11. Answers will vary.
12. Answers will vary. The mean, median, and range of each leaf characteristic should fall at or near the peak of each distribution curve.
13. Answers will vary. They should be similar.
14. Answers may vary. Students' conclusions should be consistent with their data.
15. The two graphs would probably be distinctly different.
16. The class as a whole examined many more leaves from each plant.

Leaf/ Group	PLANT A			PLANT B		
	Leaf length	Leaf width	Other	Leaf length	Leaf width	Other
1						
2						
3						
Mean						

2. Collect numerical data for one other leaf characteristic, such as number of lobes or length of petiole (leaf stalk). Record these numbers in your group's data table.

3. For each characteristic observed, make a line graph or a bar graph showing the distribution of the data for that characteristic. Label the *x*-axis of each graph with the name of a leaf characteristic, and label the *y*-axis of each graph "Frequency." Graph the data for Plants A and B separately.

4. Calculate the mean of each characteristic by adding all of the numbers in the column for a characteristic and then dividing by the number of rows (leaves measured). Record each mean in your group's data table.

5. Compile the data collected by your class in the class data table. In this table, record the mean of each lab group's data on each characteristic.

6. Repeat step 3 using the means reported by each lab group.

7. Find the mean, median, and range of the numbers in each column of the class data table. On the graph of the class data for each leaf characteristic, draw vertical lines to indicate the mean and median of the data.

8. Return your materials according to the directions from your teacher. Wash your hands before leaving the lab.

Analysis

9. **Interpreting Graphs** How does your graph for each characteristic of Plant A compare with your graph for that characteristic of Plant B?

10. **Interpreting Data** How does the mean, median, and range of each characteristic of Plant A compare with the mean, median, and range of that characteristic of Plant B?

11. **Interpreting Data** How do the mean, median, and range of each leaf characteristic compare with one another?

12. **Recognizing Relationships** How does the mean, median, and range of each leaf characteristic relate to the graph of the class data for that characteristic?

13. **Recognizing Patterns** How do the graphs of your group's data compare with the graphs of the class data?

14. **Inferring Conclusions** Based on your group's data, what does the relationship between the two plants seem to be?

15. **Predicting Patterns** How might two graphs of leaf length compare if the leaves came from two different species?

16. **Making Comparisons** How does the number of leaves from each plant examined by the class compare with the number of leaves from each plant examined by your group?

Applications

17. **Critical Thinking** Do you think that the differences between the leaves of Plants A and B were caused by genetic variation or by environmental factors? Justify your answer.

18. **Critical Thinking** After comparing your group's data with the class data, are you more certain of your conclusion about the relationship of the two plants? Why or why not?

19. **Career Connection** *Statisticians* analyze numerical data. Find out about the training and skills required to become a statistician, and discover how statisticians help biologists interpret their data.

787

Applications
17. Answers will vary.
18. Answers will vary. Students should feel more confident of their conclusions if similar trends appear in the class data.
19. Statisticians must have at least a four-year degree and often have a graduate degree. Required courses include many mathematics and computer sciences courses. Statisticians analyze data of all types to determine whether differences are significant.

Sample Class Data Table

Group	Plant A			Plant B		
	Mean leaf length	Mean leaf width	Number of lobes	Mean leaf length	Mean leaf width	Number of lobes
1	7.0 cm	3.7 cm	6	6.3 cm	5.2 cm	9
2	6.3 cm	4.0 cm	9	6.5 cm	3.0 cm	7
3	5.7 cm	5.1 cm	7	7.0 cm	5.0 cm	5
4	6.5 cm	3.5 cm	6	6.5 cm	4.9 cm	5
5	6.8 cm	3.5 cm	7	7.2 cm	4.5 cm	6
6	6.5 cm	3.8 cm	9	6.1 cm	3.9 cm	8
7	6.7 cm	4.2 cm	7	6.9 cm	4.4 cm	7
Mean	6.5	4.0	7.2	6.6	4.4	6.6
Median	6.5	3.8	7	6.5	4.5	7
Range	1.3	1.6	4	1.2	2.2	4

CHAPTER

14A

Modeling an Ecosystem

exploration

Purpose

Students will construct a micro-scale ecosystem from clear plastic soda bottles and collect data from the ecosystem over time.

Instructional Goals

Understanding Concepts

Students will

- apply principles of modeling to the construction of a microscale ecosystem.

Life/Work Skills

Students will demonstrate proficiency in

- constructing a microscale ecosystem.
- interpreting the success of this ecosystem.
- allocating resources.
- working as part of a team.
- communicating results and observations.
- using appropriate safety procedures in the laboratory.

Preparation Notes

Time Required: 2–3 lab periods to set up ecosystems, then 20 minutes every other day for at least 2–4 weeks.

Materials

Materials for this exploration can be ordered from WARD'S. See page T745-12 for catalog numbers.

Preparation Tips

- Soda bottles can be obtained from a local recycling center, or students can bring them from home. Labels and bottoms can be removed with a hair dryer or

CONTINUED ON NEXT PAGE

Skill:

Modeling an ecosystem

Objectives

- *Construct* a semiclosed, microscale ecosystem.
- *Identify* successful and unsuccessful organisms in a model ecosystem.
- *Recognize* the limitations of environmental microscale modeling.

Materials

- three 2 L clear plastic soda bottles
- wax pencil
- scissors
- 2 pieces of plastic, 5 cm square
- nail or awl
- dissecting needle
- candle or Bunsen burner
- clear waterproof tape
- algae
- *Elodea*
- *Vallisneria*
- *Myriophyllum*
- *Paramecium*
- *Daphnia*
- 2 or 3 aquatic snails
- soil
- 20–30 Rapid radish seeds
- dead organic matter (leaves, sticks, rotten fruit)
- terrestrial animals (flies, spiders, pill bugs)
- compound microscope
- slides
- coverslips
- dropping pipet

Situation

You are an ecologist who has been hired by a manufacturing company that is planning to build a new factory. The company wants to build the factory on a piece of land that is adjacent to a wilderness park. A group of citizens is trying to block construction of the factory because they believe that the factory will destroy the delicate ecosystem of the park. Your job is to perform tests that will assure the citizens that the wastes produced by the factory will not affect the park's ecosystem. First you must build a model of the park's ecosystem.

Background: An ecosystem can be studied with the aid of a **microscale model,** which is a small-scale model. A good model should include both **biotic** (living) and **abiotic** (non-living) components of the ecosystem to be studied.

Prelab Preparation

1. Define the boldface terms in the **Background** section.

2. Define the following terms: food chain, producer, consumer, scavenger, decomposer, herbivore, omnivore, carnivore.

3. Prepare a data table with four columns and the following headings: Date, Section 1 observations, Section 2 observations, and Section 3 observations.

Procedure

1. Remove the labels from three 2 L clear plastic soda bottles. Remove the bases from two of the bottles. Using a wax pencil, mark the bottles to be cut, as shown in the diagram below. Using scissors, cut the bottles along the wax-pencil lines.

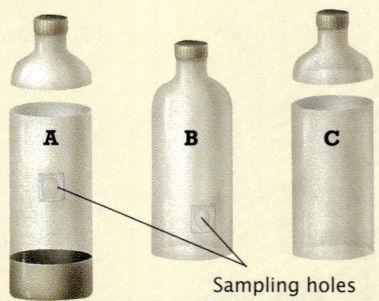

Sampling holes

ANSWERS

Prelab Preparation

1. *microscale model*—small model of a much larger system
   biotic—refers to things that are living
   abiotic—refers to things that are not living

2. *food chain*—series of organisms through which energy passes as one organism eats another
   producer—organism that produces its own nutrients from inorganic nutrients

that it takes from its environment
consumer—organism that obtains its organic nutrients by eating or digesting other organisms
scavenger—organism that eats dead animals
decomposer—organism that consumes and breaks down dead organic matter
herbivore—organism that eats only producers
omnivore—organism that eats both producers and animals

carnivore—organism that eats only animals

Analysis

12. Answers will vary. Student answers should be based on their data. Students may notice an increase in algae, protozoans, and *Daphnia*. Any of the species could decrease in number, depending on the success of the ecosystems.

13. Answers will vary. Producers should account for most biomass.

2. Cut sampling holes 4 cm in diameter in Bottles A and B, as shown in the diagram on the previous page. Make a cover for each sampling hole by placing a 5 cm square piece of plastic over each hole and attaching one side of the plastic square to the bottle with tape.

3. Using a nail or an awl, make drain holes in each of the caps from the three bottles.

4. ◆ Heat the point of a dissecting needle in the flame of a candle or Bunsen burner. Use the hot needle to make several holes in the top of Bottle A and in the sides of Bottles B and C. **CAUTION: Keep combustibles away from flames.**

5. Assemble the soda-bottle pieces into a microscale ecosystem with an aquatic community (Section 1), a lowland community (Section 2), and an upland community (Section 3), as seen in the diagram at right.

6. To make Section 1, place 5 cm of sand in the base of Bottle A, and then fill with water to within 3 cm of the sampling hole. Place aquarium plants, algae, *Daphnia*, *Paramecium*, and aquatic snails in the water.

7. To make Section 2, invert Bottle B, place it on top of Section 1, and then tape the bottles together. Fill this

Section 3

Section 2

Section 1

section one-third full with soil. Place 20 radish seeds, some dead organic matter, and two or three animals on the soil.

8. To make Section 3, place the top of Bottle A (cap up) on top of Section 2. Then invert the bottom of Bottle C and place it on top of Bottle A. Tape the bottles together. Place soil in Section 3, but do not cover the cap of Bottle A. Place seeds, dead organic matter, and two or three animals on top of the soil.

9. Invert the top of Bottle C, place it on top of Section 3, and tape these pieces together. Add water to your ecosystem, when necessary, through the opening at the top.

10. Observe your ecosystem for 2 to 3 weeks, and record any changes that you observe in your data table. Count the organisms you see. To count the microorganisms in the "pond," remove some of the water with a pipet, make a wet mount with it, and observe it under a microscope.

11. ◆ Clean up your work area and wash your hands before leaving the lab.

Analysis

12. **Interpreting Data** As your model ecosystem changed over time, which organisms increased in number? Which organisms declined in number?

13. **Drawing Conclusions** In your ecosystem, which trophic level had the most biomass?

14. **Making Inferences** Which was the most successful organism in your model ecosystem?

Applications

15. **Relating Information** Describe one food chain that you could study using your model ecosystem.

16. **Thinking Critically** How is your model ecosystem similar to a real ecosystem? How is it different?

17. **Thinking Critically** How might a microscale model of an ecosystem be useful? What are some of its limitations?

18. **Career Connection** *Wildlife biologists* study ecosystems that can't be modeled on a microscale. Find out about the training and skills required to be a wildlife biologist, and discover how they do their work.

by soaking the bottles in warm water. You will need a few extra soda bottles to make the 5 cm squares to cover sampling holes.
• Aquatic plants and snails can be obtained from a local pet store.
• Soil can be collected from around the school, brought from home, or purchased from a supermarket or garden center.
• Provide a separate container for the disposal of broken glass.

Additional Background
The balance of nutrients in an ecosystem is important to the health of the ecosystem. For example, excess nitrogen in an ecosystem can damage the balance of the ecosystem. A sudden increase in nitrogen can cause water plants and algae to multiply. When these organisms die and decay, they use up oxygen, killing other organisms in the water that need oxygen to survive.

Disposal
• Save the model ecosystems for Investigation 15A.
• Pieces of plastic soda bottles, soil, and dead leaves can be placed in the trash.

Procedural Notes
Safety Precautions
• Have students wear gloves when handling decomposing plant material.
• Discuss all safety symbols and caution statements with students.

Procedural Tip
If possible, encourage creativity by allowing students to change their ecosystems from the example given in this exploration.

789

14. Answers will vary. Student answers should be based on their data. Some possible answers are plants, algae, and protozoans.

Applications
15. Answers will vary. One food chain that would exist in the model ecosystem would be algae, *Paramecium, Daphnia*.
16. Answers will vary. The models resemble real ecosystems because they have both biotic and abiotic components and may

be self-sustaining. The models differ from real ecosystems because they are much smaller, have far fewer species, and may lack one or more trophic levels (e.g., carnivores).

17. Microscale models of ecosystems are useful for some laboratory studies. Their limitations include being unable to include large animals and plants in studies and having to base conclusions on a fraction of the biotic and abiotic components of a real ecosystem.

18. Wildlife biologists must complete at least a bachelor's degree and often complete master's or doctoral degrees. They must be observant, organized, analytical, and have a love of the outdoors. Wildlife biologists study portions of ecosystems and extrapolate their data.

Sample Data Table
Observations of a Model Ecosystem

Date	Section 1 observations	Section 2 observations	Section 3 observations
		Answers will vary.	

Investigation notes

Purpose

Students will investigate the impact of additional nutrients on an ecosystem.

Instructional Goals

Student Objectives

- Develop a laboratory procedure to determine the effects of additional nutrients on an ecosystem.
- Relate a change in an abiotic factor in an ecosystem to changes in its biotic factors.
- Predict the effect of excess nutrients on an actual ecosystem.

Life/Work Skills

- modeling an ecosystem
- allocating resources
- acquiring, organizing, and interpreting data
- communicating effectively
- working as part of a team
- using appropriate safety procedures in the laboratory

Preparation Notes

Time Required: 2–3 lab periods to set up ecosystems if students did not complete Exploration 14A; 20 minutes every other day for 2–4 weeks

Prelab Discussion

Review the concepts and procedures used in Exploration 14A. Ask students the following questions to guide their thinking:

- What will be your independent variable? *(fertilizer added to the ecosystem)*
- What will be your dependent variable? *(numbers of organisms in the ecosystem)*
- What will be your constants? *(amount of water added, soil type, temperature, light)*
- What will be your control? *(a model ecosystem with the same soil, same number and types of organisms, and same amount of water added each time)*

CONTINUED ON NEXT PAGE

15A | Modeling an Ecosystem— Fertilizer Dilemma

Prerequisites

- **Exploration 14A: Modeling an Ecosystem** on pages 788–789
- **Review** the following:
  1. independent variable
  2. dependent variable
  3. control
  4. constant

CITY ENVIRONMENTAL PLANNING COMMISSION

August 30, 1997

Rosalinda Gonzales
Director of Environmental Analysis
BioLogical Resources, Inc.
101 Jonas Salk Dr.
Oakwood, MO 65432-1101

Dear Ms. Gonzales,

I am the chairman of the City Environmental Planning Commission, which evaluates all proposed development in the local area. Our mission is to preserve the environment by intelligently managing economic development.

A large wholesale nursery is planning to relocate on the vacant farmland southeast of town. The land is very close to City Lake, which is used for recreation. The nursery will be applying a water-soluble 15-30-15 fertilizer to their plants on a regular basis. We need to know how these nutrients might affect City Lake. The city council needs our recommendation as soon as possible. Please conduct the appropriate experiments to determine any impact that the nursery may have on City Lake. Bill us when you send your report.

Sincerely,

Donald Crosby

Donald Crosby, Ph.D.
Chairman
City Environmental
Planning Commission

Safety Precautions

- Wear safety goggles and a lab apron.
- Wash your hands before leaving the laboratory.

790

SAMPLE SOLUTION

Question

How will the addition of fertilizer affect an ecosystem?

Proposed Procedure

1. Mix the fertilizer solution (or solutions) according to the directions on the label.
2. Every class period for 3 weeks, apply 10 mL of fertilizer solution to the soil in Section 2 (or Section 3) of the model ecosystem.
3. Observe the model each day for 2–4 weeks. Record observations in a data table.
4. Record the temperature of the water in the "pond" in Section 1 every other day.
5. Take samples of water from the "pond" in Section 1 every other day. Make a wet-mount slide of the water, and observe the slide under a microscope. Count the number of algal cells, protozoans, and other organisms observed.

Materials (per lab group)

- personal protective equipment
- model ecosystem from Exploration 14A
- wax pencil
- compound microscope
- microscope slide
- coverslip
- 100 mL beaker (for preparing fertilizer solution)
- 10 mL graduated cylinder

B BioLogicaL Resources, Inc., Oakwood, MO 65432-1101

MEMORANDUM

To: Team Leader, Ecology Dept.
From: Rosalinda Gonzales

Dr. Crosby is relying on us to provide quick and accurate results. His decision depends on our correctly identifying the effect that increased nutrients could have on City Lake. Make sure that your work is thorough and accurate.

The following information may be useful:

- A model ecosystem can be used to determine how excess nutrients from fertilizer might affect the ecology of a lake.
- An excess of nutrients can cause an increase in the organic matter in a lake.
- A 15-30-15 fertilizer is 15 percent nitrogen, 30 percent phosphorus, and 15 percent potassium. Different fertilizers supply different percentages of these nutrients.

Before you start your work, you must submit a proposal for my approval. **Your proposal must include the following:**

- the **question** you are seeking to answer
- the **procedure** you will use
- a detailed **data table**
- a complete, itemized list of proposed **materials** and **costs** (including use of facilities, labor, and amounts needed)

When you finish your tests, prepare a report in the form of a business letter to Donald Crosby, Ph.D. **Your report must include the following:**

- a paragraph describing the **procedure** you followed to determine how excess fertilizer might affect the lake
- a complete **data table**
- your **conclusions** about how runoff containing fertilizer nutrients will affect the lake
- a detailed **invoice** showing all materials and labor plus the total amount due

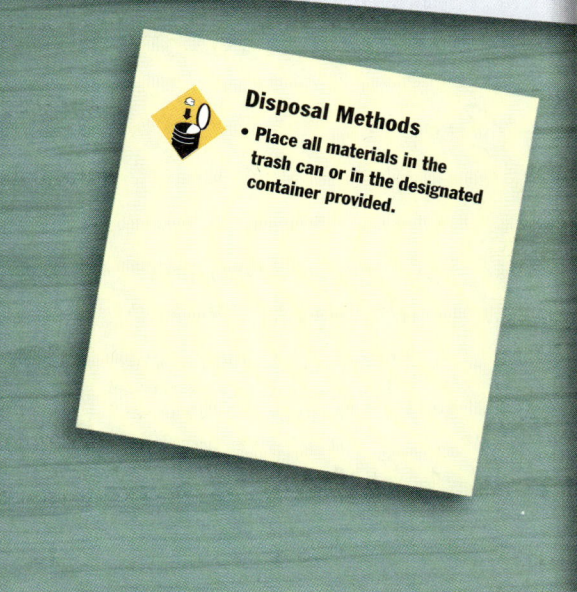

Disposal Methods
- Place all materials in the trash can or in the designated container provided.

FILE: City Environmental Planning Commission

MATERIALS AND COSTS (Select only what you'll need. No refunds.)

I. Facilities and Equipment Use

facilities	$480.00/day
personal protective equipment	$10.00/day
microscope	$100.00/day
microscope slide and coverslip	$1.00/day
forceps	$5.00/day
dropping pipet	$5.00/day
graduated cylinder	$10.00/day
beaker	$10.00/day
thermometer	$10.00/day

II. Labor and Consumables

labor	$30.00/hr
detergent	$2.00/bottle
15-30-15 fertilizer	$0.25/g
10-0-0 water-soluble fertilizer	$0.25/g
0-10-0 water-soluble fertilizer	$0.25/g
0-0-10 water-soluble fertilizer	$0.25/g
paper cups	$0.10 each
model ecosystem	$500.00 each
(from Exploration 14A)	
Fines	
OSHA safety violation	$2,000.00/incident

- 60 g of water-soluble 15-30-15 fertilizer (to mix 150 mL of fertilizer solution)
- dropping pipet
- thermometer

Estimated Cost of the Job

$8,597.00 (for 2 students for 15 days). The invoice students present to the client should include a profit. See page T745-6 for an example of how to prepare an invoice.

Results

The growth of aquatic plants and algae will increase. Numbers of protozoans and small aquatic animals may decrease as dissolved oxygen is used up. At high concentrations of fertilizer, most of the terrestrial plants will die.

Conclusions

Students' data should support their conclusions. Most students will find that eutrophication occurred. Students should relate eutrophication to excess nutrients.

- How will you measure the dependent variable? *(estimating relative amounts; microscopic observation and counting)*

Materials

Materials for this Investigation can be ordered from WARD'S. See page T745-12 for catalog numbers. Provide the items in the "Materials and Costs" list on the pupil's page. Some of these items are distracters. See "Sample Solution" to estimate what each group will use.

Preparation Tips

- Have students use the model ecosystems they prepared for Exploration 14A.
- Fertilizers can be purchased at garden-supply stores. Prepare fertilizer solutions according to the directions on the labels.
- Provide separate containers for the disposal of broken glass, plastic soda bottles, and soil and plants from model ecosystems.

Disposal

- Wrap the contents of discarded ecosystems in old newspaper, and place them in the trash.

Procedural Notes
Safety Precautions

- Discuss all safety symbols and required precautions with students.
- Have students wear safety goggles and a lab apron when mixing fertilizer solutions.
- Caution students to report any problems or odors related to their model ecosystems.

Procedural Tips

- Have students count microorganisms in four sections of their microscope slides. Then have them find the average of the counts for each organism observed and record these numbers.
- Microcomputer Based Laboratory (MBL) probes can be used to detect changes in the temperature of the ecosystem and in the pH and dissolved oxygen content of the pond water in Section 1. Comparing the beginning and ending pH will indicate any change in the CO_2 concentration of the pond water. Changes in dissolved oxygen will indicate whether eutrophication has begun.

Investigation 15A   791

Purpose

Students will test the effectiveness of antibacterial cleaning agents.

Instructional Goals

Student Objectives
- Design an experiment to identify antibacterial cleaning agents.
- Relate bacterial growth to the efficiency of antibacterial agents.

Life/Work Skills
- allocating resources
- acquiring, organizing, and interpreting data
- communicating effectively
- working as part of a team
- using appropriate safety procedures in the laboratory

Preparation Notes

Time Required: two 50-minute periods to plan and set up the experiment and two 15-minute periods to interpret results

Prelab Discussion

Review the procedures for using aseptic technique, described in **Laboratory Techniques C31** of the Holt BioSources® Lab Program, and discuss the information to include in a data table. Ask students the following question to guide their thinking:
- How can you identify an antibacterial effect? *(Clear areas in a bacterial lawn indicate that bacteria have been killed.)*

Materials

Materials for this Investigation can be purchased from WARD'S. See page T745-12 for catalog numbers. Provide the items in the "Materials and Costs" list on the pupil's page. Some of these items are distracters. See "Sample Solution" to estimate what each group will use.

CONTINUED ON NEXT PAGE

18A | Culturing Bacteria— New Antibacterial Soap

Prerequisites
- **Laboratory Techniques and Experimental Design: Using Aseptic Technique** in the Holt BioSources Lab Program
- **Review** the following:
  1. aseptic technique
  2. how to establish a bacterial lawn
  3. how to identify a positive result

Advertising Associates
New York, New York

February 14, 1997

Caitlin Noonan
Director of Research
BioLogical Resources, Inc.
101 Jonas Salk Dr.
Oakwood, MO 65432-1101

Dear Ms. Noonan,

I am heading up an advertising campaign for a new product. The product is an antibacterial, liquid soap that our client wants to market for use as a surface cleaner for the kitchen. As you are aware, foods can be contaminated with bacteria such as *Salmonella*, *Staphylococcus*, and *Escherichia coli*. These bacteria can live on kitchen counters and contaminate other foods if the counters are not cleaned before and after food preparation. Each of these bacteria can cause serious food poisoning.

All claims made in our advertisements must have research data to back them up. We want to know how the effectiveness of this new product compares with that of other antibacterial cleaning agents, such as bleach, household disinfectant, hand soap, and dishwashing soap.

Please perform the necessary tests. Bill us for your work when you send your report. Your quick action on this project will enable us to finalize our advertising campaign as soon as possible.

Sincerely,

Anda Chan

Anda Chan
Account Manager

Required Precautions
- **Wear safety goggles, gloves, and a lab apron.**
- **Do not use alcohol when there are flames in the room. Do not light burners when others are using alcohol.**
- **Do not open sealed petri dishes.**
- **Wash your hands before leaving the lab.**

792

SAMPLE SOLUTION

Question

Is the new soap an effective antibacterial agent?

Proposed Procedure

1. Clean the lab table with a disinfectant.
2. Draw lines on the bottom of a petri dish with a bacterial lawn of *E. coli* to divide the dish into six equal pie-shaped sections. Write the name of a different test solution in each section.

3. Use sterilized forceps to pick up a filter-paper disk, and dip it into one of the test solutions.
4. Carefully place the disk on the area of the culture indicated by the label.
5. Repeat steps 3 and 4 for each of the remaining test solutions and the control.
6. Seal the petri dish with tape, and place it upside down in a 37°C incubator for 24 hours.
7. Observe after 24 hours and again after 48 hours.

Materials (per lab group)
- safety goggles, gloves, and lab aprons
- disinfectant solution (5% bleach solution) and paper towels
- Petri dish with a lawn of *E. coli*
- permanent marker or wax pencil
- six 50 mL beakers
- 10 mL graduated cylinder
- 10 mL of distilled water (control)
- 10 mL of Test Soap solution
- 10 mL of bleach solution

MEMORANDUM

B BioLogical Resources, Inc., Oakwood, MO 65432-1101

To: Team Leader, Microbiology Dept.
From: Caitlin Noonan

Please get your team on this job right away. You should develop a procedure to determine whether the soap prevents new bacterial growth. Let's compare a 10 percent solution of the test soap with 10 percent solutions of four types of cleaning agents—bleach, hand soap, dishwashing detergent, and a household disinfectant. Small disks of filter paper can be used to apply the cleaning agents to cultures of *E. coli*. One petri dish of *E. coli* should accommodate a disk for each test solution, plus one for the control. Please have each of your teams perform one test with each of the cleaning agents. Compile the data from all tests into one report.

Before you start your work, you must submit a proposal for my approval. **Your proposal must include the following:**
- the **question** you are seeking to answer
- the **procedure** you will use
- a detailed **data table**
- a complete, itemized list of proposed **materials** and **costs** (including use of facilities, labor, and amounts needed)

When you finish your tests, prepare a report in the form of a business letter to Anda Chan. **Your report must include the following:**
- a paragraph describing the **procedure** you followed to test the effectiveness of each cleaning agent
- a complete **data table**
- your **conclusions** about the effectiveness of the new product
- a detailed **invoice** showing all materials and labor plus the total amount due

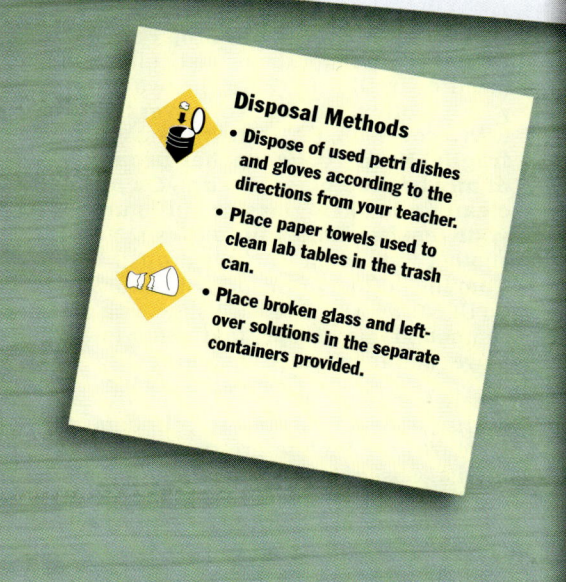

Disposal Methods
- Dispose of used petri dishes and gloves according to the directions from your teacher.
- Place paper towels used to clean lab tables in the trash can.
- Place broken glass and leftover solutions in the separate containers provided.

FILE: A to Z Advertising

MATERIALS AND COSTS (Select only what you'll need. No refunds.)

I. Facilities and Equipment Use

facilities	$480.00/day
personal protective equipment	$10.00/day
microscope	$100.00/day
incubator	$50.00/day
forceps	$5.00/day
metric ruler	$5.00/day
Bunsen burner	$10.00/day
graduated cylinder	$10.00/day
beaker	$10.00/day

II. Labor and Consumables

labor	$30.00/hr
petri dishes of *E. coli*	$10.00 each
fine-point marker	$3.00 each
tape	$0.25/m
distilled water	$1.00/L
cleaning agents	$0.50/mL
alcohol	$0.10/mL
saline solution	$0.50/mL
filter-paper disks	$0.10 each
solution of test soap	provided

Fines

OSHA safety violation	$2,000.00/incident

- 10 mL of hand-soap solution
- 10 mL of dishwashing-soap solution
- 10 mL of household disinfectant
- Bunsen burner and striker (or 5% bleach solution)
- forceps
- 6 filter-paper disks
- tape
- incubator (37°C)
- metric ruler

Estimated Cost of the Job

$1,347.70 (for two students for two days). The invoice presented to the client should include a profit. See page T745-6 for an example of how to prepare an invoice.

Results

Results will vary, depending on the types of soaps used.

Conclusions

Students' data should support their conclusions.

Preparation Tips
- Order sterile paper disks. To make them, punch holes in filter paper, place the disks in a beaker, cover with aluminum foil, and autoclave for 10 minutes.
- To prepare inoculum for a bacterial lawn, mix a loop of *E. coli* in a tube of tryptic soy agar broth. Incubate at 37°C for 24 hours.
- To prepare petri dishes for inoculation, pour heated tryptic soy agar into sterile petri dishes.
- 24 hours before the start of the lab, inoculate petri dishes to prepare bacterial lawns. Place 1 mL of inoculum in the center of the agar in a petri dish, and spread with a sterile spreader.
- To prepare 10% solutions of cleaning agents, mix 1 part of cleaning agent to 9 parts of distilled water. Mark one of the solutions "10% solution of test soap."
- Provide separate containers for the disposal of sealed petri dishes and broken glass.

Disposal
- Collect and autoclave used petri dishes to sterilize.
- Flush solutions down a sink with plenty of water.
- Paper towels used to sterilize lab tables can be thrown in the trash.

Procedural Notes
Safety Precautions
- Discuss all safety symbols and required precautions with students.
- Have students wear safety goggles, gloves, and a lab apron.

Procedural Tips
- Have each class pool its data. Help students develop a data table with heads like those below.

Solutions	Growth after 24 hours				Growth after 48 hours			
	Trial (group)				Trial (group)			
	1	2	3	4	1	2	3	4

- Have students open petri dishes by slowly lifting one side of the lid until it makes about a 45-degree angle with the bottom of the dish.
- Have students sterilize the forceps before picking up a clean filter-paper disk.
- Filter-paper disks should be 1 cm from the edge of a petri dish and at least 2 cm apart.

793

Purpose

Students will observe a variety of protists, describe them, and determine their reaction to light and temperature.

Instructional Goals

Understanding Concepts

Students will

- apply principles of microtechnique to the study of protists.
- relate environmental conditions to the behavior of protists.

Life/Work Skills

Students will demonstrate proficiency in

- making a wet mount.
- using a compound microscope.
- working as part of a team.
- using appropriate safety procedures in the laboratory.

Preparation Notes

Time Required: 50 to 75 minutes

Materials

Materials for this Exploration can be ordered from WARD'S. See page T745-12 for catalog numbers.

Preparation Tips

- Purchase cultures of the following protists: *Paramecium caudatum, Amoeba proteus, Euglena acus, Navicula,* and *Volvox globator.* Blend all of the protist cultures together to form a "protist stew" for students to examine.
- Provide a separate container for the disposal of any broken glass.

CONTINUED ON NEXT PAGE

CHAPTER

19A | Observing the Behavior of Protists

exploration

Skill:

Using a compound microscope

Objectives

- *Make* wet mounts of aquatic protists.
- *Observe* protists with a microscope.
- *Describe* the structure and behavior of aquatic protists.
- *Draw* and *label* the parts of protists.

Materials

- compound microscope
- 3 microscope slides
- 2 coverslips
- DETAIN™ (protist-slowing agent)
- aquatic protist culture
- toothpick
- 40 × 20 mm piece of black paper
- hole punch
- white paper
- light source
- forceps
- 2 capillary tubes
- WARD's silicone culture gum
- hot water
- ice water

Situation

You work for a company that installs backyard ponds. The company is developing a kit that will contain cultures of the protists necessary for a healthy aquatic ecosystem in their ponds. The kit will also have some educational literature about the protists so that customers will know what features a pond must have to ensure the survival of the protists. Your job is to observe the protists that will be included in the kit, describe the protists, and write recommendations for establishing a pond that will provide environments favorable to all of the protists.

Background: Protists are an important part of an ecosystem. They are a part of many food chains, acting as producers, consumers, decomposers, and food for other organisms.

Prelab Preparation

1. List the general characteristics of the kingdom Protista.

2. Review the procedures for using the microscope and for making a wet mount found in the Laboratory Skills section of your textbook.

3. Prepare a data table like the one at the top of the next page.

Procedure

1. Using a microscope slide, make a wet mount with one drop of liquid from the bottom of the protist culture and one drop of DETAIN™. Mix the two drops with a toothpick before you cover them with a coverslip. **CAUTION: Glassware is fragile. Notify your teacher promptly of any broken glass or cuts. Do not clean up broken glass or spills unless your teacher tells you to do so.** Make another wet mount with one drop of liquid from the bottom of the protist culture and no DETAIN™. Observe each slide with a compound microscope, first under low power and then under high power.

2. Locate five types of protists. Identify each protist, and add its name to your data table. Write a brief description of each protist. Observe the distribution of the protists. Predict whether each protist is heterotrophic or autotrophic. Record your

---

ANSWERS

Prelab Preparation

1. Protists have eukaryotic cells, are mostly unicellular, lack cell specialization, and can be autotrophic or heterotrophic.

Analysis

13. The protists adapted to change by moving. *Paramecium* and *Amoeba* move away from light. *Euglena* and *Volvox* move toward light. All but *Navicula* move away from temperature extremes.

14. *Paramecium* and *Amoeba* prefer shade. *Euglena* and *Volvox* prefer sunlight. *Navicula* should grow better in sunlight.

15. Answers will vary. Students should discuss size, depth, light, and shade.

Applications

16. Answers will vary. Students may suggest that heterotrophic protists will move to the cooler bottom of a pond, while autotrophic protists will move or float to the top of a pond, where light is available.

17. Answers will vary. This information will help in designing an ecosystem that provides light for photosynthesis and warmth and shade where protists can escape predators and heat.

18. Landscape architects earn at least a bachelor's degree. Course work emphasizes biology, chemistry, physics, and technical drawing. They must like working with plants and people, have extensive knowledge of plants and their needs, and be creative, artistic, and detail oriented.

Observations	Name of protist				
Description					
Distribution					
Autotroph or heterotroph					
Response to light					
Response to cold					
Response to warmth					

descriptions and predictions in your data table.

3. On a sheet of paper, draw and label an example of each type of protist listed in your data table.

4. Punch a hole in the center of a 40×20 mm piece of black construction paper. Wind the paper around your finger so that it has a slight curl to it.

5. Position the piece of black paper on top of the slide *without* DETAIN™ so that the hole is over the center of the coverslip. Place the slide on white paper, and leave it in a lighted area for about 10 minutes.

6. Gently place the slide on the stage of the compound microscope. **Be careful:** *Do not disturb the black paper.* Using low power, focus on the hole in the black paper. Notice which types of protists are visible through the hole. Using forceps, carefully remove the black paper. Continue observing for 2 to 3 minutes. Record what happens.

7. Hold your finger over one end of a capillary tube, and lower the open end of the tube to the bottom of the protist culture. Remove your finger from the end of the tube. Liquid from the culture will fill the tube. Plug the tube by pushing each end into silicone culture gel.

8. Place the filled and plugged capillary tube on a clean microscope slide. Roll a ball of silicone culture gum on your lab table to make a thin tube about 6 cm long, and make a well around one end of the capillary tube, as shown in the diagram above. Place the micro-observation tube you have made on the stage of your microscope.

9. Place several drops of hot tap water into the well on the microscope slide. Observe the movement of the protists in the tube first under low power and then under high power. Record your observations.

10. Repeat the procedure in step 9 using ice water instead of hot water.

11. Dispose of your materials according to the directions from your teacher.

12. Clean up your work area and wash your hands before leaving the lab.

Analysis

13. **Summarizing Data** How did the protists adapt to changes in their environment?

14. **Analyzing Data** Which of the protists preferred shade? Which preferred sunlight?

15. **Drawing Conclusions** What physical features should a backyard pond have in order to provide favorable environments for many different types of protists? Explain.

Applications

16. **Thinking Critically** Where in a pond are protists likely to be found during very hot weather? Justify your answer.

17. **Thinking Critically** Why is it important to know how protists behave when planning an aquatic ecosystem?

18. **Career Connection** *Landscape architects* design gardens and landscapes for all types of buildings. Find out about the training and skills required to become a landscape architect, and discover how landscape architects combine a variety of organisms in the landscapes they design.

795

exploration notes

SKILL BUILDING   CONTINUED

Additional Background
Diatoms, such as *Navicula*, have tiny oil droplets that allow them to float. *Paramecium, Euglena,* and *Volvox* have organelles (cilia or flagella) for locomotion. *Amoeba* moves by pseudopodia.

Disposal
• Protists and DETAIN™ may be washed down the drain.
• Follow the instructions in the supplier's MSDS for the disposal of silicone culture gum.

Procedural Notes
Safety Precautions
• Discuss all safety symbols and caution statements with students.
• Review the safety rules for working with electrical equipment.

Procedural Tip
Provide several containers of the "protist stew" and eyedroppers or plastic pipets for dispensing.

Sample Data Table

Observations	Name of Protist				
	Amoeba	**Paramecium**	**Volvox**	**Navicula**	**Euglena**
Description	bloblike, pseudopods, colorless*	slipper-shaped, cilia, colorless*	round cluster of cells, green	football-shaped, green, glasslike shell	oval-shaped, a flagellum, green
Distribution	near the bottom	all over	near surface	on debris near bottom	all over
Autotrophic/ heterotrophic	hetero-trophic	hetero-trophic	autotrophic	autotrophic	autotrophic
Response to cold (0°C)	moves away	moves away	moves away	does not move	tends to ball up
Response to warmth (60°C)	moves away	moves away	moves away	does not move	moves away
Response to	moves away	moves away	moves	does not move	moves toward

*In certain cultures, organisms are artificially colored.

CHAPTER

20A

Making a Cladogram

Purpose

Students will construct a cladogram showing the evolutionary relationship of four major plant groups.

Instructional Goals

Understanding Concepts

Students will

• relate derived characteristics to evolutionary advances in plants.

• recognize the limitations of using cladistics as a method of classification.

Life/Work Skills

Students will demonstrate proficiency in

• making a cladogram.

• following directions.

• interpreting data.

• using appropriate safety procedures in the laboratory.

Preparation Notes

Time Required: 50 minutes

Materials

Materials for this Exploration can be ordered from WARD'S. See page T745-12 for catalog numbers.

Preparation Tips

• Before students begin the Exploration, review the processes of classification and evolution. Also discuss the derived characteristics that students will use to classify plants—vascular system, seeds, and flowers.

• Provide gardening or nature magazines if you want students to cut out pictures of the plants for use in their cladograms.

CONTINUED ON NEXT PAGE

exploration

Skill:

Classifying plants by making a cladogram

Objectives

• *Identify* major characteristics of plants.

• *Determine* derived characteristics among four groups of plants.

• *Identify* the out-group among several groups of plants.

• *Construct* a cladogram that shows the evolutionary relationships of four groups of plants.

Materials

• paper
• pencil
• metric ruler
• gardening magazines (optional)
• scissors (optional)
• glue (optional)

Situation

You are the botanist for the Parks and Recreation Department of a small city. The city council recently voted to assemble an interpretive display of the plants found in the area for the city's nature preserve. The display will include a cladogram that shows the evolutionary relationships among common plants found in the local area. Your job is to make a cladogram using the following plants: spruce, horsetail, liverwort, and rose.

Background: **Cladistics** is used to determine the order in which evolutionary lines diverged, or branched. Among several groups of organisms, a group that lacks a characteristic seen in the others is called an **out-group.** The out-group is the most distantly related to the other groups because it has the fewest characteristics in common with the other groups. Any deviations from the characteristics of the out-group are considered **derived characteristics,** or evolutionary changes. Derived characteristics are used to build a **cladogram,** which shows the order in which major lines of organisms diverged from a **common ancestor.** To construct a cladogram showing the evolution of major plant groups, you can use the following derived characteristics: **flowers, seeds,** and **vascular tissue.**

Prelab Preparation

① Define the boldface terms in the **Background** section.

② Describe the process of classification.

③ Prepare a data table like the one at the top of the next page.

Procedure

1. On a separate sheet of paper, draw a diagonal line that rises from left to right and is about 18 cm long. Draw four lines, about 3 cm long and 6 cm apart, that are perpendicular to the diagonal line, as seen in the diagram at right. Your diagram will become a cladogram with four branches.

ANSWERS

Prelab Preparation

1. *cladistics*—method of classifying organisms on the basis of the derived characteristics they share

   out-group—group of organisms that does not share a particular derived characteristic with other related groups of organisms

   derived characteristic—characteristic that appears in a group of organisms due to evolutionary change

   cladogram—branching diagram that shows the evolutionary relationships among groups of organisms based on derived characteristics

   common ancestor—ancestor from which two or more groups of organisms evolved

   flower—reproductive structure of an angiosperm

   seed—plant embryo surrounded by a protective coat

   vascular tissue—specialized tissue that

   conducts water and other nutrients in plants

2. Classification is the process of grouping organisms according to shared characteristics.

Analysis

10. Liverworts and horsetails lack seeds. Liverworts, horsetails, and blue spruces lack flowers.

11. The first plants were nonvascular, like liverworts. Vascular plants evolved from

Plants	Derived Characteristics		
	Flowers	Seeds	Vascular system
Spruce			
Horsetail			
Liverwort			
Rose			
Total number of plants with characteristic (+)			

2. Using your textbook, determine whether each of the plants in your data table has a vascular system, seeds, or flowers. If the plant has a particular characteristic, mark a plus sign (+) in the column for that characteristic. If the plant does not have a particular characteristic, mark a minus sign (−) in the column for that characteristic.

3. Determine the number of groups that share each derived characteristic. To do this, count the number of plus signs (+) in each column of your data table. Write these numbers at the bottom of each column.

4. Look at your data table. The column with the greatest number of plus signs (+) indicates the derived characteristic that is shared by the most plants. In the same column, the plant with the minus sign (−) is considered the out-group. Write the name of this out-group at the end of the branch to the far left side of your cladogram.

5. To the right of the diagonal line and midway between the first two branches, write the name of the derived characteristic shared by the remaining plant groups.

6. Look at your data table again. Go to the column with the next largest number of plus signs. Determine the out-group among the remaining groups. Write the

name of this out-group at the end of the second branch from the left of your cladogram. To the right of the diagonal line and midway between the second and third branches, write the name of the derived characteristic shared by the remaining groups.

7. Determine the out-group among the remaining groups of plants. Write the name of the third out-group at the end of the third branch from the left of your cladogram. To the right of the diagonal line and midway between the third and fourth branches, write the name of the derived characteristic possessed by the last group.

8. Write the name of the last group at the end of the last branch of your cladogram.

9. Illustrate the plant groups in your cladogram with drawings, photographs, or specimens of the plants.

Analysis

10. Analyzing Diagrams According to your cladogram, which plants are in the group that lacks seeds? Which plants are in the group that lacks flowers?

11. Summarizing Information Using your cladogram, describe the sequence of events that occurred in the evolution of the four types of plants in this Exploration.

12. Evaluating Methods What are the drawbacks of using cladistics to classify organisms?

Applications

13. Thinking Critically A city council member wants you to add a favorite garden plant—the bearded iris—to your cladogram. What would be your response to this request?

14. Thinking Critically Can a cladogram be used to identify an unknown plant? Explain your answer.

15. Career Connection *Botanists* study all aspects of plants, including their structure, function, and classification. Find out about the training and skills required to become a botanist, and discover some places that employ botanists.

797

exploration notes
SKILL BUILDING   CONTINUED

Additional Background
Liverworts are nonvascular plants that have neither seeds nor flowers. Horsetails are vascular plants that have neither seeds nor flowers. Spruces are gymnosperms, vascular plants that have seeds but do not have flowers. Roses are angiosperms, which are vascular plants that have both seeds and flowers.

Disposal
none

Procedural Notes
Safety Precautions

nonvascular plants. Plants with seeds evolved from primitive vascular plants, which include horsetails. Plants with flowers, such as roses, evolved from gymnosperms, which include the spruce.

12. Cladistics shows the sequence in which groups of organisms and derived characteristics arose, but it does not show the amount of difference between the groups of organisms and cannot be used to identify unknown organisms.

Applications

13. Answers will vary. The bearded iris can be placed at the end of the cladogram because irises are monocots, which evolved from dicots.

14. No. It does not show all of the characteristics of a group of plants.

15. Botanists obtain at least a bachelor's degree and usually complete a master's degree or a Ph.D. Courses include biology, with an emphasis on plant sciences, chemistry, physics, math, and statistics.

Most botanists work outdoors or in a laboratory. Botanists work for universities, government agencies, and private industries.

Sample Data Table

Plants	Derived Characteristics		
	Vascular system	Seeds	Flowers
Liverwort	−	−	−
Horsetail	+	−	−
Spruce	+	+	−
Rose	+	+	+
Total number of plants with characteristic (+)	3	2	1

Purpose

Students will determine the best method for applying the auxin indoleacetic acid to bean plants in order to induce adventitious root growth.

Instructional Goals

Understanding Concepts

Students will

• apply principles of plant growth to an experiment using live plants.

• recognize how the concentration of plant hormones affects the growth of plants.

Life/Work Skills

Students will demonstrate proficiency in

• working with live plants.

• working as part of a team.

• collecting, recording, and analyzing data.

• communicating the results of an experiment.

• using appropriate safety procedures in the laboratory.

Preparation Notes

Time Required: 50 minutes for setup and 10 to 20 minutes a day for 10 days for observation

Materials

Materials for this Exploration can be ordered from WARD'S. See page T745-12 for catalog numbers.

Preparation Tips

• Plant bean seeds in sand 14 days before the lab is to begin. Water daily to keep the sand moist.

CONTINUED ON NEXT PAGE

---

exploration

Skills:

• **Working with living plants**

• **Graphing results**

Objectives

• *Apply* plant hormones to bean plants.

• *Compare* and *contrast* the effects of different concentrations of an auxin on root growth.

• *Evaluate* the effectiveness of two methods of applying an auxin to bean plants.

Materials

• safety goggles
• lab apron
• 5 flasks (150 mL)
• wax pencil
• 100 mL graduated cylinder
• 300 mL of water
• 5 bean seedlings
• scalpel
• cotton
• 105 mL of indoleacetic acid solution (IAA), 1:10,000
• 105 mL of indoleacetic acid solution (IAA), 1:1,000,000
• 2 small paintbrushes
• metric ruler

Situation

You have just been hired by the United States Department of Agriculture (USDA) as a lab technician for a plant physiologist. As part of your job, you will be conducting experiments to determine how the plant hormone auxin can be used to stimulate root growth. Your first assignment is to compare the effects of auxin concentration and method of application on root growth in bean plant cuttings.

Background: The auxin **indole-3-acetic acid (IAA)** is produced in the new leaves of a plant and then transported to the stem. The IAA initiates the formation of **adventitious roots,** which are roots that grow from a stem.

Prelab Preparation

1 Define the boldface terms in the **Background** section.

2 Predict which method of applying IAA will produce the best root growth.

3 List this experiment's independent variable, dependent variables, constants, and control.

4 Make a data table with six main columns and the following headings: Day, Treatment 1, Treatment 2, Treatment 3, Treatment 4, and Treatment 5. Divide each of the Treatment columns into two columns with the following headings: Number of roots, Length of roots.

Procedure

1. Put on safety goggles and a lab apron.

2. Using a wax pencil, put the initials of everyone in your group on each of the five flasks. **CAUTION: Glassware is fragile. Notify your teacher promptly of any broken glass or cuts. Do not clean up broken glass or spills unless your teacher tells you to do so.** Label the flasks as follows:

Treatment 1—water (leaves and stem)

Treatment 2—1:10,000 IAA (leaves)

Treatment 3—1:1,000,000 IAA (leaves)

Treatment 4—1:10,000 IAA (stem)

Treatment 5—1:1,000,000 IAA (stem)

ANSWERS

Prelab Preparation

1. *Indole-3-acetic Acid (IAA)*—a naturally occurring auxin
   adventitious roots—roots that grow from the stem of a plant

2. Answers will vary.

3. independent variables—IAA concentration, method of IAA application, time in days
   dependent variables—number of roots, length of roots

constants—amount of liquid in flasks, size of flasks, type of plant, amount of light, temperature
control—Treatment 1 (water applied to leaves and stem)

Analysis

12. Answers will vary but should reflect student data. Students should observe little or no root growth with Treatments 1, 3, and 4. Root growth should occur with Treatments 2 and 5.

13. Answers may vary but should reflect student data. Students should notice that IAA concentration affects root growth.

14. Answers will vary but should reflect student data. Students should give reasons to justify their choices.

15. Answers will vary. Students might suggest that increased concentrations of IAA will be more effective for foliar applications and that root growth may occur with stem applications of decreased concentrations of IAA.

3. Place 100 mL of distilled water in the flasks for Treatments 1, 2, and 3. Place 100 mL of the 1:10,000 IAA in the flask for Treatment 4. Place 100 mL of the 1:1,000,000 IAA in the flask for Treatment 5.

4. 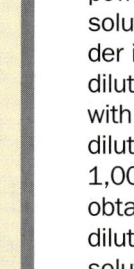 Using a scalpel, carefully cut the stems of five bean seedlings near soil level. Also remove the cotyledons from each plant. **CAUTION: Scalpels are very sharp. Be careful not to cut yourself.**

5. Place one plant in each of the five flasks. Make sure the stems are submerged in the liquid. Pack cotton at the top of each flask to keep the plants upright, as seen in the photo above. *Note: Be careful not to crush or break the stems of the plants.*

6. Using a small paintbrush, coat the leaves of the plant in the Treatment 1 flask with distilled water. Coat the leaves of the plant in the Treatment 2 flask with the 1:10,000 IAA solution. **Using a different paintbrush,** coat the leaves of the plant in the Treatment 3 flask with the 1:1,000,000 IAA solution. Repeat each day for 10 days.

7. Set the flasks in a place where the plants will receive the same light. Observe the plants daily for 10 days. Record the number of roots that appear.

8. Every day after roots appear, carefully remove each plant from its flask, and measure the length (from stem to root tip) of three typical roots. Measure the same three roots each day. Carefully replace each plant in its original flask. Find the average length of the roots for each plant, and record this average in your data table.

9. Dispose of your materials according to the directions from your teacher.

10. Clean up your work area and wash your hands before leaving the lab.

11. Make two graphs of your data. Show "Days" on the *x*-axis of both graphs. Show "Number of roots" on the *y*-axis of one graph and "Average length of roots" on the *y*-axis of the other graph. Use a different color or symbol to plot the data for each treatment.

Analysis

12. **Summarizing Data** What happened to each bean plant over the observation period?

13. **Interpreting Data** Does IAA concentration affect root growth? Explain your answer.

14. **Drawing Conclusions** Which method of applying IAA was the best? What criteria did you use in deciding which was the best method?

15. **Predicting Outcomes** What would happen if you increased the IAA concentration? What would happen if you decreased it?

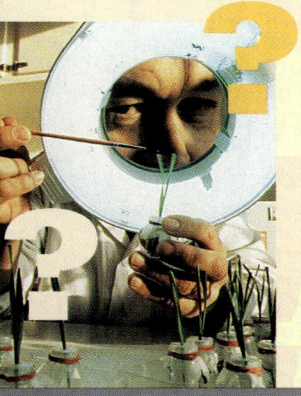

Applications

16. **Thinking Critically** Why is it important to handle living plants carefully during experiments?

17. **Designing an Experiment** Auxin produced in the buds at the tips of some plants prevents the growth of buds lower down on the stems. Design an experiment to determine the effect of removing the bud at the tip of a plant.

18. **Career Connection** *Plant physiologists* study how plant hormones affect plants. Find out about the training and skills required to become a plant physiologist, and research some of the ways that hormones are used to control the growth of plants used for food.

- Purchase Indole-3-acetic Acid (1 g powder). To obtain a 1:10,000 solution, dissolve 1 g of IAA powder in 10 mL of isopropyl alcohol, dilute that solution to 1,000 mL with distilled water, and then dilute 100 mL of that solution to 1,000 mL with distilled water. To obtain a 1:1,000,000 solution, dilute 10 mL of the 1:10,000 solution to 1,000 mL with distilled water. For each dilution, stir continuously for 5 minutes, reversing the direction of stirring every 10–20 seconds.
- Indole-3-acetic Acid crystals are unstable. Store 2–3 weeks under refrigeration. Discard the crystals if they turn brown or have a fecal smell.
- Provide a separate container for disposal of any broken glass.

Additional Background
The concentrations of IAA used in this experiment are expressed as 1:10,000, which is read "one part per ten thousand," and 1:1,000,000, which is read "one part per million."

Disposal
- Place bean plants in the laboratory trash can.
- Pour solutions containing IAA down the drain.

Procedural Notes
Safety Precautions
- Have students wear safety goggles and a lab apron.
- Discuss all safety symbols and caution statements with students.

799

Application
16. Plants must be handled carefully to prevent injuries that could kill them or alter results.

17. Answers will vary. Students could suggest removing the terminal bud and measuring the growth of lateral buds. Experiments should include a control.

18. Plant physiologists usually earn a master's degree or a Ph.D. Courses include general biology, botany, genetics, chemistry, biochemistry, physics, and plant physiology. Plant physiologists must be inquisitive, patient, detail-oriented, and good at problem solving. Auxins are applied to fruit trees to thin the fruits so that maturing fruits will be larger. Gibberellins are used to produce seedless grapes. Ethylene is used to ripen fruits that are picked before they ripen naturally.

Sample Data
Water (Treatment 1) should produce little or no root growth. Foliar application of 1:10,000 IAA (Treatment 2) should produce better root growth than foliar application of 1:1,000,000 IAA. Stem application of 1:10,000 IAA (Treatment 4) should inhibit root growth, while stem application of 1:1,000,000 IAA (Treatment 5) should promote root growth.

Purpose

Students will use indicators to test for sugar, starch, protein, and lipid in foods from plants.

Instructional Goals

Understanding Concepts

Students will

- recognize the uses and limitations of qualitative tests.

Life/Work Skills

Students will demonstrate proficiency in

- using indicators and standards to identify the presence of sugar, starch, and protein in foods.
- following directions.
- collecting, recording, and analyzing data.
- working as part of a team.
- using appropriate safety procedures in the laboratory.

Preparation Notes

Time Required: 45–60 minutes

Materials

Materials for this Exploration can be ordered from WARD'S. See page T745-12 for catalog numbers.

Preparation Tips

- Place indicator solutions in dropper bottles.
- Lugol's solution can be purchased ready-made.
- Benedict's solution can be purchased ready-made.

CONTINUED ON NEXT PAGE

exploration

Skill:

Qualitative analysis for food nutrients

Objectives

- *Prepare* standards to use in testing a food for the presence of sugar, starch, protein, and lipid.
- *Compare* tests for sugar, starch, protein, and lipid in a food to standards.
- *Identify* the nutrients present in food.

Materials

- safety goggles
- lab apron
- wax pencil
- 9 test tubes
- test-tube rack
- test-tube holder
- distilled water
- 2 mL of glucose solution
- dropper bottle of Benedict's solution
- hot-water bath
- 2 mL of 1% starch solution
- dropper bottle of Lugol's solution
- 2 mL of gelatin solution
- dropper bottle of biuret solution
- 5 in. square of brown paper
- 2 mL of vegetable oil
- food sample for four tests
- wooden splint or spatula

Peanut plant

Situation

You have applied for a job as a food technologist with a food manufacturer. If you get the job, you will be analyzing the company's new line of vegetarian foods for nutrient content. All applicants must demonstrate the ability to test a food for the presence of carbohydrates, proteins, and lipids. Obtaining accurate results, and demonstrating good lab techniques and the ability to follow instructions, will mean that you will be asked to return for the final round of interviews.

Background: When you test for *the presence of* a substance, you are performing a **qualitative analysis.** Nutrients such as carbohydrates (sugars and starch) and proteins can be detected by an **indicator,** which is a chemical that produces a characteristic color when a particular substance is present. Lipids can be detected by their ability to make paper **translucent** (able to let light shine through). Tests on substances with an unknown makeup are compared to **standards,** which are the results of tests that show a positive response for a known substance.

Prelab Preparation

1. Define the boldface terms in the **Background** section.
2. Explain how standards are used in research.
3. Prepare a data table like the one at the top of the next page.

Procedure

1. Put on safety goggles and a lab apron.
2. Using a wax pencil, label nine test tubes as follows: sugar—positive; sugar—negative; sugar—sample; starch—positive; starch—negative; starch—sample; protein—positive; protein—negative; protein—sample. Group the tubes in a test-tube rack according to the substance being tested for. Add 2 mL of distilled water to each test tube labeled "negative."
3. Pour 2 mL of glucose solution into the "sugar—positive" test tube. To test for sugar, add a dropperful of Benedict's solution to both the positive and negative test tubes. **CAUTION: If you get a chemical on your skin or clothing, wash it off while calling to your teacher.**

800

ANSWERS

Prelab Preparation

1. *qualitative analysis*—test for the presence of a substance
indicator—chemical that changes from one characteristic color to another in the presence of a particular substance
translucent—allows light to pass through
standard—result of a test on a known substance, with which tests on unknown substances are compared

2. Standards are used as a basis of comparison for identifying unknown substances.

Analysis

11. The tubes labeled "positive test" are standards.

12. sugar—Benedict's solution, starch—Lugol's solution, protein—biuret solution

13. sugar—orange or brick red, starch—dark blue or purple, protein—pink

14. The test for lipid did not involve a color change, as did the tests for the other food nutrients.

15. Natural, unsweetened peanut butter contains starch, protein, and lipid. Popular brands with added sugar contain all four nutrients.

Applications

16. Quantitative analysis tests for the amount of a substance present.

Nutrient	Indicator	Positive test (standard)	Negative test	Food sample (_____)
sugar	Benedict's solution			
starch	Lugol's solution			
protein	biuret solution			
lipid	appearance on paper			

4. 🔥 Place the test tubes in a hot-water bath using a test-tube holder. **CAUTION: Do not touch hot objects with your bare hands. Use tongs, test-tube holders, and padded gloves, as appropriate.** Heat for about 5 minutes. Record any color changes in the test tubes after heating. Using a test-tube holder, set the test tubes in the rack to cool.

5. Pour 2 mL of starch solution into the "starch—positive" test tube. To test for starch, add a dropperful of Lugol's solution to both the positive and negative test tubes. Record the colors you observe in your data table. **CAUTION: Lugol's solution will stain your skin and clothing. Promptly wash off spills to minimize staining.**

6. ☠ Pour 2 mL of gelatin solution into the "protein—positive" test tube. To test for protein, add a dropperful of biuret solution to both the positive and negative test tubes. Record your observations. **CAUTION: If you get a chemical on your skin or clothing, wash it off while calling to your teacher.**

7. Place a square of brown paper on a dry area of your lab table. Smear a drop or two of vegetable oil on the paper, and label the area "positive test" below the spot. Place a few drops of water in another area away from the oil spot. Label the area "negative test" below the water spot. Let the spots dry, and then record your observations.

8. Obtain enough food from your teacher to test for each of the four nutrients. Using a wooden splint or spatula, place a small amount of food in each of the three test tubes labeled "sample." Use the proper indicator to test for the nutrient marked on each test tube. Smear the fourth sample on an unused area of the brown paper. Compare your results with the standards you prepared earlier. Record your results in your data table.

9. 🗑 Dispose of your materials according to the directions from your teacher.

10. 🧼 Clean up your work area and wash your hands before leaving the lab.

Analysis

11. **Recognizing Patterns** Which test tubes contained standards?

12. **Analyzing Results** What indicator detects sugar? starch? protein?

13. **Analyzing Results** What color resulted when sugar was present? starch? protein?

14. **Analyzing Methods** How did the test for lipids differ from the other tests?

15. **Drawing Conclusions** What nutrients were present in the food sample?

Applications

16. **Thinking Critically** If *qualitative analysis* tests for the presence of specific substances, what do you think *quantitative analysis* tests for?

17. **Thinking Critically** Evaluate the use of qualitative tests such as these to help you plan a diet with fewer than 50 g of fat.

18. **Career Connection** *Food technologists* perform a variety of qualitative and quantitative tests on foods. Find out about the training and skills required to become a food technologist, and discover which industries employ food technologists.

801

exploration notes
SKILL BUILDING   CONTINUED

- To prepare a 1% starch solution, add 1 g soluble starch to a small amount of cold water. Dilute to 100 mL with boiling water, and stir until dissolved. Cool before using. Do not store.
- To make a 15% glucose solution, add 15 g of glucose to 100 mL of water. Stir until dissolved.
- To prepare a gelatin solution, dissolve one package of gelatin in 1000 mL of distilled water.
- Supply vegetable oil or margarine for the lipid test.
- Mix peanut butter well to suspend the oil, and thin it slightly with distilled water.
- Prepare separate containers for the disposal of sugar and protein wastes, starch wastes, lipid wastes, and broken glass.

Additional Background
Gelatin contains protein.

Disposal
- Add a few drops of a strong acid, such as 1.0 M sulfuric acid (H_2SO_4), to liquid starch wastes to make the mixture slightly acidic. Then slowly add 0.1 M sodium thiosulfate ($Na_2S_2O_3$) while stirring until the mixture is white or colorless. Pour this solution down the drain.
- Combine sugar and protein wastes. Follow the procedure for the disposal of wastes containing Benedict's solution on page 763.
- Follow the procedure for the disposal of wastes containing Lugol's solution on pages 761 or 763.
- Place pieces of brown paper used for the lipid tests in the trash.

Procedural Notes
Safety Precautions
- Discuss all safety symbols and caution statements with students.
- Have students wear safety goggles and a lab apron.
- Tell students that the iodine in Lugol's solution can cause serious damage to their eyes. If students get iodine in their eyes, they should immediately go to the laboratory eye-wash station, flush eyes with water for at least 15 minutes, and then see a doctor for further treatment.

17. Answers may vary. Students should recognize that qualitative tests indicate only that lipid is present, not how much is there. Therefore, such tests cannot be used to plan a diet that provides a certain amount of a nutrient.

18. Food technologists must obtain at least a bachelor's degree and often obtain a master's or a doctoral degree in biology, chemistry, or agriculture. They work in food and beverage industries and for many federal and state agencies.

Sample Data Table

Nutrient	Indicator	Positive test (standard)	Negative test	Food sample (peanut butter)
sugar	Benedict's solution	turns orange or brick red	stays blue-green	Answers may vary
starch	Lugol's iodine	turns deep blue or black	stays red-brown	+
protein	biuret solution	turns pink	stays light blue	+
lipid	appearance on brown paper	makes paper translucent	paper not translucent	+

Purpose

Students will identify nutrients found in foods from plants.

Instructional Goals

Student Objective

• Identify the nutrients present in several foods.

Life/Work Skills

• using indicators to test for sugar, protein, starch, and lipid
• allocating resources
• acquiring, organizing, and interpreting data
• working as part of a team
• communicating effectively
• using appropriate safety procedures in the laboratory

Preparation Notes

Time Required: 90–120 minutes

Prelab Discussion

Review the procedure used in Exploration 22A. Answer any questions students may have. Ask students the following questions to guide their thinking:

• What indicators are used to test for sugar? for starch? for protein? *(sugar— Benedict's solution; starch—Lugol's solution; protein—biuret solution)*
• What indicated the presence of lipid? *(translucency of brown paper)*
• If you were testing a food, how would you get it into a form that could be tested in a test tube and mixed readily with an indicator? *(mix with water, cut into small pieces, mash into a paste)*

Materials

Materials for this Investigation can be purchased from WARD'S. See page T745-12 for catalog numbers. Provide the items in

CONTINUED ON NEXT PAGE

22B Identifying Nutrients in Foods—School Menu

Prerequisites

• **Exploration 22A: Identifying Nutrients in Foods** on pages 800–801
• **Review** the following:
  1. indicators
  2. the use of standards

Mt. Pleasant Private Academy

March 1, 1997

Mr. John Williams, Director
Food Technology Division
BioLogical Resources, Inc.
101 Jonas Salk Dr.
Oakwood, MO 65432-1101

Dear Mr. Williams:

Our elementary students (284 in all) are busy getting ready to celebrate National Nutrition Week in April. I would love for our teachers to give them an exciting lesson on foods from plants. Young children just love colors, and I have heard that there are bright color tests for the good things in foods. Here is a list of some foods that will be served in the cafeteria during that week: potatoes, corn, white beans, whole-wheat rolls, potato chips, bananas, and peanut butter. Could you run some of those tests and let me know what good things are in these foods? Tell me how to do the tests, too, so that the teachers in our lower grades can perform the tests for their students. If the students can see some bright colors, I just know they won't forget which foods have those good carbohydrates, lipids, and proteins. The board is willing to pay your normal fee. Thank you so much.

Sincerely,

Amanda Brown

Ms. Amanda Brown, Chairperson
Education Advisory Board
Mt. Pleasant Private Academy

Required Precautions

• **Wear safety goggles and a lab apron.**
• **Do not touch hot objects with your bare hands. Use tongs, test-tube holders, and padded gloves, as appropriate.**
• **If you get a chemical on your skin or clothing, wash it off while calling to your teacher.**
• **Wash your hands before leaving the laboratory.**

SAMPLE SOLUTION

Question

What nutrients do each of the foods contain?

Proposed Procedure

1. Prepare three sets of seven test tubes. Label one set of test tubes "Sugar," one set "Starch," and one set "Protein." Label one test tube in each set with one of the seven types of foods.
2. Add a dropperful of Benedict's solution to each test tube labeled "Sugar." Place the test tubes in a hot-water bath using a test-tube holder. Heat for 5 minutes. Record any color changes in a data table.
3. Add a dropperful of Lugol's solution to each test tube labeled "Starch." Record any color changes.
4. Add a dropperful of biuret solution to each test tube labeled "Protein." Record any color changes.
5. Place a dab of each food sample on a piece of brown paper. Let each sample dry before checking for translucency.

Materials (per lab group)

• safety goggles
• lab apron
• wax pencil
• 21 test tubes
• test-tube rack
• test-tube holder
• 7 food samples
• 7 wooden splints
• sheet of wax paper

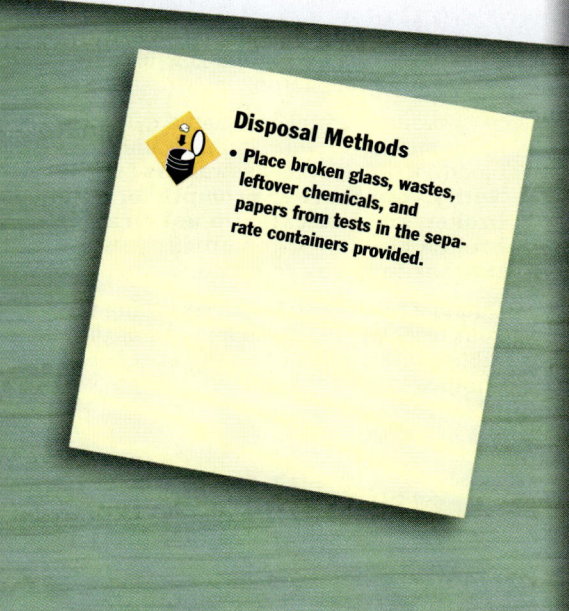

MEMORANDUM

To: Team Leader, Food Testing Dept.
From: John Williams

An education board member wants an exciting lesson for elementary students who are studying nutrition. Please analyze the foods she has listed using indicator tests, when possible, that teachers can repeat. Ms. Brown will need a list of nutrients, including lipids, in these foods and directions on repeating the tests so that teachers can show their students the colors that result when indicators are used to test for nutrients in foods. Thanks for doing this promptly.

Before you begin, you must submit a proposal for my approval. **Your proposal must include the following:**
- the **question** you are seeking to answer
- the **procedure** you will use
- a detailed **data table**
- a complete, itemized list of proposed **materials** and **costs** (including the use of facilities, labor, and amounts needed)

When you finish your tests, prepare a report in the form of a business letter to Ms. Amanda Brown. **Your report must include the following:**
- a paragraph describing the **procedure** you followed to test the food samples
- a complete **data table**
- your **conclusion** about the nutrients in the cafeteria foods being served that week
- a detailed **invoice** showing all materials and labor plus the total amount due

Disposal Methods
- Place broken glass, wastes, leftover chemicals, and papers from tests in the separate containers provided.

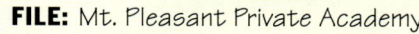

FILE: Mt. Pleasant Private Academy

MATERIALS AND COSTS (Select only what you'll need. No refunds.)

I. Facilities and Equipment Use

facilities	$480.00/day
compound light microscope	$100.00/day
personal protective equipment	$20.00/day
hot-water bath	$15.00/day
test-tube rack	$5.00/day
test-tube holder	$5.00/day
test tubes	$2.00 each

II. Labor and Consumables

labor	$30.00/hour
food samples	$5.00 each
Benedict's solution	$20.00/dropper bottle
Lugol's solution	$20.00/dropper bottle
biuret reagent	$20.00/dropper bottle
Sudan III	$20.00/dropper bottle
wax pencil	$2.00 each
wax paper	$0.50/sheet
brown paper	$0.50/square
wooden splints	$0.10 each

Fines

OSHA safety violation	$2,000.00/incident

- dropper bottle of Benedict's solution
- dropper bottle of Lugol's solution
- dropper bottle of biuret solution
- hot-water bath
- 7 pieces of brown paper

Estimated Cost of the Job

$1,355.70 (for two students for two days). The invoice students present to the client should include a profit. See page T745-6 for an example of how to prepare an invoice.

Conclusions

Answers will vary. Students' data should support their conclusions.

Results

Nutrients in Foods

Nutrient	Potato	Corn	White beans	Roll	Potato chips	Banana	Peanut butter
Sugar	–	+	–	+	–	+	–
Starch	+	+	+	+	+	+	+
Protein	–	+	–	+	–	+	+
Lipid	–	–	–	+	+	–	+

---

the "Materials and Costs" list on the pupil's page. Some of these items are distracters. See "Sample Solution" to estimate what each group will use.

Preparation Tips
- Prepare labeled containers for food samples. Moisten, mash, crush, or finely chop foods so they can be placed in a test tube with a spatula. Each group will need four samples of each food.
- Lugol's solution can be purchased ready-made.
- Benedict's solution can be purchased ready-made.
- Prepare several dropper bottles of each indicator.
- Prepare separate containers for the disposal of sugar and protein wastes, starch wastes, lipid wastes, and broken glass.

Disposal
- Follow the directions on page 801 for the disposal of liquid starch wastes and for the disposal of sugar and protein wastes.
- Pieces of brown paper used for the lipid tests can be placed in the trash.

Procedural Notes
Safety Precautions
- Discuss all safety symbols and required precautions with students.
- Have students wear safety goggles and a lab apron.
- Remind students that the iodine in Lugol's solution can cause serious damage to their eyes. If students get iodine in their eyes, they should go immediately to the laboratory eye-wash station, flush eyes with water for at least 15 minutes, and then see a doctor for further treatment.
- Remind students that test tubes being heated should never be pointed toward anyone.

Procedural Tip
Have students transfer a dime-sized dab of each food sample to labeled pieces of wax paper. They can divide each sample into four sections and use one section for each test.

Purpose

Students will construct a model that demonstrates the function of a kidney.

Instructional Goals

Understanding Concepts

Students will

- relate the function of the kidney to water conservation as an adaptation to life on land.

Life/Work Skills

Students will demonstrate proficiency in

- using a model to demonstrate a biological process.
- interpreting the results of an experiment.
- communicating the results of an experiment.
- working as part of a team.
- using appropriate safety procedures in the laboratory.

Preparation Notes

Time Required: 50 minutes (for setup and initial observations); 20 minutes 24 hours later (for observations and cleanup)

Materials

Materials for this Exploration can be ordered from WARD'S. See page T745-12 for catalog numbers.

Preparation Tips

- Purchase the "unfiltered blood" ready-made.
- Provide separate containers for the disposal of dialysis tubing, liquids, and any broken glass.

CONTINUED ON NEXT PAGE

exploration

Skill:
Modeling a biological process

Objectives

- *Construct* a model of the action of a kidney.
- *Predict* the outcome of an experiment.
- *Relate* changes in color and turgor to evidence of osmosis.
- *Evaluate* the function of the kidney as an adaptation for living on land.

Materials

- safety goggles
- lab apron
- 250 mL beaker
- graduated cylinder
- distilled water
- kidney dialysis tubing
- "unfiltered blood"
- masking tape, adhesive label, or wax pencil
- 2 pieces of string

Situation

You are an assistant to the zoologist for a natural-science museum. Part of your job is to set up demonstrations that teach museum visitors about the structure, function, and behavior of animals. The museum is building a large display that features adaptations that enabled animals such as the Iguana lizard seen below to live successfully on land. Today you will be setting up a demonstration that shows how a kidney removes nitrogen-containing wastes from the blood with little loss of water.

Background: Within a kidney, blood passes through a series of filtering units called nephrons. A nephron contains capillaries, which carry blood to be filtered, and ducts (tubes), which collect small particles of substances such as salt, water, glucose, and urea. Some of these particles are reabsorbed into the blood along with much of the water. Some of the water and the urea remain in the ducts and are excreted from the body as urine.

Prelab Preparation

1 Define the following terms: nephron, capillary, duct, diffusion, osmosis, urea.

2 Describe the function of a kidney.

3 Make a data table like the one at the top of the next page.

Procedure

1.  Put on safety goggles and a lab apron.

2. Using a 25 mL graduated cylinder, measure about 20 mL of "unfiltered blood." **CAUTION: Glassware is fragile. Notify your teacher promptly of any broken glass or cuts. Do not clean up broken glass or spills unless your teacher tells you to do so.**

3. Obtain a piece of wet dialysis tubing from your teacher. Tightly tie one end of the tubing with a piece of string, as seen in the photo at right.

ANSWERS

Prelab Preparation

1. nephron—filtering unit of the kidney
capillary—smallest type of blood vessel
duct—tube that carries body fluids
diffusion—movement of particles from an area of greater concentration to an area of lesser concentration
osmosis—diffusion of water through a selectively permeable membrane
urea—nitrogen-containing waste made during metabolism and found in urine

2. rid the body of nitrogenous wastes with little loss of water

Analysis

11. The "blood" in the bag stayed red, while the solution in the beaker turned yellow. Also, the bag became more turgid.

12. This liquid is in the cells of a nephron. Labels could say "Cytoplasm in the cells of a nephron."

13. Answers will vary. Students should mention that diffusion caused the movement of "urine" from the blood into the kidney tubule and that osmosis caused water to move from the beaker into the dialysis-tubing bag.

14. Answers will vary. One answer for the first question should state that "blood" remained inside the dialysis-tubing bag, and one answer for the second question should state that "urine" entered the solution in the beaker.

15. Answers will vary. Students' scripts should indicate that "blood" stays in the

Observations	Inside dialysis tubing	In the beaker
Initial color		
Color after 30 minutes		
Prediction		
Color after 24 hours		

4. Wet your fingers with tap water, and open the tubing by rubbing the untied end of the tubing between your fingers. Pour the 20 mL of "unfiltered blood" into the open end of the tubing. Tightly tie this end of the tubing with a piece of string. **CAUTION: Dyes in the "unfiltered blood" will stain your skin and clothing. Promptly wash off spills to minimize staining.** The dialysis-tubing bag you have made represents the blood vessels that enter a kidney.

5. Rinse the dialysis-tubing bag with tap water in the sink. Place the dialysis-tubing bag into a 250 mL beaker. Using a wax pencil, write your initials on the beaker. Fill the beaker to within 2–3 cm (about 1 in.) of the top with cold tap water. Record the beginning colors of the solutions inside the bag and in the beaker.

6. After 30 minutes, record the color of the solution in the beaker. While observing the contents of the tubing and of the beaker for the remainder of the lab period, predict what will happen in the next 24 hours. Write your prediction in your data table.

7. Clean up your work area and wash your hands before leaving the lab.

8. After 24 hours, observe any changes that have occurred in the beaker and in the dialysis-tubing bag. Record these observations in your data table.

9. Dispose of your materials according to the directions from your teacher.

10. Clean up your work area and wash your hands before leaving the lab.

Analysis

11. **Summarizing Results** Describe any changes that occurred inside the dialysis-tubing bag and in the beaker.

12. **Inferring Relationships** In what part of a kidney do you find the liquid that the water in the beaker represents? Write a label for the water in the beaker to use in your display.

13. **Relating Information** On the audiotape that will accompany your display, you have no more than 15 seconds to explain the changes you observed in your model. Write a script for what you would say, and record the time required to read the script.

14. **Drawing Conclusions** Provide four multiple-choice answers for each of the following questions, which you will include in your display: What substance remained in the dialysis-tubing bag? What substance entered the water in the beaker? Indicate the correct answer for each question.

15. **Making Inferences** For your audiotape program, write a script that explains why the "blood" remains in the dialysis-tubing bag while the "urine" passes into the beaker.

Applications

16. **Thinking Critically** What circumstances would cause water to move out of the dialysis-tubing bag (bloodstream) and into the beaker (collecting ducts of a nephron)?

17. **Thinking Critically** Complete the script for your audiotape program by writing an explanation of why the kidney is an important evolutionary advance for land animals.

18. **Career Connection** *Museum-exhibit technicians and education specialists* design and build museum exhibits. Find out about the training and skills necessary to become either an exhibit technician or an education specialist for a natural-science museum.

Disposal
• The liquids can be poured down the drain. Have students cut dialysis-tubing bags and empty their contents into the sink or a designated container.
• Used dialysis tubing can be placed in the trash.

Procedural Notes
Safety Precautions
• Have students wear safety goggles and a lab apron.
• Discuss all safety symbols and caution statements with students.

Procedural Tips
• Soak the dialysis tubing in advance to make manipulation of the tubing easier.
• Tell students that the knots at the ends of the dialysis-tubing bags must be tight so that liquid does not leak out.

dialysis-tubing bag because its particles are too large to cross the membrane and that "urine" enters the beaker because its molecules are small enough to cross the membrane.

Applications
16. Answers will vary. Water would move out of the dialysis-tubing bag (bloodstream) and into the beaker (collecting ducts of a nephron) if the salt concentration in the beaker were *higher* than the salt concentration inside the bag.

17. Answers will vary. Students should make the points that land animals are constantly losing water and that kidneys enable them to conserve water while excreting nitrogenous wastes.

18. Museum-exhibits technicians must complete high school. Course work should include algebra, geometry, biology, chemistry, and woodworking. Museum education specialists complete at least an undergraduate college degree. Course work should emphasize all of the natural sciences. Museum technicians and specialists should be creative and enjoy working with people.

Sample Data Table

Observations	Inside dialysis tubing	In the beaker
Initial observations	deep red	colorless
Color after 30 minutes	deep red	colorless to slightly yellow
Hypothesis	will be red	will be yellow
Color after 24 hours	red	yellow

Investigation notes

Purpose

Students will collect, identify, and display insects from the local area.

Instructional Goals

Student Objectives

- Collect insects from the local area.
- Use a dichotomous key to identify the order each insect belongs to.
- Construct a display showing insects that are representative of several insect orders.

Life/Work Skills

- identifying and displaying insects
- selecting and using appropriate materials and techniques
- allocating resources
- communicating effectively
- working as part of a team
- using appropriate safety procedures in the laboratory

Preparation Notes

Time Required: Two 50-minute class periods for group planning. Allow some time each day for questions and observations. Give students one to two weeks to complete projects outside of class.

Prelab Discussion

Discuss the use of a dichotomous key with students. Tell students that to use the key provided, they should start at the pair of statements marked *1*. Have students choose whether an insect is best described by 1a or 1b. Tell students that in the third column, they will find the name of an insect order or a number that directs them to the next pair of descriptive statements. Ask students the following questions to guide their thinking:

CONTINUED ON NEXT PAGE

26A Classifying Insects

Prerequisite

- **Review** the following:
  1. characteristics of insects
  2. definition and use of a dichotomous key

March 28, 1997

Shing Chun
Director of Development
BioLogical Resources, Inc.
101 Jonas Salk Dr.
Oakwood, MO 65432-1101

Dear Mr. Chun,

I can't tell you how much we have enjoyed the beautiful garden that your company donated to our school. Our students have learned a lot about gardening and plants. The garden has also attracted many insects. I want our students to be able to identify some of these insects and to understand that many garden insects are beneficial. Our PTA suggested that we add a display on insects to the garden. The following is a list of the things we would like the display to do.

- give the common name and scientific name of each insect
- indicate whether insects are harmful or beneficial to plants
- teach students how to use a key to identify an organism

I thought you might be interested in helping us provide this educational opportunity for our students. Could your staff construct an insect display like the one described above? I would appreciate any help that you can give us.

Sincerely,

Danielle Andrews

Danielle Andrews
Principal
Aldous Huxley
Elementary School

Required Precautions

- **Wear gloves when handling stinging insects.**
- **Do not attempt to collect stinging insects if you are allergic to insect stings.**
- **Wash your hands before leaving the laboratory.**

806

SAMPLE SOLUTION

Question

What is the best way to display insects so that they can be used to identify unknown insects?

Proposed Procedure

1. Collect live insects in small jars.
2. Using the dichotomous key provided, identify the order of each insect.
3. Use field guides to find the scientific name of each insect.
4. Create a display using the dichotomous key provided and the insects or sketches of insects to represent each order in the key.

Materials (per lab group)

- disposable gloves
- 20 small jars with holes in the lids
- stereomicroscope
- 2 field guides
- 5 markers or colored pencils
- 1 container of glue
- 2 sheets of poster board
- 10 m of colored string or yarn
- 10 sheets of paper

Estimated Cost of the Job

$1,438.00 (for two students for two days).* The invoice students present to the client should include a profit. See page T745-6 for an example of how to prepare an invoice.
*Materials and costs could vary widely. Allow students to be creative.

M E M O R A N D U M

To: Team Leader, Entomology Dept.
From: Shing Chun

Our board of directors has given me the go-ahead for this project. I want your team to put together a display that will be donated to the school. The display should include at least 20 insect specimens. Please collect a variety of insects from many different habitats.

I have attached a dichotomous key to the major insect orders. Use this key in constructing your display. Not all of the orders in this key are found in our area. You may also include other orders of insects that you find.

Before you start your work, you must submit a proposal for my approval. **Your proposal should include the following:**

- the **procedure** you will use
- a complete, itemized list of proposed **materials** and **costs** (including use of facilities, labor, and amounts needed)

When you finish, write a business letter to Ms. Andrews describing the procedure you used to construct your display. Your letter will accompany the completed project. Keep a careful record of the cost of all materials and labor. Because our donations are tax deductible, we will need this for our records.

Disposal Methods
- Live insects can be released.
- Place dead insects in the trash.

Dichotomous Key to Major Orders of Insects

1a	Wings lacking	Go to 2
1b	Wings present	Go to 3
2a	Abdomen narrowly joined to thorax	Hymenoptera (ants, bees, wasps)
2b	Antlike body; abdomen broadly joined to thorax	Isoptera (termites)
3a	Two wings; mouthparts adapted for sucking	Diptera (flies)
3b	Four wings	Go to 4
4a	Forewings hard, shield-like, and meeting in a straight line down the back	Coleoptera (beetles)
4b	Wings membranous, at least in part	Go to 5
5a	Wings broad and covered with scales; tubelike, sucking mouthparts	Lepidoptera (moths, butterflies)
5b	Not so	Go to 6
6a	Hindwings smaller than forewings; chewing mouthparts	Hymenoptera (wasps, ants, bees)
6b	Not so	Go to 7
7a	Hindwings as large as or larger than forewings; wings held straight	Odonata (dragonflies, damselflies)
7b	Not so	Go to 8
8a	First pair of wings thickened at base; upper thorax shield shaped	Hemiptera (true bugs)
8b	Not so	Go to 9
9a	Wings held sloping at sides when at rest; piercing and sucking mouthparts	Homoptera (cicadas, leafhoppers)
9b	Forewings straight and leathery; hindwings membranous and folded under forewings	Orthoptera (cockroaches, crickets, grasshoppers)

FILE: Aldous Huxley Elementary School

MATERIALS AND COSTS (Select only what you'll need. No refunds.)

I. Facilities and Equipment Use

facilities	$480.00/day
personal protective equipment	$10.00/day
stereomicroscope	$100.00/day
hand lens	$50.00/day
insect net	$2.00/day
small jar with lid	$2.00/day
forceps	$5.00/day
field guide for insects	$5.00/day

II. Labor and Consumables

labor	$30.00/hr
markers	$2.00 each
colored pencils	$2.00 each
glue	$2.00/bottle
poster board	$0.50/piece
paper	$0.25/piece
colored string or yarn	$0.25/m
Fines	
OSHA safety violation	$2,000.00/incident

807

Results

Students should collect a variety of insects, show an understanding of the use of a dichotomous key, and have a neatly organized and thorough display. The types of insects collected will vary depending on the time of year and your geographic location.

Conclusions

Students should recognize that there is great diversity among the insects.

- What are the major characteristics of insects? (*segmented bodies with the segments fused into three regions; specialized appendages for flying, walking, grasping, chewing, and sensing the environment; malpighian tubules; and an exoskeleton*)
- Where do orders fall in a classification system? (*Orders fall between classes and families.*)

Materials
Materials for this Investigation can be purchased from WARD'S. See page T745-12 for catalog numbers. Provide the items in the "Materials and Costs" list on the pupil's page. Some of these items are distracters. See "Sample Solution" to estimate what each group will use.

Preparation Tips
- Students can collect and keep live insects in jars with small air holes in their tops. You may want to require students to collect a minimum number of orders. If there are not enough live specimens available, provide preserved specimens for students to use in their displays.
- Provide a stereomicroscope so that students can observe the insects more closely.
- Provide students with several insect field guides.

Disposal
- Live insects can be released.
- Dead insects can be thrown in the trash.
- Mounted specimens of insects should be returned to the teacher.

Procedural Notes
Safety Precautions
- Discuss all safety symbols and required precautions with students.
- Advise students to wear protective gloves when handling live insects.

Purpose

Students will use cladistics to show evolutionary relationships among seven groups of animals.

Instructional Goals

Student Objectives

• Determine the derived characteristics of a given group of organisms.
• Construct a cladogram of seven major vertebrate groups.
• Design a display that will show the evolutionary relationships among groups of vertebrates.

Life/Work Skills

• acquiring, organizing, and interpreting data
• selecting and using appropriate materials and techniques
• allocating resources
• communicating effectively
• working as part of a team

Preparation Notes

Time Required: two 50-minute periods for planning and 1–2 weeks outside of class to complete projects

Prelab Discussion

Review the procedure in Exploration 20A and the processes of classification and evolution. Discuss the derived characteristics that students can use to classify vertebrates—spine, jaws, pectoral fins, bony skeleton, tail, lungs, four-chambered heart, feathers, hair, opposable thumb. Ask students the following questions to guide their thinking:

• What characteristic is shared by all vertebrates? *(a spine)*
• What does a cladogram indicate? *(the order in which related groups of organisms evolved)*

CONTINUED ON NEXT PAGE

28A | Making a Cladogram— Wildlife Zoo

Prerequisites

• **Exploration 20A: Making a Cladogram** on pages 796–797
• **Review** the following:
  1. characteristics of vertebrates
  2. definition and preparation of a cladogram

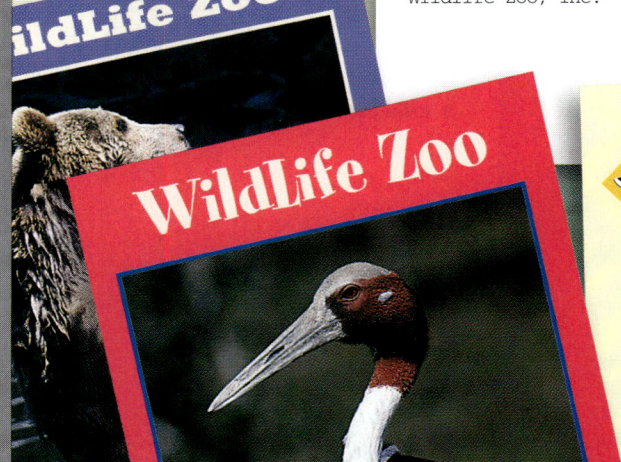

Wildlife Zoo, Inc.
Valleyview, VT 10201-2111

January 15, 1997

Shing Chun
Director of Development
BioLogical Resources, Inc.
101 Jonas Salk Dr.
Oakwood, MO 65432-1101

Dear Mr. Chun,
I am the director of a small zoo. We also do wildlife rehabilitation. Each year, hundreds of school children from the surrounding area tour our zoo. Our enthusiastic volunteers conduct educational programs for all age groups.

Recently, we received a grant from a wildlife conservation organization. The grant is to be used to provide more educational opportunities for the zoo's visitors. Our board of directors wants to use some of the grant money to build a new exhibit that shows the evolutionary relationships among the animals in the exhibit.

An architect will produce the blueprints for the exhibit. However, I need someone to "do the science" for the project. I want your company to submit a plan for displaying zoo animals in a way that shows their evolutionary relationships. We are willing to pay your normal fees. Please bill us when you finish the work.

Sincerely,

Jerome Franklin
Director,
Wildlife Zoo, Inc.

Required Precautions
• Handle scissors carefully.

SAMPLE SOLUTION

Plan

Student plans will vary. Allow students to be creative.

Proposed Procedure

1. Create a table showing the vertebrate groups that will be included in a cladogram and the derived characteristics of these groups.
2. Determine the number of groups that share each derived characteristic.
3. Starting with the derived characteristic shared by the most groups, determine the out-group for each characteristic.
4. Construct a cladogram. Write the name of each out-group above a vertical branch, and write the derived characteristic separating each out-group from the remaining groups below the diagonal line and between the branches for the out-group and the remaining groups.

Materials (per lab group)

• scissors
• 7 photographs of vertebrates
• 1 piece of particle board
• 5 markers or colored pencils
• 1 container of glue
• 10 m of colored string or yarn
• 10 pieces of paper

Estimated Cost of the Job

$1,446.00 (for two students for two days in class and five hours outside of class).*

MEMORANDUM

To: Team Leader, Zoology Dept.
From: Shing Chun

This sounds like an exciting and worthwhile project. I want your team to develop a plan for the zoo's exhibit on vertebrate evolution. Then build a model that shows what the exhibit might look like. Use preserved specimens or photographs of the animals for the model, or have one of our artists draw the animals.

I suggest that you base the exhibit on a cladogram showing the relationships among the major groups of vertebrates: jawless fish, cartilaginous fish, bony fish, amphibians, reptiles, birds, and mammals. This could be done in many ways. Be creative! Don't forget to write the description to be placed by each animal in the exhibit. Finally, produce an interpretive brochure that will guide visitors through the exhibit.

Before you build your model, you must submit a proposal for my approval. **Your proposal must include the following:**

- the **plan** you propose for the zoo's new exhibit
- the **procedure** you will use to build your model
- a detailed **data table**
- a **cladogram** showing the evolutionary relationships among vertebrates
- a complete, itemized list of proposed **materials** and **costs** (including use of facilities, labor, and amounts needed)

When you finish, prepare a report in the form of a business letter for Mr. Franklin. **Your report must include the following:**

- a paragraph describing the **plan** you propose for the zoo's new exhibit
- your **interpretive brochure**
- a detailed **invoice** showing all materials and labor plus the total amount due

Disposal Methods
- **Return preserved specimens of animals to your teacher.**

FILE: Wildlife Zoo, Inc.

MATERIALS AND COSTS (Select only what you'll need. No refunds.)

I. Facilities and Equipment Use

facilities	$480.00/day
personal protective equipment	$10.00/day
hand lens	$50.00/day
scissors	$2.00/day

II. Labor and Consumables

labor	$30.00/hr
markers	$2.00 each
colored pencils	$2.00 each
glue	$2.00/bottle
poster board	$0.50/piece
paper	$0.25/piece
colored string or yarn	$0.25/m
photographs of vertebrates	$5.00 each
particle board	$10.00/piece
preserved specimens of vertebrates	$50.00 each

Fines

OSHA safety violation	$2,000.00/incident

- What information is put into a cladogram data table? *(groups of organisms and the derived characteristics they possess)*
- What does each branch point on a cladogram indicate? *(a common ancestor shared by the out-group and the remaining groups)*
- When do derived characteristics shown on a cladogram appear in relation to the evolution of an out-group? *(after an out-group diverges from the common ancestor of the remaining groups)*

Materials

Materials for this Investigation can be purchased from WARD'S. See page T745-12 for catalog numbers. Provide the items in the "Materials and Costs" list on the pupil's page. Some of these items are distracters. See "Sample Solution" to estimate what each group will use.

Preparation Tip

Provide nature magazines or preserved specimens of the vertebrates to be classified for students to use in the construction of their displays.

Procedural Notes

Safety Precautions

- Discuss all safety symbols and required precautions with students.

The invoice students present to the client should include a profit. See page T745-6 for an example of how to prepare an invoice. *Materials and costs could vary widely. Allow students to be creative.

Conclusions

Students should conclude that the vertebrate groups evolved in the following order: lamprey, shark, salmon, frog, alligator, tiger, gorilla.

Derived Characteristics of Vertebrates

Organism	Jaws	Bony skeleton	Lungs	Heart with 4 chambers	Hair	Opposable thumb
Lamprey	–	–	–	–	–	–
Shark	+	–	–	–	–	–
Salmon	+	+	–	–	–	–
Frog	+	+	+	–	–	–
Alligator	+	+	+	+	–	–
Tiger	+	+	+	+	+	–
Gorilla	+	+	+	+	+	+
Number of shared traits	6	5	4	3	2	1

Sample Cladogram

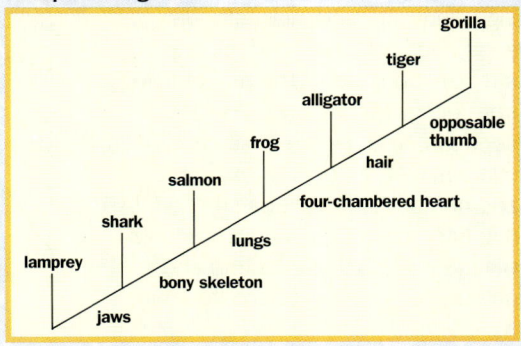

Life Span and Lifestyle

Purpose

Students will use a computer simulation to determine how life span is affected by lifestyle.

Instructional Goals

Students will
- determine how diet, exercise, and smoking affect life span.
- calculate their own life span based on their current lifestyle.

Preparation Notes

Time Required: approximately 1 hour

Preparation Tips

Students should work individually on this exercise so that each student can have the opportunity to determine his or her life span.

Prelab Discussion

Before students begin the lab, they should be able to answer the following questions:
- Why do doctors encourage their patients to eat a diet low in saturated fat? *(Diets high in saturated fat increase the likelihood of cardiovascular problems such as stroke and heart disease.)*
- Which foods contain saturated fat? *(In general, animal products such as meat, eggs, milk, and cheese are high in saturated fat. Some plant products, such as coconut oil and palm oil, also contain saturated fat.)*
- What is cancer? *(Cancer is uncontrolled cell division caused by mutations in the genes that control cell reproduction.)*

Additional Background

A century ago, infectious diseases like pneumonia and influenza were the leading causes of death in the United States. Today, the two leading killers are cardiovascular disease (including heart attack and stroke) and cancer. The risk of dying from either of these two diseases depends, to a degree, on factors such as diet, amount of exercise, and number of cigarettes smoked. In this Interactive Exploration, students will manipulate these factors and determine how they affect life span.

CONTINUED ON NEXT PAGE

interactive exploration

Objectives
- *Simulate* how weight, smoking, amount of exercise, and diet affect life span.
- *Determine* your projected life span based on your current lifestyle.

Materials
- computer with CD-ROM drive
- CD-ROM *Interactive Explorations in Biology: Human Biology*

Background: How long will you live? Although genes play a role in longevity, lifestyle and diet are also very important. Some important factors include how much exercise you get, how much you eat, and what you eat. This interactive exploration allows you to see how these and other factors affect life span.

Prelab Preparation

1. You will need to calculate the energy content of your diet and your daily energy use. Follow your teacher's instructions.

2. Load and start the program Life Span and Lifestyle. Click the Topic Information button on the Navigation Palette. Read the focus questions and review these concepts: Life Expectancy, Smoking and Health, Diet and Health, and Exercise and Health.

3. Click the word *File* at the top left of the screen, and select Interactive Exploration Help. Listen to the instructions that explain the operation of the exploration. Click the Exploration button at the bottom right of the screen to begin the investigation. You will see an animated diagram like the one below.

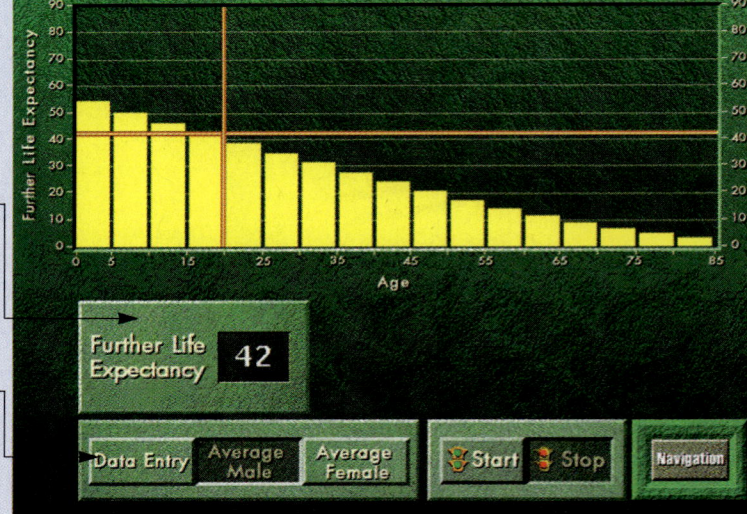

a **Feedback Meter**

Further Life Expectancy: how much longer the selected individual can expect to live

b **Variable**

Data Entry: sends you to the screen on which you can enter lifestyle data and physical characteristics

ANSWERS

Procedure

3. The life expectancy is an additional 73 years, or 88 years total.
5. The second 15-year-old is expected to die eight years sooner than the athlete.
7. The life expectancy is an additional 51 years, or a total of 69 years.

8. Smoking five cigarettes per day reduces life expectancy by about two years.
9. Smoking 20 cigarettes per day reduces life expectancy by about eight years.
10. Student life spans will vary. Among the ways they might increase their life span are exercising more, eating less, reducing the fat content of their diet, and not smoking.

Procedure

Part A: Comparing Different Lifestyles

1. Make a table like the one below in which to record your data. Now compare two 15-year-olds of the same sex who follow different lifestyles. Begin by clicking the Data Entry button.

Age	Sex	Ht.	Wt.	Exercise	Animal fat in diet	Smok-ing	Calories in diet	Expected life span

2. One 15-year-old is a female athlete who eats a low-fat diet and doesn't drink or smoke. Slide the indicator in each scale that appears on the screen to reflect her characteristics and lifestyle: height, 70 inches; weight, 130 pounds; exercise, 1500 Cals/day; animal fat in diet, 10 percent; smoking, 0 cigarettes/day; alcohol, 0 drinks/day; and diet, 2500 kcal/day. Set the age to 15 years, and click female on the Sex button. Record these values in your table, and click the Close button.

3. Click the Start button. The graph that appears is called a life expectancy histogram and indicates how many additional years this person is expected to live. What is the life expectancy for this 15-year-old athlete? Record this value in your table.

4. Compare this value with that of a female who is the same height, weight, and age but who exercises less. Click the Data Entry button. Slide the exercise scale to 750 Cals/day. Do not change any of the other variables. Record the value of each variable in your table. Click the Close button and then the Start button.

5. Record the life span in your table. Compared with the life expectancy of the 15-year-old athlete, how many years less is this 15-year-old female expected to live?

Part B: Determining the Impact of Smoking

6. Enter the following data for an 18-year-old male: height, 70 inches; weight, 165 pounds; exercise, 1000 Cals/day; animal fat in diet, 20 percent; smoking, 0 ciga-rettes/day; alcohol, 0 drinks/day; and diet, 2200 kcal/day. When you have entered all the data, record the values in your table, and click the Close button.

7. Click the Start button. What is the life expectancy for this 18-year-old?

8. Click the Data Entry button. Slide the smoking indicator to 5 cigarettes/day and record all values in your table. How does this change in lifestyle affect his life expectancy?

9. Repeat step 8, but change the number of cigarettes smoked to 20 per day. How much is life expectancy reduced by smok-ing 20 cigarettes per day?

Part C: Calculating Your Life Expectancy

10. Click the Data Entry button. Refer to the summary of your energy use and energy intake that you prepared earlier. Select the values for your age, sex, height, weight, and lifestyle. Determine your life expectancy, and record it in your table. How could you change your lifestyle to lengthen your life span?

Analysis

11. Assume that the 18-year-old described in step 6 is smoking 10 cigarettes per day. Concerned about his life expectancy, he decides to increase his exercise program to 1200 Cals per day, thinking that the additional exercise will extend his life span. Enter the data and determine if he is correct in his thinking.

12. Assume that the 18-year-old male described in the previous question is thinking about either quitting smoking or reducing the amount of animal fat in his diet to 10 percent. Enter the data for each decision, and determine which factor would have the greater impact on his life expectancy.

811

Analysis

11. Yes, he is correct, but the increase in life span only offsets the reduction caused by smoking. Smoking 10 cigarettes per day reduces life span by about four years, while increasing the amount of exercise to 1200 Cals per day increases life span by about four years.

12. Cutting his fat intake would have a greater effect, increasing his life expectancy by six years.

• The program presents two kinds of data: a single value for further life expectancy and a histogram showing the further life expectancy for each of several age classes. Students may wonder why the histogram shows values for ages above the life expectancy. Point out that the single life expectancy value is an average, meaning that some people are expected to die before they reach this age, while others are expected to live longer.

Procedural Notes
Procedural Tips

• Before beginning this exploration, students will need to calculate three values: the caloric content of their daily diet, the percentage of their caloric intake contributed by animal fat (saturated fat), and the average amount of energy they use each day. Tell students to choose an average day that is representative of their routine. On this day, students should make a detailed list of all the foods that they eat, being careful to record all snacks and the number and sizes of portions. They should also record which activities they took part in and how long they spent at each activity. Students should use a nutrition book or one of the calorie-counting guides available in bookstores to deter-mine the total number of calories in the food they ate. In the explo-ration, they should enter this value as the variable *Calories in Diet*. Have students use the same resource to calculate what percentage of their calories comes from saturated fat. They will enter this value in the pro-gram as the variable *Animal Fat in Diet*. Remind students that this value should be a percent-age. Using their log of daily activi-ties, students should determine their daily expenditure of energy. The list below shows estimates for the amount of energy used during various activities. Students can find more information in a health book or in various books on exercise.

Activity	Calories used per hour
Sleeping	130
Sitting	140
Reading	140
Classwork	160
Walking	400–480*
Cycling	360–780*
Football	860
Swimming	420*
Tennis	480–720*
Running	660–1,560*
Soccer	600

*energy expenditure varies with intensity of effort

CHAPTER **30A** | **Determining the Effect of Drugs on Heart Rate**

exploration

Purpose

Students will determine the effects of stimulant and depressant drugs on the heart rate of *Daphnia*.

Instructional Goals

Understanding Concepts

Students will

• relate changes in an indicator of central nervous system (CNS) function to the effects of stimulant and depressant drugs.

Life/Work Skills

Students will demonstrate proficiency in

• preparing a wet mount.
• monitoring heart rate.
• collecting and recording data.
• communicating the results of lab tests.
• working as part of a team.
• using appropriate safety procedures in the laboratory.

Preparation Notes

Time required: 75–100 minutes

Materials

Materials for this Exploration can be ordered from WARD'S. See page T745-12 for catalog numbers.

Preparation Tips

• All substances can be purchased from local stores and must be in liquid form for the lab.
• To prepare Solution 1, soak one high-nicotine cigarette in 100 mL of distilled water overnight. Filter the solution to remove pieces of tobacco.
• To ensure some consistency, use single-serving coffee bags and tea bags in 100 mL of distilled water to prepare Solutions 2 and 3.
• To prepare Solution 4, dissolve 1 pill or capsule containing phenylpropanolamine HCL (PPA) in 100 mL of distilled water.
• To prepare Solution 5, add 10 mL of ethyl alcohol to 90 mL of distilled water. The volume will be slightly less than 100 mL.

CONTINUED ON NEXT PAGE

Skills:

• **Measuring heart rate**
• **Graphing and analyzing numerical data**

Objectives

• *Observe* the effect of drugs on heart rate.
• *Categorize* several drugs as stimulants or depressants.

Materials

• safety goggles
• disposable gloves
• lab apron
• 5 medicine droppers
• 5 *Daphnia*
• petroleum jelly
• depression slide
• coverslip
• compound microscope
• paper towel cut into five 5 cm squares
• clock with second hand
• 100 mL beaker
• 50 mL of culture water
• Solution 1—tobacco
• Solution 2—coffee
• Solution 3—orange pekoe tea
• Solution 4—diet pill containing phenylpropanolamineHCL
• Solution 5—ethyl alcohol

Situation

As a pharmacist's assistant, you work for a clinic that helps patients recover after heart surgery. Some of these patients need to lose weight. Others need to avoid substances that make their heart beat too fast or too slowly. Your job is to develop a list of beverages and over-the-counter medications that do not cause a change in heart rate of more than 10 percent and that doctors could recommend to patients. For your first round of tests, you decide to use the invertebrate *Daphnia*.

Background: Drugs known as **stimulants** increase the body's metabolism. Others, known as **depressants,** slow the rate of metabolism. **Heart rate** (HR) is one indicator of increased or decreased metabolism. Stimulants and depressants affect the heart rate of *Daphnia* and the heart rate of humans in similar ways.

Prelab Preparation

1 Define the boldface terms in the **Background** section.

2 What is a drug?

3 Prepare a data table like the one at the top of the next page. Complete your data table by adding a row for each of the five solutions to be tested.

Procedure

1.   Put on safety goggles, gloves, and a lab apron.

2. Using a clean medicine dropper, collect one *Daphnia* in fluid from the classroom stock culture. Place the *Daphnia* into the well of a clean depression slide. Place a small dab of petroleum jelly in the well to slow the *Daphnia*'s movement. Add a coverslip, and observe under low power.

3. Collect data to serve as a control by performing step 4.

4. Count the *Daphnia*'s heartbeats for 10 seconds. Record this number under Trial 1 in your data table. Turn off the microscope light, and wait 20 seconds. Repeat the count for Trials 2 and 3, always turning off the light and waiting 20 seconds between counts.

ANSWERS

Prelab Preparation

1. *stimulant*—drug that increases metabolic rate
   depressant—drug that slows metabolic rate
   heart rate—number of times the heart beats in a minute
2. A drug is defined as a chemical that is not normally found in the body and that can alter biological structures and functions.

Analysis

13. Solution 1 (nicotine), Solution 2 (caffeine), Solution 3 (theobromine), and Solution 4 (PPA) should increase HR. Solution 5 (ethyl alcohol) should decrease HR.
14. Answers will vary. Students' data should support their conclusions.
15. Answers may vary. Nicotine, caffeine, theobromine, and PPA are stimulants, while alcohol is a depressant.
16. Previous drugs could continue to affect

| Solution | 10-second Heart Rate | | | | Formulas for calculations | | |
	Trial 1 (A)	Trial 2 (B)	Trial 3 (C)	Average 10 s HR $(A + B + C)/3$ (D)	Average 60 s HR $(D \times 6)$ (E)	Change in HR $(E_{sol} - E_{control})$ (F)	Percent difference $(E_{sol} \div E_{control}) \times 100$ (G)
Control						———	———
1							

5. Use a clean medicine dropper to place a drop of Solution 1 on the depression slide so that it touches one edge of the coverslip. Place a piece of paper towel along the opposite edge of the coverslip to draw the solution into the fluid around the *Daphnia*.

6. Wait one minute for the solution to take effect. Repeat step 4.

7. Place the *Daphnia* in the container provided. Clean the slide and coverslip with soap and water. Rinse thoroughly. Prepare a slide with a fresh *Daphnia* by repeating step 2.

8. Repeat steps 5–7 for test solutions 2–4. Repeat steps 5 and 6 for Solution 5. Use a clean dropper for each solution.

9. Complete the calculations indicated in columns D, E, F, and G of your data table.

10. Make two graphs similar to the one below. Plot the data in column E on the *y*-axis of

graph 1. Plot the data in column F on the *y*-axis of graph 2. Give each graph a title and a label for the *y*-axis. *Note: Allow for negative changes in graph 2. A bar graph would work well in this instance.*

11. 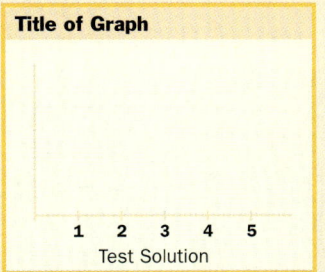 Dispose of your materials according to the directions from your teacher.

12. Clean up your work area and wash your hands before leaving the lab.

Analysis

13. **Recognizing Relationships** Which solutions increased the heart rate of *Daphnia*? decreased the heart rate of *Daphnia*? What drug does each solution contain?

14. **Analyzing Data** Which solutions caused the heart rate of *Daphnia* to differ by more than 10 percent?

15. **Interpreting Data** Based on your data, which solutions contain drugs classified as stimulants? as depressants?

16. **Analyzing Methods** Why did you need to use a fresh *Daphnia* for each solution?

17. **Drawing Conclusions** Which of the substances tested would you recommend to patients whose heart rate should not be allowed to vary by more than 10 percent?

Title of Graph

(graph with x-axis labeled 1 2 3 4 5, Test Solution)

Applications

18. **Designing an Experiment** Design an experiment that investigates the effects of different drug concentrations on heart rate.

19. **Thinking Critically** Why use the percent difference in heart rate, instead of the actual change in heart rate, when comparing the effects of drugs on the heart rate of different organisms?

20. **Career Connection** *Pharmacist's assistants* help pharmacists fill prescriptions and educate patients about their medications and how to take them properly. Find out about the training and skills required to become a pharmacist's assistant, and discover what other tasks they perform.

813

a *Daphnia*, resulting in erroneous conclusions.

17. Answers will vary. Students' data should support their conclusions.

Applications

18. Answers will vary. Students' experimental designs should include a control.

19. Since the resting heart rates of *Daphnia* and humans are so different, comparing actual HR might give a misleading picture of the magnitude of change.

20. Most pharmacist's assistants receive training in programs offered by community colleges, vocational schools, or hospital pharmacies. A high school degree or GED is required for these programs. Courses include health, health-care systems, pharmacy ethics and law, anatomy, physiology, and chemistry. Pharmacy assistants perform many tasks, such as labeling medical doses; maintaining patient records; and assembling, preparing, and delivering medications.

- **Do not use any prescription drugs for this Exploration.** You may want to have students test other drugs. Read the labels and package inserts of over-the-counter drugs carefully to be sure that a drug is appropriate for students to use in this Exploration.
- Provide separate containers for disposal of Solution 1, all other solutions, and broken glass.
- Provide a container with culture water for "used" *Daphnia*.

Additional Background
Daphnia, also called water fleas, are crustaceans found in ponds and lakes all over the world. Their transparent exoskeletons make them ideal subjects for experiments such as this one.

Disposal
- All solutions except Solution 1 (nicotine) may be poured down the drain with running water.
- Combine all Solution 1 wastes, and add 5 mL of full-strength chlorine bleach. Stir the mixture, and then heat to a gentle boil. Boil for five minutes. Let the mixture cool, and pour it down the drain.

Procedural Notes
Safety Precautions
- Discuss all safety symbols and caution statements with students.
- Have students wear safety goggles, gloves, and a lab apron.
- Tell students that nicotine is toxic and can be absorbed through the skin. Students should not be allowed to clean up spills or broken glass. Wear sturdy leather gloves over latex gloves when cleaning up broken glass and spills involving nicotine.

Procedural Tip
Tell students to select one group member to count heart rate and one to monitor time. Have them alternate tasks each time a new solution is tested.

Purpose

Students will use a computer simulation to study the effects of cocaine on the brain.

Instructional Goals

Students will

- identify the roles of neurotransmitters and transporters in a normal synapse.
- recognize how cocaine alters the functioning of a synapse.
- identify the physical basis for cocaine addiction.

Preparation Notes

Time Required: approximately 1 hour

Preparation Tips

If enough computers are available, students can work individually. Otherwise, they should work in teams of two to four.

Prelab Discussion

Before students begin the lab, they should be able to answer the following questions:

- What is a synapse? *(A synapse is the gap between two neurons.)*
- How is an impulse transmitted across a synapse? *(Neurotransmitter molecules carry the impulse across the synapse.)*
- What is the function of transporter molecules in the synapse? *(Transporter molecules remove neurotransmitters from the synapse, clearing the way for the next impulse.)*

Additional Background

The limbic system is the part of the brain that controls the sensation of pleasure. The neurotransmitter dopamine transmits signals between neurons in the limbic system. Dopamine is removed from synapses and returned for recycling by transporter molecules. Cocaine binds to these transporter molecules and blocks reabsorption of dopamine. Dopamine neurotransmitters are "trapped" in the synapses and continue to fire the post-synaptic neurons again and again, stimulating the brain's

CONTINUED ON NEXT PAGE

Objectives

- *Simulate* the effects of cocaine use on a synapse in the brain.
- *Observe* the effect of cocaine use on the number of receptors in a synapse.

Materials

- computer with CD-ROM drive
- CD-ROM *Interactive Explorations in Biology: Human Biology*

Background: This interactive exploration allows you to learn about the physical basis of drug addiction by exploring the direct consequences of using a particular addictive drug, cocaine, on a nerve. The exploration presents an animated diagram of a single nerve synapse within the limbic system of the human brain. You will explore the consequences of introducing cocaine into the synapse.

Prelab Preparation

1. Load and start the program Drug Addiction. Click the Topic Information button on the Navigation Palette. Read the focus questions and review these concepts: The Synapse, Neurotransmitters, Transporters, Neuromodulators, Desensitization, and Addiction.

2. Now click the word *File* at the top left of the screen, and select Interactive Exploration Help. Listen to the instructions that explain the operation of the exploration. Click the Exploration button at the bottom right of the screen to begin the exploration. You will see an animated diagram like the one below.

Feedback Meters

a **Addiction Meter:** the number of receptors in the synapse

b **Pleasure Meter:** the number of receptors firing

Variables

c **Frequency of Use:** changes the frequency at which cocaine is taken

d **Dosage:** varies the cocaine dosage from 0 to 5 grams

814

ANSWERS

Procedure

4. The number of receptors should not change. The synapse loses receptors only when cocaine is used.

7. **Sample Data Table**

Dosage	Addiction meter		Pleasure meter	
	Start	End	Start	End
1 g	1,000	750	100	75
2 g	1,000	500	100	50

9. The red spheres bind to the yellow "boats," the transporter molecules that remove dopamine from the synapse.

10. Because dopamine is not removed from the synapse, it continues to stimulate the post-synaptic neuron and therefore continues to create pleasurable sensations.

12. The number of receptors declines.

13. Yes, because it causes the number of receptors to decrease. Addiction may result because cocaine use stimulates the synapse and restores a normal level of synaptic firing.

Procedure

Part A: Normal Synapse
First you will investigate how the synapse works when no cocaine is present.
1. Before beginning the simulation, record the number of receptors in the synapse. As the simulation runs, observe what happens to the Pleasure Meter and the Addiction Meter. Record the highest and lowest levels reached on the Pleasure Meter.

2. Click the Start button to begin the simulation. Observe what happens when neurotransmitters (blue spheres) are released into the synapse. Each contact with a receptor on the other side of the synapse "fires" the post-synaptic neuron, producing a sensation of pleasure. Note carefully the function of the little yellow "boats," which are transporters that recycle the neurotransmitter molecules so that they don't accumulate in the synapse.

3. Allow the simulation to run for 3 to 4 minutes, noting any changes in the number of receptors (recorded by the Addiction Meter) and in the post-synaptic neuron's firing rate (recorded by the Pleasure Meter). End the simulation by clicking the Stop button.

4. Record the number of receptors in the synapse at the end of the simulation. Did the number of receptors change during the simulation? Explain why or why not.

Part B: Data Collection
Now you will explore the effects of cocaine on the synapse.
5. Click the Reset button to clear the simulation.

6. Slide the Dosage indicator to 1 gram and the Frequency of Use indicator to Weekly.

7. On a separate sheet of paper, create a four-column table like the one shown below.

Addiction meter		Pleasure meter	
Start	End	Start	End

8. Record the number of receptors in the synapse in your table in the column labeled Addiction Meter: Start. Record the post-synaptic neuron firing rate in the column labeled Pleasure Meter: Start.

9. Click the Start button. For each dose of cocaine, you will see a burst of red spheres, representing cocaine, enter the synapse. What happens to the red spheres after they enter the synapse?

10. Based on what happens to the red spheres, explain why cocaine induces pleasurable sensations.

11. The simulation will run until five doses have been taken, which should require about 5 minutes. At the end of the simulation, record in your table the number of receptors and the post-synaptic neuron's firing rate.

12. How does the number of receptors in the synapse change with repeated cocaine doses?

13. Is this dose large and frequent enough to cause addiction? Explain your answer.

14. What was the highest level reached by the Pleasure Meter? Compare this level to the highest level reached without cocaine use, and account for the difference.

15. Explain how the simulation you carried out in Part A serves as a control for this simulation.

16. Click the Reset button to clear the simulation. Set the Frequency of Use Indicator at weekly, but slide the Dosage indicator to 2 grams. Repeat steps 8–14. How do the results of this simulation differ from those obtained with a 1-gram dose?

Analysis

17. Can you conclude, based on your results, that there is a safe dose of cocaine at which addiction does not occur? Explain your answer.

18. Explain why people who are very addicted to cocaine require higher and higher doses to produce pleasure.

815

pleasure center repeatedly. This is why cocaine produces a sense of euphoria.

The nervous system responds to long-term cocaine use by reducing the number of receptors on post-synaptic neurons. Eventually, the number of receptors falls so low that, even in the presence of cocaine, the synapses fire no more often than non-drugged synapses. There are only two ways to achieve a normal rate of firing in drug-altered synapses. One way is withdrawal, waiting for the limbic system to make more receptors. The problem with withdrawal is that the pleasure center is not functioning at normal levels. The other way to reestablish a high rate of firing is to take more cocaine. Over time, however, more and more cocaine is required as the post-synaptic neurons continually reduce the number of receptors they have.

Procedural Notes
Procedural Tips

- Be sure that students are familiar with these instructions for loading and running an interactive investigation before they begin the lab.
- The animation shows a schematic cross-section of a synapse in the limbic system. When the investigation is running, dopamine neurotransmitters, represented by blue balls, diffuse across the synapse and bind to receptors on the post-synaptic neuron (represented by gray, cuplike structures), starting a pleasure-inducing nerve impulse. Transporter molecules, represented by yellow, boat-shaped structures, retrieve the neurotransmitter molecules and return them to the pre-synaptic neuron. Cocaine, represented by red balls, can be introduced into the synapse at five dosages and four frequencies of use.

14. It reached 190. The highest level reached without cocaine was 100. Because cocaine interfered with the recycling of dopamine, more dopamine remained in the synapse longer, and more receptors were stimulated.

15. The simulation in Part A shows how the synapse behaves when no cocaine is present and demonstrates that the number of receptors does not decline in the absence of cocaine.

16. The Pleasure Meter reaches a much higher value (300), and the number of receptors in the synapse falls to a lower value (500), by the end of the simulation.

Analysis
17. There is no safe dose of cocaine. Even the lowest dose taken at the lowest frequency produces the condition necessary for addiction: loss of receptors in the synapse.

18. The more cocaine is taken, the smaller the number of receptors becomes. Therefore, more cocaine is needed to restore normal sensation.

31A | Determining the Effect of Hormones—Polluted Well

Purpose

Students will design an experiment to determine the effect of epinephrine on *Daphnia*.

Instructional Goals

Student Objective

• Determine the threshold concentration at which a hormone affects the heart rate of *Daphnia*.

Life/Work Skills

• monitoring heart rate
• allocating resources
• acquiring, organizing, and interpreting data
• communicating effectively
• working as part of a team
• using appropriate safety procedures in the laboratory

Preparation Notes

Time Required: 45–60 minutes

Prelab Discussion

Review the procedure used in Exploration 30A. Answer any questions students may have. Also, discuss the distinction between the stress response and the fight-or-flight response. Ask students the following questions to guide their thinking:

• What does the term *threshold concentration* mean? *(the lowest concentration that stimulates a response)*
• Which solution has the greatest concentration of the chemical? the smallest concentration? *(C—greatest, A—smallest)*

Materials

Materials for this Investigation can be purchased from WARD'S. See page T745-12 for catalog numbers. Provide the items in the "Materials and Costs" list on the pupil's page. Some of these items are distracters. See "Sample Solution" to estimate what each group will use.

CONTINUED ON NEXT PAGE

Prerequisites

• **Exploration 30A: Determining the Effect of Drugs on Heart Rate** on pages 812–813
• **Review** the following:
  1. monitoring heart rate of *Daphnia*
  2. using *Daphnia* as a test organism
  3. how epinephrine affects the body

Aqua Test
Services
Beatrice, SD 40007

Rosalinda Gonzales
Director of Environmental Analysis
BioLogical Resources, Inc.
101 Jonas Salk Dr.
Oakwood, MO 65432-1101

Dear Ms. Gonzales,

I am a licensed water-quality engineer who owns a consulting a testing service in the rural Midwest. A rancher has hired us t test water samples from his land. His cattle have been acting strangely, and a veterinarian advised him that the cattle show signs of stress. In some of the samples, we found a chemical t appears to be similar to the hormone epinephrine, which causes the stress response. We have three samples that are different concentrations of this chemical. We want to know how these sam ples affect animals; specifically, we want to know the thresho concentration for a response.

We don't do any testing on animals, but I have heard that your company does. Could you please test the enclosed samples on a suitable animal? A rapid turn-around time is needed. FAX the results to me at 1-999-AOK-AGUA (265-2482), and invoice my com pany at the address above. Thank you for your help.

Urgently,

Henry Perales

Henry Perales

enclosures:
Three samples and their concentrations:
Sample A (0.000001%)
Sample B (0.00001%)
Sample C (0.0001%)

Required Precautions

• Wear safety goggles, gloves, and a lab apron.
• Glassware is fragile. Notify your teacher promptly of any broken glass or cuts.
• Epinephrine is toxic and is absorbed through the skin. If you get a chemical on your skin or clothing, wash it off while calling to your teacher.
• Wash your hands before leaving the lab.

SAMPLE SOLUTION

Question

How does the hormone epinephrine affect heart rate in *Daphnia*?

Proposed Procedure

1. Using a clean medicine dropper, place a fresh *Daphnia* with some fluid into the well of a clean depression slide. Add a small dab of petroleum jelly to slow the *Daphnia*'s movement. Add a coverslip, and observe under low power.

2. Perform step 3 with the *Daphnia*. Record the results in the row labeled "Control."

3. Count the heartbeats for 10 seconds. Record this number under Trial 1. Turn off the microscope light, and wait 20 seconds. Repeat the procedure for Trials 2 and 3, turning off the light and waiting 20 seconds between counts.

4. Use a clean medicine dropper to place a drop of Sample A on the depression slide so that it touches the edge of the coverslip. Place a piece of paper towel on the opposite edge to draw the solution into the well. Wait 60 seconds for the solution to take effect, and then repeat step 3.

5. Place the *Daphnia* in a beaker with culture water.

6. *(not present — see below)*

7. Repeat steps 1 and 3–6 for Samples B and C, using a new slide and coverslip and a fresh *Daphnia* for each.

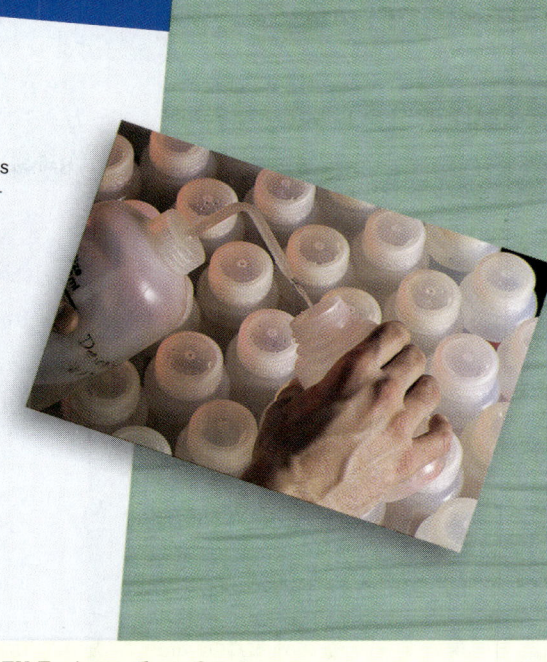

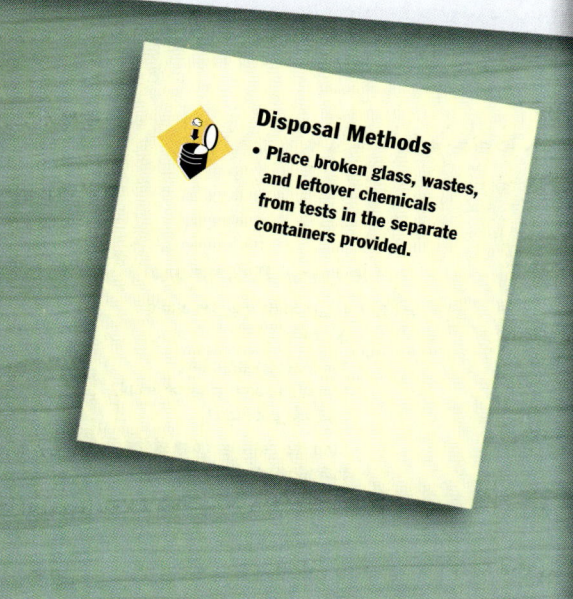

B BioLogical Resources, Inc., Oakwood, MO 65432-1101

M E M O R A N D U M

To: Team Leader, Water Quality Dept.
From: Rosalinda Gonzales

This request takes priority! The courier with this memo has samples of three different concentrations of an unknown chemical that mimics epinephrine. Start testing with the least concentrated sample. Use *Daphnia* as your test animal and, due to urgency, check only change in heart rate—the most obvious response to epinephrine. We can test for other responses later. Identify the lowest concentration of the chemical that stimulates a response. This concentration is the threshold concentration. Please send me a copy of your report. This may be a serious environmental contaminant and a danger to the livestock and people in that area.

Before you start your work, you must submit a proposal for my approval. **Your proposal must include the following:**
- the **question** you are seeking to answer
- the **procedure** you will use
- a detailed **data table**
- a complete, itemized list of proposed **materials** and **costs** (including the use of facilities, labor, and amounts needed)

When you finish your tests, prepare a report in the form of a business letter to Mr. Henry Perales. **Your report must include the following:**
- a paragraph describing the **procedure** you followed to determine the threshold concentration for the stress response
- a complete **data table**
- your **conclusions** about the threshold concentration
- a detailed **invoice** showing all materials and labor plus the total amount due

Disposal Methods
- Place broken glass, wastes, and leftover chemicals from tests in the separate containers provided.

FILE: Aqua Test Services

MATERIALS AND COSTS (Select only what you'll need. No refunds.)

I. Facilities and Equipment Use

facilities	$480.00/day
personal protective equipment	$10.00/day
compound light microscope	$100.00/day
dropper and bottle	$10.00/set
depression slide and coverslip	$2.00/day
clock with second hand	$15.00/day
beaker	$10.00/day
forceps	$5.00/day

II. Labor and Consumables

labor	$30.00/hour
Daphnia	$5.00/organism
cotton swabs	$0.10/swab
paper towels	$0.10/sheet
hot and cold water	$1.00/liter
biuret reagent	$10.00/bottle
petroleum jelly	$0.10/mL
test solutions (provided)	no charge

Fines

OSHA safety violation	$2,000.00/incident

Preparation Tips
- Order a 0.0001% solution of epinephrine.
- To make a 0.00001% solution, dilute 10 mL of 0.0001% solution with distilled water to 100 mL. To make a 0.000001% solution, dilute 10 mL of 0.00001% solution with distilled water to 100 mL. When preparing solutions, mix each solution continuously for 5 minutes, reversing the direction of stirring every 10 to 20 seconds.
- Prepare separate containers for the disposal of the solutions and broken glass.

Disposal
- Place *Daphnia* into a 100 mL beaker with 50 mL of *Daphnia* culture water to recover. Return used *Daphnia* to stock.
- Collect all wastes containing epinephrine. To the combined liquid, add 5 mL of full-strength chlorine bleach. Stir the mixture, and then heat to boiling. Boil gently for 5 minutes. Let the mixture cool, and then pour it down the drain.

Procedural Notes
Safety Precautions
- Have students wear safety goggles, gloves, and a lab apron.
- Discuss all safety symbols and required precautions with students.
- Tell students that epinephrine is toxic and is absorbed through skin. Students should not be allowed to clean up spills or broken glass. Wear sturdy leather gloves over latex gloves when cleaning up broken glass and spills involving epinephrine.

817

Materials (per lab group)
- safety goggles, gloves, and lab aprons
- 3 *Daphnia* in culture water
- beaker
- 100 mL of plain culture water
- 100 mL of 0.0001% epinephrine solution
- 100 mL of 0.00001% epinephrine solution
- 100 mL of 0.000001% epinephrine solution
- 3 medicine droppers
- 3 depression slides with 3 coverslips
- 10 mL of petroleum jelly
- compound light microscope
- paper towel
- clock with second hand

Estimated Cost of the Job

$718.20 (for two students for one day). The invoice students present to the client should include a profit. See page T745-6 for an example of how to prepare an invoice.

Conclusions

Students' data should support their conclusions. The threshold concentration for the example above was 0.0001% (Solution C).

Results

Effect of a Hormone on Heart Rate

	10-second heart rate			Formulas for calculations	
	Trial 1	Trial 2	Trial 3	Average 10 s HR (A + B + C)/3	Average 60 s HR
Solution	(A)	(B)	(C)	(D)	(E)
Control	35	34	35	34.7	208
A	34	34	35	34.3	205.8
B	33	35	35	34.3	205.8
C	44	43	45	44	264

32A | Observing the Effects of Exercise—Dance Team

Purpose

Students will determine the effect of exercise on heart rate and respiration.

Instructional Goals

Student Objectives

- Design an investigation that monitors CO_2 concentration and heart rate in response to exercise.
- Identify how exercise affects heart rate and respiration.

Life/Work Skills

- selecting and using appropriate materials and techniques
- acquiring, organizing, and interpreting data
- working as part of a team
- communicating effectively
- using appropriate safety procedures in the laboratory

Preparation Notes

Time Required: 60–100 minutes

Prelab Discussion

Discuss the procedures used in Explorations 5A and 30A. Demonstrate the procedure for finding the carotid or wrist pulse. Ask students the following questions to guide their thinking:

- What two systems are most affected by exercise? *(circulatory and respiratory)*
- How have you tested for heart rate in the past? *(counted heart rate in 10-second intervals)*
- How might this type of exercise affect respiration? *(respiration rate and CO_2 in exhaled breath would increase)*
- How could you test for exhaled CO_2? *(exhale CO_2 into water with bromothymol blue [BTB] and look for a color change)*

CONTINUED ON NEXT PAGE

Prerequisites

- **Exploration 5A: Measuring the Rate of a Process** on pages 764–765
- **Exploration 30A: Determining the Effect of Drugs on Heart Rate** on pages 812–813
- **Review** the following:
  - cellular respiration and gas exchange
  - the influence of CO_2 concentration on solvent pH
  - expiration of CO_2 and indirect measurements of CO_2 concentration
  - monitoring heart rate
  - methods for measuring pH and pulse

R H S

Roosevelt High School

Caitlan Noonan
Director of Research
Biological Resources, Inc.
101 Jonas Salk Dr.
Oakwood, MO 65432-1101

Dear Ms. Noonan:

I am an exercise physiologist working with your former high school's dance team, which is now training for a national high-kick competition. The prize money ($20,000) will be used to upgrade the training equipment used by students. Our team has a good chance to win if the girls stick to a training schedule. The team ultimately has to perform a three-minute kick routine three times in 15 minutes. I recently read about BioLogical's lab at the Olympic Training Center. Data from that lab would allow our girls to compare their physical fitness with that of other athletes. If you can provide us with a simple procedure for testing the effects of exercise on heart rate and respiration, as well as data on your athletes for comparison, we can track our progress over the next three months. Each team member can then see how her training efforts are paying off.

You know our financial position. I am hoping that you can donate your company's services for this project. We will publicize your company's name at each opportunity we get. Thank you for your consideration.

Sincerely,

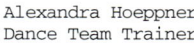

Alexandra Hoeppner
Dance Team Trainer

Required Precautions

- Wear safety goggles and a lab apron.
- Avoid hyperventilating (breathing so rapidly or deeply that you get dizzy).
- Stop the activity if any of the following occurs: chest pain, breathing difficulty, nausea, dizziness, weakness, or muscle cramping.
- Wash your hands before leaving the lab.

818

SAMPLE SOLUTION

Question

How does exercise affect heart rate and concentration of exhaled CO_2?

Proposed Procedure

1. Fill four 150 mL beakers with 50 mL of distilled water. Add 50 mL of 0.1% BTB solution, and cover with plastic wrap.
2. To establish the control, take the resting pulse and respiration rate of the test subject.
3. Have one student keep time while the test subject counts his or her pulse for 15 seconds. At the same time, have a third student count the number of breaths taken by the test subject. Record these readings in a data table.
4. Find the 60-second heart and respiration rates by multiplying each reading by 4. Record these numbers.
5. Immediately following the pulse and respiration check, partially remove the plastic wrap from one beaker, and have the test subject blow into the beaker through a straw until a color change is observed. Record the time it takes for the color change to occur.
6. Have the test subject do repeated stair steps at a consistent, fast-paced tempo for three minutes. Immediately following the exercise, begin timing a two-minute rest interval.
7. During the rest period, repeat steps 4–6 as quickly as possible. After the readings are taken, have the test subject walk

MEMORANDUM

To: Physiology Lab Director, Olympic Training Center
From: Caitlan Noonan

Please develop a simple procedure that Ms. Hoeppner can use to test the effect of exercise on the dance team, and collect sample data. Include the following in your procedure:

1. measure changes in heart rate and exhaled CO_2
2. collect data for a total of 9 minutes of intense activity using knee lifts or 12-inch step-ups
3. mimic what the dance team must do in competition—follow an interval of intense activity with an interval of light activity

Before you start your work, you must submit a proposal for my approval. **Your proposal must include the following:**

- the **question** you are seeking to answer
- the **procedure** you will use
- a detailed **data table**
- a complete, itemized list of proposed **materials and costs** (including the use of facilities, labor, and amounts needed)

When you finish your tests, prepare a report in the form of a business letter to Alexandra Hoeppner. **Your report must include the following:**

- a paragraph describing the **procedure** you followed to study the effects of exercise on heart rate and respiration
- a complete **data table**
- your **conclusions** about the effect of exercise on heart rate and respiration
- a detailed **invoice** showing all materials and labor plus the total amount due

Note: Even though our services will be donated, we need to track costs for inventory and tax records.

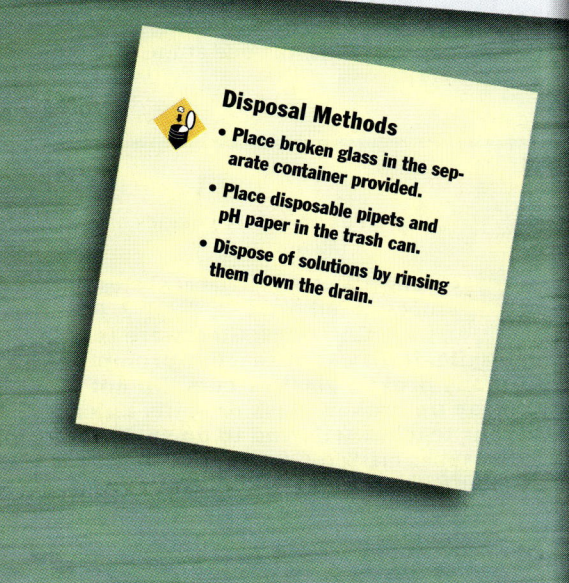

Disposal Methods
- Place broken glass in the separate container provided.
- Place disposable pipets and pH paper in the trash can.
- Dispose of solutions by rinsing them down the drain.

FILE: Roosevelt High School

MATERIALS AND COSTS (Select only what you'll need. No refunds.)

I. Facilities and Equipment Use

facilities	$480.00/day
personal protective equipment	$10.00/day
clock with a second hand	$15.00/day
150 mL beaker	$10.00/day
MBL probe (optional)	$50.00/day
thermometer	$10.00/day
metronome	$25.00/day

II. Labor and Consumables

labor	$30.00/hour
distilled water	$10.00/L
soda straw	$0.10 each
bromothymol blue solution	$5.00/mL
wax pencil	$1.00 each
plastic disposable pipet	$1.50 each
plastic wrap	$0.10 each

Fines

OSHA safety violation	$2,000.00/incident

Materials

Materials for this Investigation can be purchased from WARD'S. See page T745-12 for catalog numbers. Provide the items in the "Materials and Costs" list on the pupil's page. Some of these items are distracters. See "Sample Solution" to estimate what each group will use.

Preparation Tips

- Provide a step or other raised platform for each lab group to use for exercise periods.
- Order a 0.1% aqueous solution of BTB. To prepare this solution, follow the directions on page 764. Adjust the pH by adding two drops of ammonium hydroxide.

Disposal

- Pour water containing BTB down the drain.

Procedural Notes

Safety Precautions

- Discuss all safety symbols and required precautions with students.
- Have students wear safety goggles and a lab apron.
- Require the exercise subject to wear clothes suitable to the activity, temperature, and humidity.

Procedural Tips

- Using a metronome to pace exercise will help produce reliable results and help prevent overexertion. (A good, fast tempo is 120–140 beats per minute.)
- Students will need to develop a way to observe the breathing rate of test subjects. For example, the observer could hold a hand beneath a test subject's nose in order to feel the exhalations.

---

around for the remainder of the two-minute rest interval.

8. Immediately following the rest period, begin another three-minute exercise interval. Repeat steps 7 and 8 two more times.

Materials (per lab group)

- personal protective equipment
- four 150 mL beakers
- 200 mL of distilled water
- 200 mL of BTB solution
- 4 pieces of plastic wrap
- clock with a second hand
- 4 soda straws
- metronome

Estimated Cost of the Job

$2,282.00 (for two students for two days). The invoice students present to the client should include a profit. See page T745-6 for an example of how to prepare an invoice.

Conclusions

Students' data should support their conclusions.

Results

Heart Rate and Respiration Rate

Test	15-s heart rate	60-s heart rate	15-s respiration rate	60-s respiration rate	Seconds to a color change
Control	15	60	4	16	34
Interval 1	24	96	6	24	24
Interval 2	28	112	7	28	22
Interval 3	30	120	8	32	21

Purpose

Students will determine which of two protein digesting enzymes is most effective in the stomach.

Instructional Goals

Understanding Concepts

Students will

- relate the pH at which a digestive enzyme is effective to the conditions in the part of the digestive system where the enzyme acts.

Life/Work Skills

Students will demonstrate proficiency in

- collecting, recording, and analyzing data.
- working as part of a team.
- using appropriate safety procedures in the laboratory.

Preparation Notes

Time Required: 90–120 minutes

Materials

Materials for this Exploration can be ordered from WARD'S. See page T745-12 for catalog numbers.

Preparation Tips

- To prepare egg white (albumen), boil eggs for at least 5 minutes. Cool and cut the egg whites into 5 mm × 5 mm × 5 mm cubes. One egg provides 54 cubes.
- When preparing the solutions below, mix each solution continuously for 5 minutes, reversing the direction of stirring every 10 to 20 seconds.
- To prepare dilute (0.01 M) HCl, which has a pH of 2, dilute 50 mL of 0.1 M HCl to a volume

CONTINUED ON NEXT PAGE

exploration

Skill:

Testing the effect of pH on enzyme activity

Objectives

- *Observe* the effect of digestive enzymes on the size of a food particle.
- *Compare* the efficiency of pepsin and trypsin at two different pHs.
- *Determine* the pH at which a protease breaks down protein most completely.

Materials

- safety goggles
- lab apron
- wax pencil
- 6 test tubes
- test-tube rack
- 18 cubes of boiled egg white (protein)
- metric ruler
- 10 mL graduated cylinder
- 10 mL of distilled water
- 20 mL of pepsin
- 20 mL of trypsin
- 15 mL of dilute hydrochloric acid (HCl)
- 15 mL of dilute sodium hydroxide (NaOH)
- test-tube holder
- water bath or incubator at 37°C

HCl (pH2)   NaOH (pH8)

Situation

As a biochemist, you are well prepared to work in pharmaceutical research. Your company is developing a digestive aid for use by individuals whose stomach has been surgically removed or reduced in size. Two enzymes have been suggested. You must select one to be marketed as a digestive aid to these individuals.

Background: During digestion, food is broken down in stages by a series of chemical reactions. These chemical reactions are catalyzed by **digestive enzymes.** In the early stages of digestion, several different enzymes break down large food molecules into molecules of intermediate size. In the later stages of digestion, other enzymes break down the intermediate molecules into the final products of digestion—forms such as amino acids and simple sugars that can be used by the body. Different types of digestive enzymes work on different types of food molecules. For example, a **protease** is an enzyme that breaks down proteins. Two proteases, pepsin and trypsin, are secreted at different stages and at different sites during digestion. Each digestive enzyme works best at an **optimum pH,** the pH at which it breaks down a specific nutrient most completely.

Prelab Preparation

1. Define the boldface terms in the **Background** section.
2. Where are proteins digested in the body?
3. What is the pH of the stomach and small intestine during digestion?
4. Prepare a data table like the one at the top of the next page.

Procedure

1. Put on safety goggles and a lab apron.
2. Using a wax pencil, label six test tubes as follows: C-2, C-8, P-2, P-8, T-2, and T-8. **CAUTION: Glassware is fragile. Notify your teacher promptly of any broken glass or cuts. Do not clean up broken glass or spills unless your teacher tells you to do so.** Use the test tubes marked *C* for your controls. The letter *P* indicates pepsin, and the letter *T* indicates trypsin. The number will indicate the pH of the test tube's contents.

ANSWERS

Prelab Preparation

1. *digestive enzyme*—enzyme that catalyzes a reaction that breaks down (digests) food

   protease—enzyme that breaks down proteins

   optimum pH—the pH at which an enzyme works most completely (or is most active)
2. Proteins are digested in the stomach and small intestine. Protein digestion begins in the stomach and is completed in the small intestine.
3. The pH of the stomach is about 2, and the pH of the small intestine is between 7 and 8.

Analysis

10. Egg-white cubes in the test tubes with a protease were smaller after incubation.
11. Pepsin breaks down protein most completely at a pH of 2. Trypsin breaks down protein most completely at a pH of 8.

12. Students' answers should be consistent with their data.
13. Students' answers should be consistent with their data. Students should conclude that trypsin breaks down proteins in the small intestine because it works best at a pH of 8.
14. This temperature is comparable to normal human-body temperature—98.6°F.
15. Students' responses should be consistent with their data. Students should recommend pepsin as the digestive aid.

Test tube	Before		After	
	Food size	Food appearance	Food size	Food appearance
C-2				
C-8				
P-2				
P-8				
T-2				
T-8				

3. Place three cubes of boiled egg white in each test tube. Observe the size and appearance of the food cubes in each tube. Record your observations in your data table.

4. Add 5mL of distilled water to each test tube labeled *C*. Add 5 mL of pepsin to each test tube labeled *P*. Add 5 mL of trypsin to each test tube labeled *T*. **CAUTION: If you get a chemical on your skin or clothing, wash it off at the sink while calling to your teacher.**

5. Add 5 mL of dilute hydrochloric acid (HCl) to each tube labeled *2*. Add 5 mL of dilute sodium hydroxide (NaOH) to each tube labeled *8*. **CAUTION: If you get an acid or a base on your skin or clothing, wash it off at the sink while calling to your teacher. If you get an acid or a base in your eyes, promptly flush it out at the eye-wash station while calling to your teacher. Notify your teacher in the event of an acid or base spill.**

6. Place the test tubes in a water bath or incubator at 37°C, and leave them there overnight). Make sure the temperature remains between 35°C and 39°C.

7. After the required time, observe the tubes and note any changes in the size and appearance of the cubes of egg in each tube.

8. Dispose of your materials according to the directions from your teacher.

9. Clean up your work area and wash your hands before leaving the lab.

Analysis

10. **Analyzing Results** How did the contents of the tubes with a protease added differ from the tubes with no protease?

11. **Comparing Functions** At what pH did pepsin break down protein most completely? At what pH did trypsin break down protein most completely?

12. **Relating Concepts** How do your findings about pH and enzyme activity relate to what you know about the sites and the conditions of protein digestion?

13. **Inferring Relationships** According to today's results, what specific protease would break down protein in the small intestine? Justify your answer.

14. **Recognizing Patterns** What is the significance of using a water bath at 37°C?

15. **Relating Conclusions** What enzyme would you select as the digestive aid most useful to people with little or no stomach? Why?

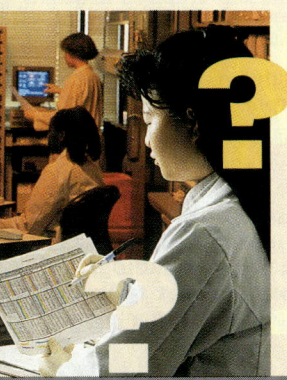

Applications

16. **Thinking Critically** If a person were taking large amounts of antacids because of excess stomach acidity, how might this affect the early stages of protein digestion?

17. **Designing an Experiment** Design an experiment that would enable you to test whether taking antacids affects protein digestion. Before conducting the experiment, discuss it with your teacher.

18. **Career Connection** *Biochemists* develop new medicines and work in many other fields of biology. Find out about the training and skills required to become a biochemist, and discover the kinds of jobs that biochemists perform.

821

Applications

16. Answers may vary. Students might suggest that antacids will raise stomach pH and hamper the early stages of protein digestion.

17. Answers will vary. *Note: If students are to perform their experiments, check their procedures for safety.*

18. Biochemists must obtain at least a bachelor's degree, and most obtain graduate degrees. Courses include biology, physics, chemistry, biochemistry, and mathematics. Biochemists must be analytical, inquisitive, and careful.

Sample Data Table

Test tube	Before		After	
	Food size	Food appearance	Food size	Food appearance
C-2	5 × 5 × 5 mm	neat cube	same	neat cube
C-8	5 × 5 × 5 mm	neat cube	same	neat cube
P-2	5 × 5 × 5 mm	neat cube	smaller	some disintegration
P-8	5 × 5 × 5 mm	neat cube	same	neat cube
T-2	5 × 5 × 5 mm	neat cube	same	neat cube
T-8	5 × 5 × 5 mm	neat cube	many small pieces	greatly disintegrated

of 500 mL with distilled water. Remember to add acid to water.

- To prepare dilute (0.001 M) NaOH, which has a pH of 8, dilute 5 mL of 0.1 M NaOH to a volume of 500 mL with distilled water.
- To prepare a 2% pepsin solution, place 4 g of dry pepsin in a flask and dilute it with 200 mL of distilled water. Use dilute HCl to adjust the pH of the solution to 2.
- To prepare a 5% trypsin solution, place 10 g of dry pancreatin (a mixture of trypsin, amylopsin, and lipase) in a flask and dilute it with 200 mL distilled water. Use dilute NaOH to adjust the pH of the solution to 8.
- Prepare separate containers for the disposal of liquids containing HCl, liquids containing NaOH, solid wastes, and broken glass.

Additional Background

Protein digestion begins in the stomach. Pepsin is a protease produced in the stomach. Hydrochloric acid is also secreted by the stomach, producing a pH of about 2. Protein digestion is completed in the small intestine. Trypsin is a protease produced by the pancreas and delivered to the small intestine. Bicarbonate of soda secreted in the small intestine results in a slightly basic environment (pH 7–8).

Disposal

- Pour pepsin and trypsin solutions down the drain.
- Wrap the egg white in an old newspaper, and place it in the trash.
- Mix liquids containing HCl and NaOH by slowly adding one to the other while stirring. Adjust the pH to between 5 and 9 by adding 1 M or less concentrated acid or base if necessary. Pour the resulting mixture down the drain.

Procedural Notes
Safety Precautions

- Discuss all safety symbols and caution statements with students.
- Have students wear safety goggles and a lab apron.

exploration

CHAPTER **34B**

Conducting a Urinalysis

Purpose

Students will use qualitative and quantitative tests to analyze artificial urine for the presence of protein, glucose, and ketones.

Instructional Goals

Understanding Concepts

Students will

- relate the presence of protein, glucose, and ketones in urine to specific conditions in the body.
- distinguish qualitative tests from quantitative tests.

Life/Work Skills

Students will demonstrate proficiency in

- qualitative analysis using indicator strips.
- collecting, recording, and analyzing data.
- working as part of a team.
- using appropriate safety procedures in the laboratory.

Preparation Notes

Time Required: 50–60 minutes

Materials

Materials for this Exploration can be ordered from WARD'S. See page T745-12 for catalog numbers.

Preparation Tips

- Purchase artificial urine, artificial urine with albumin, artificial urine with glucose, and artificial urine with ketone. Each bottle contains 500 mL of solution and will provide enough artificial urine for 100 tests.

CONTINUED ON NEXT PAGE

Skill:

Urinalysis testing

Objectives

- *Test* artificial urine for protein, glucose, and ketones.
- *Interpret* the results of a quantitative test.

Materials

- safety goggles
- lab apron
- wax pencil
- 5 test tubes
- test-tube rack
- 10 mL graduated cylinder
- 5 mL of artificial urine with glucose
- 5 mL of artificial urine with ketones
- 5 mL of artificial urine with albumin
- 5 mL of artificial urine (control)
- forceps
- 3–4 glucose test strips
- 3–4 ketone test strips
- 3–4 protein test strips
- paper towel
- 5 disposable pipets
- 5 mL of 3% sulfosalicylic acid
- 3 rubber stoppers
- 10 mL of artificial urine (unknown)

Situation

Your main task as a medical-laboratory assistant at a health clinic is to perform routine tests on urine specimens. You follow industry testing procedures, initially using test strips to detect the presence of specific substances that may be found in urine, such as glucose, ketones, and protein. When you obtain a positive result for protein in a urine sample, you perform a quantitative test to find out how much protein is present.

Background: A **urinalysis** (urine analysis) gives clues about how the body is working. Organic and inorganic chemicals that are filtered from the blood are found in urine. In the presence of disease or trauma, compounds that are not usually present in the urine may appear. For example, when the kidneys can no longer reabsorb glucose because the blood-glucose level is too high, the kidneys excrete glucose in urine. **Ketones** are organic compounds that are produced when the body uses its own tissues for energy. **Albumin** is a protein that is found in blood plasma. The presence of proteins in urine may be a sign of an abnormality because proteins are too large to pass through the filtration system of the kidney. The **turbidity** (cloudiness) of urine indicates how much protein is present.

Prelab Preparation

1. Define the boldface terms in the **Background** section.

2. Make a data table with six columns and five rows. Write the following headings for the columns: Test, Urine with glucose, Urine with ketones, Urine with protein, Control urine, and Unknown urine. Under the Test heading, write the following headings for the rows: Glucose test strips, Ketone test strips, Protein test strips, and Sulfosalicylic acid.

Procedure

1.  Wear safety goggles and a lab apron.

2. Using a wax pencil, label five test tubes as follows: P+, G+, K+, Control (P−, G−, K−), and Unknown. **CAUTION: Glassware is fragile. Notify your teacher promptly of any broken glass or cuts. Do not clean up broken glass or spills unless your teacher tells you to do so.** Place the test tubes in a test-tube rack.

822

ANSWERS

Prelab Preparation

1. *urinalysis*—analysis of the physical and chemical characteristics of urine
   ketones—organic compounds produced when the body burns fat or lean tissue to provide needed energy
   albumin—protein found in blood plasma but not normally found in urine
   turbidity—cloudiness due to the presence of suspended solids

Analysis

12. Both indicate the presence of a substance by a change in color.
13. Turbidity indicated the presence of protein in the urine. It is a quantitative test because it can be used to determine the concentration of protein in g/mL.
14. Answers will vary. Students' answers should be consistent with their data.

Applications

15. Ketones are released when the body metabolizes its fat and muscle tissue.
16. A confirmatory test reduces the risk of alarming patients by reporting false positives that may result from human error or from using out-of-date test strips.

Turbidity Grading Scale

Grade	Appearance	Protein in urine (g/100 mL)
negative	no turbidity	<0.005
trace	barely perceptible turbidity	0.010
11	distinct turbidity but no distinct granulation*	0.050
21	turbidity with granulation but no flocculation†	0.2
31	turbidity with granulation and flocculation	0.5
41	clumps of precipitated protein or solid precipitate††	1.0

*Granulation — appearance of small granules (Sugar and salt are granular.)
†Flocculation — small, individual masses resembling tufts of wool
††Precipitate — sediment at bottom

3. Using a 10 mL graduated cylinder, add 5 mL of artificial urine with albumin to the "P+" test tube. Add 5 mL of artificial urine with glucose to the "G+" test tube. Add 5 mL of artificial urine with ketones to the "K+" test tube. Add 5 mL of the artificial urine labeled Control to the "Control" test tube. Rinse the graduated cylinder well between artificial urine samples.

4. Using forceps, obtain two glucose test strips. Lay the strips on a paper towel, and label one "+" and one "−." *Note: Do not touch the strips with your fingers.* Using a pipet, place a drop of liquid from the test tube marked G+ onto the "+" strip. Use a clean pipet to place a drop of the "Control" sample on the "−" strip. Wait 60 seconds. Compare the resulting color to the color guide. Record the results in your data table.

5. Repeat step 4 using ketone test strips and the test tube marked "K+."

6. Repeat step 4 using protein test strips and the test tube marked "P+."

7. Using a clean graduated cylinder, add 5 mL of 3% sulfosalicylic acid to the "P+" and "Control" test tubes. Close each tube with a stopper, and then invert the tubes several times. Let the tubes sit for 10 minutes. Invert the tubes once more, and observe them for turbidity (cloudiness). Compare the degree of turbidity to the grading scale on this page. Record your results in your data table.

8. Obtain 5 mL of the artificial urine labeled "Unknown," and place it in the test tube marked "Unknown." Using test strips, test for glucose, ketones, and protein.

9. If you obtain a positive result for protein in step 8, repeat step 7 using the artificial urine labeled "Unknown." Record your results in your data table.

10. Dispose of your materials according to the directions from your teacher.

11. Clean up your work area and wash your hands before leaving the lab.

Analysis

12. **Analyzing Methods** How are the glucose, ketone, and protein test strips like the indicators you used in Exploration 22A?

13. **Analyzing Results** What did turbidity of the artificial urine indicate in this lab? Is this a qualitative or quantitative test? Explain.

14. **Interpreting Data** What abnormal components were present in the unknown sample?

Applications

15. **Thinking Critically** Diabetics may produce urine with ketones if their blood-glucose level is too low and their body burns proteins for energy. What body tissues are broken down in this situation?

16. **Thinking Critically** The medical testing industry recommends performing additional urinalysis tests to confirm positive results obtained with test strips. Why do you think this practice is recommended?

17. **Career Connection** *Medical-laboratory assistants* help medical technologists by performing routine tests, such as a urinalysis. Find out about the training and skills required to become a medical-laboratory assistant, and discover some other tests that they perform.

823

17. Medical-laboratory assistants help administer and analyze laboratory tests to help detect medical conditions, usually under the supervision of a lab supervisor or physician. A medical-laboratory assistant usually must complete a bachelor's degree as well as a yearlong program at a medical technology school. Some community colleges, vocational schools, and hospitals offer training programs.

Sample Data Table

Test	Urine with glucose	Urine with ketones	Urine with protein	Control	Unknown
Glucose test strips	+	−	−	−	varies
Ketone test strips	−	+	−	−	varies
Protein test strips	−	−	+	−	varies
Sulfosalicylic acid	−	−	+	trace to 4+	varies

- To provide artificial urine with a single unknown, use one of the artificial urine products with albumin, glucose, or ketone.
- To prepare an artificial urine sample with more than one unknown, mix equal amounts of artificial urine with the desired components for a total volume to meet your class size, assuming 10 mL of unknown per lab group.
- Prepare separate containers for the disposal of liquid wastes containing sulfosalicylic acid and broken glass.

Additional Background
Ketones appear in the blood during severe calorie restriction (dieting), fevers, intense activity, and diabetes. In severe calorie restriction and in fevers, the body uses both fat and protein (muscle) tissue. The condition of having ketones in the blood is called ketosis.

Disposal
- Pour sulfosalicylic acid wastes and artificial urine down the drain.
- All test strips can be thrown in the trash.

Procedural Notes
Safety Precautions
- Discuss all safety symbols and caution statements with students.
- Have students wear safety goggles and a lab apron.
- Tell students that they should not draw liquid into pipets by mouth suction. Liquid should be drawn into a pipet by squeezing the pipet bulb and then releasing the pressure on the bulb while the pipet tip is below the surface of the liquid to be drawn into the pipet.

Procedural Tips
- Instruct students not to touch the test area of a test strip with anything but forceps.
- Reinforce the importance of pipetting drops of the sample onto the test strip rather than dipping the test strip in the sample.

Purpose

Students will use a computer simulation to determine how enzymes respond to changing environmental conditions.

Instructional Goals

Students will
- determine the relationship between temperature and reaction rate for two enzymes.
- determine the relationship between pH and reaction rate for the same two enzymes.
- identify the optimal temperature and pH for each enzyme.

Preparation Notes

Time Required: approximately 1 hour

Prelab Discussion

Before students begin the lab, they should be able to answer the following questions:

- What is an enzyme? (*An enzyme is a protein that increases the rate of a reaction by reducing the activation energy necessary to start the reaction.*)

- Explain the relationship between an enzyme's shape and its function. (*An enzyme has a specific three-dimensional shape that determines its function. If the shape of an enzyme is changed, its ability to catalyze a reaction may be diminished or eliminated.*)

- What is the function of the enzyme lysozyme? (*It is a defensive enzyme that destroys bacteria.*)

CONTINUED ON NEXT PAGE

interactive **exploration**

Objectives

- *Simulate* the effect of pH, temperature, and enzyme concentration on the activity of two enzymes.
- *Determine* the optimal conditions for each enzyme.

Materials

- computer with CD-ROM drive
- CD-ROM *Interactive Explorations in Biology: Cell Biology and Genetics*
- graph paper

Background: All living things rely on enzymes to catalyze chemical reactions. Recall that an enzyme is a protein molecule that increases the rate of a chemical reaction by lowering the activation energy necessary to start the reaction. Enzyme effectiveness depends on several factors. This interactive investigation allows you to explore how three of these factors—enzyme concentration, temperature, and pH—affect the activity of the enzymes carbonic anhydrase and lysozyme.

Prelab Preparation

1. Load and start the program Thermodynamics. You will see an animated diagram like the one below. Click the Navigation button, and then click the Topic Information button. Read the focus questions and review these concepts: Reaction Rate, Enzyme Catalysis, Temperature and Reaction Rates, and pH Can Influence Enzyme Shape.

2. Now click the word *Help* at the top left of the screen, and select How to Use This Exploration. Listen to the instructions that explain the operation of the exploration. Click the Interactive Exploration button on the Navigation Palette to begin the exploration.

Feedback Meter

a **Reaction Rate:** displays reaction rate as a percentage of the maximal reaction rate (V_{max})

Variables

b **Relative Enzyme Concentration:** varies the concentration of the enzyme

c **Temperature:** varies the temperature

d **pH:** varies the pH

ANSWERS

Procedure

3. The reaction rate is 20% of the maximal rate.

5. Reaction rate increases linearly with increasing enzyme concentration.

6. **Sample Data Table**
   Enzyme: *Carbonic Anhydrase*

Temperature	Reaction rate (% of V_{max})
0°C	48%
10°C	90%
20°C	75%
30°C	32%
40°C	0%
50°C	0%

9. Students' graphs should reflect the data shown above. Reaction rate varies with temperature and peaks at 10°C.

10. The graph on the screen is smoother because it includes many more points.

13. **Sample Data Table**
    Enzyme: *Carbonic Anhydrase*

pH	Reaction rate (% of V_{max})
3	45%
4	91%
5	100%
6	91%
7	45%
8	8%

14. Reaction rate varies with pH and is highest at a pH of 5.

Procedure

Part A: Carbonic Anhydrase

1. Click the New Enzyme button until "Carbonic Anhydrase" appears at the top of the screen. Carbonic anhydrase is found in red blood cells, where it helps regulate the concentration of carbon dioxide.

2. Click and slide the indicator so that the Relative Enzyme Concentration is 0.2.

3. Click the Plot Point button and observe the point that appears on the graph. This point indicates the rate of reaction for this enzyme concentration. The rate of reaction is expressed as a percentage of V_{max}, the highest possible reaction rate. What is the reaction rate indicated by the Reaction Rate meter in the upper-left corner of the screen?

4. Repeat steps 2 and 3 until you have tested the following Relative Enzyme Concentrations: 0.4, 0.6, 0.8, and 1.0.

5. Click the Plot Graph button. How does increasing the enzyme concentration affect the rate of reaction?

6. Make a table like the one shown below.

Enzyme: _____ Temperature	Reaction rate (% of V_{max})

7. Click and slide the indicator so that the Temperature meter indicates 0°C. Click the Plot Point button and observe the point that appears on the graph. In your table, record the reaction rate.

8. Repeat step 7 until you have tested the effects of the following temperatures: 10°C, 20°C, 30°C, 40°C, and 50°C.

9. Use graph paper to make a graph of temperature versus reaction rate. Draw a curve that connects your six points. What can you conclude about the effect of temperature on the activity of carbonic anhydrase?

10. Click the Plot Graph button. Compare your graph with the one shown on the screen. Explain any differences between the two graphs.

11. Make a two-column table similar to the one you made in step 6. Label the left column "pH" and the right column "Reaction rate (% of V_{max})."

12. Click and slide the indicator so that the pH meter indicates a pH of 3. Click the Plot Point button and observe the point that appears on the graph. In your table, record the reaction rate.

13. Repeat step 12 until you have tested the following pH values: 4, 5, 6, 7, and 8.

14. After testing all the values above, make a graph of pH versus reaction rate. Draw a curve that connects your points. What can you conclude about the effect of pH on the activity of carbonic anhydrase?

15. Click the Plot Graph button. How does your graph compare with the graph on the screen? Explain any differences.

Part B: Lysozyme

16. Click the New Enzyme button until "Lysozyme" appears at the top of the screen. Lysozyme catalyzes a reaction in which polysaccharides are broken down into simple sugars.

17. Repeat steps 2–15 for the enzyme lysozyme.

Analysis

18. What is the optimal temperature for each enzyme? What is the optimal pH for each enzyme?

19. The optimal pH of pepsin, a stomach enzyme, is about 2, while the optimal pH of trypsin, an enzyme of the small intestine, is about 8. Give a functional explanation for this difference.

Additional Background

Enzymes speed up the chemical reactions in living things by bringing the reactants into close proximity and facilitating their interaction. As is true with all proteins, an enzyme's shape is crucial to its function. Each kind of enzyme catalyzes a specific reaction that is determined by its three-dimensional shape, and an enzyme's three-dimensional shape, in turn, is ultimately determined by the sequence of amino acids it contains.

The efficiency of an enzyme depends on the characteristics of its environment. One important factor is the concentration of the enzyme. The temperature and pH at which the reaction occurs are also important.

Procedural Notes
Procedural Tips

- A constraint of the program is that the variables must be tested in the following order: enzyme concentration, temperature, pH. At least five values of each variable must be tested before the computer will allow you to move to the next variable. Also remind students that they must click the Plot Point button each time they want to enter a particular value for one of the variables.

- Remind students that the values for reaction rate are expressed as a percentage of the maximum reaction rate (V_{max}).

825

---

15. Students' graphs will not be as smooth because they contain only six points.

17. **Sample Data Table**
    Enzyme: *Lysozyme*

Temperature	Reaction rate (% of V_{max})
0°C	12%
10°C	23%
20°C	40%
30°C	69%
40°C	98%
50°C	82%

Reaction rate peaks at 40°C.

Sample Data Table
Enzyme: *Lysozyme*

pH	Reaction rate (% of V_{max})
3	30%
4	84%
5	100%
6	84%
7	30%
8	4%

Reaction rate reaches a maximum at a pH of 5.

Analysis

18. The optimal temperature of carbonic anhydrase lies between 10°C and 20°C; for lysozyme, the optimal temperature is 40°C. The optimal pH for both carbonic anhydrase and lysozyme is 5.

19. The stomach is very acidic, while the small intestine is slightly basic. The optimal pH of each enzyme matches the pH at which it normally functions.

Teacher's notes

The following pages of the Reference and Skills Appendix contain **Practice Exercises** that you may wish to assign to students:

Answers to **Practice Exercises** can be found at the bottom of the pages on which they appear.

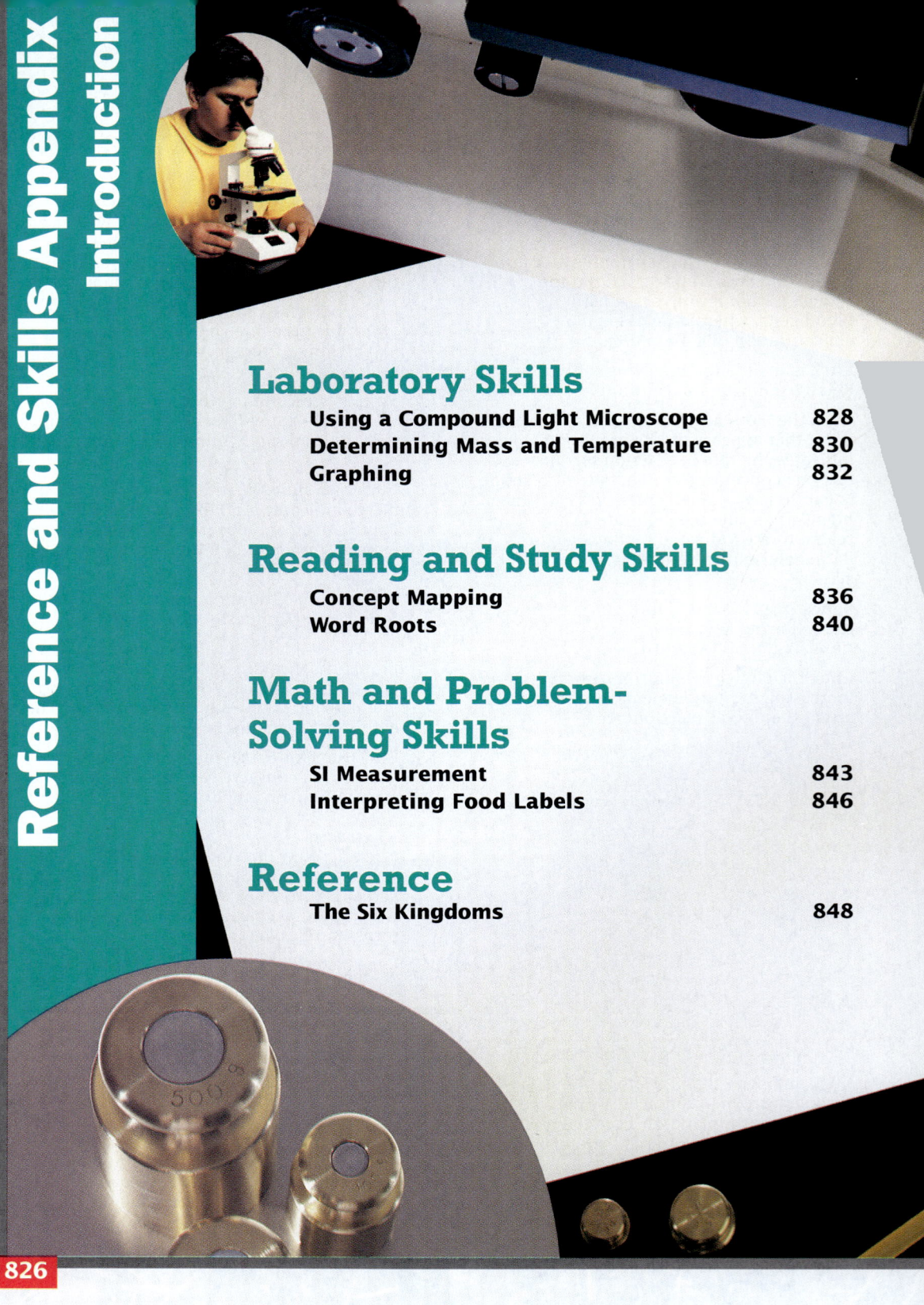

Reference and Skills Appendix Introduction

Laboratory Skills

Reading and Study Skills

Math and Problem-Solving Skills

Reference

826

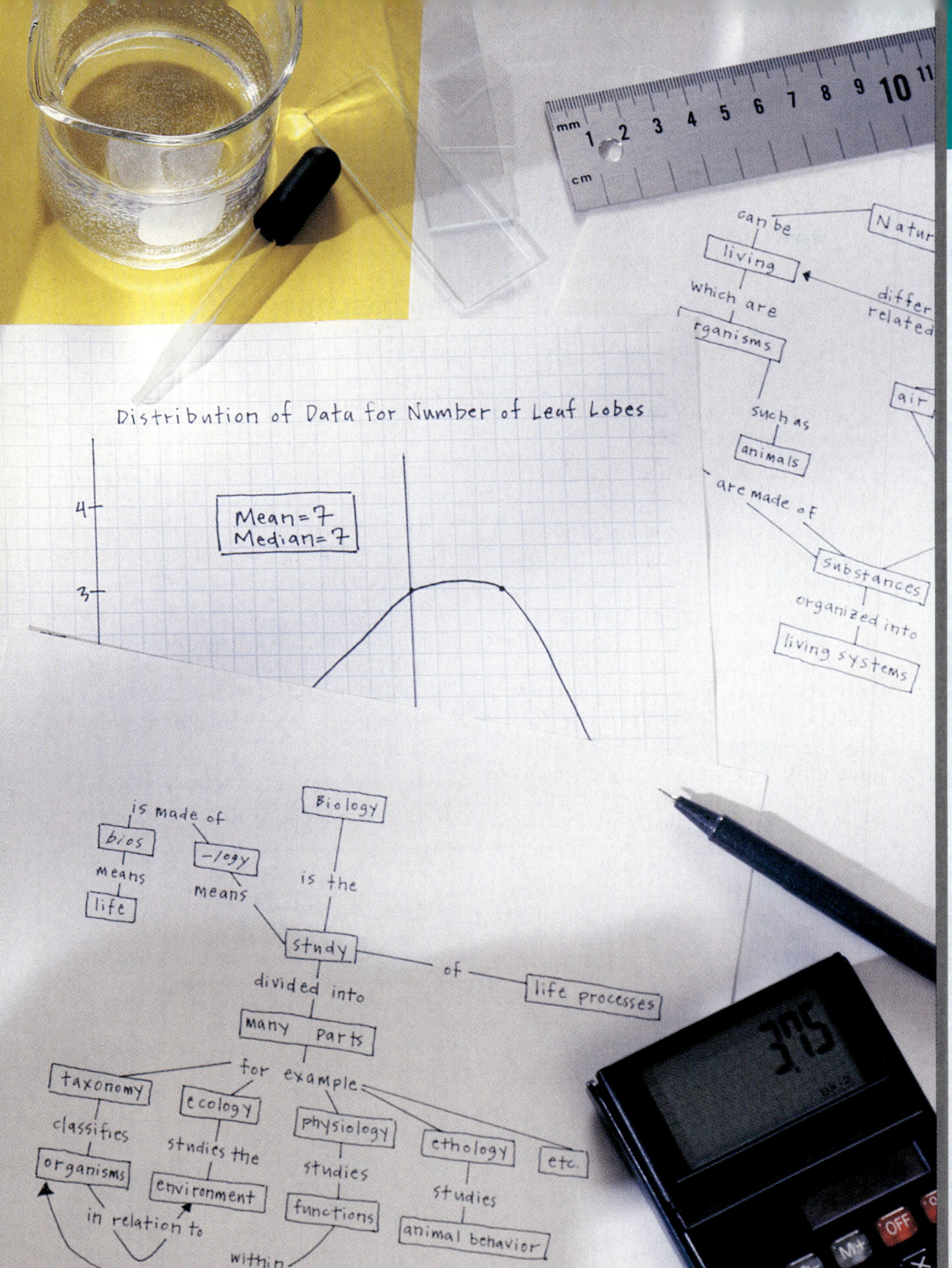

Distribution of Data for Number of Leaf Lobes

Mean = 7
Median = 7

4
3

Biology

bios — is made of — -logy

means   means

life

is the

study

of — life processes

divided into

many   parts

for example

taxonomy   ecology   physiology   ethology   etc.

classifies   studies the   studies   studies

organisms   environment   functions   animal behavior

in relation to   within

can be — living — Natur...

which are   differ...
related...

...rganisms

such as   air

animals

are made of

substances

organized into

living systems

Teacher's notes

The following additional opportunities for reinforcing student skills can be found in the **Holt BioSources Teaching Resources CD-ROM:**

Basic Skills Worksheets help students master essential skills.
1 Graphing
2 Length, Area, and Volume
3 Mass and Density
4 Measurement and Scale Drawings
5 Microscope Magnification
6 Reading a Thermometer
7 Reading a Balance
8 Temperature Conversions
9 Words and Roots

Problem-Solving Worksheets give students practice in solving problems related to biology.
1 Computing Rates and Heart Efficiency
2 Determining Percentage Composition
3 Genetics and Probability
4 Mean, Median, and Mode
5 Operations on Small and Large Numbers
6 Population Size
7 Pressure Gradients in Breathing and Calculating Respiratory Volume
8 Ratios and Proportions
9 Solution Concentration
10 Using Food Labels to Calculate Percentage of Nutrients and Calories

827

Using a Compound Light Microscope

Parts of the Compound Light Microscope

- The *eyepiece* magnifies the image, usually 10X.

- The *low-power objective* magnifies the image more, often 10X.

- The *high-power objective* magnifies the image even more, such as 43X.

- The *revolving nosepiece* holds the objectives and can be turned to change from one magnification to another.

- The *body tube* maintains the correct distance between the eyepiece and objectives. This is usually about 25 cm, the normal distance for reading and viewing objects with the naked eye.

- The *coarse adjustment* moves the body tube up and down in large increments to allow gross positioning and focusing of the low-power objective lens.

- The *fine adjustment* moves the body tube slightly to bring the image into sharp focus.

- The *stage* supports a slide.

- *Stage clips* secure the slide in position for viewing.

- The *diaphragm* (or *iris diaphragm*) controls the amount of light allowed to pass through the object being viewed.

- The *light source* provides light for viewing the image. It can be either a light reflected with a mirror or incandescent light from a small lamp.

  NEVER use direct sunlight as a light source.

- The *arm* supports the body tube.

- The *base* supports the microscope.

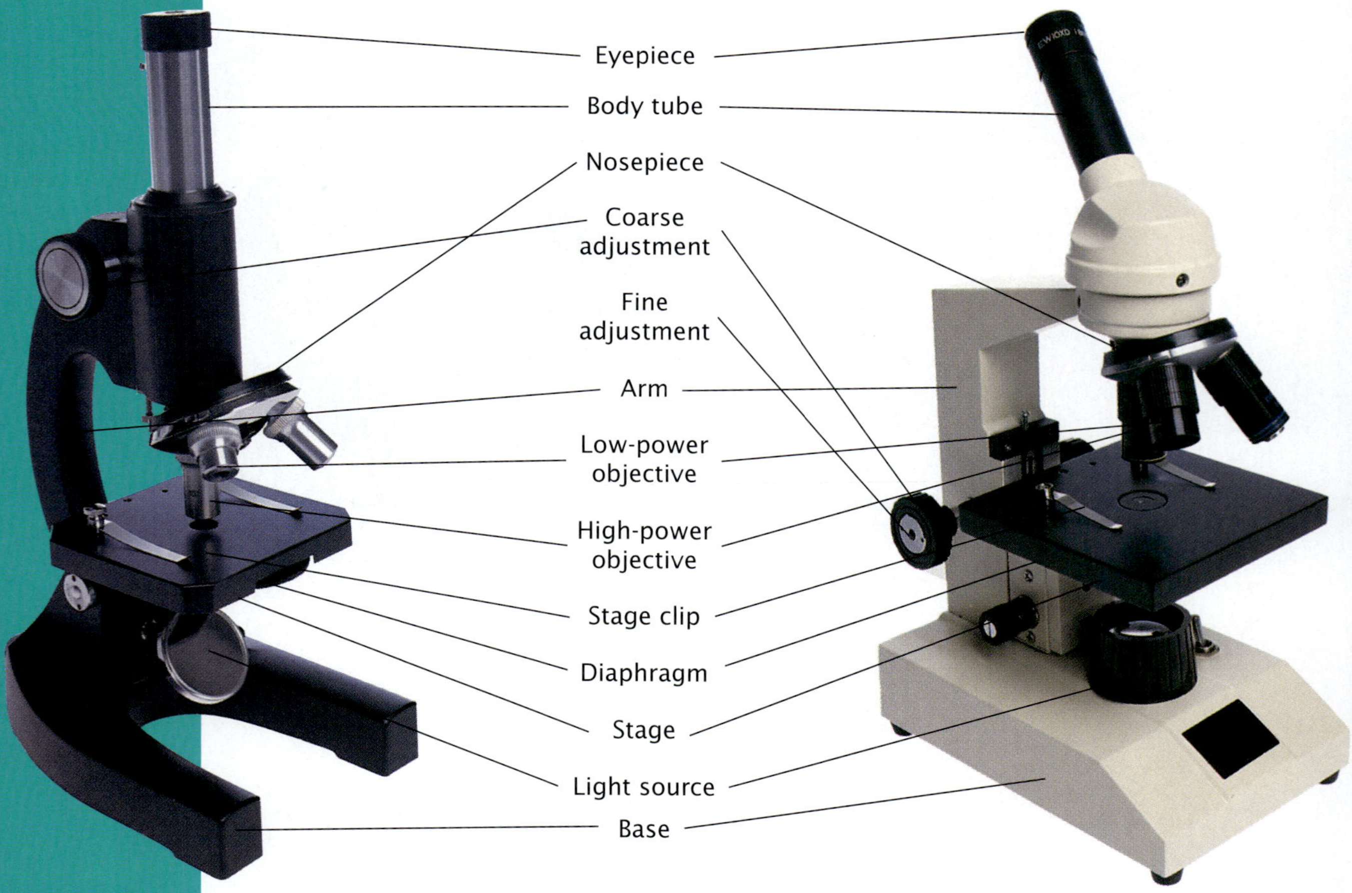

Eyepiece

Body tube

Nosepiece

Coarse adjustment

Fine adjustment

Arm

Low-power objective

High-power objective

Stage clip

Diaphragm

Stage

Light source

Base

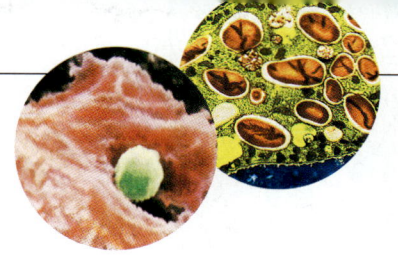
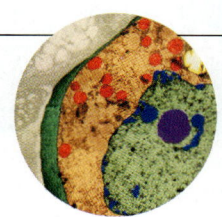

Proper Handling and Use of the Compound Light Microscope

1. Carry the microscope to your lab table using both hands, one beneath the base and the other holding the arm of the microscope. Hold the microscope close to your body.

2. Place the microscope on the lab table, at least 5 cm (2 in.) from the edge of the table.

3. Check the type of light source for the microscope. If the microscope has a lamp, plug it in, making sure that the cord is out of the way. If the microscope has a mirror, adjust it to reflect light through the hole in the stage.

CAUTION: *If your microscope has a mirror, do not use direct sunlight as a light source. Direct sunlight can damage your eyes.*

4. Adjust the revolving nosepiece so that the low-power objective is in line with the body tube.

5. Place a prepared slide over the hole in the stage and secure the slide with stage clips.

6. Look through the eyepiece and move the diaphragm to adjust the amount of light coming through the specimen.

7. Now look at the stage at eye level, and slowly turn the coarse adjustment to lower the objective until it almost touches the slide. Do not allow the objective to touch the slide.

8. While looking through the eyepiece, turn the coarse adjustment to raise the objective until the image is in focus. Never focus the objectives by moving them downward. Use the fine adjustment to raise the objective until you achieve a sharply focused image. Keep both eyes open while viewing a slide.

9. Make sure that the image is exactly in the center of your field of vision. Then, switch to the high-power objective. If necessary, increase the power of the objective to the next level. Focus the image with the fine adjustment. Never use the coarse adjustment at high power.

10. When you are finished using the microscope, remove the slide. Clean the eyepiece and objectives with lens paper and return the microscope to its storage area.

Making a Wet Mount

1. Use lens paper to clean a glass slide and coverslip.

2. Place the specimen you wish to observe in the center of the slide.

3. Using a medicine dropper, place one drop of water on the specimen.

4. Position the coverslip so that it is at the edge of the drop of water and at a 45-degree angle to the slide. Make sure that the water runs along the edge of the coverslip.

5. Lower the coverslip slowly to avoid trapping air bubbles.

6. If a stain or solution is to be added to a wet mount, place a drop of the staining solution on the microscope slide along one side of the coverslip. Place a small piece of paper towel on the opposite side of the coverslip.

7. As the water evaporates from the slide, add another drop of water by placing the tip of the medicine dropper next to the edge of the coverslip, just as you would do when adding stains or solutions to a wet mount. If you have added too much water, remove the excess by using the corner of a paper towel as a blotter. Do not lift the coverslip to add or remove water.

Reference and Skills Appendix
Laboratory Skills

Practice Exercises
Have students complete the Practice Exercises on pages 830 and 831. Answers to the Practice Exercises are found at the bottom of page 831.

Determining Mass and Temperature

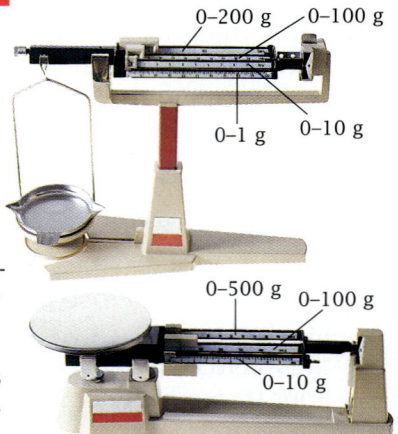

0–200 g   0–100 g

0–1 g   0–10 g

Reading a Balance

A single-pan balance has one pan and three or four beams. The scale of measure for each beam depends on the model of the balance. You can see these differences by looking at the two balances shown. When an object is placed on the pan, the riders are moved to the right as needed until the mass on the beams equals the mass of the object.

0–500 g   0–100 g

0–10 g

Measuring Mass

CAUTION: *Never place a hot object or chemical directly on a balance pan. For example, when determining the mass of a chemical or powder, use weighing or filter paper. Determine the mass of the paper and subtract that mass from the final mass.*

1. Make sure the balance is on a level surface and allow the pan to move freely. Position all the riders at zero. Use the adjustment knob (usually located under and to the left of the pan) if the pointer does not come to rest in the middle of the scale.

2. Place the mass on the pan.

3. Move the largest rider along the beam to the right until it is at the last notch that does not move the pointer below the zero point in the center of the scale.

4. Follow the same procedure with the next largest rider.

5. Move the smallest rider until the pointer rests at zero in the middle of the scale.

6. Total the readings on all the beams to determine the mass of the object.

Practice Exercises

1. Use a single-pan balance to determine the mass of each of the following items.
   a. an empty 250 mL beaker
   b. 250 mL beaker filled with 100 mL of water
   c. the same beaker filled with 100 mL of cooking oil
   d. a house key
   e. a small book
   f. a paper clip or small safety pin

2. Determine the mass of each object represented by the balance readings shown.

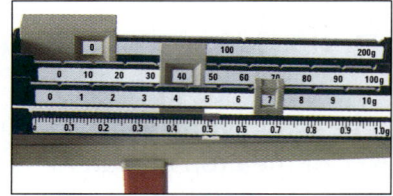

a.

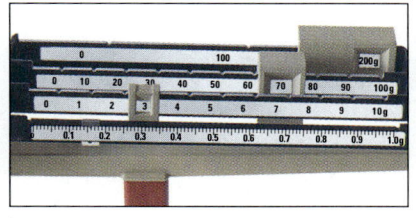

b.

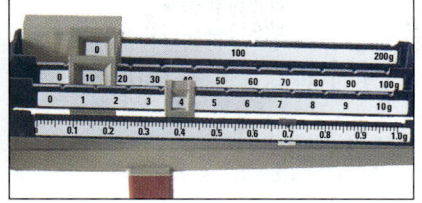

c.

Reading a Thermometer

Most laboratory thermometers are of the bulb-type illustrated at the right. The sensing bulb of the thermometer is filled with a colored liquid that expands predictably when heated. The liquid expands into a capillary tube. Most laboratory thermometers are marked in small increments in degrees Celsius.

Measuring Temperature

1. The sensing bulb of the thermometer must be carefully lowered into the material. The thermometer may rest against the side of the container but the bulb should never rest on the bottom of a container where heat is being applied. If the thermometer has an adjustable clip for the

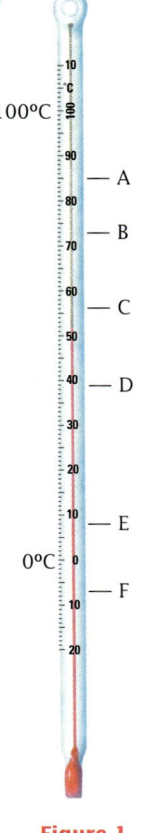

100°C

0°C

A
B
C
D
E
F

Figure 1

side of the container, the thermometer can be suspended in the liquid. For safety, never hold a thermometer in your hand while measuring the temperature of a hot substance.

2. Gently rotate the thermometer in the clip. Watch the rising colored liquid in the capillary tube. When the liquid in the capillary tube stops rising, note the whole degree increment nearest the top of the liquid column. If your thermometer is marked in tenths of a degree, count the increments up or down from the nearest whole degree to obtain your reading. For example, if the top of the colored liquid column is nearest the 52°C mark but somewhat below it, as shown, what is the accurate temperature reading?

Because the top of the column is half of a degree below the 52°C mark, the temperature is 51.5°C.

Practice Exercises

1. Examine the thermometer in **Figure 1**. Note that only 0°C and 100°C are labeled.
    a. What scale is used to mark this thermometer—Celsius or Fahrenheit?
    b. Is this thermometer marked only in whole degrees or in tenths of degrees?
    c. What is the temperature reading on this thermometer?

2. What would be the temperature reading of the thermometer shown in **Figure 1** if the top of the column were resting at
    a. point A?_____   d. point D?_____
    b. point B?_____   e. point E?_____
    c. point C?_____   f. point F?_____

Graphing

Circle Graphs

A circle graph, sometimes called a pie chart, shows groups of data in relation to all of the data. Each part of the circle represents a category of the data. The entire circle represents all of the data. For example, a biologist studying a plot of land in a hardwood forest in Wisconsin found that there were five different types of trees in the plot. The data table below summarizes the biologist's findings.

WISCONSIN HARDWOOD TREES		
Type of tree	**Number found**	**Percentage of total (rounded to nearest whole-number percent)**
Oak	539	17
Maple	758	24
Beech	319	10
Birch	1327	42
Hickory	222	7
Total	3,165	100

To aid in the interpretation of the data and to compare it with other sets of data, the biologist constructed a circle graph of the data.

Characteristics of a Circle Graph

1. The sections are accurately calculated and drawn. The number of each type of tree is divided by the total number of trees and multiplied by 100 to get the tree percentages.
2. The sections are clearly labeled.
3. Labels, colors, or shading represent each section of the circle.
4. The graph is easy to interpret.

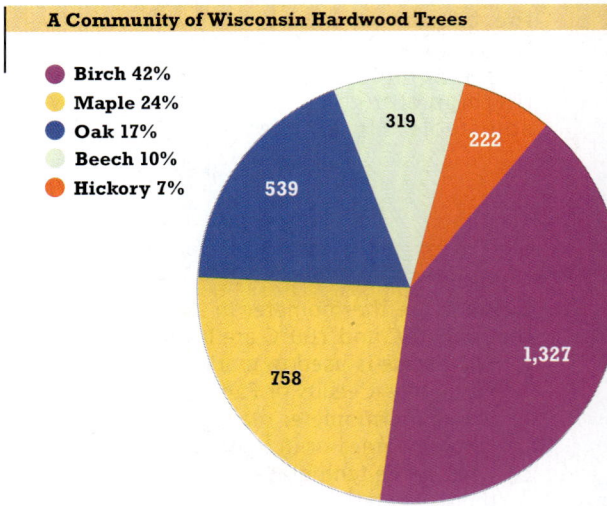

A Community of Wisconsin Hardwood Trees

- Birch 42%
- Maple 24%
- Oak 17%
- Beech 10%
- Hickory 7%

Practice Exercise

1. Construct a circle graph from the following data.

Animal	Wildlife refuge population
Baboon	20
African elephant	35
Leopard	12
Tiger	16
Giraffe	10

Line Graphs

Line graphs are most often used to demonstrate continuous change. Examine the following data.

POPULATION OF THE UNITED STATES 1880 – 1990	
Year	**Population (in millions)**
1881	50.2
1890	62.9
1900	76
1910	92
1920	105.7
1930	122.8
1940	131.7
1950	151.3
1960	179.2
1970	203.2
1980	226.5
1990	251.4

Both the year and the population are variables. The variable to which values are assigned, in this case the year, is called the **independent variable**. The population is determined by the year. The population is called the **dependent variable**. Each set of values, the independent and dependent variables, is called a **data pair**. To prepare a line graph, data pairs must first be organized in a table like that shown above.

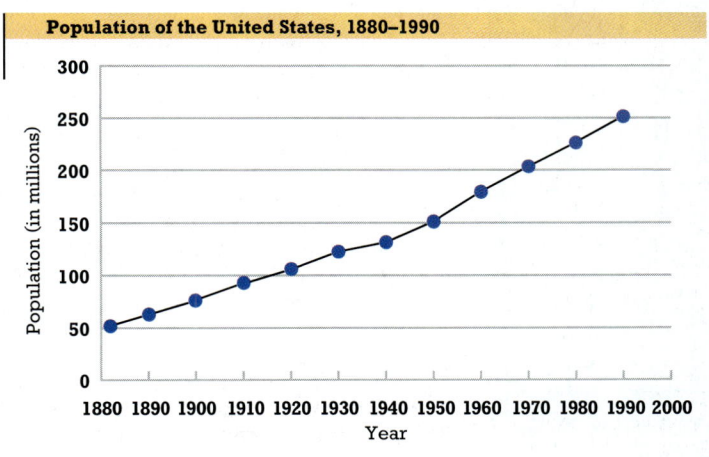

Population of the United States, 1880–1990

Teacher's notes

ANSWER TO PRACTICE EXERCISE

1.

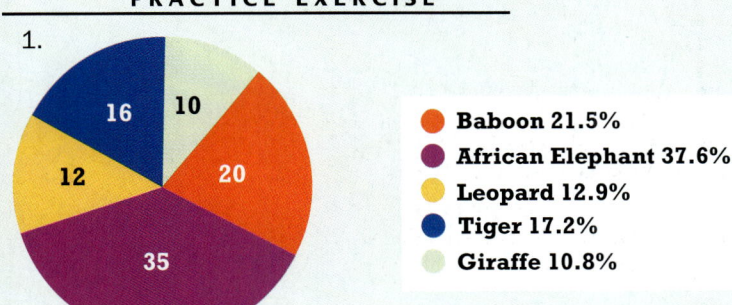

- Baboon 21.5%
- African Elephant 37.6%
- Leopard 12.9%
- Tiger 17.2%
- Giraffe 10.8%

Practice Exercises

Have students complete the Practice Exercises on pages 834 and 835. Answers to the Practice Exercises are found at the bottom of page 835.

continued

Characteristics of a Line Graph

1. The independent variable is put on the horizontal (x) axis. The dependent variable is put on the vertical (y) axis.
2. The axes are labeled and an appropriate scale and interval are used on each axis. The same scale and interval must be used for the total length of the axis. For example, if 1 cm represents an interval of 10 years, 30 years must be represented by 3 cm.
3. Reasonable starting points are used for each axis. Examine the population graph. The horizontal (x) axis goes from 1880 to 2000 and the vertical (y) axis goes from 0 to 300 million.
4. The data pairs are plotted as accurately as possible.
5. The title of the graph accurately reflects the data presented.
6. If more than one set of data is presented on a graph, a key must accompany the graph. For example, if the populations of Canada, Mexico, and the United States from 1880 to 1990 were presented on the same graph, it would be important to use a different color or type of line (solid, dotted, dashes, etc.) for each country. The key indicates what each color or type of line represents.
7. The graph is easy to interpret.

Using Graphs to Make Predictions

Examine the graph of the population of the United States from 1880 to 1990 on page 833. Do you notice any trends? Do you think you can predict the population of the United States in the year 2000? The process of going beyond the data points in a graph is called extrapolation. Scientists use extrapolation to make predictions about future data based on data patterns from the past.

We can also use graphs to find information between the data points on a data table. For example, we can use the graph to determine that the population of the United States in 1905 was approximately 84 million people. We find the point on the line that represents 1905 and then determine the position of that point on the y axis. The reading is about 84 million. Finding information between two sets of data pairs is called interpolating.

Practice Exercises

Use the population graph on page 833 to answer the following.

2. Predict what the population of the United States will be in the year 2010.
3. Determine the approximate population of the United States in 1935, 1945, and 1985.
4. What was the approximate population of the United States in 1870?
5. What will be the approximate population of the United States in 2020?
6. How certain are you of your answer? Why?

834

Bar Graphs

Consider the following information:

PRECIPITATION IN HARTFORD, CONNECTICUT APRIL 1 – 15, 1996			
Date	Precipitation (in centimeters)	Date	Precipitation (in centimeters)
April 1	0.5	April 9	0.25
April 2	1.25	April 10	0.0
April 3	0.0	April 11	1.0
April 4	0.0	April 12	0.0
April 5	0.0	April 13	0.25
April 6	0.0	April 14	0.0
April 7	0.0	April 15	6.50
April 8	1.75		

A bar graph is appropriate for data that are not continuous. A bar graph is a good indicator of trends if the data are taken over a sufficiently long period of time. Precipitation records require years of data, and even then predictions are difficult to make with reliability. The bar graph shown at the right depicts the data presented in the above table.

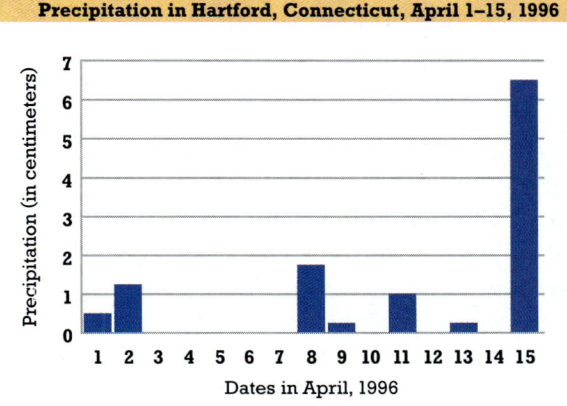

Precipitation in Hartford, Connecticut, April 1–15, 1996

Characteristics of a Bar Graph

1. An appropriate scale and reasonable starting points are used for each axis.
2. The axes are labeled and data are accurately plotted.
3. The title of the graph accurately reflects the data presented.
4. The graph is easy to interpret.

Practice Exercises

Use the bar graph above to answer the following.

7. How many centimeters of rain fell in Hartford on April 11?
8. Can a bar graph show a trend, even if the data are not continuous?
9. Can the bar graph be used to predict precipitation in Hartford on April 20?
10. Could a line graph of these data be used to make a prediction about the rainfall on April 20? Why or why not?

835

ANSWERS TO PRACTICE EXERCISES

2. 300 million

3. 127 million, 142 million, and 239 million

4. 40 million

5. 320 million

6. You cannot be certain of the answer because trends that affect population may change.

7. 1 cm

8. Yes, if the data are taken over a sufficiently long period of time.

9. No. Information about rain in Hartford on April 20 must be collected over a period of years.

10. No, the data are not continuous.

What's the Best Way to Study?

If you want to learn information that you can remember longer and use more easily, you need to move that information into your long-term memory.

Concept mapping may help you understand the meanings of ideas by showing you their connections to other ideas. If you define soccer as a team sport, you have already related the idea or concept of "soccer" to the ideas of "team" and "sport." Making an idea map may help you see the information more clearly.

This is different from taking notes or making an outline. Your map not only identifies the major ideas of interest from a chapter or your class notes, but also shows you the relationships among the ideas in much the same way that a road map illustrates how highways and other roads link cities.

Examine these words:

pool	water	biking
grass	sky	raining
tree	playing	thinking

Every one of these words is a concept. Concepts usually form a picture in your mind.

Look at the following words. Are they concepts?

the	when	with
to	was	can
has	be	

No. They don't cause a picture to form in your mind. They are linking words. They connect ideas or concepts.

Organizing Concepts

From the concept map in **Figure A**, on the next page, you can see what a concept map looks like, but we will continue to discuss the fine points of mapping and you will do some maps on your own.

Another feature of mapping ideas is that some concepts or ideas are more central, or general, and include other concepts. What is the main idea of this list of concepts: Tokyo, Mexico City, Seoul, New York, Bombay? Cities, of course. What is the main idea of this list: car, bus, train, bicycle, truck? Each of these concepts is an example of a vehicle.

Try to remember the words below after reading them once or twice:

racket	net
ellipse	helmet
starfish	mitt
tuna	bat
square	diamond
seahorse	star

You probably couldn't remember all of them. Even if you did remember almost all of them, it's a good bet that you were already categorizing them.

You shouldn't need as much time to memorize the list of words below.

square	touchdown	necklace
circle	goal	bracelet
triangle	basket	earring

Easier, wasn't it? This second list was already categorized. If you learn in a way that carries more meaning, it's easier to remember! That's how concept mapping works, too.

Making Learning Faster

You can see in **Figure A** that every concept map should have at its top the most general and all-inclusive concept. The smaller, more specific concepts and examples should go below. It might help you to capitalize the first letter of the main concept or idea. You can write the other, more specific, concepts using all lowercase letters. Your maps should show a pattern from most general to most specific, from the top of the map to the bottom of the map. Try to understand how the concept map in **Figure B** shown on the following page was made before you try one yourself. First read the following paragraph and make a list of any important words that you think should be learned.

What is life? What is the difference between living and nonliving things? If you were in a natural wilderness area, it would be easy for you to pick out the living things and nonliving things. The animals and plants are the living organisms. Organisms are made up of many substances organized into living systems. The rocks, air, water, and soil are nonliving. They contribute substances to the living organisms.

Figure A

Connecting Ideas

In the preceding paragraph, there seem to be two general ideas: living and nonliving. You can make either two separate maps, the chief concept of one being "living" and of the other being "nonliving," or one map, using "natural things" as the main idea or main concept. Capitalize the first letter of the main concept and put it at the top of the map. In this case, the main concept "natural things" did not actually appear in the paragraph, but frequently it does. Since natural things can be living or nonliving, you can make these subconcepts parts of the main one. As you read the paragraph, you learned that living things are organisms, such as plants and animals, and that they are made up of substances that are organized into living systems.

The paragraph shows that living things are different from nonliving things, but that they are related to nonliving things. You can make that connection near the top of the map. The rest of the map should explain the connection, so you can follow what you learned in the paragraph. Nonliving things such as soil, water, and rocks all contribute substances that are organized into living systems.

continued

Now you have the entire map shown in **Figure B**. If you had a choice of studying the paragraph or looking at this map, you might agree that the map shows the concepts more clearly. This map gives you the main idea more quickly, and it's easier to understand everything because you've put it in a two-dimensional form that shows how all of these things are related.

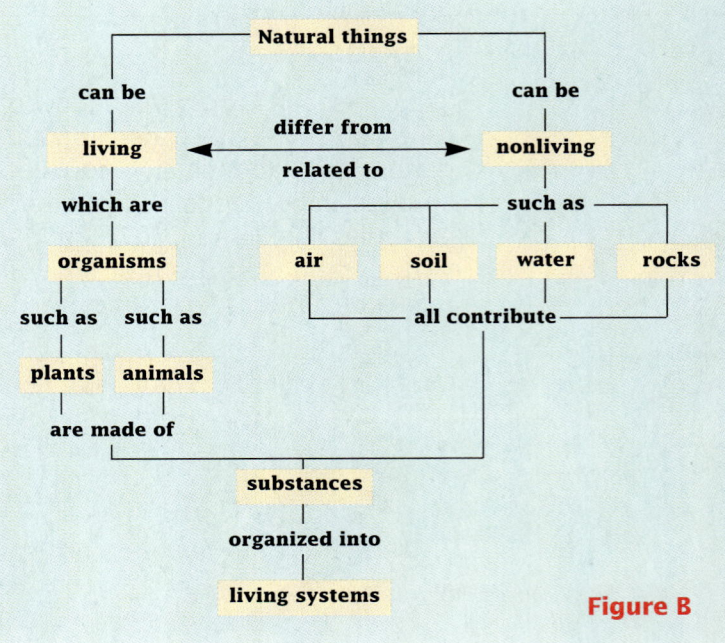

Figure B

Planning the Concept Map

Now you try it. Turn to page 52 and read the major titles in "Organelles: A Cell's Laborers."

You should have seen "The nucleus directs cell activities," "Cells manufacture and release energy," and "Cells maintain homeostasis." Of course, following those titles is quite a lot of information. Your job is to turn the information from page 52 into a concept map.

Identifying the main idea is easy—it's in the main title. It could be "Basic cell functions" or "Life functions of cells," or a similar shortened version of the title. This book is organized and written around concepts. In some other texts, the main idea may be buried in the para-graphs. So now you can put that main idea at the top of your map in a box.

Next it's time to look at the other important concepts and list them in the margin of your paper, or on another piece of paper. Use one piece of paper for each concept. Remember, your list shows how the concepts appeared in the reading, but it may not represent how the concepts are related to each other. Making those connections is your job.

Some of the concepts that should be in your list include the following: repro-duction, energy manufacture, energy release, mitochondria, chloroplasts, homeostasis, endoplasmic reticulum, and Golgi apparatus.

Building the Concept Map

The next step is to put the concepts in order, from the most general to the most specific. Some concepts will share the same rank and be equally specific. Remember that the examples are the most specific and will be at the bottom of the map.

Now begin to rearrange the concepts you've written on the pieces of paper. Start with the most general; get the main idea. Then, if there are two or more concepts that are equally specific, you're going to place them on the same level.

You probably figured out that the nucleus, mitochondria, chloroplasts, and the endoplasmic reticulum are some of the organelles described by the title. They should be placed below the main idea so that they are equally spread out across the map.

Now continue to lay out all of the other concepts under the subconcepts in the first row or layer until you have used them all. You can rearrange your pieces of paper at any time, so keep pushing them around as if they were the pieces of a jigsaw puzzle until you've arranged them the way you think they belong.

Remember not to use only the words given here. You're going to have to read the text material and add concepts to explain the major ones. For instance, your map may need to include the functions performed by the various cell organelles. Thus, under "homeostasis" you need to have "endoplasmic reticulum" and "Golgi apparatus." Under "energy manufacture" you will have "chloroplasts" and "photosynthesis," "food," "sugar," and "green plants."

Concept mapping takes some time at first; it will take about six times longer the first few times than it will after a week or two of practice.

Now you're going to make the connections among the concepts. Use lines to connect the concepts, and write linking words on the lines to show or tell why they are connected. Do this for all the lines connecting all the concepts. Glue or tape down your concept papers if you want to make the map permanent, or use a separate piece of paper to draw a sketch showing the way you've arranged the concepts.

Features of Good Concept Maps

Remember that practice is the key to good concept mapping and that you'll get better at it as you go along. Here are some things to remember as you get started.

- **A concept map does not have to be symmetrical. It can have more concepts on one side than on the other.**

- **There are no perfectly correct concept maps, only maps that come closer to the meanings you have for those concepts. As the map-maker, you must make it correct for you.**

- **Do not put more than three words in a concept box.**

- **Do not string out more than three boxes in a row or line without branching out.**

- **Write linking words to connect possible concepts using as few words as possible.**

If the relationships you have made between any two concepts are wrong, your teacher will help you sort out the misconception. Even if you are absolutely correct in your relationships, you may see another student's map that has differences. Both maps could be equally correct even though they may look nothing alike. Everyone thinks a little bit differently, and, as a result, everyone sees different relationships between certain concepts.

As you get practice in making concept maps, your teacher will examine your linking statements more closely. Since these links represent the relationships between concepts, whatever you write will tell whether you really understand how those two concepts are connected. A good concept map should always have the following characteristics:

- **It is two dimensional, not just a list of concepts. It should go from top to bottom and from general to specific, with lines that show how the concepts are related.**

- **It shows which concepts are more important by their placement on the map and by what concepts branch from them.**

- **It has many branches with no more than three concept boxes in a row and no more than three words in a concept box.**

- **It has only concepts in the boxes and only linking words on the lines.**

Word Roots

Analyzing Word Parts

A knowledge of common prefixes, roots, and suffixes can give you clues to the meaning of an unfamiliar word and help make learning new words easier. For example, each of the word parts in the chart below can be combined with the root *derm* to form another word.

Prefix	Root	Suffix
	derm	-otology
	derm	-otologist
hypo-	derm	-ic
	derm	-atitis
pachy		-derm

Example: dermatologist

derm (root):	skin
-logy (suffix):	study of
-ist (suffix):	someone who practices or deals with something

dermatologist—someone who studies or deals with skin

Following is a chart of prefixes, suffixes, and roots commonly found in the study of biology. Each is followed by its usual meaning, an example of a word in which it is used, and a definition of that word. You can use the chart to determine the meaning of a word like dermatology.

Prefix, root, or suffix	Definition	Example
a-	not, without	• asymmetrical, not symmetrical
ab-	away, apart	• abduct, move away from the middle
-able	able	• viable, able to live
ad-	to, toward	• adduct, move toward the middle
amphi-	both	• amphibian, type of vertebrate, like a frog, that lives both on land and in the water
ante-	before	• anterior, front of an organism
anti-	against	• antibiotic, substance, such as penicillin, capable of killing some disease-causing organisms
arche-	ancient	• *Archaeopteryx*, earliest known fossil bird
arthro-	joint	• arthropod, jointed-limbed organism belonging to the phylum Arthropoda
auto-	self, same, automatic	• autotrophic, able to manufacture its own food; autonomic, self-controlling, functionally independent, as in the autonomic nervous system
bi-	two	• bivalve, mollusk with two shells
bio-	life	• biology, the study of life
blast-	embryo	• blastula, hollow ball stage in the development of an embryo
carcin-	cancer	• carcinogenic, causing cancer
cereb-	brain	• cerebrum, part of the vertebrate brain

Prefix, root, or suffix	Definition	Example
chloro-	green	• chlorophyll, green pigment in plants necessary for photosynthesis
chromo-	color	• chromosome, structure found in eukaryotic cells that contains DNA
chondro-	cartilage	• Chondrichthyes, cartilaginous fish
circ-	around	• circulatory, system for moving fluids through the body
-cide	kill	• insecticide, a substance that kills insects
co-, con-	with, together	• conjoined twins, identical twins physically joined by a shared portion of anatomy at birth
-cycle	circle	• pericycle, layer of plant cells
cyt-	cell	• cytology, the study of cells
de-	remove	• dehydration, removal of water
derm-	skin	• dermatology, study of the skin
di-	two	• diploid, full set of chromosomes found in somatic cells
dia-	through	• dialysis, separation of molecules using a membrane
ecol-	dwelling, house	• ecology, the study of living things and their environments
ecto-	outer, outside	• ectoderm, outer germ layer of developing embryo
-ectomy	removal	• appendectomy, removal of the appendix
endo-	inner, inside	• endoplasm, cytoplasm within the plasma membrane
epi-	upon, over	• epiphyte, plant growing upon another plant
ex-, exo-	outside of	• exobiology, the search for life elsewhere in the universe
gastro-	stomach	• gastropod, type of mollusk
-gen	type	• genotype, genes in an organism
-gram	write or record	• climatogram, record depicting the annual precipitation and temperature for an area
hemi-	half	• hemisphere, half of a sphere
hetero-	different	• heterozygous, different alleles inherited from parents
hist-	tissue	• histology, the study of tissues
homeo-	the same	• homeostasis, maintenance of the same conditions in an organism as the environment changes
hydro-	water	• hydroponics, growing plants in water instead of soil
hyper-	above, over	• hypertension, blood pressure consistently higher than normal
hypo-	below, under	• hypothalamus, part of the brain
-ic	of or pertaining to	• hypodermic, under or below the skin
inter-	between, among	• interbreed, breed within a family or strain
intra-	within	• intracellular, inside a cell
iso-	equal	• isogenic, having an identical set of genes
-ist	someone who practices or deals with something	• biologist, someone who studies life
-logy	study of	• biology, the study of life
macro-	large	• macromolecule, large molecule such as DNA or protein

continued

Prefix, root, or suffix	Definition	Example
mal-	bad	• malnourished, poorly nourished
mega-	large	• megaspore, larger of two types of spores produced by some ferns and flowering plants
meso-	in the middle	• mesoglea, jellylike material found between outer and inner layer of coelenterates
meta-	change	• metamorphosis, change in form in insects
micro-	small	• microscopic, too small to be seen with the unaided eye
mono-	one, single	• monoploid, one set of alleles
morph-	form	• morphology, study of form of organisms
neo-	new	• neonatal, newborn
nephr-	kidney	• nephron, functional unit of the kidney
neur-	nerve	• neurotransmitter, chemical released by a neuron to stimulate or inhibit other neurons
oo-	egg	• oogenesis, gamete formation in female diploid organisms
org-	living	• organism, living thing
-oma	swelling	• carcinoma, cancerous tumor
orth-	straight	• orthodontist, dentist who straightens teeth
para-	near, on	• parasite, organism that lives on and gets nutrients from another organism
path-	disease	• pathogen, disease-causing organism
peri-	around	• pericardium, membrane around the heart
photo-	light	• phototropism, bending toward light by plants
phyto-	plants	• phytoplankton, part of plankton consisting of plant life
poly-	many	• polypeptide, sequence of amino acids joined together to form a protein
-pod	foot	• pseudopod, false foot that projects from the main part of an amoeboid cell
pre-	before	• prediction, a forecast of events before they take place; the outcome, if a hypothesis is accepted
-scope	instrument to see something	• microscope, instrument to see very small objects; telescope, instrument to see very distant objects
semi-	partially	• semipermeable, allowing some particles to move through
-some	body	• chromosome, structure found in eukaryotic cells that contains DNA
sub-	under	• substrate, molecule on which an enzyme acts
super-, supra-	above	• superficial, on or near the surface of a tissue or organ
syn-	with	• synapse, junction of one neuron with another
-tomy	to cut	• appendectomy, surgery to cut out the appendix
trans-	across	• transformation, the transfer of genetic material from one organism to another
visc-	organ	• viscera, internal organs of the body cavity

SI Measurement

Using Conversion Factors

Length

The metric system is used for making measurements in science. The official name of this system is the Système International d'Unités, or International System of Measurements (SI). SI is a decimal system. This means that all relationships between units of measurement are based on powers of 10. There are several prefixes that can be combined with an SI unit. These prefixes change the unit to mean some other power of 10. For example, the SI base unit of length is the meter. When the prefix *kilo* is added to the base unit *meter*, the word *kilometer* is formed (a derived unit meaning 1000 meters). When the prefix

centi is combined with the base unit *meter*, the word *centimeter* is formed (a derived unit meaning 1/100 of a meter).

Table 1 lists some commonly used prefixes and their meanings. The prefixes modify the value of the base to describe very small or very large measurements, like the diameter of an animal cell or distances between cities. You can easily convert from one SI derived unit to another. For example, there are 100 centimeters in a meter and there are 10 decimeters in a meter. Therefore, there are 10 centimeters in 1 decimeter. **Table 2** shows you the relationship of SI units to commonly used English units.

Table 1 SI Prefixes

Prefix	Symbol	Exponential	Rational	Meaning
tera	T	10^{12}	1,000,000,000,000	trillion
giga	G	10^{9}	1,000,000,000	billion
mega	M	10^{6}	1,000,000	million
kilo	k	10^{3}	1,000	thousand
hecto	h	10^{2}	100	hundred
deka	da	10^{1}	10	ten
deci	d	10^{-1}	1/10	one-tenth
centi	c	10^{-2}	1/100	one-hundredth
milli	m	10^{-3}	1/1,000	one-thousandth
micro	m	10^{-6}	1/1,000,000	one-millionth
nano	n	10^{-9}	1/1,000,000,000	one-billionth
pico	p	10^{-12}	1/1,000,000,000,000	one-trillionth

continued

Teacher's notes

Practice Exercises

Have students complete the Practice Exercises on page 845. Answers to the Practice Exercises are found at the bottom of page 845.

Table 2 SI Conversion Table

SI Units	From SI to English	From English to SI
Length		
kilometer (km) = 1,000 m	1 km = 0.62 mile	1 mile = 1.609 km
meter (m) = 100 cm	1 m = 3.28 feet	1 foot = 0.305 m
centimeter (cm) = 0.01 m	1 cm = 0.394 inch	1 inch = 2.54 cm
millimeter (mm) = 0.001 m	1 mm = 0.039 inch	
micrometer (μm) = 0.000 001 m		
nanometer (nm) = 0.000 000 001 m		
Area		
square kilometer (km^2) =100 hectares	1 km^2 = 0.3861 square mile	1 square mile = 2.590 km^2
hectare (ha) = 10,000 m^2	1 ha = 2.471 acres	1 acre = 0.4047 ha
square meter (m^2) = 10,000 cm^2	1 m^2 = 10.765 square feet	1 square foot = 0.0929 m^2
square centimeter (cm^2) = 100 mm^2	1 cm^2 = 0.155 square inch	1 square inch = 6.4516 cm^2
Volume		
liter (L) = 1,000 mL = 1 dm^3	1 L = 1.06 fluid quarts	1 fluid quart = 0.946 L
milliliter (mL) = 0.001 L = 1 cm^3	1 mL = 0.034 fluid ounce	1 fluid ounce = 29.57 mL
microliter (μL) = 0.000 001 L		
Mass		
kilogram (kg) = 1,000 g	1 kg = 2.205 pounds	1 pound = 0.4536 kg
gram (g) = 1,000 mg	1 g = 0.0353 ounce	1 ounce = 28.35 g
milligram (mg) = 0.001 g		
microgram (μg) = 0.000 001 g		

Temperature

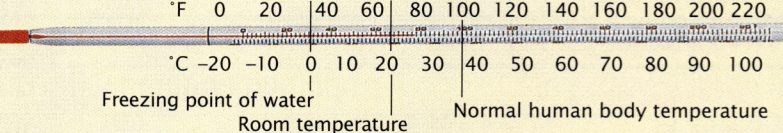

Freezing point of water
Room temperature
Normal human body temperature

The top of the thermometer is marked off in degrees Fahrenheit (˚F). To read the corresponding temperature in degrees Celsius (˚C), look at the bottom half of the thermometer. For example, 50˚F is the same temperature as 10˚C. You may also use the formulas given at the right for conversions.

Conversion of Fahrenheit to Celsius:
˚C = 5/9 (˚F − 32)

Conversion of Celsius to Fahrenheit:
˚F = (9/5 ˚C) + 32

844

Choosing the Correct Unit

Remember that every measurement may be expressed using more than one prefix. Usually, the simplest expression is best. For example, it is better to state the diameter of a cell as 5 μm rather than 0.000,0005 m, even though the two measurements are equivalent. The distance between cities is more appropriately stated in km rather than in cm.

Practice Exercises

1. What prefix and unit represents 10 meters?

2. What derived unit represents 1/100 of a meter?

3. There are 1000 millimeters in 1 meter (1 millimeter = 1/1000 of a meter). Express 500 millimeters in meters.

4. How many gigameters is 145 million kilometers?

5. The length of line segment **A** in **Figure 1** can be represented in millimeters, centimeters, and meters. All of the measures are equivalent, and all represent the length of line segment A. Estimate the length of segment A, and then measure it. Express the measurement in each of the following units.

   a. millimeters_____
   b. centimeters_____
   c. meters_____

6. Animal and plant cells are studied under a microscope. Some cells are so small that their parts are measured in micrometers. What part of a meter is a micrometer?

7. A millimeter is the smallest distance pictured on the metric ruler in **Figure 2**. Use the ruler to answer each of the following.

   a. A points to _____ mm or _____ cm
   b. B points to _____ mm or _____ cm
   c. C points to _____ mm or _____ cm
   d. D points to _____ cm or _____ mm
   e. E points to _____ cm or _____ mm

8. Choose the most appropriate metric unit for measuring each of the following:

   a. Area of a sheet of notebook paper
   b. Area of a desktop
   c. Area of an airport runway

9. A rectangular plot of land is to be seeded with grass. The plot to be seeded is 22 m by 28 m. If 1 kg of seed is needed for each 85 m² of land, how many kg of grass seed are needed?

A

Figure 1

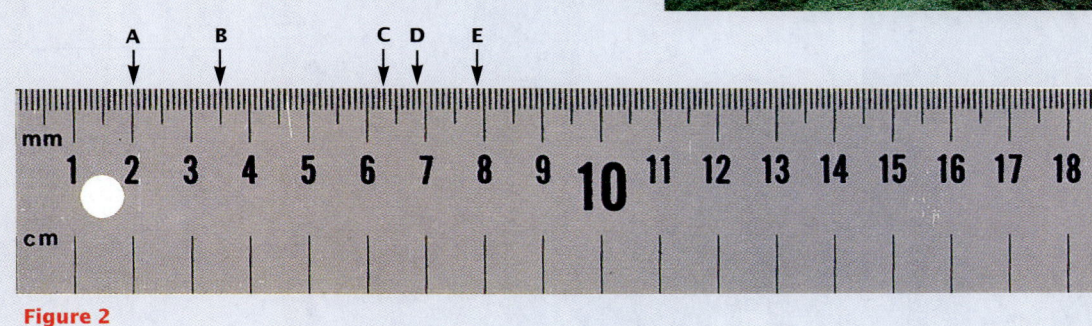

Figure 2

ANSWERS TO PRACTICE EXERCISES

1. dekameter (dam)

2. centimeter (cm)

3. 0.5 m (1/2 m)

4. 145 Gm

5. a. 93 mm
   b. 9.3 cm
   c. 0.093 m

6. 1 millionth, 10^{-6}, 1/1,000,000

7. a. 20 mm, 2 cm
   b. 35 mm, 3.5 cm
   c. 62 mm, 6.2 cm
   d. 6.8 cm, 68 mm
   e. 7.8 cm, 78 mm

8. Possible answers include the following:
   a. cm   c. m
   b. m   d. km

9. 22 m × 28 m = 616 m²,
   616 m² ÷ 85 m² = 7.25 kg of seed

Practice Exercises

Have students complete the Practice Exercises on page 847. Answers to the Practice Exercises are found at the bottom of page 847.

Interpreting Food Labels

Nutrition Facts Labels

The government now requires uniform nutrition labeling of packaged foods. The Nutrition Facts label on similar packaged foods indicates nutrition information based on similar serving sizes. The label at the right shows the nutrition information on a carton of whole milk.

The Nutrition Facts label indicates the serving size, the actual amount of a nutrient per serving, and the % Daily Value of that nutrient in one serving. We can see that one cup (236 mL) of whole milk contains 8 g of protein, which is 16 percent of the recommended daily amount (daily value) of protein we should consume. How would you determine the total amount, in grams, of protein needed each day?

The Nutrition Facts label lists *some* of the nutrients important to your health. For example, only two vitamins, vitamin A and vitamin C, and two minerals, calcium and iron, are listed.

Since vitamin D is added to milk, it is also listed on containers of milk. The Nutrition Facts label also indicates the maximum or minimum recommended daily consumption of some nutrients. We can see that on a daily basis, we should consume a maximum of 300 mg of cholesterol and a minimum of 25g of fiber.

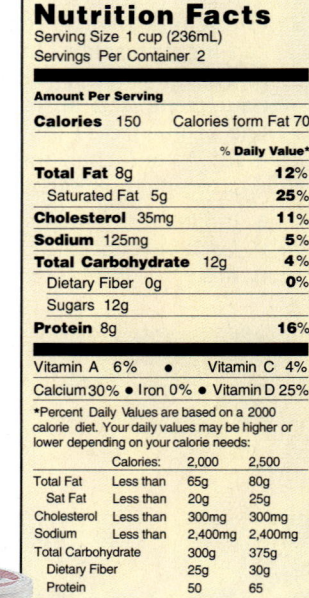

Nutrition Facts
Serving Size 1 cup (236mL)
Servings Per Container 2

Amount Per Serving

Calories 150	Calories form Fat 70

	% Daily Value*
Total Fat 8g	12%
Saturated Fat 5g	25%
Cholesterol 35mg	11%
Sodium 125mg	5%
Total Carbohydrate 12g	4%
Dietary Fiber 0g	0%
Sugars 12g	
Protein 8g	16%

Vitamin A 6%	•	Vitamin C 4%
Calcium 30%	• Iron 0% •	Vitamin D 25%

*Percent Daily Values are based on a 2000 calorie diet. Your daily values may be higher or lower depending on your calorie needs:

	Calories:	2,000	2,500
Total Fat	Less than	65g	80g
Sat Fat	Less than	20g	25g
Cholesterol	Less than	300mg	300mg
Sodium	Less than	2,400mg	2,400mg
Total Carbohydrate		300g	375g
Dietary Fiber		25g	30g
Protein		50	65

Practice Exercises

Use the Nutrition Facts label from a can of peas to answer the questions below.

Nutrition Facts	Amount /Serving	% DV*	Amount /Serving	% DV*
Serving Size 1/2cup (120g)	Total Fat 0g	0%	Total Carb.11g	4%
Servings Per Container 2	Sat.Fat 0g	0%	Fiber 4g	16%
Calories 60	**Cholest.** 0mg	0%	Sugars 3g	
Fat Cal. 0	**Sodium** 380mg	16%	**Protein** 4g	

Percent Daily Values (DV) are based on a 2,000 calorie diet.

Vitamin A 6 % • Vitamin C 10% • Calcium 2 % • Iron 6 %

1. What is the size of one serving of peas?
2. What percent of the recommended daily amount of carbohydrate consumption is in one serving of peas?
3. How many servings of these canned peas would you have to eat in order to get 50 percent of the vitamin C that you should have on a daily basis?
4. How many grams of fiber does one serving of peas provide?

Calories and Equivalents

One important piece of information listed on the Nutrition Facts label is the number of calories per serving. The calorie content of food depends on its components. Notice that the calories per gram on the label shows that fats contain more than twice as many calories as equal masses of carbohydrates and proteins.

You probably have heard the term *junk food.* Junk foods are foods that have a high caloric content and contain few or no nutrients. The amount of a specific nutrient that a food provides in relation to its calories is known as its nutrient density. A food that is high in calories and low in a spe-

Nutrition Facts
Serving Size 1oz. (28g/about 22 chips)
Servings Per Container 6

Amount Per Serving	
Calories 150	Calories form Fat 90

	% Daily Value*
Total Fat 10g	**15%**
Saturated Fat 1.5g	**8%**
Cholesterol 0mg	**0%**
Sodium 140mg	**6%**
Total Carbohydrate 14g	**5%**
Dietary Fiber 1g	**4%**
Sugars 0g	
Protein 2g	

Vitamin A 0%	•	Vitamin C 10%
Calcium 0%	•	Iron 2%

*Percent Daily Values are based on a 2000 calorie diet. Your daily values may be higher or lower depending on your calorie needs:

	Calories:	2,000	2,500
Total Fat	Less than	65g	80g
Sat Fat	Less than	20g	25g
Cholesterol	Less than	300mg	300mg
Sodium	Less than	2,400mg	2,400mg
Total Carbohydrate		300g	375g
Dietary Fiber		25g	30g

Calories per a gram:
Fat 9 • Carbohydrate 4 • Protein 4

cific nutrient is called nutrient-limited for the nutrient. Foods with greater amounts of nutrients in relation to calories are called nutrient-plus.

Practice Exercises

5. How many calories are in one serving of whole milk?
6. How many calories are in three servings of canned peas?
7. Why are the calories in junk foods often referred to as empty calories?
8. Use the Nutrition Facts label from a bag of potato chips to answer the following.
   a. Which nutrient group makes up the greatest percentage of the potato chips?
   b. How many calories are there in six servings of potato chips?
   c. Are potato chips a good source of iron? Why or why not? Are potato chips nutrient-plus or nutrient-limited for iron?
9. Keep a record of your total food intake for an entire day. Write down the name of the food, the approximate serving size, and the number of servings of the food you eat. Use the Nutrition Facts label on the packaged foods and a calorie chart to answer the following questions.
   a. What was your approximate caloric intake for the day?
   b. How did your consumption of total fat, vitamin C, fiber, and sodium compare with the recommended amounts for these nutrients?
   c. Which foods were nutrient-plus for vitamin A?
10. A type of food contains 200 calories per serving, 120 of which come from fat. It contains less than 2 percent of the % Daily Values of vitamins A and C, no calcium or iron, and 3 percent of the % Daily Value for fiber. Is it a junk food? Why or why not?
11. One serving of a food contains 20 g of fat, 14 g of protein, and 3 g of carbohydrate. Approximately how many calories are in one serving?

847

ANSWERS TO PRACTICE EXERCISES

1. 1/2 cup, 120 g
2. 4%
3. 5
4. 4 g
5. 150
6. 180
7. Junk foods are high in calories, but they provide little or no nutrients.
8. a. Fats; b. 900; c. Because one serving of

potato chips provides only 2 percent of the iron needed on a daily basis, potato chips are not a good source of iron. Potato chips are nutrient-limited for iron.

9. Answers will vary depending on the students' food choices.

10. The high number of calories per serving that come from fat and the low vitamin and mineral content indicate that it is a junk food.

11. 248 calories

Oak tree

The Six Kingdoms

Kingdom	Number of Named Species*	Description	Examples
Archaebacteria	100	Prokaryotic; unicellular; lack nucleus or other internal compartments; most primitive form of life; existed for more than 2 billion years before protists appeared; usually occupy hostile environments (extremes of temperature, salinity, no oxygen)	*Methanobacterium, Halobacterium, Thermoplasma*
Eubacteria	4,000+	Prokaryotic; unicellular; lack nucleus or other internal compartments; most primitive form of life; existed for more than 2 billion years before protists appeared; most-studied of the bacteria	*Escherichia coli, Vibrio cholerae, Salmonella typhimurium*
Protista	43,000	Eukaryotic; all but algae are unicellular; aquatic; all have nucleus and internal compartments; almost all have mitochondria and many also have chloroplasts; most have cell walls; aquatic; most diverse kingdom	*Volvox*, Paramecium, red algae
Fungi	77,000	Eukaryotic; multicellular; almost all terrestrial; cell walls of chitin; nonmotile cells; exclusively heterotrophic with nutrition by absorption; mitosis occurs within nuclear envelope	Mushrooms, yeasts
Plantae	265,350	Eukaryotic; multicellular; terrestrial; cell walls of cellulose; nonmotile cells (except gametes of a few forms); photosynthetic, with chloroplasts	Oak trees, mosses, roses, ferns
Animalia	1,203,000	Eukaryotic; multicellular; both aquatic and terrestrial; no cell walls or chloroplasts; heterotrophic with nutrition by ingestion; reproduction is predominately sexual	Humans, sea stars, earthworms, flies

* Approximate number identified

Volvox

Escherichia coli

Human

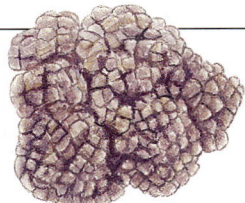
Methanosarcina

Kingdom Archaebacteria

Group*	Main Characteristics	Examples
Methanogens	Strict anaerobes that produce methane from carbon dioxide and hydrogen; die in the presence of oxygen; found in swamps and marshes	*Methanosarcina, Methanobacterium*
Thermoacidophiles	Many grow in hot, acidic environments (hot springs); use hydrogen sulfide as energy source	*Acidianus, Thermoproteus*
Halophiles	Require high concentrations of salt to survive; live in the Dead Sea and the Great Salt Lake	*Halococcus, Natronococcus*

Kingdom Eubacteria

Anabaena

Group*	Main Characteristics	Examples
Cyanobacteria	Photosynthetic bacteria; common on land and in the ocean; responsible for "blooms" in polluted waters	*Anabaena, Spirulina, oscillatoria*
Chemoautotrophs	Ancient group of bacteria that can grow without sunlight or other organisms; play critical role in Earth's nitrogen cycle	*Nitrobacteria, Nitrosomonas,* sulfur bacteria
Enterobacteria	Typically rigid, rod-shaped, heterotrophic bacteria; responsible for many diseases of animals and plants	*Salmonella typhimurium, Escherichia coli, Vibrio cholerae*
Pseudomonads	Straight or curved rods with flagella at one end; very common in soil; many are serious plant pathogens	*Pseudomonas aeruginosa*
Spirochaetes	Long spiral-shaped cells; responsible for several serious diseases	*Borrelia* (Lyme disease), *Treponema* (syphilis)
Actinomycetes	Filamentous (and thus sometimes mistaken for fungi); spore-producing; sources of several antibiotics	*Mycobacteria,* dental plaques
Rickettsias	Obligatory parasites within the cells of vertebrates and arthropods; responsible for Rocky Mountain spotted fever	*Rickettsia rickettsii*
Gliding and budding bacteria	Long rods; often aggregate into gliding masses; some members form upright spore-bearing structures of unusual complexity for bacteria	*Myxobacteria*

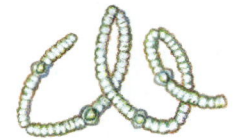

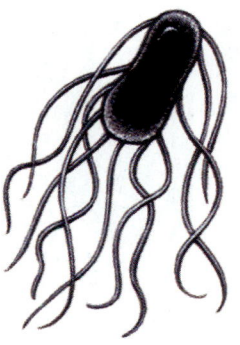
Salmonella typhimurium

Borrelia

* The bacteria are the least studied kingdoms. Since thousands of species are yet to be discovered and named, the number of species identified is not provided in this table.

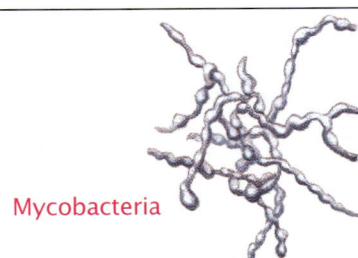
Mycobacteria

continued

Kingdom Protista

Diatom

Vorticella

Chlamydomonas

Kelp

Phylum	Number of Species*	Characteristics	Examples
Bacillariophyta "Diatoms"	11,500+	Unicellular; photosynthetic; cells within a unique shell made of opaline silica—resembles a small box with a lid; some radially symmetrical; chloroplasts resemble those of brown algae; shells often form very thick deposits called diatomaceous earth	Diatoms
Ciliophyta "Ciliates"	8,000	Very complex single cells; heterotrophic; possess rows of cilia and two types of cell nuclei; genetic code differs in several respects from that of other organisms; some scientists argue that ciliates should be assigned to a separate kingdom of their own	Vorticella, Paramecium
Chlorophyta "Green algae"	7,000	Unicellular, colonial, and multicellular species; all photosynthetic; chloroplasts very similar to those of green plants; most scientists believe that plants evolved from green algae	Chlamydomonas, Chlorella, Volvox, Ulva, Spirogyra
Rhodophyta "Red algae"	4,000	Almost all multicellular; photosynthetic; chloroplasts evolved symbiotic cyanobacteria; no cilia or centrioles; one of the most ancient groups of protists	Nori (edible algae)
Sporozoa "Sporozoans"	3,900	Unicellular; heterotrophic; nonmotile; spore-forming parasites of animals; complex life cycles, often involving alternation between different hosts; *Plasmodium* is responsible for malaria, which kills more than 1 million people each year	Plasmodium
Zoomastigina "Zoomastigotes"	3,000	Mostly unicellular; heterotrophic; flagellated; free-living or parasitic; a highly diverse phylum; similar cells exist in sponges, suggesting that animals evolved from a zoomastigote	Choanoflagellates
Phaeophyta "Brown algae"	1,500	Multicellular; photosynthetic; marine; some are the longest, fastest growing, and most photosynthetically productive species on Earth	Kelps, Sargassum

* Approximate number identified

Phylum	Number of Species*	Characteristics	Examples
Dinoflagellata "Dinoflagellates"	1,000+	Unicellular; photosynthetic; body enclosed within cellulose plates; two unequal flagella beating in grooves that encircle the body; often symbiotic with corals	*Gonyaulax*, "Red tides"
Euglenophyta "Euglenoids"	800	Unicellular; both photosynthetic and heterotrophic species; asexual; most live in fresh water; very similar to zoomastigotes; chloroplasts similar to those of green algae; thought to have evolved from the same symbiotic bacteria as algae	*Euglena*
Oomycota "Water molds"	475	Unicellular parasites on living or dead tissue; cell walls of cellulose (not chitin, like those of fungi); spores have two unequal flagella, one directed forward, the other backward; responsible for Irish potato famine of 1845–1847	*Saprolegnia*, rusts, mildews
Myxomycota "Plasmodial slime molds"	450	Heterotrophic; individuals stream along as a nonwalled multinucleate mass of "slime" cytoplasm; no centrioles; all nuclei undergo mitosis synchronously; when dry or starving, spores form to start a new individual in a more favorable environment	*Arcyria*
Foraminifera "Forams"	300	Unicellular; heterotrophic; marine; have shells of organic material with many pores through which thin cytoplasmic threads project; shells are reinforced with grains of calcium carbonate or sand; the White Cliffs of Dover and other limestone deposits are made almost entirely of foram shells	Forams
Rhizopoda "Amoebas"	300	Unicellular; heterotrophic; amorphously shaped cells that move using cytoplasmic extensions called pseudopods; asexual reproduction (fission) only	*Amoeba*
Acrasiomycota "Cellular slime molds"	65	Heterotrophic; amoeba-shaped cells that aggregate into a moving mass called a slug when deprived of food; the slug produces spores that form new amoebas elsewhere	*Dictyostelium*
Caryoblastea "Pelomyxa"	1	Unicellular; lack mitochondria and chloroplasts; have two kinds of bacterial symbionts; do not undergo mitosis; possibly an early stage in the evolution of eukaryotes	*Pelomyxa palustris*

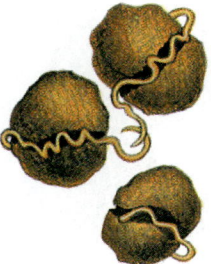

Gonyaulax

Euglena

Foram

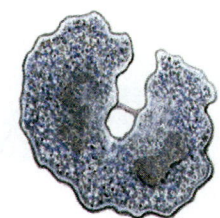

Amoeba

continued

Kingdom Fungi

Morel

Penicillium

Puffball

Rhizopus

Division	Number of Species*	Main Characteristics	Examples
Ascomycota "Sac fungi"	30,000	Fusion of hyphae leads to formation of reproductive structures of densely interwoven hyphae (visible part) that contain characteristic microscopic structures called asci (singular, ascus); two nuclei fuse within the ascus, forming a diploid zygote that undergoes meiosis; asexual reproduction is also common	Morels, yeasts, truffles, cup fungi
Deuteromycetes "Fungi imperfecti"	17,000	Sexual reproduction not observed; mostly ascomycetes that have lost the ability to reproduce sexually	*Penicillium*, *Aspergillus*
Basidiomycota "Club fungi"	16,000	Fusion of hyphae leading to formation of a densely interwoven reproductive structure (mushroom) with characteristic microscopic, club-shaped structures called basidia (singular, basidium); only the terminal cell of a basidium produces spores (all cells of an ascus do); reproduction is usually sexual	Puffballs, mushrooms, toadstools, rusts
Zygomycota "Molds"	665	Multinucleate hyphae without septa except for reproductive structures; fusion of hyphae leads directly to formation of a zygote, which divides by meiosis when it germinates; asexual reproduction is also common	*Rhizopus* (black bread mold)

Symbiotic Associations**

	Number of Species*	Main Characteristics	
Lichens	15,000	Fungi (almost always ascomycetes) that have cyanobacteria, green algae, or both, living in their cells; derive energy from their photosynthetic partners and cannot survive without them; able to survive freezing or drying out; can invade the harshest of habitats; break down rocks and set the stage for invasion by other organisms	
Mycorrhizae	5,000	Symbiotic associations between fungi and plants; 80 percent of all plants have mycorrhizae in their roots; the most common by far are endomycorrhizae, in which zygomycete fungal hyphae penetrate the cells of the plant root; some plants of temperate regions have ectomycorrhizae, in which basidiomycete (or, rarely, ascomycete) hyphae surround but do not penetrate the root	

* Approximate number identified

** Fungi can form mutualistic associations with algae to form lichens or with plants to form mycorrhizae.

Kingdom Plantae

Division	Number of Species*	Main Characteristics	Examples
Anthophyta "Flowering plants"	235,000	Angiosperms; ovules fully enclosed by carpel; after fertilization, carpel seeds mature to become fruit; flowers are re-productive structures; fertilization in-volves two sperm nuclei—one forms the gamete, the other fuses with polar bodies to form endosperm for the seed	Roses, oak trees, wheat
Bryophyta "Mosses"	16,600	No vascular tissue; lack true roots, stem, and leaves; obtain nutrients by osmosis and diffusion; found chiefly in moist habi-tats; seedless; sperm must swim to eggs; two other divisions, Hepaticophyta (liver-worts) and Antherocerophyta (hornworts), are also considered bryophytes and make up 40 percent of the bryophyte species	*Polytrichum, Sphagnum* (peat moss)
Pterophyta "Ferns"	12,000	Seedless, vascular plants; motile sperm germinate into free-living haploid individ-uals; two minor divisions, Sphenophyta (horsetails) and Psilophyta (whisk ferns), contain 21 additional species	*Sphaeropteris* (tree ferns), Azolla
Lycophyta "Lycopods"	1,000	Seedless vascular plants; motile sperm; similar in appearance to mosses, but are diploid; found chiefly in moist habitats	*Lycopodium,* club mosses
Coniferophyta "Conifers"	550	Gymnosperms; ovules exposed at time of pollination; pollen dispersed by wind; sperm lack flagella; needle-like or scale-like leaves; most species are evergreens	Fir, spruce, pine, redwood trees
Cycadophyta "Cycads"	100	Gymnosperms; sperm flagellated and motile, but reach egg by a pollen tube; palmlike trees; very slow growing	Sago palms, cycads
Gnetophyta "Shrub teas"	70	Gymnosperms; sperm nonmotile; shrubs and vines	*Welwitschia,* Mormon teas
Ginkgophyta "Ginkgo"	1	Gymnosperms; motile sperm reach egg by a pollen tube; deciduous (drop leaves in winter); fanlike leaves; fleshy and illscented seeds	Ginkgos

* Approximate number identified

Rose bush

Tree fern

Lycopodium

Fir tree

continued

Kingdom Animalia

Beetle

Oyster

Planarian

Man-of-war

Phylum	Number of Species*	Main Characteristics	Examples
Arthropoda "Arthropods"	1,000,000	Segmented bodies with paired, jointed appendages; chitinous exoskeletons; open circulatory system; many groups possess wings; most successful of all animal phyla	Beetles, spiders, flies, lobsters
Mollusca "Mollusks"	110,000	Soft-bodied animals with a true coelom; three-part body plan consisting of head-foot, visceral mass, and mantle; many have shells; 35,000 species are terrestrial; almost all have a unique rasping tongue called a radula	Oysters, snails, squids, octopuses
Chordata "Chordates"	42,500	Possess a notochord, a dorsal nerve cord, pharyngeal slits, and a tail at some stage of life; notochord is replaced during development by the spinal column in vertebrates; pharyngeal slits are lost during development of terrestrial vertebrates; 20,000 species are terrestrial	Fishes, dinosaurs, mammals
Platyhelminthes "Flatworms"	12,000	Solid worms; bilaterally symmetrical; three germ layers; digestive cavity has only one opening; no coelom or pseudocoelom; simplest animals in which organs occur	Planaria, liver flukes, tapeworms
Nematoda "Roundworms"	12,000	Tiny, parasitic, unsegmented worms; tubular; bilaterally symmetrical; complete digestive tract with mouth and anus, pseudocoelom; no cilia	*Ascaris*, pinworms, *Filaria*, hookworms
Annelida "Segmented worms"	12,000	Serially segmented worms; complete digestive tract with coelom; some have chitinous bristles (setae) on each segment that anchor them while crawling	Leeches earthworms, polychaetes
Cnidaria "Jellyfish"	10,100	Radially symmetrical; gelatinous; digestive cavity with only one opening; tentacles with stinging cells called nematocysts	Hydras, man-of-wars
Porifera "Sponges"	5,000	Asymmetrical animals; lack distinct tissues and organs; sessile; mostly marine; body consists of two layers that are supported by a stiff skeleton with many pores; internal cavity lined with unique food-filtering cells called choanocytes	Barrel sponges

Phylum	Number of Species*	Main Characteristics	Examples
Echinodermata "Echinoderms"	6,000	Deuterostomes; adults radially symmetrical; endoskeleton of calcium plates; water vascular system with tube feet; five-part body plan; able to regenerate lost body parts	Sea stars, sand dollars, sea urchins
Bryozoa "Moss animals"	4,000	Deuterostomes; microscopic, aquatic organisms that form branching colonies; U-shaped row of ciliated tentacles for feeding (the lophophore)	Plumatella, *Bowerbankia*
Rotifera "Wheel animals"	2,000	Small, wormlike or spherical animals; have digestive tract; have crown of cilia around mouth resembling a wheel; pseudocoelomates; almost all live in fresh water	Rotifers
Minor worms	980	**Rhynchocoela** (ribbon worms): bilaterally symmetrical; acoelomates; marine; long, extendible proboscis **Pognophora** (tube worms): deep-sea worms that live within chitinous tubes in ocean floor; sessile; long, beardlike tentacles **Hemichordata** (acorn worms): marine worms with dorsal and ventral nerve cords **Onychophora** (velvet worms): protostomes; chitinous exoskeleton; evolutionary relics **Chaetognatha** (arrow worms): deuterostomes; coelomates; bilaterally symmetrical; marine worms with large eyes and powerful jaws	Acorn worms, giant tube worms, velvet worms
Brachiopoda "Lamp shells"	250	Have a lophophore like bryozoans, but within two clamlike shells; more than 30,000 fossilized species known	*Lingula*
Ctenophora "Comb jellies"	100	Transparent, gelatinous marine animals; eight bands of cilia; largest animals that use cilia for locomotion; often bioluminescent; digestive tract with anal pore	Comb jellies, sea walnuts
Phoronida "Lophophores"	12	Lophophorate tube worm; U-shaped gut instead of straight digestive tube of other tube worms; protostomes; often live in dense populations	*Phoronis*
Loricifera "Sand animals"	6	Minute; bilaterally symmetrical; pseudocoelomates; live in spaces between grains of sand; mouthparts exhibit a unique flexible tube; discovered in 1983	*Nanoloricus mysticus*

* Approximate number identified

Sea star

Bowerbankia

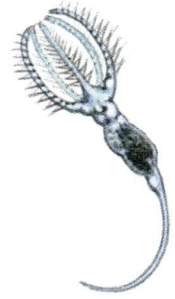

Rotifer

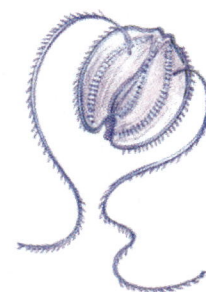

Comb jelly

Glossary

Pronunciation Key

Sound	As In	Phonetic Respelling
a	b<u>a</u>t	(BAT)
ay	f<u>a</u>ce	(FAYS)
ah	l<u>o</u>ck	(LAHK)
	<u>a</u>rgue	(AHR gyoo)
ow	<u>ou</u>t	(OWT)
ch	<u>ch</u>apel	(CHAP uhl)
eh	t<u>e</u>st	(TEHST)
ai	r<u>a</u>re	(RAIR)
ee	<u>ea</u>t	(EET)
	f<u>ee</u>t	(FEET)
	sk<u>i</u>	(SKEE)
ih	b<u>i</u>t	(BIHT)
eye	<u>i</u>dea	(eye DEE uh)
y	r<u>i</u>pe	(RYP)

Sound	As In	Phonetic Respelling
ihng	go<u>ing</u>	(GOH ihng)
k	<u>c</u>ard	(KAHRD)
	<u>k</u>ite	(KYT)
ng	a<u>ng</u>er	(ANG guhr)
oh	<u>o</u>ver	(OH vuhr)
aw	d<u>o</u>g	(DAWG)
	h<u>or</u>n	(HAWRN)
oy	f<u>oi</u>l	(FOYL)
u	p<u>u</u>ll	(PUL)
oo	p<u>oo</u>l	(POOL)
s	<u>c</u>ell	(SEHL)
	<u>s</u>it	(SIHT)
sh	<u>sh</u>eep	(SHEEP)

Sound	As In	Phonetic Respelling
th	<u>th</u>at	(THAT)
	<u>th</u>in	(THIHN)
uh	c<u>u</u>t	(CUHT)
ur	f<u>er</u>n	(FURN)
y	<u>y</u>es	(YEHS)
yoo	gl<u>o</u>bule	(GLAHB yool)
yu	c<u>u</u>re	(KYUR)
z	bag<u>s</u>	(BAGZ)
zh	trea<u>s</u>ure	(TREHZH uhr)
uh	med<u>a</u>l	(MEHD uhl)
	tal<u>e</u>nt	(TAHL uhnt)
	penc<u>i</u>l	(PEHN suhl)
	<u>o</u>ni<u>o</u>n	(UHN yuhn)
	playf<u>u</u>l	(PLAY ful)
	d<u>u</u>ll	(DUHL)
uhr	pap<u>er</u>	(PAY puhr)

acid: compound capable of donating a hydrogen ion to a water molecule; from the Latin *acere*, meaning "to be sour" (p. 291)

acid rain: any precipitation with unusually high acidity (p. 291)

acoelomate (ay SEEL oh mayt): term describing animals without a body cavity; from the Greek *a* + *koilia*, meaning "not" + "hollow" (p. 444)

activation energy: amount of energy needed to start a chemical reaction (p. 78)

active site: pocket formed in the folds of an enzyme and to which a substrate or substrates binds; site of the reaction catalyzed by the enzyme (p. 80)

active transport: one-way transport of substances across a membrane; requires energy (p. 70)

adaptation: process by which a species becomes better suited to its environment (p. 182)

adrenal gland: either of two almond-sized endocrine organs lying atop the kidney and producing more than two dozen hormones; from the Latin *ad* + *renes*, meaning "at" + "kidneys" (p. 639)

aerobic (ehr OH bihk) **exercise**: continuous, low- or moderate-intensity exercise; from the Greek *aēr* and *bias*, meaning "air" and "life" (p. 594)

AIDS: **A**cquired **I**mmune **D**eficiency **S**yndrome, the final stages of a disease in which the immune system has been disabled; caused by HIV (p. 345)

allele (uh LEEL): one of two or more alternate forms of a gene; from the Greek *allēlon* meaning "of one another" (p. 119)

allergy: immune system response to non-pathogenic antigens such as pollen; from the Greek *all* + *ergon*, meaning "different" + "work" (p. 688)

alternation of generations: describes a life cycle in which a haploid form alternates with a diploid form (p. 381)

altruism (AHL troo ihz uhm): self-sacrificing behavior; from the Latin *alter*, meaning "another" (p. 245)

alveoli (al VEE oh leye): tiny air sacs within the lungs, through which gases enter and leave the circulatory system; from the Latin *alveus*, meaning "hollow cavity" (p. 671)

amnion (AM nee ahn): thin membrane forming a closed sac around the embryo; from the Greek *amnos*, meaning "lamb" (p. 473)

amniotic egg: the egg of reptiles, birds, and mammals; the embryo develops within two protective membranes, the chorion and amnion (p. 473)

anaerobic (an uh ROH bihk) **exercise**: exercise that requires muscles to work at high intensity for a very brief period, creating a shortage of oxygen; from the Greek *an* + *aēr* and *bios*, meaning "not" + "air" and "life" (p. 594)

analogous structures: features of organisms that are similar but which have evolved independently; from the Greek *analogos*, meaning "proportionate" (p. 320)

angiosperm (AN jee oh spurm): seed plant that has flowers and produces seeds within an ovary; from the Greek *angeion* and *speirein*, meaning "case" and "to sow" (p. 386)

anorexia nervosa (an oh RECK see ah ner VOH sah): eating disorder in which sufferers starve themselves; from the Greek *an* + *oregein*, meaning "without" + "appetite" (p. 704)

anthropoid (AN thruh poyd): member of the primate suborder that contains monkeys, apes, and humans; from the Greek *anthrōpos*, meaning "man" (p. 215)

antibiotic: chemical substance with capacity to destroy or inhibit growth of bacteria; from the Greek *anti* + *bios*, meaning "against" + "life" (p. 343)

antibiotic resistance: arises when a few bacteria with mutant genes are able to survive antibiotic treatment and reproduce, passing that resistance on to the next generation (p. 344)

antibody: defensive protein produced by white blood cells in response to a foreign substance, released by B cells (pp. 163, 685)

anticodon: three-nucleotide sequence of transfer RNA (tRNA) molecule, which is complementary to an mRNA codon; from the Latin *anti* + *code*, meaning "against" + "book" (p. 144)

antigen (AN tuh juhn): molecule that can be recognized by white blood cells and that can trigger a defensive response (p. 681)

antihistamine: chemical that blocks the action of histamines thus reducing the body's reactivity to an allergen (p. 688)

anuran (uh NUR uhn): member of the order Anura, which contains frogs and toads; from the Greek *an* + *oura*, meaning "without" + "tail" (p. 536)

anus: posterior opening of the digestive tract; from the Latin *anus*, meaning "ring" (p. 445)

arachnid (uh RAK nihd): any of the animals of the class Arachnida, such as spiders, scorpions, mites, and ticks; from the Greek *arachnē*, meaning "spider" (p. 501)

archaebacteria (AHR kee bahk TIHR ee ah): distinctive group of bacteria thought to have given rise to eukaryotes; from the Greek *archaikos* + *baktērion*, meaning "ancient" + "small staff" (p. 195)

artery: blood vessel that carries blood away from the heart (p. 654)

asthma (AZ muh): respiratory disease in which airways in the lungs become restricted because of sensitivity to stimuli; from the Greek *asthma*, meaning "panting" (p. 674)

atom: smallest unit of matter that cannot be broken down by chemical means; from the Greek *a* + *tomos*, meaning "not" + "cut" (p. 26)

ATP: adenosine triphosphate; molecule used by cells to deliver energy for chemical reactions (p. 83)

atrium (AY tree uhm): chamber of the heart that receives blood from the body; from the Latin *atrium*, meaning "large room" (p. 658)

autoimmune disease: disease in which the ability of the immune system to distinguish self from non-self breaks down and the body attacks its own cells (p. 689)

autonomic nervous system: division of the nervous system that carries messages to muscles and glands, and that usually works without our noticing (p. 620)

autotroph (AWT oh trahf): organism that makes its own food; from the Greek *auto-* + *trophē*, meaning "self" + "food" (p. 257)

axon (AK sahn): long extension of a nerve cell that carries impulses away from the cell body; from the Greek *axōn*, meaning "axis" (p. 601)

balancing selection: situation in which natural selection for an allele is balanced by selection against it, and the allele remains at the same frequency (p. 183)

B cell: white blood cell that produces and releases antibodies (p. 685)

behavior: an action or series of actions performed by an animal in response to a stimulus (p. 233)

bilateral symmetry: characteristic of an animal that can be separated into nearly mirror-image halves by being cut lengthwise along the midline of the body; from the Latin *bi-* + *latus* and *symmetria*, meaning "two" + "side" and "measured together" (p. 442)

binocular vision (beye NAHK yuh luhr VIHZH uhn): vision in which both eyes simultaneously view the same object; from the Latin *bi-* + *ocularis* and *videre*, meaning "double" + "of the eye" and "to see" (p. 214)

biology: study of living things; from the Greek *bios* and *logos*, meaning "life" and "study of" (p. 5)

biome (BEYE ohm): major type of terrestrial ecological community; from the Greek *bi-* and the Latin *oma*, meaning "life" and "mass" (p. 264)

bipedal (beye PEHD uhl): walking on two legs; from the Latin *bi-* + *pedalis*, meaning "double" + "of the foot" (p. 220)

blood pressure: force exerted on the inner walls of arteries (p. 664)

blood sugar: glucose dissolved in the blood, providing energy to the cells (p. 644)

blood type: classification of blood according to the presence or absence of specific marker proteins (p. 656)

blood vessel: any of the tubes that carry blood from the heart to the organs and cells of the body and back again; from the Latin *vas*, meaning "vessel" (p. 654)

body plan: overall organization of an animal's body (p. 437)

book lung: in arachnids, highly folded sacs, used for gas exchange, that are located inside the body and that open to the outside through a spiracle (p. 467)

bulimia (buh LEEM ee uh): eating disorder in which sufferers engage in binge-purge cycles of eating followed by vomiting or intestinal elimination; from the Greek *boulimia*, meaning "ox hunger" (p. 704)

cancer: a condition in which normal restraints on cell reproduction break down, resulting in rapid, uncontrolled cell division; from the Greek *karkinōma*, meaning "crab" or "cancer" (p. 109)

capillary: one of the network of tiny blood vessels from which substances in the blood move into surrounding cells; from the Latin *capillus*, meaning "hair" (p. 654)

capillary action: movement of a liquid up a narrow tube caused by the forces of attraction between the liquid molecules and the walls of the tube (p. 396)

carbohydrate (KAHR boh HEYE drayt): compound composed of carbon, hydrogen, and oxygen in the ratio of 1:2:1; used by living things as a source of energy; from the Latin *carbon* and Greek *hydōr*, meaning "coal" and "water" (p. 30)

carcinogen (kahr SIN uh juhn): any substance that causes cancer; from the Greek *karkinōma*, meaning "crab" or "cancer" (p. 289)

cardiac muscle: muscle found in the heart; from the Greek *kardia* and the Latin *musculus*, meaning "heart" and "little mouse (muscle)" (p. 590)

cardiovascular disease: disease of the heart or blood vessels (p. 668)

carnivore (KAHR nuh vawr): flesh-eating organism; from the Latin *caro* and *vorare*, meaning "flesh" and "to devour" (p. 257)

catalyst (KAT uh lihst): material that speeds up a chemical reaction without being used itself; from the Greek *katalyein*, meaning "to dissolve" (p. 79)

cell: smallest unit that can perform all life processes; from the Latin *cella*, mean-

ing "small room" (pp. 16, 41)

cell cycle: 5-phase sequence of eukaryotic cell growth and division (p. 107)

cell membrane: bilipid layer that forms the cells outer surface, essential to the cell's metabolism; also called the plasma membrane; from the Latin *membrana*, meaning "skin" (p. 41)

cell surface marker: membrane protein that distinguishes a body's cells from foreign matter (p. 66)

cellular respiration: process by which living things obtain energy from the bonds of food molecules; from the Latin *respirare*, meaning "to breathe" (p. 84)

cell wall: thick, outer layer that encloses and supports most plant, fungal, and bacterial cells and some protist cells (p. 54)

central nervous system: brain and spinal cord (p. 611)

cephalization (sehf uh lih ZAY shuhn): evolution of a definite head end; from the Greek *kephalikos*, meaning "head" (p. 442)

cerebellum (sehr uh BEHL uhm): small structure in the rear part of the brain that controls balance, posture, and coordination; from the Latin *cerebellum*, diminutive for "brain" (p. 612)

cerebrum (suh REE bruhm): large rounded area of the brain divided into left and right hemispheres; from the Latin *cerebrum*, meaning "brain" (p. 612)

cervix: ring of strong, flexible muscles forming the lower part of the uterus; from the Latin *cervix*, meaning "neck" (p. 724)

chelicera (kuh LIHS uh ruh): one of the first pair of appendages of arachnids and their relatives; used for feeding, and in

some species as poison-delivering fangs; from the Greek *chēlē*, meaning "claw" (p. 501)

chemical bond: attractive force that holds two atoms together in a molecule; from the Latin *alchymia*, meaning "alchemy" (p. 27)

chemical reaction: the forming and breaking of covalent bonds (p. 29)

chemosynthesis: production of food using the energy contained in inorganic molecules; from the Greek *syn-* + *tithenai*, meaning "together" + "to place" (p. 335)

chitin (KY tihn): polysaccharide that makes up the tough cell walls of fungi and the exoskeletons of insects and other arthropods (p. 374)

chlamydia (KLU mih dee uh): common sexually-transmitted disease in the United States; caused by the *Chlamydia* bacterium and with symptoms similar to gonorrhea (p. 740)

chlorofluorocarbon (KLAWR oh FLOH roh KAHR buhn): any of a group of compounds that contain carbon, chlorine, and fluorine; often used as coolants, propellants, or foaming agents (p. 292)

chlorophyll (KLAWR uh fihl): the major pigment in plants that helps gather energy for photosynthesis; from the Greek *chlōros* and *phyllon*, meaning "pale green" and "a leaf" (p. 87)

chloroplast (KLAWR uh plast): carbohydrate-producing organelles found in green plants and protists; from the Greek *chlōros*, meaning "pale green" (p. 52)

chorion (KAWR ee ahn): watertight protective membrane surrounding the embryos of reptiles, birds, and mammals; from the Greek *chorion*, meaning "fetal membrane" (p. 473)

chromatin (KROH muh tihn): a threadlike complex of DNA and proteins in the nucleus of a nondividing cell (p. 101)

chromosome (KROH muh sohm): compact structure of tightly coiled DNA that forms prior to mitosis; from the Greek *chrōma*, meaning "color" (pp. 33, 101)

cilia (SIL ee uh): hairlike projections on certain cells and mobile organisms; from the Latin *celare*, meaning "to conceal" (p. 358)

circulatory system: network of blood-carrying vessels that transports nutrients, oxygen, wastes, and carbon dioxide; from the Latin *circulari*, meaning "to form a circle" (p. 446)

cladogram (KLAD uh gram): branching diagram showing evolutionary relationships among a set of organisms; from the Greek *klados*, meaning "branch" (p. 321)

class: collection of similar orders; from the Latin *classis*, meaning "class" or "division" (p. 318)

cloning (KLOHN ihng): growing a large number of genetically identical cells from one cell; from the Greek *klōn*, meaning "twig" (p. 154)

codon (KOH dahn): three-nucleotide sequence in mRNA specifying a particular amino acid; basic unit of genetic code; from the Latin *code*, meaning "book" (p. 143)

coelacanth (SEE luh kanth): any member of a group of lobe-finned bony fishes; from the Greek *koilos* and *akantha*, meaning "hollow" and "thorn" (p. 531)

coelom (SEE luhm): fluid-filled body cavity that separates the muscles of the body wall from the muscles that surround the gut (p. 446)

coevolution (KOH ev uh LOO shuhn): situation in

which two or more species evolve in response to each other; from the Latin *co-* + *evolvere*, meaning "with" + "to roll" (p. 273)

commensalism (kuh MEN suhl ihz uhm): ecological relationship between two organisms in which one benefits and the other neither benefits nor is harmed; from the Latin *com-* + *mensa*, meaning "with" + "table" (p. 277)

community: all the organisms that live in an ecosystem (p. 254)

competition: situation in which two or more organisms attempt to use the same scarce resource (p. 279)

competitive exclusion: process in which one species is outcompeted and dies out within an ecosystem (p. 279)

complete metamorphosis: series of abrupt changes in the form of young insects as they develop into adults; stages include larva, nymph, pupa (or chrysalis), adult (p. 509)

composting (KOHM pohst ihng): the process of mixing organic debris and allowing it to begin decomposition to make an organic fertilizer (p. 423)

cone: 1. in plants, clusters of scales or modified leaves that produce gametophytes (p. 385); 2. receptor cell in the retina of the eye that detects color, produces sharp images, and detects bright light; from the Greek *kōnos*, meaning "cone" (p. 624)

conjugation: the transfer of genetic material from one bacterium to another; from the Latin *conjugatus*, meaning "to join together" (p. 332)

connective tissue: bones, blood, ligaments and tendons; from the Latin *texere*, meaning "to weave" (p. 576)

consumer: organism that obtains its energy by eating other organisms; from the Latin *consumere*, meaning "to take up" (p. 256)

continental drift: movement of the continents over geologic time (p. 202)

contour feather: feathers that cover the body of a bird, giving shape to its wings and tail (p. 553)

control experiment: a comparison of an experimental group with a control group (p. 12)

control group: the group not exposed to the test condition (p. 12)

convergent evolution: process whereby organisms that are not related to each other evolve similar features (p. 320)

copepod (KOH puh pahd): very small, sometimes parasitic crustacean living in either salt water or fresh water; from the Greek *kōpē*, meaning "oar" (p. 518)

cotyledon (kaht uh LEED uhn): leaflike structure of a plant embryo that stores food or helps absorb food stored elsewhere; from the Greek *kotylēdon*, meaning "cavity" (p. 384)

covalent bond: chemical bond formed by sharing of electrons; from the Latin *co-* + *valere*, meaning "with" + "to be strong" (p. 27)

crop rotation: alternating cultivation of two or more crops in the same field (p. 422)

crossing-over: exchange of genetic material between paired homologous chromosomes during meiosis (p. 112)

cross-pollination: transfer of pollen from the anther of a flower to the stigma of a flower on another plant of the same species (p. 402)

cuticle (KYOOT ih kuhl): waxy, waterproof layer that covers the surface of most plants; from the Latin *cuticula*, meaning "skin" (p. 381)

cyanobacteria (SY ahn oh bak TIHR ee ah): group of photosynthetic bacteria thought to be the first organisms to release oxygen; from the Greek *cyano-* + *bactērion*, meaning "blue" + "small staff" (p. 196)

cytokinesis (syt oh kuh NEE sihs): division of the cytoplasm following mitosis; from the Greek *kytos* and *kinēsis*, meaning "a hollow" and "motion" (p. 105)

cytoplasm (SYT uh plaz uhm): material inside the cell membrane containing the necessary components for cell life; from the Greek *plassein*, meaning "to form" (p. 50)

cytosol (SYT uh sohl): liquid portion of the cytoplasm (p. 51)

 D

decapod (DEHK uh pahd): a crustacean with 10 legs, such as a lobster or a shrimp; from the Greek *deka* and *pous*, meaning "ten" and "foot" (p. 517)

decomposer: organism that obtains its energy by consuming organic wastes; from the Latin *de-* + *componere*, meaning "from" + "to put together" (p. 256)

dendrite (DEHN dryt): short branch of a nerve cell that carries impulses toward the cell body; from the Greek *dendron*, meaning "tree" (p. 601)

derived character: a unique characteristic, such as hair, that defines a group of organisms (p. 321)

dermis: layer of skin below the epidermis; from the Greek *derma*, meaning "skin" (p. 578)

deuterostome (DOOT uhr oh stohm): animal in which the first opening in the embryo does not form the mouth, but often becomes the anus; from the Greek *deuteros* and *stoma*, meaning "second" and "mouth" (p. 451)

development: process of growth and cell specialization (p. 17)

diabetes mellitus (deye uh BEET eez muh LYT uhs): a chronic disease in which cells are unable to absorb glucose from blood and tissue fluids; from the Latin *diabetes* and *mellitus*, meaning "siphon" and "honeyed" (p. 645)

diffusion (dif FYOO zhuhn): movement of molecules from a region of higher concentration to one of lower concentration; from the Latin *diffusus*, meaning "poured in different directions" (p. 67)

diploid (DIH ployd): describes cells that have two sets of chromosomes; from the Greek *diploos*, meaning "double" (p. 103)

direct development: developmental pattern in arthropods in which the young are miniature copies of adults (p. 509)

directional selection: situation in which selection for or against an allele in a population is unopposed (p. 183)

divergence: accumulation of differences between two or more species or populations; from the Latin *divergere*, meaning "to turn apart" (p. 185)

diversity: measure of the number of species living in an ecosystem (p. 254)

DNA fingerprint: a pattern of dark bands that reflects the composition of an organism's DNA (p. 166)

dominant: describes the allele that is expressed as a trait (p. 119)

double fertilization: fertilization in angiosperms in which one sperm fuses with an egg and a second sperm fuses with two nuclei (p. 403)

double helix: spiral of two strands, as in DNA structure; from the Greek *helissein*, meaning "to turn around" (p. 139)

down feather: fine feathers that grow underneath contour feathers and that are specialized for insulation (p. 553)

 E

ecological race: a population of a species that differs genetically from other populations of the same species because they have adapted to different environments (p. 184)

ecology: study of relationships of organisms to their environment; from the Greek *oikos* and *logos*, meaning "house" and "study of" (p. 254)

ecosystem: self-sustaining collection of organisms and their physical environment (p. 254)

ectoderm (EHK tuh durm): outer layer of cells of an embryo; from the Greek *ektos* and *derma*, meaning "outside" and "skin" (p. 441)

ectopic pregnancy: pregnancy in which the embryo grows somewhere other than in the uterus; from the Greek *ektopos*, meaning "out of place" (p. 740)

ectotherm (EHK tuh thurm): animal that uses heat from the environment to control its body temperature; from the Greek *thermē*, meaning "heat" (p. 208)

ejaculation (ee jak yoo LAY shuhn): expulsion of sperm from the male's body; from the Latin *ejaculari*, meaning "to throw out" (p. 721)

electron: elementary particle with negative electric charge; from the Greek *elektron*, meaning "amber" (p. 26)

element: matter that is made of only one kind of atom; from the Latin *elementum*, meaning "first principle" (p. 26)

embryo: fertilized egg that has begun to divide; from the Greek *en-* + *bryein*, meaning "in" + "to swell" (p. 726)

emphysema (em fuh SEE muh): condition of the lung in which it has lost its elasticity, greatly reducing the efficiency of gas exchange, often caused by smoking; from the Greek *emphysēma*, meaning "inflation" (p. 674)

endocrine (EN duh krihn) **gland**: an organ that is part of the endocrine system, which produces most of the body's hormones and which releases them without ducts directly into the bloodstream; from the Greek *krinein*, meaning "to separate" (p. 631)

endocytosis (ehn doh seye TOH sihs): process in which a cell surrounds and engulfs a particle; from the Greek *kytos*, meaning "hollow" (p. 72)

endoderm (EHN doh durm): inner layer of cells of the embryo; from the Greek *endon* and *derma*, meaning "within" and "skin" (p. 441)

endoplasmic reticulum (ehn duh PLAZ mihk rih TIK yuh luhm): organelle that consists of a network of membranes that transports substances made by the cell; from the Greek *plassein* and Latin *reticulum*, meaning "to form" and "network" (p. 52)

endoskeleton: internal supporting structure, such as bones; from the Greek *skeletos*, meaning "dried up" (p. 452)

endotherm (EHN doh thurm): animal that uses heat produced by metabolism to control its body temperature; from the Greek *thermē*, meaning "heat" (p. 208)

enzyme: protein that acts as a catalyst for a biochemical reaction; from the Greek *en-* + *zyme*, meaning "in" + "leaven" (p. 79)

epidermis: 1. in plants, the outermost layer, or

layers, of cells that cover the plant body (p. 394); 2. outermost layer of the skin, consisting of several layers of cells; from the Greek *epi-* + *derma*, meaning "upon" + "skin" (p. 578)

epididymis (ehp uh DIHD ih mihs): duct on top of and behind each testis that temporarily stores sperm; from the Greek *didymos*, meaning "testicle" (p. 720)

epithelial (ehp uh THEE lee uhl) **tissue**: tightly connected cells, arranged in flat sheets, such as the skin (p. 575)

esophagus (ih SAHF uh guhs): muscular tube from the pharynx that permits food to descend to the stomach; from the Greek *oisein* and *phagein*, meaning "to be going to carry" and "to eat" (p. 706)

essential amino acid: the nine amino acids needed by, but not produced by, the animal body and supplied by a mixed diet; in humans, one of nine specific compounds containing nitrogen (p. 415)

eubacteria (YOO bak TIHR ee ah): group of bacteria thought to have evolved more recently than the archaebacteria; from the Greek *eu-* + *baktērion*, meaning "true" + "small staff" (p. 195)

eukaryote (yoo KAR ee oht): organisms whose cells contain a membrane-bound nucleus and membrane-bound organelles, such as plants, animals, fungi, and protists; from the Greek *karyon* and *-otes*, meaning "nut (kernel)" and "inhabitant" (p. 50)

evolution (ehv uh LOO shuhn): genetic change in a species over time (p. 17)

exhalation: exit of air from the lungs during breathing, equalizing air pressure (p. 672)

exocytosis (ehk soh sye TOH sihs): process in which a cell discharges

substances or waste; from the Greek *kytos*, meaning "hollow" (p. 72)

exon: portions of DNA that code for proteins (p. 148)

exoskeleton: supporting structure that surrounds the body; from the Greek *skeletos*, meaning "dried up" (p. 451)

experiment: the controlled test of a hypothesis; from the Latin *experimentum*, meaning "a trial, test" (p. 12)

external fertilization: fertilization that takes place outside the body of either parent (p. 472)

 F

facilitated diffusion: transport of substances through channels in either direction through the cell membrane; from the Latin *facere* and *diffusus*, meaning "to do or make" and "poured in different directions" (p. 69)

fallopian tube: tube that carries eggs released from the ovaries to the uterus; named for Gabriel Fallopius, Italian anatomist (p. 723)

family: group of closely related genera (p. 318)

feedback: a system of self-regulation (p. 634)

feedback inhibition: slowing or stopping of an early reaction in a series of biochemical reactions when levels of the end product become high (p. 94)

fermentation: the incomplete breakdown of organic compounds in the absence of oxygen; from the Latin *fermentum*, meaning "leavening, yeast" (p. 91)

fertility: a soil's ability to supply plants with nutrients (p. 422)

fertilization: the fusion of gametes (p. 728)

fertilizer: substance that adds nutrients to soil (p. 423)

fetus: the embryo from the ninth week of development until birth (p. 729)

"fight or flight" reaction: reaction produced by hormones of the adrenal medulla in response to certain stresses such as fear, anger, pain, excitement, or physical exertion, enabling the body to respond to emergencies; long-term reactivity is associated with stress-related disorders and disease (p. 639)

filtration: first stage of urine formation, in which smaller solutes are forced out of the blood (p. 711)

flagellum (fluh JEHL uhm): whiplike structure of some cells, used for locomotion; from the Latin *flagellum*, meaning "whip" (p. 333)

follicle (FAHL ih kuhl): in reproductive biology, a fluid-filled chamber within the ovary in which an egg matures; from the Latin *folliculus*, meaning "small bag" (p. 726)

fracture: broken bone; from the Latin *fractus*, meaning "broken" (p. 586)

fruit: enlarged ovary of a flowering plant that contains seeds; from the Latin *fructus*, meaning "enjoyment" (p. 403)

fundamental niche: total niche that an organism could potentially use within an ecosystem (p. 278)

 G

gamete (GAM eet): a haploid reproductive cell, such as an egg or sperm cell; from the Greek *gametē*, meaning "a wife" (p. 110)

gametophyte (guh MEET uh fyt): in a plant's life cycle, the haploid plant (stage) that produces gametes and grows from a spore; from the Greek *gamein* and *phyein*, meaning "to marry" and "to grow" (p. 381)

gastrulation (gas troo LAY shuhn): process of forming layers of cells in the embryo; from the Greek *gastēr* meaning "stomach" (p. 441)

gene: segment of DNA that codes for a trait (p. 7)

gene expression: use of genetic information in DNA to make proteins (p. 141)

genetic code: the correspondence between nucleotide triplets in DNA and the amino acids in proteins; from the Greek *gignesthai* and the Latin *code*, meaning "to be born" and "book" (p. 143)

genetic disorder: the harmful effects produced by certain mutations (p. 128)

genetic engineering: the process of moving genes from the chromosomes of one organism to those of another (p. 153)

genetics (juh NEHT ihks): science of biological inheritance (p. 117)

genotype (JEE nuh typ): constitution of an organism in terms of its genes; from the Greek *genos*, meaning "race, kind" (p. 119)

genus (JEE nuhs): category in biological classification in which closely related species are grouped; from the Latin *genus*, meaning "race, kind" (p. 314)

germination: to sprout or start to grow; from the Latin *germinare*, meaning "to sprout" (p. 405)

gill: one of the structures used by aquatic animals for gas exchange (p. 464)

global warming: the increase in global temperatures (p. 293)

glycolysis (gly KAHL uh sihs): process that breaks down glucose in a cell's cytoplasm and releases a small amount of energy; from the Greek *glykys* and *lysis*, meaning "sweet" and "dissolving" (p. 90)

goiter (GOY tuhr): swollen thyroid gland caused by lack of iodine; from the Latin *guttur*, meaning "throat" (p. 642)

Golgi (GOHL jee) **apparatus**: organelle that delivers substances released by the endoplasmic reticulum to specific places in a cell; named after Camillo Golgi, Italian neurologist (p. 52)

gradualism: hypothesis that evolution occurs at a slow, constant rate (p. 186)

grain: small seedlike fruit of cereal grasses; from the Latin *granum*, meaning "seed, kernel" (p. 411)

Gram staining: use of dyes to stain bacterial cell walls to aid in identification and diagnosis; named after Hans Christian Gram, Danish physician (p. 332)

greenhouse effect: warming of Earth's atmosphere resulting from heat trapped by carbon dioxide and other gases (p. 262)

green manure: crop that is grown to be plowed back into the soil to add organic matter (p. 422)

ground tissue: tissue that makes up the bulk of a plant's body, some parts of which are for storage and the rest for strength (p. 394)

guard hair: long, thick outer hair responsible for the color of an animal's coat (p. 564)

gut: internal passage through which food passes while being digested (p. 440)

gymnosperm (JIHM noh spurm): seed plant that does not produce its seeds within a fruit; from the Greek *gymnos* and *speirein*, meaning "naked" and "to sow" (p. 385)

 H

habitat: physical location where an organism lives in an ecosystem; from the Latin *habitare*, meaning "to inhabit" (p. 254)

half-life: the time it takes for one half of the radioactive atoms in a sample to decay (p. 176)

haploid (HAH ployd): describes cells that have only one set of chromosomes; from the Greek *haploos*, meaning "single" (p. 103)

hemodialysis (hee moh deye AL uh sis): process of removing blood from an artery, purifying it by dialysis, and returning it to a vein; from the Greek *haima* and *dialyein*, meaning "flowing blood" and "to dissolve" (p. 712)

hemoglobin (HEE moh gloh bihn): an iron-containing molecule in red blood cells that gives blood its color and which carries oxygen and carbon dioxide (p. 652)

herbivore (HUR buh vawr): consumer that eats only plants; from the Latin *herba* and *vorare*, meaning "grass" and "to devour" (p. 257)

heredity (huh RED ih tee): transmission of genetic information from parent to offspring (p. 17)

hermaphrodite (huhr MAHF roh deyt): animal with both female and male sexual organs; from the Greek myth in which Hermaphroditus shared a body with a nymph (p. 483)

heterotroph (HET uhr oh trohf): organism that cannot make its own food and feeds on other organisms or organic wastes; from the Greek *hetero-* + *trophē*, meaning "different" + "food" (p. 257)

heterozygous (heht uh roh ZY guhs): having two different alleles for a trait; from the Greek *zygon*, meaning "yoke" (p. 119)

histamine (HIHS tuh meen): chemical messenger that can increase mucus production and stimulate capillaries to swell and release fluids in response to the presence of an antigen (p. 688)

HIV: Human Immunodeficiency Virus, the virus that causes AIDS and which attacks and destroys helper T-cells (p. 345)

homeostasis (hoh mee oh STAY sihs): tendency to maintain stability in an organism amid environmental change; from the Greek *homo-* + *histanai*, meaning "similar" + "to stand" (p. 16)

hominid (HAHM ih nihd): two-legged primates such as humans and australopithecines; from the Latin *homo*, meaning "man" (p. 218)

homologous (hoh MAHL uh guhs) **structures**: structures that have a common ancestry; from the Greek *homologos*, meaning "agreeing" (p. 178)

homozygous (hoh muh ZY guhs): having identical alleles for a trait; from the Greek *zygon*, meaning "yoke" (p. 119)

hormone: chemical signal, secreted by specialized glands, that travels through the bloodstream and regulates the body's activities; from the Greek *hormeinō*, meaning "to stimulate" (p. 631)

human genome: entire collection of genes within human cells (p. 166)

humus (HYOO muhs): organic component of soil (p. 421)

hybrid: offspring that results from interbreeding between members of different species (p. 323)

hydrogen bond: linkage formed when a hydrogen atom in one molecule makes an additional bond to an atom in another molecule; from the Greek *hydōr* + *genēs*, meaning "water" + "born" (p. 44)

hydroponics: cultivation of plants in nutrient solutions instead of in soil; from the Greek *ponein*, meaning "to toil" (p. 423)

hypertension: condition in which the blood pressure is continually higher than normal; from the Greek *hyper* + the Latin *tensus*, meaning "above, over" + "stretched" (p. 669)

hyperthyroidism: overproduction of thyroxine with overstimulation of the thyroid gland (p. 641)

hypha (HY fuh): one of the slender filaments that make up the body of a fungus; from the Greek *hyphē*, meaning "web" (p. 374)

hypothalamus (heye poh THAL uh muhs): part of the upper end of the brain stem that regulates activities in the nervous and endocrine systems; from the Greek *hypo-* + *thalamos*, meaning "under" + "inner chamber" (p. 613)

hypothesis: a testable explanation for an observation; from the Greek *hypotithenai*, meaning "to put under" (p. 12)

hypothyroidism: production of too little thyroxine (p. 642)

immune response: immune system's defensive action to protect itself against a specific pathogen or antigen; from the Latin *in* + *munus*, meaning "in" + "service" (p. 683)

immunity: resistance to disease either natural or acquired (p. 687)

immunological surveillance: the constant patrol of the immune system, watching for surface changes on the body's cells (p. 690)

implantation: attachment of the embryo to the uterine wall within a few days after fertilization (p. 729)

imprinting: a type of learning that enables an animal to recognize members of its own species (p. 236)

incomplete metamorphosis: in arthropods, the gradual transformation into adult form (p. 509)

inducer: molecule that binds to the repressor protein, thereby enabling DNA to be transcribed; from the Latin *inducere*, meaning "to lead into" (p. 146)

inflammatory response: the body's response to injury, indicated by redness, swelling, and fever; from the Latin *flammare*, meaning "to flame" (p. 680)

inhalation: entry of air into the lungs during breathing, equalizing air pressure (p. 672)

insulin: a peptide hormone that interacts with a receptor at the cell membrane and helps glucose cross the membrane and enter the cytoplasm of a cell (p. 644)

internal fertilization: fertilization that occurs inside the female's body (p. 473)

introns: noncoding portions of the DNA (p. 148)

ion: an atom that has lost or gained one or more electrons and therefore has a net electric charge; from the Greek *ienai*, meaning "to go" (p. 27)

ionic bond: force of attraction between oppositely charged ions (p. 27)

joint: place where two or more bones connect; from the Latin *junctus*, meaning "joined" (p. 589)

karyotype (KAH ree oh typ): array of the chromosomes found in an individual's cells arranged in order of size and shape; from the Greek *karyon*, meaning "a nut, kernel" (p. 103)

keystone species: species whose niche affects many other species in the ecosystem so that it cannot be readily replaced if lost (p. 281)

kidney: one of two organs located toward the back of the abdominal cavity that maintains homeostasis, removes wastes, regulates water in the blood, and adjusts concentrations of other substances in the blood (p. 711)

kin selection: a behavioral mechanism in which an individual helps relatives (kin) reproduce rather than producing its own offspring (p. 245)

kingdom: collection of similar phyla (p. 318)

labor: second stage of pregnancy, when the uterus contracts strongly in order to push the baby out of the mother's body (p. 736)

large intestine: organ of the digestive system that stores, compacts, and then eliminates indigestible material; from the Latin *intestinus*, meaning "inward" (p. 709)

lateral line: row of pressure-sensitive cells within a fluid-filled canal on each side of a fish; from the Latin *latus*, meaning "side" (p. 462)

learning: the development of behaviors through experience (p. 236)

legume (LEHG yoom): member of a family of plants that includes peas and beans; from the Latin *legumen*, meaning "that which can be gathered" (p. 415)

leukocyte (LOO koh syt): white blood cell, called the "soldier" of the immune system (p. 680)

lichen (LY kuhn): mutualistic relationship between a fungus and an alga; from the Greek *leichein*, meaning "to lick" (p. 378)

ligament: strong, elastic bands of connective tissue joining bones together; from the Latin *ligare*, meaning "to bind" (p. 589)

lipid (LIHP ihd): class of organic compounds that includes fats and waxes that organisms may use to store energy; from the Greek *lipos*, meaning "fat" (p. 31)

lipid bilayer: the double layer of phospholipids found in cell membranes and organelles (p. 46)

liver: large glandular organ that secretes bile and modifies substances contained in the blood; metabolizes carbohydrates, fat, and proteins, and removes toxins from the blood (p. 708)

loam: soil that is a mixture of sand, silt, and clay (p. 421)

lobe-finned fish: a group of fishes having fleshy fins supported by a series of bones (p. 531)

lumber: wood from trees that has been cut down and sawed into boards and planks (p. 417)

lung cancer: cancer in the lung (p. 674)

lymphatic system: vessels that return to the circulatory system excess fluids that bathe the cells; from the Latin *lympha*, meaning "spring water" (p. 657)

lymphocyte (LIM foh syt): specialized white blood cell of the immune system formed in the lymphatic system; from the Latin *lympho* + *kytos* meaning "spring water" + "hollow" (p. 680)

macromolecule (MAHK roh MAWL uh kyool): large molecule, such as DNA or proteins, composed of several simple structural units; from the Greek *makros* and the Latin *moles*, meaning "long" and "mass" (p. 29)

macronutrient: nutrient that plants and animals need in relatively large amounts (p. 420)

macrophage (MAHK roh fayj): white blood cell which recognizes and destroys foreign invaders of the animal body; from

the Greek *makros* + *phagein*, meaning "long" + "to eat" (p. 681)

magnification: a microscope's ability to make an object appear larger (p. 56)

Malpighian (mal PIHG ee uhn) **tubule**: in insects and spiders, organ responsible for filtering blood; named after Italian physiologist Marcello Malpighi (p. 471)

mammary gland: gland of female mammals that secretes milk for suckling the young; from the Latin *mamma*, meaning "breast" (p. 559)

mandible: jaw of certain animals; from the Latin *mandibulum*, meaning "jaw" (p. 506)

marrow: spongelike center of long bones where blood cells are produced (p. 585)

marsupial (mahr SOO pee uhl): mammal that lacks a placenta and has an external pouch for young; from the Greek *marsypos*, meaning "pouch" (p. 560)

mass extinction: an episode during which large numbers of species became extinct (p. 197)

medusa: one of the two life stages of cnidarians, the jellyfish stage; from Greek mythology, a snake-haired beast-woman called Medusa (p. 481)

meiosis (my OH sihs): a form of cell division that reduces the number of chromosomes in a cell by half; from the Greek *meioun*, meaning "to make smaller" (p. 110)

melanin (MEHL uh nihn): brownish-colored pigment of skin cells; from the Greek *melas*, meaning "black" (p. 581)

melanoma (mehl uh NOH muh): cancer arising from the melanin-producing cells, which are located in the lowest epidermal layer (p. 583)

memory cell: B cell or T-cell that remains after infection and continues to patrol the body's tissues (p. 686)

menopause: shutdown of menstrual and ovarian cycles naturally in middle age or earlier by surgery; from the Latin *mens*, meaning "month" (p. 727)

menstrual (MEHN struhl) **cycle**: the series of changes occurring in the uterus and ovaries each month (p. 725)

meristem (MEHR uh stehm): region of actively dividing cells that give rise to all of the other plant tissues; from the Greek *meristos*, meaning "divided" (p. 394)

mesoderm: layer of tissue between the endoderm and ectoderm that develops into muscle, reproductive organs, and circulatory vessels; from the Greek *mesos* and *derma*, meaning "middle" and "skin" (p. 443)

metabolism (muh TAB uh liz uhm): the sum of all the chemical processes that use of release energy in an organism; from the Greek *metabolē*, meaning "change" (p. 78)

metamorphosis (meht uh MAWR fuh sihs): change in form, structure, or function of an animal as a result of development; from the Greek *metamorphē*, meaning "change" (p. 509)

micronutrient: nutrient that plants and animals need in very small amounts (p. 420)

microvillus: any of the hairlike projections coating the villi of the small intestine; from the Greek *mikros* and the Latin *villus*, meaning "small" and "tuft of hair" (p. 708)

mineral: inorganic compound, one not made from living things; from the Latin *minera*, meaning "ore" (p. 702)

mitochondrion (myt uh KAHN dree uhn): energy-

producing organelles in eukaryotes; from the Greek *mitos* and *chondros*, meaning "thread" and "grain" (p. 52)

mitosis (my TOH sihs): nuclear division; involves copying and separating chromosomes into two new nuclei; from the Greek *mitos*, meaning "thread" (p. 105)

molecule: group of atoms that form the smallest unit of a substance that can retain its chemical properties; from the Latin *moles*, meaning "mass" (p. 28)

monotreme (MAHN oh treem): mammal that lays eggs and has a single opening for the digestive and urinary tracts and for reproduction; from the Greek *monos* and *trēma*, meaning "single" and "hole" (p. 560)

mucous (MYOO kuhs) **membrane**: epithelial layer that releases mucus and is impenetrable to most pathogens; from the Latin *mucus*, meaning "slimy secretion" (p. 679)

mulch: bark chips or other organic matter placed on top of soil and used to prevent evaporation of water from the soil around a plant (p. 426)

multicellular (MUHL tee SEHL yoo lar) **organism**: a living thing made of more than one cell (pp. 63, 196)

muscle tissue: tissue made of cells that contract and return to original length; from the Latin *musculum* and *texere*, meaning "little mouse (muscle)" and "to weave" (p. 576)

mutagen (MYOOT uh juhn): environmental agent that can alter the structure of DNA; from the Latin *mutare*, meaning "to change" (p. 140)

mutation (myoo TAY shuhn): abrupt change in genotype of an organism (pp. 17, 109, 127)

mutualism (MYOO choo uhl ihz uhm): ecological

relationship which benefits all organisms involved (pp. 199, 276)

mycorrhizae (MY koh REYE zee): mutualistic association of certain fungi with root cells of some vascular plants; from the Greek *mykes* and *rhiza*, meaning "fungus" and "root" (p. 199)

mycelium (my SEE lee uhm): tangled mass of fungal hyphae that makes up the body of a fungus (p. 374)

myelin (MY uh lihn) **sheath**: a fatty, segmented covering wrapped around axons, which increases the speed of nerve impulse transmissions (p. 604)

 N

natural selection: process by which organisms best suited to their environmental conditions are most likely to survive and reproduce (pp. 17, 175)

negative feedback: a process in which an end product inhibits the first step of a system (p. 634)

nematocyst (NEHM uh toh sihst): stinging, harpoon-like structure on the tentacles and outer body surface of cnidarians; from the Greek *nēma* and *kystis*, meaning "thread" and "sac" (p. 481)

nephridium (nee FRIHD ee uhm): tubule that collects wastes from the coelom and discharges them from the body; from the Greek *nephros*, meaning "kidney" (p. 487)

nephron (NEHF rahn): blood-cleaning unit of the kidney (p. 711)

nerve: bundles of neurons that extend throughout the body (p. 601)

nerve tissue: tissue made up of cells that generate electrical impulses and transfer them to other cells; from the Latin *nervus* and *texere*, meaning "sinew, nerve, string" and "to weave" (p. 576)

neuroendocrine system: term covering the closely-linked nervous system and endocrine system; from the Greek *neuron* and *endon* + *krinein*, meaning "nerve" and "within" + "to separate" (p. 632)

neuron (NOO rahn): basic cell of the nervous system, specialized to carry nerve impulses; from the Greek *neuron*, meaning "nerve" (p. 601)

neurotransmitter: chemical released by a neuron into a synapse that may stimulate or inhibit other neurons (p. 605)

niche (NIHCH): an organism's "profession," the sum of its interactions with its environment (p. 278)

nitrogen fixation: conversion of atmospheric nitrogen to ammonia by bacteria (pp. 159, 260)

nonpolar molecule: molecule with an even charge distribution (p. 45)

nonrenewable resource: natural resource, such as iron ore, that is not regenerated by natural processes (p. 295)

notochord (NOHT uh kawrd): rod of cartilage that extends along the back in chordates; from the Greek *nōton* and Latin *chorda*, meaning "back" and "cord" (p. 204)

nucleic (noo CLAY ihk) **acid**: DNA or RNA; large chainlike molecule containing phosphoric acid, sugar, and purine and pyrimidine bases; from the Latin *nucleus*, meaning "nut or kernel" (p. 33)

nucleotide (NOO klee oh tyd): structural unit of a nucleic acid (subunit of DNA or RNA) consisting of three parts: a sugar, a phosphate group, and a nitrogenous base (pp. 33, 139)

nucleus (NOO klee uhs): organelle that directs cell activities and stores DNA; from the Latin *nucleus*, meaning "nut or kernel" (p. 50)

nutrition: science that studies how food affects the functions of living organisms (p. 699)

nymph (NIHMF): stage in the development of an insect, which is a small but incomplete version of the adult; from the Greek *nymphe*, meaning "a young goddess" (p. 509)

 O

obesity (oh BEES ih tee): condition in which a high proportion of the body weight is stored fat; from the Latin *obesus*, meaning "devoured" (p. 697)

omnivore (AHM nih vawr): organism that eats both plants and animals; from the Latin *omni-* + *vorare*, meaning "all" + "to devour" (p. 257)

opposable thumb: digit that can be bent toward other digits (p. 213)

order: collection of similar families of organisms (p. 318)

organ: collection of different kinds of tissue that are dedicated to one or a few functions; from the Latin *organum*, meaning "instrument" or "tool" (pp. 443, 577)

organelle (awr guh NEHL): specialized compartments that carry out specific functions in eukaryotic cells (p. 51)

organic molecule: molecule with carbon-carbon bonds (p. 29)

organ system: group of interrelated organs that carry out one or a few essential body functions (pp. 443, 577)

osmosis (ahz MOH sihs): movement of water through a membrane from an area of high concentration to an area of low concentration; from the Greek *othein*, meaning "to push" (p. 68)

osmotic (ahz MAH tihk) **pressure**: pressure created by force of water pushing against a cell membrane (p. 68)

osteoporosis (ahs tee oh puh ROH sihs): condition of bone resulting from loss of bone minerals that make bone dense, causing brittleness and fractures; from the Greek *osteon* and Latin *porosis*, meaning "bone" and "porous condition" (p. 586)

ovary: one of the two female organs that produce eggs (p. 723)

overconsumption: eating too much food, a major factor leading to nutritional problems in the United States (p. 699)

ovulation (ahv yoo LAY shun): release of an egg from the ovary; from the Latin *ovum*, meaning "egg" (p. 725)

ovule (AHV yool): structure within a seed plant that contains the female gametophyte and becomes a seed when mature (p. 400)

ovum: female gamete, or egg (plural, ova) (p. 723)

oxidative (AHKS ih day tihv) **respiration**: series of chemical reactions that occur in mitochondria, and the process by which cells get most of their energy; from the Latin *respirare*, meaning "to breathe" (p. 90)

ozone: unstable pale-blue gas that absorbs ultraviolet radiation; from the Greek *ozein*, meaning "to smell" (p. 198)

 P

pacemaker: small bundle of cells near the entrance to the right atrium of the heart that emits an electrical signal to start the heartbeat (p. 659)

pancreas (PAN kree uhs): large gland situated behind the stomach that secretes digestive juices into the small intestine and that produces insulin and glucagon; from the Greek *pan-* + *kreas*, meaning "all" + "flesh" (p. 708)

parasitism: ecological relationship in which one organism lives on or in another organism and absorbs nutrients from it (p. 276)

pathogen: disease-causing agent; from the Greek *pathos*, meaning "suffering" (p. 338)

pedigree (PEHD uh gree): record that tracks the inheritance of a trait through several generations of a family (p. 130)

pedipalp: second pair of appendages on spiders and other arachnids; used to capture and manipulate prey and for courtship displays and mating; from the Latin *pes* and *palpus*, meaning "foot" and "soft palm of the hand" (p. 501)

penicillin (pen ih SIHL ihn): antibiotic compound obtained from the mold *Penicillium* (p. 343)

pepsin: enzyme present in the stomach that, with hydrochloric acid and other enzymes, breaks proteins into small chains of amino acids; from the Greek *pepsis*, meaning "digestion" (p. 707)

peptide hormone: hormone made of amino acids that send messages from outside the cell; from the Greek *peptein* and *hormeinō* meaning "to digest" and "to stimulate" (p. 638)

peripheral nervous system: the part of the nervous system that carries messages between the central nervous system and the rest of the body (p. 611)

peristalsis (pehr uh STAHL sihs): wavelike muscle contractions that propel food through the digestive tract; from the Greek *peristaltikos*, meaning "surrounding" (p. 707)

pH: term used to describe the acidity of a solution (p. 291)

phagocyte (FAG oh syt): type of white blood cell that consumes pathogens; from the Greek *phagein*, meaning "to eat" (p. 680)

phenotype (FEE nuh typ): physical characteristics of

an organism; from the Greek *phainein*, meaning "to show" (p. 119)

phloem (FLOH ehm): vascular tissue of plants that transports sugars and other dissolved nutrients; from the Greek *phloos*, meaning "bark" (p. 394)

phospholipid (fahs foh LIHP ihd): a molecule made of two nonpolar fatty acid chains joined to a short polar phosphorus-containing head (p. 46)

photosynthesis (foh toh SIHN thuh sihs): process by which organisms use the energy of light to convert inorganic molecules into organic molecules; from the Greek *synthenai*, meaning "to put together" (p. 84)

phylum (FEYE luhm): any of the broad, principal divisions of a kingdom; from the Greek *phylon*, meaning "tribe" (pp. 197, 318)

phytoplankton (feye tuh PLANK tuhn): photosynthetic plankton, usually found near the surface of a body of water; from the Greek *phyein* and *planktos*, meaning "to grow" and "wandering" (p. 362)

pigment: molecule that absorbs and reflects different colors of light; from the Latin *pingere*, meaning "to paint" (p. 86)

pistil: female part of a flower that produces ovules, which contain the female gametophyte; from the Latin *pistillum*, meaning "pestle" (p. 400)

pituitary (puh TOO uh tehr ee) **gland**: small endocrine gland that produces at least six different hormones and is attached by a stalk to the base of the brain; from the Latin *pituita*, meaning "phlegm" (p. 633)

placenta (pluh SEHN tuh): structure through which nutrients and oxygen are transferred to the fetus and which blocks some harmful agents from entering the fetal blood supply; from the Greek

plakous, meaning "flat cake" (p. 474)

placental (pluh SENT uhl) **mammal**: mammal with a placenta, through which offspring are nourished until birth (p. 560)

plankton: passively floating or weakly mobile aquatic algae, bacteria, and animals; from the Greek *planktos*, meaning "wandering" (p. 263)

plant breeding: practice of producing new varieties of plants through artificial selection (p. 430)

plasma (PLAZ muh): protein-rich fluid that makes up 55 percent of the blood; from the Greek *plassein*, meaning "to form" (p. 652)

plasmid (PLAZ mihd): small, circular DNA molecules found in cytoplasm of bacteria (p. 155)

platelet: fragment of a cell that is formed within bone marrow and helps form blood clots; from the Greek *platys*, meaning "broad, flat" (p. 653)

polar molecule: molecule in which charge is unevenly distributed (p. 44)

pollen grain: male gametophyte of a seed plant; from the Greek *palē*, meaning "dust" (p. 385)

pollination: the transfer of pollen from male to female flower structures (p. 385)

pollution: addition of harmful substances to the environment; from the Latin *polluere*, meaning "to soil" (p. 289)

polyp: one of the two life stages of cnidarians, generally attached to a hard surface; from the Greek *poly-* + *pous*, meaning "many" + "foot" (p. 481)

prediction: expected outcome if a hypothesis is proved to be accurate; from the Latin *praedicere*, meaning "to foretell" (p. 12)

primary growth: growth that results in the length-

ening of a plant's roots and shoots (p. 394)

primary immune response: immune response that occurs after the first exposure to a pathogen (p. 686)

primary succession: regular pattern of species replacement occurring where nothing has lived before (p. 280)

primate: order of mammals to which people, apes, monkeys, and prosimians belong; from the Latin *primus*, meaning "first" (p. 213)

probability: the likelihood that something will happen (p. 121)

producer: organism that is able to make its own food (p. 256)

prokaryote (pro KAR ee oht): single-celled organism lacking a true nucleus; from the Greek *pro-* and *karyon* and *otes*, meaning "before" and "nut or kernel" and "inhabitant" (p. 50)

prosimian (proh SIHM ee uhn): member of a group of tree-dwelling primates; from the Latin *pro* + *simia*, meaning "before" + "ape" (p. 214)

prostaglandins (pras tuh GLAN dihnz): a group of lipids produced in small quantities by specialized cells that function in the body as hormones; from the Greek *proístanai*, meaning "to put in front of" (p. 646)

protein (PROH teen): any of the polymers of amino acids; from the Greek *prōtos*, meaning "first" (p. 32)

proton pump: mechanism in cells that expels protons, which drives cell metabolism (p. 70)

protostome (PROHT uh stohm): animal in which the initial depression that starts gastrulation becomes the mouth of the adult organism; from the Greek *prōtos* and *stoma*, meaning "first" and "mouth" (p. 451)

pseudocoelom (SOO doh see luhm): body cavity between the mesoderm and endoderm of roundworms (nematodes); from the Greek *koilia*, meaning "hollow" (p. 445)

pseudopod (SOO doh pahd): projection of the cell body used for movement or feeding; from the Greek *podos*, meaning "foot" (p. 358)

punctuated equilibria: hypothesis that evolution occurs at an irregular rate; from the Latin *punctus*, *aequus*, and *libra*, meaning "point," "equal," and "balance" (p. 186)

purine (PYUR een): one of the two larger nucleotide bases, namely adenine and guanine (p. 139)

pyrimidine (py RIHM uh deen): one of the two smaller nucleotide bases, namely cytosine, thymine (in DNA), and uracil (in RNA) (p. 139)

pyruvic (py ROO vihk) **acid**: three-carbon organic compound; two molecules result from the splitting of a molecule of glucose during glycolysis (p. 91)

radial symmetry: wheel-like symmetry in which body parts radiate from a central axis; from the Latin *radius* and *symmetria*, meaning "spoke, ray" and "measured together" (p. 441)

radioactive dating: technique for measuring the age of an object by determining the ratio of the concentrations of a radioisotope to that of a stable isotope in it (p. 176)

radula (RAJ oo lah): flexible toothy structure in the mouth of mollusks that is used for feeding; from the Latin *radere*, meaning "to scrape" (p. 488)

ray-finned fish: bony fish whose fins are fan-shaped and supported by bony rays (p. 531)

reabsorption: second process of urine formation, in which filtered fluid passes into the nephron, returning important substances to the blood (p. 711)

realized niche: that part of a fundamental niche that an organism actually occupies as a result of competition or predation (p. 279)

receptor protein: cell membrane protein that senses chemical signals and receives other chemicals that "fit" sites on its surface (p. 64)

recessive: describes an allele that is not expressed in heterozygous individuals (p. 119)

recombinant (ree KAHM buh nuhnt) **DNA**: molecule formed when fragments of DNA from two or more different organisms are spliced together (p. 153)

red blood cell: cell containing hemoglobin that carries oxygen from the lungs to all cells of the body and carries carbon dioxide back to the lungs to be exhaled (p. 652)

reflex: sudden, involuntary response to a stimulus; from the Latin *reflexus*, meaning "reflected" (p. 619)

renewable resource: natural resource, such as water or timber, that can be replaced by a natural process (p. 295)

replication: copying of DNA before cell division (p. 140)

repressor protein: protein that blocks transcription by preventing RNA polymerase from moving along the gene; from the Latin *repressus*, meaning "held back" (p. 146)

resistance exercise: exercise that matches the force of a muscle against the force generated by a movable or an immovable object (p. 595)

resolution: the capacity of a microscope to distinguish different objects that are close to one another (p. 56)

restriction enzyme: enzyme that recognizes and binds to specific short sequences of DNA, then cuts the DNA at a specific site within that sequence; from the Greek *en-* + *zyme*, meaning "in" + "leaven" (p. 154)

retina: layer of rods and cones that covers the surface of the back of the eye (p. 624)

ribonucleic acid (RNA): a single-stranded nucleic acid containing the bases adenine, guanine, cytosine, and uracil (p. 141)

ribosome (RY buh sohm): RNA-containing organelle that is the site for protein synthesis (p. 50)

rod: receptor cell in the retina of the eye that is extremely sensitive to light and can detect shades of gray (p. 624)

root cap: thimble-like cluster of cells that covers and protects the tip of a root (p. 391)

root hair: projection from a cell in the epidermis near the end of a root of a plant, greatly increasing the surface area of a root (p. 391)

saturated fat: a type of fat in which the carbon atoms are bonded to as many hydrogen atoms as possible; usually in a solid state at room temperature (p. 31)

science: a way of investigating the world and observing nature in order to form general rules about what causes things to happen; from the Latin *scire*, meaning "to know" (p. 5)

scientific name: the unique two-word name assigned to each kind of organism on earth (p. 313)

secondary growth: growth that results in the thickening of the plant body; in woody plants, growth that produces wood through the production of rings of new xylem and phloem (p. 394)

secondary immune response: immune response to a previously encountered pathogen; usually occurs much faster and produces more antibodies than the first response (p. 686)

secondary succession: regular pattern of species replacement occurring where there has been previous growth (p. 280)

second messenger: molecule that carries information from a hormone outside the cell membrane into the cytoplasm (p. 638)

sedentary lifestyle: too little physical activity, a major factor leading to nutritional problems in the United States (p. 699)

seed: plant embryo that is surrounded by a protective coat (p. 381)

seedling: the young plant that develops from the embryo of a germinated seed (p. 384)

segmentation: characteristic of animals that are composed of repeated body units; from the Latin *segmentum*, meaning "part" (p. 448)

selective transport: process by which only one type of molecule is transported through membrane protein channels (p. 69)

self-pollination: pollination that occurs when pollen grains fall from the anther of a flower to the stigma of the same flower or another flower on the same plant (p. 402)

semen: fluid consisting of sperm mixed with the secretions of several glands, expelled from the penis during ejaculation; from the Latin *semen*, meaning "seed" (p. 721)

sensitivity: the responsiveness of an organ or an organism (p. 23)

sensory neuron: nerve cell that carries nerve impulses from sense organs to the central nervous system (p. 618)

sensory organ: a specialized organ of the body that responds to stimuli by producing nerve impulses in a sensory neuron (p. 621)

sex chromosome: either member of a pair of chromosomes responsible for sex determination (p. 103)

sex hormone: hormone responsible for the development and maintenance of sexual characteristics; from the Greek *hormeinō*, meaning "to stimulate" (p. 643)

sex-linked inheritance: a pattern of heredity in which traits are transmitted by genes located on the X chromosome (p. 129)

sexual selection: an evolutionary mechanism in which traits that enhance the ability of individuals to acquire mates increase in frequency (p. 244)

shoot: the aboveground part of a plant (p. 392)

skeletal muscle: muscle attached to the bones and responsible for movement; from the Latin *musculus*, meaning "little mouse (muscle)" (p. 590)

small intestine: digestive organ that receives partially digested food from the stomach, where it is further broken down and where nutrients are transferred to the blood; from the Latin *intestinus*, meaning "inward" (p. 708)

smooth muscle: muscle of the internal organs that is not under conscious control; from the Latin *musculus*, meaning "little mouse (muscle)" (p. 590)

sodium-potassium pump: active-transport mechanism that transports sodium out of and potassium into cells (p. 70)

species (SPEE sheez): a group of organisms that can interbreed with each other but not with members of any other group; from the Latin *species*, meaning "appearance, kind" (pp. 17, 314)

spicule (SPIHK yool): needlelike, bony structure that forms the skeleton of a sponge; from the Latin *spica*, meaning "point" (p. 479)

spinneret: nozzle-like structure on the abdomen of spiders that directs the flow of silk from glands in the abdomen (p. 502)

spore: reproductive cell capable of developing into a new organism; from the Greek *speirein*, meaning "to sow" (p. 375)

sporophyte (SPOHR uh fyt): in the life cycle of a plant, the diploid plant (stage) that produces spores and results from the fusing of two gametes; from the Greek *phyein*, meaning "to grow" (p. 381)

sprain: injury resulting from a ligament that is overstretched (p. 589)

stability: ability of an ecosystem to resist change in the face of disturbance (p. 281)

stamen (STAY mehn): male part of a flower that produces pollen grains (the male gametophytes); from the Latin *stamen*, meaning "thread" (p. 400)

steroid hormone: hormone synthesized from cholesterol, such as the sex hormones and anterior pituitary hormones testosterone or estrogen; from the Greek *hormeinō*, meaning "to stimulate" (p. 637)

stoma (STOH muh): tiny pore between two guard cells in a plant leaf; from the Greek *stoma*, meaning "mouth" (p. 392)

substrate (SUHB strayt): molecule on which an enzyme acts during a chemical reaction; from the Latin *substernere*, meaning "to strew about" (p. 80)

succession: regular progression of species replacement in a developing ecosystem; from the Latin *succedere*, meaning "to follow" (p. 280)

swim bladder: gas-filled sac in bony fishes that provides buoyancy (p. 529)

symbiosis (sihm beye OH sihs): close, long-term association between two or more species; from the Greek *syn + bios*, meaning "together" + "life" (p. 276)

synapse (SIHN ahps): junction of a neuron with another cell; from the Greek *synaptein*, meaning "to fasten together" (p. 605)

target: in the endocrine system, the specific destination (tissue or organ) of a hormone's action (p. 631)

taxonomy: science of classifying living things (p. 317)

T-cell lymphocyte: white blood cell that controls the immune response or attacks infected cells (p. 684)

tendinitis: the painful inflammation of a tendon caused by too much friction or stress (p. 596)

tendon: inelastic, strong, fibrous connective tissue attaching muscles to bones; from the Latin *tendere*, meaning "to stretch" (p. 592)

teratogens (tuh RAT oh jinz): chemicals, diseases, or other agents that cause malformation to a fetus (p. 731)

testes (TEHS tees): oval-shaped organs of the male that produce sperm; from the Latin *testis*, meaning "witness" (p. 720)

theory: explanation of several phenomena based on hypotheses that have been tested many times; from the Greek *thēorein*, meaning "to look at" (p. 13)

tissue: group of similar cells that are organized into a functional unit; from the Latin *texere*, meaning "to weave" (pp. 440, 575)

trachea (TRAY kee uh): the cartilaginous, membranous tube by which air passes to and from the lungs in humans and many vertebrates, also one of the tubes leading into an insect's body cavity from pores (spiracles) in the surface of the exoskeleton (p. 467)

transcription: first stage of gene expression, in which an RNA copy of DNA is made (p. 141)

transformation (trans fawr MAY shuhn): the transfer of genetic material from one organism to another, as when a bacterium takes up foreign DNA; first observed by Griffith (p. 137)

translation: second stage of gene expression, in which three kinds of RNA work together to assemble amino acids into a protein molecule (p. 141)

translocation: transport of organic molecules made by photosynthesis from the leaves or storage tissues throughout the body of a plant (p. 397)

transpiration: loss of water by the leaves and stem of a plant; from the Latin *trans- + spirare*, meaning "across + to breathe" (p. 397)

transposon (tranz POH zahn): "jumping gene," a gene with the ability to move from one location to another in a chromosome; from the Latin *transponere*, meaning "to transfer" (p. 148)

trimester: one of the three 3-month periods of the 9-month pregnancy; from the Latin *trimestris*, meaning "of three months" (p. 733)

trophic (TROHF ihk) **level**: group of organisms whose energy source is the same number of steps away from the sun; from the Greek *trophē*, meaning "food" (p. 257)

tropism (TROH pihz uhm): growth response of a plant that occurs toward or away from a stimulus (p. 398)

tuber: enlarged end of a rhizome that grows underground and can be used for food; from the Latin *tuber*, meaning "swelling" (p. 416)

tumor: formation of a mass of cells as a result of abnormally rapid cell division (pp. 108, 690)

underhair: shorter, thinner hairs under the guard hair coat of animals, which reduce the amount of body-heat loss (p. 564)

unsaturated fat: a type of fat in which some carbon atoms are linked by double bonds; usually in a liquid state at room temperature (p. 31)

urea: nitrogenous waste that is excreted by mammals, and requires some water for elimination; from the Greek *ouron*, meaning "urine" (p. 470)

uric acid: nontoxic solid waste eliminated by reptiles and birds (p. 470)

uterus: hollow muscular organ of the female where the fetus develops during pregnancy; from the Latin *uterus*, meaning "womb" (p. 723)

vaccine (vak SEEN): a preparation of killed or weakened pathogens introduced into the body to produce immunity; from the Latin *vacca*, meaning "cow" (pp. 163, 342)

vagina (vuh JEYE nuh): muscular tube in the female reproductive system that receives sperm ejaculated by a male during intercourse and through which the infant passes during birth; from the Latin *vagina*, meaning "sheath" (p. 724)

vascular tissue: tubes and vessels within a plant and consisting of cells that transport water and nutrients; from the Latin *vasculum*, meaning "small vessel" (p. 380)

vas deferens (vas DEHF uh REHNZ): duct that connects each epididymis to the urethra and carries sperm during ejaculation; from the Latin *vas deferentia*, meaning "deferent vessel" (p. 720)

vector: agent used to transfer genes in genetic engineering; from the Latin *vectus*, meaning "carried" (p. 156)

vegetative propagation: growing of new plants from nonreproductive plant parts, such as roots, stems, and leaves (p. 428)

vein: blood vessel that returns blood to the heart (p. 654)

ventricle (VEHN trih kuhl): chamber of the heart that pumps blood out; from the Latin *venter*, meaning "belly" (p. 658)

vertebrate: animal with a backbone; from the Latin *vertebratus*, meaning "jointed" (p. 204)

vestigial (ves TIHJ ee uhl) **structure**: structure that is a remnant of an organism's evolutionary past and has no function; from the Latin *vestigium*, meaning "footprint" (p. 178)

villus: any of the projections lining the small intestine; from the Latin *villus*, meaning "tuft of hair" (p. 708)

virulent (VEER yoo luhnt): causing disease (p. 137)

virus: any of the microscopic particles that invade cells of plants, animals, fungi, and bacteria, often destroying the cells; from the Latin *virus*, meaning "poison" (p. 345)

vitamin: organic substance needed by the body in relatively small amounts (p. 703)

voltage-sensitive channel: protein channel found in membranes of cells that respond to electrical signals (p. 65)

water vascular system: complex arrangement of water-filled tubes that function in the locomotion, feeding, and gas exchange in echinoderms; from the Latin *vasculum*, meaning "small vessel" (p. 493)

white blood cell: colorless blood cell that protects the body against invading bacteria, viruses or other foreign cells (p. 653)

wood: tissue that consists primarily of secondary xylem produced in plants that live more than one growing season (p. 417)

xylem (ZY luhm): vascular tissue of plants that transports water and minerals; from the Greek *xylon*, meaning "wood" (p. 394)

zygote (ZY goht): fertilized egg; cell that results from the fusing of an egg and a sperm (pp. 382, 729)

Index

Index

Index

Index

Index

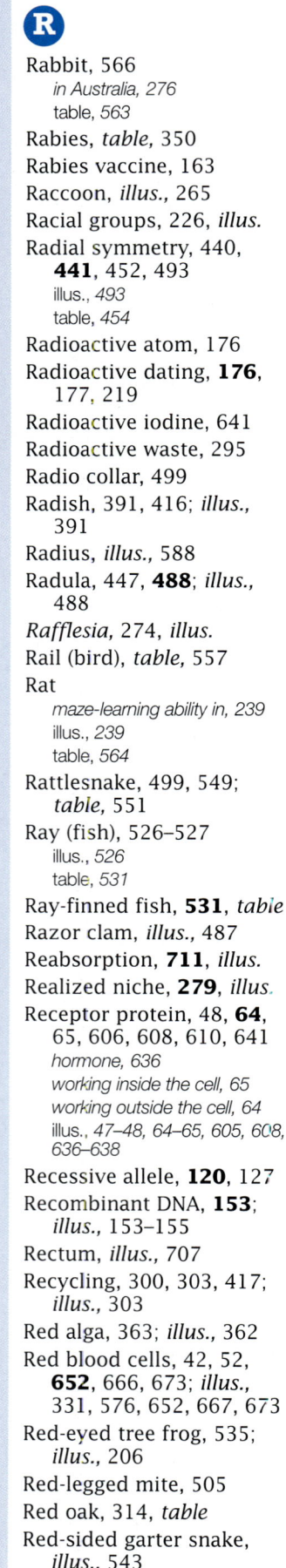
Index

Rusts, 377–378; *table,* 376
Rye, 395

 S

Saccharomyces cerevisiae, 378
Sac fungi, 376, *table*
Safety of genetic engineering, 157, *illus.*
Sage, *table,* 386
Saguaro cactus, *illus.,* 265
Sail-finned lizard, *illus.,* 543
Sake, 413
Salamander, 206, 462, 533–534, 536
  illus., *461*
  table, *536*
Saliva, 679, 706; *illus.,* 679
Salivary gland, 706
  of mosquito, *13*
Salmon, 205, 530–531; *illus.,* 205
Salmonella food poisoning, 339, *illus.*
Salmonidae, 530
Salty taste, 626, *illus.*
Sand, in soil, 421, *illus.*
Sand dollar, 493, *illus.*
Sand fly, *table,* 368
Sandpiper, *table,* 558
Sanitation, 341–342
SA node, 663; *illus.,* 659
Sarcomere, 592–593
Sargasso Sea, 363
Sargassum weed, 363
Saturated fat, **31**, 701; *illus.,* 31
Sauerkraut, 337
Sauria, 544; *table,* 551
Saurischia, *table,* 550
Sauropod, 207
Savanna, 264, *illus.*
Sawdust, 417
Scale(s)
  of birds, *552*
  of fish, *526, 528*
  of reptiles, *464, 541, 544*
  illus., *526, 528, 541*
Scale insect
  illus., *513*
  table, *427*
Scallop, 487–488; *illus.,* 487
Scanning electron microscope, 58, *illus.*
Scanning tunneling microscope, 58
Scapula, *illus.,* 588
Scarlet fever, 340
Scarlet waxy cap mushroom, *illus.,* 256

Schistosomiasis, 483, *illus.*
Schizophrenia, 607, 615
Science, **5**
Science technology, 55
Scientific method, 15
Scientific name, **313**
  how to write, *316*
  importance of, *313*
  Latin language and, *316*
  parts of, *314*
  rules for naming organisms, *315*
  illus., *313, 315–316*
  table, *314*
Scientist, 5, *illus.*
Scorpion, 450, 491, 501, 504; *illus.,* 492, 504
Scorpion fly, *illus.,* 244
Scrotum, 720
Scrub jay, 245; *illus.,* 245–246
Scurvy, *table,* 703
Scyphozoa, 402
Sea anemone, 277, 324, 440–441, 481; *illus.,* 277, 324
Sea bird, *table,* 557
Sea cucumber, 493
Seal, 566; *table,* 563
Sea lamprey, *illus.,* 524
Sea lion, *table,* 563
Sea otter, *table,* 241
Seaside sparrow, *illus.,* 184–185
Sea squirt, 494
Sea star, 281, 452, 493
  illus., *63, 281, 451–452, 493*
  table, *319, 454*
Sea turtle, 549
Sea urchin, 493
Sea wasp jellyfish, 481
Seaweed, 325, 360, 363
Secondary growth, **394**, 417
Secondary immune response, **686**, *illus.*
Secondary succession, **280**, *illus.*
Second filial (F$_2$) generation, 118–119; *illus.,* 118
Secondhand smoke, 674
Second messenger, 64, **638**, *illus.*
Second trimester, 733; *illus.,* 733, 735
Seed, **381**
  dispersal of, *384, 404*
  dormancy of, *405*
  formation of, *403*
  germination of, *405*
  growing plants from, *429*
  of gymnosperms, *385*
  naked, *385*

  planting and caring for plants, *426–427*
  survival in harsh environments, *384*
  illus., *384–385, 403–404*
Seed coat, 384, 403, 405; *illus.,* 384
Seed color
  in garden pea, *119, 124*
  illus., *124*
  table, *119*
Seedless fruit, 403
Seedless vascular plants, 382–383
Seedling, **384**, 391, 405; *illus.,* 384, 391
Seed packet, 426
Seed plants, 384–386
Seed shape
  in garden pea, *119, 124*
  illus., *124*
  table, *119*
Segmentation, **448**, 449–450, 501
  illus., *448–449, 490*
  table, *454*
Segmented worm, 448, 490–491
Segregation, law of, **119**
Selective transport, **69**
Self-fertilization, 117–118; *illus.,* 118
Self-pollination, **402**
Semen, **721**; *illus.,* 720
Semicircular canal, *illus.,* 622
Seminal vesicle, 721; *illus.,* 720
Sensitivity, **23**; *illus.,* 25
Sensory neuron, 611, **618**, 619; *illus.,* 611, 619
Sensory organ, 618, **621**
  of humans, *621–626*
  of protists, *358*
Sensory receptor, 618, 621
  illus., *622*
  table, *621*
Sepal, 400–401; *illus.,* 400
Sequestering connective tissue, *illus.,* 576
Serotonin, 606; *illus.,* 607
Serpentes, *table,* 551
Serving size, *illus.,* 701
Setae, 449
Sewage treatment, 341
Sex chromosome, **103**
Sex hormone, 31, 637, **643**, 704
  female, *726*
  male, *722*
Sex-linked inheritance, **129**

Sexual intercourse, 721, 724
  table, *692*
Sexually transmitted disease, 691–693, 737–740
  bacterial, *739–740*
  viral, *737–738*
  table, *338, 350*
Sexual reproduction, 110
  in fungi, *376*
  in plants, *385*
  in protists, *359*
  table, *181*
Sexual selection, 244, *illus.*
Shallow ocean waters, 268, *illus.*
Shark, 205, 320, 526–527, 616
  illus., *205, 320, 526*
  table, *531*
Sheep, 565; *table,* 563
Shell
  of mollusk, *447, 487–488*
  of turtle, *543, 548*
  illus., *488, 548*
Shellfish poisoning, 363, *illus.*
Shoebill, *illus.,* 322
Shoot, **392**, *illus.*
Shorebird, *table,* 556
Short-day plant, 399, *illus.*
Short-term memory, 614
Shoulder girdle, 588; *illus.,* 588–589
Shoulder joint, 589
Shrew, *table,* 562
Shrimp, 491–492, 515, 517; *illus.,* 464, 517
Shrub, 386, 395
Siamese cat, 81, *illus.*
Sickle cell anemia, 128, 166, 366
  malaria and, *128, 183*
  illus., *128, 183, 667*
Sidestream smoke, 674
Silica, 363
Silk, of spiders, 502–503; *illus.,* 503
Silk moth, 513, *illus.*
Silt particles, in soil, 421, *illus.*
Silverback, *illus.,* 244
Silverfish, 451
Single bond, 28, *illus.*
Sinus venosus, 662
Siphonaptera, *table,* 507
Six-kingdom classification system, 196, 324–326; *illus.,* 196
Skate, 526; *table,* 531
Skeletal muscle, **590**, 591–593; *illus.,* 591–592

Credits

List of Abbreviations

All photographs attributed to SP/Foca were taken by Sergio Purtell/Foca Co.

AA = Animals Animals; AP = Archive Photos; AP/WW = AP/Wide World; AT = Alexander & Turner; BPA = Biophoto Associates; BPS = BPS & Biological Photo Service; CBMI = Claire Booth Medical Illustration; CM = Custom Medical; CP = Culver Pictures; CS = Comstock; HS = Highlight Studios; ES = Earth Scenes; FPG = FPG International, Corp.; KBI = Karapelou BioMedical Illustrations; KC= Kip Carter, M.S. certified medical illustrator; LPI = Lynne Prentice Illustration; MA = rep. Mattleson Associates, Ltd.; MC = MediChrome; MMA = Margulies Medical Art; MT = rep. Melissa Turk; MHI = Mark Hallett Illustrations; NSI = Natural Science Illustration; OSF = Oxford Scientific Films; PA = Peter Arnold, Inc.; PR = Photo Researchers; RWS = rep. Richard W. Salzman S.F., CA; SPL = Science Photo Library; SS = Studio Sloth; TBA = The Bettmann Archive; TM = Teri J. McDermott, M.A., certified medical illustrator; TMMK = Teri J. McDermott, M.A., certified medical illustrator/Michael Kress-Russick, M.A., M.S.; TSA = Tom Stack & Associates; TSM = The Stock Market; TWC = The Wildlife Collection; VU = Visuals Unlimited; WCA = Woodfin Camp & Assoc.

All Safety Symbols were designed by Michael Helfenbein/Evolution Design.

Cover Frans Lanting/Minden Pictures; **ii** SP/Foca; **iii** (b) SP/Foca; (t) Claire Booth/CBMI; **iv** Courtesy of George Johnson; **v** European Space Agency/SPL/PR**; vi** (tr) R.Margulies/MMA; (b) E. Alexander/ AT; (tl) European Space Agency/SPL/PR**; vii** (t) T. Narashima/SS; (b) Daniel Kirk/BA; **viii** (tl, tr) Mark Hallet/MHI; (b) SP/ Foca; **ix** (tr, bl) SP/Foca; (tl) Laurie O'Keefe/HS; **x** (tl) Deborah Daugherty/Laurie O'Keefe/HS; (heart) Peg Gerrity/HS; (b) Wendy Smith-Griswold; (frog) SP/Foca; **xi** SP/Foca; **xii** (t) Walter Stuart/RWS; (c) E. Alexander/AT; (bl) T. McDermott/Michael Kress-Russick/TMMK; **xiii** (t) Lennart Nilsson/Bonnier Alba AB; (c) SP/Foca; calculator Permission of Texas Instruments; **xiv** (frog, vessel) Walter Stuart/RWS; (tl) Lynne Prentice/LPI; (cr) David Beck/RMF; (cell) Robert Margulies/ MMA; (turtle lung) Kip Carter/KC; (leaf, turtle) SP/Foca; **xv** (l) Kerry Klayman; (cl) Michael J. Balick/PA; (cr) Carlos Goldin/SPL/PR; (bl) Biophoto Associates/Science Source/PR; (bc) SP/Foca; **xvi** (tr) Ted Horowitz/TSM; (tl) Michel Viard/PA; (petri dishes) SP/Foca; **xvii** (tl) Ralph A. Reinhold/AA; (scientist) ©1992/CM; (br) SP/Foca; **2-3** Prof. P. Motta/Dept. of Anatomy/University "La Sapienza", Rome/SPL/PR; **3** (t) Yoav Levy/PT; (l) Simon Fraser/RVI, Newcastle-Upon-Tyne/SPL/ PR; (b) SIU/VU; **4** Kevin Schafer/PA; **5** (t) Courtesy Smithsonian Institution Photo; (b) © 1996 Discover Magazine; **06** (tl) SP/Foca; **6-7** (c) John W. Karapelou/KBI; **7** (b) Michael Minardi/PA; (tr) Tom Raymond/MediChrome; **8** (c,r) Courtesy Oil Spill Public Information Center; (tl) SP/Foca; **8-9** (c) European Space Agency/SPL/PR; **9** (l) Peter May/PA; (bc) Mark Moffett/MP; (tc) John Colwell/Grant Heilman Photography; (tr) Bruce Ando/Index Stock; **10** SP/Foca; **11** Randall Zwingler/LM; (l) Corbis-Bettmann; (c) UPI/Corbis-Bettmann; (r) Oxford Scientific Films/AA; **13** (l) Manfred Kage/PA; (c) UPI/Corbis-Bettmann; (r) Courtesy New York Academy of Medicine; **14** THE FAR SIDE cartoon by Gary Larson is reprinted by permission of Chronicle Features, San Francisco, CA. All rights reserved.; **15** Carlyn Iverson; **16** Jay Wasserman/VU; **17** (tl) James L. Amos/PA; (br) Frans Lanting/MP; (tr) Mark Newman/BC; **18** Gerard Lacz/PA; **19** (tl) Courtesy Oil Spill Public Information Center; (tr) Carlton Ray/PR; (b) Frans Lanting/MP; (cl) Oxford Scientific Films/AA; **20** (t) Kevin Schafer/PA; **21** Matt Meadows/PA; **22** Max Gibbs/Scientific Oxford Films/AA; **23** (t) Nigel Westwood/Survival Oxford Scientific Films/ES; (b) Cabisco/VU; **24** Cabisco/VU; **25** Cabisco/VU; **26** (t) Shelby Thorner/David Madison; (b) Robert Margulies/MMA; **27** (tl) SP/Foca; (cl) Dennis Kunkel/PT; (cr) Robert Margulies/MMA; (tr) Claire Booth/CBMI; **28** (tl,bl,br) Claire Booth/ CBMI; (tr) Ralph A. Reinhold/ES; **29** (br) Jeff Rotman/PA; (bl) SP/Foca; **30** SP/Foca; **31** Claire Booth/CBMI; **32** Claire Booth/CBMI; **33** Robert Margulies/ MMA; **34** (l) Claire Booth/CBMI; (hair) SP/Foca; (starch) Omikron/Science Source/PR; (fat) Manfred Kage/PA; (chromo) BPA/Science Source/PR; **35** (tl) Cabisco/VU; (b) Jeff Rotman/PA; (tr) SP/Foca; (c) Robert Margulies/MMA; **36** Max Gibbs/Scientific Oxford Films/AA; **37** Robert Margulies/MMA; **38** (bl) Sinclair Stammers/SPL/PR; (tr) Carlos Goldin/SPL/PR; (c,l) Omikron-Science Source/PR; **39** Robert Margulies/MMA; **40** © 1993 B.S.I.P./CM; **41** (tl) Nancy Kedersha/SPL/CM; (bl) M. Abbey Photo/PR; (cl,br) SP/Foca; (tr) © W. Gregory Brown/AA; **42** (tl,bl) SP/Foca; (br,tr) Claire Booth/CBMI; **43** Claire Booth/CBMI; **44** (tl,bc,br) Claire Booth/CBMI; (bl) SP/Foca; **45** (t-br) SP/Foca; (bl) Claire Booth/CBMI; **46** Catherine Twomey/Craven Design Studios,

Inc.; **47** Robert Margulies/MMA; **48** Robert Margulies/MMA; **49** Robert Margulies/MMA; **50** (l) CNRI/SPL/PR; (r) M. I. Walker/PR; **51** Robert Margulies/MMA; **53** (c) Robert Margulies/MMA; (tr) D. W. Fawcett, S. Ito/PR; (cl) BPA/PR; (br) B. Bowers/PR; (tl) David M. Phillips/The Population Council/Science Source/PR; **54** Robert Margulies/MMA; **55** (tr) Bruce Berman/TSM; (tl) Howard Sochurek/TSM; Biophoto Associates/Science Source; (bl) Gervase Pevanik/WARD'S; (bkgd) SP/Foca; **56** (r) M. Abbey Photo/PR; (l) SP/Foca; **57** (r) Electra/PT; (l) Sinclair Stammers/SPL/PR; **58** (r) Dennis Kunkel/CNRI/PT; (l) Philippe Plailly/Eurelios/SPL/PR; **59** (tl) Claire Booth/CBMI; (c,bl) Robert Margulies/MMA; (tr) SP/Foca; **60** (t) © 1993 B. S.I.P./CM; **61** Catherine Twomey/Craven Design Studios, Inc.; **62** Dr. Dennis Kunkel/PT; **63** (tl) Institut Pasteur/CNRI/PT; (r) Ed Reschke/PA; (bl) © Zig Leszczynski/AA; **64** (c) SP/Foca; (t,b) Robert Margulies/MMA; **65** (cl,tl) Claire Booth/CBMI; (bc, br) Robert Margulies/MMA; **66** (t) © 1991 Kevin Beebe/CM; (bl) T. Narashima/SS; (bc) Carolina Biological Supp/PT; (br) Robert Margulies/MMA; **67** SP/Foca; **68** (tl,tr) SP/Foca; (tc) T. Narashima/SS; **69** (l) SP/Foca; (r) Robert Margulies/MMA; **70-71** Robert Margulies/MMA; **72** (t,r) T. Narashima/SS; (bl) Secchi-Lecaque/Roussel-UCLAF/CNRI/SPL/PR; **73** (tr) HMS Images/IM; (c) Robert Margulies/MMA; (bl) SP/Foca; (br) T. Narashima/SS; **74** Dr. Dennis Kunkel/PT; **75** Robert Margulies/MMA; **76** Frans Lanting/MP; **77** (br) SP/Foca; (tl) Wayne H. Chasan/IM; **78** SP/Foca; **79** Walter H. Hodge/PA; **80** Robert Margulies/MMA; **81** (l) SP/Foca; (r) Fred Breummer/PA; **82** Dr. Arnold Brody/SPL/PR; **83** (t) Foca; (b) Claire Booth/CBMI; **84** (l) NASA; (cl) © 1991 CS; (cr) David C. Fritts/AA; (r) Mark Stouffer; **85** SP/Foca; (inset) © Colin Milkins/Oxford Scientific Films/ES; **86** SP/Foca; **86-87** SP/Foca; **87** (tl) John D. Cunningham/VU; (tr) Robert Margulies/MMA; (br) E. Alexander/AT; **88** E. Alexander/AT; **89** Claire Booth/CBMI; **90** © 1992 Bruce Fitz; **91** (tl,tr) SP/Foca; (c,bl) Claire Booth/CBMI; **92** (moclecules) Claire Booth/CMI; (grapes, boy) SP/Foca; **93** Claire Booth/CBMI; **94** Robert Margulies/MMA; **95** (tr) OSF/AA; (tl) Walter H. Hodge/PA; (tc) David C. Fritts/AA; (bc) E. Alexander/AT; (b) SP/Foca; **96** Frans Lanting/MP; **98** Omikron/Science Source/PR; **99** (t) Richard Nowitz/PT/PNI; (b) Tony Craddock/SPL/PR; **100** Ken Wagner/PT; **101** (tr) © 1992 CM; (b) Biophoto Associates/PR; **102** (c) Robert Margulies/MMA; (br) ©1995 SPL/CM; **103** (l) © 1993 Robert Becker/CM; (r) © 1990 CM; **104** (r) T. Narashima/SS; (l) Institut Pasteur/CNRI/PT; **105** Biology Media/PR; **106** T. Narashima/SS; **107** Claire Booth/CBMI; **108** (l) Dr. Tony Brain/SPL/PR; (r) Robert Margulies/MMA; **109** (l) Robert Margulies/ MMA; **110** (tl,tr,tc) SP/Foca; (bc,cl) © 1995 SPL/CM; (cr) © 1992 SPL/CM; (br) Jason Burns/Ace/PT; **111** (tl,tr) T. Narashima/SS; (bl) CNRI/PT; (br) L. Zamboni-D. Fawcett/VU; **112** T. Narashima/SS; **113** (bl) © 1995 SPL/CM; (br) © 1992 SPL/CM; (tr) Maria Taglienti/IM; (l) Biophoto Associates/PR; (c) Biology Media/PR; **114** Ken Wagner/PT; **115** (tl, tc, tr) SP/Foca; (cl,bc) © 1995 SPL/CM; (cr) © 1992 SPL/CM; (br) Jason Burns/Ace/PT; **116** David Madison; **117** (c) CP; (br) Karen Kluglein/MA; (tl) SP/Foca; **118** Karen Kluglein/MA; **119** Karen Kluglein/MA; **120** Karen Kluglein/MA; **121** Karen Kluglein/MA; **123** (c) Karen Kluglein/MA; **124** Karen Kluglein/MA; **125** (tl) SP/Foca; (bl,br) Larry Lefever/Grant Heilman Photography; **126** (t) SP/Foca; (l) Michio Hoshino/MP; (b) Jim Brandenburg/MP; **127** © David York/Medichrome; **128** (b) Al Lamke/LEN/PT; (c) © Simon Fraser/SPL/CM;**129** (l) Courtesy The Rice Family; (cr) Richard Hutchings/PR; (br) T. McDermott/Michael Kress-Russick/ TMMK; **130** Courtesy The Davidson Family; **131** (l) SP/Foca; (bkgd) Biophoto Associates/Science Source/PR; (t) Dr. Jeremy Burgess/ SPL/PR; **132** Ted Thai/Time Magazine; **133** (tr,c) SP/Foca; (tl) Karen Kluglein/MA; (b) © David York/Medichrome; **134** (b) Jim Brandenburg/MP; (t) David Madison; **136** Jean Claude Revy/PT; **137** (tl) SP/Foca; (bacteria) Claire Booth/CBMI; (mice) Susan Johnston Carlson; **138** (t) Claire Booth/CBMI; (b) Lee. D. Simon/PR; **139** (t) PA; (b) Robert Margulies/Virginia Ferrante; **140** (b) Robert Margulies/MMA; (t) SP/Foca; **141** Robert Margulies/MMA; **142** Robert Margulies/MMA; **143** SP/Foca; **144** E. Alexander/ C. Turner/AT; **145** E. Alexander/ C. Turner/AT; **146-147** Robert Margulies/Christine Schaar/MMA; **148** (l) SP/Foca; (r) D. Goldberg/Sygma; **149** (tr) PA; (tl, b) Robert Margulies/MMA; (c) E. Alexander/AT; **150** (b) Foca; (t) Jean Claude Revy/PT; **151** E. Alexander/AT; **152** Ted Horowitz/TSM; **153** (tl) Agricultural Research Service, USDA; (br) R. Kessel & G. Shih/VU; (bl) SP/Foca; (bc) Robert Margulies/MMA; **154** (bl) SP/Foca; (tl, tr, tc) Robert Margulies/MMA; (br) E. Alexander/AT; **155** (tl) David M. Phillips/VU; (c) E. Alexander/AT; (tr) R. Kessel & G. Shih/VU; **156** E. Alexander/AT; **157** Ted Horowitz/TSM; **158** E. Alexander/AT;

159 (tl, br) SP/Foca; (bc) © E. H. Newcomb & S. R. Tandon/Univ. of Wisconsin/BPS;160 B. Hansen/NSI; 161 Monsanto; 162 (c) R. Kessel & G. Shih/VU; (t) E. Alexander/AT; (b) SP/Foca; 163 (illus.) E. Alexander/AT; (tr) SP/Foca; 164 Dr. A. Liepins/SPL/SS/PR; 165 (cl) Kerry Klayman; (bkgd) Roland Seitre/PA; (tl) Karl & Kay Amman/BC; (tr) James P. Blair/National Geographic Image Collection; (bc) Michael J. Balick/PA; 166 Manfred Kage/PA; 167 (c) Monsanto; (tr) @1992 SPL/CM; (tl) E. Alexander/AT; (b) SP/Foca; 168 (t) Ted Horowitz/TSM; 169 (l) E. Alexander/AT; (tr) David M. Phillips/VU; (br) Robert Margulies/MMA; 170 (c) Monsanto; (bl) Robert Margulies/MMA; 170-171 (r) SP/Foca; 171 Robert Margulies/MMA; 172 Frans Lanting/MP; 173 (tl) Michio Hoshino/MP; (b) Lazlo Kubinyi/Rep. Gerald & Cullen Rapps, Inc.; (r) Corbis-Bettmann; 174 (tc) John S. Dunning/PR; (bl, bc) M. A. Chappell/AA; (br) Leonard Lee Rue III/AA; 175 (tl) Corbis-Bettmann; (tr) Courtesy Department of Library Services, American Museum of Natural History; (bl) Corbis-Bettmann; 176 SP/Foca; 177 (r) Chris Forsey; (l) David Beck/RMF; 178 T. McDermott/Michael Kress-Russick/TMMK; 179 T. McDermott/Michael Kress-Russick/TMMK; 180 Marius Muresanu/Foca; 181 Daniel Kirk/BA; 182 Breck P. Kent/AA; 183 C. Turner/AT; 184-185 (sparrows) Daniel Kirk/BA; (bkgd) Randall Zwingler/LM; 186 Carlyn Iverson; 187 (tr, bl) Breck P. Kent/AA; (tl) Corbis-Bettmann; (c) Chris Forsey; 188 (t) Frans Lanting/MP; 190 1993 Louis Psihoyos/Matrix; 191 (b) T. Narashima/SS; (t) SP/Foca; 192 UPI/Corbis-Bettmann; 193 Yemi; 194 (l, c) SP/Foca; (r) David M. Phillips/VU;195 (t) Corale Brierley/VU; (b) Richard Thom/VU; 196 (tl) CNRI/SPL/PR; (bl) Ralph Robinson/VU; (bc) D. Gottshall/VU; (tr, br) SP/Foca; (cr) Richard Thom/VU; 197 Lynn Prentice; 198 (l) Claire Booth/CBMI; (r) NASA/Science Source/PR; 199 (l) SP/Foca; (r) R. L. Peterson, Univ. of Guelph/BPS; 200 (tl, tc, tr) Carlyn Iverson; (bl, cc) David Beck/RMF; (bc) Pat Ortega; (cl) Lynn Prentice/LPI; (cr) Courtesy Peabody Mus. Nat. History/Yale University/painted by Rudolph F. Zallinger; (br) Robert Frank; (cr-inset) Lynn Prentice/LPI; 201 (tc) Lynn Prentice/LPI; (eukaryote) Carlyn Iverson; (cc) Courtesy Peabody Mus. Nat. History/Yale University/painted by Rudolph F. Zallinger; (tr, bl, T. Rex) Pat Ortega; (cr) John Burgoyne; (cl) David Ashby; (br) Robert Frank; (human) John Burgoyne; 202 Carlyn Iverson; 203 (bkgd) Courtesy Peabody Mus. Nat. History/Yale University/painted by Rudolph F. Zallinger; (inset) Lynn Prentice/LPI; 204 (t) David Beck/RMF; (b) © Breck P. Kent/AA; 205 (t) Robert Frank; (b) Victoria McCormick/AA; 206 (l) Stephen Dalton/AA; (r) Robert Frank; 207 (bkgd) Robert Frank; (c) Mark Hallet/MHI; (sillhouette) Kevin A. Somerville/MIS; 208 (t) AA; (r) Robert A. Tyrell/OSF/AA; (c) Steve Kauffman/TS; 209 (tc) Corale Brierley/VU; (tr) Dr. Fred Espenak/SPL/PR; (tl) David M. Phillips/VU; (bc) NASA/Science Source/ PR; (b) Steve Kauffman/TS; 210 1993 Louis Psihoyos/Matrix; 211 Yemi; 212 Gamma Press Images/Gamma Liaison; 213 (b) Todd Buck/HS; (tl) Kenneth Garrett/National Geographic Image Collection; 214 E. H. Pao/PR; 215 (bl) Patti Murray/AA; (tr) Leonard Lee Rue III/TS; 216 S. Turner/OSS/AA; 217 (gibbons) E. R. Degginger/AA; (orangutan) Christopher Arnesen/TS; (gorilla) Pat Crowe/AA; (bonobo) Michael Dick/AA; (chimpanzee, humans) SP/Foca; 218 (tl, br) Bianca Lavies/National Geographic Image Collection; (bl) Gilbert M. Grosvenor/National Geographic Image Collection; (tr) Volkmar Kurt Wentzel/National Geographic Image Collection; 219 (tl, tr) SP/Foca; (bl, br) Dana Geraths; 220 Mark Hallet/MHI; 221 (tl, br) Institute of Human Origins; (b) John Reader/SPL/PR; (jaws) Dana Geraths; 222 (l) John Reader/SPL/PR; (r) Courtesy Department of Library Services, American Museum of Natural History; 223 Mark Hallet/MHI; 224-225 (skulls) Mark Hallet/MHI; (bkgd) Randall Zwingler/LM; 226 (t) SP/Foca; (b) Randall Zwingler/LM; 227 John Burgoyne; 228 (t) Courtesy Department of Library Services, American Museum of Natural History; (b) AR, NYC; 229 (tr) Reprinted courtesy OMNI Magazine © 1991; (tl) Leonard Lee Rue III/TS; (c) Institute of Human Origins; (b) John Burgoyne; (jaw) Dana Geraths; 230 Gamma Press Images/Gamma Liaison; 231 Mark Hallet/MHI; 232 Phil Farnes; 233 (tr) Klaus Uhlenhut/AA; (b) David J. Boyle/AA; 234 (t) Robin Brandt/Natural Selection; (b) George B. Schaller; 235 Susan Johnston Carlson; 236 (tl) Susan Johnston Carlson; (br) Thomas McAvoy/Life Magazine; 237 (b) Omikron/Science Source/PR; (t) SP/Foca; 238 (l) Courtesy of Jennifer Dusek; (bkgd) SP/Foca; (tr) J. Bucher/PR; (tl) J. M. Labat/Jacana/PR; 239 (t) S. Feld/H. Armstrong Roberts; 240 (t) Gary W. Griffen/AA; (c) Peter Weimann/AA; (b) Joe McDonald/AA; 241 (b) Michael Fogden/BC; (t, bc) Ken Cole/AA; (tc) Patti Murray/AA; 242 (tl) © Bill Silker Jr./AA; (bl) IFA Bilderteam/BC; (br) Michael Fogden/Oxford Scientific Films/AA; 243 (t) J. C. Carton/BC; (b) Hans Reinhard/BC; 244 (tr) Max Gibbs/Oxford Scientific Films/AA; (br) Martin Harvey/TWC; (bl) Adrienne T. Gibson/AA; 245 (l) Patti Murray/AA; (r) B. Heinrich/University of Vermont; 246 Susan Johnston Carlson; 247 (c) Robin Brandt/Natural Selection; (b) Max Gibbs/Oxford Scientific Films/AA; (tr) feature THE FAR SIDE © 1988 FARWORKS, INC. Dist. by UNIVERSAL PRESS SYNDICATE. Reprinted with permission. All rights reserved.; 248 Phil Farnes/PR; 249 Susan Johnston Carlson; 250-251 James Randklev/TS; 251 (t) Eric Kamp/Index Stock; (c) H. Armstrong Roberts; (b) Tim Brown/Index Stock; 252 Richard Day/Panoramic Images; 253 (t) Lee Rentz/BC; (b) © 1989 Kevin Schafer/PA; 254 Lynn Prentice/LPI; 255 Carlyn Iverson; 256 (l) David Beck/RMF; (r) © Ed Reschke/PA; 257 David Beck/RMF; 258 Carlyn Iverson; 259 Carlyn Iverson; 260 (bkgd, plants, soil bacteria) Carlyn Iverson; (molecules) Claire Booth/CBMI; (roots, deer) Lynn Prentice/LPI; 261 B. Hansen/NSI; 262 (plant, jeep, bkgd) Claire Booth/CBMI; (deer, well) Lynn Prentice/LPI;263 SP/Foca; 264 (t) Klaus Uhlenhut/ES; (b) Gregory Dimijian/PR; (maps) Foca; 265 (t) Bill Bachman/PR; (c) Mickey Gibson/ES; (b) Stephen J. Krasemann/PR; (maps) Foca; (t, b) Stephen J. Krasemann/PR; 266 (maps) Foca; 267 (l, b) Courtesy Carmen R. Cid-Benevento; (bkgd) AA/ES; (tl) Stephen Dalton/AA; (tr) Zig Leszczynski/AA; 268 David Beck/RMF; 269 (tl) © Ed Reschke/PA; (c) B. Hansen/NSI; (b) Stephen J. Krasemann/PR; (tr) Raymond Mendez/AA; 270 Richard Day/Panoramic Images; 271 David Beck/RMF; 272 Gregory K. Scott/PR; 273 (t) Arthur M. Greene/BC; (b) Bill Wood/BC; 274 (b) Fletcher W. K./PR; (flies) SP/Foca; 275 SP/Foca; 276 (b) L. West/PR; (inset) V. Ahmadjian/VU; 277 (t) Fred Bavendam; (b) F. Gohier/PR; 278 Peter Weimann/AA; 279 Wendy Smith-Griswold/MT; 280 (t) Michael P. Gadomski/BC; (c) L.L. Rue III/BC; (b) Michael P. Gadomski/ES; 281 (tl) Adrienne T. Gibson/AA; (br) SP/Foca; 282 (l) Randall Zwingler/LM; (r) Alan Blank/BC; 283 (tl) Milton H. Tierney Jr./VU; (cl) Patrick Montagne/PR; (bl) Julian Baum & David Angus/SPL/PR; (r) Tom McHugh/PR; 284 (l) Bob Gossington/BC; (r) Provided by Dr. S. Bradleigh Vinson, Texas A&M University; 285 (c) Fred Bavendam; (b) Adrienne T. Gibson/AA; (t) AP/WW Photo; 286 Gregory K. Scott/PR; 288 Rafael Macia/PR; 289 (t) SP/Foca; (b) Earl Roberge/PR; 290 (t) AP/WW Photo; (b) Courtesy Oil Spill Public Information Center; 291 (l) © 1989 D. A. Glawe, Univ. of Ill./BPS; (bkgd) Randall Zwingler/LM; (tr) Master Communications; (br) 1991 Ray Pfortner/PA; 292 (l) NASA/Mark Marten/PR; 292-293 NASA/Goddard Institute for Space Studies//SPL/PR; 294 Donna Binder/Impact Visuals/PNI; 295 SP/Foca; 296 (l,r) Gene Alexander/Soil Conservation Service; (c) Tim McCabe/Soil Conservation Service; 297 (c, r) Michael J. Balick/PA; (l) R. Cramm/Okapia/PR; 299 Foca; 300 Mickey Gibson/AA; 301 SP/Foca; 302 (t) SP/Foca; magazines Courtesy Mother Earth News; Wildlife Conservation; (egret on cover) Art Wolfe; National Audubon Society; 303 SP/Foca; 304 SP/Foca; 305 (b) SP/Foca; (tr) James H. Karales/PA; (c) Michael J. Balick/PA; (tl) Courtesy Oil Spill Public Information Center; 306 Rafael Macia/PR; 308 (bl) Richard Gorbun/Leo de Wys Inc.; (t) NOAA/SPL/PR; 309 (b) Michael Newman/PhotoEdit; 310-311 Andris Apse/Panoramic Images; 311 (c) Martin Bond/SPL/PR; (b) Jim Richardson/Richardson Photography; (t) SP/Foca; 312 SP/Foca; 313 (t) SP/Foca; (b) Charles W. Mann/PR; 314 SP/Foca; 315 (tl) Ray Coleman/PR; (tc) Randall Zwingler/LM; (tr) Dan Sudia/PR; (bc) M. Fogden/OSF/AA; (br) Bridgeman, London/AR, NYC; (bl) Mark Hallet/MHI; 316 (tl, br) SP/Foca; (bl) Courtesy Paul Melancon/Univ. of Colorado, Boulder; (tc) Courtesy Alma Solis/SEL/USDA; (bc) Courtesy Lucy Bunkley-Williams, Ernest H. Williams, Univ. of Puerto Rico at Mayaguez; 317 (t) SP/Foca; (b) 1992 The Pierpont Morgan Library/AR; 319 David Beck/RMF; 320 (l, r) E. Alexander/AT; (tc) G. Soury/Jacana/PR; (bc) Chuck Davis Photography; 321 (moss) K. G. Vock/Okapia/PR; (fern, flowers, seeds) SP/Foca; (tree)1991 Tom Bean/TS; (vascular system) P. Dayanandan/PR; 322 Susan Johnston Carlson/MT; 323 Mark Boulrow/PR; 324 (b) Neil G. McDaniel/PR; (t) Eric Grave/PT; 325 (l) T. J. Reveridge/VU; (c) Oliver Meckes/PR; (r) Manfred Kage/PA; 326 (tl) Robert Lee/PR; (bl) SP/Foca; (cr) Jeremy Stafford-Deitsch/Ellis nature Photography; 327 (tr) Bob Orsillo; (tl) SP/Foca; (c) 1992 The Pierpont Morgan Library/AR; (b) Neil G. McDaniel/PR; 328 (t, cr) SP/Foca; (cl) Dan Sudia/PR; (b) Neil G. McDaniel/PR; 329 (moss) K. G. Vock/Okapia/PR; (fern, flowers, seeds) SP/Foca; (tree)1991 Tom Bean/TS; (vascular system) P. Dayanandan/PR; 331 (tl) Stanley Flegler/VU; (bl) Biophoto Associates/Science Source/PR; (cl) Oliver Meckes/Ottawa/PR; (cr) CNRI/SPL/PR; (br) CNRI/SPL/PR; 332 (tl) Manfred Kage/PA; (insets) CNRI/SPL/PR; (tr, br) T. Narashima/SS; (bl) Manfred Kage/PA; 333 (bkgd) John Coulter/VU; (c) Robert Margulies/MMA; (b) Foca; 334 (l) Michael S. Renner/BC; (r) Biophoto Associates/PR; 335 (l) Fred McConnaughey/Science Source/PR; (r) Carl O. Wirsen/VU; 336 (l) Larry Jensen/VU; (b) C. Bradley Simmons/BC; 337 (cl) SP/Foca; (c) Cabisco/VU; (cr) Martin Rotker/PT; (b) AFP/Corbis-Bettmann; 338 (t) John D. Cunningham/VU; (c) SPL/PR; (b) Ed Reschke/PA; 339 (t) SP/Foca; 340 (inset) Manfred Kage/PA; (b) Cabisco/VU; (tl) Kent Wood/PR; 341 AP/WW Photo; 342 (tl) © 1989 Cytographics/VU; (tc) David M. Phillips/VU; (bc) Genentech/VU; (b) © L. O'Shaughnessy/Medichrome; 343 (tl) National Library of Medicine/SPL/PR; (c) S. Flegler/VU; (r) SP/Foca; (l) D. Newman/VU; 344 Karen Kluglein/MA; 345 (t) National Cancer Inst./Science Source/PR; (b) © 1986 A. J. Olsen/The Scripps Research Institute; 346 (l) John W. Karapelou/KBI; (b) Foca; 347 T. Narashima/SS; 348 Lowell Georgia Science Source/PR; 349 (b) AP/WW Photo; (t) Courtesy J. Wickett/World Health Organization; 350 (viruses) Karen Kluglein/MA; (AIDS) John W. Karapelou/KBI;

BUFFALO BILL CENTER OF THE WEST

720 Sheridan Avenue, Cody, Wyoming 82414

centerofthewest.org

**BUFFALO BILL
CENTER
OF THE WEST**

ISBN 0-931618-69-X

Printed in Korea

Second printing 2016

COPYEDITER: **NANCY MCCLURE**
Buffalo Bill Center of the West, Cody, Wyoming

EDITOR: **HARLAN "HAL" CLIFFORD**
Louisville, Colorado

DESIGN AND PRODUCTION: **CAROL HARALSON**
Carol Haralson Books, Sedona, Arizona

ART SCANNING: **DONALD SIGOVICH**
Westport, Connecticut

PROJECT MANAGER: **KAREN B. MCWHORTER**
Buffalo Bill Center of the West, Cody, Wyoming

Names: Buffalo Bill Center of the West.

Title: Invisible boundaries : exploring Yellowstone's great animal migrations.

Description: Cody, Wyoming : Buffalo Bill Center of the West, 2016. |
Includes bibliographical references.

Identifiers: LCCN 2016037637 | ISBN 093161869X (pbk. : alk. paper)

Subjects: LCSH: Migratory animals--Conservation--Yellowstone National Park. |
Animal migration--Yellowstone National Park.

Classification: LCC QL754 .I586 2016 | DDC 591.56/8--dc23

LC record available at https://lccn.loc.gov/2016037637

All images of James Prosek's artwork courtesy of the artist and SCHWARTZ • WAJAHAT, NEW YORK.
All photographs by Joe Riis courtesy of the artist.
All photographs by Jenny Nichols courtesy of the artist.

Front and back cover: James Prosek. *American Elk (Wyoming)*, 2016. Oil, acrylic and mixed media on wood panel, 56 x 90 in.
Page one: Thomas Moran (American, born England, 1837–1926). *The Grand Canyon of the Yellowstone* (detail), 1872.
Oil on canvas, 84 x 144 1/4 in. Smithsonian American Art Museum, Lent by the Department of the Interior Museum,
l.1968.84.1 (Full image, page 6). **This page:** Elk on spring migration from the ranches of the Greybull
River, across the Shoshone National Forest, toward Yellowstone National Park,
late May 2015. Photograph © Joe Riis. **Contents page (overleaf):**
A mature bull elk on fall migration, near the boundary of
Yellowstone National Park in the Shoshone National
Forest, October 2014. Photograph © Joe Riis.

INVISIBLE **BOUNDARIES**

INVISIBLE BOUNDARIES

FOREWORD

THOMAS E. LOVEJOY

t was not until I was in my mid-forties that I had the privilege of visiting Yellowstone, but, like most Americans, I had been aware of—and lusted to visit—the national park from a very young age. So when invited to speak at the 1987 annual meeting of the Greater Yellowstone Coalition, not a second passed before I said, "Yes!"

I was invited because of the giant experiment I began in the Amazon in 1979 to study fragments of forest of various sizes left in the course of deforestation. The experiment was designed to resolve a huge debate about habitat fragmentation; we saw almost immediately that major changes had occurred because the fragments were no longer part of continuous forest. Although far away in equatorial South America, the initial results revealed the validity of concerns about fragmentation. Our research may have helped lead to the creation of the Greater Yellowstone Coalition and its ongoing work not only to stem the increasing isolation of the Yellowstone ecosystem, but also to restore connections to a larger wilderness spanning far beyond the park.

This may seem obvious, but in reality habitat fragmentation—and its obverse, habitat connectivity—had only recently been recognized as a major

conservation issue. Those impacts of species loss after species loss spread over time, increment by increment, so that each species disappearance seems idiosyncratic and not part of a larger trend. It took theoretical biology, looking at the question of what determines the number of species on islands, to raise the question: Do the same kinds of considerations apply to islands of habitat created when humans modify landscapes?

In retrospect it seems inevitable that David Quammen (future author of the May 2016 issue of *National Geographic* devoted exclusively to Yellowstone) and I would meet at the Old Faithful Inn's bar after my 1987 talk. David sought my views about his plan to write a book on island biogeography. I was instantly enthusiastic. What transpired became an eight-year odyssey for him; the result was *The Song of the Dodo*— a triumph of a book that did much to highlight, in general, what the *Invisible Boundaries* project is about.

In 1986, conservation biologist William Newmark applied island biogeographic theory to Yellowstone and predicted a major loss of mammal species if it were to become "isolated" as a virtual habitat island. That highlighted the issue and made connectivity an imperative. The idea of establishing and protecting a corridor of continuous nature from Yellowstone to

Yukon has since gained traction with the public, but the task of maintaining the biological integrity of Yellowstone is much more complicated than that.

Not only do many species (think grizzly bears and wolverines) need to be part of larger populations that extend beyond the park; some species only use the park for part of the year. Elk leave the park for the colder months and are then completely dependent on private lands for their winter range. In a remarkable feat of wildlife biology, Arthur Middleton has traced all the Yellowstone elk migrations. Clearly, to maintain and conserve the elk populations requires conservation while they are outside the park boundaries. This highlights an opportunity for a magnificent public-private partnership to maintain the integrity of Yellowstone and its elk in perpetuity.

But this is not just a problem about elk. Many other species also use the park for only part of the year, including migratory birds, as well as some bat and insect species. Until we truly understand their biological requirements and conservation status, they are elements of Yellowstone under threat.

More than half a century ago, a report to the Secretary of the Interior by wildlife ecologist Starker Leopold laid out the principles for management of the national parks. It has served as a hallowed guide. Two years ago, because of the extent of subsequent environmental change (land use and climate change and more), a "Revisiting Leopold" report was delivered to the Secretary of the Interior. Thoughtfully developed and exquisitely written in only fourteen small pages (like the original report fifty years prior), its purpose is to lay out the basic principles for management of national parks (they could apply equally to all federal and state public lands). The principle of connectivity is prominent in the report's statement that individual parks should be viewed as conservation anchors in larger conservation landscapes.

This is additionally important because of the obvious and growing impacts of climate change in nature almost everywhere across the globe. Glacier National Park will soon be that in name only. Species are beginning to alter their geographical ranges. Joshua trees are now growing outside of Joshua Tree National Park, for example. The more connectivity there is in the landscape, the more likely species are to make it through the changes wrought by a human-modified climate.

The lesson of *Invisible Boundaries* is that we—and nature with us—are better served by a landscape in which human aspiration is imbedded in nature rather than one in which nature survives marginally in human-dominated landscapes. That may sound very radical but there are multiple associated benefits. For example, restoring riparian vegetation not only enhances natural connectivity, but also prevents soil erosion and restores water quality. Restoring ecosystems at scale can significantly reduce climate change by pulling CO_2 back from the atmosphere—after all, living things are built with carbon.

The biology of the planet nurtured the rise of human civilization through multiple direct and indirect benefits. Beyond those, the diversity of life is made up of individual species, each with solutions to a series of biological challenges—any one of which has the potential to transform the life sciences. One of the more recent discoveries is a soil fungus from Nova Scotia that has the capacity to disarm the defenses bacterial superbugs use to resist antibiotics.

The conclusion is we would be wise to embrace nature and respect its natural fabric rather than think, with hubris, that we can dominate it.

This exhibit and this book explain and celebrate the important implications of these invisible boundaries and the multiplicity of links between humans and nature. They do so with the powerful synergy that comes of bringing science and art together, and of the resonance between the scientifically rational approach of Arthur Middleton's research and the aesthetic achievements of Joe Riis's photography and James Prosek's paintings.

It is not surprising that this collaboration is transpiring in and around Yellowstone. An icon since before it was named a park, Yellowstone always has had the capacity to inspire, whether it is experienced in person or by viewing a representation such as Thomas Moran's spectacular *The Grand Canyon of the Yellowstone* (1872), now in the Smithsonian American Art Museum. That capacity led to the establishment of the world's first national park. May it similarly lead to a recognition of invisible boundaries and linkages between humanity and nature everywhere.

THOMAS E. LOVEJOY, PH.D. is University Professor of Environmental Science and Public Policy at George Mason University as well as Conservation Fellow at the National Geographic Society and Senior Fellow at the United Nations Foundation. He was the first to use the term "Biological Diversity" in 1980 and a founder of the science of conservation biology. He started the forest fragmentation research program in the Brazilian Amazon in 1978. He and Lee Hannah are just finishing the third book on biodiversity and climate change. He is the founder of the Public Television series *Nature*. He received both his B.S. and Ph.D. in biology at Yale University.

AT THE CROSSROADS OF ART, SCIENCE, AND CONSERVATION IN YELLOWSTONE

KAREN B. MCWHORTER

Though it was not the first organized expedition into the Yellowstone region, the party led by Dr. Ferdinand V. Hayden in 1871 was the first to include fine artists in its ranks. Hayden engaged photographer William Henry Jackson, who had accompanied him into the field the year before, to help document the geological wonders of the area. When neither Albert Bierstadt nor Sanford Gifford was able to make the journey, the Northern Pacific Railroad suggested that Hayden allow painter Thomas Moran to accompany him as a guest artist. Hayden consented and Moran excitedly headed west, sketchbook and paint box in hand.

On the trail, Jackson, the photographer, and Moran, the painter, quickly established good rapport, a critical element to any successful collaboration. Historian Thurman Wilkins wrote, "The immediate cooperation between the two began the most effective teamwork between artist and photographer seen in the whole era of the Great Western Surveys." Moran assisted Jackson with the arduous process of taking photographs in the field and helped select the most compelling vantage points, recognizing the potential benefit of his colleague's photographs as source material for his planned studio paintings. The painter also frequently served as a model for his colleague, standing next to this geyser or that rock formation (as he does in the photograph on the facing page, top right) to provide a sense of scale. On a July day early in their adventure, Moran recorded in his diary, "Sketched but little but worked hard with the photographer selecting points to be taken &c."

Theirs was a collegial partnership that turned into a life-long friendship and, working side by side in the western wilderness, they successfully documented the Yellowstone area so that the world might know—might see—its breathtaking sights.

Because of the geological impetus behind Hayden's mission, the artists focused on geysers, hot springs, mountains, and canyons as principal subjects. During the course of the expedition, Jackson produced hundreds of photographs and Moran compiled a portfolio of delicate field sketches of such features. Back in Washington, Jackson's crisp black and white photographs and Moran's atmospheric, jewel-toned watercolors made tangible the awe-inspiring places Hayden and others before him had touted, but of which they couldn't quite convey the magnitude in words or statistics.

Hayden, Jackson, and Moran joined a chorus of support for acknowledging and protecting Yellowstone's geological and scenic significance upon their return from the West. Two of the most passionate advocates were Nathaniel P. Langford and Lt. Gustavus C. Doane, members of an 1870 survey of the Yellowstone area led by Gen. Henry D. Washburn. By 1871, Doane had submitted to Congress a detailed account of their expedition and Langford was busily publicizing the wonders he'd witnessed in speeches and articles. Hayden bolstered his predecessors' advocacy by writing about his own experience, but also by organizing at the U. S. Capitol an exhibition of geological samples, Jackson's photographs, and Moran's watercolors. Art historian Thomas Patin has observed that in Hayden's interdisciplinary display "the watercolor sketches, photographs, and geological specimens worked in a supportive interrelationship."

Jackson's photographs conveyed the distinctive topographical character of the area in sharp detail; Moran's sketches revealed the vivid, otherworldly palette of Yellowstone and the particular quality of light in the high country of the American West; and the specimens functioned as physical evidence of Yellowstone's unique geology. Together, the multiple media presented a more holistic view of a truly remarkable region and strengthened the cases of Hayden, Langford, Doane, and many

Right: William Henry Jackson (American, 1843-1942). *White Mountain Hot Spring, Cap of Liberty–Near View,* printed 1874. Alberttype. U.S. Geological Survey of the Territories, Hot Spring Series Plate 9. Image courtesy of Robert Enteen.
Below: Thomas Moran (American, born England, 1837–1926). *Liberty Cap and Clematis Gulch,* 1871. Watercolor (and possibly gouache) and pencil field sketch on paper, 6 7/8 x 10 in. Courtesy of National Park Service, Yellowstone National Park, YELL 8524.

WHITE MOUNTAIN HOT SPRINGS
CAP OF LIBERTY—NEAR VIEW.

others (including banks and railroads with commercial interests) whose entreaties helped inspire members of Congress to preserve the Yellowstone area as the world's first national park. In 1938, Jackson remarked that "Back in Washington that winter of 1871–72, in the proceedings before Congress for the creation of the Yellowstone National Park, the water colors [sic] of Moran and the photographs of the Geological Survey were the most important exhibits before the committees."

THE POWER OF VISUAL IMAGES, particularly in this chapter of Yellowstone's history (and American conservation history), is undeniable. Hayden's display at the Capitol spoke to both the hearts and minds of congressmen. Moran's sketches tapped the emotional power of color; his prismatic paintings were celebrations of the power and majesty of the western landscape, a uniquely American asset worthy of preserving. Jackson's photographs would have been perceived by most as truthful and unbiased depictions of the Yellowstone area, quelling any doubt that its wonders were real.

It seems Yellowstone had to be seen to be believed. Jackson's and Moran's images helped convince not only Congress, but also the American public, of the region's appeal and importance. Among the first professional images of Yellowstone to reach eastern audiences, they were reproduced in popular magazines (first as woodblock prints and later, in Moran's case, as chromolithographs) and captured the nation's attention. Their powerful visual testimony helped an incredulous public imagine Yellowstone.

THE COMBINATION of scientific inquiry and compelling imagery helped substantiate the *geological and scenic value* of the Yellowstone area in 1872. Since that time, interest in studying and preserving the *biological value* of Yellowstone has continually increased and has encouraged new avenues for

Friedrich Jüngling after Thomas Moran, "Great Hot Springs at Gardiner's River, 1872," *Scribner's Monthly* 3 [1872]: 4. McCracken Research Library, Buffalo Bill Center of the West, Cody, Wyoming.

interdisciplinary work between scientists and artists. Among the most hopeful contemporary examples of what can be accomplished when scientists and artists approach the same topic from multiple points of view is the partnership between wildlife biologist Arthur Middleton, photographer Joe Riis, and artist James Prosek. Their collaborative efforts inspired the exhibition *Invisible Boundaries: Exploring Yellowstone's Great Animal Migrations* and this namesake volume. At the heart of this project is a specific goal—to encourage stakeholders to consider the importance of elk migration in the Greater Yellowstone Ecosystem (GYE)—but it will surely have much broader resonance. *Invisible Boundaries* celebrates the enduring power of partnerships between scientists and artists and helps blur perceived distinctions between their fields.

SO WHAT CAN ART CONTRIBUTE to a conversation about elk migration? Just as Jackson's photographs and Moran's paintings persuasively illustrated Hayden's reports of Yellowstone, so too can contemporary artists' work complement and, indeed, augment, recent scientific findings. Art can narrow the lens through which we see the world, but can also broaden our view immeasurably, extending a conversation from the local to the global. In both ways, art fosters new ways of seeing. Consider the research that drives the *Invisible Boundaries* project: decades' worth of tracking collar data from elk in the Yellowstone region. These data help illuminate when, how, and why elk migrate within (and, as it turns out, well beyond) the national park. Comprising the movements of thousands of elk, it's an impressive, but daunting, set of figures. As Riis and Prosek show, using a visual vocabulary can help make these numbers and the conclusions drawn from them more convincing and relatable.

JOE RIIS is a photojournalist and biologist who has been in the Yellowstone backcountry for the better part of two years, documenting animal migrations. He roams wildlife corridors in the footsteps of the animals he photographs, allowing their daily rhythms to determine his own. Riis sets up camera traps to capture animal movements remotely and also waits patiently along newly-discovered migration routes to photograph his subjects in person. He has studied mule deer and pronghorn antelope, but for the past three years, he has turned his camera primarily toward elk while working with Middleton on the Greater Yellowstone Migrations (GYM) project, the inspiration behind the *Invisible Boundaries* exhibition and this publication. In recognition of their work on the GYM project, Riis and Middleton were named *National Geographic*'s 2016 Adventurers of the Year. The award honors "remarkable achievements in exploration, adventure sports, conservation, or humanitarianism."

For many, even those of us who live on the doorstep of Yellowstone, the concept of annual migrations of elk might be difficult to visualize. With the aid of contemporary technology, Riis helps reveal this little-known facet of Yellowstone's incredible biology. His photographs of elk and their epic journeys, and his images of the expedition team who've undertaken the field research, tell an intimate story that further enlivens the map of Greater Yellowstone elk migrations. Through his photographs, we can better comprehend the scale of elk migration in the GYE and also become acquainted

Left: Self-portrait testing camera trap lighting, June 2015. Riis eventually captured the image shown on pages 52-53 from this location. Photograph © Joe Riis.

Facing, top: Elk descending a high mountain pass on spring migration, late May 2015. Photograph © Joe Riis.

Facing, bottom: Riis in the field, June 2015. Photograph © Jenny Nichols.

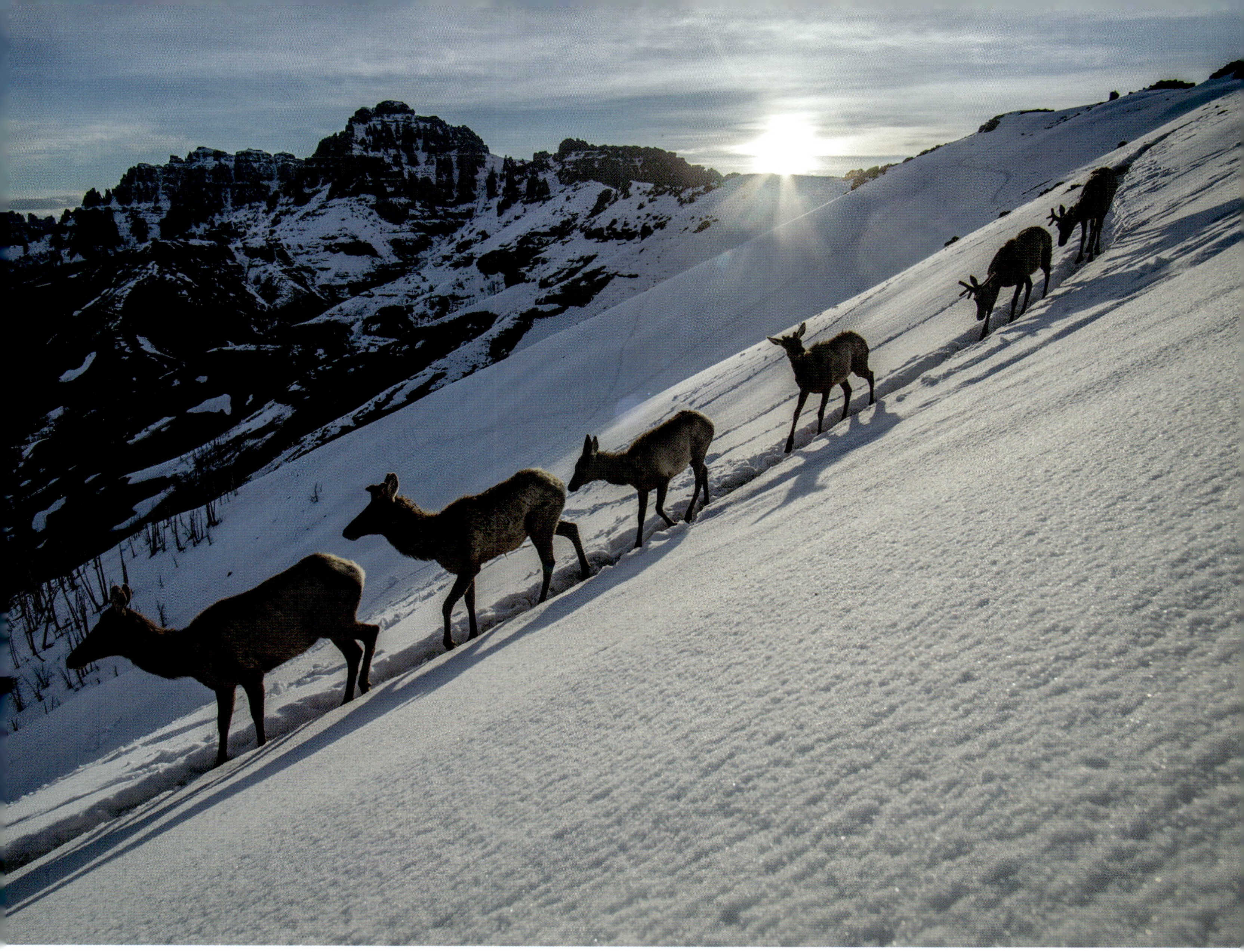

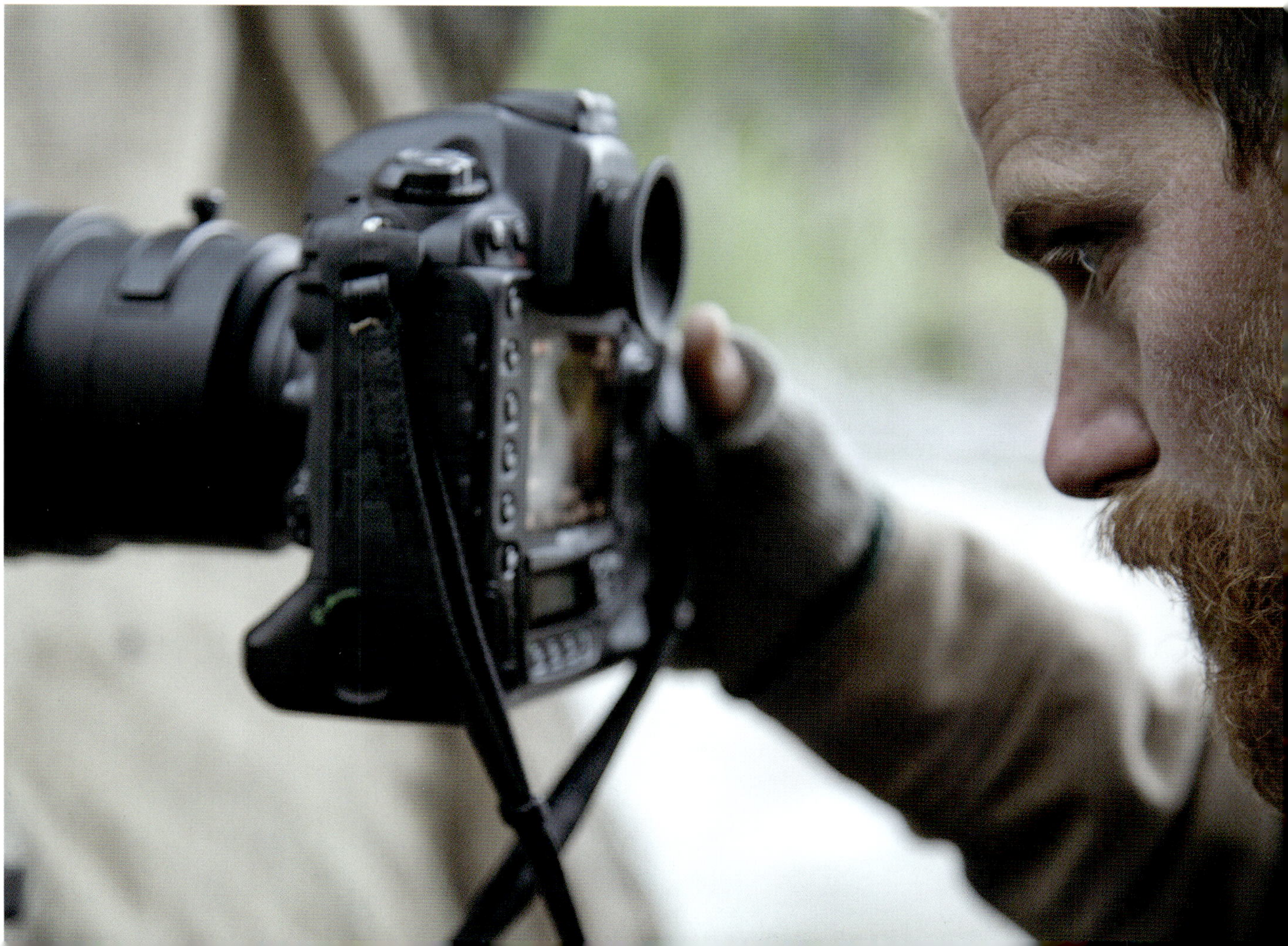

Above: Middleton, Jack the Australian Shepherd, and Riis take shelter from a storm on a ledge along the Thorofare Plateau, July 2015. Photograph by Shane Moore. **Facing:** James Prosek. *American Elk,* 2016. Watercolor, gouache, and colored pencil on tea-stained paper, 28 x 30 in.

with individual members of this mass movement. Riis invites us vicariously to stand at his vantage point and look through his camera lens onto some of the most remote terrain in the contiguous United States so as to peer into the life histories of elk, an impressive and iconic species.

Riis's photographs taken from a plane, helicopter, or distant ridge help convey the monumentality of elk migrations in the GYE and underscore the difficulty of the elk's journeys. They allow wide-angle views onto the harsh terrain migrating herds cross annually and

the obstacles they encounter along the way. Natural obstacles range from pulsing rivers that threaten to sweep all but the strongest swimmers downstream, to predation, to treacherous, snow-packed mountain passes. Man-made obstacles include fences, sprawling urbanization, and highways—imposed barriers that migrating herds must surmount to reach summer or winter ranges.

The portraits and documentary film footage Riis takes of individual or small groups of elk help us better relate to these creatures and invite empathy on their behalf. An investigative nose sniffing a trail camera, the vocalizations of a herd navigating a creek crossing, the percussion of hoof beats on a rocky, high mountain trail—these comprise unique insights into a previously unknown world. His photographs reveal the fragility and strength of elk, their vulnerability and resilience. They have the power to inspire us to care and to better understand our own impact on an increasingly fragmented but ever-important ecosystem.

JAMES PROSEK is an artist, naturalist, and author. If Riis's photographs hone our vision to the harsh realities and incredible moments along elk migration routes in and around Yellowstone, then the paintings of James Prosek extend the conversation beyond the elk's story and push us to imagine the larger implications of human-animal relations in a changing landscape. For the *Invisible Boundaries* project, Prosek turned his eye for detail and steady, expert hand to a diverse cast of characters in the Greater Yellowstone whose lives are inextricably connected. This interconnectedness among lifeforms—particularly our relationship as humans to the world around us—is central to his work in general, and poignantly applies to this project in particular. In new field sketches, watercolors, and oil paintings the artist encourages us to see the bigger picture and critically analyze our place within it.

At first glance, many of his paintings might remind viewers of carefully-rendered scientific illustrations. Their familiarity derives from Prosek's use of an artistic vocabulary codified by artist-naturalists like Titian Ramsay Peale, John James Audubon, and Olaus J. Murie. Looking to these artists and the field guides they inspired, Prosek often isolates a particular animal or plant from its natural environment, depicting it in exacting detail against a monochromatic backdrop. As in *American Elk,* Prosek might flank a central creature—in this case a single elk—with a selective sampling of plant and animal specimens of a smaller scale, here elephant's head and king's crown sprigs and a western tanager. These species' juxtaposition suggests a relationship between them, and indeed, these three all are endemic to

northwestern Wyoming. His choices of subjects and the way he orders them calls into question the hierarchies and boundaries that we create in our minds between plants and animals, between species, between anything in nature.

Prosek's frequent choice of watercolor, his preferred medium since childhood, is also reminiscent of earlier artist-naturalists. In this way, too, his work evokes associations between watercolor paintings, science, and exploration. Artists historically used watercolors in the field for practical and philosophical reasons. Watercolors are more portable and dry more quickly than oils and were, and continue to be, a popular medium for painting *en plein air* (out of doors). Watercolors can also suggest immediacy and intimacy with one's subject. A personal, one-on-one experience with his subjects has long been an important part of Prosek's process, which is fundamentally informed by close, attentive observations of nature. His desire to study his subjects in their natural habitats has taken him on journeys to remote and sometimes dangerous places across the globe and, for this project, frequently to the Yellowstone backcountry.

Though Prosek's choice of subject matter, painting style, and penchant for field work may nod to earlier artist-naturalists, his intended message is more provocative than that of his predecessors. He uses traditional representational techniques but moves beyond documentation to tackle contemporary issues, creating works of art that are engaging and often subtly subversive. Thus, Prosek creates stunningly beautiful works of art that offer lessons in environmental consciousness.

Prosek's paintings of wildlife paired with numbers suggest that there exists somewhere a corresponding enumerated list with the animals' names and perhaps more information about them (see the cover image, for example), but this is not the case. He leaves us at loose ends; there's no itemized list of the creatures he portrays. Rather than resolve this conundrum for the viewer, Prosek encourages us to reflect on our

Above: James Prosek. *Cactus with Ant, Pitchfork Ranch,* 2015. Watercolor, gouache, powdered mica and graphite on paper, 10 x 12 1/4 in.

Facing and below right: Prosek studying local flora and fauna of elk winter range, summer 2015. Photographs © Jenny Nichols.

James Prosek. *American Bison (Wyoming)*, 2014. Oil, acrylic and mixed media on wood panel, 45 x 56 in.

imposition of clean, orderly systems on a wonderfully messy world. This is a principal theme in Prosek's work: an examination of our human propensity to name and order the natural world and, as he says, "our prejudices and priorities" in such attempts at classification and control. His paintings often confront the limitations of language in describing Earth's incredible range of biological diversity. Nature is dynamic and yet we expect that a static system of names and categories can define it. We feel the need to organize nature, to chop it up, and though nature doesn't lend itself to clearly-drawn lines, we impose them nonetheless.

Here is the common ground between Prosek, the artist, and Middleton, the scientist: both are interested in, as Prosek describes, "what happens when you draw lines in a nature that doesn't have any lines." Prosek is intrigued by the conceptual lines we draw between

things in nature, like the divisions we create when we ascribe names and classifications to plants and animals. Middleton is interested in the lines we draw on maps, like the line demarcating Yellowstone National Park and what lies around it. Both Prosek and Middleton are concerned with how these manmade lines affect how we think about and act toward nature.

For the *Invisible Boundaries* project, the protagonists of Prosek's paintings are regionally-specific species, with starring roles played by Yellowstone's hooved herbivores including elk and bison, two among the most familiar species of the region. Lesser-known actors in Prosek's narratives include the western tanager, the rufous hummingbird, and the army cutworm moth, animals we might not readily identify with Yellowstone but which depend on the area as a stopover on their long-distance migrations. Prosek's inclusion of these species points to the fact that Yellowstone's reach extends further than most of us realize. Perhaps elk migrations—though sometimes more than a hundred miles long—might be considered a fairly "local" phenomenon when compared to other species that travel many hundreds or thousands of miles? Prosek's artwork, more so than documentary photography or scientific research alone, encourages us to think about Yellowstone as an ecosystem that defies its human-imposed borders.

Prosek's paintings of animal silhouettes, including an original ten-by-ten foot mural of more than five hundred animals created especially for the *Invisible Boundaries* exhibition and reproduced on page 66 of this volume, speak further to the interconnectedness of the natural world. His sampling of plants and animals and their arrangement in couplings, trios, and larger groups suggest relationships between and among them. These silhouette paintings might remind viewers of a puzzle in which the animals should fit together in one pre-determined order but don't. According to the artist, "We think that by just replacing a missing puzzle piece, like the wolf as apex predator, that the ecosystem will be "OK" again. That may be true to a certain extent but it's certainly not the whole story. In some ways we have to simplify histories and biological interactions in order to tell a narrative, to communicate, but there is a lot of nuance left behind."

At the heart of Prosek's paintings—and indeed at the heart of the *Invisible Boundaries* project—is the idea of connectivity: Yellowstone as connected to surrounding and far-flung environs; Yellowstone's plant and animal life as connected to and dependent on each other and their human neighbors.

The Hayden Survey of 1871—an early example of scientists and artists working together for the greater good of the Yellowstone area—stands as an important precedent for the *Invisible Boundaries* project. The collaborative, interdisciplinary efforts of Hayden, Jackson, Moran, and many others played an important role in Yellowstone becoming a national park, in the drawing of a roughly square perimeter around interesting geological and geothermal features of the region. Today, we understand that these boundaries encompass not only geological wonders but also biological wonders equally worthy of conservation. In the *Invisible Boundaries* exhibition, namesake publication, and ongoing outreach, art once again lends color and shape to conservation science in Yellowstone. Riis's documentary photographs and Prosek's stunning and thoughtful paintings enrich

and invigorate the data compiled by Middleton, proving art's power to clarify and popularize scientific findings. Taken as a whole, *Invisible Boundaries* reveals the challenges and opportunities in conserving migrating wildlife in Yellowstone and beyond.

KAREN B. MCWHORTER is the Scarlett Curator of Western American Art of the Whitney Western Art Museum at the Buffalo Bill Center of the West. McWhorter was previously in charge of research and publications for the Petrie Institute of Western American Art at the Denver Art Museum. She has contributed essays to *Elevating Western American Art: Developing an Institute in the Cultural Capital of the Rockies* (2012), *A Place in the Sun: The Southwest Paintings of Walter Ufer & E. Martin Hennings* (2015), and *Fur Traders and Rendezvous: The Alfred Jacob Miller Online Catalogue* and has authored numerous articles on contemporary western American art. She received her B.A. at the University of Tennessee, Knoxville and her M.A. at the University of Colorado–Boulder.

RELATED READING

Hales, Peter B. *William Henry Jackson and the Transformation of the American Landscape (*Philadelphia: Temple University Press, 1988), 108–109.

Hassrick, Peter H. *Drawn to Yellowstone: Artists in America's First National Park* (Seattle: University of Washington Press, 2002), 26–32.

Jackson, W. H. "With Moran in the Yellowstone," *Appalachia* 82 (December 1936): 157.

Moran, Thomas. Personal diary. Yellowstone Heritage and Research Center, Gardiner, Montana.

Patin, Thomas. "Western Views and Eastern Visions: National Parks, Manifest Destiny, and American Identity." In *Preserving Western History,* ed. Andrew Gulliford (Albuquerque: University of New Mexico Press, 2005), 69.

Schullery, Paul. *Searching for Yellowstone: Ecology and Wonder in the Last Wilderness* (Helena: Montana Historical Society Press, 2004), 51–67.

Wilkins, Thurman. *Thomas Moran: Artist of the Mountains,* 2nd ed., rev. & enl. (Norman, OK: University of Oklahoma Press, 1998), 79.

Prosek's studio, 2016. Photograph courtesy of the artist.

Above: James Prosek. *Bison Cow, Hoodoo Ranch, Wyoming,* 2016. Watercolor, gouache and colored pencil on tea-stained paper, 27 x 30 1/2 in.

Facing page, top: James Prosek. *Late Summer Grasses,* 2015. Watercolor, graphite and gouache on paper, 9 3/4 x 12 in.

Facing page, bottom: James Prosek. *Yellowstone Cutthroat Trout and Indian Paintbrush,* 2015. Watercolor, graphite and gouache on paper. 10 1/4 x 13 in.

Late summer grasses and sage — the smell of sagebrush is overwhelming
Meeteetse, WY 12 August 2015 Pitchfork Ranch

Native Yellowstone Cutthroat Trout in the big pool on the upper Pickett Creek. Butterfly courtesy of A. Middleton. Indian paintbrush + ladybug. Pitchfork Ranch, Wyoming. 13 July 2015. We saw a mom + 2 cub grizzlies yesterday!

THE GREATER

CHARLES R. PRESTON

YELLOWSTONE ECOSYSTEM
WHERE DO WE DRAW THE LINES?

t was one of those spectacular autumn days in northwestern Wyoming, when the golden aspen leaves and bright ruby rosehip berries contrast so beautifully with the rich green backdrop of mixed conifers. The temperature was mild, alternately warming and cooling slightly as the sun peeked through a broken blanket of lazy, gray clouds. Surprisingly for Wyoming, there was no wind. A few aspen leaves floated through the sky with no particular place to go and no deadline to meet. Armed with fly rod and elk-hair caddis fly, I had been testing the few deep runs remaining this time of year along the north fork of the upper Shoshone River, just outside Yellowstone National Park. Despite the relatively low water, I had caught and released a couple of nice trout and was walking back along the edge of a large meadow toward my car, parked a few miles up the trail.

Ever mindful of grizzly bears in this area, I called out "h-e-e-e-y bear" every few steps and kept my eyes and ears wide open and bear spray close at hand. I felt vulnerable and a little incautious for setting out in this area at this time of year without companions. But no one was available to join me, the day was too perfect, and this would be the last opportunity for me to get any significant time away from my office for several weeks. An American red squirrel announced his discontent at my presence with a series of loud, scolding, vocal rattles and tail flicks as I approached a bend in the trail between meadow and forest.

Suddenly, I heard the thrashing of shrubby willows dead ahead. All I could see through the thick branches and green-and-yellow leaves was a huge, brown, shaggy hide. The big animal was clearly in a frenzy, attacking the willows with a ferocity that quieted even the squirrel. My immediate thought was "angry grizzly," and my immediate action was to freeze. I was initially relieved to see that the huge body that emerged from the willows was not a bear—it was an adult bull bison. My relief turned to something very close to panic, however, when I realized that this nearly two-thousand-pound behemoth was running straight toward me. I didn't know how an angry bison would react to bear spray, but I steadied myself to find out. Fortunately, the big bull veered away from me just before either one of us had the chance to learn what happens when bear spray meets bison.

As he crashed through an opening in the forest, I collected my thoughts and began looking around for what might have inspired the bison's nasty mood. A small group of hikers was coming down the trail from the opposite direction, talking and laughing softly, enjoying the sights, sounds, and smells of this place. When they saw me they rushed my way and exclaimed with some excitement that one of the "park's buffaloes" had gotten out of the park, and they had tried unsuccessfully to usher it back toward "where it belonged."

The group was visiting from central Utah. After explaining how lucky they were not to have been injured or worse, I asked if they knew the exact location of the park boundaries. One of them started to produce a map until I stopped him. I asked if they knew where the boundaries were without looking at the map. When they looked around at each other and shook their heads, I asked how they thought the bison would have known about the boundaries. We all had a bit of a laugh at that point, but the incident reminded me of how easily human minds grasp the concept of political boundaries even when they are invisible on the landscape. The incident underlined for me one of the great challenges we face in managing and conserving wildlife even in one of the world's most renowned national parks and wildlife sanctuaries.

Previous pages: Hidden Creek in the Thorofare, near the southeast corner of Yellowstone National Park, August 2014. Many large elk groups from Cody, Dubois, and Jackson winter ranges spend summer grazing on the high plateaus in this region. Photograph © Joe Riis.
Above: Bison migrating outside park boundaries in winter, especially north of Yellowstone, come into conflict with area ranchers who fear the bison will transmit brucellosis to livestock. Photograph by C. R. Preston.
Facing: Some elk that spend summers in Yellowstone National Park overwinter on private lands well outside park boundaries. Photograph by C. R. Preston.

Yellowstone National Park is the world's first and arguably most famous national park. It was established in 1872 primarily to protect several important physical attributes in the area, including Yellowstone Lake, the Grand Canyon of the Yellowstone, and especially the extensive and varied geothermal features that contain roughly half of all active geysers in the world. The park's boundaries were drawn to address political considerations and encompass geological and scenic resources, but with little attention to biological resources.

As human development expanded, however, the 2.2 million acres of diverse and relatively intact native landscape became a stronghold and *de facto* refuge for an essentially complete complement of native wildlife species, including bison, elk, grizzly bear, and gray wolf, that once shared a much wider swath of the northern Rocky Mountain region. But Yellowstone National Park alone can neither contain nor sustain many of the most charismatic and wide-ranging species that inhabit the park at least part of each year. Most of the park is located at high elevation and covered with deep snow much of the year. The average elevation of the Yellowstone plateau is greater than 8,000 feet above sea level and

is virtually surrounded by higher mountain ranges, including some peaks of 13,000 feet. Therefore, many species must leave the park seasonally to find available resources in lower elevations. This understanding of the park's limitations is almost as old as the park itself. U. S. Army General Philip H. Sheridan, a strong advocate for protection of Yellowstone National Park and its wildlife, was among the first to recognize that the boundaries defining Yellowstone National Park did not include adequate habitat to support viable "game" populations throughout the year. In 1882, Sheridan argued that the park should be nearly doubled in size, extended toward the south and east to meet the requirements of migrating elk and other large ungulates.

Daniel Kingman, an Army engineer and lieutenant who helped design the major roadways in Yellowstone National Park, reinforced Sheridan's sentiments in 1886 when he suggested that the park be expanded to include both the summer and winter ranges of large game animals. Sheridan and others, including *Forest and Stream* Editor-in-Chief George Bird Grinnell and Missouri Senator George Vest, unsuccessfully fought to expand park boundaries to include additional wildlife habitat.

Nonetheless, these efforts to expand national park boundaries set the stage for Congress to eventually designate much of the lands surrounding the park as timberland reserves. In 1891, President Benjamin Harrison issued a proclamation that established the Yellowstone Park Timberland Reserve, and in 1897, President Grover Cleveland established the Teton Forest Reserve south of Yellowstone National Park. These reserves were the precursors of today's national forests, administered by the U. S. Forest Service under the U. S. Department of Agriculture. Their establishment reduced opportunities for private exploitation of public lands surrounding Yellowstone National Park, but even when expanded in subsequent years, they did not include some of the protections of national park lands administered by the National Park Service under the U. S. Department of the Interior. Recognizing the need for further protection for wildlife in 1897, acting Yellowstone Superintendent Colonel S.B.M. Young advocated expanding Yellowstone Park boundaries southward to Jackson Hole specifically to help protect migrating elk. Although Yellowstone National Park was not expanded, Grand Teton National Park was established in the Jackson Hole area in 1929 after many years of conflict and controversy.

Philip Sheridan, Daniel Kingman, and S.B.M. Young were pioneers in recognizing that large, unbroken tracts of appropriate habitat were critical for wide-ranging elk and other wildlife to persist in the Yellowstone–Grand Teton region. They understood that landscapes and wildlife in this broad region were profoundly interconnected, and that ungulate migration routes did not conform to and could not be limited to political boundaries. It was nearly a century later, in the 1970s, when grizzly bear researchers John and Frank C. Craighead coined the term Greater Yellowstone Ecosystem (GYE) to describe a contiguous geographic area including Yellowstone and Grand Teton national parks and surrounding landscapes. Where Sheridan, Kingman, and Young were primarily concerned with migratory elk, the Craigheads drew the boundaries of their GYE to encompass an area of adequate size (more than twice the area of Yellowstone National Park) and habitat resources that would sustain a viable Yellowstone grizzly bear population. As quoted by Seymour Fishbein in National Geographic Society's *Yellowstone Country: The Enduring Wonder,* Frank Craighead described the GYE as ". . . a unit that includes all the physical, chemical,

and biological elements necessary for the existence and perpetuation of a complex of animal species."

The concept of a GYE has gained wide acceptance and use, and is often described as the last large, nearly intact ecosystem in Earth's northern temperate zone. It has become a centerpiece for discussions and debates of ecosystem management and transboundary stewardship. Yet there is no universally-accepted size or boundary for the GYE, or of the specific complex of animal species to which it should be applied. Different interpretations of the area range from about 4 million acres to more than 18 million acres, depending on the species being considered and the perspective of the author.

The importance of the GYE concept is that it recognizes that the destinies of wildlife and the resources on which they depend transcend political and jurisdictional boundaries. Despite the inextricable links binding wildlife and their resources, management of the landscapes in the various versions of the GYE is segregated among several agencies and jurisdictions with often conflicting goals and objectives. The GYE as most commonly defined encompasses state lands in portions of Wyoming, Montana, and Idaho; two national parks; three national wildlife refuges; portions of six national forests; lands managed by the Bureau of Land Management; tribal lands; and private lands. More than twenty-eight federal, state, and local government agencies and thousands of private landowners manage parts of the area.

The varied jurisdictions, management objectives, and philosophies found within its imprecise borders challenge the idea of coordinated, holistic management. The Greater Yellowstone Coordinating Committee (GYCC) was formed with a Memorandum of Understanding between the National Park Service and the U. S. Forest Service in 1964 to foster communication and coordination in the management of federal lands in Yellowstone and Grand Teton national parks and adjacent landscapes. The U. S. Fish and Wildlife Service joined the Committee in 2002, and the Bureau of Land Management was added in 2012. The establishment and work of the GYCC have enhanced opportunities for transboundary federal stewardship in the region, but obstacles remain as these agencies struggle to clearly define common goals and generate adequate resources to consistently overcome bureaucratic hurdles and effectively pursue management objectives.

Even with complete agreement and synergy among

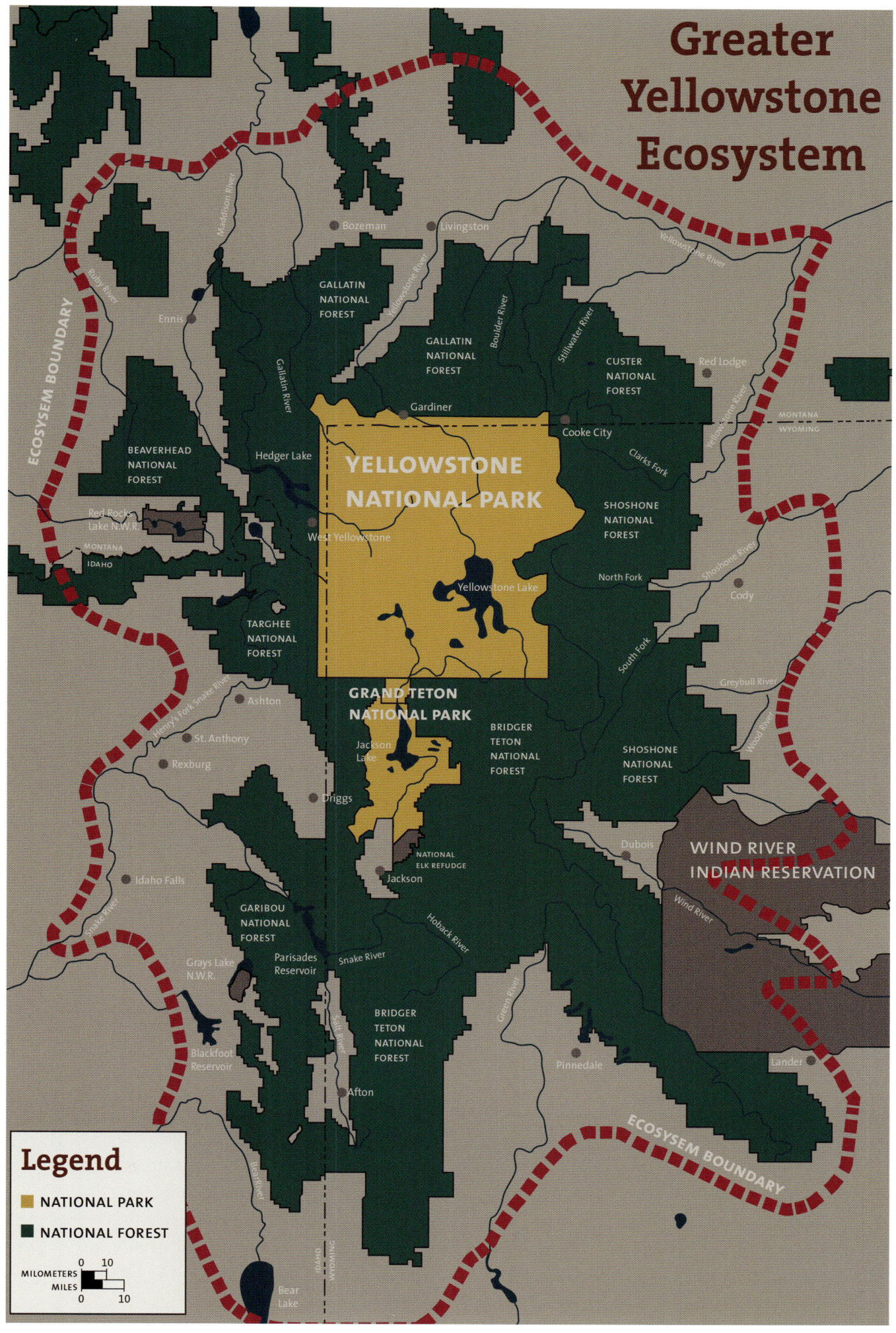

One interpretation of the Greater Yellowstone Ecosystem. Modified from Greater Yellowstone Coalition, Craighead 1979, and other sources. Image courtesy of the author.

federal agencies, a comprehensive vision and strategic plan for holistic management of the entire area must also include active cooperation of state, municipal, and tribal governments, and private landowners. Effective wildlife management across an ecosystem partitioned by so many human-imposed boundaries and so many diverse stakeholders ultimately will depend on identifying common goals that include socioeconomic and cultural considerations, as well as ecological ones. Identifying the appropriate mix of stakeholders to cooperate in a management plan requires that we delineate the area to be managed and the specific goals of management. The four- to eighteen-million-acre area identified by various authors to comprise the GYE has been heralded as the appropriate landscape for effective wildlife management in the Yellowstone region by those who claim it encompasses the resources and space needed for the perpetuation of the region's most wide-ranging wildlife. But it doesn't.

To this point, definitions, discussions, and debates surrounding wildlife conservation and management in the GYE have focused primarily on large, wide-ranging, terrestrial mammals, including grizzly bear, gray wolf, elk, bison, and other ungulates, and, to a lesser degree, Yellowstone cutthroat trout. The various published boundaries of the GYE apply reasonably well to these species, though concerns about genetic isolation and increasing habitat fragmentation have prompted some to focus more on connectivity to much broader areas, such as a Yellowstone-to-Yukon corridor for adequate grizzly bear conservation, and a western Wyoming corridor for pronghorn antelope and mule deer. But if we consider the long-distance migrations of flying animals that inhabit Yellowstone National Park and the surrounding region during part of the year, even the most expansive boundaries usually applied to the GYE are clearly inadequate.

For example, of the estimated thirteen species of bats occurring in Yellowstone National Park, at least one, the hoary bat, migrates far beyond both park boundaries and current GYE boundaries to overwinter and obtain needed resources elsewhere. Little is known about the specific movements of individual hoary bats breeding in Yellowstone, but evidence indicates that a large portion of the hoary bat population that breeds and spends summers in the western United States, including the Yellowstone region, spends the winter as far south as southern Mexico, more than 1,600 miles away.

Western tanagers nesting in Yellowstone in summer may migrate as far as Costa Rica for the winter. Photograph by C. R. Preston.

Approximately 150 to 160 species of birds nest and spend much of the spring and summer in Yellowstone National Park. Only about one-fourth to one-half of these species are year-round residents in the park or adjacent areas. The other species migrate to lower elevation landscapes outside the park or to lower latitudes far beyond the traditional boundaries of the GYE. As James Prosek describes in his essay in this book, the colorful western tanager, a common breeding bird, is a spring, summer, and early fall resident of mixed conifer and mixed aspen-conifer woodlands in Yellowstone National Park and surrounding areas. However, it spends the winter in the pine-oak woodlands of Mexico to Costa Rica. The GYE for some western tanagers may thus extend up to 3,100 miles beyond Yellowstone National Park.

For some bird species, the GYE boundaries must be stretched even farther. The Swainson's hawk is an open-country raptor that breeds through much of western North America. It is a fairly common breeding bird that nests in isolated trees and tall shrubs in large grassy and shrub-steppe areas in and around Yellowstone National Park, where the parents typically feed their nestlings a steady diet of small rodents. In September, large groups, or kettles, of the Swainson's hawks begin their southerly migration. It is not uncommon to encounter scores of these birds foraging on grasshoppers and other insects in agricultural and grassland areas along the first stage of their broad migration route, which stretches as far east as western Iowa.

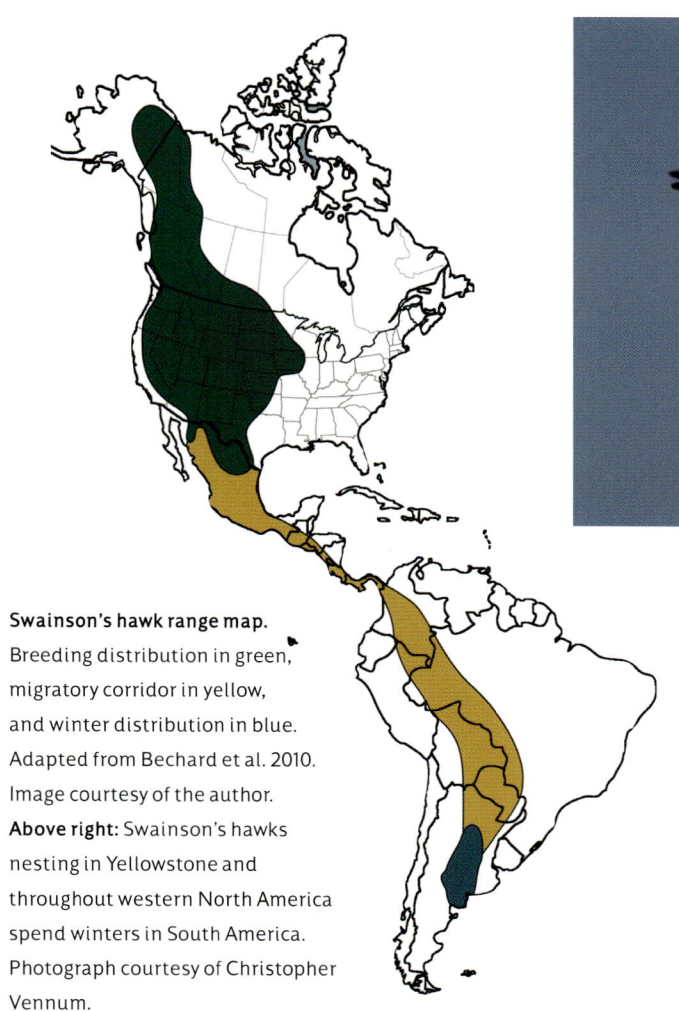

Swainson's hawk range map. Breeding distribution in green, migratory corridor in yellow, and winter distribution in blue. Adapted from Bechard et al. 2010. Image courtesy of the author. **Above right:** Swainson's hawks nesting in Yellowstone and throughout western North America spend winters in South America. Photograph courtesy of Christopher Vennum.

Although we don't have much information about the initial migratory movements of Swainson's hawks nesting in Yellowstone, we know that virtually all Swainson's hawks in existence eventually migrate to South America through the narrow Isthmus of Panama. After entering South America, these hawks follow a narrow corridor along the Andes on the way to their eventual wintering grounds in the pampas of southern Brazil, Uruguay, and Argentina. Insects comprise the bulk of the Swainson's hawk diet in winter. Large incidents of Swainson's hawk mortality were documented in the 1990s due to widespread use of pesticides applied to agricultural fields in Argentina to control grasshoppers and locusts. In one 300-acre field alone, an estimated 3,000 Swainson's hawks were killed after insecticide application. Subsequently, the U. S. and Argentinian governments cooperated to resolve the problem. Nonetheless, this episode dramatically demonstrates how events more than 6,200 miles beyond the boundaries of Yellowstone National Park can impact Yellowstone wildlife.

Many other bird species, especially shorebirds such as the black-bellied plover, semipalmated plover, black-necked stilt, American avocet, and semipalmated sandpiper, rely on Yellowstone as a stopover during migratory flights between breeding and overwintering areas far outside the park. Some semipalmated sandpipers, for example, forage for aquatic insects and small crustaceans on specific mudflats in Yellowstone each year. The mudflats are a key stopover for a portion of the western population of semipalmated sandpipers as they journey from their summer breeding range in the North American arctic tundra to their winter range along the coasts of South America. Numbers of semipalmated sandpipers have declined in recent years, and some authorities consider the species vulnerable to further declines due to their dependence on a small number of key migratory stopover sites.

In addition to bats and birds, many insect species exhibit long-distance migrations in western North America. The life history of one insect species in particular stands out as a reminder that the current concept of a Greater Yellowstone Ecosystem must be considered in a much broader context. The army cutworm moth represents a remarkable connection between the grizzly bears of Yellowstone and the distant croplands of the Great Plains. Adult army cutworm moths lay eggs in late summer and early fall in weedy areas of alfalfa, wheat, and other agricultural and overgrown fields in the plains of Nebraska, Kansas, Oklahoma, eastern Colorado, and eastern Wyoming. The eggs hatch within a few weeks, and the young caterpillars forage before hibernating through most of the winter. The partially-grown caterpillars resume foraging in early spring, damaging crops and

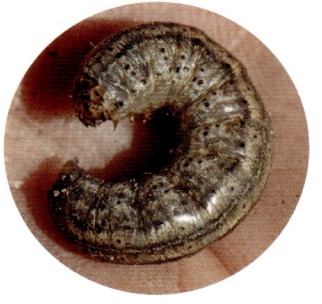

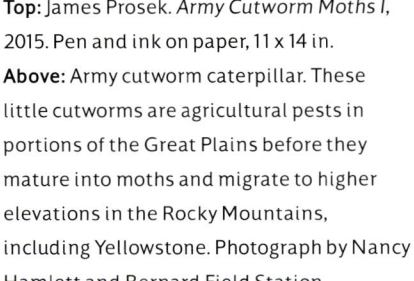

Top: James Prosek. *Army Cutworm Moths I,* 2015. Pen and ink on paper, 11 x 14 in.
Above: Army cutworm caterpillar. These little cutworms are agricultural pests in portions of the Great Plains before they mature into moths and migrate to higher elevations in the Rocky Mountains, including Yellowstone. Photograph by Nancy Hamlett and Bernard Field Station.
Above right: Army cutworm moth, also commonly referred to as miller moth. Large aggregations of these moths are an important part of the summer diet for many Yellowstone grizzly bears. Photograph by M. J. Dreiling, Bugworld.org.
Facing page: Overview of multiuse landscapes in Wyoming's Bighorn Basin, October 2015. Some of these lands are used seasonally by Yellowstone wildlife. Photograph © Joe Riis.

gardens. Some of the caterpillars become victims of pesticides. The survivors complete their growth by mid-spring and pupate in the soil. A few weeks later, the adult moths emerge and begin migrating toward the Rocky Mountains. The fine scales that cover the wings of these moths easily flake off, reminding some people of powdery flour associated with milling grain. Thus, the army cutworm moth is one of the species of moth that is commonly called a "miller moth."

Some of these 1.5- to 2-inch grayish-brown adult moths settle for the summer at high elevations in and around Yellowstone National Park. Here they feed on the nectar of alpine flowers at night, and rest in the cool temperatures under rocks of talus slopes in the day. These alpine aggregations of moths are an important food source for many grizzly and a few black bears each summer. Tens of thousands of moths may occupy a single boulder field, and each moth is packed with fat

and protein. Bears roam through the boulder fields, turning over rocks large and small. A single bear may eat thousands of nutrient-rich moths in a day, and as many as a dozen or more bears may forage in a single boulder field at the same time. By late summer, the moths that survive begin to migrate back to the plains to lay eggs and repeat the cycle.

Human-imposed boundaries mean something to humans. We can identify and trace them on maps and even recognize them on the landscape with the help of signs and fences. But animals aren't so good at recognizing or adhering to human-imposed boundaries. They tend to roam where they need to roam in order to survive and reproduce. These movements are not usually random, and many of their routes significantly predate our presence on this continent. Yet we continue to be surprised and sometimes even indignant when animals escape the little islands of habitat we graciously set aside for them with great self-satisfaction. Those of us interested in or charged with managing and conserving wide-ranging wildlife struggle to reconcile the morass of political and jurisdictional boundaries and value systems with the transboundary needs of wildlife. To make matters worse, we often complain about wildlife invading our ever-expanding neighborhoods, gardens, and recreational trails.

As I write this, there is much discussion here in Cody, Wyoming, about a fresh grizzly bear track discovered in the middle of a newly-developed mountain bike trail in the Bighorn Basin a couple of miles south of town. The site is more than fifty miles outside Yellowstone National Park and more than twenty-five miles outside the Shoshone National Forest. Prior to human settlement, the Bighorn Basin was used extensively by grizzly bears. Some people are alarmed that the recovering Yellowstone grizzly bear population is expanding its range again into the Bighorn Basin. It is true that the Yellowstone grizzly bear has expanded its range as the population has recovered from fewer than 200 bears in the mid-1970s to more than 700 bears by 2015. But the location of the recently-discovered track lies at the eastern margin of the Craigheads' proposed

GYE encompassing the area needed to support a viable grizzly bear population. The site also lies within my long-term golden eagle/sagebrush-steppe ecology research site in the Bighorn Basin, where my team and I have encountered grizzly bear spoor nearly every year during the last decade, especially when whitebark pine nuts and other foods are scarce at high elevations to the west. During the same period of my fieldwork, we've encountered very few people and no recreational trails. Is the grizzly bear suddenly expanding its range into the Bighorn Basin this year, or are the region's people continuing to expand their range and awareness of grizzly bear presence?

National parks and other land preserves provide an important foundation for constructing a long-term, sustainable strategy to manage and conserve our planet's biodiversity. But parks and preserves alone cannot conserve an area's biodiversity. They are too few, too small, too isolated, and are too often compromised by competing management goals and objectives. These challenges especially come into focus when we consider that the world's human population has more than doubled since 1950 and is expected to grow by an estimated 80 million people this year alone. The concept

of a Greater Yellowstone Ecosystem acknowledges and helps address some of these challenges. But without a cohesive, holistic vision and management strategy that involves multiple management authorities and stakeholders throughout the GYE, Yellowstone's most charismatic wildlife species remain at risk. Even if we overcome these obstacles for Yellowstone National Park and adjacent lands, Yellowstone's hoary bats, western tanagers, Swainson's hawks, semipalmated sandpipers, army cutworm moths (and thus grizzly bears), and many other species are vulnerable to events and activities hundreds and thousands of miles beyond the boundaries of Yellowstone.

Facing: A Grizzly Bear sow and cub crossing a highway in the Shoshone National Forest twenty miles east of Yellowstone National Park. Photograph by C. R. Preston. **Above:** Grizzly Bear near Yellowstone Lake. Photograph by C. R. Preston.

The long-term solutions to these conservation challenges begin with the recognition that John Muir was spot-on when he declared ". . . when we try to pick out anything by itself, we find it hitched to everything else in the Universe." Conservation of wildlife and habitat in the GYE reaches well beyond this celebrated region, just as conserving wildlife and habitat in faraway landscapes reaches into the heart of the GYE. The fundamental theme of this volume and the exhibition that inspired it is that conservation in the twenty-first century and beyond must cross jurisdictional, geopolitical, philosophical, and disciplinary boundaries to engage a wide range of stakeholders with a vision and a strategy that links human destiny with the destiny of our planet's biodiversity—a great treasure that we too often take for granted.

CHARLES R. PRESTON, PH.D., is the Willis McDonald, IV Senior Curator of Natural Science and Founding Curator of the Draper Natural History Museum at the Buffalo Bill Center of the West. He studies the influence of climate and human activities on biodiversity and is widely recognized as a leading authority on wildlife and human–wildlife relationships in Greater Yellowstone. Dr. Preston was formerly Chairman of Zoology at the Denver Museum of Nature and Science and a tenured Associate Professor of Biology at the University of Arkansas, Little Rock.

He holds or has held adjunct appointments in the Haub School for Environment and Natural Resources, University of Wyoming; Biology and Environmental Science, University of Colorado (Boulder and Denver); Environmental Policy and Management, Denver University, and Biological Sciences, University of Arkansas, Fayetteville. He has authored, co-authored, or edited seven books and more than a hundred scientific articles and popular essays covering various topics.

RELATED READING

Bechard, M. J., C. S. Houston, J. H. Sarasola, and A. S. England. Swainson's Hawk (*Buteo swainsoni*). In A. Poole, ed. *The Birds of North America* Online 265 (Ithaca: Cornell Lab of Ornithology, 2010).

Berger, J. and D. W. Smith. "Restoring Functionality in Yellowstone with Recovering Carnivores: Gains and Uncertainties." In *Large Carnivores and the Conservation of Biodiversity,* J. C. Ray, K. H. Redford, R. S. Steneck, and J. Berger, eds.(Washington, D.C.: Island Press, 2005), 100–109.

Christianson, D., R. W. Kaver, A. D. Middleton, and M. J. Kaufmann. "Confounded Winter and Spring Conditions on Temperate Herbivore Ranges," *Landscape Ecology* 28:427–437.

Clark, T. W. and S. C. Minta. *Greater Yellowstone's Future* (Moose, WY: Homestead Publishing, 1994).

Clark, T. W., E. E. Amano, D. G. Whittemore, and A. H. Harvey. "Policy and Programs for Ecosystem Management in the Greater Yellowstone Ecosystem: An Analysis," *Conservation Biology* 5:412–422.

Clark, T. W., A. P. Curlee, S. C. Minta, and P. M. Kareiva, eds. *Carnivores in Ecosystems: The Yellowstone Experience* (New Haven: Yale University Press, 1999).

Congressional Research Service. Issues surrounding the Greater Yellowstone Ecosystem. In Committee on Interior and Insular Affairs. House of Representatives Oversight Hearing on Greater Yellowstone Ecosystem (Washington, D.C.: U. S. Government Printing Office, 1986), 337–422.

Craighead, F. C., Jr. *Track of the Grizzly* (San Francisco: Sierra Club Books, 1979).

Cranshaw, W. and F. Peairs. Miller moths. Colorado State University Cooperative Extension Service, 2010. Accessed 5 October 2015. http://www.colostate.edu/Dept/CoopExt/4dmg/Pests/millers.htm.

Cryan, P. M. "Seasonal distribution of migratory tree bats (*Lasiurus* and *Lasioncteris*) in North America," *Journal of Mammalogy* 84:579–593.

Fishbein, S. L. *Yellowstone Country: The Enduring Wonder.* (Washington, D. C: National Geographic Society, 1997).

French, S. P., M. G. French, and R. R. Knight. 1994. International Conference on Bear Research and Management 9:389–399.

Glick, D. A. and T. W. Clark. "Overcoming Boundaries: The Greater Yellowstone Ecosystem." In *Stewardship Across Boundaries,* R. L. Knight and P. B. Landres, eds. (Washington, D.C.: Island Press, 1998), 237–256.

Goldstein, M. L., B. Woodbridge, M. E. Zaccaginini, S. B. Canavelli, and A. Lanusse. "An Assessment of Mortality of Swainson's Hawks on Wintering Grounds in Argentina," *Journal of Raptor Research* 30:106–107.

Gratto-Trevor, C. L. "Semipalmated Sandpiper." In *No. 6,* A. Poole, P. Stettenheim, and F. Gill, eds. (Philadelphia: The Academy of Natural Sciences; and Washington, D. C.: The American Ornithologists' Union, 1992).

Gresswell, R. E. "Yellowstone Cutthroat Trout." In *Conservation Assessment for Inland Cutthroat Trout,* M. Young, ed., General Technical Report RM-256 (Fort Collins, CO: USDA Forest Service, Rocky Mountain Forest and Range Experiment Station, 1995), 36–54.

Haines, A. L. *The Yellowstone Story: A History of Our First National Park,* Volume 1, rev. dd. The Yellowstone Association for Natural Science, History, and Education, Inc., in cooperation with University of Colorado Press, Niwot, CO, 1977.

Hudon, Jocelyn. Western Tanager (*Piranga ludoviciana*). In A. Poole, ed. *The Birds of North America* Online 432 (Ithaca: Cornell Lab of Ornithology, 1999).

Keinath, D. A. "Yellowstone's World of Bats: Taking Inventory of Yellowstone's Night Life," *Yellowstone Science* 15 (3):3–13.

Koel, T. M., P. E. Begelow, P. D. Doepke, B. D. Ertel, and D. L. Mahoney. "Nonnative Lake Trout Result in Yellowstone Cutthroat Trout Decline and Impact to Bears and Anglers," *Fisheries* 30:10–19.

McEneaney, T. *Birds of Yellowstone* (Boulder: Roberts Rhinehart, Inc., 1988).

Merrill, T. Grizzly Bear Conservation in the Yellowstone to Yukon Region. Yellowstone to Yukon Conservation Initiative, Technical Report #6, 2005.

Middleton, A. D., M. J. Kauffman, D. E. McWhirter, J. G. Cook, R. C. Cook, A. A. Nelson, M. D. Jimenez, and R. W. Klaver. "Animal Migration Amid Shifting Patterns of Predation and Phenology: Lessons from a Yellowstone Elk Herd," *Ecology* 94:1245–1256.

Muir, John. *My First Summer in the Sierra* (Cambridge: The Riverside Press, 1911).

Patten, D. T. 1991. "Defining the Greater Yellowstone Ecosystem." In *The Greater Yellowstone Ecosystem: Redefining America's Wilderness Heritage,* R. B. Keiter and M. S. Boyce, eds. (New Haven: Yale University Press, 1991) 19–26.

Preston, C. R. "Islands of Hope in a Raging Sea: Yellowstone and Serengeti." In *Beyond the Arch: Conservation and Community in Greater Yellowstone and East Africa, Proceedings of the 7th Biennial Conference on Science in the Greater Yellowstone Ecosystem,* A. Wondrak, ed. (Yellowstone National Park, Mammoth, WY: National Park Service, 2004) 244–252.

Preston, C. R. "Saving the Charmed Goose: Reconciling Human Demands with Inherent Limitations in the Greater Yellowstone Ecosystem," *Yellowstone Science* 13 (4):5–14.

Preston, C. R. "Nature's Boundaries: The Greater Yellowstone Ecosystem." In *Spectacular Yellowstone and Grand Teton National Parks,* D. Levy, L. O'Connor, and P. Vecetich, eds. (Fairfield, CT: Hugh Lauter Levin Associates, Inc., 2007) 12–19.

Reese, R. "Greater Yellowstone, the National Park and Adjacent Wildlands," *Montana Geographic,* Helena, MT, 1984.

Righter, R. W. *Crucible for Conservation: The Struggle for Grand Teton National Park* (Moose, WY: Grand Teton Natural History Association, 1982).

Sawyer, H., F. Lindzey, and D. McWhirter. "Mule Deer and Pronghorn Migration in Western Wyoming," *Wildlife Society Bulletin* 33:1266–1273.

Sawyer, H., M. J. Kauffman, A. D. Middleton, T. A. Morrison, R. M. Nielson, and T.B. Wyckoff. "A Framework for Understanding Barrier Effects on Migratory Ungulates, *Journal of Applied Ecology* 50:68–78.

Schullery, P. *The Bears of Yellowstone* (Worland, WY: High Plains Publishing, 1992).

White, P. J., R. L. Wallen, D. E. Hallac, and J. A. Jerrett. *Yellowstone Bison: Conserving an American Icon in Modern Society* (Mammoth, WY: Yellowstone Center for Resources, 2015).

Yellowstone National Park. *Birds of Yellowstone Checklist* (Mammoth, WY: Yellowstone Center for Resources, 2014).

Facing: James Prosek. *Seclusion Creek Valley—View off Sheep Mesa,* 2015. Watercolor, graphite and gouache on tea-stained paper, 8 x 12 1/4 in.

Left: James Prosek. *Blackwater Natural Bridge—View off Sheep Mesa,* 2015. Watercolor, graphite and gouache on tea-stained paper, 5 3/4 x 12 1/4 in.

SEEING YELLOWSTONE

SCIENCE AT ITS LIMITS IN A CONSERVATION CRUCIBLE

ARTHUR MIDDLETON

On the afternoon of June 6, 2015, on the airport tarmac in Cody, Wyoming, the sun was warm and the sky was clear. But to the southwest, where we needed to fly, dark clouds flickered and pulsed with lightning.

I'd gone to great lengths to line up a helicopter and a cameraman for that day. I had kept a close eye on the movements of our collared elk, and they had just started to break for the mountains. We had a chance at recording the first glimpses of a phenomenon I'd made it my mission to see and to share: the Cody elk herd's annual migration to Yellowstone National Park. This weather could ruin that chance.

"No worries!" said Mark Taylor, our pilot, chewing his gum as he surveyed the distant storm. "I'll fly that. That's the thing about helicopters. We can dodge the worst of it, set down if need be. Up to you, bud!"

I'd only met Mark a few hours earlier. He was a gentle giant in Wrangler jeans and cowboy boots, with a big, goofy smile. I don't love helicopters—they break too easily—and it takes time to trust a pilot. But I liked Mark, and he had a good reputation. I couldn't afford to lose this chance. "Sure," I said. "If you're in, I'm in."

The rotor whistled and droned as streets and lawns gave way to county roads and hayfields. Below, black Angus and white Charolais cattle dotted the open range. A few oil wells punctuated the vast Hoodoo Ranch, their pumpjacks bobbing against the velvet spring grass.

Previous pages: Bull elk of varying ages cross a river swollen with snowmelt on spring migration, June 2015. Their antlers are still developing, or "in velvet." Photograph © Joe Riis. **Above:** Middleton following migrating elk, summer 2014. Photograph © Joe Riis. **Facing page**: A large herd of elk congregate on traditional wintering grounds far outside Yellowstone National Park, March 2015. Elk retreat from higher elevations in winter to avoid even deeper snow. Photograph © Joe Riis.

Here and there pronghorn antelope sprinted along, as if to race us. At the foot of Carter Mountain, where the Rockies meet the Bighorn Basin—the edge of the great Midwestern plain—we banked west, up the Greybull River, into a building rain.

Carter Mountain stretches southwest for nearly 20 miles. More than a dozen streams drain its flanks. One by one, we crossed the ridges between them, the earth rising and falling beneath us. Patchy snow shone bright against green grass and gray sky. Down along the Greybull, to our south, I squinted to find the Pitchfork Ranch headquarters. I'd put GPS tracking collars on elk there during the past two winters.

We were heading for the first waypoint I'd given Mark, at Boulder Pass—a 10,500-foot saddle at the west end of Carter, where the elk leave the ranch country behind and enter the wilderness. As we slipped over the pass, we saw trails through the snow, darkened from muddy hooves. Dropping down the other side, we passed the gray ramparts of Castle Creek. We were into the real mountains now, and the helicopter felt small among tall sheets and spires of rock. Mark toggled to our next waypoint: Needle Mountain.

The Cody elk herd faces many obstacles on its migration—rushing rivers, hungry predators, and a series of high passes—but at 12,000 feet, Needle Mountain must be the toughest of them all. Working from local outfitters' and wardens' accounts, and more recently, from my own GPS collaring, I knew the elk crossed it. I'd even found their faint trails on a satellite image. Yet I still harbored slight disbelief. To traverse this mountain, they had to climb 5,000 feet from their winter range, then scale long knife ridges and struggle through miles of belly-deep snow—all out in the open, exposed—before dropping 5,000 feet down loose scree slopes to cross the South Fork of the Shoshone. It didn't make any sense.

The rain streaked sideways across the windshield as we approached Needle. Out ahead, through the mist, I could just make out a long, dark slash, angling up and across a steep snowfield. Mark saw it, too. "There's a trail there, but it can't be the elk trail," he said. "They would find something lower. They'd avoid a face like that."

The trail was still five hundred feet above us. Climbing toward it, Mark worked the helicopter back and forth slowly, like a hiker on switchbacks. In the thin, cold air around Needle, his machine was nearing its limits. The mountain flashed behind passing mist and clouds.

As we grew closer, the bottom lobe of a big, gray cloud cleared away in thinner and thinner wisps. Several dark shapes had appeared on the trail. "I don't believe this!" Mark said. "I… do not… BELIEVE this."

One by one, twelve cow elk pushed their way out into the snow. They would sink in, halt, then lunge forward again. Every few lunges, they would pause while the lead cow stopped them to breathe. We were seeing the vanguard of the Cody elk herd, among the first of 4,000 to start their annual journey.

More than 140 years ago, the United States Congress created Yellowstone National Park to preserve incredible geological wonders—geysers, fumaroles, canyons, and cascades. That single act, perhaps more than any other, sparked a global movement to protect the last wild places on earth. But the people who made our first park—they had never seen anything like this.

I FIRST CAME TO CODY in 2007, as a newly enrolled grad student at the University of Wyoming. For my dissertation research, I was going to work with state and federal agencies to study how re-introduced wolves were affecting the survival and behavior of their main prey—

elk—and whether those effects could explain the decline of the Clarks Fork elk herd. For three winters I would live in a place called Sunlight Basin, in the heart of the herd's expansive winter range.

Sunlight is a stunning, quiet valley of cattle and dude ranches, lined by long rows of jagged peaks, about an hour-and-a-half's drive northwest of Cody. The highway out to Sunlight snakes past big cattle ranches, then up over a high pass before dropping down into the valley. The gravel road peels west, cleaving straight up the valley bottom. About two thousand elk winter in Sunlight, and on any given day hundreds gather on the flats that flank the road, pawing a thin veneer of snow to get at the brittle, brown grass beneath it. Many a night in Sunlight in winter I've crept a truck along slowly as the herd parted around me, dozens of eyes lit yellow-green against the inky darkness. Heading back down the road at dawn, I've seen gangs of eagles and ravens hop up from a carcass into flight, leaving their crimson tracks—and the bigger, bloodier tracks of wolves—pressed into the crusty snow. From those flats, it's about thirty miles west, across the imposing Absaroka Divide, to Yellowstone National Park.

When I first arrived in Sunlight, I had never seen a wolf or an elk. This was a hard thing for me to admit. Wildlife stories can be front-page news in Wyoming, and by 2007, people in the communities that ring Yellowstone—places like Jackson and Livingston, Bozeman and Cody—had been debating the effects of wolves on elk (and cattle) for more than a decade. Elk are so familiar to people who live in northwest Wyoming that one of my colleagues refers to Jackson as "a town of 9,000 elk biologists." Cody is similar, but more insular, and with a stronger independent streak. So there I was, an Ivy League graduate from the East Coast, joining the government to help the locals around Cody better understand their wildlife.

Though it wasn't totally clear to me then, my absolute lack of personal experience with the species I'd come to study meant that I would have to rely, at least for a time, on other peoples' stories. And there were many of those. For my colleagues in agencies and universities, the elk were a conduit for the wolf's effects on a larger stage. These stories centered on dropping elk numbers—like in Sunlight Basin—that might relieve the pressure of so many hungry mouths and trampling hooves on grasses, trees, and streams. For my new friends and acquaintances in outfitting and ranching, the wolf was an aggressive invader, and the elk its innocent victim. These stories began with pitiable elk and cattle running miles to escape wolves, and ended on the cumulative impacts, emotional and financial, for local hunters and ranchers.

Over those years in Sunlight, I came to see these stories as counterplots in the battle for an overarching narrative about Yellowstone. They were less about the wolves or elk than about the wildness of the "ecosystem"—about what configuration of animals and people would make the place healthy and whole. On one side, wolves were restorative, bringing back a lost Eden. On the other side, wolves were destructive and elk were a mascot for those who felt excluded. In this light, each wolf and elk story seemed like a bid for the heart and soul of Yellowstone. But they were also terribly divisive, driving wedges deep between the people, even the neighbors, on whom the future of the place depended.

All those stories shared something else that bothered me. Their main characters, the animals, had little identify of their own. They existed in relation to other ideas and other problems. And so over my years in Sunlight Basin, I began to wonder what would happen if we could see them for themselves. Would they tell us something new about the place? Could they tell us something new about our own relationships? Something new about ourselves?

WINTERS IN SUNLIGHT were busy for me. By November, I had hired three assistants—college biology graduates willing to work hard for ten bucks an hour and a new line on their resumes. In early January I brought in a helicopter crew—a roving band of New Zealanders who make their living catching wildlife for Western agencies and universities—to catch and collar animals. I arrived in Cody before Christmas and worked through the holidays to finalize logistics: permits, ranch access, GPS collar set-up. When the helicopter arrived, and we got a lull in the wind and snow, we set about darting and collaring. I aimed to keep at least two wolves collared in each of the packs that hunted the Clarks Fork elk, and about ninety of the elk themselves. The GPS collars recorded each animal's location every three hours. The data they logged—wolves' proximity to elk, and elk responses—were the heart of my work. After the captures, by mid-January, we started our daily grind. Days in the field started and ended in the dark. We split into pairs to make circuits across a patchwork of local ranches and forest lands. We tracked elk by truck and on foot, in wind, snow, and frigid Wyoming air. Often we climbed to high points to make our observations. One of them, "the Anthill," stuck straight up in the middle of the valley. It was a near-perfect cone, draped in sagebrush and snowdrifts. We scrambled and post-holed to the top, unfolded the VHF antenna, and scanned for collars out in the folds of the valley. When we spotted our elk and their groups, we staked them out from above, watching through scopes for an hour or more. We narrated their doings into voice recorders, because it was too cold to write. "Now she's feeding… moving… now alert… feeding again… still feeding… moving… now she's bedding down…"

It turns out that wintering elk do little more than those four things. And from the accumulation of those simple behavior profiles—one every two weeks for each collared elk, for three winters—I hoped to see how wolves affected the finer details of elk feeding. Each night, we returned to a drafty state cabin we called

home. We thawed our feet, ate profusely, and transcribed the day's recordings onto paper before passing out on musty cots as close to the furnace as we could drag them.

After every winter I said farewell to the crew, packed the pickup full of my ragged gear and stacks of precious data sheets, and made the long, lonely trip to Laramie. There, back at the university, I resettled the basement cubicle where I worked through the summer and fall. I typed data into spreadsheets, caught up on my colleagues' latest work, and designed my computational analyses.

After three years cycling between the field in Cody and the desk in Laramie, I spent two more full years at work in that basement, finishing my analyses and writing a dissertation. And after five years in all—staring at elk until my face froze, and at screens until my eyes burned—the animals I saw were very different from the ones I'd been told about.

FROM AN ELK COW'S point of view, a winter's day must be a tedious proposition. In the smoky light of dawn she comes out to feed on the open ground. The grass is buried under snow, and what's left over from the summer isn't worth very much to her. Crystalline sheets of snow snake and slide across the valley like beach sands, whipping at her legs and face as she paws and noses the ground. Hour after hour, she gnashes at sharp, dry stubble. It takes hours to fill even a fraction of her big belly. Step by step by step, the group around her drifts across the flat, pulling her along in its midst. By midday she beds down with the rest of them. If it's cold, they lie in the sun on a sagebrush slope. If it's warm, or windy, they lie in the shade and the shelter of nearby timber. She chews her cud. She digests. In the afternoon, she heaves her 500-pound body up to feed all over again. All the while—as she grazes, chews, and rests—she keeps a wary eye on the world around her. The 25, 100, or 500 elk around her are watching, too.

Inevitably, a threat comes. Those 25, 100, or 500 heads pop up in unison. Their ears cock forward, locking on a noise or a movement. It can be a false alarm—a door slamming on a distant ranch, a truck rumbling by, or a scientist accidentally knocking a rock loose on a hill. But other times, it's the wolves. In three winters, I saw wolves approach elk only about a dozen times. Once, the encounter ended in a kill. Five wolves split a couple bull elk off from a group of twenty, ran them for half a mile, and dragged one down by his neck, killing him as he sank out of view into the snow. The other times were different.

One day, I was watching a collared elk in a group of sixteen when their heads all jerked upslope. A pair of black wolves with bright yellow eyes was standing there, watching the elk patiently through sparse timber. The wolves sat down on their haunches, and the elk bunched together tightly. But soon, the elk began to slacken up

Wolves, reintroduced to Yellowstone National Park in 1995 and 1996, are now the primary elk predators on many winter ranges. Photograph © Joe Riis, March 2015.

and feed again, and the wolves moved on. They had seen and reacted to something about each other—something that was invisible to me.

Another time, farther up the valley, I was watching a group of fifty elk when I noticed that a few of them kept looking behind a little hill nearby. After I finished my observation, I repositioned to see what they were looking at. There, curled up in the snow, were the twelve wolves of the Sunlight pack. Through my scope, I could see the dark fur of their backs fluttering in the whipping wind. The elk kept feeding, checking the wolves from time to time, and after a few hours I was too cold to watch the strange spectacle any longer. Neither wolves nor elk were behaving as I'd been told they would.

Scientists like me learn to discount such anecdotes in favor of more systematic observation. Yet my analyses backed up what I saw in the field. The GPS collars showed that wolves came within a half-mile of each individual elk less than once a week. After those encounters, the elk would typically drift a short distance, but they rarely abandoned the places they liked to feed. Sure, wolves killed elk, but not as many as I'd expected. Of the ninety collared elk cows I tracked over those three winters, only one was killed by wolves.

One of the most surprising things I learned was that wolves also die in the hunt. In early 2010, we collared a big male. Our capture pilot called him "Blue." His gray coat was made of black and white hairs that gave him a stunning, bluish hue. He was the breeder—the "alpha male"—in the Sunlight pack. A year later, he turned up dead in the prime of his life. We found him lifeless in the snow, with dark holes in his groin and his armpit. It seemed a bull elk had lifted him up, sunk antlers deep into his body, and tossed him down to die on the cold snow. He lay encircled by a spatter of blood from the struggle. The wolf was neither the saint nor the sinner, the hero nor the villain that I'd been told it was. The elk was coming alive for me as a graceful creature, tougher and more sophisticated than I'd ever imagined.

I had come to Sunlight to understand what was causing the decline of the Clarks Fork elk, and I was in trouble. I sought strong wolf effects because I'd been told to do so by those around me—from the most overeducated of my academic colleagues, to the most reactionary of the locals. I was looking for answers on the elk winter range because that's where the animals were easiest to see, count, and study. But I was learning that the answers weren't so simple, and would have to come from somewhere else.

ONE SINGLE INSIGHT, more than any other, opened my eyes to that "somewhere." It came from my closest collaborator on the Clarks Fork study, and on much of my work since then: Doug McWhirter. Doug is a veteran biologist for the Wyoming Game and Fish Department. He's now stationed in Cody, after serving in the same role elsewhere in Wyoming. Soon after I arrived in Cody I asked Doug an awkward question I would ask many others: "So, um, can you describe a year in the life of an elk for me?" Doug has a modesty about him that makes it feel okay to ask dumb questions, even though he can answer them with total authority. Maybe he could relate—twenty years earlier, he'd come from Kansas to ply the road between Laramie and Cody for his own grad work on bighorn sheep.

A routine part of any Game and Fish biologist's job is to survey elk herds on their winter ranges. One of the most important numbers they track, year after year, is the ratio of elk calves per hundred cows. Most mature elk cows give birth to a calf each year, so at calving time in early June, there is a potential ratio of ninety or so newborns per hundred cows. But pregnancies can be lost, and calves are born weak. Many die. When the winter calf ratio drops below thirty, biologists worry how much hunting the herd can sustain. When it drops below twenty, they cut back on hunting, and worry whether they can sustain the herd at all. Doug had watched the Clarks Fork elk herd's calf ratio drop to twelve by the year of my arrival. He was alarmed.

The recovery of wolves in Sunlight Basin coincided almost perfectly with the elk decline—which was one of several reasons it was logical to investigate wolves' role. But Doug also knew that every spring, around the middle of May, the Clarks Fork elk went somewhere else. They left Sunlight for the high country in and around Yellowstone National Park. And it was on this annual migration that most of them gave birth. They stayed in the high country, along with their calves, until the first snows of winter. A lot could happen to those little calves when they were away, behind the wilderness veil, where few of us ever go.

So in August 2007, as I was planning my first winter field season, Doug scraped the funds together for a summer helicopter survey. He came back with a surprise: the calf ratio was already down to fifteen, just three months after calving time. And he got the same result, year after year. It grew ever clearer that I was freezing my face off on elk winter range in an effort to explain something that was not happening there, but rather thirty, forty, and even sixty miles away, in the warm breezes of the summer. Back at work in my basement cubicle, I shifted focus. The depth and scale of the wilderness meant I couldn't easily go there for myself. And I couldn't fully redesign my study. So instead, I had to rely on indirect observations: weather records, satellite images, and routine agency observations.

Still, there were unmistakable patterns. The summers had grown hotter and drier. The period of spring "green-up," when the grass is young, tender, and easy for elk to digest, had grown three weeks shorter. More important, the number of grizzly bears on the summer range of the Clarks Fork elk had almost quadrupled, and the bears had lost other foods, like spawning trout, leaving them hungrier for elk. These changes in faraway places were shaping what I saw at the end of my nose in Sunlight Basin. Following the migration of Clarks Fork elk up to their summer range had led me to new answers for the questions I'd been asking. This was the closest to an "ah-ha" moment I've ever had in science. And this is how I came to see migration as a fundamental key to seeing Yellowstone. Finally, I'd found a thread that I could begin to follow into a system that for years I'd been struggling, and failing, to understand.

WHEN HARD AT WORK in the basements of our universities, grad students daydream. In the latter years of my own grad studies, one of my summer daydreams was about the elk migrations. I knew the migration of the Clarks Fork elk wasn't the only migration—that others also snaked into Yellowstone—but how many? As cold air hissed from the ceiling, fluorescent lights buzzed, and strange electrical systems hummed behind cinderblock walls, I wondered, what numbers of elk are involved? How far do they go? Where do they start, and where do they end?

I started asking agency biologists, hunting outfitters, and ranchers these questions. It's a state biologist's job to know the herds in her district, and it's a matter of pride and economics for an outfitter or a rancher to know a few of each herd's secrets. I found that nearly everyone I asked my questions had an answer, but only a partial one. I was getting somewhere, but I still had only half the pieces of a giant puzzle—and the pieces were still scattered across the floor.

Next I turned to historical reports. I read everything I could find. I quickly found that I was not, by any means, the first scientist to wonder about the migrations. Olaus Murie, a biologist for the old U. S. Biological Survey, had pioneered a long tradition of study on the Jackson elk herd. He followed the Jackson elk for years, and in 1931 he reported some of his findings to Herbert Hoover's Yellowstone Park Boundary Commission as the government considered (and rejected) an expansion of park boundaries. Then I found a journal article from the 1970s, where one of Yellowstone's most famed biologists, Frank Craighead, had reported on the migrations of five herds that summered within the park.

But through no fault of their own, my predecessors' reports were limited by the available technology. Up until the 1960s, tracking elk required luring them into a corral, clamping tags on their ears, turning them loose, and searching for them later, like needles in a fifteen-million-acre haystack. The VHF radio collars of the 70s, 80s, and 90s were an advance—given a line of sight to the collar, you could pinpoint its pulsing beacon with a handheld antenna. But finding that signal in rough country still required a plane, a bush pilot, and the funding to pay him.

The GPS revolution completely changed the game. Now, wildlife collars—like the ones I used in Sunlight—can uplink to satellites. A GPS collar creates a sort of high-tech trail of crumbs wherever a study animal goes. And many go places we'd never imagined. GPS collars opened the possibility of more comprehensive and revelatory exploration of animal movements the world over. What DNA sequencing has done for molecular biology and medicine, GPS tracking is now doing for the ecology and conservation of ecosystems.

In 2012, when I first began asking my colleagues to share GPS data from local elk herds, my calls were a shot in the dark. I suspected that many of the herds had never been collared. Five state and federal agencies manage wild animals in and around Yellowstone Park, and many universities study them. The inevitable results are fragmentation and territoriality. A biologist in Bozeman might collar 30 elk to see where they are during the hunting season, and her counterpart in Jackson might collar twenty others for a study of road crossings. Yet they work 200 miles apart, and might not like or even know each other. For all these reasons I didn't know if documenting and mapping out all the elk migrations of the Greater Yellowstone Ecosystem was a task we would ever complete.

Right: Middleton, guide Wes Livingston, and dogs Dee and Jack wait out a snow storm on the trail of migrating elk in late July 2015. The *Invisible Boundaries* project team depended heavily on the specialized horse-packing skills and backcountry knowledge of many Cody-area guides, particularly those of Livingston Outfitting, owned and operated by Lee Livingston. Photograph © Joe Riis.

To my surprise, the fragmentation was surmountable, and my colleagues were almost universally happy to help. The agencies of the Greater Yellowstone Ecosystem had generated so much GPS data—some 4 million GPS locations from hundreds of cow elk—that completing a map of the elk migrations seemed within reach. The last obstacle was a gap right in my own backyard. That gap, a few short inches on a regional map, was a vast swath of the Absaroka Range off the southeastern corner of the park, spanning the cattle ranches and the wilderness from Cody to Jackson. And no one was going to fill it for me.

IN THE FALL OF 2013, when I started my exploration of the migrations with wildlife photographer Joe Riis, I knew one thing for sure: I wanted to follow the trail of the Cody elk herd from the ranchlands all the way through the mountains up to the park. I thought we needed to experience it for ourselves. By summer 2015, the only portion of the trail that Joe and I had failed to travel together was the three-mile stretch over the top of Needle Mountain.

On our first try, in spring 2014, the slopes were so muddy that our string of pack mules couldn't get up the mountain safely. On our second try, over two eerily warm days the following November, we climbed almost 5,000 feet up the back side of Needle, mostly on foot. But as we got out on the flat top of the mountain, a frigid wind hit us with gusts so fierce that it was hard to walk. Soon we retreated to safety as a snowstorm engulfed the summit. Back at our base camp, the storm encased our tent in crackling sheets of ice.

By June 2015 we were determined to traverse that mountain. We planned to set out from the Pitchfork Ranch, following the path we'd scouted and filmed by helicopter the previous week. The first night, we'd camp near Boulder Pass. The second night, we'd camp just below Needle itself. The next morning, we'd get as high up the mountainside as we could on the horses, then send them back with our guide, Scott LaFevers, to finish the climb on foot. If we got an early start, we could get out on top and cross well before the customary afternoon thunder and lightning rolled in.

Over the first two days, we rode that same undulating terrain along Carter Mountain I had flown over with Mark Taylor. In nearly every creek basin, we saw a few dozen cow elk grazing loosely together. They were staging for the coming journey, waiting for their calves to gain strength. Twice, passing through timber, we startled grizzly bears from their daybeds. Once it was

a fat, shimmering sow with a cub almost her size, and the other time it was a young boar that streaked and splashed through a creek bottom. All of us—hunters, hunted, and curious observers—were on this migration trail together.

On the second night we slept at 10,000 feet, on one of Needle's flanking ridges. We lay side by side under a tarp, with saddles at our feet to stop us from sliding downhill. As we settled in, I complained about my aches and chills from two days' hard riding, and in his plodding way, Scott replied, "That's the thing about these mountains. You gotta take every step if you're gonna get where you wanna go."

The next morning, we woke early, packed the mules, and rode up the ridge toward Needle. Halfway along, we stopped to scope a route. The snowfields had shrunk since we'd flown over in the helicopter, but we could still make out sections of dark, braided trail. We could now see the most challenging stretch, where we'd have two options—to climb twenty or thirty yards up through a notch in a small cliff, or cross the soft snow on an open, steep face.

Scott stopped us at the last flat place we could see. "This is where we'll need to say goodbye. These mules ain't going any further." We dropped the loads and dug out our backpacks, heavy with four of Joe's camera traps.

We tired easily and moved slowly in the thin air. We followed elk trails across wet ground until they finally converged at the start of a long knife ridge approaching the face, and the summit beyond it. To one side, the rocks formed a ledge over one fork of Boulder Creek, dropping 500 feet. To the other, steep talus and scree dropped 3,000 feet or more to the South Fork of the Shoshone. We could hear the low, bass whoosh of the river as it flooded through the narrow canyon below. Here, where we could see that the elk trails were pinching together to follow the ridge, Joe began setting his camera traps.

While I waited for Joe, pale sulfur butterflies looped and flitted around in pairs and trios. Rosy finches chattered in the rocks below us, and mountain bluebirds dropped from nowhere onto sharp boulders along the ridge, cocking their heads at us. This time, the weather was perfect: a bright blue sky with only a few clouds to the east, hanging over the hazy Bighorn Basin.

As I turned to study the trail ahead of us, my gaze settled on a smooth, light-colored trough. I could see that it continued up the ridge, cutting four, five, six inches deep in the sharp brown volcanic rock of the mountainside. And in that moment, I knew I had found what I had come to see. It was the ancient trail of the Cody elk herd, formed by a hundred or a thousand generations past. As we joined the trail to set forth again, I could feel, with each breath and every step, the pain and wonder of their journey.

ALONG WITH MY COLLEAGUES, I have now completed a map of the elk migrations of the Greater Yellowstone Ecosystem. It shows the paths of nine major herds braiding in and out of Yellowstone National Park. They reach 30, 75, and 100 miles across the park, the forests, and the ranches beyond their boundaries. Altogether, they encompass an area almost five times larger than the park itself, spanning portions of Wyoming, Montana, and Idaho. It is difficult to estimate the herds' numbers for the same reasons it was difficult to map the migrations, but collectively they probably hold about 20,000 animals. That equates to something like 5,000 tons of elk, pulsing in and back out of the wilderness each year. When I look at the map, I feel I can see Yellowstone's beating heart. The routes are the veins and arteries, and the animals the blood.

Like many of the hoofed mammals, or ungulates, elk migrate to get better food. Grass is a terrible thing to eat—the same fiber that helps it stand tall makes it very hard to digest—so many ungulates migrate long distances to find tender green shoots. In Yellowstone, they are following the green-up to the high plateaus, where cool air, a gradual snowmelt, and regular afternoon storms keep the grass green until long past the browning of the foothills. This strategy can result in high rates of weight gain. We don't have good estimates from Yellowstone elk, but one classic study of Alaskan caribou showed that a 14 percent increase in grass digestibility brought a 270 percent increase in weight gain.

The nutritional advantages elk gain from migration have profound consequences for Yellowstone and the surrounding region. Every elk cow that migrates into high country each spring gains fat and muscle that help her nurse her calf, conceive anew, and survive the long, cold winter. The migration helps bull elk rebuild their strength and re-grow the antlers that they will use to defend their harems, and themselves, in fall and winter.

When other creatures harvest this productivity, the elk become the raw fuel of a great ecological engine. Inside the park, the elk become food for Yellowstone's wolves, grizzly bears, eagles, and ravens. The spectacle draws busload upon busload of visitors who come to glimpse something of a lost America. Then, when the migrants cross back outside the park each fall, they

become our prey as well. Their migrations sustain a tremendous outfitting industry, boosting hotels and restaurants that serve its out-of-state clients. Locals hunt in vast numbers as well. On winter ranges north of the park, in Montana, nearly 11,000 hunters spent 65,000 hunter-days stalking elk in late 2014. Around Cody, Bozeman, and Jackson, banks are adorned with twelve-foot bronzes of elk. For many locals, "Get your elk?" is a common greeting in the autumn. Elk may be wrapped up more tightly in the culture than any other animal.

WITH MOST OF THE SNOW melted off, the flat top of Needle Mountain was covered by a huge alpine meadow—a rich, undulating carpet of grasses intermixed with banks of yellow cinquefoil, purple elephant's head, and snowy phlox. Now that we were above 12,000 feet, we could make out the faint, jagged outline of the Grand Teton to the west, and the spine of the Wind River Range to the south. Behind us we could see to the ranchlands of the Greybull, where we'd begun our journey three days earlier. Out ahead stretched the expansive Thorofare wilderness, where the next month we would meet the herd again, jaunty in their summer coats, trailing precious, spotted young calves closely behind them. We'd soon be in the heart of Yellowstone, where sun, the rain, and the snow gather to make an ecosystem.

I believe the animals I've been following offer us a new story of Yellowstone. Though Congress created Yellowstone National Park to protect its geological features, the American public, over the past century, has come to love the place as much for its wildlife—for a grand ecological spectacle that centers on the elk, their hoofed cousins, and the complex web of life that so depends on them. That web depends on a much larger area than the park, which we've come to call the "Greater Yellowstone Ecosystem." The conundrum is that we haven't yet created a system of management that will conserve this larger landscape for another century.

We've certainly made progress. Starting in 1902, the federal government created a network of national forests and wilderness areas encircling the park, buffering the system from major threats of development and human disturbance. Over the course of the twentieth century, state wildlife agencies curtailed the excesses of unregulated hunting, the federal government slowed and in some cases reversed the loss of endangered species, and many responsible ranch owners found ways to improve their stewardship of critical lands along the ecosystem's frontiers. But this long-term effort—the integration of conservation and economic development in a beloved Western landscape—remains unfinished. The challenge is not limited to the migrations. It spans human-carnivore conflict, wildlife disease, watershed integrity, invasive species, climate change, and every other issue whose emergence or solution cuts across our many boundaries. But migrations, I think, can illuminate the challenge most clearly. When a GPS-collared elk, deer, or bison leaves her trail of crumbs across the map, she is telling us, loud and clear, that she is at our collective mercy.

What will we choose to do with this knowledge? What is our role in Yellowstone's evolution? As we work to answer these questions, science has a great deal to offer. The work my colleagues and I have done shows that we need to understand Yellowstone as a migratory system if we are to understand key wildlife populations and manage them wisely. Had I not awoken to the

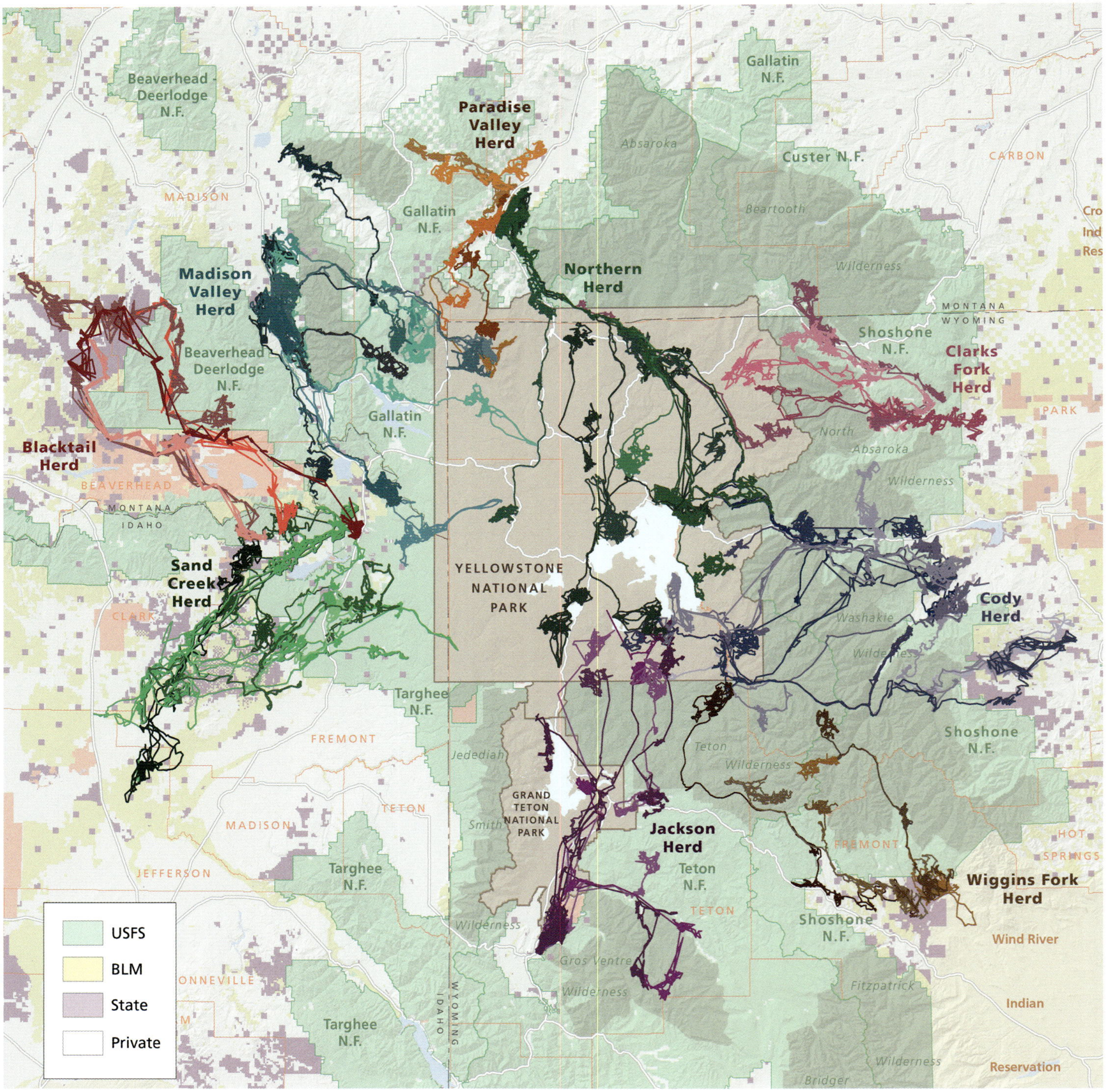

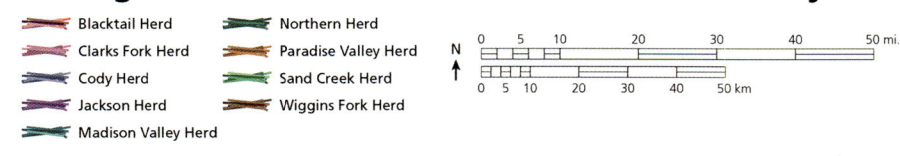

Elk Migrations of the Greater Yellowstone Ecosystem

Blacktail Herd
Clarks Fork Herd
Cody Herd
Jackson Herd
Madison Valley Herd

Northern Herd
Paradise Valley Herd
Sand Creek Herd
Wiggins Fork Herd

N

0 5 10   20   30   40   50 mi.

0 5 10   20   30   40   50 km

September 18, 2015 DRAFT

migratory behavior of the elk I study, I could have easily laid the balance of the blame on wolves, failing to notice effects of grizzly bears, drought, and invasive species. As I've followed the migrations further, traversing the ecosystem, I have seen how our system of management is weakened by divisions among the many stakeholders that these populations depend on equally.

But when it's time to act on this learning, science quickly finds its limits. That is why I have come to feel that only through the fullness of collaboration between science and art, only by enlisting all our senses and all our humanity—our minds, our eyes and ears, our sense of pride and of community and of neighborliness—will we see Yellowstone more clearly. The work of my co-contributors to this book and exhibition, Joe Riis and James Prosek, helps us do that.

Where science fails to inspire us, Joe Riis's work succeeds. Riis's photographs reveal the extraordinary beauty of the animals I have studied, and the raw power of their routine experiences. The best of his frames capture a sense of movement and of struggle that we could not otherwise see. Riis's most intimate portraits re-introduce to us an animal we have taken for granted. At once, the work stirs wonder and empathy.

Like science, though, photography can only describe what it can see. James Prosek's paintings help us move past these confines to re-imagine the ecosystem as a whole. Taking a cue from our field investigation of the elk migrations, Prosek reminds us that a whole constellation of migratory creatures experience unseen journeys, linking Yellowstone not only to nearby ranches but faraway oceans and foreign countries. His grand hybrid cow-bison crystallizes the implications of migration for Yellowstone: that this is a hybrid ecosystem, encompassing, quite beautifully, both wild and domestic (see page 20). Perhaps the sooner we can see and embrace this hybridity, the sooner we can come together around a vision for Yellowstone's future.

My hope is that through this collaborative exhibition, we can help our friends in this landscape, and our fellow Americans with shared interests, continue to re-imagine Yellowstone as a place inextricably connected to a wider world. Only then, and only working together, will we be able to secure the Greater Yellowstone Ecosystem—and its sister landscapes around the world—for another century.

ARTHUR MIDDLETON, PH.D., is a research scientist at the Yale School of Forestry and Environmental Studies and an associate of both the Wyoming Migration Initiative and the Draper Museum of Natural History. He works primarily on the ecology of large mammals, with field projects in the Rocky and Andes Ranges. He completed his Ph.D. in 2012 at the University of Wyoming, where he studied the interactions of wolves and elk in the Absaroka Range. Along with Joe Riis, Middleton was awarded the 2013 Camp Monaco Prize by Prince Albert II of Monaco for linking research and public outreach on the subject of trans-boundary wildlife migrations in the Greater Yellowstone Ecosystem.

RELATED READING

Abraham A. Anderson. *The Yellowstone Forest Reserve: Its Foundation and Development* (New Rochelle: The Knockerbocker Press, 1927).

Arthur D. Middleton and others. "Animal migration amid shifting patterns of predation and phenology: Lessons from a Yellowstone elk herd," *Ecology* 94 (2013):1245–56.

Arthur D. Middleton and others. "Linking antipredator behavior to prey demography reveals the limited risk effects of an actively hunting large carnivore" in *Ecology Letters* 16 (2013):1023–1030.

Arthur D. Middleton and others. "Grizzly bear predation links the loss of native trout to the demography of migratory elk in Yellowstone" in *Proceedings of the Royal Society* B 280 (2013): 20130870.

Arthur D. Middleton. "As wolves return to the West, greens go to court," *The Wall Street Journal*, October 2012, A11.

Arthur D. Middleton. "Is the wolf a real American hero?," *The New York Times*, March 2014, A21.

Bruce L. Smith. *Where Elk Roam: Conservation and Biopolitics of Our National Elk Herd* (Guilford: Lyons Press, 2012).

John J. Craighead, G. Atwell, and B.W. O'Gara. "Elk migrations in and near Yellowstone National Park," *Wildlife Monographs* 29 (1972):3–48.

Margaret and Olaus Murie. *Wapiti Wilderness* (Boulder: University of Colorado Press, 1987).

Olaus Murie. "Game conditions of the Upper Yellowstone-Thorofare region" in Yellowstone National Park Boundary Commission Report (Washington: Government Printing Office, 1931):52–72.

Olaus Murie. *The Elk of North America* (Washington: Wildlife Management Institute, 1951).

P.J. White, Robert A. Garrott, and Glenn E. Plumb. *Yellowstone in Transition* (Cambridge: Harvard University Press, 2013).

Facing page: This map, completed in 2015 by Middleton and federal, state, and university colleagues, displays the year-round movements of migratory elk in the Greater Yellowstone Ecosystem. New GPS collaring allowed the collaborative group to map Yellowstone's elk migrations in far greater detail than ever before. These herds, which winter in outlying areas then move to core areas of the system during summer, range in size from 2,000 to 10,000 individuals. Data provided by Wyoming Game and Fish Department; Montana Fish, Wildlife, and Parks; Idaho Department of Fish and Game; U.S. National Park Service; U.S. Fish and Wildlife Service; Wyoming Cooperative Fish and Wildlife Unit; and, Yale School of Forestry and Environmental Studies. © 2015 *Atlas of Wildlife Migration: Wyoming's Ungulates* (in production), Wyoming Migration Initiative (migrationinitiative.org). Cartography by Alethea Steingisser and Jim Meacham of InfoGraphics Lab, Department of Geography, University of Oregon.

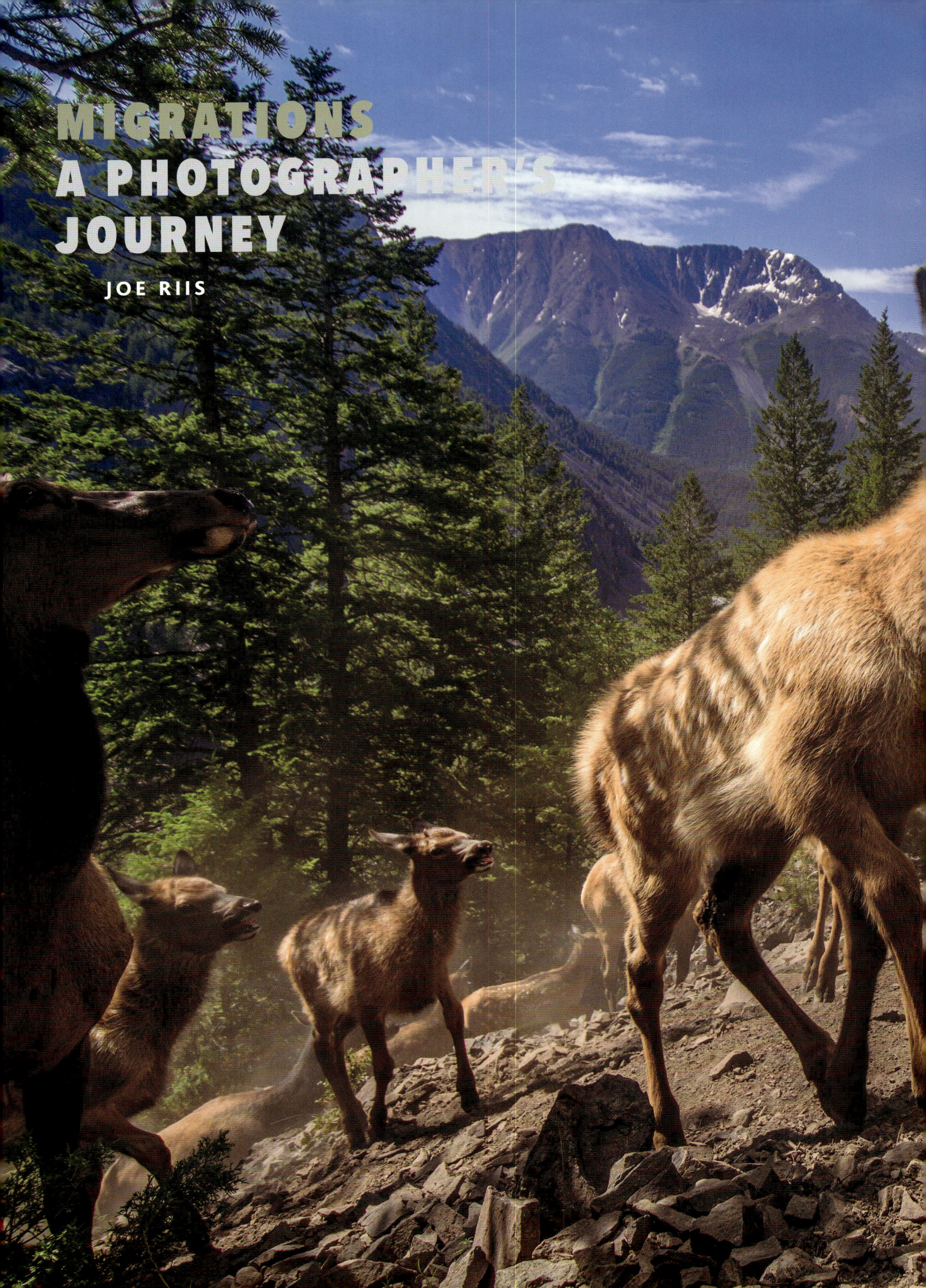

MIGRATIONS
A PHOTOGRAPHER'S
JOURNEY

JOE RIIS

When I was a kid, swarms of ducks and geese sometimes flew over our house at night, usually a few hours after the sun set. My dad would take me out onto the porch and say "Listen—hear those birds? The migration is here." He would get me excused from school and we would go out to the slough. Sometimes we shot a limit of birds by sunrise. These early memories—thousands of waterfowl migrating south in the Central Flyway—piqued my curiosity about migration. I always wondered, "Where did they come from, and where did they go?" This was my entry into the world of animal movements and migrations, a world I work in two decades later.

Imagine this with me. It's early July, hot and dusty. A dirt trail traverses a steep, rocky mountainside. Pines cling alongside it. A silhouetted peak rises in the distance. Then add a burst of life. A group of three-week-old elk calves is following their mothers up the trail on their first migration. Less than 24 hours ago, they stood near the top of a 12,000-foot mountain. From there, they dropped 5,000 feet to the South Fork of the Shoshone River, swollen with snowmelt. They swam it, and now they are climbing 5,000 feet back

up on the other side. Soon, they will drop into the Thorofare Valley of Yellowstone, one of the remotest places in the continental United States, where they will spend the summer drinking their mothers' fat-rich milk and preparing for the return journey to the winter range. The calves' mouths hang open, gasping for air. They are exhausted, but they also are built for this. Over thousands of years, the species has honed these migrations to get the best food and shelter through the seasons. The elk are on the move.

This picture, shown on the previous two pages, took me two years to make, through much trial and error. I missed it entirely my first year out there. By the time the elk calves climbed past my camera, a grizzly bear had tossed my setup off the trail. I wouldn't find that out for three weeks, after the migration had passed. I returned and reset the camera a year later. When I checked the photos after the migration, I saw that one afternoon everything had come together. A group of calves moved up the mountain right behind their mothers. Dust floated up from the trail and stuck to their legs, still wet from swimming the river. One calf bawled as it passed the camera, as if to call out both its great distress and its great purpose to the world around it. I got the photograph of my dreams.

Previous pages: On their first migration through their summer range in southeastern Yellowstone, three-week old calves follow their mothers up the mountain, July 2015. Photograph © Joe Riis.
Left: Riis and Middleton allow their horses to rest while following the Cody elk herd's spring migration, June 2015. The ruggedness of the Absaroka landscape and the need to carry photographic equipment into the backcountry required horse support on most of the project team's field expeditions. Photograph © Jenny Nichols.

THAT DREAM was a long time in the making. I have become known as a chronicler of animal migrations. That work began not far from Yellowstone, 75 miles south of the elk trail. On a blustery fall day in 2007, I stood on a knob in western Wyoming, looking north through binoculars. I did not know that what I was about to see through those lenses would change my life.

I was a senior in wildlife biology at the University of Wyoming, preparing to graduate the following spring, and I'd come here with my friend Emilene Ostlind, a creative writing student who'd read about biologists mapping a pronghorn migration in this area. Emilene wanted to follow the route on foot and write about the experience, and asked me to join the project as a photographer.

Neither of us was sure if it could be done. We had one crude, thumbnail-sized map from a scientific journal as reference, and not much else. We'd spent the previous two days hiking and driving in and around Grand Teton National Park, where we thought the pronghorn should be, but we hadn't seen anything. Even if we found the animals, I wasn't sure their migration could actually be photographed. I just didn't know how it worked—whether they traveled by day or night, in small groups or big ones, single file or scattered. I hardly knew what I was looking for.

As we started the drive back to Laramie and approached the town of Pinedale, Emilene said, "Wait. It's Trappers Point. Let's stop here. I've read about this place." I turned off the highway onto a gravel road, crossed a cattle guard, and drove to the top of a hill where a Wyoming State Historical Society sign described the fur trappers' rendezvous that happened here in the 1830s. This was Trappers Point, a geographic bottleneck formed where two rivers sweep close together and back apart, outlining an hourglass-shaped bridge of land half a mile wide. The pronghorn migration study had highlighted this place because all the animals had to pass through one narrow strip of land.

I scanned the rolling, sage-covered bluffs beyond the highway, looking for motion, a flash of white. And to my surprise, I found it: A couple of miles away, a dozen pronghorn were walking single file right at me. I ran down the hill and set up my camera and tripod near the fence that lined the highway. Emilene and I crouched together in the sagebrush near the top of the hill and waited.

The antelope moved steadily closer until they came to the fence on the far side of the highway. They stared through the wires at passing vehicles and moved back and forth along the fence line, looking for a good way through. Finally, one buck found a space under the bottom wire big enough to duck beneath. He ran out onto the highway, and the rest of the bunch followed one by one.

The animals ran across the asphalt as a truck slowed to let them pass. They came to another stop at the fence on my side of the highway, then ran back and forth looking for a way through. I held my breath, hoping they would cross the fence close to my camera. But they found an opening just downhill and out of sight, scooted under, and disappeared into a swale. I had missed the shot. All that remained to show their passing was a few hoof prints in the snow. Within an hour, another group of pronghorn came through, and again I missed the shot. We stayed until sundown, and then started the five-hour drive home to Laramie so both of us could make it to class the following day.

Despite that failure, something switched inside me. For the first time, I could imagine what a photograph of migration would look like, and what it would take to capture it. And I knew at least one specific place the animals crossed the highway and fences, a perfect place for a camera trap setup.

As soon as I graduated in the spring I bought three cameras and motion sensor triggers and moved into my pickup truck, where I lived for the next two years. I befriended Hall Sawyer, a biologist who had mapped this migration using radio collars a decade before. He explained the route and the timing of the migration. I developed a strategy, driving or walking to specific migration pinch points that I found on longer hikes through the corridor, places where I thought a motion sensor camera trap would work. I'd spend a day lugging a backpack of weather-proof boxes, cables, cameras, metal stakes, and motion sensors deep into the mountains, set up a camera, then walk back out to cook dinner and sleep in the back of the pickup. And I'd repeat it all the next day.

I spent many more days at Trappers Point. I watched desperate pronghorn fighting their way through the fences, sometimes snagging a horn or tangling in the wires. Dogs from the nearby subdivision chased the panicked animals along the highway. Sometimes I found pronghorn carcasses crumpled on the side of the road, struck by vehicles on a blind hill.

Over those two years I downloaded thousands and thousands of useless photographs. Photos with water

Above, top: Pronghorn congregate at a wildlife-friendly fence with a smooth bottom wire strung at 16 inches above the ground, which allows migrating herds to safely slide underneath. **Immediately above:** Pronghorn cross Highway 191 near the town of Pinedale, Wyoming, October 2008. **Facing page:** Built in 2012, a highway overpass allows pronghorn to safely cross over Highway 191. Photographs © Joe Riis.

or snow or ice blurring the lens. Photos out of focus or with the wrong exposure. Photos taken by a camera face down in the dirt. Photos of animals as tiny specks in the distance or as an unrecognizable blur on the edge of a frame. A black bear knocked down and bit one camera housing, shattering the lens.

However, once every month or so, I'd get a frame among those thousands that worked, and after two years, I had a body of work that I felt showed the true urgency and determination in the migration. They started to reveal a journey that until now had only been documented as a series of dots on a map. I created an exhibit and a talk with photos, video clips, and maps. Emilene and I began to travel the state, sharing the stories and images of the migration with the public, with agencies, and with schools. Eventually I traveled farther afield to Salt Lake City, Denver, Banff (in Alberta), and even to Washington, D.C.

The response was overwhelming. As the science, the pictures, and the broader story percolated through the region and state, conservation and land management groups rallied to protect the migration. The National Park Service reached out to other agencies along the corridor seeking ways to keep it open. The Forest Service designated the first "National Migration Corridor," protecting a forty-mile swath of the corridor on the Bridger-Teton National Forest. The Bureau of Land Management designated an Area of Critical Environmental Concern at Trappers Point, ensuring that the gas drilling so pervasive in nearby areas would never impede that bottleneck. The Jackson Hole Conservation Alliance took volunteer groups into the migration corridor to dismantle and carry away old, unnecessary fences. The Conservation Fund and a rancher put a critical piece of private land under a permanent easement to ensure that rural subdivisions would never block the migration there. The Green River Valley Land Trust retrofitted hundreds of miles of fence to make the journey easier for pronghorn.

And finally, the Wyoming Department of Transportation funded six wildlife underpasses and two overpasses designed especially for migrating pronghorn. One of those, at the Trappers Point bottleneck, meant that as of 2012 the animals no longer have to find their way through fences and traffic on Highway 191. Instead, without breaking pace, the migrating pronghorn flow over a big, wide, grass-covered bridge as vehicles speed by beneath.

What happened in those first ten minutes at Trapper's Point and the two years after changed my life. Pronghorn changed my life. I fell in love with them. By triggering the motion sensors on the cameras, they essentially took their own photos, sharing with me the secrets of their migration. And in seeing their ancient migration, I began to see them as leftovers from a past world. They've seen the world change around them over thousands and thousands of years.

I also learned from that project the power of the photograph. People told me they had never seen these kinds of images of pronghorn before, with the animals so close to and facing the camera, with the motion and the migration story, the landscapes, the human obstacles. While I will never know exactly how much the photographs motivated conservation actions, I am happy to know they played an important role. The pronghorn helped me find my own way—helped me discover a purpose I had been looking for.

OVER THE FOLLOWING YEARS, my pronghorn work led me to other stories on four continents. I photographed wildlife and the scientists studying different species in far corners of the world for *National Geographic*—tigers in Thailand, tropical toads in Guyana and Venezuela, Gobi bears in Mongolia, lions and hyenas in Uganda, mountain goats in Canada, vicunas and pumas in Argentina.

Then, in 2012, my friend, the biologist Hall Sawyer, called me up and described a 150-mile-long mule deer migration he'd just discovered in western Wyoming. It was an incredible discovery, and I wanted to see it and photograph it to help Hall tell the story.

The deer were different from pronghorn. The migration was more than twice as long as the pronghorn's, spanning all the way from desert to high alpine. They didn't always walk in a line like the pronghorn and they spooked easily at

Doe pronghorn ford the Green River on their migration north towards Grand Teton National Park, May 2009. Photographer Joe Riis, says "this is the best photograph I've ever made and will ever make. The shadow on the rock was a gift, a moment in time full of beauty. I couldn't believe it when I saw the image on the back of my camera." Photograph © Joe Riis.

the camera. But Hall knew the country and had a new advantage: detailed GPS collar data from individual deer. He helped me find camera sites quickly, and identified the key parts of the story: the places where the deer swim lake outlets to avoid subdivisions or where they detour around elk feeding ground fences. Photographing the migration gave me new appreciation for deer, for their tenacity and vulnerability, and for the incredible way they link a southern desert to northern mountains, stitching together distant pieces of the landscape and complicating our ideas of ecosystems.

Hall and I worked together to study and document the deer migration. It was the most direct collaboration with a scientist that I'd been involved in. Working with Hall meant that his science reached the public more quickly, and my work was not only more efficient but carried a strong message. The results of our work together—clear maps alongside striking pictures—

were almost a dare for people not to try to protect the migration. This short deer project had brought me back to Wyoming, and set the stage for my work for *Invisible Boundaries*.

FOR THE LAST TWO YEARS, I've worked with biologist Arthur Middleton documenting elk migration in the eastern Greater Yellowstone Ecosystem. Elk are, again, different from pronghorn antelope and mule deer. One of the major differences is simply their story. Elk are huge, and there are thousands upon thousands of them engaged in many migrations around Yellowstone. Their 30-, 50-, or 100-mile migrations each spring and fall are, as Arthur writes in this book, like Yellowstone's pulsing heartbeat. They sweep into the park and nearby wilderness areas in the spring, great herds trailed by speckled, bleating calves, seeking the fresh green grasses and cool high-elevation meadows where they'll spend

the summer. In fall, they surge back, dropping through immense valleys and scaling high passes again, to return to the lower-elevation winter ranges and escape from Yellowstone's impossible snowpack and bitter cold. Working on the elk, I have come to see that the migrations I photograph are not only inspiring, and a powerful connection to the past, but are all together—elk, deer, pronghorn—the engine of the landscape I have come to care so much about.

Facing: Dr. Hall Sawyer retrieves a mule deer radio collar in the Hoback Mountains, October 2012. Sawyer discovered the longest known mule deer migration in North America in 2012, the Red Desert to Hoback migration, a one-way distance of 150 miles. Photograph © Joe Riis.
Above: Mule deer, Big Sandy, November 2013. Photograph © Joe Riis.

But the most significant difference for my photography has been the challenge of simply following the elk's trail, of occupying their world. To document the pronghorn migration I usually could drive to within a few miles of any camera site. To document the deer migration I rarely had to climb high into the mountains. Not so for elk. To tell the story of the elk migrations, Arthur and I had to choose a single herd. We chose the Cody migration because it was little known, and because our friend Doug McWhirter, who works for the Wyoming Game and Fish Department, was finding success taking trail camera photographs along a few pinch points on the migration.

But I had never been in the Absaroka Mountains and I didn't have a clear idea of the terrain. My work

Top: Riis, Middleton, and Scott LaFevers work down a steep hillside.

Left and facing page, bottom: The project team with their horses and mules. Typically, the team needed between four and eight mules to support backcountry trips ranging from one to twenty-one days. Riis covered more than 1,500 miles on horseback during the course of his fieldwork. Photographs © Jenny Nichols, June 2015.

Facing page, top: Middleton, filmmaker Jenny Nichols, and Riis prepare to leave their horses behind and traverse an 11,900-foot pass crossed by the Cody elk herd on spring migration. Riis's compelling photographs prompted the project team to launch a film project in collaboration with Nichols. Photograph by Scott LaFevers, June 2015.

requires a lot of heavy equipment. I need to drive my pickup as far as possible, then backpack. The further I need to backpack, the less gear and food I can carry.

When we started our work, the first step was Arthur collaring elk to fill a gap in knowledge about the Yellowstone elk migrations. This would help me figure out where I could photograph the migration and set up camera traps. The Cody herd winters mostly on private ranchlands in the foothills and valleys east of the park, and we knew in spring the elk would leave for the Absaroka Range, but we hadn't seen the migration trails for ourselves. I knew that I needed to find locations high in the mountains where I could capture these "mountain elk" doing what they do. I had to make pictures of them climbing mountains.

AFTER TWO DAYS of the initial helicopter capture work, as we wrapped up on the TE Ranch, the pilot took Arthur and me on a thirty-minute flight up the South Fork of the Shoshone River to see the upper valley. As we approached Needle Mountain, for the first time I realized that I would not be able to do this work with a backpack; at the base of the mountain we were already seven miles from the nearest trailhead. The mountains are too big, too massive, and quite frankly just impossible to hike with all my gear. To get to locations as far as twenty miles from a trailhead, I needed to learn how to ride a horse and use pack mules.

Lee Livingston Outfitting, a horse packer with extensive experience in the Absaroka Mountains, brought us in. I know now, through experience, that the Cody elk herd's migration is among the most epic of land animal movements. They scale 12,000-foot passes and scramble through snow-choked notches in the rock. They thrash across the

Pronghorn cross the Green River in May 2014, in the same location as the image taken five years earlier shown on pages 58-59. Some of Riis's best work results from revisiting migration corridors over the course of several years. Photograph © Joe Riis. **Facing, center:** Riis holds several camera filters, June 2015 (detail). Photograph © Jenny Nichols. **Facing, right:** A buck pronghorn crossing the Green River was caught in a river snag and died, becoming a bald eagle's meal, May 2014. Photograph © Joe Riis.

raging South Fork of the Shoshone River. They face wolves and grizzlies, and they undertake some of this journey in spring with newborn calves. To follow them I've hefted cameras up steep, scree-covered mountainsides. I've been turned back by storms and lightning, learned how wonderful horses and mules are, and been awestruck by what these wild animals achieve.

I WISH TO SHOW WHAT IS AT STAKE. To show migrating elk, pronghorn, deer, and all the animals that need the freedom to roam. I hope people see the pictures, and more importantly combine what they see with the science and paintings in *Invisible Boundaries,* to gain a new understanding and appreciation of our first national park. I've had to learn entirely new approaches to my photography. As in my previous projects, I've captured thousands of useless frames. But as before, I've also found moments of perfection, frames that tell this migration story in ways words never could.

JOE RIIS is a *National Geographic Magazine* contributing photographer and Photography Fellow at the Wyoming Migration Initiative. His work explores the migrations of animals in the Greater Yellowstone region of North America, highlights science and research expeditions, and connects people to some of the most remote and rare species on the planet through his photography and video. He is the recipient of several awards including three *National Geographic* Expeditions Council grants, the 2013 Camp Monaco Prize with Arthur Middleton, the Stanford Knight-Riser Award for western environmental journalism with Emilene Ostlind, an Emmy Award for his work on pronghorn migration in the Great Migrations series, and principal support from the George B. Storer Foundation. His short films have toured in the Banff Mountain Film Festival and Telluride MountainFilm Festival. His photographs have been exhibited widely, and are included in private and public collections worldwide. Riis graduated from the University of Wyoming in 2008 with a B.S. in Wildlife Biology.

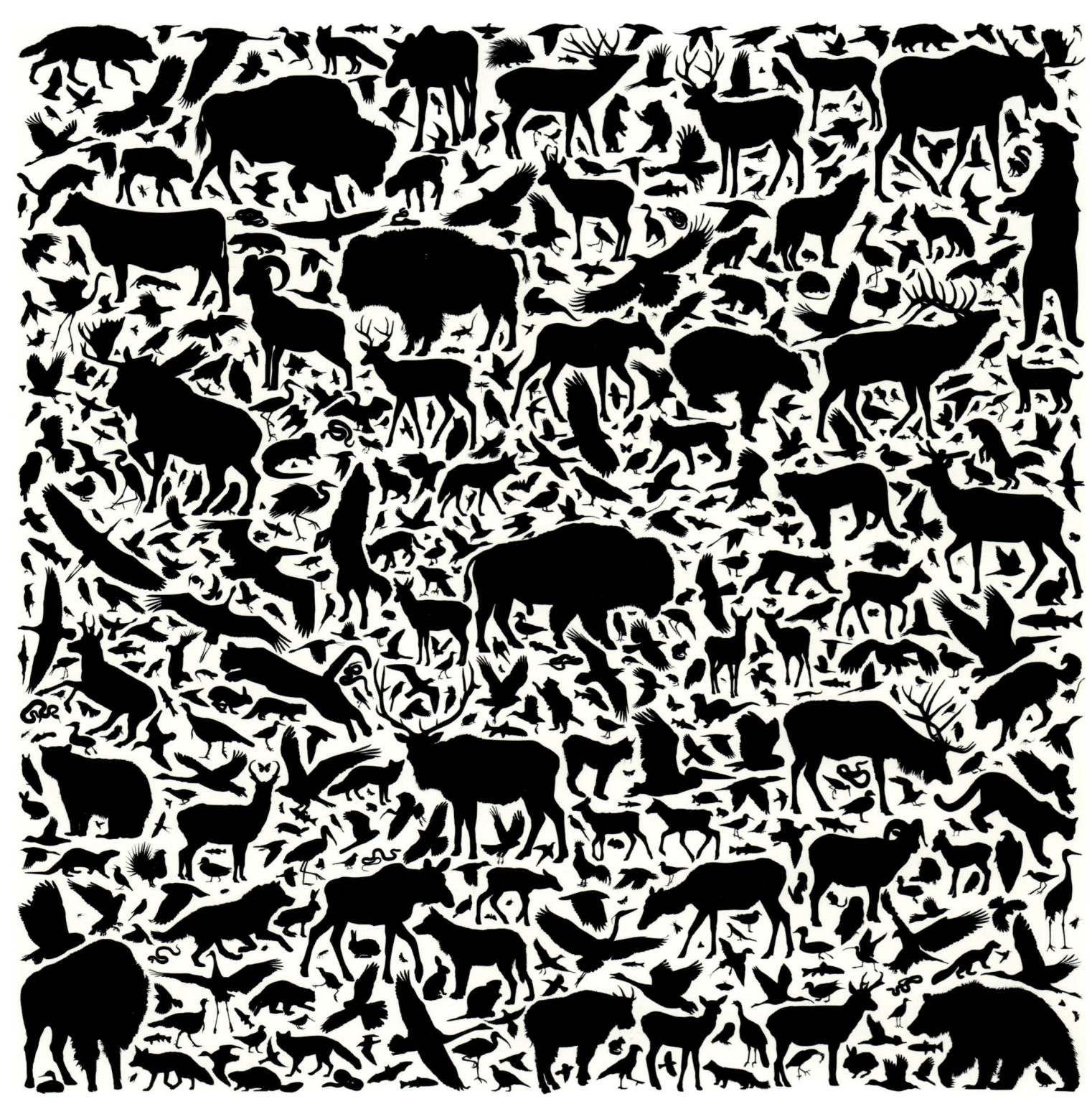

... BEHIND THE WORLD
OUR NAMES ENCLOSE
IS THE NAMELESS:
OUR TRUE ARCHETYPE AND HOME.

RAINER MARIA RILKE

YELLOWSTONE WILDERNESS IN A BOX

JAMES PROSEK

When the boundary around Yellowstone National Park was drawn in 1872, a near perfect rectangle, it was meant to encompass and protect stunning natural wonders more geological than animal. A hundred and forty-three years later, with the encroachment of man and his industry, this line, visible on a map but invisible on the landscape, has become something more concrete, and a grave problem for some of the animals that cross it seasonally.

As an artist and writer, one of my lifelong interests lies in how the lines we draw between things in our minds, such as those dividing species, can ultimately come to affect things in reality. Nature is fluid and continuous and interconnected and in a constant state of change, but in order to communicate that continuum—to say "this is this, and that is that"—we have to chop it into pieces. Fragmenting the world and labeling the parts is necessary—how would we understand and share our world without naming things and putting them into some order? And yet the process of fragmenting nature so that we can name and order it immediately gives a false impression of how nature works. We forget that language is just a tool, finding comfort in the sense of control over nature that it gives us.

In my artwork I attempt to critique, among other things, our eagerness to go out in nature and name and identify creatures. Too often, I feel, we rely on language to help us see, sometimes at the expense of having a novel experience of our own—one that doesn't involve seeing nature as an assemblage of units that fit neatly into mental boxes. In one body of work, I appropriate imagery from the endpapers of old field guides, where silhouettes of birds and numbers match up to a list of names to help us identify things in the field. I paint murals of birds and corresponding numbers, but leave out the key, so the viewer feels frustrated that they can't satisfy their urge to know "what they are." What they are, of course, goes beyond simply what we call them.

Facing page: James Prosek. *Yellowstone Composition No. 1,* 2016. Mixed media on wood panel, 120 x 120 in.
Overleaf: James Prosek. *American Elk (Wyoming)* 2016. Oil, acrylic and mixed media on wood panel, 56 x 90 in.

Middleton and Prosek study the diversity of plant life on elk winter ranges, July 2015. Photographs © Jenny Nichols.

In the course of what has become a lifelong inquiry into how and why we name and order nature, I have drawn others from varied disciplines into my maze of thoughts. In Arthur Middleton, ecologist and collaborator on this exhibition, I have found a fellow traveler and friend. We share common ground on the problem of drawing lines and boundaries on nature.

Each of us explores how lines humans draw on maps and on the land come to affect the movements and experiences of animals. Humans have become so powerful and pervasive that the classification systems and maps we create in our heads and on paper have actually, in many cases, become the terrain. ❋

The elk, the animal at the center of Arthur's work, spend their summers in Yellowstone and their winters on lands outside of it—oftentimes large, private ranches. Their fates are absolutely determined by which side of which line they are on at any given time (not only the park demarcation line but a host of other property borders both public and private). In the park they are a tourist attraction. Outside the park during hunting season they are someone's trophy or dinner. Just as the action of a chainsaw transforms forest to lumber (two different words that can apply to the very same trees), the cutting lines of Yellowstone define the identity of the elk in our minds.

As a kid, I was obsessed with the diversity of the trout of North America. I could not tire of painting their colors and forms in watercolors on paper. At ten years of age, unable to find a book of trout paintings in the local library, I set out to make my own. In the course of research for the book I learned that no two biologists could agree on how many trout species there were in our country, or even what a species was. At the same time, the decisions we make about where to draw lines between this population and that population have real world consequences. If a trout population is not deemed to be significantly different enough to name, then it cannot be protected by law. It cannot be listed as threatened or endangered, and it might as well not exist in human reality. We live in a time when a creature's being named as a species may mean the difference between existence and extinction. What markers and criteria do we use to determine what is significantly different enough to name? Morphological? Genetic? Such questions are heatedly debated amongst taxonomists (those who name things professionally). The Yellowstone cutthroat trout and the Snake River fine-spotted cutthroat (native fishes of the Greater Yellowstone Ecosystem) are genetically nearly identical and will readily hybridize. Under most definitions of species or subspecies their differences would not warrant status as a named entity. But to anglers and western economies, their very clear physical differences allow them to be loved for different reasons. ❋

Yellowstone is an important place to think about names and boundaries, because it is one of the world's greatest study sites for the relationships between human and non-human animals. The challenges in Yellowstone are paralleled in wild zones as diverse as the Serengeti and the Sargasso Sea, and people around the world look to Yellowstone for ideas and inspiration as they struggle with their own variations on its problems.

"YELLOWSTONE IS GREAT TO THINK WITH," Paul Schullery told me. "It helps us with all these fabulous and hopeless questions." Paul and I were driving with his wife Marsha from Bozeman to Gardiner, Montana, to spend a day in the park. It was January 2011. The only road open to cars was from Mammoth to Cooke City.

Paul had been a park employee for more than thirty years, and has authored more than a dozen books on Yellowstone. It was very special to spend time with him here. He

❋ In the Anthropocene, the way we think about nature, the way we talk about nature, shapes our perceptions of nature—and thus the way we treat nature and, in turn, the future of ecosystems. Consider how we selectively breed populations of animals unwittingly by harvesting trophy animals that we arbitrarily covet. We have fished out all the largest cod to eat, so the genes for beautiful big cod are now erased from the gene pool. Poachers and other hunters in Africa have targeted the bull elephants with the largest tusks, so now we are seeing fewer elephants with big tusks. Some scientific studies have shown that nature is selecting elephants with smaller tusks, or even no tusks, because they have a better chance of survival. The same has been said about other trophy animals of different species, such as bighorn sheep.

❋ The concept of a species has kept us from seeing a great deal of diversity and beauty—has allowed us to sweep much of nature's messiness under the rug. Thankfully, that is changing. One example is the native trout of Yellowstone Lake. If we thought of just preserving species and not significant local populations, then we would let the introduced lake trout eat all the native cutthroat trout that live there. Why protect them? The species itself is not in danger of extinction—there are plenty of Yellowstone cutthroats all over Wyoming. But we now recognize that the Yellowstone cutthroats that evolved in Yellowstone Lake are unique to that place. And without them running up tributaries to spawn in spring (providing food for animals as diverse as osprey and grizzly bears), the park ecosystem is disrupted.

we heard an elk bugle - a hummingbird - and the trickle of snow melting on
Carter Mountain above pitchfork
ranch, Wyoming ... 12. July. 2015

rocky mtn parnassian
butterfly.

mined from the glacier
in the meadow 10000 ft.

had invited me out West to give a talk at Montana State University in Bozeman. At that time, I was starting to think heavily about themes of naming and ordering nature—about the division and fragmentation of nature through that process—so those are the things I had spoken about the previous night. As we drove from Bozeman that next cold morning, I could see that Paul, a naturally pensive guy, was thinking particularly hard. He said our outing had taken on new meaning because of my talk. He promised he'd tell me why.

At the north entrance to Yellowstone Park at the edge of the town of Gardiner, Montana, you pass through the grand Roosevelt Arch, appropriately named for Theodore Roosevelt, who was president when it was built in 1903. It stands alone and tall, made of stone, large enough for a tourist bus to pass through, even though it was built before Yellowstone authorized motorized transportation in 1915. On either side are hills and sagebrush. It is a massive structure that lets you know without question that you've entered one place and left another behind.

Soon after passing the Roosevelt Arch, following a winding road, you come to Mammoth Hot Springs, which Thomas Moran, William Henry Jackson, and others made famous in the nineteenth century with their paintings and photographs. Mammoth is a large, calcareous mound of white residue. The steam that rises from it and occasional pits of bubbling water reveal a thin earth crust and a molten earth core dangerously close to the surface, one of the many constant reminders here that the park sits atop a giant unstable caldera, the largest volcano in the world. ❋

We know from geological evidence that the eruption of this hot spot has obliterated the landscape in the past, leaving scars on the North American tectonic plate as it moves over the earth's mantle. This swath of demolished land, called the Snake River Plain, clears a connection in a southwesterly direction between Yellowstone and the Pacific Ocean, and is a major reason why Yellowstone is lush in summer, attracting grazing animals.

Paul and Marsha pointed to the chapel in Mammoth where they were married fifteen years before. They had given a great deal of their lives to this place. The chapel,

❋ In most places in North America the earth's crust is 20 to 30 miles thick. In Yellowstone only two miles separates the surface from magma, molten and partly molten rock. This is specifically called the Yellowstone Hot Spot; the crust is thinner here than anywhere else on earth.

along with the hotel and the administrative buildings, had a quaint orderliness to them (Mammoth is the former military complex Fort Yellowstone)—rows of khaki buildings with red roofs. In summer, elk graze in the green spots in town as people stop at the gift shop and concessions (though things were very quiet here in winter). Many people, too, have migrated long distances to get here and are relieved. They made it—they are officially in the park. We could point to this as the good, perhaps, of names and boundaries. They have come to witness something, even if they don't know what, and many will leave full of wonder and inspired to protect natural things.

Not far outside of Mammoth we were passing an area called Blacktail Ponds when Paul pointed to a herd of bison running on the left side of the road, black smears across the whiteness, like in a painting by George Catlin. I'm always moved to think we almost wiped out these wooly ice age relics completely—by 1890 the millions of bison that once roamed North America had been reduced to a few hundred individuals.

Paul wondered aloud why they were running like this, with such frantic urgency. I didn't know enough to know that this was unusual, seeing bison run, but then Paul spotted something that struck him as equally if not more odd—a dark hole, almost completely black on the ground. He stopped the car at a pull-off that had been cleared of snow, enough to fit a car or two.

"What's going on over there?" Paul asked, more to himself than to me or to Marsha. He took out his binoculars and lowered the driver's side window.

A frigid wind, filled with crystalline whorls of snow, swept warmth from the car.

Paul scanned the flatness of Blacktail Ponds. "There's movement."

"Whoa," he said, and we got out of the car. It was hard to keep my eyes open it was so cold, gusts of wind driving snow horizontally over the road. Paul handed me the glasses and pointed.

As the water in my eyes cleared and I focused the lenses, I could see what Paul had seen. Three bison had fallen through the ice into one of the ponds and were using their front legs in an attempt, vain it seemed to us, to pull themselves out of the muck and the icy water. Once you knew what the black hole represented, you could discern what

Facing page: James Prosek. *On Carter Mountain above Pitchfork Ranch,* 2015. Watercolor, graphite and gouache on paper, 5 x 12 ¼ in.

Above: James Prosek. *West Fork of Blackwater Creek,* 2015. Watercolor, graphite and gouache on paper, 5 x 12 ¼ in.

was happening without the aid of the glasses. Marsha took a look, briefly, and then passed the binoculars back to Paul. "I can't look," she said. My heart wrenched too. I hoped of course that the bison would get out, but if they did could they survive? Even with their thick coats of wooly fur, with temperatures near zero degrees Fahrenheit and fierce winds, wouldn't they just freeze solid?

"I don't think they're getting out of there," Paul said, glasses raised to his eyes.

And he was right. We remained at the spot for about thirty minutes, until Paul and I could no longer stand to watch. The suction of the mud and the weight of the bison were too great. The ice continued to break from beneath their front hooves every time they tried to get on hard land.

As the frothy water in the hole grew still, the chunks of ice began to rejoin and make a solid surface. Soon, all we could see were their wet heads barely peeping above the water and tendrils of steam rising from their black nostrils like the smoke from a dying campfire. Marsha finally asked if we could move on. We got back into the car, warmed our hands and bodies, and drove away.

No one spoke for a while. Then Paul breathed deeply and said, "This is what people come to the park to see." What we had witnessed felt primal and ancient, like mammoths in tar pits. It was pure raw struggle, elements and animal engulfing each other in a realm beyond language (in a … dare we say … wilderness?). Complex organisms would be rendered to their component particles by decay, energy transferred to microbial communities of nearly infinite diversity. These visceral experiences for which there are no descriptions, which strangle the part of your brain that needs to name and tame what just happened, this is indeed what people come to a place like Yellowstone to experience—call it awe, call it wonder. There is truth to the expression "I couldn't find the words," or "I was speechless," or "It took my breath away." That is, the breath we use for speech. In such moments we have no mode to communicate the full reach and richness of emotion.

Marsha, who for eleven years had been Yellowstone's Chief of Public Affairs, said they would get calls all the time about animals in dire situations like this.

"'Can't you help them?' they would ask," Marsha said, in the voice of a mock visitor. "And we had to explain, 'no, the whole point of this place is to not control these interactions, this is what Yellowstone is all about, this kind of pure experience which is deep and timeless, as close to a world before humans as we can get today.'"

AND A WORLD WITHOUT HUMANS is a world without the imposition of language on it. No humans, no maps, no names for towns or mountains or rivers or waterfalls. That is why, as I came to find, names and ideas about wilderness can be at constant odds here.

Further up the road Paul pulled off and stopped the car. I knew this place—though it was hard to recognize at this season. Now hidden by ice and snow, a small willow-lined trout stream passed beneath the road. I had caught brook trout in this creek and had slept several nights in an old ranger cabin just upstream. It had been more than ten years since I'd been here, but I still remembered the name of the creek, Upper Blacktail, and the magical experience of being here alone. Apparently this place was also special for Paul. He had spent many days over the course of eighteen summers on top of a hill visible off the right side of the road, watching grizzly bears through binoculars and a spotting scope, making notes about the behavior of animals.

"You know," he said, "some used to call this Paul's Hill, but this name is only in the minds of a few park employees who worked in the park during that era. There was a plywood blind up there where biologists would sit and watch coyotes. During this coyote study they called this North Butte and the hill on the other side of the road South Butte. Some names are personal and come and go. The wolf biologists still call them North and South Butte. But you won't find those names on any official map."

This is how Paul's narrative started. He had promised he would tell me what was on his mind, and now he did. "Your talk last night made me think of a few things about naming in Yellowstone. Now I want you to listen, and please don't interrupt me." Paul was emphatic. He knew even from limited experience that I have a bad habit of interrupting. And then he delivered a spotless, twenty-five-minute lecture about layers of naming in Yellowstone. Layers upon layers built up in his head over many years. He spoke about everything from the challenges of naming species of bacteria and other microbial life in the thermal pools and geysers (they can evolve rapidly and don't reproduce like us), to why biologists give their study animals numbers instead of names, to a controversy over whether or not to name recently discovered waterfalls, to the overall challenges of the idea of a park with a border in a world where animals don't obey the boundaries we set for them. I was grateful and stunned and wish I'd had the foresight to record what he said. He set my mind spinning about these intertwining issues, all relevant to my personal inquiry about what changes in the mind when we join words to the world. ✻

This moment with Paul was when I began to see Yellowstone as a place at the heart of my own personal journey. I was interested in exploring what this piece of land, delineated by a line and a name, meant to the human imagination, this place commonly referred to as "Wonderland."

Toward the end of the day, as we approached Mammoth and the Roosevelt Arch again, I thought back to when I first visited Yellowstone with my family in 1979. I was four years old. We had driven across the country in an orange Volkswagen camper bus, all the way from Connecticut, over the Appalachian Mountains, through the plains to Wyoming and the foothills of the Continental Divide. My dad was a schoolteacher and had summers off. My mom was, well, a mom. We lived in the orange bus for two months, staying at KOA and other campgrounds. I have a Polaroid photo of Roosevelt Arch from that trip, and another of my mom posing way too close to a bison.

Since then, I've passed through the arch dozens of times. Each time I am affected by it. The landscape is altered in my mind. But until today I had never thought to ask why. Why is that stone structure so powerful? How can it be so critical to shaping my mood? Perhaps it creates a narrative by setting limits and giving us a border. Without limits we have no place from which to come, and nowhere to go, no acknowledgment of space. ✻ The arch has great authority. It declares, "This is no ordinary piece of land; this is a National Park." I pass through with mixed feelings. The Roosevelt Arch has a positive message engraved in it: "For the Benefit and Enjoyment of the People." But does this exceptionally unique piece of land need such an entrance? Isn't the beauty and wonder inside enough? Is the arch a celebration of wilderness or of our victory over it—it is after all, architecturally, a triumphal arch.

Later I brought up the arch with Arthur. He said he found it creepy. "It makes Yellowstone feel like the Bronx Zoo," he told me. "Like it was too expensive to get a wall put up around it, so they just settled for the gate part of a wall." I asked Arthur in jest if anyone had ever proposed a great wall around Yellowstone. He said no. ✻

✻ Here, I'm alluding to the poet Lyn Hejinian's essay "The Rejection of Closure."

We delight in our sensuous involvement with the materials of language, we long to join words to the world—to close the gap between ourselves and things—and we suffer from doubt and anxiety because of our inability to do so.

✻ Defining spaces is as essential to being human as naming and is similar in concept. We draw a border around something where a border did not exist. Space cannot exist without borders. In 700 BC the Chinese philosopher Lao Tsu wrote: *Thirty spokes came together at one hub; because of the empty spaces we have use of a carriage wheel. Mould the clay; because of the empty spaces we have use of the pot. Cut out doors and windows; because of the empty spaces we have use of a room. Thus we gain something by making use of no-thing.*

✻ Paul Schullery mentioned to me that "fences were built and experimented with over the years along the park boundary on the northern range in the general vicinity of Gardiner, Montana. These were attempts to constrain the movements of the large mammals, some or all of them."

Portrait of a specimen. Banded tagged and named. winters in mexico + central America summer in Yellowstone.

short-eared owl feather

Western tanager in the collection of the Draper Museum of Natural History Cody, WYoming 2 November 2015

DRA 304
Piranga ludoviciana
Western Tanager
Draper Museum of Natural History

And then together we imagined a Yellowstone wall as a thought experiment.

Let's say we did build a wall around Yellowstone. Which animals would live, and which would die? For the elk and other ungulates that migrate seasonally into and out of the park, a wall would be the equivalent of a dam for migrating salmon or eels. It would stop the flow of life, and render the circulatory system of the land— migrations being, in this metaphor, the lifeblood—in a state of cardiac arrest. The author-activist Todd Wilkinson calls the park border "the invisible killing line." Since the mid-1980s the government, in the guise of the Montana Department of Livestock and, at times, the National Park Service, has shot nearly 8,000 bison for crossing that line. Ranchers fear the bison will transmit an infectious disease called brucellosis to their cattle, which then would have to be culled—shot— themselves. Their fears stem in part from rules that prohibit the export of beef from a state if cattle contract the disease—a huge and real economic peril for many of those who make their living near Yellowstone. And yet, no documented case exists for the transmission of the disease from bison to cattle.

It was hard enough watching those bison die that day by means that most would describe as natural. But knowing they die at our hands by crossing a line that we impose on the landscape, simply because they are heeding an instinct to move that is ingrained in their heads through thousands of years of evolution, is harder to accept. Even when we understand the reasons behind this conundrum, it seems we ought to be able to do better to honor the creature and its needs, and retain in

our world that nameless feeling the bison had given me, and gives to so many others.

This time, because of my experience that winter day, passing under the arch changed me. I decided to take on Yellowstone and its names, largely following the outline that Paul had given me on that cold winter day when we watched the bison freeze to death.

DURING THE RESEARCH for this collaborative exhibition (and for my book on naming, in which Yellowstone is a chapter) I spent time in the backcountry with co-contributor Arthur Middleton, visiting several of his study sites. On the first trip in the field with him and Joe Riis in July 2014, we went by horse and mule up the South Fork of the Shoshone River. As Arthur and Joe describe in their essays in this book, we were headed to a place along the migration route of the Cody elk herd, where elk are forced through a narrow canyon—a pinchpoint—and then must swim across the river, which, at this time of year, was raging with snowmelt. We rode into camp and pitched our tents, went to sleep and were up at dawn to sit behind a makeshift blind by the river and watch elk attempt the crossing. As light filtered into the canyon a few cow elk and bulls came down and dipped their toes in the water, even ankles and torsos. They seemed wary, lifting their heads high to sniff the air. Perhaps they sensed our presence in the blind. Or maybe they were just too cold. Still, it was remarkable to be so close to them, to glimpse these amazing animals on an epic annual migration from their winter range on the Pitchfork Ranch, over snow-capped mountains to their summer grazing grounds in the park.

Our last morning in camp we sat by the fire where we cooked a breakfast of eggs and bacon, waiting for the outfitter to come get us, resting our heads against piles of packed-up gear. Joe set up a camera trap at the campfire site. He said that a day or two after we left a grizzly usually would come and dig through the pit for scraps. I thought back to the day we arrived. We had ambled our way up the trail in the hot sun on horseback, through meadows of wildflowers and large fields of scree. I told Arthur I had seen a western tanager fly overhead and into a Douglas fir, a flash of red and yellow, "passing like a thought," as Audubon once described the passenger pigeon gliding through the woods. The bird was already a memory by the time you acknowledged you'd seen it.

"You know that bird spends its summers here, and winters in Mexico and Costa Rica," I said to Arthur. We marveled for a moment that the Yellowstone ecosystem is somehow connected to the tropics through this small migrating bird.

"What does that mean for the idea of the Greater Yellowstone Ecosystem?" Arthur asked.

We discussed the fact that in some ways the idea of an ecosystem itself is flawed. The existence of the word suggests that an ecosystem has a beginning and an end; the word puts up walls. Although the modern and accepted term "Greater Yellowstone Ecosystem," or GYE, embraces the idea that Yellowstone doesn't end at the park border, the concept began to feel shortsighted when we considered that ecosystems overlap other ecosystems. We have yet to truly and finally embrace the visions of Humboldt, Darwin and Haeckel, Muir, Carson, Leopold, and many others, of a holistic, interconnected planet.

Perhaps it is time for a re-examination—a taking down of walls. If Yellowstone, in a word, has come to mean "a box with stuff in it…" then we have to work to make that word mean something else. And that, put simply, is the goal of our present work and of this exhibition.

Facing page: James Prosek. *Western Tanager and Short-eared Owl Feather*, 2015. Watercolor, graphite and gouache on paper, 5 x 13 in.
Above: James Prosek. *Francs Fork—Tributary of the Greybull River*, 2015. Watercolor, graphite and gouache on paper, 8 ¾ x 11 ¾ in.

Prosek sketching at Legend Rock near Thermopolis, Wyoming, 2015. Photograph © Joe Riis.

Arthur and Joe asked how I thought I could portray these concepts through art. Arthur joked that I could paint a lonely pronghorn antelope in a tropical forest, to emphasize the web-like interactions the tanager had raised. I liked the idea, a very serious one to me. Later, considering the bison, and the cows that have largely replaced them as the grazing grassland animal outside the park, I mused of painting a hybrid creature of the two. The depiction of a two-headed cow-bison could help provoke conversations about domestic versus wild, and, with humor, allow us to loosen our grip on Yellowstone and keep expanding our idea of what it is.

In time, all boundaries, even the ones we erect that seem most permanent—will come down. I believe this is what Paul was trying to tell me when he spoke of the ephemeral nature of place names in the park. Our maps, names, and boundaries won't mean much, after all, when Yellowstone's caldera again erupts—as geologists forecast that it will. Given enough time, our impositions on nature will melt away. But that time has not yet come, so we must be mindful of the dangers that the names and the lines we draw can inflict. Though they may not be visible, they do mean something to the lives of the creatures here, and that includes us. The work of embracing the fluidity and interconnectivity of nature, of fighting our urge to draw lines between this and that, is more important today than it ever has been.

I felt this most strongly, and refreshingly, when I visited Legend Rock near Thermopolis, Wyoming, in a November snowstorm. Legend Rock is largely considered to be one of the most significant Native American rock art sites in North America. It is possible that some of the figures depicted on this long, exposed stone face were chipped 10,000 years ago. As a visual artist I wanted to see how humans before us had interpreted the creatures of this region—even if I could never fully know the intent or meaning of their work. Larry Todd, an archeologist who had grown up in the vicinity of Legend Rock, explained that the Shoshone Indians saw the rock face not as something rigid and hard, but permeable, an interface between the human and spirit worlds. Some of these figures were thought to exist between these two worlds. I was struck by the frequency and number of hybrid creatures depicted on the rock face, what appeared to be bison and elk heads on bodies of men. The works were double hybrids in a sense—between here and somewhere else, between human and non-human animals. I chose to interpret this abundant hybridity as an acknowledgment of a perpetual flow and web-like interaction in nature. We ingest nature and it becomes part of us. We are elk, we are bison, we are living somewhere between birth and death on a never-ending continuum with no permanent boundaries.

YELLOWSTONE was the first national park in the world, established by an act of Congress less than ten years after the Civil War. Before that, the idea of a park for a nation did not exist except in the minds of a very few farsighted people. ✳ Parks were city parks. The designation of Yellowstone as a park created a huge perceptual shift in the minds of humans: the thinking that we should preserve some semblance of wilderness before it was too late, before wild disappeared. The park was created when a geologist named Ferdinand Hayden, a painter named Thomas Moran, and a photographer named William Henry Jackson, delivered evidence of a place that they thought was sacred and worthy of protection. ✳ A big selling point was the remarkable thermal activity—puddles, pools, bubbling mud pots, fumaroles, geysers, and hot springs in all imaginable colors. Hayden drew a big rectangle around a monumental piece of land and they named it. ✳ The name, very much like the arch, created something out of the nameless landscape, transformed this piece of land in our heads.

✳ In 1841, the artist George Catlin proposed that the entire western U. S. be made into "a nation's park, containing man and beast . . ." The historian Aubrey Haines describes this and other pre-1872 proposals for such a park in *The Yellowstone Story: A History of Our First National Park.*

✳ Of course, as is the case with any story, especially one as significant in American and world history, it's never just as simple as three people coming together to make something happen. There were other people involved, and there were other less lofty factors involved than the scientific and aesthetic aspects championed by Hayden, Moran, and Jackson. The Northern Pacific Railroad got behind the park idea at this stage, and without a doubt their commercial interests (i.e., the potential for a great tourist industry) were a major factor in the creation of the park. Paul Schullery writes about this in his book, co-authored by Lee Whittlesey, *Myth and History in the Creation of Yellowstone National Park.*

✳ Paul Schullery discusses how Yellowstone got its name in *Searching for Yellowstone: Ecology And Wonder In The Last Wilderness.*

When a place receives a name, it enters our reality, it becomes something that it wasn't before—among other things, a destination. As problematic as the border may be, it's safe to say that if that line had not been drawn (if that land had not been partitioned and labeled) this wonderland would most certainly be worse off than it is today. Four million people now cross that line every year and enter a different world, go back in time. Perhaps it shouldn't be so surprising that the border has come to mean so much—when past and present collide there are bound to be deep misunderstandings. No single guide or translation can help us. Yellowstone represents something more than a park, something less tangible, not quite definable—a state of mind. That is why Paul Schullery titled one of his many books about the park *Searching for Yellowstone.* We can search all we want for what it means, but in a sense we never find it.

All these themes, this talk, may seem self-evident, but it can't hurt to reiterate. At times, yes, Yellowstone can appear like a wilderness in a box, but then again, when you're out on the land itself, filled with the scent of sage, the visual feast of a wildflower meadow, a trout holding in a thread of current, it is not in a box at all.

I can say for certain, back here in Connecticut as I write, that Yellowstone has reached at least this far. It is part of me now.

JAMES PROSEK is an artist, writer and naturalist living and working in Easton, Connecticut. He travels widely to research his works, which depend heavily on personal experiences in nature. He has had solo presentations of his work at various institutions including the Philadelphia Museum of Art, the Smithsonian American Art Museum, the Addison Gallery of American Art, and the North Carolina Museum of Art. Prosek is the author of twelve books including *Trout of the World,* and *Ocean Fishes.* He writes frequently for *National Geographic* and *The New York Times.* In 2012 he wrote and directed *The Mystery of Eels* for the PBS series *Nature.*

James Prosek. *American Bison,* 2014. Watercolor, gouache, and colored pencil on tea-stained paper, 24 1/4 x 28 1/2 in.